HAMMOND'S
WORLD ATLAS

CLASSICS EDITION

An Encyclopedic Atlas of the World
with
Latest and most Authentic
Geographical and Statistical Information
in
Map, Word and Picture

1960

Map Publishers Since 1900

C. S. Hammond & Company
Maplewood, N. J.

New York, N. Y.   Chicago, Ill.

Contents

Alphabetic List of Maps . . . . following Contents

PART I

Understanding Maps . . . . I-VI
Space—A New Frontier . . . . VII-XVI

PART II

Gazetteer-Index of the World 1-3
Index of Principal Cities of the World 4-5
Political Maps of the World 6-7
Political Maps of the Arctic and Antarctic 8
Political Maps of Europe and Individual Countries 9-24
Political Maps of Asia and Individual Countries 24-33
Political Map of Africa 34-35
Political Map of Australia 36
Political Map of the Pacific Ocean 37
Political Maps of North America and Individual Countries 38-44
Political Maps of the West Indies and South America and Individual Countries 45-48J
Canada 40-41
   Political Maps of Individual Canadian Provinces 48K-48Q
Illustrated Gazetteer of Canada 313-320
   Political Map of Newfoundland 321
   Indexes of Individual Canadian Provinces 322-328
United States 42-43
   Political Maps of Individual States 49-96
   Index of Cities and Towns 97-159
   Commercial Airway Map 160
   Principal Highway Map 161
   Principal Railroad Map 162
   Illustrated Gazetteer of the United States and Possessions—with
      Resource Maps of the Individual States 163-208
Illustrated Geography and Gazetteer of the World 209-256
Races of Mankind 257-268
World Distribution Maps 269-276
World Statistics 277-278
Map Projections 279-280
Index of the World 281-312
Illustrated Gazetteer of Canada 313-328

PART III

Atlas of the Bible Lands B1-B32

PART IV

Historical Atlas of World Civilization C1-C16

List of Modern Maps

Name	Text Page	Map Ref. & Page
Aden	247	E7 26
Afghanistan	247	J3 26
Africa, Political	227	34-35
Africa, Resource-Relief Map		244
Alabama, U.S.A.	164	49
Alaska, U.S.A.	205	50
Albania	247	E5 21
Alberta, Canada	318	48-O
Algeria	247	G5 34
Andorra	247	G1 17
Angola	247	K14 35
Antarctica		8
Antilles	214	45
Arabia	235	26
Arctic Ocean		8
Argentina	247	48H
Arizona, U.S.A.	165	51
Arkansas, U.S.A.	166	52
Asia, Political	233	25
Asia, Resource-Relief Map		245
Australia, Political	239	36
Australia, Resource-Relief Map		246
Australian Capital Terr.		J7 36
Austria	247	20
Bahama Islands	247	C1 45
Bahrein Islands	247	F4 26
Balkan States	224	21
Barbados	247	48A
Basutoland	247	M17 35
Bechuanaland	247	L16 35
Belgian Congo	247	L12 35
Belgium	247	15
Bermuda	247	G2 45
Bhutan	247	F3 29
Bolivia	247	48F
Brazil	248	48E
British Columbia, Canada	319	48Q
British Honduras	248	C2 39
Brunei	248	E5 31
Bulgaria	248	G4 21
Burma	248	30
California, U.S.A.	167	53
Cambodia	248	E4 30
Cameroons	248	J10 34
Cameroons	248	J10 34
Canada	211	40-41
Canal Zone		G6 39
Cape Verde Islands	248	N5 6
Caroline Islands	248	E5 37
Central Africa	248	K10 34
Central America	213	39
Ceylon	248	29
Chad	248	K9 34
Channel Islands		E8 10
Chile	248	48G
China	248	32
Colombia	248	48C
Colorado, U.S.A.	168	54
Comoro Islands	248	P14 35
Congo	248	J12 35
Connecticut, U.S.A.	168	55
Cook Islands	249	K7 37
Costa Rica	249	E5 39
Cuba	249	48
Cyprus	249	28
Czechoslovakia	249	20
Dahomey	249	G10 34
Damão		B4 29
Delaware, U.S.A.	169	67
Denmark	249	13
District of Columbia, U.S.A.		F5 67
Diu		B4 29
Dominican Republic	249	D6 48
East India Islands	237	31
Ecuador	249	48D
Egypt	249	M6 34
England	249	10
Eritrea	249	O8 34
Ethiopia	249	O9 34
Europe Political	220	9
Europe, Resource-Relief Map		243
Faeroe Islands	222	D2 9
Falkland Islands	249	H14 47
Federation of Rhodesia & Nyasaland	254	M14 35
Fiji	249	H7 37
Finland	249	13
Florida, U.S.A.	170	56
Formosa (Taiwan)	248	K7 32
France	249	16
Gabon	249	J12 35
Gambia	249	C9 34
Georgia, U.S.A.	171	57
Germany	250	14
Ghana	250	F10 34
Gibralter	250	D4 17
Gilbert, Ellice and Phoenix Is.	250	H6 37
Gôa	250	B5 29
Great Britain	250	E3 9
Greece	250	F6 21
Greenland	250	D22 8
Guadeloupe	250	48A
Guam	250	E4 37
Guatemala	250	B3 39
Guiana, British	250	J2 46
Guiana, French	250	K3 46
Guiana, Neth. (Surinam)	250	J3 46
Guinea	250	O9 34
Guinea, Portuguese	250	C9 34
Guinea, Spanish	250	J11 35
Haiti	250	C5 48
Hawaii, U.S.A.	206	58
Holland (Netherlands)	252	15
Honduras	250	D3 39
Honduras, British	248	C2 39
Hong Kong	250	J7 32
Hungary	250	20
Iceland	250	C2 9
Idaho, U.S.A.	172	59
Illinois, U.S.A.	173	60
India	250	29
Indiana, U.S.A.	173	61
Indochina	236	30
Indonesia	251	F7 31
Iowa, U.S.A.	175	62
Iran (Persia)	251	27
Iraq	251	27
Ireland	251	12
Ireland, Northern	253	H2 12
Israel	251	24
Italy	251	18
Ivory Coast	251	E10 34
Jamaica	251	48
Japan	251	33
Jordan	251	24
Kansas, U.S.A.	176	63
Kentucky U.S.A.	177	64
Kenya	251	O11 35
Korea	251	33
Kuwait	251	E4 26
Laos	251	E3 30
Lebanon	251	28
Liberia	251	E10 34
Libya	251	K6 34
Liechtenstein	251	J2 19
Louisiana, U.S.A.	177	65
Loyalty Islands		G8 37
Luxembourg	251	J9 15
Macao	251	H7 32
Maine, U.S.A.	178	R15 35
Malaya, Federation of	252	66
Maldive Islands	252	30
Malgache Rep.	252	L9 25
Malta	252	E7 18
Manitoba, Canada	316	48N
Mariana Islands	252	E4 37
Maritime Provinces		48K
Marquesas Is.	252	N6 37
Marshall Islands	252	G4 37
Martinique	252	48A
Maryland, U.S.A.	178	67
Massachusetts, U.S.A.	179	68
Mauritania	252	D8 34
Mauritius	252	S19 35
Mexico	252	44
Michigan, U.S.A.	180	69
Midway Island		J3 37
Minnesota, U.S.A.	181	70
Mississippi, U.S.A.	182	71
Missouri, U.S.A.	183	72
Monaco	252	G6 16
Mongolian Republic	252	32
Montana, U.S.A.	184	73
Morocco	252	E5 34
Mozambique	252	O15 35
Near East		26
Nebraska, U.S.A.	184	74
Nepal	252	D3 29
Netherlands (Holland)	252	15
Netherlands Antilles	249	E4 45
Nevada, U.S.A.	185	75
New Brunswick, Canada	314	48K
New Caledonia	252	G8 37
New Guinea, Netherlands	252	K6 31
New Guinea, Terr. of	252	B7 31
New Hampshire, U.S.A.	186	76
New Hebrides Islands	252	G7 37
New Jersey, U.S.A.	187	77
New Mexico, U.S.A.	188	78
New South Wales, Australia		H6 36
New York, U.S.A.	189	79
New Zealand, Political	252	36
New Zealand Resource-Relief Map		246
Newfoundland, Canada	313	48K
Nicaragua	252	E4 39
Niger	253	H8 34
Nigeria	253	H10 34
Niue I.	253	K7 37
North America, Political	210	38
North America, Resource-Relief Map		241
North Borneo	253	F5 31
North Carolina, U.S.A.	190	80
North Dakota, U.S.A.	190	81
Northern Ireland	253	H2 12
Northern Rhodesia	253	M14 35
Northern Territory, Australia		E3 36
Northwest Territories, Canada	320	40
Norway	253	13
Nova Scotia, Canada	314	48K
Nyasaland Prot.	253	N14 35
Ohio, U.S.A.	191	82
Oklahoma, U.S.A.	192	83
Oman Sultanate of	253	G5 26
Ontario, Canada	316	48M
Oregon, U.S.A.	193	84
Pacific Ocean	240	37
Pakistan	253	A3&F4 29
Palau Islands	253	D5 37
Panama	253	G6 39
Papua Territory	253	B7 31
Paraguay	253	48J
Pennsylvania, U.S.A.	194	85
Persia (Iran)	251	27
Peru	253	48D
Philippines, Republic of the	253	G4 31
Pitcairn Island	253	O8 37
Poland	253	24
Portugal	253	17
Portuguese India	250	B4,5 29
Prince Edward Island, Canada	313	48K
Principe and São Tomé	254	H11 35
Puerto Rico	254	48A
Québec, Canada	315	48L
Queensland, Australia		G4 36
Réunion	254	R20 35
Rhode Island, U.S.A.	195	68
Ruanda-Urundi	254	M12 35
Rumania	254	G3 21
Russia	256	22-23
Ryukyu Islands	254	L7 33
St. Helena I.	254	E15 35
St. Pierre and Miquelon Is.	254	J4 41
Salvador, El	254	C4 39
Samoa, American	254	J7 37
Samoa, Western	254	J7 37
San Marino	254	D2 18
São Tomé and Principe	254	H11 35
Sarawak	254	E5 31
Saskatchewan, Canada	318	48P
Saudi Arabia	254	D4 26
Scotland	254	11
Senegal	254	D9 34
Seychelles	254	J10 25
Siam (Thailand)	255	30
Sierra Leone	254	D10 34
Sikkim	254	E3 29
Singapore	254	F6 30
Society Islands	254	L7 37
Solomon Islands Prot.	254	F6 37
Somaliland, French	255	P9 34
Somaliland (Italian Tr.)	254	R10 34
Somaliland Prot.	255	R10 34
South America, Political	216	46-47
South America, Resource-Relief Map		242
South Australia, Australia		E5 36
South Carolina, U.S.A.	195	86
South Dakota, U.S.A.	196	87
South West Africa		K16 35
Southeast Asia		31
Southern Rhodesia	255	M15 35
Spain	255	17
Spanish Sahara	255	D6 34
Sudan	255	M9 34
Sudanese Republic	255	E9 34
Surinam (Netherlands Guiana)	250	J3 46
Swaziland	255	N17 35
Sweden	255	13
Switzerland	255	19
Syria	255	28
Taiwan, China	248	K7 32
Tanganyika Territory	255	N13 35
Tasmania, Australia		J8 36
Tennessee, U.S.A.	197	88
Texas, U.S.A.	198	89
Thailand (Siam)	255	30
Tibet, China	255	C5 32
Timor, Portuguese	255	H7 31
Togo	255	G10 34
Tokelau (Union Group)	255	J6 37
Tonga (Friendly) Is.	255	J7 37
Trinidad and Tobago	255	48A
Trucial Oman	255	F5 26
Tuamotu (Low) Arch.	255	M7 37
Tunisia	256	H5 34
Turkey	256	28
Uganda Protectorate	256	N11 35
Union of South Africa	256	L18 35
Union of Soviet Socialist Republics	256	22-23
United Arab Republic	256	B3 26
United Kingdom	250	D3 9
United States of America	256	42-43
Upper Volta	256	F9 34
Uruguay	256	48J
Utah, U.S.A.	199	90
Vatican City	256	B6 18
Venezuela	256	48B
Vermont, U.S.A.	200	91
Victoria, Australia		G7 36
Vietnam	256	E3 30
Virgin Islands (Br.)	256	48A
Virgin Islands (U.S.A.)	256	48A
Virginia, U.S.A.	201	92
Wake Island		G4 37
Wales	249	D5 10
Washington, U.S.A.	201	93
West Indies	214	45
West Indies, Fed. of	256	H3 45
West Virginia, U.S.A.	202	94
Western Australia, Australia		C4 36
Wisconsin, U.S.A.	203	95
World		6-7
Wyoming, U.S.A.	204	96
Yemen	256	D7 26
Yugoslavia	256	C3 21
Yukon Territory, Canada	320	40
Zanzibar Prot.	256	P13 35

The Language of Maps

Maps are tools of communication which help us to understand the world. They answer a wide variety of questions related to many aspects of the world. For example: the form of the land; the location of cities; the size and shape of political divisions; or the distribution of crops. A map can be a simple diagram which tells how to get from one place to another or it may be a complex piece of cartography which shows a great deal of information about an area. Sometimes a single color will effectively present this information and sometimes the use of a variety of colors will give the answers more clearly.

The map maker tries to give the map user the information he wants most to know and which will be most helpful in understanding an area.

Just as written and spoken words are symbols for transmitting ideas and their use in combination constitutes a language, so the symbols which are used by map makers constitute a language. Of course, a language is effective only when it is understood.

The following pages give some information about the problems encountered in making maps and how these problems have been solved. A study of these pages will help you to understand the language of maps and thus enable you to gain more from all the other maps in this book.

WHAT A MAP DOES

1. A map tells you in which *direction* one object or place is from another.

You can find direction on the ground in the following ways.....

YOUR SHADOW: At noon, if you face the sun, you are looking *south*. Your shadow will point *north*. If you raise your arms, your right arm will point *west* and your left arm will point *east*.

Copyright by C. S. HAMMOND & CO., N. Y.

THE NORTH STAR: If you face the North Star, you are facing *north*.

NORTH STAR

BIG DIPPER

The two pointer stars of the Big Dipper point to the North Star.

A MAGNETIC COMPASS

The needle of a compass points toward *north*.

The compass-rose tells you where *north* is located on your map.

2. A map tells you how far away, or the *distance*, one object is from another. You can find distance in the following ways ...

... Measure with a drawing compass

and apply them to the bar scale on the map.

... or a ruler

The bar scales on maps of large areas are usually in miles instead of feet.

Scale of Feet
0   250   500   750   1000

First of all, a map tells you in which direction one place is from another, and, secondly, the distance between places.

There was a time, however, when men knew little about places away from where they lived. Most early people had only the sun and stars to tell direction. The fixed star we call the "North Star" was called "the Bear" and was used to tell direction. Instead of north or south, places were toward the Bear, or opposite the Bear. Instead of east, places were toward morning, where the sun rose, and instead of west, places were toward evening, where the sun set.

Today, there are many ways to tell direction. The magnetic compass is quite handy to use. Its needle always points north and it can be used with a map to help find your way. The stars and sun help tell direction, also. The Big Dipper constellation is easy to find in the sky. Two pointer stars form the side of the dipper farthest away from the handle. These two stars point to the North Star. At noon the sun is always due south. If it is near noon and you face the sun, north is directly behind you. Of course, if daylight-saving time is in effect, the sun will be due south at one o'clock.

You can also tell direction with your shadow. The sun always rises in the east and sets in the west. If it is before noon, your shadow will point west. If it is after noon, your shadow will point to the east.

The sun can help find direction in another way, too. When you are in the woods, look around for moss on the trees and rocks. Moss almost always grows in the shadows, on the north side where it is shaded from the bright rays of the sun.

All these ways of finding direction helped map makers. Little by little, as man ventured farther and farther from home, places were located on maps. Today, there are maps of every country in the world. By looking at these maps, one can tell quickly in what direction and how far one place is from another.

HOW TO USE A MAP

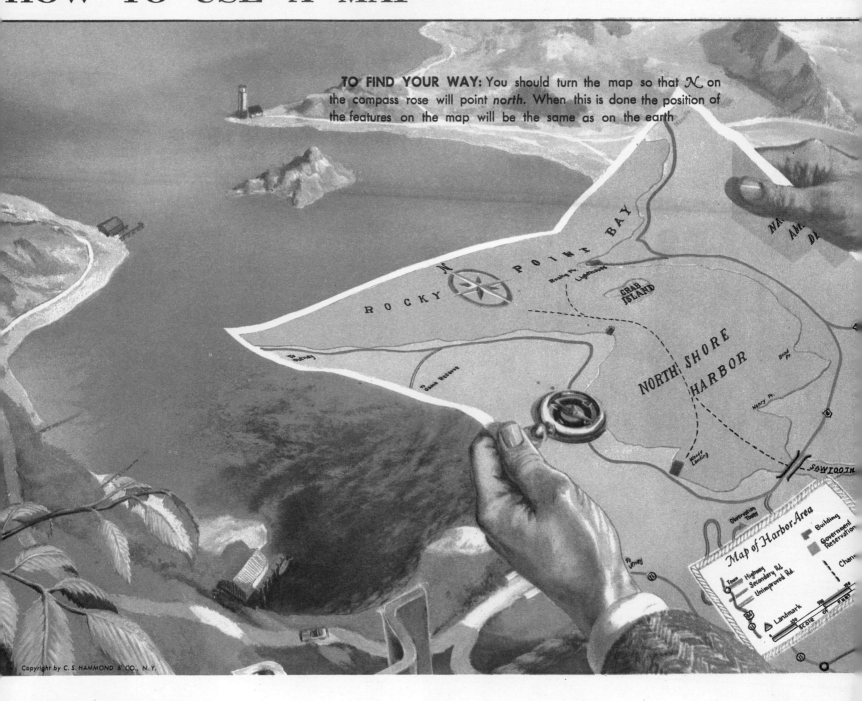

TO FIND YOUR WAY: You should turn the map so that *N* on the compass rose will point *north*. When this is done the position of the features on the map will be the same as on the earth

Copyright by C. S. HAMMOND & CO., N. Y.

TELLING DIRECTION AND DISTANCE ON A MAP

The compass-rose always shows where north is on the map. The longest "petals" of the compass-rose point toward north and south. The shorter "petals" show the other points of direction — northeast, east, southeast, southwest, west and northwest. Look at one of the maps in the atlas and find the legend box. There you will see a scale of miles, which is called a "bar scale." This scale indicates how many miles there are to an inch on that particular map. To quickly find the distance between two places, measure the distance with a drawing compass or ruler.

HOW TO USE A MAP TO FIND YOUR WAY

The illustration above shows how a person can find his way with a map. By turning the map so the features on the map and on the ground are in the same position, north can be found by looking at the compass-rose.

Next, by comparing a prominent feature on the map with one on the ground, one knows exactly where he is. For instance, in the illustration above, the person holding the map can tell by the lighthouse, or the river at the bottom of the map, that he is at "North Shore Harbor" near "Rocky Point Bay." By studying the road symbols and the scale of miles, he can easily find how far it is to the nearest town.

When taking a trip, a lot of enjoyment can be had by the whole family if road maps are studied a little ahead of time. Mark interesting spots on the map to be watched for on the trip. Then, as you go along, you can mark your progress by "sights" as well as by the speedometer. This is a good way to keep the youngsters occupied on sometimes otherwise dull trips.

MAPS — SYMBOLS

A globe is the only true map of the earth because it shows us the roundness of the earth. A globe shows us all the lands and seas in their true shapes and positions. A globe is really a *model* or small copy of our earth, just as a toy airplane is a model of a real airplane.

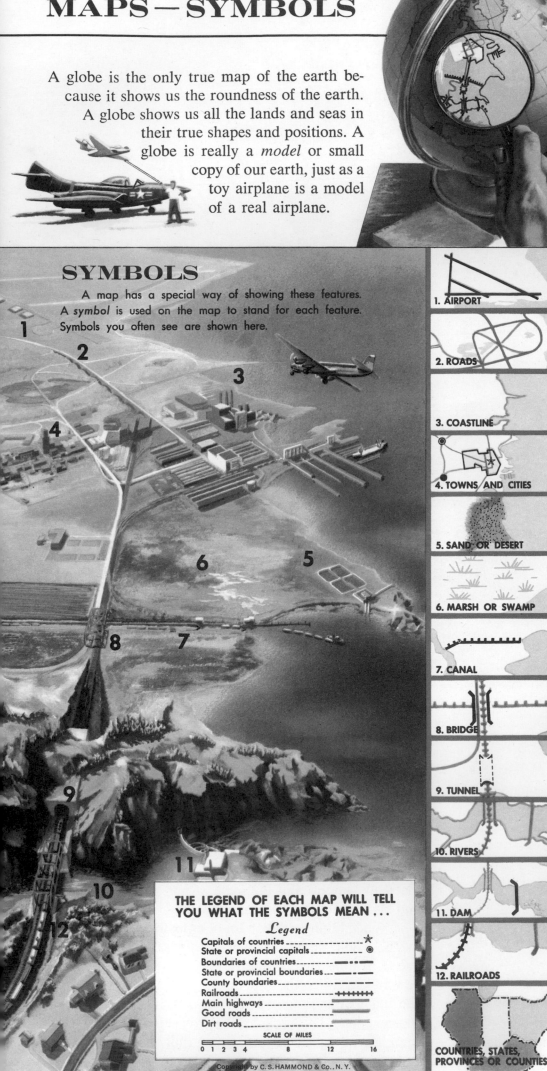

SYMBOLS

A map has a special way of showing these features. A *symbol* is used on the map to stand for each feature. Symbols you often see are shown here.

1. AIRPORT

2. ROADS

3. COASTLINE

4. TOWNS AND CITIES

5. SAND OR DESERT

6. MARSH OR SWAMP

7. CANAL

8. BRIDGE

9. TUNNEL

10. RIVERS

11. DAM

12. RAILROADS

COUNTRIES, STATES, PROVINCES OR COUNTIES

THE LEGEND OF EACH MAP WILL TELL YOU WHAT THE SYMBOLS MEAN . . .

Legend

Capitals of countries	★
State or provincial capitals	◉
Boundaries of countries	
State or provincial boundaries	
County boundaries	
Railroads	+++++
Main highways	
Good roads	
Dirt roads	

SCALE OF MILES

0 1 2 3 4   8   12   16

NATURAL FEATURES

MAN-MADE FEATURES

ROUTES

A map can show many things, including natural features and man-made features. The Legend Box will show some of these symbols to help identify places or objects on the maps. However, there is seldom room to show all of them in the Legend Box and as a great many symbols are standard on most all maps, it is really not necessary. Some of these standard symbols are shown in the illustration on the left.

WHAT SCALE MEANS

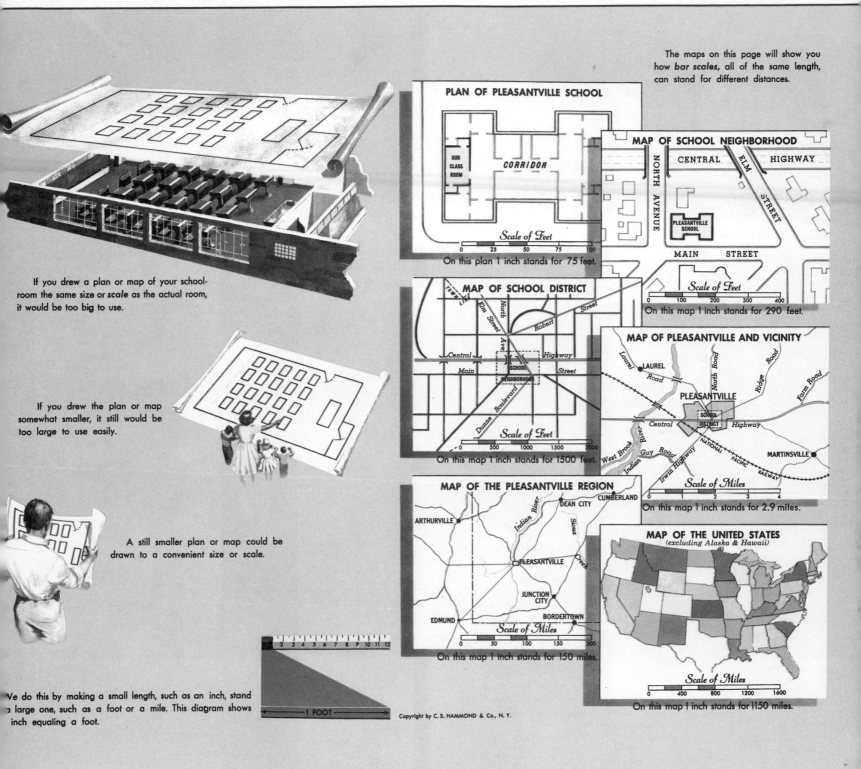

If you drew a plan or map of your school-room the same size or *scale* as the actual room, it would be too big to use.

If you drew the plan or map somewhat smaller, it still would be too large to use easily.

A still smaller plan or map could be drawn to a convenient size or scale.

We do this by making a small length, such as an inch, stand for a large one, such as a foot or a mile. This diagram shows inch equaling a foot.

The maps on this page will show you how *bar scales*, all of the same length, can stand for different distances.

PLAN OF PLEASANTVILLE SCHOOL

OUR CLASS ROOM

CORRIDOR

Scale of Feet

0   25   50   75   100

On this plan 1 inch stands for 75 feet.

MAP OF SCHOOL NEIGHBORHOOD

NORTH AVENUE   CENTRAL   ELM   HIGHWAY

STREET

PLEASANTVILLE SCHOOL

MAIN   STREET

Scale of Feet

0   100   200   300   400

On this map 1 inch stands for 290 feet.

MAP OF SCHOOL DISTRICT

TROLLEY LINE

Elm Street Ave.   North

Robert   Street

Central   Highway

Main   SCHOOL NEIGHBORHOOD   Street

Dunne Boulevard

Scale of Feet

0   500   1000   1500   2000

On this map 1 inch stands for 1500 feet.

MAP OF PLEASANTVILLE AND VICINITY

Laurel Road   LAUREL   North Road   Ridge Road   Farm Road

PLEASANTVILLE

Central   SCHOOL DISTRICT   Highway

West Brook   River   Indian   Gay Road   NATIONAL   PACIFIC   RAILWAY   MARTINSVILLE

Irwin Highway

Scale of Miles

0   1   2   3   4

On this map 1 inch stands for 2.9 miles.

MAP OF THE PLEASANTVILLE REGION

ARTHURVILLE   Indian River   DEAN CITY   CUMBERLAND

Sioux

PLEASANTVILLE   Creek

JUNCTION CITY

EDMUND   BORDERTOWN

Scale of Miles

0   50   100   150   200

On this map 1 inch stands for 150 miles.

MAP OF THE UNITED STATES
(excluding Alaska & Hawaii)

Scale of Miles

0   400   800   1200   1600

On this map 1 inch stands for 1150 miles.

Copyright by C. S. HAMMOND & Co., N.Y.

1   2   3   4   5   6   7   8   9   10   11   12

◄——— 1 FOOT ———►

Drawing or making anything to scale means to make a copy exactly like the real thing except for size. Maps are scale drawings or plans of places. To make a map of convenient size, map makers let a small length, such as an inch, stand for a large one, such as a foot or a mile. On a map of a large area, such as a continent, an inch stands for hundreds of miles.

Looking at the atlas, you will see that the scale of miles is different on each map. This means some maps are larger scale than others. For example, Asia is much larger than Europe, and although the bar scale is almost the same length on the two maps, one inch on the Asia map is equal to more than twice as many miles as on the Europe map. Thus, the Europe map is larger scale.

Large-scale maps are used to show more detail. A world map is useful because it shows all the world on one map. However, there is not enough room to show great detail on any one area.

PROJECTIONS

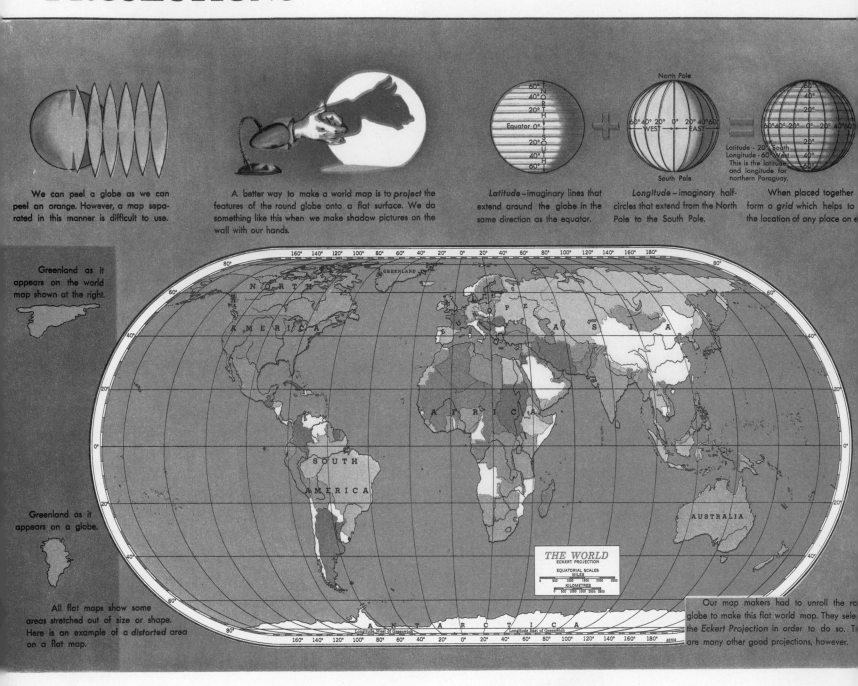

We can peel a globe as we can peel an orange. However, a map separated in this manner is difficult to use.

A better way to make a world map is to *project* the features of the round globe onto a flat surface. We do something like this when we make shadow pictures on the wall with our hands.

Latitude – imaginary lines that extend around the globe in the same direction as the equator.

Longitude – imaginary half-circles that extend from the North Pole to the South Pole.

When placed together form a *grid* which helps to the location of any place on e

Greenland as it appears on the world map shown at the right.

Greenland as it appears on a globe.

All flat maps show some areas stretched out of size or shape. Here is an example of a *distorted* area on a flat map.

THE WORLD
ECKERT PROJECTION

EQUATORIAL SCALES
MILES

KILOMETRES

Our map makers had to unroll the ro globe to make this flat world map. They sele the *Eckert Projection* in order to do so. T are many other good projections, however.

A globe is the only true map of the world. All flat maps of large areas distort some parts of the earth. If you compare a globe of the world with a flat map of the world, you can quickly see where they differ. An easy way to see why certain areas are distorted is to make an experiment with an orange.

Cut a navel orange in half and squeeze out the juice. Use the navel half of the orange and press it on a piece of paper. Press it until it is absolutely flat. Now you can see how the edges are torn and stretched out of shape. This is exactly what happens when the surface of the round earth is projected onto a flat map.

While flat maps distort parts of the world, they are very useful. The map maker uses various ways of laying out a map. Before he starts a map, he decides what he will show correctly at the expense of stretching or distorting other features. The various ways of laying out maps which are correct for one feature, such as direction, and distort another, such as area, are called "projections."

The above map uses an Eckert Projection. An important feature of this projection is the treatment of the Polar areas. The North and South Poles are represented by straight lines. These lines are half the length of the equator. If the poles were represented by single points, as they really are, the northern and southern polar regions would be pushed together in narrow triangles. Thus, the distortion of one feature (in this case, the poles) gives a truer picture of another, the shape of the polar land areas.

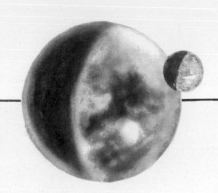

The Earth as part of the Solar System

Since many aspects of life on earth, such as climate, tides, light and cycles in time, are the result of the Earth's position in the solar system—which is just a small part of the universe—we have added to our understanding of the world by learning more about the universe.

This study was begun before recorded history and a large amount of information about the heavenly bodies has been gathered. With the advent of the modern rockets which are capable of carrying recording and communication equipment into space, the rate at which this information is accumulating is being greatly accelerated.

The following pages present some basic facts about the universe—especially the solar system—and help us to understand how the earth's size, shape and position in relation to the solar system affect us. On the following pages you will also find some facts about what we are doing to learn more about our new frontier—Outer Space.

FACTS ABOUT OUR EARTH

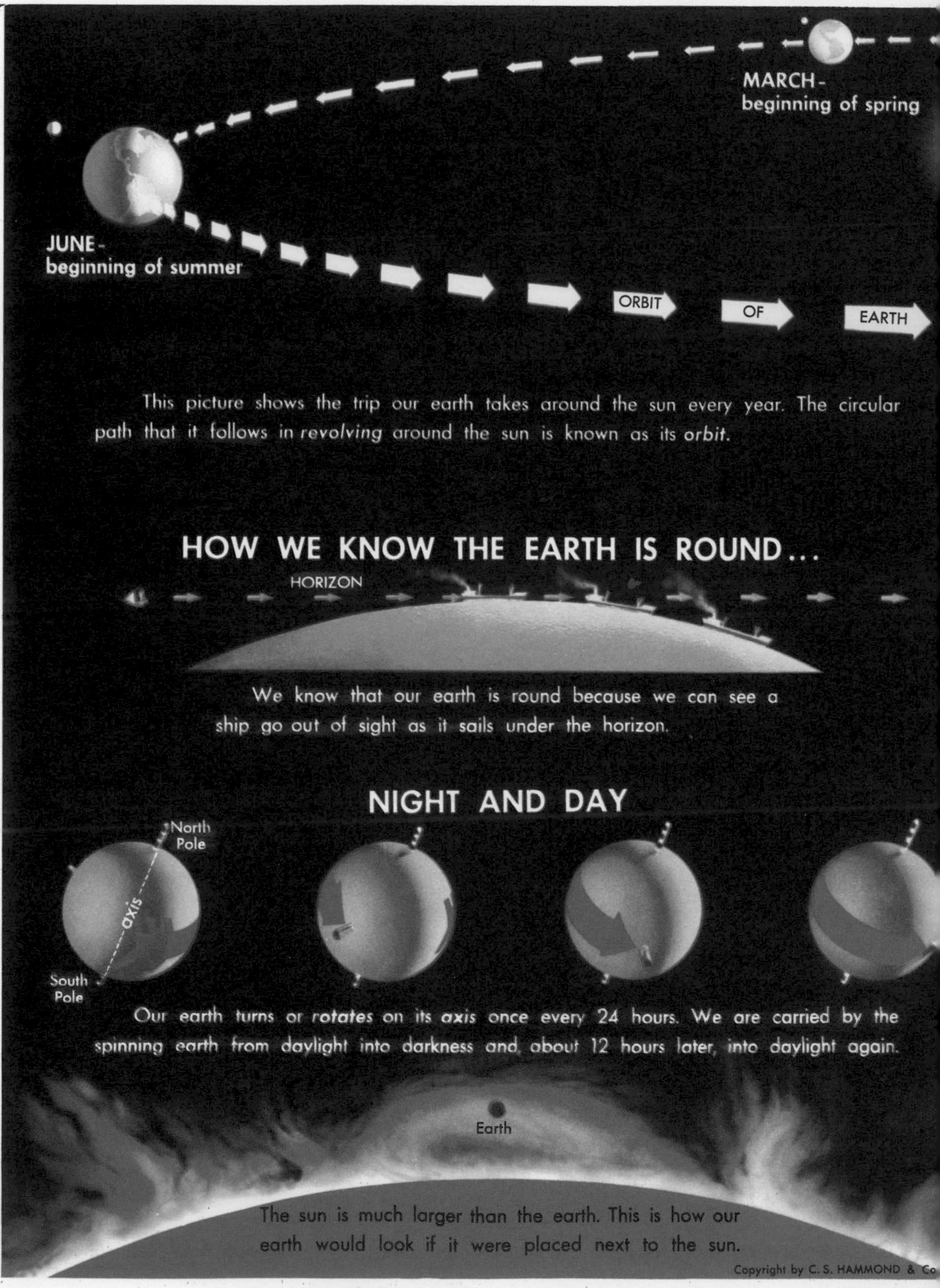

MARCH— beginning of spring

JUNE— beginning of summer

ORBIT OF EARTH

This picture shows the trip our earth takes around the sun every year. The circular path that it follows in *revolving* around the sun is known as its *orbit*.

HOW WE KNOW THE EARTH IS ROUND...

HORIZON

We know that our earth is round because we can see a ship go out of sight as it sails under the horizon.

NIGHT AND DAY

North Pole

axis

South Pole

Our earth turns or *rotates* on its *axis* once every 24 hours. We are carried by the spinning earth from daylight into darkness and, about 12 hours later, into daylight again.

Earth

The sun is much larger than the earth. This is how our earth would look if it were placed next to the sun.

Although we know the earth is round, no one has ever been high enough in the sky to see the earth as a round ball. However, photographs of part of the earth have been taken by cameras sent up in rockets. These photographs show enough of the earth to prove it is round.

The earth rotates on its axis, an imaginary line with its ends as the poles, once every 24 hours. It rotates from west to east. This rotation gives us day and night. When our part of the earth faces the sun, we have day, and when our part turns away from the sun, we have night. It is interesting to know that while the other planets also rotate on their axes, their days are all of different lengths. For instance, Mercury takes almost eighty-eight days to turn on its axis, and Jupiter's day is only about ten hours. Neptune's day is about sixteen hours and Venus', about four weeks.

As the earth spins on its axis, it also travels around the sun, thus giving us our seasons. As the earth travels around the sun, it is always tilted a little. Part of the year the northern half, the Northern Hemisphere, leans toward the sun and part of the year the southern half, the Southern Hemisphere, leans toward the sun. The part of the earth which leans toward the sun has summer while the other half has winter.

During the summer months the period of daylight is longer than in winter and the sun's rays, shining straight down on the

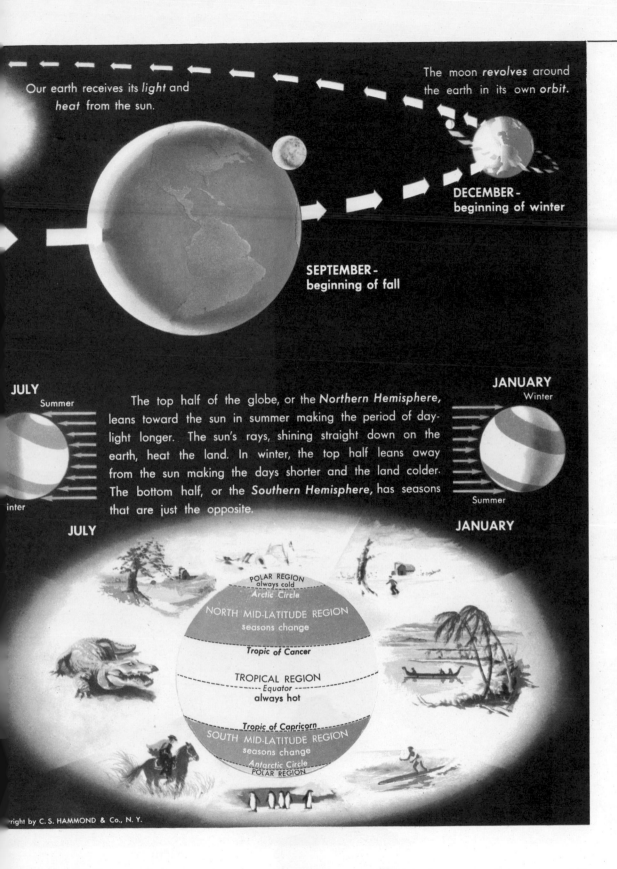

Our earth receives its *light* and *heat* from the sun.

The moon *revolves* around the earth in its own *orbit*.

DECEMBER - beginning of winter

SEPTEMBER - beginning of fall

JULY
Summer

The top half of the globe, or the *Northern Hemisphere*, leans toward the sun in summer making the period of daylight longer. The sun's rays, shining straight down on the earth, heat the land. In winter, the top half leans away from the sun making the days shorter and the land colder. The bottom half, or the *Southern Hemisphere*, has seasons that are just the opposite.

JANUARY
Winter

inter

Summer

JULY

JANUARY

POLAR REGION
always cold
Arctic Circle
NORTH MID-LATITUDE REGION
seasons change
Tropic of Cancer
TROPICAL REGION
Equator
always hot
Tropic of Capricorn
SOUTH MID-LATITUDE REGION
seasons change
Antarctic Circle
POLAR REGION

earth, heat the land and make the temperature higher. During the winter months the sun's rays are slanted toward the earth and have to go through more of the air surrounding the earth. This means the rays are more spread out and lose heat, giving us colder weather.

Between summer and winter come spring and fall, which are neither very hot nor very cold.

The region near the equator, the Tropical Region, is always hot and it is often damp and sticky there. In this region there are no seasons as we know them. Except in the arid desert areas, crops grow the year round and with little attention. There is abundant rain; in fact, during much of the year it rains almost daily. The dense forests of Africa are in this zone, as is the Panama Canal.

While near the equator it is always hot, near the poles it is always cold and almost everything is covered with ice and snow. The frozen land around the South Pole, Antarctica, is inhabited by seals and penguins. No people live there, but explorers have braved the cold to make scientific studies. The land around the North Pole, the Arctic, is inhabited by some Eskimos, polar bears, seals, walrus, some small fur-bearing animals and, of course, fish. At both poles daylight lasts for half the year and nighttime, the other half. During the daylight period it becomes a little warmer, although never warm enough to melt much ice.

THE SOLAR SYSTEM

Our sun is a star. A star with planets circling about it, with a number of satellites like our moon circling about the planets, plus a large number of asteroids, make up the solar system. We think other stars may have their own planetary systems but the only one we know about is ours. The others are too far away.

Groups of millions of stars form galaxies. Our galaxy is the Milky Way. We know there are countless galaxies in the universe. We have observed that stars are arranged in groups which seem to suggest forms. We call these groups of stars "constellations."

Imagine yourself beyond the edge of our solar system, facing the constellation, Southern Cross, and with your back toward Polaris, the North Star. This picture is an attempt to show what you would see, with certain exceptions or artistic license.

The green ellipses represent the paths or orbits of the planets. Actually, these could not be seen but they

THE SOLAR SYSTEM

are put into the picture to show how nearly in the same plane the planets move; yet certain planets move in orbits which are inclined from the others, which also is shown. If we did not use artistic license, the sun would just about fill the entire picture unless the planets were shown as tiny pin points. So the sun is shown a convenient size in relation to the planets' orbits. The nine planets themselves are drawn considerably larger than they would appear from our vantage point. Just inside

the orbit of Jupiter is the Asteroid Zone. The plane of the orbit of "Ceres," the largest asteroid, is seen to be quite inclined from the others. The orbits of two comets are also shown moving in around the sun and out again.

In the background we see part of our Milky Way. All the stars shown are in our galaxy. Behind them, shown in blue and greatly enlarged from the size they would appear, are other galaxies. These are in various forms, such as spiral, barred and elliptical.

FACTS ABOUT THE PLANETS

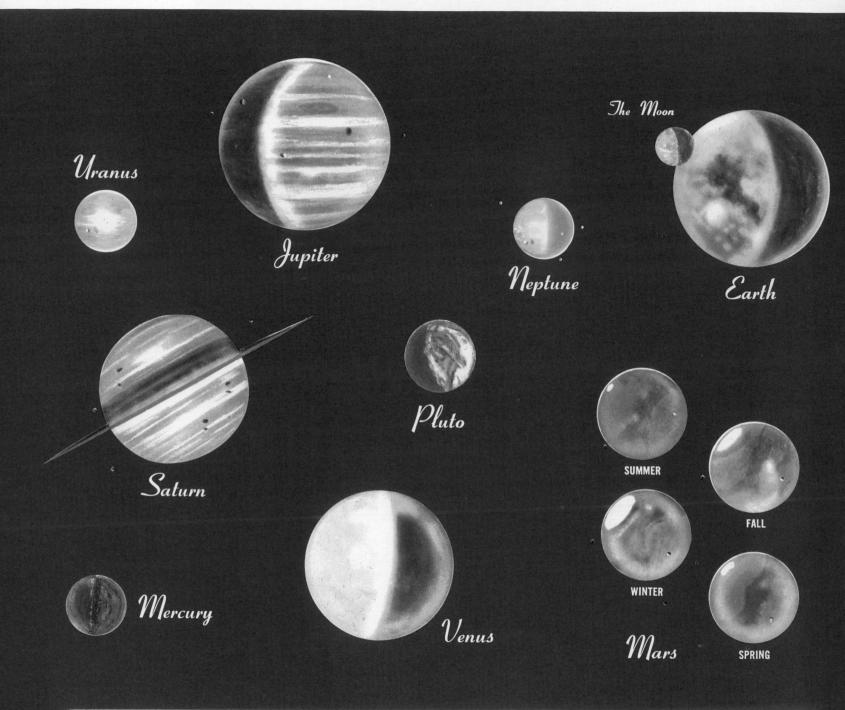

Sun and Planets	Mean Distance from Sun (Million miles)	Period of Revolution around Sun	Period of Rotation on Axis	Diameter at Equator (miles)	Density (Water=1)	Number of Known Satellites
Sun	———	———	24.7 days (equatorial)	865.390	1.4	—
Mercury	36.00	87.969 days	87.969 days	3,100	3.8	none
Venus	67.27	224.701 days	30 days approx.	7,700	5.1	none
Earth	93.00	365.256 days	23 hrs. 56 min.	7,927	5.5	one
Mars	141.71	1.881 yrs.	24 hrs. 37 min.	4,200	4.0	two
Jupiter	483.88	11.862 yrs.	9 hrs. 50 min.	88,700	1.3	twelve
Saturn	887.14	29.458 yrs.	10 mo. 14 min.	75,100	0.7	nine
Uranus	1783.98	84.013 yrs.	10.8 hrs.	32,000	1.3	five
Neptune	2795.46	164.794 yrs.	15.8 hrs.	27,700	2.2	two
Pluto	3675.27	248.430 yrs.	unknown	3,600 approx.	unknown	none

The Moon, the only natural satellite of the earth, from which her mean distance is 238,857 miles, occupies an average period, in her revolution round the earth, of 29 earth days, 12 hours, 44 minutes, 3 seconds; her diameter is 2,160 miles, and her mean density is 0.60.

THE MOON

HIDDEN SIDE OF THE MOON
AS PHOTOGRAPHED BY LUNIK III

1   Sea of Moscow
2   Gulf of the Astronauts of Sea of Moscow
3   Mare Australe
4   Crater with central peak (Tsiolkovsky)
5   Crater with central peak (Lomonosov)
6   Joliot-Curie Crater
7   Sovietsky Mountain Range
8   Sea of Dreams

———— Lunar Equator
- - - - Division between visible
         and hidden hemispheres
⬭ Definitely established features
⬭ Features requiring further study

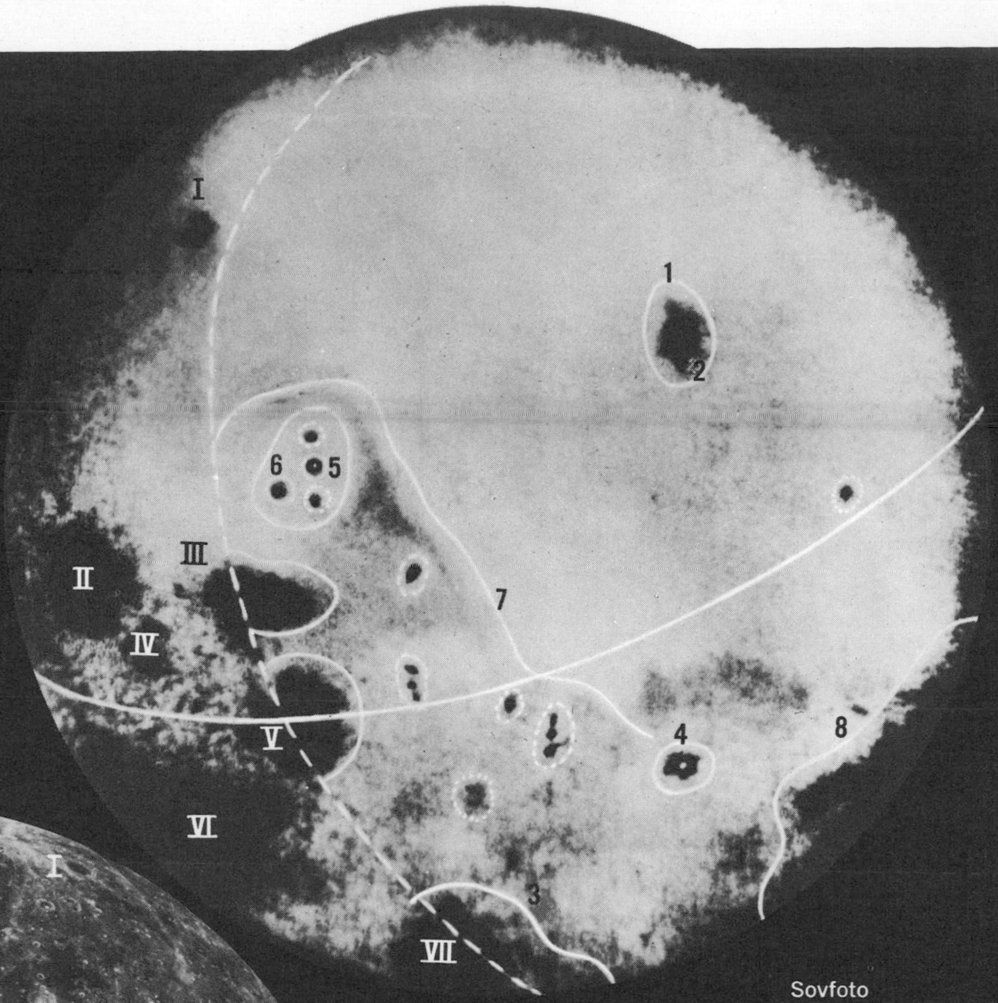

Sovfoto

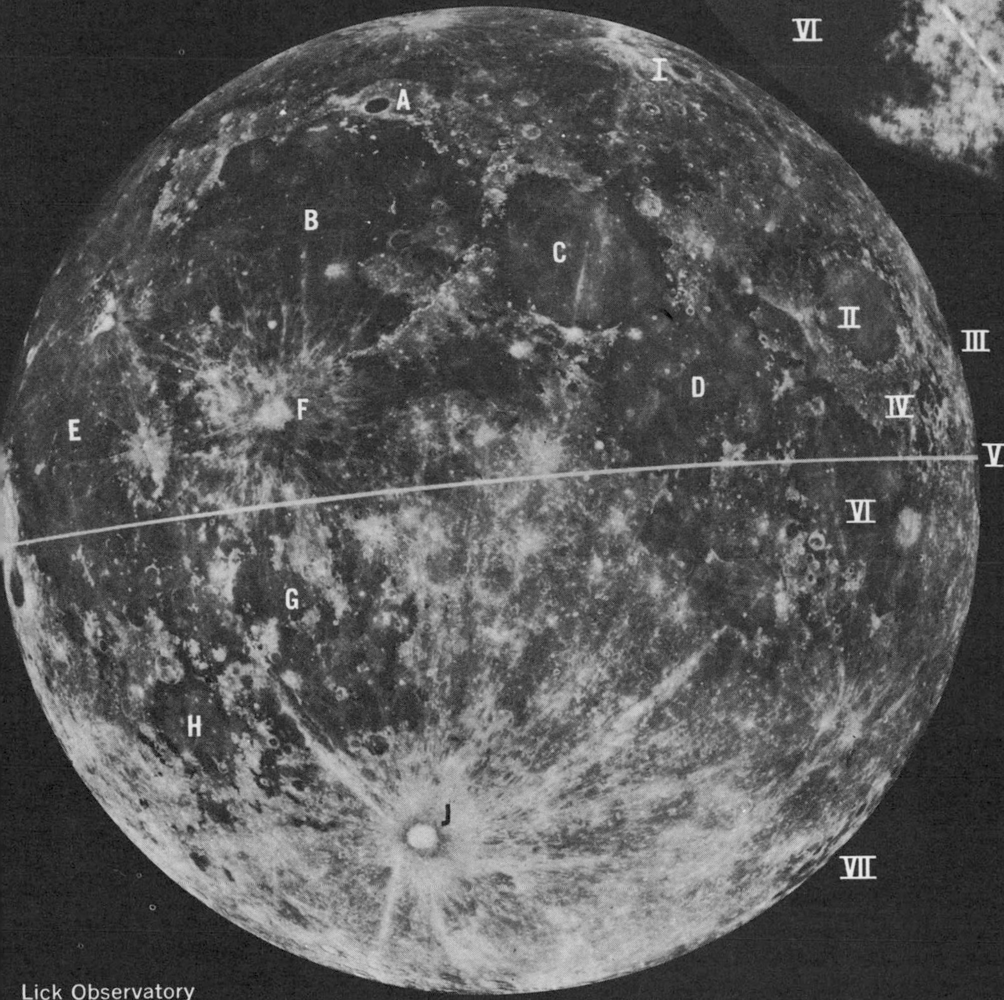

FEATURES VISIBLE ON BOTH PHOTOGRAPHS

I   Mare Humboldtianum
II   Mare Crisium
III   Mare Marginus
IV   Mare Undarum
V   Mare Smythii
VI   Mare Foecunditatis
VII   Mare Australe

Lick Observatory

VISIBLE SIDE OF THE MOON

A   Plato   F   Copernicus
B   Mare Imbrium   G   Mare Nubium
C   Mare Serenitatis   H   Mare Humorum
D   Mare Tranquilitatis   J   Tycho
E   Oceanus Procellarum

A SETTLEMENT
ON THE MOON

THE EXPLORATION OF SPACE

SPACE STATION MANNED ORBITAL SATELLITE

COMBINATION UHF RADAR ANTENNA

STABILIZING MECHANISM

VHF WAVE GUIDE ANTENNA

NUCLEAR REACTOR

REACTOR CONDENSING PIPES

HUB

SPOKES

SOLAR MIRROR A

SPECTROHELIOGRAP CAM

RIM

VHF—UHF RECEIVING ANTENN

TURRET STATIONA WHEN IN U

LANDING BERTH FOR SPACE TA

PASSENGER RETURN S

RADAR GUIDAN FOR SPACE TA

SPACE STATION — The space station is a satellite. It is a manned satellite revolving about the earth every 120 minutes at about 1000 miles above sea level, and rotating at the rate of three times a minute. It requires no power other than inertia to keep it in its orbit. The rotation once started will also continue without use of power. The rotation will give centrifugal force to the people and things inside the satellite. Centrifugal force is what keeps water in a pail when you whirl it. Its effect will cause people and things to feel and behave in a satellite as they do in the field of gravity. Man will be able to walk upright, coffee will stay in cups, and things will remain where they are placed. The centrifugal force will provide comfort and the ability to maneuver for trained space men.

Since by far the most uncertain, dangerous and costly part of a trip through space is the part that passes through the at-

mosphere, a space station 1000 miles above the earth will have an advantage.

If interplanetary ships themselve. can be more readily built out in space, the consideration for streamlining can be kep to a minimum and the ratio of power plan to pay load can be considerably decreased

TRACKING CAMERA—Mounted at ar established point in latitude and longitude these cameras are used to observe the movement of satellites. When fixed on a satellite the picture made shows it as a dot while al the stars in the picture are shown as dashe because of the earth's movement. When the camera is synchronized to the earth's movement and as a result fixed on the stars, i the picture they will appear as dots and th satellite will appear as a dash.

1. OUTER SHELL
2. INNER HOOD
3. SWEAT CAP
4. ATMOSPHERE PACK
5. ATMOSPHERE TUBE
6. AIR-PURIFICATION VALVES
7. HELMET RIM. JOINED TO SUIT BY BAYONET MOUNT AND ZIPPER
8. PRESSURE-INDICATING DISC
9. HANDLE, TV ANTENNA, FOCUSING KNOB
10. UHF RADIO RECEIVER-TRANSMITTER
11. TV CAMERA LENS
12. ADD-ON JOINT
13. COMBINED INTERNAL & EXTERNAL ZIPPERS
14. CAMERA MECHANISM AND FILM PACK
15. POLARIZED PLASTIC FACE PLATE
16. MAGNETIC SOLE PLATES

TRACKING CAMERA

RA RANGE—FINDE ANTENNA

CAMERA PACK

RANGEFIN

GUIDE TELE

GIMBAL M

HEAVY CONCRETE PLAT

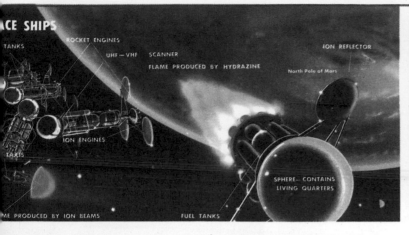

SPACE SHIPS — Space travel to the moon or to other planets will require space vehicles which can carry sufficient fuel and supplies for the round trip. Everything necessary to provide an environment in which the passengers and crew can survive must also be taken along.

While the ships are being built, fueled, loaded, manned and launched, they will of course be revolving about the earth in an orbit at about 16,000 miles per hour. The inertia which brought the parts, crew and supplies together, keeps them in orbit. Then they must depart from it and reach an orbit which will contact the orbit of their destination at the precise time their destination reaches the contact point.

SPACE TAXI—Our illustration is based on the probability that these little man-carrying satellites will be launched from earth as fuel tanks to be converted to taxis in space. It has a movable canopy of Polaroid to shield the occupants from solar and cosmic rays. At each end of the taxi a small rocket motor is installed which can be turned in any direction within 15° away from the central axis. By turning the motors and regulating the duration of a blast, the space taxi can be made to turn in any direction—even end over end—but it will remain in its orbit. If a space man steps out of the space taxi, he moves with it unless he pushes himself away.

ROCKETS

The streamlined rockets are space vehicles designed to travel through the earth's atmosphere. They are shaped to reduce atmospheric friction as much as possible. The rockets are built in stages to obtain the acceleration necessary for the orbit velocity. Each successive stage adds to the acceleration, aided by the elimination of the preceding stage.

The diagram showing how a rocket works describes the use of liquid propellent fuels. Solid fuels may be found easier to handle.

THE ATMOSPHERE AND BEYOND

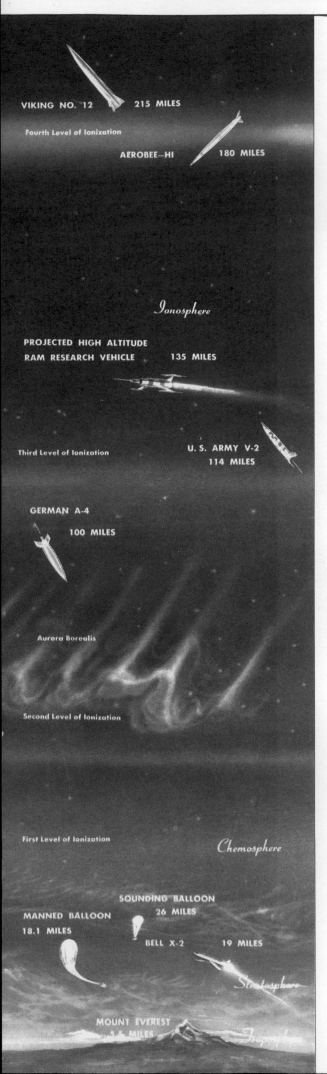

VIKING NO. 12　　215 MILES

Fourth Level of Ionization

AEROBEE—HI　　180 MILES

Ionosphere

PROJECTED HIGH ALTITUDE
RAM RESEARCH VEHICLE　　135 MILES

Third Level of Ionization

U. S. ARMY V-2
114 MILES

GERMAN A-4
100 MILES

Aurora Borealis

Second Level of Ionization

First Level of Ionization

Chemosphere

SOUNDING BALLOON
26 MILES

MANNED BALLOON
18.1 MILES

BELL X-2　　19 MILES

Stratosphere

MOUNT EVEREST
3.6 MILES

Troposphere

WHAT IS SPACE—Going up from the earth's surface we pass through the atmosphere which, as we know it, is quite dense compared to what is called outer space. The air is pressed down by the weight of the atmosphere above it. This weight at sea level is 15 pounds on every square inch. The farther up we go the less air there is pressing down and consequently it becomes less dense and the air molecules are more widely separated until there is a vacuum.

The atmosphere is made up of layers, each of which is quite different, but the change from one to the other is not sudden. The layers blend into each other.

Near the earth's surface is the Troposphere where most of the weather — wind and rain—takes place. It extends up about six miles.

Above this is the Stratosphere in which the very highest clouds and some air currents are formed. The Stratosphere extends from 6 to 20 miles high.

The next layer is the Chemosphere from 20 to 50 miles up where the sun's energy is converted for our use.

Above this is the Ionosphere which extends from 50 to 250 miles. The region is being explored with rockets and high-frequency radio. It is filled with ions which reflect radio waves.

From 250 to 600 miles is the Mesosphere which contains Mesons and other particles related to cosmic rays.

Above 600 miles is the Exosphere which is the fringe of outer space.

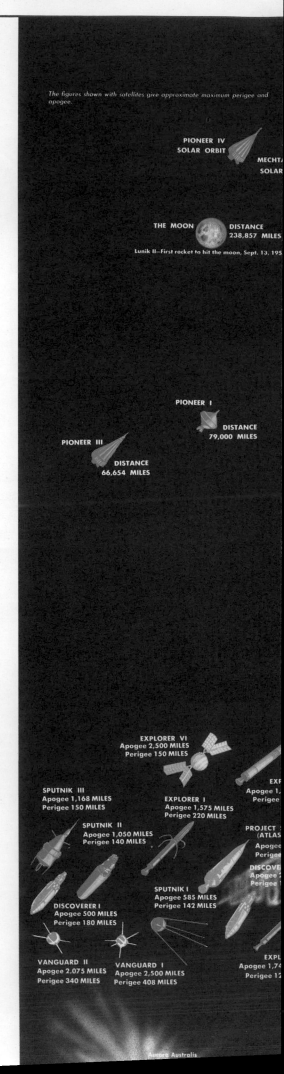

The figures shown with satellites give approximate maximum perigee and apogee.

PIONEER IV
SOLAR ORBIT

MECHTA
SOLAR

THE MOON　DISTANCE
238,857 MILES

Lunik II—First rocket to hit the moon, Sept. 13, 195

PIONEER I

DISTANCE
79,000 MILES

PIONEER III

DISTANCE
66,654 MILES

EXPLORER VI
Apogee 2,500 MILES
Perigee 150 MILES

SPUTNIK III
Apogee 1,168 MILES
Perigee 150 MILES

EXPLORER I
Apogee 1,575 MILES
Perigee 220 MILES

EXP
Apogee 1,
Perigee

SPUTNIK II
Apogee 1,050 MILES
Perigee 140 MILES

PROJECT
(ATLAS
Apogee
Perige

DISCOVE
Apogee
Perigee

SPUTNIK I
Apogee 585 MILES
Perigee 142 MILES

DISCOVERER I
Apogee 500 MILES
Perigee 180 MILES

VANGUARD II
Apogee 2,075 MILES
Perigee 340 MILES

VANGUARD I
Apogee 2,500 MILES
Perigee 408 MILES

EXPL
Apogee 1,74
Perigee 12

Aurora Australis

Hammond's
WORLD ATLAS AND GAZETTEER

GAZETTEER-INDEX OF THE WORLD

This alphabetical list of grand divisions, countries, states, colonial possessions, etc., gives area, population, capital, seat of government or chief town, and index references and numbers of plates on which they are shown on the largest scale. The mother country of colonial possessions is indicated by abbreviations in parentheses. The index reference shows the square on the respective map in which the name of the country, state or colonial possession is located.

Country	Area (Sq. Miles)	Population	Capital or Chief Town	Index Ref.	Plate No.
A					
Aden Colony (Br.)	75	138,441	Aden	E 7	26
Aden Protectorate (Br.)	112,000	650,000	Aden	E 7	26
*Afghanistan	250,000	13,000,000	Kabul	J 3	26
Africa	11,850,000	225,000,000			34, 35
Alabama, U.S.A.	51,078	3,061,743	Montgomery	M 6	43
Alaska, U.S.A.	571,065	128,643	Juneau	F 8	42
*Albania	11,096	1,391,499	Tirana (Tiranë)	E 5	21
Alberta, Canada	248,800	1,123,116	Edmonton	G 4	40
Aleutian Islands (U.S.A.)	6,800	5,600	Unalaska	F 3	6
Algeria (Fr.)	851,284	10,265,000	Algiers (Alger)	G 5	34
Andaman Is. (India)	2,508	21,316	Port Blair	F 6	29
Andorra	191	6,000	Andorra la Vella	G 1	17
Angola	481,351	4,392,000	Luanda	K14	35
Antarctica	5,500,000				8
Antigua (incl. Barbuda and Redonda)	171	56,000	St. Johns	G 3	45
Antilles, Greater, Lesser				E 3	45
Arabia	1,000,000	9,000,000		D 5	26
Arctic Ocean					8
*Argentina	1,078,266	20,438,000	Buenos Aires	H10	47
Arizona, U.S.A.	113,580	749,587	Phoenix	E 6	42
Arkansas, U.S.A.	52,725	1,909,511	Little Rock	K 6	43
Armenian S.S.R. (U.S.S.R.)	11,500	1,600,000	Erivan (Yerevan)	F 5	22
Ascension Island (Br.)	34	183	Georgetown	D13	35
Asia	16,500,000	1,596,000,000			25
*Australia, Commonwealth of.	2,974,581	9,952,000	Canberra		36
Australian Capital Territory..	939	30,315	Canberra	J 7	36
*Austria	32,369	7,021,000	Vienna (Wien)	B-C 3	20
Azerbaidzhan S.S.R. (U.S.S.R.)	33,100	3,400,000	Baku	F 5	22
Azores Islands (Port.)	890	287,091	Ponta Delgada	B 4	34
B					
Bahama Islands (Br.)	4,404	131,000	Nassau	C 1	45
Bahrein Islands	213	125,000	Manama	F 4	26
Balearic Islands (Sp.)	1,936	422,127	Palma	H 3	17
Barbados (Br.)	166	235,000	Bridgetown	G 4	45
Barbuda and Redonda Is.	63	979	Codrington	F-G 3	45
Basutoland (Br.)	11,716	641,674	Maseru	M17	35
Bechuanaland Protectorate (Br.)	275,000	327,305	Mafeking	L16	35
Belgian Congo	902,274	13,559,000	Léopoldville	L12	35
*Belgium	11,775	9,053,000	Brussels (Bruxelles)	E 7	15
Bermuda (Br.)	21	43,000	Hamilton	G 2	45
Bhutan	18,000	640,000	Bumthang	F 3	29
Bismarck Archipelago (Terr. of New Guinea)	19,660	133,465	Rabaul	E 6	37
*Bolivia	412,777	3,349,000	La Paz, Sucre	G 7	46
Bonin Is. (U.S. Adm.)	76	190		E 3	37
Borneo	208,286			E 5	31
*Brazil	3,286,170	63,511,000	Brasília	K 6	46
British Columbia, Canada	359,279	1,398,464	Victoria	F 4	40
British Honduras	8,867	59,220	Belize	C 2	39
Brunei (Br.)	2,226	75,000	Brunei	E 5	31

Country	Area (Sq. Miles)	Population	Capital or Chief Town	Index Ref.	Plate No.
*Bulgaria	42,796	7,600,525	Sofia (Sofiya)	G 4	21
*Burma	261,610	20,457,000	Rangoon	G 2	30
*Byelorussian S.S.R. (White Russian S.S.R.) (U.S.S.R.).	80,100	8,060,000	Minsk	D 4	22
C					
California, U.S.A.	156,803	10,586,223	Sacramento	C 5	42
*Cambodia	69,884	4,740,000	Phnom Penh	E 4	30
Cameroons (Br. Trust.)	34,081	1,591,000	Lagos	J10	34
Cameroons	161,787	3,200,000	Yaoundé	J10	34
*Canada	3,621,616	16,080,791	Ottawa		40, 41
Canal Zone (U.S.A.)	362	53,000	Balboa Heights	G 6	39
Canary Islands (Sp.)	2,894	776,912	Las Palmas, Santa Cruz	B 4	17
Cape of Good Hope, Union of South Africa	277,169	4,421,704	Cape Town	M18	35
Cape Verde Islands (Port.)	1,557	192,000	Praia	N 5	6
Caroline Islands (U.S. Trust)	525	36,980	Moen, Ponape	E 5	37
Cayman Islands (Br.)	104	9,000	Georgetown	B 3	45
Celebes, Indonesia	72,986	6,029,198	Makassar	G 6	31
Central Africa	239,382	1,150,000	Bangui	K10	34
Central America	217,813	8,918,547			39
*Ceylon	25,332	9,361,000	Colombo	D 7	29
Chad	455,598	2,600,000	Fort Lamy	K 9	34
Channel Islands (Br.)	75	102,776	St. Helier	E 8	10
Chatham Islands (N.Z.)	372	471	Waitangi	J10	37
*Chile	286,396	7,298,000	Santiago	F10	47
China: Mainland.	3,745,296	640,000,000	Peiping		32
*China: Taiwan.	13,885	10,039,000	Taipei		32
Christmas Island (Aust.)	60	2,620		O11	25
*Colombia	439,828	13,824,000	Bogotá	F 3	46
Colorado, U.S.A.	103,967	1,325,089	Denver	G 5	42
Comoro Is. (Is. Comores) (Fr.)	849	182,000	Dzaoudzi	P14	35
Congo	175,676	780,000	Pointe-Noire	J12	35
Connecticut, U.S.A.	4,899	2,007,280	Hartford	P 4	43
Cook Islands (N.Z.)	99	16,680	Avarua	K 7	37
Corsica (Corse) (Fr.)	3,367	204,266	Ajaccio	G 6	16
*Costa Rica	19,238	1,114,000	San José	E 5	39
Crete (Krētē), Greece	3,232	441,687	Candia (Erákleion)	G 8	21
*Cuba	42,857	6,466,000	Havana		48
Curaçao (Neth. Antilles)	173	95,195	Willemstad	E 4	45
Cyprus	3,572	528,618	Nicosia	E 5	28
*Czechoslovakia	49,356	13,522,000	Prague (Praha)	D 2	20
D					
Dahomey	42,471	1,725,000	Porto-Novo	G10	34
Daito Is. (U.S. Adm.)	18	2,691		M 6	32
Damão (Port. India)	213	69,005	Damão	B 4	29
Delaware, U.S.A.	1,978	318,085	Dover	P 5	43
*Denmark	16,556	4,448,401	Copenhagen (Köbenhavn)	E 9	13
District of Columbia, U.S.A.	61	802,178	Washington	O 5	43
Diu (Port. India)	12	21,138	Diu	B 4	29
Dominica (Br.)	305	64,000	Roseau	G 4	45
*Dominican Republic	19,129	2,791,000	Ciudad Trujillo	D 6	48

ABBREVIATIONS

Aust. = Australian.	I. = Island.	Pak. = Pakistan.	Trust. = Trust Territory.
Belg. = Belgian or Belgium.	Is. = Islands.	pen. = peninsula.	U.S.A. = United States of America.
Br. = British Commonwealth of Nations.	It. = Italian or Italy	Port. = Portugal or Portuguese.	U.S. Adm. = U.S. Administration
	Jap. = Japan or Japanese.	Rep. = Republic.	U.S.S.R. = Union of Soviet Socialist
Dan. = Danish or Denmark.	Mand. = Mandate.	So. = South.	Republics.
E. = East.	N. = North.	Sp. = Spain or Spanish.	U. of So.
Fr. = France or French.	Neth. = Netherlands.	sq. mi. = square miles.	Africa = Union of South Africa.
Gr. = Greece or Greek.	N. Z. = New Zealand.	S. S. R. = Soviet Socialist Republic.	W. = West.

© Copyright MCMLX by C. S. Hammond & Co., New York. Printed in U.S.A.

Country	Area (Sq. Miles)	Population	Capital or Chief Town	Index Ref.	Plate No.
E					
*Ecuador ....approx.	115,000	4,127,000	Quito	E 4	46
Egypt, U.A.R.	386,000	22,992,150	Cairo	M 6	34
England and Wales	58,340	45,109,000	London	.....	10
Eritrea	15,754	1,125,000	Asmara	O 8	34
Estonia (Estonian S.S.R., U.S.S.R.)	17,400	1,100,000	Tallinn (Tallin)	D 4	22
*Ethiopia (excl. Eritrea)	350,000	16,899,000	Addis Ababa	O 9	34
Europe	4,129,908	572,000,000		.....	9
F					
Faeröe Islands (Den.)	540	32,456	Thorshavn	D 2	9
Falkland Islands (Br.)	5,618	2,000	Stanley	H14	47
Fed. of Rhodesia & Nyasaland	477,482	7,650,000	Salisbury	M14	35
Fernando Pó (island, Sp. Guinea)	800	40,475	Santa Isabel	H11	34
Fiji (Br.)	7,036	345,737	Suva	H 7	37
*Finland	130,500	4,400,000	Helsinki	P 4	13
Florida, U.S.A.	54,262	2,771,305	Tallahassee	N 7	43
Formosa (Taiwan) (China)	13,885	10,039,000	Taipei	K 7	32
*France	212,736	44,600,000	Paris	.....	16
Franz Josef Land (Fridtjof Nansen Ld.)	....	....		F 1	22
G					
Gabon	90,733	410,000	Libreville	J12	35
Galápagos Islands, Ecuador	3,042	1,346	Pto. Baquerizo	D 7	46
Gambia (Br.)	4,033	277,000	Bathurst	C 9	34
Georgia, U.S.A.	58,518	3,444,578	Atlanta	N 6	43
Georgian S.S.R. (U.S.S.R.)	29,400	4,000,000	Tbilisi (Tiflis)	F 5	22
Germany, East (German Democratic Republic)	41,535	16,263,000	Berlin	.....	14
Germany, West (Federal Republic of)	95,914	52,592,000	Bonn	.....	14
*Ghana	91,844	4,836,000	Accra	F10	34
Gibraltar (Br.)	2	26,000	....	D 4	17
Gilbert, Ellice and Phoenix Islands	196	39,000	Bairiki	H 6	37
Gôa (Port. India)	1,313	547,703	Pangim	B 5	29
*Great Britain and Northern Ireland	94,279	50,211,602	London	E 3	9
*Greece	51,182	8,216,000	Athens (Athenai)	F 6	21
Greenland (Den.)	839,999	28,000	Godthaab	D22	8
Grenada (Br.)	133	91,000	St. George's	G 4	45
Guadeloupe and Dependencies (Fr.)	688	259,000	Basse-Terre	F 3	45
Guam (U.S.A.)	203	59,498	Agaña	E 4	37
Guatemala	45,452	3,546,000	Guatemala	B 3	39
Guiana, British	89,480	533,000	Georgetown	J 2	46
Guiana, French	35,135	30,000	Cayenne	K 3	46
Guiana, Netherlands (Surinam)	54,300	241,000	Paramaribo	J 3	46
*Guinea	96,525	2,650,000	Conakry	D 9	34
Guinea, Portuguese	13,948	559,000	Bissau	C 9	34
Guinea, Spanish	10,830	215,000	Santa Isabel	J11	35
H					
*Haiti	10,714	3,424,000	Port-au-Prince	C 5	48
Hawaii, U.S.A.	6,406	499,794	Honolulu	L 3	37
Hispaniola	29,843	6,215,000	....	D 2	45
*Holland (Netherlands)....land	12,883	9,625,499	The Hague, Amsterdam	F 4	15
*Honduras	45,000	1,828,000	Tegucigalpa	D 3	39
Honduras, British	8,867	85,000	Belize	C 2	39
Hong Kong (Br.)	391	2,748,000	Victoria	J 7	32
*Hungary	35,875	9,898,000	Budapest	E 3	20
I					
*Iceland	39,709	169,000	Reykjavik	C 2	9
Idaho, U.S.A.	82,808	588,637	Boise	E 3	42
Ifni (Sp.)	680	45,000	Sidi Ifni	D 6	34
Illinois, U.S.A.	55,947	8,712,176	Springfield	L 4	43
*India	1,059,342	397,540,000	New Delhi	.....	29
India, Portuguese	1,538	637,846	Pangim	B 4-5	29
Indiana, U.S.A.	36,205	3,934,224	Indianapolis	M 5	43
Indochina	285,927	27,000,000	....	E 3	30
*Indonesia (East Indies)	735,268	86,900,000	Djakarta (Batavia)	F 7	31
Iowa, U.S.A.	55,986	2,621,073	Des Moines	K 4	43
*Iran (Persia)	628,000	18,944,821	Tehran	H 4	27
*Iraq (Mesopotamia)	116,000	6,317,043	Baghdad	C 4	27
*Ireland (Eire)	26,601	2,898,264	Dublin (Baile Atha Cliath)	.....	12
Ireland, Northern	5,238	1,370,709	Belfast	H 2	12
Isle of Man (Br.)	221	55,000	Douglas	C 3	10
*Israel	7,978	2,045,000	Jerusalem	.....	24
*Italy	116,000	48,739,000	Rome (Roma)	.....	18
Ivory Coast	183,397	3,090,000	Abidjan	E10	34
J					
Jamaica (Br.)	4,411	1,630,000	Kingston	C 3	45
Jammu and Kashmir	82,258	4,410,000	Srinagar	C 2	29
*Japan	142,743	89,275,529	Tokyo	.....	33
Java and Madura, Indonesia	51,032	53,060,209	Djakarta	K 2	31
*Jordan	34,750	1,607,000	Amman	D 4	24
K					
Kansas, U.S.A.	82,113	1,905,299	Topeka	J 5	42
Kashmir and Jammu	82,258	4,410,000	Srinagar	C 2	29

Country	Area (Sq. Miles)	Population	Capital or Chief Town	Index Ref.	Plate No.
Kazakh S.S.R. (U.S.S.R.)	1,061,600	8,500,000	Alma-Ata	H 5	22
Kentucky, U.S.A.	40,109	2,944,806	Frankfort	M 5	43
Kenya (Br.)	219,730	6,351,000	Nairobi	O11	35
Kerguelen Arch. (Madag.)	....	....		T 8	6
Kirghiz S.S.R. (U.S.S.R.)	76,100	1,900,000	Frunze	J 5	22
Korea, North	49,096	7,972,000	Pyongyang	C 4	33
Korea, South	36,152	22,633,000	Seoul	C 5	33
Krētē (Crete), Greece	3,232	441,687	Candia (Erákleion)	G 8	21
Kuria Muria Is. (Aden)	28	70		G 6	26
Kuril Is. (Chishima) (U.S.S.R.)	5,700	6,000	Severo-Kuril'sk	R 5	23
Kuwait	8,000	206,177	Al Kuwait	E 4	26
L					
Laccadive Islands (India)	746	18,393	....	B 6	29
*Laos	89,343	1,690,000	Vientiane	E 3	30
Latvia (Latvian S.S.R., U.S.S.R.)	24,600	2,000,000	Riga	D 4	22
*Lebanon	3,475	1,525,000	Beirut	F 6	28
*Liberia	43,000	1,250,000	Monrovia	E10	34
*Libya	679,358	1,153,000	Tripoli, Benghazi	K 6	34
Liechtenstein	65	14,861	Vaduz	J 2	19
Lithuania (Lithuanian S.S.R., U.S.S.R.)	25,200	2,700,000	Vilna (Vil'nyus)	D 4	22
Louisiana, U.S.A.	45,177	2,683,516	Baton Rouge	K 7	43
Loyalty Islands (Fr.)	800	11,100	Chépénéhé	G 8	37
*Luxembourg	999	320,000	Luxembourg	J 9	15
M					
Macao (Port.)	6	210,000	Macao	H 7	32
Madagascar	241,094	5,050,000	Tananarive	R15	35
Madeira Islands (Port.)	308	269,179	Funchal	A 2	17
Madura I., Indonesia	1,725	1,962,462	Pamekasan	K 2	31
Maine, U.S.A.	31,040	913,774	Augusta	R 3	43
Malaya, Fed. of	50,690	6,279,000	Kuala Lumpur	E 6	30
Maldive Islands	115	81,950	Malé	L 9	25
Malgache Republic	241,094	5,050,000	Tananarive	R15	35
Malta (Br.)	122	319,656	Valletta	E 7	18
Manchuria (China)	412,801	46,893,351	Mukden	K 2	32
Manitoba, Canada	219,723	850,040	Winnipeg	L 3	40
Mariana Islands (U.S. Trust.)	142	6,286	Garapan	E 4	37
Marquesas Is. (Fr.)	480	2,976	Atuona	N 6	37
Marshall Islands (U.S. Trust)	61	11,033	Majuro	H 4	37
Martinique (Fr.)	425	265,000	Fort-de-France	G 4	45
Maryland, U.S.A.	9,887	2,343,001	Annapolis	O 5	43
Massachusetts, U.S.A.	7,907	4,690,514	Boston	P 4	43
Mauritania	328,185	640,000	Nouakchott	D 8	34
Mauritius (Br.)	720	603,000	Port Louis	S19	35
*Mexico	760,373	32,348,000	Mexico City	.....	44
Michigan, U.S.A.	57,022	6,371,766	Lansing	M 3	43
Midway Islands (U.S.A.)	2	437		J 3	37
Minnesota, U.S.A.	80,009	2,982,483	St. Paul	K 3	43
Mississippi, U.S.A.	47,420	2,178,914	Jackson	L 6	43
Missouri, U.S.A.	69,270	3,954,653	Jefferson City	K 5	43
Moldavian S.S.R. (U.S.S.R.)	13,100	2,700,000	Kishinev	D 5	22
Molucca Islands, Indonesia	30,168	683,416	Amboina	H 6	31
Monaco	370 Acres	20,442	Monaco	G 6	16
Mongolian Republic	625,946	1,000,000	Ulan Bator	F 2	32
Montana, U.S.A.	146,316	591,024	Helena	F 3	42
Montserrat (Br.)	32	14,000	Plymouth	G 3	45
*Morocco	171,583	10,330,000	Rabat	E 5	34
Mozambique	297,731	6,234,000	Lourenço Marques	O15	35
N					
Natal, Union of South Africa	35,284	2,408,563	Pieter-maritzburg	N17	35
Nauru (Austr.-N. Z.-Br. Tr. Ter.)	8	4,000		G 6	37
Nebraska, U.S.A.	76,653	1,325,510	Lincoln	H 4	42
*Nepal	54,000	9,044,000	Katmandu	D 3	29
*Netherlands (Holland)....land	12,883	11,299,000	Amsterdam, The Hague	F 4	15
Netherlands Antilles	383	193,000	Willemstad	E 4	45
Nevada, U.S.A.	109,802	160,083	Carson City	D 5	42
New Britain (island) (Terr. of New Guinea)	14,600	85,115	Rabaul	F 6	31
New Brunswick, Canada	27,473	554,616	Fredericton	G 4	41
New Caledonia (Fr.)	7,201	69,000	Nouméa	G 8	37
Newfoundland, Canada	42,734	415,074	St. John's	J 4	41
New Guinea, Terr. of (Aust. Trust.)	93,000	1,341,000	Port Moresby	B 7	31
New Guinea, Netherlands	161,514	700,000	Hollandia	K 6	31
New Hampshire, U.S.A.	9,024	533,242	Concord	R 3	43
New Hebrides Islands (Br. and Fr.)	5,700	52,000	Vila	G 7	37
New Ireland (island) (Terr. of New Guinea)	3,800	33,930	Kavieng	F 6	37
New Jersey, U.S.A.	7,522	4,835,329	Trenton	P 5	43
New Mexico, U.S.A.	121,511	681,187	Santa Fe	G 6	42
New South Wales, Australia	309,432	3,423,718	Sydney	H 6	36
New York, U.S.A.	47,929	14,830,192	Albany	P 4	43
*New Zealand	103,934	2,174,062	Wellington	M 7	36
*Nicaragua	57,143	1,378,000	Managua	E 4	39
Nicobar Islands (India)	635	12,452	Port Blair	F 7	29
Niger	501,930	2,450,000	Niamey	H 8	34
Nigeria	372,674	33,043,000	Lagos	H10	34
Niue I. (Br.)	100	4,707	Alofi	K 7	37
Norfolk Island (Australia)	15	1,000	Kingston	G 8	37
North America	9,124,000	250,000,000	....	.....	38
North Borneo (Br.)	29,387	409,000	Jesselton	F 5	31
North Carolina, U.S.A.	49,142	4,061,929	Raleigh	O 6	43
North Dakota, U.S.A.	70,054	619,636	Bismarck	J 3	42
Northern Ireland (Br.)	5,238	1,402,000	Belfast	H 2	12

Hammond's
WORLD ATLAS AND GAZETTEER

GAZETTEER-INDEX OF THE WORLD

This alphabetical list of grand divisions, countries, states, colonial possessions, etc., gives area, population, capital, seat of government or chief town, and index references and numbers of plates on which they are shown on the largest scale. The mother country of colonial possessions is indicated by abbreviations in parentheses. The index reference shows the square on the respective map in which the name of the country, state or colonial possession is located.

Country	Area (Sq. Miles)	Population	Capital or Chief Town	Index Ref.	Plate No.
A					
Aden Colony (Br.)	75	138,441	Aden	E 7	26
Aden Protectorate (Br.)	112,000	650,000	Aden	E 7	26
*Afghanistan	250,000	13,000,000	Kabul	J 3	26
Africa	11,850,000	225,000,000			34, 35
Alabama, U.S.A.	51,078	3,061,743	Montgomery	M 6	43
Alaska, U.S.A.	571,065	128,643	Juneau	F 8	42
*Albania	11,096	1,391,499	Tirana (Tiranë)	E 5	21
Alberta, Canada	248,800	1,123,116	Edmonton	G 4	40
Aleutian Islands (U.S.A.)	6,800	5,600	Unalaska	F 3	6
Algeria (Fr.)	851,284	10,265,000	Algiers (Alger)	G 5	34
Andaman Is. (India)	2,508	21,316	Port Blair	F 6	29
Andorra	191	6,000	Andorra la Vella	G 1	17
Angola	481,351	4,392,000	Luanda	K14	35
Antarctica	5,500,000				8
Antigua (incl. Barbuda and Redonda)	171	56,000	St. Johns	G 3	45
Antilles, Greater, Lesser				E 3	45
Arabia	1,000,000	9,000,000		D 5	26
Arctic Ocean					8
*Argentina	1,078,266	20,438,000	Buenos Aires	H10	47
Arizona, U.S.A.	113,580	749,587	Phoenix	E 6	42
Arkansas, U.S.A.	52,725	1,909,511	Little Rock	K 6	43
Armenian S.S.R. (U.S.S.R.)	11,500	1,600,000	Erivan (Yerevan)	F 5	22
Ascension Island (Br.)	34	183	Georgetown	D13	35
Asia	16,500,000	1,596,000,000			25
*Australia, Commonwealth of.	2,974,581	9,952,000	Canberra		36
Australian Capital Territory.	939	30,315	Canberra	J 7	36
*Austria	32,369	7,021,000	Vienna (Wien)	B-C 3	20
Azerbaidzhan S.S.R. (U.S.S.R.)	33,100	3,400,000	Baku	F 5	22
Azores Islands (Port.)	890	287,091	Ponta Delgada	B 4	34
B					
Bahama Islands (Br.)	4,404	131,000	Nassau	C 1	45
Bahrein Islands	213	125,000	Manama	F 4	26
Balearic Islands (Sp.)	1,936	422,127	Palma	H 3	17
Barbados (Br.)	166	235,000	Bridgetown	G 4	45
Barbuda and Redonda Is.	63	979	Codrington	F-G 3	45
Basutoland (Br.)	11,716	641,674	Maseru	M17	35
Bechuanaland Protectorate (Br.)	275,000	327,305	Mafeking	L16	35
Belgian Congo	902,274	13,559,000	Léopoldville	L12	35
*Belgium	11,775	9,053,000	Brussels (Bruxelles)	E 7	15
Bermuda (Br.)	21	43,000	Hamilton	G 2	45
Bhutan	18,000	640,000	Bumthang	F 3	29
Bismarck Archipelago (Terr. of New Guinea)	19,660	133,465	Rabaul	E 6	37
*Bolivia	412,777	3,349,000	La Paz, Sucre	G 7	46
Bonin Is. (U.S. Adm.)	76	190		E 3	37
Borneo	208,286			E 5	31
*Brazil	3,286,170	63,511,000	Brasília	K 6	46
British Columbia, Canada	359,279	1,398,464	Victoria	F 4	40
British Honduras	8,867	59,220	Belize	C 2	39
Brunei (Br.)	2,226	75,000	Brunei	E 5	31

Country	Area (Sq. Miles)	Population	Capital or Chief Town	Index Ref.	Plate No.
*Bulgaria	42,796	7,600,525	Sofia (Sofiya)	G 4	21
*Burma	261,610	20,457,000	Rangoon	G 2	30
*Byelorussian S.S.R. (White Russian S.S.R.) (U.S.S.R.).	80,100	8,060,000	Minsk	D 4	22
C					
California, U.S.A.	156,803	10,586,223	Sacramento	C 5	42
*Cambodia	69,884	4,740,000	Phnom Penh	E 4	30
Cameroons (Br. Trust.)	34,081	1,591,000	Lagos	J10	34
Cameroons	161,787	3,200,000	Yaoundé	J10	34
*Canada	3,621,616	16,080,791	Ottawa		40, 41
Canal Zone (U.S.A.)	362	53,000	Balboa Heights	G 6	39
Canary Islands (Sp.)	2,894	776,912	Las Palmas, Santa Cruz	B 4	17
Cape of Good Hope, Union of South Africa	277,169	4,421,704	Cape Town	M18	35
Cape Verde Islands (Port.)	1,557	192,000	Praia	N 5	6
Caroline Islands (U.S. Trust)	525	36,980	Moen, Ponape	E 5	37
Cayman Islands (Br.)	104	9,000	Georgetown	B 3	45
Celebes, Indonesia	72,986	6,029,198	Makassar	G 6	31
Central Africa	239,382	1,150,000	Bangui	K10	34
Central America	217,813	8,918,547			39
*Ceylon	25,332	9,361,000	Colombo	D 7	29
Chad	455,598	2,600,000	Fort Lamy	K 9	34
Channel Islands (Br.)	75	102,776	St. Helier	E 8	10
Chatham Islands (N.Z.)	372	471	Waitangi	J10	37
*Chile	286,396	7,298,000	Santiago	F10	47
China: Mainland	3,745,296	640,000,000	Peiping		32
*China: Taiwan	13,885	10,039,000	Taipei		32
Christmas Island (Aust.)	60	2,620		O11	25
*Colombia	439,828	13,824,000	Bogotá	F 3	46
Colorado, U.S.A.	103,967	1,325,089	Denver	G 5	42
Comoro Is. (Is. Comores) (Fr.)	849	182,000	Dzaoudzi	P14	35
Congo	175,676	780,000	Pointe-Noire	J12	35
Connecticut, U.S.A.	4,899	2,007,280	Hartford	P 4	43
Cook Islands (N.Z.)	99	16,680	Avarua	K 7	37
Corsica (Corse) (Fr.)	3,367	204,266	Ajaccio	G 6	16
*Costa Rica	19,238	1,114,000	San José	E 5	39
Crete (Krētē), Greece	3,232	441,687	Candia (Erákleion)	G 8	21
*Cuba	42,857	6,466,000	Havana		48
Curaçao (Neth. Antilles)	173	95,195	Willemstad	E 4	45
Cyprus	3,572	528,618	Nicosia	E 5	28
*Czechoslovakia	49,356	13,522,000	Prague (Praha)	D 2	20
D					
Dahomey	42,471	1,725,000	Porto-Novo	G10	34
Daito Is. (U.S. Adm.)	18	2,691		M 6	32
Damão (Port. India)	213	69,005	Damão	B 4	29
Delaware, U.S.A.	1,978	318,085	Dover	P 5	43
*Denmark	16,556	4,448,401	Copenhagen (Köbenhavn)	E 9	13
District of Columbia, U.S.A.	61	802,178	Washington	O 5	43
Diu (Port. India)	12	21,138	Diu	B 4	29
Dominica (Br.)	305	64,000	Roseau	G 4	45
*Dominican Republic	19,129	2,791,000	Ciudad Trujillo	D 6	48

ABBREVIATIONS

Aust.	= Australian.	I.	= Island.	Pak.	= Pakistan.	Trust.	= Trust Territory.
Belg.	= Belgian or Belgium.	Is.	= Islands.	pen.	= peninsula.	U. S. A.	= United States of America.
Br.	= British Commonwealth of Nations.	It.	= Italian or Italy.	Port.	= Portugal or Portuguese.	U. S. Adm.	= U. S. Administration
		Jap.	= Japan or Japanese.	Rep.	= Republic.	U. S. S. R.	= Union of Soviet Socialist Republics.
Dan.	= Danish or Denmark.	Mand.	= Mandate.	So.	= South.		
E.	= East.	N.	= North.	Sp.	= Spain or Spanish.	U. of So.	
Fr.	= France or French.	Neth.	= Netherlands.	sq. mi.	= square miles.	Africa	= Union of South Africa.
Gr.	= Greece or Greek.	N. Z.	= New Zealand.	S. S. R.	= Soviet Socialist Republic.	W.	= West.

Country	Area (Sq. Miles)	Population	Capital or Chief Town	Index Ref.	Plate No.
E					
*Ecuador ....approx.	115,000	4,127,000	Quito	E 4	46
Egypt, U.A.R.	386,000	22,992,150	Cairo	M 6	34
England and Wales	58,340	45,109,000	London	.....	10
Eritrea	15,754	1,125,000	Asmara	O 8	34
Estonia (Estonian S.S.R., U.S.S.R.)	17,400	1,100,000	Tallinn (Tallin)	D 4	22
*Ethiopia (excl. Eritrea)	350,000	16,899,000	Addis Ababa	O 9	34
Europe	4,129,908	572,000,000		.....	9
F					
Faeröe Islands (Den.)	540	32,456	Thorshavn	D 2	9
Falkland Islands (Br.)	5,618	2,000	Stanley	H14	47
Fed. of Rhodesia & Nyasaland	477,482	7,650,000	Salisbury	M14	35
Fernando Pó (island, Sp. Guinea)	800	40,475	Santa Isabel	H11	34
Fiji (Br.)	7,036	345,737	Suva	H 7	37
*Finland	130,500	4,400,000	Helsinki	P 4	13
Florida, U.S.A.	54,262	2,771,305	Tallahassee	N 7	43
Formosa (Taiwan) (China)	13,885	10,039,000	Taipei	K 7	32
*France	212,736	44,600,000	Paris	.....	16
Franz Josef Land (Fridtjof Nansen Ld.)				F 1	22
G					
Gabon	90,733	410,000	Libreville	J12	35
Galápagos Islands, Ecuador	3,042	1,346	Pto. Baquerizo	D 7	46
Gambia (Br.)	4,033	277,000	Bathurst	C 9	34
Georgia, U.S.A.	58,518	3,444,578	Atlanta	N 6	43
Georgian S.S.R. (U.S.S.R.)	29,400	4,000,000	Tbilisi (Tiflis)	F 5	22
Germany, East (German Democratic Republic)	41,535	16,263,000	Berlin	.....	14
Germany, West (Federal Republic of)	95,914	52,592,000	Bonn	.....	14
*Ghana	91,844	4,836,000	Accra	F10	34
Gibraltar (Br.)	2	26,000		D 4	17
Gilbert, Ellice and Phoenix Islands	196	39,000	Bairiki	H 6	37
Gôa (Port. India)	1,313	547,703	Pangim	B 5	29
*Great Britain and Northern Ireland	94,279	50,211,602	London	E 3	9
*Greece	51,182	8,216,000	Athens (Athenai)	F 6	21
Greenland (Den.)	839,999	28,000	Godthaab	D22	8
Grenada (Br.)	133	91,000	St. George's	G 4	45
Guadeloupe and Dependencies (Fr.)	688	259,000	Basse-Terre	F 3	45
Guam (U.S.A.)	203	59,498	Agaña	E 4	37
Guatemala	45,452	3,546,000	Guatemala	B 3	39
Guiana, British	89,480	533,000	Georgetown	J 2	46
Guiana, French	35,135	30,000	Cayenne	K 3	46
Guiana, Netherlands (Surinam)	54,300	241,000	Paramaribo	J 3	46
*Guinea	96,525	2,650,000	Conakry	D 9	34
Guinea, Portuguese	13,948	559,000	Bissau	C 9	34
Guinea, Spanish	10,830	215,000	Santa Isabel	J11	35
H					
*Haiti	10,714	3,424,000	Port-au-Prince	C 5	48
Hawaii, U.S.A.	6,406	499,794	Honolulu	L 3	37
Hispaniola	29,843	6,215,000	....	D 2	45
*Holland (Netherlands)....land	12,883	9,625,499	The Hague, Amsterdam	F 4	15
*Honduras	45,000	1,828,000	Tegucigalpa	D 3	39
Honduras, British	8,867	85,000	Belize	C 2	39
Hong Kong (Br.)	391	2,748,000	Victoria	J 7	32
*Hungary	35,875	9,898,000	Budapest	E 3	20
I					
*Iceland	39,709	169,000	Reykjavik	C 2	9
Idaho, U.S.A.	82,808	588,637	Boise	E 3	42
Ifni (Sp.)	680	45,000	Sidi Ifni	D 6	34
Illinois, U.S.A.	55,947	8,712,176	Springfield	L 4	43
*India	1,059,342	397,540,000	New Delhi	.....	29
India, Portuguese	1,538	637,846	Pangim	B 4-5	29
Indiana, U.S.A.	36,205	3,934,224	Indianapolis	M 5	43
Indochina	285,927	27,000,000		E 3	30
*Indonesia (East Indies)	735,268	86,900,000	Djakarta (Batavia)	F 7	31
Iowa, U.S.A.	55,986	2,621,073	Des Moines	K 4	43
*Iran (Persia)	628,000	18,944,821	Tehran	H 4	27
*Iraq (Mesopotamia)	116,000	6,317,043	Baghdad	C 4	27
*Ireland (Eire)	26,601	2,898,264	Dublin (Baile Atha Cliath)	.....	12
Ireland, Northern	5,238	1,370,709	Belfast	H 2	12
Isle of Man (Br.)	221	55,000	Douglas	C 3	10
*Israel	7,978	2,045,000	Jerusalem	.....	24
*Italy	116,000	48,739,000	Rome (Roma)	E 3	18
Ivory Coast	183,397	3,090,000	Abidjan	E10	34
J					
Jamaica (Br.)	4,411	1,630,000	Kingston	C 3	45
Jammu and Kashmir	82,258	4,410,000	Srinagar	C 2	29
*Japan	142,743	89,275,529	Tokyo	.....	33
Java and Madura, Indonesia	51,032	53,060,209	Djakarta	K 2	31
*Jordan	34,750	1,607,000	Amman	D 4	24
K					
Kansas, U.S.A.	82,113	1,905,299	Topeka	J 5	42
Kashmir and Jammu	82,258	4,410,000	Srinagar	C 2	29
Kazakh S.S.R. (U.S.S.R.)	1,061,600	8,500,000	Alma-Ata	H 5	22
Kentucky, U.S.A.	40,109	2,944,806	Frankfort	M 5	43
Kenya (Br.)	219,730	6,351,000	Nairobi	O11	35
Kerguelen Arch. (Madag.)	....			T 8	6
Kirghiz S.S.R. (U.S.S.R.)	76,100	1,900,000	Frunze	J 5	22
Korea, North	49,096	7,972,000	Pyongyang	C 4	33
Korea, South	36,152	22,633,000	Seoul	C 5	33
Krētē (Crete), Greece	3,232	441,687	Candia (Erákleion)	G 8	21
Kuria Muria Is. (Aden)	28	70		G 6	26
Kuril Is. (Chishima) (U.S.S.R.)	5,700	6,000	Severo-Kuril'sk	R 5	23
Kuwait	8,000	206,177	Al Kuwait	E 4	26
L					
Laccadive Islands (India)	746	18,393	.....	B 6	29
*Laos	89,343	1,690,000	Vientiane	E 3	30
Latvia (Latvian S.S.R., U.S.S.R.)	24,600	2,000,000	Riga	D 4	22
*Lebanon	3,475	1,525,000	Beirut	F 6	28
*Liberia	43,000	1,250,000	Monrovia	E10	34
*Libya	679,358	1,153,000	Tripoli, Benghazi	K 6	34
Liechtenstein	65	14,861	Vaduz	J 2	19
Lithuania (Lithuanian S.S.R., U.S.S.R.)	25,200	2,700,000	Vilna (Vil'nyus)	D 4	22
Louisiana, U.S.A.	45,177	2,683,516	Baton Rouge	K 7	43
Loyalty Islands (Fr.)	800	11,100	Chépénéhé	G 8	37
*Luxembourg	999	320,000	Luxembourg	J 9	15
M					
Macao (Port.)	6	210,000	Macao	H 7	32
Madagascar	241,094	5,050,000	Tananarive	R15	35
Madeira Islands (Port.)	308	269,179	Funchal	A 2	17
Madura I., Indonesia	1,725	1,962,462	Pamekasan	K 2	31
Maine, U.S.A.	31,040	913,774	Augusta	R 3	43
Malaya, Fed. of	50,690	6,279,000	Kuala Lumpur	E 6	30
Maldive Islands	115	81,950	Malé	L 9	25
Malgache Republic	241,094	5,050,000	Tananarive	R15	35
Malta (Br.)	122	319,656	Valletta	E 7	18
Manchuria (China)	412,801	46,893,351	Mukden	K 2	32
Manitoba, Canada	219,723	850,040	Winnipeg	L 3	40
Mariana Islands (U.S. Trust.)	142	6,286	Garapan	E 4	37
Marquesas Is. (Fr.)	480	2,976	Atuona	N 6	37
Marshall Islands (U.S. Trust)	61	11,033	Majuro	H 4	37
Martinique (Fr.)	425	265,000	Fort-de-France	G 4	45
Maryland, U.S.A.	9,887	2,343,001	Annapolis	O 5	43
Massachusetts, U.S.A.	7,907	4,690,514	Boston	P 4	43
Mauritania	328,185	640,000	Nouakchott	D 8	34
Mauritius (Br.)	720	603,000	Port Louis	S19	35
*Mexico	760,373	32,348,000	Mexico City	.....	44
Michigan, U.S.A.	57,022	6,371,766	Lansing	M 3	43
Midway Islands (U.S.A.)	2	437		J 3	37
Minnesota, U.S.A.	80,009	2,982,483	St. Paul	K 3	43
Mississippi, U.S.A.	47,420	2,178,914	Jackson	L 6	43
Missouri, U.S.A.	69,270	3,954,653	Jefferson City	K 5	43
Moldavian S.S.R. (U.S.S.R.)	13,100	2,700,000	Kishinev	D 5	22
Molucca Islands, Indonesia	30,168	683,416	Amboina	H 6	31
Monaco	370 Acres	20,442	Monaco	G 6	16
Mongolian Republic	625,946	1,000,000	Ulan Bator	F 2	32
Montana, U.S.A.	146,316	591,024	Helena	F 3	42
Montserrat (Br.)	32	14,000	Plymouth	G 3	45
*Morocco	171,583	10,330,000	Rabat	E 5	34
Mozambique	297,731	6,234,000	Lourenço Marques	O15	35
N					
Natal, Union of South Africa	35,284	2,408,563	Pieter-maritzburg	N17	35
Nauru (Austr.-N. Z.-Br. Tr. Ter.)	8	4,000		G 6	37
Nebraska, U.S.A.	76,653	1,325,510	Lincoln	H 4	42
*Nepal	54,000	9,044,000	Katmandu	D 3	29
*Netherlands (Holland)....land	12,833	11,299,000	Amsterdam, The Hague	F 4	15
Netherlands Antilles	383	193,000	Willemstad	E 4	45
Nevada, U.S.A.	109,802	160,083	Carson City	D 5	42
New Britain (island) (Terr. of New Guinea)	14,600	85,115	Rabaul	F 6	37
New Brunswick, Canada	27,473	554,616	Fredericton	G 4	41
New Caledonia (Fr.)	7,201	69,000	Nouméa	G 8	37
Newfoundland, Canada	42,734	415,074	St. John's	J 4	41
New Guinea, Terr. of (Aust. Trust.)	93,000	1,341,000	Port Moresby	B 7	31
New Guinea, Netherlands	161,514	700,000	Hollandia	K 6	31
New Hampshire, U.S.A.	9,024	533,242	Concord	R 3	43
New Hebrides Islands (Br. and Fr.)	5,700	52,000	Vila	G 7	37
New Ireland (island) (Terr. of New Guinea)	3,800	33,930	Kavieng	F 6	37
New Jersey, U.S.A.	7,522	4,835,329	Trenton	P 5	43
New Mexico, U.S.A.	121,511	681,187	Santa Fe	G 6	42
New South Wales, Australia	309,432	3,423,718	Sydney	H 6	36
New York, U.S.A.	47,929	14,830,192	Albany	P 4	43
*New Zealand	103,934	2,174,062	Wellington	M 7	36
*Nicaragua	57,143	1,378,000	Managua	E 4	39
Nicobar Islands (India)	635	12,452	Port Blair	F 7	29
Niger	501,930	2,450,000	Niamey	H 8	34
Nigeria	372,674	33,043,000	Lagos	H10	34
Niue I. (Br.)	100	4,707	Alofi	K 7	37
Norfolk Island (Australia)	15	1,000	Kingston	G 8	37
North America	9,124,000	250,000,000		.....	38
North Borneo (Br.)	29,387	409,000	Jesselton	F 5	31
North Carolina, U.S.A.	49,142	4,061,929	Raleigh	O 6	43
North Dakota, U.S.A.	70,054	619,636	Bismarck	J 3	42
Northern Ireland (Br.)	5,238	1,402,000	Belfast	H 2	12

GAZETTEER-INDEX OF THE WORLD

Country	Area (Sq. Miles)	Population	Capital or Chief Town	Index Ref.	Plate No.
Northern Rhodesia (Br.)	290,320	2,300,000	Lusaka	M14	35
Northern Territory, Australia	523,620	16,452	Darwin	E 3	36
Northwest Territories, Canada	1,258,217	19,313	Ottawa	F 1	40
*Norway	124,560	3,541,000	Oslo	F 6	13
Nova Scotia, Canada	20,743	694,717	Halifax	H 4	41
Nyasaland Protectorate (Br.)	36,829	2,710,000	Zomba	N14	35

O

Country	Area (Sq. Miles)	Population	Capital or Chief Town	Index Ref.	Plate No.
Ohio, U.S.A.	41,122	7,946,627	Columbus	N 4	43
Oklahoma, U.S.A.	69,283	2,233,351	Oklahoma City	J 6	42
Oman, Sultanate of	82,000	550,000	Masqat	J 5	26
Ontario, Canada	363,282	5,404,933	Toronto	C 3	41
Orange Free State, Union of South Africa	49,647	1,018,082	Bloemfontein	M17	35
Oregon, U.S.A.	96,350	1,521,341	Salem	C 4	42
Orkney Islands, Scotland	376	21,258	Kirkwall	J 1	11

P

Country	Area (Sq. Miles)	Population	Capital or Chief Town	Index Ref.	Plate No.
Pacific Islands (excl. Austr.)	262,718	4,313,654			37
Pacific Is., Terr. of the (U.S. Trust)	680	64,290		E-F 5	37
*Pakistan	364,218	85,635,000	Rawalpindi A 3 & F 4		29
Palau (Pelew) Islands (U.S. Trust.)	189	6,596	Koror	D 5	37
*Panama (excl. Canal Zone)	28,575	995,000	Panamá	G 6	39
Papua Territory (Austr.)	90,540	487,000	Port Moresby	B 7	31
Paraguay	150,518	1,677,000	Asunción	J 8	47
Pennsylvania, U.S.A.	45,045	10,498,012	Harrisburg	O 4	43
*Persia (Iran)	628,000	18,944,821	Teheran	H 4	27
*Peru	513,000	10,524,000	Lima	E 5	46
*Philippines, Republic of the	115,600	21,590,700	Quezon City	H 4	31
Phoenix Is. (U.S. and Br.)	16	984	Canton I.	J 6	37
Pitcairn Island (Br.)	2	143	Adamstown	O 8	37
*Poland	119,734	28,783,000	Warsaw (Warszawa)		24
*Portugal	35,413	9,040,000	Lisbon (Lisboa)	B 3	17
Prince Edward Island, Canada	2,184	99,285	Charlottetown	H 4	41
Puerto Rico (U.S.A.)	3,423	2,210,703	San Juan	G 2	45

Q

Country	Area (Sq. Miles)	Population	Capital or Chief Town	Index Ref.	Plate No.
Qatar	5,000	40,000	Doha	F 4	26
Québec, Canada	523,860	4,628,378	Québec	G 3	41
Queensland, Australia	670,500	1,318,343	Brisbane	G 4	36

R

Country	Area (Sq. Miles)	Population	Capital or Chief Town	Index Ref.	Plate No.
Réunion (Fr.)	970	318,000	St.-Denis	R20	35
Rhode Island, U.S.A.	1,050	791,896	Providence	R 4	43
Rhodesia & Nyasaland, Fed. of	477,482	7,650,000	Salisbury	M15	35
Rio de Oro, Sp. Sahara	71,585	1,304	Villa Cisneros	D 7	34
Rio Muni (Continental Sp. Guinea)	10,040	155,963	Bata	J11	35
Ruanda-Urundi (Belg. Trust.)	20,309	4,700,000	Usumbura	M12	35
*Rumania	91,671	17,489,450	Bucharest (Bucureşti)	G 3	21
Russian S.F.S.R. (U.S.S.R.)	6,501,500	112,600,000	Moscow (Moskva)	E 4	22
Ryukyu Islands (U.S. Adm.)	848	801,065	Naha	L 7	33

S

Country	Area (Sq. Miles)	Population	Capital or Chief Town	Index Ref.	Plate No.
Saguia el Hamra, Sp. Sahara	31,661	6,445	Aiún	D 6	34
St. Helena I. (Br.)	47	5,000	Jamestown	E15	35
St. Lucia (Br.)	233	91,000	Castries	G 4	45
St. Pierre and Miquelon Is. (Fr.)	93	4,827	St. Pierre	J 4	41
St. Thomas, Virgin Is. (U.S.A.)	32	13,811	Charlotte Amalie	G 1	45
St. Vincent (Br.)	150	81,000	Kingstown	G 4	45
Sakhalin (U.S.S.R.)	35,400	300,000	Yuzhno-Sakhalinsk	R 5	23
*Salvador, El	13,176	2,475,000	San Salvador	C 4	39
Samoa (U.S.A.)	76	20,154	Pago Pago	J 7	37
Samoa, Western (N.Z. Trust.)	1,133	97,327	Apia	J 7	37
San Marino	38	15,000	San Marino	D 2	18
Santa Cruz Islands			Peu	G 6	37
São Tomé e Principe (Port.)	372	62,000	São Tomé	H11	35
Sarawak (Br.)	47,071	648,000	Kuching	E 5	31
Sardinia (Sardegna, It.)	9,301	1,273,714	Cagliari	B 4	18
Saskatchewan, Canada	237,975	880,665	Regina	J 4	40
*Saudi Arabia, Kingdom of	350,000	6,036,000	Riyadh, Mecca	D 4	26
Scotland	30,405	5,169,000	Edinburgh		11
Senegal	77,401	2,300,000	Dakar	D 9	34
Seychelles (Br.)	157	41,000	Victoria	T 6	6
Shetland Islands, Scotland	550	19,343	Lerwick	L 3	11
*Siam (Thailand)	200,148	20,095,130	Bangkok (Krung Thep)	D 3	30
Sicily (It.)	9,926	4,452,773	Palermo	D 6	18
Sierra Leone (Br.)	27,925	2,120,000	Freetown	D10	34
Sikkim	2,745	150,000	Gangtok	E 3	29
Singapore (Br.)	220	1,445,929	Singapore	F 6	30
Sinkiang, China	660,977	4,873,608	Urumchi (Tihwa)	C 3	32
Society Islands (Fr.)	650	41,798	Papeete	L 7	37
Socotra (Aden)	1,400	5,000	Tamrida	J 8	25
Solomon Islands (Terr. of New Guinea)	4,070	49,067	Sohano	F 6	37
Solomon Islands Prot. (Br.)	14,600	104,000	Honiara	F 6	37
Somaliland, French	8,492	69,000	Djibouti	P 9	34
Somaliland (Italian Trust.)	194,000	1,320,000	Mogadiscio	R10	34
Somaliland Protectorate (Br.)	68,000	650,000	Hargeisa	R10	34
South America	6,894,000	131,000,000			46, 47

Country	Area (Sq. Miles)	Population	Capital or Chief Town	Index Ref.	Plate No.
South Australia, Australia	380,000	797,159	Adelaide	E 5	36
South Carolina, U.S.A.	30,594	2,117,027	Columbia	N 6	43
South Dakota, U.S.A.	76,536	652,740	Pierre	J 3	42
Southern Rhodesia (Br.)	150,333	2,640,000	Salisbury	M15	35
Southern Territories, Algeria	767,435	816,993	Algiers (Alger)	G 6	34
South-West Africa (Union of So. Africa Mand.)	317,725	535,833	Windhoek	K16	35
*Spain	195,258	29,894,000	Madrid		17
Spanish Sahara	105,022	13,000	Aiún	D 6	34
Spitzbergen (Svalbard)(Nor.)	24,294	1,539	Longyearbyen	C 2	13
*Sudan	967,500	10,262,536	Khartoum	M 9	34
Sudanese Republic	584,942	3,700,000	Bamako	E 9	34
Sumatra, Indonesia	164,148	11,605,489	Padang	C 6	31
Surinam (Netherlands Guiana)	54,300	241,000	Paramaribo	J 3	46
Swaziland (Br.)	6,704	256,000	Mbabane	N17	35
*Sweden	173,394	7,424,000	Stockholm	J 6	13
Switzerland	15,944	5,215,000	Bern		19
Syria	72,587	4,421,000	Damascus (Dimishq)	H 5	28

T

Country	Area (Sq. Miles)	Population	Capital or Chief Town	Index Ref.	Plate No.
Tadzhik S.S.R. (U.S.S.R.)	54,900	1,800,000	Stalinabad	J 6	22
Tahiti (island) (Fr.)	600	29,684	Papeete	M 7	37
Taiwan (Formosa), China	13,885	10,039,000	Taipei		32
Tanganyika Territory (Br. Trust)	342,706	8,788,466	Dar-es-Salaam	N13	35
Tasmania, Australia	26,215	308,783	Hobart	J 8	36
Tennessee, U.S.A.	41,961	3,291,718	Nashville	M 6	43
Texas, U.S.A.	263,644	7,711,194	Austin	J 7	42
*Thailand (Siam)	200,148	20,095,130	Bangkok (Krung Thep)	D 3	30
Tibet, China	469,413	2,000,000	Lhasa	C 5	32
Timor (Port.)	7,332	490,000	Dili	H 7	31
Timor Archipelago, Indonesia	24,450	1,657,376	Kupang	G 8	31
Togo	20,733	1,100,000	Lomé	G10	34
Tokelau (Union Group) (N.Z. and U.S.)	4	1,619	Fakaofo	J 6	37
Tonga (Friendly) Is. (Br.)	269	56,838	Nukualofa	J 7	37
Transvaal, Union of So. Africa	110,450	4,801,708	Pretoria	N17	35
Trinidad and Tobago (Br.)	1,980	789,000	Port of Spain	G 5	45
Tristan da Cunha (Br.)	38	230		N 7	6
Trucial Oman	12,000	86,000	Sharja	F 5	26
Tuamotu (Low) Arch. (Fr.)	332	6,692	Apataki	M 7	37
*Tunisia	48,300	3,783,169	Tunis	H 5	34
*Turkey	296,185	24,121,778	Ankara		28
Turkmen S.S.R. (U.S.S.R.)	187,200	1,400,000	Ashkhabad	G 6	22
Turks and Caicos Is. (Br.)	202	7,000	Grand Turk	D 2	45

U

Country	Area (Sq. Miles)	Population	Capital or Chief Town	Index Ref.	Plate No.
Uganda Protectorate (Br.)	80,301	5,853,000	Entebbe	N11	35
*Ukrainian S.S.R. (U.S.S.R.)	220,600	41,893,000	Kiev	E 5	22
*Union of South Africa	472,494	14,418,000	Cape Town, Pretoria	L18	35
*Union of Soviet Socialist Republics	8,570,600	208,826,000	Moscow (Moskva)		22, 23
*United Arab Republic	458,587	27,413,150	Cairo	A 4 & C 3	26
*United Kingdom	94,279	52,025,000	London	D 3	9
*United States of America.land land and water	3,554,609 3,615,221	151,325,798	Washington		42, 43
Upper Volta	105,839	3,470,000	Ouagadougou	F 9	34
*Uruguay	72,172	2,679,000	Montevideo	J10	47
Utah, U.S.A.	82,346	688,862	Salt Lake City	F 5	42
Uzbek S.S.R. (U.S.S.R.)	157,400	7,300,000	Tashkent	H 5	22

V

Country	Area (Sq. Miles)	Population	Capital or Chief Town	Index Ref.	Plate No.
Vatican City	109 Acres	1,000		B 6	18
*Venezuela	352,143	6,512,000	Caracas	G 2	46
Vermont, U.S.A.	9,278	377,747	Montpelier	P 4	43
Victoria, Australia	87,884	2,452,337	Melbourne	G 7	36
Vietnam	126,700	27,400,000	Saigon, Hanoi	E 3	30
Virgin Islands (Br.)	58	8,000	Road Town	H 1	45
Virgin Islands (U.S.A.)	132	26,665	Charlotte Amalie	H 1	45
Virginia, U.S.A.	39,899	3,318,680	Richmond	O 5	43
Volcano Is. (U.S. Adm.)	29			E 3	37

W

Country	Area (Sq. Miles)	Population	Capital or Chief Town	Index Ref.	Plate No.
Wake Island (U.S.A.)	3			G 4	37
Wales (excl. Monmouthshire)	7,466	2,172,339	Cardiff	D 5	10
Walvis Bay (So. Africa)	430	3,167		J16	35
Washington, U.S.A.	66,977	2,378,963	Olympia	C 3	42
Western Australia, Australia	975,920	639,716	Perth	C 4	36
West Indies	90,000	17,000,000			45
West Indies (Fed.)	8,000	3,055,000	Port of Spain	H 3	45
West Virginia, U.S.A.	24,090	2,005,552	Charleston	N 5	43
*White Russian S.S.R. (Byelorussian S.S.R.) (U.S.S.R.)	80,100	8,000,000	Minsk	D 4	22
Wisconsin, U.S.A.	54,715	3,434,575	Madison	L 3	43
World	57,500,000	2,795,000,000			6, 7
Wyoming, U.S.A.	97,506	290,529	Cheyenne	G 4	42

X Y Z

Country	Area (Sq. Miles)	Population	Capital or Chief Town	Index Ref.	Plate No.
Yap (U.S. Trust.)	87	2,709	Yap	D 5	37
*Yemen	75,000	4,500,000	San'a	D 7	26
*Yugoslavia	99,079	18,397,000	Belgrade (Beograd)	C 3	21
Yukon Territory, Canada	205,346	12,190	Whitehorse	C 1	40
Zanzibar Protectorate (including Pemba) (Br.)	1,020	299,111	Zanzibar	P13	35

* Members of the United Nations.   * Includes both land and water.   † Name does not appear on map.

INDEX OF PRINCIPAL CITIES OF THE WORLD

This alphabetical list of cities gives statistics of population based on the latest official reports. Each line begins with the name of a place, followed by the name of the country or state, the population, the index reference and the plate number. Different forms of names have been included to a large extent in the index.

Capitals are designated by asterisks * † Including suburbs. ‡ No room on map for name.

Place	Index	Plate
Aachen (Aix-la-Chapelle), Ger., 129,811	B3	14
Aarhus, Den., 116,167	F8	13
Aberdeen, Scot., 182,729	N5	11
Accra, *Ghana, 135,456	G11	34
Adana (Seyhan), Turk., 172,465	F4	28
Addis Ababa,* Ethiopia, 400,000	O10	34
Adelaide,* So. Aust., †483,508	D7	36
Aden,* Aden, 36,231	E7	26
Agaña,* Guam, 1,330	E4	37
Agra, India, 375,665	C3	29
Aguascalientes, Mex., 93,432	H6	44
Ahmadabad, India, 788,332	B4	29
Akron, Ohio, 274,605	N4	43
Albany,* N. Y., 134,995	O1	43
Aleppo (Haleb), Syria, 324,899	G4	28
Alessandria, It., 70,238	B2	18
Alexandria, Egypt, 925,081	M5	34
Algiers (Alger),* Alg., 329,700	G4	34
Allahabad, India, 333,362	D3	29
Allentown, Pa., 106,756	P4	43
Amboina (Ambon), Indonesia, 26,066	H6	31
Amiens, Fr., 87,126	D3	16
Amman,* Jordan, 108,304	D4	24
Amoy, China, 224,300	J7	32
Amritsar, India, 325,747	B2	29
Amsterdam,* Neth., 871,188	B4	15
Ancona, It., 68,501	D3	18
Andizhan, U.S.S.R., 115,000	U2	23
Andorra la Vieja,* Andorra, 1,100	G1	17
Angers, Fr., 93,838	C4	16
Ankara (Angora),* Turk., 453,151	E3	28
Annapolis,* Md., 10,047	P5	43
Antwerp (Antwerpen), Belg., 256,075	E6	15
Aomori, Jap., 183,747	K3	33
Apeldoorn, Neth., 97,867	H4	15
Apia,* W. Samoa	J7	37
Archangel (Arkhangel'sk), U.S.S.R., 300,000	F3	22
Arnhem, Neth., 119,814	H4	15
Asahigawa, Jap., 164,972	L2	33
Asmara,* Eritrea, 120,000	O9	34
Astrakhan', U.S.S.R., 276,000	F5	22
Asunción,* Para., 204,085	J9	47
Athens (Athēnai),* Greece, 565,084	G7	21
Atlanta,* Ga., 331,314	N6	43
Atlantic City, N.J., 61,657	P5	43
Auckland, N. Z., †381,063	L5	36
Augsburg, Ger., 185,183	D4	14
Augusta,* Me., 20,913	R3	43
Austin,* Tex., 132,459	J7	42
Avellaneda, Arg., 278,621	O12	47
Baghdad,* Iraq, 364,049	D4	27
Bahía Blanca, Arg., 112,597	H11	47
Bahia (Salvador), Braz., 398,422	N6	46
Baile Atha Cliath (Dublin),* Ireland, 539,476	J5	12
Baku, U.S.S.R., 598,000	G6	22
Baltimore, Md., 949,708	O5	43
Banaras (Varanasi), India, 355,777	D3	29
Bandjermasin, Borneo, Indon., 150,000	E6	31
Bandung, Java, Indon., 724,249	H2	31
Bangalore, India, 778,977	C6	29
Bangkok (Krung Thep),* Thai., 827,290	D4	30
Barcelona, Sp., †1,276,675	H2	17
Bari, It., 264,744	F4	18
Barnaul, U.S.S.R., 200,000	K4	22
Barnsley, Eng., 75,630	F4	10
Baroda, India, 211,407	B4	29
Barranquilla, Col., 276,199	F1	46
Barrow-in-Furness, Eng., 67,476	D3	10
Basel (Bâle, Basle), Switz., 183, 543	E1	19
Batavia (Djakarta),* Java, Indon., 1,863,139	H1	31
Bath, England, 79,294	E6	10
Bathurst,* Gambia, 19,602	C9	34
Baton Rouge,* La., 125,629	L7	43
Batumi, U.S.S.R., 75,000	F5	22
Bayonne, N. J., 77,203	R5	43
Beirut,* Lebanon, 177,780	F6	28
Belém (Pará), Braz., 225,218	L4	46
Belfast,* No. Ire., 443,670	J2	12
Belgrade (Beograd),* Yugo., 469,988	E3	21
Belize,* Br. Hond., 21,886	C2	39
Belo Horizonte, Braz., 388,585	M7	46
Benghazi,* Libya, 70,533	K5	34
Berbera, Som. Prot., 20,000	R9	34
Berdichev, U.S.S.R., 66,306	D5	22
Bergamo, It., 95,651	B2	18
Bergen, Nor., 112,845	D6	13
Berkeley, Calif., 113,805	D8	42
Berlin,* E. Ger., 3,350,785	E2	14
Bern (Berne),*Switz., 146,499	D3	19
Besançon, Fr. 61,139	G4	16
Beuthen (Bytom), Pol., 179,200	B4	24
Béziers, Fr., 58,814	E6	16
Białystok, Poland, 103,600	F2	24
Bielefeld, Ger., 153,613	C2	14
Bilbao, Sp., 229,091	E1	17
Binghamton, N. Y., 80,674	P4	43
Binh Dinh, Vietnam, 75,000	F4	30
Birkenhead, Eng., 142,501	D4	10
Birmingham, Ala., 326,037	M6	43
Birmingham, Eng., 1,112,685	F5	10
Bismarck, N. D., 18,640	H3	42
Blackburn, Eng., 111,218	E4	10
Blackpool, Eng., 147,184	D4	10
Blagoveshchensk, U.S.S.R., 58,761	O4	23
Bloemfontein,* O.F.S., †109,369	L17	35
Bobruysk, U.S.S.R., 80,000	D4	22
Bochum, Ger., 289,804	G4	14
Bogor, Java, Indon., 104,213	H2	31
Bogotá,* Col., 638,562	F3	46
Boise,* Idaho, 34,393	D4	42
Bologna, It., 323,219	C2	18
Bolton, Eng., 167,162	E4	10
Bombay, India, 2,839,270	B8	29
Bône (Bona), Alg., 88,920	H4	34
Bonn,* W. Ger., 115,394	B3	14
Bootle, Eng., 74,302	D4	10
Bordeaux, Fr., 250,306	C5	16
Boston,* Mass., 801,444	R2	43
Bottrop, Ger., 93,268	G4	14
Bournemouth, Eng., 144,845	F7	10
Bradford, Eng., 292,403	F4	10
Brăila, Rum., 95,514	H3	21
Brandenburg, Ger., 70,632	E2	14
Brasilía,* Braz.	L7	46
Bratislava (Pressburg), Czech., 246,695	D2	20
Brazzaville,* Congo, 63,023	J12	35
Bremen, Ger., 455,999	C2	14
Brescia, It., 141,808	C2	18
Breslau (Wrocław), Pol., 387,909	C3	24
Brest, Fr., 100,733	A3	16
Bridgeport, Conn., 158,709	O2	43
Bridgetown,* Barbados, 13,345	G4	45
Brighton, Eng., 156,486	G7	10
Brisbane,* Queen., 502,353	J5	36
Bristol, Eng., 442,994	E6	10
Brno (Brünn), Czech., 306,371	D2	20
Brockton, Mass., 62,860	R2	43
Brunei,* Brunei, 16,000	E4	31
Brunswick, Ger., 223,760	D2	14
Brussels, Belg., †1,371,816	F7	15
Bucharest (Bucureşti),* Rum., 1,041,807	G3	21
Budapest,* Hung., 1,783,003	E3	20
Buenos Aires,* Arg., 3,000,371	O11	47
Buffalo, N.Y., 580,132	O4	43
Bursa (Brusa), Tur., 131,336	C2	28
Bydgoszcz (Bromberg), Pol., 210,900	D2	24
Bytom (Beuthen), Pol., 179,200	B4	24
Cádiz, Sp., 100,249	C4	17
Caen, Fr., 62,887	C3	16
Cagliari, Sardinia, It., 135,658	B5	18
Cairo (El Qahira),* U.A.R., 2,100,506	N5	34
Calais, Fr., 60,160	D2	16
Calcutta, India, 2,548,677	E2	29
Calgary, Alta, 181,780	H4	40
Cali, Col., 241,357	E3	46
Calicut, India, 158,724	C6	29
Callao, Peru, 84,438	E6	46
Camagüey, Cuba, †204,254	B2	45
Cambridge, Eng., 81,500	H5	10
Cambridge, Mass., 120,740	R2	43
Camden, N. J., 124,555	P6	43
Campinas, Braz., 99,156	L8	47
Canberra,* Aust., †28,277	J7	36
Canton, China, 1,598,900	H7	32
Canton, Ohio, 116,912	N4	43
Cape Town,* U. of S. A., †577,648	C19	35
Caracas,* Venez., 495,064	G1	46
Cardiff, Wales, 243,632	E6	10
Carson City,* Nev., 3,082	D5	22
Cartagena, Col., 111,291	E1	46
Cartagena, Sp., †110,979	F4	17
Casablanca, Mor., 680,422	E5	34
Catania, Sicily, It., 296,780	E6	18
Cayenne,* Fr. Guiana, 10,961	K2	46
Ceará (Fortaleza), Braz., 205,052	N4	46
Cebu, P. I., 167,503	G3	31
Changchun, China, 855,200	K3	32
Changsha, China, 650,600	H6	32
Changteh, China, 94,800	H6	32
Charleston, S. C., 70,174	O6	43
Charleston,* W. Va., 73,501	N5	43
Charlotte, N. C., 134,042	N6	43
Chattanooga, Tenn., 131,041	M6	43
Chefoo, China, 116,000	K4	32
Chelyabinsk, U.S.S.R., 612,000	H4	22
Chemnitz, Ger., 250,188	E3	14
Chengtu, China, 856,700	F5	32
Cherbourg, Fr., 35,246	C3	16
Chernovtsy (Cernăuţi), U.S.S.R., 142,000	D5	22
Chesterfield, Eng., 68,558	F4	10
Cheyenne,* Wyo., 31,935	G4	42
Chicago, Ill., 3,620,962	L1	43
Chinkiang (Tantu), China, 201,400	K5	32
Chita, U.S.S.R., 162,000	N4	23
Chittagong, Pak., 294,046	F4	29
Chkalov (Orenburg), U.S.S.R., 226,000	G4	22
Christchurch, N. Z., 193,367	L7	36
Chungking, China, 1,772,500	G6	32
Cincinnati, Ohio, 503,998	H1	42
Ciudad Trujillo,* Dom. Rep., 181,533	E3	45
Clermont-Ferrand, Fr., 97,084	E5	16
Cleveland, Ohio, 914,808	N4	43
Cluj (Kolozsvár), Rum., 154,752	F2	21
Coblenz (Koblenz), Ger., 66,444	B3	14
Cologne (Köln), Ger., 594,941	B3	14
Colombo,* Ceylon, 423,481	C7	29
Columbia,* S. C., 86,914	N6	43
Columbus,* Ohio, 375,901	N5	43
Conakry,* Guinea, 38,000	D10	34
Concepción, Chile, 100,000	F11	47
Concord,* N. H., 27,988	P4	43
Constantine, Alg., 118,774	H4	34
Constantinople (Istanbul), Tur., 1,214,616	D6	28
Copenhagen (Köbenhavn),* Den., 768,105	G9	13
Córdoba, Arg., 369,886	G10	47
Córdoba (Cordova), Sp., 165,403	D4	17
Cork, Ire., 80,011	E8	12
Corpus Christi, Tex., 108,287	J8	42
Coruña, La., Sp., †127,618	B1	17
Coventry, Eng., 258,245	F5	10
Craiova, Rum., 96,929	F3	21
Cremona, It., 59,149	B2	18
Croydon, Eng., 249,870	G6	10
Curitiba, Braz., 141,349	L9	47
Cuttack, India, 102,505	E4	29
Częstochowa, Poland, 154,600	D3	24
Dacca, Pak., 411,279	F4	29
Dakar,* Senegal, 185,000	C9	34
Dallas, Tex., 434,462	J6	42
Damão, Port. India, 69,005	B4	29
Damascus,* Syria, 291,157	G6	28
Danzig (Gdańsk), Pol., 259,900	D1	24
Dar es Salaam,* Tang. Terr., 69,227	P13	35
Darlington, Eng., 84,886	F3	10
Darmstadt, Ger., 94,788	C4	14
Davao, P. I., 81,523	H4	31
Dayton, Ohio, 243,872	M5	43
Debrecen, Hung., 118,114	F3	20
Decatur, Ill., 66,269	L5	43
Delhi, India, 914,790	C3	29
Denver,* Colo., 415,786	G5	42
Derby, Eng., 141,267	F5	10
Des Moines,* Iowa, 177,965	K4	43
Dessau, Ger., 88,139	E3	14
Detroit, Mich., 1,849,568	M1	43
Dhahran, Saudi Arabia, 10,000	E4	26
Dijon, Fr., 106,267	F4	16
Dimishq (Damascus),* Syria, 291,157	G6	28
Djakarta, Java,* Indon., 1,863,139	H1	31
Djibouti,* Fr. Som., 17,500	P9	34
Djokjakarta, Java, Indon., 244,379	J2	31
Dnepropetrovsk, U.S.S.R., 576,000	E5	22
Doncaster, Eng., 82,054	G4	10
Dortmund, Ger., 507,349	H4	14
Dover,* Del., 6,223	P5	43
Dover, Eng., 35,215	J6	10
Dresden, Ger., 467,966	E3	14
Dublin (Baile Atha Cliath),* Ire., 539,476	J5	12
Duisburg, Ger., 410,783	F4	14
Duluth, Minn., 104,511	K3	43
Dundee, Scot., 177,340	K7	11
Dunedin, N. Z., †99,370	L7	36
Durban, Natal, †479,974	N18	35
Düsseldorf, Ger., 500,516	F5	14
Dzaudzhikau (Ordzhonikidze), U.S.S.R., 159,000	F5	22
Eastbourne, Eng., 57,821	H7	10
Edinburgh,* Scot., 466,761	K8	11
Edmonton,* Alta., 226,002	H4	40
Eindhoven, Neth., 157,621	G6	15
Elbląg (Elbing), Pol., 69,200	D1	24
Elizabeth, N. J., 112,817	R5	43
El Paso, Tex., 130,485	G7	42
Erfurt, Ger., 174,633	D3	14
Erie, Pa., 130,803	N4	43
Erivan (Yerevan), U.S.S.R., 385,000	F6	22
Essen, Ger., 605,411	G4	14
Evanston, Ill., 73,641	L1	43
Evansville, Ind., 128,636	M5	43
Exeter, Eng., 75,513	D7	10
Fall River, Mass., 111,963	R2	43
Ferrara, It., 92,385	C2	18
Fez., Mor., 179,250	F5	34
Fiume (Rijeka), Yugo., 75,112	B3	21
Flensburg, Ger., 102,832	C1	14
Flint, Mich., 163,143	N4	43
Florence (Firenze), It., 362,459	C3	18
Foochow (Minhow), China, 553,000	J6	32
Forli, It., 51,666	D2	18
Fortaleza (Ceará), Braz., 205,052	N4	46
Fort-de-France,* Mart., 66,006	G4	45
Fort Wayne, Ind., 133,607	M4	43
Fort Worth, Tex., 278,778	J6	42
Frankfort,* Ky., 11,916	M5	43
Frankfurt-am-Main, Ger., 532,037	C3	14
Frankfurt-an-der-Oder, Ger., 51,577	F2	14
Fredericton,* N. B., 18,303	G4	41
Freetown,* Sierra Leone, 64,576	D10	34
Freiburg, Ger., 109,717	B5	14
Fresno, Cal., 91,669	C5	42
Fukui, Jap., 125,304	G5	33
Fukuoka, Jap., 544,312	D7	33
Fürth, Ger., 99,890	D4	14
Fusan (Pusan), Korea, 473,619	D6	33
Galaţi, Rum., 95,646	H3	21
Galveston, Tex., 66,568	K7	43
Gander, Nfld., 3,000	K4	41
Gary, Ind., 133,911	L1	43
Gateshead, Eng., 115,039	F3	10
Gdańsk (Danzig), Pol., 191,051	D1	24
Gdynia, Poland, 117,702	D1	24
Gelsenkirchen, Ger., 367,941	G4	14
Geneva (Genève), Switz., 145,473	B4	19
Genoa (Genova), It., 668,579	B2	18
Georgetown,* Br. Guiana, 73,509	J2	46
George Town (Penang), Mal. Fed., 189,068	C6	30
Gera, Ger., 89,212	E3	14
Ghent (Gent), Belg., 166,096	D6	15
Gibraltar,* Gibr., 23,232	D4	17
Gifu, Jap., 259,047	H6	33
Gladbach (München-Gladbach), Ger., 124,879	B3	14
Glasgow, Scot., 1,089,767	D2	11
Gliwice (Gleiwitz), Pol., 128,203	A4	24
Glendale, Cal., 95,702	D8	42
Gomel', U.S.S.R., 144,000	E4	22
Goose Airport (Goose Bay), Lab., Nfld., 1,000	H3	41
Gor'kiy, U.S.S.R., 876,000	F4	22
Görlitz, Ger., 85,686	F3	14
Göteborg (Gothenburg), Sweden, 353,991	G8	13
Granada, Sp., †154,589	E4	17
Grand Rapids, Mich., 176,515	M4	43
Graz, Austria, 226,453	C3	20
Great Yarmouth (Yarmouth), Eng., 51,105	J5	10
Greenock, Scot., 76,292	A2	11
Greenwich, Eng., 91,492	H6	10
Grenoble, Fr., 102,161	G5	16
Grimsby (Great Grimsby), Eng., 94,557	H4	10
Groningen, Neth., 142,889	K2	15
Groznyy, U.S.S.R., 226,000	F5	22
Guadalajara, Mex., 378,423	H6	44
Guatemala,* Guat., 284,276	B3	39
Guayaquil, Ecu., 258,966	D4	46
Győr, Hung., 65,638	D3	20
Haarlem, Neth., 167,264	F4	15
Habana (Havana),* Cuba, 787,448	A2	45
Hagen, Ger., 146,141	H4	14
Hague, The ('s Gravenhage),* Neth., 606,728	E4	15
Haifa, Israel, 166,000	B2	24
Haiphong, Vietnam, 143,000	E2	30
Hakodate, Jap., 242,582	K3	33
Haleb (Aleppo), Syria, 324,899	G4	28
Halifax, England, 98,404	F4	10
Halifax,* N. S., 93,301	H5	41
Halle, Ger., 222,505	E3	14
Hälsingborg (Helsingborg), Swed., 71,718	H8	13
Hamamatsu, Jap., 268,792	J6	33
Hamburg, Ger., 1,605,606	D2	14
Hamilton, Ont., 239,625	E5	41
Hammond, Ind., 87,594	L1	43
Hamtramck, Mich., 43,355	N1	43
Hangchow, China, 696,600	J5	32
Hannover, Ger., 444,296	C2	14
Hanoi,* Vietnam, 237,150	E2	30
Harbin, China, 1,163,000	L2	32
Harrisburg,* Pa., 89,544	O4	43
Hartford,* Conn., 177,397	O2	43
Hastings, Eng., 65,522	H7	10
Havana. Cuba, 787,448	A2	45
Havre (Le Havre), Fr., 137,175	C3	16
Heidelberg, Ger., 116,488	C4	14
Heilbronn, Ger., 64,643	C4	14
Helena,* Mont., 17,581	E3	42
Helsinki (Helsingfors),* Fin., 436,852	O6	13
Herne, Ger., 111,591	G4	14
Hildesheim, Ger., 72,292	D2	14
Hilversum, Neth., 97,312	G4	15
Himeji., Japan, 215,315	G6	33
Hindenburg (Zabrze), Pol., 185,100	A4	24
Hiroshima, Jap., 357,287	E6	33
Hobart,* Tas., †95,223	H8	36
Hódmezövásárhely, Hung., 51,150	F3	20
Hollandia,* Neth. N. Guin.	K6	31
Holyoke, Mass., 54,661	P1	43
Honiara,* Sol. Is. Prot.	G6	37
Honolulu,* Hawaii, 248,034	L3	37
Houston, Tex., 596,163	K7	43
Howrah, India, 433,630	E2	29
Huddersfield, Eng., 129,026	F4	10
Hue, Vietnam, 407,000	E3	30
Hull, Que., 49,243	E4	41
Hull (Kingston-upon-Hull), Eng., 299,105	G4	10
Huntington, W. Va., 86,353	N5	43
Hyderabad, India, 1,085,722	C5	29
Hyderabad, Pak., 241,801	A3	29
Iaşy (Jassy), Rum., 112,989	H2	21
Ibadan, Nig., 459,196	G10	34
Ibagué, Col., 54,347	F3	46
Ichang, China, 75,000	H5	32
Inch'ŏn (Jinsen), Korea, 265,767	C5	33
Indianapolis,* Ind., 427,173	M5	43
Indore, India, 310,859	C4	29
Ipswich, Eng., 104,785	J5	10
Irkutsk, U.S.S.R., 314,000	M4	23
Irvington, N. J., 59,201	R5	43
Isfahan, Iran, 183,597	G4	27
Istanbul (Constantinople), Tur., 1,214,616	D6	28
Ivanovo, U.S.S.R., 319,000	E4	22
Ixelles, Belg., 92,657	C9	15
Izmir (Smyrna), Tur., 286,310	B3	28
Jackson,* Miss., 98,271	L6	43
Jacksonville, Fla., 204,517	N7	43
Jaffa-Tel Aviv, Israel, 363,500	B3	24
Jaipur, India, 291,130	C3	29
Jakarta (Djakarta),* Java, Indon., 1,863,139	H1	31
Jamshedpur, India, 218,162	E4	29
Jassy (Iaşi), Rum., 112,989	H2	21
Jefferson City,* Mo., 25,099	K5	43
Jena, Ger., 82,722	D3	14
Jersey City, N. J., 299,017	R5	43
Jerusalem, Jord. and *Israel, 197,000	C4	24
Jesselton,* N. Bor., 11,704	F4	31
Jinsen (Inch'ŏn), Korea, 265,767	C5	33
João Pessoa (Parahyba), Braz., 89,517	O5	46
Johannesburg, Transv., †884,007	M17	35
Juiz de Fora, Braz., 84,999	M8	46
Juneau,* Alaska, 5,956	E4	38
Kabul,* Afgh., 206,208	J3	26
Kagoshima, Jap., 274,340	E8	33
Kaifeng, China, 299,100	J5	32
Kaiserslautern, Ger., 62,761	B4	14
Kalamazoo, Mich., 57,704	M4	43
Kalgan, China, 229,300	J3	32
Kalinin, U.S.S.R., 240,000	E4	22
Kaliningrad (Königsberg), U.S.S.R., 188,000	C4	22
Kalisz, Poland, 64,300	D3	24
Kaluga, U.S.S.R., 122,000	E4	22
Kanazawa, Jap., 277,283	H5	33
Kandahar, Afgh., 77,186	A2	29
Kano, Nig., 130,173	H9	34
Kanpur, India, 705,383	D3	29
Kansas City, Kans., 129,553	K5	43
Kansas City, Mo., 456,622	K5	43
Karachi, Pak., 1,009,438	A4	29
Karlsruhe, Ger., 198,840	C4	14
Kashgar, China, 91,000	C7	32
Kassel, Ger., 162,132	C3	14
Katmandu,* Nepal, 108,805	D3	29
Katowice, Poland, 203,700	B4	24
Kaunas, U.S.S.R., 195,000	D4	22
Kawasaki, Jap., 445,520	O2	33
Kazan', U.S.S.R., 565,000	G4	22
Kecskemét, Hung., 64,297	E3	20
Kerch', U.S.S.R., 104,471	E5	22
Khabarovsk, U.S.S.R., 280,000	P5	23
Khar'kov, U.S.S.R., 877,000	E4	22
Khartoum,* Sudan, 93,103	N8	34
Kherson, U.S.S.R., 134,000	E5	22
Kiel, Ger., 254,449	C1	14
Kielce, Poland, 49,960	E3	24
Kiev, U.S.S.R., 1,102,000	E4	22
Kingston, Jam., 142,464	C3	45
Kingston-upon-Hull (Hull), Eng., 299,105	G4	10
Kingstown, St., Vin., 4,831	G4	45
Kirin, China, 435,400	L3	32
Kirov, U.S.S.R., 211,000	F4	22
Kirovabad, U.S.S.R., 111,000	F5	22
Kirovograd, U.S.S.R., 115,000	E5	22
Kishinev (Chişinău), U.S.S.R., 190,000	D5	22
Klaipéda (Memel), U.S.S.R., 48,545	D4	22
Knoxville, Tenn., 124,769	N5	43
Kobe, Jap., 979,305	H7	33
Köbenhavn (Copenhagen),* Den., 768,105	G9	13
Koblenz (Coblenz), Ger., 66,444	B3	14
Kochi, Jap., 180,146	F7	33
Kofu, Jap., 154,494	J6	33
Kokand, U.S.S.R., 75,000	T2	23
Kokura, Jap., 242,240	E7	33
Kolhapur, India, 136,835	B5	29
Köln (Cologne), Ger., 594,941	B3	14
Kolomna, U.S.S.R., 75,139	E4	22
Kolozsvár (Cluj), Rum., 154,752	F2	21
Königsberg (Kaliningrad), U.S.S.R., 188,000	C4	22
Kostroma, U.S.S.R., 156,000	F4	22
Kozhikode (Calicut), India, 158,724	C6	29
Kraków, Poland, 463,500	E3	24
Krasnodar, U.S.S.R., 271,000	E5	22
Krasnoyarsk, U.S.S.R., 238,000	L4	23
Krefeld, Ger., 171,875	F4	14
Kremenchug, U.S.S.R., 89,553	E5	22
Krung Thep (Bangkok),* Thai., 827,290	D4	30
Kuala Lumpur,* Mal. Fed., 175,961	D7	30
Kuching,* Sara., 37,949	E5	31
Kumamoto, Jap., 332,493	E7	33
Kunming, China, 698,900	F6	32
Kure, Jap., 199,304	F6	33
Kursk, U.S.S.R., 179,000	E4	22
Kutaisi, U.S.S.R., 114,000	F5	22
Kuwait,* Kuwait, 80,000	E4	26
Kuybyshev, U.S.S.R., 760,000	G4	22
Kyŏngsŏng (Seoul),* Korea, 1,446,019	C5	33
Kyoto, Jap., 1,204,084	J7	33
La Coruña, Sp., †127,618	B1	17
Lae, Territory N. G., 4,146	B7	31
Lagos,* Nig., 267,407	G10	34
Lahore, Pak., 849,476	B2	29
Lanchow, China, 397,400	F4	32
Lansing,* Mich., 92,129	M4	43
La Paz,* Bol., 321,073	G7	46
La Spezia, It., 105,301	B2	18
Lausanne, Switz., 106,807	C3	19
Lawrence, Mass., 80,536	R1	43
Leeds, Eng., 505,219	F4	10
Leghorn (Livorno), It., 134,513	C3	18
Legnica (Liegnitz), Pol., 54,600	C3	24
Le Havre (Havre), Fr., 137,175	C3	16
Leicester, Eng., 285,181	G5	10
Leiden, Neth., 94,893	E4	15
Leipzig, Ger., 607,655	E3	14
Le Mans, Fr., 103,346	C3	16
Leninakan, U.S.S.R., 103,000	F5	22
Leningrad, U.S.S.R., 2,888,000	C2	22
León, Mex., 122,585	J6	44
León, Nicar., 59,107	D4	39
Léopoldville,* Belg. Cong., 257,197	K12	35
Levallois-Perret, Fr., 61,348	A1	16
Liége, Belg., 155,670	H7	15
Liepaja, U.S.S.R., 75,000	D4	22
Lille (Lisle), Fr., 190,078	E2	16
Lima,* Peru, 628,821	E6	46
Limoges, Fr., 98,405	D5	16
Lincoln, Eng., 69,401	G4	10
Lincoln,* Nebr., 98,884	J4	42
Linz, Aust., 184,685	C2	20
Lisbon (Lisboa),* Port., 790,434	A1	17
Little Rock,* Ark., 102,213	K6	43
Liverpool, Eng., 788,659	D4	10
Livorno (Leghorn), It., 134,513	C3	18
Ljubljana, Yugo., 138,211	B3	21
Łódź, Poland, 681,900	D3	24
London,* Eng., (administrative county and city), 3,347,982, (greater city), 8,346,137	G6	10
London, Ont., 101,693	D5	41
Long Beach, Calif., 250,767	D9	42
Long Xuyen, Vietnam, 148,000	E5	30
Los Alamos, N. Mex., 9,934	G6	42
Los Angeles, Calif., 1,970,358	D8	42
Louisville, Ky., 369,129	K5	43
Lourenço Marques,* Moz., 93,303	N17	35
Lowell, Mass., 97,249	A1	43
Luanda,* Angola, 141,722	J13	35
Lübeck, Ger., 238,276	D2	14
Lublin, Poland, 142,400	F3	24
Lucca, It., 63,667	C3	18
Lucerne, Switz., 60,526	F2	19
Lucknow, India, 496,861	D3	29
Ludwigshafen, Ger., 123,869	C4	14
Lungkiang (Tsitsihar), China, 344,700	L2	32
Lüta, China, 1,200,000	K4	32
Luton, Eng., 110,381	G6	10
Luxembourg,* Lux., 61,996	J9	15
Luzern (Lucerne), Switz., 60,526	F2	19
L'vov (Łwów), U.S.S.R., 387,000	D4	22
Lynn, Mass., 99,738	R2	43
Lyon, Fr., 462,657	F5	16
McKeesport, Pa., 51,502	O4	43
Maastricht, Neth., 86,665	H7	15
Macao (Macau) (Port.), 166,544	H7	32
Maceió, Braz., 102,301	O5	46
Madison,* Wis., 96,056	L4	43
Madras, India, 1,416,056	D6	29

INDEX OF PRINCIPAL CITIES OF THE WORLD

Madrid,* Sp. 1,618,435............F4 17
Madurai, India, 361,781..........C7 29
Maebashi, Jap., 171,265..........J5 33
Magdeburg, Ger., 236,326.........D2 14
Magnitogorsk, U.S.S.R., 284,000 ....G4 22
Mainz, Ger., 88,369..................C4 14
Makassar (Macassar), Celebes, Indon., 265,263....................F7 31
Málaga, Sp., †274,847.............D4 17
Malden, Mass., 59,804.............R1 43
Malmö, Swed., 192,498............H9 13
Managua,* Nicar., 176,569.......D4 39
Manaus (Manáos), Braz., 89,612 ....H4 46
Manchester, Eng., 703,082........E4 10
Manchester, N. H., 82,732.........R4 43
Mandalay, Burma, 182,367.........C2 30
Manila, P. I., 983,906...............G3 31
Manizales, Col., 88,893.............E2 46
Mannheim, Ger., 245,634...........C4 14
Maracaibo, Venez., 235,750.......F1 46
Maranhão, (São Luís), Braz., 81,432 ....M4 46
Mariupol' (Zhdanov), U.S.S.R., 273,000 ....E5 22
Marrakech, Mor., 215,695..........F5 34
Marsala, Sicily, It., 42,488........D6 18
Marseille, Fr., 605,577..............F6 16
Matsumoto, Jap., 145,228..........H5 33
Matsuyama, Jap., 213,457..........F7 33
Mecca,* Saudi Arabia, 150,000.C5 26
Mechelen (Malines), Belg., 63,497 ....F6 15
Medan, Sumatra, Indon., 190,831 ....B5 31
Medellín, Col., 328,294.............E2 46
Meknès, Mor., 140,294..............E5 34
Melbourne,* Vic., †1,524,062.....L1 36
Memel (Klaipéda), U.S.S.R., 48,545 ....D4 22
Memphis, Tenn., 396,000...........L6 43
Mendoza, Arg., 97,496.............G10 47
Mérida, Mex., 144,793...............P6 44
Merthyr Tydfil, Wales, 61,142...D6 10
Meshed, Iran, 176,400...............L2 27
Messina, Sicily, It., 208,762.......E5 18
Metz, Fr., 81,096.......................G3 16
Mexico City,* Mex., 2,233,914...L1 44
Miami, Fla., 249,276...................N8 43
Middlesbrough, Eng., 147,276 ....F3 10
Milan (Milano), It., 1,267,040...B2 18
Milwaukee, Wis., 637,392..........M4 43
Minhow (Foochow), China, 553,000.......................J6 32
Minneapolis, Minn., 521,718.......K3 43
Minsk, U.S.S.R., 412,000...........D4 22
Miskolc, Hung., 135,231.............F2 20
Mobile, Ala., 129,009.................M7 43
Modena, It., 82,180....................C2 18
Mogadishu (Mogadiscio),* Somalia, 77,556......................R11 35
Moji, Jap., 145,027.....................E7 33
Molenbeek-Saint Jean, Belg., 62,711...........................B9 15
Molotov (Perm), U.S.S.R., 450,000 ....G4 22
Monterrey, Mex., 331,771...........J4 44
Montevideo,* Uru., 850,000......K11 47
Montgomery,* Ala., 106,525....M6 43
Montpelier,* Vt., 8,599..............P3 43
Montpellier, Fr., 83,890...............E6 16
Montreal, Que., 1,109,439...........F4 41
Montreuil-sous-Bois, Fr., 69,698 ....B2 16
Monza, It., 69,263........................B2 18
Morioka, Jap., 142,875.................K4 33
Moscow (Moskva),* U.S.S.R., †5,032,000..............B4 22
Mosul, Iraq, 203,273....................C2 27
Motherwell, Scot., 68,154............D2 11
Mt. Vernon, N. Y., 71,899............S5 43
Mukden, China, 2,299,900............K3 32
Mülheim, Ger., 149,589................G4 14
Mulhouse, Fr., 97,285...................G4 16
Multan, Pak., 190,122....................B2 29
Munich (München), Ger., 831,937 ....D4 14
Münster, Ger., 118,496..................B3 14
Murcia, Sp., †217,934....................F4 17
Murmansk, U.S.S.R., 168,000...E3 22
Mysore, India, 244,323..................C6 29
Nagano, Jap., 152,547...................J5 33
Nagaoka, Jap., 130,785..................J5 33
Nagasaki, Jap., 303,724.................D7 33
Nagoya, Jap., 1,336,780................H6 33
Nagpur, India, 449,099...................C4 29
Nairobi,* Kenya, 118,976............O12 35
Nanchang, China, 398,200............H6 32
Nancy, Fr., 120,484........................G3 16
Nanking, China, 1,091,600............J5 32
Nanning, China, 194,600................G7 32
Nantes, Fr., 197,915.......................C4 16
Naples (Napoli), It., 984,684 ....E4 18
Nashville,* Tenn., 174,307..........M5 43
Nassau,* Bahama Is., 13,231.....C1 45
Neuilly-sur-Seine, Fr., 58,658 ....A1 16
Neuss, Ger., 63,478........................F5 14
Newark, N. J., 438,776...................R5 43
New Bedford, Mass., 109,189 ....R2 43
New Britain, Conn., 73,726.........P2 43
Newcastle, N. S. W., †178,156 ....J6 36
Newcastle-on-Tyne, Eng., 291,724 ....F2 10
New Delhi,* India, 276,314.........C3 29
New Haven, Conn., 164,443.........O2 43
New Orleans, La., 570,445...........L7 43
Newport, Eng., 105,547.................E6 10
New York, N. Y., 7,891,957 ....R5 43
Niagara Falls, N. Y., 90,872......O4 43
Nice, Fr., 208,453..........................G6 16
Nictheroy (Niterói), Brazil, 170,868 ....P14 47
Niigata, Jap., 261,758....................J5 33
Nijmegen, Neth., 122,963.............H5 15
Nikolayev, U.S.S.R., 206,000........E5 22
Nîmes (Nismes), Fr., 72,274 ....F6 16
Ningpo (Ninghsien), China, 237,500 ....K6 32
Niterói, Braz., 170,868...............P14 47
Nizhni Novgorod (Gor'kiy), U.S.S.R., 876,000...................F4 22
Norfolk, Va., 213,513.....................P5 43
Norrköping, Swed., 84,939.............K7 13
Northampton, Eng., 104,432........G5 10
Nottingham, Eng., 306,055...........G5 10
Nouméa,* N. Cal., 22,238..............G8 37
Novara, It., 65,682..........................B2 18
Novi Sad, Yugo., 83,223.................D3 21
Novocherkassk, U.S.S.R., 81,286 ....F5 22
Novorossiysk, U.S.S.R., 95,280 ....E5 22
Novosibirsk, U.S.S.R., 731,000 ....K4 22
Nürnberg (Nuremberg), Ger., 362,459 ....D4 14
Oak Ridge, Tenn., 30,229.............M5 43
Oakland, Cal., 384,575....................D8 42
Oberammergau, Ger., 5,101..........D5 14
Oberhausen, Ger., 202,800............G4 14
Odense, Den., 100,940....................G9 13
Odessa, U.S.S.R., 607,000.............E5 23
Offenbach, Ger., 89,230..................C3 14
Oita, Jap., 112,429..........................E7 33
Okayama, Jap., 235,754..................F6 33
Oklahoma City,* Okla., 243,504..J6 42
Oldenburg, Ger., 122,809................B2 14
Oldham, Eng., 121,266....................E4 10
Olomouc (Olmütz), Czech., 73,899 ....D2 20
Olympia,* Wash., 15,819................C3 42
Omaha, Neb., 251,117.....................J4 42
Omdurman, Sudan, 126,650.........N8 34
Omsk, U.S.S.R., 505,000...............J4 22
Omuda, Jap., 201,737.....................E7 33
Oporto (Porto), Port., 281,406 ....B2 17
Oradea, Rum., 99,007.....................E2 21
Oran, Alg., 277,772..........................F4 34
Ordzhonikidze, U.S.S.R., 159,000 ....F5 22
Orel, U.S.S.R., 128,000..................E4 22
Orenburg, U.S.S.R., 226,000.........G4 22
Orléans, Fr., 71,533.......................D3 16
Osaka, Jap., 2,547,316....................J8 33
Oslo,* Nor., 434,047.......................D3 13
Osnabrück, Ger., 109,538...............C4 12
Ostrava, Czech., 199,206................E2 20
Otaru, Jap., 188,448.........................K2 33
Ottawa,* Canada, 222,129.............E4 41
Oxford, Eng., 98,684........................F6 10
Padova (Padua), It., 149,581 ....C2 18
Pago Pago,* Amer. Samoa, 1,586 ....J7 37
Paisley, Scot., 93,711.......................C2 11
Palembang, Sumatra, Indon., 237,616.......................D6 31
Palermo, Sicily, It., 447,421.........D5 18
Palmas, Las,* Can. Is., Sp., 153,262 ....B4 17
Panamá,* Pan., 127,874................H6 39
Paoting, China, 197,000..................H4 32
Papeete,* Tahiti, Soc. Is., 17,247 ....M7 37
Pará (Belém), Braz., 225,218 ....L4 46
Parahyba (João Pessoa), Braz., 89,517.........................O5 46
Paramaribo,* Sur., 67,381..............K2 46
Paraná, Arg., 84,153........................J10 47
Paris,* France, 2,820,534...............E3 16
Greater, 4,775,711.........E3 16
Parma, It., 95,227.............................C2 18
Pasadena, Cal., 104,577....................D8 42
Passaic, N. J., 57,702.......................R5 43
Paterson, N. J., 139,336....................R5 43
Patna, India, 283,479.........................E3 29
Pátrai (Patras), Gr., 79,014.........E6 21
Pécs, Hung., 87,909..........................E3 20
Peiraiévs (Piraeus), Gr., 186,014 ....F7 21
Peking (Peiping),* China, 2,768,149 ....J3 32
Pelotas, Braz., 78,014...................K10 47
Penang (George Town), Mal. Fed., 189,068....................C6 30
Penza, U.S.S.R., 231,000...............F4 22
Peoria, Ill., 111,856..........................L4 43
Perm, U.S.S.R., 450,000..................G4 22
Pernambuco (Recife), Braz., 512,370.........................O5 46
Perpignan, Fr., 63,863......................E6 16
Perth,* W. Aust., 348,647................B2 36
Perugia, It., 40,039.............................D3 18
Peshawar, Pak., 15,776.....................B2 29
Pforzheim, Ger., 54,153....................C4 14
Philadelphia, Pa., 2,071,605............R6 43
Phnom Penh,* Cambodia, 375,000 ....E5 30
Phoenix,* Ariz., 106,818..................E6 42
Piacenza, It., 60,114.........................B2 18
Pierre,* S. Dak., 5,715......................H3 42
Pilsen (Plzen), Czech., 134,273.B2 20
Pinkiang (Harbin), China, 1,163,000 ....L2 32
Piraeus (Peiraievs), Gr., 186,014 ....F7 21
Pisa, It., 62,310..................................C3 18
Pistoia, It., 33,526.............................C3 18
Pittsburgh, Pa., 676,806...................O4 43
Plauen, Ger., 84,778............................E3 14
Ploeşti, Rum., 114,560........................H3 21
Plovdiv, Bul., 162,518........................G4 21
Plymouth, Eng., 208,012...................D7 10
Plzen (Pilsen), Czech., 134,273 ....B2 20
Pola (Pula), Yugo., 28,089.................A3 21
Poltava, U.S.S.R., 129,000..................E5 22
Pontiac, Mich., 73,681.........................M1 43
Poole, Eng., 83,007..............................E7 10
Poona, India, 480,982.........................B5 29
Port-au-Prince,* Haiti, 152,410 ....D3 45
Portland, Me., 77,634........................R4 43
Portland, Oreg., 373,628....................C3 42
Port Elizabeth, C. of G. H., †188,987 ....M18 35
Port Louis,* Mauritius, 97,888 ....S19 35
Port Moresby,* Pap. Terr., Aust., 17,546..........................B7 31
Porto (Oporto), Port., 281,406 ....B2 17
Pôrto Alegre, Braz., 375,049 ....L10 47
Port of Spain,* Trinidad, 114,150 ....G5 45
Port Said, Egypt, 178,432..........N5 34
Portsmouth, Eng., 233,545.........G7 10
Poznan (Posen), Pol., 376,900..C2 24
Praha (Prag, Prague),* Czech., 978,634.........................C1 20
Preston, Eng., 119,250.................E4 10
Pretoria,* U. of S. A., †285,379 ....M17 35
Providence,* R. I., 248,674.........P2 43
Pskov, U.S.S.R., 59,898................D4 22
Puebla, Mex., 206,840...................N2 44
Pula (Pola), Yugo., 28,089............A3 21
Pusan, Korea, 473,619...................D6 33
P'yŏngyang,* N. Korea, 342,551 ....C4 33
Quebec,* Que., 170,703....................F4 41
Quetta, Pak., 84,348........................A2 29
Quezon City,* P. I., 107,977.....G3 31
Quincy, Mass., 83,835......................R2 43
Quito,* Ecu., 209,932.......................E3 46
Rabat,* Mor., 156,209......................E5 34
Rabaul, New Brit., Terr. N. G., 7,600........................F6 37
Racine, Wis., 71,193.........................L4 43
Radom, Poland, 118,800...................E3 24
Raleigh,* N. C., 65,679....................O6 43
Rangoon,* Burma, 711,520..............C3 30
Ravenna, It., 34,904..........................D2 18
Rawalpindi,* Pak., 237,719..............B2 29
Reading, Eng., 114,196......................F6 10
Reading, Pa., 109,320.........................P4 43
Recife (Pernambuco), Braz., 512,370.........................O5 46
Recklinghausen, Ger., 104,791....B3 14
Regensburg (Ratisbon), Ger., 117,291..........................D4 14
Reggio di Calabria, It., 120,021 ....E5 18
Reggio nell'Emilia, It., 65,360 ....C2 18
Reims, Fr., 114,682............................E3 16
Remscheid, Ger., 103,276..................G5 14
Rennes, Fr., 112,553..........................C3 16
Resht, Iran, 121,600...........................F2 27
Reykjavík,* Ice., 56,096....................B2 9
Rheydt, Ger., 78,302.........................B3 14
Rhondda, Wales, 111,389.................D6 10
Ribeirão Prêto, Braz., 63,312 ....L8 46
Richland, Wash., 21,809...................D3 42
Richmond,* Va., 230,310...................O5 43
Riga, U.S.S.R., 565,000......................D4 22
Rijeka (Fiume), Yugo., 75,112 ....B3 21
Rimini, It., 50,123..............................D2 18
Rio de Janeiro,* Braz., 2,303,063 ....P14 47
Riyadh,* Saudi Arabia, 80,000 ....E5 26
Roanoke, Va., 91,921........................N5 43
Rochester, N. Y., 332,488................O4 43
Rockford, Ill., 92,927..........................L4 43
Rome (Roma)* It., 1,610,467.....D4 18
Rosario, Arg., 467,937.....................H10 47
Rostock, Ger., 114,869.......................D1 14
Rostov, U.S.S.R., 552,000...................F5 22
Rotherham, Eng., 82,334.....................F4 10
Rotterdam, Neth., 722,718..................E5 15
Roubaix, Fr., 109,480.........................E2 16
Rouen, Fr., 101,187............................D3 16
Ryazan', U.S.S.R., 136,000.................F4 22
Rybinsk, U.S.S.R., 162,000.................E4 22
Saarbrücken, Ger., 89,700..................B4 14
Sacramento,* Cal., 137,572...............C5 42
Saginaw, Mich., 92,910......................N4 43
Saharanpur, India, 148,435................E5 30
Saigon,* S. Vietnam, 1,179,000.E5 30
St. Denis, Fr., 79,611.........................B1 16
St. Étienne, Fr., 154,283....................F5 16
St. Gallen (Sankt Gallen), Switz., 68,011............................H2 19
St. Helens, Eng., 110,260...................E4 10
Saint John, New Brunswick, 52,491 ....G4 41
St. John's* Nfld., 57,078...................K4 41
St. Joseph, Mo., 78,588.....................K5 43
St. Louis, Mo., 856,796.....................G1 43
St. Paul,* Minn., 311,349..................K3 43
Sakai, Jap., 251,793...........................H8 33
Salem,* Oreg., 43,140.........................C3 42
Salerno, It., 72,626............................E4 18
Salisbury,* Fed. of Rhod. and Nyas., †118,772........................N15 35
Salonika (Thessalonikē), Gr., 217,049..............................F5 21
Salt Lake City,* Utah, 182,121 ....F4 42
Salvador (Bahia), Brazil, 389,422 ....N6 46
Samarkand, U.S.S.R., 170,000 ....H6 22
San Antonio, Tex., 408,442..............J7 42
San Diego, Cal., 334,387....................D6 42
Sandakan, N. Bor., 14,499.................F4 31
San Francisco, Cal., 775,357.......D8 42
San Jose, Cal., 95,280........................D8 42
San José,* C. R., 118,287...................F5 39
San Juan,* P. R., 224,767..................G1 45
San Luis Potosí, Mex., 126,596 ....J6 44
San Salvador,* El Sal., 191, 393 ....C4 39
Santa Ana, El Sal., 51,702..........C4 39
Santa Cruz de Tenerife,* Can. Is., Sp., 103,446..............B4 17
Santa Fé, Arg., 168,791..................H10 47
Santa Fe,* N. Mex., 27,998.............G6 42
Santander, Sp., 102,462.....................D1 17
Santiago,* Chile, 1,348,283.......O10 47
Santiago de Cuba, Cuba, 118,266 ....C3 45
Santos, Braz., 206,920........................L8 47
São Luís (Maranhão), Braz., 81,432 ....M4 46
São Paulo, Braz., 2,041,716.......L8 47
Sapporo, Jap., 426,620......................K2 33
Saragossa (Zaragoza), Sp., 264,256..............................F2 17
Sarajevo, Yugo., 135,657..................D4 21
Saratov, U.S.S.R., 518,000...............F4 22
Sasebo, Jap., 258,211.........................D7 33
Sassari, Sardinia, It., 60,043....B4 18
Savannah, Ga., 119,638......................N6 43
Savona, It., 62,397..............................B2 18
Schaerbeek, Belg., 119,080.........C9 15
Schenectady, N. Y., 91,785.........O1 43
Schwerin, Ger., 88,164....................D2 14
Scranton, Pa., 125,536......................P4 43
Scutari (Üsküdar), Tur., 69,671.D6 28
Seattle, Wash., 467,591.....................C3 42
Semarang, Java., Indon., 334,959 ....J2 31
Sendai, Jap., 375,844.........................K4 33
Seoul,* S. Korea, 1,446,019..........C5 33
Serpukhov, U.S.S.R., 102,000....E4 22
Sevastopol', U.S.S.R., 133,000..E5 22
Sevilla (Seville), Sp., 374,138....D4 17
Seyhan (Adana), Tur., 172,465.F4 28
's Gravenhage (The Hague)* Neth., 606,728..........................E4 15
Shahjahanpur, India, 104,835....D3 29
Shanghai, China, 6,204,417..........K5 32
Shasi, China, 85,800..........................H5 32
Shcherbakov (Rybinsk), U.S.S.R., 162,000.......................E4 22
Sheffield, Eng., 512,850..................F4 10
Shenyang (Mukden), China, 2,299,900.......................K3 32
Sherbrooke, Que., 58,668..................F4 41
Shimonoseki, Jap., 230,503..............E6 33
Shizuoka, Jap., 295,172.....................H6 33
Shreveport, La., 127,206....................K6 43
Siangtan, China, 183,600...................H6 32
Simferopol', U.S.S.R., 159,000..E5 22
Singapore,* Sing., 896,800...............F6 30
Sioux City, Iowa, 83,991....................J4 42
Skopje (Skoplje, Üsküb), Yugo., 121,551.........................E5 21
Smolensk, U.S.S.R., 131,000......E4 22
Smyrna (Izmir), Tur., 286,310..B3 28
Sofia (Sofiya),* Bul., 725,756....F4 21
Solingen, Ger., 147,845....................G5 14
Somerville, Mass., 102,351..............R1 43
Soochow, China, 474,000..................K5 32
Sosnowiec, Poland, 124,200.............B4 24
Southampton, Eng., 178,326.............F7 10
South Bend., Ind., 115,911..............M4 43
Southend-on-Sea, Eng., 151,806 ....H6 10
Southport, Eng., 84,039......................E4 10
South Shields, Eng., 106,598....F3 10
Sovetsk, U.S.S.R., 57,244................D4 22
Spezia, La, It., 105,301......................B2 18
Spokane, Wash., 161,721..................D3 42
Springfield,* Ill., 81,628..................L5 43
Springfield, Mass., 162,399...............P1 43
Springfield, Ohio, 78,508..................N4 43
Srinagar,* Kash., 207,787.................C2 29
Stalingrad, U.S.S.R., 525,000....F5 22
Stalino, U.S.S.R., 625,000...............K1 23
Stanislav (Stanisławów), U.S.S.R., 60,256.........................D5 22
Stettin (Szczecin), Pol., 237,600 ....B2 24
Stockholm,* Swed., 745,936..........G1 13
Stockport, Eng., 141,650..................E4 10
Stockton-on-Tees, Eng., 74,155.................................F3 10
Stoke-on-Trent, Eng., 275,115..E4 10
Strasbourg, Fr., 192,253...................G3 16
Stuttgart, Ger., 497,677.....................C4 14
Subotica, Yugo., 115,402..................D2 21
Sucre,* Bolivia, 40,128.....................H7 46
Suez, Egypt, 108,250.........................N6 34
Sunderland, Eng., 181,524..............F3 10
Surabaja, Java, Indon., 925,617 ....K2 31
Surakarta, Java, Indon., 34,455 ....J2 31
Suva,* Fiji Is., 37,371......................H7 37
Sverdlovsk, U.S.S.R., 707,000....P6 23
Swansea, Wales, 160,988................C6 10
Swatow, China, 280,400....................J7 32
Swindon, Eng., 68,953......................E6 10
Sydney,* N. S. W., †1,863,161..L3 36
Syracuse, N. Y., 220,583..................O4 43
Syzran', U.S.S.R., 169,000.............F4 22
Szczecin (Stettin), Pol., 237,600 ....B2 24
Szeged, Hung., 93,746.......................E3 20
Tabriz, Iran, 258,865.........................E2 27
Tacoma, Wash., 143,673.....................C3 42
Taegu, Korea, 313,705.......................D6 33
Taganrog, U.S.S.R., 189,000......E5 22
Tainan, Taiwan, China, 287,797.J7 32
Taipei,* Taiwan, China, 748,510.K7 32
Taiyüan, China, 720,700....................H4 32
Takamatsu, Jap., 144,812.................G6 33
Takaoka, Jap., 131,531.......................H5 33
Tallahassee,* Fla., 27,237................M7 43
Tallinn, U.S.S.R., 168,000...............D4 22
Tambov, U.S.S.R., 150,000.............F4 22
Tampa, Fla., 124,681........................N8 43
Tampere, Fin., 119,250.....................N6 13
Tampico, Mex., 94,221......................L5 44
Tananarive,* Mada., 187,330....R15 35
Tangier, Mor., 150,000.....................E4 34
Tanjore, India, 100,680.....................C6 29
Tanta, Egypt, 139,965.......................N5 34
Taranto, It., 146,745..........................F4 18
Tartu, U.S.S.R., 50,000.....................D4 22
Tashkent, U.S.S.R., 778,000.............S1 23
Tbilisi, U.S.S.R., 635,000..................F5 22
Tegucigalpa,* Hon., 72,385..........D3 39
Tehran (Teheran),* Iran, 554,372..................................G3 27
Tel Aviv-Jaffa, Israel, 363,500..B3 24
Terni, It., 37,295.................................D3 18
Thessalonikē (Salonika), Gr., 224,748...............................F5 21
Tientsin, China, 2,693,831...............J4 32
Tiflis (Tbilisi), U.S.S.R., 635,000.........................F5 22
Tilburg, Neth., 131,277.....................G5 15
Tilsit (Sovetsk), U.S.S.R., 57,244.........................D4 22
Timişoara (Temesvár), Rum., 142,251............................E3 21
Tiranë (Tirana),* Alb., 59,887..E5 21
Tokushima, Jap., 171,419...............G7 33
Tokyo,* Jap., 6,969,104..................O2 33
Toledo, Ohio, 303,616......................M2 43
Tomsk, U.S.S.R., 224,000................K4 22
Topeka,* Kans., 78,791...................K5 43
Torino (Turin), It., 711,282..........A2 18
Toronto,* Ont., 667,706....................E5 41
Torreón, Mex., 128,548.....................H4 44
Toruń (Thorn), Poland, 96,000 ....D2 24
Toulon, Fr., 125,572..........................F6 16
Toulouse, Fr., 217,667......................D6 16
Tourcoing, Fr., 82,753......................E2 16
Tours, Fr., 80,261.............................D4 16
Toyama, Jap., 170,495......................H5 33
Toyohashi, Jap., 202,985..................H6 33
Trapani, Sicily, It., 64,135.............D5 18
Trento, It., 40,447..............................C1 18
Trenton,* N. J., 128,009...................R5 43
Treviso, It., 29,620.............................D2 18
Trier (Treves), Ger., 75,526.........B4 14
Trieste, Italy, 269,543........................D2 18
Tripoli,* Libya, 130,238....................J5 34
Trois Rivières, Que., 50,483...........F4 41
Trondheim, Nor., 56,669...................F5 13
Troy, N. Y., 72,311.............................O1 43
Troyes, Fr., 57,089.............................F3 16
Tsinan, China, 680,100......................J4 32
Tsingtao, China, 916,800...................K4 32
Tsitsihar, China, 344,700..................L2 32
Tsu, Jap., 106,754..............................H6 33
Tucumán, Arg., 194,166...................H9 47
Tula, U.S.S.R., 320,000....................E4 22
Tulsa, Okla., 182,740.........................K5 43
Tunis,* Tun., 364,593........................J4 34
Turin (Torino), It., 711,282.........A2 18
Tuticorin, India, 75,614....................C7 29
Tynemouth, Eng., 66,564.................F2 10
Udine, It., 65,199................................D1 18
Ufa, U.S.S.R., 265,000......................G4 22
Uipest, Hung., 68,530.......................E3 20
Ulan Bator (Urga),* Mongolia, 100,000 ....G2 32
Ulm, Ger., 71,132...............................C4 14
Ul'yanovsk, U.S.S.R., 183,000....F4 22
Üsküb (Skoplje, Skopje), Yugo., 121,551...........................E5 21
Üsküdar (Scutari), Tur., 69,671 ....D6 28
Utica, N. Y., 101,531..........................P4 43
Utrecht, Neth., 247,816.....................G4 15
Utsunomiya, Jap., 227,153...............K5 33
Valencia, Sp., 509,175......................F3 17
Valletta,* Malta, 18,666...................E7 18
Valparaíso, Chile, 218,829.........N10 47
Vancouver, B.C., 365,844..................F5 40
Varanasi, India, 355,777....................D3 29
Varna, Bul., 119,767..........................H4 21
Venice (Venezia), It., 291,635...D2 18
Veracruz, Mex., 101,221...................Q2 44
Verona, It., 154,931............................C2 18
Versailles, Fr., 72,038........................A2 16
Vicenza, It., 68,203.............................C2 18
Vichy, Fr., 30,099...............................E4 16
Victoria,* Hong Kong, 887,400..H7 32
Victoria,* Br. Col., 54,584...............F5 40
Vienna (Wien),* Austria, 1,766,102.........................D2 20
Vientiane,* Laos, 10,000..................D3 30
Vigo, Sp., †136,291...........................B1 17
Villeurbanne, Fr., 79,829...................F5 16
Vil'nyus, U.S.S.R., 200,000.............D4 22
Vinnitsa, U.S.S.R., 105,000..............D5 22
Vitebsk, U.S.S.R., 128,000...............E4 22
Vladivostok, U.S.S.R., 265,000 ....P5 23
Vologda, U.S.S.R., 127,000.............F4 22
Voronezh, U.S.S.R., 400,000...........F4 22
Voroshilovgrad, U.S.S.R., 251,000 ....P1 23
Vyborg (Viipuri), U.S.S.R., 56,687.........................D3 22
Wakayama, Jap., 220,021..................G6 33
Wallasey, Eng., 101,369....................D4 10
Walsall, Eng., 114,535.......................F5 10
Wanne-Eickel, Ger., 86,537..............G4 14
Warrington, Eng., 80,694..................E4 10
Warsaw (Warszawa),* Poland, 1,022,900..............................E2 24
Washington, D. C.,* U. S. A., 802,178............................O5 43
Waterbury, Conn., 104,477...............O2 43
Wattenscheid, Ger., 67,292...............G4 14
Wellington,* N. Z., 138,297.............M6 36
Wenchow (Yungkia), China, 201,600..........................K6 32
Wesermünde, Ger., 102,940..............C2 14
West Hartlepool, Eng., 72,662..G3 10
Wichita, Kans., 168,279.....................J5 42
Wien (Vienna),* Austria, 1,766,102 ....D2 20
Wiesbaden, Ger., 220,741..................B3 14
Wigan, Eng., 84,560...........................E4 10
Wilkes-Barre, Pa., 76,826.................P4 43
Willemstad,* Neth. Ant., 40,597 ....E4 45
Wilmington, Del., 110,356...............P5 43
Wimbledon, Eng., 58,141..................G6 10
Windsor, Ont., 121,980.....................D5 41
Winnipeg,* Man., 255,093................L5 40
Winston-Salem, N. C., 87,811....N5 43
Winterthur, Switz., 66,925...............G1 19
Witten, Ger., 76,312...........................G4 14
Włocławek, Pol., 58,500...................D2 24
Wolverhampton, Eng., 162,672..E5 10
Worcester, Eng., 59,703.....................F5 10
Worcester, Mass., 203,486.................P1 43
Worms, Ger., 52,237............................C4 14
Wrocław (Breslau), Pol., 387,900..............................C3 24
Wuchow (Tsangwu), China, 110,800..........................H7 32
Wuhan, China, 1,427,300....................H5 32
Wuhu, China, 242,100.........................J5 32
Wuppertal, Ger., 363,224...................G4 14
Würzburg, Ger., 78,433......................D4 14
Yarkand (Soche), China, 80,000.C7 32
Yarmouth (Great Yarmouth), Eng., 51,105..............................J5 10
Yaroslavl', U.S.S.R., 374,000.....E4 22
Yawata, Jap., 286,241........................E7 33
Yerevan (Erivan), U.S.S.R., 385,000...........................F6 22
Yokohama, Jap., 1,143,687.................O3 33
Yokosuka, Jap., 279,132......................O3 33
Yonkers, N. Y., 152,798.....................R5 43
York, Eng., 105,336..............................F4 10
York, Pa., 59,953..................................O5 43
Youngstown, Ohio, 168,330...............N4 43
Zabrze (Hindenburg), Pol., 185,100...............................A4 24
Zagreb, Yugo., 350,452.......................C3 21
Zaragoza (Saragossa), Sp., 264,256.................................F2 17
Zhdanov (Mariupol'), U.S.S.R., 273,000..........................E5 22
Zhitomir, U.S.S.R., 95,090................D4 22
Zlatoust, U.S.S.R., 143,000..............G4 22
Zürich, Switz., 390,020......................F2 19
Zwickau, Ger., 122,862........................E3 14

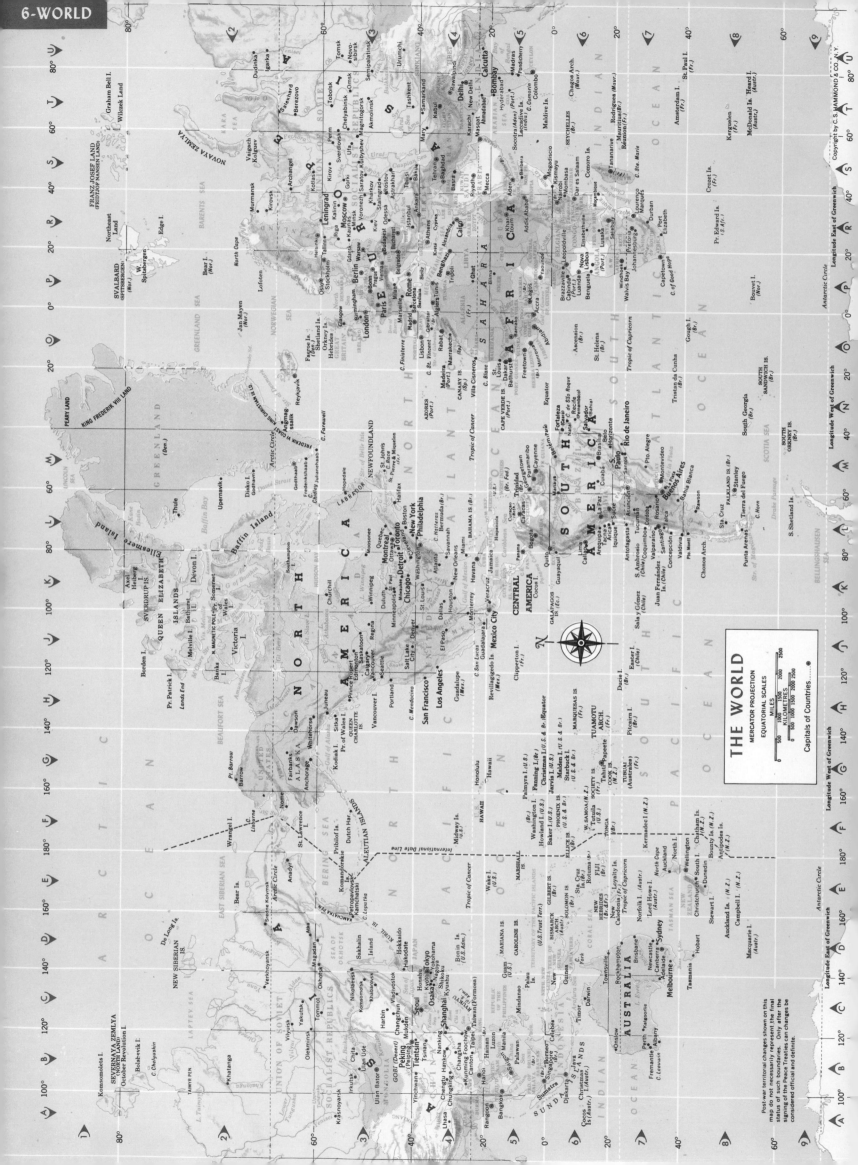

THE WORLD

MERCATOR PROJECTION

EQUATORIAL SCALES

MILES
0   500   1000   1500   2000   2500

KILOMETRES
0   500 1000 1500 2000 2500

Capitals of Countries......●

Post-war territorial changes shown on this
map do not necessarily represent the final
status of such boundaries. Only after the
signing of the Peace Treaties can changes be
considered official and definite.

This map has been prepared with the North Pole as the mathematical center. From it, distances to any part of the world may be measured. On Mercator's map of the world, the polar regions are so scattered that their relatively small area and availability for flight routes are disregarded. Today, with airplanes following great circle courses, often within the Arctic Circle, polar projection maps are indispensable to the people of this air-minded age.

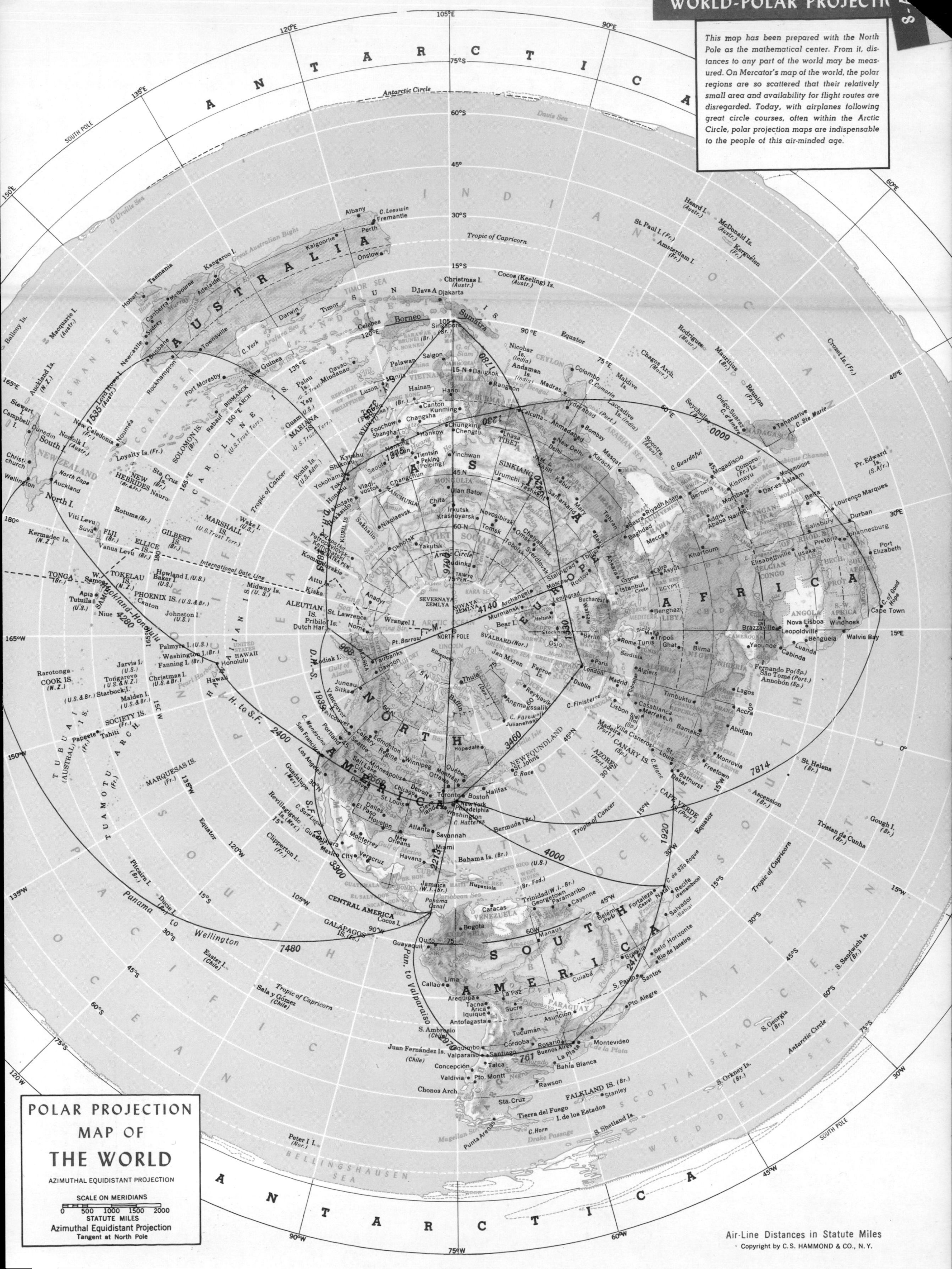

POLAR PROJECTION
MAP OF
THE WORLD

AZIMUTHAL EQUIDISTANT PROJECTION

SCALE ON MERIDIANS

0   500   1000   1500   2000
STATUTE MILES
Azimuthal Equidistant Projection
Tangent at North Pole

Air-Line Distances in Statute Miles
Copyright by C.S. HAMMOND & CO., N.Y.

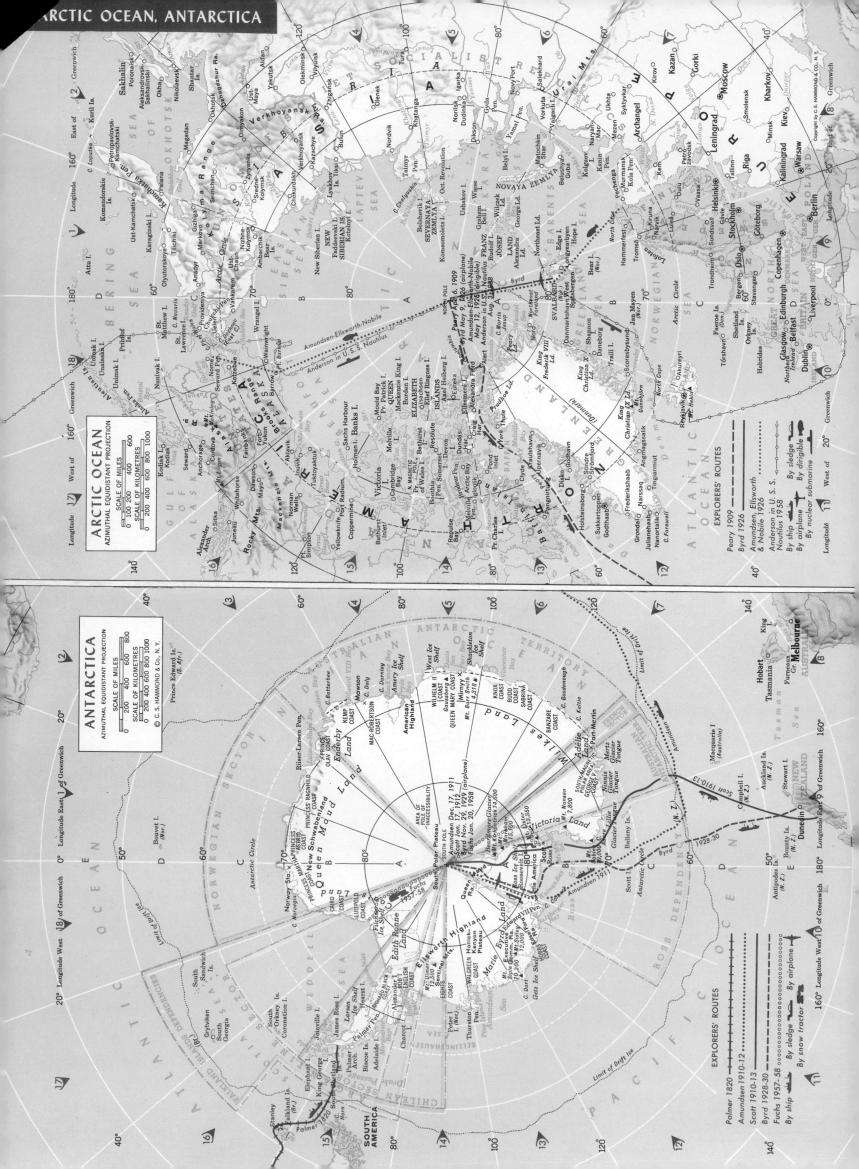

ARCTIC OCEAN
AZIMUTHAL EQUIDISTANT PROJECTION

SCALE OF MILES
0   200   400   600
SCALE OF KILOMETRES
0   200   400   600   800   1000

EXPLORERS' ROUTES

Peary 1909
Byrd 1926
Amundsen, Ellsworth & Nobile 1926
Anderson in U.S.S. Nautilus 1958

By ship — By sledge
By airplane — By dirigible
— By nuclear submarine

ATLANTIC OCEAN

ANTARCTICA
AZIMUTHAL EQUIDISTANT PROJECTION

SCALE OF MILES
0   200   400   600   800
SCALE OF KILOMETRES
0   200   400   600   800   1000

© C. S. HAMMOND & Co., N.Y.

EXPLORERS' ROUTES

Palmer 1820
Amundsen 1910-12
Scott 1910-13
Byrd 1928-30
Fuchs 1957-58

By ship — By sledge
By airplane — By snow tractor

SOUTH POLE

AREA OF GREATEST "INACCESSIBILITY"

Amundsen Dec. 17, 1911
Scott Jan. 17, 1912
Byrd Nov. 29, 1929 (airplane)
Fuchs Jan. 20, 1958

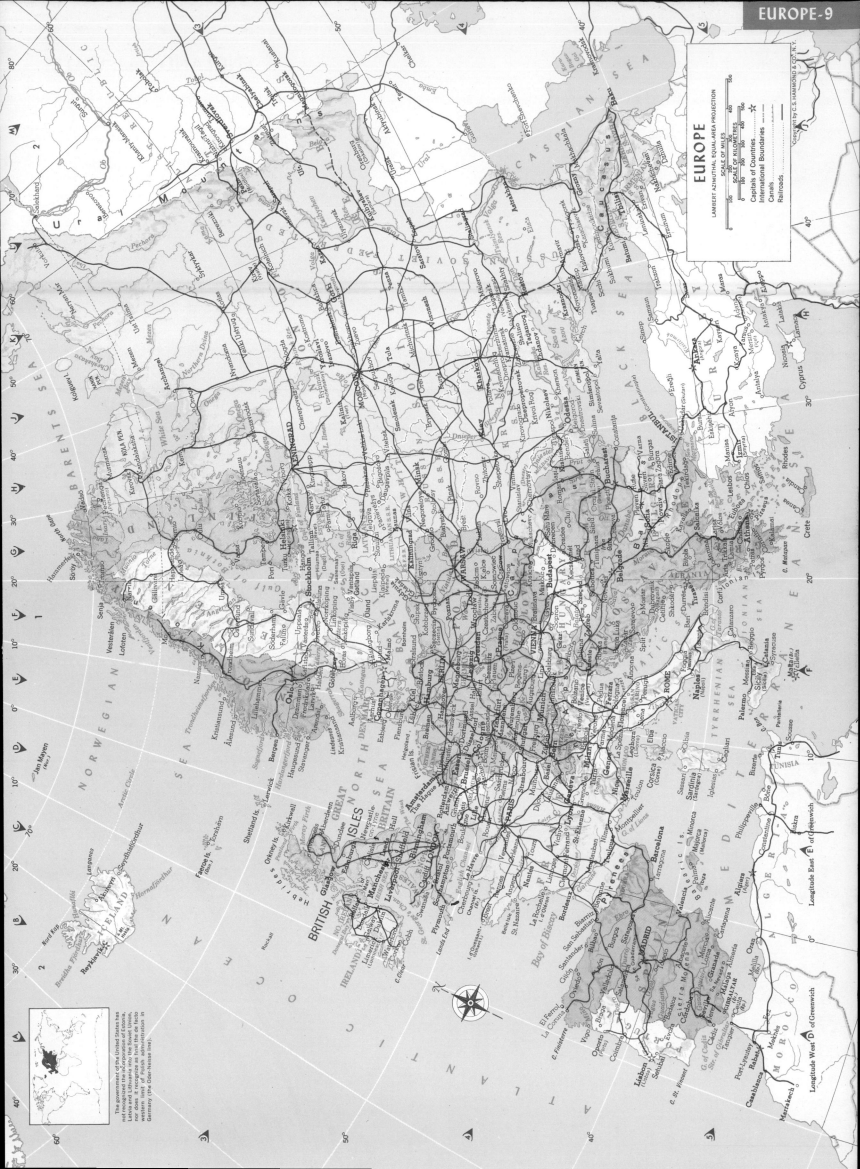

EUROPE
LAMBERT AZIMUTHAL EQUAL-AREA PROJECTION
SCALE OF MILES
SCALE OF KILOMETRES

Capitals of Countries .... ☆
International Boundaries ....
Canals ....
Railroads ....

Copyright by C. S. HAMMOND & CO., N.Y.

The government of the United States has not recognized the incorporation of Estonia, Latvia and Lithuania into the Soviet Union, nor does it recognize as final the de facto western limit of Polish administration in Germany (the Oder-Neisse line).

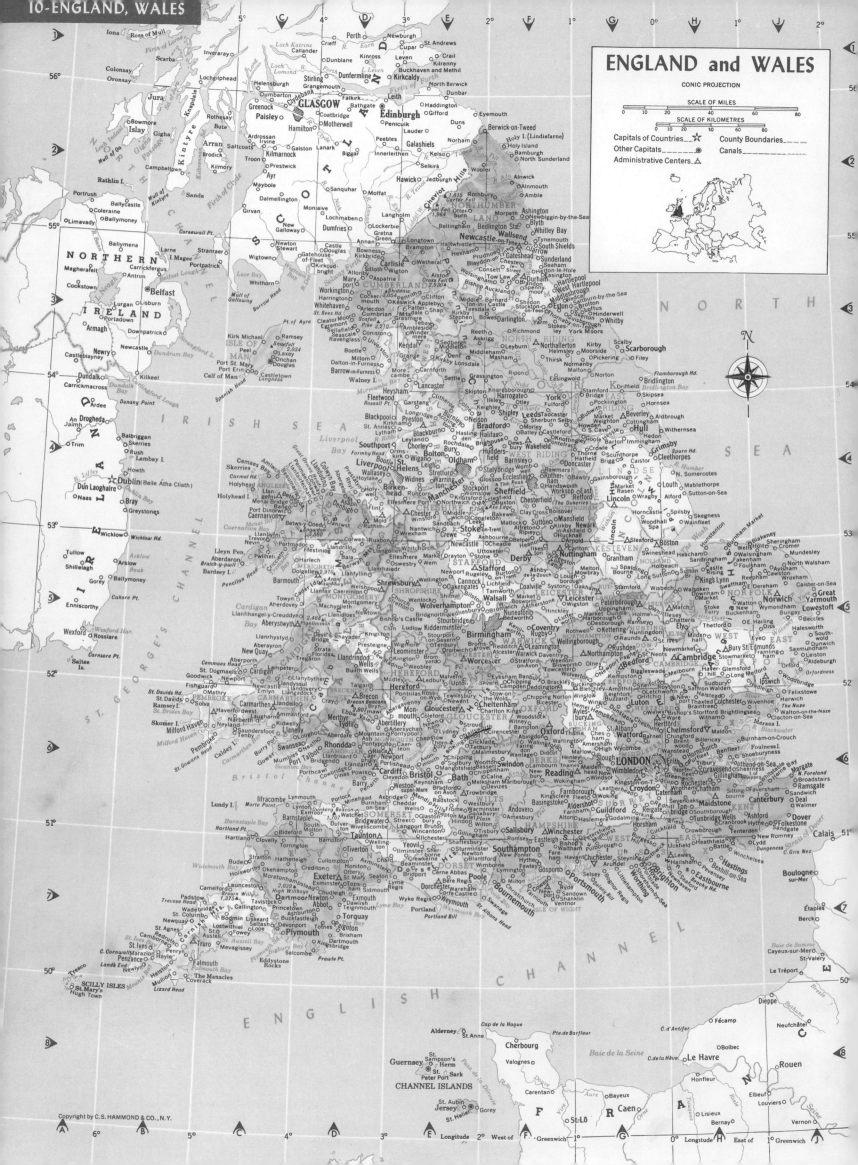

ENGLAND and WALES

CONIC PROJECTION

SCALE OF MILES

SCALE OF KILOMETRES

Capitals of Countries ☆   County Boundaries ____
Other Capitals ____ ◉   Canals ____
Administrative Centers △

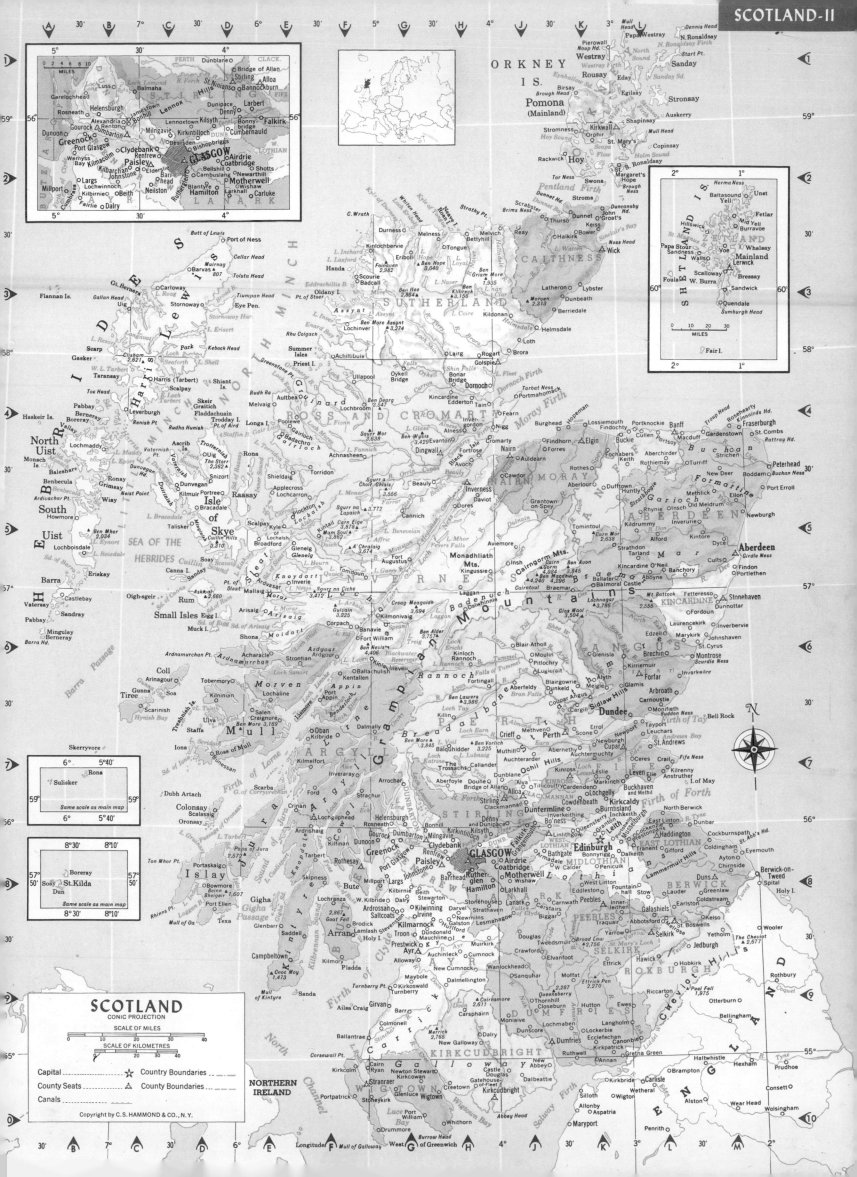

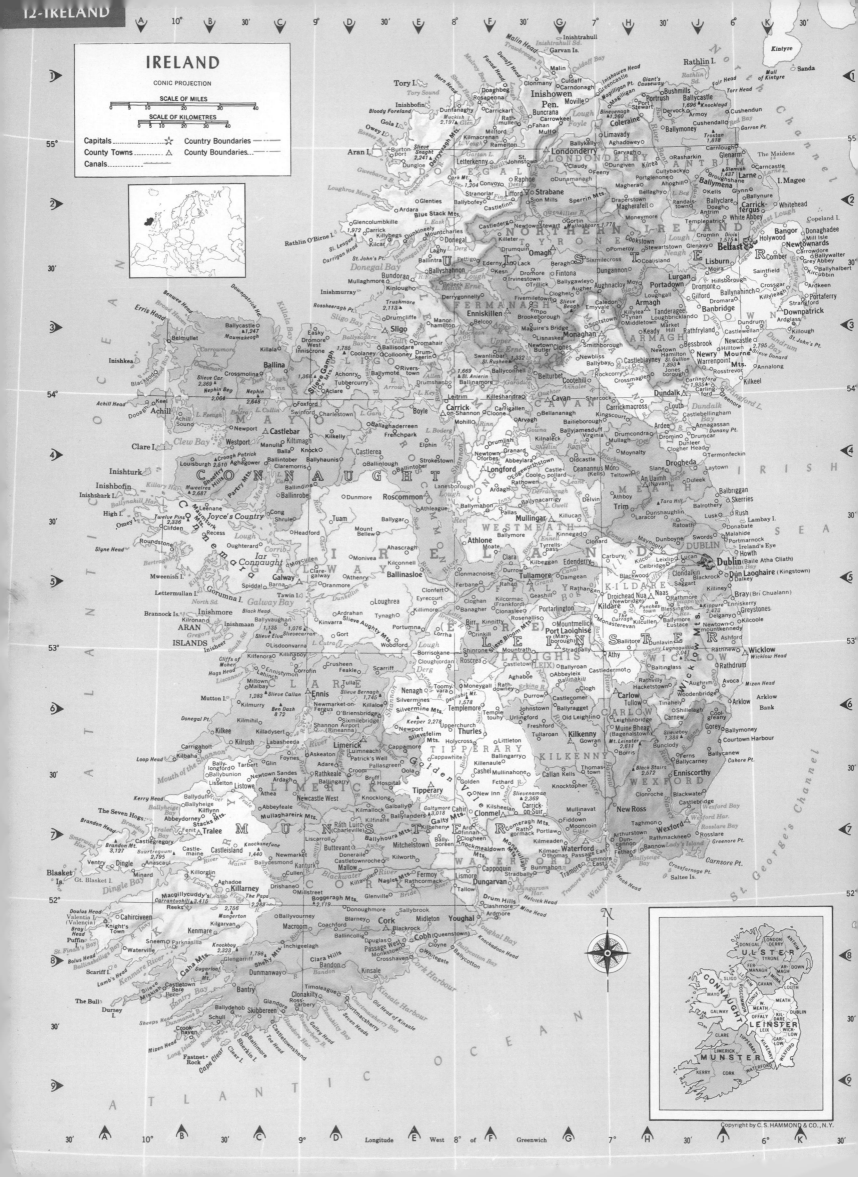

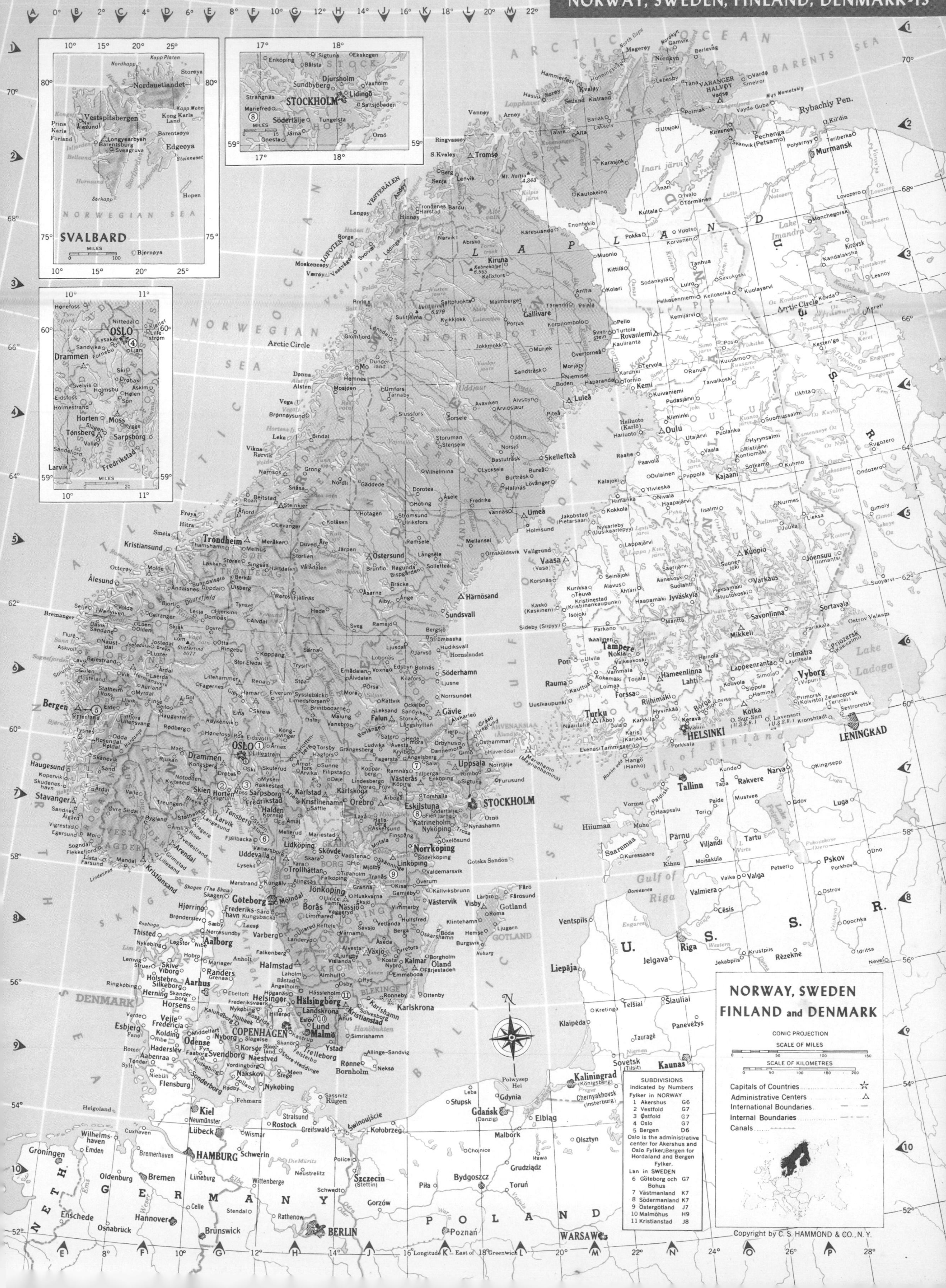

SVALBARD

Nordaustlandet · Vestspitsbergen · Ny Ålesund · Longyearbyen · Barentsburg · Sveagruva · Edgeøya · Kong Karls Land · Prins Karls Forland · Kapp Platen · Kapp Mohn · Nordkapp · Storøya · Steinneset · Hopen · Sørkapp · Hornsund · Bjørnøya

NORWEGIAN SEA

MILES 0 50 100

STOCKHOLM

Enköping · Sigtuna · Ekskogen · Bålsta · Djursholm · Sundbyberg · Vaxholm · Strängnäs · Lidingö · Saltsjöbaden · Mariefred · Södertälje · Tungelsta · Järna · Gnesta · Ornö

MILES

OSLO

Honefoss · Nittedal · Kjeller · Lillestrøm · Drammen · Sandvika · Lysaker · Fornebu · Lian · Ski · Drøbak · Svelvik · Holmsbu · Askim · Holen · Eidsfoss · Holmestrand · Horten · Moss · Rygge · Sandefjord · Tønsberg · Slagen · Sarpsborg · Valløy · Larvik · Fredrikstad

MILES

ARCTIC OCEAN · BARENTS SEA · NORWEGIAN SEA · ATLANTIC OCEAN · NORTH SEA · SKAGERRAK · KATTEGAT · BALTIC SEA · GULF OF BOTHNIA · GULF OF FINLAND · Gulf of Riga

LAPLAND · NORRBOTTEN · OULU · Arctic Circle

Selected place names: North Cape · Magerøy · Nordkyn · Vardø · Hammerfest · Alta · Kautokeino · Tromsø · Narvik · Kiruna · Murmansk · Pechenga (Petsamo) · Kirkenes · Rovaniemi · Kemi · Tornio · Oulu · Vaasa · Umeå · Sundsvall · Östersund · Trondheim · Ålesund · Kristiansund · Bergen · Haugesund · Stavanger · Kristiansand · Helsinki · Turku · Tampere · Lahti · Vyborg · LENINGRAD · Tallinn · Riga · Pärnu · Tartu · Pskov · OSLO · Drammen · Skien · Larvik · Örebro · STOCKHOLM · Uppsala · Västerås · Eskilstuna · Norrköping · Linköping · Jönköping · Göteborg · Borås · Halmstad · Gotland · Visby · Öland · Kalmar · Karlskrona · Karlshamn · Helsingborg · Malmö · Lund · COPENHAGEN · Odense · Aarhus · Aalborg · Esbjerg · Kolding · Kiel · Lübeck · HAMBURG · Bremen · Hannover · BERLIN · Szczecin (Stettin) · Gdańsk (Danzig) · Kaliningrad (Königsberg) · Kaunas · WARSAW · Poznań

DENMARK · GERMANY · POLAND · NETH. · U.S.S.R. · Lake Ladoga · Lake Onega · Inari järvi

NORWAY, SWEDEN FINLAND and DENMARK

CONIC PROJECTION

SCALE OF MILES
0   50   100   150

SCALE OF KILOMETRES
0   50   100   150   200

Capitals of Countries .... ☆
Administrative Centers .... △
International Boundaries .... — - —
Internal Boundaries .... — — —
Canals ....

SUBDIVISIONS
indicated by Numbers

Fylker in NORWAY
1 Akershus   G6
2 Vestfold   G7
3 Østfold   G7
4 Oslo   G7
5 Bergen   D6

Oslo is the administrative center for Akershus and Oslo Fylker; Bergen for Hordaland and Bergen Fylker.

Län in SWEDEN
6 Göteborg och   G7
   Bohus
7 Västmanland   K7
8 Södermanland   K7
9 Östergötland   J7
10 Malmöhus   H9
11 Kristianstad   J8

Copyright by C. S. HAMMOND & CO., N.Y.

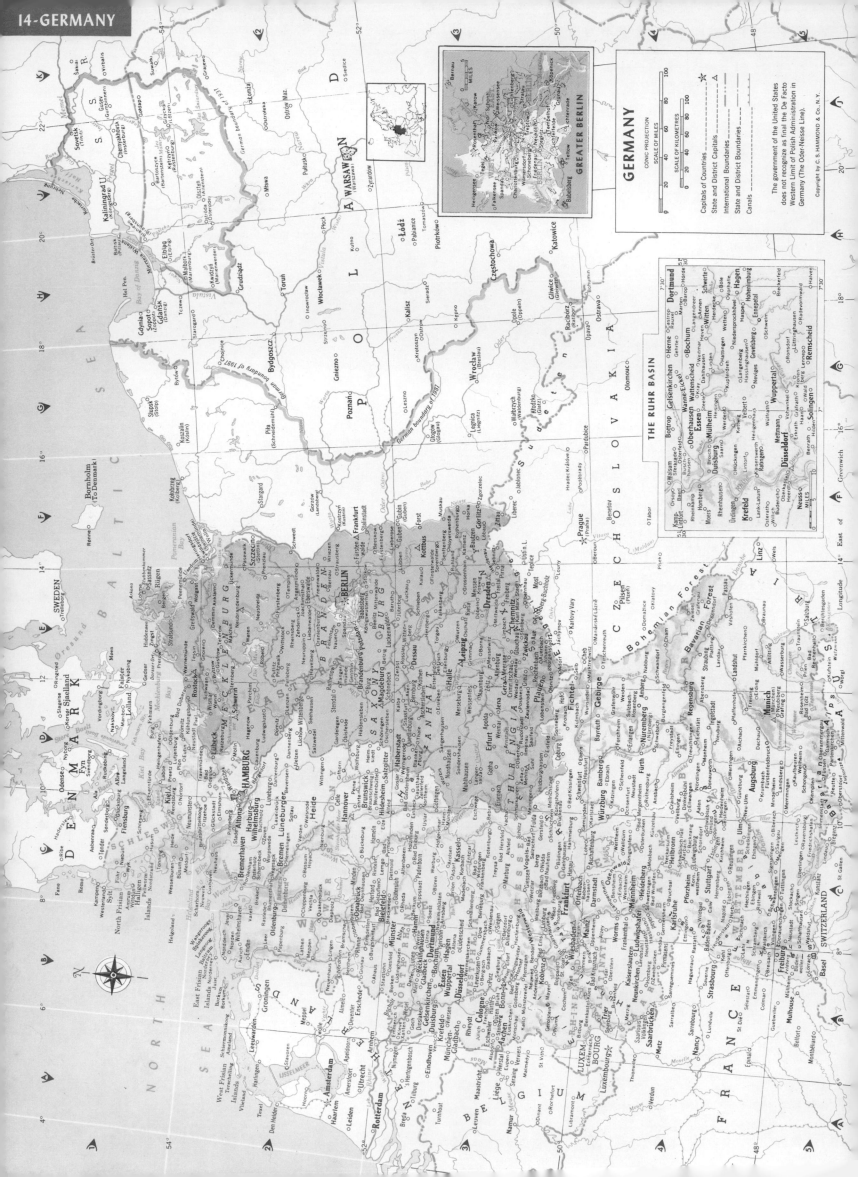

GERMANY

CONIC PROJECTION

SCALE OF MILES

SCALE OF KILOMETRES

Capitals of Countries
State and District Capitals
International Boundaries
State and District Boundaries
Canals

The government of the United States does not recognize as final the De Facto Western Limit of Polish Administration in Germany (The Oder-Neisse Line).

Copyright by C. S. HAMMOND & Co., N.Y.

GREATER BERLIN

THE RUHR BASIN

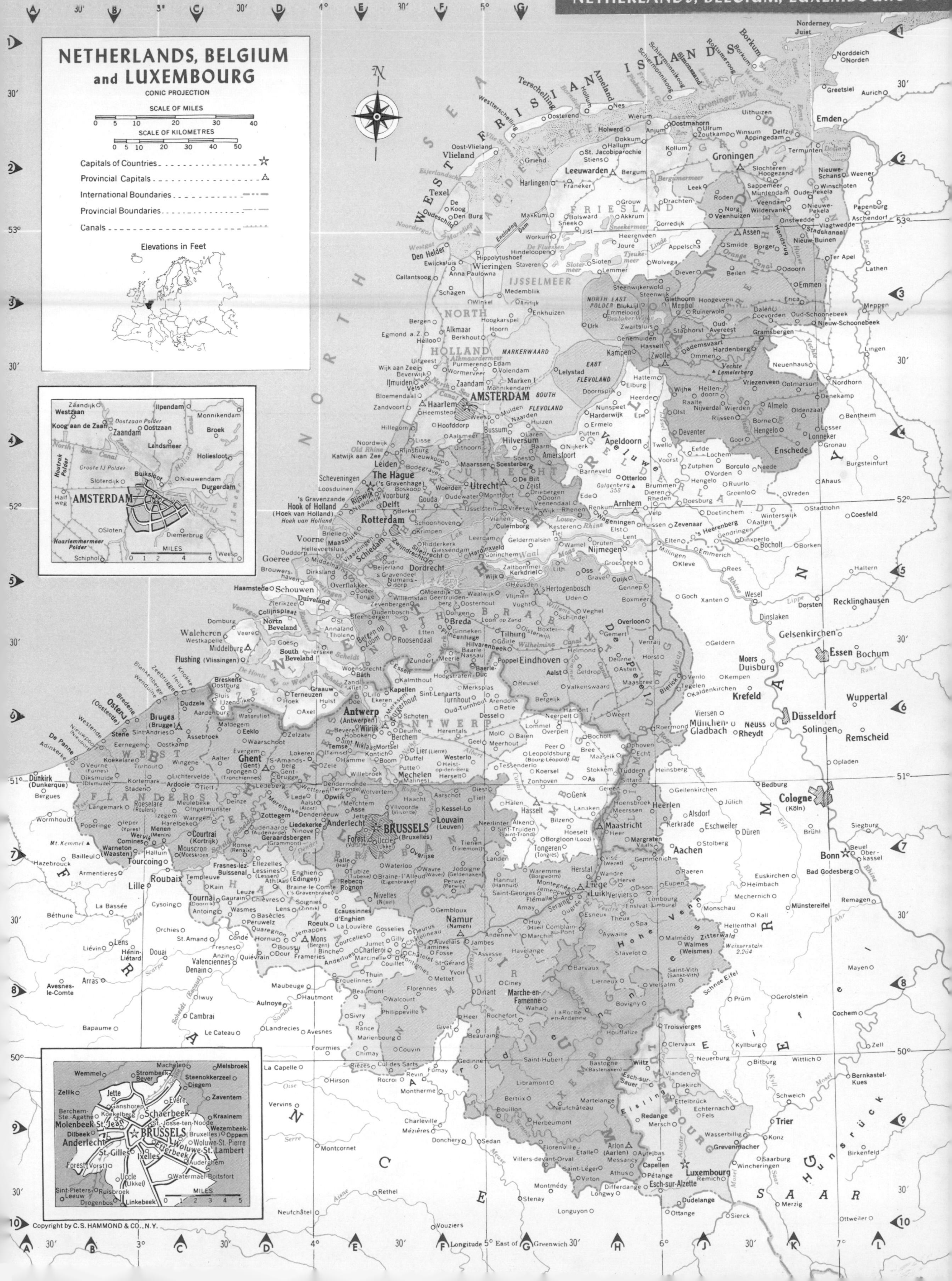
NETHERLANDS, BELGIUM
and LUXEMBOURG
CONIC PROJECTION
SCALE OF MILES
0 5 10 20 30 40
SCALE OF KILOMETRES
0 5 10 20 30 40 50
Capitals of Countries
Provincial Capitals
International Boundaries
Provincial Boundaries
Canals
Elevations in Feet
AMSTERDAM
Zaandam
Haarlemmermeer Polder
Schiphol
MILES
0 1 2 4 6
BRUSSELS
Schaerbeek
Anderlecht
Molenbeek-St.-Jean
Ixelles
Uccle (Ukkel)
MILES
0 1 2 3 4 5
NORTH SEA
WEST FRISIAN ISLANDS
IJSSELMEER
Groningen
Leeuwarden
Emden
Zwolle
Assen
Arnhem
Utrecht
The Hague
('s Gravenhage)
Rotterdam
Dordrecht
Nijmegen
Eindhoven
Breda
Tilburg
's Hertogenbosch
Middelburg
Flushing (Vlissingen)
Antwerp (Antwerpen)
Ghent (Gent)
Bruges (Brugge)
Ostend (Oostende)
Dunkirk (Dunkerque)
Lille
Roubaix
Tourcoing
Tournai (Doornik)
Mons (Bergen)
Charleroi
Namur (Namen)
Louvain (Leuven)
Mechelen (Malines)
Hasselt
Liège (Luik)
Maastricht
Aachen
Cologne (Köln)
Bonn
Düsseldorf
Essen
Krefeld
Arlon (Aarlen)
Luxembourg
Esch-sur-Alzette
Trier
FRANCE
SAAR
Copyright by C.S. HAMMOND & CO., N.Y.
Longitude 5° East of Greenwich

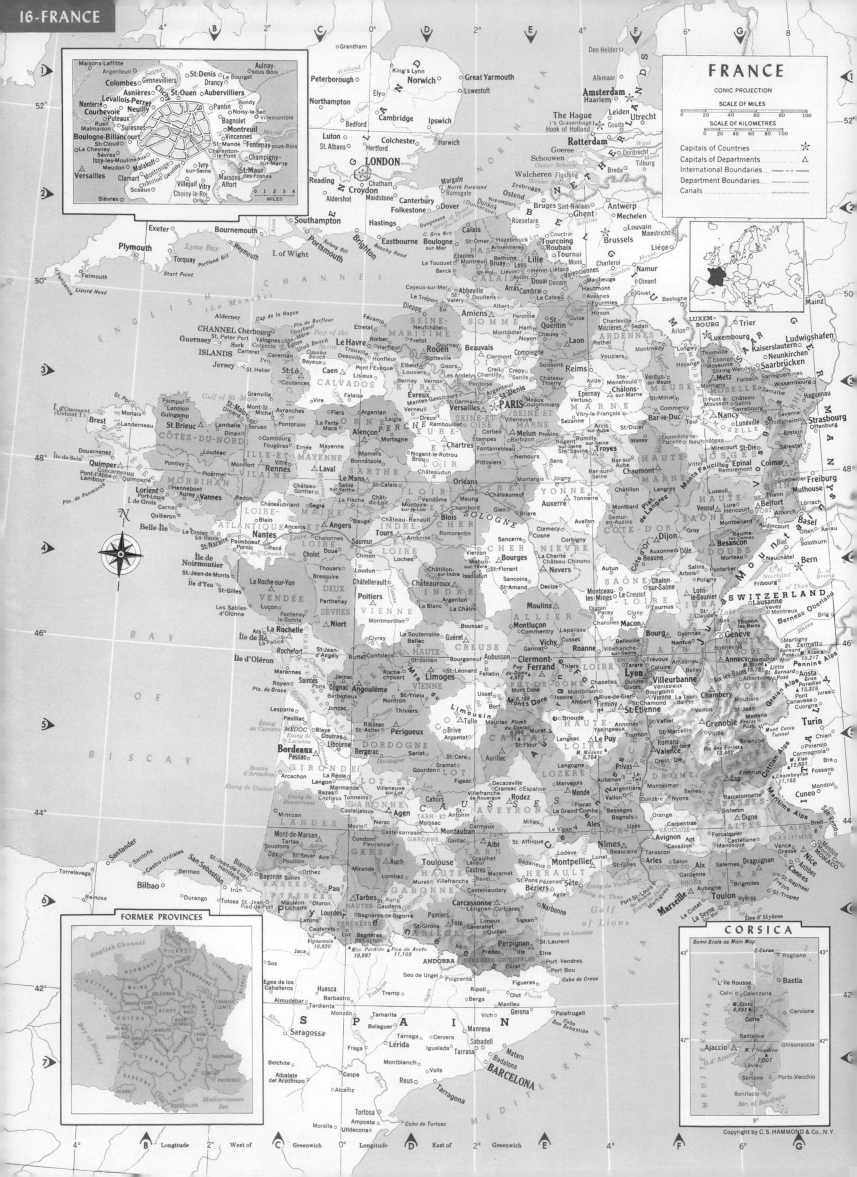

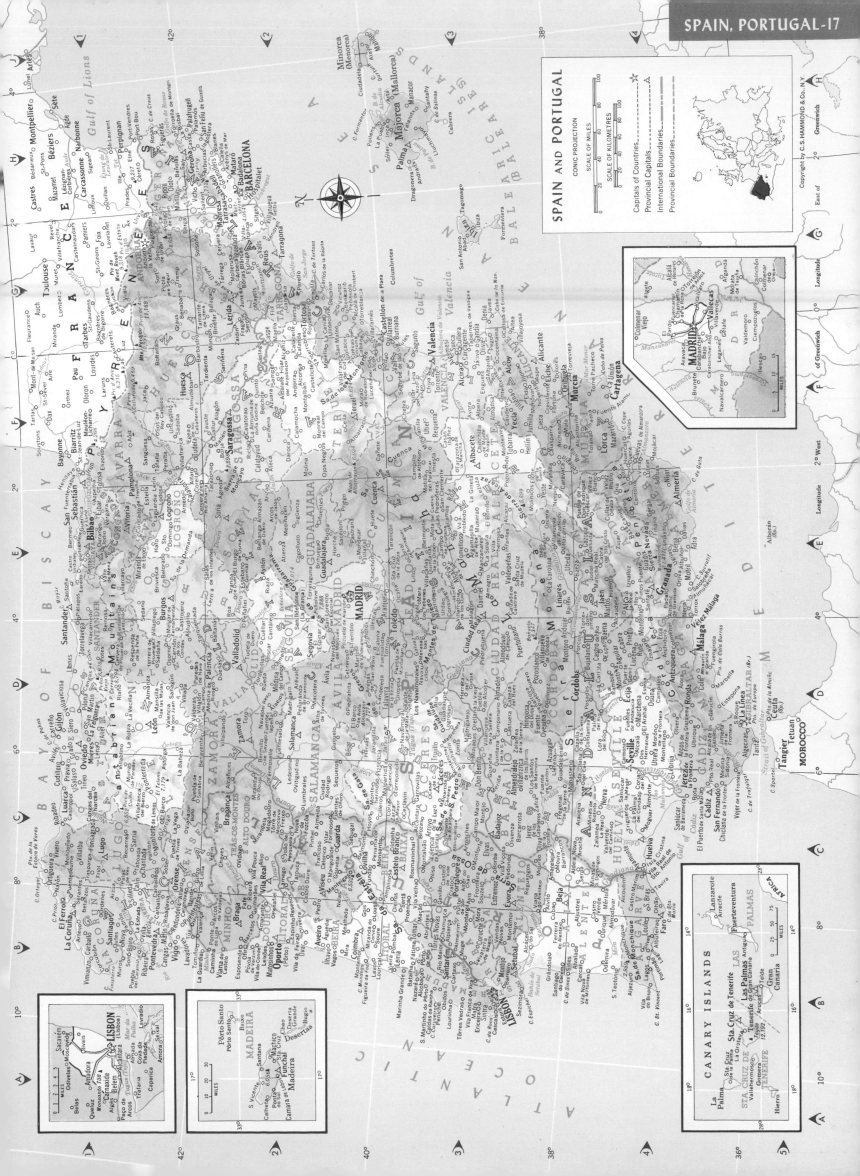

SPAIN AND PORTUGAL

CONIC PROJECTION

SCALE OF MILES

SCALE OF KILOMETRES

Capitals of Countries
Provincial Capitals
International Boundaries
Provincial Boundaries

CANARY ISLANDS

MADEIRA

LISBON (Lisboa)

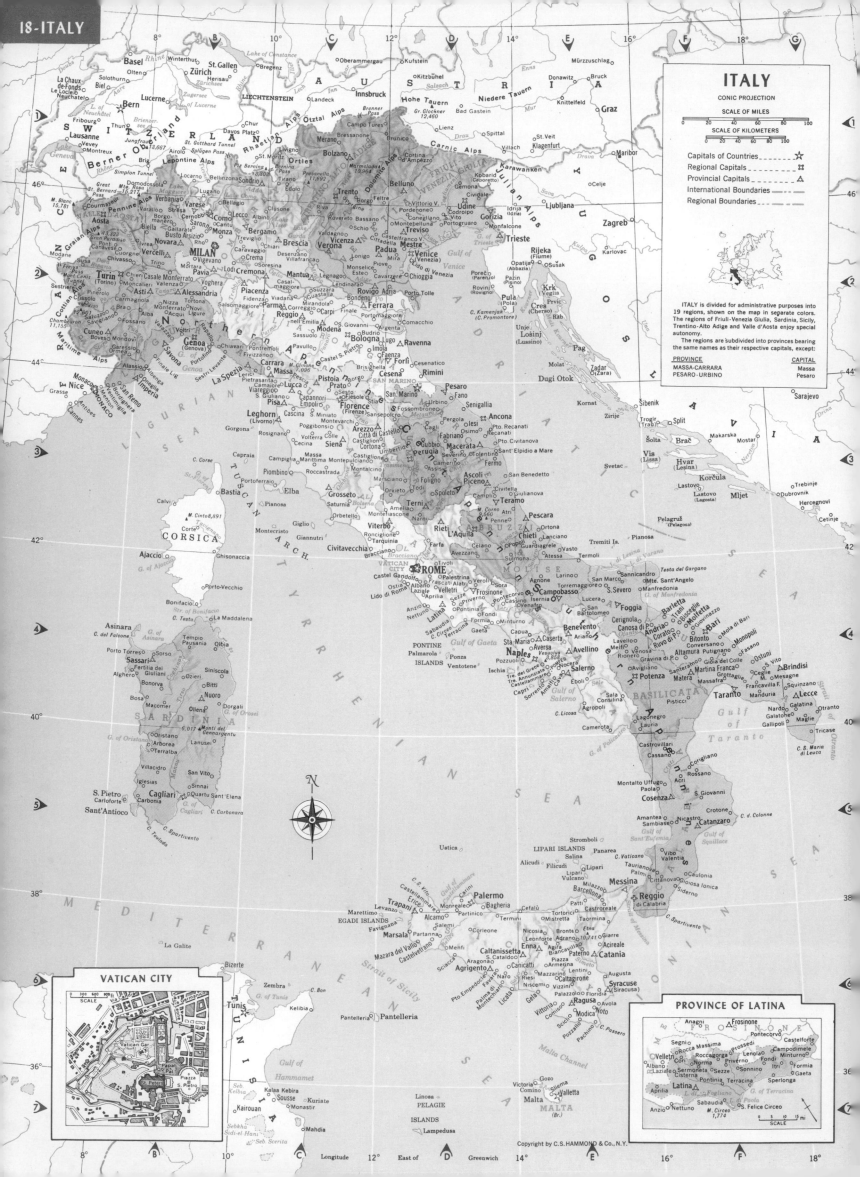

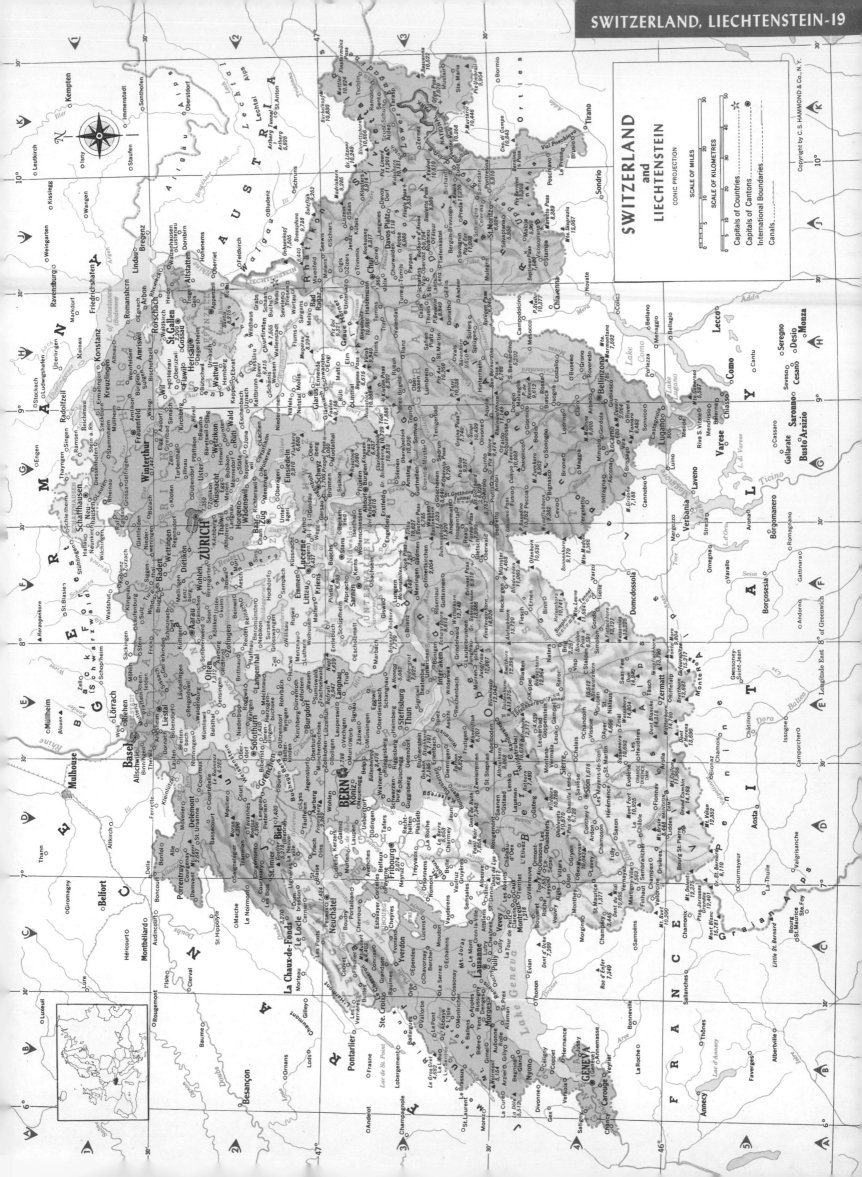

SWITZERLAND
and
LIECHTENSTEIN

CONIC PROJECTION

SCALE OF MILES

SCALE OF KILOMETRES

Capitals of Countries
Capitals of Cantons
International Boundaries
Canals

Copyright by C. S. HAMMOND & Co., N.Y.

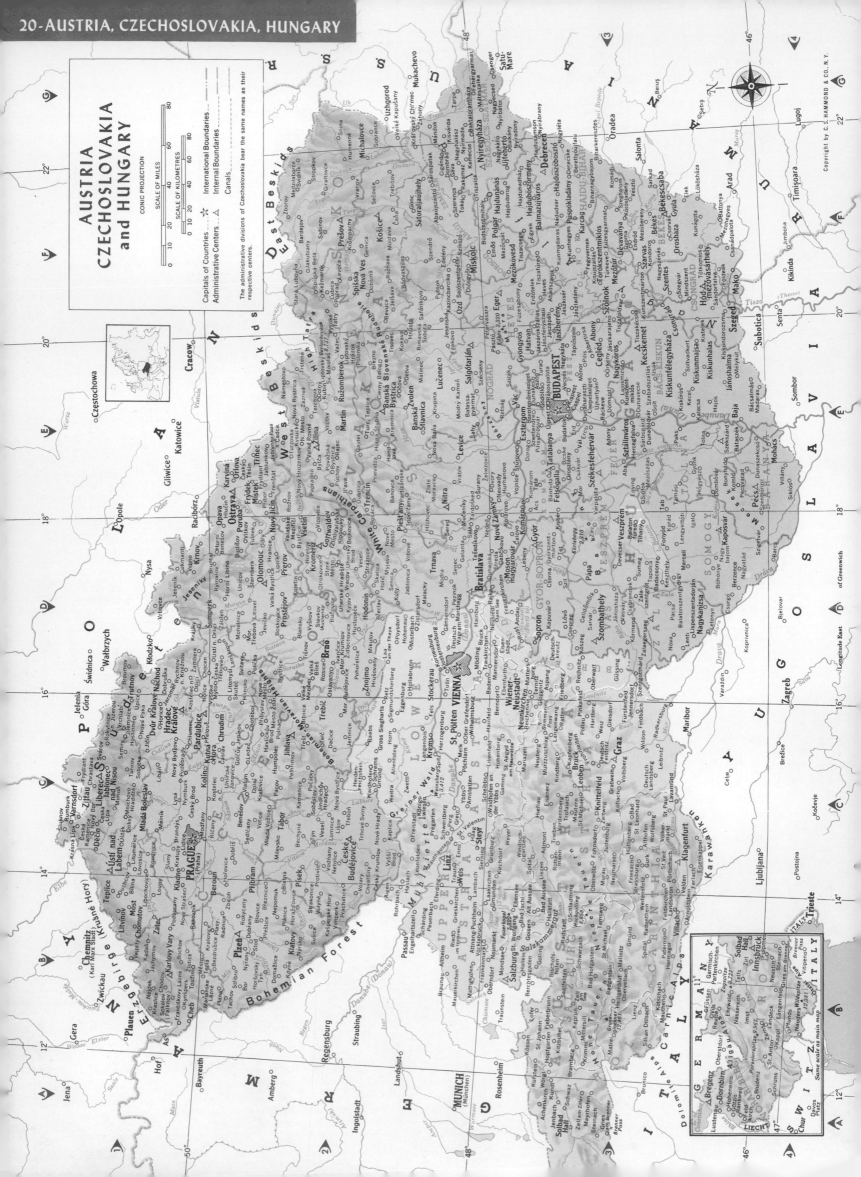

AUSTRIA CZECHOSLOVAKIA and HUNGARY

CONIC PROJECTION

SCALE OF MILES

SCALE OF KILOMETRES

Capitals of Countries ..... ★
Administrative Centers ..... △
Canals .....

The administrative divisions of Czechoslovakia bear the same names as their respective centers.

Copyright by C. S. HAMMOND & CO., N. Y.

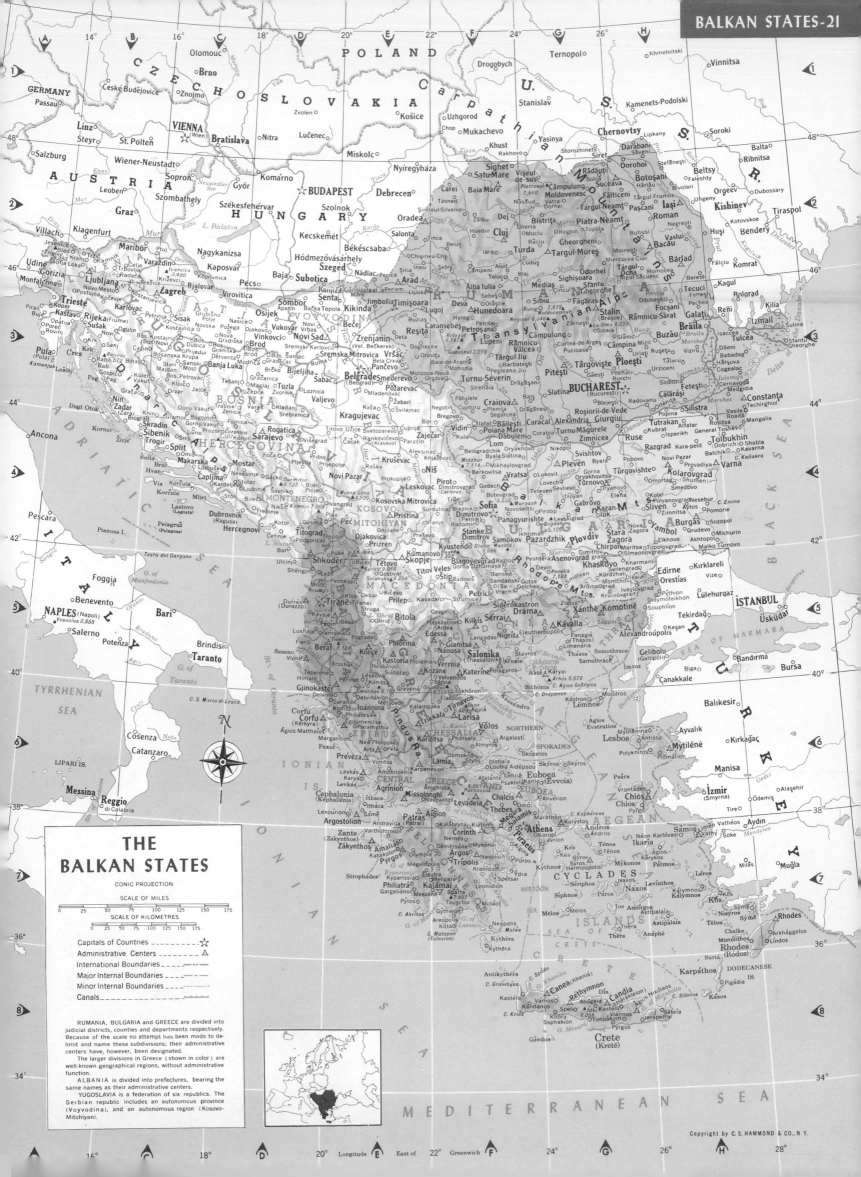

THE BALKAN STATES

CONIC PROJECTION

SCALE OF MILES

0 25 50 75 100 125 150 175

SCALE OF KILOMETRES

0 25 50 75 100 125 150 175

Capitals of Countries ⎯⎯⎯ ☆
Administrative Centers ⎯⎯⎯ △
International Boundaries ⎯ ⎯ ⎯
Major Internal Boundaries ⎯⎯⎯
Minor Internal Boundaries ⋯⋯⋯
Canals ⎯⎯⎯

RUMANIA, BULGARIA and GREECE are divided into
judicial districts, counties and departments respectively.
Because of the scale no attempt has been made to de-
limit and name these subdivisions; their administrative
centers have, however, been designated.
The larger divisions in Greece (shown in color) are
well-known geographical regions, without administrative
function.
ALBANIA is divided into prefectures, bearing the
same names as their administrative centers.
YUGOSLAVIA is a federation of six republics. The
Serbian republic includes an autonomous province
(Voyvodina), and an autonomous region (Kosovo-
Mitohiyan).

Copyright by C. S. HAMMOND & CO., N.Y.

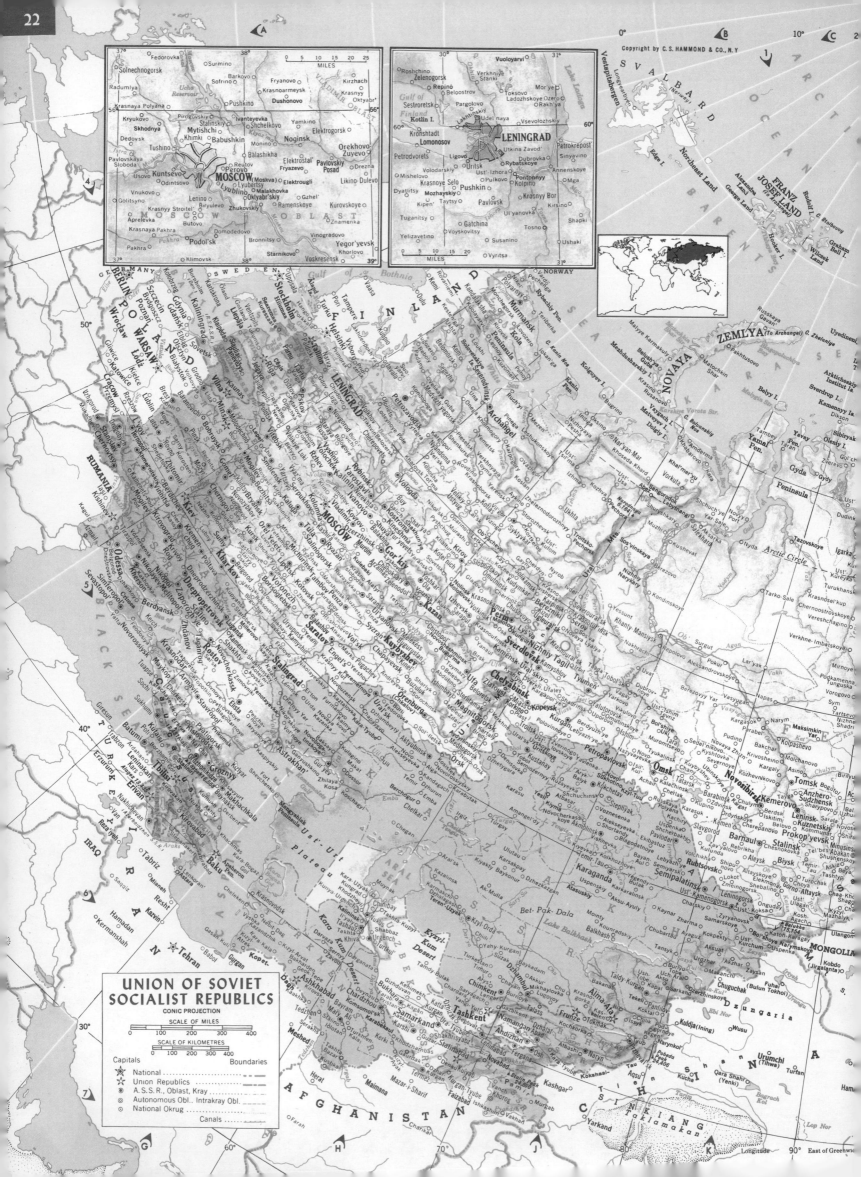

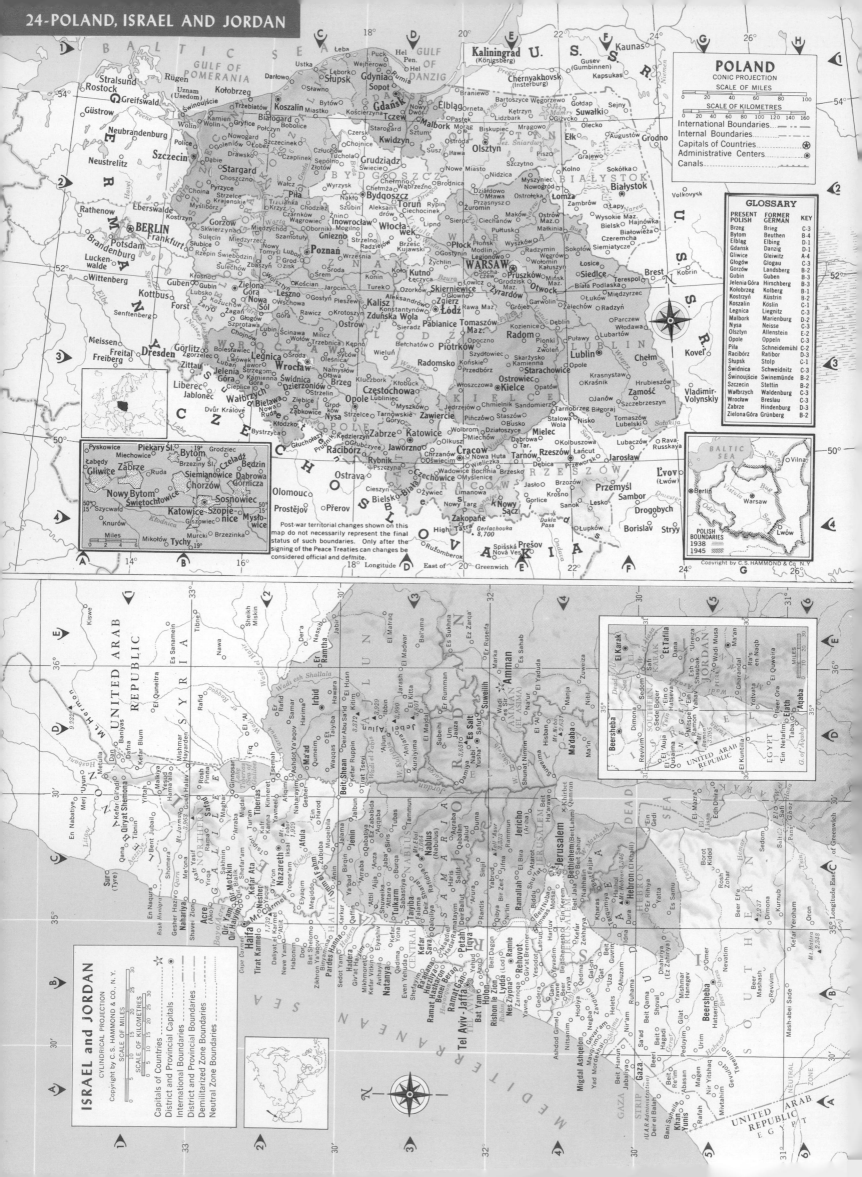

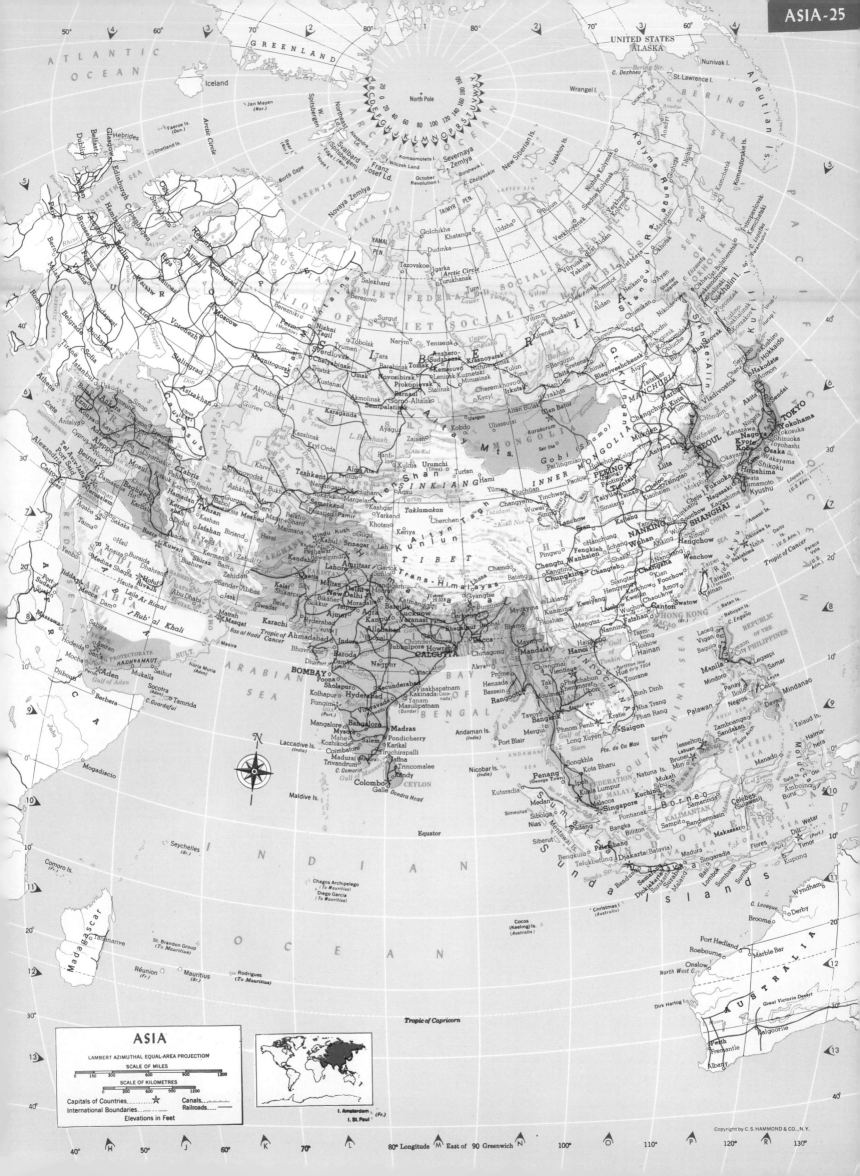

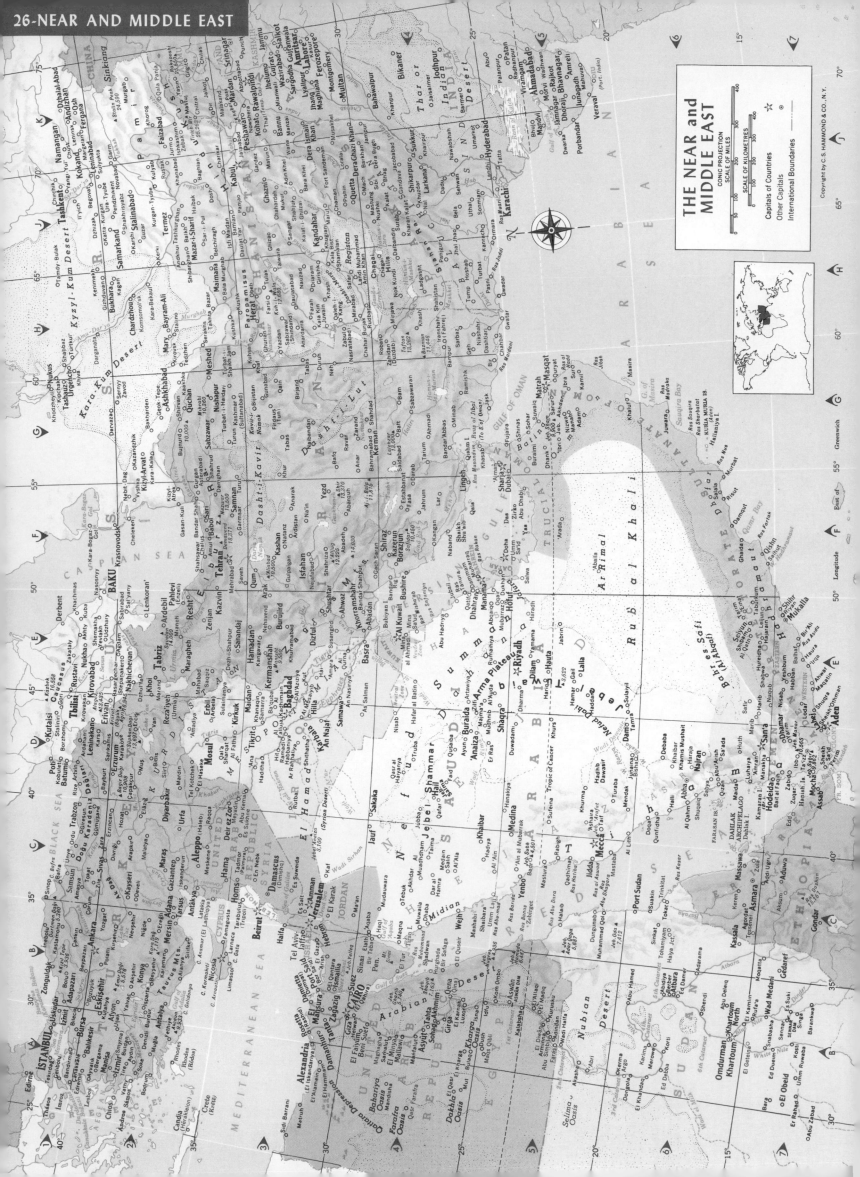

THE NEAR and
MIDDLE EAST

CONIC PROJECTION
SCALE OF MILES

SCALE OF KILOMETRES

Capitals of Countries ☆
Other Capitals ◉
International Boundaries ——

Copyright by C. S. HAMMOND & CO., N.Y.

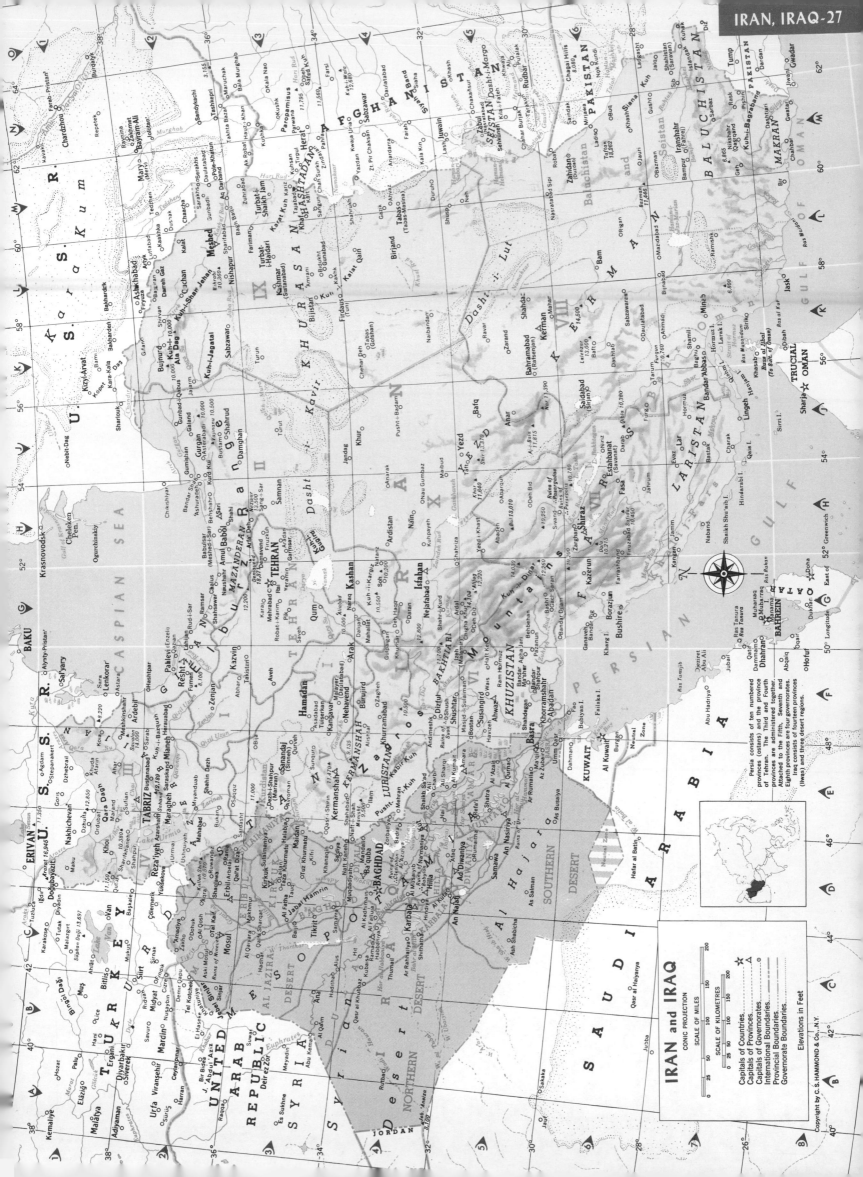

IRAN and IRAQ
CONIC PROJECTION

SCALE OF MILES

SCALE OF KILOMETRES

Capitals of Countries.........★
Capitals of Provinces.........△
Capitals of Governorates.......
International Boundaries........
Provincial Boundaries..........
Governorate Boundaries........

Elevations in Feet

Persia consists of ten numbered provinces (ostans) and the province of Tehran. The Third and Fourth provinces are administered together. Attached to the Fifth, Seventh and Eighth provinces are four governorates. Iraq consists of fourteen regions (liwas) and three desert regions.

Copyright by C. S. HAMMOND & Co., N.Y.

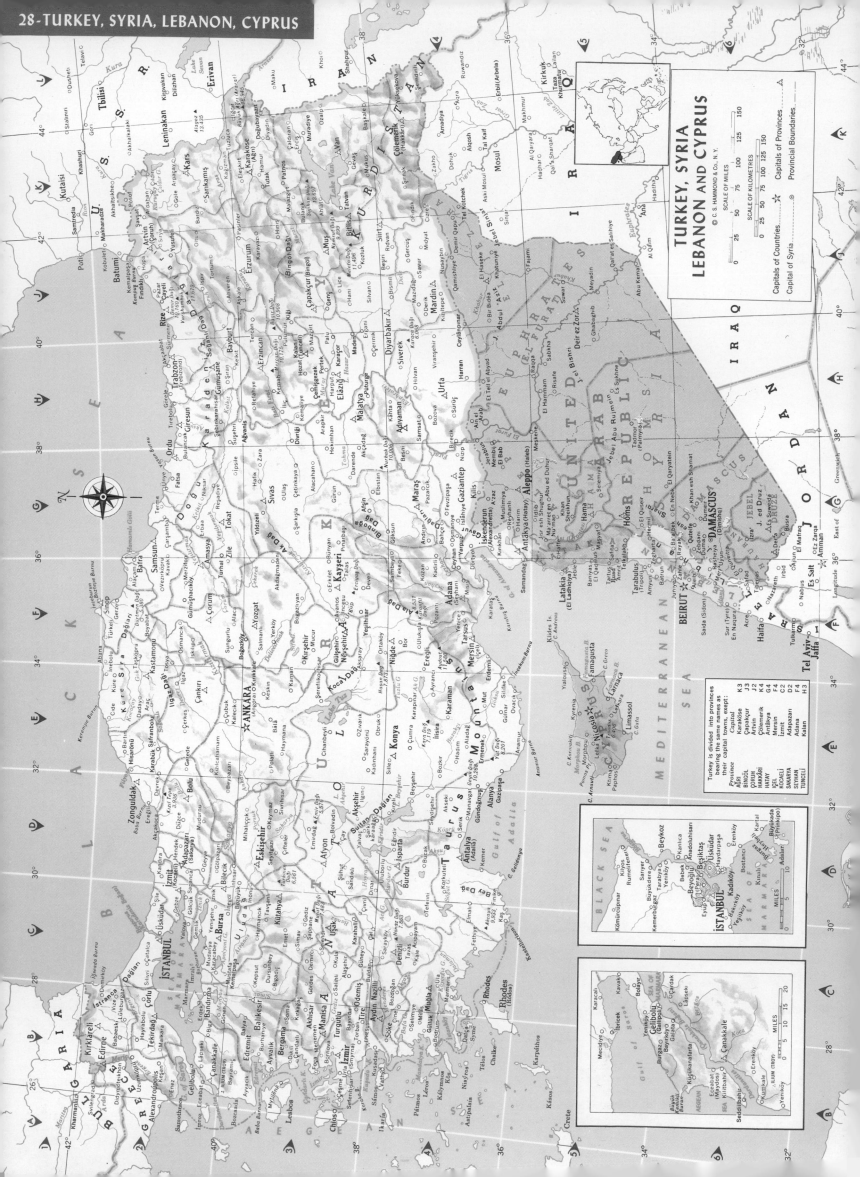

TURKEY, SYRIA LEBANON AND CYPRUS

© C. S. HAMMOND & CO., N.Y.

SCALE OF MILES
0 25 50 75 100 125 150

SCALE OF KILOMETRES
0 25 50 75 100 125 150

Capitals of Countries
Capitals of Provinces
Capital of Syria
Provincial Boundaries

Turkey is divided into provinces bearing the same names as their capital towns, except:

Province	Capital
AĞRI	Karaköse K3
BİNGÖL	Çapakçur J3
ÇORUH	Artvin J2
HAKKÂRİ	Çölemerik K4
HATAY	Antâkya G4
İÇEL	Mersin F4
KOCAELİ	İzmit C2
SAKARYA	Adapazarı D2
SEYHAN	Adana F4
TUNCELİ	Kalan H3

İSTANBUL

MILES

MILES

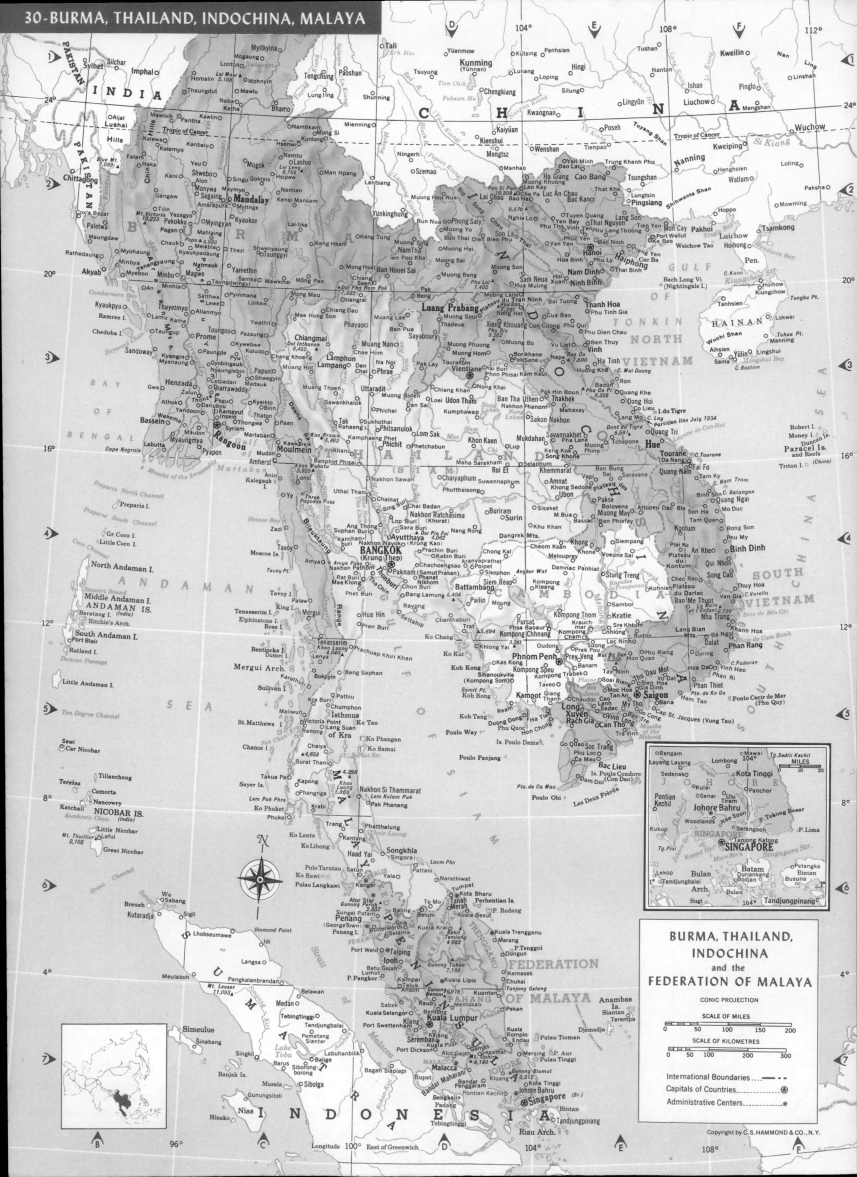

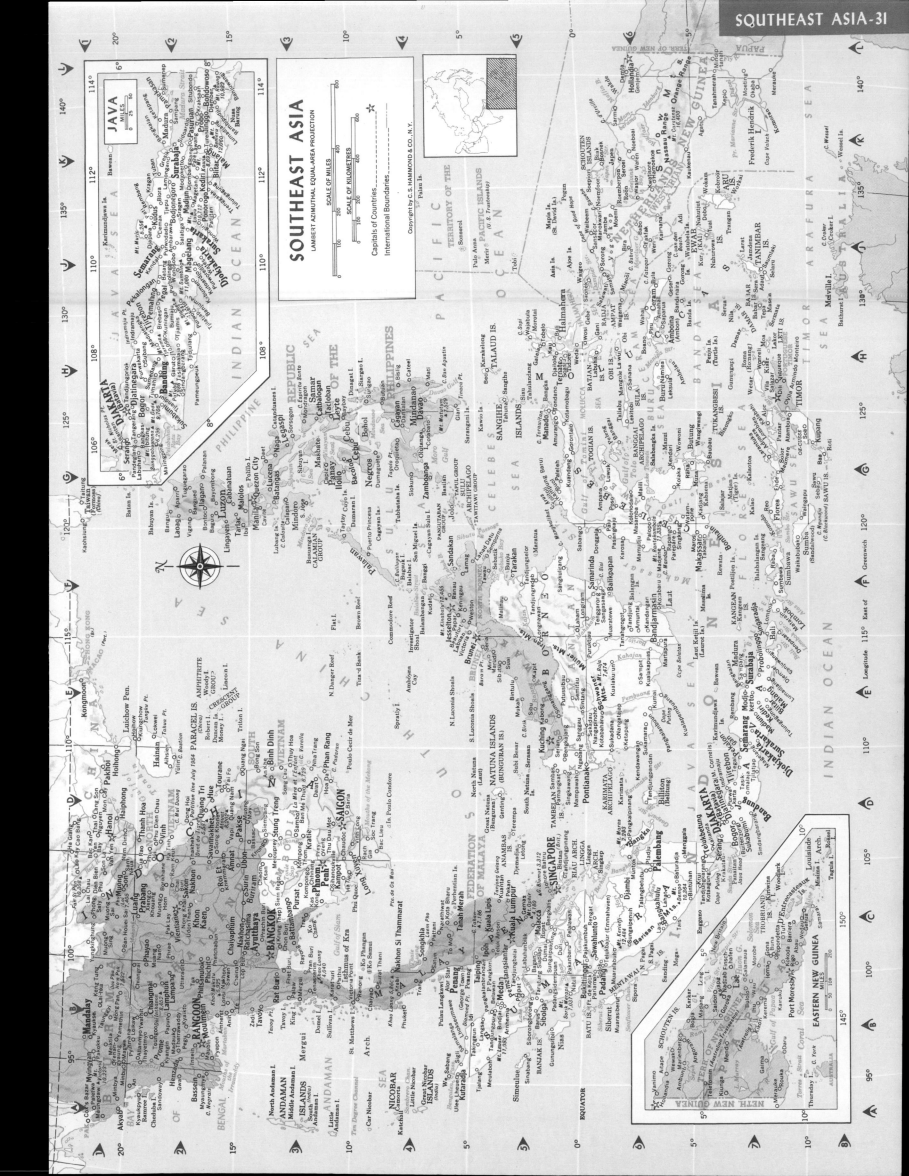

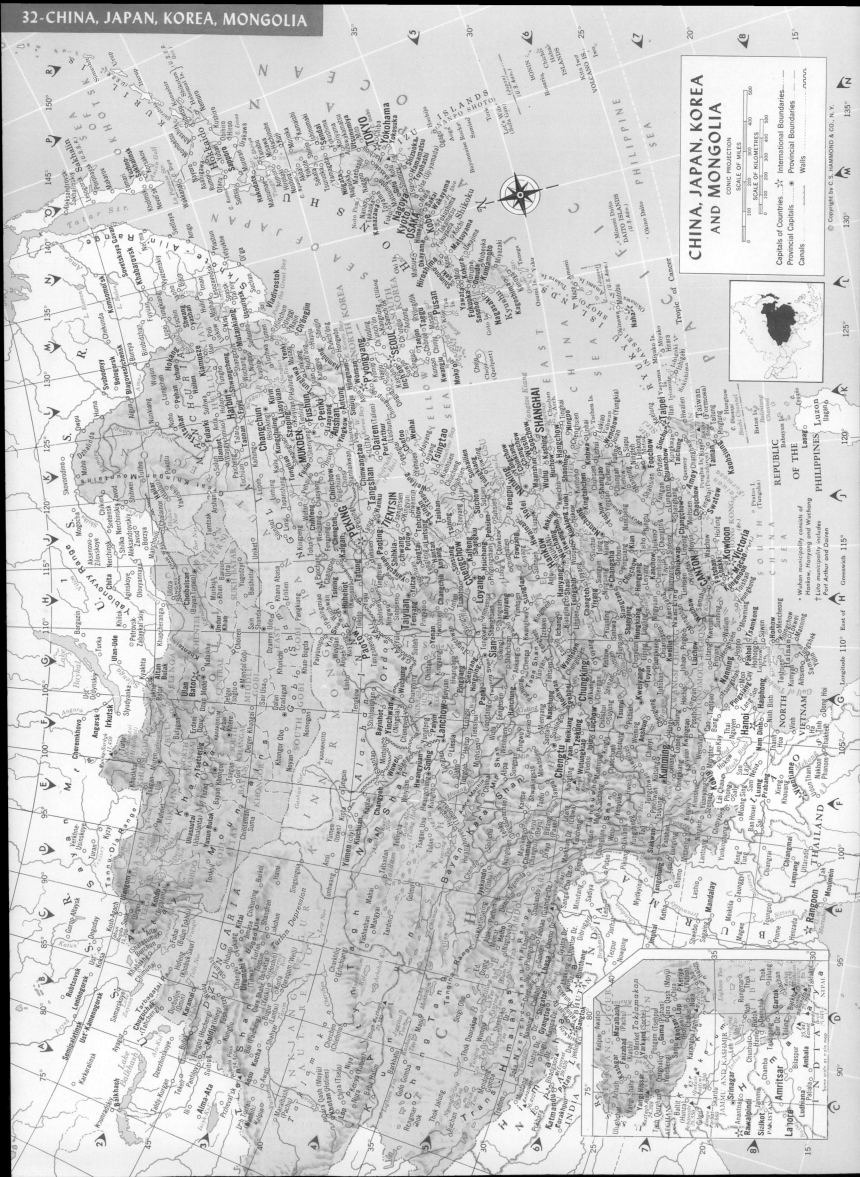

CHINA, JAPAN, KOREA
AND MONGOLIA

CONIC PROJECTION

SCALE OF MILES

SCALE OF KILOMETRES

Capitals of Countries ✯ International Boundaries
Provincial Capitals ⊙ Provincial Boundaries
Canals Walls

© Copyright by C.S. HAMMOND & CO., N.Y.

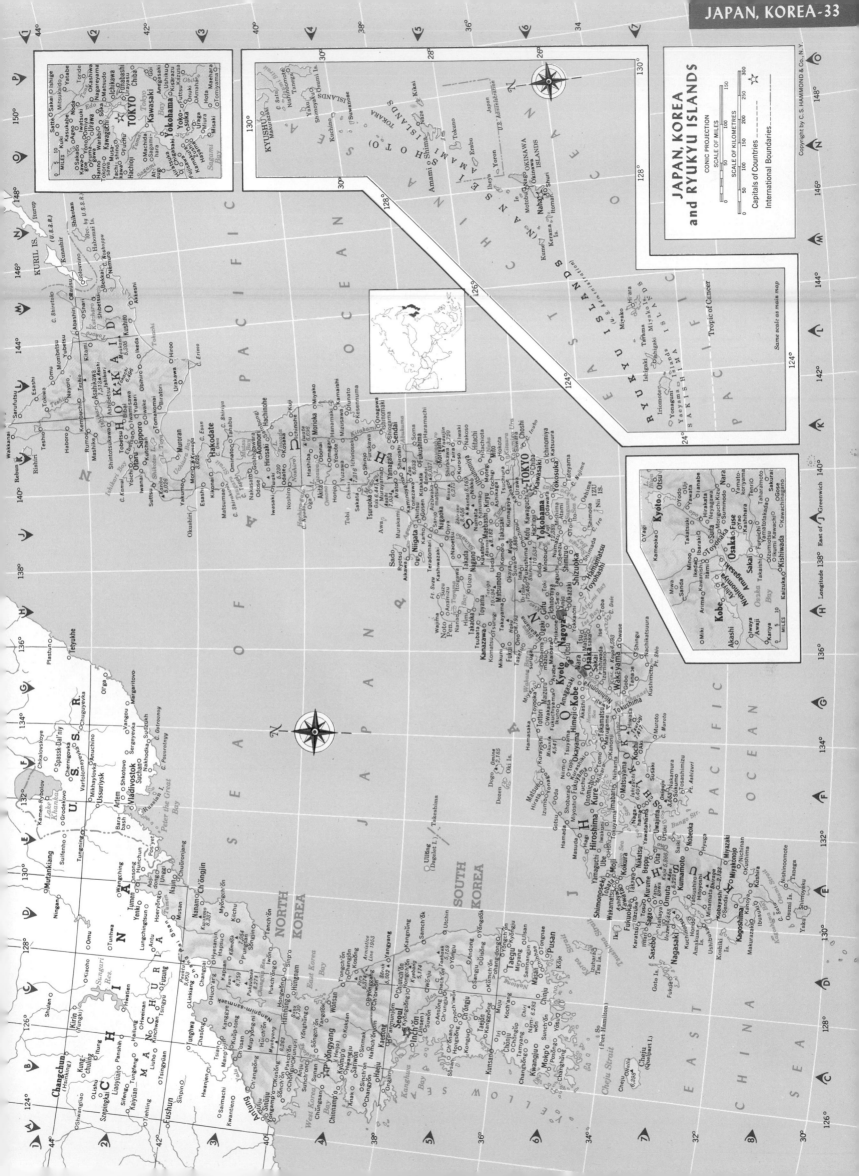

JAPAN, KOREA and RYUKYU ISLANDS

CONIC PROJECTION

SCALE OF MILES

SCALE OF KILOMETRES

Capitals of Countries

International Boundaries

Copyright by C. S. HAMMOND & Co., N.Y.

Same scale as main map

TOKYO

KYUSHU

RYUKYU ISLANDS

PACIFIC OCEAN

SEA OF JAPAN

CHINA SEA

YELLOW SEA

EAST CHINA SEA

HOKKAIDO

SOUTH KOREA

NORTH KOREA

CHINA

MANCHURIA

U.S.S.R.

KURIL IS. (U.S.S.R.)

Kyoto

Osaka

Kobe

Tropic of Cancer

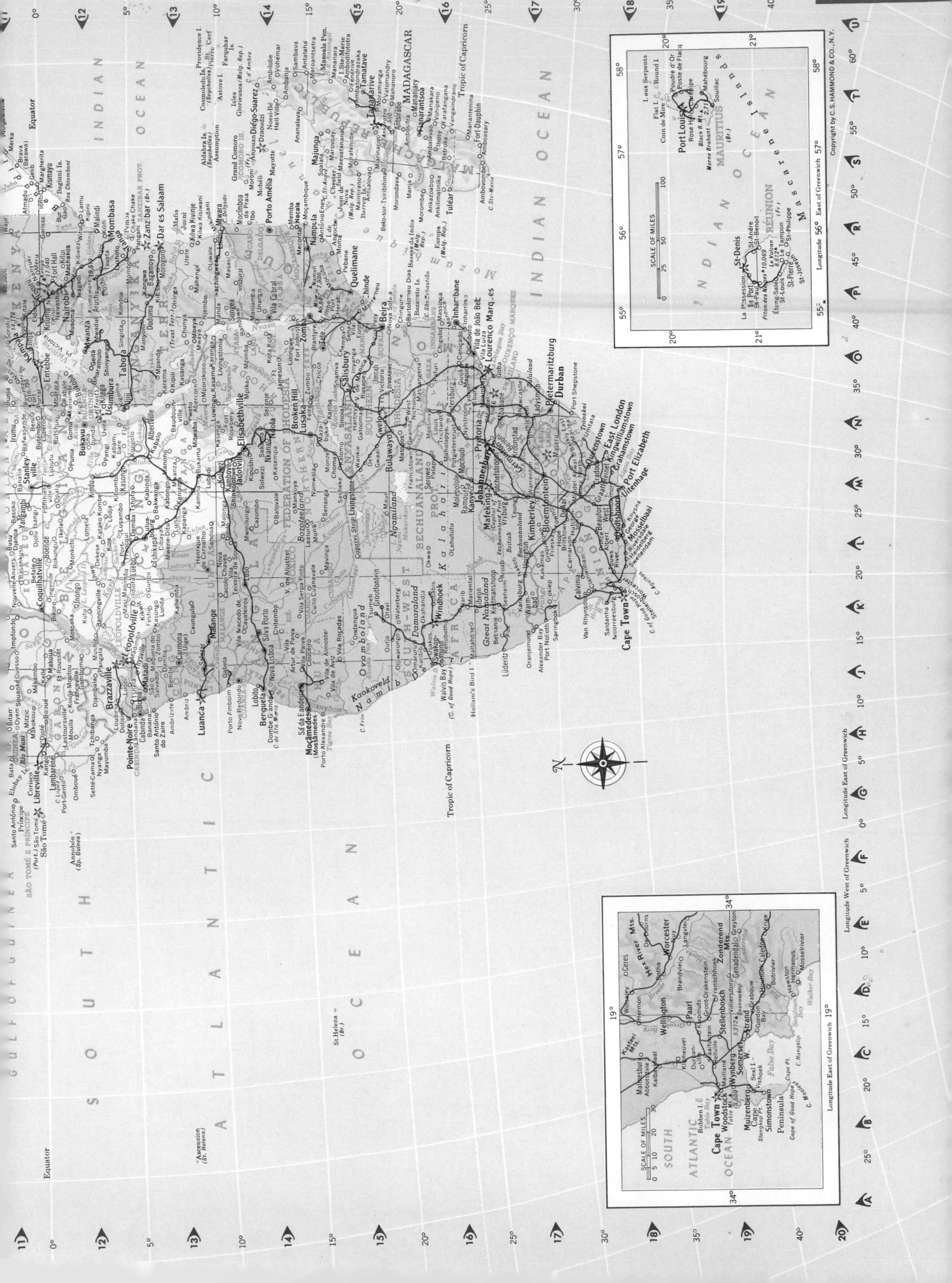

INDIAN OCEAN

ATLANTIC OCEAN

SOUTH ATLANTIC OCEAN

GULF OF GUINEA

Equator

Tropic of Capricorn

KENYA

TANGANYIKA TERR.

ZANZIBAR PROT.

MADAGASCAR

COMORO IS.

SEYCHELLES

CONGO

BELGIAN CONGO

ANGOLA

FEDERATION OF RHODESIA AND NYASALAND
NORTHERN RHODESIA
SOUTHERN RHODESIA
NYASALAND

BECHUANALAND PROT.

SOUTH-WEST AFRICA

UNION OF SOUTH AFRICA
CAPE PROVINCE
TRANSVAAL
ORANGE FREE STATE
NATAL
BASUTOLAND
SWAZILAND

MOZAMBIQUE

Kalahari Desert

Namib Desert

Nairobi • Mombasa • Dar es Salaam • Zanzibar • Bagamoyo • Tabora • Kigoma

Entebbe • Stanleyville • Bukavu • Usumbura

Leopoldville • Brazzaville • Libreville • Pointe-Noire • Coquilhatville

Luanda • Lobito • Benguela • Nova Lisboa • Mossâmedes

Elisabethville • Jadotville • Kolwezi

Lusaka • Broken Hill • Livingstone • Bulawayo • Salisbury • Gwelo • Umtali

Beira • Quelimane • Tamatave • Tananarive • Majunga

Lourenço Marques • Inhambane • Pretoria • Johannesburg • Mafeking • Kimberley • Bloemfontein • Pietermaritzburg • Durban

Windhoek • Walvis Bay • Lüderitz

Cape Town • Port Elizabeth • East London • Grahamstown • Worcester • Mosselbaai

Tropic of Capricorn

C. of Good Hope

Ascension (St. Helena)

St. Helena (Br.)

Copyright by C.S. HAMMOND & CO., N.Y.

Inset: MAURITIUS — RÉUNION
SCALE OF MILES
Port Louis • Mahébourg • St-Denis • St-Pierre
Longitude 56° East of Greenwich 57°
MASCARENE IS.
INDIAN OCEAN

Inset: Cape Town region
SCALE OF MILES
Cape Town • Woodstock • Wynberg • Simonstown • Somerset W. • Stellenbosch • Paarl • Wellington • Worcester
Hex River Mts. • Zonderend Mts.
Table Bay • False Bay
Cape of Good Hope • Cape Peninsula
Robben I. • Table Mt.
ATLANTIC OCEAN
Longitude East of Greenwich 19°

SCALE OF MILES

Longitude East of Greenwich

Longitude West of Greenwich

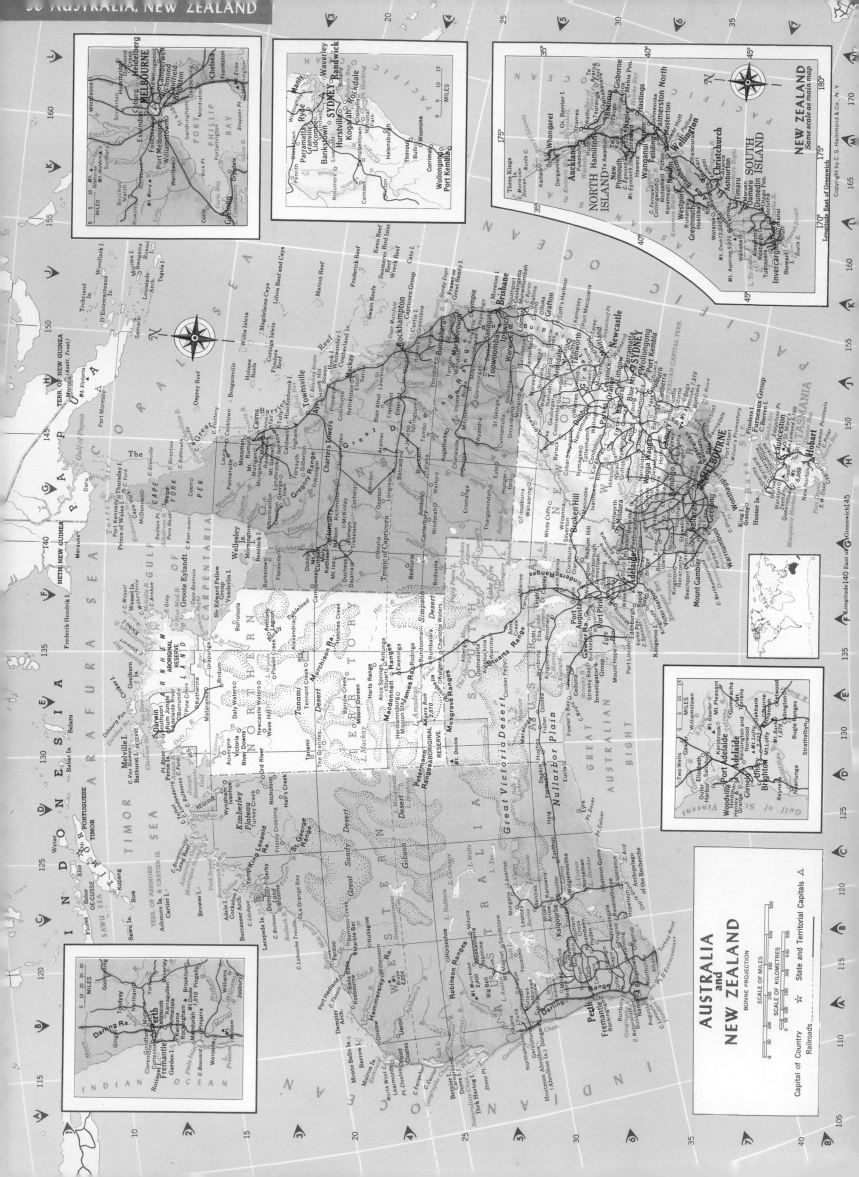

AUSTRALIA and NEW ZEALAND

BONNE PROJECTION

SCALE OF MILES

SCALE OF KILOMETRES

Capital of Country ☆ State and Territorial Capitals △

Railroads

NEW ZEALAND
Same scale as main map

NORTH ISLAND

SOUTH ISLAND

MELBOURNE

SYDNEY

Copyright by C. S. Hammond & Co., N.Y.

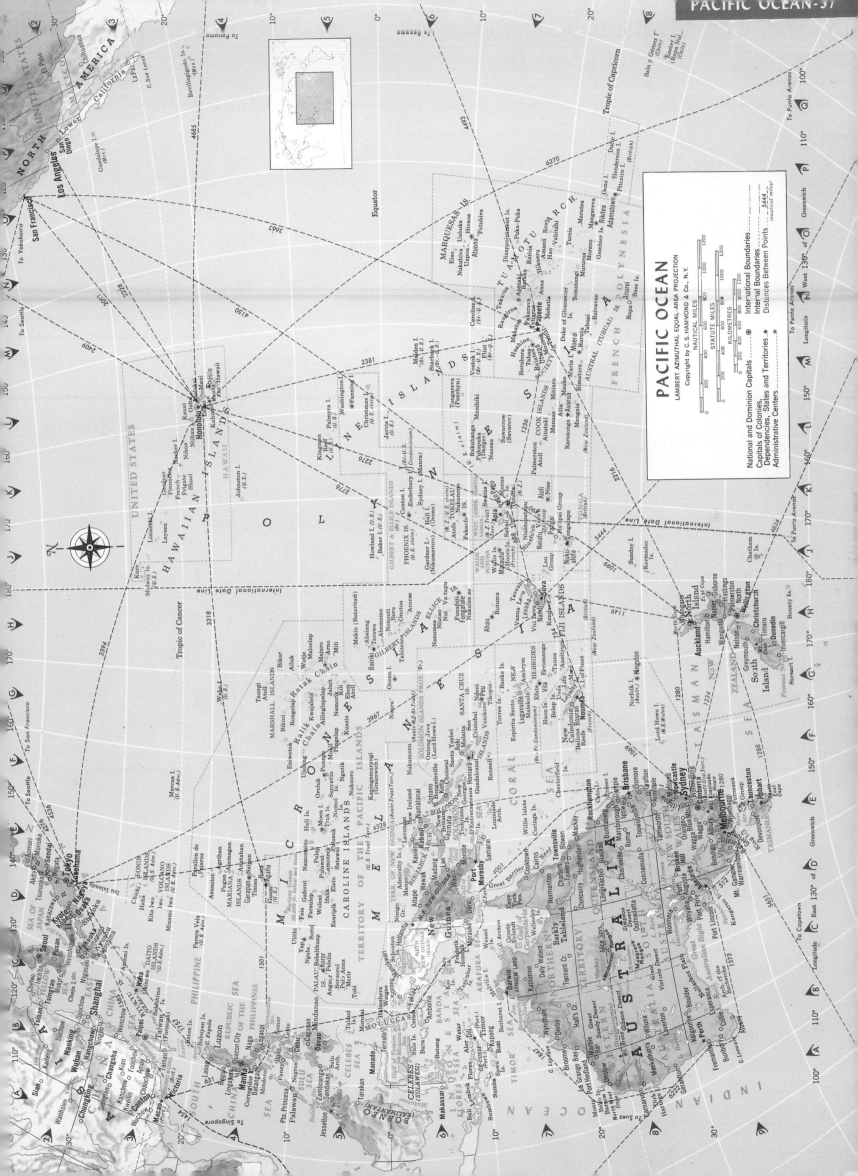

NORTH AMERICA

LAMBERT AZIMUTHAL EQUAL-AREA PROJECTION

SCALE OF MILES

0 100 200   400   600   800

SCALE OF KILOMETRES

0   200   400   600   800

Capitals of Countries..................☆
International Boundaries.............
Other Boundaries........................
Canals...
Railroads......................................

Copyright by C. S. HAMMOND & CO., N.Y.

Islands comprising THE WEST INDIES, a
federation under the British crown, are indicated by an asterisk.*

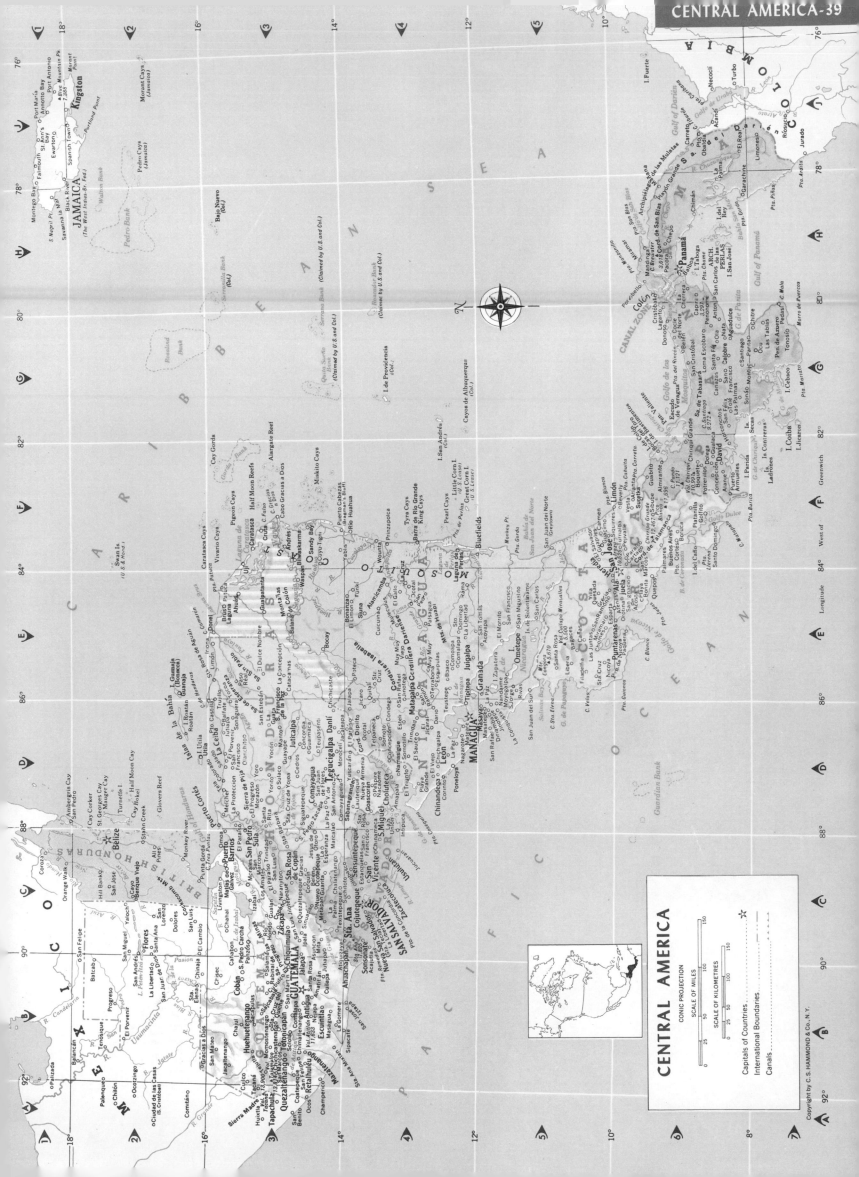

CENTRAL AMERICA

CONIC PROJECTION

SCALE OF MILES

SCALE OF KILOMETRES

Capitals of Countries .... ☆

International Boundaries ....

Canals ....

Copyright by C. S. HAMMOND & CO., N.Y.

WESTERN CANADA

Copyright by C.S. HAMMOND & Co., N.Y.

SCALE OF MILES
0   50   100   150   200

SCALE OF KILOMETRES
0   50   100   150   200

Provincial and
Territorial Capitals .... ●
International Boundaries ....
Boundaries of Provinces ....

PACIFIC OCEAN

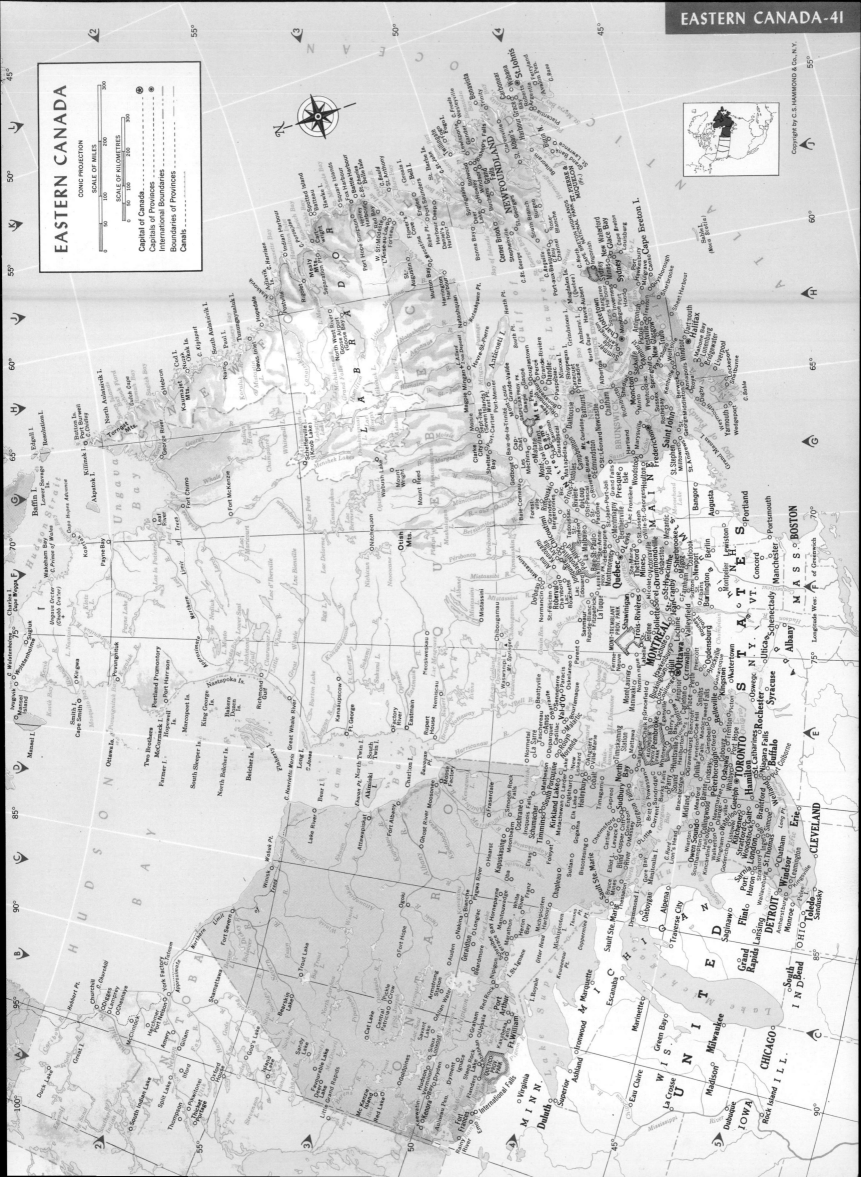

EASTERN CANADA

CONIC PROJECTION

SCALE OF MILES

SCALE OF KILOMETRES

Capital of Canada
Capitals of Provinces
International Boundaries
Boundaries of Provinces
Canals

BRITISH COLUMBIA
ALBERTA
SASKATCHEWAN
MANITOBA
CANADA
ROCKY MTS.
COAST MTS.
CASCADE RANGE
SIERRA NEVADA
COAST RANGES
BITTERROOT RANGE
PACIFIC OCEAN
GULF OF CALIFORNIA
BAJA CALIFORNIA NORTE
MEXICO
CHIHUAHUA
COAHUILA
NUEVO LEON
TAMAULIPAS
Seattle
Portland
Spokane
Boise
Salt Lake City
Denver
Phoenix
Tucson
Albuquerque
El Paso
San Francisco
Oakland
Sacramento
LOS ANGELES
San Diego
Reno
Las Vegas
Edmonton
Calgary
Vancouver
Victoria
Regina
Winnipeg
Cheyenne
Pueblo
Amarillo
Lubbock
Fort Worth
Austin
San Antonio
Wichita
Oklahoma City
Great Salt Lake Desert
YELLOWSTONE NAT'L PARK
GRAND CANYON NATIONAL PARK
Mojave Desert
Longitude West of Greenwich
Alton
St. Louis
East St Louis
MISSOURI
ILLINOIS
Cincinnati
OHIO
SCALE OF MILES
San Francisco
Oakland
Berkeley
LOS ANGELES
U.S.S.R.
Arctic Circle
Brooks Range
Fairbanks
Anchorage
Nome
Juneau
BERING SEA
Gulf of Alaska
Aleutian Is.
Kauai
Oahu
Honolulu
Molokai
Maui
Hawaii
Tropic of Cancer
120°
116°
112°
108°
104°
100°
Longitude West of Greenwich

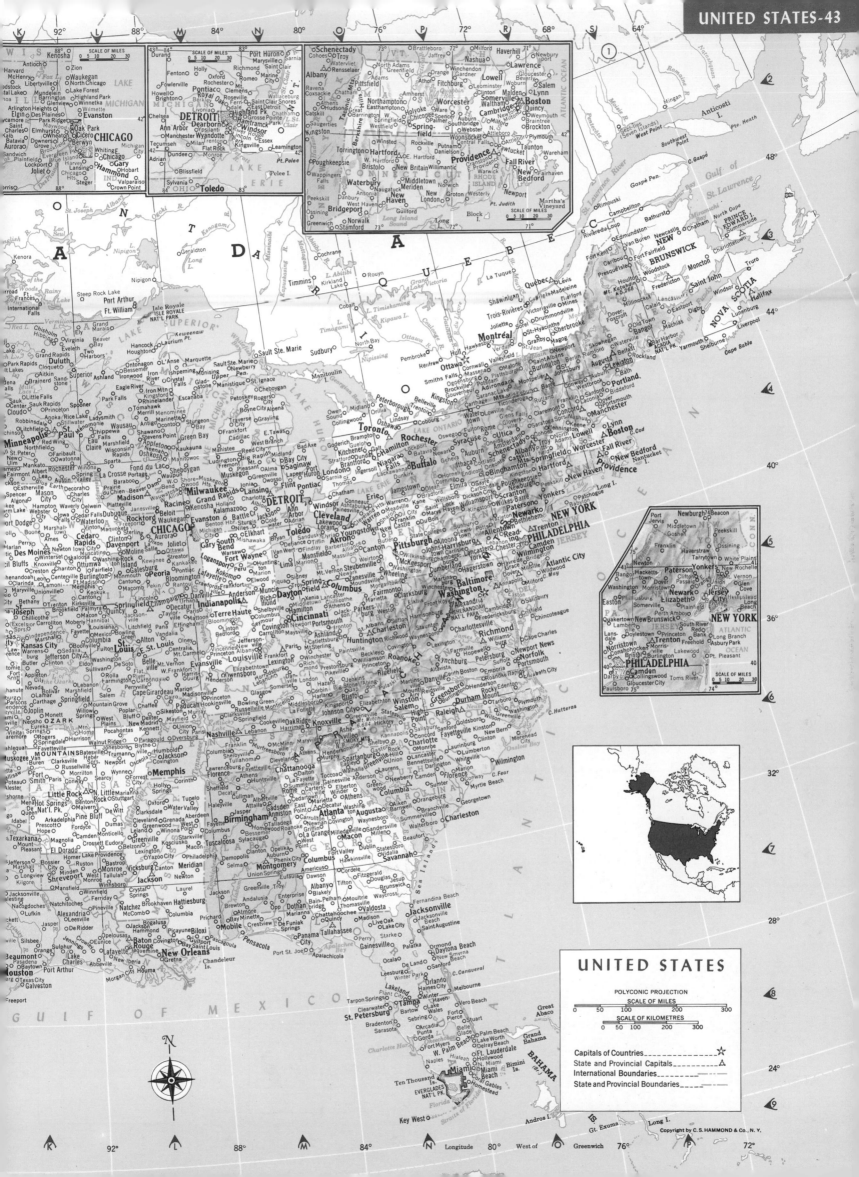

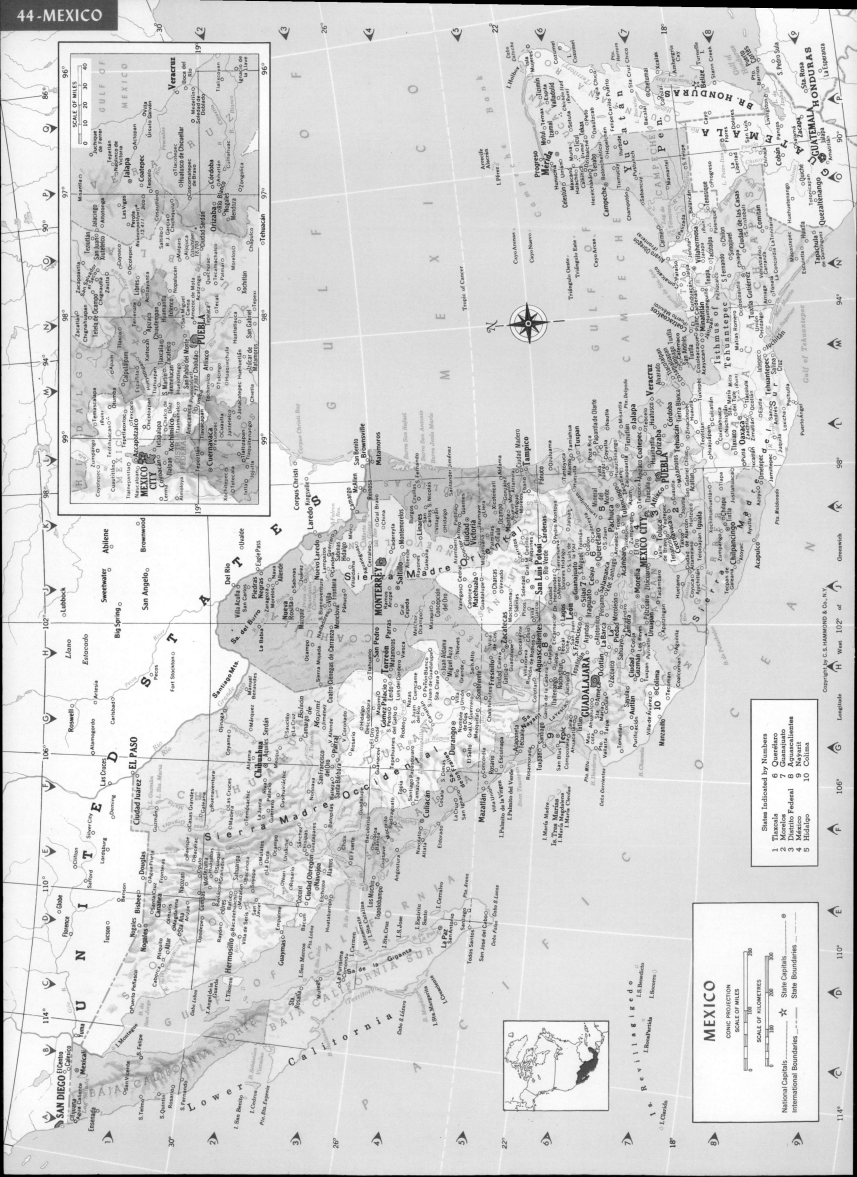

MEXICO

CONIC PROJECTION

SCALE OF MILES

SCALE OF KILOMETRES

National Capitals ⭐
State Capitals ◉
International Boundaries ────────
State Boundaries ────────

States Indicated by Numbers

1 Tlaxcala
2 Morelos
3 Distrito Federal
4 México
5 Hidalgo

6 Querétaro
7 Guanajuato
8 Aguascalientes
9 Nayarit
10 Colima

SCALE OF MILES

Copyright by C.S. HAMMOND & Co., N.Y.

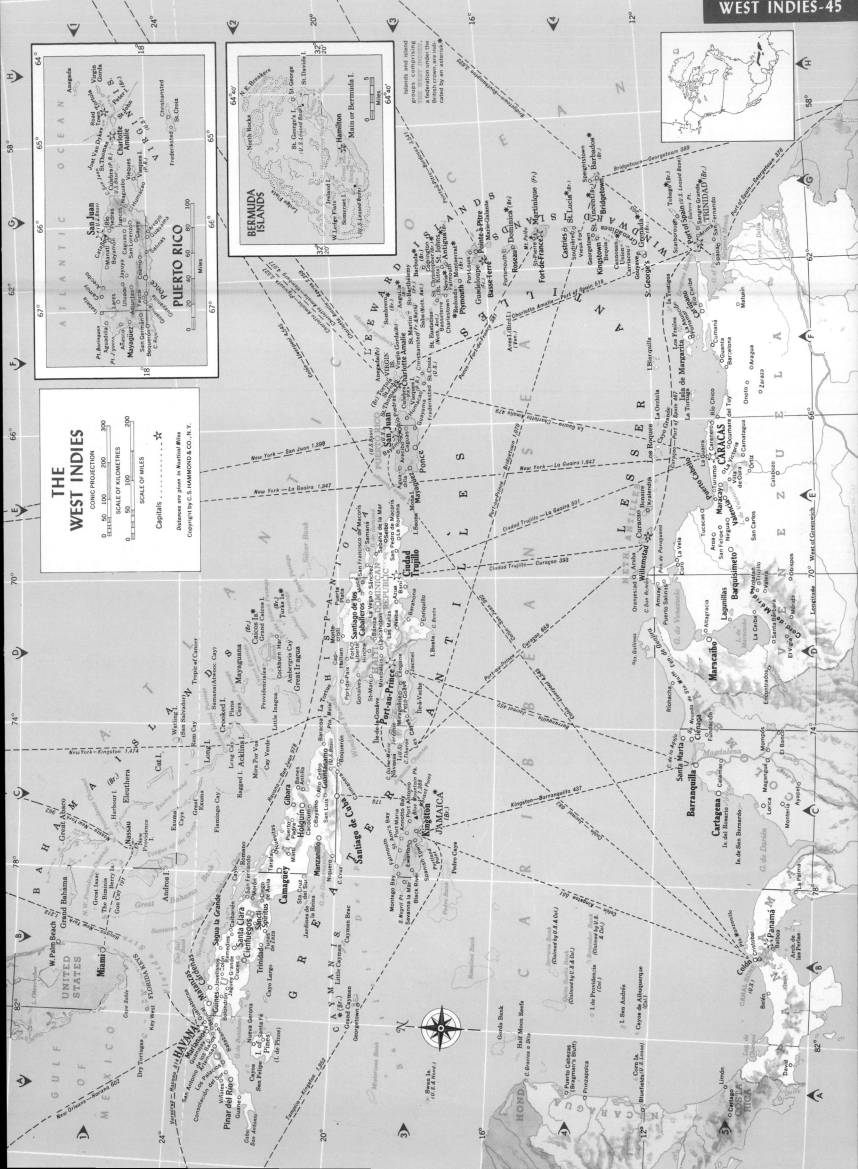

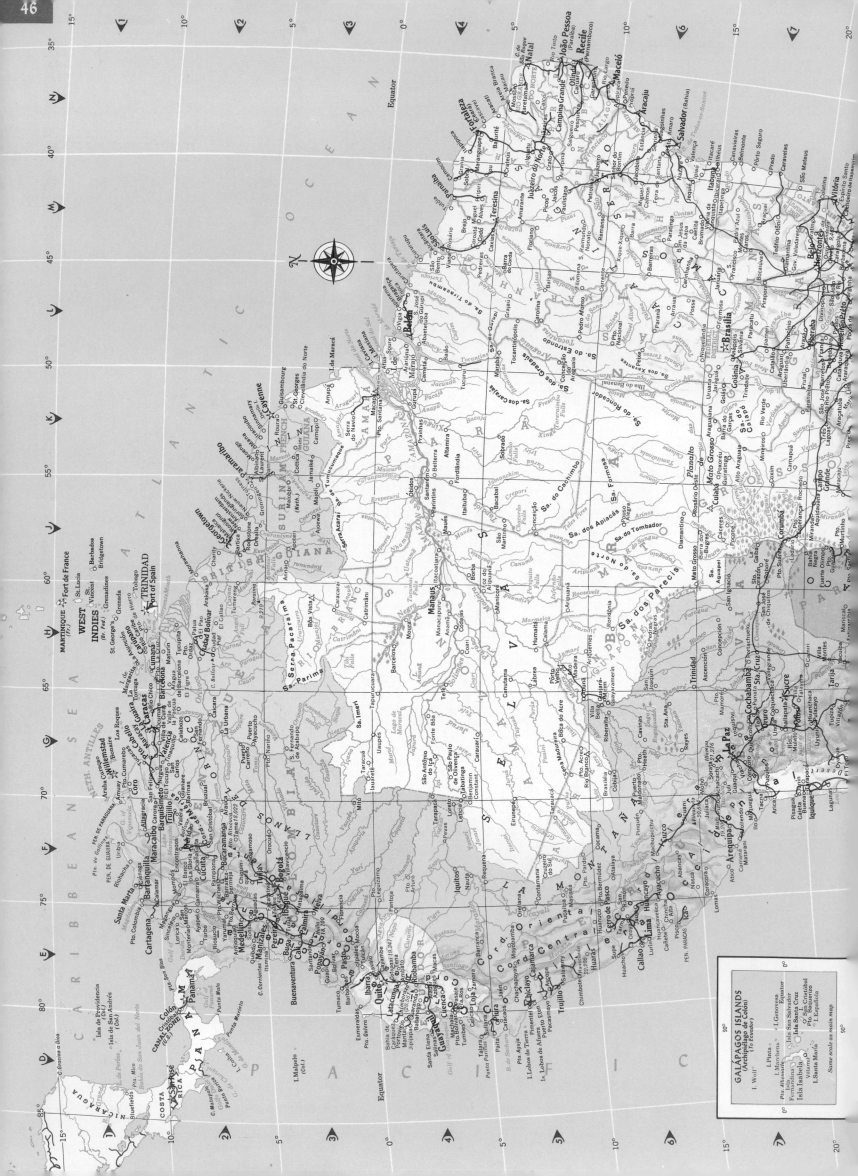

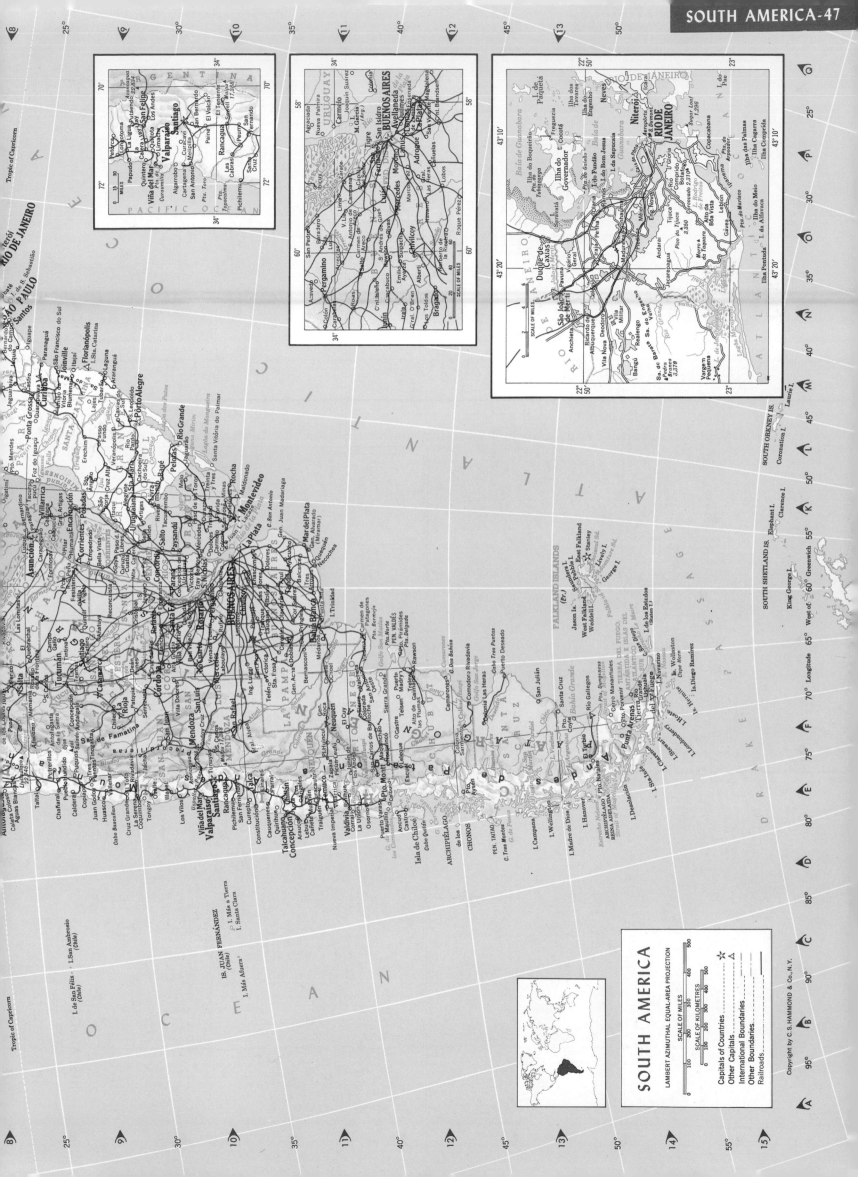

SOUTH AMERICA

LAMBERT AZIMUTHAL EQUAL-AREA PROJECTION

Copyright by C.S. HAMMOND & Co., N.Y.

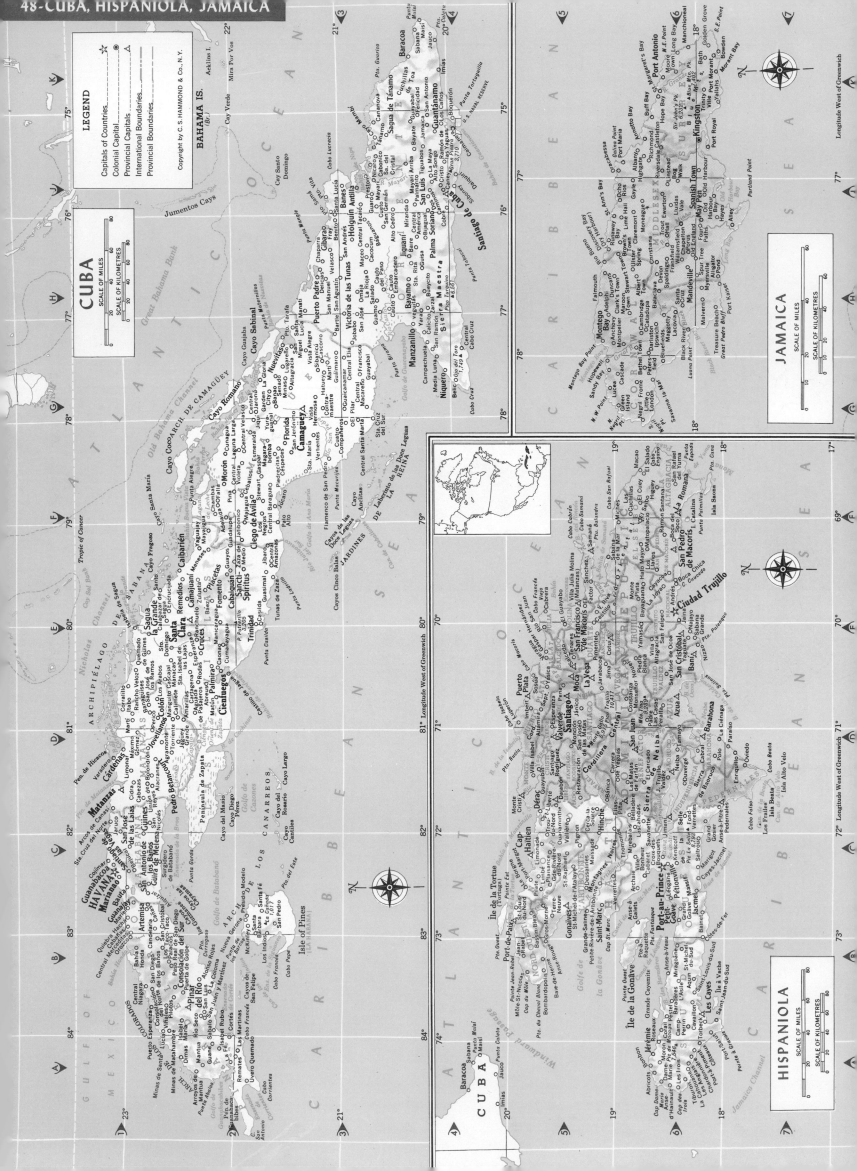

LEGEND

Capitals of Countries................ ★
Colonial Capital....................... ◉
Provincial Capitals.................... △
International Boundaries...............
Provincial Boundaries.................

Copyright by C. S. HAMMOND & Co., N.Y.

CUBA
SCALE OF MILES
SCALE OF KILOMETRES

JAMAICA
SCALE OF MILES
SCALE OF KILOMETRES

HISPANIOLA
SCALE OF MILES
SCALE OF KILOMETRES

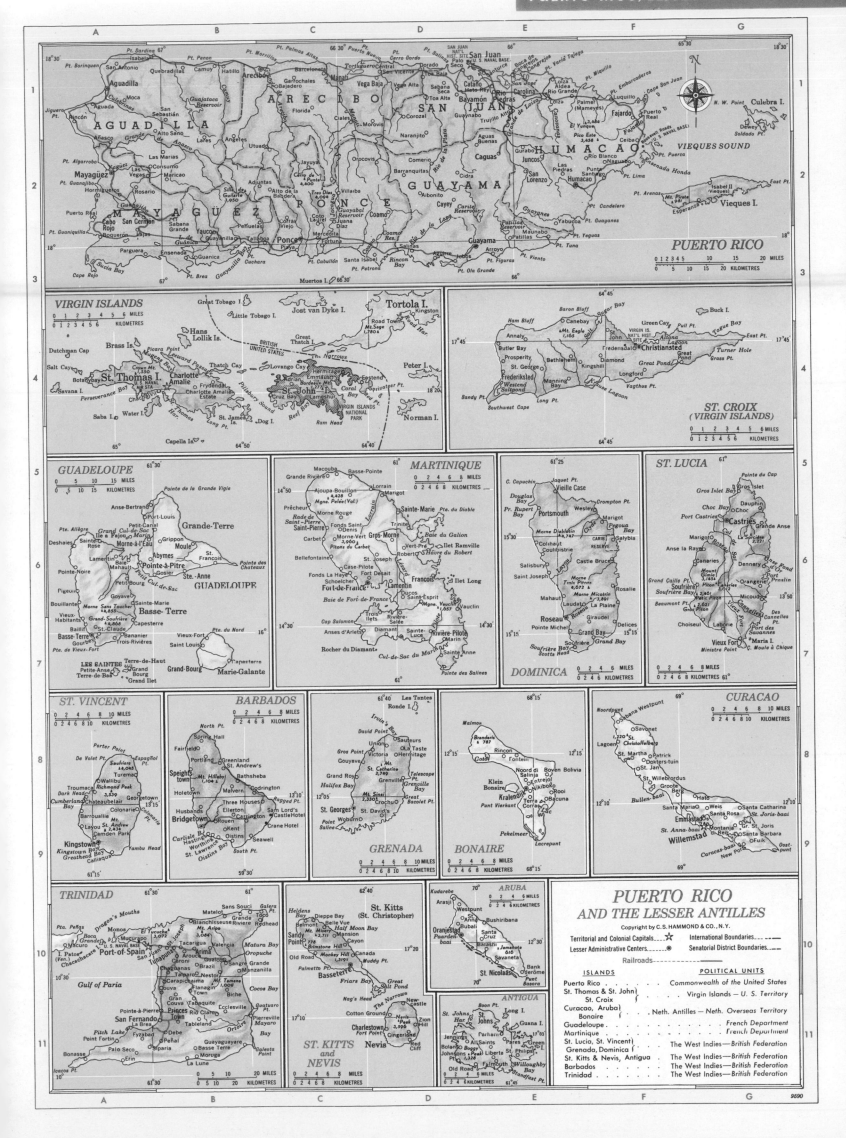

PUERTO RICO

VIRGIN ISLANDS

ST. CROIX (VIRGIN ISLANDS)

GUADELOUPE

MARTINIQUE

DOMINICA

ST. LUCIA

ST. VINCENT

BARBADOS

GRENADA

BONAIRE

CURACAO

TRINIDAD

ST. KITTS and NEVIS

ARUBA

ANTIGUA

PUERTO RICO
AND THE LESSER ANTILLES

Copyright by C.S. HAMMOND & CO., N.Y.

Territorial and Colonial Capitals .... ⭐
Lesser Administrative Centers .... ◉
International Boundaries ....
Senatorial District Boundaries ....
Railroads ....

ISLANDS	POLITICAL UNITS
Puerto Rico	Commonwealth of the United States
St. Thomas & St. John	Virgin Islands — U. S. Territory
St. Croix	
Curacao, Aruba	Neth. Antilles — Neth. Overseas Territory
Bonaire	
Guadeloupe	French Department
Martinique	French Department
St. Lucia, St. Vincent	The West Indies — British Federation
Grenada, Dominica	The West Indies — British Federation
St. Kitts & Nevis, Antigua .	The West Indies — British Federation
Barbados	The West Indies — British Federation
Trinidad	The West Indies — British Federation

9590

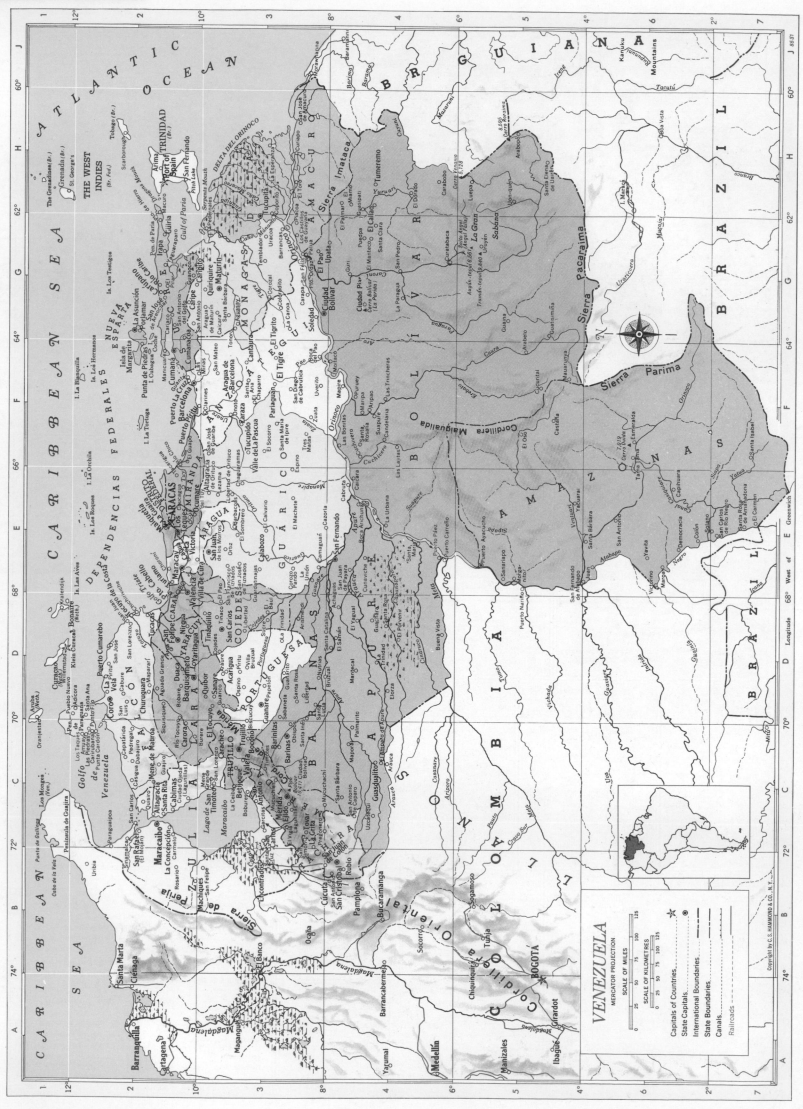

VENEZUELA

MERCATOR PROJECTION

SCALE OF MILES
0   25   50   75   100   125

SCALE OF KILOMETRES
0   25   50   75   100   125

Capitals of Countries..........★
State Capitals..........◉
International Boundaries..........
State Boundaries..........
Canals..........
Railroads..........

Copyright by C.S. HAMMOND & CO., N.Y.

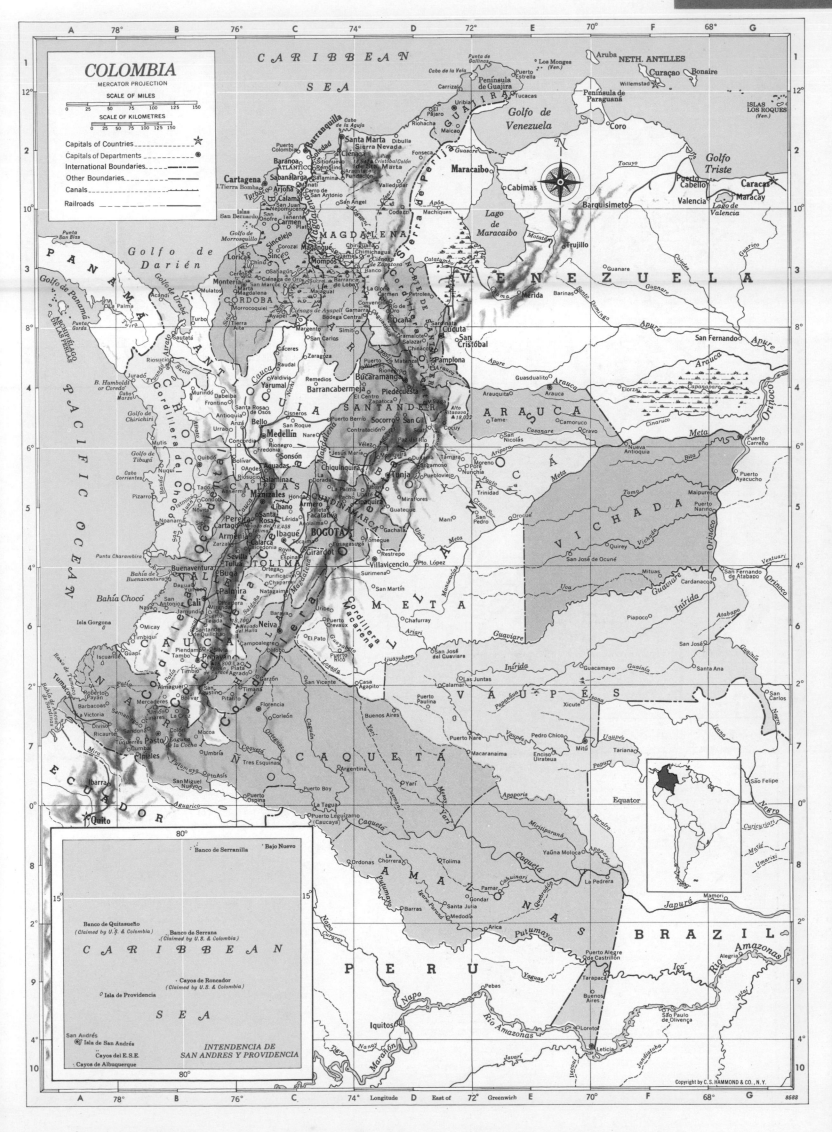

COLOMBIA

MERCATOR PROJECTION

SCALE OF MILES

0 25 50 75 100 125 150

SCALE OF KILOMETRES

0 25 50 75 100 125 150

Capitals of Countries .... ☆
Capitals of Departments .... ◉
International Boundaries ....
Other Boundaries ....
Canals ....
Railroads ....

CARIBBEAN SEA

PANAMA

Golfo de Darién

PACIFIC OCEAN

ECUADOR

VENEZUELA

BRAZIL

PERU

Cartagena
Barranquilla
Santa Marta
Maracaibo
Caracas
Medellín
Cali
BOGOTÁ
Pasto
Quito
Iquitos
Leticia

INTENDENCIA DE SAN ANDRES Y PROVIDENCIA

CARIBBEAN SEA

Banco de Serranilla
Bajo Nuevo
Banco de Quitasueño
(Claimed by U.S. & Colombia)
Banco de Serrana
(Claimed by U.S. & Colombia)
Cayos de Roncador
(Claimed by U.S. & Colombia)
Isla de Providencia
San Andrés
Isla de San Andrés
Cayos del E.S.E.
Cayos de Albuquerque

Equator

Copyright by C. S. HAMMOND & CO., N.Y.

Longitude   East of   Greenwich

8688

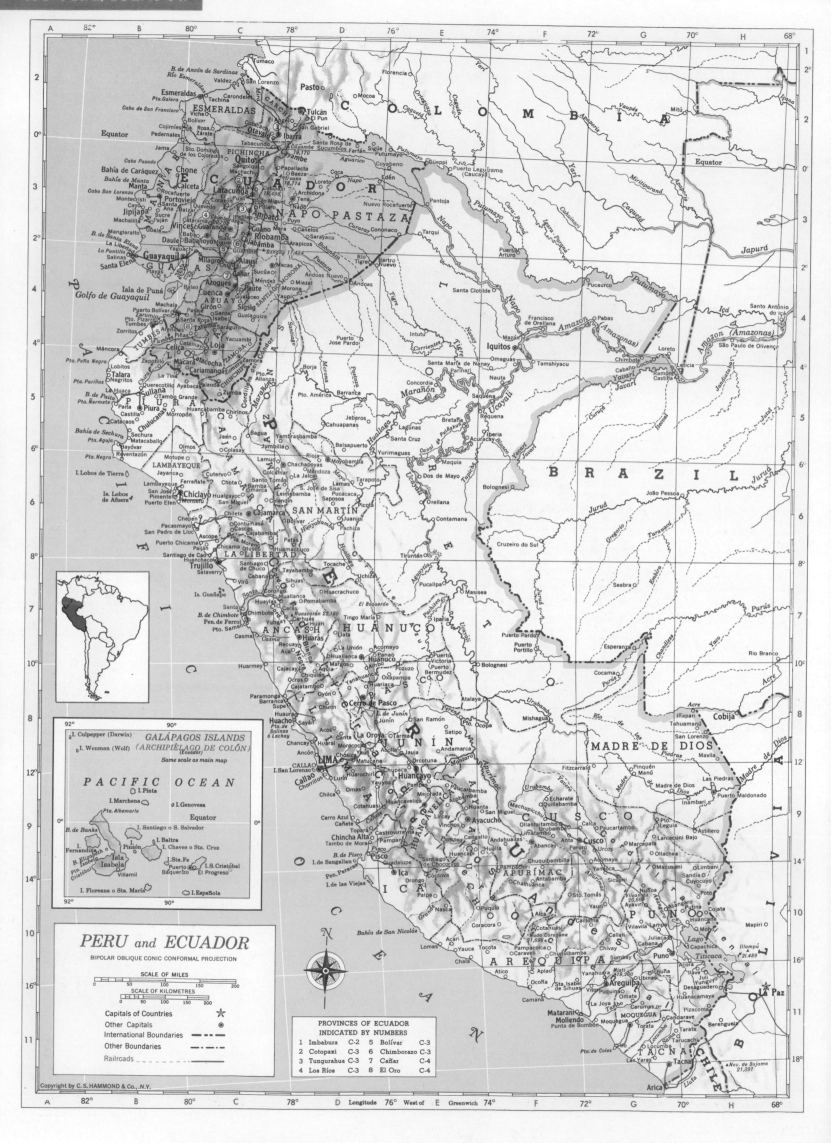

GALÁPAGOS ISLANDS
(ARCHIPIÉLAGO DE COLÓN)
(Ecuador)
Same scale as main map

PACIFIC OCEAN

PERU and ECUADOR
BIPOLAR OBLIQUE CONIC CONFORMAL PROJECTION

SCALE OF MILES
0   50   100   150   200

SCALE OF KILOMETRES
0   50   100   150   200

Capitals of Countries .... ★
Other Capitals .... ◉
International Boundaries .... — · — · —
Other Boundaries .... — ·· — ·· —
Railroads

Copyright by C. S. HAMMOND & Co., N.Y.

PROVINCES OF ECUADOR
INDICATED BY NUMBERS

1 Imbabura	C-2	5 Bolívar	C-3
2 Cotopaxi	C-3	6 Chimborazo	C-3
3 Tungurahua	C-3	7 Cañar	C-4
4 Los Ríos	C-3	8 El Oro	C-4

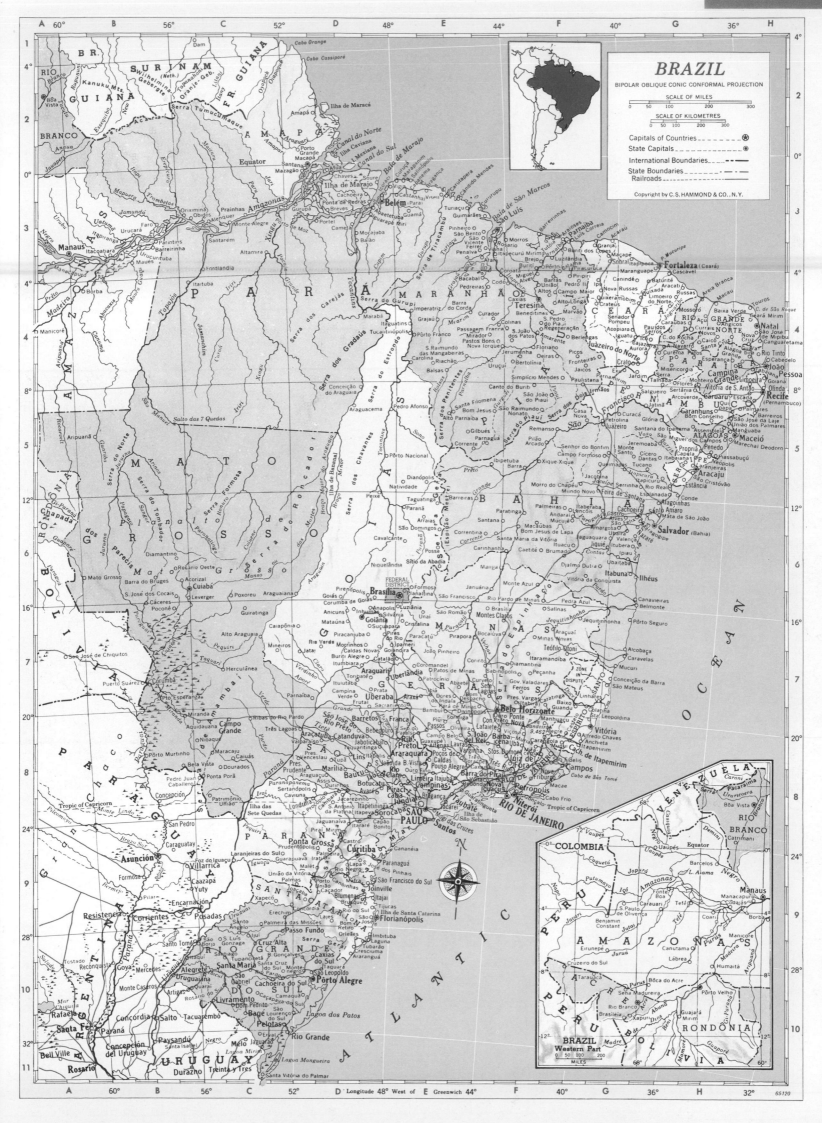

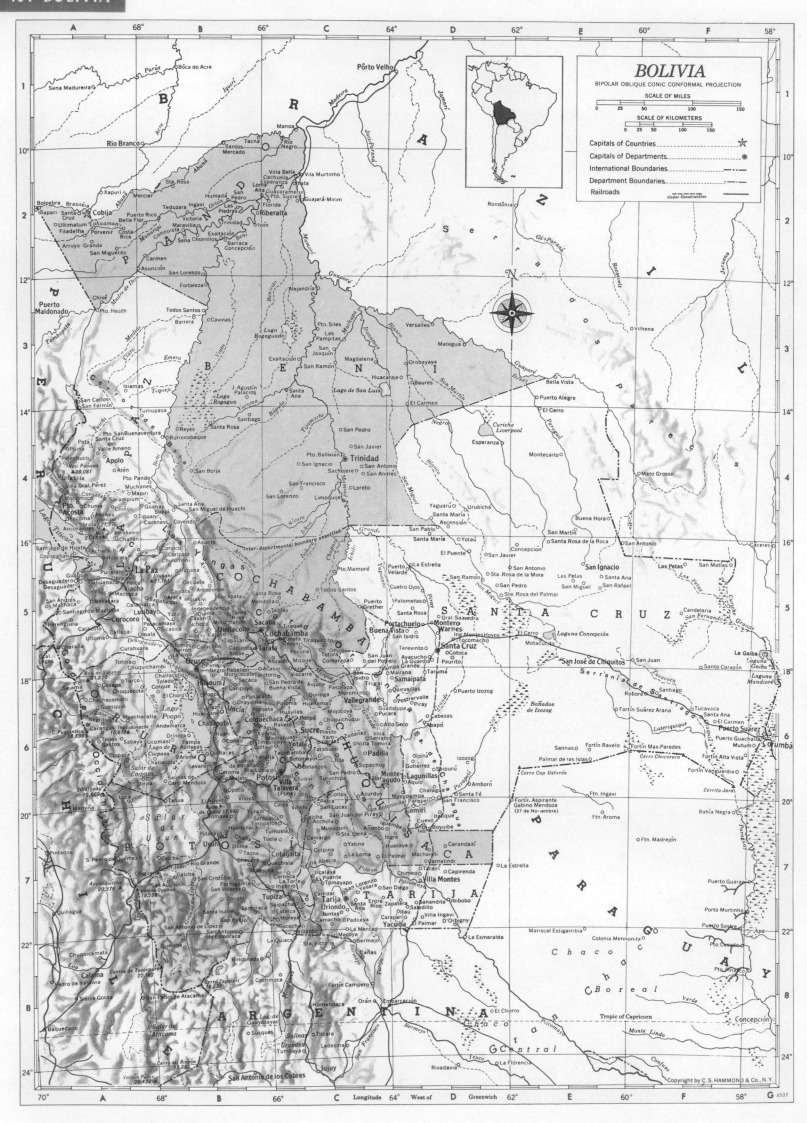

BOLIVIA
BIPOLAR OBLIQUE CONIC CONFORMAL PROJECTION

SCALE OF MILES
0 25 50   100   150

SCALE OF KILOMETERS
0 25 50   100   150

Capitals of Countries .... ☆
Capitals of Departments .... ◉
International Boundaries ....
Department Boundaries ....
Railroads ....
Under Construction

Copyright by C. S. HAMMOND & Co., N.Y.

G 1531

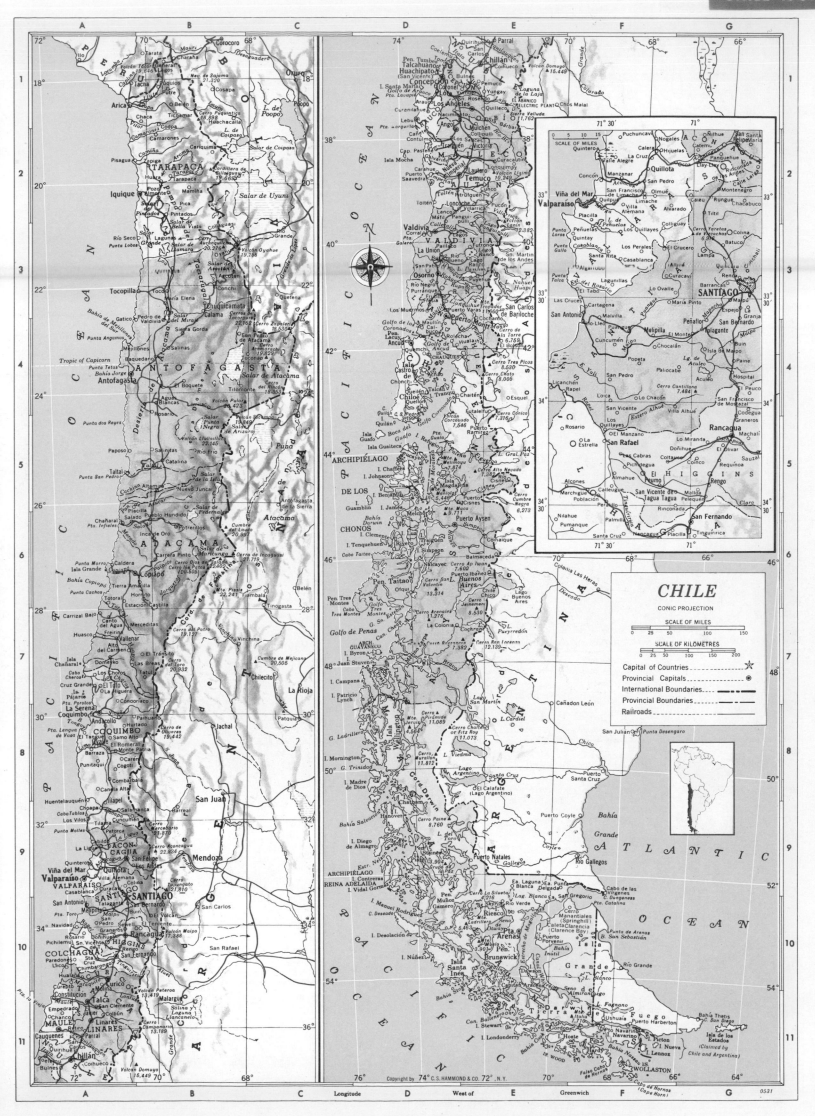

CHILE

CONIC PROJECTION

SCALE OF MILES

| 0 | 25 | 50 | 100 | 150 |

SCALE OF KILOMETRES

| 0 | 25 | 50 | 100 | 200 |

Capital of Countries .... ⭐
Provincial Capitals .... ◎
International Boundaries .... ―――――
Provincial Boundaries .... ―――――
Railroads .... ―――――

Longitude   West of   Greenwich

0531

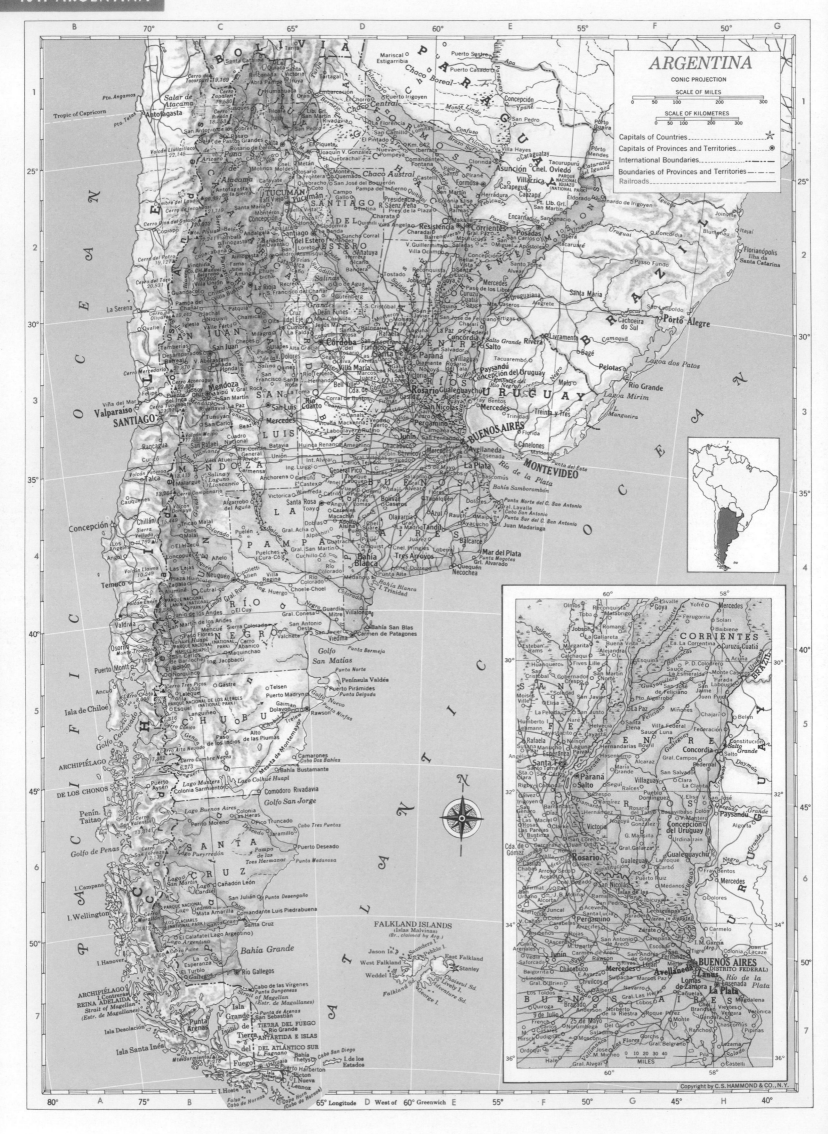

ARGENTINA

CONIC PROJECTION

SCALE OF MILES

0   50   100   200   300

SCALE OF KILOMETRES

0   50 100   200   300

Capitals of Countries .... ☆
Capitals of Provinces and Territories .... ◉
International Boundaries ....
Boundaries of Provinces and Territories ---
Railroads ....

FALKLAND ISLANDS
(Islas Malvinas)
(Br., claimed by Arg.)

Copyright by C.S. HAMMOND & CO., N.Y.

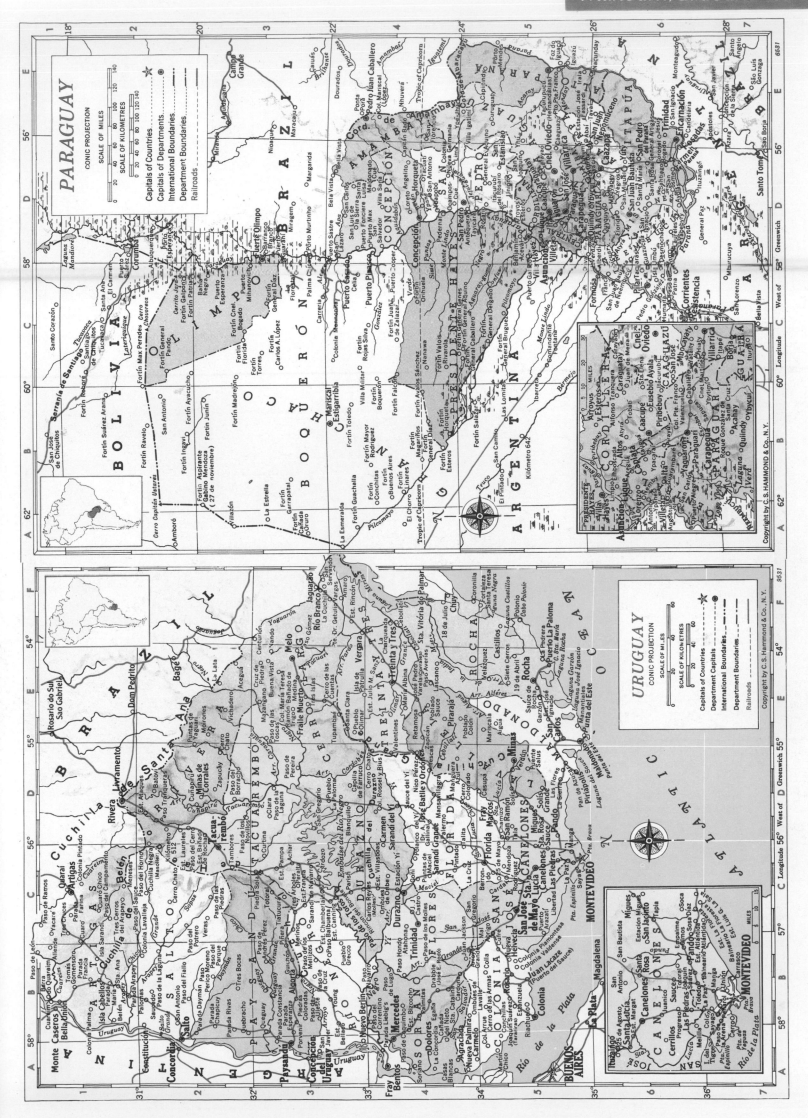

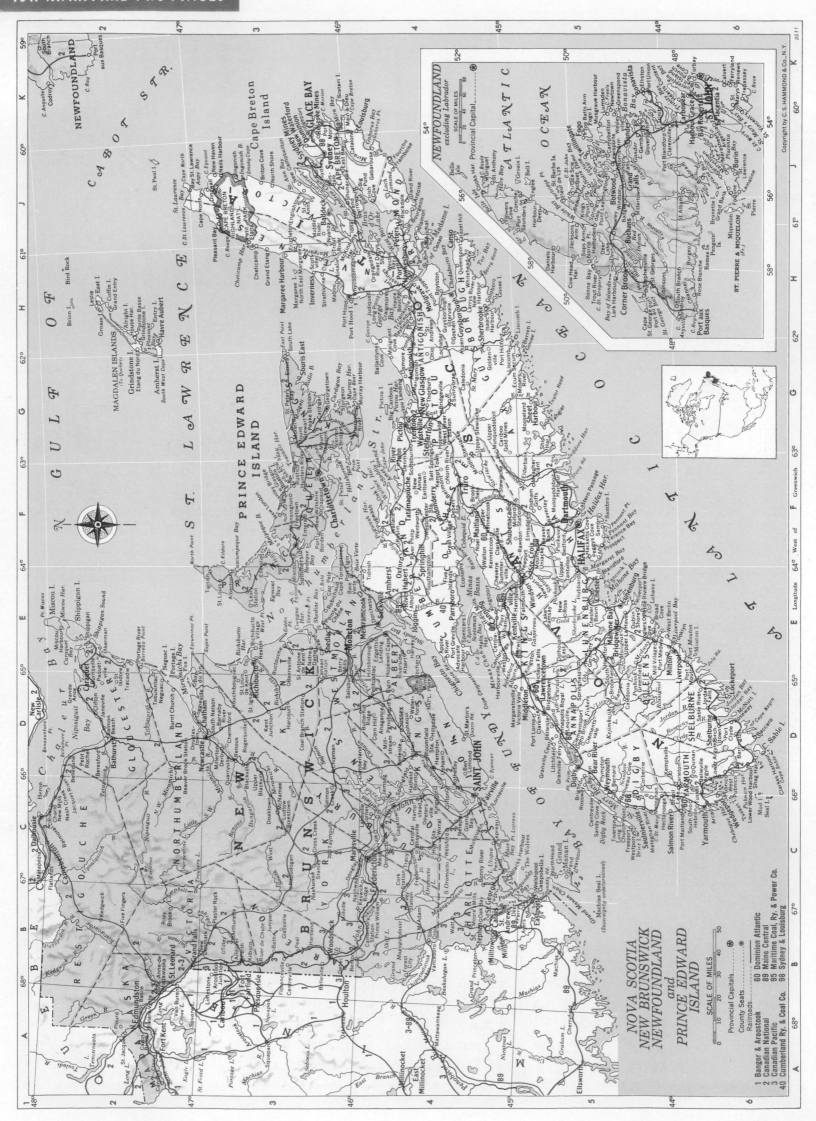

NEWFOUNDLAND
excluding Labrador

ATLANTIC OCEAN

ST. PIERRE & MIQUELON (Fr.)

NOVA SCOTIA
NEW BRUNSWICK
NEWFOUNDLAND
and
PRINCE EDWARD ISLAND

SCALE OF MILES

Provincial Capitals.........⊛
County Seats.........◎
Railroads

1 Bangor & Aroostook
2 Canadian National
3 Canadian Pacific
40 Cumberland Ry. & Coal Co.

60 Dominion Atlantic
89 Maine Central
95 Maritime Coal, Ry. & Power Co.
98 Sydney & Louisburg

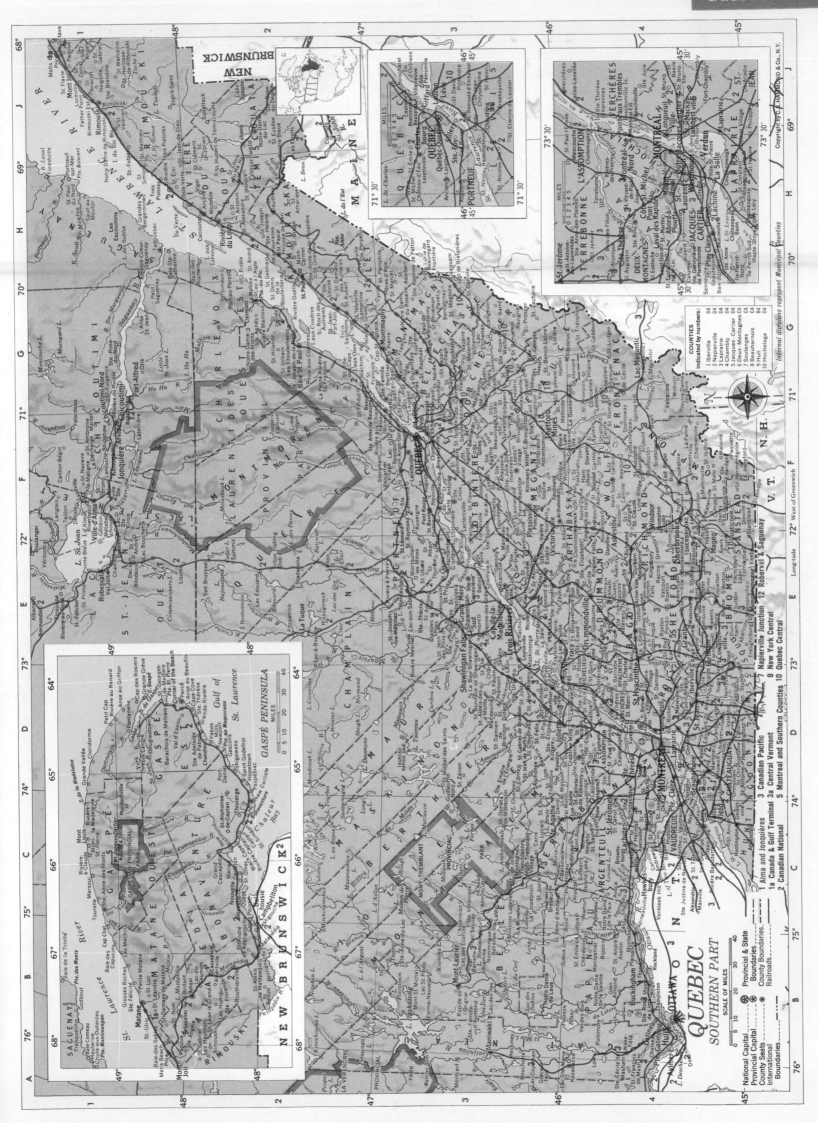

QUEBEC
SOUTHERN PART

SCALE OF MILES
0 5 10   20   30   40

National Capital .... ⊛
Provincial Capital .... ⊛
County Seats .... ⊚
Provincial & State
  Boundaries ....
County Boundaries ....
International
  Boundaries ....
Railroads ....

COUNTIES
Indicated by numbers:
1 Iberville D4
2 Napierville D4
3 Laprairie D4
4 Chambly D4
5 Jacques - Cartier C4
6 Deux - Montagnes C4
7 Soulanges C4
8 St-Catharnois B4
9 Hull A4
10 Hochelaga C4

Internal divisions represent Municipal Counties

1 Alma and Jonquières   3 Canadian Pacific
1a Canada & Gulf Terminal 3a Central Vermont
2 Canadian National   5 Montreal and Southern Counties
                           7 Napierville Junction   9 New York Central
                           10 Quebec Central

GASPÉ PENINSULA

Gulf of St. Lawrence

Chaleur Bay

NEW BRUNSWICK

MAINE

NEW BRUNSWICK

Copyright by C.S. HAMMOND & Co., N.Y.

Longitude 72° West of Greenwich F

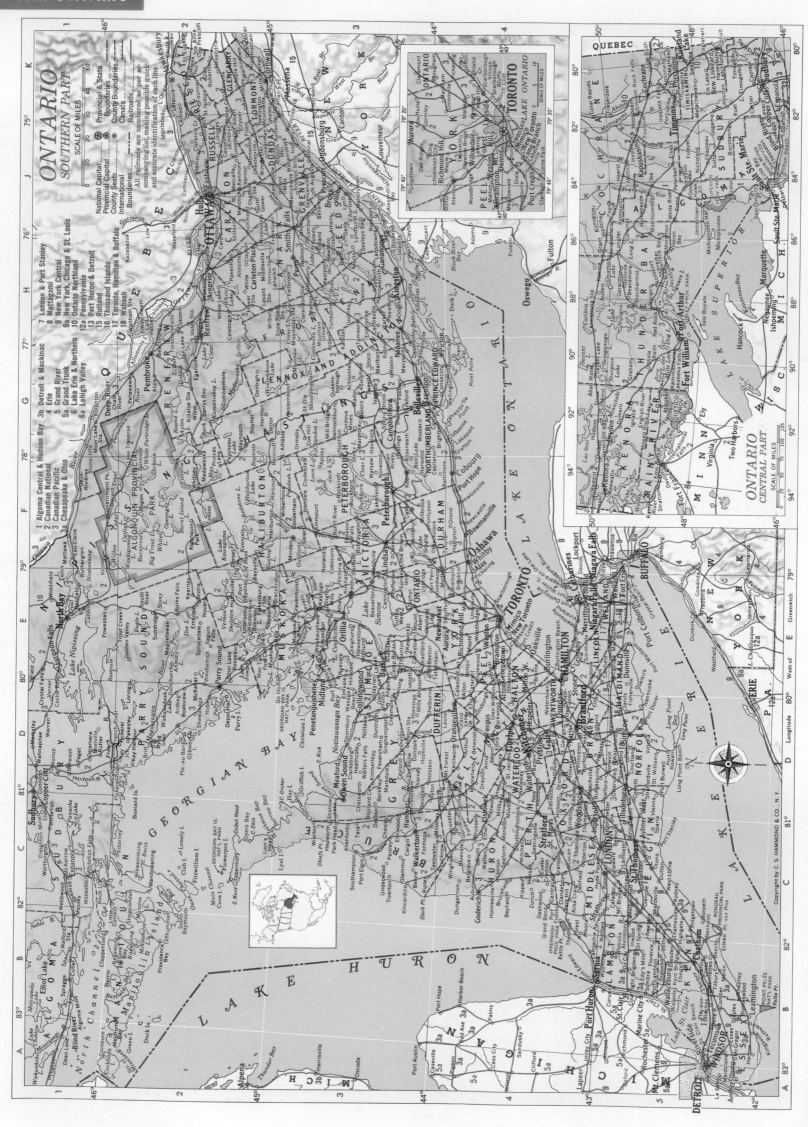

ONTARIO
SOUTHERN PART

SCALE OF MILES

National Capital
Provincial Capital
County Seats
Provincial & State Boundaries
County Boundaries
Canals
Railroads
International Boundaries

All railroads are numbered as per accompanying list, making possible quick and accurate identification of each line.

1 Canadian National
2 Canadian Pacific
3 Chesapeake & Ohio
3a
3b Detroit & Mackinac
4 Erie
5 Grand River
5a Grand Trunk
6 Lake Erie & Northern
7 London & Port Stanley
8 Mattagami
9 New York Central
9a New York, Chicago & St. Louis
10 Ontario Northland
12a Pennsylvania
13 Port Huron & Detroit
15 Rutland
16 Thousand Islands
17 Toronto, Hamilton & Buffalo
18 Wabash

Algoma Central & Hudson Bay

Copyright by C. S. HAMMOND & CO., N.Y.

TORONTO

ONTARIO
CENTRAL PART

SCALE OF MILES

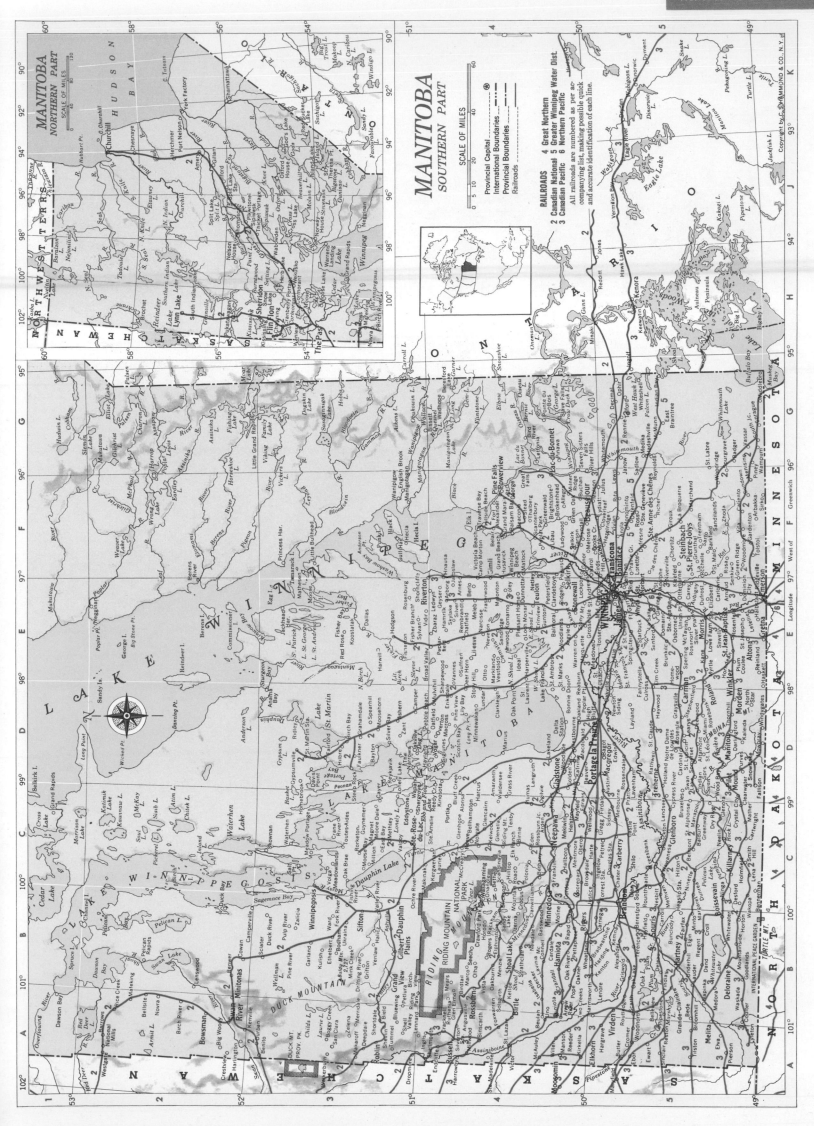

MANITOBA
NORTHERN PART
SCALE OF MILES

MANITOBA
SOUTHERN PART
SCALE OF MILES

Provincial Capital ⊛
International Boundaries
Provincial Boundaries
Railroads

RAILROADS
1 Great Northern   4 Great Northern
2 Canadian National   5 Greater Winnipeg Water Dist.
3 Canadian Pacific   6 Northern Pacific

All railroads are numbered as per accompanying list, making possible quick and accurate identification of each line.

Copyright by C. S. HAMMOND & CO., N.Y.

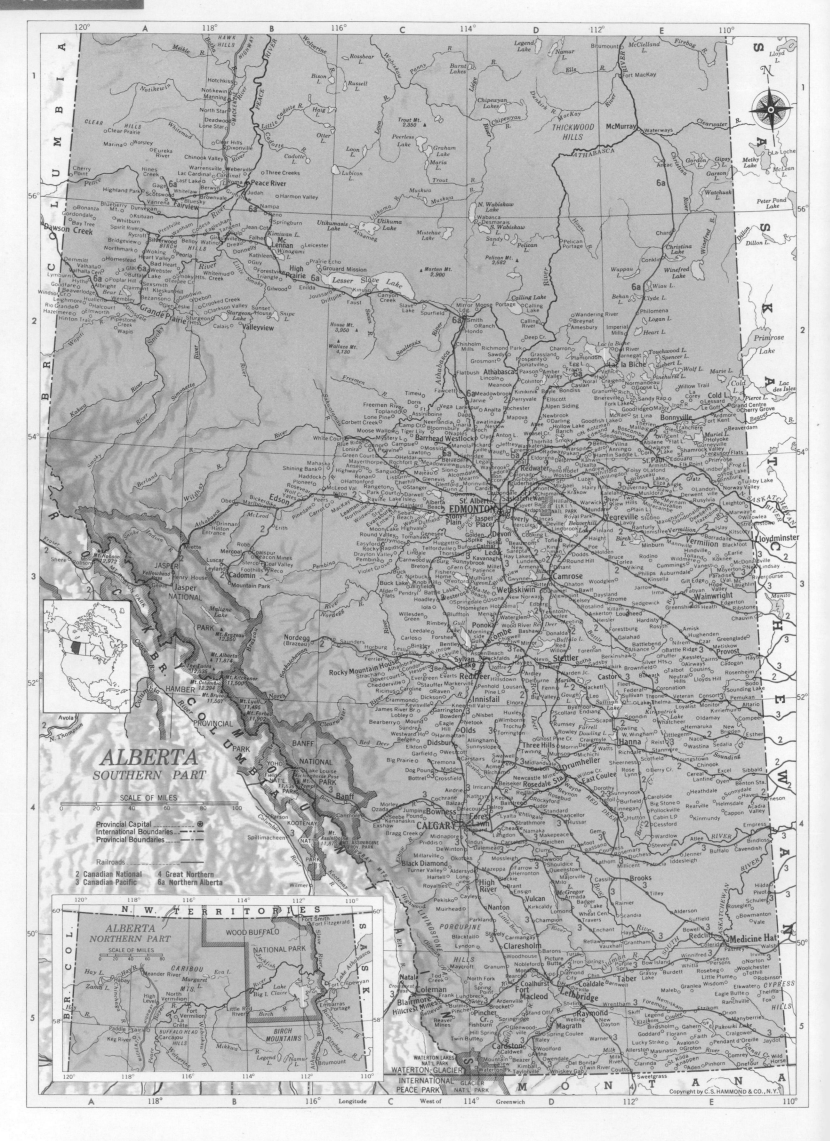

ALBERTA
SOUTHERN PART

SCALE OF MILES

0   20   40   60   80   100

Provincial Capital .... ⊛
International Boundaries .... ━ ━ ━
Provincial Boundaries .... ━━━━

Railroads ....

2 Canadian National   4 Great Northern
3 Canadian Pacific   6a Northern Alberta

ALBERTA
NORTHERN PART

SCALE OF MILES

0   20   40   60

N. W. TERRITORIES

WOOD BUFFALO

NATIONAL PARK

Copyright by C.S. HAMMOND & CO., N.Y.

Longitude   West of   Greenwich

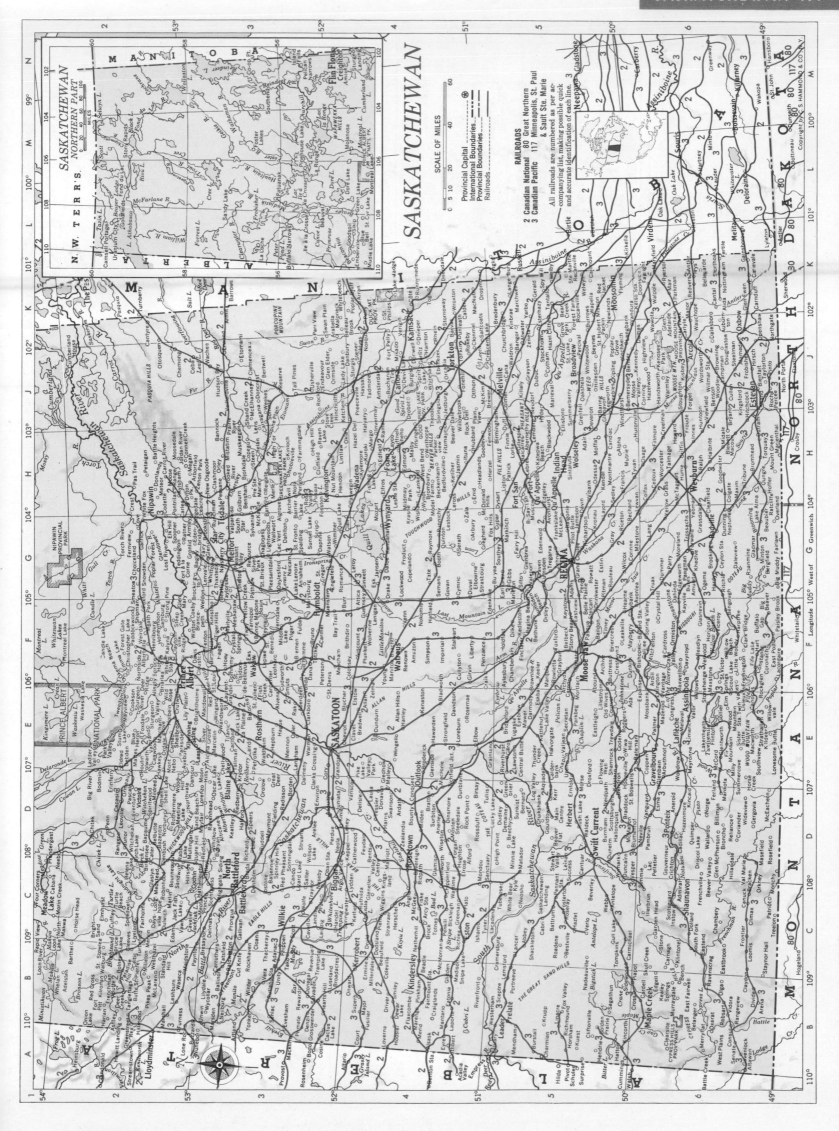

SASKATCHEWAN

SASKATCHEWAN NORTHERN PART

SCALE OF MILES

RAILROADS
2 Canadian National   80 Great Northern
3 Canadian Pacific   117 Minneapolis, St. Paul
& Sault Ste. Marie

Provincial Capital
International Boundaries
Provincial Boundaries
Railroads

All railroads are numbered as per accompanying list, making possible quick and accurate identification of each line.

Copyright by C. S. Hammond & Co., N.Y.

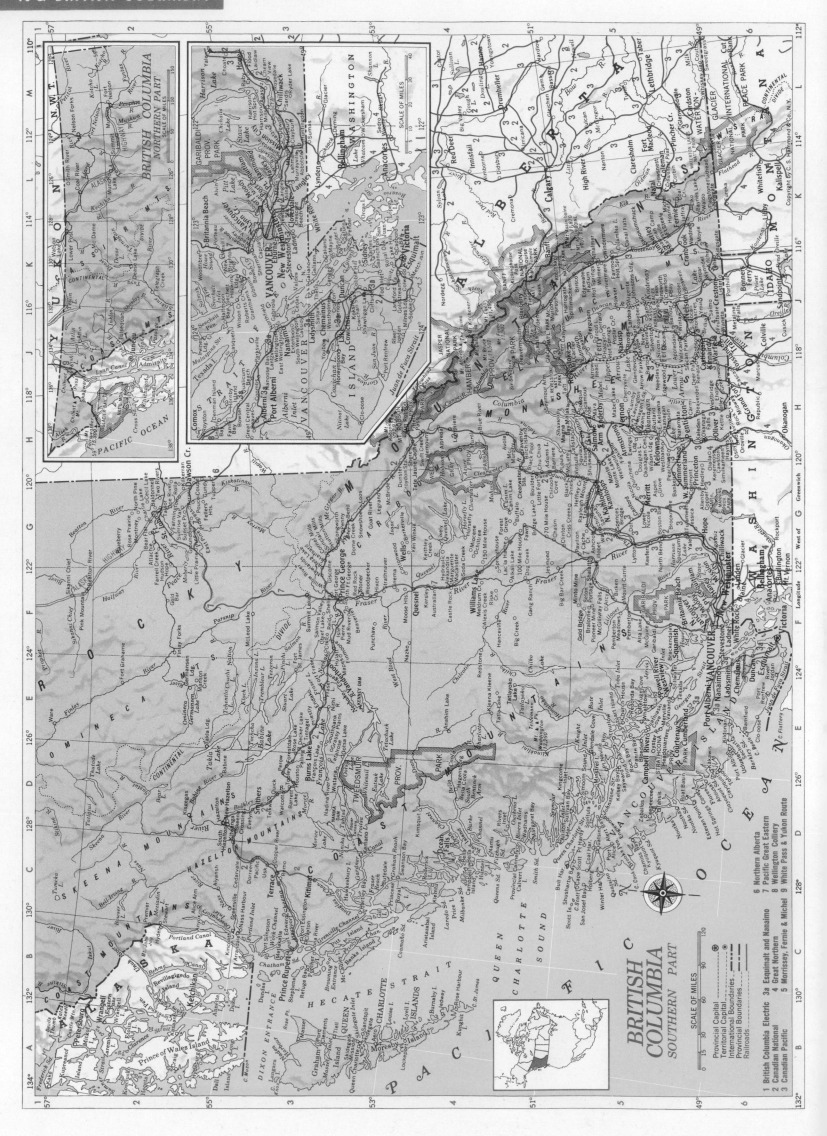

BRITISH COLUMBIA
NORTHERN PART

BRITISH COLUMBIA
SOUTHERN PART

SCALE OF MILES

Provincial Capital
Territorial Capital
International Boundaries
Provincial Boundaries
Railroads

1 British Columbia Electric 3a Esquimalt and Nanaimo
2 Canadian National 4 Great Northern
3 Canadian Pacific 5 Morrissey, Fernie & Michel

6 Northern Alberta
7 Pacific Great Eastern
8 Wellington Colliery
9 White Pass & Yukon Route

Copyright by C. S. Hammond & Co., N.Y.

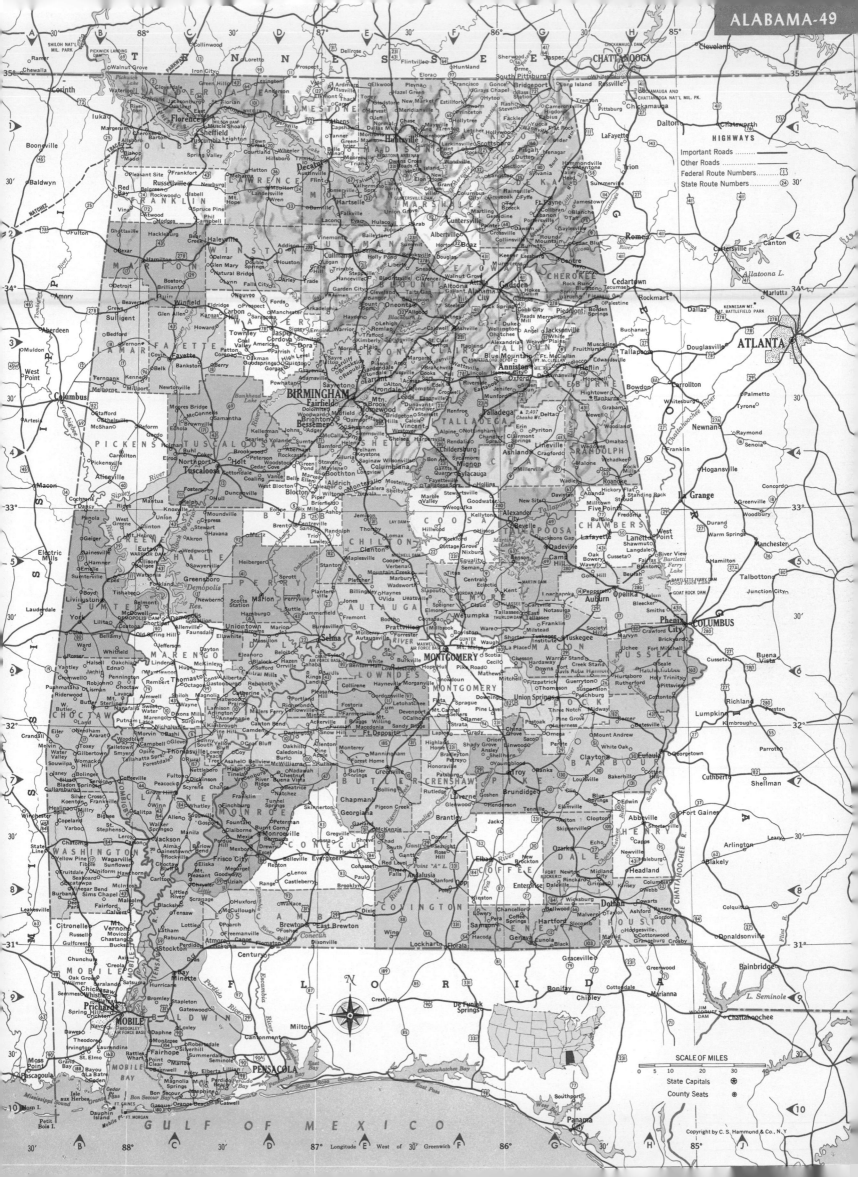

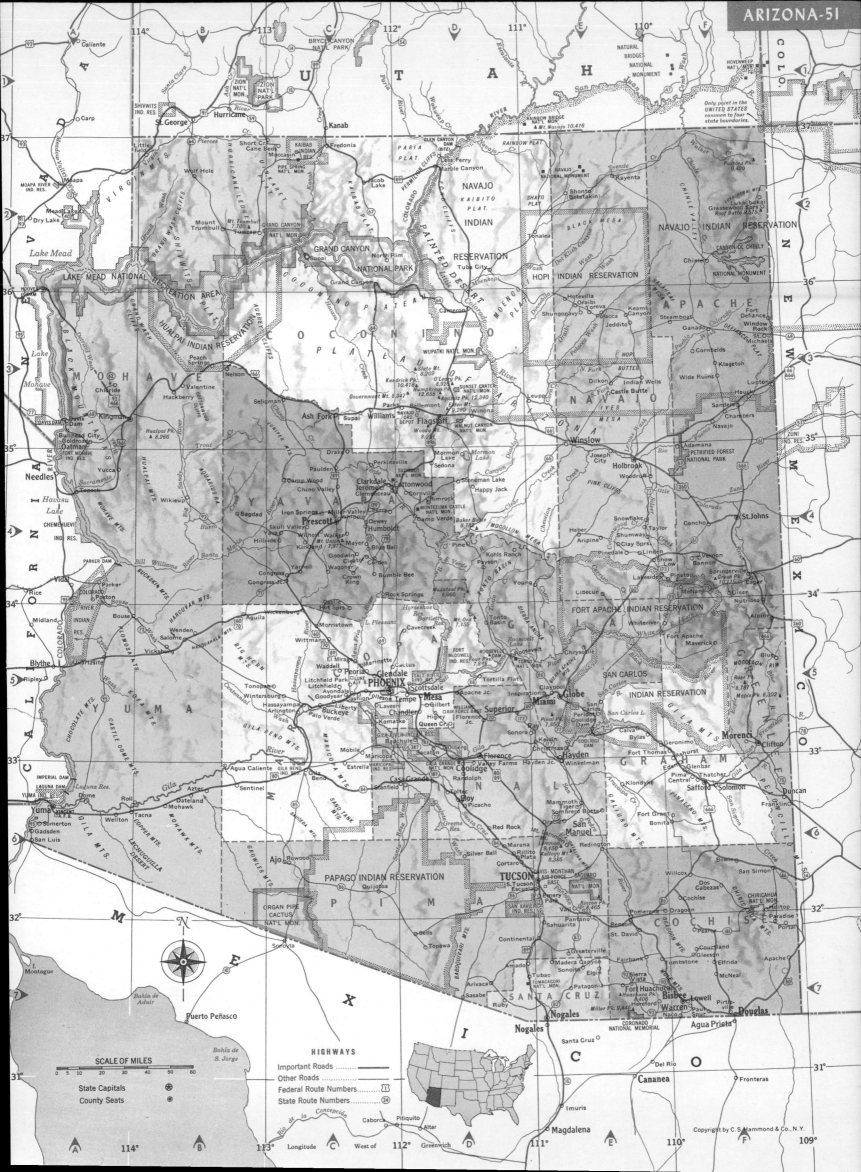

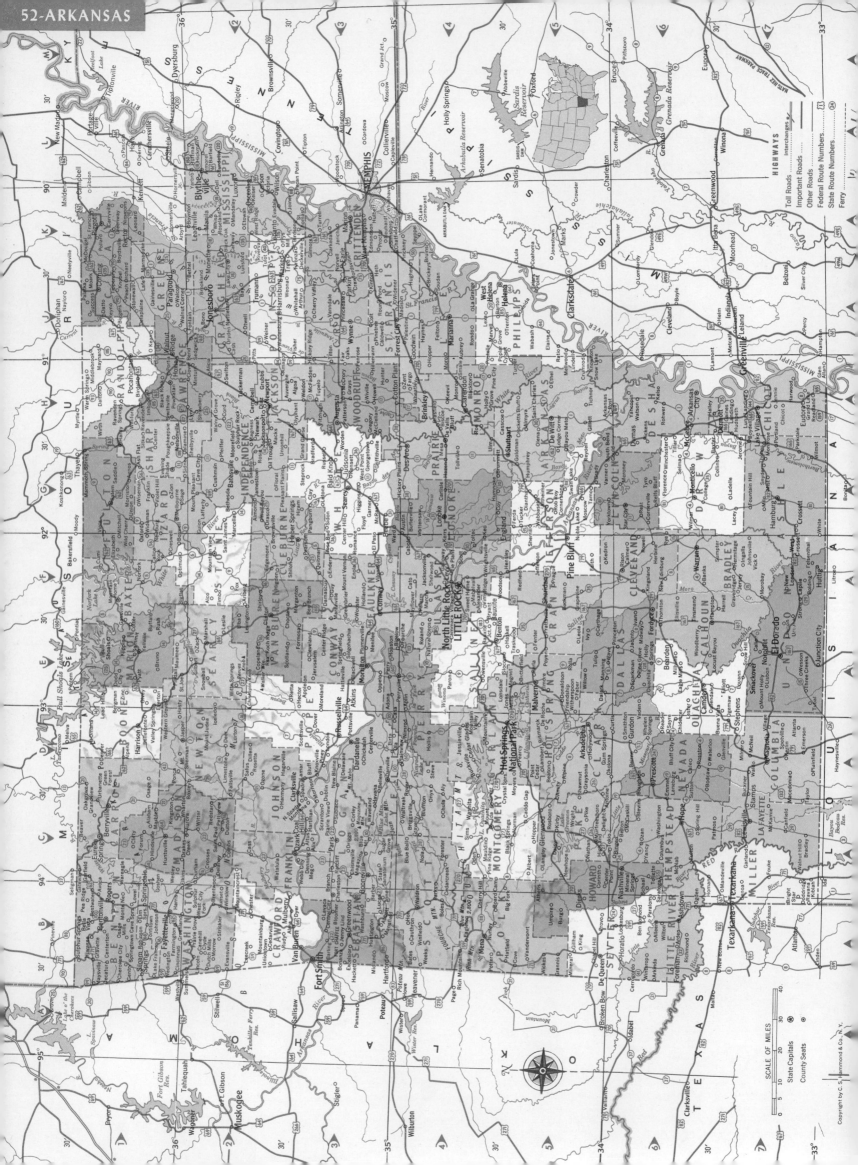

HIGHWAYS

Toll Roads · Interchanges
Important Roads
Other Roads
Federal Route Numbers
State Route Numbers

SCALE OF MILES
0 5 10 20 30 40

⊗ State Capitals
○ County Seats

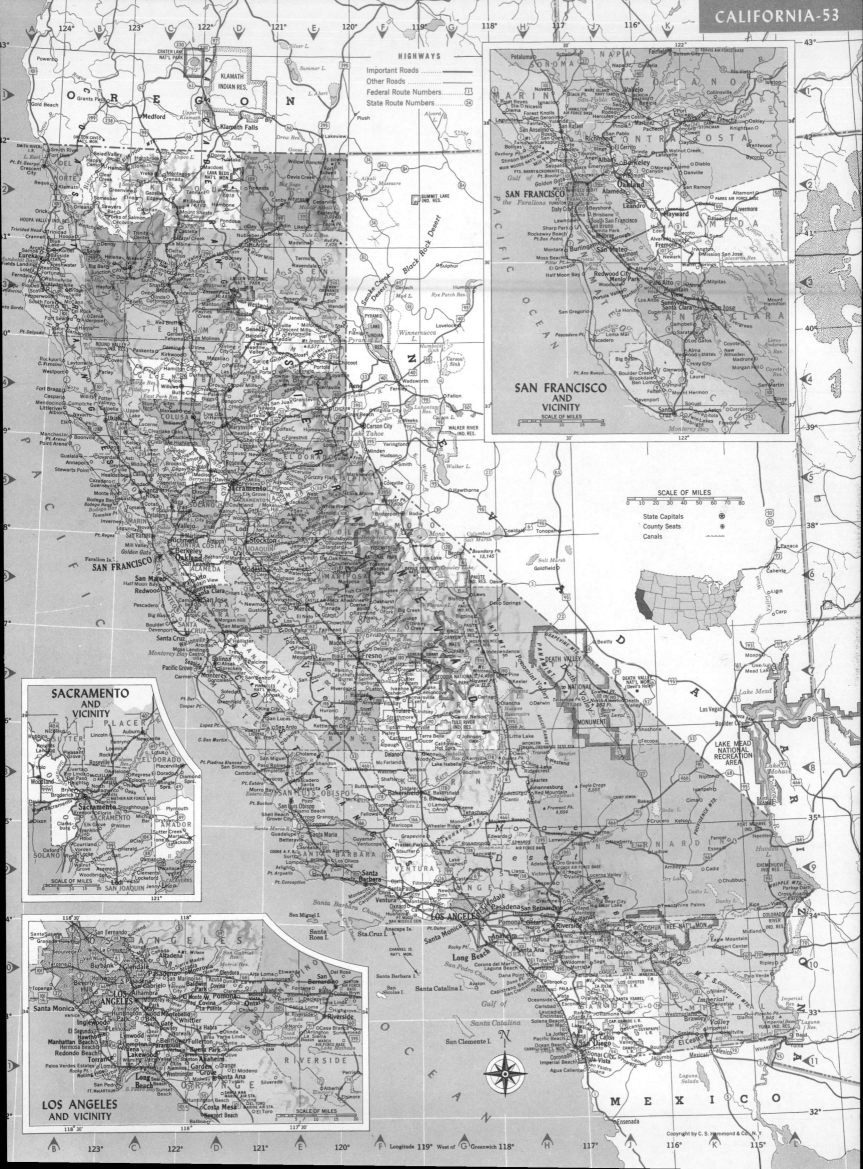

HIGHWAYS

Important Roads ....
Other Roads ....
Federal Route Numbers........ 🛡
State Route Numbers........... 🛡

SAN FRANCISCO
AND
VICINITY
SCALE OF MILES

SCALE OF MILES
0 10 20 30 40 50 60 70 80

⊛ State Capitals
⊛ County Seats
Canals

SACRAMENTO
AND
VICINITY
SCALE OF MILES

LOS ANGELES
AND VICINITY

O R E G O N

N E V A D A

P A C I F I C   O C E A N

M E X I C O

Copyright by C. S. Hammond & Co., N.Y.

Longitude 119° West of Greenwich 118°

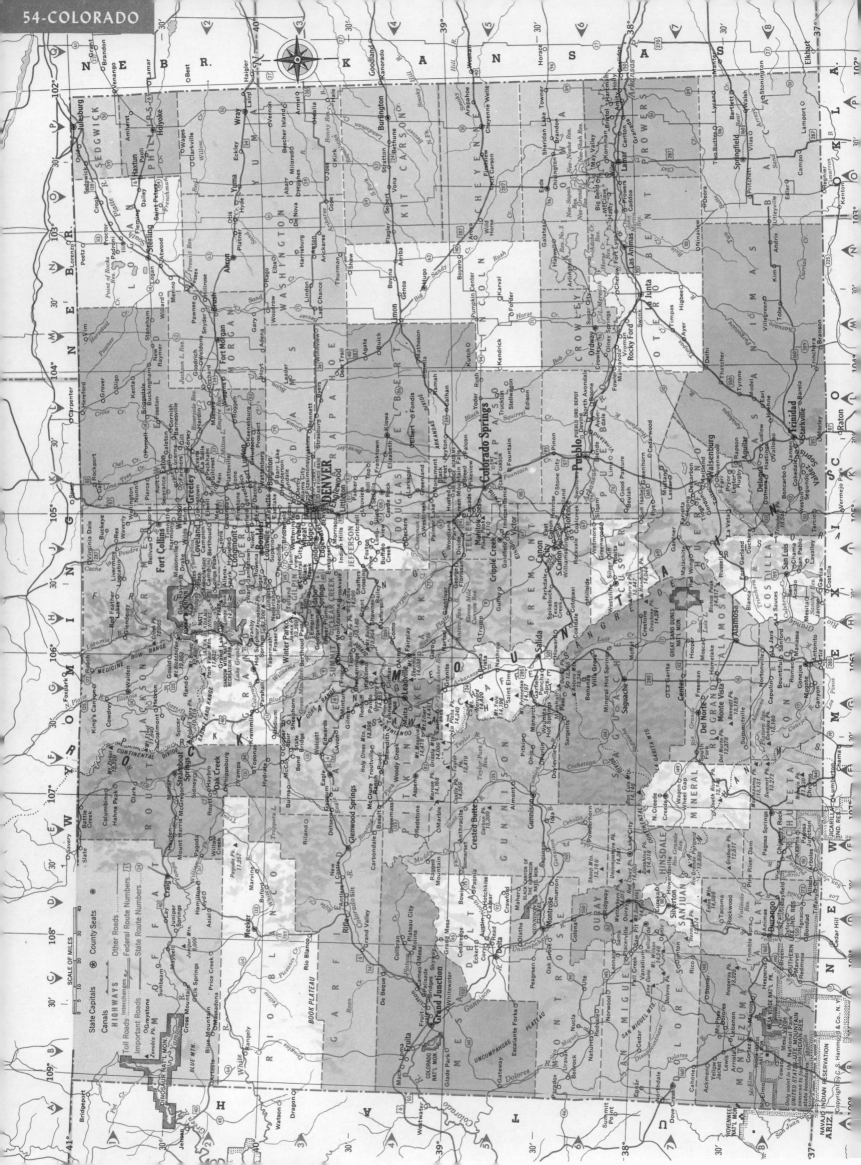

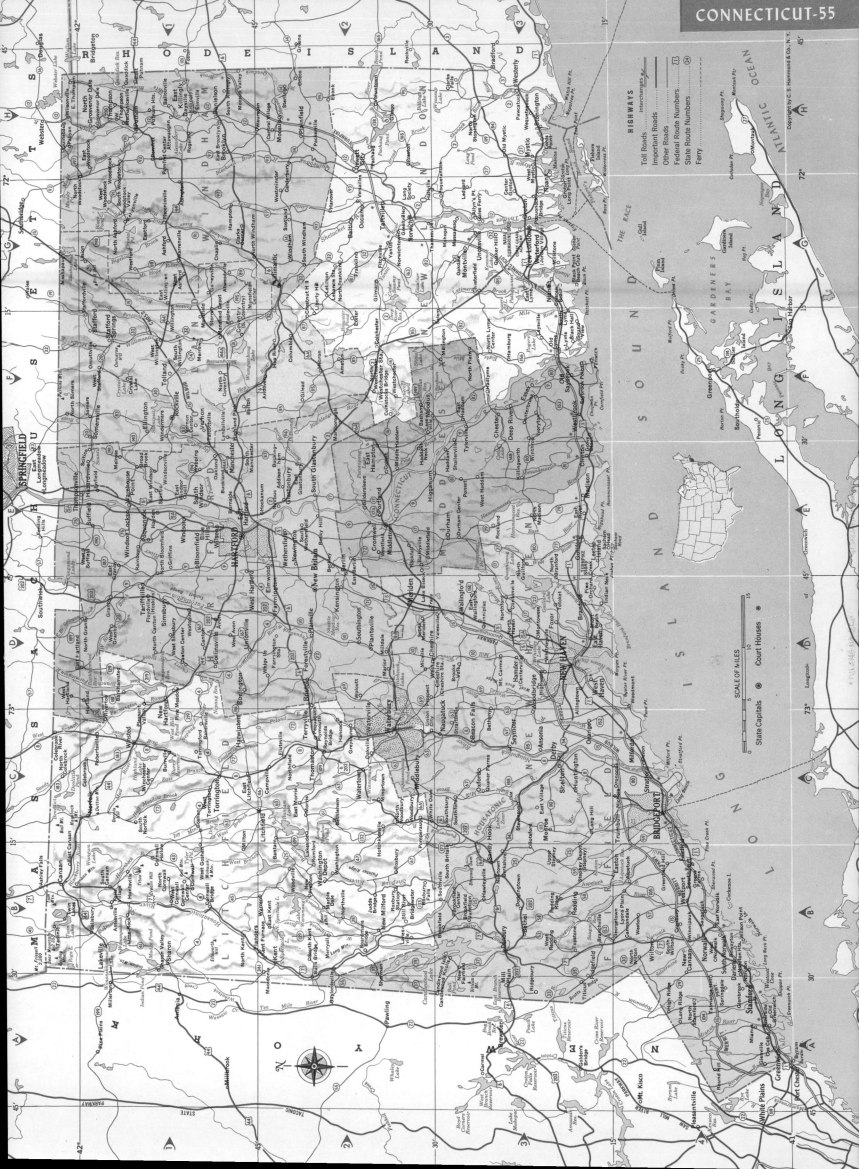

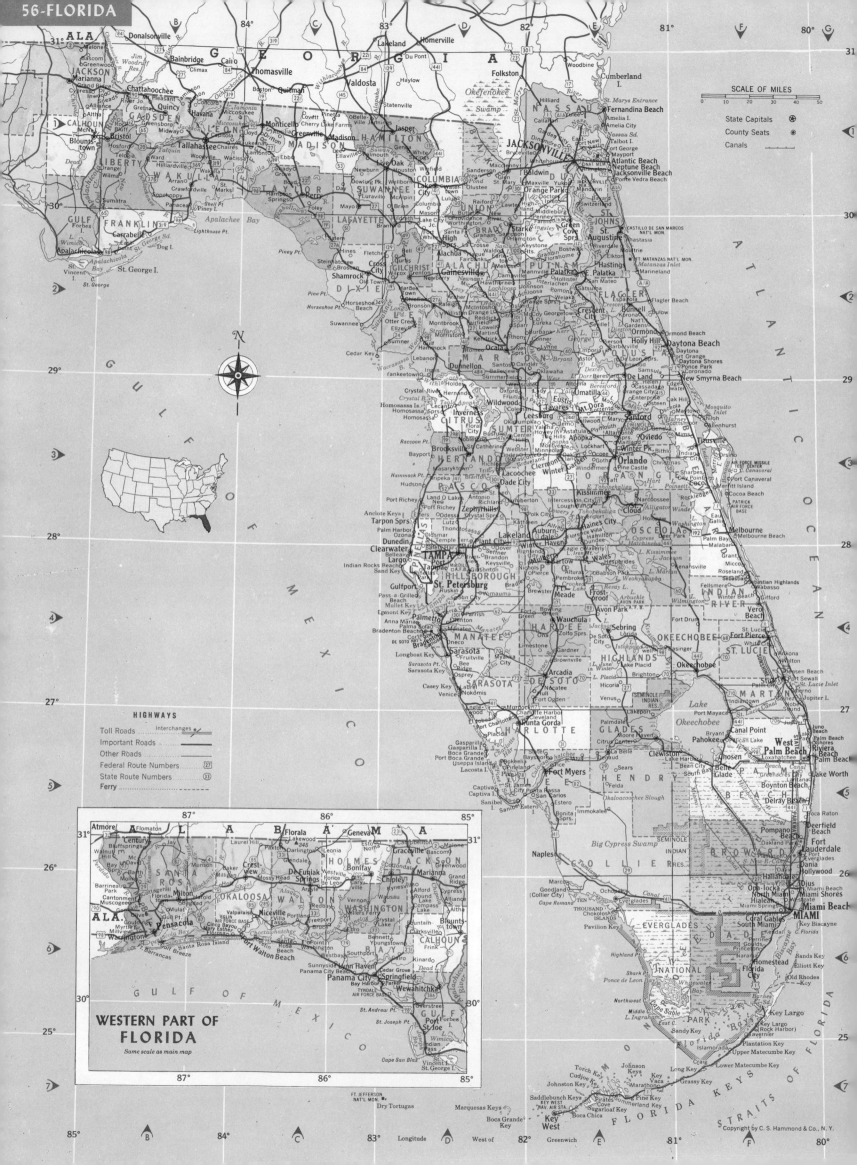

WESTERN PART OF
FLORIDA
Same scale as main map

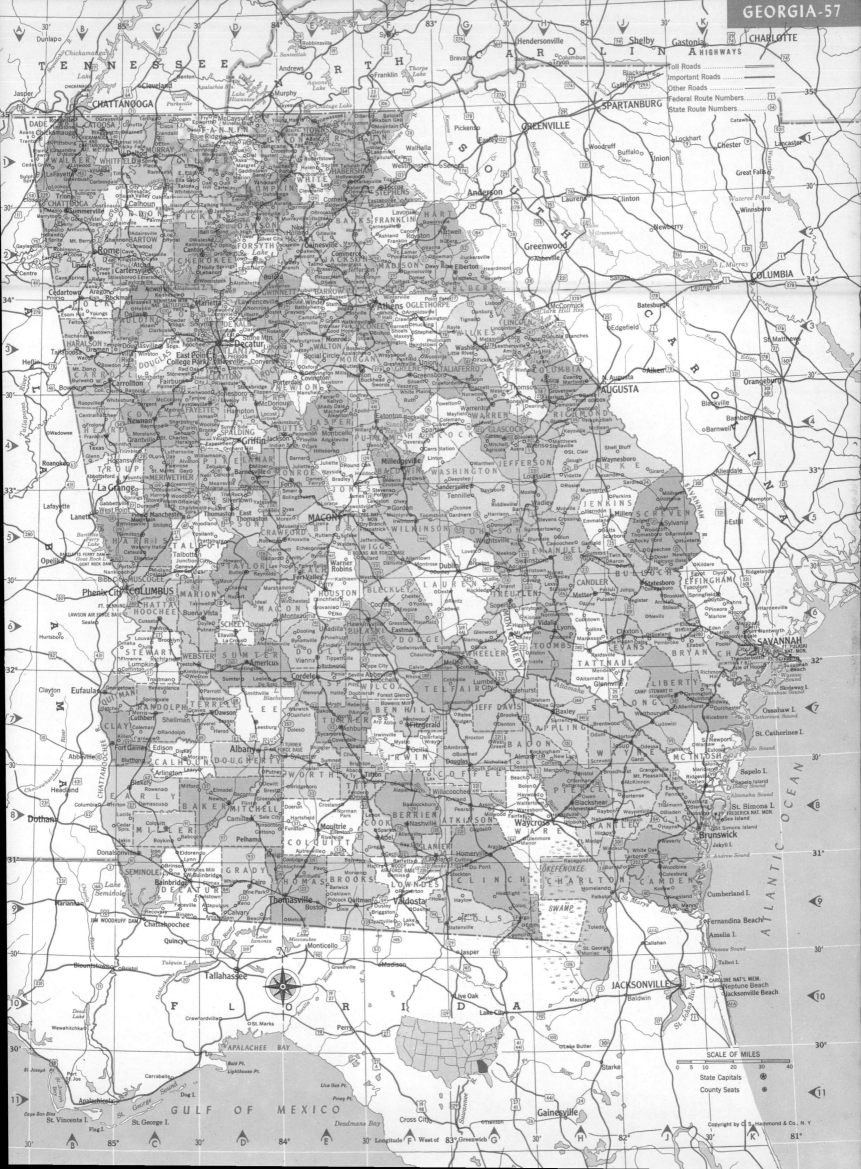

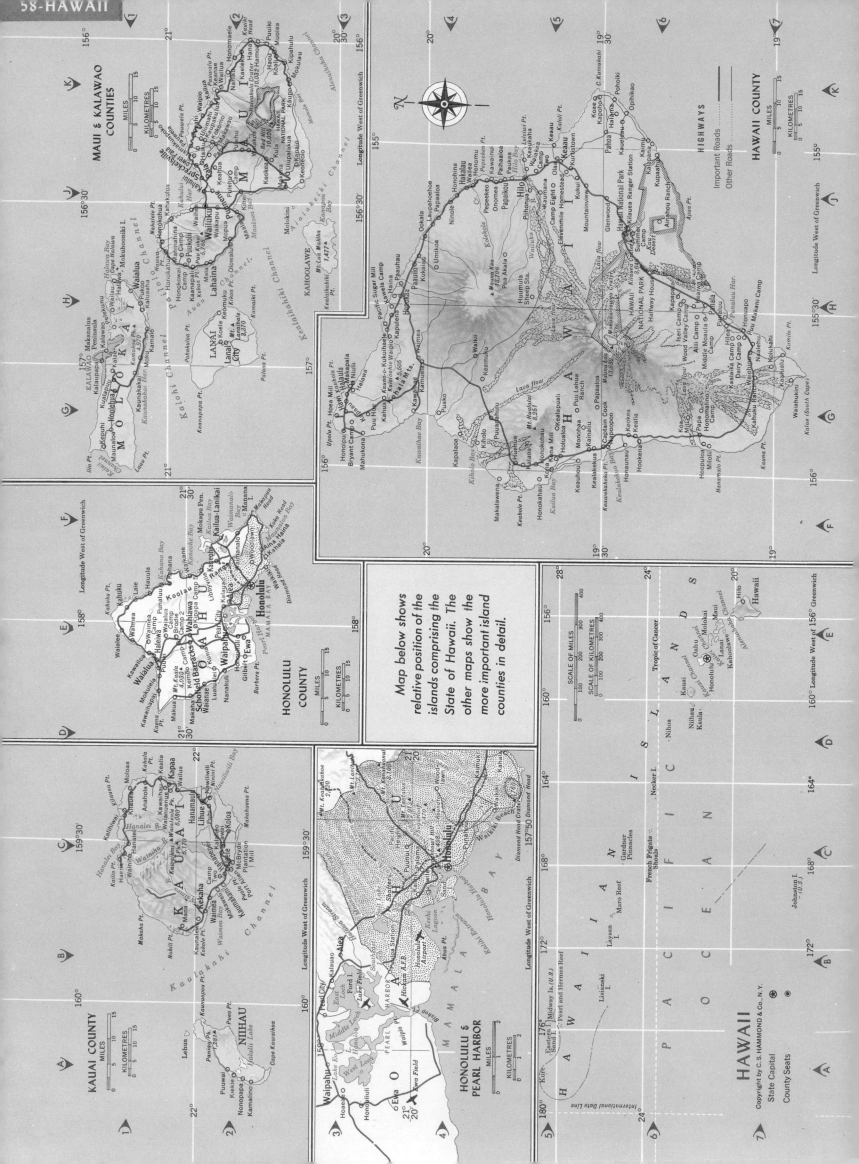

MAUI & KALAWAO COUNTIES

MILES
0 5 10 15
KILOMETRES
0 5 10 15

KAUAI COUNTY

MILES
0 5 10 15
KILOMETRES
0 5 10 15

HONOLULU COUNTY

MILES
0 5 10 15
KILOMETRES
0 5 10 15

HONOLULU & PEARL HARBOR

MILES
0 1 2
KILOMETRES
0 1 2

HAWAII COUNTY

MILES
0 5 10 15
KILOMETRES
0 5 10 15

Map below shows relative position of the islands comprising the State of Hawaii. The other maps show the more important island counties in detail.

SCALE OF MILES
0 100 200 300 400
SCALE OF KILOMETRES
0 100 200 300 400

HAWAII

Copyright by C.S. HAMMOND & Co., N.Y.

State Capital ⊛
County Seats ⊙

HIGHWAYS
Important Roads ━━━━
Other Roads ─────

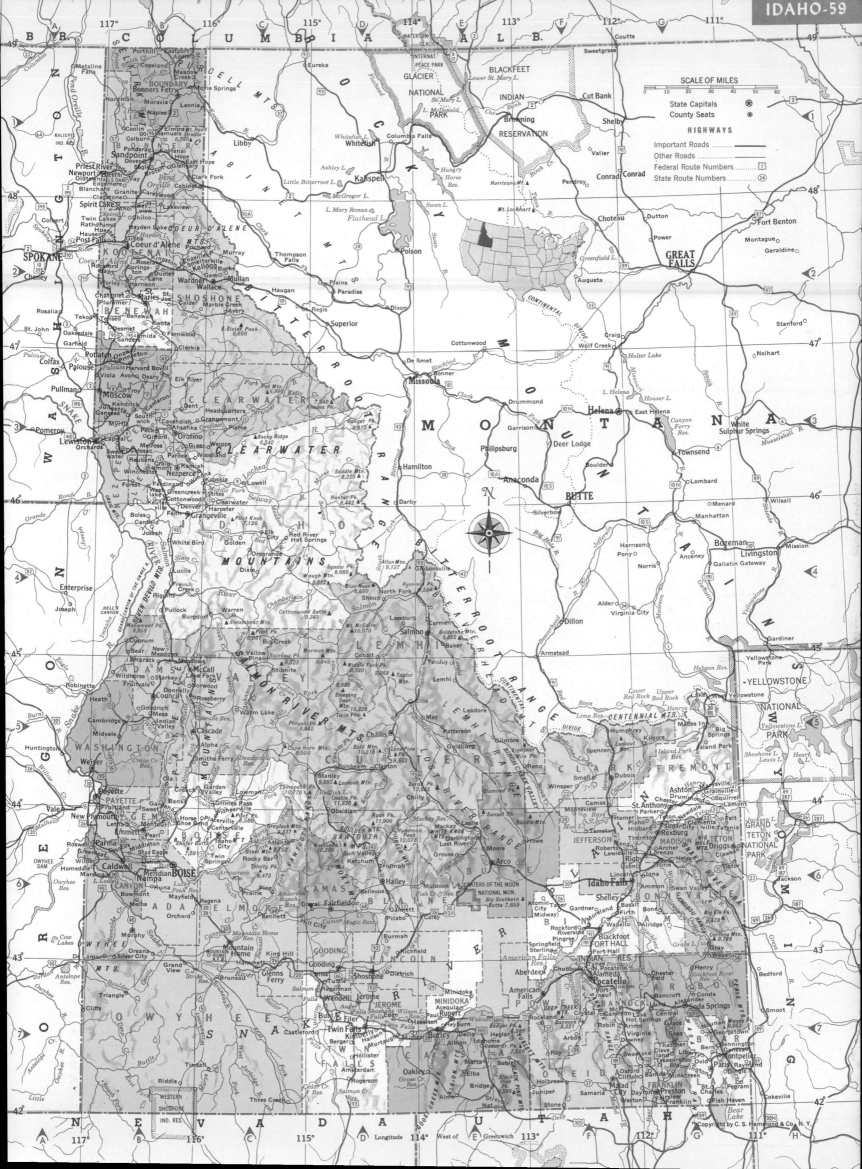

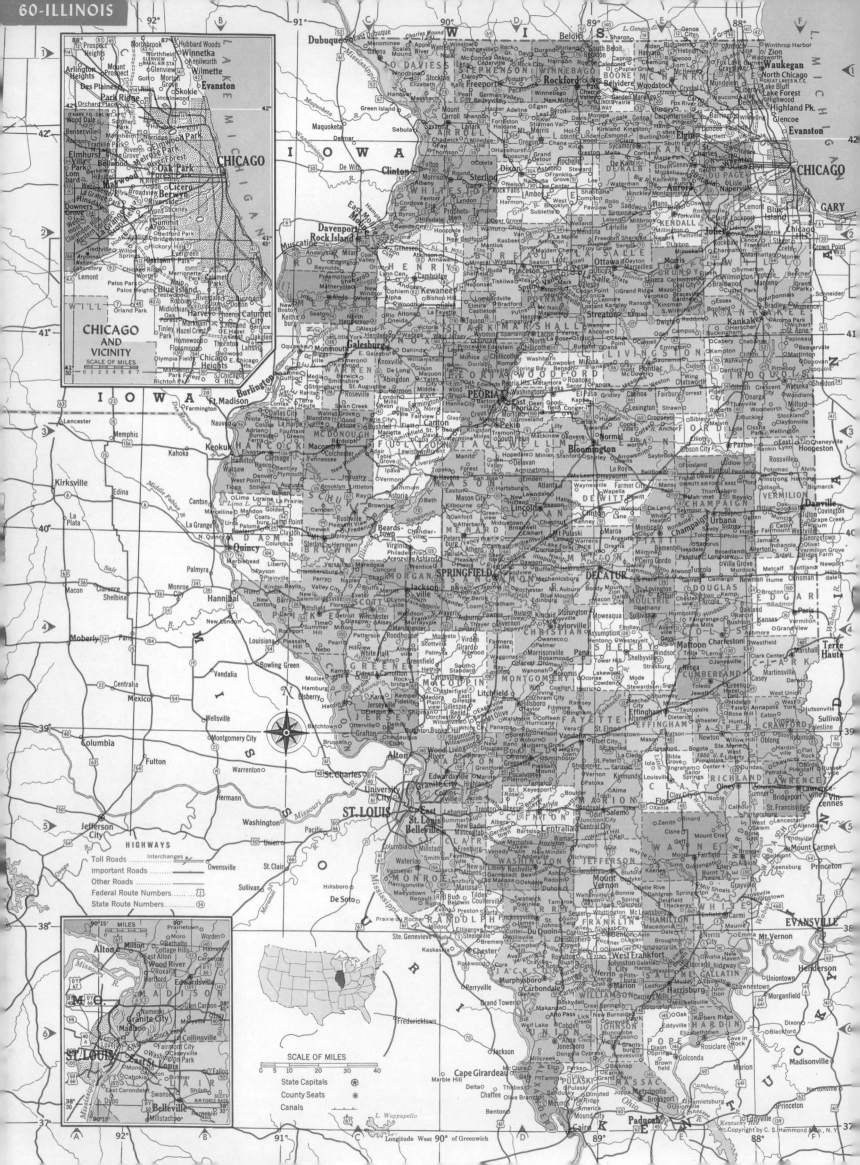

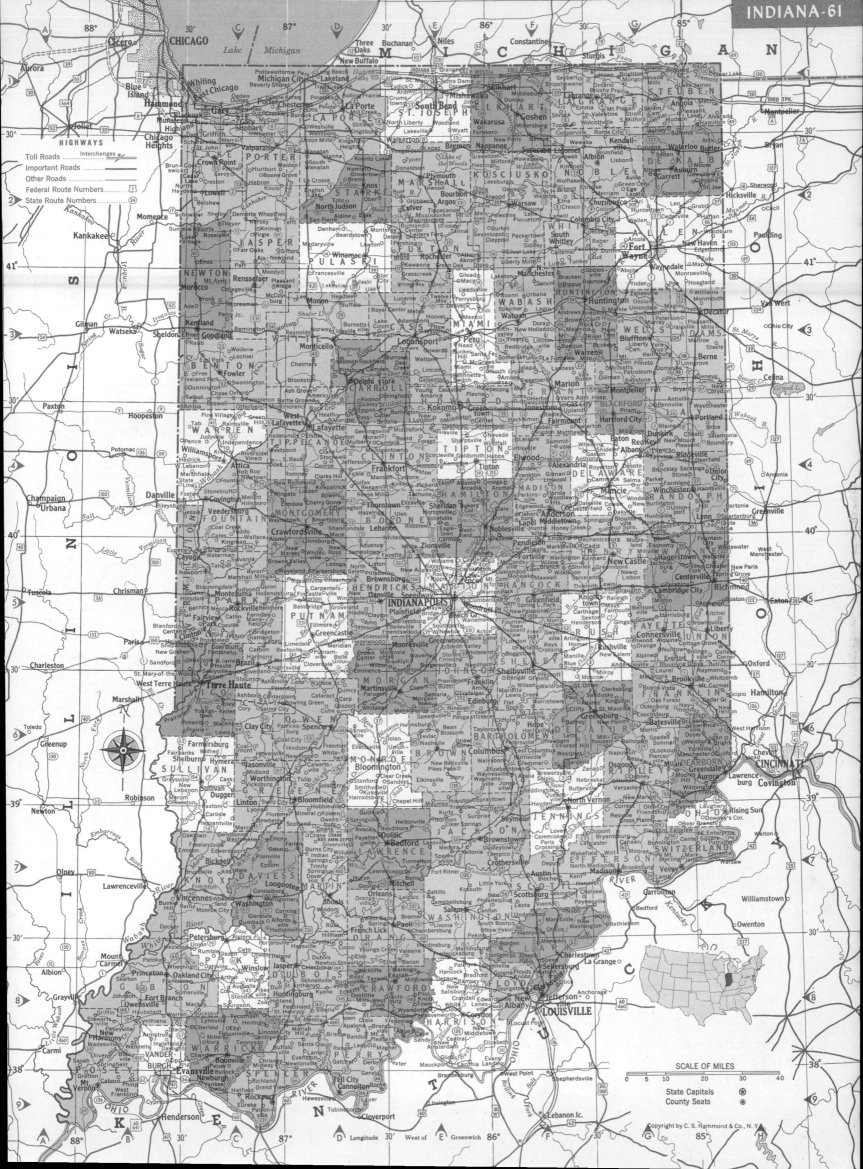

INDIANA-61

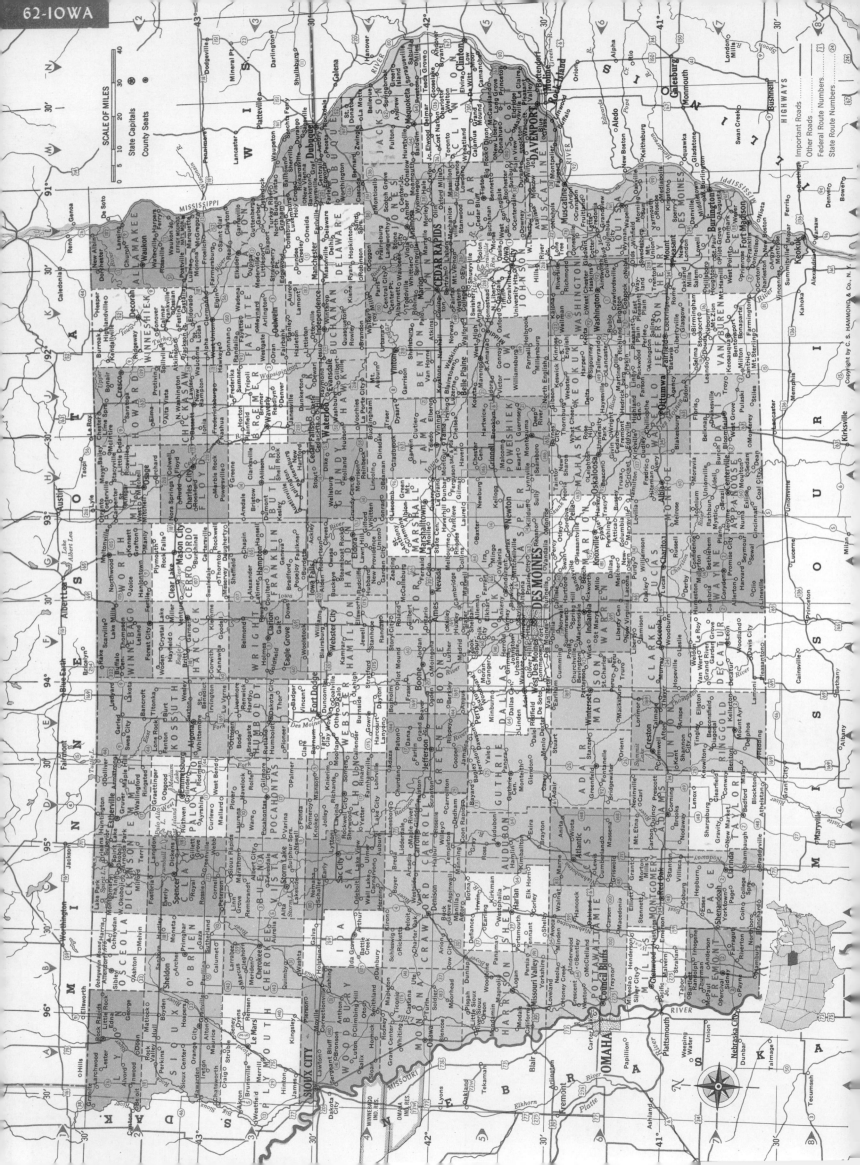

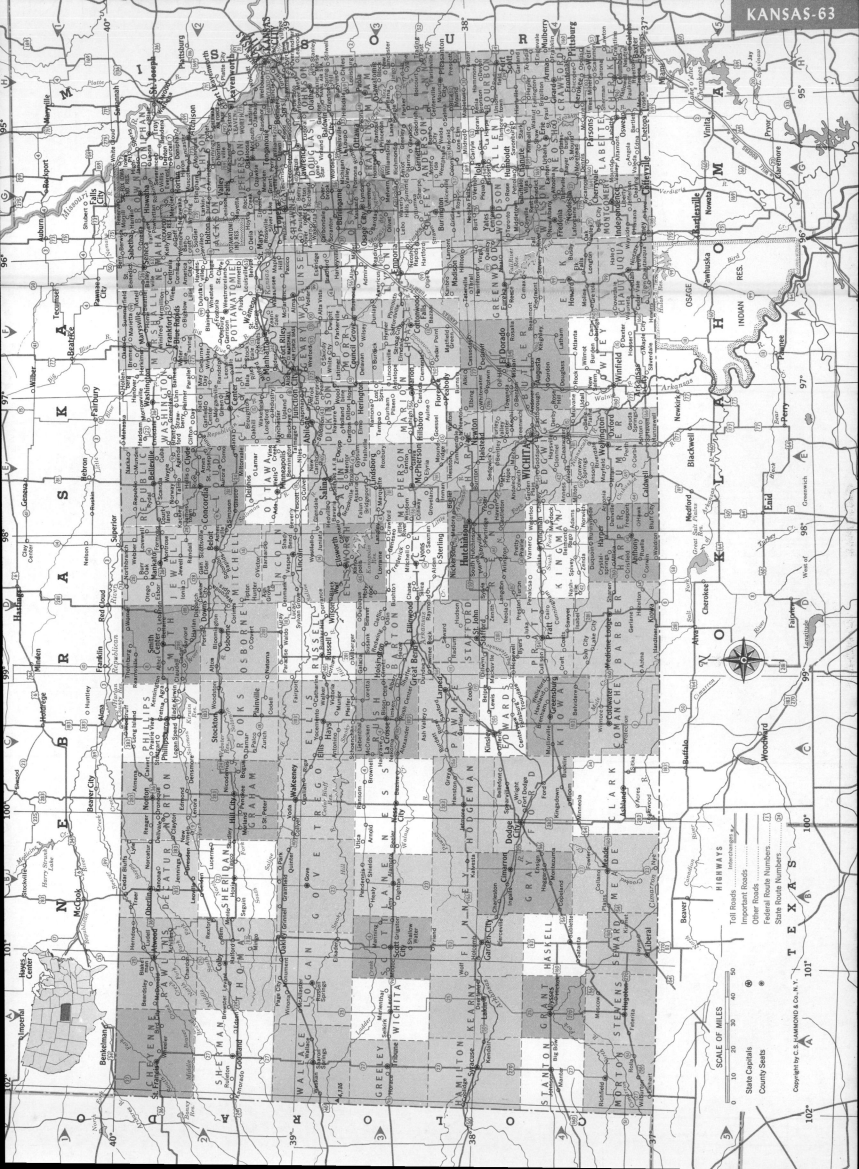

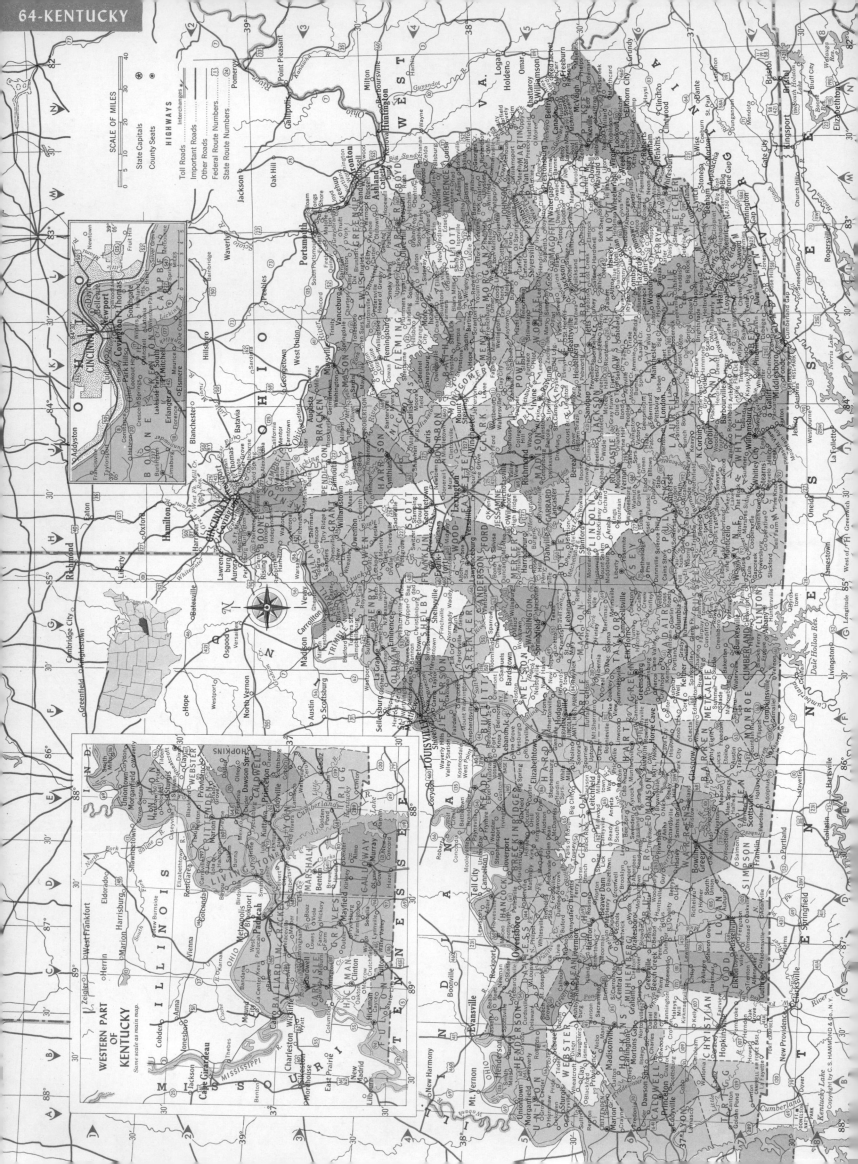

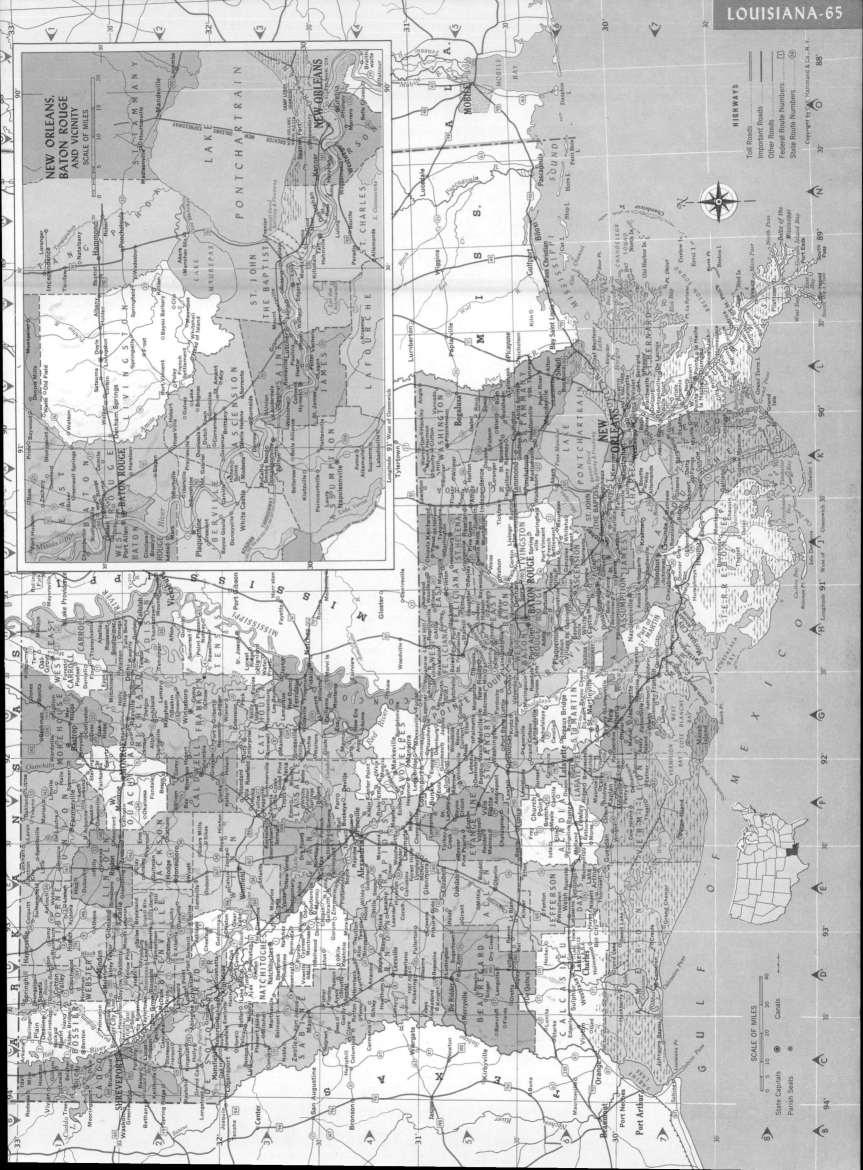

NEW ORLEANS,
BATON ROUGE
AND VICINITY
SCALE OF MILES

HIGHWAYS
Toll Roads
Important Roads
Other Roads
Federal Route Numbers
State Route Numbers

Copyright by C.S. Hammond & Co., N.Y.

SCALE OF MILES
Canals
State Capitals
Parish Seats

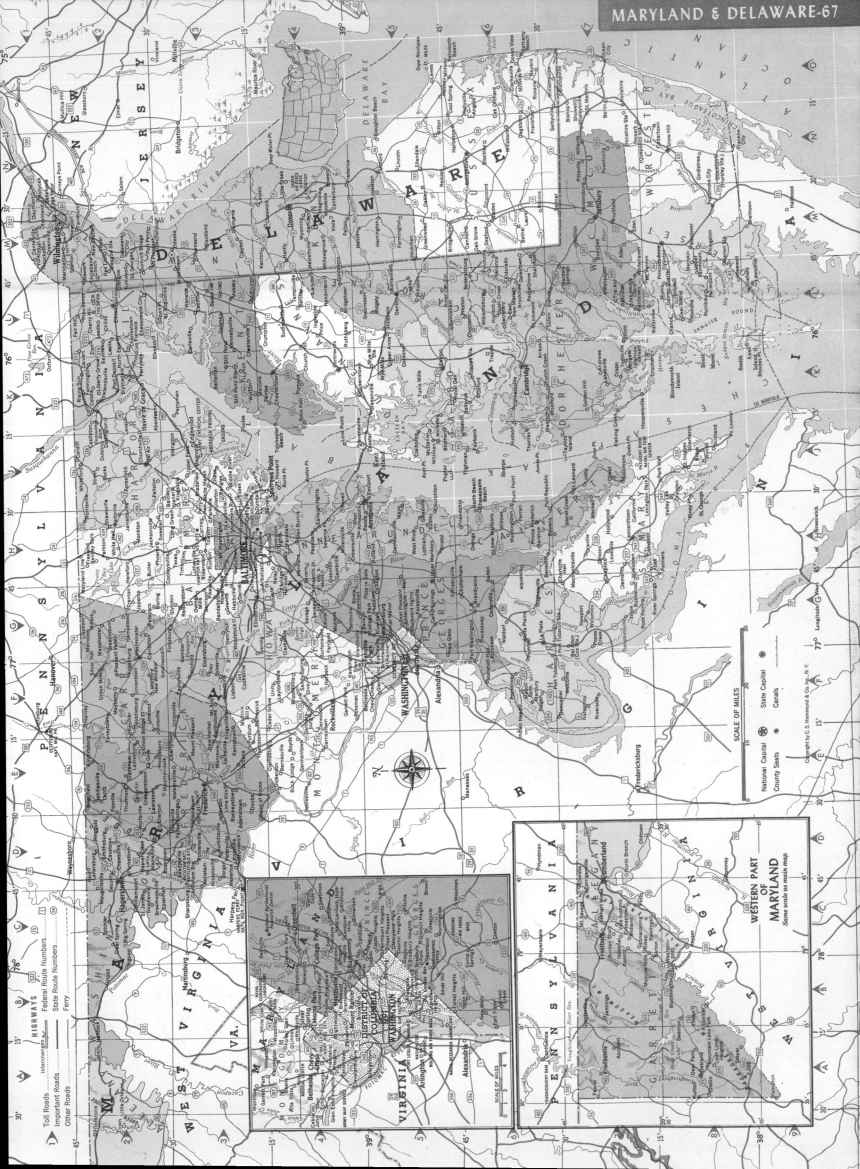

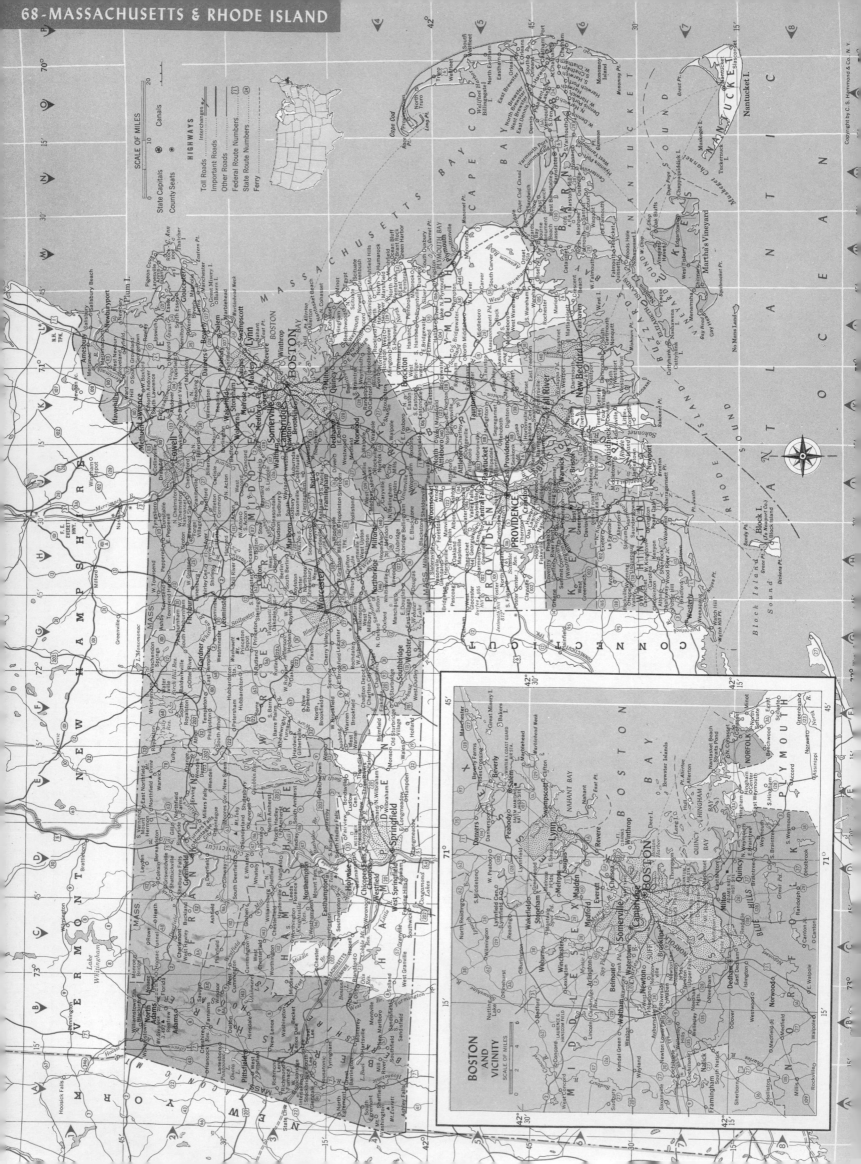

BOSTON AND VICINITY

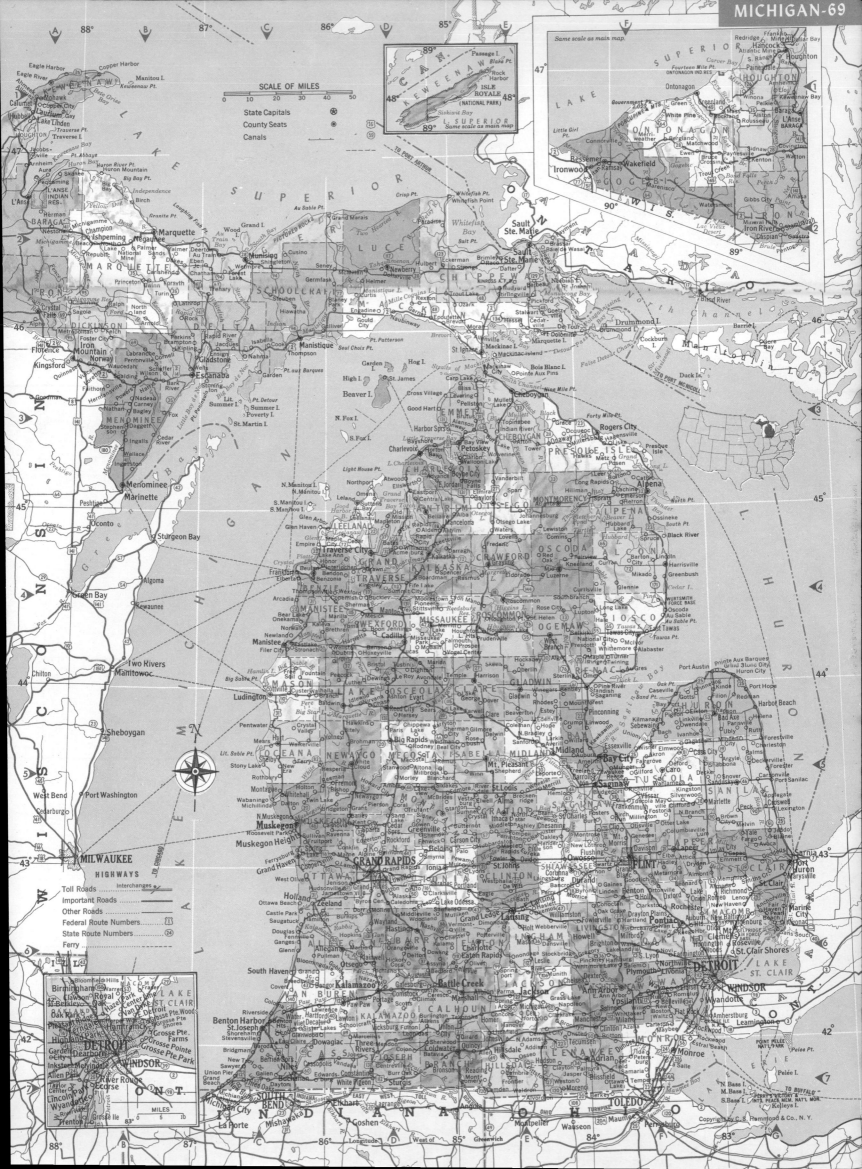

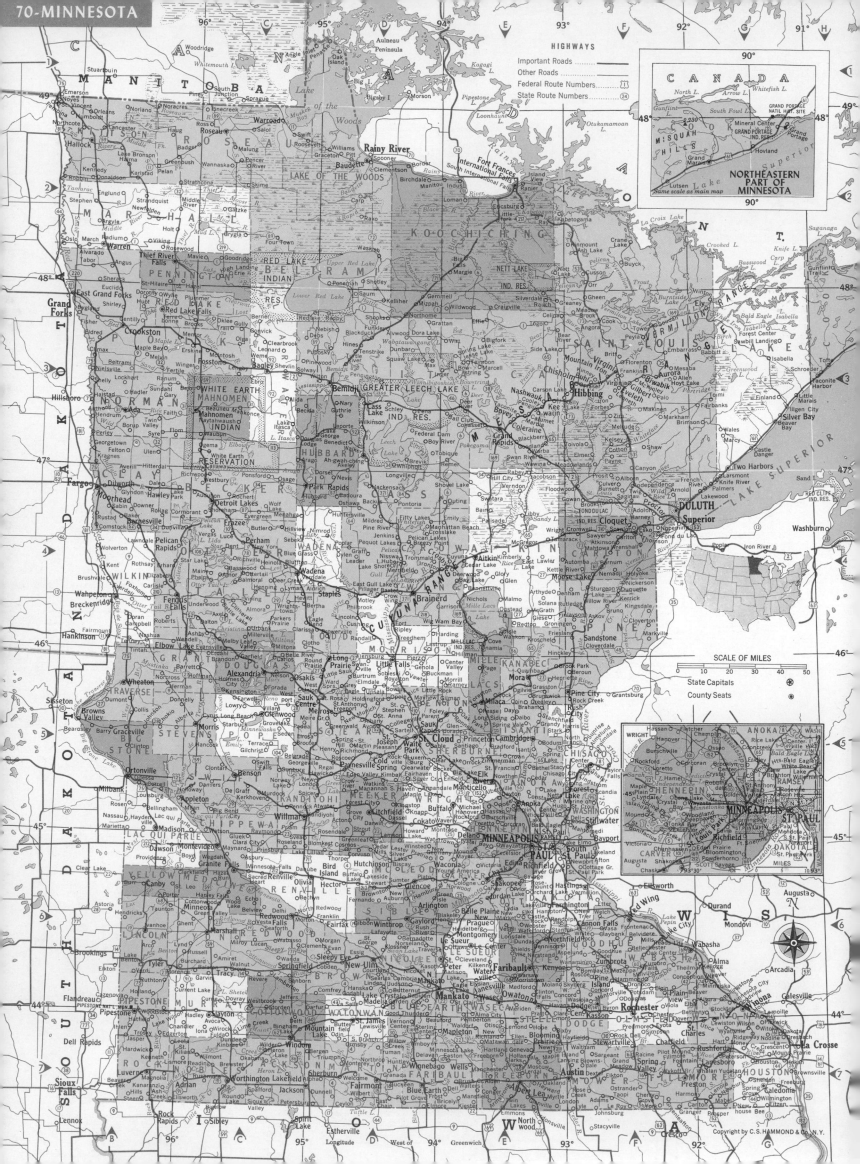

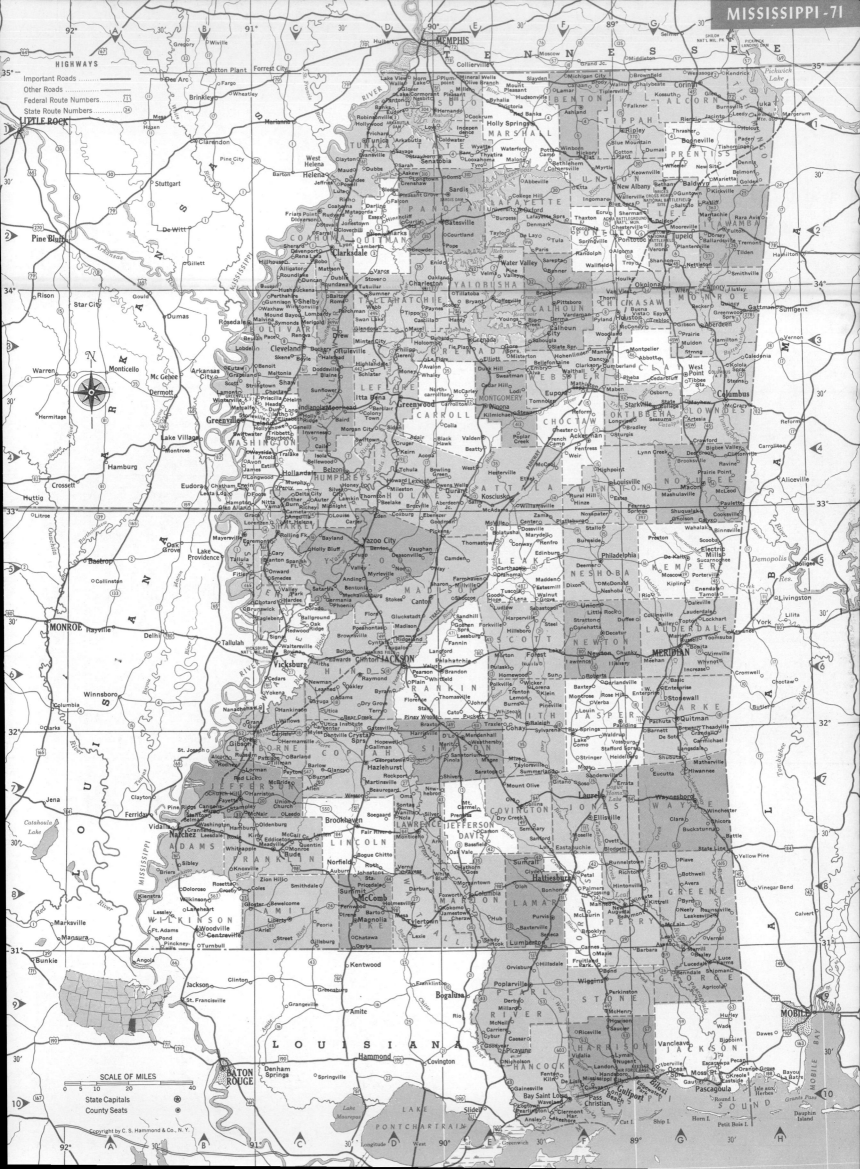

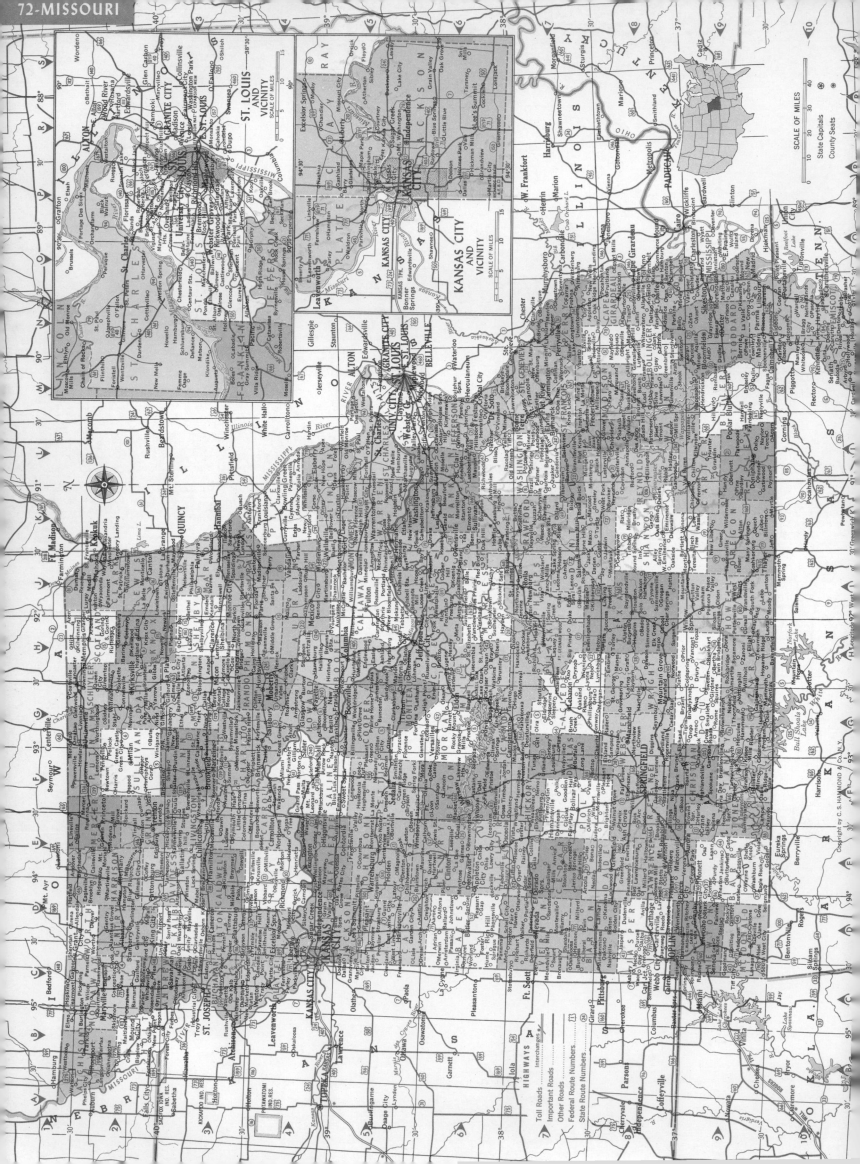

ST. LOUIS AND VICINITY
SCALE OF MILES

KANSAS CITY AND VICINITY
SCALE OF MILES

SCALE OF MILES

HIGHWAYS
Toll Roads
Interchanges
Important Roads
Other Roads
Federal Route Numbers
State Route Numbers

State Capitals
County Seats

Copyright by C. S. HAMMOND & Co., N.Y.

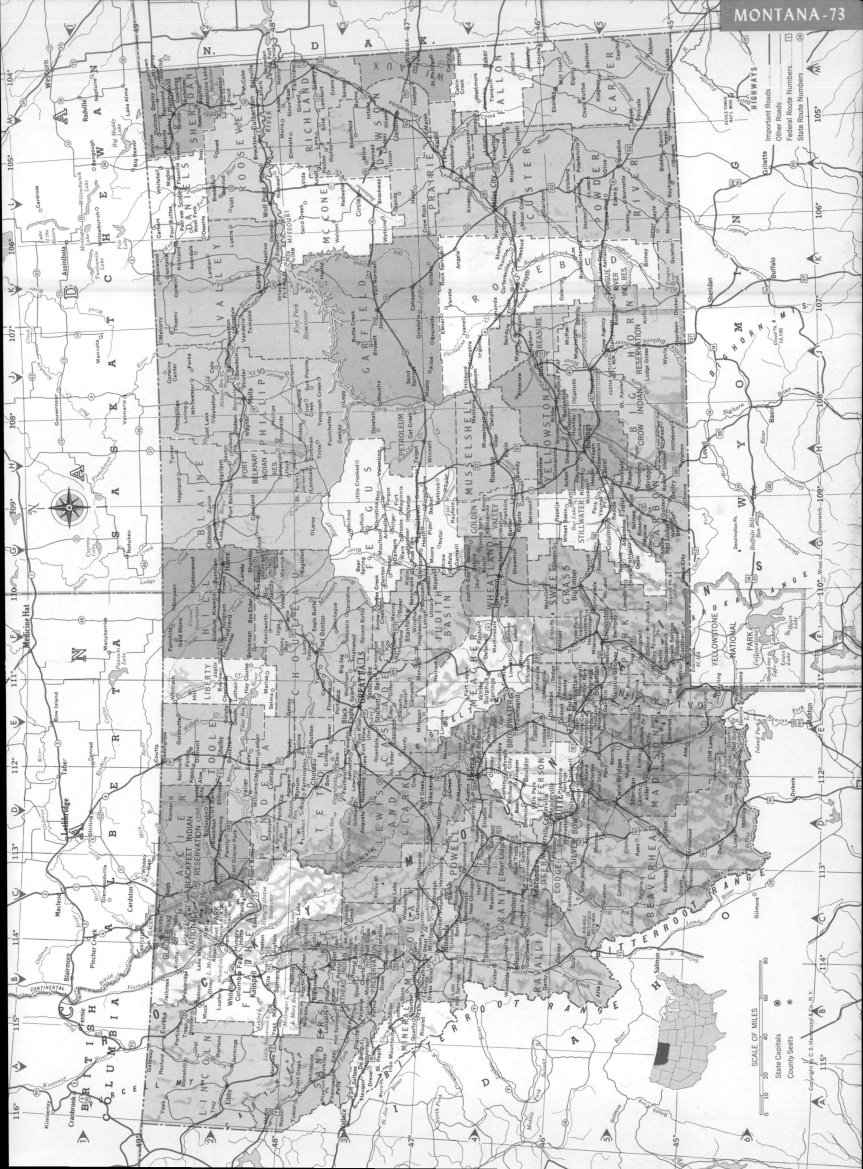

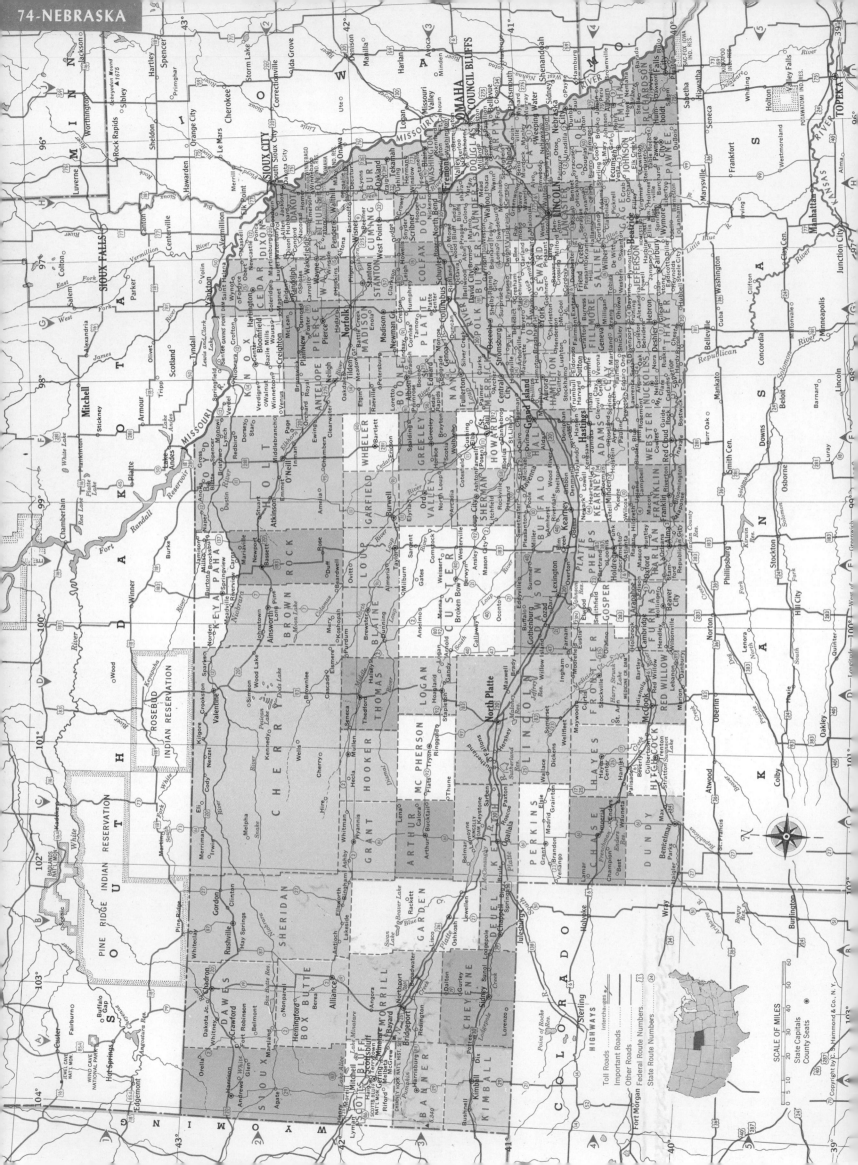

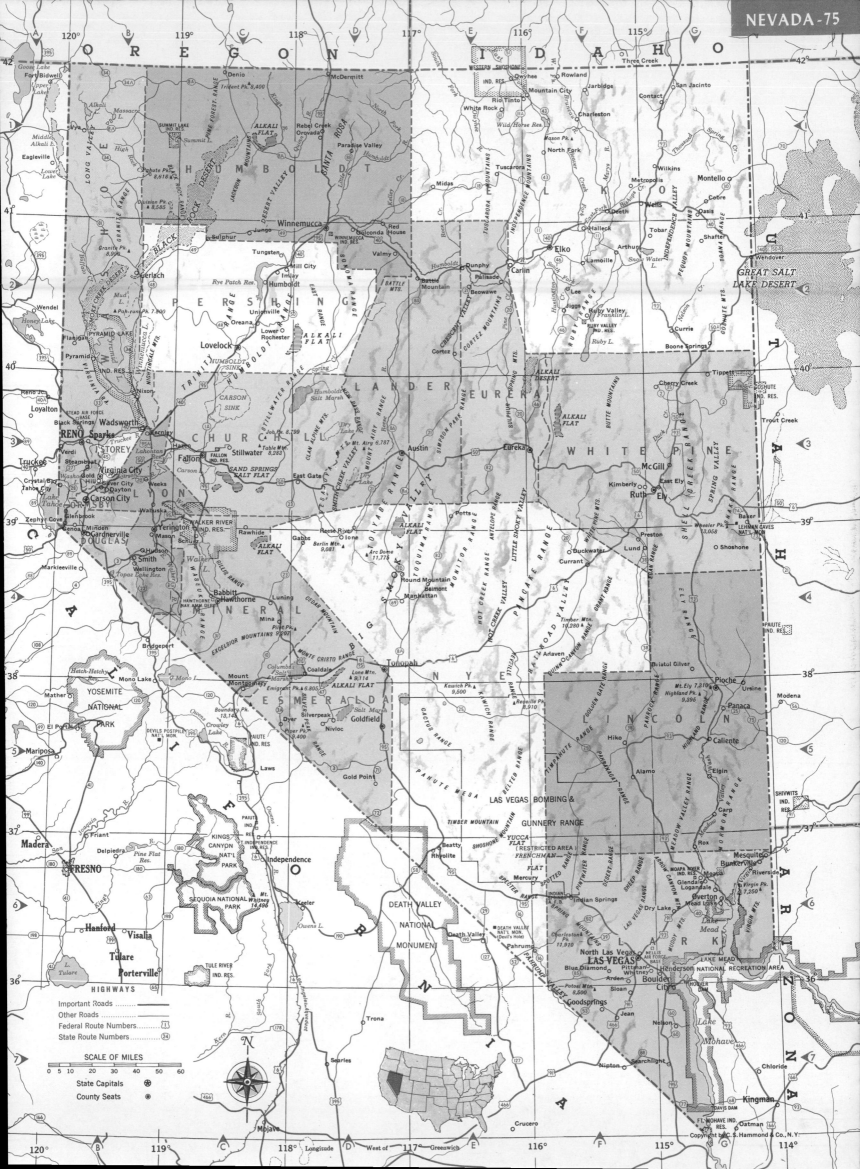

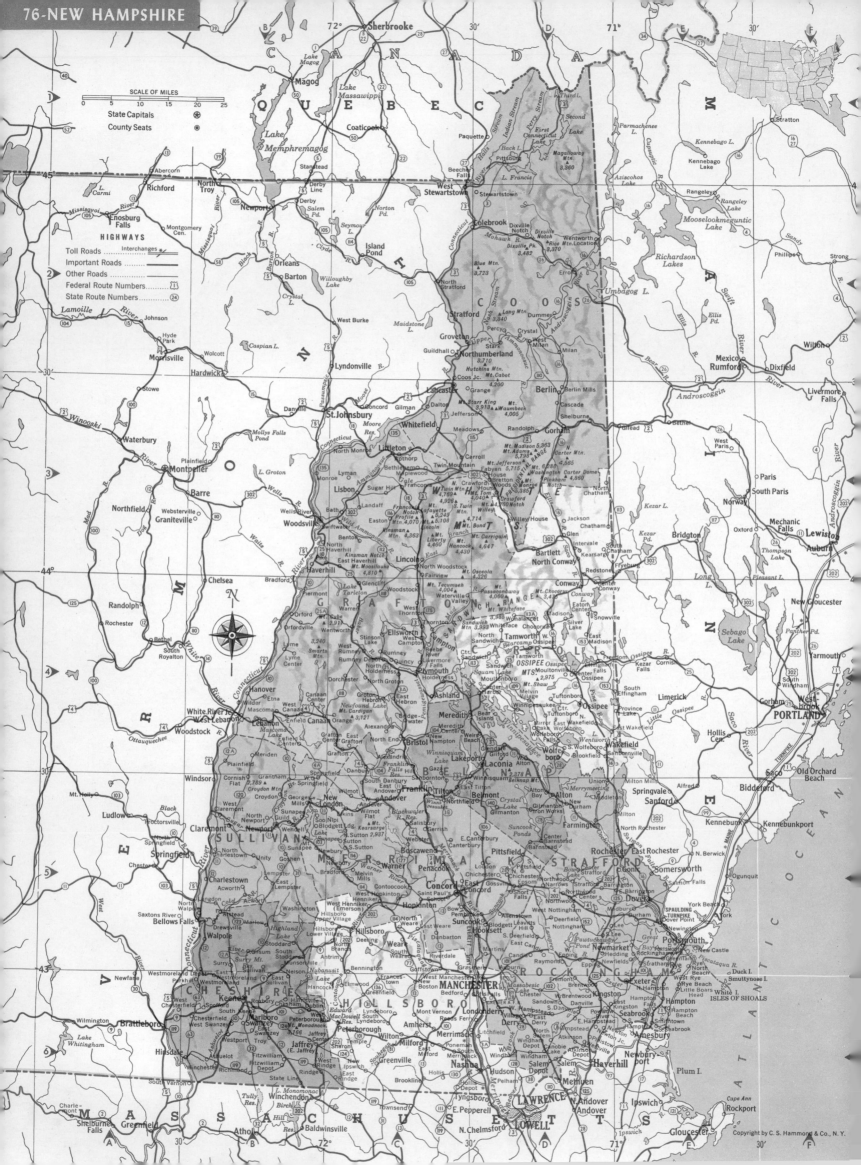

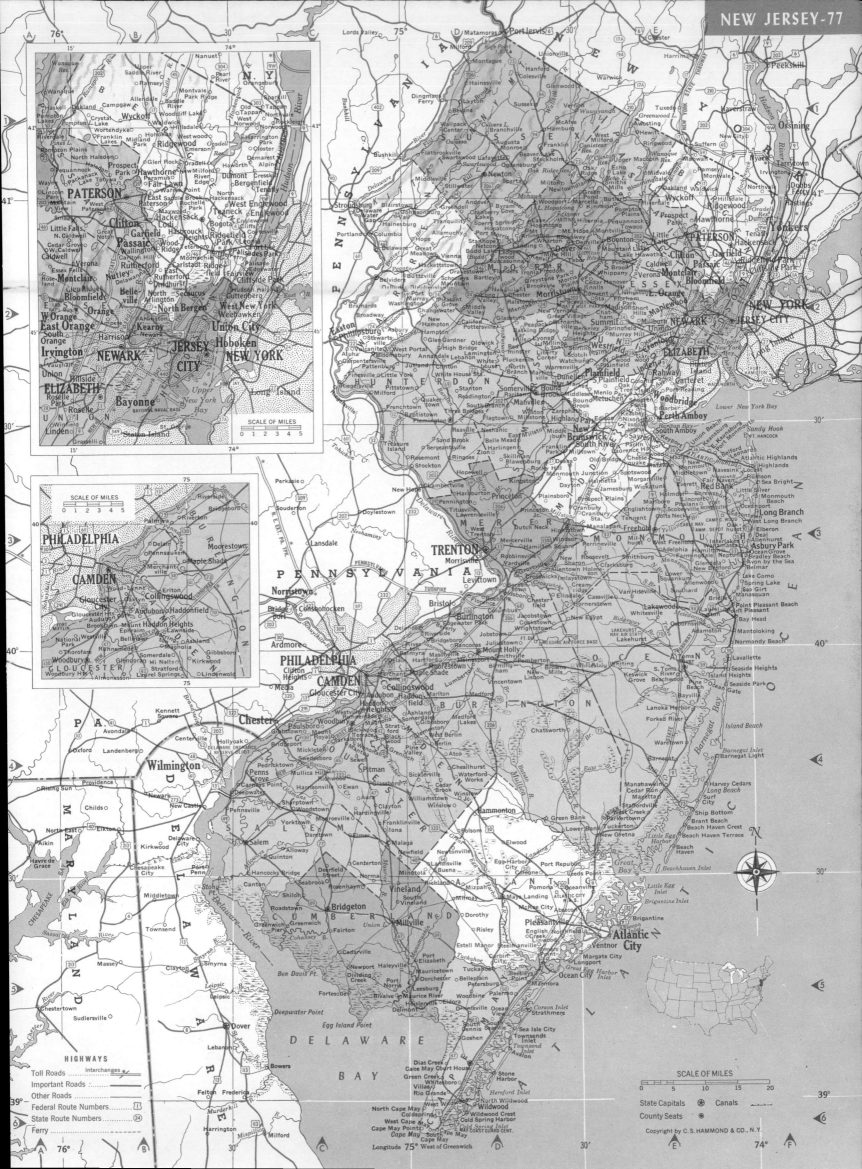

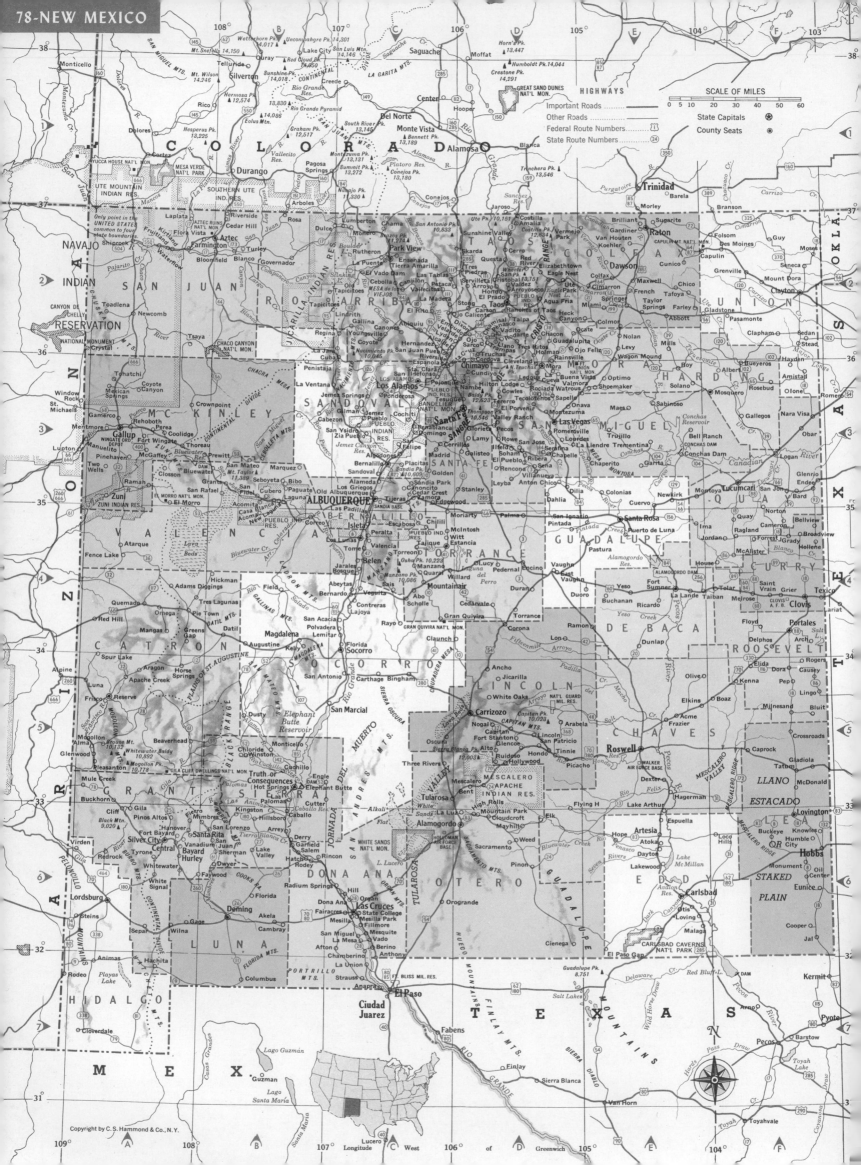

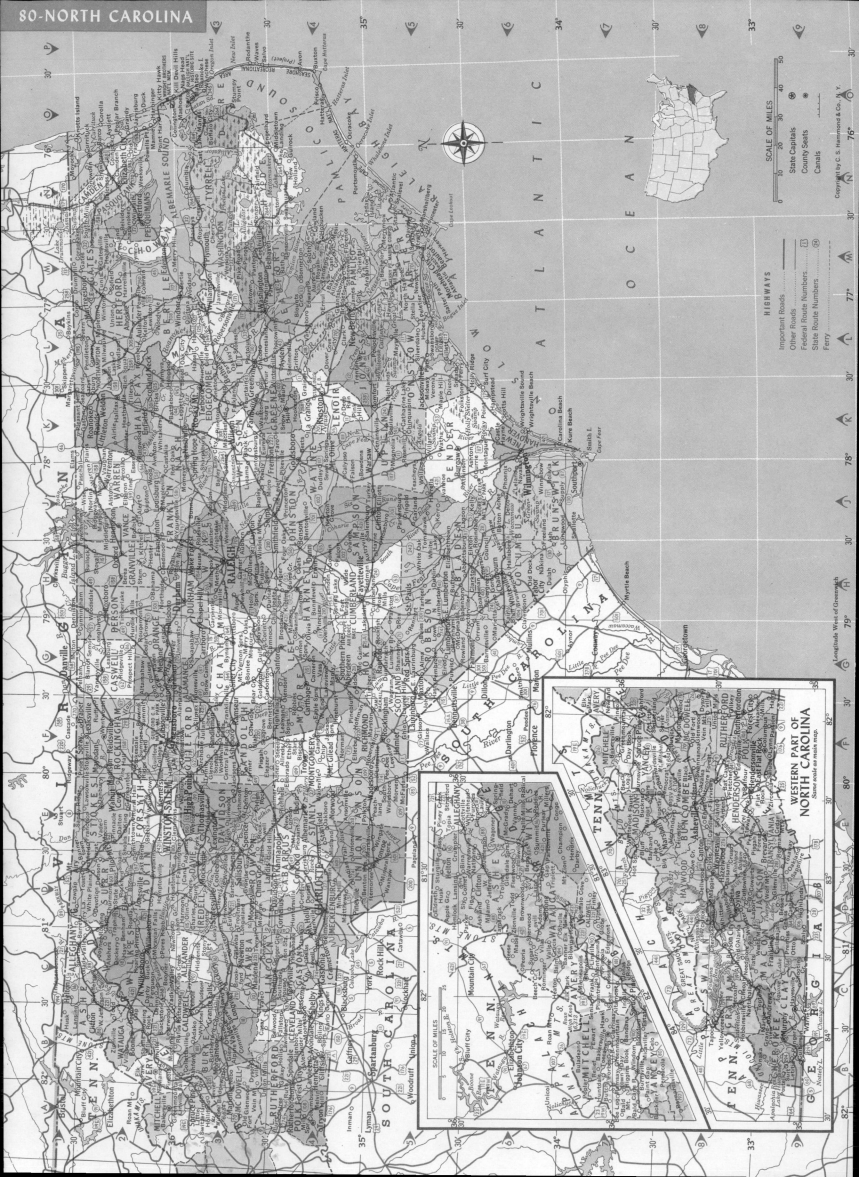

SCALE OF MILES

State Capitals
County Seats
Canals

Copyright by C. S. Hammond & Co., N. Y.

HIGHWAYS

Important Roads
Other Roads
Federal Route Numbers
State Route Numbers
Ferry

WESTERN PART OF
NORTH CAROLINA
Some scale as main map.

SCALE OF MILES

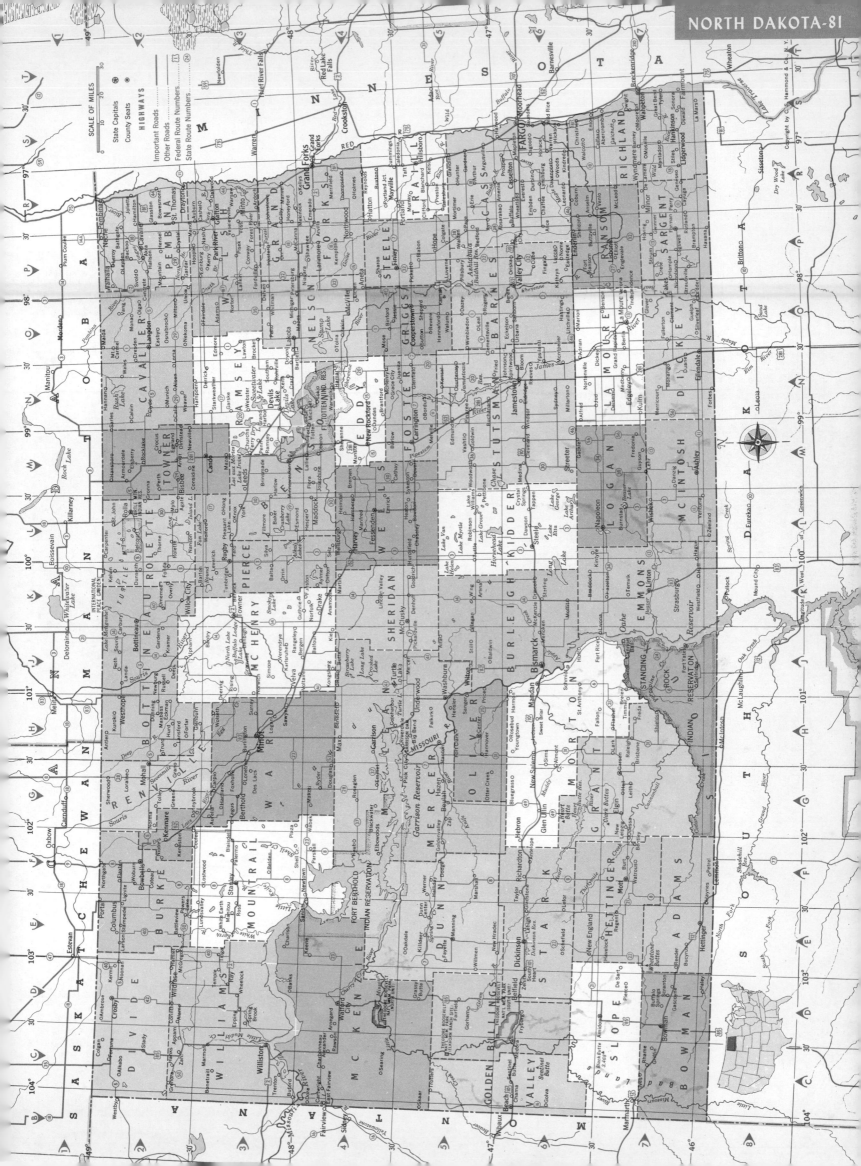

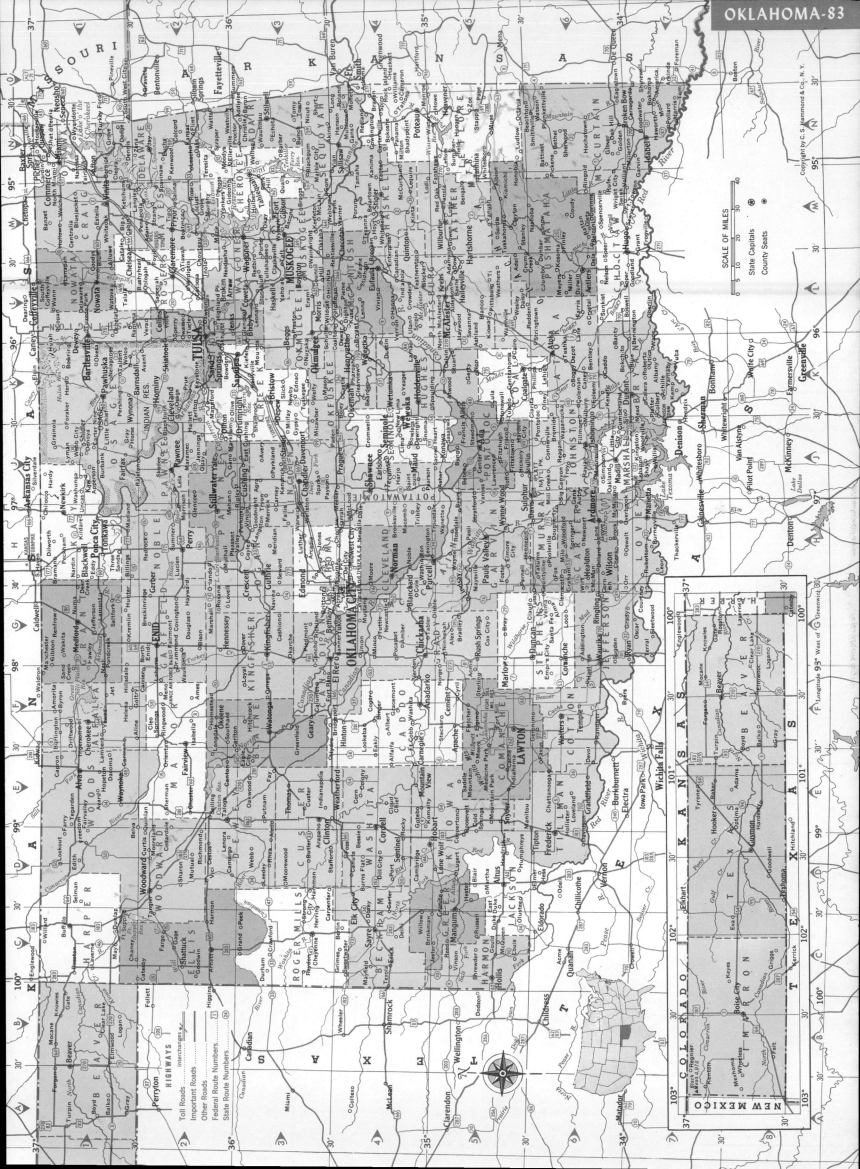

SCALE OF MILES

⊛ State Capitals
⊙ County Seats

Copyright by C. S. Hammond & Co., N.Y.

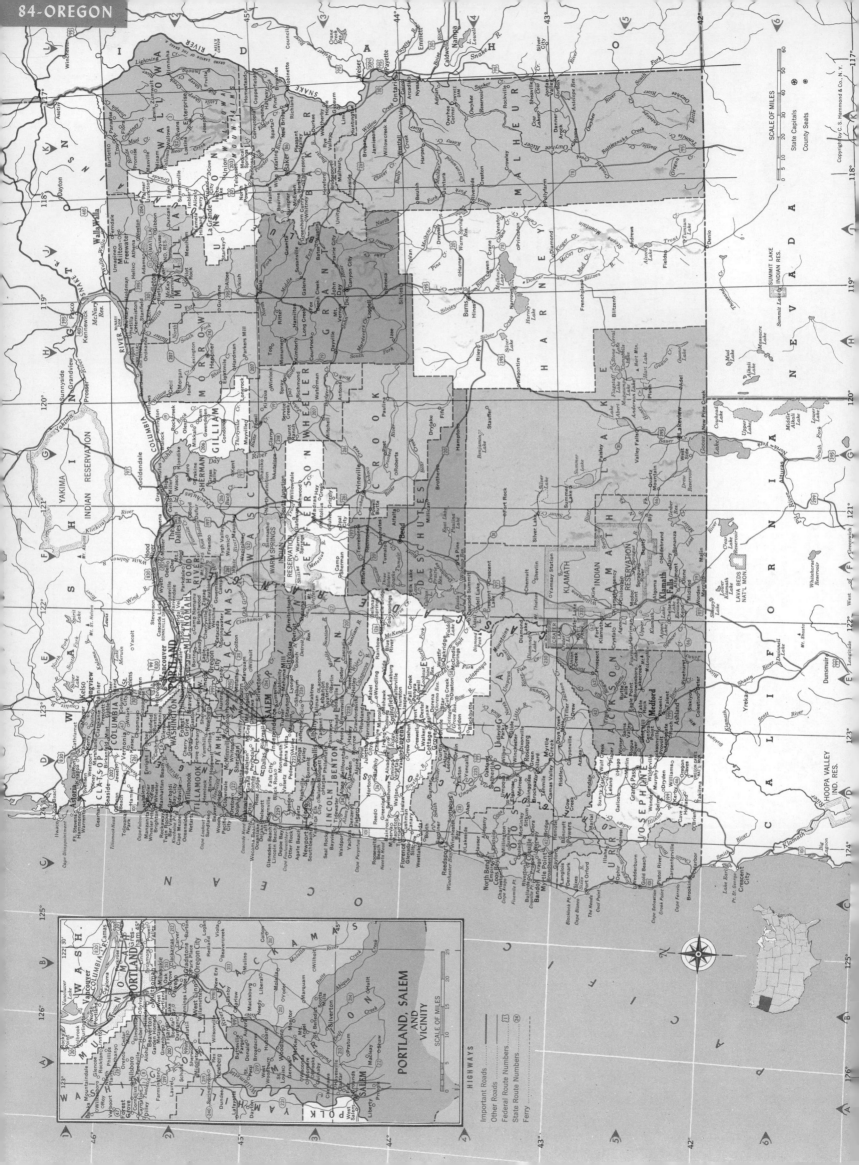

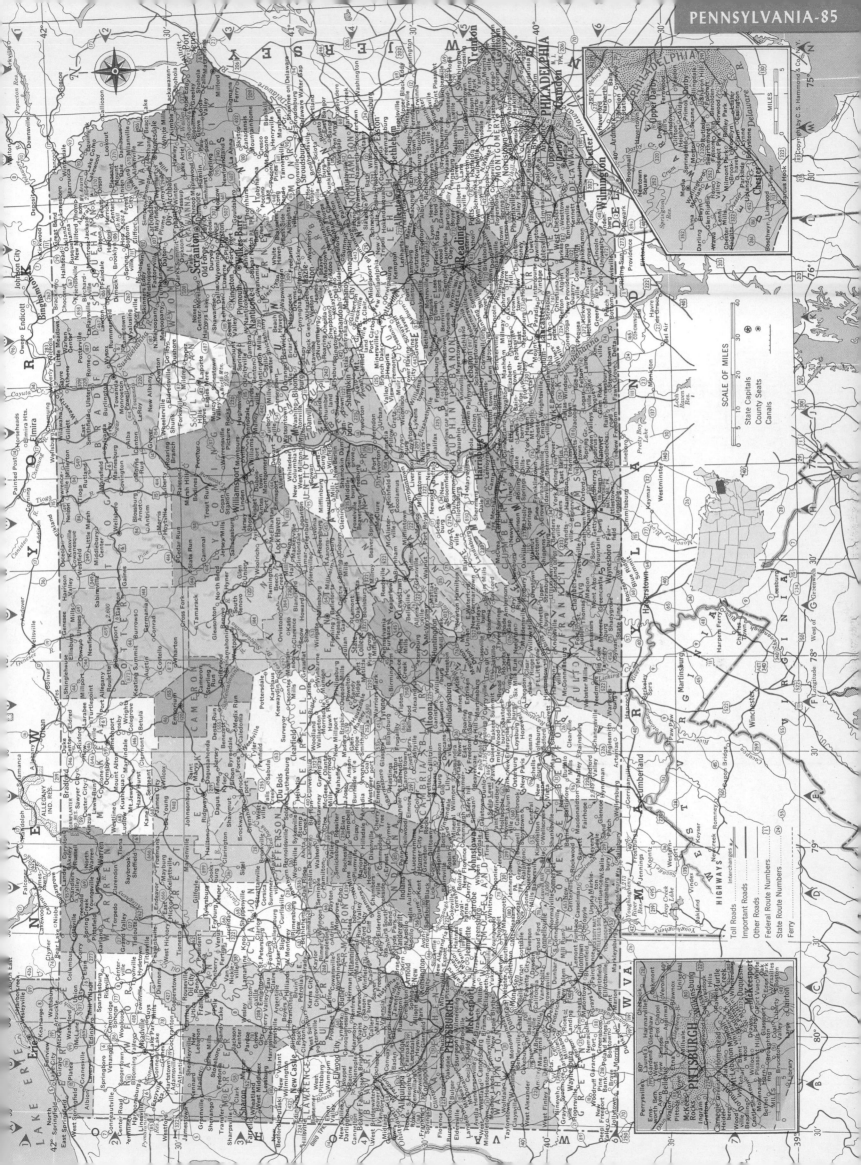

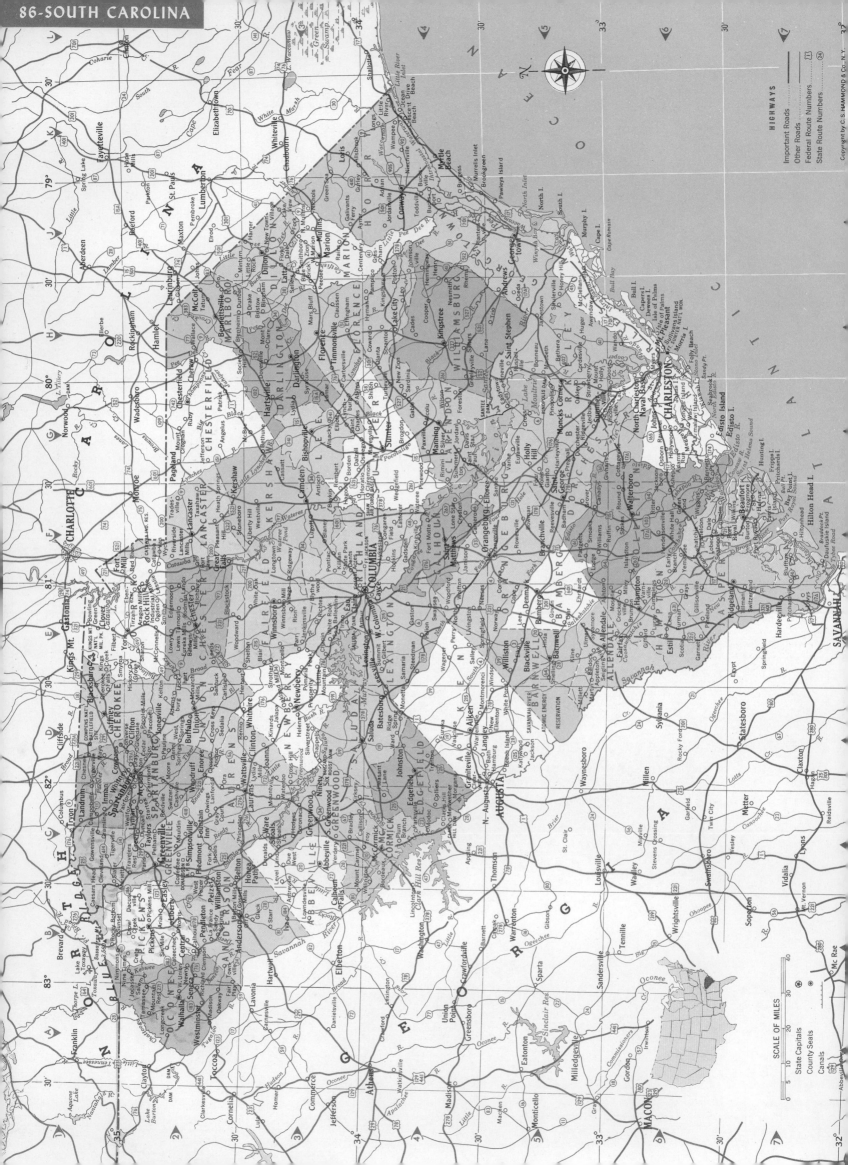

HIGHWAYS

Important Roads
Other Roads
Federal Route Numbers
State Route Numbers

SCALE OF MILES
0 5 10 20 30 40

State Capitals
County Seats
Canals

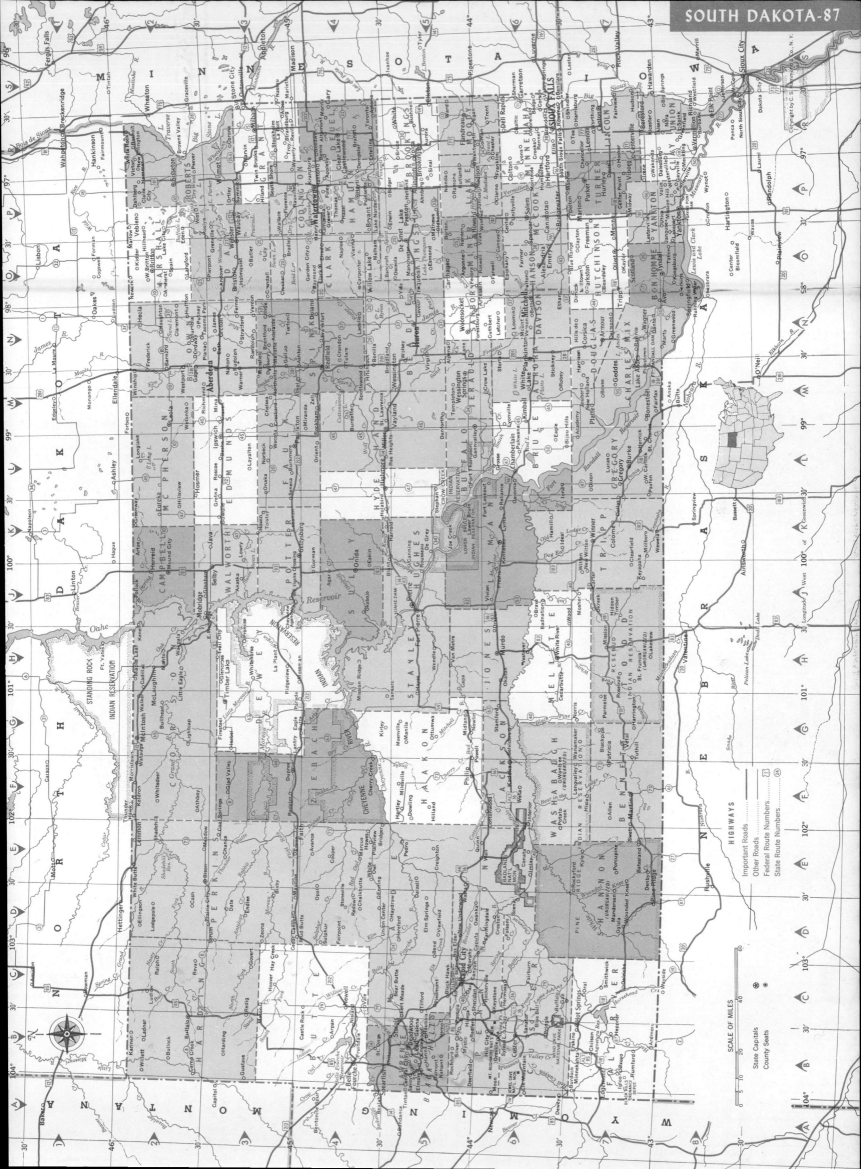

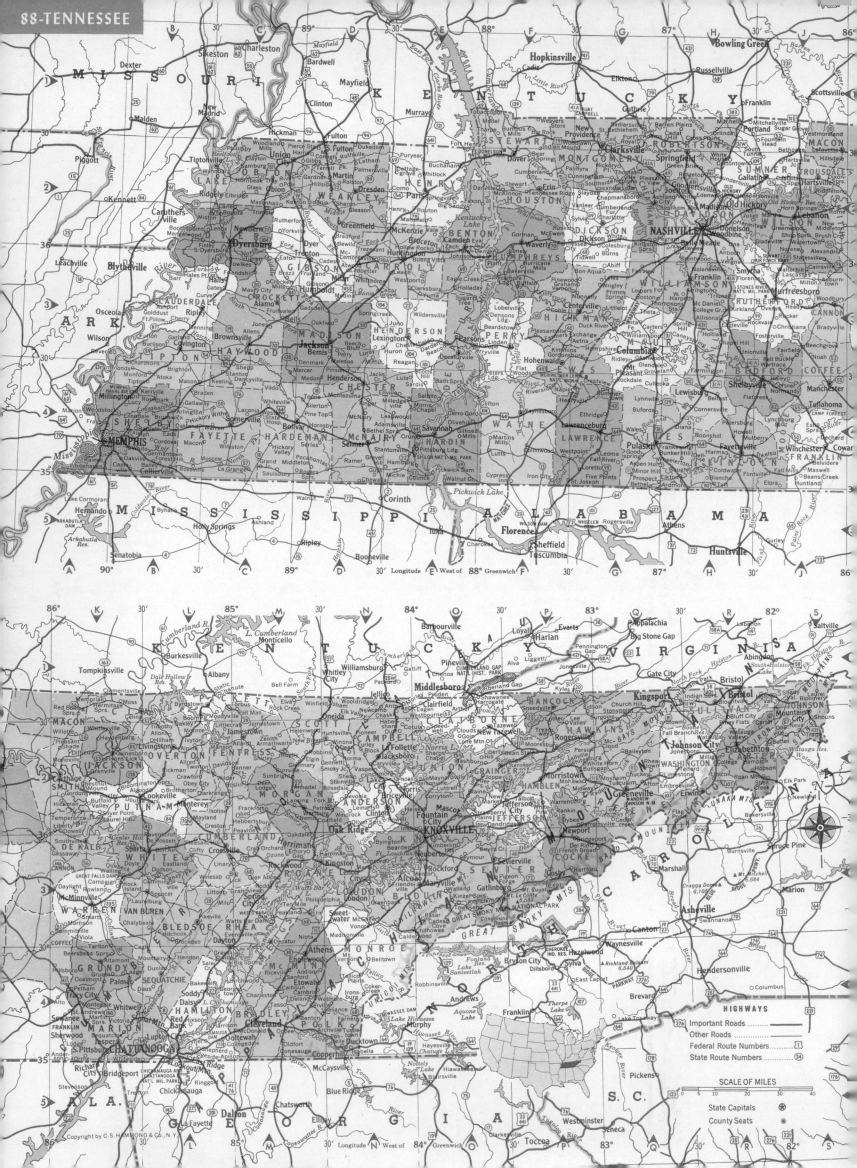

88-TENNESSEE

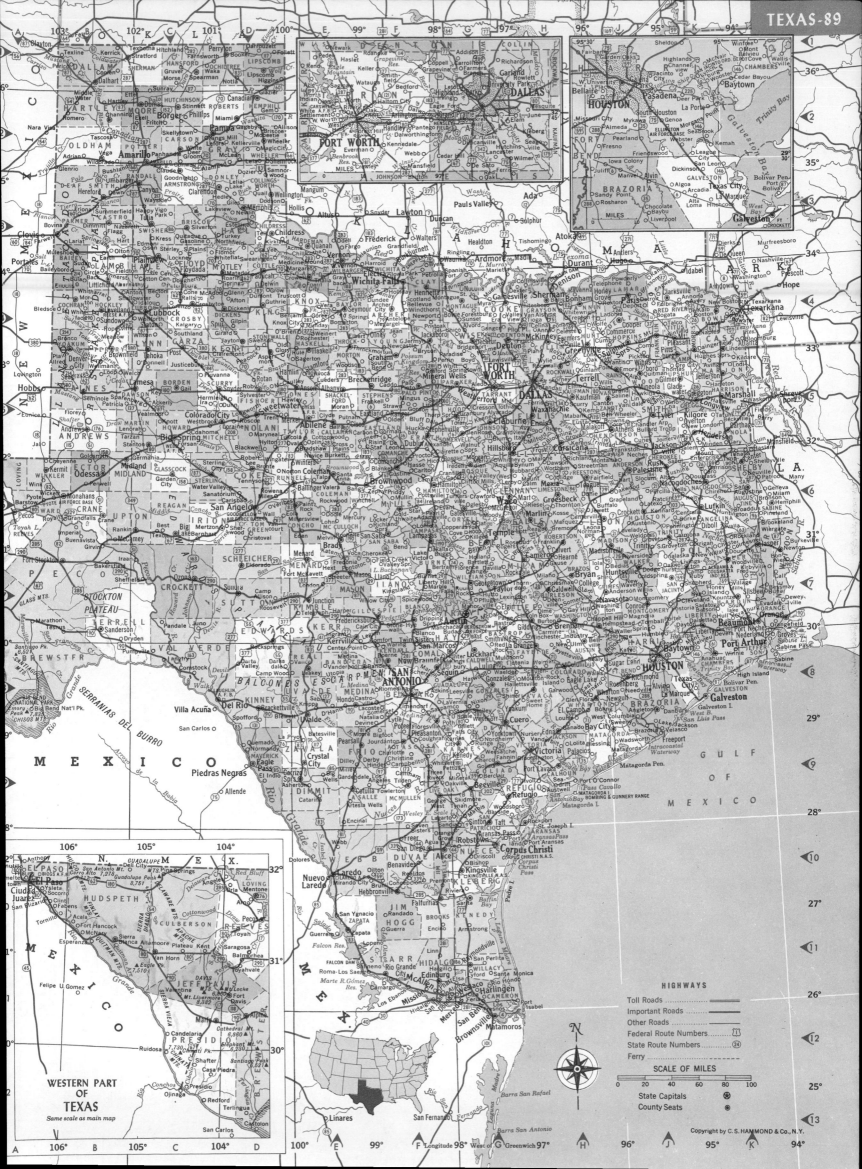

TEXAS-89

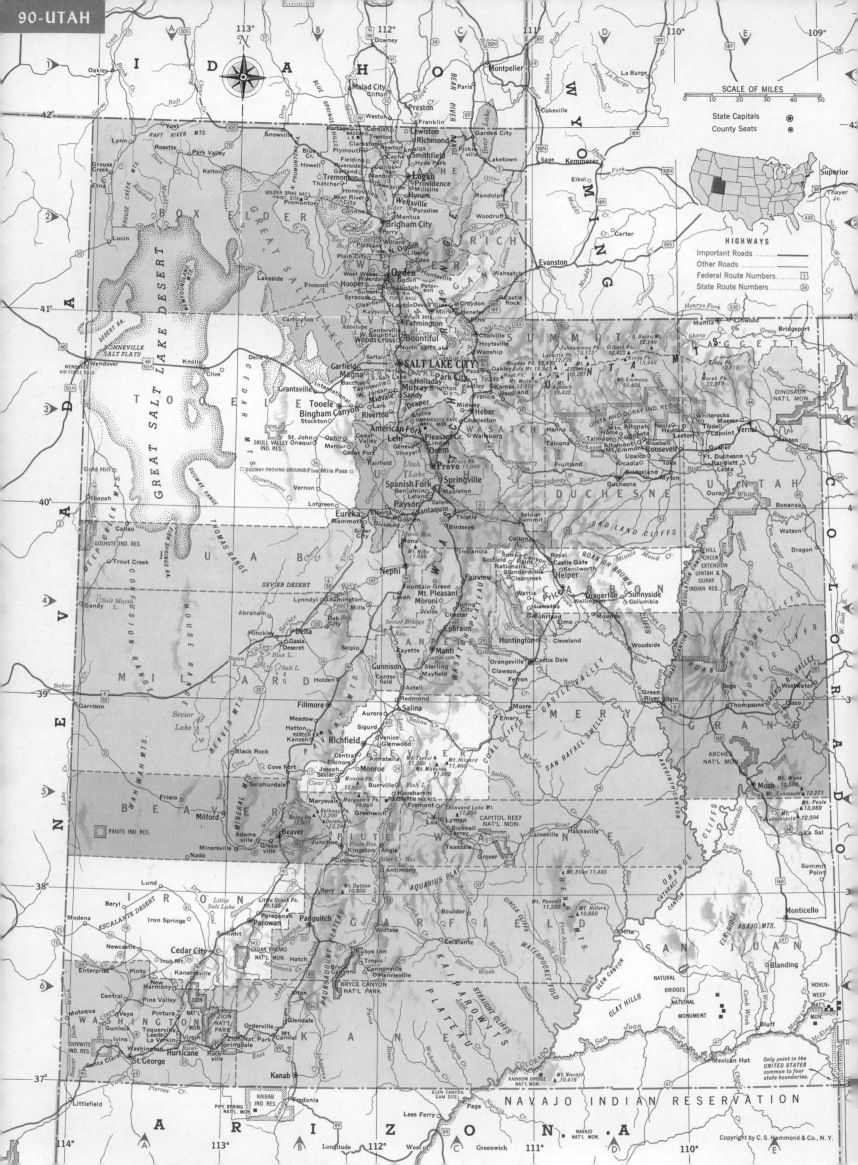

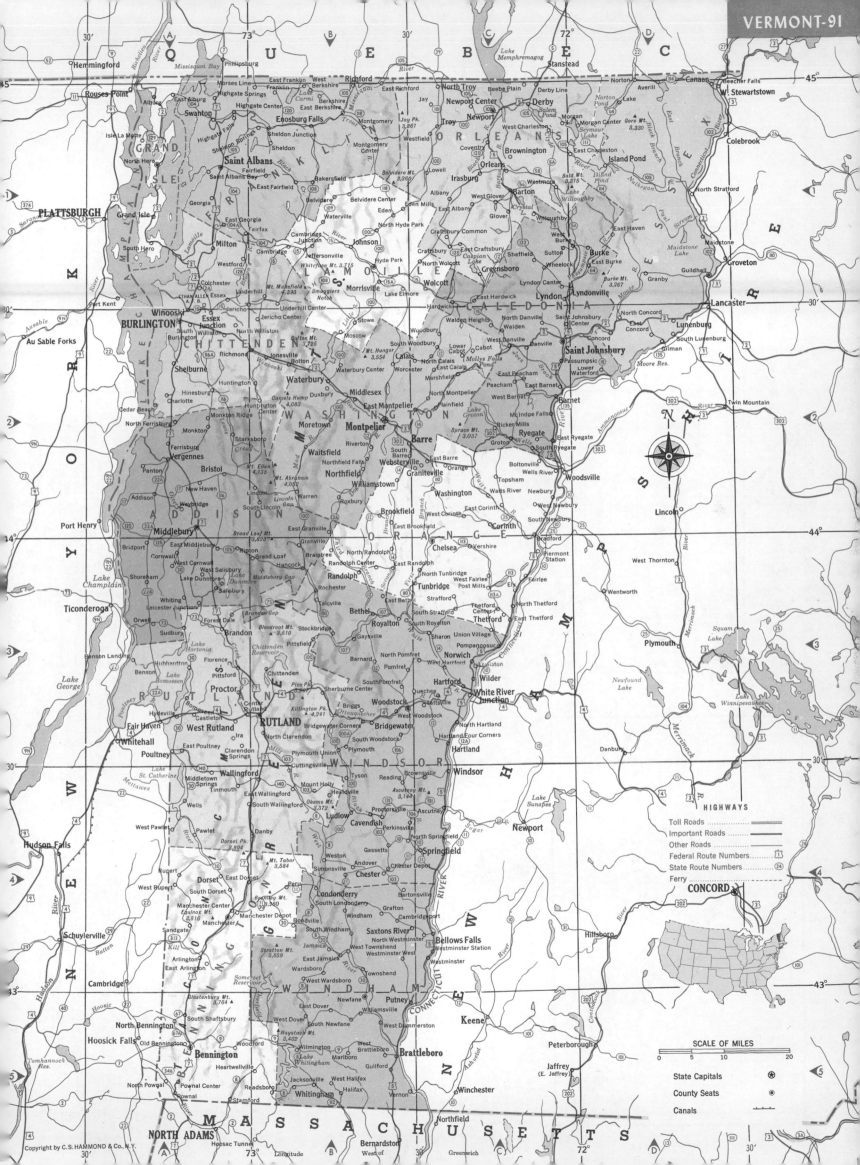

QUEBEC

Hemmingford
Rouses Point
Plattsburgh
Au Sable Forks
Ticonderoga
Hudson Falls
Whitehall
Schuylerville
Hoosick Falls
North Adams

MASSACHUSETTS

GRAND ISLE
FRANKLIN
ORLEANS
ESSEX
LAMOILLE
CALEDONIA
CHITTENDEN
WASHINGTON
ADDISON
ORANGE
RUTLAND
WINDSOR
BENNINGTON
WINDHAM

Saint Albans
Burlington
Montpelier
Barre
Saint Johnsbury
Middlebury
Rutland
White River Junction
Bennington
Brattleboro

NEW HAMPSHIRE

Concord
Keene

NEW YORK

Lake Champlain
Lake George

HIGHWAYS

Toll Roads ....
Important Roads ....
Other Roads ....
Federal Route Numbers ....
State Route Numbers ....
Ferry ....

State Capitals
County Seats
Canals

SCALE OF MILES
0   5   10   20

Copyright by C.S. Hammond & Co., N.Y.

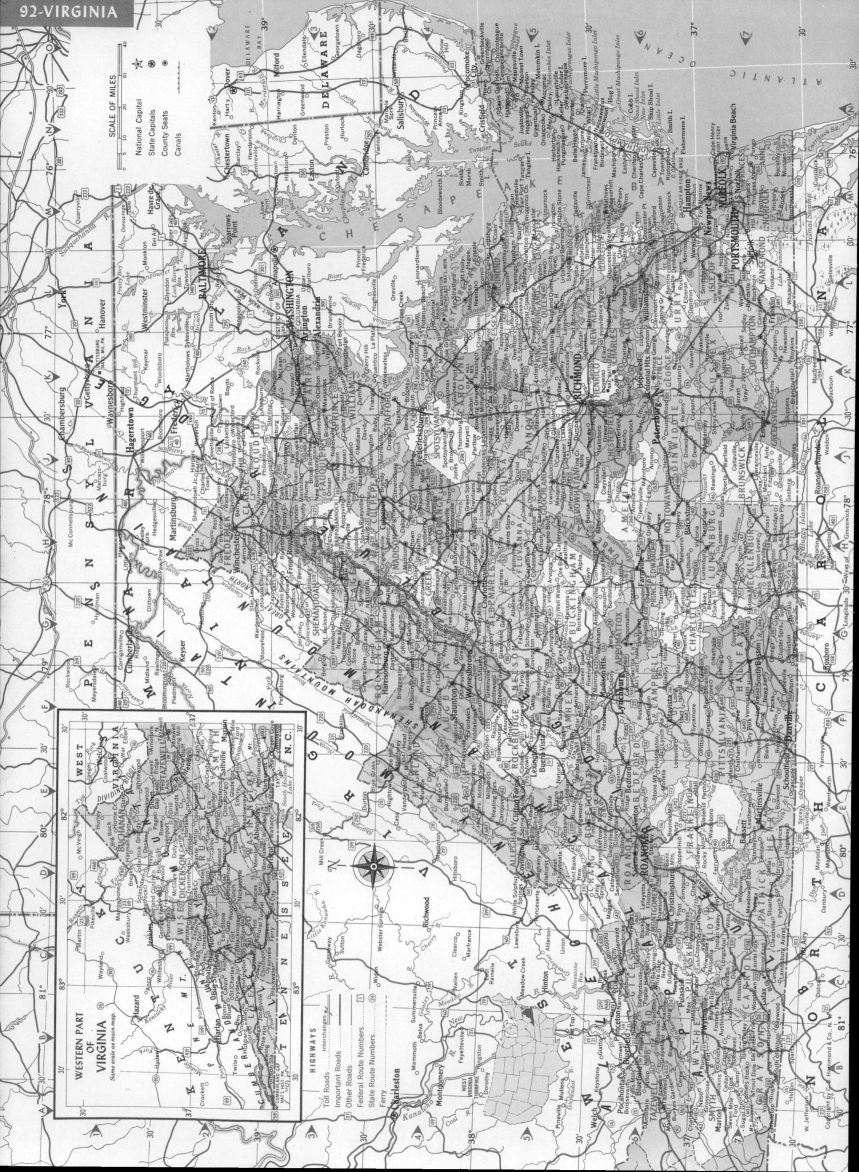

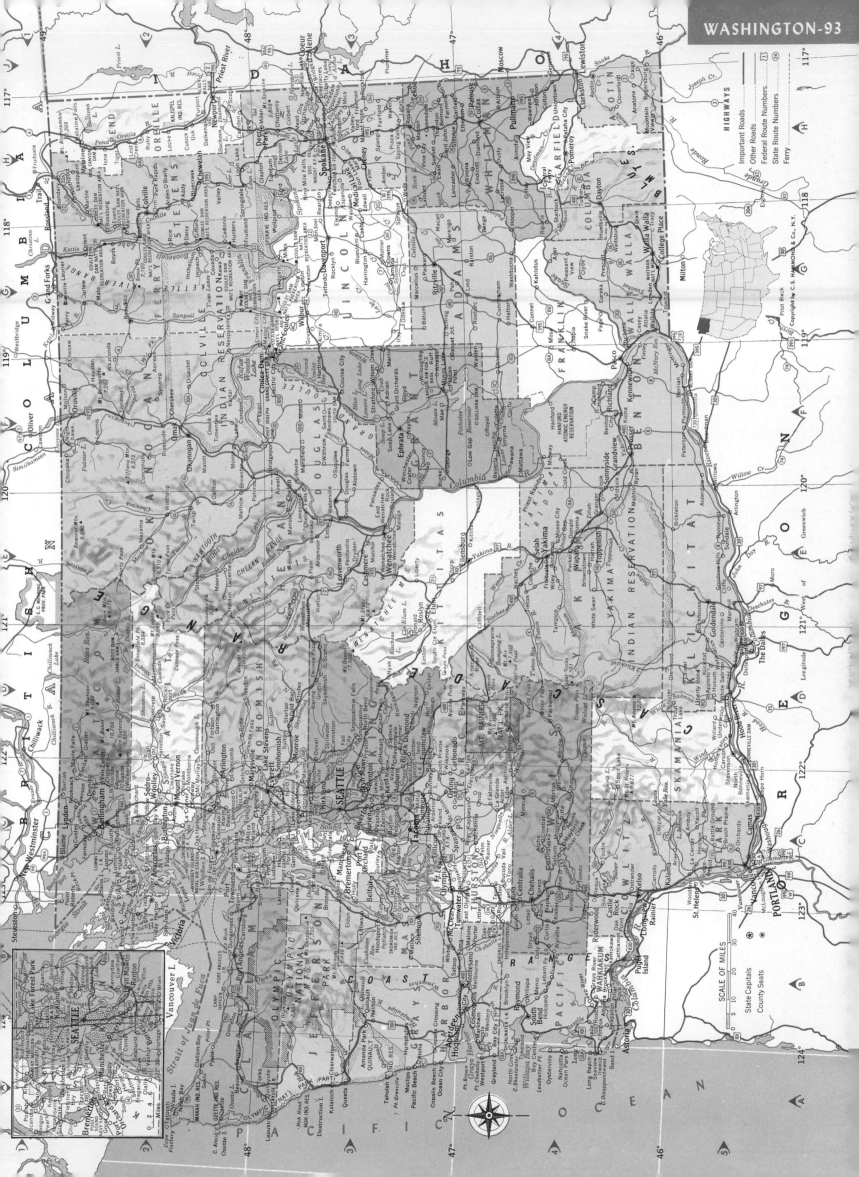

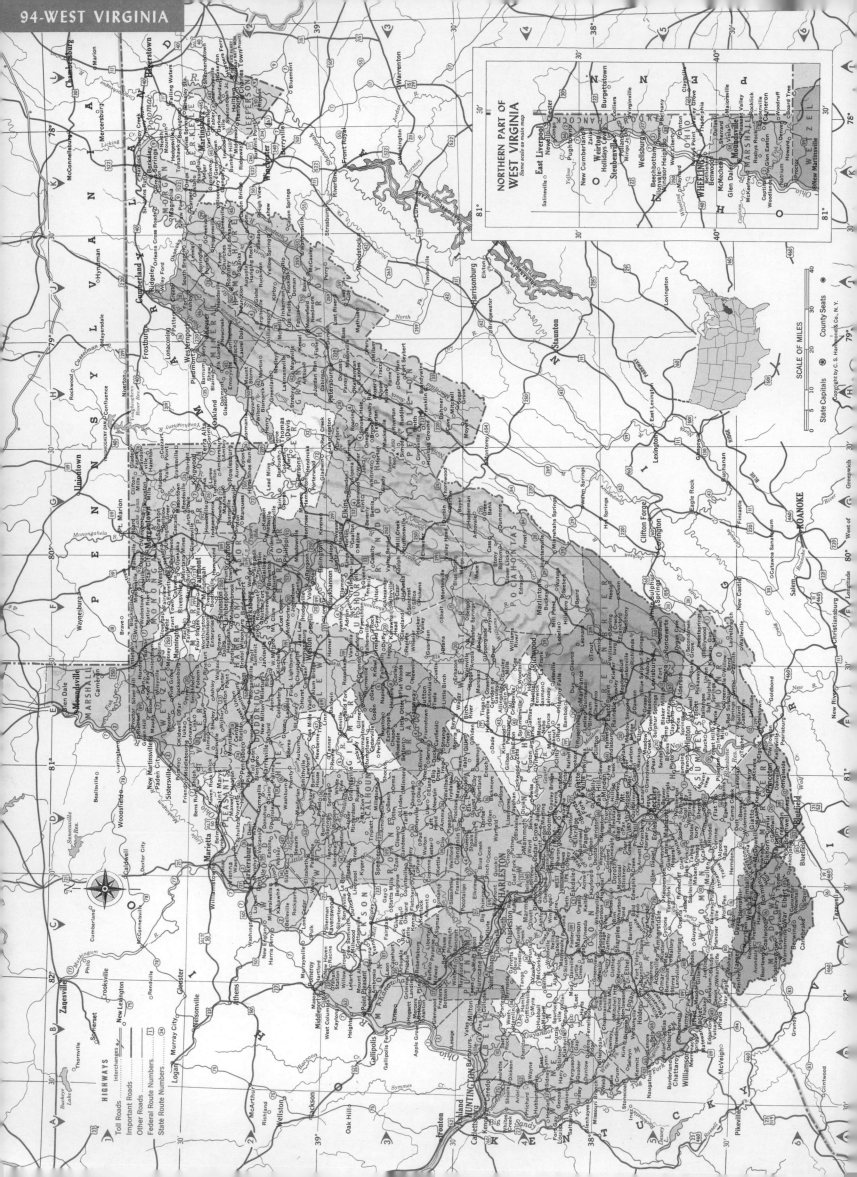

NORTHERN PART OF
WEST VIRGINIA
Same scale as main map

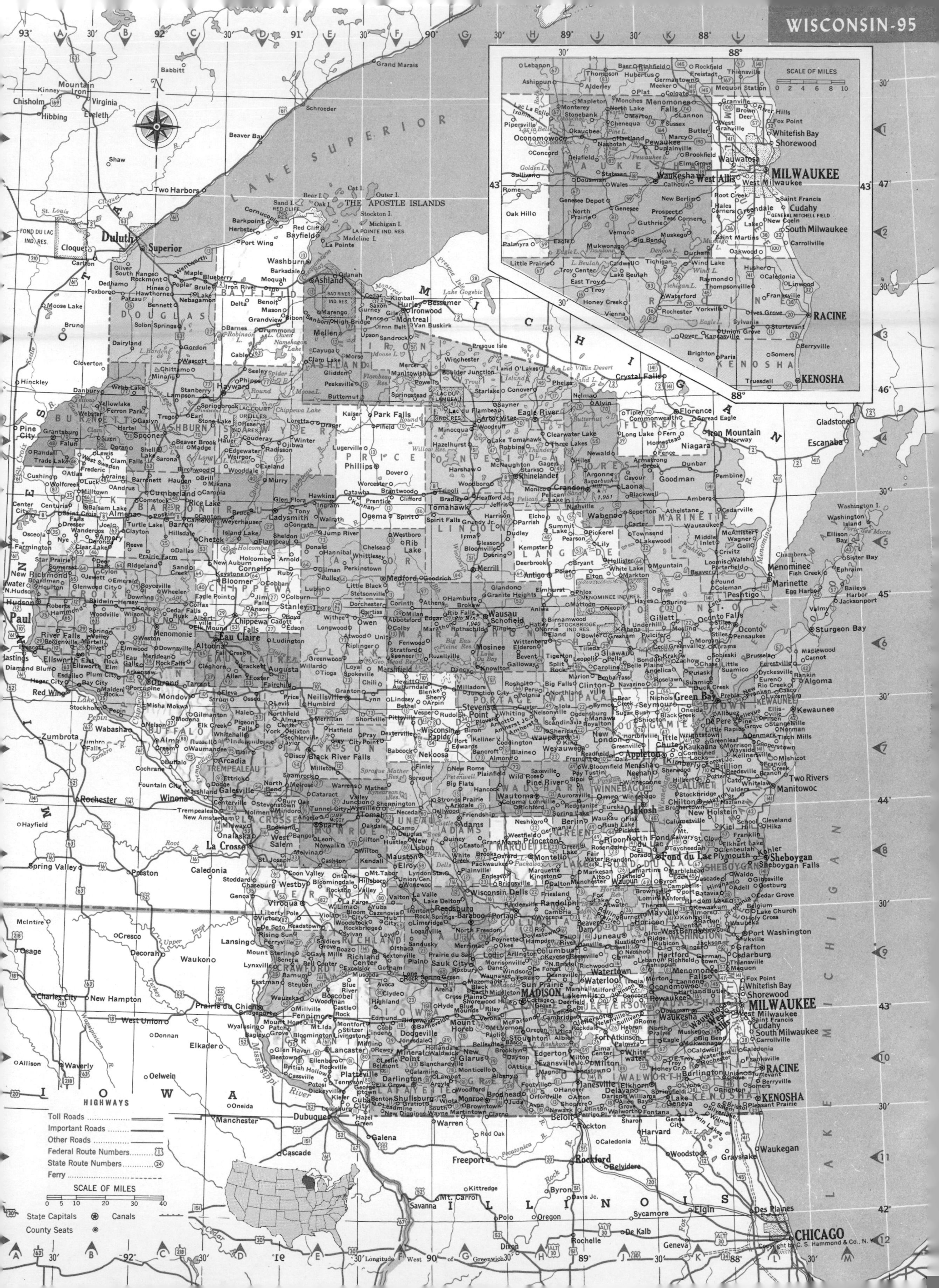

LAKE SUPERIOR

THE APOSTLE ISLANDS

MICHIGAN

MINNESOTA

IOWA

ILLINOIS

LAKE MICHIGAN

HIGHWAYS

Toll Roads ....
Important Roads ....
Other Roads ....
Federal Route Numbers 23
State Route Numbers 24
Ferry ....

SCALE OF MILES
0 5 10 20 30 40

SCALE OF MILES
0 2 4 6 8 10

State Capitals ⊛   Canals
County Seats ●

Copyright by C. S. HAMMOND & CO., N.Y.

MILWAUKEE

MADISON

Green Bay

La Crosse

Eau Claire

Superior

Duluth

Oshkosh

Fond du Lac

Sheboygan

Racine

Kenosha

Manitowoc

Wausau

Appleton

Beloit

CHICAGO

Rockford

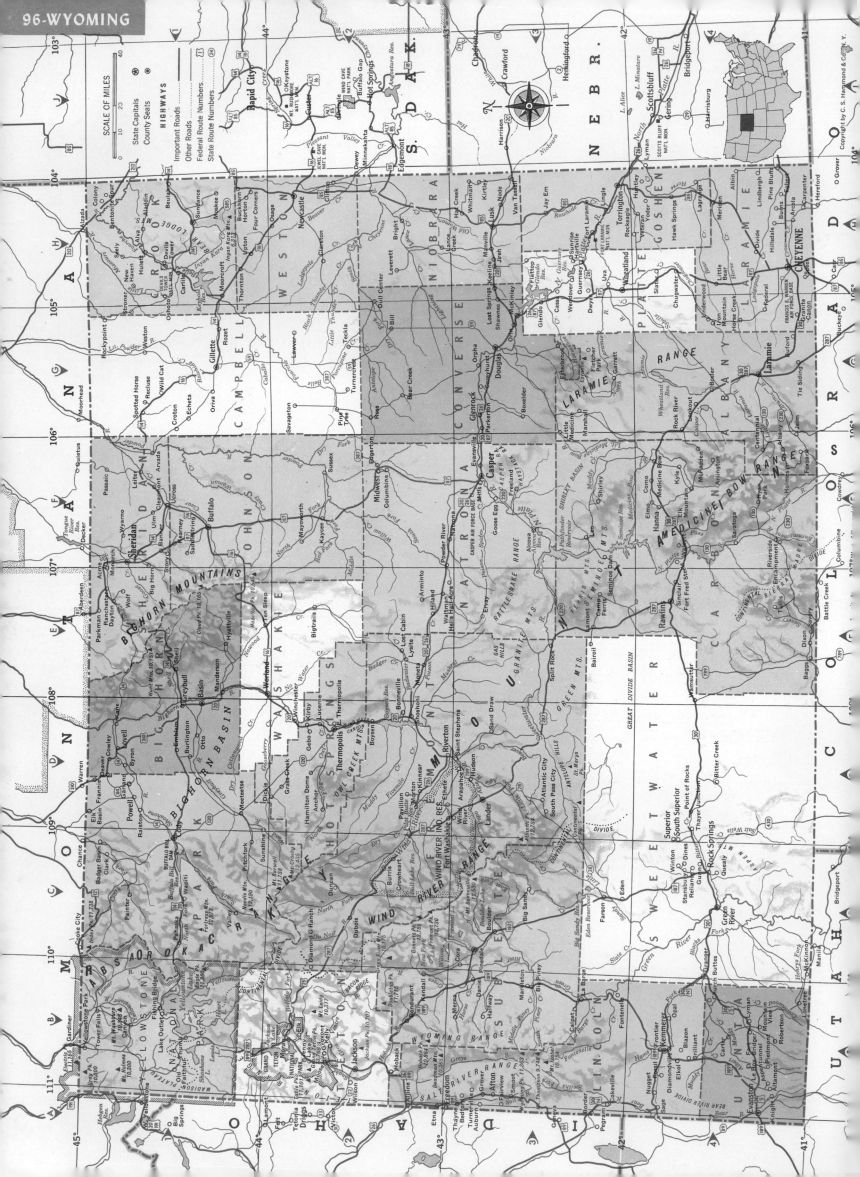

Index of the
UNITED STATES

Introduction

THE INDEX OF CITIES AND TOWNS OF THE UNITED STATES gives the location and population statistics of all cities and towns appearing on the state maps in your atlas. The index entries are arranged alphabetically by states for easy reference and the proper state map page is given at the top of each state index. Each line begins with the name of the city or town, followed by the index reference and the population. The index reference gives the location of the city or town on the state map. The name is found within the square formed by the two lines of latitude and the two lines of longitude which enclose each of the index reference coordinates — i.e., the marginal letters and numbers.

The population figures are the most up-to-date statistics to be found in any reference work. The figures for all incorporated cities and villages are taken from the latest final Federal (1950) Census. The results of a special survey taken by the publishers are given for the population of unincorporated places which are not separately enumerated by the Census. This survey was taken at the same time as the Federal Census and constitutes a major population compilation in itself. Over 25,000 questionnaires were sent to the appropriate local township, county, state or federal authorities. The resulting answers provided the most reliable population statistics available today on unincorporated communities not covered by the Federal Census.

Places listed in the index without a population figure are largely points on the map without permanent inhabitants but which may be locally important as railroad shipping points, crossroad trading centers, or even post offices. In some cases they are communities with fluctuating populations such as resorts or military installations, as for example March Field Air Force Base in California.

A feature of the index especially valuable to the business man, sales manager and advertiser is the inclusion of "urban area" populations for the larger cities according to the 1950 Federal Census. The "urban areas" are defined as consisting of most central cities of over 50,000 inhabitants plus their surrounding built-up suburbs and urban fringes. In many cases the urban area figure gives a truer picture of the relative importance of a city than does the figure for the central municipality. This has become increasingly important with the accelerating movement of population to suburban areas. An example of this is Boston, Massachusetts, with 801,444 persons in the city itself and 2,218,893 in the urban area.

The photographs used throughout this index were used through the courtesy of the various state highway, conservation and publicity bureaus and the Standard Oil Company (N. J.).

160 YEARS OF URBAN AND RURAL POPULATIONS

‡ State	Population in 1950: Urban	Population in 1950: Rural	Per Cent Urban: 1950	1940	1890	1840	1790
Alabama	1,228,209	1,833,534	40.1	30.2	10.1	2.1	.....
Arizona	273,794	475,793	36.5	34.8	9.4	.....	.....
Arkansas	617,153	1,292,358	32.3	22.2	6.5	*	.....
California	7,099,166	3,487,057	67.1	71.0	48.6	.....	.....
Colorado	759,939	565,150	57.4	52.6	45.0	.....	.....
Connecticut	1,286,817	720,463	64.1	67.8	50.9	12.6	3.0
Delaware	147,890	170,195	46.5	52.3	42.2	10.7	*
Florida	1,566,788	1,204,517	56.5	55.1	19.8	*	.....
Georgia	1,381,868	2,062,710	40.1	34.4	14.0	3.6	*
Idaho	234,138	354,499	39.8	33.7	*	.....	.....
Illinois	6,486,673	2,225,503	74.5	73.6	44.9	2.0	.....
Indiana	2,217,468	1,716,756	56.4	55.1	26.9	1.6	.....
Iowa	1,229,433	1,391,640	46.9	42.7	21.2	*	.....
Kansas	903,468	1,001,831	47.4	41.9	18.9	.....	.....
Kentucky	985,739	1,959,067	33.5	29.8	19.2	4.0	*
Louisiana	1,363,789	1,319,727	50.8	41.5	25.4	29.9	.....
Maine	374,507	539,267	41.0	40.5	28.1	7.8	*
Maryland	1,274,618	1,068,383	54.4	59.3	47.6	24.2	4.2
Massachusetts	4,122,138	568,376	87.9	89.4	82.0	37.9	13.5
Michigan	4,099,007	2,272,759	64.3	65.7	34.9	4.3	.....
Minnesota	1,607,446	1,375,037	53.9	49.8	33.8	.....	.....
Mississippi	601,772	1,577,142	27.6	19.8	5.4	1.0	.....
Missouri	2,290,149	1,664,504	57.9	51.8	32.0	4.3	.....
Montana	252,906	338,118	42,8	37.8	27.1	.....	.....
Nebraska	606,530	718,980	45.8	39.1	27.4	.....	.....
Nevada	84,079	76,004	52.5	39.3	33.8	.....	.....
New Hampshire	301,249	231,993	56.5	57.6	39.3	10.0	3.
New Jersey	3,847,771	987,558	79.6	81.6	62.6	10.6	*
New Mexico	314,636	366,551	46.2	33.2	6.2	.....	.....
New York	11,889,008	2,941,184	80.2	82.8	65.1	19.4	11.
North Carolina	1,238,193	2,823,736	30.5	27.3	7.2	1.8	*
North Dakota	164,817	454,819	26.6	20.6	5.6	.....	.....
Ohio	5,273,206	2,673,421	66.4	66.8	41.1	5.5	.....
Oklahoma	1,107,252	1,126,099	49.6	37.6	3.7	.....	.....
Oregon	732,247	789,094	48.1	48.8	27.9	.....	.....
Pennsylvania	6,906,993	3,591,019	65.8	66.5	48.6	17.9	10.
Rhode Island	700,410	91,486	88.4	91.6	85.3	43.8	19.
South Carolina	609,225	1,507,802	28.8	24.5	10.1	5.7	6.
South Dakota	216,157	436,583	33.1	24.6	8.2	.....	.....
Tennessee	1,264,159	2,027,559	38.4	35.2	13.5	0.8	*
Texas	4,612,666	3,098,528	59.8	45.4	15.6	.....	.....
Utah	412,518	276,344	59.9	55.5	35.7	.....	.....
Vermont	137,612	240,135	36.4	34.3	15.2	*	*
Virginia	1,335,944	1,982,736	40.3	35.3	17.1	5.7	1.
Washington	1,274,152	1,104,811	53.6	53.1	35.6	.....	.....
West Virginia	640,606	1,364,946	31.9	28.1	10.7	.....	.....
Wisconsin	1,906,363	1,528,212	55.5	53.5	33.2	*	.....
Wyoming	144,618	145,911	49.8	37.3	34.3	.....	.....
‡ U. S. A.	88,927,464	61,769,897	59.0	56.5	35.1	10.8	5.

* — 100% Rural ‡ Excluding Alaska and Hawaii

POPULATION OF AMERICA'S LEADING CITIES*

City	1950	1940	1890	1840	1790
New York, N. Y.	7,891,957	7,454,995	2,507,414	391,114	49,401
Chicago, Ill.	3,620,962	3,396,808	1,099,850	4,470	....
Philadelphia, Pa.	2,071,605	1,931,334	1,046,964	93,665	28,522
Los Angeles, Calif.	1,970,358	1,504,277	50,395	....	....
Detroit, Mich.	1,849,568	1,623,452	205,876	9,012	....
Baltimore, Md.	949,708	859,100	434,439	102,313	13,503
Cleveland, Ohio	914,808	878,336	261,353	6,071	....
St. Louis, Mo.	856,796	816,048	451,770	16,469	....
Washington, D. C.	802,178	663,091	188,932	23,364	....
Boston, Mass.	801,444	770,816	448,477	93,383	18,320
San Francisco, Calif.	775,357	634,536	298,997	....	....
Pittsburgh, Pa.	676,806	671,659	343,904	31,204	....
Milwaukee, Wis.	637,392	587,472	204,468	1,712	....
Houston, Texas	596,163	384,514	27,557	....	....
Buffalo, N. Y.	580,132	575,901	255,664	18,213	....
New Orleans, La.	570,445	494,537	242,039	102,193	....
Minneapolis, Minn.	521;718	492,370	164,738	....	....
Cincinnati, Ohio	503,998	455,610	296,908	46,338	....
Seattle, Wash.	467,591	368,302	42,837	....	....
Kansas City, Mo.	456,622	399,178	132,716	....	....
Newark, N. J.	438,776	429,760	181,830	17,290	....
Dallas, Texas	434,462	294,734	38,067	....	....
Indianapolis, Ind.	427,173	386,972	105,436	2,692	....
Denver, Colo.	415,786	322,412	106,713	....	....
San Antonio, Texas	408,442	253,854	37,673	....	....
Memphis, Tenn.	396,000	292,942	64,495	....	....
Oakland, Calif.	384,575	302,163	48,682	....	....
Columbus, Ohio	375,901	306,087	88,150	6,048	....
Portland, Oreg.	373,628	305,394	46,385	....	....
Louisville, Ky.	369,129	319,077	161,129	21,210	200
San Diego, Calif.	334,387	203,341	16,159	....	....
Rochester, N. Y.	332,488	324,975	133,896	20,191	....
Atlanta, Ga.	331,314	302,288	65,533	....	....
Birmingham, Ala.	326,037	267,583	26,178	....	....
St. Paul, Minn.	311,349	287,736	133,156	....	....
Toledo, Ohio	303,616	282,349	81,434	1,222	....
Jersey City, N. J.	299,017	301,173	163,003	3,072	....
Fort Worth, Texas	278,778	177,662	23,076	....	....
Akron, Ohio	274,605	244,791	27,601	....	....
Omaha, Nebr.	251,117	223,844	140,452	....	....
Long Beach, Calif.	250,767	164,271	564	....	....
Miami, Fla.	249,276	172,172	....	....	....
Providence, R. I.	248,674	253,504	132,146	23,171	6,380
Dayton, Ohio	243,872	210,718	61,220	6,067	....
Oklahoma City, Okla.	243,504	204,424	4,151	....	....
Richmond, Va.	230,310	193,042	81,388	20,153	3,761
Syracuse, N. Y.	220,583	205,967	88,143	....	....
Norfolk, Va.	213,513	144,332	34,871	10,920	2,959
Jacksonville, Fla.	204,517	173,065	17,201	....	....
Worcester, Mass.	203,486	193,694	84,655	7,497	2,095
Tulsa, Okla.	182,740	142,157	....	....	....
Salt Lake City, Utah	182,121	149,934	44,843	....	....
Des Moines, Iowa	177,965	159,819	50,093	....	....
Hartford, Conn.	177,397	166,267	53,230	9,468	2,6
Grand Rapids, Mich.	176,515	164,292	60,278	....	......
Nashville, Tenn.	174,307	167,402	76,168	6,929	......
Youngstown, Ohio	168,330	167,720	33,220	....	......
Wichita, Kans.	168,279	114,966	23,853	....	......
New Haven, Conn.	164,443	160,605	86,045	12,960	4,48
Flint, Mich.	163,143	151,543	9,803	....	......
Springfield, Mass.	162,399	149,554	44,179	10,985	1,57
Spokane, Wash.	161,721	122,001	19,922	....	......
Bridgeport, Conn.	158,709	147,121	48,866	3,294	......
Yonkers, N. Y.	152,798	142,598	32,033	....	......
Tacoma, Wash.	143,673	109,408	36,006	....	......
Paterson, N. J.	139,336	139,656	78,347	....	......
Sacramento, Calif.	137,572	105,958	26,386	....	......
Albany, N. Y.	134,995	130,577	94,923	33,721	3,49
Charlotte, N. C.	134,042	100,899	11,557	....	......
Gary, Ind.	133,911	111,719	....	....	......
Fort Wayne, Ind.	133,607	118,410	35,393	....	......
Austin, Texas	132,459	87,930	14,575	....	......
Chattanooga, Tenn.	131,041	128,163	29,100	....	......
Erie, Pa.	130,803	116,955	40,634	3,412	......
El Paso, Texas	130,485	96,810	10,338	....	......
Kansas City, Kans.	129,583	121,458	38,316	....	......
Mobile, Ala.	129,009	78,720	31,076	12,672	......
Evansville, Ind.	128,636	97,062	50,756	....	......
Trenton, N. J.	128,009	124,697	57,458	4,035	......
Shreveport, La.	127,206	98,167	11,979	....	......
Baton Rouge, La.	125,629	34,719	10,478	2,269	......
Scranton, Pa.	125,536	140,404	75,215	....	......
Camden, N. J.	124,555	117,536	58,313	3,371	......
Knoxville, Tenn.	124,769	111,580	22,535	....	......
Tampa, Fla.	124,681	108,391	5,532	....	......
Cambridge, Mass.	120,740	110,879	70,028	8,409	2,11
Savannah, Ga.	119,638	95,996	43,139	18,214	......
Canton, Ohio	116,912	108,401	26,189	....	......
South Bend, Ind.	115,911	101,268	21,819	....	......
Berkeley, Calif.	113,805	85,547	5,101	....	......
Elizabeth, N. J.	112,817	109,912	37,764	4,184	......
Fall River, Mass.	111,963	115,428	74,398	6,738	......
Peoria, Ill.	111,856	105,087	41,024	1,467	......
Wilmington, Del.	110,356	112,504	61,431	8,367	......
Reading, Pa.	109,320	110,568	58,661	8,410	......
New Bedford, Mass.	109,189	110,341	40,733	12,087	3,31
Corpus Christi, Texas	108,287	57,301	....	....	......
Phoenix, Arizona	106,818	65,414	3,152	....	......
Allentown, Pa.	106,756	96,904	25,228	....	......
Montgomery, Ala.	106,525	78,084	21,883	2,179	......
Pasadena, Calif.	104,577	81,864	4,882	....	......
Duluth, Minn.	104,511	101,065	33,115	....	......
Waterbury, Conn.	104,477	99,314	28,646	....	......
Somerville, Mass.	102,351	102,177	40,152	....	......
Little Rock, Ark.	102,213	88,039	28,874	....	......
Utica, N. Y.	101,531	100,518	44,007	12,782	......

★ U. S. Census

A closer study of the geography of the United States does much to explain the growth of the nation. For example, the stony soil of New England discouraged farming and caused the early settlers to turn to manufacturing and commerce. The swift streams furnished water power and the jagged coastline provided bays for harboring the ships from Europe. Farther south, the coastal plains widen out into broad stretches of fertile land, and the rivers are short and deep. This led to the development of the large plantations in the deep south, where the climate is favorable to crops that require long hot summers. Here the coastal plain includes half of Georgia, all of Florida, and extends alon the Gulf of Mexico. It reaches into the interior as far north as southern Illinois.

The lake and prairie region of the upper Mississippi Valley is one of the most fertil in the world, and is linked by waterways with the East and South through the Great Lake and the Mississippi River system. The Great Plains region, depending upon the natur of the topsoil and amount of rainfall, is either grain or grazing country, with valuabl deposits of oil in Texas and Oklahoma.

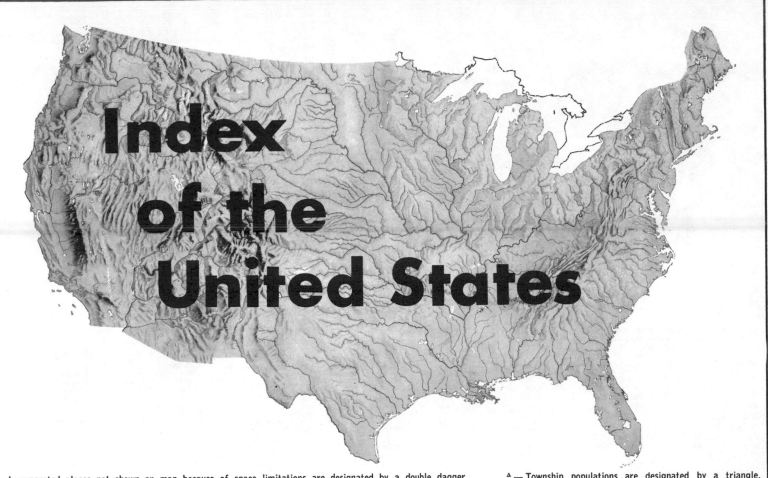

Index of the United States

‡ — Incorporated places not shown on map because of space limitations are designated by a double dagger.
* — Post Offices are designated by an asterisk.

△ — Township populations are designated by a triangle.
Capitals of States are printed in capital letters.

ALABAMA

Map on Page 49   **Total Population 3,061,743**

67 COUNTIES

utauga (E5)	18,186
aldwin (C9)	40,997
arbour (H7)	28,892
ibb (D5)	17,987
lount (E2)	28,975
ullock (G6)	16,054
utler (E7)	29,228
alhoun (G3)	79,539
hambers (H5)	39,528
herokee (G2)	17,634
hilton (E5)	26,922
hoctaw (B6)	19,152
larke (C7)	26,548
lay (G4)	13,929
leburne (G3)	11,904
offee (G8)	30,720
olbert (C1)	39,561
onecuh (E8)	21,776
oosa (F5)	11,766
ovington (F8)	40,373
renshaw (F7)	18,981
ullman (E2)	49,046
ale (G8)	20,828
allas (D6)	56,270
e Kalb (G2)	45,048
lmore (G5)	31,649
scambia (D8)	31,443
towah (F2)	93,892
ayette (C3)	19,388
ranklin (C2)	25,705
eneva (G8)	25,899
reene (C5)	16,482
ale (C5)	20,832
enry (H8)	18,674
ouston (H8)	46,522
ackson (F1)	38,998
efferson (E3)	558,928
amar (B3)	16,441
auderdale (C1)	54,179
awrence (D1)	27,128
ee (H5)	45,073
imestone (E1)	35,766
owndes (E6)	18,018
acon (G6)	30,561
adison (E1)	72,903
arengo (C6)	29,494
arion (C2)	27,264
arshall (F2)	45,090
lobile (B9)	231,105
onroe (D7)	25,732
ontgomery (F6)	138,965
organ (E2)	52,924
erry (D5)	20,439
ickens (B4)	24,349
ike (G7)	30,608
andolph (H4)	22,513
ussell (H6)	40,364
aint Clair (F3)	26,687
helby (E4)	30,362
Sumter (B5)	23,610
Talladega (F4)	63,639
Tallapoosa (G5)	35,074
Tuscaloosa (C4)	94,092
Walker (D3)	63,769
Washington (B8)	15,612
Wilcox (D7)	23,476
Winston (D2)	18,250

CITIES and TOWNS

Abanda (H4)*	125
Abbeville (H7)*	2,162
Abernant (D4)*	
Ackerville (E6)	100
Acmar (E3)*	900
Adamsville (D3)*	1,531
Addison (D2)*	590
Adger (D4)*	500
Aimwell (C6)*	150
Akron (C5)*	684
Alabama City (F2)*	
Alberta (D6)*	200
Albertville (F2)*	5,397
Aldrich (E4)*	1,000
Alexander City (G5)*	6,430
Alexandria (G3)*	300
Aliceville (B4)*	3,170
Allen (C7)*	200
Allenton (E7)*	75
Allenville (C6)	
Allgood (F3)*	350
Allison (C5)	
Allsboro (B1)*	150
Alma (C8)*	50
Alpine (F4)*	
Altoona (F2)*	860
America (D3)*	
Andalusia (E8)*	9,162
Anderson (D1)*	450
Angel (G3)	15
Annemanie (D6)*	100
Anniston (G3)*	31,066
Ansley (F7)*	
Arab (E2)*	1,592
Ararat (B7)	100
Ardmore (E1)*	408
Ariton (G7)*	620
Arkadelphia (E3)*	
Arley (D2)*	300
Arlington (C6)*	200
Asahel (D7)	
Ashby (E4)	75
Ashford (H8)*	1,400
Ashland (G4)*	1,593
Ashville (F3)*	494
Athens (E1)*	6,309
Atmore (C8)*	5,720
Attalla (F2)*	7,537
Atwood (C2)*	250
Auburn (H5)*	12,939
Austinville (D1)	1,110
Autaugaville (E6)*	459
Axis (B9)*	130
Baileyton (E2)*	200
Bakerhill (H7)*	
Bamford (E4)*	12
Bangor (E3)*	
Banks (G7)*	222
Bankston (C3)*	350
Barlow Bend (C8)*	364
Barnwell (C10)	
Barton (C1)*	250
Bashi (C7)*	
Bass Station (G1)	125
Batesville (H6)	
Battles Wharf (C10)*	300
Bay Minette (C9)*	3,732
Bayou la Batre (B10)*	2,196
Bear Creek (C2)*	223
Beatrice (D7)*	375
Beaverton (B3)*	192
Bedford (B3)	
Belgreen (C2)*	255
Belk (C3)*	152
Bellamy (B6)*	
Belle Ellen (D4)*	400
Belle Mina (E1)*	
Belleville (D8)*	300
Bellview (D7)*	50
Bellwood (G8)*	263
Belmont (C5)	153
Beloit (D6)*	250
Benson (G5)	
Benton (E6)*	
Bermuda (D8)*	240
Berry (C3)*	715
Bessemer (D4)*	28,445
Beulah (H5)	
Bevelle (G5)	
Bexar (B2)*	
Bigbee (B7)*	30
Billingsley (E5)*	158
Birmingham (D3)*	326,037
Birmingham (urban area)	438,726
Bishop (B1)	75
Black (G8)*	239
Blacksher (C8)	
Bladon Springs (B7)*	375
Blalock (D6)	15
Blanche (G2)*	104
Blanton (H5)*	
Bleecker (H5)*	250
Blocton (D4)*	1,500
Blount Springs (E3)*	
Blountsville (E2)*	695
Blue Mountain (G3)*	529
Blue Springs (G7)*	111
Bluffton (G2)	
Boaz (F2)*	3,078
Boligee (C5)*	168
Bolinger (R7)*	200
Bolling (E7)*	300
Bon Air (F4)*	360
Bon Secour (C10)*	180
Booth (E6)*	
Boothton (E4)*	814
Borden Springs (H3)*	100
Boston (C2)*	700
Boyd (B5)	300
Boylston (F6)*	500
Bradleyton (F7)*	107
Braggs (E6)*	300
Branchville (F3)*	
Brantley (F7)*	1,102
Bremen (E3)*	
Brent (D5)*	1,100
Brewton (D8)*	5,146
Brickyard (H6)	150
Bridgeport (G1)*	2,386
Bridgeton (E4)	
Brierfield (E4)*	200
Brighton (E4)*	1,689
Brilliant (C2)*	600
Bromley (C9)*	248
Brompton (F3)	
Brooklyn (E8)*	150
Brookside (E3)*	733
Brooksville (F2)*	
Brookwood (D4)*	500
Browns (D6)*	100
Brownsboro (F1)*	100
Brownville (C4)*	350
Brundidge (G7)*	2,605
Bucks (B8)*	60
Buena Vista (D7)*	200
Buffalo (H5)*	188
Buhl (C4)*	
Burbank (B8)*	
Burkville (E6)*	500
Burl (D7)*	100
Burnett (C2)	
Burnsville (E6)*	200
Burnt Corn (D7)*	250
Butler (B6)*	659
Butler Springs (E7)*	
Calcis (F3)*	
Caldwell (F3)	25
Caledonia (D7)*	150
Calera (E4)*	1,361
Calhoun (F6)*	150
Calvert (B8)*	500
Camden (D7)*	931
Cameronsville (G1)*	120
Camp Hill (G5)*	1,296
Campbell (C7)*	126
Canoe (D8)*	
Canton Bend (D6)*	300
Capps (H8)*	110
Capshaw (E1)*	275
Carbon Hill (D3)*	2,179
Cardiff (E3)*	204
Carey (F1)	25
Carlowville (D6)*	400
Carlton (C8)*	
Carrollton (B4)*	710
Carrville (G5)*	760
Carson (C8)*	200
Castleberry (D8)*	667
Caswell (D10)*	33
Catherine (D6)*	200
Cecil (F6)*	150
Cedar Bluff (G2)*	563
Cedar Cove (D4)*	100
Central (F5)*	175
Central Mills (D6)	75
Centre (G2)*	1,672
Centreville (D5)*	1,160
Champion (F3)	
Chance (C7)*	
Chancellor (G8)*	125
Chandler Springs (F4)	
Chapman (E7)*	943
Chase (E1)*	750
Chastang (B8)*	
Chatom (B8)*	609
Chavies (G2)*	250
Chelsea (E4)*	300
Cherokee (C1)*	748
Chesson (G6)*	
Chestnut (D7)*	250
Chickasaw (B9)*	4,920
Childersburg (F4)*	4,023
China Grove (G7)	
Choccolocco (G3)*	267
Choctaw (B6)*	500
Choctaw Bluff (C8)*	500
Chrysler (C8)*	
Chunchula (B9)*	300
Citronelle (B8)*	1,350
Claiborne (D7)*	175
Clairmont Spgs. (G4)*	50
Clanton (E5)*	4,640
Clarence (F2)	100
Claud (F5)	80
Clayton (G7)*	1,583
Cleveland (E3)*	400
Clinton (C5)*	200
Clio (G7)*	840
Clopton (G7)*	140
Cloverdale (C1)*	250
Coal Bluff (D7)*	150
Coal Valley (D3)*	140
Coaling (D4)*	
Coatopa (B6)*	125
Cobb City (G3)	20
Cochrane (B4)*	200
Coden (B10)*	
Coffee Springs (G8)*	173
Coffeeville (B7)*	211
Cohasset (E8)	
Coker (C4)*	325
Coleanor (E4)	25
Collbran (G2)*	109
Collinsville (G2)*	1,023
Collirene (E6)	
Columbia (H8)*	849
Columbiana (E4)*	1,761
Columbus City (F2)*	75
Comer (H6)*	150
Consul (C6)*	
Cooks Springs (F3)*	300
Cooper (E5)*	300
Coosada (F5)*	207
Copeland (B7)*	
Cordova (D3)*	3,156
Corona (C3)*	225
Cortelyou (B8)*	
Cottage Grove (F5)*	400
Cotton Hill (H7)	
Cottondale (D4)*	
Cottonton (H6)*	125
Cottonville (F2)	60
Cottonwood (H8)*	864
Courtland (D1)*	507
Covin (C3)*	110
Cowarts (H8)*	300
Coy (D7)*	
Cragford (G4)*	200
Crane Hill (D2)*	
Crawford (H6)	100
Creek Stand (G6)*	50
Creola (B9)*	25
Crews (B3)*	
Crichton (B9)*	
Cromwell (B6)*	200
Cropwell (F3)*	125
Crosby (H8)	50
Crossville (G2)*	609
Cuba (B6)*	525
Cullman (E2)*	7,523
Cullomburg (B7)*	350
Cusseta (H5)*	350
Cypress (C5)*	165
Dadeville (G5)*	2,354
Daleville (G8)*	300
Dallas Mills (E1)*	2,200
Dancy (B4)*	200
Danville (D2)*	350
Daphne (C9)*	1,041
Darlington (D7)*	150
Dauphin Island (B10)*	
Daviston (G4)*	110
Dawes (B9)*	
Dawson (G2)*	
Dayton (C6)*	85
De Armanville (G3)*	260
Deatsville (F5)*	200
Decatur (D1)*	19,974
Deer Park (B8)*	200
Delmar (C2)*	350
Delta (G4)*	150
Demopolis (C6)*	5,004
Detroit (B2)*	250
Devenport (F6)*	150
Dickinson (C7)*	250
Dixie (E8)*	50
Dixons Mills (C6)*	350
Dixonville (E8)*	
Dolomite (D4)*	4,500
Dora (D3)*	984
Dothan (H8)*	21,584
Double Springs (D2)*	524
Douglas (F2)*	200
Downing (F6)*	47
Downs (G6)	
Dozier (F7)*	362
Drewry (D8)*	
Duke (G3)*	175
Dunavant (F4)*	300
Duncanville (D4)*	10
Dutton (G1)*	
Dyas (C9)	30
Easonville (F3)*	400
East Brewton (E8)*	2,173
East Florence (C1)*	
East Tallassee (G5)*	
Eastaboga (F3)*	700
Echo (G8)	100
Echola (C4)*	120
Eclectic (F5)*	715
Eden (F3)*	621
Edna (B6)*	500
Edwardsville (H3)*	179
Edwin (H7)	170
Eiler (B7)	25
Elamville (G7)*	155
Elba (F8)*	2,936
Elberta (C10)*	350
Eldridge (C3)*	500
Eleanor (D6)	20
Eliska (C8)	75
Elkmont (E1)*	179
Elkwood (E1)	50
Ellawhite (D6)	
Elmore (F5)*	350
Elon (F1)	42
Elrod (C4)*	500
Emelle (B5)*	
Empire (D3)*	
Enterprise (G8)*	7,288
Eoline (D4)*	250
Epes (B5)*	342
Equality (F5)*	176
Erin (G4)	50
Escatawpa (B8)*	90
Estillfork (F1)*	121
Ethelsville (B4)*	135
Eufaula (H7)*	6,906
Eunola (G8)	112
Eutaw (C5)*	2,348
Eva (E2)*	200

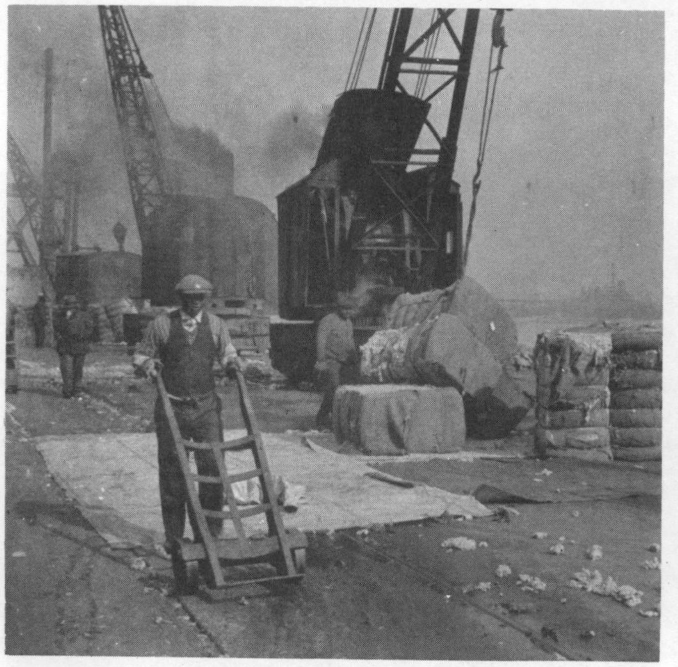

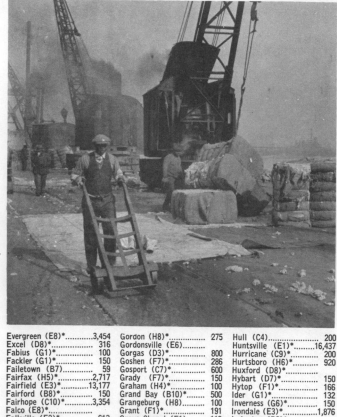

Evergreen (E8)* ... 3,454
Excel (D8)* ... 316
Fabius (G1)* ... 100
Fackler (G1)* ... 150
Failetown (B7) ... 59
Fairfax (H5)* ... 2,717
Fairfield (E3)* ... 13,177
Fairford (B8)* ... 150
Fairhope (C10)* ... 3,354
Falco (E8)* ...
Falkville (E2)* ... 613
Falls City (D2)* ... 156
Farmersville (E6)* ... 100
Faunsdale (C6)* ... 199
Fayette (C3)* ... 3,707
Fayetteville (F4)* ...
Fernbank (B3)* ...
Finchburg (D7)* ...
Fitzpatrick (G6)* ... 80
Five Points (H4)* ... 253
Flat Rock (G1)* ... 250
Flattop (E3)* ... 300
Flatwood (C6)* ... 50
Fleta (F6) ... 350
Flint (D1) ... 250
Flomaton (D8)* ... 1,036
Florala (F8)* ... 2,713
Florence (C1)* ... 23,879
Foley (C10)* ... 1,301
Fords (D3) ... 150
Forest Home (E7)* ... 250
Forestdale (C7) ... 100
Forkland (C5)* ...
Forney (H2) ... 270
Forrester (E6) ... 75
Fort Davis (G6)* ... 300
Fort Deposit (E7)* ... 1,358
Fort McClellan (G3)
Fort Mitchell (H6)* ... 150
Fort Payne (G2)* ... 6,226
Foshee (D8) ... 10
Fosters (C4)* ...
Fostoria (E6)* ... 150
Fountain (D7)* ...
Francisco (F1)* ... 87
Frankfort (C1) ... 150
Franklin (D7)* ... 350
Franklin (G6) ... 100
Frankville (B7)* ... 300
Fredonia (H5) ... 50
Freemanville (D8)* ... 250
Fremont (E6) ... 30
Frisco City (D8)* ... 1,068
Fruitdale (B8)* ... 800
Fruithurst (G3)* ... 318
Fulton (C7)* ... 696
Fultondale (E3)* ... 1,304
Furman (E6)* ... 300
Fyffe (G2)* ... 250
Gadsden (G2)* ... 55,725
Gainestown (C8)* ... 110
Gainesville (B5)* ... 319
Gallant (F2)* ...
Gallion (C6)* ... 300
Gantt (E8)* ...
Gantts Quarry (F4)* ... 426
Garden City (E2)* ... 534
Garland (E7)* ...
Gasque (C10)* ...
Gastonburg (C6)* ... 200
Gateswood (C9)
Gaylesville (G2)* ... 194
Geiger (B5)* ... 133
Geneva (G8)* ... 3,579
Georgiana (E7)* ... 1,596
Geraldine (G2)* ... 348
Gilbertown (B7)* ... 413
Gladstone (E1) ... 75
Glen Allen (C3)* ... 145
Glen Mary (C2) ... 150
Glencoe (G3)* ... 1,466
Glenwood (F7)* ... 413
Glover (C7) ... 30
Gold Hill (G5)* ...
Gonce (G1)* ... 30
Good Water (F4)* ... 1,227
Goodsprings (D3)* ... 1,000
Goodway (D8)* ... 40
Gordo (C4)* ... 952
Gordon (H8)* ... 275
Gordonsville (E6) ...
Gorgas (D3)* ... 800
Goshen (F7)* ... 286
Gosport (C7)* ... 600
Grady (F7)* ... 150
Graham (H4)* ... 100
Grand Bay (B10)* ... 500
Grangeburg (H8) ... 100
Grant (F1)* ... 191
Grays Chapel (F1) ... 119
Graysville (D3)* ... 879
Green Hill (C1) ...
Green Pond (D4)* ... 350
Greenbrier (E1) ... 120
Greensboro (C5)* ... 2,217
Greenville (E7)* ... 6,781
Gregville (E7)* ... 50
Grimes (H8) ... 60
Grove Hill (C7)* ... 1,443
Groveoak (F2)* ... 300
Guerryton (G6)* ... 200
Guin (C3)* ... 1,137
Gulfcrest (B8) ...
Guntersville (F2)* ... 5,253
Gurley (F1)* ... 700
Hackleburg (C2)* ... 534
Hacoda (F8)* ... 100
Haig (E3) ...
Haleburg (H8)* ... 93
Haleyville (C2)* ... 3,331
Halsell (B6)* ... 250
Hamburg (D5) ... 50
Hamilton (C2)* ... 1,623
Hammondville (G1) ... 94
Hamner (B5)* ...
Hanceville (E2)* ... 775
Hannon (G6)* ...
Hardaway (G6)* ... 600
Harpersville (F4)* ... 348
Hartford (G8)* ... 1,655
Hartselle (E2)* ... 3,429
Harvest (E1)* ... 250
Hatchechubbee (H6)* ... 250
Hatton (D1) ... 200
Havana (C5)* ... 100
Hawthorn (B8) ... 175
Hayden (E3)* ... 203
Haynes (E5) ... 24
Hayneville (E6)* ...
Hazel Green (E1)* ... 200
Hazen (D6)* ... 200
Headland (H8)* ... 2,091
Healing Springs (B7)* ... 205
Heflin (G3)* ... 1,982
Heiberger (D5)* ... 100
Helena (E4)* ... 421
Henagar (G1)* ... 500
Henderson (F7)
Herbert (E8)* ...
Hickory Flat (H4) ... 150
Higdon (G1)* ...
High Level (D3) ... 45
Highland Home (F7)* ... 175
Hightower (H3) ... 50
Hillsboro (D1)* ... 257
Hillwood (F5) ... 100
Hissop (F5)* ... 200
Hobbs Island (F1) ... 138
Hobson City (G3) ... 672
Hodges (C2)* ... 220
Hodgesville (H8) ... 150
Hokes Bluff (G3) ... 1,158
Hollins (F4)* ... 200
Holly Pond (E2)* ... 182
Hollytree (F1)* ...
Holywood (G1)* ... 477
Holman (C4) ... 40
Holt (D4)* ... 2,400
Holy Trinity (H6)* ... 125
Homewood (E4)* ... 12,866
Honoraville (F7)* ... 118
Hope Hull (F6)* ... 100
Hopewell (H3)* ... 95
Horton (F2)* ... 100
Houston (D2)* ... 50
Howard (C3) ... 75
Hugo (C6) ...
Hulaco (E2) ... 125
Hull (C4) ... 200
Huntsville (E1)* ... 16,437
Hurricane (C9)* ... 200
Hurtsboro (H6)* ... 920
Huxford (D8)* ...
Hybart (D7)* ... 150
Hytop (F1)* ... 166
Ider (G1)* ... 132
Inverness (G6)* ... 150
Irondale (E3)* ... 1,876
Irvington (B9)* ...
Isbell (C2) ... 200
Isney (B7)* ... 200
Jachin (B6)* ...
Jack (F7)* ...
Jackson (C8)* ... 3,072
Jacksonburg (C1) ...
Jacksons Gap (G5)* ... 400
Jacksonville (G3)* ... 4,751
Jamestown (G2)* ... 250
Jasper (D3)* ... 8,589
Jeff (E1)* ... 100
Jefferson (C6)* ... 3,200
Jemison (E5)* ... 847
Jenifer (G3)* ... 286
Johns (D4)* ... 454
Jones (E5)* ... 100
Joppa (E2)* ... 175
Josephine (C10)* ... 75
Kansas (C3)* ... 450
Keener (G2)* ... 119
Kellerman (D4)* ...
Kellyton (F5)* ... 300
Kennedy (B3)* ... 393
Kent (G5)* ... 250
Key (G2)* ...
Keystone (E4)* ... 400
Killen (D1)* ... 700
Kimberly (E3)* ... 1,100
Kimbrough (C6)* ... 132
Kings Landing (D6) ... 200
Kinsey (H8) ... 225
Kinston (F8)* ... 312
Knoxville (C4)* ...
Koenton (B7)* ...
La Place (G6) ...
Laceys Springs
(E1)* ... 150
Lacon (E2)* ... 200
Lafayette (H5)* ... 2,353
Lamison (C6)* ... 350
Land (B6)* ... 200
Landersville (D2)* ... 45
Lanett (H5)* ... 7,434
Langdale (H5)* ... 2,721
Langston (G1)* ... 280
Lapine (F7)* ... 425
Larkinsville (F1)* ... 300
Lasca (C6)* ... 62
Latham (C8)* ...
Laurendine (B9) ... 200
Lavaca (B6)* ...
Lawley (E5)* ... 175
Lebanon (G2) ...
Leeds (E3)* ... 3,306
Leesburg (G2)* ... 180
Lehigh (E3) ... 40
Leighton (D1)* ... 1,080
Lenox (D8)* ... 175
Leroy (B8)* ... 200
Letcher (F1) ... 150
Letohatchee (E6)* ... 750
Lexington (D1)* ...
Liberty (E2)* ...
Lilita (B6) ...
Lillian (D10)* ...
Lim Rock (F1)* ... 500
Lincoln (F3)* ... 547
Linden (C6)* ... 1,363
Lineville (G4)* ... 1,548
Linwood (G7)* ... 150
Lipscomb (E4)* ... 2,550
Lisman (B6)* ... 606
Little River (C8)* ...
Livingston (B5)* ... 1,681
Loachapoka (G5)* ... 400
Lockhart (F8)* ... 819
Logan (E2)* ... 129
Lomax (E5) ...
Long Island (G1)* ... 140
Longview (E4) ... 200
Lottie (C8) ... 75
Louisville (G7)* ... 622
Lower Peach Tree (C7)* 250
Lowery (F8) ... 100
Lowndesboro (E6)* ... 375
Loxley (C9)* ... 1,000
Lum (E6) ...
Luverne (F7)* ... 2,221
Lynn (C2)* ... 300
Macedonia (E6) ... 60
Madison (E1)* ... 530
Madrid (H8)* ... 312
Magazine (B9)* ...
Magnolia (C6)* ... 150
Magnolia Springs (C10)* 250
Malcolm (B8)* ... 150
Malone (G4)* ... 100
Malvern (G8)* ... 196
Manchester (D3)* ... 300
Manila (C7)* ...
Manningham (E7) ... 300
Mantua (C4)* ...
Maplesville (E5)* ... 806
Marble Valley (F4) ... 50
Marbury (E5)* ... 300
Marengo (C6) ...
Margaret (F3)* ... 1,144
Margerum (B1)* ... 160
Marion (D5)* ... 2,822
Marion Junction (D6)* .. 300
Marlow (C10) ... 75
Martling (F2)* ... 200
Marvel (D4)* ... 1,238
Marvyn (H6) ...
Massillon (D6)* ... 75
Mathews (F6)* ... 115
Maud (B1)* ... 100
Maylene (E4)* ... 210
Maysville (F1)* ... 150
Mc Calla (E4)* ... 350
Mc Connells (C4) ... 2
Mc Cullough (D8)* ...
Mc Dowell (C5) ... 275
Mc Intosh (B8)* ...
Mc Kenzie (E7)* ... 504
Mc Kinley (C6) ... 70
Mc Shan (B4)* ...
Mc Williams (D7)* ... 200
Megargel (D8)* ...
Mehama (D1) ... 75
Melborne (B3) ...
Melvin (B7)* ... 300
Mentone (G1)* ... 241
Meridianville (F1)* ... 350
Merrellton (G3) ... 40
Mertz (D5) ... 6
Mexboro (D8) ... 35
Mexia (D8)* ... 150
Midland City (H8)* ... 784
Midway (H6)* ... 544
Miflin (C10)* ... 125
Mignon (F4) ... 3,053
Millbrook (F6)* ... 300
Millers Ferry (D6)* ... 200
Millerville (G4)* ... 105
Millport (B3)* ... 682
Millry (B7)* ... 607
Milltown (H4)* ... 125
Milstead (G6)* ...
Minter (D6)* ... 250
Mitchell (G6)* ... 85
Mobile (B9)* ... 129,009
Mobile (urban area) .. 180,892
Monroeville (D7)* ... 2,772
Monrovia (E1) ... 200
Monterey (E7) ... 100
Montevallo (E4)* ... 2,150
MONTGOMERY
(F6)* ... 106,525
Montgomery (urban
area) ... 108,034
Montrose (C9)* ... 300
Moores Bridge (C4)* ...
Mooresville (E1)* ... 101
Morganville (F6) ...
Morris (E3)* ... 922
Morvin (C7)* ...
Mostellers (E4) ... 20
Moulton (D2)* ... 1,384
Moundville (C5)* ... 901
Mount Andrew (H7)* ... 300
Mount Carmel (F6) ... 275
Mount Hebron (B5)* ...
Mount Hope (D2)* ... 300
Mount Meigs (F6)* ... 200
Mount Pleasant (C8) ... 30
Mount Sterling (B6)* ... 150
Mount Vernon (B8)* ... 2,300
Mount Willing (E6)* ... 375
Mountain Brook (E4)* .. 8,359
Mountain Creek (E5)* ... 300
Movico (B8) ...
Mulberry (E6) ... 75
Mulga ‡(D3)* ... 1,743
Munford (F3)* ...
Murrycross (G2)* ... 132
Muscadine (H3)* ... 150
Muscle Shoals (C1)* ... 1,937
Myrtlewood (C6)* ... 550
Nadawah (D7)* ... 42
Nanafalia (B6)* ... 700
Natchez (D7)* ... 85
Natural Bridge (C2)* ... 85
Nauvoo (D3)* ... 416
Navco (B9)* ...
Needham (B7)* ... 140
Nettleboro (C7)* ... 76
New Brockton (G8)* ... 1,055
New Hope (F1)* ... 750
New Market (F1)* ... 500
New Site (G4) ... 200
Newala (E4) ...
Newbern (C5)* ... 367
Newburg (C1)* ... 300
Newell (H4)* ... 150
Newton (G8)* ... 745
Newtonville (C3) ... 100
Newville (H8)* ... 565
Nicholsville (C6)* ... 305
Nixburg (F5)* ... 250
Nokomis (D8)* ...
Normal (E1)* ... 1,400
North Johns (Johns*)
(D4) ... 454
Northport (C4)* ... 3,885
Notasulga (G5)* ... 816
Nottingham (F4) ...
Oak Bowery (H5) ... 75
Oak Grove (B9) ...
Oakchia (B6) ... 50
Oak Ridge ‡(F3)* ... 474
Oakhill (D7)* ... 123
Oakland (C1) ...
Oakman (D3)* ... 1,022
Ocre (H4) ... 45
Octagon (C6)* ...
Odenville (F3)* ... 302
Ohatchee (G3)* ... 750
Old Spring Hill (C6) ... 200
Omaha (H4) ... 101
Omega (G7)* ... 400
Oneonta (E3)* ... 2,802
Opelika (H5)* ... 12,295
Opine (C7) ... 40
Opp (F8)* ... 5,240
Orange Beach (C10)* ...
Orion (F7) ... 200
Orrville (D6)* ... 416
Owassa (E8)* ... 87
Owens Cross Rds. (E1)* 325
Oxford (G3)* ... 1,697
Oxmoor (E4) ... 200
Ozark (G8)* ... 5,238
Paint Rock (F1)* ... 276
Painter (F2) ... 25
Palestine (H3) ... 100
Panola (B5)* ... 350
Pansey (H8)* ... 50
Parrish (D3)* ... 757
Patsburg (F7)* ... 110
Patton (C3) ... 50
Paul (E8)* ... 200
Peachburg (G6)* ... 200
Peacock (C7) ... 36
Pelham (E4)* ...
Pell City (F3)* ... 1,189
Pennington (B6)* ... 100
Pepperell (H5)* ... 1,166
Pera (F8) ... 15
Perdido (C8)* ... 115
Perdido Beach (C10)* ...
Perdue Hill (C8)* ...
Perote (G7)* ... 500
Perryville (D5)* ... 100
Peterman (D7)* ... 400
Peterson (D4)* ...
Petrey (F7)* ... 171
Pettusville (E1) ... 100
Phenix City (H6)* ... 23,305
Phil Campbell (C2)* ... 469
Pickensville (B4)* ...
Piedmont (G3)* ... 4,498
Pigeon Creek (E7)* ...
Pike Road (F6)* ... 250
Pinckard (G8)* ... 515
Pine Apple (E7)* ... 445
Pine Grove (G6) ... 50
Pine Hill (C7)* ... 408
Pine Level (F6)* ... 300
Pinson (E3)* ... 400
Piper (D4)* ... 400
Pisgah (G1)* ... 217
Pittsview (H6)* ... 400
Plantersville (E5)* ... 550
Plateau (B9)* ...
Pleasant Gap (H3) ... 25
Pleasant Grove ‡(E3)* .. 1,802
Pleasant Hill (E6) ... 300
Pleasant Site (C1) ... 156
Pletcher (E5)* ... 60
Plevna (F1)* ... 250
Poarch (D8) ... 175
Point Clear (C10)* ...
Poley (F8) ... 50
Pollard (D8)* ... 271
Portersville (G2)* ... 150
Portland (D6) ... 30
Postoak (G6) ... 50
Powhatan (D3)* ... 400
Prairie (D6)* ... 150
Prattmont ‡(E6) ... 267
Prattville (E6)* ... 4,385
Prichard (B9)* ... 19,014
Princeton (F1)* ... 300
Prospect (D3)* ...
Pushmataha (B6)* ...
Putnam (B6)* ... 250
Pyriton (G4)* ... 50
Quinton (D3)* ... 200
Rabun (C8)* ... 50
Ragland (F3)* ... 1,008
Ralph (C4)* ... 500
Ramer (F6)* ... 500
Ranburne (H3)* ... 350
Randolph (E5)* ... 250
Range (D8)* ... 140
Rash (G1)* ... 150
Reads Mill (G3) ... 150
Red Bay (B2)* ... 1,805
Red Level (E8)* ... 656
Reform (G4)* ... 1,141
Rehoboth (D6)* ... 86
Rembert (C6) ...
Remlap (E3)* ... 150
Rendalia (F4) ...
Renfroe (F4)* ...
Repton (D8)* ... 364
Republic (E3)* ... 500
Richmond (D6) ... 300
Riderwood (B6)* ... 200
Ridge (B4) ...
River Falls (E8)* ... 376
River Ridge (D7) ... 7
River View (H5)* ... 1,322
Riverside (F3)* ... 116
Riverton (B1) ... 50
Roanoke (H4)* ... 5,392
Roba (G6)* ...
Robertsdale (C9)* ... 1,128
Robjohn (B6)* ... 150
Rock Mills (H4)* ... 550
Rock Run (G2)* ...
Rock Spring (G3) ... 350
Rockcastle (D4) ...
Rockford (F5)* ... 373
Rockville (C8) ...
Rockwood (C2) ... 250
Rogersville (D1)* ... 531
Rose Hill (F8) ... 100
Rosser (B6) ... 100
Round Mountain (G2)*.
Rural (C7) ... 50
Russell (B8) ... 130
Russellville (C2)* ... 6,012
Rutherford (H6)* ... 150
Ruthven (E7) ... 100
Rutledge (F7)* ... 370
Ryland (E1)* ... 50
Saco (G7)* ...
Safford (D6)* ... 250
Saginaw (E4)* ... 470
St. Bernard (E2)* ... 125
St. Clair (E6)* ... 200
St. Clair Springs (F3)*. 125
St. Elmo (B10)* ... 520
St. Florian (C1) ...
St. Stephens (B7)* ... 86
Salem (H5)* ... 350
Salitpa (C7)* ...
Samantha (C4)* ...
Samson (F8)* ... 2,204
Sandy (D5) ... 100
Sandy Ridge (E6) ... 350
Sanford (F8)* ... 150
Saragossa (D3)* ...
Saraland (B9)* ...
Sardis (E6)* ... 100
Satsuma (B9)* ... 1,592
Sawyerville (C5)* ... 125
Sayre (E3)* ... 500
Sayreton (E3)* ...
Scotia (F6) ... 35
Scotts Station (D5) ... 9
Scottsboro (F1)* ... 4,731
Scranage (C8) ... 50
Scyrene (C7)* ...
Seaboard (B8)* ... 56
Seale (H6)* ... 343
Searight (F8)* ... 82
Searles (D4)* ...
Section (G1)* ... 476
Sellers (F6)* ... 400
Selma (E6)* ... 22,840
Seman (F5)* ... 175
Seminole (D10)* ... 30
Semmes (B9)* ... 350
Service (B7)* ...
Shady Grove (F7)* ...
Shannon (E4)* ... 350
Shawmut (H5)* ... 3,266
Sheffield (C1)* ... 10,767
Shelby (E4)* ... 800
Shellhorn (F7)* ... 94
Shiloh (C6)* ...
Shorter (G6)* ...
Shorterville (H7)* ... 200
Shortleaf (C6)* ... 250
Shottsville (B2) ... 200
Shreve (E8) ... 100
Silas (B7)* ... 383
Siluria (E4)* ... 2,850
Silver Cross (B7)* ...
Silver Run (G3) ...
Silverhill (C9)* ... 354
Simmsville (E4) ... 100
Sims Chapel (B8)* ...
Sipsey (D3)* ... 1,000
Six Mile (D4) ... 100
Skinnerton (D7) ...
Skipperville (G7)* ... 139
Slapout (F5) ...
Slocomb (G8)* ... 1,219
Smiths (H5)* ...
Smyer (B7) ... 49
Snead (F2) ... 75
Snow Hill (E7)* ... 500
Snowdoun (F6)* ... 375
Society Hill (G6) ...
Somerville (E2)* ... 400
South (E8) ... 100
Souwilpa (B7)* ... 125
Speigner (F5)* ... 160
Sprague (F6)* ... 100
Spring Garden (G3)* ... 200
Spring Hill (B9)* ...
Spring Valley (C1) ... 523
Springville (E3)* ... 553
Sprott (D5)* ... 101
Spruce Pine (C2)* ... 495
Stafford (B4) ... 30
Standing Rock (H4)* ... 200
Stanton (E5)* ... 275
Stapleton (C9)* ... 350
Steele (F3)* ... 500
Steppville (E2)* ... 385
Sterrett (E4)* ... 400
Stevenson (G1)* ... 927
Stewart (C5)* ... 179
Stewartsville (F4) ... 300
Stockton (C9)* ...
Strata (F6) ... 150
Straven (E4) ... 43
Stroud (H4)* ... 79
Suggsville (C7)* ... 300
Sulligent (B3)* ... 1,209
Sumiton (D3)* ... 1,334
Summerdale (C10)* ... 489
Summerfield (E5) ... 300
Summit (F2)* ...
Sumter (D4) ...
Sumterville (B5)* ... 100
Sunflower (B8)* ... 185
Sunny South (C7)* ... 251
Surginer (C6)* ... 150
Suspension (G6) ... 100
Suttle (D5)* ... 210
Swaim (F1)* ...
Sweet Water (C6)* ... 575
Sycamore (F4)* ...
Sylacauga (F4)* ... 9,606
Sylvania (G1)* ...
Taff (G2) ... 90
Taits Gap (F3) ...
Talladega (F4)* ... 13,134
Talladega Spgs. (F4)* .. 222
Tallahatta Spgs. (C7) ... 150
Tallapoosa City ‡(G5) ... 168
Tallassee (G5)* ... 4,225
Tallaweka ‡(F5) ... 609
Talucah (E1)* ... 100
Tanner (E1)* ... 500
Tarrant (E3)* ... 7,571
Taylor (H8) ... 250
Tecumseh (H2) ... 45
Ten Broeck (G2) ...
Tennille (G7)* ... 70
Tensaw (C8)* ...
Thach (E1) ... 50
Thad (E8) ... 200
Theodore (B9)* ...
Thomaston (C6)* ... 1,027
Thomasville (C7)* ... 2,425
Thompson (G6)* ... 300
Thorsby (E5)* ... 828
Three Notch (G6)* ... 300
Tibbie (B8)* ...
Tinela (D7) ... 60
Tishabee (B5) ...
Titus (F5)* ... 163
Toney (E1)* ... 108
Town Creek (D1)* ... 763
Townley (D3)* ... 660
Toxey (B7)* ... 251
Trade (D2)* ... 120
Trafford (E3)* ... 551
Trenton (F1)* ... 300
Triana (E1) ... 100
Trimble (E2) ...
Trinity (D1)* ... 342
Trio (D5) ... 50
Troy (G7)* ... 8,555
Trussville (E3)* ... 1,575
Tunnel Springs (D7)* ... 150
Tuscaloosa (C4)* ... 46,396
Tuscumbia (C1)* ... 6,734
Tuskegee (G6)* ... 6,712
Tuskegee Inst. (G6)* ... 2,642
Tyler (E6)* ... 40
Uchee (H6) ... 100
Uniform (B8) ...
Union (C5) ...
Union Grove (E2)* ... 225
Union Springs (G6)* ... 3,232
Uniontown (D6)* ... 1,798
Uriah (D8)* ... 502
Valhermoso Spgs. (E2)* 180
Valley Head (G1)* ... 418
Vance (D4)* ...
Vandiver (F4)* ... 500
Verbena (E5)* ... 500
Vernon (B3)* ... 791
Veto (D1)* ... 150
Vida (E5)* ... 51
Vina (B2)* ... 313
Vincent (F4)* ... 1,240
Vinegar Bend (B8)* ... 300
Vinemont (E2)* ... 500
Vredenburgh (D7)* ... 796
Wadley (G4)* ... 535
Wadsworth (E5)* ...
Wagar (B8)* ... 250
Walker Springs (C7)* ... 200
Wallace (D8)* ...
Walnut Grove (F2)* ... 222
Wannville (G1) ... 50
Ward (B6)* ... 150
Ware (F6) ... 90
Warrior (E3)* ... 1,384
Warrior Stand (G6) ... 50
Water Valley (B7) ... 100
Waterloo (B1)* ... 327
Watsonia (C5) ...
Wattsville (F3)* ... 728
Waugh (F6)* ... 135
Waverly (G5)* ... 306
Wayne (C6)* ... 165
Weaver (G3)* ... 743
Webb (H8)* ... 344
Wedgworth (C5)* ... 300
Wedowee (H4)* ... 559
Wehadkee (H4)* ... 250
Wellington (G3)* ... 100
Weogufka (F4)* ... 400
West Blocton (D4)* ... 1,280
West Butler (B6) ...
West Greene (B5)* ... 100
Westover (E4)* ... 500
Wetumpka (F5)* ... 3,813
Whatley (C7)* ... 500
Wheeler (D1)* ... 225
Whistler (B9)* ...
White Hall (E6)* ... 200
White Oak (H7) ...
White Plains (G3) ... 375
Whitfield (B6)* ...
Whitney (F3)* ...
Wicksburg (G8) ... 100
Wilmer (B9)* ... 263
Wilsonville (E4)* ... 692
Wilton (E4)* ... 413
Winfield (C3)* ... 2,108
Winn (C7)* ... 130
Womack Hill (B7)* ... 306
Woodbluff (B7) ...
Woodland (H4)* ... 300
Woodstock (D4)* ... 200
Woodville (F1)* ... 165
Woodward (D4)* ...
Wren (D2) ... 50
Wright (C1) ... 200
Yantley (B6)* ... 250
Yarbo (B7)* ... 295
Yellow Bluff (C7)* ... 210
Yellow Pine (B8)* ... 282
Yolande (D4) ...
York (B6)* ... 1,774
Youngblood (G7)* ...
Yucca (G1) ... 50

ALASKA

Map on Page 50 — *Total Population 128,643*

Afognak (J3)... 158
Akiachak (F2)... 179
Akiak (F2)... 168
Akulurak (E2)... 197
Akutan (E4)... 86
Alaska (mt. range) (HJ2)...
Alatna (H1)... 31
Aleknagik (G3)... 153
Aleutian (isls.) (JN3)... 5,600
Aleutian (mt. range) (G3)...
Allakaket (H1)... 79
Anaktuvuk Pass (J1)... 66
Anchorage (J2)... 11,254
Angoon (N3)... 429
Aniak (G2)... 142
Anvik (F2)... 99
Arctic (K1)... 53
Atka (M4)... 85
Atkasuk (Meade)(G1)... 50
Barrow (G1)... 951
Barrow (point) (H1)...
Barter Island (Katovik) (L1)... 46
Beaver (J1)... 101
Bering (strait)(D1)
Bethel (F2)... 651
Bettles (H1)... 47
Big Delta (K2)... 155
Big Lake (J1)...
Brooks(mt. range)(GK1)
Candle, (F1)... 105
Cantwell (J2)... 67
Cape Yakataga (L3)...
Caro (J1)...
Central (K1)... 41
Chandalar (K1)...
Chaneliak (F2)... 100
Chevak (E2)... 230
Chichagof (J3)...
Chicken (L1)... 34
Chignik (G3)... 253
Chitina (K2)... 92
Circle (L1)... 83
Circle Springs (K1)... 21
Clarks Point (G3)... 128
Coal Creek (L1)... 30
Coast (mt. range) (N3)
College (J1)... 424
Cook (inlet) (H3)...
Copper Center (K2)... 90
Cordova (K2)... 1,165
Council (F1)... 41
Craig (N4)... 374
Crooked Creek (G2)... 43
Curry (J2)... 183
Cutoff (Huslia)(H1)... 65
Deering (F1)... 174
Dillingham (G3)... 577
Douglas (N3)... 699
Dutch Harbor (E4)...
Eagle (L1)... 55
Eastchester (J2)... 3,096
Eek (F2)... 141
Egegik (G3)... 119
Eielson (K1)...
Ekwak (G3)... 131
Elephant Point (F1)... 108
Endicott (mts.) (H1)...
Eureka (K2)...
Fairbanks (K1)... 5,771
False Pass (F4)... 42
Farewell (H2)...
Flat (G2)... 95
Folger (G2)...
Fort Glenn (E4)...
Fort Randall (F4)...
Fort Yukon (K1)... 446
Fortuna Ledge (Marshall) (F2)... 95
Galena (G1)... 176
Gambell (D2)... 309
Glacier Bay Nat'l Mon. (M3)...
Glenallen (K2)... 142
Golovin (F1)... 94
Gulkana (K2)... 65
Gustavus (M3)... 82
Haines (N3)... 338
Hamilton (F2)... 43
Haycock (F1)...
Healy Fork (J2)... 102
Hog River (G1)...
Holikachuk (G2)... 98
Holy Cross (G2)... 157
Homer (J3)... 307
Hoonah (N3)... 563
Hooper Bay (E2)... 307
Hope (J2)... 63
Hot Springs (J1)... 29
Hughes (H1)... 49
Hungry (G2)... 29
Huslia (Cutoff) (H1)... 65
Hydaburg (N4)... 353
Hyder (O4)... 30
Igloo (E1)... 64
Iliamna (H3)... 44
Indian Village (L1)... 45
Jonesville (J2)... 97
JUNEAU (N3)... 5,956
Kake (N3)... 376
Kaktovik (Barter Island) (L1)... 46
Kalskag (F2)... 139
Kaltag (G1)... 121
Kanatak (H3)...
Kantishna (J2)... 2
Karluk (H3)... 144
Katalla (K2)... 6
Katmai Nat'l Mon.(H3)
Kenai (J2)... 321
Ketchikan, (O4)... 5,305
Kiana (F1)... 183
King Cove (F4)... 162
Kipnuk (F2)... 185
Kivalina (E1)... 117
Klawock (N4)... 404
Kobuk (G1)... 38
Kodiak (J3)... 1,710
Kodiak (isl.)(J3)...
Kokhanok Bay (H3)... 39
Kokrines (H1)... 68
Kotzebue (F1)... 623
Koyuk (F1)... 134
Koyukuk (G1)... 79
Kuskokwim (river) (F2)
Kwethluk (F2)... 242
Kwigillingok (E3)... 245
Kwiguk (E2)... 157
Lake Minchumina (H2)... 60
Latouche (K2)... 5
Livengood (J1)... 40
Lost River (E1)... 140
Marshall (Fortuna Ledge) (F2)... 95
McCarthy (L2)... 8
McGrath (H2)... 175
McKinley (mt.) (H2)...
Meade (Atkasuk) (G1)... 50
Medfra (H2)... 25
Mekoryuk (E2)... 156
Meshik (G3)...
Metlakatla (O4)... 817
Minto (J1)... 152
Moses Point (F1)... 25
Mount McKinley Nat'l Park (K2)... 59
Mountain View (J2)... 2,880
Mountain Village (F2)... 221
Mumtrak (F3)... 100
Nabesna (L2)... 28
Naknek (G3)... 174
Napakiak (F2)... 139
Nenana (J1)... 242
Nikolai (H2)... 88
Nikolski (D4)... 64
Noatak (F1)... 326
Nome (F1)... 1,876
Nondalton (H2)... 103
Noorvik (F1)... 248
Northway (L2)... 196
Nulato (G1)... 176
Nyac (G2)... 64
Old Harbor (H3)... 121
Ophir (G2)... 68
Ouzinkie (Uzinki) (J3)... 177
Palmer (J2)... 890
Paxson (K2)...
Pelican (M3)... 180
Perryville (G3)...
Petersburg (O3)... 1,619
Pilot Point (G3)... 67
Pitkas Point (E2)... 84
Platinum (F3)... 72
Point Hope (D1)... 264
Point Lay (E1)... 75
Poorman (H1)...
Port Chilkoot (N3)... 125
Port Moller (F3)... 33
Quinhagak (F3)... 194
Rampart (J1)... 94
Ruby (H1)... 132
Russian Mission (F2)... 55
St. Elias (mt.) (L2)...
St. Elias(mt. range)(M3)
Saint Michael (F2)... 157
Salchaket (K1)... 25
Sanak (F4)...
Sand Point (G4)... 107
Savoonga (D2)... 249
Scammon Bay (E2)... 103
Selawik (G1)... 273
Seldovia (J3)... 437
Seward (J2)... 2,114
Seward (peninsula)(E1)
Shageluk (G2)... 100
Shaktoolik (F1)... 127
Shishmaref (E1)... 194
Shungnak (G1)... 141
Sitka (N3)... 1,985
Sitka Nat'l Mon. (M3)...
Skagway (N3)... 758
Skwentna (H2)... 58
Slana (K2)...
Slaterville (K1)... 611
Sleetmute (G2)... 120
Solomon (E1)... 93
Stevens Village (J1)... 84
Stony River (G2)...
Summit (J2)... 33
Suntrana (J1)... 130
Takotna (G2)... 42
Talkeetna (J2)... 106
Tanacross (L2)... 137
Tanana (H1)... 228
Taylor (E1)...
Teller (E1)... 160
Tetlin (L2)... 73
Tikikluk (G1)... 49
Tok Junction (L2)... 104
Tununak (E2)... 112
Tyonek (J2)... 132
Umiat (H1)...
Unalakleet (F2)... 469
Unalaska (E4)... 173
Unga (F4)... 107
Unimak (E4)...
Uzinki (Ouzinkie)(J3)... 177
Valdez (K2)... 554
Venetie (K1)... 81
Wainwright (F1)... 227
Wales (E1)... 141
Walkers Fork (L1)...
Wasilla (J2)... 97
White Mountain (E1)... 129
Whittier (K2)... 627
Willow (J2)...
Wiseman (J1)...
Wrangell (O3)... 1,763
Yakutat (M3)... 298
Yukon (river) (G2)...

ARIZONA

Map on Page 51 — *Total Population 749,587*

14 COUNTIES

Apache (F3)... 27,767
Cochise (F7)... 31,488
Coconino (C3)... 23,910
Gila (E5)... 24,158
Graham (E6)... 12,985
Greenlee (F5)... 12,805
Maricopa (C5)... 331,770
Mohave (A3)... 8,510
Navajo (E3)... 29,446
Pima (D6)... 141,216
Pinal (D6)... 43,191
Santa Cruz (E7)... 9,344
Yavapai (C4)... 24,991
Yuma (A5)... 28,006

CITIES and TOWNS

Adamana (F4)*... 60
Agua Caliente (B6)*... 75
Aguila (B5)*... 180
Ajo (C6)*... 5,817
Alpine (F5)*...
Amado (D7)*...
Apache (F7)... 36
Apache Junction (D5)* 50
Aripine (E4)*... 45
Arivaca (D7)*... 120
Arlington (C5)*... 500
Ash Fork (C3)*... 800
Ashurst (F5)*... 135
Avondale (C5)*... 2,505
Aztec (B6)*... 49
Bagdad (B4)*...
Bannon (F4)... 14
Bapchule (D5)*... 50
Bellemont (D3)*... 100
Benson (E7)*... 1,440
Betatakin (Shonto) (E2)
Bisbee (F7)*... 3,801
Blue (F5)*... 50
Blue Bell (C4)...
Bonita (E6)*... 100
Bouse (A5)*... 150
Bowie (F6)*... 300
Buckeye (C5)*... 1,932
Bullhead City (A3)*...
Bumble Bee (C4)*... 36
Bylas (E5)*... 750
Cactus (D5)*... 125
Calva (E5)... 25
Cameron (D3)*... 25
Camp Verde (D4)*... 550
Camp Wood (C4)*... 35
Cane Beds (B2)... 30
Casa Grande (D6)*... 4,181
Cashion (C5)*... 700
Castle Butte (E3)*...
Castle Hot Springs (C5)* 30
Cavecreek (D5)*... 250
Central (F6)*... 300
Chambers (F3)*... 106
Chandler (D5)*... 3,799
Cherry (C4)...
Chinle (F2)*... 150
Chino Valley (C4)*... 500
Chloride (A3)*... 250
Christmas (E5)... 60
Chrysotile (E5)...
Cibecue (E4)*... 35
Clarkdale (C4)*... 1,609
Clay Springs (E4)*... 199
Claypool (E5)*... 1,200
Cleator (C4)*... 66
Clemenceau (C4)*... 300
Clifton (F5)*... 3,466
Cochise (F6)*... 90
Concho (F4)*... 175
Congress (C4)*... 30
Congress Jct. (B4)... 95
Continental (D7)... 12
Coolidge (D6)*... 4,306
Coolidge Dam (E5)*... 35
Cordes (C4)...
Cornfields (F3)... 204
Cornville (D4)*... 21
Cortaro (D6)*... 360
Cottonwood (D4)*... 1,326
Courtland (F7)... 25
Crown King (C4)*... 100
Dateland (B6)*...
Davis Dam (A3)... 1,000
Dewey (C4)*... 25
Dilkon (E3)... 15
Dome (A6)*... 35
Dos Cabezas (F6)*... 80
Douglas (F7)*... 9,442
Dragoon (F6)*... 44
Drake (C4)... 5
Duncan (F6)*... 941
Eagar (F4)*... 637
Eden (F6)*... 200
Elfrida (F7)*... 277
Elgin (E7)*... 143
Eloy (D6)*... 3,580
Emery Park (E6)*... 600
Escuela (D6)... 10
Estrella (C6)... 21
Fairbank (E7)*... 50
Flagstaff (D3)*... 6,771
Florence (D5)*... 1,776
Florence Jct. (D5)*... 32
Fort Apache (F5)*... 500
Fort Defiance (F3)*... 500
Fort Grant (E6)*...
Fort Huachuca (E7)*... 100
Fort Thomas (E5)*...
Franklin (F6)*... 300
Fredonia (C2)*... 330
Fry (E7)*... 150
Gadsden (A6)*... 250
Ganado (F3)*... 450
Geronimo (F5)*... 23
Gila Bend (C6)*... 873
Gilbert (D5)*... 1,114
Gleeson (F7)... 200
Glenbar (F6)*... 170
Glendale (C5)*... 8,179
Globe (E5)*... 6,419
Goldroad (A3)... 14
Goodwin (C4)... 15
Goodyear (C5)*... 1,254
Grand Canyon (C2)*... 1,001
Greasewood Sprs. (F2).
Greaterville (E7)...
Greer (F4)*... 30
Hackberry (B3)*... 250
Hassayampa (C5)...
Hayden (E5)*... 1,494
Hayden Junction (E6)*. 71
Heber (E4)*... 250
Hereford (E7)*... 90
Higley (D5)*... 150
Hillside (B4)*... 40
Hilltop (F6)... 34
Holbrook (E4)*... 2,336
Hotevilla (E3)*... 572
Houck (F3)*...
Humboldt (C4)*... 350
Indian Wells (E3)*... 2
Inspiration (D5)*... 500
Iron Springs (C4)*... 3
Jacob Lake (C2)*... 10
Jeddito (E3)... 6
Jerome (C4)*... 1,233
Joseph City (E4)*... 500
Kayenta (E2)*... 100
Keams Canyon (E3)*... 500
Kelvin (E5)*... 35
Kingman (A3)*... 3,342
Kirkland (C4)*... 96
Klagetoh (F3)...
Klondyke (E6)*... 150
Komatke (C5)... 200
Lakeside (E4)*...
Laveen (C5)*... 300
Leupp (E3)*...
Liberty (C5)...
Linden (E4)*... 105
Litchfield (C5)... 1,000
Litchfield Park (C5)*... 450
Littlefield (B2)*... 100
Lowell (F7)*... 1,136
Lukachukai (F2)*...
Lupton (F3)*... 115
Madera Canyon (E7)... 40
Mammoth (E6)*... 275
Marana (D6)*... 1,000
Marble Canyon (D2)... 5
Maricopa (C5)*... 150
Marinette (C5)*... 500
Maverick (F5)*... 450
Mayer (C4)*... 500
Mc Nary (F4)*... 1,902
McNeal (F7)*... 101
Mesa (D5)*... 16,790
Miami (E5)*... 4,329
Miller Valley (C4)... 2,953
Mobile (C5)*... 120
Moccasin (C2)*... 55
Mohawk (B6)*... 18
Morenci (F5)*... 6,541
Mormon Lake (D4)*...
Morristown (C5)*... 185
Mount Trumbull (B2)*... 57
Naco (E7)*... 400
Navajo (F3)*... 50
Nelson (B3)*... 155
Nogales (E7)*... 6,153
North Rim (C2)*... 2
Nutrioso (F5)*... 100
Oatman (A3)*... 600
Olberg (D5)... 51
Oracle (E6)*...
Oraibi (E3)*...
Palo Verde (C5)*...
Pantano (E7)*... 40
Paradise (F7)... 14
Parker (A4)*... 1,201
Parks (C3)*... 50
Patagonia (E7)*... 700
Paul Spur (F7)*... 300
Paulden (C4)*... 25
Payson (D4)*... 350
Peach Springs (B3)*... 575
Pearce (F7)*... 150
Peoria (C5)*... 2,000
Perkinsville (C4)... 15
PHOENIX (C5)*... 106,818
Phoenix (urban area)... 214,335
Picacho (D6)*... 150
Pima (F6)*... 824
Pine (D4)*...
Pinedale (E4)*... 87
Pinetop (F4)*... 300
Pirtleville (F7)*... 1,246
Polacca (E3)*...
Pomerene (E6)*... 100
Portal (F7)*... 65
Poston (A3)*...
Prescott (C4)*... 6,764
Quartzsite (A5)*... 153
Queen Creek (D5)*... 1,200
Quijotoa (C6)... 50
Randolph (D6)*...
Ray (E5)*... 2,000
Red Rock (D6)*... 50
Redington (E6)... 51
Rillito (D6)*... 200
Rimrock (D4)*... 20
Rock Springs (C3)*...
Roll (A6)*... 66
Roosevelt (D5)*...
Rowood (C6)*... 50
Ruby (D7)...
Sacaton (D5)*... 600
Safford (F6)*... 3,756
Sahuarita (E7)*... 500
Saint David (E7)*... 750
St. Johns (F4)*... 1,469
St. Michaels (F3)*... 120
Salome (B5)*... 300
San Carlos (E5)*... 3,000
San Luis (A6)*...
San Simon (F6)*... 175
Sanders (F3)*...
Sasabe (D7)*... 75
Scottsdale (D5)*... 2,032
Sedona (D4)*... 350
Seligman (B3)*... 1,000
Sells (D7)*... 650
Sentinel (B6)*... 60
Shonto (E2)...
Short Creek (B2)*... 200
Show Low (F4)*... 1,000
Shumway (E4)*... 88
Shungopavy (E3)...
Skull Valley (C4)*... 250
Snowflake (E4)*... 929
Solomon (F6)*... 700
Sombrero Butte (E6)... 10
Somerton (A6)*... 1,825
Sonoita (E7)*... 150
Sonora (D5)*... 1,821
South Tucson (D6)... 2,364
Springerville (F4)*... 689
Steamboat (F3)...
Stoneman Lake (D4)...
Supai (C2)*... 16
Supai (C3)...
Superior (D5)*... 4,500
Tacna (B6)*... 18
Taylor (E4)*... 500
Tempe (D5)*... 7,684
Thatcher (F6)*... 1,284
Tiger (E6)*... 1,800
Tolleson (C5)*... 3,042
Toltec (D6)... 30
Tombstone (F7)*... 910
Tonalea (E2)*...
Tonopah (B5)*... 4
Tonto Basin (D5)*... 111
Topawa (D7)*... 342
Topock (A4)*... 50
Toreva (E3)...
Tortilla Flat (D5)*... 65
Tuba City (D2)*... 250
Tubac (E7)... 25
Tucson (D6)*... 45,454
Tuweep (B2)... 10
Vail (E6)*...
Valentine (B3)*... 127
Valley Farms (D6)*... 212
Vernon (F4)*... 155
Vicksburg (B5)*... 33
Waddell (C5)*...
Wagoner (C4)*... 55
Walker (C4)... 20
Warren (F7)*... 2,610
Wellton (A6)*...
Wenden (B5)*... 100
Whipple (C4)*... 650
Whiteriver (E5)*... 950
Wickenburg (C5)*... 1,736
Wide Ruins (F3)... 9
Wikieup (B4)*... 6
Wilhoit (C4)... 12
Willcox (F6)*... 1,266
Williams (C3)*... 2,152
Window Rock (F3)*...
Winkelman (E6)*... 548
Winona (D3)... 30
Winslow (E3)*... 6,518
Wintersburg (B5)... 50
Wittmann (C5)*... 170
Wolf Hole (B2)... 12
Woodruff (E4)*... 164
Yarnell (C4)*... 450
Yava (C4)*... 35
Young (D4)*... 242
Yucca (A4)*... 40
Yuma (A6)*... 9,145

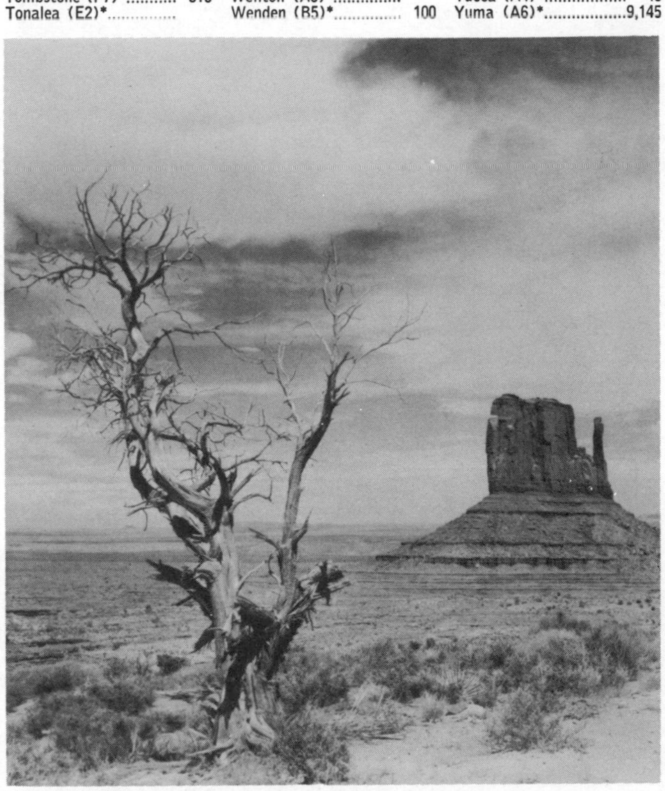

ARKANSAS

Map on Page 52 — *Total Population 1,909,511*

75 COUNTIES

Arkansas (H5)... 23,665
Ashley (G7)... 25,660
Baxter (F1)... 11,683
Benton (B1)... 38,076
Boone (D1)... 16,260
Bradley (F7)... 15,987
Calhoun (E6)... 7,132
Carroll (C1)... 13,244
Chicot (H7)... 22,306
Clark (D5)... 22,998
Clay (K1)... 26,674
Cleburne (F2)... 11,487
Cleveland (F6)... 8,956
Columbia (D7)... 28,770
Conway (E3)... 18,137
Craighead (J2)... 50,613
Crawford (B2)... 22,727
Crittenden (K3)... 47,184
Cross (J3)... 24,757
Dallas (E6)... 12,416
Desha (H6)... 25,155
Drew (G6)... 17,959
Faulkner (F3)... 25,289
Franklin (C2)... 12,358
Fulton (G1)... 9,187
Garland (D4)... 47,102
Grant (F5)... 9,024
Greene (J1)... 29,149
Hempstead (C6)... 25,080
Hot Spring (E5)... 22,181
Howard (C5)... 13,342
Independence (G2)... 23,488
Izard (G1)... 9,953
Jackson (H2)... 25,912
Jefferson (G5)... 76,075
Johnson (C2)... 16,138
Lafayette (C7)... 13,203
Lawrence (H1)... 21,303
Lee (J4)... 24,322
Lincoln (G6)... 17,079
Little River (B6)... 11,690
Logan (C3)... 20,260
Lonoke (G4)... 27,278
Madison (C1)... 11,734
Marion (E1)... 8,609
Miller (C7)... 32,614
Mississippi (K2)... 82,375
Monroe (H4)... 19,540
Montgomery (C4)... 6,680
Nevada (D6)... 14,781
Newton (D2)... 8,685
Ouachita (E6)... 33,051
Perry (E4)... 5,978
Phillips (J5)... 46,254
Pike (C5)... 10,032
Poinsett (J2)... 39,311
Polk (B5)... 14,182
Pope (D3)... 23,291
Prairie (G4)... 13,768
Pulaski (F4)... 196,685
Randolph (H1)... 15,982
Saint Francis (J3)... 36,841
Saline (E4)... 23,816
Scott (B4)... 10,057
Searcy (E2)... 10,424
Sebastian (B3)... 64,202
Sevier (B6)... 12,293
Sharp (G1)... 8,999
Stone (F2)... 7,662
Union (E7)... 49,686
Van Buren (E2)... 9,687
Washington (B2)... 49,979
White (G3)... 38,040
Woodruff (H3)... 18,957
Yell (D3)... 14,057

CITIES and TOWNS

Abbott (B3)*... 200
Adona (E3)*... 194
Agnos (G1)*... 80
Alabam (C1)*... 37
Albert (C5)... 5
Alco (F2)*...
Alexander (F4)*... 194
Algoa (H2)*... 73
Alicia (H2)*... 299
Alix (C3)*...
Alleene (B6)*...
Alma (B3)*... 1,228
Almond (G2)*... 150
Almyra (H5)*... 235
Alpena (D1)*... 304
Alpine (D5)*... 100
Altheimer (G5)*... 680
Altus (C3)*... 431
Aly (D4)*... 122
Amagon (H2)*... 181
Amity (D5)*... 591
Antoine (D5)*... 209
Aplin (E4)*... 125
Appleton (E3)*... 265

Arden (B6)*
Arkadelphia (D5)* 6,819
Arkansas City (H6)* 1,018
Arkansas Post (H5) 30
Arkinda (B6)* 92
Arlberg (F2)* 20
Armorel (L2)* 500
Arthur (J3)
Ash Flat (G1)* 265
Ashdown (B6)* 2,738
Athens (C5)* 57
Atkins (E3)* 1,291
Atlanta (D7)*
Aubrey (J4)* 300
Augusta (H3)* 2,317
Aurora (C2)* 26
Austin (G4)* 154
Auvergne (H2)*
Avoca (B1)* 200
Bald Knob (G3)* 2,022
Banks (F6)* 240
Barber (B3)* 35
Barfield (L2) 100
Barling (B3)* 325
Barton (J4)* 600
Bates (B4)* 130
Batesville (G2)* 6,414
Bauxite (F4)* 2,459
Bauxite Junction (E4)
Baxter (G6)* 75
Bay (J2)* 500
Bayou Meto (H5)* 300
Bearden (E6)* 1,300
Beaton (D5) 75
Beaver (C1)* 50
Bee Branch (F3)* 137
Beebe (G3)* 1,192
Beirne (D6)
Bellefonte (D1)* 250
Belleville (D3)* 372
Belton (C6) 50
Ben Lomond (B6)* 284
Benton (E4)* 6,277
Bentonville (B1)* 2,942
Bergman (E1)* 126
Berryville (C1)* 1,753
Bestwater (B1) 50
Bethel (K2) 50
Bethesda (G2)* 300
Big Fork (B5)* 60
Bigelow (E3)* 292
Bigflat (F1)* 197
Biggers (J1)* 333
Bingen (C6)* 50
Birdell (H1) 36
Birdsong (K3) 100
Birta (D3)* 78
Biscoe (H4)* 406
Bismarck (D5)* 150
Black Oak (K2)* 261
Black Rock (H1)* 662
Black Springs (C5)* 90
Blackton (H4)* 300
Blackwell (E3)* 240
Blevins (C6)* 271
Bloomer (B3) 250
Blue Ball (C4)* 90
Blue Mountain
(C3)* 122
Bluff City (D6)* 200
Bluffton (C4)* 400
Blytheville (L2)* 16,234
Board Camp (B4)* 75
Bodcaw (D6)* 200
Bolding (F7)* 59
Boles (B4)* 150
Bonanza (B3)* 361
Bono (J2)* 352
Bookman (F5) 50
Booneville (C3)* 2,433
Boswell (F1)*
Boughton (D6)*
Boxley (D2)*
Boydell (H7)* 100
Boydsville (K1)* 100
Boynton (K2) 15
Bradford (G3)* 720
Bradley (C7)* 444
Branch (C3)* 308
Brasfield (H4)* 100
Brentwood (B2)* 300
Brickeys (J4)* 62
Briggsville (C4)* 253
Bright Star (C7)
Brinkley (H4)* 4,173
Brookland (J2)* 334
Brownsville (G2) 100
Bruins (K4) 200
Brummitt (G4) 70
Bruno (E1)*
Bryant (F4)* 387
Buckner (D7)* 335
Buckville (D4)* 225
Buena Vista (D7)* 150
Buffalo (E1)* 52
Burdette (L2)* 122
Burg (B5) 1
Butlerville (G4) 75
Butterfield (E5)* 150
Cabot (F4)* 1,147
Caddo Gap (C5)* 150
Calamine (H1)* 24
Caldwell (J3)*
Cale (D6)* 115
Calico Rock (F1)* 963
Calion (E7)* 536
Calmer (F6) 25
Camden (E6)* 11,372
Cammack Village (E4). 987
Canehill (B2)* 150
Canfield (C7)* 125
Caraway (K2)* 970
Carlisle (G4)* 1,396
Carryville (K1)* 40
Carson (K2) 150
Carthage (E5)* 533
Casa (D3)* 184
Cash (J2)* 188
Cass (C2)*
Casscoe (H4)* 300
Cato (F4)* 125
Cauthron (B4)* 50
Cave City (G2)* 372
Cave Springs (B1)* 267
Cedar Glades (D4)* 350
Cedarcreek (C4) 50
Cedarville (B2)* 43
Center (H1)* 65
Center Hill (G3) 100
Center Point (C5)* 162
Center Ridge (E3)* 100
Centerton (B1)* 200
Centerville (D3)* 160
Central City (B3) 115
Cerrogordo (B6) 77
Chapel Hill (B5) 260
Charleston (B3)* 968
Chatfield (K3)* 200
Cherokee City (A1)* 68
Cherry Hill (B4)* 175
Cherry Valley (J3)* 521
Chester (B2)* 120
Chickalah (D3)* 97
Chicot (H7)* 100
Chidester (D6)* 425
Chismville (C3) 100
Choctaw (F2)*
Chula (C4)* 47
Cincinnati (B1) 50
Clarendon (H4)* 2,547
Clarkedale (K3)* 150
Clarksville (D3)* 4,343
Clay (G3) 40
Cleveland (E3)* 59
Clifty (C1)* 50
Clinton (F2)* 853
Clover Bend (H2) 75
Clyde (B2)* 78
Coal Hill (C3)* 873
College (G6)
Collins (G6)* 183
Colt (J3)* 267
Columbus (C6)* 200
Combs (C2)*
Conway (F3)* 8,610
Copeland (E2)*
Cord (H2)* 150
Corinth (C5) 60
Corley (C3)* 45
Cornerstone (G5) 100
Cornerville (G6)* 100
Corning (J1)* 2,045
Cotter (E1)* 1,089
Cotton Plant (H3)* 1,838
Cove (B5)* 405
Coy (G4)* 200
Crawfordsville (K3)* 680
Creswell (F1)*
Crocketts Bluff (H5)* 102
Crosses (C2)* 75
Crossett (F7)* 4,619
Crumrod (H5)* 300
Crystal Springs (D5)* 118
Cullendale (E7)* 3,225
Cumi (F1)* 3
Curtis (D6)*
Cushman (G2)* 314
Cypert (J5) 53
Daisy (C5)* 74
Dalark (E5)* 142
Dalton (H1)* 50
Damascus (F3)* 80
Danville (D3)* 829
Dardanelle (D3)* 1,772
Datto (J1)* 176
De Queen (B5)* 3,015
De Roche (D5) 200
De Valls Bluff (H4)* 830
De Witt (H5)* 2,843
Decatur (A1)* 350
Deckerville (K3) 46
Deer (D2)* 80
Delaney (C2)*
Delaplaine (J1)* 208
Delaware (D3)* 500
Delight (C5)* 574
Dell (K2)* 384
Denning (C3)* 268
Denver (D1)* 50
Dermott (H7)* 3,601
Des Arc (G4)* 1,612
Diantha (G5)
Diaz (H2)* 150
Dierks (B5)* 1,253
Dillen (D2)* 50
Dodd City (E1)
Doddridge (C7)* 128
Donaldson (E5)* 500
Douglas ‡(H5)* 1
Dover (D3)* 510
Drakes Creek (C2)*
Drasco (G2)* 100
Driggs (C3) 50
Dryden (J2) 43
Dublin (D3)
Dumas (H6)* 2,512
Durham (C2)* 110
Dutch Mills (B2)* 50
Dutton (C2)* 50
Dyer (B3)* 398
Eagle Mills (E6)* 175
Eagleton (B4)* 64
Earle (K3)* 2,375
Edgemont (F2)* 89
Edmondson (K3)* 283
El Dorado (E7)* 23,076
El Paso (F3)* 200
Elaine (J5)* 744
Elba (E2)* 32
Elizabeth (F1)* 100
Elkins (C1)* 275
Elliott (E7) 150
Ellisville (F6)
Elm Springs (B1)* 217
Elmore (E5) 45
Emerson (D7)* 523
Emmet (D6)* 482
Enders (F3) 25
England (G4)* 2,136
Enola (F3)* 250
Ethel (H5)*
Etowah (K2)* 150
Eudora (H7)* 3,072
Eureka Springs (C1)* 1,958
Evadale (K2) 100
Evansville (B2)* 2
Evening Shade (G1)* 360
Everton (E1)* 198
Excelsior (B3) 100
Faber (E5)* 215
Fair Oaks (J3)* 200
Faith (F5) 100
Fallsville (D2)*
Fargo (H4)* 200
Farmington (B1)* 300
Fayetteville (B1)* 17,071
Felsenthal (F7)*
Felton (J4) 100
Fenter (E5)* 50
Ferda (G5) 50
Fisher (J2)* 289
Fitzhugh (H3)* 165
Flippin (E1)* 646
Floral (G2)* 150
Florence (G6)* 275
Floyd (G3) 135
Fontain (J2) 250
Fordyce (F6)* 3,754
Foreman (B6)* 907
Forester (C4)* 818
Formosa (E3)* 195
Forrest City (J3)* 7,607
Fort Smith (B3)* 47,942
Fort Smith (urban
area) 55,947
Forum (C1)* 45
Fouke (C7)* 336
Fountain Hill (G7)* 320
Fourche (E4) 51
Fox (F2)*
Franklin (G1)* 100
Fredonia (Biscoe*)(H4) 406
Friendship (E5)* 179
Frys Mill (K2) 75
Fulton (C6)* 385
Gaines Landing (H7) 100
Gainesville (J1) 200
Galloway (F4) 350
Garfield (C1)* 83
Garland (C7)* 351
Garner (G3)* 175
Gassville (F1)* 273
Gateway (B1)* 97
Genoa (C7)* 100
Gentry (A1)* 729
Georgetown (G3)* 200
Gilbert (E2)* 51
Gillett (H5)* 774
Gillham (B5)* 207
Gilmore (K3)*
Glenville (D7)
Glenwood* (C5) 843
Goldman (G5) 40
Goodwin (J4)* 85
Goshen (C1)* 65
Gould (G6)* 1,076
Grady (G5)* 517
Grand Glaise (G2)*
Grand Lake (H7)*
Grandview (C1)* 86
Grannis (B5)* 193
Grapevine (F5)* 200
Gravelly (C4)* 150
Gravelridge (F7) 250
Gravette (B1)* 894
Grays (H3)*
Graysonia (D5)
Green Forest (D1)* 738
Greenbrier (F3)* 375
Greenland (B1)* 164
Greenway (K1)* 288
Greenwood (B3)* 1,634
Gregory (H3)* 250
Griffithville (G3)* 207
Grubbs (H2)* 313
Guion (G2)* 219
Gurdon (D6)* 2,390
Guy (F3)* 100
Hackett (B3)* 440
Hagarville (D2)* 195
Halley (H6)* 149
Hamburg (G7)* 2,655
Hampton (F6)* 838
Hardy (H1)* 599
Harmony (D2)* 31
Harrell (F7)* 342
Harris (B1)* 2
Harrisburg (J2)* 1,498
Harrison (D1)* 5,542
Hartford (B3)* 865
Hartman (C3)* 418
Haskell (E4)* 209
Harwood (H7)
Hasty (D1)* 25
Hatfield (B5)* 364
Hattieville (E3)* 150
Havana (D3)* 348
Haynes (J4)* 250
Hazen (G4)* 1,270
Heber Springs (G2)* 2,109
Hector (E3)* 325
Helena (J4)* 11,236
Hensley (F4)* 1,200
Herbine (F6)* 55
Hermitage (F7)* 398
Heth (K3)* 285
Hickman (L2) 150
Hickory Plains (G3)* 225
Hickory Ridge (J3)* 345
Higden (F2)* 115
Higginson (G3)* 131
Highland (C5)* 50
Hillemann (H3)* 35
Hindsville (C1)* 116
Hiram (G3)* 100
Hiwasse (B1)* 300
Holland (F3) 100
Hollis (D4)* 195
Holly Grove (H4)* 761
Holly Springs (E6)*
Hollywood (D5)* 100
Homan (C6) 75
Hon (B4)* 200
Hope (C6)* 8,605
Hopper (C5)* 200
Hopper (H4) 60
Horatio (B6)* 776
Hot Springs Nat'l
Park (D4)* 29,307
Houston (E3)* 291
Howell (H3)* 55
Hoxie (H1)* 1,855
Hudspeth (H7) 40
Huffman (L2)* 300
Hughes (J4)* 1,686
Hulbert (K3)* 750
Humnoke (G4)* 263
Humphrey (G5)* 629
Hunter (H3)* 286
Huntington (B3)* 744
Huntsville (C1)* 1,010
Huttig (F7)* 1,038
Iceledo (D2) 20
Imboden (H1)* 447
Ingalls (F7)* 300
Ione (B3)* 80
Ivan (F6)* 150
Ivy (E5)* 80
Jacinto (E6)
Jacksonport (H2)*
Jacksonville (F4)* 2,474
Jamestown (G2)* 84
Jasper (D1)* 407
Jefferson (F5)*
Jennie (H7)*
Jenny Lind (B3)* 513
Jericho (K3) 250
Jerome (G7)* 82
Jersey (F7)*
Jerusalem (E3)*
Jessieville (D4)* 100
Johnson (B1)* 350
Johnsville (F7)*
Joiner (K2)* 596
Jonesboro (J2)* 16,310
Judsonia (G3)* 1,122
Junction City (E7)* 1,013
Kedron (F5)* 100
Keevil (H4)* 350
Keiser (K2)* 522
Kelso (H6)
Kensett (G3)* 829
Keo (G4)* 200
Kerlin (D7) 50
Kerrs (F4) 100
Kiblah (C7) 55
Kimberley ‡(C5) 46
King (B5)*
Kingsland (F6)* 337
Kingston (C1)* 208
Kinton (J3)* 150
Kirby (C5)*
Knobel (J1)* 417
Knowlton (H5)
Knoxville (D3)* 367
Koch Ridge (E2) 22
La Grange (J4)* 250
Lacey (G7)
Ladelle (G7)* 38
Lafe (J1)* 400
Lafferty (G2)* 250
Lake City (K2)* 783
Lake Frances (B1) 15
Lake Village (H7)* 2,484
Lamar (D3)* 555
Lambert (D5)* 250
Laneburg (D6)* 85
Langley (C5)* 53
Lapile (F7)* 55
Lavaca (B3)* 373
Lawson (F7)* 300
Leachville (K2)* 1,230
Lead Hill (E1)* 110
Leecreek (B2)* 25
Leola (E5)* 313
Leonard (K1) 10
Lepanto (K2)* 1,683
Leslie (E2)* 610
Lester (E6)
Letona (G3)* 164
Levy (F4)*
Lewisville (C7)* 1,237
Lexa (J4)* 500
Lexington (F2) 100
Limestone (D2)*
Lincoln (B2)* 771
Lisbon (E7)
LITTLE ROCK (F4)* 102,213
Little Rock - North
Little Rock (urban
area) 150,758
Lockesburg (B6)* 714
Locust Bayou (E6) 75
Lodge Corner (H5)* 43
London (D3)* 353
Lonoke (G4)* 1,556
Lonsdale (E4)* 91
Louann (E7)* 291
Lowell (B1)* 341
Lucas (B3) 40
Luna Landing (H7) 100
Lundell (H5)* 350
Lunsford (K2) 150
Lurton (D2)*
Luxora (K2)* 1,302
Lynn (H2)*
Mabelvale (F4)* 200
Macedonia (D7) 100
Macks (H2)* 100
Madison (J4)* 718
Magazine (C3)* 503
Magness (H2)* 229
Magnet (E5)* 175
Magnolia (D7)* 6,918
Malvern (E5)* 8,072
Mammoth Spring (G1)* 870
Mandalay (K2) 15
Mandeville (C7)* 150
Manila (K2)* 1,729
Manning (E5)* 300
Mansfield (B3)* 869
Marble (C1)* 100
Marcella (G2)* 75
Marche (F4) 75
Marianna (J4)* 4,530
Marion (K3)* 883
Marked Tree (K2)* 2,878
Marmaduke (K1)* 643
Marshall (E2)* 1,189
Martinville (F3)* 450
Marvell (J4)* 1,121
Mauldin (C4)
Maumee (E1)* 25
Mayflower (F4)* 293
Maynard (J1)* 216
Maysville (A1)* 225
McCaskill (C6)* 122
McClelland (H3)* 150
McCrory (H3)* 1,115
McDougal (K1)* 250
McFadden (H3)*
McGehee (H6)* 3,854
McKamie (C7)* 109
McNab (C6)* 206
McNeil (D7)* 597
McRae (G3)* 414
Meg (C3) 10
Melbourne (G1)* 568
Mellwood (H5)* 300
Mena (B4)* 4,445
Menifee (E3)*
Meroney (G6) 50
Mesa (G4) 25
Meyers (D5)* 100
Middlebrook (H1)* 30
Midland (B3)* 356
Midway (E6)* 450
Millville (E6) 100
Milner (D7)
Milo (G7) 12
Mineral (B5)* 50
Mineral Springs (C6)* 751
Minturn (H2)* 138
Mist (G7) 15
Mitchell (G1)* 44
Moark (J1)* 125
Monette (K2)* 1,114
Monroe (H4)* 75
Montana (C3) 150
Monte Ne (B1)* 100
Monticello (G6)* 4,501
Montrose (H7)* 344
Moorefield (H2)* 107
Moreland (E3)* 50
Morganton (F3)*
Moro (H4)* 189
Morobay (F7)* 77
Morrilton (E3)* 5,483
Morrison Bluff (D3)
Morriston (G1)* 50
Morrow (B2)* 50
Moscow (G5)*
Mount Holly (E7)*
Mount Ida (C4)* 566
Mount Judea (D2)* 95
Mount Pleasant (G2)* 250
Mount Sherman (D1) 130
Mount Vernon (F3)* 200
Mountain Home (F1)* 2,217
Mountain Pine (D4)* 1,155
Mountain Valley (D4)* 160
Mountain View (F2)* 1,043
Mountainburg (B2)* 405
Mountaincrest (B2)
Mulberry (B2)* 952
Murfreesboro (C5)* 1,079
Nashville (C6)* 3,548
Nathan (C5) 100
Natural Steps (E4) 100
Nelsonville (H1)
Nettleton (J2)* 1,382
Neuhardt (K3) 190
New Blaine (D3)*
New Edinburg (F6)* 150
New London (F7) 50
New Rocky Comfort
(Foreman*) (B6) 907
Newark (H2)* 913
Newburg (G1)*
Newhope (C5)* 162
Newport (H2)* 6,254
Nimmons (K1)* 199
Nimrod (D4)* 185
Noble Lake (G5) 150
Nola (C4)* 130
Norfork (F1)* 431
Norman (C5)* 401
Norphlet (E7)* 653
No. Little Rock (F4)* 44,097
No. Little Rock-Little
Rock (urban area) 150,758
North Spadra (C3) 75
Norvell (K3) 372
Nunley (B4) 50
Oakgrove (C1)* 100
Oakhaven ‡(C6) 81
Oden (C4)* 133
Ogden (B6)* 296
Ogemaw (E7)* 75
Oil Trough (G2)* 300
O'Kean (J1)* 165
Okolona (D5)* 458
Ola (D3)* 880
Olena (H5) 39
Olvey (E1)*
Olyphant (H2)*
Omaha (D1)* 91
Oneida (J5)*
Onyx (D4)* 60
Oppelo (E3) 100
Optimus (F1)* 60
Osage (D1)* 30
Osage Mills (B1) 12
Osceola (K2)* 5,006
Otwell (J2)*
Ouachita (E6)* 75
Owensville (E4) 100
Oxford (G1)* 79
Ozan (C6)* 124
Ozark (C3)* 1,757
Ozone (D2)* 200
Palarm (F4) 25
Palatka (J1)* 40
Palestine (J4)* 420
Pangburn (G3)* 669
Paragould (J1)* 9,668
Paraloma (B6)* 186
Paris (C3)* 3,731
Parkdale (G7)* 385
Parkin (J3)* 1,414
Parks (B4)* 200
Paron (E4)* 75
Patmos (C7)* 120
Patterson (H3)* 357
Pea Ridge (B1)* 268
Peach Orchard (J1)* 327
Pearcy (D5)* 200
Pearson (F3)* 55
Pecan Point (L3) 100
Penrose (H3)* 50
Perla (E5)* 400
Perry (E3)* 284
Perryville (E3)* 674
Pettigrew (C2)*
Pfeiffer (G2) 50
Pickens (H6)* 86
Piggott (K1)* 2,558
Pike (C5)* 123
Pinckney (K4)* 175
Pindall (E1)* 160
Pine Bluff (F5)* 37,162
Pine City (H4) 55
Pine Grove (E6) 300
Pine Ridge (C4)*
Pinetree (J3) 75
Piney (D3) 50
Pitts (J2) 40
Plainfield (D7)
Plainview (D4)* 637
Pleasant Plains (G2)* 153
Plumerville (E3)* 550
Pocahontas (E1)* 3,840
Point Cedar (D5)* 63
Pollard (K1)* 165
Ponca (D1)* 42
Poplar Grove (J4)* 169
Portia (H1)* 349
Portland (G7)* 517
Postelle (J4)* 42
Potter (B4)* 175
Pottsville (D3)* 224
Poughkeepsie (H1)*
Powhatan (H1)* 120
Poyen (E5)*
Prague (F5) 39
Prairie Grove (B2)* 939
Prairie View (C3)* 300
Prattsville (F5)* 110
Prescott (D6)* 3,960
Princedale (J3) 25
Princeton (E6)* 112
Proctor (K3)* 500
Provo (B5)* 61
Pyatt (E1)* 257
Quitman (F3)* 345
Ratcliff (C3)* 213
Ratio (J5)* 375
Ravana (C7)*
Ravenden (H1)* 245
Ravenden Springs (H1)* 197
Reader (D6)* 79
Readland (H7)* 75
Rector (K1)* 1,855
Redfield (F5)* 291
Redstar (C2)*
Relfs Bluff (G6)* 50
Rest (G6) 10
Retta (E3) 10
Rex (E2) 40
Reydell (G5)* 150
Reyno (J1)* 292
Rich Mountain (B4) 57
Richmond (B6)
Rison (F6)* 953
Rivervale (K2)*
Rob Roy (G5) 50
Robinson (B1) 60
Roe (H4)* 200
Rogers (B1)* 4,962
Rohwer (H6)*
Roland (E4)* 350
Rolla (E5)* 150
Romance (F3)* 100
Rondo (J4)* 194
Rosboro (C5)* 84
Rose Bud (F3)* 181
Roseland (K2)* 75
Rosetta (D2) 50
Rosie (G2)* 300
Rosston (D6)* 200
Round Pond (J3)* 250
Rover (D4)* 182
Rowell (F6)* 50
Rudy (B2)* 97
Rush (E1)* 250
Russell (G3)* 241
Russellville (D3)* 8,166
Rye (F6)* 40
Saddle (G1)* 45
Sage (G1)* 125
Saint Charles (H5)* 313
St. Francis (K1)* 292
St. James (F2)*
St. Joe (E1)* 187
St. Paul (C2)* 136
St. Thomas (K3) 100
Salado (G2)* 200
Salem (G1)* 687
Salus (D2)* 100
Saratoga (C6)* 110
Sayre (D6)
Schaal (C6)* 25
Scotland (E2)* 200
Scott (F4)* 350
Scottsville (D3)* 150
Scranton (C3)* 283
Searcy (G3)* 6,024
Sedgwick (J2)* 196
Selma (G6)* 275
Seyppel (K4) 175
Shawmut (D5) 26
Shelbyville (H2)*
Sheridan (F5)* 1,893
Sherrill (G5)* 263
Sherwood (F4) 717
Shiloh (F2)* 41
Shirley (F2)* 259
Sidney (G1)* 120
Sidon (G3)* 75
Siloam Springs (B1)* 3,270

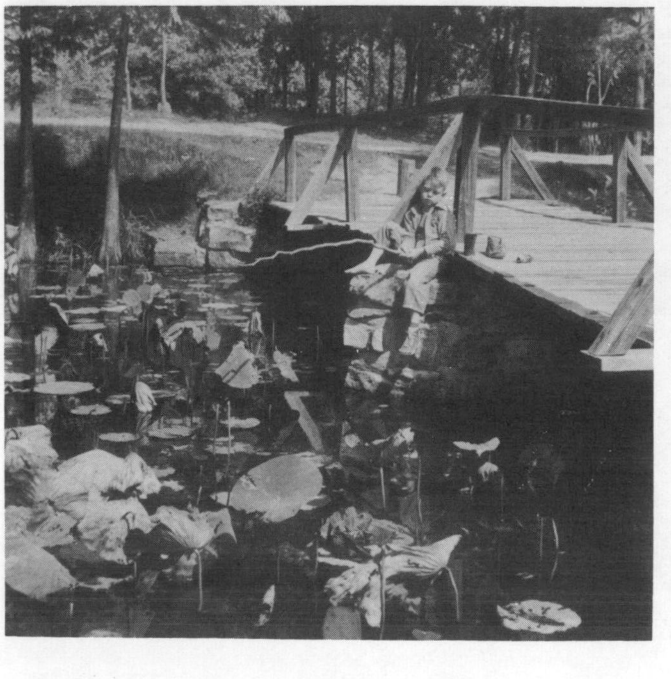

Silver (D4)*
Sims (C4)* 125
Simsboro (K3) 175
Sitka (H1)* 98
Slocomb (E4)
Smackover (E7)* 2,495
Smale (H4) 48
Smithton (D6)*
Smithville (H1)* 250
Snow Hill (E7) 150
Snow Lake (H5)* 96
Snowball (E2)* 210
Snyder (G7)* 250
Solgohachia (E3)* 125
Soudan (J4) 25
South Bend (G5) 2
Spadra (D3)* 101
Sparkman (E6)* 964
Spotville (D7) 50
Spring Hill (C6) 235
Springdale (B1)* 5,835
Springfield (E3)* 135
Springtown (B1)* 102
Stamps (D7)* 2,552
Star City (G6)* 1,296
State Sanatorium (C3)* 1,800
Stephens (E7)* 1,283
Steprock (G3)* 150
Steve (D4)*
Stonewall (J1)* 150
Strawberry (H2)* 190
Strickler (B2) 25
Strong (F7)* 839
Stuttgart (H4)* 7,276
Subiaco (C3)* 191
Success (J1)* 311
Sugar Grove (C3)* 225
Sulphur City (B2)* 60
Sulphur Rock (H2)* 179
Sulphur Springs (B1)* 543
Summers (A2)* 90
Summit (E1)* 268
Sumpter (F7)
Sunset (B2)* 93
Sutton (D6)
Swan Lake (G5) 50
Sweet Home (F4)* 750
Swifton (H2)* 539
Tamo (G5)*
Taylor (D7)* 547
Texarkana (C7)* 15,875
Thebes (G7) 250
Thornton (F6)*
Three Creeks (E7) 100
Tichnor (H5)*
Tie Plant (F4)* 300
Tillar (H6)* 239
Tilton (J3)* 25
Timbo (F2)*
Tinsman (F6)* 118
Tipperary (J1) 50
Tokio (C5)* 150
Tollette (C6) 150
Tollville (G4) 150
Toltec (F4) 130
Tontitown (B1)* 203
Traskwood (E5)* 199
Trenton (J5)
Trumann (J2)* 3,744
Tubal (E7) 25
Tucker (G5)* 200
Tuckerman (H2)* 1,253
Tulip (E5)
Tulot (K2)* 350
Tupelo (H3)* 188
Turner (H5)*
Turrell (K3)* 670
Tyro (G6)* 88
Tyronza (K3)* 656
Ulm (H4)* 131
Umpire (B5)* 83
Union (G1)* 75
Unionhill (H2)* 100
Uniontown (B2)* 66
Urbana (E7)* 800
Urbanette (D1)* 45
Vaden (E6)
Valley Springs (D1)* 110
Van Buren (B3)* 6,413
Vandervoort (B5)* 350
Vanndale (J3)* 600
Varner (G5)* 3
Vick (F7)*
Victoria (K2)* 300
Village (D7)* 500
Vilonia (F3)* 215
Vimy Ridge (F4)* 200
Vincent (K3) 75
Viola (G1)* 206
Violet Hill (G1)*
Wabash (J5)* 150
Wabbaseka (G5)* 375
Walcott (J1)* 85
Waldenburg (J2)* 150
Waldo (D7)* 1,491
Waldron (B4)* 1,292
Walnut Corner (J1) 100
Walnut Grove (H2) 28
Walnut Hill (C7) 65
Walnut Ridge (J1)* 3,106
Waltreak (C4)* 52
Ward (F3)* 364
Wareagle (C1)* 100
Warm Springs (H1)* 25
Warren (F6)* 6,319
Washburn (B3) 125
Washington (C6)* 344
Washita (D4)*
Watalula (C2)* 25
Waterloo (D6)* 250
Watson (H6)* 309
Wattensaw (G4)* 30
Wave (E5) 25
Waveland (C3)* 396
Webb City (C3)* 125
Wedington (B1) 30
Weeks (B4) 50
Weiner (J2)* 644
Weldon (H3)*
Weona (J2)* 1,500
Wesley (C1)* 100
Wesson (E7)*
West Crossett (F7) 289
West Fork (B2)* 351
West Helena (J4)* 6,107
West Memphis (K3)* 9,112
West Point (G3)* 115
West Ridge (K2)* 275
Western Grove (D1)* 184
Wharton (C1)* 200
Wheatley (H4)* 406
Whelen Springs (D6)* 192
Whisp (K2) 25
White (G7)* 300
Whitehall (J3)*
Wickes (B5)* 401
Wideman (G1)*
Widener (J3)* 187
Wild Cherry (F1)* 125
Williford (H1)* 213
Willow (E5)* 200
Wilmar (G6)* 746
Wilmot (G7)* 721
Wilson (K2)* 1,301
Wilton (B6)* 328
Winchester (G6)* 198
Winfield (B4) 50
Winslow (B2)* 248
Winthrop (B6)* 284
Wirth (H1) 50
Wiseman (G1)*
Witherspoon (E5) 45
Witter (C2)* 50
Witts Springs (E2)* 38
Wiville (H3)* 50
Wolf Bayou (G2)* 255
Woodberry (E6)* 200
Woodson (F4)* 400
Wooster (F3)* 140
Worden (H3) 50
Wright (C5)*
Wrightsville (F4)* 300
Wynne (J3)* 4,142
Yancopin (H6)* 21
Yancy (C6) 35
Yarbro (L2) 200
Yellville (E1)* 697
Yorktown (G5)* 100
Zack (E2)* 60
Zent (H4)* 30
Zinc (E1)* 99
Zion (G1)*

Map on Page 53

CALIFORNIA

Total Population 10,586,223

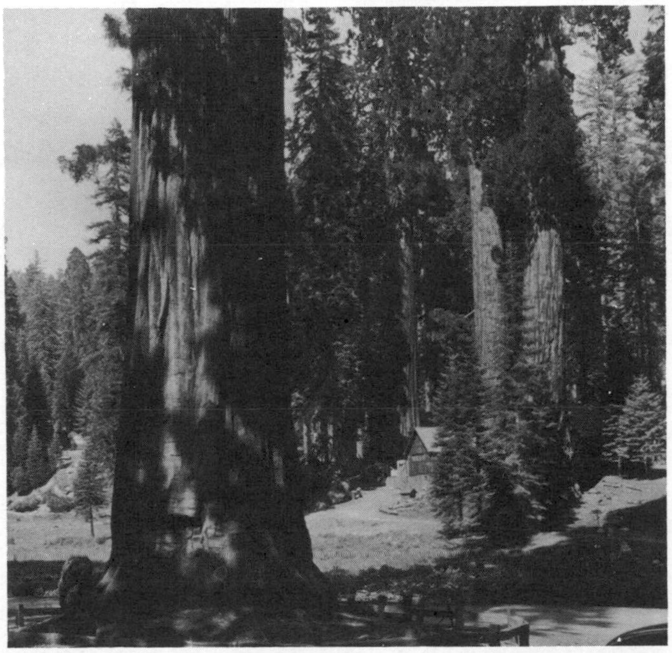

58 COUNTIES

Alameda (D6) 740,315
Alpine (F5) 241
Amador (E5) 9,151
Butte (D4) 64,930
Calaveras (E5) 9,902
Colusa (C4) 11,651
Contra Costa (D6) 298,984
Del Norte (B2) 8,078
El Dorado (E5) 16,207
Fresno (F7) 276,515
Glenn (C4) 15,448
Humboldt (B3) 69,241
Imperial (K10) 62,975
Inyo (H7) 11,658
Kern (G8) 228,309
Kings (F8) 46,768
Lake (C4) 11,481
Lassen (E3) 18,474
Los Angeles (G9) 4,151,687
Madera (F6) 36,964
Marin (C5) 85,619
Mariposa (F6) 5,145
Mendocino (B4) 40,854
Merced (E6) 69,780
Modoc (E2) 9,678
Mono (F5) 2,115
Monterey (D7) 130,498
Napa (C5) 46,603
Nevada (E4) 19,888
Orange (H10) 216,224
Placer (E4) 41,649
Plumas (E4) 13,519
Riverside (J10) 170,046
Sacramento (D5) 277,140
San Benito (D7) 14,370
San Bernardino (J9) 281,642
San Diego (J11) 556,808
San Francisco (J2) 775,357
San Joaquin (D6) 200,750
San Luis Obispo (E8) 51,417
San Mateo (C6) 235,659
Santa Barbara (E9) 98,220
Santa Clara (D6) 290,547
Santa Cruz (C6) 66,534
Shasta (C3) 36,413
Sierra (E4) 2,410
Siskiyou (C2) 30,733
Solano (D5) 104,833
Sonoma (C5) 103,405
Stanislaus (D6) 127,231
Sutter (D4) 26,239
Tehama (C3) 19,276
Trinity (B3) 5,087
Tulare (G7) 149,264
Tuolumne (F5) 12,584
Ventura (F9) 114,647
Yolo (D5) 40,640
Yuba (D4) 24,420

CITIES and TOWNS

Acampo (C9)* 800
Adelanto (H9)* 623
Adin (E2)*
Agnew (K3)* 700
Ahwahnee (F6)* 400
Alameda (J2)* 64,430
Alamo (K2)* 2,673
Albany (J2)* 17,590
Alberhill (E11)* 300
Albion (B4)* 350
Alderpoint (B3)* 200
Alhambra (C10)* 51,359
Alisal (D7)* 16,714
Alleghany (E4)* 300
Alma (K4)* 600
Almaden (L4)* 300
Alpaugh (F8)* 1,200
Alta Loma (E10) 1,200
Altadena (C10)* 37,500
Altamont (L2)* 65
Alton (A3)* 275
Alturas (E2)* 2,819
Alvarado (K2)* 2,000
Alviso (K3)* 652
Amador City ‡(E5)* 151
Amboy (K9)* 150
Anaheim (D11)* 14,556
Anderson (C3) 1,501
Angels Camp (E5)* 1,147
Angwin (C5)* 2,000
Annapolis (B5)*
Antelope (C8)* 111
Antioch (L1)* 11,051
Apple Valley (H9)* 1,400
Applegate (E5)* 300
Aptos (K4)* 2,000
Arbuckle (C4)* 1,150
Arcadia (D10)* 23,066
Arcata (A3)* 3,729
Arlight (E9)* 10
Arlington (E11)* 4,326
Armona (F7)* 1,274
Arnold (E5)* 375
Aromas (D7) 700
Arroyo Grande (E8) 1,723
Artesia (C11)* 15,920
Artois (C4) 170
Arvin (G8)* 5,007
Associated (K1)* 250
Asti (C5)* 300
Atascadero (E8)* 3,443
Atherton (K3)* 3,630
Atolia (H8) 25
Atwater (E6)* 2,856
Atwood (D11)* 500
Auberry (F6)* 477
Auburn (C8)* 4,653
Aukum (E5)*
Avalon (G10)* 1,506
Avenal (E8)* 3,982
Azusa (D10)* 11,042
Bagby (E6)* 50
Baker (J8) 300
Bakersfield (G8)* 34,784
Balboa (D11)* 3,000
Baldwin Park (D10)* 28,000
Bangor (D4)* 335
Banning (J10)* 7,034
Bard (L11)* 45
Barstow (H9)* 6,135
Bayshore (J2) 2,726
Bayside (B3)* 650
Beatrice (A3)* 100
Beaumont (J10)* 3,152
Beckwourth (E4)* 75
Belden (D3)* 500
Bell (C11)* 15,430
Bellflower (C11)* 40,000
Belmont (J3)* 5,567
Belvedere (H2)* 800
Ben Lomond (K4)* 1,500
Benicia (K1)* 7,284
Benton (G6)* 110
Berkeley (J2)* 113,805
Bethany (D6)* 25
Betteravia (E9)* 350
Beverly Hills (B10)* 29,032
Bieber (D2)* 600
Big Bar (B3)* 210
Big Basin (J4)* 60
Big Bear City (J9)* 476
Big Bear Lake (J9)* 1,434
Big Creek (F6)* 368
Big Oak Flat (E6)* 150
Biggs (D4)* 784
Bigpine (G6)* 800
Biola (E7)* 500
Bishop (G6)* 2,891
Black Point (J1)* 431
Blairsden (E4)* 90
Bloomington (E10)* 10,100
Blue Jay (H9)* 306
Blue Lake (A3)* 824
Blythe (L10)* 4,089
Bodega Bay (B5)* 350
Bodfish (G8)* 247
Bodie (F5) 20
Bolinas (H1)* 1,006
Boonville (B5)* 1,500
Boron (H8)* 236
Boulder Creek (J4)* 1,497
Boulevard (J11)* 75
Bowles (F7) 150
Bradley (E8)* 100
Brawley (K11)* 11,922
Brea (D11)* 3,208
Brentwood (L2)* 1,729
Briceland (B3)* 175
Bridgeport (F5)* 250
Bridgeville (B3)* 475
Brisbane (J2)* 4,500
Broderick (B8) 3,500
Brookdale (J4)* 150
Brooks (C5)* 75
Bryn Mawr (F10)* 300
Bryte (B8)* 3,000
Buckeye (C3) 275
Buellton (E9)* 450
Buena Park (D11)* 5,483
Burbank (C10)* 78,577
Burlingame (J3)* 19,886
Burney (D3)* 1,513
Burrel (E7)* 100
Butte City (C4)* 150
Buttonwillow (F8)* 1,000
Byron (L2)* 1,117
Cadiz (K9)* 50
Calexico (K11)* 6,433
Calipatria (K10)* 1,428
Calistoga (C5)* 1,418
Callahan (C2)* 250
Calpella (B4)* 350
Calpine (E4) 75
Camanche (C9)* 75
Camarillo (F9)* 2,500
Cambria (D8)* 1,300
Camino (E5)*
Campbell (K3)* 10,000
Campo (J11)* 550
Campo Seco (D9)* 100
Camptonville (D4)* 350
Canby (E2)* 505
Cantil (H8)* 150
Canyon (K2)* 400
Capay (C5)* 112
Capistrano Beach (H10)* 700
Capitola (K4)* 1,848
Carlsbad (H10)* 4,383
Carmel (C7)* 4,351
Carpinteria (F9)* 2,864
Cartago (G7)* 98
Caruthers (E7)* 500
Casa Blanca (E11)* 1,585
Casmalia (E9)* 300
Caspar (B4)* 400
Castaic (G9)*
Castella (C2)* 350
Castroville (D7)* 1,865
Cathay (E6)* 200
Cathedral City (J10)* 2,058
Cayucos (E8)* 1,500
Cazadero (B5)* 350
Cecilville (B2)* 50
Cedarville (E2)* 850
Centerville (K3)* 1,401
Central Valley (C3)* 2,202
Ceres (D6)* 2,351
Chambers Lodge (E4)* 25
Chester (D3)* 1,197
Chico (D4)* 12,272
Chilcoot (E4)* 75
Chinese Camp (E6)* 150
Chino (D10)* 5,784
Cholame (E8)* 500
Chowchilla (E6)* 3,893
Chrisman (F9) 4,211
Chualar (D7)* 450
Chubbuck (K9) 46
Chula Vista (J11)* 15,927
Cima (K8)* 30
Claremont (D10)* 6,327
Clarksburg (B9)*
Clay (C9)* 52
Clayton (K2)* 680
Clear Creek (B2)* 6
Clearlake Highlands (C5)* 850
Clearlake Oaks (C4)* 750
Clearwater (C11)* 8,586
Clements (C9)* 242
Clipper Mills (D4)* 100
Cloverdale (B5)* 1,292
Clovis (F7)* 2,766
Coachella (J10)* 2,755
Coalinga (E7)* 5,539
Coarsegold (F6)* 300
Coleville (F5)* 250
Colfax (E4)* 820
Collinsville (L1)* 30
Colma (J2)* 2,500
Colma (Lawndale) (H2)* 297
Coloma (D5)* 350
Colton (E10)* 14,465
Columbia (E5)* 650
Colusa (C4)* 3,031
Comptche (B4)* 150
Compton (C11)* 47,991
Concord (K1)* 6,953
Corcoran (F7)* 3,150
Cordelia (K1) 365
Corning (C4)* 2,537
Corona (E11)* 10,223
Corona del Mar (G10)* 4,500
Coronado (H11)* 12,700
Corralitos (L4) 300
Corte Madera (J2)* 1,933
Coso Junction (H7)* 40
Costa Mesa (D11)* 11,844
Cotati (C5)* 683
Cottonwood (C3)* 950
Coulterville (E6)* 350
Courtland (B9)* 750
Covelo (B4)* 550
Covina (D10)* 3,956
Cowell (K1)* 200
Coyote (L4)* 150
Crannell (A2)* 428
Crescent City (A2)* 1,706
Crescent Mills (E3)* 300
Crestline (H9)* 1,000
Creston (E8)* 85
Crockett (J1)* 6,000
Cross Roads (L9)* 42
Crows Landing (D6)* 500
Crucero (J8)
Cucamonga (E10)* 1,255
Culver City (B10)* 19,720
Cupertino (K3)* 2,438
Cutler (F7)* 1,768
Cutten (A3)* 1,340
Cypress (D11)* 1,318
Daggett (H9)* 835
Daly City (H2)* 15,191
Dana Point (H10)* 500
Danville (K2)* 3,130
Darwin (H7)* 450
Davenport (K4)* 300
Davis (B8)* 3,554
Davis Creek (E2)* 120
Day (D2)* 65
Death Valley (J7)* 100
Declezville (E10)
Decoto (K2)* 2,830
Deep Springs (H6) 50
Del Mar (H11)* 1,800
Del Paso Hts. (B8)* 15,000
Del Rey (F7)* 750
Del Rosa (E10)* 1,154
Delano (F8)* 8,717
Delhi (E6)* 1,000
Delleker (E4)* 250
Delpiedra (F7) 56
Delta (C3)* 100
Denair (E6)* 860
Denny (B3)* 55
Descanso (J11)* 400
Desert Center (K10)* 160
Diablo (K2)* 079
Diamond Spgs. (D8)* 1,200
Dinkey Creek (F6)* 90
Dinuba (F7)* 4,971
Dixon (B9)* 1,714
Dorris (D2)* 892
Dos Palos (E6)* 1,394
Douglas City (C3)* 95
Downey (C11)* 35,000
Downieville (E4)* 450
Doyle (E3)* 77
Drytown (C8)* 155
Duarte (D10)* 10,000
Dublin (K2) 200
Ducor (G8)* 155
Dunnigan (C5)* 175
Dunsmuir (C2)* 2,256
Durham (D4)* 1,600
Dutch Flat (E4)* 220
Eagle Mountain (K10)*
Earlmart (F8) 2,162
Earp (L9)* 7
East Bakersfield (G8) 38,177
Edgewood (C2)* 200
Edwards (G9)* 192
Eel Rock (B3)* 100
El Cajon (J11)* 5,600
El Centro (K11)* 12,590
El Cerrito (J2)* 18,011
El Dorado (C8)* 600
El Granada (H3)* 300
El Modeno (D11)* 1,500
El Monte (D10)* 8,101
El Nido (E6)* 765
El Portal (F6)* 279
El Segundo (B11) 8,011
El Toro (E11)* 200
Elk (B4)* 150
Elk Creek (C4)* 200
Elk Grove (B9)* 1,200
Elmira (D5)* 200
Elsinore (F11)* 2,068
Elverta (B8)* 850
Emeryville (J2)* 2,889
Empire (D6)* 1,448
Encanto (J11)* 7,300
Encinitas (H10)* 7,000
Escalon (E6)* 1,569
Escondido (H10)* 6,544
Esparto (C5)* 800
Essex (K9)* 60
Etiwanda (E10)* 1,200
Etna (C2)* 649
Eureka (A3)* 23,058
Evergreen (L3) 300
Exeter (F7)* 4,078
Fair Oaks (C8)* 5,000
Fairfax (H1)* 4,078
Fairfield (K1)* 3,118
Fairmead (E6) 250
Fall River Mills (D3)* 800
Fallbrook (H10)* 1,735
Famoso (F8) 100
Farley (B4)
Farmersville (F7)* 5,000
Farmington (E6)* 173
Fawnskin (J9)* 350
Feather Falls (D4)* 1,500
Fellows (F8)* 343
Felton (K4)* 1,200
Fenner (K9)* 25
Ferndale (A3)* 1,032
Fields Landing (A3)* 270
Fillmore (F9)* 3,884
Firebaugh (E7)* 821
Fish Camp (F6)* 25
Florin (B8)* 500
Folsom (C8)* 1,690
Fontana (E10)* 28,000
Ford City (F8) 4,347
Forest Knolls (H1)* 500
Foresthill (E4)* 1,000
Forks of Salmon (B2)* 185
Fort Bidwell (E2)* 275
Fort Bragg (B4)* 3,826
Fort Dick (A2)* 500
Fort Jones (C2)* 525
Fort Seward (B3)* 115
Fortuna (A3)* 1,762
Fowler (F7)* 1,857
Franklin (B9) 45
Freedom (L4)* 2,765
Freeport (B8) 300
French Gulch (C3)* 350
Freshwater (B3)* 186
Fresno (F7)* 91,669
Fresno (urban area) 129,275
Friant (F7)* 950
Fullerton (D11)* 13,958
Galt (C9)* 1,333
Garberville (B3)* 1,350
Garden Grove (D11)* 3,762
Gardena (C11)* 14,405
Gaviota (E9)* 125
Gazelle (C2)* 300
Georgetown (E5)* 600
Gerber (C3)* 700
Geyersville (B5)* 925
Gilroy (L4)* 4,951
Glamis (K11)* 50
Glen Ellen ‡(C5)* 1,100
Glendale (C10)* 95,702
Glendora (D10)* 3,988
Glennville (G8)* 120
Glenwood (K4)* 103
Goleta (F9)* 1,548
Gonzales (D7)* 1,821
Gorman (G9)*
Goshen (F7)* 525
Graeagle (E4)* 300
Graniteville (E4)* 25
Grapevine (F9)* 100
Grass Valley (D4)* 5,283
Greenfield (D7)* 1,309
Greenview (B2)* 200
Greenville (E3)* 1,153
Greenwood (E5)* 375
Grenada (C2)* 250
Gridley (D4)* 3,054
Grimes (C4)* 500
Grizzly Flats (E5)* 40
Groveland (E6)* 365
Grover City (E8)* 2,250
Guadalupe (E9)* 2,429
Gualala (B5)* 140
Guasti (E10)* 400
Guerneville (B5)* 1,250
Guinda (C5)* 150
Gustine (D6)* 1,984
Half Moon Bay (H3)* 1,168
Hambone (D2) 6
Hamburg (B2)* 150
Hamilton City (C4)* 900
Hammonton (D4)* 250
Hanford (F7)* 10,028
Happy Camp (B2)* 530
Harbor City (C11)* 7,500
Harris (B3)* 115
Hawthorne (B11)* 16,316
Hayfork (B3)* 1,200
Hayward (K2)* 14,272
Hazel Creek (C2)* 85
Healdsburg (B5)* 3,258
Heber (K11)* 300
Helena (B3)* 40
Hemet (J10)* 3,386
Herald (C9)*
Hercules (J1)* 343
Hermosa Beach (B11)* 11,826
Hesperia (H9)* 250
Highgrove (E10)* 553
Highland (H9)* 8,500
Hillsborough ‡(J2)* 3,552
Hilmar (E6)* 525
Hilts (C2)*
Hinkley (H9)* 75
Hollister (D7)* 4,903
Hollywood (C10)* 179,749
Holt (D6)* 150
Holtville (K11)* 2,472
Holy City (K4)* 50
Homewood (E4)* 8
Honcut (D4) 271
Hood (B9)* 250
Hoopa (B2)* 850
Hopland (B5)* 1,150
Hornbrook (C2)* 250
Hornitos (E6)* 126
Hughson (E6)* 1,816
Huntington Beach (D11)* 5,237
Huntington Park (C10)* 29,450
Huron (E7)* 1,500
Hydesville (B3)* 250
Idyllwild (J10)* 604
Ignacio (H1) 180
Imperial (K11)* 1,759
Independence (H7)* 850
Indio (J10)* 5,300
Inglewood (B11)* 46,185
Inverness (B5)* 550
Inyokern (H8)* 266
Ione (C9)* 1,071
Irvine (D11)* 150
Irvington (K3)* 2,500
Isabella (G8)* 308
Isleton (L1)* 1,597
Ivanhoe (F7)* 1,172
Ivanpah (K8)* 20
Jackson (C9)* 1,879
Jacumba (J11)* 600
Jamestown (E6)* 1,300
Janesville (E3)* 165
Jenny Lind (C9)*
Johannesburg (H8)* 200
Johnsondale (G8)* 230
Julian (J10)* 300
Junction City (B3)* 95
June Lake (G6)* 250
Keddie (E3)* 500
Keeler (H7)* 302
Keene (G8)* 300
Kelseyville (C5)* 550
Kelso (K8)* 117
Kerman (E7)* 1,563
Kernville (G8)* 475
Kettleman City (E7)* 450
King City (D7)* 2,347
Kings Beach (F4)* 500
Kingsburg (F7)* 2,310
Kirkwood (C4)* 56
Klamath (B2)* 1,012
Knights Landing (B8)* 700
Knightsen (L1)* 684
Knob (C3) 8
Korbel (B3)* 350
La Canada (C10)* 8,200
La Crescenta (C10)* 16,000
La Grange (E6)* 250
La Habra (D11)* 4,961
La Honda (J3)* 480
La Jolla (H11)* 13,000
La Mesa (H11)* 10,946
La Moine (C3)* 125
La Porte (D4)* 31
La Sierra (E11)* 3,802
La Verne (D10)* 4,198

Lafayette (K2)*...10,500
Laguna Beach (G10)*...6,661
Lagunitas (H1)*... 750
Lake Alpine (F5)*... 3
Lake Arrowhead (H9)*.. 667
Lake City (E2)*... 94
Lake Hughes (G9)*... 224
Lakeport (C4)*...1,983
Lakeside (J11)*...1,500
Lakewood (C11)*...31,000
Lamont (G8)*...3,571
Lancaster (G9)*...3,594
Larkspur (H1)*...2,905
Las Plumas (D4)*... 55
Lathrop (D6)... 600
Laton (F7)*... 881
Laurel (K4)... 64
Lawndale (C11)*...31,000
Lawndale (Colma*)(H2) 297
Laws (G6)*... 75
Laytonville (B4)*...
Le Grand (E6)*...1,000
Lebec (G9)*... 370
Leevining (F6)*... 450
Lemoncove (G7)*...1,100
Lemoore (F7)*...2,153
Lennox (C11)*...25,000
Lenwood (H9)... 250
Leucadia (H10)*... 500
Lewiston (C3)*... 300
Likely (E2)*... 200
Lincoln (B8)*...2,410
Linden (D5)*... 426
Lindsay (G7)*...5,060
Little Lake (H8)*... 50
Littleriver (B4)*... 300
Live Oak (D4)*...1,770
Livermore (L2)*...4,364
Livingston (E6)*...1,502
Llano (H9)*... 30
Locke (B9)*... 295
Lockeford (C9)*...1,000
Lodi (C9)*...13,798
Loftus (C3)*... 200
Loleta (A3)*... 500
Loma Linda (E10)*...4,000
Loma Mar (J3)*... 125
Lomita (C11)*...10,000
Lomita Park (J2)*...1,800
Lompoc (E9)*...5,520
Lone Pine (H7)*...1,415
Long Beach (C11)*...250,767
Lonoak (E7)*... 15
Lookout (D2)*... 225
Loomis (C8)*... 350
Los Alamitos (D11)*...1,800
Los Alamos (E9)*... 800
Los Altos (K3)*...11,000
Los Angeles (C10)*.1,970,358
Los Angeles (urban area)...3,970,595
Los Banos (E6)*...3,868
Los Gatos (K4)*...4,907
Los Molinos (D3)*... 600
Los Olivos (E9)*... 500
Lost Hills (F8)*... 300
Lotus (C8)*... 150
Lower Lake (C5)*... 275
Loyalton (E4)*... 911
Lucerne (C4)*... 350
Lucerne Valley (J9)*... 933
Ludlow (J9)*... 250
Lynwood (C11)*...25,823
Macdoel (D2)*... 200
Madeline (E2)*... 60
Madera (E7)*...10,497
Madison (D5)*...
Madrone (L4)*... 720
Magalia (D4)*... 200
Manchester (B5)*... 500
Manhattan Beach (B11)*...17,330
Manteca (D6)*...3,804
Manton (D3)*... 100
March Air Force Base (E11)*...
Maricopa (F8)*... 800
Mariposa (F6)*... 700
Markleeville (F5)*... 100
Martell (C9)*... 200
Martinez (K1)*...8,268
Marysville (D4)*...7,826
Maxwell (C4)*... 750
Maywood (C10)*...13,292
Mc Arthur (D2)*... 398
Mc Cann (B3)... 35
Mc Cloud (C2)*...1,394
Mc Farland (F8)*...2,183
Mc Kittrick (F8)*... 124
Meadow Valley (D4)*... 300
Mecca (K10)*... 837
Mendocino (B4)*...1,250
Mendota (E7)*...1,516
Menlo Park (J3)*...13,587
Mentone (H9)*...3,525
Merced (E6)*...15,278
Michigan Bar (C8)... 132
Middletown (C5)*... 400
Midland (L10)*... 700
Midway City (D11)*...1,421
Milford (E3)*... 55
Mill Valley (H2)*...7,331
Millbrae (J2)*...8,972
Mills (C8)... 300
Millville (C3)*... 246
Milpitas (L3)*...
Milton (E5)...
Mineral (D3)*... 125
Mira Loma (E10)*...1,555
Mission San Jose (L3)*1,080
Modesto (D6)*...17,389
Mojave (G8)*...2,055
Mokelumne Hill (E5)*.. 495
Mono Lake (F5)*... 20
Monolith (G8)*... 450
Monrovia (D10)*...20,186
Montague (C2)*... 579
Montalvo (F9)*...1,200
Montara (H3)*... 400
Monte Rio (B5)*... 750
Montebello (C10)*...21,735
Montecito (F9)...4,052
Monterey (D7)*...16,205
Monterey Park (C10)*.20,395
Monticello (C5)*...
Montrose (C10)*...8,500
Moorpark (G9)*...1,146
Moraga (K2)*... 325
Moreno (H10)*... 200
Morgan Hill (L4)*...1,627
Morro Bay (D8)*...1,659
Moss Beach (H3)*... 525
Moss Landing (C7)*... 300
Mount Eden (K2)*...1,500
Mount Hamilton (L3)*..
Mount Hermon (K4)*... 150
Mount Owen (H8)...
Mount Shasta (C2)*...1,909
Mountain Center (J10)* 40
Mountain View (K3)*...6,563
Murphys (E5)*... 650
Murray (E7)... 150
Napa (C5)*...13,579
Napa Junction (J1)... 224
National City (J11)*..21,199
Natoma (C8)*... 65
Navarro (B4)*... 117
Needles (L9)*...4,051
Nevada City (D4)*...2,505
New Cuyuma (F9)*...1,079
Newark (K3)*...1,532
Newberry (J9)*... 520
Newcastle (C8)*... 800
Newhall (G9)*...2,527
Newman (D6)*...1,815
Newport Beach (D11)*12,120
Nicasio (H1)*... 133
Nicolaus (B8)*... 400
Niland (K10)*... 700
Niles (K3)*...1,519
Nipinnawasee (F6)*...
Nipomo (E8)*...1,000
Nipton (K8)*... 15
Norco (E11)*...1,584
Norden (E4)*... 220
N. Fork (F6)*...1,453
N. Sacramento (B8)*...6,029
N. San Juan (E4)*... 250
Norwalk (C11)*...6,300
Novato (H1)*...3,496
Nubieber (D2)*... 400
Oakdale (E6)*...4,064
Oakhurst (F6)*... 325
Oakland (J2)*...384,575
Oakland-San Francisco (urban area)...1,997,303
Oakley (L1)*...2,892
Oasis (G6)... 25
Ocean Beach (H11)*...16,600
Oceano (E8)*...1,446
Oceanside (H10)*...12,881
Oildale (F8)*...16,615
Ojai (F9)*...2,519
Olancha (H7)*... 200
Olema (H1)*...
Oleum (J1)*...1,200
Olinda (C3)*... 411
Olinda (D11)... 150
Olive (D11)*... 700
Olympia (K4)... 150
O'Neals (F6)*...
Ono (C3)*... 38
Ontario (D10)*...22,872
Onyx (G8)*... 150
Orange (D11)*...10,027
Orange Cove (F7)*...2,395
Orcutt (E9)*...1,001
Orick (A2)*... 600
Orinda (K2)*...5,000
Orland (C4)*...2,067
Orleans (B2)*... 263
Oro Grande (H9)*... 556
Orosi (F7)*... 712
Oroville (D4)*...5,387
Oxford (B9)... 28
Oxnard (F9)*...21,567
Pacheco (K1)... 400
Pacific Beach (H11)*..23,600
Pacific Grove (C7)*...9,623
Paicines (D7)*... 300
Palermo (D4)*...1,200
Palm City (H11)*...3,000
Palm Springs (J10)*...7,660
Palmdale (G9)*...3,300
Palo Alto (K3)*...25,475
Palo Verde (L10)*... 200
Palos Verdes Estates (B11)*...1,963
Paradise (D4)*...4,426
Paramount (C11)*...10,006
Parker Dam (L9)*... 550
Parlier (F7)*...1,419
Pasadena (C10)*...104,577
Paskenta (C4)*... 350
Paso Robles (E8)*...4,835
Patterson (D6)*...1,343
Paynes Creek (D3)*... 35
Penryn (C8)*... 500
Pepperwood (A3)*... 300
Perkins (B8)*... 600
Perris (F11)*...1,807
Pescadero (J4)*...1,000
Petaluma (H1)*...10,315
Philo (B4)*... 700
Pico (C10)*...9,000
Piedmont (J2)*...10,132
Pine Valley (J11)*... 300
Pinecrest (F5)*... 30
Pinedale (F7)*...2,220
Pineridge (F6)... 115
Pinole (J1)*...1,147
Piru (G9)*...1,500
Pismo Beach (E8)*...1,425
Pittsburg (K1)*...12,763
Pittville (D2)*... 50
Pixley (F8)*...2,000
Placentia (D11)*...1,682
Placerville (C8)*...3,749
Planada (E6)*...1,200
Plaster City (K11)*... 205
Pleasant Grove (B8)*... 30
Pleasanton (L2)*...2,244
Plymouth (C8)*... 382
Point Arena (B5)*... 372
Point Reyes Sta. (H1)*. 500
Pollock Pines (E5)*... 850
Pomona (D10)*...35,405
Pondosa (D2)*... 400
Port Chicago (K1)*...3,000
Port Costa (J1)*... 587
Port Hueneme (F9)*...3,024
Porterville (F7)*...6,904
Portola (E4)*...2,261
Potrero (J11)*... 200
Potter Valley (B4)*...1,200
Pozo (E8)... 200
Princeton (C4)*... 300
Project City (C3)*...1,200
Puente (D10)*...3,000
Quincy (E4)*...1,330
Raisin (E7)*... 250
Ramona (J10)*...1,158
Rancho Santa Fe (H10)*... 750
Randsburg (H8)*... 300
Ravendale (E3)*... 38
Raymond (F6)*... 200
Red Bluff (C3)*...4,905
Red Mountain (H8)*... 250
Redding (C3)*...10,256
Redlands (H9)*...18,429
Redondo Beach (B11)*25,226
Redwood City (J3)*...25,544
Redwood Estates (K4)* 600
Reedley (F7)*...4,135
Represa (C8)*...3,000
Requa (A2)*...
Rialto (E10)*...3,156
Rice (L9)*... 109
Richmond (J1)*...99,545
Richvale (D4)*... 430
Ridgecrest (H8)*...2,028
Rio Dell (A3)*...1,862
Rio Linda (B8)*...5,000
Rio Vista (L1)*...1,831
Ripley (L10)*... 300
Ripon (D6)*...1,550
Riverbank (E6)*...2,662
Riverdale (E7)*... 713
Riverside (E10)*...46,764
Robbins (B8)*... 150
Rockaway Beach (H2)* 300
Rocklin (B8)*...1,155
Rockport (B4)*... 750
Rodeo (J1)*...6,500
Rohnerville (B3)*...1,500
Rosamond (G9)*... 700
Rosemead (D10)*...15,230
Roseville (B8)*...8,723
Ross (H1)*...2,179
Round Mountain (D3)*. 450
Ryde (B9)*... 397
SACRAMENTO (B8)*...137,572
Sacramento (urban area)...210,081
Sage (J10)... 52
Saint Helena (C5)*...2,297
Salinas (D7)*...13,917
Salyer (B3)*... 250
Samoa (A3)*... 600
San Andreas (E5)*...1,263
San Anselmo (H1)...9,188
San Ardo (E7)*... 500
San Benito (D7)*... 110
San Bernardino (E10)*63,058
San Bernardino (urban area)...135,394
San Bruno (J2)*...12,478
San Carlos (J3)*...14,371
San Clemente (H10)*...2,008
San Diego (J11)*...334,387
San Diego (urban area)...413,274
San Dimas (D10)*...1,840
San Fernando (C10)*..12,992
San Francisco (H2)*.775,357
San Francisco-Oakland (urban area)...1,997,303
San Gabriel (C10)*...20,343
San Geronimo (H1)*... 300
San Gregorio (J3)*... 250
San Jacinto (H10)*...1,778
San Joaquin (E7)*... 632
San Jose (L3)*...95,280
San Jose (urban area)...175,983
San Juan Bautista (D7)*...1,031
San Juan Capistrano (H10)*...1,250
San Leandro (J2)*...27,542
San Lorenzo (K2)*...10,570
San Lucas (E7)*... 400
San Luis Obispo (E8)..14,180
San Marino (D10)*...11,230
San Martin (L4)*...2,200
San Mateo (J3)*...41,782
San Miguel (E8)*... 800
San Pablo (J1)*...14,476
San Pedro (C11)*...74,000
San Quentin (H1)*...
San Rafael (J1)*...13,848
San Ramon (K2)*... 250
San Simeon (D8)*... 75
San Ysidro (J11)*...2,381
Sanger (F7)*...6,400
Sanitarium (C5)*... 750
Santa Ana (D11)*...45,533
Santa Barbara (F9)*...44,913
Santa Clara (K3)*...11,702
Santa Cruz (K4)*...21,970
Santa Margarita (E8)*. 500
Santa Maria (E9)*...10,440
Santa Monica (B10)*..71,595
Santa Paula (F9)*...11,049
Santa Rosa (C5)*...17,902
Santa Susana (B10)*...1,000
Saratoga (K4)*...1,329
Saticoy (F9)*...2,216
Sausalito (H2)*...4,828
Sawyers Bar (B2)*...
Schellville (J1)...
Scotia (A3)*...1,017
Seabright (K4)*...
Seal Beach (C11)*...3,553
Seaside (D7)...10,226
Sebastopol (C5)*...2,601
Seeley (K11)*... 500
Seiad Valley (B2)*... 41
Selby (J1)*... 403
Selma (F7)*...5,964
Seneca (D3)...
Sepulveda (B10)*...4,500
Shafter (F8)*...2,207
Shandon (E8)*... 510
Sharp Park (H2)*...3,800
Shasta (C3)*... 900
Shell Beach (E8)*...1,000
Sheridan (D5)*... 600
Shingle (C8)*... 300
Shively (B3)*... 196
Shoshome (J8)*... 150
Sierra City (E4)*... 150
Sierra Madre (D10)*...7,273
Sierraville (E4)*... 400
Signal Hill (C11)*...4,040
Silverado (E11)*...1,400
Simi (G9)*... 550
Sites (C4)*... 200
Sloat (E4)*...
Sloughhouse (C8)*...
Smartville (D4)*... 350
Smith River (A2)*... 700
Snelling (E6)*... 350
Soda Springs (E4)*... 400
Solana Beach (H11)*...1,350
Soledad (D7)*...2,441
Solvang (E9)*...1,025
Somesbar (B2)*... 200
Sonoma (C5)*...2,015
Sonora (E6)*...2,448
Soquel (K4)*...2,400
Soulsbyville (E6)*... 150
S. Bakersfield (F8)...12,120
S. Dos Palos (E7)*... 503
S. Fork (A3)*... 150
S. Gate (C11)*...51,116
S. Pasadena (C10)*...16,935
S. San Francisco (J2)*19,351
Spadra (D10)*...1,200
Spreckels (D7)*...
Spring Garden (D4)*... 180
Springville (G7)*... 735
Stacy (E3)*... 23
Standard (E6)*... 300
Standish (E3)*... 45
Stanford (J3)*...10,000
Stanton (D11)*...1,762
Stauffer (F9)... 100
Stege (J2)...
Stewarts Point (B5)*... 200
Stinson Beach (H2)*... 400
Stirling City (D4)*... 750
Stockton (D6)*...70,853
Stockton(urban area)113,362
Stonyford (C4)*... 125
Stratford (F7)*... 400
Strathmore (F7)*...2,500
Suisun City (K1)*... 946
Summerland (F9)*... 507
Summit City (C3)*...1,000
Sunland (C10)*...5,000
Sunnymead (F11)*... 885
Sunnyvale (K3)*...9,829
Sunol (L2)*... 700
Sunset Beach (C11)*...1,500
Surf (E9)*... 50
Susanville (E3)*...5,338
Sutter (D4)*...1,200
Sutter Creek (C9)*...1,151
Taft (F8)*...3,707
Tahoe City (E4)*... 250
Tahoe Valley (E5)*...
Tarzana (B10)*...10,000
Taylorsville (E3)*... 250
Tecopa (J8)*... 150
Tehachapi (G8)*...1,685
Tehama (C3)*... 314
Temecula (H10)*... 500
Temple City (C10)*...25,000
Templeton (E8)*... 586
Tennant (C2)*... 450
Termo (E3)*... 58
Terra Bella (G8)*... 850
Thermal (J10)*... 942
Thornton (B9)*...1,800
Tiburon (J2)*...1,100
Tionesta (D2)*...
Tipton (F7)*...1,000
Tomales (C5)*...
Topanga (B10)*...3,728
Torrance (C11)*...22,241
Tracy (D6)*...8,410
Tranquillity (E7)*... 500
Tres Pinos (D7)*... 180
Trigo (F7)...
Trinidad (A2)*... 188
Trinity Center (C2)*... 100
Trona (H8)*...2,450
Truckee (E4)*...1,025
Tujunga (C10)*...14,000
Tulare (F7)*...12,445
Tulelake (D2)*...1,028
Tuolumne (E6)*...1,284
Tupman (F8)*... 187
Turlock (D6)*...6,235
Tustin (D11)*...1,143
Twain (D4)*... 285
Twentynine Palms(K9)*10,22
Twin Lakes (K4)...
Twin Peaks (H9)*... 489
Ukiah (B4)*...6,120
Upland (D10)*...9,203
Upper Lake (C4)*... 600
Vacaville (D5)*...3,169
Vallejo (J1)*...26,038
Valley Center (J10)*... 50
Valley Springs (C9)*... 500
Van Nuys (B10)*...90,000
Venice (B11)*...58,871
Ventucopa (F9)*... 40
Ventura (F9)*...16,534
Verdugo City (C10)*...2,100
Vernon (C10)*... 432
Victor (C9)*...
Victorville (H9)*...3,241
Vidal (L9)*... 50
Vina (D4)*... 500
Visalia (F7)*...11,749
Vista (H10)*...1,705
Volcano (E5)*... 150
Vorden (B9)... 175
Wallace (C9)*... 55
Walnut Creek (K2)*...2,420
Walnut Grove (B9)*...1,250
Warm Springs (K3)*... 600
Wasco (F8)*...5,592
Waterford (E6)*...1,777
Watsonville (D7)*...11,572
Weaverville (C3)*...1,800
Weed (C2)*...2,739
Weitchpec (B2)*... 300
Weldon (G8)*... 196
Wendel (E3)*... 39
Weott (A3)*... 450
W. Covina (D10)...4,499
W. Point (E5)*...1,500
W. Riverside (E10)...3,798
W. Sacramento (B8)*..8,200
Westend (H8)*... 400
Westminster (D11)*...3,131
Westmorland (K10)*...1,213
Westport (B4)*... 157
Westwood (D3)*...3,618
Wheatland (D4)*... 581
Wheeler Ridge (G8)*... 250
White Plains (E5)*... 425
Whitmore (D3)... 30
Whittier (D11)*...23,820
Wildomar (H10)*... 350
Williams (C4)*...1,134
Willits (B4)*...2,691
Willow Ranch (E2)*... 275
Willows (C4)*...3,019
Wilmar (C10)*...8,000
Wilmington (C11)*...30,000
Wilton (C9)*... 263
Windsor (C5)*... 600
Winterhaven (L11)*... 400
Winters (D5)*...1,265
Winton (E6)*... 496
Woodbridge (B9)*... 850
Woodlake (G7)*...2,525
Woodland (B8)*...9,386
Woodside (J3)*...2,000
Woody (G8)*... 150
Yermo (J9)*... 775
Yettem (F7)*... 150
Yolanda (H1)*...
Yolo (B8)*... 700
Yorba Linda (D11)*...2,000
Yosemite National Park (F6)*... 900
Yountville (C5)*... 690
Yreka (C2)*...3,227
Yuba City (D4)*...7,861
Yucaipa (J9)*...1,515
Zamora (C5)*... 60
Zenia (B3)*... 100

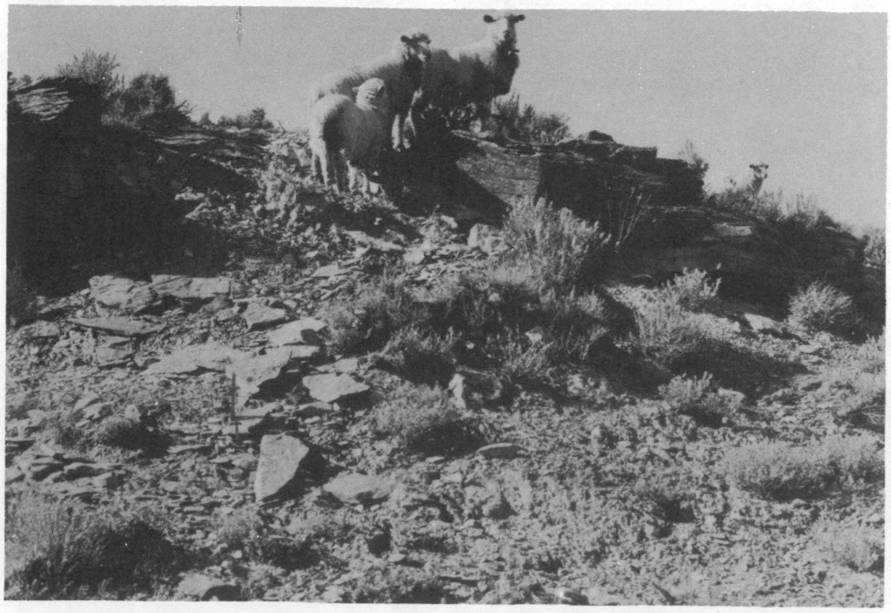

Map on Page 54

COLORADO

Total Population 1,325,089

63 COUNTIES

Adams (L3)...40,234
Alamosa (H7)...10,531
Arapahoe (L3)...52,125
Archuleta (E8)...3,030
Baca (O8)...7,964
Bent (N7)...8,775
Boulder (J2)...48,296
Chaffee (G5)...7,168
Cheyenne (O5)...3,453
Clear Creek (H3)...3,289
Conejos (G8)...10,171
Costilla (J8)...6,067
Crowley (M6)...5,222
Custer (J6)...1,573
Delta (D5)...17,365
Denver (K3)...415,786
Dolores (C7)...1,966
Douglas (K4)...3,507
Eagle (F3)...4,488
El Paso (K5)...74,523
Elbert (L4)...4,477
Fremont (J5)...18,366
Garfield (C3)...11,625
Gilpin (H3)... 850
Grand (G2)...3,963
Gunnison (E5)...5,716
Hinsdale (E7)... 263
Huerfano (K7)...10,549
Jackson (G1)...1,976
Jefferson (J3)...55,687
Kiowa (O6)...3,003
Kit Carson (O4)...8,600
La Plata (D8)...14,880
Lake (G4)...6,150
Larimer (H1)...43,554
Las Animas (L8)...25,902
Lincoln (M5)...5,909
Logan (N1)...17,187
Mesa (B5)...38,974
Mineral (F7)... 698
Moffat (C1)...5,946
Montezuma (B8)...9,991
Montrose (C6)...15,220
Morgan (M2)...18,074
Otero (M7)...25,275
Ouray (D6)...2,103
Park (H4)...1,870
Phillips (P1)...4,924
Pitkin (F4)...1,646
Prowers (P7)...14,836
Pueblo (K6)...90,188
Rio Blanco (C3)...4,719
Rio Grande (G7)...12,832
Routt (E1)...8,940
Saguache (G6)...5,664
San Juan (D7)...1,471
San Miguel (C6)...2,693
Sedgwick (P1)...5,095
Summit (G3)...1,135
Teller (J5)...2,754
Washington (N3)...7,520
Weld (L1)...67,504
Yuma (P2)...10,827

CITIES and TOWNS

Abarr (O3)... 8
Ackmen (B7)...
Adams City (K3)... 800
Adena (M2)...
Agate (M4)*... 134
Aguilar (K8)*...1,038
Akron (N2)*...1,605
Alamosa (H8)*...5,354
Allenspark (J2)*... 100
Allison (E8)*... 105
Alma (G4)*... 149
Almont (F5)*...
Amherst (P1)*... 101
Amity (P6)...
Andrix (N8)*... 10
Animas (D8)...2,500
Anthracite (E5)...
Antlers (D3)*... 150
Anton (N3)*... 50
Antonito (H8)*...1,255
Arapahoe (P5)*... 125
Arboles (E8)*... 108
Arickaree (N3)*... 13
Arlington (N6)*... 25
Armel (P3)*... 4
Aroya (N5)*...
Arriba (N4)*... 367
Arriola (B8)... 350
Artesia (B2)*... 281
Arvada (J3)*...2,359
Aspen (F4)*... 916
Association Camp (J2)*
Atwood (N1)*... 200
Ault (K1)*... 866
Aurora (K3)*...11,421
Avon (F3)*...
Avondale (L6)*... 152
Axial (D2)*...
Ayer (M7)... 7
Bailey (H4)*... 75
Barela (L8)... 9
Barnesville (L2)... 35
Barr Lake (K3)*... 100
Bartlett (P8)... 30
Basalt (E4)*... 173
Battle Creek (E1)... 18
Bayfield (D8)*... 335
Bedrock (B6)*... 15
Beecher Island (P3)*... 10
Bellvue (J1)*... 300
Bennett (L3)*... 272
Berthoud (J2)*... 867
Berthoud Pass (H3)...
Bethune (P4)*... 71
Beulah (K6)*...
Big Bend (O6)... 30
Black Forest (K4)... 10
Black Hawk (J3)*... 166
Blanca (H8)*... 376
Blende (K6)... 575
Blue Mountain (B2)*... 6
Bonanza (G6)... 51
Boncarbo (K8)*... 97
Bond (F3)*... 125
Bondad (D8)... 2
Boone (L6)*... 468
Boulder (J2)*...19,999
Bountiful (G8)... 100
Bovina (N4)*... 22
Bowie (D5)*... 250
Boyero (N5)*... 36

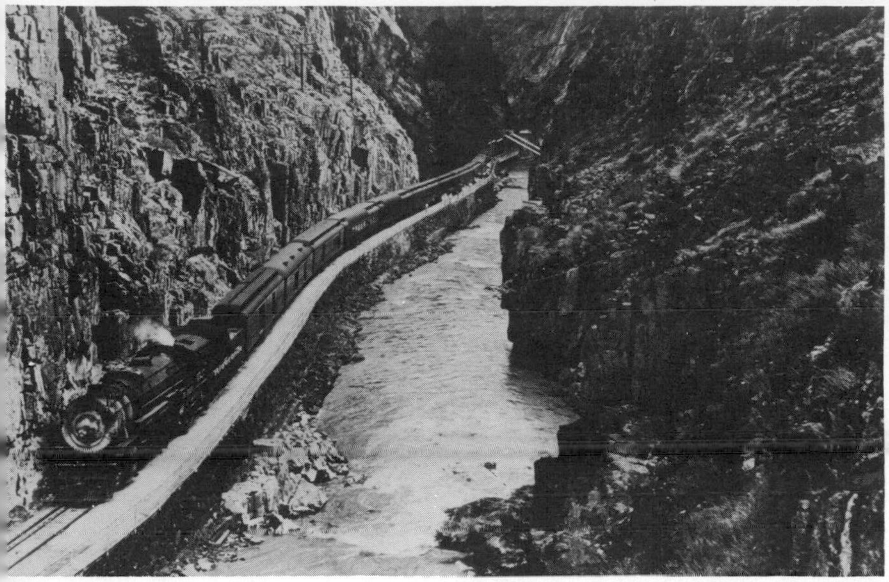

Bracewell (K2) 5
Brandon (P6)* 50
Branson (M8)* 157
Breckenridge (G4)* 296
Breed (K5) 20
Breen (C8)*
Bridges (C4) 60
Briggsdale (L1)* 200
Brighton (K3)* 4,336
Bristol (P6)* 250
Brookside (J6) 175
Brookvale (H3) 15
Broomfield (J3)* 125
Brush (M2)* 2,431
Buckeye (J1) 37
Buckingham (L1)* 36
Buena Vista (G5)* 783
Buffalo Creek (J4)* 50
Buford (D2)* 30
Buick (M4) 31
Burlington (P4)* 2,247
Burns (F3)* 200
Byers (L3)*
Caddoa (O6)* 32
Cahone (B7)* 103
Calhan (L4)* 375
Cameo (C4)* 100
Campion (J2)
Campo (O8)* 266
Canfield (J2) 65
Canon City (J6)* 6,345
Canyon (G8)
Capulin (G8)*
Carbondale (E4)* 441
Carlton (P6)* 55
Carr (K1)* 98
Cascade (K5)* 75
Castle Rock (K4)* 741
Cedar (B7)
Cedaredge (D5)* 574
Cedarwood (K7) 85
Center (G7)* 2,024
Central City (J3)* 371
Chama (J8)* 760
Cheraw (N6)* 174
Cherry Hills Village ‡(K3) 750
Cheyenne Wells (P5)* 1,154
Chimney Rock (E8)* 100
Chivington (O6)*
Chromo (F8)* 200
Cimarron (D6)* 150
Clark (F1)*
Clarkville (P2)* 4
Clifton (C4)* 920
Climax (G4)* 750
Coalcreek (J6)* 195
Coaldale (H6)* 130
Coalmont (F1)* 26
Cokedale (K8)* 214
Collbran (C4)* 237
Colona (D6) 125
Colorado Spgs. (K5)* 45,472
Columbine (E1)*
Como (H4)* 39
Conejos (G8)*
Cope (O3)* 145
Copper Spur (F3)* 36
Cornish (L2)* 140
Cortez (B8)* 2,680
Cory (C5)*
Cotopaxi (H6)* 210
Cowdrey (G1)*
Craig (D2)* 3,080
Crawford (D5)* 170
Creede (E7)* 503
Crested Butte (E5)* 730
Crestone (H7)* 72
Cripple Creek (J5)* 853

Critchell (J4) 75
Crook (O1)* 259
Cross Mountain (B2) 10
Crowley (M6)* 379
Cuchara Camps (J8)* 2
Dacono (K2)* 258
Dailey (O1)* 90
De Beque (C4)* 253
De Nova (O3)* 4
Deckers (J4)
Deer Trail (M3)* 421
Del Norte (G7)* 2,048
Delagua (K8)* 239
Delcarbon (K7)* 200
Delhi (M7)* 36
Delta (D5)* 4,097
DENVER (K3)* 415,786
Denver (urban area) 495,513
Deora (O7)* 41
Derby (K3)* 2,840
Devine (L6) 116
Dillon (H3)* 191
Divide (J5)* 50
Dolores (C8)* 729
Dotsero (E3) 58
Dove Creek (A7)* 702
Doyleville (F6)* 105
Drake (J2)* 70
Dunton (C7)*
Dupont (K3)* 400
Durango (D8)* 7,459
Eads (O6)* 1,015
Eagle (F3)* 445
Earl (L8)
East Canon (J6) 761
Eastlake (K3)* 104
Eaton (K2)* 1,276
Eckert (C5)*
Eckley (P2)* 295
Edgewater (J3)* 2,580
Edison (L5) 15
Edler (O8)
Edwards (F3)*
Egnar (B7)* 35
Elba (N3)* 25
Elbert (L4)* 200
Eldora (H3)*
Elizabeth (K4)* 253
Elk Springs (C2)* 35
Elkton (J5) 10
Elwell (K2) 40
Empire (H3)* 228
Englewood (K3)* 16,869
Erie (K2)* 937
Escalante Forks (B5)* 20
Estes Park (J2)* 1,617
Eureka (D7) 13
Evans (K2)* 862
Evergreen (J3)* 800
Fairplay (H4)* 476
Falcon (K5)
Falfa (D8)* 300
Fall Creek (C7) 25
Farisita (J7)* 125
Farmers Spur (K2) 22
Farr (K7)
Federal Heights 173
Firestone (K2)* 297
Firstview (O5)* 30
Fitzsimons (K3)* 5,000
Flagler (N4)* 793
Fleming (O1)* 377
Florence (J6)* 2,773
Florissant (J5)* 53
Fondis (L4)* 9
Forder (M5) 26
Fort Collins (J1)* 14,937
Fort Garland (J8)*

Fort Lupton (K2)* 1,907
Fort Lyon (N6)*
Fort Morgan (M2)* 5,315
Fosston (L1)
Fountain (K5)* 713
Fowler (L6)* 1,025
Foxton (J4)*
Franktown (K4)* 25
Fraser (H3)*
Frederick (K2)* 599
Freeman (G7) 100
Freshwater (Guffey*) (H5) 20
Frisco (G3)* 87
Fruita (B4)* 1,463
Fruitvale (B4)* 2,275
Galatea (N6) 10
Galeton (K1)* 200
Garcia (J8)* 350
Garden City ‡(L1) 104
Gardner (J7)* 200
Garfield (G5)* 100
Garo (H4)* 50
Gary (M2)* 6
Gateway (B5)* 250
Genoa (N4)* 257
Georgetown (H3)* 329
Gilcrest (K2)* 429
Gill (K2)* 375
Gilman (G3)* 300
Glade Park (B5)* 250
Glen Haven (H2)* 40
Glendevey (H1)* 15
Glentivar (H4)* 5
Glenwood Spgs. (E4)* 2,412
Golden (J3)* 5,238
Goldfield (J5) 81
Good Pasture (K6) 48
Goodrich (M2)* 30
Gordon (K7)
Gould (G1)* 150
Gowanda (K2) 12
Granada (P6)* 551
Granby (H2)* 463
Grand Jct. (C4)* 14,504
Grand Lake (H2)* 309
Grand Mesa (D4)*
Grand Valley (D4)* 296
Granite (G4)* 75
Grant (H4)* 25
Greeley (K2)* 20,354
Green Mt. Falls (K5)* 106
Greenhorn (K7) 20
Greenland (K4)* 75
Greenwood (J6)
Greystone (B1)* 2
Grover (L1)* 146
Guffey (Freshwater) (H5)* 20
Gulnare (K8)* 200
Gunnison (E5)* 2,770
Gypsum (F3)* 345
Hahns Peak (E1)
Hale (P3)* 240
Hamilton (D2)* 25
Hardin (L2)*
Harmony (J2) 18
Harrisburg (N3)* 6
Hartman (P6)* 181
Hartsel (H4)* 65
Hastings (K8)
Hasty (O6)*
Haswell (N6)* 163
Haxtun (O1)* 1,006
Haybro (F2)* 150
Hayden (E2)* 767
Hebron (G1) 4
Henderson (K3)* 50
Hereford (L1)* 100

Hesperus (C8)*
Higbee (M7) 6
Hill Top (K4) 10
Hillrose (N2)* 190
Hillside (H6)* 10
Hoehne (L8)* 500
Holly (P6)* 1,236
Holyoke (P1)* 1,558
Homelake (G7) 250
Hooper (H7)* 103
Hot Sulphur Spgs.(H2)* 263
Hotchkiss (D5)* 715
Howard (H6)* 210
Howardsville (E7) 20
Hoyt (L2)* 250
Hudson (K2)* 365
Hughes (O3)* 6
Hugo (N4)* 943
Husted (K4) 30
Hyde (O2)
Hydrate (F2)
Hygiene (J2)* 200
Idaho Springs (H3)* 1,769
Idalia (P3)* 74
Ignacio (D8)* 526
Iliff (N1)* 235
Independence (K5)* 20
Indian Hills (J3)* 300
Iola (E6)* 50
Ione (K2)* 100
Irondale (K5) 325
Ironton ‡(D7) 6
Ivywild (K5) 2,849
Jamestown (J2)* 118
Jansen (K8)* 1,500
Jaroso (H8)* 250
Jefferson (H4)* 75
Joes (O3)* 109
Johnstown (K2)* 897
Julesburg (P1)* 1,951
Juniper Springs (D2) 6
Karval (N5)* 90
Kearns (E8)
Keensburg (L2)* 432
Kelim (J2) 50
Kendrick (M5)* 14
Keota (L1)* 21
Kersey (L2)* 304
Kim (N8)* 475
King's Canyon (G1)
Kiowa (L4)* 173
Kirk (P3)* 125
Kit Carson (O5)* 379
Kline (C8)* 110
Kokomo (G4)* 53
Kornman (O6) 75
Kremmling (G2)* 623
Kutch (M5)* 3
La Garita (G7)*
La Jara (H8)* 912
La Junta (M7)* 7,712
La Salle (K2)* 797
La Sauces (H8)
La Veta (J8)* 701
Lafayette (K3)* 2,073
Laird (P2)* 155
Lake City (E6)* 141
Lake George (J5)* 30
Lakeside ‡(J3) 46
Lamar (O6)* 6,829
Lamport (O8)
Laporte (J1) 500
Larkspur (K4)* 200
Las Animas (N6)* 3,223
Lascar (K7)
Last Chance (M3) 25
Lavalley (J8)
Lawson (H3)*
Lay (D2)*

Lazear (D5)* 100
Leader (L3) 67
Leadville (G4)* 4,081
Lebanon (C8) 150
Leonard (C6) 10
Lester (K8) 19
Lewis (B7)* 50
Lime (K6) 22
Limon (M4)* 1,471
Lindon (N3)* 29
Littleton (K3)* 3,378
Livermore (J1)* 150
Logan (N1)
Logcabin (J1)
Loma (B4)* 400
Longmont (J2)* 8,099
Longs Peak (J2) 7
Longview (J4)
Louisville (J3)* 1,978
Louviers (K4)* 250
Loveland (J2)* 6,773
Loyd (D2)* 82
Lucerne (K2)* 100
Ludlow (L8)* 200
Lycan (P7)* 6
Lyons (J2)* 689
Mack (B4)* 185
Maher (D5)*
Maitland (K7)
Malachite (J7)
Malta (G4)* 25
Manassa (H8)* 832
Mancos (C8)* 785
Manitou Springs (J5)* 2,580
Manzanola (M6)* 543
Marble (E4) 8
Marshall Pass (G6)* 8
Marvine (D2) 25
Masonville (J2)*
Massadona (B2) 3
Masters (L2)*
Matheson (M4)* 100
May Valley (O6) 20
Maybell (C2)* 106
McClave (O6)* 125
McClure Ranch (F4) 25
McCoy (F3)*
McElmo (B8) 50
McGregor (E2) 25
McPhee (C7) 30
Mead (K2)* 186
Meeker (D2) 1,658
Meredith (F4)* 25
Merino (N2)* 209
Mesa (C4)* 300
Mesa Verde National Park (C8)* 106
Mesita (H8)*
Messex (N2) 25
Mildred (O3)* 3
Milliken (K2)* 510
Milner (F2)* 150
Mineral Hot Spgs. (G6) 10
Minturn (G3)* 509
Model (L8)* 300
Moffat (H6)* 109
Mogote (G8) 150
Molina (D4)*
Monarch (G5) 13
Monte Vista (G7)* 3,272
Montezuma (H3)* 48
Montrose (D6)* 4,964
Monument (K4)* 126
Morley (L8)* 300
Morrison (J3)* 306
Mosca (H7)* 130
Mount Harris (E2)* 700
Mountain View ‡(J3) 878
Mustang (K7) 10
Nathrop (H5)*
Naturita (B6)* 500
Nederland (H3)* 266
Nevadaville ‡(H3) 6
New Castle (E3)* 483
New Raymer (M1)* 130
Ninaview (N7)* 2
Niwot (J2)* 160
North Avondale (L6)* 22
North Creede (F7)
Northdale (B7) 50
Nortonville (G8) 25
Norwood (C6)* 294
Nucla (B6)* 457
Nunn (K1)* 182
Oak Creek (F2)* 1,488
Oak Grove (C6) 35
Ohio (F5)* 40
Olathe (D5)* 810
Olney Springs (M6)* 279
Ophir (D7)* 2
Orchard (L2)*
Ordway (M6)* 1,290
Ortiz (H8)
Otis (O2)* 532
Ouray (D6)* 1,089
Ovid (P1)* 664
Oxford (D8)*
Padroni (N1)* 153
Pagoda (E2)
Pagosa Junction (E8)*
Pagosa Springs (E8)* 1,379
Palisade (C4)* 861
Palmer Lake (J4)* 263
Pando (G4) 17
Paoli (P1)* 91

Paonia (D5)* 1,257
Paradox (B6)* 50
Parkdale (H6)* 20
Parker (K4)* 132
Parlin (F6)* 50
Parshall (G2)* 81
Pawnee (M2)
Peagreen (C5) 10
Peckham (K2) 40
Peetz (N1)* 232
Penrose (K6)* 90
Peyton (K4)*
Phippsburg (F2)*
Piedra (E8)
Pierce (K1)* 372
Pikeview (K5)* 300
Pine (J4)* 75
Pine River Dam (E8)
Pinecliffe (J3)* 25
Pinon (K6) 65
Pitkin (F5)* 152
Placerville (D6)* 50
Plainview (J3)* 100
Plateau City (D4) 20
Platner (N2)* 49
Platteville (K2)* 570
Poncha Springs (G6)* 114
Portland (K6)* 205
Portland ‡(D6) 16
Powderhorn (E6)* 90
Price Creek (C2) 2
Pritchett (O8)* 286
Proctor ((N1)* 40
Prospect (L2) 62
Prospect Heights ‡(J6). 50
Prowers (O6) 36
Pryor (K8)* 25
Pueblo (K6)* 63,685
Pueblo (urban area) 73,102
Pumpkin Center (M5)
Purcell (K1)*
Radium (F3)* 20
Ragged Mountain (E4)*
Rago (N3)
Ramah (L4)* 142
Ramona (K5)
Rand (G2)*
Rangely (B2)* 808
Rapson (K8)
Ravenwood (K7)
Raymer (New Raymer*) (M1) 130
Read (D5)
Recen (Kokomo*) (G4). 53
Red Feather Lakes(H1)* 93
Red Wing (J7)* 16
Redcliff (G4)* 556
Redmesa (C8)*
Redstone (E4) 50
Redvale (B6)* 70
Rex (J1)
Rico (C7)* 212
Ridgway (D6)* 209
Rifle (D3)* 1,525
Riland (E3) 25
Rio Blanco (C3)* 3
Roach (G1)
Rockport (K1) 2
Rockvale (J6)* 380
Rockwood (D8) 15
Rocky Ford (M6)* 4,087
Roggen (L2)* 150
Romeo (G8)* 404
Rosedale ‡(K2) 57
Rosita (J6)* 20
Roswell (K5) 1,029
Routt (E2)* 50
Rowena (J2) 3
Ruedi (F4) 25
Rugby (K8)
Rush (L5)* 18
Russell (J7)* 43
Rye (K7)* 166
Saguache (G6)* 1,024
Saint Elmo (G5)*
St. Peters (O2) 200
Salida (H6)* 4,553
Sams (D6) 15
San Acacio (H8)* 135
San Isabel (K7) 25
San Luis (J8)* 1,239
San Pablo (J8)*
Sanford (H8)* 666
Sapinero (E6)* 30
Sargents (F6)* 135
Saw Pit (D7)
Sedalia (K4)*
Sedgwick (O1)* 332
Segundo (K8)* 300
Seibert (O4)* 346
Severance (K1) 108
Shaffers Crossing (J4). 40
Shaw (N3)* 4
Shawnee (H4)*
Sheephorn (G3)*
Sheridan ‡(K3) 1,715
Sheridan Lake (P6)* 100
Sidney (F2)
Silica (J4) 3
Siloam (K6) 16
Silt (D4)* 361
Silver Cliff (J6)* 217
Silver Plume (H3)* 136
Silverton (D7)* 1,375
Simla (M4)* 424

Skyway (C4)
Slater (E1)* 15
Sligo (L1)
Snowmass (E4)*
Snyder (M2)* 250
Somerset (E5)*
Sopris (K8)* 1,330
South Canon (J6) 1,588
South Fork (F7)*
Spicer (F2)*
Spikebuck (H5)
Springfield (O8)* 2,041
Starkville (L8)* 1,000
State Bridge (F3) 2
Steamboat Spgs. (F2)* 1,913
Stellwagon (L5) 2
Sterling (N1)* 7,534
Stone City (K6)* 75
Stoneham (M1)* 75
Stoner (C7)* 2
Stonington (P8)* 44
Strasburg (L3)* 520
Stratton (O4)* 720
Strong (K7) 20
Sugar City (M6)* 527
Sugar Loaf (J2) 6
Summitville (G8) 4
Sunbeam (C1) 29
Superior (J3)* 134
Swallows (K6) 50
Swing (M7)* 336
Tabernash (H3)* 260
Tacoma (D7)* 17
Telluride (D7)* 1,101
Tennessee Pass (G4)* 25
Tercio (J8) 110
Texas Creek (H6)* 25
Thatcher (L7)*
Thurman (N3)* 10
Tiffany (D8)*
Tiger (G3) 8
Timnath (J2)* 177
Timpas (M7)* 50
Tioga (K7)* 250
Tobe (M8)*
Tolland (H3) 10
Toltec (K7)* 180
Toponas (F2)* 250
Towaoc (B8)*
Towner (P6)* 150
Trail Ridge (H2)*
Trimble Springs (D8) 30
Trinchera (M8)* 90
Trinidad (L8)* 12,204
Troutville (F4)* 16
Truckton (L5) 20
Trump (H5) 25
Tungsten (H3) 6
Twin Lakes (G4)* 60
Two Buttes (P7)* 121
Tyrone (L8)* 50
Uravan (B6)* 700
Ute (C6) 9
Utleyville (O8)* 8
Valdez (K8)* 700
Vallorso (K8)* 90
Vanadium (C7) 2
Vernon (P3)*
Victor (J5)* 684
Vilas (P8)* 132
Villa Grove (G6)* 200
Villegreen (M8)* 150
Vim (M1) 6
Vineland (K6) 200
Virginia Dale (J1)* 100
Vona (O4)* 209
Vroman (M6)*
Wages (P2) 35
Wagon Wheel Gap (F7)*
Walden (G7)* 696
Walsenburg (K7)* 5,596
Walsh (P8)* 897
Ward (H2)* 10
Watkins (K3)* 85
Wattenberg (K2)
Waunita Hot Spgs.(G6)
Waverly (J1) 20
Weldona (M2)* 300
Wellington (K1)* 541
Westcliffe (H6)* 390
Westcreek (J4)*
Westminster (J3)* 1,686
Weston (K8)* 500
Wetmore (J6)* 100
Wheat Ridge (J3)* 7,000
Whitewater (C5)* 150
Wiggins (L2)* 400
Wild Horse (N5)* 60
Wilds (J2) 25
Wiley (O6)* 417
Willard (M1)* 29
Williamsburg (J6) 65
Willow Creek (E2)
Windsor (J2)* 1,548
Winnview (M3)
Winter Park (H3)* 100
Wolcott (F3)* 50
Woodland Park (J4)* 391
Woodrow (M3)*
Woody Creek (F4)* 7
Wray (P2)* 2,198
Yampa (F2)* 421
Yellow Jacket (B8)*
Yoder (L5)* 30
Yuma (O2)* 1,908

Map on Page 55

CONNECTICUT

Total Population 2,007,280

8 COUNTIES

Fairfield (B3) 504,342
Hartford (E1) 539,661
Litchfield (C1) 98,872
Middlesex (E3) 67,332
New Haven (D3) 545,784
New London (G2) 144,821
Tolland (F1) 44,709
Windham (H1) 61,759

CITIES and TOWNS

Abington (G1)* 450
Addison (E2) 900
Allingtown (D3) 4,800
Amston (F2)* 200
Andover (F2)* ▲1,034
Ansonia (C3)* 18,706
Arnolds (E3)
Ashford (G1) ▲845
Aspetuck (B4)
Atwoodville (G1) 35
Avon (D1)* ▲3,171
Bakersville (C1)
Ballouville (H1)*
Baltic (G2)* 1,345
Bantam (B2)* 940
Barkhamsted (D1) ▲946
Beach Park (E3) 500
Beacon Falls (C3)* ▲2,067
Beckleys (E2) 100
Berkshire Junction (B3)
Berlin (E2)* ▲7,470
Bethany (C3) ▲1,318
Bethel (B3)* ▲5,104
Bethlehem (C2)* ▲1,015
Black Hall (F3)
Black Point Beach Club (G3)* 100
Bloomfield (E1)* ▲5,746
Boardmans Bridge (B2) 75
Bolton (F1) ▲1,279
Botsford (C3)*
Branchville (B3) 300
Branford (D3)* 2,552
Bridgeport (C4)* 158,709
Bridgeport (urban area) 237,954
Bridgewater (B2)* ▲639
Bristol (D2)* 35,961
Bristol-New Britain (urban area) 122,618
Broad Brook (E1)* 2,140
Brookfield (B3)* ▲1,688
Brookfield Center (B3)*
Brookfield Junction (B3)
Brooklyn (H1)* ▲2,652
Brooksvale (D3) 500
Buckingham (E2) 350
Buckland (E1)* 750
Burlington (D1) ▲1,846
Burnside (E1)*
Burrville (C1) 250
Byram (A4)* 8,000
Campbell (F1)
Campville (C2)
Canaan (B1)* 1,189
Cannondale (B4)* 300
Canterbury (H2)* ▲1,321
Canton (D1)* ▲3,613

Canton Center (D1)*... 300
Centerbrook (F3)*...... 487
Central Village (H2)*.. 800
Chaplin (G1)*...... Δ 712
Cheshire (D2)*......Δ6,295
Chester (F3)*......Δ1,920
Chesterfield (G3)...... 120
Chestnut Hill (G2)*.....
Clarks Corner (G1)...... 78
Clarks Falls (H3)...... 200
Clinton (E3)*......Δ2,466
Clintonville (D3)*...... 850
Cobalt (E2)*...... 500
Colchester (F2)*...... 1,522
Colebrook (C1)*...... Δ 592
Collinsville (D1)......2,078
Columbia (F2)*......Δ1,327
Cooper (B3)......
Cornwall (B1)*...... Δ 896
Cornwall Bridge (B1)*
Cos Cob (A4)*...... 6,800
Coventry (F1)......Δ4,043
Cranbury (B4)...... 3,000
Crescent Beach (G3)*..
Cromwell (E2)*......Δ4,286
Crystal Lake (F1)...... 350
Danbury (B3)*......22,067
Danielson (H1)*...... 4,554
Darien (B4)*......Δ11,767
Dayville (Killingly) (H1)* 1,105
Deep River (F3)*......Δ2,570
Derby (C3)*......10,259
Devon (C4)*......
Durham (E3)*......Δ1,804
Durham Center (E3)*.
Eagleville (F1)*...... 265
East Berlin (E2)*...... 1,000
E. Brooklyn (H1)...... 1,062
E. Canaan (B1)*...... 800
E. Glastonbury (E2)* 450
E. Granby (E1)*......Δ1,327
E. Haddam (F3)*......Δ2,554
E. Hampton (E2)*......Δ4,000
E. Hartford (E1)*......Δ29,933
E. Hartland (D1)*...... 400
E. Haven (D3)*......Δ12,212
E. Kent (B2)......
E. Killingly (H1)*...... 800
E. Litchfield (C1)...... 60
E. Lyme (G3)*......Δ3,870
E. Morris (C2)......
E. Norwalk (B4)...... 5,000
E. River (E3)*...... 450
E. Thompson (H1)...... 200
E. Wallingford (D3).....
E. Willington (F1)...... 50
E. Windsor (E1)......Δ4,859
E. Windsor Hill (E1)* 671
E. Woodstock (H1)*.... 275
Eastford (G1)*...... Δ 598
Easton (B4)*......Δ2,165
Ellington (F1)*......Δ3,099
Elliott (G1)......
Elmwood (D2)*...... 6,000
Enfield (E1)*......Δ15,464
Essex (F3)*......Δ3,491
Fabyan (H1)*...... 425
Fairfield (B4)*......Δ30,489
Falls Village (B1)*...... 640
Farmington (D2)*......Δ7,026
Farmington Station (D2)
Fenwick (F3)...... 16
Fitchville (G2)*...... 300
Flanders (B1)......
Florida (B3)......
Forestville (D2)*...... 6,000
Franklin (G2)...... Δ 727
Gales Ferry (G3)*...... 300
Gardner Lake (G2).....
Gaylordsville (B2)*...... 200
Georgetown (B4)*......
Gildersleeve (E2)*......
Gilead (F2)...... 70
Gilman (G2)...... 400
Glasgo (H2)*......
Glastonbury (E2)*......Δ8,818
Glenbrook (A4)*......
Glenville (A4)*...... 976
Goodyear (H1)*...... 1,000
Goshen (C1)*...... Δ 940
Granby (D1)*......Δ2,693
Greenfield Hill (B4)....
Greens Farms (B4)*.... 500
Greenville (G2)*......
Greenwich (A4)*......Δ40,835
Greystone (C2)...... 150
Griffins (E1)......
Grosvenor Dale (H1)*.. 800
Groton (G3)*...... 7,036
Groton Long Point (G3)*
Grove Beach (E3)......
Guilford (E3)*......Δ5,092
Gurleyville (G1)...... 120
Haddam (E3)*......Δ2,636
Haddam Neck (E2)...... 50
Hadlyme (F3)*...... 300
Hallville (G2)......
Hamburg (F3)*......
Hamden (D3)*......Δ29,715
Hampton (G1)*...... Δ 672
Hancock (C2)...... 25
Hanover (G2)*...... 300
HARTFORD (E1)*......177,397
Hartford (urban area) 299,676
Harwinton (C1)......Δ1,858
Hawleyville (B3)*......
Hazardville (E1)*...... 1,272
Hebron (F2)*......Δ1,320
Higganum (E2)*......
High Ridge (A4)......
Highland Park (F1).....
Highwood (D3)......
Hockanum (E2)......
Hop River (F2)......
Hotchkissville (C2)...... 300
Huntington (C3)......
Hurlbutt (B4)......
Ivoryton (F3)*...... 885
Jewett City (H2)*...... 3,702
Jordan Village (Waterford*) (G3)...Δ9,100
Judds Bridge (B2)...... 30
Kensington (D2)*...... 4,700
Kent (B2)*......Δ1,392
Kent Furnace (B2)......
Killingly (H1)...... 1,105
Killingworth (E3)...... Δ 677
Lakeside (B2)*......
Lakeville (B1)*......
Lebanon (G2)*......Δ1,654
Lebanon Station (G2)..
Ledyard (G3)......Δ1,749
Leetes Island (E3)......
Lime Rock (B1)*...... 186
Litchfield (C2)*...... 1,174
Long Hill (C3)......
Long Ridge (A4)......
Lords Point (H3)...... 400
Lyman Viaduct (F2).... 4
Lyme (F3)...... Δ 857
Madison (E3)*......Δ3,078
Manchester (E1)*......Δ34,116
Manchester Green (E1)
Mansfield (F1)*......Δ10,008
Mansfield Center (G1)* 600
Mansfield Depot (F1)*
Marble Dale (B2)*...... 150
Marion (D2)*...... 366
Marlborough (F2)...... Δ 901
Massapeag (G3)......
Mechanicsville (H1)*...
Melrose (E1)*......
Meriden (D2)*......44,088
Merrow (F1)*...... 125
Mianus (A4)......
Middle Haddam (E2)*
Middlebury (C2)*......Δ3,318
Middlefield (E2)*......Δ1,983
Middletown (E2)*......29,711
Milford (C4)*......Δ26,870
Mill Plain (A3)...... 125
Milldale (D2)*...... 1,200
Millstone (G3)......
Milton (C1)...... 200
Minortown (C2)...... 100
Mohegan (G3)......
Monroe (C3)......Δ2,892
Montowese (D3)......
Montville (G3)*......Δ4,766
Moodus (F2)*......1,400
Moosup (H2)*...... 2,909
Morris (C2)*...... Δ 799
Mount Carmel (D3)*...
Mount Hope (G1)...... 50
Mystic (H3)*...... 2,266
Naugatuck (C3)*......17,455
New Britain (E2)*......73,726
New Britain-Bristol (urban area) 122,618
New Canaan (B4)*......Δ8,001
New Fairfield (B3)......Δ1,236
New Hartford (C1)*....Δ2,395
New Haven (D3)*......164,443
New Haven (urban area) 242,589
New London (G3)*......30,551
New Milford (B2)*......Δ5,799
New Preston (B2)*...... 500
Newington (E2)*......Δ9,110
Newtown (B3)*...... 782
Niantic (G3)*...... 1,746
Nichols (C4)...... 1,171
Noank (G3)*...... 1,149
Norfolk (C1)*......Δ1,572
Noroton (B4)*...... 3,000
Noroton Heights (B4)* 3,918
North Ashford (G1)....
N. Branford (E3)......Δ2,017
N. Canton (D1)*...... 250
N. Franklin (G2)*...... 735
N. Granby (D1)*...... 650
N. Grosvenor Dale (H1)* 2,232
N. Guilford (E3)...... 1,000
N. Haven (D3)*......Δ9,444
N. Kent (B1)......
N. Madison (E3)......
N. Newington (D2)......
N. Plain (F3)......
N. Stamford (A4)......
N. Sterling (H1)......
N. Stonington (H3)*...Δ1,367
N. Westchester (F2)*.. 100
N. Wilton (B4)......
N. Windham (G1)*...... 300
N. Woodbury (C2)*......
N. Woodstock (G1)*....
Northfield (C2)*......
Northford (D3)*...... 800
Northville (B2)...... 150
Norwalk (B4)*......49,460
Norwalk-Stamford (urban area) 172,197
Norwich (G2)*......23,429
Norwichtown (G2)*...... 2,916
Oakdale (G3)*...... 150
Oakville (C2)*...... 5,100
Occum (G2)......
Old Greenwich (A4)*....5,348
Old Lyme (F3)*......Δ2,141
Old Mystic (H3)*...... 600
Old Saybrook (F3)*.....Δ2,499
Oneco (H2)*...... 450
Orange (C3)*......Δ3,032
Orcutts (F1)...... 150
Oronoque (C4)*...... 650
Oxford (C3)......Δ2,037
Pachaug (H2)...... 75
Packer (H2)*...... 65
Pawcatuck (H3)...... 5,269
Pequabuck (C2)*...... 600
Phoenixville (G1)......
Pine Meadow (D1)*.... 425
Pine Orchard (D3)*.... 5,100
Plainfield (H2)*......Δ8,071
Plainville (D2)*......Δ9,994
Plantsville (D2)*...... 1,536
Pleasant Valley (C1)*.. 325
Plymouth (C2)*......Δ6,771
Pomfret (H1)*......Δ2,018
Pomfret Center (H1)*. 675
Poquetanuck (G3)......
Poquonock (E1)*...... 1,200
Poquonock Bridge (G3) 4,050
Portland (E2)*......Δ5,186
Preston (H2)*......Δ1,775
Prospect (D2)......Δ1,896
Putnam (H1)*...... 8,181
Quaker Hill (G3)*...... 1,260
Quinebaug (H1)*...... 400
Rainbow (E1)......
Redding (B3)*......Δ2,037
Redding Ridge (B3)*...
Reynolds Bridge (C2).. 600
Ridgefield (A3)*......Δ4,356
Riverside (A4)*...... 2,000
Riverton (D1)*...... 220
Robertsville (C1)...... 130
Rockfall (E2)*...... 2,000
Rockville (F1)*...... 8,016
Rocky Hill (E2)*......Δ5,108
Romford (B2)...... 30
Round Hill (A4)...... 600
Rowayton (B4)*...... 3,200
Roxbury (B2)*...... Δ 740
Roxbury Falls (B2)......
Roxbury Station (B2)..
Sachem Head (E3)*....
Salem (F3)...... Δ 618
Salisbury (B1)*......Δ3,132
Sandy Hook (B3)*...... 1,600
Saugatuck (B4)*...... 1,500
Saybrook Point (F3)*. 250
Scitico (E1)...... 125
Scotland (G2)*...... Δ 513
Seymour (C3)*......Δ7,832
Sharon (B1)*......Δ1,889
Sharon Valley (B1)...... 174
Shelton (C3)*......12,694
Sherman (B2)*...... Δ 549
Short Beach (D3)*......
Silver Lane (E1)......
Simsbury (D1)*......Δ4,822
Somers (F1)*......Δ2,631
Somersville (F1)*...... 750
Sound View (F3)...... 100
South Britain (B3)*.... 400
S. Coventry (F1)*...... 1,617
S. Glastonbury (E2)*..
S. Kent (B2)*...... 108
S. Killingly (H1)...... 250
S. Lyme (F3)*...... 150
S. Manchester (E1).....
S. Meriden (D2)*...... 1,600
S. Norwalk (B4)*......18,000
S. Wethersfield (E2)... 200
S. Willington (F1)*....
S. Wilton (B4)......
S. Windham (G2)*...... 450
S. Windsor (E1)*......Δ4,066
S. Woodstock (G1)*.....
Southbury (C3)*......Δ3,828
Southford (C3)......
Southington (D2)*.....Δ13,061
Southport (B4)*...... 3,000
Springdale (A4)*...... 5,280
Stafford (F1)*......Δ6,471
Stafford Sprs. (F1)*.. 3,396
Staffordville (G1)*...... 1,000
Stamford (A4)*......74,293
Stamford-Norwalk (urban area) 172,197
Stepney (B3)......
Stepney Depot (B3)*.. 3,000
Sterling (H2)*......Δ1,298
Stevenson (C3)*...... 200
Still River (B2)...... 200
Stonington (H3)*...... 1,739
Stony Creek (E3)*...... 1,800
Storrs (F1)*......
Stratford (C4)*......Δ33,428
Suffield (E1)*......Δ4,895
Taconic (B1)*...... 150
Taftville (G2)*...... 3,598
Talcottville (F1)*...... 568
Talmadge Hill (A4)....
Tariffville (D1)*...... 800
Terryville (C2)*...... 6,500
Thamesville (G2)...... 5,518
Thomaston (C2)*......Δ4,896
Thompson (H1)*......Δ5,585
Thompsonville (E1)*.... 9,633
Tolland (F1)*......Δ1,659
Topstone (B3)......
Torrington (C1)*......27,820
Tracy (D2)......
Trumbull (C4)......Δ8,641
Twin Lakes (B1)......
Tyler City (D3)......
Tylerville (F3)......
Uncasville (G3)*......
Union (G1)...... Δ 261
Union City (C2)*...... 5,000
Unionville (D1)*...... 2,197
Vernon (F1)*......Δ10,115
Versailles (G2)*......
Voluntown (H2)*...... Δ 825
Wallingford (D3)*......11,994
Wapping (E1)*...... 1,000
Warehouse Point (E1)*1,283
Warren (B2)...... Δ 437
Warrenville (G1)*......
Washington (B2)*......Δ2,227
Washington Depot (B2)* 700
Waterbury (C2)*......104,477
Waterbury (urban area) 131,442
Waterford (Jordan Village) (G3)*......Δ9,100
Watertown (C2)*......Δ10,699
Waterville (C2)*......
Wauregan (H2)*...... 1,002
Weatogue (D1)*...... 800
West Ashford (G1)......
W. Avon (D1)......
W. Cheshire (D2)*...... 1,000
W. Cornwall (B1)*......
W. Goshen (B1)*......
W. Granby (D1)*......
W. Hartford (D1)*.....Δ44,402
W. Hartland (D1)*...... 196
W. Haven (D3)*......Δ32,010
W. Mystic (H3)*...... 2,362
W. Norwalk (B4)...... 724
W. Redding (B3)*...... 1,000
W. Simsbury (D1)*...... 300
W. Stafford (F1)...... 312
W. Suffield (E1)*...... 1,800
W. Thompson (H1).....
W. Torrington (C1)..... 240
W. Willington (F1)*.... 100
W. Woodstock (G1)..... 100
Westbrook (F3)*......Δ1,549
Westfield (E2)...... 1,250
Westford (G1)......
Weston (B4)......Δ1,988
Westport (B4)*......Δ11,667
Westway (F1)......
Wethersfield (E2)*....Δ12,533
Whitneyville (D3)......
Wildermere Beach (C4)
Willimantic (G2)*......13,586
Wilson (E1)*...... 3,500
Wilson Point (B4)...... 200
Wilsonville (H1)*...... 385
Wilton (B4)*......Δ4,558
Winchester Center (C1)*
Windermere (F1)...... 95
Windham (G2)*......Δ15,884
Windsor (E1)*......Δ11,833
Windsor Locks (E1)*..Δ5,221
Windsorville (E1)*......
Winnipauk (B4)...... 3,600
Winsted (C1)*...... 8,781
Wolcott (D2)......Δ3,553
Woodbridge (D3)......Δ2,822
Woodbury (C2)*......Δ2,564
Woodmont (C4)*...... 5,000
Woodstock (H1)*......Δ2,271
Woodstock Valley (G1)*
Woodville (B2)......
Yalesville (D3)*...... 1,122
Yantic (G2)*...... 800

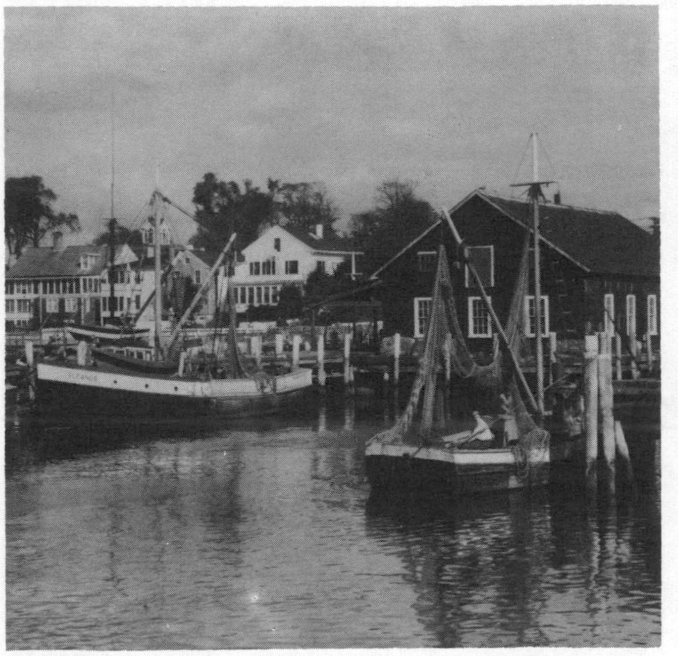

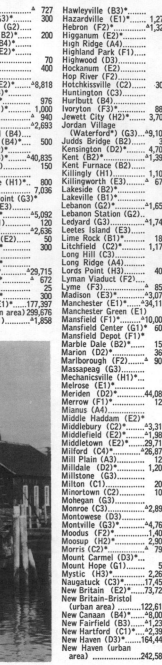

DELAWARE

Map on Page 67

Total Population 318,085

3 COUNTIES

Kent (M4)......37,870
New Castle (M2)......218,879
Sussex (N6)......61,336

CITIES and TOWNS

Angola (O6)...... 22
Arden (M1)*...... 842
Bacons (M6)...... 28
Bayard (O6)......
Bear (M2)*...... 150
Bellefonte (N1)......1,472
Bethany Beach (O6)*.... 190
Bethel (M6)*...... 271
Blackbird (M3)...... 50
Blades (M6)...... 789
Bowers (N4)*...... 284
Bridgeville (M6)*......1,468
Camden (M4)*...... 606
Cannon (M6)*...... 150
Canterbury (M4)...... 50
Centerville (M1)...... 225
Cheswold (M4)*...... 292
Christiana (M2)*...... 500
Clarksville (O6)*...... 150
Claymont (N1)*......5,370
Clayton (M3)*...... 825
Concord (M6)...... 100
Cooch (M2)...... 12
Cool Spring (O6)...... 25
Dagsboro (N6)*...... 474
Delaware City (M2)*....1,363
Delmar (M7)*......1,015
DOVER (M4)*......6,223
Edge Moor (N1)...... 25
Ellendale (N5)*...... 321
Elsmere (M2)......5,314
Farmington (M5)*...... 113
Farnhurst (M2)*...... 150
Felton (M4)*...... 455
Frankford (N6)*...... 615
Frederica (N4)*...... 675
Georgetown (N6)*......1,923
Glasgow (M2)......
Glasgow Station (M2)...
Greenville (M1)*......
Greenwood (M5)*...... 746
Harbeson (N6)*...... 142
Harrington (M5)*......2,241
Hartly (M4)*...... 139
Hazlettville (M4)...... 20
Hickman (M5)...... 200
Hockessin (M1)*......1,200
Hollyoak (N1)......1,450
Hollyville (O6)...... 20
Houston (N5)*...... 332
Kenton (M4)*...... 211
Kirkwood (M2)*......
Laurel (M6)*......2,700
Lebanon (N4)...... 150
Leipsic (N4)...... 253
Lewes (O5)*......2,904
Lincoln (N5)*...... 400
Little Creek (N4)*...... 266
Magnolia (M4)*...... 207
Marshallton (M2)*......1,600
Masten's Corner (M5).. 30
McDonough (M3)......
Middletown (M3)*......1,755
Midway (O6)...... 45
Milford (N5)*......5,179
Millsboro (N6)*...... 470
Millville (O6)*...... 270
Milton (N5)*......1,321
Mount Cuba (M1)...... 300
Mount Pleasant (M2)*.. 87
Nassau (O6)*...... 120
New Castle (M2)*......5,396
Newark (M2)*......6,731
Newport (M2)*......1,171
Oak Grove (M6)...... 50
Oak Orchards (O6)......
Oakley (M5)......
Ocean View (O6)*...... 450
Odessa (M3)*...... 467
Port Penn (M2)*......
Red Lion (M2)...... 50
Redden (N5)......
Rehoboth Beach (O6)*.1,794
Rockland (M1)*...... 350
Roxana (O6)...... 100
Saint Georges (M2)*....
Seaford (M6)*......3,087
Selbyville (N7)*......1,086
Slaughter Beach (N5)... 85
Smyrna (M3)*......2,346
Stanton (M2)*......
Stockley (N6)*......
Summit Bridge (M2)....
Townsend (M3)*...... 441
Viola (M4)*...... 134
Williamsville (O7)......
Willowgrove (M4)...... 65
Wilmington (M2)*....110,356
Wilmington (urban area) 186,265
Woodside (M4)*...... 157
Wyoming (M4)*...... 911
Yorklyn (M1)*...... 500

FLORIDA

Map on Page 56

Total Population 2,771,305

67 COUNTIES

Alachua (D2)......57,026
Baker (D1)......6,313
Bay (C6)......42,689
Bradford (D2)......11,457
Brevard (F3)......23,653
Broward (F5)......83,933
Calhoun (D6)......7,922
Charlotte (E5)......4,286
Citrus (D3)......6,111
Clay (E2)......14,323
Collier (E5)......6,488
Columbia (D1)......18,216
Dade (F6)......495,084
De Soto (E4)......9,242
Dixie (C2)......3,928
Duval (E1)......304,029
Escambia (B6)......112,706
Flagler (E2)......3,367
Franklin (B2)......5,814
Gadsden (B1)......36,457
Gilchrist (D2)......3,499
Glades (E5)......2,199
Gulf (D7)......7,460
Hamilton (D1)......8,981
Hardee (E4)......10,073
Hendry (E5)......6,051
Hernando (D3)......6,693
Highlands (E4)......13,636
Hillsborough (D4)......249,894
Holmes (C5)......13,988
Indian River (F4)......11,872
Jackson (D5)......34,645
Jefferson (C1)......10,413
Lafayette (C2)......3,440
Lake (E3)......36,340
Lee (E5)......23,404
Leon (B1)......51,590
Levy (D2)......10,637
Liberty (B1)......3,182
Madison (C1)......14,197
Manatee (D4)......34,704
Marion (D2)......38,187
Martin (F4)......7,807
Monroe (E7)......29,957
Nassau (E1)......12,811
Okaloosa (C6)......27,533
Okeechobee (F4)......3,454
Orange (E3)......114,950
Osceola (E3)......11,406
Palm Beach (F5)......114,688
Pasco (D3)......20,529
Pinellas (D4)......159,249
Polk (E4)......123,997
Putnam (E2)......23,615
St. Johns (E2)......24,998
St. Lucie (F4)......20,180
Santa Rosa (B6)......18,554
Sarasota (D4)......28,827
Seminole (E3)......26,883
Sumter (D3)......11,330
Suwannee (C1)......16,986
Taylor (C1)......10,416
Union (D1)......8,906
Volusia (E2)......74,229
Wakulla (B1)......5,258
Walton (C6)......14,725
Washington (C6)......11,888

CITIES and TOWNS

Alachua (D2)*......1,116
Alford (D6)*...... 375
Allenhurst (F3)...... 60
Alliance (A1)...... 250
Altamonte Spgs. (E3)*. 858
Altha (A1)*...... 434
Altoona (E3)*...... 500
Alturas (E4)*...... 350
Alva (E5)*...... 300
Amelia City (E1)*...... 150
Anastasia (E2)*...... 500
Ankona (F4)*...... 75
Anna Maria (D4)*...... 345
Anthony (D2)*...... 400
Apalachicola (A2)*......3,222
Apopka (E3)*......2,254
Arcadia (E4)*......4,764
Archer (D2)*...... 586
Argyle (C6)*......
Aripeka (D3)*...... 75
Arlington (E1)*......3,200
Arran (B1)*......
Artesia (F3)*......
Astatula (E3)*...... 255
Astor (E2)*......
Atlantic Beach (E1)*....1,604
Auburndale (E3)*......3,763
Aucilla (C1)*......
Avon Park (E4)*......4,612
Babson Park (E4)*......1,000
Bagdad (B6)*......1,500
Baker (C5)*......
Bal Harbour ‡(F6)...... 224
Baldwin (E1)*......1,048
Barberville (E2)*...... 350
Barrineau Park (B6)*... 200
Barth (B6)*...... 300
Bartow (E4)*......8,694
Bascom (A1)*...... 150
Basinger (F4)*...... 150
Bay Harbor (D6)*......1,676
Bay Harbor Isls. ‡(F6).. 296
Bay Springs (B6)*......
Bayard (E1)*...... 300
Bayport (D3)*...... 45
Bayshore (E5)...... 15
Bean City (F5)*...... 268
Bee Ridge (D4)*...... 500
Bell (D2)*...... 108
Belle Glade (F5)*......7,219
Belleair (D4)...... 961
Belleview (D2)*...... 595
Belleville (C1)...... 20
Benhaden (B1)...... 25
Bennett (D6)...... 100
Beresford (E2)*...... 100
Biscayne Park ‡(F6)....2,009
Bithlo (E3)*...... 50
Blanton (D3)*...... 75
Blountstown (A1)*......2,118
Bluffsprings (B5)*...... 100
Boca Ciega ‡(D4)...... 159
Boca Grande (D5)*...... 400
Boca Raton (F5)*...... 992
Bokeelia (D5)*...... 100
Bonifay (C5)*......2,252
Bonita Springs (E5)*....
Bostwick (E2)*...... 500
Bowling Green (E4)*.... 884
Boyd (C1)*...... 200
Boynton Beach (F5)*...2,542
Bradenton (D4)*......13,604
Bradenton Beach(D4)*. 500
Bradley (D4)*...... 422
Brandon (D4)*......1,250
Branford (D2)*...... 753
Brewster (E4)*...... 800
Brighton (E4)*...... 175
Bristol (B1)*......1,800
Bronson (D2)*...... 624
Brooker ‡(D2)*...... 277
Brooksville (D3)*......1,818
Broscan (C2)...... 10
Brownville (E4)*...... 200
Bruce (C6)*...... 200
Bryant (F5)*...... 400
Bryceville (D1)*...... 150
Bulow (E2)...... 25
Bunnell (E2)*......1,341
Burbank (E2)*...... 80
Bushnell (D3)*...... 536
Callahan (E1)*...... 722
Campbellton (D5)*...... 307
Campville (D2)*...... 250
Canal Point (F5)*......1,022
Canaveral (F3)......
Candler (E2)*...... 150
Cantonment (B6)*......
Capitola (B1)*...... 150
Captiva (D5)*...... 50
Carrabelle (B2)*...... 970
Caryville (C6)*...... 525

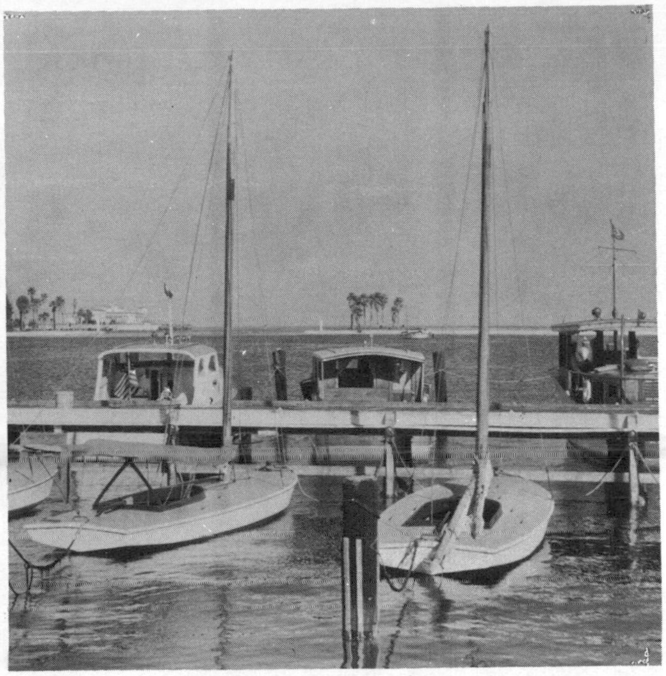

Cassadaga (E3)* 200
Casselberry ‡(E3) 407
Cedar Key (C2)* 900
Center Hill (D3)* 522
Century (B5)* 1,350
Chaires (B1)*
Charlotte Harbor (E5)* 330
Chattahoochee (B1)* 8,473
Cherry Lake Farms (C1) 600
Chiefland (D2)* 843
Chipley (D6)* 2,959
Chokoloskee (E6)* 148
Chosen (F5)* 1,873
Christmas (E3)* 250
Citra (D2)* 500
Citrus Center (E5) 15
City Point (F3)* 250
Clarksville (D6)*
Clearwater (D4)* 15,581
Clermont (E3)* 2,168
Cleveland (E5)* 104
Clewiston (E5)* 2,499
Cloud Lake ‡(F5) 132
Cocoa (F3)* 4,245
Cocoa Beach (F3)* 246
Coleman (D3)* 849
Collier City (Goodland*) (E6) 337
Columbia (D1) 75
Compass Lake (D6)*
Concord (D1)*
Conner (E2) 100
Coral Gables (F6)* 19,837
Coreytown ‡(D4) 23
Cornwell (E4)* 10
Coronado (F2)
Cortez (D4)* 600
Cottagehill (B6)* 500
Cottondale (D6)* 737
Craig (F7)* 10
Crawfordville (B1)* 525
Crescent City (E2)* 1,393
Crestview (C6)* 5,003
Cross City (C2)* 1,522
Crystal Lake (D6)* 250
Crystal River (D3)* 1,026
Crystal Springs (D3)* 250
Curtis (D2) 50
Cypress (A1)* 262
Dade City (D3)* 3,806
Dania (F5)* 4,540
Darlington (C5)*
Davenport (E3)* 760
Davie (F5) 728
Day (C1)* 300
Daytona Beach (F2)* 30,187
De Funiak Springs (C6)* 3,077
De Land (E2)* 8,652
De Leon Springs (E2)* 900
De Soto City (E4)* 220
Deer Park (F3)*
Deerfield Beach (F5)* 2,088
Delray Beach (F5)* 6,312
Denaud (E5) 100
Destin (C6)*
Dinsmore (E1)* 1,010
Doctors Inlet (E1)* 490
Dover (D4)* 1,000
Dowling Park (C1) 35
Drifton (C1)* 200
Dundee (E3)* 1,152
Dunedin (D3)* 3,202
Dunnellon (D2)* 1,110
Eagle Lake (E4)* 1,060
Earleton (D2)* 100
East Palatka (E2)* 1,367
Eastpoint (B2)* 600
Eastport (E1)
Eau Gallie (F3)* 1,554
Ebb (C1)* 100
Ebro (C6)* 200
Edgewater (F3)* 837
Edgewood ‡(E3) 217
El Jobean (D5)* 60
El Portal ‡(F6) 1,371
Elfers (D3)* 560
Elkton (E2)*
Ellaville (C1) 5
Ellenton (D4)* 700
Ellzey (D2) 150
Emporia (E2)* 420
Englewood (D5)* 1,206
Enterprise (E3)* 300
Espanola (E2)* 125
Estero (E5)* 250
Esto (C5)* 217
Eureka (E2)* 300
Eustis (E3)* 4,005
Everglades (E6)* 625
Fairbanks (D2) 35
Fairfield (D2)* 135
Fairvilla (E3) 1,000
Falmouth (C1)*
Felda (E5)* 300
Fellsmere (F4)* 649
Fernandina (E1)* 4,420
Fernandina Beach ‡(E1) 554
Flagler Beach (E2)* 374
Fletcher (C2) 100
Florahome (E2)* 400
Floral City (D3)* 700
Florence Villa (E3)* 2,500
Florida City (F6)* 1,547
Floridatown (B6) 1,200
Florosa (B6)
Foley (C1)* 1,014
Ft. Barrancas (B6) 300
Ft. Drum (F4) 50
Ft. George (E1)* 150
Ft. Green (E4)*
Ft. Lauderdale (F5)* 36,328
Ft. Mc Coy (E2)* 500
Ft. Meade (E4)* 2,803
Ft. Myers (E5)* 13,195
Ft. Ogden (E4)* 750
Ft. Pierce (F4)* 13,502
Ft. Walton (C6)* 2,463
Ft. White (D2)* 329
Fountain (D6)* 150
Freeport (C6)*
Frink (D6)* 300
Frostproof (E4)* 2,329
Fruitland Park (D3)* 551
Fruitville (D4) 900
Gainer (D6) 25
Gainesville (D2)* 26,861
Garden City (E1)* 500
Gardner (E4)* 110
Gasparilla (D5)* 250
Geneva (E3)* 600
Genoa (D1) 100
Georgetown (E2)* 300
Gibsonton (D4)*
Gifford (F4)* 1,459
Glen Ridge ‡(F5) 126
Glen Saint Mary (D1)*
Glendale (C5) 250
Glenwood (E2)* 155
Golden Beach ‡(F6)* 156
Golfview ‡(F5) 84
Gomez (F4) 65
Gonzalez (B6)* 700
Goodland (E6)* 337
Gotha (E3)* 275
Goulding (B6) 300
Goulds (F6)* 1,000
Graceville (D5)* 1,638
Graham (D2)* 50
Grand Ridge (A1)* 300
Grandin (E2)* 200
Grant (F4)*
Green Cove Spgs. (E2)* 3,291
Greenacres City (F5)* 531
Greensboro (B1)* 565
Greenville (C1)* 1,163
Greenwood (A1)*
Gretna (D1)* 305
Groveland (E3)* 1,028
Gulf Breeze (B6)* 287
Gulf Hammock (D2)* 250
Gulf Stream ‡(F5) 163
Gulfport (D4)* 3,702
Gull Point (B6)* 65
Hague (D2) 150
Haines City (E3)* 5,630
Hallandale (F6)* 3,886
Hampton (D2)* 386
Hampton Spgs. (C1) 15
Hardee Town (D2)
Harold (B6)* 75
Hastings (E2)* 577
Havana (B1)* 1,634
Hawthorne (D2)* 1,058
Hernando (D3)* 304
Hesperides (E4) 70
Hialeah (F6)* 19,676
Hicora (E4)
High Springs (D2)* 2,088
Highland (E1)* 350
Highland Beach ‡(F5) 52
Highland City (E4)* 1,600
Highland Park ‡(E4) 52
Hildreth (D2)* 22
Hillcrest Hts. ‡(E4) 91
Hilliard (E1)* 607
Hillsboro Beach ‡(F5) 84
Hines (C2) 400
Hinson (B1)* 500
Hobe Sound (F5)* 950
Holder (D3)* 75
Hollister (E2)*
Holly Hill (E2) 3,232
Hollywood (F5)* 14,351
Holmes Beach ‡(D4) 137
Holopaw (E3)*
Holt (C6)*
Homestead (F6)* 4,573
Homosassa (D3)* 500
Homosassa Spgs. (D3)* 100
Horseshoe Beach (C2)* 150
Hosford (B1)*
Houston (D1)* 140
Howey in the Hills, (E3)* 188
Hudson (D3)* 350
Hull (E4)*
Immokalee (E5)* 1,200
Indian Creek ‡(F6) 44
Indian Pass (D7) 60
Indian River City (F3)* 450
Indian Rocks Beach (D4)* 198
Indian Town (F4)*
Inglis (D2)* 200
Intercession City (E3)*
Interlachen (E2)* 297
Inverness (D3)* 1,471
Inwood (A1) 100
Islamorada (F7)* 600
Island Grove (D2)* 400
Jacksonville (E1)* 204,517
Jacksonville (urban area) 241,579
Jacksonville Beach(E1)* 6,430
Jamieson (B1)* 120
Jasper (D1)* 2,327
Jay (B5)* 547
Jennings (C1)* 549
Jensen Beach (F4)*
Johnson (E2)*
Jupiter (F5)* 313
Kathleen (D3)* 750
Kenansville (F4)* 250
Kendall (F6)* 2,100
Kendrick (D2)* 600
Key Largo (F6) 60
Key West (E7)* 26,433
Keystone Heights (E2)* 307
Keysville (D4)* 500
Kinard (D6)* 300
Kissimmee (E3)* 4,310
Korona (E2)*
Kynesville (D6) 400
La Belle (E5)* 945
La Crosse (D2)* 146
Lacoochee (D3)* 1,792
Lady Lake (E3)* 331
Lake Alfred (E3)* 1,270
Lake Butler (D1)* 1,040
Lake City (D1)* 7,571
Lake City Jct. (D2) 11
Lake Como (E2)* 250
Lake Hamilton (E3)* 604
Lake Harbor (F5)* 800
Lake Helen (E3)* 926
Lake Jem (E3)* 300
Lake Maitland ‡(E3) 889
Lake Mary (E3)* 500
Lake Monroe (E3)* 300
Lake Park (F5)* 489
Lake Placid (E4)* 417
Lake Wales (E4)* 6,821
Lake Worth (G5)* 11,777
Lakeland (D3)* 30,851
Lakeport (E5) 70
Lakewood (C5)*
Lamont (C1)*
Land O'Lakes (D3)* 75
Lantana (F5)* 773
Largo (D4)* 1,547
Laurel (D4)* 500
Lauderdale-by-the-Sea ‡(F5) 234
Laurel Hill (C5)* 327
Lawtey (D1)* 576
Lebanon (D2) 75
Lecanto (D3)* 182
Lee (C1)* 228
Leesburg (E3)* 7,395
Leonia (C5)* 105
Limestone (E4)* 150
Linden (D3)* 250
Live Oak (D1)* 4,064
Lloyd (C1)* 325
Lochloosa (E2)* 200
Lockhart (E3)* 1,200
Longwood (E3)* 717
Lorida (E4)* 225
Loughman (E3)* 350
Lovett (C1)* 18
Lowell (D2)* 150
Loxahatchee (F5)* 200
Lulu (D1)* 100
Lumberton (D3) 25
Luraville (C1) 20
Lutz (D3)* 1,800
Lynn Haven (C6)* 1,787
Lynne (E2)* 125
Macclenny (D1)* 1,177
Madeira Beach ‡(D4)* 916
Madison (C1)* 3,150
Maitland (E3)*
Malabar (F3)* 375
Malone (A1)* 521
Manalapan ‡(F5) 54
Manatee (D4)
Mandarin (E1)* 800
Mango (D4)* 350
Mangonia Park ‡(F5) 348
Mannville (E2)* 70
Marathon (E2)* 1,200
Marco (E6)* 250
Marianna (A1)* 5,845
Marineland (E2) 40
Martin (D2)* 100
Mary Esther (B6)* 332
Masaryktown (D3) 190
Mascotte (E3)* 440
Mason (D1) 20
Maxville (E1)*
Mayo (C1)* 679
Mayport (E1)* 1,300
Maytown (F3) 25
Mc Alpin (D1)* 100
Mc David (B5)* 700
Mc Intosh (D2)* 247
Mc Neal (A1) 500
Medley ‡(F6) 106
Melbourne (F3)* 4,223
Melbourne Beach (F3)* 230
Melrose (D2)* 750
Merritt Island (F3)*
Miami (F6)* 249,276
Miami (urban area) 453,004
Miami Beach (F6)* 46,282
Miami Shores (F6)* 5,086
Miami Springs (F6)* 5,108
Micanopy (D2)* 612
Micco (F4)* 250
Miccosukee (B1)* 160
Middleburg (E1)* 500
Midway (B1)* 500
Millers Ferry (C6)* 40
Milligan (C6)* 600
Millview (B6) 150
Milton (B6)* 2,040
Mims (F3)* 1,500
Minneola (E3)* 399
Molino (B6)* 600
Montbrook (D2)* 200
Monticello (C1)* 2,264
Montverde (E3)* 293
Moore Haven (E5)* 636
Morriston (D2)* 150
Mossy Head (C6)* 125
Moultrie (E2) 50
Mt. Dora (E3)* 3,028
Mt. Pleasant (B1)* 300
Mulat (B6)* 80
Mulberry (E4)* 2,024
Munson (B5)* 300
Murdock (D4)* 100
Muscogee (B6)* 165
Myakka City (D4)* 450
Myrtle Grove (B6)*
Naples (E5)* 1,465
Naranja (F6)* 500
Narcoossee (E3)* 120
National Gardens(E2)* 125
Neptune Beach (E1)* 1,767
New Berlin (E1) 100
New Port Richey (D3)* 1,512
New River (D2)* 150
New Smyrna Beach (F2)* 5,775
Newberry (D2)* 873
Newburn (C1) 10
Niceville (C6)* 2,497
Nichols (E4)* 550
Nobleton (D3)* 72
Nocatee (E4)* 1,200
Nokomis (D4)* 800
Noma (C5)*
North Bay ‡(F6) 198
North Miami (F6)* 10,734
N. Miami Beach (F6)* 2,129
O'Brien (D1)* 300
Oak Hill (F3)* 683
Oakland (E3)* 548
Oakland Park (F5)* 1,295
Ocala (D2)* 11,741
Ocean Ridge ‡(F5) 67
Ochopee (E6)* 300
Ocoee (E3)* 1,370
Odessa (D3)*
Ojus (F6)* 3,791
Okahumpka (D3)* 450
Okeechobee (F4)* 1,849
Oklawaha (E2)* 500
Old Town (C2)* 300
Oldsmar (D3)* 345
Olive (B6) 200
Olustee (D1)*
Ona (E4)* 89
Oneco (D4)* 650
Opa-Locka (F6)* 5,271
Orange (B1)*
Orange City (E3)* 797
Orange Lake (D2)* 500
Orange Park (E1)* 1,502
Orange Springs (E2)* 275
Orlando (E3)* 52,367
Orlando (urban area) 72,572
Ormond (E2)* 3,418
Ormond Beach (F2)* 900
Orsino (F3)* 55
Osceola (E3)
Osprey (D4)* 350
Osteen (E3)* 300
Otter Creek (D2)* 1,050
Overstreet (D6)* 100
Oviedo (E3)* 1,601
Oxford (D3)* 304
Ozona (D3)* 600
Pahokee (F5)* 4,472
Palatka (E2)* 9,176
Palm Bay (F3)* 300
Palm Beach (G5)* 3,886
Palm City (F4)*
Palm Harbor (D3)* 750
Palma Sola (D4)* 300
Palmdale (E5)* 82
Palmetto (D4)* 4,103
Panacea (B1)*
Panama City (C6)* 25,814
Panama City Beach(C6)*
Paola (E3)* 400
Parrish (D4)* 1,200
Parker (D6)*
Pass-a-Grille Beach (D4)* 1,000
Paxton (C5) 300
Pelican Lake (F5)*
Pembroke (E4)* 50
Penney Farms (E2)* 445
Pennsuco ‡(F6) 133
Pensacola (B6)* 43,479
Perrine (F6)* 2,859
Perry (C1)* 2,797
Pierce (E4)* 975
Pierson (E2)* 657
Pine Castle (E3)* 2,000
Pineland (D5)* 50
Pinellas Park (D4)* 2,924
Pinetta (C1)* 250
Pirates Cove (E7)
Plant City (D3)* 9,230
Plymouth (E3)* 300
Point Washington (C6)* .
Polk City (E3)* 171
Pomona Park (E2)* 443
Pompano Beach (F5)* 5,682
Ponce de Leon (C6)* 600
Ponce Park (F2) 39
Ponte Vedra Beach (E1)* 1,000
Port Boca Grande (D5) 75
Port Everglades (F5)* 100
Port Mayaca (F5)* 155
Port Orange (F2)* 1,201
Port Richey (D3)* 376
Port Saint Joe (D6)* 2,752
Port Sewall (F4) 210
Port Tampa (D4)* 1,497
Portland (C6)* 350
Princeton (F6)* 1,300
Providence (D2) 16
Punta Gorda (E5)* 1,915
Punta Rassa (E5) 25
Quincy (B1)* 6,505
Ralford (D1)* 40
Raleigh (D2)* 156
Ramrod Key (E7)* 3
Redbay (C6)* 250
Reddick (D2)* 433
Redington Beach ‡(D4) 384
Richland (D3) 100
Richloam (D3) 10
River Junction (B1)*
Riverdale (E2) 100
Riverview (D4)*
Riviera Beach (F5)* 4,065
Rock Bluff (B1)* 250
Rock Harbor (F6)* 185
Rockledge (F3)* 1,347
Romeo (D2)* 300
Roseland (F4)* 100
Round Lake (D6)* 250
Ruskin (D4)*
Safety Harbor (D4)* 894
St. Augustine (E2)* 13,555
St. Catherine (D3)* 250
St. Cloud (E3)* 3,001
St. James City (E5)* 35
St. Leo (D3)* 261
St. Lucie (F4)* 300
St. Marks (B1)* 391
St. Petersburg (D4)* 96,738
St. Petersburg (urban area) 113,378
St. Petersburg Beach ‡(D4) 722
Salem (C2)* 200
Salerno (F4)* 789
Samoset (D4)* 1,617
Sampson (D2)* 125
Samsula (E2) 500
San Antonio (D3)* 286
San Carlos (E5)
San Mateo (E2)* 750
Sanderson (D1)* 100
Sanford (E3)* 11,935
Sanibel (D5)* 125
Santa Fe (D2)* 100
Santa Rosa (C6)* 300
Santos (D2) 100
Sarasota (D4)* 18,896
Satsuma (E2)* 250
Scottsmoore (F3)* 150
Sears (E5)
Sebastian (F4)* 376
Sebring (E4)* 5,006
Seffner (D4)* 850
Seville (E2)* 427
Shady Grove (C1)* 50
Shalimar ‡(C6)* 694
Shamrock (C2)* 700
Sharpes (F3)* 300
Shiloh (F3)* 150
Silver Springs (D2)* 350
Slater (E5) 25
Sneads (B1)* 1,074
Sopchoppy (B1)*
Sorrento (E3)* 300
South Bay (F5)* 1,050
South Daytona (E2) 692
South Flomaton ‡(B5) 395
South Miami (F6)* 4,809
Southport (C6)* 825
Sparr (D2)* 450
Springfield (D6) 1,084
Starke (D2)* 2,944
Steinhatchee (C2)* 900
Stuart (F4)* 2,912
Sumatra (B1)*
Summerfield (D2)* 400
Sumner (D2) 25
Sun City (D4)* 325
Sunnyside (C6)* 85
Sunshine Beach ‡(D4) 469
Surfside ‡(F6) 1,852
Suwannee (C2)* 125
Sweetwater ‡(F6) 230
Switzerland (E1)* 350
Taft (E3)* 800
TALLAHASSEE (B1)* 27,237
Tampa (D4)* 124,681
Tampa (urban area) 178,398
Tarpon Springs (D3)* 4,323
Tavares (E3)* 1,763
Tavernier (F6)* 480
Telogia (B1)*
Temple Terrace (D3)* 433
Terra Ceia (D4)* 1,500
Thonotosassa (D3)*
Tice (E5)* 1,133
Titusville (F3)* 2,604
Treasure Island ‡(D4) 75
Trenton (D2)* 904
Trilby (D3)* 500
Uleta (F6)*
Umatilla (E3)* 1,312
Useppa Island (D5) 25
Valparaiso (C6)* 1,047
Venice (D4)* 727
Venus (E4)* 35
Vernon (C6)* 610
Vero Beach (F4)* 4,746
Virginia Gardens ‡(F6) 235
Villa Tasso (C6) 75
Wabasso (F4)* 300
Wacissa (B1)* 450
Wakulla (B1)*
Waldo (D2)* 647
Walnut Hill (B5)*
Walton (F4) 175
Ward (B1) 30
Warrington (B6)* 13,570
Watertown (D1)* 1,473
Wauchula (E4)* 2,872
Waukeenah (C1)* 200
Wausau (D6)* 350
Waverly (E4)* 1,000
Webster (D3)* 569
Weirsdale (D3)* 800
Welaka (E2)* 459
Wellborn (D1)* 450
West Miami (F6) 4,043
W. Palm Beach (F5)* 43,162
Westbay (C6)* 400
Westgate (F6) 3,303
Westville (C6)* 428
Wewahitchka (D6)* 1,289
White City (F4) 750
White Springs (D1)* 700
Whitehouse (E1)* 175
Wilcox (D2)* 125
Wildwood (D3)* 2,019
Williston (D2)* 1,323
Wilma (B1)* 50
Wilton Manor ‡(F5) 883
Wimauma (D4)* 440
Windermere (E3)* 317
Winfield (D1) 100
Winter Beach (F4)* 350
Winter Garden (E3)* 3,503
Winter Haven (E3)* 8,605
Winter Park (E3)* 8,250
Woodville (B1)*
Worthington (D2)* 30
Yalaha (E3)* 600
Yankeetown (D2)* 322
Youngstown (D6)* 500
Yukon (E1)* 2,000
Yulee (E1)* 500
Zellwood (E3)* 1,500
Zephyrhills (D3)* 1,826
Zolfo Springs (E4)* 334

Map on Page 57

GEORGIA

Total Population 3,444,578

159 COUNTIES

Appling (H7) 14,003
Atkinson (G8) 7,362
Bacon (G7) 8,940
Baker (D8) 5,952
Baldwin (F4) 29,706
Banks (E2) 6,935
Barrow (E2) 13,115
Bartow (C2) 27,370
Ben Hill (F7) 14,879
Berrien (F8) 13,966
Bibb (E5) 114,079
Bleckley (F6) 9,218
Brantley (J8) 6,387
Brooks (E9) 18,169
Bryan (K6) 5,965
Bulloch (J6) 24,740
Burke (J4) 23,458
Butts (E4) 9,079
Calhoun (C7) 8,578
Camden (J9) 7,322
Candler (H6) 8,063
Carroll (B3) 34,112
Catoosa (B1) 15,146
Charlton (H9) 4,821
Chatham (K6) 151,481
Chattahoochee (C6) 12,149
Chattooga (B1) 21,197
Cherokee (D2) 20,750
Clarke (F3) 36,550
Clay (B7) 5,844
Clayton (D3) 22,872
Clinch (G9) 6,007
Cobb (C3) 61,830
Coffee (G8) 23,961
Colquitt (E8) 33,999
Columbia (H3) 9,525
Cook (F8) 12,201
Coweta (C4) 27,796
Crawford (E5) 6,080
Crisp (E7) 17,663
Dade (A1) 7,364
Dawson (D2) 3,712
De Kalb (D3) 136,395
Decatur (C9) 23,620
Dodge (F6) 17,865
Dooly (E6) 14,159
Dougherty (D7) 43,617
Douglas (C3) 12,173
Early (C8) 17,413
Echols (G9) 2,494
Effingham (K6) 9,133
Elbert (G2) 18,585
Emanuel (H5) 19,789
Evans (J6) 6,653
Fannin (D1) 15,192
Fayette (C4) 7,978
Floyd (B2) 62,899
Forsyth (D2) 11,005
Franklin (F2) 14,446
Fulton (D3) 473,572
Gilmer (D1) 9,963
Glascock (G4) 3,579
Glynn (J8) 29,046
Gordon (C2) 18,922
Grady (D9) 18,928
Greene (F3) 12,843
Gwinnett (D2) 32,320
Habersham (E1) 16,553
Hall (E2) 40,113
Hancock (G4) 11,052
Haralson (B3) 14,663
Harris (C5) 11,265
Hart (G2) 14,495
Heard (B4) 6,975
Henry (D4) 15,857
Houston (E6) 20,964
Irwin (F7) 11,973
Jackson (E2) 18,997
Jasper (E4) 7,473
Jeff Davis (G7) 9,299
Jefferson (H4) 18,855
Jenkins (J5) 10,264
Johnson (G5) 9,893
Jones (E5) 7,538
Lamar (D4) 10,242
Lanier (F8) 5,151
Laurens (G6) 33,123
Lee (D7) 6,674
Liberty (J7) 8,444
Lincoln (H3) 6,462
Long (J7) 3,598
Lowndes (F9) 35,211
Lumpkin (D1) 6,574
Macon (D6) 14,213
Madison (F2) 12,238
Marion (C6) 6,521
Mc Duffie (H4) 11,443
Mc Intosh (K7) 6,008
Meriwether (C4) 21,055
Miller (C8) 9,023
Mitchell (D8) 22,528
Monroe (E4) 10,523
Montgomery (G6) 7,901

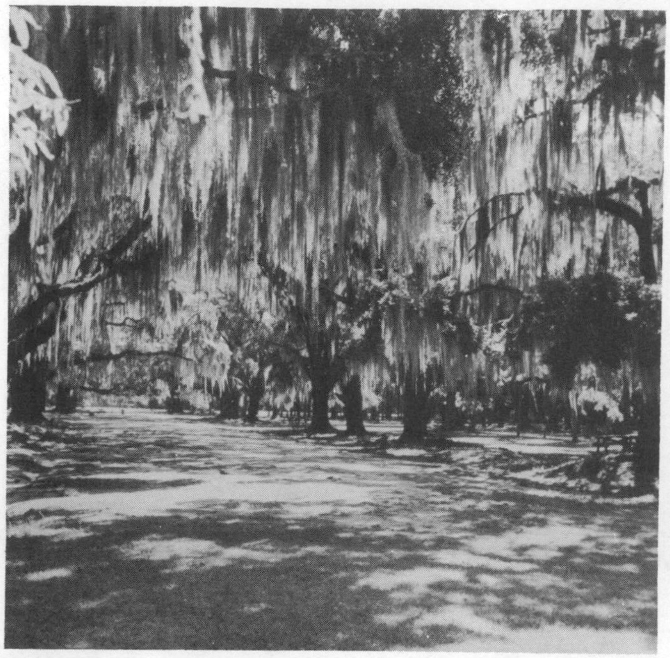

Morgan (F3)................11,899
Murray (C1)................10,676
Muscogee (C6)..........118,028
Newton (E3)................20,185
Oconee (F3)..................7,009
Oglethorpe (F3).............9,958
Paulding (C3)..............11,752
Peach (E5)..................11,705
Pickens (D2)..................8,855
Pierce (H8)..................11,112
Pike (D4)......................8,459
Polk (B3).....................30,976
Pulaski (E6)..................8,808
Putnam (F4)...................7,731
Quitman (B7)..................3,015
Rabun (F1).....................7,424
Randolph (C7)...............13,804
Richmond (H4)...........108,876
Rockdale (D3).................8,464
Schley (D6).....................4,036
Screven (J5)..................18,000
Seminole (C9)..................7,904
Spalding (D4).................31,045
Stephens (F1).................16,647
Stewart (C6)....................9,194
Sumter (D6)...................24,208
Talbot (C5).......................7,687
Taliaferro (G3).................4,515
Tattnall (J6)...................15,939
Taylor (D5)........................9,113
Telfair (G7).....................13,221
Terrell (D7)......................14,314
Thomas (E9)....................33,932
Tift (E8)..........................22,645
Toombs (H6).....................17,382
Towns (E1)..........................4,803
Treutlen (G6).......................6,522
Troup (B4).........................49,841
Turner (E7).........................10,479
Twiggs (F5)..........................8,308
Union (E1)............................7,318
Upson (D5)..........................25,078
Walker (B1).........................38,198
Walton (E3)..........................20,230
Ware (H8)............................30,289
Warren (G4)...........................8,779
Washington (G4)...................21,012
Wayne (J7)............................14,248
Webster (C6)...........................4,081
Wheeler (G6)...........................6,712
White (E1)...............................5,751
Whitfield (B1)........................34,432
Wilcox (F7)............................10,167
Wilkes (G3)............................12,388
Wilkinson (F5)..........................9,781
Worth (E8)..............................19,357

CITIES and TOWNS

Aaron (J5).................... 50
Abac (E8)....................
Abba (F7)*....................
Abbeville (F7)*............ 890
Abbottsford (B4)........... 40
Acree (D7)*................ 225
Acworth (C2)*.............1,466
Adairsville (C2)*.......... 916
Adel (F8)*...................2,776
Adgateville (E4)............ 75
Adrian (G5)*................ 503
Afton (D2).................... 7
Agnes (H3)*................. 30
Agricola (G4)................ 45
Aikenton (E4)................
Ailey (G6)*................... 508
Akes (B3)...................... 400
Alamo (G6)*.................. 800
Alapaha (F8)*................ 505
Albany (D7)*..............31,155
Aldora (D4)................... 591
Alexander (J4)*.............. 90
Aline (H6)..................... 100
Allenhurst (J7)*............ 150
Allentown (F5)*............. 450
Allenville (F8)................ 15
Alma (G7)*....................2,588
Almon (E3).................... 135
Alpharetta (D2)*............. 917
Alston (H6)*.................. 147
Altamaha (H7)..............
Alto (E2)*.................... 302
Alvaton (C4)*................. 95
Amboy (E7)..................... 50
Ambrose (G7)*................ 470
Americus (D6)*............11,389
Amity (H3)*....................
Amsterdam (D9)*............ 700
Andersonville (D6)*......... 281
Apalachee (E3)*.............. 178
Apollo (F4)...................... 25
Appling (H3)*.................. 250
Arabi (E7)*...................... 376
Aragon (B2)*.................1,272
Arcade (E2)..................... 114
Arcola (J6)....................... 78
Argyle (G8)*.................... 244
Arlington (C8)*..............1,382
Armuchee (B2)*.................
Arnoldsville (F3)*............ 150
Arp (F7)........................... 50
Ashburn (E7)*................2,918
Ashland (F2)*.................. 250
Aska (D1)*......................... 35
Atco (C2)*......................1,443
Athens (F3)*................28,180
Atkinson (J8)*.................. 500
ATLANTA (D3)*.......331,314
Atlanta (urban
area)............................502,204
Attapulgus (D9)*............ 457
Auburn (E2)*................... 301
Augusta (J4)*...............71,508
Augusta (urban area).87,823
Auraria (E1)..................... 200
Austell (C3)*..................1,413
Autreyville (E8)................ 100
Avalon (F1)*..................... 151
Avans (A1)*.....................
Avera (H4)*...................... 230
Avondale Estates
(D3)*.............................1,070
Axson (G8)*...................... 200
Babcock (C8)...................
Baconton (D8)*.................. 500
Bainbridge (C9)*............7,562
Bairdstown (F3)*................ 75
Baldwin (E2)*..................... 490
Ball Ground (D2)*............... 700
Banning (C3)...................... 225
Bannockburn (F8)................. 15
Barnesville (D4)*.............4,185
Barnett (G3)*....................... 60
Barnett Shoals (F3).........
Barney (E8)*....................... 157
Barretts (F8)*..................... 150
Bartow (G5)*....................... 347
Barwick (E9)*...................... 436
Bascom (J5).......................... 30
Baxley (H7)*....................3,409
Baxter (D1)*.....................
Beach (G8)............................ 62
Beachton (D9)....................... 50
Belair (H4)........................
Bellton (E2)*........................ 266
Bellville (H6)*...................... 245
Belmont (E2)......................... 100
Bemiss (F9)............................ 50
Benevolence (C7)*................ 157
Berlin (E8)*........................... 309
Berner (E4)*........................... 175
Berryton (B2)*....................... 520
Bethlehem (E3)*..................... 240
Between (E3)........................... 120
Beverly (G2).......................
Bibb City (B5)*..................1,452
Big Springs (C5)...................... 25
Bingen (C9)............................... 4
Bishop (F3)*............................ 253
Blackshear (H8)*..................2,271
Bladen (J8).................................. 8
Blaine (C1)................................ 95
Blairsville (E1)*........................ 430
Blakely (C8)*.........................3,234
Blalock (E1)............................... 50
Blitchton (J6)*........................... 50
Bloomingdale (K6)*.................. 350
Blue Ridge (D1)*..................1,718
Bluffton (C7)*........................... 244
Blun (H5)................................... 150
Blundale (H5)*.......................... 116
Blythe (H4)*.............................. 268
Bogart (E3)*.............................. 459
Bolen (G8)................................... 90
Bolingbroke (E5)*....................... 87
Bolton (D3)*..........................
Boneville (G4)*......................... 100
Boston (E9)*..........................1,035
Bostwick (E3)*.......................... 287
Bowdon (B3)*........................1,155
Bowdon Junction (B3)* 450
Bowens Mill (F7).................
Bowersville (G2)*...................... 303
Bowman (G2)*............................ 714
Box Springs (C5)*..................... 100
Boykin (C8)................................ 120
Bradley (E4)*............................ 100
Braselton (E2)*.......................... 165
Braswell (C3)................................ 25
Bremen (B3)*........................2,299
Brentwood (H7)............................ 50
Brest (D8)...........................
Brewton (G5)*.....................
Bridgeboro (E8)...................
Briggston (F9)................................ 35
Bright (D2).................................... 150
Brighton (E7).................................. 35
Brinson (C9)*................................. 248
Bristol (H8)*.................................. 137
Broadhurst (J8)............................... 225
Brobston (K8)..................................... 8
Bronwood (D7)*............................... 337
Brooker (G7)...................................... 50
Brookfield (F8)*............................... 350
Brooklet (J6)*.................................. 536
Brooklyn (C6)*................................. 300
Brooks (D4)*.................................... 136
Brookton (E2)................................... 200
Browns Crossing (F4)........................ 50
Broxton (G7)*................................... 890
Brunswick (K8)*........................17,954
Buchanan (B3)*................................. 651
Buckhead (F3)*................................. 220
Buena Vista (C6)*.......................1,428
Buford (D2)*................................3,812
Bullard (F5).........................
Burnt Fort (J9).................................... 75
Burtsboro (D1)..................................... 25
Burwell (B3)*.. 60
Bushnell (G7).. 27
Butler (D5)*.....................................1,182
Butts (J5)... 10
Byromville (E6)*.................................. 288
Byron (E5)*.. 379
Cadwell (G6)*...................................... 310
Cairo (D9)*.......................................5,577
Calhoun (B1)*...................................3,231
Calvary (D9)*.. 600
Calvin (F6).. 50
Camak (G4)*... 379
Camilla (D8)*......................................3,745
Camp Creek (D1)...................
Campania (H4)... 350
Campton (E3)*.. 163
Canon (F2)*.. 596
Canoochee (H5)*...................................... 62
Canton (C2)*......................................2,716
Carbondale (B1).. 75
Carl (E3)*.. 214
Carlton (F2)*.. 249
Carnegie (C7)*.. 197
Carnesville (F2)*....................................... 349
Carrollton (C3)*...................................7,753
Carrs Station (F4)...................................... 50
Cartecay (D1)*....................
Carters (C1)*.. 35
Cartersville (C2)*...................................7,270
Cass (C2)*...........................
Cassandra (B1).. 125
Cassville (C2)*......................
Cataula (C5)*... 500
Cave (C2).. 8
Cave Spring (B2)*.. 959
Cecil (F8)*.. 254
Cedar Grove (A1)*.. 75
Cedar Springs (C8)*.................
Cedartown (B2)*......................................9,470
Center (F2)*.. 112
Centralhatchee (B4)...................................... 239
Chalybeate Spgs. (C5)... 255
Chamblee (D3)*..........3,445
Charing (D6)*..................
Charles ‡(H6)..................... 20
Chatsworth (C1)*.........1,214
Chattahoochee (C3)*.......
Chauncey (F6)*.............. 348
Cherrylog (D1)*................
Chester (F6)*.................... 315
Chickamauga (B1)*.....1,747
Chipley (C5)*................... 817
Choestoe (E1)...................
Chula (E7)*....................... 210
Cisco (C1)*....................... 100
Clarkdale (C3)*................. 750
Clarkesville (F1)*..........1,106
Clarkston (D3)*.............1,165
Claxton (J6)*.................1,923
Clay Hill (H3)*...................... 17
Clayton (F1)*..................1,302
Clem (B3)*.......................... 400
Clermont (E2)*.................... 323
Cleveland (E1)*.................. 589
Climax (D9)*...................... 373
Clinchfield (E6)*................ 200
Clito (J5)............................. 25
Cloudland (A1)*.................. 100
Clyattville (F9)*.................... 75
Clyo (K6)*.......................... 600
Cobb (E7)*.......................... 150
Cobbtown (H6)*.................. 288
Cobbville (G7)..................... 126
Cobert (F2).......................
Cochran (F6)*................3,357
Coffee (H7)*........................ 200
Coffinton (C6)....................
Cogdell (G8)*.....................
Cohutta (C1)*...................... 450
Colbert (F2)*........................ 407
Coleman (C7)*...................... 295
Coleman (G4)......................... 35
Colesburg (J9)...................... 100
College Park (C3)*......14,535
Collegeboro (J6)*...........1,000
Collins (H6)*......................... 638
Colon (G9).............................. 25
Colquitt (C8)*.................1,664
Columbus (C6)*.............79,611
Columbus (urban
area)..........................118,122
Comer (F2)*........................... 882
Commerce (E2)*.............3,351
Concord (D4)*........................ 360
Conyers (D3)*..................2,003
Coolidge (E8)*........................ 764
Coosa (B2)*............................ 125
Cordele (E7)*....................9,462
Corinth (B4)........................... 135
Cork (E4)................................. 50
Cornelia (E1)*..................2,424
Cotton (D8)*........................... 146
Council (G9)*.......................... 125
Covena (H6)*.......................
Coverdale (E7)......................... 50
Covington (E3)*...............5,192
Covington Mills (E3)......
Crandall (C1)*........................ 202
Crawford (F3)*........................ 555
Crawfordville (G3)*.................. 966
Crest (D5)................................. 96
Crosland (E8)*......................... 127
Crystal Springs (B2).......
Culloden (D5)*......................... 261
Culverton (G4)*........................ 250
Cumming (D2)*...................1,264
Curryville (B2)*.......................... 54
Cusseta (C6)*............................ 571
Cuthbert (C7)*.....................4,025
Cutting (G8)............................... 100
Cyrene (C9).................................. 35
Dacula (E3)*............................... 369
Dahlonega (D1)*..................2,152
Daisy (J6)*.................................. 195
Dakota (E7).................................. 40
Dallas (C3)*..........................1,817
Dalton (B1)*........................15,968
Damascus (C8)*........................... 402
Dames Ferry (E4)*....................... 225
Danburg (G3)*............................. 181
Danielsville (F2)*......................... 298
Danville (F5)*.............................. 461
Darien (K8)*..........................1,380
Dasher (F9)*................................ 100
Davisboro (G5)*........................... 469
Dawson (D7)*.........................4,411
Dawsonville (D2)*........................ 318
De Soto (D7)*.............................. 309
Dearing (H4)*.............................. 325
Decatur (D3)*.......................21,635
Deepstep (G4)*............................ 159
Demorest (F1)*......................1,166
Dennis (F4)................................... 50
Denton (G7)*............................... 273
Devereux (F4)*............................. 170
Dewey Rose (G2)*........................ 375
Dewitt (D8)............................
Dexter (G6)*................................ 264
Dial (D1)*...................................... 89
Dickey (C7).................................. 135
Dillard (F1)*................................. 186
Dixie (E9)*.................................... 261
Doctortown (J7)*........................... 350
Doerun (E8)*................................. 902
Doles (E7)*.................................... 125
Donalsonville (C8)*...............2,569
Donovan (G5)*............................... 225
Doogan (C1)..................................... 30
Dooling (E6)*................................. 300
Doraville (D3)*............................... 472
Dorchester (K7)*............................. 150
Double Branches (H3)... 100
Doublerun (E7)...........................
Douglas (G7)*.........................7,428
Douglasville (C3)*...................3,400
Dover (J5)*..................................... 150
Doverel (D7)..................................... 25
Doyle (D6)*...............................
Draketown (B3)............................. 200
Dry Branch (F5)*........................... 250
Du Pont (G9)*................................ 285
Dublin (G5)*.........................10,232
Ducktown (D2)................................. 58
Dudley (F5)*................ 272
Due (D1)......................... 50
Duluth (D2)*.................. 842
Dunwoody (D3)*............ 240
Durand (C5)*................. 186
Dyas (E5)......................... 12
Early (B2)...................... 100
East Ellijay (C1)*.......... 549
East Juliette (E4).......... 303
East Point (C3)*........21,080
East Thomaston (D5)....3,082
Eastanollee (F1)*........... 225
Eastman (F6)*..............3,597
Eastville (F3).................... 96
Eatonton (F4)*.............2,749
Echeconnee (E5)................ 56
Eden (K6)*........................ 300
Edison (C7)*..................1,247
Edith (G9)......................... 150
Egypt (K6)*.....................
Elberton (G2)*..............6,772
Eldora (J6)......................... 50
Eldorendo (C8)*................ 250
Elko (E6)*.......................... 188
Ella Gap (C1)..................
Ellabell (K6)*..................... 100
Ellaville (D6)*..................... 886
Ellenton (E8)*..................... 429
Ellenwood (D3)*.................. 250
Ellerslie (C5)*..................... 650
Ellijay (C1)*...................1,527
Elmodel (D8)*..................... 125
Emerson (C2)*..................... 508
Emma (D1)*........................ 135
Emmalane (H5)...................... 10
Empire (F6)*........................ 157
Enigma (F8)*....................... 499
Epworth (D1)*..................... 100
Erick (G6)............................. 20
Esom Hill (B3)*.................... 175
Eton (C1)*........................... 297
Eulonia (K7)*.....................
Evans (H3)*.......................
Everett (J8)*........................ 200
Experiment (D4)*...........4,265
Faceville (C9)*..................... 700
Fairburn (C3)*................1,889
Fairfax (G8).......................
Fairmount (C2)*.................. 573
Fargo (G9)*........................
Farmdale (J5).....................
Farmington (F3)*................. 121
Farrar (E4)*.......................... 30
Fayetteville (C4)*...........1,032
Felton (B3)*......................... 250
Fender (E8)*........................ 150
Ficklin (G3)*........................ 100
Findlay (E6)........................... 50
Finleyson (F6)*...................... 79
Fish (B2)............................... 200
Fitzgerald (F7)*...............8,130
Fitzpatrick (F5)..................... 150
Fleming (K7)*........................ 200
Flemington (J7)*..................... 90
Flint (D8)...........................
Flintstone (B1)*..................... 200
Flippen (D3)*......................... 500
Florence (C6).....................
Flovilla (E4)*......................... 315
Flowery Branch (E2)*... 610
Folkston (H9)*................1,515
Forest Glen (F7)...................
Forest Park (D3)*..........2,653
Forsyth (E4)*..................3,125
Fort Gaines (C7)*...........1,339
Fort Lamar (F2)....................... 15
Fort Mudge (H8)...................... 25
Fort Oglethorpe ‡(B1)* 692
Fort Screven (L6)*................. 300
Fort Valley (E5)*............6,820
Fortson (C5)*.......................... 300
Fowlstown (D9)*..................... 300
Franklin (B4)*......................... 425
Franklin Spgs. (F2)*... 182
Frolona (B4)*.......................... 123
Fry (D1)*................................. 250
Fullerville (C3)........................ 529
Funston (E8)*........................... 233
Gabbettville (B5)*.................... 275
Gaddistown (D1)*.................... 175
Gaillard (D5)*............................ 80
Gainesville (E2)*..............11,936
Garden City (K6)*............1,557
Gardi (J7)*................................ 225
Gardners (G5)*......................... 150
Garfield (H5)*........................... 213
Gay (C4)*................................. 241
Geneva (C5)*............................ 209
Georgetown (B7)*..................... 550
Gibson (G4)*............................. 460
Gillsville (E2)*........................... 152
Girard (J4)*............................... 244
Glenmore (H8)............................ 30
Glenn (B4)*.........................
Glennville (J7)*..................2,327
Glenwood (G6)*........................ 684
Gloster (D3).............................. 100
Godfrey (F4)*............................ 168
Godwinsville (F6)...................... 100
Goggins (D4)*........................... 130
Good Hope (E3)*....................... 200
Gordon (F5)*.....................1,761
Gore (B2)*.................................. 65
Gough (H4)*.............................. 450
Gracewood (H4)*...................
Graham (H7)*............................ 160
Grangerville (J8)......................... 25
Grantville (C4)*.................1,359
Gratis (E3)................................... 70
Graves (C7)*............................... 200
Gray (F4)*.................................. 866
Graymont (Twin City)
(H5)*..................................1,018
Grayson (E3)*............................... 227
Graysville (B1)*............................ 120
Greenbush (B1)............................. 150
Greenough (D8)........................
Greensboro (F3)*....................2,688
Greenville (C4)*............................ 733
Greggs (F8)..................................... 4
Greshamville (F3)*....................... 100
Gresston (F6)*............... 200
Griffin (D4)*.............13,982
Griswoldville (F5)............
Grovania (E6)*............... 225
Groveland (J6)*.............. 140
Grovetown (H4)*............ 500
Guyton (K6)*.................. 633
Habersham (F1)*............ 750
Haddock (F4)*................ 475
Hagan (J6)*.................... 525
Hahira (F9)*...............1,010
Halcyon Dale (J5)*.......... 330
Hamilton (C5)*................ 449
Hammett (D5).................... 15
Hampton (D4)*................. 864
Hanlin (C3)....................... 50
Hapeville (D3)*............8,560
Haralson (C4)*................. 142
Hardwick (F4)*...........3,000
Harlem (H4)*...............1,033
Harris (C5)...................... 250
Harrison (G5)*................. 261
Hartsfield (E8)*............... 113
Hartwell (G2)*............2,964
Hatcher (B7)*.................... 90
Hatley (E7)...................... 100
Hawkinsville (E6)*........3,342
Haylow (G9)*...................
Hayner (J8)........................ 20
Haywood (H8).................... 20
Hazlehurst (G7)*..........2,687
Headlight (G9)...................... 4
Heardmont (G2)*................ 65
Hebardville (H8)...........1,113
Helen (E1)*........................ 191
Helena (G6)*.................1,027
Hephzibah (H4)*................ 525
Hermitage (B2).................... 25
Herndon (H5)*.................... 300
Herod (D7)......................... 126
Hiawassee (E1)*................. 375
Hickox (H8)*....................... 139
Higgston (G6)*.................... 155
High Shoals (F3)*...............
High Tower (D2)................... 75
Hill City (C1)*..................... 100
Hillsboro (E4)*.................... 300
Hilltonia (J5)*...................... 318
Hilton (C8)*.......................
Hinesville (J7)*..............1,217
Hinsonton (D8)*................
Hiram (C3)*......................... 299
Hoboken (H8)*..................... 492
Hogansville (C4)*...........3,769
Holland (B2)*........................ 300
Holly Springs (D2)*............... 386
Hollywood (E1)*.................... 100
Homeland (H9)...................... 276
Homer (F2)*.......................... 340
Homerville (G8)*..............1,787
Homestead (H8)....................... 13
Hortense (J8)*....................... 175
Hoschton (E2)*...................... 378
Howard (D5)*.....................
Howell (F9)*.......................... 169
Huching (F3).......................... 145
Hull (F2)*.............................. 153
Hunters (K5)............................ 60
Huntington (D6)..................... 100
Hurst (D1)*............................ 195
Ideal (D6)*............................. 318
Ila ((F2)*................................ 225
Inaha (E7).............................. 100
Indian Springs (E4)*.............. 200
Inman (D4)*.......................... 300
Iron City (C8)*....................... 293
Irwinton (F5)*........................ 700
Irwinville (F7)*....................... 275
Isle of Hope (K7)................... 800
Ivey (F5)................................... 46
Jackson (E4)*.................2,053
Jacksonville (G7)*.................. 300
Jakin (B8)*............................. 264
James (E5)*............................ 150
Jasper (D2)*....................1,380
Jefferson (F2)*...............2,040
Jeffersonville (F5)*................ 787
Jenkinsburg (E4)*.................. 166
Jersey (E3)*........................... 182
Jesup (J7)*.......................4,605
Jewell (E4)*............................ 200
Jimps (J6)................................ 25
Johntown (D1)............................ 8
Jonesboro (D4)*..............1,741
Julia (C6)........................
Juliette (E4)*......................... 283
Junction City (C5)*................ 259
Juniper (C6)*.......................... 150
Juno (D2)*................................ 30
Kathleen (E6)*........................ 100
Keithsburg (C2)....................... 150
Kelly (E4)*.............................. 100
Kennesaw (C2)*....................... 564
Kenwood (D3)*........................ 300
Keysville (H4)*........................ 304
Kibbee (H6)*........................... 100
Kildare (K5).............................. 75
Killen (C7)................................. 40
Kimbrough (C7)....................... 100
Kingsland (J9)*................1,169
Kingston (C2)*.......................... 675
Kinlaw (J9)................................. 35
Kirkland (G8)*.......................... 100
Kite (G5)*................................. 447
Knoxville (E5)*......................... 400
La Cross (D6)......................
La Grange (B4)*...........25,025
Ladds (C2)................................... 75
LaFayette (B1)*................4,884
Lake Park (F9)*......................... 334
Lake Tara ‡(D3)....................... 224
Lakeland (F8)*.....................1,551
Lakemont (F1)*.......................... 500
Lanier (J6)*................................ 100
Lavonia (F2)*......................1,766
Lawrenceville (D3)*.........2,932
Lax (F8)...................................... 100
Leaf (E1)*.................................. 251
Leah (H3)................................... 200
Leary (C8)*................................ 721
Leathersville (H3)*.......
Lebanon (D2)*............. 200
Lee Pope (E5)*................ 75
Leesburg (D7)*.............. 659
Lenox (F8)*.................... 789
Leslie (D7)*.................... 417
Lewiston (F5).................
Lexington (F3)*.............. 514
Lexsy (H6)*...................... 75
Lilburn (D3)*................... 567
Lilly (E6)*........................ 177
Lincolnton (H3)*.........1,315
Lindale (B2)*...............2,834
Linton (F4)*..................... 150
Linwood (B1).................... 858
Linwood (B2).................... 100
Lisbon (G3)*...................... 95
Lithia Springs (C3)*.......
Lithonia (D3)*..............1,538
Little River (G3)................ 80
Lizella (E5)*..................... 350
Loco (G3)........................
Locust Grove (D4)*.......... 405
Loganville (E3)*............... 699
Lollie (Minter) (G6)*... 143
Lone Oak (C4).................. 120
Lookout (B1)...................
Lorane (E5)......................
Louisville (H4)*...........2,231
Louvale (C6)*..................
Lovejoy (D4)*.................. 204
Lovett (G5)*....................... 80
Lucile (C8)......................... 50
Lucius (D1)......................
Ludowici (J7)*.............1,332
Ludville (C2)....................
Luella (D4)*.....................
Lula (E2)*........................ 200
Lumber City (G7)*........1,232
Lumpkin (C6)*.............1,209
Luthersville (C4)*............ 312
Lyerly (B2)*..................... 524
Lynn (J7)........................
Lynn Station (C8)............. 25
Lyons (H6)*................2,799
Machen (E4)*..................... 40
Macon (E5)*..............70,252
Macon (urban area)....93,305
Madison (F3)*..............2,489
Madras (C4)*..................... 185
Manassas (H6)*................ 128
Manchester (C5)*..........4,036
Manor (G8)*....................
Mansfield (E4)*................. 446
Marblehill (D2)*...............
Margret (D1)*.................... 145
Marietta (D3)*............20,687
Marion (D1)*...................
Marlow (K6)*..................... 250
Marshallville (D6)*.......1,121
Martin (F2)*...................... 207
Martinez (H3)*.............2,500
Matthews (H4)*................. 100
Mauk (D6)*........................ 100
Maxeys (F3)*..................... 204
Maxim (H3).......................... 25
Mayfield (G4)*.................. 250
Maysville (E2)*................. 533
Mc Bean (J4)*................... 200
Mc Caysville (D1)*.........2,067
Mc Collum (C4)................. 100
Mc Donough (D4)*.........1,635
Mc Intosh (K7)*...............
Mc Intyre (F5)*................. 194
Mc Kinnon (J8)*.................. 65
Mc Rae (G6)*................1,904
Mc Whorter (C3).................. 45
Meansville (D4)*................ 224
Meda (F4)............................ 20
Meeks (G5)*...................... 100
Meigs (D8)*..................1,125
Meinhard (K6).................... 160
Meldrim (K6)*..................... 250
Mendes (H7)*..................... 300
Menlo (B2)*........................ 453
Meridian (K8)*..................
Merrillville (E9).................. 109
Mershon (H8)*...................
Mesena (G4)*..................... 150
Metasville (G3)..................... 82
Metcalf (E9)*...................... 206
Metter (H6)*................2,091
Middleton (G2)*................... 144
Midland (C5)*...................... 200
Midville (H5)*...................... 682
Midway (K7)*....................... 228
Milan (G6)*.......................... 750
Milford (C8)*.....................
Milledgeville (F4)*.........8,835
Millen (J5)*....................3,449
Millhaven (J5)*...................... 50
Millwood (G8)*..................
Milner (D4)*......................... 345
Milstead (D3)*..............1,075
Mineral Bluff (D1)*.............. 209
Minter (Lollie*) (G6)... 143
Minter (G6)*.......................... 143
Mitchell (G4)*....................... 240
Mize (F2)................................. 75
Molena (D4)*......................... 307
Moniac (H9)*......................... 200
Monroe (E3)*................4,542
Modoc ‡(A5)............................ 32
Montezuma (E6)*...........2,921
Monticello (E4)*.............1,918
Montrose (F5)*....................... 242
Moran (E5)*........................... 250
Moreland (C4)*...................... 306
Morgan (C7)*......................... 304
Morganton (D1)*.................... 244
Morris (C7)*.......................
Morrow ‡(D3)*...................... 326
Morven (E9)*......................... 474
Moultrie (E8)*................11,639
Mount Airy (F1)*.................... 416
Mount Berry (B2)*...........1,500
Mount Pleasant (J8)................ 50
Mount Vernon (H6)*............... 990
Mount Zion (B3)*................... 141
Mountain City (F1)*............... 524
Mountain Park ‡(D3)............... 15
Mountville (C4)*..................... 142

Moxley (H5)........ 50
Munnerlyn (H5)*........ 75
Murrayville (E2)*........1,000
Musella (E5)*........ 68
Mystic (F7)*........ 281
Nacoochee (E1)*........ 250
Nahunta (H8)*........ 738
Nankipooh (C5)........ 100
Nashville (F8)*........3,414
Natal (E1)........
Naylor (F9)*........ 290
Neal (D4)........ 50
Nelson (D2)*........ 645
Nevils (J6)........ 160
New Holland (E2)*........1,618
New Lacy (H7)........ 25
Newborn (E3)*........ 298
Newington (J5)*........ 429
Newnan (C4)*........8,218
Newton (D8)*........ 503
Nicholls (G7)*........ 806
Nicholson (F2)*........ 252
Noble (B1)........ 200
Norcross (D3)*........1,340
Norman Park (E8)*........ 832
Normantown (H6)........ 78
Norristown (H5)*........ 150
North Atlanta ‡(D3)....5,930
North High Shoals †(F3) 124
Norwood (G4)*........ 268
Nuberg (G2)........ 273
Nunez (H5)*........ 82
Oak Hill (D1)........ 50
Oak Park (H6)*........ 308
Oakfield (E7)*........ 108
Oaklawn (E9)........ 75
Oakman (C1)*........ 127
Oakwood (E2)*........ 225
Oasis (C1)........ 15
Ochlochnee (E9)*........ 503
Ocilla (F7)*........2,697
Oconee (G5)*........1,500
Odessa (J7)........ 5
Odessadale (C5)*........ 55
Odum (H7)*........ 389
Offerman (H8)*........ 500
Ogeechee (J5)*........ 40
Oglesby (G2)........ 15
Oglethorpe (D6)*........1,204
Ohoopee (H6)*........ 53
Ola (4)........ 100
Oliver (J5)*........ 223
Omaha (C6)*........ 217
Omega (E8)*........ 966
Oostanaula (B1)........ 50
Ophir (D2)........ 40
Orange (D2)........ 50
Orchard Hill (D4)*........ 82
Orland (G6)........ 40
Oscarville (E2)........ 25
Osierfield (F7)*........ 147
Ousley (F9)*........ 35
Owen (H8)........ 50
Oxford (E3)*........ 817
Padena (D1)........ 105
Palmetto (C3)*........1,257
Parish (J6)........ 15
Parrott (D7)*........ 291
Patterson (H8)*........ 656
Pavo (E9)*........ 806
Payne (E5)........ 520
Pearson (G8)*........1,402
Pelham (D8)*........4,365
Pembroke (J6)*........1,171
Pendergrass (E2)*........ 189
Penfield (F3)*........ 74
Penia (E7)........ 50
Pennick (J8)........ 300
Pepperton (E4)........ 572
Perkins (J5)*........ 210
Perry (E6)*........3,849
Persimmon (E1)........
Philomath (G3)*........ 200
Pickard (D5)*........ 150
Pidcock (E9)*........ 100
Piedmont (D4)........ 34
Pike (D1)*........ 44
Pine Grove (H7)........ 135
Pine Lake ‡(D3)*........ 566
Pine Log (C2)*........
Pine Park (D9)*........ 126
Pinehurst (E6)*........ 430
Pineora (K6)*........ 450
Pineview (F6)*........ 310
Pisgah (D1)*........
Pitts (E7)*........ 397
Pittsburg (B1)........ 40
Plainfield (F6)*........ 117
Plains (D6)*........ 546
Plainville (C2)*........ 142
Pocotalago (F2)........ 68
Point Peter (F3)*........ 100
Pooler (K6)*........ 818
Pope City (F6)........
Port Wentworth (K6)*..1,500
Portal (J5)*........ 532
Porter Springs (E1)........ 125
Porterdale (E3)*........3,207
Portland (C2)........ 300
Poulan (E8)*........ 750
Powder Springs (C3)*........ 619
Powelton (G4)........ 50
Powersville (E5)*........ 100
Prattsburg (D5)........ 50
Preston (C6)*........ 260
Pridgen (G7)........ 200
Primrose (C4)........ 24
Princeton (F3)........ 100
Priors (B2)........ 50
Pulaski (J6)*........ 234
Putnam (D6)*........ 60
Putney (D8)*........ 200
Quill (D1)*........
Quitman (E9)*........4,769
Rabun Gap (F1)*........ 250
Racepond (H8)*........ 158
Rahns (K6)........
Raleigh (C5)*........ 48
Ramhurst (C1)*........ 100
Randolph (C7)........
Ranger (C2)*........ 183
Ray City (F8)*........ 576
Raybon (H8)........
Rayle (G3)........ 300
Raymond (C4)*........ 200
Rebecca (E7)*........ 295
Recovery (C9)........ 100
Red Oak (C3)*........ 675
Register (J6)*........ 300
Reidsville (H6)*........1,266
Relay (B2)........ 100
Relee (G7)........
Remerton (F9)*........ 500
Renfroe (C6)........ 56
Reno (D9)........ 108
Rentz (G6)*........ 302
Resaca (C1)*........ 300
Rest Haven ‡(D3)........ 147
Reynolds (D5)*........ 906
Rhine (F7)*........ 514
Riceboro (K7)*........ 287
Richland (C6)*........1,571
Richmond Hill (K7)*........ 500
Richwood (E6)........ 75
Riddleville (G5)........ 106
Ridgeville (K8)*........
Rincon (K6)*........ 424
Ringgold (B1)*........1,192
Rising Fawn (A1)*........ 300
Riverdale (D3)*........ 263
Riverside (E8)........ 395
Roberta (D5)*........ 673
Robertstown (E1)*........ 150
Robinson (B2)*........ 75
Rochelle (F7)*........1,097
Rockingham (H7)........ 60
Rockledge (G6)*........ 100
Rockmart (C2)*........3,821
Rockville (F4)........ 30
Rocky Face (C1)*........ 300
Rocky Ford (J5)*........ 278
Rocky Mount ‡(C4)........ 27
Rome (B2)*........29,615
Roopville (B4)*........ 202
Rosebud (D3)........ 100
Rosier (H5)*........ 125
Rossville (B1)*........3,892
Roswell (D2)*........2,123
Round Oak (E4)*........ 165
Rowell (B2)........ 45
Rowena (C8)........ 200
Roy (D1)*........ 75
Royston (F2)*........2,039
Ruckersville (G2)........ 74
Rupert (D6)*........
Russell (E3)........ 129
Ruth (F4)........ 200
Rutland (E5)........
Rutledge (E3)*........ 482
Rydal (C2)*........ 100
St. Charles (C4)........
St. Clair (H4)........ 150
St. George (H9)*........ 582
St. Marks (C4)........ 43
St. Marys (J9)*........1,348
St. Simons Isl. (K8)*....1,706
Sale City (D8)*........ 289
Sandersville (G5)*........4,480
Sapelo Island (K8)*........ 307
Sarah (D1)*........ 75
Sardis (J5)*........ 695
Sargent (C4)*........1,250
Sasser (D7)*........ 371
Satolah (F1)*........ 165
Sautee (E1)*........ 314
Savannah (L6)*........119,638
Savannah (urban area)........128,190
Savannah Beach (L7)*..1,036
Scarboro (J5)........ 150
Scotland (G6)*........ 218
Scott (G5)*........ 194
Screven (H7)*........ 752
Sea Island (K8)*........ 500
Sells (E2)........ 30
Seney (B2)........ 50
Senola (C4)*........ 770
Sessoms (G8)........ 100
Seville (E7)*........ 187
Shady Dale (E4)*........ 253
Shannon (B2)*........1,676
Sharon (G3)*........ 224
Sharpsburg (C4)*........ 133
Shell Bluff (J4)........ 20
Shellman (C7)*........1,090
Shiloh (C5)*........ 250
Shingler (E7)........
Siloam (F3)*........ 324
Silver City (D2)........ 150
Silver Creek (B2)*........ 400
Silvertown (D5)*........3,387
Smarr (E5)*........ 100
Smithonia (F2)........ 80
Smithville (D7)*........ 676
Smyrna (D3)*........2,005
Snellville (D3)*........ 309
Social Circle (E3)*........1,685
Sofkee (E5)........
Soperton (G6)*........1,667
South Georgia (G8)........ 650
South Newport (K7)........ 50
Sparks (F8)*........ 887
Sparta (F4)*........1,954
Spring Place (C1)*........ 214
Springfield (K6)*........ 627
Springvale (C7)*........ 127
Sprite (B2)........ 25
Stapleton (H4)*........ 355
Statenville (G9)*........1,000
Statesboro (J6)*........6,097
Statham (E3)*........ 626
Stellaville (H4)*........ 69
Stephens (F3)*........ 100
Sterling (K8)........ 30
Stevens Crossing (H5)...
Stevens Pottery (F5)*...
Stilesboro (B2)*........
Stillmore (H6)*........ 420
Stilson (J6)*........ 165
Stockbridge (D3)*........ 717
Stockton (G9)*........ 300
Stone Mountain (D3)*..1,899
Stonewall (C3)*........ 510
Stovall (C5)*........ 150
Stuckey (G6)*........ 150
Subligna (B1)*........ 152
Suches (E1)*........
Sugar Hill ‡(D3)........ 783
Sugar Valley (C1)*........ 214
Sulphur Springs (A1)*.. 175
Summertown (H5)*........ 137
Summerville (B2)*........3,973
Summit (Twin City) (H5)*........1,018
Sumner (E7)*........ 226
Sumter (D7)*........ 40
Sunny Side (D4)*........ 169
Suomi (G6)........ 40
Surrency (H7)*........ 295
Suwanee (E2)*........ 357
Swainsboro (H5)*........4,300
Swords (F3)*........ 35
Sycamore (E7)*........ 624
Sylvania (J5)*........2,939
Sylvester (E7)*........2,623
Talbotton (C5)*........1,175
Talking Rock (D1)*........ 94
Tallapoosa (B3)*........2,826
Tallulah Falls (F1)*........ 239
Tallulah Park (F1)........
Talmo (E2)*........ 152
Talona (C1)*........ 41
Tarboro (J8)........ 180
Tarrytown (H6)*........ 250
Tarver (G9)........
Tate (D2)*........ 100
Taylorsville (C2)*........ 260
Tazewell (D6)*........ 105
Temple (B3)*........ 676
Tennga (C1)*........ 200
Tennille (G5)*........1,713
Texas (B4)........ 40
Thalmann (J8)*........ 150
The Rock (D5)*........ 147
Thomasboro (J5)*........ 30
Thomaston (D5)*........6,580
Thomasville (E9)*........14,424
Thomson (H4)*........3,489
Thunderbolt (K6)*........1,238
Tifton (F8)*........6,831
Tiger (F1)*........ 269
Tignall (G3)*........ 502
Tilton (B1)*........ 100
Tippettville (E6)........ 50
Titus (E1)*........ 200
Toccoa (F1)*........6,781
Toledo (H9)........ 134
Toomsboro (F5)*........ 711
Towns (G7)*........ 96
Townsend (J7)*........
Trenton (A1)*........ 755
Trimble (C4)........ 150
Trion (B1)*........3,028
Troutman (C7)........ 25
Tugalo (F1)*........ 25
Tunnell Hill (C1)*........
Turin (C4)*........ 185
Tusculum (K6)*........ 100
Twin City (H5)........1,018
Ty Ty (E8)*........ 478
Tyrone (C4)*........ 156
Unadilla (E6)*........1,098
Union City (D3)*........1,490
Union Point (F3)*........1,724
Upatoi (C5)*........ 300
Uvalda (H6)*........ 511
Valdosta (K9)*........20,046
Valona (K8)*........ 50
Van Wert (B3)........
Vanna (F2)*........ 145
Varnell (C1)*........ 500
Vaughn (D4)*........ 100
Veazey (F3)........ 40
Vidalia (H6)*........5,819
Vidette (H4)*........ 159
Vienna (E6)*........2,202
Villa Rica (C3)*........1,703
Villanow (B1)........ 150
Waco (B3)*........ 328
Wade (H5)........
Wadley (H5)*........1,624
Walburg (J8)........ 4
Walden (E5)*........ 100
Waleska (D2)*........ 385
Walker Park (E3)*........ 155
Walnutgrove (E3)........ 121
Waltertown (H8)........ 2
Walthourville (J7)*........ 300
Waresboro (H8)*........
Warm Springs (C5)*........ 557
Warner Robins (E5)*..7,986
Warrenton (G4)*........1,442
Warsaw (K7)........
Warthen (G4)*........ 240
Warwick (E7)*........ 449
Washington (G3)*........3,802
Watkinsville (E3)*........ 662
Waverly (J8)*........ 100
Waverly Hall (C5)*........ 690
Waycross (H8)*........18,899
Waynesboro (J4)*........4,461
Waynesville (J8)*........
Wayside (E4)*........ 150
Wenona (E7)........ 75
Wesley (H6)*........ 66
West Bainbridge (C9)*.3,000
West Georgia College (B3)........ 700
West Green (G7)*........
West Point (B5)*........4,076
Westlake (F5)........
Weston (C7)*........ 162
Westwood (F7)........ 75
Whigham (D9)*........ 471
White (C2)*........ 454
White Hall (F3)*........ 493
White Oak (J8)*........ 150
White Plains (F4)*........ 359
White Sulphur Springs ‡(C5)........ 32
Whitepath (D1)........ 100
Whites Mill (C9)........ 5
Whitesburg (B4)*........ 400
Whitestone (D1)*........
Whitesville (C5)........ 100
Wiley (F1)*........ 125
Willacoochee (G8)*........ 987
Willard (F4)........ 25
Williamson (D4)*........ 211
Winchester (E6)........ 25
Winder (E3)*........4,604
Winfield (H3)........ 25
Winokur (H8)*........ 100
Winston (C3)*........ 154
Winterville (F3)*........ 453
Woodbine (J9)*........ 750
Woodbury (C5)*........ 985
Woodcliff (J5)*........ 175
Woodland (D5)*........ 621
Woodstock (D2)*........ 545
Woodville (F3)*........ 484
Woolsey (D4)*........ 90
Worth (E7)........
Wray (F7)*........ 45
Wrayswood (F3)........ 30
Wrens (H4)*........1,380
Wrightsville (G5)*........1,750
Yahoolah (D1)........ 125
Yatesville (D5)*........ 290
Yonkers (F6)........ 33
Young Harris (E1)*........ 450
Youngcane (E1)*........ 500
Youngs (B3)........
Ypsilanti (D5)........ 35
Zebulon (D4)*........ 539
Zeigler (J5)........ 100
Zenith (E5)........ 10

Map on Page 58

HAWAII

Total Population 499,794

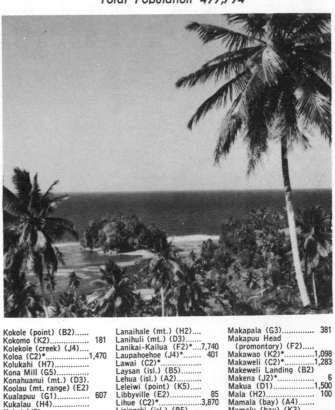

Ahua (point) (B4)........
Aiea (B3)*........3,714
Ainahou Ranch (J6)........
Alalakeiki (channel) (J3)........
Alenuihaha (channel) (E7)........
Alili Camp (H6)........
Anahola (C1)*........ 326
Apua (point) (J6)........
Auau (channel) (H2)........
Barbers (point) (E2)........
Bishop (point) (A4)........
Brodie Camp (E1)........
Bryant Camp (G3)........
Camp Eight (J5)........ 75
Camp Two (C2)........
Camp Two (J5)........ 200
Captain Cook (G5)*........ 316
Dairy Camp (G7)........
Diamond Head (crater) (C5)........
Diamond Head (promontory) (C5)........
East Loch (inlet) (B3)..
Eastern (isl.) (E4)........
Eleele (C2)*........ 993
Elevenmile Homestead (J5)........
Eo (lake) (A3)........
Ewa (A4)*........3,429
Ewa (beach) (A4)........
Ewa Field (A4)........
Ford (isl.) (B3)........
Gardner Pinnacles (isls.) (C6)........
Gilbert (E2)........
Glenwood (J5)........
Haena (C1)........ 90
Haiku (J2)*........ 729
Haina (H3)*........ 695
Hakalau (J4)*........ 688
Halalii (lake) (A2)........
Halama (K6)........
Halaula-Kapaau (G3)*..1,309
Halawa (G3)........ 900
Halawa (H1)........
Halawa (bay) (H1)........
Halawa (cape) (H1)........
Halawa (stream) (B3)..
Haleakala (crater) (K2)
Haleiwa (E1)*........2,142
Halfway House (H6)........
Hamakuapoko (J1)*........ 300
Hamoa (K2)........
Hana (K2)*........ 547
Hanalei (C1)*........ 364
Hanalei (bay) (C1)........
Hanalei (river) (C1)........
Hanaloa (lake) (A3)........
Hanamalo (point) (F7).
Hanamanioa (cape) (J3)
Hanamaulu (C2)*........1,031
Hanapepe (C2)*........1,259
Haou (K2)........
Hauula (E1)*........ 631
Hawaii (county) (K7)..68,350
Hawaii (isl.) (H5)........68,350
Hawaii National Park (J6)*........
Hawaii National (park) (K2)........
Hawaii National (park) (H6)........
Hawea (point) (H1)........
Hawi (G3)*........ 951
Hickam Field (B4)........
Hilea (H7)........ 8
Hilo (J5)*........27,198
Hilo (bay) (J5)........
Hoaeae (A3)........ 50
Hoea Mill (G3)........ 125
Holualoa (G5)*........ 475
Honaunau (G6)*........
Honohina (J4)........ 200
Honoipu (G3)........
Honokaa (H4)*........1,021
Honokahau (F5)*........ 650
Honokohau (J1)........
Honokohau (G5)........
Honokahua (H1)........ 475
Honokowai Camp (H1)..
HONOLULU (C4)*........248,034
Honolulu (county) (D3)........353,020
Honolulu (harbor) (C4)........
Honomaele (K2)........
Honomalino Camp (G6).
Honomu (J4)*........ 600
Honouliuli (A3)........
Honuapo (H7)........ 25
Hookena (G6)........ 20
Hoolehua (G1)*........ 709
Hoopuloa (G6)........
Hualalai (mt.) (G5)........
Huehue (G5)........
Huumula Sheep Station (H5)........ 6
Ilio (point) (G1)........
Iseri Camp (H6)........
Iwilei (C4)........
John Rogers Field (B4).
Johnston (isl.) (C7)........
Kaala (mt.) (E1)........
Kaalaiki Camp (G7)........ 6
Kaaluaulu (G7)........ 48
Keenapali (H2)........
Kaeleku (K2)........
Kaena (point) (D1)........
Kahakuloa (J1)........ 20
Kahala (D5)........
Kahala (point) (D1)........
Kahana (F1)........
Kahana (bay) (F1)........
Kahoolawe (isl.) (H3)...
Kahua (G3)........
Kahuku (E1)*........1,602
Kahuku (point) (E1)........
Kahuku Ranch (G7)........ 36
Kahului (J2)*........6,306
Kahului (harbor) (J1)...
Kailio (point) (C1)........
Kailua (F2)........ 326
Kailua (K2)........
Kailua-Lanikai (F5)*....7,740
Kailua (bay) (F5)........
Kailua (bay) (F2)........
Kaimu (K6)........
Kaimuli (D4)........
Kainaliu (G5)........ 510
Kaiwi (channel) (E6)...
Kakaako (C4)........
Kalae (G1)........
Kalae (South) (cape) (G7)........
Kalaheo (C2)*........ 972
Kalaoa (G5)........ 40
Kalapana (K6)........ 60
Kalaua (B3)........
Kalaupapa (G1)*........
Kalawa (G1)........
Kalawao (H1)........
Kalawao (county) (G1). 340
Kalihi (stream) (C3)........
Kalihi Entrance (strait) (B4)........
Kalihiwai (C1)........ 44
Kalohi (channel) (G1)...
Kaloli (point) (K5)........
Kaluaaha (H1)........ 300
Kamaiki (point) (H2)...
Kamakou (mt.) (H1)........
Kamalino (A2)........ 15
Kamalo (H1)........ 300
Kamilo (point) (H7)........
Kamuela-Waimea (G4)* 560
Kanaio (J3)........ 24
Kanapou (bay) (J3)........
Kaneohe (F2)*........3,208
Kaneohe (bay) (F2)........
Kapaa (D1)*........3,177
Kapaau-Halaula (G3)....1,309
Kapalaoa (G4)........
Kapapala (H6)........ 251
Kapoho (K5)*........ 335
Kapulena (H4)........
Kau (desert) (J6)........
Kauai (channel) (E6)........
Kauai (county) (A1)....29,905
Kauai (isl.) (C1)........29,683
Kaueleau (K6)........
Kauhola (point) (G3)........
Kauiki Head (promontory) (K2)........
Kaula (isl.) (D6)........
Kaulakahi (channel (B2)
Kaumalapau (harbor) (G2)........
Kaumana (J5)........
Kauna (point) (G7)........
Kaunakakai (G1)*........ 973
Kaunakakai (harbor) (G1)........
Kaunalewa (B2)........
Kauno-o-Kaleioohie(mt.) (G3)........
Kaunuopou (point) (B2)
Kaupakulua (K2)........
Kaupo (K2)........
Kawaihae (G4)*........ 152
Kawaihae (bay) (G4)........
Kawaihapai (D1)........
Kawaihau (C1)........6,290
Kawaihoa (cape) (A2)..
Kawaikini (mt.) (C1)...
Kawailoa (E1)*........
Kawainui (J4)........ 193
Kawela Camp (H3)........
Keaau (K5)........
Keaau-Olaa (J5)........1,620
Keahiakahoe (mt.) (D3)
Keahole (point) (F5)...
Keahua (J2)*........ 200
Keaiwa Camp (H6)........ 110
Kealaikahiki (channel) (H3)........
Kealaikahiki (point) (H3)........
Kealakekua (G5)*........ 325
Kealakekua (bay) (F6)..
Kealapuali (G5)........
Kealia (D1)*........ 655
Kealia (G6)........ 184
Keamuku (G4)........ 11
Keanae (K2)*........ 54
Keanapapa (point) (G2)
Keauhou (F5)*........ 196
Keaukaha (J5)........2,500
Keawekaheka (point) (F5)........
Keehi (lagoon) (B4)........
Kekaa (point) (H2)........
Kekaha (C2)*........1,989
Kemoo Camp (E2)........
Keokea (G6)........ 150
Keokea (J2)........ 698
Keomuku (H2)........ 8
Keoneoio (J3)........
Kepuhi (G1)........ 1
Kiekie (A2)........
Kihei (J2)*........1,500
Kiholo (G4)........ 1
Kiholo (bay) (F4)........
Kikoa (point) (H2)........
Kilauea (C1)*........ 757
Kilauea (crater) (H6)...
Kilauea (point) (C1)........
Kilauea Ranger Station (J6)........ 135
Kingman (reef) (C7)........
Kipahulu (K2)........
Kipapa Camp 5 (E2)........
Koa Mill (G6)........
Koae (K5)........ 65
Koali (K2)........
Koele (H2)........ 45
Kohala (mts.) (G4)........
Koko Head (promontory) (F2)........

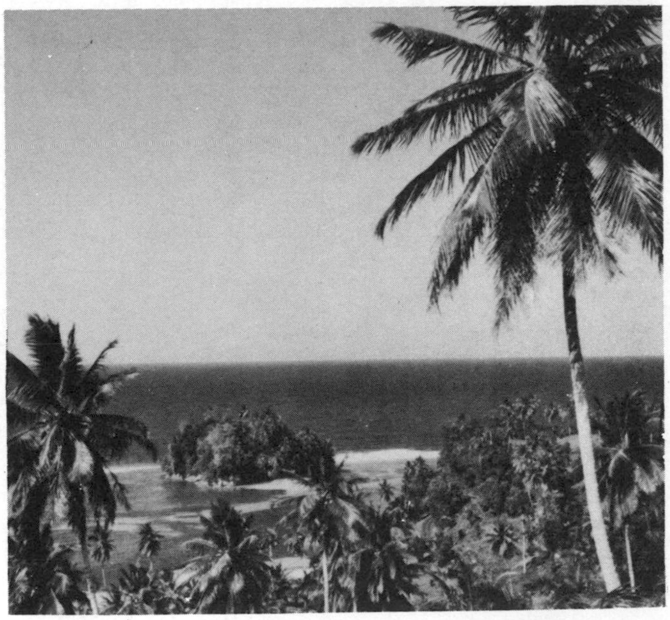

Kokole (point) (B2)......
Kokomo (K2)........ 181
Kolekole (creek) (J4)....
Koloa (C2)*........1,470
Kolukahi (H7)........
Kona Mill (G5)........
Konahuanui (mt.) (D3).
Koolau (mt. range) (E2)
Kualapuu (G1)........ 607
Kukalau (H4)........
Kukui (J5)........
Kukui (mt.) (J2)........
Kukuihaele (H3)*........ 590
Kula (J2)........
Kumukahi (cape) (K5)..
Kunia Camp (E2)*........
Kupaahu (J6)........
Kure (isl.) (A5)........
Kurtistown (J5)*........1,500
La Perouse Pinnacle (isl.) (C6)........
Laau (point) (G1)........
Lahaina (H2)*........4,025
Laie (E1)*........ 841
Lanai (isl.) (H2)........3,136
Lanai City (H2)*........2,746
Lanaihale (mt.) (H2)....
Lanihuli (mt.) (D3)........
Lanikai-Kailua (F2)*...7,740
Laupahoehoe (J4)*........ 401
Lawai (C2)*........
Laysan (isl.) (B5)........
Lehua (isl.) (A2)........
Leleiwi (point) (K5)........
Libbyville (E2)........ 85
Lihue (C2)*........3,870
Lisianski (isl.) (B5)........
Lower Paia (J1)........1,137
Lua Makika (mt.) (J3).
Lualualei (D2)........1,528
Luke Field (B3)........
Maalaea (J2)........ 500
Maalaea (bay) (J2)........
Mahinahina Camp (J1). 50
Mahukona (G3)........ 132
Makaha (D2)........1,500
Makaha (point) (B1)....
Makahuena (point) (C2)........
Makalawena (F4)........ 2
Makanalua (peninsula) (H1)........
Makapala (G3)........ 381
Makapuu Head (promontory) (F2)........
Makawao (K2)*........1,098
Makaweli (C2)*........1,283
Makeweli Landing (B2)
Makena (J2)*........ 6
Makua (D1)........1,500
Mala (H2)........ 100
Mamala (bay) (A4)........
Mamalu (bay) (K3)........
Mana (B2)........ 276
Manana (isl.) (F2)........
Maro (reef) (C6)........
Maui (county) (J1).....48,519
Maui (isl.) (J2)........46,919
Mauna Kea (mt.) (H4)
Mauna Loa (mt.) (G5).
Maunalua (bay) (F2)....
McBryde Plantation Mill (C2)........1,500
Middle Loch (inlet) (A3)
Middle Moaula Camp (H6)........
Midway (isls.) (D5)........
Milolii (G6)........ 95

Moanalua (stream) (C3)
Mokapu (peninsula) (F2)
Mokolli (isl.) (F1)
Moku (G1)
Mokuaweoweo (crater) (H6)
Mokuhooniki (isl.) (J1)
Mokulau (K3)
Mokuleia (D1) 150
Moloaa (D1)
Molokai (isl.) (G1) 5,280
Molokini (isl.) (J2)
Monohaa (G5) 2
Mopua (J2) 600
Mountainview (J5)* 747
Muolea (K2)
Naalehu (H7)* 1,004
Nahiku (K2)
Nakalele (point) (J1)
Nanakuli (D2)* 2,002
Napoopoo (G6)* 103
Nawiliwili (D2)
Nawiliwili (bay) (D2)
Necker (isl.) (D6)
Nihoa (isl.) (D6)
Niihau (isl.) (A2) 222
Ninini (point) (D2)
Ninole (J4)* 112
Niulii (G3)
Nohili (point) (B1)
Nonopapa (A2)
Nuuanu (stream) (C4)
Oahu (isl.) (E2) 353,020
Olaa-Keaau (J5)* 1,620
Olowalu (H2) 100
Onomea (J4) 300
Ookala (J4)* 662
Opihikao (K6)
Paauhau (H4)* 400
Paauilo (H4)*
Pacific Heights (C4)
Pacific Ocean (B6)
Pacific Sugar Mill (H3)
Pahala (H6)* 1,602
Pahoa (J5)* 990
Paholoi (J2) 50
Paia (J2)* 3,195
Paihaaloa (J4) 98
Pailolo (channel) (H1)
Palama (C4)
Palaoa (point) (G2)
Palmyra (isl.) (C7)
Palolo (stream) (D4)
Paniau (mt.) (A2)
Papa (G6)
Papaaloa (G5)
Papaaloa (J4)* 597
Papaikou (J5)* 1,427
Paukaa (J5) 200
Pauwalu (point) (K2)
Pauwela (K1)* 618
Pauwela (point) (K1)
Peahi (K2)
Pearl (harbor) (A3)
Pearl and Hermes (reef) (B5)
Pearl City (B3)* 2,663
Pelekunu (H1)
Pepeekeo (J4)* 1,002
Pepeekeo (point) (J4)
Piihonua (J5) 600
Pohakuloa (point) (H2)
Pohoiki (K6) 3
Port Allen (C2) 450
Pua Akala (H5)
Puako (G4)
Pueo (point) (A2)
Puhi (C2)* 765
Pukoo (H1)* 42
Pulehu (J2) 200
Pulehu Camp (J2)
Punahou (C4)
Punaluu (E1)
Punaluu (H7) 30
Punaluu (harbor) (H7)
Punchbowl (hill) (C4)
Puolo (point) (C2)
Puu Hue (G3)
Puu Lehua Ranch (G5)
Puu Makani Camp (H7)
Puuanahulu (G4) 62
Puuiki (E1) 170
Puuiki (K2)
Puukolii (J2) 689
Puuloa Station (B4)
Puunene (J2)* 5,000
Puunui (C4)
Puuwai (A2) 185
Red Hill (mt.) (K2)
Roundtop (hill) (C4)
Salt (lake) (B3)
Sand (isl.) (E4)
Sand (isl.) (C4)
Sand (isl.) (E4)
Schofield Barracks (E2)
Seward Roads (channel) (D4)
South (Kalae) (cape) (G7)
Southeast Loch (inlet) (B3)
Spreckelsville (J1)*
Sugarloaf (hill) (C4)
Summer Camp (J6) 400
Tantalus (mt.) (D4)
Ulumahi (K2)
Ulupalakua (J2)
Umikoa (J4)
Upolu (point) (G3)
Wahiawa (E2)* 8,369
Waiahukini (G7) 175
Waiakea (J5) 5,000
Waiakoa (J2)* 517
Waialee (E1) 72
Waialua (E1)* 2,602
Waialua (H1)
Waialua Camp (E1)
Waianae (D2)* 1,000
Waianuenue (C1)
Waihee (J2) 600
Waikane (F2) 85
Waikapu (J2) 549
Waikii (H4)
Waikiki (C4)* 50
Waikiki (beach) (C4)
Wailau (H1) 300
Wailea (J4) 341
Wailua (D2)
Wailua (K2)
Wailuku (J2)* 7,424
Wailuku (river) (J5)
Wailupe (F2)
Waimanalo (F2)* 868
Waimanalo (bay) (F2)
Waimea (B2)* 1,648
Waimea (E1)
Waimea-Kamuela (H4)
Waimea (bay) (B2)
Waimea (river) (C2)
Waimea Camp (E1)
Wainiha (C1) 60
Wainiha (river) (C1)
Waiohinu (G7) 163
Waipahu (A3)* 7,169
Waipio (K2)
Waipio (H3) 95
Waipio (peninsula) (A3)
Waipio (point) (A4)
Welles (harbor) (D4)
West Loch (inlet) (A3)
Wood Valley Camp (H6)
Woodlawn (D4)

Map on Page 59 IDAHO *Total Population 588,637*

45 COUNTIES

Ada (B6) 70,649
Adams (B5) 3,347
Bannock (F7) 41,745
Bear Lake (G7) 6,834
Benewah (B2) 6,173
Bingham (F6) 23,271
Blaine (D6) 5,384
Boise (C6) 1,776
Bonner (B1) 14,853
Bonneville (G6) 30,210
Boundary (B1) 5,908
Butte (E6) 2,722
Camas (D6) 1,079
Canyon (B6) 53,597
Caribou (G7) 5,576
Cassia (E7) 14,629
Clark (F5) 918
Clearwater (C3) 8,217
Custer (D5) 3,318
Elmore (C6) 6,687
Franklin (G7) 9,867
Fremont (G5) 9,351
Gem (B6) 8,730
Gooding (D6) 11,101
Idaho (C4) 11,423
Jefferson (F6) 10,495
Jerome (D7) 12,080
Kootenai (B2) 24,947
Latah (B3) 20,971
Lemhi (D4) 6,278
Lewis (B3) 4,208
Lincoln (D6) 4,256
Madison (G6) 9,156
Minidoka (E7) 9,785
Nez Perce (B3) 22,658
Oneida (F7) 4,387
Owyhee (B7) 6,307
Payette (B5) 11,921
Power (F7) 3,988
Shoshone (B2) 22,806
Teton (G6) 3,204
Twin Falls (D7) 40,979
Valley (C5) 4,270
Washington (B5) 8,576
Yellowstone Nat'l. Park† (G5)

† Part. See also Wyoming and Montana.

CITIES and TOWNS

Aberdeen (F7)* 1,486
Acequia (E7)* 125
Addie (B1)* 15
Ahsahka (B3)*
Alameda (F7)* 4,694
Albion (E7)* 610
Alexander (G7)*
Almo (E7)*
Alpha (C5)*
Alpine (G6)* 172
Alridge (G6)
American Falls (E7)* 1,874
Ammon (G6) 447
Amsterdam (D7)* 100
Arbon (F7)
Archer (G6) 400
Arco (E6)* 961
Arimo (F7)* 337
Ashton (G5)* 1,256
Athol (B2)* 226
Atlanta (C6)* 300
Atomic City (F6)* 500
Avery (C2)* 350
Avon (B3)* 6
Baker (E4)* 150
Bancroft (G7)* 495
Banida (G7)* 140
Banks (B5)*
Basalt (F6)* 227
Bayview (B2)* 150
Bear (B4)*
Bellevue (D6)* 528
Benewah (B2) 50
Bennett (C6) 10
Bennington (G7)* 200
Berger (D7)
Bern (G7)* 140
Big Creek (C4)* 24
Big Springs (G5)* 5
Blackfoot (F6)* 5,180
Blanchard (A1)* 200
Bliss (D7)* 126
Bloomington (G7)* 302
BOISE (B6)* 34,393
Boles (B4) 25
Bone (G6) 50
Bonners Ferry (B1)* 1,776
Bovill (B3)* 437
Bowmont (B6)*
Bridge (E7)*
Broten (B1)* 30
Bruneau (C7)* 100
Buhl (D7)* 2,870
Burgdorf (B4)
Burke (C2)* 800
Burley (E7)* 5,924
Burmah (D6)
Cabinet (B1)* 60
Calder (B2)* 65
Caldwell (B6)* 10,487
Camas (F5)* 40
Cambridge (B5)* 354
Cameron (B3)* 83
Canfield (B4)* 50
Carey (E6)* 1,100
Careywood (B1)* 50
Carmen (E4)*
Cascade (C5)* 943
Castleford (C7)* 500
Cavendish (B3)
Centerville (C6)* 25
Central (G7)* 120
Challis (D5)* 728
Chatcolet (B2) 92
Chester (G5)* 247
Chesterfield (F7)*
Chilco (B2)* 45
Chilly (E5)* 84
Chubbuck ‡(F7)* 120
Churchill (D7)
Clagstone (B1) 15
Clark Fork (B1)* 387
Clarkia (B2)* 150
Clarkville ‡(B2) 19
Clawson (G6) 34
Clayton (D5)* 75
Clearwater (C3)* 53
Clementsville (G6) 38
Cleveland (G7)* 135
Cliffs (B7) 32
Clifton (F7)* 201
Coeur D'Alene (B2)* 12,198
Colburn (B1)*
Conda (G7)* 330
Coolin (B1)*
Copeland (B1)* 11
Corral (D6)* 157
Cottonwood (B3)* 689
Council (B5)* 748
Craigmont (B3)* 594
Crouch (B5)* 60
Crystal (F7)
Culdesac (B3)* 175
Cuprum (B4)* 20
Dalby ‡(G6) 13
Darlington (E6)* 200
Dayton (F7)* 287
De Lamar (B6)
Deary (B3)* 320
Declo (E7)* 219
Dent (B3)*
Denver (B4) 29
Desmet (B2)*
Dietrich (D7)* 160
Dingle (G7)*
Dixie (C4)* 56
Donnelly (C5)* 595
Dover (B1)* 385
Downey (F7)* 748
Driggs (G6)* 941
Drummond (G5)* 59
Dubois (F5)* 430
Dudley (B2)*
Eagle (B6)* 500
East Hope (B1) 149
Eastport (B1)* 108
Eddiville‡ (B2) 10
Eden (D7)* 456
Edgemere (B1)* 96
Elba (E7)* 180
Elk City (C4)* 300
Elk River (B3)* 312
Ellis (D5)*
Elmira (B1)* 128
Emida (B2)* 125
Emmett (B6)* 3,067
Enaville (B2)* 60
Fairfield (D6)* 502
Fairview (G7) 398
Felt (G6)* 120
Fenn (B4)* 57
Ferdinand (B3)* 206
Fernwood (B2)* 200
Filer (D7)* 1,425
Firth (F6)* 293
Fish Haven (G7)*
Forest (B3)
Forney (D4)*
Fort Hall (F6)*
Franklin (G7)* 467
French Creek (B4) 65
Fruitland (B6)* 573
Fruitvale (B5)* 125
Gannett (D6)* 43
Garden City (B6) 764
Garden Valley (C5)* 210
Gardena (B5)*
Gardner (F6)
Gem (C2)* 500
Genesee (B3)* 552
Geneva (G7)*
Georgetown (G7)* 404
Gibbonsville (E4)* 200
Gibbs (B2)* 35
Gifford (B3)* 51
Gilmore (E5)* 50
Glengary (B1)
Glenns Ferry (C7)* 1,515
Goldburg (E5)
Golden (C4)* 100
Gooding (D7)* 3,099
Goodrich (B5)* 16
Grace (G7)* 761
Grainville (G5) 30
Grand View (B7)*
Grangemont (C3)* 130
Grangeville (B4)* 2,544
Granite (B1)* 150
Gray (G6)*
Greencreek (B3)* 51
Greenleaf (B6)*
Greer (B3)* 127
Grimes Pass (C5)
Grouse (E6)* 43
Hagerman (D7)* 520
Hailey (D6)* 1,464
Hamer (F6)*
Hammett (C7)* 350
Hansen (D7)* 463
Harpster (C4)*
Harrison (B2)* 322
Harvard (B3)* 102
Hauser (B2) 70
Hayden Lake (B2)* 39
Hazelton (E7)* 429
Headquarters (C3)* 300
Heath (B5) 15
Heglar (E7) 10
Heise (G6) 87
Henry (G7)*
Heyburn (E7)* 539
Hibbard (G6) 400
Hill City (D6)* 15
Holbrook (F7)*
Hollister (D7)* 80
Homedale (A6)* 1,411
Hope (B1)* 111
Horse Shoe Bend (B6)* 401
Howe (F6)* 200
Huetter (B2)* 84
Humphrey (F5)* 35
Idaho City (C6)* 246
Idaho Falls (F6)* 19,218
Indian Valley (B5)* 50
Inkom (F7)* 434
Iona (G6)* 502
Irwin (G6)* 147
Island Park (G5)*
Jerome (D7)* 4,523
Joseph (B4)* 23
Juliaetta (B3)* 365
Juniper (F7)
Kamiah (B3)* 812
Kellogg (B2)* 4,913
Kendrick (B3)* 409
Ketchum (D6)* 757
Keuterville (B3)* 25
Kilgore (G5)* 160
Kimberly (D7)* 1,347
King Hill (C6)*
Kingston (B2)*
Kooskia (C3)* 629
Kootenai (B1)* 199
Kuna (B6)* 534
Laclede (B1)* 200
Lago (G7)* 250
Lake (G5) 8
Lake Fork (B5)* 11
Lakeview (B2)
Lamont (G6)* 50
Lane (B2)*
Lapwai (B3)* 480
Lava Hot Springs (F7)* 591
Leadore (E5)* 159
Leesburg (D4)
Lemhi (E5)* 150
Leonia (B1)*
Leslie (E6)* 40
Letha (B6)* 376
Lewiston (A3)* 12,985
Lewisville (F6)*
Liberty (G7)
Lincoln (F6)
Lorenzo (G6)* 250
Lost River (E6) 37
Lowell (C3)
Lowman (C5)* 30
Lucile (B4)* 13
Lund (G7)* 103
Mackay (E6)* 760
Macks Inn (G5)* 100
Maland City (F7)* 2,715
Malta (E7)* 518
Marble Creek (C2) 6
Marsing (B6)* 643
Marysville (G5) 190
May (E5)* 75
Mayfield (B6)
Mc Call (C5)* 1,173
Mc Cammon (F7)* 578
Meadow Creek (B1) 15
Meadows (B5)* 190
Melba (B6)* 203
Melrose (B3) 5
Menan (F6)* 430
Meridian (B6)* 1,810
Mesa (B5)* 179
Middleton (B6)* 496
Midvale (B5)* 231
Milner (D7)
Minidoka (E7)* 113
Minkcreek (G7)* 124
Monteview (F6)*
Montour (B6)* 155
Montpelier (G7)* 2,682
Moore (E6)* 256
Moravia (B1)
Moreland (F6)* 250
Moscow (B3)* 10,593
Mountain Home (C6)* 1,887
Moyie Springs (B1)* 109
Muldoon (E6)*
Mullan (C2)* 2,036
Murphy (B6)* 37
Murray (C2)* 158
Murtaugh (D7)* 239
Myrtle (B3)* 20
Naf (E7)*
Nampa (B6)* 16,185
Naples (B1) 300
New Meadows (B4)* 621
New Plymouth (B6)* 942
Newdale (G6)* 312
Nezperce (B3)* 543
Nordman (B1)* 18
North Fork (D4)* 100
N. Pocatello (F7) 575
Norwood (C5)
Notus (B6)* 313
Nounan (G7)*
Oakley (D7)* 684
Obsidian (D6)* 11
Ola (B5)* 300
Oldtown (A1) 358
Onaway (B3) 81
Orchard (B6)*
Orchards (A3) 4,494
Oreana (B6)* 100
Orofino (B3)* 1,656
Orogrande (C4)* 12
Ovid (G7)* 200
Oxford (F7)* 110
Pardee (B3)
Paris (G7)* 774
Parker (G6)* 306
Parma (B6)* 1,369
Patterson (E5)* 112
Paul (E7)* 560
Payette (B5)* 4,032
Pearl (B6) 38
Peck (B3)* 170
Pegram (G7)* 75
Picabo (D6)* 100
Pierce (C3)* 544
Pine (C6)*
Pingree (F6)* 102
Pioneerville (C6) 8
Placerville (C6)* 17
Plano (G6) 403
Plummer (B2)* 395
Pocatello (F7)* 26,131
Polaris (B2)* 214
Pollock (B4)*
Ponderay (B1)* 248
Porthill (B1)* 68
Portneuf (F7) 65
Post Falls (A2)* 1,069
Potlatch (A3)* 1,024
Prairie (C6)* 150
Preston (G7)* 4,045
Prichard (B2) 40
Priest River (A1)* 1,592
Princeton (B3)* 84
Rathdrum (A2)* 610
Raymond (G7)* 88
Red River Hot Springs (C4) 12
Regena (C6)
Reno (F5)
Reubens (B3)* 116
Rexburg (G6)* 4,253
Richfield (D6)* 429
Riddle (B7)* 35
Rigby (G6)* 1,826
Riggins (B4)* 287
Ririe (G6)* 527
Riverside (F6)
Roberts (F6)* 341
Robin (F7)* 165
Rockford (F6)
Rockford Bay (B2)* 27
Rockland (F7)* 277
Rocky Bar (C6)
Rogerson (D7)* 75
Roseberry (C5)
Roselake (B2)* 212
Roswell (A6)* 92
Roy (F7)* 25
Rupert (E7)* 3,098
Sagle (B1)* 75
Saint Anthony (G6)* 2,695
St. Charles (G7)* 363
St. Joe (B2) 75
St. Maries (B2)* 2,220
Salmon (D4)* 2,648
Samaria (F7)*
Samuels (B1)*
Sanders (B2)* 25
Sandpoint (B1)* 4,265
Santa (B2)*
Shelley (F6)* 1,856
Shoshone (D7)* 1,420
Shoup (D4)*
Silver City (B6)
Small (F5)*
Smelterville (B2)* 76
Smiths Ferry (C5)*
Soda Springs (G7)* 1,329
Southwick (B3)* 200
Spencer (F5)* 70
Spirit Lake (A2)* 823
Springfield (F6)* 435
Springston (B2)* 57
Squirrel (G5)*
Stanley (D5)* 33
Star (B6)* 525
Starkey (B5) 3
State Line ‡(B2) 52
Sterling (F6)*
Stibnite (C5)* 717
Stites (C3)* 227
Stone (F7)* 170
Strevell (E7) 25
Sugar City (G6)* 684
Sun Valley (D6)* 428
Sunbeam (D5)* 6
Swan Valley (G6)* 203
Swanlake (F7)* 250
Sweet (B6)* 200
Sweetwater (B3)* 80
Taber (F6)
Tamarack (B5)*
Tendoy (E5)*
Tensed (B2)* 189
Terreton (F6)* 35
Teton (G6)* 463
Tetonia (G6)* 232
Thatcher (G7)* 50
Thornton (G6)* 300
Three Creek (C7) 65
Tindall (C7) 5
Treasureton (G7)
Triangle (B7)* 35
Triumph (D6)* 97
Troy (B3)* 531
Tuttle (D7)* 15
Twin Falls (D7)* 17,600
Twin Lakes (B2) 225
Twin Springs (C6)*
Tyhee (F7) 350
Ucon (F6)* 356
Ustick (B6)* 200
Vay (B1)* 80
Victor (G6)* 431
Viola (B3)* 150
Virginia (F7)* 245
Wallace (C2)* 3,140
Wapello (F6)
Wardner (B2)* 772
Warm Lake (C5)* 500
Warren (C4)* 30
Wayan (G7)*
Weippe (C3)* 1,000
Weiser (B5)* 3,961
Wendell (D7)* 1,483
Westlake (B3)* 35
Weston (F7)* 382
White Bird (B4)*
Wilder (A6)* 555
Wildhorse (B5)* 18
Winchester (B3)* 488
Winona (B3)
Winsper (F5) 62
Woodland (C3)*
Worley (B2)* 233
Yellow Pine (C4)* 35

Map on Page 60 ILLINOIS *Total Population 8,712,176*

102 COUNTIES

Adams (B4) 64,690
Alexander (D6) 20,316
Bond (D5) 14,157
Boone (E1) 17,070
Brown (C4) 7,132
Bureau (D2) 37,711
Calhoun (C4) 6,898
Carroll (D1) 18,976
Cass (C4) 15,097
Champaign (E3) 106,100
Christian (D4) 38,816
Clark (F4) 17,362
Clay (E5) 17,445
Clinton (D5) 22,594
Coles (E4) 40,328
Cook (F2) 4,508,792
Crawford (F4) 21,137
Cumberland (E4) 10,496
De Kalb (E2) 40,781
De Witt (E3) 16,894
Douglas (E4) 16,706
Du Page (E2) 154,599
Edgar (F4) 23,407
Edwards (E5) 9,056
Effingham (E4) 21,675
Fayette (D4) 24,582
Ford (E3) 15,901
Franklin (E5) 48,685
Fulton (C3) 43,716
Gallatin (E6) 9,818
Greene (C4) 18,852
Grundy (E2) 19,217
Hamilton (E5) 12,256
Hancock (B3) 25,790
Hardin (E6) 7,530
Henderson (C3) 8,416
Henry (C2) 46,492
Iroquois (F3) 32,348
Jackson (D6) 38,124
Jasper (E4) 12,266
Jefferson (E5) 35,892
Jersey (C4) 15,264
Jo Daviess (C1) 21,459
Johnson (E6) 8,729
Kane (E2) 150,388
Kankakee (F2) 73,524
Kendall (E2) 12,115
Knox (C3) 54,366
La Salle (E2) 100,610
Lake (E1) 179,097
Lawrence (F5) 20,539
Lee (D2) 36,451
Livingston (E3) 37,809
Logan (D3) 30,671
Macon (E4) 98,853
Macoupin (D4) 44,210
Madison (D5) 182,307
Marion (E5) 41,700
Marshall (D2) 13,025
Mason (D3) 15,326
Massac (E6) 13,594
Mc Donough (C3) 28,199
Mc Henry (E1) 50,656
Mc Lean (E3) 76,577
Menard (D3) 9,639
Mercer (C2) 17,374
Monroe (C5) 13,282
Montgomery (D4) 32,460
Morgan (C4) 35,568
Moultrie (E4) 13,171
Ogle (D1) 33,429
Peoria (D3) 174,347
Perry (D5) 21,684
Piatt (E4) 13,970
Pike (C4) 22,155
Pope (E6) 5,779
Pulaski (D6) 13,639
Putnam (D2) 4,746
Randolph (D5) 31,673
Richland (E5) 16,889
Rock Island (C2) 133,558
Saint Clair (D5) 205,995
Saline (E6) 33,420
Sangamon (D4) 131,484
Schuyler (C3) 9,613
Scott (C4) 7,245
Shelby (E4) 24,434
Stark (D2) 8,721
Stephenson (D1) 41,595
Tazewell (D3) 76,165
Union (D6) 20,500
Vermilion (F3) 87,079
Wabash (F5) 14,651
Warren (C3) 21,981
Washington (D5) 14,460
Wayne (E5) 20,933
White (E5) 20,935
Whiteside (D2) 49,336
Will (F2) 134,336
Williamson (E6) 48,621
Winnebago (D1) 152,385
Woodford (D3) 21,335

CITIES and TOWNS

Abingdon (C3)* 3,300
Adair (C3)* 400
Addieville (D5)* 271
Addison (A2)* 813
Adeline (D1) 1,135
Adrian (B3)* 63
Akin (E6)*
Albany (C2)* 544
Albers (D5)* 365
Albion (E5)* 2,287
Alden (E1)* 200
Aledo (C2)* 2,919
Alexander (D4)* 350
Alexis (C2)* 821
Algonquin (E1)* 1,223
Alhambra (D5)* 476
Allendale (F5)* 442
Allenville (E4)* 253
Allerton (F4)* 244
Alma (E5)* 404
Alorton (B6) 2,547
Alpha (C2)* 630
Alsey (C4)* 294
Alsip (B2) 1,228
Altamont (E4)* 1,580
Alto Pass (D6)* 462
Alton (A6)* 32,550
Altona (C2)* 462
Alvin (F3)* 287
Amboy (D2)* 2,128
America (D6)
Anchor (E3)* 175
Ancona (E2)*
Andalusia (C2)* 510
Andover (C2)* 256
Anna (D6)* 4,380
Annapolis (F4)* 147
Annawan (D2)* 592
Antioch (E1)* 1,307
Apple River (C1)* 514
Arcola (E4)* 1,700
Arenzville (C4)* 513
Argenta (E4)* 575
Argo (B2)* 9,000
Arlington (D2)* 247
Arlington Hts. (A1)* 8,768
Armington (D3)* 314
Armstrong (F3)* 325
Aroma Park (F2)* 544
Arrowsmith (E3)* 316
Arthur (E4)* 1,573
Ashkum (E3)* 420
Ashland (C4)* 1,039

Ashley (D5)*............ 738
Ashmore (F4)*.......... 406
Ashton (D2)*............ 913
Assumption (E4)*.......1,466
Astoria (C3)*............1,308
Athens (D4)*..............1,048
Athensville (C4)*........ 80
Atkinson (C2)*.......... 825
Atlanta (D3)*.............1,331
Atterberry (D3)*........ 115
Atwood (E4)*............ 661
Auburn (D4)*.............1,963
Augusta (C3)*............ 945
Aurora (E2)*.............50,576
Ava (D6)*................ 734
Aviston (D5)*............ 503
Avon (C3)*................ 870
Baileyville (D1)*........ 210
Baldwin (D5)*............ 354
Banner (D3).............. 215
Bannockburn ‡(F1)...... 249
Bardolph (C3)*.......... 246
Barrington (E1)*.........4,209
Barry (B4)*...............1,529
Bartelso (D5)*........... 304
Bartlett (E1)*............ 716
Bartonville (D3)*.........2,437
Basco (B3)*............... 220
Batavia (E2)*.............5,838
Batchtown (C4)*......... 237
Bath (C3)*................ 423
Baylis (C4)*............. 307
Beardstown (C3)*.......6,080
Beason (D3)*............ 291
Beaucoup (D5)*.......... 100
Beaverville (F3)*........ 383
Beckemeyer (D5)*.......1,045
Bedford Park (B2)....... 651
Beecher (F2)*............ 956
Beecher City (E4)*...... 437
Belgium (F3)............. 493
Belknap (E6)*............ 247
Belle Prairie ‡(E5)*..... 82
Belle Rive (E5)*......... 313
Belleville (B6)*.........32,721
Bellevue ‡(D3)*.........1,529
Bellflower (E3)*......... 413
Bellmont (F5)*........... 368
Bellwood (A2)*...........8,746
Belvidere (E1)*..........9,422
Bement (E4)*.............1,459
Benld (D4)*..............2,093
Bensenville (A1)*........3,754
Benson (D3)*............. 387
Bentley (B3)*............. 88
Benton (E6)*..............7,848
Berkeley (A2)............1,882
Berlin (D4)*.............. 218
Bernice (B2)...............
Berwick (C3)*............ 160
Berwyn (B2)*.............51,280
Bethalto (B6)*...........2,115
Bethany (E4)*............ 850
Beulah Heights (E6)....
Bible Grove (E5)*........ 186
Big Rock (E2)*........... 250
Biggsville (C3)*......... 379
Bingham (D4)*........... 170
Birds (F5)*............... 234
Birkner (B6)...............
Bishop Hill (C2)*........ 202
Bismarck (F3)*........... 400
Blandinsville (C3)*...... 918
Bloomingdale (E2)*...... 339
Bloomington (D3)*......34,163
Blue Island (B2)*.......17,622
Blue Mound (D4)*........ 886
Bluff City (E5)........... 300
Bluffs (C4)*.............. 784
Bluford (E5)*............. 477
Bogota (E5)*.............. 62
Bondville (E3)*........... 250
Bone Gap (F5)*........... 327
Bonfield (E2)*............ 143
Bonnie (E5)*.............. 257
Boody (D4)*............... 199
Boskydell (D6)............ 49
Boulder (D5)*..............
Bourbon (E4)*............. 80
Bourbonnais (F2)*.......1,598
Bowen (B3)*............... 573
Braceville (E2)*........... 384
Bradford (D2)*............ 952
Bradley (F2)*..............5,699
Braidwood (E2)*..........1,485
Breese (D5)*..............2,181
Bremen (D6)............... 123
Bridgeport (F5)*.........2,358
Bridge View (B2).........1,393
Brighton (C4)*............ 934
Brimfield (D3)*........... 648
Bristol (E2)*.............. 541
Broadlands (E4)*......... 333
Broadview (A2)*..........5,196
Broadwell (D3)*........... 149
Brocton (F4)*............. 406
Brookfield (A2)*.........15,472
Brooklyn (Lovejoy*)
(A6) 2,568
Brooklyn (C3)*............ 97
Brookport (E6)*..........1,119
Broughton (E6)*.......... 324
Brownfield (E6)*.......... 94
Browning (C3)*........... 324
Browns (F5)*.............. 336
Brownstown (E5)*........ 649
Brussels (C5)*............ 205
Bryant (C3)*.............. 396
Buckingham (E2)*........ 140
Buckley (F3)*............. 554
Buckner (E6)*............. 783
Buda (D2)*................ 761
Buffalo (D4)*............. 416
Bulpitt (D4)*.............. 376
Buncombe (E6)*........... 210
Bunker Hill (D4)*........1,238
Bureau (D2)*.............. 480
Burlington (E1)*.......... 263
Burnham (B2)..............1,331
Burnside (B3)*............ 150
Burnt Prairie (E5)*...... 172
Bush (D6)................. 504
Bushnell (C3)*............3,317
Bushton (E4)*............ 100
Butler (D4)*.............. 283
Byron (D1)*...............1,237
Cabery (E3)*.............. 290
Cahokia (B6).............. 794
Cairo (D6)*...............12,123
Caledonia (E1)*............
Calhoun (E5)*............. 215
Calumet City (B2)*....15,799
Calumet Park (B2)......2,500
Camargo (E4)*............ 236
Cambria (D6)*............ 625
Cambridge (C2)*.........1,489
Camden (C3)*............. 153
Cameron (C3)*............ 250
Camp Point (B3)*........ 969
Campbell Hill (D6)*..... 336
Campgrove (D2)*......... 125
Campus (E2)*............. 183
Canton (C3)*.............11,927
Cantrall (D4)*............ 145
Capron (E1)*.............. 572
Carbon Cliff (C2)*....... 676
Carbon Hill (E2).......... 158
Carbondale (D6)*........10,921
Carlinville (D4)*..........5,116
Carlock (D3)*............. 350
Carlyle (D5)*..............2,669
Carman (B3)*.............. 82
Carmi (E5)*................5,574
Carpenter (B6).............
Carpentersville (E1)*....1,523
Carriers Mills (E6)*.....2,252
Carrollton (C4)*..........2,437
Carterville (D6)*.........2,716
Carthage (B3)*............3,214
Cary (E1)*................ 943
Casey (F4)*...............2,734
Caseyville (B6)*..........1,209
Castleton (D2)*.......... 155
Catlin (F3)*.............. 953
Cave In Rock (E6)*...... 550
Cedar Point (D2)*........ 296
Cedarville (D1)*.......... 466
Central City (D5).........1,231
Central City ‡(E2)....... 35
Centralia (D5)*..........13,863
Cerro Gordo (E4)*.......1,052
Chadwick (D1)*........... 607
Chambersburg (C4)*..... 145
Champaign (E3)*.......39,563
Chana (D2)*............... 150
Chandlerville (C3)*...... 788
Channahon (E2)*.........1,000
Chapin (C4)*.............. 489
Charleston (E4)*..........9,164
Chatham (D4)*............ 905
Chatsworth (E3)*.........1,119
Chauncey (F5)*........... 78
Chautauqua (C5)*..........
Chebanse (F3)*........... 739
Chemung (E1)............. 200
Cheneyville (F3)*........ 98
Chenoa (E3)*..............1,452
Cherry (D2)*.............. 520
Cherry Valley (D1)*...... 741
Chester (D6)*.............5,389
Chesterfield (D4)*....... 272
Chesterville (E4)*........ 129
Chestnut (D3)*........... 296
Chicago (B2)*.........3,620,962
Chicago (urban
area)...................4,902,001
Chicago Heights (B3)*24,551
Chicago Ridge (A2)*..... 888
Chillicothe (D3)*.........2,767
Chrisman (F4)*...........1,071
Christopher (D6)*........3,545
Cicero (B2)*..............67,544
Cisco (E3)*............... 334
Cisne (E5)*............... 628
Cissna Park (F3)*........ 660
Clare (E1)*............... 118
Claremont (F5)*.......... 249
Clarendon Hills (A2)*...2,437
Clark Center (F4)..........
Clay City (E5)*...........1,103
Clayton (C3)*............. 866
Claytonville (F3)*..........
Cleveland (C2)........... 204
Clifton (F3*.............. 734
Clinton (E3)*..............5,945
Coal City (E2)*...........2,220
Coal Valley (C2)*......... 363
Coalton (D4).............. 402
Coatsburg (B3)*.......... 194
Cobden (D6)*.............1,104
Coello (D6)*.............. 513
Coffeen (D4)*............. 627
Colchester (C3)*..........1,551
Coleta (D2)*.............. 184
Colfax (E3)*.............. 819
Collinsville (B6)*........11,862
Collison (F3)*............ 94
Colona (C2)*............. 319
Colp (D6)*................ 253
Columbia (C5)*...........2,179
Columbus (B4)*.......... 83
Colusa (B3)*.............. 110
Compton (D2)*........... 321
Concord (C4)*............ 278
Congerville (D3)*........ 200
Cooks Mills (E4)......... 125
Cooksville (E3)*......... 256
Cora (D6)*.................
Cordova (C2)*............ 475
Cornell (E3)*............. 458
Cornland (D4)*........... 142
Cortland (E2)*............ 398
Cottage Hills (B6)*......3,357
Coulterville (D5)*........1,160
Cowden (E4)*............. 619
Crainville ‡(D6).......... 433
Creal Springs (E6)*..... 864
Crescent City (F3)*...... 324
Creston (D2)*............. 362
Crestwood (B2)........... 739
Crete (F2)*................2,298
Creve Coeur (D3)*........5,499
Cropsey (E3)*............ 200
Crossville (F5)*.......... 866
Crotty (Seneca*) (E2)..1,435
Crystal Lake (E1)*.......4,832
Cuba (C3)*................1,482
Cullom (E3)*.............. 492
Curran (D4)*.............. 300
Custer Park (E2)*........ 250
Cutler (D5)*.............. 520
Cypress (D6)*............ 357
Dahinda (C3)*............ 225
Dahlgren (E5)*........... 609
Dakota (D1)*.............. 318
Dale (E6)*................ 200
Dallas City (B3)*.........1,275
Dalton City (E4)*........ 384
Dalzell (D2)*............. 543
Dana (E3)*................ 246
Danforth (E3)*............ 385
Danvers (D3)*............ 762
Danville (F3)*............37,864
Darmstadt (D5)........... 90
Darwin (F4)............... 96
Davis (D1)*............... 348
Davis Junction (D1)*... 250
Dawson (D4)*............ 374
Dayton (E2)*.............. 150
De Kalb (E2)..............11,708
De Land (E3)*............ 416
De Long (C3)*............ 375
De Soto (D6)*............ 646
Decatur (E4)*............66,269
Decatur (urban area).75,148
Deer Creek (D3)*........ 501
Deer Grove (D2)*........ 72
Deerfield (F1)*...........3,288
Delafield (E5)*........... 100
Delavan (D3)*............1,248
Delhi (C4)................ 64
Denver (B3)*............. 117
Depue (D2)*..............2,163
Des Plaines (A1)*.......14,994
Detroit (C4)*............. 126
Dewey (E3)*.............. 126
Dewitt (E3)*.............. 216
Diamond ‡(E2)........... 107
Dieterich (E4)*........... 500
Divernon (D4)*...........1,013
Dix (E5)*.................. 190
Dixmoor (B2).............1,327
Dixon (D2)*..............11,523
Dixon Springs (E6)*..... 10
Dolton (B2)*..............5,558
Dongola (D6)*............ 704
Donnellson (D4)*........ 336
Donovan (F3)*............ 327
Dorchester (D4)*........ 162
Dover (D2)*.............. 191
Dow (C4)*..................
Dowell (D6)*............. 616
Downers Grove (A2)*.11,886
Downs (E3)*.............. 299
Du Quoin (D5)*...........7,147
Dubois (D5)*............. 282
Duncan (D3).............. 58
Dundas (E5)*............. 200
Dundee (E1)*.............3,414
Dunfermline (D3)*....... 292
Dunlap (D3)*............. 600
Dupo (A6)*...............2,239
Durand (D1)*............. 679
Dwight (E2)*..............2,843
Eagarville (D4)*......... 187
Earlville (E2)*............1,217
E. Alton (D6)*............7,290
E. Brooklyn ‡(E2)........ 65
E. Carondelet (A6)*..... 401
E. Chicago Hts. (B3).....1,548
E. Dubuque (C1)*........1,697
E. Dundee (Dundee*)
(E1) 1,466
E. Galesburg (C3)*...... 651
E. Gillespie (D4)......... 224
E. Hardin (C4)..............
E. Hazel Crest (B2)......1,066
E. Lynn (F3)*...............
E. Moline (C2)*..........13,913
E. Peoria (D3)*...........8,698
E. Saint Louis (B6)*..82,295
Easton (D3)*............. 371
Eaton (F4)*............... 150
Eddyville (E6)*........... 106
Edelstein (D3)*.......... 175
Edgewood (E5)*.......... 515
Edgington (C2).............
Edinburg (D4)*........... 921
Edwards (D3)*............ 150
Edwardsville (B6)*.......8,776
Effingham (E4)*...........6,892
Egan (D1)*................ 22
Eileen (E2)................ 332
El Dara (B4)*............. 137
El Paso (D3)*.............1,818
Elburn (E2)*.............. 792
Elco (D6)*................ 300
Eldorado (E6)*...........4,500
Eldred (C4)*.............. 298
Eleroy (D1)*.............. 125
Elgin (E1)*...............44,223
Elizabeth (C1)*........... 723
Elizabethtown (E6)*..... 583
Elkhart (D3)*............. 420
Elkville (D6)*............. 934
Ellery (E5)*............... 111
Elliott (E3)*.............. 337
Ellisgrove (D5)*.......... 258
Ellisville (C3)*............ 157
Ellsworth (E3)*........... 199
Elmhurst (A2)*...........21,273
Elmira (D2)............... 50
Elmwood (D3)*...........1,613
Elmwood Park (B2)*...18,801
Elsah (C5)*............... 520
Elvaston (B3)*............ 238
Elwood (E2)*............. 420
Emden (D3)*.............. 406
Emington (E3)*........... 150
Emma (E6)*.................
Energy (E6)*.............. 503
Enfield (E5)*.............. 906
Equality (E6)*............ 830
Erie (C2)*.................1,180
Esmond (E1)*............. 75
Essex (E2)*............... 284
Eureka (D3)*..............2,367
Evanston (B1)*...........73,641
Evansville (D5)*.......... 821
Evergreen Park (B2)*.10,531
Ewing (E5)*............... 330
Exeter (C4)*.............. 107
Ezra (E6).................. 100
Fairbury (E3)*............2,433
Fairdale (E1)*............ 150
Fairfield (E5)*............5,576
Fairgrange (E4)............
Fairmont City (B6)......2,284
Fairmount (F3)*.......... 618
Fairview (C3)*............ 568
Fancy Prairie (D4)*..... 110
Farina (E5)*.............. 787
Farmer City (E3)*........1,752
Farmersville (D4)*....... 485
Farmington (C3)*.........2,651
Fay (C2).................. 124
Fayetteville (D5)......... 245
Fenton (C2)*...............
Ferris (B3)*............... 226
Fiatt (C3)*................ 200
Fidelity (C4)*............. 157
Fieldon (C4)*............. 260
Fillmore (D4)*............ 384
Findlay (E4)*.............. 680
Fisher (E3)*............... 894
Fithian (F3)*.............. 414
Flanagan (E3)*............ 672
Flat Rock (F5)*........... 558
Flora (E5)*................5,255
Florence (C4)............. 107
Flossmoor (B3)*..........1,804
Foosland (E3)*............ 200
Forest City (D3)*........ 278
Forest Park (B2)*......14,969
Forest View ‡(B2)....... 291
Forrest (E3)*.............1,040
Forreston (D1)*..........1,048
Forsyth (D4)*............. 370
Fountain Green (C3)*... 145
Fowler (B3)*.............. 175
Fox Lake (E1)*............2,238
Fox River Grove (E1)*..1,313
Frankfort (F2)*........... 685
Franklin (C4)*............ 438
Franklin Grove (D2)*.... 741
Franklin Park (A2)*......8,899
Frederick (C3)*........... 175
Freeburg (D5)*...........1,661
Freedom (E2)............. 110
Freeman Spur ‡(D6)*.... 451
Freeport (D1)*...........22,467
Friendsville (F5)......... 100
Fulton (C2)*..............2,706
Fults ‡(C5)*.............. 120
Galatia (E6)*............. 933
Gale (D6)*................ 150
Galena (C1)*..............4,648
Galesburg (C3)*........31,425
Galt (D2)*..................
Galva (D2)*...............2,886
Garden Prairie (E1)*... 300
Gardner (E2)*............ 981
Garrett (E4)*............. 213
Gays (E4)*................ 261
Geff (E5)*................. 326
Geneseo (C2)*............4,325
Geneva (E2)*..............5,139
Genoa (E1)*...............1,090
Georgetown (F4)*.........3,294
German Valley (D1)*.... 206
Germantown (D5)*....... 811
Gibson City (E3)*........3,029
Gifford (E3)*.............. 350
Gilberts ‡(E1)*........... 183
Gillespie (D4)*...........4,105
Gilman (E3)*..............1,602
Gilson (C3)*.............. 250
Girard (D4)*..............1,740
Gladstone (B3)*.......... 340
Glasford (D3)*............ 922
Glasgow (C4)*............ 158
Glen Carbon (B6)*.......1,176
Glen Ellyn (F2)*..........9,524
Glencoe (F1)*.............6,980
Glenview (B1)*............6,142
Glenwood (B3)*........... 762
Godley ‡(E2).............. 102
Golconda (E6)*...........1,066
Golden (B3)*.............. 512
Goldengate (E5)*......... 199
Golf (A1)*................. 258
Good Hope (C3)*......... 392
Goodfield (D3)*........... 281
Goreville (E6)*............ 581
Gorham (D6)*............. 447
Grafton (C5)*.............1,117
Grand Chain (E6)*........ 330
Grand Detour (D2)........ 400
Grand Ridge (E2)*........ 530
Grand Tower (D6)*....... 963
Grand View (F4).......... 75
Grandview (D4)...........1,349
Granite City (B6)*.....29,465
Grant Park (F2)*......... 564
Grantfork (D5)............ 162
Grantsburg (E6)*......... 100
Granville (D2)*........... 978
Grape Creek (F3)......... 200
Graymont (E3)*.......... 132
Grayslake (E1)*..........1,970
Grayville (E5)*...........2,461
Green Valley (D3)*...... 503
Greenfield (C4)*.......... 987
Greenup (E4)*............1,360
Greenview (D3)*......... 795
Greenville (D5)*..........4,069
Gridley (E3)*............. 817
Griggsville (C4)*.........1,199
Groveland (D3)*......... 200
Gulfport (B3)............. 232
Gurnee (F1)*..............1,097
Hagarstown (D5)*........ 84
Hainesville ‡(E1)........ 154
Haldane (D1)*..............
Hallsville (D3)*.......... 123
Hamburg (C4)*........... 225
Hamel (B6)................ 250
Hamilton (B3)*...........1,776
Hamletsburg (E6)*....... 131
Hammond (E4)*.......... 405
Hampshire (E1)*......... 970
Hampton (C2)............. 706
Hanaford (Logan*)
(E5) 280
Hanna City (D3)*........ 671
Hanover (C1)*............1,643
Harco (E6)*............... 300
Hardin (C4)*.............. 928
Hardinville (F5).......... 150
Harmon (D2)*............. 208
Harper (D1)............... 45
Harrisburg (E6)*........10,999
Harrison (D1)...............
Harrisonville (C5)........ 100
Harristown (D4)*......... 200
Hartford (B6)*............1,909
Hartsburg (D3)*.......... 245
Harvard (E1)*.............3,464
Harvel (D4)*.............. 301
Harvey (B2)*.............20,683
Harwood Hts. (B1)....... 655
Havana (D3)*.............4,379
Hazel Crest (B2)*........2,129
Hazel Dell (E4)*.......... 150
Hazelhurst (D2)*......... 29
Hebron (E1)*.............. 696
Hecker (D5)*.............. 204
Henderson (C2)*.......... 166
Hennepin (D2)*........... 312
Henning (F3)*............. 283
Henry (D2)*...............1,966
Henton (E4)............... 65
Hermon (C3)*............. 67
Herrick (D4)*............. 554
Herrin (E6)*...............9,331
Herscher (E2)*............ 515
Hersman (C4)*............ 138
Hettick (C4)*.............. 268
Heyworth (E3)*...........1,072
Hidalgo (E4)*............. 167
Highland (D5)*............4,283
Highland Park (F1)*...16,808
Highwood (F1)*...........3,813
Hillsboro (D4)*...........4,141
Hillsdale (C2)*............ 425
Hillside (A2)*.............2,131
Hillview (C4)*............. 419
Hinckley (E2)*............ 774
Hindsboro (E4)*.......... 377
Hinsdale (A2)*............8,676
Hodgkins (A2)*........... 536
Holcomb (D1)*............ 200
Hollowayville ‡(D2)...... 89
Hollywood (A2)*............
Homer (F3)*...............1,028
Homewood (B3)*..........5,887
Hoopeston (F3)*..........5,992
Hooppole (D2)*........... 195
Hopedale (D3)*........... 574
Hoyleton (D5)*........... 462
Hubbard Woods (B1)*..
Hudson (E3)*.............. 339
Huey (D5)*................ 175
Hull (B4)*................. 489
Humboldt (E4)*........... 295
Hume (F4)*................ 448
Humphrey (Tovey*)
(D4) 593
Hunt (E4)*................ 104
Huntley (E1)*............. 830
Hurricane (D4)............ 32
Hurst (D6)*............... 858
Hutsonville (F4)*......... 647
Illiopolis (D4)*........... 833
Ina (E5)*.................. 432
Indianola (F4)*........... 392
Industry (C3)*............ 496
Ingalls Park (F2)........6,840
Ingraham (E5)*........... 202
Iola (E5)*................. 213
Ipava (C3)*............... 667
Iroquois (F3)*............ 232
Irving (D4)*.............. 539
Irvington (D5)*........... 379
Irwin ‡(E2)*............... 85
Itasca (F2)*...............1,274
Iuka (E5)*................. 450
Ivesdale (E4)*............ 407
Jacksonville (C4)*......20,387
Jamaica (F4)*...............
Jamestown (D5).......... 70
Janesville (E4)*.......... 165
Jeffersonville (Geff*)
(E5) 326
Jeiseyville (D4).......... 199
Jerome (D4).............. 689
Jerseyville (C4)*.........5,792
Jewett (E4)*.............. 253
Johnsonville ‡(E5)*...... 105
Johnston City (E6)*......4,479
Joliet (E2)*...............51,601
Jonesboro (D6)*..........1,607
Joppa (E6)*............... 513
Joy (C2)*.................. 505
Junction (E6)*............ 239
Junction City (D5)....... 353
Justice (B2).............. 854
Kampsville (C4)*......... 437
Kane (C4)*................ 485
Kaneville (E2)*........... 250
Kangley (E2)............. 296
Kankakee (F2)*.........25,856
Kansas (F4)*............. 835
Kappa (D3)*.............. 125
Karbers Ridge (E6)*.....
Karnak (E6)*............. 792
Kasbeer (D2)*............ 125
Kaskaskia (C6)........... 112
Keenes (E5)*...............
Keensburg (F5)*......... 302
Keithsburg (B2)*.........1,006
Kell (E5)*................. 193
Kemp (E4)*............... 60
Kemper (C4)*............. 42
Kempton (E3)*............ 255
Kenilworth (B1)*.........2,789
Kenney (D3)*............. 409
Kent (D1)*................ 103
Kernan (E2)*.............. 56
Kewanee (C2)*...........16,821
Keyesport (D5)*.......... 438
Kilbourne (D3)*........... 374
Kincaid (D4)*..............1,793
Kinderhook (B4)*......... 299
Kings (D2)*................ 250
Kingston (E1)*............. 327
Kingston Mines (D3)*.. 404
Kinmundy (E5)*........... 912
Kinsman (E2)*............. 147
Kirkland (E1)*............. 685
Kirkwood (C3)*............ 747
Knoxville (C3)*............2,209
La Clede (E5)*..............
La Fayette (D2)*.......... 301
La Grange (A2)*.........12,002
La Grange Park (A2)*..6,176
La Harpe (C3)*............1,295
La Moille (D2)*........... 505
La Place (E4)*..............
La Prairie (B3)*.......... 142
La Rose (D3)*............. 178
La Salle (D2)*...........12,083
Lacon (D2)*...............2,020
Ladd (D2)*................1,224
Lake Bluff (F1)*..........2,000
Lake City (E4)*........... 160
Lake Forest (F1)*........7,819
Lake Fork (D4)*.......... 127
Lake Villa (E1)*.......... 824
Lake Zurich (E1)*........ 850
Lakewood ‡(E1)........... 393
Lakewood (E4)*.......... 200
Lanark (D1)*..............1,359
Lancaster (F5)*.......... 134
Lane (E3)*..................
Langleyville (D4)*....... 300
Lansing (B3)*.............8,682
Latham (D4)*............. 387
Laura (D3)*............... 150
Lawndale (D3)*........... 150
Lawrenceville (F5)*.....6,328
Le Roy (E3)*..............1,820
Leaf River (D1)*......... 444
Lebanon (D5)*............2,417
Ledford (E6).............. 120
Lee (E2)*................. 251
Lee Center (D2)*........ 320
Leland (E2)*.............. 537
Lemont (A2)*..............2,757
Lena (D1)*.................1,227
Lenzburg (D5)*........... 431
Leonore (E2)*............. 204
Lerna (E4)*................ 304
Lewistown (C3)*..........2,630
Lexington (E3)*...........1,181
Liberty (B4)*.............. 300
Liberty (Burnt Prairie*)
(E5) 172
Libertyville (F1)*.........5,425
Lick Creek (D6)............
Lidice (E2).................3,000
Lilly (D3).................. 78
Lima (B3)*................ 154
Lincoln (D3)*............14,362
Lincolnwood (B1).........3,072
Lindenwood (D1)*........ 150
Lisbon (E2)*.............. 183
Lisle (E2)*.................4,500
Litchfield (D4)*...........7,208
Little York (C2)*.......... 324
Littleton (C3)*............ 215
Liverpool (C3)*.............
Livingston (D5)*.......... 999
Loami (D4)*............... 439
Lockport (F2)*............4,955
Loda (E3)*................ 559
Logan (E6)*............... 280
Lomax (B3)*.............. 490
Lombard (A2)*............9,817
Lombardville (D2)........ 101
London Mills (C3)*....... 581
Long Point (E3)*......... 286
Longview (E4)*........... 239
Loraine (B3)*............. 370
Lostant (D2)*............. 432
Louisville (E5)*........... 970
Lovejoy (A6)*.............2,568
Loves Park (E1)*.........5,366
Lovington (E4)*...........1,152
Lowder (D4)*...............
Lowpoint (D3)*........... 250
Ludlow (E3)*.............. 475
Lyndon (D2)*............. 594
Lynn Center (C2)*....... 75
Lynnville (C4)............ 101
Lyons (B2)*...............6,120
Macedonia (E5)*......... 127
Mackinaw (D3)*..........1,011
Macomb (C3)*...........10,592
Macon (E4)*.............. 942
Madison (B6)*............7,963
Maeystown (C5)*......... 137
Magnolia (D2)*........... 285
Mahomet (E3)*...........1,017
Makanda (D6)*........... 214
Malden (D2)*............. 217
Malta (E2)*............... 510
Manchester (C4)*........ 351
Manhattan (F2)*.......... 728
Manito (D3)*.............. 869
Manlius (D2)*............. 368
Mannheim (A2)..............
Mansfield (E3)*........... 665
Manteno (F2)*............1,789
Maple Park (E2)*......... 433
Mapleton (D3)*........... 300
Maquon (C3)*............. 361
Marblehead (B4)*........ 193
Marcelline (B3)........... 60
Marengo (E1)*............2,726
Marietta (C3)*............ 178
Marine (D5)*.............. 657
Marion (E6)*.............10,459
Marissa (D5)*.............1,652
Mark (D2)*................ 449
Markham (B2)*............2,753
Maroa (E3)*...............1,100
Marseilles (E2)*..........4,514
Marshall (F4)*............2,960
Martinsville (F4)*........1,440
Martinton (F3)*........... 292
Maryville (B6)*........... 539
Mascoutah (D5)*.........3,009
Mason (E5)*.............. 327
Mason City (D3)*........2,004
Massbach (C1)*........... 37
Matherville (C2)*........ 590

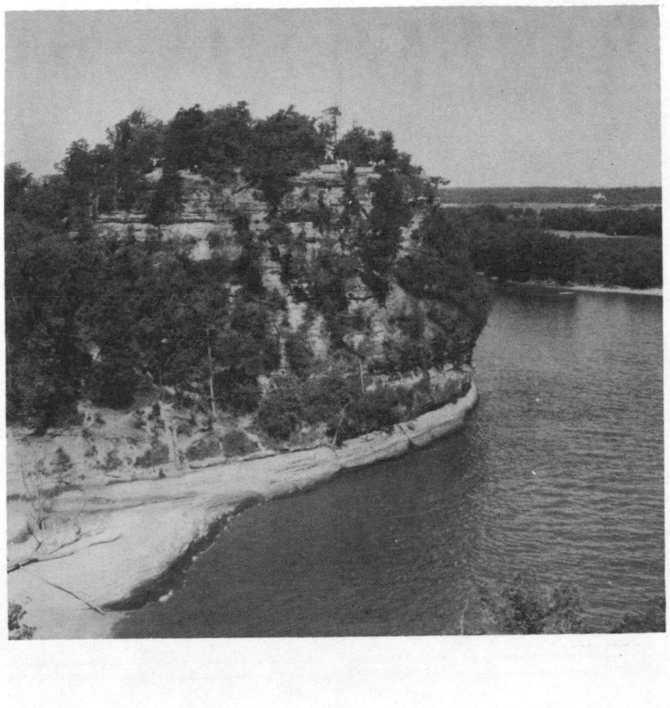

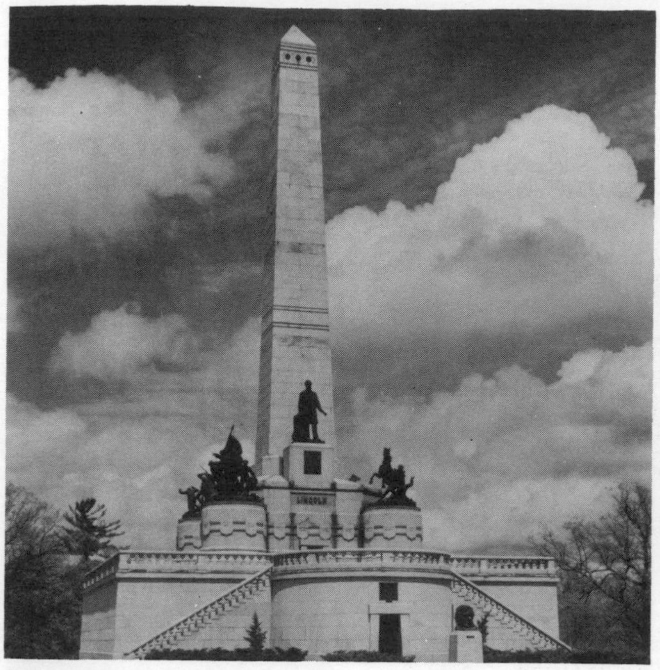

Matteson (B3)*...........1,211
Mattoon (E4)*...........17,547
Maunie (E5)*.............. 412
Maywood (A2)*..........27,473
Mazon (E2)*................ 586
Mc Clure (D6)*............ 350
Mc Connell (D1)*.......... 200
Mc Cook (A2)*............ 361
Mc Dowell (E3)............ 50
Mc Henry (E1)*...........2,080
Mc Lean (D3)*............ 667
Mc Leansboro (E5)*.....3,008
Mc Nabb (D2)*............ 190
Meadows (E3)*............ 150
Mechanicsburg (D4)*.... 464
Media (C3)*................ 148
Medora (C4)*.............. 432
Melrose Park (A2)*....13,366
Melvin (E3)*............... 535
Mendon (B3)*.............. 625
Mendota (D2)*............5,129
Menominee (C1).......... 132
Meredosia (C4)*.......... 940
Merrionette Park (B2)..1,101
Merritt (C4)................ 80
Metamora (D3)*..........1,368
Metcalf (F4)*.............. 312
Metropolis (E6)*..........6,093
Middlegrove (C3)*........ 200
Middletown (D3)*......... 480
Midlothian (B2)*..........3,216
Milan (C2)*..................1,737
Milford (F3)*..............1,648
Mill Shoals (E5).......... 417
Millbrook (E2)*........... 100
Millcreek (D6)*........... 127
Milledgeville (D1)*.......1,044
Millington (E2)*.......... 270
Millstadt (B6)*............1,566
Milmine (E4)*............. 95
Milton (C4)*................ 337
Milton (B6)..................8,232
Mineral (D2)*.............. 274
Minier (D3)*................ 780
Minonk (D3)*..............1,955
Minooka (E2)*............. 369
Mitchellsville (E6)........ 20
Mode (E4)*.................. 133
Modesto (D4)*............. 232
Modoc (C5)*................ 108
Mokena (F2)*.............. 903
Moline (C2)*..............37,397
Moline-Rock Island, Ill.-
Davenport, Iowa
(urban area).........193,733
Momence (F2)*...........2,644
Monee (F2)*............... 554
Monica (D3)*.............. 185
Monmouth (C3)*.........10,193
Monroe Center (E1)*... 215
Monsanto (B6)*........... 357
Montgomery (E2)*........ 773
Monticello (E3)*..........2,612
Montrose (E4)*........... 309
Moon (E5).................. 50
Mooseheart (E2)*........
Moro (B6)*.................. 275
Morris (E2)*................6,926
Morrison (C2)*............3,531
Morrisonville (D4)*.......1,182
Morton (D3)*..............3,693
Morton Grove (B1)*.....3,926
Mossville (D3)*............ 350
Mound City (D6)*.........2,167
Mound Station
(Timewell*) (C3)....... 184
Mounds (D6)*...............2,001
Mt. Auburn (D4)*......... 414
Mt. Carmel (F5)*.........8,732
Mt. Carroll (D1)*.........1,950
Mt. Clare ‡(D4)*......... 260
Mt. Erie (E5)*............. 149
Mt. Morris (D1)*.........2,709
Mt. Olive (D4)*............2,401
Mt. Prospect (A1)*......4,009
Mt. Pulaski (D3)*.........1,526
Mt. Sterling (C4)*........2,246
Mt. Vernon (E5)*.......15,600
Mt. Zion (E4)*............ 438
Moweaqua (E4)*...........1,475
Mozier (C4)*.............. 125
Muddy (E6)*............... 500
Mulberry Grove (D5)*.. 712
Muncie (F3)*............... 197
Mundelein (E1)*...........3,189
Murdock (E4)*............ 300
Murphysboro (D6)*.......9,241
Murrayville (C4)*......... 405
Nachusa (D2)*............ 150
Nameoki (B6)*............
Naperville (E2)*...........7,013
Naplate (E2)................ 783
Naples (C4)*............... 141
Nashville (D5)*.............2,432
Nason (D5)*................ 199
National Stock Yards
(National City)(B6)* 207
Nauvoo (B3)*...............1,242
Nebo (C4)*.................. 413
Nelson (D2)*............... 289
Neoga (E4)*.................1,125
Neponset (D2)*............ 501
New Athens (D5)*........1,518
New Baden (D5)*.........1,428
New Bedford (D2)*....... 225
New Berlin (D4)*.......... 622
New Boston (B2)*........ 767
New Burnside (E6)*..... 244
New Canton (B4)*........ 449
New Douglas (D5)*....... 359
New Grand Chain
(Grand Chain*) (D6). 330
New Haven (E6)*......... 819
New Holland (D3)*....... 343
New Lenox (F2)*..........1,235
New Memphis (D5)*..... 350
New Milford (D1)......... 340
New Minden (D5)*....... 160
New Philadelphia (C3)*
New Salem (C4)*.......... 184
New Windsor (C2)*....... 569
Newark (E2)*.............. 457
Newman (F4)*.............1,140
Newton (E5)*...............2,780
Niantic (D4)*............... 625
Niles (A1)....................3,587
Nilwood (D4)*............. 321
Niota (B3)*................. 250
Noble (E5)*................. 776
Nokomis (D4)*............2,544
Nora (D1)*.................. 208
Normal (E3)*................9,772
Norridge (B1)...............3,428
Norris (C3)*................ 319
Norris City (E6)*..........1,370
North Aurora (E2)*...... 921
N. Chicago (F1)*..........8,628
N. Chillicothe (D3)........1,741
N. City (Coello*) (E5). 513
N. Henderson (C2)*......
N. Lake (A2)*...............4,361
N. Pekin ‡(D3)............1,758
N. Quincy (B4).............2,985
N. Riverside (B2)..........3,230
N. Utica (Utica*) (E2). 985
Northbrook (A1)*.........3,348
Northfield (B1)*...........1,426
Oak (E6).......................
Oak Forest (B2)*..........1,856
Oak Hill (D3)*..............
Oak Park (B2)*..........63,529
Oakdale (D5)*.............. 570
Oakford (D3)*.............. 281
Oakglen (B3)*..............
Oakland (F4)*.............. 980
Oaklawn (B2)*.............8,751
Oakley (E4)*................ 150
Oakwood (F3)*............ 641
Oblong (F5)*................1,639
Oconee (D4)*............... 256
Odell (E2)*.................. 908
Odin (D5)*....................1,341
O'Fallon (B6)*..............3,022
Ogden (F3)*................ 436
Oglesby (D2)*...............3,922
Ohio (D2)*................... 561
Ohlman (D4)*..............
Okawville (D5)*........... 855
Old Marissa (D5).......... 200
Old Ripley (D5)............ 135
Olive Branch (D6)*.......
Olivet (F4)*.................. 325
Olmsted (D6)*.............. 525
Olney (E5)*..................8,612
Olympia Fields (B3)*.... 160
Omaha (E6)*................ 394
Onarga (F3)*................1,455
Oneida (C2)*................ 554
Opdyke (E5)*............... 200
Ophiem (C2)*............... 150
Oquawka (C3)*............. 929
Orangeville (D1)*......... 460
Oraville (D6)*.............. 200
Orchard Place (A1)....... 500
Oreana (E4)*................ 148
Oregon (D1)*................3,205
Orient (E6)*................. 801
Orion (C2)*.................. 829
Orlando Park (A2)*...... 788
Oswego (E2)*................1,220
Ottawa (E2)*.............16,957
Otterville (C4)............. 118
Owaneco (D4)*............. 343
Ozark (E6)*.................
Palatine (E1)*...............4,079
Palestine (F4)*.............1,589
Palmer (D4)*................ 335
Palmyra (C4)*.............. 746
Paloma (B3)*............... 150
Palos Heights (A2)*.....1,600
Palos Park (A2)*.......... 854
Pana (D4)*...................6,178
Panama (D4)*.............. 520
Panola (E3)*................ 52
Papineau (F3)*............ 157
Paris (F4)*....................9,460
Park Forest (B3)*..........8,138
Park Ridge (A1)*........16,602
Parkersburg (F5)*........ 288
Patoka (D5)*................ 602
Patterson (C4)*............ 147
Pawnee (D4)*.............. 974
Pawpaw (E2)*.............. 594
Paxton (E3)*.................3,795
Payson (B4)*............... 490
Pearl (C4)*.................. 472
Pearl City (D1)*........... 491
Pecatonica (D1)*..........1,438
Pekin (D3)*.................21,858
Penfield (F3)*.............. 300
Peoria (D3)*..............111,856
Peoria (urban area)..154,084
Peoria Heights (D3)*....5,425
Peotone (F2)*...............1,395
Percy (D5)*.................. 933
Perks (D6)*.................. 295
Perry (C4)*.................. 444
Peru (D2)*....................8,653
Pesotum (E4)*............. 415
Petersburg (D4)*.........2,325
Petrolia (F5)................ 200
Philadelphia (C4)*........ 110
Phillipstown (F5).......... 102
Philo (E3)*.................. 525
Phoenix (B2)................3,606
Pierron (D5)*............... 371
Pierson Station (E4)*.. 130
Pinckneyville (D5)*.......3,299
Pingree Grove (E1)....... 162
Pinkstaff (F5)*............ 235
Piper City (E3)*........... 735
Pittsburg (E6)*............ 612
Pittsfield (C4)*............3,564
Pittwood (F3)*............
Plainfield (E2)*............1,764
Plainview (C4)*............ 210
Plainville (B4)*............ 242
Plano (E2)*..................2,154
Plattville (E2)..............
Pleasant Hill (C4)*....... 856
Pleasant Mound (D5)*.. 110
Pleasant Plains (D4)*... 500
Pleasant View (C3)....... 150
Plymouth (C3)*............ 854
Pocahontas (D5)*......... 667
Polo (D1)*....................2,242
Pontiac (E3)*...............8,990
Pontoosuc (B3)*........... 214
Poplar Grove (E1)*...... 417
Port Byron (C2)*..........1,050
Posen (B2)*..................1,795
Potomac (F3)*............. 602
Prairie City (C3)*......... 500
Prairie du Rocher (C5)* 662
Prairietown (B5).......... 150
Preemption (C2)*......... 150
Prentice (C4)*.............. 60
Preston (D5)*............... 103
Princeton (D2)*............5,765
Princeville (D3)*...........1,113
Prophetstown (D2)*.....1,691
Prospect Hts. (A1)*.....1,800
Pulaski (D6)*............... 478
Putnam (D2)*............... 90
Quincy (B4)*..............41,450
Radom (D5)*................ 134
Raleigh (E6)*............... 262
Ramsey (D4)*.............. 808
Rankin (F3)*................ 737
Ransom (E2)*............... 411
Rantoul (E3)*...............6,387
Rapids City (C2)*......... 487
Rardin (E4)*................ 230
Raritan (C3)*............... 228
Ray (C3)*..................... 85
Raymond (D4)*............ 779
Red Bud (D5)*..............1,519
Reddick (E2)*.............. 208
Redmon (F4)*.............. 226
Reevesville (E6)*.......... 110
Renault (C5)*..............
Reno (D5)*.................. 224
Rentchler (B6).............
Reynolds (C2)*............. 409
Richmond (E1)*............ 623
Richton Park (B3)*...... 232
Richview (D5)*............. 352
Ridge Farm (F4)*......... 905
Ridgway (E6)*..............1,148
Ridott (D1)*................. 187
Rinard (E5)*................ 100
Ringwood (E1)*............ 175
Rio (C2)*..................... 200
Ripley (C3)*................. 177
River Forest (B2)*......10,823
River Grove (A2)*.........4,839
Riverdale (B2)*.............5,840
Riverside (B2)*.............9,153
Riverton (D4)*..............1,450
Roanoke (D3)*..............1,368
Robbins (B2)*...............4,766
Roberts (E3)*............... 416
Robinson (F5)*..............6,407
Rochelle (D2)*..............5,449
Rochester (D4)*............ 506
Rock City (D1)*............ 157
Rock Falls (D2)*...........7,983
Rock Grove (D1)........... 150
Rock Island (C2)*.......48,710
Rock Island-Moline, Ill.-
Davenport, Iowa
(urban area).........193,733
Rockbridge (C4)*.......... 243
Rockdale (E2)...............1,393
Rockford (D1)*...........92,927
Rockford (urban
area) 121,723
Rockport (B4)*............. 232
Rockton (E1)*...............1,432
Rockwood (D6)*........... 175
Rollo (E2).................... 24
Rome (D3)*................. 600
Rome (Dix*) (E5)........ 190
Romeoville (E2)........... 147
Roodhouse (C4)*..........2,368
Rosamond (D4)*.......... 300
Roscoe (D1)*............... 700
Rose Hill (E4)*............ 128
Roselle (E1)*................1,038
Roseville (C3)*..............1,080
Rosiclare (E6)*..............2,086
Rossville (F3)*..............1,382
Round Grove (D2)*.......
Round Lake ‡(E1)*....... 573
Round Lake Beach
‡(E1) 1,892
Round Lake Park ‡(E1)1,836
Roxana (B6)*................1,911
Royal (E3)*.................. 156
Royalton (D6)*..............1,506
Ruma (C5).................... 107
Rushville (C3)*..............2,682
Russellville (F5)........... 207
Rutland (D3)*.............. 486
Sadorus (E4)*.............. 388
Sailor Springs (E5)*..... 259
St. Anne (F2)*...............1,403
St. Augustine (C3)*...... 198
St. Charles (E2)*..........6,709
St. David (C3)*............ 812
St. Elmo (E4)*..............1,716
St. Francisville (F5)*....1,117
St. Jacob (D5)*............ 478
St. James (E5)*............ 60
St. Johns (D5)............. 275
St. Joseph (E3)*........... 941
St. Libory (D5)*........... 324
St. Peter (E5)*............. 354
St. Rose (D5)............... 125
Ste. Marie (E5)*........... 352
Salem (E5)*..................6,159
San Jose (D3)*............ 562
Sandoval (D5)*.............1,531
Sandusky (D6).............. 350
Sandwich (E2)*.............3,027
Saunemin (E3)*............ 338
Savanna (C1)*...............5,058
Savoy (E3)*.................. 145
Sawyerville (D4)*......... 390
Saybrook (E3)*............ 758
Scales Mound (C1)*...... 385
Schiller Park (A1)*......1,384
Schram City (D4)......... 793
Sciota (C3)*................ 128
Scottland (F4)*............ 100
Scottville (C4)*............ 200
Seaton (C2)*............... 285
Seatonville (D2)*.......... 405
Secor (D3)*.................. 375
Seneca (E2)*.................1,435
Serena (E2)*................ 165
Sesser (D5)*..................2,086
Seymour (E3)*............. 275
Shabbona (E2)*............ 667
Shannon (D1)*............. 668
Shattuc (D5)*............... 200
Shawneetown (E6)*......1,917
Sheffield (D2)*............. 995
Shelbyville (E4)*..........4,462
Sheldon (F3)*................1,114
Sheridan (E2)*............. 476
Sherman (D4)*.............
Sherrard (C2)*............. 484
Shiloh (B6).................. 453
Shipman (C4)*.............. 376
Shirland (D1)*..............
Shirley (E3)*................ 140
Shobonier (D5)*........... 315
Shumway (E4)*............ 248
Sibley (E3)*.................. 345
Sidell (F4)*................... 554
Sidney (E3)*................. 653
Sigel (E4)*.................... 296
Silvis (C2)*...................3,055
Simpson (E6)*.............. 119
Sims (E5)*.................... 408
Skokie (B1)*...............14,832
Smithboro (D5)*........... 253
Smithfield (C3)*........... 355
Smithshire (C3)*........... 150
Smithton (C5)*............. 515
Somonauk (E2)*........... 721
Sorento (D5)*............... 692
S. Beloit (E1)*..............3,221
S. Chicago Hts. (B3).....2,129
S. Elgin (E2)*...............1,220
S. Holland (B2)*............3,247
S. Jacksonville (C4)......1,165
S. Pekin (D3)*...............1,043
S. Standard (D4)*........ 192
S. Wilmington (E2)*.... 662
Southern View ‡(D4).... 898
Sparland (D2)*............ 509
Sparta (D5)*..................3,576
Spaulding (D4)............ 211
Spillertown ‡(E6)........ 196
Spring Bay (D3)........... 203
Spring Garden (E5)......
Spring Grove (E1)*....... 269
Spring Valley (D2)*......4,916
Springerton (E5)*........ 279
SPRINGFIELD (D4)*..81,628
Springfield (urban
area) 96,649
Standard (D2)*............ 290
Standard City (South
Standard*) (D4)........ 192
Stanford (D3)*............. 457
Staunton (D5)*..............4,047
Steeleville (D6)*...........1,353
Steger (F2)*..................4,358
Sterling (D2)*..............12,817
Steward (D2)*.............. 270
Stewardson (E4)*......... 666
Stickney (B2)................3,317
Stillman Valley (D1)*... 362
Stillwell (B3)*.............. 100
Stockland (F3)*............ 149
Stockton (C1)*...............1,445
Stone Park ‡(A2).........1,414
Stonefort (E6)*............ 490
Stonington (D4)*..........1,120
Stoy (F5)*.................... 161
Strasburg (E4)*............ 436
Strawn (E3)*................ 173
Streator (E2)*..............16,469
Stronghurst (C3)*........ 741
Sublette (D2)*.............. 290
Sullivan (E4)*...............3,470
Summer Hill (C4)*........ 145
Summerfield (D5)*....... 378
Summit (B2)*................8,957
Summum (C3)*............. 225
Sumner (F5)*................1,170
Sunfield (D5)...............
Swan Creek (C3)*........ 160
Swansea (B6)................1,816
Swanwick (D5)*............ 154
Sycamore (E2)*.............5,912
Symerton (F2)*............ 119
Table Grove (C3)*........ 481
Tallula (D4)*................ 527
Tamalco (D5)*.............. 50
Tamaroa (D5)*............. 849
Tamms (D6)*............... 665
Tampico (D2)*.............. 760
Taylor Spgs. (D4)*....... 627
Taylorville (D4)*...........9,188
Tennessee (C3)*........... 249
Terre Haute (C3).........
Teutopolis (E4)*........... 919
Thackeray (E5)*........... 100
Thawville (E3)*............ 267
Thayer (D4)*................ 695
Thebes (D6)*................ 541
Thomasboro (E3)*........ 330
Thompsonville (E6)*..... 530
Thomson (C2)*............. 559
Thornton (B3)*..............1,217
Tiedtville (A2)..............
Tilden (D5)*................. 906
Tilton (F3)*...................1,638
Time (C4)..................... 57
Timewell (C3)*............. 184
Tinley Park (B2)*.........2,326
Tioga (B3)*.................. 90
Tiskilwa (D2)*.............. 962
Toledo (E4)*................ 905
Tolono (E3)*..................1,065
Toluca (D2)*..................1,419
Tonica (E2)*................ 585
Tonti (E5).................... 100
Topeka (D3)*................ 72
Torino ‡(E2)................ 9
Toulon (D2)*..................1,173
Tovey (D4)*.................. 593
Towanda (E3)*............. 400
Tower Hill (E4)*........... 784
Tremont (D3)*...............1,138
Trenton (D5)*................1,432
Trilla (E4)*................... 250
Trimble (F4)*................ 165
Triumph (E2)*..............
Trivoli (D3)*................. 395
Troy (B6)*.....................1,260
Troy Grove (E2)*.......... 258
Tuscola (E4)*.................2,960
Ullin (D6)*.................... 772
Union (E1)*.................. 435
Union Hill ‡(E2)*........ 138
Unionville (E6)............. 140
Urbain ‡(E6)................ 57
Urbana (E3)*...............22,835
Ursa (B3)*.................... 400
Utica (E2)*................... 985
Valier (D5)*.................. 808
Valley City (C4)*.......... 200
Valmeyer (C5)*............ 656
Van Orin (D2)*............. 105
Vandalia (D5)*...............5,471
Varna (D2)*.................. 400
Venedy (D5)*................ 149
Venice (A6)*..................6,226
Vera (D4)..................... 125
Vergennes (D6)*........... 312
Vermilion (F4)*............. 316
Vermilion Grove (F4)*.. 200
Vermont (C3)*............... 940
Vernon (D5)*................ 243
Verona (E2)*................ 205
Versailles (C4)*............ 472
Victoria (C2)*............... 472
Vienna (E6)*..................1,085
Villa Grove (E4)*...........2,026
Villa Park (A2)*..............8,821
Villa Ridge (D6)*.......... 550
Viola (C2)*................... 826
Virden (D4)*..................3,206
Virginia (C4)*.................1,572
Wadsworth (F1)*.......... 500
Waggoner (D4)*........... 239
Walnut (D2)*..................1,093
Walnut Grove (C3)*...... 77
Walnut Hill (E5)*.......... 156
Walshville (D4)*........... 113
Waltonville (D5)*.......... 459
Wamac (D5)...................1,429
Wapella (E3)*............... 504
Warren (C1)*..................1,378
Warrensburg (D4)*....... 549
Warsaw (B3)*.................2,002
Washburn (D3)*............ 999
Washington (D3)*..........4,285
Washington Park (B6)*5,840
Wasson (E6)................. 300
Wataga (C2)*............... 550
Waterloo (C5)*...............2,821
Waterman (E2)*............ 750
Watseka (F3)*.................4,235
Watson (E4)*................ 288
Wauconda (E1)*..............1,173
Waukegan (F1)*...........38,946
Waverly (D4)*..................1,330
Wayne City (E5)*.......... 726
Waynesville (D3)*......... 516
Weldon (E3)*............... 492
Welland (D2)................ 60
Wellington (F3)*........... 300
Wenona (E2)*................1,005
Wenonah (D4).............. 125
West Brooklyn (D2)*.... 194
W. Chicago (E2)*............3,973
W. City (E5)...................1,081
W. Dundee (Dundee*)
(E1) 1,948
W. Frankfort (E6)*.....11,384
W. Jersey (D2)............. 75
W. Liberty (E5)*.......... 150
W. Point (B3)*.............. 275
W. Salem (F5)*............. 902
W. Union (F4)*............. 375
W. York (F4)................ 250
Westchester (A2).........4,308
Western Springs (A2)*.6,364
Westervelt (E4)*.......... 200
Westfield (F4)*............ 661
Westmont (A2)*.............3,402
Weston (E3)*............... 150
Westville (F3)*...............3,196
Wheaton (E2)*.............11,638
Wheeler (E4)*.............. 178
Wheeling (F1)*............. 916
White City (D4)........... 275
White Hall (C4)*............3,082
White Heath (E3)*....... 250
Whiteash ‡(E6)............ 204
Whittington (E5)*......... 200
Wichert (F2)*............... 250
Williamsfield (C3)*....... 542
Williamson (D5)........... 319
Williamsville (D4)*...... 656
Willisville (D6)*........... 635
Willow Hill (E5)*.......... 333
Willow Springs (A2)*...1,314
Wilmette (B1)*..........18,162
Wilmington (Patterson*)
(C4) 147
Wilmington (E2)*..........3,354
Wilsonville (D4)*.......... 822
Winchester (C4)*..........1,591
Windsor (E4)*................1,008
Windsor (New Windsor*)
(C2) 569
Winfield (E2)*.............. 714
Wing (E3).................... 50
Winkle (D5).................. 114
Winnebago (D1)*.......... 752
Winnetka (B1)*...........12,105
Winslow (D1)*.............. 355
Winthrop Harbor (F1)*1,765
Witt (D4)*......................1,156
Woburn (D5)................. 110
Wolf Lake (D6)*........... 135
Wood Dale (A1)*...........1,857
Wood River (B6)*........10,190
Woodbine (C1)*...........
Woodhull (C2)*............ 718
Woodland (F3)*............ 334
Woodlawn (D5)*........... 320
Woodson (C4)*............. 211
Woodstock (E1)*...........7,192
Woodworth (F3)........... 89
Woosung (D2)*............. 167
Worden (B6)*............... 968
Worth (A2)*....................1,472
Wrights (C4)*............... 150
Wyanet (D2)*............... 950
Wyoming (D2)*..............1,496
Xenia (E5)*.................. 643
Yale (E4)*..................... 153
Yates City (C3)*........... 623
Yorkville (E2)*.............. 632
Zeigler (D6)*..................2,516
Zenith (E5)................... 59
Zion (F1)*......................8,950

Map on Page 61

INDIANA

Total Population 3,934,224

92 COUNTIES

Adams (H3)...............22,393
Allen (G2)...............183,722
Bartholomew (F6)......36,108
Benton (C3)..............11,462
Blackford (G4)...........14,026
Boone (E4)................23,993
Brown (E6).................6,209
Carroll (D3)...............16,010
Cass (E3)...................38,793
Clark (F8)..................48,330
Clay (C6)...................23,918
Clinton (E4)...............29,734
Crawford (E8)..............9,289
Daviess (C7)..............26,762
De Kalb (H2)..............26,023
Dearborn (H6).............25,141
Decatur (G6)..............18,218
Delaware (G4)............90,252
Dubois (D8)................23,785
Elkhart (F1)...............84,512
Fayette (G5)...............23,391
Floyd (F8)..................43,955
Fountain (C4).............17,836
Franklin (G6)..............16,034
Fulton (E2).................16,565
Gibson (B8)................30,720
Grant (F3)..................62,156
Greene (D6)................27,886
Hamilton (E4)..............28,491
Hancock (F5)...............20,332
Harrison (E8)..............17,858
Hendricks (D5)............24,594
Henry (G5)..................45,505
Howard (E4)................54,498
Huntington (G3).........31,400
Jackson (E7)...............28,237
Jasper (C2).................17,031
Jay (G4)......................23,157
Jefferson (G7).............21,613
Jennings (F7)..............15,250
Johnson (E6)...............26,183
Knox (C7)....................43,415
Kosciusko (F2)............33,002
La Porte (D1)..............76,808
La Grange (G1)............15,347
Lake (C2)..................368,152
Lawrence (E7).............34,346
Madison (F4)..............103,911
Marion (E5)...............551,777
Marshall (E2)..............29,468
Martin (D7).................10,678
Miami (E3)..................28,201
Monroe (D6)................50,080
Montgomery (D4)........29,122
Morgan (E6)................23,726
Newton (C3)................11,006
Noble (G2)...................25,075
Ohio (H7)......................4,223
Orange (E7)................16,879
Owen (D6)...................11,763
Parke (C5)...................15,674
Perry (D8)....................17,367
Pike (C8)......................14,995
Porter (C2)...................40,076
Posey (B8)...................19,818
Pulaski (D2).................12,493
Putnam (D5).................22,950
Randolph (G4)..............27,141
Ripley (G6)...................18,763
Rush (G5).....................19,799
Saint Joseph (E1)....205,058
Scott (F7).....................11,519
Shelby (F5)...................28,026
Spencer (C9).................16,174
Starke (D2)...................15,282
Steuben (G1).................17,087
Sullivan (C6).................23,667
Switzerland (G7).............7,599
Tippecanoe (D4)............74,473
Tipton (E4)....................15,566
Union (H5)......................6,412
Vanderburgh (B8).....160,422

Vermillion (C5)..........19,723
Vigo (C6)...............105,160
Wabash (F3)..............29,047
Warren (C4)................8,535
Warrick (C8)..............21,527
Washington (E7)........16,520
Wayne (G5)...............68,566
Wells (G3).................19,564
White (D3)..................18,042
Whitley (F2)...............18,828

CITIES and TOWNS

Abington (H5)............ 200
Aboite (G3)............ 50
Acton (E5)*............
Adams (F6)*............ 350
Adamsboro (E3)............ 150
Ade (C3)............ 90
Advance (D5)*............ 413
Aix (C2)............
Akron (E2)*............ 946
Aladdin ‡(F4)............ 19
Alamo (C5)*............ 163
Albany (G4)*............1,846
Albion (G2)*............1,341
Aldine (D2)............ 75
Alert (F6)............ 110
Alexandria (F4)*............5,147
Alfordsville (C7)*............ 101
Algiers (C7)*............ 102
Alpine (G5)*............ 55
Alquina (G5)............ 114
Alton (E8)*............ 71
Altona (G2)............ 344
Alvarado (H1)............
Ambia (C4)*............ 356
Amboy (F3)*............ 414
Americus (D3)............ 105
Amity (E6)............ 150
Amo (D5)*............ 354
Anderson (F4)*............46,820
Andersonville (G5)............ 250
Andrews (F3)*............1,083
Angola (G1)*............5,081
Anthony (G4)............ 50
Antiville (G3)............ 14
Apalona (D8)*............ 14
Arba (H4)............ 84
Arcadia (E4)*............1,073
Arcola (G2)*............ 272
Ardmore (E1)............
Argos (E2)*............1,284
Ari (G2)............ 29
Arlington (F5)*............ 430
Armstrong (B8)*............ 155
Aroma (F4)............ 30
Arthur (C8)............ 225
Artic (H2)............ 50
Ash Grove (D3)............ 14
Ashboro (C6)............ 100
Asherville (C6)............
Ashley (G1)*............ 680
Athens (E2)*............ 105
Atlanta (E4)*............ 613
Attica (C4)*............3,862
Atwood (F2)*............ 300
Auburn (G2)*............5,879
Augusta (C8)............ 117
Aurora (H6)*............4,780
Austin (F7)*............2,906
Avilla (G2)*............ 669
Avoca (D7)*............ 400
Azalia (F6)............ 100
Bacon (E8)............
Bainbridge (D5)*............ 455
Bakers Corner (E4)...... 75
Ballstown (G6)............ 3
Bandon (D8)*............
Banquo (F3)............ 105
Bargersville (E5)*............ 413
Bartonia (H4)............ 26
Bass (D2)............ 40
Batesville (G6)*............3,194
Bath (H5)*............ 95
Battle Ground (D3)*...... 634
Bean Blossom (E6)............ 74
Bear Branch (G7)............ 120
Beard (E4)............ 20
Beardstown (D2)............ 50
Bedford (E7)*............12,562
Beech Grove (E5)*............5,685
Belle Union (D5)............ 75
Belleville (E5)............
Bellmore (C5)*............ 120
Belshaw (C2)............ 100
Bengal (F6)............ 35
Bennetts Switch (E3)...... 120
Bennington (G7)*............ 50
Benton (F2)*............ 225
Bentonville (G5)*............ 77
Berne (H3)*............2,277
Bethlehem (G7)*............ 200
Beverly Shores (C1)*...... 488
Bicknell (C7)*............4,572
Billingsville (H5)............ 35
Bippus (F3)*............ 200
Birdseye (D8)*............ 354
Blackhawk (C6)............ 100
Blackoak (C1)............
Blaine (G4)............ 25
Blairville (B8)............
Blanford (B5)*............ 750
Blocher (F7)*............ 250
Bloomfield (D6)*............2,086
Blooming Grove (G5)...... 105
Bloomingdale (C5)*...... 434
Bloomingport (G5)............ 60
Bloomington (D6)*......28,163
Blountsville (G4)*............ 229
Blue Ridge (F5)............ 100
Bluegrass (E3)............ 50
Bluffton (G3)*............6,076
Boggstown (F5)*............ 149
Bono (E7)............ 25
Boone Grove (C2)*............ 170
Boonville (C8)*............5,092
Borden (F8)*............ 426
Boston (H5)*............ 257
Boswell (C3)*............ 963
Boundary (H4)............ 35
Bourbon (E2)*............1,404
Bowers (D4)............ 25
Bowling Green (D6)*...... 235
Boyleston (E4)............ 110
Bracken (F3)............ 9
Bradford (E8)*............ 119
Branchville (D8)*............ 75
Brazil (C5)*............8,434
Bremen (E2)*............2,664
Brems (D2)............ 112
Brewersville (F6)............ 62
Brice (H4)............ 12
Bridgeport (E5)*............ 500
Bridgeton (C5)*............ 350
Bright (H6)............ 275
Brighton (G1)............ 100
Brimfield (G2)*............ 210
Brinckley (G4)............
Bringhurst (E3)*............ 253
Bristol (F1)*............ 738
Bristow (D8)*............
Bromer (E7)............ 75
Bronson (Losantville*) (G4)............ 247
Brook (C3)*............ 915
Brooklyn (E5)*............ 592
Brooksburg (G7)*............ 132
Brookston (D3)*............1,014
Brookville (G6)*............2,538
Browns Corner (F3)...... 35
Browns Valley (D5)...... 125
Brownsburg (E5)*............1,578
Brownstown (F7)*............1,998
Brownsville (H5)*............ 275
Bruceville (C7)*............ 800
Brunswick (B2)............ 150
Brushy Prairie (G1)...... 100
Bryant (G3)*............ 339
Bryantsburg (G7)............ 35
Buck Creek (D4)*............ 279
Buckeye (G3)............ 25
Buckskin (C8)*............ 250
Bud (E6)............ 10
Buena Vista (G6)............
Buffalo (D3)*............ 135
Buffaloville (D8)*............
Bullock (C9)............ 39
Bunker Hill (B7)............ 500
Bunker Hill (E3)*............ 659
Burdick (D1)............
Burket (F2)*............ 217
Burlington (E4)*............ 600
Burnettsville (D3)*............ 457
Burney (F6)*............ 232
Burns City (D7)*............ 242
Burnsville (F6)............
Burr Oak (E2)*............ 120
Burrows (E3)*............ 350
Butler (H2)*............1,914
Butlerville (F6)*............ 306
Byron (C5)............ 50
Caborn (B9)............ 50
Cadiz (G5)............ 222
Cale (D7)............ 60
Calvertsville (D6)............ 22
Cambria (D4)............ 70
Cambridge City (G5)*...2,559
Camden (D3)*............ 600
Cammack (G4)............ 200
Campbellsburg (E7)*...... 637
Canaan (G7)*............ 270
Cannelburg (C7)*............ 128
Cannelton (D9)*............2,027
Canton (E7)............ 125
Cape Sandy (E8)*............
Carbon (C5)*............ 480
Carlisle (C7)*............ 767
Carlos (G4)*............ 120
Carmel (E5)*............1,009
Carp (D6)............ 30
Carpentersville (D5)...... 80
Cartersburg (E5)*............ 260
Carthage (F5)*............1,065
Cass (C6)*............
Cassville (E3)............ 100
Castleton (E5)*............ 268
Cataract (D6)............ 46
Cates (C4)*............ 150
Catlin (C5)*............
Cato (C8)............
Cayuga (C5)*............1,022
Cedar Grove (H6)*............ 193
Cedar Lake (C2)*............3,907
Cedarville (G2)............ 220
Celestine (D8)*............ 120
Centenary (B5)............ 200
Center (E4)*............ 275
Center Square (H7)...... 55
Centerpoint (C6)*............ 297
Centerton (E5)*............ 125
Centerville (H5)*............1,386
Central (E8)*............ 40
Chalmers (D3)*............ 508
Chambersburg (E7)...... 200
Chandler (C8)*............1,050
Chapel Hill (E6)............ 6
Charlestown (F8)*............4,785
Charlottesville (F5)*...... 400
Chase (C3)............ 40
Chelsea (F7)............ 35
Cherry Grove (D4)............ 15
Chester (H5)............ 102
Chesterfield (F4)*............1,086
Chesterton (D1)*............3,175
Chili (F3)*............ 115
Chrisney (C8)*............ 439
Churubusco (G2)*............1,232
Cicero (E4)*............1,021
Clare (F4)............ 75
Clarks Hill (D4)*............ 493
Clarksburg (G6)*............ 325
Clarksville (F5)............ 117
Clarksville (F8)*............5,905
Clay City (C6)*............1,068
Claypool (F2)*............ 416
Claysburg (F8)............
Clayton (D5)*............ 598
Clear Creek (E6)*............ 450
Clear Lake (H1)............ 151
Clear Springs (E7)............ 205
Clermont (E5)*............ 824
Clifford (F6)*............ 232
Clifty (F6)*............ 175
Clinton (C5)*............6,462
Cloverdale (D5)*............ 649
Cloverland (C6)............ 150
Clymers (E3)............ 150
Coal Bluff (C5)*............ 128
Coal City (D6)*............ 300
Coal Creek (C4)............ 75
Coalmont (C6)*............ 595
Coatesville (D5)*............ 444
Coe (C8)............
Coesse (G2)*............ 150
Colburn (D3)*............ 234
Colfax (D4)*............ 75
Collamer (F2)............ 15
Collegeville (C3)*............ 600
Collett (H4)............ 30
Collins (G2)............
Columbia City (G2)*...4,745
Columbus (E6)*............18,370
Commiskey (F7)*............ 100
Concord (H2)............
Connersville (G5)*......15,550
Conroe (D4)............
Converse (F3)*............ 979
Cook (C2)............ 350
Cope (E6)............ 50
Corning (D7)............ 49
Correct (G7)............ 150
Cortland (F7)*............ 102
Corunna (G2)*............ 338
Cory (C6)*............ 250
Corydon (E8)*............1,944
Cosperville (F1)............ 45
Cottage Grove (H5)*...... 100
Covington (C4)*............2,235
Cowan (G4)*............ 400
Coxville (C5)............ 56
Craigville (G3)*............
Crandall (E8)*............ 149
Crane (D4)............ 21
Crane (D7)*............2,000
Crawfordsville (D4)*......12,851
Cresco (F2)............
Creston (C2)*............ 110
Crete (H4)............ 25
Crisman (C1)............ 300
Crocker (C1)............ 150
Cromwell (F2)*............ 449
Crooked Creek (G1)............
Cross Plains (G7)*............ 150
Crothersville (F7)*............1,276
Crown Center (D5)............
Crown Point (C2)*............5,839
Crows Nest ‡(E5)............ 86
Crumstown (E1)............ 200
Crystal (D8)............ 61
Cuba (D6)............ 17
Culver (E2)*............1,563
Cumback (C7)............ 50
Cumberland (F5)*............ 550
Curtisville (F4)*............ 122
Cutler (D4)*............ 165
Cuzco (D8)*............ 55
Cyclone (E4)............ 70
Cynthiana (B8)*............ 591
Cypress (B9)............
Dabney (G6)............ 50
Dale (D8)*............ 850
Daleville (F4)*............
Dana (C5)*............ 854
Danville (D5)*............2,802
Darlington (D4)*............ 711
Daylight (B8)............
Dayton (D4)*............ 650
Decatur (H3)*............7,271
Decker (B7)*............ 386
Deedsville (E3)*............ 150
Deer Creek (E3)............ 120
Deerfield (H4)............ 100
Delaware (G6)............ 229
Delong (E2)*............ 120
Delphi (D3)*............2,530
Demotte (C2)*............ 700
Denham (D2)*............ 150
Denver (E3)*............ 528
Depauw (E8)*............ 155
Deputy (F7)*............ 250
Derby (D8)*............ 73
Desoto (G4)*............ 205
Dexter (E8)............ 1
Diamond (C5)............
Dillman (G3)............ 30
Dillsboro (G6)*............ 681
Disko (E2)*............ 150
Doans (D7)*............ 30
Dolan (E6)............ 24
Domestic (G3)............ 26
Donaldson (E2)*............
Doolittle Mills (D8)*............
Dora (F3)............ 80
Dover (H6)............ 100
Dover Hill (D7)............ 150
Downey's Corner (H7)... 25
Dublin (G5)*............ 993
Dubois (D8)*............ 451
Dudleytown (F7)............ 65
Duff (C8)............ 68
Dugger (C6)*............1,204
Dundee (F4)............ 56
Dune Acres (C1)............ 86
Dunfee (G2)............ 45
Dunkirk (G4)*............3,048
Dunlap (F1)............1,154
Dunnington (C3)............ 20
Dunreith (G5)*............ 196
Dupont (G7)*............
Durbin (F4)............ 24
Dyer (C1)*............1,556
Eagletown (E4)............ 100
Earl Park (C3)*............ 488
East Chicago (C1)*....54,263
East Columbus (F6)............
East Enterprise (H7)*.. 125
East Gary (C1)*............5,635
East Germantown (Pershing*) (G5)....... 389
Eaton (G4)*............1,598
Eby (C8)............ 26
Eckerty (D8)*............ 180
Economy (G5)*............ 285
Eden (F5)............ 94
Edgerton (H2)*............ 112
Edgewood (F4)............ 796
Edinburg (E6)*............3,283
Edwardsport (C7)*............ 850
Edwardsville (F8)............ 120
Effner (C3)............ 50
Ege (G2)............ 50
Ekin (E4)............ 50
Elberfeld (C8)*............ 499
Elizabeth (F8)*............ 211
Elizabethtown (F6)*...... 323
Elizaville (E4)............ 51
Elkhart (F1)*............35,556
Elkinsville (E6)............ 25
Ellettsville (D6)*............ 855
Elmdale (D4)............ 75
Elnora (C7)*............ 849
Elon (D8)............
Elrod (G6)............ 66
Elston (D4)............ 40
Elwood (F4)*............11,362
Eminence (D5)*............ 175
Emison (C7)*............ 90
Emma (F1)............ 50
Emporia (F5)............ 65
English (E8)*............ 839
English Lake (D2)*...... 148
Enochsburg (G6)............ 40
Enos (C2)............ 25
Epsom (C7)............ 125
Etna (E8)............ 10
Etna (F2)............
Etna Green (E2)*............ 444
Eugene (B5)............ 350
Eureka (C9)............ 75
Evans Landing (F8)............
Evanston (D8)*............ 39
Evansville (C9)*............128,636
Evansville (urban area)............133,200
Everton (G5)............
Fair Oaks (C2)*............ 200
Fairbanks (B6)*............
Fairland (F5)*............ 750
Fairmount (F4)*............2,646
Fairview (G4)............ 52
Fairview (G7)............ 54
Fairview Park (C5)............ 902
Falmouth (G5)*............ 200
Farlen (D7)............ 7
Farmers Retreat (G7).. 70
Farmersburg (C6)*............1,024
Farmland (C4)*............ 943
Fayette (E5)............ 98
Fayetteville (D7)............ 50
Fenns (F6)............ 40
Ferdinand (D8)*............1,252
Ferndale (C5)............ 15
Fiat (G3)............ 50
Fickle (D4)............ 10
Fillmore (D5)*............ 375
Fincastle (D5)............ 75
Finly (F5)*............
Fishers (E5)*............ 219
Fishersburg (F4)............ 130
Flat Rock (F6)*............ 196
Flint (G1)............ 100
Flora (E3)*............1,657
Florence (H7)*............
Florida (F4)............ 100
Floyds Knobs (F8)*...... 455
Folsomville (C8)*............
Fontanet (C5)*............
Foraker (F1)*............ 144
Foresman (C3)............ 90
Forest (E4)*............ 400
Forest Hill (F6)............
Fort Branch (B8)*............1,944
Fort Ritner (E7)*............ 150
Fort Wayne (G2)*............133,607
Fort Wayne (urban area)............139,529
Fortville (F5)*............1,786
Foster (C4)............ 25
Fountain (C4)............ 50
Fountain City (H5)*...... 588
Fountaintown (F5)*...... 250
Fowler (C3)*............2,117
Fowlerton (F4)*............ 292
Francesville (D3)*............ 856
Francisco (B8)*............ 606
Frankfort (E4)*............15,028
Franklin (E6)*............7,316
Frankton (F4)*............1,047
Fredericksburg (E8)*...... 211
Fredonia (E8)*............
Free (C3)............ 4
Freedom (D6)*............ 175
Freeland Park (C3)*...... 94
Freelandville (C7)*...... 789
Freeman (D6)............ 28
Freeport (F5)............ 60
Freetown (E7)*............ 500
Fremont (H1)*............ 947
French (H6)............ 75
French Lick (D7)*............1,946
Friendship (G7)*............ 130
Friendswood (E5)............ 115
Fritchton (C7)............ 125
Fulda (D8)*............ 100
Fulton (E3)*............ 366
Galena (F8)............ 207
Galveston (E3)*............ 905
Garrett (G2)*............4,291
Gary (C1)*............133,911
Gas City (F4)*............3,787
Gaston (G4)*............ 729
Gatchel (D8)............ 20
Geetingsville (D4)............ 25
Gem (F5)............
Geneva (H3)*............ 999
Gentryville (C8)*............ 234
Georgetown (F8)*............ 449
Georgia (D7)............ 10
Gerald (D9)*............
Gessie (C4)*............ 115
Gifford (D2)............ 43
Gilead (E3)............ 75
Gilman (F4)............ 12
Gimco City ‡(F4)............ 13
Gings (G5)............ 45
Glendale (C7)............ 150
Glenn (C6)............ 75
Glenwood (G5)*............ 412
Glezen (C8)*............ 400
Glidas (E8)............ 10
Gnaw Bone (E6)............ 2
Goblesville (G3)............ 57
Goldsmith (E4)*............ 242
Goodland (C3)*............1,218
Goshen (F1)*............13,003
Gosport (D6)*............ 672
Grabill (H2)*............ 370
Grafton (B9)............ 50
Grammer (F6)*............ 125
Grand View (C9)*............ 664
Granger (E1)*............ 160
Grantsburg (E8)*............ 90
Grasscreek (E3)*............ 105
Gravelton (F2)............ 40
Graysville (B6)*............ 100
Green Center (G2)............ 20
Green Hill (C4)............ 50
Green Oak (E2)............ 4
Greencastle (D5)*............6,888
Greendale (H6)*............2,018
Greenfield (F5)*............6,159
Greenfield Mills (G1)...... 25
Greens Fork (H5)*............ 413
Greensboro (G5)*............ 241
Greensburg (G6)*............6,599
Greentown (E4)*............1,160
Greenville (F8)*............ 298
Greenwood (E5)*............3,066
Griffin (B8)*............ 249
Griffith (C1)*............4,470
Groveland (D5)............ 30
Grovertown (D2)*............ 200
Groves (G5)............
Guilford (H6)*............ 300
Guion (C5)............ 14
Guthrie (D7)............
Gwynneville (F5)*............ 244
Hackleman (F4)............ 30
Hadley (D5)............ 50
Hagerstown (G5)*............1,694
Hall (E5)*............ 125
Hamilton (H1)*............ 376
Hamlet (D2)*............ 659
Hammond (B1)*............87,594
Hancock (E8)............ 50
Hanna (D2)*............ 450
Hanover (F7)*............1,060
Hardinsburg (E8)*............ 247
Harlan (H2)*............ 500
Harmony (C5)*............ 650
Harrisburg (G5)............
Harrisville (H4)............ 83
Harrodsburg (D6)*............ 400
Hartford City (G4)*.....7,253
Hartsville (F6)*............ 340
Hastings (F2)............ 35
Hatfield (C9)*............
Haubstadt (B8)*............ 894
Hayden (F7)*............ 200
Haymond (G6)............ 20
Haysville (D8)............ 352
Hazelrigg (D4)............ 45
Hazelwood (D5)............
Hazleton (B8)*............ 498
Headlee (D3)............ 69
Heath (D4)............ 12
Hebron (C2)*............1,010
Hedrick (C4)*............ 68
Heilman (C8)............ 100
Helmer (G1)*............ 110
Helmsburg (E6)*............ 150
Heltonville (E7)*............ 500
Hemlock (F4)*............ 177
Henderson (F5)............ 68
Henryville (F7)*............
Herbst (F3)*............ 250
Hibbard (E2)*............ 100
Highland (B1)*............5,878
Highwoods ‡(F5)............ 40
Hillham (D7)............
Hillisburg (E4)*............ 225
Hillsboro (C4)*............ 526
Hillsdale (C5)*............ 250
Hoagland (H3)*............ 375
Hobart (C1)*............10,244
Hobbieville (D6)............ 125
Hobbs (F4)*............ 185
Holland (C8)*............ 501
Hollandsburg (C5)............ 25
Holton (G6)*............ 400
Home Corner (Vet's Adm. Hosp.*) (F3)....3,950
Homer (F5)*............ 105
Homestead (H6)............
Honey Creek (F4)*............ 125
Hoover (E3)............ 75
Hope (F6)*............1,215
Hortonville (E4)............ 125
Houston (E6)............ 75
Howe (G1)*............ 576
Howesville (C6)............ 75
Hudson (G1)*............ 420
Hudsonville (C7)............ 76
Huntertown (G2)*............ 500
Huntingburg (D8)*............4,056
Huntington (G3)*............15,079
Huntsville (G4)............ 50
Huntsville (F4)............ 265
Hurlburt (C2)............ 18
Huron (D7)*............
Hymera (C6)*............1,069
Idaville (D3)*............ 500
Independence (C4)............ 200
Indian Springs (D7)*...... 115
Indian Village (E1)............ 57
INDIANAPOLIS (E5)*............427,173
Indianapolis (urban area)............499,799
Ingalls (F5)*............ 666
Inglefield (B8)*............ 100
Inwood (E2)*............ 178
Ireland (C8)*............ 325
Jacksonburg (G5)............ 94
Jalapa (F3)............ 150
Jamestown (D5)*............ 718
Jasonville (C6)*............2,937
Jasper (D8)*............5,215
Jefferson (D4)............ 90
Jeffersonville (F8)*......14,685
Jessup (C5)............ 67
Jimtown (E1)............ 200
Johnson (B8)............ 250
Jolietville (E4)............ 125
Jonesboro (F4)*............1,973
Jonesville (F6)*............ 225
Judson (C5)*............ 96
Judyville (C4)*............ 90
Keller (C6)............ 25
Kempton (E4)*............ 438
Kendallville (G2)*............6,119
Kennard (G5)*............ 485
Kenneth (E3)............ 40
Kent (F7)*............ 123
Kentland (C3)*............1,633
Kersey (C2)*............ 100
Kewanna (E2)*............ 680
Keystone (G3)*............ 225
Kimmell (F2)*............ 300
Kingman (C5)*............ 509
Kingsbury (D1)*............ 281
Kingsford Heights (D2)*............1,104
Kingston (G6)............ 50
Kirklin (E4)*............ 734
Kirkpatrick (D4)............ 60
Kirksville (D6)............
Kitchel (H5)*............ 60
Knightstown (F5)*............2,486
Knightsville (C5)*............ 768
Kniman (C2)............ 150
Knox (D2)*............3,034
Kokomo (E4)*............38,672
Koleen (D7)*............
Kountz Lake (D2)............1,200
Kossuth (E7)............ 50
Kouts (C2)*............ 718
Kramer (C4)*............
Kurtz (E7)*............ 225
Kyana (D8)*............
La Crosse (D2)*............ 618
La Fontaine (F3)*............ 627
La Porte (D1)*............20,414
Laconia (E8)*............ 82
Ladoga (D5)*............ 912
Lafayette (D4)*............35,568
Lagrange (F1)*............1,892
Lagro (F3)*............ 545
Lake Bruce (E2)............ 100
Lake Cicott (D3)*............ 128
Lake James (H1)*............
Lake Village (C2)*............
Lakeland (D1)............2,172
Lakeside (D3)............ 10
Laketon (F3)*............
Lakeville (E1)*............ 736
Lamar (D8)*............ 99
Lamb (G7)............ 35
Lancaster (F7)............ 50
Landess (F3)*............ 135
Lanesville (E8)*............ 314
Laotto (G2)*............ 264
Lapaz (E2)*............ 512
Lapel (F4)*............1,389
Larwill (F2)*............ 316
Laud (G2)............
Lauer (D9)............
Laughery (H7)............
Laurel (G6)*............ 680
Lawrence (E5)............1,951
Lawrenceburg (H6)*.....4,806
Lawrenceport (D7)............ 125
Lawrenceville (H6)............ 50
Lawton (D2)............ 20
Leavenworth (E8)*............ 358
Lebanon (D4)*............7,631
Lee (D3)............
Leesburg (F2)*............ 428
Leesville (E7)............ 75
Leipsic (E7)*............ 150
Leisure (F4)............ 20
Leiters Ford (E2)*............ 250
Lena (C5)............ 75
Leo (G2)............ 385
Leopold (D8)*............ 101
Leota (F7)............ 35
Leroy (C2)*............ 350
Letts (F6)*............ 208
Lewis (C6)*............ 600
Lewis Creek (F6)............ 62
Lewisville (G5)*............ 591
Lexington (F7)*............ 350
Liberty (H5)*............1,730
Liberty Center (G3)*............ 300
Liberty Mills (F2)*............ 200
Ligonier (F2)*............2,375
Limedale (D5)............
Lincoln (E3)*............ 130
Lincoln City (C8)*............
Lincolnville (F3)............ 200
Linden (D4)*............ 590
Linngrove (H3)*............
Linnsburg (D5)............ 75
Linton (C6)*............5,973
Linwood (F4)............ 72
Lisbon (G2)............ 67
Little York (F7)*............ 146
Livonia (E7)............ 185
Lizton (D5)*............ 276
Lochiel (C3)............ 38
Locust Point (F8)*............ 18
Logan (H6)............ 125
Logansport (E3)*............21,031
London (F5)*............ 135
Long Beach (D1)............1,103
Loogootee (D7)*............2,424
Lookout (G6)............ 16
Losantville (G4)*............ 247
Lovett (F7)............ 52
Lowell (C2)*............1,621
Lucerne (E3)*............ 200
Luther (F2)............ 6
Lydick (E1)............1,175
Lyford (C5)............ 368
Lynhurst ‡(E5)............ 160
Lynn (H4)*............1,149
Lynnville (C8)*............ 404
Lyons (C7)*............ 695
Mace (D4)............ 90
Mackey (C8)*............ 170
Macy (E3)*............ 288
Madison (G7)*............7,506
Magley (G3)............ 50
Magnet (D8)*............ 73
Mahalasville (E6)............ 75
Majenica (F3)............ 97
Malden (C2)............ 50
Manchester (H6)............ 3

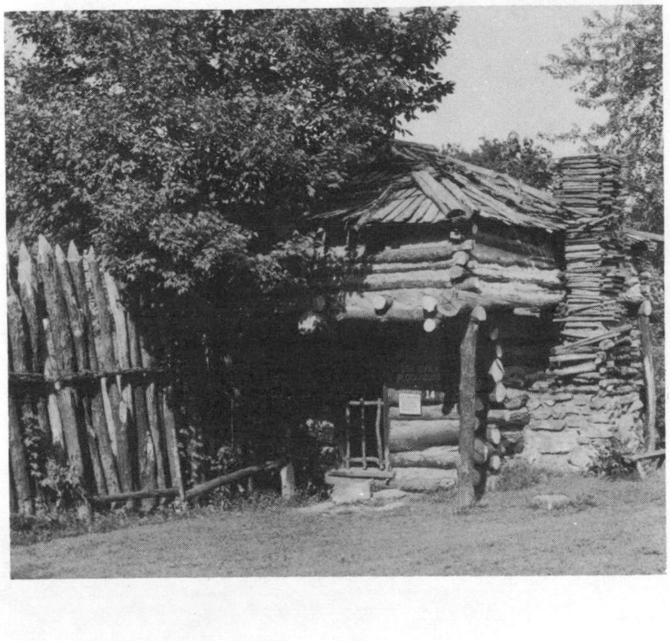

Manhattan (D5)..........
Manilla (F5)*............ 400
Mansfield (C5)............ 35
Manson (D4)............... 65
Maples (H2)............... 110
Marco (C7)*............... 195
Marengo (E8)*............ 801
Mariah Hill (D8)*........
Marietta (F6)............. 150
Marion (F3)*.............30,081
Markland (G7)............. 200
Markle (G3)*.............. 733
Markleville (F5)*......... 314
Marshall (C5)*............ 326
Marshfield (C4)*.......... 100
Martinsburg (E8).......... 125
Martinsville (D6)*........5,991
Marysville (F7)*.......... 98
Matthews (F4)*............ 501
Mauckport (E8)*........... 154
Maumee (E6)............... 25
Maxinkuckee (E2).......... 75
Maxwell (F5)*............. 285
Mays (G5)*................ 200
Maywood (E5)*............. 525
Mc Cool (C1)*............. 250
Mc Cordsville (F5)*....... 735
Mc Coysburg (C3)..........
Mc Grawsville (E3)........ 50
Mc Natts (G3)............. 25
Mecca (C5)*...............
Mechanicsburg (G5)........ 250
Medaryville (D2)*......... 833
Medora (E7)*.............. 627
Mellott (C4)*............. 266
Memphis (F8)*............. 380
Mentone (E2)*............. 798
Merom (B6)*............... 374
Merriam (G2).............. 110
Merrillville (C2)..........1,400
Metamora (G6)*............ 400
Metea (E3)................ 45
Metz (H1)*................ 175
Mexico (E3)*.............. 521
Miami (E3)*...............
Michigan City (C1)*.............28,395
Michigantown (E4)*........ 443
Middlebury (F1)*.......... 839
Middlefork (E4)........... 62
Middletown (F4)*..........1,731
Midland (C6)*.............
Midway (C8)............... 20
Mier (F3)................. 63
Milan (G6)*...............1,014
Milford (F2)*............. 952
Milford (Clifty*) (F6).... 175
Mill Creek (D1)*.......... 162
Millersburg (C8)..........
Millersburg (F1)*......... 437
Millgrove (G4)*........... 160
Millhousen (G6)*.......... 184
Milligan (C5)*............ 100
Milltown (E8)*............ 760
Millville (G5)............ 120
Milo (G3).................
Milroy (G6)*.............. 800
Milton (G5)*.............. 752
Mineral (D7).............. 55
Mishawaka (E1)*...........32,913
Mitchell (E7)*............3,245
Modoc (G4)*............... 275
Mohawk (F5)*.............. 150
Mongo (G1)*............... 225
Monitor (D4).............. 50
Monmouth (H3)............. 100
Monon (D3)*...............1,439
Monroe (H3)*.............. 428
Monroe City (C7)*......... 453
Monroeville (H3)*.........1,150
Monrovia (E5)*............ 375
Monterey (D2)*............ 250
Montezuma (C5)*...........1,220
Montgomery (C7)*.......... 538

Monticello (D3)*..........3,467
Montmorenci (D4)*......... 235
Montpelier (G3)*..........1,826
Moody (C3)................
Moore (H2)................ 30
Moorefield (G7)...........
Mooreland (G5)*........... 497
Moores Hill (G6)*......... 445
Mooresville (E5)*.........2,264
Moran (D4)*............... 140
Morgantown (E6)*.......... 838
Morocco (C3)*.............1,141
Morris (G6)*.............. 500
Morristown (F5)*.......... 679
Morton (D5)...............
Moscow (F6)...............
Mount Auburn ‡(G5)........ 164
Mt. Ayr (C3)*............. 222
Mt. Carmel (H6)........... 134
Mt. Comfort (F5)*......... 115
Mt. Etna (F3)............. 171
Mt. Meridian (D5).........
Mt. Pisgah (G1)........... 54
Mt. Pleasant (D8)*........ 24
Mt. Sterling (G7)......... 40
Mt. Summit (G4)*.......... 295
Mt. Vernon (B9)*..........6,150
Mt. Zion (G3)............. 30
Mulberry (D4)*............ 950
Muncie (G4)*..............58,479
Munster (B1)*.............4,753
Murray (G3)............... 94
Nabb (F7)*................ 110
Napoleon (G6)*............ 350
Nappanee (F2)*............3,393
Nashville (E6)*........... 526
Nead (E3)................. 48
Nebraska (F6)*............ 104
Needham (E5)*............. 110
Needmore (E7)............. 150
Nevada (F4)*.............. 45
Nevada Mills (G1)......... 75
New Albany (F8)*..........29,436
New Amsterdam (E8)........ 76
New Augusta (E5)*......... 225
New Bellsville (E6)....... 20
New Burlington (G4)....... 100
New Carlisle (E1)*........ 983
New Castle (G5)*..........18,271
New Chicago (C1).......... 921
New Corydon (H3)*......... 105
New Goshen (B5)*.......... 600
New Harmony (B8)*.........1,360
New Haven (H2)*...........2,336
New Holland (F3).......... 20
New Hope (D6)............. 11
New Lebanon (C6)*......... 125
New Lisbon (G5)*.......... 290
New London (E4)........... 210
New Marion (G6)........... 150
New Market (D5)*.......... 370
New Middletown (E8)*...... 153
New Mt. Pleasant (G4)..... 100
New Palestine (F5)*....... 504
New Paris (F2)*........... 985
New Pekin (F7)............ 543
New Philadelphia (F7)*
New Point (G6)*........... 322
New Providence (Borden*) (F8)........ 426
New Richmond (D4)*........ 391
New Ross (D5)*............ 336
New Salem (G5)............ 206
New Salisbury (E8)*....... 215
New Trenton (H6)*......... 150
New Washington (F7)*...... 750
New Waverly (E3)*......... 190
New Winchester (D5)....... 75
Newbern (F6)..............
Newberry (C7)*............ 340
Newburgh (C9)*............1,324
Newland (C2)..............
Newport (C5)*............. 660
Newton Stewart (D8)*...... 40

Newtonville (D8)*......... 123
Newtown (C4)*............. 287
Newville (H2)............. 75
Nineveh (E6)*............. 300
Noblesville (F4)*.........6,567
Norman (E7)*.............. 110
Norristown (F6)........... 75
North Grove (F3).......... 126
N. Hayden (B2)............ 150
N. Judson (D2)*...........1,705
N. Liberty (E1)*..........1,165
N. Madison (G7)*.......... 715
N. Manchester (F3)*.......3,977
N. Salem (D5)*............ 544
N. Terre Haute (C5)*......
N. Vernon (F6)*...........3,488
N. Webster (F2)*.......... 487
Norway (D3)...............
Notre Dame (E1)*..........5,000
Nulltown (G5).............
Oak (D3)*................. 150
Oak Forest (G6)........... 120
Oakford (E4)*............. 230
Oakland City (C8)*........3,539
Oaklandon (E5)*........... 346
Oaktown (C7)*............. 763
Oakville (G4)*............ 224
Oatsville (C8)............ 100
Obed (D2)*................ 100
Ockley (D4)*.............. 140
Odell (C4)................ 210
Odon (C7)*................1,177
Ogden Dunes (C1).......... 429
Oldenburg (G6)*........... 591
Olean (G7)................ 225
Oliver (B8)...............
Omega (F4)................ 50
Ontario (G1).............. 150
Onward (E3)*.............. 140
Oolitic (E7)*.............1,125
Ora (D2)*................. 140
Orange (G5)............... 200
Orangeville (D7).......... 85
Orestes (F4)*............. 482
Orland (G1)*.............. 386
Orleans (D7)*.............1,531
Osceola (E1)*.............1,091
Osgood (G6)*..............1,228
Ossian (G3)*.............. 761
Oswego (F2)...............
Otis (D1)*................
Otisco (F7)*.............. 250
Otterbein (C4)*........... 641
Otto (G7).................
Otwell (C8)*.............. 400
Owensburg (D7)*........... 400
Owensville (B8)*..........1,110
Oxford (C3)*.............. 888
Packertown (F2)........... 72
Palestine (F2)............ 90
Palmer (C2)............... 200
Palmyra (E8)*............. 327
Paoli (E7)*...............2,575
Paragon (D6)*............. 463
Paris Crossing (F7)*...... 132
Parker (G4)*.............. 915
Parkersburg (D5).......... 100
Parr (C2)*................ 132
Patoka (B8)*.............. 626
Patricksburg (D6)*........ 450
Patriot (H7)*............. 315
Patronville (C9).......... 30
Paxton (C6)*.............. 275
Paynesville (F7).......... 50
Peabody (G2)..............
Pekin (E7)*............... 553
Pelzer (C8)............... 49
Pence (C4)*............... 122
Pendleton (F5)*...........2,082
Pennville (G4)*........... 626
Peoga (E6)................ 48
Percy Junction (C3)....... 4
Perkinsville (F4)......... 250
Perrysburg (E3)........... 50

Perrysville (C4)*......... 462
Pershing (G5)*............ 389
Pershing (E2)............. 50
Peru (E3)*................13,308
Petersburg (C7)*..........3,035
Peterson (G3)............. 50
Petersville (F6)..........
Petroleum (G3)*...........
Phenix (G3)...............
Pickard (E4)..............
Pierceton (F2)*........... 973
Pierceville (G6)*.........
Pikes Peak (E6)...........
Pikeville (C8)............ 50
Pilot Knob (E8)*.......... 200
Pimento (C6)*............. 125
Pine Village (C4)*........ 311
Pinelake (D1)*............ 250
Pinola (D1)............... 50
Pittsboro (D5)*........... 599
Pittsburg (D3)............ 350
Plainfield (E5)*..........2,585
Plainville (C7)*.......... 568
Plato (G1)................ 40
Pleasant (G7)............. 15
Pleasant Lake (H1)*....... 500
Pleasant Mills (H3)*...... 175
Pleasant Ridge (C3).......
Pleasant View (F5)........ 11
Pleasantville (C7)*....... 200
Plevna (E3)............... 72
Plum Tree (G3)............ 40
Plummer (C7).............. 10
Plymouth (E2)*............6,704
Poe (G3).................. 80
Point Isabel (F4)......... 75
Poland (C6)*.............. 150
Poneto (G3)*.............. 244
Porter (C1)*..............1,458
Portersville (C8)......... 75
Portland (H4)*............7,064
Poseyville (B8)*..........1,005
Pottawattomie Park(D1).... 35
Powers (G4)............... 50
Prairie Creek (C6)*....... 225
Prairieton (B6)*..........
Preble (H3)*.............. 150
Prescott (F6)............. 30
Priam (G4)................
Princeton (B8)*...........7,673
Providence (E6)........... 100
Pulaski (D3).............. 100
Putnamville (D5)*......... 165
Pyrmont (D4).............. 100
Queensville (F6).......... 70
Quincy (D6)*.............. 320
Raber (G2)................
Raccoon (D5).............. 100
Radley (F4)............... 150
Radnor (D3)*.............. 110
Ragsdale (C7)*............ 230
Rainsville (C4)........... 130
Raleigh (G5).............. 150
Ramsey (E8)*.............. 106
Ranger (D8)*..............
Raub (C3)*................ 110
Ravenswood (E5)*.......... 498
Ray (H1)*................. 175
Raymond (H6).............. 62
Rays Crossing (F5)........ 75
Reagan (D4)............... 2
Red Key (G4)*.............1,639
Redbridge (F3)............ 75
Reddington (F6)........... 220
Reelsville (D5)*.......... 90
Reese Mill (D4)........... 130
Reiffsburg (G3)........... 43
Remington (C3)*...........1,053
Rensselaer (C3)*..........4,072
Rexville (G7)............. 60
Reynolds (D3)*............ 499
Riceville (D8)............ 4
Richland (C9)*............ 530
Richland Center (E2)...... 10
Richmond (H5)*............39,539
Richvalley (F3)*.......... 111
Ridgeview (E3)............
Ridgeville (G4)*.......... 950
Rigdon (F4)............... 80
Riley (C6)*............... 251
Rileysburg (B4)........... 40
Rising Sun (H7)*..........1,930
River (G3)................ 75
Riverside (C4)............ 120
Riverton (B6)............. 54
Roachdale (D5)*........... 918
Roann (F3)*............... 492
Roanoke (G3)*............. 905
Rob Roy (C4).............. 54
Rochester (E2)*...........4,673
Rock Creek (G3)...........
Rockfield (D3)*........... 325
Rocklane (E5).............
Rockport (C9)*............2,493
Rockville (C5)*...........2,467
Rocky Ripple (E5)......... 528
Roll (G3)*................ 150
Rolling Prairie (D1)*..... 625
Rome (D9)*................
Rome City (G1)*...........1,303
Romney (D4)*.............. 500
Rosedale (C5)*............ 673
Roseland (E1)............. 984
Roselawn (C2)*............
Rosston (E4).............. 35

Rossville (D4)*........... 739
Royal Center (E3)*........ 876
Royalton (E5)............. 50
Royerton (G4)............. 400
Rumble (C8)............... 21
Rushville (G5)*...........6,761
Rusk (D7)*................
Russellville (D5)*........ 361
Russiaville (E4)*.........1,025
Saint Anthony (D8)*....... 152
St. Bernice (C5)*.........1,200
St. Croix (D8)*........... 100
St. Henry (D8)............ 183
St. Joe (H2)*............. 479
St. John (C2)*............ 684
St. Joseph Hill (F8)...... 200
St. Leon (H6)*............ 288
St. Louis Crossing(F6)*... 150
St. Mary of the Woods (B6)*.........1,300
St. Mary's (E1)*..........
St. Maurice (G6).......... 60
St. Meinrad (D8)*......... 720
St. Omer (F6)............. 75
St. Paul (F6)*............ 669
St. Peters (H6)........... 130
St. Philip (B9)........... 200
St. Wendells (B8).........
Salamonia (H4)*........... 181
Salem (E7)*...............3,271
Salem Center (G1)......... 50
Saline City (C6)*......... 115
Saltillo (E7)*............ 122
Samaria (E6).............. 88
San Pierre (D2)*.......... 350
Sandborn (C7)*............ 572
Sanders (E6).............. 200
Sandford (B5)*............ 195
Sandusky (G6)............. 200
Santa Claus (D8)*......... 45
Santa Fe (E3)............. 92
Saratoga (H4)*............ 333
Sardinia (F6)*............ 150
Savah (B8)................ 100
Schererville (C2)*........1,457
Schneider (C2)*........... 356
Schnellville (D8)*........ 300
Scipio (H6)............... 75
Scipio (F6)*.............. 200
Scircleville (E4)*........ 181
Scotland (D7)*............ 100
Scott (F1)................ 100
Scottsburg (F7)*..........2,953
Sedalia (E4)*............. 180
Sedan (G2)................ 30
Seelyville (C6)*.......... 898
Sellersburg (F8)*.........1,664
Selma (G4)*............... 499
Selvin (C8)*..............
Servia (F3)*.............. 143
Sevastopol (F2)........... 50
Sexton (G5)............... 80
Seybert (F1).............. 30
Seymour (F7)*.............9,629
Shadeland (C4)............ 78
Shannondale (D4).......... 20
Sharpsville (E4)*......... 508
Shelburn (C6)*............1,412
Shelby (C2)*.............. 519
Shelbyville (F6)*.........11,734
Shepardsville (B5)*....... 300
Sheridan (E4)*............1,965
Shideler (G4).............
Shipshewana (F1)*......... 277
Shirley (F5)*.............1,087
Shirley City (Woodburn*) (H2)..... 540
Shoals (D7)*..............1,039
Shooters Hill ‡(E5)....... 13
Shrock (F1)...............
Siberia (D8)*............. 50
Sidney (F2)*.............. 168
Silver Lake (F2)*......... 472
Silverville (D7).......... 60
Silverwood (C5)........... 75
Simpson (G3).............. 9
Sims (F3)*................ 231
Skelton (B8).............. 50
Smartsburg (D4)........... 55
Smith Valley (E5)......... 150
Smithville (D6)*.......... 425
Snow Hill (H4)............ 15
Solon (F7)................ 137
Solsberry (D6)*........... 500
Somerset (F3)*............ 255
Somerville (C8)*.......... 353
South Bend (E1)*.........115,911
South Bend (urban area)..............167,879
S. Boston (F7)............ 125
S. Milford (G1)*.......... 350
S. Raub (D4).............. 30
S. Wanatah (D2)........... 95
S. Whitley (F2)*..........1,299
Southport (E5)*........... 730
Spades (G6)...............
Sparksville (E7)*......... 136
Spartanburg (H4).......... 200
Spearsville (E6).......... 38
Speed (F8)*...............1,000
Speedway (E5)*............5,498
Speicher (F3)............. 60
Spelterville (C5)......... 150
Spencer (D6)*.............2,394
Spencerville (G2)*........ 450

Spiceland (F5)*........... 739
Spraytown (E6)............ 63
Spring Grove (H5)......... 333
Spring Hills ‡(E5)........ 27
Spring Lake Park (F5). 156
Springfield (B8)..........
Springport (G4)*.......... 217
Springville (D7)*......... 500
Spurgeon (C8)*............ 327
Stacer (B8)...............
Stanford (D6)*............ 100
Star City (D3)*........... 600
Starlight (F8)............ 50
State Line (C4)*.......... 152
Staunton (C6)*............ 487
Steele (H3)............... 26
Stendal (C8)*............. 175
Stewartsville (B8)*....... 240
Stilesville (D5)*......... 330
Stillwell (D1)*...........
Stinesville (D6)*......... 355
Stockwell (D4)*........... 632
Stone (G4)................ 10
Stonebluff (C4)*.......... 172
Stones Crossing (E5)...... 75
Story (E6)................
Straughn (G5)*............ 345
Stroh (G1)*............... 475
Strouse (G2)..............
Sullivan (C6)*............5,423
Sulphur (E8)*............. 43
Sulphur Springs (G4)*. 351
Sumava Resorts (C2)*...... 125
Summit (G1)............... 2
Summitville (F4)*.........1,061
Sunman (G6)*.............. 358
Surprise (E7)............. 55
Swanington (C3)........... 125
Swayzee (F4)*............. 690
Sweetsers (F3)*........... 535
Switz City (C6)*.......... 328
Sycamore (F4)............. 76
Sylvania (C5)............. 35
Syracuse (F2)*............1,453
Tab (C4)*.................
Talbot (C3)*..............
Talma (E2)................ 150
Tampico (F7).............. 150
Tangier (C5)*............. 100
Taswell (D8)*............. 110
Taylorsville (F6)*........ 290
Tecumseh (C8).............
Teegarden (E2)*...........
Tefft (D2)*............... 140
Tell City (D9)*...........5,735
Templeton (C3)*........... 143
Tennyson (C8)*............ 409
Terhune (E4).............. 100
Terre Haute (C6)*.........64,214
Terre Haute (urban area)..............77,845
Thayer (C2)*.............. 250
Thorntown (D4)*...........1,380
Tiosa (E2)................ 125
Tippecanoe (E2)*.......... 400
Tipton (E4)*..............5,633
Tobinsport (D9)*.......... 205
Tocsin (G3)*.............. 175
Topeka (F1)*.............. 557
Toto (D2)................. 275
Tower (E8)................
Trafalgar (E6)*........... 439
Trail Creek (D1).......... 817
Treaty (F3)............... 90
Trevlac (E6)*............. 48
Trinity Springs (D7)...... 150
Troy (D9)*................ 537
Tulip (D6)................ 20
Tunker (F2)............... 40
Tunnelton (E7)*........... 300
Twelve Mile (E3)*......... 247
Tyner (E2)*............... 250
Ulen (E4)................. 83
Underwood (F7)*........... 328
Union (C8)*............... 209
Union City (H4)*..........3,572
Union Mills (D2)*......... 450
Uniondale (G3)*........... 293
Unionport (G4)............ 50
Uniontown (D8)*...........
Unionville (E6)*.......... 475
Universal (C5)*........... 479
Upland (F4)*..............1,565
Urbana (F3)*.............. 400
Utica (F8)................ 250
Valeene (E8)*............. 94
Valentine (G1)............ 110
Vallonia (E7)*............ 510
Valparaiso (C2)*..........12,028
Van Buren (F3)*........... 815
Veedersburg (C4)*.........1,719
Velpen (C8)*.............. 197
Vera Cruz (G3)............ 143
Verne (C7)................ 50
Vernon (F7)*.............. 480
Versailles (G6)*.......... 886
Veterans Adm. Hospital (F3)*..............3,950
Vevay (G7)*...............1,309
Vicksburg (C6)............ 390
Vienna (F7)............... 80
Vincennes (C7)*...........18,831
Vine (C4)................. 15
Virgie (C2)...............
Vistula (F1).............. 100

Wabash (F3)*..............10,621
Wadena (C3)............... 65
Wadesville (B8)*..........
Wakarusa (F1)*............1,143
Wakefield (F7)............ 45
Waldron (F6)*............. 700
Walesboro (F6)............
Walkerton (E2)*...........2,102
Wallace (C5)*............. 123
Wallace Junction (D6)..
Wallen (G2)............... 120
Walton (E3)*.............. 837
Wanamaker (E5)*........... 325
Wanatah (D2)*............. 750
Warren (G3)*..............1,247
Warren Park (F5).......... 336
Warrenton (B8)............ 100
Warrington (F5)........... 95
Warsaw (F2)*..............6,625
Washington (C7)*..........10,987
Waterloo (G2)*............1,414
Waterman (C5)............. 100
Watson (F8)............... 200
Waveland (D5)*............ 553
Waverly (E5).............. 150
Wawaka (F2)*.............. 300
Wawasee (F2)*............. 400
Wawpecong (F3)............ 84
Waymansville (E6)......... 250
Waynedale (G3)............
Waynesville (F6)..........
Waynetown (C4)*........... 658
Webster (H5)*............. 175
Weisburg (H6)*............ 148
Wellsboro (D1)*........... 170
West Baden Springs (D7)* 1,047
W. College Corner(H5). 513
W. Fork (D8)*............. 58
W. Franklin (B9).......... 100
W. Harrison (H6).......... 308
W. Lafayette (D4)*........11,873
W. Lebanon (C4)*.......... 642
W. Middleton (E4)*........ 250
W. Newton (E5)*...........
W. Terre Haute (B6)*......3,357
Westchester (H4).......... 8
Westfield (E4)*........... 849
Westphalia (C7)*.......... 250
Westpoint (C4)*........... 315
Westport (F6)*............ 658
Westville (D1)*........... 624
Wheatfield (C2)*.......... 496
Wheatland (C7)*........... 735
Wheeler (C1)*............. 400
Wheeling (G4).............
Wheeling (C8)............. 50
Whitaker (D6)............. 25
Whitcomb (H6)............. 150
White Cloud (E8).......... 50
White Lick (E5)...........
Whitehall (D6)............ 80
Whiteland (E5)*........... 465
Whitestown (E5)*.......... 550
Whitesville (D5).......... 75
Whitewater (H5)........... 104
Whiting (C1)*.............9,669
Wickliffe (D8)*........... 9
Wilbur (D5)............... 75
Wilfred (C6).............. 50
Wilkinson (F5)*........... 365
Williams (D7)*............ 400
Williams (H3)............. 75
Williams Creek (E5)....... 288
Williamsport (C4)*........1,241
Willow Branch (F5)*.......
Wilmington (H6)........... 200
Wilmot (F2)............... 100
Wilson (F6)............... 25
Winamac (D2)*.............2,166
Winchester (G4)*..........5,467
Windfall (F4)*............ 963
Windom (D7)............... 8
Windsor (G4)..............
Wingate (C4)*............. 400
Winona Lake (F2)*.........1,366
Winslow (C8)*.............1,322
Wirt (G7).................
Wolcott (C3)*............. 778
Wolcottville (G1)*........ 672
Wolflake (F2)*............ 250
Woodburn (H2)*............ 540
Woodland (E1)............. 115
Woodlawn Heights(F4)
Woodruff Place (E5)....1,557
Woodstock ‡(E5)........... 29
Worthington (C6)*.........1,627
Wyandotte (E8)*........... 50
Wyatt (E1)*............... 250
Wynnedale ‡(E5)........... 75
Yankeetown (C9)........... 323
Yeddo (C4)*............... 115
Yeoman (D3)*.............. 180
Yoder (G3)*............... 200
Yorktown (G4)*............1,109
Yorkville (H6)*........... 87
Young America (E3)*....... 250
Youngs Creek (D8)*........ 79
Youngstown (C6)........... 72
Zanesville (G3)*.......... 300
Zenas (G6)................ 44
Zionsville (E5)*..........1,536
Zipp (B8).................
Zoar (C8)................. 5
Zulu (H2)................. 175

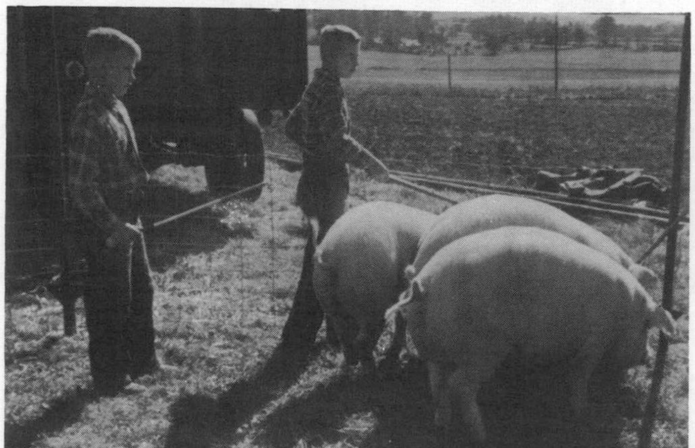

Map on Page 62

IOWA

Total Population 2,621,073

99 COUNTIES

Adair (E6)...................12,292
Adams (D6)...................8,753
Allamakee (L2)...............16,351
Appanoose (H7)...............19,683
Audubon (D5).................11,570
Benton (J4)..................22,656
Black Hawk (J4)..............100,448
Boone (F5)...................28,139

Bremer (J3)..................18,884
Buchanan (K4)................21,927
Buena Vista (C3).............21,113
Butler (H3)..................17,394
Calhoun (D4).................16,925
Carroll (D4).................23,065
Cass (D6)....................18,532
Cedar (L5)...................16,910
Cerro Gordo (G2).............46,053
Cherokee (B3)................19,052

Chickasaw (J2)...............15,228
Clarke (F6)..................9,369
Clay (C2)....................18,103
Clayton (L3).................22,522
Clinton (M5).................49,664
Crawford (C4)................19,741
Dallas (E5)..................23,661
Davis (J7)...................9,995
Decatur (F7).................12,601
Delaware (L4)................17,734

Des Moines (L7)..............42,056
Dickinson (C2)...............12,756
Dubuque (M4).................71,337
Emmet (D2)...................14,102
Fayette (K3).................28,294
Floyd (H2)...................21,505
Franklin (G3)................16,268
Fremont (B7).................12,323
Greene (E5)..................15,544
Grundy (H4)..................13,722

Guthrie (D5).................15,197
Hamilton (F4)................19,660
Hancock (F2).................15,077
Hardin (G4)..................22,218
Harrison (B5)................19,560
Henry (K6)...................18,708
Howard (J2)..................13,105
Humboldt (E3)................13,117
Ida (C4).....................10,697
Iowa (J5)....................15,835

Jackson (M4).................18,622
Jasper (G5)..................32,305
Jefferson (K6)...............15,696
Johnson (K5).................45,756
Jones (L4)...................19,401
Keokuk (J6)..................16,797
Kossuth (E2).................26,241
Lee (L7).....................43,102
Linn (K4)....................104,274
Louisa (L6)..................11,101

Lucas (G6)...................12,069
Lyon (A2)....................14,697
Madison (E6).................13,131
Mahaska (H6).................24,672
Marion (G6)..................25,930
Marshall (G4)................35,611
Mills (B6)...................14,064
Mitchell (H2)................13,945
Monona (B4)..................16,303
Monroe (H7)..................11,814

Montgomery (C6)....15,685
Muscatine (L5)....32,148
O'Brien (B2)....18,970
Osceola (B2)....10,181
Page (C7)....23,921
Palo Alto (D2)....15,891
Plymouth (A3)....23,252
Pocahontas (D3)....15,496
Polk (F5)....226,010
Pottawattamie (B6)....69,682
Poweshiek (H5)....19,344
Ringgold (E7)....9,528
Sac (C4)....17,518
Scott (M5)....100,698
Shelby (C5)....15,942
Sioux (A2)....26,381
Story (G4)....44,294
Tama (H4)....21,688
Taylor (D7)....12,420
Union (E7)....15,651
Van Buren (K7)....11,007
Wapello (J6)....47,397
Warren (F6)....17,758
Washington (K6)....19,557
Wayne (G7)....11,737
Webster (E4)....44,241
Winnebago (F2)....13,450
Winneshiek (K2)....21,639
Woodbury (B4)....103,917
Worth (G2)....11,068
Wright (F3)....19,652

CITIES and TOWNS

Abingdon (J6)....70
Ackley (G3)*....1,608
Ackworth (G6)*....95
Adair (D6)*....827
Adaza (E4)*....51
Adel (E5)*....1,799
Afton (E6)*....936
Agency (J7)*....524
Ainsworth (K6)*....396
Akron (A3)*....1,251
Albert City (C3)*....736
Albia (H6)*....4,838
Albion (H4)*....492
Alburnett (K4)*....254
Alden (G4)*....829
Alexander (G3)*....278
Algona (E2)*....5,415
Alleman (F5)*....108
Allendorf (B2)*....55
Allerton (G7)*....761
Allison (H3)*....771
Alpha (K3)*....122
Alta (C3)*....1,348
Alta Vista (J2)*....312
Alton (A3)*....1,038
Altoona (G5)*....736
Alvord (A2)*....263
Amana (K5)*....
Amber (L4)*....115
Ames (F4)*....22,898
Anamosa (L4)*....3,910
Anderson (B7)*....120
Andover (N5)*....80
Andrew (M4)*....280
Angus (E5)*....150
Anita (D6)*....1,112
Ankeny (F5)*....1,229
Anthon (B4)*....770
Aplington (H3)*....702
Arcadia (C4)*....425
Archer (B2)*....167
Ardon (L6)*....20
Aredale (H3)*....204
Argyle (K7)*....85
Arion (B5)*....220
Arispe (E7)*....110
Arlington (K3)*....661
Armstrong (D2)*....943
Arnolds Park (C2)*....1,078
Arthur (C4)*....243
Asbury (M4)....52
Ashton (B2)*....588
Aspinwall (C5)*....107
Astor (C5)....
Atalissa (L5)*....204
Athelstan (D7)*....115
Atkins (K4)*....387
Atlantic (D6)*....6,480
Attica (G6)*....
Auburn (D4)*....350
Audubon (D5)*....2,808
Augusta (L7)....50
Aurelia (C3)*....807
Aurora (K3)*....225
Austinville (H3)*....130
Avery (H6)*....175
Avoca (C6)*....1,955
Ayrshire (D2)*....334
Badger (E3)*....301
Bagley (E5)*....392
Bailey (H2)....25
Baldwin (M4)*....208
Balltown (M3)....49
Bancroft (E2)*....901
Bankston (L3)....40
Barnes City (H6)*....326
Barnum (E3)*....193
Bartlett (B7)*....88
Bassett (J2)*....125
Batavia (J7)*....524
Battle Creek (B4)*....873
Baxter (G5)*....618
Bayard (D5)*....634
Beacon (H6)*....371
Beaconsfield (E7)*....104
Beaman (H4)*....191
Beaver (E4)*....114
Bedford (D7)*....2,000
Beech (G6)*....106
Belknap (J7)*....80
Belle Plaine (J5)*....3,056
Bellevue (M4)*....1,932
Belmond (F3)*....2,169
Beloit (A2)*....90
Bennett (L5)*....357
Bentley (B6)*....50
Benton (E7)*....128
Bentonsport (K7)....60
Berkley (E5)....71
Bernard (M4)*....149
Bertram (K5)....128
Berwick (G5)*....113
Bethlehem (G7)....52
Bettendorf (N5)*....5,132
Bevington (F6)*....48
Big Rock (M5)*....106
Birmingham (K7)*....643
Blairsburg (F4)*....257
Blairstown (J5)*....523
Blakesburg (H7)*....401
Blanchard (C7)*....214
Blencoe (A5)*....328
Blockton (D7)*....407
Bloomfield (J7)*....2,688
Blue Grass (M5)*....337
Bode (E3)*....492
Bonair (J2)....80
Bonaparte (K7)*....642
Bondurant (G5)*....328
Boone (F4)*....12,164
Botna (C5)*....54
Bouton (E5)*....159
Boxholm (E4)*....304
Boyden (B2)*....541
Boyer (C4)*....70
Braddyville (D7)*....249
Bradford (G3)*....
Bradgate (E3)*....188
Brandon (K4)*....319
Brayton (D5)*....239
Brazil (H7)*....
Breda (C4)*....506
Bremer (J3)*....80
Bridgewater (D6)*....296
Brighton (K6)*....705
Bristow (H3)*....313
Britt (F2)*....1,908
Bronson (A4)*....295
Brooklyn (J5)*....1,323
Brooks (D7)*....180
Brunsville (A3)*....112
Bryant (N5)*....45
Buchanan (L5)....36
Buck Grove (C5)*....67
Buckeye (G4)*....192
Buckingham (J4)*....68
Buffalo (M6)*....695
Buffalo Center (F2)*....1,087
Bunch (H7)*....103
Burchinal (G2)*....75
Burdette (G3)....18
Burlington (L7)*....30,613
Burnside (E4)*....105
Burroak (K2)*....250
Burt (E2)*....572
Bussey (H6)*....633
Calamus (M5)*....381
California (B5)*....125
Callender (E4)*....387
Calmar (K2)*....937
Calumet (B3)*....250
Camanche (N5)*....1,212
Cambria (G7)*....125
Cambridge (G5)*....573
Cantril (J7)*....353
Carbon (D6)*....282
Carl (D6)....40
Carlisle (G6)*....903
Carnarvon (C4)*....115
Carney (F5)....
Carpenter (H2)*....165
Carroll (D4)*....6,231
Carrollton (D5)....17
Carson (C6)*....596
Carter Lake (B6)....1,183
Cartersville (G2)....25
Cascade (L4)*....1,299
Casey (D5)*....703
Castalia (K2)*....221
Castana (B4)*....265
Castle Hill (J3)....425
Cedar (H6)*....110
Cedar Bluff (L5)*....75
Cedar Falls (H3)*....14,344
Cedar Heights (H3)....
Cedar Rapids (K5)*....72,296
Cedar Rapids (urban area)....77,990
Center Junction (L4)*....153
Center Point (K4)*....987
Centerdale (L5)....34
Centerville (H7)*....7,625
Central City (K4)*....965
Central Heights ‡(G2)*....766
Centralia (M4)....78
Chapin (G3)*....200
Chariton (G6)*....5,320
Charles City (H2)*....10,309
Charleston (K7)....30
Charlotte (M5)*....427
Charter Oak (C4)*....710
Chatsworth (A3)*....102
Chelsea (J5)*....482
Cherokee (B3)*....7,705
Chester (J2)*....226
Chester Center (H5)....
Chillicothe (J6)*....196
Church (L2)....40
Churchville (F6)....25
Churdan (D4)*....593
Cincinnati (G7)*....703
Clare (E3)*....179
Clarence (M5)*....791
Clarinda (C7)*....5,086
Clarion (F3)*....3,150
Clarksville (H3)*....1,210
Clay Works (E4)....175
Clayton (L3)*....136
Clear Lake (G2)*....4,977
Clearfield (D7)*....547
Cleghorn (B3)*....246
Clemons (G4)*....202
Clermont (K3)*....625
Cleves (G4)*....50
Climbing Hill (B4)*....140
Clinton (N5)*....30,379
Clio (G7)*....162
Clive (F5)*....250
Clover Hills (F5)....408
Clutier (J4)*....302
Coal City (H7)....
Coalville (E4)....350
Coburg (C7)*....83
Coggon (L4)*....604
Coin (C7)*....407
Colesburg (L3)*....326
Colfax (G5)*....2,279
College Springs (C7)*....368
Collins (G5)*....432
Colo (G4)*....538
Columbia (G6)*....110
Columbus City (L6)*....350
Columbus Junction (L6)*....1,123
Colwell (H2)*....122
Commerce (F5)....152
Conesville (L6)*....252
Confidence (G7)....65
Conover (K2)....
Conrad (H4)*....649
Conroy (J5)*....200
Conway (D7)*....100
Coon Rapids (D5)*....1,676
Cooper (E5)*....99
Coppock (K6)*....81
Coralville (K5)....977
Cordova (G6)....15
Corley (C5)*....60
Cornell (C3)*....
Corning (D7)*....2,104
Correctionville (B4)*....992
Corwith (F3)*....480
Corydon (G7)*....1,870
Cotter (L6)*....49
Coulter (G3)*....271
Council Bluffs (B6)*....45,429
Covington (K5)....82
Craig (A3)*....142
Cranston (L6)*....
Crawfordsville (K6)*....286
Crescent (B6)*....
Cresco (J2)*....3,638
Creston (E6)*....8,317
Cricket (H6)....
Cromwell (E6)*....147
Croton (K7)....55
Crystal Lake (F2)*....286
Cumberland (D6)*....493
Cumming (F6)*....131
Curlew (D3)*....151
Cushing (B4)*....248
Cylinder (D2)*....143
Dakota City (E3)*....637
Dale (E5)....30
Dallas (G6)*....421
Dallas Center (E5)*....944
Dana (E4)*....184
Danbury (B4)*....601
Danville (L7)*....450
Davenport (M5)*....74,549
Davenport, Iowa — Rock Island, Ill.—Moline, Ill. (urban area)....193,733
Davis City (F7)*....432
Dawson (E5)*....286
Dayton (E4)*....793
De Soto (E5)*....271
De Witt (N5)*....2,644
Dean (H7)*....45
Decatur (F7)*....196
Decorah (K2)*....6,060
Dedham (D5)*....360
Deep River (J5)*....379
Defiance (C5)*....368
Delaware (L4)*....195
Delhi (L4)*....383
Delmar (M4)*....415
Deloit (C4)*....235
Delphos (E7)*....74
Delta (J6)*....562
Denison (C4)*....4,554
Denmark (L7)*....300
Denver (J3)*....635
Derby (G7)*....194
DES MOINES (F5)*....177,965
Des Moines (urban area)....198,892
Dewar (J3)*....150
Dexter (E5)*....643
Diagonal (E7)*....472
Dickens (C2)*....311
Dike (H4)*....517
Dinsdale (H4)*....80
Dixon (M5)*....208
Dolliver (D2)*....130
Donahue (M5)*....105
Donnan (K3)*....36
Donnellson (K7)*....589
Doon (A2)*....517
Dorchester (L2)*....120
Douds (K7)*....425
Dougherty (G3)*....212
Dow City (B5)*....524
Downey (L5)*....126
Dows (F3)*....948
Drakesville (J7)*....222
Dubuque (M3)*....49,671
Dudley (H6)....54
Dumont (H3)*....718
Dunbar (H5)*....80
Duncombe (E4)*....378
Dundee (L3)*....176
Dunkerton (J3)*....409
Dunlap (B5)*....1,409
Durango (M3)*....71
Durant (M5)*....1,075
Dyersville (L3)*....2,416
Dysart (J4)*....1,089
Eagle Grove (F3)*....4,176
Earlham (E6)*....771
Earling (C5)*....341
Earlville (L4)*....661
Early (C4)*....742
East Peru (F6)....204
East Pleasant Plain (K6)*....
Eddyville (H6)*....941
Edgewood (L3)*....696
Edna (A2)*....80
Elberon (J4)*....225
Eldon (J7)*....1,457
Eldora (G4)*....3,107
Eldorado (K2)*....100
Eldridge (M5)*....376
Elgin (K3)*....642
Elk Horn (C5)*....566
Elkader (L3)*....1,584
Elkhart (F5)*....222
Elkport (L3)*....99
Elliott (C6)*....482
Ellston (E7)*....158
Ellsworth (F4)*....439
Elma (J2)*....731
Elvira (N5)....210
Elwood (M4)*....125
Ely (K5)*....155
Emerson (C6)*....556
Emmetsburg (D2)*....3,760
Epworth (M4)*....536
Essex (C7)*....763
Estherville (D2)*....6,719
Evansdale (J4)*....3,571
Everly (C2)*....547
Ewart (H5)....34
Exira (D5)*....1,129
Exline (H7)*....342
Fairbank (K3)*....653
Fairfax (K5)*....335
Fairfield (J6)*....7,299
Fairport (M6)....150
Farley (L4)*....745
Farlin (E4)*....85
Farmersburg (L3)*....263
Farmington (K7)*....899
Farnhamville (D4)*....399
Farragut (C7)*....495
Farrar (G5)*....64
Farson (J6)*....100
Faulkner (G3)*....50
Fayette (K3)*....1,469
Fenton (E2)*....446
Ferguson (H5)*....178
Fernald (G4)*....100
Fertile (G2)*....397
Festina (K2)*....160
Flagler (G6)....55
Floris (J7)*....215
Floyd (H2)*....440
Fonda (D3)*....1,120
Fontanelle (E6)*....812
Forest City (F2)*....2,766
Fort Atkinson (J2)*....273
Ft. Des Moines (F5)*....
Ft. Dodge (E3)*....25,115
Ft. Madison (L7)*....14,954
Fostoria (C2)*....147
Franklin (L7)....146
Frankville (K2)....169
Fraser (E4)*....219
Fredericksburg (J3)*....701
Frederika (J3)*....210
Fredonia (L6)....133
Fredric (H6)....28
Fremont (H6)*....471
Froelich (L2)*....65
Fruitland (L6)*....150
Fulton (M4)....
Galt (F3)*....117
Galva (C3)*....492
Garber (L3)*....153
Garden City (G4)*....150
Garden Grove (F7)*....417
Garnavillo (L3)*....581
Garner (F2)*....1,696
Garrison (J4)*....457
Garwin (H4)*....518
Gaza (B2)*....85
Geneva (G3)*....242
George (B2)*....1,210
Gerled (E2)*....41
Gibson (J6)*....101
Gifford (G4)*....118
Gilbert (F4)*....237
Gilbertville (J4)*....399
Gillett Grove (C2)*....150
Gilman (H5)*....508
Gilmore City (D3)*....746
Givin (H6)*....75
Gladbrook (H4)*....862
Gladwin (L6)....50
Glasgow (K7)....85
Glendon (E5)....44
Glenwood (B6)*....4,664
Glidden (D4)*....996
Goldfield (F3)*....665
Goodell (F3)*....242
Gooselake (N5)*....148
Gowrie (E4)*....1,052
Graettinger (D2)*....1,016
Graf (M3)*....44
Grafton (G2)*....278
Graham (L3)....
Grand Junction (E4)*....1,036
Grand Mound (M5)*....526
Grand River (F7)*....350
Grandview (L6)*....311
Granger (F5)*....300
Granite (A2)....15
Grant (C6)*....237
Grant Center (A4)*....
Granville (B3)*....350
Gravity (D7)*....369
Gray (D5)*....183
Greeley (L3)*....360
Green Island (N4)*....120
Green Mountain (H4)*....199
Greene (H3)*....1,347
Greenfield (D6)*....2,102
Greenville (C3)*....173
Grimes (F5)*....582
Grinnell (H5)*....6,828
Griswold (C6)*....1,149
Grundy Center (H4)*....2,135
Gruver (D2)*....135
Guernsey (J5)*....113
Guthrie Center (D5)*....2,042
Guttenberg (L3)*....1,912
Halbur (D4)*....235
Hale (L4)*....75
Hamburg (B7)*....2,086
Hamilton (H6)*....245
Hamlin (D5)*....200
Hampton (G3)*....4,432
Hancock (C6)*....264
Hanlontown (G2)*....257
Hansell (G3)*....190
Harcourt (E4)*....303
Hardy (E3)*....139
Harlan (C5)*....3,915
Harper (J6)*....182
Harpers Ferry (L2)*....252
Harris (C2)*....319
Hartford (G6)*....221
Hartley (C2)*....1,611
Hartwick (J5)*....107
Harvard (G7)*....
Harvey (H6)*....346
Haskins (K6)*....65
Hastings (C6)*....308
Havelock (D3)*....307
Haven (H5)....50
Haverhill (H5)*....
Hawarden (A2)*....2,625
Hawkeye (J3)*....511
Hayesville (J6)*....137
Hayfield (F2)*....200
Hazleton (K3)*....550
Hedrick (J6)*....733
Henderson (B6)*....208
Hepburn (C7)*....64
Herndon (E5)*....100
Herring (C4)*....15
Herrold (F5)....45
Hesper (K2)*....
High (K5)*....130
Highland Center (J6)*....85
Highlandville (K2)*....57
Hills (K5)*....248
Hillsboro (K7)*....253
Hinton (A3)*....345
Hiteman (H6)*....250
Holbrook (K5)*....29
Holland (H4)*....221
Holmes (F3)*....65
Holstein (B4)*....1,336
Holy Cross (L3)....139
Homestead (K5)*....150
Honey Creek (B6)*....62
Hopeville (F7)....
Hopkinton (L4)*....731
Hornick (A4)*....310
Horton (J3)....66
Hospers (B2)*....604
Houghton (K7)*....
Hubbard (G4)*....836
Hudson (H4)*....613
Hull (A2)*....1,127
Humboldt (E3)*....3,219
Humeston (G7)*....750
Huntington (D2)*....39
Hurstville (M4)....83
Huxley (F5)*....422
Iconium (H7)....75
Ida Grove (B4)*....2,202
Imogene (C7)*....274
Independence (K4)*....4,865
Indianola (F6)*....5,145
Inwood (A2)*....644
Ionia (J2)*....301
Iowa City (L5)*....27,212
Iowa Falls (G3)*....4,900
Ira (G5)*....103
Ireton (A3)*....573
Irving (J5)....78
Irvington (E3)*....110
Irwin (C5)*....381
Jackson Junction (K2)*....107
Jamaica (E5)*....303
James (A3)....36
Jamison (F6)....40
Janesville (J3)*....445
Jefferson (E4)*....4,326
Jerome (G7)*....130
Jesup (J4)*....1,158
Jewell (F4)*....973
Johnston (F5)*....750
Joice (G2)*....244
Jolley (D4)*....195
Jordan (F4)*....50
Kalo (E4)....150
Kalona (K6)*....947
Kamrar (F4)*....261
Kanawha (F3)*....747
Kellerton (E7)*....483
Kelley (F5)*....244
Kellogg (H5)*....670
Kendallville (K2)....
Kensett (G2)*....424
Kent (E7)*....169
Keokuk (L8)*....16,144
Keosauqua (J7)*....1,101
Keota (K6)*....1,145
Kesley (H3)*....125
Keswick (J6)*....276
Keystone (J5)*....438
Kiene (K4)....11
Kilbourn (K7)*....73
Killduff (H5)*....145
Kimballton (D5)*....428
Kingsley (A3)*....1,098
Kingston (L7)....150
Kinross (J6)*....105
Kirkman (C5)*....131
Kirkville (H6)*....213
Kiron (C4)*....255
Klemme (F3)*....555
Knierim (D4)*....133
Knoke (D3)*....49
Knowlton (E7)....60
Knoxville (G6)*....7,625
Koszta (J5)....45
La Moille (G4)*....151
La Motte (M4)*....280
La Porte City (J4)*....1,770
Lacona (G6)*....430
Ladora (J5)*....273
Lake City (D4)*....2,308
Lake Mills (F2)*....1,560
Lake Park (C2)*....924
Lake View (C4)*....1,158
Lakeside (C3)....219
Lakota (E2)*....443
Lamoni (F7)*....2,196
Lamont (K3)*....574
Lancaster (J6)....25
Lanesboro (D4)*....280
Langdon (C2)*....60
Langworthy (L4)*....64
Lansing (L2)*....1,536
Lanyon (E4)*....120
Larchwood (A2)*....415
Larrabee (B3)*....158
Latimer (G3)*....434
Laurel (H5)*....257
Laurens (D3)*....1,556
Lavinia (D4)*....65
Lawler (J2)*....539
Lawn Hill (G4)....40
Lawton (A4)*....254
Le Claire (N5)*....1,124
Le Grand (H5)*....393
Le Mars (A3)*....5,844
Le Roy (F7)*....91
Leando (J7)....
Ledyard (E2)*....327
Lehigh (E4)*....881
Leighton (H6)*....118
Leland (F2)*....209
Lenox (D7)*....1,171
Leon (F7)*....2,139
Leslie (F7)....25
Lester (A2)*....217
Letts (L6)*....404
Lewis (C6)*....511
Liberty (F6)....56
Liberty Center (F6)*....110
Libertyville (K7)*....311
Lidderdale (D4)*....180
Lime Springs (J2)*....551
Linby (J6)....50
Lincoln (H4)*....194
Linden (E5)*....290
Lineville (G7)*....482
Linn Grove (C3)*....320
Linwood (M6)....100
Lisbon (L5)*....952
Liscomb (H4)*....278
Little Cedar (H2)*....80
Little Rock (B2)*....533
Little Sioux (B5)*....349
Littleport (L3)*....139
Littleton (K3)....75
Livermore (E3)*....615
Lockridge (K7)*....233
Logan (B5)*....1,550
Lohrville (D4)*....698
Lone Rock (E2)*....188
Lone Tree (L6)*....639
Long Grove (M5)*....156
Lorimor (E6)*....505
Lost Nation (M5)*....557
Loveland (B6)*....55
Lovilia (H6)*....619
Low Moor (N5)*....279
Lowden (M5)*....642
Lowell (L7)*....85
Luana (K2)*....220
Lucas (G6)*....420
Luther (F5)*....131
Luton (A4)*....154
Luverne (E3)*....553
Luxemburg (L3)*....120
Luzerne (J5)*....186
Lynnville (H5)*....406
Lytton (D4)*....373
Macedonia (C6)*....298
Macksburg (E6)*....220
Madrid (F5)*....1,829
Magnolia (B5)*....207
Malcom (H5)*....406
Mallard (D3)*....399
Maloy (E7)*....90
Malvern (B7)*....1,263
Manchester (L3)*....3,987
Manila (C5)*....1,035
Manly (G2)*....1,473
Manning (C5)*....1,801
Manson (D3)*....1,622
Maple Hill (D2)*....60
Maple River (D4)*....120
Mapleton (B4)*....1,857
Maquoketa (M4)*....4,307
Marathon (C3)*....565
Marble Rock (H3)*....470
Marcus (B3)*....1,263
Marengo (J5)*....2,151
Marion (K4)*....5,916
Marne (C6)*....214
Marquette (L2)*....641
Marshalltown (G4)*....19,821
Martelle (L4)*....228
Martensdale (F6)*....161
Martinsburg (J6)*....219
Marysville (G6)....165
Mason City (G2)*....27,980
Masonville (K4)*....133
Massena (D6)*....459
Massillon (L5)*....90
Matlock (A2)*....104
Maurice (A3)*....256
Maxwell (G5)*....802
Maynard (K3)*....455
Maysville (M5)....70
Mc Callsburg (G4)*....290
Mc Causland (M5)*....150
Mc Clelland (B6)*....159
Mc Gregor (L2)*....1,138
Mc Intire (H2)*....300
Mc Paul (B7)*....35
Mechanicsville (L5)*....850
Mederville (K3)....
Mediapolis (L6)*....834
Melbourne (G5)*....510
Melcher (G6)*....898
Melrose (G7)*....310
Meltonville (G2)*....
Melvin (B2)*....325
Menlo (E5)*....421
Meriden (B3)*....164
Merrill (A3)*....605
Meservey (G3)*....297
Meyer (H2)....
Middle (K5)*....
Middletown (L7)*....229
Miles (N4)*....344
Milford (C2)*....1,375
Miller (F2)*....75
Millersburg (J5)*....200
Millerton (G7)*....140
Milo (G6)*....525
Milton (J7)*....719
Minburn (E5)*....353
Minden (C6)*....328
Mineola (B6)*....145
Mingo (G5)*....227
Missouri Valley (B5)*....3,546
Mitchell (H2)*....168
Mitchellville (G5)*....906
Modale (B5)*....283
Moingona (F4)....150
Mondamin (B5)*....489
Moneta (C2)*....89
Monmouth (M4)*....198
Monona (L2)*....1,346
Monroe (G5)*....1,108
Monteith (E5)*....
Monterey (H7)....35
Montezuma (H5)*....1,460
Montgomery (C2)*....150
Monticello (L4)*....2,888
Montour (H5)*....380
Montpelier (M6)*....200
Montrose (L7)*....643
Mooar (L8)....235
Moorhead (B5)*....392
Moorland (E4)*....248
Moran (F5)....150
Moravia (H7)*....652
Morley (L4)*....157
Morning Sun (L6)*....939
Morrison (H4)*....169
Morse (L5)....
Morton Mills (C6)....70
Moscow (L5)*....195
Moulton (H7)*....985
Mount Auburn (J4)*....216
Mt. Ayr (E7)*....1,793
Mt. Etna (D6)*....90
Mt. Hamill (K7)*....44
Mt. Pleasant (L7)*....5,843
Mt. Sterling (J7)*....144
Mt. Union (L6)*....167
Mt. Vernon (K5)*....2,320
Mt. Zion (K7)*....50
Moville (A4)*....964
Murray (F6)*....767
Muscatine (L6)*....19,041
Mystic (H7)*....1,233
Nashua (J3)*....1,609
Nemaha (C3)*....184
Neola (B6)*....839
Nevada (G5)*....3,763
Nevinville (D6)*....75
New Albin (L2)*....568
New Boston (L7)*....116
New Hampton (J2)*....3,323
New Hartford (H3)*....584
New Liberty (M5)*....126
New London (L7)*....1,510
New Market (D7)*....573
New Providence (G4)*....212
New Sharon (H6)*....1,089
New Vienna (L3)*....204
New Virginia (F6)*....342
Newbern (G6)....24
Newburg (H5)*....105
Newell (D3)*....884
Newhall (K5)*....366
Newton (H5)*....11,723
Nichols (L6)*....348
Noble (K6)....34
Nodaway (D7)*....233
Nora Springs (H2)*....1,257
North Buena Vista (L3)*....148
N. English (J5)*....853
N. Liberty (K5)*....309
N. Washington (J2)*....159
Northboro (C7)*....167
Northwood (G2)*....1,767
Norwalk (F6)*....435
Norway (K5)*....441
Numa (G7)*....248
Oakdale (K5)*....650
Oakland (C6)*....1,296
Oakland Mills (K7)....37
Oakley (G6)....25
Oakville (L6)*....360
Oasis (L5)....27
Ocheyedan (B2)*....700
Odebolt (C4)*....1,279
Oelwein (K3)*....7,859
Ogden (E4)*....1,486
Okoboji (C2)*....336
Old Town ‡(C2)....40
Olds (K6)*....187
Olin (L5)*....626
Ollie (J6)*....298
Onawa (A4)*....3,498
Oneida (L3)*....75
Onslow (M4)*....244
Ontario (F4)*....140
Oran (J3)*....110
Orange City (A2)*....2,166
Orchard (H2)*....114
Orient (E6)*....427
Orillia (F6)....25
Orleans (C2)*....317
Orson (B5)*....21
Osage (H2)*....3,436
Osceola (F6)*....3,422
Osgood (D2)*....50
Oskaloosa (H6)*....11,124

Ossian (K2)*.... 804
Osterdock (L3)*.... 51
Otho (E4)*.... 403
Otley (G6)*.... 177
Oto (B4)*.... 302
Otranto (H2)*.... 75
Otterville (K3)....
Ottosen (E3)*.... 127
Ottumwa (J6)*....33,631
Owasa (G4)*.... 100
Oxford (K5)*.... 543
Oxford Junction (M4)* 663
Oxford Mills (L5).... 103
Oyens (A3)*.... 95
Pacific Junction (B6)*. 550
Packwood (J6)*.... 211
Page (C7).... 9
Palmer (D3)*.... 296
Palo (K4)*.... 285
Panama (B5)*.... 230
Panora (E5)*....1,062
Paris (K4).... 75
Parkersburg (H3)*....1,300
Parnell (J5)*.... 206
Paton (E4)*.... 404
Patterson (F6)*.... 133
Paullina (B3)*....1,289
Payne (B7)*.... 14
Pekin (J6).... 75
Pella (H6)*....4,427
Peoria (H6).... 150
Peosta (M4)*.... 60
Percival (B7)*.... 250
Percy (G6)*....
Perkins (A2).... 50
Perlee (K6).... 22
Perry (E5)*....6,174
Pershing (G6)*.... 300
Persia (B5)*.... 373
Peru (F6)*.... 250
Peterson (C3)*.... 589
Pierson (B3)*.... 453
Pilot Grove (L7)*.... 50
Pilot Mound (F4)*.... 246
Pioneer (E3)*.... 83
Pisgah (B5)*.... 327
Plain View (M5).... 42
Plainfield (J3)*.... 387
Plano (G7)*.... 106
Pleasant Plain (K6)*.... 148
Pleasant Valley (N5)*.. 500
Pleasanton (F7)*.... 130
Pleasantville (G6)*.... 893
Plover (D3)*.... 243
Plymouth (G2)*.... 395
Pocahontas (D3)*....1,949
Polk City (F5)*.... 336
Pomeroy (D3)*.... 868
Popejoy (G3)*.... 201
Portsmouth (C5)*.... 299
Postville (K2)*....1,343
Powersville (H3).... 25
Prairie City (G5)*.... 834
Prairieburg (L4)*.... 210
Prescott (D6)*.... 372
Preston (N4)*.... 684
Primghar (B2)*....1,152
Primrose (K7)*.... 65
Princeton (N5)*.... 495
Prole (F6)*....
Promise City (G7)*.... 218
Protivin (J2)*.... 283
Pulaski (J7)*.... 381
Purdy (G6)....
Quarry (H4).... 204
Quasqueton (K4)*.... 374
Quimby (B3)*.... 398
Quincy (D6)....
Radcliffe (G4)*.... 638
Rake (F2)*.... 351
Ralston (D4)*.... 166
Randalia (K3)*.... 132
Randall (F4)*.... 202
Randolph (B7)*.... 295
Rathbun (H7)*.... 229
Raymond (J4)*.... 260
Read (L3)....
Readlyn (J3)*.... 468
Reasnor (G5)*.... 227
Red Oak (C6)*....6,526
Redding (E7)*.... 200
Redfield (E5)*.... 892
Reinbeck (H4)*....1,460
Rembrandt (C3)*.... 296
Remsen (B3)*....1,280
Renwick (E3)*.... 474
Rhodes (G5)*.... 369
Riceville (H2)*.... 962
Richards (D4)*.... 48
Richland (K6)*.... 591
Richmond (K6)*.... 140
Rickardsville (M3).... 75
Ricketts (B4)*.... 166
Ridgeway (K2)*.... 307
Rinard (D4)*.... 115
Ringsted (D2)*.... 578
Rippey (E5)*.... 354
River Junction (L5).... 36
River Sioux (B5)*.... 135
Riverside (K6)*.... 631
Riverton (B7)*.... 472
Robertson (G3).... 30
Robins (K4)*.... 272
Robinson (K4).... 50
Rochester (L5).... 67
Rock Falls (G2)*.... 139
Rock Rapids (A2)*....2,640
Rock Valley (A2)*....1,581
Rockdale (M4).... 132
Rockford (H2)*.... 979
Rockwell (G3)*.... 753
Rockwell City (D4)*....2,333
Rodman (D2)*.... 123
Rodney (A4)*.... 127
Roland (F4)*.... 687
Rolfe (D3)*.... 997
Rome (K7)*.... 134
Roscoe (L6).... 2
Rose Hill (J6)*.... 243
Roselle (D5).... 82
Ross (D5).... 50
Rossie (C2)*.... 112
Rossville (L2)....
Rowan (F3)*.... 304
Rowley (K4)*.... 249
Royal (C2)*.... 495
Rubio (K6)*.... 70
Rudd (H2)*.... 398
Runnells (G5)*.... 307
Russell (G7)*.... 566
Ruthven (D2)*.... 868
Rutland (E3)*.... 225
Ryan (K4)*.... 362
Sabula (N4)*.... 888
Sac City (C4)*....3,170
Sageville (M3).... 118
Saint Ansgar (H2)*.... 981
St. Anthony (G4)*.... 175
St. Benedict (E2)*.... 135
St. Charles (F6)*.... 319
St. Donatus (M4)*.... 100
St. Lucas (K2)*.... 158
St. Marys (F6)*.... 89
St. Olaf (L3)*.... 158
St. Paul (L7).... 113
Salem (K7)*.... 473
Salina (K6).... 50
Salix (A4)*.... 337
Sanborn (B2)*....1,337
Sand Springs (L4).... 50
Sandyville (G6).... 92
Saratoga (J2)*.... 85
Saylor (F5).... 100
Scarville (F2)*.... 105
Schaller (C4)*.... 841
Schleswig (B4)*.... 751
Scotch Grove (L4)*.... 55
Scranton (D4)*.... 891
Searsboro (H5)*.... 183
Sedan (H7).... 80
Selma (J7)*.... 175
Seney (A3).... 82
Sergeant Bluff (A4)*.... 569
Sewal (G7)*.... 100
Sexton (E2)*....
Seymour (G7)*....1,223
Shambaugh (D7)*.... 251
Shannon City (E7)*.... 171
Sharpsburg (D7)*.... 147
Sheffield (G3)*....1,163
Shelby (C5)*.... 592
Sheldahl (F5)*.... 211
Sheldon (B2)*....4,001
Shell Rock (H3)*....1,013
Shellsburg (K4)*.... 632
Shenandoah (C7)*....6,938
Sherrill (M3).... 162
Sherwood (D4).... 21
Shueyville (K5).... 75
Sibley (B2)*....2,559
Sidney (B7)*....1,132
Sigourney (J6)*....2,343
Silver City (B6)*.... 311
Sioux Center (A2)*....1,860
Sioux City (A3)*....83,991
Sioux City (urban area) 90,144
Sioux Rapids (C3)*....1,010
Slater (F5)*.... 583
Sloan (A4)*.... 654
Smithland (B4)*.... 373
Soldier (B5)*.... 323
Solon (L5)*.... 527
Somers (E4)*.... 217
South Amana (J5)*.... 185
S. English (J6)*.... 248
Spechts Ferry (M3).... 10
Spencer (C2)*....7,446
Sperry (L7)*.... 65
Spillville (J2)*.... 363
Spirit Lake (D2)*....2,467
Spragueville (N4)*.... 115
Spring Hill (F6)*.... 86
Springbrook (N4)*.... 109
Springdale (L5).... 72
Springville (L4)*.... 680
Stacyville (H2)*.... 544
Stanhope (F4)*.... 420
Stanley (K3)*.... 158
Stanton (C7)*.... 570
Stanwood (L5)*.... 547
Stanzel (E6)*.... 25
State Center (G5)*....1,040
Steamboat Rock (G4)*. 395
Stennett (C6).... 28
Stiles (J7).... 50
Stockport (K7)*.... 346
Stockton (M5)*.... 165
Stone City (L4)*.... 200
Storm Lake (C3)*....6,954
Story City (F4)*....1,545
Stout (H3)*.... 135
Strahan (B7)*.... 100
Stratford (F4)*.... 673
Strawberry Point (K3)*.1,247
Struble (A3)*.... 91
Stuart (E6)*....1,500
Sully (H5)*.... 452
Sulphur Springs (C3)*.. 90
Summerset (F6)....
Summitville (K8).... 86
Sumner (J3)*....1,911
Sunbury (M5)*.... 100
Superior (D2)*.... 240
Sutherland (B3)*.... 835
Swaledale (G3)*.... 205
Swan (G6)*.... 194
Swea City (E2)*.... 869
Swedesburg (L6)*.... 104
Swisher (K5)*.... 205
Tabor (B7)*.... 869
Taintor (H6)*.... 78
Talleyrand (J6).... 24
Talmage (E6).... 44
Tama (H5)*....2,930
Tara (E4).... 70
Teeds Grove (N4)*....
Templeton (D5)*.... 385
Tennant (C5)*.... 95
Terril (C2)*.... 425
Thayer (E6)*.... 152
The Inn (C2)....
Thompson (F2)*.... 698
Thor (E3)*.... 271
Thornburg (J6)*.... 138
Thornton (G3)*.... 441
Thurman (B7)*.... 284
Ticonic (B4).... 35
Tiffin (K5)*.... 256
Tingley (E7)*.... 333
Tipton (L5)*....2,633
Titonka (E2)*.... 589
Toddville (K4)*.... 200
Toeterville (H2)*.... 75
Toledo (H4)*....2,106
Toronto (M5)*.... 165
Tracy (H6)*....
Traer (J4)*....1,627
Trenton (K6).... 104
Treynor (B6)*.... 247
Tripoli (J3)*....1,124
Troy (J7)*.... 103
Troy Mills (K4)*....
Truax (H6).... 60
Truesdale (C3)*.... 158
Truro (F6)*.... 354
Turin (B4)*.... 160
Turkey River (L3).... 9
Udell (H7)*.... 96
Ulmer (D4)*....
Underwood (B6)*.... 278
Union (G4)*.... 490
Unionville (H7)*.... 204
University Heights (K5).... 446
University Park (H6)*... 457
Urbana (K4)*.... 414
Urbandale (F5)*....1,777
Ute (B4)*.... 563
Vail (C4)*.... 532
Valeria (G5)*.... 57
Van Cleve (G5).... 25
Van Horne (J4)*.... 511
Van Meter (E5)*.... 364
Van Wert (F7)*.... 318
Vandalia (G5).... 55
Varina (D3)*.... 144
Ventura (F2)*.... 300
Victor (J5)*.... 741
Villisca (C7)*....1,838
Vincennes (K7)*.... 72
Vincent (E3)*.... 193
Vining (J5)*.... 112
Vinton (J4)*....4,307
Viola (L4)*....
Volga (L3)*.... 423
Voorhies (J4)*.... 56
Wadena (K3)*.... 316
Wahpeton ‡(C2).... 127
Walcott (M5)*.... 480
Walford (K5)*.... 165
Walker (K4)*.... 549
Wall Lake (C4)*.... 753
Wallingford (D2)*.... 229
Walnut (C6)*.... 888
Wapello (L6)*....1,755
Ware (D3)*....
Washburn (J4)*.... 132
Washington (K6)*....5,902
Washta (B3)*.... 403
Waterloo (J4)*....65,198
Waterloo (urban area)....83,551
Waterville (L2)*.... 199
Watkins (J5)*.... 130
Waubeek (K4)*.... 120
Waucoma (J2)*.... 385
Waukee (F5)*.... 501
Waukon (L2)*....3,158
Waukon Junction (L2)* 40
Waupeton (M3)*.... 11
Waverly (J3)*....5,124
Wayland (K6)*.... 600
Webb (D3)*.... 235
Webster (J6)*.... 136
Webster City (F4)*....7,611
Weldon (F7)*.... 229
Wellman (K6)*....1,071
Wellsburg (H4)*.... 744
Welton (M5)*.... 93
Wesley (E2)*.... 509
West (J5)*....
West Bend (D3)*.... 772
W. Branch (L5)*.... 769
W. Burlington (L7)*....1,614
W. Chester (K6)*.... 218
W. Des Moines (F5)*....5,615
W. Grove (J7)*.... 90
W. Liberty (L5)*....1,866
W. Mitchell (H2).... 112
W. Okoboji (C2).... 158
W. Point (K7)*.... 662
W. Union (K3)*....2,141
Western College (K5)....
Westfield (A3)*.... 172
Westgate (K3)*.... 226
Weston (B6).... 75
Westphalia (C5)*.... 160
Westside (C4)*.... 393
Wever (L7)*.... 100
What Cheer (J6)*....1,119
Wheatland (M5)*.... 568
Whiting (A4)*.... 663
Whittemore (E2)*.... 678
Whitten (H4)*.... 174
Whittier (K4)*.... 134
Wick (F6)*.... 58
Willey (D5).... 94
Williams (F3)*.... 519
Williamsburg (J5)*....1,183
Williamson (G6)*.... 294
Wilton Junction (M5)*....1,446
Winfield (L6)*.... 888
Windsor Heights (F5)...1,414
Winterset (E6)*....3,570
Winthrop (K4)*.... 604
Wiota (D6)*.... 227
Woden (F2)*.... 272
Woodbine (B5)*....1,304
Woodburn (F7)*.... 255
Woodland (F7)....
Woodward (F5)*.... 908
Woolstock (F3)*.... 255
Worthington (L4)*.... 337
Wright (J6)*.... 125
Wyman (L6)*.... 100
Wyoming (L4)*.... 724
Yale (E5)*.... 293
Yarmouth (L6)*.... 160
Yetter (D4)*.... 121
Yorkshire (B5)....
Yorktown (C7)*.... 146
Zearing (G4)*.... 514
Zook Spur (F5).... 20
Zwingle (M4)*.... 132

Map on Page 63

KANSAS

Total Population 1,905,299

105 COUNTIES

Allen (G4)....18,187
Anderson (G3)....10,267
Atchison (G2)....21,496
Barber (D4)....8,521
Barton (D3)....29,909
Bourbon (H4)....19,153
Brown (G2)....14,651
Butler (F4)....31,001
Chase (F3)....4,831
Chautauqua (F4)....7,376
Cherokee (H4)....25,144
Cheyenne (A2)....5,668
Clark (C4)....3,946
Clay (E2)....11,697
Cloud (E2)....16,104
Coffey (G3)....10,408
Comanche (C4)....3,888
Cowley (F4)....36,905
Crawford (H4)....40,231
Decatur (B2)....6,185
Dickinson (E3)....21,190
Doniphan (G2)....10,499
Douglas (G3)....34,086
Edwards (C4)....5,936
Elk (F4)....6,679
Ellis (C3)....19,043
Ellsworth (D3)....8,465
Finney (B3)....15,092
Ford (C4)....19,670
Franklin (G3)....19,928
Geary (F3)....21,671
Gove (B3)....4,447
Graham (C2)....5,020
Grant (A4)....4,638
Gray (B4)....4,894
Greeley (A3)....2,010
Greenwood (F4)....13,574
Hamilton (A3)....3,696
Harper (D4)....10,263
Harvey (E3)....21,698
Haskell (B4)....2,606
Hodgeman (C3)....3,310
Jackson (G2)....11,098
Jefferson (G2)....11,084
Jewell (D2)....9,698
Johnson (H3)....62,783
Kearny (A3)....3,492
Kingman (D4)....10,324
Kiowa (C4)....4,743
Labette (G4)....29,285
Lane (B3)....2,808
Leavenworth (G2)....42,361
Lincoln (D2)....6,643
Linn (H3)....10,053
Logan (A3)....4,206
Lyon (F3)....26,576
Marion (E3)....16,307
Marshall (F2)....17,927
Mc Pherson (E3)....23,670
Meade (B4)....5,710
Miami (H3)....19,698
Mitchell (D2)....10,320
Montgomery (G4)....46,487
Morris (F3)....8,485
Morton (A4)....2,610
Nemaha (F2)....14,341
Neosho (G4)....20,348
Ness (C3)....6,322
Norton (C2)....8,808
Osage (G3)....12,811
Osborne (D2)....8,558
Ottawa (E2)....7,265
Pawnee (C3)....11,041
Phillips (C2)....9,273
Pottawatomie (F2)....12,344
Pratt (D4)....12,156
Rawlins (A2)....5,728
Reno (D4)....54,058
Republic (E2)....11,478
Rice (D3)....15,635
Riley (F2)....33,405
Rooks (C2)....9,043
Rush (C3)....7,231
Russell (D3)....13,406
Saline (E3)....33,409
Scott (B3)....4,921
Sedgwick (E4)....222,290
Seward (B4)....9,972
Shawnee (G2)....105,418
Sheridan (B2)....4,607
Sherman (A2)....7,373
Smith (D2)....8,846
Stafford (D3)....8,816
Stanton (A4)....2,263
Stevens (A4)....4,516
Sumner (E4)....23,646
Thomas (A2)....7,572
Trego (C3)....5,868
Wabaunsee (F3)....7,212
Wallace (A3)....2,508
Washington (E2)....12,977
Wichita (A3)....2,640
Wilson (G4)....14,815
Woodson (G4)....6,711
Wyandotte (H2)....165,318

CITIES and TOWNS

Abbyville (D4)*.... 99
Abilene (E3)*....5,775
Achilles (B2)*.... 18
Acres (C4)*.... 2
Ada (E2)*.... 175
Adams (E4)*.... 45
Admire (F3)*.... 184
Aetna (D4).... 40
Agenda (E2)*.... 159
Agra (C2)*.... 354
Agricola (G3)*.... 30
Alamota (B3)*.... 39
Albert (C3)*.... 218
Alden (D3)*.... 286
Alexander (C3)*.... 188
Aliceville (G3)*.... 100
Alida (F2).... 81
Alki (F3).... 10
Allen (F3)*.... 241
Alma (F2)*.... 716
Almena (C2)*.... 616
Alta Vista (F3)*.... 420
Altamont (G4)*.... 652
Alton (D2)*.... 317
Altoona (G4)*.... 582
America City (F2).... 10
Americus (F3)*.... 339
Ames (E2)*.... 67
Amiot (G3)*....
Amy (B3)*.... 35
Andale (E4)*.... 316
Andover (E4)*.... 250
Angola (G4)*.... 50
Anness (E4)*.... 11
Anson (E4)*.... 50
Antelope (F3)*.... 40
Anthony (D4)*....2,792
Antonino (C3)*.... 75
Arcadia (H4)*.... 572
Argonia (E4)*.... 562
Arkansas City (E4)*....12,903
Arlington (D4)*.... 405
Arma (H4)*....1,334
Arnold (B3)*.... 108
Arrington (G2)*.... 50
Ash Grove (D2).... 55
Ash Valley (C3)....
Asherville (D2)*.... 105
Ashland (C4)*....1,493
Ashton (E4)*.... 45
Assaria (E3)*.... 221
Atchison (G2)*....12,792
Athol (D2)*.... 203
Atlanta (F4)*.... 309
Attica (D4)*.... 622
Atwood (B2)*....1,613
Auburn (G3)*.... 110
Augusta (F4)*....4,483
Aulne (E3)*.... 182
Aurora (E2)*.... 221
Axtell (F2)*.... 510
Baileyville (F2)*.... 150
Bala (F2)*.... 50
Baldwin City (G3)*....1,741
Bancroft (G2).... 26
Barclay (G3)*.... 47
Barker (H2).... 735
Barnard (D2)*.... 242
Barnes (F2)*.... 308
Bartlett (G4)*.... 143
Basehor (G2)*.... 275
Bassett (G4).... 117
Bavaria (E3)*.... 90
Baxter Springs (H4)*....4,647
Bazaar (F3).... 64
Bazine (C3)*.... 456
Beagle (G3)*.... 150
Beardsley (A2)*.... 30
Beattie (F2)*.... 321
Beaumont (F4)*.... 150
Beaver (D3)*.... 118
Beeler (B3)*.... 100
Bellaire (D2)*.... 55
Belle Plaine (E4)*.... 971
Bellefont (C4)*.... 35
Belleville (E2)*....2,858
Belmont (D4)*.... 48
Beloit (D2)*....4,035
Belpre (C4)*.... 231
Belvidere (C4)*.... 52
Belvue (F2)*.... 193
Bendena (G2)*.... 94
Benedict (G4)*.... 176
Bennington (E2)*.... 325
Bentley (E4)*.... 200
Benton (E4)*.... 269
Bern (F2)*.... 216
Berryton (G3)*.... 213
Berwick (G2).... 14
Beverly (E2)*.... 255
Big Bow (A4)*.... 100
Bigelow (F2)*.... 170
Bird City (A2)*.... 784
Bison (C3)*.... 326
Black Wolf (D3)*.... 23
Blaine (F2)*.... 45
Blair (H2)*.... 100
Blakeman (A2)*.... 10
Block (H3).... 21
Bloom (C4)*.... 125
Bloomington (D2)*.... 50
Blue Mound (H3)*.... 424
Blue Rapids (F2)*....1,430
Bluff City (E4)*.... 172
Bogue (C2)*.... 211
Boicourt (H3)*.... 30
Bonner Springs (H2)*...2,277
Bradford (F3).... 25
Brantford (E2).... 23
Brazilton (H4)*.... 75
Bremen (F2)*.... 80
Brenham (C4).... 21
Brewster (A2)*.... 467
Bridgeport (E3)*.... 53
Bronson (H4)*.... 415
Brookville (E3)*.... 213
Broughton (E2)*.... 96
Brownell (C3)*.... 211
Buckeye (E2).... 15
Bucklin (C4)*.... 824
Bucyrus (H3)*.... 131
Buffalo (G4)*.... 437
Buffville (G4).... 50
Buhler (E3)*.... 750
Bunker Hill (D3)*.... 271
Burden (F4)*.... 541
Burdett (C3)*.... 355
Burdick (F3)*.... 110
Burlingame (G3)*....1,065
Burlington (G3)*....2,304
Burns (F3)*.... 294
Burr Oak (D2)*.... 505
Burrton (E3)*.... 749
Burt (G4).... 35
Busby (F4).... 42
Bush City (G3)*.... 65
Bushong (F3)*.... 93
Bushton (D3)*.... 532
Byers (D4)*.... 83
Cairo (D4).... 40
Caldwell (E4)*....2,000
Calista (D4)*.... 12
Calvert (C2)*.... 22
Cambridge (F4)*.... 221
Canada (E3)*.... 38
Caney (G4)*....2,876
Canton (E3)*.... 771
Carbondale (G3)*.... 453
Carlton (E3)*.... 76
Carlyle (G4)*.... 45
Carneiro (D3)*.... 55
Carona (H4)*.... 175
Cassoday (F3)*.... 150
Castleton (E4)*.... 64
Catharine (C3)*.... 218
Cawker City (D2)*.... 691
Cedar (D2)*.... 86
Cedar Bluffs (B2)*.... 45
Cedar Point (F3)*.... 107
Cedar Vale (F4)*....1,010
Centerview (C4)*.... 30
Centerville (H3)*.... 155
Centralia (F2)*.... 574
Chanute (G4)*....10,109
Chapman (E3)*.... 990
Chardon (A2)....
Charleston (B4).... 12
Chase (D3)*.... 961
Chautauqua (F4)*.... 215
Cheney (E4)*.... 777
Cherokee (H4)*.... 849
Cherryvale (G4)*....2,952
Chetopa (G4)*....1,671
Chicopee (H4).... 250
Chiles (H3).... 20
Cimarron (B4)*....1,189
Circleville (G2)*.... 169
Claflin (D3)*.... 921
Claudell (C2)*.... 25
Clay Center (E2)*....4,528
Clayton (B2)*.... 157
Clearwater (E4)*.... 647
Cleburne (F2)*.... 150
Clements (F3)*.... 75
Clifton (E2)*.... 743
Climax (F4)*.... 91
Clonmel (E4).... 25
Cloverdale (F4)....
Clyde (E2)*....1,067
Coats (D4)*.... 255
Codell (C2)*.... 100
Coffeyville (G4)*....17,113
Colby (A2)*....3,859
Coldwater (C4)*....1,208
Collano (B4).... 25
Collyer (B2)*.... 282
Colony (G3)*.... 387
Columbus (H4)*....3,490
Colwich (E4)*.... 339
Como (E2).... 17
Concordia (E2)*....7,175
Conway (E3)*.... 101
Conway Springs (E4)*.. 816
Coolidge (A3)*.... 168
Copeland (B4)*.... 242
Corbin (E4)*.... 100
Corinth (D2).... 3
Corning (F2)*.... 254
Corwin (D4)*.... 60
Cottonwood Falls (F3)* 957
Council Grove (F3)*....2,722
Courtland (E2)*.... 367
Covert (D2)*.... 75
Coyville (G4)*.... 106
Crawford (E3)*.... 50
Crestline (H4)*.... 150
Crisfield (D4)*.... 11
Croft (D4)*.... 6
Crystalsprings (D4)*.... 73
Cuba (E2)*.... 345
Cullison (D4)*.... 174
Culver (E3)*.... 153
Cummings (G2)*.... 52
Cunningham (D4)*.... 510
Damar (C2)*.... 305
Danville (E4)*.... 122
Day (E2).... 6
De Graff (F4).... 30
De Soto (H3)*.... 518
Dearing (G4)*.... 261
Deerfield (A4)*.... 440
Delavan (F3)*.... 75
Delia (G2)*.... 164
Dellvale (B2)*.... 12
Delphos (E2)*.... 676
Denison (G2)*.... 166
Denmark (D2)*.... 50
Dennis (G4)*.... 200
Densmore (C2)*.... 61
Denton (G2)*.... 157
Derby (E4)*.... 432
Detroit (E3)*.... 124
Devon (H4)*.... 124
Dexter (F4)*.... 354
Dighton (B3)*....1,246
Dillon (E3).... 35
Dillwyn (D4).... 10
Dispatch (D2).... 17
Dodge City (B4)*....11,262
Doniphan (G2).... 50
Dorrance (D3)*.... 365
Douglass (F4)*.... 729
Dover (G3)*.... 50
Downs (D2)*....1,221
Dresden (B2)*.... 162
Dubuque (D3).... 12
Duluth (F2)*.... 70
Dundee (D3)....
Dunlap (F3)*.... 134
Duquoin (D4)*.... 15
Durham (E3)*.... 229
Dwight (F3)*.... 281
Earlton (G4)*.... 141
Eastborough (E4).... 708
Easton (G2)*.... 255
Edgerton (H3)*.... 266
Edmond (C2)*.... 110
Edna (G4)*.... 422
Edson (A2)*.... 70
Edwardsville ‡(H2)*.... 274
Effingham (G2)*.... 525
El Dorado (F4)*....11,037
Elbing (E3)*.... 98
Elgin (F4)*.... 212
Elk City (G4)*.... 524
Elk Falls (F4)*.... 276
Elkader (B3).... 5
Elkhart (A4)*....1,132
Ellinwood (D3)*....2,569
Ellis (C3)*....2,649
Ellsworth (D3)*....2,193
Elmdale (F3)*.... 180
Elmo (E3)*.... 50
Elmont (G2)*.... 65
Elsmore (G4)*.... 152
Elwood (H2)*....1,020
Elyria (E3)*.... 65
Emmett (F2)*.... 143
Emporia (F3)*....15,669
Englevale (H4)*.... 150
Englewood (C4)*.... 341
Enosdale (E2).... 11
Ensign (B4)*.... 227
Enterprise (E3)*.... 795
Erie (G4)*....1,296
Esbon (D2)*.... 278
Eskridge (F3)*.... 601
Eudora (G3)*.... 929
Eureka (F4)*....3,958
Everest (G2)*.... 368
Fact (E2).... 15
Fairport (C2)*.... 35
Fairview (G2)*.... 336
Fairway ‡(H2)....1,816
Fall River (G4)*.... 261
Falun (E3)*.... 92
Farlington (H4)*.... 96
Farlinville (H3).... 15
Faulkner (H4).... 36
Fellsburg (C4)*.... 43
Feterita (A4).... 10
Florence (E3)*....1,009
Flush (F2).... 304
Fontana (H3)*.... 168
Ford (C4)*.... 244
Formoso (D2)*.... 271
Fort Dodge (C4)*.... 500
Ft. Leavenworth (H2)*..
Ft. Riley (F2)*....2,531
Ft. Scott (H4)*....10,335
Fostoria (F2)*.... 100
Fowler (B4)*.... 778
Frankfort (F2)*....1,237
Franklin (H4)*.... 600
Frederick (D3)*.... 53
Fredonia (G4)*....3,257
Freeport (E4)*.... 30
Friend (B3)*.... 44
Frontenac (H4)*....1,569
Fulton (H4)*.... 243
Furley (E4)*.... 75
Galatia (D3)*.... 89
Galena (H4)*....4,029
Galesburg (G4)*.... 189
Galva (E3)*.... 426
Garden City (B4)*....10,905
Garden Plain (E4)*.... 323
Gardner (H3)*.... 676
Garfield (C3)*.... 297
Garfield Center (E2)....
Garland (H4)*.... 280

Garnett (G3)* 2,693
Garrison (F2)* 80
Gas (G4)* 294
Gaylord (D2)* 231
Gem (B2)* 118
Geneseo (D3)* 660
Gerlane (D4) 2
Geuda Springs (E4)* 245
Girard (H4)* 2,426
Glade (C2)* 107
Glasco (E2)* 803
Glen Elder (D2)* 582
Glendale (E3) 35
Glenloch (G3)
Goddard (E4)* 274
Goessel (E3)* 270
Goff (G2)* 315
Goodland (A2)* 4,690
Goodrich (G3) 50
Gordon (F4) 75
Gorham (D3)* 375
Gove (B3)* 206
Grainfield (B2)* 371
Grantville (G2)* 100
Gray (C3) 12
Great Bend (D3)* 12,665
Greeley (G3)* 436
Green (E2)* 219
Greenleaf (E2)* 614
Greensburg (C4)* 1,723
Greenwich (E4)* 50
Grenola (F4)* 380
Gretna (C2) 12
Gridley (G3)* 360
Grigston (B3)* 35
Grinnell (B2)* 364
Groveland (E3) 10
Gypsum (E3)* 523
Haddam (E2)* 375
Haggard (B4)* 42
Hale (F4) 8
Halford (B2)* 6
Hallowell (H4)* 223
Halls Summit (G3) 62
Hallville (E3) 5
Halstead (E4)* 1,328
Hamilton (F4)* 456
Hamlin (G2)* 118
Hammond (H4)* 62
Hanover (F2)* 854
Hanston (C3)* 286
Hardtner (D4)* 373
Hargrave (C3) 8
Harlan (D2)* 125
Harper (D4)* 1,672
Harris (G3)* 84
Hartford (F3)* 395
Harveyville (F3)* 236
Havana (G4)* 215
Haven (E4)* 720
Havensville (F2)* 208
Haviland (C4)* 606
Hawk (E4)
Hayne (B4) 6
Hays (C3)* 8,625
Haysville (E4)*
Hazelton (D4)* 250
Healy (B3)* 200
Hedville (E3) 39
Heizer (D3)* 100
Hepler (H4)* 224
Herington (E3)* 3,775
Herkimer (F2)* 120
Herndon (B2)* 321
Hesston (E3)* 686
Hewins (F4)* 200
Hiattville (H4)* 150
Hiawatha (G2)* 3,294
Hickok (A4) 37
Highland (G2)* 717
Hill City (C2)* 1,432
Hillsboro (E3)* 2,150
Hillsdale (H3)*
Hilltop (F3)* 15
Hoisington (D3)* 4,012
Holcomb (B3)* 206
Holland (E3) 50
Hollenberg (F2)* 97
Hollis (E2)* 49
Holton (G2)* 2,705
Holyrood (D3)* 748
Home (F2)* 200
Homewood (G3)* 60
Hooser (F4) 6
Hope (E3)* 480
Hopewell (D4)* 26
Horace (A3)* 258
Horton (G2)* 2,354
Howard (F4)* 1,149
Hoxie (B2)* 1,157
Hoyt (G2)* 246
Hudson (D3)* 194
Hugoton (A4)* 2,781
Humboldt (G4)* 2,308
Hunnewell (E4)* 103
Huron (G2)* 128
Hunter (D2)* 236
Hutchinson (D3)* 33,575
Hymer (F3) 10
Idana (E2)* 115
Independence (G4)* 11,335
Industry (E2) 100
Ingalls (B4)* 173
Inman (E3)* 615
Iola (G4)* 7,094
Ionia (D2)* 160
Iowa Point (G2) 110
Irving (F2)* 279
Isabel (D4)* 205
Iuka (D4)* 129
Jamestown (E2)* 494
Jarbalo (G2)* 75
Jefferson (G4)* 50
Jennings (B2)* 330
Jetmore (B3)* 988
Jewell (D2)* 593
Jingo (H3) 12
Johnson (A4)* 994
Junction City (E2)* 13,462
Juniata (D3)
Kackley (E2)* 60
Kalvesta (B3)* 49
Kanona (B2)* 25
Kanopolis (D3)* 743
Kanorado (A2)* 285
Kansas City (H2)* 129,553
Keats (F2)* 105
Kechi (E4)* 160
Keighley (F4) 21
Kelly (G2)* 150
Kenbro (F3) 50
Kendall (A4)* 125
Kensington (C2)* 635
Kimball (G4)* 67
Kincaid (G3)* 309
Kingman (D4)* 3,200
Kingsdown (C4)* 125
Kinsley (C4)* 2,479
Kiowa (D4)* 1,561
Kipp (E3)* 50
Kirwin (C2)* 374
Kismet (B4)* 180
La Crosse (C3)* 1,769
La Cygne (H3)* 794
La Harpe (G4)* 511
Labette (G4)* 145
Lafontaine (G4)* 125
Lake City (D4)* 185
Lakin (A4)* 1,618
Lamar (E2)* 100
Lamont (F3)* 100
Lancaster (G2)* 200
Lane (G3)* 200
Langdon (D4)* 128
Langley (D3)* 75
Lansing (H2)* 1,100
Larkinburg (G2)* 99
Larned (C3)* 4,447
Latham (F4)* 218
Latimer (F3)* 34
Lawrence (G3)* 23,351
Lawton (H4)* 85
Le Loup (G3)* 110
Le Roy (G3)* 695
Leavenworth (H2)* 20,579
Leawood (H3) 1,167
Lebanon (D2)* 610
Lebo (G3)* 575
Lecompton (G2)* 263
Lehigh (E3)* 240
Lenexa ‡(H3)* 803
Lenora (C2)* 511
Leon (F4)* 518
Leona (G2)* 130
Leonardville (F2)* 320
Leoti (A3)* 1,250
Leoville (B2)* 100
Levant (A2)* 130
Lewis (C4)* 475
Liberal (B4)* 7,134
Liberty (G4)* 185
Liebenthal (C3)* 211
Lillis (F2)* 50
Lincoln (D2)* 1,636
Lincolnville (F3)* 228
Lindsborg (E3)* 2,383
Linn (E2)* 395
Linwood (G2)* 261
Little River (E3)* 635
Logan (C2)* 859
Lone Elm (G3)* 82
Lone Star (G3)* 50
Long Island (C2)* 247
Longford (E2)* 178
Longton (F4)* 478
Loretta (C3) 30
Lorraine (D3)* 195
Lost Springs (E3)* 184
Louisburg (H3)* 677
Louisville (F2)* 190
Lovewell (D2)* 76
Lucas (D2)* 631
Lucerne (B2) 2
Ludell (B2)* 120
Luray (D2)* 351
Lyle (B2) 2
Lyndon (G3)* 729
Lyons (D3)* 4,545
Macksville (D4)* 624
Madison (F3)* 1,212
Mahaska (E2)* 179
Maize (E4)* 266
Manchester (E2)* 151
Manhattan (F2)* 19,056
Mankato (D2)* 1,462
Manning (B3)* 22
Manter (A4)* 200
Maple City (F4)* 50
Maple Hill (F2)* 176
Mapleton (H3)* 213
Marienthal (A3)* 110
Marietta (F2)* 49
Marion (F3)* 2,050
Marquette (E3)* 666
Marysville (F2)* 3,866
Matfield Green (F3)* 119
May Day (F2)* 27
Mayetta (G2)* 247
Mayfield (E4) 134
Mc Allaster (A3)* 35
Mc Cracken (C3)* 553
Mc Cune (G4)* 532
Mc Donald (A2)* 426
Mc Farland (F2)* 279
Mc Louth (G2)* 477
Mc Pherson (E3)* 8,689
Meade (B4)* 1,763
Medicine Lodge (D4)* 2,288
Medora (E3)* 125
Melrose (G4) 100
Melvern (G3)* 389
Menlo (B2)* 113
Mentor (E3)* 44
Mercier (G2)* 70
Meriden (G2)* 378
Merriam (H3)* 1,649
Michigan Valley (G3)* 105
Middletown (G4) 22
Midian (F4) 50
Milan (E4)* 165
Milberger (D3) 40
Mildred (G3)* 79
Milford (F2)* 284
Miller (F3)* 87
Milton (E4)* 100
Miltonvale (E2)* 911
Mingo (B2) 12
Minneapolis (E2)* 1,801
Minneola (C4)* 660
Mission (H2)* 13,000
Mission Hills ‡(H2) 1,275
Mission Woods ‡(H2) 205
Mitchell (D3)* 85
Modoc (A3)* 56
Moline (F4)* 871
Monrovia (G2)* 20
Mont Ida (G3) 50
Montezuma (B4)* 509
Montrose (D2)* 106
Monument (A2)* 160
Moran (G4)* 616
Morehead (G4)* 70
Morganville (E2)* 278
Morland (B2)* 287
Morrill (G2)* 362
Morrowville (E2)* 229
Morse (H3)* 80
Moscow (A4)* 222
Mound City (H3)* 707
Mound Valley (G4)* 566
Moundridge (E3)* 942
Mount Hope (E4)* 473
Mulberry (H4)* 779
Mullinville (C)4* 410
Mulvane (E4)* 1,387
Muncie (H2)* 60
Munden (E2)* 169
Munjor (C3) 150
Murdock (E4)* 120
Muscotah (G2)* 248
Narka (F2)* 220
Nashville (D4)* 159
Natoma (D2)* 775
Navarre (E3)* 80
Neal (F4)* 102
Nekoma (C3)* 96
Neodesha (G4)* 3,723
Neola (D4) 15
Neosho Falls (G3)* 355
Neosho Rapids (F3)* 204
Ness City (C3)* 1,612
Netawaka (G2)* 213
Neutral (H4) 23
New Albany (G4)* 152
New Almelo (B2)* 78
New Cambria (E3)* 160
New Lancaster (H3) 15
New Salem (F4)* 63
Newton (E3)* 11,590
Nickerson (D3)* 1,013
Nicodemus (C2)*
Niles (E2)* 100
Niotaze (F4)* 162
Norcatur (B2)* 368
North Newton (E3)* 566
Northbranch (D2)* 60
Norton (C2)* 3,060
Nortonville (G2)* 568
Norway (E2) 100
Norwich (E4)* 378
Nye (B4)
Oak Valley (G4)* 60
Oakhill (E2)* 92
Oakley (B2)* 1,915
Oberlin (B2)* 2,019
Odin (D3)* 115
Offerle (C4)* 269
Ogallah (C3)* 100
Ogden (F2)* 845
Oil Hill (F4)* 450
Oketo (F2)* 169
Olathe (H3)* 5,593
Olivet (G3)* 127
Olmitz (D3)* 125
Olpe (F3)* 293
Olsburg (F2)* 140
Onaga (F2)* 882
Oneida (G2)* 138
Opolis (H4)* 160
Oronoque (C2) 26
Osage City (G3)* 1,919
Osawatomie (H3)* 4,347
Osborne (D2)* 2,068
Oskaloosa (G2)* 721
Oswego (G4)* 1,997
Otego (D2)* 10
Otis (C3)* 410
Ottawa (G3)* 10,081
Ottumwa (G3) 26
Overbrook (G3)* 387
Overland Park (H3)* 10,000
Oxford (E4)* 798
Ozawkie (G2)* 204
Page City (A2)* 100
Palco (C2)* 405
Palmer (E2)* 150
Paola (H3)* 3,972
Paradise (D2)* 145
Parallel (F2) 15
Park (B2)* 223
Parker (H3)* 251
Parkerville (F3)* 78
Parsons (G4)* 14,750
Partridge (D4)* 221
Pauline (G3)* 131
Pawnee Rock (D3)* 359
Paxico (F2)* 196
Peabody (E3)* 1,194
Pearl (E3) 4
Peck (E4)* 89
Penalosa (D4)* 71
Pendennis (B3)* 10
Penokee (C2)* 90
Peoria (G3) 40
Perry (G2)* 399
Perth (E4)* 75
Peru (F4)* 368
Petrolia (G4)* 125
Pfeifer (C3)* 156
Phillipsburg (C2)* 2,589
Piedmont (F4)* 130
Pierceville (B4)* 175
Pilsen (E3)* 52
Piqua (G4)* 200
Pittsburg (H4)* 19,341
Plains (B4)* 718
Plainville (C2)* 2,082
Pleasanton (H3)* 1,178
Plevna (D4)* 200
Plymouth (F3) 80
Pomona (G3)* 453
Portis (D2)* 286
Potter (G2)* 120
Potwin (F4)* 465
Powhattan (G2)* 150
Prairie View (C2)* 192
Pratt (D4)* 7,523
Prescott (H3)* 283
Preston (D4)* 307
Pretty Prairie (D4)* 484
Princeton (G3)* 177
Protection (C4)* 814
Purcell (G2)* 50
Quenemo (G3)* 391
Quincy (F4)* 100
Quinter (B2)* 741
Radium (D3)* 64
Rago (D4)* 100
Ramona (E3)* 190
Randall (D2)* 240
Randolph (F2)* 391
Ransom (C3)* 405
Rantoul (G3)* 197
Raymond (D3)* 275
Reading (F3)* 289
Reager (B2)* 8
Reamsville (C2) 10
Redfield (H4)* 173
Redwing (D3)* 50
Reece (F4)* 250
Reno (G2) 50
Republic (E2)* 360
Reserve (G2)* 169
Rest (G4)* 10
Rexford (B2)* 304
Rice (E2)* 27
Richfield (A4)* 105
Richland (G3)* 141
Richmond (G3)* 433
Richter (G3) 25
Riga (C3) 21
Riley (F2)* 414
Riverdale (E4)* 65
Riverton (H4)* 250
Robinson (G2)* 381
Rock (F4)* 124
Rock Creek (G2)* 100
Rolla (A4)* 433
Rosalia (F4)* 100
Rose (G4)* 50
Rose Hill (E4)* 200
Roseland ‡(H4) 118
Rossville (G2)* 577
Roxbury (E3)* 145
Rozel (C3)* 233
Ruella (D4) 10
Ruleton (A2)* 52
Runnymede (E4) 5
Rush Center (C3)* 350
Russell (D3)* 6,483
Russell Springs (A3)* 161
Rydal (E2)* 42
Sabetha (G2)* 2,173
Saffordville (F3)* 110
Saint Benedict (F2) 150
St. Clere (F2)* 7
St. Francis (A2)* 1,892
St. George (F2)* 251
St. John (D3)* 1,735
St. Joseph (E2) 28
St. Marys (G2)* 1,201
St. Paul (G4)* 783
St. Peter (B2) 100
Salina (E3)* 26,176
Sanford (C3)* 50
Satanta (B4)* 667
Savonburg (G4)* 155
Sawyer (D4)* 223
Saxman (D3)* 33
Scammon (H4)* 561
Scandia (E2)* 611
Schoenchen (C3)* 170
Scott City (B3)* 3,204
Scottsville (D2)* 108
Scranton (G3)* 487
Sedan (F4)* 1,640
Sedgwick (E4)* 732
Seguin (B2) 12
Selden (B2)* 438
Selkirk (A3)* 100
Selma (G3)* 45
Seneca (F2)* 1,911
Severance (G2)* 197
Severy (F4)* 477
Seward (D3)* 130
Shady Bend (D2)* 25
Shaffer (C3) 15
Shallow Water (B3)* 105
Sharon (D4)* 278
Sharon Springs (A3)* 994
Sharpe (G3) 31
Shaw (G4)* 35
Shawnee (H3)* 845
Sherman (H4)* 100
Shields (B3)* 75
Silica (D3)* 10
Silver Lake (G2)* 331
Silverdale (F4)* 150
Simpson (E2)* 234
Sitka (C4)* 150
Skiddy (F3)* 70
Smith Center (D2)* 2,026
Smolan (E3)* 180
Soldier (G2)* 193
Solomon (E3)* 834
Solomon Rapids (D2)* 10
South Haven (E4)* 358
S. Hutchinson (D3) 1,045
S. Mound (G4)* 50
Sparks (G2)* 129
Spearville (C4)* 610
Speed (C2)* 70
Spivey (D4)* 109
Spring Hill (H3)* 619
Stafford (D4)* 2,005
Stanley (H3)* 300
Stark (G4)* 157
Sterling (D3)* 2,243
Stilwell (H3)* 209
Stockdale (F2) 80
Stockton (C2)* 1,867
Strawberry (E2) 11
Strawn (G3)* 150
Strong City (F3)* 680
Studley (B2)* 73
Stull (G3) 101
Stuttgart (C2)* 100
Sublette (B4)* 838
Summerfield (F2)* 305
Sun City (D4)* 231
Sunflower (G3)* 3,834
Susank (D3)* 100
Sycamore (G4)* 350
Sylvan Grove (D2)* 506
Sylvia (D4)* 496
Syracuse (A3)* 2,075
Talmage (E2)* 250
Talmo (E2)* 40
Tampa (E3)* 216
Tasco (B2)* 16
Tecumseh (G2)* 200
Tescott (E2)* 412
Teterville (F3)* 100
Thayer (G4)* 423
Thornburg (D2)
Thrall (F3)* 38
Timken (C3)* 138
Tipton (D2)* 246
Tonganoxie (G2)* 1,138
TOPEKA (G2)* 78,791
Topeka (urban area) 88,100
Toronto (G4)* 600
Towanda (E4)* 417
Trading Post (H3)
Traer (B2)* 69
Treece (H4)* 378
Tribune (A3)* 1,010
Trousdale (C4)* 110
Troy (G2)* 977
Turner (H2)* 1,500
Turon (D4)* 632
Tyro (G4)* 279
Udall (E4)* 410
Ulysses (A4)* 2,243
Uniontown (G4)* 232
Upland (E2) 25
Urbana (G4)* 70
Utica (B3)* 365
Valeda (G4)* 125
Valley Center (E4)* 854
Valley Falls (G2)* 1,139
Varner (D4)* 54
Vassar (G3)* 80
Vermillion (F2)* 283
Vernon (G4)* 45
Vesper (D2)* 100
Victor (D2) 6
Victoria (C3)* 988
Vilas (G4)* 34
Vine Creek (E2) 13
Vining (E2)* 168
Vinland (G3)* 68
Viola (E4)* 132
Virgil (F4)* 354
Vliets (F2)* 79
Voda (C2) 30
Volland (F3)* 20
Wabaunsee (F2) 110
Waconda Springs (D2)* 20
Wakarusa (G3)* 72
Wakeeney (C2)* 2,446
Wakefield (E2)* 591
Waldo (D2)* 216
Waldron (D4)* 83
Walker (C3)* 103
Wallace (A3)* 111
Walnut (G4)* 534
Walton (E3)* 220
Wamego (F2)* 1,869
Washington (E2)* 1,527
Waterloo (E4) 45
Waterville (F2)* 676
Wathena (H2)* 797
Wauneta (F4)* 75
Waverly (G3)* 487
Wayne (E2)* 60
Wayside (G4)* 90
Webber (D2)* 96
Webster (C2)* 130
Weir (H4)* 819
Welborn (H2)* 3,425
Welda (G3)* 214
Wellington (E4)* 7,747
Wells (E2)* 75
Wellsford (C4)* 59
Wellsville (G3)* 729
Weskan (A3)* 200
West Mineral (H4)* 349
West Plains (Plains*) (B4) 718
Westfall (D3)* 75
Westmoreland (F2)* 416
Westphalia (G3)* 254
Westwood (H2) 1,581
Westwood Hills ‡(H2) 431
Wetmore (G2)* 397
Wheaton (F2)* 134
Wheeler (A2)* 35
White City (F3)* 540
White Cloud (G2)* 308
Whitewater (E4)* 453
Whiting (G2)* 267
Wichita (E4)* 168,279
Wichita(urban area) 192,009
Wilburton (A4)* 22
Willard (G2)* 95
Williamsburg (G3)* 297
Williamstown (G2)* 60
Willis (G2)* 140
Wilmore (C4)* 172
Wilmot (F4)* 25
Wilsey (F3)* 251
Wilson (D3)* 1,039
Winchester (G2)* 355
Windom (E3)* 193
Winfield (F4)* 10,264
Winifred (F2)* 53
Winkler (F2)* 6
Winona (A2)* 382
Wolcott (H2)
Wolf (A3) 2
Womer (D2) 15
Woodbine (E3)* 195
Woodruff (C2)* 46
Woodston (C2)* 296
Worden (G3) 50
Wreford (F3) 44
Wright (C4)* 350
Xenia (G4) 24
Yates Center (G4)* 2,178
Yocemento (C3)
Yoder (E4)* 100
Zeandale (F2) 40
Zenda (D4)* 226
Zenith (D4)* 100
Zimmerdale (E3) 25
Zook (C3) 30
Zurich (C2)* 186

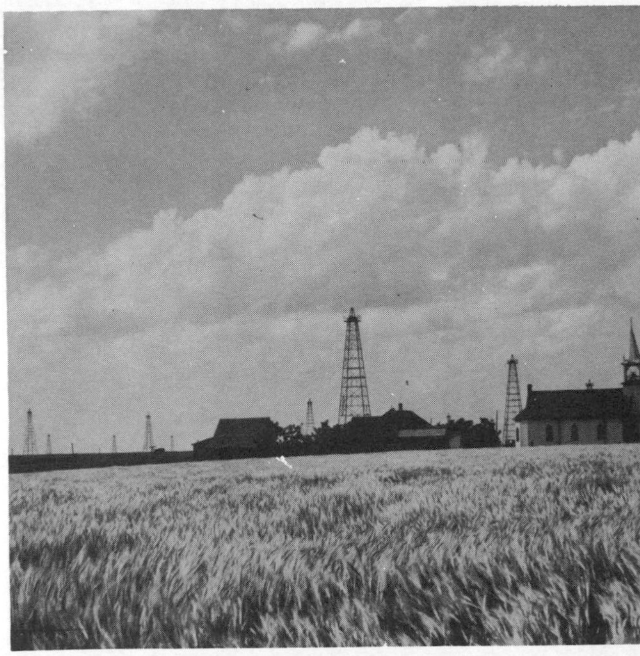

KENTUCKY

Map on Page 64

Total Population 2,944,806

120 COUNTIES

Adair (G6) 17,603
Allen (E7) 13,787
Anderson (H5) 8,984
Ballard (C3) 8,545
Barren (F7) 28,461
Bath (K4) 10,410
Bell (K7) 47,602
Boone (H3) 13,015
Bourbon (J4) 17,752
Boyd (M4) 49,949
Boyle (H5) 20,532
Bracken (J3) 8,424
Breathitt (L5) 19,964
Breckinridge (E5) 15,528
Bullitt (F5) 11,349
Butler (D6) 11,309
Caldwell (E3) 13,199
Calloway (D4) 20,147
Campbell (L2) 76,196
Carlisle (C3) 6,206
Carroll (G3) 8,517
Carter (L4) 22,559
Casey (H6) 17,446
Christian (C7) 42,359
Clark (J5) 18,898
Clay (K6) 23,116
Clinton (G7) 10,605
Crittenden (E2) 10,818
Cumberland (G7) 9,309
Daviess (C5) 57,241
Edmonson (E6) 9,376
Elliott (L4) 7,085
Estill (K5) 14,677
Fayette (J4) 100,746
Fleming (K4) 11,962
Floyd (M5) 53,500
Franklin (H4) 25,933
Fulton (C4) 13,668
Gallatin (H3) 3,969
Garrard (M5) 11,029
Grant (H3) 9,809
Graves (D3) 31,364
Grayson (E5) 17,063
Green (F6) 11,261
Greenup (M3) 24,887
Hancock (D5) 6,009
Hardin (F5) 50,312
Harlan (L7) 71,751
Harrison (J4) 13,736
Hart (F6) 15,321
Henderson (B5) 30,715
Henry (G4) 11,394
Hickman (C3) 7,778
Hopkins (B6) 38,815
Jackson (J6) 13,101
Jefferson (F4) 484,615
Jessamine (H5) 12,458
Johnson (M5) 23,846
Kenton (K2) 104,254
Knott (M6) 20,320
Knox (K7) 30,409
Larue (F5) 9,956
Laurel (J6) 25,797
Lawrence (M4) 14,418
Lee (K5) 8,739
Leslie (L6) 15,537
Letcher (M6) 39,522
Lewis (L3) 13,520

Lincoln (H6)....................18,668
Livingston (D2)..................7,184
Logan (D7).......................22,335
Lyon (E5)..........................6,853
Madison (J5)....................31,179
Magoffin (L5)...................13,839
Marion (G5).....................17,212
Marshall (D3)...................13,387
Martin (M5).....................11,677
Mason (K3).......................18,486
McCracken (D3)................49,137
McCreary (J7)...................16,660
McLean (C5).....................10,021
Meade (E5)........................9,422
Menifee (K5)......................4,798
Mercer (H5)......................14,643
Metcalfe (F7)......................9,851
Monroe (F7)......................13,770
Montgomery (K4)..............13,025
Morgan (L5)......................13,624
Muhlenberg (C6)...............32,501
Nelson (F5).......................19,521
Nicholas (J4).......................7,532
Ohio (D6)..........................20,840
Oldham (G4)......................11,018
Owen (H3)...........................9,755
Owsley (K6).........................7,324
Pendleton (J3)......................9,610
Perry (L6)..........................46,566
Pike (N6)...........................81,154
Powell (K5)..........................6,812
Pulaski (H6)......................38,452
Robertson (J3)......................2,881
Rockcastle (J6)...................13,925
Rowan (L4)........................12,708
Russell (G7)......................13,717
Scott (H4)..........................15,141
Shelby (G4)........................17,912
Simpson (D7)......................11,678
Spencer (G4)........................6,157
Taylor (G6).........................14,403
Todd (C7)...........................12,890
Trigg (E3)............................9,683
Trimble (G3).........................5,148
Union (E2)..........................14,893
Warren (E6)........................42,758
Washington (G5).................12,777
Wayne (H7)........................16,475
Webster (E2).......................15,555
Whitley (J7).......................31,940
Wolfe (K5)...........................7,615
Woodford (H4)....................11,212

CITIES and TOWNS

Aberdeen (D6)*............ 50
Adair (D5)*................. 100
Adairville (D7)*........... 800
Adams (M4)*................ 300
Adolphus (E7)*............ 500
Aflex (N5)*................. 250
Akersville (F7)*........... 152
Albany (G7)*..............1,920
Alcalde (J6)*...............
Alcorn (K5)*................ 100
Alexandria (J3)*.......... 536
Allais (L6)*................. 600
Allegre (C7)*............... 125
Allen (M5)*................. 421
Allen Springs (E7)*......
Allensville (C7)*.......... 337
Allock (L6)*................ 608
Almo (D3)*.................. 150
Alpha (G7)*................. 75
Alpine (H7)*................ 150
Alton Station (H4)*...... 75
Altro (L6)*.................. 75
Alva (L7)*.................1,341
Alvaton (E7)*.............. 250
Amburgey (M6)*..........
Ammie (K6)*...............
Anchorage (F4)*.......... 883
Anco (L6)*.................. 400
Anna (E6)*..................
Anneta (E6)*............... 100
Annville (K6)*.............. 350
Ansel (H6)*................. 195
Arabia (H6)*................ 229
Arjay (K7)*...............1,000

Arlington (C3)*........... 584
Artemus (K7)*............1,000
Arvel (K5)*..................
Ashbyburg (C5)*..........
Ashcamp (N6)*............
Ashland (M4)*..........31,131
Ashland, Ky.—Huntington, W. Va. (urban area) 156,136
Athertonville (F5)*....... 166
Auburn (D7)*.............. 994
Audubon Park (F4).......1,790
Augusta (J3)*.............1,599
Austin (F7)*................ 150
Auxier (M5)*..............1,000
Avenstoke (H4)............ 125
Bagdad (G4)*.............. 400
Baizetown (D6)*.......... 127
Bakerton (G7)*...........
Balkan (K7)*...............
Bandana (C2)*............ 300
Bangor (L4)*.............. 155
Banner (M5)*..............
Barbourville (K7)*.......2,926
Bardstown (G5)*.........4,154
Bardstown Jct. (F5)*. 75
Bardwell (C3)*...........1,033
Barlow (C3)*.............. 657
Barnrock (M5)*...........
Barretts Ferry (D5)*.... 10
Barterville (J4)*.......... 100
Baskett (B5)*............. 275
Battletown (E4)*......... 125
Bayou (D2)................ 125
Bays (L5)*..................
Beals (C5)*................ 150
Beattyville (K5)*.........1,042
Beauty (N5)*.............. 577
Beaver Dam (D6)*.......1,349
Bedford (G3)*............. 533
Bee Spring (E6)*.........
Beech Creek (C6)*.......
Beech Grove (C5)*....... 162
Belcher (N6)*.............
Belfry (N5)*...............1,315
Bell Farm (H7)*...........
Bellevue (L1)*............9,040
Belmont (F5)*............. 75
Belton (D6)*...............
Benham (M7)*............3,982
Benton (D3)*..............1,980
Berea (J5)*................3,372
Bernstadt (J6)*........... 300
Berry (J3)*................. 312
Berrys Lick (D6)*........ 50
Bertis (K4)*................ 97
Bethel (K4)*............... 225
Bethelridge (H6)*........ 190
Bethlehem (G4)*.......... 188
Betsy Layne (M5)*......1,500
Beverly (L7)*.............. 500
Bevier (C6)*............... 175
Big Branch (M6)*........
Big Clifty (E5)*............ 500
Big Creek (K6)*........... 560
Big Rock (L6)*............. 430
Big Spring (E5)*.......... 250
Billows (J6)................ 50
Birdsville (D2)*........... 113
Black Rock (E6)*......... 25
Blackey (M6)*............. 393
Blackford (B6)*........... 165
Blacks Ferry (G7)*.......
Blaine (M4)*...............
Blairs Mills (L4)*.........
Blanche (K7)*............. 455
Blandville (C3)*........... 124
Bloomfield (G5)*.......... 666
Blue Diamond (L6)*.....1,968
Bluestone (L4)*........... 60
Boaz (D3)*................. 100
Boldman (M5)*............ 300
Bolyn (M6)*............... 150
Bond (J6)*..................
Bondville (H5)*........... 91
Bonnieville (F6)*......... 300
Bonnyman (L6)*.......... 900
Boone (J5)*................ 137
Booneville (K6)*.......... 165
Boreing (J6)*.............. 250

Boston (F5)*................ 300
Botto (K6)*................. 60
Bowen (K5)*................ 150
Bowling Green (D7)*..18,347
Boyd (J3)*.................. 55
Bradford (J3)*............. 45
Bradfordsville (G6)*..... 450
Brandenburg (E4)*....... 755
Brazil (J5)*.................
Breeding (G7)*............ 100
Bremen (C6)*.............. 410
Brent (L2)...................
Brewers (D3)*............. 57
Brightshade (K7)*........ 200
Bristow (E6)*.............. 73
Brodhead (J6)*............ 808
Bromley (K1)*............. 980
Bronston (H7)*............ 300
Brooklyn (D6)*............ 50
Brooks (F4)*............... 150
Brookside (L7)*........... 600
Brooksville (J3)*.......... 622
Browder (D6)*............. 350
Brownsville (E6)*......... 447
Bruin (L4)*................. 125
Brushart (L3)*............. 50
Bryan (G7)*................ 137
Bryantsville (H5)*........ 126
Buchanan (M4)*........... 160
Buckner (G4)*............. 250
Buechel (F4)*............1,500
Buffalo (F6)*.............. 495
Buford (D5)................ 100
Bulan (L6)*................1,446
Bunch (J6)*.................
Burgin (H5)*............... 777
Burkesville (G7)*.........1,278
Burkley (C3)*.............. 340
Burlington (J2)*........... 400
Burna (D2)*................ 300
Burning Springs (K6)*.. 350
Burnside (H6)*............ 615
Burton (Bypro*) ‡(M6) 257
Burtonville (L4)*.......... 200
Bush (K6)*................. 200
Buskirk (L5)*...............
Busseyville (M4)*......... 100
Butler (J3)*................ 404
Cadiz (B7)*................1,280
Cains Store (H6)*........
Calhoun (C5)*............. 746
California (J3)*........... 117
Calvary (G6)............... 250
Calvert City (D3)*........ 900
Calvin (K7)*................
Camp Dix (L3)*............ 75
Camp Taylor (F4)*........
Campbellsburg (G3)*.... 361
Campbellsville (G6)*.....3,477
Campton (K5)*............. 431
Canada (N5)*..............1,500
Cane Valley (G6)*........ 150
Caney (L5)*................. 400
Caneyville (E6)*........... 377
Canmer (F6)*...............
Cannel City (L5)*......... 400
Canton (B7)*............... 250
Carbon Glow (M6)*...... 300
Carlisle (J4)*..............1,524
Carntown (J3)............. 100
Carpenter (K7)*...........
Carrollton (G3)*........... 226
Carrsville (D2)*........... 205
Carter (L4)*................ 84
Cartwright (G7)*.......... 110
Casey Creek (G6)*....... 117
Caseyville (B5)*.......... 73
Cash (F6)*.................. 75
Catlettsburg (M4)*.......4,750
Cave City (F6)*...........1,119
Cawood (L7)*..............1,232
Cayce (C4)*................ 200
Cecilia (F5)*............... 400
Center (F6)*................ 175
Centertown (C6)*......... 370
Central City (C6)*.......4,110
Cerulean (B7)*............ 218
Chance (G7)*............... 350
Chaplin (G5)*.............. 200
Chappell (L7)*.............

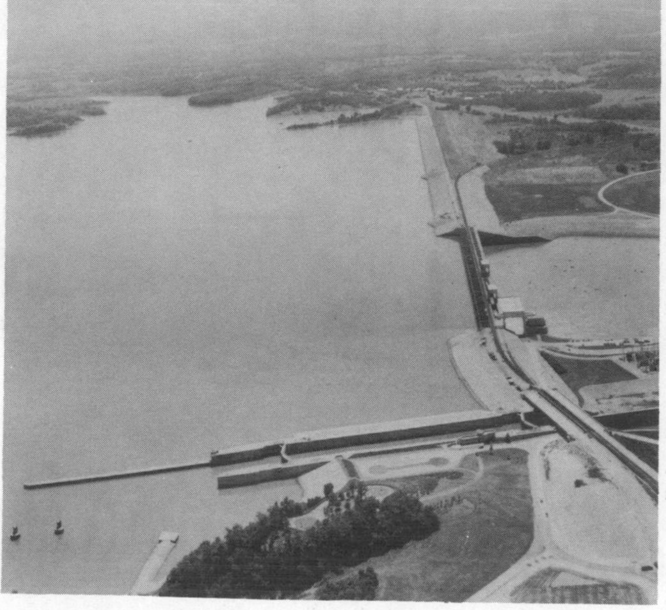

Charley (M5)*..............
Charters (L3)*............. 20
Chavies (L6)*.............. 300
Chenoa (K7)*...............
Cherokee (M4)*............
Chevrolet (L7)*............ 500
Chilesburg (J4)*.......... 50
Christianburg (G4)*...... 100
Clark Hill (L4)*............ 400
Clarkson (E6)*............ 489
Claxton (B6)*.............. 72
Clay (B6)*.................1,291
Clay City (K5)*............ 636
Claymour (C7).............. 150
Claypool (E7)*............. 50
Clearfield (L4)*............
Cleaton (C6)*.............. 450
Clermont (F5)*............. 40
Cliff (M5)*.................. 500
Clifford (N4)*.............. 50
Clifty (C7)*................. 200
Climax (J6)*................ 75
Clinton (C3)*..............1,593
Clintonville (J4)*.......... 100
Closplint (L7)*............. 600
Clover Bottom (J5)*..... 600
Cloverport (D5)*.........1,357
Co-Operative (H7)*...... 400
Coakley (F6)*.............. 150
Cobb (B6)*................. 200
Cold Spring (L2)*......... 518
Coleman (N6)*............. 200
Colesburg (F5)*........... 73
College Hill (J5)*......... 400
Collista (M5)*.............. 175
Colmar (K7)*............... 500
Colson (M6)*............... 200
Columbia (G6)*...........2,167
Columbus (C3)*............ 482
Combs (L6)*................ 800
Concord (L3)*.............. 142
Concordia (D4)*........... 75
Confluence (L6)*.......... 285
Constance (J1)*........... 150
Conway (J6)*............... 75
Cooper (H7)*............... 275
Coopersville (H7)*........ 250
Coral Ridge (F4)*........3,010
Corbin (J7)*...............7,744
Corinth (H3)*.............. 283
Cork (F6)*.................. 83
Cornishville (H5)*......... 230
Corydon (B5)*.............. 742
Cottle (L5)*.................
Cottonburg (J5)*.......... 122
Covington (K1)*.........64,452
Cowan (K4)*................ 200
Cowcreek (K6)*............ 250
Coxton (L7)*................ 700
Crab Orchard (H6)*...... 757
Crailhope (F6)*............ 50
Crane Nest (K7)*.......... 200
Crayne (A6)*............... 300
Creal (F6)*.................. 30
Creekville (L6)*............ 67
Creelsboro (G7)*.......... 50
Crescent Springs (K1)...
Creston (G6)*.............. 25
Crestwood (G4)*........... 450
Crider (B6)*................ 125
Crittenden (H3)*........... 287
Crofton (C6)*............... 500
Cromwell (D6)*............ 200
Cropper (G4)*.............. 175
Crummies (L7)*............ 400
Crutchfield (C4)*.......... 170
Cub Run (E6)*.............. 250
Cubage (K7)*............... 325
Cumberland (M6)*.......4,249
Cundiff (G7)*............... 125
Cunningham (C3)*......... 275
Curdsville (C5)*........... 169
Custer (E5)*................ 200
Cutshin (L6)*...............
Cynthiana (J4)*...........4,847
Dabney (H6)*...............
Daisy (L6)*................. 300
Dalton (B6)*................ 75
Daniel Boone (C6).........
Danville (H5)*.............8,686
David (M5)*................. 800
Dawson Springs (B6)*..2,374
Daysville (C7).............. 50
Dayton (L1)*...............8,977
De Coursey (L2)............
De Mossville (J3)*........ 104
Decoy (L5)*................. 250
Defoe (G4)*................. 142
Dekoven (B5)*..............
Delaware (C5)*............ 28
Delphia (L6)*............... 395
Denton (M4)*............... 200
Depoy (C6)*.................
Dewitt (K7)*................ 250
Dexter (D3)*................ 277
Dixon (B5)*................. 624
Donansburg (F6)*......... 200
Donerail (J4)*.............. 91
Dorton (M6)*............... 500
Dover (K3)*................. 334
Drakesboro (D6)*.........1,102
Dreyfus (J5)*............... 150
Dry Ridge (H3)*........... 640
Dublin (C3).................. 100
Duckers (H4)*.............. 50
Duncan (H5)................. 125
Dundee (D5)*............... 150
Dunham (M6)*.............1,200
Dunmor (C6)*............... 156
Dunnville (H6)*............ 140
Dwale (M5)*................ 495
Dycusburg (E3)*........... 147
Dyer (E5)*................... 39
Eadsville (H7).............. 300
Eagle Station (G3)*...... 35
Earlington (B6)*..........2,753
East Bernstadt (J6)*.... 900
East Point (M5)*.......... 200
Eby (L4)*.................... 50

Echols (D6)*................ 50
Eddyville (B6)*............1,840
Edmonton (F7)*........... 519
Edo (N6)*.................... 200
Edsel (M4)*................. 50
Eighty Eight (F7)*........ 75
Ekron (E5)*................. 188
Elamton (L5)*...............
Eli (H6)*...................... 250
Elias (K6)*...................
Elihu (H6)*...................
Elizabethtown (F5)*.....5,807
Elizaville (K4)*............ 150
Elk Creek (G4)............. 90
Elk Horn (G6)*.............
Elkatawa (K5)*............. 250
Elkfork (L5)*................
Elkhorn City (Praise*) (N6).....................1,349
Elkton (C7)*................1,312
Elliottville (L4)*........... 100
Elmrock (L6)*............... 276
Elrod (J6)*.................. 75
Elsmere (K2)...............3,483
Elva (D3)*................... 95
Eminence (G4)*...........1,462
Emlyn (J7)*.................. 700
Emma (M5)*................. 600
English (G3)*............... 150
Ennis (D6)*.................. 612
Eolia (M6)*.................. 100
Erlanger (K2)*..............3,694
Essie (L6)*...................
Estill (M6)*...................
Etoile (F7)*................... 40
Etty (M6)*.................... 200
Eubank (H6)*................ 322
Evarts (L7)*.................1,937
Evelyn (K5)*.................
Ewing (K4)*.................. 400
Ezel (L5)*.....................
Fagan (K5)*.................. 50
Fairfield ‡(G5)*............ 202
Fairplay (G7)*............... 78
Fairview (C7)*...............
Falcon (L5)*.................. 300
Falls of Rough (D5)*..... 195
Fallsburg (M4)*............. 200
Falmouth (J3)*.............2,186
Fancy Farm (C3)*.......... 419
Fariston (J6)*................ 290
Farler (L6)*.................. 200
Farmers (L4)*................
Farmington (D4)*........... 221
Faubush (H6)*............... 300
Fedscreek (N6)*.............
Felty (K6)*.................... 200
Ferguson (D7)................ 50
Ferguson (H6)*.............. 550
Field (K7)*..................... 300
Finchville (G4)*............. 75
Finley (G6)*................... 105
Finney (E7)*.................. 75
Firebrick (L3)*............... 150
Fishtrap (N6)*..............1,000
Fitchburg (K5)*............. 200
Flat (K5)*...................... 200
Flat Fork (L5)*...............
Flat Lick (K7)*..............1,000
Flat Rock (H7)*..............
Flatgap (M5)*................ 130
Fleming (M6)*................ 943
Flemingsburg (K4)*.......1,502
Flint (M6)*.................... 100
Flippin (F7)*.................. 150
Florence (J2)*...............1,325
Fonde (K7)*..................1,300
Fonthill (H6)*................ 50
Ford (J5)*..................... 250
Fordsville (D5)*............. 533
Forks of Elkhorn (H4)* 400
Fort Knox (F5)*...........10,000
Fort Mitchell (K1)......... 312
Fort Thomas (L1)*......10,870
Fort Wright ‡(K2)......... 594
Foster (J3)*................... 108
Fountain Run (F7)*........ 218
Francisville (J1)............ 25
FRANKFORT (H4)*....11,916
Franklin (D7)*...............4,343
Fredonia (B6)*.............. 395
Freeburn (N5)*.............2,200
Freedom (F7)*................ 75
Frenchburg (K5)*........... 268
Frew (L6)*..................... 162
Frogue (G7)*................. 300
Fry (G6)*....................... 50
Frymire (E5)*................ 25
Fullerton (L3)*..............1,501
Fulton (C4)*.................3,224
Furnace (K5)*................ 75
Gabbard (K6)..................
Gallup (M4)*..................
Gamaliel (F7)*............... 500
Gapcreek (H7)*.............. 300
Garfield (E5)*................ 150
Garlin (G6)*................... 150
Garrett (M6)*.................
Garrison (L3)*............... 300
Gatliff (K7)*................... 500
Gatton (F6)*................... 101
Gausdale (J7)*...............
Geneva (B5)*.................. 195
Georges Creek (M5)*..... 300
Georgetown (H4)*.........5,516
Germantown (K3)*.......... 260
Gesling (L4)*.................. 100
Gest (H4)*...................... 47
Ghent (G3)*.................... 368
Gilbertsville (D3)*.......... 700
Gimlet (L4)*.................... 100
Girdler (K7)*.................. 500
Glasgow (E6)*................7,025
Glen Dean (E5)*............. 100
Glen Springs (K3)*......... 50
Glencoe (H3)*................ 500
Glendale (F5)*................ 300
Glens Fork (G6)*............ 213
Glenwood (M4)...............
Glo (M6)*....................... 500

Glomawr (L6)*................ 800
Golden Pond (B7)*.......... 125
Goodloe (M5)*................
Gooserock (K6)*..............
Goshen (F4)*.................. 100
Gracey (B7)*...................
Gradyville (G6)*.............. 200
Graham (C6)*.................1,100
Grahn (L4)*.................... 600
Grand Rivers (E3)*.......... 234
Grange City (K4)*............ 225
Grant (H3)*..................... 100
Grassland (E6)*............... 79
Gratz (H4)*..................... 150
Gravel Switch (G5)*......... 200
Gray (K7)*...................... 300
Gray Hawk (J6)*.............. 300
Graysbranch (M3)*........... 156
Grayson (M4)*...............1,383
Green Hall (K6)*............. 120
Greenmount (J6)*............ 119
Greensburg (F6)*...........1,032
Greenup (M3)*...............1,276
Greenville (C6)*.............2,661
Greenwood (J7)*.............. 100
Grove Center (B5)*.......... 200
Guage (L5)*..................... 50
Gulnare (M5)*.................. 150
Gus (D6)*.........................
Guston (E5)*.................... 108
Guthrie (C7)*..................1,253
Guy (D6)*.........................
Haddix (L6)*..................... 500
Hadensville (C7)............... 85
Hadley (D6)*.................... 675
Haldeman (L4)*.................
Haleys Mill (C6)*...............
Halfway (E7)*.................... 200
Hall (M6)*..........................
Hamilton (H3)..................... 25
Hamlin (E4)*...................... 20
Hammond (K7)*.................. 400
Hampton (D2)*................... 120
Hanson (C6)*...................... 393
Happy (L6)*........................ 800
Hardburly (L6)*.................. 800
Hardin (D3)*....................... 324
Hardin Springs (E5)*......... 112
Hardinsburg (D5)*............. 902
Hardshell (L6)*................... 50
Hardy (N5)*.........................
Hardyville (F6)*.................. 300
Harlan (L7)*......................4,786
Harned (E5)*...................... 140
Harold (M5)*....................... 500
Harrods Creek (F4)*...........
Harrodsburg (H5)*............5,262
Hartford (D6)*...................1,564
Harveyton (L6)*................... 368
Hatcher (G6)*......................
Hatfield (N5)*...................... 250
Hawesville (D5)*.................. 925
Hazard (L6)*......................6,985
Hazel (D4)*.......................... 444
Hazel Green (K5)*................ 264
Hazle Patch (J6)*.................
Head of Grassy (L4)*.......... 50
Hebbardsville (C5)*............. 238
Hebron (J1)*........................ 250
Heidelberg (K5)*..................
Heidrick (K7)*...................... 600
Heisey (N5).......................... 150
Helechawa (L5)*.................. 120
Hellier (N6)*........................ 346
Helton (L7)*.........................
Henderson (B5)*..............16,837
Hendricks (L5)*....................
Henshaw (B5)*..................... 210
Herndon (C7)*...................... 250
Hesler (H4)...........................
Hi Hat (M6)*......................... 650
Hibernia (G6)*...................... 100
Hickman (C4)*....................2,037
Hickory (D3)*........................ 185
High Bridge (H5)*................. 350
Highland Heights (L1)...1,569
Highsplint (L7)*..................1,500
Highway (G7)*....................... 100
Hillsboro (K4)*...................... 141
Hima (K6)*............................. 200
Himlerville (Beauty*) (N5)................................ 577
Himyar (K7)*......................... 400
Hindman (M6)*...................... 521
Hinton (J4)*........................... 125
Hiram (L7)*............................ 300
Hiseville (F6)*.......................
Hitchins (M4)*.....................1,000
Hodgenville (F5)*................1,695
Holland (E7)*......................... 120
Homer (D7)*........................... 58
Hope (K4)*.............................
Hopewell (M4)*..................... 158
Hopkinsville (B7)*..............12,526
Horse Branch (D6)*............... 225
Horse Cave (F6)*.................1,545
Horton (D6)*.......................... 30
Howardstown (F5)*............... 100
Howel (B7)*........................... 50
Huddy (N5)*..........................
Hudson (E5)*......................... 133
Huntersville (G7)*................. 193
Huntsville (D6)*.................... 140
Hustonville (H6)*.................. 435
Hyden (L6)*........................... 647
Ilsley (B6)*............................ 400
Independence (H3)*.............. 285
Indian Hills ‡(F4)................ 291
Inez (N5)*............................ 622
Irad (M4)*.............................
Irvine (K5)*........................3,259
Irvington (E5)*...................... 831
Island (C6)*........................... 566
Isonville (L4)*........................ 150
Iuka (D3)*.............................. 21
Ivel (M5)*...........................1,200
Ivis (M6)*..............................
Ivyton (L5)*........................... 300
Jackson (L5)*.......................1,978
Jamestown (G7)*..................1,064

Jason (K6)*........................ 25
Jeff (L6)*...........................1,50
Jeffersontown (G4)*.........1,246
Jeffersonville (K5)*............ 47
Jellicocreek (J7)*...............
Jenkins (M6)*.....................6,92
Jericho (G4)*...................... 11
Jeriel (M4)*......................... 17
Jett (H4)*............................ 24
Jetts Creek (K6)*................ 7
Johnetta (J6)*..................... 10
Jonesville (H3)*................... 15
Joy (D2)*............................ 7
Junction City (H5)*............. 98
Kayjay (K7)*....................... 35
Keaton (L5)*........................
Keavy (J6)*..........................
Keene (H5)*........................ 50
Kehoe (L4)*......................... 17
Kelly (C7)............................ 9
Keltner (F6)*.......................
Kemp (F6)*...........................
Kenton (J3)*......................... 16
Kenvir (L7)*........................3,25
Kevil (C3)*............................ 20
King (K7).............................. 5
Kings Mountain (H6)*.......... 35
Kingsley ‡(F4)..................... 48
Kingswood (E5)*................... 22
Kirk (D5)*............................. 7
Kirkmansville (C6)*.............. 13
Kirksey (D3)*........................ 18
Kirksville (J5)*....................1,50
Kite (M6)*............................
Kitts (L7)*...........................1,43
Knifley (G6)*........................ 22
Knob Lick (F6)*....................
Knottsville (D5)................... 25
Kona (M6)*........................... 40
Kosmosdale (E4)*................. 37
Krypton (L6)*......................... 8
Kuttawa (E3)*....................... 79
Kyrock (E6)*.........................
La Center (C3)*.................... 59
La Fayette (B7)*.................. 24
La Grange (G4)*.................1,55
Lackey ‡(M6)*...................... 45
Lair (J4)................................ 6
Lake (K6)*............................. 25
Lakeside (K2)........................ 98
Lamasco (B7)*....................... 10
Lambric (L5)*......................... 7
Lancaster (H5)*..................2,40
Latonia (K2)..........................
Laurel Creek (K6)*................ 30
Lawrenceburg (H4)*............2,36
Lawton (L4)*......................... 37
Lebanon (G5)*....................4,64
Lebanon Junction(F5)*.1,24
Lecta (F6)*............................ 5
Lee (E6)*............................... 2
Lee City (L5)*........................ 12
Leeco (K5)*........................... 20
Leighton (K5)*....................... 50
Leitchfield (E6)*..................1,31
Lejunior (L7)*........................
Leon (M4)*............................ 12
Levee (K5)*...........................
Level Green (J6)*................... 7
Lewisburg (C6)*..................... 49
Lewisport (D5)*...................... 65
Lexington (J4)*..................55,53
Liberty (H6)*.......................1,29
Lida (K6)*............................. 20
Liggett (L7)*.......................... 45
Ligon (M6)*........................... 39
Lily (J6)*...............................
Limaburg (J2)........................ 4
Linton (E3)............................ 20
Linwood (F6)*........................
Lisman (B6)*......................... 17
Littcarr (M6)*.......................
Livermore (C5)*...................1,44
Livia (C5)*............................ 7
Livingston (J6)*..................... 37
Lockport (H4)*.......................
Locust Branch (J5)*............... 30
Locust Hill (E5)*.................... 5
Logansport (D6)*.................. 12
Lola (D2)*............................. 15
London (J6)*.......................3,42
Loneoak (D3)......................1,25
Lookout (N6)*......................1,30
Lookout Heights (K1)............ 60
Loretto (G5)*......................... 60
Lost Creek (L6)*.................... 25
Lothair (L6)*.......................1,31
Louellen (L7)*......................1,60
Louisa (M4)*........................2,01
Louisville (F4)*.................369,12
Louisville (urban area)....................470,39
Lovelaceville (C3)*................ 27
Lovely (N5)*.......................... 50
Lowes (C3)*........................... 15
Lomansville (M5)*.................. 50
Loyall (L7)*..........................1,54
Lucas (F7)*............................ 15
Lucile (L4).............................. 7
Ludlow (K1)*.......................6,37
Lynch (M7)*.........................3,97
Lynn Grove (D4)*.................... 7
Lynnville (D4)*....................... 10
Lyons (F5)*............................
Mac (G6)*..............................
Maceo (D5)*........................... 35
Mackville (G5)*...................... 25
Macon (E6)*...........................
Madisonville (B6)*..............11,13
Majestic (N5)*.....................1,14
Malone (L5)*.......................... 26
Maloneton (M3)*.................... 10
Manchester (K6)*.................1,70
Manitou (B6)*......................... 10
Mannington (C6)*.................... 30
Mannsville (G6)*..................... 20
Mariba (K5)*............................ 7
Marion (A6)*.........................2,37
Marrowbone (F7)*.................. 25
Marshes Siding (H7)*............ 50

Martha (M4)*
Martin (M5)* 1,170
Martinsburg (Sandy Hook*) (L4) 238
Martwick (D6)* 285
Mary (K5)* 300
Mason (H3)* 75
Matthew (L5)*
Mattingly (D5)* 40
Maud (G5)* 53
Maurice (K2)
Mayfield (D3)* 8,990
Mays Lick (K3)* 400
Maysville (K3)* 8,632
Maytown (K5)*
McAfee (H5)* 75
McAndrews (N5)*
McCarr (N5)*
McDaniels (E5)* 75
McDowell (M6)* 330
McHenry (D6)* 511
McKee (K6)*
McKinney (H6)* 500
McQuady (D5)* 100
McRoberts (M6)* 2,500
McVeigh (N5)* 1,292
Meador (E7)* 40
Mcally (M6)* 500
Means (K5)* 75
Melber (D3)* 227
Melbourne (L2)* 300
Mentor (J3)* 250
Merrimac (G6)* 175
Meta (N5)* 250
Mexico (E2)* 300
Middleburg (H6)* 250
Middlesboro (K7)* 14,482
Middletown (G4)* 1,500
Midway (H4)* 950
Milburn (C3)* 300
Milford (J3)* 150
Mill Springs (H7)* 250
Millard (N6)*
Millersburg (J4)* 828
Millerstown (E6)* 80
Mills (K7)* 300
Millstone (M6)* 700
Milltown (G6)* 250
Millwood (E6)* 175
Milo (M5)* 174
Milton (G3)* 355
Mima (L5)*
Minerva (K3)*
Mitchellsburg (H5)* 175
Mockingbird Valley ‡(F4) 150
Moct (L5)*
Monterey (H4)* 215
Monticello (H7)* 2,934
Mooleyville (D4)* 50
Moorefield (K4)* 150
Moores Creek (K6)* 214
Moorman (C6)* 300
Moree (N5)* 250
Morehead (L4)* 3,102
Moreland (H6)* 500
Morgan (J3)* 80
Morganfield (B5)* 3,257
Morgantown (D6)* 850
Morning View (J3)* 143
Morris Fork (K6)* 250
Mortons Gap (B6)* 1,081
Moscow (C4)*
Mount Eden (G4)* 300
Mount Olivet (J3)* 455
Mount Salem (H6)* 200
Mount Sherman (F6)* 150
Mount Sterling (J4)* 5,294
Mount Vernon (J6)* 1,106
Mount Washington (F4)* 40
Mountain Ash (J7)* 475
Mouthcard (N6)* 400
Muir (J4)* 400
Muldraugh (E5)* 1,100
Munfordville (F6)* 894
Murl (H7)* 400
Murray (D4)* 6,035
Myers (K4)* 150
Nancy (H6)* 500
Naomi (H6)*
Napier (L7)*
Narrows (D5)* 100
Nebo (B6)* 282
Ned (L6)* 276
Nelse (M6)* 100
Nelson (C6)*
Nelsonville (F5)* 50
Neon (M6)* 1,055
Nepton (K4)* 225
Nevisdale (J7)*
New Castle (G4)* 631
New Concord (E4)* 50
New Haven (F5)* 563
New Hope (G5)* 350
New Liberty (H3)* 225
Newfoundland (L4)* 60
Newman (C5)*
Nowport (L1)* 31,044
Newtown (J4) 100
Nicholasville (J5)* 3,406
Nick (E6)*
Noctor (L5)* 200
Nolin (F5)* 75
Norfleet (H6)* 150
Normandy (G4) 75
North Corbin (J7) 1,077
North Middletown (J4)* 319
North Pleasureville (G4)* 198
Northfield (J6)*
Nortonville (C6)* 909
Nuckols (C5)* 103
O'Bannon (G4)* 1,500
Oak Grove (C7)*
Oakland (F6)* 195
Oakton (C4)* 240
Oakville (D7)* 200
Offutt (M5)* 210
Ogle (K6)* 150
Oil Springs (L5)*
Okolona (F4)* 1,047
Old Landing (K5)* 250
Oldtown (M4)* 110
Olin (J6)* 196
Olive Hill (L4)* 1,351
Olmstead (D7)*
Olney (E2)* 75
Olympia (K4)* 250
Omer (L5)*
Oneida (K6)*
Onton (C5)* 125
Oppy (N5)
Ordinary (L4)* 100
Orlando (J6)* 150
Orville (H4)* 120
Outwood (B6)* 500
Owensboro (C5)* 33,651
Owenton (H3)* 1,249
Owingsville (K4)* 929
Packard (J7)
Pactolus (L4)* 150
Paducah (D3)* 32,828
Paint Lick (J5)* 200
Paintsville (M5)* 4,309
Palmer (J5)* 150
Panola (J5)* 200
Paris (J4)* 6,912
Park City (E6)* 448
Park Hills (K1) 2,577
Parkers Lake (H7)* 100
Parksville (H5)* 200
Parkway Village ‡(F4) 1,036
Patesville (D5)* 75
Payneville (E5)* 81
Peabody (K6)* 20
Pebworth (K5)*
Pellville (D5)* 111
Pembroke (C7)* 532
Penrod (C6)*
Peoples (J6)* 200
Perryville (H5)* 660
Petersburg (H2)* 356
Petersville (L4)* 150
Petroleum (E7)* 175
Pewee Valley (G4)* 687
Phelps (N6)* 926
Phil (H6)* 100
Philpot (D5)* 109
Pierce (F6)* 300
Pigeonroost (K6)* 250
Pike View (F6)*
Pikeville (N6)* 5,154
Pilgrim (N5)*
Pilot (K5)* 150
Pine Grove (J5)* 100
Pine Hill (J6)* 500
Pine Knot (H7)* 1,500
Pineville (K7)* 3,890
Pittsburg (J6)* 800
Place (J7)* 600
Pleasant View (J7)* 500
Pleasureville (G4)* 355
Plummers Landing (L4)* 100
Polsgrove (H4)* 44
Poole (B5)* 250
Poplarville (J6)*
Port Royal (G3)* 156
Portland (G6)* 200
Powersburg (H7)* 400
Praise (N6)* 1,349
Preece (M5)*
Premium (M6)* 500
Preston (K4)* 200
Prestonsburg (M5)* 3,585
Prestonville (G3)* 166
Priceville (F6)*
Pride (E2) 150
Princeton (B6)* 5,388
Prospect (F4)* 300
Providence (B6)* 3,905
Pryorsburg (D3)* 400
Pryse (K5)* 200
Pulaski (H6)*
Pyramid (M5)*
Quality (D6)* 55
Quicksand (L5)* 350
Quincy (L3)* 200
Quinton (H7)* 250
Raceland (M3)* 1,001
Ransom (N5)*
Ravenna (K5)* 979
Raywick (G5)* 175
Ready (E6)* 175
Redbush (L5)*
Redhouse (J5)* 500
Redwine (L4)* 138
Reed (C5)* 155
Reedyville (D6)* 50
Relief (L5)* 350
Repton (E2)* 36
Revelo (J7)*
Rexton (L3)* 20
Reynolds Station (D5)* 30
Ricetown (K6)*
Richardson (M5)* 175
Richardsville (E6)* 250
Richelieu (D7)*
Richlawn ‡(F4) 655
Richmond (J5)* 10,268
Riggs (M3)* 375
Riley (G5)* 350
Rineyville (F5)* 300
Ritner (H7)* 200
Riverside (E6)* 108
Roark (L6)*
Robards (B5)* 428
Roberta (E4)* 5
Robinson (J4)* 60
Robinson Creek (N6)*
Rochester (D6)* 372
Rockfield (E7)* 150
Rockholds (J7)* 562
Rockport (D6)* 450
Rockvale (D5)* 25
Rocky Hill ((E6)*
Rose Hill (H5)* 200
Rosewood (C6) 119
Rosine (D6)* 450
Rowena (G7)* 75
Rowland (H5) 200
Rowletts (F6)*
Royalton (M5)* 400
Rugless (L3) 25
Rumsey (C5)* 301
Rush (M4)* 500
Russell (M3)* 1,681
Russell Springs (G6)* 1,125
Russellville (D7)* 4,529
Ruth (J6)*
Sacramento (C6)* 378
Sadieville (H4)* 355
Saint Charles (B6)* 534
St. Francis (G5)* 248
St. Helens (K5)* 300
St. Joseph (C5)*
St. Mary (G5)* 212
St. Matthews (F4)*
Saldee (L6)* 75
Salem (D2)* 395
Salmons (D7)* 35
Saloma (G6)* 168
Salt Lick (K4)* 488
Salvisa (H5)* 500
Salyersville (L5)* 1,174
Samuels (G5)* 250
Sand Springs (J6)* 100
Sanders (H3)* 206
Sandgap (J6)* 800
Sandy Hook (L4)* 238
Sano (G6)* 225
Sardis (K3)* 176
Savoy (J7)* 350
Sawyer (J7)* 462
Saxton (J7)*
Scalf (K7)* 500
Science Hill (H6)* 445
Scottsburg (E3) 50
Scottsville (E7)* 2,060
Scranton (K5)* 50
Sebree (B5)* 1,158
Seco (M6)* 644
Sedalia (D4)* 240
Seneca Gardens ‡(F4) 868
Seneca Vista ‡(F4) 363
Sewell (L5)* 200
Sextons Creek (K6)* 250
Shady Grove (B6) 60
Sharon Grove (D7)* 200
Sharpsburg (K4)* 405
Shawhan (J4)* 100
Shelbiana (M6)* 500
Shelbyville (G4)* 4,403
Shepherdsville (F4)* 953
Sherburne (K4)* 100
Sherman (H3)* 160
Shively (F4)* 2,401
Sibert (K6)* 250
Sideway (L4)* 65
Siloam (M3)* 350
Silver Grove (L2)* 1,000
Silverhill (L5)* 500
Simpson (L5)*
Simpsonville (G4)* 247
Sizerock (L6)* 200
Skaggs (L4)* 171
Slade (K5)* 500
Slaughters (B6)* 326
Slemp (L6)* 150
Slickford (H7)* 450
Sloans Valley (J7)* 225
Smilax (L6)* 200
Smith Mills (B5)* 300
Smith Town (H7)* 600
Smithfield ‡(G4)* 121
Smithland (D3)* 498
Smiths Grove (E6)* 683
Smoky Valley (L4)* 100
Soft Shell (M6)* 248
Soldier (L4)* 150
Somerset (J6)* 7,097
Sonora (F5)* 292
Sophie (L4)* 70
South (E6)* 57
So. Carrollton (C6)* 289
So. Ft. Mitchell (K2)* 3,142
So. Hills ‡(K2) 412
So. Irvine (J5)* 400
So. Pleasureville (Pleasureville*) (G4) 355
So. Portsmouth (L3)* 1,196
So. Shore (M3)* 1,497
So. Union (D7)* 85
Southgate (L1) 1,903
Sparksville (G6)* 250
Sparrow (G5) 75
Sparta (H3)* 298
Spider (M6)* 211
Spottsville (C5)* 400
Spring Creek (K6) 27
Spring Lick (D6)* 140
Springdale (K3)* 30
Springfield (G5)* 2,032
Sprule (K7)* 200
Spurrier (F6)* 25
Stab (J6)* 200
Staffordsville (M5)* 350
Stamping Ground (H4)* 396
Stanford (H5)* 1,861
Stanley (C5)*
Stanton (K5)* 635
State Line (C4)* 200
Station Camp (J5)* 300
Stearns (J7)* 3,000
Stephensburg (E5)* 200
Stephensport (D5)* 155
Stepstone (K4)
Stillwater (K5)* 800
Stone (N5)*
Strathmoor Gardens ‡(F4) 329
Strathmoor Manor ‡(F4) 422
Strathmoor Village ‡(F4) 466
Stricklett (L4)* 25
Strunk (J7)* 250
Sturgis (B5)* 2,222
Sublett (L5)* 250
Subtle (F7)* 25
Sudith (K4)* 120
Sullivan (A6)* 250
Sulphur (G4)* 350
Sulphur Lick (F7)* 75
Sulphur Well (F6)*
Summer Shade (F7)* 350
Summersville (F6)* 500
Sumner (J7)* 50
Sunnydale (D5)* 75
Susie (H7)* 400
Sweeden (E6)* 130
Switzer (H4)* 246
Talbert (L6)* 25
Tateville (H7)* 500
Taylorsport (J1)* 259
Taylorsville (G4)* 888
Texas (G5)* 150
Thealka (M5)*
Threelinks (J6)* 100
Threlkel (E6)* 43
Tilden (B5) 25
Tiline (D3) 150
Tinsley (K7)* 500
Tiptop (L5)* 200
Tollesboro (K3)* 480
Tolu (E2)* 350
Tompkinsville (F7)* 1,859
Tongs (M3)* 150
Tousey (D5)* 60
Tracy (F7)* 50
Trammel (E7)* 100
Travellers Rest (K6)*
Trenton (C7)* 577
Trimble (H6)* 300
Trinity (K3)* 75
Trixie (K6)*
Truesville (H4)*
Truitt (M3)* 100
Turkey (L6)* 75
Turners Station (G3)* 89
Twila (L7)* 550
Tyner (K6)*
Tyrone (H4) 225
Ulysses (M5)* 325
Union (H3)* 155
Union Star (D5)* 57
Uniontown (B5)* 1,054
Upper Tygart (L4)* 150
Upton (F6)* 383
Urban (K6)*
Utica (C5)*
Vada (K5)*
Valley Station (F4)* 75
Valley View (J5)* 200
Van (M6)* 40
Van Lear (M5)* 1,096
Vanburen (G5) 175
Vanceburg (L3)* 1,528
Verda (L7)* 1,446
Vernon (F7)* 100
Verona (H3)* 200
Versailles (H4)* 2,760
Vicco (L6)* 1,008
Victory (J6)*
Vine Grove (F5)* 1,252
Viola (D3) 200
Virgie (M6)* 1,500
Visalia (J3) 192
Waco (J5)* 250
Waddy (G4)* 300
Walden (J7)*
Walker (K7)* 400
Wallingford (K4)* 200
Wallins Creek (K7)* 525
Wallonia (B7) 160
Wallsend (K7)
Walnut Grove (H6)*
Waltersville (J5)* 250
Walton (H3)* 1,358
Warfield (N5)* 324
Warnock (M4)* 175
Warsaw (H3)* 829
Washington (K3)* 500
Watauga (G7)* 100
Water Valley (C4)* 346
Watergap (M5)*
Waterview (G7)* 250
Waverly (B5)* 345
Waverly Hills (F4)*
Wax (E6)* 123
Wayland (M6)* 1,807
Waynesburg (H6)* 400
Webbs CrossRoads (G6)* 300
Webbville (M4)* 200
Webster (E5)* 128
Weeksbury (M6)* 1,340
Wellington (K5)* 300
Wellington ‡(F4) 656
West Irvine (J5)* 200
West Liberty (L5)* 931
West Louisville (C5)* 250
West Paducah (C3)* 135
West Point (E4)* 1,669
West Russell (M4) 1,200
West Somerset (H6)* 500
West Van Lear (M5)*
Westbend (J5)* 250
Westport (F4)* 125
Westwood (M4)* 4,000
Wheatcroft (B5)* 418
Wheatley (H3)* 85
Wheeler (K7) 400
Wheelwright (M6)* 2,037
Whick (L6)*
White Mills (E5)* 100
White Plains (C6)* 385
Whitehouse (M5)*
Whitesburg (M6)* 1,393
Whitesville (D5)* 723
Whitley City (J7)* 2,500
Wickliffe (C3)* 1,019
Wilbur (M5)*
Wild Cat (K6)* 50
Wilders (K1) 204
Wildie (J6)* 250
Willard (M4)* 124
Williamsburg (J7)* 3,348
Williamsport (M5)* 475
Williamstown (H3)* 1,466
Willisburg (G5)* 350
Wilmore (H5)* 2,337
Winchester (J4)* 9,226
Wingo (C4)* 451
Winifred (M5)*
Winston (J5)* 250
Winston Park (L2) 588
Wisdom (G7)*
Wolf Creek (E4)* 200
Wolverine (L5)* 225
Woodbine (J7)* 1,200
Woodburn (E7)* 240
Woodbury (D6)* 94
Woodlawn (G5)* 200
Woodlawn (L1) 339
Woodsbend (L5)*
Woollum (K6)* 150
Wooton (L6)* 2,725
Worthington (F4) 1,000
Worthington (M3)* 695
Worthville (G3)* 308
Wrigley (L4)* 200
Wurtland (M3)* 450
Wysox (D6)* 30
Yancey (L7)* 1,000
Yatesville (M4)* 100
Yeaddiss (L6)* 300
Yocum (L5)*
York (L3)* 150
Yosemite (H6)* 200
Youngs Creek (J7)* 94
Yuma (G6)*
Zachariah (K5)* 123
Zebulon (M5)* 100
Zelda (M4)
Zula (H7)* 400

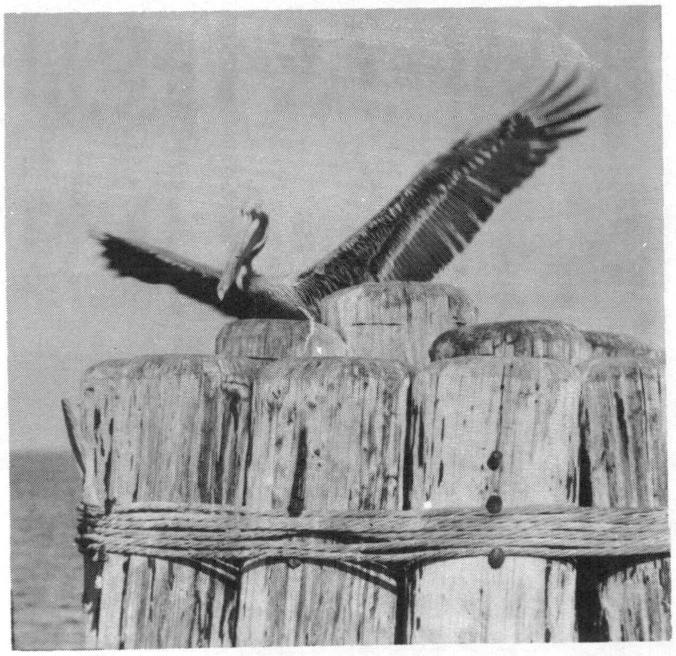

LOUISIANA

Map on Page 65

Total Population 2,683,516

64 PARISHES

Acadia (F6) 47,050
Allen (E5) 18,835
Ascension (J6) 22,387
Assumption (H7) 17,278
Avoyelles (G4) 38,031
Beauregard (D5) 17,766
Bienville (D2) 19,105
Bossier (C1) 40,139
Caddo (C1) 176,547
Calcasieu (D6) 89,635
Caldwell (F2) 10,293
Cameron (D7) 6,244
Catahoula (G3) 11,834
Claiborne (D1) 25,063
Concordia (G4) 14,398
De Soto (C2) 24,398
East Baton Rouge (K1) 158,236
East Carroll (H1) 16,302
East Feliciana (H5) 19,133
Evangeline (F5) 31,629
Franklin (G2) 29,376
Grant (E3) 14,263
Iberia (G7) 40,059
Iberville (H6) 26,750
Jackson (E2) 15,434
Jefferson (K7) 103,873
Jefferson Davis (E6) 26,298
La Salle (F3) 12,717
Lafayette (F6) 57,743
Lafourche (K7) 42,209
Lincoln (E1) 25,782
Livingston (L2) 20,054
Madison (H2) 17,451
Morehouse (G1) 32,038
Natchitoches (D3) 38,144
Orleans (L6) 570,445
Ouachita (F2) 74,713
Plaquemines (L8) 14,239
Pointe Coupee (G5) 21,841
Rapides (E4) 90,648
Red River (D2) 12,113
Richland (G2) 26,672
Sabine (C3) 20,880
Saint Bernard (L7) 11,087
St. Charles (K7) 13,363
St. Helena (J5) 9,013
St. James (L3) 15,334
St. John the Baptist (M3) 14,861
St. Landry (F5) 78,476
St. Martin (G6) 26,353
St. Mary (H7) 35,848
St. Tammany (L6) 26,988
Tangipahoa (K5) 53,218
Tensas (H2) 13,209
Terrebonne (J8) 43,328
Union (F1) 19,141
Vermilion (F7) 36,929
Vernon (D4) 18,974
Washington (K5) 38,371
Webster (D1) 35,704
W. Baton Rouge (H6) 11,738
W. Carroll (H1) 17,248
W. Feliciana (H5) 10,169
Winn (E3) 16,119

CITIES and TOWNS

Abbeville (F7)* 9,338
Abington (C2) 100
Abita Springs (L6)* 559
Acme (G4)*
Acy (L3)* 238
Addis (J2)* 505
Adeline (G7)
Afton (H2)
Aimwell (G3)* 150
Ajax (D3) 250
Akers (N2)* 500
Albany (M1)* 1,000
Albemarle (K4) 150
Alberta (D2) 35
Alco (D4)*
Alden Bridge (C1) 100
Alexandria (E4)* 34,913
Alice (H5) 20
Allemands (N4)*
Allen (D3)
Almadane (D5)
Aloha (E3)
Alsatia (H1) 65
Alto (G2)*
Alton (L6)
Ama (N4)* 650
Amelia (H7)*
Amite (K5)* 2,804
Anacoco (D4)* 500
Anchor (H5)
Andrepont (F5)
Andrew (F6)* 110
Angie (L5)* 230
Angola (G5)*
Ansley (E2)* 600
Antioch (E1)* 50
Arabi (L7)*
Arbroth (H5)*
Arcadia (E1)* 2,241
Archibald (G2)* 168
Archie (G3)* 250
Arcola (K5)* 100
Argo (G4)
Arizona (E1)* 300
Arkana (C1)
Armistead (D3)* 50
Arnaudville (G6)* 872
Ashland (D2)* 200
Ashton (G7)
Atchafalaya (G6)* 300
Athens (E1)* 487
Atkins (D2) 150
Atlanta (E3)*
Avery Island (G7)*
Avoca (K4)*
Ayers (D4)
Bains (H5)*
Baker (K1)* 762
Baldwin (H7)* 1,138
Ball (F4)*
Bancker (F7)* 75
Bancroft (C5)
Baptist (M1)* 600
Barataria (K7)*
Barton (K3)*
Basile (E5)* 1,572
Baskin (G2)* 117
Bass (K1)
Bastrop (G1)* 12,769
Batchelor (G5)* 1,936
BATON ROUGE (K2)* 125,629
Baton Rouge (urban area) 137,108
Bay (F2)
Bayou Barbary (M2) 150
Bayou Chene (G6)*
Bayou Chicot (F5) 250
Bayou Current (G5)*
Bayou Goula (J3)*
Baywood (K1)*
Beaver (E5)*
Beekman (G1) 250
Begg (F5) 20
Bel (D6)*
Belcher (C1)* 300
Bell City (D6)* 221
Belle Alliance (K3)* 200
Belle Chasse (O4)
Belle Helene (K3) 30
Belledeau (F4) 75
Bellerose (K3)*
Bellwood (D3)*
Belmont (C3)* 300
Benson (C3)* 200
Bentley (E3)*
Benton (C1)* 741
Bermuda (D3)*
Bernice (E1)* 1,524
Bertrandville (L7) 200
Berwick (H7)* 2,619
Bethany (B2)* 350
Bienville (D2)* 445
Blackburn (D1) 15
Blade (F3)* 75
Blanchard (C1)* 400
Blond (K5) 20
Bogalusa (L5)* 17,798
Bolinger (C1) 50
Bolivar (K5)
Bon Ami (D5)
Bond (E5) 60
Bonfouca (L6)
Bonita (G1)* 504
Boothville (M8)* 600
Bordelonville (G4)*
Bosco (F2)* 150
Bossier City (C1)* 15,470
Boudreaux (J8) 200
Bourg (J7)*
Boutte (N4)* 860
Boyce (E4)* 981
Braithwaite (P4)* 200
Branch (F6)* 250
Breaux Bridge (G6)* 2,492
Brignac (L2) 250
Brittany (L3)*
Brooks (H5)
Broussard (F6)* 1,237
Brusly (J2)* 493
Bryceland (E2)* 123
Buckeye (F4)*
Bunkie (F5)* 4,666

Buras (L8)*...1,200
Burnside (L3)*... 600
Burrwood (M8)*... 150
Burtville (K2)... 38
Bush (L5)*... 150
Butler (C3)...
Cabinash (K8)*... 40
Cade (G6)*... 750
Calcasieu (E4)*... 80
Calhoun (F2)*... 600
Calumet (H7)... 100
Calvin (E3)*... 300
Cameron (D7)*... 950
Camp (D1)... 8
Campti (D3)*...1,014
Caney (D4)...
Carencro (F6)*...1,587
Carlisle (L7)*... 15
Carmenia (C4)... 50
Carville (K3)*...2,200
Caspiana (C2)*... 350
Castille (F6)...
Castor (D2)*... 171
Cecelia (G6)*... 500
Cecile (C2)... 225
Center Point (F4)*...
Centerville (H7)*...
Central (L3)*...
Chacahoula (J7)*...
Chalmette (L7)*...1,695
Chamberlin (J1)*... 400
Charenton (H7)*...
Charlieville (G2)...
Chase (G2)*... 80
Chataignier (F5)*... 500
Chatham (F2)*... 833
Chauvin (J8)*...3,500
Chef Menteur (L6)... 150
Cheneyville (F4)*... 918
Chestnut (D2)*... 75
Chipola (J5)*... 18
Chopin (E4)*...
Choudrant (F1)*... 395
Church Point (F6)*...2,897
Cinclare (J2)*...
City Price (L7)...
Clare (C4)*...
Clarence (E3)*... 250
Clarks (F2)*...1,345
Clay (E2)*...
Clayton (H3)*... 657
Clear Lake (E3)... 100
Clifton (K5)*...
Clinton (J5)*...1,383
Clio (M2)*...
Cloutierville (E3)*...
Colfax (E3)*...1,651
Collinsburg (C1)... 25
Collinston (G1)*... 546
Colquitt (E1)... 30
Columbia (F2)*... 920
Columbus (C4)*... 160
Comite (K1)...
Como (G2)...
Convent (L3)*...1,200
Converse (C3)*... 311
Coon (G5)*...
Cora (E4)*...
Corbin (L1)*...
Corey (F2)...
Cornerview (K2)... 200
Cotton Valley (D1)*...1,188
Cottonport (F5)*...1,534
Couchwood (D1)... 600
Coushatta (D2)*...1,788
Covington (K5)*...5,113
Cow Island (F7)... 25
Cravens (E5)...
Creole (D7)*... 150
Crescent (J2)... 400
Creston (E3)*... 275
Crews (E3)... 25
Crichton (D2)... 10
Crowley (F6)*...12,784
Crowville (G2)*... 225
Curtis (C2)... 77
Cut Off (K7)*...
Cypress (D3)*... 325
Dalcour (P4)...
Danville (E2)*...
D'Arbonne (F1)... 30
Darlington (J5)*... 40
Darnell (G1)*... 300
Darrow (K3)*...
Davant (L7)*...
De Lacroix (L7)... 10
De Loutre (F1)...
De Quincy (D6)*...3,837
De Ridder (D5)*...5,799
Deerford (K1)*... 54
Dehlco (G2)... 75
Delcambre (F7)*...1,463
Delhi (H2)*...1,861
Delta (J2)*... 150
Delta Farms (K7)... 25
Denham Springs (L2)*.2,053
Dennis Mills (L1)...
Derry (E3)*...
Deshotels (F5)... 50
Dess (C4)... 7
Destrehan (N4)*...
Deville (F4)*...
Diamond (L7)*...
Dixie (E5)...
Dodie (C1)*...
Dodson (E2)*... 375
Donaldsonville (K3)*...4,150
Donner (J7)*...
Dorceyville (J3)... 400
Doss (G1)... 50
Downsville (F1)*... 188
Doyle (L1)*... 350
Doyline (D1)*...1,170
Dry Creek (D5)*...
Dry Prong (E3)*... 377
Dubach (E1)*... 703
Dubberly (D1)*... 173
Dulac (J8)*...
Dunn (G2)*... 280
Duplessis (K2)*...

Duson (F6)*... 707
Dutch Town (K2)*... 7
Duty (G3)...
East Point (D2)*... 200
Easton (F5)*... 250
Echo (F4)*... 500
Eden (F3)... 200
Edgard (M3)*...
Edgerly (C6)*... 500
Effie (F4)*...
Elba (G5)*...
Elizabeth (E5)*...1,113
Ellendale (J7)*...
Ellis (F6)...
Elm Park (H5)*... 300
Elmer (E4)*... 30
Elmgrove (C2)...
Elton (E6)*...1,434
Empire (L8)*... 475
Enterprise (G3)*... 35
Eola (F5)*...
Epps (G1)*... 308
Erath (F7)*...1,514
Eros (F2)*... 195
Erwinville (H5)*... 350
Esther (F7)*...
Estherwood (F6)*... 547
Ethel (H5)*...
Eunice (F6)*...8,184
Eva (G4)*...
Evangeline (F6)*... 606
Evans (D5)*...
Evelyn (D3)... 25
Evergreen (F5)*... 382
Extension (G3)*...
Fairbanks (F1)*...1,000
Fairmount (E4)...
Fairview (H4)... 30
Farmerville (F1)*...3,173
Feitel (L3)...
Fenton (E6)*... 450
Ferriday (G3)*...3,847
Fields (C5)*... 10
Fisher (D4)*... 400
Flatwoods (E4)*... 500
Flora (D3)*... 250
Florien (D4)*... 497
Floyd (H1)...
Fluker (K5)*...
Folsom (K5)*... 166
Fondale (F2)... 50
Forbing (C2)*...
Fordoche (G5)*...
Forest (H1)*... 200
Forest Hill (E4)*... 365
Fort Jessup (C3)... 45
Fort Necessity (G2)*...
Fort Saint Philip (M8) 15
Foster (H7)*...
Foules (G3)*... 35
Franklin (G7)*...6,144
Franklinton (K5)*...2,342
French Settlement(L2)* 900
Frenier (N3)*... 25
Frey (F6)...
Frierson (C2)*... 300
Frogmore (G3)*... 250
Frost (L2)*... 500
Fryeburg (D2)*... 200
Fullerton (D4)*...
Fulton (D5)...
Gaars Mills (F2)... 120
Gahagan (D2)... 5
Galbraith (E4)...
Galliano (K8)*...2,100
Gallion (G1)*...
Galvez (L2)... 500
Gandy (D4)*...
Gansville (E2)... 25
Garden City (H7)*...
Gardner (E4)*... 200
Garyville (M3)*...1,850
Ged (C6)...
Geismar (K3)*...
Georgetown (F3)*... 355
Gheens (K7)*...
Gibsland (E1)*...1,085
Gibson (J7)*... 500
Gilbert (G2)*... 452
Gilliam (C1)*...1,579
Girard (G2)*...
Glade (G4)...
Glencoe (G7)...
Glenmora (E5)*...1,556
Gloria (K7)...
Gloster (C2)*...1,000
Glynn (H5)*...
Gold Dust (F5)*... 175
Golden Meadow (K8)*..2,820
Goldonna (D2)*... 364
Gonzales (L2)*...1,642
Good Hope (N4)*... 966
Good Pine (F3)*... 500
Goodbee (K6)*... 225
Gosport (D6)...8,318
Gorum (E4)*... 250
Goudeau (G5)*... 250
Grambling (E1)*...1,100
Gramercy (M4)*...1,184
Grand Bayou (C2)*... 500
Grand Cane (C2)*... 286
Grand Chenier (E7)*... 258
Grand Coteau (G6)*...1,103
Grand Isle (L8)*...1,190
Grand Lake (D6)... 150
Grangeville (J5)*... 150
Grant (E5)*...
Gray (J7)*... 375
Grayson (F2)*... 455
Greensburg (J5)*... 423
Greenwell Springs(K1)* 500
Greenwood (B2)*... 300
Gretna (O4)*...13,813
Grosse Tete (G6)*... 548
Gueydan (E6)*...2,041
Gullett (J5)... 200
Gurley (H5)*... 211
Hackberry (D7)*...1,500
Hackley (K5)...1,100
Hahnville (N4)*...1,475

Haile (F1)*... 175
Hall Summit (D2)*...
Hammond (N1)*...8,010
Hanna (D3)*...
Happy Jack (L7)*...
Harahan (O4)*...3,394
Harelson (K2)...
Harrisonburg (G3)*... 544
Harvey (O4)*...
Haughton (C1)*... 501
Hawthorn (D4)...
Hayes (E6)*... 800
Haynesville (D1)*...3,040
Head of Island (L2)*... 443
Hebert (G2)*... 150
Hecker (D6)... 75
Heflin (D2)*... 460
Hermitage (H5)*...
Hessmer (F4)*... 500
Hester (L3)*...
Hicks (E4)*... 216
Hico (E1)*...
Highland (H2)...
Hilly (E1)*...
Hineston (E4)*...
Hinton (F2)... 20
Hobart (L2)*... 160
Hodge (E2)*...1,386
Hohen Solms (K3)*...
Holden (M1)*...
Holly (C2)...
Holly Ridge (G2)*...
Holmwood (D6)... 100
Holton (K5)*... 90
Holum (F3)*... 60
Homeplace (L8)... 300
Homer (D1)*...4,749
Hood (E4)... 150
Hope Villa (K2)...
Hornbeck (D4)*... 524
Hortman (D1)... 40
Hosston (C1)*... 750
Houltonville (K6)...
Houma (J7)*...11,505
Humphreys (J7)... 200
Hutton (D4)*... 125
Hymel (L3)*... 391
Iberville (K2)*... 480
Ida (C1)*... 525
Independence (M1)*...1,606
Indian Village (H6)... 900
Innis (G5)*...
Iota (E6)*...1,162
Iowa (D6)*...1,125
Isabel (K5)... 10
Istrouma (K1)*...
Ivan (C1)... 300
Jackson (H5)*...6,772
Jacoby (G5)*...
Jamestown (D2)*... 300
Jeanerette (G7)*...4,692
Jena (F3)*...1,438
Jennings (E6)*...9,663
Jesuit Bend (K7)...
Jigger (G2)*... 500
Johnsons Bayou (C7)... 20
Jones (G1)*... 250
Jonesboro (E2)*...3,097
Jonesville (G3)*...1,954
Joyce (E3)*...
Junction City (E1)*... 514
Kahns (J1)... 200
Kaplan (F6)*...4,562
Keatchie (C2)*... 186
Keithville (C2)*... 500
Kelly (F3)*...
Kenner (O4)*...5,535
Kentwood (J5)*...2,417
Kilbourne (H1)*... 500
Kile (D4)...
Killian (M2)*...
Killona (N4)*...
Kinder (E6)*...2,003
Kingston (C2)... 50
Kisatchie (D4)*...
Klotzville (K3)*...
Knight (D5)*... 500
Kolin (F4)*... 300
Koran (D2)...
Kraemer (M4)*...
Krotz Springs (G5)*... 866
Kurthwood (D4)*... 50
Labadieville (K4)*... 500
Lacamp (E4)*...
Lacassine (E6)*...
Lacombe (L6)*...
Lafayette (F6)*...33,541
Lafitte (K7)*...
Lafourche (J7)*...
Lagan (L4)*...
Lahoward (D2)... 120
Lake (L2)*... 300
Lake Arthur (E6)*...2,849
Lake Charles (D6)*...41,272
Lake End (D3)*... 250
Lake Providence (H1)*.4,123
Lakeland (H5)*... 100
Lamar (G2)... 500
Lamarque (G3)...
Laplace (N3)*...2,352
Laran (F1)... 50
Larose (K7)*...1,286
Larto (G4)*...
Lauderdale (L3)...
Laura (K4)...
Laurel Hill (H5)...
Lawhon (D2)*... 105
Lawrence (L7)...
Lawtell (F5)*... 700
Le Blanc (E5)*... 165
Leander (E4)*... 162
Lebeau (F5)*...
Lecompte (F4)*...1,443
Lee Bayou (G3)... 10
Leesville (D4)*...4,670
Legonier (G5)...
Leleux (F6)...
Lena (E4)*...
Leonville (G6)*... 514
Leroy (F6)*... 100

Leton (D1)...
Lettsworth (G5)*...
Levert (G6)... 10
Lewis (C1)...
Lewisburg (F6)... 100
Lewiston (K5)... 50
Liberty Hill (E2)... 150
Libuse (F4)*... 350
Lillie (E1)*... 100
Lindsay (H5)... 20
Linville (F1)*...
Lions (M3)*... 800
Lisbon (E1)*...
Lismore (G3)*... 350
Litroe (F1)*... 122
Little Creek (F3)*... 111
Liverpool (J5)*... 175
Livingston (L1)*... 600
Livonia (G5)*... 500
Lobdell (J1)*...
Loch Lomond (F1)*...
Lockhart (E1)... 25
Lockport (K7)*...1,388
Locust Ridge (H3)... 40
Logansport (C3)*...1,270
Lonepine (F5)... 500
Long Bridge (F4)*...
Longleaf (E4)*...1,200
Longstreet (B2)*... 224
Longville (D5)*... 250
Loranger (N1)*...1,000
Loreauville (G6)*... 478
Lottie (G5)*... 500
Lotus (D4)...
Louisa (G7)*... 150
Lucas (C2)...
Lucknow (G2)...
Lucky (E2)... 75
Lucy (M3)*... 520
Ludington (D5)...
Lula (C3)...
Luling (N4)*...
Lunita (C6)...
Lutcher (L3)*...2,198
Madisonville (K6)*... 861
Magda (F4)...
Magnolia (J5)*... 300
Mamou (F5)*...2,254
Manchac Station
(Akers*) (N2)... 500
Mandeville (L6)*...7,368
Mangham (G2)*... 554
Manifest (G3)*...
Mansfield (C2)*...4,440
Mansura (G4)*...1,439
Many (C3)*...1,681
Marcel (G7)...
Marco (E3)...
Maringouin (G6)*... 898
Marion (F1)*... 685
Mark (J2)...
Marksville (G4)*...3,635
Marrero (O4)*...
Marthaville (D3)*... 121
Mathews (J7)*...
Maurepas (M2)*...
Maurice (F6)*... 335
Maxie (F6)... 150
Mayna (G4)*...
Mayo (D4)... 35
Mc Call (K3)*...
Mc Dade (D2)*...
Mc Intyre (D1)... 200
Mc Nary (E5)... 267
Meeker (F4)*...
Melder (E4)*... 100
Melrose (E3)*... 850
Melville (G5)*...1,901
Mer Rouge (G1)*... 784
Mermentau (E6)*... 636
Merryville (D5)*...1,383
Midland (F6)*... 600
Millikin (H1)... 116
Milton (F6)*...
Minden (D1)*...9,787
Mineral (D3)...
Mira (C1)*...
Mitchell (C3)*... 150
Mitchiner (G1)... 15
Mittie (E5)*...
Mix (G5)*...
Modeste (K3)*... 350
Moncla (F4)*... 143
Monroe (F1)*...38,572
Montegut (J8)*...
Monterey (G4)*... 300
Montgomery (E3)*... 695
Montpelier (M1)*...
Montrose (D3)*...
Montz (M3)...
Mooringsport (B1)*... 709
Mora (E4)*... 200
Moreauville (G4)*... 835
Moreland (E4)... 300
Morgan City (H7)*...9,759
Morganza (G5)*... 817
Morrow (F5)*... 460
Morse (F6)*... 679
Morville (H4)... 60
Mound (H2)*... 105
Mount Airy (M3)*... 400
Mt. Hermon (K5)*...
Mt. Lebanon (D2)*...
Myrtle Grove (K7)*... 250
Naborton (C2)*...
Nairn (L8)*... 200
Napoleonville (K4)*...1,260
Natalbany (N1)*...
Natchez (D3)*... 300
Natchitoches (D3)*...9,914
Neame (D5)...
Nebo (F3)... 350
Negreet (C4)*...
Nero (L7)...
New Era (G4)*... 145
New Iberia (G6)*...16,467
New Orleans (O4)*...570,445
New Orleans (urban
area)...655,822
New Roads (G5)*...2,818

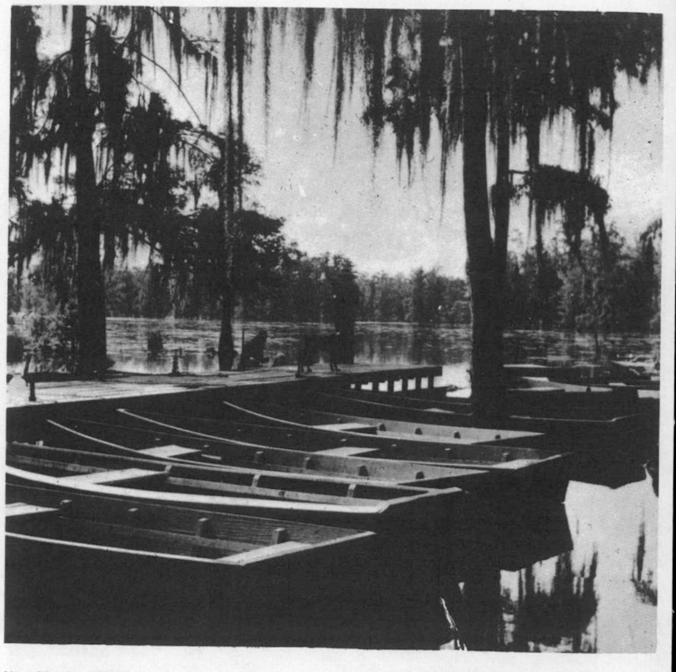

New Verda (E3)*...
Newellton (H2)*...1,280
Newlin (D5)... 25
Newllano (D4)*... 277
Niblett (E6)...
Noble (C3)*... 238
Norco (N3)*...2,400
North Baton Rouge(K1)
Norwood (H5)*... 414
Notnac (H2)... 50
Nunez (F6)*...
Oak Grove (H1)*...1,796
Oak Ridge (G1)*... 287
Oakdale (E5)*...5,598
Oakland (F1)*...
Oberlin (E5)*...1,544
Odenburg (G5)... 130
Odra (E3)... 25
Oil City (C1)*... 422
Okaloosa (F2)... 100
Old Field (L1)...
Olga (M8)... 33
Olivier (G7)*... 350
Olla (F3)*...1,115
Omega (H1)... 25
Opelousas (G5)*...11,659
Oretta (D5)... 50
Oscar (H5)*... 418
Osceola (K5)*... 200
Ostrica (L8)*...
Otis (E4)*...
Oxford (C3)*... 300
Paincourtville (K4)*...
Palmetto (G5)*... 457
Paradis (N4)*...1,500
Parcperdue (G6)... 50
Parhams (G4)*...
Parks (G6)... 460
Parr (F4)...
Patoutville (G7)... 300
Patterson (H7)*...1,938
Paulina (L3)*...
Pearl River (L6)*... 637
Peason (D4)... 8
Pecan Island (F7)*...
Peck (G3)... 25
Pelican (C3)*... 140
Perry (F7)*... 175
Perryville (G1)*...
Phoenix (L7)... 300
Pickering (D4)...
Pilottown (M8)*... 250
Pine Grove (J5)*... 500
Pine Prairie (F5)*... 575
Pineville (F4)*...6,423
Pioneer (H1)*...
Pitkin (E5)*... 475
Plain Dealing (C1)*...1,321
Plaquemine (J2)*...5,747
Plattenville (K4)*...
Plaucheville (G5)*... 277
Pleasant Hill (C3)*... 856
Point (F1)*... 100
Point Pleasant (H2)... 50
Pointe a la Hache
(L7)*...1,000
Poley (L2)...
Pollock (F3)*... 421
Ponchatoula (N2)*...4,090
Port Allen (J2)*...3,097
Port Barre (G5)*...1,066
Port Eads (M8)... 15
Port Hudson (J1)*... 50
Port Sulphur (L8)*... 978
Port Vincent (L2)*...
Potash (L8)*... 276
Powhatan (D3)*... 500
Prairieville (K2)*...
Pride (K1)*... 30
Princeton (C1)*... 500
Provencal (D3)*... 600
Quebec (H2)... 10
Quimby (H2)... 250
Quitman (E2)... 204
Raceland (J7)*...2,025
Ragley (D5)*...
Ramos (H7)... 60
Ramsay (K5)*...
Rapides (E4)...

Rattan (C4)... 6
Rayne (F6)*...6,485
Rayville (G2)*...3,138
Red Gum (G3)...
Red Oak (D3)... 10
Redcross (G5)... 7
Reddell (F5)*...
Reeves (D5)*... 106
Reggio (L7)...
Reids (E5)... 60
Reiley (J5)*...
Reisor (C2)...
Remy (L3)...1,064
Reserve (M3)*...4,465
Rhoda (H7)... 200
Ridge (F6)*... 100
Ringgold (D2)*...1,007
Rio (L5)*... 300
Rita (J7)... 500
Riverton (F2)...
Roanoke (E6)*... 500
Robeline (D3)*... 350
Robert (N1)*...
Robson (C2)...
Rochelle (F3)*...
Rocky Mount (C1)*... 130
Rodessa (B1)*...
Rogers (F3)...
Rogillioville (H5)... 15
Romeville (L3)*... 200
Roosevelt (H1)... 25
Rosa (G5)*... 100
Rosedale (G6)*... 600
Rosefield (F3)*...
Roseland (J5)*...1,038
Rosepine (D5)*... 334
Royal (F3)... 10
Ruby (F4)*...
Ruston (E1)*...10,372
Sailes (D2)*... 20
Saint Amant (L2)*... 500
St. Benedict (K5)*... 25
St. Bernard (L7)*...
St. Francisville (H5)*.. 936
St. Gabriel (K2)*... 800
St. James (L4)*... 600
St. Joseph (H3)*...1,218
St. Landry (F5)*... 800
St. Martinville (G6)*...4,614
St. Maurice (E3)*...
St. Rose (N4)*...
St. Tammany (L6)*...
Saline (E2)*... 357
Sandel (D4)...
Sarepta (D1)*... 750
Satsuma (L1)...
Schley (D4)...
Schriever (J7)*... 500
Scotlandville (J1)*...4,368
Scott (F6)*... 688
Segura (G6)...
Selma (F3)...
Shamrock (D3)... 100
Shaw (G4)... 60
Shongaloo (D1)*...
Shreveport (C1)*...127,206
Shreveport (urban
area)...148,296
Shrewsbury (O4)...
Shutts (D4)...
Sibley (D1)*... 623
Sicily Island (G3)*...
Siegen (K2)...
Sieper (E4)*...
Sikes (F2)*... 342
Simmesport (G5)*...1,510
Simms (F4)*...
Simpson (D4)*...
Simsboro (E1)*... 500
Singer (D5)*... 250
Slagle (D4)*... 300
Slaughter (H5)*... 290
Slidell (L6)*...3,464
Sligo (C2)*... 125
Smoke Bend (K3)*...
Somerset (H2)... 275
Sondheimer (H1)*... 600
Sorrento (L3)*...
South Bend (G7)...

S. Mansfield (C3)*... 276
S. Pass (M8)...
Spanish Fort (O3)... 200
Spearsville (E1)... 100
Spencer (F1)*... 160
Spring Ridge (B2)...
Springfield (M2)*...1,000
Springhill (D1)*...3,383
Springville (L2)... 50
Standard (F3)... 100
Starhill (H5)*... 150
Starks (C6)*...
Start (G2)*...
Sterlington (F1)*...
Stille (E4)...
Stonewall (C2)*...
Stonypoint (K1)...
Sugartown (D5)*... 500
Sulphur (D6)*...5,996
Summerfield (E1)*... 200
Summerville (F3)... 200
Sun (L5)*...
Sunny Hill (K5)*... 50
Sunset (F6)*...1,080
Sunshine (K2)*... 800
Supreme (K4)*...1,000
Swartz (G1)*...1,000
Sweet Lake (D7)... 40
Taft (N4)*...
Talisheek (L5)*... 250
Talla Bena (H2)... 25
Tallulah (H2)*...7,758
Tangipahoa (J5)*... 352
Taylor (D1)*... 400
Taylortown (C2)...
Temple (E4)*... 100
Tendal (H2)...
Tensinger (H2)...
Terry (H1)*... 255
Theall (F7)*...
Theriot (J8)*... 150
Thibodaux (J7)*...7,730
Thomastown (H2)...
Thornwell (E6)*...
Tickfaw (M1)*... 100
Timon (D3)... 180
Tinus (J5)*... 135
Tioga (F4)*... 338
Toro (C4)*...
Torras (G4)*...
Transylvania (H1)*...
Trees (B1)*... 75
Tremont (E1)*...
Triumph (L8)*... 600
Trout (F3)*... 550
Truxno (F1)*... 92
Tullos (F3)*... 732
Tunica (G5)*... 100
Turkey Creek (F5)*... 400
Union (L3)*...
Urania (F3)*...1,004
Utility (G3)*...
Vacherie (L3)*...4,026
Valverda (G5)*...
Varnado (L5)*... 306
Venice (M8)*...1,500
Verda (E3)*... 160
Vernon (E2)*... 65
Vick (F4)*...
Vidalia (G3)*...1,641
Vidrine (F5)... 150
Vienna (E1)*... 250
Ville Platte (F5)*...6,633
Vinton (C6)*...2,597
Violet (L7)*... 800
Vivian (B1)*...2,426
Vixen (F2)...
Vowells Mill (D3)*... 175
Wadesboro (N2)*...
Waggaman (O4)... 500
Waggoner (F3)...
Wakefield (H5)*... 200
Waldheim (L5)*... 43
Walker (L1)*... 500
Wallace (M3)*...
Walls (H5)*...
Walters (G3)*...
Warden (H1)*...
Wardville (G1)...

Warnerton (K5)*
Washington (G5)* 1,291
Water Proof (H3)* 1,180
Watson (L1)* 400
Waverly (H2)*
Waxia (G5)* 567
Weeks (G7)* 1,499
Weiss (L1)
Welcome (L3)* 300
Weldon (E1) 35
Welsh (E6)* 2,416
West Monroe (F1)* 10,302
Westlake (D6)* 1,871
Westwego (O4)* 8,281
Weyanoke (H5)*
White Castle (J3)* 1,839
White Sulphur Springs (F3) 50
Whitehall (M2)* 450
Whiteville (F5)*
Wilda (E4)*
Wildsville (G3)*
Willetts (G3)* 12
Wills Point (L7)
Wilmer (K5)* 75
Wilson (H5)* 375
Winnfield (E3)* 5,629
Winnsboro (G2)* 3,655
Wisner (G3)* 738
Woodland (J5)*
Woodlawn (E6) 210
Woodside (G5)*
Woodworth (E4)* 392
Wright (F6)* 36
Wyatt (E2)* 40
Yellow Pine (D2) 90
Youngsville (G6)* 769
Zachary (K1)* 1,542
Zenoria (F3)* 100
Zimmerman (E4)* 500
Zwolle (C3)* 1,555

MAINE

Map on Page 66

Total Population 913,774

16 COUNTIES

Androscoggin (C7) 83,594
Aroostook (F2) 96,039
Cumberland (C8) 169,201
Franklin (B5) 20,682
Hancock (G6) 32,105
Kennebec (D7) 83,881
Knox (E7) 28,121
Lincoln (D7) 18,004
Oxford (B6) 44,221
Penobscot (F5) 108,198
Piscataquis (E4) 18,617
Sagadahoc (D7) 20,911
Somerset (C4) 39,785
Waldo (E6) 21,687
Washington (H6) 35,187
York (B9) 93,541

CITIES and TOWNS

Abbot Village (E5)* △ 462
Acton (B8)* △ 473
Addison (H6)* △ 846
Albion (E6)* △ 992
Alexander (H5) △ 282
Alfred (B9)* △1,112
Allagash (F1) △ 680
Allens Mills (C6) 175
Alna (D7)* △ 350
Alton (F5) △ 314
Amherst (G6)* △ 151
Andover (B6)* △ 756
Anson (D6)* △2,199
Appleton (E7)* △ 671
Argyle (F5) △ 133
Ashdale (D8) 60
Ashland (G2)* △2,370
Ashville (G7)* 100
Athens (D6)* △ 725
Atkinson (E5) △ 400
Atlantic (G7)*
Auburn (C7)* 23,134
AUGUSTA (D7)* 20,913
Aurora (G6)* △ 91
Ayers (J6)*
Bailey Island (D8)* 175
Bancroft (H4)* △ 165
Bangor (F6)* 31,558
Bar Harbor (G7)* △3,864
Bar Mills (C8)* 800
Baring (J5)* △ 157
Bath (D8)* 10,644
Bay Point (D8)
Bayside (F7)*
Beals (H7)* △ 590
Beddington (H6) △ 26
Belfast (F7)* 5,960
Belgrade (D7)* △1,099
Belgrade Lakes (D6)* 450
Belmont (E7) △ 258
Bemis (B6)
Benedicta (G4)* △ 225
Benton (D6)* △1,421
Berry Mills (C6) 100
Berwick (B9)* △2,166
Bethel (B7)* △2,367
Biddeford (C9)* 20,836
Biddeford Pool (C9)*
Bingham (D5)* △1,354
Birch Harbor (H7)*
Birches (B6)
Blaine (H2)* △1,118
Blanchard (D5)* △ 75
Blue Hill (F7)* △1,308
Bolsters Mills (B7)* 115
Boothbay (D8)* △1,559
Boothbay Harbor (D8)* △2,290
Boundary (H3) 100
Bowdoinham (D7)* △1,039
Bowerbank (E5)* △ 20
Boyd Lake (F5)
Bradford (F5)* △ 793
Bradford Center (F5)* 150
Bradley (F6)* △ 786
Bremen (E8) △ 409
Brewer (F6)* 6,862
Bridgewater (H3)* △1,279
Bridgton (B7)* △2,950
Brighton (D5)* △ 106
Bristol (E8)* △1,476
Brooklin (F7)* △ 546
Brooks (E6)* △ 747
Brooksville (F7)* △ 751
Brookton (H4)* △ 206
Brownfield (B8)* △ 612
Brownville (E5)* △1,964
Brownville Jct. (E5)* 1,086
Brunswick (C8)* △10,996
Bryant Pond (B7)* 500
Buckfield (C7)* △ 899
Bucks Harbor (J6)* 160
Bucksport (F6)* △3,120
Burkettville (E7)* 100
Burlington (G5)* △ 425
Burnham (E6)* △ 706
Buxton (C8) △2,009
Buxton Center (B8)
Byron (B6) △ 96
Calais (J5)* 4,589
Cambridge (E5)* △ 326
Camden (F7)* △3,670
Canaan (D6)* △ 785
Canton (C7)* △ 746
Cape Neddick (B9)*
Cape Porpoise (C9)* 400
Capens (D4) 1
Caratunk (C5)* △ 96
Cardville (F5)* 200
Caribou (G2)* △9,923
Carmel (E6)* △ 996
Carrabassett (C5) 10
Carroll (G5)* △ 288
Carry Pond (C5)
Carthage (C6) △ 339
Cary (H4) △ 278
Casco (B7)* △ 881
Castine (F7)* △ 793
Cedar (J5)
Center Belmont (E7)
Center Lovell (B7)*
Center Montville (E7) 175
Centerville (H6)* △ 63
Chapman (G2) △ 381
Charleston (F5)* △ 771
Charlotte (J5) △ 252
Chebeague Island (C8)* 300
Chelsea (D7) △2,169
Cherryfield (H6)* △ 904
Chester (F5) △ 256
Chesterville (C6) △ 588
Chesuncook (D3)* 18
China (E7)* △1,375
Chisholm (C7)* 1,135
Citypoint (E7)
Clark Island (E8)* 175
Clarks Mill (B8)
Clayton Lake (E2)* 6
Cleveland (G1) 200
Cliff Island (C8)*
Clifton (G6) △ 193
Clinton (D6)* △1,623
Columbia (H6) △ 352
Columbia Falls (H6)* △ 550
Cooper (H6) △ 128
Coopers Mills (E7)* 239
Corea (H7)* 156
Corinna (E6)* △1,752
Cornish (B8)* △ 795
Cornville (D6) △ 563
Costigan (F5)* 158
Cranberry Isles (G7)* △ 228
Crawford (H5)* △ 83
Crescent Lake (C7)*
Criehaven (F8)* 60
Crouseville (G2)* 400
Crystal (G4) △ 373
Cumberland Ctr. (C8)* △2,030
Cumberland Mills (C8)*
Cundys Harbor (D8)* 80
Curtis Corner (C7)*
Cushing (E7) △ 376
Cutler (J6)* △ 483
Daigle (G1)
Damariscotta (E7)* △1,113
Danforth (H4)* △1,174
Danville (C7)*
Darkharbor (F7)*
Davidson (F4) 45
Dayton (B8) △ 502
Deblois (H6)* △ 59
Dedham (F6) △ 374
Deer Isle (F7)* △1,234
Denmark (B8)* △ 447
Dennistown (C4) △ 24
Dennysville (J6)* △ 345
Derby (E5)* 500
Detroit (E6)* △ 492
Dexter (E5)* △4,126
Dixfield (C6)* △2,022
Dixmont (E6)* △ 631
Dorman (H6)
Dover-Foxcroft (E5)* △4,218
Dover South Mills (E5)
Dresden Mills (D7)* 100
Dry Mills (C8)* 220
Dryden (C6)* 800
Dyer Brook (G3) △ 219
Eagle Lake (F1)* △1,516
East Andover (B6)* 150
E. Baldwin (B8)*
E. Blue Hill (G7)* 200
E. Boothbay (D8)* 500
E. Brownfield (B8)* 130
E. Corinth (F5)* 450
E. Dixfield (C6)* 242
E. Dixmont (E6)
E. Dover (E5)* 67
E. Eddington (F6)* 300
E. Franklin (G6)* 78
E. Hampden (F6)
E. Hiram (B8)* 350
E. Holden (F6)*
E. Jackson (E6)
E. Knox (E7)
E. Lebanon (B9)*
E. Limington (B8) 150
E. Livermore (C7)* 500
E. Lowell (G5)
E. Machias (J6)* △1,101
E. Madison (D6) 692
E. Millinocket (F4)* △1,358
E. New Portland (D6)* 43
E. Orland (F6)*
E. Otisfield (B7) 50
E. Parsonfield (B8)* 175
E. Peru (C7)
E. Pittston (D7) 1,050
E. Poland (C7)* 490
E. Sebago (B8)*
E. Stoneham (B7)* 300
E. Sullivan (G6)* 250
E. Sumner (C7)* 114
E. Union (E7)* 190
E. Vassalboro (D7)* 200
E. Waterboro (B8)* 175
E. Waterford (B7)* 175
E. Wilton (C6)* 450
E. Winn (G5) 75
Easton (H2)* △1,664
Eastport (K6)* 3,123
Eaton (H4)* 120
Eddington (F6) △ 664
Edgecomb (D8)* △ 447
Edmunds (J6) △ 288
Eliot (B9)* △2,509
Ellsworth (F6)* 3,936
Ellsworth Falls (G6)* 500
Elms (B9)
Emery Mills (B9)* 150
Enfield (F5)* △1,196
Etna (E6)* △ 458
Eustis (B5)* △ 763
Exeter (E6)* △ 734
Fairbanks (C6) 200
Fairfield (D6)* △5,811
Fairfield Center (D6) 150
Falmouth (C8) △4,342
Farmington (C6)* △4,677
Farmington Falls (D6)*
Fayette (C7)* △ 397
Five Islands (D8)* 200
Forest City (H4)* 27
Forest Station (H4)* 30
Fort Fairfield (H2)* △5,791
Fort Kent (F1)* △5,343
Fort Kent Mills (F1)* 175
Fortunes Rocks (C9) 82
Frankfort (F6)* △ 578
Franklin (G6)* △ 709
Freedom (E7)* △ 466
Freeport (C8)* △3,280
Frenchboro (G7)* 104
Frenchville (G1)* △1,528
Friendship (E7)* △ 772
Frye (B6)* 350
Fryeburg (A7)* △1,926
Gardiner (D7)* 6,649
Garland (E5)* △ 581
Georgetown (D8)* △ 510
Gerard (C5) 20
Gilbertville (C7) 100
Gilead (B7)* △ 140
Glen Cove (E7)* 200
Glenburn (F6) △ 694
Goodrich (H2)
Goodwins Mills (B8) 200
Goose Rocks Beach (C9) 135
Gorham (C8)* △4,742
Gouldsboro (H7)* 1,168
Grand Isle (G1)* △1,230
Grand Lake Stream (H5)* △ 294
Grants (B5)* 9
Gray (C8)* △1,631
Great Pond (G6) 40
Great Works (F6)*
Green Lake (F6)* 40
Greene (C7)* △ 974
Greenville (D5)* △1,889
Greenville Jct. (D5)* 780
Grindstone (F4)* 60
Grove (J5)* 125
Guerette (G1)
Guilford (E5)* △1,842
Haines Landing (B6)
Hale (B6) 60
Hallowell (D7)* 3,404
Hamlin (H1) △ 430
Hampden (F6)* △3,608
Hampden Highlands (F6)*
Hancock (G6)* △ 755
Hanover (B7)* △ 211
Harmony (D6)* △ 709
Harpswell Center (D8) 100
Harrington (H6)* △ 853
Harrison (B7)* △1,026
Hartford (C7) △ 381
Hartland (D6)* △1,310
Haynesville (G4)* △ 185
Hebron (C7)* △ 829
Hermon (F6) 1,728
Highland Lake (C8)
Highpine (B9)* 125
Hinckley (D6)* 250
Hiram (B8)* △ 804
Hodgdon (H3)* △1,162
Holeb (C4)* 54
Hollis Center (B8)* 230
Hope (E7)* △ 504
Houghton (B6)
Houlton (H3)* △8,377
Howland (F5)* △1,441
Hudson (F5)* △ 455
Hulls Cove (G7)* 450
Indian River (H6)
Intervale (C8)* 45
Island Falls (G3)* △1,237
Isle au Haut (F7)* △ 82
Islesboro (F7)* △ 529
Islesford (G7)* 150
Jackman (C4)* △ 964
Jackman Station (C4)* 980
Jacksonville (J6)* 300
Jay (C7)* △3,102
Jefferson (D7)* △1,215
Jemtland (G1) 100
Jimpond (B5) 3
Jonesboro (J6)* △ 459
Jonesport (H6)* △1,727
Katahdin Iron Works (E5) 15
Keegan (G1)* 1,100
Kellyland (H5) 23
Kenduskeag (E6)* △ 387
Kennebago Lake (B5)*
Kennebunk (B9)* △4,273
Kennebunk Beach (C9)* 125
Kennebunk Port (C9)* △1,522
Kents Hill (D7)* 170
Kezar Falls (B8)* 1,400
Kineo (D4) 40
Kingfield (C6)* △ 963
Kingman (G4)* △ 358
Kingsbury (D5)* △ 35
Kittery (B9)* △8,380
Kittery Depot (B9) 1,220
Kittery Point (B9)* 1,137
Knox (E6) △ 445
Kokadjo (E4)*
La Grange (F5)* △ 511
Lake Moxie (D5)
Lake View (F5)* △ 23
Lambert Lake (H4)*
Lamoine (G7) △ 443
Lebanon (B9) △1,499
Lee (G5)* △ 610
Leeds (C7) △ 797
Leeds Junction (C7)* 54
Levant (F6)* △ 706
Lewiston (C7)* 40,974
Liberty (E7)* △ 497
Lille (G1)*
Limerick (B8)* △ 961
Limestone (H2)* △2,427
Limington (B8)* △ 851
Lincoln (G5)* △4,030
Lincoln Center (G5)*
Lincolnville (E7)* 881
Lincolnville Ctr. (E7)*
Linneus (H3)* △ 777
Lisbon (C7)* △4,318
Lisbon Center (C7)* 300
Lisbon Falls (D7)* 2,155
Litchfield (D7)* △ 953
Little Deer Isle (F7)* 350
Littleton (H3) △1,001
Livermore (C7)* △1,313
Livermore Falls (C7)* △3,359
Locke Mills (B7)* 380
Long Island (C8)* 350
Long Pond (C4)* 84
Longcove (E8)
Loon Lake (B5) 10
Lovell (B7)* △ 640
Lowell (F5)* △ 192
Lubec (K6) △2,973
Ludlow (G3) △ 361
Machias (J6)* △2,063
Machiasport (H6)* △ 781
Macwahoc (G4) △ 131
Madawaska (G1)* △4,900
Madison (D6)* △3,639
Madrid (B6) △ 162
Mainstream (D6)
Manchester (D7)* △ 664
Mapleton (G2)* △1,367
Mariner (C8)
Mars Hill (H2)* △2,060
Masardis (G3)* △ 523
Matagamon (F3) 3
Matinicus (F8)* △ 188
Mattawamkeag (G4)* △ 803
Maysville (G2) 150
McKinley (G7)*
Mechanic Falls (C7)* △2,061
Meddybemps (J5)* △ 109
Medford (F5) △ 191
Medford Center (F5) 25
Medway (G4)* △ 725
Mercer (D6)* △ 348
Mexico (B6)* △4,762
Michaud (F1)
Middledam (B6) 25
Milbridge (H6)* △1,199
Milford (F6)* △1,435
Millinocket (F4)* △5,890
Milltown (J5)*
Milo (F5)* △2,898
Minot (C7)* △ 750
Minturn (G7)* 134
Monarda (G4)* 250
Monhegan (E8)* △ 75
Monmouth (D7)* △1,683
Monroe (E6)* △ 593
Monson (E5)* △ 855
Monticello (H3)* △1,284
Montville (E7) △ 466
Moody (B9)*
Moose River (C4)* △ 203
Moosehead (D4) 17
Morrill (E7)* △ 306
Mount Desert (G7)* △1,776
Mount Vernon (D7)* △ 653
Naples (B8)* △ 747
New Gloucester (C8)* △2,628
New Harbor (E8)* 500
New Limerick (G3)* △ 543
New Portland (C6)* △ 733
New Sharon (C6)* △ 755
New Sweden (G2)* △ 827
New Vineyard (C6)* △ 447
Newagen (D8)*
Newburgh (F6) △ 599
Newcastle (D7)* △1,021
Newfield (B8)* △ 355
Newport (E6)* △2,190
Nobleboro (D7)* △ 654
Norcross (F4) 46
Norridgewock (D6)* △1,784
North Amity (H4)* 250
N. Anson (D6)* 1,000
N. Bancroft (G4)* 71
N. Belgrade (D7)* 200
N. Berwick (B9)* △1,655
N. Bradford (F5) 25
N. Bridgton (B7)*
N. Brooksville (F7)* 190
N. Buckfield (C7)
N. Cutler (J6)
N. Dexter (E5) 60
N. Dixmont (E6)
N. East Carry (D4)* 13
N. Ellsworth (G6)
N. Fryeburg (B7)* 200
N. Gorham (C8) 500
N. Haven (F7)* △ 410
N. Islesboro (F7)
N. Jay (C6)* 550
N. Lebanon (B9)
N. Leeds (C7)* 47
N. Limington (B8) 150
N. Livermore (C7)* 145
N. Lovell (B7)* 85
N. Lubec (J6)* 150
N. Lyndon (G2) 200
N. New Portland (C6)* 350
N. Newry (B6)* 100
N. Parsonfield (A8) 67
N. Penobscot (F7)* 150
N. Perry (J5)
N. Raymond (C8)
N. Searsmont (E7) 150
N. Shapleigh (B8)* 90
N. Sullivan (G6)* 850
N. Turner (C7)* 232
N. Vassalboro (D7)* 1,000
N. Waldoboro (E7)*
N. Waterboro (B8)* 500
N. Waterford (B7)* 450
N. Wayne (C7)*
N. Whitefield (D7)* 200
N. Windham (C8)* 500
N. Yarmouth (C8) △ 942
Northeast Harbor (G7)* 700
Northfield (H6) △ 75
Northport (E7)* △ 574
Norway (B7)* △3,811
Norway Lake (B7) 150
Oakfield (G3)* △1,009
Oakland (D6)* △2,679
Ocean Park (C9)*
Ogunquit (B9)* 800
Olamon (F5)* 600
Old Orchard Beach (C9)* △4,707
Old Town (F6)* 8,261
Onawa (E5)* 25
Oquossoc (B6)*
Orient (H4)* △ 176
Orland (F6)* △1,155
Orono (F6)* △7,504
Orrington (F6)* △1,895
Orrs Island (D8)* 450
Otisfield (B7) △ 599
Otter Creek (G7)* 1,000
Ouellette (G1)
Owls Head (F7)* △ 784
Oxbow (G3)* △ 189
Oxford (C7)* △1,569
Palermo, (E7)* △ 511
Palmyra (E6)* △ 965
Paris (B7)* △4,358
Parkman (D5)* △ 590
Passadumkeag (F5)* △ 331
Patten (F4)* △1,536
Pejepscot (D8)*
Pemaquid (E8)*
Pemaquid Beach (E8)*
Pembroke (J6)* △ 998
Penobscot (F7)* △ 699
Perham (G2)* △ 572
Perkins (F4) △ 5
Perry (J6)* △ 613
Peru (C6)* △1,080
Phair (G2) 150
Phillips (C6)* △1,088
Phippsburg (D8)* △1,134
Pine Point (C8) 650
Pittsfield (E6)* △3,909
Pittston (D7) △1,258
Plaisted (F1)* 300
Pleasant Island (B5)*
Pleasant Pond (D5) 11
Plymouth (E6)* △ 496
Poland (C7)* △1,503
Poland Spring (C7)* 500
Popham Beach (D8)*
Port Clyde (E8)* 350
Portage (G2)* △ 542
Porter (B8)* △1,052
Portland (C8)* 77,634
Portland (urban area) 112,659
Pownal (C8)* △ 752
Prentiss (G5)* △ 315
Presque Isle (H2)* △9,954
Princeton (H5)* △ 865
Prospect (F6) △ 392
Prospect Harbor (H7)* 270
Prouts Neck (C9)* 2,000
Pulpit Harbor (F7) 25
Quimby (F2)*
Randolph (D7) △1,733
Rangeley (B6)* △1,228
Raymond (B8)* △ 620
Readfield (D7)* △1,022
Red Beach (J5)*
Redding (B7) 11
Richmond (D7)* △2,217
Richmond Corner (D7)* 43
Ridlonville (C6)* 2,000
Riley (C6)* 175
Ripley (E5)* △ 389
Robbinston (J5)* △ 554
Robinsons (H3)* 350
Rockland (E7)* 9,234
Rockport (F7)* △1,656
Rockville (E7) 265
Rockwood (D4)* 300
Rome (D6) △ 420
Roque Bluffs (H6)* △ 80
Round Mountain (B5) 3
Round Pond (E8)* 500
Roxbury (B6)* △ 348
Rumford (B6)* △9,954
Rumford Center (B7)* 300
Rumford Point (B6)* 200
Sabattus (C7)* 1,216
Saco (C9)* 10,324
Saint Agatha (G1)* △1,512
St. Albans (E6)* △1,035
St. David (G1)* 1,000
St. Francis (E1)* △1384
St. George (E7)* △1,482
St. John (F1) △ 569
Salem (C6) △ 67
Sandy Creek (B7)
Sandy Point (F7)* 250
Sanford (B9)* △15.177
Sangerville (E5)* △1,161
Saponac (G5)* 25
Scarboro (C8)* △4,600
Seal Cove (G7)*
Seal Harbor (G7)* 400
Searsmont (E7)* △ 558
Searsport (F7)* △1,457
Sebago (B8) △ 577
Sebago Lake (B8)* 346
Sebec (E5)* △ 442
Sebec Lake (E5)* 7
Sebec Station (E5)* 23
Seboeis (F5)* △ 70
Seboomook (D4) 18
Sedgwick (F7)* △ 614
Selden (H4)* 75
Shapleigh (B8)* △ 531
Shawmut (D6)* 1,200
Sheepscott (D7)* 100
Sheridan (F2)* 310
Sherman (G4)* △1,029
Sherman Mills (G4)* 1,030
Sherman Station (F4)* 400
Shin Pond (F3)* 17
Shirley Mills (D5)* 250
Sidney (D7) △ 918
Silvers Mills (E5)* 55
Sinclair (G1)* 800
Skinner (B4)
Skowhegan (D6)* △7,422
Small Point Beach (D8)*
Smithfield (D6)* △ 354
Smyrna Mills (G3)* 650
Soldier Pond (F1)*
Solon (D6)* △ 746
Somerville (D7) △ 227
Sorrento, (G7)* △ 201
South Acton (B9) 200
S. Addison (H6) 170
S. Bancroft (G4)
S. Berwick (B9)* △2,646
S. Blue Hill (F7) 141
S. Brewer (F6)*
S. Bridgton (B8)* 125
S. Bristol (D8)* △ 631
S. Brooksville (F7)* 140
S. Casco (B8)* 150
S. China (D7)* 310
S. Deer Isle (F7) 85
S. Eliot (B4) 1,331
S. Exeter (E6) 25
S. Harpswell (C8)* 300
S. Hiram (B8)* 250
S. Hollis (B8) 30
S. Hope (E7)* 125
S. Jefferson (D7)
S. La Grange (F5) 150
S. Lebanon (A9)
S. Levant (E6) 110
S. Liberty (E7) 47
S. Lincoln (G5) 164
S. Monmouth (D7)
S. Orrington (F6)* 300
S. Paris (C7)* 2,067
S. Penobscot (F7)*
S. Portland (C8)* 21,866
S. Robbinston (J5)
S. Sanford (B9) 600
S. Thomaston (E7)* △ 654
S. Union (E7)*
S. Waldoboro (E7)
S. Warren (E7)
S. Waterford (B7)*
S. Windham (C8)* 1,569
Southport (D8)* △ 435
Southwest Harbor (G7)* △1,534
Spencer (C5)
Springfield (G5)* △ 414
Springvale (B9)* 2,745
Squa Pan (G2) 75
Stacyville (F4)* △ 679
Standish (B8)* △1,786
Starks (D6)* △ 421
Steep Falls (B8)* 480
Stetson (E6)* △ 434
Steuben (H6)* △ 784
Stillwater (F6)* 800
Stockholm (G1)* △ 641
Stockton Springs (F7)* △ 949
Stonington (F7)* △1,660
Stow, (A7)* △ 147
Stratton (B5)* 560
Strong (C6)* △1,036
Sugar Island (D4) 4
Sullivan (G6)* △ 762
Sumner (C7) △ 526
Sunset (F7)*
Sunshine (G7) 120
Surry (F7)* △ 448
Swans Island (G7)* △ 468
Swanville (E6) △ 437
Sweden (B7) △ 212
Sweden (G2)
Tarratine (D4) 8
Temple (C6)* △ 284
Tenants Harbor (E8)* 400
The Forks (D5)* △ 45
Thomaston (E7)* △2,810
Thorndike (E6)* △ 534
Topsfield (H5)* △ 231
Topsham (D8)* △2,626
Tremont (G7) △1,115
Trenton (G7) △ 358
Trescott (J6) △ 362
Trevett (D8)* 350
Troutdale (D5) 25
Troy (E6)* △ 553
Turner (C7)* △1,712
Turner Center (C7)*
Union (E7)* △1,085
Unionville (H6) 150
Unity (E6)* △1,014
Upper Dam (B6)
Upper Frenchville (G1)* 500
Upper Gloucester (C8)* 150
Upton (B6)* △ 105
Van Buren (G1)* △5,094
Vanceboro (H4)* △ 497
Vassalboro (D7)* △2,261
Veazie (F6) △ 776
Vienna (D6)* △ 231
Vinalhaven (F7)* △1,427
Waite (H5)* △ 117
Waldo (E7) △ 324
Waldoboro (E7)* △2,536
Walnut Hill (C8) 250
Waltham (G6) △ 154
Warren (E7)* △1,576
Washburn (G2)* △1,913
Washington (E7)* △ 722
Waterboro (B8)* △1,071
Waterford (B7)* △ 828
Waterville (E6)* 18,287
Wayne (D7)* △ 459
Webhannet (C9)*
Weeks Mills (E7)* 100
Welchville (C7)*
Weld (C6)* △ 361
Wellington (D5)* 252
Wells (B9)* △2,321
Wells Beach (C9)
Wesley (H6)* △ 149
West Athens (D6) 175
W. Baldwin (B8)*
W. Bath (D8) △ 578
W. Bethel (B7)* 250
W. Boothbay Harbor (D8)*
W. Brooksville (F7)* 140
W. Buxton (B8)* 350
W. Enfield (F5)*
W. Falmouth (C8) 1,500
W. Farmington (C6)* 500
W. Franklin (G6)* 115
W. Gardiner (D7) △ 946
W. Garland (E5) 50
W. Gorham (C8)
W. Gouldsboro (G7)* 105
W. Hampden (E6)
W. Harpswell (C8) 100
W. Jonesport (H6) 850
W. Kennebunk (B9)*
W. Lebanon (B9)* 150
W. Lubec (J6)*
W. Mills (C6) 50
W. Minot (C7)* 300
W. Newfield (B8)* 175
W. Old Town (F6) 35
W. Paris (B7)* 800
W. Pembroke (J6)* 500
W. Penobscot (F7)
W. Peru (C7)* 300
W. Poland (C7)*
W. Ripley (E6)
W. Rockport (E7)* 200
W. Scarboro (C8)* 1,500
W. Seboois (F4)*
W. Sumner (C7)* 101
W. Tremont (G7)* 250
W. Winterport (E6) 30
Westbrook (C8)* 12,284
Westfield (G2)* △ 557
Weston (H4)* △ 248
Wheelock (F1)
Whitefield (D7)* △1,030
Whiting (J6)* △ 354
Whitneyville (H6)* △ 227
Willimantic (E5) △ 189
Wilsons Mills (B6)* 80
Wilton (C6)* △3,455
Windsor (D7)* △ 740
Winn (G5)* △ 497
Winnecook (E6) 35
Winslow (D6) △4,413
Winslows Mills (E7)* 200
Winter Harbor (G7)* △ 568
Winterport (F6)* △1,694
Winterville (F2)* △ 373
Winthrop (C7)* △3,026
Wiscasset (D7)* △1,584
Woodland (H5)* △1,292
Wollwich (D8)* △1,344
Wyman Dam (D5)* 451
Wytopitlock (G4)* 352
Yarmouth (C8)* △2,669
York (B9) 2,000
York Beach (B9)* 500
York Corners (B9) 100
York Harbor (B9)* 750

MARYLAND

Map on Page 67

Total Population 2,343,001

24 COUNTIES

Allegany (A2)............89,556
Anne Arundel (H4)....117,392
Baltimore (H3).........270,273
Baltimore City (H3).949,708
Calvert (H6)..............12,100
Caroline (L5).............18,234
Carroll (F2)...............44,907
Cecil (L2)..................33,356
Charles (F6)...............23,415
Dorchester (K7)..........27,815
Frederick (E3)............62,287
Garrett (A7)...............21,259
Harford (J2)...............51,782
Howard (G4)...............23,119
Kent (K3)...................13,667
Montgomery (E4)......164,401
Prince Georges (G5)..194,182
Queen Annes (L4).......14,579
Saint Marys (H7).......29,111
Somerset (M8)...........20,745
Talbot (K5).................19,428
Washington (C2).........78,886
Wicomico (M7)...........39,641
Worcester (N8)..........23,148

CITIES and TOWNS

Abell (H8)*.................. 400
Aberdeen (K2)*...........2,944
Abingdon (J3)*............ 650
Accident (A7)*............ 242
Accokeek (G6)*............
Adamstown (D3)*......... 265
Aikin (K2)....................
Aireys (K6)*................ 110
Allen (M7)*................. 350
Alta Vista (A4)...........3,000
American Corner (L5).. 15
Andrews (K7)*............
ANNAPOLIS (H5)*.....10,047
Annapolis Jct. (H4)*.... 322
Antietam (D3)............. 250
Antietam Station (D3). 50
Aquasco (G6)...............
Arbutus (H3)...............4,000
Ardmore (C4).............. 500
Arlington (H3)*..........71,750
Baden (H6).................. 150
Baldwin (J3)*.............. 350
Balnew (H4)................1,500
Baltmiore (H3)*........949,708
Baltimore (urban area) 1,151,050
Barclay (L4)*.............. 108
Barnesville (E4)*.......... 130
Barstow (H6)*............. 151
Bartholows (F3).......... 100
Barton (C7)*............... 695
Bayview (L2)...............
Beane (A4).................. 50
Beaver Creek (D2)........ 50
Bel Air (J2)*...............2,578
Bel Alton (G7)*........... 250
Bellevue (K6)*............ 300
Beltsville (C3)*............ 800
Benedict (H6)*............ 250
Bengies (J3)............... 500
Bentley Springs (H2)*.. 130
Berlin (O7)*................2,001
Berwyn (B4)*..............
Berwyn Heights (C4).... 674
Bethesda (A4)*......... 36,000
Bethlehem (L6)*..........
Betterton (K3)*........... 314
Big Spring (C2)*.......... 125
Bigpool (C2)*.............. 175
Bishop (N7)*................ 25
Bishops Head (K7)*..... 300
Bishopville (O7)*......... 375
Bivalve (L7)*............... 270
Bladensburg (C4)*........2,899
Bloomington (B8)*....... 400
Blythedale (K2)............ 100
Boonsboro (D2)*..........1,071
Borden Shaft (C7)........ 419
Boring (G2)*............... 130
Boulevard Heights (B5)
Bowens (H6)*.............. 220
Bowie (G4)*................ 860
Boyds (E4)*................ 250
Bozman (J5)*..............
Bradbury Heights (C5).1,800
Bradbury Park (C5)...... 500
Bradshaw (J3)*............ 500
Branchville (B4)*.......... 500
Brandywine (G6)*.........1,000
Breathedsville (C2)*..... 150
Brentwood (B4)*..........3,523
Bridgetown (L4).......... 16
Bristol (H5)*............... 300
Broad Creek (B6)......... 50
Brookeville (F4)*.......... 117
Brookview (L6)........... 150
Brown (C5)................. 200
Brownsville (D3)*........ 202
Brunswick (D3)*..........3,752
Buck Lodge (E4).......... 100
Buckeystown (E3)*......
Burkittsville (D3)*........ 190
Burnt Mills (B3).......... 100
Burrsville (L5)............ 200
Burtonsville (G4)*........
Bushwood (G7)*.......... 300
Butler (H2)*................ 57
Cabin Creek (L6).........
Cabin John (A4)*.........2,000
California (H7)*.......... 250
Calvert (K2)................ 150
Cambridge (K6)*........10,351
Camp Springs (C6)...... 315
Capitol Heights (C5)*..2,729
Cardiff (J2)*................ 325
Carney (H3).................1,523
Carrollton (G2)*.......... 180
Castleton (J2)*........... 343
Catoctin (E2).............. 300
Catonsville (H3)*........29,638
Cavetown (D2)*........... 300
Cecilton (L3)*............. 510
Cedar Grove (F4).......... 200
Cedar Heights (C5)....... 788
Cedartown (N8)............ 50
Cedarville (G6)............ 200
Centreville (K4)*..........1,804
Chance (L8)*................ 400
Chaptico (H7)*............ 350
Charlestown (L2)*........ 551
Charlotte Hall (H7)*.... 150
Chase (J3)*................. 900
Cheltenham (G6)*......... 500
Cherry Hill (L2)........... 300
Chesapeake Beach (J6)* 504
Chesapeake City (L2)*.1,154
Chester (J5)*...............1,100
Chestertown (K4)*.......3,143
Chesterville (L3).......... 36
Cheverly (C4)*..............3,318
Chevy Chase (A4)*........1,971
Chewsville (D2)*........... 180
Childs (L2)*................ 90
Chillum (B4)*.............15,000
Choptank (L6)*...........
Church Creek (K6)*...... 187
Church Hill (K4)*......... 271
Churchton (J5)*..........
Churchville (J2)*..........
Claiborne (J5)*............ 150
Clara (L7).................... 200
Clarksburg (E4)*.......... 367
Clarksville (G4)*........... 200
Clear Spring (C2)*....... 558
Clements (G7)*............ 300
Clinton (C6)*.............. 500
Cockeysville (H3)*........3,000
College Park (C4)*......11,170
Collington (G5).............
Colmar Manor (B4)......1,732
Colora (K2)*................ 190
Compton (H7)*............ 500
Conowingo (K2)*.......... 500
Cooksville (F3)*........... 150
Cordova (K5)*.............. 500
Cornersville (K6).......... 100
Corriganville (D7)*.......
Cottage City (B4).........1,249
Crapo (K7)*.................
Creagerstown (E2)....... 325
Crellin (A8)*................ 500
Cresaptown (C7)*.........2,000
Crisfield (L9)*..............3,688
Crocheron (K8)*...........
Crownsville (H4)*......... 350
Crumpton (L4)*...........
Cumberland (D7)*......37,679
Damascus (F3)*............1,000
Dameron (J8)*............. 250
Dames Quarter (L8)*.... 450
Daniels (G3)*.............. 800
Daniels Park (C4)......... 750
Dargan (D3)................ 300
Darlington (J2)*.......... 500
Darnestown (E4).......... 200
Davidsonville (H5)*...... 900
Day (F3)......................
Deal Island (L8)*.........1,200
Deer Park (A8)*........... 320
Delmar (M7)................1,328
Denton (L5)*...............1,806
Derwood (F4)*............. 300
Dickerson (E4)*............ 300
District Heights (C5)....1,735
Doncaster (F7)*...........
Doubs (E3)*................. 250
Downsville (C2)............ 210
Drayden (J8)*.............. 300
Dublin (J2).................. 250
Dundalk (J3)*.............40,182
Eagle Harbor ‡(F6)...... 7
Earleigh Heights (H4).. 400
Earleville (L3)*............ 42
East New Market (L6)* 264
East Riverdale (C4)......1,200
Easton (K5)*................4,836
Eastport (J5)*..............
Eckhart Mines (C7)*....2,350
Eden (M7)*.................. 150
Edgemere (J3)..............6,000
Edmonston (C4)*..........1,190
Eldersburg (G3)........... 300
Eldorado (L6).............. 79
Elk Mills (L2)*............. 300
Elkneck (L2)................
Elkridge (H4)*..............3,000
Elkton (L2)*.................5,245
Ellerslie (D7)*............. 850
Ellerton (D2)............... 41
Ellicott City (G3)*........1,500
Elliott (L7)*................ 130
Emmitsburg (E2)*........1,261
Essex (J3)*.................35,000
Ewell (K9)*................. 400
Fair Hill (L2).............. 150
Fairbank (J6).............. 300
Fairland (G4)..............
Fairlee (K4)................ 240
Fairmount (L8)*........... 600
Fairmount Heights(C5) 2,097
Fallston (J2)*.............. 300
Farmington (K2).......... 50
Fearer (A7)................. 50
Federalsburg (L6)*.......1,878
Ferndale (H4)*.............2,500
Finchville (M6)............ 3
Finksburg (G3)*........... 500
Fishing Creek (J7)*...... 700
Flint Stone (A2)*......... 170
Forest Glen (B4)..........1,500
Forest Heights (B5).....1,125
Forest Hill (J2)*.......... 300
Forestville (C5)...........1,500
Fort Foote (B6)........... 75
Ft. Howard (J4)*..........1,000
Ft. Washington (G6).... 210
Foxville (E2)............... 150
Frederick (E3)*..........18,142
Freeland (H2)*............ 200
Friendship (H6)*.......... 300
Friendship Heights (A4) 315
Friendsville (A7)*......... 607
Frizellburg (F2)........... 193
Frostburg (C7)*............6,876
Fruitland (M7)*............1,028
Fullerton (J3)*.............2,500
Funkstown (D2)*.......... 879
Gaithersburg (F4)*.......1,755
Galena (L3)*............... 259
Galestown (L6)............ 100
Galesville (H5)*........... 900
Gamber (G3)............... 600
Gambrills (H4)*........... 500
Garrett Park (A3)*...... 524
Garrison (G3)*.............1,000
Germantown (E4)*....... 200
Girdletree (N8)*........... 200
Glen Burnie (H4)*........8,000
Glen Echo (A4)*.......... 356
Glen Echo Heights (A4) 600
Glenarden (C4)*........... 492
Glenarm (J3)*.............. 350
Glenelg (G3)*.............. 40
Glenn Dale (C4)*.......... 625
Glyndon (G3)*............. 500
Golden Hill (K7)...........
Goldsboro (L4)*............ 198
Golts (L3)*.................. 100
Graceham (E2)*........... 225
Granite (G3)*............... 600
Grantsville (B7)*.......... 461
Grasonville (K5)*..........1,200
Greenbelt (C4)*............7,074
Greenmount (G2)*........ 200
Greensboro (L5)*.........1,181
Hagerstown (C2)*.......36,260
Halethorpe (H4)*.........5,000
Hall (G5)*................... 195
Hampstead (G2)*......... 677
Hancock (B2)*............. 963
Hanover (G4)*.............1,000
Harmans (H4)*............ 200
Harney (F2)................ 142
Havre de Grace (K2)*...7,809
Hebbville (G3)............. 150
Hebron (M7)*............... 723
Helen (H7)*................. 125
Henderson (L4)*.......... 106
Henryton (G3)*............ 600
Hereford (E2)*............. 310
Highfield (E2)*.............1,000
Highland Beach ‡(J6)*. 5
Hillsboro (L5)*............. 179
Hillside (C5)................3,000
Hobbs (L5)*................. 95
Hollywood (H7)*.......... 800
Hood (B2).................... 11
Hoopersville (K7)*........ 300
Hopewell (L8).............. 200
Howardville (G3).........
Hudson (J6)................ 200
Hughsville (G6)*.......... 550
Huntingtown (H6)*....... 438
Hurlock (L6)*.............. 944
Hutton (A8)*................ 350
Hyattstown (E3)*.......... 135
Hyattsville (B4)*........12,308
Ijamsville (E3)*...........
Ilchester (G4)*............ 200
Indian Head (F6)*........ 491
Ingleside (L4)*............. 150
Ironshire (O7)............... 100
Ironshire Station (N7).. 25
Island Creek (H7)*........ 250
Issue (G7)*.................. 160
Jacksonville (H2).......... 75
Jarrettsville (H2)*........ 250
Jefferson (E3)*............ 275
Jennings (B7)*............. 300
Jesterville (L7)*........... 175
Johnsonville (F2).......... 200
Keedysville (D3)*.......... 417
Kempton (A9)*............. 260
Kemptown (E3)*........... 200
Kennedyville (L3)*........ 180
Kensington (A4)*..........1,611
Keymar (F2)*...............
Kingston (M8)*............. 50
Kingsville (J3)*............
Kitzmiller (B8)*........... 652
Knoxville (D3)*............ 750
Koontz (B7)..................
La Plata (G6)*.............. 780
Ladiesburg (E2)*.......... 126
Lakesville (K7)*........... 37
Landover (C4)*............1,175
Landover Hills (C4)*.....1,661
Lanham (C4)*...............1,133
Lansdowne (H3)*..........7,500
Lantz (E2)*.................. 75
Largo (C5)................... 100
Lauraville (H3)............
Laurel (G4)*.................4,482
Lawsonia (L9).............. 800
Laytonsville (F4)*......... 132
Le Gore (E2)*............... 400
Leeds (L2).................... 40
Leitersburg (D2).......... 250
Leonardtown (H7)*.......1,017
Leslie (L2)...................
Level (K2).................... 450
Lewistown (E2)*........... 350
Lexington Park (J7)*....6,000
Liberty Grove (K2)*...... 210
Libertytown (E3)*......... 600
Lime Kiln (E3)*............ 185
Linden (A4)..................1,000
Lineboro (G2)*............. 200
Linkwood (L6)*............. 125
Linthicum Heights(H4)*3,500
Linwood (F2)*.............
Lisbon (F3)*................ 150
Little Orleans (A2)*...... 300
Loch Lynn Heights (A8) 415
Lonaconing (C7)*..........2,289
Long Green (H3)*........ 500
Lothian (H5)*..............
Love Point (J4)............ 120
Loveville (H7)*............. 500
Lower Marlboro (H6)*.. 135
Luke (B8)*.................. 820
Lusby (J7)*.................. 225
Lutherville (H3)*..........2,800
Lynch (K3)*................. 97
Mackall (H7)*..............
Madison (K6)*..............
Madonna (H2).............. 25
Magnolia (J3)*............. 500
Manchester (G2)*.........1,027
Manokin (L8)*.............. 400
Mapleville (D2)*........... 175
Marbury (F6)*.............
Mardela Springs (L7)*.. 428
Marion Station (M8)*... 475
Marshall Hall (F6)........ 50
Marydel (L4)*.............. 110
Maryland Line (H2)*..... 202
Maryland Park (C5)......1,500
Mason Springs (F6)...... 50
Massey (L3)*............... 125
Maugansville (D2)*...... 725
Mayberry (F2).............. 108
Mayo (H5)*.................. 583
Mc Daniel (J5)*............ 197
Meadows (C5).............. 350
Mechanicsville (H7)*..... 500
Medford (F2)*.............. 125
Melitota (K4)............... 100
Melrose (G2)................ 150
Middle River (J3)*.....27,500
Middleburg (F2)*.......... 150
Middletown (E3)*......... 936
Midland (C7)*............... 889
Milestown (H7)............ 400
Millers (G2)*................ 225
Millersville (H4)*.......... 250
Millington (L3)*........... 356
Monie (L8)*.................. 250
Monkton (H2)*............. 105
Monrovia (E3)*............. 112
Montrose (A3).............. 200
Morningside (C5)..........1,520
Moscow Mills (B7)........ 300
Mount Airy (F3)*.........1,061
Mt. Lena (D2).............. 150
Mt. Pleasant (E3).........
Mt. Rainier (B4)*........10,989
Mt. Savage (C7)*..........2,094
Mt. Vernon (L8)........... 400
Mt. Washington (H3)*..4,153
Mountain Lake Park(A8)*
Mountaindale (E2)........ 175
Muirkirk (G4)*............. 400
Mullinix Mill (F3)......... 25
Myersville (D3)*........... 250
Nanjemoy (F7)*............ 264
Nanticoke (L7)*............ 650
National (C7)............... 348
Neavitt (J6)*................
New Glatz (B6)............. 50
New Market (E3)*........ 301
New Windsor (F2)*....... 707
Newark (N7)*............... 500
Newport (G7)*..............
Nikep (C7)*.................. 275
Norbeck (F4)................ 500
Norrisville (J2)............. 100
North Beach (J6)*........ 314
N. Branch (D7)............. 280
N. Brentwood (B4)........ 833
N. East (L2)*...............1,517
Oakland (A8)*..............1,640
Ocean City (O7)*..........1,234
Odenton (H4)*.............1,059
Oella (G3)*..................1,500
Oldtown (D7)*.............. 500
Olivet (J7)*.................. 250
Olney (F4)*..................1,000
Orangeville (H3).......... 300
Oraville (H7)*.............. 300
Oriole (L8)*................. 268
Owings (H6)*................ 230
Owings Mills (G3)*.......1,500
Oxford (K6)*................ 757
Oxon Hill (B6).............. 280
Palmers (H8)*.............. 300
Park Hall (J8)*............ 400
Parkton (H2)*.............. 500
Parkville (H3)*.............6,500
Parole (H5)*.................1,032
Parran (H6)*................
Parsonsburg (M7)*....... 350
Pasadena (H4)*............1,500
Patapsco (G2)*............
Perry Hall (H3)............1,000
Perryman (K3)*............ 300
Perryville (K2)*............ 679
Petersville (D3)........... 250
Phoenix (H2)*.............. 150
Pikesville (G3)*..........15,000
Piney Point (H8)*.........1,000
Pinto (C7)*.................. 275
Piscataway (G6).......... 77
Pisgah (F6)*................ 450
Pittsville (N7)*............ 497
Pleasant Valley (G2).... 170
Plum Point (J6)*..........
Pocomoke City (M8)*...3,191
Point of Rocks (E3)*.... 361
Pomfret (G6)*.............. 500
Pomona (K4)................ 35
Pomonkey (F6)............ 200
Poolesville (E4)*........... 161
Popes Creek (G7)*........ 75
Port Deposit (K2)*.......1,139
Port Republic (J6)*...... 50
Port Tobacco (F6)*....... 125
Port Tobacco Station (Springhill*) (G7)..... 150
Potomac (F4)............... 250
Powellville (N7)*.......... 350
Preston (L6)*............... 353
Price (L4)*................... 245
Prince Frederick (H6)*. 500
Princess Anne (L8)*.....1,407
Principio Furnace (L2)*. 250
Providence (L2)........... 300
Purdum (E3)................ 175
Quantico (M7)*............ 250
Queen Anne (K5)*......... 396
Queenstown (K5)*......... 316
Randallstown (G3)*......1,550
Rawlings (C7)*............. 500
Reid (D2)..................... 50
Reids Grove (L6).......... 45
Reisterstown (G3)*.......1,500
Relay (H4)*..................1,000
Reliance (L6)............... 30
Revell (J4)................... 100
Rhodes Point (K9)*....... 150
Riderwood (H3)*...........
Ridge (J8)*.................. 400
Ridgely (L5)*............... 834
Ridgeville (F3)............. 150
Ringgold (D2).............. 212
Rising Sun (K2)*.......... 668
Ritchie (C5)................. 200
River Springs (G8)........ 300
Riverdale (B4)*............5,530
Riverside (F7).............. 150
Rock Hall (K4)*............ 786
Rock Point (G7)*.......... 200
Rocks (J2)*..................
Rockville (F4)*..............6,934
Rogers Heights (C4).....2,000
Rohrersville (D3)*......... 165
Roland Park (H3)*......12,000
Rosaryville (G5)............ 100
Rosedale (H3)...............3,000
Rowlandsville (K2)........
Royal Oak (K6)*...........
Rumbley (L8)*.............. 113
Ruthsberg (L4)............. 25
Rutland (H5)............... 300
Ruxton (H3)*...............
Sabillasville (E2)*......... 300
Saint Augustine (L3).... 50
St. Inigoes (J8)*........... 400
St. James (C2)*............ 100
St. Leonard (J7)*..........
St. Martin's (O7)..........
St. Michaels (J5)*........1,470
Salem (L7)*................. 42
Salisbury (M7)*..........15,141
Sandy Spring (F4)*...... 650
Sassafras (L3)............. 100
Savage (G4)*................1,238
Savage Station (G4)..... 25
Scotland (J8)*.............. 300
Seabrook (C4)*.............2,500
Seat Pleasant (C5)*......2,255
Secretary (L6)*............ 344
Security (D2)*.............. 300
Severn (H4)*................ 250
Severna Park (H4)*......1,000
Sharpsburg (C3)*......... 866
Sharptown (M6)*.......... 680
Shawsville (H2)............ 50
Shelltown (M9)*........... 28
Shipley (H4).................1,500
Showell (O7)*.............. 100
Silver Hill (B5).............1,000
Silver Run (F2)............ 325
Silver Spring (B4)*....75,0
Smallwood (F2)............ 1
Smithsburg (D2)*......... 6
Snow Hill (N8)*............2,0
Solomons (J7)*............ 2
Somerset (A4).............. 4
Sparrows Point (J4)*..12,0
Spickler (C2)...............
Spielman (C2).............. 2
Springhill (G7)*........... 1
Stemmers Run (H3)......1,2
Stevensville (J5)*......... 3
Steyer (A8)*................
Still Pond (K3)*........... 2
Still Pond Station (K3)
Stockton (N8)*............ 5
Street (J2)*................. 2
Sudlersville (L4)*......... 3
Sudley (H5)..................
Suitland (C5)*..............2,5
Swanton (A8)*............. 2
Sweetair (H2)...............
Sykesville (F3)*........... 9
T. B. (G6)................... 1
Takoma Park (B4)......13,3
Taneytown (F2)*..........1,4
Taylors Island (J7)*...... 3
Taylorsville (F3).......... 1
Templeville (L4)*.........
Texas (H3)*.................
Thomas (J6)................ 2
Thurmont (E2)*............1,6
Tilghman (J6)*.............1,2
Timonium (H3)*...........1,3
Toddville (K7)*............ 3
Tolchester Beach (J4)...
Tompkinsville (G7)*...... 5
Town Creek (A2)...........
Town Point (L3)...........
Towson (H3)*..............11,0
Trappe (K6)*............... 3
Trappe Station (K6).....
Trenton (G2)............... 1
Tunis Mills (K5)........... 1
Tuxedo (C5)*...............1,0
Tyaskin (L7)*.............. 1
Union Bridge (F2)*....... 8
Union Mills (F2)*......... 3
Uniontown (F2)*.......... 2
Unionville (F3)*........... 1
Unity (F4)...................
University Park (B4).....2,2
Upper Fairmount (L8)*. 8
Upper Falls (J3)*......... 2
Upper Marlboro (H5)*.. 7
Upperco (G2)*............. 1
Urbana (E3).................
Vale Summit (C7)......... 4
Valley Lee (H8)*........... 3
Venton (M8)*............... 1
Vienna (L7)*................ 4
Vindex (B8)*................ 1
Waldorf (G6)*...............1,1
Walkersville (E3)*......... 7
Warwick (L3)*..............
Washington Grove (F4)* 4
Waterview (L8).............
Welcome (F7)*.............. 2
Wenona (L8)*............... 3
West Annapolis (H4)*...
W. Lanham Hills (C4)*..1,2
W. River (H5)*.............
Western Port (B8)*......3,4
Westminster (G2)*........6,1
Westover (M8)*............ 4
Wetipquin (L7)............ 5
Weverton (D3)*............ 1
Whaleysville (N7)*........ 3
Wheaton (A3)*............20,0
White Hall (H2)*.......... 3
White Marsh (J3)*....... 5
White Oak (B3).............
White Plains (G6)......... 7
Whiteford (J2)*............ 3
Whitehaven (L7)*.........
Wicomico (G7)*............ 2
Willards (N7)*.............. 4
Williamsburg (L6)*....... 1
Williamsport (C2)*.......1,8
Williston (L5).............. 1
Willows (H6)*..............
Winfield (F3)...............
Wingate (K7)*..............
Wittman (J5)*..............
Wolfsville (D2).............
Woodbine (F3)*............
Woodlawn (H3).............5,0
Woodmoor (B4)*........... 5
Woodsboro (E2)*.......... 4
Woodside (B4)..............3,5
Woodstock (G3)*.......... 1
Woolford (K7)*............ 1
Worton (K3)*............... 1
Wye Mills (K5)*........... 1
Wye Mills Station (K5) 1
Wynne (J8).................. 3
Yellow Springs (D3)......
Zion (L2)......................

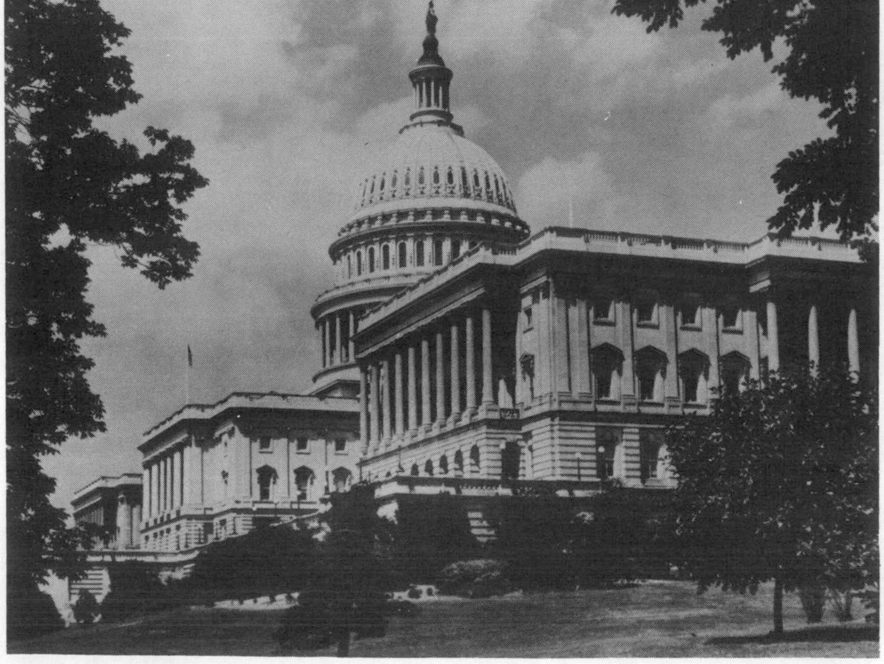

DISTRICT OF COLUMBIA

Anacostia (B5)*...........
Benning (B5)*..............
Brightwood (B4)*.........
Brookland (B4)*...........
Cleveland Park (A4)*....
Congress Heights (B5)*
Georgetown (A5)*.........
Petworth (B4)*.............
Tenleytown (A4)...........
WASHINGTON, D. C. (B5)* 802,17
Washington (urban area) 1,281,57

Map on Page 68

MASSACHUSETTS

Total Population 4,690,514

14 COUNTIES

arnstable (N6)..........46,805
erkshire (B3).........132,966
ristol (K5).............381,569
ukes (M7)................. 5,633
ssex (L2)..................522,384
ranklin (D2)...............52,747
ampden (D4)...........367,971
ampshire (D3)...........87,594
iddlesex (J3).......1,064,569
antucket (O7)........... 3,484
orfolk (K4)..............392,308
ymouth (L5)..........189,468
uffolk (K3)..............896,615
orcester (G3)..........546,401

CITIES and TOWNS

bington (L4)*...........Δ7,152
ccord (E8)*............. 150
coaxet (K7)*............ 130
cton (J3)*................Δ3,510
cushnet (L6)*..........Δ4,401
dams (B2)*.............Δ12,034
gawam (D4)*..........Δ10,166
llerton (E7)*............ 500
mesbury (L1)*........Δ10,851
mherst (E3)*..........Δ10,856
ndover (K2)*..........Δ12,437
nnisquam (M2)*.......
rlington (C6)*.........Δ44,353
shburnham (G2)*......Δ2,603
shby (G2)*...............Δ1,464
shfield (C2)*.............Δ 977
shland (J3)*..............Δ3,500
shley Falls (A4)*...... 500
ssinippi (E8)*........... 500
ssonet (K5)*............ 1,002
thol (F2)*...............Δ11,554
ttleboro (J5)*...........23,809
ttleboro Falls (J5)*.. 2,500
uburn (G4)*..............Δ8,840
uburndale (B7)*........ 6,218
von (K4)*..................Δ2,666
yer (H2)*..................Δ5,740
aldwinville (F2)*....... 1,407
allard Vale (K2)*..... 1,200
arnstable (N6)*......Δ10,480
arre (F3)*.................Δ3,406
arre Plains (F3)*...... 144
arrowsville (K5)*...... 700
ecket (B3)*..............Δ 755
edford (B6)*.............Δ5,234
eechwood (F8)*........ 200
elchertown (E3)*......Δ4,487
ellingham (J4)*........Δ4,100
elmont (C6)*...........Δ27,381
erkley (K5)...............Δ1,284
erlin (H3)*................Δ1,349
ernardston (D2)*......Δ1,117
everly (E5)*..............28,884
everly Farms (E5)*.. 2,500
illerica (J2)*...........Δ11,101
lackinton (B2)*........ 440
lackstone (H4)*.......Δ4,968
landford (C4)*..........Δ 597
olton (H3)*...............Δ 956
ondsville (E4)*......... 1,200
OSTON (D7)*..........801,444
oston (urban
area) 2,218,893
ourne (M6)*.............Δ4,720
ournedale (M5).........
oxford (K2)*.............Δ 926
oylston Center
(H3)* ....
raintree (D8)*.........Δ23,161
rant Rock (M4)*...... 350
rewster (O5)*...........Δ 987
ridgewater (K5)*......Δ9,512
rimfield (F4)*...........Δ1,182
rockton (K4)*...........62,860
rockton (urban area)92,086
rookfield (F4)*.........Δ1,567
rookline (C7)*.........Δ57,589
rookville (K4)*.......... 1,300
ryantville (L4)*........
uckland (C2)*...........Δ1,605
urlington (C5)..........Δ3,250
uzzards Bay (M5)*.. 1,459
yfield (L1)*............. 950
ambridge (C6)*.......120,740
anton (C8)*..............Δ7,465
anton Jct. (C8)........
arlisle (J2)*.............Δ 846
arver (M5)*..............Δ1,530
aryville (J4)*............ 300
ataumet (M6)*.......... 100
enterville (N6)*.........1,100
entral Village (K6)*.. 350
harlemont (C2)*........Δ 855
harlton (F4)*.............Δ3,136
harlton City (F4)*.... 1,200
harlton Depot (F4)*. 150
hartley (K5)*............ 600
hatham (P6)*............Δ2,457
hathamport (P6)....... 150
helmsford (J2)*.......Δ9,407
helsea (D6)*............38,912
herry Valley (G3)*.... 1,300
heshire (B2)*............Δ2,022
hester (C3)*..............Δ1,292
hesterfield (C3)*.......Δ 496
hicopee (D4)*..........49,211
hicopee Falls (D4)*..12,915
hilmark (M7)*...........Δ 183
hiltonville (M5).........
ity Mills (J4)*.......... 500
lifton (E6)*.............. 5,000
linton (H3)*.............Δ12,287
ochituate (A7)*........ 2,500
ohasset (F7)*...........Δ3,731
ollinsville (J2)*........ 1,500
olrain (D2)*..............Δ1,546
oncord (A6)*.............Δ8,623

Conway (D2)*.............Δ 873
Cordaville (H3)*.......... 250
Cotuit (N6)*.............. 700
Crescent Beach (M6)*
Cummaquid (N6)*....... 200
Cummington (C3)*......Δ 620
Cushing (L1)*............ 398
Cushman (D3)*.......... 250
Cuttyhunk (L7)*........ 40
Dalton (B3)*...............Δ4,772
Danvers (D5)*...........Δ15,720
Danversport (E5)........ 2,500
Dartmouth (K6)*......Δ11,115
Dedham (C7)*...........Δ18,487
Deerfield (D2)*..........Δ3,086
Dennis (O5)*..............Δ2,499
Dennis Port (O6)*....... 1,200
Dighton (K5)*.............Δ2,950
Dodge (G4)*.............. 835
Dodgeville (K5)*......... 1,500
Dorchester (D7)*.........
Douglas (H4)..............Δ2,624
Dover (B7)*................Δ1,722
Dracut (J2).................Δ8,666
Dudley (G4)*..............Δ5,261
Dunstable (J2)*..........Δ 522
Duxbury (M4)*...........Δ3,167
E. Blackstone (H4).....
E. Braintree (D8)........ 7,000
E. Brewster (O5)*....... 500
E. Bridgewater (L4)*..Δ4,412
E. Brookfield (G4)*....Δ1,243
E. Dedham (C8)*......... 5,000
E. Dennis (O5)*.......... 275
E. Douglas (G4)*........ 1,846
E. Falmouth (M6)*..... 1,405
E. Foxboro (K4)*........ 500
E. Freetown (L5)*...... 1,200
E. Harwich (O6)*........ 500
E. Lee (B3)*............... 350
E. Longmeadow (E4)*.Δ4,881
E. Milton (D7)........... 7,500
E. Northfield (E2)*..... 950
E. Norton (K5)........... 800
E. Orleans (P5)*......... 383
E. Otis (B4)*.............. 95
E. Pembroke (M4)*..... 200
E. Pepperell (H2)*...... 2,500
E. Sandwich (N6)*...... 325
E. Saugus (D6)...........
E. Taunton (K5)*........ 5,000
E. Templeton (G2)*..... 1,200
E. Village (G4)...........
E. Walpole (C8)*......... 2,000
E. Wareham (M5)*..... 500
E. Weymouth (E8)*.....10,000
E. Whately (D3).........
Eastham (O5)*...........Δ 860
Easthampton (D3)*...Δ10,694
Easton (K4)*..............Δ6,244
Eastondale (K4)*....... 600
Edgartown (M7)*........Δ1,508
Egypt (F8)*................ 600
Elmwood (L4)*........... 350
Erving (E2)*...............Δ1,322
Essex (L2)*.................Δ1,794
Everett (D6)*.............45,982
Fairhaven (L6)*.........12,764
Fairview (D4)*............ 2,108
Fall River (K6)*........111,963
Fall River (urban
area) 117,881
Falmouth (M6)*.........Δ8,662
Farnams (B2)*........... 200
Farnumsville (H4)*..... 1,427
Fayville (H3)*............ 1,000
Feeding Hills (D4)*..... 3,500
Fisherville (H4)*......... 1,167
Fiskdale (F4)*.............
Fitchburg (G2)*..........42,691
Florence (D3)*............ 4,500
Forest Hills (C7).........10,000
Forge Village (H2)*.... 1,115
Foxboro (J4)*.............Δ7,030
Framingham (A7)*....Δ28,086
Framingham Center
(J3)* 4,500
Franklin (J4)*............Δ8,037
Furnace (F3)*............ 150
Gardner (G2)*............19,581
Gay Head (L7)............Δ 88
Georgetown (L2)*.......Δ2,411
Gilbertville (F3)*........ 1,039
Gill (D2).....................Δ1,070
Gleasondale (J3)*.......
Glendale (A3)*........... 350
Gloucester (M2)*........25,167
Goshen (C3)*..............Δ 321
Grafton (H4)*.............Δ8,281
Granby (E3)*..............Δ1,861
Graniteville (J2)*........ 1,000
Granville (C4)*...........Δ 740
Great Barrington
(A4)* Δ6,712
Green Harbor (M4)*.... 300
Greenbush (F8)*......... 650
Greenfield (D2)*.......Δ17,349
Greenwood (D6)*........ 5,500
Griswoldville (D2)*...... 590
Groton (H2)*...............Δ2,889
Groveland (L1)*..........Δ2,340
Hadley (D3)*...............Δ2,639
Halifax (L5)*...............Δ 944
Hamilton (L2)*............Δ2,764
Hampden (E4)*...........Δ1,322
Hancock (A2)*.............Δ 445
Hanover (L4)*..............Δ3,389
Hanson (L4)*...............Δ3,264
Hardwick (F3)*............Δ2,348
Hartsville (B4)............
Harvard (H2)*..............Δ3,983
Harwich (O6)*.............Δ2,649
Harwich Port (O6)*.... 1,350
Hatfield (D3)*.............Δ2,179
Haverhill (K1)*...........47,280
Haydenville (C3)*....... 1,009
Heath (C2)*.................Δ 305

Hebronville (J5)*........ 754
Hingham (E8)*..........Δ10,665
Hingham Center (E8)..
Hinsdale (B3)*............Δ1,560
Holbrook (D8)*...........Δ4,004
Holden (G3)*..............Δ5,975
Holland (F4)...............Δ 377
Holliston (A8)*...........Δ3,753
Holyoke (D4)*............54,661
Holyoke-Springfield
(urban area)..........356,471
Hoosac Tunnel (C2)*... 150
Hopedale (H4)*...........Δ3,479
Hopkinton (J4)*..........Δ3,486
Hortonville (K5)..........
Housatonic (A3)*........ 1,601
Hubbardston (F3)*......Δ1,134
Hubbardston Station
(F3) 120
Hudson (H3)*..............Δ8,211
Hull (E7)*...................Δ3,379
Humarock (M4)*......... 50
Huntington (C4)*........Δ1,257
Hyannis (N6)*............ 4,235
Hyannis Port (N6)*..... 300
Hyde Park (C7)*.........
Indian Orchard (E4)*.10,000
Interlaken (A3)*......... 60
Ipswich (L2)*..............Δ6,985
Islington (C8)*.............2,300
Jamaica Plain (C7)*....
Jefferson (G3)*...........
Kendal Green (B6).....
Kingston (M5)*..........Δ3,461
Lakeville (L5).............Δ2,066
Lancaster (H3)*..........Δ3,601
Lanesboro (A2)*..........Δ2,069
Lanesville (M2)*......... 1,046
Lawrence (K2)*..........80,536
Lawrence (urban
area) 111,937
Lee (B3)*....................Δ4.820
Leeds (D3)*................ 1,700
Leicester (G4)*...........Δ6,029
Lenox (A3)*................Δ3,627
Lenox Dale (B3)*........ 500
Leominster (G2)*........24,075
Leverett (E3)*.............Δ 791
Lexington (B6)*.........Δ17,335
Leyden (D2)................Δ 306
Lincoln (B6)*..............Δ2,427
Linwood (H4)*............ 981
Littleton (H2)*............Δ2,349
Littleton Common
(J2)* 1,017
Longmeadow (D4)*.....Δ6,508
Lowell (J2)*...............97,249
Lowell (urban area)..105,783
Ludlow (E4)*..............Δ8,660
Ludlow Center (E4)... 500
Lunenburg (H2)*........Δ3,906
Lynn (D6)*..................99,738
Lynnfield (D5)*...........Δ3,927
Lynnfield Center (C5)* 2,600
Magnolia (M2)*..........
Malden (D6)*..............59,804
Manchaug (G4)*......... 790
Manchester (F5)*.......Δ2,868
Manomet (M5)*......... 350
Mansfield (J4)*...........Δ7,104
Marblehead (E5)*.....Δ13,765
Marion (L6)*...............Δ2,250
Marlboro (H3)*...........15,756
Marshfield (M4)*........Δ3,267
Marshfield Hills(M4)*. 500
Marstons Mills (N6)*. 600
Mashpee (M6)*..........Δ 438
Mattapan (C7)*..........
Mattapoisett (L6)*.....Δ2,265
Maynard (J3)*............Δ6,978
Medfield (B8)*............Δ4,549
Medfield Jct. (B8)...... 500
Medford (C6)*............66,113
Medway (J4)*.............Δ3,744
Melrose (D6)*............26,988
Melrose Highlds.(D6)*..7,713
Mendon (H4)*.............Δ1,619
Menemsha (L7)* ....
Merrimac (L1)*...........Δ2,804
Merrimacport (L1)...... 210
Methuen (K2)*..........Δ24,477
Middleboro (L5)*......Δ10,164
Middlefield (B3)*.......Δ 295
Middleton (K2)*..........Δ2,916
Milford (H4)*.............Δ15,442
Mill River (A4)...........Δ 300
Millbrook (M4)*......... 200
Millbury (H4)*............Δ8,347
Millers Falls (E2)*..... 1,134
Millis (A8)*.................Δ2,551
Millville (H4)*.............Δ1,692
Milton (D7)*..............Δ22,395
Minot (F8)*................ 150
Monroe Bridge (C2)*.. 150
Monson (E4)*.............Δ6,125
Montague (E2)*..........Δ7,812
Montague City (D2)*.. 668
Monterey (B4)*...........Δ 367
Montvale (C6).............
Montville (B4)*...........
Monument Beach
(M6)* 650
Moores Corner (E2)*..
Mt. Hermon (D2)*...... 750
Mt. Hope (C7)............ 5,000
Mt. Tom (D3)*........... 230
Mt. Washington (A4)Δ 34
Myricks (K5)............... 210
Nabnasset (J2)*......... 500
Nahant (E6)*...............Δ2,679
Nantasket Beach
(E7)* 1,900
Nantucket (O7)*.........Δ3,484
Natick (A7)*...............Δ19,838
Needham (B7)*..........Δ16,313
Needham Hts. (B7)*.. 5,500
Neponset (D7)............

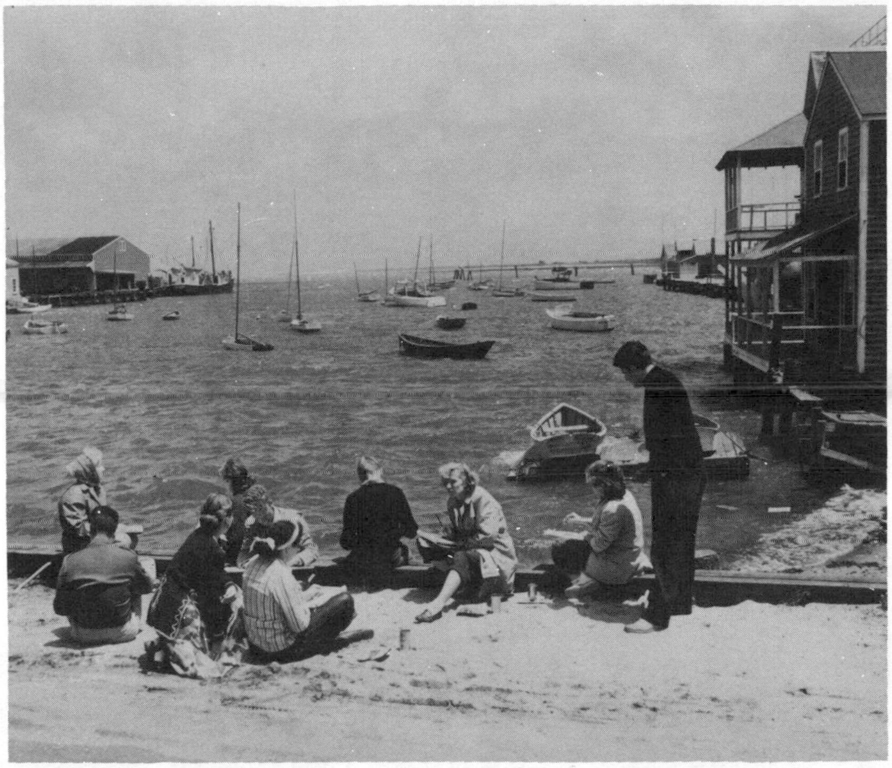

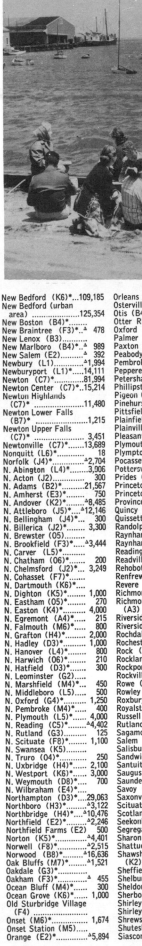

New Bedford (K6)*...109,185
New Bedford (urban
area) 125,354
New Boston (B4)*........
New Braintree (F3)*..Δ 478
New Lenox (B3)..........
New Marlboro (B4)*..Δ 989
New Salem (E2)..........Δ 392
Newbury (L1)..............Δ1,994
Newburyport (L1)*.....14,111
Newton (C7)*.............81,994
Newton Center (C7)*..15,214
Newton Highlands
(C7)* 11,480
Newton Lower Falls
(B7)* 1,215
Newton Upper Falls
(C7)* 3,451
Newtonville (C7)*.......13,689
Nonquitt (L6)*............ 18
Norfolk (J4)*...............Δ2,704
N. Abington (L4)*........3,906
N. Acton (J2).............. 300
N. Adams (B2)*..........21,567
N. Amherst (E3)*........ 750
N. Andover (K2)*........Δ8,485
N. Attleboro (J5)*....Δ12,146
N. Bellingham (J4)*... 300
N. Billerica (J2)*........ 3,300
N. Brewster (O5).........
N. Brookfield (F3)*.....Δ3,444
N. Carver (L5)*..........
N. Chatham (O6)*....... 200
N. Chelmsford (J2)*... 3,249
N. Cohasset (F7)*.......
N. Dartmouth (K6)*....
N. Dighton (K5)*........ 1,000
N. Eastham (O5)*........ 270
N. Easton (K4)*.......... 4,000
N. Egremont (A4)*..... 215
N. Falmouth (M6)*..... 800
N. Grafton (H4)*......... 2,000
N. Hadley (D3)*.......... 1,000
N. Hanover (L4)*........ 800
N. Harwich (O6)*........ 210
N. Hatfield (D3)*....... 300
N. Leominster (G2).....
N. Marshfield (M4)*... 450
N. Middleboro (L5)..... 500
N. Oxford (G4)*.......... 1,250
N. Pembroke (M4)*..... 400
N. Plymouth (L5)*...... 4,000
N. Reading (C5)*........Δ4,402
N. Rutland (G3).......... 125
N. Scituate (F8)*........ 1,100
N. Swansea (K5).........
N. Truro (O4)*............ 250
N. Uxbridge (H4)*...... 2,100
N. Westport (K6)*...... 3,000
N. Weymouth (D8)*.... 700
N. Wilbraham (E4)*....
Northampton (D3)*....29,063
Northboro (H3)*.........Δ3,122
Northbridge (H4)*....Δ10,476
Northfield (E2)*.........Δ2,246
Northfield Farms (E2) 500
Norton (K5)*..............Δ4,401
Norwell (F8)*..............Δ2,515
Norwood (B8)*..........Δ16,636
Oak Bluffs (M7)*........Δ1,521
Oakdale (G3)*............
Oakham (F3)*.............Δ 455
Ocean Bluff (M4)*...... 300
Ocean Grove (K6)*...... 1,000
Old Sturbridge Village
(F4) ....
Onset (M6)*................ 1,674
Onset Station (M5).....
Orange (E2)*..............Δ5,894

Orleans (O5)*..............Δ1,759
Osterville (N6)*........... 1,003
Otis (B4)*....................Δ 359
Otter River (F2).........
Oxford (G4)*...............Δ5,841
Palmer (E4)*...............Δ9,533
Paxton (G3)*...............Δ1,066
Peabody (E5)*...........22,645
Pembroke (L4)*..........Δ2,579
Pepperell (H2)*..........Δ3,460
Petersham (F3)*.........Δ 814
Phillipston (F2)..........Δ 638
Pigeon Cove (M2)*...... 1,011
Pinehurst (B5)*.......... 2,905
Pittsfield (A3)*..........55,348
Plainfield (C2)*..........Δ 228
Plainville (J4)*...........Δ2,088
Pleasant Lake (O6)*.. 125
Plymouth (M5)*........Δ13,608
Plympton (L5)*...........Δ 697
Pocasset (M6)*.......... 500
Pottersville (K6)........ 2,700
Prides Crossing (E5)*.. 450
Princeton (G3)*..........Δ1,032
Princeton Depot (G3).
Provincetown (O4)*....Δ3,795
Quincy (D7)*...............83,835
Quissett (M6)............. 300
Randolph (D8)*...........Δ9,982
Raynham (K5)*...........Δ2,426
Raynham Center (K5)* 1,800
Reading (C5)*..........Δ14,006
Readville (C8)*........... 6,000
Rehoboth (K5)*..........Δ3,700
Renfrew (B2).............
Revere (D6)*..............36,763
Richmond (A3)*..........Δ 737
Richmond Furnace
(A3) 250
Riverside (D2)............
Riverside (B7)............ 400
Rochdale (G4)*.............1,800
Rochester (L6)*..........Δ1,328
Rock (L5).................... 600
Rockland (L4)*............Δ8,960
Rockport (M2)*...........Δ4,231
Rockville (A8)............. 500
Rowe (C2)*..................Δ 199
Rowley (L2)*...............Δ1,768
Roxbury (C7)*.............
Royalston (F2)*...........Δ 838
Russell (C4)*...............Δ1,298
Rutland (G3)*..............Δ3,056
Sagamore (M5)*......... 1,500
Salem (E5)*.................41,880
Salisbury (L1)*............Δ2,695
Sandwich (N5)*...........Δ2,418
Santuit (N6)*............. 400
Saugus (D6)*.............Δ17,162
Saundersville (G4)*..... 380
Savoy (B2)*.................Δ 291
Saxonville (A7)*.......... 3,200
Scituate (F8)*.............Δ5,993
Scotland (L5).............
Seekonk (J5)*.............Δ6,104
Segreganset (K5)*...... 300
Sharon (K4)*...............Δ4,847
Shattuckville (D2)*..... 225
Shawsheen Village
(K2)* 2,100
Sheffield (A4)*............Δ2,150
Shelburne Falls (D2)*. 2,364
Sheldonville (J4)*....... 300
Sherborn (A8)*............Δ1,245
Shirley (H2)*...............Δ4,271
Shirley Center (H2)*.. 1,082
Shrewsbury (H3)*......Δ10,594
Shutesbury (E3)*........Δ 213
Siasconset (P7)*......... 225

Silver Lake (L5)*....... 2,024
Somerset (K5)*..........Δ8,566
Somerville (C6)*......102,351
S. Acton (J3)*........... 1,200
S. Amherst (E3).......... 750
S. Ashburnham (G2)*.. 1,000
S. Athol (F2)*............ 100
S. Attleboro (J5)*.......
S. Barre (F3)*............ 1,800
S. Berlin (H3)*.......... 200
S. Braintree (D8)*...... 5,600
S. Bridgewater (L5)*..
S. Carver (M5)*.......... 300
S. Chatham (O6)*....... 450
S. Dartmouth (L6)*.... 6,300
S. Deerfield (D3)*...... 1,418
S. Dennis (O6)*.......... 300
S. Duxbury (M4)*....... 800
S. Easton (K4)*.......... 1,500
S. Egremont (A4)*...... 415
S. Essex (L2)*............
S. Groveland (L2)....... 900
S. Hadley (D4)*........Δ10,145
S. Hadley Falls (D4)* 4,000
S. Hanover (L4)*........ 600
S. Harwich (O6)*........ 400
S. Hingham (E8)......... 650
S. Lancaster (H3)*..... 1,462
S. Lawrence (K2)........25,000
S. Lee (A3)*............... 325
S. Lincoln (J3)*..........
S. Middleboro (L5)..... 600
S. Middleton (D5).......
S. Natick (A7)*.......... 1,500
S. Orleans (O5)*.......... 89
S. Royalston (F2)*........ 415
S. Sandisfield (B4)*....
S. Sudbury (J3)*......... 900
S. Vernon (D2)*.......... 225
S. Walpole (K4)*........ 750
S. Wareham (L5)........
S. Wellfleet (P5)*....... 450
S. Westport (K6)*....... 200
S. Weymouth (E8)*.... 8,500
S. Worthington (C3)... 50
S. Yarmouth (O6)*...... 1,185
Southampton (C4)*.....Δ1,387
Southboro (H3)*.........Δ2,760
Southbridge (G4)*.....Δ17,519
Southfield (B4).......... 100
Southville (H3)*......... 300
Southwick (C4)*..........Δ2,850
Spencer (F3)*.............Δ7,027
Springfield (D4)*......162,399
Springfield-Holyoke
(urban area)..........356,471
State Line (A3)*........ 200
Sterling (G3)*.............Δ2,166
Still River (H3)*......... 150
Stockbridge (A3)*......Δ2,311
Stoneham (C6)*........Δ13,229
Stoughton (K4)*......Δ11,146
Stow (H3)*..................Δ1,700
Straits Pond (F7)*...... 250
Sturbridge (F4)*.........Δ2,805
Sudbury (A6)*.............Δ2,596
Sunderland (D3)*........Δ 905
Sutton (G4)................Δ3,102
Swampscott (E6)*.....Δ11,580
Swansea (K5)*............Δ6,121
Swansea Center (K5)..
Taunton (K5)*............40,109
Teaticket (M6)*.......... 600
Templeton (F2)*.........Δ4,757
Tewkesbury (K2)*.......Δ7,505
Thorndike (E4)*.......... 1,650
Three Rivers
(E4)* 2,359
Tolland (B4)...............Δ 107

Topsfield (L2)*...........Δ1,412
Townsend (H2)*..........Δ2,817
Townsend Harbor
(G2)* 197
Truro (O5)*................Δ 661
Tully (E2)..................
Turners Falls (D2)*..... 5,179
Tyngsboro (J2)*..........Δ2,059
Tyringham (A4)*.......Δ 235
Unionville (J4)............ 150
Upton (H4)*................Δ2,656
Uxbridge (H4)*...........Δ7,007
Vineyard Haven (M7)* 1,064
Waban (B7)*.............. 6,000
Wakefield (C5)*........Δ19,633
Wales (F4)*.................Δ 497
Walpole (B8)*..............Δ9,109
Waltham (B6)*...........47,187
Waquoit (M6)*.......... 400
Ward Hill (K2)*.......... 580
Ware (E3)*..................Δ7,517
Wareham (L5)*...........Δ7,569
Warren (F4)*................Δ3,406
Warwick (E2)*.............Δ 429
Washington (B3).........Δ 281
Watertown (C6)*......Δ37,329
Waterville (F2)*......... 450
Waverly (B6)*.............10,000
Wayland (A7)*.............Δ4,407
Webster (G4)*...........Δ13,194
Wellesley (B7)*........Δ20,549
Wellesley Hills (B7)*..18,000
Wellfleet (O5)*............Δ1,123
Wendell (E2)*..............Δ 342
Wendell Depot (E2)*..
Wenham (L2)*.............Δ1,644
W. Acton (H3)*........... 1,300
W. Auburn (G4)..........
W. Barnstable (N6)*... 750
W. Berlin (H3)*.......... 325
W. Boxford (K2)*....... 400
W. Boylston (G3)*......Δ2,570
W. Brewster (O5)........
W. Bridgewater
(K4)* Δ4,059
W. Brookfield (F4)*....Δ1,674
W. Chatham (O6)*...... 300
W. Chelmsford (J2)*... 300
W. Chesterfield (C3)*. 200
W. Concord (A6)*....... 1,285
W. Cummington (B3)* 180
W. Dennis (O6)*.......... 600
W. Dudley (F4)........... 200
W. Falmouth (M6)*.... 700
W. Granville (C4)........ 200
W. Groton (H2)*.........
W. Hanover (L4)*....... 1,200
W. Harwich (O6)*....... 400
W. Hawley (C2)*......... 56
W. Mansfield (K5)*.... 900
W. Medway (J4)*........ 1,625
W. Millbury (G4)*...... 300
W. Newbury (L1)*......Δ1,598
W. Newton (B7)*........15,000
W. Peabody (D5)*...... 1,100
W. Pittsfield (A3)....... 2,000
W. Rutland (F3)..........
W. Springfield (D4)*.Δ20,438
W. Stockbridge (A3)*Δ 1,165
W. Tisbury (M7)*.......Δ 347
W. Townsend (H2)*.... 900
W. Upton (H4)*.......... 1,400
W. Wareham (L5)*..... 800
W. Warren (F4)*......... 1,244
W. Yarmouth (N6)*.... 1,355
Westboro (H3)*...........Δ7,378
Westfield (D4)*..........20,962
Westford (J2)*............Δ4,262
Westford Station (J2). 300

Westhampton (C3)....▲ 452
Westminster (G2)*....▲2,768
Weston (B6)*....▲5,026
Westport (K6)*....▲4,989
Westport Point (K6)*. 500
Westwood (B8)*....▲5,837
Weymouth (D8)*....▲32,690
Whately (D3)*....▲ 939
Wheelwright (F3)*.... 270
Whitinsville (H4)*.... 5,662
Whitman (L4)*....▲8,413
Wilbraham (E4)*....▲4,003
Wilkinsonville (G4)*....
Williamsburg (C3)*....▲2,056
Williamstown (B2)*....▲6,194
Williamstown Station (B2) 5,000
Willimansett (D4)*.... 9,474
Wilmington (C5)*....▲7,039
Winchendon (F2)*....▲6,585
Winchendon Spgs.(G2)* 500
Winchester (C6)*....▲15,509
Windsor (B2)*....▲ 372
Winthrop (D6)*....▲19,496
Woburn (C6)*....20,492
Woods Hole (M6)*.... 750
Woodville (H4)*.... 350
Worcester (H3)*....203,486
Worcester (urban area) 217,705
Woronoco (C4)*.... 501
Worthington (C3)*....▲ 462
Wrentham (J4)*....▲5,341
Yarmouth (O6)*....▲3,297
Yarmouth Port (N6)*. 330

Map on Page 69

MICHIGAN

Total Population 6,371,766

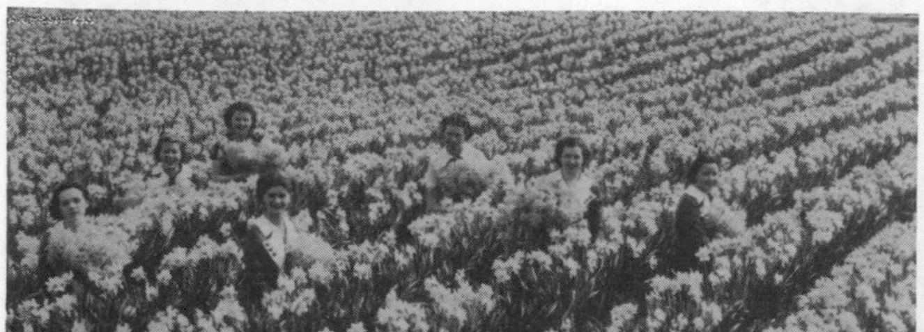

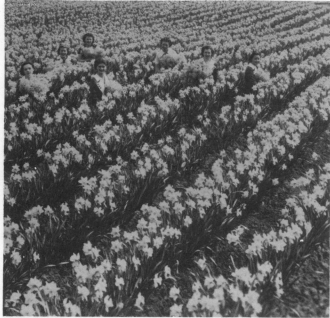

83 COUNTIES

Alcona (F4)....5,856
Alger (C2)....10,007
Allegan (D6)....47,493
Alpena (F4)....22,189
Antrim (D3)....10,721
Arenac (F4)....9,644
Baraga (A2)....8,037
Barry (D6)....26,183
Bay (E5)....88,461
Benzie (C4)....8,306
Berrien (C7)....115,702
Branch (D7)....30,202
Calhoun (D6)....120,813
Cass (C7)....28,185
Charlevoix (D3)....13,475
Cheboygan (E3)....13,731
Chippewa (E2)....29,206
Clare (E5)....10,253
Clinton (E6)....31,195
Crawford (E4)....4,151
Delta (C2)....32,913
Dickinson (B2)....24,844
Eaton (E6)....40,023
Emmet (E3)....16,534
Genesee (F5)....270,963
Gladwin (E4)....9,451
Gogebic (F2)....27,053
Grand Traverse (D4)....28,598
Gratiot (E5)....33,429
Hillsdale (E7)....31,916
Houghton (G1)....39,771
Huron (F5)....33,149
Ingham (E6)....172,941
Ionia (D6)....38,158
Iosco (F4)....10,906
Iron (G2)....17,692
Isabella (E5)....28,964
Jackson (E6)....107,925
Kalamazoo (D6)....126,707
Kalkaska (D4)....4,597
Kent (D5)....288,292
Keweenaw (A1)....2,918
Lake (D5)....5,257
Lapeer (F5)....35,794
Leelanau (D4)....8,647
Lenawee (E7)....64,629
Livingston (F6)....26,725
Luce (D2)....8,147
Mackinac (D2)....9,287
Macomb (G6)....184,961
Manistee (C4)....18,524
Marquette (B2)....47,654
Mason (C4)....20,474
Mecosta (D5)....18,968
Menominee (B3)....25,299
Midland (E5)....35,652
Missaukee (D4)....7,458
Monroe (F7)....75,666
Montcalm (D5)....31,013
Montmorency (E3)....4,125
Muskegon (C5)....121,545
Newaygo (D5)....21,567
Oakland (F6)....396,001
Oceana (C5)....16,105
Ogemaw (E4)....9,345
Ontonagon (F1)....10,282
Osceola (D5)....13,797
Oscoda (E4)....3,134
Otsego (E3)....6,435
Ottawa (C6)....73,751
Presque Isle (F3)....11,996
Roscommon (E4)....5,916
Saginaw (E5)....153,515
Saint Clair (G6)....91,591
St. Joseph (D7)....35,071
Sanilac (G5)....30,837
Schoolcraft (C2)....9,148
Shiawassee (E6)....45,967
Tuscola (F5)....38,258
Van Buren (C6)....39,184
Washtenaw (F6)....134,606
Wayne (F6)....2,435,235
Wexford (D4)....18,628

CITIES and TOWNS

Acme (D4).... 300
Ada (D6)*.... 500
Addison (E7)*.... 488
Adrian (F7)*....18,393
Advance (D3).... 50
Afton (E3)*.... 450
Ahmeek (A1)*.... 360
Akron (F5)*.... 431
Alabaster (F4)*.... 125
Alanson (E3)*.... 319
Alaska (D6).... 335
Alba (E4)*.... 500
Albion (E6)*....10,406
Alden (D4)*.... 350
Alger (E4)*.... 445
Algonac (G6)*....2,639
Allegan (D6)*....4,801
Allen (E7)*.... 340
Allen Park (B7)*....12,329
Allenville (E3)*.... 200
Allouez (A1)*.... 310
Alma (E5)*....8,341
Almont (F6)*....1,035
Alpena (F3)*....13,135
Alpha (A2)*.... 378
Alpine (D5).... 100
Alston (G1)*.... 150
Alto (D6)*.... 400
Altona (D5).... 85
Amasa (G2)*.... 700
Amble (D5)*.... 51
Amelith (F5).... 150
Anchorville (G6)*.... 950
Ann Arbor (F6)*....48,251
Antrim (D4).... 300
Applegate (G5)*.... 244
Arcadia (C4)*.... 450
Argyle (G5)*.... 400
Arlene (D4).... 86
Armada (G6)*.... 961
Arnheim (G1)*.... 50
Arnold (B2)*....
Ashley (E5)*.... 449
Ashton (D5)*.... 178
Assyria (D6).... 200
Athens (D6)*.... 768
Atlanta (E3)*.... 350
Atlantic Mine (G1)*.... 800
Attica (F5)*....
Atwood (D3).... 60
Au Gres (F4)*.... 442
Au Sable (F4).... 300
Au Train (C2)*.... 106
Auburn (F5)*.... 869
Auburn Heights (F6)*....2,500
Augusta (D6)*.... 898
Aura (A2)*.... 295
Averill (E5).... 100
Avoca (G5)*.... 300
Avondale (D4).... 50
Azalia (F6)*.... 110
Bach (F5)*.... 125
Bad Axe (G5)*....2,973
Bagley (B3).... 60
Baie de Wasai (E2).... 100
Bailey (D5)*.... 300
Baldwin (D5)*.... 835
Baltic (G1)*.... 500
Bancroft (E6)*.... 615
Bangor (C6)*....1,694
Bannister (E5)*.... 300
Baraga (G1)*.... 942
Barbeau (E2)*.... 50
Bark River (B3)*.... 500
Baroda (C7)*.... 344
Barryton (D5)*.... 445
Barton City (F4)*.... 100
Batavia (D7)*.... 124
Bates (D4).... 75
Bath (E6)*.... 600
Battle Creek (D6)*....48,666
Bay City (F5)*....52,523
Bay Port (F5)*.... 557
Bay View (E3)*.... 25
Bayshore (D3)*.... 200
Beacon (B2)*.... 300
Beal City (D5).... 338
Bear Lake (C4)*.... 364
Beaverton (E5)*.... 794
Bedford (D6)*....
Belding (D5)*....4,436
Bellaire (D4)*.... 693
Belleville (F6)*....1,722
Bellevue (E6)*....1,168
Belmont (D5)*.... 200
Bendon (D4)*.... 79
Benson (D4).... 22
Bentley (E5)*.... 150
Benton Harbor (C6)*....18,769
Benton Heights (C6)....6,160
Benzonia (D4)*.... 407
Bergland (F1)*.... 800
Berkley (B6)*....17,931
Berrien Springs (C7)*....1,761
Bessemer (F2)*....3,509
Beulah (C4)*.... 458
Big Bay (B2)*.... 670
Big Rapids (D5)*....6,736
Birch (B2).... 8
Birch Run (F5)*.... 800
Birmingham (B6)*....15,467
Bishop (D5).... 100
Bitely (D5)*.... 200
Blackriver (F4)*.... 259
Blaine (G5)*.... 108
Blanchard (D5)*.... 300
Blaney Park (D2)*.... 30
Bliss (E3).... 75
Blissfield (F7)*....2,365
Bloomfield Hills (B6)*.1,468
Bloomingdale (C6)*.... 465
Bolton (F3)*.... 25
Boon (D4)*.... 260
Boyne City (E3)*....3,028
Boyne Falls (E3)*.... 236
Brampton (B3)*.... 300
Branch (D5)*.... 150
Brant (E5)*.... 95
Brassar (E2).... 75
Breckenridge (E5)*.... 985
Breedsville (C6)*.... 239
Brethren (D4)*.... 500
Brevort (E2)*.... 80
Bridgeport (F5)*....1,200
Bridgeton (D5).... 100
Bridgman (C7)*.... 977
Brighton (F6)*....1,861
Brimley (E2)*.... 500
Bristol (D4).... 40
Britton (F6)*.... 517
Brohman (D5)*.... 150
Bronson (D7)*....2,106
Brooklyn (E6)*.... 862
Brown City (G5)*.... 878
Bruce Crossing (G2)*.... 200
Brutus (E3)*.... 200
Buchanan (C7)*....5,224
Buckley (D4)*.... 194
Burlington (D6)*.... 329
Burnips (D6)*.... 170
Burr Oak (D7)*.... 814
Burt (F5)*.... 200
Burt Lake (E3)*.... 60
Butternut (E5)*.... 128
Byron (E6)*.... 439
Byron Center (D6)*.... 650
Cadillac (D4)*....10,425
Caledonia (D6)*.... 619
Calumet (A1)*....1,256
Cambria (E7).... 210
Camden (E7)*.... 380
Capac (G5)*....1,104
Carleton (F6)*....1,039
Carlshend (B2)*.... 100
Carney (B3)*.... 325
Caro (F5)*....3,464
Carp Lake (E3)*.... 200
Carrollton (E5)*....2,000
Carson City (E5)*....1,168
Carsonville (G5)*.... 487
Caseville (F5)*.... 482
Casnovia (D5)*.... 312
Caspian (G2)*....1,608
Cass City (F5)*....1,762
Cassopolis (C7)*....1,527
Castle Park (C6)*.... 9
Cathro (F3)*.... 100
Cedar (D4)*.... 249
Cedar River (B3)*.... 75
Cedar Springs (D5)*....1,378
Cedarville (E2)*.... 250
Cement City (E6)*.... 500
Center Line (B6)*....7,659
Central Lake (D3)*.... 692
Centreville (D7)*.... 879
Ceresco (D6)*....
Champion (B2)*.... 567
Channing (B2)*.... 497
Charleston (G5).... 85
Charlevoix (D3)*....2,695
Charlotte (E6)*....6,606
Chase (D5)*.... 300
Chatham (B2)*.... 650
Cheboygan (E3)*....5,687
Chelsea (E6)*....2,580
Chesaning (E5)*....2,264
Chester (D6).... 50
Chippewa Lake (D5)*.... 125
Clare (E5)*....2,440
Clarion (E3).... 84
Clarklake (E6)*.... 500
Clarkston (F6)*.... 722
Clarksville (D6)*.... 339
Clawson (B6)*....5,196
Clayton (E7)*.... 467
Clifford (F5)*.... 330
Climax (D6)*.... 524
Clinton (F6)*....1,344
Clio (F5)*....1,963
Cohoctah (F6)*.... 150
Coldwater (D7)*....8,594
Coleman (E5)*....1,024
Coloma (C6)*....1,041
Colon (D7)*....1,000
Columbiaville (F5)*.... 789
Comins (E4)*.... 87
Comstock (D6)*....8,314
Concord (E6)*.... 730
Conklin (D5)*.... 350
Connorville (F1).... 50
Constantine (D7)*....1,514
Conway (E3)*.... 100
Cooks (C3)*.... 300
Coopersville (C5)*....1,371
Copemish (D4)*.... 255
Copper City (A1)*.... 336
Copper Harbor (B1)*.... 30
Coral (D5)*.... 300
Cornell (B3)*.... 20
Corunna (E6)*....2,358
Covert (C6)*.... 450
Covington (G2)*.... 260
Cross Village (D3)*.... 200
Croswell (G5)*....1,775
Crump (E5)*.... 75
Crystal (E5)*.... 450
Crystal Falls (A2)*....2,316
Crystal Valley (C5)*.... 250
Curran (F4)*.... 50
Curtis (D2)*.... 300
Curtisville (F4)*.... 25
Cusino (C2).... 50
Custer (C5)*.... 260
Dafter (E2)*.... 125
Daggett (B3)*.... 341
Dalton (C5).... 500
Dansville (E6)*.... 433
Darragh (E4).... 20
Davison (F5)*....1,745
Dayton (C7)*.... 125
De Witt (E6)*.... 824
Dearborn (B7)*....94,994
Decatur (C6)*....1,664
Decker (F5)*.... 100
Deckerville (G5)*.... 719
Deerfield (F7)*.... 725
Deerton (B2)*.... 225
Deford (F5)*.... 200
Delton (D6)*.... 700
Delwin (E5).... 100
Detour (F3)*.... 611
Detroit (B7)*....1,849,568
Detroit(urban area)2,644,476
Dewings (D4).... 6
Dexter (F6)*....1,307
Dighton (D4)*.... 100
Dimondale (E6)*.... 774
Dollar Bay (G1)*.... 600
Dollarville (D2).... 100
Dorr (D6)*.... 428
Douglas (C6)*.... 447
Dover (E5).... 20
Dowagiac (D6)*....6,542
Dowling (D6)*.... 126
Drayton Plains (F6)*....3,500
Drummond (F3)*.... 443
Dryden (F6)*.... 476
Dublin (D4).... 25
Dukes (B2)*.... 150
Dundee (F7)*....1,975
Durand (E6)*....3,194
Dutton (D6)*.... 150
Eagle (E6)*.... 145
Eagle Harbor (A1)*.... 75
Eagle River (A1)*.... 65
East Ann Arbor (F6)....1,826
E. Detroit (B6)*....21,461
E. Grand Rapids (D6)....6,403
E. Jordan (D3)*....1,779
E. Lansing (E6)*....20,325
E. Tawas (F4)*....2,040
Eastlake (C4)*.... 376
Eastport (D3)*.... 125
Eaton Rapids (E6)*....3,509
Eau Claire (C6)*.... 480
Eben Junction (B2)*.... 400
Eckerman (E2)*.... 300
Ecorse (B7)*....17,948
Edenville (E5)*.... 140
Edgerton (D5).... 200
Edgewood (E5).... 50
Edmore (E5)*.... 971
Edwardsburg (C7).... 616
Elba (F5)....
Elberta (C4)*.... 597
Eldorado (E4)*.... 31
Elk Rapids (D4)*.... 889
Elkton (F5)*.... 854
Ellsworth (D3)*.... 369
Elmira (E3)*.... 230
Elmwood (F5).... 100
Elo (G1)*.... 35
Eloise (F6)*....5,000
Elsie (E5)*.... 911
Elwell (E5)*.... 150
Emerson (F3)....
Emmett (G6)*.... 230
Empire (C4)*.... 251
Engadine (D2)*.... 500
Ensign (C3)*.... 446
Epoufette (D2)*.... 50
Erie (F7)*.... 800
Escanaba (C3)*....15,170
Essexville (F5)*....3,167
Estey (E5).... 50
Estral Beach (F7).... 188
Eureka (E5)*....
Evart (D5)*....1,578
Ewen (F2)*.... 817
Fair Haven (G6)*....1,200
Fairgrove (F5)*.... 570
Fairview (F4)*.... 300
Faithorn (B3)*.... 233
Falmouth (E4)*.... 300
Fargo (G5)*.... 110
Farmington (F6)*....2,325
Farwell (E5)*.... 694
Felch (B3)*.... 200
Fennville (C6)*.... 639
Fenton (F6)*....4,226
Fenwick (D5)*.... 150
Ferndale (B6)*....29,675
Ferry (C5)*.... 200
Ferrysburg (C5)*....1,454
Fife Lake (D4)*.... 347
Filer City (C4)*.... 340
Filion (G5)*.... 200
Flat Rock (F6)*....1,931
Flint (F6)*....163,143
Flint (urban area)....197,151
Flushing (F5)*....2,226
Forest Lake (C2)*.... 110
Forester (G5).... 100
Forestville (G5)*.... 124
Forsyth (B2)*.... 400
Foster City (B3)*.... 300
Fosters (F5)*.... 130
Fostoria (F5)*.... 275
Fountain (C4)*.... 247
Fowler (E5)*.... 675
Fowlerville (F6)*....1,466
Fox (B3)*.... 20
Frankenmuth (F5)*....1,208
Frankfort (C4)*....1,858
Franklin Mine (G1)*.... 90
Fraser (B6)*....1,379
Frederic (E4)*.... 250
Free Soil (C4)*.... 208
Freeland (E5)*....1,000
Freeport (D6)*.... 452
Fremont (D5)*....3,056
Frontier (E7)*.... 265
Fruitport (C5)*.... 638
Fulton (D6)*.... 200
Gaastra (G2)*.... 575
Gagetown (F5)*.... 401
Gaines (F6)*.... 352
Galesburg (D6)*....1,200
Galien (C7)*.... 610
Ganges (C6)*.... 150
Garden (C3)*.... 399
Garden City (B7)*....9,012
Garnet (D2)*.... 75
Gay (A1)*.... 156
Gaylord (E3)*....2,271
Genesee (F5)*.... 600
Germfask (C2)*.... 300
Gibbs City (G2)*.... 200
Gilford (F5)*.... 200
Gilmore (E5)....
Girard (E6).... 275
Gladstone (C3)*....4,831
Gladwin (E5)*....1,878
Glen Arbor (C4)*.... 100
Glen Haven (C4).... 25
Glenn (C6)*.... 180
Glennie (F4)*.... 250
Glenwood (C6)*.... 110
Gobles (D6)*.... 622
Goetzville (E2)*.... 150
Good Hart (D3)*.... 50
Goodells (G5)*.... 600
Goodrich (F6)*.... 525
Gotts (F5).... 50
Gould City (D2)*.... 350
Gowen (D5)*.... 200
Grace (E3).... 50
Grand Beach (C7)*.... 105
Grand Blanc (F6)*.... 998
Grand Haven (C5)*....9,536
Grand Junction (C6)*.... 350
Grand Ledge (E6)*....4,506
Grand Marais (D2)*.... 600
Grand Rapids (D5)*..176,515
Grand Rapids (urban area) 225,427
Grandville (D6)*....2,022
Grant (D5)*.... 646
Grass Lake (E6)*.... 878
Grawn (D4)*.... 175
Grayling (E4)*....2,066
Green (F1)....
Greenbush (F4)*.... 100
Greenland (G1)*.... 600
Greenville (D5)*....6,668
Gregory (E6)*.... 300
Grind Stone City (G4)*.
Grosse Ile (B7)*....2,500
Grosse Pointe (B7)*....6,283
Grosse Pointe Farms (B6) 9,410
Grosse Pointe Park (B7) 13,075
Grosse Pointe Shores (B6) 1,032
Grosse Pointe Woods (B6) 10,381
Gulliver (D2)*.... 300
Gwinn (B2)*.... 900
Hadley (F6)*.... 275
Hagensville (F3).... 100
Hale (F4)*.... 500
Hamburg (F6)*.... 350
Hamilton (C6)*.... 600
Hamtramck (B6)*....43,355
Hancock (G1)*....5,223
Hanover (E6)*.... 377
Harbor Beach (G5)*....2,349
Harbor Springs (D3)*....1,626
Harper Woods (B6)....9,148
Harrietta (D4)*.... 152
Harris (B3)*.... 150
Harrison (E4)*.... 884
Harrisville (F4)*.... 485
Hart (C5)*....2,172
Hartford (C6)*....1,838
Hartland (F6)*....
Haslett (E6)*....1,000
Hastings (D6)*....6,096
Hawkins (D5).... 50
Hawks (F3)*.... 250
Hazel Park (B6)*....17,770
Helena (G5).... 75
Helmer (D2).... 35
Hemlock (E5)*.... 700
Henderson (E5)*.... 200
Herman (A2)*.... 155
Hermansville (B3)*.... 800
Herron (F3)*....
Hersey (D5)*.... 239
Hesperia (D5)*.... 760
Hessel (E2)*.... 200
Hiawatha (C2).... 150
Hickory Corners (D6)*.... 180
Highland Park (B6)*....46,393
Hillman (F3)*.... 442
Hillsdale (E7)*....7,297
Hockaday (E4).... 5
Holland (C6)*....15,858
Holly (F6)*....2,663
Holt (E6)*....6,500
Holton (C5)*.... 350
Home Acres (D6)....20,000
Homer (E6)*....1,301
Honor (D4)*.... 269
Hope (E5)*.... 100
Hopkins (D6)*.... 531
Horton (E6)*.... 350
Horton Bay (D3).... 50
Houghton (G1)*....3,829
Houghton Lake (E4)*..
Houghton Point (E4)*..
Howard City (D5)*.... 791
Howell (E6)*....4,353
Hoxeyville (D4)*.... 128
Hubbard Lake (F4)*.... 150
Hubbardston (E5)*.... 335
Hubbell (A1)*....1,690
Hudson (E7)*....2,773
Hudsonville (D6)*....1,101
Hulbert (D2)*.... 400
Huntington Woods (F6)*....4,949
Huron City (G4).... 55
Huron Mountain (B2)*.. 20
Ida (F7)*.... 950
Idlewild (D5)*.... 450
Imlay City (F5)*....1,654
Ina (D4).... 30
Indian River (E3)*.... 600
Ingalls (B3)*.... 150
Ingallston (B3)*.... 50
Inkster (B7)*....16,728
Interlochen (D4)*.... 150
Ionia (D6)*....6,412
Iron Mountain (B3)*....9,679
Iron River (G2)*....4,048
Irons (D4)*.... 30
Ironwood (F2)*....11,466
Isabella (C3).... 2
Ishpeming (B2)*....8,962
Ithaca (E5)*....2,377
Ivanhoe (F5)
Jackson (E6)*....51,088
Jacobsville (A1)*.... 145
Jamestown (D6)*.... 300
Jasper (E7)*.... 300
Jeddo (G5)*.... 150
Jenison (D6)*.... 300
Jennings (D4)*.... 250
Johannesburg (E4)*.... 250
Jones (D7)*.... 300
Jonesville (E6)*....1,594
Kalamazoo (D6)*....57,704
Kalamazoo (urban area) 82,859
Kalamo (D6).... 135
Kaleva (C4)*.... 346
Kalkaska (D4)*....1,250
Kawkawlin (F5)*.... 500
Keego Harbor (F6)*....7,700
Kent City (D5)*.... 506
Kenton (G2)*.... 400
Keweenaw Bay (G1)*.... 300
Kilmanagh (F5).
Kinde (G5)*.... 571
Kingsford (A3)*....5,038
Kingsley (D4)*.... 425
Kingston (F5)*.... 371
Kipling (B3).... 335
Kneeland (E4).... 60
La Salle (F7)*.... 74
Labranche (B3).... 25
Lachine (F3)*.... 90
Laingsburg (E6)*.... 942
Lake (E5)*.... 300
Lake Angelus ‡(F6).. 123
Lake Ann (D4)*.... 99
Lake City (D4)*.... 719
Lake George (E5)*.... 145
Lake Leelanau (D4)*.... 400
Lake Linden (A1)*....1,462
Lake Odessa (D6)*....1,596
Lake Orion (F6)*....2,385
Lakeland (F6)*.... 300
Lakeview (D5)*.... 975
Lamont (D6)*.... 350
L'Anse (G1)*....2,376
LANSING (E6)*....92,129
Lansing (urban area) 133,625
Lapeer (F5)*....6,143
Laporte (E5).... 300
Larkin (E5).... 50
Lathrop (B2).... 46
Laurium (A1)*....3,211
Lawrence (C6)*.... 679
Lawton (D6)*....1,206
Le Roy (D4)*.... 243
Leer (F3).... 20
Leetsville (D4)*.... 35
Leland (D3)*.... 536
Lenox (G6)*.... 975
Leonard (F6)*.... 391
Leonidas (D6)*.... 225
Leslie (E6)*....1,543
Levering (E3)*.... 387
Lewiston (E4)*.... 700
Lexington (G5)*.... 594
Lincoln (F4)*.... 409
Lincoln Park (B7)*....29,310
Linden (F6)*.... 933
Linkville (F5)....
Livonia (F6)....17,534
Linwood (F5)*.... 425
Lisbon ‡(D5)....
Liske (F3).... 6
Litchfield (E6)*.... 882
Long Lake (F4)*.... 100
Long Rapids (F3).... 50
Loretto (B3)*.... 350
Lovells (E4).... 100
Lowell (D6)*....2,191
Lucas (D4)*.... 120
Ludington (C5)*....9,506
Lum (F5)*.... 300
Lupton (E4)*.... 200
Luther (D4)*.... 314
Luzerne (E4)*.... 150
Lyon Manor (E4)*.... 87
Lyons (E6)*.... 683
Mackinac Island (E3)*.. 572
Mackinaw City (E3)*.... 970
Mancelona (E4)*....1,000
Manchester (E6)*....1,388
Manistee (C4)*....8,642
Manistique (C3)*....5,086
Manton (D4)*....1,085
Maple City (D4)*.... 190
Maple Rapids (E5)*.... 645
Maple Ridge (F4).... 75
Mapleton (D4).... 60
Marcellus (D6)*....1,014
Marenisco (F2)*....1,300
Marilla (D4).... 80
Marine City (G6)*....4,270
Marion (D4)*.... 879
Marlette (G5)*....1,489
Marne (D5)*.... 600

Marquette (B2)* 17,202
Marshall (E6)* 5,777
Martin (D6)* 407
Marysville (G6)* 2,534
Mason (E6)* 3,514
Mass (G1)*
Matchwood (F1)* 100
Maybee (F6)* 428
Mayville (F5)* 888
Mc Bain (D4)* 506
Mc Brides (D5)* 223
Mc Ivor (F4)* 50
Mc Millan (D2)* 336
Mears (C5)* 262
Mecosta (D5)* 305
Melvin (G5)* 204
Melvindale (B7)* 9,483
Memphis (G6)* 800
Mendon (D7)* 844
Menominee (B3)* 11,151
Merrill (E5)* 809
Merritt (D4)* 61
Merriweather (F1)* 100
Mesick (D4)* 359
Metamora (F6)* 390
Metropolitan (A3)* 250
Metz (F3)* 35
Michiana (C7) 102
Michigamme (A2)* 600
Michigan Center (E6)* 3,012
Michillinda (C5)* 50
Middleton (E5) 450
Middleville (D6)* 1,047
Midland (E5)* 14,285
Mikado (F4)* 204
Milan (F6)* 2,768
Milford (F6)* 1,924
Millbrook (D5)* 200
Millersburg (F3)* 281
Millington (F5)* 1,043
Minden City (G5)* 359
Mineral Hills (G2) 333
Mio (E4)* 975
Missaukee Park (D4) 30
Mohawk (A1)* 900
Moline (D6)* 300
Monroe (F7)* 21,467
Montague (C5)* 1,530
Montgomery (E7)* 397
Montrose (F5)* 937
Moorestown (D4)* 53
Moran (E2)* 310
Morenci (E7)* 1,983
Morley (D5)* 413
Morrice (E6)* 401
Mount Clemens (G6)* 17,027
Mt. Morris (F5)* 2,890
Mt. Pleasant (E5)* 11,393
Mountforest (F5)* 50
Muir (D5)* 466
Mullett Lake (E3)* 75
Mulliken (E6)* 411
Munger (F5)* 250
Munising (C2)* 4,339
Munith (E6)* 500
Muskegon (C5)* 48,429
Muskegon (urban area) 84,775
Muskegon Heights (C5)* 18,828
Nadeau (B3)* 400
Nahma (C3)* 750
Napoleon (E6)* 530
Nashville (D6)* 1,374
Nathan (B3) 76
National City (F4)* 100
National Mine (B2)* 250
Naubinway (D2)* 200
Nazareth (D6)* 500
Negaunee (B2)* 6,472
Nestoria (A2)* 32
New Baltimore (G6)* 2,043
New Boston (F6)* 800
New Buffalo (C7)* 1,565
New Era (C5)* 247
New Haven (G6)* 1,082
New Lothrop (F5)* 459
New Troy (C7)* 300
Newaygo (D5)* 1,385
Newberry (D2)* 2,802
Newland (C4) 100
Niles (C7)* 13,145
Nirvana (D5)* 40
North Adams (E7)* 499
N. Bradley (E5)* 300
N. Branch (F5)* 832
N. Lake (D2) 200
N. Manitou Island (C3) 15
N. Muskegon (C5)* 2,424
Northland (B2)* 100
Northport (D3)* 582
Northstar (E5)* 285
Northville (F6)* 3,240
Norwalk (C4)* 25
Norway (B3)* 3,258
Novi (F6)* 1,000
Oak Grove (F6)* 125
Oak Park (B6) 5,267
Oakley (E5)* 333
Oberlin (E4) 5
Ocqueoc (F3)* 90
Okemos (E6)* 950
Old Mission (D4)
Olivet (E6)* 887
Omena (D3)* 80
Omer (F4)* 321
Onaway (E3)* 1,421
Onekama (C4)* 435
Onondaga (E6)* 423
Onsted (E6)* 486
Ontonagon (F1)* 2,307
Orangeville (D6) 900
Orchard Lake (F6)* 696
Ortonville (F6)* 702
Oscoda (F4)* 1,800
Oshtemo (D6)* 300
Osseo (E7)* 300
Ossineke (F4)* 150
Otisville (F5)* 592
Otsego (D6)* 3,990
Otsego Lake (E4)*
Ottawa Beach (C6) 40
Ottawa Lake (F7)* 200
Otter Lake (F5)* 523
Overisel (C6) 350
Ovid (E5)* 1,410
Owendale (F5)* 307
Owosso (E5)* 15,948
Oxford (F6)* 2,305
Ozark (E2)* 70
Painesdale (G1)* 1,100
Palmer (B2)* 825
Palms (G5)* 100
Palmyra (E7)* 250
Palo (E5)* 300
Parchment (D6)* 1,179
Paris (D5)* 225
Parisville (G5) 150
Parma (E6)* 680
Paw Paw (D6)* 2,382
Payment (E2) 100
Paynesville (G2)* 250
Peacock (D4) 25
Pearl Beach (G6)*
Peck (G5)* 471
Pelkie (G1)* 25
Pellston (E3)* 442
Pentoga (G2) 30
Pentwater (C5)* 1,097
Pequaming (A2) 21
Perkins (B3)* 500
Perrinton (E5)* 383
Perronville (B3)* 100
Perry (E6)* 1,203
Petersburg (F7)* 1,001
Petoskey (E3)* 6,468
Pewamo (E5)* 432
Pickford (E2)* 600
Pierson (D5)* 169
Pigeon (F5)* 1,015
Pinckney (F6)* 695
Pinconning (F5)* 1,223
Pine River (F5) 24
Pinnebog (F5) 100
Pioneer (D4) 10
Pittsford (E7)* 600
Plainwell (D6)* 2,767
Pleasant Ridge (B6)* 3,594
Plymouth (F6)* 6,637
Pointe Aux Barques (G4)* 9
Pointe Aux Pins (E3)* 42
Pompeii (E5)* 171
Pontiac (F6)* 73,681
Pontiac (urban area) 91,799
Port Austin (F4)* 724
Port Hope (G5)* 353
Port Huron (G6)* 35,725
Port Sanilac (G5)* 247
Portage (D6)* 1,677
Portland (E6)* 2,807
Posen (F3)* 274
Potterville (E6)* 624
Powers (B3)* 510
Prescott (F4)* 281
Presque Isle (F3)* 75
Princeton (B2)* 330
Prosper (E4) 150
Prudenville (E4)* 800
Pullman (C6)* 300
Puritan (F2)* 150
Quincy (E7)* 1,527
Quinnesec (A3)* 600
Raco (E2)* 100
Ralph (B2)* 55
Ramsay (F2)* 1,200
Rapid City (D4)* 250
Rapid River (C3)* 700
Rapson (G5)
Rasmus (E4) 40
Ravenna (D5)* 551
Reading (E7)* 1,125
Red Oak (E4) 51
Redman (G5) 40
Redridge (G1)* 94
Reed City (D5)* 2,241
Reeman (D5)* 150
Reese (F5)* 632
Remus (D5)* 600
Republic (B2)* 1,092
Rexton (D2)* 200
Rhodes (E5)* 107
Richland (D6)* 389
Richmond (G6)* 2,025
Richville (F5)* 400
River Rouge (B7)* 20,549
Riverdale (E5)* 304
Riverside (C6)* 500
Riverview (B7)* 1,432
Rives Junction (E6)* 350
Rochester (F6)* 4,279
Rock (B2)* 550
Rock Harbor (E1)* 50
Rockford (D5)* 1,937
Rockland (G1)* 500
Rockwood (F6)* 1,044
Rodney (D5)* 75
Rogers City (F3)* 3,873
Romeo (F6)* 2,985
Romulus (F6)* 1,300
Roosevelt Park (C5) 1,254
Roscommon (E4)* 877
Rose City (E4)* 446
Rosebush (E5)* 507
Roseville (G6)* 15,816
Rothbury (C5)* 350
Rousseau (G1)
Royal Oak (B6)* 46,898
Rudyard (E2)* 800
Ruth (G5)* 222
Saganing (F5) 40
Saginaw (F5)* 92,918
Saginaw (urban area) 105,358
Sagola (B2)* 300
Saint Charles (E5)* 1,469
St. Clair (G6)* 4,098
St. Clair Shores (G6)* 19,823
St. Helen (E4)*
St. Ignace (E3)* 2,946
St. Jacques (C3)*
St. James (D3)* 400
St. Johns (E6)* 4,954
St. Joseph (C6)* 10,223
St. Louis (E5)* 3,347
Salem (F6)* 350
Saline (F6)* 1,533
Samaria (F7)* 315
Sand Lake (D5)* 394
Sands (B2)* 125
Sandusky (G5)* 1,819
Sanford (E5)* 550
Sans Souci (G6)* 100
Saranac (D6)* 885
Saugatuck (C6)* 770
Sault Sainte Marie (E2)* 17,912
Sawyer (C7)* 800
Schaffer (B3)* 200
Schoolcraft (D6)* 1,078
Scotts (D6)* 375
Scottville (C5)* 1,142
Sears (D5)* 76
Sebewaing (F5)* 1,911
Selkirk (F4)* 50
Seney (C2)* 300
Shabbona (G5) 100
Shelby (C5)* 1,500
Shepherd (E5)* 899
Sheridan (D5)* 535
Sherman (D4) 100
Sherman City (D5) 25
Sherwood (D6)* 362
Shingleton (C2)* 400
Shoreham (C6) 391
Sidnaw (G2)* 400
Sidney (D5)* 100
Silverwood (F5)* 75
Sister Lakes (C6)* 175
Sixlakes (D5)* 221
Skanee (A2)* 190
Skeels (E4) 7
Smiths Creek (G6)* 400
Smyrna (D5)* 350
Snover (G5)* 350
Sodus (C6)* 300
South Boardman (D4)* 125
S. Haven (C6)* 5,629
S. Lyon (F6)* 1,312
S. Manitou Island (C3) 24
S. Range (G1)* 712
S. Rockwood (F7)* 1,100
Southbranch (E4) 70
Spalding (B3)* 600
Sparr (E3) 85
Sparta (D5)* 2,327
Spencer (D4)* 49
Spratt (F3) 52
Spring Arbor (E6)* 650
Spring Lake (C5)* 1,824
Springport (E6)* 598
Spruce (F4)* 50
Stalwart (E2)*
Stambaugh (G2)* 1,969
Standish (F5)* 1,186
Stanton (D5)* 1,123
Stanwood (D5)* 189
Stephenson (B3)* 791
Sterling (E4)* 444
Steuben (C2)* 39
Stevensville (C6)* 480
Stirlingville (E2) 100
Stittsville (D4) 10
Stockbridge (E6)* 1,098
Stonington (C3)* 408
Stony Lake (C5)* 38
Stronach (C4)* 350
Strongs (E2)* 250
Sturgis (D7)* 7,786
Sullivan (C5) 250
Summit City (D4)* 75
Sumner (E5)* 150
Sunfield (D6)* 400
Suttons Bay (D3)* 485
Swartz Creek (F6)* 1,000
Sylvan Lake (F6) 1,165
Tawas City (F4)* 1,441
Taylor Center (B7)* 20,000
Tecumseh (E7)* 4,020
Tekonsha (E6)* 647
Temperance (F7)* 1,062
Temple (E4)* 150
The Heights (E4)* 100
Thompson (C3)* 250
Thompsonville (C4)* 313
Three Oaks (C7)* 1,572
Three Rivers (D7)* 6,785
Topinabee (E3)* 390
Tower (E3)* 400
Traverse City (D4)* 16,974
Trenary (C2)* 150
Trenton (B7)* 6,222
Trout Creek (G2)*
Trout Lake (E2)* 350
Trufant (D5)* 215
Turin (B2)* 236
Turner (F4)* 193
Tuscola (F5)* 150
Tustin (D4)* 229
Twin Lake (C5)* 550
Twining (F4)* 196
Ubly (G5)* 743
Union City (D6)* 1,564
Union Pier (C7)* 700
Unionville (F5)* 531
Utica (F6)* 1,196
Van Dyke (B6)* 21,000
Vandalia (D7)* 360
Vanderbilt (E3)* 410
Vassar (F5)* 2,530
Vermontville (E6)* 707
Vernon (F6)* 678
Vestaburg (E5)* 450
Vicksburg (D6)* 2,171
Vogel Center (E4) 70
Volney (D5) 50
Vulcan (B3)* 650
Wabaningo (C5)* 12
Wahjamega (F5) 1,613
Wakefield (F2)* 3,344
Waldenburg (G6) 350
Waldron (E7)* 427
Walhalla (C5)* 210
Walkerville (C5)* 233
Wallace (B3)* 200
Walled Lake (F6)* 2,788
Walloon Lake (E3)* 214
Waltz (F6)* 350
Warren (B6)* 727
Waters (E4)* 40
Watersmeet (F2)* 600
Watervliet (C6)* 1,327
Watton (G2)* 400
Waucedah (B3) 260
Wayland (D6)* 1,591
Wayne (F6)* 9,409
Webberville (E6)* 600
Weidman (D5)* 410
Wells (B3)* 600
Wellston (D4)* 150
West Branch (E4)* 2,098
W. Olive (C6)* 81
Weston (E7)* 270
Westphalia (E6)* 459
Wetmore (C2)* 150
Wexford (D4) 50
Wheeler (E5)* 300
White Cloud (D5)* 977
White Pigeon (D7)* 1,113
Whitefish Point (E2)* 75
Whitehall (C5)* 1,819
Whitmore Lake (F6)* 1,500
Whittaker (F6)* 300
Whittemore (F4)* 452
Willard (E5) 100
Williamsburg (D4)* 200
Williamston (E6)* 2,051
Willis (F6)* 200
Willow Run (F6) 11,365
Wilson (B3)* 450
Winegars (E5)* 125
Winn (E5)* 350
Winona (G1)* 125
Wisner (F5) 98
Wolverine (E3)* 318
Woodland (D6)* 410
Wyandotte (B7)* 36,846
Yale (G5)* 1,641
Yalmer (B2) 200
Ypsilanti (F6)* 18,302
Yuma (D4)* 93
Zeeland (D6)* 3,075
Zilwaukee (F5) 1,219

Map on Page 70

MINNESOTA

Total Population 2,982,483

87 COUNTIES

Aitkin (E4) 14,327
Anoka (E5) 35,579
Becker (C4) 24,836
Beltrami (C2) 24,962
Benton (D5) 15,911
Big Stone (B5) 9,607
Blue Earth (D6) 38,327
Brown (D6) 25,895
Carlton (F4) 24,584
Carver (E6) 18,155
Cass (D4) 19,468
Chippewa (C5) 16,739
Chisago (F5) 12,669
Clay (B4) 30,363
Clearwater (C3) 10,204
Cook (H3) 2,900
Cottonwood (C6) 15,763
Crow Wing (D4) 30,875
Dakota (E6) 49,019
Dodge (F7) 12,624
Douglas (C5) 21,304
Faribault (D7) 23,879
Fillmore (F7) 24,465
Freeborn (E7) 34,517
Goodhue (F6) 32,118
Grant (B5) 9,542
Hennepin (E5) 676,579
Houston (G7) 14,435
Hubbard (D3) 11,085
Isanti (E5) 12,123
Itasca (E3) 38,321
Jackson (C7) 16,306
Kanabec (E5) 9,192
Kandiyohi (C5) 28,644
Kittson (B2) 9,649
Koochiching (E2) 16,910
Lac qui Parle (B6) 14,545
Lake (G3) 7,781
Lake of the Woods (D2) 4,955
Le Sueur (E6) 19,088
Lincoln (B6) 10,150
Lyon (C6) 22,253
Mahnomen (C3) 7,059
Marshall (B2) 16,125
Martin (D7) 25,655
McLeod (D6) 22,198
Meeker (D5) 18,966
Mille Lacs (E5) 15,165
Morrison (D4) 25,832
Mower (F7) 42,277
Murray (C6) 14,801
Nicollet (D6) 20,929
Nobles (C7) 22,435
Norman (B3) 12,909
Olmsted (F7) 48,228
Otter Tail (C4) 51,320
Pennington (B2) 12,965
Pine (F4) 18,223
Pipestone (B6) 14,003
Polk (B3) 35,900
Pope (C5) 12,862
Ramsey (E5) 355,332
Red Lake (B3) 6,806
Redwood (C6) 22,127
Renville (C6) 23,954
Rice (E6) 36,235
Rock (B7) 11,278
Roseau (C2) 14,505
Saint Louis (F3) 206,062
Scott (E6) 16,486
Sherburne (E5) 10,661
Sibley (D6) 15,816
Stearns (D5) 70,681
Steele (E7) 21,155
Stevens (B5) 11,106
Swift (C5) 15,837
Todd (D4) 25,420
Traverse (B5) 8,053
Wabasha (F6) 16,878
Wadena (D4) 12,806
Waseca (E6) 14,957
Washington (F5) 34,544
Watonwan (D7) 13,881
Wilkin (B4) 10,567
Winona (G6) 39,841
Wright (D5) 27,716
Yellow Medicine (B6) 16,279

CITIES and TOWNS

Acton (D5) 2
Ada (B3* 2,121
Adams (F7)* 663
Adolph (F4)* 53
Adrian (C7)* 1,115
Afton (F6)* 142
Ah-gwah-ching (D3)* 360
Aitkin (E4)* 2,079
Akeley (D3)* 525
Albany (D5)* 1,196
Albert Lea (E7)* 13,545
Alberta (B5)* 139
Albertville (E5)* 238
Alborn (F4)* 30
Alden (E7)* 668
Aldrich (C4)* 131
Alexandria (C5)* 6,319
Alida (C3) 6
Allen (F3) 21
Alma City (E6)* 150
Almelund (F5)* 175
Almora (C4)* 82
Alpha (D7)* 230
Altura (G6)* 269
Alvarado (B2)* 317
Alvwood (D3)* 25
Amboy (D7)* 585
Amiret (C6)* 90
Amor (C4) 20
Angle Inlet (C1)* 50
Angora (F3)* 65
Angus (B2)* 100
Annandale (D5)* 899
Anoka (E5)* 7,396
Anthony (B3) 2
Appleton (C5)* 2,256
Arago (C3)* 11
Arco (B6)* 178
Argyle (B2)* 846
Arlington (D6)* 1,313
Armstrong (E7)* 25
Arnold (F4)
Arthyde (E4)* 10
Asbury (C6) 2
Ash Creek (B7) 70
Ash Lake (F2) 15
Ashby (C4)* 443
Askov (F4)* 387
Aspelund (F6) 20
Atkinson (F4)* 20
Atwater (D5)* 880
Audubon (C4)* 275
Augusta (F6) 20
Aurora (F3)* 1,371
Austin (F7)* 23,100
Automba (F4)* 25
Averill (B4)* 46
Avoca (C7)* 281
Avon (D5)* 386
Axel (C4) 2
Babbitt (G3)* 35
Backus (D4)* 367
Badger (B2)* 448
Badoura (D4) 250
Bagley (C3)* 1,554
Bain (E4) 20
Baker (B4)* 70
Balaton (C6)* 723
Bald Eagle (E5) 1,650
Ball Club (E3)* 100
Balmoral (C4) 10
Barnesville (B4)* 1,593
Barnum (F4)* 344
Barrett (B5)* 402
Barry (B5)* 74
Basswood (C4) 22
Battle Lake (C4)* 714
Baudette (D2)* 929
Baxter (D4) 507
Bay Lake (E4) 50
Bayport (F5)* 2,502
Bear River (E3)* 75
Beardsley (B5)* 435
Beauford (D7) 250
Beaulieu (C3)* 100
Beaver (F6) 13
Beaver Bay (G3)* 100
Beaver Creek (B7)* 245
Bechyn (C6) 32
Becida (C3)* 8
Becker (E5)* 264
Bee (G7) 11
Bejou (B3)* 173
Belgrade (C5)* 659
Belle Plaine (E6)* 1,708
Belle River (C5)
Bellechester (F6)* 225
Bellingham (B5)* 388
Beltrami (B3)* 199
Belvidere Mills (F6) 10
Belview (C6)* 381
Bemidji (D3)* 10,001
Bena (D3)* 331
Benedict (D3)* 10
Bennettville (E4)
Benson (C5)* 3,398
Bergen (D7) 40
Bernadotte (D6) 19
Berner (C3) 20
Beroun (F5)* 120
Bertha (C4)* 577
Bethany (F6) 35
Bethel (E5)* 250
Big Bend City (C5) 650
Big Falls (E2)* 441
Big Lake (E5)* 480
Bigelow (C7)* 238
Bigfork (E3)* 463
Bingham Lake (C7)* 229
Birchdale (D2)* 20
Birchwood ‡(F5) 312
Bird Island (D6)* 1,333
Biscay (D6)* 90
Biwabik (F3)* 1,245
Bixby (E7)* 75
Blackberry (E3) 20
Blackduck (D3)* 732
Blakeley (E6)* 98
Blomkest (D6)* 150
Blooming Prairie (E7)* 1,442
Bloomington (G6)* 500
Blue Earth (D7)* 3,843
Blue Grass (C4) 50
Bluffton (C4)* 239
Bock (E5)* 96
Bodum (E5) 4
Bombay (F6) 28
Border (D2)* 5
Borup (B3)* 200
Bovey (E3)* 1,320
Bowlus (D5)* 233
Bowstring (E3)* 300
Boy River (D3)* 60
Boyd (C6)* 496
Bradford (E5)*
Braham (E5)* 697
Brainerd (D4)* 12,637
Brandon (C5)* 319
Breckenridge (B4)* 3,623
Breezy Point (D4)*
Brevik (D3)* 50
Brewster (C7)* 478
Bricelyn (E7)* 639
Brimson (F3)* 40
Britt (F3)* 50
Brook Park (F5)* 148
Brooklyn Center (G5) 4,284
Brooks (B3)* 184
Brookston (F4)* 180
Booten (C5)* 669
Browerville (D4)* 735
Browns Valley (B5)* 1,117
Brownsdale (F7)* 493
Brownsville (G7)* 330
Brownton (D6)* 696
Bruno (F4)* 193
Brunswick (E5) 100
Brush Creek (E7) 18
Brushvale (B4)* 16
Buckman (D5)* 173
Buffalo (E5)* 1,914
Buffalo Lake (D6)* 724
Buhl (F3)* 1,462
Burchard (C6) 25
Burnett (F4)* 68
Burr (B6)* 63
Burschville (E5) 16
Burtrum (D5)* 194
Butler (C4)* 72
Butterfield (D7)* 529
Butternut (D6) 22
Buyck (F2)* 98
Bygland (B3)
Byron (F6)* 385
Cable (D5) 10
Caledonia (G7)* 2,243
Callaway (C3)* 193
Calumet (E3)* 854
Cambria (D6)* 63
Cambridge (E5)* 2,978
Campbell (B4)* 391
Canby (B6)* 2,173
Cannon Falls (F6)* 1,831
Canton (F7)* 459
Canyon (F3)* 115
Carlisle (B4)* 24
Carlos (C5)* 233
Carlton (F4)* 650
Carp (D2) 15
Carson Lake (E3)* 700
Carver (E6)* 548
Cass Lake (D3)* 1,936
Castle Danger (G3) 75
Castle Rock (E6)* 100
Cazenovia (B6) 26
Cedar (E5)* 75
Cedar Lake (E4) 3
Cedar Mills (D6)* 99
Celina (E3)
Center City (F5)* 311
Center Valley (E5)
Centerville (E5) 209
Ceylon (D7)* 618
Champlin (E5)* 828
Chandler (C7)* 331
Chanhassen (F6)* 182
Chaska (E6)* 2,008
Chatfield (F7)* 1,605
Cherry Grove (F7) 100
Chester (F6)* 100
Chisago City (E5)* 703
Chisholm (E3)* 6,861
Chokio (B5)* 381
Clara City (C6)* 1,106
Claremont (F6)* 426
Clarissa (C4)* 650
Clarkfield (C6)* 1,012
Clarks Grove (E7)* 254
Claybank (F6) 6
Clear Lake (E5)* 297
Clearbrook (C3)* 539
Clearwater (D5)* 224
Clements (D6)* 239
Clementson (D2)* 11
Cleveland (E6)* 325
Climax (B3)* 271
Clinton (B5)* 718
Clinton Falls (E6)
Clitherall (C4)* 175
Clontarf (C5)* 206
Cloquet (F4)* 7,685
Clotho (C4) 30
Cloverdale (F4) 25
Cloverton (F4)* 26
Cobden (D6)* 118
Cohasset (E3)* 484
Coin (E5)* 3
Cokato (D5)* 1,403
Cold Spring (D5)* 1,488
Coleraine (E3)* 1,321
Collegeville (D5)* 480
Collis (B5)* 50
Cologne (E6)* 462
Columbia Heights (G5)* 8,175
Comfrey (D6)* 642
Comstock (B4)* 139
Conception (F6) 300
Concord (F6) 85
Conger (E7)* 161
Constance (E5)* 25
Cook (F3)* 482
Cooley (E3)* 113
Coon Creek (G5) 275
Corcoran (E5)* 75
Cormorant (B4) 34
Correll (B5)* 130
Corvuso (D6)* 22
Cosmos (D6)* 382
Cottage Grove (F6)* 143
Cotton (F3)* 20
Cottonwood (C6)* 709
Courtland (D6)* 251
Cove (E4) 35
Craigville (E3)* 50
Crane Lake (F2)* 93
Cromwell (F4)* 197
Crookston (B3)* 7,352
Crosby (D4)* 2,777
Crosslake (E4)* 50
Crow Wing (D4) 18
Crown (E5) 30
Crowriver (D5) 10
Crystal (G5) 5,713
Crystal Bay (E6)* 250
Culver (F4)* 45
Current Lake (C6) 20
Currie (C6)* 551
Cushing (D4)* 71
Cusson (F2) 25
Cuyuna (E4)* 112
Cyrus (C5)* 363
Dakota (G7)* 300
Dalbo (E5)* 58
Dale (B4)* 54
Dalton (C4)* 279
Danube (C6)* 437
Danvers (C5)* 162
Darfur (D6)* 150
Darwin (D5)* 273
Dassel (D5)* 962
Dawson (B6)* 1,834
Day (E5) 45
Dayton (E5)* 363
De Graff (C5)* 270
Debs (C3) 25
Deephaven (F5) 1,823
Deer Creek (C4)* 349
Deer River (E3)* 1,033
Deerwood (E4)* 572
Delano (E5)* 1,386
Delavan (D7)* 302
Delft (C7)* 125
Delhi (C6)* 152
Dell (E7) 15
Dellwood (F5) 245
Denham (F4)* 96
Dennison (E6)* 163
Dent (C4)* 187
Detroit Lakes (C4)* 5,787
Dexter (F7)* 316
Dilworth (B4)* 1,429
Dodge Center (F6)* 1,151
Donaldson (B2)* 128
Donnelly (B5)* 396
Doran (B4)* 126
Dorothy (B3) 46
Dorset (D4)* 55
Douglas (F6)* 102
Douglas Lodge (C3)* 2
Dover (F7)* 263
Dovray (C6)* 127
Downer (B4)* 135
Dresbach (G7)* 200
Duluth (F4)* 104,511
Duluth, Minn.-Superior, Wis. (urban area) 142,344

Dumont (B5)* 223
Dunbar (D3) 76
Dundas (E6)* 469
Dundee (C7)* 179
Dunnell (D7)* 242
Dunvilla (B4) 4
Duquette (F4)* 65
Eagle Bend (C4)* 691
Eagle Lake (E6)* 310
East Chain (D7) 80
East Grand Forks(B3)* 5,049
East Gull Lake (D4) 238
East Lake (E4)* 65
Easton (E7)* 379
Ebro (C3)* 70
Echo (C6)* 490
Eden Prairie (G6) 100
Eden Valley (D5)* 792
Edgerton (B7)* 961
Edina (E6)* 9,744
Effie (E3)* 202
Eitzen (G7)* 151
Elba (F6)* 147
Elbow Lake (B4)* 1,398
Eldred (B3)* 44
Elgin (F6)* 438
Elizabeth (B4)* 168
Elk River (E5)* 1,399
Elko (E6)* 111
Elkton (F7)* 141
Ellendale (E7)* 476
Ellsworth (C7)* 630
Elmdale (D5) 119
Elmer (F3)* 216
Elmore (D7)* 1,074
Elrosa (C5)* 173
Ely (G3)* 5,474
Elysian (E6)* 402
Embarrass (F3)* 450
Emily (E4)* 200
Emmons (E7)* 356
Enfield (E5)* 26
Englund (B2) 6
Erdahl (C5)* 120
Erhard (B4)* 145
Ericsburg (E2)* 210
Erie (C2) 20
Erskine (B3)* 608
Esko (F4)* 300
Essig (D6)* 88
Etter (F6)* 100
Euclid (B3)* 120
Eureka (F5) 50
Evan (D6)* 141
Evansville (C4)* 478
Eveleth (F3)* 5,872
Everdell (B4) 10
Evergreen (C4) 10
Excelsior (E6)* 1,763
Eyota (F7)* 495
Fairbanks (G3)* 12
Fairfax (D6)* 1,143
Fairhaven (D5)* 200
Fairmont (D7)* 8,193
Faith (B3) 29
Falcon Heights (G5) 3,884
Faribault (E6)* 16,028
Farmington (E6)* 1,916
Farwell (C5)* 112
Federal Dam (D3)* 225
Felton (B3)* 258
Fergus Falls (B4)* 12,917
Fernando (D6) 25
Fertile (B3)* 890
Fifty Lakes (D4)*
Fillmore (F7)
Finland (G3)* 175
Finlayson (F4)* 195
Fisher (B3)* 302
Flensburg (D5)* 281
Fletcher (F5) 70
Flom (B3)* 75
Floodwood (E4)* 667
Florence (B6)* 137
Florenton (F3)* 95
Foley (D5)* 1,089
Fond du Lac (F4)* 500
Forada (C5)* 89
Forbes (F3)* 125
Forest Center (G3) 100
Forest City (D5) 50
Forest Lake (F5)* 1,766
Foreston (E5)* 301
Fort Ripley (D4)* 88
Fort Snelling (G5)* 1,096
Fosston (C3)* 1,614
Fountain (F7)* 312
Four Town (C2) 6
Foxhome (B4)* 217
Franklin (D6)* 546
Franklin (F3) 115
Fraser (F3) 134
Frazee (C4)* 1,021
Freeborn (E7)* 300
Freeburg (G7) 58
Freedhem (D4) 30
Freeport (D5)* 558
French River (G4)
Fridley (G5) 3,796
Friesland (F4) 25
Frontenac (F6)* 151
Frost (D7)* 326
Fulda (C7)* 1,149
Funkley (D3)* 28
Garden City (D6)* 273
Garfield (C5)* 244
Garrison (E4)* 150
Garvin (C6)* 264
Gary (B3)* 278
Gatzke (C2)* 36
Gaylord (D6)* 1,229
Gemmell (D3)* 150
Geneva (E7)* 332
Genola (D5)* 79
Gentilly (B3)* 100
Georgetown (B3)* 192
Georgeville (C5)* 50
Gheen (F3)* 67
Ghent (C6)* 336
Gibbon (D6)* 830
Giese (E4)* 50
Gilbert (F3)* 2,247
Gilchrist (C5) 80
Gilman (E5)* 150
Glen (E4)* 30
Glencoe (D6)* 2,801
Glendorado (E5) 11
Glenville (E7)* 672
Glenwood (C5)* 2,666
Glory (E4) 2
Gluek (C6)* 70
Glyndon (B4)* 411
Godahl (D6) 40
Golden Valley (G5) 5,551
Gonvick (C3)* 375
Good Thunder (D6)* 476
Goodhue (F6)* 489
Goodland (E3)* 450
Goodridge (C2)* 144
Goodview (G6) 777
Gordonsville (E7)* 100
Gowan (F4)*
Graceton (D2)* 38
Graceville (B5)* 962
Graff (D4) 125
Granada (D7)* 403
Grand Marais (G2)* 1,078
Grand Meadow (F7)* 766
Grand Portage (G2)* 150
Grand Rapids (E3)* 6,019
Grandy (E5)* 175
Granger (F7)* 158
Granite Falls (C6)* 2,511
Grasston (E5)* 154
Grattan (D3) 100
Greaney (F3)* 100
Greeley (E5) 12
Green Isle (E6)* 332
Green Valley (C6)* 121
Greenbush (B2)* 713
Greenleaf (D6) 28
Greenleafton (F7) 54
Greenwald (D5)* 207
Grey Eagle (D5)* 400
Groningen (F4)* 27
Grove City (D5)* 481
Grovelake (C5) 60
Grygla (C2)* 216
Guckeen (D7)* 116
Gully (C3)* 183
Gunflint Trail (H2)
Guthrie (D3)* 60
Hackensack (D4)* 272
Hader (F6) 30
Hadler (B3) 10
Hadley (C7)* 139
Hallock (A2)* 1,552
Halma (B2)* 177
Halstad (B3)* 635
Hamburg (D6)* 184
Hamel (F5)* 200
Hammond (F6)* 192
Hampton (E6)* 275
Hancock (C5)* 852
Hanley Falls (C6)* 320
Hanover (E5)* 228
Hanska (D6)* 473
Harding (E4)* 124
Hardwick (B7)* 297
Harmony (F7)* 1,022
Harney (F4)* 75
Harris (F5)* 569
Hart (G7) 18
Hartland (E7)* 300
Hassan (E5) 50
Hastings (F6)* 6,560
Hatfield (B7)* 110
Haug (B2) 14
Havana (E6) 18
Hawick (D5)* 63
Hawley (B4)* 1,196
Haydenville (B5) 10
Hayfield (F7)* 805
Hayward (E7)* 241
Hazel (B2)* 20
Hazel Run (C6)* 129
Hector (D6)* 1,196
Heidelberg (E6) 61
Heinola (C4) 9
Henderson (E6)* 762
Hendricks (B6)* 781
Hendrum (B3)* 352
Henning (C4)* 1,004
Henriette (E5)* 57
Herman (B5)* 752
Heron Lake (C7)* 837
Hewitt (C4)* 312
Hibbing (F3)* 16,276
High Landing (C2) 7
Hill City (E4)* 501
Hillman (E4)* 85
Hills (B7)* 520
Hillview (C4) 45
Hinckley (F4)* 902
Hines (D3)* 100
Hitterdal (B4)* 262
Hoffman (C5)* 575
Hokah (G7)* 643
Holdingford (D5)* 458
Holland (B6)* 263
Hollandale (E7)* 360
Holloway (C5)* 264
Holmes City (C5)* 116
Holt (B2)* 172
Holyoke (F4)* 75
Homer (G6)* 200
Hope (E7)* 148
Hopkins (G5)* 7,595
Hopper (F3)* 175
Houston (G7)* 973
Hovland (G2)* 300
Howard Lake (D5)* 931
Hubbard (C4)* 140
Hugo (E5)* 440
Humboldt (A2)* 143
Huntersville (D4) 25
Huntley (D7)* 118
Huot (B3) 12
Hutchinson (D6)* 4,690
Ihlen (B7)* 135
Illgen City (G3) 7
Independence (F4)* 20
Indus (E2)* 55
Inger (D3)* 100
International Falls (E2)* 6,269
Inver Grove (E6)* 667

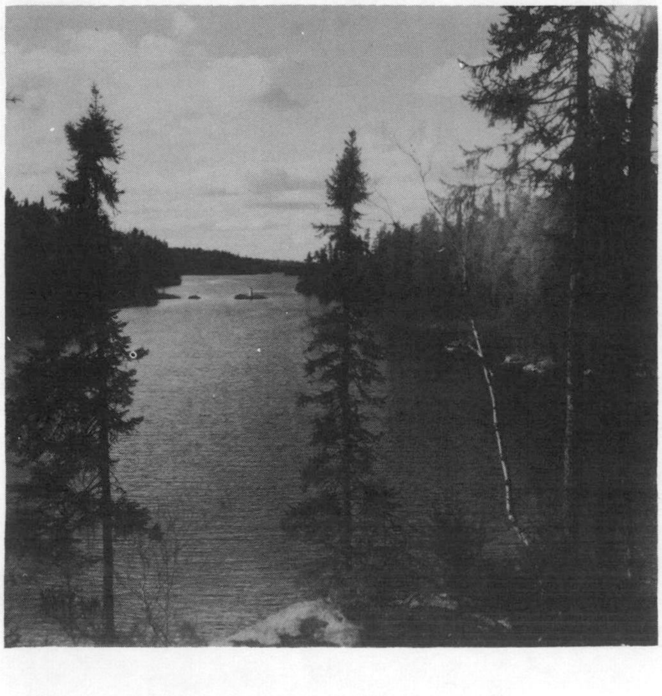

Iona (C7)* 355
Iron (F3)* 128
Ironton (D4)* 828
Isabella (G3)*
Isanti (E5)* 422
Island Park (F5)* 1,357
Island View (E2) 18
Isle (E4)* 674
Ivanhoe (B6)* 682
Jackson (C7)* 3,313
Jacobson (E4)* 106
Janesville (E6)* 1,287
Jasper (B7)* 840
Jeffers (C6)* 516
Jenkins (D4)* 170
Jesse Lake (E3)* 97
Johnsburg (F7) 31
Johnson (B5)* 54
Jordan (E6)* 1,494
Judson (D6)* 153
Kabetogama (F2)* 28
Kanaranzi (B7)* 100
Kandiyohi (D5)* 293
Karlstad (B2)* 804
Kasota (D6)* 600
Kasson (F6)* 1,353
Keewatin (E3)* 1,807
Kelliher (D3)* 336
Kellogg (G6)* 409
Kelly Lake (F3)* 700
Kelsey (F3)* 15
Kennedy (B2)* 480
Kenneth (B7)* 119
Kensington (C5)* 354
Kent (B4)* 178
Kenyon (E6)* 1,651
Kerkhoven (C5)* 664
Kerrick (F4)* 81
Kettle River (E4)* 223
Kiester (E7)* 541
Kilkenny (E6)* 174
Kimball (D5)* 479
Kimberly (E4)* 35
Kinbrae (C7)* 85
Kingsdale (F4)* 72
Kingston (D5) 140
Kinmount (F2)
Kinney (F3)* 336
Klossner (D6)* 88
Knapp (D5) 6
Knife River (G4)* 375
Kragnes (B3) 25
Kroschel (E4) 25
La Crescent (G7)* 1,229
La Prairie ‡(E3) 88
La Salle (D6)* 144
Lac qui Parle (B5) 100
Lafayette (D6)* 438
Lake Benton (B6)* 863
Lake Bronson (B2)* 438
Lake City (F6)* 3,457
Lake Crystal (D6)* 1,430
Lake Elmo (F6)* 386
Lake Fremont (Zimmerman*) (E5) 169
Lake George (D3)* 95
Lake Henry (D5) 97
Lake Hubert (D4)* 125
Lake Itasca (C3)* 50
Lake Lillian (C6)* 358
Lake Netta (E5)
Lake Park (B4)* 689
Lake Shore (D4) 326
Lake Wilson (B7)* 434
Lakefield (C7)* 1,651
Lakeland (F6)* 43
Lakeside (D6) 23
Lakeville (E6)* 628
Lakewood (G4) 917
Lamberton (C6)* 1,208
Lamoille (G6)* 50
Lamson (D5) 20
Lancaster (B2)* 536
Lanesboro (G7)* 1,100
Lansing (F7)* 100
Laporte (D3)* 189
Larsmont (G4)* 185
Lastrup (D4)* 158
Lauderdale (G5) 1,033
Lawler (E4)* 75
Lawndale (B4)* 25
Le Center (E6)* 1,314
Le Roy (F7)* 959
Le Sueur (E6)* 2,713
Leader (D4)* 20
Leaf Valley (C4)* 50
Lemond (E7) 8
Lengby (C3)* 206
Lenora (G7) 50
Leonard (C3)* 88
Leoneth (Leonidas) (F3)* 88
Leota (C7)* 250
Lerdal (E7) 26
Lester Prairie (D6)* 663
Lewiston (G7)* 786
Lewisville (D7)* 362
Libby (E4)* 17
Lime Creek (C7)* 54
Lincoln (D4)* 30
Linden (D6) 13
Lindstrom (F5)* 729
Lismore (B7)* 317
Litchfield (D5)* 4,608
Little Falls (D5)* 6,717
Little Marais (G3)* 50
Little Rock (D5) 28
Little Sauk (D5)* 100
Littlefork (E2)* 671
Lockhart (B3)* 60
Loman (E2)* 80
London (E7)* 100
Long Beach (C5) 181
Long Lake (F5)* 399
Long Prairie (D5)* 2,443
Long Siding (E5)* 48
Longville (D4)* 116
Lonsdale (E6)* 510
Loretto (F5)* 179
Louisburg (B5)* 93
Lowry (C5)* 285
Lucan (C6)* 246
Luce (C4) 32
Lutsen (F2)* 75
Luverne (B7)* 3,650
Luxemburg (D5) 66
Lydia (E6) 93
Lyle (F7)* 609
Lyman (C4) 10
Lynd (C6)* 275
Lyndale (F5)
Mabel (G7)* 788
Madelia (D6)* 1,790
Madison (B5)* 2,303
Madison Lake (E6)* 357
Magnolia (B7)* 260
Mahkonce (C3) 6
Mahnomen (C3)* 1,464
Mahtomedi (F5)* 1,375
Mahtowa (F4)* 150
Maine (C4) 14
Makinen (F3)* 255
Malmo (E4)* 58
Malung (C2)* 5
Manannah (D5) 50
Manchester (E7)* 113
Manganese ‡(D4) 41
Manhattan Beach (E4)* 72
Manitou (D2)* 50
Mankato (E6)* 18,809
Mansfield (E7) 20
Mantorville (F6)* 477
Maple Bay (B3) 110
Maple Island (E7) 175
Maple Lake (D5)* 780
Maple Plain (F5)* 479
Mapleton (E7)* 1,083
Mapleview ‡(F7) 435
Marble (E3)* 867
Marcell (E3)* 60
March (B2) 15
Marcy (G3) 18
Margie (E2)* 100
Marietta (B5)* 380
Marine on Saint Croix (F5)* 334
Markham (F3) 310
Markville (F4)* 100
Marshall (C6)* 5,923
Matawan (E7)* 59
Mavie (B2) 10
Max (D3)* 45
Mayer (E6)* 153
Mayhew Lake (D5) 24
Maynard (C6)* 507
Mazeppa (F6)* 523
McGrath (E4)* 135
McGregor (E4)* 322
McIntosh (C3)* 881
McKinley (F3)* 196
Meadow Brook ‡(F3)* 21
Meadowlands (F3)* 134
Medford (E6)* 409
Medicine Lake (G5) 284
Meire Grove (C5) 128
Melby (C4)* 75
Melrose (D5)* 2,106
Melrude (F3)* 109
Melvin (B3) 25
Menahga (C4)* 849
Mendota (G5)* 243
Mentor (B3)* 321
Meriden (E6)* 131
Merrifield (D4)* 78
Mesaba (F3)
Middle River (B2)* 356
Milaca (E5)* 1,917
Milan (C5)* 561
Mildred (D4)* 25
Millerville (C4) 173
Millville (F6)* 168
Milroy (C6)* 268
Miltona (C4)* 150
Mineral Center (G2) 6
Minneapolis (E5)* 521,718
Minneapolis-St. Paul (urban area) 977,931
Minneska (G6)* 134
Minneota (C6)* 1,274
Minnesota City (G6)* 201
Minnesota Falls (C6) 150
Minnesota Lake (E7)* 609
Minnetonka Beach ‡(F5)* 376
Mizpah (D3)* 166
Moland (E6) 23
Money Creek (G7) 150
Monterey (D7)* 315
Montevideo (C6)* 5,459
Montgomery (E6)* 1,913
Monticello (E5)* 1,231
Montrose (E5)* 300
Moorhead (B4)* 14,870
Moose Lake (E4)* 1,603
Mora (E5)* 2,018
Morgan (D6)* 949
Morningside (G5) 1,699
Morrill (E5) 40
Morris (C5)* 3,811
Morristown (E6)* 533
Morton (C6)* 794
Moscow (E7) 25
Motley (D4)* 435
Mound (E6)* 2,061
Mound Prairie (G7) 8
Mountain Iron (F3)* 1,377
Mountain Lake (D7)* 1,733
Murdock (C5)* 393
Myrtle (E7)* 136
Nary (D3) 7
Nashua (B4)* 181
Nashwauk (E3)* 2,029
Nassau (B5)* 205
Naytahwaush (C3)* 220
Nebish (D3)* 35
Nelson (C5)* 160
Nemadji (F4)* 25
Nerstrand (E6)* 228
Nett Lake (E2)*
Nevis (D4)* 332
New Auburn (D6)* 290
New Brighton (G5)* 2,218
New Germany (E6)* 286
New London (C5)* 726
New Market (E6)* 193
New Munich (D5)* 277
New Prague (E6)* 1,915
New Richland (E7) 908
New Trier (F6) 73
New Ulm (D6)* 9,348
New York Mills (C4)* 977
Newburg (G7)
Newfolden (B2)* 367
Newhouse (G7) 15
Newport (F6)* 1,672
Newry (E7) 7
Nichols (E4) 3
Nickerson (F4)* 48
Nicollet (D6)* 493
Nielsville (B3)* 189
Nimrod (D4)* 112
Nisswa (D4)* 578
Nodine (G7) 50
Nopeming (F4)* 474
Noracres (B2)
Norcross (B5)* 179
Norland (B2) 5
Norseland (D6) 75
North Branch (F5)* 769
North Mankato (D6)* 4,788
North Redwood (D6)* 215
North Saint Paul (E5)* 4,248
Northcote (A2)* 35
Northfield (E6)* 7,487
Northome (D3)* 349
Northrop (D7)* 157
Norway Lake (C5) 30
Norwood (E6)* 749
Nowthen (E5) 18
Noyes (A2)* 93
Oak Center (F6) 30
Oak Island (D1)* 40
Oak Park (E5)* 100
Oakland (E7)* 110
Odessa (B5)* 283
Odin (D7)* 208
Ogema (C3)* 249
Ogilvie (E5)* 362
Okabena (C7)* 236
Oklee (C3)* 494
Olga (C3) 7
Olivia (C6)* 2,012
Onamia (E4)* 704
Opole (D5)* 100
Opstead (E4) 18
Orchard Lake (E6) 150
Org (C7) 25
Orleans (B2)* 53
Ormsby (D7)* 190
Oronoco (F6)* 200
Orr (F2)* 309
Orrock (E5) 9
Ortonville (B5)* 2,577
Osage (C4)* 184
Osakis (C5)* 1,488
Oshawo (D4) 6
Oslo (A2)* 440
Osseo (G5)* 1,167
Ostrander (F7)* 191
Otisco (E7)* 100
Ottawa (E6)* 110
Ottertail (C4)* 237
Outing (E4)* 150
Owatonna (E6)* 10,191
Oylen (D4) 35
Padua (C5) 40
Page (E5) 22
Palisade (E4)* 212
Palmdale (F5) 12
Palmers (G4) 15
Palo (F3) 700
Parent (D5) 9
Park Rapids (D4)* 3,027
Parkers Prairie (C4)* 900
Parkville (F3)* 500
Payne (F3)* 110
Paynesville (D5)* 1,503
Pease (E5)* 179
Pelan (B2) 30
Pelican Lakes (D4) 154
Pelican Rapids (B4)* 1,676
Pemberton (E7)* 152
Penasse (C1)* 3
Pencer (C2)* 11
Pengilly (E3)* 75
Pennington (D3)* 100
Pennock (C5)* 238
Pequot Lakes (D4)* 552
Perham (C4)* 1,926
Perley (B3)* 204
Petersburg (C7) 100
Peterson (G7)* 318
Peyla (F3)*
Phelps (C4) 15
Philbrook (D4)* 100
Pickwick (G7) 122
Pierz (D5)* 856
Pillager (D4)* 362
Pilot Grove (D7) 24
Pilot Mound (F7) 18
Pine City (F5)* 1,937
Pine Island (F6)* 1,298
Pine River (D4)* 835
Pinecreek (C2)* 32
Pinewood (C3)* 60
Pipestone (B7)* 5,269
Pitt (D2)* 12
Plainview (F6)* 1,524
Plato (D6)* 263
Pleasant Lake (D5) 53
Plummer (B3)* 340
Ponemah (D2)* 200
Ponsford (C2)* 250
Pontoria (D4) 60
Poplar (D4)* 12
Porter (B6)* 291
Potsdam (F6) 50
Powderhorn (G6)* 11,118
Pratt (E6)* 43
Predmore (F7) 30
Preston (F7)* 1,399
Priam (C5) 14
Princeton (E5)* 2,108
Prinsburg (C6)* 390
Prior Lake (E6)* 536
Proctor (F4)* 2,693
Prosit (F4)* 227
Prosper (G7)* 65
Providence (B6) 8
Puposky (C3)* 100
Quamba (E5)* 100
Rabey (E4) 30
Racine (F7)* 175
Radium (B2)* 40
Rako (D2) 9
Ramey (E5) 75
Randall (D4)* 425
Randolph (E6)* 259
Ranier (E2)* 227
Ranum (B3) 2
Rapidan (D6)*
Rauch (E3)* 95
Ray (E2)* 95
Raymond (C5)* 580
Reading (C7)* 160
Reads Landing (F6)* 201
Red Lake Falls (B3)* 1,733
Red Wing (F6)* 10,645
Redby (D3)* 210
Redlake (C3)* 350
Redtop (E4)* 26
Redwood Falls (C6)* 3,813
Regal (D5)* 64
Remer (E3)* 412
Renville (C6)* 1,323
Revere (C6)* 198
Rice (D5)* 328
Rice Lake (E5) 100
Richfield (E6)* 17,502
Richmond (D5)* 700
Richville (C4)* 141
Richwood (C4)* 65
Ridgeway (G7) 50
River (C2)
Riverton (D4)* 148
Robbin (A2) 40
Robbinsdale (G5)* 11,289
Roberts (B4) 5
Rochert (C4)* 120
Rochester (F6)* 29,885
Rock Creek (F5)* 100
Rock Dell (F7) 41
Rockford (F5)* 369
Rockville (D5)* 288
Rogers (E5)* 268
Rollag (B4) 27
Rollingstone (G6)* 315
Ronneby (E5)* 72
Roosevelt (C2)* 228
Roscoe (D5)* 182
Roscoe (F6) 20
Rose Creek (F7)* 314
Roseau (C2)* 2,231
Roseland (C6)* 100
Rosemount (E6)* 567
Rosen (B5) 50
Rosendale (D5) 40
Roseville (G5) 6,437
Rosewood (B2)*
Ross (C2)* 20
Rothsay (B4)* 537
Round Lake (C7)* 435
Round Prairie (D5)* 35
Royalton (D5)* 500
Rush City (F5)* 1,175
Rush River (D6) 15
Rushford (G7)* 1,270
Rushford (Village) ‡(G7) 612
Rushmore (C7)* 368
Russell (C6)* 508
Rustad (B4)* 32
Ruthton (B6)* 534
Rutledge (F4)* 163
Sabin (B4)* 211
Sacred Heart (C6)* 745
Saginaw (F4)* 51
Saint Anna (D5) 12
St. Anthony (D5) 66
St. Anthony Falls(G5)* 1,406
St. Bonifacius (F5)* 438
St. Charles (F7)* 1,548
St. Clair (E6)* 324
St. Cloud (D5)* 28,410
St. Francis (E5)* 125
St. George (D6) 74
St. Hilaire (B2)* 276
St. James (D7)* 3,861
St. Joseph (D5)* 1,246
St. Kilian (C7)
St. Leo (C6)* 128
St. Louis Park (G5)* 22,644
St. Martin (D5)* 195
St. Michael (E5)* 487
SAINT PAUL (E6)* 311,349
St. Paul-Minneapolis (urban area) 977,931
St. Paul Park (F6)* 2,438
St. Peter (E6)* 7,754
St. Rosa (D5) 69
St. Stephen (D5) 234
St. Vincent (A2)* 155
Salol (C2)* 55
Sanborn (C6)* 613
Sandstone (F4)* 1,097
Santiago (E5)* 68
Sargeant (F7)* 121
Sartell (D5)* 662
Sauk Centre (C5)* 3,140
Sauk Rapids (D5)* 3,410
Saum (D3)* 40
Savage (E6)* 389
Sawbill Landing (G3) 25
Sawyer (F4)* 183
Scandia (F5)* 200
Scanlon (F4)* 572
Schley (D3)* 3
Schroeder (G3)* 200
Seaforth (C6)* 136
Searles (D6)* 102

Sebeka (C4)* 802
Sedan (C5)* 134
Shafer (F5)* 127
Shakopee (E6)* 3,185
Shaw (F3)* 82
Sheldon (G7) 45
Shelly (B3)* 329
Sherack (B2) 14
Sherburn (D7)* 1,221
Shevlin (C3)* 242
Shieldsville (E6) 28
Shirley (B3) 7
Shooks (D3)* 30
Shoreham (C4)* 91
Shotley (D2) 35
Shovel Lake (E4)* 10
Side Lake (E3)* 120
Silver Creek (D5)* 104
Silver Lake (D6)* 603
Silverdale (E3) 90
Simpson (F7)* 92
Sioux Valley (C7) 200
Skime (C2)*
Skyberg (F6)* 25
Slayton (C7)* 1,887
Sleepy Eye (D6)* 3,278
Sobieski (D5) 189
Solana (E4) 12
Solway (C3)* 124
Soudan (F3)* 1,190
South Branch (D7) 698
South Haven (D5)* 305
South International Falls (E2)* 1,840
South St. Paul (F6)* 15,909
Spafford (C7) 10
Spicer (C5)* 566
Spooner (D2)* 420
Spring Grove (G7)* 1,093
Spring Hill (D5) 91
Spring Lake (E3)* 24
Spring Lake (E5) 18
Spring Park (F5)* 500
Spring Vale (E5) 25
Spring Valley (F7)* 2,467
Springfield (C6)* 2,574
Squaw Lake (D3)* 132
Stacy (E5)* 150
Stanchfield (E5)* 100
Stanton (E6)* 60
Staples (D4)* 2,782
Star Lake (B4) 125
Starbuck (C5)* 1,143
Stark (E5) 39
Steen (B7)* 228
Stephen (A2)* 877
Sterling Center (D7) 22
Stewart (D6)* 695
Stewartville (F7)* 1,193
Stillwater (F5)* 7,674
Stockton (G6)* 235
Storden (C6)* 398
Strandquist (B2)* 208
Strathcona (B2)* 143
Strout (D5) 10
Sturgeon Lake (F4)* 189
Sumter (D6) 17
Sunburg (C5)* 151
Sundahl (B3) 10
Sunrise (F5)* 80
Svea (C6)* 97
Swan River (E3)* 30
Swanville (D5)* 373
Swatara (E4)* 100
Swift (C2)* 40
Swift Falls (C5) 120
Syre (B3) 10
Tabor (B2) 60
Taconite (E3)* 322
Talmoon (E3)* 25
Tamarack (E4)* 132
Taopi (F7)* 118
Taunton (B6)* 217
Taylors Falls (F5)* 520
Tenney (B4)* 62
Tenstrike (D3)* 206
Terrace (C5)* 80
Terrebonne (B3) 50
Theilman (F6)* 95
Thief River Falls (B2)* 6,926
Thomson (F4)* 170
Thorpe (D6) 7
Tintah (B5)* 235
Tobique (F3)*
Tofte (H3)* 100
Togo (E3)* 7
Toimi (G3) 100
Toivola (F3)* 312
Tonka Bay (F5) 899
Tower (F3)* 773
Tracy (C6)* 3,020
Trail (C3)* 123
Traverse (D6) 15
Triumph (D7)* 561
Trommald (D4)* 117
Trosky (B7)* 140
Truman (D7)* 1,106
Turtle River (D3) 57
Twig (F4)* 100
Twin Lakes (E7)* 124
Twin Valley (B3)* 899
Two Harbors (G3)* 4,400
Tyler (B6)* 1,121
Ulen (B3)* 525
Underwood (C4)* 336
Upsala (D5)* 366
Urbank (C4) 162
Utica (G7)* 194
Vasa (F6)* 60
Vawter (D5)
Verdi (B6)* 101
Vergas (C4)* 301
Vermillion (F6)* 112
Verndale (C4)* 576
Verndon (E4) 40
Vernon Center (D7)* 344
Veseli (E6)* 132
Vesta (C6)* 340
Victoria (E6)* 302
Viking (B2)* 130
Villard (C5)* 288
Vining (C4)* 180
Viola (F6)* 80
Virginia (F3)* 12,486
Wabasha (F6)* 2,468
Wabasso (C6)* 693
Waconia (E6)* 1,569
Wadena (C4)* 3,958
Wahkon (E4)* 202
Waite Park (D5)* 1,639
Waldorf (E7)* 266
Wales (G3)* 35
Walker (D3)* 1,192
Walnut Grove (C6)* 890
Walters (E7)* 139
Waltham (F7)* 212
Wanamingo (F6)* 496
Wanda (C6)* 178
Wannaska (C2)* 66
Warba (E3)* 125
Ward Springs (D5)* 45
Warren (B2)* 1,779
Warroad (C2)* 1,276
Warsaw (E6)* 150
Waseca (E6)* 4,927
Wasioja (F6) 150
Waskish (C2)* 40
Waterford (E6) 65
Watertown (E6)* 837
Waterville (E6)* 1,627
Watkins (D5)* 659
Watson (C5)* 284
Waubun (C3)* 426
Waverly (E5)* 493
Wawina (E3)*
Wayzata (E6)* 1,791
Weaver (G6)* 105
Webster (E6)*
Wegdahl (C6)* 51
Welch (F6)* 70
Welcome (D7)* 712
Wells (E7)* 2,475
Weme (C3)
Wendell (B4)* 284
West Concord (F6)* 770
W. Saint Paul (G5) 7,955
W. Union (C5)* 100
Westbrook (C6)* 1,017
Westbury (C4) 25
Westport (C5)* 96
Whalan (G7)* 176
Wheaton (B5)* 1,948
Whipholt (D3)* 100
White Bear Lake (G5)* 3,646
White Earth (C3)* 800
White Rock (F6) 100
Wig Wam Bay (E4) 50
Wilbert (D7) 30
Wilder (C7)* 118
Wildwood (E3) 40
Wilkinson (D3)* 200
Willernie (H5)* 592
Williams (D2)* 414
Willmar (C5)* 9,410
Willow Creek (D7) 12
Willow River (F4)* 294
Wilmington (G7) 15
Wilmont (C7)* 473
Wilson (G7)
Wilton (C3)* 108
Windom (C7)* 3,165
Winger (B3)* 283
Winnebago (D7)* 2,127
Winona (G6)* 25,031
Winsted (D6)* 941
Winthrop (D6)* 1,251
Winton (G3)* 184
Wirock (C7) 20
Wirt (E3)* 138
Witoka (G7)
Wolf Lake (C4)* 109
Wolverton (B4)* 198
Wood Lake (C6)* 504
Woodland ‡(G5) 411
Woodstock (B7)* 277
Worthington (C7)* 7,923
Wrenshall (F4)* 148
Wright (E4)* 199
Wrightstown (C4) 23
Wyattville (G7) 26
Wykoff (F7)* 509
Wylie (B3) 10
Wyoming (F5)* 325
York (F7) 6
Young America (E6)* 365
Yucatan (G7) 15
Zemple ‡(E3) 87
Zim (F3)* 110
Zimmerman (E5)* 258
Zumbro Falls (F6)* 172
Zumbrota (F6)* 1,686

Map on Page 71

MISSISSIPPI

Total Population 2,178,914

82 COUNTIES

Adams (B8) 32,256
Alcorn (G1) 27,158
Amite (C8) 19,261
Attala (E4) 26,652
Benton (F1) 8,793
Bolivar (C3) 63,004
Calhoun (F3) 18,369
Carroll (E4) 15,499
Chickasaw (G3) 18,951
Choctaw (F4) 11,009
Claiborne (C7) 11,944
Clarke (G6) 19,362
Clay (G3) 17,757
Coahoma (C2) 49,361
Copiah (D7) 30,493
Covington (E7) 16,036
De Soto (E1) 24,599
Forrest (F8) 45,055
Franklin (C8) 10,929
George (G9) 10,012
Greene (G8) 8,215
Grenada (E3) 18,830
Hancock (E10) 11,891
Harrison (F10) 84,073
Hinds (D6) 142,164
Holmes (D4) 33,301
Humphreys (C4) 23,115
Issaquena (B5) 4,966
Itawamba (H2) 17,216
Jackson (G9) 31,401
Jasper (F6) 18,912
Jefferson (B7) 11,306
Jefferson Davis (E7) 15,500
Jones (F7) 57,235
Kemper (G5) 15,893
Lafayette (E2) 22,798
Lamar (E8) 13,225
Lauderdale (G6) 64,171
Lawrence (D7) 12,639
Leake (E5) 21,610
Lee (G2) 38,237
Leflore (D3) 51,813
Lincoln (D8) 27,899
Lowndes (H4) 37,852
Madison (D5) 33,860
Marion (E8) 23,967
Marshall (E1) 25,106
Monroe (H3) 36,543
Montgomery (E4) 14,470
Neshoba (F5) 25,730
Newton (F6) 22,681
Noxubee (G4) 20,022
Oktibbeha (G4) 24,569
Panola (E2) 31,271
Pearl River (E9) 20,641
Perry (G8) 9,108
Pike (D8) 35,137
Pontotoc (F2) 19,994
Prentiss (G1) 19,810
Quitman (D2) 25,885
Rankin (E6) 28,881
Scott (E6) 21,681
Sharkey (C5) 12,903
Simpson (E7) 21,819
Smith (E6) 16,740
Stone (F9) 6,264
Sunflower (C3) 56,031
Tallahatchie (D3) 30,486
Tate (E1) 18,011
Tippah (G1) 17,522
Tishomingo (H1) 15,544
Tunica (D1) 21,664
Union (F2) 20,262
Walthall (D8) 15,563
Warren (C6) 39,616
Washington (C4) 70,504
Wayne (G7) 17,010
Webster (F3) 11,607
Wilkinson (B8) 14,116
Winston (F4) 22,231
Yalobusha (E2) 15,191
Yazoo (D5) 35,712

CITIES and TOWNS

Abbeville (F2)*
Abbott (G3)
Aberdeen (H3)* 5,290
Aberdeen Jct. (E4)
Ackerman (F4)* 1,463
Acona (D4) 250
Adair (D4)
Adams (C6)* 40
Agricola (G9)* 200
Alcorn (B7)* 500
Algoma (G2)*
Allen (C7)
Alligator (C2)* 214
Alva (F3)
Amory (H3)* 4,990
Anding (D5)* 140
Anguilla (C5)* 601
Ansley (E10) 65
Arcola (C4)* 413
Ariel (C8) 19
Arkabutla (D1)* 207
Arm (D8)* 135
Artesia (G4)* 594
Ashland (F1)* 328
Askew (D1)*
Auburn (C8)* 200
Auter (C4) 25
Avalon (D3)*
Avent (G8)
Avera (G8)*
Bailey (G6)* 35
Baird (C4)* 193
Baldwyn (G2)* 1,567
Ballardsville (H2) 30
Ballground (C5) 300
Baltzer (C3)* 250
Banks (D1)*
Banner (F2)* 125
Barbara (G9) 50
Barland (C7) 10
Barlow (C7)* 80
Barnett (G7)* 250
Barr (E1)* 275
Barto (D8) 25
Basic (G6)
Bassfield (E8)* 320
Batesville (E2)* 2,463
Battle (H8)
Baxter (F6)
Baxterville (E8)*
Bay Saint Louis (F10)* 4,621
Bay Springs (F7)* 1,302
Bayland (C5)
Bear Creek (D6)
Beatty (E4) 50
Beaumont (G8)* 1,200
Beauregard (D7)* 231
Becker (G3)* 300
Bee Lake (D4)
Belden (G2)* 360
Belen (D2)*
Bellefontaine (F3)*
Bellewood (C4) 75
Belmont (H1)* 814
Belzoni (C4)* 4,071
Benndale (G9)*
Benoit (C3)* 444
Benton (D5)* 225
Bentonia (D5)* 496
Berclair (D4) 100
Bethany (G2)*
Beulah (B3)* 342
Bewelcome (C8)
Bexley (G9)*
Big Creek (F3)* 147
Big Point (H9) 300
Bigbee Valley (H4)* 51
Biloxi (G10)* 37,425
Binnsville (H5) 50
Black Hawk (E4)* 100
Blaine (C3)* 200
Blanton (C5)*
Blodgett (F8) 5
Blue Mountain (G1)* 875
Blue Springs (G2)* 125
Bobo (C2)*
Bogue Chitto (D8)*
Bolatusha (E5) 50
Bolton (D6)* 741
Bond (F9)* 500
Bonhomie (F8)
Bonita (G6)*
Booneville (G1)* 3,295
Bothwell (G8)
Bourbon (C4)*
Bovina (C6)* 82
Bowling Green (E4) 28
Boyle (C3)* 799
Bradley (G4)
Brandon (E6)* 1,827
Braxton (D6)* 206
Brewer (G7) 50
Briers (B8)
Brody (F1)
Brookhaven (C7)* 7,801
Brooklyn (F8)* 500
Brooksville (G4)* 819
Brownfield (G1)* 300
Brownsville (D6) 50
Brozville (D4) 25
Bruce (F3)* 1,719
Brunswick (C5) 150
Bryant (E3)* 150
Buckatunna (G7)* 500
Bude (C8)* 1,195
Buena Vista (G3)* 50
Burgess (E2)
Burnell (C7)* 30
Burns (E6)* 213
Burnside (F5)* 75
Burnsville (H1)* 525
Byhalia (E1)* 581
Byram (D6)*
Byrd (G8)
Caesar (E9) 50
Caile (C4) 150
Caledonia (H3)* 252
Calhoun City (F3)* 1,319
Calyx (G5)* 150
Camden (E5)* 350
Cameta (C4)* 89
Canaan (F1)*
Cannonsburg (B7)*
Canton (D5)* 7,048
Carlisle (C7)* 350
Carmichael (G7)*
Carnes (F8)
Carpenter (C6)* 150
Carriere (E9)* 500
Carrollton (E4)* 475
Carson (E7)* 206
Carter (D5)*
Carthage (E5)* 1,925
Cary (C5)* 390
Cascilla (D3)* 108
Cato (E6)
Cayuga (C6)
Cedar Hill (E3)
Cedarbluff (G3)*
Cedars (C6) 65
Center (F5)*
Centreville (B8)* 2,025
Chalybeate (G1)*
Charleston (D2)* 2,629
Chatawa (D8)* 240
Chatham (B4)* 30
Cheraw (E8) 100
Chester (F4)*
Chesterville (G2) 40
Chicora (G7)* 500
Choctaw (C3)
Chotard (C5)
Chunky (G6)* 258
Church Hill (B7)*
Clara (G7)* 450
Clarksdale (D2)* 16,539
Clarkson (F3) 150
Clayton (D1)* 350
Clermont Harbor (F10)* 175
Cleveland (C3)* 6,747
Cliftonville (H4) 300
Clinton (D6)* 2,255
Cloverhill (C2)
Clyde (E8)
Coahoma (C2)* 300
Cockrum (E1)*
Coffeeville (E3)* 739
Cohay (E6)
Coila (E4)*
Coldwater (E1)* 949
Coles (C8)*
College Hill (E2)
Collins (E7)* 1,293
Collinsville (G6)*
Colony Town (D4)
Columbia (E8)* 6,124
Columbus (H3)* 17,172
Como (E1)* 703
Conehatta (F6)* 50
Conway (E5)*
Cooksville (H5)*
Corinth (G1)* 9,785
Cornersville (F1)
Cotton Plant (G1)* 125
Courtland (E2)* 275
Coxburg (D5)
Crandall (G7)* 145
Cranfield (B7) 20
Crawford (G4)* 374
Crenshaw (D2)* 740
Crosby (B8)* 1,152
Crowder (D2)* 476
Cruger (D4)* 494
Crupp (D5) 135
Crystal Springs (D7)* 3,676
Cuevas (F10)* 150
Cumberland (F3)*
Curtis Station (D2)
Cybur (E9)
Cynthia (D6)
Daleville (G5)* 125
Dancy (F3)
Darbun (D8)
Darling (D2)*
Davenport (C2) 75
De Kalb (G5)* 953
De Lay (F2)* 200
De Lisle (F10)* 600
De Soto (G7)*
Deasonville (D5) 50
Decatur (F6)* 1,225
Deemer (F5)*
Deerbrook (G4)
Deeson (C2)*
Delta City (C4)* 250
Denmark (F2)* 50
Dennis (H1)* 158
Dentville (C7)
Derby (E9)
Derma (F3)* 494
D'Iberville (G10) 1,429
Dickerson (C2) 100
Dixon (F5)* 100
D'Lo (E7)* 516
Dockery (C3) 25
Doddsville (C3)* 201
Doloroso (B8)*
Dorsey (H2)* 58
Dossville (E5)* 150
Drew (C3)* 1,681
Dry Creek (E7)
Dry Grove (D6)
Dubard (E3)*
Dubbs (D1)
Dublin (C2)*
Duck Hill (E3)* 537
Duffee (G6)* 65
Dumas (G1)* 187
Duncan (C2)* 436
Dundee (D1)* 250
Dunleith (C4)
Durant (E4)* 2,311
Eaglebend (C5) 38
East Side (H10) 1,215
Ebenezer (D5)* 95
Ecru (F2)* 494
Eddiceton (C8)*
Eden (D5)* 306
Edgewater Park (G10)* 500
Edinburg (F5)* 900
Edwards (C6)* 1,002
Egremont (C5)* 43
Egypt (G3)*
El Dorado (C5) 50
Electric Mills (G5)*
Elizabeth (C4)* 200
Elliott (E3)* 250
Ellisville (F7)* 3,579
Embry (F3) 300
Enid (E2)* 94
Enondale (G5) 61
Enterprise (G6)* 691
Errata (F7) 50
Erwin (B4)
Escatawpa (G10)*
Essex (D2) 25
Estabutchie (F8)* 150
Estes (F4)
Estesmill (F5) 150
Estill (C4)* 500
Ethel (F4)* 723
Etta (F2)* 75
Eucutta (G7) 50
Eudora (D1) 200
Eupora (F3)* 1,338
Eutaw (B3)*
Evansville (D1) 15
Fair River (D7)
Falcon (D2)* 200
Falkner (G1)* 600
Fannin (E6)*
Farmhaven (E5)*
Farrell (C2)*
Fayette (B7)* 1,498
Fearns Springs (G4)
Fenton (F10) 25
Fentress (F4)
Fernwood (D8)* 600
Fitler (B5)* 300
Flora (D5)* 655
Florence (D6)* 313
Foote (C4) 100
Forest (F6)* 2,874
Forkville (E6)* 145
Fort Adams (B8)* 105
Foxworth (E8)* 750
French Camp (F4)* 162
Friars Point (C2)* 916
Fruitland Park (F9)* 63
Fulton (H2)* 1,343
Gainesville (E10) 50
Gallman (D7)* 170
Garlandville (F6)* 180
Gatesville (D6)*
Gattman (H3)* 150
Gautier (G10)*
Gencill (C4)
Georgetown (D7)* 327
Geren (D3)*
Germania (C5)*
Gholson (G5)* 25
Gibson (G3)* 275
Gillsburg (C8) 50
Gitano (F7)
Glancy (C7)*
Glen (H1)*
Glen Allan (B4)* 400
Glendora (D3)* 178
Gloster (B8)* 1,467
Glover (D1)
Gluckstadt (D5)
Golden (H2)* 206
Good Hope (E5) 200
Goodman (E5)* 878
Goodyear (E9)
Goshen Springs (E6)*
Goss (E8)* 250
Grace (C5)*
Grand Gulf (B6) 25
Grapeland (B3)
Greenville (B4)* 29,936
Greenwood (D4)* 18,061
Greenwood Spgs. (H3)* 65
Grenada (E3)* 7,388
Gulfport (F10)* 22,659
Gunnison (C3)* 453
Guntown (G2)* 299
Halstead (C3)
Hamburg (B7)*
Hamilton (H3)*
Hampton (B4) 10
Handsboro (F10)* 1,275
Hankinson (C6) 10
Hardee (C5)
Hardy (E3)
Harperville (E6)*
Harriston (C7)* 150
Harrisville (D7)*
Hathorn (E8)* 350
Hatley (H3) 100
Hattiesburg (F8)* 29,474
Hazlehurst (D7)* 3,397
Heads (C4) 100
Heidelberg (F7)* 863
Helm (C4) 100
Hermanville (C7)* 255
Hernando (E1)* 1,206
Hesterville (E4)
Hickory (F6)* 614
Hickory Flat (F1)* 345
Highlandale (D3) 100
Highpoint (F4)* 300
Hillhouse (C2)* 100
Hillsboro (E6)*
Hillsdale (F9)
Hinchcliff (D2)* 50
Hintonville (F8) 150
Hinze (F4)*
Hiwannee (G7)* 300
Hohenlinden (F3) 200
Holcomb (D3)* 229
Holcut (H1)* 300
Hollandale (C4)* 2,346
Holly Bluff (C5)*
Holly Ridge (C4)* 518
Holly Springs (E1)* 3,276
Hollyknowe (C4)
Hollywood (D1)* 117
Holmesville (D8)* 70
Homewood (E6)*
Honey Island (D4)
Hopewell (D7)* 350
Horn Lake (D1)* 1,000
Houlka (G2)* 545
Houston (G3)* 1,664
Howard (D4) 25
Howison (F9)* 75
Hub (E8)* 280
Hudsonville (F1) 50
Hurley (H9)*
Hushpuckena (C2)* 200
Increase (G6) 40
Independence (E1)*
Indianola (C4)* 4,369
Ingomar (F2)*
Inverness (C4)* 1,010
Irene (D8) 100
Isola (C4)* 450
Itta Bena (D4)* 1,725
Iuka (H1)* 1,527
Jacinto (H1) 140
JACKSON (D6)* 98,271
Jackson (urban area) 99,677
James (B4)* 500
Jamestown (E8) 25
Jayess (D8)* 50
Jeffries (C2)
Johns (E6)* 800
Johnstons Station (D0)*
Jonestown (D2)* 741
Keirn (D4)*
Kendrick (H1)
Keownville (G1) 15
Kewanee (H6)* 200
Kienstra (B8)*
Kilmichael (E4)* 511
Kiln (F10)*
Kipling (G5)
Kirby (C7) 98
Kirkville (H2) 125
Kittrell (G8) 100
Klein (F6) 10
Knoxville (B8)*
Kokomo (E8)* 300

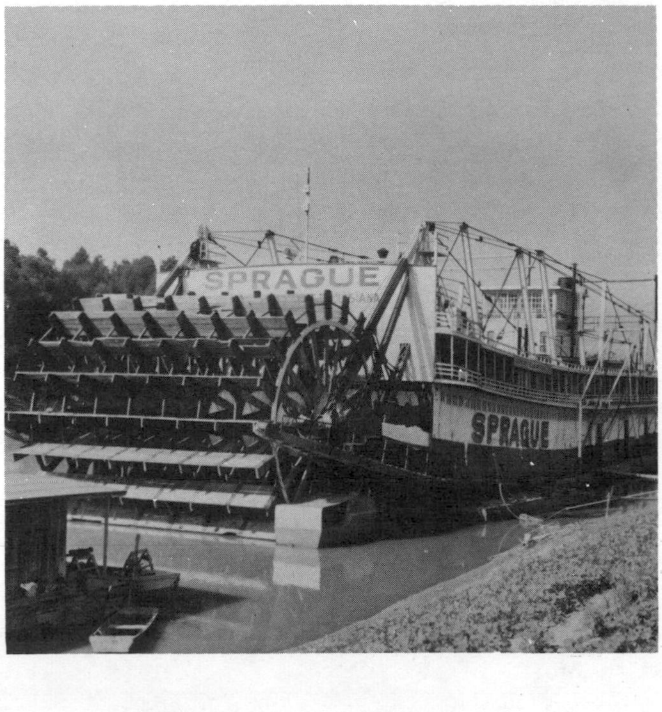

Kolola Springs (H3)* 81
Kosciusko (E4)* 6,753
Kossuth (G1)* 242
Kreole (H10)* 1,106
Lafayette Spgs. (F2)*
Lake (F6)* 345
Lake Como (F7)* 150
Lake Cormorant (D1)*
Lake View (D1) 100
Lakeshore (F10)* 107
Lamar (F1)*
Lambert (D2)* 1,023
Lamkin (D4)* 100
Lamont (B3)* 250
Landon (F10) 500
Laneheart (B8)*
Langford (E6)
Langsdale (G7)* 100
Lauderdale (G5)* 648
Laurel (F7)* 25,038
Lawrence (F6)* 300
La Flore (D3)* 75
Leaf (G8)*
Leakesville (G8)* 893
Learned (C6)* 126
Leedo (C7)*
Leedy (H1)
Leesburg (E6)
Leesdale (B7) 20
Leland (C4)* 4,736
Lemon (E6)
Lena (E5)* 353
Leota Landing (B4) 20
Lessley (B8)*
Lexie (D8)
Lexington (D4)* 3,198
Liberty (C8)* 683
Little Rock (F5)*
Lobdell (B3) 50
Lockhart (G6) 50
Lodi (E3)* 50
Logtown (E10)* 300
Lombardy (C3) 300
Long (C4) 100
Long Beach (F10)* 2,703
Longtown (D1) 82
Longview (G4)*
Longwood (C4)* 65
Looxahoma (E1)* 50
Lorena (F6)
Lorenzen (C5)*
Lorman (B7)*
Louin (F6)* 478
Louise (C5)* 479
Louisville (G4)* 5,282
Love (D1)* 75
Luce Farms (H9) 85
Lucedale (G9)* 1,631
Lucien (C7)*
Ludlow (E5)* 500
Lula (C2)* 488
Lumberton (E8)* 1,803
Lux (F8)
Lyman (F10)*
Lynn Creek (G4)
Lyon (D2)* 386
Maben (F3)* 616
Macel (D3)* 50
Macon (G4)* 2,241
Madden (F5)* 350
Madison (D6)* 540
Magee (E7)* 1,738
Magnolia (D8)* 1,984
Mahned (F8) 100
Malone (E1) 25
Malvina (C3)*
Mantachie (H2)* 178
Mantee (F3)* 189
Marietta (H2)* 125
Marion (G6)*
Marks (D2)* 2,209
Martinsville (D7)*
Marydell (F5) 200
Mashulaville (G4)* 150
Matagorda (D2)
Matherville (G7)*
Mathiston (F3)* 584
Mattson (C2)*
Maud (D1)* 102
Maxie (F9)* 80
Mayersville (B5)*
Mayhew (G4)*
Mc Adams (E4)*
Mc Bride (C7)* 35
Mc Call Creek (C7)* 300
Mc Carley (E3)* 300
Mc Comb (D8)* 10,401
Mc Condy (G3) 100
Mc Cool (F4)* 305
Mc Crary (H4) 10
Mc Donald (F5)*
Mc Henry (F9)*
Mc Lain (G8)*
Mc Laurin (F8)*
Mc Leod (H4)*
Mc Nair (C7)* 200
Mc Neill (E9)* 500
Mc Ville (E5)
Meadville (C8)* 524
Mechanicsburg (D5)* 15
Meehan (G6)* 107
Meltonia (C3)*
Mendenhall (E7)* 1,539
Meridian (G6)* 41,893
Merigold (C3)* 682
Merit (E7) 25
Merrill (G9)*
Mesa (D8)
Metcalfe (B4)* 100
Michigan City (F1)* 38
Midnight (C4)* 400
Mileston (D4)* 47
Millard (E9)
Miller (E1)* 200
Millville (E5)
Mineral Wells (E1)* 275
Minter City (D3)* 400
Mississippi City (F10)* 2,125
Misterton (E3)
Mize (E7)* 430
Money (D3)*
Monroe (C8)* 100
Monticello (D7)* 1,382
Montpelier (G3)*
Montrose (F6)* 222
Mooreville (G2)*
Moorhead (C4)* 1,749
Morgan City (D4)*
Morgantown (E8)* 300
Morton (E6)* 1,664
Moscow (G5)
Moselle (F8)* 500
Moss (F7)*
Moss Point (G10)* 3,782
Mound Bayou (C3)* 1,328
Mount Carmel (E7) 50
Mount Helena (C5)
Mount Olive (E7)* 827
Mount Pleasant (E1)* 300
Muldon (G3)* 60
Murphy (C4)* 200
Myles (C7) 50
Myrleville (D5)
Myrtle (F1)* 331
Nanachehaw (B6) 19
Natchez (B7)* 22,740
Neely (G8)* 300
Nesbit (D1)* 250
Neshoba (F5)* 300
Nettleton (G2)* 1,204
New Albany (G2)* 3,680
New Augusta (F8)* 500
New Site (H1)* 24
Newhebron (D7)* 303
Newman (C6) 12
Newton (F6)* 2,912
Nicholson (E10)* 500
Nitta Yuma (C4)*
Nod (D5) 20
Nola (D7) 120
Norfield (C8)* 123
Norris (F6)
Northcarrollton (E3)* 506
Noxapater (F5)* 615
Nugent (F10)
Oak Ridge (C6) 200
Oak Vale (E8)* 136
Oakland (E2)* 551
Oakley (D6) 205
Ocean Springs (G10)* 3,058
Ofahoma (E5)* 50
Okolona (G2)* 2,167
Oldenburg (C7)*
Olive Branch (E1)*
Oloh (E8) 50
Oma (D7)* 50
Onward (C5)*
Ora (E7)
Orange Grove (H10) 150
Orvisburg (E9)
Osborn (G3)
Osyka (D8)* 724
Ovett (F8)* 357
Owens Wells (E4)
Oxford (F2)* 3,956
Pace (C3)* 422
Pachuta (G6)* 273
Paden (H1)* 158
Palmers Crossing (F8)*
Panther Burn (C4)* 30
Parchman (D3)*
Paris (F2)* 84
Pascagoula (G10)* 10,805
Pass Christian (F10)* 3,383
Pattison (C7)* 300
Paulding (F6)* 400
Paulette (H4)* 126
Paynes (D3)*
Pearlington (E10)* 150
Pearson (D6)*
Pecan (H10) 100
Pelahatchie (E6)* 867
Penton (D1)
Peoria (C8)*
Percy (C4)*
Perkinston (F9)* 400
Perthshire (C3)*
Petal (F8)* 2,148
Pettit (C4)* 175
Peyton (C7)* 25
Pheba (G3)*
Philadelphia (F5)* 4,472
Philipp (D3)* 350
Phoenix (C5)*
Piave (G8)*
Picayune (E9)* 6,707
Pickens (E5)* 638
Pinckneyville (B8)*
Pine Ridge (B7)*
Pine Valley (E2)*
Pineville (F6)*
Piney Woods (D6)* 750
Pinola (E7)* 143
Pittsboro (F3)* 246
Plain (D6)* 500
Plantersville (G2) 479
Plattsburg (F5)
Pleasant Grove (D2)*
Pleasant Hill (E1) 200
Plumpoint (E1)
Pocahontas (D6)* 500
Polkville (E6)* 150
Pond (B8)*
Pontotoc (G2)* 1,596
Pope (E2)* 246
Poplar Creek (E4)* 350
Poplarville (E9)* 1,852
Port Gibson (B7)* 2,920
Porterville (G5)* 88
Potts Camp (F1)* 432
Powell (D2)* 80
Prairie (G3)* 654
Prairie Point (H4)*
Prentiss (E7)* 1,212
Preston (G5)* 375
Pricedale (D8)* 300
Prichard (D1)*
Priscilla (C3)* 75
Puckett (E6)* 300
Pulaski (E6)* 1,000
Purvis (F8)* 1,270
Pyland (F3) 125
Quentin (C8)* 300
Quincy (H3)*
Quitman (G6)* 1,817
Raleigh (F6)* 580
Randolph (F2)* 243
Rara Avis (H2)
Ratliff (H2) 60
Ravine (H4)
Raymond (D6)* 1,259
Red Banks (F1)* 450
Red Lick (B7)*
Redwood (C6)*
Reform (F4)* 400
Rena Lara (C2)* 50
Renfro (F5)
Renova (C3) 250
Riceville (F9) 40
Rich (D2)* 61
Richey (C4)* 86
Richton (G8)* 1,158
Ridgeland (D6)* 526
Rienzi (G1)* 468
Rio (G5)*
Ripley (G1)* 2,383
Roberts (F6)
Robinsonville (D1)* 100
Rockport (D7)*
Rodney (B7)* 209
Rolling Fork (C5)* 1,229
Rome (C3)* 189
Rose Hill (F6)* 500
Rosedale (B3)* 2,197
Rosetta (B8)*
Roundaway (C2) 150
Roundlake (C2)* 230
Rounsaville (G8) 19
Roxie (B7)* 521
Rudyard (C2)* 110
Ruleville (C3)* 1,521
Runnelstown (F8)
Rural Hill (F4) 3
Russell (G6)* 275
Russum (B7)* 350
Ruth (D8)*
Sabougla (F3) 100
Sallis (E4)* 228
Saltillo (G2)* 501
Sanatorium (E7)*
Sandersville (F7)* 681
Sandhill (E5)*
Sandy Hook (E8)*
Sanford (F8)*
Sapa (F3)
Sarah (D1)* 93
Saratoga (E7) 65
Sardis (E2)* 1,913
Sarepta (F2)* 90
Satartia (C5)* 105
Saucier (F9)*
Savage (D1)*
Schlater (D3)*
Scobey (E3)* 112
Scooba (G5)* 734
Scott (B3)* 2,000
Sebastopol (F5)* 330
Selma (B7) 2
Seminary (E7)* 345
Senatobia (E1)* 2,108
Seneca (F8) 12
Sessums (G4)*
Shannon (G2)* 520
Sharon (E5)*
Shaw (C3)* 1,892
Shelby (C3)* 2,148
Sherard (C2)* 75
Sherman (G2)* 386
Shipman (G9) 7
Shivers (E7)* 100
Shoccoe (E5)
Shubuta (G7)* 782
Shuqualak (G5)* 714
Sibley (D8)* 25
Sidon (D4)* 361
Signal (C6) 360
Silver City (C4)* 381
Silver Creek (D7)* 275
Skene (C3)* 250
Slate Spring (F3)* 134
Slayden (F1) 45
Sledge (D2)* 383
Smedes (C5)
Smithdale (C8)*
Smiths (C6)
Smithville (H2)* 419
Soegaard (D7)
Sontag (D7)*
Soso (F7)* 171
Spanish Fort (C5)* 120
Springville (F2)* 400
Stafford Springs (F7)* 200
Stallo (F5)* 500
Stampley (B7)* 23
Stanton (B7)*
Star (D6)* 300
Starkville (G4)* 7,107
State College (G4)* 4,000
State Line (G8)* 492
Steel (F6)
Steens (H3)* 95
Stewart (F4)* 311
Stokes (D5)
Stoneville (C4)* 1,015
Stonewall (G6)*
Stovall (C2)*
Stover (D2)*
Stratton (F6)*
Strayhorn (D1) 125
Street (C8) 50
Stringer (F7)* 150
Stringtown (C3)* 500
Strong (G3)* 500
Sturgis (G4)* 402
Sucarnochee (H5)*
Summerland (F7)* 112
Summit (D8)* 1,558
Sumner (D3)* 550
Sumrall (E8)* 853
Sun (F6)
Sunflower (C3)* 639
Swan Lake (D3)* 50
Sweatman (E3)*
Swiftown (D4)*
Swiftwater (B4) 10
Sylvarena (F6)* 112
Symonds (C3)*
Tallula (B5)*
Tamola (G5) 55
Taylor (E2)* 125
Taylorsville (F7)* 1,116
Tchula (D4)* 927
Terry (D6)* 497
Thaxton (F2)* 300
Theadville (G7) 75
Thomastown (E5)* 250
Thomasville (E6) 25
Thorn (F3)* 60
Thornton (D4)* 50
Thrasher (G1)* 200
Thyatira (E1)*
Tibbee Station (G3) 35
Tie Plant (E3)* 400
Tilden (H2) 150
Tillatoba (E3)* 127
Tillman (C7)* 150
Tiplersville (G1)* 110
Tippo (D3)* 80
Tishomingo (H1)* 335
Toccopola (F2)* 262
Tomnolen (F4)* 150
Toomsuba (G6)* 500
Topton (G6) 15
Tougaloo (D6)*
Tralake (C4)* 250
Traxler (E6) 75
Trebloc (G3)* 300
Tremont (H2)*
Trenton (E6)*
Tribbett (C4)* 100
Troy (G2)*
Tula (F2)*
Tunica (D1)* 1,354
Tupelo (G2)* 11,527
Turnbull (B8)*
Tuscola (E5)* 250
Tutwiler (D2)* 939
Tylertown (D8)* 1,331
Tyro (E1)* 750
Union (F5)* 1,559
Union Church (C7)* 275
University (E2)* 1,200
Utica (C6)* 824
Utica Institute (C6)*
Vaiden (E4)* 583
Valley (D5)* 125
Valley Park (C5)*
Value (D6)* 300
Van Vleet (G3)* 300
Vance (D2)*
Vancleave (G9)*
Vardaman (F3)* 686
Vaughan (D5)* 350
Velma (E2)
Verba (F6)
Verna (D8) 12
Vernal (G8)*
Verona (G2)* 589
Vicksburg (C6)* 27,948
Victoria (E1)*
Vidalia (F10) 25
Vimville (H6)*
Vossburg (F7)* 500
Wade (G9)* 300
Wahalak (G5)*
Waldrup (F7)*
Wallerville (G2)* 100
Wallfield (F2)
Walls (D1)* 318
Walnut (G1)* 481
Walnut Grove (F5)* 517
Waltersville (C6) 250
Walthall (F3)* 149
Wanilla (D7)*
Washington (B7)*
Water Valley (E2)* 3,113
Waterford (E1)* 125
Waveland (F10)* 793
Waxhaw (C3)*
Way (E5)*
Waynesboro (G7)* 3,442
Wayside (C4)*
Weathersby (E7)* 145
Webb (D3)* 680
Weir (F4)* 570
Wanasoga (G1)* 150
Wesson (D7)* 1,235
West (E4)* 354
West Enterprise (G6)*
West Point (G3)* 6,432
Whaley (D3) 15
Wheeler (G1)* 300
White Apple (B8) 25
White Bluff (E8) 25
Whitfield (E6)*
Whitfield (D3)
Whiteoak (E6) 50
Whynot (G6) 60
Wicker (E6)
Wiggins (F9)* 1,436
Wilkinson (B8)* 300
Williamsville (F4)
Willows (C6) 30
Winborn (F1)*
Winchester (G7)*
Wingate (G8) 150
Winona (E4)* 3,441
Winstonville (C3)* 322
Winterville (B4)*
Woodland (F3)* 133
Woodville (B8)* 1,609
Wren (G3) 250
Wyatte (E1)* 100
Yazoo City (D5)* 9,746
Yokena (C6)* 25
Youngs (E3) 25
Zama (F5)*
Zion Hill (C8) 50

Map on Page 72

MISSOURI

Total Population 3,954,653

115 COUNTIES

Adair (G2) 19,689
Andrew (C3) 11,727
Atchison (B2) 11,127
Audrain (J4) 23,829
Barry (E9) 21,755
Barton (D7) 12,678
Bates (D6) 17,534
Benton (F6) 9,080
Bollinger (M8) 11,019
Boone (H4) 48,432
Buchanan (C3) 96,826
Butler (M9) 37,707
Caldwell (E3) 9,929
Callaway (J5) 23,316
Camden (G6) 7,861
Cape Girardeau (N8) 38,397
Carroll (F4) 15,589
Carter (L9) 4,777
Cass (D5) 19,325
Cedar (E7) 10,663
Chariton (G3) 14,944
Christian (F9) 12,412
Clark (J2) 9,003
Clay (D4) 45,221
Clinton (D3) 11,726
Cole (H6) 35,464
Cooper (G5) 16,608
Crawford (K7) 11,615
Dade (E8) 9,324
Dallas (F7) 10,392
Daviess (E3) 11,180
De Kalb (D3) 8,047
Dent (J7) 10,936
Douglas (G9) 12,638
Dunklin (M10) 45,329
Franklin (K6) 36,046
Gasconade (J6) 12,342
Gentry (D2) 11,036
Greene (F8) 104,823
Grundy (E2) 13,220
Harrison (E2) 14,107
Henry (E6) 20,043
Hickory (F7) 5,387
Holt (B2) 9,833
Howard (G4) 11,857
Howell (J9) 22,725
Iron (L7) 9,458
Jackson (D5) 541,035
Jasper (D8) 79,106
Jefferson (L6) 38,007
Johnson (E5) 20,716
Knox (H2) 7,617
Laclede (G7) 19,010
Lafayette (E4) 25,272
Lawrence (E8) 23,420
Lewis (J2) 10,733
Lincoln (L4) 13,478
Linn (F3) 18,865
Livingston (E3) 16,532
Macon (G3) 18,332
Madison (M8) 10,380
Maries (J6) 7,423
Marion (J3) 29,765
Mc Donald (D9) 14,144
Mercer (E2) 7,235
Miller (H6) 13,734
Mississippi (O9) 22,551
Moniteau (G5) 10,840
Monroe (H3) 11,314
Montgomery (K5) 11,555
Morgan (G6) 10,207
New Madrid (N9) 39,444
Newton (D9) 28,240
Nodaway (C2) 24,033
Oregon (K9) 11,978
Osage (J6) 11,301
Ozark (H9) 8,856
Pemiscot (N10) 45,624
Perry (N7) 14,890
Pettis (F5) 31,577
Phelps (J7) 21,504
Pike (K4) 16,844
Platte (C4) 14,973
Polk (F7) 16,062
Pulaski (H7) 10,392
Putnam (F2) 9,166
Ralls (J3) 8,686
Randolph (G3) 22,918
Ray (E4) 15,932
Reynolds (L8) 6,918
Ripley (L9) 11,414
St. Charles (L5) 29,834
St. Clair (E6) 10,482
St. Francois (M7) 35,276
St. Louis (M5) 406,349
St. Louis City (M5) 856,796
Ste. Genevieve (M7) 11,237
Saline (F4) 26,694
Schuyler (G2) 5,760
Scotland (H2) 7,332
Scott (N8) 32,842
Shannon (K8) 8,377
Shelby (H3) 9,730
Stoddard (N9) 33,463
Stone (F9) 9,748
Sullivan (F2) 11,299
Taney (F9) 9,863
Texas (J8) 18,992
Vernon (D7) 22,685
Warren (K5) 7,666
Washington (L7) 14,689
Wayne (L8) 10,514
Webster (G8) 15,072
Worth (D2) 5,120
Wright (H8) 15,834

CITIES and TOWNS

Aaron (D6) 15
Abo (H7)
Acorn (L9)
Adrian (D6)* 905
Advance (N8)* 733
Affton (P3)* 5,000
Agency (C3)* 234
Aholt (G4)
Aid (M9) 55
Airport Drive ‡(D8) 225
Alanthus Grove (D2) 45
Alba (D8)* 352
Albany (D2)* 1,850
Aldrich (F7)* 198
Alexandria (K2)* 465
Allbright (M8)
Allendale (D2)* 142
Allenton (N3)*
Allenville (N8)* 125
Alley Spring (K8)*
Alma (E4)* 357
Almartha (H9)*
Alpha (F3) 25
Altamont (D3)* 178
Altenburg (O7)* 272
Alton (K9)* 571
Altona (D6) 13
Amazonia (C3)* 308
Americus (J5)*
Amity (D3)* 128
Amoret (C6)* 255
Amsterdam (C6)*
Anabel (H3)* 25
Ancell (N8)* 295
Anderson (D9)* 1,073
Andover (E1) 18
Annada (L4)* 93
Annapolis (L8)* 490
Anniston (O9)* 377
Anthonies Mill (K6)*
Anutt (J7)* 250
Apex (L4)
Appleton (Old Appleton*) (N7) 120
Appleton City (E6)* 1,150
Aquilla (N9) 50
Arab (M8)*
Arbela (H2)* 87
Arbor Terrace ‡(P3) 1,150
Arbyrd (M10)* 679
Arcadia (L7)* 414
Archie (D5)* 300
Arcola (E7)* 125
Ardmore (H3) 25
Argyle (J6)* 162
Arkoe (C2)* 48
Arlington (H7)*
Armstrong (G4)* 424
Arnica (E7) 4
Arno (G9)
Arrow Rock (F4)* 170
Asbury (C8)* 210
Ash Grove (E8)* 970
Ashburn (K3)* 153
Ashland (H5)* 416
Ashley (K4)* 205
Ashton (J2)*
Atherton (R5)* 375
Atlanta (H3)* 438
Augusta (M3)* 218
Aullville (E4)* 123
Aurora (E9)* 4,153
Austin (D5) 40
Auxvasse (J4)* 507
Ava (G9)* 1,611
Avalon (F3)* 200
Avert (N9) 45
Avilla (D8)* 142
Avondale (P5)* 532
Azen (H1)
Bachelor (J5)* 20
Bado (H8)* 15
Bagnell (G6) 74
Bakersfield (H9)*
Ballard (D6) 49
Ballwin (O3)* 600
Banner (L7)*
Bardley (K9)* 75
Baring (H2)* 274
Barnard (C2)* 275
Barnesville (G3) 12
Barnett (G6)* 200
Barry (P5) 30
Bartlett (K8) 15
Bates City (E5)* 87
Battlefield (F8)
Bay (J5)*
Beaman (F5)* 45
Bearcreek (E7)* 41
Beaufort (K6)* 250
Beck (P4)
Bedford (F3) 50
Bedison (C2) 13
Bel-Nor ‡(P3)* 1,290
Bel-Ridge ‡(P3) 1,116
Belgique (N7)* 66
Belgrade (L7)*
Bell City (N8)* 482
Bella Villa ‡(P3) 557
Bellamy (D7) 25
Belle (J6)* 906
Bellefontaine (O3)
Bellerive ‡(P3) 180
Belleview (L7)*
Bellflower (K4)* 226
Belton (C5)* 1,233
Bem (K6) 18
Bennett (L9)* 3
Benton (O8)* 546
Benton City (J4)* 141
Bentonville (F6)* 11
Berdell Hills ‡(P3) 583
Berger (K5)* 210
Berkeley (P2)* 5,268
Bernie (M9)* 1,308
Bertha (H9)* 80
Bertrand (O9)* 390
Bessville (N8)*
Bethany (E2)* 2,714
Bethel (J3)* 194
Beulah (J7)* 110
Beverly (O4)* 29
Beverly Hills ‡(P3) 938
Bevier (G3)* 838
Big Piney (H7)* 80
Bigelow (B2)* 132
Billings (F8)* 597
Billingsville (G5) 10
Billmore (K9)
Birch Tree (K9)* 409
Birdspoint (O9)
Birmingham (P5)* 236
Bismarck (L7)* 1,244
Bixby (K7)* 20
Black (L7)*
Black Jack (P2) 700
Blackburn (F4)* 306
Black Walnut (P2) 20
Blackwater (G5)* 313
Blairstown (E5)* 199
Bland (J6)* 596
Bliss (L6) 20
Blodgett (O8)* 218
Bloomfield (M9)* 1,382
Bloomington (H3) 18
Bloomsdale (M6)*
Blue Lick (F4)
Blue Ridge (D2) 27
Blue Springs (R6)* 1,068
Blythedale (E2)* 238
Boaz (F8) 26
Bogard (E4)* 285
Bois D'Arc (F8)*
Bolckow (C2)* 250
Boles (M3)
Bolivar (F7)* 3,482
Bona (E7) 12
Bonfils (O2) 125
Bonne Terre (L7)* 3,533
Bonnots Mill (J5)* 150
Boomer (F3)* 30
Boonesboro (G4)* 46
Boonville (G5)* 6,686
Boss (K7)* 108
Boston (D8)* 52
Bosworth (F4)* 503
Bourbon (K6)* 543
Bowen (E5) 30
Bowers Mill (E8) 29
Bowling Green (K4)* 2,396
Bradleyville (F9)* 69
Bragg City (N10)* 294
Braggadocio (N10)* 350
Branch (G7)*
Brandsville (J9)* 204
Branson (F9)* 1,314
Brashear (H2)* 119
Brasher (N10) 152
Braymer (E3)* 955
Brays (H6)
Brazil (K7)* 25
Brazito (H6) 25
Breckenridge (E3)* 617
Breckenridge Hills‡(P3) 4,063
Brentwood (P3)* 7,504
Brewer (N7)
Brickeys (M6)*
Bridgeton (P8)* 202
Bridgeton Terrace‡(P3) 578
Brighton (F8)* 84
Brimson (E2)* 139
Brinktown (J6)* 48
Bronaugh (C7)* 214
Brookfield (F3)* 5,810
Brooklyn (D2) 30
Brookline (F8)*
Broseley (M9)* 177
Brownbranch (G9)* 13
Browning (F2)* 492
Brownington (E6)* 179
Browns Spring (F9)
Browns Station (H4)* 75
Brumley (H6)* 78
Bruner (F8)* 85
Brunot (M8)* 31
Brunswick (F4)* 1,653
Brush Creek (G7)* 91
Brushy (K8) 14
Brushyknob (G9)*
Bryant (G8) 6
Bryson (F5) 25
Buckhart (H9)* 18
Buckhorn (M8)*
Bucklin (G3)* 783
Buckner (R5)* 639
Bucoda (M10) 20
Bucyrus (H8)* 25
Buell (K4)* 69
Buffalo (F7)* 1,213
Buick (K7)* 101
Bunceton (G5)* 556
Bunker (K8)*
Burch (M8)
Burfordville (N8)* 88
Burgess (C7) 123
Burlington Jct. (B2)* 746
Burnham (J9) 74
Burton (G4) 11
Burtville (E5) 75
Busch (K3) 3
Bute (G2)
Butler (D6)* 3,333
Butterfield (E9)* 136

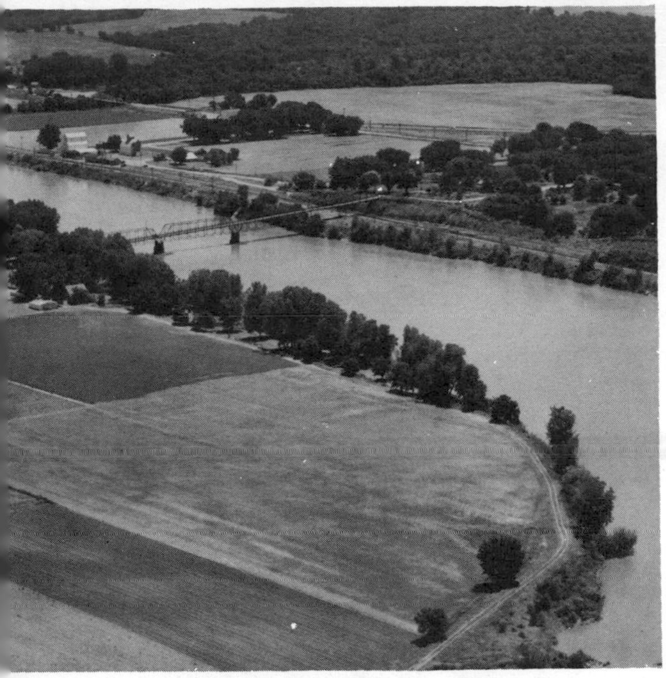

utts (K7)*........ 90
ynumville (G3)*........ 75
yrnesville (N4)........ 45
abool (H8)*........1,245
ainsville (E2)*........ 618
airo (H4)*........ 264
aledonia (L7)*........ 143
alhoun (E6)*........ 463
alifornia (H5)*........2,627
allao (G3)*........ 370
alverton Park ‡(P2)... 514
amden (D4)*........ 383
amden Point (C4)*..... 147
amdenton (G6)*........1,142
ameron (D3)*........3,570
amp Branch (F5)........ 12
ampbell (M9)*........1,931
ampbellton (K5)........ 9
analou (N9)*........ 438
ane Hill (E7)........
anton (J2)*........2,490
ape Girardeau (O8)*..21,578
aplinger Mills (E7)*.... 91
ardwell (M10)*........ 952
arl Junction (C8)*......1,006
arrington (H5)........ 18
arrollton (E4)*........4,380
arterville (D8)*........1,552
arthage (D8)*........11,188
aruth (N10)........ 150
aruthersville (N10)*....8,614
ase (K5)........ 10
assville (E9)*........1.441
astlewood (O3)........ 300
atawissa (N4)*........ 121
ato (E9)*........
atron (N9)*........ 278
aulfield (H9)*........ 58
edar City (H5)*........ 600
edar Gap (G8)*........ 45
edar Hill (L6)*........ 250
edar Springs (E7).......
edarcreek (G9)*........ 50
edargrove (J8)*........
elt (G7)*........ 50
entaur Station (N3)*.. 25
enter (J3)*........, 415
entertown (H5)*........ 248
enterview (E5)*........ 179
enterville (L8)*........ 350
entralia (H4)*........2,460
hadwick (F9)*........ 175
haffee (N8)*........3,134
hain of Rocks (M2).... 38
hamois (J5)*........ 621
handler (R4)........ 15
harity (G7)*........
harlack ‡(P3)........1,528
harleston (O9)*........5,501
herry Box (H3)........ 34
herryville (K7)*........ 25
hesterfield (O3)*........ 351
hicopee (K9)........ 100
hilhowee (E5)*........ 335
hillicothe (E3)*........8,694
hilton (L9)........ 35
hloe (E6)........
hloride (L8)*........
hula (F3)*........ 314
lair (C3)........ 10
larence (H3)*........1,123
lark (H4)*........ 276
larksburg (G5)*........ 366
larksdale (D3)*........ 282
larksville (K4)*........ 702
larkton (M10)*........1,004
laryville (N7)*........ 16
laycomo ‡(D4)........ 808
layton (P3)*........16,035
lear Springs (J8)*......
learmont (C1)*........ 283
leveland (C5)*........ 163
lever (F8)*........ 273
lifton City (G5)*........ 109
lifton Hill (G4)*........ 262
limax Springs (G6)*... 151
linton (E6)*........6,075
liquot (F7)*........ 52

Clubb (M8)*........
Clyde (C2)*........
Coal (E6)........ 33
Coatsville (G1)*........
Cockrell (R6)........ 12
Coffey (E2)*........ 253
Coffman (M7)........
Coldspring (H9)*........ 15
Cole Camp (F6)*........ 813
College Mound (G3)*.... 89
Collins (E7)*........ 199
Coloma (E3)........ 30
Colony (H2)........ 40
Columbiia (H5)*........31,974
Columbus (E5)........ 9
Commerce (O8)*........ 360
Como (N9)........ 30
Conception (C2)*........
Conception Jct. (C2)*... 285
Concordia (E5)........1,218
Connelsville (G2)........ 113
Conran (N10)*........
Converse (D4)*........ 14
Conway (G7)*........ 514
Cook Station (K7)*....... 60
Cooper Hill (J6)*........ 55
Cooter (N10)*........ 490
Cora (F2)*........ 33
Corder (E4)*........ 541
Corkery (G7)........ 5
Corning (B2)*........ 184
Cornwall (M7)*........ 100
Corridon (L8)*........ 24
Corso (K4)*........ 40
Cosby (C3)*........ 142
Cottleville (N2)*........ 162
Couch (K9)*........ 78
Country Life Acres‡(P3) 57
Country Club Hills (P2).1,731
Courtney (R5)*........ 175
Courtois (K7)*........
Cove (D9)........
Cowgill (E3)*........ 241
Cox (H3)........ 18
Coy (C9)........ 24
Craig (B2)*........ 578
Crane (E9)*........ 939
Creighton (D6)*........ 269
Crescent (O3)*........ 200
Crestwood ‡(P3)........1,645
Creve Coeur (O3)*........2,040
Crisp (E7)*........ 16
Crocker (H7)*........ 712
Cross Roads (G9)*........
Cross Timbers (F6)*..... 179
Crosstown (N7)*........ 66
Crowder (N9)*........ 133
Crown (G8)........ 23
Crystal City (M6)*........3,499
Crystal Lake Park‡(P3) 167
Cuba (K6)*........1,301
Cureall (H9)*........ 24
Curryville (K4)*........ 258
Custer (K7)........ 6
Cyclone (D9)*........ 7
Cyrene (K4)*........ 67
Dadeville (E8)*........ 208
Daisy (N7)*........ 52
Dallas (P6)........
Dalton (F4)*........ 237
Danville (J5)........ 56
Dardenne (N2)........ 26
Darien (J7)*........
Darlington (D2)*........ 217
Davis (L4)*........ 27
Davisville (K7)*........ 250
Dawn (E3)*........ 170
Dawson (H8)*........ 60
Day (F9)*........ 25
De Kalb (C3)*........ 300
De Soto (M6)*........5,357
De Witt (F4)*........ 254
Dearborn (C3)*........ 391
Decaturville (G7)*........ 25
Dederick (D7)*........ 43
Deepwater (E6)*........ 885
Deerfield (D7)*........ 200
Deering (N10)*........ 138

Defiance (N3)*........ 120
Delaware (K8)........
Dell (F6)........
Delta (N8)*........ 453
Denton (E5)*........ 150
Denton (N10)........ 126
Denver (D2)*........ 144
Des Arc (L8)*........ 376
Des Peres ‡(P3)........1,172
Deslet (K8)*........ 28
Desloge (M7)*........1,957
Deventer (O9)*........ 25
Dexter (N9)*........4,624
Diamond (D9)*........ 405
Diehlstadt (N9)*........ 165
Diggins (G8)*........ 126
Dillard (K7)*........ 51
Dillon (J7)*........ 175
Dixon (H6)*........ 988
Dodson (P6)*........1,500
Doe Run (M7)*........ 900
Doniphan (L9)*........1,611
Doolittle ‡(J7)........ 237
Dora (H9)*........ 150
Dorena (O9)*........
Dover (E4)*........ 173
Downing (H2)*........ 453
Drake (K6)........ 50
Dresden (F5)*........ 110
Drexel (C6)*........ 456
Drury (H9)*........ 24
Drynob (H7)*........
Dudenville (D8)........ 30
Dudley (M9)*........ 319
Duenweg (D8)*........ 500
Duke (H7)*........ 30
Dumas (J1)........ 5
Duncans Bridge (H3).... 65
Dunlap (F2)........ 60
Dunnegan (E7)*........
Durham (J3)*........ 264
Dutchtown (N8)*........
Eagle Rock (E9)*........ 30
Eagleville (D2)*........ 360
Easley (H5)........
East Atchison (C3)....... 110
East Kansas City (P5).. 206
East Leavenworth (O4)* 28
East Lynne (D5)*........ 204
East Prairie (O9)*.......3,033
Easton (C3)*........ 173
Ebenezer (F8)........
Economy (H3)........
Edgar Springs (J7)*.....
Edgerton (C4)*........ 408
Edina (H2)*........1,607
Edinburg (E2)........ 100
Edmundson ‡(P3)........ 621
Edwards (F6)*........ 35
Egypt Mills (O8)........ 35
El Dorado Springs
(E7)*........2,618
Eldon (G6)*........2,766
Eldridge (G7)*........ 145
Elijah (H9)*........ 33
Elk Creek (H8)*........
Elkhead (G8)*........
Elkland (F8)*........ 203
Elkton (F7)*........ 55
Ellington (L8)*........ 777
Ellisville (N3)*........ 628
Ellsinore (L9)*........ 299
Elmdale Village ‡(P3).. 641
Elmer (G3)*........ 295
Elmira (D3)*........ 128
Elmo (B1)*........ 258
Elmont (K6)........ 8
Elsberry (L4)*........1,565
Elsey (E9)*........ 105
Elston (H5)*........ 110
Elvins (L7)*........1,977
Elwood (F8)........
Ely (J3)........ 30
Embree (H8)*........ 15
Emden (J3)*........ 63
Eminence (K8)*........ 527
Emma (F5)*........ 200
Englewood (H5)*........

Enon (G6)*........ 41
Eolia (L4)*........ 476
Essex (N9)*........ 549
Estes (K4)........ 11
Esther (M7)*........2,000
Estill (G4)........ 10
Ethel (G3)*........ 226
Ethlyn (N1)*........ 50
Etlah (K5)........ 23
Eudora (E7)*........ 41
Eugene (H6)*........ 180
Eureka (N3)*........ 875
Evansville (H4)........
Eve (C7)........ 50
Eveningshade (H7)*......
Eversonville (F3)........ 23
Everton (E8)*........ 306
Ewing (J2)*........ 316
Excello (H3)*........ 95
Excelsior (G6)........
Excelsior Spgs. (R4)*...5,888
Exeter (D9)*........ 355
Fagus (M9)*........ 96
Fair Grove (F8)*........ 308
Fair Haven (D7)........ 30
Fair Play (E7)*........ 383
Fairdealing (L9)*........ 45
Fairfax (B2)*........ 806
Fairfield (F6)*........ 43
Fairmont (J2)........ 36
Fairport (D2)*........ 88
Fairview (D9)*........ 259
Fanning (K6)*........
Farber (J4)*........ 358
Farley (O4)*........ 98
Farmersville (E3)........ 40
Farmington (M7)*........4,490
Faro (M8)........ 75
Farrar (N7)*........ 71
Faucett (C3)*........ 170
Fayette (G4)*........3,144
Fayetteville (E5)*........ 100
Femme Osage (M3)...... 30
Fenton (O3)*........ 207
Ferguson (P2)*........11,573
Ferrelview (O4)*........ 126
Festus (M6)*........5,199
Fillmore (C2)*........ 284
Fisk (M9)*........ 542
Flat (J7)*........ 35
Flat River (M7)*........5,308
Flatwoods (L9)*........ 112
Flemington (F7)*........ 181
Fletcher (L6)*........ 50
Flinthill (M2)*........ 56
Flordell Hills ‡(P3)......1,214
Florence (G5)*........ 100
Florida (J4)........
Florissant (P2)*........3,737
Floyd (S5)........ 30
Foley (L4)*........ 203
Folk (H6)*........
Forbes (B3)*........ 177
Ford City (C2)*........ 59
Fordland (G8)*........ 302
Forest City (B3)*........ 484
Forest Green (G4)*........ 100
Forest Park (E9)........
Foristell (M2)*........ 165
Fornfelt (O8)*........1,539
Forsyth (F9)*........ 354
Fort Lyon (F6)........ 14
Fortescue (B2)*........ 117
Fortuna (G5)*........ 150
Foster (D6)*........ 225
Frankford (K4)*........ 449
Franklin (G4)*........ 324
Frazer (C3)........ 25
Fredericktown (M7)*....3,696
Freeburg (J6)*........ 370
Freedom (J6)*........ 35
Freeman (C5)*........ 309
Freistatt (E8)*........ 135
Fremont (K9)*........ 207
Frisco (N9)........ 31
Fristoe (F6)*........ 100
Frohna (N7)*........ 208
Frontenac (O3)........1,099
Fruitland (N8)*........ 150
Fulton (J5)*........10,052
Gads Hill (L8)........ 10
Gaines (E6)........ 2
Gainesville (G9)*........ 309
Galena (F9)*........ 439
Gallatin (E3)*........1,634
Galloway (F8)........
Galt (F2)*........ 409
Gang (K8)........ 50
Garber (F9)*........
Garden City (D5)*........ 590
Garrison (F9)*........
Garwood (L8)*........
Gasconade (J5)*........ 448
Gascondy (J6)........ 1
Gashland (P5)*........1,200
Gatewood (K9)*........ 75
Gaynor (C1)........ 12
Gentry (D2)*........ 159
Gentryville (D2)........ 70
Gerald (K6)*........ 429
Gerster (E7)*........ 47
Gibbs (H2)*........ 144
Gibson (M10)*........ 117
Gideon (N10)*........1,754
Gifford (G2)........ 16
Gilliam (F4)*........ 306
Gilman City (D2)*........ 450
Gilmore (N2)*........ 104
Gipsy (M8)*........
Girdner (G9)........ 25
Glasgow (G4)*........1,440
Glen Echo Park ‡(P3). 217
Glenallen (M8)*........ 107
Glencoe (N3)*........ 250
Glendale (P3)*........ 4,930
Glensted (G5)*........ 39
Glenwood (G1)*........ 258
Glover (L8)*........ 134
Gobler ‡(N10)*........ 116
Golden (E9)*........ 650

Golden City (D8)*........ 839
Goldsberry (G3)*........ 33
Goodfellow Ter. ‡(P3).. 503
Goodman (C9)*........ 477
Goodson (F7)*........ 60
Gordonville (N8)*........ 130
Gorin (H2)*........ 500
Goshen (E2)........ 15
Gower (C3)*........ 350
Graff (H8)*........
Graham (C2)*........ 311
Grain Valley (S6)*........ 348
Granby (D9)*........1,670
Grand Pass (F4)*........ 124
Grandin (L9)*........ 263
Grandview (P6)*........1,556
Granger (H2)*........ 122
Graniteville (L7)*........
Grant City (D2)*........1,184
Grantwood ‡(P3)........ 133
Granville (H3)........ 105
Grassy (M8)*........
Gravelton (M8)*........ 97
Gravois Mills (G6)*........ 40
Gray Summit (M3)*..... 250
Grayridge (N9)*........ 253
Grayson (D3)*........ 64
Greeley (K7)*........
Green Castle (G2)*........ 287
Green City (F2)*........ 673
Green Ridge (F5)*........ 335
Greenbrier (M8)*........ 59
Greenfield (E8)*........1,213
Greensburg (H2)*........ 40
Greentop (H2)*........ 281
Greenville (M8)*........ 270
Greenwood (R6)*........ 400
Greer (K9)........ 20
Gregory Landing (K2)*. 33
Grogan (J8)*........
Grover (O3)*........ 300
Grovespring (G8)*........ 104
Guilford (C2)*........ 164
Gunn City (D5)*........ 57
Guthrie (H5)*........ 65
Hadley (L8)........
Hahatonka (G7)........
Hale (F3)*........ 452
Half Way (F7)*........ 150
Hallsville (H4)*........ 225
Halltown (E8)*........ 99
Hamburg (N3)........ 30
Hamilton (E3)*........1,728
Hammond (G9)*........
Hampton (O4)........ 20
Hancock (H7)*........ 72
Handy (K9)*........ 65
Hanley Hills ‡(P3)......2,219
Hannibal (K3)*........20,444
Hannon (D7)*........ 43
Hardin (E4)*........ 747
Harris (F2)*........ 181
Harrisburg (H4)*........ 117
Harrisonville (D5)*.......2,530
Hart (G3)........ 32
Hartsburg (H5)*........ 171
Hartshorn (J8)*........ 63
Hartville (G8)*........ 526
Hartwell (E6)*........ 50
Harvester (O2)........ 75
Harviell (M9)*........ 190
Harwood (D7)*........ 141
Hastain (F6)*........
Hatfield (D1)*........ 64
Hattie (J8)*........ 114
Hawk Point (K5)*........ 254
Hayden (H6)*........ 11
Hayti (N10)*........3,302
Hazelwood ‡(P3)........ 336
Hazlegreen (H7)*........ 41
Helena (C3)*........
Hematite (L6)*........ 250
Hemple (D3)*........ 75
Henderson Mound (O9). 22
Hendrickson (M9)*........
Henley (H6)*........ 64
Henrietta (E4)*........ 462
Herculaneum (M6)*......1,603
Hercules (G9)........
Hermann (K5)*........2,523
Hermitage (F7)*........ 204
Hickman Mills (P6)*....1,325
Hickory Creek (E3)....... 25
Higbee (H4)*........ 674
Higginsville (E4)*........3,428
High Hill (K5)*........ 224
High Point (G5)*........
High Ridge (O4)*........
Highlandville (F9)*........ 46
Hilliard (M9)........ 75
Hillsboro (L6)*........ 390
Hillsdale ‡(P3)........2,902
Hinch (K6)*........ 50
Hinton (H4)........ 40
Hiram (M8)*........ 48
Hitt (H1)........ 15
Hoberg (E8)*........ 90
Hobson (J7)*........ 42
Hodge (E4)*........ 141
Hofflin (K6)........ 2
Hogan (L7)........ 74
Holcomb (N10)*........ 505
Holden (E5)*........1,765
Holland (N10)*........ 409
Holliday (H3)*........ 196
Hollister (F9)*........ 542
Hollow (N3)........
Hollywood (M10)*........ 79
Holmes Park (P6)*........ 100
Holstein (K5)*........
Holt (D4)*........ 270
Hooker (H7)*........ 50
Hope (J5)*........ 50
Hopewell Academy (K5) 25
Hopkins (C1)*........ 825
Horine (M6)........
Hornersville (M10)*...... 875
Horton (D7)*........ 48
House Springs (O4)*..... 151
Houston (J8)*........1,277

Houstonia (F5)*........ 309
Howards Ridge (H9)*... 4
Howell (N3)........
Howes Mill (K7)*........
Howland (F1)........ 4
Huggins (H8)*........ 14
Hughesville (F5)*........ 180
Hugo (G7)........ 10
Humansville (E7)*........ 803
Hume (C6)*........ 474
Humphreys (F2)*........ 185
Hunnewell (J3)*........ 293
Hunter (L9)*........ 134
Huntleigh ‡(P3)........ 180
Huntsdale (H5)*........ 50
Huntsville (H4)*........1,520
Hurdland (H2)*........ 268
Hurley (F9)*........ 250
Hutton Valley (J9)*...... 108
Huzzah (K7)*........
Iantha (D8)*........ 166
Iatan (C4)*........
Iberia (H6)*........ 595
Iconium (E6)*........ 40
Ilasco (K3)*........
Illmo (O8)*........1,247
Imperial (P4)........
Impo (H8)*........
Independence (R5)*....36,963
Industrial City (C3)*....
Ink (J8)*........ 35
Ionia (F6)*........ 120
Ira (G7)........
Irena (D1)........ 15
Irondale (L7)*........ 443
Ironton (L7)*........1,148
Irwin (D7)*........ 55
Isabella (G9)*........
Isbell Station (J5)........
Jack (J7)*........ 3
Jackson (N8)*........3,707
Jacksonville (G3)*........ 177
Jadwin (K8)*........ 4
Jameson (E2)*........ 185
Jamesport (E3)*........ 720
Jamestown (G5)*........ 245
Jane (D9)*........
Jasper (D8)*........ 776
Jaudon (C5)........ 30
Jeff (K9)........ 10
JEFFERSON CITY
(H5)*........25,099
Jeffriesburg (K6)........
Jenkins (E9)*........ 39
Jennings (P2)*........15,282
Jerico Springs (E7)*..... 235
Jerome (J7)*........ 250
Jewett (L8)........ 125
Jobe (K9)........
Johnstown (D6)........ 24
Jonesburg (K5)*........ 433
Joplin (D8)*........38,711
Jordan (F6)*........
Josephville (N2)........ 70
Joy (J8)*........ 25
Kahoka (J2)*........1,847
Kaiser (G6)*........ 50
Kansas City (P5)*......456,622
Kansas City (urban
area)........689,350
Kearny (D4)*........ 570
Kelso (O8)*........ 276
Kendall (J3)........ 3
Kennett (M10)*........8,685
Kenoma (D8)*........ 65
Kenwood (H2)........ 15
Keota (G3)........ 35
Kewanee (N9)*........ 96
Keysville (K7)*........ 50
Keytesville (G4)*........ 733
Kidder (D3)*........ 222
Kilwinning (H1)........ 17
Kimmswick (M6)*........ 207
Kinderpost (J7)*........
King City (D2)*........1,031
Kingston (E3)*........ 338
Kingsville (D5)*........ 207
Kinloch (P2)........5,957
Kirk (N10)........ 40
Kirksville (H2)*........11,110
Kirkwood (O3)*........18,640
Kissee Mills (G9)*........ 63
Klondike (M3)........
Knob Lick (M7)*........
Knob Noster (E5)*........ 585
Knox City (H2)*........ 362
Knoxville (E4)........ 100
Koch (P4)*........
Koenig (J6)........
Koshkonong (J9)*........ 333
Krakow (K6)*........
La Belle (J2)*........ 840
La Due (E6)*........
La Grange (K2)*........1,106
La Monte (F5)*........ 502
La Plata (H2)*........1,331
La Valle (N9)*........ 35
Labadie (N3)*........ 300
Laclede (F3)*........ 544
Laddonia (J4)*........ 599
Ladue (P3)........5,386
Laflin (N8)*........ 26
Lake City (S5)........ 25
Lake Ozark (G6)*........ 350
Lake Spring (J7)*........ 35
Lakeshire ‡(P3)........ 295
Lakeview Heights (F6)* 30
Lamar (D8)*........3,233
Lambert (O8)........ 39
Lampe (F9)*........
Lanagan (C9)*........ 368
Lancaster (H1)*........ 856
Lanes Prairie (J6)........
Langdon (A2)*........
Lanton (J9)*........ 66
Laquey (H7)*........ 39
Laredo (E2)*........ 426
Larussell (D8)*........ 82
Latham (G5)*........ 172
Lathrop (D3)*........ 888

Latour (D5)*........ 80
Lawrenceburg (E8)........ 53
Lawrenceton (M6)........
Lawson (D4)*........ 486
Leadwood (L7)*........1,479
Leann (E9)........ 25
Leasburg (K6)*........ 178
Lebanon (G7)*........6,808
Lebo (J9)........
Lecoma (J7)*........ 55
Leeper (L8)*........ 375
Lee's Summit (R6)*.....2,554
Leesville (E6)........ 72
Leeton (E5)*........ 372
Leila (E7)........ 10
Lemons (F2)*........ 176
Lenox (J7)*........ 70
Lentner (H3)*........ 65
Leonard (H3)*........ 165
Leora (M9)*........ 45
Leota (H9)*........ 15
Leslie (K6)*........ 114
Lesterville (L8)*........ 163
Levasy (S5)*........ 139
Lewis Station (E6)........ 33
Lewistown (J2)*........ 415
Lexington (E4)*........5,074
Liberal (D7)*........ 739
Liberty (R5)*........4,709
Licking (J8)*........ 733
Liege (K5)*........ 77
Lilbourn (N9)*........1,361
Lincoln (F6)*........ 316
Linden (P5)*........ 800
Linkville (P4)........ 50
Linn (J5)*........ 758
Linn Creek (G6)*........ 162
Linneus (F3)*........ 513
Lisbon (G4)........ 25
Lisle (C5)*........
Lithium (N7)*........ 57
Little Blue (R6)........ 250
Little Compton (F3).....
Livonia (G1)*........ 193
Lixville (N7)........
Lock Springs (E3)*...... 137
Lockwood (E8)*........ 791
Lodi (M8)*........ 34
Lohman (H5)*........ 123
Lonedell (L6)*........
Lonejack (S6)*........ 200
Long Lane (G7)*........
Longhorn Village ‡(K7) 41
Longtown (N7)*........ 139
Longwood (F5)*........ 52
Look Out (F5)........
Loose Creek (J5)*........
Loring (H8)*........
Louisburg (F7)*........
Louisiana (K4)*........4,389
Low Wassie (K9)........ 44
Lowndes (M8)*........ 100
Lowry City (E6)*........ 493
Lucerne (F2)*........ 227
Ludlow (E3)*........ 260
Luebbering (L6)*........
Lupus (H5)*........ 97
Luray (J2)*........ 184
Lutesville (M8)*........ 694
Luxemburg (P3)........
Lynchburg (H7)*........ 50
Lyons (H7)........
Mabel (D3)........ 10
Machens (P2)*........ 86
Mackenzie ‡(P3)........ 247
Macks Creek (G7)*........ 108
Macon (H3)*........4,152
Madison (H4)*........ 571
Madisonville (J4)........
Magnolia (E5)*........
Maitland (B2)*........ 456
Malden (M9)*........3,396
Malta Bend (F4)*........ 414
Mammoth (G9)*........
Manchester (O3)*........
Mandeville (E3)........ 25
Manes (H8)*........ 120
Manila (F5)........ 4
Manley (M10)........ 75
Mansfield (G8)*........ 963
Many Springs (K9)........ 25
Maples (J7)*........ 14
Maple Park (P5)........
Maplewood (P3)*........13,416
Marble Hill (N8)*........ 454
Marceline (F3)*........3,172
Marcoot (K7)........
Margona ‡(P3)........ 306
Marion (H5)*........ 50
Marionville (E8)*........1,167
Marlborough ‡(P3)...... 219
Marquand (M8)........ 369
Marshall (F4)*........8,850
Marshfield (G8)*........1,925
Marston (N9)*........ 610
Marthasville (L5)*........ 347
Martinsburg (J4)*........ 296
Martinsville (D2)*........ 90
Martin City (P6)*........ 350
Mary Ridge ‡(P3)........ 528
Maryland Heights (O2)*
Maryville (C2)*........6,834
Matson (N3)*........ 60
Matthews (N9)*........ 498
Maud (H3)........ 30
Maupin (L6)........
Maurine (E5)........ 9
Max (K7)*........
Mayfield (M8)*........
Maysville (D3)*........ 973
Mayview (E4)*........ 268
Maywood (J3)*........ 149
Mc Baine (H5)*........ 75
Mc Bride (N7)*........ 75
Mc Credie (J5)*........ 90
Mc Fall (D2)*........ 255
Mc Kittrick (J5)*........ 100
Meacham Park (P3).....
Meadville (F3)*........ 446
Medill (J2)*........
Melbourne (E2)*........ 102

Melrose (N3) 15
Memphis (H2)* 2,035
Mendon (F3)* 349
Mendota (G1) 2
Menfro (N7)* 80
Mercer (F2)* 377
Merwin (C6)* 88
Meta (H6)* 353
Metz (C6)* 178
Mexico (J4)* 11,623
Miami (F4)* 217
Middle Grove (H4) 48
Middletown (J4)* 240
Midridge (K8)* 75
Milan (F2)* 1,972
Milford (D7)* 100
Mill Grove (E2)*
Mill Spring (L8)*
Millard (G2) 100
Millcreek (M7)* 75
Miller (E8)* 615
Millersburg (H5)* 40
Millville (E4) 150
Milo (D7)* 124
Mincy (F9)* 6
Mindenmines (D8)* 425
Mine La Motte (M7)*
Mineola (J5)* 75
Mineral Point (L7)* 304
Mingo (M9)* 200
Minnith (M7)*
Mirabile (D3) 60
Missouri City (R5)* 344
Moberly (G4)* 13,115
Modena (E2)* 95
Mokane (J5)* 477
Moline Acres ‡(R2) 99
Molino (J4)* 31
Monett (E9)* 4,771
Monroe City (J3)* 2,093
Montauk (J8)* 20
Monterey (L7)*
Montevallo (D7)* 53
Montgomery City(K5)* 1,679
Monticello (J2)* 154
Montier (J8)* 55
Montreal (G7)* 83
Montrose (E6)* 518
Montserrat (E5)* 130
Moody (J9)* 100
Mooresville (E3)* 134
Mora (F5)* 75
Morehouse (N9)* 1,635
Morgan (G7)* 55
Morley (N8)* 494
Morrellton (K6)*
Morrison (J5)* 291
Morrisville (F8)* 296
Morse Mill (L6)*
Morton (E4) 16
Mosby (R4)* 213
Moscow Mills (M1)* 350
Moselle (M4)* 130
Mound City (B2)* 1,412
Moundville (C7)* 168
Mount Leonard (F4)* 142
Mount Moriah (E2)* 260
Mount Vernon (E8)* 2,057
Mountain Grove (H8)* 3,106
Mountain View (J8)* 892
Mount Washington (R5)
Munger (L7)
Murphy (O4) 160
Musselfork (G3) 19
Myrtle (K9)* 95
Napier (B2)
Napoleon (E4)* 143
Napton (F4)* 80
Nashua (P4)*
Nashville (D8)* 50
Nauvoo (F9) 4
Naylor (L9)* 520
Nebo (H7)* 30
Neck (C8)* 117
Neelys Landing (O7)*
Neelyville (M9)* 457
Nelson (F4)* 297
Nelsonville (J3)
Nemo (F7)
Neola (E7) 3
Neosho (D9)* 5,790
Netherlands (N10)* 72
Nevada (D7)* 8,009
New Bloomfield (J5)* 400
New Boston (G3)* 86
New Cambria (G3)* 295
New Florence (K5)* 522
New Frankfort (F4) 50
New Franklin (G4)* 1,060
New Hamburg (O8)* 156
New Hampton (D2)* 375
New Hartford (K4)* 38
New Haven (K5)* 1,009
New Hope (L4) 175
New Liberty (K9) 10
New London (K3)* 858
New Madrid (O9)* 2,726
New Market (C4)*
New Melle (M2)* 150
New Offenburg (M7)* 111
New Point (B2)* 80
New Wells (N7)* 48
Newark (H2)* 156
Newburg (J7)* 949
Newland (F5) 11
Newtonia (D9)* 190
Newtown (F2)* 231
Niangua (G8)* 344
Nind (G2) 25
Nishnabotna (B2)* 21
Nixa (F8)* 509
Noble (G9)*
Nodaway (C3)* 65
Noel (D9)* 685
Norborne (E4)* 1,114
Normandy (P3)* 2,306
North Fork (H3) 10
N. Kansas City (P5)* 3,886
North Salem (G3)*
Northmoor (P5)
Northview (G8)* 200
Northwoods ‡(P3) 1,602
Northwye (J7) 99
Norton (F4)*
Norwood (H8)*
Norwood Court ‡(P9) 72
Nottinghill (G9)* 11
Novelty (H2)* 188
Novinger (G2)* 734
Oak (C3)
Oak Grove (S6)* 761
Oak Hill (K6)
Oak Ridge (N7)* 202
Oakland (G7)* 15
Oakland (P3) 1,041
Oakside (J8)
Oakton (D8) 14
Oakville (P4)
Oakwood (K3)*
Oasis (F9)
Ocie (G9)*
Octa (M10) 20
Odessa (E5)* 1,969
Oermann (L6)*
O'Fallon (N2)* 789
Ohio (E6) 10
Olathe (H8) 20
Old Appleton (N7)* 120
Old Monroe (N1)* 268
Old Mines (L6)*
Olden (J9) 61
Olean (G6)* 165
Olivette ‡(P3) 1,761
Olney (K4)* 93
Omaha (G1) 10
Ongo (G9)
Oran (N8)* 1,156
Orchardfarm (O2)* 50
Oregon (B2)* 870
Orla (G7)* 9
Oronogo (D8)* 519
Orrick (O5)* 675
Osa (E9) 15
Osage Beach (G6) 237
Osage City (H5)* 250
Osborn (D3)* 237
Osceola (E6)* 1,082
Osgood (F2)* 173
Oskaloosa (D7)* 72
Otterville (G5)* 414
Overland (P3)* 11,566
Owensville (K6)* 1,946
Owls Bend (K8)* 75
Oxly (L9)* 150
Oyer (E7) 12
Ozark (F8)* 1,087
Pacific (N4)* 1,985
Pagedale (P3) 3,866
Palmer (L7)* 60
Palmyra (J3)* 2,295
Panama (D6)
Papinsville (D6) 55
Paradise (D4) 120
Paris (J4)* 1,407
Parker (C2)
Parkville (O5)* 1,186
Parma (N9)* 1,163
Parnell (C2)* 362
Pasadena Hills ‡(P2) 1,102
Pasadena Park ‡(P2) 682
Pascola (N10)* 242
Passaic (D6)* 75
Patterson (L8)* 125
Patton (M7)* 162
Pattonsburg (D2)* 883
Pattonville (P2)*
Paynesville (L4)*
Peace Valley (J9)* 68
Peach Orchard ‡(N10)* 59
Peculiar (D5)* 267
Peerless Park (O3) 119
Peers (K5)* 25
Pennsboro (E8) 17
Pennville (F2) 18
Perkins (N8)* 164
Perrin (D3)*
Perry (J4)* 813
Perryville (N7)* 4,591
Pershing (J5)* 36
Peruque (O2)* 85
Pevely (M6)* 416
Phelps City (A2)* 139
Phenix (F8)
Philadelphia (J3)* 200
Phillipsburg (G7)* 170
Pickering (C2)* 213
Piedmont (L8)* 1,548
Pierce City (E8)* 1,156
Pilot Grove (G5)* 635
Pilot Knob (L7)* 582
Pine (K9)* 100
Pine Lawn (P3)* 6,425
Pineville (D9)* 464
Piney Park ‡(L6) 21
Pioneer (E9) 45
Piper (D6) 25
Pittsburg (F7)* 56
Pittsville (E5)* 56
Plad (G7)* 30
Plato (H8)* 35
Platte City (C4)* 742
Platte Woods ‡(C4) 159
Plattsburg (D3)* 1,655
Pleasant Gap (D6) 15
Pleasant Green (F5)* 24
Pleasant Hill (D5)* 2,200
Pleasant Hope (F8)* 174
Plevna (H3)* 120
Plymouth (E3) 35
Pocahontas (N8)* 130
Point Pleasant (O10)* 101
Polk (F7)*
Pollock (F2)*
Polo (D3)* 549
Pomona (J9)* 300
Pond (N3) 260
Ponder (L9)* 9
Pontiac (G9)* 37
Poplar Bluff (L9)* 15,064
Portageville (N10)* 2,662
Portage Des Sioux(P2)* 264
Portia (D7) 5
Portland (J5)* 200
Postoak (E5)* 52
Potosi (L7)* 2,359
Pottersville (H9)* 25
Powe (M9) 95
Powersville (F1)* 227
Poynor (L9)* 40
Prairie Hill (G3)* 124
Prairie Home (G5)* 208
Prescott (J8)*
Preston (F7)* 109
Priceland ‡(E6) 124
Princeton (E2)* 1,506
Prior (H8) 4
Proctor (G6) 2
Prosperine (G7)* 7
Prospect Hill (R2)
Protem (G9)* 60
Purcell (D8)* 334
Purdin (F3)* 255
Purdy (E9)* 437
Pure Air (G2) 10
Purvis (G6)
Puxico (M9)* 749
Quaker (L7)*
Quarles (E6) 10
Queen City (H2)* 554
Quincy (F6)* 36
Quitman (C2)* 135
Qulin (M9)* 426
Racine (C9)* 150
Racket (F6) 27
Racola (L6)
Rader (G8)
Rainey (E7)
Randles (N8)* 169
Rat (K8)* 3
Ravanna (E2)* 132
Ravenwood (C2)* 319
Rayborn (H8)*
Raymondville (J8)* 175
Raymore (D5)* 208
Raytown (P6)*
Rayville (E4)* 193
Rea (C2)* 110
Readsville (J5)* 21
Red Bird (J6)
Red Oak (D8) 30
Redford (L8)* 60
Redtop (F7)* 50
Reeds (D8)* 136
Reeds Spring (F9)* 313
Reger (F2)* 103
Renick (H4)* 157
Rensselaer (J3)* 63
Republic (E8)* 965
Revere (J2)* 180
Reynolds (K8)*
Rhineland (J5)* 198
Rhyse (J7)* 25
Rich Fountain (J6)*
Rich Hill (D6)* 1,820
Richards (D7)* 190
Richland (H7)* 1,133
Richmond (D4)* 4,299
Richmond Hts. (P3)* 15,045
Richwoods (L6)* 250
Ridgedale (F9)*
Ridgeway (D2)* 560
Rinehart (D7)
Risco (N9)* 495
Ritchey (D9)* 137
Rivermines (L7)* 485
Rives (M10)* 166
Roanoke (G4)* 65
Robertson (P2)* 1,200
Robertsville (N4)* 117
Roby (H7)* 28
Rocheport (H5)* 376
Rock Creek (O4) 35
Rock Hill (P3)* 3,847
Rockbridge (H9)*
Rockport (B2)* 1,511
Rockville (D6)* 372
Rocky Comfort (D9)* 230
Rocky Mount (G6)* 4
Rogersville (G8)* 321
Rolla (J7)* 9,354
Rombauer (M9)*
Rome (G9)* 25
Rosati (J6)* 650
Roscoe (E7)* 128
Rosebud (K6)* 254
Rosendale (C2)* 245
Rothville (F3)* 152
Round Spring (J8)*
Rover (J9)
Ruble (L8)* 75
Ruegg (P2) 200
Rueter (G9)*
Rush Hill (J4)* 127
Rushville (B3)* 319
Russ (G7) 50
Russellville (H6)* 336
Rutledge (H2)* 217
Sabula (L8)* 60
Saco (M8)* 75
Safe (J6)* 25
Saginaw (C8)*
Sagrada (F6)
St. Albans (N3)* 30
St. Ann (P3) 4,557
St. Anthony (H6)* 30
St. Catharine (G3)* 80
St. Charles (O2)* 14,314
St. Clair (L6)* 1,779
St. Elizabeth (H6)* 59
St. Francisville (J2) 275
St. Francois (M7)* 295
St. George (H8)* 642
St. James (J6)* 1,811
St. Johns (P2)* 2,499
St. Joseph (C3)* 78,588
St. Joseph (urban area) 79,280
St. Louis (P3)* 856,796
St. Louis (urban area) 1,394,051
St. Marys (M7)* 635
St. Patrick (J2)* 53
St. Paul (N2)* 102
St. Peters (N2)* 377
Ste. Genevieve (M6)* 3,992
Salem (J7)* 3,611
Salem (Coffey*) (D2) 253
Saline (E1) 25
Salisbury (G4)* 1,676
Sammylane (F9)
Sampson (G8) 5
Sands (O2)
Sandstone (D7)
Sandyhook (G5)* 57
Sank (N8)* 6
Santa Fe (J4)* 83
Santa Rosa (D3)*
Santiago (F6)
Sappington (P3)*
Sarcoxie (D8)* 1,042
Sargent (H8)
Savannah (C3)* 2,332
Severton (K3)* 150
Schell City (D6)* 400
Schluersburg (N3) 30
Schuermann Hts.‡(P3) 306
Scopus (N8)*
Seckman (P4)
Sedalia (F5)* 20,354
Sedgewickville (N7)* 92
Seligman (D9)*
Senath (M10)* 1,528
Seneca (C9)* 1,195
Seventysix (N7)* 14
Seymour (G8)* 1,015
Shackleford (F4)* 55
Shafter (F3) 10
Shamrock (J4)* 23
Shelbina (H3)* 2,113
Shelby (F3) 32
Shelbyville (H3)* 635
Sheldon (D7)* 427
Shell Knob (E9)* 25
Sheridan (C1)* 370
Sherman (O3)* 225
Shirley (L7)*
Shook (M8)* 5
Shrewsbury (P3) 3,382
Sibley (O5)* 200
Sidney (G2) 6
Sikeston (N9)* 11,640
Silex (K4)* 188
Siloam Springs (H9)*
Silva (M8)* 66
Silver Lake (M7)* 53
Simmons (H8)* 50
Skidmore (B2)* 485
Slater (G4)* 2,836
Sleeper (G7)* 131
Sligo (K7)* 35
Smallett (G9)* 12
Smithfield (C8) 150
Smithton (F5)* 339
Smithville (D4)* 947
Sni Mills (S6) 25
Snyder (F3)* 150
Solo (J8)*
South Fork (J9)* 20
South Gifford (G3)* 128
South Gorin (H2) 303
South Greenfield (E8)* 186
South Lineville (E1) 92
South West City (D9)* 595
Spalding (J3) 25
Spanish Lake (P2)
Sparta (F9)* 244
Spencerburg (K4) 35
Spickard (F2)* 517
Splitlog (D9) 50
Spokane (F9)* 55
Spoonerville (M9) 500
Sprague (D6) 29
Spring City (C9) 140
Spring Creek (J7) 85
Spring Fork (F5)* 120
Spring Garden (H6) 46
Springfield (F8)* 66,731
Springfield (urban area) 75,117
Springhill (E3) 28
Spruce (D6)* 39
Spurgeon (C9) 25
Squires (G9)*
Stahl (G2) 5
Stanberry (C2)* 1,651
Standish (F4)* 24
Stanton (K6)* 250
Stark City (D9)* 154
Steele (N10)* 2,360
Steelville (K7)* 1,157
Steffenville (J3)* 75
Stella (D9)* 177
Stet (E4)*
Stewartsville (C3)* 414
Stickney (J6)*
Stockton (E7)* 811
Stone Hill (K7)*
Stotesbury (C7)* 71
Stotts City (E8)* 285
Stoutland (G7)* 192
Stoutsville (J3)* 146
Stover (G6)* 693
Strafford (F8)* 300
Strasburg (D5)* 180
Strother (J4)
Sturdivant (M8)* 103
Sturgeon (H4)* 544
Sturges (E3)
Sublette (G2)
Success (H8)* 45
Sudheimer (H6)
Sue City (H3)
Sugar Creek (R5)* 1,858
Sugar Tree (E4) 16
Sullivan (K6)* 3,019
Sulphur Springs (M6)* 135
Summerfield (J6)* 75
Summersville (J8)* 306
Sumner (F3)* 309
Sunnyvale ‡(D9) 28
Swart (C7) 1
Swedeborg (H7)* 150
Sweden (H9)*
Sweet Springs (F5)* 1,439
Swinton (M8)* 65
Swiss (K5) 21
Sycamore (H9)* 44
Sycamore Hills ‡(P3) 989
Syracuse (G5)* 221
Taberville (E6)* 100
Taitsville (E4) 5
Tallapoosa (N9)*
Taneyville (F9)* 132
Tarkio (B2)* 2,221
Tarsney (S6)
Tauria (F9) 25
Taylor (J3)* 60
Tea (K6) 15
Tebbetts (J5)* 150
Tecumseh (H9)* 36
Ten Brook (P4)
Teresita (J9)* 6
Thayer (J9)* 1,639
Thomasville (J9)* 70
Thompson (J4)* 70
Thornfield (G9)* 30
Tiff (L6)* 75
Tiff City (C9)*
Tiffin (E7)* 100
Tigris (G8) 15
Tilsit (N8) 53
Timber (K8)* 15
Tina (F3)* 224
Tindall (E2)* 102
Tipton (G5)* 1,234
Tolona (J2)
Topaz (H9) 4
Torch (L9)* 15
Toronto (G6)
Town and Country ‡(P3) 162
Townley (M9) 50
Tracy (C4)* 201
Trenton (E2)* 6,157
Trimble (D4)* 141
Triplett (F4)* 301
Troy (L5)* 1,738
Truesdail (K5)* 235
Truxton (K4)* 125
Tunas (F7)*
Turley (H8)
Turners (F8)*
Turney (D3)* 152
Turtle (K7)* 28
Tuscumbia (H6)* 221
Twin Bridges (H9)* 22
Twin Oaks ‡(P3) 81
Tyler (N10)* 150
Tyrone (J8)* 45
Ulman (H6)* 75
Union (L6)* 2,917
Union Star (C2)* 373
Uniontown (N7)*
Unionville (G2) 2,050
University City (P3)* 39,892
Uplands Park ‡(P3) 563
Upton (H8)*
Urbana (F7)* 359
Urbandale (G4) 35
Urich (E6)* 400
Utica (E3)* 475
Vale (R6)
Valles Mines (L6)* 225
Valley City (E5) 30
Valley Park (O3)* 2,956
Van (F7) 11
Van Buren (L8)* 708
Vancleve (H6)
Vandalia (J4)* 2,624
Vanduser (N9)* 281
Vanzant (H9)* 20
Velda ‡(P3) 480
Velda Village Hills ‡(P3) 1,527
Verona (E9)* 396
Versailles (G6)* 1,929
Vibbard (D4) 83
Viburnum (K7)* 53
Vichy (J6)* 150
Victoria (M6)* 250
Vida (J7)* 50
Vienna (H6)* 471
Vigus (O2)* 400
Villa Ridge (M4)* 1
Vineland (L6)*
Vinita Park ‡(P3) 1,8
Vinita Terrace ‡(P3) 3
Viola (E9)*
Virginia (G6)
Vista (E7)*
Vulcan (L8)* 2
Waco (C8)* 1
Wakenda (F4)* 2
Waldron (O5)*
Walker (D7)* 2
Wallace (C3)*
Walnut Grove (F8)* 3
Wappapello (M9)* 2
Wardell (N10)* 4
Warren (J3)*
Warrensburg (E5)* 6,8
Warrenton (K5)* 1,5
Warsaw (F6)* 9
Warson Woods ‡(P3) 5
Washburn (E9)* 2
Washington (K5)* 6,8
Watkins (H6)
Watson (A1)* 1
Waverly (E4)* 8
Wayland (J2)* 3
Wayne (E9)*
Waynesville (H7)* 1,0
Weatherby (D3)* 1
Weaubleau (F7)* 4
Webb City (C8)* 6,9
Webster Groves (P3)* 23,3
Weldon Spring (O2)*
Wellington (E4)* 6
Wellston (P3)* 9,3
Wellsville (K4)* 1,5
Wentworth (D8)* 2
Wentzville (M2)* 1,2
Wesco (K7)* 1
West Line (C5)*
West Eminence (J8)* 1
West Fork (K8)*
West Plains (J9)* 4,9
Westalton (R2)* 4
Westboro (B1)* 2
Weston (C4)* 1,0
Westphalia (J6)* 3
Westville (G3)
Wheatland (F7)* 2
Wheaton (E9)* 3
Wheeling (F3)*
Whiteoak (M10)*
Whiteside (K4)*
Whitesville (C2)*
Whitewater (N8)* 1
Whiting (O9) 1
Wilbur Park ‡(P3) 7
Wilcox (C2)* 1
Wilderness (K9)* 1
Willard (F8)* 3
Willhoit (H9)*
Williamsburg (J5)*
Williamstown (J2)* 1
Williamsville (L9)* 4
Willmathsville (G2)*
Willow Springs (H9)* 1,9
Winchester (J2)
Winchester ‡(O3) 1
Windsor (E5)* 2,4
Windyville (F7)*
Winfield (L5)* 4
Winigan (G2)* 1
Winkler (J7)
Winnipeg (H7)*
Winona (K8)* 4
Winston (D3)* 2
Wisdom (F6)*
Wishart (F7)*
Wittenberg (O7)*
Wolf Island (O9)*
Womack (M7)*
Woodland (J3)
Woodlawn (H3)
Woodson Terrace ‡(P3) 6
Wooldridge (G5)* 1
Worland (C6)*
Worth (C2)* 1
Worthington (G2)* 1
Wright City (K5)* 5
Wyaconda (J2)* 4
Wyatt (O9)* 3
Yancy Mills (J7)*
Yarrow (G2)*
Yates (G4)*
Youngers (H4)
Yount (M7)*
Yukon (J8)*
Zalma (N8)* 1
Zanoni (H9)*
Zeta (N9)
Zion (M8)*

MONTANA

Map on Page 73

Total Population 591,024

57 COUNTIES

Beaverhead (C5) 6,671
Big Horn (J5) 9,824
Blaine (G2) 8,516
Broadwater (E4) 2,922
Carbon (G5) 10,241
Carter (M5) 2,798
Cascade (E3) 53,027
Chouteau (F3) 6,974
Custer (L4) 12,661
Daniels (L2) 3,946
Dawson (M3) 9,092
Deer Lodge (C5) 16,553
Fallon (M4) 3,660
Fergus (G3) 14,015
Flathead (B2) 31,495
Gallatin (E5) 21,902
Garfield (J3) 2,172
Glacier (C2) 9,645
Golden Valley (G4) 1,337
Granite (C4) 2,773
Hill (F2) 14,285
Jefferson (D4) 4,014
Judith Basin (F4) 3,200
Lake (B3) 13,835
Lewis and Clark (D3) 24,540
Liberty (E2) 2,180
Lincoln (A2) 8,693
Madison (D5) 5,998
Mc Cone (L3) 3,258
Meagher (F4) 2,079
Mineral (B3) 2,081
Missoula (C3) 35,493
Musselshell (H4) 5,408
Park (F5) 11,999
Petroleum (H3) 1,026
Phillips (J2) 6,334
Pondera (D2) 6,392
Powder River (L5) 2,693
Powell (D4) 6,301
Prairie (L4) 2,377
Ravalli (B4) 13,101
Richland (M3) 10,366
Roosevelt (L2) 9,580
Rosebud (K4) 6,570
Sanders (A3) 6,983
Sheridan (M2) 6,674
Silver Bow (D5) 48,422
Stillwater (G5) 5,416
Sweet Grass (G5) 3,621
Teton (D3) 7,232
Toole (E2) 6,867
Treasure (J4) 1,402
Valley (K2) 11,353
Wheatland (G4) 3,187
Wibaux (M4) 1,907
Yellowstone (H4) 55,875
Yellowstone Nat'l. Park† (F6) 58

† Population for Montana part only. See Wyoming and Idaho.

CITIES and TOWNS

Abe (E5)
Aberdeen (J5) 8
Absarokee (G5)* 423
Accola (E5)
Acton (H5)* 14
Agawam (D2)* 17
Alberton (B3)* 326
Albion (M5)* 6
Alder (D5)* 100
Alhambra (E4) 45
Alice (J4)
Aloe (D2)
Alpine (G5)*
Alta (B5) 4
Alzada (M5)* 75
Amazon (E4) 1
Amsterdam (E5) 65
Anaconda (C4)* 11,254
Anceney (E5) 10
Andes (M3)* 32
Angela (K4)* 7
Antelope (M2)* 125
Apex (D5)
Apgar (C2) 76
Archer (M2)* 5
Arlee (B3)* 300
Armells (G3) 3
Armington (F3)* 120
Armstead (D6)* 207
Arrow Creek (F3) 25
Ashland (K5)* 150
Ashuelot (E3)
Augusta (D3)* 475
Austin (D4)* 50
Avon (D4)* 200
Avondale (K2) 5
Axtell (L3) 50
Babb (C2)* 25
Bainville (M2)* 356
Baker (M4)* 1,772
Ballantine (J5)* 298
Bannack (C5)
Barber (G4)* 60
Bascom (J4)
Basin (D4)* 300
Battrick (H4) 3
Bay Horse (L5)* 39
Bear Spring (G3) 50
Bearcreek (G5)* 162
Bearmouth (C4) 15
Beaverton (J2) 20
Becket (G4) 3
Beehive (G5)* 12
Belfry (H5)* 200
Belgrade (E5)* 663
Belknap (A3)* 72
Belltower (M5)*
Belmont (G4)* 25
Belt (E3)* 702
Benchland (F3)* 57
Benrud (L2)
Bercail (G4) 2
Bernice (D4) 2
Biddle (L5)* 5
Big Arm (B3)* 100
Big Sag (F3) 6
Big Sandy (G2)* 743
Big Timber (G5)* 1,679
Bigfork (C2)* 450
Bighorn (J4)* 21
Billings (H5)* 31,834
Birney (K5)* 35
Black Eagle (E3)* 1,449
Blackfoot (D2)* 200
Blackleaf (D2)
Blatchford (L4) 8
Bloomfield (M3)* 40
Blossburg (D4)* 35
Bole (D3)
Bonita (C4) 150
Bonner (C4)* 250
Boulder (E4)* 1,017
Bowdoin (J2)
Bowers (L5)*
Bowler (H5)
Box Elder (F2)* 2
Boyd (G5)*
Boyes (M5)*
Bozeman (F5)* 11,3
Brady (E2)*
Brandenberg (K5)*
Bredette (L2)
Brenner (C6)
Bridger (H5)* 8
Brinkman (F2)
Broadus (L5)* 5
Broadview (H4)*
Brockton (M2)* 3
Brockway (L3)*
Brooks (G3)*
Brookside (H2)
Browning (C2)* 1,6
Brunelda (J4)
Brusett (J3)*
Buelow (E2)
Buffalo (G4)* 1
Bundy (H4)

urnham (G2) 26
urns (M3) 8
usby (J5)* 20
utte (D5)* 33,251
utte Creek (J3)
ynum (D3)* 52
abin Creek (M4) 6
alkins (F4)
alvert (E3)
amas (B3)* 125
amas Prairie (B3) 5
ameron (E5)* 138
amps Pass (L5)*
ampsite (E3) 3
anton (E4) 10
anyon Creek (D4)* 76
anyon Ferry (E4)* 150
apitol (M5)* 4
arbella (F5) 5
arbert (L2)
ardwell (E5)* 98
arlyle (M4)*
arter (E3)* 100
artersville (K4)*
ascade (E3)* 447
at Creek (H3)* 65
eekay (H3)
enterville (D4) 1,800
entral Park (E5)
hadbourn (F5) 7
halk Buttes (M5) 41
hance (H5) 7
hapman (J2)* 35
harlo (B3)* 260
hester (E2)* 733
hestnut (F5) 12
hico (F5) 20
hinook (G2)* 2,307
hoteau (D3)* 1,618
hristina (G3)* 20
ircle (L3)* 856
lancey (E4)* 161
larkston (E4)* 20
asoil (E4) 8
eiv (E3)
leveland (G2)* 17
liff Lake (E6)* 21
linton (C4)* 150
lyde Park (F5)* 280
oalridge (M2)* 49
oalwood (L5)* 2
oburg (H2)
offee Creek (F3)* 50
ohagen (K3)* 36
ole (J2)
ollins (E3)* 26
olony Bay (F2)
olstrip (K5)* 300
olumbia Falls (B2)* 1,232
olumbus (G5)* 1,097
omanche (H4) 12
omertown (M2)* 50
onner (B5)* 150
onrad (D2)* 1,865
ontent (J3)
ooke (G5)* 45
oolidge (C5) 2
oram (C2)* 500
orbin (D4) 50
ordova (E3) 175
orinth (J5)* 16
orvallis (C4)* 350
orwin Springs (F5)* 2
orwine Center (J2)
ottonwood (G2) 40
ottonwood (C3)
raig (D3)* 80
rane (M3)* 50
reston (C2)* 200
row Agency (J5)* 500

Crow Rock (L4)
Culbertson (M2)* 779
Cushman (H4)* 17
Custer (J4)* 300
Cut Bank (D2)* 3,721
Dagmar (M2)* 46
Dailey (F5)
Daleview (M2)
Danvers (G3)* 32
Darby (B4)* 415
Dayton (B3)* 95
De Smet (C4) 10
Dean (G5)* 92
Deborgia (A3)* 75
Decker (K5)* 21
Deer Lodge (D4)* 3,779
Dell (D6)* 150
Delphia (H4)* 14
Delphine (F4)
Dempsey (D4) 10
Denton (G3)* 435
Devon (E2)* 50
Dillon (D5)* 3,268
Divide (D5)* 116
Dixon (B3)* 350
Dodson (H2)* 330
Dooley (M2)* 17
Dover (F3) 20
Dovetail (H3) 35
Dowd (M2)
Drexel (A3)* 9
Drummond (D4)* 531
Dryhead (H5) 4
Duderanch (F5) 3
Dunkirk (E2)* 13
Dupuyer (D2)* 125
Dutton (E3)* 431
Eagle Butte (F3) 72
Eagleton (G3)
East Glacier Park (C2)* 300
E. Helena (E4)* 1,216
Eddy (A3)* 25
Eden (E3)* 5
Edgar (H5)* 160
Ekalaka (M5)* 904
Electric (F5) 20
Elgin (M5) 15
Elk Park (D4) 80
Elliston (D4)*
Elmdale (M3) 25
Elmer (J4) 10
Elmo (B3)* 104
Emigrant (F5)* 25
Emory (G4)
Enid (M3)* 8
Ennis (E5)* 600
Epsie (L5)* 65
Essex (C2)* 75
Ethridge (D2)* 45
Eureka (B2)* 929
Evans (E3)
Evaro (C3)* 92
Fairchild (F2) 20
Fairfield (D3)* 693
Fairview (M3)* 942
Fallon (L4)* 251
Family (D2) 150
Farmington (D3) 30
Ferdig (E2)* 15
Fergus (H3)* 4
Finch (K4)
Findon (F4)
Finn (D4) 50
First Creek (J3)
Fishtail (G5)* 50
Fishtrap (C5) 10
Flaxville (L2)* 220
Florence (B4)* 350

Floweree (E3)* 60
Forestgrove (H3)* 25
Forks (J2)* 3
Forsyth (K4)* 1,906
Fort Belknap (H2)
Ft. Benton (F3)* 1,522
Ft. Browning (D2) 1,674
Ft. Logan (E4)
Ft. Maginnis (H3) 4
Ft. Peck (K2)* 1,214
Ft. Shaw (E3)* 180
Ft. Union (M2)
Fortine (A2)* 100
Foundation (L4)
Four Buttes (L2)* 50
Fourchette (H3)
Fowler (E2)
Fox (G5) 15
Francis (F4)* 10
Franklin (G4)* 7
Frazer (K2)* 575
Frenchtown (B3)* 100
Fresno (G2) 10
Froid (M2)* 555
Fromberg (H5)* 442
Gage (H4) 8
Galata (E2)* 63
Galen (D4) 220
Gallatin Gateway (E5)* 200
Gardiner (F5)*
Garland (L4) 3
Garneill (G4)* 33
Garnet (C4) 20
Garrison (D4)* 150
Garryowen (J5)* 28
Gateway (A2) 50
Genou (E2)* 25
Geraldine (F3)* 374
Geyser (F3)* 150
Gibson (G4)
Giffen (E3) 12
Gildford (F2)* 340
Gilman (D3) 15
Giltedge (G3) 8
Girard (M3) 7
Glasgow (K2)* 3,821
Glen (D5)* 100
Glendive (M3)* 5,254
Glengarry (G3) 7
Glentana (K2)* 65
Gold Stone (F2)* 9
Goldbutte (E2)
Goldcreek (D4)* 190
Golden (G5)
Grant (C5)* 25
Grantsdale (B4)* 50
Grass Valley (B4)
Grassrange (H3)* 234
Grayling (E6)* 20
Great Falls (E3)* 39,214
Greenough (C4)* 50
Gregson (D4) 35
Greycliff (G5)* 125
Grisdella (J3) 2
Gunsight (D2)
Hall (C4)* 100
Hamilton (B4)* 2,678
Hammond (M5)* 10
Hanover (G3)* 359
Hardin (J5)* 2,306
Hardy (E3)
Harlem (H2)* 1,107
Harlowton (F4)* 1,733
Harrison (E5)* 305
Hathaway (K4)* 25
Haugan (A3)* 20
Havre (G2)* 8,086
Haxby (K3)* 25
Hay Coulee (F2) 12

Hays (H2)* 150
Hazel (L3)
Heart Butte (C2)* 50
Heath (G3)* 16
Hedgesville (G4)* 25
HELENA (E4)* 17,581
Helmville (C4)* 50
Henderson (A3)
Heron (A2)* 200
Hesper (H5) 27
Hibbard (J4)
Highwood (F3)* 272
Hilger (G3)* 42
Hill (E2)*
Hillsboro (H5) 4
Hillside (K4)
Hingham (F2)* 214
Hinsdale (K2)* 350
Hobson (G4)* 205
Hodges (M4)* 40
Hogeland (H2)* 75
Holland (E5)
Homestake (D5)* 15
Homestead (M2)* 87
Hoosac (G3) 4
Horton (L4)
Hot Springs (B3)* 733
Howard (K4)
Hughesville (F3) 18
Hungry Horse (B2)*
Hunters Hotsprings (F5) 7
Huntley (H5)* 268
Huson (B3)* 75
Hysham (J4)* 410
Inga (F2)
Ingomar (J4)* 100
Intake (M3)* 8
Inverness (F2)* 360
Iron Mountain (A3) 3
Ismay (M4)* 182
Ivanell (J4)
Jackson (C5)* 82
Jardine (F5)* 40
Jeffers (E5)* 60
Jefferson City (E4)* 100
Jefferson Island (E5)* 50
Jennings (A2)* 15
Jens (D4)* 25
Joliet (G5)* 410
Joplin (F2)* 368
Jordan (J3)* 800
Judith Gap (G4)* 175
Kalispell (B2)* 9,737
Kenilworth (F2)
Kevin (D2)* 351
Kila (B2)* 100
Kinsey (L4)* 8
Kintla (B2)
Kirby (J5)* 14
Klein (H4)* 400
Knobs (M5) 33
Knowlton (L4)
Kolin (G3)* 12
Korner (D2) 50
Koyl (D3)
Kremlin (F2)* 160
Lake Mc Donald (B2)* 1
Lakeview (E6) 18
Lambert (M3)* 359
Lame Deer (K5)* 400
Lanark (M2) 3
Landusky (H3)* 65
Lane (M3) 25
Laredo (G2)* 38
Larslan (K2)* 159
Laurel (H5)* 3,663
Laurin (D5)* 110
Lavina (H4)* 195
Lebo (F4)
Ledger (E2)* 20
Lee (K5)
Legg (J3)
Lehigh (F3) 5
Lennep (F4)* 25
Leroy (G3)* 10
Lewistown (G3)* 6,573
Libby (A2)* 2,401
Lima (D6)* 483
Limestone (F5)* 43
Lincoln (D4)* 250
Lindsay (L3)* 57
Lingshire (E4)
Little Crooked (H3) 3
Living Springs (G4)* 7
Livingston (F5)* 7,683
Lloyd (G2)* 5
Locate (L4)* 4
Lockwood (H5) 200
Lodge Grass (J5)* 536
Lodgepole (H2) 50
Loesch (L5) 10
Logan (E5)* 172
Lohman (G2)*
Lolo (B4)* 210
Lolo Hot Springs (B4) 25
Loma (F3) 200
Lombard (E4)* 26
Lonepine (B3)* 9
Loring (J2)* 50
Lost Lake (H2) 25
Lothair (E2)* 72
Lothrop (B4)
Loweth (F4) 20
Lowry (D3)
Lozeau (B3)* 12
Lupfer (B2) 8
Lustre (K2)* 4
Luther (G5)* 22

Madoc (L2)* 33
Malta (J2)* 2,095
Manhattan (E5)* 716
Manicke (A2) 30
Manson (E2)
Marias (E2) 10
Marion (B2)* 47
Marsh (M4)* 100
Martinsdale (F4)* 130
Marysville (D4)*
Maschetah (J5) 25
Maudlow (E4)* 50
Maxville (C4)* 40
Mc Allister (E5)* 21
Mc Cabe (M2)* 55
Mc Elroy (M2) 2
Mc Leod (G5)* 10
Mc Rae (J5)* 5
Meaderville (D4) 250
Mecaha (J3)
Medicine Lake (M2)* 454
Meharry (J2) 4
Melrose (D5)* 130
Melstone (H4)* 195
Melville (F4)* 29
Menard (E5)
Merino (F3)* 5
Midby (M2) 7
Mike Horse (D4)* 200
Mildred (M4)* 75
Miles City (L4)* 9,243
Mill Iron (M5)* 75
Millegan (E3)
Milltown (C4)* 750
Miner (E5)* 53
Mink (L3) 30
Mission (F5)
Missoula (C4)* 22,485
Mizpah (L4)
Moccasin (F3)* 300
Mock (Radnor) (B2) 8
Moiese (B3)* 8
Molt (H5)* 25
Mona (M3) 25
Monarch (F3)* 53
Monida (D6)* 25
Montague (F3)* 20
Moon Creek (L4)
Moore (G4)* 224
Moorhead (K5)* 15
Mosby (J4)* 3
Mossmain (H5) 12
Moulton (G3)* 50
Musselshell (H4)* 250
Myers (J4)* 37
Nashua (K2)* 691
Natal (G4) 3
Navajo (M2)* 7
Neihart (F4)* 289
Nelson (E4)
New Chicago (C4) 20
Niarada (B3)* 4
Nibbe (H4)* 20
Nickwall (L2)
Nihill (G4) 2
Nimrod (C4)* 45
Ninemile (B4)*
Nohly (M3)* 57
Norris (E5)* 100
Noxon (A3)* 113
Nyack (C2) 3
Nye (G5)* 3
Oilmont (F2)* 250
Oka (G4)
Olanda (L3)
Olive (L5)* 6
Ollie (M4)*
Olney (B2)* 147
Oneill (L4)
Opheim (K2)* 383
Osborn (H5)
Ossette (L2)
Oswego (L2)* 100
Otter (K5)* 57
Outlook (M2)* 235
Ovando (D3)* 100
Oxford (G4) 10
Pablo (B3)* 150
Paola (C2)
Paradise (B3)* 300
Paragon (K4)
Park City (H5)* 450
Paxton (L3) 20
Peerless (L2)* 125
Pendroy (D2)* 80
Perma (B3)* 60
Philipsburg (C4)* 1,048
Phillips (H2)
Piedmont (D5) 21
Pineview (J4)
Piniele (M5) 10
Pioneer (D4)
Piper (G4) 6
Pipestone Hot Springs (D5) 12
Placer (E4)
Plains (B3)* 714
Plentywood (M2)* 1,862
Plevna (M4)* 247
Polaris (C5)* 25
Polebridge (B2)* 56
Polson (B3)* 2,280
Polytechnic (H5)* 250
Pompeys Pillar (J5)* 200
Pony (E5)* 185
Poplar (L2)* 1,169
Portage (E3) 22
Post Creek (C3)

Potomac (C4)* 65
Powderville (L5)* 4
Power (E3)* 75
Pray (F5)* 14
Proctor (B3)* 125
Pryor (H5)* 70
Quartz (B3) 4
Quietus (K5)* 3
Race Track (D4) 20
Radersburg (E4)*
Radio (B3)
Radnor (Mock) (B2) 8
Ramsay (D5)* 131
Ranchcreek (L5)*
Rapelje (G5)* 150
Rapids (G5)
Ravalli (B3)* 190
Rayfield (G4) 11
Raymond (M2)* 50
Raymond (M2)* 50
Raynesford (F3)* 45
Red Lodge (G5)* 2,730
Redstone (M2)* 105
Redwater (L3)
Reedpoint (G5)* 150
Regina (J3)*
Renova (D5) 6
Reserve (M2)* 215
Rexford (A2)* 200
Richey (L3)* 595
Richland (K2)*
Ridge (M5)* 50
Ridgway (M5)* 3
Riebeling (D3)
Rimini (D4)
Rimroad (L3) 20
Rimrock (H5)
Ringling (F4)* 135
Riverdale (E3) 50
Rivulet (B4)* 47
Roanwood (K2) 3
Roberts (G5)* 200
Rock Springs (K4)* 1
Rockvale (H5) 10
Rocky Boy (G2) 50
Rollins (B3)* 200
Ronan (C3)* 1,251
Roscoe (G5)* 75
Rosebud (K4)* 125
Ross Fork (G3)*
Rothiemay (G4)* 55
Round Butte (B3)*
Roundup (H4)* 2,856
Roy (H3)* 175
Rudyard (F2)* 521
Rumble Creek (C3) 30
Ryegate (G4)* 339
Saco (J2)* 539
Saint Ignatius (C3)* 781
St. Pauls (H3) 70
St. Peter (E3)
St. Phillips (M4) 6
St. Regis (A3)* 500
St. Xavier (J5)* 150
Salem (E3)
Saltese (A3)* 95
Sand Creek (L3)
Sand Springs (J3)* 12
Sandcoulee (E3)* 500
Sanders (J4)* 40
Santa Rita (D2)* 145
Sappington (E5)* 34
Sarpy (J5) 6
Savage (M3)* 300
Savoy (H2)* 15
Sayle (L5)* 10
Scobey (L2)* 1,628
Sedan (F4) 6
Seeley Lake (C3)* 250
Selma (E2) 7
Selmes (G5) 6
Selway (K5) 4
Shambo (G2)*
Shawmut (G4)* 122
Sheffield (K4)
Shelby (E2)* 3,058
Shepherd (H5)* 100
Sheridan (D5)* 572
Shirley (L4)
Shonkin (F3)* 6
Shriver (H5) 10
Sidney (M3)* 3,987
Silesia (H5)* 50
Silver Star (D5)* 55
Silverbow (D5)* 50
Simms (E3)* 250
Simpson (F2)*
Sioux Pass (M3)* 40
Sipple (G4)
Sixteen (F4) 10
Sloan (B3)
Snowden (M2) 16
Somers (B2)* 750
Sonnette (L5)* 5
Soo (L2)
Southern Cross (C4) 50
Spion Kop (F3) 10
Springdale (F5)* 75
Springhill (F5)
Square Butte (F3)* 75
Stacey (L5)* 7
Stanford (F3)* 542
Stark (B3)* 25
Stevensville (C4)* 772
Stipek (M3) 50
Stockett (E3)* 300
Stone (C4)
Stonehill (A2) 5

Strater (J2)
Straw (G4)* 25
Stryker (B2)* 60
Suffolk (G3)* 14
Sula (B5)* 112
Sumatra (J4)*
Sun Prairie (J3)
Sun River (E3)* 115
Sunburst (E2)* 845
Superior (B3)* 626
Sutherland (L4)
Swan Lake (C3)* 100
Sweetgrass (E2)*
Swingley (F5)
Taft (A3) 2
Tampico (K2)* 80
Tarkio (B4)* 75
Teigen (H3)*
Telegraph Creek (J3)* 5
Terry (L4)* 1,191
Teton (F3)
Thoeny (K2)* 10
Thompson Falls (A3)* 851
Three Forks (E5)* 1,114
Thurlow (K4)
Tonquin (M4)
Toston (E4)* 100
Townsend (E4)* 1,316
Trailcreek (B2)* 10
Trego (B2)* 48
Trident (E5)* 150
Trine (H3)
Trout Creek (A3)* 52
Troy (A2)* 770
Tunis (F3) 6
Turner (H2)* 200
Tuscor (A3)* 4
Twin Bridges (D5)* 497
Twodot (F4)* 150
Tyler (H4) 3
Ulm (E3)* 150
Union (L3) 50
Ural (A2)* 37
Utica (F4)* 60
Valentine (H3) 3
Valier (D2)* 710
Van Norman (K3)* 4
Vananda (K4)* 100
Vandalia (J2)* 25
Vanstel (K4)
Varney (E5) 12
Vaughn (E3)* 190
Verona (F2)
Victor (B4)* 350
Vida (L3)* 58
Virgelle (F2)* 20
Virginia City (E5)* 323
Volborg (L5)* 7
Volt (L2)
Wagner (H2)*
Waleston (J2)
Walkerville (D4)* 1,631
Wallum (G4)
Waltham (E3)* 25
Ware (G3)* 4
Warland (A2)* 90
Warmsprings (D4)* 2,000
Warren (H5)* 40
Warrick (G2)* 3
Washoe (G5)*
Waterloo (D5)* 95
Watkins (K3)* 10
Webster (M4)* 2
Weldon (K3)* 2
West Fork (L2)
W. Gallatin (E5)
W. Glacier (C2)* 440
W. Yellowstone (E6)* 500
Westby (M2)* 396
Westmore (M4) 16
Wheat Basin (G5) 10
Wheeler (K2)*
White Sulphur Springs (E4)* 1,025
Whitefish (B2)* 3,268
Whitehall (D5)* 929
Whitepine (A3)* 175
Whitetail (L2)* 240
Whitewater (J2)* 85
Whitlash (E2)* 18
Wibaux (M3)* 739
Wickes (D4)* 70
Wickett (H5)
Wilborn (D4)
Willard (M4)* 3
Williams (D2)* 10
Willow Creek (E5)* 300
Wilsall (F5)* 300
Windham (F3)* 116
Winifred (G3)* 217
Winnett (H4)* 407
Winston (E4)* 53
Wisdom (C5)* 125
Wise River (C5)* 50
Wolf Creek (D3)* 156
Wolf Point (L2)* 2,557
Woodside (B4) 100
Woodworth (C3) 45
Worden (H5)* 375
Wyola (J5)* 110
Yaak (A2)*
Yakt (B2) 28
Yates (M4)
Yegen (H5) 10
Youngs Point (G5)
Zero (L4)* 22
Zortman (H3)*
Zurich (G2)* 85

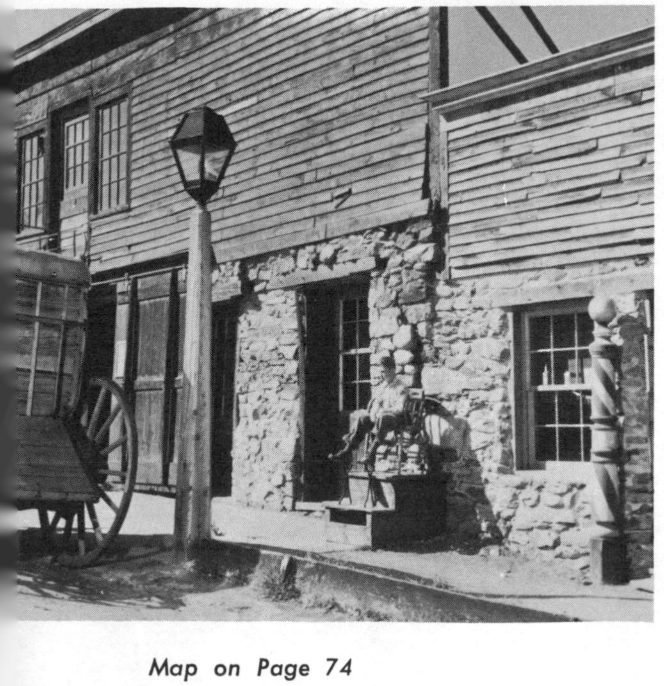

Map on Page 74

NEBRASKA

Total Population 1,325,510

93 COUNTIES

ams (F4) 28,855
elope (F2) 11,624
hur (C3) 803
nner (A3) 1,325
ine (E3) 1,203
Boone (F3) 10,721
Box Butte (A2) 12,279
Boyd (F2) 4,911
Brown (E2) 5,164
Buffalo (E4) 25,134
Burt (H3) 11,536
Butler (G3) 11,432
Cass (H4) 16,361
Cedar (G2) 13,843
Chase (C4) 5,176
Cherry (C2) 8,397
Cheyenne (A3) 12,081
Clay (F4) 8,700
Colfax (G3) 10,010
Cuming (H3) 12,994
Custer (E3) 19,170
Dakota (H2) 10,401
Dawes (A2) 9,708
Dawson (E4) 19,393
Deuel (B3) 3,330
Dixon (H2) 9,129
Dodge (H3) 26,265
Douglas (H3) 281,020
Dundy (C4) 4,354
Fillmore (G4) 9,610
Franklin (F4) 7,096
Frontier (D4) 5,282
Furnas (E4) 9,385
Gage (H4) 28,052
Garden (B3) 4,114
Garfield (F3) 2,912
Gosper (E4) 2,734
Grant (C3) 1,057
Greeley (F3) 5,575
Hall (F4) 32,186
Hamilton (F4) 8,778
Harlan (E4) 7,189
Hayes (C4) 2,404
Hitchcock (C4) 5,867
Holt (F2) 14,859
Hooker (C3) 1,061
Howard (F3) 7,226

Jefferson (G4)............13,623
Johnson (H4)............7,251
Kearney (F4)............6,409
Keith (C3)............7,449
Keya Paha (E2)............2,160
Kimball (A3)............4,283
Knox (G2)............14,820
Lancaster (H4)............119,742
Lincoln (D4)............27,380
Logan (D3)............1,357
Loup (E3)............1,348
Madison (G3)............24,338
McPherson (C3)............825
Merrick (F3)............8,812
Morrill (A3)............8,263
Nance (F3)............6,512
Nemaha (J4)............10,973
Nuckolls (F4)............9,609
Otoe (H4)............17,056
Pawnee (H4)............6,744
Perkins (C4)............4,809
Phelps (E4)............9,048
Pierce (G2)............9,405
Platte (G3)............19,910
Polk (G3)............8,044
Red Willow (D4)............12,977
Richardson (J4)............16,886
Rock (E2)............3,026
Saline (G4)............14,046
Sarpy (H3)............15,693
Saunders (H3)............16,923
Scotts Bluff (A3)............33,939
Seward (G4)............13,155
Sheridan (B2)............9,539
Sherman (F3)............6,421
Sioux (A2)............3,124
Stanton (G3)............6,387
Thayer (G4)............10,563
Thomas (D3)............1,206
Thurston (H2)............8,590
Valley (E3)............7,252
Washington (H3)............11,511
Wayne (G2)............10,129
Webster (F4)............7,395
Wheeler (F3)............1,526
York (G4)............14,346

CITIES and TOWNS

Abie (H3)*............113
Adams (H4)*............457
Agate (A2)*............10
Ainsworth (D2)*............2,150
Albion (F3)*............2,132
Alda (F4)*............190
Alexandria (G4)*............317
Allen (H2)*............374
Alliance (A2)*............7,891
Alma (E4)*............1,768
Almeria (E3)*............20
Altona (H2)............20
Alvo (H4)*............190
Amelia (F2)*............67
Ames (H3)*............80
Amherst (E4)*............219
Andrews (A2)*............14
Angora (A3)*............36
Angus (F4)*............34
Anoka (F2)*............60
Anselmo (E3)*............316
Ansley (E3)*............711
Antioch (B2)*............30
Arapahoe (E4)*............1,226
Arborville (G3)............
Arcadia (F3)*............574
Archer (F3)*............103
Arlington (H3)*............593
Arnold (D3..*............936
Arthur (C3)*............176
Ashby (C2)*............150
Ashland (H3)*............1,713
Ashton (F3)*............381
Atkinson (E2)*............1,372
Atlanta (E4)*............147
Auburn (J4)*............3,422
Aurora (F4)*............2,455
Avoca (H4)*............196
Axtell (E4)*............352
Ayr (F4)*............121
Bancroft (H2)*............596
Barada (J4)*............83
Barneston (H4)*............208
Bartlett (F3)*............145
Bartley (D4)*............399
Bassett (E2)*............1,066
Battle Creek (G3)*............630
Bayard (A3)*............1,869
Bazile Mills (G2)............46
Beardwell (E2)............6
Beatrice (H4)*............11,813
Beaver City (E4)*............913
Beaver Crossing (G4)*............425
Bee (H3)*............160
Beemer (H3)*............613
Belden (G2)*............192
Belgrade (G3)*............284
Bellevue (J3)*............3,858
Bellwood (G3)*............389
Belmar (C3)............
Belmont (A2)*............25
Belvidere (G4)*............274
Benedict (G3)*............206
Benkelman (C4)*............1,512
Bennet (H4)*............396
Bennington (H3)*............315
Berea (A2)............27
Bertrand (E4)*............584
Berwyn (E3)*............138
Best (C4)............12
Beverly (C4)............18
Big Springs (B3)*............527
Bingham (B2)*............100
Bladen (F4)*............282
Blair (H3)*............3,815
Bloomfield (G2)*............1,455
Bloomington (F4)*............293
Blue Hill (F4)*............574
Blue Springs (H4)*............581
Boelus (F3)*............167
Boone (F3*............100
Bostwick (F4)*............54
Boys Town ‡(H3)*............975
Bradish (G3)............5
Bradshaw (G4)*............352
Brady (D3)*............320
Brainard (G3)*............373
Brandon (C4)*............40
Brayton (F3)............1
Brewster (D3)*............69
Bridgeport (A3)*............1,631
Bristow (F2)*............146
Broadwater (B3)*............300
Brock (H4)*............283
Brocksburg (E2)*............15
Broken Bow (E3)............3,396
Brownlee (D2)*............38
Brownville (J4)*............357
Brule (C3)*............330
Bruning (G4)*............246
Bruno (G3)*............155
Brunswick (G2)*............260
Bucktail (C3)*............23
Buffalo (E4)*............12
Burchard (H4)*............201
Burr (H4)*............91
Burress (G4)............6
Burton (E2)*............45
Burwell (E3)*............1,413
Bushnell (A3)*............225
Butte (F2)*............614
Byron (G4)*............159
Cadams (F4)............19
Cairo (F3)*............422
Callaway (D3)*............744
Calora (C3)*............8
Cambridge (D4)*............1,352
Campbell (F4)*............412
Carleton (G4)*............291
Carns (E2)............5
Carroll (G2)*............309
Cascade (D2)*............9
Cedar Bluffs (H3)*............505
Cedar Rapids (F3)*............541
Center (G2)*............148
Central City (F3)*............2,394
Ceresco (H3)*............374
Chadron (B2)*............4,687
Chalco (H3)............32
Chambers (F2)*............395
Champion (C4)*............170
Chapman (F3)*............274
Chappell (B3)*............1,297
Charleston (G4)............
Cherry (C2)............2
Chester (G4)*............539
Clarks (G3)*............464
Clarkson (G3)*............764
Clatonia (H4)*............192
Clay Center (F4)*............824
Clearwater (F2)*............472
Clinton (B2)*............36
Cody (C2)*............296
Coleridge (G2)*............621
Colon (H3)*............127
Columbus (G3)*............8,884
Comstock (E3)*............302
Concord (H2)*............194
Cook (H4)*............332
Cordova (G4)*............147
Cornlea (G3)*............69
Cortland (H4)*............288
Cotesfield (F3)*............106
Cowles (F4)*............130
Cozad (E4)*............2,910
Crab Orchard (H4)*............120
Craig (H3)*............384
Crawford (A2)*............1,824
Creighton (G2)*............1,401
Creston (G3)*............228
Crete (G4)*............3,692
Crofton (G2)*............630
Crookston (D2)............168
Crowell (H3)............31
Culbertson (C4)*............770
Curtis (D4)*............964
Cushing (F3)*............71
Dakota City (H2)*............622
Dakota Junction (A2)............6
Dalton (B3)*............417
Danbury (D4)*............218
Dannebrog (F3)*............318
Darr (E4)............39
Davenport (G4)*............459
Davey (H4)*............112
David City (G3)*............2,321
Dawson (J4)*............309
Daykin (G4)*............157
De Witt (G4)*............528
Decatur (H2)*............806
Denman (F4)*............23
Denton (H4)*............101
Deshler (G4)*............1,063
Deweese (F4)*............115
Dickens (C4)*............60
Diller (H4)*............314
Dix (A3)*............270
Dixon (H2)*............159
Dodge (H3)*............633
Doniphan (F4)*............412
Dorchester (G4)*............478
Dorsey (F2)*............2
Douglas (H4)*............213

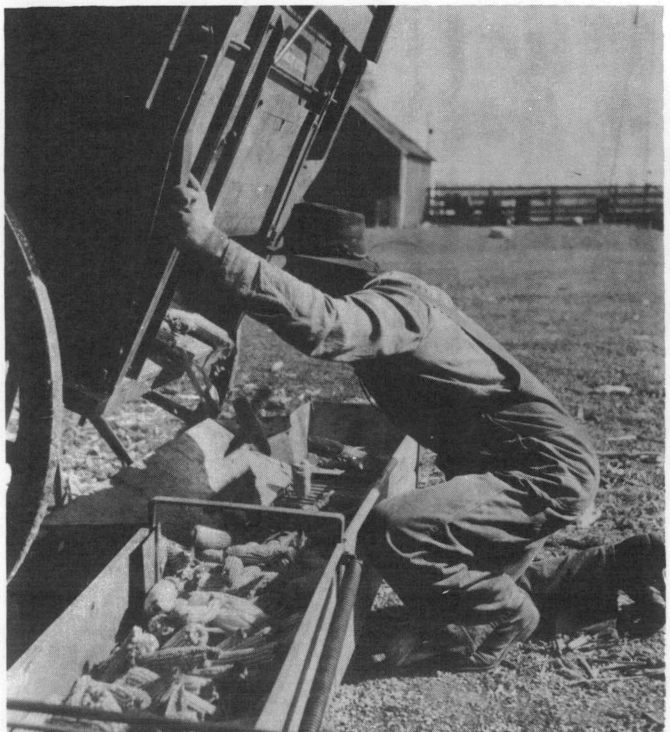

DuBois (H4)*............236
Duff (E2)*............2
Dunbar (J4)*............228
Duncan (G3)*............228
Dunning (E3)*............254
Dustin (E2)*............3
Dwight (G3)*............218
Eagle (H4)*............255
Eddyville (E3)*............188
Edgar (F4)*............724
Edison (E4)*............302
Elba (F3)*............216
Eldorado (G4)............40
Elgin (F3)*............820
Eli (C2)*............40
Elk Creek (H4)*............176
Elkhorn (H3)*............476
Ellis (H4)*............69
Ellsworth (B2)*............9
Elm Creek (E4)*............799
Elmwood (H4)*............445
Elsie (C4)*............219
Elsmere (D2)*............34
Elwood (E4)*............562
Elyria (E3)*............87
Emerson (H2)*............784
Emmet (F2)*............62
Enders (C4)*............75
Endicott (G4)*............195
Enola (G3)*............23
Ericson (F3)*............186
Eustis (D4)*............413
Ewing (F2)*............705
Exeter (G4)*............747
Fairbury (G4)*............6,395
Fairfield (G4)*............503
Fairmont (G4)*............729
Falls City (J4)*............6,203
Farnam (D4)*............323
Filley (H4)*............136
Firth (H4)*............245
Flats (C3)*............4
Fontanelle (H3)*............103
Fordyce (G2)*............165
Fort Calhoun (J3)*............314
Fort Crook (J3)*............
Fort Robinson (A2)*............36
Foster (G2)*............114
Franklin (E4)*............1,602
Fremont (H3)*............14,762
Friend (G4)*............1,148
Fullerton (F3)*............1,520
Funk (E4)*............123
Gandy (D3)*............88
Garland (G4)*............184
Garrison (G3)*............88
Gates (E3)*............14
Geneva (G4)*............2,031
Genoa (G3)*............1,026
Gering (A3)*............3,842
Gibbon (F4)*............1,063
Gilead (G4)*............109
Giltner (F4)*............284
Gladstone (G4)*............63
Glen (A2)*............19
Glenvil (F4)*............281
Goehner (G4)*............67
Goodwin (H2)............3
Gordon (B2)*............2,058
Gothenburg (D4)*............2,977
Graf (H4)*............50
Grafton (G4)*............159
Grainton (C4)*............91
Grand Island (F4)*............22,682
Grant (C4)*............1,091
Greeley (F3)*............787
Greenwood (H3)*............364
Gresham (G3)*............267
Gretna (H3)*............438
Gross (F2)*............29
Guide Rock (F4)*............676
Gurley (B3)*............219
Hadar (G2)*............129
Haig (A3)*............64
Haigler (C4)*............398
Hallam (H4)*............172
Halsey (D3)*............165
Hamlet (C4)*............154
Hampton (G4)*............289
Hansen (F4)*............50
Harbine (G4)*............85
Hardy (G4)*............348
Harrisburg (A3)*............94
Harrison (A2)*............492
Hartington (G2)*............1,660
Harvard (F4)*............774
Hastings (F4)*............20,211
Hay Springs (B2)*............1,091
Hayes Center (C4)*............361
Hayland (F4)............11
Hazard (F3)*............130
Heartwell (F4)*............125
Hebron (G4)*............2,000
Hecla (C2)............6
Hemingford (A2)*............946
Henderson (G4)*............536
Hendley (D4)*............130
Henry (A2)*............171
Herman (H3)*............380
Hershey (D3)*............573
Hickman (H4)*............279
Hildreth (E4)*............374
Hire (C2)............3
Hoagland (D3)............8
Holbrook (D4)*............301
Holdrege (E4)*............4,381
Hollinger (E4)............20
Holmesville (H4)*............110
Holstein (F4)*............187
Homer (H2)*............345
Hooper (H3)*............859
Horace (F3)............12
Hordville (G3)*............116
Hoskins (G2)*............171
Howard City (Boelus*) (F3)............167
Howe (J4)*............75
Howells (H3)*............784
Hubbard (H2)*............145
Hubbell (G4)*............199
Humboldt (J4)*............1,404
Humphrey (G3)*............761
Huntley (E4)*............98
Hyannis (C3)*............432
Imperial (C4)*............1,563
Inavale (F4)*............188
Indianola (D4)*............738
Ingham (D4)*............21
Inland (F4)*............100
Inman (F2)*............237
Irwin (C2)*............4
Ithaca (H3)*............140
Jackson (H2)*............200
Jamison (E2)*............50
Jansen (G4)*............244
Johnson (J4)*............262
Johnstown (D2)*............109
Julian (J4)*............123
Juniata (F4)*............365
Kearney (E4)*............12,115
Keene (F4)............6
Kenesaw (F4)*............584
Kennard (H3)*............273
Kennedy (D2)*............12
Keystone (C3)*............55
Kilgore (D2)*............189
Kimball (A3)*............2,048
Koshopah (E2)*............6
Kramer (H4)*............60
Lakeside (B2)*............175
Lamar (C4)*............81
Lanham (H4)*............75
Laurel (G2)*............944
Lawrence (F4)*............376
Lebanon (D4)*............213
Leigh (G3)*............551
Lemoyne (C3)*............29
Lena (C3)*............
Leshara (H3)*............61
Lewellen (B3)*............510
Lewiston (H4)*............94
Lexington (E4)*............5,068
Liberty (H4)*............246
LINCOLN (H4)*............98,884
Lincoln (urban area)............99,500
Lindsay (G3)*............247
Linwood (H3)*............168
Lisco (B3)*............150
Litchfield (E3)*............337
Lodgepole (B3)*............555
Logan (D3)............
Loma (G3)*............50
Long Pine (E2)*............567
Loomis (E4)*............218
Lorenzo (A3)............40
Loretto (F3)*............101
Lorton (H4)*............75
Louisville (H3)*............1,014
Loup City (E3)*............1,508
Lowell (F4)............49
Lushton (G4)*............60
Lyman (A3)*............666
Lynch (F2)*............440
Lyons (H3)*............1,011
Macon (E4)*............50
Macy (H2)*............356
Madison (G3)*............1,663
Madrid (C4)*............379
Magnet (G2)*............115
Malcolm (H4)*............93
Malmo (H3)*............151
Manley (H4)*............93
Mariaville (E2)*............3
Marion (D4)*............100
Marquette (G4)*............218
Marsland (A2)*............84
Martinsburg (H2)*............79
Martland (G4)............10
Mary (E2)............5
Mascot (E4)*............48
Maskell (H2)*............84
Mason City (E3)*............305
Max (C4)*............135
Maxwell (D3)*............347
Maywood (D4)*............409
McCook (D4)*............7,678
McCool Junction (G4)*............297
McGrew (A3)*............105
McLean (G2)*............67
Mead (H3)*............388
Meadow Grove (G2)*............461
Meadville (E2)*............7
Melbeta (A3)*............138
Melpha (C2)............10
Memphis (H3)*............92
Merna (E3)*............385
Merriman (C2)*............260
Middlebranch (F2)*............2
Milburn (E3)*............18
Milford (H4)*............951
Millard (H3)*............391
Miller (E4)*............179
Milligan (G4)*............367
Mills (E2)*............48
Minatare (A3)*............890
Minden (F4)*............2,120
Mitchell (A3)*............2,101
Monowi (F2)*............67
Monroe (G3)*............269
Moorefield (D4)*............58
Morrill (A3)*............849
Morse Bluff (H3)*............142
Mount Clare (F4)............35
Mullen (C2)*............652
Murdock (H4)*............225
Murphy (F4)............20
Murray (J4)*............244
Mynard (J4)............45
Nacora (H2)............
Naper (E2)*............188
Naponee (E4)*............391
Nebraska City (J4)*............6,872
Nehawka (H4)*............272
Neligh (G2)*............1,822
Nelson (F4)*............806
Nemaha (J4)*............288
Nenzel (C2)*............24
Newark (E4)*............30
Newcastle (H2)*............426
Newman Grove (G3)*............1,004
Newport (E2)*............207
Nickerson (H3)*............140
Niobrara (G2)*............577
Nonpareil (A2)............
Nora (G4)*............88
Norden (D2)*............32
Norfolk ((G2)*............11,335
Norman (F4)*............68
North Bend (H3)*............906
North Loup (F3)*............526
North Platte (D3)*............15,433
Northport (B3)*............164
Oak (G4)*............131
Oakdale (F2)*............502
Oakland (H3)*............1,456
Obert (G2)*............91
Oconto (E3)*............258
Octavia (G3)*............103
Odell (H4)*............420
Odessa (E4)*............132
O'Fallons (D3)............30
Ogallala (C3)*............3,456
Ohiowa (G4)*............253
Omaha (J3)*............251,117
Omaha (urban area)............306,291
Oneill (F2)*............3,027
Ong (G4)*............173
Orafino (D4)*............11
Orchard (F2)*............458
Ord (F3)*............2,239
Orella (A2)*............17
Orleans (E4)*............956
Osceola (G3)*............1,098
Oshkosh (B3)*............1,124
Osmond (G2)*............732
Otoe (H4)*............230
Overton (E4)*............497
Ovina (F4)............20
Ovitt (E2)............4
Oxford (E4)*............1,270
Page (F2)*............275
Palisade (C4)*............694
Palmer (F3)*............434
Palmyra (H4)*............372
Panama (H4)*............168
Papillion (J3)*............1,034
Parks (C4)*............150
Paul (J4)*............23
Pauline (F4)*............70
Pawnee City (H4)*............1,606
Paxton (C3)*............606
Pender (H2)*............1,167
Peru (J4)*............1,265
Petersburg (G3)*............508
Phillips (F4)*............190
Pickrell (H4)*............161
Pierce (G2)*............1,167
Pilger (G2)*............512
Plainview (G2)*............1,427
Platte Center (G3)*............422
Plattsmouth (J3)*............4,874
Pleasant Dale (G4)*............163
Pleasant Hill (G4)............29
Pleasanton (E4)*............188
Plymouth (G4)*............348
Polk (G3)*............508
Ponca (H2)*............893
Poole (F4)*............33
Posen (F3)*............172
Potter (A3)*............421
Powell (G4)*............70
Prague (H3)*............396
Preston (J4)*............81
Primrose (F3)*............154
Prosser (F4)*............81
Purdum (D2)*............21
Rackett (B3)............2
Raeville (F3)*............82
Ragan (E4)*............102
Ralston (J3)*............1,300
Randolph (G2)*............1,029
Ravenna (F4)*............1,451
Raymond (H4)*............196
Red Cloud (F4)*............1,744
Red Willow (D4)............10
Redbird (F2)*............13
Redington (A3)*............18
Republican City (E4)*............580
Reynolds (G4)*............166
Richland (G3)*............141
Riford (A3)............
Ringgold (D3)*............28
Rising City (G3)*............374
Riverdale (E4)*............134
Riverton (F4)*............348
Riverview (E2)*............
Roca (H4)*............105
Rockville (F3)*............164
Rogers (H3)*............113
Rohrs (J4)............8
Rosalie (H2)*............212
Roscoe (C3)*............95
Rose (E2)*............3
Roseland (F4)*............154
Rosemont (F4)*............42
Royal (F2)*............157
Rulo (J4)*............639
Rushville (B2)*............1,266
Ruskin (G4)*............214
Sacramento (E4)............7
Saint Ann (D4)*............11
St. Edward (G3)*............917
St. Helena (G2)*............77
St. Libory (F3)*............142
St. Mary (H4)*............56
St. Michael (F4)*............12
St. Paul (F3)*............1,676
Salem (J4)*............341
Santee (G2)*............175
Sarben (C3)*............100
Sargent (E3)*............818
Saronville (G4)*............87
Schuyler (G3)*............2,883
Scotia (F3)*............474
Scottsbluff (A3)*............12,858
Scribner (H3)*............913
Sedan (G4)*............10
Seneca (D2)*............219
Seward (H4)*............3,154
Shelby (G3)*............624
Shelton (F4)*............1,032
Shickley (G4)*............316
Sholes (G2)*............32
Shubert (J4)*............295
Sidney (B3)*............4,912
Silver Creek (G3)*............444
Simeon (D2)*............6
Smithfield (E4)*............102
Snyder (H3)*............369
Somerset (D4)............
South Bend (H4)*............100
South Sioux City (H2)*............5,557
Spalding (F3)*............713
Sparks (D2)*............5
Spencer (F2)*............540
Sprague (H4)*............110
Springfield (H3)*............377
Springranch (F4)............25
Springview (E2)*............298
Stamford (E4)*............265
Stanton (G3)*............1,403
Staplehurst (G4)*............224
Stapleton (D3)*............363
Star (F2)*............5
Steele City (G4)*............214
Steinauer (H4)*............141
Stella (J4)*............324
Sterling (H4)*............547
Stockham (F4)*............82
Stockville (D4)*............181
Strang (G4)*............100
Stratton (C4)*............628
Stromsburg (G3)*............1,231
Stuart (E2)*............785
Sumner (E4)*............267
Sunol (B3)*............120
Superior (G4)*............3,227
Surprise (G3)*............120
Sutherland (C3)*............856
Sutton (G4)*............1,353
Swanton (H4)*............203
Swedeburg (H3)*............54
Sweetwater (E3)*............10
Syracuse (H4)*............1,097
Table Rock (H4)*............513
Talmage (H4)*............398
Tamora (G4)*............91
Tarnov (G3)*............74
Taylor (E3)*............311
Tecumseh (H4)*............1,930
Tekamah (H3)*............1,914
Terrytown (A3)............228
Thayer (G4)*............90
Thedford (D3)*............275
Thune (C3)*............12
Thurston (H2)*............156
Tilden (G2)*............1,033
Tobias (G4)*............240
Touhy (H3)*............39
Trenton (D4)*............1,239
Trumbull (F4)*............150
Tryon (C3)*............150
Uehling (H3)*............250
Ulysses (G3)*............374
Unadilla (H4)*............216
Union (J4)*............277
Upland (F4)*............251
Utica (G4)*............550
Valentine (D2)*............2,700
Valley (H3)*............1,113
Valparaiso (H3)*............392
Venango (C4)*............233
Venus (F2)*............10
Verdel (F2)*............142
Verdigre (F2)*............570
Verdon (J4)*............366
Verona (G4)*............25
Vesta (H4)*............75
Virginia (H4)*............113
Waco (G4)*............180
Wahoo (H3)*............3,128
Wakefield (H2)*............1,027
Wallace (C4)*............361
Walnut (F2)*............25
Walthill (H2)*............958
Walton (H4)*............81
Wann (H3)............48
Washington (H3)*............55
Waterbury (H2)*............141
Waterloo (H3)*............382
Wauneta (C4)*............926
Wausa (G2)*............708
Waverly (H4)*............310
Wayne (G2)*............3,595
Wayside (A2)*............5
Weeping Water (J4)*............1,070
Weissert (E3)*............12
Wellfleet (D4)*............93
Wells (C2)............3
West Lincoln (H4)............426
West Point (H3)*............2,658
Western (G4)*............434
Westerville (E3)*............50
Weston (H3)*............345
Whiteclay (B2)*............80
Whitman (C2)*............180
Whitney (A2)*............132
Wilber (G4)*............1,356
Wilcox (E4)*............296
Willow Island (D4)*............88
Wilsonville (D4)*............327
Winnebago (H2)*............684
Winnetoon (F2)*............120
Winside (G2)*............454
Winslow (H3)*............138
Wisner (H3)*............1,233
Wolbach (F3)*............442
Wood Lake (D2)*............238
Wood River (F4)*............858
Wymore (H4)*............2,258
Wynot (G2)*............233
York (G4)*............6,178
Yutan (H3)*............287

NEVADA

Map on Page 75 — *Total Population 160,083*

17 COUNTIES

Churchill (C3) 6,161
Clark (F6) 48,289
Douglas (B4) 2,029
Elco (F1) 11,654
Esmeralda (D5) 614
Eureka (E3) 896
Humboldt (C1) 4,838
Lander (D3) 1,850
Lincoln (F5) 3,837
Lyon (B3) 3,679
Mineral (C4) 5,560
Nye (E5) 3,101
Ormsby (B3) 4,172
Pershing (C2) 3,103
Storey (B3) 671
Washoe (B2) 50,205
White Pine (F3) 9,424

CITIES and TOWNS

Adaven (F4)* 25
Alamo (F5)* 384
Arden (F6)* 43
Arthur (F2)* 3
Austin (E3)* 300
Babbitt (C4)* 2,464
Baker (G3)* 50
Battle Mountain (E2)* 850
Beatty (E6)* 485
Beowawe (E2)* 175
Black Springs (B3)* 100
Blue Diamonds (F6) 210
Bonne Springs (G2) 12
Boulder City (G7)* 3,903
Bristol Silver (G4) 25
Bunkerville (G6)* 180
Caliente (G5)* 970
Carlin (E2)* 1,203
Carp (G5)* 120
CARSON CITY (B3)* 3,082
Charleston (F1)*
Cherry Creek (G3)* 75
Coaldale (D4) 16
Cobre (G1)* 51
Contact (G1)* 20
Cortez (E2) 7
Crystal Bay (A3)* 150
Currant (F4)
Currie (G2)* 52
Dayton (B3) 300
Deeth (F1)* 75
Denio (C1)
Dry Lake (G6)* 48
Duckwater (F4)* 5
Dunphy (E2) 6
Dyer (C5)* 87
East Ely (G3)* 1,000
East Gate (D3) 10
Elgin (G5)* 50
Elko (F2)* 5,393
Ely (G3)* 3,558
Eureka (E3)* 500
Fallon (C3)* 2,400
Fernley (B3)* 650
Flanigan (B2)* 44
Gabbs (D4)* 278
Gardnerville (B4)* 600
Genoa (B4)* 75
Gerlach (B2)* 200
Glenbrook (B3)* 30
Glendale (G6) 20
Golconda (D2)* 350
Gold Hill (B3) 68
Gold Point (D5)* 100
Goldfield (D5)* 275
Goodsprings (F7)* 175
Halleck (F2)*
Hawthorne (C4)* 1,861
Hazen (C3)* 70
Henderson (G6)* 3,643
Hiko (F5)* 23
Hudson (B4) 2
Humboldt (C2) 30
Imlay (C2)* 250
Indian Springs (F6) 50
Ione (D4)*
Jarbidge (F1)* 46
Jean (F7)* 52
Jiggs (F2)* 100
Jungo (C2)* 30
Kimberly (F3)* 300
Lamoille (F2)* 200
Las Vegas (F6)* 24,624
Lee (F2)* 135
Logandale (G6)* 300
Lovelock (C2)* 1,604
Lower Rochester (C2) 5
Lund (F4)* 365
Luning (C4)* 52
Manhattan (E4)* 125
Mason (B4)* 89
Mc Dermitt (D1)* 100
Mc Gill (G3)* 2,297
Mesquite (G6)* 540
Metropolis (G1) 15
Midas (E1) 100
Mill City (D2) 35
Mina (C4)* 274
Minden (B4)* 250
Moapa (G6)* 18
Montello (G1)* 350
Mt. Montgomery (C5) 19
Mountain City (F1)* 180
Nelson (G7) 67
Nivloc (D5) 4
Nixon (B3)* 450
North Fork (F1) 31
North Las Vegas (F6)* 3,875
Oasis (G1) 25
Oreana (C2) 24
Orovada (D1)* 150
Overton (G6)* 750
Owyhee (F1)
Pahrump (E6)* 120
Palisade (E2)* 53
Panaca (G5)* 499
Paradise Valley (D1)* 95
Pioche (G5)* 1,392
Pittman (F6)* 150
Potts (E3) 35
Preston (G4)* 45
Pyramid (B2)* 27
Rawhide (C4) 10
Rebel Creek (D1) 10
Red House (D2)*
Reese River (D4)* 184
Reno (B3)* 32,497
Rio Tinto (E1) 1
Riverside (G6) 25
Round Mountain (E4)* 305
Rowland (F1) 11
Rox (G6) 20
Ruby Valley (F2)* 200
Ruth (F3)* 1,244
San Jacinto (G1) 6
Schurz (C4)* 150
Searchlight (F7)* 229
Shafter (G2)* 91
Shoshone (G4)* 25
Silver City (B3)* 200
Silverpeak (D5)* 63
Sloan (F7)* 200
Smith (B4)* 28
Sparks (B3)* 8,203
Steamboat (B3)* 94
Stillwater (C3)* 9
Sulphur (C2)* 33
Tippett (G3) 50
Tobar (G2) 10
Tonopah (D4)* 1,375
Tungsten (C2)* 300

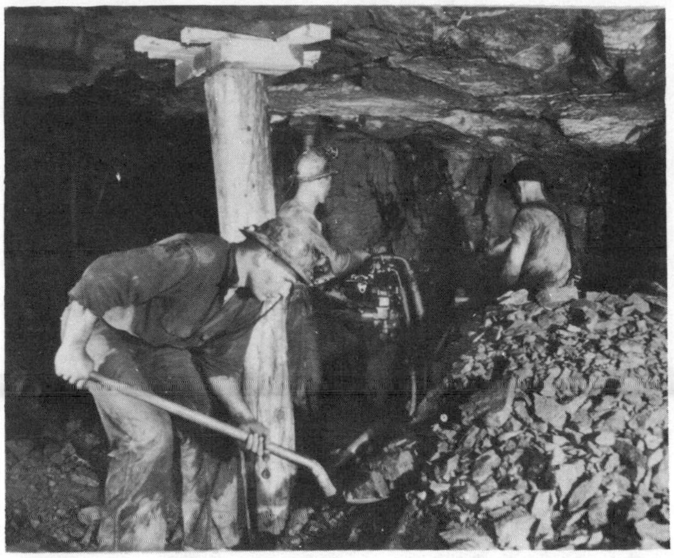

Tuscarora (E1)* 30
Unionville (C2)* 15
Ursine (G5)* 60
Valmy (D2)* 75
Verdi (B3)* 350
Virginia City (B3)* 800
Vya (B1) 30
Wabuska (B3)* 50
Wadsworth (B3)* 275
Weeks (B3) 200
Wellington (B4)* 60
Wells (G1)* 947
White Rock (E1) 26
Whitney (F6)* 200
Wilkins (G1)* 60
Winnemucca (D2)* 2,847
Yerington (B4)* 1,157
Zephyr Cove (A3)* 50

NEW HAMPSHIRE

Map on Page 76 — *Total Population 533,242*

10 COUNTIES

Belknap (D4) 26,632
Carroll (D4) 15,868
Cheshire (B6) 38,811
Coos (D2) 35,932
Grafton (C4) 47,923
Hillsboro (C6) 156,987
Merrimack (C5) 63,022
Rockingham (D5) 70,059
Strafford (D5) 51,567
Sullivan (B5) 26,441

CITIES and TOWNS

Acworth (B5)* △ 418
Alexandria (C4)* △ 402
Allenstown (D5) △1,540
Alstead (B5)* △ 851
Alton (D5)* △1,189
Alton Bay (D5)* 200
Amherst (C6)* △1,461
Andover (C5)* △1,057
Antrim (C5)* △1,030
Apthorp (C3)
Ashland (C4)* △1,599
Ashuelot (B6)* 500
Atkinson (D6) △ 492
Atkinson Depot (D6)*.
Auburn (D5)* △1,158
Barnstead (D5)* △ 846
Barrington (E5) △1,052
Bartlett (D3)* △1,074
Bath (C3)* △ 706
Bear Island (D4)*
Bedford (C6) △2,176
Beebe River (C4)* 275
Belmont (D5)* △1,611
Bennington (C5)* △ 593
Benton (C3) △ 247
Berlin (D3)* 16,615
Berlin Mills (D3)
Bethlehem (C3)* △ 882
Blodgett (D5)
Blodgett Landing (C5)*
Boscawen (C5)* △1,857
Bow (C5) △1,062
Bradford (C5)* △ 606
Brentwood (D6) △ 819
Bretton Woods (D3)* 14
Bridgewater (C4) △ 222
Bristol (C4)* △1,586
Brookfield (D4) △ 159
Brookline (C6)* △ 671
Campton (C4)* △1,149
Canaan (B4)* △14,065
Canaan Center (B4)* 179
Candia (D5)* △1,243
Canobie Lake (D6)* 778
Canterbury (C5)* △ 627
Carroll (D3) △ 359
Cascade (D3)* 1,000
CenterBarnstead (D5)* 550
Ctr. Conway (D4)* 400
Ctr. Harbor (D4)* △ 451
Ctr. Ossipee (D4)* 750
Ctr. Sandwich (C4)* 725
Ctr. Strafford (D5)*
Ctr. Tuftonboro (D4)* 500
Charlestown (B5)* △2,077
Chatham (D3) △ 177
Chesham (B6)*
Chester (D6)* △ 807
Chesterfield (B6)* △ 970
Chichester (D5) △ 735
Chocorua (D4)* 375
Claremont (B5)* 12,811
Colebrook (D2)* △2,116
CONCORD (C5)* 27,988
Contoocook (C5)* 1,000
Conway (D4)* △4,109
Coos Junction (C2)
Cornish Flat (B5)* 200
Crawford House (D3)* 6
Croydon (B5)* △ 349
Crystal (D2) 50
Dalton (C3) △ 557
Danbury (C4)* △ 496
Danville (D6)* △ 508
Deerfield (D5)* △ 706
Deering (C5) △ 392
Derry (D6)* △5,826
Dixville Notch (D2)* △ 13
Dorchester (C4) △ 133
Dover (E5)* 15,874
Drewsville (B5)* 150
Dublin (B6)* △ 675
Dummer (D2) △ 229
Dunbarton (C5)* △ 533
Durham (E5)* △4,770
East Andover (C5)*
E. Barrington (E5)*
E. Candia (D5)* 250
E. Canterbury (D5)
E. Concord (D5)*
E. Derry (D6)* 300
E. Grafton (C4) 100
E. Hampstead (D6)* 920
E. Haverhill (C3)* 150
E. Hebron (C4)*
E. Jaffrey (B6)* 1,866
E. Kingston (E6)* △ 449
E. Lempster (B5)*
E. Madison (D4)* 80
E. Milford (C6)
E. Rochester (E5)* 1,100
E. Rindge (C6)* 200
E. Sullivan (B6)* 150
E. Swanzey (B6)* 700
E. Tilton (D5)
E. Wakefield (E4)*
E. Weare (C5)* 260
E. Westmoreland (B6)* 200
E. Wolfeboro (D4)* 301
Easton (C3) △ 94
Eaton Center (D4)* △ 221
Effingham Falls (D4) △ 341
Elkins (C5)* 200
Ellsworth (C4) △ 24
Elmwood (C6)*
Emerson (West Henniker) (C5)
Enfield (B4)* △1,612
Enfield Center (B4)*
Epping (D5)* △1,796
Epsom (D5)* △ 756
Errol (D2)* △ 224
Etna (B4)*
Exeter (E6)* △5,664
Fabyan House (D3)* 300
Fairview (C3)
Farmington (D5)* △3,454
Fitzwilliam (B6)* △ 872
Fitzwilliam Depot (B6)* 250
Francestown (C6)* △ 405
Franconia (C3)* 549
Franklin (C5)* 6,552
Freedom (E4)* △ 315
Fremont (D6)* △ 698
Gaza (C4)
Georges Mills (B5)* 170
Gerrish (C5)* 275
Gilford (D4) △1,251
Gilmanton (D5)* △ 754
Gilmanton Iron Works (D5)*
Gilsum (B5)* △ 578
Glen (D3)*
Glencliff (C4)* 200
Glendale (D4)
Goffs Falls (D6)* 800
Goffstown (C5)* △5,638
Gonic (E5)* 1,000
Gorham (D3)* △2,639
Goshen (B5)* △ 356
Gossville (D5)* 300
Grafton (C4)* △ 442
Grafton Center (C4)* 93
Grange (D3) 80
Grantham (B5)* △ 359
Grasmere (D5)* 1,545
Greenfield (C6)* △ 430
Greenland (E5)* △ 719
Greenville (C6)* △1,280
Groton (C4) △ 105
Groveton (C2)* 1,918
Guild (B5)* 200
Hampstead (D6)* △ 902
Hampton (E6)* △2,847
Hampton Beach (E6)*
Hampton Falls (E6)* △ 629
Hancock (B6)* △ 612
Hanover (B4)* △6,259
Harrisville (B6)* △ 519
Haverhill (B3)* △3,357
Hedding (E5)*
Henniker (C5)* △1,675
Hill (C4)* △ 310
Hillsboro (C5)* △2,179
Hillsboro Lower Village (C5) 400
Hillsboro Upper Village (C5) 500
Hinsdale (A6)* △1,950
Holderness (C4)* △ 731
Hollis (C6)* △1,196
Hollis Depot (C6)* 380
Hooksett (D5)* △2,792
Hopkinton (C5)* △1,831
Hudson (D6)* △4,183
Intervale (D3)* 600
Jackson (D3)* △ 344
Jaffrey (B6)* △2,911
Jefferson (C3)* △ 728
Kearsarge (D3)*
Keene (B6)* 15,638
Kingston (D6)* △1,283
Laconia (D4)* 14,745
Lakeport (C4)* 3,600
Lancaster (C3)* △3,113
Landaff (C3) △ 342
Langdon (B5) 378
Leavitts Hill (D5)*
Lebanon (B4)* △8,495
Lee (E5) △ 575
Lempster (B5)* △ 309
Lincoln (C3)* △1,415
Lisbon (C3)* △2,009
Litchfield (D6) △ 427
Little Boars Head (E6)
Littleton (C3)* △4,817
Livermore Falls (C4)
Londonderry (D6)* △1,640
Loudon (D5)* △1,012
Lyme (B4)* △ 924
Lyme Center (B4)* 350
Lyndeboro (C6) △ 552
Madbury (E5)* △ 489
Madison (D4)* △ 486
Manchester (C6)* 82,732
Manchester (urban area) 84,768
Maplewood (C3)*
Marleboro (B6)* △1,561
Marlow (B5)* △ 330
Martins (D5)
Mascoma (B4)* 100
Meadows (C3)* 89
Melvin Mills (C5)* 65
Melvin Village (D4)*
Meredith (C4)* △2,222
Meredith Ctr. (C4)* 150
Meriden (B4)* 500
Merrimack (C6)* △1,908
Middleton (D5) △ 255
Milan (D2)* △ 743
Milford (C6)* △4,159
Milton (E5)* 1,510
Milton Mills (E5)* 280
Mirror Lake (D4)* 135
Monroe (B3)* △ 410
Mont Vernon (C6)* △ 405
Moultonboro (D4)* △ 880
Moultonville (D4)* 200
Mount Sunapee (B5)* 125
Munsonville (B5)*
Nashua (C6)* 34,669
Nelson (B5) △ 231
New Boston (C6)* △ 865
New Castle (E5)* △ 583
New Durham (D5)* △ 463
New Hampton (C4)* △ 723
New Ipswich (C6)* △1,147
New London (C5)* △1,484
Newbury (C5)* △ 320
Newfields (E5)* △ 469
Newington (E5) △ 494
Newmarket (D5)* △2,709
Newport (B5)* △5,131
Newton (E6)* △1,173
Newton Jct. (D6)*
North Branch (C5)
N. Charlestown (B5)* 200
N. Chatham (D3)* 177
N. Chichester (D5)* 740
N. Conway (D3)* 1,200
N. End (C4)*
N. Groton (C4) 30
N. Hampton (E6)* △1,104
N. Haverhill (C3)* 500
N. Holderness (C4)
N. Monroe (C3) 160
N. Newport (B5)* 200
N. Rochester (E5)*
N. Salem (D6)* 400
N. Sandwich (D4)*
N. Stratford (C2)*
N. Sutton (C5)*
N. Wakefield (D4)
N. Walpole (B5) 1,000
N. Weare (C5)*
N. Woodstock (C3)* 675
Northfield (C5) △1,561
Northumberland (D2)* △2,779
Northwood (D5)* △ 966
Northwood Ctr. (D5)* 120
Northwood Narrows (D5)* 325
Nottingham (D5)* △ 566
Orange (C4) △ 82
Orford (B4)* △ 726
Orfordville (B4)*
Ossipee (D4)* △1,412
Parkhill (B6) 45
Pelham (D6)* △1,317
Pembroke (D5) △3,094
Penacook (C5)* 3,100
Percy (D2)* 48
Peterborough (C6)* △2,556
Piermont (B4)* △ 511
Pike (B3)* 175
Pittsburg (D1)* △ 697
Pittsfield (D5)* △2,321
Plainfield (B4)* △1,011
Plaistow (D6)* △2,082
Plymouth (C4)* △3,039
Ponemah (C6)
Portsmouth (E5)* 18,830
Powwow River (D6) 75
Province Lake (E4)
Quincy (C4)* 125
Randolph (D3)* △ 158
Raymond (D5)* △1,428
Redstone (D3)* 250
Reeds Ferry (C6)* 500
Richmond (B6) △ 259
Rindge (B6)* △ 707
Riverdale (C5)
Rochester (D5)* 13,776
Rockingham (E5)
Roxbury (B6) △ 117
Rumney (C4)* △ 859
Rumney Depot (C4)* 165
Rye (E5)* △1,982
Rye Beach (E6)* 1,000
Rye North Beach (E5)
Saint Paul's School (C5)*
Salem (D6)* △4,805
Salem Depot (D6)* 1,637
Salisbury (C5)* △ 423
Salmon Falls (E5)* 1,290
Sanbornton (C5)* △ 755
Sanbornville (E4)* 460
Sandown (D6)* △ 315
Sandwich (D4)* △ 615
Seabrook (E6)* △1,788
Sharon (C6) △ 62
Shelburne (D3)* △ 184
Short Falls (D5)* 100
Silver Lake (D4)* 500
Smithtown (E6)* 100
Somersworth (E5)* 6,927
Snowville (D4)* 100
Soo Nipi (C5) 25
South Acworth (B5)*
S. Alexandria (C4) 100
S. Chatham (E3)* 54
S. Danbury (C5)*
S. Danville (D6)* 125
S. Deerfield (D5)*
S. Effingham (E4)*
S. Hampton (E6) △ 314
S. Keene (B6) 200
S. Lee (D5) 70
S. Lyndeboro (C6)* 552
S. Merrimack (C6)* 250
S. Newbury (C5)* 88
S. Pittsfield (D5)
S. Seabrook (E6) 1,000
S. Stoddard (B5)
S. Sutton (C5)* 139
S. Tamworth (D4)*
S. Wolfeboro (D4) 248
S. Weare (C5)
Spofford (B6)* 350
Springfield (B4)* △ 324
Stark (D2) △ 373
State Line (B6)* 125
Stewartstown (D2) △ 970
Stinson Lake (C4)*
Stoddard (B5)* △ 200
Strafford (D5)* △ 770
Stratford (C2)* △ 973
Stratham (E5)* △ 759
Sugar Hill (C3)* 250
Sullivan (B5)* △ 272
Sunapee (B5)* △1,108
Suncook (C5)*
Surry (B5)* △ 291
Sutton (C5)* △ 554
Swanzey (B6) △2,806
Swiftwater (C3)
Tamworth (D4)* △1,025
Temple (C6)* △ 330
The Weirs (D4)*
Thornton (C4) △ 460
Tilton (C5)* △2,085
Troy (B6)* △1,360
Tuftonboro (D4) △ 697
Twin Mountain (C3)* 352
Union (D5)* 550
Unity (B5)* △ 653
Village (D6)*
Wakefield (E4)* △1,267
Walpole (B5)* △2,536
Warner (C5)* △1,080
Warren (C4)* △ 581
Washington (B5)* △ 168
Waterville Valley (C4) △ 11
Weare (C4) △1,345
Webster (C5) △ 386
Wendell (B5)* 200
Wentworth (C4)* △ 413
Wentworth Location (D2)* △ 48
West Alton (D4)*
W. Andover (C5)*
W. Brentwood (D6)
W. Campton (C4)* 125
W. Canaan (B4)*
W. Chesterfield (A6)* 250
W. Claremont (B5)* 100
W. Epping (D5)
W. Hampstead (D6)*
W. Henniker (Emerson) (C5)
W. Hopkinton (C5)* 100
W. Lebanon (B4)* 1,737
W. Manchester (C6)
W. Milan (D2)* 250
W. Nottingham (D5)* 80
W. Ossipee (D4)* 175
W. Peterborough (B6)* 350
W. Rindge (C6)* 230
W. Rumney (C4)* 200
W. Rye (E6)* 55
W. Springfield (B5)* 100
W. Stewartstown (C2)* 385
W. Swanzey (B6)* 1,400
W. Thornton (C4)* 450
W. Windham (D6)
Westmoreland (B6)*△ 789
Westmoreland Depot (A6)*
Westport (B6) 328
Westville (D6)* 300
Whiteface (D4)
Whitefield (C3)* △1,677
Willey House (D3)* 10
Wilmot (C5)* △ 370
Wilmot Flat (C5)*
Wilton (C6)* △1,952
Winchester (B6)* △2,388
Windham (D6) △ 964
Windham Depot (D6)*
Winnipesaukee (D4)*
Winnisquam (D5)* 400
Wolfeboro (D4)* △2,581
Wolfeboro Falls (D4)* 600
Wonalancet (D4)* 36
Woodstock (C4)* 894
Woodsville (B3)* 1,542

NEW JERSEY

Map on Page 77 — *Total Population 4,835,329*

21 COUNTIES

Atlantic (D5) 132,399
Bergen (E2) 539,139
Burlington (D4) 135,910
Camden (D4) 300,743
Cape May (D5) 37,131
Cumberland (C5) 88,597
Essex (E2) 905,949
Gloucester (C4) 91,727
Hudson (E2) 647,437
Hunterdon (D2) 42,736
Mercer (D3) 229,781
Middlesex (E3) 264,872
Monmouth (E3) 225,327
Morris (D2) 164,371
Ocean (E4) 56,622
Passaic (E1) 337,093
Salem (C4) 49,508
Somerset (D2) 99,052
Sussex (D1) 34,423
Union (E2) 398,138
Warren (C2) 54,374

CITIES and TOWNS

Absecon (D5)* 2,355
Adamston (E3)* 450
Adelphia (E3)* 300
Allamuchy (D2)* 600
Allendale (B1)* 2,409
Allenhurst (F3)* 758
Allentown (D3)* 931
Allenwood (E3)*
Alloway (C4)* 700
Almonesson (B4)*
Alpha (C2)* 2,117
Alpine (C1)* 644
Ampere (B2)* 10,000
Andover (D2)* 560
Annandale (D2)*
Arlington (B2)* 16,000
Asbury (C2)* 300
Asbury Park (F3)* 17,094
Ashland (D4)* 1,240
Atco (D4)* 2,500
Atlantic City (E5)* 61,657
Atlantic City (urban area) 105,326
Atlantic Highlands (F3)* 3,083
Audubon (C4)* 9,531
Audubon Park (B3) 1,859
Augusta (D1)* 80
Aura (C4) 100
Avalon (D5)* 428
Avenel (E2)* 8,700
Avon by the Sea (F3)* 1,650
Awosting (E1)
Baptistown (D2)* 350
Barber (E2)*
Barnegat (E4)* 1,150
Barnegat Light (E4)* 227
Barrington (B3)* 2,651
Bartley (D2)* 500
Basking Ridge (D2)* 1,899
Bay Head (E3)* 808
Bayonne (B2)* 77,203
Bayville (E4)* 2,000
Beach Haven (E4)* 1,050
Beach Haven Crest (E4)*
Beach Haven Terrace (E4)* 350
Beachwood (E4)* 1,251
Beaver Lake (D1)* 175

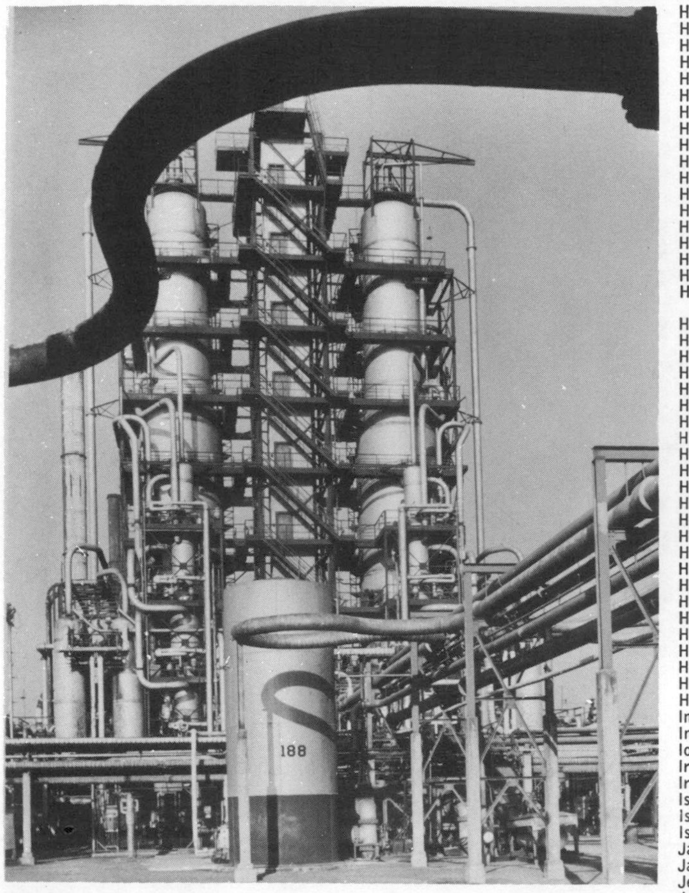

Bedminster (D2)*......... 650
Beesleys Point (D5)...... 300
Belford (E3)*..............1,832
Belle Mead (D3)*.......... 650
Belleplain (D5)............ 700
Belleville (E2)*..........32,019
Bellmawr (B3)..............5,213
Belmar (E3)*...............4,636
Belvidere (C2)*............2,406
Bergenfield (C1)*........17,647
Berkeley Heights
(E2)* 3,460
Berlin (D4)*..................2,339
Bernardsville (D2)*.......3,956
Bevans (D1)*...............
Beverly (D3)*................3,084
Birmingham (D4)*........ 250
Bivalve (C5)*................
Blackwood (C4)*...........1,344
Blackwood Terrace
(C4)* 2,100
Blairstown (C2)*.......... 875
Blawenburg (D3)*......... 200
Bloomfield (B2)*.........49,307
Bloomingdale (E1)*......3,251
Bloomsbury (C2)*......... 722
Bogota (B2)*................7,662
Boonton (E2)*...............7,163
Bordentown (D3)*.........5,497
Bound Brook (D2)*.......8,374
Bradley Beach (F3)*.....3,911
Brainards (C2)*............ 350
Branchville (D1)*.......... 810
Brant Beach (E4)*........
Bridgeboro (D3)*.......... 750
Bridgeport (C4)*........... 650
Bridgeton (C5)*..........18,378
Brielle (E3)*.................1,328
Brigantine (E5)*...........1,267
Broadway (C2)*............ 250
Brooklawn (B3).............2,262
Brookside (D2)*............
Browns Mills (D4)*.......
Budd Lake (D2)*..........1,032
Buena (D4)*.................2,640
Burlington (D3)*.........12,051
Butler (E2)*..................4,050
Buttzville (D2)*............ 300
Byram Cove (D2)*.........
Caldwell (E2)*..............6,270
Califon (D2)*................ 623
Camden (C4)*............124,555
Campgaw (B1)*............
Canton (C5)*................ 300
Cape May (D6)*............3,607
Cape May Court House
(D5)* 1,093
Cape May Point (D6)*.. 198
Carlstadt (B2)*..............5,591
Carlton Hill (B2)*.........1,000
Carneys Point (C4)*......4,000
Carpentersville (C2)*....
Carteret (E2)*.............13,030
Cassville (E3)*..............
Cedar Brook (D4)*........ 600
Cedar Grove (A2)*........7,723
Cedar Knolls (E2)*.......1,500
Cedar Run (E4)*........... 260
Cedarville (C5)*............1,009
Centerton (C4)*............ 200
Changewater (D2)*....... 225
Chatham (E2)*...............7,391
Chatsworth (D4)*.......... 350
Cheesequake (E3)*........ 300
Chesilhurst (D4)............ 314
Chester (D2)*................ 754
Chesterfield (D3).......... 500
Chews (B4)*..................1,500
Clarksboro (C4)*........... 800
Clarksburg (E3)*........... 500
Clayton (C4)*.................3,023
Clementon (D4)*............3,191
Cliffside Park (F2)*....17,116
Cliffwood (E3)*.............1,800
Clifton (E2)*................64,511
Clinton (D2)*.................1,118
Closter (C1)*..................3,376
Cold Spring (D6)........... 100
Cold Spring Harbor
(D6) 25
Colesville (D1)*............ 150
Collingswood (C4)*......15,800
Cologne (D4)*............... 672
Colonia (E2)*................
Colts Neck (E3)*.......... 200
Columbia (C2)*............. 300
Columbus (D3)*............ 600
Convent Station (E2)*..
Cookstown (D3)*.......... 450
Corbin City (D5)*.......... 238
Coytesville (C2)*...........2,500
Cranberry Lake (D2)*... 200
Cranbury (E3)*..............1,843
Cranbury Station (E3)..
Cranford (E2)*..........△18,602
Creamridge (E3)*.......... 50
Cresskill (C1)*...............3,534
Crosswicks (D3)*........... 850
Crystal Lake (B1).........
Daretown (C4)*............. 150
Dayton (D3)*................ 450
Deal (F3)*.....................1,064
Deans (D3)*.................. 300
Deepwater (C4)*............1,500
Deerfield Street (C4)*.. 500
Delair (C4)*...................2,237
Delanco (D3)*................2,494
Delawanna (B2)*..........
Delaware (C2)*............ 279
Delmont (C5)*.............. 330
Demarest (C1)*.............1,786
Dennisville (D5)*.......... 300
Denville (E2)*................6,058
Dias Creek (D5)............ 400
Dividing Creek (C5)*..... 900
Dorchester (D5)*.......... 235
Dorothy (D5)*............... 400
Dover (D2)*.................11,174
Drakestown (D2)........... 100
Dumont (F2)*...............13,013
Dunellen (D2)*..............6,291
Dutch Neck (D3)*.........
East Keansburg (E3)*...2,596
E. Millstone (D3)*........
E. Newark (B2).............2,173
E. Orange (B2)*...........79,340
E. Paterson (B2)*........15,386
E. Rutherford (B2)*......7,438
Eatontown (E3)*...........3,044
Echo Lake (E1).............
Edgewater (C2)*...........3,952
Edgewater Park (D3)*.. 150
Egg Harbor City (D4)*..3,838
Elberon (E3)*................1,200
Eldora (D5).................... 350
Elizabeth (E2)*.........112,817
Ellisdale (D3)................ 60
Elmer (C4)*...................1,460
Elwood (D4)*................ 600
Emerson (B1)*...............1,744
Englewood (C2)*.........23,145
Englewood Cliffs (C2)... 966
English Creek (D5)........ 350
Englishtown (E3)*........1,004
Erlton (B3)*...................2,000
Essex Fells (A2)*..........1,617
Estell Manor (D5)*....... 381
Everett (E3).................. 100
Ewan (C4)*................... 240
Fair Haven (E3)*...........3,560
Fair Lawn (B1)*.........23,885
Fairton (C5)*................
Fairview (C2)*..............8,661
Fanwood (E2)*..............3,228
Far Hills (D2)*............. 600
Farmingdale (E3)*........ 755
Fieldsboro (D3)*........... 589
Finesville (C2)*............ 275
Flagtown (D2)*............. 450
Flanders (D2)*.............. 450
Flatbrookville (D1)*......
Flemington (D2)*..........3,058
Florence (D3)*...............3,460
Florham Park (E2)........2,385
Folsom (D4).................. 292
Fords (E2)*....................5,200
Forked River (E4)*.......1,000
Fort Lee (C2)*.............11,648
Fortescue (C5)*............ 500
Franklin (D1)*...............3,864
Franklin Lakes (B1)......2,021
Franklin Park (D3)*..... 715
Franklinville (C4)*........1,226
Freehold (E3)*...............7,550
Frenchtown (C2)*.........1,305
Garfield (E2)*..............27,550
Garwood (E2)*...............4,622
Gibbsboro (D4)*............ 906
Gibbstown (C4)*............2,546
Gillette (E2)*.................1,300
Gladstone (D2)*............
Glassboro (C4)*.............5,867
Glasser (D2)*................ 100
Glen Gardner (D2)*....... 654
Glen Ridge (B2)*...........7,620
Glen Rock (B1)*.............7,145
Glendola (E3)................ 700
Glenwood (D1)*............ 425
Gloucester City (C4)*..14,357
Gloucester Heights
(B3)* 1,200
Goshen (D5)*................ 360
Grasselli (B3)*..............
Great Meadows (D2)*... 825
Great Notch (B2)*........1,000
Green Bank (D4)*......... 200
Green Creek (D5)*........
Green Pond (E1)*......... 105
Green Village (D2)*...... 800
Greendell (D2)*............ 100
Greenwich (C5)*........... 950
Greenwich Pier (C5)...... 25
Grenloch (C4)*..............
Greystone Park (D2)*...
Groveville (D3)*............ 700
Guttenberg (C2)*...........5,566
Hackensack (F2)*........29,219
Hackettstown (D2)*.......3,894
Haddon Heights
(C4)* 7,287
Haddonfield (D4)*.......10,495
Hainesburg (C2)*.......... 437
Hainesport (D4)*...........1,130
Hainesville (D1)............ 100
Haledon (B1).................6,204
Haleyville (C5).............. 100
Hamburg (D1)*..............1,305
Hamilton (E3)............... 750
Hamilton Square (D3)*.3,500
Hammonton (D4)*........8,411
Hampton (D2)*............. 975
Hancocks Bridge (C4)*.. 300
Hanford (D1)................
Hanover (E2)*...............
Harbourton (D3)*......... 82
Hardingville (C4)......... 75
Harlingen (D3)*............
Harrington Park (C1)*..1,634
Harrison (B2)*.............13,490
Harrisonville (C4)*........ 338
Hartford (D4)*............. 500
Harvey Cedars (E4)*..... 106
Hasbrouck Heights
(B2)* 9,181
Haskell (A1)*.................3,000
Haworth (C1)*...............1,612
Hawthorne (E2)*.........14,816
Hazlet (E3)*.................. 800
Heislerville (D5)*.......... 300
Helmetta (E3)*............. 580
Hewitt (E1)*.................
Hi-Nella (B4)................ 237
Hibernia (E2)*.............. 350
High Bridge (D2)*.........1,854
Highland Park (E2)*....9,721
Highlands (F3)*............2,959
Hightstown (D3)*..........3,712
Hillsdale (E2)*...............4,127
Hillside (B2)*.............△21,007
Hoboken (C2)*.............50,676
Hohokus (B1)*...............2,254
Holmdel (E3)*............... 500
Holmeson (E3)..............
Hopatcong (D2)*...........1,173
Hope (D2)*.................... 500
Hopewell (D3)*..............1,869
Hornerstown (E3)......... 140
Hudson Heights (C2)*...2,000
Imlaystown (D3)*.........
Interlaken (E3)............ 833
Iona (C4)*.................... 150
Ironia (D2)*.................. 300
Irvington (B2)*............59,201
Iselin (E2)*....................7,000
Island Beach ‡(E4)....... 13
Island Heights (E4)*.... 795
Jacobstown (D3)...........
Jamesburg (E3)*...........2,307
Jersey City (F2)*......299,017
Jobstown (D3)*............. 250
Johnsonburg (D2)*........ 150
Juliustown (D3)*.......... 350
Jutland (D2)*................ 120
Keansburg (E3)*............5,559
Kearny (B2)*...............39,952
Keasbey (E2)*...............
Kenilworth (E2)*...........4,922
Kenvil (D2)*...................1,361
Keswick Grove (E4)*.... 150
Keyport (E3)*................5,888
Kingston (D3)*.............. 900
Kinnelon (E2)................1,350
Kirkwood (B4)*.............. 550
Lafayette (D1)*..............1,100
Lake Como (E3)*..........
Lake Hiawatha (E2)*....
Lake Hopatcong (D2)*..5,000
Lakehurst (E3)*.............1,518
Lakewood (E3)*.............9,970
Lambertville (D3)*........4,477
Lamington (D2)............ 150
Landing (D2)*................1,500
Landisville (D4)*...........1,500
Lanoka Harbor (E4)*.... 250
Laurel Springs (B4)*....1,540
Laurelton (E3)*............ 800
Laurence Harbor (E3)*.
Lavallette (E4)*............ 567
Lawnside (B3)*..............1,566
Lawrenceville (D3)*.....1,056
Layton (D1)*................. 350
Lebanon (D2)*............... 752
Ledgewood (D2)*.......... 800
Leeds Point (E4)*........ 400
Leesburg (D5)*.............
Leonardo (E3)*..............1,887
Leonia (C2)*...................7,378
Liberty Corner (D2)*....1,500
Lincoln Park (A1)*.......3,376
Lincroft (E3)*...............
Linden (E2)*................30,644
Lindenwold (B4)*.........3,479
Linwood (D5)*...............1,925
Little Falls (E2)*...........6,600
Little Ferry (B2)*.........4,955
Little Silver (F3)*........2,595
Little York (C2)*..........
Livingston (E2)*.........10,100
Locust (F3)*.................. 500
Lodi (B2)*....................15,392
Long Branch (F3)*......23,090
Long Valley (D2)*.........
Longport (D5)*............. 618
Lower Bank (E4)*......... 118
Lower Squankum (E3).. 150
Lumberton (D4)*.......... 600
Lyndhurst (B2)*........△19,980
Lyons (D2)*..................
Madison (E2)*.............10,417
Magnolia (C4)*..............1,883
Mahwah (E1)*................3,800
Malaga (C4)*................ 425
Manahawkin (E4)*........1,200
Manalapan (E3)............
Manasquan (E3)*...........3,178
Mantoloking (E3)*........ 72
Mantua (C4)*...............
Manville (D2)*................8,597
Maple Shade (D4)*.......7,500
Maplewood (E2)*......△25,201
Marcella (E2)............... 300
Margate City (E5)*......4,715
Marlboro (E3)*............. 300
Marlton (D4)*............... 475
Marmora (D5)*............. 175
Martinsville (D2)*.........2,700
Masonville (D4)*...........1,500
Matawan (E3)*...............3,739
Maurice River (D5).......
Mauricetown (D5)*....... 500
Mayetta (E4)*.............. 150
Mays Landing (D5)*.....1,301
Maywood (B2)*..............8,667
Mc Afee (D1)*..............
Mc Kee City (D5).......... 200
Medford (D4)*...............1,300
Medford Lakes (D4)...... 461
Mendham (D2)*.............1,724
Menlo Park (E2)*.........
Mercerville (D3)*..........5,000
Merchantville (C4)*......4,183
Metuchen (E2)*.............9,879
Mickleton (C4)*............ 325
Middle Valley (D2)*...... 300
Middlebush (D2)*.........
Middlesex (E2)*.............5,943
Middletown (E3)*......... 700
Middleville (D1)*.......... 75
Midland Park (B1)*.....5,164
Midvale (E1).................2,000
Milford (C2)*.................1,012
Milhurst (E3)............... 25
Millburn (E2)*..........△14,560
Millington (D2)*........... 400
Millstone (D2)*............ 289
Milltown (E3)*...............3,786
Millville (C5)*..............16,041
Milmay (D5)*................ 294
Milton (D1)...................1,100
Mine Hill (D2)...............2,297
Minotola (D4)*.............
Mizpah (D5)*................ 875
Monmouth Beach (F3)* 806
Monmouth Jct. (D3)*.... 443
Monroe (D1)*................ 150
Monroeville (C4)*........ 500
Montague (D1)............. 600
Montclair (E2)*...........43,297
Montvale (E1)*...............1,856
Montville (E2)*............
Moonachie (B2)..............1,775
Moorestown (D4)*.........9,175
Morganville (E3)*.........
Morris Plains (D2)*.....2,707
Morristown (D2)*........17,124
Mt. Arlington (D2)*...... 639
Mt. Ephraim (B3)*........4,449
Mt. Freedom (D2)*....... 500
Mt. Holly (D4)*..............8,206
Mt. Hope (D2)................1,500
Mt. Royal (C4)*............ 850
Mountain Lakes (E2)*..2,806
Mountain View (A2)*....5,000
Mountainside ‡(E2)......2,046
Mullica Hill (C4)*......... 900
Murray Hill (E2)*......... 950
National Park (B3)*.....2,419
Naughright (D2)........... 300
Navesink (E3)*...............1,085
Neptune (E3)*................3,073
Neshanic (D3)*.............. 500
Netcong (D2)*................2,284
New Bedford (E3)......... 600
New Brunswick (E3)*..38,811
New Egypt (E3)*...........1,294
New Gretna (E4)*......... 600
New Hampton (D2)....... 200
New Lisbon (D4)*.........
New Market (D2)*.......1,500
New Milford (B1)*........6,006
New Monmouth (E3)*... 700
New Providence ‡(E2)*.3,380
New Sharon (D3).......... 50
New Vernon (D2)*........1,100
Newark (E2)*............438,776
Newfield (D4)*...............1,010
Newfoundland (D1)*.....
Newport (C5)*............... 950
Newton (D1)*.................5,781
Newtonville (D4)*.........
Nixon (E2)*....................2,500
Norma (C4)*.................
Normandy Beach (E3)*. 150
N. Arlington (B2)*......15,970
N. Bergen (B2)*........△41,560
N. Branch (D2)*........... 600
N. Caldwell (B2)...........1,781
N. Cape May (C6).........
N. Hackensack (B2)*.....
N. Haledon (B1)...........3,550
N. Plainfield (E2)*.....12,766
N. Wildwood (D6).........3,158
Northfield (D5)*............3,498
Northvale (F1)*..............1,455
Norwood (C1)*................1,792
Nutley (B2)*.................26,992
Oak Ridge (E1)*............ 75
Oak Tree (E2)................2,000
Oakhurst (E3)*...............2,388
Oakland (E1)*.................1,817
Oaklyn (B3)...................4,889
Ocean City (D5)*............6,040
Ocean Gate (E4)*......... 452
Ocean Grove (F3)*........3,806
Ocean View (D5)*......... 195
Oceanport (E3)*.............7,588
Oceanville (D5)*.............1,500
Ogdensburg (D1)*.........1,169
Old Bridge (E3)*............3,500
Old Tappan (C1)........... 828
Oldwick (D2)*............... 500
Oradell (B1)*..................3,665
Orange (B2)*................38,037
Osbornsville (E3)*........ 800
Oxford (C2)*..................1,041
Packanack Lake (B1)*..3,000
Palermo (D5)................ 150
Palisade (C2)*................3,784
Palisades Park (C2)*....9,635
Palmyra (D4)*................5,802
Paramus (B1)*...............6,268
Park Ridge (B1)*...........3,189
Parkertown (E4)*.........
Parlin (E3)*.....................2,000
Parsippany (E2)*..........
Passaic (E2)*................57,702
Paterson (E2)*.............139,336
Pattenburg (C2)*......... 200
Paulsboro (C4)*.............7,842
Peapack (D2)*..............
Pedricktown (C4)*........ 575
Pemberton (D4)*...........1,194
Pennington (D3)*...........1,682
Penns Grove (C4)*........6,669
Pennsauken (B3)*.....△22,767
Pennsville (C4)*.............3,500
Pequannock (E2)*.........2,500
Perrineville (E3)*.........
Perth Amboy (E2)*....41,330
Petersburg (D5)*.......... 250
Phalanx (E3)................
Phillipsburg (C2)*.......18,919
Pine Beach (E4)*.......... 495
Pine Brook (E2)*.......... 500
Pine Hill ‡(C4)*.............2,546
Pine Valley (D4)........... 39
Pitman (C4)*..................6,960
Pittstown (C2)*............ 273
Plainfield (E2)*............42,366
Plainsboro (D3)*............1,118
Pleasant Grove (D2)...... 75
Pleasantville (D5)*......11,938
Pluckemin (D2)*........... 300
Point Pleasant (E3)*....4,009
Point Pleasant Beach
‡(E3) 2,900
Pomona (D5)*.............. 300
Pompton Lakes (A1)*...4,654
Pompton Plains (E2)*...3,450
Port Elizabeth (D5)*.... 500
Port Monmouth (E3)*...1,767
Port Morris (D2)*..........1,735
Port Murray (D2)*........ 400
Port Norris (C5)*...........2,050
Port Reading (E2)*........3,500
Port Republic (D4)*..... 423
Pottersville (D2)*......... 350
Princeton (D3)*............12,230
Princeton Jct. (D3)*.....
Prospect Park (E2).......5,242
Prospect Plains (E3)*... 160
Quakertown (D2)*........ 148
Quinton (C4)*.................1,000
Rahway (E2)*...............21,290
Ralston (D2)*............... 500
Ramsey (E1)*..................4,670
Rancocas (D3)*............. 500
Raritan (D2)*..................5,131
Readington (D2)*......... 300
Reaville (D3)................ 219
Red Bank (E3)*............12,743
Richland (D5)*............. 800
Richwood (C4)*............ 350
Ridgefield (B2)*.............8,312
Ridgefield Park (F2)*.11,993
Ridgewood (E2)*.........17,481
Riegelsville (C2)*......... 250
Ringoes (D3)*............... 400
Ringwood (E1)*..............1,752
Rio Grande (D5)*.........
Risley (D5)...................
River Edge (B1)*...........9,204
Riverdale (E2)*..............1,352
Riverside (D3)*...............7,199
Riverton (D3)*................2,761
Roadstown (C5)*.......... 125
Robbinsville (D3)*........2,038
Rochelle Park (B2)*.....4,475
Rockaway (D2)*.............3,812
Rockleigh (C1).............. 110
Rocky Hill (D3)*........... 537
Roebling (D3)*...............3,325
Roosevelt (E3)*............ 720
Roseland (A2)*...............2,019
Roselle (B2)*................17,681
Roselle Park (A2)*......11,537
Rosemont (D3)*............ 117
Rosenhayn (C5)*...........1,000
Rumson (F3)*.................4,044
Runnemede (C4)*...........4,217
Rutherford (B2)*.........17,411
Saddle River (B1)*.......1,003
Salem (C4)*....................9,050
Sand Brook (D3)*......... 175
Sayreville (E3)*...........10,338
Schooleys Mt. (D2)*..... 250
Scobeyville (E3)*.......... 350
Scotch Plains (E2)*.....9,000
Sea Bright (F3)*........... 999
Sea Girt (E3)*.................1,178
Sea Isle City (D5)*........ 993
Seabrook (C5)*...............3,000
Seaside Heights (E4)*... 862
Seaside Park (E4)*....... 987
Secaucus (B2)*...............9,750
Sergeantsville (D3)*..... 175
Sewaren (E2)*................1,800
Sewell (C4)*.................. 600
Sharptown (C4)............ 225
Shiloh (C5)*.................. 427
Ship Bottom (E4)*........ 533
Short Hills (E2)*............7,000
Shrewsbury (E3)*...........1,613
Sicklerville (D4)*...........3,500
Singac (A2)*.................
Skillman (D3)*...............3,500
Smithburg (E3)............. 25
Smiths Mills (E1).......... 40
Smithville (D4)*............ 350
Somerdale (D4)*.............1,417
Somers Point (D5)*......2,480
Somerville (D2)*..........11,571
So. Amboy (E3)*.............8,422
So. Belmar ‡(E3)...........1,294
So. Bound Brook (E2)*.2,905
So. Branch (D2)*.......... 120
So. Cape May (D6).......
So. Dennis (D5)*.......... 372
So. Orange (A2)*.........15,230
So. Plainfield (E2)*......8,008
So. River (E3)*............11,308
So. Seaville (D5)*.........
So. Toms River (E4)..... 492
So. Vineland (D5).........
Southard (E3).............. 750
Sparta (D1)*..................3,300
Sperry Springs (D2)*... 500
Spotswood (E3)*............2,325
Spring Lake (F3)*.........2,008
Spring Lake Heights
‡(E3) 1,798
Springfield (E2)*........△7,214
Staffordville (E4)*....... 250
Stanhope (D2)*..............1,351
Stanton (D2)*............... 150
Stelton (E2)*................
Stephensburg (D2)....... 200
Stewartsville (C2)*.......1,000
Stillwater (D1)*............ 275
Stirling (E2)*.................1,076
Stockholm (D1)*........... 500
Stockton (D3)*............. 488
Stone Harbor (D5)*..... 670
Stratford (C4)*...............1,356
Strathmere (D5)*......... 110
Succasunna (D2)*.........1,022
Summit (E2)*...............17,929
Surf City (E4)*............ 291
Sussex (D1)*..................1,541
Swartswood (D1)*........ 150
Swedesboro (C4)*..........2,459
Tabor (E2)*....................2,500
Tavistock ‡(B3)............ 15
Teaneck (B2)*...........△33,772
Tenafly (F2)*..................9,651
Tennent (E3)*............... 250
Teterboro (B2)*............ 28
Thorofare (B4)*............ 500
Three Bridges (D2)*..... 700
Titusville (D3)*..............2,500
Toms River (E4)*...........2,517
Totowa (B1)*..................6,045
Towaco (E2)*..................1,500
Townsends Inlet (D5)*.. 175
Tranquility (D2)*......... 100
Treasure Island (C3)*...
TRENTON (D3)*.......128,009
Trenton (urban
area) 189,276
Tuckahoe (D5)*............ 800
Tuckerton (E4)*.............1,332
Union (E2)*..............△38,004
Union Beach (E3)*.........3,636
Union City (C2)*..........55,537
Upper Macopin (E1)..... 500
Upper Saddle River
(B1) 706
Vail (C2)....................... 75
Van Hiseville (E3)*...... 250
Vauxhall (A2)*...............7,000
Ventnor (E5)*.................8,185
Vernon (E1)*................. 360
Verona (E2)*................10,921
Vienna (D2)*................. 275
Villas (D5)*................... 700
Vincentown (D4)*.........
Vineland (C5)*...............8,155
Vulcanite (C2).............. 900
Waldwick (E1)*...............3,963
Wallington (B2)*...........8,910
Wallpack Center (D1)*. 210
Wanamassa (E3)............2,512
Wanaque (B1)*...............4,222
Waretown (E4)*............ 750
Warren Point (B1)*.....5,000
Warrenville (D2).......... 850
Washington (D2)*..........4,802
Watchung (E2)*..............1,818
Waterford Works(D4)*.1,200
Wayne (A1)*..................
Weehawken (C2)*......△14,380
Wenonah (C4)*...............1,511
W. Berlin (D4)*.............
W. Caldwell (A2)...........4,666
W. Cape May (D6)........ 897
W. Creek (E4)*............. 525
W. Englewood (C2)*....14,000
W. Freehold (E3).......... 100
W. Long Branch (F3)*..2,739
W. Milford (E1)*...........
W. New York (C2)*.....37,683
W. Norwood (C1)*.........1,900
W. Orange (A2)*..........28,605
W. Paterson (B2)...........3,931
W. Pt. Pleasant (E3)*..3,000
W. Portal (D2)*.............
W. Trenton (D3)*..........
W. Wildwood (D6)........ 237
Westfield (E2)*............21,243
Weston (D2)..................1,500
Westville (C4)*...............4,731
Westwood (B1)*..............6,766
Wharton (D2)*................3,853
Whippany (E2)*..............2,100
White House Station
(D2)* 1,750
Whitehouse (D2)*......... 600
Whitesbog (E4)*........... 175
Whitesboro (D5)*......... 700
Whitesville (E3)........... 450
Whiting (E4)*............... 350
Wickatunk (E3)*...........
Wildwood (D6)*..............5,475
Wildwood Crest (D6)....1,772
Williamstown (D4)*.......2,632
Windsor (D3)*............... 250
Winfield (B3)..................2,720
Winslow (D4)*...............
Winslow Jct. (D4).........
Wood-Lynne (B3)...........2,776
Wood-Ridge (B2)*..........6,283
Woodbine (D5)*..............2,417
Woodbridge (E2)*.....△35,758
Woodbury (C4)*............10,931
Woodbury Hts. (B4)*....1,373
Woodcliff Lake (B1)*....1,420
Woodport (D2)...............2,000
Woodstown (C4)*............2,345
Wortendyke (B1)*......... 650
Wrightstown (D3)*.........1,199
Wyckoff (E2)*.................5,400
Yardville (D3)*...............1,600
Yorktown (C4)*............. 125
Zarephath (D2)*........... 250
Zion (D3)*..................... 100

NEW MEXICO

Map on Page 78 — *Total Population 681,187*

32 COUNTIES

Bernalillo (C3)...145,673
Catron (A4)...3,533
Chaves (E5)...40,605
Colfax (E2)...16,761
Curry (F4)...23,351
De Baca (E4)...3,464
Dona Ana (C6)...39,557
Eddy (E6)...40,640
Grant (A5)...21,649
Guadalupe (E4)...6,772
Harding (F3)...3,013
Hidalgo (A7)...5,095
Lea (F6)...30,717
Lincoln (D5)...7,409
Los Alamos (C3)...10,476
Luna (B6)...8,753
Mc Kinley (A3)...27,451
Mora (E3)...8,720
Otero (D6)...14,909
Quay (F3)...13,971
Rio Arriba (B2)...24,997
Roosevelt (F4)...16,409
San Juan (A2)...18,292
San Miguel (D3)...26,512
Sandoval (C3)...12,438
Santa Fe (C3)...38,153
Sierra (B5)...7,186
Socorro (C5)...9,670
Taos (D2)...17,146
Torrance (D4)...8,012
Union (F2)...7,372
Valencia (A4)...22,481

CITIES and TOWNS

Abbott (E2)*
Abeytas (C4)
Abiquiu (C2)*
Abo (C4)
Acme (E5)
Acomita (B3)*
Adams Diggings (A4)
Afton (B6)... 15
Agua Fria (D2)
Akela (B6)... 40
Alameda (C3)*...1,792
Alamogordo (C6)*...6,783
Albert (F3)*... 35
Albuquerque (C3)*...96,815
Alcalde (C2)*
Algodones (C3)*... 250
Alma (A5)... 50
Alto (D5)*... 50
Amalia (D2)*
Amistad (F3)*... 33
Anapra (C7)
Ancho (D5)*... 100
Animas (A7)*
Anthony (C6)*... 800
Anton Chico (D3)*... 600
Apache Creek (A5)*... 85
Arabela (D5)... 60
Aragon (A5)*... 89
Arch (F4)*... 35
Arrey (B6)*... 350
Arroyo Hondo (D2)*... 500
Arroyoseco (D2)*... 400
Artesia (E6)*...8,244
Atarque (A4)*... 100
Atoka (E6)... 64
Augustine (B4)*
Aztec (B2)*... 885
Bard (F3)*... 45
Bayard (A6)*...2,119
Beaverhead (A5)
Belen (C4)*...4,495
Bell Ranch (E3)*... 20
Bellview (F4)*... 150
Bent (D5)*... 250
Berino (C6)*... 300
Bernalillo (C3)*...1,922
Bernardo (C4)... 30
Bibo (B3)
Bingham (C5)*... 7
Blanco (B2)*... 135
Bloomfield (A2)*... 500
Bluewater (A3)*... 350
Bluit (F5)
Boaz (F5)*... 30
Bosque (C4)*... 400
Brilliant (E2)*... 225
Broadview (F4)*... 80
Buchanan (E4)*
Buckeye (F6)*... 227
Buckhorn (A5)*... 500
Buena Vista (D3)*... 265
Bueyeros (F3)*... 38
Caballo (B6)*
Cabezon (B3)
Cambray (B6)*... 8
Cameron (F4)*... 18
Canjilon (C2)*... 900
Canones (C2)*... 140
Canoncito (C3)
Capitan (D5)*... 575
Caprock (F5)*... 12
Capulin (F2)*... 200
Carlsbad (E6)*...17,975
Carrizozo (D5)*...1,389
Carson (D2)*... 25
Carthage (C5)
Casa Blanca (B4)*... 493
Causey (F5)*... 50
Cebolla (C2)*...1,000
Cedar Crest (C3)*...1,000
Cedar Hill (B2)*... 130
Cedarvale (D4)*... 50
Central (A6)*...1,511
Cerrillos (D3)*
Cerro (D2)*... 600
Chacon (D2)*
Chama (C2)*...1,300
Chama (C6)*...1,000
Chamberino (C6)*...1,000
Chamisal (D2)*... 500
Chapolle (D3)... 25
Chaperito (E3)*... 125
Chico (E2)*... 6
Chilili (C4)
Chimayo (D3)*...1,550
Chloride (B5)*... 56
Cienega (D6)... 2
Cimarron (E2)*... 855
Clapham (F2)*
Claunch (C4)*
Clayton (F2)*...3,515
Cleveland (D2)*... 700
Cliff (A6)*... 250
Closson (A3)
Cloudcroft (D6)*... 251
Cloverdale (A7)
Clovis (F4)*...17,318
Cochiti (C3)... 250
Colfax (E2)
Colmor (E2)*... 80
Colonias (E3)*... 150
Columbus (B7)*... 251
Conchas Dam (E3)*... 100
Contreras (C4)
Coolidge (A3)*... 8
Cooper (F6)... 6
Cordova (D2)*
Corona (D4)*... 530
Correo (B4)*... 8
Costilla (D2)*... 300
Cowles (D3)*... 200
Coyote (C2)*
Coyote Canyon (A3)
Crossroads (F5)*... 60
Crownpoint (A3)*... 125
Crystal (A2)... 125
Cuba (B2)*... 850
Cubero (B3)*
Cuchillo (B5)*... 105
Cuervo (E3)*... 100
Cundiyo (D3)*... 160
Cunico (E2)... 60
Cutter (B5)*... 55
Dahlia (D3)*... 100
Datil (B4)*... 80
Dawson (F2)*...1,206
Dayton (E6)
Delphos (F4)... 2
Deming (B6)*...5,672
Derry (B6)*... 300
Des Moines (F2)*... 282
Dexter (E5)*... 784
Dilia (D3)*... 250
Dixon (D2)*...1,250
Domingo (C3)... 120
Dona Ana (C6)*... 400
Dora (F5)*... 120
Dulce (B2)*... 500
Dunlap (E4)*... 90
Duoro (D4)
Duran (D4)*... 300
Dusty (B5)*... 15
Dwyer (B6)
Eagle Nest (D2)*... 200
East Vaughn (D4)*...1,800
Edgewood (C3)*... 45
El Morro (A3)*... 300
El Paso Gap (E6)... 12
El Porvenir (D3)*... 350
El Prado (D2)*
El Pueblo (D3)... 175
El Rito (C2)*...1,200
El Vado Dam (C2)... 18
Elephant Butte (B5)*... 150
Elida (F5)*... 430
Elizabethtown (D2)
Elk (D6)*... 35
Elkins (E5)*... 26
Embudo (C2)*
Encino (D4)*... 408
Endee (F3)*... 50
Engle (B5)*... 65
Ensenada (C2)*... 400
Escabosa (C4)
Espanola (C3)*...1,446
Espuella (E6)... 50
Estancia (D4)*... 916
Eunice (F6)*...2,352
Fairacres (C6)*... 350
Farley (E2)*... 111
Farmington (A2)*...3,637
Faywood (B6)*
Fence Lake (A4)*... 250
Field (B4)... 300
Fierro (A6)*... 500
Fillmore (C6)
Flora Vista (A2)*... 150
Florida (B6)... 15
Florida (C4)*... 350
Floyd (F4)*... 50
Flying H (E5)*... 55
Folsom (F2)*... 206
Forrest (F4)*... 130
Fort Bayard (A6)*... 483
Fort Stanton (D5)*... 550
Ft. Sumner (E4)*...1,978
Ft. Wingate (A3)*... 250
Frazier (E5)*... 12
French (E2)... 10
Frisco (A5)
Fruitland (A2)*... 200
Gage (A6)*... 100
Galisteo (D3)*... 150
Gallegos (F3)*
Gallina (C2)*... 31
Gallup (A3)*...9,133
Gamerco (A3)*... 200
Gardiner (E2)... 50
Garfield (B6)*... 300
Garita (E3)*... 200
Gila (A6)*... 700
Gilman (C3)... 119
Gladiola (F5)*... 99
Gladstone (F2)*... 61
Glencoe (D5)*... 200
Glenrio (F3)*... 60
Glenwood (A5)*... 300
Glorieta (D3)*... 500
Golden (C3)... 75
Governador (B2)... 45
Grady (F4)*... 130
Gran Quivira (D4)*... 50
Grants (B3)*...2,251
Green Tree (D5)*... 363
Greens Gap (A4)... 25
Grenville (F2)*... 102
Grier (F4)*... 200
Guadalupita (D2)*... 475
Guy (F2)
Hachita (A7)*... 200
Hagerman (E5)*...1,024
Hanover (A6)*...1,200
Hatch (B6)*...1,064
Hayden (F3)*
Heck Canyon (D2)
Hernandez (C2)*... 400
Hickman (B4)*... 17
High Rolls (D5)*... 175
Hill (C6)... 100
Hillsboro (B6)*... 300
Hilton Lodge (D3)... 2
Hobbs (F6)*...13,875
Hollene (F4)*... 20
Hollywood (D5)*
Holman (D2)*
Hondo (D5)*... 250
Hope (E6)*... 186
Horse Springs (A5)*... 100
House (F4)*... 295
Humble City (F6)*... 42
Hurley (A6)*...2,079
Ilfeld (D3)*
Ima (E4)*... 4
Ione (F3)*... 3
Isleta (C4)*...1,400
Jal (F6)*...2,047
Jarales (C4)*...1,199
Jemez Pueblo (C3)*... 878
Jemez Springs (C3)*... 135
Jicarilla (D5)... 20
Jordan (F4)*... 93
Kelly (B4)*... 55
Kenna (F5)*... 100
Kingston (B6)*... 50
Kirtland (A2)*
Knowles (F6)... 10
Koehler (E2)*... 385
La Cueva (D3)
La Jara (B2)*...2,500
La Lande (E4)*... 35
La Liendre (E3)... 12
La Luz (C6)*... 200
La Madera (C2)*
La Mesa (C6)*... 650
La Puente (C2)... 300
La Union (C7)... 475
La Ventana (B3)
Laguna (B3)*...3,004
Lajoya (C4)*
Lake Arthur (E5)*... 380
Lake Valley (B6)*... 9
Lakewood (E6)*
Lamy (D3)*... 105
Laplata (A2)*
Las Cruces (C6)*...12,325
Las Padillas (C3)... 487
Las Palomas (B5)*... 60
Las Tablas (C2)*... 100
Las Vegas (city) (D3)*.7,494
Las Vegas (town) (D3).6,269
Ledoux (D3)*... 800
Lemitar (B4)*... 500
Levy (E2)*... 15
Leyba (D3)*
Lincoln (D5)*... 80
Lindrith (C2)*... 300
Lingo (F5)*... 20
Llano (D2)*... 550
Loco Hills (F6)*... 300
Logan (F3)*... 500
Lon (D4)
Lordsburg (A6)*...3,525
Los Alamos (C3)*...9,934
Los Griegos (C3)...3,025
Los Lunas (C4)*... 889
Lourdes (D3)*
Loving (E6)*...1,487
Lovington (F6)*...3,134
Lucy (D4)... 10
Lumberton (C2)*
Luna (A5)*... 300
Lyden (C2)*
Madrid (C3)*... 477
Maes (E3)*... 50
Magdalena (B4)*...1,297
Malaga (E6)*... 250
Mangas (A4)... 25
Manuelito (A3)*
Manzano (C4)*... 250
Marquez (B3)*... 60
Maxwell (E2)*... 404
Mayhill (D6)*
Mc Alister (F4)*
Mc Donald (F5)*... 100
Mc Gaffey (A3)... 50
Mc Intosh (D4)*... 25
Melrose (F4)*... 936
Mentmore (A3)*... 100
Mescalero (D5)*
Mesilla (C6)*...1,264
Mesilla Park (C6)*...2,000
Mesquite (C6)*... 400
Mexican Springs (A3)*
Miami (E2)*
Mills (E2)*
Milnesand (F5)*
Mimbres (B6)*... 36
Mogollon (A5)*... 26
Monero (C2)*... 207
Montezuma (D3)*...1,200
Monticello (B5)... 400
Montoya (F3)*... 75
Monument (F6)*
Mora (D3)*...1,750
Moriarty (D4)*
Moses (F2)*... 70
Mosquero (F3)*... 583
Mount Dora (F2)*... 100
Mountain Park (D6)*... 60
Mountainair (C4)*...1,418
Mule Creek (A5)*... 16
Nambe (D3)... 500
Nara Visa (F3)*... 350
New Laguna (B3)*... 150
Newcomb (A2)... 200
Newkirk (E3)*... 250
Nogal (D5)*... 25
Nolan (E2)... 11
Norton (F4)... 7
Obar (F3)*... 5
Ocate (E2)*... 105
Oil Center (F6)*... 70
Ojo Caliente (D2)*
Ojo Feliz (E2)*... 365
Ojo Sarco (D2)*... 150
Old Albuquerque (C3)*
Old Tapicitoes (C2)
Olive (E5)*... 12
Omega (A4)*... 30
Onava (D3)
Optimo (E3)
Organ (C6)*... 50
Orogrande (D6)*... 45
Oscura (C5)... 50
Otis (E6)... 150
Paguate (B3)*... 500
Palma (D4)*
Park View (C2)*... 300
Pasamonte (F2)... 12
Pastura (E4)*... 120
Pecos (D3)*...1,241
Pedernal (D4)*... 30
Penablanca (C3)*... 350
Penasco (D2)*... 700
Penistaja (B3)
Pep (F5)*... 30
Peralta (C4)*... 300
Perea (A3)
Petaca (C2)*
Picacho (D5)*... 175
Pie Town (A4)*... 135
Pinehaven (A3)
Pinon (D6)*... 100
Pinos Altos (A6)*... 250
Pintada (D4)*
Placitas (C3)*... 350
Pleasanton (A5)... 48
Pojoaque (C3)... 200
Pulvadera (B4)*
Ponderosa (C3)*... 100
Portales (F4)*...8,112
Prewitt (B3)*... 65
Puerto de Luna (E4)*... 600
Quarai (C4)... 55
Quay (F4)*... 120
Quemado (A4)*... 400
Questa (D2)*...1,400
Radium Springs (B6)*
Ragland (F4)... 12
Rainsville (D2)*... 350
Ramah (A3)*... 300
Ramon (D4)
Ranches of Taos (D2)*.1,386
Raton (E2)*...8,241
Rayo (C4)
Red Hill (A4)*
Red River (D2)*... 150
Redrock (A6)*... 17
Regina (B2)*... 100
Rehoboth (A3)*... 90
Rencona (D3)*... 32
Reserve (A5)*
Ribera (D3)*... 400
Ricardo (E4)*... 25
Rincon (C6)*... 500
Riverside (C2)
Rociada (D3)*... 40
Rodarte (D2)*... 750
Rodeo (A7)*... 250
Rodey (B6)... 250
Rogers (F5)*... 71
Romeroville (D3)... 18
Rosa (B2)... 100
Rosebud (F3)
Roswell (E5)*...25,738
Rowe (D3)*... 365
Roy (E3)*...1,074
Ruidoso (D5)*... 806
Rutheron (C2)*... 25
Sabinoso (E3)*... 125
Sacramenta (D6)*
Saint Vrain (F4)*... 48
Sais (C4)
Salem (B6)*... 350
San Acacia (B4)*... 200
San Antonio (B5)*... 900
San Cristobal (D2)*... 215
San Felipe (C3)... 500
San Fidel (B3)*... 89
San Ignacio (D4)
San Ildefonzo (C3)... 400
San Jon (F3)*... 362
San Jose (D3)*
San Juan (B6)
San Juan Pueblo (C2)*.1,200
San Lorenzo (B6)*... 350
San Marcial (C5)
San Mateo (B3)*... 150
San Miguel (C6)... 300
San Patricio (D5)*... 300
San Rafael (A3)*... 500
San Ysidro (C3)*
Sandia Park (C3)*... 100
Sandoval (C3)*
Santa Clara (C3)
Santa Cruz (D3)*
SANTA FE (C3)*...27,998
Santa Rita (B6)*...2,135
Santa Rosa (E4)*...2,199
Sapello (D3)*... 80
Scholle (C4)*
Seboyeta (B3)*
Sedan (F2)*... 100
Sena (D3)*... 190
Seneca (F2)*... 20
Separ (A6)*... 50
Serafina (D3)*... 100
Servilleta (D2)... 15
Sherman (B6)*
Shiprock (A2)*... 250
Shoemaker (E3)*... 200
Silver City (A6)*...7,022
Skarda (D2)... 25
Socorro (C4)*...4,334
Soham (D3)*... 250
Solano (E3)*... 40
Springer (E2)*...1,558
Spur Lake (A5)*... 3
Stanley (D3)*... 75
State College (C6)*...1,200
Stead (F2)*... 11
Steins (A6)
Stong (D2)
Strauss (C7)*
Sugarite (E2)... 10
Sunshine Valley (D2)... 20
Tafoya (E2)*... 325
Taiban (F4)*
Tajique (C4)*... 250
Talpa (D2)
Taos (D2)*...1,815
Tapicitoes (B2)*
Tatum (F5)*... 688
Taylor Springs (E2)... 25
Tecolotenos (D3)... 95
Tererro (D3)*... 40
Tesuque (C3)*
Texico (F4)*... 691
Thoreau (A3)*... 150
Three Rivers (C5)*... 350
Tierra Amarilla (C2)*... 800
Tijeras (C3)*
Tinnie (D5)*... 80
Toadlena (A2)*... 500
Tohatchi (A3)*... 350
Tolar (F4)
Tome (C4)*... 400
Torrance (D4)... 10
Torreon (C4)*... 100
Trampas (D2)*
Trementina (E3)*
Tres Lagunas (B4)*... 14
Tres Piedras (D2)*... 75
Tres Ritos (D2)... 50
Truchas (D2)*... 750
Trujillo (F3)*... 500
Truth or Consequences (B5)*...4,563
Tsaya (A2)... 50
Tucumcari (F3)*...8,419
Tularosa (C5)*...1,642
Turley (B2)
Two Wells (A3)
Tyrone (A6)*
Ute Park (D2)*
Vadito (D2)*... 500
Vado (C6)*... 350
Valdez (D2)*... 360
Valencia (C4)... 818
Vallecitos (C2)*... 400
Valley Ranch (D3)
Valmora (D3)*... 100
Van Houten (E2)*
Vanadium (A6)*... 450
Vaughn (D4)*...1,356
Veguita (C4)*
Velarde (C2)*... 600
Vermejo Park (D2)*... 300
Villanueva (D3)*
Virden (A6)... 146
Wagon Mound (E2)*...1,120
Waterflow (A2)*... 150
Watrous (D3)*... 250
Weed (D6)*... 100
White Oaks (D5)*... 61
White Signal (A6)
Whitewater (A6)*... 40
Willard (D4)*... 296
Wilna (A6)... 8
Winston (B5)*... 150
Witt (D4)... 12
Yeso (E4)*... 500
Youngsville (C2)*... 120
Zamora (C3)
Zuni (A3)*...2,563

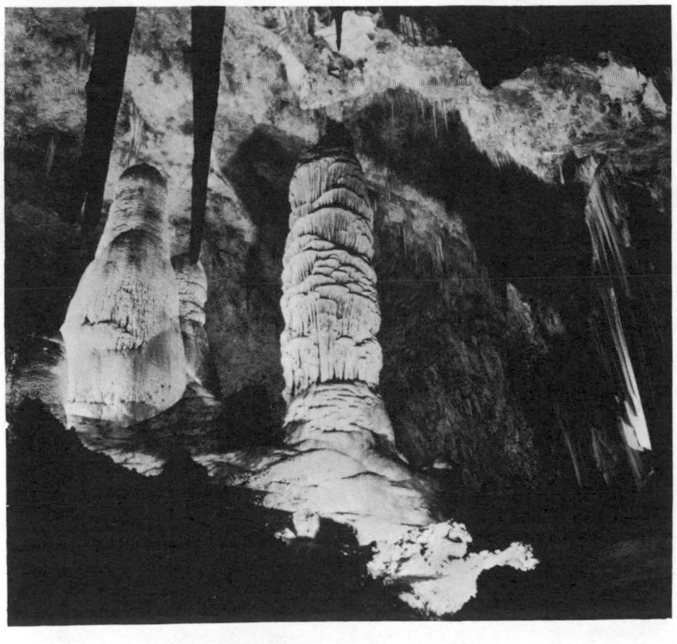

NEW YORK

Map on Page 79 — *Total Population 14,830,192*

62 COUNTIES

Albany (M5)...239,386
Allegany (D6)...43,784
Bronx (C2)...1,451,277
Broome (J6)...184,698
Cattaraugus (C6)...77,901
Cayuga (G4)...70,136
Chautauqua (B6)...135,189
Chemung (G6)...86,827
Chenango (J6)...39,138
Clinton (N1)...53,622
Columbia (N6)...43,182
Cortland (H5)...37,158
Delaware (K6)...44,420
Dutchess (N7)...136,781
Erie (C5)...899,238
Essex (N2)...35,086
Franklin (M1)...44,830
Fulton (M4)...51,021
Genesee (D4)...47,584
Greene (M6)...28,745
Hamilton (L3)...4,105
Herkimer (L4)...61,407
Jefferson (J2)...85,521
Kings (C3)...2,738,175
Lewis (K3)...22,521
Livingston (E5)...40,257
Madison (J5)...46,214
Monroe (E4)...487,632
Montgomery (M5)...59,594
Nassau (D2)...672,765
New York (C2)...1,960,101
Niagara (C4)...189,992
Oneida (J4)...222,855
Onondaga (H5)...341,719
Ontario (F5)...60,172
Orange (C1)...152,255
Orleans (D4)...29,832
Oswego (H4)...77,181
Otsego (K5)...50,763
Putnam (D1)...20,307
Queens (D2)...1,550,849
Rensselaer (O5)...132,607
Richmond (C3)...191,555
Rockland (C1)...89,276
St. Lawrence (K2)...98,897
Saratoga (N4)...74,869
Schenectady (M5)...142,497
Schoharie (M5)...22,703
Schuyler (G6)...14,182
Seneca (G5)...29,253
Steuben (F6)...91,439
Suffolk (F2)...276,129
Sullivan (L7)...40,731
Tioga (H6)...30,166
Tompkins (H6)...59,122
Ulster (M7)...92,621
Warren (N3)...39,205
Washington (O4)...47,144
Wayne (F4)...57,323
Westchester (D1)...625,816
Wyoming (D5)...32,822
Yates (F5)...17,615

CITIES and TOWNS

Accord (M7)*... 500
Adams (J3)*...1,762
Adams Center (H3)*... 850
Addison (F6)*...1,920
Adirondack (N3)*... 150
Afton (J6)*... 875
Akron (C4)*...2,481
ALBANY (N5)*...134,995
Albany-Troy (urban area)...290,209
Albion (D4)*...4,850
Alden (C5)*...1,252
Alder Creek (K4)*... 50
Alexander (D5)*... 304
Alexandria Bay (J2)*...1,688
Alfred (E6)*...2,053
Allegany (C6)*...1,738
Allentown (E6)*... 500
Almond (E6)*... 659
Alpine (G6)*... 194
Altamont (M5)*...1,127
Altmar (J3)*... 299
Alton (G4)*... 350
Altona (N1)*... 500
Amagansett (G2)*...1,000
Amber (H5)... 130
Amenia (N7)*...1,300
Ames (L5)*... 193
Amityville (E3)*...6,164
Amsterdam (M5)*...32,240
Ancram (N6)*... 200
Andes (L6)*... 430
Andover (E6)*...1,351
Angelica (E6)*... 928
Angola (C5)*...1,936
Annandale-on-Hudson (N6)*... 405
Antwerp (J2)*... 846
Apalachin (H6)*... 900
Appleton (C4)*... 100
Apulia Station (H5)*... 220
Arcade (D5)*...1,818
Ardsley (H1)*...1,744
Argyle (O4)*... 351
Arkport (E6)*... 701
Arkville (L6)*... 600
Arlington (N7)...5,374
Asharoken ‡(E2)... 116
Ashland (M6)*... 275
Ashokan (M7)*
Ashwood (D4)... 110
Athens (N6)*...1,545
Athol (N4)*... 60
Atlanta (F5)*... 500
Atlantic Beach (D3)*...2,000
Attica (D5)*...2,676
Au Sable Forks (N2)*..1,643
Auburn (G5)*...36,722
Aurora (G5)*... 711
Ava (K4)*
Averill Park (O5)*
Avoca (F6)*... 952
Avon (E5)*...2,412
Babylon (D2)*...6,015
Bainbridge (J6)*...1,505
Baldwin (B3)*...22,000
Baldwinsville (H4)*...4,495
Ballston Spa (N5)*...4,937
Bangor (M1)*... 300
Barker (C4)*... 523
Barnes Corners (J3)*... 105
Barneveld (K4)*... 331

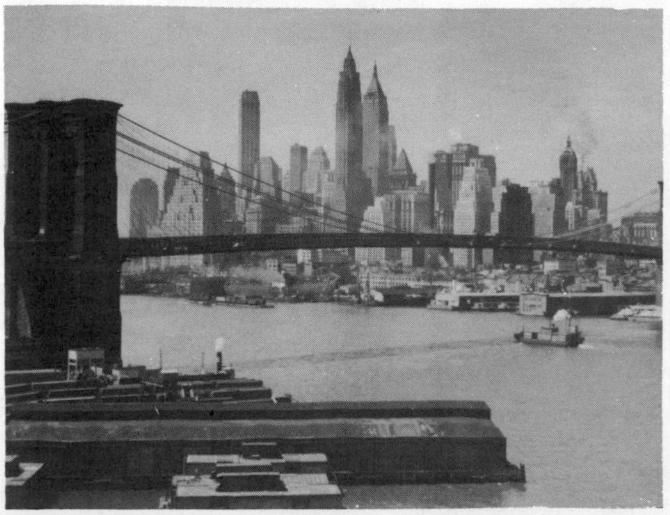

Barre Center (D4)... 350
Barryville (L7)*... 550
Bosom (D4)*... 80
Batavia (D5)*... 17,799
Bath (F6)*... 5,416
Baxter Estates ‡(D2).. 862
Bay Shore (E2)*... 9,665
Bayport (E2)*... 1,463
Bayville (B2)*... 1,981
Beach Ridge (C4)... 500
Beacon (N7)*... 14,012
Beaver Dams (F6)*... 230
Beaver Falls (K3)*... 618
Beaver River (L3)*... 20
Bedford Hills (D1)*...
Belfast (D6)*... 750
Belle Terre ‡(E2)... 120
Bellerose (A2)*... 1,134
Belleville (H3)*... 305
Bellmore (B2)*... 12,000
Bellport (F2)*... 1,449
Belmont (E6)*... 1,211
Bemus Point (B6)*... 424
Benson Mines (L2)... 400
Bergen (E4)*... 786
Berkshire (H6)*... 350
Berlin (O5)*... 900
Berne (M5)*... 225
Bernhards Bay (J4)*... 764
Bethel (L7)*... 500
Big Flats (G6)*... 523
Big Indian (M6)*... 175
Big Moose (L3)*... 105
Binghamton (J6)*... 80,674
Binghamton (urban area)... 144,570
Black River (J3)*... 1,062
Blasdell (C5)*... 3,127
Bliss (D5)*... 678
Bloomingburg (L7)*... 263
Bloomingdale (M2)*... 476
Bloomville (L6)*... 350
Blue Mountain Lake (M3)*... 275
Bolivar (D6)*... 1,490
Bolton Landing (N3)*.. 1,200
Bombay (M1)*... 500
Boonville (K4)*... 2,329
Boston (C5)*... 1,500
Bouckville (J5)*... 195
Branchport (F5)*... 1,000
Brant (B5)*... 500
Brant Lake (N3)*... 200
Brasher Falls (L1)*... 800
Breakabeen (M5)*... 165
Breesport (G6)*... 500
Brentwood (E2)*... 2,803
Brewerton (H4)*... 800
Brewster (D1)*... 1,810
Briarcliff Manor‡(D1)* 2,494
Bridgehampton (G2)*...
Bridgeport (J4)*... 1,800
Bridgewater (K5)*... 309
Brier Hill (J1)*... 200
Brightwaters ‡(E2)*... 2,336
Broadalbin (M4)*... 1,400
Brockport (D4)*... 4,748
Brocton (B6)*... 1,380
Bronx, The (D2)*... 1,451,277
Bronxville (J1)*... 6,778
Brookfield (K5)*... 400
Brooklyn (C2)*... 2,738,175
Brooktondale (H6)*... 500
Brookville ‡(D2)... 337
Brownville (H3)*... 1,013
Brushton (L1)*... 516
Buchanan (D1)*... 1,820
Buffalo (B5)*... 580,132
Buffalo (urban area). 794,747
Burdett (G6)*... 432
Burke (M1)*... 316
Burlington Flats (K5)*. 185
Burt (C4)*... 300
Busti (B6)... 210
Byron (D4)*... 300
Cadyville (N1)*... 697
Cairo (M6)*... 600
Caledonia (E5)*... 1,683
Callicoon (K7)*... 800
Callicoon Center (L7)*. 405
Cambridge (O4)*... 1,692
Camden (J4)*... 2,407
Cameron (F6)*... 200
Camillus (H4)*... 1,225
Campbell (F6)*... 600
Campbell Hall (C1)*... 251
Canaan (O6)*...
Canajoharie (L5)*... 2,761
Canadaigua (F5)*... 8,332
Canaseraga (E6)*... 693
Canastota (J4)*... 4,458
Candor (H6)*... 802
Caneadea (D6)*... 400
Canisteo (E6)*... 2,625
Canton (K1)*... 4,379
Cape Vincent (H2)*... 812
Carlisle (L5)*... 200
Carlton (D4)... 250
Carmel (D1)*... 1,526
Caroga Lake (L4)*... 325
Caroline (H6)... 35
Carthage (J3)*... 4,420
Cassadaga (B6)*... 676
Castile (D5)*... 1,072
Castleton-on-Hudson (N5)*... 1,751
Castorland (J3)*... 308
Cato (G4)*... 431
Catskill (N6)*... 5,392
Cattaraugus (C6)*... 1,190
Cayuga (G5)*... 534
Cayuga Hts. ‡(G5)... 1,131
Cazenovia (J5)*... 1,946
Cedarhurst (B3)*... 6,051
Cedarville (K5)... 149
Celoron (B6)*... 1,555
Center Moriches (F2)*.. 1,761
Central Bridge (M5)*.. 500
Central Square (H4)*... 665
Central Valley (C1)*... 1,300
Centre Island (B2)... 199
Ceres (D6)*... 350
Chadwicks (K4)*... 2,500
Chafee (C5)*... 350
Champlain (N1)*... 1,505
Charlotteville (L5)*... 200
Chase Mills (K1)*... 250
Chateaugay (N1)*... 1,234
Chatham (N6)*... 2,304
Chatham Center (N6)*. 378
Chaumont (H2)*... 513
Chautauqua (A6)*... 500
Chazy (N1)*... 600
Cheektowaga (C5)...
Chemung (G6)*... 400
Chenango Bridge (J6)* 2,500
Chenango Forks (J6)*. 400
Chepachet (K5)*... 84
Cherry Creek (B6)*... 631
Cherry Valley (L5)*... 760
Chester (B1)*... 1,215
Chestertown (N3)*... 350
Chichester (M6)*... 225
Childwold (L2)*... 200
Chittenango (J4)*... 1,307
Churchville (E4)*... 755
Churubusco (N1)*... 200
Cicero (H4)*... 1,000
Cincinnatus (H5)*... 900
Clarence (C5)*... 1,018
Clarkson (E4)*... 382
Clarksville (M5)*... 600
Claverack (N6)*... 500
Clayton (H2)*... 1,981
Clayville (K5)*... 719
Clermont (N6)*... 500
Cleveland (J4)*... 555
Clifton Springs (F4)*.. 1,838
Clinton (K4)*... 1,630
Clinton Corners (N7)*.. 300
Clintondale (M7)*... 800
Clyde (G4)*... 2,492
Clymer (A6)*... 500
Cobleskill (L5)*... 3,208
Cochecton (K7)*... 150
Coeymans (N6)*... 1,250
Cohocton (F5)*... 943
Cohoes (N5)*... 21,272
Cold Brook (L4)*... 342
Cold Spring (C1)*... 1,788
Cold Spring Harbor (E2)*... 1,500
Colden (C5)*... 700
Collins (C6)*... 500
Collins Center (C6)*... 450
Colonie ‡(N5)*... 2,068
Colton (L1)*... 250
Comstock (O4)*... 2,250
Conesus (E5)*... 200
Conewango (C6)*...
Connelly (M7)*... 350
Constable (M1)*... 200
Constableville (J3)*... 378
Constantia (H4)*... 1,250
Cooks Falls (K7)*... 200
Coopers Plains (F6)*... 304
Cooperstown (L5)*... 2,727
Copake (N6)*... 600
Copake Falls (N6)*...
Copenhagen (J3)*... 690
Corfu (D5)*... 542
Corinth (N4)*... 3,161
Corning (F6)*... 17,684
Cornwall (C1)*... 2,211
Cortland (H5)*... 18,152
Cove Neck ‡(D2)... 200
Cranberry Lake (L2)*.. 232
Croghan (K3)*... 772
Cowlesville (D5)*... 232
Coxsackie (N6)*... 2,722
Croton Falls (D1)*... 1,000
Croton-on-Hudson (C1)*... 4,837
Crown Point (N3)*... 800
Cuba (D6)*... 1,783
Cutchogue (F2)*... 1,500
Cuylerville (E5)*... 350
Dalton (E5)*... 500
Dannemora (N7)*... 4,122
Dansville (E5)*... 5,253
Darien (D5)... 90
Darien Center (D5)*... 303
Davenport (L6)*... 250
Dayton (C6)*... 300
De Kalb Junction (K2)* 500
De Peyster (K1)*... 200
De Ruyter (J5)*... 561
Deer River (J3)*... 166
Deerland (M3)*... 40
Deferiet (J2)*... 616
Degrasse (L2)*... 250
Delanson (M5)*... 430
Delevan (D6)*... 611
Delhi (L6)*... 2,223
Delmar (N5)*...
Demster (H3)... 200
Depauville (H2)*... 350
Depew (C5)*... 7,217
Deposit (K6)*... 2,016
Derby (B5)*...
Dering Harbor ‡(G2)... 4
Dexter (H2)*... 1,038
Diamond Point (N4)*... 278
Dickinson Center (M1)* 200
Dobbs Ferry (H1)*... 6,268
Dolgeville (L4)*... 3,204
Dover Plains (O7)*... 800
Downsville (L6)*... 720
Dresden (F5)*... 373
Dresden Station (O3)*.. 76
Dryden (H6)*... 976
Duanesburg (M5)*... 287
Dundee (F5)*... 1,165
Dunkirk (B5)*... 18,007
Durhamville (J4)*... 700
Eagle Bay (L3)*... 150
Eagle Bridge (O5)*...
Earlyville (J5)*... 945
E. Aurora (C5)*... 5,962
E. Bethany (D5)*... 150
E. Bloomfield (E5)*... 425
E. Branch (K7)*... 300
E. Durham (M6)*... 300
E. Greenbush (N5)*... 1,100
E. Hampton (G2)*... 1,737
E. Hills ‡(D2)... 2,547
E. Islip (E2)*... 2,834
E. Meredith (L6)*... 132
E. Moriches (F2)*... 1,500
E. Northport (E2)*... 3,842
E. Otto (C6)*... 742
E. Pembroke (D5)*... 650
E. Randolph (C6)*... 628
E. Rochester (F4)*... 7,022
E. Rockaway ‡(D2)*... 7,970
E. Springfield (L5)*... 350
E. Syracuse (H4)*... 4,766
E. Williamson (F4)*... 300
E. Williston ‡(D2)*... 1,734
E. Worcester (L5)*... 456
Eastport (F2)*... 600
Eaton (J5)*... 250
Ebenezer (C5)...
Eden (C5)*... 1,394
Edmeston (K5)*... 500
Edwards (K2)*... 584
Elba (D4)*... 569
Elbridge ‡(H4)*... 586
Elizabethtown (N2)*... 665
Ellenburg Center (N1)* 350
Ellenburg Depot (N1)*. 400
Ellenville (M7)*... 4,225
Ellicottville (C6)*... 1,073
Ellington (B6)*... 925
Ellisburg (H3)*... 285
Elmira (G6)*... 49,716
Elmira Heights (G6)*... 5,009
Elmont (B2)*... 21,125
Elmsford (J1)*... 3,147
Elnora (N5)*... 100
Endicott (H6)*... 20,050
Ephratah (L4)... 250
Erieville (J5)*... 300
Esperance (M5)*... 322
Essex (O2)*... 525
Evans (B5)...
Evans Mills (J2)*... 518
Fabius (J5)*... 369
Fair Haven (G4)*... 628
Fairport (F4)*... 5,267
Falconer (B6)*... 3,292
Farmingdale (D2)*... 4,492
Farnham (B5)*... 396
Faust (M2)*...
Fayetteville (J4)*... 2,624
Felts Mills (J3)*... 300
Fernwood (H4)*... 200
Fillmore (D6)*... 527
Findley Lake (A6)*... 500
Fine (K2)*... 350
Fishers Island (G1)*... 536
Fishkill (N7)*... 841
Fishs Eddy (K7)*... 300
Fleischmann's (L6)*... 469
Floral Park (A2)*... 14,582
Florence (J4)*... 75
Florida (B1)*... 1,376
Flower Hill ‡(D2)... 1,948
Fly Creek (K5)*... 350
Fonda (M5)*... 1,026
Forestport (K4)*... 730
Forestville (B6)*... 786
Fort Ann (N4)*... 463
Fort Covington (M1)*... 891
Fort Edward (O4)*... 3,797
Fort Jackson (L1)*... 138
Fort Johnson (M5)*... 930
Fort Plain (L5)*... 2,935
Fort Ticonderoga (O3)* 46
Frankfort (K4)*... 3,844
Franklin (K6)*... 558
Franklinville (D6)*... 2,092
Fredonia (B6)*... 7,095
Freehold (N6)*... 300
Freeport (B3)*... 24,680
Freeville (H5)*... 373
Frewsburg (B6)*... 1,383
Friendship (D6)*... 1,344
Fulton (H4)*... 13,922
Fultonville (M5)*... 840
Gainesville (D5)*... 314
Galway (N4)*... 188
Gansevoort (N4)*... 300
Garden City (B2)*... 14,486
Gardenville (C5)...
Garrison (C1)*... 1,600
Gasport (C4)*... 880
Geneseo (E5)*... 2,838
Geneva (G5)*... 17,144
Genoa (G5)*...
Germantown (N6)*...
Gerry (B6)*... 475
Ghent (N6)*... 600
Gilbertsville (K6)*... 456
Gilboa (M6)*... 125
Glasco (M6)*... 1,300
Glen Cove (B2)*... 15,130
Glen Park (J3)... 516
Glenfield (K3)*... 450
Glens Falls (N4)*... 19,610
Gloversville (M4)*... 23,634
Golden's Bridge (D1)*.. 800
Gorham (F5)*... 650
Goshen (B1)*... 3,311
Gouverneur (K2)*... 4,916
Gowanda (B6)*... 3,289
Grafton (N5)*...
Grahamsville (L7)*... 450
Grand Gorge (L6)*... 500
Grand Island (B5)*...
Grand View-on-Hudson ‡(C2)... 302
Granville (O4)*... 2,826
Great Bend (J2)*... 500
Great Neck (A2)*... 7,759
Great Neck Estates (A2)... 2,464
Great Neck Plaza (A2). 4,246
Great Valley (C6)*...
Green Island (N5)*... 4,016
Greene (J6)*... 1,628
Greenport (F1)*... 3,028
Greenville (N6)*... 376
Greenwich (O4)*... 2,212
Greenwood (E6)*... 700
Greenwood Lake (B1)*. 819
Groton (H5)*... 2,150
Groveland (E5)*... 500
Guilford (J6)*... 557
Hadley (N4)*... 500
Hagaman (M5)*... 1,114
Hague (N3)*... 400
Hailesboro (K2)*... 268
Hamburg (C5)*... 6,938
Hamden (K6)*... 250
Hamilton (J5)*... 3,507
Hamlet (B6)*... 100
Hamlin (E4)*... 400
Hammond (J2)*... 329
Hammondsport (F6)*... 1,190
Hampton (O3)*... 150
Hampton Bays (F2)*... 1,269
Hancock (K7)*... 1,560
Hannawa Falls (L1)*... 245
Hannibal (G4)*... 501
Harford (H6)*...
Harpursville (J6)*... 520
Harriman (C1)*... 676
Harrison (J1)*...
Harrisonville (K2)*... 868
Hartford (O4)*... 150
Hartwick (K5)*... 625
Hastings on Hudson (J1)*... 7,565
Haverstraw (C1)*... 5,818
Hawthorne (H1)*...
Head of the Harbor ‡(E2)... 334
Hector (G5)*... 65
Helena (L1)*...
Hemlock (E5)*... 400
Hempstead (A2)*... 29,135
Henderson (H3)*... 260
Henrietta (E4)*...
Herkimer (L4)*... 9,400
Hermitage (D5)... 100
Hermon (K2)*... 547
Herrings (J2)*... 192
Heuvelton (K1)*... 712
Hewlett Bay Park ‡(D2)... 466
Hewlett Harbor ‡(D2). 411
Hewlett Neck ‡(D2)... 369
Hicksville (B2)*... 13,000
High Falls (M7)*... 1,000
Highland (M7)*... 3,035
Highland Falls (C1)*... 3,930
Hillburn (C2)*... 1,212
Hillsdale (O6)*... 400
Hilton (E4)*... 1,036
Himrod (G5)*... 225
Hinckley (K4)*... 198
Hinsdale (D6)*... 350
Hobart (L6)*... 618
Hogansburg (L1)*... 300
Holcomb (F5)*... 313
Holland (C5)*... 980
Holland Patent (K4)*.. 400
Holley (D4)*... 1,551
Homer (H5)*... 3,244
Honeoye (F5)*... 200
Honeoye Falls (F5)*... 1,460
Hoosick Falls (O5)*... 4,297
Hopkinton (L1)*... 300
Hornell (E6)*... 15,049
Horseheads (G6)*... 3,606
Houghton (D6)*... 500
Howes Cave (M5)*...
Hubbardsville (J5)*... 300
Hudson (N6)*... 11,629
Hudson Falls (O4)*... 7,236
Hughsonville (N7)*... 250
Hulberton (D4)*... 500
Hume (D5)*... 250
Hunter (M6)*... 526
Huntington (E2)*... 9,324
Huntington Bay ‡(E2). 585
Hurleyville (L7)*... 800
Hyde Park (N7)*... 1,059
Ilion (K5)*... 9,363
Indian Lake (M3)*...
Inlet (L3)*... 250
Interlaken (G5)*... 770
Inwood (A3)*... 9,200
Ira (G4)*... 100
Irondequoit (E4)... ^34,417
Irving (B5)*... 350
Irvington (H1)*... 3,657
Ischua (D6)*... 170
Island Park (B3)*... 2,031
Islip (E2)*... 5,254
Ithaca (G6)*... 29,257
Jamaica (D2)*... 100,000
Jamestown (B6)*... 43,354
Jamesville (H5)*... 1,200
Jasper (F6)*... 600
Jay (N2)*... 425
Jefferson (L6)*... 300
Jeffersonville (L7)*... 450
Jericho (B2)*... 500
Johnsburg (M3)*... 200
Johnson City (J6)*... 19,249
Johnsonville (O5)*... 520
Johnstown (M4)*... 10,923
Jordan (H4)*... 1,295
Kanona (F6)*... 400
Katonah (D1)*...
Keene (N2)*... 550
Keene Valley (N2)*... 1,000
Keeseville (O2)*... 1,977
Kendall (E4)*... 325
Kenmore (C5)*... 20,066
Kennedy (B6)*... 508
Kensington ‡(D2)*... 978
Kerhonkson (M7)*... 1,000
Kill Buck (C6)*... 304
Kinderhook (N6)*... 853
King Ferry (G5)*... 400
Kings Park (E2)*... 10,960
Kings Point ‡(E2)*... 2,445
Kingston (M7)*... 28,817
Kirkwood (J6)*... 343
Knapp Creek (C6)*... 215
Knowlesville (D4)*... 300
Knoxboro (J5)*... 315
La Fargeville (J2)*... 425
La Fayette (H5)*... 260
Lackawanna (B5)*... 27,658
Lacona (J3)*... 540
Lake Clear Junction (M2)*... 250
Lake George (N4)*... 1,005
Lake Huntington (L7)*. 300
Lake Katrine (M7)*... 750
Lake Kushaqua (M2)*.. 300
Lake Luzerne (N4)*... 750
Lake Placid (N2)*... 2,999
Lake Pleasant (M4)*... 200
Lake Success (A2)... 1,264
Lake View (B5)*...
Lakeville (E5)*... 384
Lakewood (B6)*... 3,013
Lancaster (C5)*... 8,665
Larchmont (J1)*... 6,330
Lattingtown ‡(D2)... 745
Laurel Hollow ‡(D2)... 169
Laurens (K5)*... 261
Lawrence (A3)*... 4,681
Lawrenceville (L1)*... 236
Le Roy (E5)*... 4,721
Lebanon Springs (O6)*... 520
Lee Center (K4)*...
Leeds (N6)*... 750
Leicester (D5)*... 364
Leon (C6)*... 740
Leonardsville (K5)*... 500
Levittown (B2)*... 40,000
Lewis (N2)*... 350
Lewiston (B4)*... 1,626
Lexington (M6)*... 500
Liberty (L7)*... 4,658
Lily Dale (B6)*... 275
Lima (E5)*... 1,147
Limestone (C6)*... 601
Lincklaen (J5)*... 110
Lindenhurst (E2)*... 8,644
Lindley (F6)*... 250
Lisbon (K1)*... 300
Lisle (H6)*... 221
Little Falls (L4)*... 9,541
Little Genesee (D6)*... 300
Little Valley (C6)*... 1,287
Liverpool (H4)*... 2,933
Livingston Manor (L7)*
Livingstonville (M6)... 80
Livonia (E5)*... 837
Lloyd Harbor ‡(D2)... 945
Locke (H5)*... 275
Lockport (C4)*... 25,133
Lodi (G5)*... 362
Long Beach (B3)*... 15,586
Long Eddy (K7)*... 350
Long Lake (L3)*... 1,000
Loon Lake (N1)*... 100
Lorraine (J3)*... 250
Lowville (J3)*... 3,671
Lycoming (H3)*... 200
Lynbrook (A3)*... 17,314
Lyndonville (D4)*... 777
Lyon Mountain (N1)*... 1,053
Lyons (G4)*... 4,217
Lyons Falls (K3)*... 864
Lysander (H4)*... 250
Macedon (F4)*... 614
Machias (D6)*... 850
Madison (J5)*... 335
Madrid (K1)*...
Mahopac (D1)*...
Maine (H6)*... 600
Mallory (H4)*... 150
Malone (M1)*... 9,501
Malverne (A2)*... 8,086
Mamaroneck (J1)*... 15,016
Manchester (F5)*... 1,262
Manhasset (B2)*...
Manhattan (C2)... 1,960,101
Manlius (J5)*... 1,742
Mannsville (H3)*... 378
Manorhaven ‡(D2)... 1,819
Manorville (F2)*... 900
Marathon (J6)*... 1,057
Marcellus (H5)*... 1,382
Margaretville (L6)*... 905
Marilla (C5)*... 350
Marion (F4)*... 800
Marlboro (M7)*... 1,709
Martinsburg (J3)*... 343
Maryland (L5)*... 300
Masonville (K6)*... 370
Massapequa Park‡ (D2)*... 2,334
Massena (L1)*... 13,137
Matinecock (B2)... 507
Mattituck (F2)*... 1,089
Maybrook (B1)*... 1,316
Mayfield (M4)*... 761
Mayville (A6)*... 1,492
McConnellsville (J4)*... 300
Mc Donough (J5)*... 179
Mc Graw (H5)*... 1,197
Mc Keever (K3)*... 55
Mc Lean (H5)*... 250
Mechanicville (N5)*... 7,385
Mecklenburg (G6)*... 300
Medina (D4)*... 6,179
Menands ‡(N5)*... 2,453
Mendon (E4)*... 327
Meridian (G4)*... 334
Merrill (N1)*... 200
Mexico (H4)*... 1,398
Middle Falls (O4)*... 500
Middle Granville (O4)*.. 800
Middleburg (M5)*... 1,298
Middleport (C4)*... 1,641
Middlesex (F5)*... 300
Middletown (B1)*... 22,586
Middleville (K4)*... 647
Milford (K5)*... 502
Mill Neck ‡(D2)*... 505
Millbrook (N7)*... 1,568
Millerton (O7)*... 1,048
Millport (G6)*... 362
Milton (M7)*...
Mineola (B2)*... 14,831
Minerva (N3)*... 364
Minetto (H4)*...
Mineville (O2)*... 996
Minoa (J4)*... 1,008
Mohawk (L4)*... 3,196
Moira (M1)*... 750
Monroe (C1)*... 1,753
Montauk (G2)*... 700
Montgomery (B1)*... 1,063
Monticello (L7)*... 4,223
Montour Falls (G6)*... 1,457
Mooers (N1)*... 496
Moravia (H5)*... 1,480
Moriah (N2)*... 700
Moriah Center (N2)*... 400
Morley (K1)*... 226
Morris (K5)*... 641
Morrisonville (N1)*... 600
Morristown (J1)*... 546
Morrisville (J5)*... 1,250
Mt. Kisco (D1)*... 5,907
Mt. Morris (E5)*... 3,450
Mt. Upton (K6)*... 400
Mt. Vernon (H1)*... 71,899
Mountain Dale (L7)*... 700
Mumford (E4)*... 687
Munnsville (J4)*... 412
Munsey Park ‡(D2)... 2,048
Muttontown ‡(D2)... 382
Napanoch (M7)*... 1,094
Naples (F5)*... 1,141
Narrowsburg (L7)*... 614
Nassau (N5)*... 952
Natural Bridge (K2)*... 600
Natural Dam (J2)... 200
Nelliston (L5)*... 693
Nelsonville (C1)*... 522
New Baltimore (N6)*... 550
New Berlin (K5)*... 1,178
New Bremen (K3)*... 150
New City (C2)*... 962
New Hamburg (N7)*... 350
New Hartford (K4)*... 1,947
New Haven (H4)*... 800
New Hyde Park (A2)*... 7,349
New Lebanon (O6)*...
New Paltz (M7)*... 2,285
New Rochelle (J1)*... 59,725
New Windsor (C1)... 2,754
New Woodstock (J5)*... 500
New York (5 Boroughs) (C2)*... 7,891,957
New York-Northeastern New Jersey (urban area)... 12,222,963
New York Mills (K4)*... 3,366
Newark (G4)*... 10,295
Newark Valley (H6)*... 1,027
Newburgh (C1)*... 31,956
Newcomb (M3)*... 425
Newfane (C4)*... 1,578
Newfield (G6)*... 500
Newport (K4)*... 752
Newton Falls (K2)*... 700
Niagara Falls (C4)*... 90,872
Niagara Falls (urban area)... 97,648
Nichols (H6)*... 578
Nicholville (L1)*... 300
Nineveh (J6)*... 182
Niobe (B6)*...
Nissequogue ‡(E2)... 219
Norfolk (K1)*... 1,252
N. Bangor (M1)*... 500
N. Bay (J4)*... 500
N. Chili (E4)*... 1,000
N. Collins (C5)*... 1,325
N. Creek (M3)*... 942
N. Haven ‡(F1)... 153
N. Hills ‡(D2)... 330
N. Hornell (E6)... 605
N Hudson (N3)*... 250
N. Java (D5)*... 500
N. Lawrence (L1)*... 500
N. Pelham (H1)... 5,046
N. River (M3)*... 253
N. Rose (G4)*... 708
N. Syracuse (H4)*... 3,356
N. Tarrytown (H1)*... 8,740
N. Tonawanda (C4)*.. 24,731
Northport (E2)*... 3,859
Northville (M4)*... 1,114
Norwich (J5)*... 8,816
Norwood (L1)*... 1,995
Number Four (K3)... 50
Nunda (E5)*... 1,224
Nyack (C2)*... 5,889
Oakfield (D4)*... 1,781
Ocean Beach (E2)*... 73
Oceanside (B3)*... 15,000
Odessa (G6)*... 526
Ogdensburg (K1)*... 16,166
Olcott (C4)*... 875
Old Brookville ‡(D2)... 644
Old Field ‡(E2)... 238
Old Forge (L3)*... 900
Old Westbury (B2)*... 1,160
Olean (D6)*... 22,884
Olmstedville (N3)*... 300
Oneida (J4)*... 11,325
Oneida Castle ‡(J4)... 596
Oneonta (K6)*... 13,564
Onoville (B6)*... 400
Ontario (F4)*... 800
Orchard Park (C5)*... 2,054
Orient (G1)*... 500
Oriskany (K4)*... 1,346
Oriskany Falls (J5)*... 893
Orwell (J3)*... 425
Osceola (J3)*... 241
Ossining (D1)*... 16,098
Oswegatchie (K2)*... 500
Oswego (G4)*... 22,647
Otego (K6)*... 699
Otisco Lake (H5)...
Otisville (B1)*... 911
Otto (C6)*... 350
Ovid (G5)*... 646
Owasco (G5)*... 300
Owego (H6)*... 5,350
Oxford (J6)*... 1,811
Oyster Bay (E2)*... 5,215
Oyster Bay Cove ‡(D2). 561
Painted Post (F6)*... 2,405
Palatine Bridge ‡(L5)* 592
Palenville (M6)*... 350
Palmer (N4)*... 800
Palmyra (F4)*... 3,034
Panama (A6)*... 456
Parish (H4)*... 574
Parishville (L1)*... 450
Parksville (L7)*... 400
Patchogue (E2)*... 7,361
Patterson (D1)*... 400
Pattersonville (M5)*... 259
Paul Smiths (M2)*... 375
Pavilion (D5)*... 615
Pawling (N7)*... 1,430
Pearl River (C2)*...
Peasleeville (N1)*... 200
Peconic (F2)*... 850
Peekskill (D1)*... 17,731
Pelham ‡(H1)*... 1,843
Pelham Manor (H1)... 5,306
Pendleton (C4)...
Penfield (F4)*... 1,013
Penn Yan (F5)*... 5,481
Pennellville (H4)*... 250
Perkinsville (E5)*... 421

Perry (D5)*....4,533
Perrysburg (B6)*.... 361
Peru (N1)*....1,000
Petersburg (O5)*.... 550
Phelps (F5)*....1,650
Philadelphia (J2)*.... 870
Philmont (N6)*....1,792
Phoenix (H4)*....1,917
Piercefield (L2)*.... 240
Piermont (C2)*....1,897
Pierrepont Manor (J3)* 200
Pike (D5)*.... 286
Pine Bush (B1)*....1,100
Pine Hill (M6)*.... 233
Pine Island (B1)*.... 500
Pine Plains (N7)*.... 698
Pine Valley (G6)*.... 230
Piseco (L4)*.... 105
Pittsford (E4)*....1,668
Plandome ‡(D2)*....1,102
Plandome Hts. ‡(D2).... 882
Plandome Manor ‡(D2) 323
Plattsburg (O1)*....17,738
Pleasantville (D2)*....4,861
Plessis (J2)*....
Poland (L4)*.... 511
Pompey (J5)*.... 225
Poolville (K5)*.... 200
Poquott ‡(E2).... 136
Port Byron (G4)*....1,013
Port Chester (J1)*....23,970
Port Dickinson ‡(J6)....2,199
Port Ewen (N7)*....1,885
Port Henry (O2)*....1,831
Port Jefferson (E2)*....3,296
Port Jervis (A1)*....9,372
Port Kent (O1)*.... 175
Port Leyden (K3)*.... 841
Port Washington (A2)*15,000
Port Washington North ‡(D2) 650
Portageville (D5)*.... 350
Portland (B6)*.... 700
Portville (D6)*....1,151
Potsdam (K1)*....7,491
Pottersville (N3)*.... 400
Poughkeepsie (N7)*...41,023
Prattsburg (F5)*.... 653
Prattsville (M6)*....
Preble (H5)*.... 250
Preston Hollow (M6)*.. 200
Prospect (K4)*.... 318
Pulaski (H3)*....2,033
Pulteney (F5)*....
Pultneyville (F4)*.... 225
Pyrites (K1)*.... 240
Queens (D2)*....1,550,849
Quogue (F2)*.... 625
Randolph (C6)*....1,455
Ransomville (C4)*.... 800
Raquette Lake (L3)*.... 200
Ravena (N6)*....2,006
Raymondville (L1)*.... 500
Red Creek (G4)*.... 617
Red Hook (N7)*....1,225
Redfield (J3)*.... 500
Redwood (J2)*.... 550
Remsen (K4)*.... 483
Rensselaer (N5)*....10,856
Rensselaer Falls (K1)*. 323
Retsof (E5)*.... 500
Rexville (E6)*....
Rhinebeck (N7)*....1,923
Rhinecliff (N7)*.... 600
Richburg (D6)*.... 514
Richfield Spgs. (K5)*...1,534
Richford (H6)*.... 275
Richland (H3)*.... 450
Richmond (C3)*....191,555
Richmondville (M5)*.... 709
Richville (K2)*.... 254
Riparius (M3)*.... 100
Ripley (A6)*....1,229
Riverhead (F2)*....4,892
Riverside ‡(F6).... 818
Rochester (E4)*....332,488
Rochester (urban area) 406,923
Rock City Falls (M4)*.. 300
Rockville Centre (B2)*22,362
Rodman (J3)*.... 250
Rome (J4)*....41,682
Romulus (G5)*.... 250
Ronkonkoma (E2)*....1,334
Roosevelt (B2)*....10,500
Roscoe (L7)*....
Rose (G4)*.... 400
Roseboom (L5)*.... 115
Rosendale (M7)*.... 883
Roseton (C1)*.... 350
Roslyn (B2)*....1,612
Roslyn Estates ‡(B2).... 612
Roslyn Harbor ‡(B2).... 402
Rossie (J2)*.... 150
Rotterdam Jct. (N5)*.. 850
Round Lake (N5)*.... 876
Rouses Point (O1)*....2,001
Roxbury (L6)*.... 600
Rush (E5)*.... 500
Rushford (D6)*.... 900
Rushville (F5)*.... 465
Russell (K2)*.... 500
Russell Gardens ‡(D2). 912
Rye (J1)*....11,721
Sackets Harbor (H3)*.1,247
Saddle Rock ‡(D2).... 33
Sag Harbor (G2)*....2,373
St. George (C3)*....4,900
St. Johnsville (L5)*....2,210
St. Regis Falls (M1)*.... 850
Salamanca (C6)*....8,861
Salem (O4)*....1,067
Salisbury Center (L4)*. 300
Saltaire ‡(E3)*.. 21
Sanborn (C4)*.... 600
Sand Lake (O5)*....1,300
Sands Point ‡(D2).... 860
Sandusky (D6)*.... 275
Sandy Creek (H3)*.... 708
Saranac (N1)*.... 750
Saranac Lake (M2)*....6,913
Saratoga Spgs. (N4)*.15,478
Sardinia (C5)*.... 485
Saugerties (M6)*....3,907
Sauquoit (K5)*....1,227
Savannah (G4)*.... 582
Savona (F6)*.... 869
Sayville (E2)*....4,251
Scarsdale (J1)*....13,156
Schaghticoke (N5)*.... 687
Schenectady (M5)*....91,785
Schenectady (urban area) 123,573
Schenevus (L5)*.... 568
Schoharie (M5)*....1,059
Schroon Lake (N3)*.... 575
Schuyler Lake (L5)*.... 300
Schuylerville (N4)*....1,314
Scio (E6)*.... 640
Scotia (N5)*....7,812
Scottsville (E4)*....1,025
Sea Breeze (F4)*.... 25
Sea Cliff (B2)*....4,868
Seneca Falls (G5)*....6,634
Sharon Springs (L5)*... 361
Shelby (D4).... 200
Shelter Island Hts. (G1)* 600
Sherburne (K5)*....1,604
Sheridan (B5)*....1,050
Sherman (A6)*.... 861
Sherrill (K4)*....2,236
Shoreham ‡(E2)*.... 90
Shortsville (F5)*....1,314
Shushan (O4)*.... 325
Sidney (K6)*....4,815
Sidney Center (K6)*.... 400
Silver Creek (B5)*....3,068
Silver Springs (E5)*.... 830
Sinclairville (B6)*.... 672
Skaneateles (H5)*....2,331
Skaneateles Falls (G5)* 590
Slaterville Spgs. (H6)*. 350
Sloan (C5)*....4,698
Sloatsburg (C2)*....2,018
Smithtown Branch (E2)* 1,424
Smithville Flats (J6)*.. 200
Smyrna (J5)*.... 269
Sodus (G4)*....1,588
Sodus Point (G4)*.... 680
Solvay (H4)*....7,868
Somerset (D4).... 249
S. Bethlehem (N5)*.... 300
S. Colton (L1)*.... 500
S. Columbia (L5)*.... 325
S. Corning (F6).... 880
S. Dayton (C6)*.... 727
S. Fallsburg (L7)*....1,147
S. Floral Park ‡(D2).... 572
S. Glens Falls (N4)....3,645
S. Lansing (H5)*.... 400
S. New Berlin (K5)*....
S. Nyack ‡(C2)....3,102
S. Otselic (J5)*.... 612
Southampton (G2)*....4,042
Southfields (C1)*.... 500
Southold (F2)*....1,027
Sparrow Bush (A1)*.... 650
Speculator (M3)*.... 370
Spencer (H6)*.... 694
Spencerport (E4)*....1,595
Spring Valley (C2)*....4,500
Springville (C5)*....3,322
Springwater (E5)*.... 445
Staatsburg (N7)*.... 500
Stafford (D5)*.... 256
Stamford (L6)*....1,162
Stanard (E6).... 600
Stanfordville (N7)*.... 500
Stanley (F5)*.... 300
Starlake (K2)*.... 700
Steamburg (C6)*.... 225
Stephentown (O5)*.... 250
Stewart Manor ‡(D2)...1,879
Stillwater (N5)*....1,276
Stittville (K4)*.... 375
Stockton (B6)*.... 400
Stony Brook (E2)*....
Stony Creek (M4)*.... 465
Stony Point (C1)*....1,438
Stottville (N6)*....1,020
Stratford (L4)*.... 500
Strykersville (C5)*.... 400
Suffern (C2)*....4,010
Summitville (L7)*.... 300
Swormville (C4)*....
Sylvan Beach (J4)*.... 600
Syosset (B2)*....1,133
Syracuse (H4)*....220,583
Syracuse (urban area) 264,610
Taberg (J4)*.... 500
Tannersville (M6)*.... 639
Tarrytown (H1)*....8,851
The Glen (N3)*....
Thendara (K3)*.... 200
Theresa (J2)*.... 925
Thomaston (B2)....2,045
Thousand Island Park (J2)* 300
Three Mile Bay (H2)*.. 350
Thurman (M3)*.... 112
Ticonderoga (N3)*....3,517
Tivoli (N6)*.... 753
Tonawanda (B4)*....14,617
Trenton (Barneveld*) ‡(K4) 331
Troupsburg (F6)*.... 250
Troy (N5)*....72,311
Troy-Albany (urban area) 290,209
Trumansburg (G5)*....1,479
Truxton (H5)*.... 425
Tuckahoe (H1)*....5,991
Tully (H5)*.... 744
Tupper Lake (M2)*....5,441
Turin (K3)*.... 273
Tuxedo Park (C1)*....
Unadilla (K6)*....1,317
Union Hill (F4)*.... 436
Union Spgs. (G5)*.... 957
Unionville (B1)*.... 454
Upper Brookville ‡(D2). 469
Upper Jay (N2)*.... 175
Upper Nyack ‡(C2)....1,195
Utica (K4)*....101,531
Utica (urban area)....117,390
Valatie (N6)*....1,225
Valhalla (J1)*....
Valley Falls (N5)*.... 555
Valley Stream (A2)*...26,854
Van Etten (G6)*.... 504
Van Hornesville (L5)*... 200
Varysburg (D5)*.... 350
Vernon ‡(J4)*.... 754
Versailles (B6)*.... 192
Vestal (H6)*....5,000
Victor (F5)*....1,066
Victory Mills (N4)*.... 488
Village of the Branch ‡(E2) 163
Voorheesville (M5)*.... 895
Waddington (K1)*.... 819
Wadhams (N2)*.... 175
Wading River (F2)*.... 700
Walden (B1)*....4,559
Walker (E4)*.... 250
Wallace (E6)*.... 300
Wallkill (M7)*....1,145
Walton (K6)*....3,947
Walworth (F4)*.... 500
Wampsville (J4)*.... 379
Wanakah (C5)....
Wappingers Falls (N7)*3,490
Warners (H4)*.... 500
Warrensburg (N3)*....2,358
Warsaw (D5)*....3,713
Warwick (B1)*....2,674
Washingtonville ‡(B1)* 823
Waterford (N5)*....2,968
Waterloo (G5)*....4,438
Waterport (D4)*.... 217
Watertown (J3)*....34,350
Waterville (K5)*....1,634
Watervliet (N5)*....15,197
Watkins Glen (G6)*....3,052
Waverly (G6)*....6,037
Wayland (E5)*....1,834
Wayne (F6)*.... 195
Webster (F4)*....1,773
Weedsport (G4)*....1,588
Wells (M4)*.... 720
Wells Bridge (K6)*.... 290
Wellsburg (G6)*.... 638
Wellsville (E6)*....6,402
W. Albany (N5)*....
W. Amboy (J4).... 60
W. Carthage ‡(J3)....2,000
W. Chazy (N1)*.... 500
W. Haverstraw ‡(C1)*.3,099
W. Hurley (M6)*....1,000
W. Leyden (J4)*.... 400
W. Point (C1)*....5,000
W. Sayville (E2)*....1,370
W. Stockholm (K1)*.... 305
W. Valley (C6)*.... 500
W. Winfield (K5)*.... 832
Westbury (B2)*....7,112
Westerlo (M6)*.... 250
Westernville (K4)*.... 500
Westfield (A6)*....3,663
Westhampton (F2)*.... 950
Westhampton Beach (F2)* 1,087
Westons Mills (D6)*....
Westport (N2)*.... 733
Whallonsburg (O2)*.... 200
White Plains (J1)*....43,466
Whitehall (O3)*....4,457
Whitesboro (K4)*....3,902
Whitesville (E6)*.... 750
Whitney Point (J6)*.... 883
Willard (G5)*.... 500
Williamson (F4)*....1,520
Williamstown (J4)*.... 250
Williamsville (C5)*....4,649
Williston Park (B2)....7,505
Willsboro (N2)*.... 830
Wilmington (N2)*.... 500
Wilson (C4)*.... 962
Wilton (N4)*.... 200
Windham (M6)*.... 660
Windsor (J6)*.... 822
Wingdale (N7)*....1,300
Winthrop (L1)*.... 950
Witherbee (N2)*....1,388
Wolcott (G4)*....1,516
Wolcottsville (C4).... 450
Woodbourne (M7)*....1,600
Woodgate (K3)*.... 125
Woodhull (F6)*.... 332
Woodmere (B3)*.... 745
Woodridge (L7)*.... 951
Woodsburgh (Woodmere*) (B3).... 745
Woodstock (M6)*....1,500
Woodville (H3)*.... 115
Worcester (L5)*....1,000
Wurtsboro (L7)*.... 628
Wyoming (D5)*.... 508
Yaphank (E2)*....1,200
Yonkers (H1)*....152,798
York (E5)*....
Yorkshire (D5)*.... 400
Yorkville (K4)*....3,528
Youngstown (C4)*.... 932
Youngsville (L7)*....

Map on Page 80

NORTH CAROLINA

Total Population 4,061,929

100 COUNTIES

Alamance (G3)....71,220
Alexander (C3)....14,554
Alleghany (C1)....8,155
Anson (E4)....26,781
Ashe (D6)....21,878
Avery (C7)....13,352
Beaufort (M4)....37,134
Bertie (L2)....26,439
Bladen (H5)....29,703
Brunswick (J6)....19,238
Buncombe (E8)....124,403
Burke (B3)....45,518
Cabarrus (D4)....63,783
Caldwell (B3)....43,352
Camden (N2)....5,223
Carteret (M5)....23,059
Caswell (G2)....20,870
Catawba (C3)....61,794
Chatham (G3)....25,392
Cherokee (B9)....18,294
Chowan (M2)....12,540
Clay (C9)....6,006
Cleveland (B4)....64,357
Columbus (H6)....50,621
Craven (L4)....48,823
Cumberland (H4)....96,006
Currituck (N2)....6,201
Dare (O3)....5,405
Davidson (E3)....62,244
Davie (D3)....15,420
Duplin (K5)....41,074
Durham (H3)....101,639
Edgecombe (K3)....51,634
Forsyth (E2)....146,135
Franklin (J2)....31,341
Gaston (C4)....110,836
Gates (M2)....9,555
Graham (C8)....6,886
Granville (H2)....31,793
Greene (K3)....18,024
Guilford (F3)....191,057
Halifax (K2)....58,377
Harnett (H4)....47,605
Haywood (D8)....37,631
Henderson (E8)....30,921
Hertford (L2)....21,453
Hoke (G4)....15,756
Hyde (N3)....6,479
Iredell (D3)....56,303
Jackson (D9)....19,261
Johnston (J4)....65,906
Jones (L4)....11,004
Lee (G4)....23,522
Lenoir (K4)....45,953
Lincoln (C3)....27,459
Mc Dowell (A3)....25,720
Macon (D9)....16,174
Madison (E7)....20,522
Martin (L3)....27,938
Mecklenburg (D4)....197,052
Mitchell (B7)....15,143
Montgomery (F4)....17,260
Moore (G4)....33,129
Nash (K2)....59,919
New Hanover (K6)....63,272
Northampton (L2)....28,432
Onslow (L5)....42,047
Orange (G2)....34,435
Pamlico (M4)....9,993
Pasquotank (N2)....24,347
Pender (K5)....18,423
Perquimans (N2)....9,602
Person (H2)....24,361
Pitt (L3)....63,789
Polk (A4)....11,627
Randolph (F3)....50,804
Richmond (F4)....39,597
Robeson (G5)....87,769
Rockingham (F2)....64,816
Rowan (D3)....75,410
Rutherford (A4)....46,356
Sampson (J4)....49,780
Scotland (G5)....26,336
Stanly (E4)....37,130
Stokes (E2)....21,520
Surry (D2)....45,593
Swain (C8)....9,921
Transylvania (E9)....15,194
Tyrrell (N3)....5,048
Union (D4)....42,034
Vance (J2)....32,101
Wake (H3)....136,450
Warren (J2)....23,539
Washington (M3)....13,180
Watauga (D6)....18,342
Wayne (J4)....64,267
Wilkes (C2)....45,243
Wilson (K3)....54,506
Yadkin (D2)....22,133
Yancey (F7)....16,306

CITIES and TOWNS

Abbottsburg (H5)*....
Aberdeen (G4)*....1,603
Abner (F4)*....
Abashers (C2)*.... 83
Acme (J6)*.... 139
Adako (B3).... 50
Adams (D6).... 180
Addor (G4)*.... 110
Advance (E3)*.... 216
Ahoskie (L2)*....3,579
Airlie (K2).... 50
Alamance (F2)*.... 415
Alarka (D8)*....1,000
Albemarle (E4)*....11,798
Alert (J2).... 65
Alexander (E8)*....1,200
Alexander Mills (B4)*.. 885
Allen (B4).... 100
Alliance (M4)*.... 600
Allreds (F4)*.... 53
Almond (C8)*.... 250
Alston (J2).... 50
Altamahaw (G2)*....1,200
Altamont (C7)*....
Andrews (C9)*....1,397
Angier (H4)*....1,182
Ansonville (E4)*.... 545
Apex (H3)*....1,065
Apple Grove (D5)*.... 50
Arapahoe (M4)*.... 273
Ararat (D2)*.... 37
Archdale (F3)*....1,218
Arcola (J2)*.... 122
Arden (E8)*.... 400
Arlington ‡(D2).... 525
Ash (J6)*.... 125
Asheboro (F3)*....7,701
Asheville (E8)*....53,000
Asheville (urban area).57,658
Ashford (B3)*.... 291
Ashland (D6)*.... 50
Ashton (K6).... 200
Atkinson (J5)*.... 294
Atlantic (N5)*.... 844
Atlantic Beach (M5)*... 49
Auburn (H3).... 100
Aulander (L2)*....1,112
Aurora (M4)*.... 525
Autryville (H4)*.... 151
Aventon (K2).... 150
Avon (P4)*.... 400
Avondale (B4)*.... 769
Ayden (L4)*....2,282
Aydlett (O2).... 200
Azalea (F8)*.... 125
Bachelor (M5).... 250
Badin (E4)*....2,126
Bagley (J3).... 27
Bahama (H2)*.... 150
Bailey (J3)*.... 743
Bakersville (B7)*.... 428
Bald Creek (A7)*.... 200
Bald Mountain (A7).... 50
Balfour (F8)*.... 750
Balm (C6)*....
Balsam (D8)*.... 600
Bandana (B7)*.... 240
Banner Elk (C7)*.... 462
Bannertown (D1)....
Barber (D3)*.... 175
Barco (O2)*.... 425
Barnard (E7)*.... 100
Barnardsville (B8)*.... 500
Barnesville (G6)*.... 100
Barrett (D1).... 40
Bat Cave (F8)*.... 120
Bath (M4)*.... 381
Battleboro (K2)*.... 329
Bayboro (M4)*.... 453
Bear Creek (G3)*.... 200
Beargrass (L3).... 128
Beaufort (M5)*....3,212
Bee Log (A7).... 200
Beech Creek (C6)*.... 55
Belcross (N2)*.... 150
Belhaven (M3)*....2,528
Bellarthur (K3)*.... 190
Belmont (D4)*....5,330
Belvidere (N2)*.... 147
Belwood (B4)*.... 300
Beng (D6)*.... 50
Benham (C2)*....
Bennett (F3)*.... 236
Benson (J4)*....2,102
Benton Heights (D4)....
Bentonville (J4).... 9
Bera (H2).... 100
Bertie (M2).... 259
Bessemer City (C4)*....3,961
Bessie (D9)....
Bests (K4).... 55
Beta (D8).... 150
Bethania (E2)*.... 150
Bethel (L3)*....1,402
Beulaville (K5)*.... 724
Big Pine (E8)*.... 275
Biltmore Forest (F8).... 657
Bina (D5)*.... 100
Biscoe (F4)*....1,034
Black Creek (K3)*.... 316
Black Mountain (F8)*..1,174
Blackstone (B2).... 60
Bladenboro (H5)*.... 796
Blanch (G2)*.... 75
Blounts Creek (L4)*.... 300
Blowing Rock (C7)*.... 661
Bluff (E7)*.... 100
Boardman (H6)*.... 311
Bobbit (J2)....
Boger City (C4)*....1,733
Bogue (M5).... 150
Boiling Springs (B4)*...1,145
Bolivia (J6)*.... 215
Bolton (J6)*.... 606
Bonlee (G3)*.... 275
Bonnerton (M4).... 40
Boomer (C2)*.... 150
Boone (D6)*....2,973
Boonford (B7)*.... 200
Boonville (D2)*.... 502
Bostic ‡(B4)*.... 227
Bowdens (J4)*.... 239
Brevard (E9)*....3,908
Bricks (K2)*....
Bridgeton (M4)*.... 805
Bridgewater (B3)....
Broadway (G4)*.... 469
Brookford (C3)*.... 768
Browns Summit (F2)*... 220
Brownwood (D6)*.... 45
Brunswick (H6)*.... 190
Bryson City (D8)*....1,499
Buck (C2)*.... 75
Buckner (E7).... 100
Buffalo City (O3).... 34
Buffalo Cove (D7).... 352
Buies (G5)*....
Buies Creek (H4)*....
Buladean (B7)*.... 50
Bullock (H2)*.... 100
Bunn (J3)*.... 255
Bunnlevel (H4)*.... 177
Burgaw (J5)*....1,613
Burlington (F2)*....24,560
Burnsville (B7)*....1,341
Busick (F8).... 100
Butch (B7).... 100
Butters (H5)*.... 100
Buxton (P4)*.... 550
Bynum (G3)*.... 450
Calypso (J4)*.... 688
Camden (N2)*.... 200
Cameron (G4)*.... 284
Cana (D3)*.... 75
Candler (E8)*.... 800
Candor (F4)*.... 617
Cane River (B7)*.... 250
Canton (E8)*....4,906
Carbonton (G3).... 90
Caroleen (B4)*....1,712
Carolina Beach (K6)*...1,080
Carpenter (H3).... 150
Carrboro (G3)*....1,795
Carthage (F4)*....1,194
Cary (H3)*....1,446
Casar (B3)*.... 300
Cash Corner (M4)*.... 230
Cashiers (D9)*.... 305
Castalia (K2)*.... 421
Castle Hayne (K6)*....1,000
Catawba (C3)*.... 506
Catharine Lake (K5).... 75
Cedar Falls (F3)*.... 650
Cedar Grove (G2)*.... 350
Cedar Mountain (E9)*.. 134

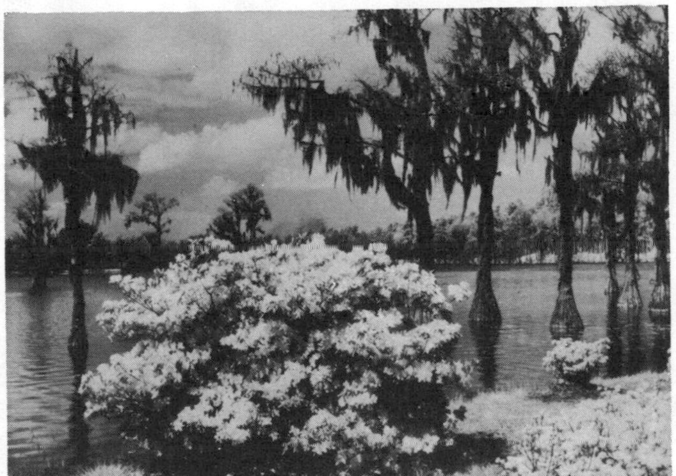

Celo (B7)*.... 150
Central Falls (F3)*.... 500
Cerro Gordo (H6)*.... 265
Chadbourn (H6)....2,103
Chalybeate Springs(H3)* 300
Champion (E6)*.... 92
Chapanoke (N2)*.... 50
Chapel Hill (H3)*....9,177
Charles (D3)*.... 75
Charlotte (D4)*....134,042
Charlotte(urban area) 140,085
Cheoah (C8)*.... 200
Cherokee (D8)*.... 500
Cherry (M3).... 73
Cherry Lane (D2)*.... 104
Cherryville (C4)*....3,492
Chicod (L3)*.... 278
China Grove (D3)*....1,491
Chinquapin (K5)*.... 800
Chip (F4).... 40
Chocowinity (L4)*.... 150
Cid (E3).... 200
Citron (E6)*.... 50
Claremont (C3)*.... 669
Clarendon (H6)*.... 200
Clark (L4)*.... 160
Clarkton (H6)*.... 589
Clarrissa (B7)*.... 250
Clayton (J3)*....2,229
Clemmons (E2)*....
Cleveland (D3)*.... 580
Cliffside (B4)*....1,388
Clifton (D6)*....
Climax (F3)*.... 225
Clinton (J5)*....4,414
Clyde (E8)*.... 598
Coats (H4)*....1,047
Cofield (M2)*.... 325
Coinjock (N2)*.... 350
Colerain (M2)*.... 367
Coleridge (F3)*.... 450
Colington (O3)....
Collettsville (B3)*.... 250
Columbia (N3)*....1,161
Columbus (F9)*.... 486
Comet (D6)*.... 50
Comfort (K5)*.... 300
Como (L1)*.... 250
Concord (D4)*....16,486
Conetoe (K3)*.... 172
Congo (E6).... 75
Connellys Springs (B3)* 550
Conover (C3)*....1,164
Conway (L2)*.... 618
Cooleemee (D3)*....1,925
Corapeake (M1)*.... 50
Corinth (G3)*.... 97
Cornelius (D4)*....1,548
Corolla (O2)*.... 75
Council (H6)*.... 64
Cove City (L4)*.... 465
Cove Creek (E8)*.... 100
Cowarts (D8)*.... 85
Cramerton (C4)*....3,211
Creedmoor (H2)*.... 852
Creswell (N3)*.... 425
Crisp (K3).... 50
Croft (D4).... 75
Crossnore (C7)*.... 240
Crouse (C4)*.... 303
Crumpler (E5)*.... 218
Cruso (E8).... 75
Culberson (B9)*.... 150
Cullasaja (D9)*.... 150
Cullowhee (D8)*.... 500
Cumberland (H5)....
Cumnock (G3)*.... 250
Cunningham (H1).... 60
Currie (J6)*.... 200
Currituck (O2)*.... 150
Cycle (D2)*.... 150
Dallas (C4)*....2,454
Dalton (E2)*.... 69
Danbury (E2)*.... 200
Darby (E7)*....
Davidson (D4)*....2,423
Davis (M5)*.... 600
Day Brook (B7)*.... 100
Daystrom (G5)*.... 116
Deep Gap (D6)*.... 150
Deep Run (K4)*.... 142
Dehart (E6).... 25
Delco (J6)*.... 257
Dellview ‡(C4).... 7
Dellwood (D8)*.... 225
Democrat (E8)*....
Denny (C2).... 100
Denton (E3)*.... 766
Denver (C3)*.... 415
Derita (D4)*.... 600
Devotion (D2)*.... 40
Dillsboro (D8)*.... 198
Dixon (K5)*.... 75
Dobson (D2)*.... 609
Dockery (C2)*.... 600
Dover (L4)*.... 638
Draper (F1)*....3,629
Drexel (B3)*.... 988
Drumhill (M1).... 75
Dublin (H5)*.... 243
Duck (O2)....
Dudley (J4)*.... 133
Dulah (H6).... 75
Duncan (H3).... 100
Dundarrach (G5).... 134
Dunn (H4)*....6,316
Durham (H2)*....71,311
Durham (urban area)...72,369
Dysortville (B3).... 100
Eagle Springs (F4)*.... 350
Earl (B4)*.... 300
East Bend (D2)*.... 475
E. Flat Rock (F9)*....

E. Lake (N3)* 100
E. Laport (D8)* 240
E. Laurinburg (G5)* 745
E. Lumberton (H5)* 1,106
E. Spencer (E3)* 2,444
Edenton (M2)* 4,468
Edgemont (D7)* 85
Edneyville (F8)* 500
Edward (M4)* 155
Efland (G2)* 500
Elams (K1)* 10
Elberon (J2)* 75
Eldorado (F4)*
Eldreth (D5) 50
Eleazer (F3)* 60
Elizabeth City (N2)* 12,685
Elizabethtown (H5)* 1,611
Elk Park (C7)* 545
Elkin (D2)* 2,842
Elkton (H6)*
Ellenboro (B4)* 537
Ellerbe (F4)* 773
Elliott (J5) 25
Elm City (K3)* 839
Elmwood (D3)* 300
Elon College (G2)* 1,109
Elrod (G5)* 135
Emerson (H6)* 85
Enfield (K2)* 2,361
Engelhard (O3)* 500
Enka (E8)* 1,792
Ernul (L4)* 150
Erwin (H4)* 3,344
Essex (J2)* 35
Estatoe (C7) 300
Ether (F4)* 50
Etowah (E8)* 400
Eufola (D3) 150
Eure (M2)* 200
Eureka (K3)* 192
Everetts (L3)* 244
Evergreen (H6)* 245
Ewart (B7)*
Fair Bluff (H6)* 1,056
Fairfield (N3)* 250
Fairmount (G6)* 2,319
Fairview (E8)* 300
Faison (J4)* 768
Faith (E3)* 490
Falcon (H4)* 245
Falkland (K3)* 174
Fallston (B4)* 500
Farmer (F3)* 125
Farmington (D3)* 300
Farmville (K3)* 2,942
Faro (K4) 140
Faust (E7) 100
Fayetteville (H4)* 34,715
Ferguson (C2)* 50
Fig (D6)* 75
Finley (D7) 100
Flat Rock (E9)* 1,000
Flats (C8)* 150
Fleetwood (D6)* 50
Fletcher (E8)* 500
Florence (M4)* 500
Folkstone (K5)* 100
Forbes (B7)* 253
Forest City (B4)* 4,971
Fork (E3)* 300
Fort Bragg (H4)* 16,000
Fountain (K3)* 451
Four Oaks (H4)* 942
Francisco (E2)*
Frank (C7)* 25
Franklin (C9)* 1,975
Franklinton (J2)* 1,414
Franklinville (F3)* 778
Freeland (J6)* 300
Fremont (J3)* 1,395
Frisco (O4)* 100
Fuquay Springs (H3)* 1,992
Furches (E6)* 150
Garland (J5)* 539
Garner (H3)* 1,180
Garysburg (K2)* 344
Gaston (K1)* 1,218
Gastonia (C4)* 23,069
Gates (M2)* 150
Gatesville (M2)* 323
Germanton (E2)* 118
Ghio (F5)* 104
Gibson (F5)* 609
Gibsonville (F2)* 1,866
Gilkey (B4)*
Glade Valley (C2)* 75
Glen Alpine (B3)* 695
Glen Raven (G2) 750
Glendale Springs (D6)* 200
Glendon (G4)* 110
Glenola (F3) 100
Glenville (D9)* 200
Glenwood (A3)*
Globe (D7)* 200
Gloucester (N5)* 130
Gneiss (D9)* 250
Godwin (H4)* 145
Gold Hill (E3)*
Gold Point (L3) 132
Goldsboro (K4)* 21,454
Goldston (G3)* 372
Graham (G2)* 5,026
Grainger (K4) 168
Grandview (B9) 75
Grandy (O2)* 500
Granite Falls (C3)* 2,286
Granite Quarry (D3) 591
Grantsboro (M4)* 1,500
Grassy Creek (E5)* 500
Greenmountain (B7)* 600
Greensboro (F2)* 74,389
Greensboro,
(urban area) 82,719
Greenville (L3)* 16,724
Grifton (L4)* 510
Grimesland (L3)* 414
Grover (C4)* 535
Guilford (F2)* 500
Guilford College (F2)* 500
Gulf (G3)* 300
Gulrock (O4)* 51
Gupton (J2) 75
Halifax (K2)* 346
Halls Mills (E6) 300
Hallsboro (H6)* 300
Hamilton (L3)* 514
Hamilton Lakes ‡(F2) 882
Hamlet (F5)* 5,061
Hampstead (K6)*
Hamptonville (D2)* 150
Hanes (E2)* 1,000
Harbinger (O2)* 250
Harkers Island (M5)* 1,244
Harmony (D3)* 374
Harrellsville (M2)* 167
Harrell Store ‡(J5) 147
Harris (G9)* 110
Harrisburg (D4)* 300
Hassell (L3)* 137
Hasty (G5) 125
Hatteras (O4)* 700
Havelock (M5)* 4,500
Haw River (G2)* 1,175
Hawk (C7)*
Hayesville (C9)* 356
Hayne (H5) 40
Hays (C2)* 400
Haywood (G3) 169
Hazelwood (D8)* 1,769
Heathsville (K2) 150
Heaton (C6)* 50
Helton (D5)* 192
Hemlock (D5) 750
Henderson (J2)* 10,996
Hendersonville (F8)* 6,103
Hendrix (E7)* 150
Henrietta (B4)* 1,013
Hertford (N2)* 2,096
Hester (H2) 110
Hickory (C3)* 14,755
Hiddenite (C3)* 600
Higgins (B7)*
High Point (E3)* 39,973
High Rock (E3) 75
Highfalls (F4)* 310
Highlands (D9)* 515
Highshoals (C4)* 875
Hildebran ‡(B3)* 529
Hillsboro (G2)* 1,329
Hobbsville (M2)* 75
Hobgood (L2)* 603
Hobucken (N4)*
Hoffman (F4)* 398
Hollifield (A3) 200
Hollis (B4)* 65
Hollister (K2)* 200
Holly Springs (H3)* 406
Hollyridge (L6)* 1,082
Hookerton (K4)* 253
Hope Mills (H5)* 1,077
Hot Springs (E7)* 721
Houstonville (D2)* 150
Hubert (L5)* 40
Hudson (C3)* 922
Huntdale (B7)*
Huntersville (D4)* 916
Hurdle Mills (G2)* 200
Husk (D5)* 78
Icard (C3)* 1,100
Icemorlee (D5)
Idlewild (E6)* 175
Indian Trail (D4)* 308
Inez (J2)* 40
Ingalls (C7)* 75
Ingold (J5)* 350
Iron Station (C4)* 232
Ivanhoe (J5)* 200
Jackson (L2)* 843
Jackson Springs (F4)* 246
Jacksons Creek (F3)* 100
Jacksonville (K5)* 3,960
James City (M4)* 750
Jamestown (F3)* 748
Jamesville (M3)* 529
Jarvisburg (O2)*
Jefferson (E6)* 359
Joe (E7)* 200
Johns (F5)* 300
Jonas Ridge (C7)*
Jonesville (D2)* 1,768
Joynes (C2)* 240
Julian (F3)* 300
Jupiter (E8) 136
Kannapolis (D4)* 28,448
Kelford (L2)* 405
Kelly (J6)* 100
Kenansville (K5)* 674
Kenly (J3)* 1,129
Kernersville (E2)* 2,396
Kerr (J5)* 40
Kill Devil Hills (O3)* 125
Kimesville (G3) 100
King (E2)* 1,000
Kings Creek (C3)* 300
Kings Mountain (C4)* 7,206
Kinston (K4)* 18,336
Kipling (H4)* 101
Kittrell (H2)* 189
Kitty Hawk (O2)* 300
Knightdale (J3)* 461
Knotts Island (O2)* 400
Kure Beach (K6)* 228
La Grange (K4) 1,852
Lagoon (J5)* 233
Lake Landing (O4)*
Lake Lure (A4)* 174
Lake Toxaway (E9)* 270
Lake Waccamaw (J6)* 575
Lakedale (H4) 4,000
Lakeview (G4)* 300
Landis (D3)* 1,827
Lansing (D5)*
Lasker (L2)* 177
Lassiter (J3) 35
Lattimore ‡(B4)* 286
Laurel Hill (F5)* 400
Laurel Park (E8) 302
Laurel Springs (E6)* 250
Laurinburg (F5)* 7,134
Lawndale (B4)* 964
Lawsonville (E2)* 200
Laxon (D6)* 61
Leaksville (F2)* 4,045
Leaman (F4)* 21
Leasburg (G2)* 400
Leechville (M3)* 200
Legerwood (B2)* 85
Leggett (K3) 200
Leicester (E7)* 750
Leland (J6)*
Lemon Springs (G4)* 200
Lenoir (C3)* 7,888
Letitia (B9)* 35
Lewarae (F5) 479
Lewiston (L2)* 339
Lexington (E3)* 13,571
Liberty (F3)* 1,342
Lilesville (F5)* 605
Lillington (H4)* 1,061
Lincolnton (C4)* 5,423
Linden (H4)* 194
Linville (C7)* 500
Linville Falls (A3)*
Linwood (E3)* 350
Little Switzerland (A3)* 400
Littleton (K2)* 1,173
Locust (E4) 216
Lola (N5)* 150
Longhurst (G2)* 1,539
Longisland (D3)* 350
Longview (C3)* 2,291
Longwood (J6)* 800
Loray (C3)* 115
Louisburg (J2)* 2,545
Lovill (D6)
Lowe (G5) 75
Lowell (C4)* 2,313
Lowgap (D1)* 500
Lowland (N4)* 200
Lucama (J3)* 405
Lumber Bridge (G5)* 154
Lumberton (G5)* 9,186
Lynn (F9)* 600
Mabel (C6)* 200
Macclesfield (K3)* 370
Mackeys (M3)* 250
Macon (J2)* 238
Madison (F2)* 1,789
Maggie (D8)*
Magnolia (K5)* 585
Maiden (C3)* 1,952
Mamers (G4)* 200
Mamie (O2)* 250
Manly (G4)* 280
Manns Harbor (O3)* 325
Manson (J2)* 40
Manteo (O3)* 635
Maple Hill (K5)* 75
Mapleton (L2)
Mapleville (J2) 50
Marble (C9)*
Margarettsville (L1)* 113
Marietta (G6)* 94
Marion (A3)* 2,740
Mars Hill (E7) 1,404
Marshall (E8)* 983
Marshallberg (N5)* 784
Marshville (E4)* 1,258
Marston (F5)* 159
Mashoes (O3)*
Matthews (D4)* 589
Maury (K4)* 251
Maxton (G5)* 1,974
Mayodan (F2)* 2,246
Maysville (L5)* 818
Mc Adenville (D4)* 1,060
Mc Cain (G4)* 900
Mc Cullers (H3) 89
Mc Donalds (G5)* 78
Mc Farlan (E5)* 136
Mc Grady (E6)* 175
Mebane (G2)* 2,068
Melvin Hill (A4)* 188
Merrimon (M5)* 250
Merry Hill (M2)* 200
Merry Oaks (G3)* 160
Mesic (M4)* 425
Method (H3)* 350
Micaville (B7)* 200
Micro (J3)* 310
Middleburg (J2)* 217
Middlesex (J3)* 446
Middletown (O4)* 200
Midland (E4)* 250
Midway Park (L5)* 3,703
Milam (D6)* 50
Mill Spring (A4)*
Millbrook (H3)* 100
Millers Creek (E6)* 500
Milton (G1)* 317
Milwaukee (L2)* 302
Mineral Springs (D5)* 135
Minneapolis (C7)* 100
Mint Hill (D4)
Mocksville (D3)* 1,909
Momeyer (J3) 200
Moncure (G3)* 500
Monroe (E5)* 10,140
Montague (K6) 100
Montezuma (C7)* 75
Mooresboro (B4)*
Mooresville (D3)* 7,121
Moravian Falls (C2)* 375
Morehead City (M5)* 5,144
Morganton (B3)* 8,311
Morrisville (H3)* 221
Mortimer (B2)* 13
Morven (E5)* 601
Mount Airy (D1)* 7,192
Mt. Gilead (F4)* 1,201
Mt. Holly (D4)* 2,241
Mt. Mourne (D3)* 232
Mt. Olive (K4)* 3,732
Mt. Pleasant (E4)* 1,019
Mt. Vernon Springs (G3)* 90
Mount Zion (D7)* 100
Moyock (N1)*
Murfreesboro (M2)* 2,140
Murphy (C9)* 2,433
Nags Head (O3)*
Nakina (H6)* 350
Nantahala (C8)* 125
Nashville (K3)* 1,302
Nathans Creek (E6)* 75
Navassa (J6)* 500
Nebo (B3)*
Needmore (C8)* 200
Neuse (H3)*
New Bern (L4)* 15,812
New Holland (N4)* 50
New London (E4)* 285
Newhill (H3)* 232
Newhope (C2)* 25
Newland (C7)* 425
Newport (M5)* 676
Newsom (E3)
Newton (C3)* 6,039
Newton Grove (J4)* 374
Norlina (J2)* 874
Norman (F4)* 300
North Cove (B3)* 500
N. Harlowe (M5)* 300
N. Lumberton (H5) 423
N. Wilkesboro (C2)* 4,379
Northside (H2)* 100
Norwood (E4)* 1,735
Oak City (L3)* 518
Oak Ridge (F2)* 500
Oakboro (E4)* 631
Oakland (E9)* 200
Oakley (L3) 58
Ocracoke (O4)* 600
Old Dock (H6) 300
Old Fort (A3)* 771
Old Trap (O2)* 380
Olin (D3)* 60
Olivia (G4)* 450
Olyphic (H7) 50
Orange (H4) 50
Oriental (M4)* 590
Orrum (G6)* 162
Oteen (E8) 1,000
Otto (C9)* 100
Overhills (G4)* 50
Oxford (H2)* 6,685
Pactolus (L3)* 265
Paint Gap (B7)* 200
Palmyra (L2)* 67
Pantego (M3)* 275
Parker (D6)* 50
Parkersburg (J5)* 114
Parkton (H5)* 527
Parmele (L3)* 406
Parsonville (E6)* 250
Paschall (J1) 75
Passion (F9) 196
Patterson (B3)* 195
Peachland (E5)* 485
Pee Dee (F5)* 50
Peletier (L5)*
Pelham (G1)* 200
Pembroke (G5)* 1,212
Pendleton (L2)* 88
Penrose (E8)* 350
Pensacola (B8)* 150
Peoria (C6) 300
Phoenix (J6)
Pike Road (M3)* 250
Pikeville (J4)* 464
Pilot Mountain (D2)* 1,092
Pine Hall (F2)* 575
Pine Level (J4)* 602
Pinebluff (F4) 575
Pinehurst (F4) 1,016
Pineola (C7)* 350
Pinetops (K3)* 1,031
Pinetown (M3)* 301
Pineview (G4) 175
Pineville (D4)* 1,373
Piney Creek (E5)* 35
Pink Hill (K4)* 386
Pinnacle (E2)* 450
Pisgah (F3)* 60
Pisgah Forest (E9)* 900
Pittsboro (G3)* 1,094
Pleasant Hill (K1)* 200
Plumtree (C7)* 300
Plymouth (M3)* 4,486
Point Harbor (O2)* 110
Polkton (E4)* 459
Pollocksville (L5)* 420
Pomona (F2)* 1,500
Ponzer (N3)* 110
Poplar (B7)* 575
Poplar Branch (O2)* 325
Pores Knob (C2)* 150
Portsmouth (N4)* 15
Postell (B9) 120
Powells Point (O2)* 375
Powellsville (M2)* 250
Prentiss (D9)* 100
Price (F1)* 175
Princeton (J4)* 608
Princeville (L3) 919
Proctorville (H6)* 232
Prospect Hill (G2)* 110
Pungo (M3)* 200
Purlear (E6)* 60
Purvis (G5)*
Quitsna (L3) 210
Radical (E6) 50
Raeford (G5)* 2,030
RALEIGH (H3)* 65,679
Raleigh (urban area) 68,190
Ramsaytown (B7)* 100
Ramseur (F3)* 1,134
Randleman (F3)* 2,066
Ranger (B9)* 150
Ransomville (M4)* 170
Raynham (G5) 30
Red Oak (J2)* 250
Red Springs (G5)* 2,245
Reddies River (E6) 175
Reese (C6)* 1,450
Reidsville (F2)* 11,708
Relief (B7)* 129
Rennert (G5)*
Rex (H5)* 180
Reynolda (E2)* 300
Rhodhiss ‡(B3)* 923
Rich Square (L2)* 971
Richfield (E4)* 237
Richlands (K5)* 877
Ridgeville (G2) 45
Ridgeway (J2)* 250
Ringwood (K2) 60
Roanoke Rapids (K2)* 8,156
Roaring Gap (D2)*
Roaring River (C2)* 350
Robbins (F4)* 1,158
Robbinsville (C8)* 515
Roberdell (F5)* 451
Robersonville (L3)* 1,414
Rockfish (G5)* 150
Rockford (D2)* 225
Rockingham (F5)* 3,356
Rockwell (E3)* 852
Rocky Mount (K3)* 27,697
Rocky Point (K6)*
Rodanthe (P3)* 86
Roe (N5)* 215
Rolesville (J3)* 288
Rominger (C6)* 200
Ronda (D2)* 545
Roper (M3)* 793
Roseboro (J5)* 1,241
Rosehill (K5)* 896
Rosindale (J6) 35
Rosman (E9)* 535
Rougemont (G2)* 300
Rowland (G5)* 1,293
Roxboro (H2)* 4,321
Roxobel (L2)* 394
Royal (M4)* 250
Royall Cotton Mills (H2) 250
Ruffin (F2)* 530
Rufus (B3) 80
Rural Hall (E2)* 1,200
Ruth (A4)* 324
Rutherford College (B3)* 750
Rutherfordton (A4)* 3,146
Ryland (H2)* 50
Saint Pauls (H5)* 2,251
Salemburg (J4)* 435
Salisbury (D3)* 20,102
Salter Path (M5)* 300
Saluda (F9)* 547
Salvo (P3)* 77
Sandy Ridge (E1)* 200
Sanford (G4)* 10,013
Sapphire (E9)* 50
Saratoga ‡(K3)* 366
Saxapahaw (G3)* 660
Scaly (D9)* 200
Scotland Neck (L2)* 2,730
Scotts (D3)* 50
Scotts Hill (K6) 150
Scottville (E5)* 180
Scranton (N4)* 125
Seaboard (K1)* 745
Seagrove (F3)* 319
Sealevel (N5)*
Selma (J3)* 2,639
Semora (G3)* 250
Senia (C7)* 25
Seven Springs (K4)* 197
Severn (L2)* 340
Sevier (A3) 130
Shallotte (J7)* 493
Shannon (G5)* 150
Sharpsburg (K3)* 415
Shawboro (N2)* 150
Shelby (C4)* 15,508
Shelmerdine (L4) 32
Sherwood (D6)* 350
Shoals (E2) 250
Shooting Creek (C9)* 260
Shulls Mills (D7)* 175
Siler City (G3)* 2,501
Siloam (D2)* 250
Silverdale (L5)*
Simpson (Chicod*) (L3) 278
Sims (J3)* 207
Skyland (E8)* 1,200
Sly (D6)*
Smithfield (J3)* 5,574
Smithtown (E2) 182
Smyrna (M5)* 200
Sneads Ferry (L5)* 125
Snow Camp (G3)* 90
Snow Hill (K4)* 946
Snowden (N2)* 85
Sophia (F3)* 200
South Creek (M4)* 108
S. Mills (N2)*
S. Wadesboro (E5) 390
S. Pines (G4)* 4,272
Southmont (E3)* 500
Southport (J7)* 1,748
Southside (C4)* 250
Sparta (C1)* 820
Spear (C7)* 445
Speed (L3)* 103
Spencer (D3)* 3,242
Spies (F4)* 100
Spindale (B4)* 3,891
Spray (F1)* 5,542
Spring Hope (K3)* 1,275
Spring Lake (H4)* 3,500
Springfield (E6)* 50
Spruce Pine (C7)* 2,280
Stacy (N5)* 302
Staley (F3)* 236
Stanfield (E4)* 350
Stanley (C4)* 1,644
Stantonsburg (K3)* 627
Star (F4)* 677
State Road (D2)* 475
Statesville (D3)* 16,901
Stecoah (C8)* 160
Stedman (H4)* 424
Steeds (F4)* 50
Stella (L5)* 100
Stem (H2)* 217
Stokes (L3)* 217
Stokesdale (F2)* 400
Stoneville (F2)* 786
Stonewall (M4)* 272
Stony Point (C3)* 1,020
Stovall (H2)* 410
Straits (M5)* 100
Stratford (E5)* 16
Stumpy Point (O3)* 300
Sturgills (D5)*
Sugar Grove (C6)* 225
Suit (B9)* 150
Summerfield (F2)* 923
Summit (E6)* 50
Sunbury (M2)* 350
Supply (J6)* 207
Surf City (L6)
Swannanoa (F8)* 1,800
Swanns (G4) 30
Swanquarter (N4)* 212
Swansboro (L5)* 559
Sylva (D8)* 1,382
Tabor City (H6)* 2,033
Tamarack (D6)* 150
Tapoco (B8)* 100
Tarboro (K3)* 8,120
Tarheel (H5)* 200
Taylorsville (C3)* 1,310
Teacheys (J5)* 226
Terrell (C3)* 200
Thomasville (E3)* 11,154
Thurmond (D2)* 77
Tillery (K2)* 250
Timberlake (H2)* 200
Timberland (G4) 11
Toast (D2)* 1,401
Todd (D6)* 89
Toecane (B7)* 250
Toliver (D6)*
Tomahawk (J5)* 30
Topia (E5)* 69
Topton (C9)* 125
Townsville (J1)* 219
Traphill (D2)* 150
Trenton (L4)* 469
Trinity (F3)* 764
Triplett (D6)* 120
Troutmans (D3)* 610
Troy (F4)* 2,213
Tryon (A4)* 1,985
Tunis (M2) 200
Turkey (J4)* 223
Turnersburg (D3)* 75
Tyner (M2)* 150
Ulah (F3)*
Unaka (B9)*
Union (L2)
Union Grove (D2)* 125
Union Mills (B3)* 200
Unionville (E4) 124
University (G2)*
Upton (D7)* 93
Uree (A4) 100
Vade Mecum (E2)*
Valdese (B3)* 2,730
Vale (C3)* 200
Valle Crucis (C6)* 200
Vanceboro (L4)* 500
Vandemere (M4)* 475
Vannoy (E6)* 25
Varina (H3)* 593
Vass (G4)* 757
Vaughan (J2)* 181
Vein Mountain (A3) 75
Verona (K5)* 125
Vilas (C6)* 60
Waco ‡(C4)* 310
Wade (H4)*
Wadesboro (E5)* 3,408
Wadeville (E4)*
Wagoner (E6)* 200
Wagram (G5)* 397
Wake Forest (H3)* 3,704
Walkertown (E2)* 1,000
Wallace (J5)* 1,622
Wallburg (E3)* 165
Walnut (E7)* 450
Walnut Cove (E2)* 1,132
Walstonburg (K3)* 177
Wanchese (O3)* 1,000
Warne (C9)* 200
Warren Plains (J2)* 100
Warrensville (E6)* 120
Warrenton (J2)* 1,166
Warsaw (J4)* 1,598
Washington (M3)* 9,698
Washington Park
(M3) 421
Watha (J5)* 222
Waves (P3)* 65
Waxhaw (D5)* 818
Waynesville (E8)* 5,295
Weaverville (E8)* 1,111
Webster (D8)* 142
Weeksville (N2)*
Welcome (E3)* 600
Weldon (K2)* 2,295
Wendell (J3)* 1,253
Wenona (M3)*
Wentworth (F2)* 100
West End (F4)* 850
W. Jefferson (D6)* 871
Westfield (D2)* 300
Wests Mill (D9)* 50
Whitakers (K2)* 962
White Lake (H5)* 400
White Oak (H5)* 125
White Plains (D2)* 500
Whitehall (Seven
Springs*) (K4) 197
Whitehead (E6)* 250
Whiterock (E7) 100
Whiteville (H6)* 4,238
Whitnel (B3)* 1,405
Whittier (D8)* 400
Wilkesboro (C2)* 1,370
Willard (J5)*
Williamston (M3)* 4,975
Wilmington (J6)* 45,043
Wilson (K3)* 23,010
Wilsons Mills (H3)* 349
Windom (B7)* 100
Windsor (L2)* 1,781
Winfall (N2)* 421
Wingate (E5)* 793
Winnabow (J6)* 250
Winston-Salem (E2)* 87,811
Winston-Salem,
(urban area) 91,493
Winterville (L3) 870
Winton (L2)* 834
Wise (J2)* 300
Wolf Mountain (D9)* 25
Wood (J2)* 128
Woodard (M3)* 325
Woodland (L2)* 590
Woodleaf (D3)* 500
Woodsdale (H2)* 200
Woodville (L2)* 387
Worthville (F3)* 550
Wrightsville Beach (K6)* 711
Wrightsville Sound (K6)* 500
Yadkin College (E3)* 82
Yadkin Valley (C2)* 12
Yadkinville (D2)* 820
Yanceyville (G2)* 1,391
Yellowcreek (B8)* 4
Youngsville (J2)* 619
Zebulon (J3)* 1,378
Zionville (D6)* 250
Zirconia (E9)*

Map on Page 81

NORTH DAKOTA

Total Population 619,636

53 COUNTIES

Adams (F7) 4,910
Barnes (O5) 16,884
Benson (M3) 10,675
Billings (D5) 1,777
Bottineau (J2) 12,140
Bowman (C7) 4,001
Burke (E2) 6,621
Burleigh (J6) 25,673
Cass (R5) 58,877
Cavalier (N2) 11,840
Dickey (N7) 9,121
Divide (C2) 5,967
Dunn (E5) 7,212
Eddy (N4) 5,372
Emmons (K7) 9,715
Foster (N5) 5,337
Golden Valley (C5) 3,499
Grand Forks (P3) 39,443
Grant (G6) 7,114
Griggs (O5) 5,460
Hettinger (E7) 7,100
Kidder (L6) 6,168
La Moure (N7) 9,498
Logan (L7) 6,357
Mc Henry (J3) 12,556
Mc Intosh (L7) 7,590
Mc Kenzie (D4) 6,849
Mc Lean (G4) 18,824
Mercer (G5) 8,686
Morton (H6) 19,295
Mountrail (E3) 9,418
Nelson (O4) 8,090
Oliver (H5) 3,091
Pembina (P2) 13,990
Pierce (K3) 8,326
Ramsey (N3) 14,373
Ransom (P7) 8,876
Renville (G2) 5,405
Richland (R7) 19,865
Rolette (L2) 11,102
Sargent (P7) 7,616
Sheridan (K4) 5,253
Sioux (H7) 3,696
Slope (C7) 2,315
Stark (E6) 16,137
Steele (P4) 5,145
Stutsman (M5) 24,158
Towner (M2) 6,360
Traill (R5) 11,359
Walsh (P3) 18,859
Ward (G3) 34,782
Wells (L4) 10,417
Williams (C3) 16,442

CITIES and TOWNS

Abercrombie (S7)* 244
Absaraka (P6)* 45
Adams (O3)* 411
Adrain (O6)* 55
Agate (L2)* 14
Akra (P2)* 25
Alamo (D2)* 192
Alexander (C4)* 302
Alfred (N6)* 150
Alice (P6)* 162
Alkabo (C2)* 70
Almont (H6)* 190
Alsen (N2)* 114
Alta (J5) 6
Ambrose (D2)* 286
Amenia (R6)* 127
Amidon (D7)* 82
Anamoose (K4)* 542
Aneta (P4)* 469
Anselm (R6) 22
Antelope (F6)* 22

Antler (H2)* 217
Appram (C2)* 55
Ardoch (R3)* 137
Arena (K5)* 8
Argusville (R5)* 126
Armourdale (M2) 7
Arndt (M2) 3
Arnegard (D4)* 206
Arthur (R5)* 380
Arvilla (P4)* 115
Ashley (M7)* 1,423
Auburn (R2) 39
Aurelia (G3)* 18
Aylmer (K4) 35
Ayr (P5)* 104
Backoo (P2)* 46
Baker (L3)* 42
Baldwin (J5)* 70
Balfour (J4)* 162
Balta (K3)* 196
Banks (D3)* 9
Bantry (J3)* 125
Barlow (M4)* 43
Barney (S7)* 145
Bartlett (N3)* 61
Barton (K3)* 102
Bathgate (P2)* 209
Battleview (E2)* 60
Beach (C6)* 1,461
Bedford (P5) 8
Belcourt (L2)* 524
Belden (F3)* 26
Belfield (D6)* 1,051
Benedict (H4)* 127
Benson (O7) 10
Bentley (F7)* 66
Berea (O6) 6
Bergen (J3)* 51
Berlin (O7)* 124
Berthold (G3)* 459
Berwick (K3)* 71
Beulah (G5)* 1,501
Big Bend (H5)* 207
Binford (O4)* 309
Bisbee (M2)* 365
BISMARCK (J6)* 18,640
Blabon (P5)* 37
Blackwater (G4) 20
Blaisdell (F3)* 80
Blanchard (R5)* 60
Bloom (N6) 10
Bluegrass (G6)* 7
Bonetraill (C3)* 20
Bordulac (N5)* 75
Bottineau (J2)* 2,268
Bowbells (F2)* 806
Bowdon (L5)* 348
Bowesmont (R2)* 150
Bowman (D7)* 1,382
Braddock (K6)* 175
Brampton (P7)* 90
Brantford (N4)* 78
Breien (H7)* 30
Bremen (M4)* 80
Brinsmade (M3)* 136
Brisbane (H7)* 24
Brocket (O3)* 212
Buchanan (N5)* 80
Bucyrus (E7)* 111
Buffalo (R6)* 261
Buffalo Springs (D7)* 23
Buford (C3)* 61
Burlington (H3)* 240
Burnstad (L7)* 68
Burt (F7)* 65
Butte (J4)* 272
Buttzville (P6)* 18
Buxton (R4)* 387
Caledonia (S5)* 150
Calio (N2)* 102
Calvin (N2)* 152
Cando (M3)* 1,530
Cannon Ball (J7)* 200
Canton (Hensel*) (P2) 139
Carbury (K2)* 37
Carpenter (L2) 3
Carpio (G3)* 194
Carrington (M5)* 2,101
Carson (H7)* 493
Cartwright (C4)* 35
Cashel (R3) 20
Casselton (R6)* 1,373
Cathay (M4)* 209
Cavalier (P2)* 1,459
Cayuga (R7)* 178
Center (H5)* 492
Chaffee (R6)* 125
Chama (C6)
Charbonneau (C4)* 22
Charlson (E3)* 25
Chaseley (L5)* 41
Christine (S6)* 150
Churches Ferry (M3)* 223
Clement (O7) 4
Clementsville (O5) 23
Cleveland (M6)* 181
Clifford (R5)* 158
Clifton (K4)* 7
Clyde (N2)* 110
Coburn (R6) 3
Cogswell (P7)* 393
Coleharbor (H4)* 315
Colfax (S7)* 116
Colgan (C2)* 31
Colgate (P5)* 72
Columbus (E2)* 525
Concrete (P2)* 54
Considine (M2) 5
Conway (P3)* 107
Cooperstown (O5)* 1,189
Corinth (D2)* 30
Coteau (F2)* 100
Coulee (F2)* 75
Courtenay (N5)* 229
Crary (N3)* 235
Crete (P7)* 50
Crocus (M2)* 20
Crosby (D2)* 1,689
Crystal (P2)* 429
Crystal Springs (L6)* 25
Cuba (P6)* 7
Cummings (S4)* 102
Dahlen (P3)* 75
Danzig (M7)* 23
Davenport (R6)* 150
Dawson (L6)* 280
Dazey (O5)* 196
De Lamere (R7)* 120
De Sart (D7)* 6
Deep (J2)
Deering (J3)* 136
Deisem (N7)
Denbigh (J3)* 27
Denhoff (K5)* 170
Derrick (N3)* 12
Des Lacs (G3)* 180
Devils Lake (N3)* 6,427
Dickey (N6)* 165
Dickinson (E6)* 7,469
Dodge (F5)* 251
Donnybrook (G2)* 207
Dore (C4)* 25
Douglas (G4)* 236
Dover (M5) 4
Doyon (O3)* 98
Drake (K4)* 831
Drayton (R2)* 875
Dresden (O2)* 165
Driscoll (K6)* 225
Duane (N7)
Dundas (N4)
Dunn Center (E5)* 246
Dunning (H2) 4
Dunseith (K2)* 713
Durbin (R6)* 34
Dwight (S7)* 129
Easby (O2)* 12
East Fairview (C4) 202
Eastedge (P6)* 14
Eckelson (O6)* 175
Eckman (H2)* 55
Edgeley (N7)* 943
Edinburg (P3)* 343
Edmore (O3)* 458
Edmunds (M5)* 60
Egeland (M2)* 248
Elbowoods (F4)* 215
Eldridge (N6)* 62
Elgin (G7)* 882
Ellendale (N7)* 1,759
Elliott (P7)* 87
Elsberry (M2) 2
Embden (R6)* 64
Emerado (R4)* 125
Emmet (G4)* 7
Emmonsburg (K7) 5
Emrick (L4)* 20
Enderlin (P6)* 1,504
Englevale (P7)* 100
Enloe (S6) 2
Epping (D3)* 158
Erie (R5)* 148
Esmond (L3)* 475
Everest (R6) 14
Fairdale (O3)* 131
Fairfield (D5)* 6
Fairmount (S7)* 660
Falkirk (H5)* 46
Fallon (H6) 3
Fargo (S6)* 38,256
Fayette (E5)* 7
Fero (L3) 4
Fessenden (L4)* 917
Fillmore (L3)* 75
Fingal (P6)* 210
Finley (P4)* 671
Flasher (H7)* 413
Flaxton (F2)* 436
Flora (M4)* 35
Fonda (K2) 16
Forbes (N8)* 204
Fordville (P3)* 376
Forest River (P3)* 236
Forfar (H2) 4
Forman (P7)* 466
Fort Clark (H5)* 30
Fort Ransom (P6)* 200
Fort Rice (J6)* 27
Fort Totten (M4)* 250
Fort Yates (J7)* 825
Fortuna (C2)* 181
Foxholm (G3)* 180
Freda (H7)* 8
Fredonia (M7)* 268
Fried (N5)* 26
Fryburg (D6)* 100
Fullerton (O7)* 206
Funston (K4) 10
Gackle (M6)* 604
Galchutt (S7)* 73
Galesburg (R5)* 169
Gardar (P2)* 81
Gardena (J2)* 116
Gardner (R5)* 136
Garrison (H4)* 1,890
Garske (N3)* 18
Gascoyne (D7)* 76
Geneseo (R7)* 135
Gilby (R3)* 350
Gladstone (F6)* 224
Glasston (R2)* 54
Glen Ullin (G6)* 1,324
Glenburn (H2)* 281
Glenfield (N5)* 165
Glover (O7) 50
Goldenvalley (F5)* 339
Goldwin (M5) 17
Golva (C6)* 174
Goodrich (K5)* 448
Gorham (D5)* 35
Grace City (N4)* 89
Grafton (R3)* 4,901
Grand Forks (R4)* 26,836
Grand Harbor (N3) 8
Grand Rapids (N7)* 45
Grandin (R5)* 156
Grano (G2)* 27
Granville (J3)* 404
Grassy Butte (D5)* 75
Great Bend (S7)* 169
Greene (G2) 20
Grenora (C2)* 525
Griffin (C7)
Gronna (L2)
Guelph (O7)* 61
Guthrie (K3) 31
Guyson (M7) 12
Gwinner (P7)* 197
Hague (L7)* 328
Haley (D8)* 9
Halliday (F5)* 477
Hallson (P2)* 3
Hamar (N4)* 79
Hamberg (L4)* 124
Hamilton (R2)* 241
Hamlet (E2)* 20
Hampden (N2)* 203
Hample (P7) 24
Hankinson (S7)* 1,409
Hanks (C2)* 115
Hannaford (O5)* 313
Hannah (N2)* 257
Hannover (H5)* 33
Hansboro (M2)* 134
Harlow (M3)* 95
Harmon (H6) 25
Hartland (G3)*
Harvey (L4)* 2,337
Harwood (S6)* 126
Hastings (O6)* 100
Hatton (R4)* 991
Havana (P8)* 267
Havelock (E7) 22
Haynes (F8)* 145
Hazelton (K7)* 453
Hazen (G5)* 1,230
Heaton (L5)* 100
Hebron (G6)* 1,412
Heil (G7)* 100
Heimdal (L4)* 120
Hensel (P2)* 139
Hensler (H5)* 43
Hesper (L4)* 20
Hettinger (E8)* 1,762
Hickson (S6)* 50
Hillsboro (S5)* 1,331
Hofflund (E3) 2
Holmes (R4)* 10
Honeyford (R3)* 50
Hong (L3) 4
Hoople (P2)* 447
Hope (P5)* 470
Horace (S6)* 190
Hoving (P7) 5
Huff (J6)* 52
Hull (K7)* 50
Hunter (R5)* 417
Hurd (H2) 2
Hurdsfield (L5)* 223
Independence (O7) 30
Inkster (P3)* 304
Ives (C7)
Jamestown (N6)* 10,697
Jessie (O4)* 83
Johnson (N6)
Johnstown (R3)* 50
Joliette (R2)* 66
Josephine (M4) 8
Juanita (N4)* 98
Jud (N6)* 175
Judson (H6)* 75
Karlsruhe (J3)* 282
Karnak (O5)* 18
Kathryn (P6)* 200
Keene (E4)* 17
Keith (N3) 4
Kellys (R4) 9
Kelso (R5)* 26
Kelvin (K2)* 10
Kempton (P4)* 55
Kenaston (F2)* 50
Kenmare (G2)* 1,712
Kensal (N5)* 376
Kermit (D2)
Kerry (P3)
Kief (J4)* 135
Killdeer (E5)* 698
Kindred (R6)* 504
Kintyre (L6)* 102
Kloten (O4)* 120
Knox (L3)* 190
Kongsberg (J4)* 14
Kramer (J2)* 198
Kulm (N7)* 707
Kuroki (H2) 20
La Mars (S8)* 5
La Moure (O7)* 1,010
Lake Williams (L5)* 50
Lakota (O3)* 1,032
Lallie (M4) 5
Landa (J2)* 132
Langdon (O2)* 1,838
Lankin (P3)* 287
Lansford (H2)* 352
Larimore (P4)* 1,374
Lark (H7)* 9
Larson (E2)* 59
Lawton (O3)* 211
Leal (O5)* 72
Leeds (M3)* 778
Lefor (F6)* 150
Lehigh (E6) 38
Lehr (M7)* 394
Leith (G7)* 160
Leonard (R6)* 325
Leroy (P2)* 70
Leverich (L3) 4
Leyden (P2)* 15
Lidgerwood (R7)* 1,147
Lignite (F2)* 230
Lincoln Valley (K4)* 79
Linton (K7)* 1,675
Lisbon (P7)* 2,031
Litchville (O6)* 408
Livona (K6)* 6
Logan (H3)
Loma (O2)* 53
Lonetree (G3)* 24
Loraine (G2)* 70
Lostwood (F3)* 30
Lucca (P6)* 37
Ludden (O7)* 96
Lundsvalley (E3)* 11
Luverne (P5)* 154
Lynchburg (R6) 27
Maddock (L4)* 741
Maida (O2)* 35
Makoti (G4)* 219
Mandan (J6)* 7,298
Mandt (R2) 20
Manfred (L4)* 74
Manitou (E3) 13
Manning (E5)* 85
Mantador (R7)* 138
Manvel (R3)* 278
Mapes (O3)* 30
Mapleton (S6)* 169
Marion (O6)* 272
Marmarth (B7)* 469
Marmon (C3)* 9
Marshall (F5)* 12
Martin (K4)* 171
Max (H4)* 465
Maxbass (H2)* 259
Mayville (R4)* 1,790
Maza (M3)* 82
Mc Canna (P3)* 41
Mc Clusky (K4)* 850
Mc Gregor (D2)* 120
Mc Henry (N4)* 189
Mc Kenzie (K6)* 81
Mc Leod (R7)* 125
Mc Ville (O4)* 626
Medberry (N7)* 5
Medina (M6)* 564
Medora (C6)* 180
Mekinock (R4)* 100
Melville (M5)* 60
Menoken (J6)* 45
Mercer (J5)* 214
Merricourt (N7)* 105
Merrifield (R4)* 27
Michigan (O3)* 486
Millarton (N6)* 31
Milnor (R7)* 674
Milton (O2)* 322
Minnewaukan (M3)* 443
Minot (H3)* 22,032
Minto (R3)* 592
Moffit (K6)* 178
Mohall (G2)* 1,073
Mona (O2)
Monango (N7)* 138
Montpelier (O6)* 105
Mooreton (S7)* 161
Mortimer (R5) 8
Mose (O4)* 20
Moselle (R7) 13
Mott (F7)* 1,583
Mount Carmel (O2)* 40
Mountain (P2)* 219
Munich (N2)* 248

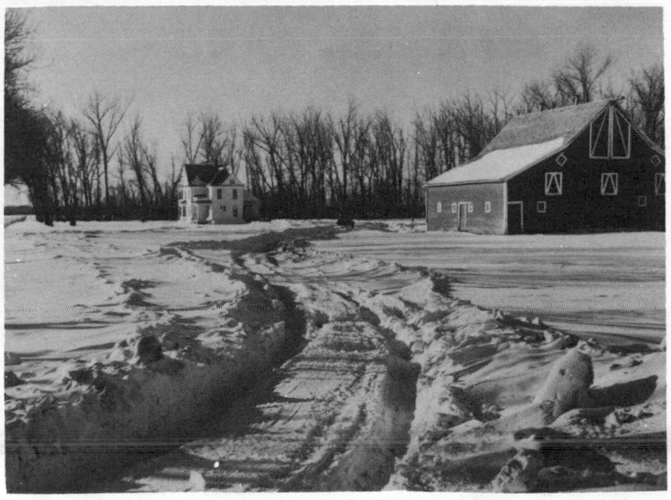

Munster (M4) 4
Murray (R5) 3
Mylo (L2)* 110
Nanson (L2)* 18
Napoleon (L6)* 1,070
Nash (P3)* 43
Neche (P2)* 615
Nekoma (O2)* 140
New England (E6)* 1,117
New Hradec (E5)* 64
New Leipzig (G7)* 447
New Rockford (N4)* 2,185
New Salem (G6)* 942
Newburg (J2)* 105
Newville (M2) 20
Niagara (P4)* 163
Nicholson (P7) 3
Niobe (F2)* 78
Nishu (G4)
Nome (P6)* 217
Noonan (D2)* 551
Norfolk (K4) 2
Norma (G2)* 100
Northgate (F2)* 85
Northwood (R4)* 1,182
Norton (O3) 3
Nortonville (N6)* 112
Norwich (J3)* 70
Oakdale (E5)* 6
Oakes (O7)* 1,774
Oakwood (R3) 66
Oberon (M4)* 238
Odessa (G7)
Olga (O2)* 145
Olmstead (M2) 24
Omemee (K2)* 60
Oriska (P6)* 135
Orr (P3)* 67
Orrin (K3)* 179
Osgood (S6) 2
Osnabrock (O2)* 284
Oswald (S7) 2
Otter Creek (G5)*
Overly (K2)* 90
Page (P5)* 482
Palermo (F3)* 150
Park River (P3)* 1,692
Parshall (F4)* 935
Pekin (O4)* 221
Pelto (O3)* 21
Pembina (R2)* 640
Penn (M3)* 67
Perry (R7)
Perth (M2)* 124
Petersburg (P3)* 318
Petrel (F8)
Pettibone (L5)* 187
Pick City (G5) 294
Pickardville (J5)* 25
Pickert (P5)* 20
Pierce (D7) 5
Pillsbury (P5)* 119
Pingree (N5)* 161
Pisek (P3)* 215
Plaza (G3)* 389
Pleasant Lake (L3)* 45
Portal (E2)* 409
Portland (R5)* 641
Portland Jct. (R4) 2
Powers Lake (E2)* 565
Preston (R5) 4
Price (H5)* 7
Prosper (R6)* 37
Raleigh (H7)* 125
Ramsey (M3) 12
Rangeley (J3) 3
Raub (F4)*
Rawson (C4)* 32
Ray (D3)* 721
Reeder (E7)* 339
Reeves (N6)
Regan (K5)* 129
Regent (E7)* 405
Revere (O5)* 22
Reynolds (R4)* 335
Rhame (C7)* 340
Richardton (F6)* 721
Rising (J3) 3
Riverdale (H5)* 2,551
Robinson (L5)* 166
Rocklake (H2)* 385
Rogers (O5)* 150
Rohrville (N3) 10
Rolette (L2)* 451
Rolla (L2)* 1,176
Rosebud (H6)
Roseglen (G4)* 40
Ross (E3)* 85
Roth (J2)* 29
Rugby (L3)* 2,907
Ruso (J4)* 37
Russell (J2)* 51
Rutland (P7)* 309
Ryder (G4)* 330
Saint Anthony (H6)* 75
St. John (L2)* 451
St. Michael (N4)* 56
St. Thomas (R2)* 566
Sanborn (O6)* 324
Sanger (H5)* 24
Sanish (F4)* 507
Sarles (N2)* 285
Saunders (S6)
Sawyer (H3)* 264
Schefield (E6) 20
Schmidt (J6) 2
Scranton (D7)* 360
Searing (C4)* 5
Selfridge (J7)* 343
Selz (L4)* 200
Sentinel Butte (C6)* 229
Sharon (P4)* 312
Shawnee (P4)*
Sheldon (P6)* 267
Shell Creek (F3) 40
Shepard (O5) 3
Sherwood (G2)* 421
Sheyenne (M4)* 469
Shields (H7)* 124
Silva (L3)* 40
Silverleaf (O7) 7
Simcoe (J3)* 24
Sims (H6) 11
Skaar (C5)* 2
Solen (J7)* 300
Sonora (S7) 15
Souris (J2)* 206
South Heart (E6)* 100
South West Fargo (S6) 1,032
Southam (N3)* 85
Spiritwood (N6)* 105
Spring Brook (D3)* 51
Stady (C2)* 7
Stampede (E2)
Stanley (F3)* 1,486
Stanton (H5)* 571
Starkweather (N3)* 229
Steele (L6)* 762
Sterling (K6)* 88
Stiles (R7) 8
Still (J5) 3
Stirum (P7)* 85
Strasburg (K7)* 733
Straubville (O7)* 22
Streeter (M6)* 602
Surrey (H3)* 175
Sutton (O5)* 125
Svold (P2) 5
Sweetbriar (H6) 5
Sydney (N6)* 22
Sykeston (M5)* 272
Taft (R5)
Tagus (G3)* 101
Tappen (L6)* 379
Taylor (F6)* 258
Temple (D3)* 20
Temvik (K7)* 71
Thompson (R4)* 270
Thorne (L2)* 37
Timmer (H7)* 6
Tioga (E3)* 456
Tokio (N4)* 100
Tolley (G2)* 248
Tolna (O4)* 281
Tower City (P6)* 292
Towner (K3)* 955
Trenton (C3)* 150
Trotters (C5)* 2
Truro (H2)
Tunbridge (K3)* 12
Turtle Lake (J4)* 839
Tuttle (L5)* 368
Tyler (S7)* 18
Underwood (H5)* 1,061
Union (O2)* 23
Upham (J2)* 403
Urbana (O6) 12
Valley City (P6)* 6,851
Van Hook (F4)* 380
Vang (O2) 10
Vashti (M5)* 15
Velva (J3)* 1,170
Venlo (R7)
Venturia (L7)* 190
Verendrye (J3)* 35
Verona (O7)* 189
Veseleyville (R3) 65
Voltaire (J3)* 72
Voss (R3)* 60
Wabek (G4)* 15
Wahpeton (S7)* 5,125
Walcott (R6)* 296
Walden (P5) 8
Wales (N2)* 235
Walhalla (P2)* 1,463
Walum (O5)* 52
Warren (S6) 10
Warsaw (R3) 89
Warwick (N4)* 155
Washburn (J5)* 913
Watford City (D4)* 1,371
Watrous (F7)
Weaver (N2)* 12
Webster (N3)* 96
Wellsburg (L4)* 42
Werner (F5)* 63
West Fargo (S6)* 159
Westfield (K7)* 52
Westhope (H2)* 575
Wheatland (R6)* 134
Wheelock (D3)* 101
White Earth (E3)* 218
Whitman (O3)* 90
Wild Rice (S6)* 42
Wildrose (D2)* 430
Williston (C3)* 7,378
Willmen (E5) 20
Willow City (K2)* 595
Wilton (J5)* 796
Wimbledon (O5)* 449
Windsor (N6)*
Wing (K5)* 312
Wishek (L7)* 1,241
Woburn (F2) 17
Wolford (L3)* 140
Wolseth (H3)* 16
Woods (R6)* 3
Woodworth (M5)* 207
Wyndmere (R7)* 627
York (L3)* 220
Youngtown (H6)* 8
Ypsilanti (O6)* 120
Zahl (C2)* 105
Zap (G5)* 425
Zeeland (L8)* 484
Zenith (D6)

Map on Page 82

OHIO

Total Population 7,946,627

88 COUNTIES

Adams (D8) 20,499
Allen (B4) 88,183
Ashland (F4) 33,040
Ashtabula (J2) 78,695
Athens (F7) 45,839
Auglaize (B4) 30,637
Belmont (J5) 87,740
Brown (C8) 22,227
Butler (A7) 147,203
Carroll (H4) 19,039
Champaign (C5) 26,793
Clark (C6) 111,661
Clermont (B7) 42,182
Clinton (C7) 25,572
Columbiana (J4) 98,920
Coshocton (G5) 31,141
Crawford (E4) 38,738
Cuyahoga (G3) 1,389,532
Darke (A5) 41,799
Defiance (A3) 25,925
Delaware (D5) 30,278
Erie (E3) 52,565
Fairfield (E6) 52,130
Fayette (D6) 22,554
Franklin (E5) 503,410
Fulton (B2) 25,580
Gallia (F8) 24,910
Geauga (H3) 26,646
Greene (C6) 58,892
Guernsey (H5) 38,452
Hamilton (A7) 723,952
Hancock (C3) 44,280
Hardin (C4) 28,673
Harrison (H5) 19,054
Henry (B3) 22,423
Highland (C7) 28,188
Hocking (F6) 19,520
Holmes (G4) 18,760
Huron (E3) 39,353
Jackson (E7) 27,767
Jefferson (J5) 96,495
Knox (F5) 35,287
Lake (H2) 75,979
Lawrence (E8) 49,115
Licking (F5) 70,645
Logan (C5) 31,329
Lorain (F3) 148,162
Lucas (C2) 395,551
Madison (D6) 22,300
Mahoning (J4) 257,629
Marion (D4) 49,959
Medina (G3) 40,417
Meigs (F7) 23,227
Mercer (A4) 28,311
Miami (B5) 61,309
Monroe (H6) 15,362
Montgomery (B6) 398,441
Morgan (G6) 12,836
Morrow (E4) 17,168
Muskingum (G5) 74,535
Noble (G6) 11,750
Ottawa (D2) 29,469
Paulding (A3) 15,047
Perry (F6) 28,999
Pickaway (D6) 29,352
Pike (D7) 14,607
Portage (H3) 63,954
Preble (A6) 27,081
Putnam (B3) 25,248
Richland (E4) 91,305
Ross (D7) 54,424
Sandusky (D3) 46,114
Scioto (D8) 82,910
Seneca (D3) 52,978
Shelby (B5) 28,488
Stark (H4) 283,194
Summit (G3) 410,032
Trumbull (J3) 158,915
Tuscarawas (H5) 70,320
Union (D5) 20,687
Van Wert (A4) 26,971
Vinton (E7) 10,759
Warren (B7) 38,505
Washington (H7) 44,407
Wayne (G4) 58,716
Williams (A2) 26,202
Wood (C3) 59,605
Wyandot (D4) 19,785

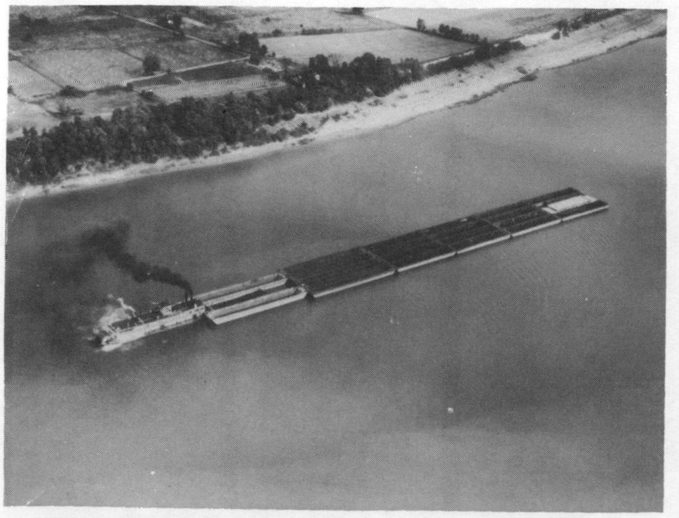

CITIES and TOWNS

Aberdeen (C8)*............ 551
Ada (C4)*...............3,640
Adams Mills (G5)*....... 150
Adamsville (G5)*......... 164
Addison (F8)*............ 120
Addyston (B9)*..........1,651
Adelphi (E7)*............ 392
Adena (J5)*..............1,517
Adrian (D3)*.............. 65
Ai (C2).................... 50
Aid (F8)*.................. 96
Akron (G3)*............274,605
Akron (urban area)....365,130
Albany (F7)*.............. 525
Alcony (B5)............... 106
Alexandria (E5)*......... 464
Alger (C4)*................ 943
Allensville (E7)*......... 105
Allentown (B4)............ 150
Alliance (H4)*..........26,161
Alpha (B6)*................ 300
Alvada (D3)*................ 89
Alvordton (A2)*........... 335
Amanda (E6)*.............. 587
Amberley (C9).............. 885
Amboy (J2).................. 300
Amelia (D10)*.............. 601
Amesville (F7)*........... 269
Amherst (F3)*...........3,542
Amity (F5).................. 100
Amsden (D3)*.............. 151
Amsterdam (J5)*.........1,048
Andover (J2)*............1,102
Anna (B5)*................. 554
Ansonia (A5)*.............. 877
Antioch (H6)*.............. 112
Antiquity (G8)............. 100
Antrim (H5)*................ 85
Antwerp (A3)*............1,162
Apple Creek (G4)*........ 548
Apple Grove (G8).......... 125
Appleton (E5)................ 75
Aquilla (H2)................ 386
Arabia (F8)................... 75
Arcadia (D3)*.............. 529
Arcanum (A6)*...........1,530
Archbold (B2)*...........1,486
Arlington (C4)*............ 825
Arlington Hts. (C9).....1,312
Armstrong Mills (J6)*.. 135
Arnheim (C8)................. 33
Ash Ridge (C8)............... 64
Ashland (F4)*...........14,287
Ashley (E5)*................ 798
Ashtabula (J2)*.........23,696
Ashville (E6)*............1,303
Assumption (B2)............ 75
Athalia (F8)*................ 307
Athens (F7)*............11,660
Atlanta (D6)*............... 180
Attica (E3)*................. 858
Attica Jct. (E3)............ 100
Atwater (H3)*.............. 750
Auburn (H3)................. 100
Augusta (J4)*.............. 300
Aultman (H4)............... 200
Aurora (H3)*................ 571
Austinburg (J2)*.........1,375
Austintown (J3)*.......... 350
Ava (G6)*.................... 300
Avery (E3)*.................. 50
Avon (F3)*.................2,773
Avon Lake (F2)*.........4,342
Ayersville (B3)............. 105
Bainbridge (D7)*.......... 964
Bairdstown (C3)............ 188
Bakersville (G5)*.......... 119
Baltic (G5)*................. 493
Baltimore (E6)*..........1,843
Bangs (F5)*.................. 125
Bantam (B7).................. 100
Barberton (G4)*.........27,820
Barlow (G7)*................ 152
Barnesville (H6)*........4,665
Barnhill (H5)................ 392
Bartlett (G7)*............... 183
Barton (J5)*...............1,300
Bascom (D3)*................ 400
Basil (E6)*
Batavia (B7)*..............1,445
Batesville (H6)*............. 149
Bay Village (G9)*.........6,917
Beach City (G4)*............ 940
Beachwood ‡(G3)..........1,073
Beallsville (J6)*............. 410
Beaver (F7)*.................. 285
Beaverdam (C4)*............ 450
Bedford (J9)*...............9,105
Belden (F3)..................... 45
Belfast (D7).................. 100
Bellaire (J5)*..............12,573
Bellbrook (C6)*.............. 425
Belle Center (C4)*.......... 889
Belle Valley (G6)*.......... 458
Bellefontaine (C5)*.....10,232
Bellevue (E3)*..............6,906
Bellville (E4)*..............1,355
Belmont (J5)*................. 638
Belmore (B3)*................. 216
Beloit (J4)*.................... 778
Belpre (G7)*.................2,451
Bennetts Corners (G10) 500
Bentleyville ‡(H3)......... 152
Benton (G4)*.................. 150
Benton (D4)................... 150
Benton Ridge (C4)*........ 337
Bentonville (C8)*........... 175
Berea (G10)*...............12,051
Bergholz (J4)*..............1,035
Berkey (C2)*.................. 239
Berlin (G4)*................... 310
Berlin Center (J3)*........ 193
Berlin Cross Roads (E7) 100
Berlin Heights (F3)*....... 613
Berne (H6)*...................... 40
Berwick (D3)*................. 100
Bethany (B7)*................. 160
Bethel (B8)*.................1,932
Bethesda (H5)*.............1,158
Bettsville (D3)*.............. 687
Beverly (G6)*................. 723
Bexley (E6)*...............12,378
Bidwell (F8)*.................. 340
Big Plain (D6)................. 146
Big Prairie (G4)*............. 250
Birmingham (F3)*............ 300
Birmingham (H5)............... 55
Blachleyville (F4).............. 85
Blackfork (E8)*................ 420
Blacklick (E6)*................. 325
Bladen (F8)*.................... 250
Bladensburg (F5)*............. 230
Blaine (J5)*..................... 400
Blakeslee (A2)*................ 142
Blanchester (B7)*..........2,109
Blissfield (G5)*................ 102
Bloomdale (D3)*............... 592
Bloomfield (G5)................... 70
Bloomfield
(Bloomingdale*) (J5) 324
Bloomingburg (D6)*........ 623
Bloomingdale (J5)*.......... 324
Bloomington (C6)............... 88
Bloomville (D3)*.............. 759
Blue Ash (C9)*.............1,420
Blue Creek (D8)*............. 100
Blue Rock (G6)*................. 70
Bluffton (C4)*...............2,423
Bogart (E3)
Bolivar (G4)*.................... 776
Bono (D2)*
Boston (H10)*.................. 350
Boston Heights (H3)........ 646
Botkins (B5)*.................. 608
Bourneville (D7)*............. 195
Bowerston (H5)*.............. 522
Bowersville (C6)*.............. 362
Bowling Green (C3)*..12,005
Bradford (B5)*...............2,055
Bradley (J5)*.................... 300
Bradner (C3)*................... 924
Brady Lake ‡(H3)*............ 444
Branch Hill (B7)*.............. 500
Brandon (F5)*
Brandt (B6)...................... 200
Bratenahl (H9)..............1,240
Brecksville (H10)*.........2,664
Bremen (F6)*.................1,187
Brewster (G4)*...............1,618
Brice (E6)*....................... 182
Bridgeport (J5)*.............4,309
Bridgetown (B9).............1,500
Brighton (F3).................... 107
Brilliant (J5)*................2,066
Brimfield (H3).................. 500
Brinkhaven (F5)*.............. 150
Bristolville (J3)*.............. 250
Broadview Hts. (H10)...2,279
Broadway (C5)*................ 210
Broadwell (G7).................... 90
Brokensword (E4).............. 100
Brook Park (G9)............2,606
Brookfield (J3)*..............1,000
Brooklyn (H9)*...............6,317
Brooklyn Hts. (H9)............ 931
Brookside (J5).................. 845
Brookville (B6)*..............1,908
Broughton (B3)................. 128
Brownhelm (F3)................ 107
Brunswick (G3)*
Bryan (A3)*...................6,365
Buchtel (F7)*.................... 569
Buckeye Lake (F6)*.......1,401
Buckland (B4)*................. 274
Bucyrus (E4)*...............10,327
Buena Vista (C7).................. 89
Buena Vista (D8)*.............. 200
Buffalo (G6)*..................... 700
Buford (C7)*...................... 250
Burbank (F4)*.................... 393
Burghill (J3)*..................... 150
Burgoon (D3)*.................... 223
Burkettsville (A5)*............. 211
Burlington (F9).................. 325
Burton (H3)*...................... 932
Bushnell (J2)..................... 100
Butler (F4)*....................... 833
Butlerville ‡(B7)................ 152
Byer (E7)*......................... 250
Byesville (G6)*.................2,236
Cable (C5)*........................ 125
Cadiz (J5)*......................3,020
Cairo (B4)*........................ 505
Calcutta (J4)...................... 200
Caldwell (G6)*.................1,767
Caledonia (D4)*................. 655
Cambridge (G5)*.............14,739
Camden (A6)*...................1,084
Cameron (J6)*................... 124
Camp Dennison (D9)*.. 350
Campbell (J3)*................12,882
Campbellstown (A6)*........... 98
Canal Fulton (H4)*..........1,258
Canal Winchester (E6)*1,194
Canfield (J3)*....................1,465
Cannelville (G6)................. 250
Canton (H4)*..................116,912
Canton (urban area)..173,215
Carbon Hill (F7)*................. 400
Carbondale (F7)*.................. 400
Cardington (E5)*..............1,465
Carey (D4)*......................3,260
Carlisle (B6)*...................... 325
Carmel (D7).......................... 40
Carpenter (F7)*..................... 45
Carroll (E6)*........................ 416
Carrollton (J4)*..................2,658
Carrothers (D3)*.................. 110
Casstown (B5)*.................... 368
Castalia (E3)*...................... 736
Castine (A6)*....................... 146
Catawba (C6)*...................... 313
Catawba Island (E2)............. 200
Cebee (F8)
Cecil (A3)*............................ 266
Cedarville (C6)*..................1,292
Celina (A4)*.......................5,703
Center Belpre (G7)*.............. 150
Center Village (E5)............... 120
Centerburg (E5)*.................. 887
Centerfield (C7)..................... 69
Centerville (B6)*.................. 827
Centerville (Thurman*)
(F8)...................................... 142
Chagrin Falls (J9)*.............3,085
Chambersburg
(F8)...................................... 225
Chandlersville (G6)*.............. 140
Chardon (H2)*.....................2,478
Charlestown (H3)..................... 50
Chatfield (E4)*...................... 204
Chatham (G3)......................... 250
Chattanooga (A4).................... 150
Chauncey (F7)*....................1,016
Cherry Fork (C8)*................... 197
Cherry Grove (C10)................ 250
Chesapeake (E9)*.................1,285
Cheshire (F8)*........................ 300
Cheshire (E5)........................... 99
Chester (G7)*......................... 184
Chesterhill (G6)*...................... 426
Chesterland (H2)*.................... 350
Chesterville (E5)*..................... 208
Cheviot (B9)..........................9,944
Chickasaw (A5)*....................... 166
Chillicothe (E7)*...................20,133
Chilo (B8)*............................... 250
Chippewa Lake (G3)*................. 107
Christiansburg (C5)*................. 666
Churchill (J3)............................ 100
Cincinnati (B9)*...................503,998
Cincinnati (urban
area)..................................808,021
Circleville (D6)*......................8,723
Claiborne (D5).......................... 112
Clarington (J6)*.......... 478
Clark (G5)*................. 250
Clarksburg (D7)*.......... 391
Clarkson (J4)................ 68
Clarksville (C7)*........... 510
Clay Center (D2)*......... 590
Claysville (G6)*.............. 55
Clayton (B6)*................ 466
Cleveland (H9)*........914,808
Cleveland (urban
area)......................1,372,274
Cleveland Hts. (J9)*...59,141
Cleves (B9)*...............1,981
Clifton (C6)*................. 220
Clinton (G4)*................ 397
Cloverdale (B3)*............ 200
Clyde (E3)*.................4,083
Coal Grove (E9)*..........2,492
Coalton (E7)*................ 628
Coldwater (A5)*............2,217
Colebrook (J2)*................ 70
College Corner (A6)*...... 468
Collins (E3)*.................. 250
Collinsville (A6)*............ 176
Colton (C3)*................... 135
Columbia Station
(G10)*............................. 58
Columbiana (J4)*...........3,369
COLUMBUS (E6)*.....375,901
Columbus (urban
area)........................436,257
Columbus Grove (B4)*..1,936
Commercial Point(E6)* 238
Condit (E5)*................... 200
Conesville (G5)*.............. 466
Congo (F6)*.................... 300
Congress (F4)................. 186
Conneaut (J2)*............10,230
Conover (B5)*................. 130
Constitution (G7)*........... 100
Continental (B3)*..........1,023
Convoy (A4)*.................. 910
Coolville (G7)*................ 469
Cooperdale (F5)*............. 50
Copley (G3)*................... 600
Corning (F6)*................1,215
Cortland (J3)*................1,259
Corwin‡ (B6).................. 326
Coshocton (G5)*...........11,675
Cove (E8)*......................... 25
Covington (B5)*.............2,172
Cozaddale (B7)*............... 180
Craig Beach ‡(J3)............ 569
Creola (E7)*...................... 150
Crescentville (C9)............ 100
Crestline (E4)*...............4,614
Creston (G3)*.................1,300
Cridersville (B4)*............. 684
Cromers (D3)*.................... 50
Crooksville (F6)*............2,960
Croton (E5)*..................... 356
Crown City (F8)*.............. 301
Cuba (C7)*........................ 150
Cumberland (G6)*............. 537
Curtice (D2)*..................... 500
Custar (C3)*....................... 263
Cutler (G7)*....................... 100
Cuyahoga Falls (G3)*..29,195
Cuyahoga Hts. (H9)............ 413
Cygnet (C3)*...................... 527
Cynthiana (D7)*.................. 110
Dalton (G4)*........................ 938
Damascus (J4)*.................... 700
Danville (F5)*...................... 853
Darbyville (D6).................... 203
Darrtown (A7)...................... 215
Dawn (A5)............................. 85
Dayton (B6)*...................243,872
Dayton (urban area)..343,781
Deavertown (G6)*
Decatur (C8)*....................... 170
Deer Park (C9)*................7,241
Deerfield (H3)*...................... 450
Deersville ‡(H5)*................... 149
Defiance (B3)*..................11,265
Degraff (C5)*......................... 972
Delaware (E5)*..................11,804
Delisle (A5)............................. 55
Dellroy (H4)*.......................... 358
Delphos (B4)*......................6,220
Delta (B2)*..........................2,120
Dennison (H5)*....................4,432
Dent (B9)................................ 640
Derby (D6)*............................ 300
Deshler (C3)*........................1,623
Deunquat (D4)............................ 97
Dexter City (G6)*..................... 170
Diamond (H3)*......................... 300
Dillonvale (J5)*.....................1,407
Dixon (A4)*.............................. 160
Dodgeville (J2)........................ 100
Dola (C4)*................................ 175
Donnelsville ‡(B6).................... 285
Dorset (J2)*.............................. 400
Dover (G4)*.........................9,852
Dowling (C3)............................ 100
Doylestown (G4)*..................1,358
Dresden (G5)*........................1,310
Dry Run (D8).............................. 300
Dublin (D5)*.............................. 289
Dunbridge (C3)*.......................... 250
Duncan Falls (G6)*..................... 575
Dundas (E7)*.............................. 300
Dunkinsville (C8).......................... 75
Dunkirk (C4)*.............................. 972
Dupont (B3)*................................ 225
E. Canton (H4)*........................1,001
E. Claridon (H2)*.......................... 350
E. Cleveland (J9)*...................40,047
E. Fultonham (F6)*......................... 565
E. Greenville (G4)........................... 450
E. Liberty (C5)*.............................. 425
E. Liverpool (J4)*.......................24,217
E. Orwell (J2)*................................ 168
E. Palestine (J4)*.........................5,195
E. Ringgold (E6).............................. 120
E. Rochester (H4)*........................... 250
E. Sparta (H4)*................................ 811
Eastlake (J8)..................................7,486
Eaton (A6)*....................................4,242
Edenton (C7)*.................................... 200
Edgerton (A3)*.............1,246
Edison (E4)*.................... 471
Edon (A2)*..................... 645
Eifort (E8)*..................... 134
Elba (H6)*....................... 150
Eldorado (A6)*................ 364
Elery (B3).......................... 50
Elgin (A4)*....................... 126
Elida (B4)*....................... 607
Elizabethtown (A9)............ 100
Ellerton (B6)..................... 160
Elliston (D2)*.................... 130
Ellsworth (J3)*.................. 200
Elmira (B2)*...................... 125
Elmore (D3)*.................1,215
Elmwood Place (B9)*...4,113
Elyria (F3)*..................30,307
Empire (J5)*...................... 610
Englewood (B6)*................ 678
Enon (C6)*......................... 462
Enterprise (F6)*................. 100
Era (D6)................................ 80
Erhart (G3)........................... 90
Etna (E6)*........................... 325
Euclid (J9)*....................41,396
Evansport (B3)*..................... 250
Ewington (F8)*......................... 64
Excello (B7)*.......................... 575
Fairborn (B6)*......................7,847
Fairhaven (A6)........................ 290
Fairpoint (J5)*........................ 500
Fairport Harbor
(Fairport) (H2)*..............4,519
Fairview (G9).........................9,311
Fairview (H5)*........................... 192
Farmdale (J3)*........................... 202
Farmer (A3)*.............................. 200
Farmersville (A6)*....................... 587
Fayette (B2)*..........................1,003
Fayetteville (C7)*......................... 401
Feesburg (B8)*............................. 150
Felicity (B8)*................................ 716
Findlay (C3)*.........................23,845
Fitchville (E3)................................ 157
Five Points (D6)
Flat Rock (E3)*............................. 325
Fletcher (B5)*................................ 515
Florida (B3).................................... 227
Flushing (J5)*..............................1,158
Fly (H6)*... 200
Footville (J2)..................................... 75
Foraker (C4)..................................... 110
Forest (C4)*...................................1,114
Forestville (C10).............................1,500
Fort Jennings (B4)*........................... 330
Fort Loramie (B5)*........................... 508
Fort Recovery (A5)*.......................1,231
Fort Seneca (D3)*.............................. 155
Foster (C9)*... 50
Fostoria (D3)*...............................14,351
Frank (E3).. 100
Frankfort (D7)*...................................... 869
Franklin (B6)*....................................5,388
Franklin Furnace (E8)* 450
Franklin Square (J4)........................... 110
Frazeysburg (F5)*................................ 689
Fredericksburg (G4)*............................ 517
Fredericktown (F5)*...........................1,467
Freedom Station (H3)* 500
Freeport (H5)*...................................... 566
Fremont (D3)*..................................16,537
Fresno (G5)*... 225
Friendship (D8)*.................................... 500
Frost (G7)*.. 29
Fruit Hill (C10)....................................... 300
Fryburg (B4)... 45
Fulda (H6)... 60
Fullertown (H2)....................................... 100
Fulton (E5)*... 269
Fultonham (F6)*.. 232
Gahanna (E5)*... 596
Galena (E5)*... 424
Galion (E4)*..9,952
Gallipolis (F8)*..7,871
Galloway (D6)*.. 300
Gambier (F5)*...1,037
Ganges (E4).. 120
Gann ‡(F5)... 177
Garfield Hts. (J9)*..................................21,662
Garrettsville (H3)*.....................................1,504
Gates Mills (J9)*..1,056
Geauga Lake (J10)*....................................1,300
Geneva (J2)*...4,718
Geneva-on-the-Lake
(H2)*.. 388
Genoa (D2)*..1,723
Georgesville (D6)... 150
Georgetown (C8)*..2,200
Germano (J5)*.. 180
Germantown (B6)*..2,478
Getaway (F9)... 100
Gettysburg (A5)*... 451
Ghent (B3).. 75
Gibsonburg (D3)*..2,281
Gilboa (C3)*.. 181
Gilmore (H5)*... 65
Girard (J3)*...10,113
Glandorf (B3)*.. 479
Glen Roy (E7).. 100
Glencoe (J6)*.. 500
Glendale (C9)*...2,402
Glenford (F6)*... 180
Glenmont (F4)*.. 242
Glenwillow (J10)*... 257
Gloria Glens Park
‡(G3)... 98
Glouster (F6)*..2,327
Gnadenhutten (G5)*.. 895
Golf Manor (C9)..3,603
Gomer (B4)*.. 300
Good Hope (D7)*.. 300
Gordon (B6)*.. 197
Gore (F6)*.. 250
Grafton (F3)*..1,194
Grand Rapids (C3)*... 657
Grand River (H2)*... 448
Grandview (H7)*... 125
Grandview Hts. (D6)...7,659
Granville (E5)*..2,653
Gratiot (F6)*.. 187
Gratis (A6)*.. 575
Graysville (H6)*.......... 138
Graytown (D2)*........... 125
Green Camp (D4)*....... 388
Green Springs (E3)*.....1,082
Greenfield (D7)*..........4,862
Greenford (J4)*............. 245
Greenhills (B9)*...........3,005
Greensburg (G4)*.......... 550
Greentown (H4)*........... 750
Greenville (A5)*...........8,859
Greenwich (E3)*...........1,204
Greer (F4)...................... 95
Grelton (C3)*................. 145
Groesbeck (B9)............... 700
Grove City (D6)*..........2,339
Groveport (E6)*............1,165
Grover Hill (B3)*............ 463
Gustavus (J3)................. 150
Guysville (G7)*............... 250
Gypsum (E2)*................. 650
Halls Corners ‡(J3)......... 254
Hallsville (E7)*............... 182
Hamden (F7)*................. 951
Hamersville (C8)*............ 380
Hamilton (A7)*............57,951
Hamilton (urban
area)........................63,021
Hamler (B3)*................... 490
Hamlet (B8)..................... 200
Hammansburg (C3)............. 81
Hammondsville (J4)*........ 475
Hanford ‡(E6).................. 922
Hanging Rock (E8)*.......... 465
Hannibal (J6)*.................. 500
Hanover (F5)*.................. 308
Hanoverton (J4)*.............. 344
Harbor View (D2)*............ 392
Hardin (B5)........................ 50
Harlem Spgs. (J4)*............ 275
Harpersfield (J2)
Harpster (D4)*.................. 236
Harriettsville (H6)*............ 175
Harrisburg (D6)*................ 344
Harrison (A9)*................1,943
Harrisonville (F7)*............. 100
Harrisville (J5)*................. 420
Harrod (C4)*..................... 482
Hartford (J3)*................... 225
Hartford (Croton*)
(E5)................................. 356
Hartsgrove (J2).................. 575
Hartville (H4)*................1,200
Harveysburg (C7)*............. 477
Haskins (C3)*..................... 469
Hatton (C3)......................... 72
Havana (E3)*....................... 93
Haverhill (E8)*.................... 150
Haviland (A3)*..................... 235
Haydenville (F7)*.................. 800
Hayesville (F4)*.................... 381
Hazelwood (C9)..................... 500
Hebbardsville (F7)................... 75
Hebron (E6)*......................... 864
Helena (D3)*.......................... 314
Hemlock (F6)*......................... 253
Hemlock Grove (F7)*.... 75
Hendrysburg (H5)*.................. 300
Hepburn (D4)........................... 120
Hicksville (A3)*...................2,629
Higginsport (C8)*.................... 385
Highland (C7)*......................... 280
Highland Hts. ‡(H2).... 762
Hill Grove (A5)........................ 85
Hilliards (D5)*.......................... 610
Hills and Dales ‡(G4).. 125
Hillsboro (C7)*......................5,126
Hinckley (G3).........................1,796
Hiram (H3)*............................. 986
Hockingport (G7)*.................... 100
Holgate (B3)*........................1,092
Holland (C2)*........................... 714
Hollansburg (A5)*...................... 295
Holloway (H5)*.......................... 654
Holmesville (G4)*...................... 392
Homer (E5)*
Homerville (F3)*........................ 110
Homeworth (J4)*........................ 600
Hooven (A9)*............................. 550
Hopedale (J5)*........................... 888
Hopewell (F6)*............................ 225
Houcktown (C4).......................... 110
Houston (B5)*............................. 150
Howard (F5)*.............................. 350
Hoytville (C3)*............................ 340
Hubbard (J3)*..........................4,560
Hudson (H3)*..........................1,538
Hume (B4)*.................................. 92
Hunting Valley ‡(H3).. 477
Huntsburg (H2)*.......................... 112
Huntsville (C5)*........................... 408
Huron (E3)*............................2,515
Iberia (E4)*................................. 250
Idaho (D7)*.................................... 50
Independence (H9)*................3,105
Indian Hill (C9).......................2,090
Irondale (J4)*................................ 775
Ironton (E8)*...........................16,333
Irwin (D5)*.................................. 183
Ithaca (A6)*.................................. 146
Ivorydale (B9)*
Jackson (E7)*...........................6,504
Jackson Center (B5)*................... 698
Jacksonburg ‡(A6)....................... 114
Jacksontown (F6)*....................... 257
Jacksonville (F7)*........................ 657
Jaite (H10)*.................................... 71
Jamestown (C6)*.......................1,345
Jasper (D7)*................................. 150
Jefferson (J2)*..........................1,844
Jeffersonville (C6)*....................... 865
Jelloway (F4)................................ 100
Jenera (C4)*.................................. 316
Jeromesville (F4)*......................... 513
Jerry City (C3)*............................. 360
Jersey (E5).................................... 140
Jerusalem (H6)*............................. 175
Jewell (B3)*.................................. 225
Jewett (H5)*...............................1,019
Johnstown (E5)*..........................1,220
Junction (A3).................................. 75
Junction City (F6)*......................... 805
Justus (G4)*.................. 325
Kalida (B4)*................... 533
Kanauga (F8)*................. 275
Kansas (D3)*................... 350
Keene (G5)*.................... 150
Kelleys Island (E2)*........ 324
Kelloggsville (J2)............ 200
Kennard (C5)..................... 75
Kensington (J4)*.............. 500
Kent (H3)*................12,418
Kenton (C4)*...............8,475
Kettlersville (B5)*........... 172
Kidron (G4)*.................... 150
Kilgore (H5)*................... 116
Killbuck (G5)*................. 767
Kimball (E3)*..................... 75
Kimbolton (G5)*............... 228
Kings Creek (C5)............... 150
Kings Mills (B7)*............... 650
Kingston (E7)*.................. 958
Kingsville (J2)*...............1,000
Kinsman (J3)*................... 350
Kipton (F3)*...................... 300
Kirby (D4)*....................... 164
Kirkersville (E6)*............... 299
Kirkpatrick (D4)................... 55
Kirtland Hills (H2).............. 235
Kitts Hill (E8)*..................... 90
Kossuth (B4)........................ 75
Kunkle (A2)*....................... 260
Kyger (F8)*......................... 110
La Fayette (C4)*.................. 444
La Rue (D4)*....................... 793
Ladd (D8)*............................ 80
Lafferty (H5)*...................... 630
Lagrange (F3)*..................... 712
Laings (J6)*........................... 65
Lakeline (J8)........................ 183
Lakemore (H3)*................2,463
Lakeside Park (E2)*.........1,034
Lakeview (C4)*..................... 966
Lakeville (F4)*...................... 190
Lakeville (J2)...................3,432
Lakewood (G9)*..............68,071
Lamartine (H5)*
Lancaster (E6)*...............24,180
Landeck (B4)........................ 119
Langsville (F7)*...................... 50
Lansing (J5)*....................2,000
Latham (D7)*......................... 100
Latty (A3)*............................ 272
Laura (B6)*........................... 380
Laurel (B8)............................ 100
Laurelville (E7)*.................... 482
Lawrenceville (C6)................. 191
Lawshe (D8)*......................... 180
Leavittsburg (J3)*..............2,533
Lebanon (B7)*....................4,618
Lees Creek (C7)*................... 150
Leesburg (D7)*...................... 841
Leesville (H5)*....................... 297
Leesville Cross Roads
(E4).................................... 214
Leetonia (J4)*...................2,565
Leipsic (C3)*.....................1,706
Lemert (D4)*............................ 50
Lemoyne (D3)*....................... 155
Lena (B5)................................ 202
Leonardsburg (D5)*................... 63
Leroy (G3)*............................ 320
Letart Falls (F8)*..................... 400
Levering (E4).............................. 75
Lewis Center (D5)*.................. 200
Lewisburg (A6)*.................1,230
Lewistown (C5)*...................... 250
Lewisville (H6)*....................... 217
Lexington (E4)*...................... 739
Liberty (B6)............................. 175
Liberty Center (B3)*................ 816
Lightsville (A5)........................... 50
Lilly Chapel (D6)*.................... 250
Lima (B4)*........................50,246
Limaville (H4)*........................ 209
Lincoln Hts. (C9)...............5,531
Lindsey (D3)*......................... 512
Linndale ‡(G3)........................ 399
Lisbon (J4)*........................3,293
Litchfield (F3)*......................... 350
Lithopolis (E6)*........................ 350
Little Hocking (G7)*
Little Sandusky (D4)...... 70
Little York (B6)........................ 150
Lockbourne (E6)*..................... 376
Lockington (B5)........................ 245
Lockland (C9)*....................5,736
Lockwood (J3)*............................ 61
Locust Grove (D8)..................... 118
Lodi (F3)*............................1,523
Logan (F6)*.........................5,972
London (C6)*.......................5,222
Londonderry (H5)....................... 46
Londonderry (E7)*.................... 210
Long Bottom (G7)*.................... 200
Lorain (F3)*.......................51,202
Lore City (H6)*......................... 495
Loudonville (F4)*................2,523
Louisville (H4)*...................3,801
Loveland (D9)*....................2,149
Lowell (H6)*............................ 638
Lowellville (J3)*..................2,227
Lower Salem (H6)*................... 126
Lucas (F4)*.............................. 573
Lucasville (E8)*
Luckey (D3)*............................ 764
Ludlow Falls (B6)*................... 277
Lynchburg (C7)*....................... 972
Lyndhurst (J9)*...................7,359
Lyndon (D7)*.............................. 50
Lyons (B2)*.............................. 511
Lytle (B6)................................ 200
Macedonia (J10)*..................... 600
Mack (B9)................................ 870
Macksburg (G6)*...................... 272
Macon (C8)*................................ 75
Madeira (C9)*....................2,689
Madison (H2)*....................1,127
Madison Mills (D6)
Madisonburg (G4).................... 135
Magnetic Spgs. (D5)*.. 321
Magnolia (H4)*......................... 901
Maineville (B7)......................... 312

Malaga (H6)* 100
Malinta (B3)* 308
Mallet Creek (G3) 200
Malta (G6)* 968
Malvern (H4)* 1,277
Manchester (C8)* 2,281
Mansfield (F4)* 43,564
Mantua (H3)* 1,059
Maple Heights (H9)* 15,586
Maplewood (B5)* 184
Marathon (C7)* 263
Marble Cliff ‡(D5) 437
Marblehead (E2)* 867
Marengo (E5)* 275
Maria Stein (A5)* 200
Mariemont (C9)* 3,514
Marietta (G7)* 16,006
Marion (D4)* 38,817
Mark Center (A3)* 158
Marr (H6)* 6
Marseilles (D4) 156
Marshall (C7) 50
Marshallville (G4)* 458
Martel (E4)* 196
Martin (D2)* 350
Martins Ferry (J5)* 13,220
Martinsburg (F5)* 264
Martinsville (C7)* 399
Marysville (D5)* 4,256
Mason (B7)* 1,196
Massillon (H4)* 29,594
Masury (J3)* 2,151
Maud (B7)* 400
Maumee (C2)* 5,548
Mayfield (J9) 805
Mayfield Hts. (J9) 5,807
Mc Arthur (F7)* 1,466
Mc Cartyville (B5) 100
Mc Clure (C3)* 508
Mc Comb (C3)* 1,026
Mc Connelsville (G6)* 1,941
Mc Cutchenville (D4)* 347
Mc Dermott (D8)* 700
Mc Donald ‡(J3)* 1,858
Mc Guffey (C4)* 639
Means (J5) 89
Mechanicsburg (C5)* 1,920
Mechanicstown (H4)* 150
Medina (G3)* 5,097
Medway (C6)* 975
Meeker (D4) 175
Melbern (A3)* 140
Melmore (D3)* 225
Melrose (B3)* 237
Mendon (A4)* 614
Mentor (H2)* 2,383
Mentor-on-the-Lake (G2)* 1,413
Mercer (A4)* 150
Mesopotamia (J3)* 310
Metamora (C2)* 532
Meyers Lake (H4) 301
Miamisburg (B6)* 6,329
Miamitown (A9)* 500
Miamiville (B7)* 250
Middle Bass (E2)* 80
Middle Point (B4)* 582
Middlebranch (H4)* 600
Middleburg (C5)* 300
Middleburg Hts. (G10) 2,299
Middlefield (H3)* 1,141
Middleport (F7)* 3,446
Middletown (A6)* 33,695
Midland (C7)* 338
Midvale (H5)* 632
Midway (Sedalia*) (D6) 276
Mifflin (F4) 186
Milan (E3)* 846
Milford (D9)* 2,448
Milford Center (D5)* 753
Millbury (D2)* 482
Milledgeville (C6)* 208
Miller (F8)* 140
Miller City (B3)* 144
Millersburg (F4)* 2,398
Millersport (E6)* 605
Millersville (D3)* 100
Millport (J4) 60
Millville (A7) 458
Millwood (F5) 200
Milton Center (C3)* 201
Miltonsburg (H6) 100
Mineral (F7)* 150
Mineral City (H4)* 831
Mineral Ridge (J3)* 1,750
Minersville (G7)* 400
Minerva (H4)* 3,280
Minerva Park (E5) 232
Minford (E8)* 300
Mingo (C5)* 130
Mingo Junction (J5)* 4,464
Minster (B5)* 1,728
Mogadore (H3)* 1,818
Monclova (C2)* 94
Monroe (B7)* 360
Monroe Center (J2) 150
Monroeville (E3)* 1,275
Montezuma (A4)* 299
Montgomery (C9)* 579
Monticello (B4) 55
Montpelier (A2)* 3,867
Montville (H2)* 200
Moreland Hills ‡(H3) 1,040
Morgantown (D7) 75
Morning Sun (A6) 102
Morral (D4)* 461
Morristown (H5)* 404
Morrow (B7)* 1,137
Moscow (B8)* 336
Mt. Blanchard (D4)* 444
Mt. Carmel (B7) 300
Mt. Cory (C4)* 302
Mt. Eaton (G4)* 203
Mt. Ephraim (G6)* 90
Mt. Gilead (E4)* 2,351
Mt. Healthy (B9)* 5,533
Mt. Hope (G4)* 158
Mt. Liberty (E5)* 300
Mt. Orab (C7)* 758
Mt. Pisgah (B8) 145
Mt. Pleasant (J5)* 760
Mt. Sterling (D6)* 1,172
Mt. Vernon (E5)* 12,185
Mt. Victory (D4)* 609
Mowrystown (C7)* 394
Moxahala (F6)* 400
Mulberry (B7)* 328
Munroe Falls (H3)* 933
Murray City (F6)* 752
Mutual (C5) 178
Nankin (F4)* 400
Napoleon (B3)* 5,335
Nashport (F5)* 180
Nashville (F4)* 234
Navarre (H4)* 1,763
Neapolis (C3)* 200
Neffs (J5)* 1,024
Negley (J4)* 500
Nellie (F5)* 165
Nelsonville (F7)* 4,845
Neptune (A4) 100
Nevada (D4)* 824
Neville (B8) 127
New Albany (E5)* 268
New Alexandria (J5) 383
New Antioch (C7) 121
New Athens (H5)* 509
New Bavaria (B3)* 132
New Bedford (G5)*
New Bloomington (D4)* 288
New Boston (E8)* 4,754
New Bremen (B5)* 1,546
New Burlington (C6)* 352
New Burlington (B9) 600
New Carlisle (C6)* 1,640
New Castle (F5) 120
New Concord (G6)* 1,797
New Dover (D5) 120
New Guilford (F5) 37
New Hampshire (C4)* 197
New Haven (E3)* 289
New Holland (D6)* 799
New Hope (A6)
New Hope (C8) 40
New Knoxville (B5)* 662
New Lebanon (B6)* 696
New Lexington (F6)* 4,233
New London (F3)* 2,023
New Lyme (J2)* 200
New Madison (A6)* 757
New Market (C7) 350
New Martinsburg (D7) 120
New Matamoras (J6)* 781
New Miami (A7)* 1,860
New Middletown (J4)* 264
New Milford (H3)* 325
New Morefield (C6) 160
New Paris (A6)* 1,046
New Petersburg (D7) 75
New Philadelphia (G5)* 12,948
New Pittsburg (F4) 150
New Plymouth (F7)* 100
New Richmond (B8)* 1,960
New Riegel (D3)* 317
New Rome (D6) 75
New Salem (E6)* 300
New Springfield (J4)* 360
New Stark (C4) 65
New Straitsville (F6)* 1,122
New Vienna (C7)* 807
New Washington (E4)* 910
New Waterford (J4)* 610
New Weston (A5)* 136
New Winchester (D4) 150
Newark (F5)* 34,275
Newburgh Hts. (H9) 3,689
Newbury (H3)* 175
Newcomerstown (G5)* 4,514
Newport (H7)* 500
Newport (C6) 225
Newton Falls (J3)* 4,451
Newtonsville (B7)* 182
Newtown (C10)* 1,462
Ney (B3)* 301
Nicholsville (B8) 50
Niles (J3)* 16,773
Nimisila (G4)*
Noble (J8)*
N. Baltimore (C3)* 2,771
N. Bend (B9)* 711
N. Bloomfield (J3)* 700
N. Canton (H4)* 4,032
N. College Hill (B9)* 7,921
N. Eaton (G3)
N. Fairfield (E3)* 468
N. Findlay (C3) 80
N. Hampton (C5)* 424
N. Industry (H4)* 1,800
N. Jackson (J3)*
N. Kenova (E9)* 200
N. Kingsville (J2)* 1,271
N. Lawrence (G4)*
N. Lewisburg (C5)* 854
N. Lima (J4)* 750
N. Madison (H2)* 200
N. Olmsted (G9)* 6,604
N. Perry (H2) 470
N. Randall (H9) 178
N. Ridgeville (F3)* 1,700
N. Robinson (E4)* 252
N. Royalton (H10)* 3,939
N. Star (A5)* 166
Northfield (J10)* 780
Norton (D5) 50
Norwalk (E3)* 9,775
Norwich (G6)* 197
Norwood (C9)* 35,001
Nova (F3)* 271
Oak Hill (E8)* 1,615
Oakharbor (D2)* 2,370
Oakwood (B6) 9,697
Oakwood (B3)* 542
Oberlin (F3)* 7,062
Obetz (E6)* 1,049
Oceola (D4)* 114
Octa (C6) 87
Ohio City (A4)* 861
Okeana (A7)* 158
Okolona (B3)* 115
Old Fort (D3)* 250
Old Washington (H5)* 322
Olive Branch (B7) 100
Olmstead Falls (G9)* 1,137
Omega (E7) 100
Oneida (H4) 150
Ontario (E4)*
Orange (J9) 897
Orangeville (J3)* 367
Oregonia (B7)* 150
Orient (D6)* 224
Orrville (G4)* 5,153
Orwell (J2)* 759
Osgood (A5)* 194
Ostrander (D5)* 408
Otsego (G5)* 117
Ottawa (B3)* 2,962
Ottawa Hills (C2) 2,333
Ottokee (B2) 143
Ottoville (B4)* 543
Otway (D8)* 229
Owensville (B7)* 419
Oxford (A6)* 6,944
Painesville (H2)* 14,432
Paintersville (C6) 110
Palestine (A5)* 207
Pancoastburg (D6) 175
Pandora (C4)* 717
Paris (H4)* 250
Parkman (H3)* 181
Parkview (G9) 661
Parma (H9)* 28,897
Parma Heights (G9) 3,901
Parral (G4) 199
Pataskala (E6)* 928
Patriot (F8)* 75
Patterson (C4)* 189
Paulding (A3)* 2,352
Payne (A3)* 1,062
Pedro (E8)* 35
Peebles (D8)* 1,498
Pemberton (B5)* 225
Pemberville (C3)* 1,099
Penfield (F3) 95
Peninsula (G3)* 636
Pennsville (G6)* 160
Peoria (D5)* 193
Pepper Pike ‡(H3) 874
Perintown (B7)* 124
Perry (H2)* 665
Perrysburg (C2)* 4,006
Perrysville (F4)* 674
Perryton (F5) 104
Pettisville (B2)* 325
Phillipsburg (B6)* 609
Philo (G6)* 881
Pickerington (E6)* 433
Piedmont (H5)* 250
Pierpont (J2)* 500
Piketon (E7)* 768
Piney Fork (J5)* 1,660
Pioneer (A2)* 696
Piqua (B5)* 17,447
Pitsburg (A6)* 359
Plain City (D5)* 1,715
Plainfield (G5)* 136
Plainville (C9)* 500
Plantsville (G7) 45
Platform (F8) 15
Pleasant Bend (B3) 77
Pleasant City (G6)* 511
Pleasant Hill (B5)* 940
Pleasant Plain (B7)* 164
Pleasantville (F6)* 618
Plumwood (D6) 200
Plymouth (E4)* 1,510
Poast Town (B6) 150
Point Isabel (B8) 76
Point Pleasant (B8)* 75
Poland (J3)* 1,652
Polk (F4)* 332
Pomeroy (G7)* 3,656
Port Clinton (E2)* 5,541
Port Homer (J4) 75
Port Jefferson (C5)* 409
Port Washington ‡(H5)* 514
Port William (C6)* 352
Portage (C3)* 437
Porter (F8)* 115
Portland (G7)* 150
Portsmouth (D8)* 36,798
Potsdam (B6)* 241
Powell (D5)* 324
Power Point (J4)* 275
Powhatan Point (J6)* 2,135
Pricetown (C7) 200
Proctorville (F9)* 737
Prospect (D5)* 1,031
Prout (E3)
Pulaski (A2) 200
Put-in-Bay (E2)* 191
Quaker City (H6)* 655
Quincy (C5)* 616
Racine (G8)* 536
Radcliff (F7)* 175
Radnor (D5)* 215
Ragersville (G5)* 100
Rainsboro (D7)* 225
Randolph (H3)* 1,000
Rarden (D8)* 251
Ravenna (H3)* 9,857
Rawson (C4)* 407
Ray (E7)* 65
Rayland (J5)* 726
Raymond (C5)* 300
Rays Corners (J2) 75
Reading (C9)* 7,836
Red Lion (B7) 150
Redhaw (F4) 150
Reedsburg (F4) 110
Reedsville (G7)* 300
Reesville (C7)* 200
Reily (A7)* 160
Reinersville (G6)* 80
Remington (C9) 412
Rendville (F6)* 301
Reno (H7)* 140
Republic (D3)* 615
Resaca (D5) 45
Reynoldsburg (E6)* 724
Rialto (C9) 70
Richmond (J5)* 579
Richmond (Grand River*) (H2) 448
Richmond Dale (E7)* 500
Richmond Hts. (J9) 891
Richwood (D5)* 1,866
Ridgeville Corners (B3)* 320
Ridgeway (C4)* 384
Rio Grande (F8)* 388
Ripley (C8)* 1,792
Risingsun (C3)* 744
Rittman (G4)* 3,810
Riverlea (D5) 324
Riverside ‡(B6) 370
Rix Mills (G6) 56
Robertsville (H4)* 465
Robins (H6)* 300
Rochester (F3)* 178
Rock Creek (J2)* 604
Rockbridge (E6)* 300
Rockford (A4)* 1,112
Rockland (G7)* 950
Rocky River (G9)* 11,237
Rockyridge (D2)* 358
Rogers (J4)* 297
Rome (J2)* 151
Rootstown (H3)* 285
Roscoe (G5)* 720
Rose Farm (F6) 250
Rosemont (J3)
Roseville (F6)* 1,808
Rosewood (C5)* 200
Ross (B9)* 275
Rossburg (A5)* 203
Rossford (C2)* 3,963
Rossmoyne (C9)* 1,660
Roswell (H5) 267
Roundhead (C4)* 185
Roxabell (D7) 103
Royalton (E6) 80
Rudolph (C3)* 500
Rush Run (J5)*
Rushmore (B4)* 84
Rushsylvania (C5)* 563
Rushtown (D8)* 75
Rushville (E6)* 252
Russells Point (C5)* 909
Russellville (C8)* 438
Russia (B5)* 200
Rutland (F7)* 554
Sabina (C7)* 1,696
Sagamore Hills (J10)
St. Bernard (B9)* 7,066
St. Clairsville (J5)* 3,040
St. Henry (A5)* 715
St. Johns (B4)* 250
St. Louisville (F5)* 336
St. Martin (C7)* 129
St. Marys (B4)* 6,208
St. Paris (C5)* 1,422
Salem (J4)* 12,754
Salesville (H6)* 187
Salineville (J4)* 2,018
Samantha (C7) 50
Sandusky (E3)* 29,375
Sandyville (H4)* 325
Santa Fe (B5)* 200
Sarahsville (H6)* 170
Sardinia (C7)* 699
Sardis (J6)* 344
Savannah (F4)* 407
Sawyerwood (G3)* 1,585
Saybrook (J2) 125
Scio (H5)* 1,152
Scioto Furnace (E8)* 275
Scott (A4)* 347
Seaman (C8)* 736
Sebring (H4)* 4,045
Sedalia (D6)* 276
Selma (C6)* 175
Senecaville (H6)* 586
Seven Hills ‡(G3) 1,350
Seven Mile (A7)* 569
Seville (G3)* 963
Shade (G7)* 60
Shadeville (D6) 110
Shadyside (J6)* 4,433
Shaker Hts. (H9) 28,222
Shalersville (H3) 150
Shandon (A9)* 250
Shanesville (G4)* 460
Sharon (G6)* 200
Sharon Center (G3)*
Sharonville (C9)* 1,318
Shauck (E4)* 300
Shawnee (F6)* 1,145
Shawnee Hills (D5)* 338
Shawtown (C3) 50
Sheffield (F3) 1,147
Sheffield Lake (F3) 2,381
Shelby (E4)* 7,971
Sherrodsville (H4)* 426
Sherwood (A3)* 570
Shiloh (E4)* 655
Short Creek (J5)* 300
Shreve (F4)* 1,287
Sidney (B5)* 11,491
Silica (C2) 75
Silver Lake (G3) 1,040
Silverton (C9) 4,827
Simons (J2) 100
Sinking Spg. (D7)* 187
Smithfield (J5)* 1,255
Smithville (G4)* 755
Solon (J9)* 2,570
Somerset (F6)* 1,383
Somerton (H6)* 200
Somerville (A6)* 383
Sonora (G6)* 200
S. Amherst (F3) 1,020
S. Bloomfield (D6) 250
S. Bloomingville (E7)* 100
S. Charleston (C6)* 1,452
S. Euclid (H9)* 15,432
S. Lebanon (B7)* 1,291
S. Olive (G6)* 200
S. Park (H10)* 75
S. Perry (E6) 125
S. Point (E9)* 804
S. Russell (H3) 349
S. Salem (D7)* 206
S. Solon (C6)* 414
S. Vienna (C6)* 424
S. Webster (E8)* 663
S. Zanesville (F6)* 1,477
Sparta (E5)* 223
Spencer (F3)* 740
Spencerville (B4)* 1,826
Spring Mountain (F5) 61
Spring Valley (C6)* 645
Springboro (B6)* 516
Springdale (B9)* 1,200
Springfield (C6)* 78,508
Springfield (urban area) 81,837
Springhills (C5) 190
Stafford (H6)* 141
Starr (F7) 50
Sterling (G4)* 500
Steuben (E3) 50
Steubenville (J5)* 35,872
Stewart (G7)* 260
Stewartsville (J6)* 350
Stillwater (H5)* 250
Stockdale (E8)* 270
Stockport (G6)* 404
Stone Creek (G5)* 225
Stout (D8)* 169
Stoutsville (E6)* 562
Stow (H3)* 2,140
Strasburg (G4)* 1,366
Stratton (J4)* 467
Strongsville (G10)* 3,504
Struthers (J3)* 11,941
Stryker (B3)* 1,026
Suffield (H3)* 200
Sugar Grove (E6)* 434
Sugar Tree Ridge (C7)* 85
Sugarcreek (G5)* 889
Sullivan (F3)* 125
Sulphur Spgs. (E4)* 300
Summerfield (H6)* 368
Summerford (D6) 250
Summersville (D5) 50
Summitville (J4)* 150
Sunbury (E5)* 936
Superior (E8)* 275
Swanders (B5) 50
Swanton (C2)* 1,740
Sycamore (D4)* 935
Sylvania (C2)* 2,433
Syracuse (G7)* 700
Tallmadge (H3)* 5,821
Tarlton (E6)* 371
Taylorsburg (B6) 50
Taylorsville (Philo*)(G6) 881
Ted (C3) 35
Tedrow (B2) 300
Temperanceville (H6)* 70
Terrace Park (D9)* 1,265
Texas (C3) 100
Thackery (C5)* 100
The Plains (F7)* 700
Thompson (H2)* 150
Thornville (F6)* 432
Thurman (F8)* 142
Thurston (E6)* 454
Tiffin (D3)* 18,062
Tiltonsville (J5)* 2,202
Timberlake (J8) 236
Tipp City (B6)* 3,304
Tippecanoe (H5)*
Tiro (E4)* 335
Tiverton (F5) 50
Tobasco (D10) 250
Toledo (D2)* 303,616
Toledo (urban area) 361,493
Tontogany (C3)* 368
Torch (G7)* 200
Toronto (J5)* 7,253
Trail (G4) 100
Tremont City (C5)* 396
Trenton (B7)* 987
Trilby (C2) 2,750
Trimble (F7)* 566
Trinway (F5)* 500
Trotwood (B6)* 1,066
Trowbridge (D2) 90
Troy (B5)* 10,661
Trumbull (J2)
Tuppers Plains (G7)* 225
Tuscarawas (H5)* 700
Twinsburg (J10)* 1,200
Uhrichsville (H5)* 6,614
Union (B6)* 370
Union City (A5) 1,622
Union Furnace (F7)* 200
Unionport (J5)* 350
Uniontown (H4)* 600
Uniontown (Fultonham*) (F6) 232
Unionville (J2)* 500
Unionville Center (D5)* 237
Uniopolis (D4)* 271
Unity (J4) 140
University Hts. (J9) 11,566
Upper Arlington (D6) 9,024
Upper Sandusky (D4)* 4,397
Urbana (C5)* 9,335
Urbancrest (D6) 823
Utica (F5)* 1,510
Utopia (B8)
Valley City (G3)* 250
Valley View ‡(D6) 611
Valley View ‡(G3) 998
Van Wert (A4)* 10,364
Vanatta (E5)* 110
Vanburen (C3)* 308
Vandalia (B6)* 927
Vanlue (C4)* 365
Vaughnsville (B4)* 216
Venedocia (B4)* 170
Venice (E3)* 300
Vermilion (F3)* 2,214
Vermilion-on-the-Lake (F3) 614
Verona (A6)* 426
Versailles (A5)* 1,812
Vickery (D3)* 200
Vienna (J3)* 500
Vienna (South Vienna*) (C6) 424
Vigo (E7) 110
Villa (C6) 70
Vincent (G7)* 300
Vinton (F8)* 378
Wabash (A4) 150
Wadsworth (G3)* 7,966
Wainwright (G5)* 500
Waite Hill (H2) 305
Wakefield (E8)* 150
Wakeman (F3)* 620
Walbridge (C2)* 1,152
Waldo (D5)* 356
Walhonding (F5)* 120
Walnut Creek (G4)* 225
Wamsley (D8) 50
Wapakoneta (B4)* 5,797
Warner (H6)* 175
Warren (J3)* 49,856
Warrensburg (D5) 80
Warrensville (H9)*
Warrensville Hts. (J9) 4,126
Warsaw (G5)* 484
Warwick (G4)* 320
Washington (Old Washington*) (H5) 322
Washington Court House (D6)* 10,560
Washingtonville ‡(J4)* 848
Waterford (G6)* 317
Waterloo (F8)* 125
Watertown (G7)* 177
Waterville (C3)* 1,110
Wauseon (B2)* 3,494
Waverly (D7)* 1,679
Wayland (H3)* 235
Wayne (C3)* 761
Waynesburg (H4)* 1,258
Waynesfield (C4)* 733
Waynesville (B6)* 1,016
Webster (B5) 210
Wellington (F3)* 2,992
Wellston (F7)* 5,691
Wellsville (J4)* 7,854
Welshfield (H3)* 125
W. Alexandria (A6)* 1,183
W. Andover (J2) 200
W. Bedford (F5)*
W. Carrollton (B6)* 2,876
W. Chester (C9)* 321
W. Clarksfield (E3) 70
W. Elkton (A6)* 297
W. Farmington (J3)* 579
W. Jefferson (D6)* 1,647
W. Lafayette (G5)* 1,346
W. Leipsic (B3) 304
W. Liberty (C5)* 1,397
W. Manchester (A6)* 469
W. Mansfield (C5)* 756
W. Millgrove ‡(C3)* 180
W. Milton (B6)* 2,101
W. Newton (B4) 45
W. Point (E4) 45
W. Portsmouth (D8)* 2,613
W. Richfield (G3)* 750
W. Rushville ‡(E6)* 152
W. Salem (F4)* 860
W. Sonora (A6) 200
W. Union (C8)* 1,508
W. Unity (B2)* 827
Westboro (C7)* 100
Westerville (D5)* 4,112
Westlake (G9)* 4,912
Westminster (B4) 270
Weston (C3)* 973
Westview (G10) 625
Wharton (D4)* 392
Wheelersburg (E8)* 1,013
Whipple (H6)* 170
White Cottage (F6)* 400
Whitehall (E6)* 4,877
Whitehouse (C2)* 849
Wickliffe (J9)* 5,002
Wilkesville (F7)* 203
Willard (E3)* 4,744
Williamsburg (B7)* 1,490
Williamsfield (J2)* 120
Williamsport (D6)* 631
Williamsport (E4) 97
Willoughby (J8)* 5,602
Willowick (G2) 3,677
Wills Creek (G5) 45
Willshire (A4)* 567
Wilmington (C7)* 7,387
Wilmot (G4)* 354
Winchester (C8)* 690
Windham (H3)* 3,968
Windsor (J2)* 170
Winesburg (G4)* 195
Winkle (C7)* 109
Winona (J4)* 200
Winterset (H5)* 122
Wintersville (J5)* 1,950
Withamsville (B7) 300
Woodington (A5) 75
Woodlawn (C9)* 1,335
Woodmere (J9) 419
Woodsfield (H6)* 2,410
Woodstock (D5)* 316
Woodville (D3)* 1,358
Wooster (G4)* 14,005
Worstville (A3) 35
Worthington (E5)* 2,141
Wren (A4)* 278
Wright View (B6) 2,500
Wyandot (D4) 75
Wyoming (C9)* 5,582
Xenia (C6)* 12,877
Yankee Lake ‡(J3) 53
Yellow Bud (D7) 300
Yellow Springs (C6)* 2,896
York (D5) 100
Yorkshire (B5)* 142
Yorkville (J5)* 1,854
Youngstown (J3)* 168,330
Youngstown (urban area) 297,084
Zaleski (F7)* 388
Zanesfield (C5) 288
Zanesville (G6)* 40,517
Zoar (H4)* 200
Zoarville (H4)* 250

OKLAHOMA

Map on Page 83

Total Population 2,233,351

77 COUNTIES

Adair (N3) 14,918
Alfalfa (F1) 10,699
Atoka (K6) 14,269
Beaver (F9) 7,411
Beckham (C4) 21,627
Blaine (F3) 15,049
Bryan (K7) 28,999
Caddo (F4) 34,913
Canadian (F3) 25,644
Carter (H6) 36,455
Cherokee (M3) 18,989
Choctaw (L6) 20,405
Cimarron (B8) 4,589
Cleveland (H4) 41,443
Coal (K5) 8,056
Comanche (F5) 55,165
Cotton (F6) 10,180
Craig (M1) 18,263
Creek (K3) 43,143
Custer (D3) 21,097
Delaware (N2) 14,734
Dewey (D2) 8,789
Ellis (C2) 7,326
Garfield (G2) 52,820
Garvin (H5) 29,500
Grady (G5) 34,872
Grant (G1) 10,461
Greer (C5) 11,749
Harmon (C5) 8,079
Harper (C1) 5,977
Haskell (M4) 13,313
Hughes (K4) 20,664
Jackson (D5) 20,082
Jefferson (G6) 11,122
Johnston (J6) 10,608
Kay (H1) 48,892
Kingfisher (G3) 12,860
Kiowa (E5) 18,926
Latimer (M5) 9,690
Le Flore (N5) 35,276
Lincoln (J3) 22,102
Logan (H3) 22,170
Love (H7) 7,721
Major (F2) 10,279
Marshall (J6) 8,177
Mayes (M2) 19,743
Mc Clain (H5) 14,681
Mc Curtain (N6) 31,588
Mc Intosh (L4) 17,829
Murray (H6) 10,775
Muskogee (M3) 65,573
Noble (H2) 12,156
Nowata (L1) 12,734
Okfuskee (K3) 16,948
Oklahoma (H3) 325,352
Okmulgee (L3) 44,561
Osage (K1) 33,071
Ottawa (N1) 32,218
Pawnee (J2) 13,616
Payne (J2) 46,430
Pittsburg (L5) 41,031
Pontotoc (J5) 30,875
Pottawatomie (J4) 43,517
Pushmataha (M6) 12,001
Roger Mills (C3) 7,395
Rogers (L2) 19,532
Seminole (J4) 40,672
Sequoyah (N3) 19,773
Stephens (G6) 34,071
Texas (D8) 14,235
Tillman (E6) 17,598
Tulsa (L2) 251,686
Wagoner (L3) 16,741
Washington (L1) 32,880
Washita (E4) 17,657
Woods (E1) 14,526
Woodward (D2) 14,383

CITIES and TOWNS

Achille (K7)* 383
Acme (F5) 115
Ada (J5)* 15,995
Adair (M2)* 299
Adams (E8)* 250
Adamson (L5)* 200
Addielee (N3)
Addington (G6)* 174
Adel (L5)* 10
Afton (N1)* 1,252
Agra (J3)* 302
Akins (N3)
Albany (K7)* 300
Albert (F4)* 120
Albion (M5)* 178

Alderson (L5)*... 311
Aledo (D3)*...
Alex (G5)*... 563
Alfalfa (E4)*... 170
Aline (F1)*... 385
Allen (K5)*... 1,215
Alluwe (M1)*... 200
Alma (G6)*...
Altus (D5)*... 9,735
Alva (E1)*... 6,505
Amber (G4)*... 300
America (N7)... 65
Ames (F2)*... 263
Amorita (F1)*... 125
Anadarko (F4)*... 6,184
Antlers (L6)*... 2,506
Apache (F5)*... 1,190
Apperson (J1)*... 21
Arapaho (D3)*... 311
Arcadia (H3)*... 350
Ardmore (H6)*... 17,890
Arkoma (O4)*... 1,691
Arnett (C2)*... 690
Asher (J5)*... 420
Ashland (K5)*... 104
Atoka (K6)*... 2,653
Atwood (K5)*... 125
Avant (K2)*... 389
Avard (E1)*... 96
Avery (J3)*... 20
Bache (L5)*... 300
Bacone (M3)*... 250
Bakersburg (E7)*... 100
Balko (A1)*... 50
Banner (G4)*... 135
Banty (K6)... 50
Banzet (M1)... 2
Barber (N3)*... 70
Barnsdall (K1)*... 1,708
Baron (N3)... 75
Bartlesville (K1)*... 19,228
Battiest (N6)*... 150
Beachton (N6)... 25
Bearden (K4)*... 250
Beaver (B1)*... 1,495
Bebee (J5)... 100
Beggs (L3)*... 1,214
Belva (D1)*... 35
Belzoni (M6)*... 25
Bengal (M5)*... 200
Bennington (L7)*... 361
Bentley (K6)*...
Berlin (C4)*... 51
Bernice (N1)*... 91
Bessie (D4)*... 205
Bethany (G3)*... 5,705
Bethel (N6)*... 165
Big Cabin (M1)*... 210
Big Canyon (J6)*... 120
Billings (H1)*... 620
Binger (F4)*... 773
Bison (G2)*... 100
Bixby (L3)*... 1,517
Blackburn (J2)*... 135
Blackgum (N3)*...
Blackwell (H1)*... 9,199
Blair (D5)*... 700
Blanchard (G4)*... 1,311
Blanco (L5)*... 200
Blocker (L4)*... 105
Blue (K7)*... 240
Bluejacket (M1)*... 274
Boatman (M2)*... 115
Boggy Depot (K6)...
Boise City (B8)*... 1,902
Bokchito (K6)*... 643
Bokhoma (N7)... 150
Bokoshe (N4)*... 589
Boley (K4)*... 646
Boswell (L6)*... 875
Bowden (K2)*... 300
Bowlegs (J4)*... 365
Bowring (K1)*... 120
Boyd (A1)*... 50
Boynton (L3)*... 718
Braden (N4)... 50
Bradley (G5)*... 248
Braggs (M3)*... 374
Braman (H1)*... 392
Bray (G5)*... 40
Breckinridge (G2)*... 67
Briartown (M4)*... 150
Bridgeport (F3)*... 199
Brinkman (C4)*... 102
Bristow (K3)*... 5,400
Britton (G3)...
Brock (H6)*... 54
Broken Arrow (L2)*... 3,262
Broken Bow (N7)*... 1,838
Bromide (J6)*... 258
Brooken (M4)*...
Brooksville (H4)*... 175
Bryant (L4)*... 88
Buffalo (C1)*... 1,544
Bunch (N3)*... 150
Burbank (J1)*... 268
Burlington (F1)*... 181
Burneyville (H7)*... 300
Burns Flat (D4)*... 250
Bushyhead (L2)*... 42
Butler (D3)*... 351
Byarns (J5)*... 284
Byng (J5)*... 50
Byron (F1)*... 131
Cache (E5)*... 677
Caddo (K6)*... 895
Cairo (K5)... 25
Calera (K7)*... 643
Calumet (F3)*... 339
Calvin (K5)*... 557
Camargo (D2)*... 312
Cambridge (D4)... 22
Cameron (O4)*... 209
Canadian (L4)*... 277
Caney (K6)*... 252
Canton (E2)*... 959
Canute (D4)*... 355
Capron (E1)*... 100
Cardin (N1)*...
Carlton (F2)*... 60
Carmen (N1)*... 654
Carnegie (E4)*... 1,719
Carney (J3)*... 227
Carpenter (D3)... 32
Carrier (F2)*... 135
Carter (D4)*... 406
Carter Nine (J1)*...
Cartersville (N4)*... 100
Cashion (G3)*... 182
Castle (K4)*... 144
Catale (M1)... 40
Catesby (C2)*... 27
Catoosa (L2)*... 438
Cedardale (D2)*... 19
Cement (F5)*... 1,076
Center (J5)... 75
Centrahoma (K5)*... 154
Centralia (M1)*... 124
Cerrogordo (N7)*... 66
Cestos (D2)... 100
Chandler (J3)*... 2,724
Chaney (C1)... 11
Chattanooga (E6)*... 333
Checotah (M4)*... 2,638
Cheek (H6)... 75
Chelsea (L1)*... 1,437
Cherokee (F1)*... 2,635
Chester (E2)*... 129
Cheyenne (C3)*... 1,133
Chickasha (G4)*... 15,842
Chilocco (H1)*... 775
Choctaw (H4)*... 355
Chouteau (M2)*... 658
Christie (N3)... 35
Claremore (M2)*... 5,494
Clarita (K6)*... 200
Clarksville (L3)...
Claud (G5)...
Clayton (M5)*... 612
Clear Lake (B1)... 30
Clearview (K4)*...
Clemscot (G6)*... 240
Cleo Springs (F2)*... 310
Cleora (N1)*... 60
Cleveland (K2)*... 2,464
Clinton (D3)*... 7,555
Cloud Chief (E4)*... 125
Cloudy (M6)*... 50
Coalgate (K5)*... 1,984
Coalton (K4)... 105
Cogar (F4)*... 67
Colbert (K7)*... 748
Colcord (N2)... 205
Cold Springs (E5)*... 40
Cole (G4)*... 100
Coleman (K6)*...
Collinsville (L2)*... 2,011
Colony (E4)*... 400
Comanche (G6)*... 2,083
Commerce (M1)*... 2,442
Concho (G3)*... 250
Connerville (J6)*...
Coodys Bluff (L1)*... 116
Cookson (N3)*...
Cooperton (E5)*... 129
Copan (L1)*... 459
Cordell (E4)*... 2,920
Corinne (M6)*... 75
Corn (E4)*... 350
Cornish (G6)... 152
Council Hill (L3)*... 166
Countyline (H6)*... 400
Courtney (G7)*... 150
Covington (G2)*... 769
Coweta (L3)*... 1,601
Cowlington (N4)*... 83
Cox City (G5)*... 250
Coyle (H3)*... 360
Crawford (C3)*... 49
Crescent (G3)*... 1,341
Cromwell (J4)*... 313
Crowder (L4)*... 267
Crum Creek (L5)... 15
Crystal (L6)*... 70
Cumberland (J6)*... 200
Curtis (D2)*... 125
Cushing (J3)*... 8,414
Custer (E3)*... 479
Cyril (F5)*... 998
Dacoma (E1)*... 256
Daisy (L5)*... 30
Dale (H4)*... 205
Darwin (L6)*... 50
Davenport (J3)*... 841
Davidson (E6)*... 490
Davis (H5)*... 1,928
Dawson (L2)...
Deer Creek (G1)*... 209
Del City (H4)... 2,504
Dela (L6)*... 20
Delaware (L1)*... 582
Delhi (C4)*...
Dennis (N1)*... 48
Denoya (J1)... 25
Depew (K3)*... 719
Devol (E6)*... 152
Dewar (L4)*... 1,015
Dewey (L1)*... 2,513
Dewright (J4)...
Dibble (G4)... 148
Dighton (L4)... 17
Dill City (D4)*... 453
Dillard (H6)*... 155
Dilworth (H1)... 63
Dodge (N1)... 12
Dougherty (H6)*... 341
Douglas (G2)*... 114
Douthat (N1)*... 700
Dover (G3)*... 400
Dow (L5)*... 300
Doxey (C4)... 75
Driftwood (F1)*... 69
Drummond (G2)*... 314
Drumright (K3)*... 5,028
Duke (C5)*... 331
Dunbar (L6)*... 85
Duncan (G5)*... 15,325
Dunlap (C1)...
Durant (K6)*... 10,541
Durham (C3)*... 84
Dustin (K4)*... 524
Eagle City (E3)*... 106
Eagletown (N6)*... 600
Eakley (E4)*... 191
Earlsboro (J4)*... 278
East Cushing (J3)... 450
East Duke (D5)... 325
Echota (N3)... 157
Eddy (H1)*... 10
Edith (D1)...
Edmond (G3)*... 6,086
Edna (K3)*... 25
El Reno (F3)*... 10,991
Eldorado (C6)*... 732
Elgin (F5)*... 428
Elk City (D4)*... 7,962
Ellerville (N2)*... 36
Elmer (D6)*... 145
Elmore City (H5)*... 743
Elmwood (B1)*... 15
Empire City (G6)...
Enid (G2)*... 36,017
Enterprise (M4)*... 200
Eram (L3)... 39
Erick (C4)*... 1,579
Estella (M1)*... 10
Eucha (N2)*...
Eufaula (L4)*... 2,540
Eva (C8)*... 24
Fairfax (J1)*... 2,017
Fairland (N1)*... 699
Fairmont (G2)*... 134
Fairvalley (E1)...
Fairview (E2)*... 2,411
Fallis (H3)*... 105
Fame (L4)... 132
Fanshawe (N5)*... 305
Fargo (C2)*... 318
Farris (L6)*... 130
Farry (E1)*... 22
Faxon (E6)*... 135
Fay (E3)*... 175
Featherston (L4)*... 75
Felt (B8)*... 53
Fillmore (J6)*... 100
Finley (M6)*... 250
Fittstown (J5)*... 350
Fitzhugh (J5)*... 200
Fleetwood (G7)*... 125
Fletcher (F5)*... 875
Flint (N2)*...
Folsom (K6)*... 16
Foraker (K1)*... 105
Forgan (A1)*... 410
Fort Cobb (F4)*... 665
Ft. Gibson (M3)*... 1,496
Ft. Reno (F3)... 35
Ft. Sill (F5)*...
Ft. Supply (C1)*... 293
Ft. Towson (M7)*... 713
Foss (D4)*... 210
Foster (H5)*... 175
Fox (H6)*... 438
Foyil (M2)*... 146
Francis (J5)*... 271
Frederick (D6)*... 5,467
Freedom (D1)*... 332
Frisco (J5)...
Frogville (M7)... 4
Gage (C2)*... 648
Gano (J2)... 4
Gans (N4)*... 300
Garber (H2)*... 957
Garden City ‡(L2)... 763
Garvin (N7)*... 155
Gate (B1)*... 197
Geary (F3)*... 1,614
Gene Autry (J6)*... 170
Geronimo (F6)*... 103
Gerty (K5)*... 155
Gibbon (G1)... 14
Gideon (M2)*... 100
Glencoe (H2)*... 309
Glenpool (L3)*... 280
Glover (N6)*... 89
Golden (N6)*... 150
Goltry (F1)*... 277
Goodland (L7)...
Goodnight (H3)... 18
Goodwater (N7)*... 25
Goodwell (D8)*... 714
Goodwin (C2)...
Gore (M3)*... 387
Gotebo (E4)*... 574
Gould (C5)*... 303
Gowen (M5)*... 525
Gracemont (F4)... 301
Grady (G6)*... 75
Graham (H6)*... 128
Grainola (J1)*... 79
Grand (C3)... 3
Grandfield (E6)*... 1,232
Granite (D5)*... 1,096
Grant (M7)*... 351
Gray (A1)*... 25
Gray Horse (J1)... 70
Greenfield (F3)*... 191
Griggs (C8)*... 10
Grimes (C4)*... 50
Grove (N1)*... 928
Guthrie (H3)*... 10,113
Guymon (D8)*... 4,718
Gypsy (J3)*... 53
Haileyville (L5)*... 1,107
Hallett (K2)*... 120
Hammon (D3)*... 621
Hanna (L4)*... 325
Hanson (N4)*...
Harden City (J5)*... 200
Hardesty (E8)*... 201
Hardy (J1)... 17
Harjo (J4)*... 112
Harmon (C2)*... 20
Harrah (H4)*... 741
Harris (N7)*... 192
Hartshorne (M5)*... 2,330
Haskell (L3)*... 1,676
Hastings (F6)*... 285
Hawley (G1)...
Haworth (N7)*... 254
Hayward (G2)*... 40
Haywood (L5)*... 200
Headrick (D5)*... 144
Healdton (H6)*... 2,578
Heavener (N5)*... 2,103
Helena (F1)*... 484
Hendrix (K7)*... 152
Hennepin (H5)*... 300
Hennessey (G2)*... 1,264
Henryetta (K4)*... 7,987
Herd (K1)... 26
Herring (C3)... 25
Hess (D6)...
Hester (D5)... 31
Hickory (J5)*... 112
Highland Park (L2)*... 476
Hillsdale (F1)*... 104
Hinton (F4)*... 1,025
Hitchcock (F3)*... 166
Hitchita (L3)*... 141
Hobart (E5)*... 5,380
Hochatown (N6)*... 180
Hockerville (N1)*...
Hodgen (N5)*... 100
Hoffman (L4)*... 302
Holdenville (K4)*... 6,192
Hollis (C5)*... 3,089
Hollister (E6)*... 172
Hollow (M1)... 1
Homestead (F2)*... 95
Hominy (K2)*... 2,702
Honobia (M5)*... 100
Hooker (E7)*... 1,842
Hopeton (E1)*... 60
Howe (N5)*... 486
Hoyt (M4)*...
Hugo (M6)*... 5,984
Hulah (K1)*...
Hulbert (M3)*... 800
Humphreys (D5)*...
Hunter (G1)*... 279
Hydro (F3)*... 714
Idabel (N7)*... 4,671
Indiahoma (E5)*... 319
Indianapolis (E3)... 10
Indianola (L4)*... 314
Ingersoll (F1)... 78
Inola (L2)*... 294
Isabella (F2)*...
Jay (N2)*... 697
Jefferson (G1)*... 179
Jenks (L2)*... 1,037
Jennings (J2)*... 338
Jester (C5)... 12
Jet (F1)*... 371
Jones (H3)*... 476
Jumbo (L6)*... 82
Kanima (N4)... 65
Kansas (N2)*...
Kaw (J1)*... 561
Keefeton (M3)*... 135
Kellyville (K3)*... 528
Kemp (K7)*... 158
Kemp City (Hendrix*) (K7)... 152
Kendrick (J3)*... 172
Kenefic (K6)*... 115
Kenton (A7)*...
Kenwood (N2)*... 115
Keota (N4)*... 619
Ketchum (M1)*... 254
Keyes (C8)*... 431
Keystone (K2)*... 228
Kiamichi (M5)*... 100
Kiefer (K3)*... 275
Kildare (H1)*... 155
Kingfisher (G3)*... 3,345
Kingston (J7)*... 677
Kinta (M4)*... 283
Kiowa (L5)*... 802
Knowles (B1)*... 91
Komalty (E4)...
Konawa (J5)*... 2,707
Kosoma (L6)*... 50
Krebs (L5)*... 1,532
Kremlin (G1)*... 143
Kusa (L4)...
Lahoma (F2)*... 190
Lamar (K4)*... 180
Lambert (E1)*... 55
Lamont (G1)*... 594
Lane (K6)*...
Langley (M2)*... 204
Langston (H3)*... 685
Laverne (C1)*... 1,269
Lawrence (J5)... 250
Lawton (F5)*... 34,757
Leach (N2)*... 200
Lebanon (J7)*... 200
Leedey (D3)*... 558
Leflore (N5)*... 400
Lehigh (K6)*... 352
Lela (J2)*...
Lenapah (L1)*... 328
Lenna (L4)*...
Lenora (D2)*... 33
Leon (H7)*... 122
Leonard (L3)*... 115
Lequire (M4)*...
Lexington (H4)*... 1,176
Lima (J4)*... 99
Lindsay (G5)*... 3,021
Little Chief (J1)... 145
Little City (J6)... 101
Loco (G6)*... 236
Locust Grove (M2)*... 730
Lodi (M4)*... 83
Logan (B1)*... 21
Lone Grove (H6)*... 285
Lone Wolf (D5)*... 660
Long (N4)... 50
Longdale (F2)*... 277
Lookeba (F4)*... 206
Lookout (D1)*...
Louis (C5)...
Loveland (E6)*... 96
Lovell (G2)*... 73
Loyal (F3)*... 125
Lucien (H2)*... 200
Ludlow (N5)*... 64
Lugert (D5)... 68
Lula (K5)*...
Luther (H3)*... 409
Lutie (M5)... 50
Lyman (J1)*... 75
Macomb (H4)*... 123
Madill (J6)*... 2,791
Manchester (G1)*... 190
Mangum (C5)*... 4,271
Manitou (E5)*... 293
Mannford (K2)*... 426
Mannsville (J6)*... 311
Maramec (J2)*... 184
Marble City (N3)*... 285
Marietta (H7)*... 1,875
Markham (J2)...
Marland (H1)*... 221
Marlow (F5)*... 3,399
Marshall (G2)*... 386
Martha (D5)*... 222
Mason (K3)*... 130
Maud (J4)*... 1,389
May (C1)*... 143
Mayfield (C4)*... 51
Maysville (H5)*... 1,294
Mazie (M2)*... 70
Mc Alester (L5)*... 17,878
Mc Curtain (M4)*... 705
Mc Lain (M3)... 100
Mc Loud (H4)*... 718
Mc Man (H6)*... 28
Mc Millan (H6)*... 150
Mc Queen (C5)*...
Mead (K7)*... 200
Medford (G1)*... 1,305
Medicine Park (E5)*... 650
Meeker (J4)*... 672
Meers (E5)*... 38
Mehan (H2)... 51
Meno (F2)*... 76
Meridian (H3)*... 187
Merrick (H3)... 21
Mexhoma (A8)...
Miami (N1)*... 11,801
Micawber (J3)*... 90
Midwest City (H4)*... 10,166
Milburn (K6)*... 350
Milfay (J3)*... 160
Mill Creek (J6)*... 299
Miller (L6)*... 32
Millerton (N7)*... 250
Milo (H6)*... 109
Milton (N4)... 100
Minco (G4)*... 978
Mocane (B1)... 7
Moffett (N4)*... 380
Monroe (N4)*... 200
Moodys (N2)*... 20
Moon (N7)... 150
Moore (H4)*... 942
Mooreland (D2)*... 867
Moorewood (D3)*... 36
Morris (L3)*... 1,122
Morrison (H2)*... 297
Mounds (K3)*... 560
Mountain Park (E5)*... 418
Mountain View (E4)*... 1,009
Moyers (L6)*... 100
Muldrow (N4)*... 828
Mulhall (H2)*... 320
Murphy (M2)*... 66
Muse (N5)*... 150
Muskogee (M3)*... 37,289
Mustang (G4)*... 210
Mutual (D2)*... 130
Narcissa (N1)... 100
Nardin (H1)*... 184
Nash (F1)*... 290
Nashoba (M6)*... 100
Navina (G3)... 15
Nelagoney (K1)*... 138
Nelson (L6)*... 45
Neodesha (L2)...
New Lima (K4)*... 52
New Marshall (Marshall*) (G2)... 386
New Woodville (Woodville*) (J7)... 78
Newcastle (G4)*... 175
Newkirk (J1)*... 2,201
Newport (H6)*... 27
Nichols Hills ‡(H3)... 2,606
Nicoma Park (H4)*... 1,200
Nicut (N3)*... 50
Ninnekah (G5)*... 250
Noble (H4)*... 724
Non (K5)*... 81
Norge (F5)*... 100
Norman (H4)*... 27,006
North Enid (G2)... 219
North Mc Alester (L5)*
North Miami (M1)*... 486
Nowata (L1)*... 3,965
Numa (G1)... 12
Nuyaka (K3)*... 40
Oak Hill (N6)... 35
Oakhurst (L2)*... 200
Oakland (J6)*... 293
Oaks (N2)*... 70
Oakwood (E3)*... 161
Oberlin (L7)... 80
Ochelata (L1)*... 357
Octavia (N5)*... 55
Oilton (J2)*... 1,109
Okarche (G3)*... 532
Okay (M3)*... 427
Okeene (F2)*... 1,170
Okemah (K4)*... 3,454
Okesa (K1)... 25
OKLAHOMA CITY (H4)*... 243,504
Oklahoma City (urban area)... 273,424
Okmulgee (K3)*... 18,317
Oktaha (M3)*... 207
Oleta (M6)*... 50
Olive (K2)... 165
Olney (K6)*... 75
Olustee (D5)*... 455
Omega (F3)*...
Oologah (L2)*... 242
Optima (E8)*... 97
Orienta (E2)*... 30
Orlando (H2)*... 262
Orr (H6)*... 70
Osage (K2)*... 425
Oscar (G7)*... 20
Oswalt (H6)... 10
Overbrook (H6)*... 100
Owasso (L2)*... 431
Paden (J3)*... 426
Page (N5)*... 90
Panama (N4)*... 1,027
Panola (M5)*... 75
Paoli (H5)*... 353
Park Hill (M3)*... 150
Parkland (J3)... 65
Pauls Valley (H5)*... 6,896
Pawhuska (K1)*... 5,331
Pawnee (J2)*... 2,861
Payson (J3)*... 80
Pearson (J4)*... 140
Peckham (H1)... 125
Peek (C3)*... 3
Peggs (M2)*... 51
Pensacola (M2)*... 48
Peoria (N1)... 201
Perkins (H3)*... 706
Pernell (H5)*... 250
Perry (H2)*... 5,137
Pershing (K1)*... 62
Pharoah (K4)*... 200
Phillips (K6)... 181
Picher (N1)*... 3,951
Pickens (N6)*...
Piedmont (G3)*... 120
Pierce (L4)*... 200
Pittsburg (L5)*... 278
Platter (K7)*... 275
Pleasant Valley (H3)... 16
Plunkettville (N6)*... 100
Pocasset (G4)*... 220
Pollard (N7)...
Ponca City (H1)*... 20,180
Pondcreek (G1)*... 1,066
Pontotoc (J6)*...
Pooleville (H6)*... 150
Port (D4)... 50
Porter (M3)*... 562
Porum (M4)*... 616
Poteau (N4)*... 4,776
Prague (J4)*... 1,546
Preston (L3)*... 525
Proctor (N3)*... 175
Prue (K2)*... 160
Pryor (M2)*... 4,486
Purcell (H4)*... 3,546
Putnam (E3)*... 106
Qualls (M3)... 10
Quapaw (N1)*... 938
Quay (J2)*... 70
Quinlan (E2)*... 107
Quinton (M4)*... 951
Ralston (J2)*... 416
Ramona (L1)*... 583
Randlett (F6)*... 396
Rattan (M6)*... 200
Ravia (J6)*... 327
Reagan (J6)...
Red Oak (M5)*... 568
Redbird (L3)*... 411
Redden (L5)*... 112
Redland (N4)... 25
Redrock (H2)*... 253
Reed (C5)*... 200
Regnier (B7)...
Renfrow (G1)*... 68
Rentiesville (M4)*... 156
Reydon (C3)*... 331
Rhea (D3)*...
Richland (G3)... 50
Richmond (D2)... 2
Ringling (G6)*... 1,092
Ringold (M6)*... 106
Ringwood (F2)*... 331
Ripley (J2)*... 292
Roberta (K7)... 65
Rock Island (O4)*... 110
Rocky (E4)*... 366
Roff (J5)*... 623
Roland (N4)*... 443
Roosevelt (E5)*... 679
Rose (M2)*... 100
Rosedale (H5)*... 136
Rosston (C1)*... 85
Roxana (G2)... 25
Rubottom (H7)*...
Rufe (M6)*... 125
Rush Springs (G5)*... 1,402
Russell (C5)*... 65
Ryan (G6)*... 1,019
Sacred Heart (J5)*... 30
Saddle Mountain (E5)* 2
Sageeyah (L2)... 50
Saint Louis (J4)*... 290
Salina (M2)*... 905
Sallisaw (N4)*... 2,885
Saltfork (G1)*... 50
Sand Creek (F1)*... 38
Sand Springs (K2)*... 6,994
Santa Fe (G6)... 8
Sapulpa (K3)*... 13,031
Sardis (M5)*... 85
Sasakwa (J5)*... 365
Savanna (L5)*... 900
Sawyer (M7)*... 200
Sayre (C4)*... 3,362
Schulter (L3)*... 700
Scipio (L4)*... 250
Scraper (N2)*... 50
Scullin (J5)*... 21
Seiling (E2)*... 700
Selman (D1)*... 58
Seminole (J4)*... 11,863
Sentinel (D4)*... 1,131
Seward (H3)*... 75
Shadypoint (N4)*... 315
Shamrock (K3)*... 263
Sharon (D2)*... 133
Shattuck (C2)*... 1,692
Shawnee (J4)*... 22,948
Shay (J7)*... 75
Sherman (E2)...
Sherwood (N6)*...
Shidler (J1)*... 840
Shinewell (O7)*...
Short (N3)*...
Shrewder (C5)...
Silo (J6)... 75
Simpson (J6)*... 150
Skedee (J2)*... 170
Skiatook (K2)*... 1,734
Slick (K3)*... 151
Smithville (N6)*... 256
Snomac (J4)*... 55
Snow (M6)*... 100
Snyder (E5)*... 1,646
Soper (L6)*... 337
South Coffeyville (L1)* 527
Southard (F2)*... 452
Sparks (J3)*... 233
Spaulding (K4)*... 75
Spavinaw (M2)*... 213
Speer (M6)*...
Spencer (H3)*... 300
Spencerville (M6)*... 100
Sperry (L2)*... 665

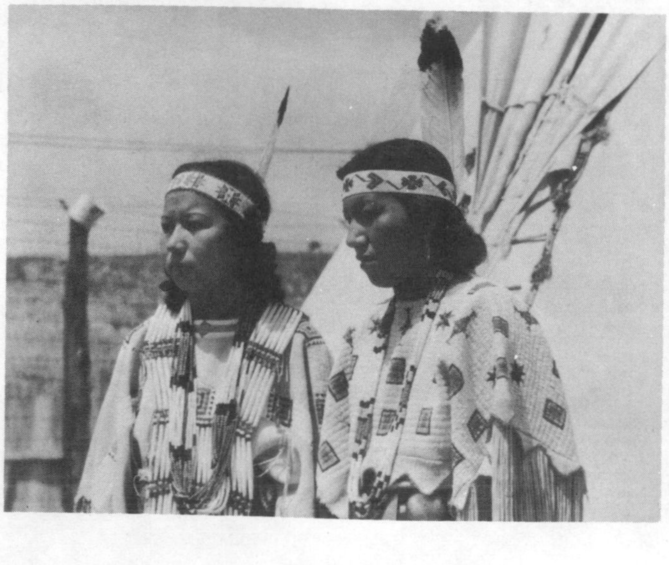

piro (N4)* 1,365
pringer (H6)* 325
tafford (D3)* 60
tanley (M5)* 50
tapp (N5)
tecker (F5)* 60
teedman (J5) 75
terling (F5)* 447
tidham (L4)* 46
tigler (M4)* 2,125
tillwater (J2)* 20,238
tilwell (N3)* 1,813
tonebluff (L3)* 300
tonewall (K5)* 634
trang (M2)* 201
tratford (H5)* 1,065
tringtown (L6)* 499
trong City (C3)* 107
troud (J3)* 2,450
tuart (K5)* 303
ugden (G6)* 105
ulphur (J5)* 4,389
ummerfield (N5)* 300
umner (H2)* 46
Sunkist (L6)* 15
Sweetwater (C4)* 60
Swink (M6)* 96
Tabler (G4)*
Taft (M3)* 541
Tahlequah (M3)* 4,750
Tahona (N4)* 45
Talala (L1)* 210
Talihina (N5)* 965
Tallant (K1)* 130
Taloga (E2)* 430
Tamaha (N4)* 117
Tangier (C2) 25
Tatums (H6)* 210
Tecumseh (J4)* 2,275
Tegarden (E1)* 14
Temple (F6)* 1,442
Teresita (N2)* 50
Terlton (K2)* 122
Terral (G7)* 616
Texanna (M4) 25
Texhoma (D8)* 1,464
Texola (C4)* 265
Thackerville (H7)* 178
Thomas (E3)* 1,171
Three Sands (H1)* 50
Ti (L5)* 23
Tiawah (L2) 100
Tip (M2)* 25
Tipton (D6)* 1,172
Tishomingo (J6)* 2,325
Tom (N7)*
Tomy Town (N3) 75
Tonkawa (H1)* 3,643
Tribbey (H4)* 100
Trousdale (H4)* 50
Troy (J6)*
Tryon (J3)* 285
Tullahassee (L3)* 209
Tulsa (K2)* 182,740
Tulsa (urban area) 203,968
Tupelo (K5)* 376
Turkey Ford (N1)* 100
Turley (L2)* 200
Turpin (A1)* 175
Tushka (K6)*
Tuskahoma (M5)* 325
Tuskegee (K3)* 84
Tussy (G6)* 96
Tuttle (G4)* 715
Tuxedo Park (L1) 1,179
Tyrone (E7)* 261
Ulan (L4)* 30
Uncas (H1)* 100
Union (G4)* 301
Utica (K7)* 100
Valliant (M6)* 661
Vanoss (J5)* 118
Velma (G6)* 1,034
Vera (L2)* 164
Verden (F4)* 508
Verdigris (L2)* 150
Vernon (L4)* 450
Veterans Village ‡(H2) 3,355
Vian (N4)* 927
Vici (D2)* 620
Vinco (H3) 25
Vinita (M1)* 5,518
Vinson (C5)* 125
Virgil (M6) 55
Vivian (L4) 75
Wade (K7)* 150
Wagoner (M3)* 4,395
Wainwright (M3)* 138
Wakita (G1)* 440
Walters (F6)* 2,743
Wanette (H5)* 594
Wann (L1)* 99
Wapanucka (J6)* 592
Wardville (L5)* 89
Warner (M4)* 382
Warr Acres (G3)* 2,378
Warwick (H3)* 132
Washington (H4)* 292
Washita (F4)* 45
Washunga (J1) 91
Watonga (F3)* 3,249
Watova (L1)* 250
Watson (N6)* 100
Watts (N2)* 267
Wauhillau (N3) 48
Waukomis (F2)* 537
Waurika (G6)* 2,327
Wayne (H5)* 501
Waynoka (E1)* 2,018
Weatherford (E4)* 3,529
Weathers (L5) 200
Webb (D3)* 33
Webb City (J1)* 284
Webbers Falls (M3)* 489
Welch (M1)* 483
Weleetka (K4)* 1,548
Welling (N3)* 77
Wellston (H3)* 643
Welty (K3)* 50
Wesley (L5)* 35
Westville (N2)* 781
Wetumka (K4)* 2,025
Wewoka (K4)* 6,747
Wheatland (G4)* 300
Wheeless (B8)* 15
Whitefield (M4)* 350
Whiteoak (M1)* 100
Whitesboro (N5)*
Wilburton (M5)* 1,939
Wildcat (L3) 147
Willard (C1) 2
Williams (O4)* 200
Willis (J7)* 115
Willow (C4)* 223
Wilson (H6)* 1,832
Wirt (G6)* 700
Wister (N5)* 729
Wolco (K1)* 100
Woodford (H6)* 105
Woodville (J7)* 78
Woodward (D2)* 5,915
Wright City (M6)* 1,121
Wyandotte (N1)* 242
Wybark (M3) 50
Wynne Wood (H5)* 2,423
Wynona (K1)* 678
Yahola (L3) 65
Yale (J2)* 1,359
Yanush (M5) 156
Yarnaby (K7)* 200
Yeager (K4)* 180
Yewed (F1)* 100
Yonkers (M2)* 20
Yuba (K7)* 108
Yukon (G3)* 1,990
Zena (N2)* 25
Zincville (N1)*
Zoe (N5)* 80

Map on Page 84

OREGON

Total Population 1,521,341

36 COUNTIES

aker (K3) 16,175
enton (D3) 31,570
lackamas (E2) 86,716
latsop (D1) 30,776
olumbia (D2) 22,967
oos (C4) 42,265
rook (G3) 8,991
urry (C5) 6,048
eschutes (F4) 21,812
ouglas (E4) 54,549
illiam (G2) 2,817
rant (J3) 8,329
arney (H4) 6,113
ood River (F2) 12,740
ackson (E5) 58,510
efferson (F3) 5,536
osephine (D5) 26,542
lamath (F5) 42,150
ake (G5) 6,649
ane (E4) 125,776
incoln (D3) 21,308
inn (E3) 54,317
alheur (K4) 23,223
arion (E3) 101,401
orrow (H2) 4,783
ultnomah (E2) 471,537
olk (D3) 26,317
herman (G2) 2,271
illamook (D2) 18,606
matilla (J2) 41,703
nion (J2) 17,962
allowa (K2) 7,264
asco (F2) 15,552
ashington (D2) 61,269
heeler (G3) 3,313
amhill (D2) 33,484

CITIES and TOWNS

da (D4)* 100
dams (J2)* 154
del (H5)* 83
drian (K4)* 170
gate Beach (C3)* 379
gness (D5)* 48
irlie (D3) 30
lbany (D3)* 10,115
lbee (J2) 7
lfalfa (F3) 25
lgoma (F5) 50
licel (J2)* 50
llegany (D4)* 220
loha (A2)* 50
lpine (D3)* 325
lsea (D3)* 130
ltamont (F5) 9,419
lvadore (D3)* 150
mity (D2)* 672
ndrews (J5)* 8
nlauf (D4) 50
ntelope (G3)* 60
ntone (H3)
pplegate (D5)* 75
rago (C4)* 117
rcadia (K4)
rlington (G2)* 686
rock (K5)* 100
sh (D4) 120
shland (E5)* 7,739
shwood (G3)* 19
storia (D1)* 12,331
thena (J2)* 750
umsville (E3)* 281
urora (A2)* 242
ustin (J3) 39
zalea (D5)* 50
aker (K3)* 9,471
allston (D2)* 100
ancroft (D5) 75
andon (C4)* 1,251
anks (A1)* 376
ar View (C2)* 200
arlow (B2)* 75
artlett (K2)
arton (B2)
ates (J3)* 500
ay City (D2)* 761
ayocean (C2)* 70
ayview (C3) 15
eatty (F5)* 50
eaver (D2)* 567
eavercreek (B2)* 60
eaverton (A2)* 2,512
eech Creek (H3)* 2
elknap Springs (F3)* 12
ellfountain (D3) 50
end (F3)* 11,409
erlin (E3)
Bethany (A2) 20
Beulah (J4) 10
Big Eddy (F2) 36
Biggs (G2)* 15
Birkenfeld (D1)* 100
Blachly (D3)* 24
Black Rock (D3) 17
Blackbutte (E4)* 50
Blaine (D2)* 75
Blalock (G2)* 21
Blitzen (H5) 7
Blodgett (D3)* 200
Blue River (E3)* 200
Bly (F5)* 800
Boardman (H2)* 120
Bonanza (F5)* 259
Bonita (A2) 50
Bonneville (F2)* 250
Booth (C4)
Boring (E2)*
Bourne (J3)
Boyd (F2)* 38
Breitenbush (F3)* 6
Bridal Veil (E2)* 120
Bridge (D4) 200
Bridgeport (K3)* 63
Brighton (C2)* 107
Brightwood (E2)* 150
Broadacres (A3) 30
Broadbent (C4)* 50
Brockway (D4)* 61
Brogan (K3)* 75
Brookings (C5)* 1,000
Brooks (A3)* 350
Brothers (G4) 15
Brownlee (L3)
Brownsboro (E5)* 100
Brownsville (E3)* 1,175
Buena Vista (D3) 160
Bullards (C4)* 25
Burlington (A1) 200
Burns (H4)* 3,093
Burnt Ranch (G3)
Butte Falls (E5)* 372
Butteville (A2) 50
Buxton (D2)* 150
Cairo (K4) 50
Camas Valley (D4)* 60
Camp Namanu (E2)* 2
Camp Sherman (F3)* 50
Canary (D4) 50
Canby (B2)* 1,671
Cannon Beach (D2)*
Canyon City (J3)* 508
Canyonville (D5)* 861
Carlton (D2)* 1,081
Carnation (A2) 100
Carpenterville (C5) 30
Carson (K3)* 100
Carver (B2) 200
Cascade Locks (F2)* 733
Cascade Summit (F4)* 5
Cascadia (E3)* 200
Cave Junction (D5)* 283
Cayuse (J2)* 48
Cecil (H2)* 20
Cedar Mill (A2) 300
Celilo (G2) 300
Central Point (D5)* 1,667
Chapman (D2) 100
Charleston (C4)* 576
Chelsea (F5) 300
Chemawa (A3)* 850
Chemult (F4)* 115
Cherry Grove (D2)* 375
Cherryville (E2)* 160
Cheshire (D3)* 73
Chiloquin (F5)* 668
Clackamas (B2)* 550
Clarno (G3)
Clatskanie (D1)* 901
Claxtar (A3) 100
Clem (G2) 12
Clifton (D1)* 68
Cloverdale (D2)* 280
Coaledo (C4) 125
Coburg (D3)* 693
Cochran (D2) 50
Colestin (E5) 7
Colton (B3)* 167
Columbia City (E2)* 405
Condon (G2)* 968
Coos Bay (C4)* 6,223
Copperfield (K3) 13
Coquille (C4)* 3,523
Cornelius (A2)* 998
Cornucopia (K3)
Corvallis (D3)* 16,207
Cottage Grove (D4)* 3,536
Courtrock (H3)* 60
Cove (K2)* 282
Cove Orchard (D2)* 140
Cow Creek (D5)
Crabtree (E3)* 350
Crane (J4)* 99
Crater Lake (E5)* 47
Crawfordsville (E3)* 250
Crescent (F4)* 300
Crescent Lake (F4)* 50
Creston (K4) 4
Creswell (D4)* 662
Crow (D4) 100
Crowley (K4) 5
Crystal (E5) 15
Culp Creek (E4)* 260
Culver (F3)* 301
Curry (J3) 4
Curtin (D4)* 70
Cushman (D4)* 150
Dairy (F5)* 50
Dale (J3)* 10
Dallas (D3)* 4,793
Danner (K5) 20
Dawson (D3) 40
Days Creek (D5)* 40
Dayton (A3)* 719
Dayville (H3)* 286
Dee (F2)* 250
Deer Island (E2)* 79
Delake (C3) 644
Denmark (C5)* 13
Denzer (D3)
Depoe Bay (C3)* 750
Deschutes (F3) 20
Deter (E5) 15
Detroit (E3)*
Dexter (E4)* 400
Diamond (J4)* 8
Diamond Lake (E4)*
Dillard (D4)* 300
Dilley (A2)* 200
Disston (E4)* 300
Divide (D4)
Dixonville (D4) 30
Dolph (D2) 50
Donald (A3)* 187
Dora (D4) 80
Dorena (E4)* 300
Drain (D4)* 1,150
Draperville (D3) 201
Drew (E5)* 265
Drewsey (J4)* 64
Dryden (D5)* 25
Drylake (G4) 18
Dufur (F2)* 422
Duncan (J2)* 18
Dundee (A2)* 308
Durham (A2) 250
Durkee (K3)* 50
Eagle Creek (E2)* 75
Eagle Point (E5)* 607
Eastside (C4)* 890
Echo (H2)* 457
Eddyville (D3)*
Eightmile (H2)
Elgarose (D4) 12
Elgin (K2)* 1,223
Elk City (D3)* 50
Elk Lake (F4)*
Elkton (D4)* 201
Elmira (D3)* 500
Elmonica (A2) 50
Elsie (D2)
Empire (C4)* 2,261
Enright (D2) 5
Enterprise (K2)* 1,718
Erskine (G2) 7
Estacada (E2)* 950
Eugene (D3)* 35,879
Eula (E4) 20
Evans (K2) 47
Fair Grounds (A3)
Fairview (B2)* 438
Fall Creek (E4)* 144
Falls City (D3)* 853
Faloma (B2) 600
Fargo (A3) 18
Farmington (A2) 20
Faubion (F2) 30
Ferndale (J2) 225
Fields (J5)* 12
Fife (G4)
Fisher (D3)
Flora (K2)* 190
Florence (C4)* 1,026
Foleysprings (E3) 4
Follyfarm (J4) 5
Forest Grove (A2)* 4,343
Fort Klamath (E5)* 350
Ft. Rock (G4)* 18
Ft. Stevens (C1) 60
Foss (D2) 50
Fossil (G2)* 645
Foster (E3)* 350
Fox (H3)* 65
Freewater (J2)* 1,489
Frenchglen (H5)* 46
Friend (F2)* 15
Fruita (L2)
Galena (J3) 1
Gales Creek (D2)* 200
Galice (D5) 40
Garden Home (A2)* 750
Gardiner (C4)* 600
Garibaldi (D2)* 1,249
Gaston (D2)* 368
Gates (E3)* 445
Gateway (F3)* 75
Gaylord (C5)* 135
Gearhart (C1)* 568
Gervais (A3)* 457
Gibbon (J2)* 52
Gladstone (B2)* 2,434
Glenada (C4) 110
Glencoe (A1) 10
Glendale (D5)* 871
Gleneden Beach (C3)* 185
Glenwood (D2)* 20
Glide (D4)* 100
Goble (E1)* 73
Gold Beach (C5)* 677
Gold Hill (D5)* 619
Gooch (E3) 25
Goshen (D4)* 250
Government Camp (F2)* 100
Grand Ronde (D2)* 800
Granite (J3)* 40
Grant (G2) 25
Grants Pass (D5)* 8,116
Grass Valley (G2)* 195
Green (D4) 60
Greenburg (A2) 25
Greenhorn (J3)
Greenleaf (D3)* 111
Gresham (B2)* 3,049
Grizzly (G3) 25
Gunter (D4) 25
Gurdane (J2) 18
Gwendolen (G2) 6
Gypsum (K3)
Haines (J3)* 321
Halfway (K3)* 312
Halsey (D3)* 388
Hamilton (H3)* 58
Hamlet (D2)* 20
Hammond (C1)* 522
Hampton (G4)* 22
Harbor (C5)* 600
Hardman (H2)* 58
Harlan (D3)* 240
Harney (J4) 6
Harper (K4)* 200
Harriman (E5)* 42
Harrisburg (D3)* 862
Hauser (C4)* 158
Hay Creek (G3) 15
Hayesville (A3) 2,697
Hebo (D2)* 250
Helix (J2)* 182
Hemlock (D2) 20
Heppner (H2)* 1,648
Hereford (K3)* 66
Hermiston (H2)* 3,804
Hershal (K3) 4
Hildebrand (F5)
Hilgard (J2) 40
Hillsboro (A2)* 5,142
Hillsdale (B2)*
Hines (H4)* 918
Holbrook (A1) 100
Holdman (J2) 30
Holland (D5)* 100
Holley (E3)* 225
Home (K3)* 10
Homestead (L2) 25
Hood River (F2)* 3,701
Hopewell (D2) 125
Hopmere (A3) 75
Horton (D3)* 168
Hot Lake (K2) 25
Hubbard (A3)* 493
Huber (A2)* 250
Hugo (D5)* 100
Hullt (B3)
Huntington (K3)* 733
Idanha (E3)* 442
Idaville (D2) 150
Idleyld Park (D4)* 100
Illahe (C5)
Imbler (J2)* 149
Imnaha (L2)* 30
Independence (D3)* 1,987
Ione (H2)* 262

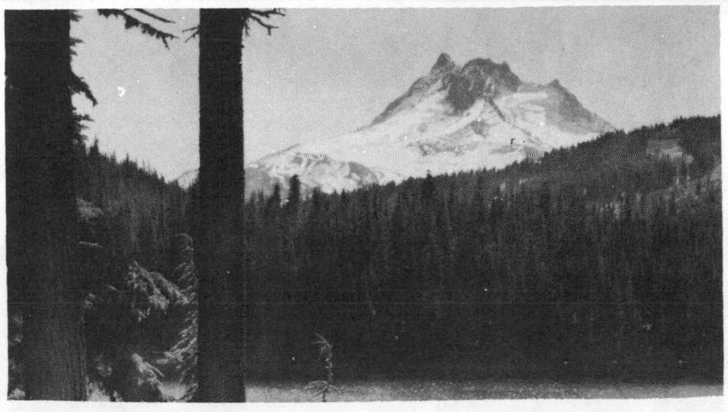

Ironside (K3)* 150
Irrigon (H2)* 75
Irving (D3) 300
Island City (K2)* 138
Izee (H3)* 4
Jacksonville (D5)* 1,193
Jamieson (K3)* 300
Jasper (E3)* 200
Jefferson (D3)* 636
Jennings Lodge (B2)* 3,500
Jewell (D2)*
John Day (J3)* 1,597
Jordan Valley (K5)* 236
Joseph (K2)* 666
Junction City (D3)* 1,475
Juntura (K4)* 107
Kamela (J2) 25
Keasey (D2)* 8
Keating (K3)* 10
Keno (F5)* 300
Kent (G2)* 60
Kerby (D5)* 150
Kernville (D3)* 105
Kerry (D1) 170
Kimberly (H3)* 60
Kings Valley (D3)* 210
Kinzua (H3)* 900
Kirk (F5) 25
Klamath Agency (F5)* 150
Klamath Falls (F5)* 15,875
Klondike (G2)* 6
Knappa (D1) 100
La Grande (J2)* 8,635
La Pine (F4)* 250
Lacomb (E3)* 100
Lafayette (A2)* 662
Lake Grove (B2)* 4,000
Lakecreek (E5)* 30
Lakeside (C4)*
Lakeview (G5)* 2,831
Langlois (C5)* 65
Latourell Falls (E2)* 72
Laurel (A2) 30
Lawen (J4)* 15
Leaburg (E3)* 106
Lebanon (E3)* 5,873
Leland (D5) 71
Leona (D4) 50
Lewis (K2) 2
Lexington (H2)* 237
Liberal (B3) 40
Liberty (A3)
Lime (K3)* 100
Lincoln Beach (C3)* 100
Linneman (B2) 550
Linnton (A2)
Linslaw (D4)* 75
Logan (B2) 50
Logdell (H3) 4
Logsden (D3)* 340
London (D4)
Lonerock (H2)* 38
Long Creek (H3)* 288
Lookingglass (D4) 100
Lostine (K2)* 178
Lowell (E4)* 700
Lyons (E3)* 600
Mabel (E3)* 85
Macksburg (B3) 50
Macleay (A3) 25
Madras (F3)* 1,258
Malheur (K3) 25
Malin (F5)* 592
Manhattan Beach (D2)*
Manning (D2)* 100
Manzanita (C2)* 339
Mapleton (C3)* 1,016
Marcola (E3)* 800
Marial (D5)* 45
Marion (D3)* 200
Marquam (B3)* 70
Marshland (D1)* 120
Maupin (F2)* 312
Maxville (K2)
Mayger (D1)* 95
Mayville (G2)* 102
Mc Coy (D2)* 75
Mc Credie Springs (E4)* 87
Mc Ewen (J3) 25
Mc Kee (A3) 75
Mc Kenzie Bridge (E3)* 105
Mc Kinley (D4)* 155
Mc Minnville (D2)* 6,635
Mc Nary (H2)*
Meacham (J2)*
Medford (E5)* 17,305
Medical Springs (K2)* 15
Mehama (E3)* 200
Melrose (D4) 150
Merlin (D5)* 225
Merrill (F5)* 835
Metolius (F3)* 157
Metzger (A2)* 2,000
Middleton (A2) 150
Midland (F5)* 85
Mikkalo (G2)* 150
Mill City (E3)* 1,792
Miller (G2)* 75
Millican (F4)* 5
Millington (C4) 300
Milo (E5)* 300
Milton (J2)* 2,362
Milwaukie (B2)* 5,253
Minam (K2)
Minerva (C3) 25
Mission (J2) 200
Mist (D1)* 269
Mitchell (G3)* 415
Modoc Point (F5)* 100
Mohawk (E3)* 20
Mohler (D2)* 100
Molalla (B3)* 1,497
Monitor (B3)* 50
Monmouth (D3)* 1,956
Monroe (D3)* 362
Monument (H3)* 228
Morgan (H2)* 10
Moro (G2)* 359
Mosier (F2)* 259
Mount Angel (B3)* 1,315
Mt. Hood (F2)* 59
Mt. Vernon (H3)* 451
Mountaindale (A1) 50
Mowich (F4) 20
Mulino (B2)* 275
Multnomah (B2)* 5,000
Murphy (D5)* 50
Myrtle Creek (D4)* 1,781
Myrtle Point (C4)* 2,033
Narrows (H4) 7
Nashville (D3)* 25
Needy (B3) 50
Nehalem (D2)* 270
Nelscott (D3)* 400
Neotsu (C2)* 300
Neskowin (D2)* 120
Netarts (C2)* 500
New Bridge (K3)* 51
New Era (B2) 100
New Pine Creek (G5)* 200
Newberg (A2)* 3,946
Newport (C3)* 3,241
North Bend (C4)* 6,099
N. Junction (G3) 2
N. Plains (A2)* 600
N. Portland (B1)* 340
N. Powder (K2)* 403
Norway (C4)* 250
Nyssa (K4)* 2,525
Oak Grove (B2)* 2,000
Oakland (D4)* 829
Oakridge (E4)* 1,562
O'Brien (D5)* 265
Oceanlake (C3)* 700
Oceanside (C2)* 150
Odell (F2)* 350
Odell Lake (F4) 50
Olene (F5)* 35
Olex (G2)* 168
Olney (D1)
Ontario (K3)* 4,465
Opal City (F3)
Ophir (C5)*
Ordnance (H2)*
Oregon Caves (D5)* 2
Oregon City (B2)* 7,682
Orenco (A2)* 313
Oretown (D2)* 60
Oswego (B2)* 3,316
Otis (D2)* 200
Otter Rock (C3)* 100
Owyhee Corner (K4)
Pacific City (C2)* 200
Paisley (G5)* 214
Palmer Junction (K2) 3
Paradise (K2) 42
Park Place (B2)* 500
Parkdale (F2)* 300
Parkers Mill (H2)
Parkrose (B2)* 3,800
Paulina (G3)*
Pedee (D3) 125
Pendleton (J2)* 11,774
Pengra (E4)
Peoria (D3) 76
Perry (J2) 125
Perrydale (D2)* 75
Phillips (A2) 3
Philomath (D3)* 1,289
Phoenix (E5)* 746
Pilot Rock (J2)* 847
Pine (K3)* 73
Pinehurst (E5) 6
Pistol River (C5)* 100
Placer (D5) 48
Plainview (D3) 20
Pleasant Valley (K3)* 30
Plush (H5)* 110
Pondosa (K2)* 150
Port Orford (C5)* 674
Portland (B2)* 373,628
Portland (urban area) 509,120
Post (G3)*
Powell Butte (G3)* 661
Powell Valley (B2) 725
Powers (D5)* 895
Prairie City (J3)* 822
Pratum (A3)* 44
Prescott (D1) 119
Princeton (J4)* 6
Prineville (G3)* 3,233
Pringle (A3) 250
Promise (K2)
Prospect (E5)* 500
Prosper (C4) 55
Provolt (D5)* 200
Quartz Mountain (G5) 12
Quinaby (A3) 100
Quincy (D1)* 400
Rainbow (E3) 65
Rainier (E1)* 1,285
Rainrock (C3)
Redland (B2) 50

Redmond (F3)*............2,956
Reed (D3)....................
Reedsport (C4)*............2,288
Reedville (A2)*............ 250
Remote (D5)*............ 60
Rex (A2)............ 5
Richland (K3)*............ 220
Richmond (H3)*............
Rickreall (D3)*............ 150
Riddle (D5)*............ 634
Rieth (J2)*............ 325
Riley (H4)*............ 5
Ritter (H3)*............ 107
Riverside (J4)*............ 38
Riverton (C4)*............ 125
Roberts (G3)............
Robinette (L3)*............ 20
Rockaway (C2)*............1,027
Rockcreek (G2)............ 19
Rockton (A2)............ 150
Rockville (K4)............ 31
Rocky Point (A1)........
Rogue River (D5)*....... 590
Rome (K5)............ 50
Roosevelt Beach (C3)....
Rose Lodge (D3)*....... 150
Roseburg (D4)*............8,390
Rowena (F2)............ 75
Rowland (D3)............ 15
Roy (A2)*............ 48
Ruch (E5)............ 50
Rufus (G2)*............ 50
Rye Valley (K3)............ 25
Saginaw (E4)*............
Saint Benedict (B3)*.... 230
St. Helens (E2)*............4,711
St. Louis (A3)............ 30
Saint Paul (A3)*............ 226
Saloda (D3)............ 12
SALEM (A3)*............43,140
Sams Valley (E5)*........
Sandlake (C2)*............ 300
Sandy (E2)*............1,003
Scappoose (E2)*............ 654
Scholls (A2)............ 70
Scio (E3)*............ 448
Scofield (D2)............ 75
Scotts Mills (B3)*....... 217
Scottsburg (D4)*............ 100
Seal Rock (C3)*............ 330
Seaside (D2)*............3,886
Selma (D5)*............ 125
Seneca (J3)*............ 760
Service Creek (G3)*.... 13
Shaniko (G3)*............ 61
Shaw (A3)............ 150
Sheaville (K4)*............ 64
Shedd (D3)*............ 165
Shelburn (E3)............ 20
Sheridan (D2)*............1,922
Sherwood (A2)*............ 575
Shevlin (F4)............ 600
Siletz (D3)*............ 570
Siltcoos (C4)*............ 28
Silver Lake (F4)*............
Silverton (A3)*............3,146
Silvies (H3)*............
Simnasho (F3)*............ 40
Siskiyou (E5)............ 50
Sisters (F3)*............ 723
Sitkum (D4)*............ 50
Sixes (C5)*............ 250
Sodaville (E3)............ 157
South Junction (G3)*.... 10
Southbeach (C3)*............ 300
Sparta (K3)*............ 25
Sprague River (F5)*....... 350
Spray (H3)*............ 375
Springbrook (A2)*............ 500
Springfield (E3)*.........10,807
Springwater (E2)............ 300
Stanfield (H2)*............ 845
Star (E4)............
Starkey (J2)............ 30
Stauffer (G4)............ 2
Stayton (E3)*............1,507
Sublimity (E3)*............ 367
Summer Lake (G5)*....... 3
Summerville (K2)*............ 73
Summit (D3)*............ 250
Sumner (C4)*............ 141
Sumpter (J3)*............ 146
Sunny Valley (D5)*....... 79
Susanville (J3)*............ 9
Sutherlin (D4)*............2,230
Svensen (D1)............ 100
Sweet Home (E3)*........3,603
Swisshome (D3)*............ 500
Sycamore (B2)............
Sylvan (B2)............1,500
Table Rock (E5)............ 200
Taft (C3)*............ 450
Takilma (D5)*............ 50
Talent (E5)*............ 739
Tallman (E3)............ 25
Tangent (D3)*............ 200
Telocaset (K2)*............ 80
Tenmile (D4)*............ 40
Terrebonne (F3)*............ 198
The Dalles (F2)*............7,676
Thompson (K3)............ 3
Thurston (E3)*............ 66
Tidewater (D3)*............ 100
Tiernan (C3)*............ 200
Tigard (A2)*............ 800
Tillamook (D2)*............3,685
Tiller (E5)*............ 150
Timber (D2)*............ 300
Toledo (D3)*............2,323
Tolovana Park (C2)*.......
Top (H3)*............ 27
Trail (E5)*............ 45
Trent (E4)*............ 300
Troutdale (E2)*............ 541
Troy (K2)*............ 150
Tualatin (A2)*............ 248
Tumalo (F3)............ 20
Turner (E3)*............ 610
Twin Rocks (C2)*............ 300
Tygh Valley (F2)*............ 449
Ukiah (J2)*............ 300
Umapine (J2)*............ 50
Umatilla (H2)*............ 883
Umpqua (D4)*............ 20
Union (K2)*............1,307
Union Creek (E5)............ 100
Unity (J3)*............ 212
Vale (K4)*............1,518
Valley Falls (G5)............ 14
Valsetz (D3)*............ 60
Van (J4)*............ 5
Vaughn (D3)............ 200
Venator (J4)............ 28
Veneta (D3)*............ 750
Verboort (A2)............ 125
Vernonia (D2)*............1,521
Vida (E3)*............ 250
Viento (F2)............ 50
Viola (B2)............ 50
Waconda (A3)............ 50
Wagontire (H4)............ 3
Waldport (C3)*............ 689
Walker (D4)............ 100
Wallowa (K2)*............1,055
Walterville (E3)*............ 100
Walton (D3)*............ 70
Wamic (F2)*............ 125
Wapinitia (F2)............ 20
Warm Springs (F3)*.... 350
Warren (E2)*............ 81
Warrendale (F2)............ 50
Warrenton (C1)*............1,896
Wasco (G2)*............ 305
Waterloo (E3)*............ 180
Waterman (H3)............
Wauna (D1)*............ 325
Weatherby (K3)............ 25
Wecoma Beach (C3)*.... 350
Wedderburn (C5)*............ 250
Welches (E2)*............ 119
Wemme (E2)*............ 109
Wendling (E3)*............ 124
West Linn (B2)*............2,945
West Portland (B2).....3,000
W. Salem (A3)............
W. Side (G5)............ 16
W. Woodburn (A3)............ 150
Westfall (K3)*............ 3
Westfir (E4)*............1,200
Westlake (C4)*............ 180
Weston (J2)*............ 679
Westport (D1)*............ 600
Wheeler (D2)*............ 291
Wheeler Heights (C2)... 125
Whiteson (D2)*............ 200
Whitney (J3)............ 3
Wilark (D2)............ 10
Wilbur (D4)*............ 150
Wilderville (D5)*............ 300
Wilhoit (B3)............ 5
Wilkesboro (A2)............ 45
Willamette (B2)*............
Willamina (D2)*............1,082
Williams (D5)*............ 100
Willowcreek (K3)*............ 300
Willowdale (G3)............ 35
Willows (G2)............ 100
Wilsonville (A2)*............ 162
Wimer (D5)............ 100
Winchester (D4)*............ 300
Winchester Bay (C4)*.... 500
Wing (K3)............
Winlock (H3)............ 12
Wolf Creek (D5)*............ 250
Wonder (D5)*............ 300
Woodburn (A3)*............2,395
Woods (C2)............ 110
Worden (F5)*............
Wyeth (F2)............ 15
Yachats (C3)*............ 300
Yamhill (D2)*............ 539
Yamsay Station (F4)....
Yaquina (C3)*............ 76
Yoder (B3)............ 150
Yoncalla (D4)*............ 626
Zigzag (F2)*............ 150
Zumwalt (L2)............ 2

Map on Page 85

PENNSYLVANIA

Total Population 10,498,012

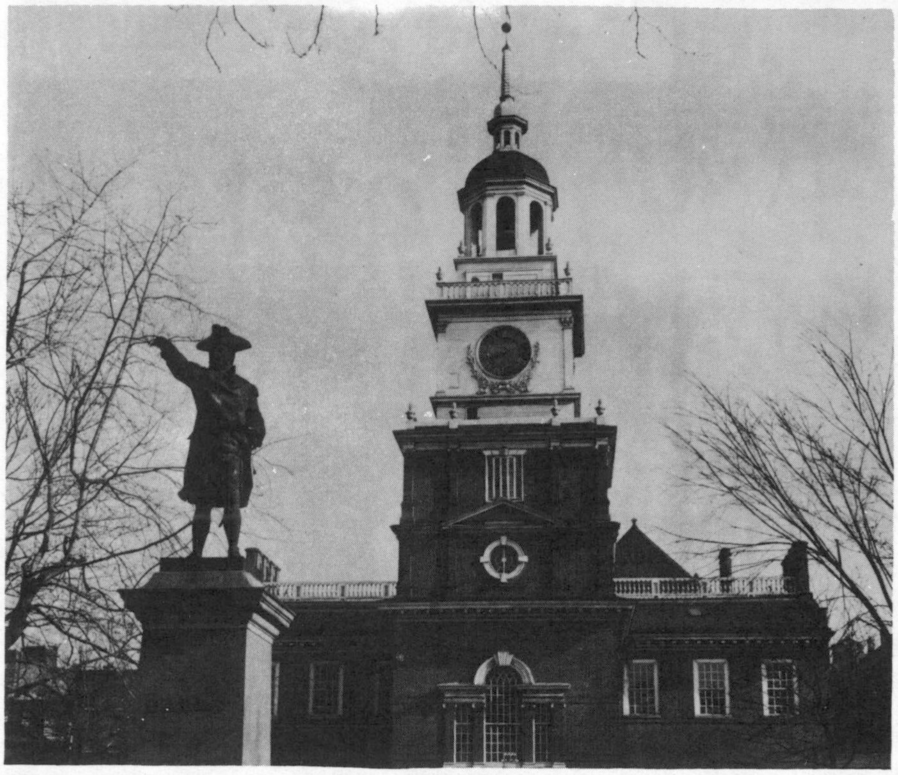

67 COUNTIES

Adams (H6)............44,197
Allegheny (B5)........1,515,237
Armstrong (D4)............80,842
Beaver (B4)............175,192
Bedford (E6)............40,775
Berks (K5)............255,740
Blair (F4)............139,514
Bradford (J2)............51,722
Bucks (M5)............144,620
Butler (C4)............97,320
Cambria (E4)............209,541
Cameron (F3)............7,023
Carbon (L4)............57,558
Centre (G4)............65,922
Chester (L6)............159,141
Clarion (D3)............38,344
Clearfield (F3)............85,957
Clinton (G3)............36,532
Columbia (K3)............53,460
Crawford (B2)............78,948
Cumberland (H5)............94,457
Dauphin (J5)............197,784
Delaware (M6)............414,234
Elk (E3)............34,503
Erie (B2)............219,388
Fayette (C6)............189,899
Forest (D2)............4,944
Franklin (G6)............75,927
Fulton (F6)............10,387
Greene (B6)............45,394
Huntingdon (F5)............40,872
Indiana (D4)............77,106
Jefferson (D3)............49,147
Juniata (H4)............15,243
Lackawanna (L3)............257,396
Lancaster (K5)............234,717
Lawrence (B4)............105,120
Lebanon (K5)............81,683
Lehigh (L4)............198,207
Luzerne (L3)............392,241
Lycoming (H3)............101,249
Mc Kean (E2)............56,607
Mercer (B3)............111,954
Mifflin (G4)............43,691
Monroe (M3)............33,773
Montgomery (M5)....353,068
Montour (J3)............16,001
Northampton (M4)....185,243
Northumberland (J4) 117,115
Perry (H5)............24,782
Philadelphia (M6)...2,071,605
Pike (M3)............8,425
Potter (G2)............16,810
Schuylkill (K4)............200,577
Snyder (H4)............22,912
Somerset (D6)............81,813
Sullivan (J3)............6,745
Susquehanna (L2)............31,970
Tioga (H2)............35,474
Union (H4)............23,150
Venango (C3)............65,328
Warren (D2)............42,698
Washington (B5)........209,628
Wayne (M2)............28,478
Westmoreland (D5)....313,179
Wyoming (K2)............16,766
York (J6)............202,737

CITIES and TOWNS

Aaronsburg (H4)*........ 350
Abbottstown (J6)*........ 538
Adamsburg ‡(C5)*........ 238
Adamstown (K5)*........1,020
Adamsville (B2)*........ 200
Addison (D6)*........ 237
Adrian (D4)*........ 130
Airville (K6)*........ 125
Aitch (F5)*........ 219
Akeley (D2)*........ 50
Akron (K5)*........1,028
Alba (J2)*........ 190
Albion (B2)*........1,729
Albrightsville (L3)*........ 150
Alburtis (L5)*........ 979
Aldan (M7)*........3,430
Aldenville (M2)*........ 100
Alexandria (F4)*........ 443
Aliquippa (B4)*........26,132
Allen (H5)*........ 395
Allenport ‡(C5)* 923
Allensville (G4)*........ 300
Allentown (L4)*........106,756
Allentown-Bethlehem (urban area)........225,155
Allenwood (H3)*........ 367
Allison Park (C4)*........2,000
Altoona (F4)*........77,177
Altoona (urban area)..86,249
Alum Bank (E5)*........ 342
Amberson (G5)*........
Ambler (M5)*........4,565
Ambridge (B4)*........16,429
Amity (B5)*........ 240
Andalusia (N5)*........1,800
Anita (D3)*........ 350
Annville (J5)*........3,564
Ansonville (E4)*........ 158
Antes Fort (H3)*........ 300
Antrim (H2)*........ 300
Apollo (D4)*........3,015
Applewold ‡(C4)*........ 500
Ararat (L2)*........ 72
Arbuckle (C1)........ 25
Arcadia (E4)*........ 500
Archbald (M2)*........6,304
Ardmore (M6)*........20,000
Arendtsville (H6)*........ 409
Argentine (C3)*........ 150
Armagh ‡(E4)*........ 176
Arnold (C4)*........10,263
Arnot (H2)*........ 300
Arona ‡(C5)*........ 482
Artemas (E6)*........ 19
Ashland (K4)*........6,192
Ashley (L3)*........5,243
Ashville (F4)*........ 441
Aspers (H6)*........ 220
Aspinwall (C6)*........4,084
Atglen (K6)*........ 668
Athens (K2)*........4,430
Athol (L5)*........ 200
Atlantic ....(B3)*........ 157
Atlas (K4)*........3,090
Atwood ‡(D4)........ 110
Auburn (K4)*........ 994
Aultman (D4)*........ 600
Austin (F2)*........ 804
Avalon (B6)*........6,463
Avella (B5)*........1,356
Avis (H3)*........1,193
Avoca (L3)*........4,040
Avondale (L6)*........ 941
Avonmore (C4)*........1,367
Baden (B4)*........3,732
Bainbridge (J5)*........ 500
Bakers Summit (F5)*.... 70
Bakerstville (D5)........ 170
Bala-Cynwyd (N6)*........
Bally (L5)*........ 753
Bangor (M4)*........6,050
Barnesboro (E4)*........3,442
Barto (L5)*........ 151
Bartonsville (M4)*........ 150
Bath (M4)*........1,824
Baxter (D3)*........ 87
Beach Haven (K3)*........ 500
Beachlake (M2)*........ 250
Beadling (B7)*........ 500
Beallsville (C5)*........ 598
Bear Creek (L3)*........ 150
Bear Lake (C1)*........ 239
Beaver (B4)*........6,360
Beaver Falls (B4)*........17,375
Beaver Meadows (L4)*.1,723
Beaver Spgs. (H4)*........ 750
Beaverdale (E5)*........2,200
Beavertown (H4)*........ 700
Bechtelsville ‡(L5)*........ 603
Bedford (F5)*........3,521
Bedford Valley (E6)........ 300
Bedminster (M5)*........ 500
Beech Creek (G3)*........ 574
Belle Vernon (C5)*........2,271
Bellefonte (G4)*........5,651
Belleville (G4)*........1,304
Bellevue (B6)*........11,604
Bellwood (F4)*........2,559
Ben Avon (B6)*........2,465
Ben Avon Hts. ‡(B5)........ 394
Bendersville (H6)*........ 409
Benezett (F3)*........ 400
Benson (Hollsopple*) (E5) 377
Bentleyville (B5)*........3,295
Benton (K3)*........ 890
Berlin (E6)*........1,507
Bermudian (J5)........ 50
Bernharts (K5)........ 760
Bernville (K5)*........ 363
Berrysburg (J4)*........ 386
Berwick (K3)*........14,010
Berwyn (L5)*........3,000
Bessemer (B4)*........1,461
Bethany (M2)........ 148
Bethel (K5)*........ 500
Bethel (B7)........11,324
Bethlehem (M4)*........66,340
Bethlehem-Allentown (urban area)........225,155
Betula (F2)*........ 90
Big Cove Tannery (F6)* 25
Big Run (E4)*........ 896
Bigler (F4)*........ 500
Biglerville (H6)*........ 870
Birchardville (L2)*........ 35
Birdsboro (L5)*........3,158
Birmingham (F4)*........ 178
Black Lick (D4)*........1,000
Blain (H5)*........ 315
Blairs Mills (G5)*........ 150
Blairsville (D5)*........5,000
Blakely ‡(L3)........6,828
Blakeslee (L3)*........ 50
Blanchard (G3)*........ 550
Blandburg (F4)*........1,200
Blawnox (C6)*........2,165
Bloomfield (New Bloomfield*) (H5).....1,098
Blooming Grove (M3)*.. 113
Blooming Valley (B2).... 256
Bloomsburg (J3)*........10,633
Blossburg (H2)*........1,954
Blue Ridge Summit (G6)* 650
Blythedale (C5)*........ 890
Boalsburg (G4)*........ 500
Bobtown (B6)*........1,553
Bodines (H3)*........ 110
Boiling Spgs. (H5)*........ 900
Bolivar (D5)*........ 828
Boltz (E5)*........ 250
Boothwyn (L7)*........4,500
Boston (C7)*........1,700
Boswell (E5)*........1,679
Bowmansdale (J5)*........ 200
Bowmanstown (L4)*........ 878
Bowmansville (L5)*........ 350
Boyers (C3)*........ 800
Boyertown (L5)*........4,074
Brackenridge (C4)*........6,178
Brackney (K2)*........ 75
Braddock (C7)*........16,488
Braddock Hills (C7)......1,965
Bradford (E2)*........17,354
Bradfordwoods ‡(B4)*.. 458
Braeburn (C5)*........ 800
Branch Dale (K4)*........1,500
Branchton (C3)*........ 130
Brave (B6)*........ 200
Brentwood (B7)*........12,535
Briar Creek (K3)*........ 348
Brickerville (K5)........ 150
Bridgeport (M5)*........5,827
Bridgeville (B5)*........5,650
Bridgewater (W. Bridgewater*) (B4)....1,316
Brisbin (F4)*........ 463
Bristol (N5)*........12,710
Broad Ford (C5)*........ 112
Broad Top (F5)*........ 483
Brockport (E3)*........ 450
Brockway (E3)*........2,650
Brodbecks (J6)*........ 50
Brodheadsville (M4)*.... 550
Brogueville (J6)*........ 55
Brookhaven (M7)........1,042
Brooklyn (L2)*........ 500
Brookville (D3)*........4,274
Broomall (M6)*........6,000
Broughton (B7)*........2,500
Brownfield (C6)*........
Brownstown (K5)........ 700
Brownstown ‡(E5)........1,508
Brownsville (C5)*........7,643
Bruceton (B7)*........ 250
Bruin (C3)*........ 717
Bryn Athyn (M5)*........ 913
Bryn Mawr (M5)*........12,000
Bucksville (M5)*........ 200
Buffalo Mills (E6)*........ 105
Bulger (B5)*........ 800
Burgettstown (A5)*........2,379
Burlington (J2)*........ 148
Burnham (H4)*........2,954
Burnside (E4)*........ 400
Burnt Cabins (G5)*........ 125
Burrows (G2)........ 15
Bushkill (M3)*........ 500
Butler (C4)*........23,482
Byrnedale (E3)*........ 500
Cadogan (C4)*........ 727
Cairnbrook (E5)*........1,504
Caledonia (F3)........ 300
California (C5)*........2,831
Callensburg (D3)*........ 261
Callery (C4)*........ 407
Cambra (K3)*........ 100
Cambridge Spgs. (C2)*.2,246
Cameron (F3)*........ 114
Cammal (H3)*........ 120
Camp Hill (H5)*........5,934
Camptown (K2)*........ 300
Canadensis (M3)*........ 400
Cannelton (A4)*........ 100
Canonsburg (B5)*........12,072
Canton (J2)*........2,118
Carbondale (L2)*........16,296
Carlisle (H5)*........16,812
Carlton (C3)*........ 50
Carmichaels (C6)*........ 895
Carnegie (B7)*........12,105
Carrolltown (E4)*........1,452
Cashtown (H6)*........ 270
Cassandra (E5)*........ 381
Casselman (D6)........ 130
Cassville (G5)*........ 158
Castle Shannon (B7)*..5,459
Catasauqua (M4)*........4,923
Catawissa (K4)*........2,000
Cecil (B5)*........1,200
Cedar Run (H2)*........ 62
Center Moreland (K3)*.. 100
Center Road (A2)........ 35
Centerport ‡(K5)*........ 226
Centerville (C2)*........ 245
Centerville (B6)........5,845
Central City (E5)*........1,935
Centralia (K4)*........1,986
Centre Hall (G4)*........ 834
Cessna (F5)........ 50
Chalfant ‡(C7)........1,381
Chalfont (M5)*........ 828
Chambersburg (G6)*...17,212
Chambersville (D4)*........ 300
Chandlers Valley (D2)* 170
Chaneysville (F6)........ 80
Chapman ‡(M4)........ 285
Charleroi (C5)*........9,872
Cheltenham (M5)*....△22,854
Cherry Tree (E4)*........ 517
Cherry Valley (C3)........ 94
Chest Springs (E4)*..... 232
Chester (L7)*........66,039
Chester Hts. (L7)*........ 474
Chester Hill ‡(F4)........ 954
Cheswick (C6)*........1,534
Cheyney (M6)*........ 289
Chicora (C4)*........1,172
Choconut (K2)........ 50
Christiana (K6)*........1,043
Churchill ‡(C7)........1,733
Churchtown (L5)*........ 250
Clairton (C7)*........19,652
Clarence (G3)*........1,700
Clarendon (D2)*........ 748
Clarington (D3)*........ 125
Clarion (D3)*........4,409
Clark (B3)*........ 345
Clarks Green ‡(L3)*.... 824
Clarks Mills (B3)*........ 100
Clarks Summit (L3)........2,940
Clarksville (B6)*........ 428
Clarksville (Clark*) (B3) 345
Claysburg (F5)*........1,355
Claysville (B5)*........ 963
Claytonia (B3)........ 50
Clear Ridge (F5)*........ 31
Clearfield (F3)*........9,357
Clearville (F6)*........ 200
Cleona ‡(K5)*........1,483
Clermont (E2)*........ 175
Clifford (L2)*........ 300
Clifton Heights (M7)*..7,549
Climax (D4)*........ 300
Clinton (B5)*........ 575
Clintondale (H3)........ 120
Clintonville (C3)*........ 307
Cloe (E4)*........ 275
Clune (D4)*........ 500
Clymer (E4)*........2,500
Coal Center ‡(C5)*........ 584
Coal Valley (C7)*........ 700
Coaldale (L4)*........5,318
Coaldale ‡(F5)........ 231
Coalmont ‡(F5)*........ 207
Coalport (E4)*........1,052
Coatesville (L5)*........13,826
Coburn (H4)*........ 280
Cochranton (B2)*........1,092
Cochranville (L6)*........ 350
Cocolamus (H4)*........
Codorus (J6)*........ 449
Cogan Station (H3)*........ 39
Cokeburg (B5)*........1,170
Cokeville (D5)*........ 50
Colegrove (F2)*........ 50
Collegeville (M5)*........1,900
Colley (K2)*........ 100
Collingdale (N7)*........8,443
Colmar (M5)........ 600
Columbia (K5)*........11,993
Columbus (C2)*........
Colver (E4)*........1,708
Colwyn ‡(M7)........2,143
Commodore (D4)*........ 450
Concord (G5)*........ 190
Concordville (M6)*........ 126
Conemaugh (E5)*........5,000
Conestoga (K6)*........ 480
Confluence (D6)*........1,037
Conneaut Lake (B2)*.... 676
Conneaut Lake Park (B2) 225
Conneautville (A2)*........1,177
Connellsville (D5)*........13,293
Conoquenessing (B4)*... 441
Conrad (G2)........ 15
Conshohocken (M5)*....10,922
Conway (B4)*........1,570
Conyngham (K3)*........ 935
Cooksburg (D3)*........ 50
Coopersburg (M5)*........1,462
Cooperstown (C2)........ 271
Coplay (L4)*........2,994
Coral (D5)*........ 675
Coraopolis (B4)*........10,498
Cornwall (K5)*........1,760
Corry (C2)*........7,911
Corsica (D3)*........ 421
Corydon (D2)*........ 250
Coryville (F2)*........ 320
Costello (G2)........ 100
Coudersport (G2)*........3,210
Courtdale ‡(L3)........ 982
Covington (J2)*........ 725
Cowan (H4)........ 105
Cowanesque (H2)*........ 200
Cowansville (C4)*........ 306
Crafton (B7)*........8,066
Cranberry (C3)*........ 450
Cranesville (B2)*........ 602
Creekside (D4)*........ 525
Creighton (C4)*........
Crenshaw (E3)*........
Cresco (M3)*........ 150
Cresson (E5)*........2,569
Cressona (K4)*........1,758
Crosby (F2)*........ 400
Cross Fork (G3)*........ 85
Cross Roads ‡(J6)........ 178
Crum Lynne (M7)*........3,500
Cuddy (B5)*........2,500
Curllsville (D3)*........ 156
Curryville (F5)*........ 150
Curwensville (E4)*........3,332
Custer City (E2)*........ 500
Cyclone (E2)*........ 700
Dagus Mines (E3)*........ 500
Daguscahonda (E3)*........ 190
Daisytown ‡(E5)........ 442
Dale ‡(E5)........3,310
Dallas (K3)*........1,674
Dallastown (J6)*........3,304
Dalmatia (J4)*........ 517

Dalton (L2)* 1,109
Damascus (M2)* 300
Danielsville (M4)*
Danville (J4)* 6,994
Darby (N7)* 13,154
Darling (L7)* 50
Darlington (A4)* 354
Dauphin (J5)* 667
Dawson (C5)* 723
Dayton (D4)* 828
De Lancey (D4)* 300
De Young (E2)* 85
Deemston ‡(B5) 775
Deep Valley (A6)* 95
Deer Lake ‡(L4) 174
Delano (K4)* 950
Delaware Water Gap (N4)* 734
Delmont (D5)* 695
Delta (K6)* 840
Denbo (C6)* 1,300
Dents Run (F3) 30
Denver (K5)* 1,658
Derry (D5)* 3,752
Devault (L5)* 300
Dewart (J3)* 350
Diamond (C2)* 100
Dickinson (H5)* 250
Dickson City (L3)* 8,948
Dillsburg (J5)* 1,146
Dilltown (E5)* 200
Dimock (L2)* 100
Dingmans Ferry (N3)* 525
Dixonville (D4)* 1,050
Donegal (D5)* 198
Donora (C5)* 12,186
Dormont (B7)* 13,405
Douglassville (L5)* 800
Dover (J6)* 809
Downingtown (L5)* 4,948
Doylestown (M5)* 5,262
Dravosburg (C7)* 3,786
Drexel Hill (M6)* 40,000
Drifton (L3)* 950
Driftwood (F3)* 289
Drums (K3)* 450
Dry Run (G5)* 200
Du Bois (E3)* 11,497
Dublin (M5)* 400
Duboistown (H3) 1,140
Dudley (F5)* 350
Duke Center (F2)* 1,200
Dunbar (C6)* 1,363
Duncannon (H5)* 1,852
Duncansville (F5)* 1,391
Dunkard (B6)*
Dunlevy ‡(C5)* 379
Dunlo (E5)* 2,200
Dunmore (L3)* 20,305
Dunns Station (B5)* 45
Dupont ‡(L3)* 4,107
Duquesne (C7)* 17,620
Duryea (L3)* 6,655
Dushore (K2)* 759
Eagles Mere (J3)* 157
E. Bangor (M4)* 988
E. Berlin (J6)* 913
E. Brady (C3)* 1,400
E. Butler (C4)* 758
E. Conemaugh ‡(E5) 4,101
E. Freedom (E5)* 325
E. Greenville (L5)* 1,945
E. Hickory (D2)* 232
E. Lansdowne ‡(M7) 3,527
E. Mauch Chunk ‡(L4)* 3,132
E. McKeesport ‡(C5)* 3,171
E. Petersburg (K5)* 1,268
E. Pittsburgh (C7)* 5,259
E. Prospect (J6)* 500
E. Rochester ‡(B4) 985
E. Side (L3)* 286
E. Smithfield (J2)* 250
E. Springfield (A2)* 499
E. Stroudsburg (M4)* 7,274
E. Vandergrift ‡(C4)* 1,665
E. Washington ‡(B5) 2,304
E. Waterford (G5)* 185
Easton (M4)* 35,632
Eastvale ‡(B4) 534
Eau Claire (C3)* 403
Ebensburg (E5)* 4,086
Echo (D4) 200
Eckley (L3)* 650
Eddington (N5)* 2,000
Eddystone (M7)* 3,014
Eden Park (C7) 1,531
Edgewood (B7)* 5,292
Edgeworth ‡(B4) 1,466
Edinboro (B2)* 1,567
Edinburg (B3)* 450
Edison (M5)* 450
Edwardsville ‡(L3) 6,686
Effort (M4)* 300
Elbon (E3)* 150
Elco ‡(C5)* 596
Eldersville (A5)* 250
Elderton (D4)* 336
Eldred (F2)* 1,199
Eldredsville (J2)* 20
Elgin (C2)* 202
Elimsport (H3)* 75
Elizabeth (C5)* 2,615
Elizabethtown (J5)* 5,083
Elizabethville (J5)* 1,506
Elkins Park (M5)* 12,000
Elkland (H1)* 2,326
Elliottsburg (H5)* 100
Elliottsville (C6) 120
Ellisburg (G2)* 100
Ellport ‡(B4) 1,122
Ellsworth (B5)* 1,670
Ellwood City (B4)* 12,945
Elmhurst (M3)* 800
Elmora (E4)* 1,850
Elrama (C5)* 1,675
Elverson (L5)* 370
Elwyn (L7)* 1,800
Elysburg (K4)* 700
Embreeville (L6)* 48
Emeigh (E4)*
Emigsville (J5)* 650
Emlenton (C3)* 945
Emmaus (M4)* 7,780
Emporium (F2)* 3,646
Emsworth (B6)* 3,128
Endeavor (D2)* 400
Enola (J5)* 2,500
Enon Valley (B4)* 392
Entriken (F5)* 101
Ephrata (K5)* 7,027
Equinunk (M2)* 300
Erie (B1)* 130,803
Erie (urban area) 151,282
Ernest (D4)* 1,170
Erwinna (N5)* 150
Espy (K4)* 700
Espyville Station (B2)* 75
Essington (M7)* 3,700
Esterly (L5)* 900
Etna (B6)* 6,750
Etters (J5)* 558
Evans City (B4)* 1,637
Evansburg (Evans City) (B4) 1,637
Evansville (L5)* 100
Everett (F5)* 97
Everson (C5)* 1,520
Exeter ‡(L3)* 5,130
Export (C5)* 1,690
Factoryville (L2)* 1,005
Fairchance (C6)* 2,091
Fairdale (L2)* 300
Fairfield (H6)* 451
Fairhope (E6)* 166
Fairmount Spgs. (K3) 50
Fairoaks (B4)* 1,600
Fairview (B1)* 697
Fairview ‡(C4) 259
Falls (L3)* 315
Falls Creek (E3)* 1,191
Fallsington (N5)* 830
Fallston ‡(B4) 511
Fannettsburg (G5)* 290
Farrell (A3)* 13,644
Fawn Grove (J6)* 397
Fayette City (C5)* 1,404
Fayetteville (H6)* 956
Felton (J6)* 429
Ferndale (M4)* 194
Ferndale (D5) 2,619
Fernwood (M7)* 400
Fertigs (C3)* 108
Finleyville (B5)* 684
Fleetwood (L5)* 2,338
Fleming (G4)* 320
Flemington (G3)* 1,446
Florence (A5)* 150
Florin (J5)* 1,319
Folcroft (M7)* 1,909
Folsom (M7)* 2,500
Force (E3)* 500
Ford City (D4)* 5,352
Ford Cliff (D4)* 597
Forest City (L2)* 3,122
Forest Hills ‡(C5)* 6,301
Fort Littleton (F5)* 117
Forestville (B3)* 150
Forksville (J3)* 145
Fort Loudon (G6)* 500
Forty Fort (L3)* 6,173
Fountain Hill ‡(M4) 5,456
Fox Chapel (C6) 1,721
Foxburg (C3)* 422
Frackville (K4)* 6,541
Frankfort Spgs. (A4) 149
Franklin (C3)* 10,006
Franklin ‡(E5) 1,833
Franklintown (H5)* 328
Fredericksburg (J5)* 850
Fredericktown (C6)* 1,000
Fredonia (B3)* 588
Freeburg (H4)* 506
Freedom (B4)* 3,000
Freehold (D2) 120
Freeland (L3)* 5,909
Freemansburg (M4)* 1,739
Freeport (C4)* 2,685
Friendsville (L2)* 65
Frugality (F4) 63
Fryburg (D3)* 300
Gaines (G2)* 125
Galeton (G2)* 1,646
Gallitzin (E4)* 3,102
Ganister (F5)* 253
Gap (L6)* 850
Garards Fort (B6)* 200
Garland (C2)* 450
Garrett (D6)* 761
Geistown (E5)* 2,148
Gelatt (L2)* 110
Genesee (G2)* 600
Geneva (B2)* 335
Georgetown (A4)* 246
Germania (G2)* 200
Gettysburg (H6)* 7,046
Gibson (L2)* 100
Gilberton (K4)* 2,641
Gilbertsville (L5)* 500
Gilfoyle (D3) 25
Gillett (J2)* 200
Gipsy (E4)* 300
Girard (B2)* 2,141
Girardville (K4)* 3,864
Glasgow (E4)* 214
Glassport (C7)* 8,707
Gleasonton (G3) 150
Glen Campbell (E4)* 510
Glen Lyon (K3)* 3,921
Glen Olden (M7)* 6,450
Glen Riddle (L7)* 300
Glen Rock (J6)* 1,477
Glen Union (G3)* 19
Glencoe (E6)* 80
Glendon ‡(M4) 601
Glenfield (B4)* 870
Glenhope (F4)* 199
Gleniron (H4)* 250
Glenshaw (C6)* 8,000
Glenside (M5)* 8,000
Glenwillard (B4)* 1,200
Goldsboro (Etters*) (J5) 558
Gordon ‡(K4)* 1,039
Gouldsboro (L3)* 462
Graceton (D4)* 500
Grampian (E4)* 589
Grand Valley (D2)*
Granville (G4)* 2,157
Grapeville (C5)* 1,563
Grassflat (F3)* 1,000
Gratz (J4)* 653
Gray (D5)* 600
Grays Landing (C6)* 450
Graysville (B6)* 300
Great Bend (L2)* 751
Greeley (N3)* 590
Green Lane (M5)* 550
Greenburr (H4)* 125
Greencastle (G6) 2,661
Greene (K6)* 75
Greensboro (B6)* 651
Greensburg (D5)* 16,923
Greentree (B7) 2,818
Greenville (B3)* 9,210
Grove City (B3)* 7,411
Grover (J2)* 200
Guys Mills (C2)* 300
Hadley (B3)* 350
Halifax (J5)* 822
Hallstead (L2)* 1,445
Hallton (E3)* 75
Hamburg (L4)* 3,805
Hamilton (D4)* 100
Hamlin (M3)* 250
Hampton (H6)* 200
Hannastown (D5)* 800
Hanover (J6)* 14,048
Harborcreek (C1)* 500
Harford (L2)* 185
Harmarville (C6)* 3,000
Harmonsburg (B2)* 350
Harmony (B4)* 912
HARRISBURG (J5)* 89,544
Harrisburg (urban area) 168,933
Harrison Valley (G2)* 400
Harrisonville (F6)* 23
Harrisville (B3)* 780
Hartleton ‡(H4) 240
Hartstown (B2)* 160
Hartsville (M5)*
Harveys Lake (L3)* 1,500
Hastings (E4)* 1,846
Hatboro (M5)* 4,788
Hatfield (M5)* 1,624
Haverford (M6)* ▲39,641
Havertown (M6)* 22,000
Hawk Run (F4)*
Hawley (M3)* 1,602
Hawthorn (D3)* 666
Haysville (B4) 177
Hazel Hurst (E1)* 600
Hazleton (L4)* 35,491
Hegins (K4)*
Heidelberg (B7) 2,250
Heilwood (E4)* 1,000
Hellam (J6)* 976
Hellertown (M4)* 5,435
Helvetia (E3) 500
Hendersonville (B5)* 600
Henryville (M3)* 100
Hereford (L5)* 225
Herman (C4)* 700
Herminie (C5)* 2,072
Herndon (J4)* 677
Herrick Center (L2)* 190
Hershey (J5)* 4,500
Hesston (F5)* 137
High Spire (J5)* 2,799
Hilliards (C3)* 230
Hillsdale (E4)* 200
Hillsgrove (J3)* 337
Hillsville (A4)*
Hokendauqua (L4)* 1,460
Hollidaysburg (F5)* 6,483
Hollsopple (E5)* 377
Holtwood (K6)* 500
Home (D4)* 82
Homer City (D4)* 2,372
Homestead (B7)* 10,046
Homewood ‡(B4)* 316
Honesdale (M2)* 5,662
Honey Brook (L5)* 864
Hookstown (B4)* 247
Hooversville (E5)* 1,240
Hop Bottom (L2)* 375
Hopeland (K5)* 400
Hopewell (F5)* 360
Horning (B7) 500
Houston (B5)* 1,957
Houtzdale (F4)* 1,306
Howard (G3)* 754
Hoytville (H2) 13
Hughestown ‡(L3) 1,888
Hughesville (J3)* 2,095
Hummelstown (J5)* 3,789
Hunkers ‡(C5)* 404
Huntingdon (G5)* 7,330
Huntingdon Mills (K3)* 300
Hustontown (F5)* 200
Hyde Park (D4)* 758
Hydetown (C2)* 530
Hyndman (E6)* 1,322
Hyner (G3)* 300
Ickesburg (H5)* 250
Idaville (H5)* 325
Imler (E5)* 175
Immaculata (L6)* 400
Imperial (B5)* 1,895
Indiana (D4)* 11,743
Industry (B4) 468
Inglesmith (F6) 14
Ingram (B7)* 4,236
Intercourse (K5)* 550
Irvine (D2)* 300
Irvona (E4)* 915
Irwin (C5)* 4,228
Iselin (D4)*
Ivyland (M5)* 358
Jackson (L2)* 100
Jackson Center (B3)* 266
Jacksonville ‡(D4) 204
Jacobus (J6)* 706
James City (E2)* 500
Jamestown (A3)* 931
Jeanesville (K4)* 500
Jeannette (C5)* 16,172
Jeddo ‡(L3)* 262
Jefferson (B6)* 575
Jefferson (Codorus*) (J6) 449
Jenkintown (M5)* 5,130
Jennerstown (D5)* 376
Jermyn (L2)* 2,535
Jerome (D5)* 1,960
Jersey Mills (H3)* 90
Jersey Shore (H3)* 5,595
Jerseytown (J3)* 165
Jessup (L3)* 6,650
Johnsonburg (E3)* 4,567
Johnstown (D5)* 63,232
Johnstown (urban area) 92,780
Jollytown (B6)* 100
Jones Mills (D5)* 150
Jonestown (K5)* 853
Josephine (D5)* 675
Julian (G4)* 196
Kane (E2)* 5,706
Karns City (C4)* 508
Karthaus (F3)* 575
Kato (G3)
Kaylor (C4)* 300
Kearsarge (B1) 375
Keating Summit (F2)* 70
Keewaydin (F3) 121
Kelayres (K4)* 1,059
Kellettville (D2)* 80
Kelly Station (C4)* 81
Kempton (L4)*
Kenhorst ‡(L5) 2,551
Kennard (B3)* 175
Kennett Square (L6)* 3,699
Kent (D4)* 175
Kerrmoor (E4)* 120
Kersey (E3)* 500
Kimble (M3) 72
Kimmelton (E5)* 156
Kingsdale (H6) 103
Kingston (K3)* 21,096
Kintnersville (M4)* 77
Kinzua (E2)* 475
Kirkwood (K6)* 102
Kistler ‡(G5) 468
Kittanning (C4)* 7,731
Knobsville (G6)* 117
Knox (C3)* 1,213
Knoxville (H2)* 656
Koppel (B4)* 1,137
Kresgeville (L4)* 250
Kulpmont (J4)* 5,199
Kulpsville (M5)*
Kunkletown (M4)* 300
Kushequa (E2)* 100
Kutztown (L4)* 3,110
Kyler (E3)
La Anna (M3) 120
La Jose (E4)* 180
La Plume (L2)* 50
Laceyville (K2)* 505
Lackawaxen (N3)* 450
Laflin ‡(L3) 256
Lairdsville (J3)* 150
Lake Ariel (M3)* 400
Lake Como (M2)* 102
Lakemont (F5)* 1,600
Lakewood (M2)* 200
Lamar (H4)* 225
Lamartine (C3)* 250
Lampeter (K6)* 443
Lancaster (K5)* 63,774
Lancaster (urban area) 76,087
Landenberg (L6)* 225
Lander (D2) 131
Landingville ‡(K4)* 230
Landisburg (H5)* 279
Lanesboro (M2)* 591
Langdondale (F5)* 300
Langeloth (A5)* 1,068
Langhorne (N5)* 1,579
Langhorne Manor ‡(N5) 781
Lansdale (M5)* 9,762
Lansdowne (M7)* 12,169
Lanse (F4)* 300
Lansford (L4)* 7,487
Laporte (K3)* 199
Larabee (F2) 50
Large (C7)* 500
Larimer (C8)* 1,057
Larksville ‡(L3) 6,360
Latrobe (D5)* 11,811
Laurel (K6)* 159
Laurel Gardens (B6)* 1,200
Laurel Run ‡(L3) 858
Laureldale (L5)* 3,585
Laurelton (H4)* 375
Lavery (B2)
Lawn (J5)* 200
Lawrenceville (H2)* 479
Lawton (K2)* 140
Le Raysville (K2)* 310
Le Roy (J2)* 125
Lebanon (K5)* 28,156
Lebanon Independent ‡(K5) 2,778
Lecontes Mills (F3)* 200
Leechburg (C4)* 4,042
Leeper (D3)* 275
Leesburg (B3) 150
Leesport (K5)* 700
Leetsdale (B4)* 2,411
Lehighton (L4)* 6,565
Lehman (K3)* 580
Lemasters (G6)* 325
Lemont (G4)* 1,100
Lemont Furnace (C6)*
Lemoyne (J5)* 4,605
Lenhartsville (L4)* 229
Lenni Mills (L7)* 200
Lester (M7)* 2,100
Levittown (N5)*
Lewis Run (E2)* 694
Lewisberry (J5)* 299
Lewisburg (J4)* 5,268
Lewistown (G4)* 13,894
Lewisville (Ulysses*)(G2) 495
Lewisville (L6)* 200
Liberty (H2)* 271
Liberty (C7) 1,900
Library (B7)* 2,124
Ligonier (D5)* 2,160
Lilly (E5)* 1,898
Lima (L7)* 580
Lincoln (K5)* 930
Lincoln University (L6)
Linden (H3)* 262
Linesville (A2)* 1,246
Linfield (L5)* 1,025
Linglestown (J5)* 400
Linwood (L7)* 5,000
Listie (D5)* 700
Listonburg (D6)* 145
Lititz (K5)* 5,568
Little Marsh (H2)* 100
Little Meadows (K2)* 196
Littlestown (H6)* 2,635
Livermore ‡(D5) 57
Liverpool (H4)* 654
Livonia (H4)* 32
Lock Haven (H3)* 11,381
Loganton (H3)* 346
Loganville (J6)* 569
Long Branch ‡(C5) 450
Long Pond (L3)* 50
Lookout (M2)* 300
Lopez (K3)* 800
Lorain ‡(E5) 1,406
Lords Valley (N3)*
Loretto (E4)* 863
Lottsville (D2) 150
Loyalhanna (D5)* 500
Loyalton (J4)* 200
Loysburg (F5)* 175
Loysville (H5)* 500
Lucernemines (D4)* 1,075
Lucinda (D3)* 350
Ludlow (E2)* 500
Lumber City ‡(E4) 262
Lumberville (N5)* 225
Luthersburg (E3)* 240
Luzerne (L3)* 6,176
Lykens (J4)* 2,735
Lyndora (B4)* 4,800
Lyon Station (Lyons) (L5)* 545
Macdonaldton (E6)* 400
Mackeyville (H3)* 200
Macungie (L4)* 983
Maddensville (G5)* 34
Madera (F4)*
Madison ‡(C5)* 386
Madley (E6) 45
Mahaffey (E4)* 646
Mahanoy City (K4)* 10,931
Mainesburg (J2)* 300
Malvern (L5)* 1,764
Mammoth (D5)* 500
Manchester (J5)* 1,264
Manheim (K5)* 4,246
Manns Choice (F6)* 313
Manor (C5)* 1,230
Manorville (C4)* 662
Mansfield (J2)* 2,657
Mapleton Depot (Mapleton) (F5)* 742
Maplewood (M3)* 130
Marcus Hook (L7)* 3,843
Marianna (B5)* 1,269
Marienville (D3)* 1,000
Marietta (J5)* 2,442
Marion (G6)* 650
Marion Center (D4)* 433
Marion Heights ‡(K4) 1,551
Marklesburg (Aitch*) (F5) 219
Markleton (D6)* 92
Markleysburg (C6)* 291
Mars (C4)* 1,385
Marsh Hill (H3) 100
Marshalls Creek (M3)* 200
Martins Creek (M4)* 1,000
Martinsburg (F5)* 1,562
Marvindale (E2) 50
Marwood (C4)* 125
Marysville (H5)* 2,158
Masontown (C6)* 4,550
Matamoras (N3)* 1,761
Mattawana (G5)* 253
Mauch Chunk (L4)* 2,959
Mayburg (D2) 39
Mayfield (L2)* 2,373
Mc Adoo (L4)* 4,260
Mc Alisterville (H4)* 515
Mc Clure (H4)* 1,000
Mc Connellsburg (F6)* 1,126
Mc Crea (H5)* 150
Mc Donald (B5)* 3,543
Mc Elhattan (H3)* 175
Mc Ewensville ‡(J3)* 297
Mc Gees Mills (E4)* 112
Mc Kean (B2)* 379
Mc Kees Rocks (B7)* 16,241
Mc Keesport (C7)* 51,502
Mc Lane (B2) 212
Mc Sherrystown (H6)* 2,510
Mc Veytown (G4)* 546
Meadow Lands (B5)* 1,059
Meadville (B2)* 18,972
Mechanicsburg (H5)* 6,786
Mechanicsville ‡(K4) 540
Media (L7)* 5,726
Medix Run (F3) 100
Mehoopany (K2)* 250
Mercer (B3)* 2,397
Mercersburg (G6)* 1,613
Merion Station (M6)* 2,000
Mertztown (L4)* 200
Meshoppen (L2)* 574
Mexico (H4)* 275
Meyersdale (E6)* 3,137
Middleboro (Mc Kean*) (B2) 379
Middleburg (H4)* 1,283
Middlebury Center (H2)* 90
Middleport (L4)* 942
Middletown (J5)* 9,184
Midland (A4)* 6,491
Midway (B5)* 993
Mifflin (H4)* 835
Mifflinburg (H4)* 2,259
Mifflintown (H4)* 1,013
Milanville (M2)* 200
Mildred (K3)* 1,000
Milesburg (G4)* 733
Milford (N3)* 1,111
Mill Creek (G5)* 417
Mill Hall (G3)* 1,677
Mill Run (C6)* 300
Mill Village (C2)* 324
Millbourne ‡(M6) 901
Millersburg (J4)* 2,861
Millerstown (H4)* 682
Millerstown (Chicora*) (C4) 1,172
Millersville (K6)* 2,551
Millerton (J2)* 250
Millheim (G4)* 750
Millmont (H4)* 250
Millport (F2)* 250
Millrift (N3)* 206
Mills (G2)* 150
Millsboro (B6)* 1,100
Millvale (B7)* 7,287
Millville (J3)* 878
Millway (K5)* 200
Milmont Park (M7)* 2,200
Milroy (G4)* 1,443
Milton (J3)* 8,578
Mineral Point (E5)* 350
Minersville (K4)* 7,783
Mines (F5) 160
Modena ‡(L6) 824
Mohnton (L5)* 2,004
Mohrsville (K5)* 600
Mollenauer (B7)* 700
Monaca (B4)* 7,415
Monessen (C5)* 17,896
Monongahela (B5)* 8,922
Monroeton (Monroe) (J2)* 466
Mont Alto (G6)* 984
Montgomery (H3)* 2,166
Montoursville (J3)* 3,293
Montrose (L2)* 2,075
Moon Run (B5)* 1,143
Moosic (L3)* 3,965
Morgantown (L5)* 415
Morris (H2)* 257
Morris Run (J2)* 600
Morrisdale (F4)* 1,000
Morrisville (N5)* 6,787
Morton (M7)* 1,352
Moscow (L3)* 1,060
Mosgrove (D4)
Moshannon (F3)* 500
Mount Alton (E2)* 105
Mt. Carbon ‡(K4) 302
Mt. Carmel (K4)* 14,222
Mt. Gretna ‡(J5)* 83
Mt. Holly Springs (H5)* 1,701
Mt. Jewett (E2)* 1,415
Mt. Joy (K5)* 3,006
Mt. Lebanon (B7)* ▲26,604
Mt. Morris (B6)*
Mt. Oliver ‡(B7)* 6,646
Mt. Penn ‡(L5) 3,635
Mt. Pleasant (D5)* 5,883
Mt. Pocono (M3)* 619
Mt. Union (G5)* 4,690
Mt. Wolf (J5)* 1,164
Mountainhome (M3)* 750
Mountville (K5)* 1,064
Moylan (L7)* 300
Muir (J4)* 950
Muncy (J3)* 2,756
Muncy Valley (J3)* 310
Munhall (C7)* 16,437
Munson (F4)* 460
Murrysville (C5)* 800
Myerstown (K5)* 3,050
Nanticoke (K3)* 20,160
Nanty Glo (E5)* 5,425
Narberth (M6)* 5,407
Natrona (C4)*
Nazareth (M4)* 5,830
Needmore (F6)* 104
Neelyton (G5)* 100
Neffs Mills (G4) 55
Nelson (H2)*
Nemacolin (B6)* 1,930
Nescopeck (K3)* 1,907
Nesquehoning (L4)*
New Albany (J2)* 365
New Alexandria (C5)* 523
New Baltimore (E6)* 221
New Bedford (A3)* 550
New Berlin (J4)* 589
New Bethlehem (D3)* 1,604
New Bloomfield (H5)* 1,098
New Brighton (B4)* 9,535
New Britain ‡(M5)* 581
New Buena Vista (E5) 300
New Buffalo (H5)* 155
New Castle (B3)* 48,834
New Centerville (D6) 145
New Columbia (H3)* 500
New Columbus ‡(K3) 152
New Cumberland (J5)* 6,204
New Eagle (B5)* 2,316
New Enterprise (F5)* 317
New Florence (D5)* 924
New Freedom (J6)* 1,271
New Freeport (B6)* 150
New Galilee (A4)* 507
New Germantown (G5)* 140
New Holland (K5)* 2,602
New Hope (N5)* 1,066
New Kensington (C4)* 25,146
New Lebanon (B3) 179
New Milford (L2)* 880
New Millport (F4)* 200
New Oxford (H6)* 1,366
New Paris (E5)* 202
New Philadelphia (K4)* 2,200
New Providence (K6)* 220
New Ringgold ‡(K4)* 302
New Salem (C6)* 1,000
New Salem ‡(York New (D5) 695
New Salem ‡(York New Salem*) (J6) 333
New Tripoli (L4)* 258
New Washington ‡(E4) 65
New Wilmington (B3)* 1,943
Newburg (G5)* 182
Newburg ‡(E4) 289
Newfield (G2) 100
Newfoundland (M3)* 650
Newport (H5)* 1,893
Newry (F5)* 412
Newton Hamilton (G5) 397
Newtown (N5)* 2,095
Newville (H5)* 1,788
Nicholson (L2)* 979
Nickleville (C3)* 100
Nineveh (B6)* 76
Nisbet (H3)* 396
Normalville (D5)* 250
Norristown (M5)* 38,126
North Apollo (D4)* 1,502
N. Belle Vernon ‡(C5) 3,147
N. Bend (G3)* 100
N. Braddock ‡(C7) 14,724
N. Catasauqua ‡(M4) 2,629
N. Charleroi ‡(C5) 2,554
N. East (C1)* 4,247
N. Girard (B1)* 1,369
N. Irwin ‡(C5) 1,076
N. Mehoopany (K2)* 120
N. Springfield (A1)*
N. Wales (M5)* 2,998
N. Warren (D2)* 900
N. York ‡(J5) 2,445
Northampton (M4)* 9,332
Northumberland (J4)* 4,207
Norvelt (D5)*
Norwood (M7)* 5,246
Noxen (K3)* 400
Nu Mine (D4)* 2,000
Nuangola ‡(C4)* 295
Nuremberg (K4)* 1,200
Oak Hall Station (G4)* 225
Oak Ridge (D3)* 800
Oakdale (B5)* 1,572
Oakford (N5)* 1,900
Oakland (L2) 871
Oakmont (C6)* 7,264
Oakville (H5)* 116
Ohiopyle (D6)* 345
Oil City (C3)* 19,581
Oklahoma ‡(C4) 930
Olanta (E4)* 125
Old Forge (L3)* 9,749
Oley (L5)* 498
Oliver (C6)* 2,180
Olyphant (L3)* 7,047
Oneida (K4)* 800
Ono (J5)* 220
Orangeville (K3)* 424
Orbisonia (G5)* 648
Ore Hill (F5) 150
Ormsby (E2)* 169
Orrstown (G5)* 295
Orrtanna (H6)* 300
Orson (M2)* 250
Orviston (G3)* 340
Orwigsburg (K4)* 3,029
Osborne ‡(B5) 496
Osceola (H2)* 300
Osceola Mills (F4)* 1,992
Osterburg (E5)* 200
Oswayo (G2)* 167
Ottsville (M5)* 817
Overton (K2)*
Oxford (K6)* 3,091
Paint (E5) 1,547
Palmerton (L4)* 6,646
Palmyra (J5)* 5,910
Palo Alto ‡(K4) 1,767
Paoli (M5)* 2,039
Paradise (K5)* 600
Pardoe (B3)* 200
Parker (C3)* 979
Parkesburg (L6)* 2,611
Parkside (M7) 1,637
Parryville ‡(L4)* 598
Patterson Heights ‡(B4) 678
Patton (E4)* 3,148
Paupack (M3)* 250
Pavia (E5) 100
Paxtang ‡(J5) 1,857
Peach Bottom (K6)* 80
Pen Argyl (M4)* 3,878
Penbrook ‡(J5) 3,691
Penfield (E3)* 831
Penn (C5)* 987
Penndel ‡(N5)* 1,100
Penn Run (D4)* 232
Pennline (A2) 25
Penns Park (N5)* 160
Pennsburg (M5)* 1,625
Pennsdale (J3)* 200
Pennsylvania Furnace (G4)* 100
Pequea (K6)* 121
Perkasie (M5)* 4,358
Perrysville (B6)* 1,500
Petersburg (G4)* 621
Petrolia (C3)* 571

Philadelphia (N6)*..2,071,605
Philadelphia (urban area)..........2,913,516
Philipsburg (F4)*........3,988
Phoenixville (L5)*......12,932
Picture Rocks (J3)*...... 569
Pillow (J4)*.............. 369
Pine Bank (B6)*.......... 25
Pine Grove (K4)*.........2,237
Pine Grove Furnace (H5)........... 40
Pine Grove Mills (G4)*.1,200
Pipersville (M5)*........ 125
Pitcairn (C5)*...........5,857
Pittock (B7)*.............2,600
Pittsburgh (B7)*.......676,806
Pittsburgh (urban area) 1,525,966
Pittsfield (D2)*...........
Pittston (L3)*............15,012
Plains (L3)*............^12,541
Platea (B2)*.............. 290
Pleasant Gap (G4)*.......1,312
Pleasant Hills (B7).......3,808
Pleasant Mount (M2)*.. 438
Pleasantville (C2)*...... 704
Pleasantville ‡(E5)....... 242
Plumsteadville (M5)*.... 312
Plumville (D4)*........... 452
Plymouth (K3)*...........13,021
Pocono Lake (L3)*........ 225
Pocono Pines (M3)*...... 475
Point Marion (C6)*.......2,197
Point Pleasant (N5)*.... 400
Poland Mines (B6)*.......
Polk (C3)*..................4,004
Pond Eddy (N3)*...........
Port Allegany (F2)*......2,519
Port Carbon (K4)*.......3,024
Port Clinton (K4)*....... 451
Port Matilda (F4)*....... 685
Port Royal (H4)*......... 800
Port Trevorton (J4)*.... 280
Port Vue (C7)..............4,756
Portage (E5)*..............4,371
Portersville (B4)*......... 294
Portland (M4)*............. 551
Pottersdale (F3)*......... 325
Potterville (K2)........... 63
Pottstown (L5)*..........22,589
Pottsville (K4)*..........23,640
Powell (J2)*............... 300
Powelton (F4)*............. 315
President (C3)............. 100
Primos (M7)*............... 500
Pringle ‡(L3)...............1,727
Proctor (J3)*............... 100
Prompton (M2)*........... 197
Prospect (B4)*............. 726
Prospect Park (M7)*....5,834
Pulaski (B3)*............... 350
Punxsutawney (E4)*....8,969
Quakertown (M5)*........5,673
Quarryville (K6)*.........1,187
Quecreek (D5)*............ 550
Queen (E5)*................. 200
Racine (B4)*................ 500
Railroad (J6)*.............. 300
Rainsburg (F6)............. 189
Ralphton (D5)*............. 225
Ralston (H2)*............... 700
Ramey (F4)*................. 696
Rankin (C7)*................6,941
Ravine (K4)*................. 600
Reading (L5)*.............109,320
Reading (urban area)..................154,571
Reamstown (K5)*.......... 950
Rebersburg (H4)*.......... 600
Red Hill ‡(M5)*............ 914
Red Lion (J6)*..............5,119
Reedsville (G4)*...........1,238
Refton (K6)*................ 235
Rehrersburg (K5)*........ 365
Renfrew (C4)*............... 400
Reno (C3)*...................1,000
Renovo (G3)*................3,751
Rew (F2)*..................... 500
Reynoldsville (D3)*.......3,569
Rices Landing (C6)*..... 796
Riceville (C2)*.............. 200
Richfield (H4)*.............. 350
Richland (K5)*..............1,090
Richlandtown (M5)*....... 762
Riddlesburg (F5)*......... 700
Ridgway (E3)*...............6,244
Ridley Park (M7)*.........4,921
Riegelsville (M4)*......... 871
Rillton (C5)*................. 875
Rimer (C4)*................... 80
Rimersburg (D3)*..........1,398
Ringtown (K4)*.............. 835
Riverside (J4)*.............. 524
Rixford (F2)*................. 650
Roaring Branch (J2)*.... 375
Roaring Creek (K4)....... 40
Roaring Spring (F5)*....2,771
Robertsdale (F5)*..........
Robesonia (K5)*............1,590
Robinson (D5)*..............
Rochester (B4)*.............7,197
Rochester Mills (D4)*.. 230
Rock Glen (K4)*............. 250
Rockhill ‡(G5)............... 567
Rockledge ‡(M5)...........2,261
Rockwood (D6)*.............1,237
Rogersville (B6)*........... 300
Rome (K2)*.................... 257
Roscoe (C5)*..................1,396
Rose Valley (L7)............ 498
Rosemont (M5)*.............2,000
Roseto (M4)*..................1,676
Roseville (Rutland*) (J2) 126
Rossiter (E4)*................1,078
Rosslyn Farms ‡(B7)..... 448
Rothsville (K5)*..............1,000
Roulette (F2)*................ 800
Rouseville (C3)*.............1,009
Rouzerville (G6)*............1,000
Roxbury (G5)*................. 400
Royalton (J5)*................1,175
Royersford (L5)*.............3,862
Rummerfield (K2)*.......... 100
Rural Valley (D4)*.......... 857
Rush (K2)*......................
Russell (D2)*.................. 800
Russellton (C4)*..............1,670
Rutland (J2)*................... 126
Rutledge (M7)*................ 919
Sabinsville (G2)*.............. 300
Sabula (E3)..................... 275
Saegerstown (B2)*........... 836
Sagamore (D4)*...............1,128
Saint Benedict (E4)*...... 500
St. Clair (K4)*..................5,856
St. Clairsville ‡(E5)*..... 127
St. Lawrence ‡(E4)*...... 810
St. Marys (E3)*...............7,846
St. Petersburg (C3)*...... 451
St. Thomas (G6)*............ 534
Salisbury (D6)*................ 865
Salladasburg (H3)*.......... 250
Salona (H3)*.................... 500
Saltillo (G5)*................... 435
Saltsburg (D4)*................1,156
Sand Patch (E6)*.............. 56
Sandy Lake (B3)*............. 767
Sandy Ridge (F4)*........... 700
Sankertown ‡(E5)............ 865
Sarver (C4)*.................... 410
Sawyer City (E2).............. 500
Saxonburg (C4)*.............. 602
Saxton (F5)*.....................1,093
Saybrook (D2)*................ 137
Saylorsburg (M4)*............ 513
Sayre (K2)*.......................7,735
Scalp Level (E5)*..............1,756
Schaefferstown (K5)*....1,000
Schellsburg (E5)*............. 305
Schnecksville (L4)*.......... 375
Schuylkill Haven (K4)*.6,597
Schwenksville (L5)*......... 563
Sciota (M4)*..................... 300
Scotland (G6)*.................. 500
Scottdale (C5)*..................6,249
Scranton (L3)*................125,536
Scranton (urban area) 235,122
Secane (M7)*.....................1,500
Seelyville (M2)*................. 600
Selinsgrove (J4)*...............3,514
Sellersville (M5)*...............2,373
Seminole (D4)*.................. 250
Seneca (C3)*..................... 700
Sergeant (E2)*................... 150
Seven Valleys (J6)*.......... 437
Seward (E5)*...................... 852
Sewickley (B4)*..................5,836
Sewickley Heights ‡(B4) 679
Shade Gap (G5)*............... 157
Shadygrove (G6)*............. 500
Shamokin (J4)*...................16,879
Shamokin Dam (J4)*........ 730
Shanksville (E5)*............... 342
Sharon (B3)*......................26,454
Sharon Hill (N7)*..............5,464
Sharpsburg (B6)*...............7,296
Sharpsville (A3)*................5,414
Shawanese (K3)*.............. 200
Shawmut (E3).....................
Shawnee on Delaware (N3)*.......... 200
Sheakleyville (B3)*............ 141
Sheffield (D2)*..................2,087
Shelocta ‡(D4)*................. 105
Shenandoah (K4)*.............15,704
Shenango (A3)*................. 200
Sheppton (K4)*...................
Shermans Dale (H5)*....... 83
Shickshinny (K3)*..............2,156
Shillington (K5)*................5,059
Shinglehouse (F2)*............1,201
Shippensburg (H5)*...........5,722
Shippenville (D3)*.............. 522
Shippingport ‡(B4)*.......... 408
Shiremanstown ‡(H5)* 887
Shirleysburg (G5)*............. 241
Shoemakersville (K4)*..1,066
Shohola (N3)*.................... 600
Shohola Falls (N3)*........... 70
Shrewsbury (J6)*................ 787
Shunk (J2)*........................ 60
Sidman (E5)*...................... 490
Sigel (D3)*.......................... 600
Silverdale ‡(M5)*............... 384
Simpson (M2)*.....................2,800
Sinking Spring (K5)*..........1,982
Sinnamahoning (G3)*........ 450
Six Mile Run (F5)*............. 400
Skinners Eddy (K2)*.......... 225
Skippack (M5)*.................. 425
Skytop (M3)*....................... 25
Slate Run (H3)*...................
Slatedale (L4)*.................. 800
Slatington (L4)*..................4,343
Slickville (C5)*...................1,266
Sligo (C3)*.......................... 913
Slippery Rock (B3)*............2,294
Smethport (F2)*..................1,797
Smicksburg (D4)*............... 92
Smithfield (C6)*..................1,066
Smithmill (F4)*...................1,500
Smithton (C5)*.................... 690
Snow Shoe (G3)*................ 670
Snydertown (J4)*............... 314
Soldier (E3)........................ 300
Somerfield ‡(D6).................
Somerset (D6)*....................5,936
Sonestown (K3)*................. 275
Souderton (M5)*.................4,521
South Bend (D4)*................ 100
S. Bethlehem ‡(D4)........... 489
S. Coatesville ‡(L6)..........1,996
S. Connellsville (D6)*...2,610
S. Fork (E5)*.......................2,616
S. Greensburg ‡(C5).....2,980
S. Heights (B4)*................. 691
S. Mountain (H6)*..............1,300
S. New Castle ‡(B4).......... 993
S. Philipsburg ‡(F4).... 512
S. Renovo (G3).................... 862
S. Waverly (J2)...................1,298
S. Williamsport (J3).......6,364
Southmont ‡(E5)................2,278
Southwest (C5)*.................. 800
Southwest Greensburg ‡(C5) 3,144
Spangler (E4)*.....................3,013
Spartansburg (C2)*............. 482
Speers ‡(C5)........................1,089
Spinnerstown (M5)*............ 400
Spring City (L5)*.................3,258
Spring Creek (D2)*............. 160
Spring Grove (J6)*..............1,238
Spring Mills (G4)*............... 720
Springboro (B2)*................. 611
Springdale (C4)*..................4,939
Springfield (M7)*.................8,000
Springtown (M4)*................ 600
Springville (L2)*................... 250
Spruce Creek (F4)*............. 150
Starrucca (M2)*................... 326
State College (G4)*....17,227
State Line (G6)*.................. 375
Steelton (J5)*......................12,574
Sterling (M3)*........................ 40
Sterling Run (F3)*................ 225
Stewartstown (K6)*............1,133
Stillwater (K3)*..................... 189
Stockdale ‡(C5)*................... 870
Stockertown (M4)*................ 757
Stoneboro (B3)*....................1,294
Stowe (L5)*............................2,524
Stowe (B7).........................^12,210
Stoystown (E5)*..................... 517
Strasburg (K6)*......................1,109
Strattanville (D3)*.................. 562
Strausstown (K5)*.................. 368
Stroudsburg (M4)*.................6,361
Stump Creek (E3)*................. 675
Sturgeon (B5)*.......................1,150
Sugar Notch (L3)*..................2,002
Sugargrove (D1)*................... 520
Summer Hill (E5)*.................. 849
Summerville (D3)*.................. 933
Summit Hill (L4)*...................4,294
Sunbury (J4)*.........................15,570
Surveyor (F3)*......................... 53
Susquehanna (L2)*.................2,646
Sutersville ‡(C5)*.................. 854
Swarthmore (M7)*..................4,825
Sweet Valley (K3)*.................. 200
Swissvale (C7)*......................16,488
Swoyersville ‡(L3)..................7,795
Sycamore (B6)*........................ 69
Sykesville (E3)*......................1,652
Sylvan (G6)*............................ 22
Sylvania (J2)*.......................... 211
Tamaqua (L4)*........................11,508
Tamarack (G3)........................ 60
Tannersville (M3)*.................. 500
Tarentum (C4)*........................9,540
Tatamy (M4)*.......................... 681
Taylor (L3)*.............................7,176
Taylorstown (A5)*.................. 400
Telford ‡(M5)*........................2,042
Temple (L5)*.............................1,460
Templeton (C4)*......................1,000
Terre Hill (L5)*........................1,000
Thomasville (J6)*.................... 320
Thompson (L2)*...................... 320
Thompsontown (H4)*.... 486
Thornburg ‡(B7)................... 335
Thornhurst (L3)*.................... 100
Three Springs (G5)*........ 417
Throop (L3)*...........................5,861
Tidioute (D2)*.......................... 998
Timblin (D4)*.......................... 327
Tioga (H2)*.............................. 544
Tiona (D2)*.............................. 350
Tionesta (C2)*.......................... 728
Tipton (F4)*.............................. 425
Tire Hill (E5)*........................... 700
Titusville (C2)*..........................8,923
Tobyhanna (M3)*...................... 825
Topton (L5)*................................1,572
Torpedo (D2)*............................ 65
Torrance (D5)*........................... 500
Toughkenamon (L6)*.............. 500
Towanda (J2)*.............................4,069
Tower City (J4)*.........................2,054
Townville (C2)*........................... 351
Trafford (C5)*..............................3,965
Trainer (L7)..................................2,001
Transfer (A3)*............................ 400
Trappe ‡(M5).............................. 773
Tremont (K4)*.............................2,102
Trevorton (J4)*...........................2,545
Trexlertown (L4*)........................ 500
Trough Creek (F5)...................... 60
Trout Run (H3)*......................... 325
Troutville ‡(E3)*........................ 223
Troxelville (H4)*........................ 130
Troy (J2)*.....................................1,371
Truemans (D2)*.......................... 80
Trumbauersville (M5)*.. 838
Tryonville (C2)*.......................... 134
Tullytown (N5)*.......................... 648
Tunkhannock (L2)*....................2,170
Tunnelhill ‡(E5)......................... 535
Turbotville (J3)*.......................... 518
Turtle Creek (C7)*....................12,363
Turtlepoint (F2)*......................... 150
Twilight ‡(C5).............................. 318
Twin Rocks (E4)*........................1,850
Tyler (F3)*.................................... 250
Tylersburg (D3)*......................... 215
Tylersville (G4)*......................... 200
Tyrone (F4)*..................................8,214
Ulster (J2)*.................................. 400
Ulysses (G2)*............................... 495
Union City (C2)*...........................3,911
Union Dale (M2)*.......................... 350
Union Deposit (J5)*.................... 550
Uniontown (C6)*..........................20,471
Uniontown ‡(J4)............................1,280
Unionville ‡(H4)*......................... 341
Unity (C4)*.................................... 700
Unityville (K3)*............................ 55
Universal (C7)*..............................3,200
Upland (L7)*....................................4,081
Upper Black Eddy (N4)* 550
Upper Darby (M6)*..^84,951
Upper Strasburg (G5)*.. 262
Urban (J4)*..................................... 100
Ursina (D6)*.................................... 334
Utica (C3)*....................................... 264
Uwchland (L5)*................................ 300
Valencia (C4)*.................................. 298
Valier (D4)*...................................... 600
Valley Forge (L5)*........................... 475
Valley View (J4)*..............................1,618
Van (C3)*.. 75
Vanderbilt (C5)*............................... 937
Vandergrift (D4)*..............................9,524
Vandling (M2)*.................................. 722
Vanport (B4)*......................................2,500
Venango (B2)*.................................... 359
Venus (C3)*.. 150
Verona (C6)*.......................................4,235
Versailles (C7)....................................2,484
Villanova (M6)*...................................1,500
Vintage (K5)....................................... 150
Vintondale (E5)*.................................1,185
Volant (B3)*.. 229
Wall (C5)*...1,850
Wallaceton (F4)*................................. 440
Wallingford (L7)*................................6,000
Walnut (G4)*.. 85
Walnut Bottom (H5)*.. 325
Walnutport (L4)*.................................1,427
Walston (D4)*...................................... 330
Wampum (B4)*....................................1,090
Wanamie (L3)*.....................................1,092
Wapwallopen (K3)*.......................... 377
Warfordsburg (F6)*.......................... 105
Warren (D2)*..14,849
Warren Center (K2)*......................... 275
Warrendale (B4)*................................ 600
Warrensville (J3)*................................ 175
Warrior Run ‡(L3)...............................1,056
Warriors Mark (F4)*.......................... 225
Washington (B5)*...............................26,280
Washington Boro ‡(K6)* 483
Washington Crossing (N5)* 300
Washingtonville (J3)*.. 194
Waterford (B2)*....................................1,195
Watsontown (J3)*................................2,327
Wattsburg (C1)*.................................... 343
Wawa (L7)*... 600
Waymart (M2)..1,068
Wayne (M6)*..6,000
Waynesboro (G6)*................................10,334
Waynesburg (B6)*.................................5,514
Weatherly (L4)*.....................................2,622
Webster (C5)*...
Webster Mills (F6)*............................ 95
Weedville (F3)*...................................... 700
Weissport ‡(L4)*..................................... 674
Wellersburg (E6)*.................................. 369
Wellsboro (H2)*.....................................4,215
Wellscreek (E5)...................................... 100
Wellsville (J5)*.. 309
Wernersville (K5)*.................................1,280
Wesley (C3)... 80
Wesleyville (C1)*.....................................3,411
West Alexander (B5)*.. 466
W. Bridgewater (B4)*..1,316
W. Brownsville (C5)*...1,610
W. Chester (L6)*.....................................15,168
W. Conshohocken ‡(M5)* 2,482
W. Easton ‡(M4)......................................1,368
W. Elizabeth (C5)*...................................1,137
W. Fairview ‡(J5)*....................................1,896
West Finley (B5)*...................................... 93
W. Grove (L6)*..1,521
W. Hazleton (K4)*.....................................6,988
W. Hickory (C2)*... 400
W. Homestead ‡(B7).....3,257
W. Kittanning ‡(C4).......... 910
W. Lawn (K5)*...2,144
W. Leechburg ‡(C4)......................................1,113
W. Leesport ‡(L5)*.. 535
W. Liberty ‡(C5).. 245
W. Mayfield ‡(B4)...1,768
W. Middlesex (B3)*......................................1,217
W. Middletown (A5)*.................................... 268
W. Mifflin (C7)*...17,985
W. Milton (J3)*.. 700
W. Monterey (C3)*... 125
W. Nanticoke (K3)*..1,780
W. Newton (C5)*..3,619
W. Pittsburg (B4)*.. 900
W. Pittston ‡(L3)*..7,230
W. Reading ‡(L5)..5,072
W. Salisbury (D6)*... 300
W. Springfield (B2)*..
W. Sunbury (B4)*.. 262
W. Union (B6).. 25
W. View (B6)*...7,581
W. Winfield (C4)*.. 600
W. Wyoming ‡(L3)..2,863
W. York ‡(J6)..5,756
Westfield (H2)*...1,357
Westford (A2)*.. 47
Westland (B5)*...1,025
Westline (E2)*.. 150
Westmont ‡(C5)...4,410
Weston (K4)*... 602
Westover (E4)*... 605
Westport (G3)*.. 221
Westtown (L6)*.. 258
Westville (E3)*... 250
Wharton (G2).. 50
Wheatland (B3)*..1,402
Wheelerville (J2)*.. 34
Whitaker (C7)*...2,149
White Haven (L3)*...1,461
White Mills (M2)*.. 600
White Oak (C7)...6,159
Whitedeer (J3)*.. 300
Whitehall (B7)..7,342
Whitney (D5)*.. 875
Wiconisco (J4)*..1,549
Widnoon (D4)*... 350
Wilawana (J2)*... 100
Wilcox (E2)*..1,000
Wilkes-Barre (L3)*....76,826
Wilkes-Barre (urban area) 270,978
Wilkinsburg (C7)*.......31,418
Williamsburg (F5)*.......1,792
Williamsport (H3)*.....45,047
Williamstown (J4)*.......2,332
Willock (B7)*................... 275
Willow Grove (M5)*.....7,000
Willow Hill (G5)*.............. 440
Wilmerding (C7)*...........5,325
Wilmore (E5)*................... 390
Wilpen (D5)*.......................
Wilson (M4)*......................8,159
Winburne (F4)*................... 785
Windber (E5)*......................8,010
Windgap (M4)*....................1,577
Windsor (J6)*.......................1,126
Winfield (J4)*........................ 320
Wingate (G4)*......................... 216
Winterdale (M2)...................... 50
Winterstown ‡(J6)................... 298
Winton (M3)............................6,280
Wolfdale (B5)*......................... 800
Wolfsburg (F5)......................... 125
Womelsdorf (K5)*...................1,549
Woodbury (F5)*......................... 254
Woodcock (C2).......................... 130
Woodland (F4)*........................1,000
Woodlyn (M7)*.........................5,000
Woodruff (B6)............................ 25
Woodville (B7)*........................3,775
Woolrich (H3)*............................ 450
Wormleysburg ‡(J5)*...1,511
Worthington (C4)*....................... 800
Worthville (D3)*.......................... 73
Wrights (F2)*............................... 250
Wrightsville (J5)*......................2,104
Wyalusing (K2)*.......................... 612
Wyoming (L3)*..........................4,511
Wyomissing (K5)*....................4,187
Wyomissing Hills ‡(K5) 646
Wysox (K2)*................................ 250
Yardley (N5)*............................1,916
Yatesboro (D4)*........................1,264
Yatesville ‡(L3)........................... 565
Yeadon (N7)*.............................11,068
Yeagertown (G4)*.....................1,628
Yoe ‡(J6)*................................... 681
York (J6)*...................................59,953
York (urban area).....................78,495
York Haven (J5)*........................ 743
York Springs (H6)*..................... 413
Yorkana ‡(J6)*............................. 229
Youngstown (D5)*....................... 577
Youngsville (D2)*.....................1,944
Youngwood (D5)*.....................2,720
Yukon (C5)*...............................1,099
Zelienople (B4)*........................2,981

Map on Page 68

RHODE ISLAND

Total Population 791,896

5 COUNTIES

Bristol (J6)................29,079
Kent (H6).....................77,763
Newport (K6).................61,539
Providence (H5)..........574,973
Washington (H7)............48,542

CITIES and TOWNS

Adamsville (K6)*........ 250
Albion (H5)*............... 800
Allenton (H6)*............. 250
Alton (G7)*................. 300
Anthony (H6)*............. 2,000
Arcadia (H6)................ 100
Arctic (J6)................... 3,000
Arnold Mills (J5)......... 300
Ashaway (G7)*............ 1,022
Ashton (J5)*............... 1,000
Barrington (J6)*.......^8,246
Block Island (H8)*...... 848
Bradford (H7)*........... 1,024
Bridgeton (G5)............. 661
Bristol (J6)*.............^12,320
Canonchet (H7)........... 150
Carolina (H7)*............. 200
Centerdale (H5)*......... 2,500
Central Falls (J5)*....23,550
Charlestown (H7)*......^1,598
Chepachet (H5)*......... 1,200
Clayville (H5)*............. 300
Conimicut (J6)*............
Coventry (H6)*...........^9,869
Cranston (J5)*...........55,060
Crompton (J6)............. 1,500
Davisville (H6)............ 1,400
East Greenwich (H6)* ....^4,923
E. Providence (J5)*...^35,871
Esmond (H5)*.............. 2,000
Exeter (H6)*...............^1,870
Farmingdale (H5).......
Fiskeville (H6)*..........
Foster (H5)...............^1,630
Foster Center (H5)*.... 225
Georgiaville (H5)*...... 1,247
Glendale (H5)*............ 243
Greene (G6)*............... 71
Greenville (H5)*......... 2,000
Hamilton (J6)*............ 950
Harmony (H5)*............ 500
Harrisville (H5)*........ 1,055
Hillsgrove (J6)*..........
Hope (H6)*.................. 800
Hope Valley (H6)*...... 1,000
Hopkinton (H7)*.........^3,676
Howard (J5)*.............. 6,000
Jamestown (J6)*.........^2,068
Kenyon (H7)*.............. 100
Kingston (J7)*............ 2,156
La Fayette (H6)*......... 550
Little Compton (K6)*.^1,556
Lonsdale (J5)*............2,500
Lymansville (J5)..........
Manton (J5)................ 2,500
Manville (H5)*............ 3,429
Mapleville (H5)*......... 1,015
Middletown (J6)..........^7,382
Narragansett (J7)*.....^2,288
Nasonville (H5)........... 677
Natick (H6)*............... 2,000
Newport (J7)*..............37,564
North Scituate (H5)*. 1,000
N. Tiverton (K6).......... 4,000
Norwood (J5)............... 2,300
Oak Lawn (H5)*........... 600
Oakland (H5)*.............. 226
Oakland Beach (J6)*..10,000
Pascoag (H5)*............. 1,760
Pawtucket (J5)*...........81,436
Peace Dale (J7)*......... 2,177
Phenix (H6)*............... 1,500
Phillipsdale (J5).......... 1,500
Pontiac (J6)*...............
Portsmouth (J6)*........^6,578
Potter Hill (H7)*........... 400
PROVIDENCE (H5)*.248,674
Providence (urban area)...................581,607
Prudence (J6)..............
Prudence Island (J6)* 80
River Point (H6).......... 1,000
Riverside (J5)*............10,000
Rockville (G6)*............ 175
Rumford (J5)*..............10,000
Saunderstown (J6)*..... 450
Saylesville (J5)*......... 3,500
Shannock (H7)*........... 300
Shawomet (J6)............ 1,500
Slatersville (H4)*........ 1,780
Slocum (H6)*.............. 100
South Foster (H5)........
Stillwater (H5).............
Summit (H6)............... 110
Tarkiln (H5)................ 191
Thornton (H5)..............
Tiverton (K6)*............^5,659
Tiverton Four Corners (K6)............. 12
Usquepaug (H6).......... 142
Valley Falls (J5)*.........2,500
Wakefield (H7)*........... 3,047
Warren (J6)................^8,513
Warwick (J6)*.............43,028
Warwick Neck (J6)*......
Washington (H6)*........ 2,800
Watch Hill (G7)*.......... 750
Weekapaug (G7)*......... 200
West Barrington (J5)* 4,250
W. Glocester (G5)........ 100
W. Greenwich (H6).....^ 847
W. Kingston (H7)*........ 500
Westerly (G7)*............^12,380
Wickford (J6)*............. 2,437
Wood River Jct. (H7)* 103
Woonsocket (J4)*.........50,211
Wyoming (H6)*............. 315

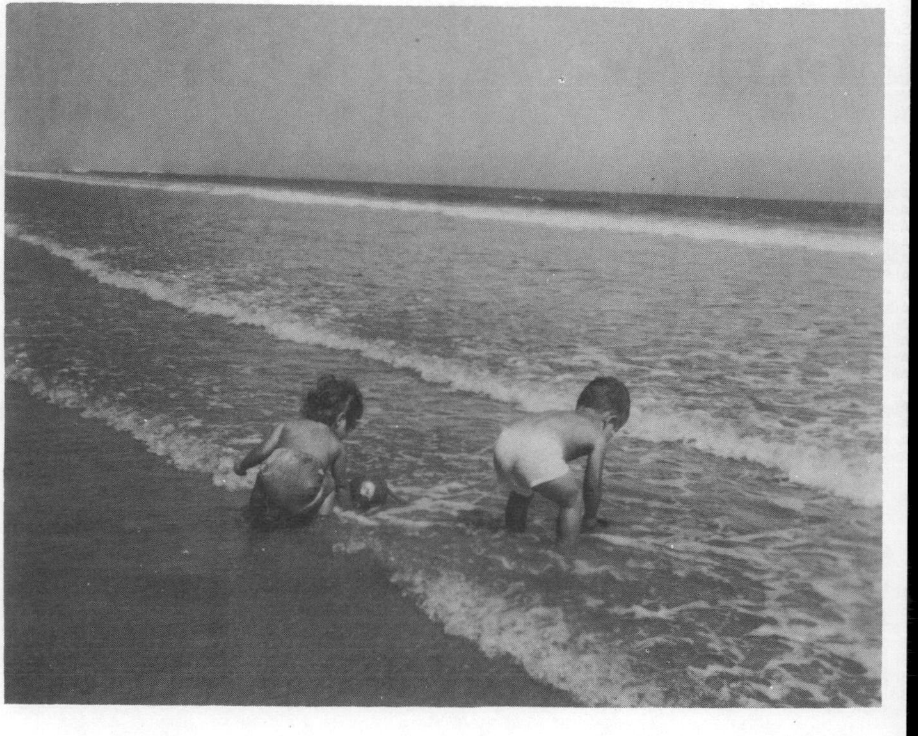

Map on Page 86

SOUTH CAROLINA

Total Population 2,117,027

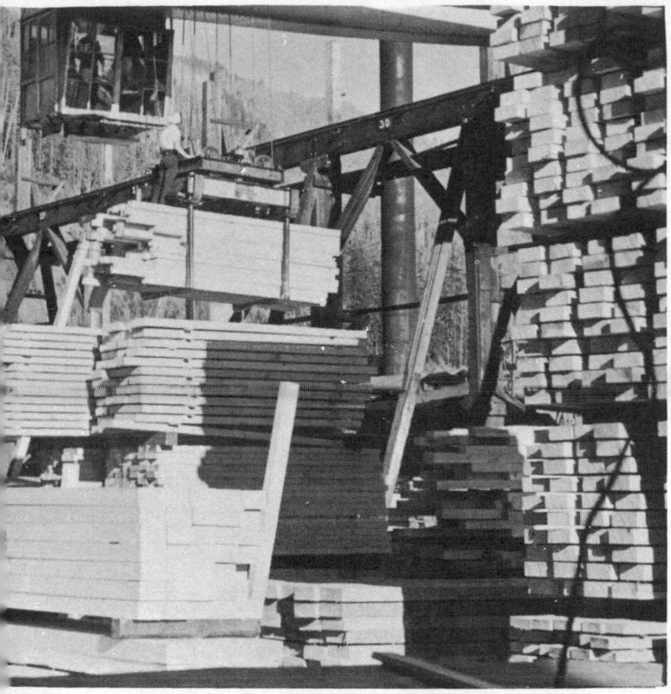

46 COUNTIES

Abbeville (B3)...22,456
Aiken (D4)...53,137
Allendale (E6)...11,773
Anderson (B2)...90,664
Bamberg (F5)...17,533
Barnwell (E5)...17,266
Beaufort (F7)...26,993
Berkeley (G5)...30,251
Calhoun (F4)...14,753
Charleston (H6)...164,856
Cherokee (D1)...34,992
Chester (E2)...32,597
Chesterfield (G2)...36,236
Clarendon (G4)...32,215
Colleton (F6)...28,242
Darlington (H3)...50,016
Dillon (J3)...30,930
Dorchester (G5)...22,601
Edgefield (D4)...16,591
Fairfield (E3)...21,780
Florence (H3)...79,710
Georgetown (J5)...31,762
Greenville (C2)...168,152
Greenwood (C3)...41,628
Hampton (E6)...18,027
Horry (J4)...59,820
Jasper (E6)...10,995
Kershaw (F3)...32,287
Lancaster (F2)...37,071
Laurens (D2)...46,974
Lee (G3)...23,173
Lexington (E4)...44,297
Marion (J3)...33,110
Marlboro (H2)...31,766
McCormick (C4)...9,577
Newberry (D3)...31,771
Oconee (A2)...39,050
Orangeburg (F5)...68,726
Pickens (B2)...40,058
Richland (F3)...142,565
Saluda (D3)...15,924
Spartanburg (D2)...150,349
Sumter (G4)...57,634
Union (D2)...31,334
Williamsburg (H4)...43,807
York (E2)...71,596

CITIES and TOWNS

Abbeville (C3)*...5,395
Adams Run (G6)*...250
Adamsburg (D2)*...150
Adrian (J4)*...150
Aiken (D4)*...7,083
Alcolu (G4)*...800
Allendale (E5)*...2,474
Allsbrook (K3)...200
Anderson (B2)*...19,770
Andrews (H5)*...2,702
Angelus (G2)*...50
Antioch (F3)...350
Antreville (B3)...300
Appleton (E5)*...
Aragon Mills (E2)...
Arcadia (C2)*...2,554
Arial (B2)*...1,098
Arthur (E3)...50
Ashepoo (G6)*...150
Ashton (E5)*...
Atkins (G3)*...50
Awendaw (H5)*...75
Aynor (J3)*...551
Badham (F5)...118
Baldock (E5)*...80
Baldwin Mills (E2)*...1,440
Ballentine (E3)*...150
Bamberg (E5)*...2,954
Barnwell (E5)*...2,005
Batesburg (D4)*...3,169
Bath (D5)*...1,232
Beaufort (F7)*...5,081
Belton (C2)*...3,371
Belton Mills (B2)...1,500
Bennetts Point (G6)*...73
Bennettsville (H2)*...5,140
Bethera (H5)*...
Bethune (G3)*...639
Bingham (H3)...169
Bishopville (G3)*...3,076
Blacksburg (D1)*...2,056
Blackstock (E2)*...
Blackville (E5)*...1,294
Blair (E3)*...74
Blaney (F3)*...183
Blenheim (H2)*...153
Blue Brick (J3)*...
Bluffton (F7)*...474
Blythewood (E3)*...400
Bonneau (H5)*...408
Bordeaux (B4)...75
Borden (G3)*...50
Bowling Green (E1)*...
Bowman (F5)*...857
Boykin (F3)*...13
Bradley (C3)*...100
Branchville (F5)*...1,353
Bristow (H3)...50
Brogdon (G4)...25
Brookgreen (K4)...
Brunson (E6)*...607
Bucksport (J4)*...800
Bucksville (J4)*...
Buffalo (D2)*...1,580
Burgess (J4)*...200
Burnettown ‡(D5)...578
Burton (F7)*...275
Cades (H4)*...150
Caesars Head (B1)*...16
Calhoun (B2)*...
Calhoun Falls (B3)*...2,396
Callison (C3)*...50
Camden (F3)*...6,986
Cameron (F4)*...630
Campobello (C1)*...394
Canadys (F5)*...150
Carlisle (D2)*...405
Cartersville (H3)*...96
Cashville (C2)...58
Cassatt (G3)*...125
Catawba (F2)*...150
Cateechee (B2)*...650
Cayce (E4)*...3,294
Cedar Springs (D2)*...1,500
Centenary (J3)*...
Central (B2)*...1,263
Chapin (E3)*...327
Chappells (D3)*...199
Charleston (G6)*...70,174
Charleston (urban area)...116,441
Cheraw (H2)*...4,836
Cherokee Falls (D1)*...
Chesnee (D1)*...1,051
Chester (E2)*...6,893
Chesterfield (G2)*...1,530
Chisolm (F6)...5
Claremont (G4)...
Clarks Hill (C4)*...
Claussen (H3)*...
Clearwater (D4)*...800
Clemson (B2)*...1,204
Cleveland (C1)*...250
Clifton (D2)*...1,707
Clinton (D3)*...7,168
Clio (H2)*...837
Clover (E1)*...3,276
Colliers (C4)...175
COLUMBIA (F4)*...86,914
Columbia (urban area)...119,747
Conestee (C2)*...750
Congaree Field (F4)...50
Converse (D2)*...1,200
Conway (J4)*...6,073
Cooper (H4)*...200
Coosawhatchie (F6)*...
Cope (E5)*...209
Cordesville (H5)*...450
Cordova (F5)*...175
Coronaca (C3)*...
Cottageville (G6)*...553
Coward (H4)*...500
Cowpens (D1)*...1,879
Crescent Beach (K4)*...540
Creston (F4)...75
Crete (B2)...
Crocketville (E6)*...120
Cross (G5)*...85
Cross Anchor (D2)*...350
Cross Hill (D3)*...543
Cross Keys (D2)...250
Crow Creek (B2)...40
Cummings (E6)...
Dacusville (B2)*...95
Dale (F6)*...300
Dalzell (G3)*...209
Darlington (H3)*...6,619
Daufuskie Island (F7)*...270
Davis Station (G4)*...200
Denmark (E5)*...2,814
Dents (F3)...1,000
Dillon (J3)*...5,171
Donalds (C3)*...332
Dorchester (G5)*...350
Dovesville (H3)*...250
Drake (H3)*...200
Drayton (D2)*...1,228
Due West (C3)*...1,033
Dunbar (H2)*...200
Duncan (C2)*...599
Eadytown (G5)...87
Early Branch (F6)*...250
Easley (B2)*...6,316
Eastover (F4)*...564
Eau Claire (E3)*...9,238
Ebenezer (E2)...680
Edgefield (C4)*...2,518
Edgemoor (E2)*...258
Edisto Island (G6)*...2,500
Effingham (H3)*...200
Ehrhardt (E5)*...510
Elko (E5)*...142
Elliott (G3)*...
Elloree (F4)*...1,127
Enoree (D2)*...1,045
Estill (E6)*...1,659
Eureka (D4)...50
Eureka Mills (E2)...1,990
Eutawville (G5)*...478
Fair Play (A2)*...250
Fairfax (E6)*...1,567
Fairforest (C2)*...800
Fairmont (D2)*...250
Filbert (E1)*...200
Fingerville (D1)*...400
Florence (H3)*...22,513
Floyd Dale (J3)*...100
Folly Beach (H6)*...800
Forest Acres (F3)...3,240
Foreston (G4)*...
Fork (J3)*...115
Fork Shoals (C2)...250
Fort Lawn (F2)*...216
Fort Mill (F1)*...3,204
Fort Motte (F4)*...350
Fountain Inn (C2)*...1,325
Four Holes (G5)*...200
Frogmore (F7)*...200
Furman (E6)*...293
Gable (G4)*...90
Gadsden (F4)*...
Gaffney (D1)*...8,123
Galivants Ferry (J3)*...150
Garnett (E6)*...100
Gaston (E4)*...250
Georgetown (J5)*...6,004
Giant (G5)...
Gifford (E6)*...
Gilbert (E4)*...172
Gillisonville (E6)...25
Givhans (G5)...100
Glendale (D2)*...1,244
Glenn Springs (D2)*...
Gluck (B3)*...1,634
Goldville (Joanna*) (D3)...1,730
Goose Creek (H6)*...600
Gossett Mills (B2)...
Govan (E5)*...109
Gowensville (C1)...100
Gramling (C1)*...200
Graniteville (D4)*...3,362
Gray Court (C2)*...479
Grays (E6)...50
Great Falls (F2)*...3,533
Greeleyville (H4)*...600
Green Pond (F6)*...
Green Sea (J3)*...500
Greenville (C2)*...58,161
Greenwood (C3)*...13,806
Greer (C2)*...5,050
Gresham (J4)*...150
Grover (F5)*...145
Gurley (J3)*...300
Hagood (F3)*...4
Hamburg (D5)...
Hamer (J3)*...500
Hampton (E6)*...2,007
Hardeeville (E7)*...546
Harleyville (G5)*...483
Hartsville (G3)*...5,658
Heath Springs (F2)*...694
Helena (D3)*...
Hemingway (J4)*...821
Hendersonville (F6)...
Henry (J4)...100
Herbert (E2)...25
Hickory Grove (E2)*...275
Hilda (E5)*...304
Hiltonhead (F7)*...1,600
Hodges (C3)*...275
Holly Hill (G5)*...1,116
Hollywood (G6)*...246
Honea Path (C3)*...2,840
Honey Hill (H5)*...69
Hopkins (F4)*...125
Horatio (G3)*...50
Huger (H5)*...500
Hyman (H4)*...150
Industrial Mills (E2)...1,868
Inman (C1)*...1,514
Irmo (E3)*...281
Islandton (F6)*...25
Isle of Palms (H6)*...1,379
Iva (B3)*...1,164
Jackson (D5)*...500
Jacksonboro (G6)*...150
Jalapa (D3)...50
Jamestown (H5)*...1,100
Jamison (F4)...75
Jedburg (G5)*...500
Jefferson (G2)*...556
Jenkinsville (E3)*...
Joanna (D3)*...1,730
Jocassee (A2)...25
Johns Island (G6)*...5,000
Johnsonville (J4)*...616
Johnston (D4)*...1,426
Jonesville (D2)*...1,345
Jordan (G4)...15
Jordanville (J4)...150
Kathwood (D5)*...30
Kelton (D2)*...90
Kershaw (G2)*...1,376
Killian (F3)...50
Kinards (D3)*...
Kings Creek (E1)*...140
Kingsburg (H4)...50
Kingstree (H4)*...3,621
Kingville (F4)...100
Kirksey (C3)...
Kline (E5)*...230
La France (B2)*...
Ladson (G6)*...500
Lake City (H4)*...5,112
Lake View (J3)*...653
Lamar (G3)*...958
Lancaster (F2)*...7,159
Lancaster Mills (F2)...4,313
Lando (E2)*...500
Landrum (C1)*...1,333
Lane (H5)*...580
Lanford (C2)*...250
Langley (D4)*...3,000
Latta (J3)*...1,602
Laurens (C3)*...8,658
Leeds (E2)*...150
Lees (E5)...25
Leesville (E4)*...1,453
Lena (E6)*...71
Leo (H4)*...350
Lesslie (E2)*...275
Level Land (C3)...230
Levys (E7)*...50
Lewis Turnout (E2)...
Lexington (E4)*...1,081
Liberty (B2)*...2,291
Liberty Hill (F3)*...200
Lincolnville (G6)...278
Little Mountain (E3)*...213
Little River (K4)*...108
Little Rock (J3)*...150
Livingston (E4)*...210
Lobeco (F6)*...137
Lockhart (D2)*...1,685
Lodge (F5)*...316
Lone Star (F4)*...50
Long Creek (A2)*...35
Longs (K4)*...300
Longtown (F3)...
Loris (K3)*...1,614
Lowndesville (B3)*...252
Lowrys (E2)*...368
Lugoff (F3)*...
Luray (E6)*...102
Lydia (G3)*...
Lydia Mills (D3)*...1,212
Lykesland (F4)*...300
Lyman (C2)*...1,365
Lynchburg (G3)*...506
Macbeth (H5)*...100
Madison (A2)*...450
Manning (G4)*...2,775
Marietta (C1)*...1,000
Marion (J3)*...6,834
Mars Bluff (H3)*...
Martin (D5)*...
Mauldin (C2)*...300
Mayesville (G4)*...706
Mayo (D1)*...500
McBee (G3)*...420
McClellanville (H5)*...417
McColl (H2)*...2,688
McConnells (E2)*...255
McCormick (C4)*...1,744
Meggett (G6)*...224
Meriwether (C4)...
Miley (E6)*...300
Millettville (D5)*...
Minturn (J2)*...47
Modoc (C4)*...150
Monarch Mills (D2)...2,158
Moncks Corner (G5)*...1,818
Monetta (D4)*...
Mont Clare (H3)*...150
Monticello (E3)*...100
Montmorenci (D4)*...425
Moore (D2)*...300
Morgana (D4)...50
Moselle (E6)...30
Mount Carmel (B3)*...84
Mount Croghan (G2)*...209
Mount Holly (H5)*...
Mount Pleasant (H6)*...1,857
Mountain Rest (A2)*...
Mountville (C3)*...
Mullins (J3)*...4,916
Murrells Inlet (K4)*...50
Myers (H6)*...
Myrtle Beach (K4)*...3,345
Naval Base (G6)*...
Neeses (E4)*...328
Nesmith (H4)*...72
New Ellenton (D5)...
New Town Village (J3)...650
New Zion (H4)*...140
Newberry (D3)*...7,546
Newry (B2)*...1,000
Nichols (J3)*...380
Nimmons (B1)*...130
Nine Times (B2)...
Ninety Six (D3)*...1,556
Nixonville (K4)*...
Norris (B2)*...325
North (E4)*...954
North Augusta (C5)*...3,659
North Charleston (G6)*...18,000
North Mullins (J3)...297
Norway (E5)*...476
Oakland Mill (D3)...621
Oakley (G5)*...150
Oakway (A2)...99
Ocean Drive Beach (K4)*...255
Oceda (H5)...300
Ogden (E2)...12
Olanta (H4)*...586
Olar (E5)*...414
Ora (D2)*...185
Orangeburg (F4)*...15,322
Orr (B3)*...2,625
Osborn (G6)*...100
Oswego (G3)*...300
Owings (C2)*...200
Pacolet (D2)*...455
Pacolet Mills (D2)*...2,170
Padgetts (F5)...35
Pageland (G2)*...1,925
Pamplico (H4)*...728
Paris (C2)*...200
Parksville (C4)*...198
Parr (E3)*...100
Paris Island (F7)*...
Patrick (G2)*...310
Pauline (D2)*...200
Pawleys Island (J5)*...2,000
Paxville (G4)*...208
Peak (E3)*...134
Peedee (H3)*...150
Pelham (C2)*...750
Pelion (E4)*...196
Pelzer (B2)*...2,692
Pendleton (B2)*...1,432
Perry (E4)*...133
Pickens (B2)*...1,961
Pickens Mill (B2)...1,000
Piedmont (C2)*...2,673
Pineland (E6)*...
Pineville (H5)*...500
Pinewood (G4)*...578
Pinopolis (G5)*...300
Plantersville (J4)*...100
Pleasant Hill (F2)...200
Pleasant Lane (D4)...102
Plum Branch (C4)*...158
Pomaria (E3)*...251
Pontiac (F3)...45
Port Royal (F7)*...793
Poston (J4)*...100
Pregnall (G5)...200
Princeton (C2)*...
Pritchardville (E7)*...200
Prosperity (D3)*...699
Rains (J3)*...50
Ravenel (G6)*...337
Red River (F2)...346
Reevesville (F5)*...285
Reidville (C2)*...236
Rembert (G3)*...300
Renno (D2)*...100
Rhems (H4)...
Richburg (E2)*...238
Richland (A2)*...75
Richtex (E3)*...85
Ridge Spring (D4)*...598
Ridgeland (E7)*...1,078
Ridgeville (G5)*...507
Ridgeway (F3)*...414
Rimini (G4)*...250
Rion (E3)*...500
Ritter (F6)*...
Riverside (F2)...30
Rock Hill (E2)*...24,502
Rocky Bottom (B1)...100
Rodman (E2)*...750
Round O (F6)*...103
Rowesville (F5)*...363
Ruby (G2)*...315
Ruffin (F6)*...500
Russellville (H5)*...300
Saint Andrews (G6)*...20,000
Saint Charles (G3)*...100
Saint George (F5)*...1,938
Saint Matthews (F4)*...2,351
Saint Paul (G4)...125
Saint Stephen (H5)*...1,341
Salem (A2)*...504
Salley (E4)*...407
Salters (H4)*...
Saluda (D4)*...1,594
Samaria (E4)*...100
Sandy Springs (B2)*...500
Santee (F5)*...107
Santuck (D2)*...300
Sardinia (G4)*...150
Scotia (E6)*...226
Scranton (H4)*...602
Seabrook (F6)*...500
Sedalia (D2)*...300
Seiglingville (E5)...
Sellers (H3)*...530
Seneca (A2)*...3,649
Sharon (E2)*...365
Sheldon (F6)*...300
Shelton (E3)*...50
Shiloh (G4)...
Shoals Junction (C3)*...85
Shulerville (H5)*...400
Silver (G4)...15
Silverstreet (D3)*...201
Simpsonville (C2)*...1,529
Six Mile (B2)*...157
Slater (C1)*...1,000
Smith (E2)*...55
Smithboro (J3)...53
Smoaks (F5)*...130
Smyrna (E1)*...105
Snelling (E5)...34
Society Hill (H2)*...645
South Greenwood (C3)*...3,712
Spartanburg (C1)*...36,795
Springfield (E4)*...782
Starr (B3)*...282
Startex (C2)*...1,638
State Park (F3)*...
Steedman (E4)...50
Stokes (F6)...80
Stoneboro (F2)...100
Strangeville (F5)...626
Strawberry (G5)...
Strother (E3)*...25
Sullivans Island (H6)*...898
Summerton (G4)*...1,419
Summerville (G5)*...3,312
Summit (E4)*...105
Sumter (G4)*...20,185
Sunset (B1)*...40
Swansea (E4)*...762
Switzer (C2)*...64
Switzerland (E7)*...74
Sycamore (E5)*...383
Syracuse (G3)...50
Tamassee (A2)*...300
Tatum (H2)*...119
Taxahaw (F2)...40
Taylors (C2)*...1,518
Tigerville (C1)*...
Tillman (E7)*...500
Timmonsville (H3)*...2,001
Tirzah (E2)...75
Toddville (J4)*...200
Townville (B2)*...250
Tradesville (F2)...125
Travelers Rest (C2)*...1,200
Trenton (D4)*...296
Trio (H5)*...187
Troy (C3)*...242
Turbeville (G4)*...271
Ulmers (E5)*...139
Union (D2)*...9,730
Van Wyck (F2)*...100
Vance (G5)*...106
Varnville (E6)*...1,180
Vaucluse (D4)*...750
Verdery (C3)*...119
Wadmalaw Island (G6)*...2,500
Wagener (E4)*...584
Walhalla (A2)*...3,104
Wallace (H2)*...
Walterboro (F6)*...4,616
Wampee (K4)*...162
Wando (H6)*...114
Ward (D4)*...122
Ware Shoals (C3)*...3,032
Warrenville (D4)*...1,604
Wateree (F4)*...100
Waterloo (C3)*...162
Wattsville (D3)*...1,649
Wedgefield (F4)*...450
Wellford (C2)*...721
West Columbia (E4)*...4,373
West Marion (J3)...175
West Pelzer (B2)...578
West Springs (D2)...300
West Union (B2)*...429
Westminster (A2)*...2,219
Westville (F3)*...350
White Hall (F6)*...
White Oak (E3)*...200
White Pond (D5)*...275
White Rock (E3)*...250
Whitmire (D3)*...3,006
Whitney (D1)*...1,611
Wiggins (F6)*...50
Wilkins (F7)*...150
Williams (F5)*...254
Williamston (B2)*...2,782
Willington (B4)*...75
Williston (E5)*...896
Wilson (G4)*...300
Windsor (D5)*...
Winnsboro (E3)*...3,267
Winnsboro Mills (E3)...2,936
Wisacky (G3)*...135
Wolfton (E4)*...40
Woodford (E4)*...179
Woodruff (D2)*...3,831
Woodward (E2)*...150
Yemassee (F6)*...712
Yonges Island (G6)*...
York (E1)*...4,181
Zion (J3)...

Map on Page 87

SOUTH DAKOTA

Total Population 652,740

67 COUNTIES

Aurora (M6)...5,020
Beadle (N5)...21,082
Bennett (F7)...3,396
Bon Homme (O7)...9,440
Brookings (R5)...17,851
Brown (N2)...32,617
Brule (L6)...6,076
Buffalo (L5)...1,615
Butte (B4)...8,161
Campbell (J2)...4,046
Charles Mix (M7)...15,558
Clark (O4)...8,369
Clay (P8)...10,993
Codington (P4)...18,944
Corson (G2)...6,168
Custer (B6)...5,517
Davison (N6)...16,522
Day (O3)...12,294
Deuel (R4)...7,689
Dewey (G3)...4,968
Douglas (N7)...5,636
Edmunds (L3)...7,275
Fall River (B7)...10,439
Faulk (L3)...4,752
Grant (R3)...10,233
Gregory (L7)...8,556
Haakon (F5)...3,167
Hamlin (P4)...7,058
Hand (L4)...7,149
Hanson (O6)...4,896
Harding (B2)...2,289
Hughes (J5)...8,111
Hutchinson (O7)...11,423
Hyde (K4)...2,811
Jackson (F6)...1,768
Jerauld (M5)...4,476
Jones (H6)...2,281
Kingsbury (O5)...9,962
Lake (P5)...11,792
Lawrence (B5)...16,648
Lincoln (R7)...12,767
Lyman (J6)...4,572
Marshall (O2)...7,835
McCook (P6)...8,828
McPherson (L2)...7,071
Meade (D5)...11,516
Mellette (H6)...3,046
Miner (O5)...6,268
Minnehaha (R6)...70,910
Moody (R5)...9,252
Pennington (C6)...34,053
Perkins (D3)...6,776
Potter (J3)...4,688
Roberts (P2)...14,929
Sanborn (N5)...5,142
Shannon (D7)...5,669
Spink (N4)...12,204
Stanley (H5)...2,055
Sully (J4)...2,713
Todd (H7)...4,758
Tripp (K7)...9,139
Turner (P7)...12,100
Union (R8)...10,792
Walworth (J3)...7,648
Washabaugh (F6)...1,551
Yankton (P7)...16,804
Ziebach (F4)...2,606

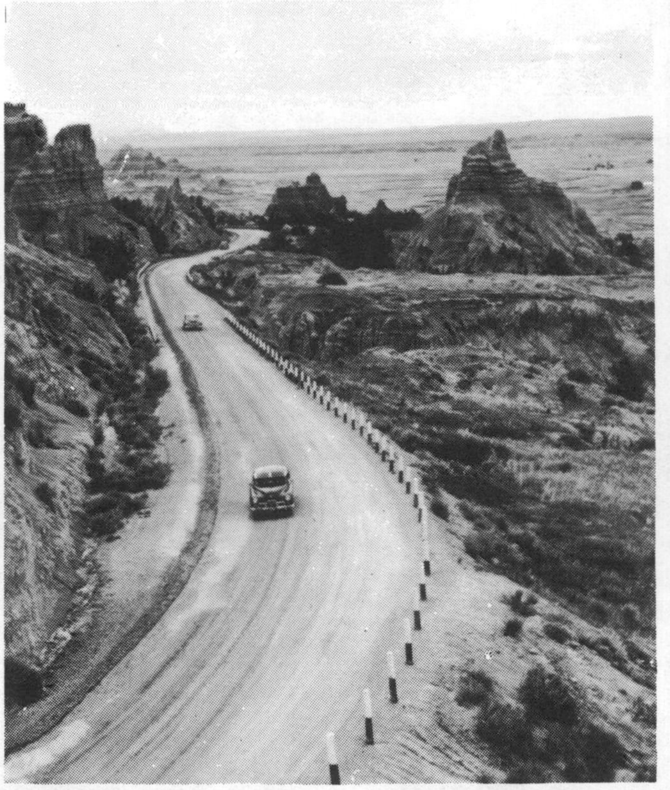

CITIES and TOWNS

Aberdeen (M3)*	21,051
Academy (M7)*	20
Adelaide (N3)	
Agar (J4)*	141
Ahnberg (P5)	3
Akaska (J3)*	84
Albee (S3)*	75
Alcester (R7)*	585
Alexandria (O6)*	714
Allen (F7)*	130
Alpena (N5)*	426
Alsen (R8)	22
Altamont (R4)*	76
Amherst (O2)*	70
Andover (O3)*	277
Appleby (R4)	8
Ardmore (B7)*	107
Argonne (O5)*	25
Arlington (P5)*	1,096
Armour (N7)*	900
Arpan (B4)	50
Artas (K2)*	172
Artesian (O6)*	429
Ashton (N3)*	222
Astoria (S4)*	206
Athboy (F2)	2
Athol (M3)*	120
Aurora (R5)*	202
Avance (E4)*	10
Avon (N8)*	692
Badger (P5)*	180
Badnation (J6)	3
Baltic (R6)*	255
Bancroft (O4)*	100
Barnard (N2)*	108
Batesland (E7)*	88
Bath (N3)*	90
Bear Butte (C5)*	50
Beardsley (O7)	4
Beebe (L3)	4
Belle Fourche (B4)*	3,540
Belvidere (G6)*	172
Bemis (R4)*	51
Benclare (R6)	15
Bend (D5)	5
Beresford (R7)*	1,686
Berton (P5)	9
Betts (N6)	5
Big Springs (S8)	21
Big Stone City (S3)*	829
Bijou Hills (L6)*	35
Bison (E2)*	457
Bixby (D3)*	1
Black Hawk (C5)*	91
Blackpipe (G7)*	
Blue Bell (C6)	4
Blue Range (O7)	
Blunt (J4)*	423
Bonesteel (M7)*	485
Bonilla (N4)*	90
Booge (R6)	10
Bovee (M7)*	25
Bowdle (K3)*	788
Box Elder (D5)*	33
Bradley (O3)*	226
Brandon (R6)*	250
Brandt (R4)*	211
Brave (J6)	2
Brentford (N3)*	132
Bridger (E4)	5
Bridgewater (P6)*	748
Bristol (O3)*	647
Britton (O2)*	1,430
Broadland (N4)*	74
Brookings (R5)*	7,764
Bruce (R5)*	305
Bryant (P4)*	624
Buffalo (B2)*	380
Buffalo Gap (C6)*	186
Bullhead (G2)*	250
Bullock (B2)*	5
Burbank (R8)*	125
Burdette (M4)	6
Burdock (B7)*	7
Burke (L7)*	829
Burkmere (L3)*	10
Bushnell (R5)*	96
Butler (O3)*	109
Cadillac (H2)	6
Camp Crook (B2)*	122
Canistota (P6)*	687
Canning (K5)*	
Canova (O6)*	340
Canton (R7)*	2,530
Capa (H5)*	49
Caputa (D5)*	30
Carpenter (O4)*	75
Carter (J7)*	16
Carthage (O5)*	458
Cash (D2)	2
Castle Rock (B4)*	11
Castlewood (R4)*	498
Cavour (N5)*	154
Cedar Canyon (D3)	3
Cedarbutte (H6)*	5
Center (P6)	18
Center Point (P7)	10
Centerville (R7)*	1,053
Central City (B5)*	218
Chalkbutte (D4)*	4
Chamberlain (L6)*	1,912
Chance (E3)*	16
Chancellor (R7)*	193
Chelsea (M3)*	41
Cherry Creek (F4)*	140
Chester (R6)*	200
Cheyenne Agency (J3)*	450
Cilson (B7)	
Claire City (P2)*	109
Claremont (N2)*	236
Clark (O4)*	1,471
Clarno (P6)	2
Clayton (O7)	10
Clearfield (K7)*	31
Clear Lake (R4)*	1,105
Coal Springs (F3)*	2
Colman (R6)*	509
Colome (K7)*	451
Colton (P6)*	521
Columbia (N2)*	270
Conata (E6)	50
Conde (N3)*	409
Cooper (E4)*	3
Corona (R3)*	191
Corsica (N7)*	551
Corson (R6)*	49
Cottonwood (F6)*	102
Crandall (O3)*	35
Crandon (N4)	10
Craven (M3)	1
Creighton (E5)*	5
Cresbard (M3)*	235
Creston (D6)	10
Crocker (O3)*	72
Crooks (R6)*	120
Crow Lake (M6)	10
Custer (B6)*	2,017
Cuthbert (N6)*	14
Dahlberg (P2)	8
Dalesburg (P8)	35
Dallas (K7)*	244
Dalzell (E5)*	62
Danforth (M5)	10
Dante (N7)*	140
Dark Canyon (C5)	50
Date (D3)*	4
Davis (P7)*	153
De Grey (K5)*	6
De Smet (O5)*	1,180
Deadwood (B5)*	3,288
Deerfield (B5)*	38
Dell Rapids (R6)*	1,650
Delmont (N7)*	405
Dempster (R4)*	99
Denby (E7)*	5
Dewey (A6)*	40
Dimock (O7)*	120
Dixon (L7)*	25
Doland (N4)*	535
Dolton (P7)*	93
Dowling (F5)*	9
Draper (J6)*	252
Dumont (B5)	6
Dupree (F3)*	438
Duxbury (M3)	5
Eagle (L6)	11
Eagle Butte (G3)*	375
Eakin (K4)	
East Mobridge (J2)	51
Eden (P2)*	149
Edgemont (B7)*	1,158
Edson (E3)	10
Egan (R6)*	347
Elk Mountain (B6)	
Elk Point (R8)*	1,367
Elkton (S5)*	657
Ellingson (D2)*	4
Ellis (R6)	21
Elm Springs (D5)*	7
Elmore (B5)	8
Elrod (O4)*	37
Emery (O6)*	480
Endlee (D3)	3
Englewood (B5)	16
Enning (E4)*	20
Epiphany (O6)	40
Erskine (B7)	5
Erwin (P5)*	153
Esmond (O5)*	49
Estelline (R4)*	760
Ethan (N6)*	319
Eureka (K2)*	1,576
Fairburn (C6)*	80
Fairfax (M7)*	301
Fairpoint (D4)*	
Fairview (R7)*	155
Faith (E4)*	599
Farmer (O6)*	114
Farmingdale (D6)*	19
Farwell (O6)	13
Faulkton (M3)*	837
Fedora (O5)*	125
Ferney (N3)*	100
Firesteel (G3)*	110
Flandreau (R5)*	2,193
Florence (P3)*	226
Foley (P4)	5
Folsom (D6)	2
Forest City (J4)	12
Forestburg (N5)*	144
Fort Lookout (K6)	
Fort Meade (C5)*	860
Fort Pierre (H5)*	951
Fort Thompson (L5)*	225
Frankfort (N4)*	331
Franklin (P6)	27
Frederick (N2)*	408
Freeman (O7)*	944
Fruitdale (B4)*	70
Fullerville (P8)	
Fulton (O6)*	139
Gage (M2)	2
Galena (B5)	10
Gallup (N3)	6
Gannvalley (L5)*	101
Garden City (O4)*	282
Garretson (S6)*	745
Gary (S4)*	558
Gayville (P8)*	271
Geddes (M7)*	502
Gettysburg (K3)*	1,555
Glad Valley (F3)*	20
Glencross (H3)*	30
Glenham (J2)*	168
Goodwin (R4)*	141
Gorman (K4)	6
Govert (C3)*	10
Greenfield (R8)	22
Greenway (K2)*	
Greenwood (N8)*	44
Gregory (L7)*	1,375
Grenville (O3)*	207
Gretna (L3)	2
Grosse (L6)	4
Groton (N3)*	1,084
Grover (P4)*	30
Gustave (B3)*	2
Hamill (K6)*	48
Hammer (R2)*	77
Hanna (B5)	12
Hanton (P4)	
Harding (B3)*	
Harrington (G7)*	3
Harrisburg (R7)*	274
Harrison (M7)*	88
Harrold (K4)*	263
Hartford (R6)*	592
Hartley (F5)	1
Hay Creek (C3)	
Haydraw (D5)*	5
Hayes (H4)*	30
Hayti (P4)*	413
Hazel (P4)*	161
Hecla (N2)*	500
Henry (P4)*	323
Heppner (B7)*	3
Hereford (D5)*	4
Hermosa (C6)*	123
Herreid (K2)*	633
Herrick (L7)*	169
Hetland (P5)*	123
Hidden Timber (J7)*	12
Highmore (L4)*	1,158
Hiland (P3)*	5
Hill City (B6)*	361
Hilland (F5)*	5
Hillhead (O2)*	100
Hillside (N7)	14
Hillsview (L2)*	68
Hisega (C5)	15
Hisle (F7)*	29
Hitchcock (M4)*	227
Holabird (K4)*	30
Holmquist (O3)*	35
Hooker (R7)*	30
Hoover (C3)*	4
Hosmer (L2)*	533
Hot Springs (C7)*	5,030
Houghton (N2)*	90
Hoven (K3)*	552
Howard (P5)*	1,251
Howes (E4)*	
Hudson (R7)*	500
Huffton (N2)*	17
Humboldt (P6)*	450
Hurley (P7)*	474
Huron (N5)*	12,788
Ideal (K6)*	10
Igloo (B7)*	1,920
Imlay (E6)*	3
Interior (F6)*	126
Iona (L6)*	17
Ipswich (L3)*	1,058
Irene (P7)*	374
Iroquois (O5)*	413
Isabel (G3)*	511
James (N3)	8
Janousek (O8)	
Java (K3)*	433
Jefferson (S8)*	466
Joe Creek (K5)*	56
Joubert (M7)	20
Junius (P6)*	30
Kadoka (F6)*	584
Kampeska (P4)	16
Karinen (B2)*	1
Kaylor (O7)*	175
Keldron (F2)*	10
Kenel (H2)*	129
Kennebec (K6)*	374
Keyapaha (J7)*	19
Keystone (C6)*	600
Kidder (O2)*	146
Kimball (M6)*	952
Kingsburg (O8)	11
Kirley (G4)*	5
Kranzburg (R4)*	135
Kyle (E7)*	89
La Bolt (R3)*	164
La Plant (H3)*	100
Ladelle (N4)	5
Ladner (B2)*	10
Lake Andes (M7)*	1,851
Lake City (O2)*	110
Lake Norden (P4)*	373
Lake Preston (P5)*	957
Lakeport (O8)	
Lakeview (H7)*	16
Lane (N5)*	145
Langford (O2)*	456
Lantry (G3)*	26
Lead (B5)*	6,422
Lebanon (K3)*	215
Lemmon (E2)*	2,760
Lennox (R7)*	1,218
Leola (M2)*	772
Lesterville (O7)*	192
Letcher (N6)*	291
Lightcap (G2)	2
Lily (O3)*	139
Little Eagle (H2)*	575
Lodgepole (D2)*	30
Longlake (L2)*	175
Longvalley (F7)*	10
Loomis (N6)*	67
Lower Brule (K5)*	162
Lowry (K3)*	70
Loyalton (L3)*	57
Lucas (L7)*	25
Ludlow (C2)*	6
Lyman (K6)*	16
Lyons (R6)*	77
Lyonville (M6)	
Madison (P6)*	5,153
Mahto (H2)*	55
Manchester (O5)*	40
Manderson (D7)*	110
Manila (G5)	5
Mansfield (M3)*	200
Mapleleaf (H2)	
Marcus (E4)*	11
Marion (P7)*	794
Marlow (P2)	8
Martin (F7)*	989
Marty (N8)*	600
Marvin (R3)*	110
Mason (B3)	1
Mathews (P5)	
Maurine (E3)*	11
McCook (S8)	300
McIntosh (G2)*	628
McLaughlin (H2)*	713
Meadow (E2)*	37
Meckling (R8)*	111
Melham (O4)	
Mellette (N3)*	250
Menno (P7)*	868
Midland (G5)*	387
Midway (P7)	15
Milbank (R3)*	2,982
Milesville (F5)*	19
Millboro (K7)*	33
Miller (L4)*	1,916
Milltown (O7)*	39
Mina (M3)*	46
Minnekahta (B7)	6
Miranda (M4)*	79
Mission (H7)*	388
Mission Hill (P8)*	169
Mission Ridge (H4)*	2
Mitchell (N6)*	12,123
Mobridge (J2)*	3,753
Moenville (G4)*	4
Monroe (P7)*	160
Montrose (P6)*	448
Moon (B6)*	4
Morefield (R6)	7
Moritz (S4)	16
Morristown (F2)*	190
Mosher (J7)*	18
Mossman (H3)	7
Mound City (K2)*	177
Mount Vernon (N6)*	387
Mud Butte (D4)*	16
Murdo (H6)*	739
Murphy (C5)	10
Mystic (B5)*	40
Nahant (B5)	
Nahon (N3)	4
Nansen (O5)	2
Naples (O4)*	62
Nemo (B5)*	100
New Effington (R2)*	367
New Holland (M7)*	125
New Underwood (D5)*	268
New Witten (K7)	198
Newark (O2)*	80
Newell (C4)*	784
Nisland (C4)*	216
Nora (R8)	10
Norbeck (L3)*	16
Norris (G7)*	111
Northville (M3)*	220
Nowlin (G5)*	20
Nunda (P5)*	102
Oacoma (L6)*	231
Oahe (J5)	32
Oelrichs (C7)*	168
Oglala (D7)*	
Okaton (H6)*	137
Okobojo (J4)	2
Okreek (J7)*	260
Oldham (P5)*	349
Olivet (O7)*	202
Onaka (L3)*	158
Onida (K4)*	822
Opal (D4)*	50
Oral (C7)*	100
Ordway (N2)	6
Oreville (B6)	
Orient (L4)*	206
Ortley (P3)*	144
Osceola (O5)*	37
Ottumwa (G5)*	4
Owanka (D5)*	50
Pactola (C5)*	85
Parade (G3)*	8
Parker (P7)*	1,148
Parkston (O7)*	1,354
Parmelee (G7)*	116
Patricia (G7)*	10
Paxton (L7)	11
Pedro (E5)*	19
Peever (R2)*	221
Perkins (O8)	14
Philip (F5)*	810
Pickstown (M7)*	2,217
Piedmont (C5)*	200
Pierpont (O3)*	326
PIERRE (J5)*	5,715
Pine Ridge ((E7)*	2,000
Plainview (E4)*	7
Plana (N2)	15
Plankinton (N6)*	754
Platte (M7)*	1,069
Poinsette (P4)	50
Pollock (J2)*	395
Porcupine (E7)*	25
Potato Creek (F6)*	8
Powell (G5)*	15
Presho (J6)*	712
Pringle (B6)*	193
Promise (H3)*	7
Provo (B7)*	100
Pukwana (L6)*	302
Putney (N2)*	14
Quinn (E5)*	214
Ralph (C2)*	2
Ramona (P5)*	278
Randolph (N3)*	29
Rapid City (C5)*	25,310
Rauville (P3)	8
Ravinia (N7)*	200
Raymond (O4)*	174
Redelm (F3)*	6
Redfern (B5)	
Redfield (N4)*	2,655
Redig (C3)*	10
Redowl (D4)*	11
Ree Heights (L4)*	254
Reliance (K6)*	215
Renner (R6)*	99
Reva (C2)*	6
Revillo (R3)*	249
Richland (R8)	30
Richmond (M2)	7
Ridgeview (H3)*	60
Robey (M6)	100
Rochford (B5)*	50
Rockerville (C6)	30
Rockham (M4)*	113
Rockyford (E7)*	11
Roscoe (L3)*	726
Rosebud (H7)*	
Rosholt (R2)*	387
Roslyn (P2)*	222
Roswell (O6)*	69
Roubaix (B5)	
Rouseau (K5)	41
Rowena (R6)*	70
Rudolph (N3)	4
Rumford (B7)*	8
Running Water (O8)	23
Rutland (P5)*	100
Saint Charles (L7)*	50
St. Francis (H7)*	241
St. Lawrence (M4)*	261
St. Onge (B4)*	104
Salem (P6)*	1,119
Sanator (B6)*	251
Sansarc (H5)*	4
Savoy (B5)	16
Scenic (D6)*	75
Scotland (O7)*	1,188
Selby (J3)*	706
Seneca (L3)*	204
Shadehill (E2)*	21
Sheridan (C5)	8
Sherman (S6)*	120
Shindler (R7)*	50
Silver City (B5)*	35
Sinai (P5)*	181
Sioux Falls (R6)*	52,696
Sisseton (R2)*	2,871
Smithwick (C7)*	100
Sorum (D3)*	3
South Shore (P3)*	269
So. Sioux Falls (R6)	1,586
Spain (O2)	
Spearfish (B5)*	2,755
Spencer (O6)*	552
Spink (R8)	41
Spottswood (M4)	
Springfield (N8)*	801
Stamford (G6)*	10
Stephan (K5)*	150
Stevens (R8)*	300
Stickney (M6)*	388
Stockholm (R3)*	114
Stoneville (D4)*	5
Storla (M6)	36
Strandburg (R3)*	144
Stratford (N3)*	164
Strool (D3)*	75
Sturgis (B5)*	3,471
Sulphur (D4)*	3
Summit (P3)*	431
Swett (E7)	12
Sylvan Lake (B6)*	
Tabor (O8)*	373
Tacoma Park (N2)*	15
Tea (R7)*	151
Templeton (M5)	5
Terry (B5)	70
Thomas (P4)*	37
Thunder Hawk (F2)*	82
Tilford (C5)*	85
Timber Lake (H3)*	552
Tinton (A5)*	10
Tolstoy (K3)*	180
Toronto (R4)*	322
Trail City (H3)*	200
Trent (R6)*	213
Tripp (N7)*	913
Trojan (B5)*	200
Troy (R3)*	44
Tulare (N4)*	212
Turton (N3)*	201
Tuthill (G7)*	50
Twin Brooks (R3)*	113
Tyndall (O8)*	1,292
Union Center (D4)*	10
Unityville (P6)*	85
Utica (P8)*	84
Vale (C4)*	152
Valley Springs (S6)*	389
Van Metre (H5)*	10
Vayland (M5)*	24
Veblen (P2)*	476
Verdon (N3)*	34
Vermillion (R8)*	5,337
Vetal (G7)*	38
Viborg (P7)*	644
Victor (R2)*	35
Vienna (O4)*	306
Viewfield (D5)*	3
Vilas (O6)*	71
Virgil (N5)*	124
Vivian (J6)*	250
Volga (R5)*	578
Volin (P8)*	197
Wagner (N7)*	1,528
Wakonda (P7)*	454
Wakpala (H2)*	350
Walker (G2)*	27
Wall (E6)*	556
Wallace (P3)*	188
Wanamaker (G7)*	5
Wanblee (F6)*	325
Ward (R5)*	96
Warner (M3)*	115
Wasta (D5)*	144
Watauga (G2)*	96
Watertown (P4)*	12,699
Waubay (P3)*	879
Waverly (R3)*	50
Webster (P3)*	2,503
Wecota (L3)*	40
Wendte (H5)*	40
Wentworth (R6)*	270
Wessington (M5)*	467
Wessington Spgs. (M5)*	1,453
West Britton (O2)	
West Carlock (L7)	3
Westerville (P8)	17
Westover (H6)*	2
Westport (M2)*	116
Weta (F6)	
Wetonka (M2)*	115
Wewela (K7)*	29
White (R5)*	525
White Butte (E2)*	154
White Lake (M6)*	395
White Owl (E4)*	19
White River (H6)*	465
White Rock (R2)*	113
Whitedeer (F2)	
Whitehorse (H3)*	67
Whitewood (B5)*	304
Whitlocks Cross'g (J3)*	2
Willett (B2)*	
Willow Lake (O4)*	48
Wilmot (R3)*	59
Winfred (P6)*	17
Winner (K7)*	3,25
Winship (M2)	
Wist (P2)	
Witten (J7)*	
Wolsey (N5)*	39
Wood (J6)*	26
Woonsocket (N5)*	1,05
Worthing (R7)*	27
Wounded Knee (D7)*	15
Yale (O5)*	16
Yankton (P8)*	7,70
Zell (M4)*	9
Zeona (D3)*	

Map on Page 88

TENNESSEE

Total Population 3,291,718

95 COUNTIES

Anderson (N2)	59,407
Bedford (J3)	23,627
Benton (E2)	11,495
Bledsoe (L3)	8,561
Blount (O3)	54,691
Bradley (M4)	32,338
Campbell (N2)	34,369
Cannon (J3)	9,174
Carroll (E3)	26,553
Carter (R2)	42,432
Cheatham (G2)	9,167
Chester (D4)	11,149
Claiborne (O2)	24,788
Clay (K1)	8,701
Cocke (P3)	22,991
Coffee (J3)	23,049
Crockett (C3)	16,624
Cumberland (M3)	18,877
Davidson (H2)	321,758
De Kalb (K3)	11,680
Decatur (F3)	9,442
Dickson (G2)	18,805
Dyer (C2)	33,473
Fayette (C4)	27,535
Fentress (M2)	14,917
Franklin (J4)	25,431
Gibson (D3)	48,132
Giles (G4)	26,961
Grainger (O2)	13,086
Greene (Q2)	41,048
Grundy (K4)	12,558
Hamblen (P2)	23,976
Hamilton (L4)	208,255
Hancock (P1)	9,116
Hardeman (C4)	23,311
Hardin (E4)	16,908
Hawkins (P2)	30,494
Haywood (C3)	26,212
Henderson (E3)	17,173
Henry (E2)	23,828
Hickman (G3)	13,353
Houston (F2)	5,318
Humphreys (F2)	11,030
Jackson (K2)	12,348
Jefferson (P2)	19,667
Johnson (S2)	12,278
Knox (O3)	223,00
Lake (B2)	11,65
Lauderdale (B3)	25,04
Lawrence (G4)	28,81
Lewis (F3)	6,07
Lincoln (H4)	25,62
Loudon (N3)	23,18
Macon (J1)	13,59

Madison (D3) 60,128
Marion (K4) 20,520
Marshall (H4) 17,768
Maury (G3) 40,368
Mc Minn (M4) 32,024
Mc Nairy (D4) 20,390
Meigs (M3) 6,080
Monroe (N4) 24,513
Montgomery (G2) 44,186
Moore (J4) 3,948
Morgan (M2) 15,727
Obion (C2) 29,056
Overton (L2) 17,566
Perry (F3) 6,462
Pickett (M1) 5,093
Polk (N4) 14,074
Putnam (K2) 29,869
Rhea (M3) 16,041
Roane (M3) 31,665
Robertson (H1) 27,024
Rutherford (J3) 40,696
Scott (M2) 17,362
Sequatchie (L4) 5,685
Sevier (O3) 23,375
Shelby (B4) 482,393
Smith (K2) 14,098
Stewart (F1) 9,175
Sullivan (R1) 95,063
Sumner (J2) 33,533
Tipton (B3) 29,782
Trousdale (J2) 5,520
Unicoi (R2) 15,886
Union (O2) 8,670
Van Buren (L3) 3,985
Warren (K3) 22,271
Washington (Q2) 59,971
Wayne (F4) 13,864
Weakley (D2) 27,962
White (L3) 16,204
Williamson (H3) 24,307
Wilson (J2) 26,318

CITIES and TOWNS

Abiff (G3) 12
Adams (G1)* 525
Adamsville (E4)* 927
Addison (M4) 40
Aetna (G3)* 100
Afton (Q2)* 150
Alamo (C3)* 1,501
Alcoa (N3)* 6,355
Alexandria (J2)* 372
Algood (K2)* 729
Allardt (M2)* 800
Allens (C3)
Allisona (H3)* 75
Allons (L2)* 270
Allred (L2)* 300
Alpine (L2)* 200
Altamont (K4)* 296
Alto (K4) 125
Anderson (K4)* 375
Andersonville (O2)* 525
Anes (H3) 35
Annadel (M2) 25
Anthras (N1) 100
Antioch (H2)* 298
Apison (L5)*
Archville (N4)* 150
Ardmore (H4)* 157
Arlington (B4)* 463
Armathwaite (M2)* 350
Arrington (H3)* 250
Arthur (O1)* 450
Ashland City (G2)* 1,024
Ashport (B3)*
Ashwood (G3)* 80
Aspen Hill (G4)* 225
Athens (M4)* 8,618
Atoka (B4)* 334
Atwood (D3)* 1,000
Auburntown (J3)* 273
Bailey (B4)* 207
Baileyton (Q2)* 224
Bakerville (F3)* 68
Bakewell (L4)* 250
Banner Springs (M2)* 406
Barr (B3)* 100
Barren Plains (H1) 100
Bartlett (B4)* 489
Bath Springs (E4)* 50
Baugh (H4) 25
Baxter (K2)* 861
Beacon (E3)* 200
Bean Station (P2)*
Beans Creek (J4)* 50
Bear Spring (F2) 100
Bearden (N3) 1,600
Beardstown (F3)* 100
Beech Bluff (D3)* 180
Beechgrove (J3)* 250
Beersheba Springs (K4)* 300
Belfast (H4)* 150
Bell Buckle (J3)* 341
Belle Meade (H2) 2,831
Belleview (H2)* 250
Bells (C3)* 1,225
Belltown (N4) 100
Belvidere (J4)* 250
Bemis (D3)* 3,248
Benton (M4)* 650
Berry Hill ‡(H2)* 1,248
Bethel (G4)* 150
Bethel Springs (D4)* 623
Bethpage (J1)* 280
Big Lick (L3)* 150
Big Rock (F1)* 250
Big Sandy (E2)* 621
Big Spring (M4)* 68
Birchwood (M4)* 800
Blaine (O2)* 300
Blanche (H4)* 250
Block (N2)* 160
Bloomington Springs (K2)* 200
Blountville (R1)* 500
Bluff City (R2)* 1,074
Bogota (C2)* 300
Bolivar (C4)* 2,429
Bon Air (L3)* 300
Bon Aqua (G3)* 120
Boom (L1)* 121
Boonshill (H4) 35
Boothspoint (B2)* 200
Boston (G3) 100
Boyds Creek (O3)* 485
Braden (B4)* 250
Bradford (D2)* 599
Bradyville (J3)* 98
Brazil (C3) 140
Brentwood (H2)*
Briceville (N2)* 2,500
Bridgeport (P3)*
Brighton (B4)* 306
Bristol (R1)* 16,771
Brockdell (L3)*
Brotherton (L2)* 600
Brownsville (C3)* 4,711
Bruceton (E2)* 1,204
Brunswick (B4)* 500
Brush Creek (J2)* 200
Buchanan (E2)* 100
Buena Vista (E3)* 60
Buffalo (F3)* 25
Buffalo Valley (K2)* 300
Buford (G4)
Bullsgap (P2)* 558
Bumpus Mills (F1)* 225
Bunker Hill (H4) 100
Burlison (B3)* 75
Burns (G2)*
Burrville (M2)* 230
Bybee (P2)* 250
Byington (N3)* 125
Byrdstown (L1)* 379
Cades (D3)* 68
Cades Cove (O3) 40
Cagle (L4) 165
Cainsville (J3)
Calderwood (N3)* 245
Calhoun (M4)* 450
Cambria (M4) 100
Camden (E2)* 2,029
Campaign (K3)* 100
Caneyspring (H3) 55
Capleville (B4)* 950
Carderview (S2)*
Carter (R2) 600
Carters Creek (G3)* 250
Carthage (K2)* 1,604
Caryville (N2)* 1,234
Castalian Springs (J2)* 129
Cedar Grove (D3)* 25
Cedar Hill (H1)* 872
Cedarcreek (Q2)* 175
Celina (K1)* 1,136
Centerville (G3)* 1,532
Cerro Gordo (E4)* 10
Chalybeate (K3)
Chanute (L1) 450
Chapel Hill (H3)* 603
Chapmansboro (G2)* 26
Charleston (M4)*
Charlotte (G2)* 478
Chaska (N1)* 121
Chattanooga (K4)* 131,041
Chattanooga (urban area) 167,031
Cherry (B3)
Chesterfield (E3)* 150
Chestnut Mound (K2)* 150
Chewalla (D4)* 150
Chilhowee (O3)* 150
Christiana (J3)* 300
Chuckey (Q2)* 300
Church Hill (Q1)* 1,741
Clairfield (O1)* 2,000
Clarkrange (L2)*
Clarksburg (E3)* 350
Clarksville (G1)* 16,246
Clayton (C2) 30
Clementsville (K1) 25
Cleveland (M4)* 12,605
Clifton (F4)* 818
Clifty (L3)* 51
Clinchmore (N2)*
Clinton (N2)* 3,712
Clouds (O2)* 50
Coalfield (M2)*
Coalmont (K4)* 800
Coble (F3) 100
Cokercreek (N4)* 366
Coldwater (H4) 85
Colesburg (G2) 150
College Grove (H3)* 300
Collegedale (M4)* 1,200
Collierville (B4)* 1,153
Collinwood (F4)* 589
Columbia (G3)* 10,911
Como (E2)* 120
Conasauga (M4)* 475
Concord (N3)* 294
Cookeville (L2)* 6,924
Copperhill (N4)* 924
Cordova (B4)* 250
Cornersville (H4)* 358
Corryton (O2)* 1,275
Cortner (J4) 63
Cosby (P3)*
Cottagegrove (E2)* 126
Cottontown (H2)* 250
Cotula (O2) 250
Counce (E4)*
Covington (B3)* 4,379
Cowan (J4)* 1,835
Crab Orchard (M3)* 315
Crawford (L2)* 100
Creston (L2) 125
Crestview (G4) 356
Crockett Mills (C3)* 148
Cross Plains (H1)* 200
Crossville (L3)* 2,291
Crump (E4)* 500
Culleoka (G4)* 300
Cumberland City (F2)* 500
Cumberland Furnace (G2)* 350
Cumberland Gap (O1)* 403
Cummingsville (L3) 50
Cunningham (G2)* 250
Curve (B3)
Cypress Inn (F4)* 1,000
Daisy (L4)* 1,336
Dale Hollow ‡(K1) 5
Dancyville (C4) 80
Dandridge (O2)* 690
Danville (F2)
Darden (E3)* 250
Daus (L4)*
Davidson (L2)
Daylight (K8)* 250
Dayton (L3)* 3,191
De Rossett (L3)* 250
Dean (N2)* 130
Decatur (M3)* 235
Decaturville (E3)* 514
Decherd (J4)* 1,435
Deer Lodge (M2)* 275
Del Rio (P3)* 300
Delano (M4)* 350
Dellrose (H4)* 350
Denmark (D3)* 69
Densons Landing (F3)
Denver (F2)* 130
Devonia (N2)* 250
Diana (H4)*
Dickson (G2)* 3,348
Difficult (K2)* 500
Dixon Springs (J2)* 200
Dodson (L3) 98
Doeville (S2)* 125
Donelson (H2)* 1,765
Double Springs (K2)* 200
Dover (F2)* 800
Dowelltown (K2)* 262
Doyle (K3)* 500
Dresden (D2)* 1,509
Drummonds (A4)* 160
Duck River (G3)*
Ducktown (N4)* 1,064
Duff (N2)*
Dukedom (D2)* 115
Dunlap (L4)* 873
Dyer (D2)* 1,864
Dyersburg (C2)* 10,885
Eads (B4)* 250
Eagan (O1)* 300
Eagle Creek (E3)*
Eagleville (H3)* 378
East Jamestown (M2)* 100
East Ridge (L5)* 9,645
Eastland (L3)*
Eaton (C3)*
Edenwold (H2)* 500
Eidson (P1)* 300
Elbridge (C2)* 89
Elgin (M2)* 350
Elizabethton (R2)* 10,754
Elk Valley (N1)* 300
Elkmont (O3) 35
Elkton (H4)* 168
Ellendale (B4)* 700
Elora (J4)* 225
Elva (M1) 15
Embreeville (Q2)* 1,273
Emory Gap (M3)* 350
Englewood (M4)* 1,545
Enville (E4)* 350
Erie (M3)* 25
Erin (F2)* 858
Erwin (R2)* 3,387
Estill Springs (J4)* 496
Ethridge (G4)* 500
Etowah (M4)* 3,261
Eva (E2)* 250
Evensville (M3)* 450
Fairfield (J3) 100
Fairview (G3)*
Fall Branch (Q2)* 300
Fall Mills (J4) 34
Fall River (G4) 50
Farmers Exchange (F3)* 134
Farmington (H3) 200
Farner (N4)* 200
Faxon (E2)* 120
Fayetteville (H4)* 5,447
Finger (D4)* 130
Finley (B2)* 1,000
Five Points (G4)* 125
Flag Pond (Q2)* 300
Flat Woods (F4)* 275
Flatcreek (J4)
Flintville (J4)* 100
Florence (H3) 125
Flynns Lick (K2) 50
Forbus (M1)* 200
Fordtown (Q2)*
Forest Hill (B4)* 200
Fork Mountain (N2)* 900
Fort Henry (E1)* 10
Fort Pillow (B3)* 150
Fosterville (J3)* 200
Fountain City (O2)* 15,000
Fountain Head (J1)* 252
Fowlkes (C3)* 150
Frankewing (H4)* 90
Frankfort (M2)
Franklin (H3)* 5,475
Frayser (A4)*
French Broad (P3)* 154
Friendship (C3)* 452
Friendsville (N3)* 625
Fruitland (D3)*
Fruitvale (C3)* 50
Fulton (B3)* 150
Gadsden (D3)* 255
Gainesboro (K2)* 992
Gallatin (H2)* 5,107
Gallaway (B4)* 200
Gardner (D2)
Garland (B3) 157
Gassaway (K3)* 80
Gates (C3)* 234
Gatlinburg (O3)* 1,301
Gennett (N2) 25
Georgetown (L4)* 100
Germantown (B4)* 408
Gibbs (D2) 100
Gibson (D3)* 308
Gillises Mills (E4)
Gladeville (J2)* 114
Glass (C2) 75
Gleason (D2)* 1,063
Glen Alice (M3) 300
Glendale (G3) 130
Glenmary (M2)* 300
Goin (O2)* 300
Golddust (B3)* 50
Goodlettsville (H2)* 1,590
Goodspring (G4)* 31
Gordonsburg (F3)
Gordonsville (K2)* 304
Gorman (F2) 80
Graham (G3)* 25
Grand Junction (C4)* 477
Grandview (M3)* 250
Granville (K2)* 130
Gravel Hill (D4) 42
Graysville (L4)* 820
Green Brier (H2)* 890
Greenback (N3)* 1,200
Greeneville (Q2)* 8,721
Greenfield (D2)* 1,706
Greenwood (J2) 200
Groveland (G3) 25
Gruetli (K4)* 600
Guys (D4)* 100
Habersham (N2)* 500
Hales Point (B3) 25
Haley (J4)* 150
Halls (C3)* 1,808
Hamburg (E4) 350
Hampshire (G3)* 200
Hampton (R2)* 1,164
Harms (H4) 75
Harriman (M3)* 6,389
Harris (C2) 75
Harrison (L4)* 500
Harrogate (O1)*
Hartford (P3)* 200
Hartsville (J2)* 1,130
Hartsville Junction (J2) 40
Haydenburg (K2)* 100
Hebbertsburg (M2) 110
Heiskell (O2)* 130
Helenwood (M2)* 500
Henderson (D4)* 2,532
Hendersonville (J2)* 1,000
Hendon (L4)* 125
Henning (B3)* 493
Henry (E2)* 200
Henryville (G4)* 150
Hermitage (H2)* 800
Hermitage Springs (K1) 200
Hickman (K2)* 175
Hickory Point (G2)* 100
Hickory Valley (C4)* 400
Hickory Withe (C4)* 50
Highland Park (R1) 3,500
Hilham (L2)* 177
Hillsboro (K4)* 200
Hillsdale (J2)*
Hillside (D2) 160
Hitchcox (L3)* 98
Hixon (L4)* 2,100
Hohenwald (F3)* 1,703
Holladay (E3)* 200
Hollow Rock (E2)* 397
Holston Valley (R1) 125
Holtland (H3)* 400
Hopson (R2) 300
Horn Springs (J2) 200
Hornbeak (C2)* 309
Hornsby (D4)* 280
Howell (H4)* 150
Humboldt (D3)* 7,426
Huntingdon (E2)* 2,043
Huntland (J4)* 285
Huntsville (N2)* 1,400
Huron (E3)* 70
Hurricane Mills (F3)* 35
Idlewild (D2)* 200
Indian Mound (F1)* 375
Indian Springs (R1)* 300
Inskip (N2) 5,000
Iron City (F4)* 750
Ironsburg (N4) 100
Isabella (N4)* 400
Isham (N1) 75
Isoline (L2) 275
Ivyton (L2)*
Jacks Creek (D4)* 75
Jacksboro (N2)* 1,500
Jackson (D3)* 30,207
Jamestown (M2)* 2,115
Jasper (K4)* 1,198
Jefferson City (P2)* 3,633
Jellico (N1)* 1,556
Joelton (H2)* 2,500
Johnson City (R2)* 27,864
Johnsonville (F2)* 100
Jones (C3)* 140
Jonesboro (Q2)* 1,126
Joppa (O2) 85
Juno (E3)* 80
Keeling (C4) 100
Kelso (J4)* 85
Kenton (C2)* 899
Kerrville (B4)* 300
Kimberlin Heights (O3)* 120
Kimmins (F3)* 78
Kingsport (Q1)* 19,571
Kingston (N3)* 1,627
Kingston Springs (G2)* 390
Kinzel Springs (O3) 100
Kirkland (H3) 225
Knoxville (O3)* 124,769
Knoxville (urban area) 148,174
Kodak (O3)* 1,670
Kyles Ford (P1)* 75
La Follette (N2)* 5,797
La Grange (C4)* 241
La Vergne (H2)* 500
Laager (K4)* 650
Laconia (C4)* 75
Lafayette (J1)* 1,195
Lake City (N2)* 1,827
Lancing (M2)* 250
Lane (C2)* 150
Lascassas (J3)* 250
Latham (D2) 85
Laurel Bloomery (S1)* 208
Laurel Hill (K2)*
Laurelburg (L3)*
Lavinia (D3)* 88
Lawrenceburg (G4)* 5,442
Leach (E3)* 15
Leapwood (E4)* 110
Lebanon (J2)* 7,913
Ledbetter (D3) 25
Lee Valley (P2)* 200
Leinarts (N2)* 32
Leipers Fork (G3) 325
Lenoir City (N3)* 5,159
Lenox (C2)* 500
Leoma (G4)* 398
Lewisburg (H4)* 5,164
Lexington (E3)* 3,566
Liberty (K2)* 314
Liberty Hill (O2)*
Limestone (Q2)* 450
Linary (L3)* 160
Linden (F3)* 854
Littlecrab (L2)* 100
Littlelot (G3)* 150
Litton (L3)* 25
Livingston (L2)* 2,082
Lobelville (F3)* 600
Lodge (K4)*
Lone Mountain (O2)* 175
Lonely (F2) 76
Lookout Mountain (L5)* 1,675
Loretto (G4)* 706
Loudon (N3)* 3,567
Louisville (N3)* 130
Lucy (B4)* 600
Lula (E4)*
Lupton City (L4)* 1,250
Luray (D3)* 300
Luther (P2)*
Luttrell (O2)* 382
Lutts (F4)* 250
Lyles (G3)* 500
Lynchburg (J4)* 401
Lynnville (G4)* 356
Macon (B4)* 215
Madison (H2)* 7,000
Madisonville (N3)* 1,487
Malesus (D3)* 500
Manchester (J4)* 2,341
Mansfield (E2)* 110
Manson (L2)*
Martel (N3)* 95
Martha (J2)* 25
Martin (D2)* 4,082
Martin Springs (K4) 200
Martins Mills (F4) 33
Maryville (O3)* 7,742
Mascot (O2)* 2,500
Mason (B4)* 414
Masonhall (C2) 175
Maury City (C3)* 553
Maxwell (J4)* 85
Mayland (L2)* 175
Maynardville (O2)*
Mc Cloud (Q2)* 100
Mc Connell (D2)
Mc Daniel (H3) 100
Mc Donald (M4)* 150
Mc Ewen (F2)* 710
Mc Ghee (N3) 75
Mc Kenzie (E2)* 3,774
Mc Kinnon (F2)* 250
Mc Lemoresville (D3)* 242
Mc Minnville (K3)* 7,577
Mc Nairy (D4)* 90
Medina (D3)* 690
Medon (D4)* 115
Memorial (K1)* 300
Memphis (B4)* 396,000
Memphis (urban area) 404,033
Mengelwood (B2) 200
Mentor (O3)* 425
Mercer (D4)* 400
Michie (E4)*
Middleton (D4)* 362
Midway (P2)* 200
Mifflin (D3) 250
Milan (D3)* 4,938
Milledgeville (E4)* 300
Milligan College (R2)* 213
Millington (B4)* 4,696
Milo (L3)* 300
Milton (J3)* 75
Minor Hill (G4)* 292
Miston (B2)* 350
Mitchell (H1)
Mitchellville (J1)* 202
Model (F1)* 140
Mohawk (P2)* 200
Monoville (K2)* 75
Monroe (L2)*
Monteagle (K4)* 865
Monterey (L2)* 2,043
Montezuma (D4)* 130
Moodyville (L1)* 400
Mooresburg (P2)* 500
Morley (O1)* 300
Morris Chapel (E4)*
Morrison (K3)* 301
Morristown (P2)* 13,019
Moscow (C4)* 394
Mosheim (Q2)* 350
Moss (K1)* 200
Mount Juliet (H2)*
Mount Pleasant (G3)* 2,931
Mount Vernon (N4)* 250
Mountain City (S2)* 1,405
Mountairy (L4)* 140
Mulberry (H4)* 220
Munford (B4)* 976
Murfreesboro (J3)* 13,052
Napier (F4) 75
NASHVILLE (H2)* 174,307
Nashville (urban area) 257,898
Nemo (M2) 8
Neptune (G2)* 125
Neubert (O3)* 2,800
Neva (S2)* 50
New Market (O2)* 600
New Middleton (J2)* 150
New Providence (G1) 1,825
New River (M2)* 650
New Tazewell (O2)* 1,400
Newbern (C2)* 1,734
Newcomb (N1)*
Newport (P3)* 3,892
Niota (M3)* 956
Noah (J3) 100
Nolensville (H3)*
Norene (J2)* 250
Norma (N2)*
Normandy (J4)* 159
Norris (N2)* 1,134
Nunnelly (G3)*
Oak Ridge (N2)* 30,229
Oakdale (M3)* 718
Oakfield (D3)* 125
Oakland (B4)* 236
Oakley (L2) 50
Oakville (A4) 1,500
Obey City (L2)
Obion (C2)* 1,212
Ocoee (M4)* 225
Old Hickory (H2)* 10,000
Oldfort (M4)* 133
Olivehill (E4)* 140
Olive Springs (N2)* 1,089
Oneida (N1)* 1,304
Only (F3)*
Ooltewah (M4)* 900
Orlinda (H1)* 275
Orme (K4)* 230
Overall (J3)* 135
Ozone (M3)* 140
Pall Mall (M1)* 100
Palmer (K4)* 871
Palmersville (D2)* 100
Palmyra (G2)* 200
Paris (E2)* 8,826
Parrottsville (P2)* 115
Parsons (E3)* 1,640
Peakland (M3)*
Peavine (M2) 35
Pegram (H2)* 325
Pelham (K4)*
Perry (D3) 100
Perryville (F3)* 150
Persia (P2)* 50
Peters Landing (F4)* 40
Petersburg (H4)* 497
Petros (M2)* 800
Philadelphia (M3)* 600
Phillippy (C2)* 375
Pickwick Dam (E4)* 250
Pierce Station (C2)* 50
Pigeon Forge (O3)* 1,500
Pikeville (L3)* 882
Pine Top (D4) 15
Pinewood (F3) 5
Piney Flats (R2)* 300
Pinson (D4)* 300
Pioneer (N2)*
Pittsburg Landing (E4)* 114
Plant (F3) 250
Pleasant Hill (L3)* 152
Pleasant Shade (K2)* 125
Pleasant View (G2)* 300
Pleasantville (F3)*
Pocahontas (D4)* 250
Polk (C2)* 50
Pope (F3)* 30
Port Royal (G1)
Portland (H1)* 1,660
Postelle (N4)* 232
Powder Springs (O2)* 110
Powell (N2)* 400
Primm Springs (G3)* 4
Prospect Station (G4)* 350
Pruden (O1)* 250
Pulaski (G4)* 5,762
Puryear (E2)* 430

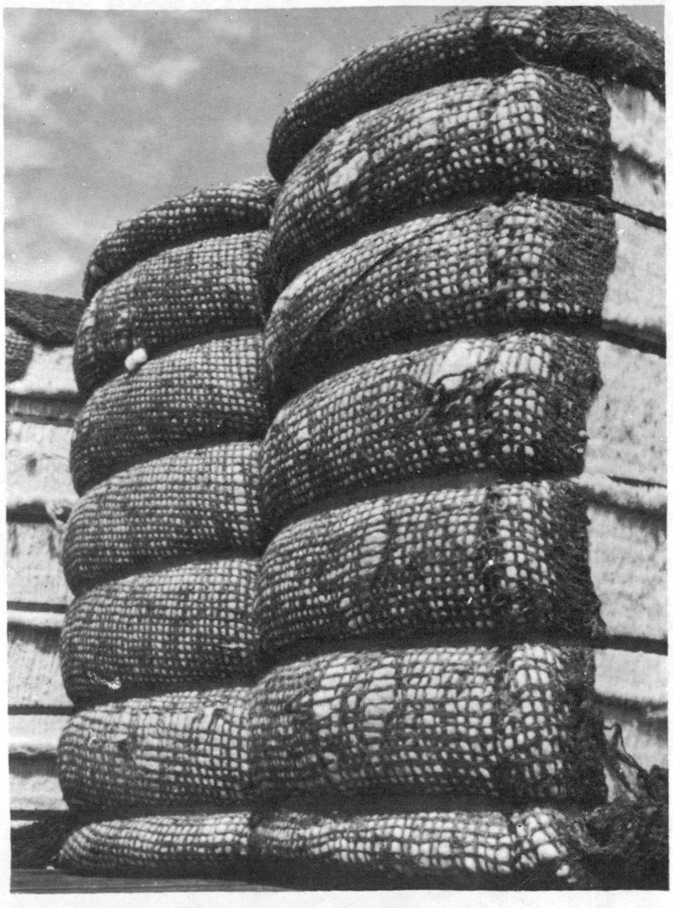

Quebeck (K3)*............ 200
Rader (Q2)................. 72
Raines (A4)................
Raleigh (B4)*..............1,100
Ralston (D2)*............. 78
Ramer (D4)*............... 400
Rankin (P2)................
Rasar (O3)*............... 200
Ravenscroft (L3)*........ 96
Readyville (J3)*.......... 250
Reagan (E3)*.............. 250
Red Bank (L4)*............
Red Boiling Springs (K1)* 1,000
Reliance (N4)*............
Reverie (A3)*.............. 250
Rheatown (Q2)*........... 107
Riceville (M4)*............ 450
Richard City (K5)*........ 300
Richardsons (B4).......... 50
Rickman (L2)*............. 500
Riddleton (J2)*........... 150
Ridgely (B2)*..............1,504
Ridgeside (L4)............. 337
Ridgetop (H2)*............ 354
Ridley (G3)................ 150
Ripley (B3)*................3,318
Riverside (F4).............. 80
Rives (C2)*................ 413
Roan Mountain (R2)*...1,000
Robbins (M2)*............ 900
Rock Creek (M1).......... 20
Rock Island (K3)*........ 150
Rockdale (G4).............. 25
Rockford (O3)*............1,500
Rockvale (J3)*............ 139
Rockwood (M3)*..........4,272
Roddy (M3)................ 200
Rogers Springs (D4)*... 100
Rogersville (P2)*..........2,545
Rome (J2).................. 125
Rosedale (N2)*............
Rosemark (B4)............ 300
Roslin (M2)*.............. 300
Rossville (B4)*............ 175
Routon (E2)................ 150
Rowland (K3).............. 35
Rucker (J3)................ 78
Rugby (M2)*...............
Ruskin (F2)................ 26
Russellville (P2)*......... 608
Rutherford (C2)*......... 994
Ruthville (D2)..............
Rutledge (P2)*............ 600
Sadlersville (G1)*......... 100
Saint Andrews (K4)*....
St. Bethlehem (G1)*..... 275
St. Joseph (G4)*.......... 550
Sale Creek (L4)*.......... 650
Saltillo (E4)*............... 400
Samburg (C2)*............ 378
Sanford (M4)...............
Santa Fe (G3)*........... 250
Sardis (E4)*............... 299
Saulsbury (C4)*........... 143
Saundersville (J2)........ 200
Savannah (E4)*............1,698
Scotts Hill (E4)*.......... 299
Selmer (D4)*...............1,759
Sequatchie (K4)*.........
Serles (D4)*............... 50
Servilla (M4)*............. 100
Sevierville (P3)*...........1,620
Sewanee (K4)*.............1,407
Seymour (O3)*............. 120
Shady Valley (S1)*.......2,238
Sharon (D2)*............... 880
Sharps Chapel (O2)*.... 50
Shawanee (O1)*........... 350
Shea (N2).................. 150
Shelbyville (H4)*..........9,456
Shell Creek (R2)*......... 200
Shepherd (L4)*.............1,000
Shepp (C4)*................
Sherwood (K4)*...........
Shirley (M2)*.............. 171
Shop Spring (J2)*......... 150
Shouns (S2)*.............. 350
Sidonia (D2)*.............. 175
Signal Mountain (L4)*.1,786
Silerton (D4)*............. 121
Silver Point (K2)*........ 150
Slayden (G2)*.............. 90
Smartt (K3)*............... 300
Smithville (K3)*............1,558
Smokey Junction (N2)* 200
Smyrna (H3)*..............1,544
Sneedville (P1)*........... 500
Soddy (L4)*..................2,157
Somerville (C4)*...........1,760
South Dyersburg (C2)...
S. Fulton (D2)..............2,119
S. Harriman (M3).........2,761
S. Pittsburg (K4)*........2,573
S. Tunnel (H2)*........... 500
Southside (G2)*........... 200
Sparta (K3)*.................4,299
Speedwell (O2)*..........
Spencer (L3)*.............. 721
Spring City (M3)*........1,725
Spring Hill (H3)*......... 541
Springcreek (D3)*........
Springfield (H2)*..........6,506
Springville (E2)*.......... 30
Stainville (N2)*........... 800
Stanton (C4)*.............. 503
Stantonville (E4)*........ 300
Statesville (J2)*........... 150
Static (L1)*................. 40
Stewart (F2)*..............
Stonypoint (Q1)*..........
Strawberry Plains (O2)*
Sugar Grove (J1).......... 25
Sugar Tree (E3)*..........
Summertown (G4)*....... 300
Summitville (K3)*........ 400
Sunbright (M2)*........... 600
Surgoinsville (Q2)*........ 800
Sweetwater (N3)*........4,199
Sycamore Landing (F3)* 53
Sylvia (G2)*................ 186
Taft (H4)*................... 225
Talbott (P2)*............... 250
Tarlton (K3)................. 75
Tasso (M4)*................ 150
Tazewell (P2)*..............1,000
Telford (R2)*............... 300
Tellico Plains (N4)*...... 833
Temperance Hall (K2).. 100
Ten Mile (M3)*............
Tennessee City (F2)*.... 180
Tennessee Ridge (F2)*.. 275
Terrell (D2)*................ 70
Tharpe (F1)................. 30
Theta (G3).................. 250
Thomasville (G2).......... 27
Thompsons Station (H3)* 150
Thorn Hill (P2)*........... 35
Tidwell (G2)................. 50
Tigrett (C3)*................ 175
Timothy (L2)*..............
Tipton (B4)*................. 35
Tiptonville (B2)*...........1,953
Tobaccoport (F1).......... 30
Toone (D4)*................. 231
Townsend (O3)*............ 328
Tracy City (K4)*..........1,414
Trade (S2)*.................. 75
Treadway (P2)*............
Trenton (D3)*................3,868
Trezevant (D2)*........... 765
Trimble (C2)*............... 674
Triune (H3).................. 225
Troy (C2)*................... 593
Tullahoma (J4)*...........7,562
Turley (N2).................. 40
Turtletown (N4)*......... 200
Tusculum (Q2)............. 250
Twinton (L2)................ 75
Tyner (L4)*...................1,000
Una (H2)...................... 500
Unicoi (R2)*..................1,500
Union City (C2)*..........7,665
Unionville (H3)*........... 176
Vale (E2)*.................... 50
Vanleer (G2)*............... 243
Vasper (N2)*................
Vernon (F3)*................ 150
Victoria (K4)*..............
Vildo (C4)*.................. 75
Viola (K3)*.................. 223
Vonore (N3)*................ 478
Wales (G4)*.................. 50
Walland (O3)*.............. 300
Walling (K3)*............... 200
Walnut Grove (E4).......
Walterhill (J3)*............ 200
Warren (C4)*................ 75
Warrensburg (P2)........ 75
Wartburg (M2)*............ 400
Wartrace (J3)*............. 545
Washburn (O2)*........... 170
Watauga (R2)*............. 500
Watauga Valley (R2).... 200
Watertown (J2)*.......... 933
Watts Bar Dam (M3)*.. 110
Waverly (F2)*...............1,892
Waynesboro (F4)*........1,147
Weavers Store (F1).......
West Harpeth (H3)....... 30
Westbourne (O1)*........ 600
Western State Hospital (C4)* 3,000
Westmoreland (J1)*.... 895
Westpoint (G4)*........... 350
Westport (E3)*............. 175
Wetmore (N4).............. 125
Wheelerton (H4)*......... 65
White (B4)....................
White Bluff (G2)*........ 506
White Horn (Q2)..........
White House (H2)*.......
White Pine (P2)*.......... 78
Whitehaven (A4)*.........1,311
Whites Creek (H2)*...... 10
Whitesburg (P2)*......... 50
Whiteside (K5)*............ 50
Whiteville (C4)*........... 794
Whitleyville (K2)*........ 7
Whitlock (E2)*............. 142
Whitthorne (D3)........... 1
Whitwell (K4)*.............1,586
Wilder (L2)*................ 30
Wildersville (E3)*........ 27
Willette (K2)............... 10
Williamsport (G3)*....... 14
Williston (C4)*............ 17
Winchester (J4)*..........3,974
Windrock (N2)*............ 337
Winesap (L3)*.............. 8
Winfield (M1)*............ 35
Winona (N2)*..............
Woodbine (H2)*...........
Woodbury (J3)*............1,00
Woodland Mills (C2)*... 17
Woodlawn (G1)*.......... 3
Woodstock (A4)........... 30
Wooldridge (N1)*........
Wrigley (G3)*..............
Wynnburg (C2)*........... 20
Yorkville (C2)*............ 50
Yuma (E3)*..................
Zach (E2).................... 10
Zenith (M2).................. 4

Map on Page 89

TEXAS

Total Population 7,711,194

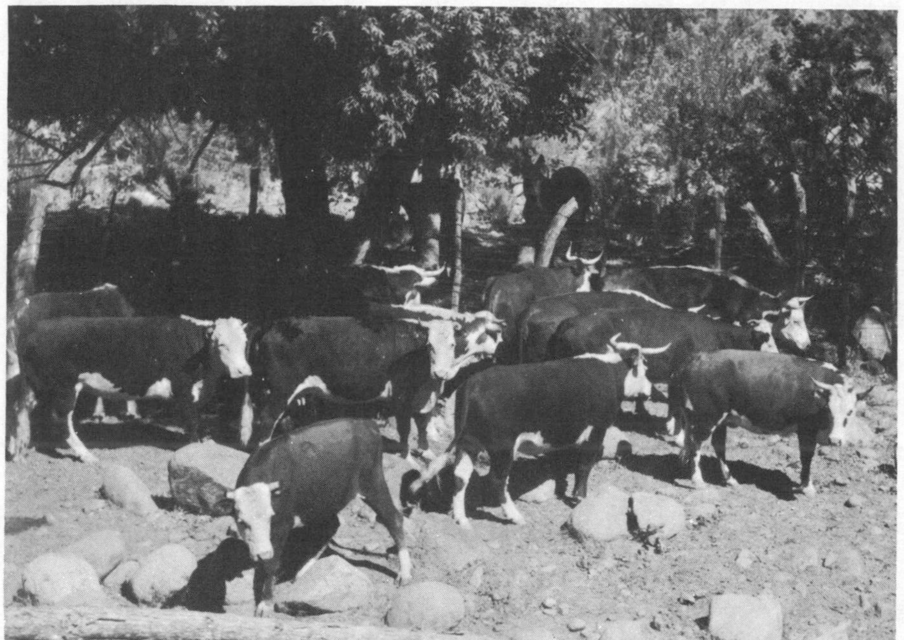

254 COUNTIES

Anderson (J6)............31,875
Andrews (B5)...............5,002
Angelina (K6).............36,032
Aransas (H10)..............4,252
Archer (F4)..................6,816
Armstrong (C3)............2,215
Atascosa (F9)..............20,048
Austin (H8).................14,663
Bailey (B3)...................7,592
Bandera (E8)................4,410
Bastrop (G7)...............19,622
Baylor (E4)...................6,875
Bee (G9)......................18,174
Bell (G6)......................73,824
Bexar (F8)..................500,460
Blanco (F7)...................3,780
Borden (C5)..................1,106
Bosque (G6).................11,836
Bowie (K4)...................61,966
Brazoria (J3)...............46,549
Brazos (H7)..................38,390
Brewster (D12)..............7,309
Briscoe (C3)...................3,528
Brooks (F11)..................9,195
Brown (F6)...................28,607
Burleson (H7)...............13,000
Burnet (F7)..................10,356
Caldwell (G8)...............19,350
Calhoun (H9)..................9,222
Callahan (E5)..................9,087
Cameron (G11)..........125,170
Camp (K5)......................8,740
Carson (C2)....................6,852
Cass (K4).....................26,732
Castro (B3).....................5,417
Chambers (L1)................7,871
Cherokee (J6)..............38,694
Childress (D3)..............12,123
Clay (F4)........................9,896
Cochran (B4)...................5,928
Coke (D6)........................4,045
Coleman (E6)................15,503
Collin (H4)....................41,692
Collingsworth (D3).......9,139
Colorado (H8)...............17,576
Comal (F8)...................16,357
Comanche (F5)............15,516
Concho (E6)...................5,078
Cooke (G4)..................22,146
Coryell (G6)................16,284
Cottle (D3)....................6,099
Crane (B6).....................3,965
Crockett (C7).................3,981
Crosby (C4)....................9,582
Culberson (C11)..............1,825
Dallam (B1).....................7,640
Dallas (G2)..................614,799
Dawson (C5)..................19,113
De Witt (G9).................22,973
Deaf Smith (B3) 9,111
Delta (J4)........................8,964
Denton (G4)...................41,365
Dickens (D4)....................7,177
Dimmit (E9)...................10,654
Donley (D2)......................6,216
Duval (F10).....................15,643
Eastland (F5)..................23,942
Ector (B6)........................42,102
Edwards (D7)....................2,908
El Paso (A10)................194,968
Ellis (H5).........................45,645
Erath (F5).......................18,434
Falls (H6)........................26,724
Fannin (H4).....................31,253
Fayette (H8)....................24,176
Fisher (D5)......................11,023
Floyd (C3)........................10,535
Foard (E3).........................4,216
Fort Bend (J2)..................31,056
Franklin (J4).......................6,257
Freestone (H6)..................15,696
Frio (E9)............................10,357
Gaines (B5).........................8,909
Galveston (K3)..................113,066
Garza (C4)...........................6,281
Gillespie (F7).....................10,520
Glasscock (C6).....................1,089
Goliad (G9)..........................6,219
Gonzales (G8).....................21,164
Gray (D2)...........................24,728
Grayson (H4).......................70,467
Gregg (K5)..........................61,258
Grimes (J7)..........................15,135
Guadalupe (G8)....................25,392
Hale (C3).............................28,211
Hall (D3)..............................10,930
Hamilton (F6).......................10,660
Hansford (C1)........................4,202
Hardeman (E3)......................10,212
Hardin (K7)...........................19,535
Harris (J1)...........................806,701
Harrison (K5).........................47,745
Hartley (B2)............................1,913
Haskell (E4)...........................13,736
Hays (F7)...............................17,840
Hemphill (D2)...........................4,123
Henderson (J5)........................23,405
Hidalgo (F11).........................160,446
Hill (G5)..................................31,282
Hockley (B4)............................20,407
Hood (G5).................................5,287
Hopkins (J4)............................23,490
Houston (J6)............................22,825
Howard (C5).............................26,722
Hudspeth (B10)..........................4,298
Hunt (H4).................................42,731
Hutchinson (C2)........................31,580
Irion (C6)...................................1,590
Jack (F4)....................................7,755
Jackson (H9)..............................12,916
Jasper (K7)................................20,049
Jeff Davis (C11)...........................2,090
Jefferson (K8)...........................195,083
Jim Hogg (F11).............................5,389
Jim Wells (F10)...........................27,991
Johnson (G5)..............................31,390
Jones (E5)..................................22,147
Karnes (G9)................................17,139
Kaufman (H5)..............................31,170
Kendall (F8)..................................5,423
Kenedy (G11)................................. 632
Kent (D4)......................................2,249
Kerr (E7).....................................14,022
Kimble (E7)...................................4,619
King (D4).. 870
Kinney (D8)....................................2,668
Kleberg (G10).................................21,991
Knox (E4).......................................10,082
La Salle (E9)....................................7,485
Lamar (J4)......................................43,033
Lamb (B3).......................................20,015
Lampasas (F6)...................................9,929
Lavaca (H8).....................................22,159
Lee (H7)...10,144
Leon (J6)...12,024
Liberty (K7).....................................26,729
Limestone (H6).................................25,251
Lipscomb (D1)..................................3,658
Live Oak (F9)....................................9,054
Llano (F7)..5,377
Loving (D10).. 227
Lubbock (C4)...................................101,048
Lynn (C4)..11,030
Madison (J6).......................................7,996
Marion (K5).......................................10,172
Martin (C5)...5,541
Mason (E7)..4,945
Matagorda (H9)...................................21,559
Maverick (D9).....................................12,292
Mc Culloch (E6)..................................11,701
Mc Lennan (G6).................................130,194
Mc Mullen (F9)......................................1,187
Medina (E8)..17,013
Menard (E7)...4,175
Midland (B6)..25,785
Milam (H7)..23,585
Mills (F6)..5,999
Mitchell (D5)..14,357
Montague (G4)..17,070
Montgomery (J7).....................................24,504
Moore (C2)...13,349
Morris (K4)...9,433
Motley (D3)...3,963
Nacogdoches (K6)....................................30,326
Navarro (H5)..39,916
Newton (L7)...10,832
Nolan (D5)...19,808
Nueces (G10)...165,471
Ochiltree (D1)..6,024
Oldham (B2)..1,672
Orange (L7)..40,567
Palo Pinto (F5)...17,154
Panola (K5)...19,250
Parker (G5)...21,528
Parmer (B3)..5,787
Pecos (B7)...9,939
Polk (K7)...16,194
Potter (C2)..73,366
Presidio (C12)...7,354
Rains (J5)...4,266
Randall (C2)...13,774
Reagan (C6)..3,127
Real (E8)...2,479
Red River (J4)..21,851
Reeves (D11)...11,745
Refugio (G9)..10,113
Roberts (D2)..1,031
Robertson (H6)...........19,908
Rockwall (H5)................6,156
Runnels (E6)...............16,771
Rusk (K5)....................42,348
Sabine (L6)...................8,568
San Augustine (K6).....8,837
San Jacinto (J7)...........7,172
San Patricio (G10)......35,842
San Saba (F6)...............8,666
Schleicher (D7).............2,852
Scurry (D5).................22,779
Shackelford (E5)...........5,001
Shelby (K6).................23,479
Sherman (C1)...............2,443
Smith (J5)....................74,701
Somervell (G5)..............2,542
Starr (F11)..................13,948
Stephens (F5)..............10,597
Sterling (C6).................1,282
Stonewall (D4)..............3,679
Sutton (D7)...................3,746
Swisher (C3)..................8,249
Tarrant (F2)...............361,253
Taylor (E5)..................63,370
Terrell (B7)....................3,189
Terry (B4)....................13,107
Throckmorton (E4)........3,618
Titus (K4).....................17,302
Tom Green (D6)............58,929
Travis (G7)..................160,980
Trinity (J6)...................10,040
Tyler (K7).....................11,292
Upshur (K5)..................20,822
Upton (B6).....................5,307
Uvalde (E8)...................16,015
Val Verde (C8)...............16,635
Van Zandt (J5)...............22,593
Victoria (H9)..................31,241
Walker (J7)....................20,163
Waller (J8).....................11,961
Ward (A6).......................13,346
Washington (H7).............20,542
Webb (E10)......................56,141
Wharton (H8)...................36,077
Wheeler (D2)....................10,317
Wichita (F3).....................98,493
Wilbarger (E3)..................20,552
Willacy (G11)...................20,920
Williamson (G7)................38,853
Wilson (F8).......................14,672
Winkler (A6)......................10,064
Wise (G4)..........................16,141
Wood (J5).........................21,308
Yoakum (B4)........................4,339
Young (F4).........................16,810
Zapata (E11)........................4,405
Zavala (E9).........................11,201

CITIES and TOWNS

Abbott (H6)*............. 345
Abernathy (B4)*..........1,692
Abilene (E5)*..............45,570
Acala (B10)*.............. 150
Ackerly (C5)*............. 550
Acme (E3)*................ 200
Adamsville (F6)*......... 300
Addison (G1)*............ 258
Adkins (F8)*.............. 20
Adrian (B2)*.............. 205
Afton (D4)*................ 115
Agua Dulce (F10)*...... 660
Alamo (F11)*...............3,017
Alamo Hts. ‡(F8)*........8,000
Alanreed (D2)*........... 200
Alba (J5)*.................. 547
Albany (E5)*...............2,241
Aledo (G5)*................ 260
Alexander (F5)*.......... 96
Algoa (K3)*................ 250
Alice (F10)*................16,449
Allamoore (C11)*........ 50
Allison (D2)*.............. 150
Allred (B4)*................ 30
Almeda (J2)*...............1,800
Alpine (D11)*..............5,261
Alta Loma (K3)*..........1,400
Alto (J6)*.....................1,021
Alvarado (G5)*.............1,656
Alvin (J3)*....................3,701
Alvord (G4)*................ 735
Amarillo (C2)*............74,246
Amarillo (urban area).74,450
Amherst (B4)*............. 922
Anahuac (K8)*.............1,284
Anderson (J7)*............ 500
Andrews (B5)*..............3,294
Angeles (C10)..............
Angleton (J8)*..............3,399
Anna (H4)*.................. 525
Annona (K4)*............... 392
Anson (E5)*..................2,708
Antelope (F4)*............. 125
Anthony (A10)*............1,200
Anton (B4)*................. 934
Aquilla (G6)*............... 450
Aransas Pass (G10)*....5,396
Arcadia (K3)*.............. 865
Archer City (K4)*.........1,901
Arlington (F2)*.............7,692
Armstrong (G11)*......... 97
Arp (J5)*..................... 909
Artesia Wells (E9)*...... 200
Asherton (E9)*..............2,425
Aspermont (D4)*..........1,062
Athens (J5)*.................5,194
Atlanta (K4)*................3,782
Aubrey ‡(H4)*.............. 491
AUSTIN (G7)*..........132,459
Austin (urban area)..135,465
Austonio (J6)*.............
Austwell (H9)*............. 228
Avalon (H5)*................ 400
Avery (K4)*.................. 442
Avinger (K5)*............... 546
Avoca (E5)*.................. 210
Azle (E1)*.....................1,700
Bagwell (J4)*................ 400
Bailey ‡(H4)*............... 198
Baileyboro (B3)*........... 50
Baird (E5)*....................1,821
Bakersfield (B7)*......... 150
Balcones Hts. ‡(F8)..... 376
Ballinger (E6)*..............5,302
Balmorhea (D11)*......... 500
Bandera (F8)*...............1,036
Bangs (E6)*.................. 935
Bardwell ‡(H5)*........... 229
Barksdale (D8)*............ 300
Barnhart (C6)*............. 357
Barstow (A6)*.............. 683
Bartlett (G7)*...............1,727
Bastrop (G7)*................3,176
Batesville (E9)*............ 500
Batson (K7)*................ 800
Bay City (H9)*...............9,427
Bayside (G9)*............... 300
Baytown (L2)*............22,983
Beaumont (K7)*..........94,014
Beaumont (urban area) 94,050
Beckville (K5)*............ 550
Becton (C4).................. 50
Bedford (F2)*............... 150
Bedias (J7)*................. 575
Beeville (G9)*...............9,348
Belcherville ‡(G4)*....... 31
Bellaire (J2)*.............10,173
Bellevue (F4)*............. 418
Bells (H4)*.................. 614
Bellville (H8)*...............2,112
Belton (G7)*..................6,246
Ben Wheeler (J5)*...... 400
Benavides (F10)*..........3,016
Benbrook (E2)*............ 617
Bend (F7)*................... 228
Benjamin (E4)*............ 530
Berclair (G9)*.............. 300
Bertram (F7)*.............. 900
Bessmay (L7)*..............1,800
Best (C6)*.................... 26
Beverly Hills ‡(G6)*..... 701
Big Bend National Park (A8)*................
Big Lake (C6)*..............2,152
Big Sandy (J5)*........... 689
Big Spring (C5)*.........17,286
Big Foot (F9)................ 150
Big Wells (E9)*.............1,077
Bishop (G10)*...............2,731
Blackwell (D5)*............ 600
Blanco (F7)*................ 71
Blanket (F6)*............... 361
Bledsoe (A4)*.............. 10
Blessing (H9)*............. 60
Blewett (D8)*.............. 20
Bloomburg (L4)*.......... 47
Blooming Grove (H5)*.. 73
Bloomington (H9)*......1,50
Blossom (J4)*.............. 78
Blue Ridge (H4)*......... 30
Bluff Dale (F5)*..........
Blum (G5)*.................. 36
Boerne (F8)*................1,80
Bogata (J4)*................ 93
Boling (H8)*.................1,20
Bomarton (E4)*............ 30
Bon Wier (L7)*.............1,20
Bonham (H4)*...............7,04
Booker (D1)*................ 61
Borger (C2)*................18,05
Boston (K4)*................ 20
Bovina (A3)*................ 61
Bowie (G4)*..................4,54
Boyd (G4)*................... 55
Brackettville (D8)*......1,85
Bradshaw (E5)*............ 10
Brady (E6)*...................5,94
Brandon ‡(H5)*............ 18
Brazoria (J9)*.............. 77
Breckenridge (F5)*......6,61
Bremond (H6)*..............1,14
Brenham (H7)*..............6,94
Bridgeport (G4)*...........2,04
Briggs (F7)*.................
Briscoe (D2)*............... 10
Britton (F3)*................ 13
Broaddus (K6)*............ 15
Bronco (B4)*................ 4
Bronson (L6)*.............. 25
Bronte (D6)*..................1,02
Brookeland (L6)*......... 35
Brookshire (J8)*...........1,01
Brownfield (B4)*...........6,16
Brownsboro (J5)*......... 51
Brownsville (G12)*......36,06
Brownwood (F6)*.........20,18
Bruni (F10)*................. 70
Bryan .(H7)*.................18,10
Bryson (F4)*................ 58
Buckholts (H7)*........... 70
Buda (G7)*................... 48
Buenavista (B6)*.........
Buffalo (J6)*................ 97
Bula (B4)*...................
Bullard (J5)*................ 31
Buna (L7)*...................
Burkburnett (F3)*........4,55
Burke (K6)*.................. 50
Burkett (E5)*................ 22
Burkeville (L7)*............ 50
Burleson ‡(G5)*........... 79
Burnet (F7)*..................2,39
Burton (H7)*................ 51
Bushland (B2)*............. 8
Byers (F3)*.................. 54
Bynum (H6)*................ 32
Caddo (F5)*.................
Caddo Mills ‡(H4)*...... 50
Cain City (E7)*............ 3
Caldwell (H7)*..............2,10
Call (L7)*......................1,50
Calliham (F9)*............. 16
Calvert (H7)*.................2,54
Cameron (H7)*...............5,05
Camp Allison (D7)*......
Camp Ruby (K7)*......... 10
Camp Wood (D8)*........ 78
Campbellton (F9)*........ 36
Canadian (D2)*..............2,70
Candelaria (C12)*......... 25
Canton (J5)*................. 88
Canutillo (A10)*............1,32
Canyon (C3)*.................4,36
Carbon (F5)*................ 44
Carlsbad (D6)*.............
Carlton (F6)*................ 25
Carmine (H7)*.............. 49
Carmona (K6)*............. 30
Caro (K6)*................... 22
Carrizo Spgs. (E9)*......4,31
Carrollton (G1)*............1,61

arta Valley (D8)*........
arthage (K5)*............4,750
asa Piedra (C12)*....... 50
astolon (D13)*.......... 20
astroville (E8)*........ 985
atarina (E9)*........... 380
ayuga (J6)*.............1,200
edar Bayou (L2)*........1,000
edar Hill (G2)*......... 732
ee Vee (D3)*............ 27
eleste (H4)*............ 729
elina (H4)*.............1,051
ement (G2)...............
enter (K6)*.............4,323
enter Point (E8)*....... 900
enterville (H6)*........ 961
entralia (K6)*.......... 130
handler (J5)*...........
hannelview (K1)*........
hanning (B2)*........... 400
hapel Hill (H7)*........ 500
harco (G9)*............. 135
harlotte (F9)*..........1,272
herokee (F7)*........... 311
hester (K7)*............ 700
heyenne (B6)............ 10
hico (G4)*.............. 850
hildress (D3)*..........7,619
hillicothe (E3)*........1,415
hireno (K6)*............ 500
hocolate Bayou (J3).... 50
hriesman (H7)*.......... 100
hristine (F9)*.......... 289
hristoval (D6)*......... 650
ircle Back (B3)*........
isco (E5)*..............5,230
lairmont (D4)*.......... 130
lairette (G5)*.......... 100
larendon (C3)*..........2,577
larksville (K4)*........4,353
laude (C2)*............. 820
leburne (G5)*...........12,905
leveland (K7)*..........5,183
lifton (G6)*............1,837
lint (A10)*.............
lyde (E5)*.............. 908
oahoma (C5)*............ 802
ockrell Hill (G2).......2,207
oldspring (J7)*.........
oleman (E6)*............6,530
ollege Station (H7)*....7,925
ollinsville (H4)*....... 561
olmesneil (K7).......... 750
olorado City (C5)*......6,774
olumbus (H8)*...........2,878
omanche (F6)*...........3,840
omfort (F7)*............1,200
ommerce (J4)*...........5,889
omo (J4)*............... 356
omstock (C8)*........... 300
onception (F10)*........
one (C4)*............... 105
onlen (B1)*............. 40
onroe (J7)*.............7,298
onway (C2)*............. 75
oolidge (H6)*...........1,062
ooper (J4)*.............2,350
oppell (F1)*............ 250
opperas Cove (G6)*......1,052
orpus Christi(G10)*.108,287
orpus Christi (urban
area) 122,354
orrigan (K7)*...........1,417
orsicana (H5)*..........1,921
otton Center (C4)*...... 45
ottonwood (E5)*......... 175
otulla (E9)*............4,418
oughran (F9)*........... 50
ove (L1)................ 50
randall (H5)*........... 727
rane (B6)*..............2,154
ranfills Gap (G6)*...... 435
rawford (G6)*........... 423
resson (G5)*............ 355
rockett (J6)*...........5,932
rosby (J8)*.............
rosbyton (C4)*..........1,879
ross Plains (E5)*.......1,305
rowell (E4)*............1,912
rowley (E2)*............ 300
rystal City (E9)*.......7,198
uero (G8)*..............7,498
umby (J4)*.............. 504
uney (J5)*.............. 500
ushing (J6)*............ 479
aingerfield (K4)*.......1,668
aisetta (K7)*...........1,764
alhart (B1)*............5,918
allas (H2)*...........434,462
allas (urban area).536,864
alworth Park (F2).......
alworthington (F2)..... 267
anbury (J8)*............ 700
arrouzett (D1)*......... 328
avilla (G7)*............ 300
awn (B3)*............... 75
awson (H6)*.............1,107
ayton (J7)*.............1,820
e Berry (L5)*........... 475
e Kalb (K4)*............1,928
e Leon (F5)*............2,241
e Soto (G2)*............ 298
eanville (H7)*.......... 175
ecatur (G4)*............2,922
eer Park (K2)*.......... 736
el Rio (D8)*............14,211
ell City (C10)..........
elwin (D4)*............. 23
enison (H4)*............17,504
enton (G4)*.............21,372
enver City (B4)*........1,855
eport (J4)*............. 734
erby (E9)*.............. 400
etroit (J4)*............ 679
evers (K8)*............. 700
evine (E8)*.............1,672
eweyville (L7)*.........
exter (H4)*............. 50
'Hanis (E8)*............1,000
iboll (K6)..............2,391
ickens (D4)*............ 420
Dickinson (K3)*..........2,704
Dilley (E9)*.............1,809
Dime Box (H7)*........... 700
Dimmitt (B3)*............1,461
Dodd City ‡(H4)*......... 329
Dodge (J7)*.............. 350
Dodson (D3)*............. 336
Dolores (E10)............ 20
Donie (H6)............... 300
Donna (F11)*.............7,171
Doole (E6)*..............
Doucette (K7)*........... 300
Dougherty (C4)*.......... 100
Douglass (K6)*........... 400
Dozier (D2)*............. 34
Dripping Spgs. (F7)*..... 150
Driscoll (G10)*.......... 700
Dryden (C7)*............. 210
Dublin (F5)*.............2,761
Dumas (C2)*..............6,127
Dumont (D4)*............. 65
Duncanville (G2)*........ 841
Dundee (F4)*............. 146
Dunn (D5)*............... 66
Eagle Ford (G2)*.........4,679
Eagle Lake (H8)*.........2,787
Eagle Pass (D9)*.........7,276
Earth (B3)*.............. 539
East Bernard (H8)*....... 900
Eastland (F5)*...........3,626
Easton ‡(K5)*............ 203
Ector ‡(H4)*............. 430
Edcouch ‡(H11)*..........2,925
Eddy (G6)*............... 450
Eden (E6)*...............1,993
Edgewood ‡(J5)*.......... 834
Edinburg (F11)*..........12,383
Edmonson (C3)*........... 82
Edna (H9)*...............3,855
El Campo (H8)*...........6,237
El Indio (D9)*........... 150
El Paso (A10)*...........130,485
El Paso (urban area).136,430
Elam (H2)................ 500
Elbert (E4)*............. 75
Eldorado (D7)*...........1,663
Electra (F4)*............4,970
Elgin (G7)*..............3,168
Elkhart (J6)*............ 776
Ellinger ‡(H8)*.......... 219
Elmendorf (F8)*.......... 500
Elmo (H5)*............... 150
Elsa (G11)*..............3,179
Elysian Fields (L5)*..... 305
Emhouse ‡(H5)*........... 198
Emory (J5)*.............. 648
Encinal (E9)*............1,071
Encino (F11)*............ 500
Enloe ‡(J4)*............. 186
Ennis (H5)*..............7,815
Enochs (B4)*.............
Eola (E6)*...............
Era (G4)*................ 175
Esperanza (B11)*......... 200
Estelline (D3)*.......... 464
Etter (B2)............... 30
Eustace (H5)*............ 700
Evadale (L7)*............ 500
Evant (G6)*.............. 500
Everman (E2)*............ 451
Exell (C2)*.............. 300
Fabens (A10)*............3,089
Fairbanks (J1)*.......... 730
Fairfield (H6)*..........1,742
Falfurrias (F10).........6,712
Falls City (G9)*......... 422
Fannin (G9)*............. 110
Fargo (E3)............... 50
Farmers Branch (G1)*.. 915
Farmersville (H4)*.......1,955
Farnsworth (C1)*......... 150
Farwell (A3)*............ 500
Fate ‡(H5)*.............. 141
Fayetteville (H8)*....... 462
Ferris (G2)*.............1,735
Field Creek (F7)*........ 80
Fieldton (B3)*........... 70
Flagg (B3)............... 25
Flat (G6)*............... 350
Flatonia (G8)*...........1,098
Flomot (D3)*............. 200
Florence (G7)*........... 561
Floresville (F9)*........1,949
Florey (B5)*............. 5
Floydada (C3)*...........3,210
Fluvanna (D5)*........... 205
Foard City (E4)*......... 20
Follett (D1)*............ 540
Forest Hill (F2).........1,519
Forestburg (G4)*......... 200
Forney (H5)*.............1,425
Forsan (C5)*............. 200
Fort Davis (D11)*........1,200
Fort Hancock (B11)*......1,000
Fort Mc Kavett (E7)*....
Fort Stockton (A7)*......4,444
Fort Worth (E2)*.........278,778
Ft. Worth (urban
area) 313,872
Fostoria (J7)*........... 950
Fowlerton (F9)*.......... 300
Frankell (F5)*........... 27
Franklin (H6)*...........1,209
Frankston (J5)*..........1,050
Fred (K7)*............... 500
Fredericksburg (E7)*.....3,854
Fredonia (E7)*........... 200
Freeport (J9)*...........6,012
Freer (F10)*.............2,280
Fresno (J2)*.............
Friendswood (J2)*........ 400
Friona (B3)*.............1,202
Frisco (H4)*............. 736
Fritch (C2)*.............
Frost (H5)*.............. 585
Fruitdale ‡(G2).......... 876
Fulbright (J4)*.......... 150
Gageby (D2)*............. 10
Gail (C5)*............... 70
Gainesville (G4)*........11,246
Galena Park (J1)*........7,186
Galveston (L3)*..........66,568
Galveston (urban
area) 71,000
Ganado (H8)*.............1,258
Garden City (C6)*........ 274
Garden Oaks (J1)*........
Gardendale (E9)*......... 45
Garland (H1)*............10,571
Garrison (K6)*........... 699
Garwood (H8)*............ 975
Gary (K5)*............... 475
Gasoline (C3)............ 25
Gatesville (G6)*.........3,856
Gause (H7)*.............. 500
Gay Hill (H7)*........... 125
Gem (D2)*................ 3
Geneva (L6)*............. 125
Genoa (K2)*.............. 500
George West (F9)*........1,533
Georgetown (G7)*.........4,951
Germania (C5)............ 35
Giddings (H7)*...........2,532
Giles (D3)*.............. 25
Gillett (G8)*............
Gilmer (J5)*.............4,096
Gilpin (D4)*............. 30
Girard (D4)*............. 450
Girvin (B6)*............. 35
Gladewater (K5)*.........5,305
Glazier (D2)*............ 107
Glen Flora (H8)*......... 650
Glen Rose (G5)*..........1,254
Glenn (D4)*.............. 25
Godley ‡(G5)*............ 424
Goldsmith (B5)*..........1,200
Goldthwaite (F6)*........1,566
Goliad (G9)*.............1,584
Gonzales (G8)*...........5,659
Goodnight (C3)*.......... 100
Gordon (F5)*............. 404
Goree (E4)*.............. 640
Gorman (F5)*.............1,317
Graford (F5)*............ 655
Graham (F4)*.............6,742
Granbury (G5)*...........1,683
Grand Prairie (G2)*...14,594
Grand Saline (J5)*.......1,810
Grandfalls (B6)*......... 995
Grandview (G5)*.......... 886
Granger (G7)*............1,637
Grapeland (J6)*..........1,358
Grapevine (F1)*..........1,824
Grayback (E4)*........... 100
Grayburg (K7)*........... 500
Greenville (H4)*.........14,727
Greggton (K5)*...........2,168
Griffing Park ‡(K8).....2,096
Groesbeck (H6)*..........2,182
Groom (C2)*.............. 678
Groves (L8)*.............
Groveton (J6)*........... 805
Grow (D4)*............... 23
Grulla (F11)*............1,013
Gruver (C1)*............. 813
Guerra (F11)*............ 115
Gunter ‡(H4)*............ 463
Gustine (F6)*............ 421
Guthrie (D4)*............ 200
Hale Center (C4)*........ 1626
Hallettsville (G8)*......2,000
Hallsville (K5)*......... 617
Haltom City (F2).........5,760
Hamilton (G6)*...........3,077
Hamlin (E5)*.............3,569
Handley (F2).............
Happy (C3)*.............. 690
Hargill (F11)*........... 900
Harleton (K5)*........... 350
Harlingen (G11)*.........23,229
Harper (E7)*............. 360
Harrold (F3)*............ 250
Hart (B3)*............... 500
Hartley (B2)*............ 425
Harwood (G8)*............ 157
Haskell (E4)*............3,836
Haslam (L6)*.............
Haslet (F1)*............. 180
Hasse (F6)*.............. 400
Hawkins (J5)*............ 493
Hawley (E5)*............. 325
Hearne (H7)*.............4,872
Hebbronville (F10)*......4,302
Hedley (D3)*............. 588
Hemphill (L6)*........... 972
Hempstead (J7)*..........1,395
Henderson (K5)*..........6,833
Henrietta (F4)*..........2,813
Hereford (B3)*...........5,207
Hermleigh (D5)*.......... 671
Hext (E7)*...............
Hico (F6)*...............1,212
Hidalgo (F11)*........... 560
Higgins (D1)*............ 675
High Island (K8)*........1,000
Highland Park (G2).......11,405
Highlands (K1)*..........2,723
Hillcrest (H8)...........2,826
Hillsboro (G5)*..........8,363
Hindes (F9).............. 123
Hitchcock (K3)*..........1,105
Hitchland (C1)*.......... 25
Holland (G7)*............ 674
Holliday (F4)*...........1,007
Hondo (E8)*..............4,188
Honey Grove (J4)*........2,340
Honey Island (K7)*.......1,250
Hooks (K4)*..............2,319
Houston (J2)*............596,163
Houston(urban area).697,287
Howe ‡(H4)*.............. 572
Hubbard (H6)*............1,768
Huckabay (F5)*........... 130
Hughes Spgs. (K5)*.......1,445
Hull (K7)*...............1,200
Humble (J7)*.............1,388
Hunter (G8)*............. 150
Huntington (K6)*.........1,039
Huntsville (J7)*.........9,820
Hutchins (H2)*........... 743
Hutto (G7)*.............. 529
Hye (F7)*................ 85
Hylton (D5)*............. 25
Idalou (C4)*.............1,014
Imperial (B6)*........... 400
Indian Oaks (E2)......... 800
Industry (H7)*........... 500
Ingram (E7)*............. 475
Iola (H7)*............... 500
Iowa Colony (J2)*........ 642
Iowa Park (F4)*..........2,110
Ira (C5)*................ 118
Iraan (B7)*..............1,196
Iredell (G6)*............ 394
Ireland (F6)*............ 100
Irving (G2)*.............2,621
Italy (H5)*..............1,185
Itasca (G5)..............1,718
Jacksboro (F4)*..........2,951
Jacinto City ‡(J1).......6,856
Jacksonville (J5)*.......8,607
Jasper (L7)*.............4,403
Jayton (D4)*............. 635
Jean (F4)*............... 120
Jefferson (K5)*..........3,164
Jermyn (F4)*............. 300
Jewett (H6)*............. 598
Joaquin (L5)*............ 579
Johnson City (F7)*....... 648
Joinerville (J5)*........ 500
Jourdanton (F9)*.........1,481
Juliff (J3)*.............
Junction (E7)*...........2,471
Juno (C7)*............... 50
Justiceburg (C5)*........ 86
Justin (G5)*............. 496
Kalgary (E4)*............
Kamay (F4)*.............. 500
Kanawha (J4)*............ 300
Karnes City (G9)*........2,588
Katemcy (E7)*............ 85
Katy (J8)*............... 849
Kaufman (H5)*............2,714
Keene (G5)*..............1,200
Keller (F1)*............. 800
Kellerville (D2)*........ 250
Keltys (K6)*.............1,091
Kemah (K2)*..............1,000
Kemp (H5)*............... 881
Kenedy (G9)*.............4,234
Kennard (J6)*............ 550
Kennedale (F2)*..........1,046
Kent (C11)*.............. 93
Kerens (H5)*.............1,198
Kermit (B6)*.............6,912
Kerrick (B1)*............ 20
Kerrville (E7)*..........7,691
Key (C5)................. 30
Kildare (K5)*............ 350
Kilgore (K5)*............9,638
Killeen (G6)*............7,045
Kings Mill (D2)*......... 250
Kingsbury (G8)*.......... 500
Kinksland (F7)*.......... 100
Kingsville (G10)*........16,898
Kirbyville (K7)*.........1,150
Kirkland (D3)*........... 250
Kirvin (H6)*............. 152
Kleberg (H2)*............
Knippa (E8)*............. 360
Knott (C5)*.............. 200
Knox City (E4)*..........1,489
Kosse (H6)*.............. 566
Kountze (K7)*............1,651
Kress (C3)*.............. 350
Krum (G4)*............... 450
Kyle (G8)*............... 888
La Feria (G11)*..........2,952
La Grange (G8)*..........2,738
La Porte (K2)*...........4,429
La Pryor (E9)*........... 500
La Vernia (G8)*..........
Lacoste (E8)*............
Ladonia (J4)*............1,104
Lagarto (F9)............. 210
Lake Jackson (J9)*.......2,897
Lake June (H2)...........1,517
Lake Victor (F7)*........ 50
Lake Worth (E2)..........2,351
Lakeview (D3)*........... 287
Lakeview ‡(K8)...........3,091
Lamarque (K3)*...........7,359
Lamesa (C5)*.............10,704
Lamkin (F6)*............. 100
Lampasas (F6)*...........4,869
Lancaster (G2)*..........2,632
Langtry (C8)*............ 135
Laredo (E10)*............51,910
Lariat (B3)*............. 50
Larue (J5)*.............. 75
Latexo (J6)*............. 500
Lawn ‡(E5)*.............. 311
League City (K2)*........1,341
Leakey (E8)*............. 800
Leesville (G8)*.......... 285
Lefors (D2)*............. 577
Legion (F7)*............. 200
Lela (D2)*............... 130
Lelia Lake (D3)*......... 150
Lenorah (B5)*............ 108
Leona (H6)*.............. 300
Leonard (H4)*............1,211
Leroy (G6)*.............. 275
Letot (G2)...............
Levelland (B4)*..........8,264
Lewisville (G5)*.........1,516
Lexington (G7)*.......... 603
Liberty (K7)*............4,163
Liberty Hill (F7)*....... 700
Lincoln (H7)*............ 103
Lindale (J5)*............1,105
Linden (K4)*.............1,744
Linn (F11)*.............. 150
Lipan (F5)*.............. 650
Lipscomb (D1)*........... 100
Littlefield (B4)*........6,540
Liverpool (J3)*.......... 200
Livingston (K7)*.........2,865
Llano (F7)*..............2,954
Locker (F6)*............. 70
Lockhart (G8)*...........5,573
Lockney (C3)*............1,692
Lodi (K5)*............... 190
Lohn (E6)*...............
Lolita (H9)*............. 268
Lometa (F6)*............. 951
London (E7)*............. 175
Lone Oak (H5)*........... 571
Longview (K5)*...........24,502
Longworth (D5)*.......... 101
Loop (B5)*............... 120
Lopeno (E11)*............ 500
Loraine (D5)*............1,045
Lorenzo (C4)*............ 939
Los Angeles (F9)*........
Los Ebanos (F11)*........ 300
Los Fresnos (G11)*.......1,113
Lott (H6)*............... 956
Louise (H8)*............. 700
Lovelady (J6)*........... 541
Lubbock (C4)*............71,747
Lueders (E5)*............ 708
Lufkin (K6)*.............15,135
Luling (G8)*.............4,297
Lyford (G11)*............1,473
Lynchburg (K1)...........
Lytle (F8)*..............1,000
Mabank (K6)*............. 896
Madisonville (J7)*.......2,393
Magic City (D2)*......... 25
Magnolia (J7)*........... 525
Malakoff (H5)*...........1,286
Malone (H6)*............. 352
Manchaca (G7)*........... 200
Manor (G7)*.............. 820
Mansfield (F2)*.......... 964
Manvel (J3)*............. 350
Marathon (A7)*........... 800
Marble Falls (F7)*.......2,044
Marfa (C12)*.............3,603
Margaret (E3)*........... 75
Marion (F8)*............. 439
Marlin (H6)*.............7,099
Marquez (H6)*............ 287
Marshall (K5)*...........22,327
Mart (H6)*...............2,269
Maryneal (D5)*........... 150
Mason (E7)*..............2,456
Matador (D3)*............1,335
Matagorda (J9)*.......... 700
Mathis (G9)*.............4,050
Maud (K4)*............... 713
May (F5)*................
Maypearl ‡(H5)*.......... 373
Mc Adoo (C4)*............ 108
Mc Allen (F11)*..........20,067
Mc Camey (B6)*...........3,121
Mc Caulley (E5)*......... 200
Mc Dade (G7)*............ 400
Mc Gregor (G6)*..........2,669
Mc Kinney (H4)*..........10,560
Mc Lean (D2)*............1,439
Mc Nair (K1)*............1,313
Mc Nary (B11)*........... 250
Meadow (B4)*............. 490
Medicine Mound (E3)*. 150
Medina (E8)*............. 400
Megargel (F4)*........... 347
Melvin (E6)*............. 386
Memphis (D3)*............3,810
Menard (E7)*.............2,685
Mentone (D10)*........... 145
Mercedes (F12)*..........10,081
Mercury (E6)*............ 100
Meridian (G6)*...........1,146
Merkel (E5)*.............2,338
Mertens ‡(H5)*........... 210
Mertzon (C6)............. 768
Mesquite (H2)*...........1,696
Mexia (H6)*..............6,627
Miami (D2)*.............. 646
Middle Water (B2)*....... 15
Midland (C6)*............21,713
Midlothian (G5)*.........1,177
Milam (L6)*.............. 75
Milano (H7)*............. 500
Miles (D6)*.............. 739
Milford (H5)*............ 690
Millersview (E6)*........ 200
Millett (E9)*............ 300
Millsap (G5)*............ 287
Minden (K5)*............. 275
Mineola (J5)*............3,626
Mineral (G9)*............ 260
Mineral Hts. ‡(H4)....... 552
Mineral Wells (F5)*......7,801
Mingus (F5)*............. 310
Mirando City (E10)*...... 800
Mission (F11)*...........10,765
Missouri City (J2)*...... 150
Mobeetie (D2)*........... 350
Monahans (B6)*...........6,311
Mont Belvieu (L1)*....... 600
Montague (G4)*........... 402
Montalba (J6)*...........
Montgomery (J7)*......... 800
Moody (G6)*..............1,084
Moore (E9)*..............
Moran (E5)*.............. 610
Morgan (G5)*............. 424
Morgans Point (K2)....... 656
Morse (C1)*.............. 150
Morton (B4)*.............2,274
Moulton (H8)*............ 692
Mt. Calm (H6)*........... 456
Mt. Enterprise (K6)*..... 504
Mt. Pleasant (K4)*.......6,342
Mt. Vernon (J4)*.........1,433
Muenster (G4)*........... 896
Muldoon (G8)*............ 250
Muleshoe (B3)*...........2,477
Mullin (F6)*............. 326
Munday (E4)*.............2,280
Mykawa (J2).............. 200
Myra (G4)*............... 70
Nacogdoches (J6)*........12,327
Naples (K4)*.............1,346
Nash (K4)*............... 550
Natalia (F8)*............1,175
Navasota (J7)*...........5,188
Nazareth (B3)*........... 104
Neches (J6)*............. 350
Nederland (K8)*..........3,805
Needville (J8)*.......... 609
Neuville (L6)*........... 500
New Boston (K4)*.........2,688
New Braunfels (K8)*...12,210
New London (K5)*.........1,800
New Salem (K6)*.......... 250
New Ulm (H8)*............ 400
New Waverly (J7)*........ 500
New Willard (K7)*........ 500
Newark (E1)*.............
Newcastle (F4)*.......... 743
Newgulf (J8)*............1,803
Newlin (D3)*.............
Newport (F4)*............ 256
Newton (L7)*............. 929
Nixon (G8)*..............1,875
Nocona (G4)*.............3,022
Nordheim (G9)*........... 477
Normandy (D9)*........... 350
Normangee (H6)*.......... 657
N. Pleasanton ‡(F9)*..... 832
N. Texarkana (L4)........1,328
Northfield (D3)*......... 150
Norton (E6)*............. 100
Notla (D1)*.............. 5
Novice (E5)*............. 252
Nursery (H9)*............ 200
Oak Knoll (F2)...........3,930
Oakalla (F7)*............
Oakhurst (J7)*........... 500
Oakville (G9)*........... 400
Oakwood (J6)*............ 759
O'Brien (E4)*............ 550
Odell (E3)*.............. 238
Odem ‡(G10)*.............1,680
Odessa (B6)*.............29,495
O'Donnell (C4)*..........1,473
Oglesby (G6)*............ 450
Oilton (F10)*............ 500
Oklaunion (E3)*.......... 129
Old Glory (D4)*.......... 125
Olden (F5)*.............. 500
Olmos Park ‡(F8).........2,841
Olney (F4)*..............3,765
Olton (B3)*..............1,201
Omaha ‡(K4)*............. 735
Onalaska (J7)*........... 200
Oplin (E5)*.............. 100
Orange (L7)*.............21,174
Orange Grove (F10)*...... 935
Orangefield (L7)*........1,500
Ore City (K5)*........... 342
Orla (D10)*..............
Ovalo (E5)*.............. 161
Overton (K5)*............2,001
Ozona (C7)*..............2,885
Paducah (D4)*............2,952
Paige (G7)*.............. 350
Paint Rock (E6)*.........
Palacios (H9)*...........2,799
Palestine (J6)*..........12,503
Palmer ‡(H5)*............ 647
Palo Pinto (F5)*......... 500
Pandale (C7)*............ 50
Panhandle (C2)*..........1,406
Pantego (F2)............. 646
Paradise (G5)*...........
Paris (J4)*..............21,643
Pasadena (K2)*...........22,483
Patricia (B5)*........... 60
Patroon (L6)*............
Peacock (D4)*............ 165
Pear Ridge ‡(K0).........2,020
Pearl (F6)*.............. 126
Pearland (J2)*...........1,250
Pearsall (E9)*...........4,481
Pecan Gap ‡(J4)*......... 319
Pecos (D10)*.............8,054
Peden (E1)............... 200
Penelope ‡(H6)*.......... 243
Pennington (J6)*......... 250
Penwell (B6)*............
Percilla (J6)*........... 60
Perico (B1)*............. 36
Perrin (G5)*............. 387
Perryton (D1)*...........4,417
Petersburg (C4)*......... 777
Petrolia (F4)*........... 606
Pettus (G9)*.............
Pflugerville (G7)*....... 450
Pharr (F11)*.............8,690
Phillips (C2)*...........4,105
Pickton (J4)*............ 673
Pilot Point (H4)*........1,176
Pine Springs (C10)*...... 2
Pineland (L6)*...........1,454
Pioneer (F5)*............ 82
Pittsburg (J4)*..........3,142
Plains (B4)*............. 470
Plainview (C3)*..........14,044
Plano (H4)*..............2,126
Plateau (C11)............ 20
Pleasanton (F9)*.........2,913
Point (J5)*.............. 450
Pontotoc (E7)*........... 100
Port Aransas (H10)*...... 551
Port Arthur (K8)*........57,530
Port Arthur (urban
area) 81,763
Port Bolivar (L3)*....... 410
Port Isabel (G11)*.......2,372
Port Lavaca (H9)*........5,599
Port Neches (K7)*........5,448
Port O'Connor (H9)*...... 600
Porter (J7)*............. 840
Portland (G10)*..........1,292
Post (C4)*...............3,141
Postoak (F4)*............ 8
Poteet (F8)*.............2,487
Poth (F8)*...............1,089
Pottsboro ‡(H4)*......... 383
Pottsville (F6)*......... 200
Powderly (J4)*........... 380
Premont (F10)*...........2,619
Presidio (C12)*..........2,000
Priddy (F6)*............. 300
Princeton ‡(H4)*......... 540
Proctor (F5)*............ 90
Prosper ‡(H4)*........... 243
Pumpville (C8)*.......... 75
Purdon ‡(H5)*............ 203
Putnam (E5)*............. 289
Pyote (A6)*..............
Quail (D3)*.............. 150
Quanah (E3)*.............4,589
Queen City ‡(K4)*........ 511
Quemado (D9)*............
Quinlan (H5)*............ 599
Quitaque (C3)*........... 647
Quitman (J5)*............ 927
Ralls (C4)*..............1,779
Randado (F10)*...........
Ranger (F5)*.............3,989
Rankin (B6)*.............1,139
Ratcliff (J6)*........... 250
Ravenna (H4)*............ 185
Raymondville (G11)*.....9,136
Reagan (H6)*.............
Realitos (F10)*..........
Red Oak (G3)*............ 400
Red Rock (G8)*........... 97
Red Springs (E4)*........ 95
Redford (C12)*........... 297
Redwater (K4)*........... 451
Refugio (G9)*............4,666
Reno (E1)................ 300
Rhome (G4)*.............. 461
Rice (H5)*............... 396
Richardson (H1)*.........1,289
Richland (H6)*........... 308
Richland Spgs. (F6)*..... 584
Richmond (J8)*...........2,030
Riesel (H6)*............. 409
Ringgold (G4)*...........
Rio Grande City (F11)*.3,992
Rio Hondo (G11)*.........1,125
Riomedina (F8)*..........
Rising Star (F5)*........1,289
River Oaks (E2)*.........7,097
Riverside (J7)*.......... 300
Riviera (F10)*........... 600
Roanoke (F1)*............ 511
Roaring Spgs. (D4)*...... 435
Robert Lee (D5)*.........1,069
Robstown (G10)*..........7,278
Roby (D5)*...............1,051
Rochelle (E6)*........... 300
Rochester (E4)*.......... 773
Rock Island (H8)*........ 435
Rockdale (G7)*...........2,321
Rockland (K6)*........... 300
Rockport (H9)*...........2,266
Rocksprings (D8)*........1,436
Rockwell (H5)*...........1,501
Rockwood (E6)*........... 200
Rogers (G6)*............. 948
Roma-Los Saenz
(E11)* 1,576
Romero (B2)*............. 25
Roosevelt (D7)*.......... 200
Ropesville (B4)*......... 391
Roscoe (D5)*.............1,584
Rosebud (G6)*............1,730
Rosenberg (J8)*..........6,210
Rosharon (J3)*........... 200
Rotan (D5)*..............3,163
Round Rock (G7)*.........1,438
Round Top ‡(H8)*......... 126
Rowena (D6)*............. 435
Rowlett (H1)*............ 275
Roxton (J4)*.............1,000
Royalty (B6)*............
Royse City (H4)*.........1,266
Ruidosa (C12)*........... 200
Rule (E4)*...............1,251
Runge (G9)*..............1,055
Rusk (J6)*...............6,598
Rye (K7)*................ 185
Sabinal (E8)*............1,974
Sabine (L8)*............. 200
Sabine Pass (L8)*........ 816
Sacul (J6)*.............. 700
Sagerton (E4)*........... 102
Saginaw (E2)*............ 561
Saint Joe (G4)*..........1,147
Salineno (E11)*.......... 400
Samnorwood (D2)*......... 75
San Angelo (D6)*.........52,093
San Antonio (F8)*....408,442
San Antonio (urban
area) 447,365
San Augustine (K6)*.....2,510
San Benito (G12)*........13,271
San Diego (F10)*.........4,397
San Elizario (A10)*......1,200
San Felipe ‡(H8)*........ 296
San Juan (F11)*..........3,413
San Leon (K2)............
San Marcos (F8)*.........9,980
San Perlita (G11)*....... 200
San Saba (F6)*...........3,400
San Ygnacio (E10)*.......1,800
Sanatorium (D6)*.........1,275
Sanderson (B7)*..........2,500
Sandia (F9)*............. 517
Sansom Park Village
‡(E2) 1,611
Sandy Point (J3)*........ 100
Sanger (G4)*.............1,170
Santa Anna (E6)*.........1,605
Santa Monica (G11)....... 200
Santa Rosa ‡(G11)*....... 400
Santo (F5)*.............. 350
Saragosa (D11)*.......... 200
Saratoga (K7)*...........1,500
Sarita (G10)*............ 250
Saspamco (F8)*........... 500
Savoy ‡(H4)*............. 314
Schertz (F8)*............
Schulenburg (H8)*........2,005
Scotland (F4)*........... 400
Scurry (H5)*............. 500
Seabrook (K2)*...........1,800
Seadrift (H9)*........... 567
Seagoville (H2)*.........1,927
Seagraves (B5)*..........2,101
Sealy (H8)*..............1,942
Seguin (G8)*.............9,733
Seminole (B5)*...........3,479
Seven Sisters (F9)*...... 350
Seymour (E4)*............3,779
Shafter (C12)*........... 259

Shallowater (B4)* 500
Shamrock (D2)* 3,322
Sheffield (B7)* 350
Shelbyville (L6)*
Sheldon (K1)* 200
Shepherd (K7)*
Sherman (H4)* 20,150
Sherwood (D6)* 247
Shiner (G8)* 1,778
Shiro (J7)* 300
Shore Acres ‡(J8) 783
Sierra Blanca (B11)* 900
Silsbee (K7)* 3,179
Silverton (C3)* 857
Sinton (G9)* 4,254
Skellytown (C2)* 700
Skidmore (G9)* 800
Slaton (C4)* 5,036
Slocum (J6)* 200
Smeltertown (A10)* 3,500
Smiley (G8)* 503
Smithfield (F1)* 500
Smithville (G7)* 3,379
Snyder (D5)* 12,010
Socorro (A10)*
Somerset (F8)* 920
Somerville (H7)* 1,425
Sonoma ‡(H5) 210
Sonora (D7)* 2,633
Sourlake (K7)* 1,630
South Bend (F5)* 325
South Groveton (J7)
South Houston (J2)* 4,126
South Plains (C3) 100
Southland (C4)* 210
Southside Place (J2) 1,436
South Texarkana ‡(K4) 317
Spanish Fort (G4)* 203
Sparenberg (B5)*
Spearman (C1)* 1,852
Spicewood (F7)*
Spofford (D8)* 246
Spring (J7)* 500
Springlake (B3)*
Springtown (G5)* 650
Spur (D4)* 2,183
Stamford (E5)* 5,819
Stanton (C5)* 1,603
Star (F6)*
Stephenville (F5)* 7,155
Sterley (C3)* 96
Sterling City (D6)* 846
Stinnett (C2)* 1,170
Stockdale (G8)* 1,105
Stonewall (F7)* 135
Stratford (C1)* 1,385
Strawn (F5)* 922
Streeter (E7)* 26
Streetman (H6)* 419
Sudan (B3)* 1,348
Sugar Land (J8)* 2,285
Surphur Spgs. (J4)* 8,991
Summerfield (B3)*
Sundown (B4)* 1,492
Sunray (C1)* 1,530
Sunset (G4)*
Swearingen (D3)* 45
Sweeny (J8)* 1,393
Sweet Home (H8)* 500
Sweetwater (D5)* 13,619
Swenson (D4)* 175
Sylvester (D5)*
Taft (G9)* 2,978
Tahoka (C4)* 2,848
Talco (K4)* 917
Talpa (E6)* 234
Tarzan (B5)* 79
Tascosa (B2)* 125
Tatum (K5)* 599
Taylor (G7)* 9,071
Teague (H6)* 2,925
Tehuacana ‡(H6)* 389
Telegraph (E7)* 17
Telephone (J4)* 275
Tell (D3)* 100
Temple (G6)* 25,467
Tenaha (K6)* 715
Tennyson (D6)*
Terlingua (D12)* 20
Terrell (H5)* 11,544
Terrell Hills ‡(F8) 2,708
Tesnus (B7)* 8
Texarkana (L4)* 24,753
Texas City (K3)* 16,620
Texhoma (C1) 299
Texline (B1)* 437
Texon (C6)* 500
Thalia (E4)* 223
Thomas (J5)* 200
Thorndale (G7)* 855
Thornton (H6)* 623
Thorp Spring (F5)* 200
Thrall ‡(G7)* 585
Three Rivers (F9)* 2,026
Throckmorton (F4)* 1,320
Tilden (F9)* 425
Timpson (K6)* 1,455
Tioga (H4)* 529
Tivoli (H9)* 300
Tokio ((B4)* 200
Tolar (G5)* 338
Tom Bean ‡(H4)* 286
Tomball (J7)* 1,065
Tornillo (A10)* 400
Toyah (D11)* 409
Toyahvale (D11)* 16
Trent (D5)* 296
Trenton (H4)* 603
Trinidad (J5)* 950
Trinity (J7)* 2,054
Troup (J5)* 1,539
Truscott (E4)* 255
Tulia (C3)* 3,222
Turkey (D3)* 1,005
Turnersville (G6)* 150
Tuscola (E5)* 497
Twin Sisters (F7) 50
Tyler (J5)* 38,968
Tynan (G9)* 70
Umbarger (B3)* 465
University Park (H2)* 24,275
Utopia (E8)* 350
Uvalde (E8)* 8,674
Valentine (C11)* 510
Valera (E6)* 300
Valley Mills (G6)* 1,037
Valley Spg. (F7)*
Valley View (H4)* 500
Van (J5)* 610
Van Alstyne (H4)* 1,649
Van Horn (C11)* 1,161
Vance (E8)* 100
Vancourt (D6)* 11
Vanderbilt (H9)* 400
Vanderpool (E8)* 150
Vealmoor (C5)* 35
Vega (B2)* 620
Velasco (J9)* 2,260
Venus ‡(H5)* 357
Vera (E4)* 270
Veribest (D6)* 33
Vernon (E3)* 12,651
Victoria (H9)* 16,126
Vigo Park (C3)*
Village Mills (K7)* 267
Voca (E7)* 100
Voth (K7)* 1,200
Waco (G6)* 84,706
Waco (urban area) 92,299
Wadsworth (J9)* 250
Waelder (G8)* 1,275
Waka (D1)* 100
Wake ‡(K4)* 1,066
Wall (D6)* 200
Waller (J7)* 715
Wallis (H8)* 1,500
Wallisville (L1)* 300
Walnut Spgs. (G5)* 626
Waring (F8)* 176
Washington (J7)* 300
Waskom (L5)* 719
Watauga (F1) 150
Water Valley (C6)* 300
Waxahachie (H5)* 11,204
Wayside (C3)* 43
Weatherford (G5)* 8,093
Webb (E10)* 17
Webb (F2) 45
Webster (K2)*
Weesatche (G9)* 250
Weimar (H8)* 1,663
Weinert (E4)* 288
Welch (B5)*
Weldon (J6)* 250
Wellington (D3)* 3,676
Wellman (B5)* 165
Wells (J6)* 718
Weslaco (G11)* 7,514
West (G6)* 2,130
W. Columbia (J8)* 2,100
W. University Pl. (J2) 17,074
W. Vernon (E3)
W. Worth (E2) 529
Westbrook (C5)* 220
Westhoff (G8)* 610
Westminster ‡(H4)* 192
Westover Hills (E2) 266
Wharton (J8)* 4,450
Wheeler (D2)* 904
White Deer (C2)* 629
White Settlement (E2) 10,827
Whiteface (B4)* 579
Whiteflat (D3)* 100
Whitesboro (H4)* 1,854
Whitewright (H4)* 1,372
Whitharral (B4)* 275
Whitney (G6)* 1,383
Whitsett (F9)* 100
Whitt (G5)* 150
Wichita Falls (F4)* 68,042
Wickett (B6)*
Wiergate (L6)* 1,
Wildorado (B2)*
Willis (J7)* 1,
Willow City (F7)*
Wills Point (J5)* 2,
Wilmer (H2)*
Wilson (C4)*
Winchell (E6)*
Winchester (H7)*
Windom ‡(H4)*
Windthorst (F4)*
Winfield (K4)*
Winfree (L1)
Wingate (D5)*
Wink (A6)* 1,
Winnie (K8)*
Winnsboro (J5)* 2,
Winona (J5)*
Winters (E6)* 2,
Wolfe City (J4)* 1,
Wolfforth (C4)*
Woodsboro (G9)* 1,
Woodson (E5)*
Woodville (K7)* 1,
Wooster (K2)
Wortham (H6)* 1,
Wylie (H5)* 1,
Yantis (J5)*
Yoakum (G8)* 5,
Yorktown (G9)* 2,
Ysleta (A10)* 4,
Zapata (E11)* 1,
Zavalla (K6)*
Zephyr (F6)*

Map on Page 90

UTAH

Total Population 688,862

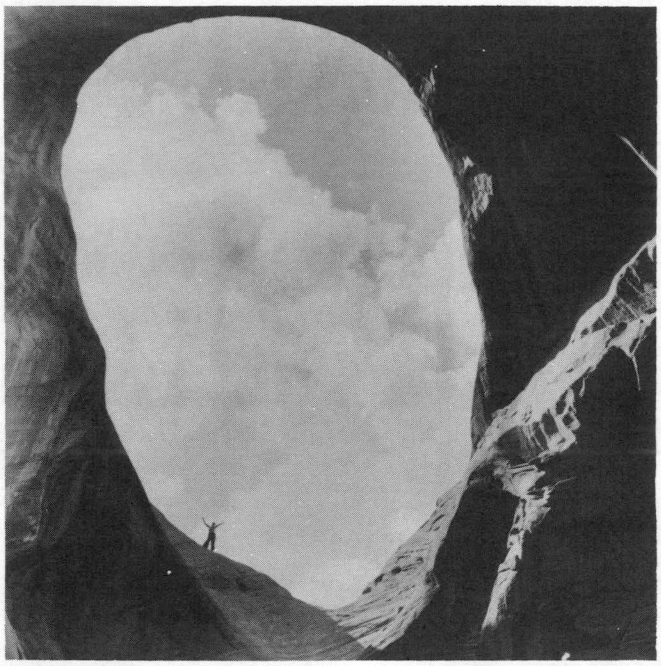

29 COUNTIES

Beaver (A5) 4,856
Box Elder (A2) 19,734
Cache (C2) 33,536
Carbon (D4) 24,901
Daggett (E3) 364
Davis (B3) 30,867
Duchesne (D3) 8,134
Emery (D4) 6,304
Garfield (C6) 4,151
Grand (E5) 1,903
Iron (A6) 9,642
Juab (A4) 5,981
Kane (B6) 2,299
Millard (A4) 9,387
Morgan (C2) 2,519
Piute (B5) 1,911
Rich (C2) 1,673
Salt Lake (B3) 274,895
San Juan (E6) 5,315
Sanpete (C4) 13,891
Sevier (C5) 12,072
Summit (D3) 6,745
Tooele (A3) 14,636
Uintah (E3) 10,300
Utah (C3) 81,912
Wasatch (C3) 5,574
Washington (A6) 9,836
Wayne (C5) 2,205
Weber (B2) 83,319

CITIES and TOWNS

Abraham (B4)* 100
Adamsville (B5)* 50
Alpine (C3) 571
Alton (B6)* 154
Altonah (D3)* 363
Amalga (C2) 225
American Fork (C3)* 5,126
Angle (C5) 30
Annabella (C5)* 263
Antimony (C5)* 187
Arcadia (D3)* 168
Aurora (B5)* 614
Axtell (C4)* 155
Bacchus (B3)* 94
Bear River City (B2)* 438
Beaver (B5)* 1,685
Benjamin (C3) 450
Beryl (A6)* 26
Bicknell (C5)* 373
Bingham Canyon (B3)* 2,569
Birdseye (C4)* 75
Black Rock (B5)* 19
Blanding (E6)* 1,177
Blue Creek (B2) 43
Bluebell (D3)* 218
Bluff (E6)* 100
Bonanza (E4)*
Boneta (D3)* 134
Bothwell‡ (B2) 317
Boulder (C6)* 166
Bountiful (C3)* 6,004
Bridgeland (D3)* 240
Bridgeport (E3) 6
Brigham City (C2)* 6,790
Brighton (C3)*
Bryce Canyon (B6)* 200
Burrville (C5) 35
Cache Junction (C2)* 80
Caineville (D5) 12
Callao (A4)* 65
Cannonville (C6)* 205
Castle Dale (D4)* 715
Castle Gate (D4)* 701
Castle Rock (C2) 20
Cedar City (A6)* 6,106
Cedar Fort (B3) 213
Cedar Valley (B3)* 82
Centerfield (C4)* 601
Centerville (C3)* 1,262
Central (A6)* 49
Central (B5) 100
Charleston (C3) 201
Chester (C4)* 153
Circleville (B5)* 603
Cisco (E5)* 41
Clarkston (B2)* 526
Clawson (C4)* 136
Clearcreek (C4)* 168
Clearfield (B2)* 4,723
Cleveland (D4)* 343
Clinton ‡(B2) 670
Clive (A3) 10
Clover (B3) 110
Coalville (C3)* 850
Collinston (B2)* 145
Colton (C4) 21
Columbia (D4)* 412
Corinne (B2)* 427
Cornish (B2)* 181
Cove Fort (B5) 10
Croydon (C2)* 90
Delle (B3)* 35
Delta (B4)* 1,703
Deseret (B4)* 332
Devils Slide (C2)* 200
Deweyville (B2)* 233
Dividend (C4)* 30
Dragerton (D4)* 3,453
Dragon (E4)
Draper (C3)* 2,000
Duchesne (D3)* 804
East Layton‡ (C2) 217
Echo (C3)* 175
Eden (C2)* 235
Elberta (B4)* 138
Elmo (D4)* 170
Elsinore (B5)* 657
Elwood ‡(B2) 393
Emery (C5)* 488
Enterprise (A6)* 790
Ephraim (C4)* 1,987
Escalante (C6)* 773
Etna (A2) 22
Eureka (B4)* 1,318
Fairfield (B3) 37
Fairview (C4)* 974
Farmington (C3)* 1,468
Fayette (C4)* 200
Ferron (C4)* 478
Fielding (B2)* 249
Fillmore (B5)* 1,890
Five Mile Pass (B3)
Fort Duchesne (E3)* 200
Fountain Green (C4)* 767
Francis (C3) 276
Fremont (C5)* 224
Frisco (A5)
Fruit Heights (C2) 124
Fruitland (D3)* 127
Gandy (A4) 48
Garden City (C2)* 164
Garfield (B3)* 2,079
Garland (B2)* 1,008
Garrison (A5)* 34
Geneva (C3)
Genola (C4) 314
Glendale (B6)* 226
Glenwood (C5)* 338
Gold Hill (A3) 4
Goshen (C4)* 525
Grantsville (B3)* 1,537
Green River (D4)* 583
Greenville (B5)* 128
Greenwich (B5)* 50
Grouse Creek (A2)* 167
Grover (C5)* 53
Gunlock (A6)* 89
Gunnison (C4)* 1,144
Gusher (E3)* 125
Hanksville (D5)* 100
Hanna (D3)* 175
Hatch (B6)* 244
Hatton (B5) 9
Hayden (D3)* 52
Heber (C3)* 2,936
Helper (D4)* 2,850
Henefer (C2)* 346
Henrieville (C6)* 114
Hiawatha (D4)* 1,421
Hinckley (B4)* 589
Hite (D6)
Holden (B4)* 476
Holladay (C3) 3,100
Honeyville (B2)* 599
Hooper (B2)* 1,243
Howell (B2)* 176
Hoytsville (C3) 330
Huntington (C4)* 1,029
Huntsville (C2)* 494
Hurricane (A6)* 1,271
Hyde Park (C2)* 644
Hyrum (C2)* 1,704
Ibapah (A3)* 150
Indianola (C4) 50
International (B3)
Ioka (D3) 238
Iron Mountain (A6)
Iron Springs (A6) 20
Ivins (A6)* 95
Jensen (E3)*
Joseph (B5)* 208
Junction (B5)* 285
Kamas (C3)* 721
Kanab (B6)* 1,287
Kanarraville (A6)* 263
Kanosh (B5)* 476
Kaysville (B2)* 1,898
Keetley (C3)*
Kelton (A2)
Kenilworth (D4)* 932
Kingston (B5)* 138
Knolls (A3) 12
Koosharem (C5)* 300
La Sal (E5)* 75
La Verkin (A6)* 387
Lakeside (B2) 25
Laketown (C2)* 217
Lapoint (E3)* 400
Lark (B3)* 750
Latuda (C4)* 200
Layton (C2)* 3,456
Laytona ‡(C2) 405
Leamington (B4)* 214
Leeds (A6)* 160
Leeton (D3) 50
Lehi (C3)* 3,627
Leland (C3) 175
Leota (E3) 124
Levan (C4)* 521
Lewiston (C2)* 1,533
Liberty (C2) 196
Lindon (C3) 801
Linwood (E3)* 22
Loa (C5)* 437
Lofgreen (B3)* 20
Logan (C2)* 16,832
Lucin (A2)* 51
Lund (A5)* 42
Lyman (C5)* 276
Lynn (A2)* 50
Lynndyl (B4)* 241
Maeser (E3) 643
Magna (B3)* 3,502
Mammoth (B4)* 137
Manila (E3)* 147
Manti (C4)* 2,051
Mantua (C2) 271
Mapleton (C3) 1,175
Marysvale (B5)* 520
Mayfield (C4)* 390
Meadow (B5)* 378
Mendon (B2)* 369
Mercur (B3) 2
Mexican Hat (E6)
Midvale (B3)* 3,996
Midway (C3)* 711
Milford (A5)* 1,673
Mills, (B4) 42
Millville (C2)* 401
Minersville (A5)* 593
Moab (E5)* 1,274
Modena (A6)* 130
Mohrland (D4)
Mona (C4)* 328
Monroe (B5)* 1,214
Monticello (E6)* 1,172
Moore (C5)* 41
Morgan (C2)* 1,064
Moroni (C4)* 1,076
Motoqua (A6) 25
Mounds (D4) 15
Mount Carmel (B6)* 158
Mount Emmons (D3)* 276
Mount Pleasant (C4)* 2,030
Mountain Home (D3)* 300
Murray (C3)* 9,006
Myton (D3)* 435
Nada (A5)
National (C4)*
Neola (D3)* 400
Nephi (C4)* 2,990
New Harmony (A6)* 126
Newcastle (A6)* 229
Newton (C2)* 497
Nibley (C2) 304
North Logan (C2) 535
North Ogden (C2) 1,105
North Salt Lake (C3)* 255
Oak City (B4)* 334
Oakley (C3)* 264
Oasis (B4)* 190
Ogden (C2)* 57,112
Onaqui ‡(B3) 333
Ophir (B3)* 199
Orangeville (C4)* 589
Orderville (B6)* 371
Orem (C3)* 8,351
Ouray (E3)* 111
Panguitch (B6)* 1,501
Paradise (C2)* 401
Paragonah (B6) 404
Park City (C3)* 2,254
Park Valley (A2)* 142
Parowan (B6)* 1,455
Payson (C3)* 3,998
Peoa (C3)* 210
Perry (C2) 449
Peterson (C2) 275
Pickleville (C2) 96
Pine Valley (A6) 16
Pinto (A6)
Pintura (A6)* 40
Plain City (B2) 899
Pleasant Grove (C3)* 3,195
Pleasant View (B2) 420
Plymouth (B2)* 228
Portage (B2)* 254
Price (D4)* 6,010
Promontory (B2) 72
Providence (C2)* 1,055
Provo (C3)* 28,937
Randlett (E3)* 400
Randolph (C2)* 562
Redmond (C4)* 600
Richfield (B5)* 4,212
Richmond (C2)* 1,091
River Heights ‡(C2) 468
Riverdale (C2) 871
Riverside (B2)* 281
Riverton (B3)* 1,666
Rockville (A6)* 180
Roosevelt (D3)* 1,628
Rosette (A2) 68
Roy (B2)* 3,723
Royal (D4)* 195
Rubys Inn (B6)*
Saint George (A6)* 4,562
St. John (B3)* 130
Salem (C3)* 781
Salina (C5)* 1,789
SALT LAKE CITY (C3)* 182,121
Salt Lake City (urban area) 226,880
Saltair (B3)* 75
Sandy (C3)* 2,0
Santa Clara (A6)* 3
Santaquin (C4)* 1,2
Scipio (B4)* 4
Scofield (C4)* 2
Sego (E4)*
Sevier (B5)* 1
Sigurd (B5)* 4
Silver City (B4)*
Smithfield (C2)* 2,3
Snowville (B2)* 1
Soldier Summit (C4)*
South Jordan (C3) 1,0
S. Ogden (C2) 3,7
S. Salt Lake (C3)* 7,7
S. Weber (C2) 2
Spanish Fork (C3)* 5,2
Spring Canyon (C4)* 4
Spring City (C4)* 7
Springdale (B6)* 1
Springville (C3)* 6,4
Spry (B5)*
Standardville (C4)* 3
Sterling (C4)* 1
Stockton (B3)* 4
Sulphurdale (B5)
Summit (B6)* 1
Summit Point (E5)*
Sunnyside (D4)* 1,8
Sunset (B2) 9
Syracuse (B2) 8
Tabiona (D3)* 1
Talmage (D3)* 1
Taylorsville (B3)
Teasdale (C5)* 2
Thatcher (B2) 2
Thistle (C4)* 2
Thompson (E5)* 1
Tooele (B3)* 7,2
Toquerville (A6)* 2
Torrey (C5)* 2
Tremonton (B2)* 1,6
Trenton (B2)* 4
Tridell (E3)* 3
Tropic (B6)* 4
Trout Creek (A4)*
Uintah (C2) 3
Upalco, (D3)* 1
Venice (C5)* 2
Vernal (E3)* 2,8
Vernon (B3)* 1
Veyo (A6)*
Vineyard (C3) 1
Virgin (A6)* 1
Wahsatch (C2)*
Wales (C4)* 1
Wallsburg (C3)* 2
Wanship (C3) 1
Washington (A6)* 4
Watson (E4)
Wattis (C4)* 2
Wellington (D4)* 8
Wellsville (C2)* 1,2
Wendover (A3)* 2
West Bountiful (C3) 6
W. Jordan (C3)* 2,1
W. Point ‡(B2) 4
W. Weber (B2) 2
Westwater (E4)*
Whiterocks (E3)* 3
Whitsoe (C6)
Willard (C2)* 5
Woodland (C3) 2
Woodruff (C2)* 1
Woods Cross (B3)* 2
Woodside (D4)*
Yost (A2)* 1
Zion Nat'l. Park (B6)*

Map on Page 91

VERMONT

Total Population 377,747

14 COUNTIES

Addison (A2) 19,442
Bennington (A4) 24,115
Caledonia (C1) 24,049
Chittenden (A2) 62,570
Essex (D1) 6,257
Franklin (B1) 29,894
Grand Isle (A1) 3,406
Lamoille (B1) 11,388
Orange (C3) 17,027
Orleans (C1) 21,190
Rutland (A3) 45,905
Washington (B2) 42,870
Windham (B5) 28,749
Windsor (B4) 40,885

CITIES and TOWNS

Addison (A2) △628
Albany (C1)* 196
Alburg (A1)* 563
Andover (B4) △185
Arlington (A4)* △1,463
Ascutney (C4)* 200
Averill (D1)* △20
Bakersfield (B1)* △779
Barnard (B3)* △439
Barnet (D2)* △1,425
Barre (C2)* 10,922
Barton (C1)* 1,267
Bartonsville (B4)* 200
Beebe Plain (C1)* 173
Beecher Falls (D1)* 500
Bellows Falls (C4)* 3,881
Belvidere (B1) 207
Belvidere Center (B1)* 50
Bennington (A5)* 8,002
Benson (A3)* △573
Benson Landing (A3) 2
Berkshire (B1)* △1,063
Bethel (B3)* △1,534
Bolton (B2) △301
Boltonville (C2)* 50
Bomoseen (A3)* 275
Bondville (B4)* 229
Bradford (C3)* 725
Braintree (B3)* △626
Brandon (A3)* △3,304
Brattleboro (C5)* △11,5
Bread Loaf (B3)*
Bridgewater (B3)* △9
Bridgewater Corners* (B3) 1
Bridport (A3)* △6
Briggs (B3) 1
Bristol (A2)* 1,3

rookfield (B2)* Δ 762
rownington (C1) Δ 673
rownsville (C4)* 125
urke (D1) Δ1,042
urlington (A2)* 33,155
abot (C2)* 219
alais (B2)* Δ 778
ambridge (B1)* 244
ambridge Jct. (B1)* 80
ambridgeport (C4)* 48
anaan (D1)* Δ 969
astleton (A3)* Δ1,748
avendish (B4)* Δ1,374
edar Beach (A2)*
enter Rutland (A3)* 540
harlotte (A2)* Δ1,215
helsea (C2)* Δ1,025
hester (C4)* 796
hester Depot (C4)* 600
hittenden (B3)* Δ 424
larendon Springs (A3) 75
olchester (A1)* Δ3,897
oncord (D2)* 348
orinth (C2)* Δ 786
ornwall (A3) Δ 728
oventry (C1)* Δ 497
raftsbury (C1)* Δ 709
raftsbury Common* (C1) 225
uttingsville (B3)* 164
anby (B4)* Δ 990
anville (C2)* Δ1,312
erby (Derby Center) (C1)* 383
erby Line (C1)* 767
orset (A4)* Δ1,150
uxbury (B2) Δ 489
ast Albany (C1) 148
. Alburg (A1) 20
. Arlington (A4)* 500
. Barnet (D2)* 166
. Barre (C2)* 600
. Berkshire (B1)* 225
. Bethel (B3)* 64
. Brookfield (C2)* 175
. Burke (D1)* 330
. Calais (C2)* 140
. Charleston (D1)* 350
. Concord (D2)* 220
. Corinth (C2)* 185
. Craftsbury (C1)* 43
. Dorset (A4)* 350
. Dover (B5)* 150
. Fairfield (B1)* 500
. Franklin (B1)* 80
. Georgia (B1)* 60
. Granville (B2)* 65
. Hardwick (C1)* 267
. Haven (D1)* Δ 85
. Jamaica (B4)* 100
. Middlebury (A3)* 300
. Montpelier (B2)* Δ1,128
. Peacham (C2) 70
. Poultney (A3)* 500
. Randolph (C3)* 175
. Richford (C1)* 160
. Ryegate (D2)* 225
. Thetford (C3)* 50
. Wallingford (B4)* 300
den (B1)* Δ 496
den Mills (C1)* 225

Ely (C3)* 51
Enosburg Falls (B1)* 1,289
Essex (A1)* Δ3,931
Essex Junction (A2)* 2,741
Fair Haven (A3)* 2,058
Fairfax (B1)* Δ1,129
Fairfield (B1)* Δ1,428
Fairlee (C3)* 571
Ferrisburg (A2)* Δ1,387
Florence (A3)* 300
Forest Dale (A3)* 400
Franklin (B1)* Δ 878
Gassetts (B4)* 50
Gaysville (B3)* 172
Georgia (A1) Δ1,055
Gilman (D2)* 900
Glover (C1)* 228
Grafton (B4)* Δ 422
Granby (D1)* Δ 74
Grand Isle (A1)* Δ 735
Graniteville (C2)* 1,500
Granville (B3)* Δ 213
Greensboro (C1)* Δ 737
Groton (C2)* 435
Guildhall (D1)* Δ 270
Guilford (B5) Δ 796
Halifax (B5)* Δ 343
Hancock (B3)* Δ 391
Hardwick (C2)* 1,696
Hartford (C3)* Δ5,827
Hartland (C3)* Δ1,559
Hartland Four Corners (C3)* 300
Healdville (B4)* 124
Highgate Center (B1)* 350
Highgate Falls (A1)* 218
Highgate Springs (A1)* 300
Hinesburg (A2)* Δ1,120
Hubbardton (A3)* Δ 332
Huntington (A2)* Δ 601
Huntington Ctr. (B2)* 150
Hyde Park (B1)* 440
Hydeville (A3)* 400
Irasburg (C1)* 711
Island Pond (D1)* 1,252
Isle La Motte (A1)* Δ 295
Jacksonville (B5)* 220
Jamaica (B4)* Δ 597
Jay (C1) Δ 243
Jeffersonville (B1)* 387
Jericho (A2)* Δ1,135
Jericho Center (B2)* 125
Johnson (B1)* 900
Jonesville (B2)* 156
Lake (D1) 6
Lake Dunmore (A3)* 35
Lake Elmore (B1)* 75
Leicester Jct. (A3)* 97
Lewiston (C3)* 55
Lincoln (B2)* Δ 577
Londonderry (B4)* Δ 953
Lowell (C1)* Δ 643
Lower Cabot (C2) 120
Lower Waterford (D2)* 550
Ludlow (B4)* 1,678
Lunenburg (D2)* Δ1,299
Lyndon (C1)* Δ3,360
Lyndon Center (C1)* 321
Lyndonville (D1)* 1,506
Maidstone (D1) Δ 81
Manchester (A4)* 454

Manchester Center (A4)* 900
Manchester Depot (B4)* 561
Marlboro (B5)* Δ 311
Marshfield (C2)* 274
Mc Indoe Falls (C2)* 200
Middlebury (A2)* 3,614
Middlesex (B2)* Δ 887
Middletown Springs (A4)* Δ 496
Milton (A1)* 739
Monkton (A2)* Δ 520
Monkton Ridge (A2) 150
Montgomery (B1)* Δ1,091
Montgomery Center (B1)*
MONTPELIER (B2)* 8,599
Moretown (B2)* Δ 883
Morgan (D1)* Δ 296
Morgan Center (D1)* 130
Morrisville (B1)* 1,995
Morses Line (B1) 25
Moscow (B2)* 245
Mount Holly (B4)* Δ 567
New Haven (A2)* Δ 932
Newbury (C2)* Δ1,667
Newfane (B4)* 156
Newport (C1)* 5,217
Newport Center (C1)* 235
North Bennington (A5)* 1,327
N. Calais (C2)* 20
N. Clarendon (B3)* 226
N. Concord (D2)* 108
N. Danville (C2) 250
N. Ferrisburg (A2)* 500
N. Hartland (C3)* 268
N. Hero (A1)* Δ 407
N. Hyde Park (B1)* 250
N. Montpelier (C2)* 136
N. Pomfret (B3)* 200
N. Pownal (A5)* 650
N. Randolph (C3) 36
N. Springfield (C4)* 450
N. Thetford (C3)* 110
N. Troy (C1)* 1,057
N. Tunbridge (C3) 50
N. Westminster (C4) 404
N. Williston (B2) 75
N. Wolcott (C1) 100
Northfield (B2)* 2,262
Northfield Falls (B2) 340
Norton (C1)* Δ 279
Norwich (C3)* Δ1,532
Old Bennington (A5) 198
Orange (C2) Δ 410
Orleans (C1)* 1,261
Orwell (A3)* Δ 902
Panton (A2) Δ 332
Passumpsic (C2)* 180
Pawlet (A4)* Δ1,156
Peacham (C2)* Δ 501
Perkinsville (B4)* 142
Peru (B4)* Δ 197
Piermont Station (C3). 75
Pittsfield (B3)* Δ 225
Pittsford (A3)* 622
Plainfield (C2)* 604
Plymouth (B3)* Δ 348
Plymouth Union (B3)* 130
Pomfret (B3)* Δ 586
Pompanoosuc (C3) 50
Post Mills (C3)* 200

Poultney (A3)* 1,685
Pownal (A5)* Δ1,453
Pownal Center (A5) 300
Proctor (A3)* 1,813
Proctorsville (B4)* 349
Putney (B4)* Δ1,019
Quechee (C3)* 330
Randolph (B3)* 2,223
Randolph Center (B3)* 141
Reading (B4)* Δ 470
Readsboro (A5)* 654
Richford (B1)* 1,916
Richmond (A2)* 731
Ricker Mills (C2) 10
Ripton (B3)* Δ 207
Riverton (B2)* 125
Rochester (B3)* Δ 937
Roxbury (B2)* Δ 465
Royalton (B3)* Δ1,331
Rupert (A4)* Δ 713
Rutland (B3)* 17,659
Ryegate (C2)* Δ 996
Saint Albans (A1)* 8,552
St. Albans Bay (A1)* 335
St. Johnsbury (D2)* 7,370
St. Johnsbury Ctr. (D2) 350
Salisbury (A3)* Δ 573
Saxtons River (B4)* 715
Sharon (C3)* Δ 470
Sheffield (C1)* Δ 451
Shelburne (A2)* Δ1,365
Sheldon (B1)* Δ1,352
Sheldon Junction (B1)* 70
Sheldon Springs (A1)* 325
Sherburne Center (B3)* 70
Shoreham (A3)* Δ 829
Simonsville (B4)* 100
South Barre (B2)* 675
S. Burlington (A2) Δ3,279
S. Dorset (A4)* 173
S. Hero (A1)* Δ 567
S. Lincoln (B2)* 80
S. Londonderry (B4)* 400
S. Lunenburg (D2)* 78
S. Newbury (D2)* 105
S. Newfane (B5)* 119
S. Pomfret (B3)* 100
S. Royalton (C3)* 700
S. Ryegate (C2)* 340
S. Shaftsbury (A5)* 480
S. Strafford (C3)* 300
S. Wallingford (B4)* 350
S. Windham (B4)* 40
S. Woodbury (B2)* 62
S. Woodstock (B3)* 250
Springfield (C4)* 4,940
Stamford (A5) Δ 514
Starksboro (A2)* Δ 576
Stockbridge (B3)* Δ 427
Stowe (B2)* 556
Strafford (C3)* Δ 680
Sudbury (A3)* Δ 263
Sutton (C1)* Δ 528
Swanton (A1)* 2,275
Taftsville (C3)* 125
Talcville (B3) 70
Thetford (C3)* Δ1,046
Thetford Center (C3)* 125
Tinmouth (B4) Δ 248
Topsham (C2)* Δ 733
Townshend (B4)* 178

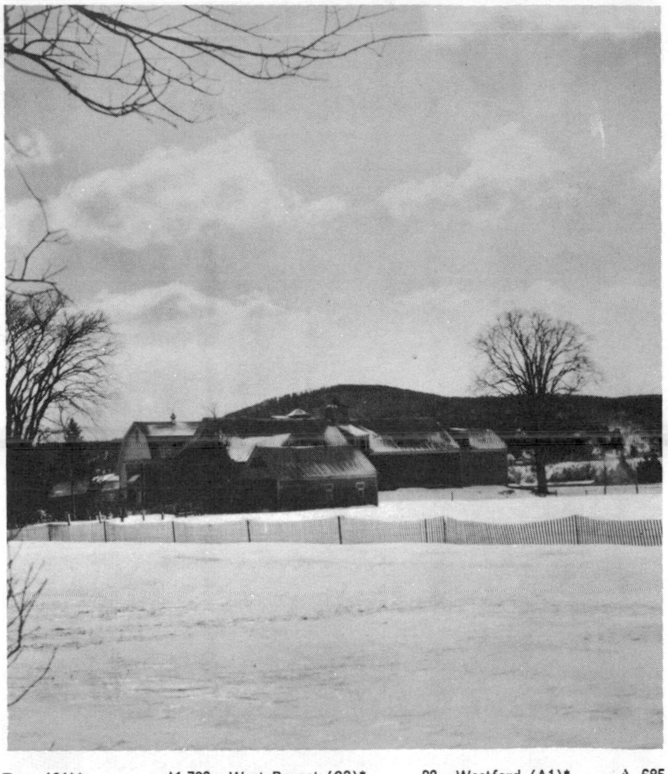

Troy (C1)* Δ1,786
Tunbridge (C3)* Δ 774
Tyson (B4) 175
Underhill (B1)* Δ 698
Underhill Center (B2)*
Union Village (C3)* 45
Vergennes (A2)* 1,736
Vernon (B5)* Δ 712
Vershire (C3)* Δ 284
Waits River (C2)* 76
Waitsfield (B2)* Δ 661
Walden (C2)* Δ 481
Walden Heights (C2)* 60
Wallingford (A4)* Δ1,482
Wardsboro (B4)* Δ 377
Warren (B2)* Δ 498
Washington (C2)* Δ 650
Waterbury (B2)* 3,153
Waterbury Center (B2)* 650
Waterville (B1)* Δ 409
Websterville (C2)* 975
Wells (A4)* Δ 487
Wells River (D2)* 570

West Barnet (C2)* 88
W. Berkshire (B1)* 70
W. Brattleboro (B5)*
W. Burke (C1)* 414
W. Charleston (C1)* 185
W. Corinth (C2)* 52
W. Cornwall (A3) 50
W. Danville (C2)* 131
W. Dover (B5)* 45
W. Dummerston (C5)* 200
W. Fairlee (C3)* Δ 363
W. Glover (C1)* 58
W. Halifax (B5)* 200
W. Hartford (C3)* 225
W. Newbury (C2)* 100
W. Pawlet (A4)* 500
W. Rupert (A4)* 300
W. Rutland (A3)* Δ2,487
W. Salisbury (A3) 145
W. Townshend (B4)* 200
W. Wardsboro (B4)* 82
W. Woodstock (B3)* 80
Westfield (C1)* Δ 358

Westford (A1)* Δ 685
Westminster (C4)* 298
Westminster Sta. (C4)* 70
Westminster West (B4)* 150
Westmore (C1) Δ 210
Weston (B4)* Δ 468
Wheelock (C1)* Δ 287
White River Jct. (C3)* 2,365
Whiting (A3)* Δ 282
Whitingham (B5)* Δ 816
Wilder (C3)* 1,097
Williamstown (B2)* Δ1,600
Williamsville (B5)* 150
Williston (A2)* Δ1,182
Willoughby (C1) 150
Wilmington (B5)* 571
Windham (B4)* Δ 146
Windsor (C4)* 3,467
Winooski (A2)* 6,734
Wolcott (C1)* Δ 766
Woodbury (C2)* Δ 449
Woodford (A5) Δ 198
Woodstock (B3)* 1,326
Worcester (B2)* Δ 445

VIRGINIA

Map on Page 92 — *Total Population 3,318,680*

100 COUNTIES

ccomack (N5) 33,832
lbemarle (G5) 26,662
lleghany (D5) 23,139
melia (H6) 7,908
mherst (F5) 20,332
ppomattox (G6) 8,764
rlington (K3) 135,449
ugusta (F4) 34,154
ath (E4) 6,296
edford (E6) 29,627
land (B6) 6,436
otetourt (E5) 15,766
runswick (J7) 20,136
uchanan (D1) 35,748
uckingham (G5) 12,288
ampbell (F6) 28,877
aroline (K4) 12,471
arroll (C7) 26,695
harles City (K6) 4,676
harlotte (G6) 14,057
hesterfield (J6) 40,400
larke (H2) 7,074
raig (D6) 3,452
ulpeper (H3) 13,242
umberland (H6) 7,252
ickenson (D2) 23,393
inwiddie (J6) 18,839
ssex (L5) 6,530
airfax (K3) 98,557
auquier (J3) 21,248
loyd (D7) 11,351
luvanna (H5) 7,121
ranklin (E6) 24,560
rederick (H2) 17,537
iles (C6) 18,956
loucester (L6) 10,343
oochland (J5) 8,934
rayson (B7) 21,379
reene (H4) 4,745
reensville (J7) 16,319
alifax (G7) 41,442
anover (J5) 21,985
enrico (K6) 57,340
enry (E7) 31,219
ighland (E4) 4,069
sle of Wight (L7) 14,906
James City (L6) 6,317
King and Queen (L5) 6,299
King George (K4) 6,710
King William (K5) 7,589
ancaster (M5) 8,640

Lee (B2) 36,106
Loudoun (J2) 21,147
Louisa (J5) 12,826
Lunenburg (H7) 14,116
Madison (H4) 8,273
Mathews (M6) 7,148
Mecklenburg (H7) 33,497
Middlesex (M5) 6,715
Montgomery (D6) 29,780
Nansemond (L7) 25,238
Nelson (G5) 14,042
New Kent (L5) 3,995
Norfolk (M7) 99,937
Northampton (N6) 17,300
Northumberland (M5) 10,012
Nottoway (H6) 15,479
Orange (H4) 12,755
Page (H3) 15,152
Patrick (D7) 15,642
Pittsylvania (F7) 66,096
Powhatan (J5) 5,556
Prince Edward (H6) 15,398
Prince George (K6) 19,679
Prince William (K3) 22,612
Princess Anne (M7) 42,277
Pulaski (C6) 27,758
Rappahannock (H3) 6,112
Richmond (L5) 6,189
Roanoke (D6) 41,486
Rockbridge (F5) 23,359
Rockingham (G4) 35,079
Russell (E2) 26,818
Scott (D2) 27,640
Shenandoah (G3) 21,169
Smyth (E2) 30,187
Southampton (K7) 26,522
Spotsylvania (J4) 11,920
Stafford (K4) 11,902
Surry (L6) 6,220
Sussex (K7) 12,785
Tazewell (B6) 47,512
Warren (H3) 14,801
Washington (E2) 37,536
Westmoreland (L4) 10,148
Wise (C2) 56,336
Wythe (B7) 23,327
York (L6) 11,750

CITIES and TOWNS

Abingdon (E2)* 4,709
Accomac (N5)* 500
Achilles (M6)*
Acorn (L4)* 100
Adams Grove (K7)* 75
Adner (L5)* 71
Advance Mills (G4) 25
Afton (G4)* 370
Agricola (F5)* 65
Airpoint (D6)* 150
Alanthus (H3)
Alberene (G5)* 500
Alberta (J7)* 430
Alexandria (L3)* 61,787
Allegheny (D5)*
Allisonia (C7)* 400
Alpha (H5)*
Altavista (F6)* 3,332
Alto (F5) 75
Alton (F7)* 53
Alvarado (E2)* 50
Amelia Court House (J6)* 800
Amherst (F5)* 1,038
Amissville (H3)* 100
Ammon (J6)* 50
Amonate (A6)* 1,800
Andersonville (G6)* 50
Andover (C2)*
Ante (J7)*
Appalachia (C2)* 2,915
Apple Grove (J5) 50
Appomattox (G6)* 1,094
Ararat (C7)*
Arcadia (E5)* 125
Arcanum (G6)*
Arlington (L3)* 135,449
Arrington (G5)* 200
Artrip (D2)* 350
Arvonia (H5)*
Ashburn (K2)* 210
Ashland (J5)* 2,610
Atkins (B7)* 500
Atlee (K5) 207
Augusta Springs (F4)* 300
Austinville (B7)*
Avalon (M5)* 25
Axton (E7)* 166
Aylett (K5)* 100
Backbay (M7)* 150
Bacons Castle (L6)* 75
Ballsville (H6)* 95
Balty (K5)* 50
Banco (H4)* 90
Banner (D2)* 700
Barboursville (H4)* 250

Barren Springs (C7) 300
Bartlick (D1)* 275
Baskerville (H7)* 51
Bassett (E7)* 3,421
Bastian (B6)* 1,200
Batesville (G5)* 150
Baywood (C7)* 91
Beach (J6)* 40
Bealeton (J3)* 350
Beaverdam (J5)* 500
Beaverlett (M6)* 188
Beckham (G6)* 35
Bedford (E6)* 4,061
Belle Haven (N5)* 453
Belona (H5)* 80
Belspring (C6)* 300
Ben Hur (B2)* 400
Benhams (D2)* 148
Benns Church (L7)* 100
Bent Creek (G5)* 60
Bent Mountain (D6)* 88
Bentonville (H3)* 600
Berea (J4)* 22
Bergton (G3)* 100
Berryville (J2)* 1,401
Bertrand (L5)* 27
Big Island (F5)* 500
Big Rock (D1)* 250
Big Stone Gap (C2)* 5,173
Birchleaf (D1)* 500
Birdsnest (N6)* 200
Blackridge (H7)* 10
Blacksburg (D6)* 3,358
Blackstone (J6)* 3,536
Blackwater (B2)* 500
Blairs (F7)* 300
Bland (B6)* 600
Bloxom (N5)* 400
Blue Grass (E3)* 105
Blue Ridge (E6)* 765
Bluefield (B6)* 4,212
Bluemont (J2)* 180
Bluff City (C6)* 225
Bohannon (M6)* 250
Boissevain (B6)* 1,197
Bolar (E4)* 111
Bon Air (J5)* 1,500
Bondtown (C2)* 240
Bonny Blue (B2)* 930
Boones Mill (E6)* 335
Boonesville (H4)* 400
Boulevard (L6)* 100
Bowers Hill (M7)* 400
Bowling Green (K4)* 616
Boxwood (E7) 18

Boyce (H2) 372
Boydton (H7)* 501
Boykins (K7)* 811
Branchville (K7)* 169
Brandon (K6)* 100
Brandy (J4)* 350
Breaks (D1)* 300
Bremo Bluff (H5)* 300
Bridgewater (F4)* 1,537
Brightwood (H4)* 250
Bristol (D3)* 15,954
Bristow (J3)* 75
Broad Run (J3)* 30
Broadford (E2)* 800
Broadway (G3)* 561
Brodnax (J7)* 499
Brokenburg (J4)* 100
Brooke (K4)* 450
Brookneal (G6)* 883
Brownsburg (F5)* 360
Browntown (H3)* 150
Brucetown (H2)* 265
Buchanan (E5)* 1,300
Buckhorn (L7)* 100
Buckingham (G5)* 264
Buckner (J5)* 100
Buena (H4)
Buena Vista (F5)* 5,214
Buffalo Junction (G7)* 15
Buffalo Springs (G7)* 55
Bula (H5)*
Bumpass (J5)* 75
Burdette (L7)* 250
Burgess (M5)*
Burkes Garden (B6)*
Burkeville (H6)* 695
Burnleys (H4)* 125
Burnsville (E4)* 20
Caledonia (H5)* 100
Callands (E7)* 35
Callao (L5)* 400
Callaville (J7)*
Callaway (D7)*
Calverton (J3)* 200
Calvin (C2)* 800
Cambria (D6)* 853
Camp (B7)* 100
Cana (C7)*
Capahosic (L6)*
Cape Charles (M6)* 2,427
Cape Henry (N7)
Capeville (M6)* 300
Capron (K7)* 281
Carbo (D2)* 50
Cardwell (J5)* 130

Carloover (E5)* 65
Carrie (D1)* 500
Carrsville (L7)* 200
Carson (K6)* 105
Carters Bridge (H5)* 8
Cartersville (H5)* 109
Carthage (D6)* 25
Carysbrook (H5)* 70
Casanova (J3)* 105
Cascade (E7)* 275
Castlewood (D2)* 250
Catawba Sanatorium (D6)* 500
Catlett (J3)* 250
Cedar Bluff (E2)* 1,083
Cedar Springs (B7) 97
Cedarville (H3)*
Cedon (K4)* 45
Center Cross (L5)* 100
Central Point (K4)*
Ceres (B6)* 200
Champlain (L4)* 65
Chancellor (J4)* 150
Charles City (K6)*
Charlotte Court House (G6)* 397
Charlottesville (H4)* 25,969
Chase City (H7)* 2,519
Chatham (F7)* 1,456
Chatham Hill (A7)*
Check (D6)* 40
Cheriton (M6)* 1,000
Cherry Hill (K3) 250
Chester (K6)* 1,168
Chesterfield (J6)* 200
Childress (D6)* 73
Chilhowie (E2)* 1,022
Chincoteague (O5)* 2,724
Christiansburg (D6)* 2,967
Chuckatuck (L7)* 500
Chula (J6)* 200
Church Road (J6)* 150
Church View (L5)*
Churchville (F4)*
Cismont (H4)* 250
Claremont (L6)* 374
Clarksville (H7)* 1,035
Clarkton (G7)* 50
Claudville (D7)*
Clay Bank (L6)* 100
Clayville (J6)* 50
Cleveland (D2)* 388
Clifford (F5)* 175
Clifton (K3)* 262
Clifton Forge (E5)* 5,795

Clinch (D2)* 166
Clinchburg (E2)* 250
Clinchco (D1)* 1,390
Clinchport (C2)* 359
Clintwood (D2)* 1,366
Clover (G7)* 274
Clover Creek (E4) 50
Cloverdale (E6)* 350
Cluster Springs (G7)* 100
Coan (M5) 10
Cobbs Creek (M6)* 200
Cobham (H4)* 400
Coeburn (D2)* 760
Cohasset (H5)* 100
Coke (L6)*
Collierstown (E5)* 300
Colonial Beach (L4)* 1,464
Colonial Heights (K6)* 6,077
Colony (F6)* 250
Columbia (H5)* 119
Columbia Furnace (G3)* 100
Comers Rock (B7)* 50
Comorn (K4)*
Concord (F6)* 600
Conicville (G3)* 82
Cootes Store (G3) 50
Copper Hill (D6)* 153
Copper Valley (C7)* 86
Cornwall (F5)* 20
Coulwood (E2)* 100
Courtland (K7)* 443
Covesville (G5)* 300
Covington (D5)* 5,860
Craig Healing Springs (D6)* 50
Craigsville (E4)* 1,200
Crandon (C6)* 135
Crewe (H6)* 2,030
Criglersville (H4)* 50
Crimora (G4)* 250
Cripple Creek (B7)* 200
Critz (D7)* 150
Crockett (B7)* 150
Cropp (J4)
Cross Junction (H2)* 50
Crozet (G4)* 1,000
Crozier (J5)* 200
Crystal Hill (G7)* 50
Cuckoo (J5)* 200
Cullen (G6)* 160
Culpeper (H4)* 2,527
Cumberland (H6)* 300
Curdsville (G6)*
Dahlgren (K4)* 500
Daleville (E6)* 200

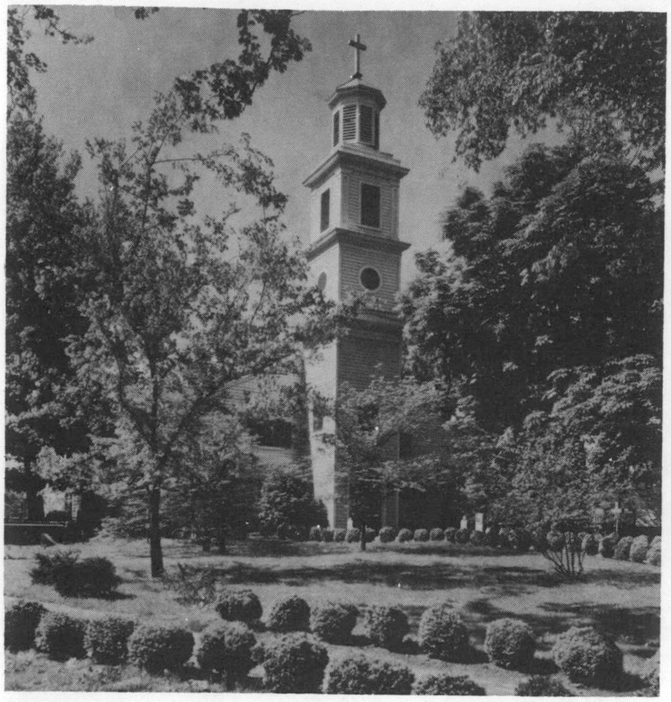

Damascus (E2)*............1,726
Dante (D2)*..................2,405
Danville (F7)*............35,066
Darlington Heights
(G6)* 50
Darwin (C1)*............... 500
Davenport (D1)*..........
David (J3)..................... 100
Dayton (G4)*................ 788
De Jarnette (K5)..........
Delaplane (J3)*............ 75
Deltaville (M5)*...........1,000
Denbigh (L6)*..............1,500
Dendron (L6)*.............. 476
Denniston (G7)*........... 100
Deskins (D1)*............... 225
Dewitt (J6)*................. 80
Dillwyn (H5)*............... 556
Dinwiddie (J6)*............ 200
Disputanta (K6)*.......... 500
Doe Hill (F4)*.............. 40
Dorchester (C2)*..........1,129
Doswell (J5)*................ 500
Downings (L5)*............ 84
Drakes Branch (G7)*.... 410
Draper (C7)*................ 258
Drewrys Bluff (J6)*..... 160
Drewryville (K7)*......... 185
Drill (E1)*.................... 200
Dry Fork (F7)*............ 250
Dryden (B2)*................ 350
Duane (K5)*.................
Dublin (C6)*.................1,313
Duffield (C2)*............... 176
Dugspur (C7)*.............. 26
Dumbarton (J5)............ 400
Dumfries (K3)*.............1,300
Dunbar (C2)*................
Dunbrooke (L5)*........... 25
Dundas (H7)*................ 139
Dungannon (D2)*.......... 431
Dunnsville (L5)*............ 100
Duty (D1)*.................... 104
Eagle Rock (E5)*.......... 700
Earlehurst (D5).............
Earls (J6)*.................... 150
Earlysville (H4)*........... 91
East Lexington (F5)*.... 300
East Stone Gap (C2)*...
Eastville (N6)*.............. 311
Eclipse (M7)*................ 300
Edgehill (K4)*............... 150
Edgerton (J7)*.............. 112
Edinburg (H3)*.............. 533
Edom (G3)*................... 90
Eggleston (C6)*............ 350
Elberon (L6)*................
Elk Creek (B7)*............ 150
Elk Garden (E2)*.......... 150
Elko (K6)*....................
Elkton (G4)*.................1,361
Ellerson (K5)*............... 140
Elliston (D6)*................ 600
Elmington (G5)*........... 100
Emmerton (L5)*............ 30
Emory (E2)*.................. 300
Emporia (J7)*...............5,664
Enfield (K5)*.................
Esmont (G5)*................ 750
Esserville (C2)*.............1,000
Etlan (H3)*................... 300
Ettrick (K6)*.................3,030
Evergreen (G6)*............ 100
Evington (F6)*.............. 145
Ewing (B2)*..................1,000
Exmore (N5)*................1,362
Faber (G5)*.................. 100
Fair Port (M5)*............. 100
Fairfax (K3)*.................1,946
Fairfield (F5)*............... 265
Fairview (C2)*............... 200
Falls Church (K3)*........7,535
Falls Mills (B6)*............ 300
Falmouth (K4)*.............1,176
Farmville (H6)*..............4,375
Farnham (L5)*............... 100
Fentress (M7)*.............. 500

Ferrum (D7)*................ 350
Fieldale (D7)*..............1,295
Fincastle (E6)*............ 405
Fine Creek Mills (J5)*.. 10
Fishersville (F4)*.......... 500
Fitzhugh (J7)*.............. 30
Flint Hill (H3)*............. 250
Floyd (D7)*.................. 493
Ford (J6)*.................... 75
Fordwick (F4)*.............
Forest (F6)*................. 300
Forestville (G3)*........... 63
Fork Union (H5)*.......... 800
Forks of Buffalo (F5)*. 25
Fort Belvoir (K3)*........
Fort Blackmore (C2)*.... 250
Fort Defiance (G4)*......
Fort Mitchell (H7)*...... 25
Fort Monroe (M6)*.......2,500
Fort Myer (K3)*...........
Fosters Falls (C7)*....... 160
Fox (B7)*..................... 200
Franklin (L7)*..............4,670
Franktown (N6)*........... 100
Fredericksburg (J4)*...12,158
Fredericks Hall (J4)*.... 102
Free Union (G4)*.......... 80
Fremont (D1)*.............. 150
Fries (B7)*...................1,442
Front Royal (H3)*........8,115
Gainesboro (H2)*.......... 110
Gainesville (J3)*........... 200
Gala (E5)*....................
Galax (C7)*...................5,248
Gasburg (J7)*............... 200
Gate City (C3)*............2,126
Gaylord (H2)*............... 25
Georges Fork (C1)........ 500
Gholsonville (J7)*.........
Gibson Station (A2)*.... 250
Glade Spring (E2)*....... 827
Gladehill (E7)*............. 50
Gladys (F6)*................. 220
Glamorgan (C1)...........
Glasgow (F5)*............... 810
Glen Lyn (C6)*.............. 240
Glen Wilton (E5)*......... 350
Glenallen (J5)*............. 600
Gloucester (L6)*........... 600
Gloucester Point (M6)*
Goldbond (C6)*............
Goochland (J5)*........... 125
Goode (F6)*................. 150
Gordonsville (H4)*........1,118
Gore (H2)*.................... 150
Goshen (F5)*................ 125
Grafton (L6)*................ 100
Grapefield (B6)*........... 75
Gray (K7)*.................... 50
Green Bay (H6)*........... 200
Green Cove (E2)*.......... 585
Green Springs (H4)*.....
Greenbackville (O5)*..... 400
Greenbush (N5)*........... 300
Greenfield (G5)*........... 200
Greenville (F5)*...........
Greenwood (G4)*.......... 500
Gretna (F7)*................. 803
Grimsted (M5)*............
Groseclose (B7)*........... 25
Grottoes (G4)*............. 908
Grundy (D1)*................1,947
Guinea (K4)*................ 325
Guinea Mills (H6)*....... 40
Gum Spring (J5)*......... 200
Hacksneck (N5)*........... 200
Hagan (B2)*.................. 125
Hague (L4)*.................. 100
Halifax (G7)*................ 791
Hallsboro (J6)*............. 100
Hallwood (N5)*............ 500
Hamilton (J2)*.............. 351
Hampden Sydney (G6)* 500
Hampton (M6)*............5,966
Handsom (K7)*............. 200
Hanover (K5)*.............. 500
Hansonville (D2)*.......... 350

Happy Creek (H3)*.......
Harborton (N5)*........... 300
Hardy (E6)*..................
Harman (D1)*...............
Harrisonburg (F4)*.....10,810
Harriston (G4)*............ 98
Haymakertown (D6)*....
Haymarket (J3)*........... 213
Haysi (D1)*.................. 476
Head Waters (F4)*... 34
Healing Springs (E5)*.. 400
Healys (M5)*................ 30
Heathsville (L5)*........... 350
Hebron (J6)*................ 40
Henry (E7)*.................. 200
Herndon (K3)*..............1,461
Hewlett (J5)*................ 200
Hickory (M7)*............... 170
Highland Springs(K5)*.3,171
Hightown (E4)*............ 25
Hill (C2).......................
Hillsboro (J2)*............. 129
Hillsville (C7)*............. 764
Hilton Village (L6)*.....4,486
Hiltons (D2)*...............
Hiwassee (C7)*............ 300
Hoadly K3)*.................. 200
Hobson (L7)*................ 200
Holcombs Rock (F6)*... 82
Holland (L7)*................ 289
Hollins (E6)*................ 800
Holston (D2)*................ 80
Home Creek (D1)*........ 150
Homeville (K7)*............ 85
Honaker (D1)*.............. 847
Hopeton (N5)*.............. 324
Hopewell (K6)*...........10,219
Hopkins (N5)*.............. 80
Horntown (O5)*............ 400
Hot Springs (E4)*........1,500
Howardsville (G5)*........ 50
Hubbard Springs (B2)*
Huddleston (F6)*..........
Hume (J3)*................... 300
Huntley (H3)*...............
Hurley (D1)*................ 225
Hurt (F6)*.................... 500
Hylas (J5)*................... 95
Independence (B7)*...... 486
Indian (E1)*................. 750
Indian Neck (K5)*........ 203
Indian Rock (E5)*......... 98
Indian Valley (C7)*....... 20
Ingram (F7)*................ 30
Iron Gate (E5)*............ 725
Irvington (M5)*............ 800
Irwin (J5)*................... 50
Isle of Wight (L7)*...... 100
Ivanhoe (C7)*...............
Ivor (L7)*..................... 377
James Store (L6)*........
Jamestown (L6)*.......... 10
Jamesville (N5)*...........
Jarratt (K7)*................ 574
Java (F7)*.................... 100
Jefferson (J5)*............. 40
Jeffersonton (J3)*........ 300
Jeffress (G7)*............... 65
Jennings Ordinary(H6)* 50
Jerome (G3)*................ 225
Jetersville (H6)*........... 150
Jewel Ridge (E1)*......... 465
Jones (J4)*................... 150
Jonesville (B3)*............ 597
Joplin (K3).....................
Joyner (K7)*................. 75
Justisville (N5)*........... 100
Keeling (F7)*................
Keezletown (G4)*......... 150
Keller (N5)*.................. 500
Kenbridge (H7)*...........1,176
Kents Store (H5)*......... 50
Keokee (C2)*................ 700
Kernstown (H2)*........... 300
Keswick (H4)*.............. 200
Keysville (H6)*............. 690
Kilmarnock (M5)*......... 689

Kimball (H3)*............... 20
King and Queen Court
House (L5)*............... 150
King George (K4)*....... 246
King William (K5)*...... 125
Kinsale (L4)*................ 350
Kiptopeke (M6)............ 25
Konnarock (E2)*........... 500
La Crosse (H7)*............ 675
Lacey Spring (G3)*...... 300
Ladysmith (J4)*...........
Lafayette (D6)*............ 150
Lahore (J4)*.................
Lakeside (J5)*..............9,000
Lambsburg (C7)*..........
Lancaster (M5)*........... 100
Lanesville (L5)*............ 36
Laurel Fork (C7)*......... 31
Lawrenceville (J7)*......2,239
Leatherwood (E7)*....... 60
Lebanon (D2)*.............. 672
Lebanon Church (G2)*.. 107
Leesburg (J2)*..............1,703
Leesville (F6)*.............. 50
Lennig (G7)*................. 50
Lexington (F5)*............5,976
Lightfoot (L6)*.............
Lilian (M5)*.................. 40
Limeton (H3)*.............. 250
Linden (H3)*................
Lithia (E6)*..................
Little Plymouth (L5)*.. 110
Littleton (K7)*............. 67
Lively (L5)*.................. 275
Locustville (N5)*.......... 200
Long Island (F6)*......... 100
Longshoal (C7)*............ 75
Loretto (K4)*................ 10
Lorton (K3)*................ 132
Lottsburg (M5)*........... 350
Louisa (H4)*................. 344
Lovesmill (H7)*............ 10
Lovettsville (J2)*.......... 341
Lovingston (G5)*.......... 350
Lowesville (F5)*........... 200
Lowmoor (E5)*............ 750
Lowry (F6)*.................. 125
Lucketts (J2)*............... 35
Lunenburg (H7)*.......... 100
Luray (H3)*...................2,731
Lurich (C6)................... 150
Lyells (L5)*.................. 15
Lynch Station (F6)*..... 300
Lynchburg (F6)*.........47,727
Lynnhaven (M7)*.......... 300
Maces Spring (D2)*...... 50
Machipongo (N6)*........
Madison (H4)*.............. 308
Madison Heights (F6)*.2,830
Maggie (D6)*............... 100
Maidens (J5)*.............. 26
Mallow (E5)*................
Manakin (J5)*.............. 382
Manassas (K3)*............1,804
Mangohick (K5)*.......... 250
Mannboro (J6)*............ 75
Mappsville (O5)*.......... 175
Marion (A7)*................6,982
Markham (J3)*............. 50
Marshall (J3)*.............. 500
Martinsville (E7)*......17,251
Marye (J4).................... 150
Massaponax (K4).......... 40
Massies Mill (F5)*........ 175
Mathews (M6)*.............1,500
Matoaca (J6)*...............1,027
Mattoax (J6)*............... 150
Maurertown (G3)*........ 150
Max Meadows (C6)*....1,000
Maxwell (A6)*.............. 150
McClure (D2)*..............1,000
McCoy (C6)*................. 125
McCrady (E2)............... 350
McDowell (E4)*............ 107
McGaheysville (G4)*..... 450
McKenney (J7)*............ 476
McLean (K3)*...............1,094
McMullen (H4)*............ 100
Meadows of Dan (D7)*. 450
Meadowview (E2)*........ 722
Mechanicsburg (C6)*....
Mechanicsville (K5)*.....1,500
Mechum River (G4)*..... 50
Meherrin (H6)*............. 250
Melfa (N5)*.................. 300
Mendota (D2)*.............
Merchant (J7)*.............
Messick (M6)*..............2,000
Middlebrook (F4)*........ 175
Middleburg (J3)*.......... 663
Middletown (H2)*......... 386
Midland (J3)*............... 145
Milford (K4)*................ 300
Millboro (E5)*.............. 500
Millboro Spring (E4)*... 300
Millwood (H2)*............. 700
Mine Run (J4)*............. 80
Mineral (J4)*................ 414
Mitchells (J4)*............. 83
Modest Town (O5)*...... 150
Moffatts Creek (F4)*.... 60
Moneta (E6)*................ 200
Monroe (F6)*................ 800
Monroe Hall (K4)*........ 200
Montague (L5)*............ 50
Monterey (F4)*............ 262
Montross (L4)*............. 331
Montvale (E6)*............. 400
Morattico (L5)*............ 250
Morrison (L6)*..............2,357
Morrisville (J4)*........... 120
Moseley (J6)*............... 100
Mount Crawford (G4)*.. 303
Mount Holly (L4)*........ 238
Mount Jackson (G3)*.... 732
Mount Sidney (G4)*...... 500
Mount Solon (F4)*........ 115
Mount Vernon (K3)*.....
Mouth of Wilson (B7)*. 100
Munden (M7)*.............. 65

Mustoe (E4)*................ 12
Myrtle (L7)................... 100
Nace (E6)*.................... 50
Narrows (C6)*..............2,520
Naruna (G6)*................ 200
Nassawadox (N6)*........
Nathalie (G7)*.............. 200
Natural Bridge (E5)*....
Natural Bridge Station
(F5)* 950
Natural Tunnel (C2)*.... 300
Naxera (M6)*............... 207
Nebo (B7)*................... 216
Neenah (L4)*................ 125
New Baltimore (J3)...... 60
New Castle (D5)*.......... 239
New Church (N5)*........ 379
New Glasgow (G5)*....... 110
New Hope (G4)*............ 200
New Kent (L5)*............ 50
New Market (G3)*........ 701
New River (C6)*............ 400
Newbern (C6)*.............. 175
Newport (D6)*.............. 247
Newport News (M7)*..42,358
News Ferry (F7)*......... 21
Newsoms (K7)*............. 392
Nickelsville (D2)*......... 268
Niday (B6)*.................. 150
Nokesville (J3)*............ 300
Norfolk (M7)*............213,513
Norfolk-Portsmouth
(urban area)...........351,342
Norge (L6)*.................. 100
Norland (C1)................ 500
North Garden (G5)*...... 500
North Tazewell (B6)*... 816
North View (H7)*......... 5
Northwest (M7)*.......... 145
Norton (C2)*.................4,315
Norwood (G5)*............. 200
Nottoway (H6)*............ 100
Nutbush (H6)*.............. 100
Oak Grove (K4)*........... 80
Oak Hall (N5)*............. 160
Oakpark (H4)*.............. 150
Oakwood (E1)*.............
Occoquan (K3)*............ 317
Oceana (N7)*................1,500
Ocoonita (B2)*.............
Odd (M6)*.................... 300
Omega (G7).................. 30
Onancock (N5)*............1,353
Onley (N5)*.................. 650
Orange (H4)*................2,571
Orchid (J5)*................. 35
Ore Bank (H5)*............
Oriskany (E5)*.............. 240
Orlean (J3)*................. 200
Othma (J5)*.................
Owenton (K5)*............. 190
Oyster (N6)*................ 250
Ozeana (L5)*................ 10
Paces (F7)*.................. 70
Page (D1)*...................
Paint Bank (D5)*.......... 75
Painter (N5)*............... 250
Palls (K5)*................... 150
Palmyra (H5)*.............. 300
Pamplin (G6)*.............. 370
Pardee (C1)*................ 300
Paris (J3)* 110
Parksley (N5)*.............. 883
Partlow (J4)*................ 37
Passing (K4)*...............
Patrick Springs (D7)*... 300
Patterson (D1)*........... 500
Peaks (K5)*.................. 200
Pearisburg (C6)*...........2,005
Peary (M6)*................. 225
Pedlar Mills (F5)*........ 150
Pembroke (C6)*............1,010
Pendletons (J5)*........... 150
Penhook (E7)*.............. 55
Pennington Gap (C2)*...2,090
Penola (K5)*................
Perrin (M6)*................. 200
Petersburg (J6)*.........35,054
Phenix (G6)*................ 290
Philomont (J2)*............ 157
Phoebus (M6)*..............3,694
Pilot (D6)*.................... 100
Piney River (G5)*......... 325
Plasterco (E2)*............. 350
Pocahontas (B6)*..........2,410
Poindexter (H5)*.......... 25
Poplar Hill (C6)*.......... 28
Poquoson (M6)*............ 300
Port Republic (G4)*...... 340
Port Richmond (L5)*.... 900
Port Royal (K4)*........... 139
Portlock (M7)................3,809
Portsmouth (M7)*.......80,039
Portsmouth-Norfolk
(urban area)...........351,342
Potomac Beach (L4)*... 125
Pound (C1)*..................1,193
Pounding Mill (E1)*..... 350
Powcan (L5)................. 80
Powhatan (J5)*............ 275
Prince George (K6)*..... 50
Princess Anne (M7)*.... 500
Prospect (G6)*............. 300
Providence Forge (L6)* 250
Pulaski (C6)*.................9,202
Pungo (N7)*................. 175
Pungoteague (N5)*....... 250
Purcellville (J2)*........... 945
Purdy (J7)*................... 250
Putnam (E1)*................ 75
Quantico (K3)*..............1,240
Quicksburg (G3)*.......... 170
Quinby (N5)*................ 450
Quinton (K5)*............... 34
Radford (C6)*...............9,026
Radiant (H4)*............... 224
Randolph (G7)*............ 200
Ransons (G5)*.............. 200
Raphine (F5)*............... 325
Rapidan (H4)................

Raven (E1)*.................. 750
Rawlings (J7)*.............. 500
Reams (K6).................... 18
Rectortown (J3)*.......... 300
Rectory (K4)................. 100
Red Ash (E2)*.............. 750
Red House (G6)*.......... 50
Redoak (G7)*................ 125
Reedville (M5)*............ 400
Rehoboth (H7)*............ 16
Reliance (H3)*.............. 150
Remington (J3)*........... 309
Republican Grove (F7)* 100
Rest (H2)...................... 60
Reusens (F6)*............... 450
Rice (H6)*..................... 215
Rich Creek (C6)*.......... 740
Richlands (E1)*.............4,648
RICHMOND (K5)*....230,310
Richmond (urban
area) 257,423
Ridgeway (E7)*............ 440
Riner (D6)*................... 180
Ringgold (F7)*..............
Ripplemead (C6)*......... 450
Riverton (H3)*.............. 500
Riverville (G5)*............. 75
Rixeyville (H3)*............
Roanoke (D6)*.............91,921
Roanoke (urban
area) 105,883
Rockingham (G4)*........ 150
Rockville (J5)*.............. 100
Rocky Gap (B6)*........... 350
Rockymount (E7)*........1,432
Rolling Hill (G6)*.......... 32
Rose Hill (B3)*............. 750
Roseland (F5)*............. 60
Round Hill (J2)*........... 403
Rowe (D1)*...................
Ruby (J3)*.................... 50
Rugby (B7)*.................. 150
Rural Retreat (B7)*..... 478
Rushmere (L6)*............. 150
Rustburg (F6)*............. 650
Ruther Glen (K5)*........ 50
Ruthville (L6)*.............. 122
Saint Brides (M7)*....... 400
St. Charles (C2)*........... 550
St. Paul (D2)*...............1,014
St. Stephens Church
(K5)* 50
Salem (D6)*..................6,823
Saltville (E2)*...............2,678
Saluda (L5)*................. 300
Salvia (K5)*.................. 75
Sandidges (F5)*........... 200
Sandston (K5)*..............3,500
Sandy Hook (J5)*......... 75
Savedge (K6)*.............. 45
Saxe (G7)*................... 100
Saxis (N5)*.................. 600
Schoolfield (E7)*..........
Schuyler (G5)*............. 900
Scottsburg (G7)*.......... 222
Scottsville (G5)*........... 396
Seaford (M6)*..............1,500
Sebrell (K7)*................ 175
Sedley (L7)*................. 225
Selma (E5)*..................1,200
Seven Mile Ford (A7)*.. 150
Shacklefords (L5)*........ 150
Shanghai (L5)*............. 60
Sharps (L5)*................. 300
Shawsville (D6)*........... 500
Shenandoah (G4)*.........1,903
Sheppards (H6)*........... 60
Shiloh (K4)*.................
Shipman (G5)*.............. 500
Shortt Gap (E1)*..........
Simpsons (D6)*............ 102
Singers Glen (F3)*........ 126
Skeetrock (D1)*............ 300
Skippers (K7)*.............. 400
Skipworth (G7)*........... 35
Slant (C2)*................... 75
Slate (E1)*...................
Slate Mills (H3)*..........
Smithfield (L7)*...........1,180
Snowville (C6)*............. 200
Somerset (H4)*............
Soudan (H7)*................ 50
South Boston (G7)*......6,057
South Hill (H7)*............2,153
South Norfolk (M7)*...10,434
Sparta (K4)*................. 200
Speedwell (B7)*............ 700
Speers Ferry (C2)*........
Spencer (E7)*............... 500
Sperryville (H3)*........... 800
Splashdam (D1)*.......... 200
Spotsylvania (J4)*........ 75
Spottswood (F5)*......... 111
Spring Grove (L6)*....... 28
Spring Valley (B7)........ 300
Springfield (K3)*.........
Springwood (E5)*......... 300
Stafford (K4)*..............
Staffordsville (C6)*...... 200
Stampers (L5)*............
Stanardsville (G4)*....... 182
Stanley (G3)*................ 399
Stanleytown (E7)*........
Star Tannery (G2)*....... 175
Starkey (E6)*............... 750
Staunton (F4)*............19,927
Steeles Tavern (F5)*.... 146
Stella (D7)....................
Stephens City (H2)*...... 676
Sterling (K2)*............... 100
Stevensburg (J4)*......... 80
Stone Mountain (E6)*..
Stonega (C2)*...............1,400
Stony Creek (J7)*......... 482
Stony Point (H4)*.........
Strasburg (H3)*............2,022
Stratford (L4)*............. 150
Stuart (D7)*................. 849
Stuarts Draft (G4)*..... 600
Studley (K5)*............... 125

Suffolk (L7)*..............12,33
Sugar Grove (B7)*........ 50
Sunset Hills (K3)*........ 10
Surry (L6)*................... 24
Sussex (K7)*................ 4
Sutherlin (F7)*............. 5
Sweet Briar (F5)*........ 20
Sweet Chalybeate (D5)* 15
Swimley (J2)*............... 1
Swords Creek (E1)*...... 40
Sycamore (F6)*............ 12
Sylvatus (C7)*.............. 50
Tacoma (C2)*............... 50
Tangier (M5)*............... 91
Tappahannock (K5)*.....1,01
Taylors Valley (E2)*..... 10
Taylorstown (J2).......... 9
Tazewell (B6)*..............1,34
Temperanceville (O5)*... 30
Tetotum (K4)*..............
Thaxton (E6)*............... 50
The Plains (J3)*........... 40
Thornburg (J4)*............ 10
Thornhill (J4)*..............
Tignor (K5)*................. 10
Timberville (G3)*.......... 27
Tiptop (B6)*................. 20
Toano (L6)*.................. 25
Toms Brook (G3)*......... 25
Toms Creek (D2)*......... 65
Toshes (F7)*................. 10
Townsend (M6)*........... 20
Trammel (D1)*.............
Trevilians (H4)*............ 3
Triangle (K3)*............... 28
Trout Dale (B7)*........... 25
Troutville (E6)*............ 60
Troy (H5)*.................... 3
Tunstall (K5)*............... 3
Turbeville (F7)*............ 6
Tye River (G5)*............ 10
Tyro (F5)*.................... 3
Union Hall (E6)*........... 6
Union Level (H7)*......... 19
Unionville (J4)*............. 25
Upperville (J2)*............. 40
Urbanna (L5)*............... 50
Valentines (J7)*............ 20
Vanderpool (E4)*..........
Venia (D1)*.................. 20
Vera (G6)*.................... 4
Vernon Hill (G6)*......... 15
Vesta (D7)*.................. 15
Vesuvius (F5)*.............. 30
Vicker (C6)*.................. 7
Victoria (H6)*...............1,60
Vienna (K3)*.................2,02
Vinton (E6)*..................3,62
Virgilina (G7)*.............. 32
Virginia Beach (N7)*....5,39
Volney (B7)*................. 10
Wachapreague (N5)*.... 55
Wadesville (H2)*........... 1
Waidsboro (E7)*..........
Wakefield (K7)*............ 94
Waldrop (H4)*............... 8
Wallace (D2)*............... 12
Ware Neck (M6)*......... 50
Warfield (J7)*............... 8
Warm Springs (E4)*..... 30
Warren (G5)*................ 30
Warrenton (J3)*............1,79
Warsaw (L5)*................ 43
Warwick (L6)* 39,87
Washington (H3)*........ 24
Water View (L5)*......... 15
Waterfall (J3)*.............. 2
Waverly (K6)*...............1,50
Waynesboro (F4)*.......12,35
Wealthia (H5)*.............. 7
Weems (L5)*................. 25
Weirwood (N6)*............ 5
Well Water (G5)........... 5
Wellville (J6)*............... 2
West Augusta (F4)*......
West Norfolk (M7)*...... 80
West Point (L5)*...........1,91
West View (J5)*............ 2
Weyers Cave (G4)*........ 50
Whaleyville (L7)*.......... 50
White Gate (C6)*.......... 24
White Hall (G4)*........... 5
White Plains (J7)*........
White Post (H2)*.......... 15
White Stone (M5)*....... 80
Whitetop (A7)*............. 30
Whitewood (E1)*..........
Whitmell (F7)*.............. 15
Wicomico Church (M5)* 10
Widewater (K4)*........... 5
Wilder (D1)*................. 13
Wilderness (J4)............ 10
Williamsburg (L6)*.......6,73
Williamsville (E4)*....... 13
Willis (D7)*.................. 6
Willis Wharf (N5)*....... 52
Wilsons (J6)*................ 25
Winchester (H2)*........13,84
Windsor (L7)*............... 45
Winterpock (J6)*.......... 20
Wirtz (E6)*................... 10
Wise (C2)*....................1,57
Wolftown (H4)*............ 7
Wood (C2)*...................
Woodberry Forest(H4)* 4
Woodbridge (K3)*......... 60
Woodlawn (C7)*........... 37
Woodstock (G3)*..........1,81
Woodville (H3)*............ 7
Woodway (C2)*............ 50
Woolwine (D7)*............ 6
Wren (G6)*................... 2
Wylliesburg (G7)*........ 10
Wyndale (D2)*.............. 30
Wytheville (C7)*...........5,51
Yale (K7)*..................... 3
Yancey Mills (G4)*....... 17
Yorktown (M6)*............ 38
Zepp (G3)*.................... 11
Zuni (L7)*..................... 15

Map on Page 93

WASHINGTON

Total Population 2,378,963

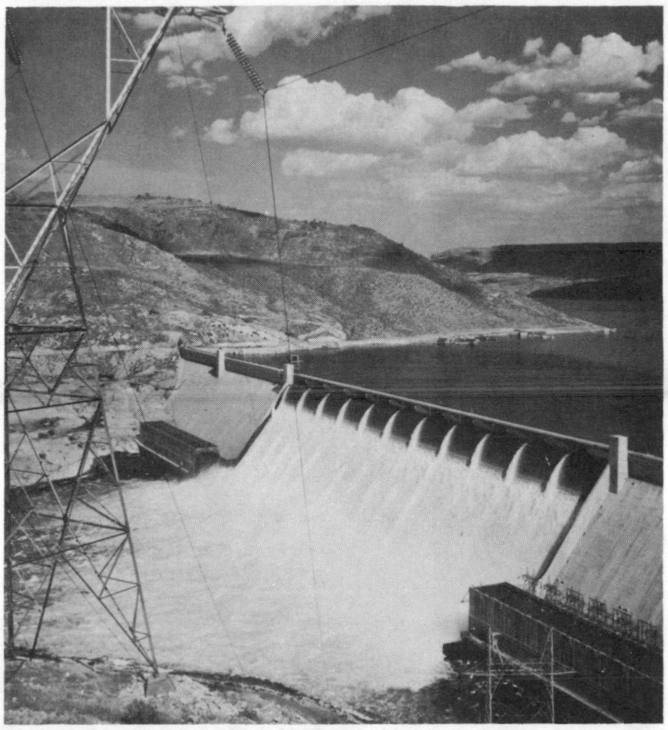

39 COUNTIES

dams (G3)....6,584
sotin (H4)....10,878
enton (F4)....51,370
helan (E3)....39,301
lallam (B2)....26,396
lark (C5)....85,307
olumbia (H4)....4,860
owlitz (C4)....53,369
ouglas (F3)....10,817
erry (G2)....4,096
ranklin (G4)....13,563
arfield (H4)....3,204
rant (F3)....24,346
rays Harbor (B3)....53,644
land (C2)....11,079
efferson (B3)....11,618
ing (D3)....732,992
itsap (C3)....75,724
ittitas (E3)....22,235
lickitat (E5)....12,049
ewis (C4)....43,755
incoln (G3)....10,970
ason (B3)....15,022
kanogan (F2)....29,131
acific (B4)....16,558
end Oreille (H2)....7,413
ierce (C3)....275,876
an Juan (C2)....3,245
kagit (D2)....43,273
kamania (D5)....4,788
nohomish (D2)....111,580
pokane (H3)....221,561
tevens (H2)....18,580
hurston (C4)....44,884
ahkiakum (B4)....3,835
alla Walla (G4)....40,135
hatcom (D2)....66,733
hitman (H4)....32,469
akima (E4)....135,723

CITIES and TOWNS

berdeen (B3)*....19,653
cme (C2)*.... 300
ddy (H2)*.... 387
dna (B4)*.... 110
drian (F3)*.... 20
eneas (F2)*.... 5
ntanum (E4).... 45
lune (C4)*.... 6
bion (H4)*.... 256
der (C4)*....
derdale (E5)*.... 20
derton (C3)*.... 300
derwood Manor (C3)* 250
gona (C3)*....1,400
lyn (C3)*.... 275
mira (G3)*.... 395
mota (H4)*.... 33
oha (A3)*.... 150
pha (C4)*....
stown (F3)....
toona (B4)*.... 81
manda Park (A3)*.... 150
mber (H3)*.... 20
mboy (C5)*.... 225
merican River (D4).... 10
nacortes (C2)*....6,919
natone (H4)*.... 60
nnapolis (A2).... 800
ppleton (D5)*.... 50
ppleyard (South
Wenatchee*) (E3)....1,479
rden (H2).... 25
rdenvoir (E3)*.... 350
riel (C5)*.... 95
rlington (C2)*....1,635
shford (C4)*.... 350
sotin (H4)*.... 740
ttalia (G4)*.... 75
uburn (C3)*....6,497
ustin (C3).... 12
von (C2).... 150
zwell (F3)*.... 105
aldi (D3).... 5
angor (A1).... 124
aring (D3)*.... 150
attle Ground (C5)*.... 750
atum (G3)....
ay Center (A4)*.... 200
ay City (B4)....
ay View (C2)*.... 200
eaver (A2)*.... 125
eebe (F3)....
elfair (C3)*.... 450
ellevue (B2)*....14,182
ellingham (C2)*....34,112
elmont (H3)*.... 72
enge (G4)*.... 50
enton City (F4)*.... 863
errian (F5)....
everly (F4)*.... 75
everly Park (C3)*....
arly (H2).... 5
ckleton (E5)*.... 125
glake (C2).... 120
ngen (D5)*.... 736
lack Diamond (D3)*....1,500
aine (C2)*....1,693
anchard (C2)*.... 150
ockhouse (E5).... 8
luecreek (H2)*.... 62
luestem (G3)*.... 23
lyn (B3).... 200
onney Lake (C3).... 275
ossburg (H2)....
othell (B1)*....1,019
oundary (H2)*.... 3
ow (C2)*.... 100
oyds (G2)*.... 61
remerton (A2)*....27,678
rewster (F2)*.... 851
ridgeport (F3)*.... 802
Brief (E3).... 20
Brinnon (B3)*.... 150
Brookfield (B4)*.... 13
Brooklyn (B4)*.... 85
Brownstown (E4)*.... 80
Brownsville (A2).... 75
Brush Prairie (C5)*.... 60
Bryant (C2)*....
Bryn Mawr (B2)*....4,781
Buckley (D3)*....2,705
Bucoda (C4)*.... 473
Buena (E4)*.... 600
Burbank (G4)*.... 150
Burien (A2)*....4,387
Burley (C3)*.... 350
Burlington (C2)*....2,350
Burton (C3)*....1,400
Byron (F4)*.... 50
Camas (C5)*....4,725
Camden (H2)*.... 12
Cape Horn (C5)....
Carbonado (D3)*.... 412
Carlsborg (B2)*.... 350
Carlton (F2)*.... 200
Carnation (D3)*.... 446
Carrolls (C4)*.... 400
Carson (D5)*.... 450
Casey (G4)*.... 75
Cashmere (E3)*....1,768
Castle Rock (B4)*....1,255
Cathlamet (B4)*.... 501
Cedar Falls (D3)*.... 300
Cedonia (G2)*.... 26
Centerville (D5)*.... 125
Central Ferry (H4).... 10
Centralia (C4)*....8,657
Chattaroy (H3)*.... 141
Chehalis (C4)*....5,639
Chelan (E3)*....2,157
Chelan Falls (E3)*.... 350
Cheney (H3)*....2,797
Chesaw (G2)*.... 45
Chewelah (H2)*....1,683
Chico (A2)....1,151
Chimacum (C3)*....
Chinook (B4)*.... 390
Chopaka (F2)....
Cinebar (C4)*.... 160
Clallam Bay (A2)*.... 350
Clarkston (H4)*....5,617
Clayton (H3)*.... 280
Cle Elum (E3)*....2,206
Clearlake (C2)*.... 400
Clearwater (A3)*.... 100
Cliffdell (E4).... 10
Cliffs (E5).... 16
Clinton (C3)*....1,623
Clipper (C2)*.... 70
Cloverland (H4).... 10
Clyde (G4).... 10
Coalfield (B2).... 150
Colbert (H3)*.... 52
Colby (A2)*.... 200
Cold Creek (F4)....
Colfax (H4)*....3,057
College Place (G4)*....3,174
Colton (H4)*.... 207
Colville (H2)*....3,033
Conconully (F2)*.... 141
Concrete (D2)*.... 760
Connell (G4)*.... 465
Conway (C2)*.... 150
Cook (D5)*.... 20
Copalis Beach (A3)*.... 500
Copalis Crossing (B3)*.. 100
Corfu (F4).... 11
Cosmopolis (B4)*....1,164
Cougar (C4)*.... 70
Coulee City (F3)*.... 977
Coulee Dam (F2)*....
Coupeville (C2)*.... 379
Covada (G2)*.... 31
Cove (A2)*.... 150
Cowiche (E4)*.... 200
Craige (H4).... 40
Creosote (A2)*.... 225
Creston (G3)*.... 268
Cumberland (D3)*.... 175
Cunningham (G4)*.... 23
Curlew (G2)*.... 100
Curtis (B4)*.... 46
Cusick (H2)*.... 360
Custer (C2)*.... 250
Dabob (C3)*.... 102
Daisey (G2)*.... 180
Dalkena (H2).... 25
Dallesport (D5)*.... 25
Danville (G2)*.... 155
Darrington (D2)*.... 921
Davenport (G3)*....1,417
Dayton (H4)*....2,979
Deep Creek (H3)*.... 95
Deep River (B4)*.... 45
Deer Harbor (B2)*.... 145
Deer Park (H3)*....1,167
Deming (C2)*.... 500
Denison (H3)*.... 26
Des Moines (B2)*....2,694
Diamond (H4)*.... 98
Disautel (F2)*.... 121
Dishman (H3)*....1,500
Dixie (G4)*.... 250
Doebay (C2)*.... 60
Donald (E4).... 100
Doty (B4)*.... 350
Douglas (F3)*.... 50
Dryad (B4)*.... 400
Dryden (E3)*.... 300
Dungeness (B2).... 300
Dusty (H4).... 65
Duvall (D3)*.... 236
Duwamish (B2).... 900
Earlington (B2).... 175
East Olympia (B4)*.... 300
E. Stanwood (C2)*.... 378
E. Wenatchee (E3)*.... 389
Easton (D3)*.... 300
Eastsound (B2)*.... 125
Eatonville (C4)*....1,048
Edgecomb (C2)*.... 75
Edison (C2)*.... 150
Edmonds (C3)*....2,057
Edwall (H3)*.... 143
Elbe (C4)*.... 250
Elberton (H4)*.... 145
Eldon (B3).... 50
Eleanor (G3)....
Electric City (F3)*....1,484
Electron (C4)....
Elk (H2)*.... 97
Ellensburg (E3)*....8,430
Elma (B4)*....1,543
Elmer City (G2)*.... 513
Eltopia (G4)*.... 61
Endicott (H4)*.... 397
Entiat (E3)*.... 420
Enumclaw (D3)*....2,789
Ephrata (F3)*....4,589
Espanola (H3)*.... 35
Ethel (C4)*....
Eureka (G4)*.... 25
Evans (H2)*.... 326
Everett (C3)*....33,849
Everson (C2)*.... 345
Ewan (H3)*.... 100
Fairchild (H3)....10,000
Fairfax (C4).... 70
Fairfield (H3)*.... 369
Fall City (D3)*.... 850
Farmer (F3)*.... 125
Farmington (H3)*.... 239
Ferndale (C2)*.... 979
Ferry (G2)....
Finley (F4).... 25
Fircrest ‡(C3)....1,459
Fletcher Bay (A2)....
Florence (C2).... 20
Ford (H3)*.... 20
Forest (C4).... 62
Forest City (A2)*.... 300
Forks (A3)*....1,120
Fort Lewis (C3)*....35,000
Fortson (D2)*....
Foster (B2).... 400
Four Lakes (H3)*.... 200
Fragaria (A2)*.... 20
Frances (B4)*.... 250
Freeland (C2)*....
Freeman (H3)*.... 100
Friday Harbor (B2)*.... 783
Fruitland (G2)*.... 75
Fruitvale (E4)....3,654
Furport (H2).... 40
Galvin (B4)*.... 250
Gardiner (B2)*.... 150
Garfield (H3)*.... 674
Gate (B4)*....
Getchell (C2).... 35
Gifford (G2)*.... 74
Gig Harbor (C3)*.... 803
Glacier (D2)*.... 114
Glenoma (C4)*....
Glenwood (D4)*....
Gold Bar (D3)*.... 305
Goldendale (E5)*....1,907
Goodnoe Hills (E5)*.... 114
Gooseprairie (D4)*.... 20
Gorst (A2)*.... 550
Govan (G3)*.... 22
Graham (C3)*.... 95
Grand Coulee (G3)*....2,741
Grand Mound (C4)*.... 55
Grandview (F4)*....2,503
Granger (E4)*....1,164
Granite Falls (D2)*.... 635
Grant Orchards (F3)*.... 102
Grapeview (C3)*.... 150
Grayland (A4)*.... 600
Grays River (B4)*.... 300
Greenacres (J3)*....1,287
Greenbank (C2)*.... 200
Grotto (D3)*.... 90
Guler (D4).... 87
Haas (G4)*....
Hadlock (C2)*.... 250
Hamilton (D2)*.... 294
Hanford (F4)....
Hansville (C3)*.... 127
Harper (A2)*.... 478
Harrah (E4)*.... 297
Harrington (G3)*.... 620
Hartline (F3)*.... 205
Hatton (G4)*.... 42
Havillah (F2).... 20
Hay (H4)*.... 130
Heisson (C5)*.... 50
Hellgate (G3).... 15
Hillyard (H3)*....
Hobart (D3)*.... 350
Holcomb (B4).... 150
Holden (E2)*.... 601
Holly (C3).... 60
Home Valley (D5)*.... 175
Hoodsport (B3)*.... 500
Hooper (G4)*.... 200
Hoquiam (A3)*....11,123
Hot Springs (D3)....
Houghton (B2)*....1,005
Humptulips (A3)*.... 100
Hunters (G2)*.... 350
Huntsville (G4)*.... 113
Husum (D5)*.... 75
Hyak (D3)*.... 20
Ilwaco (A4)*.... 628
Impach (G2)*.... 30
Inchelium (G2)*.... 97
Independence (B4)....
Index (D3)*.... 211
Ione (H2)*.... 714
Irby (G3)*.... 30
Issaquah (C3)*.... 955
Johnson (H4)*.... 200
Joyce (B2)*.... 350
Juanita (B1).... 900
Junction City (B4)*.... 176
Kahlotus (G4)*.... 151
Kalaloch (A3)*.... 24
Kalama (C4)*....1,121
Kapowsin (C4)*....
Kartar (F2)....
Keller (G2)*.... 75
Kelso (C4)*....7,345
Kendall (C2).... 72
Kenmore (B1)*....2,500
Kennewick (F4)*....10,106
Kennydale (B2)*....2,200
Kent (C3)*....3,278
Kettle Falls (H2)*.... 714
Kewa (G2)*.... 5
Keyport (A2)*.... 500
Kingston (C3)*.... 500
Kiona (F4)*.... 102
Kirkland (B2)*....4,713
Kitsap (A1)*.... 200
Kittitas (E4)*.... 586
Klaber (B4)*....
Klickitat (D5)*.... 800
Knappton (B4).... 20
Kosmos (C4)....
Krupp (Marlin*) (F3).... 98
La Center (C5)*.... 204
La Conner (C2)*.... 594
La Grande (C4)*.... 102
Lacey (C3)*....1,952
Lacrosse (H4)*.... 457
Lafleur (F2).... 28
Lake City (B1)*....2,800
Lake Forest Park (B1).3,500
Lake Stevens (D3)*....2,586
Lakebay (C3)*.... 250
Lakeside (E3)*.... 288
Lakewood (C2)*.... 40
Lamona (G3)*.... 44
Lamont (H3)*.... 101
Lancaster (H3)*.... 65
Langley (C2)*.... 427
Lapush (A3)*.... 248
Latah (H3)*.... 244
Laurel (D5)*.... 200
Laurier (G2)*.... 29
Leadpoint (H2).... 10
Leavenworth (E3)*....1,503
Lebam (B4)*.... 400
Leland (C3)*.... 115
Lester (D3)*.... 150
Liberty (E3).... 30
Liberty Bond (D5).... 6
Liberty Lake (J3)*.... 600
Lilliwaup (B3)*.... 200
Lincoln (G3)*.... 200
Lind (G4)*.... 796
Littell (B4).... 68
Littlerock (B4)*.... 250
Locke (H2)*.... 6
Long Beach (A4)*.... 783
Longbranch (C3)*.... 495
Longmire (D4)*.... 85
Longview (B4)*....20,385
Loomis (F2)*.... 210
Loon Lake (H2)*.... 300
Lopez (C2)*.... 33
Lost Creek (H2).... 20
Lowden (G4)*.... 30
Lowell (C3)*....1,754
Lucerne (E2)*.... 142
Lummi Island (C2)*.... 232
Lyle (D5)*.... 250
Lyman (D2)*.... 378
Lynden (C2)*....2,161
Lynnwood (C3)*.... 650
Mabton (E4)*.... 831
Macall (G3)....
Mae (F3)*.... 14
Malaga (E3)*.... 70
Malden (H3)*.... 332
Malo (G2)*.... 27
Malone (B4)*.... 340
Malott (F2)*.... 250
Maltby (C3)*.... 385
Manchester (A2)*.... 500
Mansfield (F3)*.... 414
Manson (E3)*....2,000
Maple Falls (D2)*.... 105
Maple Valley (C3)*....1,800
Marble (H2).... 25
Marblemount (D2)*.... 80
Marcellus (G3).... 15
Marcus (H2)*.... 149
Marengo (G3)*.... 35
Marietta (C2)*.... 200
Markham (B4)....
Marlin (F3)*.... 98
Marshall (H3)*.... 115
Maryhill (E5)*.... 120
Marysville (C2)*....2,259
Mason City (G3)....2,606
Matlock (B3)*.... 100
May View (H4)*.... 16
Mayfield (C4)*.... 70
Mazama (E2)*.... 4
Mc Cleary (B3)*....1,175
Mc Kenna (C4)*.... 95
Mc Loughlin Heights
(C5)*....14,500
Mc Millin (C3)*.... 100
Mc Murray (C2).... 70
Mead (H3)*.... 520
Medical Lake (H3)*....4,488
Medina (B2)*.... 500
Melbourne (B4).... 100
Menlo (B4)*....
Mercer Island (B2)*....6,000
Merritt (E3).... 25
Mesa (G4)*.... 105
Metaline (H2)*.... 547
Metaline Falls (H2)*....
Methow (E2)*....
Mica (H3)*.... 155
Midlakes (B2).... 20
Midvale (E4)....
Midway (F4)*.... 500
Milan (H3)*.... 95
Miles (G3)*.... 25
Millwood (H3)*....1,240
Milton (C3)*....1,374
Mineral (C4)*.... 600
Moclips (A3)*.... 425
Mohler (G3)*.... 30
Mold (F3)*.... 6
Molson (F2)*....
Mondovi (G3)*.... 150
Monitor (E3)*.... 308
Monroe (D3)*....1,556
Monse (F2)*.... 62
Montborne (C2).... 66
Montesano (B4)*....2,328
Moore (E2)*.... 40
Morton (C4)*....1,140
Moses Lake (F3)*....2,679
Mossyrock (C4)*.... 356
Mottinger (F5).... 12
Mount Hope (H3)*.... 28
Mt. Vernon (C2)*....5,230
Mountain View (H4)*.... 31
Moxee City (E4)*.... 543
Mukilteo (C3)*.... 826
Naches (E4)*.... 633
Nagrom (D3)....
Nahcotta (A4)*.... 250
Napavine (C4)*.... 242
Naselle (B4)*.... 750
National (D4)*.... 350
Neah Bay (A2)*....1,000
Neilton (B3)*.... 100
Nesika (C4)....
Nespelem (G2)*.... 425
Newman Lake (J3)*.... 64
Newport (H2)*....1,385
Nighthawk (F2)*.... 36
Nine Mile Falls (H3)*... 130
Nisqually (C3)*.... 250
Nooksack (C2)*.... 323
Nordland (C2)*.... 500
North Bend (D3)*.... 787
N. Bonneville (C5)*.... 564
N. Cove (A4)....
N. Richland (F4)*....3,067
Northport (H2)*.... 487
Oak Harbor (C2)*....1,193
Oak Point (B4)....
Oakesdale (H3)*.... 576
Oakville (B4)*.... 372
O'Brien (B2).... 350
Ocean City (A3)*....
Ocean Park (A4)*.... 550
Ocosta (B4)....
Odessa (G3)*....1,127
Ohop (C4)*....
Okanogan (F2)*....2,013
Olalla (A2)*.... 800
Olequa (C4)....
Olga (C2)*.... 100
OLYMPIA (C3)*....15,819
Omak (F2)*....3,791
Onalaska (C4)*.... 280
Opportunity (H3)*....10,000
Orchards (C5)*.... 600
Orient (G2)*.... 200
Orillia (B2)*.... 135
Orin (H2).... 37
Orondo (E3)*.... 250
Oroville (F2)*....1,500
Orting (C3)*....1,299
Osborne (G3).... 100
Oso (D2)*.... 250
Ostrander (C4)....
Othello (F4)*.... 526
Otis Orchards (H3)*....1,500
Outlook (F4)*.... 308
Ovington (B2).... 10
Oysterville (A4)*.... 140
Ozette (A2).... 21
Pacific ‡(C3)*.... 755
Pacific Beach (A3)*.... 600
Packard (G3)....
Packwood (D4)*.... 650
Page (G4)*.... 31
Paha (G3).... 12
Palisades (E3)*.... 120
Palmer (D3)*.... 80
Palouse (H4)*....1,036
Paradise Inn (D4)*....
Park Rapids (H2).... 11
Parker (E4)*.... 200
Parkland (C3)*....3,000
Parkwater (H3)*....1,000
Parkway (D3).... 25
Pasco (F4)*....10,288
Pataha City (H4).... 60
Pateros (E2)*.... 866
Paterson (F5)*.... 100
Pe Ell (B4)*.... 787
Pearl (F2)....
Pearson (A2).... 50
Peshastin (E3)*.... 675
Pillar Rock (B4).... 31
Pine City (H3)*.... 75
Pinehurst (C3)*....4,260
Plain (E3).... 30
Plaza (H3)*.... 55
Plymouth (F5)*.... 325
Point Roberts (B2)*.... 230
Pomeroy (H4)*....1,775
Port Angeles (B2)*....11,233
Port Blakely (A2)*....
Port Gamble (C3)*.... 500
Port Ludlow (C3)*.... 275
Port Madison (A1)....
Port Orchard (A2)*....2,320
Port Townsend (C2)*....6,888
Portage (A2)*.... 200
Porter (B4)*.... 200
Potlatch (B3)*.... 150
Poulsbo (A1)*....1,014
Prescott (G4)*.... 244
Preston (D3)*.... 500
Prevost (B2)*.... 8
Prosser (F4)*....2,636
Puget Island (B4).... 735
Pullman (H4)*....12,022
Puyallup (C3)*....10,010
Pysht (A2).... 15
Queets (A3).... 200
Quilcene (B3)*.... 600
Quillayute (A3).... 10
Quinault (B3)*.... 450
Quincy (F3)*.... 804
Rainier (C4)*.... 331
Ralston (G4)*.... 27
Randle (D4)*.... 500
Ravensdale (D3)*.... 300
Raymond (B4)*....4,110
Reardan (H3)*.... 410
Redmond (B1)*.... 573
Redondo (C3)*.... 540
Renton (B2)*....16,039
Republic (G2)*.... 895
Retsil (A2)*.... 738
Rice (G2)*.... 40
Richardson (B2)*.... 10
Richland (F4)*....21,809
Richmond Beach (A1)*..1,900
Richmond Highlands
(A1)*....11,081
Ridgefield (C5)*.... 762
Riffe (C4)*.... 750
Riparia (G4)*.... 37
Ritzville (G3)*....2,145
Riverside (F2)*.... 149
Riverton (A2)*....2,000
Riverton Heights (B2)...3,060
Robe (D2)*.... 55
Roche Harbor (B2)*.... 98
Rochester (C4)*.... 325
Rock Island (E3)*.... 152
Rockdale (D3).... 12
Rockford (H3)*.... 360
Rocklyn (G3)*.... 24
Rockport (D2)*.... 100
Rogersburg (H4).... 3
Rollingbay (A2)*.... 800
Ronald (E3)*....
Roosevelt (E5)*.... 75
Rosalia (H3)*.... 660
Rosburg (B4)*.... 300
Roslyn (E3)*....1,537
Roxboro (G4)*.... 9
Roy (C4)*.... 263
Ruby (H2).... 10
Ruff (F3)*.... 75
Ruston ‡(C3).... 838
Ryderwood (B4)*....
Saint Andrews (F3)*.... 120
St. John (H3)*.... 542
Salkum (C4)*.... 360
San de Fuca (C2)*.... 90
Sappho (A2)*.... 250
Satsop (B3)*.... 125
Sauk (D2).... 75
Saxon (C2).... 149
Scandia (A1).... 50
Scenic (D3).... 25
Schrag (G3).... 5
Scotia (H2).... 2
Seabeck (C3)*.... 300
Seabold (A1).... 250
Seahurst (A2)*....2,305
Seattle (A2)*....467,591
Seattle (urban area) 616,047
Seaview (A4)*.... 600
Sedro Woolley (C2)*....3,299
Sekiu (A2)*.... 211
Selah (E4)*....2,489
Selleck (D3)*.... 250
Sequim (B2)*....1,044
Sharon (H3).... 95
Shaw Island (B2)*.... 80
Shelton (B3)*....5,045
Silvana (C2)*.... 300
Silver Creek (C4)*.... 312
Silverdale (A2)*.... 750
Silverlake (C4)*....1,500
Silverton (D2).... 16
Skamania (C5)*....
Skamokawa (B4)*.... 562
Skykomish (D3)*.... 497
Smyrna (F4)*.... 21
Snake River (G4)*.... 35
Snohomish (D3)*....3,094
Snoqualmie (D3)*.... 806
Snoqualmie Falls (D3)*
Soap Lake (F3)*....2,091
South Bellingham (C2)*
S. Bend (B4)*....1,857
S. Cle Elum (D3)*.... 442
S. Colby (A2)*.... 280
S. Prairie (D3)*.... 207
S. Wenatchee (E3)*....1,479
Southworth (A2)*.... 250
Spanaway (C3)*.... 600
Spangle (H3)*.... 242
Spirit Lake (C4).... 20
Spokane (H3)*....161,721
Spokane (urban area)174,853
Spokane Bridge (J3)*.... 50
Sprague (G3)*.... 598
Spring Valley (H3)....
Springdale (H2)*.... 268
Stanwood (C2)*.... 710
Starbuck (G4)*.... 194
Startup (D3)*.... 386

Stehekin (E2)* 37
Steilacoom (C3)* 1,233
Stella (B4)
Steptoe (H3)* 110
Stevenson (C5)* 584
Stillwater (D3)
Stratford (F3)* 112
Sultan (D3)* 814
Sumas (C2)* 658
Sumner (C3)* 2,816
Sundale (E5) 72
Sunnydale (B2) 1,296
Sunnyside (F4)* 4,194
Sunset (H3)* 65
Supplee (F3)
Suquamish (A1)* 1,000
Synarep (F2)* 3
Tacoma (C3)* 143,673
Tacoma (urban area) 166,910
Tahola (A3)* 380
Tahuya (B3)* 60
Tampico (E4) 50
Tatoosh (A2) 30
Tekoa (H3)* 1,189
Telma (E3) 12
Tenino (C4)* 969
Thatcher (C2) 4
Thornton (H3)* 225
Thorp (E3)* 350
Tieton (E4)* 620
Tiger (H2)* 79
Tillicum (C3)* 3,000
Timentwa (F2)
Tokeland (A4)* 150
Toledo (C4)* 602
Tolt (Carnation*) (D3). 446
Tonasket (F2)* 957
Tono (C4) 1
Toppenish (E4)* 5,265
Touchet (G4)* 350
Toutle (C4)*
Tracy (G4)
Tracyton (A2)* 500
Trinidad (F3)* 25
Troutlake (D5)* 350
Tukwila (B2)* 800
Tulalip (C2)*
Tumtum (H3)* 100
Tumwater (B3)* 2,725
Turner (H4) 25
Twisp (E2)* 776
Tyler (H3)* 25
Underwood (D5)* 370
Union (B3)* 350
Union Gap (E4)* 1,766
Uniontown (H4)* 254
Urban (C2)* 11
Usk (H2)* 300
Vader (B4)* 426
Vail (C4)* 175
Valley (H2)* 250
Valleyford (H3)* 213
Van Zandt (C2)* 62
Vancouver (C5)* 41,664
Vantage (E4)* 67
Vashon (A2)* 550
Vaughn (C3)* 280
Veradale (H3)* 1,700
Wahkiacus (D5)* 40
Waitsburg (G4)* 1,015
Waldron (B2)* 40
Walla Walla (G4)* 24,102
Wallula (G4)* 400
Walville (B4) 15
Wapato (E4)* 3,185
Warden (F4)* 322
Warm Beach (C2)*
Washougal (C5)* 1,577
Washtucna (G4)* 316
Waterville (E3)* 1,013
Wauconda (F2)* 3
Waukon (H3)* 40
Wauna (C3)* 100
Waverly (H3)* 120
Wawawai (H4)* 6
Wellpinit (G3)* 60
Wenatchee (E3)* 13,072
West Wenatchee (E3) 2,690
Western (B4)
Westport (A4)* 731
Wheeler (F3)* 30
White Center (A2)* 30,000
White Salmon (D5)* 1,353
White Swan (E4)* 200
Whites (B3) 75
Wickersham (C2)* 135
Wilbur (G3)* 1,043
Wiley (E4) 450
Wilkeson (D3)* 386
Willapa (B4)* 230
Willard (D5) 245
Wilson Creek (F3)* 337
Winchester (F3)* 30
Winesap (E3)
Winlock (C4)* 878
Winona (H4)* 75
Winslow (A2)* 637
Winthrop (E2)* 396
Winton (E3) 23
Wishram (D5)* 678
Withrow (F3)* 53
Woodinville (B1)* 1,500
Woodland (C5)* 1,292
Yacolt (C5)* 411
Yakima (E4)* 38,486
Yardley (H3)* 500
Yelm (C4)* 470
Zenith (C3)* 600
Zillah (E4)* 911

Map on Page 94

WEST VIRGINIA

Total Population 2,005,552

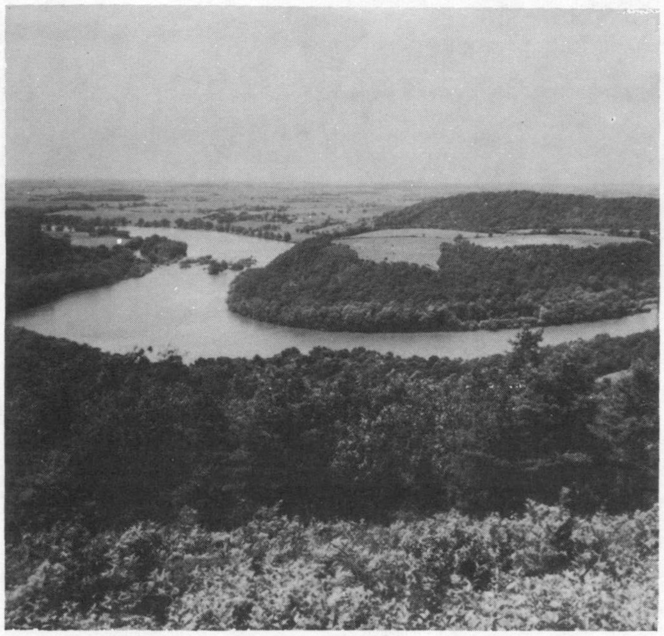

55 COUNTIES

Barbour (F2) 19,745
Berkeley (K2) 30,359
Boone (C4) 33,173
Braxton (E3) 18,082
Brooke (K5) 26,904
Cabell (B4) 108,035
Calhoun (D3) 10,259
Clay (D4) 14,961
Doddridge (E2) 9,026
Fayette (D4) 82,443
Gilmer (E3) 9,746
Grant (H2) 8,756
Greenbrier (F5) 39,295
Hampshire (J2) 12,577
Hancock (K4) 34,388
Hardy (J2) 10,032
Harrison (F2) 85,296
Jackson (C3) 15,299
Jefferson (L2) 17,184
Kanawha (C4) 239,629
Lewis (E2) 21,074
Lincoln (B4) 22,466
Logan (C5) 77,391
Marion (F2) 71,521
Marshall (K6) 36,893
Mason (B3) 23,537
Mc Dowell (C6) 98,887
Mercer (D6) 75,013
Mineral (J2) 22,333
Mingo (B5) 47,409
Monongalia (F1) 60,797
Monroe (E5) 13,123
Morgan (K1) 8,276
Nicholas (E4) 27,696
Ohio (K5) 71,672
Pendleton (H3) 9,313
Pleasants (D2) 6,369
Pocahontas (F4) 12,480
Preston (G1) 31,399
Putnam (C4) 21,021
Raleigh (D5) 96,273
Randolph (G3) 30,558
Ritchie (D2) 12,535
Roane (D3) 18,408
Summers (E5) 19,183
Taylor (F2) 18,422
Tucker (G2) 10,600
Tyler (E2) 10,535
Upshur (F3) 19,242
Wayne (B4) 38,696
Webster (F4) 17,888
Wetzel (E1) 20,154
Wirt (D2) 5,119
Wood (C2) 66,540
Wyoming (C5) 37,540

CITIES and TOWNS

Accoville (C5)* 1,400
Acme (D4)* 200
Ada (D6)* 300
Addison (Webster Springs*) (F4) 1,313
Adolph (F3)* 85
Adrian (F3)* 400
Advent (C3)* 100
Albert (G2)*
Albion (D4)
Albright (G1) 396
Alderson (E5)* 1,489
Alexander (F3)* 250
Algoma (D6)*
Alkol (C4)* 125
Allen (B4)*
Allingdale (E4)
Alma (E2)*
Alpena (G3)* 125
Alpoca (D5)* 550
Alton (F3)* 156
Alum Bridge (E2) 125
Alum Creek (C4)* 249
Alvon (F5)* 100
Alvy (E2)* 155
Amblersburg (G2) 4
Amboy (G2)* 75
Ambrosia (C3) 100
Ameagle (D5)*
Amherstdale (C5)
Amma (D3)* 500
Anawalt (D6)* 1,383
Angerona (C3) 10
Anmoore (F2)* 1,388
Ansted (D4)* 1,543
Anthony (F5)* 82
Antioch (H2)* 50
Apple Grove (B3)* 22
Arbovale (G4)* 80
Arbuckle (C3)* 50
Arcola (F4)* 125
Ardel (A4) 200
Arden (G2)* 250
Arlee (B3)* 100
Arnett (D5)*
Arnoldsburg (D3)* 130
Arthur (H2)* 30
Arthurdale (G1)* 900
Asbury (E5)* 320
Asco (C6)* 200
Ashford (C4)* 350
Ashley (E2)* 90
Ashton (B3)* 66
Athens (E6)* 935
Auburn (E2)* 149
Augusta (J2)* 250
Aurora (G2)* 337
Avon (E2) 50
Avondale (C6)* 975
Backus (E5) 200
Baileysville (C5)* 1,127
Baisden (C5)*
Baker (J2)* 75
Bakerton (L2)* 300
Bald Knob (C5)* 500
Baldwin (E3)* 95
Ballard (E6)* 300
Ballengee (E5)*
Bamboo (E4) 25
Bancroft (C3)* 700
Barboursville (B4)* 1,943
Bardane (L2) 120
Barnabus (C5)* 1,500
Barnum (H2)* 95
Barrackville (F1)* 2,500
Barrett (C5)*
Bartley (C6)* 1,275
Bartow (G3)* 200
Bass (J3) 25
Bath (Berkeley Sprs.*) (K1) 1,213
Bayard (H2)* 589
Bays (E3)*
Beard (F4)* 50
Beards Fork (D4)* 750
Bearsville (E2) 30
Beaver (Glen Hedrick) (D5)* 1,484
Bebee (E1)* 200
Beckley (D5)* 19,397
Bedington (L1)* 150
Beech (D3)* 41
Beechbottom (K5)* 1,100
Beechwood (G1)
Beeson (D6)*
Belfont (E3) 25
Belgrove (C3)*
Belington (F2)* 1,699
Belle (C4)* 2,350
Belleville (C2)* 101
Belmont (D2)* 215
Belo (B5) 150
Belva (D4)* 301
Bemis (G3)* 75
Benbush (G2)* 135
Bens Run (D2)* 135
Benwood (K5)* 3,485
Berea (E2)* 66
Bergoo (F4)* 800
Berkeley Springs (K1)* 1,213
Berkeley Station (L2) 75
Berlin (F2) 66
Bernie (C4)*
Berryburg (F2) 200
Berwind (C6)* 1,354
Beryl (H2)* 150
Bethany (L5)* 1,063
Bethlehem (K5) 1,146
Beverly (G3)* 515
Bias (B5)
Bickmore (D4)*
Big Chimney (C4)* 500
Big Creek (B5)* 500
Big Four (C6) 200
Big Isaac (E2)* 30
Big Otter (D3)* 200
Big Springs (D3)* 150
Bigbend (D3)* 100
Bim (C5)* 750
Bingham (E4) 90
Birch River (E4)* 200
Bismarck (H2)*
Blacksville (F1)* 241
Blaine (H2) 300
Blair (C5)* 624
Blakeley (D4)*
Blaker Mills (E5)* 115
Bloomery (K2)*
Blue Creek (D4)* 140
Blue Spring (F3)
Blue Sulphur Springs (E5)* 400
Bluefield (D6)* 21,506
Board Tree (L6) 25
Boaz (D2) 50
Boggs (E4)* 211
Bolair (F4)* 300
Bomont (D4)* 206
Booher (E2)
Boomer (D4)*
Boothsville (F2) 200
Borderland (B5)* 270
Bowden (G3)* 150
Bower (E3) 35
Bownemont (C4) 400
Boyer (G3)* 150
Bradshaw (C6)* 1,062
Bramwell (D6)* 1,587
Brandonville (G1)* 100
Brandywine (H3)* 150
Braxton (E3)* 67
Breeden (B5)* 300
Bridgeport (F2)* 2,414
Bristol (F2)* 300
Brohard (D2)* 400
Brood (H3)
Brooklyn (E1)* 500
Brooks (E5)*
Brounland (C4)* 50
Brown (F2)* 250
Brownton (F2)* 928
Bruce (E4)* 175
Bruceton Mills (G1)* 165
Brushy Run (H3)* 300
Buck (E5) 50
Buckeye (F4)* 40
Buckhannon (F3)* 6,016
Bud (D5)* 500
Buffalo (C3)* 333
Bunker Hill (K2)* 350
Burlington (J2)* 300
Burning Springs (D3)*
Burnsville (E3)* 731
Burnt House (D2)* 40
Burnwell (D4)* 1,000
Burton (F1)* 219
Byrnside (C4)
Cabell (C4)
Cabins (H2)* 120
Cairo (D2)* 500
Caldwell (F5)* 600
Caloric (D5) 320
Calvin (E4)*
Camden (E2)* 150
Camden on Gauley (E4)* 373
Cameron (L6)* 1,736
Camp Creek (D5)* 150
Canebrake (C6)* 568
Canfield (E3)* 65
Canton (E2)
Canvas (E4)* 500
Capehart (C3) 15
Capon Bridge (K2)* 223
Capon Springs (K2)* 220
Captina (K6)* 200
Carbon (D4)* 500
Cascade (G1)* 200
Cashmere (E6)* 100
Cass (G4)* 417
Cassie (B5)* 350
Cassity (G3)* 250
Cassville (F1)*
Catawba (F1)*
Cave (H3)* 50
Cedar Grove (D4)* 1,738
Cedarville (E3)* 103
Center Point (E2)* 200
Central Station (E2)* 350
Centralia (E3)*
Century (F2)* 500
Ceredo (B4)* 1,399
Chapel (E3)* 50
Chapmanville (B5)* 1,349
Charles Town (L2)* 3,035
CHARLESTON (D4)* 73,501
Charleston (urban area) 130,122
Charmco (E4)* 700
Chattaroy (B5)* 1,484
Chelyan (C4)*
Cherry Run (L1)* 150
Chesapeake (D4)* 2,566
Chester (L4)* 3,758
Christian (C5)*
Churchville (E2) 125
Cicerone (D3)*
Cinco (D4)*
Cinderella (B5)* 600
Circleville (H3)* 250
Clarksburg (F2)* 32,014
Clay (D4)* 500
Clayton (E5) 135
Clear Creek (D5)*
Clearco (F4)* 120
Clendenin (D3)* 1,475
Cleveland (F3)* 150
Clifftop (E4)* 400
Clifton (B3)* 355
Clifton Mills (G1)* 51
Clifty (E4)*
Clinton (K5)
Clintonville (E5)*
Clio (D3)*
Clothier (C5)* 636
Clover (D3)*
Clover Lick (F4)* 324
Coal City (D5)* 1,000
Coal Fork (D4)* 1,185
Coalton (G3)* 407
Coalwood (C6)* 1,310
Coburn (F1)*
Coco (D4)* 200
Coe (F4)
Coketon (G2)* 200
Colcord (D5)* 1,800
Cold Stream (J2)* 50
Coldwater (E2)* 27
Colliers (L5)* 425
Conaway (E2) 10
Congo (K4) 100
Copen (E3)* 309
Corinne (D5)*
Corinth (H2)* 175
Corley (E3)* 15
Cornwallis (D2)* 124
Costa (C4)* 168
Cottageville (C3)* 250
Countsville (C3)* 6
Cove Gap (B4)* 125
Cowen (E4)* 632
Coxs Mills (E2)* 50
Craigsville (E4)*
Cranberry (D5)* 750
Craneco (C5) 596
Cranesville (G1) 25
Crawford (F3)* 100
Crawley (E5)* 150
Creekvale (K2) 30
Cressmont (E4)
Creston (D3)*
Crow Summit (C3) 25
Crum (B5)* 350
Crystal (D6)* 400
Cucumber (C6)* 350
Culloden (B4)* 250
Curry (C5)*
Custis (E3)
Cuzzart (H1)* 75
Cuzzie (B4)* 100
Cyclone (C5)* 265
Czar (F3)*
Dahmer (H3) 125
Dallas (K5)* 110
Daniels (D5)* 800
Danville (C4)* 544
Darkesville (L2) 275
Davis (H2)* 1,271
Davisville (C2)* 45
Davy (C6)* 1,650
Dawes (D4)* 700
Dawson (E5)* 100
Dean (E1) 15
Decota (D4)* 1,300
Deer Run (H3)*
Deer Walk (D2) 75
Delbarton (B5)* 1,353
Dellslow (G1)*
Denver (K6) 50
Diamond (C4)*
Diana (F3)*
Dickson (B4)
Dille (E4)* 500
Dingess (B5)* 400
Dixie (D4)* 50
Dola (F2)* 110
Doman (J2) 50
Donohue (D2) 75
Dorcas (H3)* 60
Dorfee (D4) 19
Dorothy (D5)* 3,000
Dott (D6)* 400
Douglas (D3) 25
Dry Creek (D5)* 489
Dryfork (H3)* 200
Duck (E3)*
Duffy (F3)* 40
Dulin (D2) 3
Dunbar (C4)* 8,032
Duncan (C3)* 50
Dundon (D4)* 125
Dunlow (B4)* 125
Dunmore (G4)* 65
Dunns (D5)* 35
Duo (E4)*
Durbin (G3)* 540
Durgon (J3) 50
Dyer (F4) 25
East Lynn (B4)* 300
E. Rainelle (E5)* 1,695
Eastbank (D4)* 735
Eatons (D2)*
Eccles (D5)* 1,885
Eckman (C6)* 1,574
Edgarton (B5)* 500
Edray (F4) 32
Edwight (C5)*
Egeria (D5)* 300
Eglon (G2)* 110
Elana (D3)* 145
Elbert (C6)* 1,565
Elgood (E6)* 75
Elizabeth (D2)* 755
Elk Garden (H2)* 318
Elkhorn (D6)* 1,035
Elkhurst (D4)* 66
Elkins (G3)* 9,121
Elkridge (D4)* 475
Elkview (C4)* 400
Elkwater (G3)* 75
Ellamore (F3)* 600
Ellenboro (D2)* 307
Elm Grove (K5)* 8,000
Elmira (E3)* 200
Elton (E5)* 200
Emoryville (H2)* 100
English (C6)* 890
Enoch (E4)* 282
Enon (E4)
Enterprise (F2)* 1,200
Erbacon (E3)* 210
Eskdale (C4)*
Ethel (C5)* 1,032
Eureka (D2)* 125
Evans (C3)* 150
Evansville (G2) 45
Evenwood (G3) 25
Everettville (F1)* 750
Everson (F2) 50
Exchange (E3)* 25
Fabius (J2)* 30
Fairmont (F2)* 29,346
Fairplain (C3)*
Fairview (F1)* 775
Falling Springs (Renick*) (F4) 307
Failing Waters (L1)* 75
Fallsmill (E3)* 50
Fame (H3) 15
Far (E1) 20
Farmington (F1)* 824
Farmington (F1)* 824
Fayetteville (D4)* 1,952
Fellowsville (G2) 120
Fenwick (E4)* 500
Ferguson (B4)*
Ferrellsburg (B4)* 275
Fink (E2) 8
Fire Creek (E5) 30
Fireco (D5)*
Fisher (H2)* 20
Flat Top (D5)* 150
Flat Woods (E3)* 288
Flemington (F2)* 572
Fletcher (C3)
Flint (G3)
Follansbee (K5)* 4,435
Folsom (E2)* 485
Forest Hill (E5)* 45
Fort Ashby (J2)* 800
Ft. Branch (C5)
Ft. Gay (A4)* 714
Ft. Seybert (H3)* 200
Ft. Spring (E5)* 225
Foster (C4)*
Four States (F2)* 470
Frame (C3)* 98
Frametown (E3)* 500
Frankford (F5)* 185
Franklin (H3)* 777
Fraziers Bottom (B3)* 75
Freed (D2)*
Freeman (D6)* 400
Freemansburg (F2) 21
French Creek (F3)* 175
Frenchton (F3)* 221
Friendly (D1)* 216
Frost (G4)* 99
Gallipolis Ferry (B3)* 100
Galloway (F2)* 1,000
Gandeeville (D3)* 328
Ganotown (K2) 75
Gap Mills (F5)*
Garretts Bend (C4)* 125
Gary (C6)* 1,600
Gassaway (E3)* 1,306
Gauley Bridge (D4)* 1,134
Gauley Mills (E4)* 200
Gay (C3)*
Gem (E3)* 22
Genoa (B4)*
Gerrardstown (K2)* 205
Ghent (D5)* 488
Giatto (D6)* 550
Gilbert (C5)* 722
Gilboa (E4)* 275
Gill (B4)* 50
Gilmer (E3)* 250
Given (C3)* 250
Glade Farms (G1)
Gladesville (G2) 100
Gladwin (G2) 30
Glady (G3)* 300
Glasgow ‡(D4)* 881
Gleason (H2) 40
Glebe (J2) 50
Glen (D4)* 200
Glen Dale (K5)* 1,467
Glen Daniel (D5)*
Glen Easton (K6)* 200
Glen Ferris (D4)* 500
Glen Jean (D5)* 1,800
Glen Hedrick (Beaver*) (D5) 1,484
Glen Rodgers (D5)* 1,593
Glen White (D5)* 300
Glenalum (C5)* 600
Glengary (K2)* 50
Glenhayes (A4)* 300
Glenray (E5) 75
Glenville (E3)* 1,789
Glenwood (B3)* 150
Glovergap (F1)* 150
Good (K2) 100
Goodwill (D6)* 800
Goose Creek (D2) 100
Gordon (C5)* 800
Gormania (H2)* 185
Grace (D3) 3
Grafton (G2)* 7,365
Grandview (D5)* 175
Grant Town (F1)* 1,273
Grantsville (D3)* 959
Granville (Mona*)(G3) 1,004
Grassy (B4)*
Grassy Meadows (E5)* 100
Great Cacapon (K1)* 550
Green Bank (G4)* 200
Green Hill (E1) 175
Green Sulphur Springs (E5)*
Greenland (H2)* 14
Greenview (C4)* 400
Greenville (E5)* 65
Greenwood (E2)* 366
Greer (G1)*
Griffithsville (B4)* 500
Grimms Landing (B3)*. 420
Grove (E2)
Guardian (F3)* 600
Guyan (C5)* 300
Hacker Valley (F3)* 150
Hall (F2)* 43
Halltown (L2)* 250
Hambleton (G2)* 283
Hamlin (B4)* 841
Hammond (F2)* 102
Hampden (C5)* 50
Hancock (K1)* 131
Handley (D4)* 1,007
Hanging Rock (J2)* 75
Hanover (C5)* 500
Hany (B4) 350
Harding (G3)* 250
Harman (G3)* 146
Harmony (D3)* 13
Harper (D5)* 1,700
Harpers Ferry (L2)* 822
Harris Ferry (C2) 25
Harrisville (E2)* 1,387
Hartford (C2)* 366
Hartland (D4) 50
Harts (B4)* 160
Harvey (D5)* 503
Havaco (C6)*
Hazelton (G1)* 80
Headsville (J2)* 240
Heaters (E3)*
Hebron (D2)* 50
Hedgesville (K1)* 419
Heights (B3)* 300
Helvetia (F3)* 94
Hemphill (C6)* 2,300
Henderson (B3)* 483
Hendricks (G2)* 492
Henlawson (B5)* 1,750
Henry (H2) 5
Hepzibah (F2)* 1,800
Herndon (D5)* 500
Hewlet (A4) 75
Higginsville (J2) 150
Hico (D4)* 300
High View (K2)* 50
Highcoal (C5)* 500
Highland (D2)* 100
Hillsboro (F4)* 241
Hilltop (D5)* 615
Hinton (E5)* 5,780
Hoard (G1) 6
Hodgeville (F2) 100
Hogsett (B3)* 25
Holcomb (E4)* 50
Holden (B5)*
Hollidays Cove (K5)
Hollywood (F5)* 75
Hominy Falls (E4)* 310
Hookersville (E4)*
Horner (F3)* 97
Horse Shoe Run (G2)* 125
Horton (G3)
Hosterman (G4) 25
Howard (K6) 25
Howesville (G2)* 250
Hubball (B4) 200
Hubbardstown (A4) 400
Hudson (G1) 40
Hundred (E1)* 587
Huntersville (G4)* 80
Hunting Ground (H3) 75

Huntington (A4)* 86,353
Huntington, W. Va. — Ashland, Ky. (urban area) 156,136
Hurricane (C4)* 1,463
Hurst (E2)*
Hutchinson (F2)* 600
Huttonsville (G3)* 227
Iaeger (C6)* 1,271
Independence (G2)* 175
Indian Mills (E5)* 65
Indore (D4)* 1,000
Ingleside (E6)* 200
Ingo (F3) 32
Inkerman (J2)* 26
Institute (C4)* 500
Inwood (K2)* 375
Ira (E3)
Ireland (F3)* 60
Irona (G2) 30
Itmann (D5)* 500
Iuka (E1) 30
Ivan (D3)
Ivanhoe (F3)* 150
Ivydale (D3)*
Jacksonburg (E1)* 350
Jane Lew (F2)* 491
Jarvisville (F2) 150
Jeffery (C5)* 2,000
Jenkinjones (D6)* 1,859
Jenningston (H3) 30
Jerryville (F4)* 300
Jesse (C5)* 150
Jetsville (E4)* 108
Job (G3)*
Jodie (D4)* 600
Johnstown (F2) 650
Joker (D3)* 50
Jones Springs (K2)* 100
Jordan Run (H2)* 1,000
Jumping Branch (E5)* 500
Junction (J2)* 35
Junior (G3)* 729
Justice (C5)* 405
Kanawha Falls (D4)* 149
Kanawha Head (F3)* 150
Kanawha Station (C2) 50
Kasson (G2)* 45
Kayford (C4)* 500
Kaylong (B3) 8
Kearneysville (L2)* 500
Keenan (F5)* 60
Kegley (D6)*
Keith (C4)* 310
Kellysville (E6)* 150
Kemper (E3) 55
Kenna (C3)* 85
Kenova (A4)* 4,320
Kentuck (C3)*
Kerens (G2)*
Kermit (B5)* 964
Kessel (H2)*
Kester (D3)
Ketterman (H3)
Kettle (D3)*
Keyser (J2)* 6,347
Keystone (D6)* 2,594
Kiahsville (B4)* 85
Kidwell (E1) 65
Kieffer (E5)*
Killarney (D5)* 300
Kilsyth (D5)* 500
Kimball (C6)* 1,359
Kincheloe (F2)* 33
Kingston (D5)* 1,098
Kingsville (F3) 85
Kingwood (G2)* 2,186
Kirby (J2)* 45
Kirk (B5)*
Kirkwood (E4)
Kistler (C5)* 1,072
Kline (H3)* 30
Knawl (E3) 6
Knob Fork (E1)* 50
Kopperston (C5)* 1,112
Kyger (D3)* 300
La Frank (F4)* 150
Lahmansville (H2)* 50
Lanark (D5)*
Landes (H3)* 125
Landisburg (E5)* 150
Landville (C5)* 400
Lantz (F3)* 50
Larew (G2) 25
Largent (K2)*
Laurel Dale (H2)*
Laurelbranch (F5) 25
Lavalette (B4)*
Lawford (E2) 25
Lawton (E5)* 800
Layland (E5)* 900
Layopolis (Sand Fork) (E3) 273
Le Roy (C3)* 54
Lead Mine (G2)* 25
Leet (B4)* 40
Left Hand (D3)* 500
Lehew (K2)* 200
Leivasy (E4)*
Lenore (B5)* 350
Leon (C3)* 244
Leonard (F4) 25
Leopold (E2)* 38
Lerona (D6)* 200
Lesage (B3)* 60
Leslie (E4)*
Lester (D5)* 780
Letart (C3)* 150
Levels (J2)*
Lewisburg (E5)* 2,192
Lex (C6)* 250
Liberty (C3)* 60
Lightburn (E2) 40
Linden (D3)*
Lindside (E6)* 100
Link (E2)* 45
Linn (E2)* 53
Little Birch (E3)* 350
Little Otter (E3)* 200
Littleton (F1)* 448
Liverpool (C3)* 60
Lizemores (D4)*
Lobelia (F4)* 25
Lochgelly (D4)* 650
Lockney (E3)* 46
Lockwood (D4)* 500
Logan (B5)* 5,079
London (D4)* 350
Lone Cedar (C2) 9
Lookout (E4)* 950
Loom (K2) 50
Looneyville (D3)*
Lorado (C5)* 1,087
Lorentz (F2)* 250
Lost City (J3)* 125
Lost Creek (F2)* 798
Lost River (J3)* 25
Loudenville (L6) 40
Lowell (E5)* 150
Lowgap (C4) 30
Lowney (B5)
Lubeck (C2) 35
Lumberport (F2)* 1,198
Lundale (C5)* 500
Maben (D5)*
Mabie (G3)* 750
Mabscott (D5)* 1,665
Mace (F4)* 100
Macfarlan (D2)* 200
Macksville (H3)* 14
Madison (C4)* 2,025
Magnolia (K1)
Maidsville (F1)* 500
Majorsville (L5) 75
Malden (C4)* 600
Mallory (C5)* 1,286
Mammoth (D4)* 1,000
Man (C5)* 1,632
Manheim (G2)* 270
Manila (C5)* 500
Mannington (F1)* 3,241
Marcus (E4)* 400
Marfrance (E4)*
Marie (E5)* 150
Marlinton (F4)* 1,645
Marmet (C4)* 2,515
Marquess (G2) 20
Martin (H2)* 35
Marting (D4)*
Martinsburg (K2)* 15,621
Marytown (C6)* 1,268
Mason (B2)* 924
Masontown (G1)* 941
Masonville (H3) 30
Matewan (B5)* 989
Mathias (J3)* 100
Matoaka (D6)* 1,003
Maud (E1)*
Maxwell (D2) 50
Maybeury-Switchback (D6)* 1,646
Maysel (D3)* 200
Maysville (H2)* 105
Mc Cauley (J2) 50
Mc Corkle (C4)* 225
Mc Dowell (D6)*
Mc Keefrey (K6) 150
Mc Mechen (K5)* 3,518
Mc Neill (J2) 50
Mc Whorter (F2)* 277
Meador (B5)*
Meadow Bluff (E5)* 55
Meadow Bridge (E5)* 597
Meadow Creek (E5)* 500
Meadowbrook (F2)* 500
Meadowville (G2)
Medley (H2)* 51
Mercers Bottom (B3) 25
Merrimac (B5)* 150
Metz (F1)* 350
Middlebourne (E1)* 741
Middleway (K2) 350
Midkiff (B4)* 121
Midway (C3)* 150
Milam (H3)* 70
Miletus (E2) 20
Mill Creek (G3)* 800
Mill Point (F4)* 50
Millstone (D3)*
Millwood (C3)* 82
Milton (B4)* 1,552
Minden (D5)* 2,200
Mineralwells (C2)* 50
Mingo (F3)* 200
Minnehaha Springs (G4)* 100
Minnora (D3)* 57
Missouri Branch (A3)* 100
Mitchell (H3)
Mitchell Heights (C5) 185
Moatsville (G2)* 110
Mobley (F1) 25
Mohawk (C5)* 225
Mona (G1)* 1,004
Monaville (B5)* 650
Monclo (C5) 500
Monongah (F2)* 1,622
Montana Mines (F1)* 300
Montcoal (D5)*
Monterville (F3)*
Montgomery (D4)* 3,484
Montrose (G2)* 79
Moore (G2) 25
Moorefield (J2)* 1,405
Mooresville (F1)*
Morgansville (E2)* 50
Morgantown (G1)* 25,525
Morris (E3)* 37
Morrisvale (C4)*
Moundsville (K6)* 14,772
Mount Alto (C3)* 70
Mt. Carbon (D5)* 500
Mt. Clare (F2)* 1,236
Mt. Gay (B5)* 676
Mt. Hope (D5)* 2,588
Mt. Lookout (E4)* 575
Mt. Nebo (E4)* 75
Mt. Storm (H2)* 150
Mt. Zion (D3)* 25
Mountain (E2)* 165
Mountview (D5)* 230
Moyers (H4)* 78
Mozer (H3)* 25
Mud (C4)*
Mullens (D5)* 3,470
Murphytown (D2) 75
Murraysville (C2)* 30
Myra (B4)* 128
Nallen (E4)*
Napier (E3)* 115
National (G1) 500
Naugatuck (B5)* 400
Neals Run (K2) 16
Nebo (D3)*
Needmore (J2)* 75
Nellis (C4)* 1,200
Neola (F5)*
Nestorville (G2)* 200
Nettie (E4)* 600
New Cumberland (K4)* 2,119
New England (C2)* 75
New Haven (C3)* 969
New Martinsville(E1)* 4,084
New Milton (E2)*
Newark (D2)* 70
Newberne (E2)* 55
Newburg (G2)* 657
Newcreek (J2)*
Newell (K4)* 2,101
Newhall (C6)* 750
Newton (D3)* 375
Newville (E3)* 175
Nitro (C4)* 3,314
Nolan (B5)* 600
Normantown (E3)* 89
North Mountain (K1) 175
Northfork (D6)* 994
Norton (G3)* 600
Nutter Fort (F2)* 2,285
Oak Hill (D4)* 4,518
Oakland (K2)* 125
Oakmont (H2) 125
Oakvale (D6)* 239
Oceana (C5)* 1,373
Odd (D5)*
Ohley (D4)* 250
Oka (D3)*
Okeefe (B5)* 150
Okonoko (J1)* 30
Olcott (C4)* 550
Old Fields (J2)* 100
Olympia (D2) 4
Omar (C5)* 1,500
Omps (K2)* 100
Ona (B4)* 100
Onego (H3)*
Opekiska (G1)* 100
Organ Cave (F5) 500
Orgas (C4)* 175
Orlando (E3)* 300
Orleans Cross Roads (J1) 75
Orma (D3)*
Osage (F1)* 800
Oswald (D5)* 350
Otsego (D5)*
Otto (D3)* 5
Oxford (E2)* 41
Packsville (C5)* 365
Pad (D3)
Paden City (D1)* 2,588
Page (D4)* 800
Palestine (D2)* 348
Pansy (H3)
Panther (C6)* 475
Paradise (C3) 78
Park (F2)*
Parkersburg (D2)* 40,492
Parsons (G2)* 2,009
Pattersons Creek (J1)* 100
Paw Paw (K1)* 820
Pax (D5)* 561
Peach Creek (C5)* 800
Pear (E5)
Pecks Mill (B5) 810
Pemberton (D5)* 1,000
Pence Springs (E5)* 85
Pennsboro (E2)* 1,753
Pentress (F1)* 500
Perkins (E3)* 2
Perry (J3)* 80
Persinger (E4)*
Peru (H3) 25
Petersburg (H3)* 1,898
Peterstown (E6)* 571
Petroleum (D2)* 100
Peytona (C4)* 650
Philippi (G2)* 2,531
Pickaway (E5)* 100
Pickens (F3)* 300
Pie (B5)* 250
Piedmont (H2)* 2,565
Pierce (H2)* 288
Pigeon (D3)*
Pike (D2)* 87
Pinch (D4)*
Pine Grove (E1)* 877
Pineville (C5)* 1,082
Piney (E1)* 150
Pipestem (E5)* 132
Pleasant Valley (L6) 25
Pliny (B3)* 55
Plum Orchard (C3)
Pluto (E5)*
Plymouth (C3) 300
Poca (C4)* 465
Pocotaligo (C4) 150
Point Pleasant (B3)* 4,596
Points (J2)*
Polk (C2)
Pond (C5)
Portersville (B4)
Porterwood (G2)* 100
Powellton (D4)* 1,477
Power (K5)* 558
Powhatan (D6)* 550
Poynette (D2) 10
Pratt (D4)* 457
Premier (C6)* 1,000
Price Hill (D5)* 350
Prichard (A4)* 400
Priestley (C4) 50
Princeton (D6)* 8,279
Procious (D3)* 900
Proctor (E1)* 217
Prunty (D2)* 51
Pruntytown (F2) 300
Pughtown (K4)* 250
Pullman (D2)* 210
Purgitsville (J2)* 30
Pursley (D1) 110
Putney (D4)*
Quaker (B4) 150
Queen Shoals (D4)* 150
Queens (F3)* 300
Queens Ridge (B4) 15
Quick (D4)*
Quincy (C4)* 360
Quinnimont (D5)* 250
Quinwood (E4)* 838
Rachel (F1)* 1,200
Racine (C4)* 700
Radnor (A4)* 70
Rainelle (E5)* 853
Raleigh (D5)* 1,164
Ramage (C5)* 100
Ramp (E5) 100
Ranger (B4)* 275
Rangoon (F2)* 100
Ranson (L2)* 1,436
Raven Rock (D2)* 83
Ravencliff (C5)* 150
Ravenswood (C3)* 1,175
Raymond City (C4)* 300
Reader (E1)* 600
Red Creek (H2)* 150
Red House (C3)* 250
Red Jacket (B5)* 1,575
Red Sulphur Sprs. (E5)* 100
Redstar (D5)*
Reed (C4)* 750
Reedsville (G1)* 321
Reedy (D3)* 352
Renick (F4)* 307
Replete (F3)*
Revere (E3)* 75
Rhodell (D5)* 829
Richardson (D3)* 46
Richlands (F5) 83
Richwood (F4)* 5,321
Ridgeley (J1)* 1,754
Ridgeway (K2)* 100
Rinehart (E2)* 150
Rio (J2)* 150
Ripley (C3)* 1,813
Rippon (L2)* 130
Riverton (H3)* 300
Rivesville (F1)* 1,343
Roanoke (E3)* 250
Roaring (H3) 162
Robertsburg (C3) 120
Rock Castle (C3)
Rock Cave (F3)* 175
Rocklick (L6) 150
Rockoak (J2)* 75
Rockport (C2)* 200
Roderfield (C6)*
Romance (C3)*
Romney (J2)* 2,059
Ronceverte (F5)* 2,301
Roneys Point (K5)* 150
Rosbys Rock (K6) 135
Rosedale (E3)* 400
Rosemont (F2)* 300
Rossmore (C5)* 544
Rowlesburg (G2)* 1,299
Ruckman (J2) 50
Ruddle (H3)* 103
Runa (E4)* 175
Rupert (E5)* 952
Russellville (E4)* 225
Russet (D3) 50
Ryan (D3)* 150
Sabraton (G1)*
Saint Albans (C4)* 9,870
St. Clara (E2) 18
St. George (G2)* 210
St. Marys (D2)* 2,196
Salem (E2)* 2,578
Salt Rock (B4)* 200
Salt Sulphur Sprs.(E5)* 20
Saltpetre (A4)* 75
Sand Fork (E3)* 273
Sandstone (E5)* 500
Sandyville (C3)* 450
Sanoma (D3)*
Sardis (F2)
Saulsville (C5)*
Saxman (E4) 35
Scarbro (D5)* 244
Schultz (D2) 75
Scott Depot (C4)* 500
Seacoal (C5) 100
Secondcreek (F5)* 100
Seebert (F4)* 156
Selbyville (F3)* 240
Selwyn (B5) 200
Servia (E3)* 175
Seth (C4)* 1,033
Sewell (E5)*
Shanghai (K2) 75
Shanks (J2)* 200
Sharon (D4)* 650
Sharples (C5)* 465
Shaw (H2)* 225
Shenandoah Jct. (L2)* 400
Shepherdstown (L2)* 1,173
Sheridan (B4) 75
Sherman (C3)* 35
Sherrard (K5)* 500
Shiloh (D2)
Shinnston (F2)* 2,793
Shirley (E2)* 129
Shoals (B4)* 550
Shock (D3)*
Shrewsbury (D4)*
Sidney (B4)*
Sigman (C3) 50
Silica (F3)
Silush (C4)
Silver Hill (E1)*
Silverton (C3) 56
Simoda (G3)*
Simpson (F2)* 375
Sinks Grove (F5)* 120
Sir Johns Run (K1) 50
Sissonville (C3)* 200
Sistersville (D1)* 2,313
Skelt (F3)
Slab Fork (D5)* 824
Slagle (C5)* 625
Slanesville (K2)* 50
Slate (D2)* 150
Sleepy Creek (K1)* 300
Smith (B4) 100
Smith Creek (H3) 300
Smithburg (E2)* 350
Smithers ‡(D4)* 2,208
Smithfield (E2)* 390
Smithville (D2)* 250
Smoke Hole (H3)*
Smoot (E5)*
Sophia (D5)* 1,430
South Branch (J1) 20
S. Charleston (C4)* 16,686
Spanishburg (D6)* 200
Sparks (E4)* 158
Spencer (D3)* 2,587
Sprague (D5)* 2,626
Sprigg (B5)* 450
Spring Creek (F5)* 101
Springfield (J2)* 500
Spurlockville (B4)* 100
Squire (C6)* 1,240
Star City (F1)* 1,205
Statler Run (F1) 300
Statts Mills (C3)*
Steelton (E1) 200
Stickney (D5)* 250
Stiltner (B4)* 400
Stirrat (C5)* 700
Stonecoal (B5)*
Stonewood (F2) 2,066
Stony Bottom (F4)* 92
Stotesbury (D5)* 950
Strange Creek (E3)* 75
Streby (H2) 25
Stumptown (E3)* 92
Sugar Grove (H3)* 125
Sullivan (D5)*
Summersville (E4)* 1,628
Summit Point (K2)* 280
Suncrest (F3)
Surveyor (D5)* 125
Sutton (E3)* 1,070
Swandale (E3)* 354
Sweetsprings (F5)* 100
Swiss (D4)* 150
Switzer (B5)* 940
Tabler (L2) 125
Talcott (E5)* 600
Tallmansville (F3)*
Tams (D5)*
Tango (C4)* 200
Tanner (E3)* 88
Tariff (D3)* 20
Teays (B4)* 300
Tenmile (F3)* 300
Terra Alta (H2)* 1,649
Tesla (E3)* 400
Teterton (H3)*
Thacker (B5)* 400
Thayer (E5)* 400
Thomas (H2)* 1,146
Thornton (G2)* 250
Thornwood (G3) 75
Thorpe (D6)* 1,362
Three Churches (J2)* 50
Thurmond (D5)* 219
Tioga (E4)* 200
Tipton (E4) 65
Toll Gate (E2)* 75
Tomahawk (K1) 65
Toneyfork (C5) 265
Tophet (E6) 12
Tralee (D5)*
Triadelphia (L5)* 741
Tribble (C3) 35
Triplett (D3)
Trout (F4)* 100
Troy (E2)*
Tunnelton (G2)* 544
Turtle Creek (C4)*
Uffington (G1)* 50
Uler (D3)* 164
Uneeda (C4)* 550
Unger (K2)* 50
Union (E5)* 300
Uniontown (F1)*
Upper Tract (H3)*
Upperglade (F4)*
Urland (B5) 50
Vadis (E2)* 200
Valley Bend (F3)* 500
Valley Grove (L5)*
Valley Head (G3)* 800
Valley Point (G1) 150
Van (C5)*
Van Clevesville (L2) 65
Vandalia (F3) 150
Vanvoorhis (G1)* 82
Varney (B5)*
Vaughan (D4)* 215
Verdunville (B5)*
Vicars (D3)*
Victor (D4)* 200
Vienna (D2)* 6,020
Vinton (E4) 30
Viola (K5) 45
Virginville (L5)* 90
Vivian (D6)*
Volcano (D2) 50
Volga (F2)* 565
Vulcan (B5)*
Wadestown (F1)* 61
Waggy (E3) 15
Wainville (E4)* 175
Waiteville (F6)*
Wake Forest (D4) 200
Walker (D2)* 75
Walkersville (F3)* 180
Wallace (E2)* 600
Wallback (D3)*
Walton (D3)* 350
Wana (F1)* 203
War (C6)* 3,992
War Eagle (C5)* 500
Ward (D4)* 2,055
Wardensville (J2)* 171
Warfield (D4)
Warriormine (C6)* 500
Washburn (D2)* 50
Washington (C2)* 50
Watoga (F4)* 35
Watson (F2)* 1,200
Waverly (D2)* 325
Wayne (B4)* 1,257
Weaver (G3) 73
Webb (B5)*
Webster Springs (F4)* 1,313
Weirton (K5)* 24,005
Welch (C6)* 6,603
Welcome (K6)
Wellford (D3) 105
Wellsburg (K5)* 5,787
Wendel (F2)* 233
West Columbia (B3)* 200
W. Hamlin (B4)* 793
W. Liberty (K5) 600
W. Milford (F2)* 401
W. Union (E2)* 1,341
Weston (F2)* 8,945
Westover (F1)* 4,318
Wevaco (D5)* 200
Wharncliffe (C5)* 250
Wharton (C5)* 881
Wheeler (F3)*
Wheeling (K5)* 58,891
Wheeling (urban area) 106,151
Whirlwind (B5)*
White Pine (D3) 50
White Sulphur Springs (F5)* 2,643
Whites Creek (A4)* 100
Whitesville (C4)* 1,017
Whitmer (G3)* 250
Wick (E2)*
Wickham (D5)
Widemouth (D6)* 500
Widen (E4)* 1,274
Wikel (E5)*
Wilbur (E2)* 75
Wiley Ford (J1)* 400
Wileyville (E1)*
Wilkinson (B5)* 750
Williams River (F4) 25
Williamsburg (F5)* 200
Williamson (B5)* 8,624
Williamsport (J2) 25
Williamstown (C2)* 2,001
Willow Bend (F5)*
Willow Grove (C3)
Willowton (E6)* 300
Wilson (H2)* 40
Wilsonburg (F2)*
Wilsondale (B5)* 450
Winding Gulf (D5)* 989
Windsor Heights (K5)* 1,230
Windy (C2)* 15
Winfield (C3)* 346
Winifrede (C4)* 100
Winona (E4)* 1,050
Wolf Pen (C5)*
Wolf Summit (F2)* 200
Womelsdorf (Coalton*) (G3) 407
Woodbine (E4) 30
Woodlands (K6)* 100
Woodruff (L6)*
Woodville (C4)*
Worthington (F2)* 544
Wriston (D4)
Wymer (G3)*
Yates (B4) 150
Yawkey (C4)*
Yellow Spring (J2)* 100
Yolyn (C5)*
Yukon (C6)*
Zalia (K4) 45
Zela (E4)*
Zenith (F5)* 25
Zona (D3)*

WISCONSIN

Map on Page 95

Total Population 3,434,575

71 COUNTIES

Adams (G8) 7,906
Ashland (E3) 19,461
Barron (C5) 34,703
Bayfield (D3) 13,760
Brown (L7) 98,314
Buffalo (C7) 14,719
Burnett (B4) 10,236
Calumet (K7) 18,840
Chippewa (D5) 42,839
Clark (E6) 32,459
Columbia (H9) 34,023
Crawford (E9) 17,652
Dane (H9) 169,357
Dodge (J9) 57,611
Door (M6) 20,870
Douglas (C3) 46,715
Dunn (C6) 27,341
Eau Claire (D6) 54,187
Florence (K4) 3,756
Fond du Lac (K8) 67,829
Forest (J4) 9,437
Grant (E10) 41,460
Green (G10) 24,172
Green Lake (H8) 14,749
Iowa (F9) 19,610
Iron (F3) 8,714
Jackson (E7) 16,073
Jefferson (J9) 43,069
Juneau (F8) 18,930
Kenosha (K10) 75,238
Kewaunee (L6) 17,366
La Crosse (D8) 67,587
Lafayette (F10) 18,137
Langlade (H5) 21,975
Lincoln (G5) 22,235
Manitowoc (L7) 67,159
Marathon (G6) 80,337
Marinette (K5) 35,748
Marquette (H8) 8,839
Milwaukee (L9) 871,047
Monroe (E8) 31,378
Oconto (K6) 26,238
Oneida (G4) 20,648
Outagamie (K7) 81,722
Ozaukee (L9) 23,361
Pepin (C6) 7,462
Pierce (B6) 21,448
Polk (B5) 24,944
Portage (G6) 34,858
Price (F4) 16,344
Racine (K10) 109,585
Richland (F9) 19,245
Rock (H10) 92,778
Rusk (D5) 16,790
Saint Croix (B5) 25,905
Sauk (G9) 38,120
Sawyer (D4) 10,323
Shawano (J6) 35,249
Sheboygan (L8) 80,631
Taylor (E5) 18,456
Trempealeau (D7) 23,730
Vernon (E8) 27,906
Vilas (G3) 9,363
Walworth (J10) 41,584
Washburn (C4) 11,665
Washington (K9) 33,902
Waukesha (K9) 85,901
Waupaca (J6) 35,056
Waushara (H7) 13,920
Winnebago (J7) 91,103
Wood (F7) 50,500

CITIES and TOWNS

Abbotsford (F6)* 1,013
Abrams (L6)* 278
Adams (G8)* 1,425
Adell (L8)* 366
Afton (H10)* 175
Albany (G10)* 839
Albertville (C6) 75
Albion (H10)* 200
Alderley (J1) 60
Algoma (M6)* 3,384
Allen (C6) 92
Allen Grove (J10)* 250
Allenton (K9)* 382
Allouez (K7)* 4,094
Alma (C7)* 1,068
Alma Center (E7)* 441
Almena (B5)* 406
Almond (G7)* 435
Alto (J8) 200
Altoona (C6)* 1,713
Alvin (J4)* 108
Amberg (K5)* 560
Amery (B5)* 1,625
Amherst (H7)* 608
Amherst Junction (H7)* 185
Andrus (B4)
Angelica (K6) 100
Angelo (E8) 123
Aniwa (H6)* 257
Anson (D6) 120
Antigo (H5)* 9,902
Appleton (J7)* 34,010
Arbor Vitae (G4)* 175
Arcadia (D7)* 1,949
Arena (G9)* 296
Argonne (J4)* 350
Argyle (G10)* 702
Arkansaw (B6)* 237
Arkdale (G7)*
Arlington (H9)* 255
Armstrong Creek (K4)* 145
Arnold (D5) 100
Arnott (G7) 117
Arpin (G6)* 325
Ashford (K8) 50
Ashippun (H1)* 278
Ashland (E2)* 10,640
Athelstane (K5)* 58
Athens (G5)* 823
Atlas (A4) 27
Attica (H10) 100
Atwater (J8) 50
Atwood (E6)
Auburndale (F6)* 325
Augusta (D6)* 1,458
Auroraville (H7)* 95
Avoca (F9)* 424
Avon (H10) 60
Babcock (F7)* 250
Baer (J1) 15
Bagley (D10)* 329
Baileys Harbor (M5)* 250
Baldwin (B6)* 1,100

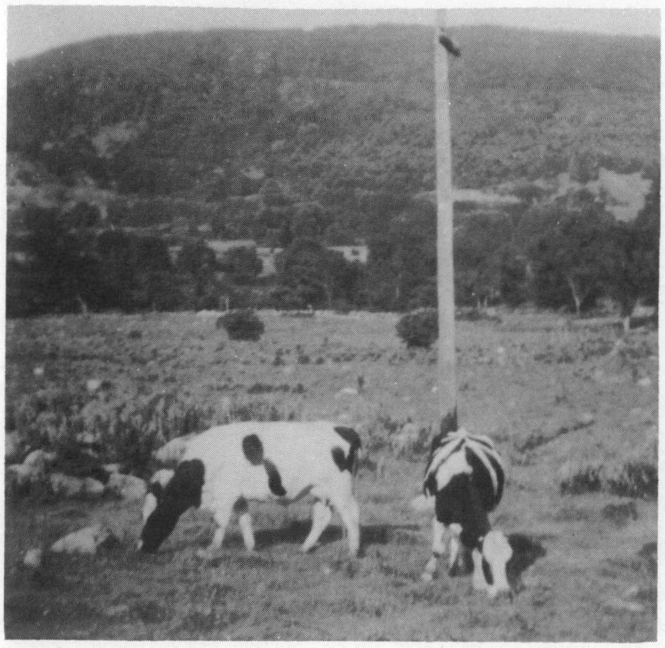

Balsam Lake (B5)* 488
Bancroft (G7)* 185
Bangor (E8)* 941
Baraboo (G8)* 7,264
Barkpoint (D2) 10
Barksdale (D2)* 40
Barnes (D3) 20
Barneveld (F10)* 373
Barnum (E9)* 75
Barron (C5)* 2,355
Barronett (B4)* 116
Barton (K9)* 1,039
Basco (H10)* 60
Batavia (K8) 120
Bay City (B6)* 326
Bayfield (E2)* 1,153
Bear Creek (J6)* 476
Beaver (K5)* 500
Beaver Brook (C4)
Beaver Dam (J9)* 11,867
Beetown (E10)* 175
Beldenville (A6)* 106
Belgium (L8)* 460
Bell Center (E9) 195
Belle Plaine (J6) 50
Belleville (G10)* 735
Bellevue (L7) 30
Belmont (F10)* 474
Beloit (J11)* 29,590
Bennett (C3)* 100
Benoit (D3)* 350
Benton (F10)* 842
Berlin (H8)* 4,693
Berryville (M3)
Bethel (F6) 50
Bevent (H6) 65
Bibon (E3) 15
Big Bend (K2)* 480
Big Falls (H6)* 146
Big Flats (G7) 25
Birchwood (C4)* 502
Birnamwood (H6)* 561
Biron (G7) 528
Black Creek (K7)* 650
Black Earth (G9)* 655
Black River Falls (E7)* 2,824
Blackwell (J4)* 100
Blaine (H7) 25
Blair (D7)* 873
Blanchardville (G10)* 707
Blenker (F6)* 85
Bloom City (E8)* 92
Bloomer (D5)* 2,556
Bloomingdale (E8) 90
Bloomington (E10)* 631
Bloomville (G5) 15
Blue Mounds (G9)* 207
Blue River (E9)* 425
Blueberry (C2) 30
Boardman (A5) 30
Boaz (E9)* 188
Bonduel (K6)* 742
Boscobel (E9)* 2,347
Boulder Junction (G3)* 150
Bowler (J6)* 344
Boyceville (C5)* 645
Boyd (E6)* 619
Brackett (D6) 35
Bradley (G4)
Branch (L7)* 119
Brandon (J8)* 728
Brantwood (F4)*
Breed (K5)* 12
Bridgeport (D9)* 15
Briggsville (H8)* 150
Brighton (K3) 50
Brill (C4)* 105
Brillion (L7)* 1,390
Bristol (L10)*
British Hollow (E10) 10
Brodhead (G10)* 2,016
Brokaw (G5)* 380
Brookfield (K1)* 539
Brooklyn (H10)* 479
Brooks (G8)* 125
Brothertown (K7) 48
Brown Deer (L1) 350
Brownsville (J8)* 275
Browntown (G10)* 279
Bruce (D5)* 867
Brule (C2)* 120
Brussels (L6)* 182
Bryant (J5)* 75
Buffalo (C7) 319
Burlington (K10)* 4,780
Burnett (J8)* 300
Burr Oak (E7) 75
Butler (K1)* 1,047
Butternut (E3)* 522
Byron (K8)* 85
Cable (D3)* 250
Cadott (D6)* 791
Calamine (F10)* 100
Caldwell (J2) 90
Caledonia (L2)* 45
Calhoun (K1) 800
Calumetville (K8) 56
Cambria (H8)* 633
Cambridge (H9)* 552
Cameron (C5)* 963
Camp Douglas (F8)* 556
Campbellsport (K8)* 1,254
Campia (C4) 50
Canton (C5)* 125
Carnot (M6) 25
Caroline (J6)* 280
Carrollville (M2)* 1,240
Carter (J5)* 200
Cascade (K8)* 403
Casco (L6)* 389
Cashton (E8)* 836
Cassville (E10)* 984
Castle Rock (E9) 30
Cataract (E7)* 200
Catawba (E4)* 233
Cato (L7)* 250
Cavour (J4)* 200
Cayuga (E3)* 55
Cazenovia (F8)* 403
Cecil (K6)* 395
Cedar (F2)* 41
Cedar Falls (C6) 50
Cedar Grove (L8)* 1,010
Cedarburg (L9)* 2,810
Cedarville (L5) 50
Centerville (D7) 125
Centuria (A5)* 521
Chase (K6) 35
Chaseburg (D8)* 219
Chelsea (F5)* 100
Chenequa (J1) 270
Chetek (C5)* 1,585
Chili (F6)* 250
Chilton (K7)* 2,367
Chippewa Falls (D6)* 11,088
Chittamo (C3) 64
City Point (F7)* 60
Clam Falls (B4)* 67
Clam Lake (E3)* 100
Clarno (G10)* 46
Clay (E7)
Clayton (B5)* 350
Clear Lake (B5)* 695
Clearwater Lake (H4)* 152
Cleghorn (C6) 69
Cleveland (L8)* 350
Clifford (F4)
Clifton (F8) 50
Clinton (J10)* 1,138
Clintonville (J6)* 4,657
Clyde (F9)
Clyman (J9)* 250
Cobb (F10)* 284
Cobban (D5)
Cochrane (C7)* 444
Coddington (H7)*
Colburn (E5) 15
Colby (F6)* 989
Coleman (L5)* 668
Colfax (C6)* 1,044
Colgate (K1)* 65
Coloma (H7)* 338
Columbus (H9)* 3,250
Combined Locks (K7)* 720
Commonwealth (K4)* 125
Comstock (C5)* 84
Concord (H1)
Conover (H3)*
Conrath (E5)* 114
Coon Valley (E8)* 466
Cooperstown (L7) 75
Corinth (F5) 30
Cornell (D5)* 1,944
Cornucopia (D2)* 175
Cottage Grove (H9)* 372
Couderay (D4)* 133
Crandon (J4)* 1,922
Cream (C7) 30
Crivitz (L5)* 825
Cross Plains (G9)* 464
Cuba City (F10)* 1,333
Cudahy (M2)* 12,182
Cumberland (C4)* 1,872
Curtiss (F6)* 139
Cushing (A4)* 138
Custer (H6)* 104
Cylon (B5)* 85
Dairyland (B3)
Dale (J7)* 400
Dallas (C5)* 370
Dalton (H8)* 250
Danbury (B3)* 383
Dancy (G6)* 110
Dane (G9)* 305
Danville (J9) 100
Darien (J10)* 695
Darlington (F10)* 2,174
Dayton (H10) 127
DeForest (H9)* 805
DePere (K7)* 8,146
DeSoto (D9)* 367
Deansville (H9) 54
Dedham (B2)
Deer Park (B5)* 226
Deerbrook (H5)* 45
Deerfield (H9)* 614
Delafield (J1)* 2,000
Delavan (J10)* 4,007
Dellwood (G7)* 74
Delta (D3)* 158
Denmark (L7)* 1,012
Deronda (B5)* 50
Dexterville (F7) 64
Diamond Bluff (A6)* 220
Dickeyville (E10)* 269
Disco (E7) 40
Dodge (D7)* 211
Dodgeville (F10)* 2,532
Doering (G5) 25
Donald (E5) 65
Doran (B4)
Dorchester (F5)* 457
Dousman (J1)* 328
Dover (F4) 70
Dover (K3)
Downing (B5)* 295
Downsville (C6)* 300
Doylestown (H9)* 261
Draper (E4) 60
Dresser (A5)* 365
Drummond (D3)* 150
Duck Creek (K6) 350
Dudley (H5) 20
Dunbar (K4)*
Duplainville (K1) 10
Durand (C6)* 1,961
Durham (K2) 76
Dyckesville (L6)
Eagle (H2)* 460
Eagle Point (C5) 250
Eagle River (H4)* 1,469
Earl (C4)* 73
East Ellsworth (B6)* 360
East Farmington (A5) 54
East Troy (J2)* 1,052
Eastman (D9)* 359
Easton (G8)
Eau Claire (D6)* 36,058
Eau Galle (B6)* 225
Eden (K8)* 234
Edgar (G6)* 705
Edgerton (H10)* 3,507
Edgewater (D4)* 30
Edmund (F9)* 150
Edson (E6) 25
Egg Harbor (M5)* 210
El Dorado (J8)* 200
Eland (H6)* 232
Elcho (H5)* 700
Elderon (H6)* 212
Eleva (D6)* 479
Elk Creek (C7) 40
Elk Grove (F10)
Elk Mound (C6)* 390
Elkhart Lake (L8)* 587
Elkhorn (J10)* 2,935
Ellenboro (E10) 90
Ellison Bay (M5)* 147
Ellisville (L7)
Ellsworth (A6)* 1,475
Elm Grove (K1)* 2,000
Elmhurst (H5) 35
Elmwood (B6)* 772
Elroy (F8)* 1,654
Elton (J5)* 250
Embarrass (J6)* 303
Emerald (B5)* 130
Endeavor (G8)* 314
Ephraim (M5)* 244
Esdaile (A6) 75
Ettrick (D7)* 415
Eureka (J7)* 250
Euren (L6) 55
Evansville (H10)* 2,531
Excelsior (E9)*
Exeland (D4)* 211
Fair Water (J8)* 311
Fairchild (D6)* 592
Fall Creek (D6)* 584
Fall River (H9)* 479
Falun (A4) 60
Fence (K4)* 300
Fennimore (E9)* 1,696
Fenwood (F6)* 139
Fern (K4)*
Ferron Park (B4) 10
Ferryville (D9)* 216
Fifield (F4)* 450
Fillmore (K9) 50
Finley (F7) 25
Fish Creek (M5)* 300
Fisk (J8) 125
Flambeau (D5) 50
Florence (K4)* 1,400
Fond du Lac (K8)* 29,936
Fontana (J10)* 726
Footville (H10)* 562
Forest Junction (K7)* 150
Forestville (L6)* 259
Fort Atkinson (J10)* 6,280
Foster (D6) 30
Fountain City (C7)* 934
Fox Lake (J8)* 1,153
Fox Point (M1) 2,585
Foxboro (B2)* 26
Francis Creek (L7)* 225
Franklin (L8) 100
Franksville (M3)* 260
Frederic (B4)* 893
Fredonia (L8)* 471
Freistadt (K1)
Fremont (J7)* 504
Friendship (G8)* 566
Friesland (H8)* 311
Gagen (H4) 50
Galesville (D7)* 1,193
Galloway (H6)* 220
Gaslyn (B4)
Gays Mills (E9)* 662
Genesee (J2) 500
Genesee Depot (J2)* 190
Genoa (D8)* 340
Genoa City (K11)* 866
Georgetown (F10)* 50
Germania (H8) 75
Germantown (K1)* 357
Gibbsville (L8) 200
Gile (F3)* 557
Gillett (K6)* 1,410
Gilman (E5)* 402
Gilmanton (C7)* 230
Glandon (H5) 6
Gleason (G5)* 200
Glen Flora (E4)* 91
Glen Haven (E10)* 175
Glenbeulah (L8)* 384
Glenwood City (B5)* 778
Glidden (E3)* 1,221
Goll (L5) 26
Goodman (K4)* 1,020
Goodrich (G5)* 17
Gordon (C3)* 250
Gotham (F9)* 300
Grafton (L9)* 1,489
Grand Marsh (G8)* 170
Grandview (D3)* 250
Granite Heights (H5)* 60
Granton (E6)* 299
Grantsburg (A4)* 931
Granville (L1)* 305
Gratiot (F10)* 323
Green Bay (K6)* 52,735
Green Lake (H8)* 728
Greendale (L2)* 2,752
Greenleaf (L7)* 250
Greenvalley (K6)* 125
Greenville (J7)* 250
Greenwood (E6)* 956
Gresham (J6)* 427
Grundy Junction (G5) 15
Gurney (F3)* 159
Guthrie (K2)
Hager City (A6)* 100
Hale (D7) 10
Hales Corners (L2)* 1,200
Hamburg (G5)* 50
Hammond (A6)* 554
Hampden (H9) 25
Hancock (G7)* 449
Hannibal (E5)* 120
Hanover (H10)* 160
Harrison (G5) 40
Harshaw (G4)* 30
Hartford (K9)* 4,549
Hartland (J1)* 1,190
Hatfield (E7) 50
Hatley (H6)* 299
Hauer (D4)*
Haugen (C4)* 246
Hawkins (E4)* 414
Hawthorne (C3)* 120
Hayes (J5) 20
Hayton (K7) 40
Hayward (D3)* 1,577
Hazel Green (F11)* 635
Hazelhurst (G4)*
Heafford Junction (G4)* 25
Hebron (J10) 115
Helenville (J10)* 185
Herbster (D2)* 75
Hersey (B6)*
Hertel (B4)* 50
Hewitt (F6)* 200
High Bridge (E3)* 50
Highland (F9)* 785
Hika (L8)* 200
Hilbert (K7)* 648
Hiles (J4)* 132
Hillsboro (F8)* 1,341
Hillsdale (C5)* 200
Hines (C2)* 50
Hingham (K8)* 200
Hixton (E7)* 315
Holcombe (D5)* 350
Hollandale (G10)* 281
Hollister (J5)*
Holmen (D8)* 584
Holy Cross (L9) 65
Homestead (K4) 50
Honey Creek (J3)* 200
Horicon (J9)* 2,664
Hortonville (J7)* 1,081
Houlton (A5) 250
Hub City (F9) 50
Hubertus (K1)* 78
Hudson (A6)* 3,435
Humbird (E6)* 380
Hurley (F3)* 3,034
Husher (L2) 50
Hustisford (J9)* 622
Hustler (F8)* 194
Hyde (G9) 25
Independence (D7)* 1,088
Ingram (E5)* 146
Ino (D2) 10
Iola (H6)* 867
Irma (G5)* 65
Iron Belt (F3)* 650
Iron Ridge (K9)* 341
Iron River (D2)* 895
Ironton (F8)* 176
Island Lake (D5) 300
Ithaca (F9) 55
Ives Grove (L3) 75
Ixonia (H1)* 200
Jackson (K9)* 361
Jacksonport (M6)* 152
Janesville (J10)* 24,899
Jefferson (J10)* 3,625
Jeffris (G5) 20
Jewett (B5) 25
Jim Falls (D5)* 237
Joel (B5)* 41
Johnson Creek (J9)* 575
Johnstown (J10) 80
Jonesdale (F10) 28
Juda (H10)* 320
Jump River (E5)* 100
Junction City (G6)* 330
Juneau (J9)* 1,444
Kaiser (E4)
Kansasville (L3)* 135
Kaukauna (K7)* 8,337
Kellner (G7) 30
Kellnersville (L7)* 135
Kempster (H5)* 45
Kendall (F8)* 558
Kennan (F5)* 194
Kenosha (M3)* 54,368
Keshena (J6)* 97
Kewaskum (K8)* 1,183
Kewaunee (M7)* 2,583
Keyeser (H9) 25
Keystone (D5)
Kiel (L8)* 2,129
Kieler (E10)* 177
Kimball (F2)
Kimberly (K7)* 3,179
King (H7)* 665
Kingston (H8)* 334
Knapp (B6)* 424
Knowlton (G6)*
Kohler (L8)* 1,716
Kohlsville (K9) 135
Krakow (K6)* 150
La Crosse (D8)* 47,535
La Farge (E8)* 905
La Pointe (E2)* 236
La Valle (F8)* 448
Lac du Flambeau (G4)*
Lac la Belle (H1) 174
Ladysmith (D5)* 3,924
Lake (L2)
Lake Beulah (J2)* 107
Lake Church (L9) 72
Lake Delton (G8)* 350
Lake Geneva (K10)* 4,300
Lake Nebagamon (C3)* 340
Lake Tomahawk (H4)* 200
Lakemills (H9)* 2,516
Lakewood (K5)* 109
Lamartine (J8)
Lamont (G10) 40
Lampson (C3)* 86
Lancaster (E10)* 3,266
Land o' Lakes (H3)*
Lannon (K1)* 438
Leona (J4)* 1,113
Leadmine (F10)* 150
Lebanon (H1)* 160
Lena (K6)* 526
Leon (E8) 103
Leopolis (J6)* 105
Leslie (F10) 10
Levis (D6) 10
Lewis (B4)* 155
Liberty Pole (D8) 45
Lily (J5)* 150
Lima Center (J10)* 150
Limeridge (F9)* 183
Linden (F10)* 463
Lindsey (F6)* 51
Linwood (M2)
Little Black (F5) 25
Little Chute (K7)* 4,152
Little Prairie (H2) 50
Little Rapids (L7)
Little Suamico (L6)* 150
Livingston (E10)* 452
Lodi (G9)* 1,416
Loganville (F9)* 250
Lohrville (H7)* 206
Lomira (J8)* 746
London (H9)* 140
Lone Rock (F9)* 570
Long Lake (J4)* 229
Longwood (E6) 12
Loomis (K5)* 35
Loraine (B4)* 100
Loretta (E4)* 115
Louisburg (E10) 35
Lowell (J9)* 319
Loyal (E6)* 1,104
Loyd (F9) 56
Lublin (E5)* 161
Luck (B4)* 803
Ludington (D6) 15
Lugerville (E4) 42
Luxemburg (L6)* 519
Lyndon Station (F8)* 377
Lynn (F6) 35
Lynxville (D9)* 217
Lyons (K10)* 400
Madge (C4)
MADISON (H9)* 96,056
Madison (urban area) 109,577
Magnolia (H10) 20
Maiden Rock (B6)* 269
Manawa (J7)* 990
Manchester (J8)* 150
Manitowish (F3)* 75
Manitowoc (L7)* 27,598
Maple (C2)* 75
Maple Bluff ‡(H9) 1,361
Mapleton (J1) 75
Maplewood (M6)* 150
Marathon (G6)* 853
Marblehead (K8) 125
Marcy (K1) 100
Marengo (E3)* 110
Marinette (L5)* 14,178
Marion (J6)* 1,118
Markesan (J8)* 1,010
Markton (J5)*
Marquette (H8)* 350
Marshall (H9)* 541
Marshfield (F6)* 12,394
Marshland (C7) 70
Martell (B6)* 125
Martintown (G10) 45
Mason (D3)* 140
Mather (F7)* 75
Mattoon (J5)* 510
Mauston (F8)* 3,171
Mayville (K9)* 3,010
Mazomanie (G9)* 962
McAllister (L5)* 41
McFarland (H10)* 593
McNaughton (H4)* 22
Medford (F5)* 2,799
Meeker (K1) 55
Mellen (E3)* 1,306
Melrose (E7)* 497
Melvina (E8)* 121
Menasha (J7)* 12,385
Menomonee Falls(K1)* 2,469
Menomonie (C6)* 8,245
Mequon (L1)*
Mercer (F3)* 800
Meridean (C6) 40
Merrill (G5)* 8,951
Merrillan (E7)* 579
Merrimac (G9)* 317
Merton (K1)* 343
Middle Inlet (K5)*
Middleton (G9)* 2,110
Midway (D8) 113
Mifflin (F10)* 90
Mikana (C4)* 125
Milan (F6)* 153
Milford (J9) 150
Milladore (G6)* 247
Millston (E7)* 175
Milltown (B4)* 580
Millville (E9) 50
Milton (J10)* 1,549
Milton Junction (H10)* 1,104
Milwaukee (M1)* 637,392
Milwaukee (urban area) 823,430
Mindoro (D7)*
Miner (F7) 15
Mineral Point (F10)* 2,284
Minocqua (G4)*
Minong (C3)* 357
Misha Mokwa (C7) 32
Mishicot (L7)* 583
Modena (C7)* 116
Monches (J1) 53
Mondovi (C6)* 2,285
Monico (H4)* 375
Monona ‡(H9) 2,544
Monroe (G10)* 7,037
Montello (H8)* 1,069
Monterey (J1) 85
Montfort (E10)* 576
Monticello (G10)* 792
Montreal (F3)* 1,439
Moquah (D2)* 31
Morgan (K6) 29
Morrison (L7) 100
Morrisonville (G9)* 236
Morse (E3)* 135
Mosinee (G6)* 1,453
Mosling (K6) 42
Mount Calvary (K8)*
Mt. Hope (D10)* 232
Mt. Horeb (G10)* 1,716
Mt. Ida (E10) 60
Mt. Sterling (D9)* 205
Mt. Tabor (F8) 18
Mt. Vernon (G10) 105
Mountain (K5)* 200
Mukwonago (J2)* 1,207
Murry (D4) 15
Muscoda (F9)* 1,046
Muskego (K2)* 1,968
Nashotah (J1)* 400
Nashville (J5) 50
Navarino (J6)* 100
Necedah (F7)* 862
Neenah (J7)* 12,437
Neillsville (E6)* 2,663
Nekoosa (G7)* 2,352
Nelma (J3) 77
Nelson (C7)* 325
Nelsonville (H7)* 188
Neopit (J6)* 1,257
Neosho (J9)* 287
Neshkoro (H8)* 361
New Amsterdam (C8) 55
New Auburn (D5)* 371
New Berlin (K2) 100
New Coeln (L2) 30
New Diggings (F10)* 300
New Franken (L6)* 115
New Glarus (G10)* 1,224
New Hulstein (K8)* 1,831
New Lisbon (F8)* 1,482
New London (J7)* 4,922
New Richmond (A5)* 2,886
New Rome (G7)
Newald (J4)* 280
Newark (H10) 20
Newburg (K9)* 288
Niagara (K4)* 2,022
Nichols (K6)* 150
Norman (L7) 22
Norrie (H6)* 48
North Bend (D7)* 125
North Bristol (H9) 88
N. Fond du Lac (J8)* 2,291
North Freedom (G9)* 611
North Hudson (A5) 787
North Lake (J1)* 300
North Prairie (J2)* 424
Northfield (D7)* 50
Northland (H6) 56
Norwalk (E8)* 519
Nye (A5)* 35
Oak Hill (H2) 16
Oakdale (F8)* 190
Oakfield (J8)* 697
Oakwood (L2)* 125
Oconomowoc (H1)* 5,345
Oconto (L6)* 5,055
Oconto Falls (K6)* 2,050
Odanah (E2)*
Ogdensburg (J7)* 221
Ogema (F5)* 300
Ojibwa (D4)*
Okauchee (J1)* 1,673
Okee (H9)*
Oliver (B2) 210
Olivet (B6) 38
Omro (J7)* 1,470
Onalaska (D8)* 2,561
Oneida (K7)* 150
Ontario (E8)* 527
Oostburg (L8)* 895
Oregon (H10)* 1,341
Orfordville (H10)* 543
Osceola (A5)* 700
Oshkosh (J8)* 41,084
Osseo (D6)* 1,126
Owen (F6)* 1,034
Oxford (H8)* 509
Packwaukee (G8)* 275
Palmyra (H2)* 862
Paoli (G10) 108
Pardeeville (H8)* 1,112
Paris (L3)
Park Falls (F4)* 2,924
Park Ridge ‡(G6) 314
Parrish (H5)* 95
Patch Grove (D10)* 203
Patzau (B3)* 350
Pearson (H5)* 25
Peeksville (E3) 25
Pelican Lake (H4)* 200
Pella (J6) 95
Pembine (L4)* 665
Pence (F3)* 375
Pensaukee (L6)* 200
Pepin (B7)* 840
Perkinstown (E5)* 160
Perrigo Place (H10) 3,315
Peru (H6) 60
Peshtigo (L5)* 2,279
Pewaukee (K1)* 1,792
Phelps (H3)* 600
Phillips (E4)* 1,775
Phipps (D3) 20
Phlox (J5)* 200
Pickerel (J5)* 300
Pickett (J8)*
Pigeon Falls (D7)* 300
Pilsen (L7)
Pine Grove (L7) 50
Pine River (H7)* 102
Pipersville (H1) 50
Pittsville (F7)* 636
Plain (F9)* 512
Plainfield (G7)* 680
Plainville (G8)
Plat (K1) 45
Platteville (F10)* 5,751
Pleasant Prairie (L10)* 274
Plover (G7)* 515
Plum City (B6)* 355
Plymouth (L8)* 4,543
Polar (H5)* 200

Polley (E5)... 20
Polonia (H6)...
Poplar (C2)*... 489
Porcupine (C6)... 73
Port Edwards (G7)*...1,336
Port Washington (L9)*.4,755
Port Wing (D2)*... 250
Portage (G8)*...7,334
Porterfield (L5)*... 37
Poskin (C5)*... 87
Potosi (E10)*... 556
Potter (K7)*... 210
Pound (L5)*... 354
Powell (F3)... 12
Poy Sippi (J7)*... 450
Poynette (G9)*... 969
Prairie du Chien (D9)*...5,392
Prairie du Sac (G9)*...1,402
Prairie Farm (C5)*... 343
Pray (F7)... 12
Preble (L6)...5,092
Prentice (F4)*... 477
Prescott (A6)*...1,005
Price (E6)...
Princeton (H8)*...1,371
Prospect (K2)... 150
Pulaski (K6)*...1,210
Pulcifer (K6)*... 140
Quincy (G8)...
Racine (M3)*...71,193
Racine (urban area)....76,101
Radisson (D4)*... 200
Randall (A4)*... 54
Randolph (H8)*...1,350
Random Lake (K8)*... 679
Rankin (M6)... 200
Raymond (L2)...
Readfield (J7)*... 200
Readstown (E9)*... 541
Red Cliff (E2)... 80
Redgranite (J7)*... 648
Reedsburg (G8)*...4,072
Reedsville (L7)*... 691
Reeseville (J9)*... 470
Reeve (B5)... 27
Reserve (D4)... 175
Rewey (F10)*... 252
Rhinelander (H4)*...8,774
Rib Falls (G6)... 125
Rib Lake (F5)*... 853
Rice Lake (C5)*...6,898
Richfield (K1)*... 276
Richford (H7)... 51
Richland Center (F9)*...4,608
Richwood (J9)*... 60
Ridgeland (B5)*... 273
Ridgeway (F10)*... 410
Riley (G9)... 40
Ringle (G6)*... 100
Rio ((H9)*... 741
Rio Creek (L6)*... 100
Riplinger (E6)*... 92
Ripon (J8)*...5,619
Rising Sun (D9)... 40
River Falls (A6)*...3,877
River Hills (M1)... 567
Robbins (H4)...
Roberts (A6)*... 290
Rochester (K3)*... 333
Rock Elm (B6)*... 225
Rock Falls (C6)*... 100
Rock Springs (F8)*... 442
Rockbridge (F9)*... 96
Rockdale (J10)*... 161
Rockfield (L1)*... 150
Rockland (D8)*... 216
Rockmont (B2)...
Rockton (E8)...
Rockville (E10)... 25
Rolling Prairie (J9)... 100
Rome (H1)*... 285
Root Creek (L2)...
Rose Lawn (K6)... 50
Rosendale (J8)*... 388
Rosholt (H6)*... 508
Rothschild (G6)*...1,425
Roxbury (G9)... 150
Royalton (J7)*... 375
Rozellville (G6)... 128
Rubicon (K9)*... 132
Ruby (D5)... 35
Rudolph (G7)*... 225
Rush Lake (J8)*... 48
Rusk (C6)*... 80
Russell (C7)... 7
Saint Cloud (K8)*... 408
St. Croix Falls (A5)*...1,065
St. Francis (M2)*...
St. Joseph (D8)... 41
St. Martins (L2)... 150
St. Nazianz (L7)*... 450
Salem (K10)*... 450
Sanborn (E3)*... 102
Sand Creek (C5)*... 175
Sandrock (F3)...
Sandusky (F9)... 20
Sarona (C4)*... 95
Sauk City (G9)*...1,755
Saukville (L9)*... 699
Sawyer (M6)*... 539
Saxeville (H7)*... 59
Saxon (F3)*... 450
Sayner (H4)*... 300
Scandinavia (H7)*... 286
Schofield (H6)*...1,948
School Hill (L8)... 75
Sechlerville (E7)*... 60
Seeley (D3)...
Seneca (E9)*... 207
Sextonville (F9)*... 195
Seymour (K6)*...1,760
Shamrock (E7)... 40
Sharon (J11)*...1,013
Shawano (J6)*...5,894
Sheboygan (L8)*...42,365
Sheboygan Falls (L8)*..3,599
Sheldon (D5)*... 271
Shell Lake (C4)*... 954
Shennington (F7)... 41
Sheridan (H7)*... 50
Sherry (G6)*... 82
Sherwood (K7)*... 350
Shiocton (K7)*... 673
Shopiere (H10)*... 300
Shorewood (M1)*...16,199
Shorewood Hills (G9)...1,594
Shortville (F7)... 30
Shullsburg (F10)*...1,306
Silverlake (K10)*... 603
Siren (B4)*... 613
Sister Bay (M5)*... 429
Slinger (K9)*... 919
Sobieski (L6)*... 82
Soldiers Grove (E9)*... 781
Solon Springs (C3)*... 480
Somers (M3)*... 175
Somerset (A5)*... 531
Soperton (J5)*... 334
South Milwaukee (M2)*...12,855
South Range (B2)*... 104
South Wayne (G10)*... 328
Sparta (E8)*...5,893
Spencer (F6)*... 757
Spirit (F5)... 85
Spirit Falls (G5)*... 32
Split Rock (H6)... 55
Spokeville (E6)... 50
Spooner (B4)*...2,597
Sprague (F7)... 10
Spread Eagle (K4)*...
Spring Green (G9)*...1,064
Spring Lake (H8)... 150
Spring Valley (B6)*... 975
Springbrook (C4)*... 150
Springfield (K10)*... 175
Springstead (F3)...
Stanberry (C3)... 50
Stangelville (L7)... 60
Stanley (E6)*...2,014
Star Prairie (A5)*... 288
Starks (H4)... 150
Starlake (G3)*... 100
Statesan (J1)*... 275
Stetsonville (F5)*... 334
Steuben (E9)*... 264
Stevens Point (G7)*...16,564
Stevenstown (D7)... 33
Stiles (L6)*... 200
Stiles Junction (L6)... 15
Stitzer (E10)*... 200
Stockbridge (K7)*... 409
Stockholm (B7)*... 124
Stoddard (D8)*... 459
Stone Lake (C4)*... 250
Stonebank (J1)... 100
Stoughton (H10)*...4,833
Stratford (F6)*... 982
Strongs Prairie (G7)*... 103
Strum (D6)*... 542
Sturgeon Bay (M6)*...7,054
Sturtevant (M3)*...1,176
Suamico (K6)*... 400
Sugar Bush (J7)*... 150
Sullivan (H1)*... 349
Summit Lake (H5)*... 180
Sun Prairie (H9)*...2,263
Superior (city) (C2)*..35,325
Superior, Wis.-Duluth, Minn.(urban area).142,344
Superior (village) ‡(C2)... 339
Suring (K5)*... 546
Sussex (K1)*... 679
Sylvan (E9)... 25
Sylvania (L3)... 75
Symco (J6)... 175
Tarrant (C6)... 8
Taycheedah (K8)*... 150
Taylor (E7)*... 350
Tennyson (E10)... 211
Tess Corners (K2)...
Theresa (K8)*... 461
Thiensville (L1)*... 897
Thompson (J1)... 15
Thompsonville (L2)...
Thorp (E6)*...1,383
Three Lakes (H4)*... 850
Tichigan (K2)...
Tigerton (H6)*... 827
Tilleda (J6)*... 120
Tioga (E6)*... 30
Tipler (J4)*...
Tisch Mills (L7)*... 250
Token (H9)... 64
Tomah (F8)*...4,760
Tomahawk (G5)*...3,534
Tony (E5)*... 182
Townsend (K5)*...
Trade Lake (A4)... 100
Trego (C4)*... 250
Trempealeau (C8)*... 645
Tripoli (G4)*... 190
Troy (J2)... 77
Troy Center (J2)*... 161
Truesdell (L3)*... 85
Tunnel City (E7)*... 190
Turtle Lake (B5)*... 696
Tustin (J7)... 100
Twin Lakes (K11)*... 637
Two Rivers (M7)*...10,243
Underhill (K6)*... 110
Union Center (F8)*... 261
Union Grove (L3)*...1,358
Unity (F6)*... 355
Upson (F3)*...
Utica (H10)...
Valders (L7)*... 560
Valley (F8)*... 120
Valley Junction (E7)... 60
Valmy (M6)... 100
Valton (F8)... 71
Van Buskirk (G3)...
Vernon (J2)... 40
Verona (G9)*... 748
Vesper (F7)*... 342
Victory (D9)*... 118
Vienna (J3)...
Viola (E8)*... 785
Viroqua (D8)*...3,795
Wabeno (J5)*... 668
Wagner (L5)...
Waldo (L8)*... 367
Waldwick (G10)... 86
Wales (J1)*... 237
Walrath (E5)... 30
Walsh (L5)... 23
Walworth (J10)*...1,137
Wanderoos (B5)*... 100
Warrens (E7)*... 275
Wascott (C3)*... 42
Washburn (D2)*...2,070
Washington Isl. (M5)*.. 800
Waterford (K3)*...1,100
Waterloo (J9)*...1,667
Watertown (J9)*...12,417
Waubeka (L9)*... 200
Waukau (J8)*... 150
Waukesha (K1)*...21,233
Waumandee (C7)*... 110
Waunakee (G9)*...1,042
Waupaca (H7)*...3,921
Waupun (J8)*...6,725
Wausau (G6)*...30,414
Wausaukee (K5)*... 612
Wautoma (H7)*...1,376
Wauwatosa (L1)...33,324
Wauzeka (E9)*... 564
Wayside (L7)*... 177
Webb Lake (B3)*... 10
Webster (B4)*... 552
Weirgor (D4)... 87
Wentworth (C2)*... 31
West Allis (L1)*...42,959
West Bend (K9)*...6,849
West Bloomfield (J7)*.. 65
West Granville (L1)...
West Lima (E8)*... 110
West Milwaukee (L1)...5,429
West Salem (D8)*...1,376
West Sweden (B4)... 150
Westboro (F5)*... 500
Westby (E8)*...1,491
Westfield (H8)*... 935
Weston (C6)*... 56
Weyauwega (H7)*...1,207
Weyerhauser (D5)*... 331
Wheeler (C5)*... 235
White Creek (G8)...
White Lake (J5)*... 408
Whitefish Bay (M1)*...14,665
Whitehall (D7)*...1,379
Whitelaw (L7)*... 386
Whitewater (J10)*...5,101
Whiting (H7)... 854
Whittlesey (F5)*... 31
Wild Rose (H7)*... 582
Willard (E6)*... 110
Williams Bay (J10)*...1,118
Wilmot (K11)*... 381
Wilson (B6)*... 174
Wilton (F8)*... 533
Winchester (G3)*... 250
Wind Lake (K2)...1,067
Windsor (H9)*...
Winegar (G3)*... 250
Winnebago (J7)*...
Winneconne (J7)*...1,078
Winter (E4)*... 440
Wiota (G10)... 112
Wisconsin Dells (G8)*...1,957
Wisconsin Rapids (G7)*...13,496
Withee (E6)*... 421
Wittenberg (H6)*... 874
Wolfcreek (A4)... 25
Wonewoc (F8)*... 961
Woodboro (G4)... 50
Wooddale (D4)... 4
Woodford (G10)*... 115
Woodman (E9)*... 149
Woodruff (G4)*... 600
Woodstock (E9)... 75
Woodville (B6)*... 410
Worcester (F4)...
Wrightstown (K7)*... 761
Wyalusing (D10)*... 100
Wyeville (F7)*... 195
Wyocena (H9)*... 714
Yellowlake (B4)*...
York (D7)... 22
Yorkville (K3)... 50
Yuba (F8)*... 119
Zachow (K6)*... 130

Map on Page 96

WYOMING

Total Population 290,529

24 COUNTIES

Albany (G4)...19,055
Big Horn (E1)...13,176
Campbell (G1)...4,839
Carbon (F4)...15,742
Converse (G3)...5,933
Crook (H1)...4,738
Fremont (D2)...19,580
Goshen (H4)...12,634
Hot Springs (D2)...5,250
Johnson (F1)...4,707
Laramie (H4)...47,662
Lincoln (B3)...9,023
Natrona (F3)...31,437
Niobrara (H2)...4,701
Park (C1)...15,182
Platte (H4)...7,925
Sheridan (F1)...20,185
Sublette (C3)...2,481
Sweetwater (D4)...22,017
Teton (B2)...2,593
Uinta (B4)...7,331
Washakie (E2)...7,252
Weston (H2)...6,733
Yellowstone National Park (B1).... 353

CITIES and TOWNS

Acme (E1)*... 200
Afton (B3)*...1,319
Akwensa (B4)*... 50
Aladdin (H1)*... 10
Albany (F4)*... 50
Albin (H4)*... 208
Alcova (F3)*... 36
Alva (H1)*... 51
Anchor (D2)...
Arapahoe (D3)*... 193
Arcola (H4)... 15
Arlington (F4)...
Arminto (E2)*... 30
Arvada (F1)*... 85
Aspentunnel (B4)... 20
Atlantic City (D3)*... 20
Auburn (A3)*... 400
Badger Basin (C1)*...
Baggs (E4)*... 206
Bairoil (E3)*... 300
Banner (F1)*... 4
Basin (E1)*...1,220
Bear Creek (G2)... 6
Bedford (A3)*... 268
Bentonite Spur (H1)... 12
Beulah (H1)*... 50
Big Horn (E1)*... 200
Big Piney (B3)*... 206
Big Sandy (C3)... 20
Bigtrails (E2)...
Bill (G2)*... 6
Bitter Creek (D4)*... 150
Blazon (B4)...
Bondurant (B2)*... 6
Bonneville (E2)*... 75
Border (B3)... 35
Bosler (G4)*... 75
Boulder (C3)*... 20
Boxelder (G3)...
Boysen (D2)... 100
Bright (H2)*... 4
Brilliant (B4)... 15
Buckhorn (H1)... 5
Buffalo (F1)*...2,674
Buford (G4)*... 62
Burlington (D1)*... 150
Burns (H4)*... 216
Burris (C2)*... 90
Byron (D1)*... 350
Calpet (B3)*... 79
Camp Ferris (E3)... 20
Canyon (B1)*...
Careyhurst (G3)...
Carlile (H1)*... 2
Carpenter (H4)*... 104
Carter (B4)*... 75
Casper (F3)*...23,673
Cassa (G3)*... 10
Centennial (F4)*... 68
CHEYENNE (H4)*...31,935
Chugwater (H4)*... 283
Church Buttes (B4)... 75
Clareton (H2)... 3
Clark (C1)*... 100
Clearmont (F1)*... 225
Clifton (H2)... 5
Cody (D1)*...3,872
Cokeville (B3)*... 440
Colony (H1)*...
Columbine (F2)... 40
Como (F4)... 6
Cora (C3)*... 4
Cowley (D1)*... 463
Croton (G1)...
Crowheart (C2)*... 4
Daniel (B3)*... 75
Dayton (E1)*... 316
Deaver (D1)*... 118
Devils Tower (H1)*... 30
Diamond G Ranch (C2)*
Diamondville (B4)*... 415
Dickie (D1)... 35
Dines (C4)*... 237
Divide (H4)... 2
Dixon (E4)*... 124
Douglas (G3)*...2,544
Dubois (C2)*... 279
Dull Center (H2)*... 8
Duncan (C2)*... 17
Dwyer (G3)*... 16
East Thermopolis (D2). 246
Echeta (G1)...
Eden (C3)*... 200
Edgerton (F2)*... 203
Egbert (H4)*... 50
Elk (B2)*... 34
Elk Basin (D1)*... 200
Elk Mountain (F4)*... 196
Elkol (B4)*... 40
Elmo (F4)... 213
Emblem (D1)*... 250
Encampment (F4)*... 288
Ervay (E3)... 3
Esterbrook (G3)*... 15
Ethete (D2)*... 50
Etna (A2)*... 450
Evanston (B4)*...3,863
Evansville (F3)*... 393
Fairview (B3)*... 400
Farson (C3)*... 150
Federal (H4)*... 10
Fishing Bridge (B1)*...
Flattop (H3)*... 2
Fletcher Park (G3)*... 5
Fontenelle (B3)... 35
Fort Bridger (B4)*... 100
Fort Fred Steele (E4)* 40
Fort Laramie (H3)*... 300
Fort Washakie (C2)*...1,500
Fossil (B4)... 10
Four Corners (H1)*... 30
Foxpark (F4)*... 110
Frannie (D1)*... 180
Freedom (B3)*... 510
Freeland (F3)*... 5
Frontier (B4)*... 500
Garland (D1)*... 60
Garrett (G3)*... 29
Gebo (D2)*... 200
Gillette (G1)*...2,191
Glendo (G3)*... 215
Glenrock (G3)*...1,110
Goose Egg (F3)... 20
Granger (C4)*... 122
Granite Canon (G4)*... 120
Grass Creek (D2)*... 150
Green River (C4)*...3,187
Greybull (E1)*...2,262
Grover (B3)*... 350
Grovont (B2)...
Guernsey (H3)*... 721
Gunn (C4)...
Halfway (B3)... 25
Hamilton Dome (D2)*... 187
Hanna (F4)*...1,326
Hartville (H3)*... 229
Hat Creek (H3)*... 1
Hawk Springs (H4)*... 163
Hells Half Acre (E2)*..
Hiland (E2)*... 7
Hillsdale (H4)*... 78
Hoback (B2)... 5
Holmes (F4)... 25
Horse Creek (G4)*... 10
Horton (H1)...
Hudson (D3)*... 293
Hulett (H1)*... 236
Huntley (H4)*... 69
Hyattville (E1)*... 125
Iron Mountain (G4)*... 23
Jackson (B2)*...1,244
Jay Em (H3)*... 30
Jelm (G4)*... 2
Jenny Lake (B2)*... 7
Jireh (H3)... 7
Kane (D1)*... 21
Kaycee (F2)*... 211
Kearney (F1)... 11
Keeline (H3)*... 17
Kelly (B2)*... 18
Kemmerer (B4)*...1,667
Kendall (B2)... 8
Kinnear (D2)*...
Kirby (D2)*... 99
Kirtley (H3)...
Knight (B4)... 12
Kyle (F4)... 30
La Barge (B3)*... 110
Lagrange (H4)*... 221
Lake Outlet (B1)*...
Lamont (E3)*... 100
Lance Creek (H2)*...2,000
Lander (D3)*...3,349
Laramie (G4)*...15,581
Lawver (G2)*... 2
Le Roy (B4)... 15
Leiter (F1)*... 3
Leo (F3)*... 41
Leverett (H2)...
Lindbergh (H4)... 5
Lingle (H3)*... 403

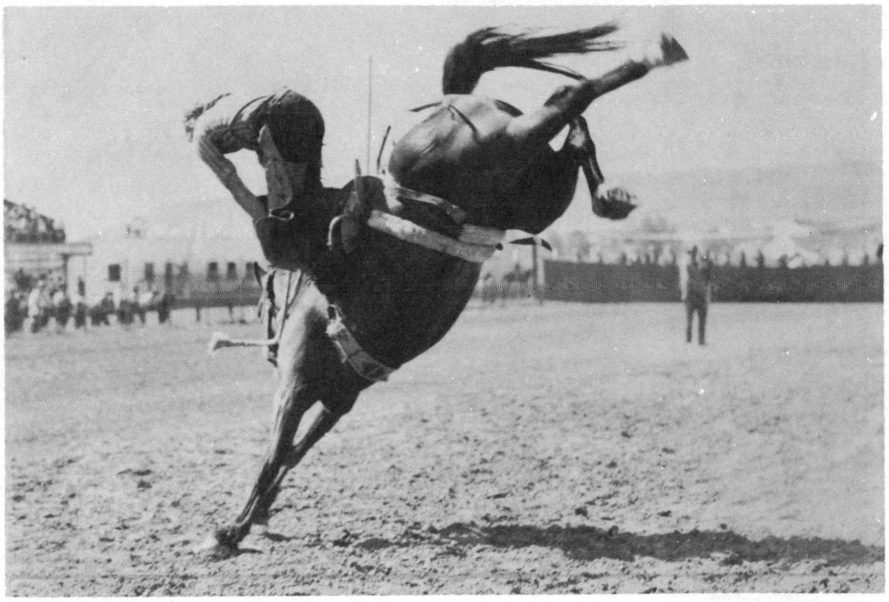

Little Bear (H4)*...
Little Medicine (G3)... 6
Lonetree (B4)*... 70
Lookout (G4)... 15
Lost Cabin (E2)*... 73
Lost Springs (G3)*... 9
Lovell (D1)*...2,508
Lucerne (D2)*... 13
Lusk (H3)*...2,089
Lyman (B4)*... 483
Lysite (E2)*... 50
Manderson (E1)*... 107
Manville (H3)*... 154
Marbleton (B3)... 20
Marshall (G3)... 20
Mayoworth (F2)... 5
Mc Fadden (F4)*... 225
Mc Kinley (G3)*... 21
Mc Kinnon (C4)*... 154
Medicine Bow (F4)*... 328
Meeteetse (D1)*... 404
Meriden (H4)*... 16
Merna (B3)... 50
Midwest (F2)*...2,000
Mills (F3)*... 866
Monarch (F1)*... 500
Moneta (E2)*... 12
Moorcroft (H1)*... 517
Moose (B2)*... 65
Moran (B2)*... 120
Morton (D2)*... 18
Moskee (H1)... 70
Mountainview (B4)*...
Natrona (F2)*...
New Haven (H1)*...
Newcastle (H2)*...3,395
Node (H3)*... 4
Nugget (B4)... 10
Old Faithful (B1)*...
Opal (B4)*... 67
Orin (G3)*... 50
Oriva (G1)...
Orpha (G3)*... 40
Osage (H2)*... 284
Oshoto (G1)*... 7
Otto (D1)*... 400
Pahaska (C1)... 50
Painter (C1)... 35
Parkerton (G3)*... 90
Parkman (E1)*... 75
Passaic (F1)... 5
Pavillion (D2)*... 241
Piedmont (B4)*... 29
Pine Bluffs (H4)*... 846
Pine Tree (G2)...
Pinedale (C3)*... 770
Pitchfork (C1)*... 50
Point of Rocks (D4)*... 46
Powder River (F2)*... 42
Powell (D1)*...3,804
Quealy (C4)*... 147
Ralston (D1)*... 64
Ranchester (E1)*... 251
Rawlins (E4)*...7,415
Recluse (G1)*... 21
Reliance (C4)*... 700
Riverside (F4)... 50
Riverton (D2)*...4,142
Robertson (B4)*... 24
Rock River (G4)*... 424
Rock Springs (C4)*...10,857
Rockeagle (H3)*... 2
Rockypoint (G1)*... 4
Ross (G2)*... 25
Rozet (G1)*... 50
Ryan Park (F4)*... 150
Saddlestring (F1)*... 10
Sage (B4)*... 25
Saint Stephens (D3)*... 150
Saratoga (F4)*... 926
Savageton (G2)...
Savery (E4)*... 55
Seely (H1)*... 5
Seminole Dam (E3)*... 59
Shawnee (G3)*... 25
Shell (E1)*... 61
Sheridan (F1)*...11,500
Shirley (F3)... 20
Shoshoni (D2)*... 891
Sinclair (E4)*... 775
Slater (H4)*... 12
Smoot (B3)*... 280
South Pass City (D3)*... 15
S. Superior (D4)... 780
Speer (H4)... 10
Spotted Horse (G1)*... 4
Story (F1)*... 335
Stroner (H1)*... 3
Sundance (H1)*... 893
Sunrise (H3)*... 450
Sunshine (C1)*...
Superior (D4)*...1,580
Sussex (F2)*...
Teckla (G2)*... 9
Ten Sleep (E1)*... 289
Thayer Junction (D4)... 37
Thayne (A3)*... 229
Thermopolis (D2)*...2,870
Thornton (H1)...
Thumb (B1)*...
Tie Siding (G4)*... 50
Torrington (H4)*...3,247
Tower Falls (B1)*...
Tullis (E4)... 3
Turnercrest (G2)*... 10
Turnerville (A3)*... 73
Ucross (F1)... 45
Ulm (F1)*... 45
Underwood (G4)... 10
Upton (H1)*... 951
Urie (B4)... 25
Uva (H3)*... 35
Valley (C1)*... 100
Van Tassell (H3)*... 34
Veteran (H4)*... 48
Walcott (F4)*... 25
Waltman (E2)... 6
Wamsutter (E4)*... 103
Wapiti (C1)*... 13
Wendover (H3)*... 30
Weston (G1)... 2
Wheatland (H3)*...2,286
Whitman (H3)*... 2
Wild Cat (G1)... 2
Wilson (B2)*... 200
Winchester (D2)*... 57
Wind River (D3)... 300
Winton (C4)*... 665
Wolf (E1)*... 75
Worland (E1)*...4,202
Wyarno (F1)*... 6
Yellowstone Park (B1)*... 250
Yoder (H4)*... 128

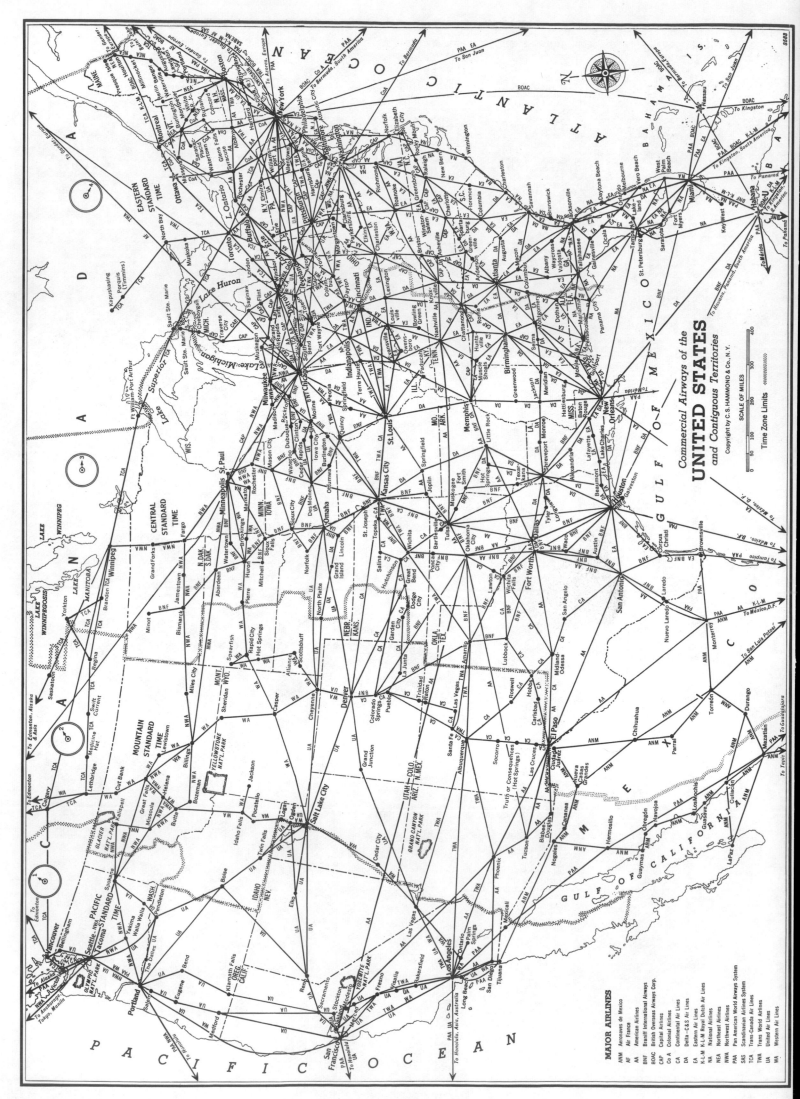

Commercial Airways of the
UNITED STATES
and Contiguous Territories

Copyright by C. S. HAMMOND & Co., N.Y.

SCALE OF MILES

Time Zone Limits

MAJOR AIRLINES

ANM	Aeronaves de Mexico
AF	Air France
AA	American Airlines
BNF	Braniff Airways
BOAC	British Overseas Airways Corp.
CAP	Capital Airlines
Co A	Colonial Airlines
CA	Continental Air Lines
DA	Delta-C&S Air Lines
EA	Eastern Air Lines
K-L-M	K-L-M Royal Dutch Air Lines
NA	National Airlines
NEA	Northeast Airlines
NWA	Northwest Airlines
PAA	Pan American World Airways
SAS	Scandinavian Airlines System
TCA	Trans-Canada Air Lines
TWA	Trans World Airlines
UA	United Air Lines
WA	Western Air Lines

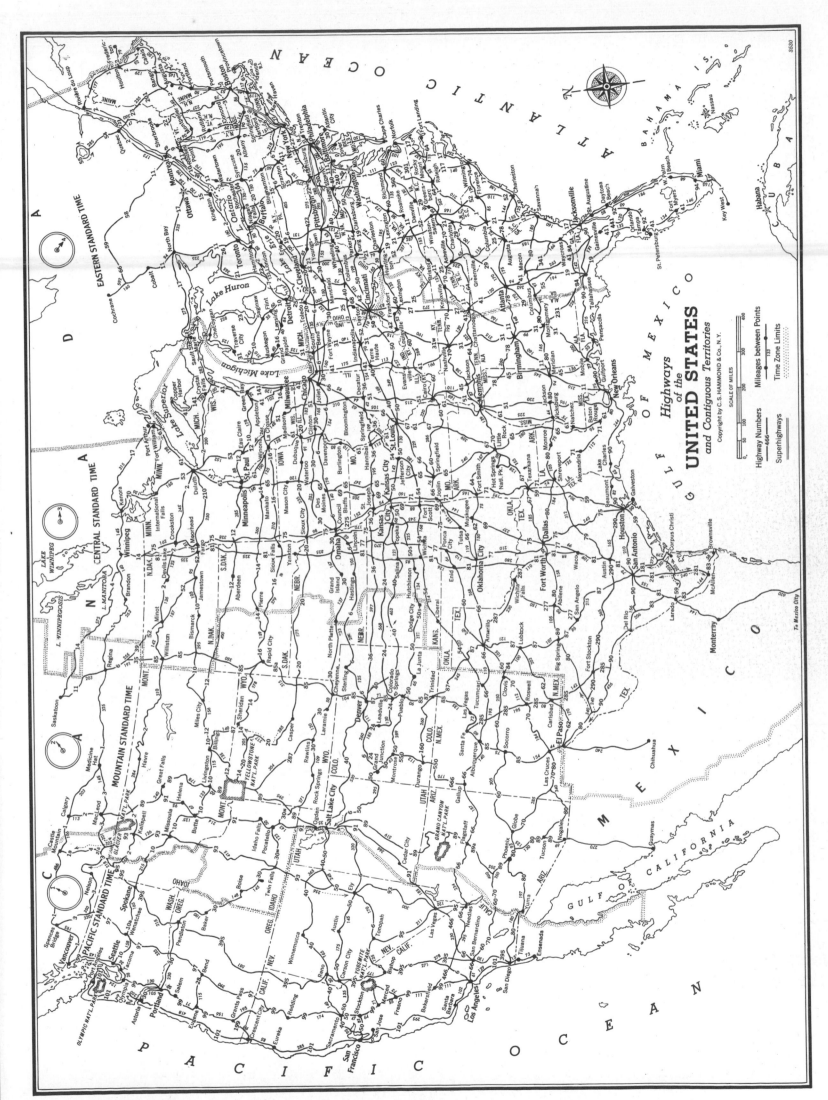

Highways
of the
UNITED STATES
and Contiguous Territories

Copyright by C. S. HAMMOND & CO., N.Y.

SCALE OF MILES

Highway Numbers
466
Superhighways

Mileages between Points
133
Time Zone Limits

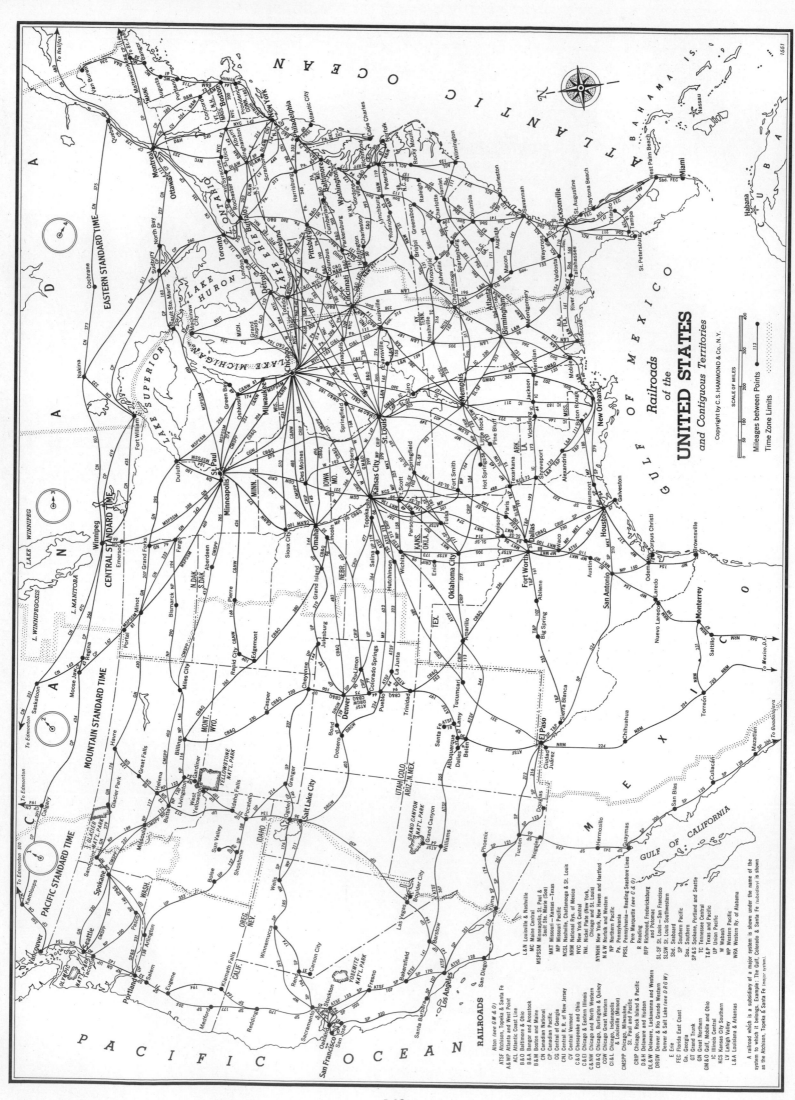

Railroads of the
UNITED STATES
and Contiguous Territories

Copyright by C. S. HAMMOND & Co. N.Y.

SCALE OF MILES

Mileages between Points
Time Zone Limits

RAILROADS

Alton (see *G M & O*)
ATSF Atchison, Topeka & Santa Fe
A&WP Atlanta and West Point
ACL Atlantic Coast Line
B&O Baltimore & Ohio
B&A Bangor and Aroostook
BM Boston and Maine
CN Canadian National
CP Canadian Pacific
CG Central of Georgia
CNJ Central R. R. of New Jersey
CV Central Vermont
C&O Chesapeake and Ohio
C&EI Chicago & Eastern Illinois
C&NW Chicago and North Western
CB&Q Chicago, Burlington & Quincy
CGW Chicago Great Western
C&IL Chicago, Indianapolis
   & Louisville (Monon)
CMSPP Chicago, Milwaukee,
   St. Paul and Pacific
CRIP Chicago, Rock Island & Pacific
D&H Delaware and Hudson
DL&W Delaware, Lackawanna and Western
DRGW Denver & Rio Grande Western
   Denver & Salt Lake (see *D R G W*)
E Erie
FEC Florida East Coast
Ga. Georgia
GT Grand Trunk
GN Great Northern
GM&O Gulf, Mobile and Ohio
IC Illinois Central
KCS Kansas City Southern
LV Lehigh Valley
L&A Louisiana & Arkansas

L&N Louisville & Nashville
MC Maine Central
MSPSSM Minneapolis, St. Paul &
   Sault Ste. Marie (Soo)
MKT Missouri—Kansas—Texas
MP Missouri Pacific
NCSL Nashville, Chattanooga & St. Louis
NRM National Rys. of Mexico
NYC New York Central
NKL Nickel Plate (New York,
   Chicago and St. Louis)
NYNHH New York, New Haven and Hartford
N&W Norfolk and Western
NP Northern Pacific
Pa. Pennsylvania
PRSL Pennsylvania—Reading Seashore Lines
   Pere Marquette (see *C & O*)
R Reading
RFP Richmond, Fredericksburg
   and Potomac
SLSF St. Louis-San Francisco
SLSW St. Louis Southwestern
Sbd. Seaboard
Sou. Southern
SP Southern Pacific
SP&S Spokane, Portland and Seattle
TC Tennessee Central
T&P Texas and Pacific
UP Union Pacific
W Wabash
WP Western Pacific
WRA Western Ry. of Alabama

A railroad which is a subsidiary of a major system is shown under the name of the system to which it belongs. Example: The Gulf, Colorado & Santa Fe (*subsidiary*) is shown as the Atchison, Topeka & Santa Fe (*major system*).

Illustrated Gazetteer of the
UNITED STATES
and Possessions

Introduction

THE AMERICAN PEOPLE are blessed with the richest and most productive homeland on the globe. Nowhere else in the world do *all* the important factors of favorable climate, level terrain, plentiful mineral resources and rich soil interract so favorably. Because of its huge size, America enjoys a climatic range that permits the growth of citrus fruit in Florida and California, wheat on the Great Plains and potatoes along the northern frontier — all within the same borders. The nation's mineral storehouse is a repository containing a vast variety of the metals and fuels so vital to an industrial economy.

This treasure house would have been worthless, however, without the brain and brawn that the American people have given with such vitality to its exploitation. The epic labors of the pioneers in transforming our homeland from an undeveloped wilderness to its present magnificent stature among the nations are familiar to all. As important as the actual physical conquest of the continent, however, is the story of the vast increase in the productivity of agriculture, mining and industry through the ever-growing use of machinery. Each person in the United States has at his command the resources of many mechanical slaves — a situation unequalled elsewhere. This has been brought about through American initiative and inventiveness which derives from the basic enterprise of our people and the unmatched productivity of our economic system.

On the following pages you will find a graphic summary of the American achievement in map, picture and text. The state resource and product maps give a vivid picture of the state's economic life, while carefully chosen illustrations present scenes of human interest. Short descriptions of the states' histories present the background to the present economic and social development of the area.

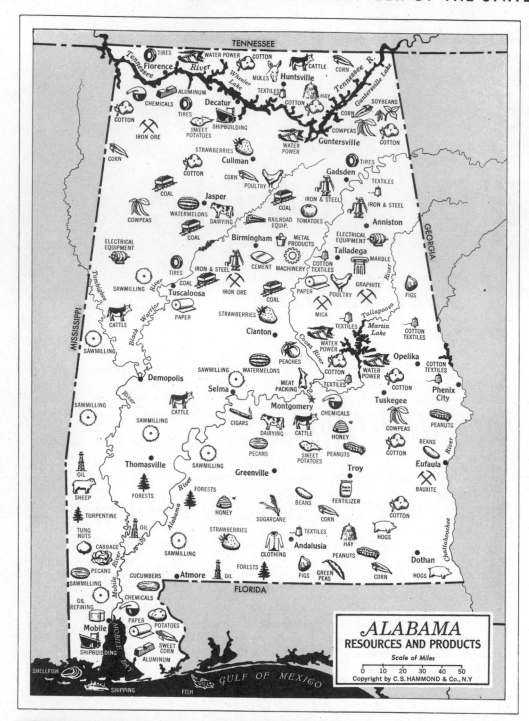

ALABAMA
RESOURCES AND PRODUCTS

Scale of Miles

0   10   20   30   40   50

Copyright by C. S. Hammond & Co., N.Y

ALABAMA

Alabama was settled by the French in 1702. Mobile, the first important town, was founded by them in 1711 as the base of operations in tapping the rich fur-bearing region of the Tombigbee and Alabama Rivers. As English traders and trappers moved in from the east, they displaced the French by offering guns and other valuable implements to the Indians. The region was ceded to the United States in 1783. The Mobile Bay area was added in 1817 by the purchase of Spanish Florida, and Alabama became a territory in the same year. It was admitted to the Union in 1819. Encroachment of the settlers and the violation of Indian rights led to the Bloody Creek wars in which Andrew Jackson gained further fame. The defeated Indians were settled in Oklahoma Territory. The state seceded from the Union on January 11, 1861, but Northwest Alabama attempted to secede from Alabama and set up the state of Nickajack. Though defeated, the "Free Winstons" sent 2,500 white and 10,000 negro soldiers to the Union Army. Of 120,000 troops mobilized in Alabama, 75,000 were lost. The defeated state was readmitted in July 1868.

Standard Oil Co. (N. J.)

▲ COTTON PICKER. Cotton is still the chief crop of Alabama.

◄ WHEELER DAM. The value of flood-control projects was dramatically shown soon after Wheeler Dam was completed in 1937. Floods of that winter swelled the Tennessee River into a mighty instrument of destruction, but Wheeler and Norris Dams held back the flood by storing millions of gallons and regulated runoff. Though agriculture is still the chief industry of Alabama, TVA is affording rapid gains in manufacturing, especially since the failure of a one-crop (cotton) system threatened the economy of the state.

Tennessee Valley Authority

ARIZONA

Pueblo ruins and aboriginal remains are found in the river basins of Arizona, notably in those of the Colorado, Little Colorado, and Gila. Arizona was explored by Spaniards from Mexico in the 16th Century. Jesuit and Franciscan missionaries labored among the Indians from the days of the early explorers until about 1820, when they finally abandoned the country because of Indian wars, and there was little attempt on the part of the Spaniards to settle the country for the same reason. American traders and explorers began to visit Arizona about 1820. As a result of the Mexican War, New Mexico, which then included all of Arizona north of the Gila, was ceded to the United States. The strip of territory known as the Gadsden Purchase was added to New Mexico in 1854. The progress of American settlement was slow and the removal of troops during the Civil War, led to the outbreak of Indian hostilities and prolonged wars. In 1861, Arizona was occupied by a Texan force and joined the Confederacy. In 1862, the Texans were driven out. In 1863, Congress organized Arizona as a territory, with the meridian of 109° W. longitude as its eastern boundary. It was admitted as a state on February 14, 1912.

HOOVER DAM. Though the largest, ▲ Hoover Dam is only one of many extensive power and irrigation projects in Arizona. In no other state is water so vitally important. Nearly all agriculture is on irrigated land.

▼ A TEEN-AGE COWBOY. The Arizona cowboy shuns the ornate regalia of California "Vaqueros" and adopts the simple habit of Texas cowhands. His riding skill is amply demonstrated in numerous rodeos, such as the annual powwow at Flagstaff.

Arizona State Highway Dep't

Arizona State Highway Dep't

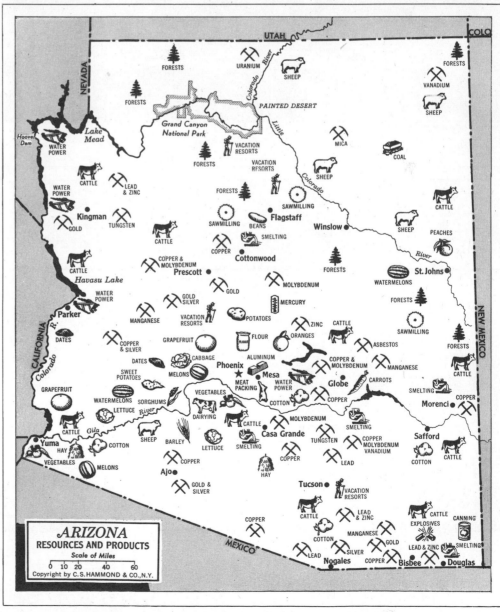

ARIZONA
RESOURCES AND PRODUCTS
Scale of Miles
0 10 20 40 60
Copyright by C.S. HAMMOND & CO., N.Y.

Arkansas Resources and Development Comm.

ARKANSAS

The first settlement of Europeans in what is now Arkansas was made by the French (1686) at Arkansas Post, important as a trading post in the earlier days of the American occupation, and the first territorial capital, 1819-20. In 1717, a grant on the Arkansas was made to John Law as a part of what turned out to be the "Mississippi Bubble"; in 1763, the territory passed to Spain; in 1800, it reverted to France, and formed a part of the French Colony of Louisiana which was purchased by the United States in 1803. It was organized as a territory in 1819, became a state in 1836, seceded in 1861, and was readmitted in 1868.

◄ HOT SPRINGS, ARKANSAS. Famed Central Avenue, winding its way through the foothills of the Ouachita Mountains, is the mecca for tourists and visitors to the spa and park area in America's oldest National Park. Its sidewalks are lined with gift and curio shops, luxurious hotels and bathhouses. Hot Springs boasts that it bathes the world, recording more than 1,000,000 baths in its hot, thermal waters annually.

▼ SACRAMENTO VALLEY ORANGE GROVES. Oranges were introduced into California in 1804, and are now the most intensively developed crop-culture in the world. The present giant industry dates from the coming of the navel orange in 1873. Today 47 million crates of oranges from 20 million trees are produced annually in California. Pest control, frost protection, irrigation and wind protection are only some of the problems accounting for the intensiveness of the industry.

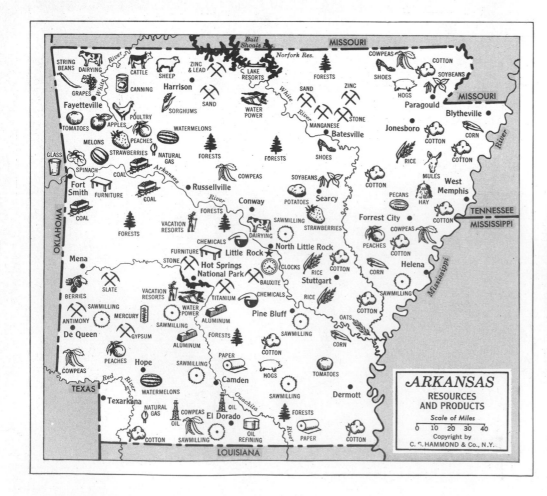

United Air Lines

CALIFORNIA

California was formerly a part of Mexico, and the Franciscan Fathers made several settlements here between 1769 and 1776. In 1846, during the war between the United States and Mexico, it was occupied by the former country and annexed by it in 1848. The gold discoveries later in 1848, caused a rush of immigrants to the territory, which in 1850 was admitted to the Union. The prosperity of the state was greatly stimulated by the opening of the Union Pacific Railway in 1869. In April, 1906, a disastrous earthquake and the resultant fires destroyed a great part of San Francisco and injured many other towns. Visitors to the Panama-Pacific Exposition, held in San Francisco in 1915, found a new and more beautiful city built upon the ruins of the old town.

TWA-Trans World Airlines

➡ GOLDEN GATE BRIDGE. Golden Gate Channel, entrance to San Francisco Bay, the world's largest landlocked harbor, is spanned by the world's longest single-span bridge (6,450 ft.). It typifies one of America's most dramatic cities.

⬇ HOLLYWOOD NIGHT VIEW. Hollywood Boulevard mirrors the splendor and wealth of the world's movie capital. The city was annexed to Los Angeles in 1910 and now forms a district in the latter metropolis. Other large industries connected with the movies and also major broadcasting companies have moved to Hollywood. California's natural grandeur in mountains, canyons, deserts and valleys is fully exploited by the movie industry.

TWA-Trans World Airline

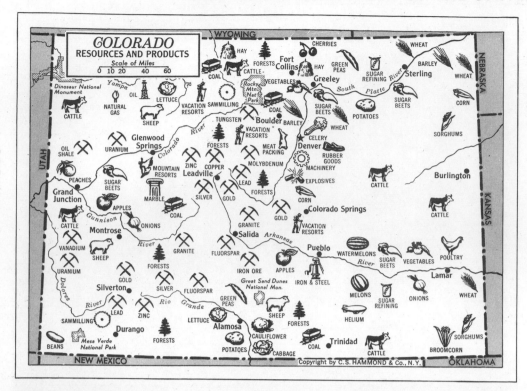

COLORADO

Within Colorado are pueblos and cave dwellings which are survivals of the Indian period and culture of the southwest. Coronado may have entered Colorado in 1540. There are records of Spanish exploration in the south in the latter half of the 18th century. In 1806, while exploring for the Federal government, Zebulon M. Pike discovered the famous peak that bears his name. From 1804 to 1854, the whole or parts of Colorado were included nominally under some half dozen territories carved successively out of the trans-Mississippi country. It was practically an unknown region when, in 1858, gold was discovered on the tributaries of the South Platte near Denver. During 1860, '61 and '62, it received a continuous stream of immigration. The territory was organized in 1861, and was admitted as a state in 1876.

Denver Rio Grande Railroad

◄ ROYAL GORGE. Perhaps the best known of Colorado's scenic and engineering wonders is Royal Gorge of the Arkansas River, spanned by the world's highest suspension bridge, 1,053 feet above the floor of the gorge. Here a colorful, violent chapter in Colorado history was written by steel rails. The Denver Rio Grande Western fought bitterly with the "Sante Fe" for control of this passage. Both lines laid rails for half the day and spent the other half ripping up their opponent's tracks. The history of settlement in Colorado is, indeed, largely the history of Colorado's railroads. Today the state is exploiting its mineral wealth, its land and great scenic beauty vigorously and progressively. Colorado looks forward to a prosperous future.

CONNECTICUT

The first settlement in Connecticut was made by English colonists on the site of Hartford in 1633. Trading and exploring parties from Massachusetts soon opened the way for the immigration into the Connecticut Valley of Puritan colonists from Dorchester, Watertown, and New Town (now Cambridge). This colony may be said to date from the secession in 1634 of the more democratic element from Massachusetts. Its constitution of 1639 was "the first written democratic constitution on record." The Royal Charter of 1662, mainly a confirmation of the older one, was superseded only in 1818 when the present state constitution was framed and adopted. Prominent events in Connecticut history were the bloody war with the Pequot Indians, 1637; the governorship of Sir Edmond Andros (during a part of which, 1687-88, the colonial charter was in abeyance), and the abolition of slavery in 1818.

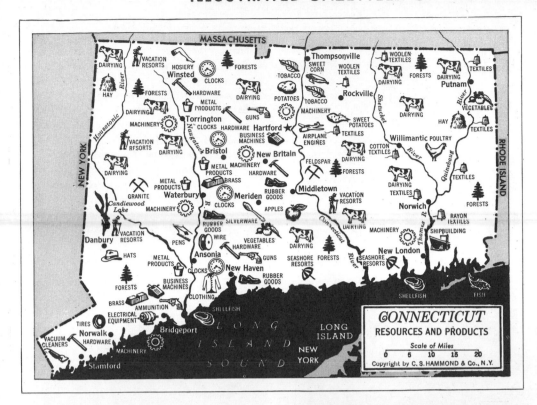

CONNECTICUT RESOURCES AND PRODUCTS
Scale of Miles
0 5 10 15 20
Copyright by C. S. HAMMOND & Co., N.Y.

▶ **SILVERCRAFT.** The skilled workmanship which goes into the making of metal ware has long been traditional in Connecticut, dating back to Revolutionary days. Supplied with a great quantity of mineral resources, Connecticut is a leader in metal products. Waterbury's clocks and Danbury's hats are nationally known. Astonishing growth has been realized in the aircraft industry, and shipbuilding continues to break records.

Connecticut Development Comm.

DELAWARE

Delaware River and Bay was explored by Henry Hudson in 1609. As a result of that voyage, the territory was claimed by the Dutch who planted a settlement near the present town of Lewes in 1631. The Dutch settlement was soon destroyed by the Indians, and the first permanent white settlements were made by Swedes and Finns in 1638; Dutch and Swedes contended for this region until 1655 when it passed under Dutch sway. After the transfer of New Netherland (New York) to the English in 1664, Delaware became English also. Though a slave state until the Civil War, Delaware took no part in the secession movement. During the Reconstruction Period Delaware entered a phase of general prosperity which resulted in the expansion of industry and transportation. Throughout its history "The First State" has contributed many outstanding figures to the national scene.

Connecticut Development Comm.

▲ **SPLITTING ROLLED BRASS.** Rolled metal is split into narrow strips from which many coins and small articles are stamped by machines. Waterbury is the U. S. center for the brass industry. Many Latin American coins, the majority of shell-casings and thousands of smaller brass or copper articles are made here. Leadership in metal working, skill and design accounts for Connecticut's industrial success.

▼ **PIGMENTS FOR PAINTS.** Delaware is dotted with chemical factories manufacturing a multitude of chemical products for industrial use throughout the country. This picture shows a hill of Ilmenite, widely used in the preparation of quality white paint. Wilmington, Delaware, is one of the chief chemical centers of the world. For such a small state, Delaware has a great diversity of important industries, including textiles, leather, canning, machinery, shipbuilding, iron and steel, buttons, paper, dental supplies and rubber hose. Of great importance to the State's commerce is the Chesapeake and Delaware Canal, built in 1829 and enlarged to accommodate ocean liners in 1919.

E. I. du Pont de Nemours & Co.

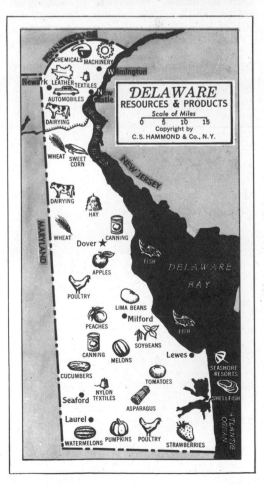

DELAWARE RESOURCES & PRODUCTS
Scale of Miles
0 5 10 15
Copyright by C. S. HAMMOND & Co., N.Y.

FLORIDA
RESOURCES AND PRODUCTS
Scale of Miles
0   20   40   60   80   100
Copyright by C. S. HAMMOND & Co., N.Y.

FLORIDA

Florida was discovered by Ponce de Leon in 1513, settled by Huguenots in 1562, and permanently settled by Spaniards in St. Augustine in 1565. It was ceded to Great Britain in 1763 and to Spain in 1783. In 1818, General Jackson invaded Florida, attacked the Seminoles, and captured Pensacola which was then restored to Spain. It was ceded to the U. S. A. in 1819. The state was admitted to the Union in 1845; seceded in 1861; was readmitted in 1868.

Florida State News Bureau

▼ **FLORIDA PHOSPHATES.** The world's largest phosphate works is at Bartow, Florida, pictured below. Phosphate production in Florida has been the highest in the country for over forty years, amounting to 79% of the national volume. Phosphate rock yields bone phosphate of lime for fertilizers; phosphoric acid, used in preserves and jellies, soft drinks, and rust-proof metals; and compound derivatives.

▲ **SHRIMPING.** Shrimp fishermen quickly toss back to the sea all the crabs, fish, seashells and even octopuses from their nets. Of 700 species of fish in Florida over 100 are edible.

▼ **BEACH SCENE.** Known as the foremost vacation spot in the eastern half of the United States, Miami Beach yearly receives thousands of tourists who stream to her health-giving shore line.

Florida State News Bureau

Florida State News Bureau

GEORGIA

Georgia, named in honor of George the Second, was settled by a chartered company of English colonists under Oglethorpe in 1733, as a refuge for poor whites and persons seeking religious freedom. Georgia became a Royal Province in 1763, and was the fourth state to ratify the Federal Constitution (January 2, 1788). It seceded in January, 1861, and was readmitted to the Union in 1870. It has experienced a rapid industrial growth.

Georgia Dept. of Commerce

▲ GRANITE QUARRY AT ELBERTON. Georgia is noted for her granite and marble quarries. At Stone Mountain is the largest exposed mass of granite in North America. This huge mountain, over a mile long and about 800 feet high, is the site of a massive Confederate memorial which is being carved into its face. Granite and marble are shipped all over the world from Georgia's quarries. One seventy-six ton block of marble was shipped from Tate to be used in the Buckingham Fountain in Chicago. Georgia also produces vast amounts of fuller's earth and commercial quantities of talc, manganese, bauxite, iron and coal. Her steady industrial growth has been made possible because of the state's diversity of raw materials.

Standard Oil Co. (N. J.)

▲ PAPER ON DRYING MACHINE. Georgia's huge yellow and slash pine forests provide raw material for an expanding paper and pulp industry.

Georgia Dept. of Commerce

▲ UNLOADING SUGAR CANE. Sugar, another of Georgia's many products, is important to her canning and preserving industries.

Standard Oil Co. (N. J.)

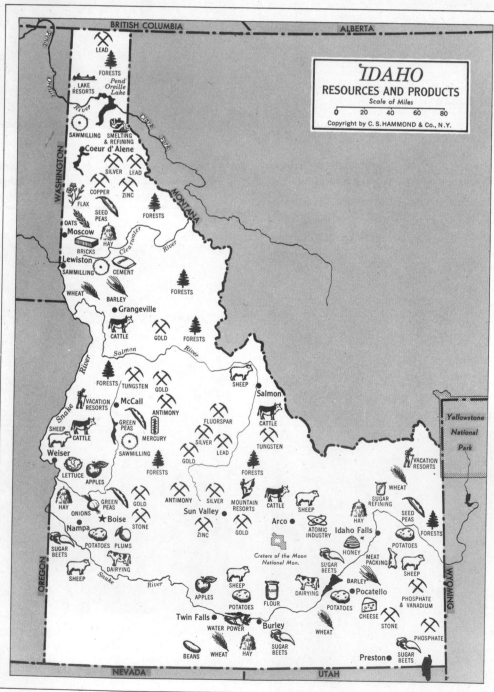

▲ PEAK IN THE LOST RIVER RANGE. The Lost River Mountains lie in a primitive area, a 1,000,000 acre tract of wilderness which is entered only by pack and by foot. This vast undeveloped playground is heavily forested with 50 lakes, countless canyons, buttes, glaciers, water falls and snow-capped peaks.

➡ SHEEP HERDER AND HIS FLOCK. Idaho provides grazing for a million sheep and four million head of cattle. Although rich in agricultural products, the state's greatest asset is in its beautiful recreational areas. Containing more lakes than have been counted or explored and high peaks perennially crowned with snow, Idaho has few scenic rivals.

IDAHO

The first recorded exploration of Idaho was made by Lewis and Clark in 1805. In 1810, Ft. Henry on the Snake River was established by the Missouri Fur Company. In 1834, Ft. Hall in east Idaho was founded. Missions for the Indians were established by both Catholics and Protestants about the same time. The territory now constituting Idaho was comprised in the territory of Oregon from 1848-53; from 1854-59, the southern portion of the present state was a part of Oregon, and the northern portion, a part of Washington Territory; from 1859-63, the territory was within the bounds of Washington Territory. Idaho was organized as a territory on March 3rd, 1863, but at that time included both Montana and Wyoming. In May, 1864, a part was set aside as Montana and in 1868, Wyoming was organized, and Idaho assumed its present boundaries. Gold was discovered in 1860, and the population of the territory rapidly increased. From 1857 to 1877 there were many serious Indian outbreaks. Later there were frequent conflicts among the miners. Idaho became a state in 1890.

ILLINOIS

The first Europeans to explore the country were French traders and missionaries. In 1675 Father Marquette founded a mission at the Indian town of Kaskaskia near the present Utica. In 1679 La Salle built Creve Coeur, a fort, not far from Lake Peoria. After 1682 the French made a number of permanent settlements which had originated in missions, or in trading posts. By the Treaty of Paris of 1763, France ceded to Great Britain her claims to the country between the Ohio and Mississippi Rivers. Owing to Indian resistance, the English were unable to take possession until 1765. The Northwest Territory, of which Illinois was a part, was secured to the United States by the Treaty of Paris of 1783. Illinois was a part of Indiana Territory in 1800; was made a separate territory in 1809; and became a state in 1818. Black Hawk's War occurred in 1832, and the Mormon troubles culminated in 1844. Slavery existed in the state until 1848. Illinois bore a notable part in the Civil War.

Standard Oil Co. (N. J.)

▼ CATTLE FEEDING. Two-thirds of farm income in Illinois is derived from livestock and three-fourths of the land is in feed crops.

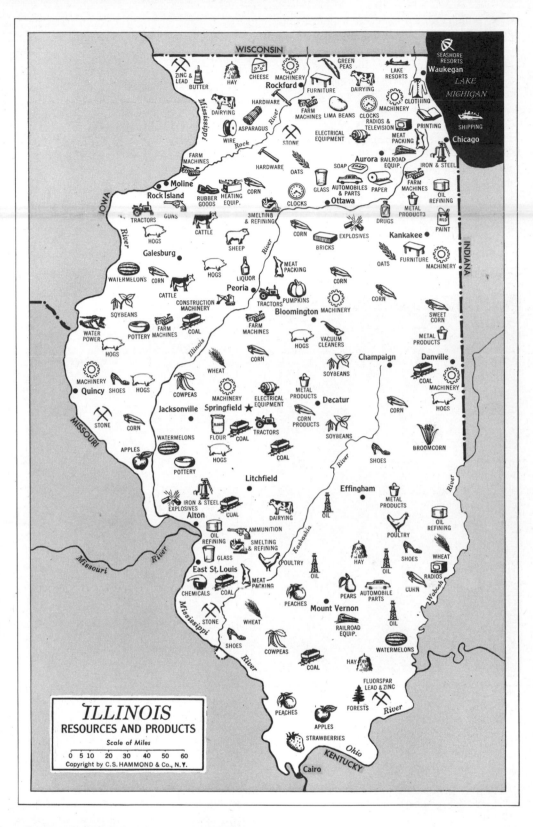

ILLINOIS RESOURCES AND PRODUCTS
Scale of Miles
0 5 10   20   30   40   50   60
Copyright by C.S. HAMMOND & Co., N.Y.

Standard Oil Co. (N. J.)

INDIANA

Extensive remains (mounds and fortifications) of the prehistoric inhabitants of Indiana are numerous in Knox and Sullivan Counties. The first Europeans to enter the state found it occupied chiefly by the tribes of the Miami Confederacy, a league of Algonquin Indians formed to oppose the advance of the Iroquois. La Salle undoubtedly passed through Indiana during his journeys of 1669 and succeeding years. Vincennes, founded in 1731, was the first permanent

white settlement; no other was made until after the War of Independence. Indiana was a part of the Northwest Territory which passed under the control of the United States in 1779, and an American settlement was made at Clarksville in 1784. The Northwest Territory was governed under the Ordinance of 1787. Indiana assumed its present limits in 1809 when it was organized as a territory. Indian wars were frequent. In 1810 began the last great Indian war in Indiana, which ended in November, 1811, with the battle of Tippecanoe when Gen. Harrison defeated the confederated Indians under Tecumseh. The territory was admitted to statehood in 1816. Slavery existed until 1830. Indiana took the Union side in the Civil War.

TWA-Trans World Airline

⬆ WRIGLEY BUILDING. Overlooking Lake Michigan, the Wrigley Building is a familiar landmark of the "Windy City", Chicago, Ill.

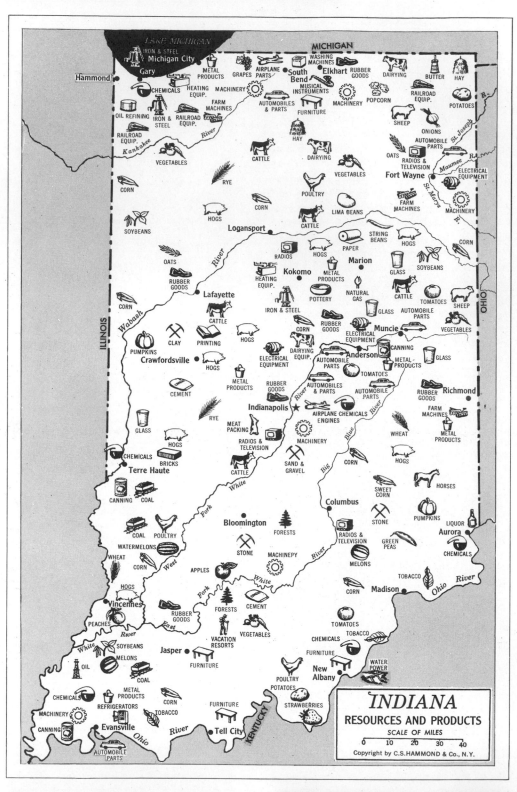

INDIANA
RESOURCES AND PRODUCTS
SCALE OF MILES
0   10   20   30   40
Copyright by C.S.HAMMOND & Co., N.Y.

Indiana Dept. of Comm. & Public Rel.

◀ WEEDING PEPPERMINT. Indiana produces more peppermint oil than any other state. Much hand labor is required to keep the fields free of obnoxious weeds.

➡ PREPARING TILE FOR THE KILN. The State's almost unlimited deposits of clay, sand and gravel are used in the making of cement, glass, pottery and brick. The topography of Indiana is marked by definite contrasts. The roll of the western prairie begins in "The Hoosier State," while the northern and central portions are fertile farm regions. Lakes and sloping hills grace the northeastern area. Such physical diversity creates a happy balance between agriculture and industry.

Indiana Dept. of Comm. & Public Rel.

Iowa Development Comm.

Iowa Development Comm.

Iowa Development Comm.

▲ SPLITTING BEEF INTO SIDES. Excepting general farming and livestock raising, meat packing is Iowa's largest industry with thirty-eight packing plants employing over 15,000 workers. The annual income of the industry is over $500,000,000.

◄ IOWA CORN. Iowa produces 20% of the nation's total corn yield. In 1952 Iowa farmers realized their biggest corn crop in history, over 680 million bushels or their first billion dollar crop.

▲ GYPSUM MINING. The United States is the world's leading producer of gypsum. Plentiful natural deposits, in Iowa and elsewhere, make it the least expensive of raw materials. Its uses are chiefly confined to the manufacture of plaster and other building materials. Iowa's mineral resources and fertile soil provide the basis for a continually growing economy. In recent years an attempt to stem the injurious effects of erosion has resulted in the reclamation of much unarable land.

IOWA

The first white men to visit Iowa were the Frenchmen, Marquette and Joliet, in 1673, and Hennepin in 1680. They found the country occupied by a tribe of Sioux Indians from which came the name of the state, "Iowa." With the Louisiana Purchase, 1803, the territory became the property of the United States. From 1804-05, as part of the District of Louisiana, it was under the government of Indiana Territory; from 1805-12, it was part of Louisiana Territory; from 1812-21, part of Missouri Territory; from 1821-34, part of the unorganized territory of the United States; from 1834-36, part of Michigan Territory; and from 1836-38, part of Wisconsin Territory. In 1838, the western portion of Wisconsin Territory was named "Iowa" and out of this, the state, with its present boundaries, was carved in 1846.

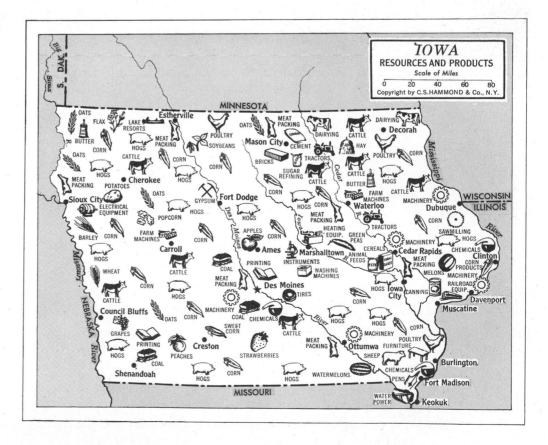

IOWA
RESOURCES AND PRODUCTS
Scale of Miles
0   20   40   60   80
Copyright by C.S.HAMMOND & Co., N.Y.

Standard Oil Co. (N. J.)

KANSAS

Kansas was a part of the Louisiana Purchase (1803), and was colonized by both free and slave state settlers. It was made a territory in 1854, and at once became the battleground between the partisans of slavery and freedom. A bloody civil war broke out, in which many almost-battles took place. One of the most ardent of the anti-slavery partisans was John Brown. The Topeka Constitution, prohibiting slavery, was framed in 1855 and the Lecompton Constitution, sanctioning slavery, in 1857. The Wyandotte Constitution, forbidding slavery, was adopted in 1859, and Kansas was admitted as a free state in 1861. It took a prominent part in the Civil War.

◄ AERIAL VIEW OF KANSAS CITY. Railroad freight cars wait alongside filled grain elevators. Kansas, after the first decade of immigration, was settled by means of a railroad expansion plan. Because of this, the State has always had adequate transportation from farm to market. Grain elevators form the point of convergence for the scattered wheat-growing areas. The grain is stored in the elevators until freight cars carry it to the mills.

▼ PORTABLE DRILLING RIG. The state of Kansas is fourth in the output of oil and great industries have arisen near its source. The land is equally rich in deposits of zinc, coal, salt and building stone. Such raw materials are converted into a thousand commercial items by over three thousand manufacturing plants.

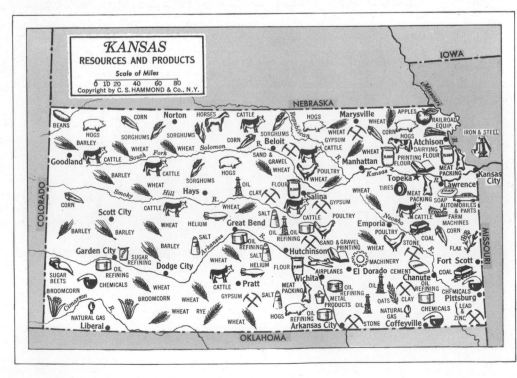

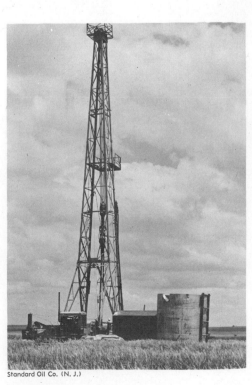

Standard Oil Co. (N. J.)

KENTUCKY

Numerous historic remains indicate that the mound-builders once lived in this territory. The name Kentucky, meaning "dark and bloody ground," commemorates the conflicts between various tribes of Indians. Kentucky was explored by Dr. Thomas Walker in 1750, by John Finley in 1767, and by Daniel Boone in 1769; was settled at Harrodsburg in 1774; was formed into a county of Virginia in 1776; was admitted to the Union in 1792; was distinguished in the War of 1812 and in the Mexican War; was a slave state, but did not secede; was occupied by Federals and Confederates in 1861; was the scene of campaigns and raids.

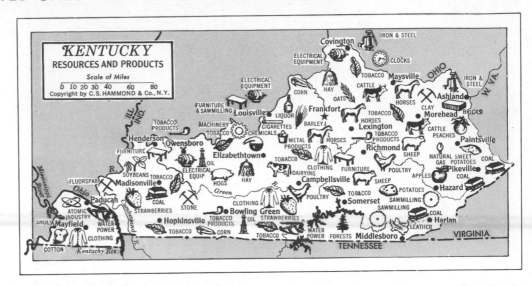

KENTUCKY RESOURCES AND PRODUCTS

E. L. du Pont de Nemours & Co.

◀ SYNTHETIC RUBBER. Neoprene (man-made rubber) is processed in Louisville, Kentucky. Other world-famous Kentucky products are tobacco products, hemp and cotton.

▼ RAW SUGAR. The raw sugar shown here is a product of Louisiana's cane fields. Ninety per cent of the nation's cane sugar is from the "sugar bowl" of southeastern Louisiana.

Standard Oil Co. (N. J.)

LOUISIANA RESOURCES AND PRODUCTS

LOUISIANA

Louisiana was explored by De Soto in 1541, and by La Salle in 1682; was settled by the French under Iberville and Bienville about 1700. The latter founded the city of New Orleans on its present site in 1718. In 1717, Louisiana was granted to a company, of which John Law was the head, but in 1731, reverted to the crown; was ceded by France to Spain in 1763, but in 1800 again became French territory. It was purchased by the United States in 1803 and was created the Territory of Orleans in 1804; had the portion east of the Mississippi annexed in 1810; was admitted to the Union in 1812; seceded in January, 1861; occupied by the Federals 1862-63; readmitted in 1868.

MAINE
RESOURCES AND PRODUCTS
Scale of Miles
0   10   20   30   40   50
Copyright by C. S. HAMMOND & Co., N.Y.

Standard Oil Co. (N. J.)

▲ TURTLES. Familiar natives of Louisiana are these small turtles commonly sold as household pets. Their eggs are deposited and hatched beneath the earth which makes discovery of the nests difficult. Each year thousands are shipped to different parts of the U. S.

MARYLAND

Maryland, through the grant made by Charles I to George Calvert, first Lord Baltimore, became a proprietary colony, and its settlement was begun at St. Mary's, in 1634. During colonial times, it was involved in the Claiborne rebellion and in boundary and other disputes. In 1649, religious toleration was enacted for all sects and churches which acknowledged a belief in the Trinity. For many years, the colony was torn by quarrels between the proprietary party and Puritan settlers. There was a time when Roman Catholics were denied the privileges which Lord Baltimore had granted to Protestants. The city of Baltimore was founded in 1729. The boundary with Pennsylvania was finally settled, 1763-69, by Charles Mason and Jeremiah Dixon, who established the line named after them, which runs along the parallel 39° 43' 26.3" N. lat.

MAINE

Maine was visited by many of the early explorers, including the Cabots, Verrazano, Gomez, Gosnold, Pring, du Guast, De Monts, and others. The first permanent settlement, at Bristol, dates from 1624. The eastern part of the state was a part of Acadia or Nova Scotia until 1691, at which time the whole region was merged in the "province of Massachusetts Bay." Maine became a separate state in 1820. A dispute with Great Britain over the northern boundary of the state was settled by the Webster-Ashburton Treaty in 1842. The Maine liquor law, the first state law on the subject, was passed in 1851. In World War I, Maine contributed a larger proportion of men (on a population basis) than any other state.

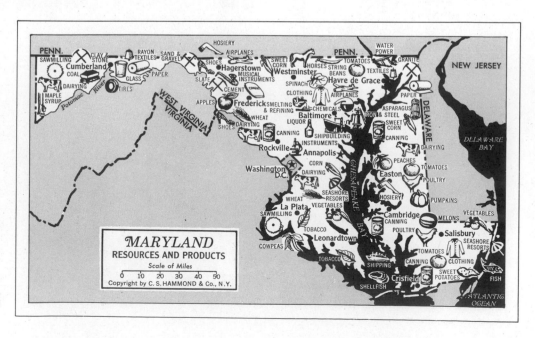

MARYLAND
RESOURCES AND PRODUCTS
Scale of Miles
0   10   20   30   40   50
Copyright by C. S. HAMMOND & Co., N.Y.

▲ MAINE HARBOR. The rocky coast of Maine, with its various vacation spots, is provided with many natural harbors. Known for its invigorating climate, the State offers ideal facilities for the sportsman and tourist.

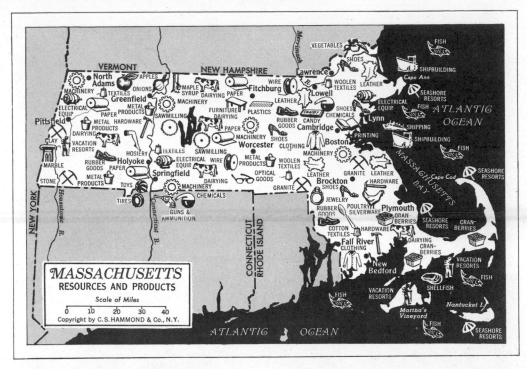

MASSACHUSETTS
RESOURCES AND PRODUCTS
Scale of Miles
0   10   20   30   40
Copyright by C. S. HAMMOND & Co., N.Y.

MASSACHUSETTS

The coast of Massachusetts is supposed to have been visited by the Norsemen about 1000 A.D.; but the first permanent white settlement was made by the Pilgrim Fathers at Plymouth, on the coast north of Cape Cod, in December, 1620. This was known as the Plymouth Colony. In 1628, a company of Puritans settled at Salem, and from that beginning was formed the Massachusetts Bay Colony which included the settlements of Boston, Lynn, and other towns. In 1692, the two colonies were united.

The early history of Massachusetts is the inspiring heritage of much of America. The state was settled by men seeking liberty for tneir own form of religious worship and intolerant of all other forms. However, they were far ahead of their European contemporaries; gradually that bigotry diminished and religious tolerance grew; the state became a leader in all that stood for liberty. The War of Independence began in Massachusetts in 1775, with the battles of Lexington and Bunker Hill.

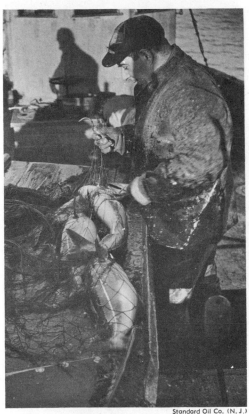

Standard Oil Co. (N. J.)

▲ FISHING IN GLOUCESTER. The fishermen above are busy freeing fish from the nets. Their boats, battered by the stormy seas of the iceberg-infested Grand Banks, bring in codfish for food, fertilizer, glue and isinglass. Once the leading industry of Massachusetts, fishing has left the foreground to be supplanted by a wide variety of other industries.

➤ OIL REFINERY. Not a Martian city, but the propane section of a Baltimore oil refinery. Oil refining, like other huge industries, has come to Baltimore because it is a key transportation center. Chesapeake Bay, in turn, provides the international outlet.

Standard Oil Co. (N. J.)

The Kellogg Co.

MICHIGAN

What is now the state of Michigan was probably visited by Jean Nicolet in 1634 at Sault Ste. Marie where the first permanent white settlement was made by Father Marquette in 1668. In 1701 Detroit was founded as a fur trading center by the French. The country was ceded to Great Britain in 1763; later was the scene of Pontiac's War; was surrendered to the United States in 1796; formed part of the Northwest Territory and later of Indiana Territory; and was constituted Michigan Territory in 1805. Detroit was taken by the British during the War of 1812, Michigan was recovered by the United States in 1813, and was admitted to the Union in 1837.

◄CEREAL PLANT. Much of Michigan's cereal grain is converted into the nation's traditional breakfast foods. The commercial need for cereal grain by such a company as Kellogg has accounted for an ever-increasing rise in the State's agricultural output. Other staple foods like corn, oats and beans form the mainstay of the State's agrarian economy. Additional crops of celery, onions and an abundant yield of strawberries and cantaloupes place Michigan among the leading farm areas of the United States.

▼ STEEL MILLS. A view of the steel mills in Dearborn, Michigan. Michigan, surrounded by the greatest inland waterway in the world and containing large mineral and timber resources, has become one of the most highly industrialized regions in the world. Michigan has created more manufacturing industries than could be named here. Probably the best known is that of the automobile. Of approximately 60 other industries, furniture, paper, chemicals, cereals, stoves and machinery are the largest.

MICHIGAN
RESOURCES AND PRODUCTS
Scale of Miles
Copyright by C.S. HAMMOND & Co., N.Y.

Standard Oil Co. (N. J.)

MINNESOTA

Before the coming of Europeans, Minnesota was occupied by two powerful Indian tribes, the Ojibways (or Chippewas) in the north and along the Mississippi River, and the Sioux (or Dakotas) in the south and west. The region was first explored by the French near the end of the 17th century. That part of Minnesota which lies east of the Mississippi River belonged to the Northwest Territory, acquired by the United States in 1783. West of the Mississippi, it was a part of the Louisiana Purchase of 1803. In 1838, the Chippewa Indians surrendered the land east of the Mississippi. Immigration began: Minnesota became a territory in 1849, and a state in 1858. In 1862 occurred a terrible massacre by the Sioux Indians, finally defeated in 1864.

Standard Oil Co. (N. J.)

▲ IRON ORE MINE. The Susquehanna mine near Hibbing, Minnesota is the largest in the world. It is a mile wide and has 55 miles of track. Minnesota supplies nearly three-quarters of the total production of iron ore of the United States. The State also has millions of acres of forest and 10,000 lakes which makes it one of the nation's major vacation areas.

➤ LOADING GRAIN. Grain-loading from elevators in the Duluth-Superior harbor. Minnesota is a world center for flour-milling. The State is also famous for its meat, butter and cheese. With much tillable land, it is one of the world's great agricultural regions. Strangely enough, coffee roasting is a large industry in Minnesota. Other products include paper, machinery, cement and glass.

Standard Oil Company (N. J.)

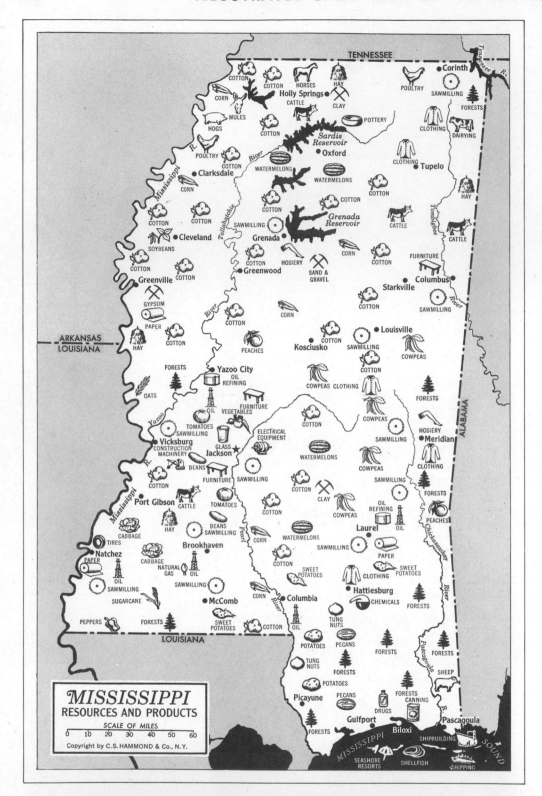

MISSISSIPPI
RESOURCES AND PRODUCTS
SCALE OF MILES
0 10 20 30 40 50 60
Copyright by C.S. HAMMOND & Co., N.Y.

Standard Oil Company (N. J.)

MISSISSIPPI

Mississippi was visited by De Soto in 1540. The Mississippi River was explored by Marquette and La Salle in 1681. An attempt was made at settlement by the French at Iberville in 1699, and a settlement was made on the site of Natchez in 1716. It was ceded by France to Great Britain in 1763; part was ceded to the United States in 1783; the remainder was acquired in 1811. Mississippi was organized as a territory in 1798, and was admitted to the Union as a state in 1817. It seceded in 1861; was the scene of various conflicts during the Civil War; was readmitted to the Union in 1870. In the Mississippi River flood of 1927 more than $45,000,000 worth of property and crops was destroyed.

Mississippi A. & I. Board

▲ THE GULF COAST. Few areas of the South have a more colorful and varied history than the Gulf Coast. Seven flags have flown over the territory since 1699. The influence of the French, Spanish and English is still evident in architecture, customs and Old World symbols of its two and a half centuries of history. Early Spanish and Civil War forts, presidential homes, legendary pirate hide-outs and Indian myths are all part of the highly interesting Gulf Coast story. Today, Biloxi, a major city on the Gulf Coast, is the scene of an annual regatta in which many outstanding yachtsmen participate to vie for its coveted trophies.

◄ MECHANICAL PICKER. The mechanical cotton-pickers, shown operating in Delta County, Mississippi, have set off the spark of much dispute among the hand-pickers of cotton. The machine requires an evenly-grown crop and dry fields. Because of its high cost, it can only be used on large plantations. Recent improvement may bring about its wider use.

MISSOURI

The territory included in the present state of Missouri formed part of the French colony of Louisiana. Ste. Genevieve was settled in 1735, and Ft. Orleans on the Missouri River, had been temporarily established in 1720, but few others were made before the transfer of Louisiana to Spain in 1763. St. Louis was founded in 1764. It was ceded back to France in 1800; formed part of the Louisiana Purchase of 1803; and was included in Louisiana Territory in 1805. Missouri Territory was formed in 1812, and admitted to the Union as a slave state in 1821. The state did not receive its present limits until 1835. In the Kansas troubles of 1855, the citizens of the western border took an active part against the free state movement. At the outbreak of the Civil War in 1861, the people of Missouri were divided with regard to secession, but the unionists finally prevailed. A world's fair was held in St. Louis in 1904 to commemorate the Louisiana Purchase.

Standard Oil Company (N. J.)

▲ FARMLANDS. The undulating upland region of Missouri rises to the west and forms a level land which is devoted to the raising of wheat and livestock. Winding rivers from the highlands cut across the fertile plains.

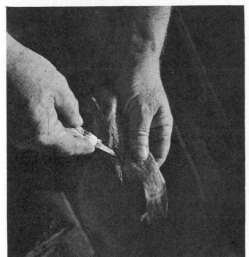

Standard Oil Co. (N. J.)

▲ CAT FISH. Quiet waters of Missouri's Ozark Hills provide a catch for an old-fashioned fish-fry.

▼ MISSOURI MULE. The Missouri mule is known for its exceptional quality and fine breeding.

Standard Oil Co. (N. J.)

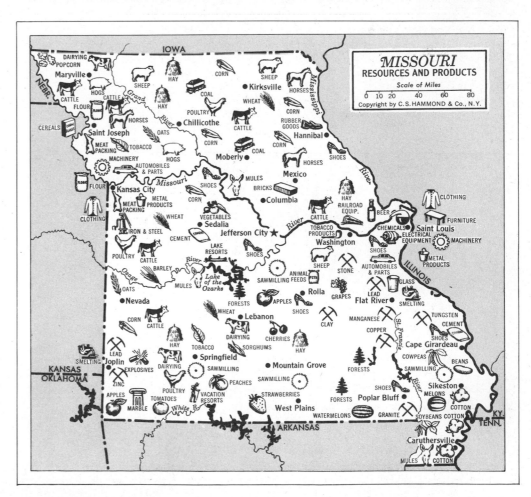

MONTANA

The portion of Montana east of the Rocky Mountains was part of the Louisiana Purchase (1803); that to the west was part of Oregon and Washington. It was first visited by the French in 1742, and by Lewis and Clark in 1804-06; these explorers were followed by fur traders, trappers and Jesuit missionaries. The part of Montana which was included in the Louisiana Purchase became successively a part of Missouri Territory (1812), of Nebraska Territory (1854), of Dakota Territory (1861), and of Idaho Territory (1863); that which lies west of the mountains became successively a part of Oregon (1848), of Washington Territory (1853), and of Idaho Territory (1863). Gold was discovered in 1861. In 1864, the territory was organized and in 1889 Montana became a state of the Union.

Montana Highway Dept.

Montana Highway Dept.

▲ LEWIS AND CLARK CAVERN. The beautiful Lewis and Clark Cavern, near Bozeman, was discovered when a prospector decided to find out how an eagle disappeared into a mountainside. The Paradise Room is shown above Montana's varied topography ranges from emerald-like meadows in the east to raging cascades and towering mountains in the west.

▲ COPPER SMELTER. Montana and copper are so closely associated that often injustice is done to all the other vast wealth of the "Treasure State." One-sixth of the world's copper and one-third of the United States' supply is Montana-mined. The smelter shown above is in the Butte-Anaconda area where nearly all the copper is located. Montana yields half of the nation's supply of arsenic, and ranks next to the continent of Australia in sapphire production. It leads all other states in manganese. Of the latter, Montana's mines produce forty-three per cent of the nation's supply.

➤ WHITEFACED STEERS. Western Nebraska is a cattleman's country. Cattle is the State's leading product. Often livestock are grazed in the west but later sent east to the Omaha area for fattening.

NEBRASKA

French explorers followed the Platte River (or the Nebraska) to the Forks, in 1739. Nebraska passed to the United States in 1803 as part of the Louisiana Purchase, and was explored by several American expeditions. Several trading posts were probably established between 1795 and 1812. In 1823 Bellevue became an Indian agency, and later was the first postoffice in the state. Nebraska was one of the two territories created by the Kansas-Nebraska Bill of 1854. Slaves were within its borders from the beginning, but a territorial law of 1861 excluded slavery. As organized in 1854, Nebraska extended from 40° N. latitude to British America, and from the Missouri and White Earth Rivers to the summit of the Rockies; it was reduced to its present boundaries in 1861 and 1863. The state was torn by bitter factional quarrels over the location of the capital and admission to statehood, and during part of 1866 and 1867, there were two de facto governments—the territorial and the state. It was admitted to the Union in 1867.

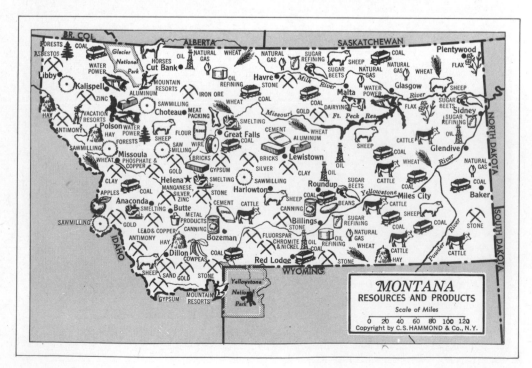

MONTANA
RESOURCES AND PRODUCTS
Scale of Miles
0 20 40 60 80 100 120
Copyright by C.S. HAMMOND & Co., N.Y.

NEVADA

Francisco Garces, a Franciscan monk, passed through the state on his way to California in 1775. Some fifty years later, American and Canadian trappers worked along the Humboldt River. Many overland immigrants, on their way to California, crossed Nevada in the early '40's. In 1843-45, Fremont made a series of explorations in this region. In 1848, by the Treaty of Guadalupe-Hidalgo which concluded the war with Mexico, Nevada became United States territory. It was known as the Washoe Country, California, until September, 1850, when most of the present state was included in the territory of Utah. The first settlement in what is now the state of Nevada was made at Genoa in the valley of the Carson River in 1849. In 1859 the discovery of the fabulous "Comstock Lode" brought thousands of people into the territory. In March, 1861, the territory of Utah was divided at 39° west of Washington, and the western portion called Nevada was admitted as a state in 1864. In 1931, the legislature passed a bill permitting divorces to those establishing a six-weeks residence, and another bill legalizing gambling. The famous Hoover Dam was built across the Colorado River in 1936.

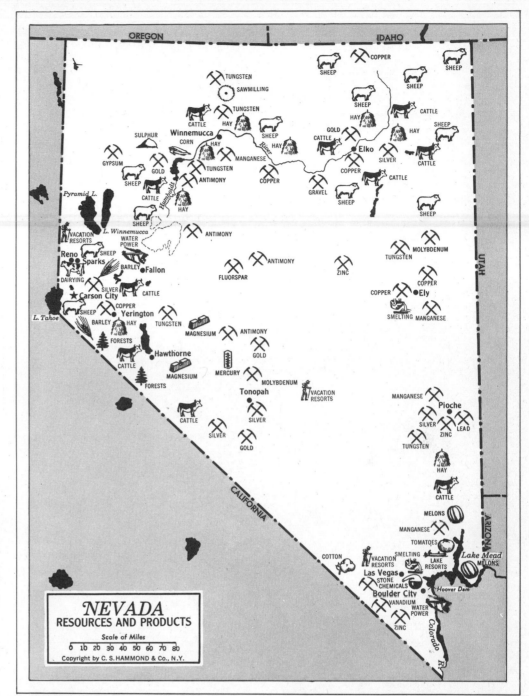

NEVADA
RESOURCES AND PRODUCTS
Scale of Miles

0 10 20 30 40 50 60 70 80

Copyright by C. S. HAMMOND & Co., N.Y.

Standard Oil Co. (N. J.)

➤ INDUSTRIAL SCENE at Henderson, Nev.

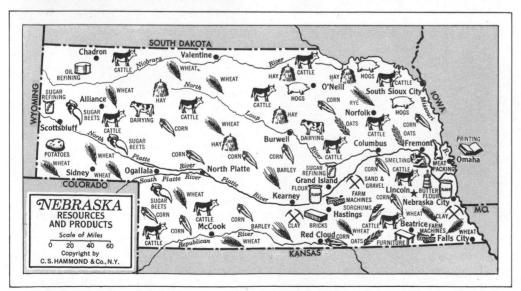

NEBRASKA
RESOURCES AND PRODUCTS
Scale of Miles

0 20 40 60

Copyright by
C. S. HAMMOND & Co., N.Y.

Nevada Dept. of Highways

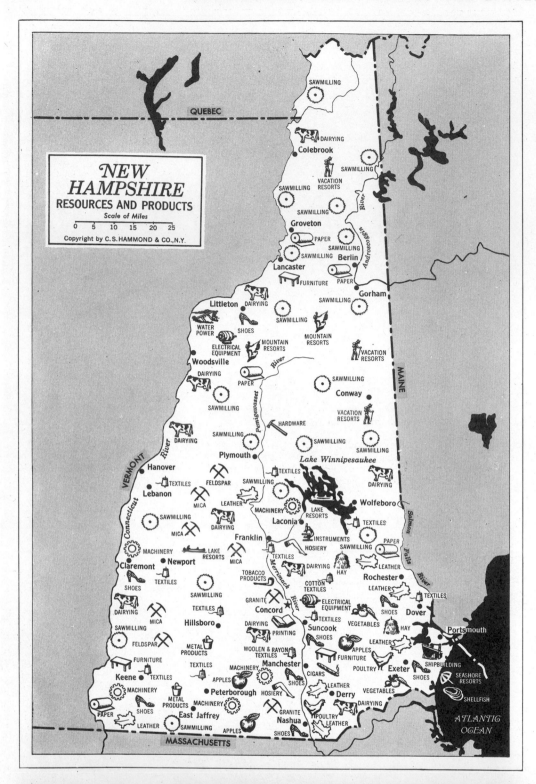

NEW HAMPSHIRE
RESOURCES AND PRODUCTS
Scale of Miles
0 5 10 15 20 25
Copyright by C.S. HAMMOND & CO., N.Y.

NEW HAMPSHIRE

Among the early explorers who visited New Hampshire were Martin Pring (1603), Samuel de Champlain (1605), and Captain John Smith (1614). The first settlement, of which there is positive evidence, was made in 1623 by David Thomson at Little Harbor, now in the town of Rye. In 1641-79, 1689-92, and 1699-1741, New Hampshire was joined to the Massachusetts Colony; but during the intervening dates and until 1775, it was under royal governors of its own. A provisional government was formed in 1776, a state constitution adopted in 1784, and New Hampshire was the ninth state to ratify the National Constitution in 1788. During the 19th century the state became involved in the Northeastern Boundary Dispute with Great Britain, which was finally settled by Daniel Webster in the famous Webster-Ashburton Treaty of 1842. New Hampshire gained national attention in 1852, when Franklin Pierce was elected president, the first and only chief executive to come from New Hampshire.

White Mts. Region Ass'n

▲ AERIAL TRAMWAY. The Cannon Mountain Aerial Tramway carries passengers 2,000 feet up for high-level skiing near Franconia Notch, N. H. The State is one of the most popular winter recreational areas in the world. "Snowtrains" run from Eastern cities to bring huge out-of-state crowds to attend winter carnivals, ice-boating, sled-dog racing and ski meets.

Standard Oil Company (N. J.)

◄ NEW HAMPSHIRE COWS. Rich pasturage affords New Hampshire with ideal facilities for raising dairy cows. Milk and by-products are shipped by rail to eastern markets where they are purchased in wholesale quantities. Hay, too, is an important crop and is harvested in large amounts.

► **CHEMICAL PLANT.** Typical of New Jersey's expanding industry is this chemical plant at Deepwater which manufactures organic compounds for the many other industrial companies of the state.

▼ **AERONAUTICAL PRODUCTION.** New Jersey is among the nation's foremost producers of aircraft engines. Factories in northern New Jersey, such as this one at Wood-Ridge, turn out some of the country's finest precision-built aeronautical parts and equipment.

E. I. du Pont de Nemours & Co.

Curtiss-Wright Corp.

NEW JERSEY

Voyages made with a view to exploration and settlement of the region now called New Jersey may be said to have begun with the voyage of Henry Hudson in 1609. The English claim to the territory was founded on the voyage of Cabot in 1498. The Dutch settled at Bergen in 1617. Soon after, some Swedes settled on the lower Delaware but were expelled by the Dutch in 1655. In 1664, New Netherland passed to the English, and the Duke of York gave the portion included in the present New Jersey to Lord Berkeley and Sir George Carteret. The latter had been administrator of the Island of Jersey, so the American province was named New Jersey. In 1676 the province was divided into West and East New Jersey, the former being under a Quaker proprietorship and the latter under Carteret. West New Jersey soon passed to William Penn who, in 1682, purchased East New Jersey also. In 1702 the government of both colonies passed to the Crown and the two were united. Until 1736, New Jersey was under the governor of New York, but had a separate assembly. New Jersey was one of the original thirteen states and was the scene of stirring events in the struggle for independence. The Morristown National Historical Park, established by Congress in 1933, commemorates some of these events.

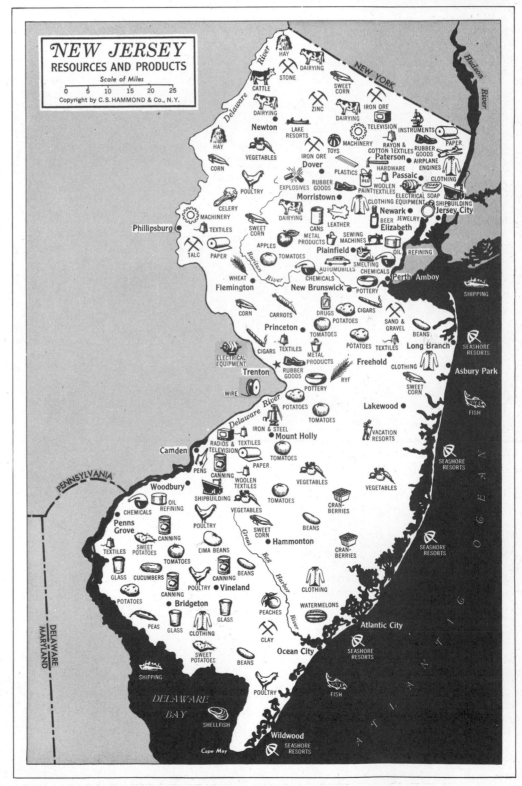

NEW JERSEY RESOURCES AND PRODUCTS

Scale of Miles

Copyright by C.S. HAMMOND & Co., N.Y.

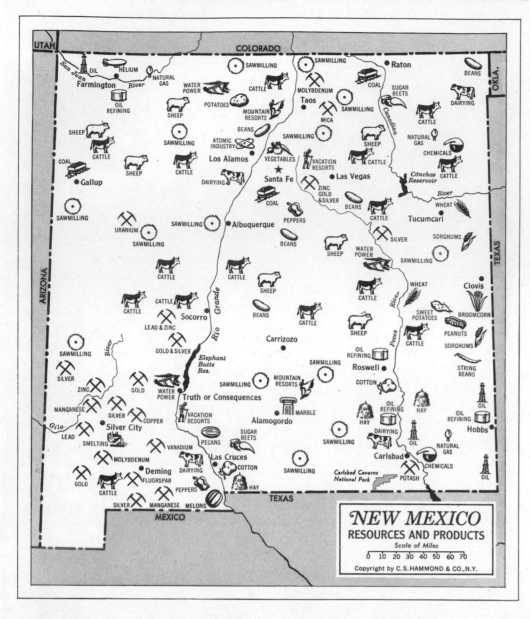

NEW MEXICO
RESOURCES AND PRODUCTS
Scale of Miles
0 10 20 30 40 50 60 70
Copyright by C.S. HAMMOND & CO., N.Y.

NEW MEXICO

New Mexico was explored by Spaniards from Mexico at various times between 1536 and 1581. Between 1583 and 1595, several attempts at the conquest and occupation of New Mexico were made but were unsuccessful. Santa Fe, which occupies a site nearly 7,000 ft. in elevation, is, after St. Augustine, Florida, the oldest town in the United States, dating from 1605. An Indian revolt in 1680 resulted in the massacre of over 400 Spanish settlers and the capture of Santa Fe but in 1692 the Spaniards regained their hold on the territory, and European occupation was assured. The history of New Mexico, during the 18th century, was uneventful. After the achievement of Mexican independence in 1821, New Mexico became successively a province, a territory, and a department of that country. It was ceded to the United States by the Treaty of Guadalupe-Hidalgo in 1848. Previous to that time, American traders had been active in the territory and after that date, the settlement of the region by Americans progressed steadily. The territorial form of government was provided by Congress in 1850 and was inaugurated on the 3rd of March, 1851. Its area was increased by the Gadsden Purchase from Mexico and by the Texan cession of the country lying east of the Rio Grande. New Mexico assumed its present boundaries in 1863. It was admitted to the Union as a state in January, 1912. In 1915 and 1916, frequent raids of New Mexico villages by Mexican bandits caused strained relations between Mexico and the United States.

New Mexico State Tourist Bur.

▲ COPPER MINE. The Santa Rita, one of New Mexico's most productive copper mines, was worked as far back as 1800 by the Spaniards. The State's mineral deposits are abundant, and include zinc, silver and some iron ore.

➤ WHITE SANDS. A wide desert area of 270 square miles, White Sands has become the site of our national rocket experimentation program. The Sands, situated west of Alamagordo, is one of New Mexico's numerous natural wonders.

New Mexico State Tourist Bur.

NEW YORK

Before the coming of Europeans, the territory now known as New York was occupied by the Iroquois Indians (Five Nations). New York Bay was entered by Verrazano in 1524. In 1609, Samuel de Champlain, the French explorer, penetrated the northeastern part of the state, and Henry Hudson, an Englishman in the service of the Netherlands, explored the Hudson River as far as the present site of Albany. A few years later (1613-14) settlements were made by the Dutch on Manhattan Island, and the region was called New Netherlands. Among the early Dutch governors were Minuit, Wouter van Twiller, Kieft, and Stuyvesant. New Amsterdam (New York City) was founded in 1623. The Dutch colony was devastated by an Indian war in 1641. England, basing her demands on the Cabot voyages, claimed New Netherlands, forced its surrender and renamed it New York. New York, New Jersey, and New England were consolidated under Andros in 1686-89. New York was the scene of many events in the French and Indian Wars, and of Burgoyne's surrender (1777) and other events in the Revolutionary War and the War of 1812. The completion of the Erie Canal in 1825 led to a rapid development of western New York and all of the states carved from the old Northwest Territory. New York City was the capital of the United States from 1785-90, and the state capital from 1784-97.

▼ NEW YORK SKYLINE. Truly an American mecca, New York City, cultural and commercial focal point of the nation, is an example of the dynamism which is expressive of American civilization. With a population of almost eight million, it counts among its inhabitants the most diversified elements of any American city. Both artisan and artist find the great metropolis the logical center for the full employment and appreciation of their respective talents.

Standard Oil Co. (N. J.)

▲ BROOKLYN BRIDGE. Familiar landmark for New Yorkers is Brooklyn's famous bridge. At one time the longest suspension bridge in the world, it has been superseded by the more modern structures of which it was a forerunner.

TWA-Trans World Airline

NORTH CAROLINA

Unsuccessful attempts were made to colonize the Carolina region under the auspices of Sir Walter Raleigh in 1584-87. The first permanent English settlement was made by Virginians at Albemarle on the Chowan River, about 1660. The territory was granted to proprietors in 1663 and 1665. An attempt was made to introduce a constitution framed by Shaftsbury and Locke in 1669 but it ended in failure. A Royal Province was formed in 1728 when North and South Carolina were separated. The "Mecklenburg Declaration of Independence" was passed in 1775; it is claimed that this document formed the model for the Declaration of 1776. North Carolina was the scene of several battles in the Revolution (1780-81); rejected the United States Constitution in 1788, but adopted it in 1789; seceded May 20, 1861. It was the scene of various engagements and military operations in the Civil War. It was readmitted to the Union in July, 1868.

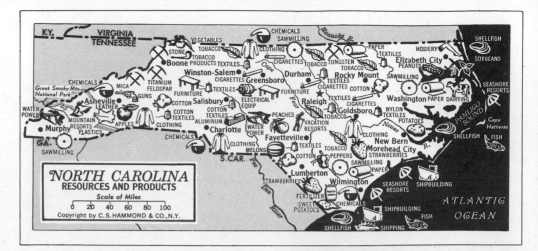

NORTH CAROLINA
RESOURCES AND PRODUCTS
Scale of Miles
0   20   40   60   80   100
Copyright by C.S. Hammond & Co., N.Y.

Standard Oil Co. (N. J.)

HANGING TOBACCO. As one of the principal commercial crops, tobacco has long been one of North Carolina's agricultural assets. Contributing greatly to the South's tobacco monopoly, the local producers are proud of their "bright leaf" variety. The flue-cured tobacco is taken from the curing barn as shown in the picture on the right, is graded, tied into bundles, and then sold at auction. The buyer re-dries the tobacco and stores it for aging. North Carolina is the world's largest producer of tobacco.

PULP MILL. Among North Carolina's other industries lumber-processing is notable. Through a well-planned forestry program, the State has managed to develop an adequate lumber supply; and takes special precautions to replace and cultivate all trees which are essential to proper soil conservation. Forests cover fifty per cent of North Carolina and furnish many different wood types. Oak, poplar, ash and hickory grow in the mountain region, while pine predominates on the coastal plain.

Standard Oil Co. (N. J.)

NORTH DAKOTA

North Dakota was visited by traders of the Hudson Bay Company late in the 18th Century. It was part of the region ceded by France in the Louisiana Purchase of 1803. It was successively a part of the District of Louisiana, of the Louisiana Territory, the Missouri Territory, the Territory of Michigan, Wisconsin Territory, Iowa Territory, and Minnesota Territory. The first permanent settlement was made by Scottish Highlanders at Pembina in 1812. They had formerly been located at Winnipeg and thought their new settlement was in British territory. The Territory of Dakota was created in 1861 and included the present Dakotas and portions of Wyoming and Montana. In 1863, the boundaries of the Dakotas were fixed at practically their present limits. The settlement of the territory was impeded by the Civil War and by Indian hostilities. Rapid development began in 1872; the territory was divided into North and South Dakota, and both entered the Union as states in 1889. Many advanced social and economic experiments have been made in North Dakota, since the organization in 1915 of the Non-Partisan League. Among these are a state-owned grain elevator and mill, and a state bank at the capital.

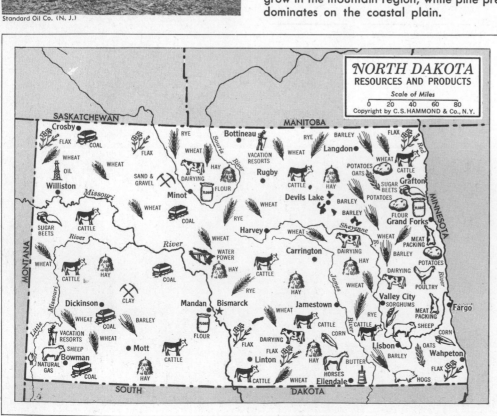

NORTH DAKOTA
RESOURCES AND PRODUCTS
Scale of Miles
0   20   40   60   80
Copyright by C.S. Hammond & Co., N.Y.

▲ WHEAT FIELD. North Dakota is second only to Kansas in total wheat production. Other crops include potatoes and a large yield of barley.

OHIO

Ohio was part of the Northwest Territory which, besides Ohio, included the present states of Michigan, Indiana, Illinois, Wisconsin, and the NE. part of Minnesota. Discovered late in the first half of the 17th Century, it was claimed by both France and England. France founded her claim on exploration and occupation covering the period between the middle and the close of the 17th Century; England based her claim to the same territory on the discovery of the Atlantic coast by the Cabots, and upon the Virginia, Massachusetts, and Connecticut charters, under which these grants extended westward to the Pacific Ocean. New York also had a claim to the territory. The contest between France and England, known as the Seven Years' War, ended in the cession of the entire Northwest to Great Britain. After winning the Northwest Territory, however, Great Britain no longer recognized those claims of her colonies to this territory, which she had asserted against France, and finally annexed the region to the Province of Quebec. This embittered the colonies and was one of the grievances which brought on the War of Independence and during that war, the Northwest was won for the Americans by George Rogers Clark. Marietta (founded in 1788) at the mouth of the Muskingum, is regarded as the oldest permanent settlement of the state, and the first territorial government was established there. The state was admitted to the Union in 1803. Ohio was the scene of many important actions during the War of 1812, among them Commodore Perry's victory on Lake Erie, in 1813. In no other state have been found so many antique implements of stone, copper, bone, and clay, and such extensive systems of earthworks.

▲ SNOW FENCES. The expansive land of North Dakota, which is bordered on the north by Canada, is exposed to cold and blustering winters. The fences above are constructed to serve as barriers against snowdrifts.

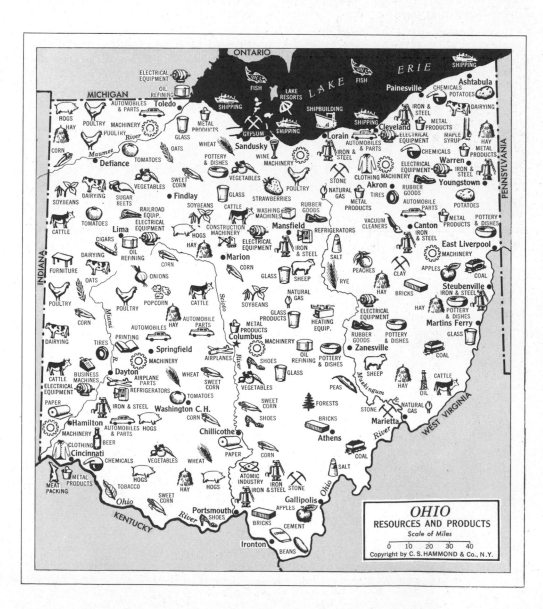

OHIO
RESOURCES AND PRODUCTS
Scale of Miles
0 10 20 30 40
Copyright by C. S. HAMMOND & Co., N. Y.

Toledo Scale Co.

▲ SCALES. Synonymous with the city of Toledo is its famous scales. Cleveland, Cincinnati and Youngstown combine with the "scale city" to form the chain of industrial centers which lie along the periphery of the state.

Ohio Development and Pub. Comm.

OKLAHOMA

With the exception of the strip comprising the Counties of Beaver, Texas, and Cimarron, the territory included in the present state of Oklahoma was set apart by Congress in 1834 under the name of Indian Territory, for the possession of certain Indian tribes. Oklahoma, the western part of Indian Territory, was ceded by the Indians to the United States in 1866. The treaties under which these lands were transferred stipulated that they were to be used by the government for the settlement of other Indian tribes or freedmen, but not for whites. Many parties of "Boomers" entered the territory, and military forces were required to eject them. In 1889 arrangements were made with certain Indian tribes by which, in consideration of the payment by the government of several million dollars, the clause forbidding settlement by white citizens on this land was cancelled, and it was thrown open for settlement at noon on April 22, 1889. In 1890, this portion of Indian Territory, together with the narrow strip north of Texas, became Oklahoma Territory. In 1893, Congress opened negotiations with the Indians, which led to the passage of the Curtis Act in 1898. That act provided for individual allotment of land to the Indians of Indian Territory, and for a government administered from Washington. When the allotments were nearly all made, Congress, in 1906, authorized Oklahoma and Indian Territories to qualify for admission to the Union as one state, and the state was admitted on the 16th of November, 1907.

◄ OHIO FARM. Favored by its advantageous position, the farms that are scattered along western Ohio are assured a profitable market.

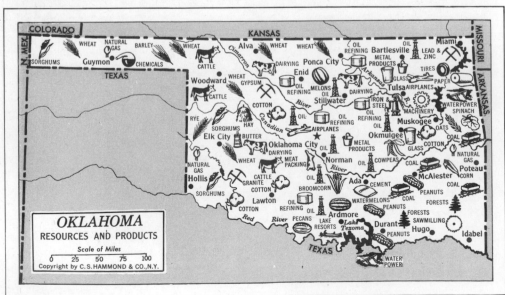

OKLAHOMA
RESOURCES AND PRODUCTS
Scale of Miles
0   25   50   75   100
Copyright by C.S. HAMMOND & CO., N.Y.

Libbey-Owens-Ford Glass Co.

▲ GLASS CUTTER. Lured in the '80s by the inexpensive fuel provided by large gas fields, the glass industry, among others, came to the growing state of Ohio. Since then glass-making has been a prominent industry and manufactures some of the finest plate-glass in the world.

▶ HOPPER CARS. The transportation of Oklahoma's principal crop, wheat, is the job of its efficient railway system. The rich soil of the State is highly adaptable to most grain crops. The climate is consistently mild so that no shelter is required for livestock. The state's various soils are cultivated to raise many staple crops among which cotton, wheat, potatoes, corn, oats and alfalfa figure predominantly. Cotton, once Oklahoma's leading crop, has been replaced in recent years by wheat. Diversified farming has added considerably to the state's agricultural production.

Rock Island Lines

OREGON

In 1579, Francis Drake sailed along the Pacific coast of the United States as far as 43° N. latitude. He took possession of the country in the name of Queen Elizabeth and called it New Albion. Between the date of Drake's voyage and 1774, the coast was visited by a number of Spanish explorers, the most successful of all being Juan Perez. Among others who sailed along the coast was Bruno Heceta who landed off what is called Point Granville and took formal possession of the country, and later, in latitude 46° 9', discovered a bay whose swift currents indicated that he was in the mouth of a large river or strait. The Spaniards made no effort to colonize North America or to develop trade with the Indians. In 1778, the English Captain James Cook sighted the coast of Oregon in the latitude 44°, and explored it between 47° and 48°, in the hope of finding the Straits of Juan de Fuca of Spanish accounts. The mouth of the Columbia River was discovered by the American Captain Gray in 1792. It was partly explored by Lewis and Clark in 1804-05. A trading post was founded in Astoria in 1811. The territory between latitudes 42° and 54° 40' N. was long in dispute between Great Britain and the United States. The claims were finally settled by treaty in 1846. Oregon Territory was organized in 1849, and admitted to statehood in 1859.

Oregon State Highway Comm.

▲ PORTLAND, OREGON. Different from many Eastern centers, Portland, largest city in Oregon, is noticeably free of smoke. Most factories are operated by electric power.

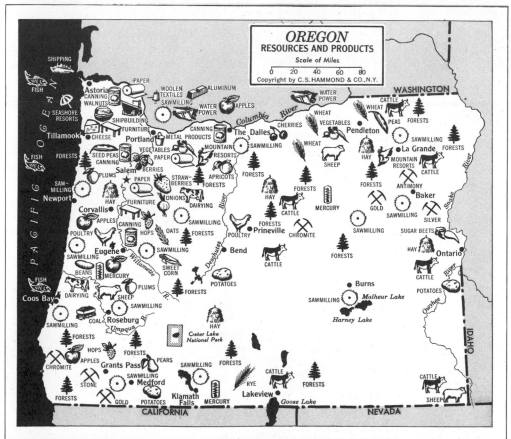

Oregon State Highway Comm.

▲ ALPINE FORESTS. Vast source of the country's timber supply, almost 30 million acres of forests constitute one-fourth of the United States lumber resources. Mount Hood stands in the distance.

➤ PITTSBURGH. Foremost producer of the life-blood of American industry, the steady flow of Pittsburgh steel surges through the nation's commercial arteries to be transformed into everything from tools to railway cars. This great steel center ranks among the highest producers in the world.

Standard Oil Company (N. J.)

▲ THE BETSY ROSS HOUSE. Philadelphia, "cradle of the Revolution," is filled with historic landmarks. Notable among them is the alleged birthplace of Betsy Ross, reputed designer of the first American flag.

➤ COAL STRIP MINE. Large coal deposits are found throughout Pennsylvania. Veins of coal near the surface are extracted by means of "strip mining." Deposits which are deep in the earth are mined by shaft.

Standard Oil Company (N. J.)

PENNSYLVANIA

The earliest European settlements (1643-81) within the present limits of Pennsylvania were made by Swedish and Dutch traders in the lower valley of the Delaware River. In 1664, the English obtained possession of the territory and in 1681, it was granted by Charles the Second to William Penn, a prominent member of the Society of Friends. In colonial days, Quaker influence was very strong, but religious freedom was given to all. The colony had serious boundary disputes with Maryland, Virginia, and New York, and a dispute with Connecticut over the Wyoming Valley, which was settled in favor of Pennsylvania in 1782. A strong anti-proprietary sentiment grew among the people after the death of William Penn, the great leaders of the movement being Joseph Galloway and Benjamin Franklin. The people of the colony were not united in sentiment over the War of Independence. There were not only many loyalists and many who were opposed to war on religious grounds, but the people generally were satisfied with the liberal and free government which they already enjoyed. The liberty party, however, became dominant, and Pennsylvania bore a creditable part in the struggle which ended in the establishment of independence. Philadelphia, where the Declaration of Independence was adopted in 1776, became the seat of the Federal Government, except for a brief period in 1789-90, until the removal to Washington in 1800. The state bore a notable part in the Civil War. Many of the miners and ironworkers are of foreign birth, and serious industrial disturbances have occured at intervals since 1865.

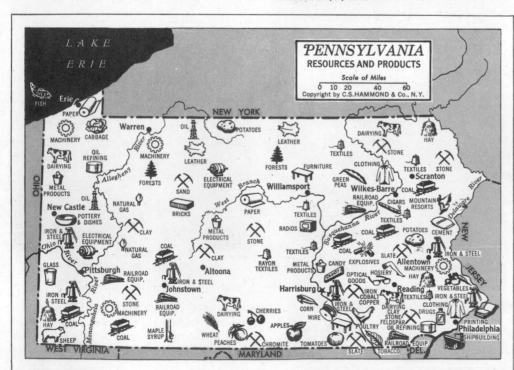

PENNSYLVANIA
RESOURCES AND PRODUCTS
Scale of Miles
0   10   20   40   60
Copyright by C.S. HAMMOND & Co., N.Y.

RHODE ISLAND

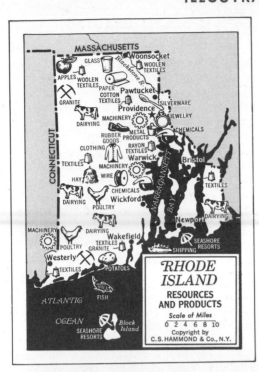

Rhode Island was founded by religious and political exiles from Massachusetts. Roger Williams planted the first settlement at Providence in 1636 William Coddington and others settled on Aquidneck or Rhode Island in 1638. Newport was founded in 1639. The Royal Charter for Rhode Island and Providence Plantations was issued in 1663. The government of Rhode Island permitted complete freedom in religious matters. Rhode Island did not ratify the federal constitution until 1790. The first successful cotton mill in the country was established at Pawtucket in 1790. In 1842 occurred the Dorr Rebellion, a revolt against conditions which were the outgrowth of the charter of 1663, which served in place of a constitution, gave undue power to country towns, and restricted suffrage. As a result of this revolt, a constitution was adopted. There were two centers of government until 1900.

Standard Oil Company (N. J.)

▲ PAPER MILL. South Carolina uses some of its timber supply for the processing of paper. The wood is first converted into pulp and then filtered through screens. The pulp is then chemically bleached, and later the thin, fibrous mass is rolled smooth. Pictured above is the filtering stage where the paper is drained of excess moisture.

Rhode Island Dept. of Agr. and Conservation

◄ RHODE ISLAND TURKEYS. Comparatively small but known for quality is Rhode Island's poultry. The State's name has become associated with the type of fowl produced. At the left, is a typical Rhode Island turkey farm.

SOUTH CAROLINA

An unsuccessful attempt was made by the French to colonize what is now South Carolina in 1562. The first permanent English settlement was made in 1670. Charleston was founded in 1680. The territory remained under a proprietary government with North Carolina until 1729, when it became a separate colony. Many of the early colonists were French Huguenots, Scotch, Irish, Swiss, and Germans. South Carolina was the scene of many battles during the Revolution, those of Ft. Moultrie, Charleston, Camden, King's Mountain, Cowpens, and Eutaw Springs being among the most notable. It was held by the British 1780-1781. Its advocacy of nullification nearly led to civil war in 1832-33. It was foremost among the southern states in the advocacy of the states' rights doctrine, and was the first state to secede (Dec. 20, 1860). It opened the Civil War by the bombardment of Fort Sumter (April 12, 1861), suffered severely by the blockade attacks at Charleston Harbor and near the close of the war (in 1865) by the march of Sherman's army. It was readmitted to the Union in 1868. The state was visited by a severe earthquake in 1886.

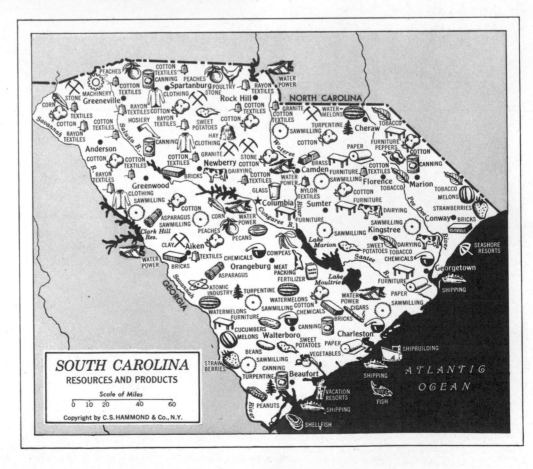

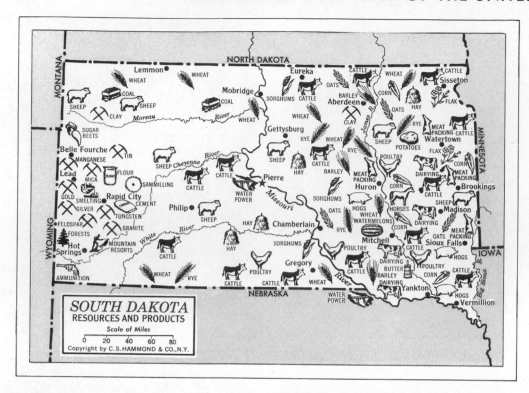

SOUTH DAKOTA
RESOURCES AND PRODUCTS
Scale of Miles
0   20   40   60   80
Copyright by C.S. HAMMOND & CO., N.Y.

SOUTH DAKOTA

The territory included within the present limits of the state was a part of the District of Louisiana from 1803-05; of the Territory of Louisiana from 1805-20, and of the Territory of Missouri from 1812-20. The section east of the Missouri was successively a part of the Territories of Louisiana, Wisconsin, Iowa, and Minnesota; and the western section a part of the Territory of Nebraska. In 1861, the Territory of Dakota was created, including the present Dakotas and portions of Wyoming and Montana. The Dakotas acquired their present territorial limits in 1882. The territory was divided into two states in November, 1887, and both were admitted to the Union on November 2, 1889. After admission, South Dakota underwent a period of Indian resistance which culminated in the so-called Wounded Knee Massacre. In 1905, after much debate, Pierre was selected as the state's capital. The state contains a national shrine at Mount Rushmore where the likenesses of four presidents have been carved from the natural rock.

▼ GRAZING SHEEP. In some parts of South Dakota sheep-raising is carried on in addition to farming. Such flocks are known as "farm flocks." Sheep that are raised as a sole occupation are known as "range flocks." South Dakota possesses many miles of natural range country for grazing. The rich natural grasses and a facilitative soil for growing alfalfa and other feeds make South Dakota important in stock-raising.

➤ HAY STACK. South Dakota's agricultural wealth undoubtedly resides in its fertile soil, half of which still remains to be cultivated by tractor and plow. The land is equally divided into grazing and farm areas, thus offering facilities for both farmer and cattleman alike. An irrigation program has been put into operation so that increased productivity may be obtained in the drier sections of the State.

U. S. Bureau of Reclamation

South Dakota State Highway Comm.

➤ TEXTILES. Textile mills have long been a prominent industry in Tennessee. During the Civil War, the manufacture of cotton thread was seriously affected, but throughout the Reconstruction Period new possibilities were discovered for textile production. Synthetic yarn is one of the State's more recent developments.

➤ SMOKY MOUNTAINS. Rising more than 6,000 feet, "The Smokies" form one of the landmarks of Tennessee. Because of varied climatic conditions, this mountain area possesses a wide variety of flora and therefore furnishes a playground for the explorer, amateur or professional.

➤ BAD LANDS. First named by aboriginal Indians, the Bad Lands are an isolated and barren region devoid of any great amount of vegetation. Close by lie the Black Hills of South Dakota which hold a magnetic attraction for the archaeologist who finds himself amidst a superabundance of fossil-bearing rock. It is also a haven for writers, artists and engineers whose presence adds a note of urbanity to an otherwise primitive setting. These hills were formally the site of a gold rush in 1875. Weather-beaten prospectors arrived in swarms to claim a portion of the rich earth. Such activity soon transformed a hitherto unknown locality into a familiar mining town with its traditionally colorful characters. Even today the State's mining is concentrated in the Black Hills, gold being a principal source of South Dakota's wealth.

Standard Oil Company (N. J.)

E. I. du Pont de Nemours Co.

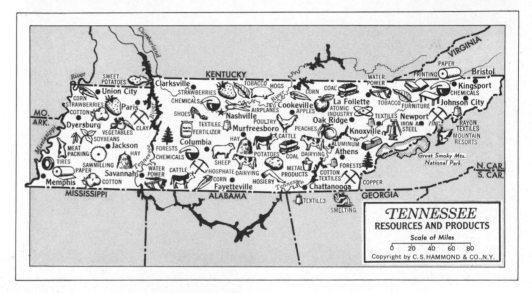

Copyright by C. S. HAMMOND & CO., N.Y.

TENNESSEE
RESOURCES AND PRODUCTS
Scale of Miles

Standard Oil Company (N. J.)

TENNESSEE

Tennessee was included in the English grant to Sir Walter Raleigh in 1584, and in the later Stuart grants including that of North Carolina in 1663. The region was claimed in early times by North Carolina and by the French and Spanish. The leading settlement was made from Virginia and North Carolina in 1769. North Carolina ceded its claim to the United States, and the territory was formed in 1790. It was admitted to the Union as a state in 1796. It seceded June 8, 1861 and next to Virginia, was the chief battleground during the Civil War. Among the stirring events of that period were the capture of Fort Henry and Fort Donelson and of Island No. 10; the battles of Shiloh, Memphis, Murfreesboro, Lookout Mountain, and Chickamauga; the relief of Chattanooga and Knoxville; and the battles of Franklin and Nashville. The state was re-admitted to the Union in 1866.

Standard Oil Company (N. J.)

▲ CANTALOUPES. Over 100 crops are grown in "The Lone Star State" varying from almonds to avocados. Citrus fruit production constantly maintains its leadership in the State's agricultural market. Recent steps have been taken to insure a greater horticultural yield than has been previously possible. The amount of rainfall is sufficient to guarantee the growing of all important crops.

▼ OIL WELL. Mineral wealth, above all oil, is part of the foundation upon which the reputation of Texas rests. Great reserves of natural gas, including those in the well-known Panhandle, make up the largest single supply that is found in any area in the United States. Underdeveloped though potential deposits of iron ore exist in the northeast, while in other sections a good supply of marble, asphalt and granite is present. Texas has attained undoubted superiority in the extent of its mineral assets as well as in its quality of beef cattle.

Standard Oil Company (N. J.)

TEXAS

An attempt at settlement was made by Sieur de la Salle about 1685 and several missions were established by the Spaniards in the 18th Century. The region was invaded by various adventurers early in the 19th century. It formed, with Coahuila, a state of Mexico, and was settled rapidly about 1820-30 by American colonists. Most of these colonists came from the southern states of the Union and brought their slaves with them. A rebellion against Mexico broke out in 1835; the garrisons at Alamo and Goliad were massacred by the Mexicans in 1836; and the Mexicans were finally defeated by Houston at San Jacinto, April 21, 1836. Texas was a republic from 1836-45 when it was annexed to the United States. It was largely the cause of the Mexican War of 1846 and the scene of many of the conflicts in that struggle. By the terms of the treaty which terminated the conflict, the Rio Grande River became the boundary between Texas and Mexico. Texas seceded in 1861. Because of its isolated position, there was little military action in the state during the Civil War. However, the last battle of that conflict was fought on its soil at Palmito, more than a month after the surrender at Appomatox. Texas was readmitted to the Union in 1870.

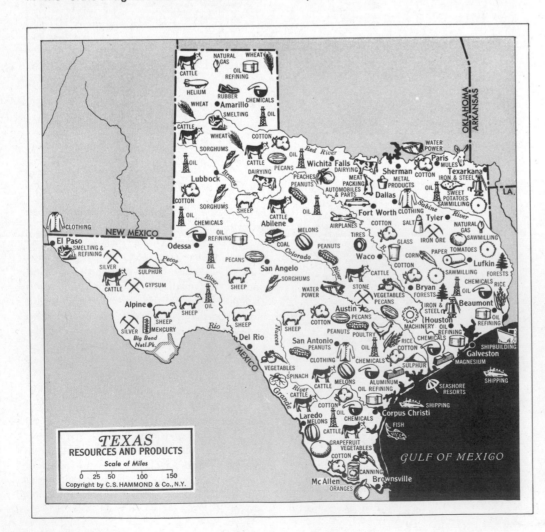

TEXAS
RESOURCES AND PRODUCTS
Scale of Miles
0   25   50   100   150
Copyright by C.S. HAMMOND & Co., N.Y.

UTAH

This arid desert country, part of the area ceded by Mexico in 1848, was colonized by Mormons in the first large-scale use of irrigation in this country. Driven from Missouri and Illinois by mobs because of their religious beliefs, the Mormons, under the direction of Brigham Young, sought refuge in the Salt Lake Valley. They were without federal government until organized as a territory in 1850. Until then the Church acted as the only authority. Now only three-fifths of Utah is Mormon. It was admitted as a state in 1896.

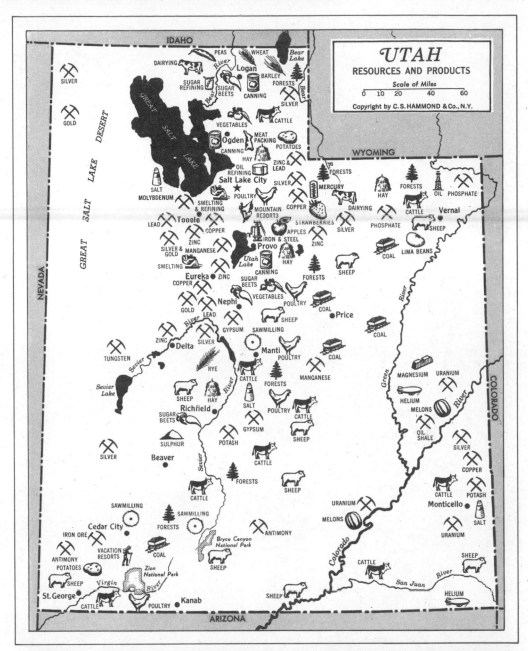

Dow Chemical Co.

⬆ CHEMICAL MANUFACTURE. Texas' soil offers itself to the exploitation of many chemical deposits.

Salt Lake City C. of C.

⬆ SALT. Endowed by nature with an almost inexhaustible supply of salt, the Salt Lake City vicinity is the location for many refining companies.

➤ COPPER MINE. Mining the great untapped mineral reservoirs of Utah accounts for at least fifty per cent of the State's livelihood.

Salt Lake City C. of C.

VERMONT
RESOURCES AND PRODUCTS
Scale of Miles
0 5 10 15 20 25
Copyright by C.S. HAMMOND & Co., N.Y.

VERMONT

Samuel de Champlain, the French governor of Quebec, discovered the lake which bears his name in 1609, and thus laid the basis for the French claim to the region. The French built a fort on Isle La Motte in 1665. Part of the country was claimed by Massachusetts which planted the first permanent white settlement (1724) at Fort Dummer in the present town of Brattleboro. Soon after 1750, numerous settlements were made under the auspices of New Hampshire which also claimed jurisdiction in the region. New York laid claim to the country as far east as the Connecticut River, by virtue of the charter granted to the Duke of York. George the Third decided in favor of New York in 1764, and discord continued until 1771 when the people declared themselves independent and drew up a state constitution. In 1791, Vermont was admitted into the Union, the first state added to the original thirteen. The "Green Mountain Boys" bore a notable part in the War of the Revolution; and in the War of 1812, and again in the Civil War, the sons of Vermont distinguished themselves by their bravery and devotion to the Union.

Standard Oil Company (N. J.)

▲ SNOW SCENE. Vermont is a blend of the rural and the modern. Its farm and mountain regions serve to breed a thrifty individualism which is so typical of the Vermonter. Like most of the northern states its climate is varied with deep snows in the central section during the winter.

◄ WILLIAM AND MARY COLLEGE. Many of the famous figures of American history were from Virginia and the state has many historic shrines. The homes of Jefferson, Washington and Lee, as well as the easily recollected names of Williamsburg and Yorktown, are a reminder to the state of its great historic past. The picture shows the Wren building at William and Mary College. The college, founded in 1693, is the second oldest one in the United States.

Virginia Conservation Comm.

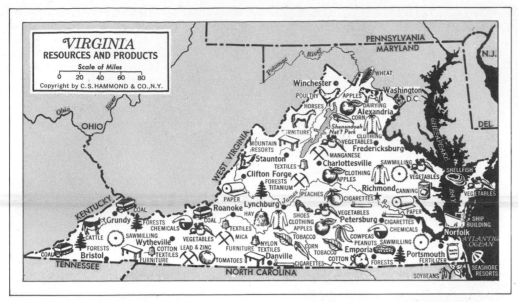

Washington State Adv. Comm.

VIRGINIA

At Jamestown, in Virginia, in 1607, was planted the first permanent English settlement in North America. Capt. John Smith became the head of the government there, established law and order and laid the foundations of industrial life. Slavery in America had its beginnings in the Virginia colony in 1619. At the close of the colonial period, Virginia was the most populous and the wealthiest of the thirteen colonies. In the protest against the Stamp Act and the encroachment of Great Britain, Virginia took the lead, and in the Revolutionary struggle furnished such noted sons as Washington, Jefferson, Patrick Henry, the Lees, and Madison. At Yorktown, Cornwallis's surrender put an end to the contest. In the Civil War, Virginia furnished the great commander, Rob-

PLYWOOD. Lumbering in Washington is a thriving industry. The production of plywood, made by compressing several thin layers of wood together to form a strong panel, has greatly stimulated the lumber output. The cultivation of tree farms safeguards against possible depletion of forest reserves. Douglas fir, birch, maple, spruce and hemlock constitute the State's timber resources.

ert E. Lee. Of the first twenty-one presidents of the United States, seven were Virginians, as was also President Woodrow Wilson. The part played by Virginia in the history of the country has endeared it to all Americans, and the national shrines at Mt. Vernon, Monticello, and the Arlington National Cemetery are visited by hundreds of thousands annually.

WASHINGTON

The Strait of Juan de Fuca was discovered in 1592, and explored in 1789. The mouth of the Columbia River was explored by the American Captain Gray in 1792, and further explorations were conducted by Lewis and Clark in 1805. A settlement at the mouth of the Columbia was founded by John Jacob Astor in 1811. The boundary question was settled with Great Britain in 1846. Washington formed part of the territory of Oregon; was organized as a territory in 1853; and was admitted to the Union in 1889.

Washington State Adv. Comm.

CRAB BOAT. To the west of Washington is the open expanse of the North Pacific. It is these waters and those of the Columbia River which offer up to the fishing and canning industry the catches of salmon, halibut and tuna.

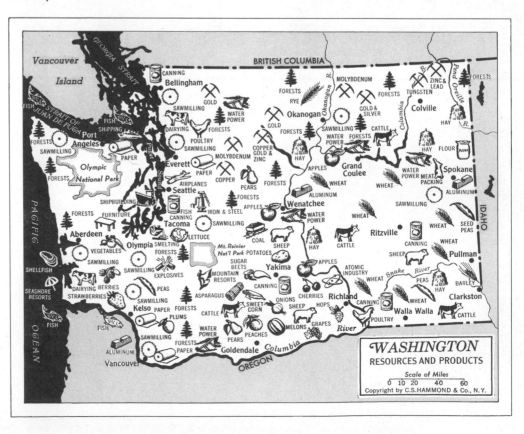

Washington State Adv. Comm.

West Virginia Ind. & Pub. Comm.

← MOUNT SHUKSAN. Washington abounds in facilities for winter sports. For the less active, the lakes, coast and forests provide unusual scenic beauty. Innumerable streams attract fishing enthusiasts from all sections of the country, and for the hunter the uplands and mountains afford a wide variety of game. Such natural accommodations make Washington the vacation spot of the West.

WEST VIRGINIA

West Virginia was a part of Virginia until the beginning of the secession movement in 1861. The separation of these states had, however, been agitated before the adoption of the Federal Constitution. West Virginia was settled largely by immigrants who entered by way of Pennsylvania, and the population included Germans, Protestant Irish, and people from the states farther north.

Slavery was rendered unprofitable by the difficulties in agriculture, caused by the rugged nature of the country and the climate. Social conditions were, therefore, entirely unlike those of the eastern part of the state, and little sympathy existed between the two sections. At the outbreak of the Civil War, the inhabitants of the northern and western counties remained loyal to the United States and in 1863 West Virginia was admitted to the Union.

▲ WHITE SULPHUR SPRINGS. A nationally-known spa, these springs are visited by people from all over the country. Consequently, hotel accommodations are offered to the many visitors seeking the curative possibilities of the springs. This hotel, built in Georgian style, is situated near by.

▼ COAL CARS. The great binder of industries, coal is one of the most important elements in West Virginia's earth. Iron, one of the principal needs of steel-making, follows a close second. The prosperity of industry depends in large amount on the railroads.

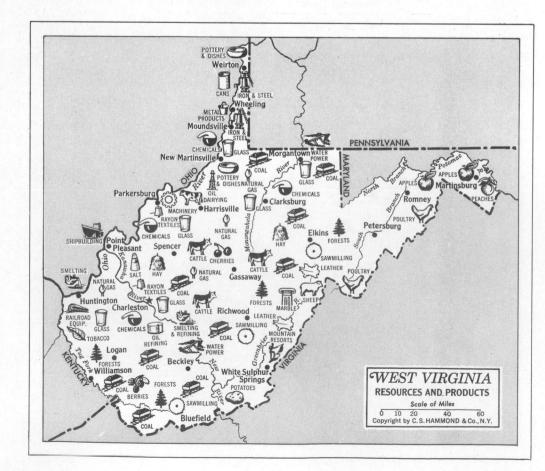

WEST VIRGINIA
RESOURCES AND PRODUCTS
Scale of Miles
0 10 20   40   60
Copyright by C. S. HAMMOND & Co., N.Y.

Standard Oil Co. (N. J.)

WISCONSIN

Wisconsin was opened to wide settlement by French explorers, missionaries, and traders. Among the Frenchmen whose names are associated with its early history are those of Jean Nicollet, Sieur de Radisson, Sieur des Groseilliers, Jacques Marquette, Louis Joliet, Rene Menard, Claude Allouez, La Salle, Henri de Tonty, Duluth, and Louis Hennepin. The French claimed, and to a greater or less extent, occupied the territory from 1634 until the close of the Seven Years' War in 1760 when it passed to Great Britain. British occupation was brief and in 1783, it became a part of the United States, and was included in 1787 in the Northwest Territory; afterward in Indiana Territory; in 1809 in Illinois Territory; and in 1818 in Michigan Territory. Wisconsin Territory was organized in 1836 and was admitted as a state in 1848.

▼ WISCONSIN'S WOODS. Wisconsin's many rivers, lakes and forests enhance the state's scenic value, making it a beautiful vacation spot as well as a lucrative area for valuable lumber resources. A land covered by forests, it furnishes a large amount of timber yearly. The typical beauty of Wisconsin's forest lakes—and there are many— is the natural result of prehistoric glaciers which imperceptibly gouged out large indentations in the earth's surface. Geologically, Wisconsin's boundaries encompass some of the oldest land to be found anywhere in the world.

Philip Gendreau, N. Y.

▲ INLAND SHIPPING. Unusual facilities are supplied by the waters of Lake Superior for commercial shipping. This waterway is of prime importance in providing an ideal means of transportation for Wisconsin's natural and manufactured products. The picture shows a freighter being loaded with ore cargo.

Philip Gendreau, N. Y.

WYOMING
RESOURCES AND PRODUCTS
Scale of Miles
0 10 20 30 40 50 60
Copyright by C. S. HAMMOND & Co., N. Y.

Standard Oil Co. (N. J.)

▲ THE WIND RIVER MOUNTAINS. The Wind River Mountains are one of many ranges that form the Continental Divide. Three large rivers have their origins in Wyoming; the Columbia, Colorado and Missouri. In the northwest of the State is Yellowstone National Park. The mountains, serried with timber, make a natural storage place for the winter's snows which, in summer, drain off into the adjacent streams or lakes.

WYOMING

Fort Laramie, near the mouth of the Laramie River, was established in 1834 to control the fur trade of the Arapahoes, Cheyennes, and Sioux. The United States exploring expedition, commanded by John C. Fremont, explored the Wind River Mountains and the South Pass in 1842. From this time, the favorite route to the Pacific led through Wyoming, but the aridity of the land and the pronounced hostility of the Indians were not conducive to settlement. For the protection of immigrant trains, the United States government built Fort Kearney in 1848, and purchased Fort Laramie in 1849. A Mormon settlement was made on the Green River in 1853. These Mormons afterwards retired to Salt Lake City. Indian hostilities were active from 1851 to 1868. Gold was discovered on the Sweetwater River in 1867, and population increased rapidly. The Territory of Wyoming, with its present boundaries, was organized in 1868. The state was admitted to the Union in 1890.

Wyoming Comm. & Ind. Comm.

◄ DUDE RANCH. Ranching has changed from what it used to be at one time. Most large ranches, many of which were converted into "dude ranches," have been reduced in size. This has been so because the cattleman is no longer able to compete merely on the basis of spacious lands. Cattle must be raised in strict proportion to the amount of feed which the land furnishes.

ALASKA

Alaska, formerly called Russian-America, was first visited by Vitus Bering in 1742. In 1799, the whole country passed under the control of the Russian-American Company. In 1867, the United States purchased the entire territory from Russia for $7,200,000 in gold. When Mr. Seward, our Secretary of State, concluded the negotiations for the purchase of Alaska, there were many critics who felt that the country was paying a great price for comparatively valueless territory. As a return for the $7,200,000 purchase money, the United States received untold wealth in mineral resources, farming lands, furs and fisheries. Alaska became, in 1912, a Territory and, in 1959, the 49th State.

➡ ALASKAN VOLCANO. Alaska's thick snows coat mountainsides and form glaciers which slowly descend into the fiords below and break up into icebergs. But Alaska is not all frozen waste. In the valleys of the Yukon thousands of acres of fertile soil await proper cultivation.

U. S. Navy Photo

Philip Gendreau, N. Y.

▲ SALMON LOADING. The center of the salmon industry in Alaska is located at Bristol Bay. After the fish are caught, they are brought in to the canning plants where they are prepared for shipment.

➡ PLANTING PINEAPPLES. Pineapples do not usually bear seeds. In Hawaii they are sometimes planted from "slips"—tufts of leaves from the base of the fruit. Because the planting of pineapples is not mechanized, the operation must be carried on by hand. From 15,000 to 20,000 plants are cultivated per acre.

➡ CATTLE LOADING AT KAILUA. About half of the land of Hawaii is used as pasturage for livestock. Cattle are raised on the larger sections and tended by Paniolas (Hawaiian cowboys). At Kailua the waters of the bay are so shallow the Paniolas must swim out with the steers to the freighter to load the stock aboard.

Hawaiian Pineapple Co.

Hawaii Visitors Bureau

HAWAII

The islands are said to have been discovered in 1542 by Gaetano, and rediscovered in 1778 by Captain Cook who lost his life in a conflict with natives the following year. In 1790, Kamehameha formed the islands into one kingdom. Missionaries came from America in 1820 and in less than forty years, they gave to the whole Hawaiian people the rudiments of a common school education and taught them something of domestic science. In 1843, the independence of the kingdom was guaranteed by the French and English governments. Kalakaua, elected king in 1874, died in 1891 and was succeeded by his eldest sister, Liliuokalani who was dethroned in January, 1893, and a provisional republican government set up. The islands were finally annexed by the United States in 1898, and in 1900 were organized as one of the Territories. In 1959 they became the 50th State of the Union.

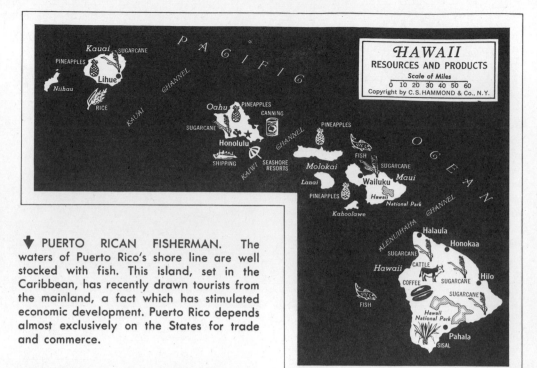

▼ PUERTO RICAN FISHERMAN. The waters of Puerto Rico's shore line are well stocked with fish. This island, set in the Caribbean, has recently drawn tourists from the mainland, a fact which has stimulated economic development. Puerto Rico depends almost exclusively on the States for trade and commerce.

Hamilton Wright

▼ JIBARO ON HORSEBACK. From the 16th century on, the export of sugar has been the most valuable source of revenue for the island of Puerto Rico. Other cash crops on which the internal economy is based are tobacco, coffee and citrus fruits.

Hamilton Wright

PUERTO RICO

Puerto Rico was discovered by Columbus in 1493, and Ponce de Leon founded a settlement there in 1510. The island was ceded by Spain to the United States after the war of 1898 and in 1900, civil government was given to the Territory. Since then, the island has prospered greatly. In 1947 the Territory won the right to elect its own governor and, in 1952, achieved full commonwealth status as an Associated Free State.

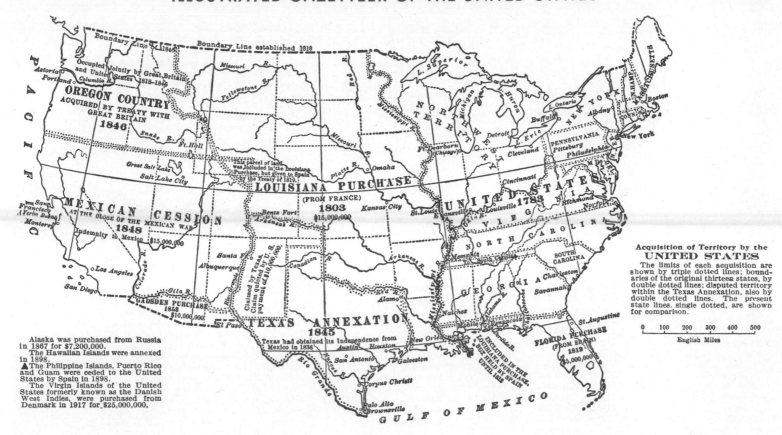

Acquisition of Territory by the
UNITED STATES

The limits of each acquisition are shown by triple dotted lines; boundaries of the original thirteen states, by double dotted lines; disputed territory within the Texas Annexation, also by double dotted lines. The present state lines, single dotted, are shown for comparison.

0   100   200   300   400   500
English Miles

Alaska was purchased from Russia in 1867 for $7,200,000.
The Hawaiian Islands were annexed in 1898.
△The Philippine Islands, Puerto Rico and Guam were ceded to the United States by Spain in 1898.
The Virgin Islands of the United States formerly known as the Danish West Indies, were purchased from Denmark in 1917 for $25,000,000.

State or Territory	Admitted to the Union	Setted at	Date	State Nickname	State Flower
Alabama	Dec. 14, 1819	Mobile	1702	Cotton State	Golden Rod
Alaska	Jan. 3, 1959	Sitka	1801	The Great Land	Forget-me-not
Arizona	Feb. 14, 1912	Tucson	1580	Baby State	Saguaro Cactus
Arkansas	June 15, 1836	Arkansas Post	1685	Wonder State	Apple Blossom
California	Sept. 9, 1850	San Diego	1769	Golden State	Golden Poppy
Colorado	Aug. 1, 1876	Near Denver	1858	Centennial State	Columbine
Connecticut	†Jan. 9, 1788	Windsor	1635	Nutmeg State	Mountain Laurel
Delaware	†Dec. 7, 1787	Cape Henlopen	1627	Diamond State	Peach Blossom
District of Columbia	** 1790-1791		1790	------------	American Beauty Rose
Florida	Mar. 3, 1845	St. Augustine	1565	Peninsula State	Orange Blossom
Georgia	†Jan. 2, 1788	Savannah	1733	Cracker State	Cherokee Rose
Guam	‡Dec. 10, 1898	Agana	....	------------	------------
Hawaii	Aug. 21, 1959		....	Aloha State	Red Hibiscus
Idaho	July 3, 1890	Coeur d'Alene	1842	Gem State	Syringa
Illinois	Dec. 3, 1818	Kaskaskia	1720	Sucker State	Violet
Indiana	Dec. 11, 1816	Vincennes	1730	Hoosier	Zinnia
Iowa	Dec. 28, 1846	Burlington	1788	Hawkeye State	Wild Rose
Kansas	Jan. 29, 1861		1831	Sunflower State	Sunflower
Kentucky	June 1, 1792	Harrodsburg	1774	Blue Grass State	Goldenrod
Louisiana	April 30, 1812	Iberville	1699	Pelican State	Magnolia
Maine	Mar. 15, 1820	Bristol	1624	Pine Tree State	Pine Cone
Maryland	†April 28, 1788	St. Mary's	1634	Free State	Blackeyed Susan
Massachusetts	†Feb. 6, 1788	Plymouth	1620	Bay State	Mayflower
Michigan	Jan. 26, 1837	Near Detroit	1650	Wolverine State	Apple Blossom
Minnesota	May 11, 1858	St. Peter's River	1805	North Star State	Lady Slipper
Mississippi	Dec. 10, 1817	Natchez	1716	Magnolia State	Magnolia
Missouri	Aug. 10, 1821	St. Louis	1764	Show Me State	Hawthorn
Montana	Nov. 8, 1889		1809	Treasure State	Bitter Root
Nebraska	Mar. 1, 1867	Bellevue	1847	Tree Planter's State	Goldenrod
Nevada	Oct. 31, 1864	Genoa	1850	Battle Born State	Sage Brush
New Hampshire	†June 21, 1788	Dover and Portsmouth	1623	Granite State	Purple Lilac
New Jersey	†Dec. 18, 1787	Bergen	1617	Garden State	Violet
New Mexico	Jan. 6, 1912	Sante Fe	1605	Sunshine State	Yucca
New York	†July 26, 1788	Manhattan Island	1614	Empire State	Rose
North Carolina	†Nov. 21, 1789	Albemarle	1650	Tar Heel State	Dogwood
North Dakota	Nov. 2, 1889	Pembina	1780	Sioux State	Wild Prairie Rose
Ohio	Nov. 29, 1802	Marietta	1788	Buckeye State	Scarlet Carnation
Oklahoma	Nov. 16, 1907		1889	Sooner State	Mistletoe
Oregon	Feb. 14, 1859	Astoria	1810	Beaver State	Oregon Grape
Pennsylvania	†Dec. 12, 1787	Delaware River	1682	Keystone State	Mountain Laurel
Puerto Rico	‡Dec. 10, 1898	Caparra	1510	------------	------------
Rhode Island	†May 29, 1790	Providence	1636	Little Rhody	Violet
South Carolina	†May 23, 1788	Port Royal	1670	Palmetto State	Yellow Jessamine
South Dakota	Nov. 2, 1889	Sioux Falls	1856	Coyote State	The Pasque
Tennessee	June 1, 1796	Ft. Loudon	1757	Volunteer State	Iris
Texas	Dec. 29, 1845	Matagorda Bay	1686	Lone Star State	Bluebonnet
Utah	Jan. 4, 1896	Salt Lake City	1847	Beehive State	Sego Lily
Vermont	Mar. 4, 1791	Ft. Dummer	1764	Green Mountain State	Red Clover
Virgin Islands	***Mar. 31, 1917		....	------------	------------
Virginia	†June 26, 1788	Jamestown	1607	Old Dominion State	American Dogwood
Washington	Nov. 11, 1889	Astoria	1811	Evergreen State	Rhododendron
West Virginia	June 19, 1863	Wheeling	1774	Mountain State	Rhododendron
Wisconsin	May 29, 1848	Green Bay	1670	Badger State	Violet
Wyoming	July 10, 1890	Ft. Laramie	1834	Equality State	Indian Paintbrush

† Ratified the Constitution.   ‡ Treaty of Peace with Spain. In 1952 became an Associated Free State.   ** Established under Acts of Congress.   *** See Virgin Is. note above left.
Philippines became independent in 1946.

State or Territory	Area (Sq. Mi.)	Population	Inhabitants per Sq. Mi.	Capital or Chief Town	Geographic Centers	Page No.
Alabama	51,078	3,061,743	59.9	Montgomery	Chilton Co., 12 miles southwest of Clanton	164
Alaska	586,400	128,643	.2	Juneau	12 miles south of Lake Minchumina	205
Arizona	113,580	749,587	6.6	Phoenix	Yavapai Co., 55 miles southeast of Prescott	165
Arkansas	52,725	1,909,511	36.2	Little Rock	Pulaski Co., 12 miles north of west of Little Rock	166
California	156,803	10,586,223	67.5	Sacramento	Madera Co., 35 miles northeast of Madera	167
Canal Zone	379	51,827	....	Balboa Heights		...
Colorado	103,967	1,325,089	12.7	Denver	Park Co., 30 miles northwest of Pikes Peak	168
Connecticut	4,899	2,007,280	409.7	Hartford	Hartford Co., at East Berlin	168
Delaware	1,978	318,085	160.8	Dover	Kent Co., 11 miles south of Dover	169
District of Columbia	61	802,178	....	Washington	Near corner of Fourth and L streets, N.W.	178
Florida	54,262	2,771,305	51.1	Tallahassee	Citrus Co., 12 miles west of north of Brooksville	170
Georgia	58,518	3,444,578	58.9	Atlanta	Twiggs Co., 18 miles southeast of Macon	171
Guam	206	58,754		Agana		...
Hawaii	6,434	499,794	78.0	Honolulu		206
Idaho	82,808	588,637	7.1	Boise	Custer Co., 24 miles south of west of Challis	172
Illinois	55,947	8,712,176	155.7	Springfield	Logan Co., 28 miles northeast of Springfield	173
Indiana	36,205	3,934,224	108.7	Indianapolis	Boone Co., 14 miles west of north of Indianapolis	173
Iowa	55,986	2,621,073	46.8	Des Moines	Story Co., 5 miles northeast of Ames	175
Kansas	82,113	1,905,299	23.2	Topeka	Barton Co., 15 miles northeast of Great Bend	176
Kentucky	40,109	2,944,806	73.4	Frankfort	Marion Co., 3 miles west of north of Lebanon	177
Louisiana	45,177	2,683,516	59.4	Baton Rouge	Avoyelles Parish, 3 miles southeast of Marksville	177
Maine	31,040	913,774	29.4	Augusta	Piscataquis Co., 18 miles north of Dover	178
Maryland	9,887	2,343,001	237.0	Annapolis	Anne Arundel Co., 3 miles east of Collington	178
Massachusetts	7,907	4,690,514	593.2	Boston	Worcester Co., in northern part of City of Worcester	179
Michigan	57,022	6,371,766	111.7	Lansing	Wexford Co., 5 miles west of north of Cadillac	180
Minnesota	80,009	2,982,483	37.3	St. Paul	Crow Wing Co., 10 miles southwest of Brainerd	181
Mississippi	47,420	2,178,914	45.9	Jackson	Leake Co., 9 miles north of west of Carthage	182
Missouri	69,270	3,954,653	57.1	Jefferson City	Miller Co., 20 miles southwest of Jefferson City	183
Montana	146,316	591,024	4.0	Helena	Fergus Co., 12 miles west of Lewistown	184
Nebraska	76,653	1,325,510	17.3	Lincoln	Custer Co., 10 miles northwest of Broken Bow	184
Nevada	109,802	160,083	1.5	Carson City	Lander Co., 23 miles southeast of Austin	185
New Hampshire	9,024	533,242	59.1	Concord	Belknap Co., 3 miles east of Ashland	186
New Jersey	7,522	4,835,329	642.8	Trenton	Mercer Co., 5 miles southeast of the State Capital	187
New Mexico	121,511	681,187	5.6	Sante Fe	Torrance Co., 12 miles west of south of Willard	188
New York	47,929	14,830,192	309.4	Albany	Madison Co., 6 miles east of South of Oneida	189
North Carolina	49,142	4,061,929	82.7	Raleigh	Chatham Co., 10 miles northwest of Sanford	190
North Dakota	70,054	619,636	8.8	Bismarck	Sheridan Co., 5 miles southwest of McClusky	190
Ohio	41,122	7,946,627	193.2	Columbus	Delaware Co., 25 miles east of north of Columbus	191
Oklahoma	69,283	2,233,351	32.2	Oklahoma City	Oklahoma Co., 8 miles north of Oklahoma City	192
Oregon	96,350	1,521,341	15.8	Salem	Crook Co., 25 miles east of south of Prineville	193
Pennsylvania	45,045	10,498,012	233.1	Harrisburg	Center Co., 2.5 miles southwest of Bellefonte	194
Puerto Rico	3,435	2,210,703	....	San Juan		206
Rhode Island	1,058	791,896	748.5	Providence	Kent Co., 1 mile west of south of Crompton	195
St. Croix, Virgin Is.	82	12,103	....	Christiansted		206
St. John, Virgin Is.	19	749	....			206
St. Thomas, Virgin Is.	32	13,813	....	Charlotte Amalie		206
Samoa	76	18,937	....	Pago-Pago		206
South Carolina	30,594	2,117,027	69.2	Columbia	Richland Co., 13 miles southeast of Columbia	195
South Dakota	76,536	652,740	8.5	Pierre	Hughes Co., 8 miles northeast of Pierre	196
Tennessee	41,961	3,291,718	78.4	Nashville	Rutherford Co., 5 miles northeast of Murfreesboro	197
Texas	263,644	7,711,194	29.2	Austin	McCulloch Co., 15 miles northeast of Brady	198
United States	3,615,221	151,325,798	....	Washington	Butte Co., S. Dak., c. 17 miles west of Castle Rock (town)	...
Utah	82,346	688,862	8.4	Salt Lake City	Sanpete Co., 3 miles north of Manti	199
Vermont	9,278	377,747	40.7	Montpelier	Washington Co., 3 miles east of Roxbury	200
Virgin Islands	133	26,665	....	Charlotte Amalie		206
Virginia	39,899	3,318,680	83.2	Richmond	Appomattox Co., 11 miles south of east of Amherst	201
Wake Island						...
Washington	66,977	2,378,963	35.5	Olympia	Chelan Co., 10 miles south of west of Wenatchee	201
West Virginia	24,090	2,005,552	83.3	Charleston	Braxton Co., 4 miles east of Sutton	202
Wisconsin	54,715	3,434,575	62.8	Madison	Wood Co., 9 miles southeast of Marshfield	203
Wyoming	97,506	290,529	3.0	Cheyenne	Fremont Co., 58 miles north of east of Lander	204

TEMPERATURES AND PRECIPITATION OF PRINCIPAL CITIES

States	Cities	Jan. Aver.	July Aver.	Max.	Min.	Annual Precip.	States	Cities	Jan. Aver.	July Aver.	Max.	Min.	Annual Precip.
Ala.	Mobile	53	82	103	−1	60.67	Mont.	Helena	20	66	103	−42	12.54
Alaska	Anchorage	11	57	92	−36	14.32	Nebr.	Omaha	24	78	114	−32	25.49
Ariz.	Phoenix	52	90	118	16	7.62	Nev.	Winnemucca	28	72	108	−36	8.20
Ark.	Little Rock	43	81	110	−12	46.12	N. H.	Concord	22	70	102	−37	36.24
Calif.	San Francisco	50	59	101	27	20.23	N. J.	Atlantic City	35	73	104	−9	40.91
Colo.	Denver	32	73	105	−29	13.99	N. Mex.	Sante Fe	29	69	97	−13	14.19
Conn.	New Haven	30	73	101	−15	44.96	New York	New York	32	74	102	−14	41.63
Del.	Wilmington	33	76	107	−15	44.58	N. C.	Charlotte	41	78	103	−5	44.22
Fla.	Miami	68	82	96	27	59.18	N. Dak.	Bismarck	9	71	114	−45	15.43
Ga.	Atlanta	44	79	103	−8	47.58	Ohio	Cincinnati	33	77	108	−17	37.21
Hawaii	Honolulu	71	78	90	52	25.28	Okla.	Oklahoma City	38	82	113	−17	31.15
Idaho	Boise	30	74	121	−28	12.47	Oreg.	Portland	39	67	107	−2	39.43
Ill.	Chicago	26	74	105	−23	31.85	Pa.	Philadelphia	34	77	106	−11	41.86
Ind.	Indianapolis	30	76	106	−25	38.26	R. I.	Block Island	32	69	92	−10	38.81
Iowa	Dubuque	20	75	110	−32	31.32	S. C.	Charleston	50	81	104	7	40.26
Kans.	Wichita	32	80	114	−22	29.64	S. Dak.	Pierre	18	76	115	−40	16.21
Ky.	Louisville	35	79	107	−20	40.58	Tenn.	Nashville	40	79	106	−13	44.77
La.	New Orleans	54	80	102	7	59.72	Texas	Galveston	55	83	101	8	44.36
Me.	Portland	23	68	103	−39	42.05	Utah	Salt Lake City	30	77	105	−20	15.79
Md.	Baltimore	36	78	107	−7	41.94	Vt.	Burlington	19	69	100	−29	31.87
Mass.	Boston	30	72	104	−18	38.94	Va.	Norfolk	42	78	105	2	40.45
Mich.	Detroit	26	73	105	−24	31.04	Wash.	Seattle	40	63	98	3	31.80
Minn.	Minneapolis	13	73	108	−34	27.31	W. Va.	Parkersburg	33	75	106	−27	37.89
Miss.	Vicksburg	50	81	104	−1	49.40	Wis.	Milwaukee	21	70	105	−25	29.64
Mo.	St. Louis	33	80	110	−22	36.67	Wyo.	Cheyenne	27	67	100	−38	15.82

Illustrated GEOGRAPHY and GAZETTEER of the WORLD

THE HEADLINE EVENTS of the last half-century have made the average American acutely curious of the vast world beyond the national borders of the American homeland. Constant repetition has tended to make this thought a cliché, yet it is one of the most significant truths of our times. This new national concern for the external world and its problems is one of the hopeful signs pointing to a better future for mankind. However, no matter how well-intentioned our concern for international relations may be, it is of no value unless it is grounded on an intelligent appreciation for the great diversity of social, economic and political forms extant throughout the globe.

On the following pages the editors have presented a treasure-trove of information on the world's nations, resources, peoples and governments. Salient facts regarding the many countries of our Mother Earth have been arranged in easily-found tabular form. This arrangement by tables makes comparison between political units a simple task. Striking photographs lend a sense of immediacy to the equally engaging text descriptions of countries and continents. Highlighting the gazetteer and geography are the Resource-Relief maps which locate at a glance the major relief and resource features of the continental land masses.

Canadian National Railways

Small fishing fleets like this one in Prince Rupert, British Columbia, support Canada's important fishing industry.

NORTH AMERICA — Lying across the wide expanse of the Atlantic Ocean, was a new World waiting discovery and recognition. Europe was completely unaware of its existence for many centuries. Its discovery was destined to change the whole course of history and affect the fortunes of men and nations the world over. More than that, its discovery ushered in a whole new era of civilization, and marked the first faltering steps towards the exploration and charting of all lands and waters of the world.

No discovery, before or since, has added more to man's opportunities and the wealth of the world; or played a more important part in shaping a world's destiny.

Compared with the other continents of the world, North America is perhaps the most favored for natural wealth, climate and position on the earth. Being situated between the two largest oceans has protected the people of North America from enemy invasion, and also enabled them to develop an extensive commerce. The millions of square miles of fertile soil and untold mineral wealth has provided a standard of living unknown elsewhere in the world.

The principal geographical features of North America are its two mountain ranges and the intervening central plains. The high and rugged mountains to the westward extend from the tip of Alaska to the base of the Isthmus of Panama, or from the northern to the southern extremity of the continent. These mountain ranges include the coastal system that hugs the Pacific Coast, and the Rocky Mountains that branch out eastward and southward across the United States to become, in Mexico and Central America, the Sierra Madres. The Cascade Mountains, which farther south become the Sierra Nevada, are separate ranges that work inland from the coastal mountains. These diverging mountain chains in the east and west form the bulwark for a number of high plateaus that lie between. The land adjoining the Cascade Mountains is the Columbia Plateau, while farther south lies the Colorado Plateau. In between is the arid region of the Great Basin. The Great Salt Lake is a remnant of an inland sea which once covered this vast area.

In the east, extending from the Gulf of Saint Lawrence to the Gulf of Mexico is the Appalachian Range. These mountains are older and less rugged than the Rockies. Time has worn them down and rounded their peaks. On the side toward the Atlantic Ocean, they merge with the Piedmont Plateau, which slopes off into a coastal plain.

The great central plains that slope towards the center, and lie between the Rocky Mountains and Appalachian Highlands describe a giant "V" which extends from the Arctic Ocean to the Gulf of Mexico.

More varieties of climate prevail in North America than in any other land in the world. The greater part of the continent, however, enjoys a temperate and invigorating climate. The inhabitants of the far north must adjust themselves to the rigors of Arctic weather, Mexico endures sub-tropical temperatures, and Central America a tropical heat. Even from east to west there is a wide variety of climate due to difference in altitude and other conditions not affected by latitude.

On the western coast, the great Pacific Ocean, generally a protective barrier, separating most of North America from the shores of Asia, offers little promise of isolation at its far northwest corner. While eight thousand miles separate the peoples of China from the United States, Russia and Alaska almost meet at the Bering Strait, which is only fifty-five miles wide.

Quidi Vidi Gut, Newfoundland, is typical of the many inlets along Canada's eastern coast.

Trans Canada Airlines

CANADA—The over 5,000 mile boundary between the United States and Canada is convincing proof that two great nations may live side by side in peace and harmony. For over a hundred years this boundary line —the longest in the world—has been free from fortification of any kind by either nation.

Canada is the largest domain of the British Commonwealth. It extends from the icy waters of the Arctic to the borders of the United States, and from east to west its greatest distance is 3,700 miles. Its area is greater than that of the United States and nearly as large as the continent of Europe. Like the United States, Canada can be roughly divided into three sections: the eastern highlands, a great level central plain, and mountain ranges extending from the Rockies to the Pacific.

In the east the Appalachian region is a beautiful land of hilly or mountainous terrain with very heavily forested sections and fertile farm lands. Just west of the highlands lies the St. Lawrence Valley including the Ontario peninsula, the hub of Canada's industry. In this area, rich in minerals, forests, water power and fertile land, is the highest concentration of population. Moderate climate combined with valuable accessible resources have made this a section of the greatest economic importance. Northwest of the Valley is the Canadian Shield, an area characterized by low hills, countless lakes connected by streams and rapids. Here is Canada's greatest store of resources, minerals, forests, furs and water power. In the interior Plains is the great wheat belt. In the west, parallel to the Pacific, is the magnificent mountain country formed by the Cordilleran Mountain System. In addition to minerals and valuable forests, this area, in the fertile valleys, produces much of Canada's fruit and vegetable crops.

Wheat is the principal crop of the prairie provinces, and Canada is one of the biggest producers and exporters of this grain. Lumbering is of great importance, which is to be expected, for the forests of Canada are among the largest in the world. Furs have been a great source of wealth since the early

Drumlins, elongated mounds of glacial drift, as seen from the air over Labrador.

Walter Nebiker

U.S. Air Forces

Like a wide river of ice with side-streams, Ribbon Glacier descends from high peaks near Mt. McKinley, Alaska.

days of the Hudson's Bay Company, and the fishing grounds of Canada are the largest and most productive on earth.

Canada's mineral resources are of the richest in the world and include uranium, petroleum, gold, nickel, iron, lead, zinc and copper. Since the expansion of railroads and, more recently, the development of air service, their exploitation is rapidly increasing. As over six per cent of Canada's area is water, the country's potential hydroelectric power is almost limitless.

About half of the population is of British origin and one third is French. The rest are Germans, Russians, Scandinavians and others. Indians number some hundred thousands; in the Arctic region live a few thousand Eskimo.

UNITED STATES—Within the last two hundred years the United States of America has written an amazing chapter in history. In that brief period a wilderness has been tamed, and a powerful nation has arisen to take its place among the foremost countries of the world. A land populated by people of every race and creed, and a haven of refuge for the oppressed, its phenomenal growth has never been equalled. Far removed from the traditions and hampering fetters of the Old World, it has charted a new course in government. Its freedom loving people have devoted their energies to

developing the riches that Nature has so lavishly supplied.

The United States has reached its present position of economical and industrial importance because of a number of reasons. It is blessed with a favorable climate and is rich in mineral resources. With a coastline on three sides well supplied with harbors, it is ideally situated for trade with the rest of the world. Many of its rivers and lakes are navigable and give easy access into the interior of the country. The variety of climate and the fertility of the soil make a great diversity of crops possible.

Climate has made the people of the United States energetic, and Nature has endowed the land with more than enough to meet their needs. This country's way of life has provided the incentive for continually bettering the standards of living of its people. All this has brought continued economic, cultural and scientific progress.

The United States is the greatest manufacturing nation in the world, with about one third of the population depending upon industry for a living. It has the finest systems of transporation and communication, including the great majority of the automobiles in the world. About one third of the coal, and a quarter of the iron in the world, as well as large deposits of almost all important minerals are found here.

TWA-Trans World Airlines
Modern, many-storied office buildings characterize the sky line of New York City.

The three principal geographical features are a continuation of those in Canada. They are the eastern highlands, comprising the Appalachian Range, the broad central plains, and the Rockies and coastal ranges in the Far West.

A closer study of the geography of the United States does much to explain the growth of the nation. For example, the stony soil of New England discouraged farming and caused the early settlers to turn to manufacturing and commerce. The swift streams furnished water power and the jagged coastline provided bays for harboring ships from Europe. Farther south, the coastal plains widen out into broad stretches of fertile land, and the rivers are short and deep. The climate is favorable to crops that require long hot summers. This led to the development of large plantations. Here the coastal plain includes half of Georgia, all of Florida, and extends along the Gulf of Mexico. It reaches into the interior as far as southern Illinois.

The lake and prairie region of the upper Mississippi Valley is one of the most fertile in the world. It is linked by waterways with the East and South through the Great Lakes and the Mississippi River system. The Great Plains region, depending upon the nature of the topsoil and the amount of rainfall, is either grain or grazing country, with valuable deposits of oil in Texas and Oklahoma.

To the west of the Rocky Mountains, in the valleys and along the coast of California, the soil is fertile and the climate favorable for the growing of a great variety of fruits and vegetables.

With Alaska becoming a state (in 1958), the United States now embraces land reaching into the Arctic, while the statehood of Hawaii, voted for by Congress in March, 1959, adds a region of tropical island climate and vegetation.

Purchased from Russia in 1867 for a pittance, Alaska became a most valued U.S. possession and it is now the 49th state. Although Alaska is partially in the Arctic Circle, it is by no means the frozen and inhospitable land its latitude would suggest. Alaska has a wide area of equable climate. Along its mountainous and island-fringed coast, the warm Japanese Current keeps the temperature almost always above zero. This rises in the summer to a seasonal heat of 80°. These sections endure drenching rain, caused by the condensation of warm winds striking the snow-capped peaks of the mountains. In the center of Alaska is a broad upland where grasses, flowers and mosses grow.

The Yukon River, rising in Canada, swings across Alaska for 1,265 miles, all of which are navigable. Although frozen for two-thirds of the year, this river is a main artery of travel. Dog sled teams replace the large steamers when it is icebound. Even though the growing season is short, the Arctic days provide long hours of sunshine.

Walter Nebiker
Spanish-style church on Watling I., Bahamas, where Columbus first landed in 1492.

The popular conception of the Arctic does, however, exist in the northern regions. Here the ground thaws only a few inches at the surface during the summer. Except for a few Eskimo and reindeer, there is comparatively no life or vegetation able to survive the rigors of the frigid climate.

First known as "Seward's Folly," Alaska justified its purchase within a few short years and has proved a veritable storehouse of treasure. Each year it produces more than twice its purchase price, in minerals alone. Its population is increasing and its industries are expanding. In this development, the 1,525 miles long Alaska Highway and improved air service play a major part.

The Aleutian Islands are strung out in a broad arc off the tip of Alaska for a thousand miles and separate the Bering Sea from the North Pacific. Numbering about one hundred and fifty islands, they are the tops of submerged mountains. Included in the purchase of Alaska, they have great strategic value as air bases and weather observing stations for the United States.

Small towns like Peacham, Vermont, add to the rural charm of the New England countryside.

Winston Pote

MEXICO — Beyond the southern border of the United States and across the Rio Grande, where North America begins to taper sharply to a point, lies Latin America. It is difficult to conceive of the contrast to be found beyond this man-made boundary with the rest of the continent. It is another world, with a totally different culture, another language, and traditions and customs which set it apart from its northern neighbors.

Over one fifth the area of the United States, Mexico swings south for about eighteen hundred miles, ending in the narrow hook of the peninsula of Yucatan.

While half of Mexico lies in the torrid zone, its climate is determined more by elevation than latitude. Along the coast the weather is hot and humid, with luxuriant

Picturesque Taxco, in Mexico, founded by Cortes In 1529

Constance Larson

Charles Perry Weimer
Farm and farmhouse in El Salvador.

between. The average altitude of this plateau is about 6,500 feet. Mexico's highest concentration of population is here where the fertile land, ideal climate and favorable rainfall afford excellent conditions for agricultural crops. Although industrial development has increased rapidly in recent years and most of Mexico's wealth is derived from her mines and petroleum, the great majority of the people are still employed in agricultural pursuits. Except for the coastal plain bordering the Gulf of Mexico, mountains and plateaus occupy the greater part of Mexico. Lying in both the temperate and torrid zones allows the country to produce a greater variety of crops than is possible in most other countries.

Mexico is a beautiful and picturesque country with ancient ruins of pyramids and temples still standing as mute evidence of a flourishing civilization that existed before the coming of the Spanish invaders in the early fifteenth century.

bors on both coasts, with the principal seaports on the Caribbean Sea. Most of the rivers that flow into the Caribbean are navigable.

Charles Perry Weimer
Volcano Santiago near Managua, Nicaragua.

tropical vegetation. As the land rises the climate changes to temperate and the mountain peaks are snow-clad. Two mountain chains, that are a continuation of those in the United States, converge and meet at the southern tip, leaving a high plateau

Guatemalan Indians, descendants of the Mayas, selling their wares in Chichicastenango.

E. L. Jordan

CENTRAL AMERICA — As North America decreases in size from a land of magnificent distance to a slender neck of land where the Isthmus of Panama joins South America, the sizes of its nations shrink to even greater extent. In Central America a string of six small countries, Guatemala, Honduras, El Salvador, Nicaragua, Costa Rica and Panama, is confined to an area less than that of the State of Texas. Their total population does not equal that of New York City.

The Cordilleras, a continuation of the mountain chains starting far north in Alaska, extend the entire length of the land. Many of the peaks are volcanic and frequent eruptions occur. These mountains have formed many high and fertile plateaus which provide fine pasturage for livestock and rich soil for a diversity of crops. As in Mexico, the tropical climate of the lower regions is tempered by the elevation of the high plateaus. There are a number of har-

These agricultural nations have become increasingly important in the past few years. With the organizing of the Pan American Union, the growth of air travel, and the fostering of a new spirit of co-operation between the republics of North and South

Natives displaying their attractive woven goods in Santiago Atitlán, Guatemala.

E. L. Jordan

Hamilton Wright

El Morro fortress, centuries-old sentinel guarding the harbor of San Juan, Puerto Rico.

America, Central America's future became one of promise. When global war shut off supplies of many important crops to the Western world from the East, it was found that here in the Americas could be grown many necessities that formerly had been imported from afar. Great variation in soils, rainfall, and terrain afford an enormous variety of tropical, semi-tropical and temperate crops. Experiments have successfully produced important quantities of spices, fibers, and essential oils for medicinal and industrial purposes that were introduced from the East. Among the important crops exported almost exclusively to the United States are bananas, natural rubber, coffee, rope fibers, cacao and sugar.

Although there is potential mineral wealth in most of the countries of Central America, this resource, for the most part, has been unexploited. Much of the land is heavily forested and some of the world's most valuable woods such as mahogany, rosewood, teak and ebony are found here. However, only a very small part of the forests have been as yet cut for commercial purposes.

ISLANDS OF THE CARIBBEAN—The Caribbean Sea is a vital water link between the Americas and the West Indies. With the opening of the Panama Canal it took on added importance as a trade route for the ships of the world.

The Caribbean islands, which Columbus named the Indies in the belief he had reached India, extend in a wide arc beginning near southern Florida and ending off the coast of Venezuela. The upper part of this arc is called the Greater Antilles and includes Jamaica, Cuba, Hispaniola, Puerto Rico and some smaller islands. The lower part of the arc from Virgin Islands to Curacao and Aruba is made up of many small islands known as the Lesser Antilles.

Cuba, the largest island of the Greater Antilles, and Haiti and the Dominican Republic, which share Hispaniola, the second largest of this island group, are independent countries, and Puerto Rico is a free commonwealth associated with the United States. Jamaica and most of the islands of the Lesser Antilles are united in the Federation of the West Indies within the British Commonwealth. The small islands east of Puerto Rico comprise the Virgin Islands. Some of them are British but do not belong to the West Indies Federation; the rest form a territory of the United States.

Although most of the Caribbean islands are mountainous, there is sufficient arable land to permit the raising of a great variety of tropical products. The climate is hot but tempered by the trade winds. All the islands are subject to hurricanes and in many regions occur occasional volcanic eruptions.

The original Carib Indians have for the most part disappeared from the islands. In Cuba, Puerto Rico and the Dominican Republic, the descendants of the white Spanish settlers form a large part of the population. In the other islands, the majority of the peoples are Negro or of mixed descent.

All the Caribbean islands depend on farming, and since they are very densely populated, the available crops are insufficient. Many of the natural resources are underdeveloped. In recent years a more extensive utilization of the natural wealth has set in, as modern agricultural planning helps to improve the crops, industrial manufacture is encouraged, and better transportation opens up wider markets.

CUBA — This largest of the Caribbean islands is also the most fertile, often called the "Pearl of the Antilles." Its actual name is of Indian origin. After its discovery by Columbus in 1492, it was ruled by Spain until 1898 and in 1902 became a republic under United States direction, which ended in 1934. The population contains minorities of Negroes, native Indians and mixed groups, but the majority (about 66%) are white, of Spanish descent. Customs and traditions have a distinctly Spanish flavor.

In Central and South America, sugar cane is cut by hand and large numbers of seasonal workers are required for its harvest.

Hamilton Wright

Cuba has a coast line of about 2500 miles and many excellent harbors. Only one of its rivers is navigable, but it has extensive railroad and highway systems. Cuba exports more cane sugar than any other country, and its tobacco is of the finest. It also grows coffee, corn and bananas and exports fresh fruits and vegetables mainly to the United States. There are large iron deposits, and other minerals, such as copper and gold, are mined. The trade winds bring coolness in the summer, and the winters are mild. Ferryboat service with Florida and air service with North and South America assist commerce and the important tourist trade.

HAITI — The western portion of the island of Hispaniola, where the Gulf of Gonaives reaches far inland, is occupied by Haiti. This

Dominican Information Center

Central American countries produce sugar mainly for export. This sugar factory is in the Dominican Republic.

Publishers Photo Service

The raising and export of tropical fruit is an important activity in Central America.

was the first of the Latin American countries to gain independence. In 1804 it shook off French rule, retaining, however, one important heritage, the French language; it is the only French-speaking republic in the Americas. The majority of the population is Negro.

Trade winds from the northeast bring rain and fertility to Haiti's tropical valleys. Coffee, which grows wild on its slopes, is the chief product for export. Haiti is also known for its sisal fiber, obtained from the leaves of the agave plant, which is used for lariats and other tough cordage, and its logwood, which furnishes an important dye.

DOMINICAN REPUBLIC — This comprises the eastern and larger part of the island of Hispaniola, bordering on the Atlantic Ocean and the Caribbean Sea. During its turbulent past, the country saw Spanish and Haitian rule and was temporarily occupied by the

United States (1916-1924). Its capital, Ciudad Trujillo, formerly called Santo Domingo, was founded by Columbus' brother Bartholomew and is the oldest surviving European town in the Americas.

The island's Monte Tina, 10,301 feet high, is the highest peak in the Caribbean. The country is mainly agricultural, cattle are extensively raised, the mineral resources include gold, and the forests abound in valuable timber. The most important products for export are sugar and molasses.

PUERTO RICO — This island, crisscrossed by craggy mountains and deep valleys, rises close to the greatest known depth of the Atlantic Ocean, and its southern shore is washed by the Caribbean Sea. In the West Indies group, it is the easternmost island of the Greater Antilles, of which Cuba, Hispaniola and Jamaica are the other larger units. Roughly rectangular in shape, it is about 100 miles long by 35 miles wide.

Puerto Rico was discovered by Columbus in 1493. Morro Castle, which guards the entrance to the harbor of San Juan, the capital, was built by the Spaniards, who ruled the island until 1898, when it was ceded to the United States. Puerto Rico has been a free commonwealth associated with the United States since 1952.

The island has over 2 million inhabitants and an area of 3,435 square miles; it is thus very densely populated with more than 643

inhabitants to the square mile. Its major agricultural crop is sugar. Tobacco, coffee and fruits are also extensively raised. By 1956, manufacturing had gained ground and the income from it exceeded that from agriculture. The climate is mild the year around with a mean winter temperature of 73° and a summer temperature of about 79°. This fine climate and excellent shipping and air connections attract many tourists.

THE WEST INDIES—A FEDERATION —This young nation was born on January 3, 1958. It is within the British Commonwealth. It has a population of about 3 million people, of whom the majority are Negroes, but there are many thousands of mixed descent, and Trinidad has a large minority of East Indians. With a land area of about 8,000 square miles, the West Indies Federation ranges in a huge sweep of over 1,500 miles of the Caribbean Sea—from Jamaica in the northwest to Trinidad in the southwest, off the South American coast. Jamaica accounts for more than half of the land area and half of the population. The islands are widely scattered, small and heavily overpopulated. They depend mostly on agricultural products, with sugar as the chief export. Trinidad's rich oil fields make it the most industrial and valuable part of the Federation. The other islands base their economy largely on sugar, rum, bauxite and the tourist trade.

Air view of English Harbour, Antigua, in the West Indies.

Hamilton Wright
Children in native costume in Medellín, Colombia.

Charles Perry Weimer
Sparkling bays and jagged hills form Rio de Janeiro's impressive natural setting.

SOUTH AMERICA — It is a common error to think of South America as being directly south of the United States. A glance at the globe will show that this is far from the truth. Except for the bulge to the west and the southern tip, all of South America is east of the Atlantic coast boundary of the United States. This places South America much closer to Africa than North America is to Europe. A theory has been advanced, though never proved, that at one time Africa and South America were joined.

Smaller than North America by nearly two million square miles, and representing one-seventh of the world's total land area, South America is the fourth largest continent.

With the equator crossing South America on a line with the Amazon River, two thirds of this southern neighbor is in the tropics and the balance in the temperate zone. In

common with other lands situated in the Southern Hemisphere, it has the further disadvantage of being far removed from the principal world markets. These factors, together with the history of the continent, explain why it has not developed as rapidly as the United States, although discovered at the same time. But in spite of the handicaps of climate, position and history, South America has an extensive trade with the United States and Europe. And, although for centuries the Spaniards robbed it of its buried treasures, South America still possesses great mineral wealth.

South of the Isthmus of Panama, the great line of mountains which extends the entire length of North America becomes the mighty Andes. Second only to the Himalayas, they follow the western coast to Cape Horn, rising steeply from the Pacific in long ranges of snow-capped peaks and wide plateaus. Mount Aconcagua is the highest peak in the Americas and rises to nearly twenty-three thousand feet. Several lesser peaks are active volcanos. To the south the range begins to narrow and the coast is bordered by a tattered fringe of islands clothed with pines and swept by fierce northwesterly winds.

In the east are two broad plateaus, the Guiana and Brazilian highlands, which might be compared with the Laurentian highlands and the Appalachian chain of North America. Between the eastern slope of the Andes and these plateaus lie broad lowlands. The grassy, tree-dotted plains, or *llanos,* of the Orinoco Basin in Venezuela and Colombia, provide fine pasturage between the dry and rainy seasons. In the dry season they practically revert to desert. To the south are the dry plains, or *pampas,* of Northern Argentina, which is the great cattle country of the continent.

The Amazon—largest river system in the world—drains over one third of the continent. This area is equal to two thirds that of the United States. This mighty river is

four thousand miles long and in some places is over fifty miles wide. It flows through the densest tropical forest in the world and much of it is unexplored.

The La Plata River is actually the estuary for three rivers, the Paraná, with a drainage area almost as large as that of the Mississippi, the Uruguay and the Paraguay.

Don Murray
Native children in Brazil doing their share of the farmwork.

Buenos Aires, metropolis of the Southern Hemisphere, is situated on the south bank of the La Plata 175 miles from the Atlantic.

The only important indentations on the Pacific are found along the rugged coast of southern Chile and the Gulf of Guayaquil in Ecuador.

The high temperature and humidity of the tropical regions, together with many insects and diseases, discourage the activity of white people and even sap the strength of the natives. Large areas of swamp and rugged mountains have made the development of transportation difficult and expensive. Only with the growth of air travel has it been possible for the Andean countries to contact one another with relative ease.

In the main, South America is sparsely settled, with the greatest density of popula-

The backdrop for Caracas' baroque churches and modern apartment buildings is formed by the slopes of an eastern spur of the Andes.

Hamilton Wright

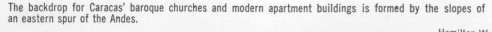

tion along the coasts. The original inhabitants were Indians, but, due to the early colonization by the Spanish and Portuguese, many of the present inhabitants are *mestizos*, a mixture of Indian and Spanish or Portuguese blood. The remainder is largely composed of Italian and German immigrants. Except in Brazil, where the official language is Portuguese, Spanish is spoken in all the other independent countries.

Since the early coming of the Spaniards, South America has continued to yield great stores of precious metals. The Andes are rich in minerals, and the eastern highlands contain iron, gold, and diamonds. Some coal is found in Brazil, Chile and Colombia, but

Moore-McCormack

Its extensive port facilities have helped to make Buenos Aires one of the largest and most important trade centers in the western hemisphere.

Charles Perry Weimer

Llamas in the highlands of Bolivia serving as beasts of burden.

Charles Perry Weimer

Ruins of an ancient Indian citadel at Machu Picchu high in the Peruvian mountains.

not in great quantity. Water-power and oil are being utilized to make up for this lack.

Ecuador, Peru and Chile are all west coast countries, which, until the opening of the Panama Canal, were practically isolated from the rest of the world. Bolivia, having no outlet to the sea, moves nearly all of her exports through the seaports of Chile and Peru.

CHILE — Sometimes called the "Shoestring Republic," Chile stretches along the west coast for twenty-six hundred miles, from the borders of Peru to Cape Horn. It has a

variety of climate ranging from frigid to torrid. This long, narrow and mountainous country is one of the most progressvie in South America. It is one of the three republics where there are more white people than natives. The other two are Argentina and Uruguay.

From north to south Chile is divided into three regions: the desert, a dry sub-tropical region which is densely populated, and a section that is forested. The greatest mineral region lies between Santiago and the Peruvian border. In the northern half of this area are the nitrate fields which have produced almost the entire world's supply of this important fertilizer. The nitrate beds located in the Pacific coastal desert (Atacama) were wrested from Peru during the War of the Pacific (1879-83) from which Chile emerged victorious. Chile's fame as a nitrate region has waned with the introduction of synthetic nitrate into world industry. The country is now seeking to stimulate the export of wine, honey and livestock. In the southern half there are deposits of copper, iron, gold and silver. Chile ranks next to the United States in the mining of copper and supplies about 20 per cent of the world's output.

PERU—This country is an extension of the narrow and arid coastal plain in northern Chile, with the Andes occupying fully half of the land. A densely wooded tropical region drops down in the east to meet the low-plains of Brazil.

About a fourth of the population is white, most of whom are Spanish. The balance are *mestizos* (mixed) or Indians. Descendants of the ancient Incas, the Indians of Peru are found principally living on the high mountain slopes of the Andes, and sailing their strange fiber craft on Lake Titicaca. These Indians have domesticated the llama and the alpaca, two animals which are native to this region, and which have never been raised successfully elsewhere. The llama is a sure-footed animal upon which the Indians depend for food, clothing and transportation. Used as a beast of burden in this lofty arid country, the llama, like the camel, can go several days without water. The alpaca is too small to carry loads and is raised for its very long wool.

Once famous for its precious metals, Peru today produces in its mountains besides silver and gold other important minerals such as copper, zinc and vanadium. In the coastal lowlands, cotton and sugar are grown on

Not Panama but Ecuador is the place where the original, hand-woven "Panama" hats are made.

Hamilton Wright

large plantations (haciendas). In the head-lands of the Amazon River, shut off from the rest of the country by the Andes, oil has recently been discovered, which may hasten their development.

ECUADOR—Peru and Ecuador have a similar climate and topography except for the northern part of the coastal plain of Ecuador. This plain is as fertile as any area in South America and is the principal agricultural section of Ecuador. The chief crops are cacao, coffee and bananas. Ecuador's coffee and bananas have been increasing in importance since its cacao, blighted by witches'-broom, has suffered an appreciable decrease in export. Tagua, a substitute for ivory, is produced in limited quantities. Ecuador is world-famous for its amazing variety of wild birds. The country contains one-fourth of all recorded species in South America.

BOLIVIA—Shut off from the sea by Chile and Peru, Bolivia is one of the most sparsely populated countries in the world. It consists of a high plateau in the southwest that is cold and dry, and wet tropical lowlands in the north and east. Though Bolivia's surface is three fifths lowlands, the country includes one of the highest inhabitable regions in the world. The Andes spread out into two great chains of mountains which enclose a plateau nearly as high as the peaks themselves. On this plateau, on the border between Peru and Bolivia, lies Lake Titicaca, the highest navigable lake in the world.

While its scenery is tropical, Brazil's climate is tempered in many parts by altitude and sea breezes.

Brazilian Government Trade Bureau

Oil refinery at Cochabamba, second largest city in Bolivia. Bolivia's young oil industry promises to become important.

Bolivia ranks next to the Malay Peninsula and the Indonesian islands in its tin deposits, and is well supplied with nearly all the known metals. Strangely enough, although having local supplies of coal, necessary in smelting, it is usually cheaper to import coal.

Lack of capital, the high cost of transportation, and the scarcity of labor, have retarded mining in all the countries of the Andes. Only the natives can do manual labor in the high altitudes and the people are not inclined toward mining.

BRAZIL—Covering nearly half the continent and with half the population, Brazil lies almost entirely in the tropics. This republic is nearly as large as the United States and has three times the area of Argentina.

The Amazon and its tributaries have a total length of over nineteen thousand miles, of which thirteen thousand are navigable. This huge system extends through more than half the country's area.

The Brazilian Highlands, a great plateau country, extend to the south and east of the Amazon River. The capital, Brasilia, is located in this region. At the Atlantic shore lies Rio de Janeiro with its famous harbor. It is the second largest city on the continent.

Brazil at one time was the greatest rubber-producing country. Brazil has embarked on a program of intensified manufacturing. Silk, cotton and woolen mills have sprung up all over the eastern seaboard. Shoes and hats

are becoming major products. Many paper mills are being built to utilize some of the billion acres of forests that cover half the land area. Its greatest mineral wealth has yet to be exploited, though one of the largest estimated deposits of iron ore in the world is now being developed. The country produces nearly fifty percent of the world's coffee. Efforts to do away with the one-crop system are gaining success and coffee is no longer the economic tyrant that it was. A growing cacao industry now ranks second in the world, while tobacco, rice, cotton and sugar are attaining commercial significance.

URUGUAY—This is the smallest republic in South America. It has a fine climate with the winds of the ocean modifying the temperature.

Since the Spanish brought sheep and cattle to the grassy plains of Uruguay in the 17th century, it has been a stock raising country. Today it is one of the leading meat exporters of the world. Only a small percentage of the arable land is devoted to the raising of crops and it is limited in both minerals and manufacturing.

PARAGUAY—One of the two republics of South America that is completely surrounded by other nations. Little has been done to develop its natural resources.

Most of the surface of western Paraguay is a low, swampy and unhealthy plain. The climate in the north is hot and unsuited to

the white man. Most of the people live in the southern area east of the Paraguay River. It is a country of small villages, grazing and farm lands, which depends upon the rivers for means of transportation.

Extending from Bolivia across the western third of Paraguay and south into Argentina, is the Gran Chaco, a great plain.

THE ARGENTINE REPUBLIC — The early colonists' anticipation of finding silver and gold in Argentina prompted them to name the country for the Latin word meaning silver. Although the colonists' search for great mineral wealth was in vain, the fertile soil and temperate climate have fostered the country's great economic progress. The Republic is the second largest of the South American countries.

The Gran Chaco, in the northern part, is a land of forests, lakes and swamps, which is largely unexplored. The grassy plains of the *Pampas* occupy a large area of Argentina. This cattle country and farm land extends from the Atlantic coast to the Andes in the west, and northwest to the highlands which reach into Brazil. The rich grazing lands, which have led to Argentina becoming a large exporter of meat and wool, are in the center of the *Pampas*.

Argentina is an agricultural and commercial, rather than an industrial country. It has been hindered in the development of manufacture by a shortage of coal, the lack of water power, and an inadequate supply of minerals.

Descendants of the Spanish settlers are the leaders of the country, with most of the farm population consisting of Italians. Immigrants from the British Isles have taken to sheep raising, and many Germans have migrated to Argentina. Today most of the population are foreign-born or descendants of immigrants.

COLOMBIA—The only South American country having a coastline along both the Atlantic and Pacific oceans. Half the country is high in the rugged Andes; the other half lies in unhealthy tropical plains. Three cordilleras of the Andes traverse it in parallel lines from north to south forming a barrier between the seacoast and the rich inland valleys. The chief source of wealth is coffee. Colombian coffee is the finest in the world and the bean is jealously guarded. Ninety percent of the exported coffee is shipped to the United States. A type from the area around Medellín commands the highest price per pound in the world. Surpassed by Brazil in quantity, Colombia's coffee yields to none in quality. Next to coffee in export value is oil. The fields are to a large extent a continuation of those in Venezuela. Other resources include gold, platinum, emeralds and coal.

VENEZUELA—One of the most productive oil regions in the world is on the coast of the Caribbean. Easy access to this coast from the interior affords great possibilities for commercial and industrial development. Venezuela's land area is distinguished by its llanos or wide lowlands along the Orinoco River. The river is navigable for a course of 700 miles and is connected to the Amazon system by the Casiquare River, a natural canal. Coffee, chiefly from the basin of the Maracaibo, is second only to that of Colombia. A ranking producer of petroleum, Venezuela's exploitation of oil is fraught with difficulties which have never been successfully surmounted. Virgin forests cover the country and include about 600 species of wood. At Margarita is located a profitable pearl in-

The large oil deposits beneath the waters of Lake Maracaibo make Venezuela one of the most productive oil regions in the world.

dustry. Salt, asphalt, coal and gold figure as the main mineral resources.

THE GUIANAS — On the north coast of South America are the only European possessions on the continent. The climate is tolerable except in the south where the northeast trade winds do not prevail. Mineral resources in the form of gold and diamonds are about equally divided among the three Guianas.

Long stretches of the Pan American Highway pass through elevated highlands in sight of snow-capped peaks and extinct volcanoes.

Hamilton Wright

The Rock of Gibraltar guards the western entrance to the Mediterranean Sea.

Walter Nebiker

E. L. Jordan

On the Balearic Islands, as elsewhere in Europe, windmills were an important source of power before motors were invented.

EUROPE — Eurasia is the world's largest land mass and includes both Europe and Asia. Europe occupies about a third of the western end of Eurasia, and, with the exception of Australia, is the smallest continent.

the Balkan Peninsula is surrounded by the Black Sea and the Adriatic, Ionian and Aegean Seas of the Mediterranean.

Great Britain is prevented from being a peninsula only by the narrow English Channel, and was once a part of the mainland. The entire course of history has been changed by this strip of water which made England an island. The same may be said for the Straits of Gibraltar separating Europe from Africa. But for this eight-mile passage, the Mediterranean would have had no outlet to the Atlantic.

Europe may be divided into five natural regions: (1) the Northwest Highlands, (2) the Central Plains, (3) the Central Highlands, (4) the Southern Mountains and Plateaus, and (5) the Southern Lowlands.

Most of the British Isles, a section of France, and a good part of the Scandinavian Peninsula are included in the Northwest Highlands. This is the coastal region with excellent harbors where men have made

a cool, temperate climate and people are energetic.

The great Central Plains extend from the British Isles to the Ural Mountains that separate Europe from Asia. These plains range from the tundra regions of the Far North to the Caspian Sea, the Caucasus Mountains, and the Black Sea of the Southeast. In the Southwest they reach into southern France. Within such an extensive area there are naturally great differences in climate. There is also great diversity of vegetation and the occupations of the people.

The Central Highlands include the plateau in central France and take in parts of Belgium, southern Germany, Austria, and the Czecho-Slovakian area. It is the region of forest, water-power, and varied mineral resources. The industrial districts of Central Europe are the outgrowth of the great deposits of coal and iron found here.

The impressive peaks of the Alps rise south of the Central Highlands, forming one of the many ranges of Southern Europe. The Apennines extend the length of Italy, and other ranges follow the eastern coast of the Adriatic through Yugoslavia and Albania to the southern tip of Greece. Spreading out to the east they include most of the Balkan Peninsula. To the north the Carpathian Mountains swing northeast and then southeast around

The world's northernmost city, Hammerfest in Norway, lies in the region of the midnight sun. A warm ocean drift keeps the port ice-free.

E. L. Jordan

It is the most densely populated for its size and no other continent has so many separate nations. Nearly all of these countries have distinctive customs and speak different languages. This does much to explain Europe's turbulent history.

Actually Europe is a huge peninsula, subdivided into a number of lesser peninsulas, caused by the oceans and inland seas which encroach upon it. Its irregular form, together with the mountain barriers, and the presence of important islands near the continent, have contributed to the growth of individual nations.

In the northwest, two peninsulas are formed by the Baltic Sea. The countries of Norway and Sweden occupy the Scandinavian Peninsula. Denmark is on the Jutland Peninsula between the Baltic and North Seas. To the south, Portugal and Spain comprise the Iberian Peninsula. The peninsular boot of Italy thrusts out into the Mediterranean, and

their living by the sea, and commerce has become most important. In those places where coal and iron are found it has led to an industrial life. This highland region enjoys

Rome is the seat of the Vatican City State with the beautiful Renaissance basilica of St. Peter's.

TWA-Trans World Airlines

the valley of the Danube, forming with the Transylvanian Alps in Rumania a kind of semicircle around the Plain of Hungary. Farther to the east, the Caucasus Mountains reach from the Black to the Caspian Sea. Separating France and Spain are the Pyrenees, and the Sierra Nevadas are in southern Spain bordering the Mediterranean.

The Southern Lowlands of the Danube Valley and the Plain of Hungary represent some of the finest farming and grazing land in the world.

The extreme irregularity of the European coastline has been of great importance to the life of the people. With the North and Baltic Seas, the Mediterranean and Black Seas penetrating far into the interior, only Central Europe and Eastern Russia are very far from the coast. Although the combined areas of South America and Africa are nearly five times that of Europe, the coastline of Europe is longer.

TWA-Trans World Airlines
The Arch of Triumph, begun by Napoleon I, is a landmark of Paris.

A majority of the great seaports of the world are in Western Europe. Its people have led the world in seafaring.

Europe has a generally mild, temperate climate, particularly in the western areas,

Canals thread their way through the center of Amsterdam, capital of the Netherlands.

Karletta

British Information Services

The soil yields little and rural life is simple on the Isle of Skye, Scotland.

which are warmed by ocean currents and the winds blowing over these waters. Even the British Isles have a mild climate in spite of being in the same latitude as Labrador. Greater extremes of temperature exist in eastern Europe where these winds lose their moderating effect.

Due to the Alps blocking the cold north winds, and the influence of the warm waters of the Mediterranean, the southern shores of Europe enjoy a mild year-round climate. Except in eastern Europe, where the rainfall is light, there is generally sufficient moisture for agriculture.

GREAT BRITAIN AND NORTHERN IRELAND

GREAT BRITAIN AND NORTHERN IRELAND—The British Isles and the British Commonwealth of Nations owe much of their commercial and industrial growth to the daring and initiative of their early mariners. Although we usually think of the British Isles as comprising Great Britain and Ireland, it actually consists of nearly five thousand islands. Within the small compass of the islands there is a considerable variety of topography.

In Northern Ireland there are many lakes, including the largest one of the island, Lough Neagh, as well as a range known as the Mourne Mountains. A large portion of the country consists of the basalt plateau of Antrim.

Northern Ireland, or Ulster, as the six counties are sometimes called, is the seat of a very extensive lace and linen industry. In County Down and County Antrim there are highgrade deposits of granite and bauxite which are being exploited. Shipbuilding is a major industry centered in the capital, Belfast.

In Scotland the three well-marked divisions stand out, the highlands, the southern uplands, and between these two, the central lowlands, into which four fifths of the population is crowded. The lowlands contain the richest agricultural land as well as the coal fields. They are penetrated by three great estuaries, the Firths of Tay and Forth on the east, and of Clyde on the west, so that communication coastwise or overseas is everywhere easy.

Scotland has some of the largest shipbuilding yards in the world on the Firth of Clyde. Sheep and cattle are raised in large numbers since the land is not well suited to agriculture.

The Welsh cliffy upland is flanked to the north and east by small coal fields, but the greatest field lies to the south. A belt of limestone running from Bill of Portland to Tees Bay, and bearing at many points valuable iron ores, serves as a rough boundary of industrial England, for to the south and east of it, apart from the metropolis, agricultural interests predominate. Lying to the west of the limestone band is the Devon-Cornwall peninsula, where great bosses of granite and slate form the famous moors.

Wales, after 700 years as a part of the English kingdom, retains its individuality and is nationalistic in speech, dress and customs. The Welsh language is Celtic, akin to the Gaelic of Ireland. It is the only speech of nearly one tenth of the people.

Because of the density of population Great Britain is far from self-sustaining and must depend upon the raw materials and products

The colorful uniforms of the "Yeomen of the Guard," also called "Beefeaters," attest to England's tendency to preserve old customs.

British Information Services

Typical Irish landscape in County Donegal, Ireland.

of other countries. This has led to the development of her world-wide commerce, a large part of which is carried on with the other members of the British Commonwealth. Agriculture is intensive with much importance placed on livestock. Many of the world's most valuable breeds of farm animals have been developed on English farms.

IRELAND—Except for coastal hills and mountains, the country is largely an ill-drained plain dotted with lakes and peat-bogs, and crossed by the sluggish Shannon. In the southwest is the beautiful Killarney Lakes region which attracts many tourists each year. Although little of the land is suitable for large scale agriculture, grass and fodder crops are abundant and provide stockraising needs which is the major in-

dustry of the country. The Shannon River, Royal Canal, and the Grand Canal provide an excellent inland waterway system of transportation. Shannon airport, near Limerick, is a major international airway terminal. Horse-breeding is the most famous of Irish farm industries. A prosperous tourist trade is developing.

NORWAY AND SWEDEN—With its saw-toothed coast, great fiords, and neighboring islands, it is natural that Norway, occupying the western part of the Scandinavian peninsula, would be a maritime country. Norway's long coast line, facing the Atlantic, is edged with lofty cliffs and seamed with deep fiords. Islands, countless in number, fringe the coast. Most of the country is a rocky, rugged and barren land, about 20 per cent of which is forested. The rivers are short and torrential, but provide the finest salmon fishing in Europe. The Kjolen Mountains which form the backbone of the peninsula separate Norway from Sweden. These mountains rise in many parts to over 6,000 feet, the highest peaks being over 8,000 feet.

Norway is the land of the "midnight sun". From Trondheim northward at least a part of the disk of the sun is visible from May through July. But the winter nights are 17 hours long and midday seems like twilight during the winter months. Another striking feature is that much of the area above the Arctic Circle is warmer than some regions further south. Northeast Norway is the warmest part of the country in the summer.

Sweden consists primarily of a tableland sloping from the Kjolen Range to the Baltic. No less than 8 per cent of the surface of Sweden is water, the immense number of lakes covering almost 15,000 square miles. The two largest, Vänern and Vättern, in the southern portion of the country, are connected by a system of canals. Besides the

large number of small islands which fringe the coast, Sweden includes the two large Baltic islands of Gotland and Oland.

In Sweden, iron deposits are among the richest in the world. Swedish steel is universally famous for its fine qualities. The making of machinery for export is a major industry. Swedish agriculture is in a very high state of development, and exports wheat, bacon and butter in large quantities. In forestry and sawmilling the nation has evolved advanced methods and nearly half of her exports are in pulp and paper products.

DENMARK — Denmark occupies a peninsula and numerous islands lying at the entrance to the Baltic. It is a lowland country characterized by many lakes, ponds and short rivers. Its sandy shores are shallow, with lagoons shut in by shifting sand bars. Most of Denmark is farm land, about half of which is used for grazing. The Faeroe Islands produce fish, mutton and wool for the homeland.

Dairy farming is the country's chief industry, the products of which comprise nearly all her exports. Greenland, the largest island in the world, is a part of Denmark.

ICELAND — The republic is an island in the north Atlantic consisting of a great tableland averaging 2,000 feet above sea level. Of its whole area barely a quarter is habitable. The surface is dotted by over 100 volcanic peaks. There are many boiling springs and the geysers are world-famous. It is too cold for agriculture but has rich grazing land for sheep and cattle. Fishing provides the chief products for export.

FINLAND—Finland consists of a great plateau, ranging from 400 to 600 feet in elevation. The southern half of the plateau has about 25 per cent of its area occupied by thousands of shallow lakes, many of them linked by short natural or artificial channels, providing many miles of navigable waterways. Forests cover the greater part of the country which has led to lumbering, paper-making and the manufacture of woodenware. Over half the population is engaged in agricultural pursuits which are carried on under great difficulties.

THE NETHERLANDS — The tiny kingdom of the Netherlands, lacking natural resources, has been largely a nation of seafarers for centuries. Along the canals, the meadows are often ten or twelve feet below the water line, and between the land and the sea at high tide there may be a difference of twenty-five feet or more. The land is protected by embankments and dikes, and it may be pictured as a great trough, the floor of which slopes down from east and southeast toward the North Sea. The rivers which flow across the country from the

The picturesque old part of Stockholm lies on an island in Lake Mälaren.

Swedish National Travel Office

Belgian Government Information Center

Some of the atmosphere of the Middle Ages
can still be felt in Bruges, Flanders.

higher continent beyond, are at their mouths
frequently below the level of the sea, into
which they have to be lifted by canals and
locks across the dams or dikes. A large part
of the land has been reclaimed from the sea
and little by little it has become a fertile
country.

BELGIUM — Smaller than Holland, Belgium
is one of Europe's most densely populated
countries. Situated between England, Holland,
France and Germany, it is in the very center
of industrial Europe. The country is well
watered, and has two principal rivers, the
Scheldt and the Maas. Four fifths of the
land are under cultivation, and although over
half the people are engaged in either farming or stock raising the country still does
not raise sufficient food to feed her people.
Belgium's intensive industrialization has been
at the expense of its agriculture, for the valley of the Sambre-Meuse, the chief industrial
center, is also the richest farming land.
Metals from the Katanga region of the
Belgian Congo are intensifying industrial ac-
tivities. The textile industry is also important.
The nation furnishes a great variety of farm
products and is known for its world-famous
breed of horses.

LUXEMBOURG—The Grand Duchy of Luxembourg, smaller than the state of Rhode
Island, is one of Europe's oldest states. An
abundant store of iron ore has encouraged
mining, smelting and some manufacturing.
International trade of the duchy has been
carried on through a customs union with
Belgium.

LIECHTENSTEIN—Only 27 miles larger than
San Marino, Liechtenstein is a part of the
Swiss customs union. Switzerland also ad-
ministers its postal facilities.

FRANCE—France is largely an agricultural
country where the farmers, instead of living
on their farms usually live in nearby villages.
Although rich in minerals, it has lagged behind both England and Germany as an industrial country. France does not mine sufficient coal to make full use of its large iron
ore deposits. The country's supply of energy
has recently been supplemented by hydro-
electric power obtained mainly in the alpine
regions. It is a leading producer of textiles
and has an important silk and rayon industry
at Lyon. The business and traffic center of
the entire country is Paris.

A large part of southeastern France is
taken up by the Massif Central, a roughly
triangular plateau with peaks reaching
above 6,000 feet. Its eastern edge is formed
by the Cevennes, and from them to the Vos-
ges extend other mountain ranges. There is
a mountainous area in Brittany, but the
greatest heights are on the frontiers, the
Jura, the Pyrenees, and the Alps separating
France respectively from Switzerland, Spain
and Italy. The Ardennes in the northeast are
less lofty. The Seine drains the north, the
Loire and the Garonne the west, and the
Rhône the east and south. France has an
extensive network of canals and much of its
freight travels by waterway.

France enjoys a delightful climate. Only
in the region of the Alps is real winter encountered. Protected by the mountains to
the north, the balmy area along the Mediterranean is a magnet that has drawn countless vacationers. Many semi-tropical plants
and fruits are grown in this section. Here
also lies Grasse, an important center of the
French perfume industry. In other parts of
the country, notably around Paris and in
Flanders, an abundant wheat crop is obtained. A great number of livestock are
raised in many regions, particularly in Normandy and the Massif Central. Favored by
a mild climate and fertile soils, French

viticulture has reached a high standard of
excellency. France produces more wine than
any other country, and the names of many
of its vineyards and wine cellars have become famous throughout the world.

MONACO—The Principality of Monaco is
one of the smallest states in the world. It
possesses the administrative organs and in-
stitutions of larger nations in miniature. It
has no taxes for it is supported by the
gambling casino of Monte Carlo from which
its own citizens are barred. The most striking
feature of this 370 acre state is the Mon-
agasque Acropolis on a headland 200 feet
above the water. The Prince's Palace, a
magnificent structure, is located on it.

SWITZERLAND—This rugged little country
is a completely land-locked republic
nestling among the beautiful Alps. It has
succeeded in maintaining its neutrality and
independence while the rest of Europe engaged in costly and devastating wars. Cap-
italizing upon its wonderful mountain and
lake scenery, Switzerland has been the playground of Europe for many years. Although it has only very limited natural resources, the country has harnessed its great
water power and is producing high-quality
manufactured goods. On the slopes of the
Alps and in the high valleys, dairying and
cattle raising provide the chief occupation.

GERMANY—There are two natural regions in
Germany, the low northern plains and the
central and southern highlands. During the
glacial period, sand was deposited over the
plains region and the soil in many parts is
not fertile, requiring the heavy use of fertilizers. Potatoes, sugar beets and rye are
the chief crops, and cattle and horses are
raised on large farms. In the central and
southern highlands, a variety of fruits, vege-

River traffic on Rhine near St. Goar. On terraced hillsides are famous vineyards.

Rapallo on the Italian Riviera attracts vacationers from many parts of the world.

Walter Nebiker

tables and grains are grown on small farms. In Bavaria, where the Alps reach German soil, dairy farming prevails.

Germany's major rivers flow from the southern highlands northward, emptying into the North and Baltic Seas. Long stretches of them are navigable, and their lower courses are connected by canals providing cheap river traffic across the country and to the ocean. The Rhine carries more than half of this traffic, being the only river whose water supply remains adequate during the summer months. A system of canals enables German Rhine shipping to reach the ocean at a German seaport, Emden. Ships from the Baltic have a short route to the North Sea through the Kiel canal.

Germany is devoid of many important natural resources. However, she has an exceptionally large supply of coal. This formed the basis for the development of the country into one of the world's leading industrial nations. The chief coal fields are in the Ruhr Basin. Together with the adjacent part of

Mittenwald, Bavaria, is typical of places in the Bavarian and Austrian Alps.

Karletta

the Rhine valley, it is Germany's main industrial center. Germany also has sizable supplies of potash and petroleum and possesses some iron ore. The hydroelectric power obtained mainly in the southern highlands furnishes energy to a growing number of industries.

Germany's location in the center of Europe has meant both cultural stimulation and political tension. After the Second World War, the country was divided into an eastern and western part, each belonging to a different political sphere. This division upset the balance between Germany's various industrial and agricultural regions and required a far-reaching economic reorientation.

AUSTRIA AND HUNGARY — Austria is characterized by its beautiful mountain scenery, over 90 percent of the land is classified as mountainous, which has contributed to development of one of its largest industries—tourist and resort trade. However, over 80 per cent of the land is productive and half of this is under cultivation. In contrast, Hungary is largely comprised of a low fertile plain. The country is primarily agricultural and is a great grain and wine producer.

CZECHOSLOVAKIA — This land-locked country contains strategic routes between north and south Europe of economic and political value. The country has two large mountain ranges, the Carpathian in the east and the Sudeten in the west. Czechoslovakia is famous for its subterranean caverns and its spas and mineral springs. The people are energetic and progressive and there are valuable forest resources, fertile soil and varied mineral deposits.

THE BALKANS—They include Rumania, Yugoslavia, Bulgaria, Albania, Greece and European Turkey. Located at the gateway to Asia, and on a natural route connecting the two continents, this region has been a battleground for centuries. Repeated invasions from various directions have resulted in a

number of racial groups and religious beliefs. The rugged nature of the country has isolated the people into many rival factions with intense racial and national spirit.

YUGOSLAVIA—It consists essentially of a mountainous core, which stretches from the Dinaric Alps in the northwest to the Balkan Mountains on the Bulgarian frontier. The only valley which cuts the mountains and forms a passageway is that of the Marava River, which, with that of the Vardar, leads from Belgrad to Thessalonike. Beyond the Sava-Danube, as far as the northern boundary, the land is low and swampy near the rivers, with a few minor elevations. The chief concentrations of people are around Zagreb and Belgrad. Yugoslavia's greatest problem is the lack of communications between its regions. The more highly developed coastal areas have access to outside markets, but further inland the mountains impose a rugged barrier between the provinces.

E. L. Jordan

Canals lined with trees are frequently seen in many European countries.

RUMANIA—In eastern Rumania the Carpathian Mountains from the northwest and the Transylvanian Alps from the southwest meet in the center to form a crescent. To the north and west of this crescent is the Transylvanian plateau; to the south and east are

The sounds of the Alphorn, a peculiar Swiss instrument, carry far across the valleys.

E. L. Jordan

The gleaming marbles of the Parthenon temple crown the Acropolis above Athens, Greece.

E. L. Jordan

Italy's colorful history, scenery and balmy climate have attracted many tourists which has in some measure offset an unfavorable balance of trade.

SAN MARINO—San Marino is one of the oldest republics in the world and is the smallest. It has always been on good terms with its big neighbor, Italy, by whom it is surrounded. The state was founded in the fourth century by Marinius of Dalmatia, a stonecutter. Except for a few invasions, its liberty has been respected, even by Napoleon. Much of its revenue is obtained through the sale of its postage stamps issued for the benefit of collectors.

the plains of Moldavia and Walachia. The principal rivers are the Danube in the south which enters the Black Sea at Sulina, and the Prut in the northeast and the Siret in the southeast—both of which connect with the Danube. At the southern and eastern edge of the Carpathian Mountains are Rumania's rich oil fields.

BULGARIA — The country is hilly and well watered by numerous streams, of which the Isker, Struma and Maritza are the most important. Although nearly one third of the country's area is in forests, only a small part of the wood is used commercially since about one fourth of the forest area is completely unproductive. Many of the forests consist of scrub timber and a sizeable portion of the good forests are inaccessible. Eighty percent of Bulgaria's population is employed in agriculture, the chief crops being tobacco and cereals. Attar of roses and silk are important products.

ALBANIA—Albania is a mountainous country on the western side of the Peninsula. In the center, part of the plateau is cultivable,

The donkey, once its chief beast of burden, is seen less often in modern, motorized Italy.

Hamilton Wright

and in the south there is fertile alluvial soil with grazing land on the slopes.

GREECE—With a very long coast line on the Aegean and Ionian Seas, and a large number of islands, including Crete, Mitylene, Chios, and the Dodecanese islands, the area is generally mountainous. The mountains, though not very high, divide the country into a number of small districts, between which communication is difficult. It is the sea which links the different regions of Greece.

ITALY—Once the hub of the known world, Italy's importance declined as the age of exploration and discovery opened up the ocean routes of the world. Taking no part in this period of conquest and empire building, she did not acquire colonies. Lacking unity she was in no position to demand her share of the rich prizes of newly discovered land being acquired by other European nations.

With the opening of the Suez Canal and tunnels through the Alps, her trade somewhat improved, but the absence of the necessary minerals prevented her from keeping pace with industrial development elsewhere in Europe.

The south slope of the Alps belongs to Italy. At the point where the Alps reach the Mediterranean, the Apennines begin. These mountains follow the length of Italy and form a rugged backbone which extends through the island of Sicily. The southern and western parts of the peninsula have been subjected to volcanic eruptions, and Vesuvius, Etna, and Stromboli are still active volcanoes. The chief lowlands are in the Po Valley with narrow coastal plains east and west of the Apennines. The majority of the people, and most of the agriculture and manufacturing, are located in the Po Valley. Consequently Northern Italy does not experience the poverty to be found in Southern Italy. It is from the south that most of the immigrants to the United States have come.

SPAIN AND PORTUGAL — About three fourths of the Iberian Peninsula is a granite plateau with a range of mountains dividing it in the center. The rivers that flow through this region through deep gorges block transportation and are unsuited for navigation, waterpower or irrigation. The dry climate, lack of water, a rugged land formation, poor soil and an absence of transportation have been great obstacles standing in the way of the economic development of both Spain and Portugal. A portion of the land in the valleys and plains has been made fertile through irrigation, and farming is the main industry. Fishing is important along the Portugal coast, although a great part of the coast is too rugged for harbors. There are forests in most of the higher areas where half the world's supply of cork is produced.

The beautiful Alhambra, rising above Granada in Spain, was a fortress-palace of the Moors.

E. L. Jordan

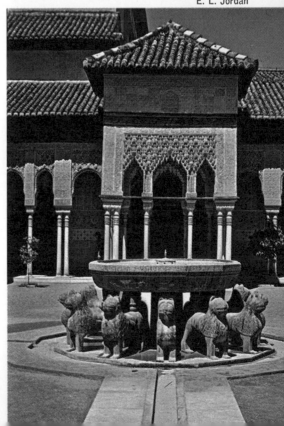

The High Tatra, on the Polish-Czechoslovakian border, is famous for its alpine scenery.

ANDORRA — Tiny Andorra is in the Pyrenees Mountains between France and Spain. It is not a republic, as is often supposed, but a joint dependency of France and the Bishops of Urgel in Spain. Its mountains are high and arid, and its valleys contain poor soil so that the people are nearly all engaged in pastoral pursuits. The one product of the soil is tobacco.

POLAND — Lying between the western European nations and Russia, Poland has changed its boundaries many times. It was for centuries a chiefly agricultural country. More recently, her resources of coal, iron, lead and zinc have helped her industrial progress. Since World War II the rich coal fields of Upper Silesia, formerly German, have become a part of Poland. Most of the land is comprised of a plain. The lower regions of the Vistula have marshes, sand dunes and lakes. The central plain of Poland with an elevation of about 500 feet is traversed by great rivers, the most important being the Oder and the Vistula. The Baltic seaports Swinoujscie and Gdansk were joined to Poland after World War II. In the south, the country reaches into the Sudeten and Carpathian mountains.

U.S.S.R.—Almost two and a half times the size of the United States and comprising more than one seventh of the world's land surface, the Union of Soviet Socialist Republics sprawls across two continents. A large part of European Russia and western Siberia is a great plain. Russia's position in northern latitudes and the absence of protecting barriers result in an extreme climate with long, cold winters. The port of Murmansk to the north of Finland, lying within the Arctic Circle, is kept ice-free throughout the year by warm ocean currents. Kaliningrad on the

Sovfoto

Blast furnaces of the iron and steel works at Magnitogorsk on the Ural River, Russia.

Baltic Sea is also ice-free the year around. All other northern seaports of Russia are frozen for many months each year. Vladivostok on the Pacific coast, however, is kept open by icebreakers. In no part of the land is the rainfall heavy, and there are frequent and widespread droughts.

To the east of the Ural mountains is Siberia, Russia's Asiatic part. In the far north the ground has been found to be frozen to a depth of over six hundred feet. This presents peculiar problems which make it difficult to exploit the resources in the Arctic region. Here in the tundra country the moss, upon which the reindeer of the nomadic tribes feed, is often five feet thick.

South of the tundra belt is a great evergreen forest covering billions of acres, where lumbering and fur-trapping are the chief occupations.

Russia's supply of minerals is so great and widely scattered that the extent of many of the deposits is still unknown. There are immense reserves of coal in both European and Asiatic Russia. Copper, platinum, iron, gold, manganese and other minerals are found in the Urals. Some of the richest petroleum deposits in the world are located in the Baku region of the Caspian Sea.

Great strides have been made in industrial development, with the manufacture of iron and steel, machinery, textiles and leather goods in the lead.

In spite of climate, high cost of manufacture and difficulties of transportation, the U. S. S. R. is a country that is largely self-sustaining. Its rapidly expanding industrialization and advancement in modern science have made it one of the leading world powers.

Within the walls of the Kremlin in Moscow stands the bell tower of Ivan the Great. Its construction was begun by Boris Godunov in 1600.

Catharine de Bary

Rocky hills rising from the desert sands near Wadi Halfa, Sudan.

AFRICA—In its steady conquest of the world, the technical age has reached Africa, and across the second largest continent great changes are taking place. As the difficulties of climate, communications and diseases are overcome and education increases, Africa with its rich natural resources and its remarkably vital peoples is rapidly joining the modern world.

Lying astride the equator, large parts of Africa extend through the torrid zone. Its coastline is steep and regular, offering few places for ships to anchor. The rivers, although numerous and many of them large, are not so important to transportation as the great rivers of Europe, Asia and the Americas.

The deltas of the Niger and the Zambezi are choked by silt, and on nearly all the other rivers navigation is impeded by shoal or cataract. Nevertheless, the Congo and the Nile with their tributaries have many thousands of miles of navigable waterways, as have the Niger, the Benue and the Zambezi.

To the north, the Sahara Desert proved an effective barrier of sand and intense heat, which for hundreds of years prevented any important exchange of ideas or trade between the north and the south. Extending from the Atlantic to the River Nile, and reaching from the Mediterranean to the Sudan, the dry Sahara is a region of desolation. What trade existed between Asia, Europe and Africa followed caravan routes which led from oasis to oasis. The only life to be found there is at these scattered oases.

Africa is a great plateau, about five thousand miles long from north to south. The average height of the entire continent is over two thousand feet above sea level. Its loftiest peak is nearly twenty thousand feet high (Kilimanjaro in Tanganyika Territory), while

the Qattara Depression in the Libyan Desert sinks to four hundred feet below sea level

The Atlas Mountains parallel the north coast of Africa, with their southern slopes dropping down to the Sahara. The Sudan Belt, which extends south from the Sahara to the Gulf of Guinea, is a lower region of hills, valleys and plains. To the south is the Cameroon Massif and in the East rise the Plateau of Ethiopia and the mountain ridges of the lake region.

The geological formation of the Great Rift, which on the Asian continent caused the deep trench of the Dead Sea, has its continuation in East Africa. Here a series of deep trenchlike valleys extend from the Red Sea into Mozambique, and between the mountain ridges lie Africa's large lakes. Lake Victoria is the second largest body of fresh water, Lake Tanganyika the second deepest in the world. In this lake region rise three of Africa's great rivers. The Nile flows north toward the Mediterranean, the Congo twists and turns to finally reach the Atlantic to the west, and the Zambezi flows east to empty into the Indian Ocean. Each river follows a winding course through the mountains before finding a way over the edge of the plateau to reach the sea. This results in many falls and rapids which interrupt transportation. The Victoria Falls on the Zambezi, the rapids of the Congo, and the cataracts of the Nile are typical.

The Congo, winding through the gloomy depths of fever-infested forests, is three thousand miles long. It is second only to the Amazon of South America in the volume of water it empties into the sea. The Nile, the longest river in the world, travels four thousand miles before reaching the Mediterranean, and today, as in ancient times,

makes Egypt a habitable country. As the Nile winds slowly through the Sahara, the evaporation is so great that the river would dry up before reaching the sea were it not joined by rivers from the Ethiopian Highlands. It is these waters of the Blue Nile which bring the great Nile floods. They also supply water for irrigation, making Egypt a fertile strip of land hemmed in by cliffs and burning sands. Africa's fourth large river, the Niger, while rising only one hundred and fifty miles from the ocean, flows twenty-five hundred miles before reaching the Atlantic.

Africa is a land of climatic contradictions. At the equator the temperature ranges from typical jungle weather at the lower levels to a climate similar to that found well over a thousand miles to the north. This occurs in the high altitudes of the mountains. Along the Mediterranean, the weather compares with that of southern Europe. The weather in the Congo Basin is always hot and humid. However, to the east, in the mountain and lake region, it is tempered by the higher altitudes. In the far south, around Cape Town the weather is mild and sunny like the climate of southern California. The same extremes exist in rainfall. At the equator it is excessive, with periods of torrential rains. Traveling north or south from this wet center there is less and less rain, with parts of the Sahara never getting a drop.

Plant life varies with the rainfall. The dense, matted tropical jungles, which are exceeded only in size by the forests of the Amazon, give way to grassy plains and open forests, the savannas. The only vegetation in the Sahara is around the springs that nourish the oases. Because the hot winds of the south are blocked by the Atlas Mountains, the entire coastal area of North Africa from

Sailboats on the River Nile pass through the heart of modern Cairo.

Egypt. State Tourist Admin.

East Africa Tourist Travel Assoc.

The giraffe, tallest of mammals, lives in the savannas of southeastern Africa.

the Atlantic to the Nile River is agriculturally productive.

Sorghum and other grains are staple foods in Africa. Other important products, especially for export, are coffee, cocoa, tea and

Africa still has many wild animals, especially in its deep jungles. These teem with monkeys, among them gorillas and chimpanzees, and there are snakes and many birds. In the open woods and semi-arid grasslands of the savanna (called veldt in South Africa) live elephants, lions, giraffes, rhinoceroses, zebras and antelopes. Crocodiles and hippopotamuses are found in the rivers. The savanna is also the region for the raising of cattle. The desert has a very sparse animal population of a special kind, such as camels and jackals.

Some of Africa's mineral resources are of the richest in the world. Almost all gem diamonds for the world market are found here; gold is mined on a large scale, and one of the world's richest uranium mines lies in this continent (Shinkolobwe mine in the Bel-

months, bringing fertile silt with the life-giving water. In recent years, several dams have been built on the river, and the large water reservoirs thus obtained make possible continuous irrigation. Crops can now be harvested three times a year. The exploitation of the hydroelectric power of the Nile has been started; it will increase the industrial and manufacturing possibilities of Egypt. In spite of the rich crops, the Egyptian farmer is very poor. Attempts are being made to improve farming methods, many of which have not changed since the time of the pharaohs. In 1958, Egypt and Syria joined to form the United Arab Republic.

SUDAN — Since 1899 under joint Anglo-Egyptian rule, the Sudan became independent in 1956. This land, inhabited in the north by Arabs, in the south by Negro tribes, embraces the Upper Nile basin to the borders of Uganda and Ethiopia. Its wild Acacia trees furnish most of the world's supply of gum arabic, important in the manufacture of adhesives. Cotton is raised in the fertile areas between the Blue and the White Nile. Dates, ivory and livestock are also exported. Khartoum on the Blue Nile is capital and trade center.

ETHIOPIA — Three different zones of climate, depending on altitude, are typical for this mountainous country. The lowest zone, mainly comprising the lowlands in the west and the deep valleys, is tropical and unhealthy. The middle zone, of 6000-8000 feet elevation, favors agriculture and is most densely populated. In the higher regions, cattle are raised. In its federation with Eritrea in 1952, Ethiopia obtained access to the Red Sea, but its main outlet is Djibouti in Somaliland opposite Aden, where the railroad from the capital, Addis Ababa, terminates. An excellent coffee, growing wild on the slopes especially of the Jimma area, is chief export. With the exception of a few years of

South African Tourist Corp.

Large-eared African elephants in Kruger National Park, South Africa. The young remain with their mothers for four years.

tobacco. Cotton is grown in many places, and from various regions hides, ivory and timber are exported. The rain forests furnish rubber, mahogany and teakwood.

Gezira cotton, the "white gold" of the Sudan.

Br. Information Services

gian Congo). Other minerals such as tin, copper, chromium, vanadium and manganese are also found. There is very little oil, which poses a serious problem for modern transportation needs. However, Africa has a great potential source of industrial power in its mighty rivers.

EGYPT — Between the Arabian and the Libyan desert extends what might be called a huge river oasis, the valley and delta of the Nile. Here flourished the civilization of ancient Egypt, one of the oldest in the world. It was important in Greek and Roman times and became a stronghold of Islamic faith in the 7th century A.D. Mameluks and Turks held it during the Middle Ages. In modern times, Egypt became important because of the Suez Canal, opened in 1869. This artificial waterway, used by almost all shipping between Europe and the Orient, lies in Egyptian territory. Since antiquity the Nile waters flooded this land during the summer

Giant Protea, national flower of the Union of South Africa.

South African Tourist Corp.

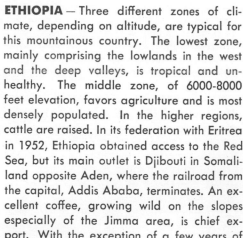

East Africa Tourist Travel Assoc.

In contrast to its cooler uplands, Kenya's lowlands are tropically hot.

Italian occupation (1936-41), this country has always been independent. Its population is partly pagan, partly Moslem and partly Christian, belonging to the old Christian Coptic church.

SOMALILAND — A group of countries on the Gulf of Aden consisting of French Somaliland, Somaliland Protectorate (British) and Somalia, an Italian trust territory scheduled to become independent in 1960. The climate in these lands is hot and dry. Djibouti, the chief town in French Somaliland, is a free port and outlet for Ethiopia. The capital of British Somaliland is Hargeisa, the chief port Berbera. Somalia is the largest country in the group, reaching from the Gulf of Aden to Kenya. Its capital is Mogadishu. Somalia supplies half of the world's frankincense.

KENYA — This eastern gateway to Central Africa abounds in big game. The lowlands bordering the Indian Ocean are fertile, the climate is bearable. Western Kenya is a high plateau with isolated towering peaks, snowcapped the year around. The chief harbor is Mombasa. A large part of the Europeans and Asians in the country live in Nairobi, the capital, situated in the highlands.

UGANDA — Between Mount Elgon (14,136 ft.) in the east and the Ruwenzori range (highest peak 16,787 ft.) in the west lie wide

Dancer at Shembe festival, Durban, South Africa.

South African Tourist Corp.

lakes and huge swamps, where rises the Nile River. The British administer this prosperous colony from the capital, Entebbe, on Lake Victoria. Cotton, raised exclusively by the natives, is the main source of income. This land is the home of the Baganda people, who attained a higher degree of development before the white man came than any other African tribe. Their kings can be traced back through several centuries.

TANGANYIKA—Part of a former German territory, it is now administered by Great Britain as a United Nations trust territory. In its northern highlands rises Kilimanjaro, Africa's highest peak. Also in the north, near Arusha, is Ngorongoro, a large inhabited crater with the strange appearance

East Africa Tourist Travel Assoc.

Masai warriors, Tanganyika. The Masai, of Nilo-Hamitic origin, have a well-developed tribal organization.

of a portion of the moon. Tanganyika's forests abound in wildlife of a greater number and variety than anywhere else in Africa. The main harbor is Dar es Salaam, capital and largest city.

ZANZIBAR—During the Middle Ages, this island off the east coast of Africa was ruled by Arabs and for a time by the Portuguese. The Germans occupied it in the 1880's but turned it over to England in exchange for Helgoland in the North Atlantic. Zanzibar is a very fertile island; together with the nearby island of Pemba it supplies most of the world's cloves.

MOZAMBIQUE — Several large rivers, among them the Zambezi, drain this Portuguese territory, which has a coast line of 1500 miles along the Indian Ocean. Vasco da Gama, the Portuguese who discovered the sea route to India around the Cape of Good Hope, visited it in 1498. Its natural re-

sources have not been developed to any great extent. The country sends laborers to the South African mines. Mozambique's several harbors are important outlets for South African minerals. Because of malaria and yellow fever, a large part of the country is unhealthful. Few Europeans live there.

UNION OF SOUTH AFRICA — Cool summers and mild winters make the southern tip of Africa an ideal land for European settlers. In the generally dry central tableland, crops are planted and cattle and sheep are raised. To the north extends the Witwatersrand with its rich gold mines. The outlet for this mining region is Durban, an artificial port on the Indian Ocean. The only large natural harbor is at Cape Town. In the low veldt (savanna) of Transvaal is the world-

famous Kruger National Park, an extensive reserve for African wildlife.

The population of the Union of South Africa consists of a white minority made up

These fishermen near Cape Town are Afrikaners, of Dutch descent.

South African Tourist Corp.

Union of S.A. Gov't. Inform. Office

The towering headgear of gold mines is a familiar sight around the city of Johannesburg.

BECHUANALAND, BASUTOLAND AND SWAZILAND — When the Boers extended their settlements into the interior of South Africa, the opposition of native tribes caused continuous friction. These tribes finally sought the protection of the British, and three protectorates were established: Basutoland and Swaziland within the Union of South Africa, Bechuanaland to the north between South-West Africa and Southern Rhodesia. Although most of the land is reserved for the natives, they have remained poor and many seek work in South African mines.

MADAGASCAR—The world's fourth largest island is separated from the east coast of Africa by the channel of Mozambique. In the mountains of the interior are found graphite, mica and other minerals, but only a small part of these resources has been developed. In the forests live the lemurs, shy monkey-like animals mostly confined to this island. There are no large wild animals on Madagascar. The native population are the Malagasy who as a race are related to the islanders of the Pacific. During the 19th century, Madagascar was ruled by the Howa, an educated tribe, many of whom became Christians. The numerous Negroes living on the island are mostly descendants of freed slaves. The French conquered Madagascar in 1896, but today it has regained its independence. Tananarive in the highlands is the capital. Main ports are Tamatave on the east coast and Diego Suarez at the northern tip. The country is now called Malgache Republic.

MAURITIUS — Negroes, East Indians and Chinese live on this fertile, very densely populated island in the Indian Ocean. Many tropical crops are produced. Sugar is the chief export. The island lies in the path of tropical hurricanes. It was discovered by the Portuguese and then in turn occupied by the Dutch and the French. In 1815, Napoleon

Philip Gendreau

Diamond mine near Pretoria. Mining goes on underground, shafts reaching the diamond-rich "blue rock."

lost it to England. French is still spoken there. The capital is Port Louis.

FEDERATION OF RHODESIA AND NYASALAND — In 1953, Northern Rhodesia, Southern Rhodesia and Nyasaland were joined in a federation.

NYASALAND — This narrow strip of land stretching along the west coast of Lake Nyasa has a healthy climate because of its elevation. The chief activity is in agriculture.

NORTHERN RHODESIA — Lying between the forests of Central Africa and the wide plains of South Africa, it is separated from Southern Rhodesia by the Zambezi River and its famous Victoria Falls. This is more than twice as high as Niagara Falls. Copper, lead and cattle provide Northern Rhodesia's principal source of wealth.

SOUTHERN RHODESIA — Most of the land consists of two plateaus ranging from 2000 to 6000 feet in altitude. It is suited to European settlement. Agriculture and mining are the chief occupations. The country's main resources are gold, asbestos and chrome.

ANGOLA (Portuguese West Africa) — Although the central elevated plateau of Angola is a great African watershed, where rise important tributaries to the Congo and

of English and Dutch stock, a considerable group of East Indians, a large Negro majority, and a smaller group of mixed people.

Dutch settlers came to this land in the 17th century; their descendants call themselves Afrikaners. When the English began to occupy the country, many Dutch left for the interior (in the so-called Boer Trek in 1836), where they founded the republic of Transvaal, the Orange Free State, and Natal. After the Boer War (1899-1902), these republics were combined with the Cape Colony to form the Union of South Africa.

Sheep farm in South Africa's high veldt. The Union is one of the world's chief wool producers.

the Zambezi Rivers, the country as a whole is arid and exposed to constant dry winds. Export of coffee, largely to the United States, provides the chief income. Luanda, the capital at the mouth of the Kuanza, was founded in 1575. It is today the third largest Portuguese city in the world.

BELGIAN CONGO — King Leopold II of Belgium, who supported Stanley's explorations of the Congo region, took a personal interest in this territory. It was called the Congo Free State. But because of misrule it was turned over to the state of Belgium in 1908. Its many natural resources make this one of the richest regions in Africa. Stretching on either side of the equator, it has a large area of tropical rain forests which furnish valuable tropical products including timber. These and the ores from the colony's rich mines are transported on its many waterways to the country's only seaport, Matadi, at the mouth of the Congo River. Attempts to improve farming methods and to combat erosion are being made on a large scale. Leopoldville, the capital, on the lower Congo, is a growing modern town and important trade center, with an airport, radio station and a noted institute for tropical medicine. Independence is scheduled for 1960.

Philip Gendreau

Victoria Falls on the Zambezi River were discovered by Livingstone. They demonstrate Africa's potential in hydroelectric power.

RUANDA-URUNDI — A very densely populated country in the heart of Africa, administered by Belgium as a United Nations trust territory. Its frequent dry spells sometimes cause famines. The capital, Usumbura, on the northern tip of Lake Tanganyika, is on the site where Stanley and Livingstone landed in 1871. Due to its high elevation, the country has a healthy, cool climate.

The hippopotamus, one of Africa's large wild animals, lives along rivers and lakes near the equator.

Philip Gendreau

FORMER FRENCH EQUATORIAL AFRICA —These countries, which became independent in 1958, comprise Chad, Central Africa, Congo and Gabon. They lie in a belt extending from the tropical rain forest region along the Atlantic coast north of the Congo River to the desert region of the Southern Sahara. Chief cities are Point-Noire and Libreville on the Atlantic coast, Brazzaville and Bangui on the Congo, and Fort-Lamy near Lake Chad. Modernization has not penetrated far beyond these towns.

SPANISH GUINEA — Small territory on the Gulf of Guinea embracing also the islands of Fernando Po and Annobón.

CAMEROONS—Former German territory to the east of Nigeria, stretching from the Gulf of Guinea to Lake Chad. It is now divided into three parts: Northern Cameroons and Southern Cameroons administered by Great Britain as United Nations trust territories, and the Cameroons, a former French trust territory which is now independent.

NIGERIA — From the forest-covered coast of the gulf of Guinea at the huge delta of the Niger River, this country extends northward into dry savanna regions and finally to the desert around Lake Chad. Its highest elevation is the Bauchi plateau. The tin found there is approaching exhaustion. Nigeria is one of the most densely populated countries in Africa. Its capital and main port is Lagos. The largest town is Ibadan, seat

of an African university. The independence of Nigeria within the British Commonwealth is scheduled for 1960.

TOGO — The eastern part of a former German territory. From a narrow, coastal strip the country rises to interior highlands, finally extending into desert. Independence is scheduled for 1960. The western part of the territory, British Togoland, became part of independent Ghana in 1957.

GHANA — Independent within the British Commonwealth, this republic comprises the former Gold Coast and British Togoland. Once known for its gold alone, the country is today a leading producer of cocoa. Its manganese export, especially to the United States, is considerable. It is also an important producer of diamonds.

LIBERIA — This is the oldest independent African republic. In 1822 the American Colonization Society established a small settlement for freed American Negroes at the site of the present capital, Monrovia (named after President James Monroe). In 1847 Liberia became an independent state with its constitution modeled after that of the United States. The land is handicapped by a hot and unhealthful climate. Its economic condition was improved in recent years by American government aid and private enterprise. Rubber, mainly produced on plantations of the Firestone Company, is the chief export. A valuable iron ore is also exported.

British Information Services

Mosque at Kano, Nigeria. Mohammedan influence is strong in northwestern and northeastern Africa.

SIERRA LEONE — The country was visited by early navigators and became a British possession in 1787. Rain forest covers the coastlands, savanna the arid interior. The country has an excellent natural harbor.

British Information Services
The Wana of Wa, a chieftain of Ghana.

Native weaving in Sierra Leone.

British Information Services

Here Freetown, the capital is located. It began as an English settlement for freed slaves. Today it is an active trade center.

GUINEA—To the north and east of Sierra Leone stretches this land, which until 1958 was a part of French West Africa. Its main town and port is Conakry. Bananas, bauxite and iron ore are the chief exports.

PORTUGUESE GUINEA — An unhealthful region of tropical forest and savanna, in the hands of the Portuguese since the time of Prince Henry the Navigator (middle of 15th century). When England claimed a part of the territory, President Grant of the United States was asked to settle the dispute (1870). He decided in favor of Portugal.

GAMBIA—British possession since the early 17th century. Extends along both banks of the Gambia River. Capital is Bathurst on an island at the river's mouth. Peanuts are the chief crop.

SÃO TOMÉ AND PRINCIPE — Portuguese islands off the coast of Guinea, of volcanic origin. Climate and vegetation are tropical.

FORMER FRENCH WEST AFRICA — This group of former French colonies which are now independent includes Mauritania, Senegal, the Sudanese Republic, Ivory Coast, Upper Volta, Niger and Dahomey. The region comprises tropical rain forest near the coast and savanna and desert land in the interior. The most important city is Dakar, located at the westernmost point of the African continent. Its airport serves as a stepping stone in transatlantic flying between Europe and South America.

MOROCCO — Three chains of the Atlas Mountains traverse this country from southwest to northeast. Although agriculture and manufacturing are handicapped in this rugged land, it is active in several industries. It has attractive old towns like Marrakech

and Fez, seat of an old Islamic university, while Casablanca is one of the most modern cities on the African continent. At the northern shore of Morocco is the Strait of Gibraltar, separating Africa from Europe. At its narrowest point it is 8 miles wide.

For about half a century, Morocco was ruled by France, with a small portion under Spanish control. In 1956, it became independent and the formerly international city of Tangier was joined with it.

ALGERIA—The rugged, arid ranges of the Atlas Mountains divide Northern Algeria into three zones roughly parallel to the coast: the Tell Atlas, the High Plateau, and the Saharan Atlas. To the north of the Tell Atlas, the climate is Mediterranean and fruits and vegetables are abundantly grown. The High Plateau is an arid region with several landlocked salt lakes. From the heights of the Saharan Atlas, the land falls off abruptly to the desert of the Sahara. Southern Algeria lies in the Sahara and has a typical desert climate.

TUNISIA—In Ancient times, during Phoenician and later Roman rule, this land furnished grains and excellent fruits to the other countries around the Mediterranean. Then came centuries of neglect, and during the Middle Ages this coastal land was feared for its pirates. Today Tunisia is again very fertile. Olives grow along the coast, grains and tropical fruits, especially dates, are raised inland. There are several important towns, among them Tunis, the capital, and Bizerte, a naval base. Turkish rule over Tunisia was replaced by French protectorate in 1881. In 1956, Tunisia became independent.

LIBYA — This is the least valuable of the North African regions, being relatively unprotected from the scorching desert winds. However, the coastal areas are cultivated with the aid of artificial irrigation. The chief towns are Tripoli and Benghazi.

Market scene at Moulay Idris, ancient town and Islamic shrine in Morocco.

Philip Gendreau

E. L. Jordan

Arab street scene.

ASIA — Although there is no separating ocean between Europe and Asia, the great steppes and deserts of central and eastern Asia served as an effective barrier through thousands of years. Some of the oldest civilizations in the world developed in eastern and southeast Asia in almost complete isolation. In modern times, with the spreading of science and technology, Asia's old traditions and customs are receding as industrialization expands, based on the continent's rich resources and carried out by its great masses of populations.

This huge continent is the largest in the world. It is more than a million square miles larger than the combined areas of North and South America and covers one third of the world's land area. It extends from the ice-bound regions of the Arctic Circle to the sunburnt islands of the tropics. In the Himalayas it rises to the highest elevation in the world — Mount Everest — and in Palestine it sinks to the world's lowest surface —the Dead Sea.

Asia forms with Europe one continuous land mass, Eurasia. The boundary between Asia and Europe follows the Ural Mountains, the Ural River to the Caspian Sea, and the Greater Caucasus Mountains to the Black Sea. A man-made canal, the Suez Canal, separates the continent of Asia from Africa. Washed by three oceans, Asia has a coastline over thirty thousand miles in length. Deep indentations form seas, such as the Bay of Bengal and the Arabian Sea. Twisting and pointed peninsulas reach far out into the oceans, which are dotted with island groups. Among these are Japan, the Philippines, and Indonesia, all of which have become as important as mainland countries.

The belt of high mountains which extends across Europe from west to east finds its con-

tinuation in the high mountain ranges of Asia. They reach their greatest height in the Himalayas, which have been called "the roof of the world." These mountain chains extend eastward to the plateau of Tibet, then turn sharply south and traverse the Malay Peninsula in long mountain lines separated by deep, forested ravines. They terminate in the mountainous backbone of the Indonesian (Sunda) Islands.

The Himalayas represent the southern edge of Central Asia's high plateaus and mountain ranges. To the north extends the great tableland of northern Asia, which descends slowly to the Arctic Ocean. To the south are the peninsular plateaus of Arabia and India.

This enormous continent is drained by many large rivers. In Siberia, the Ob, Yenisei and Lena Rivers, rising in Central Asia, flow northward into the Arctic Ocean. They are blocked with ice for several months each year and flood the surrounding country in thaw. China's large rivers also have their headlands in the Central Asian mountains. They wind their way eastward to the sea through alluvial plains made fertile by the silt they carry. They are the Amur on the border between Siberia and China, the Hwang-Ho, or Yellow River, and the Yangtse Kiang or Blue River. These rivers often overflow in disastrous floods and have changed their courses many times.

India's holy river, the Ganges, rising in the western Himalayas, flows eastward through the plain which bears its name. Shortly before emptying into the Bay of Bengal, it receives another mighty river from the Himalayas, the Brahmaputra. In southwest Asia, two rivers, the Euphrates and Tigris, water the alluvial plain of ancient Mesopotamia in Iraq.

Covering so many degrees of latitude, the climate of Asia would naturally show great variation. Some of the coldest inhabited

Aramco

Onions growing in the irrigated Arabian desert.

Walter Nebiker

Where the Mediterranean reaches furthest east lies Iskenderun, Turkey.

Modern and traditional transportation—train and camel—meet in the desert of Arabia.

Aramco

TWA-Trans World Airlines

The state of Israel is commercially very active.

places on earth, Verkhoyansk and Oimyakon, lie in northeastern Siberia. Great areas in the center of the continent, far from the sea, are dry; tropical conditions prevail in the south. The heaviest rainfall anywhere in the world is in some localities of southeast Asia. In Assam, India, the rainfall averages about 40 feet a year.

The great continuous landmass of Asia cools off more in the winter and gets hotter in the summer than the surrounding oceans. The resulting changes in air pressure cause streams of air to flow from the continent to the oceans during the winter and from the oceans to the continent during the summer. In India and southeast Asia, these winds are known as monsoons; from April to October they bring the heavy, life-giving rains.

There is every type of vegetation, ranging from tundra mosses in the extreme north to tropical plant life in the south. There are extensive desert areas with very scant vegetation such as the famous Gobi desert in

The Dead Sea with the alluvial mouth of the Jordan.

Mongolia and the deserts in Arabia, Iran, south central U.S.S.R., and Sinkiang. Across Siberia stretches a wide belt of coniferous forest called the taiga. To the south of it are Siberia's steppelands. The slopes of the Himalayan foothills and the hills of the East Indian Islands are covered with tropical forest.

Of the many wild animals living in Asia, the giant panda is found only in Tibet. Here also lives one of the largest wild oxen, the black Yak. Another purely Asiatic animal, the tiger, is found over a wide range, from Persia (Iran) to the Amur, and from the island of Sakhalin to the forests of Bali. Birds of Paradise, who have the most brilliant plumage of any birds on earth, are confined to New Guinea and the Moluccas. In India and countries of southeast Asia, the Asiatic elephant has been tamed and is used for various types of work, such as hauling of logs. In agriculture, tamed water buffaloes are widely used.

Although Asia is very rich in resources, many of them have not yet been developed. They are unevenly distributed and often at great distances from trade and shipping centers. The greatest variety of resources has been found in the Ural Mountains on the borderline between Siberia and European Russia. Another important industrial center is the Kuznetsk Basin southeast of Novosibirsk in Siberia. In these regions, industrialization has attained a modern level. China's coal supply is one of the largest in the world. China is also rich in iron ore and other minerals, such as antimony and tungsten. Antimony is important in the making of steel, and tungsten is needed to harden metals. Japan has no ample mineral supplies, but water power obtained from its many swift rivers has helped manufacturing. India, long known for its wealth in precious stones, has an abundance of coal, copper, iron ore and sheet mica. There are large oil fields in southwest Asia—Arabia, Iran, Iraq and the Kuwait—as well as in southeast Asia—Burma, Indonesia and Borneo. Tin occurs in the Malay Peninsula in great amounts, and much of the world's natural rubber comes from

Malaya and Sumatra. Cotton and jute are exported by India, Pakistan and Japan, which also exports silk. Tea is grown in many parts of southern and southeastern Asia; the main exporting countries are India and Ceylon. Indochina produces great quantities of rice for export.

In the past, transportation in Asia was on rivers, canals and by coastwise shipping, or by slow caravan across the deserts and over the mountain passes. A great change was brought about when railroads were built, and today India, China and Japan have fairly extensive railroad systems. European Russia is connected with Siberia, the Mongolian Republic and Manchuria (China) by the Trans-Siberian Railroad, which has branches to the larger towns and industrial centers of adjacent regions. In the East Indies, transportation by bus and truck has become important in modern times. Many major cities in Asia are linked by airlines.

TURKEY—Once a vast empire, Turkey now comprises roughly the rectangular peninsula

Philip Gendreau

Small barges form the foreground for the Maquan Mosque in Baghdad, Iraq.

between the eastern Mediterranean and the Black Sea. It is a dry plateau surrounded by mountain ranges, which reach to considerable heights. (Mt. Ararat, highest peak, 16,-945 ft.) Along the Mediterranean and Aegean seas, the land is fertile. The capital, Ankara, lies in the central highlands. Istanbul, on the European side of the Sea of Marmara, is an important seaport and a trade and university center. Another large port is Izmir (Smyrna). A republic since 1923, Turkey encourages modern industry and western style of life. At the same time, adhering to the Mohammedan religion, it retains many Turkish and Asiatic traits and traditions.

LEBANON—On the slopes along the coast and in the valley between the Lebanon and Anti-Lebanon mountains the country is fertile. It is mainly agricultural, and on its steep, terraced hillsides grow abundant crops. Besides the Philippines, Lebanon is the only country in Asia with a large Christian population (about 50 per cent). It obtained complete independence in 1946. The capital and

U.S. Air Force Photo

Philip Gendreau

Modern bank and bazaar building in Tehran, Iran.

main port, Beirut, is one of the most important trade centers in the Near East.

JORDAN—When the Turkish empire broke apart after the First World War, Jordan became a British mandate. It gained its independence in 1946. Only a small area in the northwest of the country is fertile. Here lies Amman, the capital. The country has many relics from Biblical times.

ISRAEL—After 2000 years the Jewish people realized their dream of an independent homeland with the establishment of the new state of Israel in 1948. Lying between Egypt and Jordan on the eastern shores of the Mediterranean, the country is a hot and arid land. Modern irrigation, however, has made large regions fertile, and orchards and forests begin to give the land a green appearance. The new nation's economy is based on agriculture, but oil refining, chemical production and light industry are also important. Tel Aviv-Jaffa is the center of the manufacturing industries, while heavy industry is located at the seaport of Haifa. Many of the people, immigrants from all over the world, live together in modern cooperative settlements. The Hebrew language, formerly used only in religious rites and Bible studies, is the official language of the young republic. The frontier with Jordan divides Jerusalem; the modern part is Israel's capital and the old city belongs to Jordan.

SYRIA—Between Syria's mountain ranges in the west and its wide desert regions in the east lies a strip of land famous for its fertility. In ancient times, Syria was crossed by caravan trails connecting Mesopotamia with Egypt. In our time, it is an important passageway between the oil fields of Iraq and Arabia and the Mediterranean. The country is still mainly agricultural. The capital is Damascus, the oldest continuously inhabited city known today. Syria emerged from the First World War as a French mandate and became independent in 1946. On February 1, 1958, it joined with Egypt to form the United Arab Republic.

IRAQ—The Euphrates and Tigris Rivers flow from the northwest to the southeast through the middle of Iraq. To the west and southwest extend the Syrian and Arabian deserts and to the north the mountains of Kurdistan. Agriculture depends on irrigation. Since the time of the ancient Babylonians, who had extensive irrigation systems, the land was neglected. In modern times, the income from the rich oil fields near Mosul permits extensive new efforts to irrigate the land. Important towns beside Baghdad, the capital, are Mosul, the oil center, and Basra, the country's port town near the mouth of the two rivers. Iraq was part of Turkey until after the First World War, when it became an independent constitutional monarchy. As a result of the revolution in July, 1958, it was declared a republic.

IRAN (Persia)—Although more than half of the country is desert, it has been the seat of flourishing empires in antiquity and the Middle Ages. Today it is an independent monarchy. In the region near the Caspian Sea, the country is fertile with a subtropical climate and abundant rainfall. Here lies the capital, Tehran. Nearby rises Mt. Demavend, the highest peak (18,550 ft.). The desert stretches in a vast belt through most of the interior. In the fertile regions, agriculture is the main occupation. Sheep are raised in the more arid parts. A source of wealth are the country's oil fields, and the refinery at Adaban is one of the largest in the world.

ARABIA—The Arabian Peninsula is a land composed almost entirely of desert, mostly of a barren and stony type, with an abundance of sand in the southeast. Besides scattered oases there are only a few small areas in Arabia with enough rainfall to permit the growing of crops. In the mountains of Yemen in the southeast corner of the peninsula, there is sufficient rain and the soil is fertile. A high-quality coffee is grown here. It received its name from the Red Sea port, Mocha, which used to handle its export. In some parts of Saudi Arabia, modern methods of irrigation are used. Recent discovery of immense oil fields along the Persian Gulf fostered new economic development, and many local sheikhs or tribal rulers have become suddenly rich. Roads are being built and cars and trucks are beginning to replace the camel. A railroad runs from Riyadh to the Persian Gulf. Saudi Arabia, a unified kingdom since 1932, comprises about two thirds of the peninsula. It has two capitals, Riyadh and Mecca. Mecca is the center of worship for all Mohammedans.

AFGHANISTAN—Lying as a barrier between Siberia and India, Afghanistan has been the scene of many invasions and conquests but was never completely vanquished. Barren tablelands, deep ravines and snow-covered mountains leave it an unproductive country. However, the crops raised in small, irrigated areas are of high quality. The country is noted for its fine rugs and sheepskins, major export items. Attempts are made to develop water power and oil resources. Kabul is the capital.

PAKISTAN—In 1949 Pakistan was created to give the Mohammedans of India their own homeland. Its two sections are about 1000 miles apart and differ greatly. West Pakistan comprises the Indus valley and adjacent areas, stretching from the Himalayas to the Arabian Sea. It has vast desert regions and is not densely populated. Cereal raising and cotton growing are concentrated in the Indus valley, irrigated through an ancient but still efficient canal system and huge modern dams. East Pakistan occupies most of the Ganges-Brahmaputra delta and the foothills of the Assam highlands. It is very humid and densely populated. Here, rice

Palace in the hills at Junagadh, India. Nearby is Forest of Gir, only place in India where the lion survives.

Philip Gendreau

Remnant from British rule: traffic is "left-handed" in Indian lands. This traffic officer is at Srinagar, Kashmir.

E. L. Jordan

and jute are the chief crops. The separation from India entailed great human, economic and political problems which have only in part been solved.

Both Pakistan and India claim Kashmir (officially called Jammu and Kashmir), a largely Mohammedan state to the north and east of Pakistan.

SIKKIM, NEPAL and BHUTAN — These three small independent states are shut off from the outside world by the Himalayas. Several of the World's highest mountains, including Mount Everest, are in southern Nepal or on its border. The inhabitants are known for their courage. The Gurkhas of Nepal were famous soldiers in the Indian army, while the Nepalese Sherpas furnished reliable guides in the ascent of Himalayan peaks.

INDIA — India has an average population density of 300 people per square mile. Although there are many large cities and some very sizeable industries, the majority of the people depend on agriculture. The Indian farmers live in small villages surrounded by tilled fields. In spite of primitive methods and equipment, crops are usually large. But India's harvest depends on seasonal rains (monsoons), and if they do not arrive in time,

disastrous droughts result. At such times, large groups of the population may be exposed to famine made more serious because transportation is often inadequate, so that food cannot be rushed to stricken areas. Within the last several decades, the government has sponsored irrigation works and the construction of railroads and motor roads to decrease the danger of famines.

For over four thousand years, India has been at the mercy of marauding and conquering races. Unlike many lesser countries, who have successfully thrown off the yoke of oppression, India has for many centuries been subject to foreign rule. As a result, it is a confusion of races and traditions. Throughout its history, the Hindu religion, especially the caste system, has had a strong influence on life in India, even under English rule. The caste system has prevented a gradual decrease in social differences, and great wealth and extreme poverty exist side by side.

India received its independence in 1947 and in 1950 became a republic. The capital is at New Delhi. By expanding its industries and modernizing its farming methods, it hopes to improve the lot of its people. To combine modern ideas and industrial requirements with age-old traditions in a densely populated country is India's major problem.

CEYLON — This island, whose capital is Colombo, lies in the Indian Ocean near India's southern tip. Ruled by kings since antiquity, Ceylon became an English colony in 1802 and obtained its independence in 1948. Mountains rise in the interior of the southern part of the island. Here is grown Ceylon's famous tea. In the lowlands of the north and along the coast, rice is the chief crop. Precious stones are found in the gravel of the rivers. Sea breezes temper the heat.

INDOCHINESE PENINSULA — Lying in South Asia between the Bay of Bengal and the South China Sea, it includes parts of Burma, Thailand, Vietnam, Laos, Cambodia and the Federation of Malaya. Most of the peninsula is characterized by densely forested valleys and mountain ridges. Rainfall is heavy and the land is very productive. In

Hamilton Wright

Rice is cultivated throughout the lowlands of southeastern Asia.

the forests are valuable stands of prize woods, such as teak, ebony and other trees used for their wood or gum. Most of the world's natural rubber comes from this area. In the river plains and deltas, rice is harvested twice a year and much of it is exported. The villages are built on the dams between the rice fields. Chief harbors are the Burmese capital and great seaport, Rangoon, Bangkok (Krung Thep), the capital of Thailand, Saigon, capital of South Vietnam, and Singapore. The latter lies on an island at the tip of the peninsula and commands one of the most important sea routes in the world. A new port is being constructed in the bay of Kompong Som in Cambodia — Sihanoukville.

THE MALAY ARCHIPELAGO — The world's largest group of islands extends from Su-

Busy docks at Singapore, one of the crossroads of the world.

British Information Services

matra to the Philippine islands off the coast of China and includes many thousands of islands. With the exception of the Philippines and parts of Timor, Borneo and New Guinea, the archipelago was ruled for hundreds of years by the Netherlands.

INDONESIA — Colonization and development begun by the Dutch in the seventeenth century has resulted in the richest and most important island group in the world.

Most of the islands are mountainous and of volcanic origin. At one time they were a part of the mainland connecting Asia with Australia. Java is the most productive and highly developed of the East Indies. It is one of the most densely populated regions in the world.

After Greenland, New Guinea and Borneo are the largest islands in the world. Sumatra and Celebes are next in size in the East Indies. Much of the mineral wealth of these islands is yet untouched. Borneo is crossed almost in the middle by the equator and few white people occupy the island because of the humidity and heat. Petroleum is an important resource of Borneo, Sumatra and Java, and two small islands adjoining Su-

Hamilton Wright

Spring and Autumn Temple at Kaohsiung, Taiwan. The city is a major port and industrial center of southern Taiwan.

E. L. Jordan

Floating market at Bangkok, Thailand.

Market scene at Kokura, Japan.

Ronald Tolles

matra have valuable deposits of tin. Bali, one of the lesser islands, is known for its tropical charm.

After an extended struggle, Indonesia became independent in 1949. To mold the vast region of islands and islets into a unified country is no small task. An even greater problem lies in the fact that the education of the Indonesian people, neglected in the centuries of colonization, has as yet to be brought up to a more modern level.

PHILIPPINE ISLANDS — Numbering over seven thousand islands, the Philippines, like other islands of the Malay Archipelago, are the tops of drowned mountains protruding from the sea. There are well watered fertile plains between the mountains. The islands are near the equator and the temperature is never very low. Some of the many volcanoes in the Philippines are still active and the islands are subject to earthquakes.

Magellan, the great Portuguese sailor, discovered the Philippines in 1521. He was killed on Cebu Island. The Spaniards settled in the islands in 1565 and held them for 333 years. Their influence is still felt in many traditions. Most Filipinos are Christians (Catholics), but there are pagan tribes in the hills, and Mohammedans live on Mindanao and the Sulu Islands. During the nearly five decades of American rule (1898-1946), modern education, industry and land reform were introduced to the Philippines.

CHINA — The Chinese civilization is of greater antiquity than any other existent world culture. In the past it was able to absorb all foreign influences without changing basically. The Chinese people are patient, industrious and have great physical endurance. A large part of the country has a moderate climate. Agriculture supports the majority of the people. Few animals are raised, which conserves acreage for food crops. Rice is most widely grown, but almost every known crop is raised.

During the last three centuries, China's population increased from about 60 million in the 16th century to about 600 million to-

day. At the same time, the country remained almost completely agricultural, retaining its antiquated farming methods. As a result, famines were frequent and the living standard of the people as a whole remained low. In 1912, in an attempt to improve conditions, China became a democracy. However, quiet development was frustrated when Japan occupied Manchuria in 1931 and invaded China in 1937. When the Japanese were finally defeated, Communism had spread throughout the land, and in 1949 the mainland of China fell under Communist rule. Since then, industrialization and the establishment of cooperative farms on a large scale are changing the face of China.

Inner Mongolia, Tibet and Sinkiang are outer provinces of China. These regions have extreme temperatures and are largely desert.

The island of Taiwan (Formosa) has remained free of Communist rule and is the seat of the Nationalist Chinese government. The central and eastern part of the island is mountainous, the highest peak, Mt. Morri-

Street scene in Hong Kong.

E. L. Jordan

An airplane brings medical aid to tent dwellers in the desert of Mongolia.

Eastfoto

son, rising to 13,595 feet. Valuable timber grows on the slopes and rivers furnish electrical power. The western part of the island is a fertile plain. Economically, Taiwan is almost self-supporting. Recently, a modern land reform has been introduced.

SIBERIA—The Asiatic part of Russia is a vast low plain in the west, rising to rugged plateaus and mountain chains in the east. Siberia has a "continental" (inland) climate, which means little rainfall and high temperatures in the summer, scant snow cover and low temperatures in the winter. In the Arctic region, the subsoil is permanently frozen. This land, where trees cannot grow, is called tundra. South of it is a wide belt of coniferous forests, the taiga, and these in turn merge into steppelands. Some of the steppe is dry, supporting only sheep and goats. But in southwestern Siberia, where the fertile "black soil" of the steppe receives sufficient rainfall, crops are abundant. The highest peak in Siberia is Klyuchevskaya Sopka, a volcano on Kamchatka peninsula. Lake Baikal, near the Mongolian border, is the deepest lake in the world (5,712 ft.).

For centuries, Russia sent its criminals and political exiles to Siberia to make up for the lack of voluntary settlers. In modern times, industry and large-scale agriculture have been developed in some regions, especially in the southwest, around the capital, Novosibirsk, and in the Kuznetsk basin. Huge dams are being built to furnish electrical power. The railway system is steadily expanded. Some isolated towns have air service. But the harsh climate, generally poor soil and enormous distances still remain major obstacles to a rapid development of the country.

MONGOLIAN REPUBLIC — The greater part of this country consists of an arid plateau composed mainly of the Gobi Desert. In the northwest are high mountains whose streams flow into numerous sizable lakes. The people are mostly nomads who wander from place to place seeking new pastures for their herds. In 1921, the country became a "People's Republic" and has since then been under the influence of Communist Russia. Attempts are being made to settle the nomads in cooperative farms. Ulan Bator is the capital.

JAPAN—Since Japan opened its doors to Western trade in the middle of the last century, it took over Western technical achievements and became in a very short time a modern industrialized state. Simultaneously, it increased its military power and was victorious in wars against China and Russia. Formosa (Taiwan today) and Korea were occupied in 1905, Manchukuo in 1932, and finally, in 1937, China was invaded. During the Second World War, Japan controlled Indonesia and Indochina. Defeat at the end of the war reduced the empire to the area of the Japanese islands.

Rising from great depths of the sea, the islands of Japan are largely mountainous (Fujiyama, 12,395 ft.). The Inland Sea or Japanese Mediterranean is almost entirely landlocked and surrounded by chains of volcanoes, of which few are now active. Because earthquakes are frequent, houses and factories are low structures mostly built of wood. The climate is temperate and healthful, with abundant rainfall. About 80 per cent of the land is too steep to be cultivated. Every effort is made to obtain large crops from the 20 per cent of arable land, as Japan is very densely populated. Fisheries and canneries add to the food supply and are important for export.

The Japanese are a hardworking people with great technical ability who require little for themselves. They have been able to build up important textile, manufacturing and heavy industries, although most of the raw materials have to be imported. More recently, electrical power plants have been constructed to supplement available coal supplies. Japan's merchant fleet is one of the largest in the world.

For centuries, Japan had been controlled by a few powerful families. After the Second World War, it assumed a democratic constitution. The duties of the Emperor are merely ceremonial.

KOREA — Forming a kind of land bridge between the Asian mainland and Japan, Korea has been an historic pathway for invasion. Coveted at different times by China, Russia and Japan, it lost its independence early in the century to the Japanese. During the Second World War, Korea was promised independence. But the end of the fighting brought division and renewed conflict. Today, the country is divided by the 38th parallel into a northern Communist republic and a southern democracy following western ideas. Seoul is the capital of South Korea and Pyongyang is capital of North Korea.

In its climate the peninsula of Korea is influenced by the surrounding seas and the large continent of Asia, to which it is attached. In the summer, seasonal winds blow from the sea, bringing heat and humidity. In the winter, the winds blow from inner Asia, often bringing bitterly cold, dry weather.

Physically and economically, Korea is divided into two contrasting natural regions. The agricultural heart of the nation is south of the 38th parallel, producing rice, barley, cotton and other crops. North of the parallel, industry and mining of coal and iron predominate.

Seoul, capital of South Korea, lies in a setting of rocky hills.

I. L. P. Korea

AUSTRALIA — This island continent of the South Seas is the smallest, and last to be discovered of all the continents.

The United States and Australia are nations of about the same age and size, and in other respects have much in common. The loss of America as a British Colony directly led to the settling of Australia. It was first claimed for the British Crown in 1788 as a settlement for British convicts who had previously been sent to America. Landing in a virgin country, the early pioneers of the two countries had to conquer the wilderness before creating a nation. In the process of so doing the people of both lands developed similar characteristics. In later years Australia even patterned its constitution after that of the United States.

But, whereas the United States became a melting pot for all the races and creeds in the world, Australia has been peopled almost entirely by British stock. Today 97 per cent of the population are descendants of British colonists, and 86 per cent are Australian born. Strict laws have confined immigration to the white race. Few of the natives who originally inhabited Australia remain. These aborigines are similar to the African Negro but not so intelligent, and are believed to be a separate race.

Almost half of Australia lies within the tropics, but being surrounded by great oceans, the continent has a mild climate throughout the year. Snow normally falls only in the high mountains in the winter. Since the seasons are the reverse of those in the United States, this occurs in their winter months of June, July, and August.

Australia is said to be most level in surface and regular in outline of all the continents. There is an entire absence of towering mountains. The highest peak is only about seventy-three hundred feet above sea level. The mountains parallel the east coast, with, by far, the greater part of the continent a vast, irregular, and undulating plateau.

Australia can be regarded as falling into four well-defined regions: (1) The Great Plateau in the west extends over about half of the continent; (2) The Eastern Highlands follow along the whole of the eastern coastline, rarely exceeding a distance of a hundred miles inland; (3) The Central Basin is a lowland area much of which was once a sea-bed; and (4) the Coastal Plains, which form a rim of varying width surrounding most of the continent.

Despite rich coastal lands and an immense grazing area in the interior, much of this interior is unsuited for agriculture. It is a great arid region of desert and semi-desert which is sparsely settled and will never support a dense population. The heaviest rainfall is in the tropical regions of the north, and there is adequate moisture along the south coast and southern part of the highlands. Elsewhere there is insufficient rain.

One of the world's greatest bridges spans the harbor of Sydney, Australia.

But for the presence of innumerable artesian wells scattered over wide areas, much more of the country would be without water. It is these wells that make stock-raising possible, but because of its mineral content, the water is seldom used for agriculture or human use.

The major rivers of Australia are of two types—those which flow toward the coast and are similar to such rivers in other parts of the world; and the inland rivers which gradually lose their water as they flow away from the coastal regions. The headwaters of most of these inland rivers are in the Eastern Highlands.

The Murray River with its tributaries is the main river system and flows into the ocean on the south coast. The Gilbert, Norman and Flinders are the principal streams flowing into the Gulf of Carpentaria in the north. On the west the Murchison, Gascoyne, Ashburton and Fitzroy empty into the Indian Ocean.

The rivers which flow inland vary greatly in volume during the year. For long periods they are mere strings of waterholes, but during floods their waters spread out over the flat country for many miles. Most of their waters evaporate or soak into the ground before they flow very far. In the center of the continent the rivers flow into Lake Eyre when there is sufficient water in them, but generally they are merely beds of dry sand.

The lakes that appear to be scattered so liberally over the land are also a disappointment as they are little more than shallow basins that carry water only after rains.

Great Barrier Reef, the largest of all coral formations, follows the northeast coast for twelve hundred miles of Australia's twelve-thousand-mile coastline. Except in a few places this reef is impassable to ships, but it does provide an inner passage for coastal navigation. There are good harbors on the southeastern coast.

Wherever there is sufficient moisture for grass to grow, the land is especially adapted to grazing. This land has proved the most suitable in the world for raising sheep. Merino sheep, which produce a very fine quality of wool, comprise most of the flocks. The heavy fleece from these sheep exceeds that of breeds raised elsewhere, so, although Australia produces less than one sixth of the world's sheep, the wool yield is more than a quarter of the world's requirement.

Convenient transportation for a young Koala. The Koala lives in the eucalyptus trees of eastern Australia.

Philip Gendreau

Rawlinson Range, a flat tableland, typical of central Australia.

Australian News Bur.

Lacking navigable rivers, most of the transportation is by railways. These have been of first importance in developing the country, but one great drawback of railroad transportation is that there are several gauges. During the last fifty years there has been a steady expansion of motor roads, and air routes are rapidly increasing.

In addition to the mainland and the island of Tasmania, Australia has extensive territorial interests. These comprise the Trust Territory of New Guinea, Papua, Nauru and Norfolk Island.

The Trust Territory of New Guinea includes the northeastern section of New Guinea, the Bismarck Archipelago, and the northern islands of the Solomon group. Scattered over a sea area of more than one million square miles, these islands are mountainous with limited coastal areas suitable for cultivation.

NEW ZEALAND — Two large islands and several small ones make up New Zealand. Situated about twelve hundred miles southeast of Australia, New Zealand is a lonely

Queenstown, at Lake Wakatipu, lies in the shadow of the Remarkables, New Zealand.

N. Z. Gov't. Travel Comm.

member of the British Commonwealth of Nations.

The two principal islands, North and South Island are separated by Cook Strait which is ninety miles wide. Close as they are to each other, these islands have little in common except that they are both mountainous. North Island is of volcanic origin and consists chiefly of forested hills and plateaus. South Island is more rugged with glaciers and snow-clad peaks that rival the Alps of Switzerland.

PACIFIC ISLANDS — The Pacific Islands fall into three major regions: Polynesia, Micronesia and Melanesia.

Polynesia, or "many islands," consists of widely scattered groups and a few isolated islands forming a rough triangle. The Hawaiian Islands are at the northern point, twenty degrees north of the Equator. The Fiji Islands, at the western point of the triangle, are the meeting place of Polynesian and Melanesian cultures, the people being of mixed stock. The easternmost point lies in the Gambier group of the Tuamotu Archipelago, although isolated Pitcairn Island, inhabited by Anglo-Tahitian descendants of the mutinous crew of the "Bounty," is generally included geographically. Within this area lives the most highly developed group of Pacific peoples, a mixture of white, black and yellow racial stocks, the Polynesians. Famous as navigators, they crossed the Pacific from Asia hundreds of years ago, and sailed their canoes eastward to their present homes. For the most part, the islands are mountainous, volcanic and covered with dense vegetation, often fringed by coral reefs. Along the equator and in the southeast, low coral atolls predominate, often only a few feet above sea level, and frequently torn by hurricanes.

The people, often easy-going to the point of idleness, are not always used in local production, some Chinese having been

hired to do manual work. Famous for dancing and feasting, the generally happy Polynesians strive to maintain their early customs against the inroads of European traders, missionaries and government regulations.

In the western Pacific, for the most part north of the equator, lies Micronesia, or "little islands," confined to the Marianas, Carolines, Marshall Islands, and Gilbert and Ellice Islands. Except for the latter islands, they are mostly volcanic and coral-fringed, and are peopled by a light-skinned group—the latest arrivals in the Pacific. These inhabitants show more evidence of a recent black and yellow mixture.

The earliest inhabited area of the Pacific, New Guinea and the islands spreading to the southeast of it, is known as Melanesia, the "black islands." Of early Negroid stock, this area was generally by-passed by the later Polynesians and Micronesians, as settlement was already established. Melanesia is a rapidly developing area, rich in minerals

House with grass roof, Fiji Islands.

Jean LeRoy

as well as the usual coconuts. Today the people range from Europeanized workers in the plantations of New Caledonia and Fiji, and the missions of the New Guinea coast, to half-naked savages, often head-hunters and cannibals, in the higher regions of New Guinea.

Colorful sailboat at Waikiki Beach, Hawaii, with Diamond Head in the background.

A. N. Dupay

RESOURCE - RELIEF MAP
of
NORTH AMERICA

Copyright by C.S. HAMMOND & CO., N.Y.

RESOURCE-RELIEF MAP
of
SOUTH AMERICA

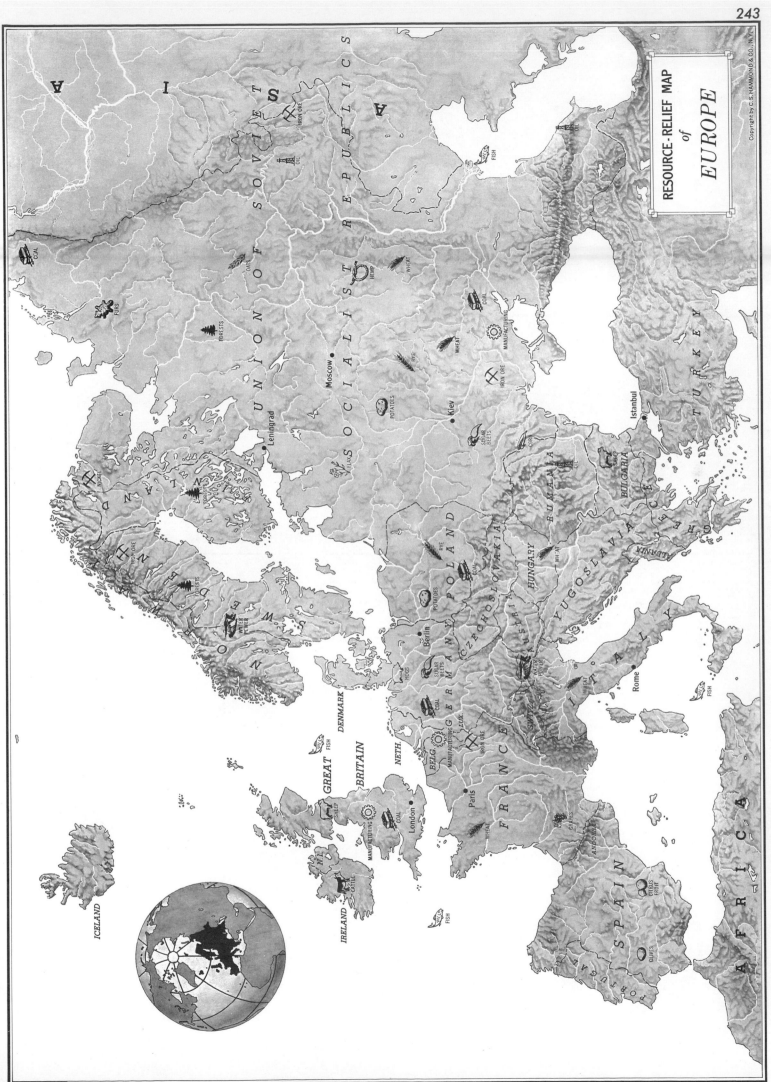

RESOURCE · RELIEF MAP
of
EUROPE

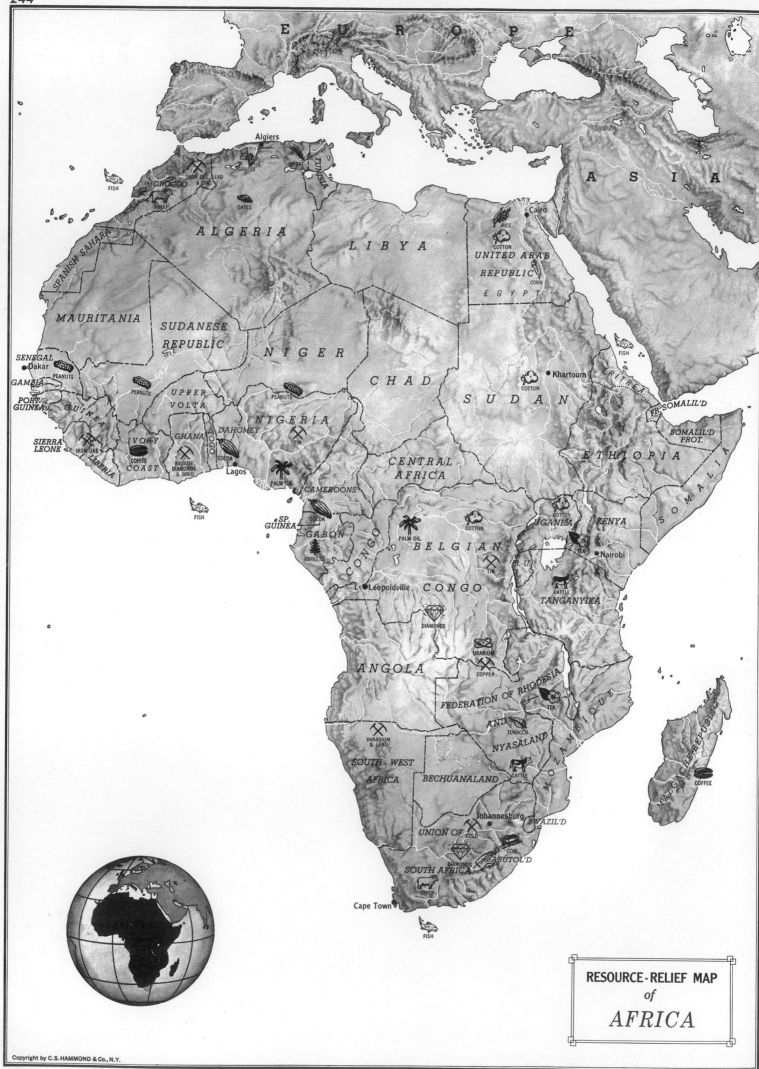

EUROPE

ASIA

FISH

Algiers

GRAPES

WHEAT

TUNISIA

IRON ORE, LEAD
& ZINC

MOROCCO

SHEEP

DATES

ALGERIA

LIBYA

Cairo

RICE

COTTON

UNITED ARAB

REPUBLIC

EGYPT

CORN

FISH

MAURITANIA

SUDANESE

REPUBLIC

NIGER

CHAD

SUDAN

Khartoum

COTTON

ERITREA

FR. SOMALIL'D

SENEGAL
Dakar

PEANUTS

GAMBIA

PEANUTS

PEANUTS

SOMALIL'D
PROT.

PORT.
GUINEA

UPPER
VOLTA

GUINEA

SIERRA
LEONE

IRON ORE

LIBERIA

IVORY
COAST

COFFEE

GHANA

BAUXITE,
DIAMONDS
& GOLD

DAHOMEY

TOGO

NIGERIA

TIN

COCOA

ETHIOPIA

SOMALIA

Lagos

PALM OIL

CAMEROONS

SP.
GUINEA

COCOA

CENTRAL

AFRICA

COTTON

UGANDA

KENYA

FISH

GABON

PALM OIL

BELGIAN

COTTON

TEA

Nairobi

FORESTS

CONGO

Leopoldville

CONGO

TIN

CATTLE

TANGANYIKA

DIAMONDS

URANIUM

COPPER

ANGOLA

FEDERATION OF RHODESIA

TEA

MOZAMBIQUE

MALGACHE REPUBLIC

AND

TOBACCO

NYASALAND

VANADIUM
& LEAD

SOUTH - WEST

AFRICA

BECHUANALAND

CATTLE

COFFEE

SWAZIL'D

Johannesburg

GOLD

UNION OF

COAL

BASUTOL'D

DIAMONDS

SOUTH AFRICA

SHEEP

Cape Town

FISH

RESOURCE - RELIEF MAP
of
AFRICA

RESOURCE - RELIEF MAP
of
ASIA

246

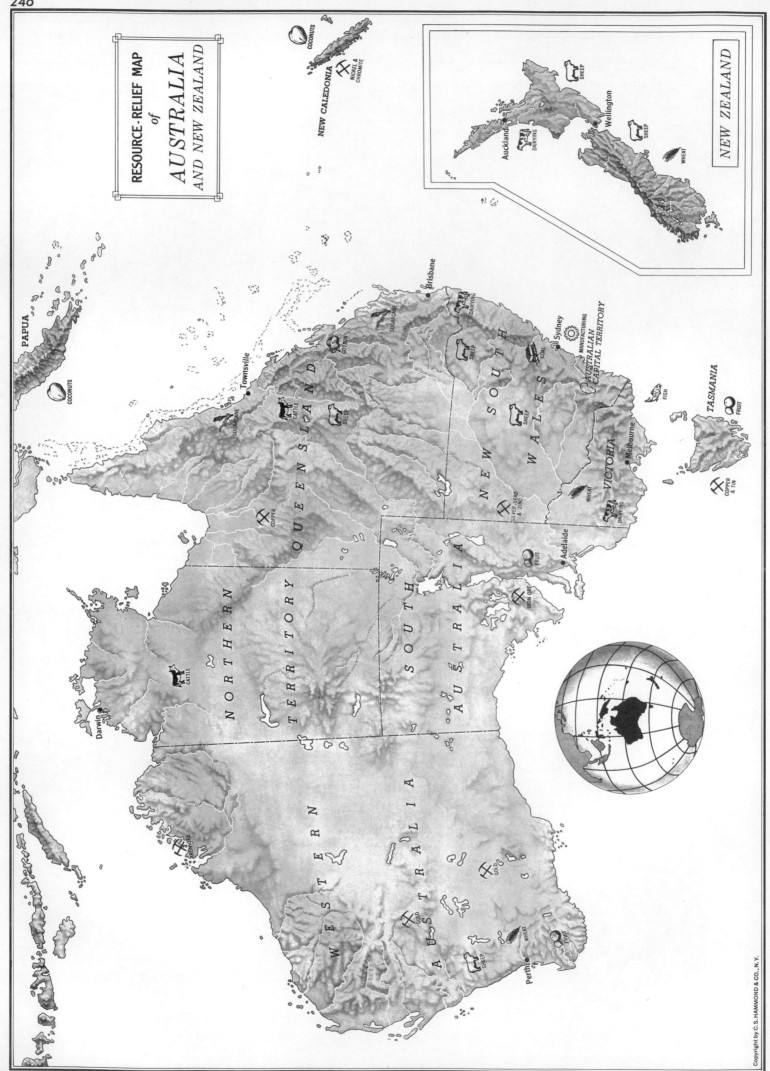

RESOURCE-RELIEF MAP
of
AUSTRALIA
AND NEW ZEALAND

NEW ZEALAND

NEW CALEDONIA

COCONUTS

NICKEL & CHROMITE

SHEEP

Auckland
DAIRYING
Wellington
SHEEP
WHEAT

PAPUA

COCONUTS

Brisbane

SUGAR CANE

COTTON

DAIRYING

Townsville

SUGAR CANE

CATTLE

SHEEP

QUEENSLAND

SHEEP

COAL
Sydney

MANUFACTURING
AUSTRALIAN
CAPITAL TERRITORY

NEW SOUTH WALES

FISH

TASMANIA

FRUIT

COPPER

SHEEP

SILVER, LEAD & ZINC

WHEAT

VICTORIA

Melbourne

COPPER & TIN

DAIRYING

NORTHERN TERRITORY

SOUTH AUSTRALIA

FRUIT
Adelaide

IRON ORE

CATTLE

Darwin

WESTERN AUSTRALIA

IRONSTONE

GOLD

GOLD

WHEAT

FRUIT

SHEEP

Perth

Copyright by C.S. HAMMOND & CO., N.Y.

Gazetteer of the World
SOCIAL AND ECONOMIC TABLES

POLITICAL DIVISION	GOVERNMENT	MONETARY UNIT	LANGUAGE	RELIGION	MAJOR PRODUCTS
ADEN	British colony administered by a governor and an executive and legislative council.	East African shilling	Arabic Hindu	Mohammedan	Salt, cigarettes, dhow building, fish cloth, dyeing, seasame oil, soap, sorghum, ship-bunkering.
ADEN PROTECTORATE	Ruled by native sultans and sheikhs advised by a British agent responsible to the governor of Aden.	East African shilling	Arabic	Mohammedan	Dates, gums, tobacco, fish oil, butter, wheat, barley, sesame, millet, sorghum, aloes, ghee; goats, sheep, camels, cattle.
AFGHANISTAN	A constitutional monarchy ruled by a king, a cabinet and a bi-cameral legislative assembly.	Afghani rupee	Afghan (Pushta) Persian	Mohammedan	Wheat, barley, millet, corn, sorghum, lentils, vegetables, fruits, nuts, castor beans, madder, asafetida, cotton, tobacco, fat-tailed sheep (karakul), camels, zebus; wool, skins; sheepskin, textiles, leather, carpets, rugs; gold, iron, lapis lazuli, coal, copper, lead, silver.
ALBANIA	A Soviet-type republic with president, cabinet and one house legislature. Actually ruled by the Communist party politburo.	lek	Albanian	Moslem, Orthodox, Roman Catholic	Corn, tobacco, wheat, flax, oats, barley, rye, rice, olives, fruit; cattle, sheep; fish; wool, hides; dairy products, furs; bitumen, salt, lignite, aluminum, petroleum, copper, chromite; flour, olive oil, cheese, cement, leather.
ALGERIA	It is composed of 15 departments of France. The former Southern Territories of Algeria now form 2 separate departments of France, Saoura and Oasis.	franc	Arabic French Berber	Mohammedan Roman Catholic Jewish	Wheat, barley, oats, corn, grapes, olives, tobacco, dates, figs, flax, pomegranates, prunes, apricots, legumes, potatoes; sheep, goats, cattle, mules, horses, pigs, camels; sardines, anchovies, tuna; forestry products; iron phosphates, zinc, petroleum; wine, olive oil, distilling, flour, carpet weaving, alcohol, cotton weaving, tobacco products, wool, cork.
ANDORRA	A republic under the joint suzerainty of the French State and the Bishop of Urgel, with a council general of 24 elective members. Executive authority is vested in the First Syndic.	franc and peseta	Catalan	Roman Catholic	Tobacco, potatoes, barley; sheep, cattle; lumber.
ANGOLA	Portuguese overseas province with a governor-general.	angolar	Bantu languages Portuguese	Tribal religions	Coffee, corn, sugar, palm oil and kernels, cotton, sisal, wax, tobacco; diamonds; whale oil, fish oil, sugar, palm oil.
ARGENTINA	A republic with a president, vice-president, appointive cabinet, elective senate and house of deputies.	peso	Spanish	Roman Catholic	Wheat, corn, oats, barley, linseed, rye, grapes and other fruit, tobacco, vegetables; yerba maté; cattle, sheep; quebracho, lumber; petroleum, natural gas, gold, lead, silver, tungsten; vegetable oils, wines, hides, wool, meats, textiles, metal products, vehicles and machinery, chemicals, wood and paper products, leather, clothing and shoes.
ASCENSION ISLAND	Possession of Great Britain administered through the government of St. Helena by a resident magistrate and a Justice of the Peace.	pound	English	Protestant	
AUSTRALIA	Member of the British Commonwealth of Nations with a governor-general, prime minister and cabinet. Parliament consists of a senate and house of commons.	Australian pound	English	Protestant Roman Catholic	Wheat, oats, rice and other grains, fruits, vegetables, honey; sheep, cattle; gold, coal, copper, iron, lead, silver, tin, zinc; iron and steel, wool, textiles, electrical and radio equipment and appliances, drugs and chemicals, paints, optical instruments, agricultural implements and machinery, metal work and machinery, clothing, leather, furniture, airplanes, engines, ships, processed fruit and vegetables, building materials, confectionery, automobiles.
AUSTRIA	Republic with a president, chancellor and vice-chancellor, cabinet of ministers, and two-house assembly.	schilling	German	Roman Catholic	Rye, wheat, oats, barley, corn, potatoes, sugar beets, hops, grapes, rapeseed, flax, hemp, tobacco; iron, copper, lead, magnesite, graphite, coal, aluminum, petroleum, lignite, salt; timber, pulp, poultry and livestock; steel, machinery, machine tools, chemicals, textiles, paper, building materials, processed foods, leather.
BAHAMAS	British colony with governor, executive and legislative council and house of assembly.	pound	English	Roman Catholic and Protestant	Tomatoes, pineapples, okra, vegetables, citrus fruits, bananas, sisal; crawfish, shells; lumber; salt; handcraft products.
BAHREIN	Arab Sheikhdom protected by Great Britain and advised by British political agent.	rupee	Arabic	Mohammedan	Pearl fishing, petroleum, boat building, fishing; reed mats, dates, lucerne; donkeys; textiles.
BARBADOS*	British colony with governor, executive and legislative council and house of assembly.	B.W.I. dollar	English	Protestant	Sugar cane, cotton; flying fish; manjak (asphalt); sugar, molasses, rum, edible oil, margarine.
BASUTOLAND	British colony. Governed by a resident commissioner under High Commissioner for Basutoland, Bechuanaland and Swaziland.	pound	Bantu languages Afrikaans English	Tribal religions Christian missions	Corn, wheat, sorghum, barley, oats, beans, peas; cattle, sheep, goats, horses, donkeys, pigs, mules; wool, mohair.
BECHUANALAND	British protectorate. Governed by a resident commissioner under High Commissioner for Basutoland, Bechuanaland and Swaziland.	pound	Bantu languages Bushman English	Tribal religions Protestant	Kaffir, wheat and wheatmeal; cattle, sheep, goats, pigs; hides, gold.
BELGIAN CONGO	Belgian colony administered by a governor-general.	franc	Bantu languages French Flemish	Tribal religions Roman Catholic	Palm oil and kernels, cotton, coffee, oil cakes, copal, rice, groundnuts; rubber, manioc, fibers; copper, cement, coal, silver, cassiterite (tin), diamonds, gold, cobalt, radium, uranium, tantulum, zinc.
BELGIUM	Constitutional, hereditary monarchy. King appoints a cabinet of ministers. Parliament consists of a senate and chamber of deputies.	franc	French and Flemish	Roman Catholic	Wheat, rye, oats, barley, potatoes, sugar beets, flax, tobacco, vegetables, fruit, hops, hemp, bulbs, livestock, fish; coal, iron, zinc, lead, copper, tin, silver; coke, steel, machinery, textiles, lace, glass, chemicals, uranium refining, sugar, margarine, cheese, vinegar, alcohol, beer, matches, paper, foods, beverages, wool, cut diamonds, dairy products.
BERMUDA	British colony with governor, executive and legislative council and house of assembly.	pound	English	Protestant	Lily bulbs, onions, bananas, cabbage, tomatoes, beans; coral; fish; perfume.
BHUTAN	Ruled by a Maharaja and advised by India in foreign relations.	rupee	Bhutanese (Tibetan dialect)	Lamaist Hindu	Rice, corn, millet, lac, wax, musk; elephants, ponies, chowries; cloth, baskets, mats, metalwork, guns, swords.
BISMARCK ARCHIPELAGO	A part of the territory of New Guinea administered by Australia as a U.N. trust territory.	Australian pound	Papuan English Chinese	Tribal religions Roman Catholic Protestant	Coconuts, cocoa, coffee, kapok, rubber, grains; cattle, goats, pigs; fish.
BOLIVIA	A republic with a president, vice-president, appointive ministers of state, and an elective senate and chamber of deputies.	boliviano	Spanish, Indian	Roman Catholic	Potatoes, corn, barley, quinoa, nuts, coca, vanilla, rubber, quinine; tin, zinc, lead, copper, silver, antimony, tungsten, sulphur, petroleum; cattle; textiles, flour, cement, tobacco products, hides, beer, earthenware.

*Member of the West Indies (British Caribbean Federation)

POLITICAL DIVISION	GOVERNMENT	MONETARY UNIT	LANGUAGE	RELIGION	MAJOR PRODUCTS
BONIN ISLANDS	Administered by the United States.	dollar yen	Japanese	Shinto-Buddhist	Vegetables, sugar, coca; poultry, pigs, cattle; fish.
BRAZIL	Federal republic with a president, vice-president, appointive secretaries of state and a bicameral legislature.	cruzeiro	Portuguese	Roman Catholic	Coffee, corn, rice, cotton, cacao, sugar cane, cassava, beans, carnauba wax, medicinal plants, oranges, balata, tobacco, fibers, castor oil; livestock; timbo, brazil nuts; iron, manganese, gold, rutile, zirconium, diamonds, mica, bauxite, quartz, beryllium, chrome, tungsten, silver; foods, textiles, chemicals, pharmaceuticals, metallurgical products, paper and wood products, hides, vegetable oils, machinery.
BRITISH HONDURAS	British colony with governor, executive council and legislative assembly.	Br. Honduras dollar	English and Spanish	Protestant and Roman Catholic	Rice, maize, beans, bananas, coconuts, citrus fruits, sugar cane; mahogany, chicle, pine, cedar; fish; rum, food products.
BRUNEI	A sultanate with a chief minister, executive and legislative councils and British High Commissioner.	Malayan dollar	Malay English	Mohammedan	Rice, sago, rubber, jelutong, cutch, sugar cane, tapioca, bananas, pineapples; timber; domestic birds, buffalo, pigs, cattle; petroleum, natural gas; boat building, cloth, brass and silverware.
BULGARIA	Soviet-type republic with a one-house legislature, which elects a presidium whose president is the nominal chief of state. Actual power is Communist politburo.	lev	Bulgarian	Eastern Orthodox	Wheat, corn, barley, oats, rye, tobacco, fruit, cotton, sugar beets, potatoes; livestock, silkworm cocoons; fish; coal, salt, bauxite, copper, iron, lead, manganese, silver, kaolin; tobacco products, attar of roses, sugar, flour, textiles, leather goods, shoes, lead concentrates, wines and spirits.
BURMA, UNION OF	A republic with a president elected by a bicameral legislature.	kyat	Burmese Khaner Shan	Buddhist Tribal religions	Rice, sesame, peanuts, corn, cotton, millet, tobacco, sugar, beans, fruit, vegetables, pulses, rubber; teak wood, lumber; cattle, buffalo, pigs, goats, sheep; petroleum, silver, lead, zinc, tin, copper, tungsten, rubies, sapphires, amber, jade, nickel, gold, antimony, cobalt, salt; textiles, hides, matches, lacquer ware.
CAMBODIA	Constitutional monarchy with a national assembly.	riel	Khmer Tao	Buddhist	Rice, tobacco, kapok, cotton, pepper, coin, sugar, rubber; timber; cattle; fish; silk, cotton, textiles, pottery, rush mats, precious stones, phosphates.
CAMEROONS	Two United Nations trusteeships, Northern and Southern Cameroons, administered by Great Britain.	pound	Bantu and Sudanese languages	Mohammedan Tribal religions Christian	Cocoa, coffee, rubber, bananas, palm oil and kernels; cattle, goats, sheep, horses.
CAMEROONS	Former French U.N. trusteeship, Cameroun; now independent republic.	franc	Sudanese and Bantu languages Arabic French	Tribal religions Mohammedan Roman Catholic	Cocoa, palm kernels, bananas, caoutchouc, coffee, cacao, palm oil; timber; cattle, sheep, pigs, horses, asses; rubber, tobacco.
CANADA	Member of the British Commonwealth with a governor-general, prime minister and cabinet. Parliament consists of a senate and house of commons.	dollar	English	Protestant Roman Catholic	Wheat, oats, barley, flax, rye, potatoes, turnips, vegetables, sugar beets, tobacco, fruits, dairy products, livestock; fish; forestry products; furs; gold, copper, nickel, zinc, lead, silver, platinum, iron ore, titanium, cobalt, radium, uranium, petroleum, natural gas, coal, asbestos, salt, gypsum, quartz, sulphur, cement, clay; hydro-electric power; foods, beverages, transportation equipment, iron and steel products, aluminum, metal products, pulp, paper and wood products, textiles, electrical apparatus, chemicals.
CANARY ISLANDS	Islands forming two provinces of Spain, each governed by a governor.	peseta	Spanish	Roman Catholic	Bananas, cochineal, potatoes, sugar cane, onions, fruits; fish; wine, sugar.
CAPE VERDE ISLANDS	Portuguese overseas province, ruled by a governor.	escudo	Portuguese	Roman Catholic	Coffee, castor beans, corn, fruit, grains, tobacco; goats, oxen, pigs, asses; hides, skins; preserved fish, salt, lime, sugar.
CAROLINE ISLANDS	A group in the United States trust territory of the Pacific Islands and administered by a high commissioner.	dollar	Micronesian dialects Malayo-Polynesian languages	Tribal religions Protestant Roman Catholic	Copra, breadfruit, cassava, taro, sweet potatoes; pigs, cattle, poultry, fish; phosphates.
CENTRAL AFRICA	Equatorial African republic within the French Community with a legislative assembly.	franc	Bantu and Sudanese languages Arabic, French	Mohammedan Tribal religions Roman Catholic	Coffee, cotton, sisal, groundnuts, millet, sorghum; gold, diamonds; rubber; palm products, beeswax.
CEYLON	Dominion of the British Commonwealth ruled by a governor-general, a prime minister, a cabinet and a bicameral legislature.	rupee	Singhalese Tamil	Buddhist Hindu	Tea, coconuts, rubber, rice, millet, tobacco, cacao, cinnamon, citronella, cloves, fruits, palmyra, fish; cattle, buffalo, goats, swine, sheep; graphite, plumbago, mica, ilmenite, monazite, iron ore; salt, pearls, zircon, glass sands, copra, plywood, leather, shoes, glass, steel, acetic acid, ceramics, quinine, strychine, shark-liver oil, coconut oil, textiles.
CHAD	Equatorial African republic within the French Community with a legislative assembly.	franc	Bantu and Sudanese languages Arabic, French	Mohammedan Tribal religions Roman Catholic	Millet, sesame, vegetables; livestock, hides; ivory, ostrich feathers; cotton, dates.
CHILE	A republic with a president, vice-president, appointive cabinet of ministers of state, elective senate and chamber of deputies.	escudo	Spanish	Roman Catholic	Wheat, potatoes, oats, rice, barley, corn, kidney beans, lentils, fruits; fish; livestock; copper, silver, nitrates, iodine, iron, sulphur, gold, manganese, coal; foods, textiles, leather, wood products, cement, chemicals and pharmaceuticals, wines and beer, wool.
CHINA: MAINLAND (COMMUNIST)	In theory, governmental power resides in the National People's Congress and the State Council. In practice, power resides in the Communist Party's Central Committee.	Chinese dollar	Chinese Mongol Turki	Confucianist Buddhist Taoist Mohammedan	Rice, wheat, sweet potatoes, corn, barley, millet, kaoliang, soybeans, cotton, tea, sugar cane, tobacco, peanuts, peas, beans, opium, tung, silk; pigs, oxen, sheep, goats, buffalo, donkeys, horses, mules, poultry; timber; fish; iron, coal, tungsten, tin, antimony, mercury, copper, lead, zinc, silver, salt, soda, gold, petroleum, bismuth, molybdenum; foodstuffs, textiles, chemicals, machinery, metal work, metallurgical products, bristles, cement, clothing, embroideries, ceramics.
CHINA: TAIWAN (NATIONALIST)	A republic whose supreme organ of government is the popularly elected National Assembly. The Assembly elects the president and vice-president. Legislative powers reside with the Legislative Yuan.	dollar	Chinese (Amoy dialect) Formosan	Confucianist Buddhist Taoist Christian Tribal religions	Rice, tea, sugar, sweet potatoes, ramie, jute, tumeric, pineapples, bananas, camphor; pigs, buffalo, cattle, goats, horses.
COLOMBIA	A centralized federal republic with a president, vice-president, appointive cabinet, elective senate and house of representatives.	peso	Spanish	Roman Catholic	Coffee, sugar cane, corn, rice, root crops, cotton, bananas, cacao, wheat, tobacco, cinchona; cattle; rubber, fibers; petroleum, gold, silver, platinum, emeralds, salt; textiles, beer, sugar, cement, flour, tobacco products.
COMORO ISLANDS	An overseas territory of France with an administrator, privy council and an elective general council.	franc	Arabic French	Mohammedan	Sugar cane, vanilla, rice, sweet potatoes, yams, copra, sisal, cacao, perfume plants; rum distilling.
CONGO	Equatorial African republic within the French Community with a legislative assembly.	franc	Bantu and Sudanese languages Arabic, French	Mohammedan Tribal religions Roman Catholic	Palm oil and kernels, hardwoods, kola nuts, copal, rubber, tobacco; lead, gold; livestock; rice.

POLITICAL DIVISION	GOVERNMENT	MONETARY UNIT	LANGUAGE	RELIGION	MAJOR PRODUCTS
COOK ISLANDS	Territory of New Zealand administered by a resident commissioner.	New Zealand pound	Polynesian dialects English	Protestant Tribal religions	Citrus fruits, coconuts, copra, tomatoes, arrowroot, pineapples, breadfruit, taro, kumaras, plantains, yams; mother-of-pearl.
COSTA RICA	Republic with president, cabinet and one-house legislature.	colon	Spanish	Roman Catholic	Coffee, bananas, cocoa, abaca, sugar cane, maize, rice, tobacco; cattle; tuna; gold, silver; cigars and cigarettes, textiles, furniture and woodwork, sugar.
CUBA	Republic with president, vice-president, cabinet and a two-house legislature.	peso	Spanish	Roman Catholic	Sugar cane, tobacco, coffee, pineapples, citrus fruits, bananas, henequen; cattle; cedar, mahogany and other woods; fish; chromite, iron, manganese, copper, nickel, asphalt; sugar, textiles, alcohol, molasses, chemicals, tobacco products, electrical goods, clothing.
CURACAO (NETH. ANTILLES)	Self-governing part of Netherlands Union with governor, executive council and one-house legislature.	guilder	Dutch and Papiamento	Protestant	Fish; dividivi (tannin), crude salt, phosphates; refined petroleum.
CYPRUS	British colony ruled by a governor with the assistance of an executive council. An independent government is being established.	pound	Greek Turkish	Greek Orthodox Mohammedan	Wheat, barley, oats, grapes, raisins, olives, fodder crops, potatoes, carobs, cotton, tobacco, linseed, hemp, flax, citrus fruits, bread beans, corn, sesame, melons; sponges, fish; sheep, goats, donkeys, cattle, pigs, horses, mules; copper pyrites, asbestos, chromite, gypsum, amber, copper concentrates; tobacco products, buttons, wines, spirits, false teeth, lace, gum, boots and shoes, dried fruits, cheese.
CZECHOSLOVAKIA	Soviet-type republic with a president and a one-house elective parliament. Actual power resides in politburo, highest body of Communist party.	koruna	Czech and Slovak	Roman Catholic	Wheat, rye, barley, oats, corn, hops, sugar beets, grapes, potatoes; poultry, livestock; timber; coal, lignite, iron, graphite, garnets, silver, copper, lead, salt, manganese, zinc; beer, spirits, malt, metals, munitions, machinery, iron and steel, porcelain, shoes, textiles, wood products, pulp and paper, sugar, leather, foods, chemicals, rubber products.
DAHOMEY	West African republic within the French Community with a legislative assembly.	franc	Sudanese languages French	Tribal religions Mohammedan	Palm oil, shea nuts, groundnuts, cotton fiber, copra, castor oil, kapok, millet; gold, diamonds, bauxite, iron ore.
DENMARK	Constitutional, hereditary monarchy with a two-house, elective legislature and an appointive council of ministers.	krone	Danish	Protestant	Barley, mixed grains, oats, rye, wheat, potatoes, sugar beets; livestock, fish; clay; ships and transportation equipment, butter, bacon, eggs, cheese, milk, footwear, clothing, machines, chemicals, tobacco products, metal goods, leather goods, beverages; stone, earthenware and glassware, electrical goods.
DOMINICAN REPUBLIC	Republic with president, cabinet and two-house legislature.	peso	Spanish	Roman Catholic	Sugar cane, cacao, coffee, tobacco, bananas, rice, corn; cattle; lumber; gold; starch, alcohol, molasses, sugar, chocolate, meats, cigars, cigarettes, leather.
ECUADOR	A centralized republic with a president, a cabinet and an elective bicameral legislature, the senate including representatives of various social, economic and governmental groups.	sucre	Spanish, Indian	Roman Catholic	Rice, cacao, coffee, bananas, rubber, kapok, cotton, tagua (ivory) nuts, cinchona; livestock; gold, petroleum, salt, balsa wood; textiles, toquilla (panama) hats, buttons, sugar, flour, shoes, beer and liquors, chemicals, pharmaceuticals, cement, soap, candles.
EGYPT	Province of United Arab Republic.	Egyptian pound	Arabic	Mohammedan Christian minorities	Cotton, barley, wheat, rice, sugar cane, onions, corn, millet, fruits, vegetables; sheep, goats, cattle, buffalo, donkeys, pigs, horses, mules; fish; petroleum, cement, phosphates, asbestos, chromite, cotton ginning, milling, pottery, perfume, soap.
ENGLAND AND WALES	England is governed directly by the government of Great Britain and Northern Ireland. Executive power resides nominally in the Crown but actually in the prime minister and cabinet. Parliament consists of two houses.	pound	English and Welsh (Celtic)	Protestant	Potatoes, turnips, beets, oats, wheat, barley, rye, hay, beans, peas, cabbage, vetches, hops, fruits; sheep, cattle, pigs, horses, poultry; fish; coal, coke, gas, iron, copper, lead, nickel, tin, clay; dairy products, wool, cotton and linen textiles; electrical goods, vehicles, steel, scientific instruments, cutlery, foods and beverages, tobacco products, clothing and shoes, chemicals, pottery, china, machinery, locomotives, carpets, knitwear, lace, pharmaceuticals.
ERITREA	Autonomous state federated with Ethiopia. Administered locally by a representative legislature.	Ethiopian dollar	Hamitic languages Arabic	Coptic Christian Mohammedan	Coffee, barley, sisal, bananas, legumes, gum arabic, wheat, tobacco, dates, dom nuts, senna; goats, sheep, camels, horses, mules, donkeys, cattle; hides, skins; fish-meal; pearls, mother-of-pearl; gold, salt, potassium salts, matting.
ETHIOPIA	Constitutional monarchy with an emperor assisted by a council of ministers and a bicameral legislature (See Eritrea)	Ethiopian dollar	Amharic Hamitic languages Arabic	Coptic Christian Mohammedan	Coffee, teff, barley, durra, wheat, cotton, sugar cane; cattle, sheep, goats, horses, mules; hides, skins; wax, gold, rocksalt.
FALKLAND ISLANDS	British colony with a governor and an executive and a legislative council.	pound	English	Protestant, Roman Catholic	Forage crops, sheep; wool, skins, tallow, whale oil, whale-meat meal.
FIJI	British colony ruled by a governor with an executive and legislative council.	Fiji pound	English Fijian Hindustani Chinese	Protestant Roman Catholic Moslem Hindu	Sugar cane, coconuts, bananas, pineapples, rice, root vegetables, citrus fruits, cotton, rubber, castor oil seeds, taro, yams, cassava, sweet potatoes, groundnuts, pulses, corn, fodder crops, tobacco; cattle, pigs; tuna, bêche-de-mer, trochus shell; gold, silver; sugar, copra, coconut oil, soap, biscuits, molasses, paint, butter, ghee, candlenut oil.
FINLAND	A republic with a president, a one-house elective diet and appointive council of state.	marhka	Finnish and Swedish	Protestant	Hay, potatoes, wheat, oats, barley, rye, sugar beets, flax, hemp, vegetables; cattle, horses, sheep, pigs, poultry, reindeer; wood and timber; fish; copper; lumber, plywood, furniture, pulp and paper, cardboard, textiles, butter, eggs, cheese, flour, leather, chemicals, china and glass, foodstuffs.
FRANCE	A republic with a president, a two-house elective parliament and an appointive council of ministers.	franc	French	Roman Catholic	Sugar beets, potatoes, wheat, oats, barley, rye; corn, turnips, fruits, nuts, wine grapes, buckwheat; cattle, sheep, pigs, horses; fish; coal, iron ore, lignite, salt, bauxite, pyrites, potash salts, leeks, kaolin, natural gas, iron and steel, chemicals; silk, cotton, rayon, wool and linen, textiles; clothing, lace, perfumes and cosmetics, automobiles, machinery, dairy products, beet sugar, wines, porcelain, aluminum, foods, leather, spirits.
GABON	Equatorial African republic within the French Community with a legislative assembly.	franc	Bantu and Sudanese languages Arabic, French	Mohammedan Tribal religions Roman Catholic	Mahogany, ebony, okumé wood; gold; fishing; cocoa; rubber, kapok, waxes, kola nuts; manioc, sweet potatoes, corn, plantains.
GAMBIA	Crown colony and protectorate of Great Britain administered by a governor, executive and legislative councils.	pound	Sudanese languages English	Mohammedan Tribal religions Christian	Groundnuts, palm kernels; hides and skins; beeswax.
GAMBIER ISLANDS	A group of islands in French Polynesia governed from Tahiti	franc	Polynesian dialects	Roman Catholic Tribal religions	Coconuts, copra, oranges, breadfruit; pearls, pearl shell, fish.

POLITICAL DIVISION	GOVERNMENT	MONETARY UNIT	LANGUAGE	RELIGION	MAJOR PRODUCTS
GERMANY	Country is divided between two governments—a democratic **Federal Republic of Germany** in the west and a Soviet-dominated **German "Democratic" Republic** in the east. **Federal Republic** has an elected federal diet and council who jointly elect the president. **German "Democratic" Republic** has a communist-controlled legislative branch which selects the president, cabinet and prime minister.	East German and West German Deutsch mark.	German	Protestant Roman Catholic	Wheat, rye, barley, oats, potatoes, sugar beets, fruits, hops; pigs, cattle, poultry, horses; fish; forest products; coal, lignite, iron, copper, potash, sulphur, salt, uranium, lead, zinc, fluor spar, gypsum, vanadium, aluminum; automobiles, steel, cement, diesel oil, gasoline, cotton yarn, woolen yarn, rayon fiber, beet sugar, beer, wines, optical instruments, sulphuric acid, sodium bicarbonate, chemicals.
GHANA	Independent member of British Commonwealth headed by a prime minister and a national assembly.	pound	Sudanese languages English	Mohammedan Tribal religions Christian	Cocoa, palm oil and kernes, sorghum, millet, corn, yams, cassava, groundnuts, cotton; gold, diamonds, manganese, bauxite.
GIBRALTAR	British Crown Colony administered by a governor, executive council, and a legislative council.	pound	English and Spanish	Roman Catholic	Fish for export and processing of commodities for local consumption.
GILBERT AND ELLICE ISLS.	British colony administered by a resident commissioner.	Australian pound	English Gilbertese Samoan	Tribal religions Protestant Roman Catholic	Coconuts, copra, phosphate of lime; pearl shell, fish; hats, mats.
GÕA	Portuguese overseas province ruled by a governor assisted by executive and legislative councils.	rupia	Portuguese Marathi	Hindu Roman Catholic Mohammedan	Rice, cashew nuts, betel nuts, grains, vegetables, coconuts, mangoes; teak, bamboo, blackwood; fish; salt, manganese, asbestos, asphalt, guano, silica, coal, petroleum; sugar, textiles, distilling, dessicated coconut, tobacco products, rice milling, cocoa, coconut oil, embroideries.
GREAT BRITAIN	(see England, N. Ireland and Scotland)				
GREECE	A constitutional hereditary monarchy with a prime minister, cabinet of ministers and an elective assembly.	drachma	Greek	Greek Orthodox	Wheat, barley, corn, oats, rye, tobacco, currants, sultana raisins, olives, figs, grapes, cottonseed, sesame seed; sheep, goats, cattle, pigs, horses, mules; fish; iron ore, sulphur, emery, magnesite, zinc, lead, lignite, marble, bauxite; textiles, olive oil, foods, wines, chemicals, leather, wood and paper, metal products, machinery.
GREENLAND	An integral part of the Danish kingdom, with representation in Parliament.	krone	Danish and Greenlandic	Protestant	Grass for fodder; cod and other fish; sheep, furs; cryolite; processed fish, hides.
GUADELOUPE	Overseas department of France with a prefect and elective general council.	franc	French, French Patois	Roman Catholic	Sugar cane, bananas, coffee, cocoa, vanilla, cassava; fish; alcohol, rum.
GUAM	Territory of the United States administered by a governor and advisory and legislative bodies.	dollar	English Chamorro Spanish	Roman Catholic	Copra, coconut oil, corn, taro, bananas, citrus fruits, mangoes, papayas, breadfruit, sweet potatoes, cocoa, cassava, sugar cane, pineapples; cattle, pigs, poultry, buffalo.
GUATEMALA	Republic with a president, cabinet and one-house legislature.	quetzal	Spanish	Roman Catholic	Coffee, bananas, sugar cane, rubber, chicle, cacao, abaca, cattle; mahogany and dye woods; essential oils; gold; textiles.
GUIANA, BRITISH	A British colony with a governor and partly nominated, partly elected legislative and executive councils.	B.W.I. dollar	English	Protestant	Sugar cane, rice, coconuts, coffee, citrus fruits, cacao; balata, rubber, green heart and other timber; livestock; bauxite, diamonds, gold; textiles, milled rice, beer and rum, lime rum and oil, sugar, woods, molasses, charcoal, matches.
GUIANA, FRENCH	Overseas department of France governed by a prefect, with an elective council-general.	franc	French	Roman Catholic	Rice, cacao, bananas, sugar cane, corn, cassava, woods; gold; hides, rosewood essence, shoes, rum, fish glue.
GUIANA, NETH. (SURINAM)	Self-governing part of the Netherlands Union with an appointed governor, an appointive council of ministers, an advisory council and an elective legislative body.	guilder	Dutch	Christian Moslem Hindu	Rice, citrus fruits, coconuts, coffee, bananas, sugar cane, cacao, balata, corn, tobacco; lumber; gold, bauxite; sugar, rum, plywood, molasses.
GUINEA	Independent republic.	franc	Sudanese languages French	Tribal religions Mohammedan	Rice, groundnuts, palm oil and nuts, wax, honey, bananas, indigo, kola, orange products, coffee; cattle, sheep, goats, pigs; hides and skins; bauxite, iron ore, gold.
GUINEA, PORTUGUESE	Portuguese overseas province ruled by a governor.	escudo	Sudanese languages Portuguese	Tribal religions Roman Catholic	Rice, palm kernels and oil, wax, groundnuts; hides.
GUINEA, SPANISH	Spanish colony ruled by a governor.	peseta	Bantu languages Spanish	Tribal religions Roman Catholic	Cocoa, coffee, vegetables and fruit; wood.
HAITI	Republic with a president, cabinet and a two-house legislature.	gourde	Creole, French	Roman Catholic	Coffee, sugar, fig bananas, sisal, cotton, rice, cocoa; logwood; molasses, sisal products.
HONDURAS	Republic with a president, council of ministers and a one-house legislature.	lempira	Spanish	Roman Catholic	Bananas, coffee, coconuts, tobacco, grapefruit, rice, henequen; mahogany; cattle; gold, silver.
HONG KONG	A British colony ruled by governor assisted by executive and legislative council.	Hong Kong dollar	Chinese English	Confucianist Buddhist Christian	Rice, sugar, ginger; fish; poultry, pigs; kaolin, lead, iron, wolfram, granite, silver, cement; shipbuilding; enameled hollow-ware, textiles.
HUNGARY	Soviet-type republic with a president and a presidential council selected by the national assembly. Actual power in hands of politburo, highest organ of Communist party.	forint	Hungarian	Catholic Protestant	Wheat, corn, rye, barley, oats, potatoes, sugar beets, tobacco, grapes and other fruits, peppers, hemp, flax; pigs, cattle, sheep, horses, poultry; fish; coal, lignite, petroleum, natural gas, iron ore, bauxite, manganese; flour, sugar, distilling, brewing, iron and steel, wines, textiles, paprika, chemicals, leather, metal products, wood and paper products.
ICELAND	A republic with a president, an elective, two-house legislature and an appointive cabinet of ministers.	krona	Icelandic	Protestant	Hay, potatoes, turnips, hothouse fruits and vegetables; sheep, poultry, horses, cattle; fish; dairy products, meats, animal and vegetable oils, hides, skins, leather, clothing, textiles, frozen fish, herring oil, herring meal.
IFNI	Spanish province ruled by a governor.	peseta	Berber Arabic Spanish	Mohammedan	Barley, alfalfa, corn, tomatoes, argan oil, wheat; fish.
INDIA	An independent republic within the British Commonwealth with a president, cabinet and a bicameral legislature.	rupee	Indo-Aryan (Hindi, Bengali, Urdu, Gujarati, Punjab, etc.) and Dravidian (Tamil, Kanarese, Telugan) English	Hindu Mohammedan Buddhist Animist Christian Sikh Jain Parsi	Rice, wheat, legumes, groundnuts, oilseeds, tea, tobacco, jute, cotton, rubber, coffee, sugar cane, barley, millet, corn; cattle, goats, buffalo, sheep, pigs; fish; coal, manganese, gold, petroleum, salt, mica, iron, copper, chromite, ilmenite, diamonds, silver, bauxite; textiles, shawls, carpets, jute manufacturers, wood-carving and metal work, leather, chemicals, shipbuilding, petroleum refining, sugar refining, cotton ginning, iron and steel mills, glass, soap, matches.

POLITICAL DIVISION	GOVERNMENT	MONETARY UNIT	LANGUAGE	RELIGION	MAJOR PRODUCTS
INDONESIA	Republic with president, cabinet and unicameral legislature.	rupiah	Indonesian (Malay, Javanese, etc.)	Mohammedan Tribal religions Christian Hindu	Rice, sugar cane, rubber, palm oil, tobacco, corn, coconuts copra, cassava, sweet potatoes, groundnuts, soya beans cotton, kapok, coffee, cinchona, cocoa, pepper, fruits, vegetables; cattle, buffalo; tin, coal, petroleum, bauxite, manganese; rubber goods, chemicals, shipyards, textiles, paper, breweries, glass, handicrafts.
IRAN	Constitutional monarchy governed by a shah, prime minister, cabinet and a bicameral legislature.	rial	Persian Arabic Kurdish	Mohammedan Parsi	Wheat, cotton, gums, opium, fruit, rice, barley, sugar beets, tobacco, tea, corn, millet, legumes, vegetables, nuts; sheep, goats, cattle, asses, horses, mules; fish; petroleum oil, red oxide, copper, sulphur, arsenic, coal, salt, marble, nickel, manganese, lead, cobalt, turquoise, iron ore; carpets, rugs, textiles, leather, glass, matches, chemicals, jute, tobacco products, oil refining, casings, wood, oils.
IRAQ	Independent republic.	dinar	Arabic Turkish Kurdish	Mohammedan	Dates, other fruits, barley, wheat, rice, tobacco, cotton, beans, corn, sorghum, sesame; sheep, goats, asses, camels, horses, buffalo; oil, salt, wool, textiles, cigarettes, distilling.
IRELAND	A republic with a president, premier and an elective, two-house parliament.	pound	English and Gaelic	Roman Catholic	Hay, potatoes, turnips, fodder, beets, sugar beets, oats, wheat, barley, cabbage, rye, flax; cattle, sheep, pigs, horses, poultry; fish; coal, peat, gypsum; tobacco, dairy products, foodstuffs, beer, malt, clothing, meats, textiles, boots and shoes, wood and paper products.
ISRAEL	Republic with president, prime minister, cabinet and elective unicameral legislature.	Israeli pound	Hebrew Arabic	Judaist Mohammedan	Dairy products, vegetables, eggs, fruits, green fodder, wheat, hay, barley, corn, durra; goats, sheep, cattle, camels, poultry; fish; textiles, clothing, foods, beverages, tobacco, diamond polishing, shoes, metal and woodwork, furniture, building materials, leather, dairy products, electrical products, paper, printing, false teeth, pharmaceuticals, chemicals, dyes, soap, radios, oil refining, wines.
ITALY	A republic with a president, a two-house, elective legislature and an appointive cabinet.	lira	Italian	Roman Catholic	Wheat, corn, oats, sugar beets, potatoes, tomatoes, rice, olives, grapes, lemons and other fruits, hemp, tobacco, nuts; fish; sheep and goats, cattle, pigs, horses, donkeys; iron ore, sulphur, zinc, bauxite, lead, mercury, barite, copper, marble, manganese, lignite; textiles, chemicals, wines, automobiles and machinery, electrical goods, beet sugar, olive oil, cheese, clothing, processed foods.
IVORY COAST	West African republic within the French Community with a legislative assembly.	franc	Sudanese languages French	Tribal religions Mohammedan	Coffee, cocoa, bananas, manioc, corn, rice, yams, kola, coconuts, palm oil, groundnuts, cotton, millet, tobacco; mahogany, caoutchouc; sheep, cattle, goats, pigs; gold, diamonds, manganese, iron ore, ilmenite.
JAMAICA*	British colony with a governor, executive and legislative councils and house of representatives.	pound	English	Protestant, Roman Catholic	Sugar cane, bananas, tobacco, coconuts, cacao, pimentoes, coffee, ginger; bauxite; honey; logwood; rum, textiles, cigars.
JAPAN	Constitutional monarchy with the executive power vested in prime minister and cabinet, the legislative power residing in a two-house parliament. The duties of the emperor are merely ceremonial.	yen	Japanese	Buddhist Shinto	Rice, wheat, barley, mulberry trees, potatoes, sweet potatoes, fruits, rape, vegetables, oats, tobacco, soy beans, tea, flax, hemp, camphor; timber; bamboo; horses, cattle, sheep, goats, pigs, rabbits; fish, agar, pearl oysters; silk worms; coal, pyrites, gold, copper, pyrethrum, manganese, silver, sulphur, chromite, zinc, salt, tin, lead, iron, petroleum; textiles, steel, paper, porcelain, earthenware, lacquer ware, vegetable oil, toys, slippers, shoes, machinery.
JORDAN	Constitutional monarchy with cabinet and bicameral legislature.	Jordan dinar	Arabic	Mohammedan	Wheat, barley, legumes, vegetables, fruits, olives; sheep, goats, camels; salt, phosphate, potash; wool, tobacco products, flour milling, building materials, olive oil.
KENYA	Colony and protectorate of Great Britain with a governor, a council of ministers, an appointive executive and a partly elective legislative council.	East African shilling	Swahili English Sudanese Hamitic Bantu	Tribal religions Mohammedan	Sisal, wheat, tea, coffee, pyrethrum, cotton, corn, sugar cane, sesame, groundnuts, wattle; hides and skins; sodium carbonate, gold, kyanite, salt, silver, lime, bags, butter, sugar, sisal products.
KOREA	Divided into two parts by Armistice Line of August, 1953, pending final decisions of peace treaty. Communist "people's republic" in North Korea; South Korea headed by a president, a prime minister, a cabinet and a bicameral legislature.	hwan	Korean	Confucianist Buddhist Christian	Rice, barley, millet, wheat, soya beans, red beans, cotton, tobacco, hemp, ginseng, fruit, radishes; timber; draft cattle, pigs, horses, mules, donkeys, sheep, goats, rabbits; fish; gold, iron ore, coal, tungsten, copper, silver, graphite, salt, kaolin, talc, bismuth, flourite, minerals (N. Korea), textiles, fertilizer, chemicals, cement, heavy industries (N. Korea); textiles, cement, tobacco, silkworms, chemicals, machinery, metal, rubber, wood, paper and tobacco products (S. Korea).
KUWAIT	Arab sheikhdom protected by Great Britain and advised by British political agent.	Indian rupee	Arabic	Mohammedan	Petroleum, shipbuilding (dhows), pearls, skins, wool.
LAOS	Constitutional monarchy with a cabinet and a national assembly.	kip	Khmer (Annamese) Lao	Buddhist	Rice, coffee, tea, citrus fruits, corn, cinchona, gum, benzoin, cardamon; stick-lac; teak; tin.
LEBANON	Independent republic governed by a president, cabinet and an elective legislature.	Lebanese pound	Arabic French	Christian Mohammedan	Wheat, barley, corn, potatoes, citrus and other fruits, onions, olives, tobacco (Latakia); goats, asses, cattle, buffalo, sheep, horses, mules; iron, lignite; textiles, cement, olive oil, tobacco products, soap, matches, petroleum refining, gasoline, leather.
LIBERIA	Republic with president, cabinet, senate and house of representatives.	dollar	English Sudanese languages	Christian Tribal religions Mohammedan	Rubber, rice, coffee, cassava, sugar cane, cacao, palm oil and kernels, piassava, groundnuts; rum; iron ore.
LIBYA	A federal kingdom with a bicameral legislature, constituted under U. N. auspices and comprising the three provinces of Cyrenaica, Tripolitania and the Fezzan.	Libyan pound	Arabic	Mohammedan	Barley, wheat, olives, grapes, dates, almonds, figs, tobacco, esparto; goats, sheep, camels, cattle, donkeys, mules and horses; sponge and tuna fishing; matting, carpets, leather articles, embroidered fabrics.
LIECHTENSTEIN	A principality headed by a prince and an elective, one-house legislature.	Swiss franc	German	Roman Catholic	Grain, fruit, grapes, wood; cattle, pigs, chickens; cotton textiles, wine, leather, false teeth, pottery, wood-carving.
LUXEMBOURG	A grand duchy and hereditary, constitutional monarchy with an elective chamber of deputies and appointive minister of state and cabinet.	franc	Mosel-frankisch (German dialect)	Roman Catholic	Oats, potatoes, wheat, rye, grapes; livestock; iron ore, slate, gypsum, sand and gravel; iron, steel and metal working; chemicals, non-metallic minerals, beverages, tobacco, leather, wines, dairy products, quarrying.
MACAO	Portuguese overseas province ruled by a governor.	pataca	Chinese Portuguese	Confucianist Buddhist Taoist Christian	Fish; preserves, firecrackers, vegetable oil, cement, metal work, lumber, tobacco (processed), matches, wine.

*Member of the West Indies (British Caribbean Federation)

POLITICAL DIVISION	GOVERNMENT	MONETARY UNIT	LANGUAGE	RELIGION	MAJOR PRODUCTS
MALAYA, FEDERATION OF	Federation of nine sultanates and two settlements, within Br. Commonwealth. It is a constitutional monarchy with cabinet and two-house legislature.	Malayan dollar	Malay Chinese English	Mohammedan Confucianist	Rubber, rice, coconuts, pineapples, tapioca, pepper, spices, tobacco, fibers, gambier, vegetables, tea; buffalo, swine, oxen, goats, sheep; fish; guano, tin, coal, iron ore, bauxite, manganese, copra, palm oil, timber, gold, rubber products, gutta percha, wood products, canned pineapples, textiles.
MALDIVE ISLANDS	An independent sultanate, under British protection, with a bicameral legislature.	rupee	Singhalese Arabic Dravidian	Mohammedan	Coconuts, copra, coir, fruit, nuts; fish, cowries; cloth, mats, boats.
MALGACHE REPUBLIC	Autonomous republic within the French Community.	franc	French Malagasy and Bantu languages	Tribal religions Roman Catholic Protestant	Cassava, rice, corn, potatoes, coffee, sugar cane, haricot beans, groundnuts, sisal, castor oil, tobacco, raffia; cattle, pigs, goats, sheep; graphite, mica, gold, rock crystal, corundum, phosphates, agate; textiles, sugar and rice factories, tapioca.
MALTA	A self-governing colony of Great Britain with a governor, Lt. governor and an elective legislative assembly.	pound	Maltese and English	Roman Catholic	Wheat, barley, potatoes, onions, grapes and other fruits, cumin seed, cotton; goats, sheep, pigs, cattle; fish; lace, filigree, wine, footwear, beer, cigarettes, buttons, pipes, gloves.
MARIANA ISLANDS	A group of islands in the United States trust territory of the Pacific administered by a high commissioner.	dollar	Micronesian dialects Spanish	Tribal religions	Fruits, corn, sweet potatoes, vegetables, breadfruit, cacao; fish; phosphates.
MARQUESAS ISLANDS	A group of islands in French Polynesia administered from Tahiti.	franc	Marquesan French	Tribal religions Roman Catholic	Bananas, breadfruit, yams, bamboo, coconuts, sugar cane.
MARSHALL ISLANDS	A group of islands in the United States trust territory of the Pacific administered by a high commissioner.	dollar	Micronesian dialects	Tribal religions Protestant	Arrowroot, breadfruit, coconuts, pandanus, taro, vegetables, copra, bananas; poultry, pigs; fish.
MARTINIQUE	Overseas department of France with a prefect and elective general council.	franc	Creole, French	Roman Catholic	Sugar cane, cocoa, pineapples, bananas, coffee; rum, sugar.
MAURITANIA	West African republic within the French Community with a legislative assembly.	franc	Arabic Hamitic and Sudanese languages French	Mohammedan	Millet, gum, dates, corn, watermelons, wheat, henna; sheep and goats, cattle, camels, asses, horses; hides and skins; salt.
MAURITIUS	British colony ruled by a governor, an executive council and a legislative council.	rupee	English Hindustani French	Roman Catholic	Sugar, aloe fiber, rice, vanilla beans, hemp, sisal, groundnuts, tea, yams, manioc, pineapples, tobacco, coconuts; alcohol, molasses, rum, copra.
MEXICO	Federative republic with a president, council of ministers and a two-house legislature.	peso	Spanish	Roman Catholic	Corn, wheat, beans, chick peas, sugar bananas, barley, cotton, coffee, vegetables; cattle; henequen; fish; silver, petroleum, lead, gold, zinc, copper; textiles, sugar, alcohol, foundry products.
MONACO	A principality. The prince's authority exercised through a state ministry and 3 government counsellors. The one-house legislative body is elective.	franc	French	Roman Catholic	Principal revenue derived from Monte Carlo gambling casino. Tobacco, postage stamps, perfume, liqueurs, olive oil, oranges.
MONGOLIAN REPUBLIC	Communist republic, whose prime minister is also head of Communist party politburo, which is the actual ruler.	Tugrik	Mongolian Russian	Lamaist Tribal religions	Stock raising (sheep, goats, cattle, horses, camels); milk, butter, cheese; wool, hides, skins, horns, bricks, machinery; coal, lead, gold.
MOROCCO	Constitutional monarchy with a cabinet and a consultative national assembly.	Moroccan franc	Arabic Berber French	Mohammedan Roman Catholic Jewish	Wheat, barley, olives, almonds, citrus fruits, dates, beans, grapes, vegetables, linseed; cork, cedar; sheep, goats, cattle, asses, camels, horses, mules, pigs; fish; phosphate, iron ore, anthracite, manganese, lead, zinc, cobalt, copper, antimony; leather, carpets.
MOZAMBIQUE	Portuguese overseas province ruled by a governor and a government council.	escudo	Bantu languages Portuguese	Tribal religions Roman Catholic	Sugar, corn, cotton, copra, sisal, cashew nuts, bananas, coffee, kapok, sorghum, manioc, beeswax, tea, tobacco, vegetable oils; mangrove bark, timber; oxen, goats, pigs, sheep, cattle; gold, silver, asbestos, uranium, bauxite, samerskite.
NEPAL	An independent kingdom governed by a maharaja, prime minister and a bicameral legislature.	Nepalese rupee	Indo-Aryan languages Tibetan	Hindu Buddhist Lamaist	Rice, grains, jute, sugar cane, tea, vegetables, tobacco, cotton, potatoes, medicinal herbs; timber; cattle, hides, skins, ghee; iron, coal, copper, lead, zinc; cotton cloth, pottery, paper.
NETHERLANDS	A constitutional, hereditary monarchy governed by the queen, her ministers and a two-house legislature, partly elective and partly chosen by provincial councils.	guilder	Dutch	Roman Catholic Protestant	Potatoes, sugar beets, rye, wheat, oats, barley, flax, legumes, flower bulbs, seeds, vegetables, fruit; cattle, pigs, sheep, horses, poultry; fish; coal, petroleum, salt; leather, rubber, footwear; metal products, textiles, paper, building materials, chemicals, foods and beverages, clothing, ship-building, cheese and other dairy products, fertilizers, ceramics, cement, tobacco products.
NEW CALEDONIA	French overseas territory administered by high commissioner assisted by an appointive executive council and an elective general council.	franc	Melanesian dialects French	Roman Catholic Tribal religions	Coconuts, copra, coffee, cotton, manioc, corn, tobacco, bananas, pineapples, wheat, rice, kauri logs; cattle, pigs, horses, goats, sheep, hides; guano, trochus shell; nickel, chrome, manganese, iron, cobalt, copper, lead, platinum; canned meat.
NEW GUINEA, NETHERLANDS	A Dutch colony, its status undetermined pending negotiations with Indonesian government.	guilder	Papuan Dutch Negrito	Tribal religions	Sago, coconuts, sweet potatoes, wild nutmeg, mace, copra; bird of paradise plumes; petroleum.
NEW GUINEA, TERR. OF	Trust territory of Australia governed by administrator of Papua.	Australian pound	Papuan Pidgin English English	Tribal religions Roman Catholic Protestant	Coconuts, copra, cocoa, dairying; timber; gold, silver, platinum; boat making.
NEW HEBRIDES	British and French condominium administered by British and French resident commissioners.	Australian currency Bank of Indo-china Notes	Melanesian dialects Pidgin English English French	Tribal religions Protestant Roman Catholic	Coconuts, copra, cocoa, coffee, yams, taro, manioc, fruits; kauri pine; cattle, pigs; trochus shells.
NEW ZEALAND	A member of the British Commonwealth with dominion status governed by a governor-general, cabinet and unicameral assembly.	New Zealand pound	English Maori	Protestant	Wheat, oats, barley, seeds, kauri, gum; sheep, cattle, pigs, horses; hides, skins; fish; gold, silver, coal, copper, limestone, manganese, iron, tungsten; dairy products, meats, wool, clothing, lumber, woodwork, furniture, electrical and radio goods, motor assembly, printing, publishing, biscuits, confections, footwear, rubber products, chemical fertilizers, tobacco products, brewing.
NICARAGUA	Republic with a president, cabinet and a two-house legislature.	córdoba	Spanish	Roman Catholic	Coffee, sugar cane, sesame, corn, bananas, rice, cacao, cotton, beans; cattle; hardwoods; gold, silver; sugar, wood products.

POLITICAL DIVISION	GOVERNMENT	MONETARY UNIT	LANGUAGE	RELIGION	MAJOR PRODUCTS
NIGER	West African republic within the French Community with a legislative assembly.	franc	Sudanese Hamitic Arabic French	Mohammedan Tribal religions	Millet, manioc, groundnuts, rice, wheat, cotton, gum arabic, kapok, kidney beans, corn, onions, sorghum, dates, sugar cane; goats, sheep, cattle, asses, camels, horses; hides and skins, leather; natron, sodium sulphate, salt.
NIGERIA	A federated colony and protectorate of Great Britain with a governor-general, a council of ministers and a federal house of representatives.	pound	Sudanese languages Arabic English	Mohammedan Christian	Palm oil and kernels, cacao, groundnuts, cotton, rubber, bananas, benni seeds, shea nuts, yams, cassava, corn, rice, fruits, millet, coffee; cattle, sheep, goats; hides and skins; timber; tin, coal, columbite, lead, gold, silver, zinc; cigarettes, soap, sugar.
NIUE	Dependency of New Zealand administered by a resident commissioner.	New Zealand pound	Mixed Melanesian and Polynesian dialects English	Protestant	Copra, sweet potatoes, bananas; hats, baskets.
NORFOLK ISLAND	Administered by Australia.	Australian pound	English	Protestant	Citrus, passion fruits, bananas, cherry guavas; hides; fish.
NORTH BORNEO	British colony ruled by a governor and assisted by executive and legislative councils.	Malayan dollar	Malay Indonesian languages English Chinese	Tribal religions Mohammedan	Rubber, coconuts, copra, tobacco, manila hemp, sago, rice, cutch, sugar, pepper, kapok, groundnuts, derris root, vegetables; timber; fish.
NORTHERN IRELAND	Executive power vested in appointed governor and cabinet responsible to legislative two-house parliament.	pound	English and Gaelic	Protestant Roman Catholic	Potatoes, oats, flax, turnips, hay; cattle, sheep, pigs, poultry; basalt and igneous rocks, sand and gravel, grit and conglomerate, chalk, clays; linen, rayon, woolen goods, carpets, hosiery, cotton goods, shirts, collars, underwear, shipbuilding, aircraft, marine machinery, rope, tobacco, whiskey.
NORTHERN RHODESIA*	British protectorate administered by a governor and executive and legislative council.	pound	Bantu languages English	Tribal religions	Corn, wheat, potatoes, tobacco, sorghum, millet, groundnuts, cassava, rice, beans, cow-peas, cotton; lumber; cattle and other livestock.
NORWAY	A constitutional, hereditary monarchy headed by the king, his council of state and a two-house, elective legislature.	krone	Norwegian	Protestant	Hay, potatoes, oats, barley, wheat, rye, fruits, vegetables; dairy products, livestock; herring, cod and other fish; sulphur, iron, copper, zinc, silver, nickel, molybdenum; timber, pulp, cellulose, paper, canned foods, electro-chemical products, transportation equipment, salted, dried and canned fish, leather, basic metals, textiles, fertilizers, shipbuilding.
NYASALAND*	British protectorate administered by a governor and executive and legislative council.	pound	Bantu languages English	Tribal religions	Tobacco, tea, cotton, pulses, tung-oil, sisal, corn, cassava, wheat, rice, millet, groundnuts, rubber, beeswax; timber; goats, cattle, pigs, sheep; hides, skins, meat, ghee, soap; gold, mica, corundum.
OMAN AND MUSCAT	An independent sultanate.	rupee (official) Maria Theresa dollar	Arabic	Mohammedan	Dates, pomegranates, limes and other fruits, sugar cane; dried fish.
PAKISTAN	Self-governing republic within the British Commonwealth ruled by a president, cabinet and unicameral legislature.	Pakistani rupee	Indo-Aryan languages (Urdu, Bengali, Punjabi, etc.)	Mohammedan Hindu Christian Sikh	Rice, wheat, corn, jute, cotton, sugar cane, fruit, oilseeds, tobacco, tea, fibers; timber; cattle, goats, sheep, horses, camels, poultry; hides, skins, wool; fish; salt, copper, petroleum, chromite, gypsum, magnisite, sulphur, antimony; textiles, flour milling, cement, iron and steel foundries, sugar, leather, chemicals, glass, sportsgoods, handicrafts, surgical instruments.
PALAU ISLANDS	A civil administrative district in the Western Carolines and part of the United States Pacific trust territory.	dollar	Micronesian dialects	Tribal religions Christian	Coconuts, manioc, taro, pineapples, sweet potatoes, papayas; poultry, pigs, goats; fish; phosphate; handcrafts.
PANAMA	Republic with a president, two vice-presidents, and a one-house legislature.	balboa	Spanish	Roman Catholic	Bananas, cacao, abaca, coconuts, rice, sugar cane, coffee, pineapples; cattle; hardwoods; gold; hides, sugar, wood products.
PAPUA TERRITORY	Australian colony governed by an administrator.	Australian pound	Papuan Pidgin English English	Tribal religions Protestant Roman Catholic	Coconuts, rubber, sweet potatoes, yams, taro, sago, rice, bananas, coffee, kapok, bamboo, sisal hemp, copra; shells; sponges; cattle, goats, poultry; gold, copper, manganese.
PARAGUAY	A centralized republic with a president, an appointed cabinet and a one-house legislature.	guarani	Spanish, Indian	Roman Catholic	Cotton, tobacco, sugar cane, rice, cassava, yerba maté, corn, citrus fruits; cattle, hides; lumber, quebracho; iron, manganese, copper; canned meats, vegetable oils, petit-grain oil, tobacco products.
PERU	A republic with a president, two vice-presidents, appointive cabinet and a two-house legislature.	sol	Spanish, Indian	Roman Catholic	Cotton, sugar, potatoes, barley, corn, rice, wheat, coca, quinoa, cacao, tobacco, coffee, quinine, flax, rubber, balata, guano; fish; livestock; petroleum, lead, zinc, copper, silver, gold, vanadium; textiles, foodstuffs, cement, leather, wool, hides, pharmaceuticals, paper products, clothing, metal products.
PHILIPPINES	Republic governed by a president, cabinet and a bicameral legislature.	peso	Malayan languages (Tagalog, Visayan, etc.) English Spanish	Roman Catholic Mohammedan Tribal religions	Rice, sugar cane, copra, manila hemp (abacá), corn, tobacco, maguey, rubber, bananas, pineapples, mangoes, papaya, citrus fruits, other fruits; hogs, carabaos, cattle, horses, goats, sheep; fish; timber, gum resins, tan and dye barks, dye woods; gold, iron, copper, chromite, silver, manganese, asbestos, asphalt, guano, silica, coal, petroleum; sugar, textiles, distilling, dessicated coconuts, tobacco products, rice milling, cocoa, coconut oil, embroideries.
PITCAIRN ISLAND	British colony administered by a chief magistrate responsible to the governor of Fiji.	Fiji pound	English Tahitian	Protestant (Seventh Day Adventist)	Fruits, vegetables, goats, poultry; handicraft.
POLAND	A Soviet-type "People's Republic" headed by a one-party legislative Sejm which elects an executive Council of Ministers. Actual power in the hands of politburo, highest organ of Communist party.	zloty	Polish	Roman Catholic	Potatoes, straw and hay, rye, sugar beets, mangolds, oats, barley, wheat, peas, beans, flax, hemp, rapeseed; livestock; fish; zinc, lead, coal, salt, iron ore, petroleum, natural gas, phosphates, lignite; iron and steel products, coke, foods and beverages, textiles, cement, lime, bricks, electrical goods, chemicals, wood, timber, paper, cellulose, leather and leather products, glass.
PORTUGAL	A "unitary corporative republic" with a president, premier, and a one-house elective legislature.	escudo	Portuguese	Roman Catholic	Wheat, corn, oats, barley, rye, rice, French beans, potatoes, grapes, olives; livestock; cork, lumber, resin; sardines, tuna and other fish; copper pyrites, coal, copper, tin, kaolin, cement, wolfram, sulphur, tungsten, iron; wines, olive oil, canned sardines, textiles, porcelain, tiles, embroideries, lace.

*Member of Federation of Rhodesia and Nyasaland

POLITICAL DIVISION	GOVERNMENT	MONETARY UNIT	LANGUAGE	RELIGION	MAJOR PRODUCTS
PRINCIPE AND SÃO TOMÉ	Portuguese overseas province administered by a governor.	escudo	Bantu languages Portuguese	Tribal religions Roman Catholic	Cacao, coffee, coconuts, copra, palm oil, cinchona, bananas.
PUERTO RICO	A self-governing commonwealth associated with the United States, with a governor, an executive council and a bicameral legislature.	dollar	Spanish, English	Roman Catholic	Sugar cane, tobacco, fruits, pineapples, grapefruit, coconuts, coffee, cotton, livestock, vegetables; molasses, embroideries, rum, canned fruit and juice, alcohol, cordials, tobacco products.
QATAR	Sheikhdom under British protection.	rupee riyal	Arabic	Mohammedan	Dates; pearl fishing, dried fish; camels; petroleum.
RÉUNION	French overseas department administered by a prefect and a council-general.	franc	French	Roman Catholic	Sugar, rum, vanilla, tapioca, essences, fruit and vegetable preserves.
RHODESIA AND NYASALAND, FED. OF	Br. Commonwealth Federation of Northern and Southern Rhodesia and Nyasaland Protectorate, with governor-general, cabinet and federal assembly.	pound	See member countries	See member countries	See member countries.
RUANDA—URUNDI	Under United Nations trusteeship, administered by Belgium and governed by a vice-governor-general.	franc	Bantu languages Flemish French	Tribal religions Roman Catholic	Foods; cattle; hides.
RUMANIA	A Soviet-type "People's Republic" with a 17-member presidium, cabinet of ministers and a one-house legislature. Supreme power resides in Communist party politburo.	leu	Rumanian	Rumanian Orthodox	Wheat, barley, rye, corn, oats, potatoes, sugar beets, hemp, flax, grapes, fruits, tobacco; lumber; sheep, cattle, pigs, horses; petroleum, natural gas, salt, coal, lignite, iron and copper ores, gold, silver, bauxite, lead, manganese, zinc; flour, brewing and distilling, iron and steel, metal products, textiles, wood and paper products.
RYUKYU IS.	Administered by the United States.	yen	Luchuan Japanese English	Animistic Shinto	Sweet potatoes, sugar cane, rice, fruits, mulberries; swine, cattle, goats, horses, poultry; silkworms; fish; Panama hats, textiles, lacquer, pottery, china, glassware, tiles.
ST. HELENA	British colony with a governor, an executive and an advisory council.	lira	English	Protestant	Hemp, lily bulbs, potatoes, tow, rope and twine, lace; sheep, goats, cattle, donkeys, poultry.
ST. PIERRE AND MIQUELON	French overseas territory with a governor, privy council and elective general council.	franc	French	Roman Catholic	Fish, silver fox; dried cod and cod liver oil; sienna earth, yellow ocher.
SALVADOR, EL	Republic with a president and a one-house legislature.	colón	Spanish	Roman Catholic	Coffee, cotton, corn, tobacco, henequen, sugar cane, rice; balsam and other woods; gold, silver; cotton textiles, henequen bags, sugar.
SAMOA, EASTERN	Possession of the United States with a governor and a bicameral legislature.	dollar	English Samoan	Protestant	Copra, taro, breadfruit, yams, bananas, arrowroot, pineapples, oranges; mats.
SAMOA, WESTERN	Under United Nations trusteeship administered by New Zealand.	New Zealand pound	Samoan English	Protestant Tribal religions	Copra, cocoa beans, bananas, taro; fish; pigs, poultry.
SAN MARINO	Republic with two regents, council of state, one-house legislature.	pound	Italian	Roman Catholic	Cattle, hides, wines, quarrying.
SARAWAK	British colony administered by a governor and an executive and legislative council.	Malayan dollar	Malay Indonesian languages Chinese English	Mohammedan Tribal religions	Rice, rubber, sago, pepper, coconuts, pineapples, tobacco, coffee, fruits, vegetables; timber, rattan cane, guttas; buffalo, cattle, pigs, goats; fish; petroleum, gold, antimony, phosphate, cutch.
SAUDI ARABIA	Absolute monarchy, with premier and cabinet responsible to the king and advisory councils.	riyal	Arabic	Mohammedan	Dates, sorghum, wheat, rice, henna, coffee, fruits, nuts, vegetables, honey, gum, sesame oil; fish; camels, sheep, goats, cattle, donkeys, poultry, horses; hides, wool, clarified butter, charcoal, pottery, tile, salt, soap, weaving; petroleum, gold, pearls.
SCOTLAND	A secretary of state for Scotland in the British cabinet has in his charge four departments for Scotland (agriculture, education, health and home.) Authority in other matters is exercised by other members of the British cabinet.	pound	English and Gaelic	Protestant	Turnips, potatoes, wheat, barley, sugar beets, flax, vegetables, forage crops, fruits; sheep, cattle, pigs, horses; coal, iron ore, granite, sandstone, limestone, slate, lead, clay; steel, machinery, tools, locomotives, electronic equipment, linoleum, shipbuilding and repair, watches, clocks, jute, bagging, burlap, textiles, hosiery, thread, lace, carpet, yarn, chemicals, whiskey, ale, paper, bricks and other clay products, preserves, boots and shoes, furniture.
SENEGAL	West African republic within the French Community with a legislative assembly.	franc	Sudanese languages Arabic French	Mohammedan Tribal religions Roman Catholic	Millet, groundnuts, manioc, rice, corn, gum arabic, palm nuts, honey, sweet potatoes, sisal, indigo; sheep, goats, cattle, asses, horses; fish; titanium, zircon; brick, pottery, weaving, jewelry, oil cakes.
SEYCHELLES	A British colony ruled by a governor and a legislative and executive council.	rupee	English French	Roman Catholic	Coconuts, cinnamon, patchouli, copra, vanilla, corn; guano; salted fish, tortoise shell, calipee.
SIERRA LEONE	A British colony and protectorate ruled by a governor and a legislative and executive council.	pound	Sudanese languages English	Tribal religions Mohammedan Christian	Palm oil and kernels, kola nuts, ginger, piassava, groundnuts, cocoa; diamonds, iron ore, chrome ore.
SIKKIM	A protectorate of India ruled by a maharaja and a council.	rupee	Nepali Tepcha Bhutia	Hindu Buddhist	Millet, corn, pulse, rice, fruits; cattle; woolen cloth.
SINGAPORE	Br. Commonwealth state with internal self-government, headed by appointed prime minister and cabinet and elective legislative assembly.	Malayan dollar	Chinese Malay Hindi English	Confucianist Buddhist Taoist Mohammedan Hindu Christian	Rubber, coconuts, fruits, vegetables, rice, coffee, tapioca, tobacco, sweet potatoes, pepper, pineapples; pigs, poultry, cattle; fish; tin, tin smelting, rubber milling, coconut milling, soap, beer, pineapple canning, biscuits, brick making, shipping, textiles, palm oil, cigarettes, gasoline, kerosene.
SOCIETY ISLANDS	Part of French Polynesia governed from Tahiti.	franc		Roman Catholic Tribal religions	Copra, vanilla, pearls, mother of pearl, vanilla, phosphates, sugar, rum.
SOLOMON ISLANDS	A protectorate administered by the British high commissioner of the Western Pacific.	Australian pound	Melanesian Pidgin English English	Tribal religions Protestant Roman Catholic	Copra, pigs, poultry; trochus shell, turtle shell, bêche-de-mer.
SOLOMON ISLANDS (NORTHERN)	Part of the territory of New Guinea and governed as an Australian trust territory.	Australian pound	Melanesian Pidgin English English	Tribal religions Protestant Roman Catholic	Coconuts, copra, bananas, yams, taro, fruits; trochus shell, green snail shell, rubber.
SOMALIA	Under U.N. trusteeship, administered by Italy. Independence is planned for July, 1960.	Somalo	Somali Arabic Italian	Mohammedan Roman Catholic	Sugar, cotton, tobacco, bananas, aromatic gums, resin, kapok, grains, beans; camels, goats, sheep, cattle; skins, hides; tunny, mother-of-pearl.

POLITICAL DIVISION	GOVERNMENT	MONETARY UNIT	LANGUAGE	RELIGION	MAJOR PRODUCTS
SOMALILAND, BRITISH	British protectorate ruled by a governor with a legislative council.	Indian rupee East African shilling	Somali Arabic	Mohammedan	Millet, sorghum, corn; sheep, goats, camels, cattle; skins, hides; gums, salt.
SOMALILAND, FRENCH	Overseas territory of France with a governor and an elective representative assembly.	Djibouti franc	Hamitic languages Arabic French	Mohammedan	Boats, sheep; salt.
SOUTHERN RHODESIA †	A self-governing colony and member of Br. Commonwealth with governor and elective executive and legislative councils.	pound	Bantu languages English	Tribal religions Protestant	Corn, tobacco, groundnuts, wheat, potatoes, citrus and other fruits; cattle, sheep, pigs, goats; meats, hides; gold, asbestos, chromite, coal; footwear, apparel, cigarettes, flour, groundnut oil, wood products.
SPAIN	A nominal monarchy governed by a chief of state. The legislative Cortés prepares laws subject to the veto of the chief of state. A king is to be chosen by a regency council upon the death or incapacitation of the chief of state.	peseta	Spanish, Catalan	Roman Catholic	Wheat, barley, potatoes, oranges, olives, oats, rye, rice, corn, peas, beans, grapes, onions, sugar beets, esparto, flax, hemp, pulse, cork, nuts; pigs, sheep, goats, donkeys, mules, horses, poultry; sardines, tuna, cod and other fish; coal, lignite, iron ore, lead, iron pyrites, potash, zinc, mercury, sulphur, copper; textiles, wines, olive oil, paper, cement, hides, preserved and canned fish and shellfish, paper products.
SPANISH SAHARA	Spanish province consisting of Saguia el Hamra and Río de Oro, ruled by a governor-general.	peseta	Arabic Spanish	Mohammedan	Barley, corn; goats, sheep, camels; fish.
SUDAN	A republic with a bicameral parliament and council of ministers. Executive power resides temporarily in a council of state.	Egyptian pound	Arabic Sudanese Hamitic languages English	Mohammedan Tribal religions	Cotton, cotton seed, gum arabic, Senna leaves and pods, groundnuts, sesame, millet, dates, dom nuts (vegetable ivory), wheat, shea nuts; sheep, goats, cattle, camels, asses; mahogany; hides and skins, ivory, gold, salt, trochus shell, mother-of-pearl.
SUDANESE REPUBLIC	West African republic within the French Community with a legislative assembly.	franc	Sudanese languages Hamitic languages Arabic French	Mohammedan Tribal religions	Millet, rice, groundnuts, corn, sweet potatoes, cotton, manioc, tobacco, karite, shea nuts, yams, kopak, sisal; cattle, goats, sheep, horses, asses, camels; hides and skins; pottery, bricks, jewelry, weaving, leather, rice mills, soap.
SWAZILAND	British protectorate governed by a resident commissioner under the High Commissioner for Basutoland, Bechuanaland and Swaziland.	pound	Bantu languages English	Tribal religions Christian missions	Tobacco, corn, groundnuts, kaffir-corn, wheat, oats, rye, barley, fruits; cattle, goats, sheep, pigs; butter; hides, skins; asbestos, gold, tin.
SWEDEN	A constitutional hereditary monarchy with a prime minister, council of state and a two-house elective legislature.	krona	Swedish	Protestant	Hay, sugar beets, potatoes, fodder crops, oats, wheat, rye, barley; forest products, cattle, pigs, sheep, horses, poultry; fish; iron ore, sulphur, arsenic, zinc, copper, silver, gold, lead, manganese; lumber and wood products, machinery, textiles, iron and steel and metal goods, chemicals, dairy products, electric power, tobacco products, brick, porcelain and glass, shipbuilding, matches.
SWITZERLAND	A republic with a president, vice-president, an executive federal council and a two-house, elective legislature.	franc	German, French, Italian, Romansch	Protestant Roman Catholic	Wheat, potatoes, sugar beets, rye, oats, barley, fruits, tobacco; livestock; salt, iron, manganese; dairy products, textiles, watches and clocks, chemicals, foods, wines, dyes, instruments.
SYRIA	Province of United Arab Republic.	Syrian pound	Arabic Turkish Kurdish	Mohammedan Christian	Wheat, barley, sorghum, corn, cotton, lentils, chickpeas, sesame, vegetables, olives, grapes, tobacco (Latikia); sheep, goats, cattle, donkeys, camels, horses, poultry; wool, hides, skins; gypsum; leather, textiles, food, tobacco, wine, flour.
TANGANYIKA TERRITORY	Under United Nations trusteeship and administered by Great Britain. Ruled by a governor and a legislative and executive council.	East African shilling	Bantu languages Swahili English	Tribal religions Mohammedan Christian missions	Sisal, cotton, coffee, bananas, tobacco, papain, beeswax, grains, sugar; cattle, goats, sheep; hides, skins; wood, timber, wax, gum arabic; diamonds, gold, tin, mica, salt, camphor, tungsten.
THAILAND (SIAM)	Constitutional monarchy ruled by a king, prime minister and a legislative assembly.	baht	Thai Khmer	Buddhist Tribal religions	Rice, rubber, coconuts, tobacco, cotton, corn, beans; teak and other woods; bullocks, buffalo, horses, elephants; fish; tin, wolfram.
TIBET	Theocracy. Nominally independent but under effective Chinese Communist control. Religious affairs are directed by the Dalai Lama.	sang	Tibetan	Lamaist	Barley, wheat, pulse, corn, vegetables, rice; yaks, asses, sheep, goats, donkeys; hides, wool, furs, musk; borax, salt, gold; cult objects.
TIMOR, PORTUGUESE	Portuguese overseas province ruled by a governor.	escudo	Malay Portuguese	Mohammedan Tribal religions Roman Catholic	Coffee, copra, sandalwood, wax, cocoa; hides, shells.
TOGO	Independent republic. Under French trusteeship until April 1960.	franc	Sudanese languages French	Tribal religions Mohammedan Roman Catholic	Palm oil and kernels, tapioca, cocoa, yams, coffee, plantains, corn, groundnuts, cotton, copra, kola, cassava, rubber; sheep, goats, pigs, cattle, asses, horses.
TOKELAU ISLANDS	An island territory of New Zealand administered by a high commissioner.	New Zealand pound	Samoan	Protestant Roman Catholic	Coconuts, fiber, taro, copra; pigs, chickens; fish; hats, mats.
TONGA	Constitutional monarchy under British protection ruled by queen with cabinet and legislative assembly.	Tongan pound	Tongan English	Protestant Roman Catholic	Copra, bananas, fungus, candlenuts; pigs, cattle, goats.
TRINIDAD AND TOBAGO*	British colony with a governor and executive and legislative councils.	B.W.I. dollar	English	Roman Catholic Protestant Hindu	Coffee, cocoa, sugar cane, citrus fruits; cattle; petroleum, asphalt; rum, canned grapefruit juice, sugar.
TRISTAN DA CUNHA	Possession of Great Britain governed by an administrator and an island council responsible to St. Helena.	pound	English	Protestant	Potatoes, fruit; cattle, sheep; fish.
TRUCIAL OMAN	Seven sheikhdoms under British protection with a British agent.	rupee riyal	Arabic	Mohammedan	Dates, grains, vegetables; fishing, pearl fishing.
TUAMOTU ARCHIPELAGO	Part of French Polynesia governed from Tahiti.	franc	Polynesian dialects French	Tribal religions Roman Catholic	Copra, pearls, pearl shell.
TUBUAI ARCHIPELAGO	Part of French Polynesia governed from Tahiti.	franc	Polynesian	Roman Catholic Tribal religions	Copra, arrowroot.

† Member of new Federation of Rhodesia and Nyasaland.   * Member of the West Indies (British Caribbean Federation)

POLITICAL DIVISION	GOVERNMENT	MONETARY UNIT	LANGUAGE	RELIGION	MAJOR PRODUCTS
TUNISIA	A republic with a president, a cabinet of secretaries of state, and an assembly.	franc	Arabic French Berber	Mohammedan Roman Catholic	Wheat, barley, oats, corn, sorghum, beans, grapes, olives, citrus fruits, dates, alfa grass, almonds, oranges, shaddocks, pistachios, cork; sheep, goats, cattle, horses, asses, mules, camels, pigs; fish, sponges; flour milling, oil refining, wool spinning, pottery, leather, silk weaving; phosphates, iron ore, lignite, lead, zinc.
TURKEY	A republic with a president and a one-house, elective legislature.	pound	Turkish	Moslem	Tobacco, cereals, olives, cotton, figs, nuts, fruits; cattle, livestock; fish; chromium, iron ore, copper, coal, lignite, meerschaum, manganese; textiles, iron and steel, paper, rugs, olive oil.
UGANDA	British protectorate controlled by a governor with executive and legislative councils. Native kings and their assemblies rule locally.	East African shilling	Bantu and Sudanese languages English	Tribal religions Christian	Cotton, coffee, plantains, millet, cotton seed, tobacco, chilies, sugar cane, rubber; cattle, sheep, goats; hides, skins; tin; cigarettes.
UNION OF SOUTH AFRICA	Member of British Commonwealth with a governor-general, cabinet, elective senate and house of assembly.	pound	Afrikaans English Bantu languages Bushman	Protestant Roman Catholic Mohammedan Hindu Buddhist	Corn, wheat, potatoes, oats, kaffir-corn, barley, tobacco, sugar cane, tea, citrus fruits, rye, groundnuts, grapes, pineapples; cattle, sheep, goats, pigs, horses, donkeys, mules; gold, coal, diamonds, copper, asbestos, manganese, lime, limestone, platinum, chrome, iron, silver, tungsten, mercury, vanadium, tin, antimony, silver, scheelite, talc; hides, chemicals, wool, footwear, rubber, machinery, clothing, textiles, food, vehicles, printing, furniture, building materials.
U.S.S.R.	A federation of 15 socialist republics with a two-chamber legislative assembly (Supreme Soviet) which elects the executive presidium and council of ministers. The policy of the state is largely defined by the Central Committee of the Communist party, the only legal party.	ruble	Russian, Ukrainian, White Russian, Uzbek, Tatar, Azerbaizhani, Georgian, Lithuanian, Armenian, Yiddish, Latvian, Mordvinian, Chuvash, Tadzhik, Esthonian, Kazakh.	Russian Orthodox	Wheat, rye, oats, barley, corn, sugar beets, sunflower seeds, cotton, forage crops, flax, hemp, potatoes, tobacco; cattle, sheep, goats, pigs, horses; lumber, furs; fish; coal, peat, petroleum, iron, lignite, copper, lead, zinc, nickel, aluminum, phosphates, manganese, gold, sulphur, potash, asbestos, platinum, salt, chromite; steel, machinery, textiles, sugar, flour, meats, automobiles, paper, synthetic rubber, foods, wines, chemicals.
UNITED ARAB REPUBLIC	A republic combining Egypt and Syria, with a president, cabinet and unicameral legislature.	Egyptian and Syrian pound	See Egypt and Syria	See Egypt and Syria	See Egypt and Syria.
UNITED STATES	Federal republic with a president, vice-president and two-house legislature.	dollar	English	Protestant, Roman Catholic	Corn, hay, tobacco, wheat, cotton, oats, soy beans, potatoes, barley, sorghums, peanuts, rye, rice, citrus fruits, fruits, sugar beets, sugar cane, vegetables, tree nuts, feed grains and hay; livestock; fish; lumber; petroleum, coal, cement, iron, natural gas, copper, sand and gravel, zinc, lead, stone, gold, silver, molybdenum, bauxite, phosphates, mica, sulphur; foods, transportation equipment, machinery, primary metal products, electrical machinery, textiles, chemicals, paper and wood products, beverages, dairy products.
UPPER VOLTA	West African republic within the French Community with a legislative assembly.	franc	Sudanese languages French	Tribal religions Mohammedan	Millet, groundnuts, corn, karite nuts and butter (shea nut), vegetables, rice, tapes, cotton, kapok, sesame, sorghum, tea; sheep, goats, cattle, asses, pigs; gold, manganese, copper, silver, chrome, lignite, iron.
URUGUAY	A republic governed by a National Council, an appointed cabinet and a two-house elective legislature.	peso	Spanish	Roman Catholic	Wheat, corn, linseed, oats, sunflower seeds, peanuts, barley, rice, citrus fruits, peaches, grapes, vegetables, tobacco; sheep, cattle; gold; meat, hides, wool, textiles, leather, boots and shoes, wines.
VATICAN CITY	The Pope, who is elected for life by the cardinals of the Roman Catholic Church, exercises absolute legislative, executive and judicial power. He appoints a governor of the state and delegates diplomatic and judicial power.	lira	Italian Latin	Roman Catholic	
VENEZUELA	A republic with a president, appointive cabinet, and elective two-house legislature.	bolivar	Spanish	Roman Catholic	Coffee, cacao, sugar cane, cotton, tobacco, coconuts, tonka beans; balata, dividivi, rubber; livestock; fish and pearls; petroleum, iron, gold, coal, copper, phosphates, magnesite, asphalt, salt, diamonds; textiles, leather, sugar, cement, wood products, foodstuffs, beverages, soap, tobacco products, meats, milk; refined petroleum.
VIETNAM	Divided in two parts by Armistice Line Sept. 1954. North of 17th parallel is Communist controlled "republic." South is a republic with a president and an assembly.	piaster	Khmer (Annamese) Lao	Buddhist	Rice, corn, sugar, tobacco, coffee, fruits, manioc, betel nuts, arrowroot, tea, cotton, areca nut, medicinal plants, cardamom, soya, rubber, copra, groundnuts, haricots, sweet potatoes, cinnamon; mulberries, bamboo, silk; cattle, buffalo, pigs; lumber; gold, tin, copper, coal, zinc, iron, cement, limestone, calamine, tungsten, manganese, phosphate, lead, bauxite.
VIRGIN ISLANDS (BR.)	British colony with an administrator, an executive and a legislative council.	B.W.I. dollar	English, Creole	Protestant	Poultry and livestock, fish, fruit, vegetables.
VIRGIN ISLANDS (U. S.)	Territory of the U. S. with an appointed governor.	dollar	English, Creole	Roman Catholic, Protestant	Sugar cane, vegetables, citrus fruits, coconuts; cattle; fish; rum, bay rum, bay oil, molasses, handicrafts, sugar, lime juice, hides, bitters.
VOLCANO ISLANDS	Administered by the United States.	dollar yen	Japanese	Shintoist Buddhist	Sugar cane; fish; sulphur.
WEST INDIES	A federation of colonies within the Br. Commonwealth with a governor-general, council of state and bicameral legislature.	B.W.I. dollar	English	See member countries	See member countries.
YAP	Administered by a civil administrator of the Palau district as a part of the United States Pacific trust territory.	dollar	Micronesian dialects	Tribal religions Christian	Coconuts, breadfruit, sweet potatoes, taro, manioc, vegetables; poultry, pigs; fish.
YEMEN*	Independent kingdom.	riyal	Arabic	Mohammedan	Coffee, barley, wheat, millet, sesame; cattle, hides; fish.
YUGOSLAVIA	A Soviet-type republic combining six republics under a central government with a president, fed. executive council and two-house elective legislature. Actually ruled by Communist League.	dinar	Serbian-Croatian, Slovenian Macedonian	Eastern Orthodox Roman Catholic	Wheat, barley, rye, oats, corn, sugar beets, hemp, hops, opium, tobacco, flax, alfalfa, vegetables, fruits; sheep, cattle, pigs, goats, horses, poultry; coal, lignite, iron, copper, lead, salt, zinc, mercury, antimony, petroleum, bauxite, chrome, cement; lumber, textiles, foods, beverages, sugar, wood-distillates, wines.
ZANZIBAR	British protectorate nominally ruled by a sultan but under the effective control of a governor and a legislative and executive council.	East African shilling	Bantu languages Swahili English	Tribal religions Mohammedan Christian missions	Sisal, cotton, coffee, bananas, tobacco, papain, beeswax, grains, sugar; cattle, goats, sheep; hides, skins; wood, gum arabic; diamonds, gold, tin, mica, salt, camphor, tungsten.

* Allied member of the United Arab Republic.

THE RACES OF MANKIND

BY DR. HENRY FIELD FORMERLY CURATOR OF PHYSICAL ANTHROPOLOGY

Revised by DR. W. D. HAMBLY CURATOR OF AFRICAN ETHNOLOGY

CHICAGO NATURAL HISTORY MUSEUM

FORMERLY FIELD MUSEUM OF NATURAL HISTORY

MONGOLOID WHITE NEGRO

GROUP SYMBOLIZING UNITY OF MANKIND
SCULPTURE BY MALVINA HOFFMAN

TEXT AND ILLUSTRATIONS COPYRIGHTED MCMXLVI BY CHICAGO NATURAL HISTORY MUSEUM

PUBLISHED BY C. S. HAMMOND & CO., INC., NEW YORK

DESCRIPTION OF RACES

FOR MANY YEARS THE WORD "RACE" WAS FREELY AND UNCRITICALLY USED BY ANTHROPOLOGISTS; IT HAS EVEN BEEN MADE TO INCLUDE PSYCHOLOGICAL AND SOCIAL QUALITIES, AND HAS OFTEN BEEN CONFUSED WITH NATIONALITY; ALSO, IT HAS BEEN ALLIED WITH IDEAS OF INHERENT SUPERIORITY OR INFERIORITY. LET IT BE CLEAR THAT BY "RACE" WE MEAN A CERTAIN COMBINATION OF HERITABLE PHYSICAL TRAITS, WITHOUT ANY IMPLICATION OF SOCIAL STATUS OR PSYCHOLOGICAL ATTRIBUTES.

AFRICA

The continent of Africa covers an area of 12,000,000 square miles, almost four times the size of the United States. The total population has been estimated at 150,000,000, but this is a vague approximation. About two-thirds of the continent—the forest zone comprising a western coastal strip and a large central area—is the habitat of typical Negroes. These show many important local variations in physical appearance. The general physique of the African is well represented in the Negro's statue in the group symbolizing the unity of mankind.

TYPICAL NEGROES OF THE WEST COAST

The Negro is characterized by a dark skin color varying from extremely dark brown to almost black, though perhaps the skin is never jet black, and the stature varies considerably according to locality. The Kru of Liberia, the Ibo of Nigeria, and the Ijaw of the Niger Delta are often mentioned as exemplary Negro types. The West African coastal Negro is long-headed, of medium stature, extremely well developed, with a heavy torso and massive limbs. The arms are long and the legs short in comparison with the length of the trunk. In all Negroes the face is usually broad and massive, sometimes with a projecting chin. The nose is broad, and the lips are thick and everted. Dark eyes and woolly hair likewise are constant Negro features. The problems as to the origin of Negro types are too complex to be discussed here, yet the main branches of Negro stock may be mentioned.

NEGROES OF THE UPPER NILE

In order to account for this type, which is usually called Nilotic, a hypothesis regarding the intrusion of a foreign race is helpful. Anthropologists believe that migratory waves of people, called Hamites, have been penetrating northeast Africa from a remote time long before the period of recorded history. It is thought also that the crossing of these Hamitic intruders with the true Negro produced the Nilotic type. The Nilotic Negros, if compared with typical Negroes of West Africa, show greater stature, a far more slender build, and heads longer in relation to their breadth (more dolichocephalic).

NEGROES OF NORTHEAST AFRICA

In Kenya Colony are tribes whose physical type has been affected by intrusive Hamites. Here, as among the Nilotic Negroes, the true Negro physique has been modified in the direction of greater stature, less massive build, and refinement of the nose and mouth. These "Hamiticized" Negroes, of whom the Suk, the Masai, and the Nandi are examples, are referred to by some anthropologists as Half-Hamites.

HAMITES

The Hamites, who inhabit north and northeast Africa, belong to the Caucasian branch of mankind. They possess dark brown or black hair, which is either curly or wavy in form, and the skin varies in color from reddish brown to dark brown. Their average stature varies from very tall to medium and their build is slender. The typical Hamite possesses a long head, an oval, elongated face with no forward protrusion, thin lips, pointed chin, and a prominent, well-shaped, narrow nose. Two main divisions of Hamites must be recognized, northern and eastern. The principal northern Hamites are the Berbers and the Tuareg, who are confined to the Sahara region. The eastern group of Hamites comprises the Somali, Hadendoa, and Bisharin peoples.

BERBER MAN
MOROCCO
NORTH AFRICA
WHITE STOCK

SOME NOTES ON MALVINA HOFFMAN. *Malvina Hoffman may be called the leading portrayer, in plastic form, of the world's racial types. Before Miss Hoffman was commissioned to create her racial studies in bronze, she was a recognized sculptor. After having studied under Gutzon Borglum and Auguste Rodin, she was awarded first prize at the Paris Salon for "Russian Dancers." Her works may be seen in the Metropolitan Museum of Art, New York, the Luxembourg Musée, Paris, the Carnegie Institute, Pittsburgh, and the American Academy, Rome. In 1929 Miss Hoffman was commissioned by the Field Museum of Chicago to record in bronze certain selected racial types. In her journeys to the native habitats of these races, she travelled in all of the continents and visited many out-of-the-way tribes. Accompanying the articles on The Races of Mankind are photographs of the bronzes resulting from Miss Hoffman's work in the service of anthropology.*

ETHIOPIAN MAN
ETHIOPIA
NORTHEAST AFRICA
WHITE STOCK

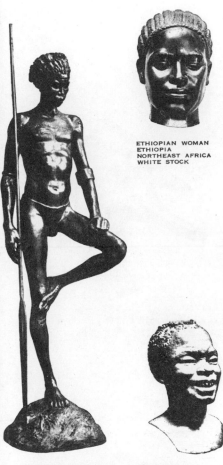

NUER WARRIOR
NUER TRIBE
UPPER WHITE NILE
NORTHEAST AFRICA
NEGRO STOCK

ETHIOPIAN WOMAN
ETHIOPIA
NORTHEAST AFRICA
WHITE STOCK

BATWA
PYGMY BOY
BELGIAN CONGO
CENTRAL AFRICA
NEGRO STOCK

SOMALI MAN
SOMALI TRIBE
NORTHEAST AFRICA
WHITE STOCK

SEMITES

The words Semitic and Hamitic have a definite linguistic connotation in the minds of anthropologists. The two languages, of which there are many dialects, were long ago split off from the original Hamitico-Semitic stock. But in addition to a linguistic meaning the terms bring to mind physical types which differ greatly from Negroes. Some characteristics of Hamites were mentioned in the preceding paragraph, and in a measure the physical traits of Hamites resemble those of Semites. Members of the Semitic group now living chiefly in the extreme north of Africa migrated from Arabia at early dates. One great migration and conquest occurred in the seventh and another in the eleventh century of the Christian Era. The Arabs, who are typical Semites in both physique and language, are usually medium in stature, are dark-haired, and generally have oval faces with long, narrow, straight noses. There are two typical head-forms among the Arabs—one is long, the other broad. For centuries the Arabs enslaved and sometimes intermarried with Negroes, consequently many Arab-Negro types may be seen in the north and the northeast of Africa. The Jews, of whom there are many in North Africa, speak Semitic languages, and in physiognomy some of them are not unlike the Arabs. We must regard the Semites as a big ethnic family which anciently split up into physical and linguistic types such as Arabs, Jews, and many of the tribes and nations so often mentioned in the Old Testament.

PYGMIES

It has not yet been determined what genetic relationship exists between typical Negroes, Pygmies (sometimes misnamed Negrillos), Bushmen, and Hottentots. It must be noted that many small Negroid tribes of the central forest region are referred to as Pygmies. But some of these, for example, the Batwa Pygmy boy represented in a bronze bust, have probably issued from a crossing of Pygmies with Negroes.

There are, however, groups of true Pygmies, the most typical of which are the Wambuti of the Ituri Forest in the Belgian Congo. Their dark brown hair is usually short. Their skin color varies from light brown with a yellow tinge to a very dark chocolate color. The average male stature is four feet six inches, and both body and legs are short. There is a peculiar development of the buttocks similar to that of the Kalahari Bushmen. In shape the head is typically round and there is some protrusion of the face. The lips are full, and the root of the nose is flat and broad.

BUSHMEN AND HOTTENTOTS

From a racial standpoint the Bushmen are the most interesting people south of equatorial Africa. At present they are confined mainly to the Kalahari Desert. The Bushmen possess short, frizzly hair which grows in separate tufts coiled into balls and because of its appearance is known as "peppercorn" hair. There is very little hair on the face and body. The skin ranges in color from yellow to olive, and becomes markedly wrinkled at an early age. The head is extremely small, low in the crown, and in shape intermediate between long and round. The width of the cheekbones combined with the narrowness of the forehead gives the face a lozenge-shaped appearance. The forehead is slightly protruding, and the nose is broader and flatter than in any other race. The dark eyes are often narrow and slightly oblique. The average male is below five feet in stature. In both sexes there is excessive development of the buttocks, which is often extremely accentuated among the women. The racial mixture of the Bushmen with Negroes and possibly with early invading Hamites resulted in a slightly taller people called Hottentots, who possess a longer and narrower head and a more protruding face. The Hottentots formerly inhabited the western part of South Africa, but their tribal organization is preserved at present only in southwestern Africa.

MANGBETU WOMAN
MANGBETU TRIBE
NORTHEASTERN
BELGIAN CONGO
NEGRO STOCK

NUBIAN MAN
NUBIA
NILE VALLEY
EGYPT
WHITE STOCK

SARA GIRL
SARA TRIBE
LAKE CHAD DISTRICT
FRENCH EQUATORIAL
AFRICA
NEGRO STOCK

SENEGAL MAN
SENEGAL
FRENCH WEST
AFRICA
NEGRO STOCK

SUDANESE WOMAN
NORTHEAST AFRICA
NEGRO STOCK

ZULU WOMAN
ZULU TRIBE
SOUTHEAST AFRICA
NEGRO STOCK

We now proceed to a review of the sculptures pictured in this article, beginning two pages back. The Hamitic peoples from the north and northeast of Africa are represented by four examples. The bronze bust of a Hamite from Ethiopia shows the fine, delicate features characteristic of the group. There is also the head of an Ethiopian woman carved out of black Belgian marble. The regularity of the features and the peculiar method of dressing the hair are particularly well portrayed by the medium employed. The bust of a Somali also exhibits typical Hamitic features, while the Nubian shows a mixture of Hamitic and Negro blood. This man is from Luxor in Egypt, but the thickness of his lips differentiates him slightly from the typical Fellah of the Nile Valley.

The Negroes of the Upper Nile Valley are represented by a full-length statue—a dark-skinned Nuer warrior who is six feet eight inches in height. He is standing on one leg in the peculiar pose characteristic of these people. The Mangbetu of the northeastern Congo region are primarily a true Negro type; but the light brown skin of the aristocratic class suggests some Hamitic mixture. The bust of a Mangbetu woman is interesting for the peculiar mode of hairdressing and the deformation of the skull. The heads of some children are bound tightly with bandages which force them to grow both long and narrow. The resulting deformation is considered a mark of beauty and social distinction. The profile of this woman clearly shows the effects of this treatment.

The Negro type is illustrated by two full-length figures which are complementary: a Senegalese drummer and a dancing girl of the Sara tribe. These bronzes, patinated with a rich, black sheen, are shown in poses characteristic of the rhythmic movements associated with Negro music. The vivacious and graceful figure of the girl in dancing posture contrasts strikingly with the dreamy expression of the drummer.

In Dahomey, West Africa, there exists, as illustrated, a modified Negro type with features and hair suggesting Hamitic mixture. A Dahomey man is shown in a bust. The head of a woman from the Sudan illustrates the remarkable coiffure which is fashionable among her people. The head of a Ubangi duck-billed girl portrays one of the most remarkable artificial deformations in existence. A girl's lips are perforated, and small studs are inserted in order to broaden them. At intervals the size of the lip studs is increased. For many years, this custom has been prohibited by the French government. The central or equatorial peoples of Africa are represented by a life-size family group of Ituri Forest Pygmies. While the man beats rhythmically on the drum, his wife, carrying her small baby, listens attentively.

The realistic Bushman family group shows a woman carrying a baby strapped to her back. In addition, there is the head of an aged man. All three portray in detail the racial characters of this primitive desert dwelling people. The Zulu woman is a Negro type found in the far southeastern part of Africa.

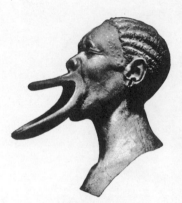

UBANGI WOMAN
UBANGI TRIBE
LAKE CHAD
FRENCH EQUATORIAL
AFRICA
NEGRO STOCK

DAHOMEY MAN
DAHOMEY
WEST AFRICA
NEGRO-WHITE
MIXTURE

BUSHMAN MAN
KALAHARI DESERT
SOUTH AFRICA
NEGRO-MONGOLOID
MIXTURE

WAMBUTI PYGMY
FAMILY
ITURI FOREST
NORTHEAST
BELGIAN CONGO
NEGRO STOCK

BUSHMAN WOMAN
AND BABY
KALAHARI DESERT
SOUTH AFRICA
NEGRO-MONGOLOID
MIXTURE

EUROPE

The modern inhabitants of Europe can be divided into three groups—Mediterranean (southern European), Alpine (central European), and Nordic (northern European). While there has been untold interbreeding of these basic stocks since Paleolithic times, it is still possible to adopt this general classificatory system. Terminology tends toward change and elaboration. The Dinarics are broad-headed people of Alpine type; the Baltics are part of the Nordic or northern stock. Under "Mediterranean" stock are southern Europeans and north Africans (northern Hamites).

The Mediterranean race is exemplified by a Sicilian, who is short in stature and stocky in build, with an olive complexion, dark hair and eyes, long head, narrow oval face, and a small mouth. This group is now confined mainly to the Iberian Peninsula, western Mediterranean islands, southern France and Italy, and the western parts of Wales and Ireland.

The Alpine race comprises the majority of the round-headed peoples of Europe. They extend from the central plateau of France, Switzerland, and Czechoslovakia southward into the Balkans and eastward into the Soviet Union. A typical member of this group possesses a fairly dark complexion, brown wavy hair, thick eyebrows over brown eyes, heavy body hair, a broad face, sometimes a thick neck, and a medium to heavy build. The bust of an Austrian man is a good example of this group.

The Nordic peoples inhabit Scandinavia, northern Germany, and part of Holland and Belgium. There is also a strong Nordic element in Great Britain. A tall Swede, with light complexion and hair, blue eyes, long head, and a face with a prominent nose and chin, is a typical member of this group.

The racial divisions of Europe are represented by the full-length figures of a Sicilian fisherman, who is shown with his fishing net, and a Nordic man. In this section are also displayed busts of a Breton woman from Brittany, France, with her picturesque headdress, and of a Basque from northern Spain. There are also heads of an Englishman, a Frenchman, a Russian, a Turk and a Lapp.

SICILIAN MAN
SICILY
WHITE STOCK

LAPP MAN
LAPP TRIBE
EXTREME NORTHWEST
EUROPE
WHITE-MONGOLOID
MIXTURE

RUSSIAN MAN
GEORGIA U.S.S.R.
WHITE STOCK

FRENCHMAN
FRANCE
WHITE STOCK

ENGLISHMAN
GREAT BRITAIN
WHITE STOCK

TURKISH MAN
TURKEY
WHITE STOCK

ITALIAN MAN
NORTHERN ITALY
WHITE STOCK

BRETON WOMAN
BRITTANY
NORTHWESTERN
FRANCE
WHITE STOCK

BASQUE MAN
NORTHERN SPAIN
WHITE STOCK

AUSTRIAN MAN
CENTRAL EUROPE
WHITE STOCK

NORDIC MAN
NORTHERN EUROPE
WHITE STOCK

ARAB MAN
HILLA
IRAQ
WHITE STOCK

BEDOUIN MAN
NORTH AFRICA
WHITE STOCK

VEDDA MAN
VEDDA TRIBE
CEYLON
AUSTRALOID STOCK
WHITE-NEGRO
MIXTURE

ASIA

The study of the peoples of Asia is beset with numerous difficulties and presents many complex problems. In view of the evidence available it seems probable that man originated somewhere on this vast continent. A general survey of Asia is presented here, based on six large geographical divisions: southwest, south, southeast, east, central, and north.

SOUTHWESTERN ASIA

This area was inhabited originally by early members of the Mediterranean stock, which forms the basic population at the present time. The northern and southern extremities of this section are inhabited by round-headed peoples. For example, in Armenia and Anatolia (Asiatic Turkey) the characteristic individual possesses dark hair, a tawny-white skin, medium stature, and a prominent aquiline nose with a depressed tip and large wings. Along the southern coast of Arabia the dominant type is round-headed, and there are also smaller brachycephalic (round-headed) groups, such as the Druze of Syria and part of the basic element in Iraq (Mesopotamia) on the east. As a representative of the great Arab group there was selected one of the workmen at Kish, in Iraq, where the Field Museum—Oxford University Joint Expedition conducted archaeological excavations from 1922 to 1933.

The Jewish people, who are a section of the larger Semitic group, form part of the great Mediterranean stock and are divided into two groups—the Ashkenazim and the Sephardim. The former includes the Jews of the U.S.S.R. and of central and western Europe, while the latter comprises those of Spain, Portugal, Asia Minor, Egypt, and Arabia. According to Haddon, the original Jews were racially akin to the modern Beduins of northern Arabia and blended at an early date with Amorites, Philistines, and Hittites, from whom they acquired the so-called "Jewish" nose. This entire region, with the exception of certain isolated zones, has been overrun in historic times by numerous invasions so that the modern population is extremely mixed.

In Iran (Persia) there are direct descendants of the ancient dwellers on the Iranian plateau together with Mediterranean elements on the west and Mongoloid traits on the northeast. There are also intrusive elements, such as the Kurds, Arabs, Armenians, and others who have settled in the country. Afghanistan is essentially the homeland of the Indo-Afghan stock, which is characterized by black, wavy hair, light, transparent brown complexion, long heads and faces, prominent, narrow noses, and dark eyes. An Afghan money lender pictured in the article, possesses the features

typical of this group. The inhabitants of Baluchistan are closely related to the Afghans. Among the Baluchi, however, the head is rounder in shape; therefore they may be classified among Indo-Iranian peoples.

SOUTHERN ASIA

There are three main geographical regions in India which appear to have influenced the principal racial groups. In the north lies the Himalayan chain of mountains; in the central northern portion are the sweeping plains of Hindustan; and to the south extends the great plateau, in many places jungle-covered, called the Deccan. With a varied population of about 350,000,000, racial origins in India are incapable of exact definition. In prehistoric times India was probably inhabited by a primitive Negroid population related to the aborigines of Ceylon, Sumatra, and possibly even Australia. It is believed also that at an early date Dravidian stocks entered India from the North-West Frontier region and Mongoloid races from the northeast territory. Dravidian is a general term used for the main population of the Deccan. The physical characters are a long head, abundant, wavy hair, brownish black skin, and medium stature.

The Veddas of Ceylon are one of the most interesting primitive groups in India. They belong to the pre-Dravidian division, and their physical characters comprise long, black hair which is coarse and wavy, dark brown skin, and short stature. The form of the head is long and narrow and the forehead slightly retreating, with prominent brow ridges, a relatively broad face and nose, thin lips, and pointed chin. The Veddas are modern survivors of the earliest inhabitants of India.

Among the photographic illustrations is shown a sculpture of a typical young Vedda with a bow by his side; also the full-length figure of a Tamil (linguistic term) and the head of a man from Kashmir, India. The Tamil occupy the northern half of the island of Ceylon and part of the mainland of southern India. In physique they belong to the Dravidian group. A Tamil is shown in the act of climbing a large palm tree—a feat which is performed with remarkable skill. The Kashmiri possess a light, transparent, brown skin, and are usually of relatively tall stature. The head is long with a well-developed forehead, a long, narrow face, regular features, and prominent, finely chiseled, narrow nose. Except for their skin color, many people of northern India closely resemble Europeans.

Other figures in this section represent a Singhalese from Kandy in Ceylon; a woman from Rajputana, belonging to the "untouchable" caste; a Brahman from

TAMIL MAN
SOUTHERN INDIA
WHITE-NEGRO
MIXTURE

KASHMIRI MAN
KASHMIR PROVINCE
NORTHWEST INDIA
WHITE STOCK

TODA MAN
TODA TRIBE
VERY OLD
EAST INDIAN TYPE
SOUTHERN INDIA
AUSTRALOID STOCK
WHITE-NEGRO
MIXTURE

AFGHAN MAN
PESHAWAR
NORTHWEST INDIA
WHITE STOCK

Benares; and a man and a woman from Bengal. These sculptures show the refined features of the people of northern India. There is also the head of a beautiful Jaipur lady carved from limestone. It is exceptional for the regularity of her pleasing features.

The Andaman Islands, located in the Indian Ocean, are inhabited by members of the Negrito group, which comprises the Semang of the Malay Peninsula and eastern Sumatra, the Aëta of the Philippine Islands, and the Tapiro of New Guinea. The Andamanese are represented by a Pygmy hunter seated on a rock with his large bow held in his left hand and an arrow drawn back to his right cheek. He possesses the characteristic features of his group, which are short, black hair (sometimes with a reddish tinge), black skin, well-proportioned body, a small, round head, and small hands. The face is broad, the lips full but not everted, and there is no projection of the jaws.

The inhabitants of Burma represent southern Mongoloid types, possessing black hair (almost absent on the face and body), round heads, broad faces and noses, and frequently oblique eyes. The color of the skin varies from yellow to brown according to locality. For example, the farther removed from China, the less yellow is the color of the skin. As a representative of these people, the head of a Burmese man is interesting in comparison with the peoples of India and China.

SOUTHEASTERN ASIA
MALAY PENINSULA AND MALAY ARCHIPELAGO

The population of this region may be divided into two sections—a large southern Mongoloid group and a group not included in this classification. In the dense jungles of the Malay Peninsula live the Semang and the Sakai. The former belong to the Negrito or Pygmy group, since they are five feet or less in stature. The hair is short and frizzy, black in color with a reddish tinge and sparse on the face and body. The skin is dark chocolate brown in color. The shape of the head tends to be round; the lips are generally thin; the nose is short, flat, and extremely broad. The Semang also inhabit the eastern portion of the island of Sumatra. The representative of this group is a Pygmy hunter with his long blow-gun held upright beside him.

In the southern part of the Malay Peninsula also live the Sakai, who represent the second element among the aboriginal tribes of this region. They have intermarried considerably with the Negritos in the north and the Proto-Malays in the south. They differ from the Negritos in the lighter color of their skins, in their greater stature, and in their long, wavy, or curly hair, which is black with a reddish tinge. The Sakai belong to the pre-Dravidian group, being related to the Veddas of Ceylon and to the primitive jungle tribes of southern India.

RAJPUTANA WOMAN
RAJPUTANA PROVINCE
NORTH WESTERN INDIA
WHITE STOCK

SINGHALESE MAN
CEYLON
WHITE STOCK

BENARES MAN
BENARES
NORTH CENTRAL INDIA
WHITE STOCK

JAIPUR WOMAN
RAJPUTANA PROVINCE
NORTHWEST INDIA
WHITE STOCK

BENGALI WOMAN
BENGALI MAN
BENGAL PROVINCE
NORTHEASTERN
INDIA
WHITE STOCK

BURMESE MAN
BURMA
MONGOLOID STOCK

PADAUNG WOMAN
PADAUNG TRIBE
UPPER BURMA
MONGOLOID STOCK

SAKAI MAN
SAKAI TRIBE
TAPAH
MALAY PENINSULA
AUSTRALOID STOCK
WHITE-NEGRO
MIXTURE

PYGMY MAN
SEMANG TRIBE
MALAY PENINSULA
NEGRO STOCK

PYGMY HUNTER
ANDAMAN ISLANDS
INDIAN OCEAN
NEGRO STOCK

JAKUN GIRL
JAKUN MAN
JAKUN TRIBE
MALAY PENINSULA
MONGOLOID STOCK

MALAY MAN
MALAY PENINSULA
MONGOLOID STOCK

BONTOC IGOROT
MAN
LUZON
PHILIPPINES
MONGOLOID STOCK

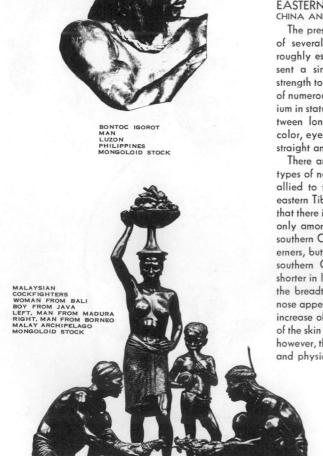

MALAYSIAN
COCKFIGHTERS
WOMAN FROM BALI
BOY FROM JAVA
LEFT, MAN FROM MADURA
RIGHT, MAN FROM BORNEO
MALAY ARCHIPELAGO
MONGOLOID STOCK

There is still a third primitive group in the Malay Peninsula. The Jakun, sometimes called "Savage Malays," possess a dark red or copper-brown skin and straight, dark, coarse hair. The head is round with high cheekbones and dark eyes with a tendency to obliquity. Busts of a Jakun man and girl are shown.

In marked contrast to these primitive types, there is a pure type of Malay, whose features express a high grade of intelligence compared with the Jakun.

The Malayan family (or, as it is also called, Indonesian) is distributed over the greater portion of the Malay Archipelago. It may be divided into the following groups: the Malay proper of the Malay Peninsula; the aborigines of the Philippines, Borneo, and Celebes; the Javanese and Sundanese of Java and Bali; and the Bataks of Sumatra. There are also scattered members of this family in Formosa and Madagascar. A typical Malayan is rather short in stature and has dark, wavy hair, tawny yellow-colored skin, lozenge-shaped face, prominent cheekbones, and slight-projecting jaws. The shape of the head varies markedly from long to round, with the former as the probable basic shape.

The types selected from the peoples of the Malay Archipelago represent a Dyak from Sarawak in Borneo, and a boy and a young girl from Java. There is also a composite group of figures representing various people of the Archipelago. These are two cockfighters intent on their national sport, watched by a girl from Bali who balances a platter of fruit on her head, and a small boy from Java eating a banana. In physical type the two men are similar, although one is from Borneo and the other from the island of Madura, situated off the north coast of Java.

EASTERN ASIA
CHINA AND JAPAN

The present Republic of China extends over an area of several million square miles, with a population roughly estimated at 400,000,000. The Chinese represent a single racial unit, which has had sufficient strength to maintain its culture and traditions in the face of numerous invaders. The Chinese as a whole are medium in stature. The shape of the head is intermediate between long and round, the skin yellowish brown in color, eyes oblique with the Mongolian fold, and hair straight and black.

There are, according to L. H. Dudley Buxton, two types of northern Chinese, one of which appears to be allied to the southern Chinese, and the other to the eastern Tibetans. From statistical data it can be shown that there is a tall element in the population, paralleled only among the neighboring Tibetans. The people of southern China belong to the same group as the northerners, but there are certain remarkable differences. In southern China the stature is less, and the head is shorter in length, which increases the cephalic index as the breadth remains fairly constant. The width of the nose appears slightly greater, which may be due to the increase of heat and moisture of the climate. The color of the skin becomes darker in the south. We must admit, however, that the effects of climate on general physique and physiognomy are not well understood.

CANTONESE WOMAN
CANTON
SOUTH CHINA
MONGOLOID STOCK

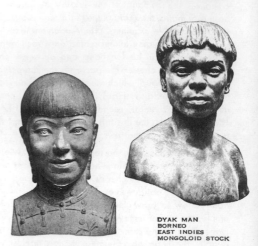

CHINESE WOMAN
SOUTHERN CHINA
MONGOLOID STOCK

DYAK MAN
BORNEO
EAST INDIES
MONGOLOID STOCK

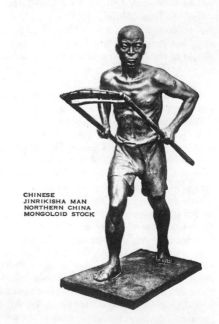

CHINESE
JINRIKISHA MAN
NORTHERN CHINA
MONGOLOID STOCK

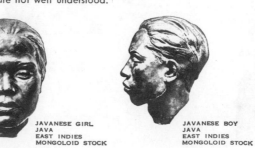

JAVANESE GIRL
JAVA
EAST INDIES
MONGOLOID STOCK

JAVANESE BOY
JAVA
EAST INDIES
MONGOLOID STOCK

CHINESE MAN
SHANGHAI
CHINA
MONGOLOID STOCK

JAPANESE MAN
TOKYO
JAPAN
MONGOLOID STOCK

AINU MAN
NORTHERN JAPAN
WHITE-MONGOLOID
MIXTURE

AINU MAN
NORTHERN JAPAN
WHITE-MONGOLOID
MIXTURE

TIBETAN WOMAN
LHASA
TIBET
MONGOLOID STOCK

JAPANESE WOMAN
TOKYO
JAPAN
MONGOLOID STOCK

As representatives of the racial types of China, the following are shown: the full-length figure of a Chinese coolie posed between the shafts of his jinrikisha; and the bust of a Cantonese woman of the peasant class, with a bamboo pole, which is used for carrying loads, over her shoulder. There are also a bronze bust of a Chinese student and a stone bust of an attractive lady in her ornamented robe.

In prehistoric times the Ainus inhabited the islands which now comprise the Japanese Empire. At present confined to the northern island of Hokkaido, the Kuriles, and the southern portion of Sakhalin Island, they differ from all Mongolian races in their luxuriant black beards, the bushy and wavy head hair, and the general hairiness of other parts of the body. The color of the skin resembles that of the tanned Central European. Medium in stature, the average Ainu is thickset, with a head intermediate in shape between long and round, and a broad face, which does not project markedly. The narrow nose is short and concave. The large horizontal eyes are usually dark brown in color. The racial position of the Ainus is a question of considerable interest. They represent an ancient prehistoric stock, which has been greatly specialized.

There are two distinct types of modern Japanese, one of which possesses relatively fine features, while the other is more coarse in type. Both possess certain traits in common. The hair is always black and may be curly in form, where influenced by Ainu blood. In general, the stature is short, although there is considerable variation. The cephalic index and skin color are also variable characters. The color of the eyes is dark brown.

The fine or aristocratic type is taller and more slender, with an elongated face, and a prominent, narrow, arched nose. The eyes are either straight or oblique, and the epicanthic fold may be present. The coarse type, which may represent immigrants from southeastern Asia, is short and stocky, with a broad face, short, concave nose, and rounded nostrils, oblique eyes, usually an epicanthic fold, and a darker complexion than the other group.

As representatives of these islands are shown the busts of a Japanese man and a young woman. The life-size statue of an Ainu is an important contribution to the study of this racial type. Miss Hoffman modeled an aged Ainu and the head of a young man of this primitive tribe.

CENTRAL AND NORTHERN ASIA

Central Asia comprises Tibet, Chinese Turkestan, and Mongolia. Northern Asia is practically identical with Siberia, which covers approximately one-quarter of the entire continent. The vast area of northern Asia is divided by the Yenisei River into western and eastern Siberia. The inhabitants may be grouped as Paleo-Siberians and Neo-Siberians. The latter, who inhabit chiefly the western geographical division, are a miscellaneous group including the Finnish-speaking tribes.

Among the Paleo-Asiatics are the Chukchi of northeastern Siberia; the Koryaks, who live between the Anadyr River and Kamchatka; and the Kamchadales. The Giliaks, Ainus, and those Eskimos who live on the Asiatic side of Bering Strait, are sometimes included in this division. The physical characters are black hair, brown- or reddish-colored sparse beard, yellowish white or brown skin, sometimes with a flat face, prominent cheekbones, oblique eyes, and a straight or concave nose. The head form varies from intermediate to round, although traces of a very ancient long-headed stock are present.

Included in this section is a seated figure of a Tibetan merchant from Lhasa. There are also the head of a Tibetan woman from Lhasa, and that of a Mongol priest from Outer Mongolia.

MONGOL MAN
CENTRAL ASIA
OUTER MONGOLIA
MONGOLOID STOCK

CHINESE MAN
NORTHERN CHINA
MONGOLOID STOCK

KOREAN MAN
NORTHEASTERN ASIA
MONGOLOID STOCK

TIBETAN MAN
LHASA
TIBET
MONGOLOID STOCK

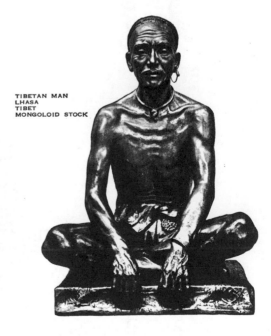

AMERICA

Before the advent of European peoples the population of the Americas consisted of aborigines, called Indians by Columbus. From a historical point of view they are the true Americans. Moreover, up to the present time, there is no definite archaeological evidence for the existence of any pre-Indian peoples or cultures. It is generally conceded that the Indians are of Mongoloid stock. They entered the New World possibly 15,000 years ago, or even more remotely, in a series of migrations extending over many years. Small groups probably crossed Bering Strait, either because of pressure from hostile tribes or in search of new hunting grounds. Traveling south and east, they gradually spread over North, Central, and South America. The theory of waves of migration is corroborated by the fact that on either side of Bering Strait the country is incapable of supporting a large population, and by the fact that the American Indians, while possessing many traits in common, often show great variability in physical characters. And again we may speculate on the effects of climate and other environmental factors in producing physical differences.

The constant physical characters of the American Indians consist of a brown skin which frequently bears a reddish or yellowish tinge; dark eyes; straight, coarse, black hair; a minimum of beard and body hair; and a broad face with high and prominent cheekbones. The head is usually round, although there are certain groups in which long heads predominate. The stature also varies in different groups. The nose varies from flat to aquiline. The tallest people inhabited the region of the Mississippi Valley and extended for some distance to the north and east.

Among the Plains Indians and the tribes of the Northern and Eastern Woodlands there is little variation of the above characters. The Northwest Coast Indians, however, possess lighter skin and hair than do the other groups. They are medium in stature, with short bodies and long arms, and apparently are closely allied to the natives of northeastern Asia. The tribes north of this general region, including the Tlingit, Haida, and Tsimshian, are above the average in stature. They have large heads with extremely broad faces and concave or straight noses. In the southern part of this region, as, for example, among the Kwakiutl, the people are less tall, and are round-headed, with broad, high faces, and very long, narrow noses, which are frequently convex in shape. These Indians inhabit the Northwest Coast from latitude 60° north to the northern boundary of the state of Washington. Among the accompanying pictures are shown a magnificent Blackfoot Indian in the pose he adopts at the end of a successful hunt, and the head of a Sioux brave. To illustrate additional types of North American Indians several individuals from New Mexico have been portrayed, including a full-length figure of a Navaho, a Pueblo woman from San Ildefonso, New Mexico, and a Jicarilla Apache.

SAN ILDEFONSO
INDIAN WOMAN
NEW MEXICO U.S.A.
MONGOLOID STOCK

JICARILLA
APACHE INDIAN
MAN
NEW MEXICO U.S.A.
MONGOLOID STOCK

NAVAHO MAN
NAVAHO INDIANS
NEW MEXICO U.S.A.
MONGOLOID STOCK

BLACKFOOT
INDIAN MAN
MONTANA U.S.A.
MONGOLOID STOCK

SIOUX INDIAN
MAN
SOUTH DAKOTA U.S.A.
MONGOLOID STOCK

SIOUX INDIAN
MAN
SOUTH DAKOTA U.S.A.
MONGOLOID STOCK

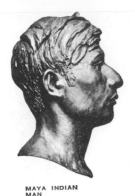

MAYA INDIAN
MAN
YUCATAN
MEXICO
MONGOLOID STOCK

CARIB INDIAN
MAN
AMAZON BASIN
SOUTH AMERICA
MONGOLOID STOCK

The Eskimos form a definite group, clearly of Asiatic origin. In many respects they are the most Mongoloid of all Americans. They are distinguished by a short, stocky build, markedly long heads combined with very broad faces (an unusual feature in a people with a long skull), massive jaws, and moderately narrow noses. The sides of the head are often flat, and a ridge may be present along the dome of the skull. The eyes frequently show the Mongoloid fold. The head of an Eskimo man and that of an Eskimo woman are shown.

In Mexico and Central America the average stature is medium to short, and round heads predominate, although the evidence suggests that the first inhabitants were long-headed and were conquered by these later invaders. The head of a Yucatecan Maya is shown as an example.

The Indians of South America bear, in general, the physical characters common to the whole race. It is believed that they entered that continent through a succession of migrations by way of the Isthmus of Panama. The bust of a Tehuelche from Patagonia and the head of a Carib of the Amazon Basin illustrate two types from South America.

From time to time it has been asserted that ancient pre-Indian human remains have been discovered in America; for example, in Argentina, primitive types of Tertiary fossil man were reported to have been found. All alleged evidence of this character has so far been discredited.

OCEANIA

Oceania is the area which extends from Australia to Easter Island and from New Zealand northward to Hawaii, including all the island groups of the Pacific Ocean. The consensus of opinion is that man first entered the Pacific area from southeastern Asia. There have also been several important waves of migration, which add to the complexity of the racial problems involved. The six principal racial divisions in Oceania include the inhabitants of Australia, Tasmania, Melanesia, New Guinea, Polynesia, and Micronesia.

AUSTRALIA

Australia is the smallest continent, with an area approximately the same size as the United States. In general, the physical traits of the Australian aborigines are uniform throughout the continent, although there are numerous minor variations. Archaeological evidence suggests that man entered this continent at a very early date and that he remained but little changed by outside factors until the arrival of the first Europeans in 1606.

The physical characters of the aboriginal Australian are jet black, wavy or curly hair, which is often heavy on the face; dark chocolate brown skin; medium stature with slim limbs; and a long head with a flat, retreating forehead, prominent brow ridges, projecting face, and a deeply set, broad nose.

TASMANIA

The Tasmanians became extinct during the latter part of the nineteenth century. They were of medium height, had black to dark brown skins, woolly hair, and heavy brow ridges. The face was long, and oval or pentagonal in shape, while the head was sloping and small in size. The nose was short and broad, and the teeth were large. Tasmanian skulls and living heads show resemblance to Negritos, Melanesians, and Australian aborigines. In general, the physical characters of the Tasmanians were similar to those of the Australians. But Tasmanians were more Negroid than are the Australians. The original migratory route of these people is still under discussion.

ESKIMO WOMAN
NORTH AMERICA
MONGOLOID STOCK

ESKIMO MAN
NORTH AMERICA
MONGOLOID STOCK

TEHUELCHE
INDIAN MAN
PATAGONIA
SOUTH AMERICA
MONGOLOID STOCK

AUSTRALIAN
ABORIGINAL WOMAN
AND BOY
NORTHEASTERN
AUSTRALIA
AUSTRALOID STOCK
WHITE-NEGRO
MIXTURE

AUSTRALIAN
ABORIGINAL MAN
NORTHEAST
AUSTRALIA
AUSTRALOID STOCK
WHITE-NEGRO
MIXTURE

SOLOMON ISLANDER
SOLOMON ISLANDS
MELANESIA
NEGRO STOCK

MELANESIA

The name is derived from the dark skin color of the peoples who inhabit these islands. This area embraces the Bismarck Archipelago, northeast of New Guinea, the Louisiade, Solomon, Santa Cruz, New Hebrides and Loyalty Islands, New Caledonia, Fiji, and small intervening groups. While a large Papuan element prevails throughout the population of Melanesia, there have also been several movements of racial stocks from Indonesia. The result of this mingling of peoples is that the modern population shows considerable variation and is by no means homogenous in character. The hair of the Melanesians is usually woolly, but may be either curly or wavy. The skin ranges from very dark to light brown. The stature varies from short to medium. The head is usually long in shape, but there are isolated round-headed groups. The forehead is commonly rounded, and the brow ridges are fairly prominent. The nose is broad, sometimes straight, and broader than that of the Papuan. In Melanesians there are Australoid and Negroid elements.

NEW GUINEA

The inhabitants of New Guinea and the adjacent island groups belong to the woolly-haired (Negro) branch of mankind. There is considerable variety of racial type, which is subdivided into Negritos, Papuans, and Melanesians. Typical Negritos are the Tapiro Pygmies of the western mountains in Dutch New Guinea, who can be compared with the inhabitants of the Andaman Islands, the Semang Pygmies of the central part of the Malay Peninsula and eastern Sumatra, and the Negritos of the Philippines.

The hair of the Tapiro is short, black in color, and abundant on face and body. The skin is yellowish brown in color. In stature the average Tapiro is four feet nine inches. The head shows considerable variation in shape, the nose is straight and of medium breadth. A trait frequent among them and among other Negritos is a deep and convex upper lip.

The Papuans are dark-skinned, medium in stature, and long-headed. The black hair is often long and may be abundant on the face. The forehead is retreating, the brow ridges are prominent, and the lower part of the face projects. The broad nose is often prominent and convex, while the tip is sometimes turned down. The Papuans now inhabit the greater part of New Guinea, and were originally distributed throughout Melanesia. The words Papuan and Melanesian have geographical, linguistic, and physical connotations. We may speak of Papua and of Melanesia, of a Papuan and of a Melanesian. Both are of basic Negro stock with Australoid elements here and there.

MICRONESIA

To the north of Melanesia lie countless islands including the Marianas, Caroline, Marshall, and Gilbert groups, which together form the area known as Micronesia. The population is extremely mixed, containing certain Melanesian, Polynesian, and Malaysian influences. The skin color ranges from brown to nearly yellow, and the hair is wavy or straight, but in the west some individuals are very dark-skinned with frizzly hair, while others are light-skinned with wavy or straight hair. The eyes are almost black and the cheekbones relatively prominent. In stature the Micronesians are medium and are not as robust as the Polynesians.

Among the illustrations various individuals of the peoples of Oceania are shown. Australia is represented by the full-length figures of a man, a woman and child. The man is shown in a characteristic pose as though throwing a spear. On his body are deep scars caused by cutting the flesh with a stone implement. The Solomon Islander in the act of climbing a date palm represents the Melanesian group. Around his neck is a crescent-shaped shell, and he wears a nose ring.

Two men from Hawaii and the bust of a Samoan are characteristic of the Polynesian group. There is a full-length Hawaiian on his surf-board as he speeds toward the beach. The Samoan, who holds a large knife against his right shoulder, also illustrates the well-developed physique of the Polynesian.

POLYNESIA

This area of the central Pacific region includes the numerous groups and small islands situated mostly south of the equator. The two islands of New Zealand are the largest of the entire area, which also includes the Hawaiian, Society, and Marquesan groups, as well as Tonga and Samoa. The origin of the Polynesians remains in considerable doubt, but it is believed that at an early date they migrated into this large area from southeastern Asia. The Polynesian is average to tall in stature, the hair being straight or wavy in form and black in color. The skin varies from that of a South European to several shades of brown. The shape of the head is round, but there are smaller divisions of people with long or intermediate-shaped heads. In general form the face is elliptical with relatively prominent cheekbones, and a prominent nose, generally straight as among the Maori, but sometimes convex. Skull measurements show very few close resemblances to those of Melanesians and Australian aborigines.

HAWAIIAN MAN
HAWAII
POLYNESIA
WHITE-MONGOLOID-
NEGRO MIXTURE

HAWAIIAN MAN
HAWAII
POLYNESIA
WHITE-MONGOLOID-
NEGRO MIXTURE

SAMOAN MAN
SAMOA
POLYNESIA
WHITE-MONGOLOID-
NEGRO MIXTURE

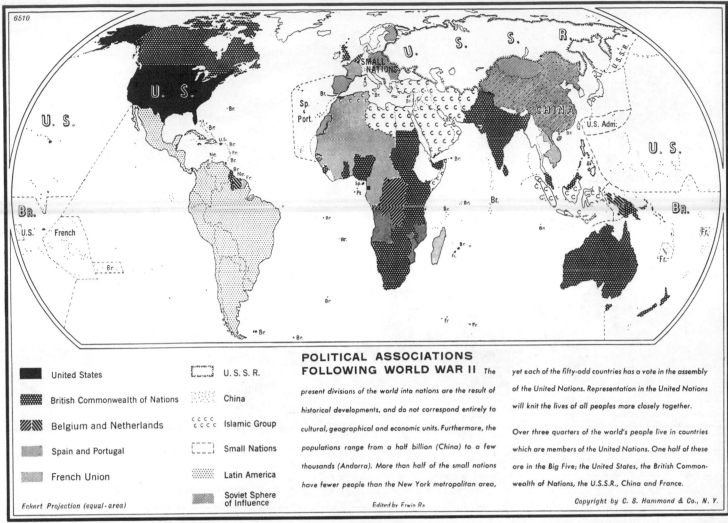

6510

Legend

Symbol	Label	Symbol	Label
■	United States	▦	U. S. S. R.
▓	British Commonwealth of Nations	░	China
▨	Belgium and Netherlands	cccc	Islamic Group
▒	Spain and Portugal	┄	Small Nations
▥	French Union	⠂	Latin America
▦		▨	Soviet Sphere of Influence

Eckert Projection (equal-area)

POLITICAL ASSOCIATIONS FOLLOWING WORLD WAR II

The present divisions of the world into nations are the result of historical developments, and do not correspond entirely to cultural, geographical and economic units. Furthermore, the populations range from a half billion (China) to a few thousands (Andorra). More than half of the small nations have fewer people than the New York metropolitan area, yet each of the fifty-odd countries has a vote in the assembly of the United Nations. Representation in the United Nations will knit the lives of all peoples more closely together.

Over three quarters of the world's people live in countries which are members of the United Nations. One half of these are in the Big Five; the United States, the British Commonwealth of Nations, the U.S.S.R., China and France.

Edited by Erwin Ra—

Copyright by C. S. Hammond & Co., N. Y.

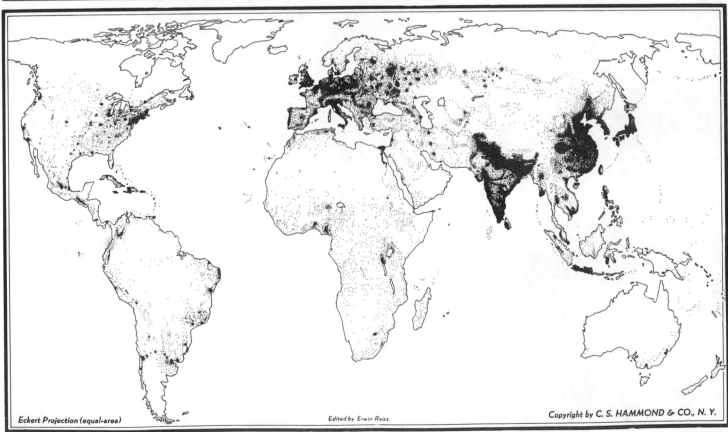

Eckert Projection (equal-area)

Edited by Erwin Raisz

Copyright by C. S. HAMMOND & CO., N. Y.

DENSITY OF POPULATION. One of the most outstanding facts of human geography is the extremely uneven distribution of people over the Earth. One-half of the Earth's surface has less than 3 people per square mile, while in the lowlands of India, China, Java and Japan rural density reaches the incredible congestion of 2000-3000 per square mile. Three-fourths of the Earth's population live in four relatively small areas; Northeastern United States, North-Central Europe, India and the Far East.

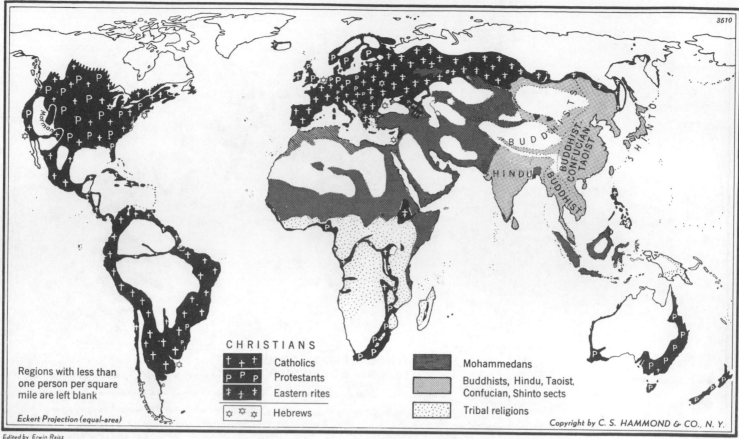

Edited by Erwin Raisz

RELIGIONS. Most people of the Earth belong to four major religions: Christians, Mohammedans, Brahmans, Buddhists and derivatives. The Eastern rites of the Christians include the Greek Orthodox, Greek Catholic, Armenian, Syrian, Coptic and more minor churches. The lamaism of Tibet and Mongolia differs a great deal from Buddhism in Burma and Thailand. In the religion of China the teachings of Buddha, Confucius and Tao are mixed, while in Shinto a great deal of ancestor and emperor worship is added. About 11 million Hebrews live scattered over the globe, chiefly in cities and in the state of Israel.

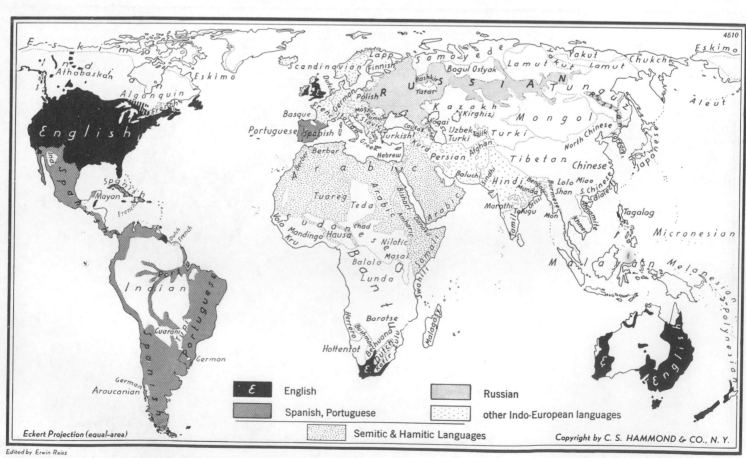

Edited by Erwin Raisz

LANGUAGES. Several hundred different languages are spoken in the World, and in many places two or more languages are spoken, sometimes by the same people. The map above shows the dominant languages in each locality. English, French, Spanish, Russian, Arabic and Swahili are spoken by many people as a second language for commerce or travel.

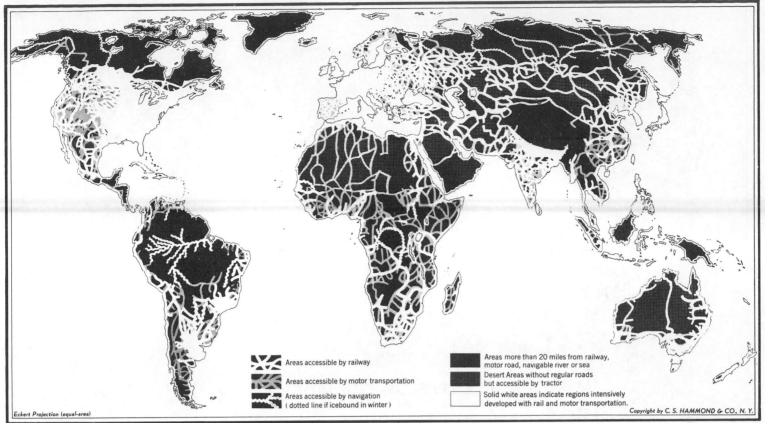

Eckert Projection (equal-area)

Areas accessible by railway

Areas accessible by motor transportation

Areas accessible by navigation (dotted line if icebound in winter)

Areas more than 20 miles from railway, motor road, navigable river or sea

Desert Areas without regular roads but accessible by tractor

Solid white areas indicate regions intensively developed with rail and motor transportation.

Copyright by C. S. HAMMOND & CO., N. Y.

Edited by Erwin Raisz

ACCESSIBILITY. *Many regions in the world are far from railways, roads, navigable rivers or the seas. Their economic development is retarded because their products can be brought to the world's markets only at great expense. Such areas are in the tundra (alpine), the boreal forest and in the equatorial rain* *forest regions. Desert areas, if not too mountainous, can be crossed by tractors. The largest inaccessible area is in Tibet, on account of high mountains, the alpine climate and isolationist attitude of the people. Airplane transportation will help to bring inaccessible areas into the orbit of civilization.*

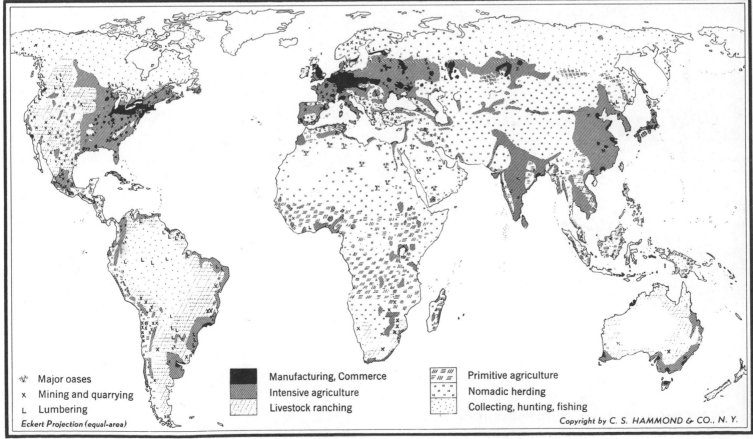

⚷ Major oases

x Mining and quarrying

L Lumbering

Manufacturing, Commerce

Intensive agriculture

Livestock ranching

Primitive agriculture

Nomadic herding

Collecting, hunting, fishing

Eckert Projection (equal-area)

Copyright by C. S. HAMMOND & CO., N. Y.

Edited by Erwin Raisz

OCCUPATIONS. *Correlation with the density of population shows that the most densely populated areas fall into the regions of manufacturing and intensive farming. All other economies require considerable space. The most* *sparsely inhabited areas are those of collecting, hunting and fishing. Areas with practically no habitation are left blank.*

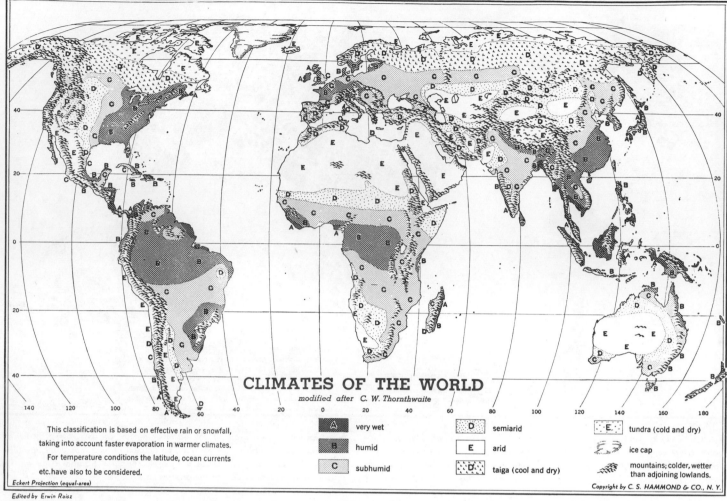

CLIMATES OF THE WORLD
modified after C. W. Thornthwaite

This classification is based on effective rain or snowfall, taking into account faster evaporation in warmer climates. For temperature conditions the latitude, ocean currents etc. have also to be considered.

Eckert Projection (equal-area)

Edited by Erwin Raisz

A	very wet	
B	humid	
C	subhumid	
D	semiarid	
E	arid	
D	taiga (cool and dry)	
E	tundra (cold and dry)	
	ice cap	
	mountains; colder, wetter than adjoining lowlands.	

Copyright by C. S. HAMMOND & CO., N. Y.

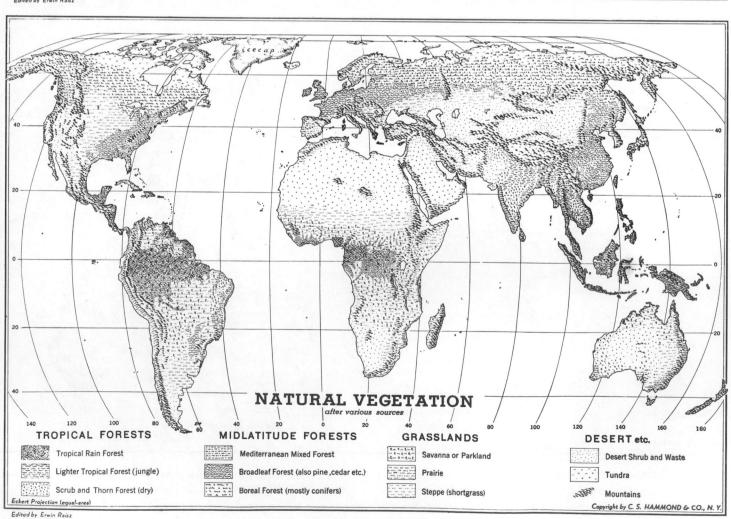

NATURAL VEGETATION
after various sources

TROPICAL FORESTS
- Tropical Rain Forest
- Lighter Tropical Forest (jungle)
- Scrub and Thorn Forest (dry)

MIDLATITUDE FORESTS
- Mediterranean Mixed Forest
- Broadleaf Forest (also pine, cedar etc.)
- Boreal Forest (mostly conifers)

GRASSLANDS
- Savanna or Parkland
- Prairie
- Steppe (shortgrass)

DESERT etc.
- Desert Shrub and Waste
- Tundra
- Mountains

Eckert Projection (equal-area)

Edited by Erwin Raisz

Copyright by C. S. HAMMOND & CO., N. Y.

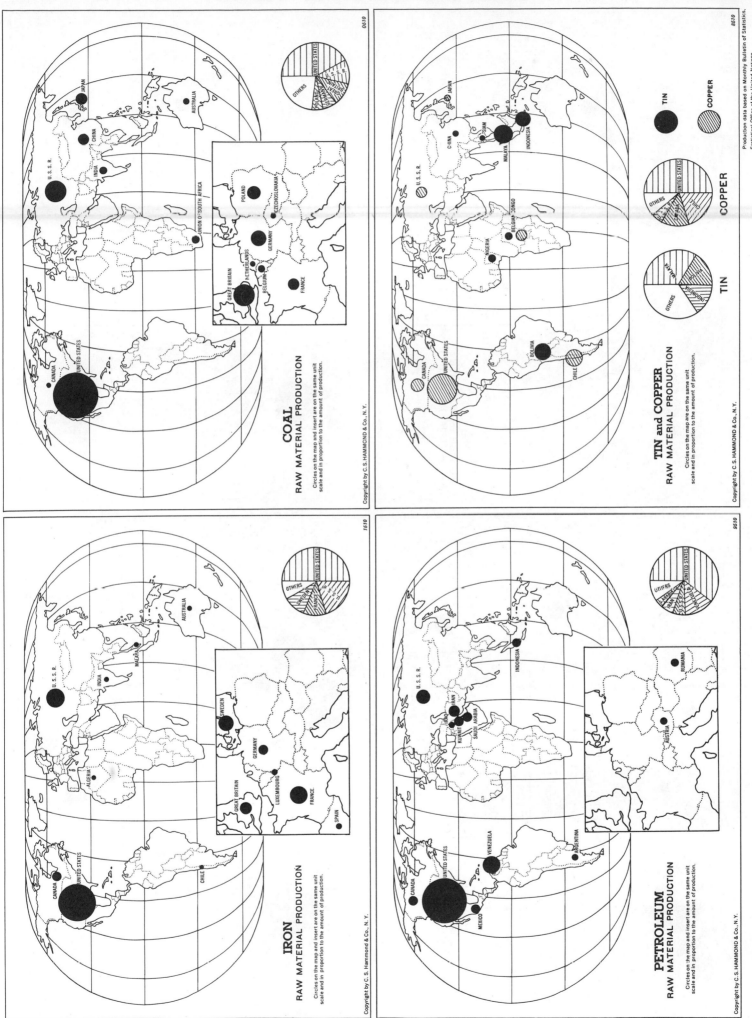

COAL
RAW MATERIAL PRODUCTION

Circles on the map and insert are on the same unit scale and in proportion to the amount of production.

Copyright by C. S. HAMMOND & Co., N. Y.

TIN and COPPER
RAW MATERIAL PRODUCTION

Circles on the map are on the same unit scale and in proportion to the amount of production.

Copyright by C. S. HAMMOND & Co., N. Y.

Production data based on Monthly Bulletin of Statistics, Statistical Office of the United Nations.

IRON
RAW MATERIAL PRODUCTION

Circles on the map and insert are on the same unit scale and in proportion to the amount of production.

Copyright by C. S. Hammond & Co., N. Y.

PETROLEUM
RAW MATERIAL PRODUCTION

Circles on the map and insert are on the same unit scale and in proportion to the amount of production.

Copyright by C. S. HAMMOND & Co., N. Y.

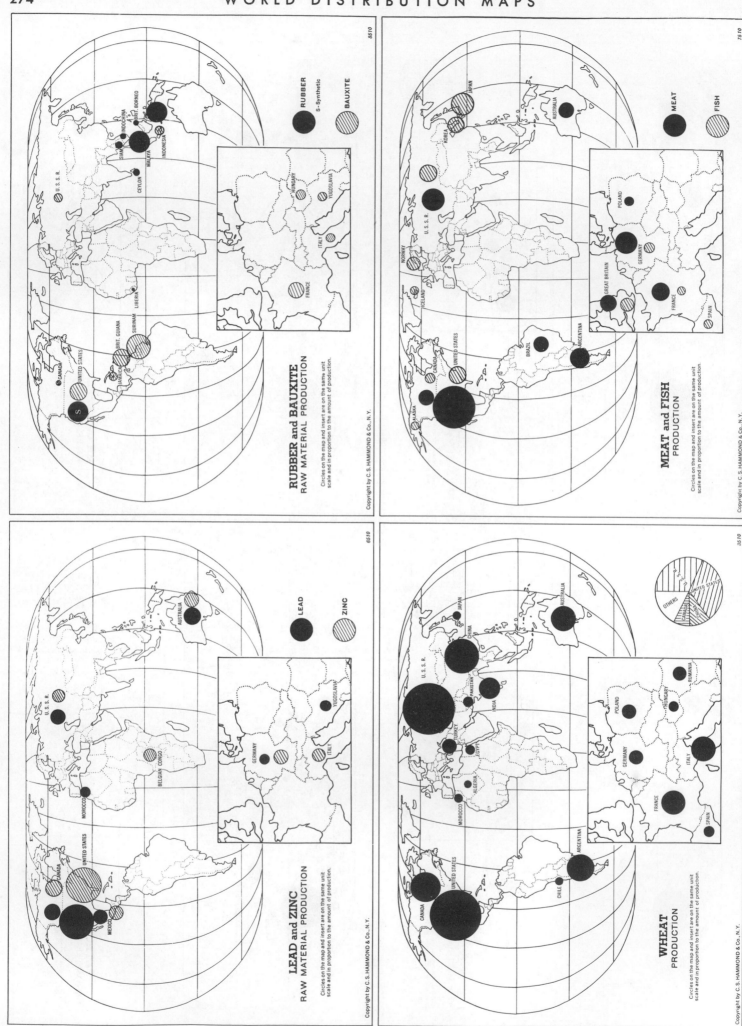

RUBBER and BAUXITE
RAW MATERIAL PRODUCTION

Circles on the map and insert are on the same unit scale and in proportion to the amount of production.

RUBBER
S-Synthetic
BAUXITE

Copyright by C. S. HAMMOND & Co., N. Y.

MEAT and FISH
PRODUCTION

Circles on the map and insert are on the same unit scale and in proportion to the amount of production.

MEAT
FISH

Copyright by C. S. HAMMOND & Co., N. Y.

Production data based on Monthly Bulletin of Statistics, Statistical Office of the United Nations.

LEAD and ZINC
RAW MATERIAL PRODUCTION

Circles on the map and insert are on the same unit scale and in proportion to the amount of production.

LEAD
ZINC

Copyright by C. S. HAMMOND & Co., N. Y.

WHEAT
PRODUCTION

Circles on the map and insert are on the same unit scale and in proportion to the amount of production.

Copyright by C. S. HAMMOND & Co., N. Y.

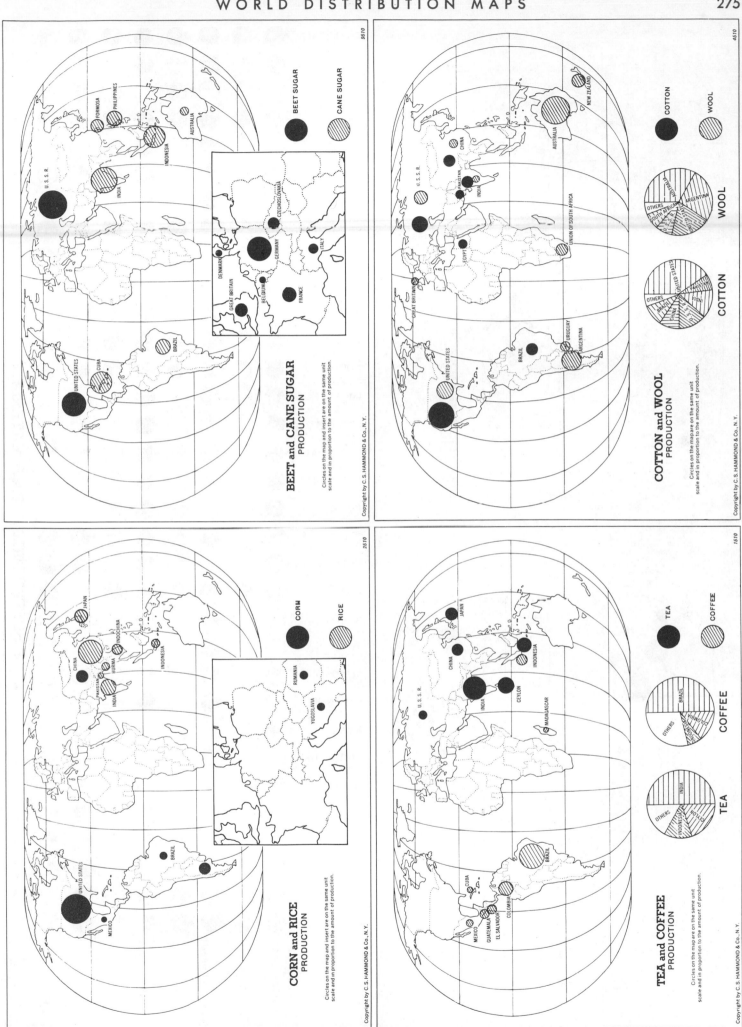

BEET and CANE SUGAR
PRODUCTION

Circles on the map and insert are on the same unit scale and in proportion to the amount of production.

Copyright by C. S. HAMMOND & Co., N. Y.

COTTON and WOOL
PRODUCTION

Circles on the map are on the same unit scale and in proportion to the amount of production.

Copyright by C. S. HAMMOND & Co., N. Y.

Production data based on Monthly Bulletin of Statistics, Statistical Office of the United Nations.

CORN and RICE
PRODUCTION

Circles on the map and insert are on the same unit scale and in proportion to the amount of production.

Copyright by C. S. HAMMOND & Co., N. Y.

TEA and COFFEE
PRODUCTION

Circles on the map are on the same unit scale and in proportion to the amount of production.

Copyright by C. S. HAMMOND & Co., N. Y.

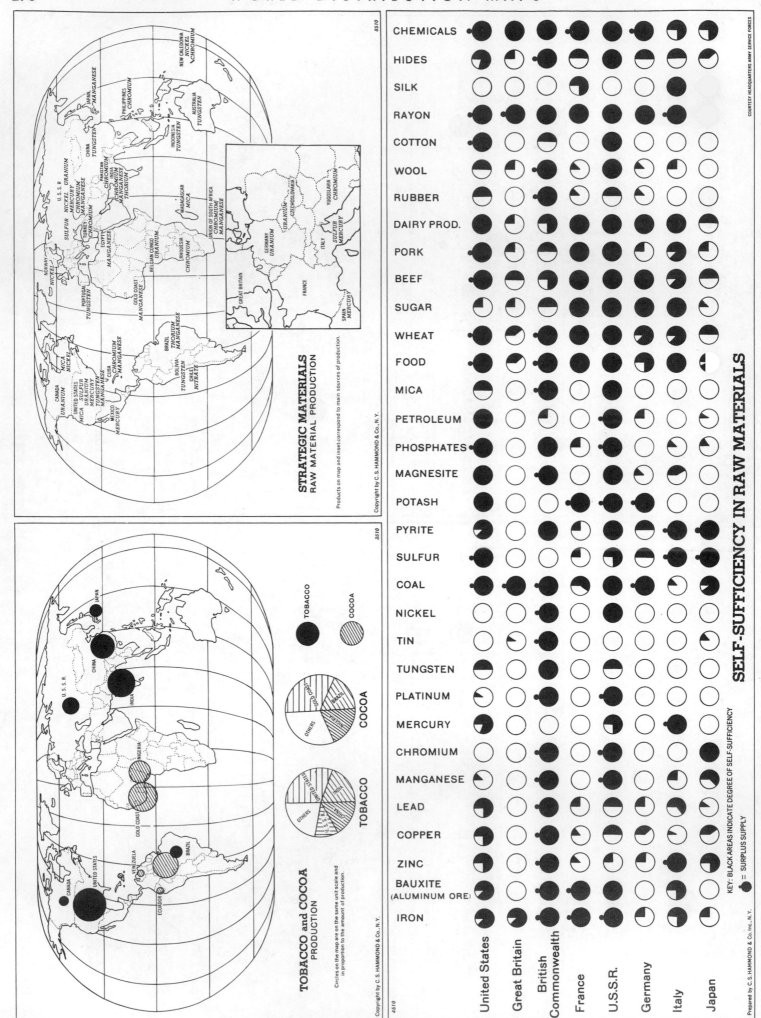

STRATEGIC MATERIALS
RAW MATERIAL PRODUCTION

Products on map and inset correspond to main sources of production.

Copyright by C. S. HAMMOND & Co., N.Y.

TOBACCO and COCOA
PRODUCTION

Circles on the map are on the same unit scale and in proportion to the amount of production.

Copyright by C. S. HAMMOND & Co., N.Y.

TOBACCO

COCOA

SELF-SUFFICIENCY IN RAW MATERIALS

KEY: BLACK AREAS INDICATE DEGREE OF SELF-SUFFICIENCY

= SURPLUS SUPPLY

Prepared by C. S. HAMMOND & Co. Inc., N.Y.

COURTESY HEADQUARTERS ARMY SERVICE FORCES

CHEMICALS · HIDES · SILK · RAYON · COTTON · WOOL · RUBBER · DAIRY PROD. · PORK · BEEF · SUGAR · WHEAT · FOOD · MICA · PETROLEUM · PHOSPHATES · MAGNESITE · POTASH · PYRITE · SULFUR · COAL · NICKEL · TIN · TUNGSTEN · PLATINUM · MERCURY · CHROMIUM · MANGANESE · LEAD · COPPER · ZINC · BAUXITE (ALUMINUM ORE) · IRON

United States · Great Britain · British Commonwealth · France · U.S.S.R. · Germany · Italy · Japan

EARTH AND SOLAR SYSTEM

PRINCIPAL LAKES AND INLAND SEAS

Elements of the Solar System

PLANETS	DISTANCE FROM SUN IN MILES MAXIMUM	MINIMUM	PERIOD OF REVOLUTION AROUND SUN IN DAYS	DIAMETER IN MILES	DENSITY (EARTH=1)
Sun . .	....	....	....	865,390	0.26
Mercury .	43,404,000	28,599,000	87.87	3,009	0.68
Venus . .	67,730,000	66,814,000	224.70	7,575	0.94
Earth . .	94,560,000	91,446,000	365.26	7,927	1.00
Mars . .	154,936,000	128,476,000	686.98	4,216	0.71
Jupiter .	507,289,000	460,465,000	4,332.59	88,698	0.24
Saturn .	936,637,000	837,655,000	10,759.20	75,060	0.12
Uranus .	1,868,930,000	1,700,745,000	30,685.93	30,878	0.25
Neptune .	2,820,610,000	2,773,510,000	60,187.64	27,700	0.41
Pluto . .	4,585,000,000	2,753,000,000	90,470.23	3,600 approx.	0.7

Dimensions of the Earth

Superficial area	196,950,000	sq. miles
Land surface	57,510,000	" "
North America	8,500,000	" "
South America	6,814,000	" "
Europe	3,872,000	" "
Asia	16,990,000	" "
Africa	11,500,000	" "
Australia	2,974,581	" "
Water surface	139,440,000	" "
Atlantic Ocean	31,830,000	" "
Pacific Ocean	63,801,000	" "
Indian Ocean	28,356,000	" "
Arctic Ocean	5,440,000	" "
Equatorial circumference	24,902	miles
Meridional circumference	24,860	"
Equatorial diameter	7,926.677	"
Polar diameter	7,899.988	"
Equatorial radius	3,963.34	"
Polar radius	3,949.99	"
Volume of the Earth	260,000,000,000 cubic miles	
Mass, or weight	6,592,000,000,000,000,000,000,000 tons	
Mean distance from the Sun	92,897,416 miles	

The Moon, the only satellite of the Earth, from which her mean distance is 238,857 miles, occupies an average period, in her revolution round the earth, of 29 days, 12 hours, 44 minutes, 3 seconds; her diameter is 2,160 miles, and her mean density 0.60.

	AREA IN SQ. MILES
Caspian Sea	163,800
Lake Superior	31,820
Lake Victoria	26,828
Lake Aral	24,900
Lake Huron	23,010
Lake Michigan	22,400
Lake Tanganyika	12,700
Lake Baikal	12,150
Great Bear Lake	12,000
Great Slave Lake	11,170
Lake Nyasa	11,000
Lake Erie	9,940
Lake Winnipeg	9,398
Lake Ontario	7,540
Lake Ladoga	7,100
Lake Balkhash	6,700
Lake Tchad (Chad)	6,500
Lake Onega	3,765
Lake Titicaca	3,200
Lake Nicaragua	3,100
Lake Athabaska	3,058
Reindeer Lake	2,444
Issyk-kul	2,276
Vänern	2,149
Lake Urmia	1,795
Great Salt Lake	1,700
Lake Albert	1,640
Lake Van	1,453
Lake Peipus	1,400
Lake Tana	1,219
Lake Bangweulu . . . . . . Approx.	1,000
Vättern	733
Dead Sea	405
Lake Balaton	266
Lake Geneva	225
Lake Constance	208
Lough Neagh	153
Lake Garda	143
Lake Neuchâtel	83
Lake Maggiore	82
Lough Corrib	71
Lake Como	56
Lake Lucerne	44½
Lake Zürich	34

OCEANS AND SEAS OF THE WORLD

GREAT SHIP CANALS

	AREA IN SQ. MILES	GREATEST DEPTH FEET	VOLUME IN CUBIC MILES
Pacific Ocean . . .	63,801,000	35,400	162,870,600
Atlantic Ocean . . .	31,830,000	30,246	75,533,900
Indian Ocean . . .	28,356,000	22,968	69,225,200
Arctic Ocean . . .	5,440,000	17,850	4,029,400
Mediterranean Sea . .	1,145,000	15,197	1,019,400
Bering Sea	876,000	13,422	788,500
Caribbean Sea . . .	750,000	23,748	2,298,400
Sea of Okhotsk . . .	590,000	11,070	454,700
East China Sea . . .	482,000	10,500	52,700
Hudson Bay	475,000	1,500	37,590
Japan Sea	389,000	13,242	383,200
North Sea	222,000	2,654	12,890
Red Sea	169,000	7,254	53,700
Black Sea	165,000	7,200	....
Baltic Sea	163,000	1,506	5,360

	LENGTH IN MILES	DEPTH IN FEET
Baltic-White Sea, U.S.S.R.	141	....
Suez, Egypt	100.76	34
Albert, Belgium	81	16.5
Moscow-Volga, U.S.S.R.	80	18
Kiel, Germany	61	37
Göta, Sweden	54	10
Panama, Canal Zone, U.S.A.	50.72	41
Houston, U.S.A.	50	36
Amsterdam-Rhine, Netherlands	45	41
Beaumont-Port Arthur, U.S.A.	40	32
Manchester, England	35.5	28
Chicago Sanitary and Ship, U.S.A. . . .	30	22
Welland, Canada	27.6	25
Juliana, Netherlands	21	11.8
Chesapeake-Delaware, U.S.A.	19	27
Cape Cod, U.S.A.	13	25
Lake Washington, U.S.A.	8	30
Corinth, Greece	4	26.25
Sault Ste. Marie, U.S.A.	1.6	24.5
Sault Ste. Marie, Canada	1.4	18.25

	AREA IN SQ. MILES		AREA IN SQ. MILES		AREA IN SQ. MILES		AREA IN SQ. MILES
Greenland	839,999	Devon	22,000	Canary Islands	2,894	Martinique	425
New Guinea	345,054	Bismarck Arch.	19,660	Wrangel	2,819	Pemba	380
Borneo	289,859	Solomon Islands	18,670	Kerguelen	2,700	Orkney Islands	376
Madagascar	241,094	Tierra del Fuego	18,500	Prince Edward	2,184	Madeira Islands	308
Baffin	201,600	Southampton	16,936	Balearic Islands	1,935	Dominica	305
Sumatra	164,148	Melville	16,503	Trinidad	1,864	Tonga or Friendly Islands	269
Philippines	115,600	New Britain	14,600	Madura	1,752	Molokai	261
New Zealand, North and South Islands	103,934	Formosa (Taiwan)	13,885	South Georgia	1,600	St. Lucia	233
England-Scotland-Wales	88,745	Kyushu	13,770	Cape Verde Islands	1,557	Corfu	229
Honshu	87,426	Prince of Wales	13,736	Long I., New York	1,401	Bornholm	227
Victoria	80,450	Vancouver	13,020	Socotra	1,400	Isle of Man	221
Ellesmere	77,392	Hainan	13,000	Gotland	1,225	Singapore	220
Celebes	72,986	Sicily	9,926	Samoa	1,209	Isle Royale	209
Java	49,280	Somerset	9,594	Isle of Pines	1,180	Guam	203
Cuba	42,857	Sardinia	9,301	Réunion	970	Virgin Islands	190
Newfoundland	42,734	New Caledonia	7,202	Azores	890	Curacao	173
Luzon	40,420	Fiji Islands	7,036	Fernando Poo	810	Barbados	166
Iceland	39,709	New Hebrides	5,700	Tenerife	785	Seychelles	157
Mindanao	36,537	Kuril Islands	5,700	Maui	728	St. Vincent	150
Sakhalin	35,400	Falkland Islands	4,618	Mauritius	720	Isle of Wight	147
Novaya Zemlya	35,000	Jamaica	4,411	Zanzibar	640	Lanai	141
Ireland	31,839	Bahama Islands	4,404	Tahiti	600	Grenada	133
Molucca Islands	30,168	Hawaii	4,021	Oahu	589	Malta	122
Hispaniola	29,843	Cape Breton	3,975	Guadeloupe	583	Martha's Vineyard	120
Hokkaido	29,600	New Ireland	3,800	Ahvenanmaa (Aland Is.)	564	Tobago	116
Tasmania	26,219	Cyprus	3,572	Kauai	551	Channel Islands	75
Banks	26,000	Puerto Rico	3,423	Shetland Islands	550	Nantucket	60
Ceylon	25,332	Corsica	3,367	Rhodes	542	St. Helena	47
Timor Arch	24,450	Crete	3,235	Faeröe Islands	540	Ascension	34
Svalbard (Spitsbergen)	24,294	Galápagos Islands	3,042	Caroline Islands	525	Hong Kong	32
		Hebrides	3,000	Marquesas Islands	480	Manhattan, New York	22
						Bermudas	21

PRINCIPAL MOUNTAINS OF THE WORLD

LONGEST RIVERS OF THE WORLD

	FEET		FEET
Mt. Everest, Nepal-Tibet	29,028	Dikh-Tau, U.S.S.R.	17,085
Mt. Godwin Austen (K2), India	28,250	Mt. Kenya, Kenya	17,040
Kanchenjunga, Nepal-Ind.	28,146	Mt. Ararat, Turkey	16,916
Mt. Makalu, Tibet-Nepal	27,790	Ruwenzori, Uganda	16,787
Dhaulagiri, Nepal	26,795	Klyuchevskaya Volcano, U.S.S.R.	15,912
Nanga Parbat, India	26,620	Mont Blanc, France	15,781
Annapurna, Nepal	26,492	Carstensz Toppen, New Guinea	15,709
Nanda Devi, India	25,645	Mt. Kazbek, U.S.S.R.	15,545
Mt. Kamet, India	25,447	Monte Rosa, Switzerland	15,217
Tirich-Mir, Pakistan	25,263	Mt. Belukha, U.S.S.R.	15,154
Anne Machin, China	25,000	Mt. Markham, Antarctica	15,102
Minya Konka, China	24,900	Matterhorn, Switzerland	14,780
Stalin Peak, U.S.S.R.	24,589	Ras Dashan, Ethiopia	14,760
Pobedy Peak, U.S.S.R.	24,403	Mt. Morrison, Formosa	14,720
Mt. Chomo Lhari, Bhutan	23,997	Mt. Whitney, California	14,495
Muztagh, Sinkiang	23,885	Mt. Elbert, Colorado	14,431
Tengri Khan, U.S.S.R.	23,600	Mt. Rainier, Washington	14,408
Aconcagua Volcano, Arg.	23,080	Mt. Shasta, California	14,162
Cerro Ojas del Salado, Argentina	22,402	Pikes Peak, Colorado	14,110
Cerro Huascarán, Peru	22,180	Finsteraarhorn, Switzerland	14,026
Llullaillaco Volcano, Chile	22,145	Mauna Loa, Hawaii	13,680
Cerro Mercedario, Arg.	21,870	Jungfrau, Switzerland	13,667
Tupungato, Chile	21,810	Jebel Toubkal, Morocco	13,665
Mt. Illampú, Bolivia	21,489	Mt. Kinabalu, No. Borneo	13,451
Sajama Volcano, Bolivia	21,320	Cameroon Mt., Cameroon	13,349
Mt. Illimani, Bolivia	21,151	Gran Paradiso, Italy	13,323
Chimborazo, Ecuador	20,702	Mt. Robson, Br. Columbia	12,972
Mt. McKinley, Alaska	20,300	Gross Glockner, Austria	12,461
Mt. Logan, Yukon	19,850	Fujisan, Japan	12,395
Cotopaxi Volcano, Ecuador	19,498	Mt. Cook, New Zealand	12,349
Kilimanjaro, Tanganyika Terr.	19,319	Pico de Teyde, Tenerife	12,200
Misti Volcano, Peru	19,200	Mt. Semeru, Java	12,057
Citlaltepetl, Mexico	18,696	Mulhacén, Spain	11,417
Mt. Demavend, Iran	18,550	Mt. Leuser, Sumatra	11,093
Mt. Elbrus, U.S.S.R.	18,468	Mt. Etna, Sicily	10,741
Mt. Tolima, Colombia	18,438	Lassen Peak, California	10,453
Mt. St. Elias, Alaska	18,008	Mt. Tina, Dominican Rep.	10,301
Mt. Popocatepetl, Mexico	17,888	Volcano Irazu, Costa Rica	10,525
		Mt. Kosciusco, Australia	7,352
		Mt. Mitchell, No. Carolina	6,684

	LENGTH IN MILES		LENGTH IN MILES
Nile, Africa	4,149	Japurá, S. A.	1,500
Amazon, S. A.	4,000	Arkansas, U.S.A.	1,450
Mississippi-Missouri, U.S.A.	3,892	Dneiper, U.S.S.R.	1,418
Ob-Irtish, U.S.S.R.	3,200	Rio Negro, S. A.	1,400
Yangtze, China	3,100	Colorado, Ariz., U.S.A.	1,360
Congo, Africa	2,900	Kolyma, U.S.S.R.	1,335
Amur, Asia	2,704	Ohio, U.S.A.	1,306
Hwang (Yellow), China	2,700	Orange, Africa	1,300
Lena, U.S.S.R.	2,648	Red, Texas, U.S.A.	1,300
Mekong, Asia	2,600	Kama, U.S.S.R.	1,262
Niger, Africa	2,600	Irrawaddy, Burma	1,250
Mackenzie, Canada	2,514	Don, U.S.S.R.	1,222
Paraná, S. A.	2,450	Columbia, U.S.-Canada	1,214
Yenisei, U.S.S.R.	2,364	Saskatchewan, Canada	1,205
Murray, Australia	2,310	Darling, Australia	1,160
Volga, U.S.S.R.	2,290	Angara, U.S.S.R.	1,151
Madeira, S. A.	2,000	Tigris, Iraq	1,150
Yukon, Alaska	1,979	Sungari, Asia	1,130
St. Lawrence, Canada	1,900	Pechora, U.S.S.R.	1,111
Purus, S. A.	1,850	Peace, Canada	1,054
Rio Grande, U.S.A.	1,800	Snake, U.S.A.	1,038
São Francisco, S. A.	1,800	Churchill, Canada	1,000
Salween, Burma	1,750	Pilcomayo, S. A.	1,000
Danube, Europe	1,725	Uruguay, S. A.	1,000
Euphrates, Iraq	1,700	Magdalena, S. A.	950
Indus, Pakistan	1,700	Platte, U.S.A.	928
Orinoco, S. A.	1,700	Oka, U.S.S.R.	918
Tocantins, S. A.	1,700	Canadian, U.S.A.	906
Brahmaputra, India	1,680	Tennessee, U.S.A.	900
Syr Darya, U.S.S.R.	1,680	Brazos, U.S.A.	870
Si, China	1,650	Dneister, U.S.S.R.	852
Nelson, Canada	1,600	Frazer, Canada	850
Zambezi, Africa	1,600	Colorado, Tex., U.S.A.	840
Ural, U.S.S.R.	1,574	Northern Dvina, U.S.S.R.	803
Amu Darya, U.S.S.R.	1,550	Tisza, Europe	800
Ganges, India	1,540	Athabaska, Canada	765
Olenek, U.S.S.R.	1,500	North Canadian, U.S.A.	760
Paraguay, S. A.	1,500	North Saskatchewan, Can.	760

MAP PROJECTIONS

by Erwin Raisz

Our earth is rotating around its *axis* once a day. The two end points of its axis are the *poles*; the line circling the earth midway between the poles is the *equator*. The arc from either of the poles to the equator is divided into 90 *degrees*. The distance, expressed in degrees, from the equator to any point is its *latitude* and circles of equal latitude are the *parallels*. On maps it is customary to show parallels of evenly-spaced degrees such as every fifth or every tenth.

The equator is divided into 360 degrees. Lines circling from pole to pole through the degree points on the equator are called *meridians*. They are all equal in length but by international agreement the meridian passing through the Greenwich Observatory in London has been chosen as *prime meridian*. The distance, expressed in degrees, from the prime meridian to any point is its *longitude*. While meridians are all equal in length, parallels become shorter and shorter as they approach the poles. Whereas one degree of latitude represents everywhere approximately 69 miles, one degree of longitude varies from 69 miles at the equator to nothing at the poles.

Each degree is divided into 60 minutes and each minute into 60 seconds. One minute of latitude equals a nautical mile.

The map is flat but the earth is nearly spherical. Neither a rubber ball nor any part of a rubber ball may be flattened without stretching or tearing unless the part is very small. To present the curved surface of the earth on a flat map is not difficult as long as the areas under consideration are small, but the mapping of countries, continents, or the whole earth requires some kind of *projection*. Any regular set of parallels and meridians upon which a map can be drawn makes a map projection. Many systems are used.

In any projection only the parallels or the meridians or some other set of lines can be *true* (the same length as on the globe of corresponding scale); all other lines are too long or too short. Only on a globe is it possible to have both the parallels and the meridians true. The scale given on a flat map can not be true everywhere. The construction of the various projections begins usually with laying out the parallels or meridians which have true lengths.

RECTANGULAR PROJECTION.

This is a set of evenly-placed meridians and horizontal parallels. The central or *standard parallel* and all meridians are true. All other parallels are either too long or too short. The projection is used for simple maps of small areas, as city plans, etc.

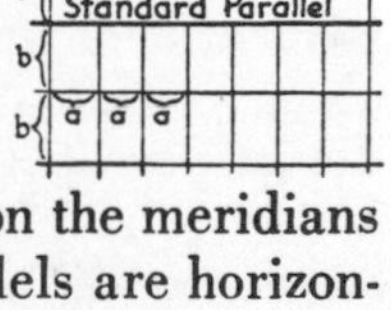

MERCATOR PROJECTION.

In this projection the meridians are evenly spaced vertical lines. The parallels are horizon-tal, spaced so that their length has the same relation to the meridians as on a globe. As the meridians converge at higher latitudes on the globe, while on the map they do not, the parallels have to be drawn also farther and farther apart

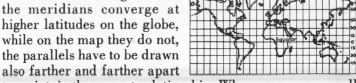

to maintain the correct relationship. When every very small area has the same shape as on a globe we call the projection *conformal*. The most interesting quality of this projection is that all *compass directions* appear as straight lines. For this reason it is generally used for marine charts. It is also frequently used for world maps in spite of the fact that the high latitudes are very much exaggerated in size. Only the equator is true to scale; all other parallels and meridians are too long. The Mercator projection did *not* derive from projecting a globe upon a cylinder.

SINUSOIDAL PROJECTION.

The parallels are truly-spaced horizontal lines. They are divided truly and the connecting curves make the meridians. It does not make a good world map because the outer regions are distorted, but the central portion is good and this part is often used for maps of Africa and South America. Every part of the map has the same area as the corresponding area on the globe. It is an *equal-area* projection.

MOLLWEIDE PROJECTION.

The meridians are equally-spaced ellipses; the parallels are horizontal lines spaced so that every belt of latitude should have the same area as on a globe. This projection is popular for world maps, especially in Euro-pean atlases.

GOODE'S INTERRUPTED PROJECTIONS.

Only the good central part of the Mollweide or sinusoidal (or both) projection is used and the oceans are cut. This makes an equal-area map with little distortion of shape. It is commonly used for world maps.

ECKERT PROJECTIONS.

These are similar to the sinusoidal or the Mollweide projections, but the poles are shown as lines half the length of the equator. There are several variants; the meridians are either sine curves or ellipses; the parallels are horizontal and spaced either evenly or so as to make the projection equal area. Their use for world maps is increasing. The figure shows the elliptical equal-area variant.

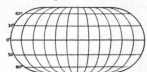

CONIC PROJECTION.

The original idea of the conic projection is that of capping the globe by a cone upon which both the parallels and meridians are projected from the

center of the globe. The cone is then cut open and laid flat. A cone can be made tangent to any chosen *standard parallel*.

The actually-used conic projection is a modification of this idea. The radius of the standard parallel is obtained as above. The meridians are straight radiating lines spaced truly on the standard parallel. The parallels are concentric circles spaced at true distances. All parallels except the standard are too long. The projection is used for maps of countries in middle latitudes, as it presents good shapes with small scale error.

There are several variants: The use of *two standard parallels,* one near the top, the other near the bottom of the map, reduces the scale error. In the *Albers projection* the parallels are spaced unevenly, to make the projection equal-area. This is a good projection for the United States. In the *Lambert conformal conic projection* the parallels are spaced so that any small quadrangle of the grid should have the same shape as on the globe. This is the best projection for air-navigation charts as it has relatively straight azimuths.

An *azimuth* is a great-circle direction reckoned clockwise from north. A *great-circle direction* points to a place along the shortest line on the earth's surface. This is not the same as compass direction. The center of a great circle is the center of the globe.

BONNE PROJECTION. The parallels are laid out exactly as in the conic projection. All parallels are divided truly and the connecting curves make the meridians. It is an equal-area projection. It is used for maps of the northern continents, as Asia, Europe, and North America.

POLYCONIC PROJECTION. The central meridian is divided truly. The parallels are non-concentric circles, the radii of which are obtained by drawing tangents to the globe as

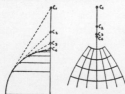

though the globe were covered by several cones rather than by only one. Each parallel is divided truly and the connecting curves make the meridians. All meridians except the central one are too long. This projection is used for large-scale topographic sheets—less often for countries or continents.

THE AZIMUTHAL PROJECTIONS. In this group a part of the globe is projected from an eyepoint onto a plane. The eyepoint can be at different distances, making different projections. The plane of projection can be tangent at the equator, at a pole, or at any other point on which we want to focus attention. The most important quality of all azimuthal projections is that they show every point at its true direction (azimuth) from the center point and all points equally distant from the center point will be equally distant on the map also.

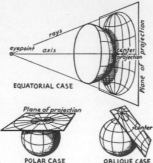

In the **GNOMONIC PROJECTION** the eyepoint is at the center of the globe. Only the central part is good; the outer regions are badly distorted. Yet the projection has one important quality, all great circles being shown as straight lines. For this reason it is used for laying out the routes for long range flying or trans-oceanic navigation.

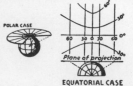

The **ORTHOGRAPHIC PROJECTION** has the eyepoint at infinite distance and the projecting rays are parallel. The polar or equatorial varieties are rare but the oblique case became very popular on account of its visual quality. It looks like a picture of a globe. Although the distortion on the peripheries is extreme, we see it correctly because the eye perceives it not as a map but as a picture of a three-dimensional globe. Obviously only a hemisphere (half globe) can be shown.

Some azimuthal projections do not derive from the actual process of projecting from an eyepoint, but are arrived at by other means:

AZIMUTHAL EQUIDISTANT PROJECTION. This is the only projection in which every point is shown both at true great-circle direction and at true distance from the center point, but all other directions and distances are distorted. The principle of the projection can best be understood from the polar case. Most polar maps are in this projection. The oblique case is used for radio direction finding, for earthquake research, and in long-distance flying. A separate map has to be constructed for each central point selected.

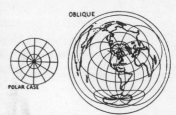

LAMBERT AZIMUTHAL EQUAL-AREA PROJECTION. The construction of this projection can best be understood from the polar case. All three cases are widely used. It makes a good polar map and it is often extended to include the southern continents. It is the most common projection used for maps of the Eastern and Western Hemispheres, and it is a good projection for continents as it shows correct areas with relatively little distortion of shape. Most of the continent maps in this atlas are in this projection.

IN THIS ATLAS, on almost all maps, parallels and meridians have been marked because they are useful for the following:

(a) They show the north-south and east-west directions which appear on many maps at oblique angles especially near the margins.

(b) With the help of parallels and meridians every place can be exactly located; for instance, New York City is at 41° N and 74° W on any map.

(c) They help to measure distances even in the distorted parts of the map. The scale given on each map is true only along certain lines which are specified in the foregoing discussion for each projection. One degree of latitude equals nearly 69 statute miles or 60 nautical miles. The length of one degree of longitude varies (1° long. = 1° lat. × cos lat.).

Index of
THE WORLD

Introduction

*T*HE INDEX OF THE WORLD gives the principal cities, towns and geographical features of the world (such as mountains, rivers, bays and islands) exclusive of the cities of the United States which are covered in THE INDEX OF THE UNITED STATES.

Each entry gives the index reference and the plate number on which the name is found. The name is found within the square formed by the two lines of latitude or longitude which enclose each of the co-ordinates — i.e. the marginal letters and numbers. In the case of maps consisting entirely of insets, the name is found near the intersecting point of the imaginary lines connecting the co-ordinates.

Where space on the map has not permitted giving the complete form of a name, the extended form is shown in the index. Where a place may be known under different names or by various spellings of the name, the different forms have been included to a large extent in the index.

The population figures given are the latest census figures or the latest official estimates.

In the belief that a geographical index should primarily serve to enable the reader to locate names quickly and accurately, we have employed the system of indexing followed in all government publications and telephone directories. All indexes sorted by mechanical means, such as the I. B. M. method, employ this system. Therefore, in alphabetizing, all those compound names with a common first part are grouped together, even though the first letter of the second part of the name may succeed the corresponding letter in a simple name. The three examples shown below are offered to illustrate this system in comparison with the less convenient alternate system of indexing.

INDEXING SYSTEM USED IN THIS ATLAS

San Cristobal	La Ceiba	Bac Kan
San Francisco	La Spezia	Bac Lieu
San Jose	Labe	Bac Ninh
Sanchez	Lachlan	Bacabal
Sandakan		Backang

ALTERNATE INDEXING SYSTEM

Sanchez	Labe	Bacabal
San Cristobal	La Ceiba	Bac Kan
Sandakan	Lachlan	Backang
San Francisco	La Spezia	Bac Lieu
San Jose		Bac Ninh

As a special feature translations of foreign geographical terms have been incorporated directly into the body of the index. For example: Rio will be found in the index with its English translation. All physical features are listed under their proper names and not according to their generic terms; that is to say, Rio Negro will be found under Negro and not under Rio Negro.

© Copyright MCMLX by

C. S. HAMMOND & CO.
Maplewood, N. J.   New York, N. Y.

Printed in U. S. A.

INDEX OF THE WORLD

Capitals of Countries, States and Provinces are designated by asterisks (*). Dagger (†) designates Population figure including suburbs.

Index Ref. Plate No.

A

Aabenraa, Denmark, 13,017.......F 9 13
Aachen (Aix la Chapelle), Germany, 129,811.......B 3 14
Aalborg, Denmark, 79,806.......G 8 13
Aalen, Germany, 25,375.......D 4 14
Aalst (Alost), Belgium, 43,835.......D 7 15
Aarau, Switzerland, 14,280.......F 2 19
Aarhus, Denmark, 116,167.......F 8 13
Aarlen (Arlon), Belgium, 12,415.......H 9 15
Aba, Nigeria, 57,787.......H10 34
Abadan with Khorramshahr, Iran 64,889.......F 5 27
Abadeh, Iran, 8,000.......H 5 27
Abakan, U.S.S.R., 56,000.......L 4 22
Abancay, Peru, 5,332.......F 6 46
Abashiri, Japan, 39,218.......M 1 33
Abau, Papua.......C 7 31
Abaya (lake), Ethiopia.......O10 34
Abbazia (Opatija) Yugo., 11,737.......A 3 21
Abbeville, France, 18,932.......D 2 16
Abbotsdale, C. of Good Hope, 618.......D18 35
Abbottabad, Pakistan, 27,602.......B 2 29
Abdulino, U.S.S.R., 13,636.......G 4 22
Abécher, Chad.......L 9 34
Abeokuta, Nigeria, 56,600.......G10 34
Abercorn, N. Rhodesia, 1,177.......N13 35
Aberdare, Wales, 40,916.......D 6 10
Aberdeen (lake), Canada.......L 2 40
Aberdeen, Scotland, 182,729.......N 5 11
Abertillery, England, 27,617.......E 6 10
Abha, Saudi Arabia, 15,000.......D 6 26
Abidjan,* Ivory Coast, 56,000.......F10 34
Abitibi (lake), Canada.......D 4 41
Abitibi (river), Canada.......D 3 41
Åbo (Turku), Finland, 117,464.......N 6 13
Abomey, Dahomey, 16,906.......G10 34
Abony, Hungary, 15,299.......E 3 20
Abu 'Arish, Saudi Arabia, 5,000.......D 6 26
Abu Dhabi, Tr. Oman, 5,000.......F 5 26
Abu Road, India, 9,935.......B 4 29
Abunã, Brazil.......H 5 46
Acadia Valley, Alta., 99.......H 4 40
Acambaro, Mex., 23,038.......J 7 44
Acapulco, Mexico, 28,512.......J 8 44
Accra,* Ghana, 135,192.......G11 34
Accrington, England, 40,671.......E 4 10
Achill (island), Ireland.......A 4 12
Achill Head (cape), Ireland.......A 4 12
Achinsk, U.S.S.R. ....L 4 22
Acireale, Italy 34,330.......E 6 18
Acklins (island), Bahama Is., 1,744.......C 2 45
Aconcagua (mountain), Arg. F10 47
Acqui, Italy, 12,328.......B 2 18
Acre (Ako), Israel, 21,400.......C 2 24
Acre (river), Brazil.......G 6 46
Adalia (gulf), Turkey.......D 4 28
Adana (Seyhan), Turkey, 172,465.......F 4 28
Adapazari, Turkey, 55,116.......D 2 28
Adaut, Indonesia.......J 7 31
Addanki, India, 11,310.......C 5 29
Addis Ababa,* Ethiopia, 250,000.......O10 34
Addis Alam, Ethiopia, 1,000.......O10 34
Adelaide, Australia, †483,508.......D 7 36
Adelboden, Switzerland, 2,873.......E 3 19
Aden,* Aden, †97,760.......E 7 26
Adilabad, India, 11,128.......C 5 29
Adirondack (mountains), U.S. ....P 3 43
Adiyaman, Turkey, 14,017.......H 4 28
Admiralty (gulf), Australia.......C 2 36
Admiralty (islands), Territory N.G., 14,420.......E 6 37
Adoni, India, 35,431.......C 5 29
Adrano, Italy, 26,952.......E 6 18
Adrar, Saoura, 1,722.......G 6 34
Adrar (reg.), Mauritania, 49,000.......D 7 34
Adria, Italy, 22,990.......D 2 18
Adrianople (Edirne), Turkey 33,591.......B 2 28
Adriatic (sea).......E 3 18
Adrogué, Arg., 37,588.......O12 47
Aduwa, Ethiopia, 6,000.......O 9 34
Aegean (sea).......G 6 21
Afmadu, Somalia, 2,000.......P11 35
'Afula, Israel, 12,900.......C 2 24
Afyon, Turkey, 31,385.......D 3 28
Agadès, Niger, 4,300.......H 8 34
Agadir, Morocco, 29,879.......D 5 34
Agaña,* Guam, 1,330.......E 4 37
Agartala, India, 17,693.......F 4 29
Agen, France, 28,591.......D 5 16
Aginskoye, U.S.S.R. ....N 4 23
Agira, Italy, 15,677.......E 6 18
Agordat, Eritrea, Ethiopia, 2,000.......O 8 34
Agra, India, 375,665.......C 3 29
Ağri (Karaköse), Turkey, 17,022.......K 3 28
Agrigento, Italy, 37,506.......D 6 18
Agrínion, Greece, 20,981.......E 6 21
Agua Prieta, Mexico, 10,471.......E 1 44
Aguadas, Colombia, 7,631.......F 2 46
Aguadilla, P.R., 18,181.......F 1 45
Aguascalientes, Mexico, 93,432.......H 6 44
Aguilar, Spain, 15,275.......D 4 17
Aguilas, Spain, 11,829.......F 4 17
Aguju (point), Peru.......D 5 47
Agulhas (cape), U.S. Africa.......K19 35
Ahaggar (mts.), Oasis.......H 7 34
Ahar, Iran, 20,047.......E 1 27
Ahlen, Germany, 33,141.......B 3 14
Ahmadabad, India, 788,333.......B 4 29
Ahmadnagar, India, 70,418.......B 5 29
Ahmadpur East, Pakistan, 20,404.......B 3 29
Ahuachapán, El Salvador, 10,294.......B 4 39
Ahvenanmaa (Aland) (isls.), Finland, 21,650.......L 6 13
Ahwar, Aden Pr., 5,000.......E 7 26
Ahwaz, Iran, 49,336.......F 5 27
Aígion, Greece, 15,070.......F 6 21
Aigun, China.......L 1 32
Aïn-Sefra, Algeria, 3,500.......G 5 34
Aioun el Atrous, Mauritania, 900.......E 8 34
Aïr (Asben) (mountains), Niger.......H 8 34
Airdrie, Scotland, 30,308.......D 2 11
Aire (river), England.......F 4 10
Aitape, Terr. N. G. 161.......B 6 31
Aitutaki (island), Pacific, 2,356.......K 7 37
Aiud, Rumania, 9,535.......F 2 21
Aiún,* Sp. Sahara, Spain, 3,142.......D 6 34
Aix, France, 32,076.......F 6 16
Aix-les-Bains, France, 10,720.......G 5 16
Aizuwakamatsu, Japan, 97,885.......J 5 33
Ajaccio, France, 28,732.......F 7 16
Ajana, Australia, 80.......B 5 36
Ajedabia, Libya, 7,000.......L 5 34
'Ajlun, Jordan, 2,518.......D 3 24
Ajmer, India, 196,633.......B 3 29
Akaroa, New Zealand, 560.......L 7 36
Akashi, Japan, 65,642.......H 8 33
Aken, Germany, 14,624.......D 3 14
Aketi, Belgian Congo, 6,616.......L11 35
Akhdar (mts.), Oman.......G 5 26
Akhisar, Turkey, 30,156.......B 3 28
Akhmim, Egypt, 32,071.......N 6 34
Akhty, U.S.S.R., 3,886.......F 5 22
Akimiski (island), Canada.......D 3 41
Akita, Japan, 126,074.......J 4 33
Akjoujt, Mauritania, 2,000.......D 7 34
Aklavik, N. W. Territories, 900.......C 1 40
Akmolinsk, U.S.S.R., 101,000.......J 4 22
Akola, India, 62,564.......C 4 29
Akpatok (island), Canada.......G 1 41
Aksaray, Turkey, 14,363.......F 3 28
Aksehir, Turkey, 15,387.......D 3 28
Aksum, Ethiopia, 10,000.......O 9 34
Aktyubinsk, U.S.S.R., 97,000.......G 4 22
Akureyri, Iceland 7,143.......C 2 9
Akyab, Burma, 41,589.......B 2 30
Al Kadhimain, Iraq, 65,000.......C 4 27
Al Kuwait,* Kuwait, 80,000.......E 4 26
Alabama (river), U.S. ....M 7 43
Alagir, U.S.S.R., 4,192.......F 5 22
Alagoinhas, Brazil, 21,283.......N 6 46
Alajuela, Costa Rica, 13,903.......E 6 39
Aland (isls.), Finland, 21,650.......L 6 13
Alanya, Turkey, 8,055.......D 4 28
Alapayevsk, U.S.S.R., 30,000.......P 6 23
Alaşehir, Turkey, 11,537.......C 3 28
Alaska (peninsula), U. S. ....F 8 42
Alaska (mtn. range), U.S. ....F 8 42
Alatyr', U.S.S.R., 25,567.......F 4 22
Alausí, Ecuador, 4,812.......E 4 46
Alba, Italy, 13,807.......B 2 18
Alba Iulia, Rumania, 14,420.......F 2 21
Albacete, Spain, 71,822.......F 3 17
Albany, Australia, 8,265.......B 6 36
Albany (river), Canada.......D 3 41
Albatross (bay), Australia.......G 2 36
Alberga (river), Australia.......E 5 36
Alberni, B. C., 3,947.......E 5 40
Albert, France, 8,742.......E 2 16
Albert (lake), Africa.......M11 35
Alberton, P.E.I., 820.......H 4 41
Albertville, Belgian Congo, 27,931.......M13 35
Albi, France, 27,768.......E 6 16
Albina, Surinam, 370.......K 2 46
Albury, Australia, 16,726.......H 7 36
Alcalá de Guadaira, Spain, 17,844.......D 4 17
Alcalá de Henares, Spain, 14,651.......G 4 17
Alcamo, Italy, 41,471.......D 6 18
Alcântara, Brazil, 1,453.......M 4 46
Alcázar de San Juan, Spain, 22,964.......E 3 17
Alcira, Spain, 21,059.......F 3 17
Alcobaça, Brazil, 1,307.......K 4 46
Alcoy, Spain, 39,417.......F 3 17
Aldabra (islands), Seychelles, 47.......R13 35
Aldan, U.S.S.R. ....O 4 23
Aldan (river), U.S.S.R. ....O 4 23
Aldershot, England, 36,184.......G 6 10
Aleg, Mauritania, 352.......D 8 34
Alegrete, Brazil, 20,160.......J 9 47
'Aleih, Lebanon, 5,271.......F 6 28
Aleksandrovsk-Sakhalinskiy, U.S.S.R., 40,000.......R 4 23
Aleksandrovskiy Zavod, U.S.S.R., 2,097.......N 4 23
Aleksinac, Yugoslavia, 7,383.......E 4 21
Alençon, France, 19,427.......D 3 16
Aleppo, Syria, 371,897.......G 4 28
Alès, France, 20,259.......E 5 16
Alessandria, Italy, 70,238.......B 2 18
Ålesund, Norway, 18,527.......D 5 13
Aleutian (islands), U. S. ....F 8 42
Alexandra, New Zealand, 1,823.......K 7 36
Alexandretta (Iskenderun), Turkey, 48,084.......G 4 28
Alexandria, Egypt, 925,081.......M 5 34
Alexandria, Rumania, 17,840.......G 3 21
Alexandroúpolis, Greece, 17,081.......H 5 21
Alfeld, Germany, 12,287.......C 2 14
Alfreton, England, 23,388.......F 4 10
Algeciras, Spain, 20,610.......D 4 17
Algemesí, Spain, 15,510.......F 3 17
Algés, Portugal, 9,826.......A 1 17
Alghero, Italy, 18,602.......B 4 18
Algiers (Alger),* Algeria, 329,700.......G 4 34
Alicante, Spain, †101,741.......F 3 17
Alice Arm, Br. Columbia, 75.......E 3 40
Alice Springs, Aust., 2,785.......E 4 36
Aligarh, India, 141,618.......C 3 29
Alipore, India, 46,332.......E 2 29
Aliwal North, C. of G.H., 8,754.......M18 35
Alkmaar, Netherlands, 42,060.......F 3 15
Allahabad, India, 332,295.......D 3 29
Allen (lake), Ireland.......E 3 12
Allen, Bog of, Ireland.......H 5 12
Allenstein (Olsztyn), Poland, 60,400.......E 2 24
Alleppey, India, 116,278.......C 7 29
Alloa, Scotland, 13,436.......E 1 11
Alma, Quebec, 10,748.......F 4 41
Alma-Ata, U.S.S.R., 455,000.......J 5 22
Almada, Portugal, 11,995.......A 1 17
Almadén, Spain, 12,069.......D 3 17
Almansa, Spain, 14,942.......F 3 17
Almeirim, Portugal, 7,104.......B 3 17
Almelo, Netherlands, 48,018.......K 4 15
Almendralejo, Spain, 21,363.......C 3 17
Almería, Spain, 75,861.......E 4 17
Almora, India, 10,995.......C 3 29
Alofi,* Niue, 884.......K 7 37
Alon, Burma.......B 2 30
Alor Star, Mal. Fed., 32,424.......D 6 30
Alsask, Sask., 232.......J 4 40
Alsdorf, Germany, 22,205.......B 3 14
Alta Gracia, Argentina, 11,570.......H10 47
Altagracia, Venezuela, 3,987.......F 1 46
Altamira, Brazil, 1,988.......K 4 46
Altamura, Italy, 38,231.......F 4 18
Altan Bulak, Mon. Rep., 8,000.......G 2 32
Altay (mountains), Asia.......D 2 32
Altayskoye, U.S.S.R., 7,555.......K 4 22
Altena, Germany, 22,162.......B 3 14
Altenburg, Germany, 51,805.......E 3 14
Altiplano (plateau), S. A. ....F 7 46
Altona, Germany.......C 2 14
Altona, Man., 1,698.......L 5 40
Alty-Aryk, U.S.S.R., 5,706.......T 2 23
Altyn Tagh (mt. range), China.......C 4 32
Alula, Som., 2,000.......S 9 34
Älv (means river) (Swedish).......
Alvaro Obregón (Frontera), Mex., 8,466.......N 7 44
Alwar, India, 54,143.......C 3 29
Amadeus (lake), Australia.......E 4 36
Amadjuak (lake), Canada.......F26 8
Amagasaki, Japan, 279,264.......H 8 33
Amakusa (islands), Japan, 183,044.......D 7 33
Amaliás, Greece, 15,189.......E 7 21
Amalner, India, 34,694.......B 4 29
Amami (islands), Japan, 167,887.......N 5 33
Amapá, Brazil, 1,267.......K 3 46
Amapala, Honduras, 2,934.......D 4 39
'Amara, Iraq, 48,915.......E 5 27
Amarante, Brazil, 2,545.......M 5 46
Amarapura, Burma.......B 2 30
Amasya, Turkey, 17,549.......F 2 28
Amatitlán, Guat., 6,683.......B 3 39
Amazon (river), Brazil.......K 4 46
Ambala, India, 107,383.......C 2 29
Ambalavao, Malg. Rep., 2,183.......R16 35
Ambarawa, Indonesia, 19,480.......J 2 31
Ambarchik, U.S.S.R. ....T 3 23
Ambato, Ecuador, 33,908.......E 4 46
Ambatondrazaka, Malg. Rep., 2,919.......S15 35
Amberg, Germany, 37,920.......E 4 14
Ambodifototra, Malg. Rep., 2,194.......S15 35
Amboina (Ambon), Indonesia, 23,066.......H 6 31
Ambositra, Malg. Rep., 4,516.......R16 35
Ambre (cape), Malg. Rep. R14 35
Ambriz, Angola, 2,196.......J13 35
Ambrizete, Angola, 1,147.......J13 35
Ambunti, Terr. N.G. ....B 6 31
Amderma, U.S.S.R. ....H 3 22
Ameca, Mexico, 13,589.......H 6 44
American Falls (res.), U.S. ....E 4 42
Amersfoort, Neth., 66,403.......G 4 15
Amery, Manitoba, 25.......M 3 40
Amherst, Burma.......C 3 30
Amherst, N. S., 10,301.......H 4 41
Amherstburg, Ont., 4,099.......D 5 41
Amiens, France, 87,126.......D 3 16
Amman,* Jordan, 108,304.......D 4 24
Amne Machin (mts.), China.......F 5 32
Amos, Quebec, 5,145.......E 4 41
Amoy, China, 224,300.......J 7 32
Ampana, Indonesia.......G 6 31
'Amran, Yemen, 5,000.......D 6 26
Amravati, India, 61,971.......C 4 29
Amreli, India, 25,485.......B 4 29
Amritsar, India, 325,747.......B 2 29
Amsterdam,* Neth., 871,188.......B 4 15
Amstetten, Austria, 11,341.......C 2 20
Amu-Dar'ya (river), U.S.S.R. ....H 5 22
Amul, Iran, 16,119.......H 2 27
Amundsen (gulf), Canada.......D31 8
Amuntai, Indonesia.......F 6 31
Amur (river), Asia.......P 5 23
Amurang, Indonesia.......G 5 31
Amya, Burma.......C 4 30
An Khe, Vietnam.......F 4 30
An Najaf, Iraq, 35,000.......C 5 27
An Nasiriya, Iraq, 15,000.......D 5 27
An Uaimh (Navan), Ireland, 3,643.......H 4 12
Anadyr', U.S.S.R. ....U 3 23
Anadyr' (mt. range), U.S.S.R. ....U 3 23
Anagni, Italy, 14,262.......F 6 18
'Anaiza, Saudi Arabia, 20,000.......D 4 26
Anakapalle, India, 29,249.......D 5 29
Ananalava, Malg. Rep., 1,170.......R14 35
Anantapur, India, 21,482.......C 6 29
Anantnag, Kash., 11,985.......C 2 29
Anápolis, Brazil, 18,350.......L 7 46
Anatolia (plateau), Turkey.......C 3 28
Añatuya, Arg., 9,310.......H 9 47
Anchieta, Brazil, 1,328.......M14 47
Ancona, Italy, 68,501.......D 3 18
Ancud, Chile, 6,410.......F12 47
Andaman (islands), India, 21,316.......F 6 29
Anderlecht, Belgium, 92,062.......B 9 15
Andermatt, Switz., 1,231.......G 3 18
Andernach, Germany, 15,879.......B 3 14
Anderson (river), Canada.......E 1 40
Andheri, India, 38,493.......B 7 29
Andizhan, U.S.S.R., 129,000.......U 2 23
Andkhui, Afghan., 18,438.......J 2 26
Andong, Korea, 35,275.......D 5 33
Andorra la Vella,* Andorra, 1,100.......G 1 17
Andria, Italy, 63,937.......F 4 18

	Index Ref.	Plate No.
Andros (island), Bahamas, 6,718..	B 1	45
Andújar, Spain, 22,906.	D 3	17
Aneto (mountain), Spain.	G 1	17
Anécho, Togo, 7,000.	G10	34
Ang Thong, Thai., 8,527.	C 4	30
Angara (river), U.S.S.R.	M 4	23
Angarsk, U.S.S.R., 134,000.	M 4	23
Angel (fall), Venezuela.	H 2	46
Angermünde, Germany, 10,813.	E 2	14
Angers, France, 93,838.	C 4	16
Anglesey (island), Wales, 40,068..	C 4	10
Angliers, Quebec, 442.	E 4	41
Angmagssalik, Greenland, 1,121..	E22	8
Angora (Ankara),* Turkey, 453,151.	E 3	28
Angoram, Terr. N.G.	B 6	31
Angoulême, France, 38,060.	D 5	16
Angren, U.S.S.R., 55,000.	T 1	23
Anguilla (island), W.I., 5,073..	F 3	45
Anín, Burma.	C 4	30
Aniva, U.S.S.R., 7,404.	R 5	23
Ankang, China.	G 5	32
Ankara,* Turkey, 453,151.	E 3	28
Ankazoabo, Malg. Rep., 3,571.	P16	35
Anking, China, 105,300.	J 5	32
Ankober, Ethiopia, 3,000.	O10	34
Annaberg-Buchholz, Ger., 19,584..	E 3	14
Annapolis Royal, N.S., 765.	H 5	41
Annecy, France, 30,196.	G 5	16
Annobón (island), Sp. Guin., 1,403.	G12	35
Annonay, France, 13,092.	F 5	16
Annotto Bay, Jamaica, 2,805.	C 3	45
Ansbach, Germany, 33,170.	D 4	14
Anshan, China, 548,900.	K 3	32
Anshun, China.	G 6	32
Anson (bay), Australia.	D 2	36
Ansŏng, Korea, 17,740.	C 5	33
Antåkya, Turkey, 37,484.	G 4	28
Antalaha, Malg. Rep., 7,533.	S14	35
Antalya, Turkey, 35,923.	D 4	28
Antarctic Circle.	E 9	6
Antequera, Spain, 29,855.	D 4	17
Antibes, France, 13,778.	G 6	16
Anticosti (island), Canada, 856..	H 4	41
Antigonish, N.S., 3,592.	H 4	40
Antigua, Guatemala, 10,691.	B 3	39
Antigua (island), W.I., 40,778..	G 3	45
Antilles, Greater (islands), 14,686,446.	D 3	45
Antilles, Lesser (islands), 1,833,000.	F 4	45
Antioch (Antåkya), Turkey, 30,385.	G 4	28
Antioquia, Colombia, 3,810.	E 2	46
Antofagasta, Chile, 62,272.	F 8	47
António Enes, Moz., 11,979.	P15	35
Antsalova, Malg. Rep., 1,000.	P15	35
Antsirabe, Malg. Rep., 14,097.	R16	35
Antung, China, 360,000.	K 3	32
Antwerp (Antwerpen), Belgium, 256,075.	E 6	15
Anuradhapura, Ceylon, 12,287.	D 7	29
Anyang, China, 124,900.	H 4	32
Anyox, British Colombia.	E 3	40
Anzhero-Sudzhensk, U.S.S.R., 116,000.	O 5	23
Anzio, Italy, 9,084.	E 7	18
Aomori, Japan, 106,417.	K 3	33
Aoji-dong, Korea, 39,616.	E 2	33
Aosta, Italy, 24,214.	A 2	18
Aoulef, Oasis, 3,143.	G 6	34
Apalachee (bay), U.S.	M 7	43
Apaporis (river), Colombia.	F 3	46
Aparri, Phil. Islands, 10,125.	G 2	31
Apatin, Yugoslavia, 13,537.	D 3	21
Apeldoorn, Netherlands, 97,867..	H 4	15
Apia,* W. Samoa, 10,000.	J 7	37
Apizaco, Mexico, 12,710.	N 1	44
Apolda, Germany, 33,439.	D 3	14
Appalachian (mountains), U.S.	M 6	43
Apure (river), Venezuela.	F 2	46
'Aqaba, Jordan, 931.	C 4	26
Aqsu, China.	B 3	32
Aquidauana, Brazil, 7,582.	J 8	46
Aquila (L'Aquila), Italy, 24,843..	D 3	18
Aquin, Haiti, 1,799.	B 6	48
'Arab (river), Sudan.	M10	34
Arabian (desert), Egypt.	N 6	34
Arabian (pen.).	D 5	26
Arabian (sea).	H 5	26
Aracaju, Brazil, 67,539.	N 6	46
Aracati, Brazil, 8,952.	N 4	46
Araçatuba, Brazil, 27,692.	K 8	46
Arad, Rumania, 87,291.	E 2	21
Aragona, Italy, 16,628.	D 6	18
Araguaya (river), Brazil.	K 6	46
Araguari, Brazil, 24,616.	L 7	46
Arak, Iran, 61,393.	F 4	27
Arakan (mountains), Burma.	B 2	30
Aral (sea), U.S.S.R.	G 5	22
Aral'sk, U.S.S.R.	H 5	22

	Index Ref.	Plate No.
Aramac, Australia, 532.	H 4	36
Aran (island), Ireland.	D 2	12
Aran (islands), Ireland.	B 5	12
Aranjuez, Spain, 19,627.	E 2	17
Aranyaprathet, Thai., 5,124.	D 4	30
Araranguá, Brazil, 4,340.	L 9	47
Araraquara, Brazil, 34,671.	L 8	46
Ararat, Australia, 7,414.	G 7	36
Ararat (mountain), Turkey.	L 3	28
Arauca, Colombia, 2,028.	F 2	46
Arauca (river), S. A.	G 2	46
Araxa, Brazil, 14,997.	L 7	46
Arbela (Erbil), Iraq, 26,086.	D 2	27
Arborfield, Sask., 557.	K 4	40
Arborg, Man., 450.	L 4	40
Arbroath, Scotland, 19,503.	L 6	11
Arcachon, France, 13,931.	C 5	16
Archangel, U.S.S.R., 256,000.	F 3	22
Arcola, Sask., 609.	K 5	40
Arcot, India, 16,583.	C 6	29
Arctic Circle.	M 2	6
Arctic Red River, N.W. Terr.	D 1	40
Ardebil, Iran, 81,382.	F 1	27
Ardistan, Iran, 8,956.	H 4	27
Arecibo, P. R., 28,500.	G 1	45
Areia Branca, Brazil, 7,665.	N 4	46
Arendal, Norway, 11,751.	F 7	13
Arequipa, Peru, 97,110.	F 7	46
Arezzo, Italy, 39,213.	C 3	18
Argenteuil, France, 53,513.	A 1	16
Argentia, Newfoundland, 900.	K 4	41
Argentino (lake), Argentina.	F14	47
Árgos, Greece, 13,440.	F 7	21
Argostólion, Greece, 8,205.	E 6	21
Argun (river), U.S.S.R.-China.	O 4	23
Ariano Irpino, Italy, 11,442.	E 4	18
Arica, Chile, 18,947.	F 7	46
Arid (cape), Australia.	C 6	36
Arinos (river), Brazil.	J 6	46
Aripuanã (river), Brazil.	H 5	46
Arkaig (lake), Scotland.	F 6	11
Arkansas (river), U.S.	H 5	42
Arkhangel'sk (Archangel), U.S.S.R., 256,000.	F 3	22
Arkhara, U.S.S.R. 2,147.	P 5	23
Arles, France, 23,409.	F 6	16
Arlon (Aarlen), Belgium, 12,415..	H 9	15
Armadale, Australia, 1,496.	B 2	36
Armavir, U.S.S.R., 111,000.	F 5	22
Armentières, France, 18,691.	E 2	16
Armidale, Australia, †8,662.	J 6	36
Armstrong, British Col., 1,197..	G 4	40
Armstrong Station, Ont., 375.	C 3	41
Arnhem, Netherlands, 119,814.	H 4	15
Arnhem (cape), Australia.	F 2	36
Arnhem Land (region) Aust.	E 2	36
Arnhemia, Indonesia.	B 5	31
Arnold, England, 21,474.	G 4	10
Arnprior, Ont., 5,137.	E 4	41
Arnsberg, Germany, 18,884.	C 3	14
Arnstadt, Germany, 27,846.	D 3	14
Arrah, India, 53,122.	D 3	29
Arran (island), Scotland, 4,506..	F 8	11
Arras, France, 32,298.	E 2	16
Arrecifes, Argentina, 7,635.	M11	47
Arrowhead, British Col., 200.	G 4	40
Artá, Greece, 12,947.	E 6	21
Artem, U.S.S.R., 55,000.	P 5	23
Artemisa, Cuba, 13,081.	B 1	48
Artemovsk, U.S.S.R., 61,000.	K 1	23
Artemovsk, U.S.S.R.	L 4	23
Artigas, Uruguay, 16,500.	J10	47
Artur Bernardes, Brazil.	K 8	47
Artvin (Çoruh), Turkey, 5,845..	J 2	28
Arua, Uganda, 6,389.	N11	35
Aruba (isl.), Neth. Ant., 55,912..	G 1	46
Arucas, Canary Isls., Spain, 22,737.	B 5	17
Aruppukkottai, India, 35,001.	C 7	29
Arusha, Tan. Territory, 5,320.	O12	35
Aruwimi (river), Belg. Congo.	M11	35
Arvi, India, 16,228.	C 4	29
Arvida, Quebec, 12,919.	F 4	41
Arvika, Sweden, 15,154.	H 7	13
Arzamas, U.S.S.R., 19,203.	F 4	22
Aš, Czech., 10,524.	B 1	20
Asahikawa, Japan, 123,238.	L 2	33
Asansol, India, 55,797.	E 4	29
Asben (Aïr) (mts.), Niger.	H 8	34
Asbest, U.S.S.R., 60,000.	P 6	23
Asbestos, Quebec, 8,969.	F 4	41
Ascension (island), 196.	D13	35
Aschaffenburg, Germany, 45,499..	C 4	14
Aschersleben, Germany, 42,196..	D 3	14
Ascoli Piceno, Italy, 29,657.	D 3	18
Ascope, Peru, 3,727.	E 5	46
Asenovgrad, Bulgaria, 20,920.	G 5	21
Ashburton, New Zealand, 10,176..	L 7	36
Ashburton (river), Australia.	B 4	36
Ashcroft, British Colombia, 950..	F 4	40
Ashern, Man., 333.	L 4	40
Ashford, England, 24,777.	H 6	10
Ashibetsu, Japan, 68,091.	L 2	33

	Index Ref.	Plate No.
Ashikaga, Japan, 52,810.	J 5	33
Ashington, England, 28,723.	F 2	10
Ashiya, Japan, 42,951.	H 8	33
Ashkhabad, U.S.S.R., 170,000.	G 6	22
Ashmore (isls.), Australia.	C 2	36
Askiz, U.S.S.R., 741.	L 4	22
Asmara,* Eritrea, Eth., 132,000..	O 9	34
Asnières, France, 72,035.	A 1	16
Assab, Eritrea, Ethiopia, 8,000..	P 9	34
Assen, Netherlands, 27,941.	K 3	15
Assiniboia, Sask., 2,027.	J 5	40
Assiniboine (river), Canada.	K 4	40
Asterabad (Gurgan), Iran, 21,555.	J 2	27
Asti, Italy, 38,412.	B 2	18
Astorga, Spain, 13,952.	C 1	17
Astrakhan', U.S.S.R., 294,000.	F 5	22
Asunción,* Para., 204,085.	J 9	47
Aswân, Egypt, 25,397.	N 7	34
Asyût, Egypt, 90,378.	N 6	34
Atacama (desert), S. A.	G 8	47
Atakpame, Togo, 3,250.	G10	34
Atambua, Indonesia.	G 7	31
Atar, Mauritania, 4,019.	D 7	34
Atbara, Sudan, 34,700.	N 8	34
Atbara (river), Sudan.	O 8	34
Atbasar, U.S.S.R., 6,746.	H 4	22
Athabasca, Alta., 1,293.	H 4	40
Athabasca (lake), Canada.	J 3	40
Athabasca (river), Canada.	H 3	40
Athens,* Greece, 565,084.	F 7	21
Athlone, Ireland, 9,393.	F 5	12
Áthos (mountain), Greece.	G 5	21
Atikokan, Ontario, 2,400.	B 4	41
Atkarsk, U.S.S.R., 19,348.	F 4	22
Atlas (mountains), Africa.	E 5	34
Atlin, British Colombia, 500.	D 3	40
'Atlit, Israel, 4,000.	B 2	24
Atlixco, Mexico, 15,622.	M 2	44
Atotonilco, Mexico, 11,038.	H 6	44
Attawapiskat (river), Canada.	C 3	41
Atuel (river), Argentina.	G11	47
Aubervilliers, France, 52,766.	B 1	16
Auch, France, 11,489.	D 6	16
Auckland, New Zealand, 381,063..	L 5	36
Auden, Ontario, 444.	C 3	41
Audincourt, France, 8,656.	G 4	16
Aue, Germany, 25,567.	E 3	14
Auerbach, Germany, 18,708.	E 3	14
Augsburg, Germany, 185,183.	D 4	14
Augusta, Australia, 217.	A 6	36
Augusta, Italy, 22,107.	E 6	18
Augustów, Poland, 11,300.	F 2	24
Aujila, Libya, 1,502.	L 6	34
Aulnay-sous-Bois, France, 32,223.	B 1	16
Aurangabad, India, 66,725.	C 5	29
Auray, France, 8,038.	B 4	16
Aurich, Germany, 11,284.	B 2	14
Aurillac, France, 19,375.	E 5	16
Austin (lake), Australia.	B 5	36
Austral (Tubuai) (islands), Pacific, 3,915.	L 8	37
Australian Alps (mountains) Australia.	H 7	36
Autlán, Mexico, 11,356.	G 7	44
Autun, France, 11,767.	F 4	16
Auxerre, France, 23,100.	E 4	16
Avalon (peninsula), Canada.	K 4	41
Avarua,* Cook Islands, 270.	L 8	37
Avdeyevka, U.S.S.R., 8,767.	J 1	23
Aveiro, Portugal, 13,423.	B 2	17
Avellaneda, Argentina, 278,621..	O12	47
Avellino, Italy, 28,597.	E 4	18
Aversa, Italy, 33,809.	E 4	18
Avezzano, Italy, 21,983.	D 3	18
Avignon, France, 51,863.	F 6	16
Ávila de los Caballeros, Spain, 22,577.	D 2	17
Avion, France, 16,072.	E 2	16
Avola, Br. Columbia, 97.	G 4	40
Avola, Italy, 24,304.	E 6	18
Avon (river), England.	F 6	10
Avon (river), England.	F 5	10
Avranches, France, 7,176.	C 3	16
Awe (lake), Scotland.	F 7	11
Ayabe, Japan, 33,573.	G 6	33
Ayacucho, Peru, 16,642.	F 6	46
Ayaguz, U.S.S.R., 30,000.	K 5	22
Ayapel, Colombia, 1,624.	E 2	46
Aydin, Turkey, 27,706.	B 4	28
Aykino, U.S.S.R., 560.	F 3	22
Aylesbury, England, 21,054.	G 6	10
Aylmer (lake), Canada.	J 2	40
Ayr, Australia, 7,082.	H 3	36
Ayr, Scotland, 42,377.	G 9	11
Ayre (point), Isle of Man.	C 3	10
Aytos, Bulgaria, 9,972.	H 4	21
Ayutthaya (Krung Kao), Thai., 15,821.	D 4	30
Ayvalik, Turkey, 16,755.	B 3	28
Azamgarh, India, 24,307.	D 3	29
Azcapotzalco, Mexico, 48,650.	L 1	44
Azogues, Ecuador, 6,579.	E 4	46

	Index Ref.	Plate No.
Azores (islands), 318,686.	B 4	34
Azov (sea), U.S.S.R.	E 5	22
Azua, Dominican Rep., 7,419.	D 6	48
Azul, Argentina, 28,609.	J11	47

B

	Index Ref.	Plate No.
Baa, Indonesia.	G 8	31
Ba'albek, Lebanon, 8,691.	G 5	28
Baarn, Netherlands, 19,324.	G 4	15
Babadag, Rumania, 4,022.	J 3	21
Babaeski, Turkey, 11,035.	B 2	28
Babahoyo, Ecuador, 9,045.	D 4	46
Babelthuap (island), Pacific, 3,672.	D 5	37
Babol (Barfrush), Iran, 36,590..	H 2	27
Babushkin, U.S.S.R., 112,000.	B 4	22
Babushkin, U.S.S.R., 2,570.	M 4	23
Babuyan (islands), Phil. Isls.	G 2	31
Bac Kan, Vietnam.	E 2	30
Bac Lieu, Vietnam, 20,638.	E 5	30
Bac Ninh, Vietnam.	E 2	30
Bacabal, Brazil, 4,877.	J 5	46
Bacău, Rumania, 34,461.	H 2	21
Bacchus Marsh, Australia, 2,825..	K 1	36
Back (river) Canada.	J 1	40
Bačka Topola, Yugoslavia, 14,177.	D 3	21
Backnang, Germany, 18,189.	C 4	14
Bacolod, Philippine Isls., 42,820..	G 3	31
Bácsalmás, Hungary, 13,310.	E 3	20
Bad Godesberg, Germany, 44,627..	B 3	14
Bad Homburg, Germany, 27,971..	C 3	14
Bad Ischl, Austria, 13,441.	B 3	20
Bad Kissingen, Germany, 14,318..	D 3	14
Bad Kreuznach, Germany, 30,063..	B 4	14
Bad Nauheim, Germany, 13,019..	C 3	14
Bad Oldesloe, Germany, 14,944..	D 2	14
Bad Reichenhall, Germany, 13,351.	E 5	14
Bad Wildungen, Germany, 11,379..	C 3	14
Badagara, India, 17,924.	C 6	29
Badajoz, Spain, 76,098.	C 3	17
Badalona, Spain, 40,983.	H 2	17
Baden, Austria, 21,382.	D 2	20
Baden, Switzerland, 11,575.	F 2	19
Baden-Baden, Germany, 36,582..	C 4	14
Badulla, Ceylon, 13,213.	D 7	29
Badung (Denpasar), Indonesia, 16,639.	F 7	31
Baena, Spain, 20,084.	D 4	17
Baeza, Spain, 16,506.	E 4	17
Baffin (bay), Canada.	D25	8
Baffin (island), Canada.	F25	8
Bafoulabé, Sudanese Rep., 1,037..	D 9	34
Bafra, Turkey, 17,588.	F 2	28
Baft, Iran, 2,554.	K 6	27
Bagalkot, India, 24,521.	C 5	29
Bagamoyo, Tan. Terr., 5,000.	O13	35
Bagan Siapiapi, Indonesia.	C 5	31
Bagé, Brazil, 34,525.	K10	47
Baghdad,* Iraq, 364,049.	D 4	27
Bagheria, Italy, 30,782.	D 5	18
Baghlan, Afghanistan, 24,410.	J 2	26
Bagnères de Bigorre, France, 8,499.	D 6	16
Bagnolet, France, 25,059.	B 2	16
Bagrach (lake), China.	C 3	32
Baguio, Philippine Islands, 29,262.	G 2	31
Bahama (islands), 68,846.	C 1	45
Bahamas (islands).		
Bahawalnagar, Pakistan, 18,373..	B 3	29
Bahawalpur, Pakistan, 41,646.	B 3	29
Bahía (means bay) (Sp.).		
Bahía (Salvador), Brazil, 389,422.	N 6	46
Bahía, Ecuador, 7,993.	D 4	46
Bahía Blanca, Argentina, 112,597.	H11	47
Bahr (means river) (Arab.).		
Bahraich, India, 39,963.	D 3	29
Bahramabad, Iran, 9,184.	K 5	27
Baia de Aramá, Rumania, 1,513..	F 3	21
Baia Mare, Rumania, 20,959.	F 2	21
Baidyabati, India, 25,825.	E 1	29
Baie (means bay) (Fr.).		
Baie-Comeau, Quebec, 4,332.	G 4	41
Baie-de-la-Trinité, Quebec, 913..	G 4	41
Baie-Saint-Paul, Quebec, 4,052..	F 4	41
Baikal (Baykal) (lake), U.S.S.R..	M 4	23
Baile Átha Cliath (Dublin), *Ireland, 539,476.	K 5	12
Bãilești, Rumania, 15,289.	F 3	21
Bairnsdale, Australia, 5,718.	H 7	36
Bait al Faqih, Yemen, 12,000.	D 7	26
Baja, Hungary, 28,216.	E 3	20
Baja (Lower) California (pen.), Mexico, 287,308.	C 2	44
Bakel, Senegal, 2,400.	D 9	34
Baker (island), Pacific, 3.	J 5	37

Index Ref. Plate No.

Baker (lake), Canada ... L 2 40
Bakirköy, Turkey, 82,590 ... D 6 28
Baku, U.S.S.R., 636,000 ... G 6 22
Balagansk, U.S.S.R., 1,179 ... M 4 23
Balaghat, India, 11,482 ... D 4 29
Balakhna, U.S.S.R. ... F 4 22
Balakhta, U.S.S.R., 3,027 ... L 4 22
Balashikha, U.S.S.R., 58,000 ... B 3 22
Balashov, U.S.S.R., 64,000 ... F 4 22
Balasore, India, 19,405 ... E 4 29
Balaton (lake), Hungary ... D 3 20
Balboa, Canal Zone, 4,162 ... H 6 39
Balboa Heights,* Canal Zone, 363 ... H 6 39
Balcarce, Argentina, 15,210 ... J11 47
Balclutha, New Zealand, 3,323 ... L 7 36
Bâle (Basel), Switz., 183,543 ... E 1 19
Balearic (Baleares) (islands), Spain, 422,089 ... H 3 17
Balhannah, Australia, 414 ... E 8 36
Bali (island), Indon., 1,101,393 ... F 7 31
Balikesir, Turkey, 46,556 ... B 3 28
Balikpapan, Indonesia, 29,843 ... F 6 31
Balkan (mountains), Bulgaria ... G 4 21
Balkh, Afghanistan, 12,488 ... J 2 26
Balkhash, U.S.S.R., 53,000 ... J 5 22
Balkhash (lake), U.S.S.R. ... J 5 22
Ballarat, Australia, †48,030 ... G 7 36
Ballia, India, 23,520 ... D 3 29
Ballina, Australia, 3,558 ... J 5 36
Ballina, Ireland, 6,091 ... C 3 12
Ballinasloe, Ireland, 5,489 ... E 5 12
Bally, India, 50,397 ... E 1 29
Ballymena, N. Ireland, 14,165 ... J 2 12
Balmazújváros, Hungary, 16,318 ... F 3 20
Balonne (river), Australia ... H 5 36
Balrampur, India, 35,461 ... D 3 29
Balranald, Australia, 1,273 ... G 6 36
Bals, Rumania, 6,128 ... G 3 21
Baltic (sea), Europe ... K 9 13
Bam, Iran, 15,224 ... L 6 27
Bamako,* Sudanese Rep., 60,000 ... E 9 34
Bamberg, Germany, 76,180 ... D 4 14
Bamenda, So. Cameroons, 2,264 ... H10 34
Ban Houei Sai, Laos ... D 2 30
Ban Me Thuot, Vietnam ... F 4 30
Banana, B. Congo ... J13 35
Banbury, England, 18,916 ... F 5 10
Banco, Colombia, 5,626 ... F 2 46
Bancroft, Ontario, 1,669 ... E 5 41
Banda, India, 27,070 ... D 3 29
Banda (sea), Indonesia ... H 7 31
Bandanaira, Indonesia ... H 6 31
Bandar (Masulipatnam), India, 59,146 ... D 5 29
Bandar 'Abbas, Iran, 15,233 ... J 7 27
Bandar Maharani, Malayan Fed., 32,228 ... D 7 30
Bandar Penggaram, Malayan Fed., 26,506 ... D 7 30
Bandeira (peak), Brazil ... M 8 46
Bandiagara, Sudanese Rep., 3,700 ... F 9 34
Bandirma, Turkey, 25,515 ... B 2 28
Bandjarmasin, Indonesia, 150,219 ... E 6 31
Bandra, India, 71,789 ... B 8 29
Bandung, Indonesia, 724,249 ... H 2 31
Banes, Cuba, 14,097 ... J 3 48
Banff, Alta, 2,518 ... G 4 40
Banff (park), Alta., 3,069 ... G 4 40
Bangalore, India, 778,977 ... C 6 29
Bangassou, Central Africa, 9,000 ... L10 34
Banggai, Indonesia ... G 6 31
Bangil, Indonesia, 20,236 ... K 2 31
Bangka (island), Indon., 230,000 ... D 6 31
Bangkahulu, Indonesia, 13,418 ... C 6 31
Bangkalan, Indonesia, 12,359 ... K 2 31
Bangkok,* Thailand, 827,290 ... D 4 30
Bangor, N. Ireland, 20,615 ... K 2 12
Bangor, Wales, 12,822 ... C 4 10
Bangú, Brazil, 5,626 ... M14 47
Bangued, Philippine Isls., 5,663 ... G 2 31
Bangui,* Central Africa, 41,100 ... K10 34
Bangui, Philippine Islands, 3,323 ... G 2 31
Bangweulu (lake), N. Rhodesia ... N14 35
Baní, Dominican Rep., 10,048 ... E 6 48
Bani (river), Sudanese Rep. ... E 9 34
Baniara, Papua ... C 7 31
Banja Luka, Yugoslavia, 37,770 ... C 3 21
Banjumas, Indonesia, 6,686 ... J 2 31
Banjuwangi, Indonesia, 25,185 ... L 2 31
Banks (islands), Canada ... D31 8
Banks (strait), Tas., Australia ... H 8 36
Bankstown, Australia, 102,384 ... L 3 36
Bankura, India, 46,617 ... E 4 29
Bann (river), Ireland ... H 2 12
Banningville, Belg. Congo, 3,947 ... K12 35
Bannu, Pakistan, 27,199 ... B 2 29
Bansberia, India, 23,716 ... E 1 29
Banská Bystrica, Czech., 18,806 ... E 2 20
Banská Stiavnica, Czech., 10,381 ... E 2 20
Banswara, India, 12,772 ... B 4 29
Bantry (bay), Ireland ... B 8 12
Bao Lac, Vietnam ... E 2 30
Bar-le-Duc, France, 14,015 ... F 3 16
Barabinsk, U.S.S.R. ... J 4 22
Baracoa, Cuba, 10,397 ... K 4 48
Baradero, Argentina, 10,194 ... N11 47
Barahona, Dom. Rep., 14,690 ... D 6 48
Baramati, India, 16,366 ... B 5 29
Baramula, Kash., 12,724 ... B 2 29
Baranagore, India, 54,451 ... E 1 29
Baranchinskiy, U.S.S.R., 9,500 ... P 6 23
Baranof (island), Alaska ... C 3 40
Baranovichi (Baranowicze), U.S.S.R., 58,000 ... D 4 22
Barasat, India, 11,230 ... E 1 29
Barbacena, Brazil, 24,718 ... M 8 46
Barbacoas, Colombia, 3,739 ... E 3 46
Barbados (island), West Indies, 192,841 ... G 4 45
Barbuda (island), West Indies, 979 ... G 3 45
Barcaldine, Australia, 1,705 ... G 4 36
Barce (El Marj), Libya, 8,000 ... L 5 34
Barcellona Pozzo di Gotto, Italy, 23,685 ... E 5 18
Barcelona, Spain, †1,276,675 ... H 2 17
Barcelona, Venezuela, 25,341 ... H 2 46
Barcelos, Brazil, 904 ... H 4 46
Barcelos, Portugal, 7,875 ... B 2 17
Barcoo (Cooper's Creek) (river), Australia ... F 5 36
Bardai, Chad ... K 7 34
Bardera, Somalia, 3,500 ... P11 35
Bardsey (island), Wales ... B 5 10
Bareilly, India, 208,083 ... C 3 29
Barents (sea) ... R 2 6
Barfrush (Babol), Iran, 36,590 ... H 2 27
Barguzin, U.S.S.R., 2,263 ... N 4 23
Bari, Italy, 264,744 ... F 4 18
Baria, Vietnam, 3,307 ... E 5 30
Barinas, Venezuela, 8,672 ... G 2 46
Barisal, Pakistan, 89,278 ... F 4 29
Barisan (mountains), Indonesia ... C 6 31
Barito (river), Indonesia ... E 6 31
Barkly East, Cape of Good Hope 2,483 ... M18 35
Barkol, China ... D 3 32
Bârlad, Rumania, 24,035 ... H 2 21
Barlee (lake), Australia ... C 5 36
Barletta, Italy, 63,692 ... F 4 18
Barmer, India, 12,051 ... B 3 29
Barnagore, India, 54,451 ... E 1 29
Barnaul, U.S.S.R., 320,000 ... K 4 22
Barnet, England, 25,019 ... G 6 10
Barnsley, England, 75,630 ... F 4 10
Barnstaple, England, 16,299 ... D 6 10
Barnstaple (bay), England ... C 6 10
Baroda, India, 211,407 ... B 4 29
Barotseland (region), N. Rhod. ... L14 35
Barpeta, India, 18,466 ... F 3 29
Barquisimeto, Venezuela, 105,108 ... F 2 46
Barra, Brazil, 5,737 ... M 6 46
Barra (islands), Scotland, 1,728 ... A 5 11
Barra do Corda, Brazil, 2,969 ... M 5 46
Barra Head (cape), Scotland ... A 6 11
Barraba, Australia, 1,521 ... J 6 36
Barrackpore, India, 59,717 ... E 1 29
Barranca, Peru, 3,873 ... E 4 46
Barrancabermeja, Colombia, 9,307 ... F 2 46
Barranquilla, Colombia, 276,199 ... F 1 46
Barraute, Quebec, 500 ... E 4 41
Barreiras, Brazil, 5,932 ... M 6 46
Barreiro, Portugal, 22,190 ... A 1 17
Barretos, Brazil, 23,683 ... L 8 46
Barrhead, Alta., 1,610 ... H 4 40
Barrhead, Scotland, 12,971 ... C 2 11
Barrie, Ontario, 16,851 ... E 5 41
Barrow (island), Australia ... A 4 36
Barrow (river), Ireland ... H 7 12
Barrow (strait), Canada ... D28 8
Barrow-in-Furness, England, 67,476 ... D 3 10
Barry, Wales, 40,990 ... D 6 10
Barry's Bay, Ont., 1,366 ... E 4 41
Barsi, India, 36,870 ... C 5 29
Bartica, Br. Guiana, 2,352 ... J 2 46
Bartin, Turkey, 10,057 ... E 2 28
Barus, Indonesia, 9,615 ... B 5 31
Barwani, India, 12,569 ... B 4 29
Barwon (river), Australia ... H 5 36
Basel, Switz., 183,543 ... E 1 19
Bashi (channel) ... K 7 32
Basim, India, 17,928 ... C 4 29
Basingstoke, England, 16,979 ... F 6 10
Basirhat, India, 26,348 ... E 4 29
Basra, Iraq, 93,889 ... E 5 27
Bass (strait), Australia ... H 7 36
Bassac, Laos ... E 4 30
Bassano, Alta., 753 ... H 4 40
Bassano del Grappa, Italy, 18,834 ... C 2 18
Basse-Terre,* Guad., 10,086 ... F 4 45
Bassein, Burma, 77,382 ... B 2 30
Basseterre,* St. Christopher, 12,194 ... F 3 45
Bastia, France, 24,356 ... G 6 16
Bastogne (Bastenaken), Belg., 5,854 ... H 9 15
Bat Yam, Israel, 18,250 ... B 3 24
Batala, India, 44,458 ... C 2 29
Batan (islands), Philippine Isls., 10,705 ... G 1 31
Batang, China ... E 5 32
Batang, Indonesia, 28,655 ... J 2 31
Batangas, Philippine Isls., 10,326 ... G 3 31
Batavia (Djakarta),* Indonesia, 2,800,000 ... H 1 31
Bath, England, 79,294 ... E 6 10
Bathgate, Scotland, 11,291 ... J 8 11
Bathurst, Australia, 16,089 ... H 6 36
Bathurst, Gambia, 19,602 ... C 9 34
Bathurst, N. B., 5,267 ... G 4 41
Bathurst (island), Australia ... D 2 36
Batley, England, 40,192 ... F 4 10
Batlow, Australia, 1,114 ... H 7 36
Battambang, Cambodia ... D 4 30
Batticaloa, Ceylon, 12,948 ... D 7 29
Battle Harbour, Lab., Newf., 106 ... K 3 41
Battleford, Saskatchewan, 1,498 ... J 4 40
Battonya, Hungary, 13,297 ... F 3 20
Batumi, U.S.S.R., 82,000 ... F 5 22
Baturadja, Indonesia, 2,955 ... C 6 31
Baturité, Brazil, 5,563 ... N 4 46
Baubau, Indonesia, 2,493 ... G 7 31
Bauchi, Nigeria, 10,000 ... H 9 34
Bauld (cape), Canada ... J 3 41
Bauru, Brazil, 53,126 ... L 8 46
Bautzen, Germany, 38,524 ... F 3 14
Bay Roberts, Newf., 1,306 ... K 4 41
Bayamo, Cuba, 20,245 ... H 4 48
Bayamón, P. R., 20,171 ... G 1 45
Baybay, Philippine Islands, 9,414 ... H 3 31
Bayburt, Turkey, 13,332 ... H 2 28
Bayeux, France, 9,077 ... C 3 16
Bayindir, Turkey, 10,693 ... B 3 28
Baykal (Baikal)(lake), U.S.S.R. ... M 4 23
Baykonur, U.S.S.R. ... H 5 22
Bayombong, Phil. Isls., 6,929 ... G 2 31
Bayonne, France, 26,897 ... C 6 16
Bayram-Ali, U.S.S.R. ... H 6 22
Bayreuth, Germany, 58,800 ... D 4 14
Baza, Spain, 14,071 ... E 4 17
Beachport, Australia, 382 ... F 7 36
Beachy Headland (prom.), Eng. ... H 7 10
Beardmore, Ontario, 450 ... C 4 41
Beatrice (cape), Australia ... F 2 36
Beaufort West, C. of G. Hope 10,882 ... L17 35
Beaune, France, 11,022 ... F 4 16
Beauséjour, Man., 1,523 ... L 4 40
Beauvais, France, 24,645 ... E 3 16
Beaver (river), Canada ... H 4 40
Beawar, India, 36,720 ... B 3 29
Bebedouro, Brazil, 11,642 ... L 8 46
Bečej, Yugoslavia, 22,923 ... E 3 21
Beckum, Germany, 17,551 ... C 3 14
Bedford, England, 53,075 ... G 5 10
Bedlington Station, Eng., 28,932 ... F 2 10
Bedworth, England, 24,932 ... F 5 10
Będzin, Poland, 38,800 ... C 4 24
Beer Tuvya, Israel, 1,119 ... B 4 24
Beersheeba, Israel, 32,000 ... D 4 24
Beeston and Stapleford, England, 49,849 ... F 5 10
Bega, Australia, 3,518 ... J 7 36
Begovat, U.S.S.R. ... P 1 23
Behbehan, Iran, 23,232 ... G 5 27
Behrens (river), Canada ... L 4 40
Beira, Mozambique, 42,539 ... O15 35
Beirut,* Lebanon, 183,738 ... F 6 28
Beit Dagon, Israel, 2,100 ... B 3 24
Beit Jala, Jordan, 3,710 ... C 4 24
Beit Lahm (Bethlehem), Jordan, 19,155 ... C 4 24
Beit Shean, Israel, 6,400 ... D 3 24
Beiuş, Rumania, 5,807 ... F 2 21
Beja, Portugal, 14,058 ... C 4 17
Békés, Hungary, 29,283 ... F 3 20
Békéscsaba, Hungary, 45,901 ... F 3 20
Bela Crkva, Yugoslavia, 9,373 ... E 3 21
Belawan, Indonesia ... B 5 31
Belaya (river), U.S.S.R. ... G 4 22
Belcher (islands), Canada ... D 2 41
Belebey, U.S.S.R., 11,320 ... G 4 22
Belém, Brazil, 225,218 ... L 4 46
Belet Uen, Somalia, 9,400 ... P11 34
Belfast,* N. Ireland, 443,670 ... J 2 12
Belfast (bay), N. Ireland ... K 2 12
Belfort, France, 41,197 ... G 4 16
Belgard (Bialogard), Poland, 16,700 ... B 2 24
Belgaum, India, 75,482 ... B 5 29
Belgorod, U.S.S.R., 71,000 ... E 4 22
Belgorod-Dnestrovskiy, U.S.S.R., 7,766 ... E 5 22
Belgrade,* Yugoslavia, 469,988 ... E 3 21
Belitung (Billiton) (island), Indonesia, 80,000 ... D 6 31
Belize,* Br. Honduras, 21,886 ... C 2 29
Bell (island), Canada, 11,724 ... J 3 41
Bell (river), Canada ... E 4 41
Bell Island, Newf., 7,873 ... K 4 41
Bell Ville, Argentina, 15,796 ... H10 47
Bella Coola, B. C., 350 ... E 4 40
Bellary, India, 56,148 ... C 5 29
Belle (island), Canada ... K 3 41
Belle-Île (island), France, 4,670 ... B 4 16
Belle Isle (strait), Canada ... J 3 41
Belleoram, Newfoundland, 570 ... J 4 41
Belleville, Ontario, 20,605 ... E 5 41
Bellinzona, Switz., 12,060 ... H 4 19
Belluno, Italy, 19,604 ... D 1 18
Bellville, Cape of G. Hope, 9,968 ... D19 35
Belmonte, Brazil, 5,204 ... N 7 46
Belo Horizonte, Brazil, 338,585 ... M 7 46
Belogorsk, U.S.S.R. ... O 4 23
Belomorsk, U.S.S.R. ... E 3 22
Beloretsk, U.S.S.R., 59,000 ... G 4 22
Belovo, U.S.S.R., 107,000 ... O 5 23
Beloye (lake), U.S.S.R. ... E 3 22
Belozersk, U.S.S.R., 6,990 ... E 4 22
Belper, England, 15,714 ... F 4 10
Belterra, Brazil, 3,602 ... K 4 46
Belyy, U.S.S.R., 6,882 ... E 4 22
Ben Lomond (mountain), Tas., Australia ... H 8 36
Ben More Assynt (mountain), Scotland ... G 3 11
Ben Nevis (mountain), Scotland ... F 6 11
Ben Thuy, Vietnam ... E 3 30
Ben Tre, Vietnam, 9,300 ... E 5 30
Benadir (region), Somalia ... P11 35
Benares (Varanasi), India, 355,777 ... D 3 29
Benbecula (island), Scotland, 924 ... A 5 11
Bender Kassim, Som., 3,000 ... R 9 34
Bendigo, Australia, †36,918 ... G 7 36
Bendorf, Germany, 11,980 ... B 3 14
Benei Beraq, Israel, 33,000 ... B 3 24
Benevento, Italy, 34,405 ... E 4 18
Bengal (bay) ... E 5 29
Benghazi,* Libya, 79,533 ... K 5 34
Bengkajang, Indonesia ... D 5 31
Bengkalis, Indonesia, 3,291 ... C 5 31
Bengkulu (Bangkahulu), Indon., 13,418 ... C 6 31
Benguela, Angola, 14,690 ... J14 35
Beni (river), Bolivia ... G 6 46
Beni-Abbès, Saoura, 3,268 ... F 5 34
Beni Suef, Egypt, 57,464 ... N 6 34
Beni Ulid, Libya, 30,000 ... J 5 34
Benin (bay), Nigeria ... G11 34
Benin City, Nigeria, 53,753 ... H10 34
Benito, Man., 406 ... K 4 40
Benoni, Transvaal, 74,176 ... M 7 35
Bensberg, Germany, 22,584 ... B 3 14
Bensheim, Germany, 22,279 ... C 4 14
Bentinck (island), Australia ... F 3 36
Benue (river), Nigeria ... H10 34
Beo, Indonesia ... H 5 31
Beograd (Belgrade),* Yugoslavia, 469,988 ... E 3 21
Beppu, Japan, 93,033 ... E 7 33
Berat, Albania, 11,872 ... D 5 21
Berber, Sudan, 16,550 ... N 8 34
Berbera, Som. Pr., 30,000 ... R 9 34
Berbérati, Cent. Afr. ... K11 34
Berchem-Ste. Agathe, Belgium, 47,104 ... F 6 15
Berchtesgaden, Germany, 5,752 ... E 5 14
Berck, France, 10,059 ... D 2 16
Berdichev, U.S.S.R., 53,000 ... D 5 22
Berdyansk, U.S.S.R., 65,000 ... E 5 22
Berens River, Man., 200 ... L 4 40
Berettyóújfalu, Hungary, 11,781 ... F 3 20
Berezniki, U.S.S.R., 106,000 ... G 4 22
Berezovskiy, U.S.S.R., 16,500 ... P 6 23
Berg (means mt.) (Ger. & Dutch)
Bergama, Turkey, 18,085 ... B 3 28
Bergamo, Italy, 95,651 ... B 2 18
Bergen (Mons), Belgium, 25,625 ... E 8 15
Bergen, Norway, 112,845 ... D 6 13
Bergen op Zoom, Neth., 33,855 ... E 5 15
Bergerac, France, 18,286 ... D 5 16
Bergisch Gladbach, Ger., 32,681 ... B 3 14
Berhampore, India, 41,558 ... E 4 29
Berhampur, India, 43,536 ... D 5 29
Bering (sea) ... U 4 23
Berlin,* East Germany, 3,350,785 ... E 2 14
Bermejo (river), Argentina ... H 9 47
Bermuda (islands), 40,450 ... G 2 45
Bern (Berne),* Switz., 146,499 ... D 3 19
Bernau, Germany, 12,984 ... K 3 14
Bernburg, Germany, 53,367 ... D 3 14
Berndorf, Austria, 9,486 ... C 3 20
Bernier (island), Australia ... A 4 36
Beroun, Czech., 15,473 ... B 2 20
Berthierville, Quebec, 3,504 ... F 4 41
Berwick, Nova Scotia, 1,134 ... G 4 41
Berwick-on-Tweed, Eng., 12,554 ... F 2 10

Place	Index Ref.	Plate No.
Berwyn (mountains), Wales	D 5	10
Besançon, France, 61,139	G 4	16
Beşiktaş, Turkey, 84,791	D 6	28
Besni, Turkey, 11,452	G 4	28
Bethanie, S. W. Africa, 625	K17	35
Bethlehem, Jordan, 19,155	C 4	24
Bethlehem, O. F. S., 13,532	M17	35
Béthune, France, 20,521	E 2	16
Bettegiri (Gadag), India, 56,283	C 5	29
Bettiah, India, 30,309	D 3	29
Betul, India, 11,841	C 4	29
Beuel, Germany, 24,730	B 3	14
Beuthen (Bytom), Poland, 93,179	B 4	24
Beverley, Australia, 852	B 2	36
Beverley, England, 15,504	G 4	10
Beverwijk, Neth., 24,009	F 4	15
Bexhill-on-Sea, England, 25,693	H 7	10
Beykoz, Turkey, 31,931	D 5	28
Beyoğlu (Pera), Turkey, 208,853	D 6	28
Béziers, France, 58,814	E 6	16
Bezwada (Vijayavada), India, 161,198	D 5	29
Bhadgaon, Nepal, 93,176	E 3	29
Bhadrakh, India, 19,550	E 4	29
Bhadravati, India, 19,585	C 6	29
Bhadreswar, India, 27,673	E 1	29
Bhagalpur, India, 114,530	E 4	29
Bhamo, Burma	C 1	30
Bhandara, India, 19,708	D 4	29
Bharatpur, India, 35,541	C 3	29
Bhatinda, India, 24,833	B 2	29
Bhatkal, India, 10,718	B 6	29
Bhatpara, India, 134,916	E 1	29
Bhavnagar, India, 137,951	B 4	29
Bhawani Patna, India, 10,863	D 5	29
Bhera, Pakistan, 16,632	B 2	29
Bhilsa, India, 14,472	C 4	29
Bhilwara, India, 15,169	B 3	29
Bhimavaram, India, 21,049	D 5	29
Bhiwandi, India, 18,776	B 5	29
Bhiwani, India, 43,921	C 3	29
Bhopal, India, 102,333	C 4	29
Bhuj, India, 26,331	A 4	29
Bhusaval, India, 36,352	C 4	29
Biafra (bay), Africa	H11	35
Biała Podlaska, Poland, 16,700	F 2	24
Białogard (Belgard), Poland, 16,700	B 2	24
Białystok, Poland, 103,600	F 2	24
Biancavilla, Italy, 17,770	E 6	18
Biarritz, France, 21,542	C 6	16
Bibai, Japan, 88,667	L 2	33
Biberach, Germany, 14,984	C 4	14
Bic, Quebec, 1,142	G 4	41
Bida, Nigeria, 50,000	H10	34
Bidar, India, 20,514	C 5	29
Bidh, India, 15,222	C 5	29
Biel (Bienne), Switz., 49,342	D 2	19
Bielawa, Poland, 25,700	C 3	24
Bielefeld, Germany, 153,613	C 2	14
Biella, Italy, 39,438	B 2	18
Bielsko-Biała, Poland, 68,800	D 4	24
Bien Hoa, Vietnam, 6,690	E 5	30
Bienfait, Sask., 802	K 5	40
Bienne (Biel), Switz., 49,342	D 2	19
Big Beaver, Saskatchewan, 100	J 5	40
Big Bell, Australia, 854	B 5	36
Big River, Saskatchewan, 904	J 4	40
Biga, Turkey, 8,767	B 2	28
Biggar, Saskatchewan, 2,424	J 4	40
Bighorn (mountains), U. S.	G 3	42
Bighorn (river), U. S.	G 3	42
Bihać, Yugoslavia, 8,330	B 3	21
Bihar, India, 54,551	E 3	29
Bijapur, India, 48,968	C 5	29
Bijar, Iran, 7,920	E 3	27
Bijeljina, Yugoslavia, 15,614	D 3	21
Bijnor, India, 27,900	C 3	29
Bikaner, India, 117,113	B 3	29
Bikini (island), Pacific	G 4	37
Bilaspur, India, 37,460	D 4	29
Bilbao, Spain, 212,974	E 1	17
Bilimbay, U.S.S.R., 4,435	P 6	23
Billericay, England, 43,352	H 6	10
Billiton (Belitung) (island), Indonesia, 80,000	D 6	31
Bilma, Niger, 1,100	J 8	34
Bilston, England, 33,458	E 5	10
Bimlipatam, India, 9,914	D 5	29
Bindjai, Indonesia, 9,176	B 5	31
Bingara, Australia, 1,465	H 5	36
Bingen, Germany, 16,803	B 4	14
Bingerville, Ivory Coast, 700	F10	34
Bingöl (Çapakçur), Turkey, 7,114	J 3	28
Binh Dinh, Vietnam, 75,000	F 4	30
Bintuhan, Indon., 1,918	C 6	31
Binyamina, Israel, 3,269	B 2	24
Biograd, Yugoslavia, 8,668	B 4	24
Bir (Bidh), India, 15,222	C 5	29
Bir (means well) (Arab.)		
Bira, U.S.S.R., 2,092	P 5	23
Bird (isl.), Australia	K 4	36
Birecik, Turkey, 10,421	G 4	28
Birjand, Iran, 14,504	L 4	27
Birkenhead, England, 142,501	D 4	10
Birmingham, England, 1,112,685	F 5	10
Birobidzhan, U.S.S.R., 41,000	P 5	23
Birsk, U.S.S.R., 17,500	G 4	22
Birtle, Man., 806	K 4	40
Biryulevo, U.S.S.R., 2,018	C 4	22
Biscay (bay)	B 5	16
Bisceglie, Italy, 38,151	F 4	18
Bischofshofen, Austria, 7,923	B 3	20
Biscotasing, Ontario, 200	D 4	41
Bisert', U.S.S.R., 8,080	P 6	23
Bishop Auckland, England, 36,351	F 3	10
Bishops Falls, Newf., 2,522	K 4	41
Biskra, Algeria, 52,511	H 5	34
Bislig, Philippine Isls., 1,086	H 4	31
Bismarck (archipelago), Terr. N.G., 145,000	E 6	37
Bissagos (isls.), Port Guinea, 9,314	C 9	34
Bissau,* Port Guinea, 6,000	D 9	34
Bissett, Manitoba, 250	L 4	40
Bistrița, Rumania, 15.801	G 2	21
Bitlis, Turkey, 14,022	J 3	28
Bitola (Bitolj), Yugo., 31,131	E 5	21
Bitonto, Italy, 35,122	F 4	18
Bitterfeld, Germany, 32,833	E 3	14
Bitterroot (mt. range), U.S.	E 3	42
Biwa (lake), Japan	H 6	33
Biysk, U.S.S.R., 146,000	K 4	22
Bizerte, Tunisia, 39,327	J 4	34
Bjelovar, Yugoslavia, 13,147	C 3	21
Björneborg (Pori), Finland, 50,417	M 6	13
Black (hills), United States	H 3	42
Black (sea)	H 4	9
Black (Schwarzwald) (forest), Germany	C 5	14
Black Diamond, Alberta, 991	H 4	40
Black River, Jamaica, 1,263	B 3	45
Black Rock (desert), U.S.	D 4	42
Black Volta (river), Africa	F 9	34
Blackall, Australia, 1,885	G 4	36
Blackburn, England, 111,218	E 4	10
Blackpool, England, 147,184	D 4	10
Blacktown, Australia, 25,417	K 3	36
Blackwater (river), Ireland	D 7	12
Blagodarnoye, U.S.S.R.,12,209	F 5	22
Blagoveshchensk, U.S.S.R., 94,000	O 4	23
Blagoyevgrad, Bulgaria, 14,066	F 5	21
Blaine Lake, Saskatchewan, 638	J 4	40
Blair Athol, Australia, 532	H 4	36
Blairmore, Alberta, 1,973	H 5	40
Blaj, Rumania, 6,641	G 2	21
Blanc (cape), Africa	C 7	34
Blanc (mountain), France	G 5	16
Blanca Peak (mountain), U.S.	G 6	42
Blanco (cape), U.S.	B 4	42
Blankenburg, Germany, 18,445	D 3	14
Blantyre and Limbe, Nyas. Pr., 24,380	N15	35
Blasket (isls.), Ireland	A 7	12
Blaydon-on-Tyne, England, 30,764	F 3	10
Blaze (point), Australia	D 2	36
Blenheim, New Zealand, 9,219	L 6	36
Blida, Algeria, 30,170	G 4	34
Blind River, Ontario, 3,633	D 4	41
Blitar, Indonesia, 27,846	K 2	31
Bloemfontein,* O.F.S., †100,180	L17	35
Blois, France, 24,352	D 4	16
Bloody Foreland (prom.), Ireland	D 1	12
Blora, Indonesia, 18,451	K 2	31
Bludenz, Austria, 10,130	B 4	20
Blue Mountains, Aust., †23,089	J 6	36
Blue (mountains), U.S.	D 3	42
Blue Mud (bay), Australia	F 2	36
Blue Nile (river), Africa	N 9	34
Blue River, Br. Columbia, 500	G 4	40
Bluefields, Nicaragua, 7,463	F 4	39
Bluff, New Zealand, 2,693	L 7	36
Blumenau, Brazil, 22,919	L 9	47
Blyth, England, 34,747	F 2	10
Bôa Vista, Brazil, 5,132	H 3	46
Bobbili, India, 22,090	D 5	29
Bobo-Dioulasso, Upper Volta, 38,000	F 9	34
Bobruysk, U.S.S.R., 97,000	D 4	22
Bôca do Acre, Brazil, 1,723	G 5	46
Bochnia, Poland, 11,700	E 4	24
Bocholt, Germany, 37,674	B 3	14
Bochum, Germany, 289,804	G 4	14
Bodaybo, U.S.S.R.	N 4	23
Bodenbach (Podmokly), Czech., 21,134	C 1	20
Bodensee (Constance) (lake)	H 1	19
Bodhan, India, 19,443	C 5	29
Bodinayakkanur, India, 28,435	C 7	29
Bodjonegoro, Indonesia, 19,784	J 2	31
Bodö, Norway, 6,344	J 3	13
Bogazi (means strait) (Turk.)		
Boggeragh (mountains), Ireland	D 7	12
Bogia, Terr. N. G.	B 6	31
Bognor Regis, England, 25,647	G 7	10
Bogor, Indonesia, 104,213	H 2	31
Bogotá,* Colombia, 638,532	F 3	46
Bogra, Pakistan, 24,996	E 4	29
Boguchar, U.S.S.R., 7,958	E 4	22
Bohemian (forest), Czech.	B 2	20
Boileau (cape), Australia	C 3	36
Bois (lake), Canada	F 1	40
Boissevain, Manitoba, 1,115	L 5	40
Bojador (cape), Sp. Sahara	C 6	34
Boké, Guinea, 3,600	D 9	34
Bolama, Port. Guinea, 4,895	D 9	34
Bolangir, India, 11,105	D 4	29
Bolbeck, France, 10,238	D 3	16
Bolesławiec, Poland, 18,300	B 3	24
Bolívar, Argentina, 14,010	H11	44
Bolívar, Colombia, 2,495	E 3	46
Bolívar (peak), Venezuela	F 2	46
Bolligen, Switz., 9,841	E 3	19
Bologna, Italy, 323,219	C 2	18
Bologoye, U.S.S.R., 10,863	E 4	22
Bol'shevik (island), U.S.S.R.	M 2	23
Bolsón de Mapimí (dep.) Mexico	G 3	44
Bolton, England, 167,167	E 4	10
Bolu, Turkey, 11,884	D 2	28
Bolus Head (cape), Ireland	A 8	12
Bolvadin, Turkey, 12,604	D 3	28
Bolzano, Italy, 67,859	C 1	18
Boma, Belg. Congo, 10,677	J13	35
Bombala, Australia, 1,258	H 7	36
Bombay, India, 2,839,270	B 8	29
Bomu (river), Belg. Congo	L11	34
Bonaire (island), Neth. Antilles, 5,356	C 1	46
Bonaventure, Que., 2,500	G 4	41
Bonavista, Newfoundland, 4,000	K 4	41
Bondoukou, Ivory Coast, 5,489	F10	34
Bondowoso, Indonesia, 18,751	L 2	31
Bondy, France, 19,473	B 1	16
Bône, Algeria, 88,920	H 4	34
Bong Son, Vietnam	F 4	30
Bonin-Volcano (islands), Pacific, 146	E 3	37
Bonn,* West Germany, 111,287	B 3	14
Bonne Bay, Newfoundland, 800	J 4	41
Bonnyville, Alberta, 1,495	H 4	40
Bonthain, Indonesia, 6,711	F 7	31
Bontoc, Philippine Isls., 4,471	G 2	31
Boom, Belgium, 18,292	E 6	15
Boothia (gulf), Canada	E27	8
Boothia (peninsula), Canada	D28	8
Bootle, England, 74,302	D 4	10
Bor, Turkey, 12,235	F 4	28
Bor, Yugoslavia, 12,261	E 3	21
Borah Peak (mountain), U.S.	E 3	42
Borås, Sweden, 58,076	H 8	13
Borazjun, Iran, 8,744	G 6	27
Borba, Brazil, 1,030	J 4	46
Bordeaux, France, 250,306	C 5	16
Bordertown, Australia, 1,315	G 7	36
Borgerhout, Belgium, 50,118	E 6	15
Borisoglebsk, U.S.S.R., 54,000	F 4	22
Borisov, U.S.S.R., 59,000	D 4	22
Borlänge, Sweden, 21,614	J 6	13
Bornholm (island), Denmark 47,185	J 9	13
Borovichi, U.S.S.R., 28,400	E 4	22
Borovskoye, U.S.S.R., 5,149	O 1	23
Bosanska Gradiška, Yugo., 5,573	C 3	21
Bosporus (Karadeniz) (strait), Turkey	C 2	28
Boston, England, 24,454	H 5	10
Botany, Australia, 29,491	L 3	36
Bothnia (gulf)	N 4	13
Botoşani, Rumania, 29,145	H 2	21
Bottrop, Germany, 93,268	G 4	14
Botucatu, Brazil, 23,692	L 8	47
Botwood, Newfoundland, 2,744	J 4	41
Bouaké, Ivory Coast, 22,200	F10	34
Boucaut (bay), Australia	E 2	36
Bougainville (cape), Australia	D 2	36
Bougainville (island), Australia	H 3	36
Bougainville (island), Territory N.G., 37,000	F 6	37
Bougie, Algeria, 21,011	G 4	34
Bougouni, Sudanese Rep., 2,265	E 9	34
Boulder, Australia, 6,279	C 6	36
Boulia, Australia, 179	G 4	36
Boulogne-Billancourt, France, 78,925	A 2	16
Boulogne-sur-Mer, France, 34,389	D 2	16
Boultoum, Niger, 1,700	H 9	34
Boundary Peak (mountain), U.S.	D 5	42
Bourem, Sudanese Rep., 1,732	G 8	34
Bourg, France, 21,169	F 4	16
Bourges, France, 45,372	E 4	16
Bourke, Australia, 2,642	H 6	36
Bourlamaque, Quebec, 3,018	E 4	41
Bournemouth, England, 144,845	F 7	10
Boutilimit, Mauritania, 35,000	C 8	34
Bow (river) Canada	H 4	40
Bow Island, Alberta, 1,001	H 5	40
Bowen, Australia, 3,571	H 3	36
Bowling Green (cape), Australia	H 3	36
Boyne (river), Ireland	J 4	12
Bozen (Bolzano), Italy, 67,859	C 1	18
Bozüyük, Turkey, 8,227	C 3	28
Bra, Italy, 12,135	A 2	18
Bracebridge, Ontario, 2,849	D 4	41
Brackwede, Germany, 21,486	C 3	14
Bradford, England, 292,403	F 4	10
Braga, Portugal, 32,153	B 2	17
Bragado, Argentina, 16,104	M12	47
Bragança, Brazil, 5,580	L 4	46
Bragança, Portugal, 8,250	C 2	17
Brahmaputra (river)	F 3	29
Braich-y-pwll (cape), Wales	B 5	10
Brăila, Rumania, 95,514	H 3	21
Braintree, England, 10,048	H 6	10
Brake, Germany, 15,641	C 2	14
Bralorne, Br. Columbia, 500	F 4	40
Branco (river), Brazil	H 3	46
Brandenburg, Germany, 70,632	E 2	14
Brandon (mountain), Ireland	A 7	12
Brandon, Manitoba, 24,796	K 5	40
Brandon and Byshottles, England, 19,749	F 3	10
Brandvlei, Cape of G. H., 994	E19	35
Brantford, Ontario, 51,869	D 5	41
Brasília,* Brazil	L 7	46
Braşov (Stalin), Rumania, 82,984	G 3	21
Bratislava, Czech., 246,695	D 2	20
Bratsk, U.S.S.R., 51,000	M 4	23
Braunau, Austria, 11,559	B 2	20
Braunschweig (Brunswick), Germany, 223,760	D 2	14
Brava (Barawa), Somalia, 6,100	P11	35
Bravo (river), Mexico	H 2	44
Bray (Brí Chualann), Ireland, 10,856	K 6	12
Brazos (river), U.S.	J 7	42
Brazzaville,* Congo, 63,023	K12	35
Brčko, Yugoslavia, 9,305	D 3	21
Brebes, Indonesia, 13,707	H 2	31
Brecon Beacons (mt.), Wales	D 6	16
Breda, Netherlands, 101,781	F 5	15
Bregenz, Austria, 20,318	A 3	20
Breidha (fiord) Iceland	B 2	9
Brejo, Brazil, 2,635	M 4	46
Bremen, Germany, 499,780	C 2	14
Bremerhaven, Germany, 114,070	C 2	14
Brentwood, England, 18,160	H 6	10
Brescia, Italy, 126,507	C 2	18
Breslau (Wrocław), Poland, 387,900	C 3	24
Bressay (island), Scotland, 335	N 3	11
Brest, France, 100,733	A 3	16
Brest (Brześć-nad-Bugiem), U.S.S.R., 73,000	D 4	22
Brewarrina, Australia, 905	H 5	36
Brí Chualann (Bray), Ireland, 10,856	K 5	12
Bridgend, Wales, 13,646	D 6	10
Bridgetown,* Barbados, 13,345	G 4	45
Bridgewater, Nova Scotia, 4,445	H 5	41
Bridgwater, England, 22,202	D 6	10
Bridlington, England, 24,661	G 3	10
Bridlington (bay), England	G 3	10
Brighouse, England, 30,587	F 4	10
Bright, Australia, 803	H 7	36
Brighton, Australia, 13,018	D 8	36
Brighton, Australia, 40,458	L 2	36
Brighton, England, 156,486	G 7	10
Brijnagar, India, 11,549	C 4	29
Brindisi, Italy, 53,437	G 4	18
Brisbane, Australia, †502,320	J 5	36
Bristol, England, 442,994	E 6	10
Bristol (channel), England	C 6	10
Britstown, Cape of G. H., 2,103	L18	35
Britt, Ontario, 225	D 4	41
Brive-la-Gaillarde, France, 32,041	D 5	16
Brno (Brünn), Czech., 306,371	D 2	20
Broach, India, 55,810	B 4	29
Broad (sound), Australia	H 4	36
Broad Arrow, Australia, 82	C 6	36
Broadstairs-Saint Peter's, Eng., 15,082	J 6	10
Brockville, Ontario, 13,885	E 5	41
Brod, Yugoslavia, 21,547	D 3	21
Brodeur (peninsula), Canada	D27	8
Brodnica, Poland, 13,600	D 2	24
Broken Hill, Australia, †31,451	G 6	36
Broken Hill, N. Rhodesia, †6,472	M14	35
Bromberg (Bydgoszcz), Poland, 210,900	D 2	24
Bromma, Sweden, 72,293	H 1	13
Bromsgrove, England, 27,918	E 5	10
Bronnitsy, U.S.S.R., 3,797	C 4	22
Bronte, Italy, 19,202	E 6	18
Brooks, Alberta, 2,320	H 4	40
Brooks (mtn. range), U.S.	F 7	42
Brookton, Australia, 685	B 2	36
Broome, Australia, 1,095	C 3	36

Index Plate
Ref. No.

Browse (island), Australia....C 2 36
Bruay, France, 31,664....E 2 16
Bruce (mountain), Australia....B 4 36
Bruce Mines, Ontario, 451....D 4 41
Bruchsal, Germany, 16,282....C 4 14
Bruck an der Mur, Austria, 14,709....C 3 20
Bruges (Brugge), Belg., 52,098....C 6 15
Brühl, Germany, 29,791....B 3 14
Brumado, Brazil, 3,098....M 6 46
Brunei,* Brunei, 10,619....E 4 31
Brunswick (bay), Australia....C 3 36
Brunswick (Braunschweig), Germany, 223,760....D 2 14
Brussels,* Belgium, 172,009....C19 15
Brussels, Greater, Belgium, 1,371,816....C 9 15
Brux (Most), Czech., 35,770....B 1 20
Bruxelles (Brussels),* Belgium, 172,009....C 9 15
Bryansky, U.S.S.R, 206,000....E 4 22
Brzeg, Poland, 20,300....C 3 24
Bucaramanga, Colombia, 102,887...F 2 46
Buccaneer (arch.), Australia....C 3 36
Buchan Ness (prom.) Scotland....N 5 11
Buchans, Newfoundland, 1,800....J 4 41
Bucharest (București),* Rumania, 1,041,807....G 3 21
Buckhaven and Methil, Scotland, 20,152....L 7 11
Buckingham, Quebec, 6,781....E 4 41
Buckleboo, Australia, 118....F 6 36
București (Bucharest),* Rumania, 1,041,807....G 3 21
Budapest,* Hungary, 1,058,288....E 3 20
Budaun, India, 52,077....C 3 29
Budennovsk (Prikumsk), U.S.S.R., 15,776....F 5 22
Budge-Budge, India, 32,394....D 2 29
Budszentmilhály, Hungary, 12,008....F 3 20
Budweis (České Budějovice), Czech., 64,104....C 2 20
Buea,* So. Cameroons (Br. Trust), 3,000....H11 34
Buenaventura, Colombia, 35,087....E 3 46
Buenos Aires,* Argentina, 2,982,580....O11 47
Buenos Aires (lake), S. A. F13 47
Bug (river)....F 3 24
Buga, Colombia, 19,595....E 3 46
Bugle Ranges, Australia, 67....E 8 36
Bugul'ma, U.S.S.R., 61,000....G 4 22
Buguruslan, U.S.S.R., 17,646....G 4 22
Buhuși, Rumania, 8,198....H 2 21
Buitenzorg (Bogor), Indonesia, 104,213....H 2 31
Bujalance, Spain, 14,589....D 4 17
Bujnurd, Iran, 19,432....K 2 27
Bukama, Belgian Congo, 300....M13 35
Bukavu, B. Congo, 26,792....M12 35
Bukhara, U.S.S.R., 69,000....H 6 22
Bukittinggi, Indonesia, 14,657....B 6 31
Bukoba, Tan. Terr., 2,500....N12 35
Bula, Indonesia....J 6 31
Bulagan, Mong. Rep., 10,000....F 2 32
Bulawayo, S. Rhodesia, †92,168....M16 35
Buldan, Turkey, 10,287....C 3 28
Bulli, Australia, 3,997....L 4 36
Bulloo (lake), Australia....G 5 36
Bulloo (river), Australia....G 5 36
Bulo Burti, Somalia, 3,000....P11 34
Bulolo, Terr. New Guinea, 1,689...B 7 31
Bulun, U.S.S.R. ....O 2 23
Bulun Tokhoi, China....C 2 32
Bumba, Belgian Congo, 3,531....L11 35
Bumiaju, Indonesia, 9,879....H 2 31
Bumthang,* Bhutan....F 3 29
Buna, Papua....C 7 31
Bunbury, Australia, 9,869....A 6 36
Bundaberg, Australia, 19,951....J 5 36
Bundi, India, 20,846....C 3 29
Bungo (strait), Japan....F 7 33
Buraida, Saudi Arabia, 30,000....D 4 26
Burao, Som. Prot., 10,000....R10 34
Burdur, Turkey, 19,235....D 4 28
Burdwan, India, 62,910....E 4 29
Burg, Germany, 27,088....E 2 14
Burgas, Bulgaria, 43,684....H 4 21
Burgdorf, Switzerland, 11,586....E 2 19
Burgeo, Newfoundland, 1,138....J 4 41
Burgos, Spain, †61,789....E 1 17
Burgsteinfurt, Germany, 11,837....B 2 14
Burhanpur, India, 53,987....C 4 29
Burin, Newfoundland, 796....J 4 41
Buriram, Thai., 6,581....D 4 30
Burketown, Australia, 79....F 3 36
Burks Falls, Ontario, 902....E 4 41
Burnie, Australia, 11,193....H 8 36
Burnley, England, 84,987....E 4 10
Burns Lake, Br. Colombia, 1,016..E 4 40
Burriana, Spain, 15,472....G 3 17
Bursa, Turkey, 131,336....C 2 28
Burton-on-Trent, England, 49,167....F 5 10
Buru (island), Indonesia, 19,625..H 6 31
Burujird, Iran, 47,055....F 4 27
Bury, England, 50,838....E 4 10
Bury Saint Edmunds, England, 20,033....H 5 10
Bushire, Iran, 24,799....G 6 27
Busselton, Australia, 2,449....A 6 36
Bussum, Neth., 38,064....G 4 15
Busto Arsizio, Italy, 50,356....B 2 18
Buta, Belg. Congo, 11,261....M11 35
Butiaba, Uganda, 624....N11 35
Butt of Lewis (prom.) Scotland..C 2 11
Butterworth, Mal. Fed., 13,450....D 6 30
Butuan, Philippine Islands, 9,162.H 4 31
Buvaydy, U.S.S.R., 2,274....T 2 23
Buxton, England, 19,568....F 4 10
Buy, U.S.S.R. ....F 4 22
Buynaksk, U.S.S.R., 10,923....F 5 22
Büyükada (Prinkipo), Turkey, 16,347....D 6 28
Buzău, Rumania, 43,365....H 3 21
Buzuluk, U.S.S.R., 55,000....G 4 22
Byala Slatina, Bulgaria, 9,357....F 4 21
Bydgoszcz (Bromberg), Poland, 210,900....D 2 24
Bylot (island), Canada....D26 8
Byrock, Australia, 89....H 6 36
Byron (cape), Australia....J 5 36
Bystrzyca-Kłodzka, Poland, 9,564.C 3 24
Bytom, Poland, 179,200....B 4 24

C

Ca Mau, Vietnam....E 5 30
Ca Mau (point), Vietnam....E 5 30
Cabaiguán, Cuba, 9,853....F 3 48
Cabantuan, Philippine Is., 15,691.G 2 31
Cabinda, Angola, 46,284....J13 35
Cabo (means cape) (Sp. & Port.)
Cabo Juby (Tarfaya), Morocco, 2,000....D 6 34
Cabot (strait), Canada....H 4 41
Cabra, Spain, 15,026....D 4 17
Cabri, Saskatchewan, 627....J 4 40
Čačak, Yugoslavia, 18,050....E 4 21
Cáceres, Spain, 45,429....C 3 17
Cachoeira do Sul, Brazil, 23,827..K10 47
Cachoeiro de Itapemirim, Brazil, 24,611....N 8 46
Cader Idris (mountain), Wales....D 5 10
Cadillac, Quebec, 1,281....E 4 41
Cádiz, Spain, 100,249....C 4 17
Cádiz (gulf), Spain....C 4 17
Cadomin, Alberta, 800....G 4 40
Caen, France, 62,887....C 3 16
Caernarvon (bay), Wales....C 4 10
Caerphilly, Wales, 35,189....D 6 10
Caetité, Brazil, 3,778....M 6 46
Cagayan, Philippine Is., 15,159....G 4 31
Cagliari, Italy, 135,658....B 5 18
Caguas, P. R., 33,733....G 1 45
Caha (mountains), Ireland....B 8 12
Cahors, France, 12,706....D 5 16
Cahul (Kagul), U.S.S.R., 7,375....D 5 22
Caibarién, Cuba, 21,382....F 2 48
Cairn Gorm (mountain), Scotland.J 5 11
Cairns, Australia, †21,020....H 3 36
Cairo (El Qahira),* U.A.R., 2,100,506....N 5 34
Cajamarca, Peru, 14,290....E 5 46
Cajazeiras, Brazil, 9,832....N 5 46
Calabar, Nigeria, 15,000....H10 34
Calabozo, Venezuela, 4,257....G 2 46
Călafat, Rumania, 8,251....F 3 21
Calahorra, Spain, 13,003....E 1 17
Calais, France, 60,160....D 2 16
Calama, Chile, 12,955....G 8 46
Calamar, Colombia, 6,934....F 1 46
Calapan, Philippine Is., 6,113....G 3 31
Călărași, Rumania, 24,448....H 3 21
Calatayud, Spain, 15,234....F 2 17
Calcutta. India, 2,548,677....E 2 29
Caldas da Rainha, Port., 10,039...B 3 17
Caledon, Cape of G. H., 3,249....E20 35
Calf of Man (island)....B 3 10
Calgary, Alberta, 181,780....H 4 40
Calgary, Greater, Alta., 196,152....H 4 40
Cali, Colombia, 241,357....E 3 46
Calicut (Kozhikode), India, 158,724....C 6 29
California (gulf), Mexico....D 3 44
Callander, Ontario, 750....E 4 41
Callao, Peru, 84,438....E 6 46
Callington, Australia, 157....E 8 36
Caltagirone, Italy, 35,976....E 6 18
Caltanissetta, Italy, 47,610....D 6 18
Caluire, France, 16,846....F 5 16
Calvinia, Cape of G. H., 4,123....K18 35
Camagüey, Cuba, †204,254....G 3 48
Camaná, Peru, 2,253....F 7 46
Camargo, Mexico, 11,945....G 3 44
Cambay, India, 34,941....B 4 29
Cambay (gulf), India....B 4 29
Camberwell, Australia, 90,391....L 2 36
Camborne, England, 13,949....B 7 10
Cambrai, France, 28,230....E 2 16
Cambridge, England, 81,500....H 5 10
Camden, Australia, 4,847....K 4 36
Cametá, Brazil, 3,630....K 4 46
Camiri, Bolivia, 4,969....H 8 46
Camocim, Brazil, 8,299....M 4 46
Camooweal, Australia 178....F 4 36
Campana, Argentina, 14,452....N11 47
Campbell River, Br. C., 3,069....E 4 40
Campbellford, Ontario, 3,425....E 5 41
Campbellpur, Pakistan, 17,671....B 2 29
Campbellton, N.B., 8,389....G 4 41
Campbelltown, Austrailia, 9,690....L 3 36
Campeche, Mexico, 31,274....O 7 44
Campeche (gulf), Mexico....M 7 44
Câmpina, Rumania, 16,963....H 3 21
Campina Grande, Brazil, 73,835....N 5 46
Campinas, Brazil, 99,156....L 8 47
Campo de Criptana, Spain, 14,863.E 3 17
Campo Grande, Brazil, 31,708....K 8 46
Campo Maior, Portugal, 8,086....C 3 17
Campobasso, Italy, 22,635....E 4 18
Campos, Brazil, 61,633....M 8 46
Câmpulung, Rumania, 18,174....G 3 21
Câmpulung-Moldovenesc, Rumania, 11,041....G 2 21
Camrose, Alberta, 5,870....H 4 40
Can Tho, Vietnam, 22,186....E 5 30
Cañada de Gómez, Argentina, 12,353....H10 47
Canadian (river), U.S. ....H 6 42
Çanakkale, Turkey, 16,074....B 6 28
Cananea, Mexico, 17,892....D 1 44
Canary (Canarias) (islands), Spain, 793,328....B 5 17
Canaveral (cape), U.S. ....N 7 43
Canberra,* Australia, †28,277....H 7 36
Candia (Hērákleion), Greece, 51,144....G 8 21
Canea (Khaniá), Greece, 33,211....G 8 21
Canelones, Uruguay, 27,000....J10 47
Cañete, Peru, 4,794....E 6 46
Canicatti, Italy, 30,239....E 6 18
Çankiri, Turkey, 18,084....E 2 28
Canmore, Alberta, 754....G 4 40
Canna (island), Scotland, 8....C 5 11
Cannanore, India, 34,649....B 6 29
Cannes, France, 40,540....G 6 16
Cannock, England, 40,917....E 5 10
Canora, Saskatchewan, 1,783....K 4 40
Canosa di Puglia, Italy, 34,044....E 4 18
Canso, Nova Scotia, 1,261....H 4 41
Cantabrian (Cantábrica) (mt. range), Spain....D 1 17
Canterbury, England, 27,795....J 6 10
Canton, China, 1,598,900....H 7 32
Canton (island), Pacific, 61....J 6 37
Cantù, Italy, 18,759....B 2 18
Canuelas, Argentina, 5,614....O12 47
Canutama, Brazil, 947....H 5 46
Cao Bang, Vietnam....E 2 30
Cap-Chat, Quebec, 1,954....G 4 41
Cap-Haïtien, Haiti, 24,957....C 5 48
Cap Saint Jacques (Vung Tau), Vietnam, 8,935....E 5 30
Çapakçur (Bingöl), Turkey, 7,114..J 3 28
Cape Breton (island), Canada, 154,674....J 4 41
Cape Coast, Ghana, 23,206....F11 34
Cape Town,* U.of S. Afr., †577,211....C19 35
Capilla del Señor, Argentina, 3,521....N11 47
Capiz, Philippine Is., 11,673....G 3 31
Capreol, Ontario, 2,394....D 4 41
Caprivi Strip (region), S.W. Afr. ..L15 35
Capua, Italy, 14,380....E 4 18
Caquetá (river), Colombia....F 3 46
Carabanchel Bajo, Spain, 13,002...F 4 17
Carabelas, Argentina, 3,024....M11 47
Caracal, Rumania, 17,892....G 3 21
Caracas,* Venezuela, 495,064....G 1 46
Carangola, Brazil, 9,339....M 8 46
Caransebeș, Rumania, 10,106....F 3 21
Caraquet, New Brunswick, 1,500..H 4 41
Caratinga, Brazil, 13,149....M 7 46
Carauarí, Brazil, 651....G 4 46
Caravelas, Brazil, 2,726....N 7 46
Carberry, Manitoba, 1,065....L 5 40
Carbonear, Newfoundland, 3,955...K 4 41
Carbonia, Italy, 41,187....B 5 18
Carcagente, Spain, 15,117....F 3 17
Carcassonne, France, 31,305....D 6 16
Carcross, Yukon, 150....C 2 40
Cárdenas, Cuba, 37,059....D 1 48
Cárdenas, Mexico, 11,160....K 6 44
Cardiff, Wales, 243,632....E 6 10
Cardigan (bay), Wales....C 5 10
Cardston, Alberta, 2,607....H 5 40
Cardwell, Australia, 320....H 3 36
Carei, Rumania, 15,425....F 2 21
Caribbean (sea)....C 4 45
Caribou (mountains), Canada....F 4 40
Carini, Italy, 16,115....D 5 18
Carleton Place, Ontario, 4,790....E 4 41
Carlingford (bay), N. Ireland....J 3 12
Carlisle, England, 67,798....D 3 10
Carlow, Ireland, 7,465....H 6 12
Carlsbad (Karlovy Vary), Czech., 42,639....B 1 20
Carlton, England, 34,248....G 5 10
Carlyle, Saskatchewan, 829....K 5 40
Carmacks, Yukon, 15....C 2 40
Carman, Manitoba, 1,884....L 5 40
Carmarthen, Wales, 12,114....C 6 10
Carmarthen (bay), Wales....C 6 10
Carmaux, France, 9,648....E 5 16
Carmelo, Uruguay, 12,000....J10 47
Carmen, Mexico, 11,603....N 7 44
Carmen de Areco, Argentina, 4,411....N11 47
Carmen de Patagones, Arg., 5,423.H12 47
Carmona (Uige), Angola, 1,474....K13 35
Carmona, Spain, 21,498....D 4 17
Carnarvon, Australia, 1,453....A 4 36
Carnarvon, Cape of G.H., 2,895....L18 35
Carnduff, Saskatchewan, 823....K 5 40
Carnsore (point), Ireland....J 7 12
Carolina, Brazil, 4,861....L 5 46
Caroline (isls.), Pacific, 36,980....E 5 37
Carora, Venezuela, 13,699....F 1 46
Carpathos (Karpáthos) (island), Greece, 7,416....H 8 21
Carpentras, France, 11,044....F 5 16
Carpi, Italy, 20,363....C 2 18
Carrara, Italy, 27,225....C 2 18
Çarşamba, Turkey, 10,418....G 2 28
Carson Sink (depr.), U.S. ....D 5 42
Cartagena, Colombia, 111,291....E 1 46
Cartagena, Spain, 110,979....F 4 17
Cartago, Costa Rica, 12,933....F 6 39
Cartier, Ontario, 507....D 4 41
Cartwright, Labrador, Newf., 175.J 3 41
Carúpano, Venezuela, 30,395....H 1 46
Casablanca, Morocco, 682,388....E 5 34
Casale Monferrato, Italy, 32,403..B 2 18
Cascade (mountains), U.S. ....C 4 42
Cascais, Portugal, 7,887....B 3 17
Caserta, Italy, 43,247....E 4 18
Casino, Australia, 7,844....J 5 36
Casiquiare, Brazo (river), Venezuela....G 3 46
Caspian (sea)....J 4 9
Cassel (Kassel), Ger., 162,132....C 3 14
Cassino, Italy, 8,852....E 4 18
Castellammare del Golfo, Italy, 17,905....D 5 18
Castellammare di Stabia, Italy, 51,395....E 4 18
Castellón de la Plana, Spain, 52,778....G 3 17
Castelo Branco, Portugal, 13,056..C 3 17
Castelvetrano, Italy, 29,007....D 6 18
Casterton, Australia, 2,391....G 7 36
Castleford, England, 43,116....F 4 10
Castlegar, Br. Columbia, 1,705....G 5 40
Castlereagh (bay), Australia....F 2 36
Castor, Alberta, 958....H 4 40
Castres, France, 26,759....E 6 16
Castries,* St. Lucia, 7,056....G 4 45
Castro, Brazil, 6,158....L 8 47
Castro, Chile, 6,283....F12 47
Castro del Río, Spain, 16,152....D 4 17
Castrop-Rauxel, Germany, 69,960....G 4 14
Castrovillari, Italy, 12,054....F 5 18
Cat (island), Bahamas, 3,870....C 1 45
Catacáos, Peru, 8,526....D 5 46
Cataguases, Brazil, 8,972....M 8 46
Catalão, Brazil, 6,327....L 7 46
Catamarca, Argentina, 31,067....H 9 47
Catanduva, Brazil, 22,186....L 8 46
Catania, Italy, 296,780....E 6 18
Cataño, Puerto Rico, 7,924....G 1 45
Catanzaro, Italy, 49,786....F 5 18
Catbalogan, Philippine Is., 10,757.H 3 31
Cateel, Philippine Is., 2,333....H 4 31
Caterham and Warlingham, England, 31,290....G 6 10
Cato (island), Australia....K 4 36
Catskill (mountains), U.S. ....P 4 43
Cauca (river), Colombia....E 2 46
Caucasus (mts.), U.S.S.R. ....F 5 22
Caulfield, Australia, 75,217....L 2 36
Cauquenes, Chile, 12,987....F11 47

Index Ref. Plate No.

Causapscal, Quebec, 2,957............G 4 41
Cava de'Tirreni, Italy, 27,625........E 4 18
Cavaillon, France, 9,412................F 6 16
Cavarzere, Italy, 10,097.................D 2 18
Caviana (island), Brazil..................L 3 46
Cavite, Philippine Is., 35,052........G 3 31
Cawnpore (Kanpur), India, 705,383 ....D 3 29
Caxias, Brazil, 14,445...................M 4 46
Caxias do Sul, Brazil, 31,561.......K 9 47
Cayambe, Ecuador, 7,364...............E 4 46
Cayenne,* Fr. Guiana, 10,961.......K 2 46
Cayey, Puerto Rico, 18,402...........G 1 45
Cazombo, Angola, 2,212................L14 35
Ceará (Fortaleza), Brazil, 205,052 ....N 4 46
Cebu, Philippine Is., 167,503.........G 3 31
Cedros (island), Mexico, 1,003......A 2 44
Cegléd, Hungary, 37,971................E 3 20
Ceglie Messapico, Italy, 16,194.....F 4 18
Celaya, Mexico, 34,424..................J 6 44
Celebes (island), Indonesia, 6,029,198 ....G 6 31
Celebes (sea)..................................G 5 31
Celia, Ecuador, 1,627.....................D 4 46
Celje, Yugoslavia, 25,455...............B 2 21
Celle, Germany, 59,667...................D 2 14
Central (mt. range), S. A. ....E 2 46
Central Patricia, Ontario, 230.......B 3 41
Ceres, Cape of G. H., 4,067............E18 35
Cerignola, Italy, 46,977..................E 4 18
Cernăuti (Chernovtsy), U.S.S.R., 145,000 ....D 5 22
Cernavodă, Rumania, 6,100.............J 3 21
Cerritos, Mexico, 8,758..................K 5 44
Cerro (means hill) (Sp.)..............
Cerro de Pasco, Peru, 17,882.......E 6 46
Cesena, Italy, 34,047......................D 2 18
Cēsis, U.S.S.R., 8,748.....................D 4 22
Česká Budějovice, Czech., 64,104..C 2 20
Česká Lípa, Czech., 12,621............C 1 20
Český Těšín, Czech., 14,243...........E 2 20
Cessnock, Australia, 14,417............J 6 36
Cetatea-Albă (Belgorod-Dnestrovskiy), U.S.S.R., 7,766..E 5 22
Cetinje, Yugoslavia, 11,094............D 4 21
Cette (Sète), France, 29,914...........E 6 16
Ceuta, Spain, 59,936.......................F 4 34
Cevennes (mt. range), France......E 5 16
Ceyhan, Turkey, 23,284..................F 4 28
Ceylon (island) 6,657,339..............D 7 29
Chacabuco, Argentina, 12,917.......M12 47
Chachapoyas, Peru, 5,145..............E 5 46
Chaco (region), S. A. ....H 9 47
Chad (lake), Chad...........................K 9 34
Chagos (arch), Mauritius, 1,048....L10 25
Chahbar, Iran, 3,122.......................M 8 27
Chaibasa, India, 13,052..................E 4 29
Chaiyaphum, Thai., 6,446...............D 4 30
Chake Chake, Pemba, Zanzibar Prot., 2,469..................................P13 35
Chalcis, Greece, 23,786...................F 6 21
Chalk River, Ontario, 986...............E 4 41
Challapata, Bolivia, 2,529...............G 7 46
Chalon-sur-Saône, France, 29,851..F 4 16
Châlons-sur-Marne, France, 28,257 ....F 3 16
Chamartín de la Rosa, Spain, 64,874 ....G 4 17
Chambal (river), India...................C 3 29
Chambéry, France, 28,872................F 5 16
Chambord, Quebec, 1,091................F 4 41
Chamdo, China.................................E 5 32
Champagne, Yukon, 30.....................C 2 40
Champdani, India, 31,833.................E 1 29
Champigny-sur-Marne, France, 29,207 ....C 2 16
Champlain (lake), U.S. ....M 2 43
Chanda, India, 35,730......................C 4 29
Chandernagore, India, 47,785..........E 1 29
Chandler, Quebec, 3,338...................H 4 41
Changchih, China, 97,800.................H 4 32
Changchow, China, 87,200.................J 7 32
Changchow, China, 296,500...............K 5 32
Changchun, China, 855,200...............K 3 32
Changhwa, China...............................J 6 32
Changpeh, China...............................H 3 32
Changsha, China, 650,600.................H 6 32
Changsŏng, Korea, 21,767.................C 6 33
Changteh, China, 94,800...................H 6 32
Changting, China..............................J 6 32
Channel-Port aux Basques, Newf., 3,320 ....J 4 41
Chanthaburi, Thailand, 6,711..........D 4 30
Chao Phraya (river), Thailand.......D 4 30
Chaochow, China, 101,300................J 7 32
Chaotung, China, 50,000....................F 6 32
Chaoyang, China................................J 3 32
Chapayevsk, U.S.S.R., 83,000...........F 4 22
Chapleau, Ontario, 2,750..................D 4 41
Chapra, India, 55,142........................E 3 29
Charcas, Mexico, 9,320.....................J 5 44
Chardzhou, U.S.S.R., 66,000.............H 6 22
Charenton-le-Pont, France, 20,891 ....B 2 16
Charikar, Afghanistan, 21,070.......J 2 26
Charleroi, Belgium, 26,006..............E 8 15
Charles (cape), U.S. ....P 5 43
Charleville, Australia, 4,517...........H 5 36
Charleville, France, 19,454..............F 3 16
Charlotte (harbor), U.S. ....N 8 43
Charlotte Amalie,* Virgin Is. (U. S.), 11,463.............................H 1 45
Charlottenburg, Germany, 221,012 ....J 3 14
Charlottetown,* P.E.I., 16,707.......H 4 41
Charlton (island), Canada................D 3 41
Charters Towers, Australia, 6,961.G 4 36
Chascomús, Argentina, 9,105..........J11 47
Château-Thierry, France, 7,939......E 3 16
Châteauroux, France, 34,016............D 4 16
Châtellerault, France, 20,764..........D 4 16
Chatham, England, 44,424...............H 6 10
Chatham, New Brunswick, 6,332...G 4 41
Chatham, Ontario, 22,262................D 5 41
Châtillon-sous-Bagneau, France, 12,281 ....B 2 16
Chaudoc, Vietnam, 6,875...................E 5 30
Chaumont, France, 16,945.................F 3 16
Chauny, France, 9,206.......................E 3 16
Chaux des Fonds, La, Switz., 33,154 ....C 2 19
Chaves, Portugal, 11,286..................C 2 17
Cheb, Czech., 20,136..........................B 1 20
Cheboksary, U.S.S.R., 83,000...........F 4 22
Chefoo, China, 116,000......................K 4 32
Cheju, Korea, 57,573..........................C 7 33
Cheju (island), Korea, 254,589.........L 5 32
Chekhov, U.S.S.R., 7,846...................R 5 23
Cheleken, U.S.S.R., 2,728..................G 6 22
Chelkar, U.S.S.R. ....G 5 22
Chełm, Poland, 26,700.......................F 3 24
Chelmno, Poland, 15,200....................D 2 24
Chelmsford, England, 37,891.............H 6 10
Chelmsford, Ontario, 2,142................D 4 41
Chełmża, Poland, 12,700....................D 2 24
Chelsea, Aust., 16,857........................L 2 36
Cheltenham, England, 62,850............F 6 10
Chelyabinsk, U.S.S.R., 688,000..........H 4 22
Chelyuskin (cape), U.S.S.R. ....M 2 23
Chemnitz, Germany, 250,188..............E 3 14
Chenab (river), Pakistan...................B 2 29
Chengchow, China, 594,700................H 4 32
Chengkiang, China..............................F 7 32
Chengteh, China, 92,900....................J 3 32
Chengtu, China, 856,700.....................F 5 32
Chenyüan, China................................G 6 32
Cher (river), France..........................D 4 16
Cherbourg, France, 35,246..................C 3 16
Cherdyn', U.S.S.R., 3,884..................G 3 22
Cheremkhovo, U.S.S.R., 123,000...M 4 23
Cherepovets, U.S.S.R., 92,000...........E 4 22
Cheribon (Tjirebon), Indonesia, 54,079 ....H 2 31
Cherkassy, U.S.S.R., 83,000...............E 5 22
Cherkessk, U.S.S.R., 41,000...............F 5 22
Cherlak, U.S.S.R., 2,862......................J 4 22
Chernigov, U.S.S.R., 89,000...............E 4 22
Chernovtsy, U.S.S.R., 145,000............D 5 22
Chernyy Yar, U.S.S.R., 3,387..............F 5 22
Chesapeake (bay), U.S. ....O 5 43
Cheshunt, England, 23,019..................G 6 10
Chester, England, 48,237.....................E 4 10
Chester-le-Street, England, 18,538 ....F 3 10
Chesterfield, England, 68,558.............F 4 10
Chesterfield Inlet, N. W. Terr. ....M 2 40
Cheviot (hills)....................................L 9 11
Cheyenne (river), U.S. ....H 3 42
Chhatarpur, India, 13,210...................C 4 29
Chhindwara, India, 21,916...................C 4 29
Chiang Dao, Thailand, 5,179................C 3 30
Chiangmai, Thailand, 60,942................C 3 30
Chiangrai, Thailand, 5,330...................C 3 30
Chiari, Italy, 18,868.............................C 2 18
Chiavari, Italy, 19,087..........................B 2 18
Chiba, Japan, 133,844...........................P 2 33
Chicacole, India, 22,249.......................D 5 29
Chichagof (island), Alaska..................C 3 40
Chichester, England, 19,127..................G 7 10
Chichibu, Japan, 31,510........................J 6 33
Chichicastenango, Guat., 1,622.......B 3 39
Chiclana de la Frontera, Spain, 14,451 ....C 4 17
Chiclayo, Peru, 31,539...........................E 5 46
Chico (river), Argentina......................G13 47
Chicoutimi, Quebec, 24,878...................F 4 41
Chidambaram, India, 26,212..................D 6 29
Chidley (cape), Canada..........................H 1 41
Chieti, Italy, 29,394...............................E 3 18
Chigasaki, Japan, 47,013.......................O 3 33
Chihfeng, China, 430,000.......................J 3 32
Chihli (Po Hai) (gulf), China..............K 4 32
Chihuahua, Mexico, 86,962....................G 2 44
Chik Ballapur, India, 14,989.................C 6 29
Chikmagalur, India, 15,383....................C 6 29
Chilecito, Argentina, 6,121...........G 9 47
Chillán, Chile, 52,576....................F11 47
Chilliwack, Br. Columbia, 7,297....F 5 40
Chiloé (island), Chile, 78,335.......E12 47
Chilpancingo, Mexico, 12,673........K 8 44
Chilwa (lake), Africa......................O14 35
Chimaltenango, Guatemala, 6,059.B 3 39
Chimbay, U.S.S.R., 5,720.................G 5 22
Chimborazo (mountain), Ecuador.E 4 46
Chimbote, Peru, 4,243.....................E 5 46
Chimkent, U.S.S.R., 153,000............V 1 23
Chinabad, U.S.S.R., 1,704................U 2 23
Chinandega, Nicaragua, 13,172........D 4 39
Chinaz, U.S.S.R., 3,191....................R 1 23
Chincha Alta, Peru, 12,446..............E 6 46
Chinchow, China, 352,200.................J 3 32
Chinde, Mozambique, 1,142..............O15 35
Chingford, England, 48,330...............H 6 10
Chingleput, India, 17,829.................D 6 29
Chinhae, Korea, 36,449.....................D 6 33
Chiniot, Pakistan, 39,042..................B 2 29
Chinju, Korea, 77,473........................D 6 33
Chinkiang, China, 201,400.................K 5 32
Chinnamp'o, Korea, 82,162................B 4 33
Chinsura and Hooghly, India, 49,081 ....E 1 29
Chinwangtao, China, 186,800..............K 4 32
Chioggia, Italy, 39,915.........................D 2 18
Chios, Greece, 24,361...........................G 6 21
Chiplun, India, 15,528..........................B 5 29
Chiquimula, Guatemala, 8,848.............C 3 39
Chiquinquirá, Colombia, 10,143...........F 2 46
Chiquita (lake), Argentina.................H10 47
Chirala, India, 27,086...........................D 5 29
Chirchik, U.S.S.R., 65,000.....................T 1 23
Chirmiri, India, 10,044..........................D 4 29
Chirpan, Bulgaria, 13,231......................G 4 21
Chirskiy (mt. range), U.S.S.R. ....R 3 23
Chisinău (Kishinev), U.S.S.R., 214,000 ....D 5 22
Chistopol', U.S.S.R., 51,000...................G 4 22
Chistyakovo, U.S.S.R., 92,000................M 1 23
Chita, U.S.S.R., 171,000..........................N 4 23
Chitaldroog, India, 14,528.....................C 6 29
Chitorgarh, India, 9,300..........................B 4 29
Chitre, Panama, 7,476..............................G 7 39
Chittagong, Pakistan, 294,046...............F 4 29
Chittoor, India, 27,835............................C 6 29
Chivilcoy, Argentina, 23,386..................N12 47
Chkalov (Orenburg), U.S.S.R., 260,000 ....G 4 22
Choch'iwŏn, Korea, 16,109.....................C 5 33
Choibalsan, Mong. Rep., 10,000..............H 2 32
Choisy-le-Roy, France, 27,213................B 2 16
Chojnice, Poland, 18,400.........................C 2 24
Chokurdakh, U.S.S.R. ....R 2 23
Cholet, France, 23,214.............................C 4 16
Cholula, Mexico, 11,615...........................M 1 44
Choluteca, Honduras, 7,075.....................D 4 39
Chomutov, Czech., 32,752.........................B 1 20
Chon Buri, Thailand, 18,743.....................D 4 30
Ch'ŏnan, Korea, 22,661.............................C 5 33
Ch'ŏngjin, Korea, 184,301.........................E 3 33
Chŏngju, Korea, 18,633..............................B 4 33
Ch'ŏngju, Korea, 51,522.............................C 5 33
Chŏnju, Korea, 100,624...............................C 6 33
Chonos, Los (arch.), Chile..........................E13 47
Chorley, England, 32,640............................E 4 10
Chorzów, Poland, 143,800...........................B 4 24
Choshi, Japan, 73,512..................................K 6 33
Chott (means lake) (Arab.)........
Chowkow, China, 85,500..............................J 5 32
Christchurch, England, 20,511....................F 7 10
Christchurch, N.Z., †193,367.....................L 7 36
Christiansted, Virg. Isls., 4,110.................H 1 45
Christmas (island), Australia, 866..O11 25
Christmas (island), Pacific, 52.....L 5 27
Chrudim, Czech., 15,234..............................C 2 20
Chrzanów, Poland, 19,000.............................D 3 24
Chu (river), U.S.S.R. ....J 5 22
Chu Chua, Br. Columbia, 77........................G 4 40
Chüanchow, China, 107,700............................J 6 32
Chubut (river), Argentina...........................G12 47
Chuchow, China, 127,300...............................H 6 32
Chukchi (sea), U.S.S.R. ....V 2 23
Chulym (river), U.S.S.R. ....K 4 22
Chumikan, U.S.S.R. ....P 4 23
Chumphon, Thailand, 5,219..........................C 5 30
Ch'unch'ŏn, Korea, 54,539.............................D 5 33
Chunghsien, China..G 6 32
Ch'ungju, Korea, 64,571.................................C 5 33
Chungking, China, 1,772,500..........................G 6 32
Chur (Coire), Switzerland, 19,382.J 3 19
Churchill, Manitoba, 500...............................M 3 40
Churchill (cape), Canada...............................M 3 40
Churchill (river), Canada..............................K 3 40
Churu, India, 28,269.......................................B 3 29
Chusovoy, U.S.S.R., 60,000...........................G 4 22
Chust, U.S.S.R., 18,400...................................U 2 23
Ciechanów, Poland, 18,400..............................E 2 24
Ciego de Ávila, Cuba, 23,802..........................F 2 48
Ciénaga, Colombia, 24,358...............................F 1 46
Cienfuegos, Cuba, 52,910..................................D 2 48
Cieplice Zdrój, Poland, 12,800.......B 3 24
Cieszyn, Poland, 22,000....................D 4 24
Cieza, Spain, 18,913..........................F 3 17
Cimarron (river), U.S. ....J 5 42
Cinto (mountain), Corsica, France ....F 7 16
Città del Vaticano, 1,010..................B 6 18
Cittanova, Italy, 13,680.....................F 5 18
Ciudad Bolívar, Venezuela, 31,009 ....H 2 46
Ciudad de las Casas (San Cristóbal), Mexico, 17,472.........O 8 44
Ciudad García, Mexico, 10,397......H 5 44
Ciudad Guzmán, Mexico, 23,630....H 7 44
Ciudad Juárez, Mexico, 122,598....F 1 44
Ciudad Madero, Mexico, 41,110.....L 5 44
Ciudad Mante (Juárez), Mexico, 21,291 ....K 5 44
Ciudad Obregón, Mexico, 30,991 ..E 3 44
Ciudad Real, Spain, †33,375.........D 3 17
Ciudad Serdán, Mexico, 8,926.........O 2 44
Ciudad Trujillo,* Dom. Rep., 181,533 ....E 6 48
Ciudad Victoria, Mexico, 31,815....K 5 44
Civitavecchia, Italy, 29,165..............C 3 18
Clacton-on-Sea, England, 24,065..J 6 10
Clamart, France, 32,638....................A 2 16
Clanwilliam, Cape of G. H., 1,452.L18 35
Clare (island), Ireland......................A 4 12
Claremont, Australia, 8,643...............B 2 36
Clarence (strait), Australia...............E 2 36
Clarenville, Newfoundland, 1,195..K 4 41
Claresholm, Alberta, 2,431..................H 4 40
Clarke City, Quebec, 700....................G 3 41
Clausthal-Zellerfeld, Germany, 16,851 ....D 3 14
Clear (cape), Ireland..........................B 9 12
Clear (lake), U.S. ....C 5 42
Clearwater (lake), Canada..................E 2 41
Cleethorpes, England, 29,557...............H 4 10
Clermont, Australia, 1,587...................H 4 36
Clermont-Ferrand, France, 97,084.E 5 16
Cleves (Kleve), Germany, 17,825..B 3 14
Clew (bay), Ireland...............................B 4 12
Clichy, France, 52,652.............................B 1 16
Climax, Saskatchewan, 402....................J 5 40
Clipperton (island)..................................H 8 38
Clogher, N. Ireland, 10,687....................G 3 12
Cloncurry, Australia, 1,955.....................G 4 36
Clonmel, Ireland, 10,697..........................F 7 12
Cluj, Rumania, 117,915.............................F 2 21
Clyde (firth), Scotland.............................G 9 11
Clyde (river), Scotland.............................G 8 11
Clydebank, Scotland, 44,638.....................C 2 11
Coalville, England, 25,739.......................F 5 10
Coamo, Puerto Rico, 11,561......................G 1 45
Coast (mountains), Canada.......................D 3 40
Coast (mt. range), U.S. ....C 5 42
Coatbridge, Scotland, 47,541....................D 2 11
Coatepec, Mexico, 13,747..........................P 1 44
Coatepeque, Guatemala, 6,714...................A 3 39
Coaticook, Quebec, 6,492..........................F 4 41
Coats (island), Canada.............................P 2 40
Coatzacoalcos (Puerto México), Mexico, 19,501...................................M 7 44
Cobalt, Ontario, 2,367...............................E 4 41
Cobán, Guatemala, 6,854...........................B 3 39
Cobar, Australia, 2,224..............................H 6 36
Cóbh, Ireland, 5,169..................................E 8 12
Coblenz (Koblenz), Germany, 66,444 ....B 3 14
Cobourg, Ontario, 9,399..............................E 5 41
Cobourg (peninsula), Australia.................E 2 36
Coburg, Australia, 62,077............................L 1 36
Coburg, Germany, 44,929.............................D 3 14
Cocanada (Kakinada), India, 100,054 ....D 5 29
Cochabamba, Bolivia, 80,795........................G 7 46
Cochin, India, 26,320....................................C 6 29
Cochrane, Ontario, 3,695...............................D 4 41
Cockburn, Australia, 101..............................F 6 36
Cocos (island), C. R. ....K 9 38
Cocos (Keeling) (islands), (Australia) N11 25
Cocula, Mexico, 7,854....................................G 6 44
Cod (cape), U.S. ....N 2 43
Codajás, Brazil, 1,322....................................H 4 46
Codó, Brazil, 6,027..M 4 46
Coe Hill, Ontario, 288....................................E 5 41
Coeur d'Alene (lake), U.S. ....D 3 42
Coff's Harbour, Australia, 6,215...................J 6 36
Cognac, France, 16,843...................................C 5 16
Coimbatore, India, 197,755.............................C 6 29
Coimbra, Portugal, 41,977...............................B 2 17
Coire (Chur), Switzerland, 19,382.J 3 19
Cojímar, Cuba, 1,846..C 1 48
Cojutepeque, El Salvador, 10,015.C 4 39
Colchester, England, 57,449.............................H 6 10
Coleman, Alberta, 1,566..................................H 5 40
Coleraine, Australia, 1,393.............................G 7 36
Coleraine, N. Ireland, 10,748..........................H 1 12
Colima, Mexico, 28,656.....................................H 7 44
Coll (island), Scotland, 210...............................C 6 11

Index Plate Ref. No.

Collie, Australia, 8,667...B 6 36
Collier (bay), Australia...C 3 36
Collingwood, New Zealand, 167...L 6 36
Collingwood, Ontario, 7,978...D 5 41
Collinsville, Australia, †1,856...H 4 36
Colmar, France, 43,514...G 3 16
Colne, England, 20,670...E 4 10
Cologne (Köln), Germany, 594,941...B 3 14
Colomb-Béchar,* Saoura, 16,650...F 5 34
Colombes, France, 60,997...A 1 16
Colombo,* Ceylon, 355,374...C 7 29
Colón, Cuba, 11,534...D 1 48
Colón, Panama, 52,204...H 6 39
Colonia, Uruguay, 8,000...J10 47
Colonsay (island), Scotland, 227...D 7 11
Colorado (river), Argentina...H11 47
Colorado (river), U.S....E 6 42
Colorado (river), U.S....J 7 42
Columbia (river), Canada...G 4 40
Columbia (river), U.S....C 3 42
Colwyn Bay, Wales, 22,283...D 4 10
Comalapa, Guat., 7,404...B 3 39
Comayagua, Honduras, 5,192...D 3 39
Comeragh (mountains), Ireland...F 7 12
Comet (river), Australia...H 4 36
Comilla, Pakistan, 47,195...F 4 29
Comiso, Italy, 24,561...E 6 18
Comitán, Mexico, 11,753...O 8 44
Como, Italy, 65,390...B 2 18
Comodoro Rivadavia, Arg., 25,651...G13 47
Comoé (river), Ivory Coast...F10 34
Comorin (cape), India...C 7 29
Comoro (islands), 156,150...P14 35
Compiègne, France, 17,701...E 3 16
Con Cuong, Vietnam...E 3 30
Conakry,* Guinea, 38,000...D10 34
Conceição do Araguaia, Brazil, 1,389...L 5 46
Concepción, Argentina, 12,338...G 9 47
Concepción, Chile, 119,887...F11 47
Concepción, Paraguay, 14,640...J 8 47
Concepción del Uruguay, Argentina, 31,498...J10 47
Conception (point), U.S....C 6 42
Conchas (reservoir), U.S....H 6 42
Conchos (river), Mexico...G 2 44
Concordia, Argentina, 52,213...J 10 47
Condobolin, Australia, 2,840...H6 36
Conegliano, Italy, 11,549...D 2 18
Congleton, England, 15,502...F 4 10
Congo (river), Africa...L11 35
Coniston, Ontario, 2,478...D 4 41
Conjeeveram (Kanchipuram), India, 74,635...D 6 29
Conn (lake), Ireland...C 3 12
Consett, England, 39,456...F 3 10
Constance (lake)...H 1 19
Constance (Konstanz), Germany, 42,934...C 5 14
Constanţa, Rumania, 78,586...J 3 21
Constantina, Spain, 11,773...D 4 17
Constantine, Algeria, 111,315...H 4 34
Constantinople (Istanbul), Turk., 1,214,616...D 6 28
Constitución, Chile, 8,285...F11 47
Consul, Saskatchewan, 166...J 5 40
Contamana, Peru, 2,860...F 5 46
Conversano, Italy, 15,050...F 4 18
Cooch Behar, India, 16,000...E 3 29
Cook (islands), Pacific, 14,088...K 7 37
Cooktown, Australia, 448...H 3 36
Coolangatta, Aust., 2,343...J 5 36
Coolgardie, Australia, 952...C 6 36
Cooma, Australia, 6,503...H 7 36
Coonamble, Australia, 2,910...H 6 36
Coondapur, India, 9,537...B 6 29
Cooper's (creek), Australia...G 5 36
Cootamundra, Australia, 5,760...H 6 36
Copacabana, Brazil...P15 47
Copenhagen (København), *Denmark, 768,105...G 9 13
Copiapó, Chile, 19,535...F 9 47
Coplay, Australia, 86...F 6 36
Copper Cliff, Ontario, 3,801...D 4 41
Coppermine, N. W. Terr....G 1 40
Coppermine (river), Canada...H 1 40
Coquet (river), England...F 2 10
Coquilhatville, Belg. Congo, 25,457...L11 35
Coquimbo, Chile, 24,962...F10 47
Corabia, Rumania, 10,772...G 4 21
Coracora, Peru, 3,671...F 7 46
Coral (sea), Pacific...F 7 37
Corato, Italy, 44,601...F 4 18
Corbeil, France, 10,797...E 3 16
Cordillera (means mt. range) (Sp.)
Córdoba, Argentina, 369,886...G10 47
Córdoba, Mexico, 32,888...P 2 41
Córdoba, Spain, 165,403...D 4 17
Corfield, Australia, 34...G 4 36
Corfu, Greece, 27,431...D 6 21
Corigliano Calabro, Italy, 17,396...F 5 18
Corinda, Aust., 9,668...K 2 36
Coringa (isls.), Australia...H 3 36
Corinth, Greece, 17,728...F 7 21
Corinthia (gulf), Greece...F 6 21
Corio, Aust., 12,998...K 2 36
Cork, Ireland, 80,011...E 8 12
Cork (harbor), Ireland...E 8 12
Corleone, Italy, 16,161...D 6 18
Corlu, Turkey, 17,025...B 2 28
Corner Brook, Newf., 23,225...J 4 41
Corno (mountain), Italy...D 3 18
Cornwall, Ontario, 18,158...E 4 41
Coro, Venezuela, 29,341...G 1 46
Corocoro, Bolivia, 4,431...G 7 46
Coroico, Bolivia, 2,235...G 7 46
Coronation, Alberta, 784...H 4 40
Coronation (gulf), Canada...H 1 40
Coronel Brandsen, Arg., 3,803...O12 47
Coronel Pringles, Arg., 12,844...H11 47
Coronel Suárez, Arg., 11,133...H11 47
Corpus Christi (bay), U.S....J 8 42
Corrib (lake), Ireland...C 5 12
Corrientes, Argentina, 56,544...J 9 47
Corrientes (cape), Colombia...E 2 46
Corrientes (cape), Mexico...G 6 44
Corrigin, Australia, 785...B 6 36
Corsica (Corse) (island), France, 244,286...G 6 16
Cortona, Italy, 8,744...C 3 18
Çoruh (Artvin), Turkey, 5,845...J 2 28
Çorum, Turkey, 25,827...F 2 28
Corumbá, Brazil, 18,725...J 7 46
Coruña, La, Spain, †127,618...B 1 17
Cosenza, Italy, 48,172...F 5 18
Cosmoledo (islands), Seychelles, 51...R13 35
Cotabato, Philippine Is., 8,909...G 4 31
Cotonou, Dahomey, 23,000...G10 34
Cotopaxi (mountain), Ecuador...E 4 46
Cotswold (hills), England...E 6 10
Cottbus (Kottbus), Germany, 49,131...F 3 14
Cottesloe, Australia, 8,092...B 2 36
Courbevoie, France, 54,025...A 2 16
Courtenay, Br. Columbia, 3,025...F 5 40
Courtrai, Belgium, 41,569...C 7 15
Coutts, Alberta, 350...H 5 40
Coventry, England, 258,245...F 5 10
Covilhã, Portugal, 20,423...C 2 17
Cowan (lake), Australia...C 6 36
Cowdenbeath, Scotland, 13,151...K 7 11
Cowes, England, 17,158...F 7 10
Cowra, Australia, 6,097...H 6 36
Coxim, Brazil, 884...K 7 46
Coyoacán, Mexico, 45,893...L 1 44
Cozumel (island), Mexico, 2,905...Q 6 44
Cracow (Kraków), Poland, 463,500...E 3 24
Cradle (mountain), Australia...H 8 36
Cradock, Cape of G. H., 14,839...M18 35
Craik, Saskatchewan, 607...J 4 40
Craiova, Rumania, 84,574...F 3 21
Cranbrook, Br. Columbia, 4,562...G 5 40
Crateús, Brazil, 7,391...N 5 46
Crato, Brazil, 16,030...N 5 46
Cree (lake), Canada...J 3 40
Creil, France, 9,476...E 3 16
Crema, Italy, 22,698...B 2 18
Cremona, Italy, 59,149...B 2 18
Creston, Br. Columbia, 1,844...G 4 40
Crete (island), Greece, 460,844...G 8 21
Crewe, England, 52,423...E 4 10
Crimea (pen.), U.S.S.R. ...E 5 22
Crimmitschau, Germany, 30,504...E 3 14
Croker (island), Australia...E 2 36
Cromarty (inlet), Scotland...H 4 11
Cronulla, Australia, 7,330...L 3 36
Crook and Willington, England, 27,606...F 3 10
Cross (lake), Canada...L 4 40
Cross Fell (mountain), England...E 3 10
Crotone, Italy, 30,788...F 5 18
Croydon, Australia, 127...G 3 36
Croydon, England, 249,870...G 6 10
Cruz Alta, Brazil, 19,375...K 9 47
Cruz del Eje, Argentina, 15,563...H10 47
Cruzeiro do Sul, Brazil, 3,824...F 5 46
Csepel, Hungary, 46,171...E 3 20
Csongrád, Hungary, 24,660...E 3 20
Cua Rao, Vietnam...E 3 30
Cuanza (river), Angola...K13 35
Cuba (island), 4,778,583...B 2 45
Cuckfield, England, 16,506...G 6 10
Cúcuta, Colombia, 70,375...F 2 46
Cuddalore, India, 60,632...D 6 29
Cuddapah, India, 28,246...C 6 29
Cudgewa, Australia, 257...H 7 36
Cudworth, Saskatchewan, 582...J 4 40
Cue, Australia, 467...B 5 36
Cuenca, Ecuador, 39,983...E 4 46
Cuenca, Spain, 24,836...E 2 17
Cuernavaca, Mexico, 30,597...L 2 44
Cufra (Kufra) (oasis), Libya, 4,600...L 7 34
Cuiabá, Brazil, 23,745...J 7 46
Cuillin (sound), Scotland...D 5 11
Cuito (river), Angola...K15 35
Culgoa (river), Australia...H 5 36
Culiacán, Mexico, 48,983...F 4 44
Cullera, Spain, 14,214...F 3 17
Culver (point), Australia...D 6 36
Cumaná, Venezuela, 46,350...H 1 46
Cumberland (islands), Australia...H 4 36
Cumberland (sound), Canada...F25 8
Cumbum, India, 22,177...C 5 29
Çumra, Turkey, 8,805...E 4 28
Cunene (river), Africa...J15 35
Cuneo, Italy, 27,902...A 2 18
Cunnamulla, Australia, 1,955...H 5 36
Ćuprija, Yugoslavia, 9,819...E 4 21
Curaçao (island), Neth. Antilles, 115,929...G 1 46
Curacautín, Chile, 5,740...F11 47
Curepipe, Maur., 27,468...S19 35
Curitiba, Brazil, 138,178...L 9 47
Curtea de Argeş, Rumania, 9,180...G 3 21
Curtis (island), Australia...J 4 36
Curuzú Cuatia, Arg., 15,440...J 9 47
Cuttack, India, 102,505...E 4 29
Cuvier (cape), Australia...A 4 36
Cuxhaven, Germany, 46,861...C 2 14
Cuyuni (river), S. A. ...H 2 46
Cuzco, Peru, 45,158...F 6 46
Cyclades (islands), Greece, 125,959...G 7 21
Cygnet, Australia, 878...H 8 36
Cyprus (island), 450,114...E 5 28
Cyrene (Shahat), Libya, 494...L 5 34
Czechowice, Poland, 21,000...D 4 24
Czeladź, Poland, 26,000...B 4 24
Częstochowa, Poland, 154,610...D 3 24

D

Dąbrowa Górnicza, Poland, 41,400...C 4 24
Dabhoi, India, 21,139...B 4 29
Dabola, Guinea, 3,788...D 9 34
Dabou, Ivory Coast, 4,500...F11 34
Dacca, Pakistan, 411,279...F 4 29
Dachau, Germany, 23,552...D 4 14
Dadu, Pakistan, 13,716...A 3 29
Dăeni, Rumania, 4,015...J 3 21
Daet, Phil. Islands, 11,355...G 3 31
Dag, Dagh (means mt.) (Turk.)...
Dagabur, Ethiopia, 2,000...P10 34
Dagana, Senegal, 4,132...D 8 34
Dăglari (means mt.) (Turk.)
Daimiel, Spain, 18,820...E 3 17
Dairen (incl. in Lüta), China, 766,400...K 4 32
Daito (islands), Pacific, 2,691...D 3 37
Dajarra, Australia, 199...F 4 36
Dakar,* Senegal, 185,000...C 9 34
Dalat, Vietnam, 5,200...F 5 30
Dalby, Australia, 6,182...J 5 36
Dalhousie, N. B., 5,468...G 4 41
Daloa, Ivory Coast, 5,163...E10 34
Daltonganj, India, 13,943...D 4 29
Daly (river), Australia...E 2 36
Damão, P. India, 9,027...B 4 29
Damaraland (region), S. W. Afr. ..K16 35
Damascus,* Syria, U.A.R., 345,237...G 6 28
Damba, Angola, 1,367...K13 35
Damghan with Shahrud, Iran, 17,837...J 2 27
Damietta, Egypt, 53,620...N 5 34
Damoh, India, 26,795...C 4 29
Dampier (arch.), Australia...B 4 36
Dampier Land (peninsula), Aust. .C 3 36
Dandenong, Australia, 27,748...L 2 36
Daniels Harbour, Newf., 257...J 3 41
Dannevirke, New Zealand, 5,294...M 6 36
Dansalan, Phil. Islands, 4,882...G 4 31
Dante (Hafun), Somalia, 2,000...S 9 34
Danube (delta), Rumania...J 3 21
Danube (Donau, Dunav) (river)...D 2 20
Danzig (Gdańsk) Poland 259,900...D 1 24
Dar es Salaam,* Tan. Terr., 69,227...P13 35
Darab, Iran, 6,637...J 6 27
Darabani, Rumania, 11,379...H 1 21
Darbhanga, India, 69,203...E 3 29
Dardanelles (strait), Turkey...A 1 26
Darende, Turkey, 6,647...G 3 28
Darganata, U.S.S.R. ...H 5 22
Dargaville, New Zealand, 3,306...L 5 36
Darien (gulf), S.A. ...E 2 46
Darjeeling, India, 25,873...E 3 29
Darling (mountain range), Aust. ..B 6 36
Darling (river), Australia...G 6 36
Darlington, England, 84,886...F 3 10
Darmstadt, Germany, 94,788...C 4 14
Dartmoor (plateau), England...C 7 10
Dartmouth, N. S., 21,093...H 5 41
Daru, Papua, 237...E 6 31
Darwin, Australia, †8,071...E 2 36
Dashan (mountain), Ethiopia...O 9 34
Dasht (means desert, plain) (Persian)...
Datia, India, 22,086...C 3 29
Dattein, Germany, 24,476...D 3 14
Daugavpils, U.S.S.R., 65,000...D 4 22
Daulatabad (Malayer), Iran 19,749...F 3 27
Dauphin, Manitoba, 6,190...K 4 40
Davangere, India, 31,759...C 6 29
Davao, Philippine Islands, 81,523..H 4 31
David, Panama, 14,969...F 6 39
Davidson, Saskatchewan, 851...J 4 40
Davis (strait), Canada...F24 8
Davos (Dorf and Platz), Switz., 10,433...J 3 19
Dawa (river), Ethiopia...O11 34
Dawson, Yukon, 851...C 2 40
Dawson Creek, British Columbia, 7,521...F 3 40
Dax, France, 12,551...C 6 16
Daysland, Alta., 499...H 4 40
DeAar, C. of G. H., 11,069...L18 35
DeDoorns, C. of G. H., 1,534...F18 35
D'Entrecasteaux (islands), Papua, 35,000...F 6 37
D'Entrecasteaux (point), Aust. ..B 7 36
De Grey (river), Australia...C 4 36
Dead (sea)...C 4 24
Deal, England, 24,309...J 6 10
Deán Funes, Argentina, 13,840...H10 47
Dease (strait), Canada...J 1 40
Dease Lake, British Columbia...E 3 40
Death Valley (depr.), U.S. ...D 5 42
Deauville, France 5,438...C 3 16
Debal'tsevo, U.S.S.R., 13,112...M1 23
Dębica, Poland, 14,500...E 3 24
Dęblin, Poland, 12,300...E 3 24
Debra Markos, Ethiopia, 10,000...O 9 34
Debra Tabor, Ethiopia, 9,000...O 9 34
Debrecen, Hungary, 119,635...F 3 20
Decazeville, France, 10,751...E 5 16
Deccan (plateau), India...C 6 29
Děčín, Czechoslovakia, 34,930...C 1 20
Dedougou, Upper Volta, 2,720...F 9 34
Dee (river), England...D 4 10
Dee (river), Scotland...M 5 11
Deer Lake, Newfoundland, 3,481...J 4 41
Deggendorf, Germany, 16,328...E 4 14
Dehra Dun, India, 144,216...C 2 29
Dej, Rumania, 14,681...F 2 21
Delagoa (bay), Moz....N17 35
Delft, Netherlands, 69,865...E 4 15
Delgado (cape), Moz. ...P14 35
Delhi, India, 914,790...C 3 29
Delisle, Saskatchewan, 482...J 4 40
Delitzsch, Germany, 25,148...E 3 14
Delmenhorst, Germany, 57,273...C 2 14
Deloraine, Australia, 1,772...H 8 36
Deloraine, Manitoba, 900...K 5 40
Demak, Indonesia, 8,783...J 2 31
Demavend (mountain), Iran...F 2 27
Dembidollo, Ethiopia, 8,000...N10 34
Demirci, Turkey, 7,664...C 3 28
Demmin, Germany, 18,006...E 2 14
Den Helder, Netherlands, 46,102...F 3 15
Denain, France, 22,299...E 2 16
Dendermonde (Termonde), Belgium, 9,532...E 6 15
Deniliquin, Australia, 4,704...H 7 36
Denizli, Turkey, 29,934...C 4 28
Denpasar, Indonesia, 16,639...F 7 31
Deodoro, Brazil...M14 47
Deoghar, India, 19,792...E 4 29
Deoria, India, 15,198...D 3 29
Dera Ghazi Khan, Pak., 35,909...B 3 29
Dera Ismail Khan, Pak., 41,813...B 2 29
Dérac, Haiti, 4,767...C 5 48
Derbent, U.S.S.R., 27,476...F 5 22
Derby, Australia, 478...C 3 36
Derby, England, 14,267...F 5 10
Derg (lake), Ireland...E 6 12
Derna, Libya, 15,218...L 5 34
Derryveagh (mt. range), Ireland..E 2 12
Derventa, Yugo., 9,085...C 3 21
Derwent (river), England...D 4 10
Deseado (river), Argentina...G13 47
Desna (river), U.S.S.R. ...E 4 22
Desolación (island), Chile...E14 47
Dessalines, Haiti, 3,745...C 5 48
Dessau, Germany, 88,139...E 3 14

Index Plate
Ref. No.

Dessye, Ethiopia, 36,000..............O 3 34
Detmold, Germany, 30,178..............C 3 14
Deurne, Belgium, 62,469..............F 6 15
Deutsch Brod. (Havlíčkuv B.), Czech., 14,068..............C 2 20
Deva, Rumania, 12,959..............F 3 21
Dévaványa, Hungary, 15,202..............F 3 20
Develi, Turkey, 11,662..............F 3 28
Deventer, Netherlands, 52,678..............J 4 15
Devils (Diable) (island), French Guiana..............K 2 46
Devlali, India, 16,292..............B 5 29
Devon (island), Canada..............C28 8
Devonport, Australia, 10,597..............H 8 36
Dewas, India, 22,949..............C 4 29
Dewsbury, England, 53,487..............F 4 10
Dezhnev (East) (cape), U.S.S.R. ....W 3 23
Dhahran, Saudi Arabia, 10,000..............E 4 26
Dhamar, Yemen, 5,000..............D 7 26
Dhamtari, India, 14,071..............D 4 29
Dhar, India, 22,015..............C 4 29
Dharamsala, India, 9,653..............C 2 29
Dharwar, India, 47,992..............B 5 29
Dholpur, India, 21,311..............C 3 29
Dhond, India, 12,828..............B 5 29
Dhoraji, India, 37,647..............B 4 29
Dhubri, India, 12,699..............E 3 29
Dhulia, India, 54,406..............B 4 29
Diable (Devils) (island), French Guiana..............K 2 46
Diamantina (river), Australia..............G 4 36
Diamantina, Brazil, 9,837..............M 7 46
Diamantino, Brazil, 540..............J 6 46
Dibrugarh, India, 23,191..............G 3 29
Didsbury, Alta., 1,227..............H 4 40
Didymóteikhon, Greece, 8,136..............H 5 21
Diego Garcia (island), Mauritius, 619..............L10 25
Diégo-Suarez, Malg. Rep., 32,217..............R14 35
Dien Bien Phu, Vietnam..............D 2 30
Dieppe, France, 25,983..............D 3 16
Differdange, Lux., 15,179..............H 9 15
Digby, N. S., 2,145..............G 5 41
Dijon, France, 106,267..............F 4 16
Dikson, U.S.S.R...............K 2 22
Dikwa, No. Cam., 5,242..............J 9 34
Dili,* Port. Timor, 1,795..............H 7 31
Dimbokro, Ivory Coast, 1,238..............F10 34
Dimishq (Damascus),* Syria, U.A.R., 345,237..............G 6 28
Dimitrovo, Bulgaria, 28,504..............F 4 21
Dinajpur, Pakistan, 34,271..............E 3 29
Dinan, France, 11,111..............B 3 16
Dinaric Alps (mt. range), Yugo. ....B 3 21
Dindigul, India, 56,275..............C 6 29
Dingle (bay), Ireland..............A 7 12
Dinguiraye, Guinea, 2,914..............D 9 34
Dinslaken, Germany, 31,947..............B 3 14
Diomede (isls.)..............W3 23
Diósgyőr, Hungary, 26,538..............F 2 20
Diourbel, Senegal, 16,000..............C 9 34
Dire Dawa, Ethiopia, 20,000..............P10 34
Diriamba, Nicaragua, 7,566..............D 5 39
Dirk Hartog (island), Australia..............A 5 36
Dirranbandi, Australia, 870..............H 5 36
Dirschau (Tczew), Poland, 30,900..............D 1 24
Disappointment (cape), U.S. ....B 3 42
Disappointment (lake), Australia..............C 4 36
Discovery (bay), Australia..............F 7 36
Disko (island), Greenland..............E24 8
Diu, Port. India, 5,215..............B 4 29
Divinópolis, Brazil, 20,550..............L 8 47
Divnoye, U.S.S.R., 7,127..............F 5 22
Dixon Entrance (strait), Canada..............D 4 40
Diyarbakir, Turkey, 63,180..............H 4 28
Dizful, Iran, 47,705..............F 4 27
Djailolo, Indonesia..............H 5 31
Djakarta,* Indonesia 2,800,000..............H 1 31
Djakovica, Yugoslavia, 14,497..............E 4 21
Djakovo, Yugoslavia, 8,942..............D 3 21
Djambi, Indonesia, 22,071..............C 6 31
Djapara, Indonesia, 8,356..............J 2 31
Djatinegara, Indonesia..............H 2 31
Djebel (means mt.) (Arab.)........
Djelfa, Algeria, 6,212..............G 5 34
Djember, Indonesia, 20,222..............K 2 31
Djenné, Sudanese Rep., 5,000..............F 9 34
Djerid (lake), Tunisia..............H 5 34
Djibouti,* Fr. Somaliland, 17,300..............P 9 34
Djiring, Vietnam..............F 5 30
Djokjakarta, Indonesia, 244,379..............J 2 31
Djombang, Indonesia, 20,380..............K 2 31
Djougou, Dahomey, 5,446..............G10 34
Dneprodzerzhinsk, U.S.S.R., 194,000..............E 5 22
Dnepropetrovsk, U.S.S.R., 658,000..............E 5 22
Dnieper (Dnepr) (river), U.S.S.R. ....E 4 22
Dniester (Dnestr) (river), U.S.S.R. ....D 5 22
Döbeln, Germany, 28,841..............E 3 14
Dobo, Indonesia..............J 7 31
Dobrich (Tolbukhin), Bulgaria 31,049..............H 4 21
Dodecanese (islands), Greece, 121,100..............H 8 21
Dodoma, Tan. Terr., 9,414..............N13 34
Doetinchem, Netherlands, 24,867..............J 5 15
Dog Creek, British Columbia, 35..............F 4 40
Doha,* Qatar, 7,500..............F 4 26
Dohad, India, 12,666..............B 4 29
Dolbeau, Quebec, 5,079..............F 4 41
Dôle, France, 19,785..............F 4 16
Dolinsk, U.S.S.R., 22,295..............R 5 23
Dolisie, Congo, 7,495..............J12 35
Dolo, Ethiopia, 400..............P11 34
Dolores, Uruguay, 11,500..............J10 47
Dominica (isl.), W.I., 61,358..............G 4 45
Don (river), England..............F 4 10
Don (river), Scotland..............L 5 11
Don (river), U.S.S.R. ....E 4 22
Don Benito, Spain, 21,852..............C 3 17
Doncaster, England, 82,054..............G 4 10
Dondra Head (cape), Ceylon..............D 7 29
Donegal (bay), Ireland..............D 2 12
Donets (river), U.S.S.R. ....E 5 22
Dong Hoi, Vietnam..............E 3 30
Dongara, Australia, 381..............A 5 36
Donggala, Indonesia, 3,821..............F 6 31
Dongola, Sudan, 3,800..............M8 34
Doornik (Tournai), Belg., 33,326..............C 7 15
Dordogne (river), France..............D 5 16
Dordrecht, Netherlands, 77,624..............F 5 15
Dore (mountain), France..............E 5 16
Dori, Upper Volta, 3,600..............G 9 34
Dorking, England, 20,252..............G 6 10
Dornbirn, Austria, 22,508..............A 3 20
Dornoch (firth), Scotland..............J 4 11
Dorohoi, Rumania, 15,036..............H 2 21
Dorre (island), Australia..............A 5 36
Dorset Heights (hills), England..............E 7 10
Dortmund, Germany, 507,349..............H 4 14
Dos Bahías (cape), Argentina..............H12 47
Dos Hermanas, Spain, 16,502..............D 4 17
Dossor, U.S.S.R., 12,000..............G 5 22
Douai, France, 41,649..............E 2 16
Douala, Cam., 35,362..............J11 34
Douarnenez, France, 18,519..............A 3 16
Douglas,* Isle of Man, 20,288..............C 3 10
Douglastown, Quebec, 779..............H 4 41
Dour, Belgium, 11,581..............D 8 15
Douro (river), Portugal..............C 2 17
Dover, England, 35,215..............J 6 10
Dover (point), Australia..............D 6 36
Dover (strait), England..............J 6 10
Drăgăşani, Rumania, 9,737..............F 3 21
Draguignan, France, 8,879..............G 6 16
Drake (passage), S.A. E15 47
Dráma, Greece, 29,498..............F 5 21
Drammen, Norway, 27,297..............C 4 13
Drancy, France, 42,096..............B 1 16
Drava (river), Yugoslavia..............C 3 21
Dresden, Germany, 467,966..............E 3 14
Dreux, France, 11,528..............D 3 16
Drina (river), Yugoslavia..............D 3 21
Drogheda, Ireland, 17,008..............J 4 12
Drogobych (Drohobycz), U.S.S.R., 42,000..............D 5 22
Drumheller, Alta., 2,632..............H 4 40
Drummondville, Quebec, 26,284..............F 4 41
Druzhkovka, U.S.S.R. ....H 1 23
Dryden, Ontario, 4,428..............B 4 41
Dubai, Tr. Oman, 24,000..............F 5 26
Dubawnt (lake), Canada..............K 2 40
Dubawnt (river), Canada..............K 2 40
Dubbo, Australia, 12,009..............H 6 36
Dublin (Baile Átha Cliath), *Ireland, 522,183..............K 5 12
Dublin (bay), Ireland..............J 5 12
Dubrovka, U.S.S.R., 2,070..............C 2 22
Dubrovnik (Ragusa), Yugoslavia, 19,063..............C 4 21
Duchess, Australia, 52..............F 4 36
Duck Lake, Saskatchewan, 585..............J 4 40
Dudinka, U.S.S.R. ....K 3 22
Duero (river), Spain..............C 2 17
Duifken (point), Australia..............G 2 36
Duisburg, Germany, 410,783..............F 4 14
Dum Dum, India, 39,434..............E 1 29
Dumaguete, Phil. Is., 9,366..............G 4 31
Dumai, Indonesia..............C 5 31
Dumbarton, Scotland, 23,702..............B 2 11
Dumfries, Scotland, 26,322..............J 9 11
Dumyât (Damietta), Egypt, 53,620..............N 5 34
Dún Laoghaire (Kingston), Ireland, 47,553..............K 5 12
Duncan, British Columbia, 3,247..............F 5 40
Duncansby Head (prom.), Scotland..............L 2 11
Dundalk, Ireland, 20,154..............H 3 12
Dundalk (bay), Ireland..............J 4 12
Dundas (strait), Australia..............E 2 36
Dundee, Scotland, 177,340..............K 7 11
Dundrum (bay), North. Ireland..............K 3 12
Dunedin, New Zealand, 99,370..............L 7 36
Dunfermline, Scotland, 44,719..............J 7 11
Dungarvan, Ireland, 5,394..............F 7 12
Dungarvan (harbor), Ireland..............F 7 12
Dungeness (prom.), England..............J 7 10
Dunkerque (Dunkirk), France, 20,735..............E 3 16
Dunnet Headland (prom.), Scotland..............J 2 11
Dunstable, England, 17,109..............G 6 10
Duparquet, Quebec, 1,144..............E 4 41
Duque de Caxias, Brazil, 74,557..............N13 47
Durango, Mexico, 59,498..............G 4 44
Durazno, Uruguay, 27,000..............J10 47
Durban, Natal, †476,236..............N18 35
Durbanville, C. of G. H., 1,667..............D19 35
Düren, Germany, 35,234..............B 3 14
Durg, India, 16,766..............D 4 29
Durham, England, 19,287..............F 3 10
Duri, Indonesia..............C 5 31
Durmitor (mountain), Yugoslavia..............D 4 21
Durrës (Durazzo), Albania, 14,031..............D 5 21
Düsseldorf, Germany, 500,516..............F 5 14
Düzce, Turkey, 12,810..............D 2 28
Dvina, Northern (river), U.S.S.R..............F 3 22
Dvina, Western (river), U.S.S.R., ...D 4 22
Dvinsk (Daugavpils), U.S.S.R. 65,000..............D 4 22
Dvůr Kralové, Czech., 15,179..............C 1 20
Dwarka, India, 10,876..............A 4 29
Dyer (cape), Canada..............E25 8
Dyment, Ontario, 158..............B 4 41
Dzaudzhikau (Ordzhonikidze), U.S.S.R., 164,000..............F 5 22
Dzaoudzi,* Comoro Is., 168..............R14 35
Dzerzhinsk, U.S.S.R., 163,000..............F 4 22
Dzerzhinsk, U.S.S.R., 12,806..............J 1 22
Dzhalal-Abad, U.S.S.R., 14,961..............V 2 23
Dzhambeyty, U.S.S.R., 2,388..............G 4 22
Dzhambul, U.S.S.R., 67,000..............J 5 22
Dzhankoy, U.S.S.R. ....E 5 22
Dzhizak, U.S.S.R., 17,500..............H 5 22
Dzierżoniów, Poland, 16,646..............C 3 24

E

Earn (lake), Scotland..............H 7 11
East Anglian Ridge (hills), Eng. ....H 6 10
East China (sea)..............L 6 32
East London, C. of G. H., †91,190..............M18 35
East Retford, England, 16,316..............G 4 10
East Siberian (sea), U.S.S.R. ....S 2 23
Eastbourne, England, 57,821..............H 7 10
Eastend, Saskatchewan, 706..............J 5 40
Easter (Rapa Nui) (island), Chile, 270..............P 8 37
Eastern Ghats (mt. range), India..............C 6 29
Eastleigh, England, 30,559..............F 7 10
Eastmain (river), Canada..............E 3 41
Ebbw Vale, England, 29,220..............D 6 10
Ebensee, Austria, 10,329..............B 3 20
Eberswalde, Germany, 30,186..............E 2 14
Ebingen, Germany, 17,076..............C 4 14
Eboli, Italy, 16,315..............E 4 18
Ebolowa, Cam., 9,232..............J11 35
Echuca, Australia, 5,407..............G 7 36
Écija, Spain, 25,276..............D 4 17
Eckernförde, Germany, 23,356..............D 1 14
Ed Damer, Sudan, 7,650..............N 8 34
Ed Dueim, Sudan, 12,319..............N 9 34
Eddystone (point), Australia..............H 8 36
Eddystone Rock (island), Eng. ....C 7 10
Ede, Netherlands, 54,253..............H 4 15
Édessa, Greece, 14,935..............F 5 21
Edinburgh,* Scotland, 466,761..............K 8 11
Edirne, Turkey, 33,591..............B 2 28
Edithburgh, Australia, 477..............F 6 36
Edjeleh, Oasis..............H 6 34
Edmonton,* Alta., 226,002..............H 4 40
Edmonton, Greater, Alta., 248,949..............H 4 40
Edmundston, N.B., 10,753..............G 4 41
Edremit, Turkey, 17,829..............B 3 28
Edson, Alta., 2,518..............G 4 40
Edward (lake), Africa..............M12 35
Eeklo, Belgium, 17,841..............D 6 15
Eganville, Ontario, 1,598..............E 4 41
Eger, Hungary, 29,434..............F 3 20
Eger (Cheb), Czech., 20,136..............B 1 20
Eidsvold, Australia, 485..............J 5 36
Eigg (island), Scotland, 115..............D 6 11
Eil, Somalia, 350..............S10 34
Eilam, Iran, 6,203..............E 4 27
Eileen (lake), Canada..............J 2 40
Eilenburg, Germany, 19,980..............E 3 14
'Ein Harod, Israel, 1,230..............C 2 24
Einbeck, Germany, 17,759..............C 3 14
Eindhoven, Netherlands, 157,621..............G 6 15
Eirunepé, Brazil, 1,757..............F 5 46
Eisenach, Germany, 51,834..............D 3 14
Eisenerz, Austria, 12,759..............C 3 20
Eisleben, Germany, 29,095..............D 3 14
Eltorf, Germany, 11,611..............B 3 14
Ekibastuz, U.S.S.R., 10,000..............J 4 22
El Aghelia, Libya, 1,000..............L 5 34
El 'Alamein, Egypt..............M 5 34
El Arahal, Spain, 12,133..............D 4 17
El Bur, Somalia, 600..............R11 34
El Callao, Venezuela, 4,069..............H 2 46
El Faiyûm, Egypt, 73,314..............M 6 34
El Fasher, Sudan, 23,250..............M 9 34
El Ferrol del Caudillo, Spain, 47,388..............B 1 17
El Goléa, Oasis, 7,452..............G 5 34
El Husn, Jordan, 4,510..............D 3 24
El Iskandariya (Alexandria), Egypt, 925,081..............M 5 34
El Jauf, Libya, 2,500..............L 7 34
El Karak, Jordan, 5,539..............E 4 24
El Khalil (Hebron), Jordan, 35,933..............C 4 24
El Kharga, Egypt, 6,686..............N 6 34
El Ladhiqiya (Latakia), Syria 102,832..............F 5 28
El Marj, Libya, 8,000..............L 5 34
El Minya, Egypt, 76,412..............M 6 34
El Obeid, Sudan, 72,300..............N 9 34
El Oro, Mexico, 8,638..............K 7 44
El Oued, Oasis, 13,489..............H 5 34
El Progreso, Honduras, 9,150..............D 3 39
El Puerto de Santa María, Spain, 28,376..............C 4 17
El Qahira (Cairo),* U.A.R., 2,100,506..............N 5 34
El Quseir, Egypt, 5,388..............O 6 34
El Salto, Mexico, 6,070..............G 5 44
El Tigre, Venezuela, 20,655..............H 2 46
El Tocuya, Venezuela, 5,519..............G 2 46
Elâziğ, Turkey, 41,915..............H 3 28
Elba (island), Italy, 31,641..............C 3 18
Elbasan, Albania, 14,968..............E 5 21
Elbe (river), Germany..............D 2 14
Elbert (mountain), U.S. ....G 5 42
Elbeuf, France, 15,341..............D 3 16
Elbistan, Turkey, 8,536..............G 3 28
Elbląg (Elbing), Poland, 21,100..............D 1 24
Elbow, Saskatchewan, 281..............J 4 40
El'brus (mtn.), U.S.S.R...............F 5 22
Elburz (mountains), Iran..............F 2 27
Elche, Spain, 31,191..............F 3 17
Elcho (island), Australia..............F 2 36
Elda, Spain, 18,785..............F 3 17
Elektrostal', U.S.S.R., 97,000..............B 3 22
Elephant Butte (res.), U.S. ....G 6 42
Eleuthera (island), Bahama Is., 6,430..............C 1 45
Elgin, Scotland, 10,624..............K 4 11
Elgon (mountain), Africa..............N11 35
Elisabethville, Belgian Congo, 117,879..............M14 35
Elista, U.S.S.R., 22,000..............F 5 22
Ełk, Poland, 21,100..............F 2 24
Elk Island Park, Alta., 55..............H 4 40
Elk Lake, Ont., 350..............D 4 41
Elkhorn, Manitoba, 673..............K 5 40
Elko, British Columbia, 200..............G 5 40
Ellesmere Port, England, 32,653..............E 4 10
Ellice (islands), Pacific, 4,487..............H 6 37
Ellichpur, India, 31,475..............C 4 29
Ellore (Eluru), India, 64,911..............D 5 29
Elmshorn, Germany, 36,186..............C 2 14
Elrose, Saskatchewan, 538..............J 4 40
Elsas, Ontario, 150..............D 4 41
Elsinore (Helsingör), Denmark, 21,010..............H 8 13
Eluru, India, 64,911..............D 5 29
Elvas, Portugal, 10,821..............C 3 17
Emba (river), U.S.S.R. ....G 5 22
Embarcación, Argentina, 3,303..............G 8 47
Emden, Germany, 37,252..............B 2 14
Emerald, Australia, 1,633..............H 4 36
Emerson, Manitoba, 896..............L 5 40
Emi Koussi (mtn.), Chad..............K 8 34
Emmahaven (Telukbajur,), Indon. ....C 6 31
Emo, Ontario, 653..............B 4 41
Empalme, Mexico, 10,375..............D 2 44
Empedrado, Argentina, 3,715..............J 9 47
Empoli, Italy, 23,509..............C 3 18
Empress, Alta., 480..............H 4 40
En Nahud, Sudan, 30,200..............M 9 34
Encarnación, Paraguay, 13,321..............J 9 47
Encounter (bay), Australia..............F 7 36
Ende, Indonesia, 7,226..............G 7 31

Index Ref. Plate No.

Endeavour (strait), Australia........G 2 36
Engel's, U.S.S.R., 90,000..............F 4 22
Englee, Newfoundland, 677...........J 3 41
Englehart, Ontario, 1,705.............D 4 41
English Bazar, India, 23,333........E 3 29
English (channel)..........................E 8 10
Eniwetok (island), Pacific............G 4 37
Enna, Italy, 25,784.........................E 6 18
Ennepetal, Germany, 27,422..........G 4 14
Ennis, Ireland, 5,741.....................D 6 12
Enniscorthy, Ireland, 5,445............J 7 12
Enns, Austria, 8,206......................C 2 20
Enschede, Neth., 118,671..............K 4 15
Ensenada, Argentina, 24,925.........O12 47
Ensenada, Mexico, 18,150.............A 1 44
Enshih, China.................................G 5 32
Entebbe,* Uganda, 7,942...............N12 33
Entwistle, Alberta, 354..................G 4 40
Enugu, Nigeria, 62,964..................H10 34
Enzeli (Pahlevi), Iran, 45,726.......F 2 27
Epernay, France, 19,527................E 3 16
Épinal, France, 26,288...................G 3 16
Equator ....N 5 6
Er Ramtha, Jordan, 6,410..............E 2 24
Erbaa, Turkey, 8,537......................G 2 28
Erbil (Arbela), Iraq, 26,086.........D 2 27
Erd, Hungary, 13,062.....................E 3 20
Erechim, Brazil, 14,663..................K 9 47
Ereğli, Turkey, 7,880......................D 2 28
Ereğli, Turkey, 24,098....................F 4 28
Erfurt, Germany, 174,633...............D 3 14
Erg Iguidi (desert).........................E 6 34
Ericht (lake), Scotland...................H 6 11
Erie (lake), U.S.-Canada................N 4 43
Eriksdale, Manitoba, 260...............L 4 40
Erith, England, 46,270....................H 6 10
Erivan, U.S.S.R., 509,000 ....F 6 22
Erlangen, Germany, 50,001.............D 4 14
Ermenek, Turkey, 7,498..................E 4 28
Ernakulam, India, 46,790...............C 6 29
Erne (lake), Ireland........................F 3 12
Erode, India, 39,483.......................C 6 29
Eromanga, Australia, 25..................G 5 36
Erris Head (cape), Ireland..............H 3 12
Erzgebirge (mt. range), Ger. ....E 3 14
Erzincan, Turkey, 26,664.................H 3 28
Erzurum, Turkey, 69,499..................J 3 28
Es Salt, Jordan, 15,478...................D 3 24
Esbjerg, Denmark, 48,205................F 9 13
Esch-sur-Alzette, Lux., 26,851.....J 9 15
Eschwege, Germany, 23,544............D 3 14
Eschweiler, Germany, 35,500...........B 3 14
Escuintla, Guatemala, 9,822............B 3 39
Esk (river), Scotland.......................L 9 11
Eskilstuna, Sweden, 53,577.............K 7 13
Eskimo Point, N. W. Terr. ....M 2 40
Eskişehir, Turkey, 122,755...............D 3 28
Esmeraldas, Ecuador, 13,169............D 3 46
Esperance, Australia, 706.................C 6 36
Esperanza, Argentina, 10,035.........H10 47
Espinho, Portugal, 7,989..................B 2 17
Esquel, Argentina, 5,584..................F12 47
Essendon, Australia, 57,873.............K 1 36
Essequibo (river), Br. Guiana.........J 2 46
Esslingen, Germany, 70,633.............C 4 14
Estados, Los (Staten) (island), Argentina H14 47
Estância, Brazil, 14,215....................N 6 46
Este, Italy, 11,773...........................C 2 18
Estelí, Nicaragua, 5,525...................D 4 39
Estevan, Saskatchewan, 5,264..........K 5 40
Eston, England, 33,308.....................F 3 10
Eston, Saskatchewan, 1,624..............J 4 40
Estoril, Portugal, 5,545....................B 3 17
Estrecho (means strait) (Sp.)......
Estrêla (mt. range), Portugal..........C 2 17
Esztergom, Hungary, 20,128.............E 3 20
Et Tafila, Jordan..............................E 5 24
Étampes, France, 9,952......................E 3 16
Etawah, India, 53,114........................C 3 29
Etna (volcano), Sicily, Italy.............E 6 18
Eton, Australia, 263...........................H 4 36
Etosha Pan (dry lake), S.W. Africa K15 35
Etterbeek, Belgium, 51,252...............C 9 15
Ettlingen, Germany, 16,451...............C 4 14
Euboea (island), Greece, 164,542..G 6 21
Eulo, Australia, 60.............................G 5 36
Eupen, Belgium, 14,010......................J 7 15
Euphrates (river)...............................E 3 26
Euskirchen, Germany, 16,805.............B 3 14
Eutin, Germany, 19,100.......................D 1 14
Evans (mountain), U.S. ....G 5 42
Evans (strait), Canada.......................P 2 40
Even Yehuda, Israel, 2,050.................B 3 24
Everard (lake), Australia....................E 6 36
Everest (mt.), Asia.............................E 3 29
Évora, Portugal, 25,678......................C 3 17
Évreux, France, 20,441.......................D 3 16
Ewab (Kai) (isls.), indonesia, 50,648 ....J 7 31
Ewarton, Jamaica, 2,900.....................C 3 45

Exe (river), England...........................D 7 10
Exeter, England, 75,513......................D 7 10
Exmoor (plateau), England.................D 6 10
Exmouth, England, 17,222..................D 7 10
Exmouth (gulf), Australia...................A 4 36
Eyasi (lake), Tan. Terr. O12 35
Eyre (lake), Australia.........................F 5 36
Eyre's (peninsula), Australia..............F 6 36
Eyüp, Turkey, 50,984...........................D 6 28
Ez Zarqa', Jordan, 3,000......................E 3 24

F

Fabriano, Italy, 20,987.......................D 3 18
Facatativá, Colombia, 9,779................F 3 46
Fada-N'Gourma, Upper Volta, 4,121 ....G 9 34
Faenza, Italy, 26,365...........................C 2 18
Făgăras, Rumania, 9,296......................G 3 21
Faguibine (lake), Sudanese Rep. ....E 8 34
Fahrej (Iranshahr), Iran, 4,063.....M 7 28
Fai Fo, Vietnam...................................F 4 30
Fair (island), Scotland, 73.................M 3 11
Fairview, Alberta, 1,260......................G 3 40
Fairweather (mountain), Alaska-Canada ....C 3 40
Faizabad, Afghanistan, 25,770.........K 2 26
Faizabad, India, 57,632.......................D 3 29
Fakfak, Neth. N. G. ....J 6 31
Falaise, France, 5,289...........................C 3 16
Falam, Burma.......................................B 2 30
Fălçiu, Rumania, 5,124........................J 2 21
Falher, Alberta, 802..............................G 3 40
Falkensee, Germany, 28,275..................J 3 14
Falkirk, Scotland, 37,535......................E 2 11
Falkland (islands), S.A., 2,239.......H14 47
Falmouth, England, 16,975...................C 7 10
Falmouth, Jamaica, 2,561.....................C 3 45
Falso (cape), Mexico............................D 5 44
Fălticeni, Rumania, 10,563...................H 2 21
Falun, Sweden, 16,858..........................J 6 13
Famagusta, Cyprus, 16,500...................F 5 28
Fanning (island), Pacific, 259..............L 5 37
Fano, Italy, 25,428...............................D 3 18
Farafangana, Malg. Rep., 7,036...R16 35
Farafra (oasis), Egypt, 749..................M 6 34
Farah, Afghanistan, 15,258..................H 3 26
Fareham, England, 45,520....................F 7 10
Faridpur, Pakistan, 25,287....................F 4 29
Farneborough, England, 26,271.........G 6 10
Farnham, England, 23,928....................G 6 10
Farnham, Quebec, 5,843.......................F 4 41
Faro, Portugal, 17,631..........................B 4 17
Farquhar (cape), Australia...................A 4 36
Farrukhabad (Fatehgarh), India, 69,418 ....C 3 29
Fasa, Iran, 10,228..................................H 6 27
Fasano, Italy, 20,899.............................F 4 18
Fatehgarh, India, 69,418.......................C 3 29
Fatehpur, India, 23,253.........................B 3 29
Fatehpur, India, 27,436.........................D 3 29
Fatih, Turkey, 284,621...........................D 6 28
Fátima, Portugal, 4,719.........................B 3 17
Fatsham, China, 122,500........................H 7 32
Favara, Italy, 25,331...............................D 6 18
Faversham, England, 12,299...................J 6 10
Fawn (river), Canada.............................C 3 41
Fear (cape), U.S. ....O 6 43
Fécamp, France, 17,193...........................D 3 16
Feilding, New Zealand, 6,784................L 6 36
Feira de Santana, Brazil, 27,285 ....N 6 46
Feldkirch, Austria, 15,045......................A 3 20
Felixstowe, England, 15,081...................J 6 10
Felsögalla, Hungary, 17,110....................E 3 20
Feltre, Italy, 13,717................................C 1 18
Fenelon Falls, Ontario, 1,137.................E 5 41
Fénérive, Malgache Rep., 2,347.....S15 35
Fengkieh, China......................................G 5 32
Fenyang, China.......................................H 4 32
Feodosiya, U.S.S.R., 28,656...................E 5 22
Fergana, U.S.S.R., 80,000.......................T 2 33
Ferkessédougou, Ivory Coast, 7,614 ....E10 34
Ferme-Neuve, Quebec, 1,891.................E 4 41
Fermo, Italy, 12,343...............................D 3 18
Fernando Po (island), Sp. Guin., 40,475 ....H11 34
Fernie, Br. Columbia, 2,808....................G 5 40
Ferozepore, India, 82,502.......................B 2 29
Ferrara, Italy, 92,385..............................C 2 18
Ferryland, Newfoundland, 500..............K 4 41
Feteşti, Rumania, 11,946.........................H 3 21
Fetlar (island), Scotland, 161................N 2 11
Fez, Morocco, 179,372............................F 5 34

Fianarantsoa, Malg. Rep., 26,515..R16 35
Fife Ness (prom.), Scotland.........M 7 11
Figueira da Foz, Portugal, 10,486 ....B 2 17
Figueras, Spain, 15,393...........................H 1 17
Figuig, Morocco, 9,490.............................F 5 34
Fiji (isls.), Pacific, 333,389.....................H 7 37
Finisterre (cape), Spain............................B 1 17
Finland (gulf), Europe..............................P 7 13
Finlay (river), Canada...............................E 3 40
Finschhafen, Terr. N.G., 1,564...............C 7 31
Finsterwalde, Germany, 20,766.............E 3 14
Firenze (Florence), Italy, 362,459 ....C 3 18
Firminy, France, 17,941............................F 5 16
Firozabad, India, 40,572...........................C 3 29
Firubabad, Iran, 4,337..............................H 6 27
Fisher (strait), Canada..............................P 2 40
Fitzpatrick, Quebec, 300...........................F 4 41
Fitzroy (river), Australia..........................C 3 36
Fiume (Rijeka), Yugoslavia, 75,112 ....B 3 21
Flamborough Headland (prom.) England ....H 3 10
Flanders, Ontario, 188...............................B 4 41
Flannan (islands), Scotland, 3.............A 3 11
Flathead (lake), U.S. ....E 3 42
Flattery (cape), Australia..........................H 2 36
Flattery (cape), U.S. ....B 2 42
Fleetwood, England, 27,525......................D 4 10
Flensburg, Germany, 102,832....................C 1 14
Flers, France, 9,651.....................................C 3 16
Flin Flon, Manitoba, 10,234......................K 4 40
Flinders (bay), Australia............................A 6 36
Flinders (islands), Tas., Australia ....H 7 36
Flinders (mt. range), Australia.................F 6 36
Flinders (reef), Australia...........................H 3 36
Flinders (river), Australia..........................G 3 36
Flint, Wales, 14,257.....................................D 4 10
Florence, Italy, 362,459..............................C 3 18
Florencia, Colombia, 4,164.........................F 3 46
Flores (island), Indonesia, 494,851 ....G 7 31
Flores (sea)..F 7 31
Floriano, Brazil, 9,588.................................M 5 46
Florianópolis, Brazil, 48,264........................L 9 47
Florida, Italy, 15,519.....................................E 6 18
Florida, Uruguay, 16,000.............................J10 47
Florida (bay), U.S. ....N 8 43
Florida (peninsula), U.S. ....N 7 43
Florida (strait), U.S. ....N 8 43
Flowers Cove, Newf., 800...............................J 3 41
Flushing, Neth., 29,148..................................C 6 15
Foam Lake, Saskatchewan, 841.......................K 4 40
Focşani, Rumania, 27,960...............................H 3 21
Foggia, Italy, 85,582.......................................E 4 18
Fogo, Newfoundland, 1,184.............................K 4 41
Fogo (island), Canada, 4,488.........................K 4 41
Fohnsdorf, Austria, 11,190.............................C 3 20
Foleyet, Ontario, 500.......................................D 4 41
Foligno, Italy, 33,474.......................................D 3 18
Folkestone, England, 45,203...........................J 6 10
Fond-du-Lac (river), Canada..........................K 3 40
Fontainebleau, France, 17,218........................E 3 16
Fontenay-sous-Bois, France, 30,225 ....C 2 16
Fontenay-le-Comte, France, 8,139.C 4 16
Foochow, China, 553,000 ....J 6 32
Foothills, Alberta, 250....................................G 4 40
Footscray, Australia, 57,915.........................K 2 36
Forbes, Australia, 6,514..................................H 6 36
Forchheim, Germany, 16,599..........................D 4 14
Forecariah, Guinea, 4,356..............................D10 34
Forest (Vorst), Belgium, 49,142.....................B 9 15
Forestville, Quebec, 1,117...............................G 4 41
Forlì, Italy, 51,666...D 2 18
Formia, Italy, 15,192..F 6 18
Formosa, Argentina, 16,506.............................J10 47
Formosa (Taiwan)(island), China, 8,212,213 ....K 7 32
Formosa (Taiwan)(strait), China.K 7 32
Forst, Germany, 29,829....................................F 3 14
Fort-Archambault, Chad, 5,000.....K10 34
Fort-Coulonge, Quebec, 1,633.........................E 4 41
Fort-Dauphin, Malg. Rep., 8,364..R17 35
Fort-de-France,* Martinique, 66,006 ....G 4 45
Fort de Kock (Bukittinggi), Indonesia, 14,657...................................B 6 31
Fort-Flatters, Oasis, 6,992...............................H 6 34
Fort Frances, Ontario, 9,005...........................B 4 41
Fort George (river), Canada............................E 3 41
Fort Jameson, N. Rhod., 5,739......N14 35
Fort-Lamy,* Chad, 18,465..............................K 9 34
Fort-Laperrine (Tamanrasset) Oasis, 1,846 ....H 7 34
Fort Macleod, Alta., 2,103..............................H 5 40
Fort McPherson, N. W. Terr., 20..D 1 40
Fort Nelson, B. C., 350....................................F 3 40
Fort Norman, N. W. Terr., 70..........................E 2 40
Fort Peck, (res.) U.S. ....G 3 42
Fort Portal, Uganda, 5,527..............................N11 35

Fort Qu'appelle, Saskatchewan, 1,130 ....K 4 40
Fort Reliance, N.W. Terr. ....J 2 40
Fort Resolution, N. W. Terr., 140.H 2 40
Fort Rosebery, N. Rhod., 1,170........M14 35
Fort Saint James, B. C., 615............F 4 40
Fort Saint John, B.C., 1,908..............F 3 40
Fort Sandeman, Pakistan, 9,353...A 2 29
Fort Saskatchewan, Alberta, 2,582 ....H 4 40
Fort Shevchenko, U.S.S.R. ....F 5 22
Fort Simpson, N. W. Terr., 80.........F 2 40
Fort Smith, N. W. Terr., 250............H 2 40
Fort Vermilion Alberta, 350..............G 3 40
Fort Victoria, S. Rhodesia, 3,587..N15 35
Fort William, Ontario, 39,464...........C 4 41
Fortaleza (Ceará), Brazil, 205,052 ....N 4 46
Forteau, Labrador, Newf., 250..........J 3 41
Fortescue (river), Australia................B 4 36
Forth (firth), Scotland..........................L 7 11
Fougères, France, 18,599......................C 3 16
Fourmies, France, 11,805......................F 2 16
Fowler's Bay, Australia, 59...................E 6 36
Fowning, China, 62,144.........................K 5 32
Fox Valley, Saskatchewan, 395.............J 4 40
Foxe (basin), Canada..............................E26 8
Foxe (channel), Canada..........................P 1 40
Foxe (peninsula), Canada.......................L 3 38
Foyle (bay), N. Ireland...........................G 1 12
Foz do Iguaçú, Brazil, 2,949.................K 9 47
Franca, Brazil, 26,629.............................L 8 46
Francavilla Fontana, Italy, 24,743.F 4 18
Frankenstein (Ząbkowice Śląskie), Poland, 10,100......................................C 3 24
Frankenthal, Germany, 25,417...............C 4 14
Frankfurt am Main, Germany, 532,037 ....C 3 14
Frankfurt an der Oder, Germany, 51,577 ....F 2 14
Franz, Ontario, 75.......................................D 4 41
Franz Josef Land (isls.), U.S.S.R. .F 1 22
Frascati, Italy, 11,067.................................D 4 18
Fraser (river), Canada................................F 4 40
Fraser (Great Sandy) (island), Australia ....J 5 36
Fraserburgh, Scotland, 10,444...................N 4 11
Fraserdale, Ontario, 150............................D 4 41
Fray Bentos, Uruguay, 9,500......................J10 47
Frechen, Germany, 20,490..........................B 3 14
Fredericia, Denmark 25,981.......................F 9 13
Fredericton,* New Brunswick, 18,303 ....G 4 41
Frederikshaab, Greenland, 634..................F24 8
Frederikshavn, Denmark, 18,394...............G 8 13
Frederiksted, Virg. Isls., 1,925..................G 1 45
Fredrikstad, Norway, 14,326.....................D 4 13
Freetown,* S. Leone, 64,576.....................D10 34
Freiberg, Germany, 42,303..........................E 3 14
Freiburg, Germany, 109,717........................B 5 14
Freienwalde, Germany, 10,667....................E 2 14
Freising, Germany, 25,491...........................D 4 14
Freital, Germany, 39,159.............................E 3 14
Fréjus, France, 5,587....................................G 6 16
Fremantle, Australia, †47,269.....................B 2 36
Frenchman Butte, Sask., 106......................J 4 40
Fresnillo, Mexico, 29,931............................H 5 44
Freudenstadt, Germany, 10,689..................C 4 14
Fribourg, Switzerland, 29,005....................D 3 19
Friedberg, Germany, 15,175.........................C 3 14
Friedrichshafen, Germany, 20,501..C 5 14
Friendly (Tonga) (islands), Pacific, 46,870...J 7 37
Frio (cape), Brazil..M 8 47
Frio (cape), S. W. Africa...............................J15 35
Frisian (islands), Netherlands.......................G 1 15
Frobisher (bay), Canada.................................F25 8
Frome (lake), Australia..................................G 6 36
Frontera (Alvaro Obregón), Mexico, 8,466...N 7 44
Frozen (strait), Canada..................................P 1 40
Frunze, U.S.S.R., 217,000............................J 5 22
Frutal, Brazil, 3,270......................................L 7 46
Fryanovo, U.S.S.R., 2,582............................B 3 22
Frýdek-Místek, Czech., 24,736....................E 2 20
Fuchu, Japan, 30,308.....................................O 2 33
Fuerte Olimpo, Paraguay, 1,113...J 8 46
Fuji (volcano), Japan.....................................J 6 33
Fujisawa, Japan, 84,581.................................O 3 33
Fukuchiyama, Japan, 45,085..........................G 6 33
Fukui, Japan, 100,691.....................................G 5 33
Fukuoka, Japan, 392,649................................D 7 33
Fukushima, Japan, 93,435..............................K 5 33
Fukuyama, Japan, 67,063...............................F 6 33
Fulda, Germany, 42,213.................................C 3 14
Funabashi, Japan, 83,348..............................P 2 33
Funchal,* Madeira, Portugal, 37,035 ....A 2 17
Fundy (bay), Canada......................................G 5 41
Fürstenwalde, Germany, 21,782.....F 2 14
Fürth, Germany, 99,890..................................D 4 14
Fusan (Pusan), Korea, 473,619....D 6 33
Fuse, Japan, 150,129......................................J 8 33

	Index Ref.	Plate No.
Fushun, China, 678,600	K 3	32
Fusin, China, 188,600	K 3	32
Fuyü, China, 64,969	L 2	32
Fyne (lake), Scotland	F 7	11
Fyzabad (Faizabad), India, 57,632	D 3	29

G

	Index Ref.	Plate No.
Gabès, Tunisia, 22,512	H 5	34
Gabès (gulf), Tunisia	J 5	34
Gablonz (Jablonec), Czech., 25,820	C 1	20
Gabrovo, Bulgaria, 21,268	G 4	21
Gadag, India, 56,283	C 5	29
Gadwal, India, 14,716	C 5	29
Găeşti, Rumania, 7,726	G 3	21
Gafsa, Tunisia, 11,320	H 5	34
Gagnoa, Ivory Coast, 15,000	E10	34
Gaiman, Argentina, 4,000	G12	47
Gainsborough, England, 17,513	G 4	10
Gairdner (lake), Australia	F 6	36
Galana (river), Kenya	O12	35
Galashiels, Scotland, 12,496	L 8	11
Galaţi, Rumania, 80,411	H 3	21
Galatina, Italy, 20,975	G 4	18
Galatone, Italy, 12,878	F 4	18
Galilee (sea), Israel	D 2	24
Galkayu, Som., 6,000	R10	34
Gallarate, Italy, 27,261	B 2	18
Galle, Ceylon, 49,038	C 7	29
Gallipoli, Italy, 15,416	F 4	18
Gallipoli (Gelibolu) Turkey, 12,481	C 5	28
Gällivare, Sweden, 3,626	M 3	13
Galt, Ontario, 19,207	D 5	41
Galty (mountains), Ireland	E 7	12
Galway, Ireland, 21,219,	C 5	12
Galway (bay), Ireland	C 5	12
Gamarra, Colombia, 1,963	F 2	46
Gambaga, Ghana, 1,952	G 9	34
Gambela, Ethiopia, 600	N10	34
Gambier (Mangareva) (islands), Pacific, 554	N 8	37
Gamlakarleby (Kokkola), Finland, 15,993	N 5	13
Gananoque, Ontario, 4,981	E 5	41
Ganchi, U.S.S.R., 1,284	P 2	23
Gand (Ghent), Belgium, 162,366	D 6	15
Gander, Newfoundland, 3,000	K 4	41
Gandia, Spain, 15,997	F 3	17
Gandzha (Kirovabad), U.S.S.R., 116,000	F 5	22
Ganges (river), India	E 3	29
Gangtok,* Sikkim	E 3	29
Gani, Indonesia	H 6	31
Gannett Peak (mountain), U.S.	F 4	42
Gao, Sudanese Rep., 8,000	G 8	34
Gaoua, Upper Volta, 2,013	F 9	34
Gap, France, 13,338	G 5	16
Garanhuns, Brazil, 20,718	N 5	46
Gardelegen, Germany, 12,322	D 2	14
Garden Reach, India, 109,160	E 2	29
Gardez, Afghanistan, 17,540	J 3	26
Gardula, Ethiopia, 4,000	O10	34
Garmisch-Partenkirchen, Germany, 24,624	D 5	14
Garonne (river), France	C 5	16
Garoua, Cam., 7,000	J10	34
Garry (lake), Canada	L 1	40
Garulia, India, 20,150	E 1	29
Garut, Indonesia, 24,219	H 2	31
Gasan-Kuli, U.S.S.R., 3,471	G 6	22
Gascoyne (river), Australia	A 5	36
Gasmata, Terr. N. G.	F 6	37
Gaspé, Quebec, 2,194	H 4	41
Gaspé (peninsula), Canada	G 4	41
Gatchina, U.S.S.R., 18,589	D 3	22
Gateshead, England, 115,039	F 3	10
Gatooma, S. Rhodesia, 6,122	M15	35
Gauhati, India, 29,598	F 3	29
Gävle, Sweden, 46,894	K 6	13
Gawler, Australia, 5,117	D 7	36
Gawler (mt. range), Australia	F 6	36
Gaya, Niger, 3,109	G 9	34
Gaya, India, 133,700	E 4	29
Gaza, Egypt, 34,170	A 5	24
Gaziantep, Turkey, 97,144	G 4	28
Gdańsk (Danzig), Poland, 259,900	D 1	24
Gdynia, Poland, 133,300	D 1	24
Gedaref, Sudan, 30,950	O 9	34
Gedera, Israel, 2,530	B 4	24
Geel, Belgium, 25,113	F 6	15
Geelong, Australia, 72,595	K 2	36
Geelvink (channel), Australia	A 5	36
Geislingen, Germany, 22,535	C 4	14
Gela, Italy, 43,326	E 6	18
Gelib, Somalia, 2,000	P11	35
Gelibolu, Turkey, 12,481	C 5	28
Gelsenkirchen, Germany, 367,941	G 4	14
Gemlik, Turkey, 10,403	C 2	28
Genadendal, Cape of G.H., 2,626	E19	35
General Acha, Argentina, 4,709	G11	47
General Alvear, Argentina, 2,548	G11	47
General Madariaga, Arg., 7,073	J11	47
General Pico, Argentina, 11,121	H11	47
Geneva (lake), Switzerland	C 4	19
Geneva (Genève), Switz., 145,473	B 4	19
Genk, Belgium, 43,618	H 7	15
Gennargentu (mountain), Italy	B 5	18
Gennevillers, France, 25,159	B 1	16
Genoa (Genova), Italy, 668,579	B 2	18
Gent (Ghent), Belgium, 162,366	D 6	15
Genthin, Germany, 17,776	F 2	14
Gentilly, France, 16,256	B 2	16
Geographe (bay), Australia	A 6	36
Geographe (channel) Australia	A 4	36
Geok-Tepe, U.S.S.R.	G 6	22
George, Cape of G. H., 11,992	L18	35
George (river), Canada	G 2	41
George Town (Penang), Malayan Fed., 189,068	C 6	30
Georgetown, Australia, 151	G 3	36
Georgetown,* Br. Guiana, 73,509	J 2	46
Georgetown, Gambia, 841	C 9	34
Georgian (bay), Canada	D 4	41
Georgina (river), Australia	F 4	36
Gera, Germany, 89,212	E 3	14
Geraardsbergen (Grammont), Belgium, 10,141	D 7	15
Geraldton, Australia, 8,309	A 5	36
Geraldton, Ontario, 3,263	C 4	41
Germiston, Transv., †166,310	M17	35
Gerona, Spain, †26,163	H 2	17
Géryville, Algeria, 7,210	G 5	34
Geser, Indonesia	J 6	31
Gevelsberg, Germany, 27,918	G 4	14
Ghadames, Libya, 2,758	J 6	34
Ghaghra (river), India	D 3	29
Ghardaia, Oasis, 14,046	G 5	34
Gharian, Libya, †43,747	J 5	34
Ghat, Libya, 732	J 6	34
Ghat Kopar, India, 18,176	B 7	29
Ghazal (river), Chad	K 9	34
Ghazipur, India, 31,326	D 3	29
Ghazni, Afghanistan, 27,084	J 3	26
Ghent, Belgium, 162,366	D 6	15
Gheorgheni, Rumania, 10,031	G 2	21
Gherla, Rumania, 6,663	G 2	21
Gia Dinh, Vietnam, 8,696	E 5	30
Gianitsá, Greece, 16,640	F 5	21
Gibeon, S. W. Africa, 541	K17	35
Gibraltar, 23,232	D 4	17
Gibraltar (strait)	D 5	17
Gibson (desert), Australia	C 4	36
Giessen, Germany, 46,712	C 3	14
Gifu, Japan, 211,845	H 6	33
Gigha (passage), Scotland	E 8	11
Gijón, Spain, †108,564	D 1	17
Gila (river), U.S.	E 6	42
Gilbert (isls.), Pacific, 27,824	H 5	37
Gilbert (river), Australia	G 3	36
Gilbert and Ellice (isls.), Pacific, 37,120	H 6	37
Gillam, Manitoba, 95	M 3	40
Gillingham, England, 68,099	H 6	10
Gilly, Belgium, 24,967	E 8	15
Gimli, Manitoba, 1,660	L 4	40
Gingin, Australia, 382	B 1	36
Ginir, Ethiopia, 3,500	P10	34
Gioia del Colle, Italy, 27,094	F 4	18
Gioiosa Ionica, Italy, 11,675	F 5	18
Giovinazzo, Italy, 13,978	F 4	18
Girdle Ness (prom.), Scotland	N 5	11
Giresun, Turkey, 15,260	H 2	28
Giridih, India, 25,326	E 4	29
Gisborne, New Zealand, †22,622	M 6	36
Giurgiu, Rumania, 30,197	G 3	21
Giv'at Brenner, Israel, 1,685	B 4	24
Givors, France, 12,653	F 5	16
Gizhduvan, U.S.S.R., 4,900	H 5	22
Gizhiga, U.S.S.R.	T 3	23
Giżyeko, Poland, 14,100	E 1	24
Gjinokastër, Albania, 10,910	D 5	21
Gjövik, Norway, 5,723	G 6	13
Glace Bay, Nova Scotia, 24,416	J 4	41
Gladbach (München-Gladbach), Germany, 124,879	B 3	14
Gladbeck, Germany, 71,612	B 3	14
Gladstone, Australia, 6,944	J 4	36
Glasgow, Scotland, 1,089,767	D 2	11
Glatz (Kłodzko), Poland, 20,700	C 3	24
Glauchau, Germany, 34,996	E 3	14
Glazov, U.S.S.R., 59,000	G 4	22
Gleichen, Alberta, 581	H 4	40
Glen Innes, Australia, 5,842	J 5	36
Glenelg, Australia, 12,966	D 8	36
Glenmorgan, Australia, 143	H 5	36
Glittertind (mountain), Norway	F 6	13
Gliwice (Gleiwitz), Poland, 132,500	A 4	24
Gloggnitz, Austria, 7,068	D 3	20
Glomma (river), Norway	G 6	13
Glossop, England, 18,004	F 4	10
Gloucester, England, 67,280	E 6	10
Głowno, Poland, 10,500	D 3	29
Głuchołazy, Poland, 10,000	C 3	24
Glückstadt, Germany, 12,551	C 2	14
Glukhov, U.S.S.R., 16,000	E 4	22
Gmünd, Germany, 33,448	C 4	14
Gmunden, Austria, 12,912	B 3	20
Gniezno (Gnesen), Poland, 41,200	C 2	24
Gnjilane, Yugoslavia, 8,287	E 4	21
Go Cong, Vietnam, 2,760	E 5	30
Goba, Ethiopia, 3,000	O10	34
Gobabis, S. W. Africa, 2,051	K16	35
Gobi (Shamo) (desert)	G 3	32
Goch, Germany, 12,989	B 3	14
Godavari (river), India	C 5	29
Godbout, Quebec, 663	G 4	41
Goderich, Ontario, 5,886	D 5	41
Godhavn, Greenland, 319	E24	8
Godhra, India, 41,986	B 4	29
God's Lake, Manitoba, 200	M 4	40
Godthaab,* Greenland 1,021	F24	8
Godwin Austen (mtn.), Kash.	C 1	29
Gogama, Ontario, 500	D 4	41
Goiânia, Brazil, 14,093	L 7	46
Goiás, Brazil, 5,606	K 7	46
Gölcük, Turkey, 14,176	C 2	28
Golden (valley), Ireland	E 6	12
Golfo (means gulf) (Sp., It., Port.)		
Golitsyno, U.S.S.R., 1,500	B 4	22
Gomel', U.S.S.R., 166,000	E 4	22
Gómez Palacio, Mexico, 45,872	G 4	44
Gona, Papua	C 7	31
Gonaïves, Haiti, 13,534	B 5	48
Gonda, India, 21,567	D 3	29
Gondar, Ethiopia, 14,000	O 9	34
Gönen, Turkey, 9,609	B 2	28
Good Hope (cape), U. of S. Afr.	K18	35
Goole, England, 19,234	G 4	10
Goomalling, Australia, 804	B 1	36
Goondiwindi, Australia, 2,950	H 5	36
Goose (lake), U.S.	C 4	42
Goose Airport (Goose Bay), Lab., Newfoundland, 1,000	H 3	41
Göppingen, Germany 39,329	C 4	14
Gorakhpur, India, 132,436	D 3	29
Gordon's Bay, Cape of G. H., 1,020	D20	35
Gore, Ethiopia, 25,000	O10	34
Gore, New Zealand, 6,567	L 7	36
Gore Bay, Ontario, 731	D 4	41
Gori, U.S.S.R., 15,000	F 5	22
Gorinchem (Gorkum), Neth., 19,306	G 6	15
Gorizia, Italy, 38,497	D 2	18
Gor'kiy, U.S.S.R., 942,000	F 4	22
Gorlice, Poland, 10,000	E 4	24
Görlitz, Germany, 85,686	F 3	14
Gorlovka, U.S.S.R., 293,000	L 1	23
Gorna Dzhumaya (Blagoyevgrad), Bulgaria, 14,066	F 5	21
Gorna Oryakhovitsa, Bulgaria, 10,303	G 4	21
Gorno-Altaysk, U.S.S.R., 27,000	K 4	22
Goroka, Terr. N. G., 1973	B 7	31
Gorontalo, Indonesia, 15,603	G 5	31
Gorzów Wielkopolski (Landsberg), Poland, 46,300	B 2	24
Goslar, Germany, 40,689	D 3	14
Gospić, Yugoslavia, 5,287	B 3	21
Gosport, England, 56,279	F 7	10
Göteborg (Gothenburg), Sweden, 353,991	G 8	13
Gotha, Germany, 57,639	D 3	14
Gotland (island), Sweden, 59,054	L 8	13
Goto (islands), Japan, 116,363	D 7	33
Gotse Delchev, Bulgaria, 11,061	F 5	21
Göttingen, Germany, 78,680	D 3	14
Gottwaldov (Zlín), Czech., 57,974	D 2	20
Gouda, Netherlands, 42,181	F 4	15
Gouin (res.), Canada	F 4	41
Goulburn, Australia, 19,183	J 7	36
Goulburn (islands), Australia	E 2	36
Goundam, Sudanese Rep., 6,500	F 8	34
Governador Valadares, Brazil, 20,864	M 7	46
Goya, Argentina, 20,804	J 9	47
Goyders (lagoon), Australia	F 5	36
Graaf-Reinet, Cape of G. H., 14,088	M18	35
Gračanica, Yugoslavia, 5,651	D 3	21
Gracefield, Quebec, 639	E 4	41
Gracias a Dios (cape), Nicaragua	F 3	39
Grafton, Australia, 9,759	J 5	36
Graham, Ontario, 49	B 4	41
Grahamstown, Cape of G. H., 23,767	M18	35
Grammont, Belgium, 10,141	D 7	15
Grampians (mountains), Scotland	G 7	11
Gran Chaco (region), S.A.	H 9	47
Gran Sirte (Sidra) (gulf), Libya	K 5	34
Granada, Nicaragua, 21,743	E 5	39
Granada, Spain, †154,859	E 4	17
Granby, Quebec, 27,095	F 4	41
Grand (canal), China	J 4	32
Grand (cape), Australia	C 6	36
Grand Bank, Newfoundland, 2,435	J 4	41
Grand-Bassam, Ivory C., 4,770	F11	34
Grand Cayman (island), West Indies, 5,311	B 3	45
Grand Coulee (dam), U.S.	D 3	42
Grand Falls, New Brunswick, 3,675	G 4	41
Grand Falls, Newfoundland, 5,508	J 4	41
Grand Forks, Br. Columbia, 1,995	G 5	40
Grand-Lahou, Ivory C., 4,703	E11	34
Grand Rapids, Manitoba, 300	L 4	40
Grande (bay), S.A.	G14	47
Grande (river), Brazil	L 8	46
Grande Prairie, Alberta, 6,302	G 3	40
Grande-Rivière, Quebec, 1,024	H 4	41
Grande-Valléé, Quebec, 459	H 4	41
Grandes-Bergeronnes, Quebec, 810	G 4	41
Grangemouth, Scotland, 15,432	J 8	11
Granollérs, Spain, 12,662	H 2	17
Grantham, England, 23,555	G 5	10
Granville, Australia, 26,949	L 3	36
Granville, France, 9,858	C 3	16
Granville, Yukon	C 2	40
Granville (lake), Canada	L 3	40
Gras (lake), Canada	J 2	40
Grasse, France, 13,731	G 6	16
Graudenz (Grudziadz), Poland, 59,800	D 2	24
Gravelbourg, Saskatchewan, 1,434	J 5	40
Gravenhurst, Ontario, 3,014	E 5	41
Gravesend, England, 44,560	H 6	10
Gravina di Puglia, Italy, 29,895	F 4	18
Graz, Austria, 226,453	C 3	20
Great Abaco (island), Bahama Is.	C 1	45
Great Australian (bay), Australia	D 6	36
Great Bahama (island), Bahama Is., 4,095	B 1	45
Great Barrier, The (reef), Australia	H 3	36
Great Bear (lake), Canada	F 1	40
Great Dividing (mt. range), Australia	H 4	36
Great Exuma (island), Bahama Is., 2,919	C 2	45
Great Inagua (island), Bahama Is., 999	D 2	45
Great Khingan (mt. range), China	K 2	32
Great Salt (lake), U.S.	E 4	42
Great Sandy (desert), Australia	C 4	36
Great Sandy (Fraser) (island), Australia	J 5	36
Great Slave (lake), Canada	H 2	40
Great Victoria (desert), Australia	D 5	36
Great Wall, China	G 4	32
Great Whale (river), Canada	E 2	41
Great Yarmouth, England, 51,105	J 5	10
Greater Antilles (islands)	B 2	45
Green (river), U. S.	F 5	42
Greenland (island), 25,302	F23	8
Greenock, Scotland, 76,292	A 2	11
Greenwich, England, 89,846	H 6	10
Gregory (mt. range), Australia	G 3	36
Greifswald, Germany, 43,590	E 1	14
Greiz, Germany, 45,410	E 3	14
Grenada (island), W. I., 72,055	G 4	45
Grenchen, Switzerland, 12,650	D 2	19
Grenfell, Saskatchewan, 1,080	K 4	40
Grenoble, France, 111,054	G 5	16
Grenville (cape), Australia	G 2	36
Gresik, Indonesia, 25,621	K 2	31
Gretna, Manitoba, 603	L 5	40
Grey (cape), Australia	F 2	36
Greymouth, N. Z., 8,948	K 7	36
Greyton, Cape of G. H., 1,094	F19	35
Griffith, Australia, 6,608	H 6	36
Grimma, Germany, 14,310	E 3	14
Grimsby, England, 94,557	H 4	10
Grimshaw, Alberta, 904	G 3	40
Grindelwald, Switzerland, 3,053	E 3	19
Griquatown, Cape of G. H., 2,893	L17	35
Grodekovo, U.S.S.R., 4,066	P 5	23
Grodno, U.S.S.R., 72,000	D 4	22
Grodzisk Mazowiecki, Poland, 18,200	E 2	24
Gronau, Germany, 24,403	B 2	14
Groningen, Neth., 142,889	K 2	15
Groote Eylandt (island), Australia	F 2	36
Grootfontein, S. W. Afr., 1,550	K15	35

Index Plate
Ref. No.

Grossenhain, Germany, 17,708......E 3 14
Grossglockner (mtn.), Australia...B 3 20
Grosseto, Italy, 29,364.................C 3 18
Grottaglie, Italy, 18,819.................F 4 18
Grouard Mission, Alberta, 328.........G 3 40
Groznyy, U.S.S.R., 240,000............F 5 22
Grudziądz (Graudenz), Poland, 59,800 ....D 2 24
Grünberg (Zielona Góra), Poland, 43,600 ....B 3 24
Gryfice, Poland, 10,200....................F 2 24
Guadalajara, Mexico, 378,423.........H 6 44
Guadalajara, Spain, †18,748..........E 2 17
Guadalcanal (island), Pacific, 14,500 ....F 6 37
Guadalquivir (river), Spain..........C 4 17
Guadalupe (island), Mexico..........F 7 38
Guadarrama (mt. range), Spain...E 2 17
Guadeloupe (island), 278,864........F 3 45
Guadiana (river), Spain.................C 4 17
Guadix, Spain, 17,465.....................E 4 17
Guajará-Mirim, Brazil, 2,687........H 6 46
Guajira (peninsula), Colombia.......F 1 46
Guam (island), Pacific, 59,498.......E 4 37
Guanabacoa, Cuba, 30,287...............C 1 48
Guanajay, Cuba, 10,527....................B 1 48
Guanajuato, Mexico, 30,575...........J 6 44
Guanare, Venezuela, 8,062...............G 2 46
Guanica, Puerto Rico, 4,833............F 1 45
Guantánamo, Cuba, 42,423..............K 4 48
Guapi, Colombia, 1,348....................E 3 46
Guaporé (river), S.A. ....H 6 46
Guaranda, Ecuador, 7,287...............E 4 46
Guarapuava, Brazil, 5,657...............K 9 47
Guarda, Portugal, 7,704...................C 2 17
Guardafui (cape), Somalia..............S 9 34
Guatemala,* Guat., 284,276.............B 3 39
Guaviare (river), Colombia.............F 3 46
Guayama, Puerto Rico, 19,408.....G 1 45
Guayaquil, Ecuador, 258,966...........D 4 46
Guayaquil (gulf), S.A. ....D 4 46
Guaymas, Mexico, 18,890.................D 3 44
Guben, Germany, 25,297...................F 3 14
Gudiyatam, India, 32,671.................C 6 29
Gudur, India, 12,105.........................C 6 29
Guebwiller, France, 9,695.................G 4 16
Guelph, Ontario, 33,860....................D 5 41
Guéret, France, 8,239.......................D 4 16
Guildford, Australia, 2,134..............B 2 36
Guildford, England, 47,496...............G 6 10
Guimarães, Portugal, 18,294............B 2 17
Güines, Cuba, 22,669.........................C 1 48
Gujranwala, Pakistan, 114,193.......B 2 29
Gujrat, Pakistan, 46,971...................B 2 29
Gull Lake, Saskatchewan, 1,052.....J 4 40
Gulpaigan, Iran, 19,889...................F 4 27
Gumeracha, Australia, 471..............E 7 36
Gummersbach, Germany, 31,079....B 3 14
Gümüşhaciköy, Turkey, 8,592.........F 2 28
Guna, India, 15,328...........................C 4 29
Gunnedah, Australia, 5,129.............H 6 36
Guntakal, India, 20,414....................C 5 29
Gunto (means archipelago) (Jap.)
Guntur, India, 125,255.....................D 5 29
Gunungsitoli, Indonesia, 3,124.......B 5 31
Gurgan, Iran, 7,457..........................J 2 27
Gurgan (Asterabad), Iran, 21,555..J 2 27
Gurgueia (river), Brazil...................M 5 46
Gurupá, Brazil, 667...........................K 4 46
Gurupi (river), Brazil.......................L 4 46
Gur'yev, U.S.S.R., 78,000.................G 5 22
Gusau, Nigeria, 40,202.....................H 9 34
Gusinje, Yugoslavia, 5,777...............D 4 21
Güstrow, Germany, 32,899...............E 2 14
Gütersloh, Germany, 43,111.............C 3 14
Guysborough, Nova Scotia, 800.....H 5 41
Gwa, Burma...B 3 30
Gwabegar, Australia, 378.................H 6 36
Gwalior, India, 34,488.......................C 3 29
Gwanda, S. Rhodesia, 1,034...........M16 35
Gwelo, S. Rhodesia, 12,356.............M15 35
Gyangtse, China...................................C 6 32
Gydan (Kolyma) (mt. range), U.S.S.R. ....S 3 23
Gympie, Australia, 9,964...................J 5 36
Gyöngyös, Hungary, 22,033..............E 3 20
Györ, Hungary, 55,200.......................D 3 20
Gypsumville, Manitoba, 212.............L 4 40
Gýtheion, Greece, 7,112.....................F 7 21
Gyula, Hungary, 23,579......................F 3 20

H

Ha Giang, Vietnam..............................E 2 30
Ha Tien, Vietnam, 2,710.....................E 5 30
Ha Tinh, Vietnam.................................E 3 30

Index Plate
Ref. No.

Haad Yai, Thailand, 19,426...............D 6 30
Haan, Germany, 14,524......................G 5 14
Haarlem, Netherlands, 167,264.........F 4 15
Habiganj, Pakistan, 19,378...............F 4 29
Hachinohe, Japan, 104,335...............K 3 33
Hachioji, Japan, 82,539......................O 2 33
Hadar Ramatayim, Israel, 7,000....B 3 24
Hadd (cape), Oman..............................G 5 26
Hadera, Israel, 23,500.......................B 3 24
Haderslev, Denmark, 18,276.............F 9 13
Hadhramaut (region), Aden Prot. .E 7 26
Haeju, Korea, 82,135..........................B 4 33
Hafun (Dante), Som., 2,000..............S 9 34
Hafun (cape), Somalia........................S 9 34
Hagen, Germany, 146,141.................H 4 14
Hagi, Japan, 41,613.............................E 6 33
Hague, The ('s Gravenhage), *Netherlands, 606,728......................E 4 45
Haguenau, France, 15,103..................H 3 16
Haifa, Israel, 166,000..........................B 2 24
Haig, Australia, 65..............................D 6 36
Hail, Saudi Arabia, 15,000.................D 4 26
Hailar (Hulun), China, 43,200..........K 2 32
Haileybury, Ontario, 2,654.................D 4 41
Hailun, China, 344,700.......................L 2 32
Hailuoto (island), Finland..................O 4 13
Hainan (island), China........................G 8 32
Hainburg, Austria, 7,077.....................D 2 20
Haiphong, Vietnam, 143,000..............E 2 30
Hajduböszörmény, Hungary, 30,612 ....F 3 20
Hajdunánás, Hungary, 18,217............F 3 20
Hajduszoboszló, Hungary, 18,506..F 3 20
Hajmówka, Poland, 10,900..................F 2 24
Hakata, Japan, 392,649.......................D 7 33
Hakodate, Japan, 228,994..................K 3 33
Halberstadt, Germany, 45,410...........D 3 14
Halden, Norway, 9,419........................G 7 13
Haldensleben, Germany, 22,016........D 2 14
Haleb (Aleppo), Syria, 371,897.........G 4 28
Haliburton, Ontario, 983.....................E 4 41
Halifax, England, 98,404.....................F 4 10
Halifax,* Nova Scotia, 93,301...........H 5 41
Halifax, Greater, N.S., 162,700........H 5 41
Hall, Germany, 19,266.........................C 4 14
Hall (Solbad Hall), Austria, 10,031 ....B 3 20
Halle (Hal), Belgium, 18,045.............E 7 15
Halle, Germany, 222,505.....................E 3 14
Hallein, Austria, 14,849.......................B 3 20
Hall's Creek, Australia, 74..................D 3 36
Halmahera (isl.), Indonesia, 83,882 ....H 5 31
Halmstad, Sweden, 35,276..................H 8 13
Hälsingborg, Sweden, 71,718.............H 8 13
Halver, Germany, 12,482.....................H 5 14
Hama, Syria, 150,892..........................G 5 28
Hamada, Japan, 40,440.......................E 6 33
Hamadan, Iran, 104,000......................F 3 27
Hamamatsu, Japan, 152,028...............H 6 33
Hamar, Norway, 11,507.......................G 6 13
Hamburg, Germany, 1,605,606...........D 2 14
Hämeenlinna, (Tavastehus), Finland, 26,723...................................O 6 13
Hameln, Germany, 48,122...................C 2 14
Hamhŭng, Korea, 112,184.....................C 4 33
Hami, China..D 3 32
Hamilton, Australia, 8,507..................G 7 36
Hamilton,* Bermuda, 2,978..................H 3 45
Hamilton (inlet), Canada......................J 3 41
Hamilton, New Zealand, †40,646...L 6 36
Hamilton, Ontario, 239,625..................E 5 41
Hamilton, Greater, Ontario, 327,600 ....E 5 41
Hamilton, Scotland, 40,174..................D 2 11
Hamm, Germany, 59,866......................C 3 14
Hammerfest, Norway, 3,538................N 1 13
Hammersley (mt. range), Australia ....B 4 36
Hanamaki, Japan, 61,728....................K 4 33
Hanamkonda, India, 133,130...............C 5 29
Hanau, Germany, 30,702......................C 3 14
Hangchow, China, 696,600..................K 5 32
Hangö (Hanko), Finland, 6,791.....N 7 13
Hankow (incl. in Wuhan), China, 750,000 ....H 5 32
Hanna, Alberta, 2,327..........................H 4 40
Hanno, Japan, 34,839..........................O 2 33
Hannover (Hanover), Germany, 444,296 ....C 2 14
Hannoversch-Münden, Germany, 21,114 ....C 3 14
Hanoi,* N. Vietnam, 237,150..........E 2 30
Hanover (island), Chile......................E14 47
Hanover, Ontario, 3,943......................D 5 41
Hansard, Br. Columbia, 92.................F 4 40
Hanyang (incl. in Wuhan), China, 101,357 ....H 5 32
Harar, Ethiopia, 45,000......................P10 34
Harbin, China, 1,163,000....................L 2 32
Harbour Deep, Newf., 214..................J 3 41
Harbour Grace, Newf., 2,545.............K 4 41
Harburg-Wilhelmsburg, Germany..C 2 14

Index Plate
Ref. No.

Harda, India, 15,120............................C 4 29
Hardanger (fjord), Norway..................D 7 13
Hardisty, Alberta, 628.........................H 4 40
Hardoi, India, 24,252...........................C 3 29
Hardwar, India, 40,823........................C 3 29
Hargeisa,* Somaliland Prot., 20,000 ....P10 34
Hariq, Saudi Arabia, 5,000..................E 5 26
Hârlău, Rumania, 4,172.......................H 2 21
Harney (lake), U.S. ....D 4 42
Harney Peak (mountain), U.S. ....H 4 42
Härnösand, Sweden, 15,263.................L 5 13
Harrington Harbour, Quebec, 163 ....H 3 41
Harris (lake), Australia.......................E 6 36
Harris (district), Scotland...................C 4 11
Harris (sound), Scotland.....................C 4 11
Harrogate, England, 50,494.................F 4 10
Hârşova, Rumania, 3,762.....................J 2 21
Hartland (point), England...................C 6 10
Hartland, New Brunswick, 1,022...G 4 41
Hartlepool, England, 17,217...............F 3 10
Hartley, S. Rhodesia, 999..................M15 35
Hartney, Manitoba, 554......................K 5 40
Harwich, England, 14,069...................J 6 10
Hassan, India, 14,596..........................C 6 29
Hasselt, Belgium, 33,902....................G 7 15
Hassi-Messaoud, Oasis.......................H 5 34
Hassloch, Germany, 12,291.................C 4 14
Hastings, England, 65,522...................H 7 10
Hastings, New Zealand, †27,787...M 6 36
Hatay (Antâkya), Turkey, 37,484..G 4 28
Hateg, Rumania, 3,210.........................F 3 21
Hathras, India, 46,994.........................C 3 29
Hatteras (cape), U.S. ....P 6 43
Hattingen, Germany, 19,400................G 4 14
Hatvan, Hungary, 16,442.....................E 2 20
Haugesund, Norway, 18,407................D 7 13
Hauta, Saudi Arabia, 12,000................E 5 26
Hautmont, France, 14,127....................F 2 16
Havana (La Habana),* Cuba, 787,448 ....C 1 48
Havant and Waterloo, England, 32,453 ....G 7 10
Havasu (lake), U.S. ....E 6 42
Havlíčkuv Brod, Czech.. 14,068......C 2 20
Havre (Le Havre), France, 137,175 ....C 3 16
Havre-Aubert, Magdalen Is., Quebec, 1,200...................................H 4 41
Havre-Saint-Pierre, Quebec, 1,000 ....H 4 41
Hawaii (island), U. S., 68,350.......H 8 42
Hawera, New Zealand, 5,620..............L 6 36
Hawick, Scotland, 16,717.....................L 9 11
Hawkesbury, Ontario, 7,929................E 4 41
Hawston, Cape of G.H., 787..............D20 35
Hay, Australia, 3,009............................H 6 36
Hay (river), Australia..........................F 4 36
Hay (river), Canada..............................G 3 40
Hay River, N. W. Terr., 942..............G 2 40
Hayange, France, 10,266......................F 3 16
Hazaribagh, India, 24,918....................E 4 29
Hazebrouck, France, 11,896.................E 2 16
Hazelton, Br. Columbia, 279...............E 3 40
Heanor, England, 24,395.......................F 5 10
Hearst, Ontario, 2,214...........................D 4 41
Hebrides (islands), Scotland, 35,591 ....A 5 11
Hebron (El Khalil), Jordan, 35,983 ....C 4 24
Hecate (strait), Canada.......................D 4 40
Heemstede, Netherlands, 25,458.....F 4 15
Heerlen, Netherlands, 67,162.............J 7 15
Heide, Germany, 22,169........................C 1 14
Heidelberg, Australia, 60,007..............L 1 36
Heidelberg, Cape of G. H., 7,131..L19 35
Heidelberg, Germany, 116,488.............C 4 14
Heidenau, Germany, 18,694..................F 3 14
Heidenheim, Germany, 40,142..............D 4 14
Heijo (P'yŏngyang),* N. Korea, 342,551 ....C 4 33
Heilbronn, Germany, 64,643................C 4 14
Heiligenhaus, Germany, 13,248........G 4 14
Heinsburg, Alberta, 135......................H 4 40
Hekla (mountain), Iceland...................C 2 9
Helensburgh, Australia, 2,000............L 4 36
Helgoland (island), Germany.............B 1 14
Hell-Ville, Malgache Rep., 3,463 ....R14 35
Hellín, Spain, 13,257............................F 3 17
Helmand (river), Afghanistan......J 3 26
Helmond, Netherlands, 40,888.............H 6 15
Helmstedt, Germany, 28,041...............D 2 14
Helsingör, Denmark, 21,010................H 8 13
Helsinki (Helsingfors),* Finland, 436,852 ....O 6 13
Hemel Hempstead, England, 23,437 ....G 6 10
Hendek, Turkey, 7,717.........................D 2 28
Hengelo, Neth., 56,765........................K 4 15
Hengyang, China, 235,000...................H 6 32
Hénin-Liétard, France, 22,347.......E 2 16

Index Plate
Ref. No.

Henley and Grange, Australia, 7,012 ....D 7 36
Henrietta Maria (cape), Canada...D 2 41
Henzada, Burma, 60,666.....................B 3 30
Hērákleion (Candia), Greece, 51,144 ....G 8 21
Herat, Afghanistan, 75,642..................H 3 26
Herbert, Saskatchewan, 958...............J 4 40
Hercegnovi, Yugoslavia, 13,329......D 4 21
Herdecke, Germany, 13,757.................H 4 14
Heredia, Costa Rica, 11,967................E 5 39
Hereford, England, 32,501...................E 5 10
Herentals, Belgium, 16,740..................F 6 15
Herford, Germany, 50,107....................C 2 14
Herisau, Switzerland, 13,407..............H 2 19
Hermanus, Cape of G. H., 4,488...E20 35
Hermil, Lebanon, 4,796........................G 5 28
Hermosillo, Mexico, 43,522.................D 2 44
Herne, Germany, 111,591.....................G 4 14
Herne Bay, England, 18,298................J 6 10
Herning, Denmark, 19,439....................F 8 13
Heron Bay, Ontario, 175......................C 4 41
Hersfeld, Germany, 21,285...................C 3 14
Herstal, Belgium, 28,801......................H 7 15
Herten, Germany, 35,704......................B 3 14
Hertogenbosch, 's (Bois le Duc), Neth., 67,394...................................G 5 15
Hervey (bay), Australia.......................J 4 36
Herzliya, Israel, 22,800........................B 3 24
Hetton-le-Hole, England, 18,511...F 3 10
High Prairie, Alberta, 1,743................G 3 40
High River, Alberta, 2,102...................H 4 40
High Wycombe, England, 40,702...G 6 10
Hikone, Japan, 49,207..........................H 6 33
Hilda, Alberta, 285................................J 4 40
Hilden, Germany, 27,304......................G 5 14
Hildesheim, Germany, 72,292..............D 2 14
Hilla, Iraq, 51,361.................................C 4 27
Hilleröd, Denmark, 10,023...................H 9 13
Hillston, Australia, 1,019.....................G 6 36
Hilversum, Netherlands, 97,312.....G 4 15
Himalaya (mt. range)..........................L 6 25
Himeji, Japan, 212,100.........................G 6 33
Himi, Japan, 68,611...............................H 5 33
Hinche, Haiti, 4,511..............................C 5 48
Hinchinbrook (island), Australia...H 3 36
Hinckley, England, 39,094...................F 5 10
Hindenburg (Zabrze), Poland, 185,100 ....A 4 24
Hindmarsh, Australia, 13,561..............D 7 36
Hindu Kush (mt. range)......................J 2 26
Hindupur, India, 19,049......................C 6 29
Hines Creek, Alberta, 360...................G 3 40
Hinganghat, India, 28,040....................C 4 29
Hingoli, India, 14,601...........................C 5 29
Hinojosa del Duque, Spain, 13,684 ....D 3 17
Hirakata, Japan, 43,970.......................J 7 33
Hiratsuka, Japan, 52,381......................O 3 33
Hirosaki, Japan, 65,597........................K 3 33
Hiroshima, Japan, 285,712...................E 6 33
Hirschberg (Jelenia Góra) Poland, 46,100 ....B 3 24
Hirson, France, 10,208..........................F 3 16
Hispaniola (island), 5,233,056.........D 2 45
Hissar, India, 28,618.............................C 3 29
Hit, Iraq, 8,000......................................C 4 27
Hitachi, Japan, 131,011.........................K 5 33
Hitchin, England, 19,963......................G 6 10
Hitoyoshi, Japan, 45,169.......................E 7 33
Hjörring, Denmark, 14,093..................F 8 13
Ho, Ghana, 5,852..................................G10 34
Hoa Binh, Vietnam................................E 2 30
Hobart, Australia, †95,206....................H 8 36
Hoboken, Belgium, 30,683....................E 6 15
Hodeida, Yemen, 26,000.......................D 7 26
Hodh (reg.), Mauritania, 169,000..E 8 34
Hódmezővásárhely, Hungary, 59,340 ....F 3 20
Hodonín, Czech., 16,141.......................D 2 20
Hodur, Som., 2,500................................P11 34
Hof, Germany, 61,033...........................D 3 14
Hofei, China, 183,600............................J 5 32
Hofu, Japan, 96,821..............................E 6 33
Hofuf, Saudi Arabia, 100,000..............E 4 26
Hohenems, Austria, 6,994......................A 3 20
Hohenlimburg, Germany, 23,862....H 4 14
Hohensalza (Inowrocław), Poland, 45,600 ....C 2 24
Hoihow, China, 135,300........................H 8 32
Hokitika, New Zealand, 3,032..............L 7 36
Hokkaido (island), Japan, 4,295,567 ....L 2 33
Holbaek, Denmark, 14,417.................G 9 13
Holbrook, Australia, 1,210....................H 7 36
Holguín, Cuba, 35,865..........................J 3 48
Hollandia,* Neth. N. G. ....K 6 31
Holmes (reefs), Australia.....................H 3 36
Holon, Israel, 37,000............................B 3 24
Holstebro, Denmark, 14,711................F 8 13
Holy (island), England.........................F 2 10
Holyhead (island), Wales......................C 4 10
Holzminden, Germany, 22,151.............C 3 14

Index Plate
Ref. No.

Homalin, Burma....B 1 30
Homberg, Germany, 27,971....F 4 14
Hombori, Sudanese Rep., 3,263....F 8 34
Home Hill, Australia, 2,793....H 3 36
Homs, Libya, †12,918....J 5 34
Homs, Syria, 250,915....G 5 28
Hon, Libya, †3,681....K 6 34
Honduras (gulf)....D 2 39
Hongsŏng, Korea, 15,718....C 5 33
Hongwŏn, Korea, 25,663....C 3 33
Honiara, *Sol. Is. Prot., 2,000....G 6 37
Honshu (island), Japan, 58,769,968....H 6 33
Hood (mountain), U.S. ....C 3 42
Hooghly and Chinsura, India, 49,081....E 1 29
Hook (island), Australia....H 4 36
Hoorn (islands), Pacific, 2,005....J 7 37
Hope, Br. Columbia, 2,226....F 5 40
Hope Town, Cape of G.H., 2,695....L17 35
Hopedale, Lab., Newf., 167....J 2 41
Hopetown, Australia, 55....C 6 36
Hopfgarten, Austria, 3,908....B 3 20
Hopkins (lake), Australia....D 4 36
Hoppo, China, 80,000....G 7 32
Horn (Hornos) (cape), S. A....G 5 47
Hornchurch, England, 104,128....H 6 10
Hornepayne, Ontario, 1,400....C 4 41
Horqueta, Paraguay, 2,634....J 8 47
Horsens, Denmark, 35,898....F 9 13
Horsham, Australia, 7,767....G 7 36
Horsham, England, 16,682....G 6 10
Horten, Norway, 11,418....D 4 13
Hoshangabad, India, 13,290....C 4 29
Hospet, India, 26,023....C 5 29
Hospitalet, Spain, 66,637....H 2 17
Hoste (island), Chile....F15 47
Hotien (Khotan), China....B 4 32
Hottah (lake), Canada....G 1 40
Houhoek, Cape of G.H. E20 35
Houtman Abrolhos (Abrolhos Is.), Australia....A 5 36
Hove, England, 69,535....G 7 10
Howe (cape), Australia....J 7 36
Howland (island), Pacific, 4....J 5 37
Howley, Newfoundland, 500....J 4 41
Howrah, India, 433,630....E 2 29
Hoy (island), Scotland, 957....K 2 11
Hoylake, England, 30,936....D 4 10
Hradec Králové, Czech., 55,250....C 1 20
Hranice, Czech., 10,786....D 2 20
Hrubieszów, Poland, 11,600....F 3 24
Hsinking (Changchun) China, 855,200....K 3 32
Hsipaw, Burma....C 2 30
Huacas (point), Peru....E 6 46
Huacho, Peru, 12,993....E 6 46
Huamantla, Mexico, 7,287....N 1 44
Huamatla, Mexico, 8,526....N 1 44
Huancavelica, Peru, 7,497....E 6 47
Huancayo, Peru, 26,729....F 6 46
Huanchaca, Bolivia....G 8 46
Huanuco, Peru, 11,966....E 6 46
Huarás, Peru, 11,054....E 5 46
Huascarán (mountain), Peru....E 5 46
Huasco, Chile, 1,537....F 9 47
Hubli, India, 129,609....B 5 29
Hucknall, England, 23,213....F 4 10
Huddersfield, England, 129,026....F 4 10
Hudson, Ontario, 700....B 3 41
Hudson (bay), Canada....C 2 41
Hudson (strait), Canada....F 1 41
Hudson Bay, Saskatchewan, 1,421..K 4 40
Hue, S. Vietnam, †407,000....E 3 30
Huedin, Rumania, 5,134....F 2 21
Huelva, Spain, †63,002....C 4 17
Huesca, Spain, †20,003....F 1 17
Hughenden, Australia, 1,772....G 4 36
Huhehot, China, 148,400....H 3 32
Huixtla, Mexico, 10,221....N 9 44
Hull (Kingston-upon-Hull), England, 299,105....G 4 10
Hull, Quebec, 49,243....E 4 41
Hulun (Hailar), China, 43,200....K 2 32
Humacao, Puerto Rico, 10,823....G 1 45
Humaitá, Brazil, 828....H 5 46
Humber (estuary), England....H 4 10
Humboldt, Saskatchewan, 2,916....J 4 40
Humboldt (river), U.S. ....D 4 42
Humphreys Peak (mountain), U.S. ....F 6 42
Húnaflói (fjord), Iceland....B 2 9
Hunchun, China, 13,246....M 3 32
Hunedoara, Rumania, 7,018....F 3 21
Hŭngnam, Korea, 143,600....C 4 33
Huntly, New Zealand, 4,187....L 6 36
Huntsville, Ontario, 3,051....E 4 41
Huon (gulf), Terr. N. G. ....E 6 37
Huong Khê, Vietnam....E 3 30
Huron (lake), U.S.-Canada....N 3 43
Hurstbridge, Australia, 824....L 1 36
Hurstville, Australia, 50,336....L 3 36
Huşi, Rumania, 16,605....J 2 21
Husum, Germany, 24,858....C 1 14
Hutchinson, Cape of G. H., 638....L18 35
Huy (Hoei), Belgium, 13,142....G 8 15
Hwainan, China, 286,900....J 5 32
Hwang Ho (river), China....H 5 32
Hwangju, Korea, 16,993....B 4 33
Hwangshih, China, 110,500....J 5 32
Hyden, Australia, 261....B 6 36
Hyderabad, India, 1,085,722....C 5 29
Hyderabad, Pakistan, 241,801....A 3 29
Hyères, France, 15,649....G 6 16
Hythe, Alberta, 481....G 3 40
Hyvinkää (Hyvinge), Finland, 18,756....O 6 13

I

Iaco (river), Brazil....F 6 46
Iar Connaught (region), Ireland....C 5 12
Iaşi, Rumania, 94,075....H 2 21
Iba, Philippine Islands, 3,064....F 2 31
Ibadan, Nigeria, 327,284....G10 34
Ibagué, Colombia, 54,347....F 3 46
Ibar (river), Yugo....E 4 21
Ibaraki, Japan, 34,820....J 7 33
Ibarra, Ecuador, 14,037....E 3 46
Ibbenbüren, Germany, 13,763....B 2 14
Ibo, Moz., 3,769....P14 35
Ica, Peru, 20,896....E 6 46
Içá (river), Brazil....G 4 46
Icaraí, Brazil....P14 47
Içel (Mersin), Turkey, 51,251....F 4 28
Ichang, China, 75,000....H 5 32
Ichchapuram, India, 11,159....E 5 29
Ichikawa, Japan, 102,506....P 2 33
Ichinomiya, Japan, 71,431....H 6 33
Idar-Oberstein, Germany, 24,875....B 4 14
Idfu, Egypt, 18,404....N 7 34
Idi, Indonesia....B 4 31
Ieper (Ypres), Belgium, 17,363....B 7 15
Iesi, Italy, 21,598....D 3 18
Igarka, U.S.S.R., 20,000....K 3 22
Igdir, Turkey, 9,646....L 3 28
Iglau (Jihlava), Czech., 34,939....C 2 20
Iglesias, Italy, 20,816....B 5 18
Ignace, Ontario, 300....B 4 41
Iguacú (river), Brazil....K 9 47
Iguala, Mexico, 19,422....K 7 44
Igualada, Spain, 15,684....G 2 17
Iguassú (falls), S. A. ....K 9 47
Iguatu, Brazil, 10,063....N 5 46
Ihosy, Malg. Rep., 2,517....R16 35
Iida, Japan, 32,684....H 6 33
IJmuiden, Netherlands, 22,121....E 4 15
IJsselmeer (lake), Netherlands....G 3 15
Ijuí (river), Brazil....K 9 47
Ikeda, Japan, 45,177....H 7 33
Ikryanoye, U.S.S.R., 2,296....F 5 22
Ilagan, Philippine Islands, 7,436....G 2 31
Ile à la Crosse, Sask., 25....J 3 40
Ilford, Manitoba, 97....L 3 40
Ilhéus, Brazil, 22,593....N 6 46
Ili (river)....J 5 22
Ilkeston, England, 33,677....F 5 10
Ilkley, England, 17,265....F 4 10
Illapel, Chile, 6,085....F10 47
Il'men (lake), U.S.S.R. ....D 4 22
Ilmenau, Germany, 18,603....D 3 14
Ilo, Peru, 1,043....F 7 46
Iloilo, Philippine Is., 46,416....G 3 31
Ilorin, Nigeria, 54,700....G10 34
Il'yaly, U.S.S.R., 1,500....G 5 22
Imabari, Japan, 60,191....F 6 33
Iman, U.S.S.R. ....P 5 23
Imandra (lake), U.S.S.R. ....E 3 22
Imari, Japan, 81,625....D 7 33
Imatra, Finland, 29,242....Q 6 13
Imi, Ethiopia, 300....P10 34
Imola, Italy, 26,982....C 2 18
Imperia, Italy, 28,295....B 3 18
Imphal, India, 99,716....F 4 29
Inari (lake), Finland....P 2 13
Inawashiro (lake), Japan....K 5 33
Inca, Bal. Is., Spain, 12,852....H 3 17
Inch'ŏn (Jinsen), Korea, 265,767..C 5 33
Indian (peninsula)....C 5 29
Indian (Thar) (des.), India....B 3 29
Indian Head, Sask., 1,721....K 4 40
Indigirka (river), U.S.S.R. ....R 3 23
Indochina (peninsula)....E 4 30
Indore, India, 310,859....C 3 29
Indramaju, Indonesia, 21,190....H 2 31
Indus (river)....B 2 29
Inegöl, Turkey, 19,262....C 2 28
Ingersoll, Ontario, 6,811....D 5 41
Ingham, Australia, 3,943....H 3 36
Ingolstadt, Germany, 40,523....D 4 14
Ingonish, N. S., 400....J 4 41
Inhambane, Moz., 5,134....O16 35
Inhauma, Brazil, 1,086....O14 47
Inini (region), Fr. Guiana....K 3 46
Inishbofin (island), Ireland....A 4 12
Inishturk (island), Ireland....A 4 12
Injune, Australia, 416....H 5 36
Inn (river)....B 2 20
Innisfail, Alberta, 1,883....H 4 40
Innisfail, Australia, 6,649....H 3 36
Innsbruck, Austria, 95,055....B 3 20
Inny (river), Ireland....F 4 12
Inowrocław, Poland, 45,600....C 2 24
Insein, Burma, 20,487....C 3 30
Interlaken, Switzerland, 4,368....E 3 19
International Date Line....E 4 6
Inubo (cape), Japan....K 6 33
Inuvik, N.W. Territories....D 1 40
Invercargil, N. Z., †35,107....K 7 36
Inverell, Australia, 7,514....J 5 36
Inverie, Scotland....E 5 11
Inverness, N.S., 2,026....H 4 41
Inverness, Scotland, 28,107....H 5 11
Investigator (strait), Aust. ....F 7 36
Investigator's (islands), Aust. ....E 6 36
Ioánnina, Greece, 32,315....E 6 21
Iolotan', U.S.S.R., 3,160....H 6 22
Ioma, Papua....C 7 31
Iona (island), Scotland, 173....D 7 11
Ionian (sea)....D 7 21
Ipiales, Colombia, 8,343....E 3 46
Ipin, China, 177,500....F 6 32
Ipoh, Malayan Fed., 80,894....D 6 30
Ipswich, Australia, 38,953....J 5 36
Ipswich, England, 104,785....J 5 10
Ipu, Brazil, 5,957....M 4 46
Iquique, Chile, 39,576....F 8 46
Iquitos, Peru, 31,828....F 4 46
Iracoubo, French Guiana, 1,109....K 2 46
Iran (mountains)....E 5 31
Iranshahr (Fahrej), Iran, 4,063....M 7 27
Irapuato, Mexico, 49,426....J 6 44
Irbid, Jordan, 23,157....D 3 26
Irbit, U.S.S.R., 23,500....H 4 22
Iri, Korea, 46,674....C 6 33
Iriri (river), Brazil....K 5 46
Irish (sea), Ireland....K 4 12
Irkutsk, U.S.S.R., 365,000....M 4 23
Iron Knob, Australia, 628....F 6 36
Iroquois Falls, Ontario, 1,478....D 4 41
'Irqa, Aden Prot. ....E 7 26
Irrawaddy (river), Burma....B 3 30
Irtysh (river), U.S.S.R. ....H 4 22
Irvine, Scotland, 14,745....H 8 11
Isaacs (river), Australia....H 4 36
Isabela (bay), Dom. Rep. ....D 5 48
Isaccea, Rumania, 4,653....J 3 21
Isahaya, Japan, 65,593....E 7 33
Ise, Japan, 97,223....H 6 33
Iserlohn, Germany, 46,221....B 3 14
Isfahan, Iran, 183,597....G 4 27
Isha Baidoa, Somalia, 10,000....P11 34
Ishim, U.S.S.R., 34,500....H 4 22
Ishim (river), U.S.S.R. ....H 4 22
Ishimbay, U.S.S.R. ....G 4 22
Ishinomaki, Japan, 52,351....K 4 33
Iskenderun, Turkey, 48,084....G 4 28
Iski-Naukat, U.S.S.R., 5,000....U 2 23
Iskilip, Turkey, 10,925....F 2 28
Island (lake), Canada....M 4 40
Islay (island), Scotland, 4,267....D 8 11
Ismailia, Egypt, 53,594....N 5 34
Isparta, Turkey, 24,491....D 4 28
Issoudun, France, 11,794....D 4 16
Issy-les-Moulineaux, Fr. 39,818....A 2 16
Issyk-Kul' (lake), U.S.S.R. ....J 5 22
Istanbul, Turkey, 1,214,616....D 6 28
Istonio (Vasto), Italy, 14,036....E 3 18
Itabuna, Brazil, 26,312....M 6 46
Itacoaí (river), Brazil....F 5 46
Itacoatiara, Brazil, 5,275....J 4 46
Itaituba, Brazil, 628....J 4 46
Itajaí, Brazil, 20,017....L 9 47
Itajubá, Brazil, 21,255....L 8 47
Itala (El Athale), Somalia, 800....R11 35
Itami, Japan, 56,348....H 7 33
Itapecuru (river), Brazil....M 5 46
Itapicuru (river), Brazil....N 6 46
Itapipoca, Brazil, 4,666....N 4 46
Itaqui, Brazil, 9,152....J 9 46
Itaretama, Brazil, 1,726....N 5 46
Itarsi, India, 14,269....C 4 29
Ithaca (island), Greece, 7,275....E 6 21
Iturup (island), U.S.S.R. ....R 5 23
Ituxí (river), Brazil....G 5 46
Itzehoe, Germany, 37,153....C 2 14
Ivanhoe, Australia, 546....G 6 36
Ivanovka, U.S.S.R., 4,590....N 1 23
Ivanovo, U.S.S.R., 332,000....E 4 22
Ivry-sur-Seine, France, 40,377....B 2 16
Iwakuni, Japan, 90,607....E 6 33
Iwamisawa, Japan, 55,774....L 2 33
Iwo (island), Pacific....D 3 37
Ixelles, Belgium, 92,657....C 9 15
Ixtapalapa, Mexico, 17,372....L 1 44
Ixtepec, Mexico, 11,288....L 8 44
Izhevsk, U.S.S.R., 283,000....G 4 22
Izmail (Ismail), U.S.S.R., 17,569....D 5 22
Izmir (Smyrna), Turkey, 246,619....B 3 28
Izmit, Turkey, 56,702....C 2 28
Izu (islands), Japan, 20,382....J 6 33
Izucar de Matamoros, Mexico, 10,597....M 2 44
Izumiotsu, Japan, 33,341....H 8 33
Izumisano, Japan, 32,153....G 6 33

J

Jabalpur (Jubbulpore), India, 256,998....D 4 29
Jablonec nad Nisou, Czech., 25,820....C 1 20
Jacarèzinho, Brazil, 8,343....K 8 47
Jacmel, Haiti, 8,545....C 6 48
Jacobabad, Pakistan, 22,827....A 3 29
Jacobina, Brazil, 7,850....N 6 46
Jadotville, B. Congo, 55,960....M14 35
Jaén, Spain, †61,247....E 4 17
Jaffa Tel Aviv, Israel, 380,000....B 3 34
Jaffna, Ceylon, 76,664....D 7 29
Jagdalpur, India, 11,304....D 5 29
Jagtial, India, 16,294....C 5 29
Jaguarão, Brazil, 9,941....K10 47
Jaguaribe (river), Brazil....N 5 46
Jahrum, Iran, 23,978....H 6 27
Jaicós, Brazil, 905....M 5 46
Jaina, Dom. Rep. ....E 6 48
Jaipur, India, 291,130....C 3 29
Jajce, Yugoslavia, 5,177....C 3 21
Jajpur, India, 11,188....E 4 29
Jakarta (Djakarta),* Indonesia 2,800,000....H 1 31
Jakobstad (Pietarsaari), Finland, 12,400....N 5 13
Jalalabad, Afghan., 14,756....K 3 26
Jalapa, Guatemala, 6,605....B 3 39
Jalapa, Mexico, 51,123....P 1 44
Jalgaon, India, 48,596....C 4 29
Jalna, India, 48,423....C 4 29
Jalpaiguri, India, 27,766....E 3 29
Jaluit (island), Pacific, 1,093....G 5 37
Jamaica (island), 1,503,047....C 3 45
Jamalpur, India, 39,401....E 4 29
Jamalpur, Pakistan, 26,952....E 4 29
Jamanchim (river), Brazil....J 5 46
James (bay), Canada....D 3 41
James (mt. range), Australia....E 4 36
James (river), U. S. ....J 3 42
James (river), U. S. ....O 5 43
Jamestown, Australia, 1,489....F 6 36
Jammu, Kash., 50,379....C 2 29
Jamnagar, India, 104,419....A 4 29
Jamshedpur, India, 218,162....E 4 29
Jan Mayen (island), Norway....D 7 9
Jandowae, Australia, 1,028....J 5 36
Jánoshalma, Hungary, 15,933....E 3 20
Januária, Brazil, 7,123....M 7 46
Jaora, India, 25,501....C 4 29
Japan (sea)....E 4 33
Japurá (river), Brazil....G 4 46
Jarabub (Jaghbub), Libya, 215....L 5 34
Jarash, Jordan, 2,614....D 3 24
Jarí (river), Brazil....K 3 46
Jarocin, Poland, 14,600....C 3 24
Jaroměr, Czech., 12,292....C 1 20
Jarosław, Poland, 23,400....F 3 24
Jarrow, England, 28,635....F 3 10
Järvi (means lake) (Finnish)....
Jarvis (island), Pacific, 3....K 6 37
Jasberény, Hungary, 27,515....E 5 20
Jask, Iran, 3,584....K 8 27
Jasper, Alberta, 2,105....G 4 40
Jasper (park), Alberta, 2,322....G 4 40
Jassy (Iaşi), Rumania, 94,075....H 2 21
Jászárokszállás, Hung., 14,310....E 3 20
Játiva, Spain, 17,164....F 3 17
Jaú, Brazil, 18,936....L 8 46
Jauf, Saudi Arabia, 7,500....C 4 26
Jauja, Peru, 7,713....E 6 46
Jaunpur, India, 44,833....D 3 29
Java (island), Indonesia, 51,097,747....D 7 31
Java (sea)....D 6 31
Javarí (Yavarí) (river), S.A. ....F 4 36

Index Ref. *Plate No.*

Jawor (Jauer), Poland, 11,900......C 3 24
Jaworzno, Poland, 35,600......D 3 24
Jebel (means mt.) (Arab.)..........
Jedrzejów, Poland, 11,800......E 3 24
Jelenia Góra, Poland, 46,100......B 3 24
Jelgava, U.S.S.R., 34,099......D 4 22
Jemappes, Belg., 12,966......D 8 15
Jena, Germany, 82,722......D 3 14
Jenin, Jordan, 12,663......C 3 24
Jequié, Brazil, 20,652......M 6 46
Jérémie, Haiti, 11,138......A 6 48
Jerez de la Frontera, Spain, †107,770......C 4 17
Jerez de los Caballeros, Spain, 12,738......C 3 17
Jericho, Australia, 263......H 4 36
Jericho (Ariha), Jordan, 41,593....C 4 24
Jerusalem (New City),* Israel, 152,500......C 4 24
Jerusalem (Old City), Jordan, 46,700......C4 24
Jesenice, Yugoslavia, 15,811......A 2 21
Jesselton,* No. Borneo, 11,704....F 4 31
Jessore, Pakistan, 23,867......E 4 29
Jette, Belgium, 31,337......B 9 15
Jever, Germany, 10,720......B 2 14
Jeypore, India, 12,504......D 5 29
Jhang-Maghiana, Pak., 73,397....B 2 29
Jhansi, India, 127,365......C 3 29
Jhelum, Pakistan, 38,567......B 2 29
Jhunjhunu, India, 16,874......C 3 29
Jibhalanta (Uliassutai), Mon. Rep., 6,000......E 2 32
Jidda, Saudi Arabia, 80,000......C 5 26
Jihlava, Czech., 34,939......C 2 20
Jijiga, Ethiopia, 11,000......P10 34
Jima (means island) (Jap.)..........
Jimma, Ethiopia, 15,000......O10 34
Jind, India, 14,909......C 3 29
Jinja, Uganda, 8,410......N11 35
Jinotepe, Nicaragua, 7,128......D 5 39
Jinsen (Inch'ŏn), Korea, 265,767..C 5 33
Jiparaná (river), Brazil......H 6 46
Jirgalanta (Kobdo), Mon. Rep. 10,000......D 2 32
João Pessoa (Paraíba), Brazil, 89,517......O 5 46
Jódar, Spain, 11,980......E 4 17
Jodhpur, India, 180,717......B 3 29
Jogjakarta (Djokjakarta), Indonesia, 244,379......J 2 31
Johannesburg, Transv., †880,573..M17 35
Johnston (island), Pacific, 69......K 4 37
Johnstone, Scotland, 16,660......B 2 11
Johore Bahru, Mal. Fed., 38,826......B 2 11
Joinville, Brazil, 20,915......L 9 47
Joki (means river) (Finnish)........
Joliette, Quebec, 16,940......F 4 41
Jones (cape), Canada......D 3 41
Jönköping, Sweden, 44,685......H 8 13
Jonquière, Quebec, 25,550......F 4 41
Jordan (river)......D 3 24
Jorhat, India, 11,664......F 3 29
Jos, Nigeria, 11,854......H10 34
Joseph Bonaparte (gulf), Aust. ..D 2 36
Juan de Fuca (strait), No. Amer......B 2 42
Juan Fernández (islands), Chile...D10 47
Juárez (Ciudad Mante), Mexico, 21,291......K 5 44
Juàzeiro do Norte, Brazil, 41,999......N 5 46
Juba, Sudan, 7,900......N11 34
Juba (river), Somalia......P11 35
Jubbulpore, India, 256,998......D 4 29
Juchitán, Mexico, 13,819......M 8 44
Judenburg, Austria, 9,821......C 3 20
Juiz de Fora, Brazil, 84,999......M 8 46
Jujuy, Argentina, 31,091......G 8 46
Juli, Peru, 2,266......G 7 46
Juliaca, Peru, 6,034......F 7 46
Julianehaab, Greenland, 954......F23 8
Jülich, Germany 6,831......B 3 14
Jullundur, India, 168,816......C 2 29
Jumet, Belgium, 29,004......E 8 15
Jumilla, Spain, 15,745......F 3 17
Jumna (river), India......C 3 29
Junagadh, India, 58,111......B 4 29
Juncos, Puerto Rico, 8,285......G 1 45
Jundiaí, Brazil, 39,560......L 8 47
Junee, Australia, 4,064......H 6 36
Junín, Argentina, 36,149......M12 47
Junín, Chile......G 7 46
Juquiá, Brazil, 899......L 8 47
Jur (river), Sudan......M10 34
Jura (island), Scotland, 258......E 8 11
Jura (mountains)......F 4 16
Juruena (river), Brazil......J 5 46
Jutaí (river), Brazil......G 4 46
Jüterbog, Germany, 15,137......E 3 14
Jutiapa, Guatemala, 5,141......B 3 39
Jyväskylä, Finland, 35,666......O 5 13

K

K 2 (Godwin Austen) (mt.), Kash......C 1 29
Kaakhka, U.S.S.R., 2,072......G 6 22
Kabala, S. Leone, 3,064......D10 34
Kabale, Uganda, 2,469......N12 35
Kabansk, U.S.S.R., 2,233......M 4 23
Kabul,* Afghanistan, 206,208......J 3 26
Kadayanallur, India, 29,652......C 7 29
Kadiköy, Turkey, 61,745......D 6 28
Kadina, Australia, 1,808......F 6 36
Kadiri, India, 11,885......C 6 29
Kadiyevka, U.S.S.R., 180,000......M 1 23
Kadjang, Indonesia......G 7 31
Kaduna, Nigeria, 10,628......H 9 34
Kaédi, Mauritania, 5,030......D 8 34
Kaesŏng, Korea, 88,708......C 5 33
Kafr Kanna, Israel, 2,478......C 2 24
Kafue (river), N. Rhodesia......M15 35
Kagoshima, Japan, 229,462......E 8 33
Kagul, U.S.S.R., 7,375......D 5 22
Kaiapit, Terr. N.G......B 7 31
Kaiapoi, New Zealand, 2,738......L 7 36
Kaifeng, China, 299,100......J 5 32
Kaikoura, New Zealand, 1,535......L 6 36
Kairouan, Tunisia, 32,299......H 4 34
Kairuku, Papua......B 7 31
Kaiserslautern, Germany, 62,761......B 4 14
Kaitaia, New Zealand, 2,358......L 5 36
Kaizuka, Japan, 53,586......H 8 33
Kajaani, Finland, 11,040......P 4 13
Kakabeka Falls, Ontario, 422......B 4 41
Kakhk, Iran, 4,978......L 3 27
Kakinada, India, 100,054......D 5 29
Käkisalmi (Priozersk), U.S.S.R. 4,132......D 3 22
Kalabahi, Indonesia......G 7 31
Kalachinsk, U.S.S.R., 4,243......J 4 22
Kalámai, Greece, 37,781......F 7 21
Kalannie, Australia, 114......B 6 36
Kalat, Pak., 2,009......A 3 29
Kalbe, Germany, 15,161......D 3 14
Kalewa, Burma......B 2 30
Kalgan, China, 229,300......J 3 32
Kalgoorlie, Australia, †22,837......C 6 36
Kalianda, Indonesia......D 7 31
Kalinin, U.S.S.R., 261,000......E 4 22
Kaliningrad, U.S.S.R., 202,000......D 4 22
Kalisz, Poland, 64,300......D 3 24
Kalmar, Sweden, 27,049......K 8 13
Kalmykovo, U.S.S.R., 1,329......G 5 22
Kaluga, U.S.S.R., 133,000......E 4 22
Kalutara, Ceylon, 18,801......C 7 29
Kalyan, India, 31,356......B 5 29
Kálymnos, Greece, 9,683......H 7 21
Kama (river), U.S.S.R......G 4 22
Kamaishi, Japan, 35,231......L 4 33
Kamakura, Japan, 85,391......O 3 33
Kamarhati, India, 42,545......E 1 29
Kambove, B. Congo, 9,195......M14 35
Kamchatka (peninsula), U.S.S.R., 135,000......S 4 23
Kamen', U.S.S.R., 22,982......K 4 22
Kamenets-Podol'skiy, U.S.S.R., 33,035......D 5 22
Kamensk-Shakhtinskiy, U.S.S.R., 58,000......F 5 22
Kamensk-Ural'skiy, U.S.S.R., 141,000......G 4 22
Kamenskoye, U.S.S.R., 216......T 3 23
Kamenz, Germany, 13,862......F 3 14
Kamienna Góra, Poland, 14,900......C 3 24
Kamina, B. Congo, 1,020......L13 35
Kamloops, British Col., 9,096......F 4 40
Kamo, Japan, 27,741......J 5 33
Kampala, Uganda, 22,094......N11 35
Kampar, Malayan Fed., 15,302......D 6 30
Kampen, Netherlands, 25,847......H 3 15
Kampot, Cambodia......E 5 30
Kamptee, India, 26,930......C 4 29
Kamsack, Saskatchewan, 2,843......K 4 40
Kamyshin, U.S.S.R., 55,000......F 4 22
Kamyshlov, U.S.S.R., 20,000......H 4 22
Kanazawa, Japan, 252,017......H 5 33
Kanchanaburi, Thailand, 7,342......C 4 30
Kanchenjunga (mt.), Asia......E 3 29
Kanchipuram, India, 74,635......D 6 29
Kanchow, China, 98,600......H 6 32
Kandagach, U.S.S.R......G 5 22
Kandahar, Afghan., 77,186......J 3 26
Kandalaksha, U.S.S.R., 7,799......E 3 22
Kandangan, Indonesia, 9,774......F 6 31
Kandi, Dahomey, 5,917......G 9 34
Kandukur, India, 10,396......C 5 29
Kandy, Ceylon, 57,013......D 7 29
Kangaroo (island), Australia......F 7 36
Kangavar, Iran, 7,037......F 3 27
Kanggye, Korea, 30,013......C 3 33
Kanggyŏng, Korea, 20,327......C 5 33
Kanghwa (bay), Korea......B 5 33
Kangnŭng, Korea, 31,820......D 5 33
Kaniapiskau (river), Canada......G 2 41
Kanibadam, U.S.S.R., 16,450......S 2 23
Kanin (peninsula), U.S.S.R......F 3 22
Kanjiža, Yugoslavia, 12,404......D 2 21
Kankan, Guinea, 16,000......E 9 34
Kannauj, India, 21,994......C 3 29
Kano, Nigeria, 130,173......H 9 34
Kanoya, Japan, 75,488......E 8 33
Kanpur, India, 705,383......D 3 29
Kansas (river), U.S......J 5 42
Kansk, U.S.S.R., 74,000......L 4 23
Kanuma, Japan, 80,771......J 5 33
Kanye, Bech. Pr., 22,922......L16 35
Kaohsiung, China, 371,225......J 7 32
Kaokoveld (mts.), S.W. Africa......J15 35
Kaolack, Senegal, 33,000......C 9 34
Kapfenberg, Austria, 23,843......C 3 20
Kapingamarangi (Greenwich) (atoll), Pacific, 454......F 5 37
Kaposvár, Hungary, 33,076......D 3 20
Kapsan, Korea, 58,077......C 3 33
Kapuskasing, Ontario, 5,463......D 4 41
Kara (sea), U.S.S.R......H 2 22
Kara- Bogaz-Gol, U.S.S.R., 4,000......G 5 22
Kara-Kum (des.), U.S.S.R......G 5 22
Karabük, Turkey, 15,558......E 2 28
Karacabey, Turkey, 13,321......C 2 28
Karachayevsk, U.S.S.R., 2,848......F 5 22
Karachi, Pakistan, 1,409,138......A 4 29
Karad, India, 17,996......B 5 29
Karadeniz (Bosporus) (strait), Turkey......C 2 28
Karaganda, U.S.S.R., 398,000......J 5 22
Karaginskiy (island), U.S.S.R. ....T 4 23
Karaikudi, India, 28,908......C 7 29
Karakorum (mts.), Asia......C 1 29
Karaköse (Ağri), Turkey, 17,022...K 3 28
Karaman, Turkey, 17,209......E 4 28
Karanja, India, 18,126......C 4 29
Karapinar, Turkey, 9,682......E 4 28
Karasburg, S.W. Africa, 1,092......K17 35
Karasuk, U.S.S.R., 2,682......J 4 22
Karatsu, Japan, 51,820......D 7 33
Karauli, India, 19,177......C 3 29
Karbala, Iraq, 122,719......D 2 27
Karcag, Hungary, 25,031......F 3 20
Kardítsa, Greece, 18,543......E 6 21
Kargopol', U.S.S.R., 3,449......E 3 22
Kariba (lake), Africa......M15 35
Karibib, South-West Africa, 875..K16 35
Karikal, India, 70,541......D 6 29
Karimata (strait), Indonesia......D 6 31
Karisimbi (mt.), Africa......M12 35
Karkala, India, 9,012......B 6 29
Karkur, Israel, 2,900......C 3 24
Karlö (Hailuoto) (island), Finland......O 4 13
Karlovac, Yugoslavia, 31,738......B 3 21
Karlovy Vary, Czech., 42,639......B 1 20
Karlshamn, Sweden, 10,691......J 9 13
Karlskoga, Sweden, 31,303......J 7 13
Karlskrona, Sweden, 30,997......K 8 13
Karlsruhe, Germany, 198,840......C 4 14
Karlstad, Sweden, 35,651......H 7 13
Karmakchi, U.S.S.R., 2,280......H 5 22
Karnal, India, 37,444......C 3 29
Karonga, Nyas. Pr., 300......N13 35
Karosa, Indonesia......F 6 31
Karpinsk, U.S.S.R......R 5 23
Karpogory, U.S.S.R., 684......F 3 22
Karragullen, Australia, 287......B 2 36
Kars, Turkey, 30,920......K 2 28
Karsakpay, U.S.S.R., 15,000......H 5 22
Karshi, U.S.S.R., 19,000......H 6 22
Kartaly, U.S.S.R., 13,500......G 4 22
Karur, India, 27,575......C 6 29
Karviná, Czech., 44,190......E 2 20
Karwar, India, 15,812......B 6 29
Kasai (river), Belgian Congo......L13 35
Kasama, N. Rhodesia, 1,383......N14 35
Kasaragod, India, 11,566......B 6 29
Kasba (lake), Canada......K 2 40
Kaschau (Košice), Czech., 79,460..F 2 20
Kasganj, India, 28,465......C 3 29
Kashan, Iran, 53,525......G 3 27
Kashgar, China, 91,000......C 4 32
Kashing, China, 78,300......K 5 32
Kashiwazaki, Japan, 38,142......J 5 33
Kashmar, Iran, 12,298......K 3 27
Kasimov, U.S.S.R., 13,007......F 4 22
Kaslo, British Columbia, 669......G 4 40
Kassa (Košice), Czech., 79,460......F 2 20
Kassala, Sudan, 39,074......O 8 34
Kassan, U.S.S.R., 6,224......H 6 22
Kassansay, U.S.S.R., 18,705......U 2 23
Kassel, Germany, 162,132......C 3 14
Kastamonu, Turkey, 13,688......E 2 28
Kastoría, Greece, 9,468......E 5 21
Kastrup, Denmark, 5,343......H 9 13
Kasur, Pakistan, 63,086......B 2 29
Katahdin (mountain), U.S. ......R 3 43
Katanning, Australia, 2,864......B 6 36
Kateríne, Greece, 24,604......F 5 21
Katha, Burma......B 1 30
Katherine, Australia, 555......E 2 36
Katihar, India, 26,326......E 3 29
Katmandu,* Nepal, 108,805......D 3 29
Katni, India, 24,630......D 4 29
Katowice, Poland, 203,700......B 4 24
Katrineholm, Sweden, 14,492......K 7 13
Katsena Ala, Nigeria, 1,138......J10 34
Katsina, Nigeria, 52,672......H 9 34
Katta-Kurgan, U.S.S.R., 18,500...H 5 22
Kattegat (strait)......G 8 13
Kattowitz (Katowice), Poland, 203,700......B 4 24
Katwijk aan Zee, Netherlands, 27,143......E 4 15
Kau, Indonesia......H 5 31
Kauai (island), U.S., 29,683......G 7 42
Kaufbeuren, Germany, 19,866......D 5 14
Kaulakapuas, Indonesia, 8,682......E 6 31
Kaulakurun, Indonesia......E 6 31
Kaunas, U.S.S.R., 214,000......D 4 22
Kaura Namoda, Nigeria, 13,068....H 9 34
Kavadarci, Yugoslavia, 6,053......E 5 21
Kavaje, Albania, 9,689......D 5 21
Kavali, India, 11,969......D 6 29
Kávalla, Greece, 42,102......G 5 21
Kavieng, Terr. N.G., 715......E 6 37
Kavir (desert), Iran......J 3 27
Kawagoe, Japan, 52,820......O 2 33
Kawaguchi, Japan, 124,783......O 2 33
Kawasaki, Japan, 319,226......O 2 33
Kaya, Upper Volta, 3,610......F 1 34
Kayes, Sudanese Rep., 25,000......D 9 34
Kayseri, Turkey, 65,489......F 3 28
Kazalinsk, U.S.S.R......H 5 22
Kazan (river), Canada......K 2 40
Kazan', U.S.S.R., 643,000......G 4 22
Kazandzhik, U.S.S.R., 2,600......G 6 22
Kazanlŭk, Bulgaria, 19,386......G 4 21
Kazbek (mtn.), U.S.S.R......F 5 22
Kazerun, Iran, 25,831......G 6 27
Kazvin, Iran, 77,269......F 2 27
Kebumen, Indonesia, 14,102......J 2 31
Kecskemét, Hungary, 88,374......E 3 20
Kediri, Indonesia, 48,567......K 2 31
Kédougou, Senegal, 822......D 9 34
Kędzierzyn, Poland, 15,700......D 3 24
Keele (peak), Canada......E 2 40
Keelung, China, 197,029......K 6 32
Keeper (mountain), Ireland......E 6 12
Keer-weer (cape), Australia......G 2 36
Keetmanshoop, S. W. Afr., 4,447......K17 35
Keewatin, Ontario, 1,949......B 3 41
Kefar Ata, Israel, 12,600......C 2 24
Kefar Sava, Israel, 17,000......B 3 24
Keighley, England, 56,944......F 4 10
Keijo (Seoul),* S. Korea, 1,446,019......C 5 33
Kellett (cape), Canada......D31 8
Kelliher, Saskatchewan, 461......K 4 40
Kelmscott, Aust., 1,250......B 2 36
Kelowna, Br. Columbia, 9,181......G 5 40
Kelvington, Saskatchewan, 819.....K 4 40
Kem', U.S.S.R., 16,700......E 3 22
Kemerovo, U.S.S.R., 277,000......O 5 23
Kemi, Finland, 26,448......O 4 13
Kemi (river), Finland......O 3 13
Kempsey, Australia, 7,489......J 6 36
Kempten, Germany, 39,821......D 5 14
Kenadsa, Saoura, 7,840......F 5 34
Kendal, England, 18,541......E 3 10
Kendal, Indonesia, 13,804......J 2 31
Kendari, Indonesia......G 6 31
Kendawangan, Indonesia......D 6 31
Kendrapara, India, 11,880......E 4 29
Keng Tung, Burma......C 2 30
Kenitra (Port-Lyautey), Morocco, 55,954......E 5 34
Kenmare (river), Ireland......A 8 12
Kenn (reef), Australia......K 4 36
Kennet (river), England......F 6 10
Keno Hill, Yukon, 100......C 2 40
Kénogami, Quebec, 11,309......F 4 41
Kenora, Ontario, 10,278......B 4 41
Kensington, P.E.I., 854......H 4 41
Kensington and Norwood, Australia, 14,159......D 8 36
Kentville, Nova Scotia, 4,937......H 4 41
Kenya (mountain), Kenya......O12 35
Keonjhargarh, India, 9,004......E 4 29
Kepsut, Turkey, 33,696......C 3 28
Kerang, Australia, 3,227......G 7 36
Kerch', U.S.S.R., 99,000......E 5 22

	Index Ref.	Plate No.
Kerema, Papua, 292	B 7	31
Keren, Eritrea, Ethiopia, 8,000	O 8	34
Kerintji (mountain), Indonesia	C 6	31
Kerki, U.S.S.R., 14,200	H 6	22
Kerkrade, Netherlands, 47,347	J 7	15
Kérkyra (Corfu), Greece, 27,431	D 6	21
Kerman, Iran, 53,464	K 5	27
Kermanshah, Iran, 102,759	E 3	27
Kerrobert, Saskatchewan, 1,037	J 4	40
Kersbrook, Australia, 402	D 7	36
Kerulen (river), Mon. Rep.	H 2	32
Keşan, Turkey, 11,089	B 2	28
Keta, Ghana, 11,380	G10	34
Ketapang, Indonesia, 4,385	E 6	31
Ketapang, Indonesia	K 2	31
Kete Krachi, Ghana, 2,022	F10	34
Kettering, England, 36,817	G 5	10
Kettwig, Germany, 15,573	G 4	14
Kew, Australia, 31,518	L 2	36
Khabarovsk, U.S.S.R., 322,000	P 5	23
Khachmas, U.S.S.R., 3,280	F 5	22
Khaipur, Pakistan, 18,184	A 3	29
Khalkhal, Iran, 6,170	F 2	27
Khalturin, U.S.S.R., 4,722	F 4	22
Khamgaon, India, 26,402	C 4	29
Khammam (Khammamett), India, 18,982	C 5	29
Khan Yunis, Egypt, 11,220	A 5	24
Khanabad, Afghanistan, 18,042	J 2	26
Khandwa, India, 38,493	C 4	29
Khanewal, Pakistan, 37,915	B 2	29
Khaniá (Canea), Greece, 33,211	G 8	21
Khanka (lake)	P 5	23
Khanpur, Pakistan, 15,197	B 3	29
Khanty-Mansiysk, U.S.S.R.	H 3	22
Kharagpur, India, 129,636	E 4	29
Khardah, India, 9,568	E 1	29
Kharga (oasis), Egypt, 11,155	N 6	34
Khar'kov, U.S.S.R., 930,000	E 4	22
Kharmanlii, Bulgaria, 9,240	H 5	21
Kharovsk, U.S.S.R., 2,830	F 3	22
Khartoum,* Sudan, 75,000	N 8	34
Khartoum North, Sudan, 37,450	N 8	34
Khaskovo, Bulgaria, 27,394	G 5	21
Khatanga, U.S.S.R.	M 2	23
Khenifra, Morocco, 11,549	E 5	34
Kherson, U.S.S.R., 157,000	E 5	22
Khingan, Great (mt. range), China	K 2	32
Khiva, U.S.S.R., 23,700	G 5	22
Khmel'nitskiy, U.S.S.R., 62,000	D 5	22
Khodzheyli, U.S.S.R., 4,820	G 5	22
Khoi, Iran, 36,476	D 1	27
Kholm, U.S.S.R., 5,533	E 4	22
Kholmsk, U.S.S.R., 18,151	R 5	23
Khon Kaen, Thailand, 10,385	D 3	30
Khorat (Nakhon Ratchasima), Thailand, 21,774	D 4	30
Khorog, U.S.S.R., 8,000	J 6	22
Khorramshahr with Abadan, Iran, 64,889	F 5	27
Khotan (Hotien), China	B 4	32
Khulna, Pakistan, 41,409	E 4	29
Khurja, India, 35,376	C 3	29
Khurramabad, Iran, 17,933	F 4	27
Khushab, Pakistan, 20,467	B 2	29
Khyber (pass), Pakistan	B 2	29
Kiama, Australia, 2,400	J 6	36
Kiamusze, China, 146,000	L 2	32
Kian, China, 52,800	J 6	32
Kiang (means river) (Chinese)		
Kiaochow (bay), China	K 4	32
Kidal, Sudanese Rep., 800	G 8	34
Kidderminster, England, 37,406	E 5	10
Kiel, Germany, 254,449	C 1	14
Kielce, Poland, 77,500	E 3	24
Kienteh, China	J 6	32
Kieta, Terr. New Guinea, 242	F 6	37
Kiev, U.S.S.R., 1,102,000	E 4	22
Kiffa, Mauritania, 4,655	D 8	34
Kigali, Ru.-Urun., 1,850	M12	35
Kigoma, Tanganyika Terr., 1,000	N12	35
Kikinda, Yugoslavia, 29,607	E 3	21
Kikori, Papua, 113	B 7	31
Kikwit, Belgian Congo, 5,081	K13	35
Kilimanjaro (mountain), Tanganyika Territory	O12	35
Kilis Turkey, 30,247	G 4	28
Kilkenny, Ireland, 10,607	G 6	12
Kilkís, Greece, 9,702	F 5	21
Killarney, Ireland, 6,464	C 7	12
Killarney, Manitoba, 1,410	L 5	40
Killarney (lakes), Ireland	C 7	12
Kilmarnock, Scotland, 42,123	G 8	11
Kilosa, Tan. Terr., 4,500	O13	35
Kilwa Kivinje, Tan. Terr., 3,000	P13	35
Kim, U.S.S.R., 1,029	S 2	23
Kimberley, Br. Columbia, 5,774	G 5	40
Kimberley, Cape of G. H., †62,445	L17	35
Kinabalu (mountain), No. Borneo	F 4	31
Kincardine, Ontario, 2,667	D 5	41
Kindersley, Saskatchewan, 2,572	J 4	40
Kindia, Guinea, 12,600	D 9	34
Kindu, Belgian Congo, 13,076	M12	35
Kineshma, U.S.S.R., 84,000	F 4	22
King (island), Tas., Australia, 954	G 7	36
King (sound), Australia	C 3	36
King Leopold (mt. range), Australia	D 3	36
King William (island), Canada	E28	8
Kingaroy, Australia, 4,464	J 5	36
Kingoonya, Australia, 113	E 6	36
King's Lynn, England, 26,176	H 5	10
Kings Peak (mountain), U.S.	F 4	42
Kingscote, Australia, 739	F 7	36
Kingsgate, Br. Columbia, 35	G 5	40
Kingston, Australia, 806	F 7	36
Kingston,* Jamaica, 142,464	C 3	45
Kingston, Ontario, 48,618	E 5	41
Kingston, Greater, Ontario, 58,000	E 5	41
Kingston-on-Thames, Eng., 40,172	G 6	10
Kingston-upon-Hull (Hull), England, 299,105	G 4	10
Kingstown, W. I., 4,831	G 4	45
Kingstown (Dún Laoghaire), Ireland, 47,553	K 5	12
Kingsville, Ontario, 2,884	D 5	41
Kingswood, England, 18,921	E 6	10
Kingtehchen, China, 92,000	J 6	32
Kingwilliamstown, Cape of G. H., 12,456	M18	35
Kinhwa, China, 46,200	K 6	32
Kinistino, Saskatchewan, 654	J 4	40
Kinnairds Head (prom.), Scotland	N 4	11
Kinsale, Ireland, 1,612	D 8	12
Kintampo, Ghana, 2,829	F10	34
Kintyre (peninsula), Scotland	E 9	11
Kinuso, Alberta, 306	G 3	40
Kioga (lake), Uganda	N11	35
Kirchheim, Germany, 20,133	C 4	14
Kirensk, U.S.S.R.	M 4	23
Kirikkale, Turkey, 27,071	E 3	28
Kirin, China, 435,400	L 3	32
Kirkağaç, Turkey, 9,438	B 3	28
Kirkby-in-Ashfield, England, 20,131	F 4	10
Kirkcaldy, Scotland, 49,050	K 7	11
Kirkee, India, 26,285	B 5	29
Kirkintilloch, Scotland, 14,826	C 2	11
Kirkland Lake, Ontario, 18,459	D 4	41
Kirklareli, Turkey, 19,312	B 2	28
Kirkuk, Iraq, 69,035	D 3	27
Kirkwall, Orkney Islands, 4,348	K 2	11
Kirov, U.S.S.R., 252,000	F 4	22
Kirovabad, U.S.S.R., 116,000	F 5	22
Kirovakan, U.S.S.R., 14,000	F 5	22
Kirovgrad, U.S.S.R., 34,700	P 6	23
Kirovo, U.S.S.R., 4,874	T 2	23
Kirovograd, U.S.S.R., 127,000	E 5	22
Kirovsk, U.S.S.R., 29,000	E 3	22
Kirsanov, U.S.S.R., 23,546	F 4	22
Kirşehir, Turkey, 16,606	F 3	28
Kiruna, Sweden, 19,023	L 3	13
Kiryu, Japan, 95,533	J 5	33
Kirzhach, U.S.S.R., 5,035	B 3	22
Kisarazu, Japan, 37,901	P 3	33
Kiselevsk, U.S.S.R., 130,000	O 6	23
Kishangarh, India, 14,459	C 3	29
Kishinev, U.S.S.R., 214,000	D 5	22
Kishiwada, Japan, 98,821	J 8	33
Kishorganj, Pakistan, 19,034	F 4	29
Kiskundorozsma, Hungary, 19,670	E 3	20
Kiskunfélegyháza, Hungary, 31,879	E 3	20
Kiskunhalas, Hungary, 24,281	E 3	20
Kiskunmajsa, Hungary, 18,282	E 3	20
Kislovodsk, U.S.S.R., 79,000	F 5	22
Kismayu, Somalia, 4,500	P12	35
Kississing, Manitoba, 500	K 3	40
Kisújszállás, Hungary, 14,441	F 3	20
Kisumu, Kenya, 10,899	N12	35
Kita, Sudanese Rep., 3,200	E 9	34
Kitale, Kenya, 6,338	O11	35
Kitami, Japan, 45,952	L 2	33
Kitchener, Ontario, 59,562	D 5	41
Kitchener, Greater, Ontario, 79,500	D 5	41
Kitega, Ru.-Urundi, 2,000	N12	35
Kitimat, Br. Columbia, 8,000	E 4	40
Kitwanga, Br. Columbia, 175	E 3	40
Kitzbühel, Austria, 7,120	B 3	20
Kitzingen, Germany, 16,489	D 4	14
Kiuchüan, China, 246,873	E 4	32
Kiukiang, China, 64,600	J 5	32
Kivu (lake), Africa	M12	35
Kizel, U.S.S.R., 60,000	G 4	22
Kizlyar, U.S.S.R., 14,800	F 5	22
Kizyl-Arvat, U.S.S.R., 12,630	G 6	22
Kizyl-Atrek, U.S.S.R.	G 6	22
Kizyl-Kiya, U.S.S.R., 15,104	U 2	23
Kjölen (mt. range)	K 3	13
Kladno, Czech., 49,701	C 1	20
Klagenfurt, Austria, 62,782	C 3	20
Klaipėda, U.S.S.R., 89,000	D 4	22
Klamath (river), U.S.	C 4	42
Klang, Malayan Fed., 33,500	D 7	30
Klar (river), Sweden	H 6	13
Klatovy, Czech., 14,333	B 2	20
Klaypeda (Klaipėda), U.S.S.R., 89,000	D 4	22
Klemtu, Br. Columbia, 150	E 4	40
Kletskaya, U.S.S.R., 2,622	F 5	22
Kleve (Cleves), Germany, 17,825	B 3	14
Klin, U.S.S.R., 53,000	E 4	22
Klinsty, U.S.S.R., 22,229	E 4	22
Kłodzko (Glatz), Poland, 20,700	C 3	24
Kloppenburg, Germany, 13,822	C 2	14
Kluane (lake), Canada	C 2	40
Kluang, Malayan Fed., 15,954	D 7	30
Kluczbork, Poland, 12,900	D 3	24
Klukhori (Karachayevsk), U.S.S.R., 2,848	F 5	22
Klyuchevsk, U.S.S.R., 5,500	P 6	23
Klyuchevskaya Sopka (volcano), U.S.S.R.	T 4	23
Knittelfeld, Austria, 13,143	C 3	20
Knong, Laos	E 4	30
Knurów, Poland, 13,600	A 4	24
Knysna, Cape of G. H., 7,354	L18	35
Kobayashi, Japan, 41,410	E 8	33
Kobdo, Mongolian Rep., 10,000	D 2	32
Kobe, Japan, 765,435	H 7	33
Köbenhavn (Copenhagen), *Denmark, 768,105	G 9	13
Koblenz (Coblenz), Germany, 66,444	B 3	14
Kobrin (Kobryn), U.S.S.R., 10,101	D 4	22
Koburg (Coburg), Germany, 44,929	D 3	14
Kocaeli (Izmit), Turkey, 56,702	C 2	28
Kochevo, U.S.S.R., 600	G 4	22
Kochi, Japan, 161,640	F 7	33
Koesfeld, Germany, 14,579	B 3	14
Koforidua, Ghana, 17,806	G10	34
Kofu, Japan, 121,645	J 6	33
Kogaluk (river), Canada	E 2	41
Kogarah, Australia, 43,618	L 3	36
Köge, Denmark, 10,602	H 9	13
Kohat, Pakistan, 40,534	B 2	29
Koi (river), Vietnam	E 2	30
Koil (Aligarh), India, 141,618	C 3	29
Kok-Yangak, U.S.S.R., 8,416	V 2	23
Kokan-Kishlak, U.S.S.R., 2,011	V 2	23
Kokand, U.S.S.R., 105,000	T 2	23
Kokchetav, U.S.S.R., 40,000	J 4	22
Kokiu, China, 159,700	F 7	32
Kokkola (Gamlakarleby), Finland, 15,993	N 5	13
Koko Nor (lake), China	E 4	32
Kokoda, Papua	C 7	31
Kokopo, Terr. N. G.	F 6	37
Kokura, Japan, 199,397	E 7	33
Kola (Kol'skiy) (peninsula), U.S.S.R.	E 3	22
Kolaka, Indonesia	G 6	31
Kolar, India, 19,006	C 6	29
Kolar Gold Fields, India, 159,084	C 6	29
Kolarovgrad (Shumen), Bulgaria, 31,169	H 4	21
Kolding, Denmark, 31,017	F 9	13
Kolguyev (island), U.S.S.R., 300	F 3	22
Kolhapur, India, 136,835	B 5	29
Kolín, Czech., 21,743	C 1	20
Köln (Cologne), Germany, 594,941	B 3	14
Kołobrzeg, Poland, 10,600	B 1	24
Kolomna, U.S.S.R., 100,000	E 4	22
Kolonodale, Indonesia	G 6	31
Kolozsvár (Cluj), Rumania, 117,915	F 2	21
Kolpashevo, U.S.S.R.	K 4	22
Kolpino, U.S.S.R., 17,317	C 2	22
Kolwezi, B. Congo, 47,772	M14	35
Kolyma (river), U.S.S.R.	S 3	23
Kolyma (Gydan) (mt. range), U.S.S.R.	S 3	23
Komandorskiye (islands), U.S.S.R.	T 4	23
Komárno (Komorn), Czech., 23,996	D 3	20
Komatsu, Japan, 72,378	H 5	33
Komodo (isl.), Indonesia	F 7	31
Komotau (Chomutov), Czech., 26,697	B 1	20
Komotinē, Greece, 29,734	G 5	21
Kompong Chhnang, Cambodia	E 4	30
Kompong Speu, Cambodia	E 5	30
Komsomol'sk, U.S.S.R., 177,000	P 4	23
Konakry (Conakry),* Guinea, 38,000	D10	34
Konan (Hungnam), Korea, 143,600	C 4	33
Kondopoga, U.S.S.R., 14,000	E 3	22
Kongju, Korea, 20,394	C 5	33
Kongmoon, China, 85,000	H 7	32
Kongolo, Belgian Congo, 2,322	M13	35
Kongsberg, Norway, 8,324	F 7	13
Königgrätz (Hradec Králové), Czech., 55,250	C 1	29
Königsberg (Kaliningrad), U.S.S.R., 202,000	D 4	22
Königshütte (Chorzów), Poland, 143,800	B 4	24
Konin, Poland, 14,900	D 2	24
Köniz, Switzerland, 20,742	D 3	19
Konnagar and Rishra, India, 37,432	E 1	29
Könniggrätz (Hradec Králové), Czech., 55,250	C 1	29
Konotop, U.S.S.R., 53,000	E 4	22
Konstantinovka, U.S.S.R., 89,000	J 1	23
Konstantinovskoye, U.S.S.R., 2,988	O 5	23
Konstanz (Constance), Germany, 42,934	C 5	14
Kontagora, Nigeria, 3,826	H 9	34
Kontum, Vietnam	E 4	30
Konya, Turkey, 93,125	E 4	28
Kopbal, India, 13,970	C 5	29
Kopenick, Germany, 113,851	K 3	14
Kopeysk, U.S.S.R., 160,000	H 4	22
Koprivnica, Yugoslavia, 9,105	C 2	21
Korat (Nakhon Ratchasima), Thai., 21,744	D 4	30
Korbach, Germany, 10,403	C 3	14
Korçë, Albania, 24,035	E 5	21
Korea (peninsula)	C 4	33
Korea (strait)	L 5	32
Korhogo, Ivory Coast, 4,069	E10	34
Koriyama, Japan, 70,866	K 5	33
Korkino, U.S.S.R., 85,000	H 4	22
Korneuburg, Austria, 7,867	D 2	20
Kornwestheim, Germany, 15,686	C 4	14
Koror, Palau Islands, 1,207	D 5	37
Korosten', U.S.S.R., 12,012	D 4	22
Korsakov, U.S.S.R., 23,600	R 5	23
Korsör, Denmark, 11,885	G 9	13
Kortkeros, U.S.S.R., 1,472	G 3	22
Kortrijk (Courtrai), Belgium, 41,569	C 7	15
Koryak (mtn. range), U.S.S.R.	T 3	23
Koschagyl, U.S.S.R.	G 5	22
Kościan, Poland. 15,400	C 2	24
Kosciusko (mountain), Australia	H 7	36
Košice, Czech., 79,460	F 2	20
Koslan, U.S.S.R., 598	F 3	22
Köslin (Koszalin), Poland, 37,400	C 1	24
Kosovska Mitrovica, Yugoslavia, 13,947	E 4	21
Kosti, Sudan, 29,900	N 9	34
Kostroma, U.S.S.R., 171,000	F 4	22
Koswig, Germany, 11,705	E 3	14
Koszalin (Köslin), Poland, 37,400	C 1	24
Kota Bharu, Mal. Fed., 22,765	D 6	30
Kota Kota, Nyas. Pr., 7,500	N14	35
Kotaagung, Indonesia, 2,822	C 7	31
Kotabaharu, Indonesia	E 6	31
Kotabaru, Indonesia, 3,756	F 6	31
Kotah, India, 45,032	C 3	29
Kotamobagu, Indonesia	G 5	31
Kotel'nich, U.S.S.R.	F 4	22
Kothen, Germany, 42,588	E 3	14
Kotka, Finland, 28,776	P 6	13
Kotlas, U.S.S.R.	F 3	22
Kotor, Yugoslavia, 5,402	D 4	21
Kotovsk, U.S.S.R.	F 4	22
Kotrang, India, 9,401	E 1	29
Kotri, Pakistan, 15,154	A 3	29
Kottayam, India, 33,364	C 7	29
Kottbus (Cottbus), Germany, 49,131	F 3	14
Kotto (river), Central Africa	L10	34
Koudougou, Upper Volta, 15,929	F 9	34
Koulikoro, Sudanese Rep., 4,500	E 9	34
Kouroussa, Guinea, 5,500	E 9	34
Koutiala, Sudanese Rep., 2,942	F 9	34
Kouvola, Finland, 16,209	P 6	13
Kovel' (Kowel), U.S.S.R., 27,650	D 4	22
Kovrov, U.S.S.R., 100,000	F 4	22
Kovur, India, 10,601	D 6	29
Kowloon, Hong Kong, 699,500	H 7	32
Kozan, Turkey, 11,382	F 4	28
Kozáne, Greece, 17,651	F 5	21
Kozhikode (Calicut), India, 158,724	C 6	29
Kraaifontein, Cape of G. H., 2,932	D19	35
Kragan, Indonesia	K 2	31
Kragujevac, Yugoslavia, 32,528	E 3	21
Kraków (Cracow), Poland, 463,500	E 3	24
Kraksaan, Indonesia, 4,738	K 2	31
Kraljevo (Rankovičevo), Yugoslavia, 12,503	E 4	21
Kramatorsk, U.S.S.R., 115,000	H 1	23
Kranj, Yugoslavia, 17,753	B 2	21
Krasnaya Polyana, U.S.S.R., 4,360	B 4	22
Kraśnik, Poland, 11,700	F 3	24

Name	Index Ref.	Plate No.
Krasnoarmeysk, U.S.S.R., 4,444	B 3	22
Krasnoborsk, U.S.S.R., 989	F 3	22
Krasnodar, U.S.S.R., 312,000	E 5	22
Krasnokamsk, U.S.S.R., 54,000	G 4	22
Krasnoslobodsk, U.S.S.R., 7,176	F 4	22
Krasnotur'insk, U.S.S.R., 62,000	R 5	23
Krasnoufimsk, U.S.S.R., 21,600	G 4	22
Krasnoural'sk, U.S.S.R., 35,000	P 6	23
Krasnovishersk, U.S.S.R., 14,000	G 3	22
Krasnovodsk, U.S.S.R., 30,000	G 5	22
Krasnoyarsk, U.S.S.R., 409,000	L 4	23
Krasnystaw, Poland, 10,700	F 3	24
Krasnyy Bor, U.S.S.R., 3,623	D 2	22
Krasnyy Liman, U.S.S.R.	H 1	23
Krasnyy Luch, US.S.R., 94,000	O 1	23
Kratié, Cambodia	E 4	30
Krefeld, Germany, 171,875	F 4	14
Kremenchug, U.S.S.R., 86,000	E 5	22
Krems, Austria, 20,353	C 2	20
Krētē (Crete) (island), Greece, 460,844	G 8	21
Kribi, Cam., 2,056	J11	35
Krishna (river), India	C 5	29
Krishnagar, India, 32,016	E 4	29
Kristiansand, Norway, 25,815	F 8	13
Kristianstad, Sweden, 25,036	J 9	13
Kristiansund, Norway, 13,152	E 5	13
Kristinehamn, Sweden, 19,084	H 7	13
Krivoy Rog, U.S.S.R., 386,000	E 5	22
Križevci, Yugoslavia, 5,248	C 2	21
Krnov, Czechoslovakia, 22,029	D 1	20
Kroměříž, Czechoslovakia, 21,014	D 2	20
Kronshtadt, U.S.S.R., 45,000	B 3	22
Kroonstad, O. F. S., 21,087	M17	35
Kropotkin, U.S.S.R., 54,000	F 5	22
Krosno, Poland, 18,500	E 4	24
Krotoszyn, Poland, 17,300	C 3	24
Krui, Indonesia, 3,860	C 7	31
Krung Kao (Ayutthaya), Thailand, 15,821	D 4	30
Krung Thep (Bangkok),* Thailand, 827,290	D 4	30
Kruševac, Yugoslavia, 13,788	E 4	21
Kryukovo, U.S.S.R., 957	B 4	22
Ksar-es-Souk, Morocco, 5,484	F 5	34
Kuala Lumpur,* Malayan Fed., 175,961	D 7	30
Kuala Trengganu, Malayan Fed., 27,004	D 6	30
Kuandang, Indonesia	G 5	31
Kuban' (river), U.S.S.R.	E 5	22
Kubeno (Kubenskoye) (lake), U.S.S.R.	F 4	22
Kuching,* Sara., 37,949	E 5	31
Kudat, No. Borneo, 1,895	F 4	31
Kudus, Indonesia, 54,524	J 2	31
Kudymkar, U.S.S.R., 10,200	G 4	22
Kufra (oasis), Libya, 4,600	L 7	34
Kufstein, Austria, 10,962	B 3	20
Kukawa, Nigeria, 20,000	J 9	34
Kukmor, U.S.S.R., 7,900	G 4	22
Kuldja, China, 108,200	B 3	32
Kulebaki, U.S.S.R., 15,142	F 4	22
Kulmbach, Germany, 24,193	D 3	14
Kulyab, U.S.S.R., 6,700	H 6	22
Kuma (river), U.S.S.R.	F 5	22
Kumagaya, Japan, 65,487	J 5	33
Kumamoto, Japan, 267,506	E 7	33
Kumanovo, Yugoslavia, 19,798	E 4	21
Kumasi, Ghana, 77,689	F10	34
Kumbakonam, India, 67,008	C 6	29
Kumta, India, 12,466	B 6	29
Kungrad, U.S.S.R., 3,125	G 5	22
Kungur, U.S.S.R., 65,000	G 4	22
Kuningan, Indonesia	H 2	31
Kunlun (mt. range), China	B 4	32
Kunming, China, 698,900	F 6	32
Kunsan, Korea, 74,447	C 6	33
Kuntsevo, U.S.S.R., 128,000	B 4	22
Kuolayarvi (Kuolajärvi), U.S.S.R.	E 3	22
Kuopio, Finland, 40,209	Q 5	13
Kupang, Indonesia, 7,171	G 8	31
Kupyansk, U.S.S.R., 15,156	E 5	22
Kurashiki, Japan, 53,301	F 6	33
Kurdzhali, Bulgaria, 10,480	G 5	21
Kure, Japan, 187,775	F 6	33
Kuressaare (Kuressare), U.S.S.R., 4,478	D 4	22
Kurgan, U.S.S.R., 145,000	H 4	22
Kurgan-Tyube, U.S.S.R., 6,000	H 6	22
Kuria Muria (islands) (Aden), 70	G 6	26
Kuril (isls.), U.S.S.R., 6,000	R 5	23
Kurla, India, 39,066	B 8	29
Kurnool, India, 45,250	C 5	29
Kursk, U.S.S.R., 203,000	E 4	22
Kurume, Japan, 100,997	E 7	33
Kurunegala, Ceylon, 13,510	D 7	29
Kusaie (island), Pacific, 1,865	G 5	37
Kushiro, Japan, 93,357	M 2	33
Kushka, U.S.S.R., 3,450	H 6	22
Kushva, U.S.S.R., 35,200	P 6	23
Kuskokwim (river), U.S.	F 8	42
Kustanay, U.S.S.R., 86,000	H 4	22
Kut, Iraq, 56,294	E 4	27
Kütahya, Turkey, 27,180	C 3	28
Kutaisi, U.S.S.R., 128,000	F 5	22
Kutaradja, Indonesia, 19,235	A 4	31
Kutch (region), India	A 4	29
Kutna Hora (Kuttenberg), Czech., 14,565	C 2	20
Kutno, Poland, 24,500	D 2	24
Kutoardjo, Indonesia, 11,496	J 2	31
Kuva, U.S.S.R., 5,907	T 2	23
Kuybyshev, U.S.S.R., 806,000	G 4	22
Kuybyshevka-Vostochnaya (Belogorsk), U.S.S.R.	O 4	23
Kuybyshevo, U.S.S.R., 5,536	N 1	23
Kuybyshevo, U.S.S.R., 5,424	T 2	23
Kuzino, U.S.S.R., 5,000	P 6	23
Kuznetsk, U.S.S.R., 57,000	F 4	22
Kuzomen', U.S.S.R., 533	E 3	22
Kwajalein (island), Pacific, 1,081	G 5	37
Kwando (river), Africa	L15	35
Kwangju, Korea, 138,883	C 6	33
Kweilin, China, 145,100	G 6	32
Kweisui (Huhehot), China, 148,400	H 3	32
Kweiyang, China, 270,900	G 6	32
Kwilu (river), Belg. Congo	K13	35
Kyaikto, Burma	C 3	30
Kyakhta, U.S.S.R., 12,300	M 5	23
Kyangin, Burma	B 3	30
Kyaukpadaung, Burma	B 2	30
Kyaukpyu, Burma	B 3	30
Kyaukse, Burma, 8,117	C 2	30
Kyŏmip'o, Korea, 53,035	C 4	33
Kyŏngju, Korea, 33,260	D 6	33
Kyŏngsŏng (Seoul),* S. Korea, 1,446,019	C 5	33
Kyoto, Japan, 1,101,854	J 7	33
Kyshtovka, U.S.S.R., 1,430	J 4	22
Kyshtym, U.S.S.R., 38,400	G 4	22
Kytlym, U.S.S.R., 6,500	P 5	23
Kyushu (island),Japan, 11,398,976	E 7	33
Kyustendil, Bulgaria, 19,309	F 4	21
Kywebwe, Burma	C 3	30
Kyzyl, U.S.S.R., 34,000	L 4	23
Kyzyl-Kum (desert), U.S.S.R.	H 5	22
Kzyl-Orda, U.S.S.R., 66,000	H 5	22
L		
L'Aquila, Italy, 24,843	D 3	18
La Barca, Mexico, 13,868	H 6	44
La Caleri, Chile, 8,426	N 9	47
La Carolina, Spain, 13,112	E 3	17
La Ceiba, Honduras, 16,645	D 3	39
La Chaux-de-Fonds, Switz., 33,154	C 2	19
La Chorrera, Panama, 8,652	H 6	39
La Ciotat, France, 10,819	F 6	16
La Coruña, Spain, †127,618	B 1	17
La Flèche, France, 8,380	C 4	16
La Gloria, Colombia, 1,331	F 2	46
La Grand' Combe, France, 9,689	E 5	16
La Guaira, Venezuela, 16,271	G 1	46
La Línea, Spain, 35,446	D 4	17
La Malbaie, Quebec, 2,789	F 4	41
La Mancha (region), Spain	E 3	17
La Orotava, Canary Is., Spain, 17,906	B 4	17
La Paz, Argentina, 15,006	J10	47
La Paz,* Bolivia, 321,073	G 7	46
La Paz, Mexico, 13,081	D 5	44
La Pérouse (strait), Asia	O 2	32
La Piedad, Mexico, 17,843	H 6	44
La Plata, Argentina, 207,031	O12	47
La Plata (river), S.A.	J11	47
La Quiaca, Argentina, 6,768	G 8	46
La Rioja, Argentina, 23,164	G 9	47
La Roche-sur-Yon, France, 16,735	C 4	16
La Rochelle, France, 56,056	C 4	16
La Romana, Dominican Rep., 11,587	F 6	48
La Ronge, Saskatchewan, 639	J 3	40
La Sarre, Quebec, 3,132	E 4	41
La Serena, Chile, 37,618	F 9	47
La Seyne-sur-Mer, France, 11,086	F 6	16
La Solana, Spain, 13,653	E 3	17
La Spezia, Italy, 105,301	B 2	18
La Tuque, Quebec, 11,096	F 4	41
La Unión, Chile, 7,234	F12	47
La Unión, El Salvador, 7,890	D 4	39
La Vega, Dominican Rep., 14,445	E 5	48
Labé, Guinea, 3,472	D 9	34
Łabędy, Poland, 13,800	A 4	24
Labelle, Quebec, 1,150	E 4	41
Laboulaye, Argentina, 9,032	H10	47
Labrador (terr.), Newf., 10,814	H 3	41
Lábrea, Brazil, 1,247	H 5	46
Labuha, Indonesia	H 6	31
Labuhan, Indonesia	G 2	31
Labuhanbilik, Indonesia	C 5	31
Lac (means lake) (Fr.)		
Lac-au-Saumon, Quebec, 1,681	G 4	41
Lac-Bouchette, Quebec, 781	F 4	41
Lac-Edouard, Quebec, 250	F 4	41
Lac-Frontière, Quebec, 619	G 4	41
Lac-la-Biche, Alberta, 967	H 4	40
Laccadive (islands), India, 18,393	B 6	29
Lacepede (bay), Australia	F 7	36
Lacepede (islands), Australia	C 3	36
Lachine, Quebec, 34,494	F 4	41
Lachlan (river), Australia	G 6	36
Lachute, Quebec, 6,911	F 4	41
Lacombe, Alberta, 2,747	H 4	40
Ladoga (Ladozhskoye) (lake), U.S.S.R.	E 3	22
Ladysmith, Br. Columbia, 2,107	F 5	40
Ladysmith, Natal, 16,639	N17	35
Lae, Terr. N. Guinea, 4,146	B 7	31
Laflèche, Saskatchewan, 661	J 5	40
Laghouat, Oasis, 11,058	G 5	34
Lago (means lake) (Sp.)		
Lagos, Mexico, 13,190	J 6	44
Lagos,* Nigeria, 267,407	G10	34
Lagos, Portugal, 7,143	B 4	17
Laguna, Brazil, 9,459	L 9	47
Laham, Indonesia	F 5	31
Lahat, Indonesia	C 6	31
Lahej, Aden Protectorate, 11,000	E 7	26
Lahore, Pakistan, 849,476	B 2	29
Lahr, Germany, 19,530	B 4	14
Lahti, Finland, 61,712	O 6	13
Lai Chau, Vietnam	D 2	30
Lais, Indonesia	C 6	31
Laiwui, Indonesia	H 6	31
Lajes, Brazil, 14,774	L 9	47
Lake Cargelligo, Australia, 988	H 6	36
Lake Louise, Alberta, 113	G 4	40
Lakhdenpokh'ya (Lahdenpohja), U.S.S.R., 1,832	D 3	22
Lakhtinskiy, U.S.S.R., 1,229	B 2	22
Lal'sk, U.S.S.R., 1,784	F 3	22
Lambay (island), Ireland	K 4	12
Lamego, Portugal, 7,449	C 2	17
Lamía, Greece, 22,353	F 6	21
Lammermuir (hills), Scotland	L 8	11
Lamongan, Indonesia, 11,012	K 2	31
Lampang, Thai., 22,405	C 3	30
Lampertheim, Germany, 15,953	C 4	14
Lamphun, Thailand, 7,896	C 3	30
Lamu, Kenya, 5,868	P12	35
Lanai (island), U.S., 3,136	H 8	42
Lanark, Scotland, 6,219	J 8	11
Lancaster, England, 51,661	E 3	10
Lancaster (sound), Canada	D27	8
Lanchow, China, 397,400	F 4	32
Lanciano, Italy, 12,000	E 3	18
Łańcut, Poland, 9,106	F 3	24
Lândana, Angola, 819	J13	35
Landau, Germany, 23,188	B 4	14
Lander, The (river), Australia	E 4	36
Landerneau, France, 9,363	B 3	16
Landeshut (Kamienna Góra), Poland, 14,900	C 3	24
Lands End (cape), England	B 7	10
Landsberg, Germany, 11,733	D 4	14
Landsberg (Gorzów Wielkopolski), Poland, 46,300	B 2	24
Landshut, Germany, 46,785	E 4	14
Landskrona, Sweden, 25,089	H 9	13
Lang Son, Vietnam	E 2	30
Langenbielau (Bielawa), Poland, 25,700	C 3	24
Langenburg, Germany, 14,796	G 4	14
Langenburg, Saskatchewan, 668	K 4	40
Langensalza, Germany, 16,013	D 3	14
Langsa, Indonesia, 4,749	B 5	31
Lanús, Argentina, 244,473	O12	47
Lao Kay, Vietnam	E 2	30
Laoag, Philippine Is., 22,218	F 2	31
Laon, France, 19,295	E 3	16
Lappeenranta, Finland, 20,621	P 6	13
Laptev (sea), U.S.S.R.	N 2	23
Lar, Iran, 13,917	J 7	27
Larache, Morocco, 41,917	E 4	34
Laramie (mt. range), U.S.	G 4	42
Larantuka, Indonesia	G 7	31
Larder Lake, Ontario, 1,455	E 4	41
Lárisa, Greece, 41,016	F 6	21
Larkana, Pakistan, 33,247	A 3	29
Larnaca, Cyprus, 17,500	E 5	28
Larne, N. Ireland, 11,976	K 2	12
Larvik, Norway, 10,311	C 4	13
Las Flores, Argentina, 9,287	J11	47
Las Lomitas, Argentina, 4,000	H 8	47
Las Palmas, *Canary Is., Spain, 153,262	B 4	17
Lascahobas, Haiti, 2,191	C 6	48
Lashio, Burma	C 2	30
Lashkar, India, 113,718	C 3	29
Lassen Peak (mountain), U.S.	C 4	42
Latacunga, Ecuador, 10,340	E 4	46
Latakia Syria, 102,832	F 5	28
Latouche Treville (cape), Aust.	C 3	36
Latur, India, 24,985	C 5	29
Lauban (Lubań), Poland, 13,100	B 3	24
Launceston, Australia, †49,303	H 8	36
Lauria, Italy, 4,530	E 4	18
Lauritsala, Finland, 10,539	Q 6	13
Lausanne, Switzerland, 106,807	C 3	19
Laval, France, 30,119	C 3	16
Lavello, Italy, 14,563	E 4	18
Laverton, Australia, 179	C 5	36
Lavongai (island), Territory N. G., 5,500	F 6	37
Lawang, Indonesia	K 2	31
Le Chesnay, France, 8,315	A 2	16
Le Creusot, France, 27,394	F 4	16
Le Havre, France, 137,175	C 3	16
Le Locle, Switzerland, 11,979	C 2	19
Le Mans, France, 103,346	C 3	16
Le Port, Réunion, 7,232	P20	35
Le Puy, France, 19,636	F 5	16
Leader, Saskatchewan, 1,085	J 4	40
Leaf (river), Canada	F 2	41
Leamington, England, 36,344	F 5	10
Leamington, Ontario, 7,856	D 5	41
Leatherhead, England, 27,203	G 6	10
Lębork (Lauenburg), Poland, 19,600	C 1	24
Lebrija, Spain, 12,903	D 4	17
Lebyazh'ye, U.S.S.R., 2,307	H 4	22
Lecce, Italy, 56,937	G 4	18
Lecco, Italy, 41,684	B 2	18
Ledesma, Argentina, 4,476	H 8	47
Ledo, India	G 3	29
Leduc, Alberta, 2,008	H 4	40
Lee (river), Ireland	D 8	12
Leech (lake), U.S.	K 3	43
Leeds, England, 505,219	F 4	10
Leek, England, 19,356	E 4	10
Leer, Germany, 20,616	B 2	14
Leeuwarden, Netherlands, 81,458	H 2	15
Leeuwin (cape), Australia	A 6	36
Legaspi, Philippine Is., 18,987	G 3	31
Leghorn, Italy, 134 513	C 3	18
Legionowo, Poland, 17,600	E 2	24
Legnica (Liegnitz), Poland, 54,600	C 3	24
Lehrte, Germany, 19,172	D 2	14
Leiah, Pakistan, 14,913	B 2	29
Leicester, England, 285,181	G 5	10
Leichhardt (river), Australia	F 3	36
Leiden, Netherlands, 94,893	E 4	15
Leigh, England, 48,728	E 4	10
Leipzig, Germany, 607,655	E 3	14
Leiria, Portugal, 7,123	B 3	17
Lekitobi, Indonesia	G 6	31
Leksula, Indonesia	H 6	31
Lemberg (L'vov), U.S.S.R., 410,000	D 4	22
Lemgo, Germany, 20,088	C 2	14
Lēmnos (island), Greece, 24,507	G 6	21
Lena (river), U.S.S.R.	O 3	23
Lenger, U.S.S.R.	V 1	23
Leninabad, U.S.S.R., 77,000	R 1	23
Leninakan, U.S.S.R., 108,000	F 5	22
Leningrad, U.S.S.R., 2,888,000	C 2	22
Leninogorsk, U.S.S.R., 67,000	K 4	22
Leninsk, U.S.S.R., 14,808	F 5	22
Leninsk-Kuznetskiy, U.S.S.R., 132,000	O 5	23
Lenkoran', U.S.S.R., 24,000	F 6	22
Lens, France, 34,134	E 2	16
Lentini, Italy, 28,999	E 6	18
Leoben, Austria, 35,319	C 3	20
Léogane, Haiti, 3,608	C 6	48
León, Mexico, 122,585	J 6	44
León, Spain, †59,403	D 1	17
Leonforte, Italy, 17,699	E 6	18
Leonora, Australia, 358	C 5	36
Léopold II (lake), Belg. Congo	K12	35
Léopoldville,* Belg. Congo, 257,197	K12	35
Leoville, Saskatchewan, 397	J 4	40
Lepaya (Liepāja), U.S.S.R., 71,000	D 4	22
Lepel', U.S.S.R., 6,776	D 4	22
Lerdo, Mexico, 13,389	H 4	44
Lérida, Spain, †51,432	G 2	17
Les Cayes, Haiti, 11,835	B 6	48
Les Méchins, Quebec, 600	G 4	41
Les Sables d'Olonne, France, 17,411	B 4	16
Lesbos (island), Greece, 126,928	G 6	21
Leskovac, Yugoslavia, 21,763	E 4	21
Lesogorsk, U.S.S.R., 18,618	R 5	23
Lesozavodsk, U.S.S.R., 10,500	P 5	23
Lesser Antilles (islands)	E 4	45
Lesser Slave (lake), Canada	G 3	40
Leszno, Poland, 27,600	C 3	24
Letchworth, England, 20,321	G 6	10
Lethbridge, Alberta, 29,462	H 5	40

Index Ref. / Plate No.

Leticia, Colombia, 1,898 F 4 46
Letpadan, Burma C 3 30
Leuser (mountain), Indon. B 5 31
Leuven (Louvain), Belgium, 34,122 F 7 15
Levac, Ontario, 1,833 D 4 41
Levádeia, Greece, 12,517 F 6 21
Levallois-Perret, France, 61,348 A 1 16
Lévêque (cape) Australia C 3 36
Leverkusen, Germany, 65,531 B 3 14
Levice, Czech., 15,832 E 2 20
Levikha, U.S.S.R., 2,100 P 6 23
Lévis, Quebec, 13,644 F 4 41
Levskigrad, Bulgaria, 8,862 G 4 21
Levuka, Fiji Islands, 1,944 H 7 37
Lewis (island), Scotland, 26,465 C 3 11
Lewisporte, Newf., 2,076 K 4 41
Lhasa, China, 50,000 D 6 32
Lhokseumawe, Indonesia, 2,043 B 4 31
Liaoyang, China, 150,000 K 3 32
Liaoyüan, China, 120,100 L 3 32
Liard (river), Canada E 3 40
Liberec, Czech., 66,796 C 1 20
Libourne, France, 14,581 C 5 16
Libreville,* Gabon, 17,868 H11 35
Libyan (desert) L 6 34
Licata, Italy, 35,871 D 6 18
Lice, Turkey, 6,725 J 3 28
Lichtenberg, Germany, 157,721 J 3 14
Lida, U.S.S.R., 19,490 D 4 22
Lidcombe, Australia, 20,286 L 3 36
Lidice, Czech. C 1 20
Lidingö, Sweden, 20,798 H 1 13
Lidköping, Sweden, 14,542 H 7 13
Lidzbark Warminski, Poland, 10,200 E 1 24
Liège (Luik), Belgium, 155,670 H 7 15
Liegnitz (Legnica), Poland, 54,600 C 3 24
Lienz, Austria, 10,024 B 3 20
Liepāja, U.S.S.R., 71,000 D 4 22
Lier (Lierre), Belgium, 29,010 F 6 15
Liévin, France, 15,272 E 2 16
Liffey (river), Ireland H 5 12
Ligurian (sea) B 3 18
Lihou (reef and cays), Australia J 3 36
Lille, France, 190,078 E 2 16
Lillehammer, Norway, 6,634 F 6 13
Lillooet, Br. Columbia, 1,083 F 4 40
Lima,* Peru, 628,821 E 6 46
Limassol, Cyprus, 23,500 B 3 28
Limay (river), Argentina G11 47
Limbach, Germany, 17,693 E 3 14
Limbe-Blantyre, Nyas. Pr., 24,380 N15 35
Limburg, Germany, 15,419 C 3 14
Limeira, Brazil, 27,962 L 8 46
Limerick, Ireland, 50,886 D 6 12
Limmen Bight (bay), Australia F 2 36
Limoges, France, 98,405 D 5 16
Limón, Costa Rica, 11,310 F 6 39
Limonade, Haiti, 1,209 C 5 48
Limpopo (river), Africa N16 35
Linares, Chile, 17,108 F11 47
Linares, Spain, 44,093 E 3 17
Lincoln, Argentina, 12,695 H10 47
Lincoln, England, 69,401 G 4 10
Lindau, Germany, 20,308 C 5 14
Lindesnes (cape), Norway E 8 13
Lindi, Tan. Terr., 8,577 P13 35
Lindsay, Ontario, 10,110 E 5 41
Linfen, China H 4 32
Lingayen, Philippine Is., 6,350 F 2 31
Lingeh, Iran, 8,871 J 7 27
Lingen, Germany, 20,164 B 2 14
Linguère, Senagal, 1,324 D 8 34
Linköping, Sweden, 54,552 K 7 13
Lins, Brazil, 24,170 L 8 46
Linz, Austria, 184,685 C 2 20
Lions (gulf), France E 6 16
Lion's Head, Ontario, 413 D 4 41
Lipari (islands), Italy, 11,799 E 5 18
Lipetsk, U.S.S.R., 156,000 E 4 22
Lipno, Poland, 8,389 D 2 24
Lipova, Rumania, 6,556 E 2 21
Lippstadt, Germany, 31,462 C 3 14
Lisbon (Lisboa),* Portugal, 790,434 A 1 17
Lisburn, N. Ireland, 14,778 J 2 12
Lisieux, France, 14,511 D 3 16
Lismore, Australia, 17,372 J 5 36
Listowel, Ontario, 3,644 D 5 41
Lithgow, Australia, 15,128 J 6 36
Litoměrice, Czech., 14,491 C 1 20
Little Colorado (river), U.S. F 6 42
Little Current, Ontario, 1,514 D 4 41
Little Minch (channel), Scotland C 4 11
Little Missouri (river), U.S. H 3 42
Litvinow, Czech., 24,149 B 1 20
Liuchow, China, 158,800 G 7 32
Liverpool, Australia, 26,610 K 3 36
Liverpool, England, 788,659 D 4 10
Liverpool, Nova Scotia, 3,500 H 5 41
Liverpool (bay), England D 4 10
Livingstone, N. Rhodesia, 12,278 M15 35
Livny, U.S.S.R., 19,873 E 4 22
Livorno (Leghorn), Italy, 134,513 C 3 18
Livramento, Brazil, 29,099 K10 47
Lizard Head (point), England B 8 10
Ljubljana, Yugoslavia, 138,211 B 3 21
Llandudno, Wales, 16,715 D 4 10
Llanelly, Wales, 34,476 C 6 10
Llanos (means plains) (Sp.)
Llera, Mexico, 1,653 K 4 44
Lleyn (peninsula), Wales C 5 10
Lloydminster, Sask., 5,077 J 4 40
Llullaillaco (mountain), Chile F 8 47
Loange (river), Angola K13 35
Löbau, Germany, 15,361 F 3 14
Lobaye (river), Central Africa K10 34
Lobito, Angola, 23,897 J14 35
Lobos, Argentina, 8,372 O12 47
Lobos de Afuera (islands), Peru D 5 46
Lobos de Tierra (island), Peru D 5 46
Lobva, U.S.S.R., 5,200 R 5 23
Loc Ninh, Vietnam E 5 30
Locarno, Switzerland, 7,767 G 4 19
Lochy (lake), Scotland G 6 11
Lockeport, Nova Scotia, 1,207 H 5 41
Lod (Lydda), Israel, 18,600 B 4 24
Lodi, Italy, 30,217 B 2 18
Łódź, Poland, 681,900 D 3 24
Lofoten (islands), Norway, 29,375 H 2 13
Logan (mountain), Canada B 2 40
Logone (river) K 9 34
Logroño, Spain, †50,090 E 1 17
Loheia (Luhaiya), Yemen, 6,000 D 6 26
Loikaw, Burma C 3 30
Loire (river), France C 4 16
Loja, Ecuador, 23,757 E 4 46
Lokeren, Belgium, 25,986 D 6 15
Lokoja, Nigeria, 8,085 H10 34
Lokot', U.S.S.R., 5,675 K 4 22
Lom, Bulgaria, 15,182 F 4 21
Lom Sak, Thailand, 6,243 D 3 30
Lomami (river), Belg. Congo L12 35
Lomas de Zamora, Argentina, 125,943 O12 47
Lombok (island), Indonesia, 701,290 F 7 31
Lomé,* Togo, 28,000 G10 34
Lomela (river), Belg. Congo L12 35
Lomond (lake), Scotland G 7 11
Lomonosov, U.S.S.R. C 3 22
Łomża, Poland, 18,900 F 2 24
London (Adm. County-City), England, 3,347,982 G 6 10
London, Greater,* England, 8,346,137 G 6 10
London, Ontario, 101,693 D 5 41
London, Greater, Ont., 154,500 D 5 41
Londonderry (cape), Australia D 2 36
Londonderry, N. Ireland, 50,099 G 2 12
Londrina, Brazil, 33,095 K 8 47
Long (island), U.S. M 2 43
Long (island), Bahama Is., 4,564 C 2 45
Long (reef), Australia C 2 36
Long Eaton, England, 28,638 F 5 10
Long Island (sound), U.S. M 2 43
Long Xuyen, Vietnam, 148,000 E 5 30
Longford, Australia, 1,411 H 8 36
Longiram, Indonesia F 6 31
Longlac, Ontario, 250 C 4 41
Longnawan, Indonesia F 5 31
Longreach, Australia, 3,350 G 4 36
Longwy, France, 4,420 F 3 16
Lons-le-Saunier, France, 14,247 F 4 16
Loop Head (cape), Ireland A 6 12
Lop Nor (lake), China D 3 32
Lop Buri, Thai., 7,779 D 4 30
Lopatka (cape), U.S.S.R. S 4 23
Lopez (cape), Gabon H12 35
Lorca, Spain, 21,057 F 4 17
Lorica, Colombia, 6,146 E 2 46
Lorient, France, 37,981 B 4 16
Lorne (firth), Scotland E 7 11
Lörrach, Germany, 22,689 B 5 14
Los Angeles, Chile, 20,979 F11 47
Los Mochis, Mexico, 21,552 E 4 44
Los Toldos, Arg., 5,342 M12 47
Lota, Chile, 31,087 F11 47
Louga, Senegal, 14,240 C 8 34
Lough Swilly (inlet), Ireland F 1 12
Loughborough, England, 34,731 F 5 10
Louis Trichardt, Transv., 5,668 M16 35
Louisburg, Nova Scotia, 1,314 J 4 41
Louisiade (archipelago), Papua, 10,384 F 7 37
Lourdes, France, 14,110 C 6 16
Lourenço Marques,* Mozambique, 93,303 O17 35
Louvain, Belgium, 34,122 F 7 15
36,640 F 7 15
Louviers, France, 8,720 D 3 16
Lovat' (river), U.S.S.R. E 4 22
Lovech, Bulgaria, 11,730 G 4 21
Low (cape), Canada N 2 40
Lower California (pen.), Mexico, 287,308 C 2 44
Lower Post, Br. Columbia E 3 40
Lower Tunguska (river), U.S.S.R. L 3 23
Lowestoft, England, 42,834 J 5 10
Łowicz, Poland, 16,800 E 2 24
Loxton, Australia, 2,321 G 6 36
Loyalty (islands), Pacific, 11,100 G 8 37
Loyang, China, 171,200 H 5 32
Lualaba (river), Belg. Congo M13 35
Luanda,* Angola, 141,722 J13 35
Luang Prabang, Laos D 3 30
Luangwa (river), N. Rhodesia N14 35
Luapula (river), Africa M14 35
Lubań, Poland, 13,100 B 3 24
Lübeck, Germany, 238,276 D 2 14
Lublin, Poland, 142,400 F 3 24
Lubliniec, Poland, 11,000 D 3 24
Lubny, U.S.S.R., 21,302 E 4 22
Luc An Chau, Vietnam E 2 30
Lucca, Italy, 63,667 C 3 18
Luce (bay), Scotland G10 11
Lucena, Philippine Is., 18,085 G 3 31
Lucena, Spain, 22,797 D 4 17
Lucenec, Czech, 15,083 E 2 20
Lucera, Italy, 22,271 E 4 18
Lucerne, Switz., 60,526 F 2 19
Luchow, China, 289,000 G 6 32
Łuck (Lutsk), U.S.S.R., 49,000 D 4 22
Luckenwalde, Germany, 30,979 E 2 14
Lucknow, India, 496,861 D 3 29
Lüdenscheid, Germany, 51,705 B 3 14
Lüderitz, S. W. Africa, 3,451 J17 35
Ludhiana, India, 153,795 C 2 29
Ludwigsburg, Germany, 58,489 C 4 14
Ludwigshafen, Germany, 123,869 C 4 14
Ludwigslust, Germany, 12,487 D 2 14
Luebo, Belg. Congo, 17,826 L13 35
Luga, U.S.S.R., 24,200 E 4 22
Lugano, Switzerland, 18,122 G 4 19
Lugansk, U.S.S.R., 274,000 P 1 23
Luganville (Segond), New Hebrides G 7 37
Lugenda (river), Mozambique O14 35
Lugh, Somalia, 5,000 P11 34
Lugo, Italy, 16,084 D 2 18
Lugo, Spain, †52,093 C 1 17
Lugoj, Rumania, 26,707 F 3 21
Luhaiya, Yemen, 6,000 D 6 26
Luik (Liège), Belgium, 155,670 H 7 15
Luilaka (river), Belg. Congo L12 35
Luimneach (Limerick), Ireland, 50,886 D 6 12
Luján, Argentina, 19,176 N12 47
Lukenie (river), Belg. Congo L12 35
Lukovit, Bulgaria, 7,755 G 4 21
Łuków, Poland, 10,000 F 3 24
Lukuga (river), Belg. Congo M13 35
Luleå, Sweden, 22,515 N 4 13
Luleälv (river), Sweden M 3 13
Lüleburgaz, Turkey, 18,355 B 2 28
Lulua (river), Belg. Congo L13 35
Luluabourg, Belg. Congo, 27,252 L13 35
Lumadjang, Indonesia, 18,838 K 2 31
Lumsden, Saskatchewan, 512 J 4 40
Lund, Sweden, 33,954 H 9 13
Lundy (island), England, 43 C 6 10
Lüneburg, Germany, 58,139 D 2 14
Lünen, Germany, 61,305 B 3 14
Lunenburg, Nova Scotia, 2,859 H 5 41
Lunéville, France, 20,512 G 3 16
Lungchen, China, 14,000 L 2 32
Luque, Paraguay, 5,519 J 8 47
Lurin, Peru, 2,141 E 6 46
Lusaka,* N. Rhodesia, 19,825 M15 35
Lusambo, Belg. Congo, 7,558 L12 35
Luscar, Alberta, 500 G 4 40
Lüshun (Port Arthur), China, 126,000 K 4 32
Luso, Angola, 2,821 L14 35
Lustenau, Austria, 10,309 A 3 20
Lut (desert), Iran L 5 27
Lüta, China, 1,200,000 K 4 32
Luton, England, 110,381 G 6 10
Lutsk, U.S.S.R., 49,000 D 4 22
Luwingu, N. Rhodesia, 540 N13 35
Luwuk, Indonesia G 6 31
Luxembourg (Luxemburg), *Luxembourg, 61,996 J 9 15
Luxor, Egypt, 24,118 N 6 34
Luzern (Lucerne), Switz., 60,526 F 2 19
Luzon (island), Phil. Islands, 9,074,974 G 2 31
L'vov (Lwów), U.S.S.R., 410,000 D 4 22
Lyakhov (islands), U.S.S.R. R 2 23
Lyallpur, Pakistan, 179,127 B 2 29
Lydda (Lod), Israel, 18,600 B 4 24
Lydenburg, Transv., 3,846 N16 35
Lyme (bay), England D 7 10
Lymington, England, 22,699 F 7 10
Lynn Lake, Manitoba, 1,444 K 3 40
Lyon, France, 462,657 F 5 16
Lyons (river), Australia B 4 36
Lys'va, U.S.S.R., 73,000 G 4 22
Lytton, Br. Columbia, 329 F 4 40
Lyubertsy, U.S.S.R., 93,000 B 4 22
Lyublino, U.S.S.R., 86,000 B 4 22

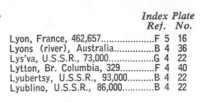

M

Ma'ad, Jordan, 8,629 D 2 24
Ma'an, Jordan, 4,509 D 2 24
Maastricht, Netherlands, 86,665 H 7 15
Macaé, Brazil, 10,818 M 8 46
Macao (Macau),* Macao, 166,544 H 7 32
Macapá, Brazil, 9,748 K 3 46
Macas, Ecuador, 1,079 E 4 46
Macclesfield, England, 35,999 F 4 10
Macdonald (lake), Australia D 4 36
Macdonnell (mt. ranges), Aust. E 4 36
Maceió, Brazil, 99,088 O 5 46
Macerata, Italy, 21,875 D 3 18
Machala, Ecuador, 7,491 D 4 46
Mackay, Australia, 14,762 H 4 36
Mackay (lake), Australia D 4 36
Mackenzie (bay), Canada D32 8
Mackenzie (river), Canada F 2 40
Macklin, Saskatchewan, 561 J 4 40
Maclear, C. of G.H., 2,161 M18 35
Mâcon, France, 20,226 F 4 16
Macquarie (harbor), Tas., Aust. G 7 36
Macumba, The (river), Aust. F 5 36
Ma'daba, Jordan, 8,545 D 4 24
Madagascar (island), 4,463,801 R16 35
Madang, Terr. N.G., 1,550 B 7 31
Madaripur, Pakistan, 21,005 F 4 29
Madeira (island), Port., 266,752 A 2 17
Madeira (river), Brazil H 5 46
Madhubani, India, 20,272 E 3 29
Madiun, Indonesia, 41,872 J 2 31
Madjalengka, Indonesia, 8,596 H 2 31
Madjene, Indonesia F 6 31
Madoc, Ontario, 1,325 E 5 41
Madras, India, 1,416,056 D 6 29
Madre (lagoon), U.S.-Mex. J 8 42
Madre de Dios (island), Chile E14 47
Madre de Dios (river), S.A. F 6 46
Madre del Sur (mt. range), Mex. K 8 44
Madre Occidental (mt. range), Mexico E 3 44
Madre Oriental (mt. range), Mexico J 5 44
Madrid,* Spain, 1,618,435 F 4 17
Madurai (Madura), India, 361,781 C 7 29
Mae Klong, Thailand, 9,332 D 4 30
Maebashi, Japan, 97,394 J 5 33
Maestricht (Maastricht), Netherlands, 86,665 H 7 15
Maevatanana, Malg. Rep., 2,693 R15 35
Mafeking,* Bech. Prot., 6,870 L17 35
Mafeking, Manitoba, 278 K 4 40
Mafia (island), Tan. Terr., 9,000 P13 35
Magadan, U.S.S.R., 62,000 S 4 23
Magangué, Colombia, 9,770 E 2 46
Magdalen (islands), Canada, 9,999 H 4 41
Magdalena, Argentina, 4,114 P12 47
Magdalena (river), Colombia E 1 46
Magdeburg, Germany, 236,326 E 2 14
Magdelaine (cays), Australia J 3 36
Magdiel, Israel, 5,100 B 3 21
Magelang, Indonesia, 52,944 J 2 31
Magellan (strait), S.A. G14 47
Magetan, Indonesia, 15,152 K 2 31
Maglie, Italy, 12,404 G 4 18
Magnitogorsk, U.S.S.R., 311,000 G 4 22
Magog, Quebec, 12,720 F 4 41
Magpie, Quebec, 155 H 3 41
Magrath, Alberta, 1,382 H 5 40
Magwe, Burma, 9,353 B 2 30
Maha Sarakham, Thai., 11,816 D 3 30
Mahabad, Iran, 15,971 D 2 27
Mahaica, British Guiana, 486 J 2 46
Mahanadi (river), India D 4 29
Mahbubnagar, India, 16,462 C 5 29
Mahe, India, 18,293 C 6 29
Mahébourg, Maur., 6,020 T19 35
Mahoba, India, 17,224 C 3 29
Mahón, Balearic Is., Spain, 14,237 J 3 17
Mahone Bay, N.S., 1,109 H 5 41
Mährisch Ostrau (Ostrava), Czech., 199,206 E 2 20
Mahuva, India, 22,058 B 4 29
Maida, Yemen, 2,500 D 6 26
Maidenhead, England, 27,155 G 6 10
Maidstone, England, 54,035 H 6 10

Index Ref. Plate No.
Maidstone, Saskatchewan, 555 J 4 40
Maiduguri, Nigeria, 24,359 J 9 34
Maimana, Afghan., 25,698 H 2 26
Main (river), Germany C 4 14
Maintirano, Malg. Rep., 2,482 P15 35
Mainz, Germany, 88,369 C 4 14
Maipu (mountain), Argentina G10 47
Maisons-Alfort, France, 35,578 B 2 16
Maisons-Laffitte, France, 13,074 A 1 16
Maitland, Australia, †21,331 J 6 36
Maitland, C. of G.H., 5,000 C19 35
Maizuru, Japan, 91,914 G 6 33
Maji, Ethiopia, 3,000 O10 34
Majunga, Malg. Rep., 48,073 R15 35
Makarikari (salt lake), Bech. Prot. L16 35
Makassar, Indonesia, 265,263 F 7 31
Makassar (strait), Indonesia F 6 31
Makeni, S. Leone, 7,500 D10 34
Makeyevka, U.S.S.R., 358,000 K 1 23
Makhachkala, U.S.S.R., 119,000 F 5 22
Makhnevo, U.S.S.R., 540 R 6 23
Makin (island), Pacific, 969 H 5 37
Makó, Hungary, 32,591 F 3 20
Maku, Iran, 6,668 D 1 27
Makurdi, Nigeria, 7,655 H10 34
Malacca, Malay. Fed., 54,507 D 7 30
Malacca (strait) D 7 30
Malad, India, 12,212 B 7 29
Málaga, Spain, †274,847 D 4 17
Malaita (island), Pacific, 40,000 G 6 37
Malakal, Sudan, 12,150 N10 34
Malakoff, France, 27,424 A 2 16
Malamir, Iran, 2,001 F 5 27
Malang, Indonesia, 500,000 K 2 31
Malange, Angola, 22,390 K13 35
Malartic, Quebec, 6,818 E 4 41
Malatya, Turkey, 64,880 H 3 28
Malay (peninsula) D 6 30
Malayer (Daulatabad), Iran, 19,749 F 3 27
Malbork (Marienburg), Poland, 22,500 D 2 24
Maldive (islands), 82,086 L 9 25
Maldonado, Uruguay, 8,000 K10 47
Malegaon, India, 39,924 B 4 29
Maler Kotla, India, 29,321 C 2 29
Malheur (lake), U.S. D 4 42
Malili, Indonesia G 6 31
Malin Head (cape), Ireland F 1 12
Malinau, Indonesia F 5 31
Malindi, Kenya, 3,292 P12 35
Malines (Mechelen), Belgium, 63,497 F 6 15
Malingping, Indonesia G 2 31
Malkapur, India, 20,598 C 4 29
Mallow, Ireland, 5,729 D 7 12
Malmesbury, C. of G. H., 5,751 D18 35
Malmö, Sweden, 192,498 H 9 13
Malolos, Philippine Is., 2,894 G 2 31
Malpelo (island), Colombia D 3 46
Maltahöhe, S. W. Africa, 706 K16 35
Malvan, India, 25,677 B 5 29
Malvern, England, 21,505 E 5 10
Mam Soul (mountain), Scotland F 5 11
Mamoré (river), Bolivia G 6 46
Mampawah, Indonesia D 5 31
Mamudju, Indonesia F 6 31
Man (island), 55,213 C 3 10
Mana, Fr. Guiana, 1,443 K 2 46
Manacor, Balearic Is., Spain, 12,823 H 3 17
Manado, Indonesia, 61,982 G 5 31
Managua,* Nicaragua, 176,569 D 4 39
Manakara, Malg. Rep., 6,775 R16 35
Manakha, Yemen, 3,000 D 6 26
Manama,* Bahrein, 39,648 F 4 26
Mananara, Malg. Rep., 11,182 S15 35
Mananjary, Malg. Rep., 11,747 R16 35
Manar (gulf), India C 7 29
Manatí, P.R., 10,075 G 1 45
Manaus, Brazil, 89,612 H 4 46
Manchester, England, 703,082 E 4 10
Manchouli, China, 45,000 J 2 32
Mandalay, Burma, 182,367 C 2 30
Mandi, India, 9,033 C 2 29
Mandla, India, 12,209 D 4 29
Mandsaur, India, 21,972 B 4 29
Mandurah, Australia, 1,623 B 2 36
Manduria, Italy, 21,584 F 4 18
Mandvi, India, 28,750 A 4 29
Manfalût, Egypt, Egypt, 20,939 M 6 34
Manfredonia, Italy, 26,682 F 4 18
Mangalia, Rumania, 4,547 J 4 21
Mangalore, India, 117,083 B 6 29
Mangareva (Gambier) (islands), Pacific, 554 N 8 37
Mangotsfield, England, 17,784 E 6 10
Mangrol, India, 18,818 A 4 29
Mangueira (lake), Brazil K10 47
Manicoré, Brazil, 2,241 H 5 46
Manicouagan (river), Canada G 3 41
Manifold (cape), Australia J 4 36
Manila, Philippine Is., 983,906 G 3 31
Manilla, Australia, 1,972 J 4 36
Manisa, Turkey, 45,484 B 3 28
Manitoba (lake), Canada L 4 40
Manitoulin (isl.), Canada D 4 41
Maniwaki, Quebec, 5,399 E 4 41
Manizales, Colombia, 88,893 E 2 46
Manly, Australia, 32,473 L 3 36
Manmad, India, 16,838 B 4 29
Mannargudi, India, 23,288 C 6 29
Mannheim, Germany, 245,634 C 4 14
Mannville, Alberta, 599 H 4 40
Manokwari, Neth. N. G. J 6 31
Manresa, Spain, 36,934 G 2 17
Mansel (island), Canada D 1 41
Mansfield, England, 51,352 F 4 10
Manta, Ecuador, 19,028 D 4 46
Mantes-Gassicourt, France, 13,055 D 3 16
Mantua (Mantova), Italy, 48,250 C 2 18
Manyberries, Alberta, 130 H 5 40
Manzanares, Spain, 18,428 E 3 17
Manzanillo, Cuba, 36,395 H 4 48
Manzanillo, Mexico, 13,006 G 7 44
Mao, Chad, 3,000 K 9 34
Maple Creek, Sask., 1,974 J 5 40
Mapuera (river), Brazil J 4 46
Maquela do Zombo, Angola, 1,103 K13 35
Mar (means sea) (Sp. & Port.)...
Mar del Plata, Arg., 114,729 J11 47
Maraba, Brazil, 4,937 L 5 46
Maracá (island), Brazil L 3 46
Maracaibo, Venezuela, 235,750 F 1 46
Maracaibo (lake), Venezuela F 2 46
Maracaju, Brazil, 1,323 K 8 46
Maracay, Venezuela, 65,761 G 1 46
Maragheh, Iran, 35,308 E 2 27
Marajó (island), Brazil L 4 46
Marand, Iran, 13,868 D 1 27
Maranguape, Brazil, 5,467 N 4 46
Maranón (river), Peru E 4 46
Maraş, Turkey, 44,306 G 4 28
Marathôn, Greece, 2,401 G 6 21
Marathon, Ontario, 3,500 C 4 41
Marble (island), Canada M 2 40
Marble Bar, Australia, 168 C 4 36
Marburg, Germany, 39,530 C 3 14
Marchena, Spain, 17,030 D 4 17
Marcos Paz, Argentina, 4,115 N12 47
Marcus (island), Pacific F 3 37
Mardan, Pakistan, 48,827 B 2 29
Mardee (lake), Scotland F 4 11
Mardin, Turkey, 24,338 J 4 28
Margão, Port. India, 17,933 B 5 29
Margaree Harbour, N.S., 300 H 4 41
Margaret Bay, Br. Columbia, 50 E 4 40
Margarita (island), Venezuela 76,035 H 1 46
Margate, England, 42,512 J 6 10
Margelan, U.S.S.R., 68,000 T 2 23
Margherita, Somalia, 5,000 P12 35
Mariana (islands), Pacific, 6,286 E 4 37
Marianao, Cuba, 120,163 C 1 48
Maribor, Yugoslavia, 77,124 B 2 21
Marienberg, Terr. N.G. B 6 31
Marienburg (Malbork), Poland, 22,500 D 2 24
Mariinsk, U.S.S.R., 21,000 O 5 23
Marion (reef), Australia J 3 36
Mariscal Estigarribia, Para., 2,698 H 8 46
Maritsa (river) G 4 21
Mariupol' (Zhdanov), U.S.S.R., 284,000 E 5 22
Markhamat, U.S.S.R., 3,468 U 2 23
Marks, U.S.S.R., 12,461 F 4 22
Marktredwitz, Germany, 15,953 E 3 14
Marmande, France, 8,536 C 5 16
Marmara (sea), Turkey J 5 21
Maroantsetra, Malg. Rep., 4,261 S15 35
Maroni (river), S.A. K 3 46
Maros, Indonesia F 7 31
Maroua, Cam., 14,029 J 9 34
Marovoay, Malg. Rep., 11,898 R15 35
Marquesas (isls.), Pacific, 2,976 N 6 37
Marra (mountain), Sudan L 9 34
Marrakech, Morocco, 215,312 E 5 34
Marree, Australia, 206 F 5 36
Marsala, Italy, 42,488 D 6 18
Marseille, France, 605,577 F 6 16
Marshall (islands), Pacific, 11,033 H 4 37
Martaban, Burma C 3 30
Martapura, Indonesia F 6 31
Martin, Czech., 23,855 E 2 20
Martina Franca, Italy, 24,609 F 4 18
Martinique (isl.), 261,595 G 4 45
Marton, New Zealand, 4,001 L 6 36
Martos, Spain, 17,481 E 4 17
Martre (lake), Canada G 2 40
Marugame, Japan, 37,312 G 6 33
Mary, U.S.S.R., 48,000 H 6 22
Maryborough, Australia, 6,827 G 7 36
Maryborough, Australia, 17,952 J 5 36
Marysville, N.B., 2,538 G 4 41
Más Afuera (island), Chile D10 47
Más Atierra (island), Chile E10 47
Masamba, Indonesia G 6 31
Masan, Korea, 91,291 D 6 33
Masaya, Nicaragua, 16,765 D 5 39
Mascara, Algeria, 26,086 G 4 34
Mascarene (islands), Africa S20 35
Maseru,* Basutoland, 2,600 M17 35
Masindi, Uganda, 989 N11 35
Masira (island), Oman G 5 26
Masisea, Peru, 1,742 F 5 46
Mask (lake), Ireland C 4 12
Masqat,* Oman, 5,500 G 5 26
Massa, Italy, 45,108 C 2 18
Massafra, Italy, 16,106 F 4 18
Massawa, Eritrea, Ethiopia, 9,000 O 8 34
Massey, Ontario, 1,068 D 4 41
Masterton, New Zeauand, 13,000 M 6 36
Masulipatnam, India, 59,146 D 5 29
Matachewan, Ontario, 1,000 D 4 41
Matadi, B. Congo, 48,351 J13 35
Matagalpa, Nicaragua, 10,362 E 4 39
Matam, Senegal, 2,425 D 8 34
Matamoros (Coahuila), Mexico, 10,154 H 4 44
Matamoros (Tamaulipas), Mexico, 45,776 L 4 44
Matane, Quebec, 8,069 G 4 41
Matanzas, Cuba, 54,844 C 1 48
Matapédia, Quebec, 500 G 4 41
Matara, Ceylon, 23,434 D 7 29
Mataram, Indonesia F 7 31
Matarani, Peru F 7 46
Mataranka, Australia, 102 E 2 36
Mataró, Spain, 28,797 H 2 17
Matehuala, Mexico, 14,163 J 5 44
Matera, Italy, 30,009 F 4 18
Matheson, Ontario, 758 D 4 41
Mathura, India, 105,773 C 3 29
Mati, Philippine Islands, 2,899 H 4 31
Matlock, England, 17,756 F 4 10
Mato Grosso, Brazil, 427 J 6 46
Mato Grosso (plateau), Brazil K 7 46
Matochkin Shar, U.S.S.R. G 2 22
Matosinhos, Portugal, 29,078 B 2 17
Matrah, Oman, 8,500 G 5 26
Matruh, Egypt, 3,047 M 5 34
Matsudo, Japan, 52,531 P 2 33
Matsue, Japan, 74,018 F 6 33
Matsumoto, Japan, 86,005 H 5 33
Matsuyama, Japan, 163,859 F 7 33
Matsusaka, Japan, 48,743 H 6 33
Mattancheri, India, 53,346 C 7 29
Mattawa, Ontario, 3,208 E 4 41
Maturín, Venezuela, 25,350 H 2 46
Mau, India, 29,357 D 3 29
Maubeuge, France, 20,310 F 2 16
Maubin, Burma, 9,637 B 3 30
Maués, Brazil, 2,128 J 4 46
Maui (island), U.S., 40,103 H 8 42
Maumere, Indonesia G 7 31
Maun, Bech. Pr., 2,500 L15 35
Mauna Kea (mtn.), U.S. H 8 42
Mauna Loa (mtn.), U.S. J 8 42
Maurice (lake), Australia E 5 36
Mauritius (island), 501,471 S19 35
Mawlaik, Burma B 2 30
May (cape), U.S. P 5 43
Mayaguana (isl.), Bah. Is., 591 D 2 45
Mayagüez, Puerto Rico, 58,944 F 1 45
Mayavaram (Mayuram), India, 32,670 D 6 29
Mayen, Germany, 14,370 B 3 14
Mayerthorpe, Alberta, 563 G 4 46
Maykop, U.S.S.R., 82,000 E 5 22
Mayo, Yukon, 249 C 2 40
Mayuram, India, 32,670 D 6 29
Mazabuka, N. Rhodesia, †1,720 M15 35
Mazagan, Morocco, 34,781 E 5 34
Mazamet, France, 13,705 E 6 16
Mazar-i-Sharif, Afghan., 41,960 J 2 26
Mazara del Vallo, Italy, 31,744 D 6 18
Mazatenango, Guatemala, 10,735 B 3 39
Mazatlán, Mexico, 41,470 F 5 44
Mazzarino, Italy, 17,844 E 6 18
M'Bout, Mauritania, 1,800 D 8 34
Mbabane,* Swaz., 2,000 N17 35
Mbarara, Uganda, 2,047 N12 35
McBride, Br. Columbia, 582 F 4 40
McClintock (channel), Canada D29 8
McCreary, Manitoba, 365 L 4 40
McKenzie Island, Ont., 1,450 B 3 41
McKinlay, Australia, 43 G 4 36
McKinley (mountain), U.S. F 8 42
McLennan, Alberta, 1,092 G 3 40
McMurray, Alta., 1,110 H 3 40
Mead (lake), U.S. E 5 42
Meadow Lake, Sask., 2,477 J 4 40
Meaford, Ontario, 4,643 D 5 41
Meaux, France, 13,030 E 3 16
Mecca,* Saudi Arabia, 150,000 C 5 26
Mechelen (Malines), Belgium, 63,497 F 6 15
Méchéria, Algeria, 5,121 F 5 34
Mechigmen, U.S.S.R. V 3 23
Mechtal (Miechowice), Poland B 4 24
Medan, Indonesia, 500,000 B 5 31
Medellín, Colombia, 328,294 E 2 46
Médenine, Tunisia, 3,564 J 5 34
Medgidia, Rumania, 6,916 J 3 21
Mediaş, Rumania, 23,247 G 2 21
Medicine Bow (mt. range), U.S. G 4 42
Medicine Hat, Alberta, 20,826 H 4 40
Medina, Saudi Arabia, 15,000 D 5 26
Medina del Campo, Spain, 13,480 D 2 17
Mediterranean (sea) A 3 26
Mednogorsk, U.S.S.R. G 4 22
Medvezh'yegorsk, U.S.S.R., 13,400 E 3 22
Meekatharra, Australia, 585 B 5 36
Meerane, Germany, 26,804 E 3 14
Meerut, India, 233,183 C 3 29
Meester Cornelis (Djatinegara), Indonesia H 2 31
Mégantic, Quebec, 6,864 F 4 41
Mégara, Greece, 13,863 F 6 21
Megiddo, Israel, 82 C 2 24
Mehsana, India, 16,986 B 4 29
Meiktila, Burma, 12,321 B 2 30
Meiningen, Germany, 23,700 D 3 14
Meissen, Germany, 48,348 E 3 14
Meknes, Morocco, 140,380 E 5 34
Mekong (river) D 3 30
Melanesia (isls.), Pacific G 6 37
Melbourne, Australia, †1,524,111 L 1 36
Melekess, U.S.S.R., 51,000 G 4 22
Meleuz, U.S.S.R., 5,724 G 4 22
Melfort, Saskatchewan, 2,919 K 4 40
Melilla, Spain, 84,599 F 4 34
Melipilla, Chile, 9,316 N10 47
Melita, Manitoba, 926 K 5 40
Melitopol', U.S.S.R., 95,000 E 5 22
Melo, Uruguay, 23,000 K10 47
Melrhir (lake), Algeria H 5 34
Melun, France, 18,391 E 3 16
Melville, Saskatchewan, 4,948 K 4 40
Melville (bay), Australia F 2 36
Melville (cape), Australia H 2 36
Melville (island), Australia E 2 36
Melville (lake), Canada H 3 41
Melville (peninsula), Canada E27 8
Memel (Klaipėda), U.S.S.R., 89,000 D 4 22
Memmingen, Germany, 25,343 D 5 14
Menai (strait), Wales C 4 10
Mendi, Papua B 7 31
Mendip (hills), England E 6 10
Mendocino (cape), U.S. B 4 42
Mendoza, Argentina, 97,496 G10 47
Mendoza, Mexico, 15,189 O 2 44
Menemen, Turkey, 14,323 B 3 28
Menfi, Italy, 16,644 D 6 18
Menggala, Indonesia, 14,174 D 6 31
Mengtsz, China, 193,004 F 7 32
Menindee, Australia, 644 G 6 36
Menton, France, 16,421 G 6 16
Menzel Bourguiba, Tunisia, 29,353 H 4 34
Menzies, Australia, 147 C 5 36
Merak, Indonesia G 1 31
Merano, Italy, 26,551 C 1 18
Merauke, Neth. N. G. K 7 31
Mercedes, Argentina, 30,575 G10 47
Mercedes, Argentina, 16,932 N12 47
Mercedes, Uruguay, 35,000 J10 47
Mergui, Burma, 33,604 C 4 30
Mérida, Mexico, 144,793 P 6 44
Mérida, Spain, 23,001 C 3 17
Mérida, Venezuela, 25,064 F 2 46
Mérida (mt. range), Venezuela F 2 46
Merka, Somalia, 12,000 R11 35
Merksem, Belgium, 32,103 E 6 15
Merredin, Australia, 2,342 B 6 36
Merritt, Br. Columbia, 1,790 F 4 40
Merseburg, Germany, 33,978 D 3 14
Mersin (Içel), Turkey, 51,251 F 4 28
Merthyr Tydfil, Wales, 61,142 D 6 10
Merv (Mary), U.S.S.R., 48,000 H 6 22
Merzifon, Turkey, 20,012 F 2 28
Mesagne, Italy, 20,486 G 4 18
Meshed, Iran, 176,400 L 2 27
Mesopotamia (region), Iraq B 3 27
Messina, Italy, 208,762 E 5 18
Messina (strait), Italy E 5 18
Messina, Transv., 7,770 M16 35
Mestre, Italy, 73,435 D 2 18
Meta (river), S.A. G 2 46
Mettmann, Germany, 18,694 F 4 14
Metz, France, 81,096 G 3 16
Meudon, France, 20,106 A 2 16
Meulaboh, Indonesia, 2,575 B 5 31
Meuse (river) F 8 15

Index Plate Ref. No.
Mexico (gulf)....K 7 38
Mexico City (México),* Mexico, 2,233,914 ....L 1 44
Mezen', U.S.S.R., 2,952....F 3 22
Mezen, (river), U.S.S.R. ....F 3 22
Mezőberény, Hungary, 14,578....F 3 20
Mezőkovesd, Hungary 20,838....F 3 20
Mezőtúr, Hungary, 23,798....F 3 20
Mhow, India, 34,823....C 4 29
Mianeh, Iran, 15,958....E 2 27
Mianwali, Pakistan, 23,340....B 2 29
Miarinarivo, Malg. Rep., 1,338....R15 35
Miass, U.S.S.R., 19,378....H 4 22
Michigan (lake), U.S. ....M 4 43
Michikamau (lake), Canada....H 3 41
Michipicoten Harbour, Ont., 164....C 4 41
Michurinsk, U.S.S.R., 80,000....E 4 22
Micronesia (isls.), Pacific....G 5 37
Middelburg, C. of G.H., 5,787....M18 35
Middelburg, Netherlands, 21,968....C 6 15
Middelburg, Transv., 8,006....N17 35
Middlesbrough, England, 147,276..F 3 10
Middleton, Nova Scotia, 1,769....G 5 41
Midland, Ontario, 8,250....D 5 41
Midland Junction, Aust., 8,496....B 2 36
Midnapore, India, 43,171....E 4 29
Midway (isls.), Pacific....G 8 42
Miechowice, Poland....B 2 24
Międzyrzec Podlaski, Poland, 8,696 ....F 3 24
Mielec, Poland, 20,300....E 3 24
Miercurea Ciuc, Rumania, 6,143...H 2 21
Migdal Ashqelon, Israel, 21,000....A 4 24
Mihara, Japan, 70,650....F 6 33
Mikhaylovgrad, Bulg., 8,067....F 4 21
Mikhaylovka, U.S.S.R., 12,944....F 4 22
Mikindani, Tanganyika Terr., 3,000 ....P14 35
Mikkeli (Sankt Michel), Finland, 18,655 ....P 6 13
Mikołów, Poland, 16,700....B 4 24
Milan (Milano), Italy, 1,267,040...B 2 18
Milâs, Turkey, 10,145....B 4 28
Milazzo, Italy, 16,129....E 5 18
Mildura, Australia, 10,972....G 6 36
Miles, Australia, 1,193....H 5 36
Milestone, Saskatchewan, 488....K 5 40
Milford Haven (inlet), Wales....B 6 10
Miling, Australia, 384....B 6 36
Milk (river), Canada....H 5 40
Milk (river), U.S. ....G 2 42
Milk River, Alberta, 642....H 5 40
Millau, France, 16,990....E 5 16
Mille Lacs (lake), U.S. ....K 3 43
Millerovo, U.S.S.R., 12,822....F 5 22
Milltown, New Brunswick, 1,975....G 4 41
Minamata, Japan, 46,233....E 7 33
Minas, Uruguay, 32,000....K10 47
Minatitlán, Mexico, 22,455....M 8 44
Minbu, Burma, 6,404....B 2 30
Mindanao (island), Philippine Islands, 2,427,587....H 4 31
Minden, Germany, 41,527....C 2 14
Mindoro (island), Philippine Islands, 167,705....G 3 31
Mineral del Monte, Mex., 12,552..K 6 44
Mingan, Quebec, 60....H 3 41
Mingenew, Australia, 633....B 5 36
Minho (river), Portugal....B 2 17
Minitonas, Manitoba, 663....K 4 40
Minna, Nigeria, 2,590....H10 34
Minnedosa, Manitoba, 2,306....K 4 40
Miño (river), Spain....B 1 17
Minsk, U.S.S.R., 509,000....D 4 22
Mińsk Mazowiecki, Pol., 16,400....E 2 24
Minto, New Brunswick, 850....G 4 41
Minto (lake), Canada....E 2 41
Minton, Saskatchewan, 191....K 5 40
Minusinsk, U.S.S.R., 21,427....L 4 22
Minya Konka (mountain), China...F 6 32
Miraj, India, 32,455....B 5 29
Miranda, Brazil, 1,642....J 8 46
Miranda de Ebro, Spain, 15,922....E 1 17
Miri, Sarawak, 10,951....E 5 31
Mirim (lake), South America....K10 47
Mirpur, Kash., 8,556....B 2 29
Mirpur Khas, Pakistan, 40,412....A 3 29
Mirtóön (sea), Greece....F 7 21
Mirzachul' U.S.S.R., 4,600....R 1 23
Mirzapur, India, 70,944....D 4 29
Mishima, Japan, 47,333....J 6 33
Miskolc, Hungary, 135,231....F 2 20
Missinaibi (river), Canada....D 4 41
Mississippi (delta), U.S. ....K 7 38
Mississippi (river), U.S. ....L 4 43
Missolonghi, Greece, 12,179....E 6 21
Missouri (river), U.S. ....J 4 42
Mistassini, Quebec, 2,912....F 4 41
Mistassini (lake), Canada....F 3 41
Místek-Frýdek, Czech., 26,573....E 2 20
Misti (mountain), Peru....F 7 46
Mistretta, Italy, 11,638....E 6 18
Misurata, Libya, †34,451....K 5 34

Index Plate Ref. No.
Mitchell, Australia, 1,407....H 5 36
Mitchell (river), Australia....G 3 36
Mitchell (mountain), U.S. ....N 6 43
Mito, Japan, 67,163....K 5 33
Mittweida, Germany, 22,794....E 3 14
Mitú, Colombia, 312....F 3 46
Miyako, Japan, 39,255....L 4 33
Miyakonojo, Japan, 75,114....E 8 33
Miyazaki, Japan, 103,443....E 8 33
Mizda, Libya, 1,000....J 5 34
Mizen Head (cape), Ireland....B 9 12
Mizil, Rumania, 6,528....H 3 21
Mladá Boleslav, Czech., 24,389....C 1 20
Mladenovac, Yugoslavia, 5,159....E 3 21
Mlanje (mountain), Nyasa. Prot..O15 35
Mława, Poland, 14,600....E 2 24
Moca, Dominican Rep., 9,739....D 5 48
Moçambique, Mozambique, 12,500.P15 35
Moçâmedes, Angola, 13,591....J15 35
Mocha, Yemen, 600....D 7 26
Mochudi, Bech. Pr., 11,767....M16 35
Mocoa, Colombia, 1,446....E 3 46
Moçoró (Mossoró), Brazil, 20,576 ....N 5 46
Modasa, India, 11,598....B 4 29
Modena, Italy, 82,180....C 2 18
Modica, Italy, 27,730....E 6 18
Modjokerto, Indonesia, 23,600....K 2 31
Mödling, Austria, 17,054....D 2 20
Moengo, Surinam, 1,890....K 2 46
Mogadishu,* Somalia, 63,272....R11 35
Mogador, Morocco, 22,391....D 5 34
Mogilev, U.S.S.R., 121,000....E 4 22
Mogilev-Podol'skiy, U.S.S.R., 22,993 ....D 5 22
Mogok, Burma....C 2 30
Mohács, Hungary, 18,297....E 4 20
Moineşti, Rumania, 5,868....H 2 21
Moisie, Quebec, 351....G 3 41
Moisie (river), Canada....G 3 41
Mojave (desert), U.S. ....D 6 42
Moji, Japan, 124,399....E 7 33
Moknine, Tunisia, 15,699....J 4 34
Mokp'o, Korea, 111,128....C 6 33
Mola di Bari, Italy, 22,402....F 4 18
Molchanovo, U.S.S.R., 794....K 4 22
Molenbeek-Saint-Jean, Belgium, 62,711 ....B 9 15
Molepolole, Bech. Pr., 14,805....M16 35
Molfetta, Italy, 55,150....F 4 18
Mollendo, Peru, 12,259....F 7 46
Mölln, Germany, 13,721....D 2 14
Mölndal, Sweden, 20,857....H 8 13
Molodechno (Molodeczno), U.S.S.R., 26,000....D 4 22
Molokai (island), U.S., 5,280....H 8 42
Molopo (river), Africa....L17 35
Molotov (Perm), U.S.S.R., 628,000 ....G 4 22
Molotovsk (Severodvinsk), U.S.S.R., 79,000....E 3 22
Molotovsk (Nolinsk), U.S.S.R., 5,517 ....G 4 22
Mombasa, Kenya, 84,746....P12 35
Mominabad, India, 16,250....C 5 29
Momostenango, Guat., 7,956....B 3 39
Mompós, Colombia, 9,192....F 2 46
Mon Cay, Vietnam....E 2 30
Mona (passage)....E 3 45
Monaco,* Monaco, 19,242....G 6 16
Monchegorsk, U.S.S.R., 30,000....E 3 22
Monclova, Mexico, 19,049....J 3 44
Moncton, New Brunswick, 36,003..G 4 41
Mondovi, Italy, 13,736....A 2 18
Mondragon, Philippine Is., 3,781...H 3 31
Monfalcone, Italy, 24,160....D 2 18
Monghyr, India, 63,150....E 3 29
Mongolian (plateau), Mon. Rep. ..F 2 32
Mongu, N. Rhodesia, 1,761....L15 35
Monopoli, Italy, 23,233....F 4 18
Monreale, Italy, 21,396....D 5 18
Monrovia,* Liberia, 14,000....D10 34
Mons (Bergen), Belgium, 25,625....E 8 15
Mont (means mt.) (Fr.)....
Mont-de-Marsan, France, 11,929.C 6 16
Mont-Joli, Quebec, 6,179....G 4 41
Mont-Laurier, Quebec, 5,486....E 4 41
Mont-Louis, Quebec, 500....G 4 41
Montague, P.E.I., 1,152....H 4 41
Montague (sound), Australia....C 2 36
Montargis, France, 14,154....E 3 16
Montauban, France, 24,664....D 5 16
Montbéliard, France, 13,596....G 4 16
Monte Bello (islands), Australia...A 4 36
Monte-Carlo, Monaco, 7,967....G 6 16
Monte Caseros, Arg., 11,409....J10 47
Monte Cristi, Dom. Rep., 4,600....C 5 48
Monte Sant'Angelo, Italy, 26,700.F 4 18
Montego Bay, Jamaica, 11,547....B 3 45
Montélimar, France, 10,567....F 5 16
Monterey (bay), U.S. ....C 5 42
Montería, Colombia, 12,804....E 2 46
Monterrey, Mexico, 331,771....J 4 44

Index Plate Ref. No.
Montes Claros, Brazil, 20,370....M 7 46
Montevideo,* Uruguay, 850,000....K11 47
Montgomery, Pakistan, 50,185....B 2 29
Montigny, France, 12,726....G 3 16
Montilla, Spain, 18,541....D 4 17
Montluçon, France, 46,994....E 4 16
Montmagny, Quebec, 6,405....G 4 41
Montmorency, Quebec, 5,817....F 4 41
Montpellier, France, 83,890....E 6 16
Montréal, Quebec, 1,109,439....F 4 41
Montréal, Greater, Quebec, 1,595,330 ....F 4 41
Montreal Lake, Saskatchewan, 25 ....J 4 40
Montreuil, France, 69,698....B 2 16
Montreux-le-Châtelard, Switzerland, 11,614....C 4 19
Montrose, Scotland, 10,762....M 6 11
Montrouge, France, 34,508....B 2 16
Monumbo, Terr. N.G. ....B 6 31
Monywa, Burma, 13,414....B 2 30
Monza, Italy, 69,263....B 2 18
Monze, N. Rhodesia, 616....M15 35
Moonbeam, Ontario, 500....D 4 41
Moonta, Australia, 1,220....F 6 36
Moora, Australia, 829....B 6 36
Moore (lake), Australia....B 5 36
Moorreesburg, C. of G.H., 2,920....K18 35
Moose (lake), Canada....L 4 40
Moose Factory, Ontario, 400....D 3 41
Moose Jaw, Sask., 29,603....J 4 40
Moosehead (lake), U.S. ....R 3 43
Moosomin, Saskatchewan, 1,390...K 4 40
Moosonee, Ontario, 300....D 3 41
Mopti, Sudanese Rep., 8,564....F 9 34
Moquegua, Peru, 3,718....F 7 46
Moradabad, India, 161,854....C 3 29
Moramanga, Malg. Rep., 3,626....R15 35
Moratuwa, Ceylon, 50,093....C 7 29
Morava (river), Yugoslavia....E 3 21
Moravská Ostrava (Ostrava), Czech., 199,206....E 2 20
Morawa, Australia, 713....B 5 36
Morawhanna, Br. Guiana, 305....J 2 46
Moray (firth), Scotland....J 4 11
Morden, Manitoba, 2,237....L 5 40
Mordialloc, Australia, 21,025....L 2 36
Morecambe, England, 15,877....E 3 10
Morecambe (bay), England....D 3 10
Moree, Australia, 5,502....H 5 36
Morelia, Mexico, 63,248....J 7 44
Morena (mt. range), Spain....E 3 17
Morgans, Australia, 68....C 5 36
Moriguchi, Japan, 68,204....J 8 33
Morinville, Alberta, 957....H 4 40
Morioka, Japan, 117,578....K 4 33
Morlaix, France, 12,929....B 3 16
Morley, England, 39,783....F 4 10
Mormugão (Vasco da Gama), Port. India, 14,140....B 5 29
Mornington, Australia, 3,589....L 2 36
Mornington (island), Australia....F 3 36
Morobe, Terr. N.G. ....C 7 31
Morogoro, Tan. Terr., 1,500....O13 35
Moroleón, Mexico, 13,801....J 6 44
Morombe, Malg. Rep., 2,067....P16 35
Morón, Arg., 25,000....O12 47
Morón, Cuba, 13,954....F 2 48
Morón de la Frontera, Spain, 22,091 ....D 4 17
Morondava, Malg. Rep., 7,863....P16 35
Moroni, Comoro Is., 5,108....P14 35
Morphou, Cyprus, 4,335....E 5 28
Morris, Manitoba, 1,260....L 5 40
Mörs, Germany, 34,832....F 4 14
Morshansk, U.S.S.R., 27,779....F 4 22
Mortara, Italy, 11,074....B 2 18
Mortes (river), Brazil....K 6 46
Morvi, India, 37,048....B 4 29
Moscow (Moskva),* U.S.S.R., 5,032,000 ....B 4 22
Moselle (river), France....G 3 16
Moshi, Tanganyika Terr., 8,048....O12 35
Moskva (river), U.S.S.R. ....E 4 22
Mosonmagyaróvár, Hungary, 16,870 ....D 3 20
Mosquitos (gulf), Panama....G 6 39
Moss, Norway, 18,489....D 4 13
Mossâmedes (Moçâmedes), Angola, 13,591....J15 35
Mossbank, Saskatchewan, 593....J 5 40
Mosselbaai, C. of G.H., 9,290....L19 35
Mossoró, Brazil, 20,576....N 5 46
Most, Czech., 35,770....B 1 20
Mostaganem, Algeria, 56,446....F 4 34
Mostar, Yugoslavia, 31,608....D 4 21
Mosul, Iraq, 203,273....C 2 27
Motala, Sweden, 24,723....J 7 13
Motherwell and Wishaw, Scotland, 68,154 ....D 2 11
Motril, Spain, 19,185....E 4 17
Motueka, New Zealand, 2,824....L 6 36
Moulins, France, 22,677....E 4 16

Index Plate Ref. No.
Moulmein, Burma, 101,720....C 3 30
Moundou, Chad....K10 34
Mount Gambier, Australia, 10,331 ....F 7 36
Mount Garnet, Australia, 383....G 3 36
Mount Hope, Australia, 50....E 6 36
Mount Isa, Australia, 7,433....F 4 36
Mount Lofty, Australia, 355....D 8 36
Mount Magnet, Australia, 648....B 5 36
Mount Morgan, Australia, 4,152....H 4 36
Mount Mulligan, Australia, 359....G 3 36
Mount Pleasant, Australia, 405....E 7 36
Mount Torrens, Australia, 272....E 7 36
Mountain Ash, Wales, 31,521....D 6 10
Mountain Park, Alberta, 400....G 4 40
Moura, Brazil....H 4 46
Moura, Portugal, 9,509....C 3 17
Mourne (mountains), Ireland....J 3 12
Mouscron (Moeskroen), Belgium, 36,393 ....C 7 15
Moyale, Kenya....O11 35
Moyamba, S. Leone, 2,500....D10 34
Moyeuvre, France, 8,422....G 3 16
Moyobamba, Peru, 7,046....E 5 46
Mozambique (channel), Africa....O17 35
Mozyr', U.S.S.R. ....D 4 22
Mtsensk, U.S.S.R., 10,142....E 4 22
Muang Nan, Thailand, 10,041....D 3 30
Muang Phayao, Thailand, 8,253...C 3 30
Muang Thoen, Thailand, 5,192....C 3 30
Muaralabuh, Indonesia....C 6 31
Muarasiberut, Indonesia....B 6 31
Muaratewe, Indonesia....F 6 31
Muck (island), Scotland, 42....D 6 11
Mudgee, Australia, 5,294....J 6 36
Muğla, Turkey, 12,081....C 4 28
Muharraq, Bahrein, 25,577....F 4 26
Mühlhausen, Germany, 48,013....D 3 14
Muiron (islands), Australia....A 4 36
Muizenberg, C. of G.H., 10,000....C19 35
Mukachevo (Mukačevo), U.S.S.R., 26,123 ....D 5 22
Mukalla, Aden Prot., 19,000....E 7 26
Mukdahan, Thailand, 6,847....E 3 30
Mukden, China, 2,299,900....K 3 32
Mulchén, Chile, 6,892....F11 47
Mulgrave, Nova Scotia, 1,227....H 4 41
Mulhacén (mountain), Spain....E 4 17
Mülheim, Germany, 149,589....G 4 14
Mulhouse, France, 97,285....G 4 16
Mull (island), Scotland, 2,420....D 7 11
Mull of Galloway (cape), Scotland F10 11
Mull of Oa (cape), Scotland....D 8 11
Mullewa, Australia, 806....B 5 36
Mullingar, Ireland, 5,884....G 4 12
Multan, Pakistan, 190,122....B 2 29
München (Munich), Germany, 831,937 ....D 4 14
München-Gladbach, Germany, 124,879 ....B 3 14
Mundare, Alberta, 650....H 4 40
Munich, Germany, 831,937....D 4 14
Munkacs (Mukachevo), U.S.S.R., 26,123 ....D 5 22
Münster, Germany, 118,496....B 3 14
Muntok, Indonesia, 6,929....D 6 31
Muong May, Laos....E 4 30
Muonio (river), Sweden....M 2 13
Muradiye, Turkey, 1,431....K 3 28
Murchison (mountain), Australia..B 5 36
Murchison (mt. range) Australia..E 4 36
Murchison (river), Australia....B 5 36
Murcia, Spain, †217,934....F 4 17
Murmansk, U.S.S.R., 226,000....E 3 22
Murom, U.S.S.R., 73,000....F 4 22
Muroran, Japan, 110,443....K 2 33
Murray (river), Australia....G 6 36
Murray Bridge, Australia, 4,362...F 7 36
Murree, Pakistan, 9,398....B 2 29
Murrumbidgee (river), Australia..G 6 36
Murwara (Katni), India, 24,630....D 4 29
Murwillumbah, Australia, 6,748....J 5 36
Mürzzuschlag, Austria, 11,202....C 3 20
Muş, Turkey, 10,487....J 3 28
Musala (Stalin) (mountain), Bulgaria ....F 4 21
Musashino, Japan, 73,149....O 2 33
Muscat (Masqat),* Oman, 5,500..G 5 26
Musgrave (mt. ranges), Australia.E 5 36
Musselburgh, Scotland, 17,010....L 8 11
Musselshell (river), U.S. ....F 3 42
Mustafa Kemalpaşa, Turkey, 16,867 ....C 3 28
Muswellbrook, Australia, 5,635....J 6 36
Mutankiang, China, 151,400....M 3 32
Mutton Bay, Quebec, 110....J 3 41
Muttra (Mathura), India, 105,773.C 3 29
Muzaffarpur, India, 54,139....D 3 29
Múzquiz, Mexico, 8,225....J 3 44
Mwanza, Tanganyika Terr., 11,296 ....N12 35
Mweru (lake), Africa....M13 35

Index Ref. Plate No.

My Tho, Vietnam, 12,034 E 5 30
Myaungmya, Burma, 10,066 B 3 30
Myingyan, Burma, 26,895 B 2 30
Myitkyina, Burma, 12,382 C 1 30
Mymensingh, Pakistan, 44,527 F 4 29
Myslowice (Myslowitz), Poland, 39,500 B 4 24
Mysore, India, 244,323 C 6 29
Myszków, Poland, 12,500 D 3 24
Myszyniec, Poland E 2 24
Mytilēnē, Greece, 25,518 H 6 21
Mytishchi, U.S.S.R., 99,000 B 4 22

N

Nablus (Nabulus), Jordan, 42,499 C 3 24
Náchod, Czechoslovakia, 18,620 D 1 20
Nadiad, India, 46,510 B 4 29
Nadzab, Terr. New Guinea B 7 31
Naestved, Denmark, 17,557 G 9 35
Naga, Philippine Is., 8,136 G 3 31
Nagahama, Japan, 46,722 H 6 33
Nagano, Japan, 101,426 J 5 33
Nagaoka, Japan, 66,818 J 5 33
Nagasaki, Japan, 241,805 D 7 33
Nagaur, India, 14,714 B 3 29
Nagercoil, India, 51,657 C 7 29
Nagina, India, 26,077 C 3 29
Nagoya, Japan, 1,030,635 H 6 33
Nagpur, India, 449,099 C 4 29
Naguabo, Puerto Rico, 4,442 G 1 45
Nagykanizsa, Hungary, 30,119 D 3 20
Nagykörös, Hungary, 26,413 E 3 20
Naha,* Ryukyu Islands, 34,338 N 6 33
Nahanni (river), Canada E 2 40
Nahariya, Israel, 12,600 C 1 24
Nahuel Huapi (lake), Argentina F12 47
Naihati, India, 42,200 E 1 29
Na'in, Iran, 5,995 H 4 27
Nain, Labrador, Newf., 283 H 2 41
Naini Tal, India, 9,539 C 3 29
Nairne, Australia, 547 E 8 36
Nairobi,* Kenya, 118,976 O12 35
Najin, Korea, 34,338 E 2 33
Nakatsu, Japan, 51,410 E 7 33
Nakhichevan', U.S.S.R., 25,000 F 6 42
Nakhodka, U.S.S.R., 63,000 P 5 23
Nakhon Nayok, Thailand, 6,121 D 4 30
Nakhon Pathom, Thailand, 16,348 C 4 30
Nakhon Phanom, Thai., 8,526 D 3 30
Nakhon Ratchasima, Thai., 21,774 D 4 30
Nakhon Sawan, Thai., 12,499 D 4 30
Nakhon Si Thammarat, Thai., 15,344 D 5 30
Nakina, Ontario, 500 C 3 41
Nakło nad Notecią, Poland C 2 24
Nakskov, Denmark, 16,074 G 9 13
Nakuru, Kenya, 17,625 O11 35
Nakusp, Br. Columbia, 1,750 G 4 40
Nal'chik, U.S.S.R., 87,000 F 5 22
Nalgonda, India, 12,674 C 5 29
Nam Tso (lake), China D 5 32
Nam Dinh, Vietnam, 40,000 E 2 30
Namangan, U.S.S.R., 122,000 U 2 23
Namatanai, Terr. N. Guinea, 315 F 6 37
Namib (desert), S.W. Afr. J15 35
Namlea, Indonesia, 707 H 6 31
Nampula, Mozambique, 3,416 P15 35
Namuli (mountain), Mozambique O15 35
Namur (Namen), Belgium, 32,307 F 8 15
Namwŏn, Korea, 24,736 C 6 33
Nanaimo, Br. Columbia, 12,705 F 5 40
Nanam, Korea, 20,936 D 3 33
Nanango, Australia, 1,353 J 5 36
Nanchang, China, 398,200 J 6 32
Nancheng, China, 50,000 J 6 32
Nanchung, China, 164,700 G 5 32
Nancy, France, 120,484 G 3 16
Nanded, India, 65,018 C 5 29
Nandurbar, India, 22,139 B 4 29
Nandyal, India, 25,886 C 5 29
Nangapinoh, Indonesia, 16,069 E 6 31
Nangatajap, Indonesia E 6 31
Nanking, China, 1,091,600 J 5 32
Nanning, China, 194,600 G 7 32
Nannup, Australia, 869 B 6 36
Nanping, China, 53,445 J 6 32
Nansei (Ryukyu) (islands), 917,400 L 7 33
Nanterre, France, 39,565 A 1 16
Nantes, France, 197,915 C 4 16
Nanton, Alberta, 1,047 H 4 40
Nantucket (island), U.S., 3,484 N 2 43
Nanyang, China, 75,000 H 5 32
Nanyuki, Kenya, 4,090 O11 35
Náousa, Greece, 12,584 F 5 21
Napier, New Zealand, 27,507 L 6 36
Naples (Napoli), Italy, 984,684 E 4 18
Napo (river), S. A. E 4 46
Nara, Sudanese Rep., 2,227 E 8 34
Nara, Japan, 77,866 J 8 33
Naracoorte, Australia, 3,329 F 7 36
Naradhan, Australia, 85 H 6 36
Narathiwat, Thailand, 11,352 D 6 30
Narayanganj, Pakistan, 68,373 F 4 29
Narayanpet, India, 16,396 C 5 29
Narbada (river), India C 4 29
Narbonne, France, 27,896 E 6 16
Nardò, Italy, 21,891 F 4 18
Narembeen, Australia, 363 B 6 36
Narnaul, India, 23,063 C 3 29
Naro, Italy, 16,309 D 6 18
Narrabri, Australia, 3,722 H 6 36
Narrandera, Australia, 4,418 H 6 36
Narrogin, Australia, 3,768 B 6 36
Narromine, Australia, 1,975 H 6 36
Narsinghgarh, India, 11,036 C 4 29
Narsinghpur, India, 12,908 C 4 29
Narva, U.S.S.R., 23,512 D 4 22
Narvik, Norway, 10,281 K 2 13
Nar'yan-Mar, U.S.S.R. G 3 22
Narym, U.S.S.R., 1,000 K 4 22
Naryn, U.S.S.R., 15,000 J 5 22
Naryn, U.S.S.R., 2,029 U 2 23
Nasaud, Rumania, 3,716 G 2 21
Nasca, Peru, 2,175 F 6 46
Nasik, India, 55,524 B 5 29
Nasirabad, India, 17,804 B 3 29
Nasratabad (Zabul), Iran, 13,401 M 5 27
Nassau,* Bahamas, 13,231 C 1 45
Nässjö, Sweden, 15,675 J 8 13
Natagaima, Colombia, 4,066 F 3 46
Natal, Brazil, 97,736 O 5 46
Natanya, Israel, 37,000 B 3 24
Natashquan, Quebec, 100 H 3 41
Natashquan (river), Canada H 3 41
Natuna (islands), Indonesia, 13,077 D 5 31
Naturaliste (cape), Australia A 6 36
Naturaliste (channel), Australia A 5 36
Nau, U.S.S.R., 2,314 R 1 23
Nauen, Germany, 13,106 E 2 14
Naumburg, Germany, 41,379 E 3 14
Na'ur, Jordan, 4,650 D 4 24
Nauru (island), Pacific, 2,855 G 6 37
Navan (An Uaimh), Ireland, 3,643 H 4 12
Navanagar (Jamnagar), India, 104,419 A 4 29
Navarino (island), Chile G15 47
Navojoa, Mexico, 17,348 E 3 44
Navrongo, Ghana, 1,170 F 9 34
Navsari, India, 35,445 B 4 29
Nawabganj, Pakistan, 23,311 E 4 29
Nawabshah, Pakistan, 34,201 A 3 29
Nazareth, Israel, 23,500 C 2 24
Naze, The (prom.), England J 6 10
Nazilli, Turkey, 31,986 C 4 28
Ndola, N. Rhodesia, 16,206 M14 35
Neagh (lake), Ireland J 2 12
Neath, Wales, 32,284 D 6 10
Necochea, Argentina, 17,808 J11 47
Neemuch, India, 17,074 C 4 29
Neepawa, Manitoba, 3,109 L 4 40
Nefta, Tunisia, 14,167 H 5 34
Nefud (desert), Saudi Arabia D 4 26
Negapattinam, India, 52,937 D 6 29
Negev (region), Israel D 5 24
Negoiul (mountain), Rumania F 3 21
Negombo, Ceylon, 32,632 C 7 29
Negotin, Yugoslavia, 6,633 F 3 21
Negrais (cape), Burma B 3 30
Negro (river), Argentina H11 47
Negro (river), S.A. G 3 46
Negros (island), Phil. Is., 1,218,710 G 4 31
Neheim-Hüsten, Germany, 29,130 C 3 14
Neikiang, China, 190,200 F 6 32
Neisse (Nysa), Poland, 19,800 C 3 24
Neiva, Colombia, 33,040 F 3 46
Nellore, India, 56,315 D 6 29
Nelson, Br. Columbia, 7,226 G 5 40
Nelson, England, 34,384 E 4 10
Nelson, New Zealand, †22,503 L 6 36
Nelson (river), Canada L 3 40
Néma, Mauritania, 1,994 E 8 34
Německý Brod (Havlíčkuv B.), Czech., 14,068 C 2 20
Nene (river), England H 5 10
Nerchinsk, U.S.S.R., 15,300 N 4 23
Nerchinskiy Zavod, U.S.S.R., 3,186 O 4 23
Nerva, Spain, 10,374 C 4 17
Nes Ziyona (Nes Tsiyona), Israel, 11,000 B 4 24
Nesher, Israel, 7,000 C 2 24
Ness (lake), Scotland H 5 11
Netherdale, Australia, 122 H 4 36
Nettilling (lake), Canada E26 8
Nettuno, Italy, 12,084 F 7 18
Neu-Ulm, Germany, 14,866 D 4 14
Neubrandenburg, Germany, 20,446 E 2 14
Neuburg, Germany, 13,966 D 4 14
Neuchâtel, Switzerland, 27,998 C 3 19
Neuilly, France, 58,658 A 1 16
Neukölln, Germany, 285,283 J 3 14
Neumünster, Germany, 73,481 C 1 14
Neunkirchen, Austria, 9,771 C 3 20
Neunkirchen, Germany, 37,250 B 4 14
Neuquén, Argentina, 7,498 G11 47
Neuruppin, Germany, 26,040 E 2 14
Neuss, Germany, 63,478 F 5 14
Neustadt (Prudnik), Poland, 10,866 C 3 24
Neustadt (Rhein-Pfalz), Germany, 26,764 B 4 14
Neustettin (Szczecinek), Poland, 12,413 C 2 24
Neustrelitz, Germany, 24,692 E 2 14
Neuwied, Germany, 24,284 B 3 14
Neva (river), U.S.S.R. C 2 22
Nevada (mt. range), Spain E 4 17
Nevel', U.S.S.R., 12,923 D 4 22
Nevel'sk, U.S.S.R., 11,180 R 5 23
Nevers, France, 33,918 E 4 16
Neves, Brazil, 53,052 P13 47
Neviges, Germany, 13,804 G 4 14
Nevşehir, Turkey, 16,820 F 3 28
Nev'yansk, U.S.S.R., 24,300 P 6 23
New (forest), England F 7 10
New Amsterdam, Br. Guiana, 9,567 J 2 46
New Britain (island), Territory N.G., 87,505 F 6 37
New Caledonia (island), Pacific, 64,461 G 8 37
New Delhi,* India, 276,314 C 3 29
New Georgia (island,) Pacific, 10,000 F 6 37
New Glasgow, Nova Scotia, 9,998 H 4 41
New Guinea (island), Pacific, 2,475,000 E 6 37
New Hebrides (islands), Pacific, 47,000 G 7 37
New Ireland (island), Territory N.G., 33,930 F 6 37
New Liskeard, Ontario, 4,619 E 4 41
New Norfolk, Australia, 4,756 H 8 36
New Plymouth, New Zealand, †28,292 L 6 36
New Richmond, Quebec, 1,000 G 4 41
New Siberian (islands), U.S.S.R. R 2 23
New Waterford, Nova Scotia, 10,381 J 4 41
New Westminster, Br. Columbia, 31,665 F 5 40
New Windsor, England, 23,299 G 6 10
Newark, England, 22,917 G 4 10
Newbury, England, 17,782 F 6 10
Newcastle, Australia, †178,144 J 6 36
Newcastle, England, 70,036 E 5 10
Newcastle, Natal, 9,747 N17 35
Newcastle, New Brunswick, 4,670 G 4 41
Newcastle-on-Tyne, England, 291,724 E 2 10
Newcastle Waters, Australia, 82 E 3 36
Newdegate, Australia, 222 B 6 36
Newmarket, Ontario, 7,368 D 5 41
Newport (Hampshire), England, 20,430 F 7 10
Newport (Monmouthshire), England, 105,547 E 6 10
Newry, N. Ireland, 13,264 J 3 12
Newton Abbot, England, 16,403 D 7 10
Newtownards, N. Ireland, 12,237 K 2 12
Nezhin, U.S.S.R., 41,406 E 4 22
Ngami (salt lake), Bech. Prot. L16 35
N'Gaoundéré, Cam., 9,000 J10 34
Ngabang, Indonesia, 2,324 E 5 31
N'Guigmi, Niger, 2,538 J 9 34
Nguru, Nigeria, 23,084 J 9 34
Nha Trang, Vietnam F 4 30
Nhamunda (river), Brazil J 4 46
Niafounké, Sudanese Rep., 4,142 F 8 34
Niagara (falls), Canada E 5 41
Niagara (falls), U.S. O 4 43
Niagara Falls, Ontario, 23,563 E 5 41
Niamey,* Niger, 9,000 G 9 34
Nias (island), Indonesia, 187,199 B 5 31
Nicaragua (lake), Nicaragua E 5 39
Nicastro, Italy, 25,121 F 5 18
Nice, France, 208,453 G 6 16
Nichinan, Japan, 41,432 E 8 33
Nicobar (islands), India, 12,452 F 7 29
Nicolet, Quebec, 3,762 F 4 41
Nicosia,* Cyprus, 25,000 E 5 28
Nicosia, Italy, 17,950 E 6 18
Niemen (river), U.S.S.R. D 4 22
Nienburg, Germany, 21,533 C 2 14
Nieuw-Nickerie, Surinam, 3,141 J 2 46
Niğde, Turkey, 14,693 F 4 28
Niger (river), Africa G 9 34
Nigríta, Greece, 8,335 F 5 21
Niigata, Japan, 220,901 J 5 33
Niihama, Japan, 107,234 F 6 33
Niitsu, Japan, 37,370 J 5 33
Nijmegen, Netherlands, 122,963 H 5 15
Nikko, Japan, 29,363 J 5 33
Nikolayev, U.S.S.R., 224,000 E 5 22
Nikolayevsk, U.S.S.R. R 4 23
Nikolayevskiy, U.S.S.R., 19,225 F 5 22
Nikol'sk, U.S.S.R., 3,100 F 4 22
Nikol'skoye, U.S.S.R., 6,418 F 5 22
Nikopol', U.S.S.R., 81,000 E 5 22
Niksar, Turkey, 8,459 G 2 28
Nikšic, Yugoslavia, 6,686 D 4 21
Nile (delta) N 5 34
Nimach (Neemuch), India, 17,074 C 4 29
Nîmes, France, 72,274 F 6 16
Ningpo, China, 237,500 K 6 32
Ningsia (Yinchwan), China, 84,000 F 4 32
Ninh Binh, Vietnam E 2 30
Nioro, Sudanese Rep., 5,488 E 8 34
Nioro-du-Rip, Senegal, 1,923 C 9 34
Niort, France, 30,199 C 4 16
Nipawin, Saskatchewan, 3,337 K 4 40
Nipigon, Ontario, 700 C 4 41
Nipigon (lake), Canada C 4 41
Nipissing (lake), Canada D 4 41
Nirgua, Venezuela, 4,778 G 2 46
Niriz, Iran, 14,946 J 6 27
Nirmal, India, 14,499 C 5 29
Niš (Nish), Yugoslavia, 50,692 F 4 21
Niscemi, Italy, 23,114 E 6 18
Nishapur, Iran, 27,378 L 2 27
Nishinomiya, Japan, 126,783 H 8 33
Nishinoomote, Japan, 32,527 O 4 33
Niterói, Brazil, 170,868 P14 47
Nith (river), Scotland J 9 11
Nitra, Czech., 22,589 E 2 20
Niue (island), Pacific, 4,253 K 7 37
Nizamabad, India, 55,202 C 5 29
Nizhneudinsk, U.S.S.R., 10,342 L 4 23
Nizhni Novgorod (Gor'kiy), U.S.S.R., 942,000 F 4 22
Nizhniy Tagil, U.S.S.R., 338,000 P 6 23
Nizhnyaya Salda, U.S.S.R., 15,166 P 6 23
Nizhnyaya Tura, U.S.S.R., 5,428 P 5 23
Nizip, Turkey, 15,132 G 4 28
Noakhali, Pakistan, 16,657 F 4 29
Noarlunga, Australia, 265 D 8 36
Nobeoka, Japan, 88,117 E 7 33
Nocera Inferiore, Italy, 32,472 E 4 18
Noda, Japan, 38,875 P 2 33
Noda (Chekhov), U.S.S.R., 7,846 R 5 23
Nogales (Sonora), Mexico, 24,478 D 1 44
Nogales (Veracruz), Mexico, 7,524 P 2 44
Noginsk, U.S.S.R., 93,000 B 3 22
Nogoa (river), Australia H 4 36
Noisy-le-Sec, France, 16,103 B 1 16
Nokia, Finland, 17,251 N 6 13
Nokomis, Saskatchewan, 516 J 4 40
Nolinsk, U.S.S.R., 5,517 G 4 22
Nominingue, Quebec, 738 E 4 41
Nong Khai, Thai., 11,757 D 3 30
Nonni (river), China K 2 32
Noranda, Quebec, 10,323 E 4 41
Nordegg, Alberta, 1,014 G 4 40
Norden, Germany, 18,012 B 2 14
Nordenham, Germany, 28,146 C 2 14
Nordhausen, Germany, 32,848 D 3 14
Nordhorn, Germany, 33,633 B 2 14
Nördlingen, Germany, 13,425 D 4 14
Nordvik, U.S.S.R. N 2 23
Nore (river), Ireland G 7 12
Norfolk (island), Pacific, 938 G 8 37
Noril'sk, U.S.S.R., 108,000 K 3 23
Norman (river), Australia G 3 36
Norman Wells, N. W. Terr., 600 E 1 40
Normandin, Quebec, 1,918 F 4 41
Normanton, Australia, 238 G 3 36
Normetal, Quebec, 600 E 4 41
Norrköping, Sweden, 84,939 K 7 13
Norseman, Australia, 2,539 C 6 36
North (Nord) (cape), Iceland B 2 9
North (Nordkapp) (cape), Norway P 1 13
North (channel), England A 2 10
North (sea) E 3 9
North Battleford, Sask., 8,924 J 4 40
North Bay, Ontario, 21,020 E 4 41
North Foreland (prom.), England J 6 10
North Minch (channel), Scotland E 3 11
North Platte (river), U.S. H 4 42
North Ronaldsay (islands), Scotland 224 M 1 11
North Saskatchewan (river), Canada J 4 40

Index Plate Ref. No.

North Truchas Peak (mountain), U.S.........G 6 42
North Uist (island), Scotland, 1,890.........A 4 11
North Vancouver, Br. Columbia, 15,687.........F 5 40
North West (cape) Australia...A 4 36
North West River, Lab., Newf., 400.........H 3 41
North York Moors (plateau), England.........G 3 10
Northam, Australia, 5,725.........B 2 36
Northampton, Australia, 992...A 5 36
Northampton, England, 104,432..G 5 10
Northcliffe, Australia, 508.........B 6 36
Northeim, Germany, 18,651......D 3 14
Northern Dvina (river), U.S.S.R. ..F 3 22
Northfleet, England, 18,803.......H 6 10
Northumberland (cape), Australia.........F 7 36
Northwich, England, 17,489.......E 4 10
Norton (sound), U.S.........E 8 42
Norway House, Manitoba, 1,200..L 4 40
Norwich, England, 121,236......J 5 10
Noshiro, Japan, 49,027.........J 3 33
Nosob (river), S. W. Africa...L17 35
Nossi-Bé (isl.), Malg. Rep., 25,825.........R14 35
Noto, Italy, 21,982.........E 6 18
Noto (peninsula), Japan.........H 5 33
Notodden, Norway, 6,653.........F 7 13
Nottaway (river), Canada.........E 3 41
Nottingham, England, 306,055....G 5 10
Nouakchott,* Mauritania.........C 8 34
Nouasseur, Morocco.........E 5 34
Nouméa,* New Caledonia, 22,238..G 8 37
Nova Goa (Pangim),* P. India, 31,950.........B 5 29
Nova Gradiška, Yugoslavia, 5,852..C 3 21
Nova Lisboa, Angola, 28,297......K14 35
Nova Scotia (peninsula), Canada..G 5 41
Nova Zagora, Bulgaria, 11,031...H 4 21
Novabad, U.S.S.R.........J 6 22
Novara, Italy, 65,682.........B 2 18
Novaya Lyalya, U.S.S.R., 15,000..R 5 23
Novaya Zemlya (islands), U.S.S.R., 400.........G 2 22
Nové Zámky, Czech., 23,533......D 3 20
Novgorod, U.S.S.R., 61,000......E 4 22
Novgorod-Severskiy, U.S.S.R., 10,075.........E 4 22
Novi Ligure, Italy, 18,698.......B 2 18
Novi Pazar, Yugoslavia, 12,196...E 4 21
Novi Sad, Yugoslavia, 83,223.....D 3 21
Novi Vrbas, Yugoslavia, 15,562...D 3 21
Novo-Aydar, U.S.S.R., 5,225.....R 1 23
Novo Mesto, Yugoslavia, 5,404...B 3 21
Novo-Orsk, U.S.S.R., 3,935......G 4 22
Novo Redondo, Angola, 1,016....J14 35
Novocherkassk, U.S.S.R., 94,000..F 5 22
Novorossiysk, U.S.S.R., 93,000...E 5 22
Novosheshminsk, U.S.S.R., 5,317..G 4 22
Novosibirsk, U.S.S.R., 887,000...K 4 22
Novouzensk, U.S.S.R., 13,943....F 4 22
Novozybkov, U.S.S.R., 19,345....E 4 22
Nový Jičín, Czech., 16,706.......D 2 20
Novyy Port, U.S.S.R.........J 3 22
Nowa Ruda, Poland, 16,600......C 3 24
Nowa Sól, Poland, 23,400.......B 3 24
Nowgong, India, 12,972.........F 3 29
Nowra, Australia, 5,981.........J 6 36
Nowshera, Pakistan, 23,114......B 2 29
Nowy Bytom, Poland, 81,500.....B 4 24
Nowy Sącz, Poland, 31,800......E 4 24
Nowy Targ, Poland, 14,200......E 4 24
Nubian (desert), Sudan.........N 7 34
Nudo de Albarracín (mountain), Spain.........E 2 17
Nueva Imperial, Chile, 6,643....F11 47
Nueva San Salvador (Santa Tecla), El Salvador, 18,313.........C 4 39
Nuevitas, Cuba, 11,303.........G 2 48
Nuevo Laredo, Mexico, 57,699...J 3 44
Nukha, U.S.S.R., 26,262.........F 5 22
Nuku'alofa,* Tonga, 6,500.......J 8 37
Nukus, U.S.S.R., 39,000.........H 5 22
Nullagine, Australia, 131.........C 4 36
Nullarbor (plain), Australia......D 6 36
Numazu, Japan, 101,976.........J 6 33
Nuneaton, England, 54,407......F 5 10
Nunkiang, China.........L 2 32
Nuoro, Italy, 16,667.........B 4 18
Nürnberg (Nuremberg), Germany, 362,459.........D 4 14
Nuyts (cape), Australia.........E 6 36
Nyala, Sudan, 4,100.........L 9 34
Nyandoma, U.S.S.R.........F 3 22
Nyasa (lake), Africa.........N14 35
Nyaunglebin, Burma.........C 3 30
Nyborg, Denmark, 10,775.......G 9 13
Nyíregyháza, Hungary, 52,584...F 3 20
Nyköbing, Denmark, 17,192......H 9 13
Nyköping, Sweden, 20,477......K 7 13

Index Plate Ref. No.

Nylstroom, Transvaal, 4,666......M16 35
Nymagee, Australia, 243.........H 6 36
Nyngan, Australia, 2,257.........H 6 36
Nysa (Neisse), Poland, 19,800....C 3 24
Nyslott (Savonlinna), Finland, 13,425.........Q 6 13
N'Zerekore, Guinea, 10,500......E10 34

O

Oahu (island), U.S., 353,020......H 8 42
Oakbank, Australia, 311.........E 8 36
Oamaru, N.Z., 9,801.........L 7 36
Oaxaca, Mexico, 46,150.........L 8 44
Ob' (gulf), U.S.S.R.........J 3 22
Ob' (river), U.S.S.R.........J 3 22
Oba, Ontario, 75.........D 4 41
Oban, Scotland, 6,226.........F 7 11
Obbia, Somalia, 3,000.........R10 34
Oberammergau, Germany, 5,101...D 5 14
Oberhausen, Germany, 202,800...G 4 14
Obidos, Brazil, 3,487.........J 4 46
Obihiro, Japan, 51,794.........L 2 33
Ob'yachevo, U.S.S.R., 275.......F 3 22
Ocaña, Colombia, 9,937.........F 2 46
Occidental (mt. range), S.A. ..E3, F 6 46
Ocean (island), Pacific, 2,060....G 6 37
Ocean Falls, Br. Columbia, 2,650..E 4 40
Ochil (hills), Scotland.........J 7 11
Ocotlán, Mexico, 16,824.........H 6 44
October Revolution (island), U.S.S.R.........L 2 23
Ocumare del Tuy, Venezuela, 9,517.........G 1 46
Odawara, Japan, 75,334.........J 6 33
ödemiş, Turkey, 25,560.........C 3 28
Odense, Denmark, 100,940.......G 9 13
Oder (Odra) (river), Europe......F 2 14
Odessa, U.S.S.R., 667,000.......E 5 22
Odienné, Ivory C., 6,500.........E 10 34
Odobeşti, Rumania, 4,482.......H 3 21
Odorhei, Rumania, 10,366.......G 2 21
Oels, (Oleśnica), Poland, 15,000..C 3 24
Offenbach, Germany, 89,230.....C 3 14
Offenburg, Germany, 22,560.....B 4 14
Ogaki, Japan, 74,811.........H 6 33
Ogbomosho, Nigeria, 139,535....H10 34
Ogema, Saskatchewan, 455......K 5 40
Ogooué (river), Gabon.........J11 35
O'Higgins (lake), Chile.........F13 47
Ohio (river), U.S.........M 5 43
Ohrid, Yugoslavia, 11,119.......E 5 21
Oirot Tura (Gorno-Altaysk), U.S.S.R., 27,006.........K 4 22
Oita, Japan, 94,455.........E 7 33
Ojiya, Japan, 25,724.........J 5 33
Oka (river), U.S.S.R.........F 4 22
Okahandja, S. W. Africa, 1,739...K16 35
Okayama, Japan, 162,904.......F 6 33
Okazaki, Japan, 96,030.........H 6 33
Okeechobee (lake), U.S.........N 8 43
Okene, Nigeria, 32,602.........H10 34
Okha, U.S.S.R.........R 4 23
Okhotsk, U.S.S.R.........R 4 23
Okhotsk (sea), U.S.S.R.........R 4 23
Oki (islands), Japan, 43,814......F 5 33
Okinawa (island), 517,634......N 6 33
Okovanggo (river), Africa.........K15 35
Oktyabr'skiy, U.S.S.R., 65,000....C 4 22
Ola, U.S.S.R., 271.........S 4 23
Oława (Ohlau), Poland, 10,200...C 3 24
öland (island), Sweden, 25,900...K 8 13
Olary, Australia, 99.........F 6 36
Olavarría, Argentina, 24,204.....H11 47
Olbernhau, Germany, 11,133.....E 3 14
Olbia, Italy, 12,900.........B 4 18
Old Lop (dry salt lake), China....D 4 32
Oldenburg, Germany, 122,809....B 2 14
Oldham, England, 121,266.......E 4 10
Olds, Alberta, 1,980.........H 4 40
Olekminsk, U.S.S.R., 2,285......N 3 23
Olenek, U.S.S.R.........N 3 23
Olenek (river), U.S.S.R.........O 2 23
Oléron (island), France, 12,820...C 5 16
Oleśnica, Poland, 15,000.........C 3 24
Olhão, Portugal, 16,592.........C 4 17
Olinda, Brazil, 38,981.........N 5 46
Oliva, Spain, 17,801.........F 3 17
Oliva de la Frontera, Spain, 11,575.........C 3 17
Oliver, Br. Columbia, 1,147......F 5 40
Olkusz, Poland, 10,900.........D 3 24
Olomouc (Olmütz), Czech., 73,899.........D 2 20
Olonets, U.S.S.R., 1,766.........E 3 22
Oloron, France, 8,601.........C 6 16
Olot, Spain, 12,925.........H 1 17

Index Plate Ref. No.

Ölsnitz, Germany, 20,034.........E 3 14
Olsztyn, Poland, 60,400.........E 2 24
Olt (river), Rumania.........G 3 21
Olten, Switzerland, 16,485.......E 2 19
Olympic (mountains), U.S.........B 3 42
Olympus (mt.), Greece.........F 5 21
Om' (river), U.S.S.R.........J 4 22
Oman (gulf), Asia.........G 5 26
Omaruru, S.W. Africa, 1,947....K16 35
Omdurman, Sudan, 126,650......N 8 34
Omiya, Japan, 100,093.........O 2 33
Omolon (river), U.S.S.R.........T 3 23
Omsk, U.S.S.R., 579,000.........J 4 22
Omuta, Japan, 191,978.........E 7 33
Omutninsk, U.S.S.R.........G 4 22
Onega, U.S.S.R.........E 3 22
Onega (river), U.S.S.R.........E 3 22
Onega (Onezhskoye) (lake), U.S.S.R.........E 3 22
Ongrup, Australia, 118.........B 6 36
Ongole, India, 21,184.........C 5 29
Onitsha, Nigeria, 65,000.........H10 34
Onomichi, Japan, 61,411.........F 6 33
Onslow, Australia, 242.........B 4 36
Ontario (lake), U.S.-Canada......O 4 43
Onteniente, Spain, 11,878.......F 3 17
Oodnadatta, Australia, 126......E 5 36
O'okiep, C. of G.H., 1,015.......K17 35
Oostende (Ostend), Belgium, 53,752.........B 6 15
Ootacamund, India, 29,850......C 6 29
Ootsa Lake, British Columbia, 50..E 4 40
Opatija, Yugoslavia, 9,280.......A 3 21
Opava, Czech., 42,308.........E 2 20
Opole (Oppeln), Poland, 56,400...C 3 24
Opole Lubelskie, Poland.........F 3 24
Oporto (Pôrto), Port., 281,406...B 2 17
Opua, New Zealand.........L 5 36
Oradea, Rumania, 82,282.......E 2 21
Orai, India, 17,242.........C 3 29
Oran, Algeria, 277,772.........F 4 34
Orán, Argentina, 6,706.........H 8 46
Orange, Australia, 18,247.......H 6 36
Orange, France, 10,515.........F 5 16
Orange (river), Africa.........M18 35
Orangeville, Ontario, 3,887......D 5 41
Oranienbaum (Lomonosov), U.S.S.R.........C 3 22
Oranienburg, Germany, 18,633...E 2 14
Orăştie, Rumania, 8,817.........F 3 21
Oraşul Stalin (Stalin), Rumania, 82,984.........G 3 21
Oravita, Rumania, 6,974.........E 3 21
Orbost, Australia, 2,214.........H 7 36
Ord (river), Australia.........D 3 36
Ordu, Turkey, 14,962.........G 2 28
Ordynskoye, U.S.S.R., 3,333.....K 4 22
Ordzhonikidze, U.S.S.R., 2,505...T 1 23
Ordzhonikidze, U.S.S.R., 164,000..F 5 22
Ordzhonikidze (Yenakiyevo), U.S.S.R., 92,000.........M 1 23
örebro, Sweden, 66,548.........J 7 13
Orekhovo-Zuyevo, U.S.S.R., 108,000.........B 3 22
Orel, U.S.S.R., 152,000.........E 4 22
Orenburg, U.S.S.R., 260,000.....G 4 22
Orense, Spain, †55,030.........C 1 17
Orestiás, Greece, 7,719.........H 5 21
Oriental (mt. range), S.A.........F 3 46
Orillia, Ontario, 13,827.........E 5 41
Orinoco (plains), S. A.........G 2 46
Orinoco (river), Venezuela.......H 2 46
Oristano, Italy, 13,914.........B 5 18
Orizaba, Mexico, 55,522.........O 2 44
Orkney (islands), Scotland, 21,255.........J 1 11
Orléans, France, 71,533.........D 3 16
Orléansville, Algeria, 12,455.....G 4 34
Orlová, Czech., 22,522.........E 2 20
Ormskirk, England, 20,482.......E 4 10
Orocué, Colombia, 598.........F 3 46
Oroquieta, Philippine Is., 7,233...G 4 31
Orosháza, Hungary, 31,063......F 3 20
Oroya, Peru, 14,492.........E 6 46
Orsha, U.S.S.R., 64,000.........E 4 22
Orsk, U.S.S.R., 176,000.........G 4 22
Ortona, Italy, 13,697.........E 3 18
Oruro, Bolivia, 62,975.........G 7 46
Oryakhovo, Bulgaria, 6,972......F 4 21
Osa, U.S.S.R., 5,876.........G 4 22
Osaka, Japan, 1,956,136.........J 8 33
Oschatz, Germany, 15,331.......E 3 14
Oschersleben, Germany, 21,011...D 2 14
Osh, U.S.S.R., 65,000.........U 2 23
Oshawa, Ontario, 50,412.........E 5 41
Oshawa, Greater, Ontario, 64,128..E 5 41
Oshogbo, Nigeria, 123,000......H10 34
Osijek, Yugoslavia, 57,320.......D 3 21
Osimo, Italy, 10,444.........D 3 18
Osinniki, U.S.S.R., 68,000.......O 6 23
Osipenko (Berdyansk), U.S.S.R., 65,000.........E 5 22
Oskelaneo, Quebec, 250.........E 4 41

Index Plate Ref. No.

Oslo,* Norway, 434,047.........D 3 13
Osmanabad, India, 14,414.......C 5 29
Osmaniye, Turkey, 19,701.......G 4 28
Osnabrück, Germany, 109,538....C 2 14
Osorno, Chile, 25,075.........F12 47
Osoyoos, British Columbia, 860...F 5 40
Osprey (reef), Australia.........H 2 36
Oss, Netherlands, 27,520.........H 5 15
Ostend (Oostende), Belgium, 53,752.........B 6 15
östersund, Sweden, 21,378......J 5 13
Ostrava, Czech., 199,206.........E 2 20
Ostróda (Osterode), Poland, 15,600..D 2 24
Ostrogozhsk, U.S.S.R., 22,990...F 4 22
Ostrołęka, Poland, 12,600.......E 2 24
Ostrov, U.S.S.R.........D 4 22
Ostrów Mazowiecka, Poland, 11,600.........E 2 24
Ostrow Wielkopolski, Poland, 40,000.........C 3 24
Ostrowiec Świętokrzyski, Poland, 34,700.........E 3 24
Ostuni, Italy, 24,020.........F 4 18
Osumi (islands), Japan, 86,968...O 4 33
Osuna, Spain, 19,575.........D 4 17
Oświęcim (Auschwitz), Poland, 26,400.........D 3 24
Otaru, Japan, 178,330.........K 2 33
Otavalo, Ecuador, 8,379.........E 3 46
Otavi, S. W. Africa, 762.........K15 35
Otjiwarongo, S. W. Africa, 2,487..K16 35
Otranto (strait), Italy.........G 5 18
Otsu, Japan, 85,251.........J 7 33
Ottawa,* Canada, 222,129......E 4 41
Ottawa, Greater, Ont., 342,507...E 4 41
Ottawa (islands), Canada.........D 2 41
Ottawa (river), Canada.........E 4 41
Otway (cape), Australia.........G 7 36
Otwock, Poland, 30,700.........E 2 24
Ouagadougou,* Upper Volta, 20,000.........F 9 34
Ouahigouya, Upper Volta, 7,100...F 9 34
Ouanaminthe, Haiti, 2,378.......C 5 48
Ouargla,* Oasis, 6,456.........G 5 34
Oudtshoorn, C. of G.H., 18,722...L18 35
Ouessant (island), France, 2,223..A 3 16
Ouezzane, Morocco, 23,509.....E 5 34
Ouidah, Dahomey, 14,657.......G10 34
Oujda, Morocco, 80,646.........F 5 34
Oullins, France, 17,728.........F 5 16
Oulu (Uleåborg), Finland, 51,073..O 4 13
Oulu (lake), Finland.........P 4 13
Oulu (river), Finland.........O 4 13
Ounas (river), Finland.........O 3 13
Ourinhos, Brazil, 13,829.........K 8 47
Ouro Prêto, Brazil, 8,751.........M 8 46
Ouse (river), England.........H 5 10
Outjo, S.W. Africa, 1,412.......K15 35
Outlook, Saskatchewan, 885......J 4 40
Ovalle, Chile, 17,573.........F10 47
Ovamboland (region), S.W. Afr. ..K15 35
Ovar, Portugal, 7,298.........B 2 17
Oviedo, Spain, †100,813.........C 1 17
Owen Sound, Ontario, 16,976....D 5 41
Owyhee (river), U.S.........D 4 42
Oxbow, Saskatchewan, 783......K 5 40
Oxford, England, 98,684.........F 6 10
Oxus (Amu-Dar'ya) (river), U.S.S.R.........H 5 22
Oyapock (river), S.A.........K 3 46
Oymakon, U.S.S.R.........R 3 23
Oyo, Nigeria, 72,133.........G10 34
Oyonnax, France, 9,694.........F 4 16
Oyster (bay), Tas., Australia.....H 8 36
Ozark (mountains), U.S.........K 5 43
Ozd, Hungary, 24,616.........F 2 20
Ozero (means lake), (Russian)....
Ozorków, Poland, 14,900.........D 2 24

P

Paan (Batang), China.........E 5 32
Paarl, C. of G.H., 30,037.........E14 35
Pabianice, Poland, 53,100.......D 3 24
Pabna, Pakistan, 31,924.........E 4 29
Pacasmayo, Peru, 6,615.........D 5 46
Pachino, Italy, 24,830.........E 6 18
Pachuca, Mexico, 58,653.........K 6 44
Padang, Indonesia, 108,728.....B 6 31
Padangsidempuan, Indon., 5,709..B 5 31
Padany, U.S.S.R., 363.........E 3 22
Paderborn, Germany, 40,270.....C 3 14
Padre (island), U.S.........J 8 42
Padua, Italy, 149,581.........C 2 18
Pago Pago,* Amer. Samoa, 1,586..J 7 37
Pahlevi (Enzeli), Iran, 45,726....F 2 27

Index Ref. Plate No.

Paignton, England, 25,553 D 7 10
Pailin, Cambodia D 4 30
Paisley, Scotland, 93,711 C 2 11
Paita, Peru, 6,797 D 5 46
Pajakumbuh, Indon., 5,914 C 6 31
Pakamburu, Indonesia C 5 31
Pakch'on, Korea, 17,184 B 4 33
Pakhoi, China, 75,000 G 7 32
Paknam (Samut Prakan), Thailand, 11,633 D 4 30
Pakokku, Burma, 23,558 B 2 30
Pakse, Laos, 130,060 E 4 30
Palamcottah, India, 30,967 C 7 29
Palana, U.S.S.R. S 4 23
Palanpur, India, 21,643 B 4 29
Palapye, Bech. Pr., 1,042 M16 35
Palau (islands), Pacific, 6,596 D 5 37
Palaw, Burma C 4 30
Palawan (isl.), Phil. Is., 54,807 E 4 31
Palazzolo Acreide, Italy, 12,078 E 6 18
Paldiski, U.S.S.R., 851 D 4 22
Paleleh, Indonesia G 5 31
Palembang, Indonesia, 237,616 D 6 31
Palencia, Spain, †41,122 D 2 17
Palermo, Italy, 447,421 D 5 18
Paletwa, Burma B 2 30
Palghat, India, 55,160 C 6 29
Pali, India, 12,356 B 3 29
Palimé, Togo, 2,797 G10 34
Palk (strait), Asia C 7 29
Palma (river), Brazil L 6 46
Palma, Bal. Is., Spain, †133,397 H 3 17
Palma del Río, Spain, 12,323 D 4 17
Palma di Montechiaro, Italy, 18,569 D 6 18
Palma Soriano, Cuba, 15,743 J 4 48
Palmas (cape), Liberia E11 34
Palmas, Las,* Canary Islands, Spain, 153,262 B 4 17
Palmerston North, N.Z., †37,775 M 6 36
Palmi, Italy, 15,786 E 5 18
Palmira, Colombia, 24,881 E 3 46
Palmyra (island), Pacific, 32 K 5 37
Palni, India, 24,706 C 6 29
Palopo, Indonesia, 4,208 F 6 31
Palu, Indonesia F 6 31
Pamangkat, Indonesia, 4,292 D 5 31
Pamekasan, Indonesia, 13,403 L 2 31
Pameungpeuk, Indonesia H 2 31
Pamiers, France, 9,641 D 6 16
Pamir (plateau), U.S.S.R. J 6 22
Pamlico (sound), U.S. O 6 43
Pampas (means plains) (Sp.)
Pamplona, Colombia, 16,396 F 2 46
Pamplona, Spain, 68,288 F 1 17
Panagyurishte, Bulg., 12,015 F 4 21
Panamá (gulf), Panama H 7 39
Panamá,* Panama, 127,874 H 6 39
Panay (isl.), Phil. Is., 1,423,836 G 3 31
Pančevo, Yugoslavia, 30,816 E 3 21
Panciu, Rumania, 4,523 H 3 21
Pandeglang, Indonesia G 1 31
Pandharpur, India, 33,329 C 5 29
Panevėžys (Panevezhis), U.S.S.R., 23,947 D 4 22
Panfilov, U.S.S.R., 11,148 J 5 22
Pangani, Tanganyika Terr., 3,000 O13 35
Pangani (river), Tan. Terr. O12 35
Pangim,* P. India, 31,950 B 5 29
Pangkalanbrandan, Indonesia B 5 31
Pangkalanbuun, Indonesia E 6 31
Pangkalpinang, Indonesia, 11,970 D 6 31
Panihati, India, 27,410 E 1 29
Panipat, India, 37,837 C 3 29
Pankow, Germany, 143,962 J 3 14
P'anmunjŏm, Korea C 5 33
Panna, India, 13,375 D 4 29
Panruti, India, 16,429 C 6 29
Pantelleria (isl.), Italy, 10,306 D 6 18
Pantin, France, 35,969 B 1 16
Paoki, China, 130,100 G 5 32
Paoting, China, 197,000 J 4 32
Paotow, China, 149,400 G 4 32
Pap, U.S.S.R., 3,049 T 2 23
Pápa, Hungary, 24,748 D 3 20
Papa Stour (island), Scotland, 68 M 3 11
Papa Westray (island), Scotland, 184 L 1 11
Papantla, Mexico, 11,359 L 6 44
Papeete,* Fr. Oceania, 17,247 M 7 37
Papenburg, Germany, 15,108 B 2 14
Paphos, Cyprus, 5,500 E 5 28
Papua (gulf), Pacific E 6 37
Papun, Burma C 3 30
Pará (Belém), Brazil, 225,218 L 4 46
Paracatu, Brazil, 5,975 L 7 46
Paraćin, Yugoslavia, 10,120 E 4 21
Paradis, Quebec, 200 E 4 41
Paraguai (river), Brazil J 7 46
Paraguari, Para., 4,297 J 9 47
Paraguay (river) J 8 47
Paraíbo (João Pessoa), Brazil, 89,517 O 5 46
Parakou, Dahomey, 5,061 G10 34
Paramaribo,* Surinam, 67,381 K 2 46
Paramushir (island), U.S.S.R. S 4 23
Paraná, Argentina, 84,153 J10 47
Paranã, Brazil, 594 L 6 46
Paraná (river), Argentina J 9 47
Paranaguá, Brazil, 15,803 L 9 47
Paranaíba (river), Brazil L 7 46
Paranapanema (river), Brazil K 8 46
Paratinga, Brazil, 2,873 M 6 46
Parbhani, India, 21,683 C 5 29
Parchim, Germany, 19,948 D 2 14
Pardes Hanna, Israel, 6,200 B 2 24
Pardo (river), Brazil M 7 46
Pardubice, Czech., 54,077 C 1 20
Pare, Indonesia, 22,388 K 2 31
Parent, Quebec, 1,443 E 4 41
Parepare, Indonesia, 6273 F 6 31
Pargolovo, U.S.S.R., 4,187 B 2 22
Paria (gulf), S.A. H 1 46
Pariaman, Indonesia B 6 31
Parintins, Brazil, 5,855 J 4 46
Paris,* France, 2,820,534 E 3 16
Parkent, U.S.S.R., 7,722 T 1 23
Parkes, Australia, 7,973 H 6 36
Parlakimidi, India, 21,042 D 5 29
Parma, Italy, 95,227 C 2 18
Parnaíba, Brazil, 30,174 M 4 46
Parnaíba (river), Brazil M 5 46
Parnassus (mountain), Greece F 6 21
Pärnu (Pyarnu), U.S.S.R., 20,334 D 4 22
Parral, Chile, 10,225 F11 47
Parral, Mexico, 32,063 G 3 44
Parramtta, Australia, 76,117 K 3 36
Parras, Mexico, 18,547 H 4 44
Parrsboro, N.S., 1,849 H 4 41
Parry Sound, Ontario, 5,378 E 4 41
Partanna, Italy, 13,706 D 6 18
Partapgarh, India, 13,505 B 4 29
Partinico, Italy, 24,000 D 6 18
Parvatipuram, India, 19,456 D 5 29
Pasaje, Ecuador, 4,864 E 4 46
Pasangkaju, Indonesia F 6 31
Paşcani, Rumania, 10,857 H 2 21
Pasewalk, Germany, 10,977 F 2 14
Pasinler, Turkey, 6,922 J 3 28
Paso de los Libres, Arg., 11,665 J 9 47
Paso de los Toros, Uruguay, 9,000 C 3 46
Paspébiac, Quebec, 800 H 4 41
Passau, Germany, 34,351 E 4 14
Passo Fundo, Brazil, 25,232 K 9 47
Passos, Brazil, 14,307 L 8 46
Pasto, Colombia, 48,843 E 3 46
Pasuruan, Indonesia, 36,973 K 2 31
Patan, India, 39,549 B 4 29
Patan, Nepal, 104,928 E 3 29
Patchewollock, Australia, 326 G 7 36
Paternion, Austria, 7,676 B 3 20
Paterno, Italy, 34,026 E 6 18
Pathfinder (res.), U.S. G 4 42
Pati, Indonesia, 22,444 J 2 31
Patiala, India, 69,850 C 2 29
Patjitan, Indonesia J 2 31
Patna, India, 283,479 E 3 29
Patos (lake), Brazil K10 47
Patras (Pátrai), Greece, 79,014 E 6 21
Patrocíni, Brazil, 7,345 L 7 46
Pattani, Thailand, 8,969 D 6 30
Pátzcuaro, Mexico, 10,327 J 7 44
Pau, France, 41,730 C 6 16
Paulis, Belgian Congo, 5,025 M11 35
Paulistana, Brazil, 1,042 M 5 46
Pavda, U.S.S.R., 1,695 P 5 23
Pavia, Italy, 59,487 B 2 18
Pavlodar, U.S.S.R., 90,000 J 4 22
Pavlovsk, U.S.S.R., 20,844 D 3 22
Pavlovskaya Sloboda, U.S.S.R., 2,399 B 4 22
Pavlovskiy Posad, U.S.S.R., 55,000 B 3 22
Pavuna, Brazil N13 47
Payne (lake), Canada F 2 41
Paysandú, Uruguay, 46,000 J10 47
Paytok, U.S.S.R., 4,993 U 2 23
Pazardzhik, Bulgaria, 30,430 G 4 21
Peace (river), Canada G 3 40
Peace River, Alberta, 2,034 G 3 40
Pearl Harbor (bay), U.S. H 8 42
Peć, Yugoslavia, 17,175 E 4 21
Pechenga, U.S.S.R., 5,198 E 2 22
Pechora (river), U.S.S.R. G 3 22
Pecos (river), U.S. H 7 42
Pécs, Hungary, 87,909 E 3 20
Pedro Alfonso, Brazil, 1,723 L 5 46
Peebinga, Australia, 54 G 6 36
Peebles, Scotland, 6,013 K 8 11
Peel (river), Canada C 1 40
Peera Peera (lake), Australia F 5 36
Pegu, Burma, 21,712 C 3 30
Pegu (mountains), Burma B 2 30
Pehpei, China, 150,000 G 6 32
Pehuajo, Argentina, 13,537 H11 47
Peine, Germany, 27,404 D 2 14
Peiping (Peking),* China, 2,768,149 J 3 32
Peipus (lake), U.S.S.R. D 4 22
Peixe, Brazil, 557 L 6 46
Pekalongan, Indonesia, 65,982 J 2 31
Peking,* China, 2,768,149 J 3 32
Pelalawan, Indonesia C 5 31
Pelee Island, Ontario, 644 D 5 41
Peleliu (island), Pacific, 846 D 5 37
Pelly, Saskatchewan, 477 K 4 40
Pelly (lake), Canada K 1 40
Pelly (river), Canada D 2 40
Pelotas, Brazil, 78,014 K10 47
Pemalang, Indonesia, 29,249 J 2 31
Pematangsiantar, Indonesia, 15,328 B 5 31
Pemba (isl.), Zanz. Prot., 114,587 P12 35
Pemberton, British Columbia, 25 F 4 40
Pembroke, Ontario, 15,434 E 4 41
Pembroke, Wales, 12,296 B 6 10
Penang (George Town), Malayan Federation, 189,068 C 6 30
Peñarroya-Pueblonuevo, Spain, 19,572 D 3 17
Penarth, Wales, 18,528 D 6 10
Penas (gulf), Chile E13 47
Pend Oreille (lake), U.S. D 2 42
Pendembu, S. Leone, 2,203 D10 34
Penedo, Brazil, 14,664 N 6 46
Pengpu, China, 253,000 J 5 32
Penha, Brazil N14 47
Peniche, Portugal, 10,057 B 3 17
Penki, China, 449,000 K 3 32
Pennine (mt. range), Eng. E 3 10
Penong, Australia, 98 E 6 36
Penrhyn (Tongareva) (island), Pacific, 654 L 6 37
Penrith, Australia, 17,924 K 3 36
Penticton, Br. Columbia, 11,894 G 5 40
Pentland (channel), Scotland J 2 11
Penza, U.S.S.R., 254,000 F 4 22
Penzance, England, 20,626 B 7 10
Pera (Beyoğlu), Turkey, 208,853 D 6 28
Pera Head (cape), Australia G 2 36
Percé, Quebec, 700 H 4 41
Perdido (mt.), Spain G 1 17
Perdue, Saskatchewan, 413 J 4 40
Pereira, Colombia, 30,762 E 3 46
Pergamino, Argentina, 32,382 M11 47
Péribonca (river), Canada F 3 41
Périgueux, France, 37,168 D 5 16
Perleberg, Germany, 13,701 E 2 14
Perm, U.S.S.R., 628,000 G 4 22
Pernambuco (Recife), Brazil, 512,370 O 5 46
Pernik (Dimitrovo), Bulgaria, 28,504 F 4 21
Peron (islands), Australia D 2 36
Perovo, U.S.S.R., 143,000 B 4 22
Perpignan, France, 63,863 E 6 16
Persian (gulf), Asia E 4 26
Perth, Australia, †348,647 B 2 36
Perth, Ontario, 5,145 E 5 41
Perth, Scotland, 40,547 J 7 11
Perugia, Italy, 40,039 D 3 18
Pervomaysk, U.S.S.R., 10,028 M 1 23
Pervoural'sk, U.S.S.R., 90,000 P 6 23
Pesaro, Italy, 34,647 D 3 18
Pescadores (Penghu) (isls.), China J 7 32
Pescara, Italy, 49,721 E 3 18
Peshawar, Pakistan, 151,435 B 2 29
Peshtera, Bulgaria, 8,946 G 4 21
Pesqueira, Brazil N 5 46
Pessac, France, 14,969 C 5 16
Petah Tiqva, Israel, 48,000 B 3 24
Peterborough, Australia, 3,473 F 6 36
Peterborough, England, 53,412 G 5 10
Peterborough, Ontario, 42,698 E 5 41
Peterborough, Greater, Ontario, 45,200 E 5 41
Peterhead, Scotland, 12,763 N 4 11
Pétionville, Haiti, 9,417 C 6 48
Petit-Goâve, Haiti, 5,536 B 6 48
Petitcodiac, New Brunswick, 900 G 4 41
Petite-Rivière-de-L'Artibonite, Haiti, 4,377 B 5 48
Petrich, Bulgaria, 13,456 F 5 21
Petrinja, Yugoslavia, 5,261 B 3 21
Petrodvorets, U.S.S.R., 28,000 C 3 22
Petrokrepost', U.S.S.R., 6,412 C 2 22
Petrolina, Brazil, 7,478 M 5 46
Petropavlovsk, U.S.S.R., 131,000 H 4 22
Petropavlovsk-Kamchatskiy, U.S.S.R., 86,000 T 4 23
Petrópolis, Brazil, 61,011 M 8 47
Petroşani, Rumania, 14,138 F 3 21
Petrovsk-Zabaykal'skiy, U.S.S.R., 12,100 M 4 23
Petrovskoye, U.S.S.R., 14,732 F 5 22
Petrozavodsk, U.S.S.R., 135,000 E 3 22
Petsamo (Pechenga), U.S.S.R., 5,198 E 2 22
Pforzheim, Germany, 54,143 C 4 14
Phalodi, India, 17,689 B 3 29
Phan Rang, Vietnam F 5 30
Phan Ri, Vietnam F 5 30
Phan Thiet, Vietnam F 5 30
Phatthalung, Thailand, 5,180 C 6 30
Phet Buri, Thailand, 16,279 C 4 30
Philiatrá, Greece, 11,057 E 7 21
Philippeville, Algeria, 48,773 H 4 34
Philippine (sea) D 3 37
Philippine Islands, 19,234,182 H 4 31
Phitsanulok, Thailand, 14,494 D 3 30
Phlórina, Greece, 12,270 E 5 21
Phnom Penh,* Cambodia, 375,000 E 5 30
Phoenix (islands), Pacific, 984 J 6 37
Phong Saly, Laos D 2 30
Phrae, Thailand, 11,900 D 3 30
Phu Lang Thuong, Vietnam E 2 30
Phu Ly, Vietnam E 2 30
Phu Tho, Vietnam E 2 30
Phuc Yen, Vietnam E 2 30
Phuket, Thailand, 18,759 C 6 30
Piacenza, Italy, 60,114 B 2 18
Piatra-Neamţ, Rumania, 26,303 G 2 21
Piazza Armerina, Italy, 25,558 E 6 18
Pico (means peak) (Sp.)
Picos, Brazil, 4,670 M 5 46
Picton, Australia, 1,234 K 4 36
Picton, New Zealand, 2,079 L 6 36
Picton, Ontario, 4,998 E 5 41
Pictou, Nova Scotia, 4,564 H 4 41
Pidurutalagala (mt.), Ceylon D 7 29
Piedras Negras, Mexico, 27,581 J 2 44
Piekary Śląskie, Poland, 29,200 B 4 24
Pielinen (lake), Finland Q 5 13
Piešt'any, Czech., 19,215 D 2 20
Pietarsaari (Jakobstad), Finland, 12,400 N 5 13
Pietermaritzburg,* Natal, †74,407 N17 35
Pietersburg, Transvaal, 20,360 N16 35
Pikes Peak (mountain), U.S. G 5 42
Pikwitonei, Manitoba, 150 L 3 40
Piła (Schneidemühl), Poland, 29,300 C 2 24
Pilar, Para., 5,141 J 9 47
Pilcomayo (river), S.A. H 8 47
Pilibhit, India, 44,709 C 3 29
Pillar (cape), Tas., Australia H 8 36
Pilsen (Plzeň), Czech., 134,273 B 2 20
Pimental, Peru, 4,125 D 5 46
Pinar del Río, Cuba, 26,241 B 2 48
Pincher Creek, Alberta, 1,729 H 5 40
Pindigheb, Pakistan, 10,150 B 2 29
Pindus (mt. range), Greece E 6 21
Pine Creek, Australia, 83 E 2 36
Pine Falls, Manitoba, 600 L 4 40
Pinega, U.S.S.R., 1,376 F 3 22
Pinega (river), U.S.S.R. F 3 22
Pinerolo, Italy, 20,856 A 2 18
Pines (island), Cuba, 9,812 A 2 45
Pingliang, China, 75,000 G 4 32
Pingrup, Australia, 128 B 6 36
Pinjarra, Australia, 906 B 2 36
Pinnaroo, Australia, 752 G 7 36
Pinneberg, Germany, 26,426 C 2 14
Pinsk, U.S.S.R., 31,913 D 4 22
Piombino, Italy, 28,122 C 3 18
Pionki, Poland, 10,100 E 3 24
Piotrków Tribunalski, Poland, 49,400 D 3 24
Piracicaba, Brazil, 46,611 L 8 46
Piraeus, Greece, 186,014 F 7 21
Pirapora, Brazil, 8,531 L 7 46
Pirenópolis, Brazil, 2,220 L 7 46
Pirmasens, Germany, 41,972 B 4 14
Pirna, Germany, 37,426 E 3 14
Pirogovskiy, U.S.S.R., 4,200 B 4 22
Pirot, Yugoslavia, 13,033 F 4 21
Pirovskoye, U.S.S.R., 1,443 L 4 23
Piru, Indonesia H 6 31
Pisa, Italy, 62,310 C 3 18
Pisco, Peru, 14,240 E 6 46
Písek, Czech., 20,297 C 2 20
Pisticci, Italy, 13,147 F 4 18
Pistoia, Italy, 33,526 C 2 18
Pitcairn (island), Pacific, 138 O 8 37
Piteşti, Rumania, 29,007 G 3 21
Piura, Peru, 19,027 D 5 46
Placentia, Newfoundland, 1,233 K 4 41
Placetas, Cuba, 19,693 E 2 48
Pladju, Indonesia D 6 31
Plasencia, Spain, 14,224 C 2 17
Plastun, U.S.S.R., 1,500 P 5 23
Platte (river), U.S. J 4 42
Plattling, Germany, 10,713 E 4 14
Plauen, Germany, 84,778 E 3 14
Plav, Yugoslavia, 5,961 D 4 21
Plei Ku, Vietnam E 4 30

Index Ref. Plate No.

Plenița, Rumania, 6,735........F 3 21
Pleszew, Poland, 10,300........C 3 24
Pletipi (lake), Canada........F 3 41
Pleven, Bulgaria, 38,997........G 4 21
Płock, Poland, 39,800........D 2 24
Ploești, Rumania, 95,632........H 3 21
Plovdiv, Bulgaria, 125,440........G 4 21
Plymouth, England, 208,012........D 7 10
Plymouth, W. I., 2,500........F 3 45
Plynlimmon (mountain), Wales....D 5 10
Plzeň, Czech., 134,273........B 2 20
Po (river), Italy........B 2 18
Pobé, Dahomey, 3,927........G10 34
Pobeda (mountain)........K 5 22
Poços de Caldas, Brazil, 19,680....L 8 46
Podgorica (Titograd), Yugo., 16,333........D 4 21
Podkamennaya Tunguska, U.S.S.R. ....K 3 22
Podol'sk, U.S.S.R., 124,000........C 4 22
Podor, Senegal, 3,996........D 8 34
P'ohang-dong, Korea, 45,147........D 5 33
Pointe-à-Pitre, Guadeloupe, 41,823 ....G 3 45
Pointe-Noire, Congo, 29,818........J12 35
Poitiers, France, 45,805........D 4 16
Pola (Pula), Yugo., 28,089........A 3 21
Polatli, Turkey, 16,271........E 3 28
Polgár, Hungary, 15,167........F 3 20
Polotsk, U.S.S.R., 24,816........D 4 22
Polovinnoye, U.S.S.R., 2,551........H 4 22
Poltava, U.S.S.R., 141,000........E 5 22
Polyanovgrad, Bulgaria, 10,225....H 4 21
Polyarnyy, U.S.S.R. ....E 3 22
Polynesia (islands), Pacific........K 6 37
Pomona (island), Scotland, 14,198.K 1 11
Ponape (island), Pacific, 6,316......F 5 37
Ponce, Puerto Rico, 99,492........F 1 45
Pond (inlet), Canada........D26 8
Pondicherry, India, 59,835........D 6 29
Ponnani, India, 17,838........C 6 29
Ponoka, Alberta, 3,387........H 4 40
Ponorogo, Indonesia, 21,680........J 2 31
Ponoy, U.S.S.R., 291........F 3 22
Pont-à-Mousson, France, 9,899....G 3 16
Pont-l'Evêque, France, 1,967........D 3 16
Ponta Grossa, Brazil, 44,130........K 9 47
Ponta Porã, Brazil, 5,554........K 8 46
Pontarlier, France, 12,130........G 4 16
Pontecorvo, Italy, 13,100........F 6 18
Pontefract, England, 23,173........F 4 10
Ponteix, Saskatchewan, 794........J 5 40
Pontevedra, Spain, †41,828........B 1 17
Pontianak, Indonesia, 45,196........D 6 31
Pontine (islands), Italy, 4,483......D 4 18
Pontivy, France, 6,764........B 3 16
Pontoise, France, 9,658........E 3 16
Pontypool, England, 42,683........E 6 10
Pontypridd, Wales, 38,633........D 6 10
Poole, England, 83,007........E 7 10
Poona, India, 480,982........B 5 29
Poopó (lake), Bolivia........G 7 46
Popayán, Colombia, 31,866........E 3 46
Popondetta, Papua........C 7 31
Porbandar, India, 48,493........A 4 29
Porcuna, Spain, 12,755........D 4 17
Porcupine (river), Canada........C 1 40
Porcupine Plain, Sask., 472........K 4 40
Pordenone, Italy, 23,625........D 2 18
Poreč, Yugoslavia, 5,982........A 3 21
Pori (Björneborg), Finland, 50,417 ....M 6 13
Porkkala, Finland........O 7 13
Poronaysk, U.S.S.R., 27,935........R 5 23
Porsanger (fjord), Norway........O 1 13
Porsgrunn, Norway, 9,456........G 7 13
Port Adelaide, Australia, 38,377....D 7 36
Port Alberni, Br. Columbia, 10,373.E 5 40
Port Albert, Australia, 333........H 7 36
Port-Alfred, Quebec, 7,968........F 4 41
Port Alice, Br. Columbia, 350........E 4 40
Port-à-Piment, Haiti, 2,328........A 6 48
Port Arthur, Ontario, 38,136........E 5 41
Port Arthur (incl. in Lüta), China, 126,000........K 4 32
Port Augusta, Australia, 6,704......F 6 36
Port-au-Prince,* Haiti, 152,410....C 6 48
Port-aux-Basques-Channel, Newfoundland, 3,320........J 4 41
Port Burwell, N.W. Terr. ....H 1 41
Port-Cartier, Quebec........G 4 41
Port Colborne, Ontario, 14,028.....E 5 41
Port-de-Paix, Haiti, 6,309........B 5 48
Port Elizabeth, C. of G.H., †188,982 ....M18 35
Port-Étienne, Mauritania, 1,500....C 7 34
Port Fairy, Australia, 2,265 .....G 7 36
Port Francqui, B. Congo, 3,607.....L12 35
Port-Gentil, Gabon, 9,313........H12 35
Port Glasgow, Scotland, 21,618....A 2 11
Port Harcourt, Nigeria, 71,634.....H11 34
Port Hardy, B.C., 175........E 4 40
Port Hawkesbury, N.S., 1,078.......H 4 41
Port Hedland, Australia, 613........B 3 36
Port Hood, Nova Scotia, 800........H 4 41
Port Hope, Ontario, 7,522........E 5 41
Port Laoighise (Maryborough), Ireland, 3,196........G 5 12
Port Lincoln, Australia, 5,871......E 6 36
Port Louis,* Mauritius, 97,888.......S19 35
Port-Lyautey (Kenitra), Morocco, 55,905 ....E 5 34
Port Macquarie, Australia, 4,408..J 6 36
Port Melbourne, Aust., 13,104.....K 2 36
Port-Menier, Anticosti Island, Quebec, 125........H 4 41
Port Moresby,* Papua, 17,546.......B 7 31
Port Nolloth, C. of G.H., 1,943....K17 35
Port of Spain,* Trinidad,* W.I. Fed., 114,150........G 5 45
Port Phillip (bay), Australia........G 6 36
Port Pirie, Australia, 14,223........F 6 36
Port Radium, N.W. Territories.....G 1 40
Port Said, Egypt, 178,432........N 5 34
Port Saunders, Newf., 350........J 3 41
Port Shepstone, Natal, 4,204........N18 35
Port Simpson, Br. Columbia, 750..E 4 40
Port Sudan, Sudan, 53,800........O 8 34
Port Talbot, Wales, 44,115........D 6 10
Port Wakefield, Australia, 478......F 6 36
Port Wallut, Vietnam........E 2 30
Portadown, N. Ireland, 17,202........H 3 12
Portage la Prairie, Man., 10,525..L 4 40
Portalegre, Portgual, 10,510........C 3 17
Portarlington, Australia, 841........K 2 36
Portimão, Portugal, 12,066........B 4 17
Portland, Australia, 4,759........G 7 36
Portland Bill (prom.), England....E 7 10
Pôrto (Oporto), Portugal, 281,406.B 2 17
Pôrto Alegre, Brazil, 375,049........L10 47
Porto Alexandre, Angola, 2,894.....J15 35
Porto Amboim, Angola, 1,537........J14 35
Porto Amélia, Moz., 5,095........P14 35
Porto Civitanova (Civitanova Marche), Italy, 23,625........D 3 18
Porto Empedocle, Italy, 15,632.....D 6 18
Pôrto Murtinho, Brazil, 2,826........J 8 46
Pôrto Nacional, Brazil, 2,935........L 6 46
Porto Novo, India, 14,175........D 6 29
Porto-Novo,* Dahomey, 31,000.....G10 34
Pôrto Santana, Brazil........K 4 46
Porto Tolle, Italy, 19,403........D 2 18
Pôrto Velho, Brazil, 10,026........H 5 46
Portoviejo, Ecuador, 18,082........D 4 46
Portsmouth, England, 233,545........G 7 10
Poruba, Czech., 21,179........D 2 20
Posadas, Argentina, 37,588........J 9 47
Posen (Poznań), Poland, 376,900..C 2 24
Poso, Indonesia, 2,875........G 6 31
Possneck, Germany, 20,247........D 3 14
Poste de Flacq, Maur., 1,085........T19 35
Potchefstroom, Transv., 27,153....M17 35
Potenza, Italy, 22,371........F 4 18
Potgietersrust, Transvaal, 5,676...M16 35
Poti, U.S.S.R., 16,671........F 5 22
Potiskum, Nigeria, 4,227........J 9 34
Potosí, Bolivia, 45,758........H 7 46
Potsdam, Germany, 113,568........E 2 14
Pouce-Coupé, Br. Columbia, 585...F 3 40
Poudre d'Or, Maur., 1,504........S19 35
Póvoa de Varzim, Port., 16,913......B 2 17
Powassan, Ontario, 935........E 4 41
Powder (river), U.S. ....G 3 42
Powell River, Br. Col., 5,174........F 4 40
Poyang (lake), China........J 6 32
Poyarkovo, U.S.S.R., 2,617........O 5 23
Poza Rica, Mexico, 14,901........L 6 44
Požarevac, Yugoslavia, 16,108......E 3 21
Požega, Yugoslavia, 8,854........C 3 21
Poznań (Posen), Poland, 376,900..C 2 24
Pozoblanco, Spain, 14,066........D 3 17
Pozzallo, Italy, 11,645........E 6 18
Pozzuoli, Italy, 35,216........D 4 18
Prado, Brazil, 1,595........N 7 46
Prague (Praha),* Czech., 978,634........C 1 20
Prainhas, Brazil, 445........K 4 46
Prapat, Indonesia........B 5 31
Prato, Italy, 44,626........C 3 18
Prawle (point), England........D 6 10
Preeceville, Saskatchewan, 807.....K 4 40
Preetz, Germany, 12,218........D 1 14
Prelate, Saskatchewan, 632........J 4 40
Premier, Br. Columbia, 400........E 3 40
Prenzlau, Germany, 17,699........F 2 14
Přerov, Czechoslovakia, 24,730......D 2 20
Prescott, Ontario, 4,920........E 5 41
Presidente Epitacio, Brazil, 2,609.K 8 46
Presidente Prudente, Brazil, 27,312........K 8 46
Presidente Roque Sáenz Peña, Argentina, 23,100........J 9 47
Prešov, Czechoslovakia, 31,100......F 2 20
Pressburg (Bratislava), Czech., 246,695........D 2 20
Preston, England, 119,250........E 4 10
Prestwick, Scotland, 11,387........G 9 11
Pretoria,* U. of S. Afr., †285,379.M17 35
Préveza, Greece, 11,008........E 6 21
Prey Veng, Cambodia........E 5 30
Pribilof (islands), U.S. ....E 8 42
Příbram, Czech., 14,653........B 2 20
Priego de Córdoba, Spain, 12,276.D 4 17
Prieska, Cape of G.H., 3,442........L17 35
Prijedor, Yugoslavia, 8,152........C 3 21
Prikumsk, U.S.S.R., 15,776........F 5 22
Prilep, Yugoslavia, 25,996........E 5 21
Primorsk, U.S.S.R. ....D 3 22
Prince Albert, C. of G.H., 2,520....L18 35
Prince Albert, Sask., 20,366........J 4 40
Prince Albert (peninsula), Canada D30 8
Prince Albert (park), Sask. ....J 4 40
Prince Edward (island), Canada, 99,285 ....H 5 41
Prince George, Br. Columbia, 10,536 ....F 4 40
Prince Regent (inlet), Canada......D28 8
Prince Rupert, Br. Columbia, 10,498 ....D 4 40
Prince of Wales (island), Alaska...D 3 40
Prince of Wales (island), Australia ....G 2 36
Prince of Wales (island), Canada..D28 8
Princess Charlotte (bay), Australia ....G 2 36
Princeton, Br. Columbia, 2,245......F 5 40
Príncipe (island), S. Tomé and Príncipe, 4,332........H11 35
Priozersk, U.S.S.R., 4,132........D 3 22
Pripet (Pripyat') (river), U.S.S.R. ....D 4 22
Priština, Yugoslavia, 19,822........E 4 21
Priverno, Italy, 9,154........F 6 18
Prizren, Yugoslavia, 19,838........E 4 21
Probolinggo, Indonesia, 37,009......K 2 31
Proddatur, India, 26,961........C 6 29
Progreso, Mexico, 13,338........P 6 44
Prokop'yevsk, U.S.S.R., 282,000....O 6 23
Prokuplje, Yugoslavia, 9,842........E 4 21
Prome, Burma, 36,762........B 3 30
Propriá, Brazil, 12,962........N 6 46
Proserpine, Australia, 2,187........H 4 36
Prostějov, Czechoslovakia, 33,853..D 2 20
Provadiya, Bulgaria, 8,730........F 4 21
Provideniya, U.S.S.R. ....V 3 23
Provost, Alberta, 878........H 4 40
Prudnik, Poland, 14,900........C 3 24
Pruszków, Poland, 35,700........E 2 24
Prut (river), Europe........J 2 21
Przemyśl, Poland, 42,900........F 4 24
Przeworsk, Poland, 8,569........F 3 24
Przheval'sk, U.S.S.R., 21,173........J 5 22
Pskent, U.S.S.R., 7,218........S 1 23
Pskov, U.S.S.R., 81,000........D 4 22
Pszczyna, Poland, 13,600........D 4 24
Ptuj, Yugoslavia, 7,906........C 2 21
Pucallpa, Peru, 2,468........E 5 46
Pucioasa, Rumania, 4,643........G 3 21
Pudukkottai, India, 34,188........C 6 29
Puebla, Mexico, 206,840........N 2 44
Puente Genil, Spain, 22,699........D 4 17
Puerto Armuelles, Panama, 5,808..F 6 39
Puerto Ayacucho, Ven., 2,991........G 2 46
Puerto Aysén, Chile, 3,767........F13 47
Puerto Barrios, Guatemala, 15,659.C 3 39
Puerto Berrio, Colombia, 5,487......E 2 46
Puerto Cabello, Venezuela, 34,382.G 1 46
Puerto Carreño, Colombia, 540.......G 2 46
Puerto Colombia, Colombia, 4,896.E 1 46
Puerto Cortés, Honduras, 12,228...D 2 39
Puerto Cumarebo, Ven., 4,757.......G 1 46
Puerto Deseado, Arg. 3,392........H13 47
Puerto Eten, Peru, 2,576........D 5 46
Puerto Madryn, Arg., 3,441........G12 47
Puerto Maldonado, Peru, 1,032.....G 2 46
Puerto México (Coatzacoalcos), Mexico, 19,501........M 7 44
Puerto Montt, Chile, 28,944........F12 47
Puerto Plata, Dominican Rep., 14,419 ....D 5 48
Puerto Princesa, Phil. Is., 3,326...F 4 31
Puerto Real, Spain, 12,726........D 4 17
Puerto Rico (island), 2,210,703.....E 3 45
Puerto Wilches, Colombia, 2,055..F 2 46
Puertollano, Spain, 29,468........D 3 17
Pugachev, U.S.S.R., 17,411........F 4 22
Puget (sound), U.S. ....C 3 42
Pukch'ŏng, Korea, 30,709........C 3 33
Pukekohe, New Zealand, 4,689......L 5 36
Pula (Pola), Yugoslavia, 28,089...A 3 21
Pulacayo, Bolivia, 7,984........G 8 46
Puławy, Poland, 12,600........F 3 24
Pułtusk, Poland, 10,200........E 2 24
Punakha, Bhutan........F 3 29
Punch, Kashmir, 8,608........B 2 29
Puno, Peru, 13,786........F 7 46
Punta (means point) (Sp. & It.)..
Punta Alta, Argentina, 19,852......H11 47
Punta Arenas, Chile, 34,440........F14 47
Puntarenas, Costa Rica, 13,272.....E 6 39
Purbolinggo, Indonesia, 16,435......J 2 31
Puri, India, 41,055........E 5 29
Puruándiro, Mexico, 9,713........J 7 44
Purnea, India, 19,036........E 3 29
Puruktjau, Indonesia........E 6 31
Purulia, India, 30,445........E 4 29
Purús (river), Brazil........H 5 46
Purwakarta, Indonesia, 15,141.......H 2 31
Purwodadi, Indonesia, 10,840........J 2 31
Purwokerto, Indonesia, 33,266.......H 2 31
Purworedjo, Indonesia, 24,645.......J 2 31
Pusan, Korea, 473,619........D 6 33
Pushkin, U.S.S.R., 45,700........C 3 22
Pushkino, U.S.S.R. ....B 4 22
Püspökladány, Hungary, 15,204.....F 3 20
Puteaux, France, 37,233........A 2 16
Putignano, Italy, 14,721........F 4 18
Puttur, India, 9,563........C 6 29
Putumayo (river), S.A. ....F 4 46
Putussibau, Indonesia........E 5 31
Pyapon, Burma, 15,501........B 3 30
Pyarnu (Pärnu), U.S.S.R., 20,334.D 4 22
Pyatigorsk, U.S.S.R., 69,000........F 5 22
Pyinmana, Burma........C 3 30
P'yŏngyang (Heijo),* N. Korea, 342,551........C 4 33
Pyramid (lake), U.S. ....C 4 42
Pyrenees (mt. range), Europe.....C 6 16
Pýrgos, Greece, 17,996........E 7 21
Pyrmont, Germany, 16,264........C 2 14
Pyskowice, Poland, 18,400........A 4 24
Pytalovo, U.S.S.R., 1,242........D 4 22

Q

Qattara (depression), Egypt........M 6 34
Qena, Egypt, 42,037........N 6 34
Qiryat Bialik, Israel, 6,000........C 2 24
Qiryat Haiyim, Israel, 11,000........B 2 24
Qiryat Motzkin, Israel, 8,000........C 2 24
Qiryat Shemona, Israel, 6,000........C 1 24
Qiryat Yam, Israel, 9,200........C 2 24
Qizan, Saudi Arabia, 5,000........D 6 26
Qu'Appelle (river), Canada........K 4 40
Quang Nam, Vietnam........E 4 30
Quang Ngai, Vietnam........F 4 30
Quang Tri, Vietnam........E 2 30
Quang Yen, Vietnam........E 2 30
Quartu Sant' Elena, Italy, 17,324..B 5 18
Quatsino, Br. Columbia, 300........E 4 40
Quchan, Iran, 28,031........L 2 27
Québec,* Quebec, 170,703........F 4 41
Québec, Greater, Quebec, 305,700..F 4 41
Quedlinburg, Germany, 35,142........D 3 14
Queen Charlotte (islands), Canada, 3,082 ....D 4 40
Queen Charlotte (sound), Canada.D 4 40
Queen Maud (gulf), Canada........K 1 40
Queenstown, Australia, 3,458........G 8 36
Queenstown, C. of G.H., 25,846....M18 35
Queenstown (Cóbh), Ireland, 5,169.E 8 12
Quelimane, Mozambique, 4,451....O15 35
Quequén, Argentina, 4,627........J11 47
Querétaro, Mexico, 49,428........K 6 44
Quesnel, Br. Columbia, 4,384........F 4 40
Quetta, Pakistan, 84,343........A 2 29
Quezaltenango, Guat., 36,209........B 3 39
Quezon City,* Phil. Is., 107,977....G 3 31
Qui Nhon, Vietnam........F 4 30
Quibdó, Colombia, 5,278........E 2 46
Quillacollo, Bolivia, 9,123........G 7 46
Quillota, Chile, 17,232........N 9 47
Quilmes, Argentina, 115,113........O12 47
Quilpie, Australia, 860........G 5 36
Quimili, Argentina, 3,686........H 9 47
Quimper, France, 15,629........A 4 16
Quirindi, Australia, 2,735........H 6 36
Quito,* Ecuador, 209,932........E 3 46
Qum (means desert) (Arab.)........
Qum, Iran, 83,200........G 3 27
Qunfidha, Saudi Ar., 4,500........D 6 26
Quorn, Australia, 869........F 6 36
Qurveh, Iran, 4,636........E 3 27

R

Ra'anana, Israel, 9,000........B 3 24
Raba, Indonesia, 6,781........F 7 31
Rabat,* Morocco, 156,209........E 5 34

Index Plate
Ref. No.

Rabaul, Terr. New Guinea, 7,600...F 6 37
Rača, Yugoslavia, 6,335...E 3 21
Race (cape), Canada...K 4 41
Rach Gia, Vietnam, 17,785...E 5 30
Racibórz (Ratibor), Poland, 30,500...C 3 24
Rădăuţi, Rumania, 14,530...G 2 21
Radevormwald, Germany, 18,067...G 5 14
Radhanpur, India, 11,959...B 4 29
Radium Hot Springs, B. C., 75...G 4 40
Radom, Poland, 118,800...E 3 24
Radomsko, Poland, 24,700...D 3 24
Radville, Sask., 1,087...K 5 40
Rae, N. W. Terr. ...G 2 40
Rae (isthmus), Canada...N 1 40
Rafaela, Argentina, 23,665...H10 47
Ragusa, Italy, 42,429...E 6 18
Ragusa (Dubrovnik), Yugo., 19,063...C 4 21
Raha, Indonesia...G 6 31
Rahaeng (Tak), Thailand, 8,246...C 3 30
Rahimyar Khan, Pakistan, 14,919.B 3 29
Raichur, India, 53,858...C 5 29
Raigarh, India, 20,327...D 4 29
Rainier (mountain), U.S. ...C 3 42
Rainy (lake), U.S.-Canada...K 2 43
Rainy (river), U.S.-Canada...K 2 43
Rainy River, Ontario, 1,354...B 4 41
Raipur, India, 63,465...D 4 29
Rajahmundry, India, 105,276...D 5 29
Rajapalaiyam, India, 46,289...C 7 29
Rajkot, India, 132,069...B 4 29
Rajnandgaon, India, 19,039...D 4 29
Rajpipla, India, 15,855...B 4 29
Rajshahi, Pakistan, 39,662...E 4 29
Rákospalota, Hungary, 48,379...E 3 20
Ram Hormuz, Iran, 7,854...F 5 27
Ramadi, Iraq, 92,474...C 4 27
Ramallah, Jordan, 17,145...C 4 24
Ramat Gan, Israel, 71,500...B 3 24
Ramat, Hasharon, Israel, 7,200...B 3 24
Rambipudji, Indonesia...K 2 31
Ramenskoye, U.S.S.R., 20,100...C 3 22
Ramle, Israel, 23,300...B 4 24
Ramnad, India, 18,152...C 7 29
Râmnicu-Sărat, Rumania, 19,267.H 3 21
Râmnicu-Vâlcea, Rumania, 17,238.F 3 21
Ramoutsa, Bech. Pr., 8,256...L16 35
Rampur, India, 134,277...C 3 29
Ramsgate, England, 35,801...J 6 10
Ranan (Nanam), Korea, 20,936...D 3 33
Rancagua, Chile, 31,018...N10 47
Ranchi, India, 107,286...E 4 29
Randers, Denmark, 40,098...G 8 13
Randwick, Australia, 99,080...L 3 36
Rangiora, New Zealand, 3,150...L 7 36
Rangkasbitung, Indonesia...G 2 31
Rangoon,* Burma, 711,520...C 3 30
Rangpur, Pakistan, 30,501...E 3 29
Rankovičevo, Yugoslavia, 12,503...E 4 21
Rannes, Australia, 65...J 4 36
Rannoch (lake), Scotland...H 6 11
Rapa Nui (Easter) (island), Chile, 270...P 8 37
Rapide-Blanc, Quebec, 190...F 4 41
Rarotonga (isl.), Pacific, 5,828...K 8 37
Ras (means cape, mt.) (Arab.)...
Rastatt, Germany, 16,390...C 4 14
Rastede, Germany, 14,439...B 2 14
Rat Buri, Thailand, 9,173...C 4 30
Ratangarh, India, 20,961...B 3 29
Rathenow, Germany, 27,566...E 2 14
Rathlin (island), Ireland...J 1 12
Ratibor (Racibórz), Poland, 30,500...C 3 24
Ratingen, Germany, 25,245...F 4 14
Ratlam, India, 44,939...B 4 29
Ratnagiri, India, 17,904...B 5 29
Ratnapura, Ceylon, 12,367...C 7 29
Ratzeburg, Germany, 12,502...D 2 14
Rauma (Raumo), Finland, 20,256...M 6 13
Ravenna, Italy, 34,904...D 2 18
Ravensburg, Germany, 25,889...C 5 14
Ravenshoe, Australia, 860...G 3 36
Ravensthorpe, Australia, 158...C 6 36
Rawalpindi,* Pakistan, 237,219...B 2 29
Rawicz, Poland, 11,900...C 3 24
Rawmarsh, England, 18,793...F 4 10
Rawson (Chubut), Arg., 1,745...H12 47
Ray (cape), Canada...J 4 41
Raymond, Alberta, 2,399...H 5 40
Razgrad, Bulgaria, 15,023...H 4 21
Ré (island), France, 7,908...C 4 16
Reading, England, 114,196...F 6 10
Real (mt. range), S.A. ...E 4 46
Ream, Cambodia...D 5 30
Reboly, U.S.S.R., 168...E 3 22
Rebrikha, U.S.S.R., 5,554...K 4 22
Recherche (arch.), Australia...C 6 36
Rechitsa, U.S.S.R., 16,559...D 4 22
Recife (Pernambuco), Brazil, 512,370...O 5 46
Recklinghausen, Germany, 104,791.B 3 14
Reconquista, Argentina, 12,729...H 9 47
Red (lake), U.S. ...K 3 43
Red (river), U.S. ...J 3 42
Red (river), U.S. ...K 6 43
Red (sea)...C 5 26
Red Deer, Alberta, 12,338...H 4 40
Red Deer (river), Canada...H 4 40
Red Lake, Ontario, 1,100...B 3 41
Red Rock, Ontario, 1,200...C 4 41
Red Volta (river), Upper Volta...F 9 34
Redcar, England, 27,516...G 3 10
Redcliff, Alberta, 2,001...H 4 40
Redditch, England, 28,183...F 5 10
Redruth, England, 9,704...B 7 10
Ree (lake), Ireland...F 4 12
Regensburg, Germany, 117,291...D 4 14
Reggan, Saoura...G 6 34
Reggio di Calabria, Italy, 120,021.E 5 18
Reggio nell'Emilia, Italy, 65,360...C 2 18
Reghin, Rumania, 9,599...G 2 21
Regina,* Saskatchewan, 89,755...K 4 40
Rehoboth, S. W. Africa, 1,782...K16 35
Rehovot, Israel, 29,500...B 4 24
Reichenbach, Germany, 34,708...E 3 14
Reichenbach, (Dzierżonión), Poland, 24,100...C 3 24
Reichenberg (Liberec), Czech., 66,796...C 1 20
Reigate, England, 42,248...G 6 10
Reims, France, 114,682...E 3 16
Reina Adelaida (arch.), Chile...E14 47
Reindeer (lake), Canada...K 3 40
Reinosa, Mexico, 34,087...K 3 44
Remanso, Brazil, 4,464...M 5 46
Rembang, Indonesia, 13,791...K 2 31
Remedios, Cuba, 10,485...E 2 48
Remiremont, France, 8,562...G 3 16
Remscheid, Germany, 103,276...G 5 14
Renaix (Ronse), Belg., 25,295...D 7 15
Rendsburg, Germany, 36,991...C 1 14
Renfrew, Ontario, 8,634...E 4 41
Renfrew, Scotland, 17,091...C 2 11
Rengat, Indonesia, 1,949...C 6 31
Renmark, Australia, 1,979...G 6 36
Rennes, France, 112,553...C 3 16
Reo, Indonesia...G 7 31
Repelen-Baerl, Germany, 15,405...F 4 14
Republican (river), U.S. ...J 5 42
Resht, Iran, 121,600...F 2 27
Resistencia, Argentina, 52,385...J 9 47
Reşiţa, Rumania, 24,895...E 3 21
Resolution (island), Canada...H 1 41
Retalhuleu, Guatemala, 7,677...B 3 39
Réthymnon, Greece, 11,057...G 8 21
Retto (means archipelago) (Jap.)
Réunion (island), 274,370...P20 35
Reus, Spain, 31,739...G 2 17
Reutlingen, Germany, 45,735...C 4 14
Revda, U.S.S.R., 55,000...P 6 23
Revelstoke, Br. Columbia, 3,469...G 4 40
Revillagigedo (islands), Mexico...C 7 44
Rewa, India, 26,008...D 4 29
Rewari, India, 30,673...C 3 29
Reyhanli, Turkey, 9,354...G 4 28
Reykjavík,* Iceland, 56,096...B 2 9
Reza'iyeh (Urmia), Iran, 50,171...D 2 27
Rēzekne, U.S.S.R., 13,139...D 4 22
Rheden, Netherlands, 36,428...J 4 15
Rheine, Germany, 40,363...B 2 14
Rheinhausen, Germany, 51,542...F 4 14
Rheydt, Germany, 78,302...B 3 14
Rhine (river), Europe...B 3 14
Rho, Italy, 22,137...B 2 18
Rhodes, Greece, 23,599...J 7 21
Rhodes (Ródos) (island), Greece, 55,181...H 7 21
Rhodope (mountains), Bulgaria...F 5 21
Rhondda, Wales, 111,389...D 6 10
Rhône (river)...F 5 16
Rhyl, Wales, 18,745...D 4 10
Ribe, Denmark, 7,219...F 9 13
Ribble (river), England...D 4 10
Ribeirão Prêto, Brazil, 63,312...L 8 46
Riberalta, Bolivia, 6,549...G 6 46
Richibucto, New Brunswick, 1,158.G 4 41
Richmond, Australia, 806...G 4 36
Richmond, Australia, 35,213...L 2 36
Riding Mountain (park), Man. ...K 4 40
Ried im Innkreis, Austria, 9,540...B 2 20
Riehen, Switzerland, 12,402...E 1 19
Riesa, Germany, 34,406...E 3 14
Riesi, Italy, 19,976...E 6 18
Rieti, Italy, 17,865...D 3 18
Riga, U.S.S.R., 605,000...D 4 22
Riga (gulf), U.S.S.R. ...D 4 22
Rigo, Papua...C 7 31
Riihimäki, Finland, 18,923...O 6 13
Rijeka, Yugoslavia, 75,112...B 3 21
Rijswijk, Neth., 28,913...E 4 15
Rimbey, Alberta, 3,387...H 4 40
Rimini, Italy, 50,123...D 2 18
Rimouski, Quebec, 14,630...G 4 41
Ringwood, Australia, 12,951...L 2 36
Río (means river) (Sp., It., Port.)
Río Blanco, Mexico, 8,412...P 2 44
Rio Branco, Brazil, 9,371...G 5 46
Río Caribe, Venezuela, 6,659...H 1 46
Río Cuarto, Argentina, 48,706...H10 47
Rio de Janeiro, Brazil, 2,303,063.M 8 46
Río Gallegos, Argentina, 5,880...G14 47
Rio Grande, Brazil, 63,235...K10 47
Rio Grande (river), U.S.-Mex. ...H 7 42
Rio Pardo, Brazil, 8,517...K 9 47
Río Piedras, Puerto Rico, 132,438.G 1 45
Rio Tinto, Brazil, 20,352...O 5 46
Rio Verde, Mexico, 10,100...J 6 44
Riobamba, Ecuador, 29,611...E 4 46
Riohacha, Colombia, 5,651...F 1 46
Rionero in Vulture, Italy, 13,500..E 4 18
Riosucio, Colombia, 648...E 2 46
Ripley, England, 18,194...F 4 10
Risca, England, 15,131...D 6 10
Rishon le Zion, Israel, 23,600...B 4 24
Rishra and Konnagar, India, 37,432...E 1 29
Rive-de-Gier, France, 13,786...F 5 16
Rivera, Uruguay, 30,000...J10 47
Riverhurst, Saskatchewan, 251...J 4 40
Rivers Inlet, Br. Columbia, 250...E 4 40
Riversdale, Cape of G.H., 4,530...L18 35
Riverton, Manitoba, 795...L 4 40
Rivière-Bleue, Quebec, 1,481...G 4 41
Rivière-du-Loup, Quebec, 9,965...G 4 41
Riyadh,* Saudi Arabia, 80,000...E 5 26
Rize, Turkey, 17,868...J 2 28
Roanne, France, 45,262...E 4 16
Robertsport, Liberia...D10 34
Roberval, Quebec, 6,648...F 4 41
Robson (mountain), Canada...G 4 40
Roca (cape), Portugal...B 3 17
Rocha, Uruguay, 25,000...K11 47
Rochdale, England, 88,429...E 4 10
Rochefort, France, 23,753...C 4 16
Rochester, England, 43,934...H 6 10
Rockbank, Australia, 241...K 2 36
Rockdale, Australia, 75,995...L 3 36
Rockglen, Saskatchewan, 543...J 5 40
Rockhampton, Australia, †40,670..J 4 36
Rockingham, Australia, 1,022...B 2 36
Rocky (mountains), U.S.-Canada.D 2 42
Rocky Mountain House, Alberta, 1,285...G 4 40
Rodakovo, U.S.S.R., 1,469...O 1 23
Rodez, France, 17,136...E 5 16
Rodrigues (islands), Maur., 13,333...K11 25
Roebourne, Australia, 182...B 4 36
Roebuck (bay), Australia...C 3 36
Roermond, Netherlands, 25,840...J 6 15
Roes Welcome (sound), Canada...N 2 40
Roeselare (Roulers), Belgium, 34,304...C 7 15
Rogaguado (lake), Bolivia...G 6 46
Rohri, Pakistan, 13,243...A 3 29
Roi Et, Thailand, 8,105...D 4 30
Rojas, Argentina, 6,608...M11 47
Roma, Australia, 4,248...H 5 36
Romaine (river), Canada...H 3 41
Roman, Rumania, 23,701...H 2 21
Romans-sur-Isère, France, 18,865.F 5 16
Rome (Roma),* Italy, 1,610,467...D 4 18
Romilly-sur-Seine, France, 12,925.F 3 16
Ron, Vietnam...E 3 30
Rona (island), Scotland...B 7 11
Ronda, Spain, 17,131...D 4 17
Rondorf, Germany, 18,828...B 3 14
Ronge (lake), Canada...J 3 40
Rönne, Denmark, 12,696...J 9 13
Ronse (Renaix), Belgium, 25,295..D 7 15
Roosevelt (res.), U.S. ...F 6 42
Roosevelt (river), Brazil...H 5 46
Roosendall, Netherlands, 33,984...F 5 15
Roper (river), Australia...E 2 36
Roques, Los (islands), Venez., 562...G 1 46
Roraima (mountain), S.A. ...H 2 46
Rorschach, Switz., 11,325...H 2 19
Rosa (mountain)...A 2 18
Rosario, Argentina, 467,937...H10 47
Rosario, Mexico, 7,624...G 5 44
Rosario de la Frontera, Arg., 4,927...H 9 47
Rosário Oeste, Brazil, 1,603...J 6 46
Roscommon, Ireland, 1,697...E 4 12
Rose-Blanche, Newf., 950...J 4 41
Rose Hill, Maur., 11,838...S19 35
Roseau, Dominica, 12,000...G 2 45
Rosenheim, Germany, 29,937...D 5 14
Rosetown, Saskatchewan, 2,265...J 4 40
Rosignol, Br. Guiana, 1,204...J 2 46
Roşiorii-de-Vede, Rumania, 14,905...G 3 21
Roskilde, Denmark, 26,355...G 9 13
Roslavl', U.S.S.R., 28,974...E 4 22
Ross, New Zealand, 549...L 7 36
Ross River, Yukon, 30...D 2 40
Rossano, Italy, 12,948...F 5 18
Rossland, Br. Columbia, 4,344...G 5 40
Rosslau, Germany, 17,473...E 3 14
Rossosh', U.S.S.R., 16,270...F 4 22
Rosthern, Saskatchewan, 1,268...J 4 40
Rostock, Germany, 114,869...D 1 14
Rostov, U.S.S.R., 597,000...F 5 22
Rothenburg, Germany, 11,214...D 4 14
Rotherham, England, 82,334...F 4 10
Rothesay, New Brunswick, 802...G 4 41
Rothesay, Scotland, 10,141...F 8 11
Roto, Australia, 158...G 6 36
Rotorua, New Zealand, 12,302...M 6 36
Rotterdam, Neth., 722,718...E 5 15
Rottweil, Germany, 15,140...C 4 14
Rotuma (island), Pacific, 2,929...H 7 37
Roubaix, France, 109,480...E 2 16
Rouen, France, 113,062...D 3 16
Rouleau, Saskatchewan, 1,402...K 4 40
Rousay (island), Scotland, 342...K 1 11
Rouyn, Quebec, 17,076...E 4 41
Rovaniemi, Finland, 13,183...O 3 13
Rovereto, Italy, 20,196...C 2 18
Rovigo, Italy, 17,588...C 2 18
Rovinj (Rovigno), Yugoslavia, 9,438...A 3 21
Rovno (Równe), U.S.S.R., 57,000..D 4 22
Rowsley, Australia, 125...K 2 36
Roxburgh, New Zealand, 794...K 7 36
Royale (island), U.S. ...M 2 43
Rtishchevo, U.S.S.R., 11,409...F 4 22
Rubʻ al Khali (desert), Saudi A. .F 5 26
Rubtsovsk., U.S.S.R., 111,000...J 4 22
Ruda, Poland, 39,200...B 4 24
Rudolf (lake), Kenya...O11 34
Rudolstadt, Germany, 22,100...D 3 14
Rueil-Malmaison, France, 17,103..A 2 16
Rufiji (river), Tan. Terr. ...O13 35
Rufino, Argentina, 10,987...H10 47
Rufisque, Senegal, 30,000...C 8 34
Rugby, England, 45,428...F 5 10
Rügen (island), Germany...E 1 14
Rugozero, U.S.S.R., 487...E 3 22
Rukwa (lake), Tan. Terr. ...N13 35
Rulhieres (cape), Australia...D 2 36
Rum (island), Scotland, 25...D 6 11
Ruma, Yugoslavia, 14,049...D 3 21
Rumia, Poland, 12,100...D 1 24
Rumoe, Japan, 32,513...K 2 33
Rumula, Australia, 53...G 3 36
Runanga, New Zealand, 1,804...L 7 36
Runcorn, England, 22,931...E 4 10
Rupert (river), Canada...E 3 41
Rusape, S. Rhodesia, 1,134...N15 35
Ruse, Bulgaria, 53,420...H 4 21
Rushden, England, 16,370...G 5 10
Russell, Manitoba, 1,227...K 4 40
Rute, Spain, 13,387...D 4 17
Rutherglen, Scotland, 24,225...C 2 11
Ruvo di Puglia, Italy, 25,662...F 4 18
Ruvuma (river), Africa...O14 35
Ruwenzori (mountain), Africa...N11 35
Ružomberok, Czech., 22,483...E 2 20
Ryazan', U.S.S.R., 213,000...F 4 22
Ryazhsk, U.S.S.R., 20,000...E 4 22
Rybinsk, U.S.S.R., 181,000...E 4 22
Rybinsk (res.), U.S.S.R., ...E 4 22
Rybnik, Poland, 31,100...D 3 24
Rychbach (Dzierżoniów), Poland, 16,646...C 3 24
Ryde, Australia, 54,101...L 3 36
Ryde, England, 20,105...F 7 10
Ryukyu (Nansei) (islands), 917,400.L 7 33
Rzeszów, Poland, 55,900...E 3 24
Rzhev, U.S.S.R., 45,000...E 4 22

S

's Gravenhage,* Neth., 606,728...E 4 15
's Hertogenbosch, Neth., 67,394...G 5 15
Saʻada, Yemen, 4,000...D 6 26
Sá da Bandeira, Angola, 11,657...J14 35
Saalfeld, Germany, 26,387...D 3 14
Saalfelden, Austria, 8,274...B 3 20
Saarbrücken, Germany, 89,700...B 4 14
Saarlautern, Germany, 26,088...B 4 14
Šabac, Yugoslavia, 19,987...D 3 21
Sabadell, Spain, 51,306...H 2 17
Sabang, Indonesia, 6,855...B 4 31
Sabang, Indonesia...F 5 31
Sabi (river), S. Rhodesia...N16 35
Sabinas, Mexico, 11,249...J 3 44
Sabine (river), U.S. ...K 7 43
Sabirabad, U.S.S.R., 2,480...F 6 22
Sable (cape), Canada...G 5 41

Index Ref. Plate No.
Sable (island), Canada J 5 41
Sabya, Saudi Ar., 5,000 D 6 26
Sabzawar (Shindand), Afghan., 12,500 H 3 26
Sabzawar, Iran, 33,217 K 2 27
Sackville, New Brunswick, 2,849 H 4 41
Sacramento (river), U.S. C 5 42
Sadec, Vietnam, 9,205 E 5 30
Safad, Israel, 8,500 C 2 24
Safi, Jordan E 5 24
Safi, Morocco, 51,751 E 5 33
Saga, Japan, 66,807 E 7 33
Sagaing, Burma, 13,631 B 2 30
Sagamihara, Japan, 83,841 O 2 33
Sagua la Grande, Cuba, 24,044 E 1 48
Saguenay (river), Canada F 4 41
Saharanpur, India, 148,435 C 3 29
Sahuayo, Mexico, 12,511 H 6 44
Saïda, Algeria, 13,292 G 4 34
Saïda (Sidon), Lebanon, 17,730 F 6 28
Saidabad, Iran, 9,020 J 6 27
Saidapet, India, 41,347 D 6 29
Saidor, Terr. N.G. B 7 31
Saigon,* S. Vietnam, 1,179,000 E 5 30
Saihut, Aden Pr., 10,000 F 6 26
Saiki, Japan, 51,226 E 7 33
Sain Qal'eh, Iran, 3,603 E 2 27
Saint Abbs Headland (prom.), Scotland M 8 11
Saint Albans, England, 44,098 G 6 10
Saint Albans, Newf., 800 J 4 41
Saint-Amand-Montrond, France, 9,831 E 4 16
Saint Andrews, N.B., 1,534 G 5 41
Saint Annes, Eng., 30,343 D 4 10
Saint Anthony, Newf., 1,761 K 3 41
Saint-Augustin, Quebec, 393 J 3 41
Saint Austell, England, 23,634 C 7 10
Saint-Benoit, Réunion, 8,175 R20 35
Saint Boniface, Man., 28,851 L 5 40
Saint Brandon (islands), Maur., 136 J11 25
Saint Brides (bay), Wales B 6 10
Saint-Brieuc, France, 32,965 B 3 16
Saint Catharines, Ontario, 39,708 E 5 41
Saint Catharines, Greater, Ontario, 84,493 E 5 41
Saint-Chamond, France, 14,546 F 5 16
Saint Christopher (isl.), West Indies, 29,818 F 3 45
Saint-Claude, France, 9,865 F 4 16
Saint-Cloud, France, 17,101 A 2 16
Saint Davids Headland (prom.), England B 6 10
Saint-Denis, France, 79,611 B 1 16
Saint-Denis,* Réunion, 41,863 P20 35
Saint-Dié, France, 18,033 G 3 16
Saint Dizier, France, 22,542 F 3 16
Saint Elias (mt.), Can.-U.S. B 2 40
Saint-Étienne, France, 154,283 F 5 16
Saint-Félicien, Quebec, 4,152 F 4 41
Saint George, Australia, 1,698 H 5 36
Saint George, N.B., 1,322 G 5 41
St. George (mt. range), Aust. D 3 36
Saint Georges, Newf., 750 J 4 41
Saint George's, W.I., 5,774 F 5 45
Saint Georges (channel), Eng. B 6 10
Saint-Germain, France, 25,394 D 3 16
Saint-Gilles, Belgium, 56,532 B 9 15
Saint Helena (island), 4,748 E15 35
Saint Helens, England, 110,260 E 4 10
Saint Helier (*Jersey), Channel Is., 25,360 E 8 10
Saint-Hyacinthe, Quebec, 20,439 F 4 41
Saint Ives (bay), England B 7 10
Saint-Jean, Quebec, 24,367 F 4 41
Saint-Jean (lake) Quebec F 4 41
Saint-Jean-de-Luz, France, 8,476 C 6 16
Saint-Jean-Port-Joli, Quebec, 900 G 4 41
Saint-Jérôme, Quebec, 20,645 F 4 41
Saint John, N.B., 52,491 G 4 41
Saint John, Greater, N. B., 85,500 G 4 41
Saint John (river), Canada G 4 41
Saint Johns, W.I., 10,965 G 3 45
Saint John's,* Newf., 57,078 K 4 41
Saint-Joseph, Quebec, 2,484 F 4 41
Saint-Joseph, Réunion, 5,508 P20 35
Saint Joseph (lake), Canada M 4 40
Saint-Josse-ten-Noode, Belgium, 25,502 C 9 15
Saint-Junien, France, 8,103 D 5 16
Saint Kilda, Australia, 53,301 L 2 36
Saint Kilda (island), Scotland B 8 11
St. Kitts (St. Christopher)(island), W.I., 29,818 F 3 45
St.-Laurent, Fr. Guiana, 2,095 K 2 46
Saint Lawrence, Australia, 290 H 4 36
Saint Lawrence, Newf., 1,837 J 4 41
Saint Lawrence (gulf), Canada H 4 41
Saint Lawrence (isl.), U.S. E 8 42
Saint Lawrence (river), Canada F 4 41
Saint-Léonard, N.B., 1,593 G 4 41
Saint-Lô, France, 11,287 C 3 16
Saint-Louis, Senegal, 63,000 C 8 10
Saint-Louis, Réunion, 25,220 P20 35
Saint Lucia (island), W.I., 86,219 G 4 45
Saint Magnus (bay), Scotland M 3 11
Saint-Malo, France, 13,515 B 3 16
Saint-Malo (gulf), France B 3 16
Saint-Mandé, France 22,279 B 2 16
Saint-Marc, Haiti, 10,485 B 5 48
Saint Mary's, Australia, 592 H 8 36
Saint-Maur-des-Fossés, France, 55,079 B 2 16
Saint-Michel-de-l'Atalaye, Haiti, 2,328 C 5 48
Saint Moritz, Switz., 2,558 J 3 19
Saint-Nazaire, France, 33,513 B 4 16
Saint-Nicolas (Sint-Niklaas), Belgium, 46,474 E 6 15
Saint-Omer, France, 15,785 E 2 16
Saint-Ouen, France, 45,360 B 1 16
Saint-Pacôme, Quebec, 1,283 G 4 41
Saint-Pascal, Quebec, 1,962 G 4 41
Saint Paul, Alberta, 2,229 H 4 40
Saint-Paul, Réunion, 28,681 P20 35
Saint Peter Port (*Guernsey), Channel Is., †16,799 E 8 10
Saint-Philippe, Réunion, 1,065 K20 35
Saint-Pierre, Réunion, 27,573 P20 35
Saint-Pierre,* St. P. and Miquelon, 3,636 J 4 41
Saint-Quentin, France, 52,148 E 3 16
Saint-Servan, France, 10,815 C 3 16
Saint-Siméon, Quebec, 1,114 F 4 41
Saint Stephen, N.B., 3,491 G 4 41
Saint Thomas, Ontario, 19,129 D 5 41
Saint Vincent (cape), Portugal B 4 17
Saint Vincent (isl.), W.I., 75,190 G 4 45
Saint Walburg, Sask., 618 J 4 40
Sainte-Anne-de-Beaupré, Quebec, 1,865 F 4 41
Sainte-Marie, Quebec, 3,094 F 4 41
Ste.-Marie (cape), Malg. Rep. P17 35
Sainte Rose du Lac, Man., 740 L 4 40
Sainte-Savine, France, 9,874 E 3 16
Saintes, France, 21,154 C 5 16
Saipan (island), Pacific, 4,943 E 4 37
Sakai, Japan, 213,688 J 8 33
Sakarya (Adapazari), Turkey, 55,116 D 2 28
Sakata, Japan, 54,291 J 4 33
Sakhalin (island), U.S.S.R., 500,000 R 5 23
Sakhnin, Israel, 3,477 C 2 24
Saki (means cape), (Jap.)
Sakishima (islands), Ryukyu Is. K 7 33
Sakon Nakhon, Thailand, 5,975 E 3 30
Salado (river), Argentina G11 47
Salado (river), Argentina H 9 47
Salaga, Ghana, 3,156 F10 34
Salair, U.S.S.R., 21,500 O 5 23
Salamanca, Mexico, 20,610 J 6 44
Salamanca, Spain, †74,773 D 2 17
Salamat (river), Chad K10 34
Salamís, Greece, 8,347 F 6 21
Salatiga, Indonesia, 24,274 J 2 31
Salaverry, Peru, 3,403 E 5 46
Salazar, Angola, 2,105 K13 35
Saldanha, C. of G.H., 1,469 K18 35
Sale, Australia, 6,537 H 7 36
Salé, Morocco, 46,582 E 5 34
Salekhard, U.S.S.R., 8,800 H 3 22
Salem, India, 202,335 C 6 29
Salemi, Italy, 13,755 D 6 18
Salerno, Italy, 72,626 E 4 18
Salgótarján, Hungary, 23,814 E 2 20
Sali, Saoura, 1,821 G 6 34
Salihli, Turkey, 18,043 C 3 28
Salina Cruz, Mexico, 8,243 M 9 44
Salinas, Ecuador, 2,868 D 4 46
Salisbury, Australia, 2,619 D 7 36
Salisbury, England, 32,911 F 6 10
Salisbury (plain), England E 6 10
Salisbury,* S. Rhodesia, †118,772 N15 35
Salmon (river), U.S. E 3 42
Salmon Arm, B.C., 1,344 G 4 40
Salmon Gums, Australia, 172 C 6 36
Salon, France, 10,625 F 6 16
Salonika, Greece, 217,049 F 5 21
Salonta, Rumania, 14,447 E 2 21
Salt (lake), Australia B 5 36
Salt (lake), Australia A 4 36
Salt (lakes), Australia D 5 36
Salta, Argentina, 67,403 H 8 46
Saltcoats, Saskatchewan, 506 K 4 40
Saltcoats, Scotland, 13,108 G 8 11
Saltillo, Mexico, 69,874 J 4 44
Salto, Argentina, 7,771 M11 47
Salto, Uruguay, 60,000 J10 47
Salton (sea), U.S. D 4 42
Salûm, Egypt, 1,011 M 5 34
Saluzzo, Italy, 11,312 A 2 18
Salvador (Bahia), Brazil, 389,422 N 6 46
Salween (river), Burma C 2 30
Salzburg, Austria, 100,096 B 3 20
Salzkammergut (region), Austria B 3 20
Salzwedel, Germany, 24,564 D 2 14
Sam Neua, Laos E 2 30
Samalkot, India, 22,349 D 5 29
Samandağ, Turkey, 11,197 F 4 28
Samar (isl.), Phil. Is., 470,678 H 3 31
Samara (Kuybyshev), U.S.S.R. 806,000 G 4 22
Samarai, Papua, 777 C 8 31
Samarinda, Indonesia, 11,086 F 6 31
Samarkand, U.S.S.R., 195,000 H 6 22
Samarra, Iraq, 33,000 C 3 27
Samarskoye, U.S.S.R., 2,211 K 5 22
Sambalpur, India, 17,079 D 4 29
Sambas, Indonesia D 5 31
Sambhal, India, 53,887 C 3 29
Sambiase, Italy, 13,761 F 5 18
Sambre (river) D 8 15
Samch'ŏk, Korea, 28,117 D 5 33
Samnan, Iran, 30,770 H 3 27
Samoa (isls.), Pacific, 113,065 J 7 37
Samokov, Bulgaria, 12,784 F 4 21
Sámos (island), Greece, 47,877 H 7 21
Sampang, Indonesia, 12,673 K 2 31
Sampit, Indonesia E 6 31
Samsun, Turkey, 62,648 F 2 28
San (means hill) (Jap.)
San, Sudanese Rep., 6,883 F 9 34
San Ambrosio (island), Chile E 9 47
San Andreas (mountains), U.S. G 6 42
San Andrés de Giles, Arg., 5,392 N12 47
San Andrés Tuxtla, Mex., 15,150 M 7 44
San Antonio (cape), Argentina J11 47
San Antonio, Chile, 11,859 N10 47
San Antonio de Areco, Arg., 7,436 N11 47
San Antonio de los Baños, Cuba, 16,512 C 1 48
San Benedetto del Tronto, Italy, 18,015 E 3 18
San Bernardino (mts.), U.S. E 6 42
San Bernardo, Chile, 20,673 O10 47
San Carlos, Venezuela, 7,174 G 2 46
San Carlos (lake), U.S. F 6 42
San Carlos de Bariloche, Arg., 6,562 G12 47
San Cataldo, Italy, 23,828 D 6 18
San Clemente (island), U.S. D 6 42
San Cristóbal, Argentina, 9,071 H10 47
San Cristóbal, Dom. Rep., 9,668 E 6 48
San Cristóbal, (Ciudad de las Casas), Mexico, 17,472 O 8 44
San Cristobal (island), Pacific, 8,000 G 7 37
San Cristóbal, Venezuela, 53,933 F 2 46
San Diego (cape), Argentina H14 47
San Felipe, Chile, 13,168 O 9 47
San Felipe, Venezuela, 18,060 G 1 46
San Félix (island), Chile D 9 47
San Fernando, Arg., 44,666 N12 47
San Fernando, Chile, 14,419 O10 47
San Fernando, Spain, 31,811 C 4 17
San Fernando, Venezuela, 13,377 G 2 46
San Francisco, Argentina, 24,354 H10 47
San Francisco, Mexico, 18,193 H 6 48
San Francisco de Macorís, Dom. Republic, 16,152 E 5 48
San Francisco del Oro, Mexico, 11,465 F 3 44
San Germán, Puerto Rico, 8,872 F 1 45
San Giovanni in Fiore, Italy, 17,443 F 5 18
San Isidro, Arg., 25,070 O11 47
San Joaquin (river), U.S. C 5 42
San Jorge (gulf), Chile G13 47
San José,* Costa Rica, 118,287 F 5 39
San Jose, Philippine Isls., 2,259 G 3 31
San José de Chiquitos, Bolivia, 1,933 H 7 46
San José de Mayo, Uraguay, 30,000 J10 47
San Juan, Argentina, 82,410 G10 47
San Juan, Dom. Rep., 10,093 D 6 48
San Juan, Mexico, 7,501 K 6 44
San Juan,* Puerto Rico, 224,767 G 1 45
San Juan (river), U.S. F 5 42
San Julián, Argentina, 3,050 G13 47
San Luis, Argentina, 25,147 G10 47
San Luis Potosí, Mex., 126,596 J 6 44
San Marco in Lamis, Italy, 21,592 E 4 18
San Marcos, Colombia, 2,482 E 2 46
San Marino,* San Marino, 2,418 D 3 18
San Martín (lake), Argentina F13 47
San Martín Texmelucan, Mexico, 11,343 M 1 44
San Matías (gulf), Argentina H12 47
San Miguel, El Salvador, 26,702 D 4 39
San Miguel, Mexico, 11,629 J 6 44
San Miguel (river), Bolivia H 6 46
San Nicolás, Argentina, 25,029 J10 47
San Nicolas (island), U.S. C 6 42
San Pablo del Monte, Mex., 9,297 M 1 44
San Pedro, Argentina, 12,778 M11 47
San Pedro, Mexico, 19,258 H 4 44
San Pedro de Macorís, Dom. Rep., 19,994 E 6 48
San Pedro Sula, Hond., 21,139 C 3 39
San Rafael, Argentina, 28,847 G10 47
San Ramón, Peru, 1,275 F 6 46
San Remo, Italy, 30,705 A 3 18
San Salvador,* El Salvador, 191,393 C 4 39
San Sebastián, Spain, †110,687 E 1 17
San Severo, Italy, 47,875 E 4 18
San Vicente, El Salvador, 12,204 C 4 39
San Vito dei Normanni, Italy, 17,351 F 4 18
San'a,* Yemen, 28,000 D 6 26
Sanaga (river), Cameroons J11 34
Sanana, Indonesia H 6 31
Sanandaj, Iran, 32,104 E 3 27
Sánchez, Dom. Republic, 3,135 E 3 45
Sancti-Spiritus, Cuba, 28,262 E 2 48
Sandakan, No. Borneo, 14,499 F 4 31
Sandanski, Bulgaria, 7,422 F 5 21
Sanday (island), Scotland, 866 L 1 11
Sandefjord, Norway, 6,302 C 4 13
Sandgate, Australia, 16,889 J 5 36
Sandikli, Turkey, 8,110 D 3 28
Sandomierz, Poland, 10,200 E 3 24
Sandoway, Burma B 3 30
Sandringham, Australia, 31,758 L 2 36
Sandstone, Australia, 59 B 5 36
Sandviken, Sweden, 18,784 K 6 13
Sandy (cape), Australia J 4 36
Sandy (lake), Canada M 4 40
Sangamner, India, 18,730 B 5 29
Sangerhausen, Germany, 16,220 D 3 14
Sanggau, Indonesia E 5 31
Sangju, Korea, 41,983 D 5 33
Sangkulirang, Indonesia F 5 31
Sangli, India, 37,756 B 5 29
Sangorodok, U.S.S.R. H 3 22
Sangre de Cristo (mts.), U.S. G 6 42
Sanjo, Japan, 46,646 J 5 33
Sankt Gallen, Switz., 68,011 H 2 19
Sankt Michel (Mikkeli), Finland, 18,655 P 6 13
Sankt Pölten, Austria, 40,203 C 2 20
Sankt Valentin, Austria, 7,134 C 2 20
Sankt Veit, Austria, 9,212 C 2 20
Sankuru (river), Belg. Congo L12 35
Sanlúcar de Barrameda, Spain, 28,741 C 4 17
Sanmaur, Quebec, 163 F 4 41
Sannicandro Garganico, Italy, 15,773 E 4 18
Sânnicolaul-Mare, Rum., 9,789 E 2 41
Sanok, Poland, 13,700 F 4 24
Sansanné-Mango, Togo, 11,000 G 9 34
Santa Ana, Bolivia, 2,225 G 6 46
Santa Ana, El Salvador, 51,702 C 4 39
Santa Bárbara, Honduras, 3,218 D 3 39
Santa Bárbara, Mexico, 14,808 F 3 44
Santa Barbara (channel), U.S. C 6 42
Santa Catalina (island), U.S. D 6 42
Santa Clara, Cuba, 53,981 E 2 48
Santa Cruz, Bolivia, 42,746 H 7 46
Santa Cruz (island), U.S. D 6 42
Santa Cruz (islands), Pacific, 5,000 G 6 37
Santa Cruz de la Palma, Canary Islands, Spain, 11,013 B 4 17
Santa Cruz de Tenerife,* Canary Islands, Spain, 103,446 B 4 17
Santa Elena, Ecuador, 2,764 O 4 46
Santa Fe, Argentina, 168,791 H10 47
Santa Inés (island), Chile F14 47
Santa Isabel,* Sp. Guinea, 11,261 H11 34
Santa Isabel (island), Pacific, 5,500 G 6 37
Santa Maria, Brazil, 45,907 K 9 47
Santa Maria Capua Vetere, Italy, 27,943 E 4 18
Santa Marta, Colombia, 37,005 F 1 46
Santa Rosa, Argentina, 14,623 H11 47
Santa Rosa, Ecuador, 4,672 E 4 46
Santa Rosa (island), U.S. C 6 42
Santa Rosa de Copán, Honduras, 6,417 C 3 39
Santa Vitória do Palmar, Brazil, 5,925 K10 47
Santa Tecla (Nueva San Salvador), El Salvador, 18,313 C 4 39
Santai, China, 70,000 F 5 32
Santander, Colombia, 4,421 E 3 46
Santander, Spain, †102,462 D 1 17
Santarém, Brazil, 14,061 J 4 46
Santarém, Portugal, 13,114 B 3 17
Santeramo in Colle, Italy, 19,360 F 4 18
Santiago,* Chile, 1,348,283 O10 47
Santiago, Dom. Rep., 56,192 D 5 48
Santiago, Mexico, 9,092 G 6 44
Santiago, Panama, 5,886 G 6 39

Index Ref. Plate No.

Santiago, Spain, 31,140...B 1 17
Santiago (mountains), U.S. ...H 7 42
Santiago (river), Mexico...G 6 44
Santiago de Cuba, Cuba, 118,266..J 4 48
Santiago del Estero, Arg., 60,039.H 9 47
Santipur, India, 29,892...E 4 29
Santo Amaro, Brazil, 12,265...N 6 46
Santo Ângelo, Brazil, 13,742...K 9 47
Santo Antônio, Brazil, 2,475...H 5 46
Santo António do Zaire, Angola, 528 ...J13 35
Santo Domingo (Ciudad Trujillo),* Dom. Rep., 181,533...E 6 48
Santos, Brazil, 206,920...L 8 47
São Antônio do Içá, Brazil...G 4 46
São Borja, Brazil, 11,971...J 9 47
São Francisco, Brazil, 3,108...M 7 46
São Francisco (river), Brazil...N 5 46
São Francisco do Sul, Brazil, 9,982 ...L 9 47
São João da Bôa Vista, Brazil, 15,837 ...L 8 46
São João de Meriti, Brazil, 44,146 ...M13 47
São João del Rei, Brazil, 25,228...M 8 46
São José do Rio Prêto, Brazil, 37,717 ...K 8 46
São Leopoldo, Brazil, 19,735...K 9 47
São Lourenço (river), Brazil...J 7 46
São Luís, Brazil, 81,432...M 4 46
São Mateus, Brazil, 3,060...N 7 46
São Paulo, Brazil, 2,041,716...L 8 47
São Paulo de Olivença, Brazil, 1,016 ...G 4 46
São Salvador, Angola, 2,965...J13 35
São Sebastião (island), Brazil, 1,815 ...M 8 47
São Tomé,* S.T. and Pr., 5,607...H11 35
São Tomé (island), S.T. and Pr., 55,827 ...H11 35
Saône (river), France...F 4 16
Saparua, Indonesia...H 6 31
Sapporo, Japan, 313,850...K 2 33
Saqqiz, Iran, 8,698...E 2 27
Sar-i-Pul, Afghan., 14,000...J 2 26
Sarab, Iran, 14,820...E 2 27
Saragossa, Spain, 264,256...F 2 17
Sarajevo, Yugoslavia, 135,657...D 4 21
Saransk, U.S.S.R., 90,000...F 4 22
Sarapul, U.S.S.R., 68,000...G 4 22
Saratov, U.S.S.R., 581,000...F 4 22
Saravane, Laos...E 4 30
Sardarshahr, India, 26,048...B 3 29
Sardinia (Sardegna) (island), Italy, 1,276,023...B 4 18
Sargodha, Pakistan, 78,447...B 2 29
Sari, Iran, 25,927...H 2 27
Sari Buri, Thailand, 7,112...D 4 30
Sarikamiş, Turkey, 17,566...K 2 28
Sarina, Australia, 1,983...H 4 36
Sariwŏn, Korea, 42,957...C 4 33
Sariyer, Turkey, 40,173...D 5 28
Sarnia, Ontario, 43,447...D 5 41
Sarnia, Greater, Ontario, 52,500..D 5 41
Sarny, U.S.S.R., 7,587...D 4 22
Saronno, Italy, 20,710...B 2 18
Sárospatak, Hungary, 13,213...F 2 20
Sarpsborg, Norway, 13,234...D 4 13
Sarreguemines, France, 12,876...G 3 16
Sasaram, India, 27,201...D 4 29
Sasebo, Japan, 194,453...D 7 33
Saskatchewan (river), Canada...K 4 40
Saskatoon, Saskatchewan, 72,858 ...J 4 40
Sassandra, Ivory Coast, 1,922 ...E11 34
Sassandra (river), Ivory Coast...E10 34
Sassari, Italy, 60,043...B 4 18
Sata (cape), Japan...E 8 33
Satadougou, Sudanese Rep., 1,291.D 9 34
Satara, India, 36,405...B 5 29
Satna, India, 11,575...D 4 29
Sátoraljaújhely, Hung., 15,272...F 2 20
Satpura (mountain range), India.B 4 29
Satu-Mare, Rumania, 46,519...F 2 21
Saugor, India, 63,933...C 4 29
Sault Sainte Marie, Ont., 37,329..D 4 41
Sault Sainte Marie, Greater, Ontario, 50,400...D 4 41
Saumarez (reef), Australia...J 4 36
Saumlaki, Indonesia...J 7 31
Saumur, France, 15,528...D 4 16
Sava (river), Yugoslavia...D 3 21
Savaii (island), Pacific, 21,000...J 7 37
Savanna la Mar, Jamaica, 4,046...B 3 45
Savannah (river), U.S. ...N 6 43
Savannakhet, Laos...E 3 30
Savant Lake, Ontario, 97...B 3 41
Savantvadi, India, 10,024...B 5 29
Savanur, India, 12,628...C 6 29
Savé, Dahomey, 5,128...G10 34
Saveh, Iran, 12,905...G 3 27
Săveni, Rumania, 6,470...H 1 21
Saverne, France, 8,218...G 3 16
Savona, Italy, 62,397...B 2 18
Savonlinna, Finland, 13,425...Q 6 13
Sawahlunto, Indonesia, 15,146...C 6 31
Sawankhalok, Thailand, 5,205...C 3 30
Say, Niger, 2,202...G 9 34
Sayaboury, Laos...D 3 30
Sayan (mountains), U.S.S.R. ...L 4 23
Sayram, U.S.S.R., 12,791...V 1 23
Sayula, Mexico, 10,090...H 7 44
Scarborough, England, 43,985...G 3 10
Sceaux, France, 8,320...A 2 16
Schaerbeek, Belgium, 119,080...C 9 15
Schaffhausen, Switz., 25,971...G 1 19
Scharmbeck, Germany, 12,059...C 2 14
Schefferville, Quebec...G 3 41
Scheveningen, Neth., 65,998...E 4 15
Schiedam, Netherlands, 77,383...E 5 15
Schiltigheim, France, 22,168...G 3 16
Schio, Italy, 19,466...C 2 18
Schleswig, Germany, 36,247...C 1 14
Schmalkalden, Germany, 12,663...D 3 14
Schneidemühl (Piła), Pol., 29,300.C 2 24
Schönebeck, Germany, 44,578...D 2 14
Schöneberg, Germany, 188,739...J 3 14
Schöningen, Germany, 15,583...D 2 14
Schorndorf, Germany, 13,813...C 4 14
Schramberg, Germany, 16,458...C 4 14
Schreiber, Ontario, 1,850...C 4 41
Schuler, Alberta, 188...H 4 40
Schumacher, Ontario, 3,002...D 4 41
Schwabach, Germany, 19,376...D 4 14
Schwandorf, Germany, 13,400...E 4 14
Schwaner (mountains), Indonesia.E 6 31
Schwaz, Austria, 8,911...A 3 20
Schweidnitz (Świdnica), Poland, 33,100 ...C 3 24
Schweinfurt, Germany, 46,140...D 3 14
Schwelm, Germany, 28,720...G 4 14
Schwenningen, Germany, 23,440...C 4 14
Schwerin, Germany, 88,164...D 2 14
Schwerte, Germany, 22,940...H 4 14
Schwetzingen, Germany, 14,068...C 4 14
Sciacca, Italy, 22,333...D 6 18
Scicli, Italy, 19,916...E 6 18
Scilly (islands), Eng., 2,194...A 8 10
Scone, Australia, 3,351...J 6 36
Scunthorpe, England, 54,255...G 4 10
Scutari (Shkodër), Albania, 33,852 ...E 5 21
Scutari (Üsküdar), Turkey, 69,671 ...D 6 28
Sea (islands), U.S. ...N 7 43
Seaham, England, 26,142...F 3 10
Seba, Indonesia...G 8 31
Sebeş, Rumania, 10,080...F 3 21
Sebha, Libya, †7,193...J 6 34
Şebinkarahisar, Turkey, 7,576...H 2 28
Sebnitz, Germany, 13,653...F 3 14
Secunderabad, India, 225,127...C 5 29
Sedan, France, 16,684...F 3 16
Sedel'nikovo, U.S.S.R., 570...J 4 22
See (means sea, lake) (Ger.)...
Segezha, U.S.S.R., 5,400...E 3 22
Segond (Luganville), New Hebrides ...G 7 37
Ségou, Sudanese Rep., 15,000...E 9 34
Segovia, Spain, †29,568...D 2 17
Séguéla, Ivory Coast, 3,543...E10 34
Sehore, India, 16,831...C 4 29
Seine (river), France...D 3 16
Sekadau, Indonesia...E 6 31
Sekondi, Ghana, 26,416...F11 34
Selb, Germany, 18,802...E 3 14
Selenga (river)...F 2 32
Sélestat, France, 10,225...G 3 16
Selkirk, Manitoba, 7,413...L 4 40
Selkirk (mountains), Canada...G 4 40
Sella, Libya, 2,450...K 6 34
Selsey Bill (prom.), England...G 7 10
Selukwe, S. Rhodesia, 1,001...M15 35
Semarang, Indonesia, 334,959...J 2 31
Sembiyam, India, 37,625...D 6 29
Seminoe (res.), U.S. ...G 4 42
Semiozernyy, U.S.S.R., 3,144...H 4 22
Semipalatinsk, U.S.S.R., 155,000...J 4 22
Semitau, Indonesia...E 5 31
Sena Madureira, Brazil, 1,799...G 5 46
Sendai, Japan, 341,685...K 4 33
Senegal (river)...D 8 34
Senftenberg, Germany, 17,783...F 3 14
Senhor do Bonfim, Brazil, 10,113.N 6 46
Senigallia, Italy, 20,600...D 3 18
Sennar, Sudan, 10,700...N 9 34
Senneterre, Quebec, 2,197...E 4 41
Sens, France, 17,184...E 3 16
Senta, Yugoslavia, 24,916...D 3 21
Seoni, India, 20,570...C 4 29
Seoul,* S. Korea, 1,446,019...C 5 33
Sept-Îles, Quebec, 5,592...G 3 41
Seraing, Belgium, 42,383...G 7 15
Serampore, India, 55,339...E 1 29
Serang, Indonesia, 11,163...G 1 31
Serangoon, Singapore, 10,481...F 6 30
Serdobol' (Sortavala), U.S.S.R., 13,000 ...E 3 22
Serdobsk, U.S.S.R., 18,616...F 4 22
Seremban, Malayan Fed., 35,274..D 7 30
Sergo (Kadiyevka), U.S.S.R., 180,000 ...M 1 23
Seria, Brunei...E 5 31
Serian, Sarawak...E 5 31
Sernyy Zavod, U.S.S.R., 1,812...G 5 22
Serov, U.S.S.R., 98,000...R 5 23
Serowe, Bech. Pr., 15,935...M16 35
Serpa, Portugal, 7,273...C 4 17
Serpents Mouth (strait), S.A. ...H 2 46
Serpukhov, U.S.S.R., 105,000...E 4 22
Serra (means mt. range) (Port.).
Serra do Navio, Brazil...K 3 46
Sérrai, Greece, 36,760...F 5 21
Sestao, Spain, 17,950...E 1 17
Sestroretsk, U.S.S.R. ...B 3 22
Sète, France, 29,914...E 6 16
Sétif, Algeria, 40,168...H 4 34
Setit (river), Africa...O 9 34
Seto, Japan, 45,752...H 6 33
Setúbal, Portugal, †44,235...B 3 17
Seul (lake), Canada...M 4 40
Sevastopol', U.S.S.R., 148,000...E 5 22
Seven Islands (Sept-Îles), Quebec, 5,592 ...G 3 41
Seventy Mile House, Br. Columbia, 25 ...F 4 40
Severn (river), Canada...C 3 41
Severn (river), England...E 6 10
Severnaya Zemlya (islands), U.S.S.R. ...M 1 23
Severo-Kuril'sk, U.S.S.R. ...S 4 23
Severo-Yeniseyskiy, U.S.S.R., 5,100 ...L 3 23
Severodvinsk, U.S.S.R., 79,000...E 3 22
Severoural'sk, U.S.S.R., 30,000...H 3 22
Sevier (lake), U.S. ...E 5 42
Sevier (river), U.S. ...E 5 42
Seville (Sevilla), Spain, †374,138.D 4 17
Sevlievo, Bulgaria, 9,856...F 4 21
Sèvres, France, 15,112...A 2 16
Sexsmith, Alberta, 345...G 3 40
Seychelles (islands), 34,632...J10 25
Seyhan (Adana), Turkey, 172,465.F 4 28
Seymchan, U.S.S.R. ...S 3 23
Sfantu Gheorghe, Rum., 14,224...G 3 21
Sfax, Tunisia, 54,637...J 5 34
Shadrinsk, U.S.S.R., 52,000...H 4 22
Shahat, Libya, 494...L 5 34
Shahjahanpur, India, 104,835...D 3 29
Shahriza, Iran, 24,138...H 4 27
Shahrud with Damghan, Iran, 17,837 ...J 2 27
Shajapur, India, 10,757...C 4 29
Shakhrisyabz, U.S.S.R., 14,200...H 6 22
Shakhty, U.S.S.R., 196,000...F 5 22
Shamo (Gobi) (desert)...G 3 32
Shamva, S. Rhodesia, 577...N15 35
Shan (means hill, mt. range)... (Chinese, Jap.)...
Shanghai, China, 6,204,417...K 5 32
Shangjao, China, 75,000...J 6 32
Shangkiu, China, 134,400...J 5 32
Shanhaikwan, China...K 3 32
Shannon (estuary), Ireland...B 6 12
Shannon (river), Ireland...E 6 12
Shaohing, China, 130,600...J 6 32
Shaoyang, China, 117,700...H 6 32
Shaqra, Saudi Arabia, 16,000...D 4 26
Sharasume (Altai), China...C 2 32
Shari (Chari) (river), Chad...K 9 34
Sharja,* Tr. Oman, 9,000...F 4 26
Shark (bay), Australia...A 5 36
Sharlyk, U.S.S.R., 4,577...G 4 22
Shasi, China, 85,800...H 5 32
Shasta (mountain), U.S. ...C 4 42
Shatt-al-Arab (river)...F 5 27
Shaulyay (Šiauliai), U.S.S.R., 60,000 ...D 4 22
Shaunavon, Saskatchewan, 1,959..J 5 40
Shawinigan, Quebec, 28,597...F 4 41
Shchelkovo, U.S.S.R., 12,330...B 3 22
Shcherbakov (Rybinsk), U.S.S.R., 181,000 ...E 4 22
Shchigry, U.S.S.R., 7,043...E 4 22
Shediac, New Brunswick, 2,173...H 4 41
Sheerness, England, 15,796...H 6 10
Sheet Harbour, Nova Scotia, 1,500 ...H 5 41
Shefar'am, Israel, 5,600...C 2 24
Sheffield, England, 512,850...F 4 10
Sheikh 'Othman, Aden Pr., 19,407 ...E 7 26
Sheikh Sa'id, Yemen, 1,000...D 7 26
Shelburne, Nova Scotia, 2,337...H 5 41
Shellbrook, Saskatchewan, 907...J 4 40
Shelter Bay, Quebec, 450...G 3 41
Shendi, Sudan, 15,050...N 8 34
Shenkursk, U.S.S.R., 2,536...F 3 22
Shenyang (Mukden), China, 2,299,900 ...K 3 32
Shepetovka, U.S.S.R., 14,693...D 4 22
Sherbro (island), Sierra Leone, 107,962 ...D10 34
Sherbrooke, Nova Scotia, 500...H 5 41
Sherbrooke, Quebec, 58,668...F 4 41
Sherridon, Manitoba, 1,500...K 3 40
Shetland (islands), Scotland, 19,352 ...M 3 11
Shibam, Aden Pr., 6,000...E 6 26
Shibarghan, Afghan., 22,464...H 2 26
Shiel (lake), Scotland...E 6 11
Shigatse, China...C 6 32
Shihr, Aden Pr., 11,000...E 7 26
Shikarpur, Pakistan, 45,376...A 3 29
Shikoku (island), Japan, 4,245,243.F 7 33
Shilka (river), U.S.S.R. ...N 4 23
Shillong, India, 38,192...F 3 29
Shimanovsk, U.S.S.R., 2,703...O 4 23
Shimizu, Japan, 88,472...J 6 33
Shimoga, India, 27,712...C 6 29
Shimonoseki, Japan, 193,572...E 6 33
Shin (lake), Scotland...G 3 11
Shindand (Sabzawar), Afghanistan, 12,500 ...H 3 26
Shingu, Japan, 33,827...H 7 33
Shinjo, Japan, 31,140...K 4 33
Shinko (Chinko) (river), Central Africa ...L10 34
Shipley, England, 32,585...F 4 10
Shirane (mountain), Japan...H 6 33
Shiraz, Iran, 129,023...H 6 27
Shire (river), Africa...N15 35
Shivpuri, India, 15,490...C 3 29
Shizuoka, Japan, 238,629...H 6 33
Shkodër (Scutari), Albania, 33,852 ...E 5 21
Shkotovo, U.S.S.R., 2,522...P 5 23
Shoal Lake, Manitoba, 751...K 4 40
Sholapur, India, 266,050...C 5 29
Shorapur, India, 11,836...C 5 29
Shrewsbury, England, 44,919...E 5 10
Shumen (Kolarovgrad), Bulgaria, 31,169 ...H 4 21
Shurab, U.S.S.R., 3,000...S 2 23
Shuri, Ryukyu Islands, 20,006...N 6 33
Shushenskoye, U.S.S.R., 3,104...L 4 22
Shushtar, Iran, 25,119...F 4 27
Shuya, U.S.S.R., 64,000...F 4 22
Shwebo, Burma, 13,590...F 2 30
Shwegyin, Burma...C 3 30
Shwenyaung, Burma...C 2 30
Si Kiang (river), China...H 7 32
Sialkot, Pakistan, 156,378...B 2 29
Siam (gulf)...D 5 30
Sian (Siking), China, 787,300...G 5 32
Siangtan, China, 183,600...H 6 32
Šiauliai, U.S.S.R., 60,000...D 4 22
Šibenik, Yugoslavia, 18,959...C 4 21
Siberut (island), Indonesia, 9,314.B 6 31
Sibiu, Rumania, 60,602...G 3 21
Sibolga, Indonesia, 10,765...B 5 31
Siborongborong, Indonesia, 3,076..B 5 31
Sibu, Sara., 9,983...E 5 31
Sicily (island), Italy, 4,486,749...D 6 18
Sicuani, Peru, 6,335...F 6 46
Sidcup and Chislehurst, England, 83,837 ...G 6 10
Siderno, Italy, 9,735...F 5 18
Sidērókastron, Greece, 7,754...F 5 21
Sidhpur, India, 24,565...B 4 29
Sidi Barrani, Egypt, 3,308...M 5 34
Sidi-bel-Abbès, Algeria, 72,985...F 4 34
Sidi Ifni,* Ifni Spain, 7,651...D 6 34
Sidlaw (hills), Scotland...K 7 11
Sidmouth (cape), Australia...G 2 36
Sidoardjo, Indonesia, 12,082...K 2 31
Sidon (Saida), Lebanon, 17,739...F 6 28
Sidra (gulf), Libya...K 5 34
Siedlce, Poland, 30,200...F 2 24
Siegburg, Germany, 27,076...B 3 14
Siegen, Germany, 38,787...B 3 14
Siemianowice Śląskie, Poland, 57,200 ...B 4 24
Siena, Italy, 40,722...C 3 18
Sieradz, Poland, 12,300...D 3 24
Sierning, Austria, 7,005...C 2 20
Sierpc, Poland, 10,100...D 2 24
Sierra (means mt. range) (Sp.)..
Sierra Nevada (mountains), U.S. .C 5 42
Sighet, Rumania, 18,329...F 2 21
Sighişoara, Rumania, 18,284...G 2 21
Sigli, Indonesia, 3,327...B 4 31
Siguiri, Guinea, 11,003...E 9 34
Sihanoukville (Kompong Som), Camb. ...D 5 30
Siirt, Turkey, 20,895...J 4 28
Sikar, India, 32,334...C 3 29
Sikasso, Sudanese Rep., 14,300...E 9 34
Sikhote-Alin' (mt. range), U.S.S.R. ...P 5 23
Siking (Sian), China, 787,300...G 5 32

Index Ref. / Plate No.

Silao, Mexico, 18,463 J 6 44
Silchar, India, 16,601 F 4 29
Siliguri, India, 10,487 E 3 29
Silistra, Bulgaria, 16,180 H 3 21
Silkeborg, Denmark, 23,372 F 8 13
Silva Porto, Angola, 32,754 K14 35
Silvânia, Brazil, 1,778 L 7 46
Silverton, Australia, 141 G 6 36
Simcoe, Ontario, 8,087 D 5 41
Simeulue (island), Indonesia, 19,302 A 5 31
Simferopol', U.S.S.R., 189,000 E 5 22
Simla, India, 18,348 C 2 29
Simleul-Silvaniei, Rumania, 7,931 F 2 21
Simonstown, Cape of G.H., 7,307 C19 35
Simpson (desert), Australia F 5 36
Sinabang, Indonesia B 5 31
Sinaia, Rumania, 6,537 G 3 21
Sincelejo, Colombia, 11,014 E 2 46
Sindangbarang, Indonesia H 2 31
Sing Buri, Thailand, 5,430 D 4 30
Singa, Sudan, 16,950 N 9 34
Singapore,* Singapore, 679,650 F 6 30
Singaradja, Indonesia, 12,345 F 7 31
Singen, Germany, 21,706 C 5 14
Singkang, Indonesia, 5,847 F 6 31
Singkawang, Indonesia, 7,127 D 5 31
Singleton, Australia, 4,506 J 6 36
Singora (Songkhla), Thailand, 17,842 D 6 30
Sinhailien, China, 207,600 K 5 32
Sining, China, 93,700 F 4 32
Sinj, Yugoslavia, 19,973 C 4 21
Sinnamary, Fr. Guiana, 1,373 K 2 46
Sinoia, S. Rhodesia, 1,465 M15 35
Sinsiang, China, 170,500 H 4 32
Sint-Niklaas, Belgium, 46,474 E 6 15
Sintang, Indonesia, 4,474 E 5 31
Sintra, Portugal, 7,150 B 3 17
Sinŭiju, Korea, 118,414 B 3 33
Siocon (Siokun), Phil. Is., 2,922 G 4 31
Sioux Lookout, Ontario, 2,504 B 3 41
Sir Edward Pellew (islands), Australia F 3 36
Siracusa (Syracuse), Italy, 67,224 E 6 18
Sirajganj, Pakistan, 37,545 E 4 29
Siret, Rumania, 8,058 G 1 21
Siret (river), Rumania H 2 21
Sirohi, India, 9,501 B 3 29
Sironj, India, 13,906 C 4 29
Sirsa, India, 20,718 C 3 29
Sirsi, India, 10,451 B 6 29
Sisak, Yugoslavia, 19,125 C 3 21
Sisaket, Thailand, 6,520 E 4 30
Sisophon, Cambodia D 4 30
Sitapur, India, 35,249 D 3 29
Sittard, Netherlands, 28,262 H 6 15
Sittingbourne and Milton, England, 21,904 H 6 10
Situbondo, Indonesia, 15,238 L 2 31
Sivas, Turkey, 66,350 G 3 28
Siverek, Turkey, 21,147 H 4 28
Sivrihisar, Turkey, 6,257 D 3 28
Siwa, Egypt, 878 M 6 34
Siwa (oasis), Egypt, 3,799 M 6 34
Sjö (means lake)(Nor., Swed.).....
Skagerrak (strait), Europe E 8 13
Skarżysko-Kamienna, Poland, 32,800 E 3 24
Skeena (river), Canada E 4 40
Skellefteå, Sweden, 14,065 M 4 13
Skerries (islands), Wales C 4 10
Skien, Norway, 15,006 F 7 13
Skierniewice, Poland, 20,800 D 2 24
Skive, Denmark, 14,497 F 8 13
Skopje (Skoplje), Yugoslavia, 91,557 E 5 21
Skövde, Sweden, 17,723 H 7 13
Skovorodino, U.S.S.R. O 4 23
Skye (island), Scotland, 8,267 D 5 11
Slagelse, Denmark, 19,184 G 9 13
Slaney (river), Ireland H 7 12
Slănic, Rumania, 6,495 H 3 21
Slatina, Rumania, 13,136 G 3 21
Slave (river), Canada H 2 40
Slavgorod, U.S.S.R., 4,420 E 4 22
Slavgorod, U.S.S.R., 18,000 J 4 22
Slavonski Brod (Brod), Yugoslavia, 21,547 D 3 21
Slavyanoserbsk, U.S.S.R., 3,170 N 1 23
Slavyansk, U.S.S.R., 83,000 H 1 23
Sliedrecht, Netherlands, 16,703 F 5 15
Slieve Aughty (mountains), Ireland D 5 12
Slieve Bloom (mountains), Ireland F 5 12
Sligo, Ireland, 12,947 E 3 12
Sligo (bay), Ireland D 3 12
Sliven, Bulgaria, 35,553 H 4 21
Slobodskoy, U.S.S.R., 18,600 G 4 22
Slobozia, Rumania, 7,714 H 3 21
Slocan, Br. Columbia, 326 G 5 40
Slough, England, 66,471 G 6 10
Słupsk (Stolp), Poland, 49,300 C 1 24
Slyne Head (cape), Ireland A 5 12
Smederovo, Yugoslavia, 15,455 E 3 21
Smidovich, U.S.S.R., 2,495 P 5 23
Smith, Alberta, 350 H 3 40
Smithers, Br. Columbia, 1,962 E 4 40
Smiths Falls, Ontario, 8,967 E 5 41
Smoky (river), Canada G 4 40
Smoky Hill (river), U.S. H 5 42
Smoky Lake, Alberta, 663 H 4 40
Smolensk, U.S.S.R., 146,000 E 4 22
Smooth Rock Falls, Ontario, 1,102 D 4 41
Smyrna (Izmir), Turkey, 246,619 B 3 28
Snaefell (mountain), Isle of Man C 3 10
Snake (river), U.S. D 3 42
Sneek, Netherlands, 19,881 H 2 15
Snow Lake, Manitoba, 300 K 4 40
Snowdon (mountain), England D 4 10
Snowdrift, N. W. Terr. H 2 40
Soalala, Malg. Rep., 673 P15 35
Sobrado, Brazil, 1,373 K 5 46
Sobral, Brazil, 23,003 M 4 46
Soc Trang, Vietnam, 13,736 E 5 30
Sochaczew, Poland, 15,000 E 2 24
Soche (Yarkand), China, 80,000 C 7 32
Sochi, U.S.S.R., 95,000 E 5 22
Society (islands), Pacific, 41,798 L 7 37
Socuellamos, Spain, 11,818 E 3 17
Söderhamn, Sweden, 11,514 K 6 13
Södertälje, Sweden, 25,266 G 1 13
Soë, Indonesia G 7 31
Soerabaja (Surabaja), Indonesia, 847,843 K 2 31
Soerakarta (Surakarta), Indonesia, 500,000 J 2 31
Soest, Germany, 28,939 C 3 14
Sofala (gulf), Mozambique O16 35
Sofia,* Bulgaria, 437,000 F 4 21
Sogamosa, Colombia, 5,216 F 2 46
Sogne (fjord), Norway D 6 13
Sohag, Egypt 43,234 N 6 34
Sohar, Oman, 7,000 G 5 26
Soissons, France, 18,901 E 3 16
Söke, Turkey, 21,465 B 4 28
Sokna, Libya, 1,250 K 6 34
Sokode, Togo, 3,666 G10 34
Sokolo, Sudanese Rep., 3,200 E 9 34
Sokoto, Nigeria, 47,643 H 9 34
Sol'-Iletsk, U.S.S.R., 11,096 G 4 22
Solbad Hall, Austria, 10,031 B 3 20
Solca, Rumania, 2,212 G 2 21
Solikamsk, U.S.S.R., 47,000 G 4 22
Solingen, Germany, 147,845 G 5 14
Solnechnogorsk, U.S.S.R., 14,600 A 4 22
Solo (Surakarta), Indonesia, 500,000 J 2 31
Solok, Indonesia 6,214 C 6 31
Solomon (isls.), Pacific, 139,232 F 6 37
Solothurn (Soleure), Switzerland, 16,743 E 2 19
Soltau, Germany, 14,560 C 2 14
Soluk, Libya, 2,500 L 5 34
Solway (firth), England D 3 10
Soma, Turkey, 9,924 B 3 28
Sombor, Yugoslavia, 26,586 D 3 21
Somerset (island) Canada D28 8
Somerset West, Cape of G. H. 5,041 D19 35
Son (river), India D 4 29
Son La, Vietnam D 2 30
Sŏnch'on, Korea, 22,725 B 4 33
Sönderborg, Denmark, 16,204 G 9 13
Sondershausen, Germany, 13,118 D 3 14
Sonepur (Sonpur Raj), India, 9,065 D 4 29
Song Cau, Vietnam F 4 30
Sŏngjin, Korea, 67,778 D 3 33
Songkhla, Thailand, 17,842 D 6 30
Sonneberg, Germany, 21,534 D 3 14
Sonpur Raj, India, 9,065 D 4 29
Sonsonate, El Salvador, 17,949 C 4 39
Soochow, China, 474,000 K 5 32
Sopot (Zoppot), Poland, 44,000 D 1 24
Sopron, Hungary, 40,391 D 3 20
Sora, Italy, 9,193 D 4 18
Sorata, Bolivia, 2,087 G 7 46
Sorel, Quebec, 16,476 F 4 41
Soria, Spain, †15,798 E 2 17
Sorocaba, Brazil, 68,811 L 8 47
Sorochinsk, U.S.S.R., 11,179 G 4 22
Sorong, Neth. N. G. J 6 31
Sorrenton, Italy, 7,947 E 4 18
Sorsogon, Philippine Islands, 9,971 G 3 31
Sortavala, U.S.S.R., 4,528 E 3 22
Sosnowiec, Poland, 124,200 B 4 24
Sos'va, U.S.S.R., 2,334 R 5 23
Sotteville, France, 18,271 D 3 16
Souillac, Mauritius, 1,905 S19 35
Souphlíon, Greece, 7,435 H 5 21
Souris, Manitoba, 1,759 K 5 40
Souris (river), U.S.-Canada H 2 42
Souris East, P.E.I., 1,449 H 4 41
Sousse, Tunisia, 36,566 J 4 34
South Branch, Newf., 200 J 4 41
South China (sea), Asia E 3 31
South Downs (hills), England G 7 10
South Junction, Manitoba, 250 L 5 40
South Melbourne, Australia, 37,995 L 2 36
South Orkney (islands) L16 47
South Platte (river), U.S. H 4 42
South Porcupine, Ontario, 5,618 D 4 41
South Ronaldsay (island), Scotland, 1,128 L 2 11
South Saskatchewan (river), Canada J 4 40
South Shetland (islands) J16 47
South Shields, England, 106,598 F 3 10
South Suburban, India, 104,055 E 2 29
South Uist (island), Scotland, 2,462 A 5 11
South West (cape), Tas., Australia G 8 36
Southampton, England, 178,343 F 7 10
Southampton, Ontario, 1,640 D 5 41
Southampton (island), Canada N 2 40
Southend-on-Sea, England, 151,806 H 6 10
Southern Cross, Australia, 625 B 6 36
Southern Indian (lake), Canada L 3 40
Southport, Australia, 8,134 J 5 36
Southport, England, 84,039 D 4 10
Sovetsk, U.S.S.R., 40,000 D 4 22
Sovetsk, U.S.S.R., 4,827 F 4 22
Sovetskaya Gavan', U.S.S.R. R 5 23
Soya (cape), Japan L 1 33
Spalato (Split), Yugo., 75,377 C 4 21
Spalding, Australia, 301 F 6 36
Spandau, Germany, 165,509 J 3 14
Spanish Town, Jamaica, 12,007 C 3 45
Sparta, Greece, 7,900 F 7 21
Spassk-Dal'niy, U.S.S.R., 23,000 P 5 23
Spencer (cape), Australia F 7 36
Spencer's (gulf), Australia F 6 36
Spennymoor, England, 19,784 F 3 10
Sperrin (mountains), Ireland G 2 12
Spey (river), Scotland K 4 11
Speyer, Germany, 31,841 C 4 14
Spezia, La, Italy, 105,301 B 2 18
Spirit River, Alberta, 743 G 3 40
Spišská Nová Ves, Czech., 18,017 F 2 20
Spittal, Austria, 8,682 B 3 20
Split, Yugoslavia, 75,377 C 4 21
Split Lake, Manitoba, 500 L 3 40
Spoleto, Italy, 21,659 D 3 18
Spremberg, Germany, 17,498 F 3 14
Springbok, Cape of G.H., 1,812 K17 35
Springdale, Newfoundland, 800 J 4 41
Springhill, Nova Scotia, 7,348 H 4 41
Springlands, Br. Guiana, 1,199 J 2 46
Springsure, Australia, 728 H 4 36
Spurn Headland (prom.), England H 4 10
Squamish, Br. Columbia, 1,292 F 5 40
Squinzano, Italy, 13,277 G 4 18
Sragen, Indonesia, 15,382 J 2 31
Srebrenica, Yugoslavia, 5,751 D 3 21
Sredne-Kolymsk, U.S.S.R., 2,000 S 3 23
Sredne-Ural'sk, U.S.S.R., 8,800 P 6 23
Śrem, Poland, 8,308 C 2 24
Sremska Mitrovica, Yugoslavia, 15,416 D 3 21
Sremski Karlovici, Yugo., 5,670 D 3 21
Sretensk, U.S.S.R., 12,800 N 4 23
Sri Ganganagar, India, 16,136 B 3 29
Srinagar,* Kashmir, 207,787 C 2 29
Środa, Poland, 12,100 C 2 24
Staaten (river), Australia G 3 36
Stade, Germany, 30,009 C 2 14
Stafford, England, 40,295 F 5 10
Stalin, Rumania, 82,984 G 3 21
Stalin (mountain), U.S.S.R. J 6 22
Stalin (Musala) (mountain), Bulgaria F 4 21
Stalinabad, U.S.S.R., 224,000 H 6 22
Stalingrad, U.S.S.R., 591,000 F 5 22
Staliniri, U.S.S.R., 22,000 F 5 22
Stalino, U.S.S.R., 701,000 K 1 23
Stalino, U.S.S.R., 10,206 U 2 23
Stalinogorsk, U.S.S.R., 107,000 E 4 22
Stalinsk, U.S.S.R., 377,000 O 6 23
Stalinskiy, U.S.S.R., 4,650 B 4 22
Stalinstadt, Germany, 15,000 F 2 14
Stalowa Wola, Poland, 21,400 E 3 24
Stalybridge, England, 22,541 F 4 10
Stanichno-Luganskoye, U.S.S.R., 3,139 P 1 23
Stanislav (Stanisławów), U.S.S.R., 66,000 D 5 22
Stanke Dimitrov, Bulg., 19,239 F 4 21
Stanley, Australia, 789 H 8 36
Stanley,* Falkland Islands, 1,252 J14 46
Stanley (falls), Belgian Congo M11 35
Stanleyville, Belg. Congo, 47,315 M11 35
Stanovoy (mt. range), U.S.S.R. O 4 23
Stanthorpe, Australia, 2,907 J 5 36
Stara Kanjiža (Kanjiža), Yugo., 12,404 D 2 21
Stara Zagora, Bulgaria, 37,057 G 4 21
Starachowice, Poland, 32,400 E 3 24
Staraya Lyalya, U.S.S.R., 708 P 5 23
Staraya Russa, U.S.S.R., 26,700 E 4 22
Stargard Szczeciński, Poland, 25,400 B 2 24
Starobel'sk, U.S.S.R., 13,973 E 5 22
Starogard Gdański, Poland, 15,081 D 2 24
Staroutkinsk, U.S.S.R., 5,900 P 6 23
Staryy Oskol, U.S.S.R., 26,697 E 4 22
Stassfurt, Germany, 29,762 D 3 14
Stavanger, Norway, 50,647 D 7 13
Stavropol', U.S.S.R., 140,000 F 5 22
Stawell, Australia, 5,463 G 7 36
Steep (point), Australia A 5 36
Steep Rock, Manitoba, 88 L 4 40
Steep Rock Lake, Ontario, 1,450 B 4 41
Stefăneşti, Rumania, 7,770 H 2 21
Steglitz, Germany, 153,747 J 3 14
Steinbach, Manitoba, 2,688 L 5 40
Stellenbosch, Cape of G.H., 15,292 D19 35
Stendal, Germany, 40,325 E 2 14
Stepanakert, U.S.S.R., 20,000 F 6 22
Stephenville, Newfoundland, 3,762 J 4 41
Stepnoy (Elista), U.S.S.R., 22,000 F 5 22
Stepnyak, U.S.S.R., 25,000 J 4 22
Sterlitamak, U.S.S.R., 111,000 G 4 22
Stettin (Szczecin), Poland, 237,600 B 2 24
Stettler, Alberta, 3,359 H 4 40
Stewart, Br. Columbia, 435 E 3 40
Stewart (cape), Australia F 2 36
Stewart (river), Canada C 2 40
Steyr, Austria, 36,818 C 2 20
Stikine (river), Canada D 3 40
Štip, Yugoslavia, 11,519 F 5 21
Stirling, Scotland, 26,962 D 1 11
Stockerau, Austria, 11,112 D 2 20
Stockholm,* Sweden, 745,936 G 1 13
Stockport, England, 141,650 E 4 10
Stockton-on-Tees, England, 74,155 F 3 10
Stoke-on-Trent, England, 275,115 E 4 10
Stolberg, Germany, 31,742 B 3 14
Stolp (Słupsk), Poland, 49,300 C 1 24
Stony Tunguska (river), U.S.S.R. L 3 23
Storm (bay), Tasmania, Australia H 8 36
Storozhevsk, U.S.S.R., 2,045 G 3 22
Stour (river), England H 6 10
Stourbridge, England, 37,247 E 5 10
Stralsund, Germany, 50,389 E 1 14
Strand, Cape of G.H., 8,676 D19 35
Strangford (bay), N. Ireland K 2 12
Strasbourg, France, 192,253 H 3 16
Strasbourg, Sask., 589 K 4 40
Stratford, New Zealand, 4,811 L 6 36
Stratford, Ontario, 19,972 D 5 41
Stratford-on-Avon, Eng., 14,982 F 5 10
Strathalbyn, Australia, 1,334 D 8 36
Strathfield, Australia, 25,829 L 3 36
Strathmore, Alberta, 727 H 4 40
Strathmore (valley), Scotland J 7 11
Strathroy, Ontario, 4,240 D 5 41
Strathy (point), Scotland H 2 11
Straubing, Germany, 36,147 E 4 14
Streaky (bay), Australia E 6 36
Streaky Bay, Australia, 652 E 6 36
Strehaia, Rumania, 7,776 F 3 21
Stretford, England, 61,532 E 4 10
Stromboli (island), Italy, 546 E 5 18
Stronsay (island), Scotland, 638 L 1 11
Stroud, England, 15,972 E 6 10
Struga, Yugoslavia, 5,243 E 5 21
Strumica, Yugoslavia, 10,649 F 5 21
Strzelce Opolskie, Poland, 10,800 D 3 24
Stuart (Alice Springs), Australia, 2,785 E 4 36
Stuarts (mt. range), Australia E 5 36
Stung Treng, Cambodia E 4 30
Sturgeon Falls, Ontario, 5,874 D 4 41
Stuttgart, Germany, 497,677 C 4 14
Suakin, Sudan, 6,900 O 8 34
Subang, Indonesia, 10,539 H 2 31
Subotica, Yugoslavia, 115,402 D 2 21
Suceava, Rumania, 10,123 G 2 21
Suchan, U.S.S.R., 40,000 P 5 23
Süchow, China, 373,200 J 5 32
Suck (river), Ireland E 5 12
Sucre,* Bolivia, 40,128 H 7 46
Sudau, Papua C 8 31
Sudbury, Ontario, 46,482 D 4 41
Sudbury, Greater, Ontario, 93,750 D 4 41
Sueca, Spain, 17,024 F 3 17
Suez, Egypt, 108,250 N 6 34
Sufi-Kishlak, U.S.S.R., 1,602 U 2 23
Suhl, Germany, 24,598 D 3 14

Index Ref. Plate No.
Suihwa, China, 36,000 L 2 32
Suir (river), Ireland G 7 12
Suita, Japan, 78,415 J 7 33
Suiteh, China G 4 32
Sukabumi, Indonesia, 34,191 G 2 31
Sukadana, Indonesia, 5,838 E 6 31
Sukamara, Indonesia E 6 31
Sukhothai, Thailand, 9,979 D 3 30
Sukhumi, U.S.S.R., 64,000 F 5 22
Sukkertoppen, Greenland, 933 F24 8
Sukkur, Pakistan, 77,057 A 3 29
Sulaiman (mt. range), Pakistan A 3 29
Sulaimaniya, Iraq, 41,114 D 3 27
Sulina, Rumania, 3,373 J 3 21
Sulisker (island), Scotland B 7 11
Sulitjelma (mountain), Norway K 3 13
Sullana, Peru, 21,159 D 4 46
Sulmona, Italy, 19,847 E 3 18
Sultan, Ontario, 125 D 4 41
Sulu (arch.), Phil. Is., 240,826 G 4 31
Sulu (sea), Asia E 4 31
Sulyukta, U.S.S.R., 10,078 R 2 23
Sumatra (island), Indonesia, 11,605,489 B 5 31
Sumba (Sandalwood) (island), Indonesia, 182,326 F 7 31
Sumbawa, Indonesia F 7 31
Sumbawa (island), Indonesia, 314,843 F 7 31
Sumburgh Headland (prom.), Scotland M 3 11
Sumedang, Indonesia, 12,448 H 2 31
Sumenep, Indonesia, 17,824 L 2 31
Summer (lake), U.S. C 4 42
Summerland, Br. Columbia, 3,567 F 5 40
Summerside, P.E.I., 7,272 H 4 41
Šumperk, Czech., 21,595 D 1 20
Sumy, U.S.S.R., 97,000 E 4 22
Sunbury, Australia, 2,385 K 1 36
Sunda (strait), Indonesia C 7 31
Sundarbans (swamp), India-Pakistan E 4 29
Sundbyberg, Sweden, 24,488 G 1 13
Sunderland, England, 181,524 F 3 10
Sundown, Manitoba, 600 L 5 40
Sundridge, Ontario, 697 E 4 41
Sundsvaal, Sweden, 25,775 K 5 13
Sungaipakning, Indonesia C 5 31
Sungapenuh, Indonesia C 6 31
Sungari (river), China M 2 32
Sungei Patani, Malayan Fed., 13,175 C 6 30
Sungurlu, Turkey, 7,739 F 2 28
Suoyarvi (Suojärvi), U.S.S.R. E 3 22
Supe, Peru, 2,180 E 6 46
Superior (lake), U.S.-Canada L 3 43
Suphan Buri, Thailand, 7,980 C 4 30
Sur (Tyre), Lebanon, 9,455 F 6 28
Surabaja, Indonesia, 847,843 K 2 31
Surakarta, Indonesia, 500,000 J 2 31
Surat, India, 223,182 B 4 29
Surat Thani, Thailand, 10,423 C 5 30
Surendranagar, India, 21,622 B 4 29
Suresnes, France, 31,775 A 2 16
Surigao, Philippine Is., 12,870 H 4 31
Surin, Thailand, 8,768 D 4 30
Sussex, New Brunswick, 3,403 G 4 41
Sutherland, Saskatchewan, 1,329 J 4 40
Sutlej (river), Pakistan B 2 29
Sutton, Quebec, 1,407 F 4 41
Sutton-in-Ashfield, England, 40,518 F 4 10
Suva,* Fiji Isls., 37,371 H 7 37
Suwa, Japan, 35,480 H 6 33
Suwałki, Poland, 18,800 F 1 24
Suweilih, Jordan, 5,070 D 3 24
Suwŏn, Korea, 42,173 C 5 33
Suzak, U.S.S.R., 4,050 H 5 22
Svendborg, Denmark, 23,069 G 9 13
Sverdlovsk, U.S.S.R., 777,000 P 6 23
Sveti Vrach (Sandanski), Bulgaria, 7,422 F 5 21
Svetozarevo, Yugoslavia, 10,007 E 4 21
Svilajnac, Yugo., 5,398 E 3 21
Svilengrad, Bulgaria, 9,918 G 5 21
Svir' (river), U.S.S.R. E 3 22
Svishtov, Bulgaria, 12,949 G 4 21
Svobodnyy, U.S.S.R., 57,000 O 4 23
Swain (reefs), Australia J 4 36
Swakopmund, S. W. Africa, 2,877 J16 35
Swale (river), England F 3 10
Swan Hill, Australia, 5,197 G 7 36
Swan River, Manitoba, 2,644 K 4 40
Swansea, Wales, 160,988 C 6 10
Swansea (bay), Wales C 6 10
Swatow, China, 280,400 J 7 32
Swellendam, Cape of G.H., 4,004 L19 35
Swidnica (Schweidnitz), Poland, 33,100 C 3 24
Świebodzin, Poland, 11,200 B 2 24
Świecie, Poland, 11,500 D 2 24
Świetochłowice, Poland, 58,300 B 4 24
Swift Current, Saskatchewan, 10,612 J 4 40
Swindon, England, 68,953 F 6 10
Sydney, Australia, 1,863,161 L 3 36
Sydney, Nova Scotia, 32,162 H 4 41
Sydney Mines, Nova Scotia, 8,731 H 4 41
Syktyvkar, U.S.S.R., 64,000 G 3 22
Sylhet, Pakistan, 32,773 F 4 29
Sylt (island), Germany C 1 14
Sylva, U.S.S.R., 4,428 P 6 23
Sylvan Lake, Alberta, 1,114 H 4 40
Syr-Dar'ya (river), U.S.S.R. H 5 22
Syracuse (Siracusa), Italy, 67,224 E 6 18
Syrian (desert), Asia A 4 27
Sýros, Greece, 16,971 G 7 21
Syzran', U.S.S.R., 148,000 F 4 22
Szamotuły, Poland, 11,000 C 2 24
Szarvas, Hungary, 25,023 F 3 20
Szczecin (Stettin), Poland, 237,600 B 2 24
Szczecinek, Poland, 19,800 C 2 24
Szczytno, Poland, 11,400 E 2 24
Szeged, Hungary, 93,746 E 3 20
Székesfehérvár, Hungary, 49,620 E 3 20
Szekszárd, Hungary, 16,933 E 3 20
Szentes, Hungary, 32,778 F 3 20
Szeping, China, 125,900 K 3 32
Szolnok, Hungary, 40,093 F 3 20
Szombathely, Hungary, 51,132 D 3 20
Szopienice, Poland, 54,100 B 4 24
Sztálinváros, Hungary, 27,507 E 3 20

T

Tabas, Iran, 8,116 K 4 27
Tabatinga, Brazil, 1,746 G 4 46
Tabelbala, Saoura, 1,009 F 6 34
Taber, Alberta, 3,688 H 5 40
Tábor, Czech., 16,975 C 2 20
Tabora, Tanganyika Terr., 12,768 N12 35
Tabou, Ivory Coast, 1,787 E11 34
Tabriz, Iran, 258,865 E 2 27
Tachikawa, Japan, 51,651 O 2 33
Tacloban, Philippine Is., 31,155 H 3 31
Tacna, Peru, 11,025 F 7 46
Tacuarembo, Uruguay, 18,000 J10 47
Tademait (plateau) G 6 34
Tadoussac, Quebec, 1,066 F 4 41
Taegu, Korea, 313,705 D 6 33
Taejŏn, Korea, 126,704 C 5 33
Taganrog, U.S.S.R., 201,000 E 5 22
Tagant (region), Mauritania, 41,000 D 8 34
Tagus (river) B 3 17
Tahan (mountain), Malayan Fed. C 5 31
Tahat (mountain), Oasis H 7 34
Tahiti (island), Pacific, 29,684 M 7 37
Tahoe (lake), U.S. C 5 42
Tahoua, Niger, 12,621 H 9 34
Tahuna, Indonesia H 5 31
Taichung, China, 249,946 K 7 32
Taif, Saudi Arabia, 15,000 D 5 26
Taimyr (Taymyr)(peninsula), U.S.S.R. M 2 23
Tainan, China, 287,797 J 7 32
Taipei,* China, 748,510 K 6 32
Taiping, Malayan Fed., 41,361 D 6 30
Taira, Japan, 42,891 K 5 33
Tais, Indonesia C 6 31
Taitao (peninsula), Chile E13 47
Taiwan (island), China, 8,212,213 K 7 32
Taiwan (strait), China R 7 32
Taiyiba, Israel, 6,103 C 3 24
Taiyüan, China), 720,700 H 4 32
Ta'izz, Yemen, 3,500 D 6 26
Tajo (Tagus) (river) D 3 17
Tak (Rahaeng), Thailand, 8,246 C 3 30
Takada, Japan, 36,255 J 5 33
Takamatsu, Japan, 124,545 G 6 33
Takaoka, Japan, 142,046 H 5 33
Takasaki, Japan, 92,964 J 5 33
Takatsuki, Japan, 43,321 J 7 33
Takawa, Japan, 100,071 E 7 33
Takayama, Japan, 42,823 H 5 33
Takeo, Cambodia E 5 30
Takingeun, Indonesia, 1,411 B 5 31
Taklamakan (desert), China B 4 32
Takoradi, Ghana, 17,734 F11 34
Talangbetutu, Indonesia C 3 31
Talara, Peru, 12,985 D 4 46
Talass, U.S.S.R. J 5 22
Talavera de la Reina, Spain, 21,228 D 2 17
Talbot (cape), Australia D 2 36
Talca, Chile, 55,059 F11 47
Talcahuano, Chile, 54,782 F11 47
Taldy-Kurgan, U.S.S.R., 41,000 J 5 22
Tali, China E 6 32
Talien (Dairen), China, 766,400 K 4 32
Tallinn (Tallin), U.S.S.R., 280,000 D 4 22
Taltal, Chile, 4,901 F 9 47
Tamale, Ghana, 16,164 F10 34
Tamanrasset, Oasis, 1,846 H 7 34
Tamar (river), England C 7 10
Tamatave, Malg. Rep., 39,843 S15 35
Tambacounda, Senegal, 3,766 D 9 34
Tambo, Australia, 481 H 4 36
Tambov, U.S.S.R., 170,000 F 4 22
Tambovka, U.S.S.R., 3,113 O 4 23
Tame, Colombia, 1,154 F 2 46
Tampere (Tammerfors), Finland, 119,250 N 6 13
Tampico, Mexico, 94,221 L 5 44
Tamrida,* Socotra, Aden Prot. J 8 25
Tamworth Australia, 13,641 J 6 36
Tana (lake), Ethiopia O 9 34
Tana (river), Europe P 1 13
Tanabe, Japan, 37,602 G 7 33
Tanahgrogot, Indonesia F 6 31
Tanana (river), U.S. F 8 42
Tananarive,* Malg. Rep., 187,330 R15 35
Tanda, India, 26,128 D 3 29
Tandil, Argentina, 32,309 J11 47
Tandjung, Indonesia F 6 31
Tandjungbalai, Indonesia, 6,823 C 5 31
Tandjungkarang, Indonesia C 7 31
Tandjungpandan, Indonesia, 15,708 D 6 31
Tandjungpinang, Indonesia, 5,789 C 5 31
Tandjungpriok, Indonesia H 1 31
Tandjungpura, Indonesia B 5 31
Tandjungredeb, Indonesia, 1,672 F 5 31
Tandjungselor, Indonesia, 1,991 F 5 31
Tando Adam, Pakistan, 21,260 A 3 28
Tanga, Tanganyika Terr., 20,619 O12 35
Tanganyika (lake), Africa N13 35
Tangerang, Indonesia G 1 31
Tangermünde, Germany, 16,480 E 2 14
Tangier, Morocco, 79,906 E 4 34
Tangshan, China, 693,300 J 4 32
Tanjong Katong, Singapore, 25,951 F 6 30
Tanjore, India, 100,680 C 6 29
Tannu (mountains), Asia D 1 32
Tanta, Egypt, 139,816 N 5 34
Tantan, Morocco, 877 D 6 34
Taonan, China, 56,315 K 2 32
Tapachula de Domínguez, Mexico, 29,990 N 9 44
Tapajós (river), Brazil J 5 46
Tapanshang, China J 3 32
Taquarí (river), Brazil J 7 46
Tara, U.S.S.R. J 4 22
Tarabulus (Tripoli), Lebanon, 59,001 F 5 28
Tarakan, Indonesia, 11,589 F 5 31
Taranto, Italy, 146,745 F 4 18
Taranto (gulf), Italy F 5 18
Tarare, France, 9,130 F 5 16
Tarawa (island), Pacific, 3,582 H 5 37
Tarbat Ness (prom.), Scotland J 4 11
Tarbes, France, 37,018 D 6 16
Taree, Australia, 7,408 J 6 36
Tarfaya, Morocco, 1,981 D 6 34
Târgovişte, Rumania, 26,038 G 3 21
Târgul-Frumos, Rumania, 4,665 H 2 21
Târgul-Jiu, Rumania, 17,698 F 3 21
Târgul-Mures, Rumania, 47,043 G 2 21
Târgul-Neamt, Rumania, 8,948 G 2 21
Târgul-Ocna, Rumania, 9,796 H 2 21
Târgul-Săcuesc, Rumania, 5,424 H 2 21
Tarija, Bolivia, 16,869 H 8 46
Tarim (river), China C 3 32
Tarkwa, Ghana, 7,840 F10 34
Tarlac, Philippine Is., 20,818 G 2 31
Tarma, Peru, 7,340 E 6 46
Tarnopol (Ternopol'), U.S.S.R., 52,000 D 5 22
Tarnów, Poland, 60,200 E 3 24
Tarnowskie Góry, Poland, 26,700 D 3 24
Taroom, Australia, 560 H 5 36
Taroudant, Morocco, 9,320 E 5 34
Tarragona, Spain, †36,807 G 2 17
Tarrasa, Spain, 54,949 G 2 17
Tarsus, Turkey, 39,622 F 4 28
Tartagal, Argentina, 8,539 H 8 46
Tartu, U.S.S.R., 74,000 D 4 22
Tarutung, Indonesia, 3,436 B 5 31
Taschereau, Quebec, 1,000 E 4 41
Tashauz, U.S.S.R., 37,000 G 5 22
Tashkent, U.S.S.R., 911,000 S 1 23
Tashkumyr, U.S.S.R., 3,198 V 2 23
Tashkurghan, Afghan., 20,000 J 2 26
Tashtyp, U.S.S.R., 2,667 L 4 22
Tasikmalaja, Indonesia, 25,605 H 2 31
Tasman (peninsula), Tas., Australia H 8 36
Tasman (sea), Pacific G 9 37
Tatabánya, Hungary, 40,268 E 3 20
Tatar (strait), U.S.S.R. R 5 23
Tatarsk, U.S.S.R. J 4 22
Tateyama, Japan, 37,291 K 6 33
Tatnam (cape), Canada M 3 40
Tatta, Pakistan, 9,716 A 4 29
Tatung, China, 228,500 H 3 32
Taunggyi, Burma C 2 30
Taung, Cape of G.H., 1,923 L17 35
Taunton, England, 33,620 D 6 10
Tauranga, New Zealand, 9,572 L 5 36
Taurianova, Italy, 17,212 E 5 18
Taurus (mountains), Turkey D 4 28
Tavani, N. W. Terr. M 2 40
Tavas, Turkey, 7,501 C 4 28
Tavastehus (Hämeenlinna), Finland, 26,723 O 6 13
Tavda, U.S.S.R., 25,266 H 4 22
Tavda (river), U.S.S.R. H 4 22
Tavira, Portugal, 7,496 C 4 17
Tavoy, Burma, 40,066 C 4 30
Tavşanli, Turkey, 9,702 C 3 28
Tawau, N. Borneo, 4,282 F 5 31
Taxco de Alarcón, Mexico, 10,023 K 7 44
Tay (firth), Scotland L 7 11
Tay (lake), Scotland H 7 11
Tay (river), Scotland K 7 11
Tay Ninh, Vietnam, 5,543 E 5 30
Tayga, U.S.S.R., 33,800 O 5 23
Taymyr (peninsula), U.S.S.R. M 2 23
Tayshet, U.S.S.R., 17,000 L 4 23
Taytay, Philippine Is., 506 G 3 31
Tayü, China H 6 32
Taza, Morocco, 28,457 F 5 34
Tbilisi, U.S.S.R., 694,000 F 5 22
Tczew, Poland, 30,900 D 1 24
Te Awamutu, New Zealand, 3,878 L 6 36
Te Kuiti, New Zealand, 3,781 L 6 36
Tébessa, Algeria, 18,293 H 4 34
Techirghiol, Rumania, 2,136 J 3 21
Tecuala, Mexico, 8,975 G 5 44
Tecuci, Rumania, 20,292 H 3 21
Tedzhen, U.S.S.R. G 6 22
Tees (river), England F 3 10
Tefé, Brazil, 2,220 H 4 46
Tegal, Indonesia, 43,015 J 2 31
Tegucigalpa,* Honduras, 72,385 D 3 39
Tehachapi (mountains), U.S. D 6 42
Tehran,* Iran, 554,372 G 3 27
Tehuacán, Mexico, 23,209 L 7 44
Tehuantepec, Mexico, 10,093 M 8 44
Teifi (river), England C 5 10
Tejo (Tagus) (river) C 3 17
Tekirdağ, Turkey, 17,804 B 2 28
Tel Aviv-Jaffa, Israel, 380,000 B 3 24
Tela, Honduras, 12,614 D 3 39
Telde, Canary Is., Spain, 22,675 B 5 17
Telefomin, Terr. N. G. A 7 31
Telegraph Creek, Br. Columbia, 75 D 3 40
Teles Pires (river), Brazil J 5 46
Tellicherry, India, 36,320 B 6 29
Teltow, Germany, 10,950 J 3 14
Teluk Anson, Malayan Fed., 23,055 D 6 30
Telukbajur, Indonesia C 6 31
Telukbetung, Indonesia, 25,170 D 7 31
Temassinin (Ft.-Flatters), Oasis, 6,992 H 6 34
Temir, U.S.S.R., 4,126 G 5 22
Temir-Tau, U.S.S.R., 54,000 J 4 22
Temora, Australia, 4,567 H 6 36
Tempelhof, Germany, 119,825 J 3 14
Temuco, Chile, 51,497 F11 47
Temuka, New Zealand, 2,254 L 7 36
Ten Thousand (islands), U.S. N 8 43
Tenali, India, 40,639 D 5 29
Tenasserim, Burma C 5 30
Tenggarong, Indonesia F 6 31
Tengiz (lake), U.S.S.R. H 4 22
Tenkodogo, Upper Volta, 6,047 G 9 34
Tennant Creek, Australia, 662 E 3 36
Tennessee (river), U.S. L 6 43
Tenterfield, Australia, 3,268 J 5 36
Teocaltiche, Mexico, 9,575 H 6 44
Teófilo Otôni, Brazil, 20,204 M 7 46
Tepa, Indonesia H 7 31
Tepatitlán, Mexico, 15,053 H 6 44
Tepic, Mexico, 24,595 G 6 44
Teplaya Gora, U.S.S.R., 2,400 P 5 23
Teplice, Czech., 37,940 B 1 20
Teramo, Italy, 25,984 D 3 18
Terek (river), U.S.S.R. F 5 22
Teresina, Brazil, 51,418 M 4 46
Terijoki (Zelenogorsk), U.S.S.R. B 3 22
Termez, U.S.S.R., 22,000 H 6 22
Termini Imerese, Italy, 24,978 D 6 18
Ternate, Indonesia, 7,126 H 5 31
Terni, Italy, 53,163 D 3 18
Ternopol', U.S.S.R., 52,000 D 5 22
Terrace, Br. Columbia, 1,473 E 4 40
Terracina, Italy, 17,474 F 7 18

Index Ref. Plate No.

Terranova di Sicilia (Gela), Italy, 43,326 E 6 18
Teruel, Spain, †18,745 F 2 17
Teschen (Ceský Těšín), Czech., 14,243 E 2 20
Teschen (Cieszyn), Poland, 22,000 D 4 24
Teslin, Yukon D 2 40
Teslin (lake), Canada D 3 40
Tete, Mozambique, 2,733 N15 35
Tetovo, Yugoslavia, 16,919 E 5 21
Tetuan, Morocco, 93,658 F 4 34
Tetyukhe, U.S.S.R. P 5 23
Tetyushi, U.S.S.R., 8,500 F 4 22
Teulon, Manitoba, 634 L 4 40
Teziutlán, Mexico, 13,536 O 1 44
Tezpur, India, 11,879 F 3 29
Tha Chin, Thailand, 20,316 D 4 30
Thai Binh, Vietnam E 2 30
Thai Nguyen, Vietnam E 2 30
Thakhek, Laos E 3 30
Thale, Germany, 18,082 D 3 14
Thames, Mouth of (estuary), Eng. H 6 10
Thames (river), England H 6 10
Thames, New Zealand, 5,001 L 5 36
Thana, India, 29,751 B 7 29
Thangool, Australia, 165 J 4 36
Thanh Hoa, Vietnam E 3 30
Thar (desert), India B 3 29
Thargomindah, Australia, 108 G 5 36
Tharrawaddy, Burma, 8,326 C 3 30
Thaton, Burma, 18,220 C 3 30
Thayetmyo, Burma, 11,847 B 3 30
Thazi, Burma C 2 30
The Cheviot (mountain), England M 9 11
The Hague ('s Gravenhage),* Neth., 606,728 E 4 15
The Pas, Manitoba, 3,971 K 4 40
The Peak (mountain), England F 4 10
Thebes, Greece, 12,582 F 6 21
Thelon (river), Canada K 2 40
Theodore, Australia, 378 H 4 36
Thessalon, Ontario, 1,716 D 4 41
Thessalonikē (Salonika), Greece, 217,049 F 5 21
Thetford Mines, Quebec, 19,511 F 4 41
Thiers, France, 11,180 E 5 16
Thiès, Senegal, 35,000 C 9 34
Thionville, France, 21,009 G 3 16
Thomson (river), Australia G 4 36
Thonburi, Thailand, 194,185 D 4 30
Thongwa, Burma C 3 30
Thonon-les-Bains, France, 11,267 G 4 16
Thorn (Toruń), Poland, 96,000 D 2 24
Thornaby-on-Tees, England, 23,416 F 3 10
Thouars, France, 9,903 C 4 16
Thouin (cape), Australia B 4 36
Three Hills, Alberta, 1,095 H 4 40
Three Rivers (Trois-Rivières), Quebec, 50,483 F 4 41
Thu Daumot, Vietnam, 11,147 E 5 30
Thule, Greenland, 125 C25 8
Thun, Switzerland, 24,157 E 3 19
Thurles, Ireland, 6,363 F 6 12
Thursday (island), Australia G 2 36
Thysville, Belg. Congo, 5,026 K13 35
Tiaret, Algeria, 22,344 G 4 34
Tibagi, Brazil, 1,444 L 8 47
Tiber (Tevere) (river), Italy D 3 18
Tiberias, Israel, 19,000 C 2 24
Tibet (plateau), China C 5 32
Tibooburra, Australia, 138 G 5 36
Tichitt, Mauritania, 3,100 E 8 34
Ticul, Mexico, 10,326 P 6 44
Tidjikja, Mauritania, 5,700 D 8 34
Tiehling, China, 52,945 K 3 32
Tien Shan (mt. range), China A 3 32
Tien Yen, Vietnam E 2 30
Tienen (Tirlemont), Belgium, 22,587 F 7 15
Tienshui, China, 63,000 F 5 32
Tientsin, China, 2,693,831 J 4 32
Tierra Blanca, Mexico, 12,012 L 7 44
Tierra del Fuego (isl.), S.A. G14 47
Tietê (river), Brazil L 8 46
Tiflis (Tbilisi), U.S.S.R., 694,000 F 5 22
Tigre, Arg., 24,809 O11 47
Tigre (river), Peru E 4 46
Tigris (river) E 3 26
Tihwa (Urumchi), China, 140,700 C 3 32
Tijuana, Mexico, 60,740 A 1 44
Tikhoretsk, U.S.S.R., 34,700 E 5 22
Tikhvin, U.S.S.R., 16,400 E 4 22
Tiksi, U.S.S.R. O 2 23
Tilburg, Netherlands, 131,277 G 5 15
Tilemsi (valley), Sudanese Rep. G 8 34
Tilichiki, U.S.S.R., 164 T 3 23
Tillabéri, Niger, 1,008 G 9 34
Tilsit (Sovetsk), U.S.S.R., 40,000 D 4 22
Timagami, Ontario, 500 D 4 41
Timaru, New Zealand, †24,695 L 7 36
Timbuktu, Sudanese Rep., 7,000 F 8 34
Timimoun, Saoura, 5,683 F 6 34
Timiskaming (lake), Canada E 4 41
Timiskaming Station, Quebec, 2,668 E 4 41
Timişoara, Rumania, 111,987 E 3 21
Timmins, Ontario, 27,551 D 4 41
Timor (island), Asia H 7 31
Tinaquillo, Venezuela, 5,458 G 2 46
Tindouf, Saoura, 1,412 E 6 34
Tinian (island), Pacific, 368 E 4 37
Tinnevelly (Tirunelveli), India, 60,676 C 7 29
Tipperary, Ireland, 4,790 E 7 12
Tiranë (Tirana),* Albania, 59,887 E 5 21
Tiraspol', U.S.S.R., 62,000 E 5 22
Tirat Karmel, Israel, 12,800 B 2 24
Tire, Turkey, 23,721 B 3 28
Tiree (island), Scotland, 1,216 C 7 11
Tiruchendur, India, 11,110 C 7 29
Tiruchirapalli, India, 218,921 C 6 29
Tirunelveli, India, 60,676 C 7 29
Tirupati, India, 20,143 C 6 29
Tiruppattur, India, 23,008 C 6 29
Tiruvannamalai, India, 33,575 C 6 29
Tisdale, Saskatchewan, 2,104 K 4 40
Tisul', U.S.S.R., 3,925 O 5 23
Tisza (river) E 3 21
Titagarh, India, 57,416 E 1 29
Titicaca (lake), S.A. F 7 46
Titograd (Podgorica), Yugoslavia, 16,333 D 4 21
Titov Veles, Yugo., 14,866 E 5 21
Titovo Užice, Yugoslavia, 13,268 D 4 21
Tivoli, Italy, 22,035 D 4 18
Tiv'on, Israel, 2,250 C 2 24
Tixtla, Mexico, 7,097 K 8 44
Tizi-Ouzou, Algeria, 4,700 G 4 34
Tiznit, Morocco, 6,476 D 5 34
Tjalang, Indonesia B 5 31
Tjepu, Indonesia, 21,861 J 2 31
Tjiamis, Indonesia, 13,864 H 2 31
Tjiandjur, Indonesia, 20,812 H 2 31
Tjidjulang, Indonesia H 2 31
Tjilatjap, Indonesia, 28,309 H 2 31
Tjimahi, Indonesia, 21,994 H 2 31
Tjirebon, Indonesia, 54,079 H 2 31
Tlalnepantla, Mexico, 10,332 L 1 44
Tlalpan, Mexico, 18,140 L 1 44
Tlaxiaco, Mexico, 8,229 L 8 44
Tlemcen, Algeria, 53,233 F 5 34
Tobata, Japan, 87,885 E 6 33
Tobelo, Indonesia H 5 31
Tobol (river), U.S.S.R. H 4 22
Tobol'sk, U.S.S.R., 32,200 H 4 22
Tobruk, Libya, 4,130 L 5 34
Tocantinópolis, Brazil, 3,736 L 5 46
Tocantins (river), Brazil L 5 46
Tochigi, Japan, 42,248 J 5 33
Tocopilla, Chile, 19,353 F 8 46
Todos-os-Santos (bay), Brazil N 6 46
Tofino, Br. Columbia, 389 E 5 40
Tokanui, New Zealand, 237 L 7 36
Tokat, Turkey, 26,716 G 2 28
Tokelau (Union) (islands), Pacific, 1,388 J 6 37
Tokmak, U.S.S.R., 19,431 J 5 22
Tokorosawa, Japan, 42,559 O 2 33
Tokushima, Japan, 121,416 G 7 33
Tokuyama, Japan, 70,987 F 6 33
Tokyo,* Japan, 5,385,071 O 2 33
Tolbukhin, Bulgaria, 31,049 H 4 21
Toledo, Spain, †38,136 D 3 17
Tolitoli (Kampung Baru), Indon. G 5 31
Tollygunge, India, 150,527 E 2 29
Toluca, Mexico, 52,789 K 7 44
Tölz, Germany, 12,786 D 5 14
Tomakomai, Japan, 39,226 L 2 33
Tomar, Portugal, 8,034 B 3 17
Tomari, U.S.S.R., 11,381 R 5 23
Tomaszów Mazowiecki, Poland, 45,000 E 2 24
Tomazina, Brazil, 967 K 8 47
Tombigbee (river), United States L 6 43
Tombouctou (Timbuktu), Sudanese Rep., 7,000 F 8 34
Tomelloso, Spain, 30,208 E 3 17
Tomini (gulf), Indonesia G 6 31
Tommot, U.S.S.R., 2,800 O 4 23
Tompkins, Saskatchewan, 399 J 4 40
Tomsk, U.S.S.R., 249,000 O 5 23
Tonalá, Mexico, 10,100 N 8 44
Tonbridge, England, 19,237 H 6 10
Tondano, Indonesia, 15,007 H 5 31
Tönder, Denmark, 7,031 F 9 13
Tonga (Friendly) (islands), Pacific, 46,870 J 7 37
Tongareva (Penrhyn) (isl.), Pacific, 654 L 6 37
Tongatapu (island), Pacific, 20,000 J 8 37
Tonk, India, 38,650 C 3 29
Tonkin (gulf) E 3 30
Tonle (lake), Cambodia D 4 30
Tönsberg, Norway, 12,211 D 4 13
Tontonicapán, Guat., 9,492 B 3 39
Toowoomba, Australia, †43,149 J 5 36
Top (lake), U.S.S.R. S 4 13
Torbay Head (cape), Australia B 7 36
Torgau, Germany, 18,455 E 3 14
Torino (Turin), Italy, 711,282 A 2 18
Torne (river), Sweden M 3 13
Tornio (Tornea), Finland, 5,085 O 4 13
Törökszentmiklós, Hung., 23,391 F 3 20
Toronto,* Ontario, 667,706 E 5 41
Toronto, Greater, Ont., 1,347,905 E 5 41
Toropets, U.S.S.R., 10,733 E 4 22
Torquay, England, 53,281 D 7 10
Torre Annunziata, Italy, 51,170 E 4 18
Torre del Greco, Italy, 54,677 E 4 18
Torredonjimeno, Spain, 14,833 D 4 17
Torremaggiore, Italy, 17,665 E 4 18
Torrens (lake), Australia F 6 36
Torrente, Spain, 12,856 F 3 17
Torreón, Mexico, 128,548 H 4 44
Torres (strait) G 2 36
Tôrres Novas, Port., 7,291 B 3 17
Tórshavn,* Faeroe Isls., 4,390 D 2 9
Tortona, Italy, 17,496 B 2 18
Tortorici, Italy, 2,443 E 6 18
Tortosa, Spain, 15,150 G 2 17
Tortuga, La (island), Ven. G 1 46
Toruń (Thorn), Poland, 96,000 D 2 24
Tory (island), Ireland E 1 12
Tosno, U.S.S.R., 13,000 D 2 22
Tosya, Turkey, 11,963 F 2 28
Tot'ma, U.S.S.R., 10,000 F 3 22
Totness, Surinam, 1,019 J 2 46
Tottenham, Australia, 527 H 6 36
Tottori, Japan, 61,721 G 6 33
Touggourt, Oasis, 17,305 H 5 34
Toul, France, 8,971 F 3 16
Toulon, France, 125,572 F 6 16
Toulouse, France, 268,863 D 6 16
Toungoo, Burma, 25,960 B 3 30
Tourane (Da Nang), S .Vietnam, 50,900 E 3 30
Tourcoing, France, 73,772 E 2 16
Tournai (Doornik), Belg., 33,326 C 7 15
Tours, France, 80,261 D 4 16
Touws River, C. of G.H., 2,411 L18 35
Townsville, Australia, †40,471 H 3 36
Towy (river), England D 6 10
Toy-Tyube, U.S.S.R., 2,453 T 1 23
Toyama, Japan, 154,484 H 5 33
Toyanaka, Japan, 86,203 J 7 33
Toyohara (Yuzhno-Sakhalinsk), U.S.S.R., 86,000 R 5 23
Toyohashi, Japan, 145,855 H 6 33
Toyooka, Japan, 31,677 G 6 33
Tozeur, Tunisia, 12,464 H 5 34
Tra Vinh, Vietnam, 7,069 E 5 30
Trabzon, Turkey, 42,273 H 2 28
Tracadie, New Brunswick, 1,500 H 4 41
Traiguén, Chile, 8,829 F11 47
Trail, Br. Columbia, 11,395 G 5 40
Tralee, Ireland, 10,928 B 7 12
Tralee (bay), Ireland B 7 12
Trang, Thailand, 8,622 C 6 30
Trani, Italy, 33,204 F 4 18
Tranquebar, India, 11,111 D 6 29
Transcona, Manitoba, 8,312 L 5 40
Trans-Himalayas (mt. range), Tibet, China C 5 32
Transylvanian Alps (mt. range), Rumania F 3 21
Trapani, Italy, 64,945 D 5 18
Traun, Austria, 9,648 C 2 20
Traunstein, Germany, 14,611 E 5 14
Trautenau (Trutnov), Czech., 14,244 D 1 20
Travnik, Yugoslavia, 8,132 C 3 21
Trbovlje, Yugoslavia, 16,595 B 2 21
Trebíč, Czech., 19,149 C 2 20
Trebizond (Trabzon), Turkey, 42,273 H 2 28
Treherne, Manitoba, 551 L 5 40
Treinta y Tres, Uruguay, 18,500 K10 47
Trelleborg, Sweden, 17,126 H 9 13
Tremadoc (bay), Wales C 5 10
Trenčín, Czech., 22,970 E 2 20
Trenggalek, Indonesia, 8,571 K 2 31
Trenque Lauquen, Arg., 10,671 H11 47
Trent (river), England G 4 10
Trento, Italy, 39,287 C 1 18
Trenton, N.S., 3,240 H 4 41
Trenton, Ontario, 11,492 E 5 41
Treptow, Germany, 108,035 J 3 14
Tres Arroyos, Argentina, 29,996 J11 47
Três Lagoas, Brazil, 7,730 K 8 46
Tres Puntas (cape), Argentina H13 47
Trèves (Trier), Germany, 75,526 B 4 14
Treviglio, Italy, 17,031 B 2 18
Treviso, Italy, 52,988 D 2 18
Trichinopoly (Tiruchirapalli), India, 218,921 C 6 29
Trichur, India, 57,524 C 6 29
Trier (Trèves), Germany, 75,526 B 4 14
Trieste, Italy, 269,543 B 3 21
Triglav (mountain), Yugoslavia A 2 21
Tríkkala, Greece, 23,385 E 6 21
Trincomalee, Ceylon, 29,146 D 7 29
Třinec, Czech., 14,716 E 2 20
Trinidad, Bolivia, 8,695 H 6 46
Trinidad, Cuba, 15,453 E 2 48
Trinidad, Uruguay, 18,700 J10 47
Trinity, Newfoundland, 800 K 4 41
Trinity (bay), Australia H 3 36
Trinity (river), U.S. K 7 43
Tripoli (Tarabulus), Lebanon, 59,001 F 5 28
Tripoli,* Libya, 128,714 J 5 34
Trípolis, Greece, 17,585 F 7 21
Trivandrum, India, 186,931 C 7 29
Trnava, Czech., 32,507 D 2 20
Trois-Pistoles, Quebec, 4,039 G 4 41
Trois-Rivières (Three Rivers), Quebec, 50,483 F 4 41
Troitsk, U.S.S.R., 76,000 H 4 22
Troitsko-Pechorsk U.S.S.R., 558 C 3 22
Troitskoye, U.S.S.R., 2,171 O 5 23
Trollhättan, Sweden, 21,143 H 7 13
Tromsö, Norway, 10,990 L 2 13
Trondheim, Norway, 56,669 F 5 13
Trondheims (fjord), Norway G 5 13
Troon, Scotland, 10,063 G 8 11
Tropic of Cancer E 4 6
Tropic of Capricorn O 7 6
Troppau (Opava), Czech., 42,308 E 2 20
Trou-du-Nord, Haiti, 2,918 C 5 48
Trout (lake), Canada F 2 40
Trouville, France, 6,781 C 3 16
Troyes, France, 57,089 F 3 16
Trujillo, Honduras, 3,016 E 3 39
Trujillo, Peru, 36,958 E 5 46
Trujillo, Venezuela, 11,773 F 2 46
Truk (islands), Pacific, 10,252 F 5 37
Truro, Australia, 291 F 6 36
Truro, England, 12,860 C 7 10
Truro, N.S., 12,250 H 4 41
Trutnov, Czech., 22,703 D 1 20
Tsaidam (marsh), China E 4 32
Tsamkong, China, 166,000 H 7 32
Tsangpo (river), China C 6 32
Tsentral'nyy, U.S.S.R. O 5 23
Tsesis (Cēsis), U.S.S.R., 8,748 D 4 22
Tshikapa, Belg. Congo, 21,631 L13 35
Tsinan, China, 680,100 J 4 32
Tsingkiang, China, 77,000 J 5 32
Tsingtao, China, 916,800 K 4 32
Tsining, China, 86,200 J 4 32
Tsitsihar, China, 344,700 K 2 32
Tsu, Japan, 76,077 H 6 33
Tsu (islands), Japan, 67,140 D 6 33
Tsuchiura, Japan, 62,246 J 5 33
Tsumeb, S.W. Africa, 931 K15 35
Tsunyi, China, 97,500 G 6 32
Tsuruga, Japan, 31,092 G 6 33
Tsuruoka, Japan, 44,019 J 4 33
Tsushima (strait), Japan D 7 33
Tsuyama, Japan, 51,645 F 6 33
Tual, Indonesia J 7 31
Tuamotu (arch.), Pacific Ocean, 6,138 M 7 37
Tuapse, U.S.S.R., 29,600 E 5 22
Tuban, Indonesia, 23,285 K 2 31
Tubarão, Brazil, 11,947 L 9 47
Tübingen, Germany, 37,506 C 4 14
Tubuai (Austral) (islands), Pacific, 3,915 L 8 37
Tucumán, Argentina, 194,166 H 9 47
Tucupita, Venezuela, 8,546 H 2 46
Tudela, Spain, 12,449 F 1 17
Tufi, Papua C 7 31
Tuguegarao, Phil. Is., 12,378 G 2 31
Tukums, U.S.S.R., 8,144 D 4 22
Tula, U.S.S.R., 345,000 E 4 22
Tulancingo, Mexico, 18,529 K 7 44
Tulare (lake), United States C 6 42
Tulcán, Ecuador, 10,658 E 3 46
Tulcea, Rumania, 21,642 J 3 21
Tuléar, Malg. Rep., 12,004 P16 35
Tulkarm, Jordan, 21,872 C 3 24
Tullamore, Ireland, 6,147 G 5 12
Tulle, France, 15,813 D 5 16
Tully, Australia, 2,808 H 3 36
Tuluá, Colombia, 12,017 E 3 46
Tulun, U.S.S.R., 30,000 M 4 23
Tulungagung, Indon., 31,767 K 2 31
Tumaco, Colombia, 12,692 E 3 46
Tumbarumba, Australia, 1,293 H 7 36
Tumbes, Peru, 6,172 D 4 46
Tumkur, India, 21,893 C 6 29
Tunbridge Wells, England, 38,400 H 6 10
Tunghwa, China, 129,100 L 3 32
Tungkiang, China, 96,652 M 2 32
Tungliao, China, 44,110 K 3 32
Tungting (lake), China H 6 32

Index Ref. Plate No.

Tunguska, Lower (river), U.S.S.R. ... L 3 23
Tunguska, Stony (river), U.S.S.R. ... L 3 23
Tunguska, Upper (river), U.S.S.R. L 4 23
Tuni, India, 13,060 ... D 5 29
Tunis,* Tunisia, 364,593 ... J 4 34
Tunja, Colombia, 23,008 ... F 2 46
Tupiza, Bolivia, 8,248 ... G 8 46
Tura, U.S.S.R. ... L 3 23
Turbat-i-Haidari, Iran, 20,457 ... L 3 27
Turbat-i-Shaikh Jam, Iran, 5,520 M 3 27
Turbo, Colombia, 2,636 ... E 2 46
Turda, Rumania, 25,905 ... G 2 21
Turen, Indonesia ... K 2 31
Turfan, China ... C 3 32
Tŭrgovishte, Bulgaria, 10,505 ... H 4 21
Turgutlu, Turkey, 27,424 ... B 3 28
Turhal, Turkey, 13,228 ... F 2 28
Turin, Italy, 711,282 ... A 2 18
Turkestan, U.S.S.R., 44,000 ... H 5 22
Túrkeve, Hungary, 13,626 ... F 3 20
Turku (Åbo), Finland, 117,464 ... N 6 13
Turnhout, Belgium, 34,488 ... F 6 15
Tŭrnovo, Bulgaria, 16,182 ... G 4 21
Turnu-Măgurele, Rumania, 11,493 ... G 4 21
Turnu-Severin, Rumania, 31,296 ... F 3 21
Turrialba, Costa Rica, 5,449 ... F 6 39
Turtkul', U.S.S.R., 19,600 ... H 5 22
Turtleford, Saskatchewan, 367 ... J 4 40
Tushino, U.S.S.R., 90,000 ... B 4 22
Tuticorin, India, 75,614 ... C 7 29
Tutrakan, Bulgaria, 7,203 ... H 4 21
Tuttlingen, Germany, 21,271 ... C 5 14
Tutuila (island), Pacific, 15,556 ... K 7 37
Tuwaiq (mountain range), Saudi Arabia ... E 5 26
Tuxpan (Jalisco), Mex., 8,206 ... H 7 44
Tuxpan (Nayarit), Mex., 11,642 ... G 6 44
Tuxpan (Veracruz), Mex., 16,096 ... L 6 44
Tuxtla Gutiérrez, Mex., 28,243 ... N 8 44
Tuyen Quang, Vietnam ... E 2 30
Tuzla, Yugoslavia, 31,227 ... D 3 21
Tver (Kalinin), U.S.S.R., 261,000 ... E 4 22
Tweed, Ontario, 1,634 ... E 5 41
Tweed (river), Scotland ... M 8 11
Twillingate, Newfoundland, 2,100 ... K 4 41
Two Wells, Australia, 387 ... D 7 36
Tychy, Poland, 31,200 ... B 4 24
Tyne (river), England ... F 3 10
Tynemouth, England, 66,564 ... F 2 10
Tyre (Sur), Lebanon, 9,455 ... F 6 28
Tyrrhenian (sea), Italy ... C 4 18
Tyumen', U.S.S.R., 150,000 ... H 4 22
Tyurya-Kurgan, U.S.S.R., 1,260 ... U 2 23
Tzekung, China, 291,300 ... F 6 32
Tzepo, China, 184,200 ... J 4 32

U

Ubangi (river), Africa ... K12 35
Ube, Japan, 128,569 ... E 6 33
Ubeda, Spain, 28,611 ... E 3 17
Uberaba, Brazil, 43,915 ... L 7 46
Ubon, Thailand, 9,690 ... E 4 30
Ubsa (lake), Mon. Republic ... D 1 32
Ucayali (river), Peru ... E 5 46
Uccle (Ukkel), Belgium, 66,410 ... B 9 15
Uch-Kurgan, U.S.S.R., 4,422 ... V 2 23
Uckermünde, Germany, 11,177 ... E 2 14
Udaipur, India, 59,648 ... B 4 29
Uddevalla, Sweden, 24,922 ... G 7 13
Udine, Italy, 65,199 ... D 1 18
Udipi, India, 18,043 ... B 6 29
Udon Thani, Thailand, 11,995 ... D 3 30
Ueda, Japan, 51,572 ... J 5 33
Uele (river), Belgian Congo ... L11 34
Uelen, U.S.S.R. ... V 3 23
Uelzen, Germany, 23,666 ... D 2 14
Ufa, U.S.S.R., 546,000 ... G 4 22
Uglegorsk, U.S.S.R., 35,115 ... R 5 23
Uherské Hradiště, Czech., 10,884 D 2 20
Uige (Carmona), Angola, 1,474 ... K13 35
Ŭiju (Gishu), Korea, 27,378 ... B 3 33
Uitenhage, C. of G.H., 38,724 ... M18 35
Ujfehértó, Hungary, 15,154 ... F 3 20
Ujiji, Tanganyika Terr., 25,000 ... N12 35
Ujjain, India, 129,959 ... C 4 29
Újpest, Hungary, 68,530 ... E 3 20
Ukhta, U.S.S.R. ... G 3 22
Ulan Bator,* Mon. Rep., 100,000 G 2 32
Ulan-Ude, U.S.S.R., 174,000 ... M 4 23
Ulanhot, China, 51,400 ... K 2 32
Uleåborg (Oulu), Finland, 51,073 O 4 13
Ulee Lheue, Indonesia, 626 ... A 4 31
Uliassutai, Mon. Rep., 6,000 ... E 2 32
Ulm, Germany, 71,132 ... C 4 14
Ulverstone, Australia, 5,005 ... H 8 36
Ul'yanovka, U.S.S.R., 3,732 ... D 2 22
Ul'yanovsk, U.S.S.R., 205,000 ... F 4 22
Ume (river), Sweden ... L 4 13
Umeå, Sweden, 17,113 ... M 5 13
Umm el Fahm, Israel, 6,114 ... C 2 28
Umrer, India, 19,361 ... C 4 29
Umtali, S. Rhodesia, 17,170 ... N15 35
Umtata, C. of G.H., 9,163 ... M18 35
Unao (Unnao), India, 20,107 ... D 3 29
Uncía, Bolivia, 4,507 ... G 7 46
Ungava (bay), Canada ... G 2 41
Ungvár (Uzhgorod), U.S.S.R., 47,000 ... D 5 22
Union (Tokelau) (islands), Pacific, 1,388 ... J 6 37
Unity, Saskatchewan, 1,607 ... J 4 40
Unley, Australia, 40,077 ... D 8 36
Unna, Germany, 26,332 ... B 3 14
Unnao, India, 20,107 ... D 3 29
Unst (island), Scotland, 1,101 ... N 2 11
Upernavik, Greenland, 321 ... D24 8
Upington, C. of G.H., 10,122 ... L17 35
Upolu (island), Pacific, 54,000 ... J 7 37
Upper Erne (lake), Ireland ... F 3 12
Upper Hutt, New Zealand, 12,226 ... L 6 36
Upper Klamath (lake), U.S. ... C 4 42
Upper Tunguska (river), U.S.S.R. L 4 23
Uppsala, Sweden, 63,072 ... L 7 13
Upsala, Ontario, 190 ... C 4 41
Ura-Tyube, U.S.S.R., 24,300 ... P 1 23
Ural (mountain range), U.S.S.R. ... C 3 22
Ural (river), U.S.S.R. ... G 5 22
Ural'sk, U.S.S.R., 105,000 ... G 4 22
Uranium City, Sask, 1,794 ... J 3 40
Uraricuera (river), Brazil ... H 3 46
Urawa, Japan, 115,019 ... O 2 33
Urda, U.S.S.R., 4,282 ... F 5 22
Ure (river), England ... F 3 10
Urfa, Turkey, 48,013 ... H 4 28
Urga (Ulan Bator),* Mon. Rep., 100,000 ... G 2 32
Urgench, U.S.S.R., 43,000 ... H 5 22
Urla, Turkey, 10,969 ... B 3 28
Urlati, Rumania, 6,661 ... H 3 21
Urmia (Reza'iyeh), Iran, 50,171 ... D 2 27
Urmia (lake), Iran ... D 2 27
Uruapan, Mexico, 31,420 ... H 7 44
Uruguaiana, Brazil, 32,639 ... J 9 47
Uruguay (river), S.A. ... J 9 47
Urumchi, China, 140,700 ... C 3 32
Urup (island), U.S.S.R. ... S 5 23
Uryupinsk, U.S.S.R., 14,409 ... F 4 22
Urziceni, Rumania, 4,425 ... H 3 21
Usa (river), U.S.S.R. ... H 3 22
Uşak, Turkey, 23,366 ... C 3 28
Usakos, S.W. Africa, 2,389 ... K16 35
Ushuaia, Argentina, 2,198 ... G14 47
Üsküb (Skopje), Yugo., 91,557 ... E 5 21
Üsküdar, Turkey, 88,599 ... D 6 28
Usman', U.S.S.R., 13,456 ... E 4 22
Usol'ye-Sibirskoye, U.S.S.R. ... M 4 23
Uspenka, U.S.S.R., 3,680 ... P 1 23
Ussuri (river), Asia ... P 5 23
Ussuriysk, U.S.S.R., 104,000 ... P 5 23
Ust'-Kamenogorsk, U.S.S.R., 117,000 ... K 4 22
Ust'-Koksa, U.S.S.R., 360 ... K 4 22
Ust'-Kulom, U.S.S.R., 2,479 ... G 3 22
Ust'-Ordynskiy, U.S.S.R. ... M 4 23
Ust'-Tsil'ma, U.S.S.R., 3,264 ... G 3 22
Ust'-Urt (plateau), U.S.S.R. ... G 5 22
Ust'-Uyskoye, U.S.S.R., 4,195 ... H 4 22
Uster, Switzerland, 12,350 ... G 2 19
Ustí nad Labem, Czech., 64,798 ... C 1 20
Usulután, El Salvador, 9,481 ... C 4 39
Usumacinta (river), Mexico ... O 8 44
Usumbura,* Ruanda-Urundi, 27,294 ... N12 35
Utah (lake), United States ... E 4 42
Uthai Thani, Thailand, 7,364 ... C 4 30
Utrecht, Netherlands, 247,816 ... G 4 15
Utrera, Spain, 26,279 ... D 4 17
Utsonomiya, Japan, 107,210 ... K 5 33
Uttaradit, Thailand, 5,494 ... D 3 30
Uttarpara, India, 13,610 ... E 1 29
Uusikaarlepyy (Nykarleby), Finland, 14,407 ... N 5 13
Uusikaupunki (Nystad), Finland, 4,355 ... M 6 13
Uvat, U.S.S.R., 637 ... H 4 22
Uwajima, Japan, 56,570 ... F 7 33
'Uweinat (mountain), Libya ... L 7 34
Uyuni, Bolivia, 6,968 ... G 8 46
Uzgen, U.S.S.R., 13,120 ... V 2 23
Uzhgorod (Užhorod), U.S.S.R., 47,000 ... D 5 22
Uzunköprü, Turkey, 15,465 ... B 2 28

V

Vaal (river), Union of So. Africa ... M17 35
Vaasa (Vasa), Finland, 42,860 ... M 5 13
Vác, Hungary, 23,409 ... E 3 20
Vaduz,* Liecht., 2,735 ... H 2 19
Vakh (river), U.S.S.R. ... K 3 22
Val-Brillant, Quebec, 931 ... G 4 41
Val-d'Or, Quebec, 9,876 ... E 4 41
Val Marie, Saskatchewan, 383 ... J 5 40
Valdepeñas, Spain, 26,276 ... E 3 17
Valdés (peninsula), Argentina ... H12 47
Valdivia, Chile, 45,138 ... F11 47
Valença, Brazil, 11,628 ... N 6 46
Valence, France, 36,659 ... F 5 16
Valencia, Spain, †509,075 ... F 3 17
Valencia, Venezuela, 88,701 ... G 2 46
Valenciennes, France, 37,716 ... E 2 16
Valentia (island), Ireland, 1,015 ... A 8 12
Valenza, Italy, 11,740 ... B 2 18
Valera, Venezuela, 20,529 ... F 2 46
Valga, U.S.S.R., 10,842 ... D 4 22
Valjevo, Yugoslavia, 15,091 ... D 3 21
Valkeakoski, Finland, 13,569 ... N 6 13
Valladolid, Mexico, 8,165 ... P 6 44
Valladolid, Spain, †119,499 ... D 2 17
Valle de Santiago, Mexico, 15,628 ... J 6 44
Valle Grande, Bolivia, 5,094 ... H 7 46
Vallecas, Spain, 4,218 ... G 4 17
Vallenar, Chile, 9,677 ... F 9 47
Valletta,* Malta, 18,666 ... E 7 18
Valleyfield, Quebec, 23,584 ... F 4 41
Valognes, France, 2,997 ... C 3 16
Valparaíso, Chile, 218,829 ... N10 47
Valuyki, U.S.S.R., 10,243 ... E 4 22
Valverde, Dom. Rep., 6,600 ... D 5 48
Van, Turkey, 17,408 ... K 3 28
Van (lake), Turkey ... K 3 28
Van Diemen (cape), Australia ... D 2 36
Van Diemen (gulf), Australia ... E 2 36
Van Gia, Vietnam ... F 4 30
Van Rhynsdorp, C. of G.H., 1,597 K18 35
Vancouver, B. C., 365,844 ... F 5 40
Vancouver, Greater, B.C., 662,500 ... F 5 40
Vancouver (island), B.C. ... E 5 40
Vanderhoof, B. Columbia, 1,085 ... F 4 40
Vänern (lake), Sweden ... H 7 13
Vänersborg, Sweden, 15,655 ... G 7 13
Vanimo, Terr. New Guinea ... B 6 31
Vaniyambadi, India, 31,281 ... C 6 29
Vankarem, U.S.S.R. ... V 3 23
Vannes, France, 23,377 ... B 4 16
Vanua Levu (island), Pacific, 39,958 ... H 7 37
Varanasi, India, 355,777 ... D 3 29
Varanger (fjord), Norway ... Q 2 13
Varaždin, Yugoslavia, 19,397 ... B 2 21
Varberg, Sweden, 12,524 ... G 8 13
Vardar (river) ... E 5 21
Varel, Germany, 13,939 ... B 2 14
Varese, Italy, 36,882 ... B 2 18
Varginha, Brazil, 13,404 ... M 8 46
Varkaus, Finland, 19,717 ... Q 5 13
Varna, Bulgaria, 77,792 ... H 4 21
Varnsdorf, Czech., 15,356 ... C 1 20
Vasile Roaită, Rumania, 1,075 ... J 3 21
Vaslui, Rumania, 13,738 ... H 2 21
Västerås, Sweden, 59,990 ... J 7 13
Västervik, Sweden, 15,741 ... K 8 13
Vasto (Istonio), Italy, 14,036 ... E 3 18
Vatican City, 1,010 ... B 6 18
Vatomandry, Malg. Rep., 2,445 ... S15 35
Vatra-Dornei, Rumania, 7,078 ... G 2 21
Vättern (lake), Sweden ... J 7 13
Vaupés (river), Colombia ... F 3 46
Växjö, Sweden, 20,104 ... J 8 13
Vaygach (Vaigach) (isl.), U.S.S.R. ... G 3 22
Vechta, Germany, 13,097 ... C 2 14
Vecsés, Hungary, 18,491 ... E 3 20
Vegreville, Alberta, 2,574 ... H 4 40
Vejle, Denmark, 29,448 ... F 9 13
Velbert, Germany, 41,421 ... G 4 14
Velika Kikinda (Kikinda), Yugoslavia, 29,607 ... E 3 21
Velikaya Guba, U.S.S.R., 171 ... E 3 22
Veliki Bečkerek (Zrenjanin), Yugoslavia, 40,517 ... E 3 21
Velikiy Ustyug, U.S.S.R., 23,382 ... F 3 22
Velikiye Luki, U.S.S.R., 59,000 ... E 4 22
Velletri, Italy, 15,870 ... F 6 18
Vellore, India, 106,603 ... C 6 29
Velp, Netherlands, 15,598 ... J 5 15
Velsen, Neth., 59,948 ... F 4 15
Vel'sk, U.S.S.R., 3,499 ... F 3 22
Venado Tuerto, Arg., 15,947 ... H10 47
Venezuela (gulf) ... F 1 46
Vengurla, India, 21,663 ... B 5 29
Venice (Venezia), Italy, 291,635 ... D 2 18
Venissieux, France, 15,006 ... F 5 16
Venkatagiri, India, 16,408 ... D 6 29
Venlo, Netherlands, 51,719 ... J 6 15
Venosa, Italy, 13,154 ... E 4 18
Ventspils, U.S.S.R., 15,679 ... D 4 22
Veracruz, Mexico, 101,469 ... Q 1 44
Veranópolis, Brazil, 2,664 ... K 9 47
Veraval, India, 30,275 ... B 4 29
Verbania, Italy, 24,493 ... B 2 18
Vercelli, Italy, 39,647 ... B 2 18
Verde (cape), Senegal ... C 9 34
Verde (river), U.S. ... F 6 42
Verden, Germany, 18,821 ... C 2 14
Verdun-sur-Meuse, France, 16,411 ... F 3 16
Verkh-Chebula, U.S.S.R., 2,616 ... O 5 23
Verkhne-Neyvinskiy, U.S.S.R., 4,057 ... P 6 23
Verkhne-Ural'sk, U.S.S.R., 10,005 ... H 4 22
Verkhne-Usinskoye, U.S.S.R., 2,242 ... L 4 23
Verkhneye, U.S.S.R., 11,153 ... L 1 23
Verkhniy Ufaley, U.S.S.R., 12,671 H 4 22
Verkhnyaya Pyshma, U.S.S.R., 10,800 ... P 6 23
Verkhnyaya Salda, U.S.S.R., 10,500 ... P 6 23
Verkhnyaya Sinyachikha, U.S.S.R., 2,272 ... P 6 23
Verkhnyaya Tura, U.S.S.R., 15,200 ... P 6 23
Verkhotur'ye, U.S.S.R., 4,689 ... R 5 23
Verkhoyansk, U.S.S.R. ... P 3 23
Verkhoyansk (mountain range), U.S.S.R. ... O 3 23
Verlo, Saskatchewan, 134 ... J 4 40
Vermilion, Alberta, 2,196 ... H 4 40
Vermilion (lake), United States ... K 2 43
Vermilion Bay, Ontario, 98 ... B 3 41
Vernon, Br. Columbia, 8,998 ... G 4 40
Vernon, France, 10,033 ... D 3 16
Verona, Italy, 154,931 ... C 2 18
Verrettes, Haiti, 1,541 ... C 5 48
Véroia, Greece, 21,844 ... F 5 21
Versailles, France, 72,038 ... A 2 16
Verviers, Belgium, 37,401 ... H 7 15
Vesoul, France, 10,744 ... F 4 16
Vest (fjord), Norway ... H 3 13
Vesterålen (islands), Norway, 33,375 ... J 2 13
Vesuvius (vol.), Italy ... E 4 18
Veszprém, Hungary, 22,644 ... D 3 20
Vevey, Switzerland, 14,264 ... C 4 19
Viacha, Bolivia, 23,200 ... G 7 46
Viana, Brazil, 5,054 ... M 4 46
Viana do Castelo, Portugal, 14,023 B 2 17
Viareggio, Italy, 39,341 ... C 3 18
Vibo Valentia, Italy, 19,100 ... F 5 18
Viborg, Denmark, 21,522 ... F 8 13
Vicenza, Italy, 68,203 ... C 2 18
Vich, Spain, 13,678 ... H 2 17
Vichada (river), Colombia ... F 3 46
Vichy, France, 30,099 ... E 4 16
Victor Harbor, Australia, 1,914 ... F 7 36
Victoria, Argentina, 17,711 ... J10 47
Victoria, So. Cam., 7,657 ... H11 34
Victoria,* Br. Columbia, 54,584 ... F 5 40
Victoria, Greater, Br. Columbia, 124,500 ... F 5 40
Victoria, Guinea, 1,269 ... D 9 34
Victoria,* Hong Kong, 887,400 ... H 7 32
Victoria (falls), Africa ... M15 35
Victoria (isl.), Canada ... B29 8
Victoria (lake), Africa ... N12 35
Victoria (river), Australia ... E 3 36
Victoria de las Tunas, Cuba, 12,754 ... H 3 48
Victoria Point, Burma ... C 5 30
Victoriaville, Quebec, 13,031 ... F 4 41
Vidin, Bulgaria, 18,580 ... F 4 21
Viedma, Argentina, 4,683 ... H12 47
Viedma (lake), Argentina ... F13 47
Vienna,* Austria, 1,766,102 ... D 2 20
Vienne, France, 21,926 ... F 5 16
Vienne (river), France ... D 4 16
Vientiane,* Laos, 10,000 ... D 3 30
Viersen, Germany, 36,974 ... B 3 14
Vierzon, France, 26,808 ... D 4 16
Vigan, Philippine Is., 7,424 ... F 2 31
Vigevano, Italy, 39,030 ... B 2 18
Vigo, Spain, †136,291 ... B 1 17
Viipuri (Vyborg), U.S.S.R., 51,000 ... D 3 22
Vijayavada, India, 160,831 ... D 5 29
Vila,* New Hebrides, 1,500 ... G 7 37
Vila de João Belo, Mozambique, 3,243 ... O17 35

	Index Ref.	Plate No.
Vila de Manica, Moz., 9,000	N15	35
Vila do Conde, Portugal, 7,772	B 2	17
Vila Franca de Xira, Portugal, 8,296	B 3	17
Vila Macedo de Cavaleiros, Angola, 2,631	K14	35
Vila Real, Portugal, 9,285	C 2	17
Vila Teixeira de Sousa, Angola, 870	L14	35
Vilcanota (mountain), Peru	F 6	46
Villa Acuña, Mexico, 11,372	J 2	44
Villa Ángela, Argentina, 7,375	H 9	47
Villa Cisneros, Sp. Sahara, 1,011	C 7	34
Villa de Cura, Venezuela, 9,910	G 2	46
Villa Dolores, Argentina, 13,385	G10	47
Villa Frontera, Mexico, 9,441	J 3	44
Villa María, Argentina, 30,362	H10	47
Villa Montes, Bolivia, 3,105	H 8	46
Villa Sanjurjo, Mor., 10,770	F 4	34
Villabruzzi, Somalia, 10,500	R11	35
Villacarrillo, Spain, 11,928	E 3	17
Villach, Austria, 30,066	B 3	20
Villafranca de los Barros, Spain, 15,165	C 3	17
Villahermosa, Mexico, 33,578	N 8	44
Villanueva de Córdoba, Spain, 16,256	D 3	17
Villanueva de la Serena, Spain, 18,396	D 3	17
Villanueva y Geltrú, Spain, 16,382	G 2	17
Villarreal, Spain, 16,793	G 3	17
Villarrica, Chile, 4,679	F11	47
Villarrica, Paraguay, 14,680	J 9	47
Villarrobledo, Spain, 24,405	E 3	17
Villavicencio, Colombia, 6,074	F 3	46
Ville-Marie, Quebec, 1,409	E 4	41
Ville-Saint-Georges, Quebec, 3,142	G 4	41
Villefranche-sur-Saône, France, 21,101	F 4	16
Villejuif, France, 23,542	C 1	16
Villemomble, France, 18,617	C 1	16
Villena, Spain, 15,065	F 3	17
Villeneuve, France, 18,279	E 3	16
Villeneuve-sur-Lot, France, 13,305	D 5	16
Villeurbanne, France, 79,829	F 5	16
Villiersdorp, Cape of G.H., 1,487	D19	35
Villingen, Germany, 20,127	C 4	14
Villupuram, India, 23,829	C 6	29
Vilna (Vil'nyus), U.S.S.R., 235,000	D 4	22
Vilvoorde (Vilvorde), Belgium, 29,771	F 7	15
Vilyuy (mt. range), U.S.S.R.	N 3	23
Vilyuy (river), U.S.S.R.	M 3	23
Vilyuysk, U.S.S.R.	O 3	23
Viña del Mar, Chile, 85,281	N 9	47
Vincennes, France, 48,851	B 2	16
Vindhya (hills), India	C 4	29
Vinh, Vietnam	E 3	30
Vinh Long, Vietnam, 11,853	E 5	30
Vinh Yen, Vietnam	E 2	30
Vinkovci, Yugoslavia, 20,670	D 3	21
Vinnitsa, U.S.S.R., 121,000	D 5	22
Viramgam, India, 27,834	B 4	29
Virden, Manitoba, 3,225	K 5	40
Vire, France, 3,179	C 3	16
Virgin (islands)	F 3	45
Virovitica, Yugoslavia, 10,161	C 3	21
Visakhapatnam, India, 108,042	D 5	29
Visby, Sweden, 14,770	L 8	13
Viscount Melville (sound), Canada	D29	8
Viseu, Portugal, 13,190	C 2	17
Visim, U.S.S.R., 6,809	P 6	23
Visimo-Utkinsk, U.S.S.R., 3,081	P 6	23
Vistula (Wisła) (river), Poland	B 2	24
Vitebsk, U.S.S.R., 148,000	E 4	22
Viterbo, Italy, 35,438	C 3	18
Viti Levu (island), Pacific, 176,822	H 7	37
Vitim (river), U.S.S.R.	N 4	23
Vitória, Brazil, 51,329	N 8	46
Vitoria, Spain, †48,900	E 1	17
Vitória da Conquista, Brazil, 18,017	M 6	46
Vitry, France, 52,540	B 2	16
Vittoria, Italy, 42,230	E 6	18
Vittorio Veneto, Italy, 20,113	D 1	18
Vizagapatam (Visakhapatnam), India, 108,042	D 5	29
Vizianagaram, India, 51,749	D 5	29
Vizinga, U.S.S.R., 321	F 3	22
Vizzini, Italy, 13,396	E 6	18
Vlaardingen, Netherlands, 62,188	E 5	15
Vladimir, U.S.S.R., 154,000	E 4	22
Vladivostok, U.S.S.R., 283,000	P 5	23
Vlissingen (Flushing), Neth., 29,148	C 6	15
Vlonë (Valona), Albania, 14,640	D 5	21
Vöcklabruck, Austria, 8,942	B 2	20
Voghera, Italy, 27,712	B 2	18
Vohémar, Malg. Rep., 2,481	S14	35
Voiron, France, 9,847	F 5	16
Volchikha, U.S.S.R., 6,731	J 4	22
Volga (river), U.S.S.R.	F 5	22
Völklingen, Germany, 35,570	B 4	14
Volkovysk, U.S.S.R., 15,027	D 4	22
Volodarskiy, U.S.S.R., 3,960	C 3	22
Vologda, U.S.S.R., 138,000	F 4	22
Vólos, Greece, 51,144	F 6	21
Vol'sk, U.S.S.R., 62,000	F 4	22
Volta (river)	G10	34
Volta Redonda, Brazil, 33,110	M 8	47
Volterra, Italy, 11,166	C 3	18
Voorburg, Netherlands, 40,073	E 4	15
Vordingborg, Denmark, 11,231	G 9	13
Vorkuta, U.S.S.R., 65,000	H 3	22
Voronezh, U.S.S.R., 454,000	F 4	22
Voroshilov (Ussuriysk), U.S.S.R., 104,000	P 5	23
Voroshilovgrad (Lugansk), U.S.S.R., 274,000	P 1	23
Voroshilovsk, U.S.S.R., 98,000	N 1	23
Vorst (Forest), Belgium, 49,142	B 9	15
Voskresensk, U.S.S.R.	C 3	22
Votkinsk, U.S.S.R., 59,000	G 4	22
Voznesensk, U.S.S.R., 7,830	E 5	22
Voznesenskoye, U.S.S.R., 2,239	P 4	23
Vranje, Yugoslavia, 12,404	F 4	21
Vratsa, Bulgaria, 19,448	F 4	21
Vršac, Yugoslavia, 24,571	E 3	21
Vryburg, Cape of G.H., 7,211	L17	35
Vsetín, Czechoslovakia, 18,451	D 2	20
Vsevolozhskiy, U.S.S.R., 1,324	C 2	22
Vuadil', U.S.S.R., 5,232	T 2	23
Vukovar, Yugoslavia, 14,813	D 3	21
Vulcan, Alberta, 1,204	H 4	40
Vyatka (Kirov), U.S.S.R., 252,000	F 4	22
Vyaz'ma, U.S.S.R., 20,814	E 4	22
Vyborg, U.S.S.R., 51,000	D 3	22
Vyritsa, U.S.S.R., 2,920	D 3	22
Vyshka, U.S.S.R.	G 6	22
Vyshniy Volochek, U.S.S.R., 66,000	E 4	22
Vytegra, U.S.S.R., 5,090	E 3	22

W

	Index Ref.	Plate No.
Wa, Ghana, 5,165	F 9	34
Wabash (river), U.S.	M 5	43
Waboden, Manitoba, 88	L 3	40
Wąbrzeźno, Poland, 10,100	D 2	24
Wad, Wadi (means river) (Arab.)		
Wad Medani, Sudan, 61,450	N 9	34
Waddington (mountain), Canada	E 4	40
Wadena, Saskatchewan, 1,154	K 4	40
Wadhwan (Surendranagar), India, 21,622	B 4	29
Wadi Halfa, Sudan, 11,006	N 7	34
Wageningen, Netherlands, 21,305	H 5	15
Wager (bay), Canada	M 1	40
Wagga Wagga, Australia, 19,235	H 7	36
Wagin, Australia, 1,526	B 6	36
Wagrowiec, Poland, 11,600	C 2	24
Wahai, Indonesia	H 6	31
Waihi, New Zealand, 3,075	L 5	36
Waikabubak, Indonesia	F 7	31
Waikerie, Australia, 909	G 6	36
Waingapu, Indonesia, 2,127	G 7	31
Wainwright, Alberta, 2,655	H 4	40
Wairoa, New Zealand, 3,796	M 6	36
Wajabula, Indonesia	H 5	31
Wakamatsu, Japan, 89,574	E 7	33
Wakaw, Saskatchewan, 898	J 4	40
Wakayama, Japan, 191,337	G 6	33
Wake (island), Pacific, 349	G 4	37
Wakefield, England, 60,371	F 4	10
Wakkanai, Japan, 34,529	K 1	33
Wałbrzych (Waldenburg), Poland, 110,300	C 3	24
Wałcz, Poland, 14,700	C 2	24
Waldenburg (Wałbrzych), Poland, 110,300	C 3	24
Walgett, Australia, 1,348	H 6	36
Walker (lake), U.S.	D 5	42
Walkerton, Ontario, 3,698	D 5	41
Wallaceburg, Ontario, 7,892	D 5	41
Wallaroo, Australia, 2,403	F 6	36
Wallasey, England, 101,369	D 4	10
Wallis (islands), Pacific, 4,765	J 7	37
Wallsend, Australia, 2,240	J 6	36
Wallsend, England, 48,645	F 2	10
Walney (island), England	D 3	10
Walsall, England, 114,535	F 5	10
Walsrode, Germany, 13,603	C 2	14
Walsum, Germany, 27,929	F 4	14
Walvis (bay), Africa	J16	35
Walvis Bay, C. of Good Hope, 2,263	J16	35
Wan (means bay, gulf) (Jap.)		
Wandoan, Australia, 589	H 5	36
Wandsbek, Ger., 46,210	D 2	14
Wanganui, New Zealand, †32,100	L 6	36
Wangaratta, Australia, 10,715	H 7	36
Wangyehmiao (Ulanhot), China, 51,400	K 2	32
Wanhsien, China, 75,000	G 5	32
Wankie, S. Rhodesia, 9,901	M15	35
Wanless, Manitoba, 100	K 4	40
Wanne-Eickel, Germany, 86,537	G 4	14
Wanstead and Woodford, England, 61,620	H 6	10
Warabi, Japan, 29,846	O 2	33
Warangal (Hanamkonda), India, 133,130	D 5	29
Waratah, Australia, 320	G 8	36
Warburton (river), Australia	F 5	36
Wardha, India, 28,359	C 4	29
Ware, Br. Columbia, 75	E 3	40
Waren, Germany, 19,807	E 2	14
Warmbad, S. W. Africa, 546	K17	35
Warrenton, Cape of G.H., 3,557	M17	35
Warri, Nigeria, 10,726	H10	34
Warrington, England, 80,694	E 4	10
Warrnambool, Australia, 10,850	G 7	36
Warsaw (Warszawa),* Poland, 1,022,100	E 2	24
Warta (Warthe) (river), Poland	C 2	24
Warwick, Australia, 9,151	J 5	36
Warwick, England, 15,349	F 5	10
Wasatch (mt. range), U.S.	F 5	42
Wash, The (bay), England	H 5	10
Washington (island), Pacific, 158	L 5	37
Watampone, Indonesia, 2,515	G 6	31
Waterford, Ireland, 28,878	G 7	12
Waterford (harbor), Ireland	G 7	12
Watergraafsmeer, Neth., 28,972	C 5	15
Waterloo, Belg., 9,854	E 7	15
Waterloo, Ontario, 16,373	D 5	41
Waterton Lakes (park), Alberta, 300	H 5	40
Waterways, Alberta, 400	H 3	40
Wates, Indonesia, 7,784	J 2	31
Watford, England, 73,130	G 6	10
Watrous, Saskatchewan, 1,340	J 4	40
Watsa, Belg. Congo, 2,391	N11	35
Watson, Saskatchewan, 783	K 4	40
Watson Lake, Yukon, 100	E 2	40
Wattenscheid, Germany, 67,292	G 4	14
Wau, Sudan, 6,600	M10	34
Wau, Terr. New Guinea, 1,865	B 7	31
Waveney (river), England	J 5	10
Waverley, Australia, 67,474	L 3	36
Weda, Indonesia	H 5	31
Wedau, Papua	C 7	31
Wedgeport, Nova Scotia, 1,322	G 5	41
Wednesbury, England, 34,759	E 5	10
Weida, Germany, 13,511	D 3	14
Weiden, Germany, 37,715	D 4	14
Weidenau, Germany, 15,026	C 3	14
Weifang, China, 148,900	J 4	32
Weihai, China, 45,000	K 4	32
Weilheim, Germany, 11,145	D 5	14
Weimar, Germany, 66,659	D 3	14
Weinheim, Germany, 25,199	C 4	14
Weissenfels, Germany, 50,995	D 3	14
Weissensee, Germany, 82,017	J 3	14
Wejh, Saudi Arabia, 2,000	C 4	26
Wejherowo, Poland, 22,000	D 1	24
Wekusko, Manitoba, 150	L 4	40
Welland, Ontario, 16,405	E 5	41
Wellesley (islands), Australia	F 3	36
Wellingborough, England, 28,222	G 5	10
Wellington, Australia, 5,213	H 6	36
Wellington, Cape of G. H., 8,202	D18	35
Wellington,* New Zealand, †138,297	L 6	36
Wellington (island), Chile	E13	47
Wels, Austria, 38,078	C 2	20
Welwyn, England, 18,314	G 6	10
Wenchow, China, 201,600	K 6	32
Wenlock, England, 15,095	E 5	10
Wentworth, Australia, 4,034	G 6	36
Werdau, Germany, 27,041	E 3	14
Wermelskirchen, Germany, 20,859	B 3	14
Werne, Germany, 17,717	B 3	14
Wernigerode, Germany, 33,800	D 3	14
Wesel, Germany, 18,244	B 3	14
Weser (river), Germany	C 2	14
Wesleyville, Newfoundland, 1,313	K 4	41
Wessel (cape), Australia	F 2	36
Wessel (islands), Australia	F 2	36
West Bromwich, England, 87,981	F 5	10
West Hartlepool, England, 72,662	G 3	10
West Irian (region)	K 6	31
Western Ghats (mt. range), India	B 5	29
Westlock, Alberta, 1,136	H 4	40
Weston-super-Mare, England, 40,165	E 6	10
Westport, New Zealand, 5,522	L 6	36
Westray (island), Scotland, 1,091	K 1	11
Westville, Nova Scotia, 4,247	H 4	41
Wetaskiwin, Alberta, 4,476	H 4	40
Wetter, Germany, 13,335	G 4	14
Wettingen, Switzerland, 11,667	F 2	19
Wetzlar, Germany, 26,252	C 3	14
Wewak, Terr. New Guinea, 879	B 6	31
Wexford, Ireland, 10,838	H 7	12
Wexford (harbor), Ireland	J 7	12
Weyburn, Saskatchewan, 7,684	K 5	40
Weymouth, Nova Scotia, 1,500	G 5	41
Weymouth-Melcombe Regis, England, 37,099	E 7	10
Whakatane, New Zealand, 5,445	M 6	36
Whale (river), Canada	G 2	41
Whalsay (island), Scotland, 859	N 3	11
Whangarei, New Zealand, 13,363	L 5	36
Wharfe (river), England	F 4	10
Whitby, Ontario, 9,995	E 5	41
White (bay), Canada	J 3	41
White (sea), U.S.S.R.	E 3	22
White Nile (river), Africa	N10	34
White Pass, Br. Columbia	C 3	40
White River, Ontario, 401	C 4	41
White Volta (river), Upper Volta	F 9	34
Whitecourt, Alberta, 130	G 4	40
Whitehaven, England, 24,629	D 3	10
Whitehorse,* Yukon, 2,570	D 2	40
Whitley Bay, England, 32,260	F 2	10
Whitney, Ontario, 247	E 4	41
Whitney (mountain), U.S.	D 5	42
Whitstable, England, 17,459	J 6	10
Whitsunday (island), Australia	H 4	36
Whittlesea, Australia, 601	L 1	36
Wiarton, Ontario, 1,954	D 5	41
Wicklow (mt. range), Ireland	J 6	12
Wicklow Head (cape), Ireland	K 6	12
Widnes, England, 48,785	E 4	10
Wieliczka, Poland, 11,800	E 3	24
Wieluń, Poland, 10,900	D 3	24
Wien (Vienna),* Austria, 1,766,102	D 2	20
Wiener Neustadt, Austria, 30,509	D 3	20
Wierzbnik, Poland, 18,569	E 3	24
Wiesbaden, Germany, 220,741	B 3	14
Wigan, England, 84,560	E 4	10
Wight (island), England, 95,625	F 7	10
Wigston (Wigston Magna), England, 15,452	G 5	10
Wigtown (bay), Scotland	H10	11
Wilberforce (cape), Australia	F 2	36
Wilcannia, Australia, 821	G 6	36
Wilhelmshaven, Germany, 101,210	B 2	14
Wilkie, Saskatchewan, 1,630	J 4	40
Willemstad,* Neth. Antilles, 40,597	E 4	45
Williams, Australia, 430	B 2	36
Williams Lake, Br. Columbia, 1,790	F 4	40
Williamstown, Australia, 575	E 7	36
Williamstown, Australia, 29,313	K 2	36
Willis (islets), Australia	J 3	36
Willoughby, Australia, 52,090	L 3	36
Willow Bunch, Saskatchewan, 745	J 5	40
Willowmore, Cape of G.H., 2,533	L18	35
Wilmersdorf, Germany, 141,310	J 3	14
Wilmington, Australia, 377	F 6	36
Wilmslow, England, 19,536	E 4	10
Wilno (Vilna), U.S.S.R., 235,000	D 4	22
Wilson's (promontory), Australia	H 7	36
Wiluna, Australia, 158	C 5	36
Wimbledon, England, 58,141	G 6	10
Winchester, England, 25,721	F 6	10
Wind River (mt. range), U.S.	F 4	42
Windhoek,* S. W. Africa, 14,929	K16	35
Windorah, Australia, 70	G 5	36
Windsor, Newfoundland, 4,520	J 4	41
Windsor, Nova Scotia, 3,651	H 5	41
Windsor, Ontario, 121,980	D 5	41
Windsor, Greater, Ontario, 185,045	D 5	41
Windward (passage), W.I.	C 3	45
Wingham, Ontario, 2,766	D 5	41
Winkler, Manitoba, 1,634	L 3	40
Winnemucca (lake), U.S.	D 4	42
Winnipeg,* Manitoba, 255,093	L 5	40
Winnipeg, Greater, Manitoba, 409,687	L 5	40
Winnipeg (lake), Canada	L 4	40
Winnipegosis, Manitoba, 984	K 4	40
Winnipegosis (lake), Canada	K 4	40
Winterthur, Switz., 66,925	G 1	19
Winton, Australia, 1,398	G 4	36
Wisbech, England, 17,432	G 5	10
Wismar, Germany, 42,018	D 2	14
Witham (river), England	G 4	10
Witten, Germany, 76,312	G 4	14
Wittenberg, Germany, 41,304	E 3	14
Wittenberge, Germany, 31,485	E 2	14

	Index Plate Ref.	No.
Włocławek, Poland, 58,500	D 2	24
Woking, England, 47,591	G 6	10
Wolfenbüttel, Germany, 34,401	D 2	14
Wolfsberg, Austria, 8,050	C 3	20
Wolfville, Nova Scotia, 2,497	H 4	41
Wollaston (lake), Canada	K 3	40
Wollongong, Australia, †90,852	K 4	36
Wołomin, Poland, 19,500	E 2	24
Wolseley, Cape of G.H., 1,654	E18	35
Wolseley, Saskatchewan, 1,001	K 4	40
Woluwe-Saint-Lambert, Belgium, 33,565	C 9	15
Woluwe-St.-Pierre, Belg., 26,951	C 9	15
Wolverhampton, England, 162,672	E 5	10
Wombwell, England, 18,837	F 4	10
Wonju, Korea, 20,429	D 5	33
Wonogiri, Indonesia	J 2	31
Wonosobo, Indonesia, 10,710	J 2	31
Wonreli, Indonesia	H 7	31
Wŏnsan, Korea, 112,952	C 4	33
Wonthaggi, Australia, 4,461	G 7	36
Wood Buffalo (park), Canada	H 3	40
Woodridge, Manitoba, 600	L 5	40
Woods (lake), Australia	E 3	36
Woods (lake), Canada	M 5	40
Woodstock, New Brunswick, 4,308	G 4	41
Woodstock, Ontario, 18,347	D 5	41
Woodville, Aust., 57,538	D 7	36
Wooramel (river), Australia	A 5	36
Worcester, Cape of G.H., 25,388	F18	35
Worcester, England, 59,703	F 5	10
Workington, England, 28,891	D 3	10
Worksop, England, 31,034	F 4	10
Worms, Germany, 52,239	C 4	14
Worthing, England, 69,431	G 7	10
Wosi, Indonesia	H 6	31
Wrangel (island), U.S.S.R.	V 2	23
Wrath (cape), Scotland	F 2	11
Wreck (reef), Australia	J 4	36
Wrexham, Wales, 30,967	E 4	10
Wrocław (Breslau), Poland, 387,900	C 3	24
Września, Poland, 12,500	C 2	24
Wuchang (incl. in Wuhan), China, 199,000	J 5	32
Wuchow, China, 110,800	H 7	32
Wuhan, China, 1,427,300	H 5	32
Wuhu, China, 242,100	J 5	32
Wukari, Nigeria, 7,869	J10	34
Wülfrath, Germany, 16,794	G 4	14
Wun, India, 12,225	C 4	29
Wuppertal, Germany, 363,224	G 4	14
Würzburg, Germany, 78,433	D 4	14
Wurzen, Germany, 22,234	E 3	14
Wusih, China, 581,500	K 5	32
Wutungkiao, China, 199,100	F 6	32
Wuwei, China	F 4	32
Wyalong, Australia, 604	H 6	36
Wyandra, Australia, 217	H 5	36
Wye (river), England	D 5	10
Wynberg, Cape of G.H., 1,646	C19	35
Wyndham, Australia, 613	D 3	36
Wynyard, Australia, 2,185	H 8	36
Wynyard, Saskatchewan, 1,522	K 4	40
Wyoming (mt. range), U.S.	F 4	42

X Y Z

	Index Plate Ref.	No.
Xánthē, Greece, 25,700	G 5	21
Xieng Khouang, Laos	E 2	30
Xingu (river), Brazil	K 4	46

	Index Plate Ref.	No.
Xochimilco, Mexico, 20,685	L 1	44
Yaan, China, 55,200	F 6	32
Yaapeet, Australia, 146	G 7	36
Yablonovyy (mountains), U.S.S.R.	N 4	23
Yacuiba, Bolivia, 5,027	H 8	46
Yakutsk, U.S.S.R., 74,000	O 3	23
Yala, Thailand, 7,100	D 6	30
Yalgoo, Australia, 180	B 5	36
Yallourn, Aust., 5,580	H 7	36
Yalta, U.S.S.R., 28,838	E 5	22
Yalutorovsk, U.S.S.R.	H 4	22
Yama (means mt.) (Jap.)		
Yamagata, Japan, 104,891	K 4	33
Yamaguchi, Japan, 77,759	E 6	33
Yamal (peninsula), U.S.S.R.	H 2	22
Yamatotakada, Japan, 31,499	J 8	33
Yambol, Bulgaria, 30,311	H 4	21
Yamethin, Burma, 10,126	C 2	30
Yampol', U.S.S.R., 3,431	H 1	23
Yanac, Australia, 92	G 7	36
Yangambi, B. Congo, 17,948	L11	35
Yangchow China, 180,200	K 5	32
Yangchüan, China, 177,400	H 4	32
Yangi-Kurgan, U.S.S.R., 2,481	U 2	23
Yangi-Yul', U.S.S.R., 30,000	S 1	23
Yangtze Kiang (river), China	F 6	32
Yao, Japan, 66,698	J 8	33
Yaounde,* Cam., 25,000	J11	34
Yap (islands), Pacific, 2,700	D 5	37
Yaraka, Australia, 66	G 4	36
Yare (river), England	J 5	10
Yariga (mountain), Japan	H 5	33
Yarim, Yemen, 5,000	D 7	26
Yarkand, China, 80,000	C 7	32
Yarkovo, U.S.S.R., 741	H 4	22
Yarmouth, Nova Scotia, 8,095	G 5	41
Yaroslavl', U.S.S.R., 406,000	E 4	22
Yartsevo, U.S.S.R., 18,703	E 4	22
Yarumal, Colombia, 8,693	E 2	46
Yass, Australia, 3,662	H 7	36
Yathyed (lake), Canada	L 2	40
Yatsushiro, Japan, 90,303	E 7	33
Yauco, Puerto Rico, 9,801	F 1	45
Yavne, Israel, 1,540	B 4	24
Yavneel, Israel, 1,540	D 2	24
Yawata, Japan, 210,051	E 7	33
Yawatahama, Japan, 39,932	F 7	33
Yaya, U.S.S.R.	O 5	23
Ye, Burma	C 4	30
Yecla, Spain, 21,257	F 3	17
Yegor'yevsk, U.S.S.R., 59,000	C 3	22
Yehud, Israel, 6,000	B 3	24
Yelan', U.S.S.R., 13,283	F 4	22
Yelets, U.S.S.R., 78,000	E 4	22
Yelgava (Jelgava), U.S.S.R., 34,099	D 4	22
Yell (island), Scotland, 1,483	M 2	11
Yellamanchili, India, 9,054	D 5	29
Yellandlapad, India, 15,907	C 5	29
Yellow (Hwang Ho) (river), China	H 5	32
Yellow (sea)	K 4	32
Yellow Grass, Saskatchewan, 490	K 5	40
Yellowknife, N. W. Terr., 3,100	H 2	40
Yellowstone (river), U.S.	G 3	42
Yen Bay, Vietnam	E 2	30
Yenangyaung, Burma	B 2	30
Yenakiyevo, U.S.S.R., 92,000	M 1	23
Yenbo, Saudi Arabia, 10,000	C 5	26
Yendi, Ghana, 7,694	G10	34
Yenişehir, Turkey, 8,702	C 2	28
Yenisey (river), U.S.S.R.	K 3	22
Yeniseysk, U.S.S.R.	L 4	23
Yenki, China, 70,000	L 3	32
Yenotayevka, U.S.S.R., 3,798	F 5	22

	Index Plate Ref.	No.
Yeola, India, 17,817	B 4	29
Yeotmal, India, 26,555	C 4	29
Yeovil, England, 23,337	E 7	10
Yerevan (Erivan), U.S.S.R., 509,000	F 6	22
Yerwa, Nigeria, 54,646	J 9	34
Yezd, Iran, 60,000	J 5	27
Yinchwan, China, 84,000	F 4	32
Yingkow, China, 131,400	K 3	32
Yoichi, Japan, 26,396	K 2	33
Yokkaichi, Japan, 123,870	H 6	33
Yokohama, Japan, 951,189	O 3	33
Yokosuka, Japan, 250,533	O 3	33
Yola, Nigeria, 5,310	J10	34
Yonago, Japan, 58,661	F 6	33
Yonezawa, Japan, 55,008	J 5	33
Yŏngch'ŏn, Korea, 25,487	D 6	33
Yŏngju, Korea, 21,056	D 5	33
Yono, Japan, 29,072	O 2	33
York, Australia, 1,720	B 2	36
York, England, 105,371	F 4	10
York (cape), Australia	G 2	36
York (sound), Australia	C 2	36
Yorkton, Saskatchewan, 8,256	K 4	40
Yoshkar-Ola, U.S.S.R., 88	F 4	22
Youghal (bay), Ireland	F 8	12
Young, Australia, 5,503	H 6	36
Youngstown, Alberta, 305	H 4	40
Yoyang, China, 4,800	H 6	32
Yozgat, Turkey, 14,784	F 3	28
Ypres (leper), Belg., 17,363	B 7	15
Ystad, Sweden, 13,002	H 9	13
Yubari, Japan, 99,530	L 2	33
Yucatán (channel)	K 7	38
Yucatán (peninsula), Mexico	Q 6	44
Yukon (river), N. Amer.	C 3	38
Yule (river), Australia	B 4	36
Yülin, China	G 4	32
Yuna, Australia, 156	B 5	36
Yungkia (Wenchow), China, 201,600	K 6	32
Yuzhno-Kuril'sk, U.S.S.R.	R 5	23
Yuzhno-Sakhalinsk, U.S.S.R., 86,000	R 5	23
Yverdon, Switzerland, 12,266	C 3	19
Zaandam, Netherlands, 46,814	B 4	15
Zabid, Yemen, 8,000	D 7	26
Ząbkowice Śląskie, Poland, 10,100	C 3	24
Zabrze (Hindenburg), Poland, 185,100	A 4	24
Zabul (Nasratabad), Iran, 13,401	M 5	27
Zacapa, Guatemala, 8,282	C 3	39
Zacatecas, Mexico, 24,257	H 5	44
Zacatecoluca, El Salvador, 9,190	C 4	39
Zacatelco, Mexico, 9,126	M 1	44
Zadâr (Zara), Yugoslavia, 18,913	B 3	21
Zagań, Poland, 16,200	B 3	24
Zagreb, Yugoslavia, 350,452	C 3	21
Zahle, Lebanon, 25,153	F 6	28
Zaječar, Yugoslavia, 12,300	E 4	21
Zaki (means cape) (Jap.)		
Zakopane, Poland, 24,000	D 4	24
Zákynthos, Greece, 11,126	E 7	21
Zalaegerszeg, Hungary, 17,082	D 3	30
Zălău, Rumania, 11,652	F 2	21
Zalesovo, U.S.S.R., 2,379	N 5	23
Zambezi (river), Africa	M15	35
Zamboanga, Philippine Is., 17,001	G 4	31
Zamora, Mexico, 23,397	H 7	44
Zamora, Spain, †35,392	D 2	17
Zamość, Poland, 26,300	F 3	24
Zante (Zákynthos)(isl.), Greece, 38,062	E 7	21

	Index Plate Ref.	No.
Zanzibar,* Zanzibar Prot., 44,350	P13	35
Zapala, Argentina, 3,387	F11	47
Zaporozh'ye, U.S.S.R., 435,000	E 5	22
Zara, Turkey, 6,627	G 3	28
Zara (Zadar), Yugoslavia, 18,193	B 3	21
Zaragoza (Saragossa), Spain, 264,256	F 2	17
Zárate, Arg., 12,692	N11	47
Zaria, Nigeria, 54,000	H 9	34
Zary, Poland, 20,700	B 3	24
Žatec, Czechoslovakia, 15,114	B 1	20
Zavitaya, U.S.S.R.	P 4	23
Zav'yalovo, U.S.S.R., 3,217	K 4	22
Zawiercie, Poland, 31,400	D 3	24
Zaysan, U.S.S.R., 8,245	K 5	22
Zduńska Wola, Poland, 23,700	D 3	24
Zeballos, Br. Columbia, 154	E 4	40
Zeehan, Australia, 698	G 8	36
Zegharta, Lebanon, 9,553	F 5	28
Zehdenick, Germany, 13,246	E 2	14
Zeila, Somaliland Prot., 5,000	P 9	34
Zeist, Netherlands, 49,198	G 4	15
Zeitz, Germany, 39,581	E 3	14
Zelenodol'sk,, U.S.S.R., 60,000	F 4	22
Zelenogorsk, U.S.S.R.	B 3	22
Zella-Mehlis, Germany, 17,352	D 3	14
Zelten (mts.), Libya	K 6	34
Zenica, Yugoslavia, 21,809	C 3	21
Zenjan, Iran, 50,476	F 2	27
Zerbst, Germany, 19,237	E 3	14
Zermatt, Switz., 1,395	E 4	19
Zeulenroda, Germany, 14,039	D 3	14
Zgierz, Poland, 32,600	D 3	24
Zhdanov, U.S.S.R., 284,000	E 5	22
Zherdevka, U.S.S.R., 574	F 4	22
Zhitomir, U.S.S.R., 105,000	D 4	22
Zielona Góra (Grünberg), Poland, 15,738	B 3	24
Ziguinchor, Senegal, 16,000	C 9	34
Zikhron Ya'aqov, Israel, 3,000	B 2	24
Zilair, U.S.S.R., 5,624	G 4	22
Zile, Turkey, 21,399	G 2	28
Žilina, Czechoslovakia, 31,123	E 2	20
Zima, U.S.S.R., 15,100	M 4	23
Zimbabwe (ruins), S. Rhod.	N16	35
Zimnicea, Rumania, 11,056	G 4	21
Zimovniki, U.S.S.R., 2,885	F 5	22
Zinder, Niger, 14,000	H 9	34
Zitácuaro, Mexico, 19,943	J 7	44
Zittau, Germany, 45,084	F 3	14
Zlatoust, U.S.S.R., 161,000	G 4	22
Zlín (Gottwaldov), Czech., 57,974	D 2	20
Zliten, Libya, †21,033	K 5	34
Znojmo (Znaim), Czechoslovakia, 22,681	D 2	20
Zomba,* Nyasaland Prot., 4,111	N15	35
Zonguldak, Turkey, 46,902	D 2	28
Zoppot (Sopot), Poland, 44,000	D 1	24
Zrenjanin (Vel. Bečkerek), Yugoslavia, 40,517	E 3	21
Zug, Switzerland, 14,488	G 2	19
Zürich, Switzerland, 390,020	F 2	19
Zushi, Japan, 35,908	O 3	33
Zutphen, Netherlands, 24,220	J 4	15
Zverevo, U.S.S.R., 2,388	K 2	22
Zverinogolovskoye, U.S.S.R., 5,133	H 4	22
Zvolen, Czechoslovakia, 19,921	E 2	20
Zwara, Libya, 10,816	J 5	34
Zweibrücken, Germany, 25,766	B 4	14
Zwickau, Germany, 122,862	E 3	14
Zwolle, Netherlands, 54,087	J 3	15
Żyrardów, Poland, 20,186	E 2	24
Żyryanovsk, U.S.S.R., 54,000	K 5	22
Żywiec, Poland, 17,700	D 4	24

ILLUSTRATED
GAZETTEER

Ottawa, seat of the Canadian Government, is dominated by the splendid Gothic Parliament Buildings.

of Canada

A DESCRIPTION OF THE PROVINCES AND TERRITORIES GIVING FACTS ABOUT THE AREA,

CLIMATE, NATURAL RESOURCES, OCCUPATIONS AND INDUSTRIAL DEVELOPMENT.

PRINCE EDWARD ISLAND

Prince Edward Island is the smallest of the Canadian provinces. Extending only 140 miles in length and from 4 to 40 miles in width, with a total area of 2,184 square miles, it lies in a great semi-circle in the Gulf of St. Lawrence.

Charlottetown, the capital, is the only city on the island and there are only seven towns. Of the total population almost three-fourths live in rural communities.

The island's situation close to the mainland on the west and Nova Scotia on the south and east affords it protection from the full fury of Atlantic storms. The well protected harbours, mild climate and fertile soil have made fishing and agriculture the two main industries of Prince Edward Island. A large amount of canned lobster is exported. The chief agricultural crops are oats and potatoes. Fox farming and ship-building are also important sources of income to the province.

The island, which was called St. Jean during the French regime, was later named Prince Edward in honour of the Duke of Kent, father of Queen Victoria. It joined with the other provinces in 1873.

NEWFOUNDLAND

Newfoundland, the oldest colony in the British Empire and once a dominion itself, became in 1949, the tenth province of Canada, moving the easternmost point of Canada 200 miles nearer England. With an area of 155,364 square miles, Newfoundland lies one-third of the way on the airline route from New York to London. Gander, one of the great airports established on it, has come to be a well-known news dateline. St. John's, the capital, is the most easterly city of the North American continent. It has a harbour completely free of ocean swell.

GAZETTEER OF CANADA

NOVA SCOTIA

Drying codfish is one of Newfoundland's major industries.

Nova Scotia, rich in historical interest, is one of the most picturesque of the provinces. The peninsula, jutting out into the Atlantic Ocean from the southeastern tip of the mainland, has a total land area of 20,743 square miles which includes Cape Breton Island. The population is almost equally divided between rural and urban life.

The province is divided approximately in half by a low, mountainous ridge. The coast along the Atlantic, although broken and rocky, affords innumerable harbours for the famous fishing fleets of Nova Scotia. During the summer months this coast is often engulfed in heavy rainstorms accompanied by severe gales which are caused by semi-tropical air currents sweeping north along the Atlantic seaboard. But, for the most part, the peninsula enjoys a cool, healthy climate.

The northern slope of the land has many fertile plains and rich, alluvial valleys. This area is dotted with many farms. There are large orchards as well as general farms. In the Annapolis Valley are grown apples that are world famous for their flavour and quality. Halifax, the capital, with its six mile long, year 'round harbour, is Canada's chief eastern winter port and point of entry.

The four main industries of Nova Scotia are shipbuilding, iron and steel production, fishing and allied industries, and agriculture, which includes fruit production and dairy output. The fishing industries of Nova Scotia are second in importance only to those of British Columbia among the provinces. There are also many sawmills and a quantity of pulp and paper is produced.

Close to the coast are abundant fishing grounds, which make Nova Scotia a fisherman's paradise for the amateur as well as the professional. The supply of swordfish and tuna have attracted big game anglers from all over the globe.

Just a mile from the mainland is Cape Breton

Waterfront scene at Halifax, Nova Scotia.

Island which abounds in wild, natural beauty.

The province was called Acadia under the French occupation. It was first named Nova

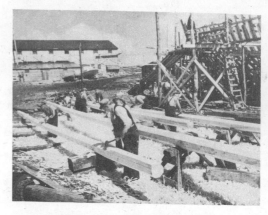

Shipbuilding is an essential industry in Nova Scotia, as in the other Maritime Provinces.

Scotia, Latin for New Scotland, in a patent granted to Sir William Alexander in 1621 by James I. The right to an elective, representative government was granted it in 1758.

NEW BRUNSWICK

New Brunswick, almost as large as Scotland, has a total land area of 27,473 square miles. Its population is about two-thirds rural. Much of the land is wild and rugged, covered with forests, rushing streams, and lakes. However, there is fertile farm land in the valleys and coastal plains in the south and east.

New Brunswick has three cities. Fredericton, the smallest of these, is the capital and seat of the University of New Brunswick. Saint John is the largest city in the province. It is an important port, and like Halifax, has a year 'round harbour. Moncton, a port on the Petitcodiac River, is the home of the main offices and workshops of the Canadian National Railway. All three cities are important to the commerce of the province.

Production of pulp and paper, and sawmilling are the leading industries of New

Newfoundland's inhabitants are mostly of western English stock, with an admixture of Scottish and Irish elements. They are skilled in open-air crafts, and their talents are in great demand in New England and the St. Lawrence Valley.

The new province gives Canada easier access to one of the world's greatest fishing grounds, and adds its lumber resources and its paper mills to the country's wood and pulp industry.

Labrador, Newfoundland's bleak coastal dependency, stretches along the North American mainland to Hudson Strait. Along the Quebec border are fields of iron ore more extensive and at least as rich as the famous Minnesota Mesabi range. Although the deposits are now coming into initial production, cod-fishery remains the staple industry of the 7,000 inhabitants.

A typical Newfoundland fishing community stands on the rocky coast.
Fishing is the major industry of the region.

1. A raft of logs being floated to the mill.

2. Charlo River Falls in northern New Brunswick, typical of the many beautiful scenes in the province.

3. Potatoes are one of the chief crops of New Brunswick.

4. Logs entering the mill to be converted into pulp.

5. Along the Restigouche, an excellent salmon stream.

6. Southern Cross Cape, Grand Manan, New Brunswick.

7. Pulp logs being ground at the paper mill.

Brunswick. Other industries of importance are shipbuilding and repairs, production of miscellaneous foods, and fishing and allied industries.

Excellent hunting and fishing grounds which are easily accessible from the modern cities of the province attract sportsmen throughout the year. Red deer and black bear are plentiful. It is an ideal vacation place for those who love the outdoors, and the good modern highway system gives one the advantage of being able to reach the wild, beautiful country without the inconvenience of travelling over slow country roads.

New Brunswick, part of the territory origin-ally called Acadia became a separate province in 1784.

QUEBEC

As a mirror of the past, Québec, the largest of the provinces, remains, to-day, full of old world flavour. Throughout the province—despite the constant growth of modern cities, excellent highways, and marked industrial progress—the quaint and picturesque customs of old have been retained. The population is about 60% urban and is concentrated in the southern part of the province.

The total area of Québec is 594,860 square miles, 71,000 of which is fresh water area. This water area, formed mainly by many big rivers, represents the tremendous water-power available to serve the province in her great pulp and paper industry.

Québec City, capital, is an old city built on two levels, the upper and lower level being connected by steeply inclined, twisting streets and by an elevator. The older, lower part of the city with its irregular, narrow streets, reminiscent of old French provincial towns, is still the financial centre and main business section.

Montreal, an important port on the St. Lawrence River, is the largest city of Canada, and remains the second greatest French speaking

Bread is still baked in open-air ovens in the picturesque Gaspe region of Quebec.

city in the world. Amid modern skyscrapers and the busy whirl of a large manufacturing centre, the traveller sees landmarks of the day of Maisonneuve, founder of the first permanent colony on Montreal Island, and many historical buildings and monuments.

The province is richly endowed in natural resources. Its hydro-electric power development, greatest of all the provinces, is equal to that of Ontario and Manitoba combined. This great source of power, combined with the good supply of timber, forms the basis of Québec's dominant industry—pulp and paper production.

Montreal on the St. Lawrence river is one of the world's largest inland ports.

Québec is responsible for approximately fifty percent of the total value of this industry in Canada. Non-ferrous metal smelting and refining and petroleum refining have become the leading industries. Production of miscellaneous chemicals is important. Québec manufactures over 70% of the country's cotton yarn and cloth. The manufacture of railway rolling-stock and shipbuilding and repairs are two other important industries of the province. Extensive deposits of high quality asbestos and gold are found in its southeastern part. In this area many modern cities have developed as a result of the increase in mineral production. Iron mining is important in the northeast.

In the upper St. Lawrence Valley, as well as in the eastern sections, the climate and soil provide excellent farming country. There are many dairy farms and many commercial vegetable farms throughout this area. Québec

produces about 87% of the country's tobacco products.

Québec is unique in its mixture of the old and the new. In some sections, oxen are still being used to some extent as draught animals. In many districts country-women use hand looms and spinning wheels, and outdoor clay or stone bake ovens are still employed.

From the time of its founding, when it was called New France, the name of the province underwent many changes before it became officially known as the Province of Québec in 1867.

Fraser Falls in Québec, which has the greatest hydro-electric power development of all the provinces.

ONTARIO

Between the Great Lakes on the south and Hudson and James Bays on the north, lies Ontario, the greatest manufacturing province of Canada. It covers a total land area of 333,835 square miles. The population is about 60% urban.

In the southwest, fertile soil and an ideal climate for farming provide one of the richest agricultural districts in Canada. The seasons here are comparatively mild and pleasant, and there is abundant rainfall. The cultivation of fruit has been highly and successfully developed, especially throughout the Niagara Belt on the Ontario Peninsula. Ontario is second in fruit production among the provinces.

Toronto, the second largest city in Canada, and capital of the province, is a beautiful, spreading city covering an area of about forty

square miles. It is the home of the University of Toronto and has many other important schools and colleges. The city is spaciously laid out. Toronto is the publishing centre of the country, and is the financial centre for the northern mining district. It has the largest mining exchange in the world.

In the northeast, is Ottawa, the capital of Canada, built on a group of hills overlooking the Ottawa River. From Parliament Hill, where the government buildings are located, one gets a magnificent view up and down the river, from the Chaudière Falls to the Rideau Falls. The city is divided approximately in half by the Rideau Canal—Upper Town being occupied by the English and Lower Town, by the French.

Ontario has a wider range of industrial activity than any other province. By virtue of its position on the Great Lakes which gives ready accessibility to the coal and iron ore from the United States, its large, industrious population, and a wealth of natural resources — minerals, forests, agriculture and water power, it has steadily maintained its leadership in Canadian industry.

The leading industries of Ontario include the manufacture of automobiles and parts, smelting and refining of non-ferrous metals, and primary iron and steel production and manufactures. Slaughtering and meat-packing and pulp and paper production are also important. In addition to these, Ontario produces almost the entire supply of Canada's agricultural implements and starch; operates about 80% of the country's leather tanneries; and supplies two-thirds of the fruit and vegetable preparations. It produces about one-half of the minerals of Canada.

All of southern Ontario enjoys a healthy invigorating climate. The climate in the north and northwest, where most of the good timberland is located, varies from that of the remainder of the province. During the winter there is an extremely heavy snowfall, which accumulates on the ground and often reaches a depth of as much as one hundred and forty inches before the late spring thaws. This heavy snow is of great value in hauling timber from the forest.

MANITOBA

Manitoba, originally a part of the old district called Assiniboia, is known as the Keystone province. Located in the centre of Canada, it has a land area of 219,723 square miles.

Grain elevators at Winnipeg store the golden harvest of Manitoba's fertile prairies.

1. Pulp logs being loaded for shipment to one of Ontario's many papermills.

2. A gold mine in operation at Kirkland Lake, Ontario, one of the world's great gold producing areas.

3. Twin locks in the Welland Ship Canal which connects Lake Erie with Lake Ontario.

4. The supplying of dairy products to the large urban centres is a major industry of southern Ontario.

5. Heavy snows are valuable in hauling timber from the northern forests.

6. Cultivating peach trees near Grimsby in the Niagara Belt.

7. Scene on the Rideau Canal, Ottawa.

Although regarded principally as agricultural, Manitoba has an appreciable amount of ready water-power — ranking fourth in this resource — and large forests in the north. In recent years, the discovery of rich mineral deposits in the north and northwest have enabled the province to take its place in the great mining industry of Canada.

Manitoba has a continental type climate. The average precipitation is less than twenty inches annually. However, about 70% of this occurs during the summer months and is, thus, profitably used for the growing of crops. Strong gales and blizzards often occur during the cold winter months. The one redeeming feature of the extreme weather is its dryness.

Winnipeg, the capital of Manitoba, is an important distribution centre, forming the link between eastern and western Canada. All the grain from the western provinces passes through Winnipeg before being shipped east. It is also a big fur centre, and buyers from all over the North American continent go each year to the fur auctions held there. Both the Canadian National and the Canadian Pacific Railways have their western headquarters in this city.

The development of inexpensive electric

Excellent grazing land throughout the Prairie Provinces makes livestock raising a major industry.

power on the Winnipeg River has fostered the city's industrial progress. There are now many factories and plants and it is rapidly developing into an industrial centre.

Agriculture is still one of the leading occupations of Manitoba's people. The soil in the Red River Valley, in the southern part of the province, is exceptionally fertile, and long, sunny days facilitate the rapid growth of vegetation. Hard spring wheat is the leading crop. Oats, rye and barley are the next important ones.

The raising of livestock provides a great portion of Manitoba's income. Slaughtering and meat-packing recently attained first place among Manitoba's industries. Butter and cheese production is second. Close to these in importance is the manufacture of railway rolling stock, milling of flour and feed, and the making of chemical products.

The development of the mineral industry dates back to 1915 when the great Flin Flon mine was discovered in northern Manitoba. Since that time, there have been extensive mining operations and the province now mines quantities of gold, silver, copper, nickel and zinc.

A large part of the forest area of Manitoba

is classed as unproductive land, being covered with scrub growth. However, the province still possesses large, valuable forests and obtains much of its wealth from this resource. Fur trapping is carried on in the north.

Sheep farming in western Canada is an important part of the livestock industry.

SASKATCHEWAN

Saskatchewan, named for the river, the full Indian name of which, *Sis-Sis-Katche-Wan-Sepie*, means the Big Angry Water, lies between Alberta and Manitoba, and has an area of 251,700 square miles. Almost all of the population, which is predominately rural, lives in the southern part of the province.

This is the most completely agricultural of all the provinces. Very little of the potential water power has been developed, but the discovery of large ore bodies along the Manitoba border has greatly increased the mineral output of the province.

The climate of Saskatchewan is continental in type, but the temperature does not reach quite the extremes found in Manitoba. The average precipitation is under twenty inches annually, 60% of it in the growing season.

Regina, the capital of Saskatchewan, formerly capital of the Northwest Territories, has a large distributing trade and is a central market

for its agricultural region. It contains many mills, banks, factories, wholesale houses, and a large oil refinery. Here is the western headquarters of the Royal Canadian Mounted Police. Both the Canadian Pacific and Canadian National Railways pass through Regina, and there are twelve radiating lines.

There are over 125,000 square miles—more than half the total land area—of prairie land in the province suitable for agriculture. Spring wheat is the leading crop, and oats comes second. Manufacturing has materially increased, but still consists chiefly of localized industries.

Although almost half of the entire wooded area is unproductive, there are many sawmills and planing mills in the province. The leading industry is slaughtering and meat-packing. Flour and feed milling and butter and cheese production and petroleum production are other important industries of the province.

Prince Albert National Park, a recreational area of 1,869 square miles of forested slopes, lakes with fine beaches, and streams is one of the many parks in the province.

ALBERTA

Alberta, the furthest west of the three prairie provinces, contains a large and picturesque part of the Canadian Rockies. It has a land area of 248,800 square miles. Of its total population, 52% is rural.

The climate of Alberta is continental, modified somewhat by the Rocky Mountains. The winter climate in Alberta is one of the most variable in the world. Annual precipitation averages about twenty inches, or slightly higher than Manitoba and Saskatchewan, and occurs largely in summer.

Edmonton, the capital of the province, was originally the head of navigation on the North Saskatchewan River, and a centre of the fur trade for both the Hudson's Bay and North West Fur companies. Now, it is a centre of an important coal mining and mixed farming area and a distribution point for both these and the extensive mining areas to the north. It is also a railway centre, served by both transcontinental lines, and is the site of the

Perhaps the most exciting scenery in Canada's National Parks is found in Alberta.

University of Alberta. Edmonton was the first city of Canada to establish a municipal airport, and now has one of the most modern in the country. It is on the great circle air route to the Orient and connects directly by both railway and plane with the Alaska highway.

Agriculture in Alberta has been greatly aided by extensive irrigation, the chief crop being spring wheat, with oats second and barley third. Some rye is planted; and the sugar beet is beginning to be raised successfully. The provincial department of agriculture gives extensive aid to farmers. There are 85,560 square miles of non-forested land, suitable for agriculture.

Alberta is well suited to the development of ranches, and livestock is an important source of wealth. Meat-packing is first among the industries. Other important industries are the production of petroleum products, flour and feed, bread and bakery goods, and sawn lumber.

Alberta contains a coal reserve estimated at over a trillion tons, produces 97% of the Canadian output of petroleum, and leads in the production of natural gas.

At Fort McMurray are immense tar sands deposits, largest known reservoir of oil in the British Commonwealth of Nations. Natural gas comes from the coal fields of Viking, Kinsella and Fabyan in the eastern part of the province.

There are over 100,000 square miles of forested land. Five of the most famous national parks of Canada are located in Alberta, including Jasper, Banff, and Waterton Lakes.

BRITISH COLUMBIA

Almost all of British Columbia, the third largest province, is mountainous. It covers 366,255 square miles including Vancouver, Queen Charlotte and other islands in the Pacific. Over

The rocks of Canada's mines yield a king's ransom in valuable minerals daily.

Farm scene in the rich oil lands at Redwater, Alberta.

half the population is urban.

The climate varies according to the geographical position of the various sections of the province. Vancouver, off the coast, has a climate very like England—the winters are warm and the summers, long, and cool. The western coast of the island has an average of more than 100 inches of precipitation annually. On the eastern side the precipitation is considerably lighter, averaging only about 29 inches.

On the southeast tip of Vancouver Island is Victoria, the capital of British Columbia. It is one of the most beautiful cities in Canada. There are many fine gardens, which because of the exceptionally mild climate, bloom most of the year. It has a good harbour and is the fourth important port of Canada. The Royal Canadian Navy has its headquarters here.

Victoria is an industrial centre and maintains a steady trade with other coastal cities, Australia, and the East.

Vancouver is the largest city in British Columbia and one of the principal ports of Canada. The University of British Columbia is located here. This city is also a large industrial centre and exports great quantities of lumber, wheat, flour, fish and apples.

British Columbia leads in the production of the following: lumber, shingles, fish, silver and fruit.

Shipbuilding and repairs is one of the chief industries of the province. Other leading industries are: Sawmilling; fish curing and packing; pulp and paper production; slaughtering and meat packing; mining and manufacture of petroleum products; aluminum refining.

The coastal area of the mainland enjoys a mild and wet climate. In the fertile valleys between the parallel mountain ranges, the climate is ideal and, although the rainfall is light there are numerous mountain streams which afford irrigation for the extensive fruit farming in this area. Almost all the common fruits such

British Columbia is the leading producer of lumber among the provinces.

as apples, cherries, plums, pears, peaches, etc. are grown here with great success. Cattle and

View of Mt. Robson, British Columbia, showing the tumbling glacier.

sheep are raised in some areas, and fur farming has been increasing steadily. Throughout the farming country, there are grains and mixed vegetable crops.

Salmon from the waters around British Columbia is famous the world over and this one fish accounts for a large portion of the value of the province's fishing industry. The main salmon waters are around Vancouver and Queen Charlotte Islands and the Fraser River. Other important fish are: halibut, herring and cod.

The province has an immense mineral wealth. Gold, silver, lead, copper, coal and zinc are found in large deposits.

The scenery of British Columbia is magnificent; 20,000 miles of highway lead through this beautiful country of majestic mountains and fertile valleys.

Intensive settlement began with the discovery of gold and led to British Columbia becoming a British colony in 1858. United with the colony of Vancouver, British Columbia became a province of Canada in 1871.

Cleaning fish for market at Prince Rupert, British Columbia.

YUKON TERRITORY

The Yukon Territory has a total land area of 205,346 square miles.

Until the great Klondike gold strike in 1896, the Territory was inhabited by only a few tribes of Indians. During the boom years in the gold-mining industry there was a great influx of people to the area. In 1898, two years after the big strike, it was created a separate Territory and Dawson was selected as its capital. In 1953, however, the territorial capital was transferred to White Horse.

The climate of the Yukon is similar to that of the Northwest Territories. The summers are short, but the days are long and sunny, often averaging as much as twenty hours of light making possible farming on a small scale; the winters are about seven months long and are quite cold—the temperature often dropping as low as sixty-five degrees below zero.

There is great potential mineral wealth in this Territory. Gold is still mined in considerable quantity. Since the great placer deposits were depleted, lode mining has been the principal method of production.

The interior of the Yukon is principally a large plain surrounded by the St. Elias Mountain Range on the southwest and the Rocky Mountains on the south and southeast. Through the whole Territory runs the mighty Yukon River, and in the valleys and sand flats formed by it and its tributaries, are many dense forests. In the forest areas are many fur bearing animals and a variety of big game. Fox farming has become one of the important industries of the Territory.

The construction of the Alaska highway now links the great northwest areas, which were formerly inaccessible, with the cities of the Prairie Provinces and other parts of Canada. Opening of this highway and the advent of air traffic, have made the Yukon and Northwest Territories new frontiers for industrial development. Already new mining operations and prospecting expeditions have been planned and are being put into operation.

NORTHWEST TERRITORIES

The Northwest Territories, by far the largest section of Canada, with 1,304,903 square miles, includes the many large islands between the mainland and the North Pole. The North Magnetic Polar Area has been located just north of Boothia Peninsula.

Very little land is fitted for agriculture, most of it being in the Mackenzie basin, but it is usual to raise the more common vegetables at most posts, taking advantage of the long daylight of summer. The broad northeastern stretch is known as the Barren Lands, or the Arctic Prairies. The shallow, tundra soil grows almost 800 species of flowering plants, and in a few sheltered spots, mainly along rivers, are found stunted willows. A sparse, Arctic forest of balsam, spruce, tamarack, poplar, white birch and Jack pine cover most of the rest of the mainland of the Territories.

There is great potential wealth of natural resources. At Great Bear Lake is the silver pitchblend mine, important as a source of radium and uranium. Silver, copper, cobalt and lead are also recovered from the ores dug at Port Radium. Gold and silver are mined at Yellowknife, on Great Slave Lake. Underlying the lower Mackenzie Valley are extensive oil and natural gas deposits. Expansion of the mining industry has been increased through the development of hydro-electric power.

South of Great Slave Lake is the northern part of Wood Buffalo National Park, a sanctuary for the North American bison. Muskoxen are protected throughout the Territories, and reindeer herding, as a native industry, has been introduced principally along the Mackenzie River.

The origin of the Territories is the 1670 grant of land to the Hudson's Bay Company. This area was much larger than the present one, and included almost all of Canada from the Rocky Mountains to the St. Lawrence watershed. The Territories as they exist today were practically unexplored, and most of the company's posts were entirely within the present borders of Manitoba and Saskatchewan.

Samuel Hearne and Alexander Mackenzie, travelling for the Hudson's Bay and Northwest Fur Companies, respectively, explored the Arctic regions in the latter part of the eighteenth century. Important trading posts in the present Territories were set up soon thereafter. By 1869 Canada gained total jurisdiction, and the province of Manitoba was cut from the Territories in 1870. The Northwest Mounted Police was established shortly thereafter and a lieutenant governor and council set up for the Territories.

By 1882, the area below the 60th parallel had become the provisional districts of Assiniboia, Saskatchewan, Athabaska and Alberta. From these, the three prairie provinces were later carved.

The Yukon Territory was separated in 1898. By 1906 Alberta and Saskatchewan became provinces, and Manitoba was extended to Hudson Bay in 1912, while Ontario and Quebec received the rest of the southern and eastern shores of the bay.

Recent discoveries of uranium are opening the vast regions of northern Canada to development.

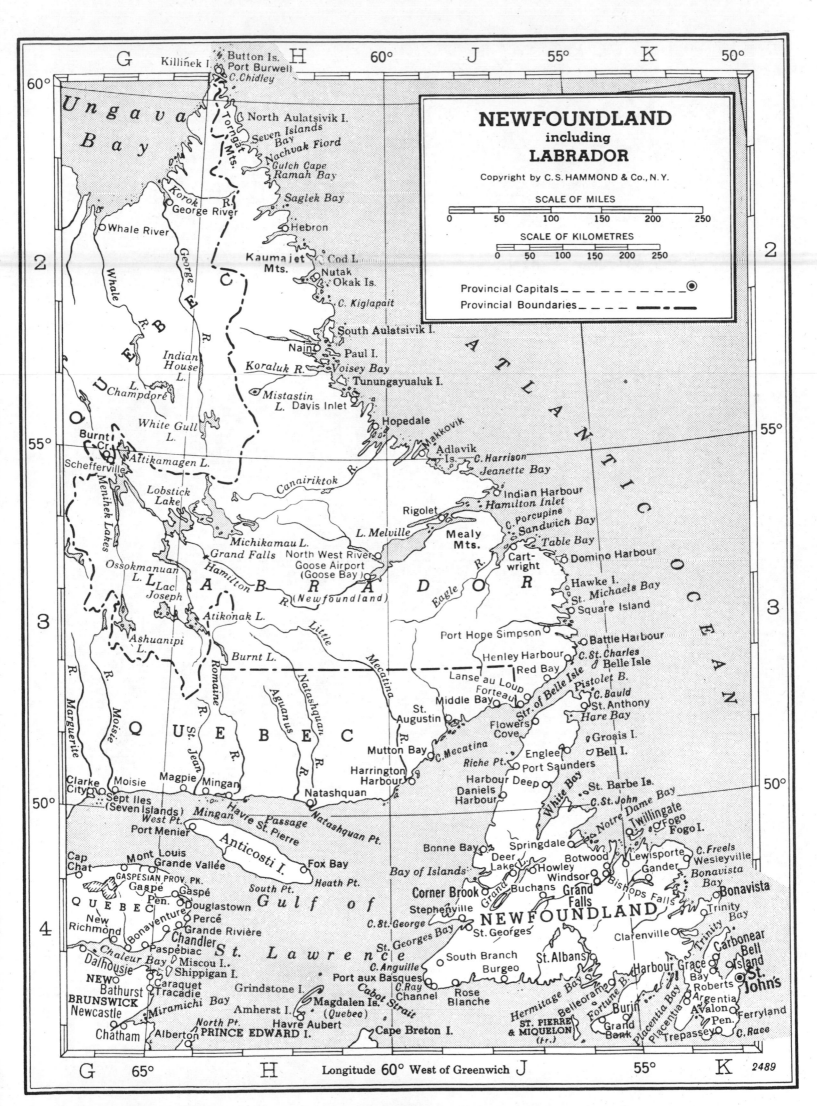

NEWFOUNDLAND
including
LABRADOR

Copyright by C.S. HAMMOND & Co., N.Y.

SCALE OF MILES
0   50   100   150   200   250

SCALE OF KILOMETRES
0   50   100   150   200   250

Provincial Capitals _ _ _ _ _ ◉
Provincial Boundaries _ _ _ _ _ _

NEW BRUNSWICK

NOVA SCOTIA

PRINCE EDWARD I.

NEWFOUNDLAND

MARITIME PROVINCES AND NEWFOUNDLAND

MAGDALEN ISLANDS
Total Population 11,556

Etang du Nord (G2) 300
Grand Entry (H2)... 714
Grindstone Island (H2) 738
Havre Aubert (H2).1,200
House Harbour (H2) 425
Leslie (H2).......... 140
Pointe Basse (H2)...

NEW BRUNSWICK
Total Population 559,616

Albert (E4).......... 250
Alma (D4).......... 500
Anagance (D4)........ 150
Andover (B3).......... 321
Apohaqui (D4)........ 200
Arthurette (B3)....... 125
Baie Verte (E3)....... 100
Balmoral (C2)......... 300
Barnaby River (D3) 300
Bath (B3).......... 400
Bathurst ◉(D2).......5,267
Bay du Vin (D2).... 25
Beaver Brook Sta. (D2) 54
Beersville (E3)......... 100
Belledune (D2)........ 125
Belleisle Creek (D4) 125
Belleville (B3)......... 50
Ben Lomond (D4)..
Benton (B3).......... 100
Beresford (D2)........ 127
Berry Mill Sta. (E3) 150
Black's Harbour (C4) 600
Blackville (D3) 500
Bloomfield Sta. (D4) 100
Boiestown (C3)....... 225
Bonney River (C4).. 25
Buctouche (E3)....... 800
Burnsville (D2)........ 100
Burnt Church (D2) 100
Burton ◉(C4)..........
Butternut Ridge (D4) 1,000
Campbellton (C2)...8,389
Canaan Station (E3) 88
Canterbury Sta. (B4) 400
Cap Pele (E3).......... 250
Sape Tormentine (E3) 127
Caraquet (D2).........1,500
Caron Brook (A2).. 200
Central Blissville (C4) 45
Centreville (B3)....... 250
Chatham (D2).........6,332
Chelmsford (D3).... 30
Chipman (D3).........1,200
Clair (A2).......... 400
Clifton (D2).......... 150
Clifton (C4).......... 100
Coal Branch Sta. (D3) 188
Cocagne (E3).......... 200
Connors (A2).......... 150
Cork Station (C4)... 15
Corn Hill (D4)........ 100
Cross Creek (C3).... 200
Cumberland Bay (D3) 70
Dalhousie ◉(C1).....5,468
Debec (B3) 139
Derby (D3).......... 100
Doaktown (C3)....... 270
Dorchester ◉(E4)...1,080
Douglas (C3).......... 209
Douglastown (D2).. 481
Edgett's Landing (E4) 150
Edmundston ◉(A2) 11,997
Elgin (D4).......... 280
Fairville (C4)........12,307
Five Fingers (B2).... 15
Flatlands (B2)......... 300
Florenceville (B3)... 490
Forest City (B4).....
FREDERICTON (C4) 18,303
Fredericton Junction (C4) 175
Gagetown ◉(C4)..... 312
Glassville (B3)........ 150
Grand Bay (C4)...... 207
Grand Falls (B2)....3,672
Grand Harbour (C5) 200
Grande Anse (D2).. 400
Hampstead (C4)..... 200
Hampton ◉(D4)...... 175
Harcourt (D3)......... 250
Hartland (B3).........1,022
Harvey (E4).......... 200
Harvey Station (B4) 200
Hatfield Point (D4) 150
Hillsborough (E4)...1,000
Hillsdale (D4)......... 125
Hopewell Cape ◉(E4) 25
Hoyt Station (C4)... 75
Inkerman (E2)......... 300
Jacquet River (C2). 316
Janeville (D2)......... 30
Jemseg (C4).......... 100
Juniper (B3).......... 96
Kedgwick (B2)....... 500
Kent Junction (D3) 77
Keswick Ridge (B4) 25
Kilburn (B3).......... 177
Kingston (C4)......... 125
Kouchibouguac (D3) 200
Lakeville Corner (C4) 250
Lepreau (C4).......... 125
Little Rocher (E4).. 25
Loggieville (D2)...... 437
Lorneville (C4)........ 50
Ludlow (C3).......... 100
Marysville (C3).......2,538
Maugerville (C4)..... 50
Mc Adam (B4).........2,100
McNamee (C3)....... 150
Memramcook (E4). 400
Millerton (D3)......... 300
Millstream (D4)...... 250
Milltown (B4).........1,975
Millville (B3).......... 350
Moncton (Metropolitan Area) (E3).........49,496
Moore's Mills (B4). 150
Musquash (C4)....... 188
Napudogan (C3)..... 180
Nash Creek (C2).... 175
Nashwaaksis (C3)... 238
Neguac (D2).......... 400
Nerepis (C4).......... 25
New Denmark (B3) 90
New Mills (C2)....... 250
Newcastle ◉(D2).....4,670
North Head (C5).... 800
Norton (D4).......... 550
Notre-Dame (E3).... 335
Oak Bay (B4).......... 100
Oromocto (C4)........ 661
Paquetville (D2)...... 233
Peel (B3).......... 125
Pennfield (C4)......... 200
Penobsquis (D4)...... 150
Perth ◉(B3).......... 706
Petersville (C4)........ 100
Petit Rocher (D2)... 500
Petitcodiac (D4)...... 900
Plaster Rock (B3)... 900
Plourd (A2).......... 50
Pointe du Chêne (E3) 250
Port Elgin (F3)....... 717
Portage River (E2). 150
Prince William (B4) 80
Quarryville (D3)..... 150
Renous (D3).......... 100
Rexton (E3).......... 400
Richibucto ◉(D3)...1,158
Richibucto Village (E3) 50
Riley Brook (B2).... 50
River Charlo (C2).. 200
River de Chute (B3) 100
Riverside (E4)......... 125
Rivière Verte (A2).. 700
Robichaud (E3)...... 300
Rogersville (D3)..... 700
Rothesay (D4)......... 802
Sackville (E4).........2,849
Saint Andrews ◉(B4) 1,534
Saint Antoine de Kent (E3)....... 300
Saint Basile (A2)..... 250
Saint George (C4)...1,322
Saint Ignace (D3)... 50
Saint Isidore (D2).. 300
Saint Jacques (A2).. 200
Saint John ◉(D4)..52,491
Saint John (Metropolitan Area) (D4)........77,553
Saint Leonard (B2).1,593
Saint Louis de Kent (D3) 500
Saint Martin's (D4) 547
Saint Stephen (B4)..3,491
Sainte Anne de Madawaska (B2).1,750
Sainte Croix (B4).... 90
Salisbury (D3)......... 340
Salmon Beach (D2). 100
Salmon Creek (C3).
Shediac (E3)..........2,173
Sheffield (C4).......... 250
Shippigan (E2).........1,362
South Nelson (D3). 477
Springleld (D4)........ 66
Stanley (C3).......... 300
Sussex (D4)..........3,403
Tabusintac (D2)..... 150
Taymouth (C3)....... 97
Tilley (B3).......... 25
Tracadie (D2)..........1,500
Tracy (C4).......... 100
Upham (D4).......... 100
Upper Blackville (C3) 200
Waterford (D4)....... 125
Watt (B4).......... 40
Welsford (C4).......... 300
Welshpool (C5)....... 400
Wirral (C4).......... 50
Woodstock ◉(B3)...4,308

NOVA SCOTIA
Total Population 694,717

Advocate Harbour (E4) ....
Amherst ◉(E4)....10,301
Annapolis Royal (D5) 765
Antigonish ◉(G4)...3,592
Apple River (E4).... 300
Arcadia (C6).......... 200
Argyle (D6).......... 30
Arichat ◉(J4).......... 700
Aspen (G4).......... 50
Athol (E4).......... 50
Auburn (E4).......... 100
Aylesford (E4)........ 500
Baccaro (D6).......... 75
Baddeck ◉(J3)........ 650
Ballantyne's Cove (G4) 200
Barrington (D6)...... 400
Barton (D5).......... 300
Bass River (F4)....... 450
Bay Saint Lawrence (J3) 200
Bayfield (H4)..........
Bear River (D5)......1,200
Beaver Bank (F5)... 250
Bedford (F5).......... 925
Belleisle (D5).......... 400
Belleville (D6)......... 75
Belliveau Cove (D5) 350
Belmont (F4).......... 300
Berwick (E4)..........1,134
Big Pond (J4).......... 150
Birchtown (D6)....... 250
Blandford (E5)........ 350
Boisdale (J3).......... 125
Boylston (H4).......... 500
Brazil Lake (C5)..... 75
Bridgeport (K3)...... 500
Bridgetown ◉(D5)..1,041
Bridgeville (G4)...... 200
Bridgewater (E5).....4,445
Brighton (C5)......... 75
Briton Cove (J3).... 40
Broad Cove (E5).... 250
Brookfield (F4)....... 175
Caledonia (G4)........ 100
Caledonia (D5)....... 482
Cambridge Sta. (E4) 200
Canning (E4).......... 800
Canso (H4)..........1,261
Cape North (J3)..... 350
Cariboo Gold Mines (G4) ....
Carleton (D5).......... 450
Catalone (J4).......... 100
Centreville (C5)...... 300
Centreville (E4)....... 222
Chester (E5)..........1,000
Chester Basin (E5).. 300
Cheticamp (H3)...... 600
Cheverie (E4).......... 200
Church Point (C5). 500
Clarence (D5).......... 100
Clark's Harbour (D6) 945
Clarksville (F4)....... 83
Clementsport (D5).. 290
Clementsvale (D5).. 550
Corberrie (D5)........ 125
Craigmore (H4)...... 30
Dalhousie East (E5) 140
Dartmouth (F5)....21,093
Debert Station (F4) 300
Deep Brook (D5).... 400
Denmark (F4).......... 200
Digby ◉(D5)..........2,145
Dingwall (J3).......... 132
Dominion (K3)........2,964
Dublin Shore (E5).. 200
Earltown (F4)......... 250
East Bay (J3).......... 300
Eastern Passage (F5) 750
Economy (E4)......... 200
Ecum Secum (G4).. 300
Elderbank (F5)........ 200
Elmsdale (F5).......... 300
Englishtown (J3)..... 125
Falmouth (E5)......... 300
Five Islands (E4).... 400
Fourchu (J4).......... 343
Framboise (J4)........ 275
Frankville (H4)....... 300
Freeport (C5)......... 700
Frizzleton (J3)......... 100
Gabarouse (J4)........ 500
Glace Bay (K3).....24,416
Glace Bay-Sydney (Metropolitan Area) (K3).....107,124
Goffs (F5)..........
Goldsboro (H4)....... 354
Goldenville (G4)..... 800
Goshen (H4).......... 150
Grand Etang (H3)... 300
Grand Narrows (J4) 100
Grand River (J4).... 300
Granville Centre (D5) 100
Granville Ferry (D5) 344
Great Village (F4).. 654
Greenfield (D5)....... 250
Guysborough ◉(H4) 800
Guysborough Intervale (H4)..... 250
Hackett's Cove (F5) 150
HALIFAX (F5)....93,301
Halifax (Metropolitan Area) (F5)......159,678
Hall's Harbour (E4) 105
Hantsport (E4)........1,298
Harbourville (D4)... 175
Havre Boucher (H4) 300
Hazel Hill (J4)......... 300
Hebron (C6).......... 500
Hectanooga (C5)..... 100
Miscou Harbour (E2) 30
Moncton (E3)........36,003
Hemford (E5).......... 130
Hopewell (G4)........ 365
Hubbards (E5)........ 450
Ingonish (J3).......... 400
Inverness (H3).........2,026
Iona (J3).......... 160
Irish Cove (J4)........ 50
Isaac's Harbour (H4) 377
Joggins (E4)..........1,102
Jordan Bay (D6)..... 100
Jordan Falls (D6)... 225
Judique (H4).......... 400
Kempt (D5).......... 225
Kempt Town (F4)... 110
Kemptville (D5)...... 75
Kennetcook (F4)..... 200
Kentville ◉(E4).......4,937
Kingsport (E4)........ 200
Kingston (E5).......... 500
Lake Ramsay (E5).. 20
L'Ardoise (J4)......... 450
Larry's River (H4).. 400
Lawrencetown (D5) 600
Lequille (D5).......... 350
Liscomb (G4).......... 209
Lismore (G4).......... 100
Litchfield (D5)........ 125
Liverpool ◉(E5)......3,500
Lochaber (G4)......... 200
Lockeport (D6).......1,207
Londonderry (F4)... 625
Long Point (H4)..... 80
Louisburg (K4).......1,314
Lower Argyle (D6). 125
Lower Wood Harbour (C6)...... 482
Lunenburg ◉(E5)....2,859
Mabou (H3).......... 600
Mahone Bay (E5)...1,109
Main-à-Dieu (K4).. 216
Maitland (F4).......... 400
Malignant Cove (H4) 20
Margaree Harbour (H3) 400
Margaretsville (D4) 200
Mc Kinnon's Harbour (J3)........ 100
Meagher's Grant (F5) 150
Merigomish (G4).... 200
Meteghan (C5)........ 750
Meteghan River (C5) 400
Middle River (J3).... 300
Middle Stewiacke (F4) 200
Middleton (D5).......1,769
Milford Sta. (F4).... 300
Mill Village (E5).... 150
Milton (E5)..........1,000
Mooseland (G5)...... 50
Moser's River (G5) 230
Mount Uniacke (F5) 230
Mulgrave (H4).........1,227
Musquodoboit Harbour (F5)....... 500
Neil's Harbour (J3) 300
New Annan (F4)..... 350
New Campbellton (J3) 68
New Germany (E5). 900
New Glasgow (G4).9,998
New Harbour (H4). 100
New Haven (J3)...... 100
New Ross (E5)........ 500
New Waterford (K3) 10,381
Newport (F5).......... 400
Newport Sta. (E5).. 300
Nictaux Falls (E5).. 250
Noel (F4).......... 500
North East Margaree (H3) 700
North River (F4)... 800
North Shore (J3)..... 225
North Sydney (J3)...8,125
Nyanza (J3).......... 50
Ohio (G4).......... 150
Oldham (F5)..........
Orangedale (H4)..... 233
Oxford (E4)..........1,545
Parrsboro (E4).........1,849
Peggy's Cove (F5).. 75
Petit Etang (J3)....... 360
Petite Rivière Bridge (E5) 350
Pictou ◉(G4)..........4,564
Pictou Landing (G4) (G4) 240
Pleasant Bay (H3).. 200
Plympton (D5)........ 300
Point Tupper (H4). 290
Pomquet (H4).......... 160
Port Clyde (D6)...... 200
Port Greville (E4)... 350
Port Hastings (H4).. 300
Port Hawkesbury (H4) 1,078
Port Hillford (H4).. 125
Port Hood ◉(H3).... 636
Port Lorne (D5)...... 200
Port Maitland (C6) 500
Port Medway (E5).. 369
Port Morien (K3).... 800
Port Mouton (E6)... 200
Port Williams (E4).. 500
Poulamon (J4)......... 350
Prospect (F5).......... 50
Pubnico (D6).......... 331
Pugwash (F4).......... 930
Queensport (H4)..... 250
Quinan (D6).......... 500
Rawdon (F4).......... 250
Reserve Mines (K3).1,300
River Bourgeois (J4) 300
River Denys Sta. (H4) 75
River Hébert (E4)..1,100
River John (G4).... 700
River Philip (F4).... 75
Riverport (E5)........ 200
Rockdale (J4).......... 600
Roseway (D6).......... 50
Roslin (F4).......... 15
Rossway (C5).......... 190
Round Hill (D5).... 100
Sable River (D6)..... 100
Saint Andrews (H4) 400
Saint Anns (J3)........ 100
Saint Bernard (D5).1,000
Saint Peter's (J4).... 812
Sainte Croix (F5)....1,200
Salmon River (C5).. 800
Salt Springs (F4).... 150
Sambro (F5).......... 150
Sandy Cove (C5).... 400
Saulnierville (C5)... 200
Scotsburn (F4)........ 200
Scotsville (H3)........ 75
Shag Harbour (D6) 200
Sheet Harbour (G5).1,500
Sheffield Mills (E4) 266
Shelburne ◉(D6)....2,337
Sherbrooke (H4)..... 500
Ship Harbour (G5) 500
Shubenacadie (F4).. 785
Shunacadie (J3).......
South Brookfield (D5) 250
South Ohio (C6)..... 350
Southampton (E4).. 150
Spencer's Island (E4) 188
Springfield (D5)...... 200
Springhill (F4)........7,348
Stellarton (G4)........5,445
Stewiacke (F4)........1,024
Strathlorne (H3)...... 100
Summerville (E4).... 350
Sunnybrae (G4)....... 260
Sydney ◉(J3)........32,162
Sydney-Glace Bay (Metropolitan Area) (J3).....107,124
Sydney Mines (J3).8,731
Tangier (G5).......... 300
Tatamagouche (F4) 1,000
Terence Bay (F5)... 300
Thorburn (G4)........1,200
Tidnish (E4).......... 350
Tiverton (C5).......... 400
Tracadie (H4).......... 200
Trenton (G4)..........3,240
Trout River (H3)....
Truro ◉(F4)..........12,250
Tusket (C6).......... 400
Upper Kennetcook (F4) 97
Upper La Have (E5) 300
Upper Musquodoboit (G4) 475
Upper Stewiacke (G4) 800
Upper Tantallon (E5) 132
Victoria Vale (D4). 25
Voglers Cove (E5).. 300
Wallace (F4).......... 300
Walton (F4).......... 250
Waverly (F5).......... 350
Wedgeport (C6)......1,322
Wentworth (F4)...... 95
West Bay (H4)......... 100
West Berlin (E5)..... 30
West Pubnico (D6). 200
West River Sta. (G4) 50
Westchester Sta. (F4) 100
Weston (E4)..........
Westport (C5)......... 400
Westville (G4).........4,247
Weymouth (D5)......1,500
Whitehead (H4)....... 132
Whycocomagh (H4) 400
Windsor ◉(E5)........3,651
Wolfville (E4).........2,497
Yarmouth ◉(C6)....8,095

NEWFOUNDLAND
Total Population 415,074

Argentia (J6).......... 900
Badger (J5).......... 500
Bay Roberts (J6)....1,306
Beaumont (J5)........ 400
Bell Island (Wabana) (K6)...7,837
Belleoram (J6)......... 570
Bishop's Falls (J5)..2,522
Bonavista (K5)........4,078
Bonne Bay (H5)...... 800
Botwood (J5)..........2,744
Buchans (H5)..........1,800
Burgeo (H6)..........1,138
Burin (J6)..........1,116
Calvert (K6).......... 350
Campbellton (J5).... 350
Cape Saint George (H5) ....
Carbonear (K6).......3,955
Channel-Port aux Basques (H6).......3,320
Clarenville (J6).......1,195
Codroy (H6).......... 450
Conche (J5).......... 25
Cook's Harbour (J4) 250
Corner Brook (H5) 23,225
Cow Head (H5)...... 343
Daniel's Harbour (H5) 257
Deer Lake (H5)......3,481
Elliston (K5).......... 750
Englee (J5).......... 677
Ferryland (K6)........ 500
Fleur de Lys (J5).... 300
Flower's Cove (J4).. 800
Fogo (J5)..........1,184
Fortune (J6)..........1,194
Fortune Harbour (J5) 275
Gambo (J5).......... 600
Gander (J5)..........3,000
Garnish (J6).......... 666
Glovertown (J5)...... 604
Grand Bank (J6)....2,430
Grand Falls (J5).....5,508
Greenspond (K5).... 784
Griguet (J4).......... 300
Hampden (H5)........ 150
Harbour Deep (J5). 214
Harbour Grace (J6) 2,545
Heart's Content (K6) 1,000
Howley (J5).......... 500
Humbermouth (H5) 1,914
Jackson's Arm (H5) 350
Joe Batt's Arm (K5) 800
King's Point (J5).... 275
La Scie (J5).......... 450
Lamaline (J6).......... 500
Lark Harbour (H5) 400
Lewisporte (J5).......2,076
Lumsden (K5)......... 470
Marystown (J6).......1,460
Merasheen (J6)........ 346
Millertown (J5)....... 400
Musgrave Harbour (K5) 385
Newtown (K5)......... 450
Norris Arm (J5)......1,000
Norris Point (H5)... 464
Pacquet (J5).......... 175
Placentia (K6).........1,223
Point Leamington (J5) 500
Port au Port (H5).. 500
Port aux Basques-Channel (H6).......3,320
Port Blandford (J5). 600
Port Saunders (J5).. 350
Port Union (K5)..... 625
Pouch Cove (K6)....1,090
Renews (K6).......... 450
Robinsons (H5)....... 200
Rose Blanche (H6). 950
Saint Alban's (J6).... 800
Saint Anthony (J4).1,761
Saint George's (H5) 750
SAINT JOHN'S (K6) 57,078
Saint John's (Metropolitan Area) (K6)......85,121
Saint Lawrence (J6) 1,837
Saint Mary's (K6)... 660
Saint Vincent's (J6). 400
Sop's Arm (H5)...... 100
South Branch (H6).. 200
Springdale (J5)........ 800
Stephenville (H5)....3,762
Torbay (K6)..........1,475
Trepassey (K6)........ 570
Trinity (K5).......... 250
Trout River (H5).... 500
Twillingate (J5).......2,100
Wesleyville (J5).......1,313
Windsor (J5)..........4,520

PRINCE EDWARD ISLAND
Total Population 99,285

Alberton (E3).......... 820
Cardigan (G3)......... 210
CHARLOTTETOWN (F3) 16,446
Crapaud (F3).......... 178
Ellerslie (E3).......... 125
Elmira (G3).......... 100
Emerald (F3).......... 100
Freetown (F3)......... 300
Georgetown ◉(G3). 754
Hunter's River (F3). 375
Kensington (F3)...... 855
Midgell (G3).......... 75
Miscouche (E3)....... 175
Montague (G3).......1,152
Morell (G3).......... 309
Mount Albion (G3). 75
Mount Stewart (G3) 439
Murray Harbour (G4) 405
Murray River (G3). 450
New Glasgow (F3). 150
New London (F3).. 50
New Wiltshire (F3). 175
O'Leary Sta. (E3)... 639
Peake Station (G3) 100
Port Borden (F3).... 695
Port Hill (F3)......... 150
Pownal (G3).......... 60
Rustico (F3).......... 40
Saint Louis (E3)..... 200
Saint Peter's Bay (G3) 308
Souris East (G3).....1,449
South Lake (G3).... 75
Stanley Bridge (F3) 65
Sturgeon (G3).......... 100
Summerside ◉(E3)..7,242
Tignish (E3).......... 914
Vernon Bridge (G3) 100

◉ County Seat

QUEBEC

1956 Total Population 4,628,378

Abbotsford (E4)..... 533
Abord-à-Plouffe (H4) 8,068
Acton Vale (E4).....3,547
Albertville (B2)....... 500
Alma (Ville-d'Alma) (F1) 10,822
Amqui ◉(B2)..........3,247
Ancienne-Lorette (H3) 1,000
Ange-Gardien (F3). 333
Ange-Gardien-de-Rouville (E4)....... 387
Anse-au-Griffon (D1) 500
Armagh (G3).......... 839
Arthabaska ◉(F3)..2,399
Arundel (C4).......... 350
Arvida (F1)..........12,919
Asbestos (F4)..........8,969
Aston Jct. (E3)........ 401
Athelstan (C4)........ 325
Ayer's Cliff ◉(E4).. 718
Aylmer (lake) (F4).
Aylmer East (B4)....5,294
Bagotville (G1).......4,822
Baie-Comeau (A1)..4,332
Baie-des-Capucins (B1) 300
Baie-des-Sables (A1) 735
Baie-d'Urfé (G4).....1,838
Baie-Saint-Paul ◉ (G2) 4,052
Barachois-de-Malbaie (D1)...... 515
Barré (G3)..........1,000
Baskatong (lake) (B3) ....
Batiscan (E3).......... 750
Batiscan (riv.) (E2)
Beaconsfield (H4)....5,496
Beauceville-Est ◉ (G3) 1,709
Beauceville-Ouest (G3) 1,459
Beauharnois ◉(D4).6,774
Beauport (J3)..........6,735
Beaupré (G2)..........2,377
Beaurepaire (G4).....2,500
Beaurivage (F3)....... 396
Bécancour ◉(E3).... 312
Bedford ◉(E4).........2,272
Beebe (E4)..........1,363
Beloeil (D4)..........3,966
Berthierville ◉(D3).3,504
Bic (J1)..........1,142
Black Lake (F3)......3,685
Boischatel (J3).........1,461
Boisvert (point) (J1)
Bolduc (G4)..........1,000
Bonaventure (C2)...2,500
Boucherville (J4)....3,911
Bouchette (A3)........ 400
Breakeyville (J3)..... 500
Brébeuf (C3).......... 500
Brome (lake) (E4).
Brompton (lake) (E4)
Bromptonville (F4).2,316
Brownsburg (C4)....3,412
Buckingham (B4)....6,781
Buckland (G3)......... 500
Bury (F4).......... 600
Cabano (J2)..........2,350
Cacouna (H2).......... 782
Calumet (C4).......... 826
Canrobert (Ange-Gardien-de-Rouville) (E4)... 387
Canton-Bégin (F1)..1,000
Cap-a-l'Aigle (G2).. 595
Cap-Chat (B1).........1,954
Cap-de-la-Madeleine (E3) 22,943
Cap-Rouge (H3)..... 350
Cap-Saint-Ignace (G2) 915
Cap-Santé ◉(F3)..... 528
Cascapédia (riv.) (C1) ....
Caughnawaga (H4).2,240
Causapscal (B2)......2,957
Chaleur (bay) (C2).
Chambly (J4)..........2,817
Chambord (E1).......1,091
Champlain (E3)...... 710
Champlain (lake) (D4) ....
Chandler (D2).........3,338
Charette (D3).......... 800
Charlemagne (H4)..2,428
Charlesbourg (J3)...8,202
Charny (J3)..........3,622
Château-Richer ◉ (F3) 700
Châteauguay (H4)..3,265
Châteauguay-Basin (H4) 3,250
Chaudière (riv.) (G4)
Chénéville (B4)........ 706
Chicoutimi ◉(G1).24,878
Chicoutimi (riv.) (F2) ....
Clermont (G2).........2,628
Cloridorme (D1)..... 600
Coaticook (F4).......6,441
Commissioners (lake) (E1)..........
Compton (F4).......... 481
Contrecoeur (D4)...1,662
Cookshire ◉(F4).....1,315
Corner of the Beach (D1) 300
Côte-St.-Michel (H4) 24,706
Coteau-Landing ◉ (C4) 551
Coudres (isl.) (G2).
Courcelles (G4)...... 498
Cowansville (E4).....5,242
Crabtree Mills (D4) 1,103
Danville (E4)..........2,296
Dartmouth (riv.) (D1) ....
Daveluyville (E3).... 591
Delisle (F1)..........1,261
Delson (H4).......... 816
Desbiens (F1)..........2,021
Deschaillons (E3) 1,759
Deschambault (E3).1,002
Deschênes (lake) (A4) ....
Deux-Rivières (St.-Stanislas-de-Champlain) (E3) 628
Disraeli (F4)..........2,437
Dixville (F4).......... 458
Donnacona (F3)......4,147
Dosquet (F3).......... 600
Douglastown (D1).. 779
Drummondville ◉ (E4) 26,284
Dunham (E4).......... 399
East Angus (F4)......4,239
East Broughton (F3) 1,868

QUEBEC (Continued)

East Broughton Station (F3) 1,060
Eastman (E4) 651
Edouard (lake) (E2)
Farnham (E4) 5,843
Fassett (C4) 500
Ferme-Neuve (B3) 1,891
Fontenelle (D1) 430
Forestville (H1) 1,117
Fort-Chambly (J4) 1,864
Fortierville (F3) 600
Foster (E4) 436
Frampton (G3) 888
Garthby Sta. (F4) 497
Gaspé (D1) 2,194
Gaspé (bay) (D1)
Gaspé (cape) (D1)
Gaspé (pen.) (D2)
Gaspesian Prov. Park (C1)
Gatineau (B4) 8,423
Gatineau (riv.) (B3)
Gentilly (E3) 664
Giffard (J3) 9,964
Godbout (B1) 663
Gracefield (A3) 639
Granby (E4) 27,095
Grande-Cascapédia (C2) 513
Grand Mère (E3) 14,023
Grande-Ligne (D4). 600
Grand-Rivière (D2) 1,024
Grande-Vallée (D1) 459
Grandes-Bergeronnes (H1) 810
Grandes-Piles (E3) 650
Grenville (C4) 1,277
Grosses-Roches (B1) 501
Ha! Ha! (riv.) (G1)
Ham-Nord (F4) 800
Hébertville (F1) 1,509
Hébertville-Station (F1) 1,189
Hemmingford (D4). 682
Henryville (D4) 644
Hérouxville (E3) 500
Honfleur (G3) 388
Howick (D4) 560
Huberdeau (C4) 900
Hudson (C4) 1,549
Hull ◉(B4) 49,243
Huntingdon ◉ (C4) 2,995
Iberville ◉(D4) 6,270
Ile-Bizard (H4) 900
Ile-Maligne (F1) 1,761
Ile-Perrot-Nord (G4) 450
Ile-Perrot-Sud (H4) 2,600
Iles (lake) (B3)
Inverness ◉(F3) 321
Isle-aux-Grues (H1) 1,000
Isle-Verte (H1) 1,000
Jacques-Cartier (Ville-Jacques-Cartier) (J4) 33,132
Jacques-Cartier (mt.) (C1)
Jacques-Cartier (riv.) (F2)
Jesus (isl.) (H4)
Joliette ◉(D3) 16,940
Jonquière (F1) 25,550
Kamouraska (H2) 506
Kénogami (F1) 11,309
Kénogami (lake) (F1)
Kiamika (B3) 400
Kiamika (lake) (B3)
Kildare (D3) 450
Kingsey Falls (E4) 596
Knowlton ◉(E4) 1,328
La Baie (E3) 658
La Conception (C3) 400
La Decharge (F1) 400
La Durantaye (G3). 412
La Guadeloupe (F4) 1,482
La Malbaie ◉(G2) 2,817
La Minerve (C3) 350
La Patrie (F4) 535
La Petite Rivière St. François (G2) 450
La Salle (H4) 18,867
La Tuque (E2) 11,096
La Vérendrye Prov. Park (A3)
Labelle (C3) 1,150
Lac-au-Saumon (B2) 1,681
Lac-aux-Sables (E3) 500
Lac-Bouchette (E1). 781
Lac-Carré (C3) 601
Lac-Edouard (E2) 250
Lac-Etchemin (G3) 1,380
Lac-Frontière (H3). 619
Lac-Humqui (B2) 500
Lac-Masson (D3) 650
Lac-Mégantic ◉ (G4) 6,864
Lac-Saguay (B3) 295
Lac-Sainte-Marie (B4) 450
L'Acadie (J4) 550
Lachine (H4) 34,494
Lachute ◉(C4) 6,866
Lachute Mills (C4) 3,000
Lacolle (D4) 1,141
Lamartine (G2) 1,000
Lambton (F4) 701
Langevin (G3) 552
L'Annonciation (C3) 783
Lanoraie (D4) 900
L'Anse-Saint-Jean (G1) 250
Laprairie ◉(J4) 5,271
Larochelle (St.-Grégoire) (E3) 625
Larouche (F1) 350

L'Assomption ◉ (D4) 3,683
L'Assomption (riv.) (D3)
Laterrière (F1) 658
Laurentides Prov. Park (F2)
Laurierville (F3) 767
Lauzon (F3) 10,265
Laval-des-Rapides (H4) 11,248
Lavaltrie (D4) 917
L'Avenir (E4) 357
Leeds Village (F3) 500
Lennoxville (F4) 3,149
L'Epiphanie (D4) 2,671
Les Eboulements (G2) 500
Les Escoumins (H1) 750
Les Etroits (J2) 500
Les Hauteurs de Rimouski (J1). 750
Les Méchins (B1) 600
Lévis (J3) 13,644
Lièvre (riv.) (B4)
Linière (G3) 1,149
L'Islet (G2) 823
Longueuil ◉(J4) 14,332
Loretteville ◉(H3) 4,957
Louiseville ◉(E3) 4,392
Loup (riv.) (H2)
Low (B4) 500
Luceville (J1) 1,265
Lyster Station (F3) 1,010
Madeleine (cape) (D1)
Magog (E4) 12,638
Malbaie (riv.) (G2)
Manicouagan (point) (B1)
Maniwaki ◉(B3) 5,399
Manseau (E3) 846
Mansonville (E4) 700
Marbleton (F4) 750
Maria (C2) 500
Marieville ◉(D4) 3,478
Mascouche (H4) 1,000
Maskinongé (E3) 800
Maskinonge (riv.) (D3)
Masson (B4) 1,656
Massueville (St.-Aimé) (E4) 644
Matane ◉(B1) 8,069
Matapédia (B2) 500
Matapédia (lake) (B1)
Mattawin (riv.) (D3)
Mégantic (Lac-Mégantic) ◉(G4) 6,864
Mégantic (lake) (G4)
Mekinac (lake) (E2)
Melocheville (C4) 1,422
Memphremagog (lake) (E4)
Metabetchouan (riv.) (F1)
Mille Isles (riv.) (H4)
Mistassini (riv.) (E1)
Mont-Joli (J1) 6,179
Mont-Laurier ◉ (B3) 5,486
Mont-Louis (C1) 500
Mont-Rolland (C4) 1,000
Mont-Saint-Grégoire (D4) 594
Mont-Tremblant Prov. Park (C3)
Montauban (E3) 336
Montebello (B4) 1,287
Montmagny ◉(G3) 6,405
Montmorency (J3) 6,077
Montmorency (riv.) (F2)
Montréal ◉ (H4) 1,109,439
Montréal (Metropolitan Area) (H4) 1,395,400
Morin Heights (C4) 600
Mount Royal (H4) 16,990
Namur (C4) 300
Napierville ◉(D4) 1,510
Neuville (F3) 727
New Carlisle ◉ (D2) 1,000
New Richmond (C2) 1,000
Newport (D2) 500
Nicolet (E3) 4,084
Nicolet (riv.) (E3)
Nominingue (B3) 733
Normandin (E1) 1,918
North (riv.) (C4)
North Coaticook (F4) 500
North Hatley (E4) 671
Notre-Dame-de-Ham (F4) 500
Notre-Dame-des-Bois (G4) 822
Notre-Dame-du-Lac ◉(J2) 1,512
Notre-Dame-du-Laus (B3) 650
Notre-Dame-du-Rosaire (G3) 800
Oies (isl.) (G2)
Oka (C4) 1,084
Orléans (isl.) (F3)
Ormstown (D4) 1,347
Ottawa (riv.) (B4)
Ouareau (riv.) (D3)
Outremont (H4) 29,990
Panet (G3) 2,100
Papineau (lake) (C4)
Papineauville ◉ (C4) 1,141
Parisville (F3) 500
Pespébiac (D2) 800

Patapedia (riv.) (B2)
Percé ◉(D1) 700
Péribonca (E1) 500
Petit-Saguenay (G1) 500
Petite-Nation (riv.) (B4)
Pierreville (E3) 1,589
Plaisance (B4) 500
Plessisville (F3) 5,829
Pointe-au-Pic (G2) 1,220
Pointe-aux-Trembles (J4) 11,981
Pointe-Claire (H4) 15,208
Pointe-Garleau (B4) 6,175
Poisson-Blanc (lake) (B4)
Poltimore (B4) 400
Pont-Rouge (F3) 2,631
Pont-Viau (H4) 8,218
Pontbriand (F3) 450
Port-Alfred (G1) 7,986
Port-Daniel (D2) 800
Portneuf (F3) 1,256
Prairies (riv.) (H4)
Price (A1) 3,140
Princeville (F3) 2,841
QUÉBEC (H3) 170,703
Québec (Metropolitan Area) (H3) 301,108
Ravignan (G3) 807
Rawdon (D3) 2,049
Restigouche (C2) 532
Restigouche (riv.) (B2)
Richelieu (Village-Richelieu) (D4) 1,398
Richmond ◉(E4) 3,849
Rigaud (C4) 1,784
Rimouski ◉(J1) 14,630
Rimouski (riv.) (J1)
Rimouski Est (J1) 1,209
Ripon (B4) 549
Rivière-à-Pierre (E3) 817
Rivière-au-Doré (E1)
Rivière-au-Renard (D1) 850
Rivière-Beaudette (C4) 270
Rivière-Bleue (J2) 1,481
Rivière-Caplan (C2) 317
Rivière-des-Prairies (H4) 6,806
Rivière-du-Loup ◉ (H2) 9,964
Rivière-du-Moulin (G1) 4,138
Rivière-la-Madeline (C1) 225
Rivière-Mailloux (G2) 550
Rivière-Ouelle (G2). 600
Rivière-Trois-Pistoles (J1) 400
Robertsonville (F3) 1,030
Roberval ◉(E1) 6,643
Rock Island (E4) 1,608
Rouge (riv.) (C3)
Roxton Falls (E4) 1,023
Roxton Pond (E4) 735
Saguenay (riv.) (G1) 53
St.-Adalbert (H3) 600
St.-Adelphe-de-Champlain (E3) 750
St.-Adolphe-de-Howard (C4) 350
St.-Adolphe-de-Dudswell (F4) 400
St.-Aimé (E4) 644
St.-Alban (E3) 815
St.-Albert (E3) 375
St.-Alexandre-d'Iberville (D4) 375
St.-Alexandre-de-Kamouraska (H2) 904
St.-Alexis-de-Montcalm (D4) 489
St.-Alexis-de-Matapédia (B2) 500
St.-Alexis-des-Monts (D3) 700
St.-Alphonse-de-Caplan (C2) 600
St.-Ambroise-de-Chicoutimi (F1) 1,305
St.-Anaclet (J1) 800
St.-André-de-Kamouraska (H2) 539
St. Andrews (C4) 811
St.-Anselme (F3) 1,086
St.-Antoine-Abbé (D4) 275
St.-Antoine-Lotbinière (F3) 300
St.-Antoine-sur-Richelieu (D4) 500
St.-Antonin (H2) 500
St. Apollinaire (F3) 824
St.-Arsène (H2) 400
St.-Athanase (H2) 250
St.-Aubert (G2) 550
St.-Augustin (G4) 393
St.-Augustin-de-Québec (H3) 550
St.-Barnabé-Sud (D4) 300
St.-Barthélémy (D3) 900
St.-Basile (J4) 700
St.-Basile (F3) 1,635
St.-Benjamin (G3) 700
St.-Benoît (C4) 467
St.-Benoît-Labre (G3) 600
St.-Bernard-de-Dorchester (F3) 500
St.-Bonaventure (E4) 500
St.-Boniface-de-Shawinigan (D3). 880
St.-Bruno (J4) 800
St.-Bruno-de-Kamouraska (H2) 800

St.-Calixte-de-Kilkenny (D4) 400
St.-Camille (F4) 375
St.-Camille-de-Bellechasse (G3) 650
St.-Casimir (E3) 1,447
St.-Césaire (D4) 1,739
St.-Charles-de-Bellechasse (G3). 946
St.-Charles-River-Richelieu (D4) 287
St.-Chrysostome (D4) 866
St.-Clément (H2) 500
St.-Clet (C4) 308
St.-Côme (D3) 525
St.-Constant (H4) 500
St.-Cuthbert (D3) 600
St.-Cyprien (J2) 575
St.-Cyrille-de-Wendover (E4) 1,198
St.-Cyrille-de-L'Islet (G3) 700
St.-Damase (D4) 450
St.-Damase-de-Matane (B1) 700
St.-Damase-des-Aulnaies (G2) 737
St.-Damien-de-Brandon (D3) 400
St.-Damien-de-Buckland (G3) 500
St.-David-de-Lévis (J3) 400
St.-David-d'Yamaska (E4) 800
St.-Denis-Rivière-Richelieu (D4) 944
St.-Denis-de-la-Bouteillerie (G2). 450
St.-Didace (D3) 472
St.-Dominique-de-Bagot (E4) 483
St.-Donat-de-Rimouski (J1) 476
St.-Edouard-de-Napierville (D4). 350
St.-Eleuthère (H2) 650
St.-Elie (E3) 775
St.-Eloi (H1) 650
St.-Emile-de-Québec (H3) 1,645
St.-Emile-de-Suffolk (B4) 450
St.-Emilien (Desbiens) (F1) 2,021
St.-Ephrem-de-Beauce (G3) 831
St.-Esprit (D4) 850
St.-Etienne-des-Grès (E3) 500
St.-Eugène-de-Grantham (E4) 400
St.-Eusèbe (J2) 308
St.-Eustache (H4) 3,740
St.-Fabien (J1) 1,200
St.-Félicien (E1) 4,152
St.-Félix-de-Valois (D3) 1,323
St.-Ferdinand (F3) 2,431
St.-Féréol (G2) 330
St.-Fidèle (H2) 390
St. Flavien (F3) 634
St.-Fortunat (F4) 400
St.-Francis (riv.) (E4)
St.-François-Montmagny (G3). 600
St.-François (lake) (C4)
St.-François (lake) (F4)
St.-François-du-Lac ◉(E3) 826
St.-Frédéric (G3) 375
St.-Fulgence (G1) 1,054
St.-Gabriel-de-Brandon (D3) 3,265
St.-Gabriel-de-Rimouski (J1) 575
St.-Gédéon (F1) 873
St.-Gédéon-de-Beauce (G4) 857
St.-Georges-de-Cacouna (Cacouna) (H2) 782
St.-Georges-de-Windsor (F4) 400
St.-Georges-Ouest (G3) 3,597
St.-Gérard (F4) 665
St.-Germain-de-Grantham (E4) 919
St.-Gervais (G3) 1,000
St.-Gilles (F3) 400
St.-Godefroi (D2) 400
St.-Grégoire (E3) 625
St.-Guillaume (E4) 802
St.-Henri (J3) 661
St.-Hermas (C4) 400
St.-Herménégilde (F4) 236
St.-Hilarion (G2) 400
St.-Hilaire-Village (D4) 2,000
St.-Honoré (G4) 650
St.-Honoré-de-Témiscouta (H2). 891
St. Hubert (J4) 400
St.-Hubert-de-Temiscouata (J2). 800
St.-Hugues (E4) 487
St.-Hyacinthe ◉ (D4) 20,439
St.-Irénée (G2) 500
St.-Isidore-d'Auckland (F4). 468
St.-Isidore-Dorchester (F3) 688
St.-Jacques (D4) 1,979

St.-Janvier (H4) 650
St.-Jean ◉(D4) 24,367
St.-Jean (G3) 600
St.-Jean-Chrysostome-de-Lévis (J3) 500
St.-Jean-de-Boischatel (Boischatel) (J3) 1,461
St.-Jean-de-Dieu (J1) 998
St.-Jean-de-Matha (D3) 1,016
St.-Jean-des-Piles (E3) 350
St.-Jean-Port-Joli ◉ (G2) 900
St.-Jérôme ◉(H4) 20,645
St.-Joachim-de-Montmorency (G2) 568
St.-John (lake) (E1)
St.-Joseph (lake) (F3)
St.-Joseph-de-Beauce (G3) 2,484
St.-Joseph-de-la-Rivière-Bleue (J2) 1,481
St.-Joseph-de-Sorel (D3) 3,530
St.-Joseph-du-Lac (C4) 400
St.-Jovite (C3) 1,613
St.-Jude (E4) 700
St.-Just-de-Bretenières (H3) 400
St.-Justin (D3) 588
St.-Lambert (J4) 12,224
St.-Laurent (H4) 38,291
St.-Laurent-d'Orléans (G3) 450
St.-Lawrence (gulf) (D2)
St.-Lawrence (riv.) (H1)
St.-Lazare-Village (G3) 466
St.-Léandre (B1) 450
St.-Léon-le-Grand (B2) 500
St.-Léonard-de-Portneuf (F3) 636
St.- Léonard-d'Aston E3 752
St.-Liboire ◉(E4) 613
St.-Liguori (D3) 250
St.-Louis (lake) (H4)
St.-Louis-de-Gonzague (D4) 500
St.-Louis-du-Ha!-Ha! (H2) 800
St.-Luc-de-Matane (B1) 624
St.-Ludger (G4) 301
St.-Magloire (G3) 772
St.-Malachie (G3) 500
St.-Marc (D4) 322
St.-Marc-des-Carrières (E3) 2,457
St.-Marcel-de-l'Islet (G3) 495
St.-Marcellin (J1) 350
St.-Martin (H4) 6,440
St.-Mathieu (J1) 550
St.-Maurice (riv.) (E2)
St.-Méthode-de-Frontenac (F3) 1,000
St.-Michel-de-Bellechasse (G3) 660
St.-Michel (Côte-St.-Michel) (H4) 24,706
St.-Michel-des-Saints (D3) 800
St.-Modeste (H2) 300
St.-Nazaire (E4) 500
St.-Nérée (G3) 530
St.-Nicolas (H3) 350
St.-Noël (B1) 1,027
St.-Norbert-d'Arthabaska (F3) 248
St.-Octave (B1) 500
St.-Odilon (G3) 450
St.-Omer (C3) 275
St.-Ours (D4) 691
St.-Pacôme (G2) 1,283
St.-Pamphile (H3) 1,000
St.-Pascal ◉(H2) 1,962
St. Paul-de-Chester (F4) 267
St. Paul-de-Montminy (G3) 850
St. Paul-du-Nord (H1) 300
St.-Paul-l'Ermite (J4) 2,002
St.-Paulin (D3) 943
St.-Peter (lake) (E3)
St.-Philémon (G3) 500
St.-Philippe-de-Laprairie (J4) 498
St.-Philippe-de-Néri (H2) 635
St.-Pie (E4) 1,229
St. Pierre-Baptiste (F3) 750
St.-Pierre-Les-Becquets (E3) 393
St.-Pierre-Montmagny (G3) 1,200
St.-Pierre (point) (D1)
St.-Placide (C4) 305
St.-Polycarpe (C4) 554
St.-Prime (E1) 629
St.-Prosper (E3) 418
St.-Prosper-de-Dorchester (G3) 998
St.-Raphaël-Bellechasse ◉(G3) 1,059
St.-Raymond (F3) 3,502
St.-Rémi (D4) 2,303
St.-Rémi-d'Amherst (C3) 750

St.-Robert (E4) 500
St.-Roch-des-Aulnaies (G2) 350
St.-Roch-de-l'Achigan (D4) 700
St.-Roch-de-Richelieu (D4) 700
St.-Romain (F4) 800
St.-Romuald-d'Etchemin (J3) 4,502
St.-Samuel-de-Gayhurst (G4) 550
St.-Sauveur-des-Montagnes (C4) 1,316
St.-Sébastien-de-Beauce (G4) 473
St.-Sévère (E3) 250
St.-Siméon (G2) 1,114
St.-Simon (E4) 436
St.-Simon (H1) 528
St. Stanislas-de-Champlain (E3) 620
St.-Sylvestre (F3) 476
St.-Télesphore (C4). 275
St.-Théophile (G4). 388
St.-Thuribe (E3) 500
St.-Timothée (D4) 688
St.-Tite (E3) 3,183
St.-Tite-des-Caps (G2) 650
St.-Ubald (E3) 775
St.-Ulric (B1) 980
St.-Urbain-de-Charlevoix (G2) 690
St.-Valère-de-Bulstrode (E3) 300
St.-Valérien (E4) 348
St.-Valérien-de-Charlevoix (J1) 450
St.-Vallier (G3) 533
St.-Victor-de-Beauce (G3) 684
St.-Vincent-de-Paul (H4) 6,784
St.-Wenceslas (E3) 315
St.-Zacharie (G3) 400
St.-Zénon (D3) 850
St.-Zéphirin (E3) 430
Ste.-Adelaide-de-Pabos (D2) 300
Ste.-Adèle (C4) 1,309
Ste.-Agathe-de-Lotbinière (F3) 559
Ste.-Agathe-des-Monts (C3) 5,173
Ste.-Agnès-de-Charlevoix (G2) 500
Ste.-Angèle-de-Monnoir (D4) 580
Ste.-Angèle-de-Mérici (J1) 655
Ste.-Angèle-de-Laval (E3) 542
Ste.-Anne (riv.) (G2)
Ste.-Anne (riv.) (F3)
Ste.-Anne-de-Beaupré (F2) 1,865
Ste.-Anne-de-Bellevue (H4) 3,647
Ste.-Anne-de-la-Pérade (E3) 1,282
Ste.-Anne-de-la-Pocatière (H2) 300
Ste.-Anne-des-Monts (C1) 1,000
Ste.-Anne-des-Plaines (H4) 949
Ste.-Anne-du-Lac (B3) 528
Ste.-Apolline-de-Patton (H3) 650
Ste.-Béatrix (D3) 375
Ste.-Blandine (J1) 508
Ste.-Catherine (F3) 450
Ste.-Cécile-de-Frontenac (G4) 375
Ste.-Cécile-de-Masham (B4) 300
Ste.-Claire (G3) 828
Ste.-Clothilde (E4) 450
Ste.-Croix ◉(F3) 1,241
Ste.-Edwidge (F4) 450
Ste.-Elizabeth (D3). 554
Ste.-Emélie-de-l'Energie (D3) 700
Ste.-Emmélie (F3) 500
Ste.-Eulalie (E3) 450
Ste.-Euphémie (G3) 500
Ste.-Famille (G3) 300
Ste.-Félicité (B1) 812
Ste.-Florence (B2) 370
Ste.-Flore (E3) 500
Ste.-Foy (H3) 14,615
Ste.-Geneviève-de-Batiscan ◉(E3) 550
Ste.-Geneviève-de-Pierrefonds (H4) 2,041
Ste.-Gertrude (E3) 379
Ste.-Hélène-de-Kamouraska (H2) 800
Ste.-Hélène-de-Bagot (E4) 290
Ste.-Hénédine ◉ (F3) 606
Ste.-Julie-de-Verchères (J4) 400
Ste.-Julienne ◉(D4) 700
Ste.-Justine-de-Newton (C4) 487
Ste.-Louise (G2) 558
Ste.-Lucie-de-Beauregard (H3). 350
Ste.-Lucie-de-Doncaster (C3) 484
Ste.-Marguerite-de-Dorchester (G3) 350
Ste.-Marie-Beauce (G3) 3,094

Ste.-Marthe (C4) 773
Ste.-Martine (D4) 573
Ste.-Perpétue (E3) 488
Ste.-Perpétue-de-l'Islet (H2) 500
Ste.-Pudentienne (Roxton Pond) (E4) 735
Ste.-Rosalie (D4) 1,120
Ste.-Rose ◉(H4) 4,948
Ste.-Rose-de-Lima (B4) 1,714
Ste.-Rose-de-Watford (G3) 450
Ste.-Rose-du-Dégelé (J2) 1,400
Ste.-Sabine (G3) 400
Ste.-Scholastique ◉ (C4) 865
Ste.-Sophie-de-Lévrard (E3) 450
Ste.-Sophie-de-Mégantic (F3) 575
Ste.-Thérèse-de-Blainville (H4) 8,266
Ste.-Thérèse (isl.) (J4)
Ste.-Ursule (D3) 486
Ste.-Véronique (C3) 400
Ste.-Victoire (D4) 450
Salmon (riv.) (F4).
Sault-au-Mouton (H1) 873
Sawyerville (F4) 823
Sayabec (B2) 2,281
Scotstown (F4) 1,347
Scott-Jonction (F3) 477
Senneville (G4) 979
Shawbridge (C4) 680
Shawinigan (riv.) (E3)
Shawinigan Falls (D3) 28,597
Shawinigan Falls (Metropolitan (Area) (D3) 58,328
Sherbrooke ◉(E4) 58,668
Sherbrooke (Metropolitan Area) (E4) 63,694
Sillery (J3) 13,154
Sorel ◉(D4) 16,342
South Durham (E4) 416
South Roxton (E4). 480
Squatteck (J2) 300
Stanstead (Stanstead Plain) (F4) 1,134
Stoneham (F2) 472
Stratford Centre (F4) 400
Sully (H2) 500
Sutton (E4) 1,407
Sweetsburg (E4) 879
Tadoussac ◉(H1) 1,066
Taureau (res.) (D3)
Témiscouata (lake) (H2)
Templeton (B4) 2,475
Terrebonne (H4) 4,097
Thetford Mines (F3) 19,511
Thirty One Mile (lake) (B3)
Thurso (B4) 2,324
Ticouape (E1) 600
Tingwick (F4) 500
Tourelle (C1) 700
Tourville (H2) 713
Tring Jonction (F3) 1,083
Trois-Pistoles (H1) 4,039
Trois-Rivières (F3) 50,483
Trois-Rivières (Metropolitan Area) (E3) 77,961
Two Mountains (lake) (C4)
Upton (E4) 797
Val-Alain (F3) 600
Val-Barrette (B3) 568
Val-Brilliant (B1) 939
Val-David (C3) 1,016
Valcartier-Village (F3) 800
Valcourt (E4) 753
Vallée-Jonction (G3) 1,340
Valleyfield (C4) 23,584
Valmont (E3) 520
Varennes (J4) 2,047
Vaudreuil ◉(C4) 778
Verchères ◉(J4) 1,412
Verdun (H4) 78,262
Victoriaville (E3) 16,031
Viger (H2) 450
Village Richelieu (D4) 1,398
Ville-d'Alma ◉ (F1) 10,822
Ville-Jacques-Cartier (J4) 33,132
Ville-St. Georges (G3) 3,142
Villeneuve (J3) 1,417
Villers (Ste.-Gertrude) (E3) 379
Wakefield (B4) 376
Warwick (F4) 1,498
Waterloo ◉(E4) 4,266
Waterville (F4) 1,373
Weedon (F4) 1,287
West Shefford (E4). 369
Westmount (H4) 24,800
Wickham Ouest (E4) 393
Windsor (F4) 5,886
Wotton (F4) 751
Yamachiche ◉(E3). 900
Yamaska (riv.) (E4)

◉ County Seat

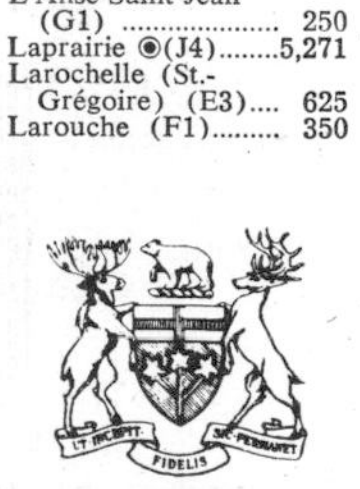

ONTARIO

1956 Total Population 5,404,933

Abitibi (riv.) (J5)
Actinolite (G3) 200
Acton (D4) 3,578
Agincourt (J4) 350
Ailsa Craig (C4) 533
Ajax (F4) 5,683

Alexandria (K2) 2,487
Alfred (K2) 1,257
Algoma Mills (B1) 100
Algonquin Park (F2) 100
Algonquin Prov. Park (F2)

Allenford (C3) 200
Alliston (E3) 2,426
Alma (D4) 195
Almonte (H2) 2,960
Alton (E4) 500
Alvinston (B5) 652

Amherst (isl.) (H3)
Amherstburg (A5) 4,099
Angus (E3) 400
Ansonville (K5) 3,167
Appin (C5) 125
Apple Hill (K2) 370

Apsley (F3) 175
Arden (G3) 300
Arkona (C4) 447
Armstrong Sta. (H4) 375
Arnprior (H2) 5,137
Arthur (D4) 1,124

Athens (J3) 935
Atherly (E3) 250
Atikokan (G5) 2,400
Atwood (D4) 600
Auburn (C4) 175
Auden (H4) 444

Aultsville (J3) 350
Aurora (J3) 3,957
Avening (D3) 94
Avonmore (K2) 500
Aylmer West (C5) 4,201
Ayr (D4) 939

Ayton (D3)............ 500
Baden (D4)............1,000
Bala (E2)............ 452
Balsam (lake) (F3).
Baltimore (F3)........ 200
Bancroft (G2)..........1,669
Bannockburn (G3).. 200
Baptiste (lake)(G2)
Barrie ◉(E3).........16,851
Barrys Bay (G2).....1,366
Bath (H3)............ 637
Battersea (H3)........ 100
Bayfield (C4)......... 321
Bayfield (sound) (B2) ......
Bays (lake) (F2).....
Baysville (E2)........ 125
Beachburg (H2)........ 450
Beachville (D4)....... 700
Beamsville (E4).......2,198
Beardmore (H5)........ 450
Beaverton (E3).........1,099
Beeton (E3)........... 675
Belgrave (C4)......... 125
Bellamys (J3)......... 96
Belle River (B5)......1,814
Belleville ◉(G3)......20,605
Belmont (C5).......... 500
Belwood (D4).......... 200
Berkeley (D3)......... 200
Bervie (C3)........... 300
Bethany (F3).......... 294
Birch Cliff (K4)......1,000
Biscotasing (J5)...... 200
Bishops Mills (J3) ...150
Blackstock (F3)....... 300
Blenheim (C5).........2,844
Blind River (A1)......3,633
Bloomfield (G4)....... 769
Bluevale (C4)......... 235
Blyth (C4)............ 757
Blytheswood (B5)...... 100
Bobcaygeon (F3).......1,242
Bolton (J4)...........1,093
Bonfield (E1)......... 609
Bothwell (C5)......... 765
Bourget (J2).......... 612
Bowmanville (F4)...6,544
Bracebridge ◉(E2)..2,849
Bradford (E3).........2,010
Braeside (H2)......... 506
Brampton ◉(J4)....12,587
Brantford ◉(D4)..51,869
Brantford (Metropolitan Area) (D4)......55,740
Brechin (E3).......... 225
Brigden (B5).......... 500
Brighton (G3)..........2,182
Britt (D2)............ 225
Brockville ◉(J3)....13,885
Bronte (E4)...........2,024
Brooklin (E4)......... 650
Brougham (K3)......... 300
Bruce Mines (J5)... 451
Brucefield (C4)....... 200
Brussels (C4)......... 782
Buckhorn (F3)......... 150
Burford (D4).......... 700
Burgesville (D4)...... 300
Burks Falls (E2)...... 902
Burlington (E4).......9,127
Burlington Beach (E4) 3,314
Burnt (riv.) (F3)...
Burnt River (F3)..... 200
Burwash (D1).......... 125
Byng Inlet (D2)....... 647
Cabot Head (prom.) (C2) ...
Cache Bay (D1)........ 894
Calabogie (H2)........ 428
Caledon East (E4).. 337
Caledonia (E4).........2,078
Callander (E1)........ 750
Camlachie (B4)........ 147
Camp Borden (E3).1,000
Campbellford (G3).3,425
Canfield (E4)......... 138
Cannington (E3)....... 926
Capreol (K5)..........2,394
Caradoc (C5).......... 477
Cardinal (J3)..........1,994
Cargill (C3).......... 300
Carleton Place (H2) 4,790
Carp (H2)............. 400
Carrying Place (G3) 150
Cartier (J5)................. 507
Casselman (J2).......1,241
Castleton (F3)........ 400
Cavan (F3)............ 95
Cayuga ◉(E5)......... 772
Centralia (C4)........ 230
Centreville (H3)...... 100
Ceylon (D3)........... 150
Chalk River (G1).... 946
Chapleau (J5).........2,750
Charing Cross (B5) 135
Chatham ◉(B5).....22,262
Chatsworth (D3).... 410
Chelmsford (K5).....2,142
Cherry Valley (G4) 125
Chesley (C3)..........1,672
Chesterville (J2).....1,169
Chippawa (E4).........2,039
Christian (isl.) (D3)
Chute à Blondeau (K2) 225
Clandeboye (C4)..... 175
Claremont (K3)........ 400
Clarence (J2)......... 175
Clarence Creek (J2) 335
Clarendon Sta. (H3) 66
Clarksburg (D3)....... 478
Clarkson (J4)..........1,450
Clear (lake) (F3)...
Clifford (D4)......... 533
Clinton (C4)..........2,896
Cobalt ◉(K5)..........2,367
Cobden (H2)........... 913
Coboconk (F3)......... 500
Cobourg ◉(F4).........9,399
Cockburn Island (A2) 210
Cochrane ◉(K5).....3,695
Cockburn (isl.) (A2)
Coe Hill (G3)......... 288
Colborne (G4).........1,240
Coldwater (E3)........ 693
Collingwood (D3)...7,978
Comber (B5)........... 608
Combermere (G2).. 150
Coniston (D1).........2,478
Consecon (G3)......... 500
Cookstown (E3)........ 600
Cooksville (J4).......1,800
Copetown (E4)......... 300
Copper Cliff (D1)...3,801
Coral Rapids (J4).. 51
Cordova Mines (G3) 10
Corinth (D5).......... 200
Cornwall ◉(K2)....18,158
Corunna (B5).......... 232
Couchiching (lake) (E3) ....
Courtland (D5)........ 341
Courtright (B5)....... 581
Craighurst (E3)....... 190
Crediton (C4)......... 500
Creemore (D3)......... 838
Creighton Mine (C1) 1,240
Crosby (H3)........... 125
Crysler (J2).......... 333
Crystal Beach (E5).1,850
Crystal Falls (D1)..
Cumberland (J2)....... 300
Cutler (B1)........... 175
Dashwood (C4)......... 500
Dean Lake (A1)........ 80
Deep River (G1).....1,750
Delamere (D1)........
Delaware (C5)......... 257
Delhi (D5).............3,002
Deloro (G3)........... 253
Delta (H3)............ 500
Denbigh (G2).......... 100
Denfield (C4).........
Depot Harbour (D2) 457
Desbarats (J5)........ 200
Desboro (C3).......... 100
Deseronto (G3)........1,729
Detlor (G2)........... 90
Deux Rivières (F1).
Devlin (F5)........... 262
Dixie (J4)............ 325
Dorchester Sta. (C5) 400
Dorset (F2)........... 131
Douglas (H2).......... 500
Drayton (D4).......... 573
Dresden (B5)..........2,260
Drumbo (D4)........... 500
Dryden (G4)...........4,428
Dublin (C4)........... 300
Dunchurch (E2)........ 200
Dundalk (D3).......... 847
Dundas (D4)...........9,507
Dungannon (C4)........ 435
Dunnville (E5)........4,478
Duntroon (D3)......... 166
Durham (D3)...........2,067
Dutton (C5)........... 784
Dyment (G5)........... 158
Eastview (J2).........1,909
Eastwood (D4)......... 150
Eau Claire (F1)....... 150
Echo Bay (J5)......... 290
Edy's Mills (B5)...... 75
Eganville (G2)........1,598
Elgin (H3)............ 300
Elk Lake (K5)......... 350
Elmira (D4)...........2,916
Elmvale (E3).......... 897
Elmwood (C3).......... 406
Elora (D4)............1,457
Elsas (J5)............ 150
Embro (C4)............ 529
Embrun (J2)........... 500
Emo (F5).............. 653
Emsdale (E2).......... 180
Englehart (K5)........1,705
English River (G5).
Enterprise (H3)....... 400
Erie (lake) (E5)....
Erieau (C5)........... 475
Erin (D4)............. 885
Espanola (C1).........4,000
Essex (B5)............3,348
Ethel (C4)............ 250
Everett (E3).......... 190
Exeter (C4)...........2,655
Falkenburg Station (E2) 60
Fallbrook (H3)........ 250
Farran's Point (K3) 296
Fauquier (J5)......... 500
Fenelon Falls (F3) 1,137
Fergus (D4)...........3,677
Fesserton (E3)........ 150
Feversham (D3)........ 200
Field (E1)............ 372
Finch (J2)............ 389
Fingal (C5)........... 350
Fisherville (E5)...... 200
Fitzroy Harbour (H2) 150
Fitzwilliam (isl.) (C2) ....
Flanders (G5)......... 188
Flesherton (D3)....... 471
Florence (B5)......... 350
Flowerpot (isl.) (C2)
Foleyet (J5).......... 500
Fonthill (E4).........1,845
Fordwich (C4)......... 400
Forest (C4)...........2,035
Forest Hill (J4).....19,480
Foresters Falls (H2) 150
Formosa (C3).......... 300
Fort Erie (E5)........8,632
Fort Frances ◉(F5) 9,005
Fort William (G5) 39,464
Fort William-Pt. Arthur (Metropolitan Area) (G5)......83,597
Fournier (K2)......... 250
Foxboro (G3).......... 319
Frankford (G3).......1,491
Franktown (H2)........ 100
Fraserdale (J5)....... 150
French (riv.) (D1).
Galetta (H2).......... 177
Galt (D4)............23,738
Gananoque (H3).....4,981
Gelert (F3)........... 200
Georgetown (E4).....5,942
Georgian (bay) (D2)
Georgian Bay Is. Nat'l Park (D3)..
Geraldton (H5).......3,263
Glammis (C3).......... 150
Glen Huron (D3)....... 95
Glen Robertson (K2) 560
Glen Williams (D4) 394
Glencoe (C5)..........1,044
Goderich ◉(C4).......5,886
Gogama (J5)........... 500
Golden Lake (G2)..... 100
Gooderham (F3)........ 100
Goodwood (E3)......... 333
Gore Bay ◉(B2)....... 731
Gormley (J3).......... 75
Gorrie (C4)........... 500
Goudreau (J5)......... 135
Grafton (G4).......... 430
Grand (riv.) (D4)..
Grand Bend (C4) ... 939
Grand Valley (D4). 655
Granton (C4).......... 306
Gravenhurst (E4)....3,014
Grimsby (E4)..........3,805
Guelph ◉(D4).......33,860
Guelph (Metropolitan Area) (D4)........36,641
Hagersville (D5)......1,964
Haileybury (K5)......2,654
Haley Sta. (H2)....... 300
Haliburton (F2)....... 983
Haliburton (lake) (F2) ....
Hamilton ◉(E4)..239,625
Hamilton (Metropolitan Area) (E4)....325,579
Hammond (J2).......... 200
Hampton (F4).......... 233
Hanover (C3)..........3,943
Harriston (D4)........1,592
Harrow (B5)...........1,851
Harrowsmith (H3).. 400
Harty (J5)............ 200
Harwood (F3).......... 190
Hastings (G3)......... 816
Hatchley (D4)......... 100
Havelock (G3).........1,205
Hawk Jct. (J5)........ 195
Hawkesbury (K2)...7,929
Hawkestone (E3)....... 195
Hearst (J5)...........2,214
Heathcote (D3)........ 100
Hensall (C4).......... 829
Hepworth (C3)......... 356
Heron Bay (H5)........ 175
Hespeler (D4).........3,876
Hickson (D4).......... 250
Highgate (C5)......... 378
Highland Creek (K4) 1,200
Hillsburgh (D4)....... 500
Hillsdale (E3)........ 413
Holland Centre (D3) 300
Holland Landing (E3) 326
Holstein (D3)......... 300
Hornepayne (J4).....1,400
Hornings Mills (D3) 311
Hudson (G4)........... 700
Huntsville (E2).......3,051
Hurd (cape) (C2)...
Huron (lake) (B3)..
Hyde Park (C4)........ 200
Ignace (G5)........... 300
Ilderton (C4)......... 200
Ingersoll (C4)........6,811
Inglewood (E4)........ 400
Inkerman (J2)......... 250
Innerkip (D4)......... 335
Inwood (C5)........... 395
Iona (C5)............. 100
Ipperwash Prov. Park (C4) ....
Iroquois (J3) 1,078
Iroquois Falls (K5).1,478
Islington (J4)........2,735
Ivanhoe (G3).......... 130
Jamestown (H5)........1,400
Jarvis (D5)........... 733
Jasper (J3)........... 300
Jeannettes Creek (B5) 138
Jellicoe (H5)......... 344
Joseph (lake) (E2).
Kagawong (B2)......... 200
Kakabeka Falls (G5) 422
Kaladar (H3).......... 200
Kaministikwia (G5) 120
Kapuskasing (J5)....5,463
Kapuskasing (riv.) (J5) ....
Kearney (E2).......... 454
Keene (F3)............ 333
Keewatin (F5).........1,949
Kemptville (J2).......1,730
Kenilworth (D4)....... 200
Kenmore (J2).......... 200
Kenogami (riv.) (H4)
Kenora ◉(F4).........10,278
Kent Bridge (B5)...... 166
Kerwood (C5).......... 166
Keswick (E3).......... 248
Killaloe Sta. (G2).... 854
Kimberley (D3)........ 200
Kinburn (H2).......... 174
Kincardine (C3)......2,667
King City (J3)........ 530
Kingston ◉ (H3)..................48,618
Kingston (Metropolitan Area) (H3)......57,600
Kingsville (B5)........2,884
Kinmount (F3)......... 488
Kippen (C4)........... 112
Kirkfield (E3)........ 412
Kirkland Lake (K5) 18,459
Kitchener ◉(D4)...59,562
Kitchener (Metropolitan Area) (D4)......79,429
Kleinburg (J4)........ 227
Komoka (C5)........... 188
La Passe (H2)......... 137
La Salle (A5).........2,703
Lake of the Woods (lake) (F5)........
Lake Superior Prov. Park (J5).........
Lakefield (F3)........1,938
Lakeport (G4)......... 200
Lakeview (J4).........1,400
L'Amable (G3)......... 88
Lambeth (C5).......... 333
Lanark (H2)........... 871
Lancaster (K2)........ 594
Lansdowne (H3)........ 490
Lansing (J4)..........4,000
Latchford (K5)........ 508
Laurel (D4)........... 130
Leamington (B5).....7,856
Leaside (J4)..........16,538
Lefaivre (K2)......... 200
Levack (J5)...........2,929
Limoges (J2).......... 329
Lindsay ◉(F3)........10,110
Linwood (D4).......... 503
Lion's Head (C2).... 413
Listowel (D4).........3,644
Little Britain (F3)... 300
Little Current (B2).1,514
Lloydtown (J3)........ 200
Lochalsh (J5)......... 300
Lombardy (H3)......... 125
London ◉(C5)....101,693
London (Metropolitan Area) (C5).....153,491
Long (point) (D5).
Long Branch (J4).10,249
Longford Mills (E3) 360
Longlac (H5).......... 250
L'Original ◉(K2)....1,067
Loring (D2)........... 200
Lorne Park (J4)....... 500
Low Bush River (K5) 150
Lucan (C4)............ 924
Lucknow (C4).......... 908
Lyn (J3).............. 255
Lynden (D4)........... 500
Lyndhurst (H3)........ 295
Mac Tier (E2)......... 500
Madawaska (F2)........ 400
Madawaska (riv.) (G2) ....
Madoc (G3)............1,325
Magnetawan (E2)....... 197
Maidstone (B5)........ 190
Mallorytown (J3)...... 300
Malton (J4)...........1,500
Malvern (J4).......... 175
Manitouwadge (H5)
Manitoulin (isl.) (B2)
Manitowaning (C2). 726
Manotick (J2)......... 500
Maple (J4)........... 400
Marathon (H5)........3,500
Markdale (D3)......... 986
Markham (K4).........2,873
Markstay (D1)......... 375
Marlbank (G3)......... 350
Marmora (G3)..........1,428
Martintown (K2)....... 357
Massey (C1)...........1,068
Matachewan (J5)......1,000
Matheson (K5)......... 758
Mattagami (riv.) (J5)
Mattawa (F1)..........3,208
Mattice (J5).......... 225
Maxville (K2)......... 782
Maynooth (G2)......... 290
Mc Gregor (B5)........ 175
Mc Kellar (D2)........ 697
Mc Kerrow (C1)........ 190
Meadowvale (J4)...... 150
Meaford (D3)..........3,643
Melbourne (C5)........ 360
Merlin (B5)........... 500
Merrickville (J3)..... 859
Merritton (E4)........5,404
Metcalfe (J2)......... 400
Michipicoten (isl.) (H5) ....
Michipicoten Harbour (H5)....... 164
Middleville (H2)...... 192
Midhurst (E3)......... 166
Midland (D3)..........8,250
Mildmay (C3).......... 860
Mill Bridge (G3)...... 150
Millbank (D4)......... 450
Millbrook (F3)........ 807
Mille Lacs (lake) (G5) ....
Mille Roches (K2).. 729
Milton West ◉(E4).4,294
Milverton (C4)........1,070
Mimico (J4)..........13,687
Minaki (F4)........... 150
Minden ◉(F3).......... 600
Missinaibi (riv.) (J5)
Missisagi (str.) (A2)
Mississippi (lake) (H2) ....
Mississippi Station (H3) 88
Mitchell (C4).........2,146
Monkton (C4).......... 350
Moonbeam (J5)......... 500
Moorefield (D4)....... 400
Moose Creek (K2).. 600
Morewood (J2)......... 195
Morpeth (C5).......... 200
Morrisburg (J3).......2,131
Morton (H3)........... 109
Moulinette (K2)....... 250
Mount Albert (E3). 600
Mount Brydges (C5) 577
Mount Dennis (J4).9,000
Mount Forest (D4).2,438
Mount Pleasant (D4) 300
Mountain Grove (H3) 200
Muncey (C5)........... 83
Muskoka (lake) (E2) 130
Myrtle (E3)........... 130
Nakina (H4)........... 500
Nanticoke (E5)........ 100
Napanee ◉(G3)........4,273
Neustadt (D3)......... 490
New Hamburg (D4) 1,939
New Liskeard (K5).4,619
New Lowell (E3)....... 300
New Toronto (J4).11,560
Newboro (H3).......... 270
Newburgh (H3)......... 603
Newbury (C5).......... 331
Newcastle (F3)........1,098
Newington (K2)........ 300
Newmarket (E3).....7,368
Newtonbrook (J4)..1,500
Newtonville (F4)...... 733
Niagara (riv.) (E4).
Niagara Falls (E4) 23,563
Niagara-on-the-Lake (E4) 2,740
Nipigon (H5).......... 700
Nipigon (lake) (H5)
Nipissing (lake) (E1)
Nobel (D2)............ 600
Nobleton (J3)......... 200
Noelville (D1)........ 200
North (chanl.) (A1)
North Augusta (J3).. 500
North Bay ◉(E1).21,020
North Gower (J2).. 469
Norval (E4)........... 300
Norwich (D5)..........1,611
Norwood (F3)..........1,017
Nottawa (D3).......... 211
Nottawasaga (bay) (D3) ....
Novar (E2)............ 250
Oak Ridges (J3)...... 150
Oakville (E4).........9,983
Oakwood (F3).......... 250
Odessa (H3)........... 600
Oil City (B5)......... 175
Oil Springs (B5)...... 481
Omemee (F3)........... 837
Ontario (lake) (G4)
Opeongo (lake) (F2)
Orangeville ◉(D4)..3,887
Orillia (E3)..........13,857
Orono (F4)............ 800
Osgoode Sta. (J2).. 390
Oshawa (F4)........50,412
Oshawa (Metropolitan Area) (F4)......64,428
OTTAWA (J2)....222,129
Ottawa (Metropolitan Area) (J2)......335,507
Ottawa (riv.) (H2)..
Otterville (D5)....... 500
Owen Sound ◉ (D3) 16,976
Oxford Mills (J3)... 225
Paisley (C3).......... 730
Pakenham (H2)......... 500
Palmerston (D4).......1,550
Paris (D4)............5,504
Park Hill (C4)........1,043
Parry (isl.) (D2).....
Parry Sound ◉(E2).5,378
Pefferlaw (E3)........ 184
Pelée (point) (B5)..
Pembroke ◉(G2)..15,434
Penetanguishene (D3) 5,420
Perth ◉(H3)...........5,145
Petawawa (G2)......... 300
Peterborough ◉ (F3) 42,698
Peterborough (Metropolitan Area) (F3)......45,410
Petrolia (B5)..........3,426
Pickering (K4)........1,150
Picton ◉(G3)..........4,998
Plantagenet (J2)...... 583
Plattsville (D4)...... 700
Point Edward (B4).2,558
Point Pelée Nat'l Park (B5)..........
Pointe-au-Baril (D2) 200
Pointe-aux-Roches (B5) 240
Pontypool (F3)........ 190
Porcupine (J5)........ 500
Port Arthur ◉ (H5) 38,136
Port Arthur-Ft. William (Metropolitan Area) (H5)......83,597
Port Burwell (D5).... 722
Port Carling (E2)..... 510
Port Colborne (E5) 14,028
Port Credit (J4)......6,350
Port Dalhousie (E4) 3,087
Port Dover (D5) 2,790
Port Elgin (C3).......1,558
Port Hope ◉(F4).......7,522
Port Lambton (B5). 300
Port Maitland (E5) 150
Port McNicoll (E3) 932
Port Perry (E3).......2,121
Port Rowan (D5)...... 766
Port Stanley (C5).....1,480
Port Sydney (E2)...... 185
Port Union (K4)....... 500
Portland (H3)......... 250
Powassan (E1)......... 935
Prescott ◉(J3).........4,920
Preston (D4)...........9,387
Priceville (D3) 231
Princeton (D4)........ 450
Proton Station (D3) 130
Providence Bay (B2) 350
Queensborough (G3) 188
Quetico Prov. Park (G5) ....
Quibell (F4).......... 170
Rainy (lake) (G5)...
Rainy River (F5).....1,354
Red Rock (H5)........1,200
Redditt (F4).......... 300
Renfrew (H2)..........8,634
Rice (lake) (F3).....
Richmond (J2)......... 772
Richmond Hill (J4) 6,677
Rideau (lake) (H3).
Rideau (riv.) (J2)...
Ridgetown (C5)........2,483
Ridgeway (E5)......... 864
Ripley (C3)........... 450
Riverside (B5).......13,325
Rockland (J2).........2,757
Rockcliffe Park (H2) 2,097
Rockport (J3)......... 200
Rockwood (D4)......... 600
Rodney (C5)...........1,026
Rondeau Prov. Park (C5) ....
Roseneath (G3)........ 200
Rosseau (E2).......... 223
Rosseau (lake) (E2)
Rossport (H5)......... 190
Rostock (C4).......... 100
Russell (J2).......... 600
Rutherglen (F1)....... 300
Ruthven (B5).......... 275
Saint Albert (J2)..... 222
Saint Catharines ◉ (E4) 39,708
Saint Catharines (Metropolitan Area) (E4)......84,493
Saint Clair (lake) (B5) ....
Saint Clair (riv.) (B5)
Saint Clair Beach (B5) 831
Saint Davids (F4)..... 250
Saint Eugene (K2).. 791
Saint George (D4)..... 569
Saint Isidore (K2)... 450
Saint Jacobs (D4)..... 548
Saint Lawrence (riv.) (J3)..........
Saint Marys (C4).....4,185
Saint Thomas ◉ (C5) 19,129
Saint Williams (D5) 377
Sainte Anne de Prescott (K2)....... 250
Salem (D4)............ 244
Salford (D4).......... 150
Sarnia ◉(B5)..........43,447
Sarnia (Metropolitan Area) (B5)......52,493
Saugeen (riv.) (C3).
Sault Sainte Marie◉ (J5) 37,329
Sault Ste. Marie (Metropolitan Area) (J5)......50,436
Savant Lake (G4)... 97
Scarborough Village (K4) ......
Scarborough Bluffs (K4) 1,475
Schreiber (H5)........1,850
Schumacher (K5)......3,002
Scotia (E2)........... 98
Scotland (D4)......... 444
Scugog (lake) (F3).
Seaforth (C4).........2,128
Sebringville (C4)..... 546
Seeleys Bay (H3)...... 285
Selkirk (E5).......... 421
Seul (lake) (G4)....
Severn (riv.) (E3)...
Severn Bridge (E3). 333
Shallow Lake (C3).. 366
Shannonville (G3)..... 237
Sharbot Lake (H3). 533
Shedden (C5).......... 209
Sheguiandah (C2)... 250
Shelburne (D3)........1,245
Simcoe ◉(D5)..........8,078
Simcoe (lake) (E3).
Singhampton (D3)... 177
Sioux Lookout (G4) 2,504
Smiths Falls (H3)...8,967
Smithville (E4)...... 754
Smooth Rock Falls (J5) 1,104
Sombra (B5)........... 388
South Mountain (J3) 278
South Porcupine (K5) 5,618
South River (E2)...... 995
Southampton (C3)..1,640
Spanish (B1) 194
Spanish (riv.) (C1)
Sparta (C5)........... 330
Spencerville (J3)..... 400
Spring Brook (G3).. 200
Springfield (C5)...... 482
Sprucedale (E2)....... 266
Stayner (E3)..........1,429
Steep Rock Lake (G5) 1,450
Stella (H3)........... 200
Stirling (G3).........1,191
Stittsville (J2)...... 250
Stonecliffe (F1)...... 158
Stoney Creek (E4)..4,506
Stony (lake) (G3)...
Stouffville (J3).......2,307
Straffordville (D5).. 267
Stratford ◉(C4)....19,972
Strathroy (C5)........4,240
Stratton (F5)......... 450
Streetsville (J4)......2,643
Sturgeon Falls (D1).5,874
Sudbury ◉(C1)......46,482
Sudbury (Metropolitan Area) (C1)......93,755
Sulphide (G3)......... 198
Sultan (J5)........... 125
Sunderland (E3)...... 793
Sundridge (E2)........ 697
Superior (lake) (H5)
Sutton West (E3).....1,310
Swansea (J4)..........8,595
Swastika (K5)......... 935
Sydenham (H3)......... 550
Tamworth (H3)......... 500
Tara (C3)............. 515
Tavistock (D4)........1,155
Tecumseh (B5).........4,177
Teeswater (C3)........ 852
Terrace Bay (H5).... 600
Thames (riv.) (B5).
Thamesford (C4)...... 500
Thamesville (C5).....1,074
Thedford (C4)......... 717
Thessalon (J5)........1,716
Thornbury (D3)........1,037
Thorndale (C4)........ 290
Thornhill (J4)........ 850
Thornton (E3)......... 288
Thorold (E4)..........8,053
Thousand (isls.) (H3)
Tillbury (B5)..........3,138
Tillsonburg (D5).....6,216
Timagami (K5)......... 500
Timagami (lake) (K5) ....
Timmins (J5).........27,551
Tiverton (C3)......... 252
Tobermory (C2)........ 400
Toledo (H3)........... 275
TORONTO (K4).667,706
Toronto (Metropolitan Area) (K4)..1,347,905
Tottenham (E3)........ 702
Trenton (G3)..........11,492
Trout Creek (E2)..... 389
Tweed (G3)............1,634
Tyrone (F3)........... 145
Underwood (C3)........ 250
Unionville (K4)....... 565
Upsala (G5)........... 190
Utterson (E2)......... 300
Uxbridge (E3).........2,065
Vankleek Hill (K2) 1,647
Varney (D3)........... 100
Vars (J2)............. 300
Vermillion Bay (G4) 98
Verner (D1)........... 800
Vernon (J2)........... 200
Vernon (lake) (E2).
Verona (H3)........... 275
Victoria Harbour (E3) 1,012
Victoria Road (F3). 228
Vienna (D5)........... 362
Vineland (E4)......... 475
Vittoria (D5)......... 300
Wahnapitae (D1)...... 269
Wales (K2)............ 250
Walford Sta. (B1).... 140
Walkerton ◉(C3)......3,698
Wallaceburg (B5).....7,892
Walters Falls (D3).. 193
Walton (C4)........... 200
Wanup (D1)............ 133
Wardsville (C5)....... 318
Warren (D1)........... 500
Warsaw (F3)........... 233
Wasaga Beach (D3) 529
Washago (E3).......... 332
Waterdown (D4).......1,754
Waterford (D5)........1,908
Watford (C5)..........1,217
Waterloo (D4)........16,373
Waubaushene (E3).. 557
Webbwood (C1)........ 600
Welland ◉(E4)........16,405
Wellesley (D4)........ 750
Wellington (G4).......1,077
West Hill (K4)........2,000
West Lorne (C5).....1,088
Westmeath (H2)...... 375
Weston (J4) 9,543
Westport (H3)......... 704
Wheatley (B5).........1,196
Whitby ◉(F4)..........9,995
White Lake (H2)...... 150
White River (J5)..... 401
Whitefish (C1)........ 137
Whitney (F2).......... 247
Wiarton (C3)..........1,954
Widdifield (E1)...... 96
Wikwemikong (C2). 452
Wilberforce (F3)..... 100
Williamsburg (J3).. 350
Williamstown (K2).. 531
Willowdale (J4).......9,500
Wilno (G2)............ 166
Winchester (J2).......1,338
Windermere (E2)...... 158
Windsor ◉(B5)......121,980
Windsor (Metropolitan Area) (B5)......184,045
Wingham (C4)..........2,766
Wolfe Island (H3).. 300
Woodbridge (J4)......1,958
Woodstock ◉(D4).16,347
Woodville (F3)........ 406
Wooler (G3)........... 250
Worthington (C1).... 150
Wroxeter (C4)......... 437
Wyevale (E3).......... 145
Wyoming (B5)......... 792
Yarker (H3)........... 365
York (E4)............. 150
Zephyr (E3)........... 150
Zurich (C4)........... 549

◉County Seat

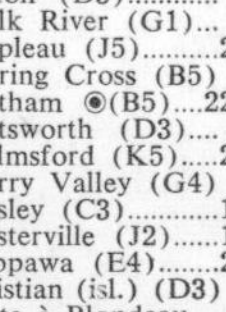

MANITOBA

1956 Total Population 850,040

Aikens (lake) (G3).
Alexander (B5)......... 500
Alexander Slough (marsh) (B5)......
Allegra (F4)........... 10
Alonsa (C4)........... 132
Altamont (D5)......... 125
Altona (E5)...........1,698
Amaranth (D4)......... 100
Amery (J2)............ 25
Anderson (lake) (D2)
Angusville (A4)....... 452
Anola (F5).....
Arbakka (F5).....
Arborg (E4).......... 450
Arden (C4)........... 300
Argyle (E4)........... 100
Armit (lake) (A2)...
Arnaud (E5)........... 590
Arnes (E4)............ 10
Arrow River (B4).... 150
Ashern (D3).......... 333
Ashville (B3)......... 20
Assapan (riv.) (G2)
Assiniboine (riv.) (C5) ....
Assinika (lake) (G2)

Aubigny (E5) 150
Austin (D5) 300
Badger (G5) 110
Bagot (D5) 100
Baldur (C5) 550
Balmoral (E4) 200
Balsam Bay (F4) 100
Bannerman (C5) 118
Baralzon (lake) (J1)
Barkfield (F5)
Barrows (A2)
Basket (lake) (C3)
Basswood (B4) 144
Bayton (D3)
Beaconia (F4)
Beauséjour (F4) 1,523
Beaver (D4)
Beaverhill (lake) (J3)
Bede (B5)
Belair (F4)
Belleview (B5)
Bellhampton (C4)
Bellsite (A2) 300
Belmont (C5) 350
Bénard (E5)
Benito (A3) 487
Berens (isl.) (E2)
Berens (riv.) (F2)
Berens River (F2) 200
Beresford (B5) 55
Beresford Lake (G4)
Berlo (E4)
Bethany (C4) 133
Bethel (C4)
Beulah (A4) 74
Bield (A3)
Big Stone (point) (E2)
Bigstone (riv.) (J3)
Binscarth (A4) 452
Birch (isl.) (C2)
Birch Bay (D3)
Birch River (A2) 273
Birchview (B3)
Bird River (G4)
Birds Hill (F4) 190
Birdtail (B4)
Birnie (C4) 97
Birtle (B4) 806
Bissett (G4) 250
Black (isl.) (F3)
Bloodvein (riv.) (F3)
Bluewing (A3)
Bluff Creek (D4)
Bodhan (B3)
Boggy Creek (A3) 350
Boissevain (C5) 1,115
Bonnet (lake) (G4)
Bonnie Doon (D4)
Bowsman (A2) 519
Bradwardine (B5) 100
Brandon (C5) 24,796
Brightstone (F4)
Broad Valley (E3) 150
Brochet (H2) 100
Brokenhead (F4)
Brookdale (C4) 100
Broomhill (B5) 30
Brunkild (E5) 77
Bruxelles (C5) 150
Buchan (F4)
Buffalo (bay) (G5)
Bunclody (B5) 12
Burntwood (riv.) (J2)
Butler (A5) 32
Caliento (F5)
Camp Morton (F4) 350
Camper (D3) 30
Camperville (B2) 25
Carberry (C5) 1,065
Cardale (B4) 77
Cardinal (D5) 117
Carey (E5) 47
Carlowrie (E5) 50
Carman (D5) 1,884
Carnegie (B5)
Carroll (B5) 88
Carroll (lake) (G3)
Cartwright (C5) 459
Castle Point (C5) 16
Cayer (D3)
Cedar (lake) (B1)
Channel (isl.) (B2)
Channing (H3)
Charron (lake) (G2)
Chater (C5) 44
Chatfield (E4) 100
Childs (lake) (A3)
Chitek (lake) (C2)
Chortitz (F5) 150
Churchill (K2) 500
Churchill (cape) (K2)
Churchill (riv.) (J2)
Clandeboye (E4)
Clanwilliam (C4) 188
Clarkleigh (D4)
Clear (lake) (C4)
Clearwater (D5) 500
Clematis (E4)
Cloverleaf (F5)
Cochrane (riv.) (H2)
Commissioner (isl.) (E3)
Cooks Creek (F4)
Cordova (C4)
Cormorant (H3)
Cormorant (lake) (H3)
Coulter (B5) 48
Cowan (B2)
Cracknell (A4) 10
Cranberry Portage (H3) 350
Crandall (B4) 190
Crane River (C3) 750
Crocus (C4)
Croll (B5)
Cromer (A5) 88
Cross (lake) (C1)
Cross (lake) (J3)
Crow Duck (lake) (G4)
Crystal City (C5) 505
Culross (E5)
Cypress River (D5) 505
Dallas (E3) 480
Dand (B5) 20
Darlingford (D5) 190
Dauphin (B3) 6,190
Dauphin (lake) (C3)
Davis Point (D3)
Dawson (bay) (B2)
Decimal (G5)
Decker (B4) 95
Deepdale (A3) 77
Deer Horn (E4)
Deerwood (D5)
Deleau (B5) 188
Deloraine (B5) 900
Delta Station (D4) 70
Dennis (lake) (E4)
Desford (C5)
Dog (lake) (D3)
Dogskin (lake) (G3)
Domain (E5) 47
Dominion City (E5) 700
Douglas Sta. (C5) 150
Drifting River (B3)
Dropmore (A3) 47
Dry River (C5)
Duck (mt.) (B3)
Duck River (B3) 73
Dufresne (F5)
Dufrost (E5) 150
Dunnottar (E4) 178
Dunrea (C5) 250
Durban (A3) 77
Eardley (lake) (F2)
East Bay (C3)
East Braintree (G5)
East Selkirk (F4) 390
East Shoal (lake) (E4)
Ebb and Flow (lake) (C3)
Ebor (A5) 25
Eddystone (C3)
Eden (C4) 175
Edrans (C4) 67
Edwin (D5)
Egg (isl.) (E3)
Ekhart (E4)
Elbow (lake) (G4)
Elgin (B5) 400
Elie (E5) 150
Elk (isl.) (F4)
Elk Ranch (C4)
Elkhorn (A5) 673
Elliot (lake) (G2)
Elm Creek (E5) 400
Elphinstone (B4) 275
Elva (A5) 97
Emerson (E5) 896
Endcliffe (A4)
Erickson (C4) 488
Eriksdale (D4) 260
Erinview (E4)
Etawney (lake) (J2)
Ethelbert (B3) 505
Ewart (A5)
Fairfax (B5) 63
Fairford (D3) 25
Falcon (lake) (G5)
Fallison (D6)
Family (lake) (G3)
Fannystelle (E5) 166
Faulkner (D3)
Findlay (B5) 25
Firdale (C5)
Fisher (bay) (E3)
Fisher Branch (E3) 637
Fisherton (E3)
Fishing (lake) (G2)
Fishing River (C3)
Flin Flon (H3) 10,234
Flintstone (lake) (G4)
Foley (E4)
Fork River (B3) 174
Forrest Station (C5) 66
Fort Alexander (F4) 1,000
Fort Garry (E5) 1,485
Fort Whyte (E5) 800
Fortier (E5)
Fox (riv.) (K2)
Foxwarren (A4) 270
Franklin (C4) 166
Fraserwood (E4) 94
Gammon (riv.) (G3)
Gardenton (F5) 500
Garland (B3)
Garner (lake) (G4)
Garson (F4) 277
Geillini (lake) (J1)
Gem (lake) (G4)
Genthon (F5) 150
George (isl.) (E2)
George (lake) (G4)
Geyser (E4)
Gilbert Plains (B3) 859
Gilchrist (lake) (G2)
Gillam (K2) 95
Gimli (F4) 1,660
Giroux (F5) 95
Gladstone (D4) 882
Glen Elmo (B4)
Glen Souris (C5)
Glenboro (C5) 765
Glencairn (C4)
Glenella (C4) 195
Glenhope (C4)
Glenlea (E5) 22
Glenora (C5) 35
Gods (lake) (K3)
Gods (riv.) (K3)
God's Lake (J3) 200
Golden Stream (D4)
Gonor (F4)
Goodlands (B5) 120
Grahamdale (D3)
Grand Beach (F4)
Grand Marais (F4)
Grand Rapids (C1) 300
Grand View (B3) 963
Grande Clairière (B5)
Granville (lake) (H2)
Grass (riv.) (J3)
Grass River (D4)
Graysville (D5) 115
Great Falls (F4) 150
Green Ridge (F5)
Greenwald (F4)
Greenway (C5) 133
Gregg (C5) 36
Gretna (E5) 603
Grifton (B3)
Griswold (B5) 200
Grosse Isle (E4) 63
Grunthal (F5) 870
Gunton (E4) 178
Guynemer (C3)
Gypsum (lake) (D3)
Gypsumville (D3) 212
Hadashville (G5)
Halbstadt (E5) 450
Halicz (B3)
Hallboro (C4) 86
Hamiota (B4) 690
Hamrlik (E4)
Harcus (D4) 20
Harding (B5) 67
Hargrave (A5) 75
Harlington (A2)
Harmsworth (B5)
Harperville (E4)
Harrop (lake) (G2)
Harrowby (A4) 70
Harte (C4)
Hartney (B5) 554
Harwill (E3)
Haskett (E5) 72
Hayes (riv.) (K3)
Hayfield (B5) 87
Hayland (D3)
Haywood (D5) 134
Hazelridge (F5) 95
Heaslip Sta. (C5)
Hecla (F3) 300
Hecla (isl.) (F3)
Helston (C4)
Herb Lake (H3) 225
High Bluff (D4) 96
Hilbre (D3)
Hillside Beach (F4)
Hilltop (C4)
Hilton (C5)
Hnausa (F4) 250
Hodgson (E3) 600
Holland (D5) 361
Holmfield (C5) 175
Homebrook (C3)
Homewood (E5) 63
Horndean (E5)
Horod (B4)
Horseshoe (lake) (G2)
Horton (B5) 12
Hubbart (point) (K2)
Hudson (bay) (K2)
Hudwin (lake) (G1)
Husavick (F4)
Ideal (E4)
Ile des Chênes (F5)
Ilford (J2) 97
Indian Bay (G5)
Indian Springs (D5)
Ingelow (C5)
Inglis (A4) 212
Inland (lake) (C2)
International Peace Garden (B5)
Inwood (E4) 95
Isabella (B4) 86
Island (lake) (K3)
Janow (G5) 230
Jaroslaw (F4)
Julius (F5) 54
Justice (C4) 45
Kaleida (D5)
Kane (E5)
Katimik (lake) (C2)
Katrime (D4)
Kawinaw (lake) (C2)
Kazanjerri (lake) (H2)
Kelloe (B4) 86
Kelwood (C4) 222
Kemnay (B5) 66
Kenton (B5) 126
Kenville (A3) 139
Kergwenan (C4)
Keyes (C4) 64
Killarney (C5) 1,434
Kinosota (D4)
Kinwow (bay) (E2)
Kirkella (A4) 65
Kississing (H3) 500
Kississing (lake) (H2)
Kleefeld (F5) 625
Knee (lake) (J3)
Komarno (E4) 133
Koostatak (E3)
Kulish (B3)
La Broquerie (F5) 800
La Rivière (D5) 256
La Rochelle (F5) 120
La Salle (E5) 99
Lac du Bonnet (G4) 523
Ladywood (F4) 25
Lake Francis (E4)
Lake of the Woods (lake) (H5)
Lakeland (D4)
Landseer (C5) 8
Langruth (D4) 150
Lauder (B5) 184
Laurie (lake) (A3)
Laurier (C4) 225
Lavenham (D5)
Lavinia (B4)
Layland (D5)
Learys (D5)
Ledwyn (E4)
Lena (C5) 25
Lennard (A3)
Lenore (B5) 166
Lenswood (B2) 300
Letellier (E5) 772
Lettonia (G4)
Lewis (F5)
Lewis (lake) (G2)
Libau (F4) 162
Lillesve (E4)
Lily Bay (D4)
Little Bullhead (F3)
Loch Monar (E4)
Lockport (E4) 250
Lonely (lake) (C3)
Lonely Lake (D3)
Long (lake) (G4)
Long (point) (D1)
Long (point) (D4)
Lorette (F5) 500
Lowe Farm (E5) 150
Lundar (D4) 800
Lyditt (F5) 50
Lyleton (A5) 150
Lynn Lake (H2) 1,700
Macdonald (D4) 200
MacGregor (D5) 611
Macross (D4)
Mafeking (B2) 278
Magnet (C3) 60
Makaroff (A3) 25
Makinak (C4) 130
Malonton (E4) 55
Manigotagan (F3)
Manigotagan (lake) (G4)
Manitoba (lake) (D4)
Manitou (D5) 795
Manson (A4) 30
Mantagao (riv.) (E3)
Marchand (F5) 96
Marco (B4)
Margaret (C5) 70
Mariapolis (C5) 100
Marius (D4) 800
Markland (E4)
Marquette (E4) 50
Marshy (lake) (B5)
Mather (C5) 150
Matheson Island (E3) 150
Matlock (F4) 500
Mayfeld (C4)
Mc Auley (A4) 158
Mc Connell (B4) 65
Mc Creary (C4) 365
Mc Kay (lake) (C2)
Mc Munn (G5)
Mc Phail (riv.) (F2)
Mc Tavish (E5) 139
Meadow Portage (C3)
Meadowlands (C3)
Meadows (E4) 65
Mears (B4)
Medika (G5) 450
Medora (B5) 150
Mekiwin (C4)
Melbourne (C5) 78
Meleb (E4) 97
Melita (A5) 926
Melrose (F4) 300
Menisino (F5)
Mentmore (C4) 20
Menzie (B4)
Merridale (A3)
Methley (C3)
Methven (C5) 50
Miami (D5) 390
Middle Church (E5)
Middlebro (G5)
Million (C3)
Millwood (A4)
Milner Ridge (F4)
Miniota (B4) 300
Minitonas (B2) 663
Mink Creek (B3)
Minnedosa (B4) 2,306
Minnedosa (riv.) (B4)
Minnewakan (D4)
Minto (B5) 175
Moar (lake) (G2)
Moline (B4)
Molson (F4) 95
Molson (lake) (J3)
Monominto (F5)
Moore Dale (C3)
Moorepark (C4) 166
Moose (isl.) (E3)
Moose (lake) (H3)
Moose Bay (C3)
Moose Lake (H3)
Moosehorn (D3) 223
Morden (D5) 2,237
Morris (E5) 1,260
Morrison (lake) (C1)
Mossy (riv.) (C3)
Mountain Road (C4)
Mountainside (B5)
Mowbray (D5) 75
Muir (D4)
Mukutawa (riv.) (E1)
Mulvihill (D4) 169
Myrtle (E5) 110
Napinka (B5) 181
Narcisse (E4)
Narol (F4)
National Mills (A2)
Neelin (C5) 86
Neepawa (C4) 3,109
Nejanilini (lake) (J2)
Nelson (riv.) (J2)
Nesbitt (C5) 100
Netley (E4)
Neveton (E4)
Newdale (B4) 350
Newton Siding (D5)
Ninette (C5) 160
Ninga (C5) 300
Niverville (F5) 600
Norgate (C4)
North Birch (lake) (E3)
North Indian (lake) (J2)
North Shoal (lake) (E4)
Norway House (J3) 1,200
Notre Dame de Lourdes (D5) 400
Novra (A2)
Nueltin (lake) (J1)
Oak (lake) (B5)
Oak Brae (C3)
Oak Island (lake) (E4)
Oak Lake (B5) 471
Oak Point (D4) 138
Oak River (B4) 175
Oakbank (F5) 150
Oakburn (B4) 266
Oakland (D4) 10
Oakner (B4) 120
Oakview (D3)
Oakville (D5) 190
Oatfield (D4)
Oberon (C4) 10
Obukowin (lake) (G3)
Ochre River (C3) 300
Ogilvie (D4) 20
Oiseau (riv.) (G4)
Olha (B4)
Onanole (C4) 210
Osborne (E5)
Ostenfeld (F5)
Otterburne (E5) 335
Otto (E4)
Overflowing (riv.) (A1)
Overton (D4)
Owl (riv.) (K2)
Oxford (lake) (J3)
Ozerna (B4)
Paint (lake) (J2)
Palsen (riv.) (G2)
Pebble Beach (D3)
Peguis (F4)
Pelican (lake) (B2)
Pelican (lake) (C5)
Pelican Rapids (B2)
Pembina (mt.) (D5)
Pembina (riv.) (C5)
Peonan (pen.) (D3)
Petersfield (E4) 200
Petlura (B3)
Petrel (C5)
Pettapiece (M4) 30
Pickerel (lake) (C2)
Pierson (A5) 200
Pigeon (riv.) (F2)
Pikwitonei (J3) 150
Pilot Mound (D5) 785
Pinawa (G4) 75
Pine Falls (F4) 600
Pine River (B3) 150
Pine View (D4)
Piney (F5) 350
Pipestone (B5) 230
Pipestone (creek) (A5)
Pleasant Home (E4)
Plum (lake) (B5)
Plum Coulee (E5) 498
Plumas (D4) 300
Pointe du Bois (G4) 222
Polonia (C4)
Pope (B4) 50
Poplar (point) (E2)
Poplar Park (F4) 300
Poplar Point (D4) 98
Poplarfield (E4) 116
Port Nelson (K2)
Portage (bay) (D3)
Portage la Prairie (D4) 10,525
Powerview (F4) 1,078
Prairie Grove (F5) 300
Pratt (D5)
Pulp River (B3)
Punk (isl.) (F3)
Purves (D5) 66
Quesnel (lake) (G4)
Rackham (B4)
Rapid City (B4) 434
Rat (riv.) (F5)
Rathwell (D5) 250
Reaburn (E4) 10
Red (riv.) (E5)
Red Deer (lake) (A2)
Red Rose (E3) 50
Reedy Creek (C4)
Regent (B5) 50
Reindeer (isl.) (E2)
Reindeer (lake) (H2)
Reinland (E5)
Rembrandt (E4) 25
Rennie (G5) 100
Renwer (B2)
Reston (A5) 516
Reykjavik (D3)
Rice Creek (A2)
Richer (F5) 500
Ridgely (E4)
Ridgeville (E5) 500
Riding (mt.) (B4)
Riding Mountain (C4) 50
Riding Mountain Nat'l Park (B4)
Riding Park (B3)
Ridley (D3)
Riel (E5)
Rita (F5)
Rivers (B4) 1,422
Riverton (E3) 795
Roblin (A3) 1,173
Rock (lake) (C5)
Roland (D5) 500
Rorketon (C3) 150
Rosa (F5)
Rosebank (D5) 44
Roseisle (D5) 166
Rosenburg (E3)
Rosenfeld (E5) 175
Rosenort (E5) 148
Ross (F5)
Rossburn (B4) 589
Rossburn Junction (C4)
Rossendale (D5) 137
Rosser (E5) 117
Rounthwaite (C5) 7
Routledge (B5)
Russell (A4) 1,227
Ruthenia (A4)
Sadlow (G5) 100
Saint Adolphe (E5) 500
Saint Alphonse (C5) 40
Saint Ambroise (E4) 400
Saint Andrew (lake) (E3)
Saint Andrews (E4) 850
Saint Boniface (F5) 28,851
Saint Charles (E5) 500
Saint Claude (D5) 300
Saint Eustache (E5) 122
Saint François Xavier (E5) 450
Saint George (F4) 40
Saint George (lake) (E3)
Saint James (E5) 26,502
Saint Jean-Baptiste (E5) 1,200
Saint Joseph (E5)
Saint Labre (G5)
Saint Laurent (D4) 281
Saint Lazare (A4) 323
Saint Léon (D5)
Saint Lupicin (D5) 268
Saint Malo (F5) 500
Saint Marks (E4) 80
Saint Martin (lake) (D3)
Saint Martin Station (D3)
Saint Norbert (E5) 813
Saint Pierre-Jolys (F5) 838
Sainte Agathe (E5) 500
Sainte Amelie (C4) 100
Sainte Anne des Chênes (F5) 800
Sainte Elizabeth (E5) 300
Sainte Geneviève (F5)
Sainte Madeleine (A4)
Sainte Rose du Lac (C3) 740
Sale (riv.) (E5)
San Clara (A3) 300
Sandilands (F5)
Sandridge (E4)
Sandy Lake (B4) 287
Sanford (E5) 98
Sarto (F5)
Sasaginnigak (lake) (G3)
Scandinavia (C4)
Scanterbury (F4) 97
Scarth (B5) 94
Sclater (B3)
Scotch Bay (D4)
Seal (riv.) (J2)
Seech (B4)
Selkirk (F4) 7,413
Senkiw (F5) 150
Setting (lake) (H3)
Seven Sisters Falls (G4)
Sewell (E5) 50
Sharpewood (E4)
Shell Valley (A3)
Shellmouth (A4) 86
Shergrove (C3) 150
Sherridon (H3) 1,500
Shevlin (A3)
Shoal (lake) (B4)
Shoal (lake) (G5)
Shoal Lake (B4) 751
Shorncliffe (E3)
Shortdale (A3)
Sidney (C5) 162
Sifton (B3) 1,000
Siglunes (D4)
Silver (E4)
Silver Bay (D3)
Silver Plains (E5)
Silverton Sta. (A4) 6
Sinclair (A5) 92
Sipiwesk (lake) (J3)
Sirko (F5) 5
Sisib (lake) (C2)
Skownan (C3)
Skylake (E4) 140
Sleeve (lake) (E3)
Slemon (lake) (G1)
Smith Hill (C5)
Snowflake (D5) 122
Snowshoe (lake) (G4)
Solsgirth (B4) 85
Somerset (D5) 600
Souris (B5) 1,759
Souris (riv.) (B5)
South Junction (G5) 250
Southern Indian (lake) (H2)
Spearhill (D3)
Sperling (E5) 214
Split (lake) (J2)
Split Lake (J2) 500
Sprague (G5) 400
Springstein (E5)
Spruce (isl.) (B1)
Spurgrave (G5) 140
Starbuck (E5) 230
Stead (F4)
Steep Rock (D3) 88
Steinbach (F5) 2,688
Stephenfield (D5) 10
Stevenson (lake) (J3)
Stockton (C5) 124
Stonewall (E4) 1,110
Stony Hill (E4)
Stony Mountain (E4) 200
Strathclair (B4) 245
Sturgeon (bay) (E3)
Suffren (E4)
Sundown (F5) 600
Swan (lake) (B2)
Swan (lake) (D5)
Swan Lake (D5) 325
Swan River (A2) 2,644
Sylvan (E3) 250
Tamarac (isl.) (F3)
Tatnam (cape) (K2)
Tenby (C4) 20
Terence (B5) 41
Teulon (E4) 634
Thalberg (F4)
The Narrows (D3)
The Pas (H3) 3,971
Thicket Portage (J3)
Thornhill (D5) 133
Tilston (A5) 125
Todatara (lake) (J1)
Tolstoi (F5) 572
Toutes-Aides (C3)
Transcona (F5) 8,312
Traverse Bay (F4) 120
Treesbank (C5)
Treherne (D5) 551
Trentham (F5) 500
Tummel (A3)
Turtle (mt.) (B5)
Turtle (riv.) (C3)
Two Creeks (B4) 86
Tyndall (F4) 270
Ukraina (B3)
Underhill (B5) 4
Union Point (E5) 78
Uno (B4)
Valley (riv.) (B3)
Valley River (B3)
Valpoy (C3)
Vannes (E4)
Vassar (G5) 95
Venlaw (B3)
Vestfold (E4)
Vickers (lake) (F3)
Victoria Beach (F4)
Vidir (E3)
Viking (lake) (G3)
Virden (A5) 3,225
Vista (B4) 88
Vita (F5) 404
Vivian (F5) 333
Vogar (D4)
Volga (C3)
Wabowden (J3) 88
Wakopa (C5) 62
Waldersee (D4)
Walkerburn (A3)
Wallace (lake) (G3)
Wampum (G5)
Wanipigow (riv.) (G3)
Wanless (H3) 100
Wapah (D3)
Ward (B3)
Warrenton (E4) 122
Wasagaming (C4)
Washow (bay) (F3)
Waskada (B5) 357
Waterhen (C3)
Waterhen (lake) (C2)
Wawanesa (C5) 440
Weaver (lake) (F2)
Weiden (C3)
Wekusko (H3) 150
Wellman (lake) (B3)
Wellwood (C4) 160
West Hawk (lake) (G5)
West Shoal (lake) (E4)
Westbourne (D4) 150
Westgate (A2)
Wheatland (B4) 60
Whitemouth (G5) 300
Whitemouth (lake) (G5)
Whitemouth (riv.) (G5)
Whitewater (B5) 93
Whitewater (lake) (B5)
Wicked (point) (D2)
Willen (A4)
Windygates (D5)
Winkler (E5) 1,634
WINNIPEG (E5) 255,093
Winnipeg (Metropolitan Area) (E5) 409,687
Winnipeg (lake) (E2)
Winnipeg (riv.) (G4)
Winnipeg Beach (F4) 805
Winnipegosis (B3) 984
Winnipegosis (lake) (C2)
Wood Bay (D5) 10
Woodlands (E4)
Woodmore (F5)
Woodnorth (A5) 55
Woodridge (G5) 600
Woodside (D4)
Wrong (lake) (F2)
York Factory (K2)
Zalicia (B3)
Zant (D3)
Zbaraz (E4)
Zelena (A5)
Zhoda (F5)

SASKATCHEWAN

1956 Total Population 880,665

Abbey (C5) 305
Aberdeen (E3) 284
Abernethy (H5) 290
Abound (F5) 30
Adanac (B3) 47
Admiral (C6) 152
Alameda (J6) 304
Albertown (D3) 5
Albertville (F2) 35
Alida (K6) 168
Allan (E4) 337
Allan (hills) (E4)
Alsask (B4) 232
Altawan (B5)
Alticane (D3) 75
Alvena (E3) 176
Amisk (lake) (M4)
Amulet (G6) 91
Anerley (D4) 44
Aneroid (D6) 350
Anglia (C4) 110

SASKATCHEWAN (Continued)

Antelope (C5) 150
Antelope (lake) (C5)
Antler (K6) 143
Antler (riv.) (K6)
Arborfield (H2) 557
Archerwill (H3) 230
Archydal (F5)
Arcola (J6) 609
Ardath (D4) 68
Ardill (F6) 34
Arm (riv.) (F5)
Armit (K3) 10
Armley (G2) 112
Arran (K4) 183
Artland (B3) 55
Ashley (B2)
Asquith (D3) 288
Assiniboia (E6) 2,027
Assiniboine (riv.) (J3)
Athabasca (lake) (L2)
Atwater (J5) 106
Avonhurst (G5) 20
Avonlea (G5) 342
Aylesbury (F5) 180
Aylsham (H2) 320
B-Say-Tah (G5) 21
Bad (lake) (C4)
Balcarres (H5) 640
Baldwinton (B3) 155
Balgonie (G5) 215
Bangor (J5) 104
Bankend (H4) 50
Bannock (H3) 15
Bapaume (D2) 20
Barford (H3) 15
Basin (lake) (F3)
Bateman (E5) 161
Batoche (E3) 200
Battle (creek) (B6)
Battle (riv.) (B3)
Battleford (C3) 1,498
Battrum (C5) 25
Bay Trail (F3) 10
Beadle (B4) 75
Bear (hills) (C4)
Bear Creek (K5) 5
Beatty (G3) 141
Beaufield (C4) 5
Beaver (hills) (H4)
Beaver (riv.) (L4)
Beaver Lodge (lake) (L2)
Beechy (D5) 358
Belle Plaine (F5) 81
Bender (J5) 45
Bengough (F6) 573
Benson (J6) 164
Bents (D4)
Bertwell (J3) 20
Bestville (C5)
Bethune (F5) 288
Beverley (C5) 68
Bienfait (J6) 802
Big Beaver (F6) 100
Big Muddy (lake) (G6)
Big River (D2) 904
Biggar (C3) 2,424
Bigstick (lake) (B5)
Birch (lake) (C2)
Birch Hills (F3) 562
Birkensee (C2)
Birmingham (H5) 36
Birsay (D4) 142
Bishopric (F5) 120
Bitter (lake) (B5)
Bjorkdale (H3) 100
Black (lake) (M2)
Bladworth (E4) 178
Blaine Lake (D3) 638
Blucher (E3) 63
Blumenhof (D5) 125
Bodmin (D2) 151
Boharm (F5) 50
Borden (D3) 208
Bounty (D4) 87
Bournemouth (C2) 15
Bracken (C6) 107
Brada (C3) 27
Bradwell (E4) 134
Brancepeth (F3) 112
Bratton (D4) 25
Bredenbury (K5) 456
Bremen (F3) 5
Bresaylor (C3) 50
Briarlea (F2)
Bridgeford (E5) 40
Briercrest (F5) 174
Brightsand (lake) (B2)
Broadacres (B3) 33
Broadview (J5) 978
Brock (C4) 240
Brockington (G2)
Broderick (E4) 130
Bromhead (H6) 117
Bronson (lake) (B2)
Brooking (G6) 118
Brooksby (G2) 212
Browning (J6) 66
Brownlee (F5) 115
Bruno (F3) 646
Bryant (H6) 75
Buchanan (J4) 460
Buffalo Gap (F6) 77
Bulyea (G5) 172
Burr (F3) 15
Burstall (B5) 222
Buzzard (B2) 20
Cabri (C5) 627
Cabri (lake) (B4)
Cactus Lake (B3) 20
Cadillac (D6) 300
Calder (K4) 227
Cana (J5) 25
Candiac (H5) 99
Candle (lake) (F2)
Cando (C3) 150
Canoe (lake) (L3)
Canora (J4) 1,873
Cantuar (D5) 64
Canuck (C6)
Canwood (E2) 310
Carieyale (K6) 271
Carlton (E3) 100
Carlyle (J6) 829
Carmel (F3) 133
Carmichael (C5) 84
Carnduff (K6) 823
Caron (F5) 125
Carpenter (F3) 5
Carragana (J3) 268
Carrot (riv.) (J2)
Carrot River (H2) 819
Carruthers (B3) 95
Cavell (C3) 36
Cedoux (H6) 86
Central Butte (E5) 318
Ceylon Station (G6) 355
Chamberlain (F5) 154
Chaplin (E5) 488
Chaplain (lake) (E5)
Chelan (H3) 152
Cheviot (E3) 33
Chipman (riv.) (M2)
Chitek (lake) (D2)
Choiceland (G2) 478
Christopher Lake (F2) 75
Churchbridge (J5) 257
Churchill (riv.) (M3)
Clair (G3) 150
Clarkboro (E3) 10
Clashmoor (H3) 20
Clavet (E4) 52
Claydon (B6) 112
Clearwater (riv.) (L3)
Cleeves (C2) 62
Cliftonville (B5) 15
Climax (C6) 402
Cloan (C3) 20
Cochin (C2) 50
Cochrane (riv.) (N2)
Coderre (E5) 132
Codette (H2) 194
Coleville (B4) 472
Colfax (H6) 77
Colgate (H6) 103
Colonsay (F3) 295
Congress (E6) 89
Conquest (D4) 292
Consul (B6) 166
Cookson (E2) 42
Coppen (E6) 50
Corinne (G5) 53
Corning (J6) 122
Coronach (F6) 358
Cory (E3) 27
Coteau, The (hills) (D4)
Court (B4) 15
Courval (E5) 100
Cowan (lake) (D2)
Craik (F4) 607
Crane (lake) (B5)
Crane Valley (F6) 89
Craven (G5) 189
Crean (lake) (E1)
Cree (lake) (L3)
Cree (riv.) (M2)
Creelman (H6) 215
Creighton (N4) 1,646
Crestwynd (F5) 55
Crooked River (H3) 175
Crystal Springs (F3) 150
Cudworth (F3) 582
Cumberland (lake) (J1)
Cumberland House (J2) 20
Cupar (G5) 519
Cut Knife (B3) 453
Cypress (hills) (B6)
Cypress (lake) (B6)
Cypress Hills Prov. Park (B6)
D'Arcy Station (C4) 188
Dafoe (G4) 95
Dahinda (G6) 40
Dalmeny (E3) 352
Dana (F3) 75
Darmody (E5) 39
Davidson (E4) 851
Davin (H5) 100
Davis (F2) 200
Daylesford (G3) 25
Daysville (C2) 10
Debden (E2) 379
Delaronde (lake) (E1)
Delisle (D4) 482
Delmas (C3) 137
Demaine (D5) 122
Denholm (C3) 104
Denzil (B3) 259
Dewar Lake (B4) 63
Dilke (F5) 168
Dinsmore (D4) 388
Disley (F5) 78
Dnieper (J4) 15
Dodsland (C4) 323
Dollard (C6) 193
Domremy (F3) 226
Donavon (D4) 77
Donwell (J4) 40
Doonside (K6) 23
Doré (lake) (L3)
Drake (G4) 232
Drinkwater (F5) 163
Driver (B4) 5
Druid (C4) 61
Dubuc (J5) 200
Duck Lake (E3) 585
Duck Mountain Prov. Park (K4)
Duff (H5) 102
Dulwich (C2) 10
Dumas (J6) 25
Dummer (G6) 150
Dunblane (D4) 132
Dundurn (E4) 421
Dunkirk (F5) 62
Dunleath (K4) 15
Duval (G4) 218
Dysart (H5) 341
Eagle (hills) (C3)
Eaglehill (creek) (D4)
Ear (lake) (B3)
Earl Grey (G5) 258
Eastend (C6) 706
Eatonia (B4) 565
Ebenezer (J4) 151
Edam (C2) 264
Edenwold (G5) 190
Edfield (H4) 10
Edgeley (H5) 250
Edgeworth (G6) 10
Edmore (H4) 8
Elbourne (G4) 6
Elbow (E4) 281
Eldersley (H3) 105
Eldred (E2) 14
Elfros (H4) 308
Elk Hill (G2)
Ellisboro (H5) 20
Elrose (D4) 538
Elstow (E4) 111
Endeavour (J3) 208
Englefeld (G3) 153
Environ (D3) 15
Erinferry (D2) 6
Ernfold (D5) 156
Erwood (J3) 150
Esk (G4) 30
Eskbank (E5) 97
Esterhazy (K5) 748
Estevan (J6) 5,264
Estlin (G5) 75
Eston (C4) 1,625
Estuary (B5) 98
Ethelton (G3) 103
Etomami (J3) 25
Etomami (riv.) (J3)
Evesham (B3) 90
Expanse (F6) 76
Eyebrow (E5) 286
Eyebrow (lake) (E5)
Eyehill (creek) (B3)
Fairholme (C2) 102
Fairlight (K6) 194
Fairmount Sta. (B4) 188
Fairy Glen (G2) 114
Fenwood (H4) 191
Fielding (D3) 78
Fife (lake) (E6)
Fife Lake (F6) 166
File (hills) (H5)
Fillmore (H6) 342
Findlater (F5) 95
Fir (riv.) (J2)
Fir Mountain (E6) 125
Fishing Lake (H4) 25
Fiske (C4) 168
Flaxcombe (B4) 147
Fleming (K5) 193
Flintoft (E6) 80
Foam Lake (H4) 841
Fond du Lac (L2) 35
Fond du Lac (riv.) (M2)
Forgan (D4) 93
Forget (J6) 166
Forrest (lake) (L3)
Fort Qu'Appelle (H5) 1,130
Forward (G6) 33
Fosston (H3) 122
Foster (riv.) (M3)
Fox Valley (B5) 395
Foxford (F2) 85
Francis (H5) 179
Frenchman (riv.) (C6)
Frenchman Butte (B2) 106
Frobisher (J6) 315
Frobisher (lake) (L3)
Frontier (C6) 306
Froude (H6) 50
Frys (K6) 66
Fulda (F3) 40
Furness (B2) 72
Fusilier (B4) 300
Gainsborough (K6) 400
Galilee (F6) 25
Gap (creek) (B6)
Garrick (G2) 450
Geikie (riv.) (M3)
Gerald (K5) 84
Gilroy (E5) 100
Girvin (F4) 142
Gladmar (G6) 250
Glamis (D4) 50
Glaslyn (C2) 250
Glen Elder (J3) 148
Glen Ewen (K6) 272
Glenavon (J5) 335
Glenbain (E6) 100
Glenbush (D2) 89
Glenside (E4) 135
Glentworth (E6) 145
Glidden (B4) 131
Golden Prairie (B5) 244
Good Spirit (lake) (J4)
Good Spirit Lake Prov. Park (J4)
Goodeve (H4) 211
Goodsoil (L4) 200
Goodwater (H6) 76
Gouverneur (D6) 75
Govan (G4) 442
Govenlock (B6) 188
Grand Coulee (G5) 92
Gravelbourg (E6) 1,434
Gray (G5) 94
Grayson (J5) 355
Great Sand (hills) (B5)
Green (lake) (D1)
Greenstreet (A2) 40
Greenwater Lake Prov. Park (H3)
Grenfell (J5) 1,080
Griffin (H6) 136
Gronlid (G2) 400
Guernsey (F4) 94
Gull Lake (C5) 1,052
Gunnworth (C4) 40
Hafford (D3) 453
Hagen (F3) 77
Hague (E3) 413
Halbrite (H6) 214
Hallonquist (D5) 96
Handel (C3) 115
Hanley (E4) 425
Hardy (G6) 75
Harlan (B2) 12
Harris (D4) 282
Hart (F6) 19
Hatherleigh (C2) 50
Hatton (B5) 92
Haultain (riv.) (L3)
Hawarden (E4) 174
Hazel Dell (H4) 50
Hazelwood (J6)
Hazenmore (D6) 186
Hazlet (C5) 175
Hearne (F5) 43
Hearts Hill (B3) 25
Hendon (H3) 100
Hendrie (B5)
Henribourg (F2) 100
Hepburn (E3) 286
Herbert (D5) 958
Herschel (C4) 203
Herzel (H4)
Heward (H6) 134
Hillmond (B2) 40
Hillside (C2)
Hinchcliffe (J3) 10
Hitchcock (J6) 60
Hodgeville (E5) 312
Hoey (F3) 150
Hoffer (H6)
Holbein (E2) 30
Holdfast (F5) 303
Honeymoon (F2)
Hoosier (B4) 20
Horizon (F6) 70
Hubbard (H4) 187
Hudson Bay (J3) 1,421
Hughton (D4) 100
Humboldt (F3) 2,916
Hyas (J4) 267
Iffley (C3) 10
Ile à la Crosse (L3) 25
Ile à la Crosse (lake) (L3)
Imperial (F4) 566
Indian Head (H5) 1,721
Insinger (H4) 135
Instow (C6) 42
Invermay (J4) 300
Ironspring (creek) (G3)
Isham (C4) 5
Ituna (H4) 627
Jack Fish Lake (C2) 20
Jackfish (lake) (C2)
Jameson (G5) 55
Jansen (G4) 249
Jasmin (H4) 70
Jedburgh (J4) 87
Juniata (D3) 40
Kamsack (K4) 2,843
Kandahar (G4) 98
Kayville (F6) 100
Keatley (D3) 10
Kedleston (F5) 45
Keeler (F5) 90
Kelfield (C4) 60
Kelliher (H4) 461
Kelso Station (K6) 98
Kelstern (E5) 127
Kelvington (H3) 819
Kenaston (E4) 385
Kendal (H5) 162
Kennedy (J5) 268
Keppel (D3) 82
Kerrobert (C4) 1,037
Ketchen (J3) 50
Keystown (F5) 88
Khedive (G6) 153
Killaly (J5) 206
Kilwinning Siding (E2) 10
Kincaid (D6) 306
Kincorth (B5) 44
Kindersley (B4) 2,572
Kingsmere (lake) (E1)
Kinistino (F3) 654
Kinley (D3) 116
Kipling (J5) 684
Kisbey (J6) 276
Kiyiu (lake) (C4)
Kronau (G5) 86
Krydor (D3) 169
Kuroki (H4) 190
Kyle (C5) 467
Kylemore (H4) 30
La Ronge (L3) 639
La Ronge (lake) (M3)
Lac Vert (G3) 150
Lacadena (C5) 100
Lady Lake (J3) 25
Laflèche (E6) 661
Laird (E3) 312
Lajord (G5) 100
Lake Alma (G6) 170
Lake Lenore (G3) 461
Lake Valley (E5) 77
Lampman (J6) 506
Lancer (C5) 215
Landis (C3) 240
Lang (G6) 281
Langbank (J5) 88
Langenburg (K5) 668
Langham (E3) 390
Lanigan (F4) 462
Laporte (B4) 100
Lashburn (B2) 394
Last Mountain (lake) (F4)
Laura (D4) 97
Lawson (E5) 77
Leacross (H2) 66
Leader (B5) 1,085
Leaf (lake) (J2)
Leask (E2) 412
Lebret (H5) 335
Leech (lake) (J4)
Leipzig (C3) 123
Lemberg (H5) 525
Lemsford (B5) 54
Leney (D3) 50
Lenore (lake) (G3)
Leoville (D2) 397
Leross (H4) 100
Leroy (G4) 514
Leslie Station (H4) 123
Lestock (G4) 354
Lewvan (H5) 92
Liberty (F4) 182
Lilac (D3) 10
Limerick (E6) 239
Lintlaw (H3) 338
Lipton (H5) 412
Lisieux (E6) 100
Little Manitou (Lake) (F4)
Livelong (C2) 122
Lloydminster (A2) 2,571
Lockwood (G4) 113
Lodge (creek) (B6)
Lone Rock (A2) 60
Long (creek) (H6)
Loomis (C6) 66
Loon (creek) (G4)
Loon Lake (B1) 272
Loon River (B1) 15
Loreburn (E4) 197
Lorlie (H5) 95
Love (G2) 148
Loverna (B4) 129
Lucky Lake (D5) 432
Lumsden (G5) 512
Luseland (B3) 591
Macdowall (E2) 35
Macklin (A3) 661
MacNutt (K4) 228
Macoun (H6) 191
Macrorie (E4) 152
Madison (B4) 107
Maidstone (B2) 555
Major (B4) 131
Makwa (lake) (B1)
Makwa (riv.) (B1)
Manito (lake) (B3)
Manitou Beach (F4) 138
Mankota (D6) 461
Manor (K6) 275
Mantario (B4) 115
Maple (creek) (B5)
Maple Creek (B6) 1,974
Marcelin (E3) 267
Marengo (B4) 130
Margo (H4) 257
Markinch (G5) 131
Marquis (F5) 157
Marsden (B3) 176
Marshall (B2) 138
Maryfield (K6) 456
Mawer (E5) 84
Mayfair (D2) 92
Maymont (D3) 197
Mazenod (E6) 173
McCord (E6) 160
McFarlane (riv.) (L2)
McGee (C4) 58
McKague (G3) 144
McLean (G5) 150
McMahon (D5) 150
McTaggart (H6) 73
Meacham (F3) 193
Meadow (lake) (C1)
Meadow Lake (C1) 2,477
Meath Park (F2) 198
Medstead (C2) 202
Melaval (E6) 96
Melfort (G3) 3,322
Melville (J5) 4,948
Mendham (B5) 211
Mennon (E3) 25
Meota (C2) 240
Merid (B4) 44
Mervin (C2) 207
Meskanaw (F3) 102
Meyronne (E6) 220
Midale (H6) 703
Middle Lake (F3) 166
Mikado (J4) 160
Milden (D4) 390
Mildred (D2) 122
Milestone (G5) 488
Millerdale (B4) 20
Ministikwan (lake) (B1)
Minton (G6) 191
Missouri Coteau (hills) (F6)
Mistatim (H3) 187
Mitchellton (F6) 57
Mont Nebo (E2) 40
Montmartre (H5) 425
Montreal (lake) (F1)
Montreal Lake (F1) 25
Moose (mt.) (J6)
Moose Jaw (F5) 29,603
Moose Jaw (creek) (G5)
Moose Mountain (creek) (J6)
Moose Mountain Prov. Park (J6)
Moose Range (H2) 25
Moosomin (K5) 1,390
Morse (D5) 459
Mortlach (E5) 251
Mossbank (E6) 593
Mossy (riv.) (H1)
Mozart (G4) 75
Muddy (lake) (B3)
Mudjatik (riv.) (L3)
Muenster (F3) 147
Mullingar (D2) 25
Naicam (G3) 529
Naseby (C3) 10
Neidpath (D5) 222
Neilburg (B3) 264
Netherhill (C4) 111
Neudorf (J5) 442
Neville (D6) 199
New Osgoode (H3) 150
Nipawin (H2) 3,337
Nipawin Prov. Park (G1)
Nokomis (F4) 516
Nora (H3) 25
Norquay (J4) 448
North Battleford (C3) 8,924
North Portal (J6) 253
North Saskatchewan (riv.) (D3)
Northgate (J6) 30
Northside (F2) 10
Notukeu (creek) (D6)
Nut Mountain (H3) 200
Oban Station (D3) 55
Odessa (H5) 252
Ogema (G6) 455
Okla (H3) 25
Old Wives (lake) (E5)
Oldman (riv.) (L2)
Onion Lake (B2) 90
Opuntia (lake) (C4)
Orkney (D6) 121
Ormiston (F6) 125
Osage (H6) 102
Osler (E3) 209
Otthon (J4) 42
Outlook (E4) 885
Overflowing (riv.) (K2)
Oxbow (J6) 783
Paddockwood (F2) 225
Palmer (E6) 97
Palo (C3) 10
Pambrun (D6) 18
Pangman (G6) 231
Paradise Hill (B2) 251
Parkbeg (E5) 86
Parkman (K6) 50
Parkside (E2) 125
Pas Trail (H2) 10
Pasqua (F5) 45
Pasquia (hills) (J2)
Pasquia (riv.) (K2)
Paswegin (H4) 100
Pathlow (G3) 100
Paynton (B2) 241
Peebles (J5) 30
Peesane (H3) 116
Pelican (lake) (E5)
Pelly (K4) 477
Penn (D2) 15
Pennant Sta. (C5) 306
Pense (G5) 301
Penzance (F4) 122
Percival (J5) 15
Perdue (D3) 413
Perigord (H3) 25
Peter Pond (lake) (L3)
Peterson (F3) 30
Pheasant (hills) (J5)
Phippen (C3) 44
Piapot (B6) 268
Pilger (F3) 175
Pilot Butte (G5) 129
Pinkham (B4) 77
Pinto (creek) (D6)
Pipestone (creek) (K6)
Pipestone (riv.) (L2)
Plato (C4) 185
Plenty (C4) 212
Plunkett (F4) 117
Ponass (lake) (H3)
Ponteix (D6) 794
Pontrilas (H2) 100
Poplar (riv.) (E6)
Porcupine (mt.) (K3)
Porcupine Plain (H3) 572
Portreeve (B5) 128
Prairie River (J3) 88
Pré Sainte Marie (H3) 20
Preeceville (J4) 807
Prelate (B5) 632
Primate (B3) 120
Primrose (lake) (L3)
Prince (C3) 40
Prince Albert (F2) 17,149
Prince Albert Nat'l Park (E1)
Prud'Homme (F3) 290
Punnichy (G4) 349
Qu'Appelle (H5) 595
Qu'Appelle (riv.) (J5)
Quill (lakes) (G4)
Quill Lake (G3) 458
Quinton (G4) 184
Rabbit Lake (D2) 197
Radisson (D3) 500
Radville (G6) 1,087
Rama (H4) 262
Ravenscrag (C6) 94
Raymore (G4) 434
Readlyn (F6) 127
Red Deer (riv.) (A5)
Red Deer (riv.) (K3)
Redberry (lake) (D3)
Redfield (D2) 20
Redvers (K6) 561
Reflex (lake) (A3)
REGINA (G5) 89,755
Regina Beach (F5) 301
Reindeer (lake) (N3)
Reindeer (riv.) (M3)
Renown (F4) 90
Reserve (J3) 33
Revenue (B3) 120
Reward (B3) 50
Reynaud (F3) 150
Rhein (J4) 384
Riceton (G5) 150
Richard (D3) 101
Richardson (G5) 30
Richlea (C4) 120
Richmound (B5) 196
Ridgedale (H2) 208
Ridpath (C4) 50
Riou (lake) (M2)
Riverhurst (E5) 251
Rivers (lake) (F6)
Robsart (B6) 115
Rocanville (K5) 491
Roche Percée (J6) 200
Rockglen (F6) 543
Rockhaven (B3) 100
Rokeby (J4) 50
Ronge, La (lake) (M3)
Rose Valley (H3) 537
Rosetown (D4) 2,262
Rosthern (E3) 1,268
Rouleau (G5) 402
Ruddell (D3) 61
Runnymede (K4) 99
Rush Lake (D5) 186
Ruthilda (C4) 92
Rutland Sta. (B3) 99
St. Benedict (F3) 200
St. Boswells (D5) 101
St. Brieux (G3) 411
St. Front (G3) 40
St. Gregor (G3) 170
St. Louis (F3) 159
St. Walburg (B2) 618
Salt (lake) (K2)
Saltcoats (J4) 506
Salvador (B3) 145
Saskatchewan (riv.) (H2)
Saskatoon (E3) 72,858
Saskeram (riv.) (K2)
Sceptre (B5) 254
Scotsguard (C6) 88
Scott (C3) 339
Scott (lake) (M2)
Scout Lake (F6) 88
Secretan (E5) 47
Sedley (H5) 352
Selwyn (lake) (M2)
Semans (G4) 402
Senate (B6) 47
Senlac (B3) 121
Shackleton (C5) 105
Shamrock (E5) 101
Shaunavon (C6) 1,959
Sheho (H4) 407
Shell Lake (D2) 258
Shellbrook (E2) 907
Sikip (L4)
Silton (G5) 93
Silver Park (G3) 20
Simmie (C6) 123
Simpson (F4) 371
Sinnett (G4) 15
Sintaluta (H5) 402
Smeaton (G2) 275
Smiley (B4) 219
Smuts (F3) 50
Snowden (G2) 244
Sonningdale (D3) 225
Souris (riv.) (H6)
South Fork (C6) 76
South Saskatchewan (riv.) (C5)
Southey (G5) 460
Sovereign (D4) 161
Spalding (G3) 378
Speedwell (C2)
Speers (D3) 155
Spinney Hill (C3) 10
Spiritwood (D2) 488
Spooner (G2)
Spring Valley (F6) 115
Springside (J4) 308
Springwater (C4) 118
Spruce Home (F2) 40
Spruce Lake (B2) 104
Spy Hill (K5) 172
Stalwart (F4) 92
Star City (G3) 619
Stenen (J4) 301
Stewart Valley (D5) 125
Stockholm (J5) 199
Stonehenge (F6)
Stony Beach (F5) 75
Stony Rapids (M2)
Stornoway (K4) 115
Storthoaks (K6) 234
Stoughton (H6) 562
Stove Creek (J3)
Stranraer (C4) 106
Strasbourg (G4) 589
Stripe (lake) (C4)
Strongfield (E4) 164
Sturgeon (riv.) (E2)
Sturgeon Valley (E2)
Sturgis (J4) 729
Success (D5) 98
Summerberry (J5) 95
Superb (B4) 77
Swan (riv.) (J3)
Swanson (D4) 40
Swift Current (D5) 10,612
Swiftcurrent (creek) (D5)
Sylvania (G3) 177
Tadmore (J4) 40
Talmage (H6) 55
Tantallon (K5) 132
Tarnopol (F3) 96
Tate (G4) 30
Tazin (lake) (L2)
Tessier (D4) 104
Theodore (J4) 418
Thickwood (hills) (D2)
Tichfield (D4) 50
Tisdale (H3) 2,104
Togo (K4) 302
Tompkins (C5) 399
Torch (riv.) (H2)
Torquay (H6) 526
Totzke (F3) 40
Touchwood (hills) (G4)
Tramping (lake) (C3)
Tramping Lake (B3) 262
Traynor (C3) 92
Tregarva (G5) 47
Tribune (H6) 129
Trossachs (G6) 200
Trout (riv.) (L2)
Truax (G6) 90
Tuberose (C5) 60
Tuffnell (H4) 75
Tugaske (E5) 218
Turtle (lake) (C2)
Turtleford (B2) 367
Tuxford (F5) 133
Tway (F3) 200
Twelvemile (lake) (E6)
Tyvan (H5) 109
Unity (B3) 1,607
Unwin (B3) 53
Uranium City (L2) 900
Val Marie (D6) 383
Valley Centre (D4) 98
Valor (E6) 44
Valparaiso (G3) 68
Vanguard (D6) 443
Vanscoy (D4) 107
Vantage (F6) 65
Vawn (C2) 74
Venn (F4) 91
Verigin (K4) 278
Verlo (C5) 134
Verwood (F6) 122
Vibank (H5) 253
Viceroy (F6) 289
Vidora (B6) 75
Viscount (F4) 302
Vonda (F3) 246
Wadena (H4) 1,154
Wakaw (F3) 898
Waldeck (D5) 128
Waldheim (E3) 495
Waldron (J5) 119
Walpole (K6) 70
Wapawekka (hills) (M4)
Wapella (K5) 530
Warman (E3) 88
Wartime (C4) 95
Waseca (B2) 132
Waskana (creek) (G5)
Waskesiu (lake) (E2)
Waskesiu Lake (E2) 100
Wathaman (riv.) (M3)
Watrous (F4) 1,340
Watson (G3) 783
Wauchope (K6) 78
Wawota (J6) 441
Webb (C5) 179
Weed (hills) (J5)
Weekes (J3) 286
Weirdale (F2) 112
Weldon (F2) 220
Welwyn (K5) 224
West Bend (H4) 95
Westerham (B5) 75
Weyburn (H6) 7,684
White Bear (C5) 98
White Fox (H2) 366
White Gull (creek) (G2)
Whitefox (riv.) (G2)
Whiteshore (lake) (C3)
Whiteswan (lakes) (F1)
Whitewood (J5) 789
Whitkow (D3) 93
Wilcox (G5) 221
Wilkie (C3) 1,630
William (riv.) (L2)
Wilmar Station (J6) 65
Willow Bunch (F6) 742
Willow Bunch (lake) (F6)
Willowbrook (J4) 106
Windthorst (J5) 212
Wirr (B3) 60
Wiseton (D4) 215
Wishart (H4) 252
Witchekan (lake) (D2)
Wollaston (lake) (N2)
Wolseley (H5) 1,001
Wood (mt.) (E6)
Wood (riv.) (E6)
Wood Mountain Station (E6) 117
Woodrow (E6) 161
Wordsworth (J6) 72
Wroxton (K4) 129
Wymark (D5) 157
Wynyard (G4) 1,522
Yellow Creek (F3) 178
Yellow Grass (H6) 490
Yonker (B3) 25
Yorkton (J4) 8,256
Young (F4) 431
Zealandia (D4) 186
Zelma (E4) 103
Zenon Park (H2) 411

ALBERTA

1956 Total Poulation 1,123,116

Abee (D2)	75
Abilene (E2)	30
Acadia Valley (E4)	99
Acme (D4)	292
Aden (E5)	150
Aetna (D5)	64
Airdrie (C4)	327
Airways (E3)	
Alberta (mt.) (B3)	
Alberta Beach (C3)	127
Alcomdale (C3)	100
Alder Flats (C3)	53
Alderson (E4)	81
Aldersyde (C4)	50
Alexo (C3)	
Alhambra (C3)	
Alix (D3)	517
Allerston (E5)	
Alliance (E3)	313
Alpen Siding (D2)	
Altario (E4)	75
Amber Valley (D2)	
Amesbury (D2)	
Amisk (E3)	151
Analta (D2)	
Andrew (D3)	602
Angle Lake (E3)	
Anton Lake (D2)	
Anzac (E1)	
Ardley (D3)	88
Ardmore (E2)	120
Ardrossan (D3)	41
Armada (D4)	65
Armena (D3)	37
Arrowwood (D4)	240
Ashmont (E2)	100
Aspen Beach (D3)	
Assiniboine (mt.) (C4)	
Athabasca (D2)	1,293
Athabasca (lake) (C5)	
Athabasca (riv.) (D1)	
Atikameg (C2)	
Atlee (E4)	65
Bad Heart (A2)	
Badger Lake (D4)	
Balzac (C4)	
Banff (C4)	2,518
Banff Nat'l Park (B-C4)	
Barich (D2)	
Barnegat (E2)	
Barnwell (D5)	200
Barons (D4)	352
Barrhead (C2)	1,610
Bashaw (D3)	597
Bassano (D4)	753
Battle (riv.) (D3)	
Battle Lake (C3)	
Battle Ridge (E3)	
Battlebend (E3)	4
Bawlf (D3)	287
Bay Tree (A2)	3
Beacon Mines (B3)	
Beaumont (D3)	75
Beauvallon (E3)	175
Beaver Mines (C5)	
Beaverdam (E2)	
Beaverhill (lake) (D3)	
Beaverlodge (A2)	768
Beazer (D5)	
Beiseker (D4)	321
Bellevue (C5)	863
Bellis (D2)	127
Belloy (A2)	100
Benalto (C3)	100
Bentley (C3)	536
Benton Station (E4)	87
Berkinshaw (E3)	
Berry Creek (E4)	
Berwyn (B1)	342
Beverly (D3)	4,602
Beynon (D4)	
Bezanson (A2)	
Biche (lake) (E2)	
Bickerdike (B3)	190
Big Prairie (C4)	
Big Valley (D3)	354
Bitumount (E1)	
Birch (lake) (E3)	
Bindloss (E4)	100
Birch (mt.) (B5)	
Bircham (D4)	25
Bittern (lake) (D3)	
Bittern Lake (D3)	45
Black Diamond (C4)	991
Blackfalds (D3)	340
Blackfoot (E3)	100
Blackie (D4)	198
Blacktail (C4)	
Blairmore (C5)	1,973
Bloomsbury (C2)	
Blue Ridge (C2)	
Blueberry Mt. (A2)	
Bluesky (A1)	315
Bluffton (C3)	400
Bodo (E3)	
Bon Accord (D3)	125
Bonanza (A2)	
Bondiss (D2)	
Bonnyville (E2)	1,495
Boscombe (E2)	
Botha (D3)	102
Bottrel (C4)	
Bow (riv.) (D4)	
Bow Island (E5)	1,001
Bowden (C4)	296
Bowell (E4)	15
Bowmanton (E4)	
Bowness (C4)	6,217
Boyle (D2)	304
Bragg Creek (C4)	
Brant (D4)	100
Brazeau (mt.) (B3)	
Brazeau (riv.) (B3)	
Breton (C3)	500
Breynat (D2)	50
Brightview (D3)	
Brocket (D5)	100
Brooks (E4)	2,320
Brosseau (D3)	
Brownvale (B1)	200
Bruce (E3)	150
Bruderheim (D3)	290
Buck Lake (C3)	
Buffalo (E4)	75
Buffalo (lake) (D3)	
Buffalo Head (hills) (B5)	
Burdett (E5)	225
Burmis (C5)	166
Busby (C3)	150
Byemoor (D4)	80
Cabin Lake (E4)	
Cadogan (E3)	97
Cadomin (B3)	800
Cadron (D2)	
Cairns (E3)	
Calais (B2)	
Caldwell (D5)	
Calgary (C4)	181,780
Calgary (Metropolitan Area) (C4)	196,152
Calling (lake) (D2)	
Calmar (D3)	730
Camp Creek (C2)	
Campsie (C2)	12
Camrose (D3)	5,817
Canmore (C4)	754
Canyon Creek (C2)	
Cappon (E4)	
Carbon (D4)	354
Carbondale (D3)	60
Carcajou (B5)	
Cardiff (D3)	150
Cardston (D5)	2,607
Caribou (mts.) (B5)	
Carmangay (D4)	299
Caroline (C3)	296
Carolside (E4)	3
Carrot Creek (B3)	
Carseland (D4)	125
Carstairs (D4)	449
Caslan (D2)	25
Cassils (D4)	
Castor (D3)	958
Cavendish (E4)	66
Cayley (D4)	146
Cereal (E4)	154
Cessford (E4)	150
Champion (D4)	402
Chancellor (D4)	
Chard (E2)	
Chauvin (E3)	353
Cheadle (D4)	50
Chedderville (C3)	
Cherhill (C3)	100
Cherry Grove (E2)	150
Cherry Point (A1)	
Chigwell (D3)	25
Chin (D5)	40
Chinook (E4)	154
Chinook Valley (B1)	
Chipman (D3)	192
Chisholm Mills (C2)	200
Claire (lake) (B5)	
Clairmont (A2)	98
Clandonald (E3)	350
Claresholm (D4)	2,431
Clarkson Valley (B2)	
Clear Prairie (A1)	
Clive (D3)	249
Clover Bar (D3)	
Cluny (D4)	197
Clyde (D2)	221
Coal Valley (B3)	
Coaldale (D5)	2,327
Coalhurst (D5)	105
Coalspur (B3)	
Cochrane (C4)	707
Codesa (B2)	50
Cold (lake) (E2)	
Cold Lake (E2)	1,097
Coleman (C5)	1,566
Coleridge (E4)	188
Colinton (D2)	200
Columbia (mt.) (B3)	
Compeer (E4)	138
Condor (C3)	175
Conklin (E2)	130
Connor Creek (C2)	
Consort (E3)	434
Cooking Lake (D3)	
Cork (E2)	
Coronado (D3)	
Coronation (E3)	784
Countess (D4)	8
Cousins (E3)	
Coutts (D5)	350
Cowley (D5)	92
Craigend (E2)	300
Craigmyle (D4)	138
Craigower (E5)	
Crammond (C3)	
Cremona (C4)	192
Crooked Creek (B2)	
Crossfield (C4)	459
Crowfoot (D4)	
Crowsnest (pass) (C5)	
Czar (E3)	153
Dalemead (D4)	36
Dalroy (D4)	45
Dapp (C2)	150
Darling (D2)	
Darwell (C3)	25
Daysland (D3)	499
DeWinton (C4)	100
Deadwood (B1)	
Delacour (D4)	
Delburne (D3)	429
Delia (D4)	282
Delph (D3)	
Demmitt (A2)	
Derwent (E3)	289
Desmarais (D2)	
Deville (D3)	
Devon (D3)	1,429
Dewberry (E3)	150
Diamond City (D5)	143
Dickson (C3)	
Didsbury (C4)	1,227
Dimsdale (A2)	
Dixonville (B1)	
Dodds (D3)	35
Dog Pound (C4)	
Donalda (D3)	256
Donatville (D2)	
Donnelly (B2)	265
Dorenlee (D3)	66
Doris (C2)	
Dorothy (D4)	
Dowling (E4)	
Drayton Valley (C3)	2,588
Dreau (B2)	
Driftpile (C2)	
Drinnan (B3)	
Drumheller (D4)	2,632
Duchess (E4)	177
Duffield (C3)	
Duhamel (D3)	
Dunvegan (A2)	
Duvernay (E3)	
Eagle Butte (E5)	68
Eagle Hill (C4)	
Eaglesham (B2)	250
Earlie (E3)	
East Coulee (D4)	1,350
Easyford (C3)	13
Eckville (C3)	456
Edberg (D3)	167
Edgerton (E3)	292
EDMONTON (D3)	226,002
Edmonton (Metropolitan Area) (D3)	248,949
Edson (B3)	2,560
Edwand (D2)	99
Egg Lake (D2)	135
Egremont (D2)	122
Eldorena (D2)	300
Elk Island Nat'l Park (D3)	
Elk Point (E3)	594
Elmworth (A2)	
Elnora (D3)	177
Embarrass Portage (C5)	
Empress (E4)	480
Enchant (D4)	73
Endiang (D4)	165
Enilda (B2)	350
Ensign (D4)	60
Entrance (B3)	50
Entwistle (C3)	354
Erith (B3)	
Erskine (D3)	164
Etzikom (E5)	95
Etzikom Coulee (riv.) (E5)	
Eureka River (A1)	
Evansburg (C3)	350
Evergreen (C3)	
Excel (E4)	95
Exshaw (C4)	250
Fabyan (E3)	
Fairview (A1)	1,260
Faith (E5)	
Falher (B2)	802
Faust (C2)	600
Fawcett (C2)	
Federal (E3)	20
Fedorah (D3)	
Ferguson Flats (E2)	
Ferintosh (D3)	195
Fern Creek (C3)	
Ferrier (C3)	
Finnegan (E4)	
Fifth Meridian (B5)	
Flat Lake (E2)	
Flatbush (C2)	125
Fleet (E3)	100
Florann (E5)	
Foothills (B3)	250
Forbes (mt.) (B4)	
Foreman (D3)	
Foremost (E5)	456
Forest Lawn (D4)	3,150
Forestburg (E3)	552
Forestview (B2)	
Fork Lake (E2)	
Forshee (C3)	
Ft. Assiniboine (C2)	75
Ft. Chipewyan (C5)	
Ft. Fitzgerald (C4)	
Ft. Kent (E2)	
Ft. Macleod (D5)	2,103
Ft. MacKay (E1)	
Ft. Saskatchewan (D3)	2,582
Ft. Vermilion (B5)	350
Fox (E5)	
Frains (D2)	73
Franchere (E2)	36
Frank (C5)	221
Freemen River (C2)	
Frog (lake) (E3)	
Gadsby (D3)	145
Gage (A1)	
Gahern (E5)	
Gainford (C3)	75
Galahad (E3)	215
Garfield (C4)	
Garrington (C4)	
Gelkie (A3)	
Genesee (C3)	
Ghost Pine Creek (D4)	
Gibbons (D3)	100
Gilt Edge (E3)	
Gilwood (B2)	2
Girouxville (B2)	300
Gleichen (D4)	581
Glen Leslie (A2)	
Glendon (E2)	314
Glenevis (C3)	
Glenford (C3)	
Glenwoodville (D5)	96
Golden Spike (D3)	
Goodfish Lake (D2)	
Goose Lake (E2)	
Gordon (lake) (E1)	
Gordondale (A2)	171
Graham (lake) (C1)	
Grainger (D4)	45
Grand Centre (E2)	
Grande Prairie (A2)	6,302
Granlea (E5)	
Grantham (E4)	25
Granum (D5)	322
Granum (E2)	
Grassland (D2)	
Grassy Lake (E5)	282
Gratz (E3)	
Green Court (C2)	60
Greenshields (E3)	
Grimshaw (B1)	904
Grosmont (D2)	
Groton (E5)	
Grouard Mission (C2)	328
Gull (lake) (C3)	
Guy (B2)	
Gwynne (D3)	100
Habay (A5)	450
Hackett (D3)	
Haddock (B3)	
Haight (D3)	
Hairy Hill (D3)	183
Halcourt (A2)	
Halkirk (D3)	209
Hamlin (D2)	
Hanna (E4)	2,327
Hardieville (D5)	100
Hardisty (E3)	628
Harmattan (C4)	
Hartell (C4)	500
Hattonford (C3)	
Hay (lake) (A5)	
Hay (riv.) (A5)	
Hay Lakes (D3)	193
Haynes (D3)	94
Hays (E4)	
Hayter (E3)	95
Hazeldine (E3)	75
Hazelmere (A2)	
Heart Valley (A2)	
Heath (E3)	31
Heathdale (E4)	
Heinsburg (E3)	135
Heisler (D3)	166
Heldar (C2)	100
Helmsdale (E4)	
Hemaruka (E4)	61
Henry House (B3)	
Hercules (D3)	18
Herronton (D4)	
Hespero (C3)	
High Level (A5)	
High Prairie (B2)	1,743
High River (D4)	2,102
Highland Park (A1)	
Highridge (D2)	50
Highvale (C3)	
Highway (C3)	
Hilda (E4)	285
Hill Spring (D5)	350
Hillcrest Mines (C5)	1,000
Hilliard (D3)	178
Hillsdown (D3)	
Hindville (E3)	
Hines Creek (A1)	360
Hinton (B3)	
Hinton Trail (A2)	
Hoadley (C3)	
Hobbema (D3)	122
Holden (D3)	544
Holyoke (E2)	
Homeglen (D3)	
Hondo (D2)	
Hope Valley (E3)	
Horburg (C3)	
Hotchkiss (B1)	
Huallen (A2)	
Hubalta (D4)	350
Huggett (C3)	
Hughenden (E3)	212
Hussar (D4)	168
Hutton (E4)	
Huxley (D4)	87
Hylo (D2)	
Hythe (A2)	481
Idamay (E4)	
Iddesleigh (E4)	35
Imperial Mills (E2)	
Indus (D4)	46
Inland (D3)	
Innisfail (D3)	1,883
Innisfree (E3)	318
Iola (C3)	
Irma (E3)	421
Iron River (E2)	
Iron Springs (D5)	
Irricana (D4)	158
Irvine (E5)	232
Islay (E3)	125
James River Bridge (C4)	10
Jarrow (E3)	66
Jarvie (D2)	145
Jasper (B3)	2,105
Jasper Nat'l Park (A-B3)	
Jasper Place (D3)	15,957
Jaydot (E5)	
Jean-Coté (B2)	
Jenner (E4)	24
Joffre (D3)	
Jumping Pound (C4)	
Kahwin (D3)	
Kaleland (D3)	
Kathleen (B2)	
Kathryn (D4)	44
Kavanagh (D3)	
Keg River (A5)	
Kelsey (D3)	55
Keoma (D4)	
Kickinghorse (pass) (B4)	
Killam (E3)	524
Kimball (D5)	
Kingman (D3)	97
Kinikinik (D2)	
Kinmundy (E4)	
Kinsella (E3)	93
Kinuso (C2)	306
Kipp (D5)	88
Kirkcaldy (D4)	47
Kirriemuir (E4)	77
Kitchener (mt.) (B3)	
Kitscoty (E3)	283
Kleskun Hill (A2)	
Knob Hill (C3)	
Koknee (E3)	
Ksituan (A2)	
La Corey (E2)	
La Crête (B5)	
La Glace (A2)	
Lac Cardinal (A1)	
Lac la Biche (E2)	967
Lacombe (D3)	2,747
Lafond (E3)	
Lake Eliza (E3)	
Lake Isle (C3)	
Lake Louise (C4)	113
Lake Majeau (C3)	
Lake Thelma (E3)	
Lamont (D3)	632
Landonville (E3)	
Lanfine (E4)	44
Langdon (D4)	92
Larkspur (D2)	
Last Lake (A1)	
Lathom (D4)	
Lavoy (E3)	127
Lawton (C2)	
Le Goff (E2)	
Leaman (C3)	
Leduc (D3)	2,008
Leedale (C3)	
Legal (D3)	457
Legend (lake) (D1)	
Leicester (B2)	
Leighmore (A2)	
Leighton (E3)	
Leslieville (C3)	153
Lessard (E2)	
Lesser Slave (lake) (C2)	
Lethbridge (D5)	29,462
Leyland (B3)	53
Lindbergh (E3)	
Lindbrook (D3)	
Lisburn (C3)	
Little Plume (E5)	
Little Red River (B5)	
Lloydminster (E3)	2,506
Lloyds Hill (E3)	
Lobley (C4)	
Lomond (D4)	189
Lone Pine (C2)	
Lone Star (B1)	
Lonebutte (E4)	
Longview (C4)	1,250
Lonira (C2)	
Looma (D3)	
Lougheed (E3)	201
Lousana (D3)	93
Loyalist (E4)	69
Lucky Strike (E5)	
Lundbreck (C5)	100
Lundemo (D3)	
Luscar (B3)	500
Luzan (D3)	
Lyell (mt.) (B4)	
Lyndon (C4)	
Ma-Me-O Beach (D3)	137
MacKay (C3)	
Mackenzie Highway (B1)	
Madden (C4)	
Magrath (D5)	1,382
Mahaska (B3)	
Majorville (D4)	
Makepeace (D4)	
Maligne (lake) (B3)	
Mallaig (E2)	450
Maloy (E2)	
Manning (B1)	726
Mannville (E3)	599
Manola (C2)	
Manyberries (E5)	130
Mapova (D2)	
Marina (A1)	
Markerville (C3)	
Marlboro (B3)	75
Marwayne (E3)	337
Masinasin (E5)	
Maughan (E3)	
Maycroft (C5)	
Mayerthorpe (C3)	563
Mazeppa (D4)	48
McDonaldville (E3)	
McLaughlin (E3)	95
McLennan (D2)	1,002
McMurray (E1)	1,110
McRae (E2)	
McLeod Valley (C3)	
Meadowbrook (D2)	
Meadowview (C3)	
Meander River (A5)	265
Meanook (D2)	
Medicine Hat (E4)	20,826
Meeting Creek (D3)	150
Menaik (D3)	
Mercoal (B3)	600
Metiskow (E3)	95
Michichi (D4)	100
Midlandvale (D4)	700
Midnapore (C4)	250
Miette (B3)	
Milk (riv.) (D5)	
Milk River (D5)	642
Millet (D3)	427
Millicent (E4)	77
Milo (D4)	167
Minburn (E3)	150
Mirror (D3)	591
Mirror Landing (D2)	344
Monarch (D5)	74
Monitor (E4)	79
Moon Lake (C3)	
Moose Portage (D2)	
Morecambe (E3)	
Morinville (D3)	957
Morley (C4)	75
Morningside (D3)	
Morrin (D4)	267
Mosside (C2)	
Mossleigh (D4)	50
Mound (C4)	
Mountain Park (B3)	400
Mountain View (D5)	250
Moyerton (E3)	
Muirhead (C4)	
Mundare (D3)	650
Munson (D4)	82
Muriel (lake) (E2)	
Musidora (E3)	
Myrnam (E3)	440
Mystery Lake (C2)	
Naco (E4)	
Namaka (D4)	34
Nampa (B1)	
Nanton (D4)	1,047
Neerlandia (C2)	
Nemiskam (E5)	
Nestow (D2)	
Neutral Hills (E3)	
Nevis (D3)	75
New Brigden (E4)	96
New Dayton (D5)	100
New Kiew (E3)	
New Lindsay (E3)	
New Norway (D3)	273
New Sarepta (D3)	
Newbrook (D2)	129
Newcastle Mine (D4)	1,078
Nightingale (D4)	
Nilrem (E3)	
Nisbet (D4)	
Nisku (D3)	250
Niton (C3)	
Nobleford (D5)	263
Noral (D2)	
Norbuck (C3)	
Nordegg (B3)	1,014
Normandeau (E2)	
North Fork (D5)	
N. Saskatchewan (riv.) (E3)	
North Star (B1)	
N. Wabiskaw (lake) (D1)	
Norton (E5)	
Norway Valley (E3)	
Obed (B3)	
Ohaton (D3)	46
Okotoks (C4)	764
Oldman (riv.) (D5)	
Olds (D4)	1,980
Onefour (E5)	
Onoway (C3)	190
Opal (D3)	128
Oras (C3)	
Orion (E5)	75
Owl River (E2)	
Owlseye Lake (E2)	
Oyen (E4)	562
Ozada (C4)	250
Pakan (D2)	
Paradise Valley (E3)	200
Park Court (C3)	
Parkland (D4)	130
Pashley (E5)	
Patience (D3)	
Patricia (E4)	130
Paxson (D2)	
Peace (riv.) (B1)	
Peace River (B1)	2,034
Pearce (D5)	60
Peavine (C2)	
Peerless (lake) (C1)	
Peers (B3)	55
Pembina (riv.) (C3)	
Pemukan (E3)	
Pendant d'Oreille (E5)	
Pendryl (C3)	
Penhold (D3)	213
Peno (D3)	
Peoria (A2)	
Philips (E3)	
Philomena (E2)	
Pibroch (D2)	122
Pickardville (D2)	425
Picture Butte (D5)	881
Pigeon (lake) (D3)	
Pincher (C5)	98
Pincher Creek (D5)	1,729
Pine Lake (D3)	
Pinedale (B3)	
Pinhorn (E5)	
Pipestone Creek (A2)	
Pivot (E4)	
Plain Lake (E3)	
Plamondon (D2)	100
Poe (D3)	
Pollockville (E4)	66
Ponoka (D3)	3,387
Poplar Hill (A2)	
Porcupine (hills) (C4)	
Prairie Echo (B2)	
Prestville (A2)	
Priddis (C4)	
Primrose (E3)	
Prosperity (D2)	
Provost (E3)	878
Puffer (E3)	
Purple Springs (E5)	40
Queenstown (D4)	166
Radway (D2)	203
Rainier (E4)	
Raley (D5)	
Ranch (D2)	
Ranchville (E5)	
Ranfurly (E3)	222
Rangeton (C3)	
Ravine (C3)	
Raymond (D5)	2,399
Rearville (E4)	
Red Deer (D3)	12,338
Red Deer (riv.) (D4)	
Red Willow (D3)	54
Redcliff (E4)	2,001
Redland (D4)	39
Redwater (D3)	1,065
Reist (E4)	
Reno (B2)	
Retlaw (D4)	60
Ribstone (E3)	90
Rich Lake (E2)	
Richdale (E4)	38
Richmond Park (D2)	
Ricinus (C3)	
Rimbey (C3)	980
Rio Grande (A2)	
Robinson (E5)	
Rochester (D2)	195
Rochfort Bridge (C3)	150
Rocky (mts.) (B-C4)	
Rocky Mountain House (C3)	1,285
Rocky Rapids (C3)	
Rockyford (D4)	226
Rodef (D3)	
Rodino (E3)	
Roma (B1)	
Rosalind (D3)	96
Rose Lynn (E4)	
Rosebeg (E5)	
Rosebud (D4)	93
Rosedale (D4)	1,400
Roseglen (E4)	
Rosemary (E4)	158
Rosenheim (E3)	
Rosevear (B3)	
Rosyth (E3)	
Round Hill (D3)	177
Round Valley (C3)	
Rowley (D4)	95
Royal Park (D3)	
Royalties (C4)	600
Rumsey (D4)	104
Rusylvia (E3)	
Rycroft (A2)	424
Ryley (D3)	495
Saddle Lake (E2)	
Saint Albert (D3)	1,320
Saint Edouard (E3)	
Saint Kilda (E5)	
Saint Lina (E2)	
Saint Michael (D3)	200
Saint Paul (E3)	2,229
Saint Vincent (E2)	
Sandy Rapids (E2)	
Sangudo (C3)	331
Saunders (C3)	159
Sawdy (D2)	130
Scandia (E4)	
Scapa (D4)	
Schuler (E4)	188
Scollard (D4)	66
Scotfield (E4)	
Scotswood (A1)	
Seba Beach (C3)	141
Sedalia (E4)	66
Sedgewick (E3)	608
Seebe (C4)	
Seven Persons (E5)	97
Sexsmith (A2)	345
Shamrock Valley (E2)	
Sheerness (E4)	100
Shepard (D4)	114
Shining Bank (B3)	
Shouldice (D4)	
Sibbald (E4)	88
Silver Heights (E3)	
Sion (C3)	
Slave (riv.) (C5)	
Slave Lake (C2)	90
Smith (D2)	
Smoky (riv.) (A2)	
Smoky Heights (A2)	
Smoky Lake (D2)	563
S. Saskatchewan (riv.) (E4)	
S. Wabiskaw (lake) (D2)	
Sounding Lake (E3)	
Spedden (E2)	150
Spirit River (A2)	743
Spring Coulee (D5)	125
Springburn (B2)	
Spruce Grove (C3)	309
Stand Off (D5)	
Standard (D4)	230
Stanger (C3)	
Stanmore (E4)	45
Star (D3)	
Stauffer (C3)	
Stavely (D4)	338
Sterco (B3)	175
Stettler (D3)	3,359
Steveville (E4)	
Stirling (D5)	430
Stony Plain (C3)	1,098
Strachan (C3)	
Strathmore (D4)	727
Streamstown (E3)	90
Strome (E3)	306
Stubno (E3)	
Sturgeon Heights (B2)	
Styal (C3)	
Suffield (E4)	76
Sullivan (lake) (D3)	
Sundre (C4)	923
Sunnybrook (C3)	200
Sunnydale (E4)	
Sunnynook (E4)	100
Sunnyslope (D4)	97
Sunset House (B2)	
Swalwell (D4)	117
Sylvan Lake (C3)	1,114
Taber (E5)	3,688
Talbot (E3)	50
Tawatinaw (D2)	125
Teepee Creek (A2)	
Tees (D3)	69
Temple (mt.) (B4)	
The Twins (mt.) (B3)	
Thérien (E2)	520
Thickwood (hills) (D1)	
Thorhild (D2)	288
Thorsby (C3)	411
Three Hills (D4)	1,095
Throne (E3)	
Tiger Lily (C2)	
Tilley (E4)	240
Timeu (C2)	
Tod Creek (C5)	
Tofield (D3)	800
Tolland (E3)	
Tomahawk (C3)	
Torlea (E3)	
Torrington (D4)	125
Tothill (E5)	
Travers (D4)	66
Trefoil (D4)	
Triangle (B2)	
Trochu (D4)	680
Tudor (D4)	
Tulliby Lake (E3)	
Turin (D5)	132
Turner Valley (C4)	704
Twin Butte (C5)	
Twin River (D5)	
Twining (D4)	
Ukalta (D3)	
Usona (D3)	
Utikuma (lake) (C2)	
Vanesti (E3)	
Vanrena (A1)	
Vauxhall (D4)	713
Vega (C2)	
Vegreville (E3)	2,574
Venice (E2)	
Vermilion (E3)	2,196
Veteran (E3)	241
Viewpoint (D3)	
Viking (E3)	897
Vilna (E2)	374
Violet Grove (C3)	
Vulcan (D4)	1,204
Wabamun (C3)	198
Wabasca (D2)	
Wabiskaw (riv.) (C1)	
Wainwright (E3)	2,653
Wallace (mt.) (C2)	
Walsh (E5)	142
Wanham (A2)	162
Wapiti (A2)	
Warburg (C3)	257
Warden Jc. (D3)	76
Wardlow (E4)	
Warner (D5)	450
Warrensville (B1)	
Warspite (D2)	159
Warwick (D3)	

ALBERTA (Continued)

Waskatenau (D2) 289
Wastina (E4)
Waterglen (D3)
Waterton Lakes Nat'l Park (C5)
Waterton Park (D5) 300
Waterways (E1) 400
Watino (B2) 62
Watts (D4)
Waybrook (D3)
Wayne (D4) 700
Weasel Creek (D2) 20
Webster (A2)
Welling (D5)
Wembley (A2) 272
West Wingham (E4)
Westcott (C4)
Westlock (C2) 1,136
Westward Ho (C4)
Wetaskiwin (D3) 4,476
Whatcheer (E4)
Wheat Centre (D4)
Whiskey Gap (D5) 100
Whitburn (A2)
White Court (C2) 130
Whitelaw (A1) 477
Whitemud Creek (B2)
Whitla (E5) 67
Wild Horse (E5)
Wildmere (E3)
Wildwood (C3) 547
Willesden Green (C3)
Willingdon (E3) 431
Willow Creek (D4)
Willow Trail (E2)
Willowlea (E3)
Wimborne (D4) 88
Windsor Creek (A2)
Winefred (lake) (E2)
Winfield (C3) 362
Winnifred (E5) 96
Withrow (C3)
Woking (A2) 325
Wolf Creek (B3)
Wood Buffalo (Nat'l Park) (B5).
Wood River (D3)
Woodhouse (D5)
Woolchester (E5)
Wostok (D3) 150
Wrentham (D5) 87
Yates (B3)
Yellowhead (pass) (A3)
Yeoford (C3)
Youngstown (E4) 305

BRITISH COLUMBIA

1956 Total Population 1,398,464

Abbotsford (L3) 830
Aero (B3)
Agassiz (M3) 600
Ainsworth (J5) 250
Aiyansh (C2) 250
Alberni (H3) 3,947
Alberni (inlet) (H3).
Albert Canyon (J4). 50
Albreda (H4) 50
Alert Bay (D5) 695
Alexandria (F4) 70
Alexis Creek (F4) 50
Aleza Lake (G3) 250
Alice Arm (C2) 75
Alkali Lake (F4) 125
Allenby (G5) 250
Alta Lake (F5) 50
Alvin (L2)
Anahim Lake (E4)
Anvil Island (K2)
Anyox (C2)
Appledale (J5) 275
Argenta (J5)
Aristazabal (isl.) (C4)
Armstrong (H5) 1,197
Arrow Park (H5)
Arrowhead (H5) 200
Ashcroft (G5) 805
Aspen Grove (G5) 50
Assiniboine (mt.) (K5)
Athalmer (K5) 225
Atlin (J2) 500
Atlin (lake) (J1)
Attachie (G2)
Australian (F4)
Avola (H4) 97
Babine (D2) 10
Babine (lake) (E3)
Babine (riv.) (D2)
Baldonnel (G2)
Balfour (J5) 100
Bamfield (E6) 250
Bankeir (G5)
Banks (isl.) (B3)
Barkerville (G3) 300
Barkley (sound) (E6)
Barrett Lake (D3)
Barriere (H4) 50
Baynes Lake (K5) 100
Bear Flat (G2)
Beaton (J5) 100
Beatton (riv.) (G1)
Beatton River (F1).
Beavermouth (J4)
Beaver Creek (H3)
Beaverdell (H5) 98
Beaverley (F3)
Bella Bella (D4)
Bella Coola (D4) 350
Bella Coola (riv.) (D4)
Birch Island (H4) 72
Birken (F5) 50
Blind Channel (E5). 50
Bloedel (E5)
Blue River (H4) 500
Blueberry (G2)
Boat Basin (D5)
Boston Bar (G5) 135
Boswell (J5) 205
Boulder (G4)
Bowen Island (K3) 98
Bowser (H2) 50
Brackendale (F5) 175
Bralorne (F5) 500
Bridesville (H6) 113
Bridge Lake (G4) 200
Brilliant (J5) 712
Brisco (J5) 100
Britannia Beach (K2) 1,500
Brookmere (G5) 127
Brooks (pen.) (D5)
Brouse (J5) 150
Bryce (mt.) (J4)
Bulkley (mts.) (D3).
Bull Harbour (C5)
Burns Lake (D3) 1,016
Burton (H5) 250
Bute (inlet) (E5)
Butedale (C3) 350
Caamaño (sound) (C4)
Cache Creek (G5) 45
Calvert (isl.) (C4)
Campbell Island (C4) 200
Campbell River (E5) 3,069
Canal Flats (K5) 175
Canford (G5) 50
Canim Lake (G4) 50
Canoe (H5) 166
Cape Scott (C5)
Capilano (K3) 950
Cariboo (mts.) (G3)
Carmi (H5) 50
Cascade (H6) 175
Cassiar (mts.) (K2)
Cassidy (J3) 400
Castlegar (J5) 1,705
Cawston (H5) 350
Cecil Lake (G2)
Cedar (J3) 200
Cedarvale (C2) 100
Ceepeecee (D5) 100
Celista (H5) 175
Chamiss Bay (D5)
Chapman Camp (J5) 560
Chase (H5) 700
Chatham (sound) (B3)
Cheam View (M3) 35
Chemainus (J3) 2,250
Chief Lake (F3) 84
Chilkat (mt.) (H1)
Chilko (lake) (F4)
Chilkoot (pass) (J1).
Chilliwack (M3) 7,297
Chu Chua (H4) 77
Cinema (F3) 30
Claxton (C3)
Clayburn (L3) 350
Clayoquot (D5) 10
Clearwater Station (G4) 300
Cliffside (J3) 50
Clinton (G4) 300
Cloverdale (L3) 1,300
Coal Creek (K5) 150
Coal Harbour (D5). 20
Coal River (L2)
Coalmont (G5) 244
Coast (mts.) (D3)
Cobble Hill (K3) 300
Colquitz (K3) 150
Columbia (mt.) (J4).
Columbia (riv.) (H4)
Colwood (J4) 350
Comox (H2) 1,151
Continental Divide (D2)
Coombs (H3) 150
Copper Mountain (G5) 200
Copper River (C3)
Cornel Mills (G3)
Cottonwood (G3) 10
Courtenay (E5) 3,025
Cowichan Station (J3) 214
Cranbrook (K5) 4,562
Creston (J5) 1,844
Criss Creek (G4)
Crofton (J3) 100
Crowsnest (K5) 250
Crowsnest (pass) (K5)
Croydon Station (G3)
Cumberland (E5) 1,039
D'Arcy (F5) 50
Dawson Creek (G2) 7,531
Dean (chan.) (D4)
Dean (riv.) (D4)
Dease Lake (K2)
Dease (lake) (K2)
Decker Lake (E3) 250
Deer Park (H5) 100
Denman Island (H2) 150
Deroche (L3) 150
Devil's Thumb (mt.) (A1)
Dewdney (L3) 300
Dixon Entrance (str.) (A3)
Doe River (G2) 280
Dog Creek (G4) 35
Dome Creek (G3) 110
Dorreen (C3) 75
Douglas Lake (H5) 65
Duncan (J3) 3,247
Dunster (G3) 125
East Arrow Park (J5) 60
East Kelowna (H5). 350
East Pine (G2)
East Wellington (J3) 200
Eburne (K3) 1,100
Edgewater (J5) 55
Edgewood (H5) 190
Eholt (H5) 80
Elko (K5) 200
Endako (E3) 74
Enderby (H5) 965
Engen (E3)
Englewood (D5) 150
Esquimalt (K4) 10,353
Eutsuk (lake) (D3)
Ewings Landing (H5) 85
Extension (J3) 178
Fairmont Hot Springs (J5)
Fairweather (mt.) (H1)
Falkland (H5) 203
Fanny Bay (H2) 200
Farmington (G2)
Farrell Creek (G2)
Fawn (G4) 150
Ferguson (J5)
Fernie (K5) 2,808
Field (J4) 400
Finlay (riv.) (E1)
Finmoore (F3) 100
Flagstone (K5) 225
Flathead (K5) 68
Forest Grove (G4) 100
Fort Fraser (E3) 325
Fort Langley (L3) 560
Fort Nelson (M2) 350
Fort Saint John (G2) 1,908
Fort Saint James (E3) 615
Fort Steele (K5) 276
François (lake) (D3)
François Lake (D3) 250
Fraser (riv.) (F4)
Fraser Lake (E3) 250
Fraser Mills (K3) 633
Fruitvale (J5) 870
Fulford Harbour (K3) 205
Gabriola (J3) 200
Galiano (K3) 100
Gang Ranch (F4) 75
Ganges (K3) 500
Gardner (canal) (C3)
Garibaldi (F5) 50
Garibaldi Park (L2)
Georgia (str.) (J3)
Germansen Landing (E2)
Gerrard (J5) 30
Gibsons (J3) 990
Giscome (F3) 90
Glacier (J4) 50
Glacier Nat'l Pk. (J4)
Glendale Cove (E5)
Gold Bridge (F5) 400
Golden (J4) 750
Goldstream (J4) 100
Graham (isl.) (A3)
Grand Forks (H6) 1,995
Granite Bay (E5) 50
Granthams Landing (J3) 40
Grassy Plains (E3) 100
Great Central (H2). 200
Greenville (C2)
Greenwood (H5) 815
Gundy (G2)
Hagensborg (D4) 250
Halcyon Hot Springs (J5) 30
Halfmoon Bay (J2)
Hamber Park (J4).
Hanceville (F4) 50
Haney (L3) 2,250
Hansard (G3) 92
Harrison (lake) (M2)
Harrison Hot Springs (M3) 613
Harrison Mills (L3). 200
Harrogate (J5)
Hatzic (L3) 500
Haynes (H5)
Haysport (C3) 50
Hazelton (D2) 279
Headquarters (E5)
Hecate (str.) (B3)
Hedley (G5) 600
Heffley Creek (G5) 140
Holberg (C5) 50
Honeymoon Bay (J3)
Hope (M3) 2,226
Hopkins Landing (K2) 50
Hornby Island (H2) 150
Horsefly (G4) 110
Horseshoe Bay (K3) 150
Hosmer (K5) 100
Hot Springs Cove (D5) 66
Houston (D3) 200
Howser (J5) 36
Hudson Hope (F2) 50
Hulatt (F3) 50
Huntingdon (L3) 200
Hutton Mills (G3)
Hydraulic (F4) 50
Invermere (J5) 543
Ioco (K3) 900
Irvine's Landing (J2) 500
Iskut (riv.) (B2)
Isle Pierre (F3) 150
Jaffray (K5) 110
James Island (K3) 500
Johnson's Landing (J5) 35
Juan de Fuca (str.) (J4)
Kaleden (H5) 109
Kamloops (G5) 9,096
Kaslo (J5) 669
Kates Needle (mt.) (A1)
Keefer's (G5) 50
Keithley Creek (G4) 75
Kelowna (H5) 9,181
Kemano (D2)
Keremeos (G5) 666
Kettle Valley (H5) 100
Kickinghorse (pass) (J4)
Kimberley (K5) 5,774
Kincolith (B2) 125
King (isl.) (D4)
Kingsgate (K5) 35
Kinnaird (J5) 1,267
Kisgegas (D2)
Kitchener (J5) 185
Kitimat (C3) 8,000
Kitwanga (C2) 175
Klemtu (C4) 150
Klinaklini (riv.) (E4)
Knight Inlet (E5) 40
Kokanee Glacier Park (J5)
Koksilah (J3) 200
Kootenay (lake) (J5)
Kootenay (Nat'l Park) (J4)
Kootenay (riv.) (K5)
Kyuquot (D5) 125
Lac la Hache (G4) 50
Ladner (K3) 2,000
Ladysmith (J3) 2,107
Laidlaw (M3) 60
Lake Cowichan (J3) 1,949
Lake Hill (K3)
Langford Station (J3) 450
Langley (L3) 2,131
Lantzville (J3)
Lardeau (J5) 175
Lavington (H5) 150
Lempriere (H4)
Liard (riv.) (L2)
Lillooet (G5) 1,083
Lister (J5)
Little Fort (G4) 150
Longworth (G3) 175
Loos (G3) 50
Louis Creek (H4) 240
Lower Arrow (lake) (H5)
Lower Post (K1)
Lumby (H5) 786
Lund (E5) 210
Lyell (mt.) (J4)
Lynn Creek (K3) 1,000
Lytton (G5) 329
Mabel Lake (H5)
Macalister (F4) 85
Magna Bay (H4) 100
Malakwa (H5) 178
Manning, E. C., Park (G5)
Manson Creek (E2) 285
Mapes (E3)
Mara (H5) 150
Margaret Bay (D4) 50
Marguerite (F4) 10
Marysville (K5) 918
Masset (B3) 400
Matsqui (L3) 250
Mayne (K3) 250
McBride (G3) 489
McDame (K2)
McGuire (F5)
McLeod Lake (F2)
McLure (H4)
McMurdo (J4)
McMurphy (H4)
Merritt (G5) 1,790
Merville (E5) 175
Metchosin (K4) 250
Metlakatla (B3) 30
Michel (K5) 800
Midway (H5) 250
Milner (L3) 366
Milne's Landing (J4) 50
Minstrel Island (D5) 50
Minto Mine (F5) 50
Miocene (G4)
Mission City (L3) 3,010
Monashee (mts.) (H4)
Monte Creek (G5) 75
Monte Lake (G5)
Montney (G2)
Moose Heights (F3)
Moresby (isl.) (B4)
Mount Assiniboine Park (K5)
Mount Cartier (J5)
Mount Currie (F5).
Mount Lehman (L3) 150
Mt. Revelstoke Nat'l Park (H4)
Mount Robson (H3)
Mount Robson Park (H4)
Moyie (K5) 200
Mud River (F3)
Murrayville (L3) 390
Muskwa (M2)
Nadina River (D3) 100
Nakusp (J5) 1,750
Namu (D4) 100
Nanaimo (J3) 12,705
Nanika (dam) (D3).
Nanoose Bay (J3) 250
Naramata (H5) 450
Nass (riv.) (C2)
Nass Harbour (C3)
Natal (K5) 1,200
Nazko (F3)
Needles (H5) 100
Nelson (J5) 7,226
Nelson Forks (M2)
New Brighton (K2).
New Denver (J5) 736
New Hazelton (D2). 200
New Westminster (K3) 31,665
Newgate (K5) 60
Newlands (F3) 125
Newton Station (K3) 650
Nicola (G5) 170
Nithi River (E3)
North Bend (G5) 276
North Galiano (K3) 50
North Kamloops (G5) 4,351
North Pine (G2)
North Vancouver (K3) 19,951
Northfield (J3) 175
Notch Hill (H5) 75
Observatory (inlet) (C2)
Ocean Falls (D4) 2,650
Okanagan (lake) (H5)
Okanagan Centre (H5) 150
Okanagan Falls (H5) 125
Okanagan Landing (H5) 175
Okanagan Mission (H5) 250
Oliver (H5) 1,147
150 Mile House (G4) 177
Oona River (C3)
Ootsa Lake (E3) 50
Osoyoos (H6) 860
Oyama (H5) 100
Pacific (C3) 50
Parksville (J3) 1,112
Parsnip (riv.) (F2)
Parson (J4) 100
Pavilion (G5) 50
Peace (riv.) (F2)
Peachland (G5) 500
Pemberton (F5) 25
Pemberton Meadows (F5) 100
Pender Island (K3) 300
Penny (G3) 100
Penticton (H5) 11,894
Perow (D3) 50
Pink Mountain (F1)
Pioneer Mine (F5) 450
Pitt (isl.) (C3)
Pitt (lake) (L3)
Poplar Creek (J5) 33
Porcher (isl.) (B3)
Port Alberni (H3) 10,373
Port Albion (E6)
Port Alice (D5) 350
Port Clements (B3). 250
Port Coquitlam (L3) 4,632
Port Edward (B3) 250
Port Essington (C3) 225
Port Hammond (L3) 2,000
Port Hardy (D5) 175
Port Mann (L3) 500
Port Moody (L3) 2,713
Port Renfrew (J3) 100
Port Simpson (B3) 750
Portland (canal) (B2)
Pouce-Coupé (G2) 585
Powell River (E5) 5,174
Premier (C2) 400
Price (isl.) (C4)
Prince George (F3) 10,563
Prince Rupert (B3) 10,498
Princess Royal (isl.) (C3)
Princeton (G5) 2,245
Procter (J5) 250
Provincial Cannery (C4)
Punchaw (F3)
Purcell (mts.) (J5)
Qualicum Beach (J3) 726
Quathiaski Cove (E5) 175
Quatsino (D5) 300
Quatsino (sound) (C5)
Queen Charlotte (A3) 250
Queen Charlotte (isls.) (B3)
Queen Charlotte (sound) (C4)
Queen Charlotte (str.) (D5)
Quesnel (F4) 1,941
Quesnel (lake) (G4).
Quick (D3) 200
Quilchena (G5) 100
Radium Hot Springs (J5) 75
Red Pass (H4) 36
Redstone (F4) 10
Refuge Cove (E5) 300
Reid Lake (F3) 100
Remo (C3)
Renata (H5) 125
Revelstoke (J5) 3,469
Riske Creek (F4) 100
Rivers Inlet (D4) 250
Roberts Creek (J3) 150
Robson (J5) 200
Robson (mt.) (H3)
Rock Bay (E5) 100
Rock Creek (H6) 100
Rocky (mts.) (G3)
Rolla (G2) 950
Rose Lake (E3) 50
Rosebery (J5) 130
Rosedale (M3) 337
Rossland (H6) 4,344
Royal Oak (K3) 100
Royston (H2) 250
Ruby Creek (M3) 77
Ruskin (L3) 190
Rutland (H5) 500
Ryder Lake (M3)
Saanichton (K3) 500
Salmo (J5) 846
Salmon Arm (H5) 1,344
Salmon Valley (F3).
Saltair (J3)
San Josef Bay (C5).
Sandon (J5) 200
Sandspit (B3) 25
Sardis (M3) 500
Saturna (K3) 50
Savona (G5) 194
Sayward (D5)
Sechelt (J2) 439
Seechelt (pen.) (J2)
Selkirk (mts.) (J4)
Seton Portage (F5) 50
Seventy Mile House (G4) 25
Seymour (inlet) (D4)
Seymour Arm (H4).
Shalalth (F5) 250
Shawnigan Lake (J3) 398
Telkwa (D3) 580
Shelley (F3) 100
Shere (H4)
Shoreacres (J5) 500
Shushartie Bay (C5) 25
Shuswap (H5) 90
Shuswap (lake) (H4)
Sicamous (H5) 200
Sidmouth (J5) 100
Sidney (K3) 1,371
Sikanni Chief (F1)
Silverdale (L3) 250
Silverton (J5) 347
Similkameen (G5)
Simoom Sound (D5) 244
Sinclair Mills (G3)
Sir Sandford (mt.) (H4)
Sirdar (J5) 76
Skeena (riv.) (C3)
Skeena Crossing (D2) 15
Skidegate (B3) 400
Slocan (J5) 326
Slocan Park (J5) 100
Smith (sound) (C4)
Smith River (L1)
Smithers (D3) 1,962
Snowshoe (G3)
Soda Creek (G4) 50
Sointula (D5) 450
Solsqua (H5) 150
Somenos (J3) 200
Sooke (J4) 500
South Fort George (F3) 250
South Hazelton (C2) 150
South Pender (K3) 25
South Slocan (J5) 190
South Wellington (J3) 200
Southbank (E3) 100
Spences Bridge (G5). 400
Spuzzum (G5) 150
Squamish (K2) 1,292
Squilax (H5) 200
Stave (lake) (L3)
Steveston (K3) 1,100
Stewart (C2) 435
Stikine (mts.) (K2)
Stikine (riv.) (B1)
Stillwater (E5) 150
Stoner (F3)
Strathcona Park (E5)
Strathnaver (F3)
Stuart (lake) (E3)
Stuart Island (E5) 75
Sullivan Bay (D5) 150
Summerland (G5) 3,000
Summit Lake (F3).
Swift Creek (H4)
Taft (H4) 40
Tagish (lake) (J1)
Tahsis (D5)
Takla (lake) (D2)
Takla Landing (E2)
Taku (riv.) (J2)
Tatalrose (D3)
Tatla Lake (E4)
Taylor (G2)
Teidemann (peak) (E4)
Telegraph Creek (K2) 75
Terrace (C3) 1,473
Tête Jaune Cache (H4)
Texada (isl.) (J2)
Thetis Island (J3) 25
Thompson (riv.) (G5)
Thurlow (E5) 75
Tintagel (E3) 50
Tlell (B3)
Tofino (E5) 389
Topley (D3) 75
Trail (J6) 11,395
Trout Lake (J5) 100
Tulameen (G5) 100
Tupper (G2) 250
Tweedsmuir Park (D3)
Two Rivers (G2)
Ucluelet (E6) 520
Union Bay (H2) 500
Upper Arrow (lake) (H5)
Usk (C3) 150
Valemount (H4) 200
Vallican (J5) 50
Vananda (E5) 150
Vancouver (K3) 365,844
Vancouver (Metropolitan Area) (K3) 530,728
Vancouver (isl.) (J3)
Vanderhoof (E3) 1,085
Vavenby (H4) 75
Vernon (H5) 8,998
VICTORIA (K4) 54,584
Victoria (Metropolitan Area) (K4) 104,303
Waddington (mt.) (E4)
Wadhams (D4)
Waldo (K5) 100
Walhachin G5) 100
Waneta (J5) 75
Wardner (K5) 175
Ware (E1)
Warfield (J5) 2,051
Wellington (J3) 391
Wells (G3) 1,250
West Summerland (G5) 3,000
West Vancouver (K3)
Westbank (H5) 575
Westbridge (H5)
Westholme (J3) 150
Westview (E5) 3,499
Westwold (G5) 200
Whaletown (E5) 50
White Rock (K3) 2,000
Whonock (L3) 695
Williams Lake (F4) 1,790
Willow River (F3) 200
Wilmer (J5) 225
Wilson Creek (J2) 25
Windermere (K5) 95
Winlaw (J5) 248
Woodfibre (K2) 560
Woodpecker (F3) 75
Wynndel (J5) 200
Yale (M2) 176
Yellowhead (pass) (H4)
Ymir (J5) 190
Yoho Nat'l Park (J4)
Youbou (J3) 266
Zeballos (D5) 154

ATLAS
of the
BIBLE LANDS

C. S. HAMMOND & CO.
MAPLEWOOD, N. J.

List of Maps

	PAGE
Physical Map of the Holy Land	B-3
The Nations According to Genesis 10	B-4
The Biblical World at the Time of the Patriarchs (2000-1600 B.C.)	B-5
Canaan Before the Conquest	B-6
The Route of the Exodus and the Conquest of Canaan	B-7
Canaan as Divided Among the Twelve Tribes (c. 1200-1020 B.C.)	B-8
The Kingdom of Saul (c. 1020-1000 B.C.)	B-9
The Empire of David and Solomon (c. 1000-925 B.C.)	B-10
The Kingdoms of Israel and Judah (c. 925-842 B.C.)	B-11
Israel and Judah at the Time of the Syrian Conquests (c. 840-800 B.C.)	B-12
Israel and Judah at the Time of Jeroboam II (c. 785-745 B.C.)	B-13
The Assyrian Empire (824-625 B.C.)	B-14
Judah After the Fall of Israel (c. 700 B.C.)	B-15
Great Empires of the Sixth Century B.C.	B-16
The Restoration of Judah (c. 445 B.C.)	B-17
The Empire of Alexander the Great (323 B.C.) and the Kingdoms of Alexander's Successors (c. 305 B.C.)	B-18
Palestine Under the Maccabees (166 to 63 B.C.)	B-19
The Roman World in the Time of Caesar (60-44 B.C.)	B-20
The Dominions of Herod the Great (37 to 4 B.C.)	B-21
Palestine in the Time of Christ	B-22
The Journeys of Christ	B-23

a. Early Journeys
b. Galilean Ministry
c. Later Ministry

The Journeys of the Apostles	B-24
St. Paul's First and Second Journeys	B-25
St. Paul's Third Journey and His Journey to Rome	B-25
Dominions of Herod Agrippa I (37-44 A.D.)	B-26
Palestine at the Time of the Jewish-Roman War (66-73 A.D.)	B-27
The Roman Empire at its Greatest Extent (c. 117 A.D.)	B-28
The Spread of Christianity	B-29
Jerusalem in Old Testament Times	B-30

a. The City of David (c. 1000 B.C.)
b. Temple Area of Jerusalem as Built by Solomon
c. Jerusalem Under Nehemiah (c. 445 B.C.)

| Jerusalem in New Testament Times (20 B.C. - 70 A.D.) | B-31 |
| The Holy Land Today | B-32 |

Title page picture of Nazareth by E. L. Jordan.

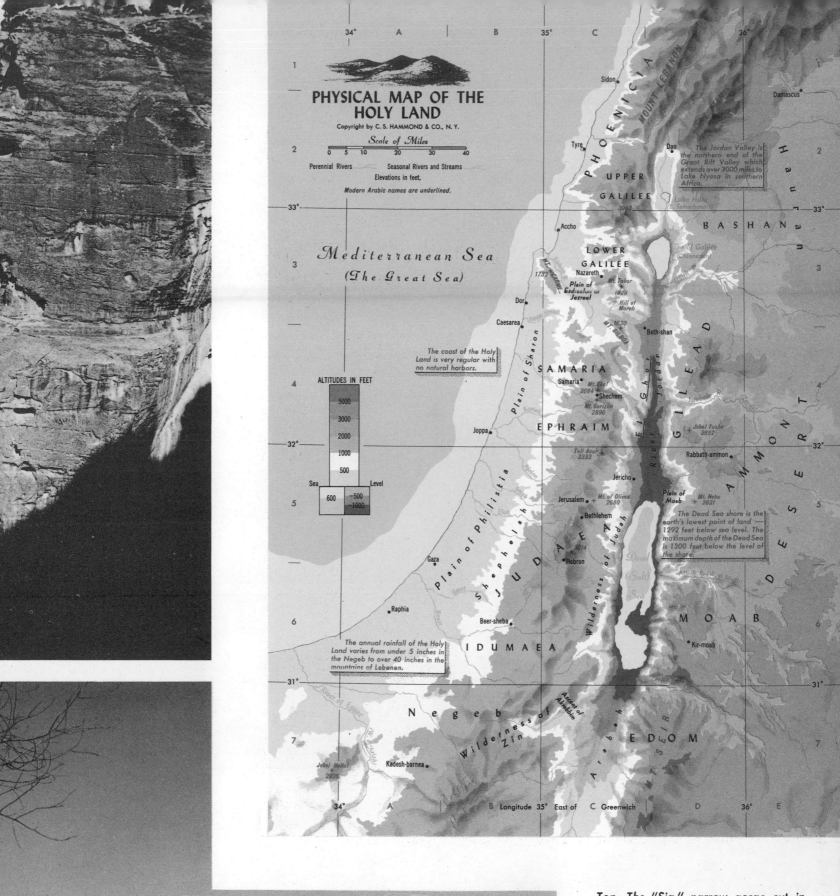

PHYSICAL MAP OF THE HOLY LAND

Copyright by C. S. HAMMOND & CO., N. Y.

Scale of Miles

0 5 10   20   30   40

Perennial Rivers   Seasonal Rivers and Streams

Elevations in feet.

Modern Arabic names are underlined.

ALTITUDES IN FEET

5000
3000
2000
1000
500
Sea Level
600   −500
       −1000

Mediterranean Sea
(The Great Sea)

PHOENICIA

Sidon

Damascus

Tyre

Dan

The Jordan Valley is the northern end of the Great Rift Valley which extends over 3000 miles to Lake Nyasa in southern Africa.

UPPER
GALILEE

Lake Huleh
L. Semechonitis

BASHAN

Accho

LOWER
GALILEE

Sea of Galilee
(Chinnereth)

Mt. Carmel
1732

Nazareth
Mt. Tabor
1829
Plain of
Esdraelon or
Jezreel
Hill of
Moreh

Dor

Mt. 1630
GILBOA
Beth-shan

Caesarea

GILEAD

El Ghor

River Jordan

The coast of the Holy Land is very regular with no natural harbors.

Plain of Sharon

SAMARIA

Samaria
Mt. Ebal
3084
Shechem
Mt. Gerizim
2890

Joppa

EPHRAIM

Tell Asur
3333

Rabbath-ammon

AMMON

DESERT

Jericho

Jerusalem
Mt. of Olives
2680
Bethlehem

Plain of
Moab
Mt. Nebo
2631

The Dead Sea shore is the earth's lowest point of land — 1292 feet below sea level. The maximum depth of the Dead Sea is 1300 feet below the level of the shore.

Plain of Philistia

Shephelah

JUDAEA

Wilderness of Judah

3514

Hebron

Dead
(Salt)
Sea

Gaza

MOAB

Raphia

Beer-sheba

IDUMAEA

Kir-moab

The annual rainfall of the Holy Land varies from under 5 inches in the Negeb to over 40 inches in the mountains of Lebanon.

Ascent of
Akrabbim

River el Egypt

Negeb

Wilderness of
Zin

Arabah

EDOM

MT. SEIR

Jebel Helal
2826

Kadesh-barnea

B Longitude 35° East of C Greenwich

Top: The "Siq," narrow gorge cut in sandstone leads to the Nabataean rock city of Petra in ancient Edom.
Jordan Tourist Attaché, N.Y.

The River Jordan lined with vegetation winds through the semi-desert valley of El Ghor.
TWA—Trans World Airlines

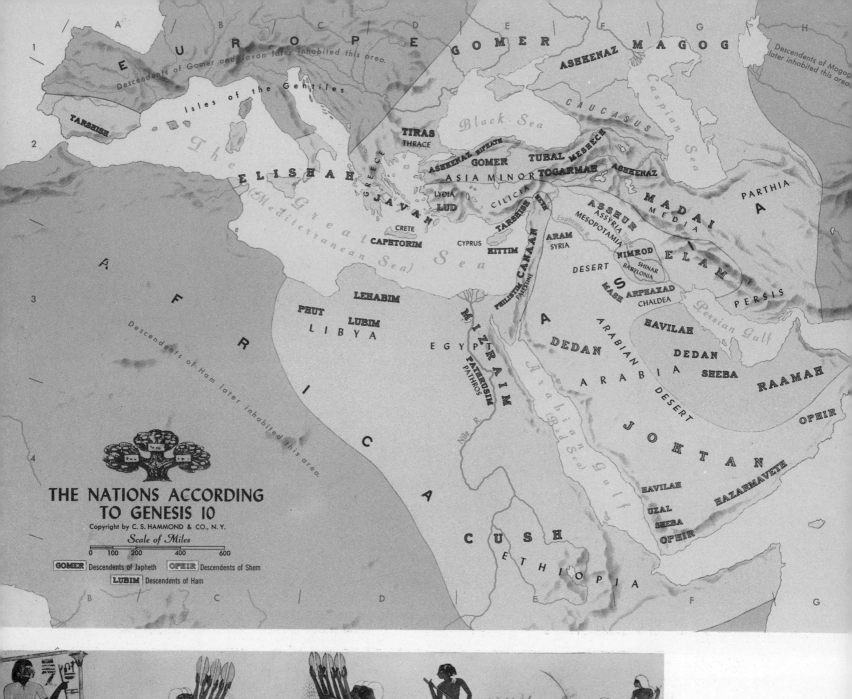

THE NATIONS ACCORDING TO GENESIS 10

Copyright by C. S. HAMMOND & CO., N. Y.

Scale of Miles

0   100   200   400   600

GOMER Descendents of Japheth   **OPHIR** Descendents of Shem

LUBIM Descendents of Ham

Egyptian wall painting of about 1500 B.C. showing harvester working under supervision of an estate inspector who appears at the upper left.
Davies, "Ancient Egyptian Wall Painting," pl. L1

Egyptian mural from about 1450 B.C. showing Asiatic captives making bricks as the Israelites were forced to do during the bondage in Egypt.
Lepsius, "Denkmaeler," part 3, pl. 40

B-4

Queen Nefertiti, about 1375 B.C.
Metropolitan Museum of Art

The Great Sphinx and pyramids at Gizeh, Egypt, built about 2500 B.C.
TWA—Trans World

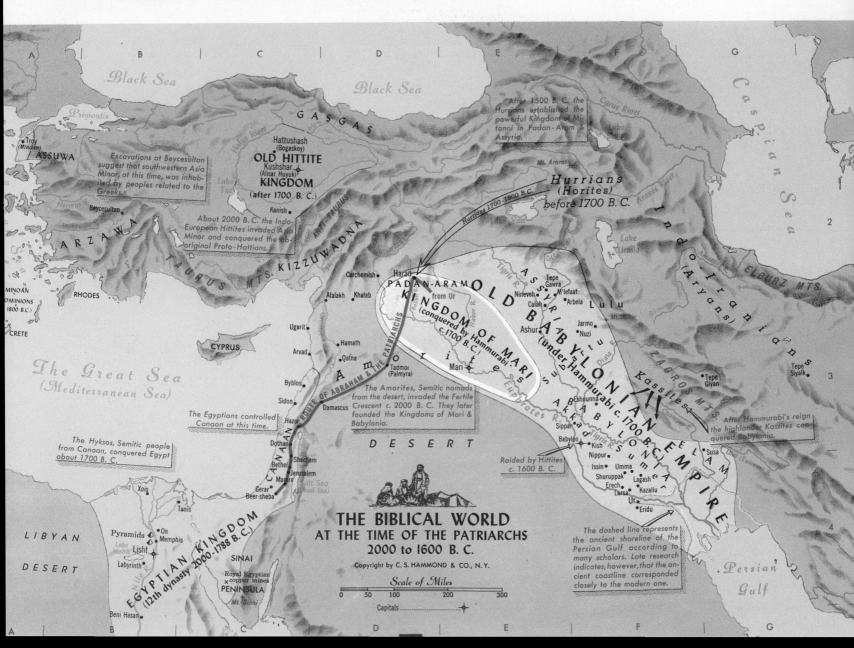

THE BIBLICAL WORLD
AT THE TIME OF THE PATRIARCHS
2000 to 1600 B.C.

Copyright by C. S. HAMMOND & CO., N.Y.

Scale of Miles
0   50   100   200   300

Capitals .... ✦

Black Sea

Black Sea

GASGAS

Propontis

Troy (Hissarlik)

ASSUWA

Sangarius R.

Hattushash (Bogazkoy)
OLD HITTITE
Kushshar (Alisar Huyuk)
KINGDOM
(after 1700 B.C.)

Halys River

Lake Tuz

Kanish

Excavations at Beycesultan suggest that southwestern Asia Minor, at this time, was inhabited by peoples related to the Greeks.

Beycesultan

ARZAWA

Hermus R.

Maeander R.

About 2000 B.C. the Indo-European Hittites invaded Asia Minor and conquered the aboriginal Proto-Hattians.

TAURUS MTS.

KIZZUWADNA

ANTI-TAURUS

MINOAN DOMINIONS 1800 B.C.

RHODES

CRETE

The Great Sea
(Mediterranean Sea)

CYPRUS

Ugarit

Arvad

Byblos

Sidon

Carchemish

Alalakh   Khalab

Hamath

Qatna

Tadmor (Palmyra)

Damascus

Hazor

PADAN-ARAM
KINGDOM
from Ur
(conquered by Hammurabi c. 1700 B.C.)

Haran

Balikh R.

Khabur R.

KINGDOM OF MARI

Mari

Amorites

Euphrates R.

ROUTE OF ABRAHAM & THE PATRIARCHS

The Egyptians controlled Canaan at this time.

CANAAN

Dothan

Shechem

Bethel

Jerusalem

Mamre

(Salt Sea/Dead Sea)

Gerar

Beer-sheba

The Hyksos, Semitic people from Canaan, conquered Egypt about 1700 B.C.

Xois

Tanis

LIBYAN DESERT

Pyramids

On   Memphis

Lake Moeris

Lisht

EGYPTIAN KINGDOM
(12th dynasty 2000-1788 B.C.)

SINAI

Royal Egyptian
copper mines
PENINSULA

Mt. Sinai

Beni Hasan

Labyrinth

The Amorites, Semitic nomads from the desert, invaded the Fertile Crescent c. 2000 B.C. They later founded the Kingdoms of Mari & Babylonia.

DESERT

After 1500 B.C. the Hurrians established the powerful Kingdom of Mitanni in Padan-Aram & Assyria.

Cyrus River

Mt. Ararat

Hurrians (Horites)
before 1700 B.C.

Hurrians 1700-1600 B.C.

Lake Van

Araxes River

Caspian Sea

ELBURZ MTS.

Indo-Iranian (Aryans)

Lake Urmia

Great Zab R.

Tigris R.

ASSYRIA

Tepe Gawra

Nineveh   M'lefaat

Calah   Arbela

Ashur   Nuzi

Jarmo

Lulu

Little Zab R.

Diala R.

OLD BABYLONIAN EMPIRE
(under Hammurabi c. 1700 B.C.)

AKKAD

BABYLONIA

Eshnunna

Babylon   Kish

Sippar

Nippur

Issin

Umma

Shuruppak   Lagash

Erech   Larsa   Kazallu

Ur

Eridu

SUMER

Raided by Hittites c. 1600 B.C.

ZAGROS MTS.

Kassites

Tepe Giyan

Tepe Siyalk

After Hammurabi's reign the highlander Kassites conquered Babylonia.

ELAM

Susa

Karun R.

The dashed line represents the ancient shoreline of the Persian Gulf according to many scholars. Late research indicates, however, that the ancient coastline corresponded closely to the modern one.

Persian Gulf

CANAAN BEFORE THE CONQUEST

Copyright by C. S. HAMMOND & CO., N.Y.

Scale of Miles

0   5   10   20   30   40

Perennial Rivers

Seasonal Rivers & Streams

Capitals ....

Phoenicians from the cities of Sidon and Tyre traded throughout the Mediterranean.

Sidon
Zarephath
Tyre
Kanah
Misrephoth-maim
Achzib
Accho
Achshaph
Chinnereth
Madon
Shimron
Jokneam
Dor
Megiddo
Taanach
Ibleam
Dothan
Sochoh
Tirzah
Shechem
Jacob's Well
Aphek
Tappuah
Joppa
Ono
Lod
Bethel
Ai
Beeroth
Gezer
Gibeon
Jericho
Ekron
Chephirah
Kirjath-jearim
Gilgal
Ashdod
Beth-shemesh
Makkedah
Jarmuth
Libnah
Ashkelon
Gath
Adullam
Lachish
Bethlehem
Eglon
Kirjath-arba (Hebron)
Mamre
Gaza (Azzáh)
Kirjath-sepher (Debir)
Hazeon-tamar (En-gedi)
Gerar
Raphia
Sharuhen
Beer-sheba
Arad
Hormah
Rehoboth
Zoar
Ascent of Akrabbim
Kadesh-barnea (En-mishpat)

Laish (Dan)
Kedesh
Hazor
Merom
Karnaim
Ashtaroth
Edrei
Ramoth-gilead
Ham
Beth-shan
Pella
Jabesh-gilead
Mahanaim
Succoth
Penuel (Peniel)
Adam
Jazer
Rabbath-ammon
Heshbon
Medeba
Jahaz
Dibon
Aroer
Kiriathaim
Ar
Kir-moab (Kir-hareseth)
Bozrah
Oboth
Punon

HITTITE EMPIRE
Ubi
Damascus

BASHAN (KINGDOM OF OG)

KINGDOM OF SIHON

AMMON

MOAB

EDOM

The Great Sea (Mediterranean Sea)

Sidonians (Phoenicians)
MOUNT LEBANON
MT. HERMON
MT. CARMEL
Mt. Tabor
Mt. Ebal
Mt. Gerizim
Canaanites
Hittites
Jebusites
Hittites
Amorites
Amalekites
Kenites
Wilderness of Zin
Plain of Sharon
MTS. SEIR
Arabah
Sea of Chinnereth
Yarmuk R.
Jabbok R.
Plains of Moab
Mt. Nebo (Pisgah)
Salt Sea (Dead Sea)
River of Egypt
Kidron
Arnon
Besor
Gerar

Jerusalem (Jebus, Salem)

The 13th and 12th century kingdoms of Bashan, Ammon, Moab and Edom displaced the Rephaim, Zuzim, Emim and Horites respectively.

Canaan at this time was an Egyptian province organized on a city-state system. The local kings were only required to pay tribute and to furnish labor for Egyptian royal projects.

The destroyed cities of Sodom and Gomorrah are believed to be beneath the shallow waters of the Dead Sea which now cover the Vale of Siddim (shaded portion).

Ivory female head from Canaanite palace at Megiddo, c. 1300 B.C.
Oriental Institute

Libation vase in the form of a bearded Semite, found at Beth-shemesh.
Handcocke, "Archaeology of the Holy Land," pl. 19-20

Tell el-Judeideh in Syria with "step trench" showing layers of occupation. Cultural levels are indicated by typical objects. Earliest occupation c. 5000 B.C., latest c. 600 A.D.
Oriental Institute

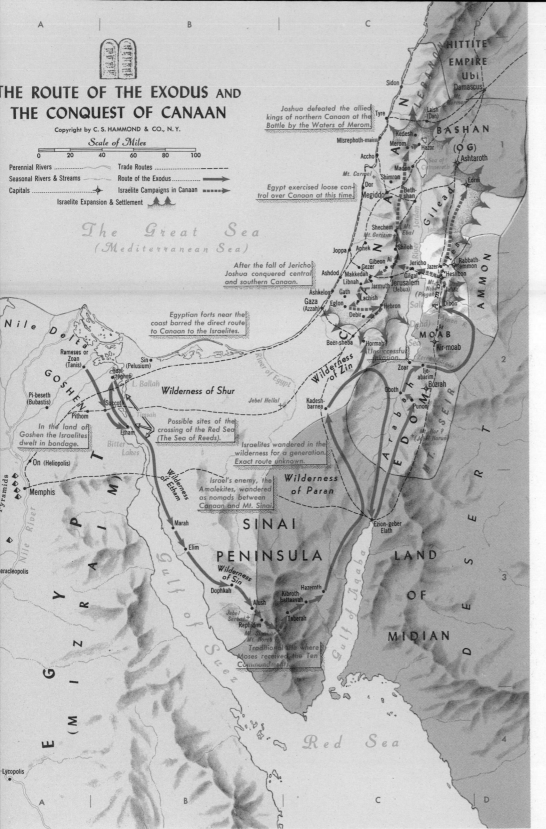

THE ROUTE OF THE EXODUS AND THE CONQUEST OF CANAAN

Copyright by C. S. HAMMOND & CO., N.Y.

Scale of Miles

0 20 40 60 80 100

Perennial Rivers ....
Seasonal Rivers & Streams ....
Capitals ....
Trade Routes ....
Route of the Exodus ....
Israelite Campaigns in Canaan ....
Israelite Expansion & Settlement

The Great Sea
(Mediterranean Sea)

Joshua defeated the allied kings of northern Canaan at the Battle by the Waters of Merom.

Egypt exercised loose control over Canaan at this time.

After the fall of Jericho Joshua conquered central and southern Canaan.

Egyptian forts near the coast barred the direct route to Canaan to the Israelites.

In the land of Goshen the Israelites dwelt in bondage.

Possible sites of the crossing of the Red Sea (The Sea of Reeds).

Israelites wandered in the wilderness for a generation. Exact route unknown.

Israel's enemy, the Amalekites, wandered as nomads between Canaan and Mt. Sinai.

Traditional site where Moses received the Ten Commandments.

Nile Delta
GOSHEN
Rameses or Zoan (Tanis)
Pi-beseth (Bubastis)
Pithom
On (Heliopolis)
Memphis
Heracleopolis
Lycopolis
Pyramids
Nile River
EGYPT (MIZRAIM)

Wilderness of Shur
Wilderness of Etham
Gulf of Suez
Wilderness of Sin
SINAI PENINSULA
Marah
Elim
Dophkah
Alush
Rephidim
Kibroth-hattaavah
Taberah
Hazeroth
Jebel Serbal
Mt. Sinai / Mt. Horeb

Gulf of Aqaba
LAND OF MIDIAN
DESERT

Wilderness of Paran
Wilderness of Zin
Kadesh-barnea
Ezion-geber / Elath

Sidon
Tyre
Kedesh
Misrephoth-maim
Accho
Merom
Madon
Hazor
Shimron
Mt. Carmel
Dor
Megiddo
Beth-shan
Shechem
Mt. Ebal / Mt. Gerizim
Shiloh
Joppa
Aphek
Gibeon Ai
Gezer
Ashdod
Makkedah
Libnah
Gath
Ashkelon
Eglon
Gaza (Azzah)
Debir
Hebron
Beer-sheba
Hormah
Unsuccessful Invasion
Jericho
Gilgal
Jerusalem (Jebus)
Jarmuth
Lachish

HITTITE EMPIRE
Ubi
Damascus
Laish (Dan)
BASHAN (OG)
Ashtaroth
Edrei
Sea of Chinnereth
Gilead
Jabbok R.
AMMON
Rabbath-ammon
Jazer
Heshbon
Mt. Nebo (Pisgah)
Salt (Dead) Sea
MOAB
Kir-moab
Zoar
Oboth
Bozrah
Ije-abarim
Punon
EDOM
Mt. SEIR
Mt. Hor (Jebel Harun)
Arabah

Jebel Hellal
River of Egypt
L. Ballah
Bitter Lakes
Succoth
Etham
Baal-zephon
Sin (Pelusium)

The traditional Mount Sinai where Moses received the Ten Commandments.
Underwood and Underwood

The remains of the walls of the Canaanite fortress of Jericho.
TWA—Trans World Airlines

Watering well in present day Jericho a short distance from the Biblical site.
TWA—Trans World Airlines

Typical Philistine pottery found at Beth-shemesh, c. 1200 B.C.
Palestine Exploration Fund

Ivory box with cherubs and lions in relief from Megiddo, c. 13th century B.C.
Oriental Institute

CANAAN AS DIVIDED AMONG THE TWELVE TRIBES
c. 1200-1020 B.C.
Copyright by C. S. HAMMOND & CO., N.Y.
Scale of Miles
Perennial Rivers   Seasonal Rivers & Streams

Part of the tribe of Dan unable to secure its inheritance migrated north and capture Laish, renaming it Dan.

Although all of Bashan w assigned to the half tribe Manasseh, it is doubtful th settlement reached beyond t Yarmuk Valley.

The Israelites were unable to capture the fortified towns of the plains during the early period of settlement.

During the period Judges, invading Ammo ites, Moabites and Midia ites were repulsed by t Israelites.

The Israelites were under constant attack from Philistine invaders who occupied the coastal area at about this time.

The cities assigned to Simeon were also a part of the inheritance of Judah. Simeon as a tribe was later absorbed by Judah.

The priestly tribe of Levi did not receive a definite territory but instead was allotted 48 cities distributed over the tribal areas.

Mt. Tabor in Lower Galilee where the prophetess Deborah directed Barak to gather his forces and attack the Canaanite army under Sisera.
Bonfils

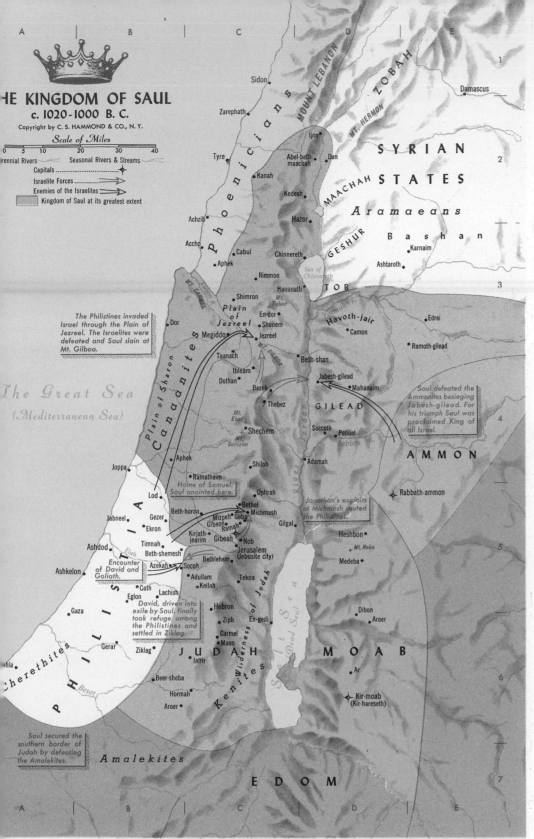

THE KINGDOM OF SAUL
c. 1020-1000 B.C.
Copyright by C. S. HAMMOND & CO., N.Y.

Scale of Miles

0 5 10 20 30 40

Perennial Rivers — Seasonal Rivers & Streams

Capitals ....
Israelite Forces ——→
Enemies of the Israelites ——→
Kingdom of Saul at its greatest extent

ZOBAH

Sidon

Zarephath

Damascus

SYRIAN

MT. HERMON

MAACHAH

STATES

Tyre

Ijon

Abel-beth-maachah

Dan

Aramaeans

Kanah

Achzib

Kedesh

GESHUR

Bashan

Hazor

Karnaim

Accho

Cabul

Aphek

Chinnereth

Ashtaroth

Rimmon

Sea of Chinnereth

TOB

Shimron

Hammath

Plain of Jezreel

En-dor

Mt. Tabor

Havoth-jair

Dor

The Philistines invaded Israel through the Plain of Jezreel. The Israelites were defeated and Saul slain at Mt. Gilboa.

Megiddo

Shunem

Jezreel

MT. GILBOA

Camon

Edrei

Ramoth-gilead

Taanach

Beth-shan

Ibleam

Jabesh-gilead

Mahanaim

The Great Sea
(Mediterranean Sea)

Plain of Sharon

Canaanites

Dothan

Bezek

GILEAD

Saul defeated the Ammonites besieging Jabesh-gilead. For his triumph Saul was proclaimed King of all Israel.

Mt. Ebal

Thebez

Shechem

Succoth

Penuel

Mt. Gerizim

Jabbok R.

Joppa

Aphek

Shiloh

Adamah

AMMON

Ramathaim
Home of Samuel. Saul anointed here.

Ophrah

Rabbath-ammon

Lod

Bethel

Michmash

Jonathan's exploits at Michmash routed the Philistines.

Jabneel

Beth-horon

Gezer

Mizpeh

Geba

Gibeon

Gilgal

Heshbon

Ekron

Kirjath-jearim

Ramah

Mt. Nebo

Timnah

Gibeah

Nob

Medeba

Ashdod

Beth-shemesh

Jerusalem (Jebusite city)

Encounter of David and Goliath.

Azekah

Socoh

Bethlehem

Ashkelon

Adullam

Tekoa

Keilah

PHILISTIA

Gath

Lachish

Hebron

Dibon

Eglon

Ziph

En-gedi

Aroer

David, driven into exile by Saul, finally took refuge among the Philistines and settled in Ziklag.

Gaza

Gerar

Carmel

Maon

Ziklag

JUDAH

Jattir

MOAB

Cherethites

Wilderness of Judah

Salt Sea (Dead Sea)

Ar

Beer-sheba

Kir-moab (Kir-hareseth)

Hormah

Kenites

Saul secured the southern border of Judah by defeating the Amalekites.

Aroer

Amalekites

EDOM

Model of an Egyptian royal harp of about 1090 B.C. On perhaps a cruder version of such a harp young David played for King Saul.
Oriental Institute

Ruins at Beth-shan, which served as a fortress to Egyptians, Canaanites and Philistines. Saul was slain at nearby Gilboa and his body taken to Beth-shan.
Frances Jenkins Olcott

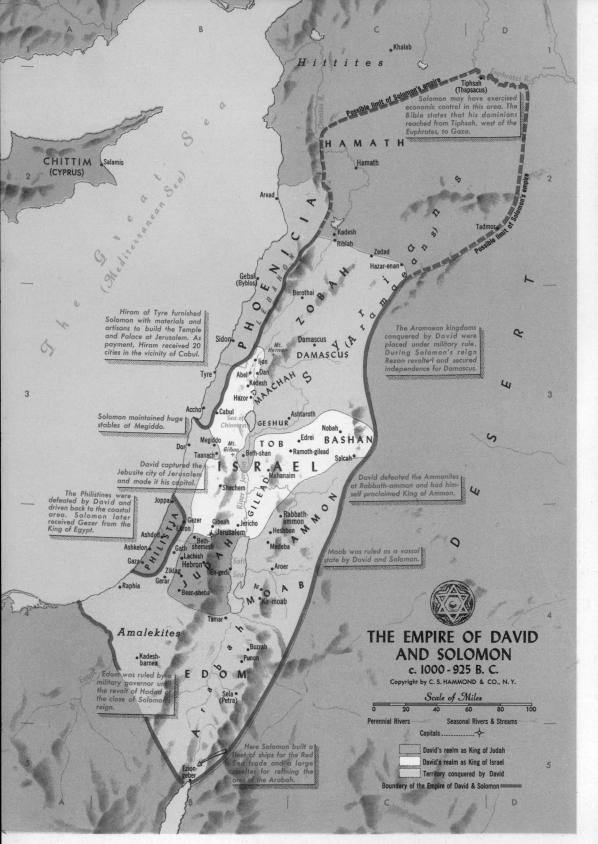

THE EMPIRE OF DAVID AND SOLOMON
c. 1000 - 925 B.C.

Copyright by C. S. HAMMOND & CO., N.Y.

Scale of Miles

| 0 | 20 | 40 | 60 | 80 | 100 |

Perennial Rivers   Seasonal Rivers & Streams

Capitals

David's realm as King of Judah

David's realm as King of Israel

Territory conquered by David

Boundary of the Empire of David & Solomon

Possible limit of Solomon's empire. *Solomon may have exercised economic control in this area. The Bible states that his dominions reached from Tiphsah, west of the Euphrates, to Gaza.*

Hiram of Tyre furnished Solomon with materials and artisans to build the Temple and Palace at Jerusalem. As payment, Hiram received 20 cities in the vicinity of Cabul.

The Aramaean kingdoms conquered by David were placed under military rule. During Solomon's reign Rezon revolted and secured independence for Damascus.

Solomon maintained huge stables at Megiddo.

David captured the Jebusite city of Jerusalem and made it his capital.

The Philistines were defeated by David and driven back to the coastal area. Solomon later received Gezer from the King of Egypt.

David defeated the Ammonites at Rabbath-ammon and had himself proclaimed King of Ammon.

Moab was ruled as a vassal state by David and Solomon.

Edom was ruled by a military governor until the revolt of Hadad at the close of Solomon's reign.

Here Solomon built a fleet of ships for the Red Sea trade and a large smelter for refining the ores of the Arabah.

Model of the Stables of Solomon at Megiddo
Oriental Institute

Solomon's Pool which supplies water for Jerusalem even today.
Jordan Tourist Attaché, N.Y.

Hittite hunting scene of later Hittite time (9th cent. B.C.) from Tell Halaf. In the 14th cent. B.C. the Hittite Empire rivaled those of Egypt and Babylonia.
Metropolitan Museum of Art

A Cedar of Lebanon. The monarchs of ancient empires drew heavily from these forests for their luxurious palaces.
Religious News Service

View of Haifa from Mt. Carmel, the mountain where Elijah challenged the priests of Baal.
Israel Gov't Tourist Office, N.Y.

THE KINGDOMS OF ISRAEL AND JUDAH
c. 925-842 B.C.

Copyright by C. S. HAMMOND & CO., N.Y.

Scale of Miles

10   20   30   40

Perennial Rivers ....   Capitals ....
Seasonal Rivers & Streams   Egyptian & Syrian Attacks ⟶

Elijah took refuge in Zarephath and brought back to life the widow's son.

In the reign of Baasha the cities of northern Israel were raided by the King of Damascus in league with Asa, King of Judah.

Aram waged almost constant war against Israel. The Syrians were held in check by Ahab until his death in battle at Ramoth-gilead.

Elijah challenged the prophets of Baal at Mt. Carmel.

The introduction of Phoenician cults following the marriage of Ahab with Jezebel caused violent reactions in Israel that eventually wiped out the house of Omri.

Samaria, fortress capital of Israel was built by Omri c. 870 B.C.

Moab was ruled as a vassal kingdom during the Omri dynasty. The Dibon stele commemorates the victory of Mesha, King of Moab, over Israel and the return of Moabite independence.

Shishak (Sheshonk), Egyptian Pharaoh, raided the divided kingdoms, plundering Jerusalem c. 925 B.C.

During the reign of Jehoshaphat Judah regained control over Edom.

Map labels: Sidon, Damascus, Zarephath, Tyre, Ijon, Abel-beth-maachah, Dan, Kedesh, Hazor, Accho, Cabul, Chinnereth, Karnaim, Ashtaroth, Aphek, Hammath, Mt. Tabor, Edrei, Dor, Megiddo, Shunem, Jezreel, Ramoth-gilead, Taanach, Beth-shan, Dothan, Ibleam, Jabesh-gilead, Mahanaim, Sochoh, Abel-meholah, Tishbe, Samaria, Mt. Ebal, Tirzah, Shechem, Mt. Gerizim, Penuel, Aphek, Janohah, Shiloh, Joppa, Jeshanah, Lod, Zemaraim, Beth-horon, Bethel, Rabbath-ammon, Jabneel, Gezer, Aijalon, Mizpeh, Geba, Jericho, Ekron, Gibbethon, Ramah, Gilgal, Ashdod, Timnah, Zorah, Beth-shemesh, Jerusalem, Elealeh, Heshbon, Azekah, Etam, Bethlehem, Ashkelon, Shoco, Mt. Nebo, Medeba, Jahaz, Libnah, Adullam, Tekoa, Baal-meon, Gath, Mareshah, Beth-zur, Gaza, Lachish, Hebron, Ataroth, Debir, Adoraim, Ziph, En-gedi, Dibon, Aroer, Gerar, Ziklag, Ar, Raphia, Beer-sheba, Kir-moab (Kir-hareseth), Valley of Salt

Region labels: PHOENICIA, MOUNT LEBANON, MT. HERMON, ARAM, ASSYRIA, GESHUR, BASHAN, The Great Sea (Mediterranean Sea), MT. CARMEL, Plain of Jezreel, Plain of Sharon, ISRAEL, Havoth-jair, GILEAD, AMMON, PHILISTIA, JUDAH, Wilderness of Judah, Salt Sea (Dead Sea), MOAB, EDOM

A replica of the Dibon stele erected by Mesha, King of Moab, to commemorate his successful revolt against Israel and the "House of Omri," around 845 B.C. (2 Kings 3:4 ff.)
Oriental Institute

Ivory carving of the Israelite period found at Samaria.
Oriental Institute

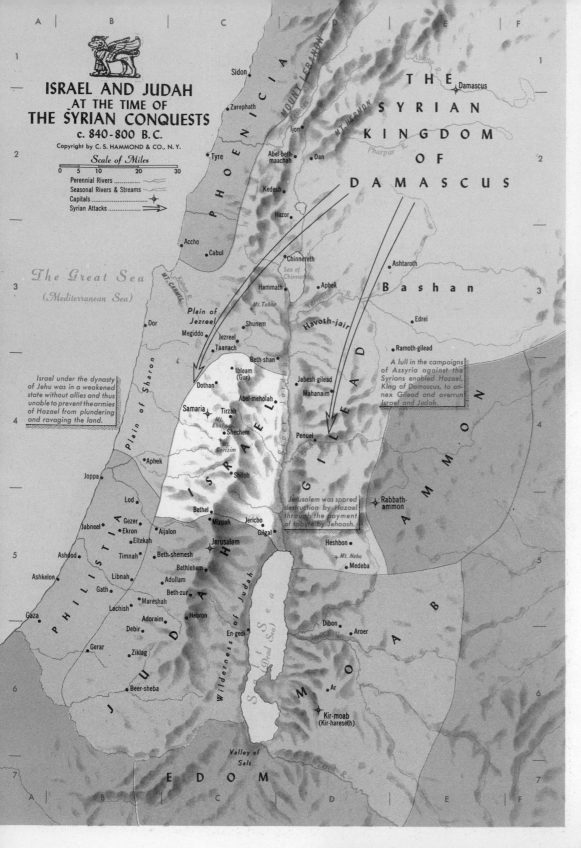

ISRAEL AND JUDAH
AT THE TIME OF
THE SYRIAN CONQUESTS
c. 840-800 B.C.
Copyright by C. S. HAMMOND & CO., N. Y.

Scale of Miles
0 5 10   20   30

Perennial Rivers	....
Seasonal Rivers & Streams	~~~~
Capitals	............⋆
Syrian Attacks	⟶

THE
SYRIAN
KINGDOM
OF
DAMASCUS

The Great Sea
(Mediterranean Sea)

PHOENICIA

Sidon
Zarephath
Ijon
Tyre
Abel-beth-maachah
Dan
Accho
Cabul
Kedesh
Hazor
Chinnereth
Ashtaroth
Bashan
Hammath
Aphek
Dor
Plain of Jezreel
Shunem
Edrei
Megiddo
Jezreel
Havoth-jair
Taanach
Beth-shan
Ramoth-gilead
Ibleam (Gur)
Jabesh-gilead
Dothan
Abel-meholah
Mahanaim
Samaria
Tirzah
Shechem
Penuel
GILEAD
Aphek
Shiloh
Joppa
Lod
Bethel
AMMON
Gezer
Mizpah
Jericho
Jabneel
Ekron
Aijalon
Gilgal
Eltekah
Jerusalem
Rabbath-ammon
Ashdod
Timnah
Beth-shemesh
Heshbon
Libnah
Bethlehem
Medeba
Ashkelon
Gath
Adullam
Gaza
Lachish
Mareshah
Beth-zur
Debir
Adoraim
Hebron
Dibon
Aroer
Gerar
Ziklag
En-gedi
MOAB
Beer-sheba
Ar
Kir-moab (Kir-hareseth)
Valley of Salt
EDOM

PHILISTIA
JUDAH
ISRAEL
Wilderness of Judah
Salt Sea (Dead Sea)

Israel under the dynasty of Jehu was in a weakened state without allies and thus unable to prevent the armies of Hazael from plundering and ravaging the land.

A lull in the campaigns of Assyria against the Syrians enabled Hazael, King of Damascus, to annex Gilead and overrun Israel and Judah.

Jerusalem was spared destruction by Hazael through the payment of tribute by Jehoash.

Typical Jordan countryside.
Jordan Tourist Attaché, N.Y.

View of modern Damascus, the world's oldest continuously inhabited city. The Aramaean kingdom of Damascus founded by Rezon dominated Palestine and southern Syria until it was wiped out by the Assyrians about 732 B.C. Damascus continued to be an important trade center and rich prize for succeeding conquerors down through the ages.
Philip Gendreau

B-12

Port of Aqaba on the Red Sea near the
Biblical Elath and Ezion-geber.
Jordan Tourist Attaché, N.Y.

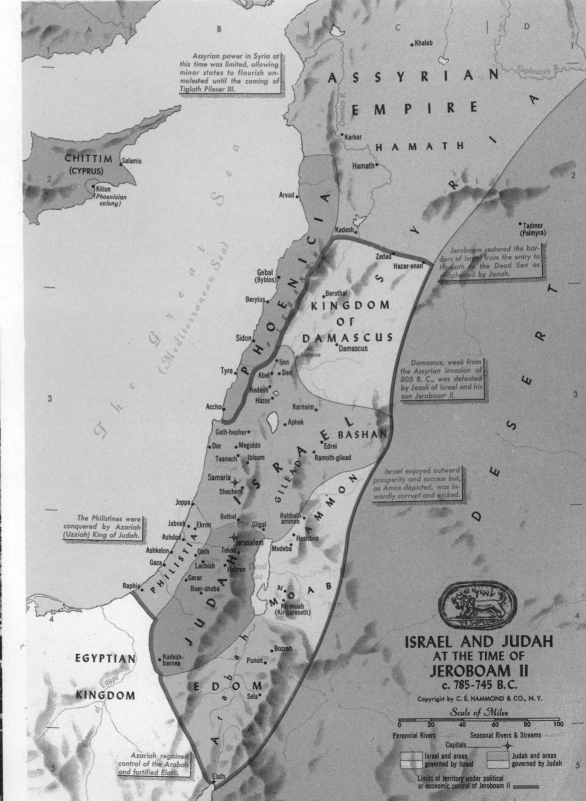

Assyrian power in Syria at
this time was limited, allowing
minor states to flourish un-
molested until the coming of
Tiglath Pileser III.

A S S Y R I A N

E M P I R E

HAMATH

• Khalab

Euphrates R.

Orontes R.

• Karkar

• Hamath

CHITTIM
(CYPRUS)

• Salamis

The
Great
Sea
(Mediterranean Sea)

• Kition
(Phoenician
colony)

• Arvad

• Kadesh

• Zedad

Hazar-enan

Jeroboam restored the borders of Israel from the entry to
Hamath to the Dead Sea as
prophesied by Jonah.

• Tadmor
(Palmyra)

S Y R I A

P H O E N I C I A

Gebal
(Byblos)

• Berytus

• Berothai

KINGDOM
OF
DAMASCUS

• Damascus

Mt. Hermon

Damascus, weak from
the Assyrian invasion of
805 B.C., was defeated
by Joash of Israel and his
son Jeroboam II.

D
E
S
E
R
T

• Sidon

• Tyre

• Ijon

Abel • • Dan

Kedesh •

• Hazor

• Accho

Karnaim •

• Aphek

• Gath-hepher

• Dor

• Megiddo

Taanach • • Ibleam

• Samaria

• Shechem

I S R A E L

BASHAN

• Edrei

Ramoth-gilead

G
I
L
E
A
D

A
M
M
O
N

Israel enjoyed outward
prosperity and success but,
as Amos depicted, was in-
wardly corrupt and wicked.

• Joppa

The Philistines were
conquered by Azariah
(Uzziah) King of Judah.

• Bethel

• Jabneh • Ekron

• Gilgal

Rabbath-
ammon •

• Ashdod

• Gath

Jerusalem

• Heshbon

• Ashkelon

• Tekoa

• Medeba

• Gaza

• Lachish

• Hebron

Dead
Sea

P
H
I
L
I
S
T
I
A

• Gerar

• Beer-sheba

J U D A H

• Ar

M
O
A
B

• Kir-moab
(Kir-hareseth)

• Raphia

EGYPTIAN

KINGDOM

• Kadesh-
barnea

Arabah

• Bozrah

• Punon

E D O M

• Sela

ISRAEL AND JUDAH
AT THE TIME OF
JEROBOAM II
c. 785-745 B.C.

Copyright by C. S. HAMMOND & CO., N.Y.

Scale of Miles

0   20   40   60   80   100

Perennial Rivers   Seasonal Rivers & Streams

Capitals

Israel and areas   Judah and areas
governed by Israel   governed by Judah

Limits of territory under political
or economic control of Jeroboam II

Azariah regained
control of the Arabah
and fortified Elath.

• Elath

B-13

THE ASSYRIAN EMPIRE
824 to 625 B. C.

Copyright by C. S. HAMMOND & CO., N.Y.

Scale of Miles

0   50   100   200   300

Capitals..........................✦

Assyrian Empire – 824 B.C.   Assyrian Empire – 671 B.C.

Site of Assyrian trading post 1850 B.C.

Greek colonization of the Mediterranean world began in this period.

Shalmaneser III's victory over Ahab 854 B.C.

Sargon II destroyed the Kingdom of Israel in 721 B.C.

Sennacherib's great capital

Destroyed by Sennacherib 689 B.C.

The Medes & Babylonians destroyed the Assyrian Empire in 612 B.C.

Home of Assyrian colonists of Samaria

The dashed line represents the ancient shoreline of the Persian Gulf according to many scholars. Late research indicates, however, that the ancient coast corresponded closely to the modern one.

The Assyrians held Egypt from 671 B.C. to 652 B.C.

Destroyed by Ashurbanipal 663 B.C.

Assyrian winged bull from the Palace of Sargon at Khorsabad, 15 miles north of Nineveh.
Oriental Institute

Right: Assyrian relief sculpture from the palace of Ashurnasirpal II (885-859 B.C.)
Metropolitan Museum of Art

Ashurnasirpal II attacking a city (885-859 B.C.)
Metropolitan Museum of Art

A section of this prism of Sennacherib describes his campaign against Judah in 701 B.C. He says:

"As for Hezekiah the Jew, who did not submit to my yoke, 46 of his strong walled cities, as well as the small cities in their neighborhood, which were without number—by constructing a ramp out of trampled earth and by bringing up battering-rams, by the attack of infantry, by tunnels, breaches, and (the use of) axes I besieged and took (those cities). Two hundred thousand one hundred and fifty people great and small, male and female, horses, mules, asses, camels, cattle, and sheep, without number, I brought away from them and counted as spoil. Himself like a caged bird I shut up in Jerusalem, his royal city."

Oriental Institute

JUDAH AFTER THE FALL OF ISRAEL
c. 700 B.C.
Copyright by C. S. HAMMOND & CO., N. Y.

Scale of Miles

Perennial Rivers ....
Seasonal Rivers & Streams ....
Capitals ....

Sennacherib conquered Phoenicia, with the exception of Tyre, in 701 B.C.

After Samaria fell, Sargon II exiled most of the influential people. The Ten Tribes were moved to various parts of Mesopotamia and disappeared forever from the pages of history.

With the conquest of Samaria in 721 B.C. by Sargon II, the Kingdom of Israel came to an end.

In 701 B.C. Sennacherib captured 46 cities of Judah as he pushed down toward the Egyptians, defeating them at Eltekeh.

In 701 B.C. Jerusalem was besieged, though not taken, by Sennacherib.

Ammon, Moab and Edom fell to the Assyrian Esarhaddon in 690 B.C., but they were never held long enough to be organized as regular provinces of the empire.

Here Sargon II defeated the Egyptian army in 720 B.C.

Judah was never a province of Assyria. Throughout Assyrian domination, it preserved a nominal independence under its own king, though paying tribute regularly and homage when it was required.

R-15

These reconstructions show Babylon's architectural splendor at the time of its political and cultural zenith during the reign of Nebuchadnezzar II, c. 600 B.C. In the first picture, the Tower of Babel can be seen to the left across the Euphrates River. In the second picture, a royal procession passes through the Ishtar Gate toward the Hanging Gardens, behind which is visible the Tower of Babel.
Oriental Institute

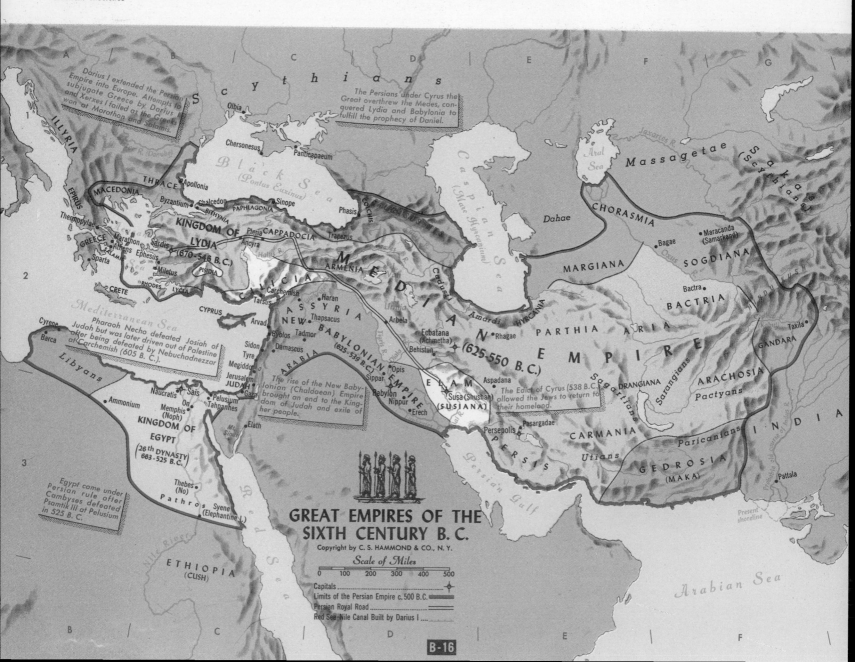

Darius I extended the Persian Empire into Europe. Attempts to subjugate Greece by Darius and Xerxes I failed as the Greeks won at Marathon and Salamis.

The Persians under Cyrus the Great overthrew the Medes, conquered Lydia and Babylonia to fulfill the prophecy of Daniel.

Pharaoh Necho defeated Josiah of Judah but was later driven out of Palestine after being defeated by Nebuchadnezzar at Carchemish (605 B.C.).

The rise of the New Babylonian (Chaldean) Empire brought an end to the Kingdom of Judah and exile of her people.

The Edict of Cyrus (538 B.C.) allowed the Jews to return to their homeland.

Egypt came under Persian rule after Cambyses defeated Psamtik III at Pelusium in 525 B.C.

GREAT EMPIRES OF THE SIXTH CENTURY B.C.

Copyright by C. S. HAMMOND & CO., N. Y.

Scale of Miles

0   100   200   300   400   500

Capitals .... ✦
Limits of the Persian Empire c. 500 B.C. ▬▬▬
Persian Royal Road ▬▬▬▬
Red Sea-Nile Canal Built by Darius I ▬▬▬

Ruins of Susa, ancient capital of
Elam and winter residence of
Persian kings.
Aerial Survey—Oriental Institute

A Mede bringing two horses as tribute to
King Sargon II of Assyria (722-705 B.C.)
Metropolitan Museum of Art

Relief from Persepolis showing King Darius
seated on his throne and his son Xerxes
standing behind him.
Oriental Institute

THE RESTORATION OF JUDAH
c. 445 B.C.

Copyright by C. S. HAMMOND & CO., N. Y.

Scale of Miles

0   5   10   20   30   40

Perennial Rivers   Seasonal Rivers & Streams

Route of the Returning Exiles ➝

After Cyrus the Persian
issued a decree permitting the
exiles to return to their homeland in 538 B. C., many exiles
took the long journey back to
Judah.

In 458 B. C. (398 B. C.?) Ezra
led a group of the exiles back to
Judah to reform conditions there
according to the laws of God.

Judah was a small province in the
Fifth Persian Satrapy which extended
from the borders of Syria and Cilicia to
the borders of Egypt, including all
Phoenicia, Palestine, Syria and Cyprus.

In 445 B. C. Nehemiah led a
group of exiles back to Judah to
rebuild the walls and gates of
Jerusalem.

After the reformation in Judah,
the priests became the dominating
power and influence among the
Jews. They kept the Jews a distinct race by forbidding marriage
with other tribes and peoples.

Lod, Ono and Hadid were Jewish
cities outside the province of Judah.

Sheshbazzar, who brought with him from
Babylon the sacred vessels carried away by
Nebuchadnezzar, started the rebuilding of
the Temple in Jerusalem. The Temple was
completed by Zerubbabel in 515 B. C.

The Edomites were driven north from
their land into the southern half of the old
territory of Judah by the Arabs.

The Great Sea

(Mediterranean Sea)

The ruins of Persepolis give impressive evidence of the height which Persian culture attained. This city was begun by Darius I, the Great, around 522 B.C. and later completed by his successors. In 331 B.C. Alexander the Great conquered the Persian Empire and sealed his conquest by setting fire to the palaces which symbolized the power of the Achaemenids.
New York Public Library

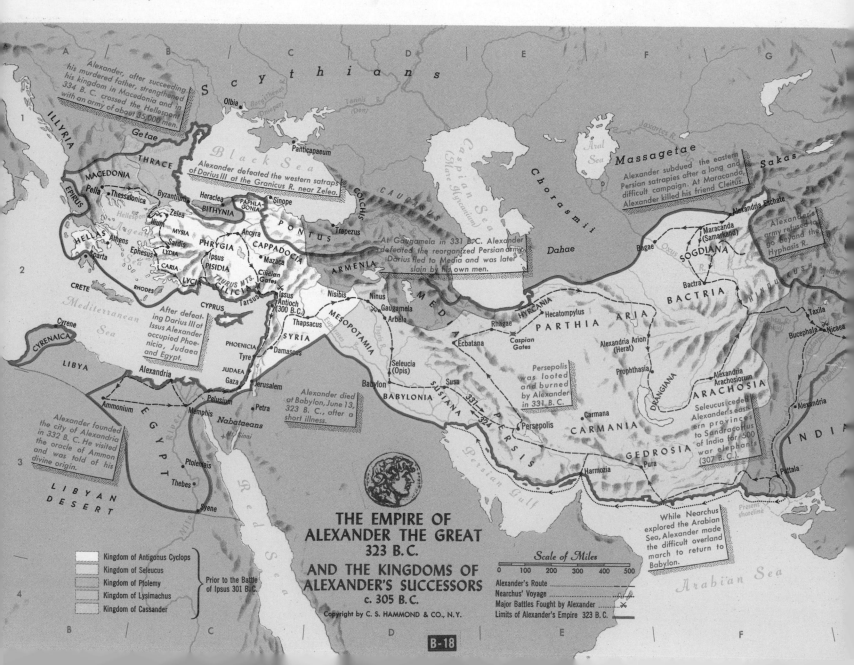

Alexander, after succeeding his murdered father, strengthened his kingdom in Macedonia and in 334 B.C. crossed the Hellespont with an army of about 35,000 men.

Alexander defeated the western satraps of Darius III at the Granicus R. near Zelea.

At Gaugamela in 331 B.C. Alexander defeated the reorganized Persian army. Darius fled to Media and was later slain by his own men.

Alexander subdued the eastern Persian satrapies after a long and difficult campaign. At Maracanda, Alexander killed his friend Cleitus.

Alexander's army refused to go beyond the Hyphasis R.

After defeating Darius III at Issus Alexander occupied Phoenicia, Judaea and Egypt.

Alexander died at Babylon, June 13, 323 B.C., after a short illness.

Persepolis was looted and burned by Alexander in 331 B.C.

Seleucus ceded Alexander's eastern provinces to Sandragotus of India for 500 war elephants (307 B.C.).

Alexander founded the city of Alexandria in 332 B.C. He visited the oracle of Ammon and was told of his divine origin.

While Nearchus explored the Arabian Sea, Alexander made the difficult overland march to return to Babylon.

Prior to the Battle of Ipsus 301 B.C.

THE EMPIRE OF ALEXANDER THE GREAT
323 B.C.
AND THE KINGDOMS OF ALEXANDER'S SUCCESSORS
c. 305 B.C.

Copyright by C. S. HAMMOND & CO., N.Y.

Kingdom of Antigonus Cyclops
Kingdom of Seleucus
Kingdom of Ptolemy
Kingdom of Lysimachus
Kingdom of Cassander

Scale of Miles
0   100   200   300   400   500

Alexander's Route
Nearchus' Voyage
Major Battles Fought by Alexander
Limits of Alexander's Empire 323 B.C.

Silver stater with its design of lion and bull in combat, from the treasury at Persepolis.
Oriental Institute

Coin of Alexander the Great minted in Persia a few years after his death, also from the treasury at Persepolis.
Oriental Institute

Coin of Ptolemy II (285-246 B.C.) with his wife (also his sister).
Metropolitan Museum of Art

Tetradrachm of Antiochus III, the Great, King of Syria (222-187 B.C.)
Metropolitan Museum of Art

PALESTINE UNDER THE MACCABEES
166 TO 63 B.C.
Copyright by C. S. HAMMOND & CO., N. Y.

Scale of Miles

0 5 10 20 30 40

Perennial Rivers .... Seasonal Rivers & Streams
Capitals .... ⊹

GROWTH OF MACCABAEAN JUDAEA

Judaea at the start of the revolt, 166 B. C.
Acquisitions under Jonathan, 161-142 B. C.
Acquisitions under Simon, 142-134 B. C.
Acquisitions under John Hyrcanus, 134-104 B. C.
Acquisitions under Aristobulus I, 104-103 B. C.
Acquisitions under Alexander Jannaeus, 103-76 B. C.
Maximum extent of the Maccabaean dominions ▬▬▬

The Maccabaean revolt arose from the attempt of the Seleucid monarch, Antiochus IV (Epiphanes) to force Hellenization upon the Jews.

SELEUCID EMPIRE

The Great Sea (Mediterranean Sea)

Besieged and razed by John Hyrcanus.

John Hyrcanus destroyed the Samaritan Temple on Mt. Gerizim.

Original home of the Maccabees or "Hasmonaeans."

Death place of Alexander Jannaeus.

In 63 B. C. Jerusalem fell before the forces of Pompey and Judaea came under Roman control.

Feast of Hanukkah is celebrated by the Jews in memory of the cleansing of the Temple by Judas Maccabaeus.

Unique bronze lamp from Syria decorated with Jewish religious symbols.
Miriam Schloessinger, N.Y.—Frank J. Darmstaedter Photo

THE ROMAN WORLD
IN THE TIME OF CAESAR
60 TO 44 B. C.

Copyright by C. S. HAMMOND & CO., N.Y.

Scale of Miles

0   100   200   400   600

Roman territory at the beginning
of the 1st Triumvirate-60 B.C.

Territory acquired under the
Triumvirate and Caesar

Dependencies and client kingdoms

Limits of Roman control at
the death of Caesar-44 B.C.

Major battles fought by Caesar .... ✕
Capitals .... ✦

Caesar raided Britain
in 55 and 54 B.C.

Caesar conquered
Gaul in 58-51 B.C.

In 49 B.C. Caesar
crossed the Rubicon,
the boundary of his
province of Cisalpine
Gaul, precipitating
civil war.

Caesar "came, saw and
conquered" Pharnaces II at
Zela in 47 B.C.

Crassus killed
by Parthian
at Carrhae in
53 B.C.

Caesar defeated Pompey
at Pharsalus in
48 B.C.

Under Caesar the
Jews enjoyed semi-in-
dependent rule with
religious freedom and
deferral from military
service.

Pompey was murdered
at Alexandria in 48
B.C. Caesar defeated
the Egyptians and placed
Cleopatra on the throne
in 47 B.C.

Bust of Julius Caesar.
Museo Nazionale, Naples

The Emperor Augustus (27 B.C.-14 A.D.)
Vatican Museum

The "Treasury" at Petra, built by the great Nabataean King Aretas, father-in-law of Herod Antipas.
Jordan Tourist Attaché, N.Y.

Roman ruins of the 2nd century A.D. at Jarash, ancient Gerasa, important Decapolis town.
Jordan Tourist Attaché, N.Y.

Right: The fortress of Masada built by the Hasmonaeans and fortified by Herod the Great. In the Jewish-Roman War the Israelites defended it against the Romans until 73 A.D.
Israel Gov't Tourist Office, N.Y.

Ulatha and Panias were placed under Herod's control in 20 B.C.

Herod's first territory was Galilee, given to him by his father, Antipater.

Hippos and Gadara were cities of the Decapolis given to Herod by Augustus.

City and port were rebuilt by Herod.

Herod rebuilt Samaria, giving it the new name of Sebaste.

The Decapolis was a league of neighboring city districts united for mutual protection against marauding tribes. It was not a compact geographical or political unit with definite boundaries.

Herod gained control of Jerusalem in 37 B.C., defeating Antigonus, and became King of Judaea.

Birthplace of Herod.

THE DOMINIONS OF
HEROD THE GREAT
37 to 4 B.C.
Copyright by C. S. HAMMOND & CO., N.Y.

Scale of Miles
0 5 10 20 30 40

Perennial Rivers
Seasonal Rivers & Streams
Capitals
Cities of the Decapolis

Kingdom of Herod the Great - 4 B.C.
Decapolis
Autonomous city state of Ascalon
Roman province of Syria
Kingdom of Lysanias

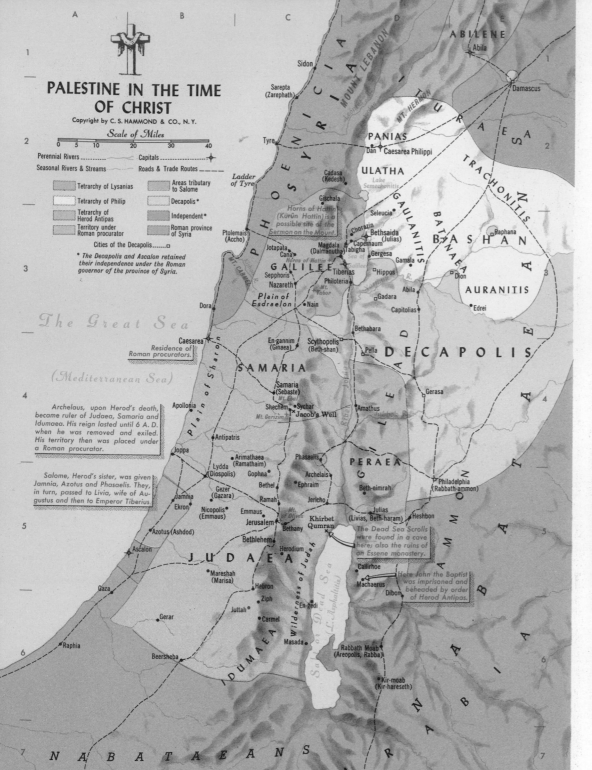

PALESTINE IN THE TIME OF CHRIST

Copyright by C. S. HAMMOND & CO., N.Y.

Scale of Miles

0 5 10 20 30 40

Perennial Rivers ——— Capitals ✦
Seasonal Rivers & Streams ——— Roads & Trade Routes ———

Tetrarchy of Lysanias
Tetrarchy of Philip
Tetrarchy of Herod Antipas
Territory under Roman procurator
Areas tributary to Salome
Decapolis *
Independent *
Roman province of Syria

Cities of the Decapolis ———

* The Decapolis and Ascalon retained
their independence under the Roman
governor of the province of Syria.

*Archelaus, upon Herod's death,
became ruler of Judaea, Samaria and
Idumaea. His reign lasted until 6 A.D.
when he was removed and exiled.
His territory then was placed under
a Roman procurator.*

*Salome, Herod's sister, was given
Jamnia, Azotus and Phasaelis. They,
in turn, passed to Livia, wife of Augustus and then to Emperor Tiberius.*

*The Dead Sea Scrolls
were found in a cave
here; also the ruins of
an Essene monastery.*

*Here John the Baptist
was imprisoned and
beheaded by order
of Herod Antipas.*

The Great Sea

(Mediterranean Sea)

Fishermen on the Sea of Galilee.
TWA—Trans World Airlines

*Ruins of a synagogue (2nd or 3rd century
at site of Biblical Capernaum.*
Philip Gendreau

*The Church of the Nativity,
Bethlehem, built on what is
claimed to be the site of the
Inn where Christ was born.*
TWA—Trans World Airlines

Below: The traditional Mount of Temptation, modern Jebel Quruntul.
Jordan Tourist Attaché, N.Y.

e Mount of Olives seen from the Temple Terrace
Jerusalem.
ordan Tourist Attaché, N.Y.

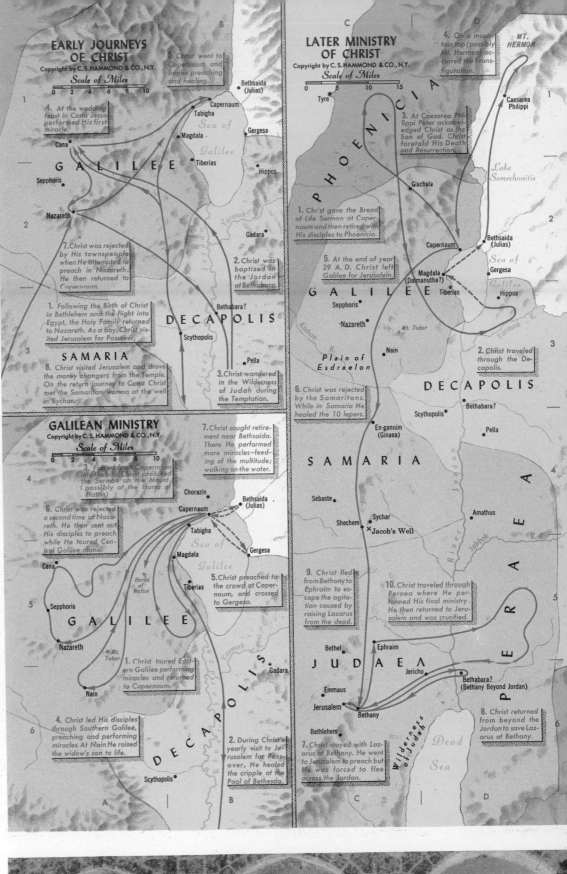

EARLY JOURNEYS OF CHRIST
Copyright by C. S. HAMMOND & CO., N.Y.
Scale of Miles
0 2 4 6 8 10

4. At the wedding feast in Cana Jesus performed His first miracle.

5. Christ went to Capernaum and began preaching and healing.

7. Christ was rejected by His townspeople when He attempted to preach in Nazareth. He then returned to Capernaum.

1. Following the Birth of Christ in Bethlehem and the flight into Egypt, the Holy Family returned to Nazareth. As a boy, Christ visited Jerusalem for Passover.

8. Christ visited Jerusalem and drove the money changers from the Temple. On the return journey to Cana Christ met the Samaritan woman at the well in Sychar.

2. Christ was baptized in the Jordan at Bethabara.

3. Christ wandered in the Wilderness of Judah during the Temptation.

GALILEE — Sea of Galilee — SAMARIA — DECAPOLIS

Bethsaida (Julias), Capernaum, Tabigha, Magdala, Gergesa, Tiberias, Hippos, Cana, Sepphoris, Nazareth, Gadara, Bethabara?, Scythopolis, Pella

GALILEAN MINISTRY
Copyright by C. S. HAMMOND & CO., N.Y.
Scale of Miles
0 2 4 6 8 10

3. Forced from Capernaum into the hills, Christ preached the Sermon on the Mount. (possibly at the Horns of Hattin)

6. Christ was rejected a second time at Nazareth. He then sent out His disciples to preach while He toured Central Galilee alone.

7. Christ sought retirement near Bethsaida. There He performed more miracles—feeding of the multitude; walking on the water.

5. Christ preached to the crowd at Capernaum, and crossed to Gergesa.

1. Christ toured Eastern Galilee performing miracles and returned to Capernaum.

4. Christ led His disciples through Southern Galilee, preaching and performing miracles. At Nain He raised the widow's son to life.

2. During Christ's yearly visit to Jerusalem for Passover, He healed the cripple at the Pool of Bethesda.

Chorazin, Bethsaida (Julias), Capernaum, Tabigha, Magdala, Gergesa, Sea of Galilee, Tiberias, Cana, Horns of Hattin, Sepphoris, Nazareth, Mt. Tabor, Nain, GALILEE, DECAPOLIS, Gadara, Scythopolis

LATER MINISTRY OF CHRIST
Copyright by C. S. HAMMOND & CO., N.Y.
Scale of Miles
0 5 10 15

4. On a mountain top (possibly Mt. Hermon) occurred the Transfiguration.

3. At Caesarea Philippi Peter acknowledged Christ as the Son of God. Christ foretold His Death and Resurrection.

1. Christ gave the Bread of Life Sermon at Capernaum and then retired with His disciples to Phoenicia.

5. At the end of year 29 A.D. Christ left Galilee for Jerusalem.

2. Christ traveled through the Decapolis.

6. Christ was rejected by the Samaritans. While in Samaria He healed the 10 lepers.

9. Christ fled from Bethany to Ephraim to escape the agitation caused by raising Lazarus from the dead.

10. Christ traveled through Peraea where He performed His final ministry. He then returned to Jerusalem and was crucified.

7. Christ stayed with Lazarus at Bethany. He went to Jerusalem to preach but He was forced to flee across the Jordan.

8. Christ returned from beyond the Jordan to save Lazarus at Bethany.

MT. HERMON, Caesarea Philippi, Tyre, PHOENICIA, Lake Semechonitis, Gischala, Capernaum, Bethsaida (Julias), Magdala (Dalmanutha?), Gergesa, Tiberias, Hippos, Sea of Galilee, GALILEE, Sepphoris, Nazareth, Mt. Tabor, Nain, Plain of Esdraelon, DECAPOLIS, En-gannim (Ginaea), Scythopolis, Bethabara?, Pella, SAMARIA, Sebaste, Shechem, Sychar, Jacob's Well, Amathus, River Jabbok, PERAEA, Bethel, Ephraim, JUDAEA, Jericho, Bethabara? (Bethany Beyond Jordan), Emmaus, Jerusalem, Bethany, Bethlehem, Wilderness of Judah, Dead Sea

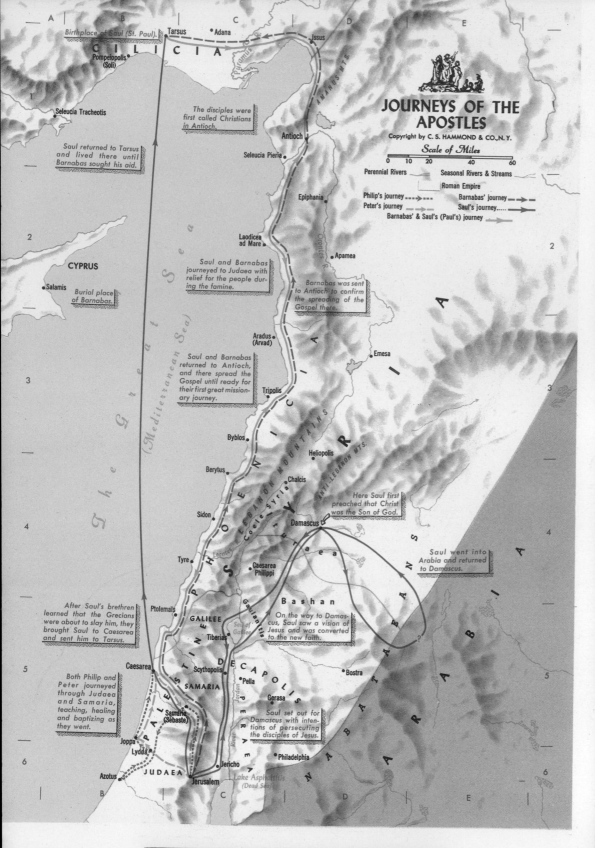

JOURNEYS OF THE APOSTLES

Copyright by C. S. HAMMOND & CO., N. Y.

Scale of Miles
0   10   20   40   60

Perennial Rivers ———   Seasonal Rivers & Streams

Roman Empire

Philip's journey ----▶   Barnabas' journey ——▶
Peter's journey ⇒⇒   Saul's journey ·····▶
Barnabas' & Saul's (Paul's) journey ⟹

Birthplace of Saul (St. Paul). Tarsus

The disciples were first called Christians in Antioch.

Saul returned to Tarsus and lived there until Barnabas sought his aid.

Saul and Barnabas journeyed to Judaea with relief for the people during the famine.

Barnabas was sent to Antioch to confirm the spreading of the Gospel there.

Burial place of Barnabas.

Saul and Barnabas returned to Antioch, and there spread the Gospel until ready for their first great missionary journey.

Here Saul first preached that Christ was the Son of God.

Saul went into Arabia and returned to Damascus.

After Saul's brethren learned that the Grecians were about to slay him, they brought Saul to Caesarea and sent him to Tarsus.

On the way to Damascus, Saul saw a vision of Jesus and was converted to the new faith.

Both Philip and Peter journeyed through Judaea and Samaria, teaching, healing and baptizing as they went.

Saul set out for Damascus with intentions of persecuting the disciples of Jesus.

Greek inscription from the synagogue in Jerusalem built by Theodotus before the Roman destruction of Jerusalem in 70 A.D. In such a synagogue the preaching of Stephen was disputed by Jewish leaders (Acts 6:9).
Sukenik, "Ancient Synagogues in Palestine and Greece," pl. XVI:A

St. Stephen's Gate in the fortress-like wall which surrounds the Old City of Jerusalem. The gate derives its name from the fact that St. Stephen was stoned to death in the vicinity.
Jordan Tourist Attaché, N.Y.

View of the Taurus Mountains near Tarsus, birthplace of St. Paul.
New York Public Library

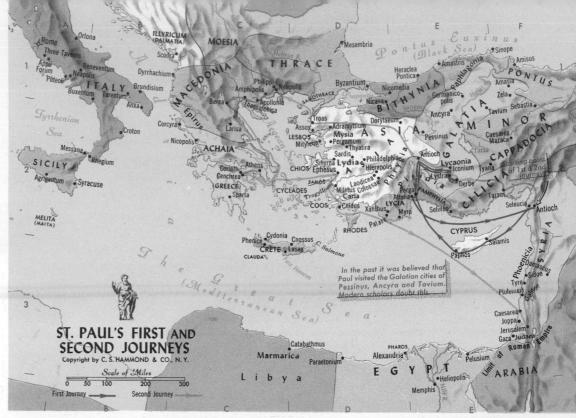

ST. PAUL'S FIRST AND SECOND JOURNEYS
Copyright by C. S. HAMMOND & CO., N.Y.

Scale of Miles

0 50 100 200 300

First Journey ⟶   Second Journey ⟶

In the past it was believed that Paul visited the Galatian cities of Pessinus, Ancyra and Tavium. Modern scholars doubt this.

The Temple of Erechtheum at Athens. When Paul visited Athens, the city was the world's most important center for philosophy, architecture and art.
TWA—Trans World Airlines

The Appian Way near Rome.
Italian State Tourist Office, N.Y.

ST. PAUL'S THIRD JOURNEY AND HIS JOURNEY TO ROME
Copyright by C. S. HAMMOND & CO., N.Y.

Scale of Miles

0 50 100 200 300

Third Journey ⟶   Journey to Rome ⟶

An ancient tradition states that Paul traveled extensively throughout the Mediterranean world after his journey to Rome.

Starting point of journey to Rome.

View of Tiberias on the shore of the Sea of Galilee. The city was founded by Herod Antipas and was the capital city of Galilee. After the destruction of Jerusalem in 70 A.D. it became the center of Jewish learning.
Israel Gov't Tourist Office, N.Y.

Agrippa received the tetrarchies of Philip and Lysonias in 37 A.D.

Agrippa received the tetrarchy of Antipas (Galilee and Peraea) in 39 A.D.

Agrippa died after a sudden and dramatic illness at Caesarea in 44 A.D.

Agrippa was given Judaea and Samaria by Claudius in 41 A.D.

Agrippa persecuted the disciples of Christ, as recorded in Acts 12:1-19.

DOMINIONS OF HEROD AGRIPPA I
37 to 44 A.D.
Copyright by C. S. HAMMOND & CO., N.Y.

Scale of Miles

Perennial Rivers .... Capitals
Seasonal Rivers & Streams ..... Cities of the Decapolis □

Kingdom of Herod Agrippa I -41 A.D.
Decapolis
Autonomous city state of Ascalon
Roman province of Syria

B-26

Roman theatre at the Decapolis city of Phi[la]delphia, present day Amman and Rabba[th] ammon of Old Testament times. At Caesarea, a similar theatre while attending games, Her[od] Agrippa I was seized with a fatal disease.
Jordan Tourist Attaché, N.Y.

The Wailing Wall in Jerusalem. It [is part] of the western wall of the Temp[le] closure and was built by Herod the [Great.] Here the Jews lamented the loss o[f the] Temple and independence.
TWA—Trans World Airlines

... e of the jars which contained the Dead
... Scrolls, ancient Biblical manuscripts of
... Essene community at Khirbet Qumran.
...tal Institute

The Great Sea
(Mediterranean Sea)

**PALESTINE
AT THE TIME OF THE
JEWISH - ROMAN WAR
66 to 73 A.D.**
Copyright by C. S. HAMMOND & CO., N. Y.

Scale of Miles

0   5   10   20   30   40

Perennial Rivers..............   Capitals..............
Seasonal Rivers & Streams   Cities of the Decapolis □

Territory under Roman procurator
Kingdom of Herod Agrippa II
Decapolis
Autonomous city state of Ascalon
Roman province of Syria

Vespasian led the Roman
armies in crushing the Jewish
rebellion. Resistance in the
north crumbled after the fall of
Jotapata. Roman legions then
swept south through Samaria,
Peraea and Judaea.

Opposition to Roman
rule and violence moun-
ted until in 66 A. D. the
Jews openly rebelled
and gained control of
their homeland.

Siege and de-
struction of Jerusalem
by Titus in 70 A. D.

The fall of Masada
in 73 A. D. marked the
end of the Jewish-
Roman War.

A final effort to throw off
Roman rule occurred in 132-
135 A. D. when Bar Cochba
led the Jews in a hopeless
struggle against the might of
Rome.

Bronze cast from the Arch of Titus showing Temple treasures from Jerusalem
being carried in triumphal procession.
The Jewish Museum, N.Y.—Frank J. Darmstaedter Photo

THE ROMAN EMPIRE
AT ITS GREATEST EXTENT
c. 117 A.D.

Copyright by C. S. HAMMOND & CO., N.Y.

Scale of Miles

0   100   200   400   600

Capital .... ✦
Maximum extent of Roman control
in the time of Trajan, 98-117 A. D. _____

Roman walls .... ▪▪▪▪▪▪▪▪

The Germanic tribes exerted constant pressure on the Rhine-Danube frontier, placing the Empire on the defensive. The western provinces and Italy were overrun by Germanic invaders in the 5th cent. A.D.

Trajan's conquests east of the Euphrates were abandoned by Hadrian in 118 A.D.

In 395 A. D. the Roman world was divided into separate eastern and western empires.

The Arch of Constantine in Rome. It was built to commemorate the victory of Constantine, the first Christian emperor, over Maxentius in 312 A.D. To the right is a portion of the Colosseum completed by Titus in 70 A.D. During times of persecution, Christians were forced to fight wild animals in the huge arena.
TWA—Trans World Airlines

...corated vault of the San Sebastian catacomb in Rome. Early ...ristians used such underground chambers for burial vaults and ...imes of persecution as places of secret worship.

...an State Tourist Office, N.Y.

Silver chalice known as "The Chalice of Antioch." The figures in relief are of Christ and the Apostles. The cup was once claimed to be the "Holy Grail" but is now dated from about the 4th or 5th century A.D.

Metropolitan Museum of Art

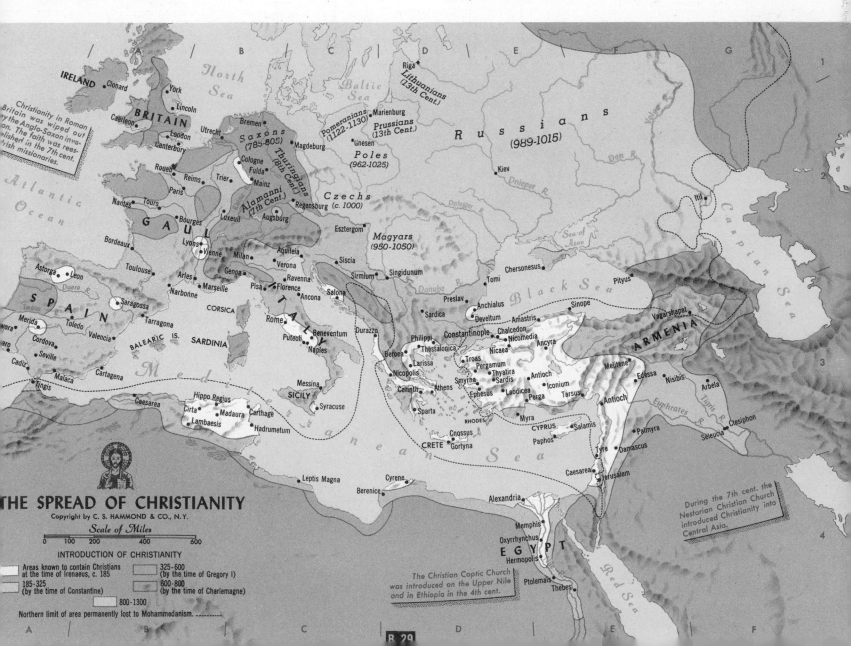

THE SPREAD OF CHRISTIANITY

Copyright by C. S. HAMMOND & CO., N.Y.

Scale of Miles

0   100   200   400   600

INTRODUCTION OF CHRISTIANITY

Areas known to contain Christians at the time of Irenaeus, c. 185

185-325 (by the time of Constantine)

325-600 (by the time of Gregory I)

600-800 (by the time of Charlemagne)

800-1300

Northern limit of area permanently lost to Mohammedanism. - - - - -

Christianity in Roman Britain was wiped out by the Anglo-Saxon invasion. The faith was reestablished in the 7th cent. ...rish missionaries.

During the 7th cent. the Nestorian Christian Church introduced Christianity into Central Asia.

The Christian Coptic Church was introduced on the Upper Nile and in Ethiopia in the 4th cent.

IRELAND • Clonard
York
Lincoln
BRITAIN
Caerleon
London
Canterbury
Utrecht
Bremen
Saxons (785-805)
Magdeburg
Thuringians (8th Cent.)
Cologne
Fulda
Mainz
Alamanni (7th Cent.)
Regensburg (c. 1000)
Rouen
Reims
Trier
Paris
Nantes
Tours
GAUL
Bourges
Luxeuil
Augsburg
Bordeaux
Lyons
Vienne
Milan
Aquileia
Verona
Genoa
Ravenna
Toulouse
Arles
Pisa
Florence
Ancona
Narbonne
Marseille
Astorga • Leon
Duero R.
SPAIN
Saragossa
Merida
Toledo
Tarragona
CORSICA
Rome
Beneventum
Cordova
Valencia
Puteoli
Seville
BALEARIC IS.
SARDINIA
Naples
Cadiz
Malaca
Cartagena
SICILY
Messina
Syracuse
Caesarea
Cirta
Hippo Regius
Madaura
Carthage
Lambaesis
Hadrumetum
Leptis Magna
Cyrene
Berenice
Riga
Lithuanians (13th Cent.)
Marienburg
Pomeranians (1122-1130)
Prussians (13th Cent.)
Gnesen
Poles (962-1025)
Russians (989-1015)
Kiev
Czechs
Esztergom
Magyars (950-1050)
Siscia
Sirmium
Singidunum
Chersonesus
Tomi
Preslav
Sardica
Anchialus
Develtum
Sinope
Durazzo
Philippi
Constantinople
Chalcedon
Amastris
Thessalonica
Nicomedia
Nicaea
Ancyra
Berhoea
Larissa
Troas
Pergamum
Vagarshapat
ARMENIA
Nicopolis
Thyatira
Sardis
Antioch
Iconium
Melitene
Edessa
Athens
Smyrna
Ephesus
Laodicea
Perga
Tarsus
Nisibis
Corinth
Sparta
Myra
Antioch
Arbela
RHODES
CYPRUS
Salamis
Euphrates R.
Tigris R.
Cnossus
CRETE
Gortyna
Paphos
Palmyra
Seleucia
Ctesiphon
Tyre
Damascus
Caesarea
Jerusalem
Alexandria
Memphis
Oxyrrhynchus
EGYPT
Hermopolis
Ptolemais
Thebes

North Sea
Baltic Sea
Atlantic Ocean
Mediterranean Sea
Black Sea
Sea of Azov
Caspian Sea
Red Sea
Danube R.
Dnieper R.
Dniester R.
Don R.
Volga R.
Itil
Pityus

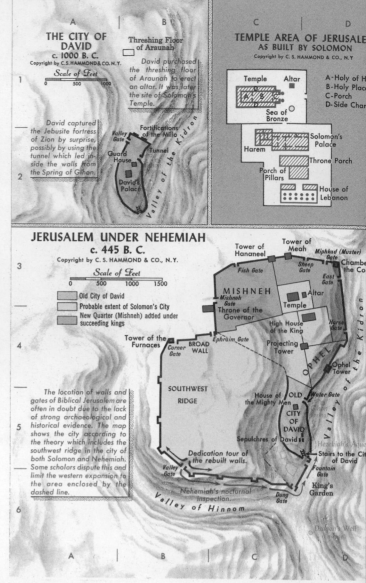

The Dome of the Rock, Jerusalem. This shrine is built over the site of the ancient Jewish Temple. The site is sacred to Moslems as well as Christians and Jews. The present-day mosque dates from the late 7th century.
Jordan Tourist Attaché, N.Y.

Air view of Jerusalem looking to the northeast. The walled rectangle encloses the Temple terrace and the Dome of the Rock. To the right is the Valley of the Kidron and the Mt. of Olives.
Jordan Tourist Attaché, N.Y.

King David's Tower, Jerusalem. On this site once stood one of the towers built by Herod the Great to protect his palace.
TWA—Trans World Airlines

Via Dolorosa within the Old City of Jerusalem. Tradition claims this street as the one used by Jesus on His way to the crucifixion.
Jordan Tourist Attaché, N.Y.

The Church of the Holy Sepulchre, Jerusalem. This site has been the traditional location for the crucifixion and entombment of Jesus since the time of Constantine.
Jordan Tourist Attaché, N.Y.

JERUSALEM
NEW TESTAMENT TIMES
20 B.C. - 70 A.D.
Copyright by C. S. HAMMOND & CO., N.Y.

Scale of Feet
0   500   1000   1500

Ancient Walls
Location of walls according to theory
Biblical site based on tradition

To Shechem & Damascus

THIRD NORTH WALL?

Gordon's Calvary †

Psephinus Tower ?

BETHESDA

Pool of Bethesda

Fortress of Antonia

Sheep Gate

Garden of Gethsemane

To Mount of Olives and Bethany

Second North Wall

Golgotha Calvary (Church of the Holy Sepulchre)

SUBURB

Court of Women

Herod's Temple

Solomon's Porch

Altar

Beautiful Gate ?

Pool of Amygdalon

Council House

Court of Gentiles

Gennath Gate

Xystus (Market)

Bridge

Huldah Gates

Herod built the towers of Hippicus (1), Phasael (2) and Mariamne (3) to guard the western entrance to the city and his palace.

Palace of Herod

Hasmonaean Palace

UPPER CITY

LOWER CITY

Tyropoeon Valley

Valley of the Kidron

Serpent Pool

House of Caiaphas

House of the Last Supper

Pool of Siloam

Pool of Old Pool

Essene Gate

Valley of Hinnom

Aceldama or Field of Blood

To Bethlehem and Hebron

To the Dead Sea

Old man in the bazaar at Mosul, Iraq.
Courtesy of James H. Breasted, Jr.

Jordanian Arab boy with wheat.
Jordan Tourist Attaché, N.Y.

"Sabra" or native-born Israeli girl.
Israel Gov't Tourist Office, N.Y.

Arabs learning to use modern agricultural machines.
Israel Office of Information, N.Y.

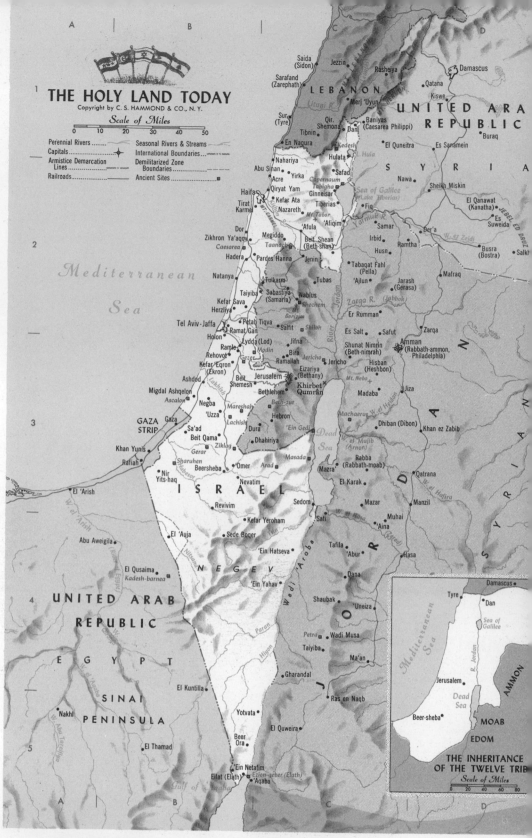

THE HOLY LAND TODAY
Copyright by C. S. HAMMOND & CO., N. Y.

Scale of Miles
0   10   20   30   40   50

Perennial Rivers ....
Capitals ....
Armistice Demarcation Lines ....
Railroads ....
Seasonal Rivers & Streams
International Boundaries ....
Demilitarized Zone Boundaries ....
Ancient Sites ....

LEBANON

UNITED ARAB REPUBLIC

SYRIA

Mediterranean Sea

ISRAEL

NEGEV

UNITED ARAB REPUBLIC

EGYPT

SINAI PENINSULA

JORDAN

Dead Sea

Gulf of Aqaba

THE INHERITANCE OF THE TWELVE TRIBES
Scale of Miles
0   20   40   60   80

Mediterranean Sea
Tyre   Damascus
Dan
Sea of Galilee
R. Jordan
AMMON
Jerusalem
Dead Sea
Beer-sheba
MOAB
EDOM

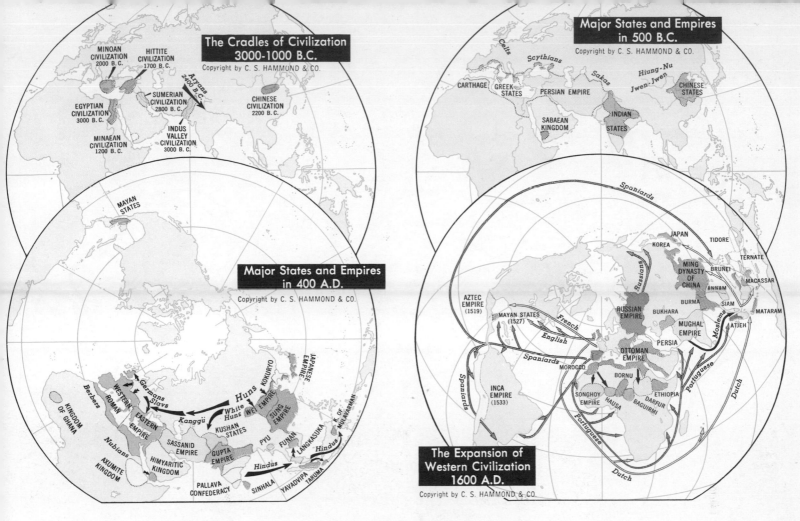

Hammond's

HISTORICAL ATLAS
of WORLD CIVILIZATION

**A collection of maps covering man's history
in the Old and New Worlds
from 3000 B.C. to the present century.**

CONTENTS

The Cradles of Civilization, 3000-1000 B.C. ....C - 1

Major States and Empires in 500 B.C. ....C - 1

Major States and Empires in 400 A.D. ....C - 1

The Expansion of Western Civilization, 1600 A.D. ....C - 1

The Persian Empire about 500 B.C. and the
    Empire of Alexander the Great, 323 B.C. ....C - 2

The Roman Empire at its Greatest Extent,
    about 117 A.D. ....C - 2

Europe Showing Barbaric Migrations in the
    Fourth and Fifth Centuries....................................C - 3

Europe c. 800 A.D. ....C - 4

Mediterranean Lands in 1097.....................................C - 5

Mediterranean Lands after 1204.................................C - 5

Historical Map of Asia ....C - 6

Europe in 1648 at the Peace of Westphalia ....C - 7

Europe in 1803 ....C - 8

Europe in 1914 ....C - 9

Europe, 1919-1938 ....C - 9

The Principal Voyages of Discovery to America,
    1492 to 1611 ....C-10

King James' Grants to the Plymouth and London
    Companies, 1606, 1609 and 1620 ....C-11

Early Colonial Grants, 1609 to 1744 ....C-11

Changing Ownership of the Continent, 1682 to 1783..C-11

French and Indian War, 1756 to 1763.........................C-11

Colonial America, 1770....................................C-12

Routes to the West, 1760-1860...........................C-13

The Growth of the United States from 1776 to 1867...C-14

Slavery in the United States, 1775-1865 ....C-14

The West, 1860-1910.......................................C-15

Exploration of Canada C-16

The Growth of Canada from 1791 to 1949................C-16

© C. S. Hammond & Co.

Maplewood, New Jersey

MCMLX

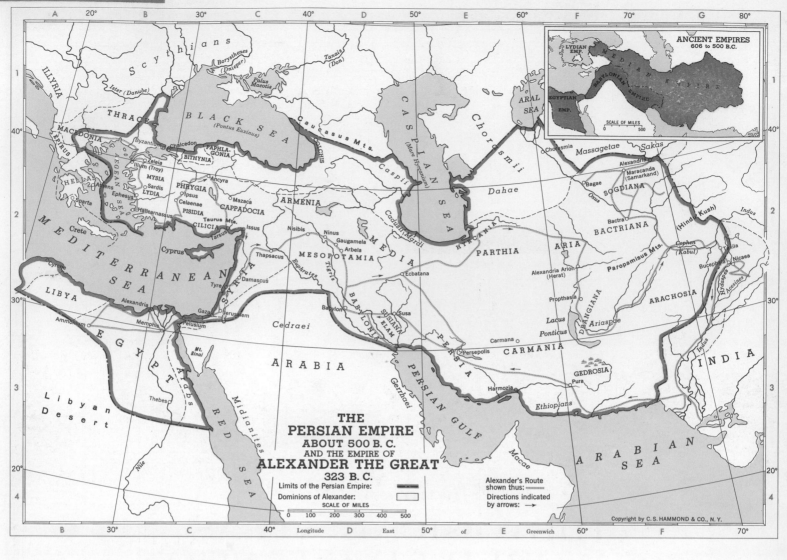

THE PERSIAN EMPIRE
ABOUT 500 B.C.
AND THE EMPIRE OF
ALEXANDER THE GREAT
323 B.C.

Limits of the Persian Empire: ▬▬▬

Dominions of Alexander: ▭

SCALE OF MILES
0 100 200 300 400 500

Alexander's Route shown thus: ·············

Directions indicated by arrows: →

Copyright by C. S. HAMMOND & CO., N.Y.

ANCIENT EMPIRES
606 to 500 B.C.
SCALE OF MILES
500

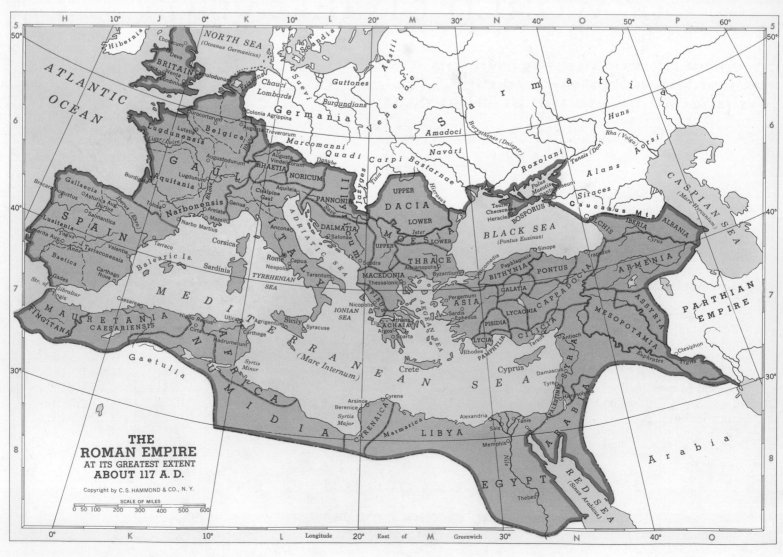

THE ROMAN EMPIRE
AT ITS GREATEST EXTENT
ABOUT 117 A.D.

Copyright by C.S. HAMMOND & CO., N.Y.

SCALE OF MILES
0 50 100 200 300 400 500 600

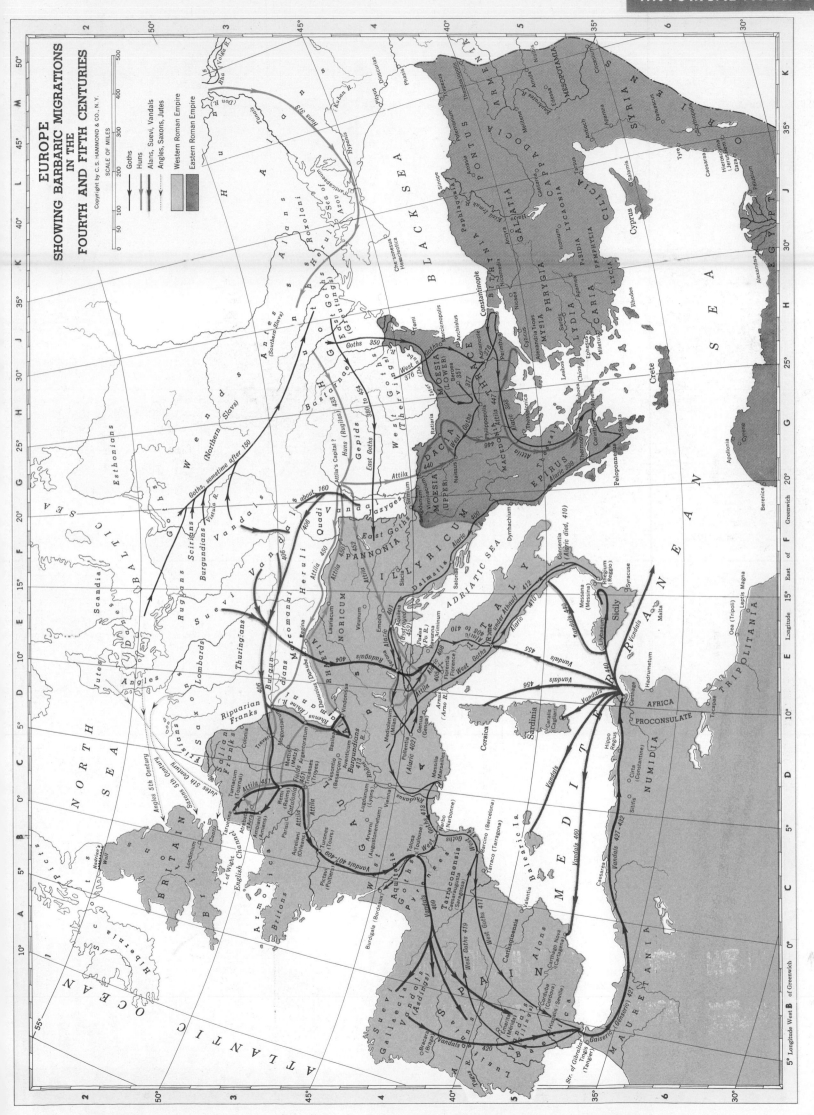

EUROPE
SHOWING BARBARIC MIGRATIONS IN THE FOURTH AND FIFTH CENTURIES

Copyright by C.S. HAMMOND & CO. N.Y.

SCALE OF MILES

Goths
Huns
Alans, Suevi, Vandals
Angles, Saxons, Jutes
Western Roman Empire
Eastern Roman Empire

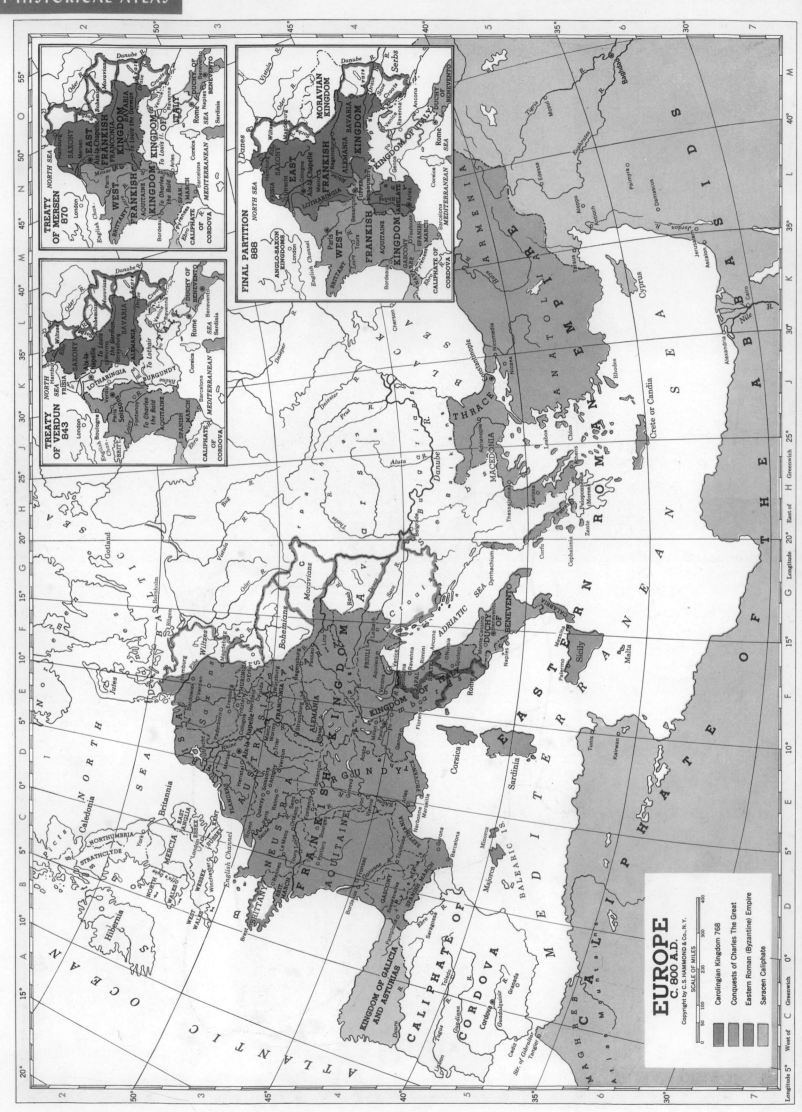

TREATY OF MERSEN 870

TREATY OF VERDUN 843

FINAL PARTITION 888

EUROPE
C. 800 A.D.

Copyright by C. S. HAMMOND & Co., N.Y.

SCALE OF MILES

Carolingian Kingdom 768
Conquests of Charles The Great
Eastern Roman (Byzantine) Empire
Saracen Caliphate

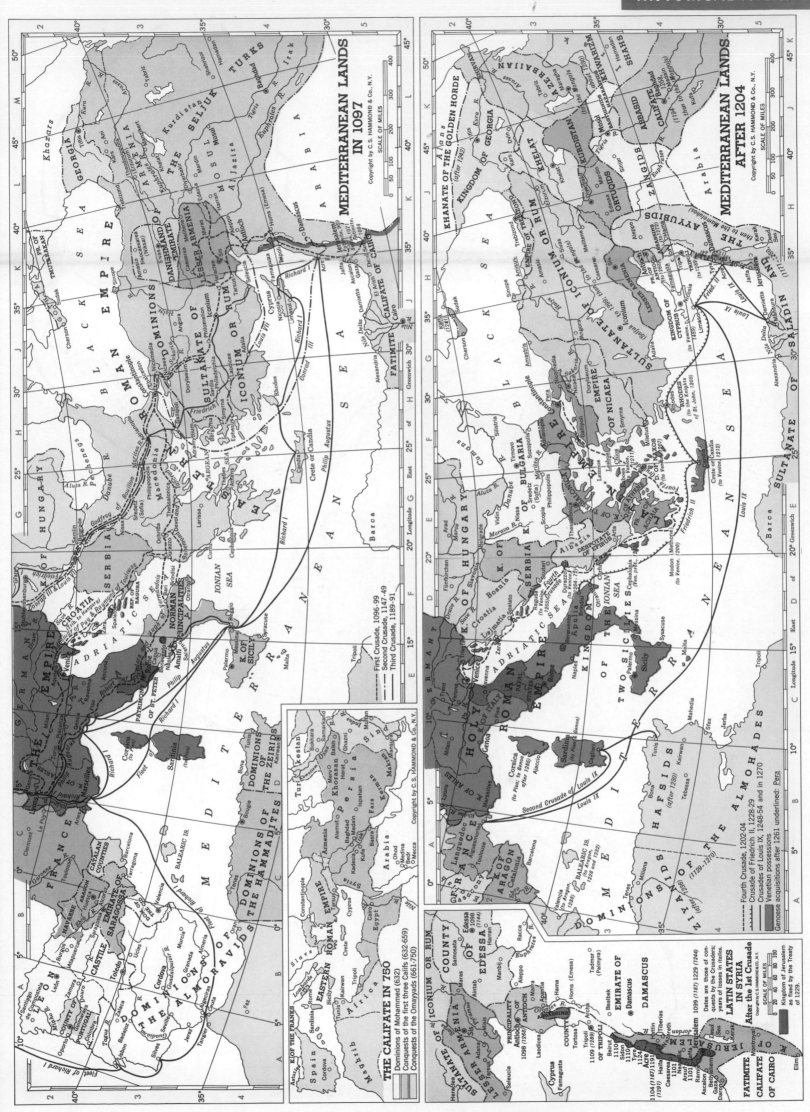

MEDITERRANEAN LANDS IN 1097

Copyright by C.S. HAMMOND & Co., N.Y.

SCALE OF MILES

First Crusade, 1096-99
Second Crusade, 1147-49
Third Crusade, 1189-91

THE CALIFATE IN 750

Dominions of Mohammed (632)
Conquests of the first three Califs (632-659)
Conquests of the Omayyads (661-750)

Copyright by C.S. HAMMOND & Co., N.Y.

MEDITERRANEAN LANDS AFTER 1204

Copyright by C.S. HAMMOND & Co., N.Y.

SCALE OF MILES

Fourth Crusade, 1202-04
Crusade of Friedrich II, 1228-29
Crusades of Louis IX, 1248-54 and in 1270
Venetian possessions
Genoese acquisitions after 1261 underlined: Pera

LATIN STATES IN SYRIA
After the 1st Crusade

SCALE OF MILES

Dates are those of conquests by the Crusaders; years of losses in italics.

Kingdom of Jerusalem as fixed by the Treaty of 1229.

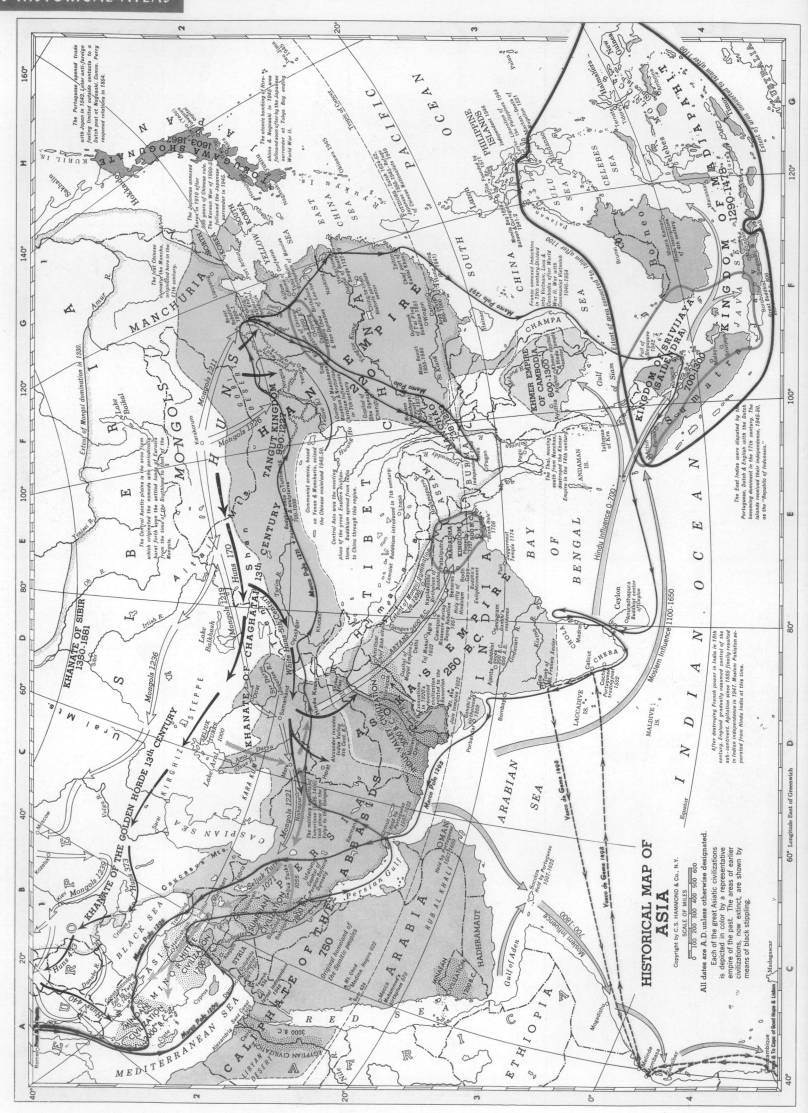

HISTORICAL MAP OF ASIA

Copyright by C.S. Hammond & Co., N.Y.

SCALE OF MILES

0 100 200 300 400 500 600

All dates are A.D. unless otherwise designated.
Each of the great Asiatic civilizations
is depicted in color by a representative
empire of the past. The areas of earlier
civilizations, now extinct, are shown by
means of black stippling.

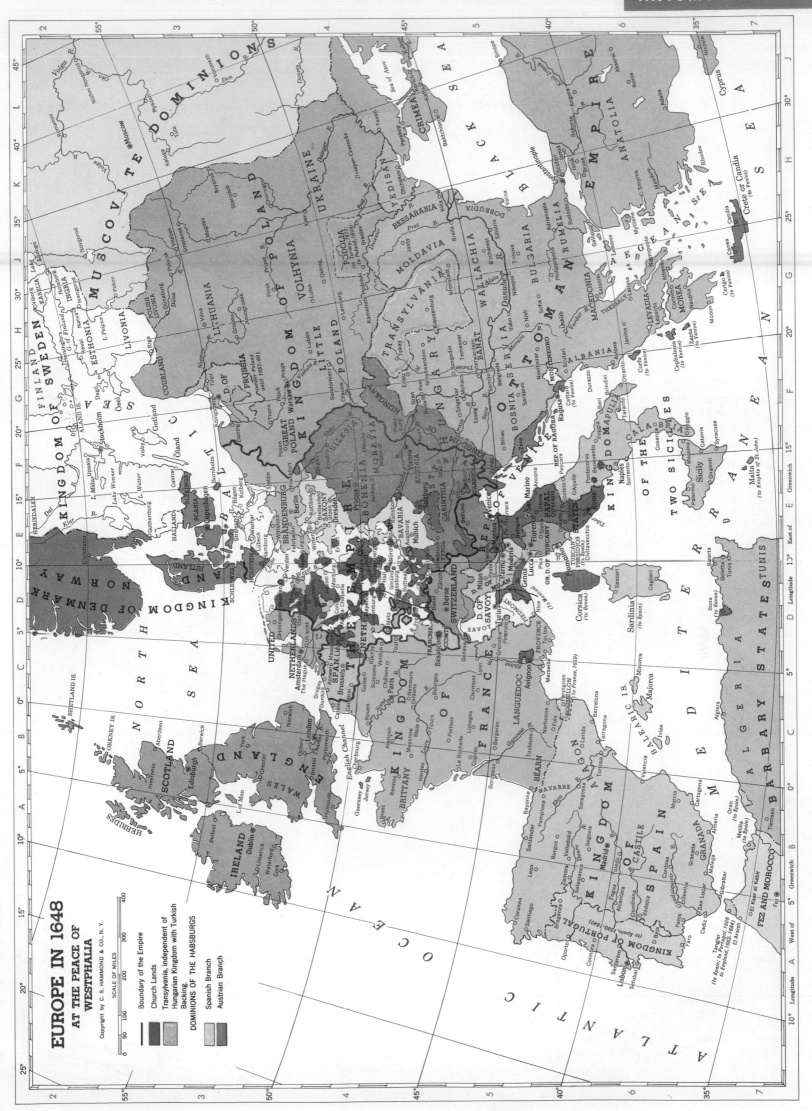

EUROPE IN 1648
AT THE PEACE OF
WESTPHALIA

Copyright by C. S. HAMMOND & CO., N.Y.

SCALE OF MILES
0 50 100 200 300 400

Boundary of the Empire
Church Lands
Transylvania, independent of
Hungarian Kingdom with Turkish
Backing.
DOMINIONS OF THE HABSBURGS
Spanish Branch
Austrian Branch

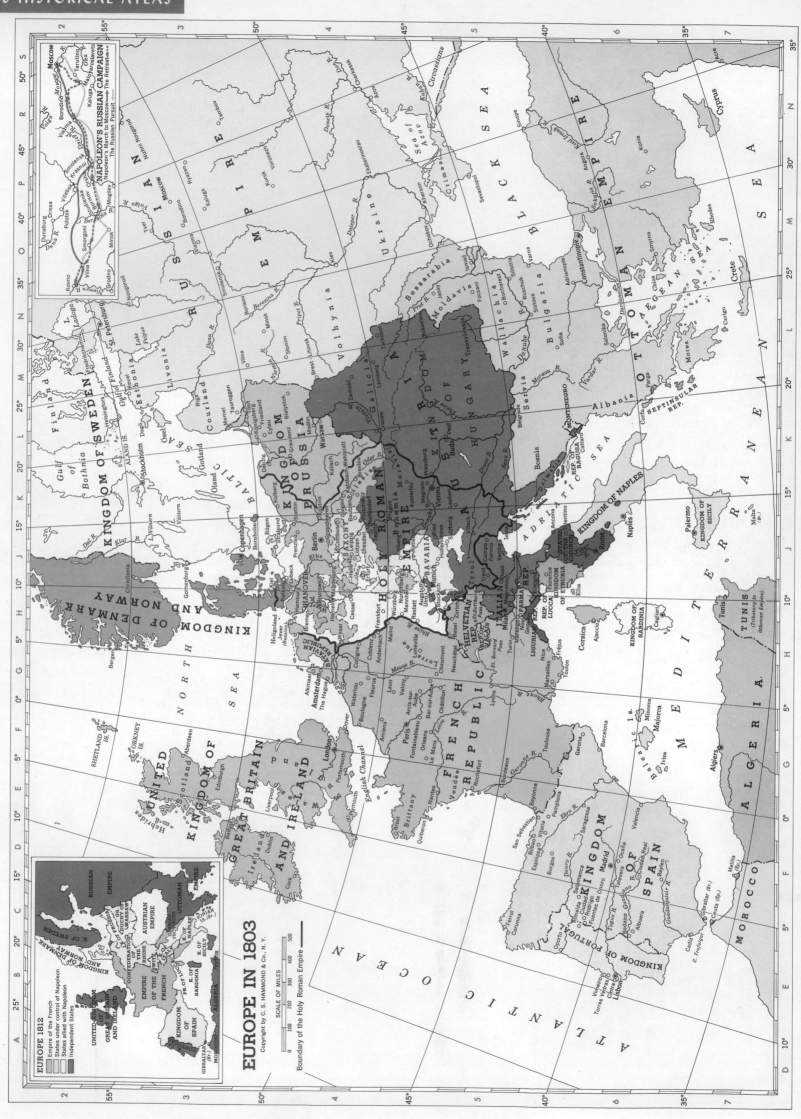

NAPOLEON'S RUSSIAN CAMPAIGN
Napoleon's March to Moscow ---- The Retreat
The Russian Pursuit

EUROPE 1812

EUROPE IN 1803

Copyright by C. S. HAMMOND & Co., N.Y.

SCALE OF MILES

0   100   200   300   400   500

Boundary of the Holy Roman Empire

Empire of the French (Napoleon)
States under control of Napoleon
States allied with Napoleon
Independent States

EUROPE IN 1914
Copyright by C. S. HAMMOND & Co., N.Y.

SCALE OF MILES
0   100   200   300   400   500

———— The Central Powers in World War I

EUROPE 1919-1938
Copyright by C. S. HAMMOND & Co., N.Y.

SCALE OF MILES
0   100   200   300   400   500

———— The Rome-Berlin Axis

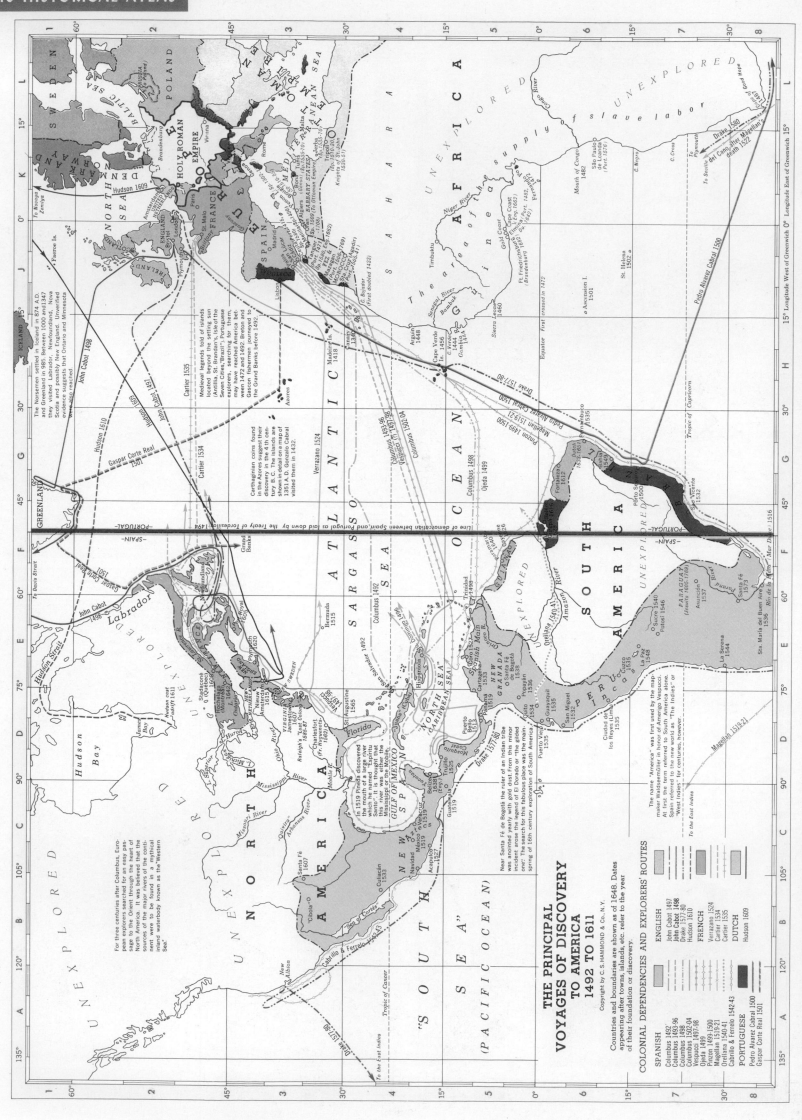

THE PRINCIPAL VOYAGES OF DISCOVERY TO AMERICA 1492 TO 1611

Copyright by C. S. Hammond & Co., N.Y.

Countries and boundaries are shown as of 1648. Dates appearing after towns, islands, etc. refer to the year of their foundation or discovery.

COLONIAL DEPENDENCIES AND EXPLORERS' ROUTES

SPANISH
Columbus 1492
Columbus 1493-96
Columbus 1498
Vespucci 1502-04
Ojeda 1499
Pinzon 1499-1500
Magellan 1519-21
Orellana 1540-41
Cabrillo & Ferrelo 1542-43

ENGLISH
John Cabot 1497
John Cabot 1498
Drake 1577-80
Hudson 1610

FRENCH
Verrazano 1524
Cartier 1534
Cartier 1535

DUTCH
Hudson 1609

PORTUGUESE
Pedro Alvarez Cabral 1500
Gaspar Corte Real 1501

The Norsemen settled in Iceland in 874 A.D. and Greenland in 985. Between 1000 and 1347 they visited Labrador, Newfoundland, Nova Scotia and possibly New England. Unverified evidence suggests that Ontario and Minnesota were also reached.

Medieval legends told of islands located beyond the setting sun (Antilla, St. Brandan's, Isle of the Seven Cities, "Brazil"). Portuguese explorers, searching for them, may have reached America between 1472 and 1492. Breton and Gascon fishermen journeyed to the Grand Banks before 1492.

Carthaginian coins found in the Azores suggest their discovery in the 4th century B.C. The islands are shown in detail on a map of 1351 A.D. Gonzalo Cabral visited them in 1432.

For three centuries after Columbus, European explorers searched for an easy passage to the Orient through the heart of North America. It was believed that the sources of the major rivers of the continent were to be found in a mythical inland waterbody known as the Western Sea.

In 1519 Pineda discovered the mouth of a large river which he named "Espiritu Santo". It is thought that this river was either the Mississippi or the Mobile.

Near Santa Fé de Bogotá the ruler of an Indian tribe was anointed yearly with gold dust. From this minor incident arose the legend of El Dorado or "the gilded one". The search for this fabulous place was the mainspring of 16th century exploration of South America.

The name "America" was first used by the mapmaker Waldseemüller in honor of Amerigo Vespucci. At first the term referred to South America alone. Spain referred to the new world as "The Indies" or "West Indies" for centuries, however.

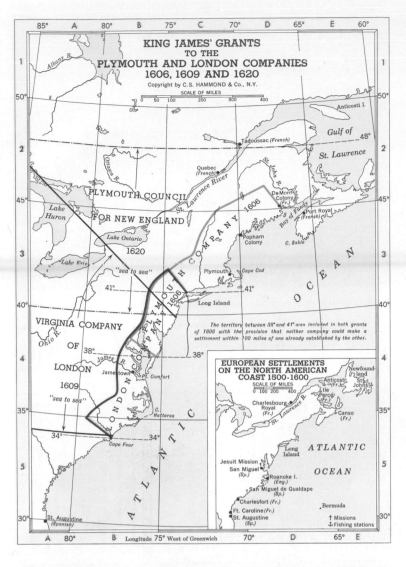

KING JAMES' GRANTS
TO THE
PLYMOUTH AND LONDON COMPANIES
1606, 1609 AND 1620
Copyright by C.S. Hammond & Co., N.Y.

EUROPEAN SETTLEMENTS
ON THE NORTH AMERICAN
COAST 1500-1600

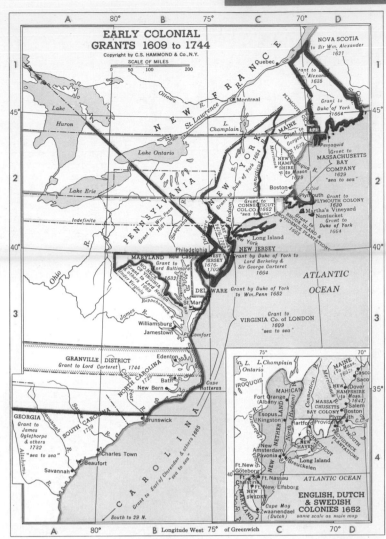

EARLY COLONIAL
GRANTS 1609 to 1744
Copyright by C.S. Hammond & Co., N.Y.

ENGLISH, DUTCH
& SWEDISH
COLONIES 1652
same scale as main map

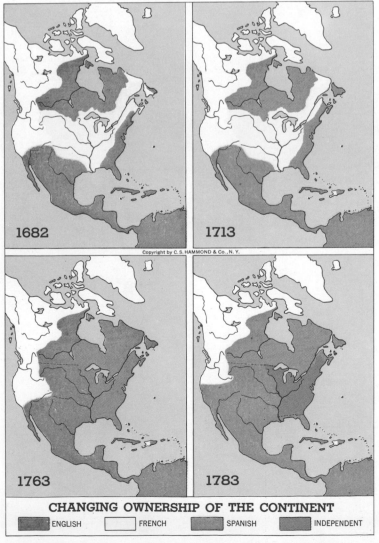

CHANGING OWNERSHIP OF THE CONTINENT

ENGLISH   FRENCH   SPANISH   INDEPENDENT

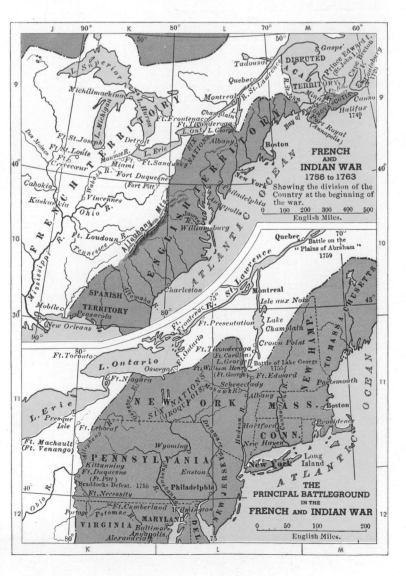

FRENCH
AND
INDIAN WAR
1756 to 1763
Showing the division of the
Country at the beginning of
the war.

THE
PRINCIPAL BATTLEGROUND
IN THE
FRENCH AND INDIAN WAR

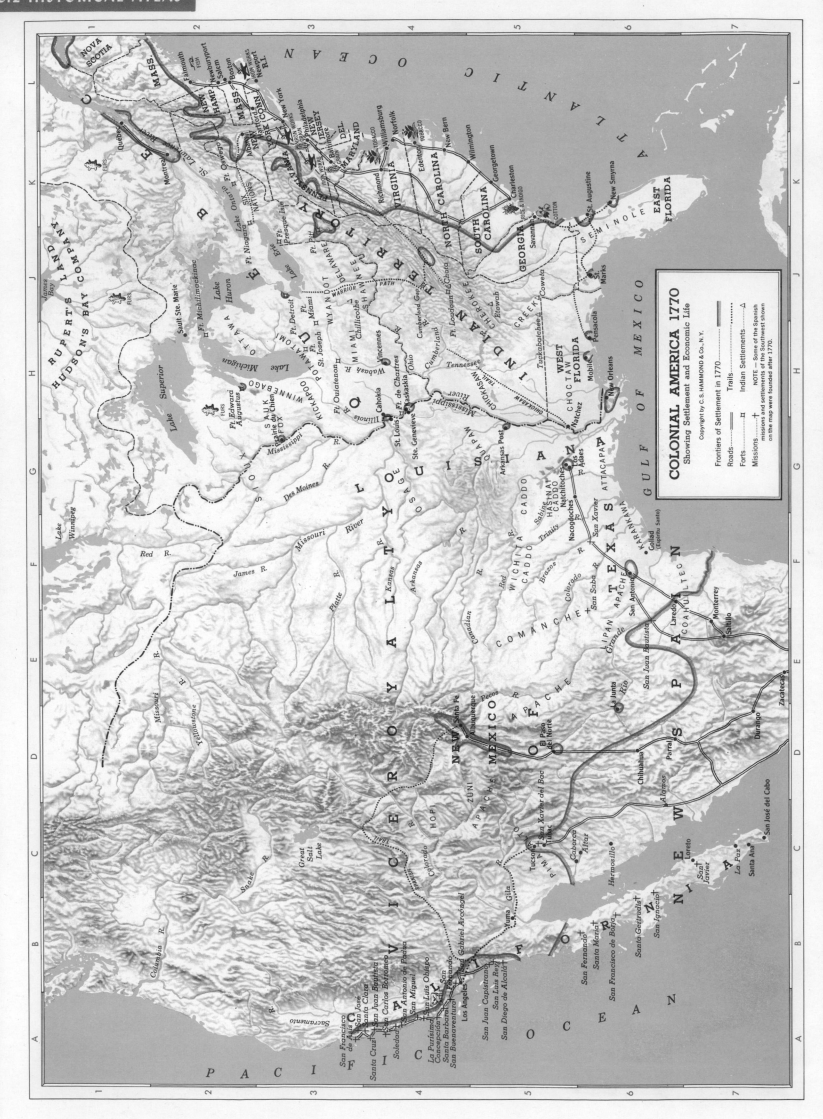

COLONIAL AMERICA 1770
Showing Settlement and Economic Life

Copyright by C.S.HAMMOND & Co. N.Y.

Frontiers of Settlement in 1770...........
Roads...........
Forts...........
Trails...........
Indian Settlements...........
Missions...........

NOTE — Some of the Spanish missions and settlements of the Southwest shown on the map were founded after 1770.

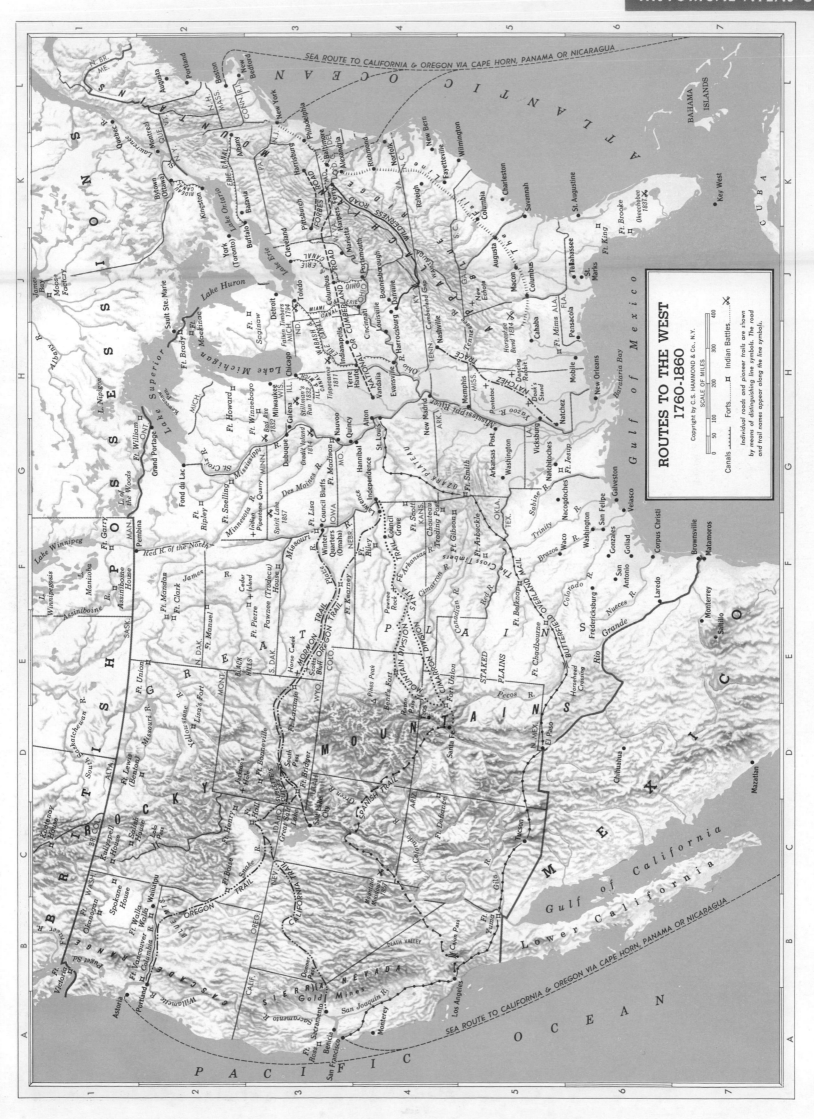

ROUTES TO THE WEST
1760-1860

Copyright by C.S. HAMMOND & Co. N.Y.

SCALE OF MILES
0 50 100 200 300 400

Canals........ Forts.... ⊠ Indian Battles....✕

*Individual roads and pioneer trails are shown
by means of distinguishing line symbols. The road
and trail names appear along the line symbols.*

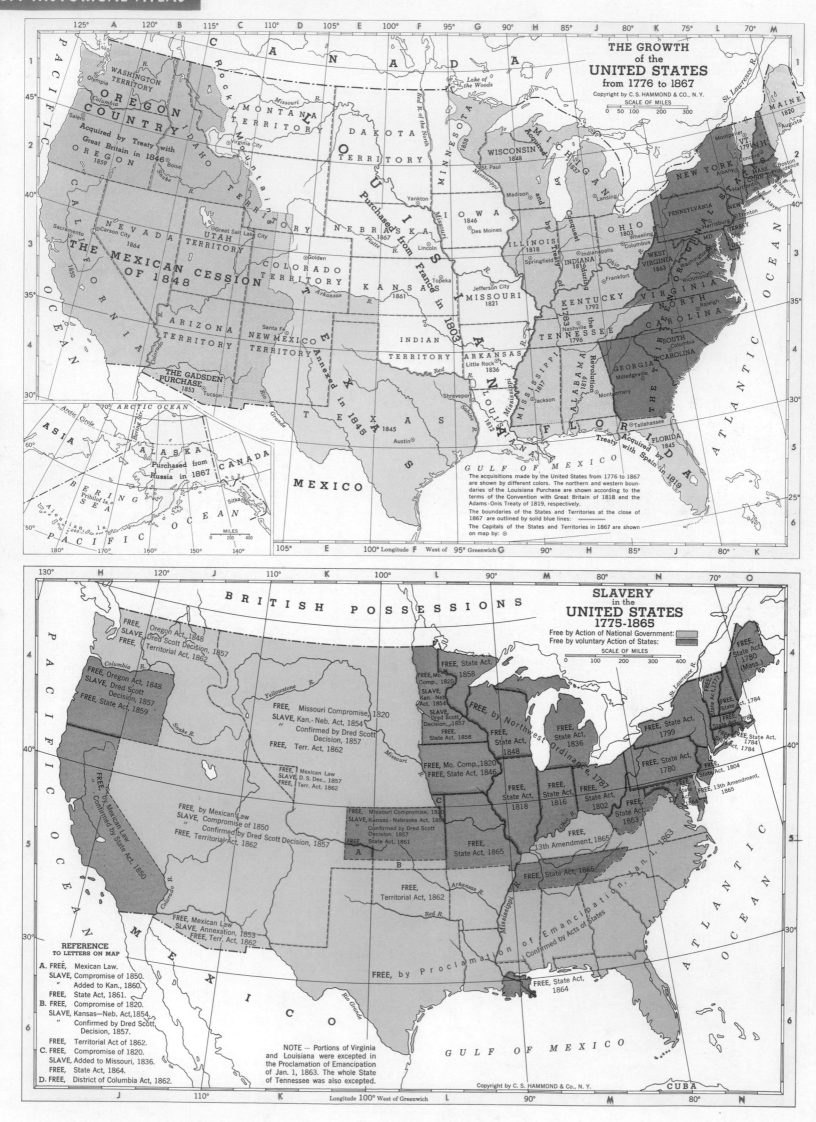

THE GROWTH of the UNITED STATES from 1776 to 1867

Copyright by C. S. HAMMOND & CO., N. Y.

SCALE OF MILES
0 50 100 200 300

The acquisitions made by the United States from 1776 to 1867 are shown by different colors. The northern and western boundaries of the Louisiana Purchase are shown according to the terms of the Convention with Great Britain of 1818 and the Adams-Onis Treaty of 1819, respectively.

The boundaries of the States and Territories at the close of 1867 are outlined by solid blue lines: ———

The Capitals of the States and Territories in 1867 are shown on map by: ⊙

SLAVERY in the UNITED STATES 1775-1865

Free by Action of National Government:
Free by voluntary Action of States:

SCALE OF MILES
100 200 300 400

Copyright by C. S. HAMMOND & Co., N. Y.

REFERENCE TO LETTERS ON MAP

A. FREE, Mexican Law.
   SLAVE, Compromise of 1850.
   " Added to Kan., 1860.
   FREE, State Act, 1861.
B. FREE, Compromise of 1820.
   SLAVE, Kansas—Neb. Act, 1854.
   " Confirmed by Dred Scott Decision, 1857.
   FREE, Territorial Act of 1862.
C. FREE, Compromise of 1820.
   SLAVE, Added to Missouri, 1836.
   FREE, State Act, 1864.
D. FREE, District of Columbia Act, 1862.

NOTE — Portions of Virginia and Louisiana were excepted in the Proclamation of Emancipation of Jan. 1, 1863. The whole State of Tennessee was also excepted.

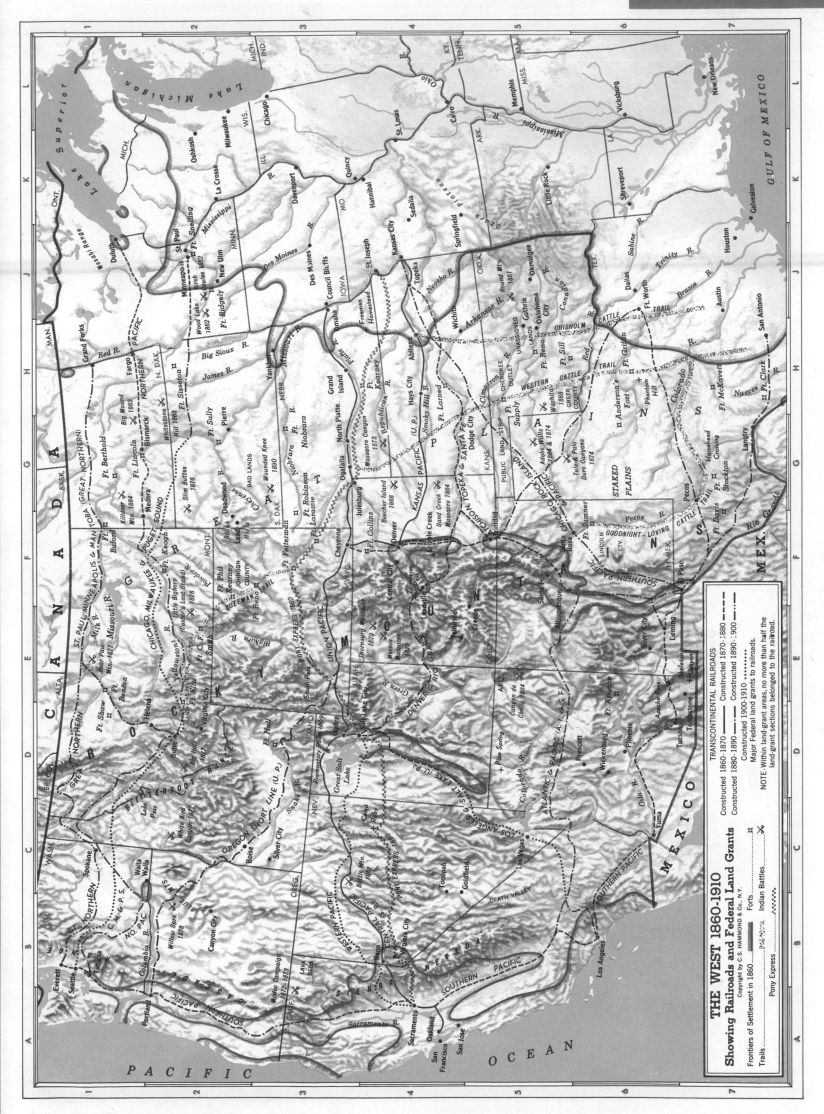

THE WEST 1860-1910
Showing Railroads and Federal Land Grants
Copyright by C.S. HAMMOND & Co., N.Y.

Frontiers of Settlement in 1860	
Forts........	Ħ
Trails........	
Pony Express........	

TRANSCONTINENTAL RAILROADS
Constructed 1860-1870 ———
Constructed 1870-1880 ———
Constructed 1880-1890 ———
Constructed 1890-1900 —·—·
Constructed 1900-1910 ·······
Major Federal land grants to railroads.
NOTE: Within land-grant areas, no more than half the land-grant sections belonged to the railroad.

Indian Battles........ ⚔

PACIFIC OCEAN

GULF OF MEXICO

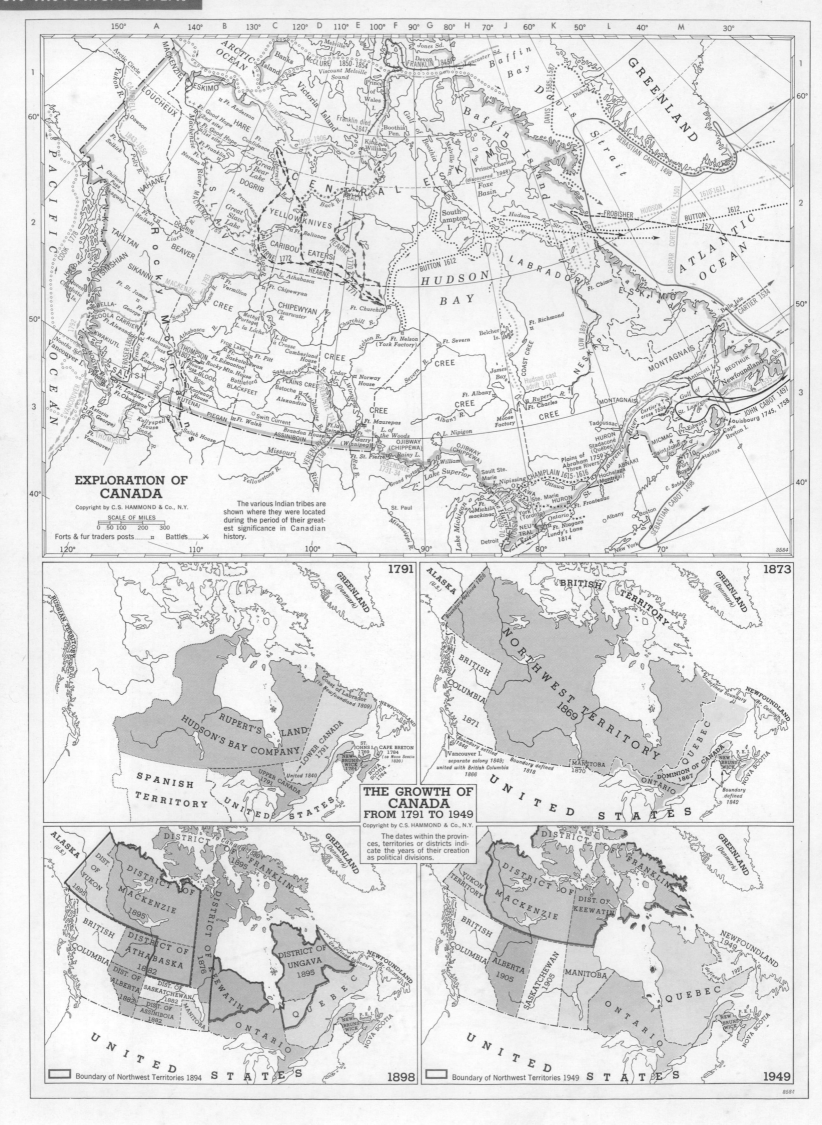

EXPLORATION OF CANADA

Copyright by C.S. HAMMOND & Co., N.Y.

SCALE OF MILES
0 50 100 200 300

Forts & fur traders posts ......□   Battles ....✗

The various Indian tribes are shown where they were located during the period of their greatest significance in Canadian history.

THE GROWTH OF CANADA
FROM 1791 TO 1949

Copyright by C.S. HAMMOND & Co., N.Y.

The dates within the provinces, territories or districts indicate the years of their creation as political divisions.

1791

1873

1898   Boundary of Northwest Territories 1894

1949   Boundary of Northwest Territories 1949